THE YALE EDITION

OF

HORACE WALPOLE'S

CORRESPONDENCE

EDITED BY W. S. LEWIS

(1895–1979)

VOLUME FORTY-THREE

HORACE WALPOLE'S CORRESPONDENCE

ADDITIONS AND CORRECTIONS

SUBJECT INDEX TO ILLUSTRATIONS

INDEX OF HORACE WALPOLE'S

CORRESPONDENTS

CHRONOLOGICAL LIST OF LETTERS

COMPILED BY
EDWINE M. MARTZ
WITH THE ASSISTANCE OF
RUTH K. McCLURE *AND* WILLIAM T. LA MOY

NEW HAVEN
YALE UNIVERSITY PRESS
OXFORD · OXFORD UNIVERSITY PRESS

1983

TABLE OF CONTENTS

INTRODUCTION

Our principle in compiling the Additions and Corrections has been to bring the footnotes up to date as far as possible, by using the many biographical studies which have been published during the last forty-three years. For members of Parliament we have checked dates against Romney Sedgwick, *The History of Parliament: The House of Commons 1715–1754*, London, 1970, and Sir Lewis Namier and John Brooke, *The History of Parliament: The House of Commons 1754–1790*, London, 1964. For actors and actresses, as well as theatrical performances, we have added new material from the *Enciclopedia dello spettacolo*, Rome, 1954–62, and *The London Stage 1660–1800 . . .*, ed. W. Van Lennep, E. L. Avery, A. H. Scouten, G. W. Stone, Jr, and C. B. Hogan, 1960–68, and *A Biographical Dictionary of Actors, Actresses . . . in London, 1660–1800*, ed. P. H. Highfill, Jr, K. A. Burnim, and E. A. Langhans, Carbondale, Illinois, 1973– . For musicians we have used *The New Grove Dictionary of Music and Musicians*, ed. Stanley Sadie, London, 1980.

For every book in Walpole's library we have added the reference to Allen T. Hazen, *A Catalogue of Horace Walpole's Library*, New Haven, Connecticut, 1969, where full bibliographical information is given. We have tried to incorporate all the corrections and suggestions which have been sent to us by our friendly readers, and acknowledgment has been made in individual footnotes. Mr John Brooke read through all our volumes and sent detailed corrections, and Professor Gilbert Bagnani corrected our translations of Italian phrases in parts of the Mann correspondence. The designation 'now WSL' means now in the Lewis-Walpole Library, Farmington, Connecticut, which was bequeathed to Yale University by Mr Lewis, who died in 1979.

We have added a cumulative list of Cue-Titles, since each correspondence has used some different short titles. There is also a complete index to the illustrations and a chronological list of all letters to and from Walpole in the edition. Corrections to the indices of each correspondence have not been included, since the final overall index incorporates all corrections in dates and biographical material.

Some manuscripts of letters already printed in our earlier volumes have come to light. Of these the text is here reprinted from the manuscript if there are many variants; otherwise the variants, chiefly in punctuation, are recorded. If parts of letters have been omitted in previous printings, we have restored the omitted sections from the manuscripts.

The manuscripts of ten unpublished letters have recently been discovered and are here printed for the first time as additions to volumes 41 and 42, which comprise miscellaneous letters arranged chronologically. The 'new' letters from Walpole include three letters to Lord Bessborough in 1764 and 1766, one letter to an unknown correspondent in 1769, four letters to Treadway Russell Nash in 1782, 1787, ca 1787–91, and 1792, and two letters to the Hon. William Waldegrave in 1789.

CUE-TITLES AND ABBREVIATIONS

CUE-TITLES AND ABBREVIATIONS

Unless otherwise stated, all English books are assumed to be published in London and all French books in Paris.

acq.	purchase (*acquisizione* in Italian MS sources).
ADD. AND CORR. . .	*The Yale Edition of Horace Walpole's Correspondence: Additions and Corrections*, New Haven, Connecticut, 1982.
Ædes Walpolianæ, Works ii . . *Ædes, Works* ii	Horace Walpole, *Ædes Walpolianæ: or, A Description of the Collection of Pictures at Houghton Hall in Norfolk, the Seat of . . . Sir Robert Walpole*; in *The Works of Horatio Walpole, Earl of Orford*, 1798, vol. ii.
aff.	collection or dossier (*affare* in Italian MS sources).
Alderson . . .	Mason's unpublished letters (1763–95) to Christopher Alderson, in the possession of Canon Rowland A. Wilson, Hartlebury, Worcs; photostats in the possession of W. S. Lewis.
Alumni Cantab. . .	*See* Venn, *Alumni Cantab.*
Alumni Oxon. . .	*See* Foster, *Alumni Oxon.*
Anecdotes[1] . .	Horace Walpole, *Anecdotes of Painting in England*, Strawberry Hill, vols i and ii, 1762; vol. iii, 1763; vol. iv, 1771.
Anecdotes[2] . .	Horace Walpole, *Anecdotes of Painting in England*, 2d edn, Strawberry Hill, 1765, 4 vols.
Anecdotes, ed. Dallaway	Horace Walpole, *Anecdotes of Painting in England*, ed. Rev. James Dallaway, 1828, 5 vols.
Anecdotes, ed. Wornum, 1876 .	Horace Walpole, *Anecdotes of Painting in England*, ed. Ralph N. Wornum, 1876, 3 vols.
Anecdotes, Works iii .	Horace Walpole, *Anecdotes of Painting in England*, in *The Works of Horatio Walpole, Earl of Orford*, 1798, vol. iii.

Anson, *Mary Hamilton* .   *Mary Hamilton, afterwards Mrs John Dicken-son, at Court and at Home. From Letters and Diaries 1756 to 1816*, ed. Elizabeth and Florence Anson, 1925.

Army Lists (*or Army Lists*) . . .   [Great Britain, War Office,] *A List of the General and Field Officers as they Rank in the Army*, 1740–1841.

Arneth . . .   Alfred, Ritter von Arneth, *Maria Theresia's Erste Regierungsjahre*, Vienna, 1863–5, 3 vols.

B . . . .   Mary Berry.

B [with page reference] .   *Letters of the Marquise du Deffand to the Hon. Horace Walpole . . .* , ed. Mary Berry, 1810, 4 vols.

Baker, *History of St John's College* .   Thomas Baker, *History of the College of St John the Evangelist, Cambridge*, ed. John E. B. Mayor, Cambridge, 1869, 2 vols.

Beauties of England .   John Britton and Edward W. Brayley, *The Beauties of England and Wales*, 1801–16, 18 vols.

Bedford Corr. . .   John Russell, Duke of Bedford, *Correspondence of John Fourth Duke of Bedford*, ed. Lord John Russell, 1842–6, 3 vols.

Bentham, *Ely*[2] . .   James Bentham, *The History and Antiquities of the Conventual & Cathedral Church of Ely*, 2d edn, Norwich, 1812.

BERRY . . .   *The Yale Edition of Horace Walpole's Correspondence: The Correspondence with Mary and Agnes Berry*, New Haven, 1944, 2 vols.

'Berry-Damer' . .   Four notebooks containing extracts made by Mrs Damer from Mary Berry's letters to her, 1789–1804. The originals are not known to exist, and the extracts have never been published. In vol. i, p. 2, is the note, 'These 4 vols found among Mrs Damer's papers and in her own handwriting.' They are now WSL.

Berry, *Journals* . .   See MBJ.

Berry Papers . .   *The Berry Papers: Being the Correspondence Hitherto Unpublished of Mary and Agnes Berry (1763–1852)*, ed. Lewis Melville, 1914.

Betham, *Baronetage* . William Betham, *The Baronetage of England,* 1801–5, 5 vols.

Bibl. Nat. Cat.
(or *Bibl. Nat. Cat.*) . *Catalogue générale des livres imprimés de la Bibliothèque nationale,* 1897– .

Bibliothèque
Nationale Catalogue . *See* Bibl. Nat. Cat.

Biddulph . . . Violet Biddulph, *The Three Ladies Waldegrave,* 1938.

Blecheley Diary . . *The Blecheley Diary of the Rev. William Cole* ... *1765–67,* ed. Francis G. Stokes, 1931.

Blomefield, *Norfolk²* . Francis Blomefield and Charles Parkin, *An Essay towards a Topographical History of the County of Norfolk,* 2d edn, 1805–10, 11 vols.

BM Add. MSS . . Additional Manuscripts, British Museum.

BM, *Bibl. Birch.* . . British Museum, *Bibliotheca Birchiana.*

BM Cat. . . . Catalogue of Printed Books in the British Museum.

BM Cat. of Engraved British Portraits . British Museum, Department of Prints and Drawings. *Catalogue of Engraved British Portraits Preserved in the Department of Prints and Drawings in the British Museum,* by Freeman O'Donoghue and Henry M. Hake, 1908–25, 6 vols.

BM Egerton MSS . . Egerton Manuscripts, British Museum.

BM *Satiric Prints* . . British Museum, Department of Prints and Drawings. *Catalogue of Prints and Drawings in the British Museum. Division I. Political and Personal Satires,* 1870–1954, 11 vols.

'Book of Materials' . Three manuscript volumes, the first two entitled by Walpole 'Book of Materials,' the third entitled 'Miscellany,' begun in 1759, 1771 and 1786 respectively; now in the possession of W. S. Lewis.

'Book of Visitors' . . See 'Visitors' below for full entry.

Boswell, *Johnson* . . Boswell's *Life of Johnson,* ed. George Birkbeck Hill, revised by L. F. Powell, Oxford, 1934–51, 6 vols.

Boswell Papers . .	*Private Papers of James Boswell*, ed. Geoffrey Scott and Frederick A. Pottle, privately printed, 1928–34, 18 vols.
Brydges, *Restituta* .	Sir Samuel Egerton Brydges, *Restituta; or, Titles, Extracts, and Characters of Old Books in English Literature, Revived*, 1814–16, 4 vols.
Burke, *Commoners* .	John Burke, *A Genealogical and Heraldic History of the Commoners of Great Britain and Ireland*, 1833–8, 4 vols.
Burke, *Landed Gentry* .	Sir John Bernard Burke, *A Genealogical and Heraldic History of the Landed Gentry of Great Britain*.
Burke, *Peerage* . .	Sir John Bernard Burke and Ashworth P. Burke, *A Genealogical and Heraldic History of the Peerage and Baronetage*.
Burnet, *Hist. of His Own Times* . .	Gilbert Burnet, *History of His Own Times*, 1723–34, 2 vols.
Burney, *Diary* . .	*Diary and Letters of Madame d'Arblay (1778–1840)*, ed. Charlotte Barrett with preface and notes by Austin Dobson, 1904–5, 6 vols.
Burney, *Hist. of Music* .	Charles Burney, *A General History of Music*, 1776–89, 4 vols.
c., cc.	leaf; leaves (*carte*, in Italian MS sources).
Camden, *Britannia*[2] .	William Camden, *Britannia*, revised by Edmund Gibson, 1722, 2 vols.
Carlisle MSS . .	[Great Britain] Historical Manuscripts Commission, Fifteenth Report, Appendix, Part VI, *The Manuscripts of the Earl of Carlisle*, 1897.
CBEL	*The Cambridge Bibliography of English Literature*, ed. F. W. Bateson, New York and Cambridge, 1941, 4 vols.
C-D	*See* La Chenaye-Desbois.
CHBE	*The Cambridge History of the British Empire*, Cambridge, 1929–59.
Chatham Corr. . .	William Pitt, Earl of Chatham, *Correspondence*, ed. W. S. Taylor and J. H. Pringle, 1838–40, 4 vols.

Chatsworth MSS . .	Devonshire MSS, first series, at Chatsworth, Derbyshire.
CHATTERTON . .	*The Yale Edition of Horace Walpole's Correspondence: The Correspondence with Thomas Chatterton . . .*, New Haven, 1951.
Chatterton's *Works* .	*The Works of Thomas Chatterton*, ed. Robert Southey and Joseph Cottle, 1803, 3 vols.
CHUTE . . .	*The Yale Edition of Horace Walpole's Correspondence: The Correspondence with John Chute . . .*, New Haven, 1973.
Cobbett, *Parl. Hist.* .	*The Parliamentary History of England*, ed. William Cobbett, John Wright, and T. C. Hansard, 1806–20, 36 vols.
cod.	codex (*codice* in Italian MS sources).
Coke, *Journals* . .	*The Letters and Journals of Lady Mary Coke*, ed. James A. Home, Edinburgh, 1889–96, 4 vols.
Coke, 'MS Journals' (*or* Coke, Lady Mary, *MS Journals, or* Coke, MS Journals) .	Photostats of unpublished journals (1775–91) of Lady Mary Coke in the possession of Lord Home.
COLE	*The Yale Edition of Horace Walpole's Correspondence: The Correspondence with the Rev. William Cole*, New Haven, 1937, 2 vols.
Cole, *Jour. to Paris* (*or* Cole, *Journey to Paris*) . . .	William Cole, *A Journal of my Journey to Paris in the Year 1765*, ed. Francis Griffin Stokes, 1931.
Collins, *Peerage*, 1812 (*or* Collins, *Peerage*) .	Arthur Collins, *The Peerage of England*, ed. Sir Samuel Egerton Brydges, 1812, 9 vols.
Commonplace Book I and *II* . . .	Sir David Dalrymple's manuscript commonplace books, in the library of Sir Mark Dalrymple, Bt, at Newhailes.
Conti, *Firenze dopo i Medici* . .	Giuseppe Conti, *Firenze dopo i Medici*, Florence, 1921.
CONWAY . . .	*The Yale Edition of Horace Walpole's Correspondence: The Correspondence with Henry Seymour Conway, Lady Ailesbury, Lord and Lady Hertford, Mrs Harris*, New Haven, 1974.

Cooper, *Annals*	Charles Henry Cooper, *Annals of Cambridge*, 4 vols, 1842–52; vol. v, ed. John William Cooper, Cambridge, 1908.
Cooper, *Memorials*	Charles Henry Cooper, *Memorials of Cambridge*, Cambridge, 1860–66, 3 vols.
Corr. Geo. III	*See* Geo. III's *Corr.*, ed. Fortescue.
Country Seats	'Horace Walpole's Journals of Visits to Country Seats, etc.,' ed. Paget Toynbee, in *The Walpole Society 1927–1928*, vol. xvi, Oxford, 1928.
Coxe, *Pelham Administration*	William Coxe, *Memoirs of the Administration of . . . Henry Pelham*, 1829, 2 vols.
Croker, *Letters of Lady Hervey*	*Letters of Mary Lepel, Lady Hervey*, ed. John Wilson Croker, 1821.
Croker, *Letters of Lady Suffolk*	*Letters to and from Henrietta, Countess of Suffolk . . . from 1712 to 1767*, ed. John Wilson Croker, 1824, 2 vols.
Cunningham	*The Letters of Horace Walpole, Earl of Orford*, ed. Peter Cunningham, 1857–59, 9 vols.
D	Madame du Deffand.
DAB	*Dictionary of American Biography*, ed. Allen Johnson and Dumas Malone, 1943, 22 vols.
Daily Adv.	*The Daily Advertiser*, 1731–95. Film in the Yale University Library from the file in the Library of Congress.
DALRYMPLE	*The Yale Edition of Horace Walpole's Correspondence: The Correspondence with Sir David Dalrymple . . .*, New Haven, 1951.
Damer-Waller	The MS passed on HW's death to Mrs Damer, who bequeathed it to Sir Wathen Waller, 1st Bt.
Davies, *York Press*	Robert Davies, *A Memoir of the York Press, with Notices of Authors, Printers, and Stationers*, Westminster, 1868.
Debrett's Peerage	*Debrett's Peerage, Baronetage, Knightage, and Companionage*, ed. Arthur G. M. Hesilrige.
Delany Corr. (or *Delany Correspondence*)	*The Autobiography and Correspondence of Mary Granville, Mrs Delany*, ed. Lady Llanover, 1861, 3 vols; 2d series, 1862, 3 vols.

Designs, 1753 . .	*Designs by Mr R. Bentley for Six Poems by Mr T. Gray*, 1753.
Des. of SH, 1774 . .	Horace Walpole, *A Description of the Villa of Horace Walpole . . . at Strawberry-Hill . . . With an inventory . . .*, Strawberry Hill, Printed by Thomas Kirgate, 1774.
Des. of SH, 1784 . .	Horace Walpole, *A Description of the Villa of Mr Horace Walpole . . .* , Strawberry Hill, Printed by Thomas Kirgate, 1784.
'Des. of SH,' *Works* ii (*or* 'Description of SH') .	Horace Walpole, 'A Description of the Villa of Mr Horace Walpole at Strawberry Hill near Twickenham,' in *The Works of Horatio Walpole, Earl of Orford*, 1798, vol. ii.
Dict. de Paris . .	*Dictionnaire historique de la ville de Paris*, by Pierre-Thomas-Nicolas Hurtaut and —— Magny, 1779, 4 vols.
Dictionary of English Church History .	*A Dictionary of English Church History*, ed. Sidney L. Ollard, London, Oxford, and Milwaukee, 2d edn, [1919].
Dictionnaire de biographie française (*or Dict. de biographie française*) . . .	*Dictionnaire de biographie française*, sous la direction de J. Balteau . . . M. Barroux . . . M. Prévost . . . avec le concours de nombreux collaborateurs . . . , 1933– .
Directory to the Nobility, Gentry . . . for 1793 . . .	*Directory to the Nobility, Gentry, and Families of Distinction, in London, Westminster, &c. Being a Supplement to the British Directory of Trade, Commerce, and Manufacture, for 1793.*
DNB	*Dictionary of National Biography*, ed. Leslie Stephen and Sidney Lee, reissue, 1908–9, 22 vols.
Doran	John Doran, *'Mann' and Manners at the Court of Florence, 1740–1786*, 1876, 2 vols.
Draper, *Mason* . .	John W. Draper, *William Mason: A Study in Eighteenth-Century Culture*, New York, 1924.
D's Journal . . .	Madame du Deffand's Journal (*see* vol. 7, p. 421).
DU DEFFAND . . .	*The Yale Edition of Horace Walpole's Correspondence: The Correspondence with Mme du Deffand*, New Haven, 1939, 6 vols.

Dugald Stewart, *Bio-graphical Memoirs* . Dugald Stewart, *Biographical Memoirs of Adam Smith, LL.D., of William Robertson, D.D., and of Thomas Reid, D.D.*, Edinburgh, 1811.

Dugdale, *Baronage* . Sir William Dugdale, *The Baronage of England*, 1675–76, 3 vols in 2.

EBP . . . . *See BM Cat. of Engraved British Portraits.*

Effemeridi . . . Dr Antonio Cocchi, *Effemeridi*. MS in the Biblioteca della Facoltà di Medicina e Chirurgia, at Careggi.

Enciclopedia italiana . *Enciclopedia italiana*, ed. Gentile and Tumminelli, Milan and Rome, 1929–39, 36 vols.

Engravers[1] . . . Horace Walpole, *A Catalogue of Engravers*, Strawberry Hill, 1763.

Engravers[2] . . . *Idem*, 1765.

Engravers, Works . . Horace Walpole, *A Catalogue of Engravers*, in *The Works of Horatio Walpole*, 1798, vol. iv.

Espasa . . . . *Enciclopedia universal ilustrada Europeo-Americana*, Espasa, Barcelona, [1905–30] 70 vols; *Apéndice*, [1930–33] 10 vols.

Eton Coll. Reg. . . R. A. Austen-Leigh, *Eton College Register 1698–1752*, Eton, 1927; *1753–1790*, Eton, 1921.

FAMILY . . . *The Yale Edition of Horace Walpole's Correspondence: The Correspondence with the Walpole Family*, New Haven, 1973.

fasc. . . . . instalment or part (*fascicule* in French sources).

filza . . . . series (in Italian MS sources).

F. O. . . . . Foreign Office. Film in the Yale University Library from the MSS in the Foreign Office in London. The class numbers are followed by volume numbers in arabic numerals.

Fortescue, *British Army* Sir John William Fortescue, *A History of the British Army*, 2d edn, 1910–30, 13 vols.

Foster, *Alumni Oxon.* . Joseph Foster, *Alumni Oxonienses: The Members of the University of Oxford, 1500–1714*, Oxford and London, 1891–2, 4 vols; *1715–1886*, London, 1887–8, 4 vols.

Fox, *Memorials and Correspondence*	*Memorials and Correspondence of Charles James Fox*, ed. Lord John Russell, 1853–7, 4 vols.
Frederick II, *Politische Correspondenz* . .	*Politische Correspondenz Friedrich's des Grossen*, Berlin, 1879–1939, 46 vols.
Fugitive Verses . .	See *HW's Fugitive Verses*.
Funzioni di corte . .	*Descrizione delle funzioni riguardanti la real corte di Toscana dall' epoca dell' arrivo in Firenze di S. A. R. Pietro Leopoldo I Granduca fino alla renunzia del granducato da esso fatta a favore del suo figlio l'Arciduca Ferdinando III cioè dal dì 13 settembre 1765 a tutto l'anno 1790*. Film in the Yale University Library from the MS at Florence.
Gaskell . . .	Philip Gaskell, *The First Editions of William Mason*, Cambridge, 1951 (Cambridge Bibliographical Society, Monograph No. 1).
Gazette de Leyde . .	*Journal politique, publié à Leyde* . . . [ca 1680–].
GEC	George Edward Cokayne, *The Complete Peerage*, revised by Vicary Gibbs *et al.*, 1910–59, 13 vols.
GEC, *Baronetage* . .	George Edward Cokayne, *The Complete Baronetage*, Exeter, 1900–9, 6 vols.
Genealog. hist. Archivarius . .	Michael Ranft, *Der genealogische Archivarius . . . welcher alles, was sich in diesem Jahre unter den itztlebenden hohen Personen in der Welt an Geburten, Vermählungen, Avancements und Todesfällen veränderliches zugetragen hat . . .*, Leipzig, 1733–8, Parts 1–50 in 6 vols. With Part 37 (vol. vii) the title changed to *Der genealogisch-historische Archivarius*.
Genealog. hist. Nachrichten 1st ser. .	Michael Ranft, *Genealogisch-historische Nachrichten von den allerneuesten Begebenheiten, welche sich an den europäischen Höfen zutragen . . .*, Leipzig, 1739–52, Parts 1–145 in 12 vols.
Genealog. hist. Nachrichten 2d ser. .	*Idem, Neue genealogisch-historische Nachrichten . . .*, Leipzig, 1750–63, Parts 1–160 in 13 vols.

Genealog. hist. Nachrichten 3d ser. .	*Idem, Fortgesetzte neue genealogisch-historische Nachrichten* . . . , Leipzig, 1762–77, Parts 1–168 in 14 vols.
'Genesis of SH' . .	W. S. Lewis, 'The Genesis of Strawberry Hill,' *Metropolitan Museum Studies*, vol. v, pt i, New York, June, 1934.
Genest . . .	John Genest, *Some Account of the English Stage*, Bath, 1832, 10 vols.
Geo. III's *Corr.*, ed. Fortescue . . .	*The Correspondence of King George the Third from 1760 to December 1783* . . . , ed. Sir John Fortescue, 1927–8, 6 vols.
ɢᴍ	*The Gentleman's Magazine.*
Gough, *British Topography*² .	Richard Gough, *British Topography*, 2d edn, 1780, 2 vols.
Gough, *Sepulchral Monuments* .	Richard Gough, *Sepulchral Monuments in Great Britain*, 1786–96, 2 vols in 5.
Granger¹ . .	James Granger, *A Biographical History of England*, 1769, 2 vols (with *Supplement*, 1774).
Granger⁵ . .	James Granger, *A Biographical History of England*, 5th edn, 1824, 6 vols.
Granger, *Correspondence* .	*Letters between the Rev. James Granger* . . . *and* . . . *Eminent Literary Men of His Time*, ed. J. P. Malcolm, 1805.
Graves and Cronin .	Algernon Graves and William Vine Cronin, *A History of the Works of Sir Joshua Reynolds, P. R. A.*, 1899–1901, 4 vols.
ɢʀᴀʏ . . .	*The Yale Edition of Horace Walpole's Correspondence: The Correspondence with Thomas Gray, Richard West, and Thomas Ashton*, New Haven, 1948, 2 vols.
Gray-HW-West-Ashton Corr. .	*The Correspondence of Gray, Walpole, West and Ashton (1734–1771)*, ed. Paget Toynbee, Oxford, 1915, 2 vols.
Gray's Commonplace Book . .	Gray's MS Commonplace Book in three volumes, covering approximately the years from 1737 to 1761. Contains notes of Gray's reading and copies of poems by himself, Walpole, and West. Left by Mason to Stonhewer, and by Stonhewer to Pembroke College, Cambridge.

Gray's Corr. . .	*Correspondence of Thomas Gray*, ed. Paget Toynbee and Leonard Whibley, Oxford, 1935, 3 vols.
Gray's MS Journal 1739–41 . . .	Gray's notebook of his travels in France and Italy, owned by Sir John Murray; photostatic copy owned by W. S. Lewis. Printed in part in Gosse, *The Works of Thomas Gray* (1884, 4 vols), i. 237–46.
Gray's *Naturalist's Journal* . .	Gray's copy, with MS notes, of *The Naturalist's Journal*, London, 1767, a diary or memorandum book in which Gray entered notes, chiefly on natural phenomena, from 1 Jan. 1767 to 16 May 1771. Now in the collection of Carl H. Pforzheimer of New York City.
Grenville Papers . .	*The Grenville Papers, being the Correspondence of Richard Grenville, Earl Temple, K. G., and the Right Hon. George Grenville, their Friends and Contemporaries*, ed. William James Smith, 1852–3, 4 vols.
Grimm (*or* Grimm, *Correspondance*) .	Friedrich Melchior, Freiherr von Grimm, *Correspondance littéraire, philosophique et critique par Grimm, Diderot, Raynal, Meister, etc.*, ed. Maurice Tourneux, 1877–82, 16 vols.
Grove's *Dictionary of Music* . .	*The New Grove Dictionary of Music and Musicians*, 6th edn, ed. Stanley Sadie, 1980, 20 vols.
Hadley . . .	Horace Walpole, *Selected Letters*, ed. William Hadley, 1926.
Halkett and Laing .	Samuel Halkett and John Laing, *Dictionary of Anonymous and Pseudonymous English Literature*, ed. James Kennedy, W. A. Smith and A. F. Johnson, Edinburgh, 1926–[62], 9 vols.
Harcourt Papers . .	*The Harcourt Papers*, ed. Edward William Harcourt, Oxford, n.d., 14 vols.
Hardwicke Corr. . .	Philip C. Yorke, *The Life and Correspondence of Philip Yorke, Earl of Hardwicke*, Cambridge, 1913, 3 vols.
Hardwicke, *State Papers*	Philip Yorke, 2d Earl of Hardwicke, *Miscellaneous State Papers*, 1778, 2 vols.

Hazen, *Bibl. of HW* (or Hazen, *Bibliography of Walpole*) .	Allen T. Hazen, *A Bibliography of Horace Walpole*, New Haven, 1948.
Hazen, *Cat. of HW's Lib.* . . .	Allen T. Hazen, *A Catalogue of Horace Walpole's Library*, New Haven, 1969, 3 vols.
Hazen, *SH Bibl.* (or Hazen, *SH Bibliography*) . .	Allen T. Hazen, *A Bibliography of the Strawberry Hill Press*, New Haven, 1942; new edn, 1973.
Hertford Corr. . .	*Correspondence between Frances, Countess of Hartford, and Henrietta Louisa, Countess of Pomfret, between the years 1738 and 1741*, 1805, 3 vols.
Hervey, *Memoirs* . .	John, Lord Hervey, *Some Materials towards Memoirs of the Reign of King George II*, ed. Romney Sedgwick, 1931, 3 vols.
Hist. MSS Comm. .	Historical Manuscripts Commission.
Historic Doubts[1] (or *Historic Doubts*) .	Horace Walpole, *Historic Doubts on the Life and Reign of King Richard the Third*, 1768.
Horn, *Diplomatic Representatives* .	David B. Horn, *British Diplomatic Representatives 1689–1789*, 1932, Camden Society, 3d ser. xlvi.
HW	Horace Walpole.
HW, 'MS Commonplace Book of Verses'	*See MS Commonplace Book of Verses.*
HW, Waldegrave MSS	*See MS Commonplace Book of Verses; MS Poems; MS Political Papers*
HW's England . .	Alfred B. Mason, *Horace Walpole's England as His Letters Picture It*, 1930.
HW's Fugitive Verses .	*Horace Walpole's Fugitive Verses*, ed. W. S. Lewis, New York and Oxford, 1931.
HW's 'Journal . . . 1769 [and 1770, 1771]'	'Journal of the most remarkable events of the reign of King George the Third, from the beginning of the year 1769, being a supplement to the memoires of Mr Horace Walpole, carried on by himself,' 148 pp., in HW's hand; now in the possession of W. S. Lewis. '1770' starts at p. 30; '1771' at p. 90. A preliminary draft for the end of *Mem. Geo. III*.

HW'S Letters to Hertford and Zouch .	*Letters from . . . Horace Walpole to the Earl of Hertford . . .* [and to] *Henry Zouch*, 1825.
HW's MS *Journal of the Most Remarkable Events of . . . 1769* [*and 1770, 1771*] .	*See* HW's 'Journal . . . 1769 [and 1770, 1771].'
HW's *Private Correspondence*, 1820 .	*Private Correspondence of Horace Walpole, Earl of Orford. Now First Collected*, 1820, 4 vols.
Ilchester, *Hanbury-Williams* . . .	Earl of Ilchester and Mrs Langford-Brooke, *The Life of Sir Charles Hanbury-Williams*, 1929.
Ilchester, *Henry Fox* .	Earl of Ilchester, *Henry Fox, First Lord Holland*, 1920, 2 vols.
ins. . . .	bundle of documents (*inserto* in Italian MS sources).
Isenburg, *Stammtafeln* .	Wilhelm Karl, Prinz von Isenburg, *Stammtafeln zur Geschichte der europaeischen Staaten*, Berlin, 1936, 2 vols.
Jesse, *Selwyn* . .	John Heneage Jesse, *George Selwyn and His Contemporaries*, new edn, 1882, 4 vols.
Johnson, *Lives of the Poets* . . .	Samuel Johnson, *Lives of the English Poets*, ed. George Birkbeck Hill, Oxford, 1905, 3 vols.
'Journal Geo. 3d 1772' .	*Journal of the Reign of King George the Third, from the beginning of the year 1772; by Horace Walpole; being a supplement to his Memoires*, HW's transcript in his MS of *Last Journals*, in the possession of Lord Waldegrave.
Journal of the Printing-Office . .	Horace Walpole, *Journal of the Printing-Office at Strawberry Hill*, ed. Paget Toynbee, 1923.
Journals of the House of Commons . .	[Great Britain, Parliament, House of Commons,] *Journals of the House of Commons . . . Reprinted by Order of the House of Commons*, 1803, 51 vols.
Journals of the House of Lords . . .	[Great Britain, Parliament, House of Lords,] *Journals of the House of Lords*, [ca 1777–] 1891, 123 vols.

Jour. Print. Off. . .	*See Journal of the Printing-Office.*
Judd, *Members of Parliament* . .	Gerrit P. Judd, *Members of Parliament 1734–1832*, New Haven, 1955.
Ketton-Cremer, *Walpole* (*or* Ketton-Cremer) .	Robert W. Ketton-Cremer, *Horace Walpole. A Biography*, 1940.
LA	*See* Nichols, *Lit. Anec.*
La Chenaye-Desbois .	François-Alexandre Aubert de la Chenaye-Desbois and —— Badier, *Dictionnaire de la noblesse*, 3d edn, 1863–76, 19 vols.
La Fontaine, *Fables* .	Jean de la Fontaine, *Fables*, Boston, 1841, 2 vols.
La Grande encyclopédie . .	*La Grande encyclopédie*, ed. Berthelot, Hartwig, Devenbourg, 1886–1902, 31 vols.
Lalanne . . .	Marie-Ludovic-Chrétien Lalanne, *Dictionnaire historique de la France*, 1872.
Last Journals . .	Horace Walpole, *The Last Journals of Horace Walpole during the Reign of George III from 1771–1783*, ed. A. Francis Steuart, 1910, 2 vols.
LC Cat. . . .	Library of Congress Catalogue.
Leinster Corr. . .	*Correspondence of Emily, Duchess of Leinster*, ed. Brian Fitzgerald, Dublin, 1949–57, 3 vols.
Le Neve, *Knights* . .	*Le Neve's Pedigrees of the Knights*, ed. George W. Marshall, 1873 (Publications of the Harleian Society, vol. viii).
Lennox, *Life and Letters* . . .	*The Life and Letters of Lady Sarah Lennox, 1745–1826* . . . , ed. the Countess of Ilchester and Lord Stavordale, 1901, 2 vols.
Letters of David Hume .	*The Letters of David Hume*, ed. J. Y. T. Grieg, Oxford, 1932, 2 vols.
Letters to Henry Fox .	*Letters to Henry Fox, Lord Holland*, ed. Earl of Ilchester, Roxburghe Club, 1915.
Letter to the Editor .	Horace Walpole, *A Letter to the Editor of the Miscellanies of Thomas Chatterton*, Strawberry Hill, 1779.
Lévis, *Souvenirs* . .	Gaston-Pierre-Marc, Duc de Lévis, *Souvenirs et portraits 1780–1789*, 1813.

LI	*See* Nichols, *Lit. Illus.*
Libro d'oro . . .	Archivio di Stato di Firenze, *Libro d'oro dei Patrizi di Firenze* (with name of the Quarter of the city).
Litta	Pompeo Litta, *Famiglie celebri italiane*, Milan, Turin, and Naples, 1819–1923, 13 vols.
Lodge, *Irish Peerage*, 1789 . . .	John Lodge, *The Peerage of Ireland*, revised by Mervyn Archdall, [Dublin,] 1789, 7 vols.
Lond. (London), sold .	*See* sold London.
London Past and Present . . .	*London Past and Present; Its History, Associations, and Traditions*, ed. Henry B. Wheatley and Peter Cunningham, 1891, 3 vols.
London Stage . .	*The London Stage 1660–1800* . . . , Pt I: 1660–1700, ed. W. Van Lennep, Carbondale, Illinois, 1965; Pt II: 1700–1729, ed. E. L. Avery, 1960; Pt III: 1729–1747, ed. A. H. Scouten, 1961; Pt IV: 1747–1776, ed. G. W. Stone, Jr, 1962; Pt V: 1776–1800, ed. C. B. Hogan, 1968.
Lort's Sale Cat. . .	*A Catalogue of the . . . Library of the Late Rev. Michael Lort . . . Which Will Be Sold by Auction, by Leigh and Sotheby . . . April 5, 1791 and the Fourteen Following Days . . . and . . . May 4, 1791, and . . . the Nine Following Days* [1791].
Lucas	*Letters of Horace Walpole*, ed. C. B. Lucas [1904].
Lugt	Frits Lugt, *Répertoire des catalogues de ventes publiques intéressant l'art ou la curiosité: tableaux, dessins, estampes* . . . , La Haye, 1938–64.
Luynes, *Mémoires* .	Charles-Philippe d'Albert, Duc de Luynes, *Mémoires sur la cour de Louis XV*, 1860–5, 17 vols.
Lysons, *Mag. Brit.* .	Daniel and Samuel Lysons, *Magna Britannia*, vol. ii containing *Cambridgeshire*, 1808; vol. iii containing *Cambridgeshire and . . . Chester*, 1810.
Lysons's *Environs* .	Daniel Lysons, *The Environs of London*, 1792–96, 4 vols.

McMahan . . . *The Best Letters of Horace Walpole,* ed. Anna B. McMahan, 1909.

MANN . . . . *The Yale Edition of Horace Walpole's Correspondence: The Correspondence with Sir Horace Mann,* New Haven, 1954–71, 11 vols.

MASON . . . *The Yale Edition of Horace Walpole's Correspondence: The Correspondence with William Mason,* New Haven, 1955, 2 vols.

Mason, *Gray*[1] . . See Mason, *Mem. Gray.*

Mason, *Mem. Gray* . William Mason, *The Poems of Mr Gray to which are prefixed Memoirs of his Life and Writings,* York, 1775.

Mason, *Satirical Poems* (*or* Mason's *Satirical Poems*) . . . *Satirical Poems Published Anonymously by William Mason, with Notes by Horace Walpole, Now First Printed from His Manuscript,* ed. Paget Toynbee, Oxford, 1926. The MS of Walpole's commentary and notes is now in the Harvard Library. An incomplete draft in Walpole's hand, headed 'Notes to Mr W. Mason's later poems, by Mr Horace Walpole, 1779,' is now in the possession of W. S. Lewis.

Mason's *Works* . . *The Works of William Mason, M. A.,* 1811, 4 vols.

Masters, *History of CCCC,* 1831 . . Robert Masters, *History of the College of Corpus Christi and the Blessed Virgin Mary in the University of Cambridge,* 1831.

MBJ . . . . *Extracts from the Journals and Correspondence of Miss Berry from the Year 1783 to 1852,* ed. Lady Theresa Lewis, 1865, 3 vols; 2d edn, 1866, 3 vols.

'Mem. 1783–91' . . Horace Walpole's manuscript journal 1783–1791 in the possession of W. S. Lewis.

Members of Parliament [Great Britain, Parliament, House of Commons], *Members of Parliament,* 1878, part ii.

Mem. Geo. II . . Horace Walpole, *Memoirs of the Reign of King George the Second,* 2d edn, ed. Henry R. V. Fox, Lord Holland, 1847, 3 vols.

Mem. Geo. III . . Horace Walpole, *Memoirs of the Reign of King George the Third,* 2d edn, ed. G. F. Russell Barker, 1894, 4 vols.

Mem. Gray . . . *See* Mason, *Mem. Gray.*

Mem. of Geo. III . . *See Mem. Geo. III.*

Mem. of the Reign of   *See Mem. Geo. II*
  George II . . .

Mem. of the Reign of   *See Mem. Geo. III.*
  George III . .

Memorials and Letters,   Sir David Dalrymple, *Memorials and Letters*
  Reign of James I .   *Relating to the History of Great Britain in the*
                         Reign of James the First, Glasgow, 1762; 2d
                         edn, 1766.

Meyerstein, *Chatterton*   E. H. W. Meyerstein, *A Life of Thomas Chat-*
                         terton, 1930.

Middleton's   Conyers Middleton, *Germana quædam anti-*
  Monumenta . . *quitatis eruditæ monumenta,* 1745.

MISC. CORR. . . *The Yale Edition of Horace Walpole's Corre-*
                         spondence: Horace Walpole's Miscellaneous
                         Correspondence, New Haven, 1980.

Mitford . . . *The Correspondence of Horace Walpole, Earl*
                         of Orford, and the Rev. William Mason, Now
                         First Published from the Original MSS, ed.
                         John Mitford, 1851, 2 vols. Mitford's own
                         copy, including his MS corrections, margin-
                         alia, and related correspondence, is now in
                         the possession of W. S. Lewis.

Mitford, 1816 . . *The Works of Thomas Gray,* ed. John Mit-
                         ford, 1816, 2 vols.

Mitford, 1835–43 . . *The Works of Thomas Gray,* ed. John Mit-
                         ford, 1835–36, 4 vols; vol. v containing the cor-
                         respondence of Gray and the Rev. Norton
                         Nicholls, 1843.

Mme de Sévigné,   Marie de Rabutin-Chantal, Marquise de Sé-
  Lettres . . . vigné, *Lettres,* ed. Louis-Jean-Nicolas Mon-
                         merqué, 1862–66, 14 vols.

Moniteur . . . *Gazette nationale, ou le Moniteur universel.*

MONTAGU . . . *The Yale Edition of Horace Walpole's Corre-*
                         spondence: The Correspondence with George
                         Montagu, New Haven, 1941, 2 vols.

MORE	*The Yale Edition of Horace Walpole's Correspondence: The Correspondence with Hannah More* . . . , New Haven, 1961.
MS Cat. . . .	Horace Walpole, 'Catalogue of the Library of Mr Horace Walpole at Strawberry Hill, 1763,' unpublished MS in the possession of Lord Walpole, Wolterton Park, Norfolk; photostatic copy in the possession of W. S. Lewis.
MS Commonplace Book	*See MS Commonplace Book of Verses*; *MS Poems*; *MS Political Papers*.
MS Commonplace Book of Verses . . .	Horace Walpole, 'A Common Place Book of Verses, Stories, Characters, Letters, &c. &c. with some Particular Memoirs of a Certain Parcel of People' [1740], MS in the possession of W. S. Lewis.
MS in Society of Antiquaries . .	Manuscript letter in the Cely-Trevilian Collection, Society of Antiquaries, London.
MS Newhailes . .	Manuscript in the possession of Sir Mark Dalrymple, Bt, of Newhailes.
MS Poems . .	Horace Walpole, 'Poems and Other Pieces by Horace Walpole, Youngest Son of Sir Robert Walpole, Earl of Orford,' MS in the possession of W. S. Lewis.
MS Political Papers .	Horace Walpole, 'Political Papers Written by Horace Walpole son to Sir Robert Walpole Earl of Orford,' MS in the possession of W. S. Lewis.
Musgrave, *Obituary* .	*Obituary Prior to 1800 . . . Compiled by Sir William Musgrave*, ed. Sir George J. Armytage, Harleian Society Publications, 1899–1901, 6 vols.
n.	number (*numero* in Italian MS sources).
n., nn. . . .	note, notes (in English sources).
N&Q	*Notes and Queries*.
Namier, *Structure* .	Sir Lewis B. Namier, *The Structure of Politics at the Accession of George III*, 1929, 2 vols.
Namier and Brooke .	Sir Lewis B. Namier and John Brooke, *The History of Parliament: The House of Commons 1754–1790*, 1964, 3 vols.

NBG . . . . *Nouvelle biographie générale*, ed. Jean-Chrétien-Ferdinand Hoefer, 1852–66, 46 vols.

Nichols, *Lit. Anec.* . John Nichols, *Literary Anecdotes of the Eighteenth Century*, 1812–15, 9 vols.

Nichols, *Lit. Illus.* . John Nichols, *Illustrations of the Literary History of the Eighteenth Century*, 1817–58, 8 vols.

Nicoll, *Drama 1700–50* Allardyce Nicoll, *A History of Early Eighteenth Century Drama, 1700–1750*, Cambridge, 1929.

Nouv. Biog. Gén. . See NBG.

now WSL . . . In the possession of W. S. Lewis.

OED . . . . *A New English Dictionary on Historical Principles*, ed. Sir James A. H. Murray *et al.*, Oxford, 1888–1928, 10 vols.

Oesterr. Erbfolge-Krieg *Oesterreichischer Erbfolge-Krieg 1740–1748 nach den Feld-Acten und anderen authentischen Quellen bearbeitet in der kriegsgeschichtlichen Abtheilung des K. und k. Kriegs-Archivs*, Vienna, 1896–1914, 9 vols.

Office de documentation Information supplied by the Office de documentation of the Amis de la Bibliothèque Nationale, Paris.

Old Westminsters . *The Record of Old Westminsters*, ed. G. F. Russell Barker and Alan H. Stenning, 1928, 2 vols. *A Supplementary Volume*, ed. J. B. Whitmore and G. R. Y. Radcliffe [1938?].

Ossory . . . *The Yale Edition of Horace Walpole's Correspondence: The Correspondence with the Countess of Upper Ossory*, New Haven, 1965, 3 vols.

Paget Toynbee . . See Toynbee, *Supp.*

Palmer, *Monumental Inscriptions* . . *Monumental Inscriptions and Coats of Arms from Cambridgeshire*, ed. William M. Palmer, Cambridge, 1932.

Palmer, *William Cole* . William M. Palmer, *William Cole of Milton*, Cambridge, 1935.

'Paris Journals' (*or Paris Jour.*) . . Horace Walpole, 'Paris Journals,' in *The Yale Edition of Horace Walpole's Correspondence:*

	The Correspondence with Mme du Deffand, New Haven, 1939, v. 255–417.
Pastor, *Geschichte der Päpste* . . .	Ludwig, Freiherr von Pastor, *Geschichte der Päpste*, Freiburg, 1886–1933, 16 vols.
P. C. C. . . .	Prerogative Court of Canterbury.
Peck, *Desid. Cur.*[1] .	Francis Peck, *Desiderata Curiosa*, 1779, 2 vols in 1.
Pennant, *Tour in Scotland* . . . *1769* .	Thomas Pennant, *A Tour in Scotland; MDCCLXIX* (3d edn; 1st in quarto), Warrington, 1774.
Pennant, *Tour in Scotland* . . . *1772* .	Thomas Pennant, *A Tour in Scotland, and Voyage to the Hebrides; MDCCLXXII*, Chester, 1774.
Pinkerton MSS, Farmington . .	Four volumes of manuscripts, chiefly letters addressed to John Pinkerton 1775–1815. Formerly in the possession of Dawson Turner; now in the possession of W. S. Lewis.
Plomer . . .	Henry Robert Plomer *et al., A Dictionary of the Printers and Booksellers . . . in England, Scotland and Ireland from 1726 to 1775* [Oxford], 1932.
Pope, *Works*, ed. Elwin and Courthope . .	*The Works of Alexander Pope,* ed. Whitwell Elwin and W. J. Courthope, 1871–89.
prot.	insertion (*protesi* in Italian MS sources).
Public Adv. . .	*The Public Advertiser* [1752–94].
R&NA[1]	Horace Walpole, *A Catalogue of the Royal and Noble Authors of England*, Strawberry Hill, 1758, 2 vols.
R&NA[2]	*Idem*, R. and J. Dodsley, London, 1759, 2 vols.
R&NA, *Works* . .	*Idem*, in *The Works of Horatio Walpole, Earl of Orford*, 1798, vol. i.
Ranfft . . .	Michael Ranft (or Ranfft), *Merkwürdige Lebensgeschichte aller Cardinäle der Röm. Cathol. Kirche*, Regensburg, 1768–73, 4 vols.
Redgrave, *Dict. of Artists* . .	Samuel Redgrave, *A Dictionary of Artists of the English School*, 1878.
reg.	register (*registro* in Italian MS sources).

Reminiscences .	.	*Reminiscences Written by Mr Horace Walpole in 1788*, ed. Paget Toynbee, Oxford, 1924.
Rép. de la Gazette	.	Anatole, Marquis de Granges de Surgères, *Répertoire historique et biographique de la Gazette de France, depuis l'origine jusqu'à la Révolution*, 1902–6, 4 vols.
Roberts, *Memoirs of Hannah More* .	.	William Roberts, *Memoirs of the Life and Correspondence of Mrs Hannah More*, 1834, 4 vols.
Rockingham Memoirs .		George Thomas Keppel, 6th Earl of Albemarle, *Memoirs of the Marquis of Rockingham and his Contemporaries*, 1852, 2 vols.
Royal and Noble Authors, Works i (or *Roy. & Nob. Authors, Works* i) .	. .	See R&NA, *Works*.
Royal Calendar .	.	*The Royal Kalendar; or Complete and Correct Annual Register for England, Scotland, Ireland, and America* . . . [1767–1813].
S-A . .	. .	The Marquis de Sainte-Aulaire.
S-A [with page reference]	. .	Louis-Camille-Joseph de Beaupoil, Marquis de Sainte-Aulaire, *Correspondance complète de Mme du Deffand*, 1866, 3 vols.
St-Allais .	. .	Nicolas Viton de Saint-Allais and Ange-Jacques-Marie Poisson de la Chabeaussière, *Nobiliaire universel de France*, 1872–75, 20 vols.
Sandwich Papers .	.	*The Private Papers of John, Earl of Sandwich, First Lord of the Admiralty 1771–1782*, ed. G. R. Barnes and J. H. Owen, 1932–38, 4 vols (Publications of the Navy Records Society, vols 69, 71, 75, and 78).
Scots Peerage .	.	*The Scots Peerage*, ed. Sir James Balfour Paul, Edinburgh, 1904–14, 9 vols.
Sedgwick .	. .	Romney Sedgwick, *The History of Parliament: The House of Commons 1715–1754*, 1970, 2 vols.
SELWYN . .	.	*The Yale Edition of Horace Walpole's Correspondence: The Correspondence with George Selwyn* . . . , New Haven, 1961.

Sexagenarian	. .	William Beloe, *The Sexagenarian; or, the Re-collections of a Literary Life*, 1817, 2 vols.
SH . . .	.	Strawberry Hill.
SH Accounts	.	*Strawberry Hill Accounts . . . Kept by Mr Horace Walpole from 1747 to 1795*, ed. Paget Toynbee, Oxford, 1927.
'Short Notes'	.	Horace Walpole, 'Short Notes of the Life of Horatio Walpole,' in *The Yale Edition of Horace Walpole's Correspondence: The Correspondence with Thomas Gray, Richard West, and Thomas Ashton*, New Haven, 1948, i. 3–51.
Sir Spencer Walpole	.	*Some Unpublished Letters of Horace Walpole*, ed. Sir Spencer Walpole, 1902.
sold London	.	*A Catalogue of the Collection of Scarce Prints* [also MSS and books] *Removed from Strawberry Hill*, 13–23 June 1842. The number following each entry is the lot number in the sale.
sold SH . .	.	*A Catalogue of the Classic Contents of Strawberry Hill Collected by Horace Walpole*, 25 April–21 May 1842. The roman and arabic numerals which follow each entry indicate the day and lot number in the sale.
Soleinne . .	.	Charles Brunet, *Tables des pièces de théâtre décrites dans le catalogue de . . . M. de Soleinne*, 1914.
S.P. . . .	.	State Papers. Film in the Yale University Library from the MSS in the Public Record Office in London. The class numbers (78, 98 or 105) are followed by the volume numbers in arabic numerals.
T . . .	.	Mrs Paget Toynbee *or The Letters of Horace Walpole*, ed. Mrs Paget Toynbee, Oxford, 1903–5, 16 vols.
taf. . . .	.	table (*tafel* in German sources).
tav. . . .	.	table (*tavola* in Italian sources).
Thieme and Becker	.	Ulrich Thieme and Felix Becker, *Allgemeines Lexikon der bildenden Künstler von der An-*

tike bis zur Gegenwart, Leipzig, 1907–50, 37 vols.

Times Lit. Supp.	.	*See* TLS.
TLS (*or TLS*)	. .	*The Times* (London) *Literary Supplement.*
to. . .	.	vol. (*tomo* in Italian MS sources).
Tovey, *Gray and His Friends* . .	.	Duncan C. Tovey, *Gray and His Friends*, Cambridge, 1890.
Toynbee . .	.	*The Letters of Horace Walpole*, ed. Mrs Paget Toynbee, Oxford, 1903–5, 16 vols, *or Lettres de la Marquise du Deffand à Horace Walpole*, ed. Mrs Paget Toynbee, Londres, 1912, 3 vols.
Toynbee, *Supp.* (*or* Toynbee Supp.)	.	*Supplement to the Letters of Horace Walpole*, ed. Paget Toynbee, Oxford, 1918–25, 3 vols.
Tracts of Geo. 3 .	.	'A collection of tracts and pamphlets, historical and political, published during the reign of King George III,' 1760–90, 59 vols (2 vols numbered 47), collected by HW; sold SH iii. 110; now in the possession of W. S. Lewis (Hazen, *Cat. of HW's Lib.* No. 1609).
tratte reg. . .	.	extracts from the register (*tratte registro* in Italian MS sources).
T-W . . .	.	Paget Toynbee and Leonard Whibley, editors of the *Correspondence of Thomas Gray*, Oxford, 1935.
Venn, *Alumni Cantab.*		*Alumni Cantabrigienses*, Part I to 1751, compiled by John Venn and J. A. Venn, Cambridge, 1922–27, 4 vols; Part II 1752–1900, ed. J. A. Venn, Cambridge, 1940–54, 6 vols.
Vernon Smith .	.	*Letters Addressed to the Countess of Ossory, from the Year 1769 to 1797. By Horace Walpole*, ed. R. Vernon Smith, 2d edn, 1848, 2 vols.
Vertue Notebooks	.	George Vertue, *Vertue Note Books*, 6 vols (Index, vol. vi), in *The Walpole Society*, vols xviii, xx, xxii, xxiv, xxvi, xxix, Oxford, 1932–47.
Vetusta Monumenta	.	Society of Antiquaries of London, *Vetusta Monumenta: quae ad rerum britannicarum memoriam conservandam*, 1747, 7 vols, 1906.

Vict. Co. Hist. (or Vict. Co. Hist.) . .	*The Victoria History of the Counties of England* [with name of county].
'Visitors' . .	Horace Walpole's manuscript list of visitors to Strawberry Hill, printed in *The Yale Edition of Horace Walpole's Correspondence: The Correspondence with Mary and Agnes Berry*, New Haven, 1944, ii. 221–74.
Voltaire, *Œuvres* . .	*Œuvres complètes de Voltaire*, ed. Louis-Émile-Dieudonné Moland, 1877–85, 52 vols.
Waldegrave MSS . .	*See MS Commonplace Book of Verses; MS Poems; MS Political Papers.*
Walpole-Mason Corr. .	*The Correspondence of Horace Walpole and the Rev. William Mason*, ed. John Mitford, 1851, 2 vols.
Walpole Society . .	The annual volumes of *The Walpole Society*, Oxford, 1911/12– .
Walpoliana . . .	John Pinkerton, *Walpoliana* [1799], 2 vols.
Warton, *An Enquiry* .	Thomas Warton, *An Enquiry into the Authenticity of the Poems Attributed to Thomas Rowley*, 1782.
Warton, *Hist. of English Poetry* . .	Thomas Warton, *History of English Poetry*, 1774–81, 3 vols.
Waterbeach Diary .	William Cole, *The Waterbeach Diary 1768–69*; proof sheets of the forthcoming edition edited by Francis Griffin Stokes; the last portion of Cole's MS is referred to as Add. MS 5835. Published in 1933.
Wheatley, *London Past and Present* . .	See London Past and Present.
Williams, *Works* . .	*The Works of the Right Honourable Sir Chas. Hanbury Williams, K. B. . . . with Notes by Horace Walpole, Earl of Orford*, 1822, 3 vols.
Williams's MSS (*or* Williams MSS) . .	A collection of Sir Charles Hanbury Williams's manuscripts and correspondence owned by W. S. Lewis. The citations are to volumes and folios or pages.
Willis and Clark . .	Robert Willis and John W. Clark, *The Architectural History of the University of Cambridge*, Cambridge, 1886, 4 vols.

Winstanley, *Unre-formed Cambridge* .	D. A. Winstanley, *Unreformed Cambridge. A Study of Certain Aspects of the University in the Eighteenth Century*, Cambridge, 1935.
W. O. . . .	War Office.
Woelmont de Brumagne	Henri de Woelmont, Baron de Brumagne, *Notices généalogiques*, 1923–35, 8 vols.
Works . . .	Horace Walpole, *The Works of Horatio Walpole, Earl of Orford*, 1798, 5 vols.
Wright . . .	*The Letters of Horace Walpole, Earl of Orford*, ed. John Wright, 1840, 6 vols.
wsl (now wsl) . .	In the possession of W. S. Lewis.
wsl, *Selection of HW's Letters* . . .	*A Selection of the Letters of Horace Walpole*, ed. W. S. Lewis, 1926.
Wurzbach, *Biogra-phisches Lexikon* .	Constant von Wurzbach, *Biographisches Lexikon des Kaiserthums Oesterreich*, Vienna, 1856–91, 60 vols.
Wyvill, *Political Papers*	*Political Papers, Chiefly Respecting the Attempt of the County of York . . . to Effect a Reformation of the Parliament of Great Britain*, ed. Christopher Wyvill, York [1794–1802], 4 vols.

ADDITIONS AND CORRECTIONS

ADDITIONS AND CORRECTIONS

VOLUME 1

Page xvii, List of illustrations, *sub* William Cole by John Gooch, *for* now in the Spencer Collection, New York Public Library *read* now wsL.

Page xx, last line, *after* riddles' *add* (*Quarterly Review* June 1848, vol. lxxxiii, no. 165, pp. 112–13).

Page xxxvi, line 13, *for* Foster *read* Forster   *after* 110. *insert* An autograph note signed 'H.W.', about the MSS of Cole's letters, was sold Sotheby's 27–28 Oct. 1981, lot 694.

Page xli, line 27, *after* New York City; *add* Guildhall Library;

Page li, line 3, *after* 1803.* *insert* The text of Walpole's letters is taken from the original manuscripts, now Add. MSS 5952–5953. Cole made copies of Walpole's letters interspersed with copies of his own letters in his notebooks. We use Cole's copies to fill in illegible phrases and missing addresses in letters from Walpole. The text of Cole's letters is taken from the manuscripts in the Forster collection, Victoria and Albert Museum, from manuscripts at Nostell Priory, Wakefield, Yorks, or from Cole's own copies in his notebooks.

Selected letters from Walpole and other extracts from Cole's manuscripts, bequeathed to the British Museum, were printed in the *Monthly Magazine* 1803–1804 as follows:

HW to Cole 22 June 1771	1803, xvi pt ii. 12–13
HW to Cole 12 Oct. 1771	13
HW to Cole 25 Aug. 1772	308–9
HW to Cole 16 April 1776	539
HW to Cole 9 March 1765	1804, xvii pt i. 33
HW to Cole 18 Jan. 1766 (1 paragraph)	33
HW to Cole 7 April 1776 (1 paragraph)	33–4
HW to Cole 22 Feb. 1782 ('I doubt you are again in error . . . Yours ever. H.W.')	141
HW to Cole 6 March 1780 ('Mr Pennicott has . . . partner with Wise')	141
HW to Cole 19 June 1777	253
HW to Cole 30 Dec. 1781 ('You will be surprised . . . H. Walpole')	253–4
HW to Cole 11 Oct. 1774	1804, xviii pt ii. 127
HW to Cole 11 April 1775	127–9
HW to Cole 5 Jan. 1780 (2 paragraphs)	302–3
HW to Cole 1 June 1776	407–8

Letters between ... Rev. James Granger ... and ... Literary Men of his Time, 1805, pp. 375–6, prints HW to Cole 16 April 1776 (without PS). Isaac Disraeli, in 'The Pains of Fastidious Egotism,' *Calamities of Authors*, 1812, prints passages from HW to Cole 3 June 1778, 21 July 1774, 22 May 1777, 24 July 1776, 27 April 1773 (i. 113–14, 114, 115–16, 117–18, 121–3).

John Nichols, *Literary Anecdotes of the Eighteenth Century*, 1812–15, prints:

HW to Cole 9 March 1765	i. 659
HW to Cole 4 May 1781 (extract)	i. 696
Cole to HW 7 May 1781 (extract)	i. 697
HW to Cole 19 Aug. 1762	iii. 483–4
HW to Cole 12 Aug. 1769 (misdated)	iv. 706–8
HW to Cole, Cole to HW, 1772 (2 fragments)	viii. 385
HW to Cole 15 Aug. 1774	ix. 711–14

Blackwood's Magazine, 1818–19, prints (some extracts undated or misdated):

HW to Cole 14 Oct. 1778	iv. 40–1
HW to Cole 9 March 1765 (1st and last paragraphs)	iv. 148–9
HW to Cole 11 Oct. 1774 (last paragraph plus 2 sentences)	iv. 149
HW to Cole 1 June 1776 (1st paragraph)	iv. 149
HW to Cole 28 Jan. 1772 (3d paragraph to end)	iv. 149–50
HW to Cole 11 April 1775 (2 paragraphs)	iv. 150
HW to Cole 25 April 1775 (1 paragraph)	iv. 150
Cole to HW 20 April 1775 (extract)	iv. 151
HW to Cole 22 May 1777 (2 paragraphs)	iv. 151
HW to Cole 5 Nov. 1782 (extract attached to 22 May 1777)	iv. 151
HW to Cole 28 March 1779 (1st paragraph omitted)	iv. 151–2
HW to Cole 5 Feb. 1780	iv. 152
HW to Cole 13 March 1780 (last 3 paragraphs omitted)	iv. 153–4
HW to Cole 15 June 1780	iv. 154

Page li, 1st paragraph, last line, *add* (The manuscript of Walpole's letter to Cole of 19 Aug. 1762 is now WSL.)

Page li, note *, right column, line 9, *after* Add MSS *add* 33498

Page lii, 6th paragraph, line 5, *after* publishing them. *add* Colburn died in 1855 and in the following year his widow married John Forster, who died in 1876, leaving his literary collection to the Victoria and Albert Museum. The manuscripts of four original letters have been found at Nostell Priory, Wakefield, Yorks: from Cole 16 May 1762, 31 July 1762, 20 July 1768; and from Robert Masters Aug. 1762 (enclosure).

Page lii, last paragraph, line 3, *after* Walpole, *add* 2 vols,

Page 1, From Cole 16 May 1762, headnote, line 1, *for* The original is missing. *read* The manuscript of the original letter is at Nostell Priory,

Wakefield, Yorks. [The MS contains many variations from Cole's draft; the text is printed here for the first time from a photostat of the MS:]
    Address: To the Honourable Horace Walpole, Esqr. Present.[1]

Blecheley, near Fenny Stratford
May 16, 1762.

Dear Sir,

The extreme pleasure and entertainment I have received from your two late volumes on Painting in England call for my most grateful acknowledgments: indeed it was a continual feast from the beginning to the end: and it is no small satisfaction to think that we are to be favoured with another volume before the entertainment is to be over.

After having said thus much, which truth and gratitude force from me, I must apologize for the present intrusion, and inform you, that in the course of my reading your book, I met with two or three errata, or false printings, which I hope you will excuse me for pointing out, if you have not done it already; as is more probable. With these I have put down two or three trifling observations of another sort; which perhaps might as well have been let alone: yet such as they are I submit them to your candour, where I well know I am safe, and so shall put them down without further ceremony.

Vol. 1, p. 148. In the article of Petruccio Ubaldini, one of his books is there thus entitled, *Le Vite et i Fatti di sei Donne illustri*. Perhaps this may be a different book from one in my possession, which is thus entitled at large,

Le Vite delle Donne illustri del Regno d'Inghilterra & del Regno di Scotia, & di quelle, che d'altri Paesi ne i due detti Regni sono stato maritate. Scritte in Lingua Italiana da Petruccio Ubaldino Cittadin Fiorentino. Londra. Appresso Giovanni Volfio. 1591.—4to. If this is a different book from that which you have given us the title of, my observation is impertinent, as I was apt to suppose it might be the same: however to make the best apology for it, whether right or wrong, if you have not the book already, shall think myself much honoured if you will give it a place in your library: and at the same time will do myself the further honour of bringing it and staying a day or two with you at Strawberry Hill some time before the summer is concluded: a pleasure I should long ago have embraced, as you have been so kind more than once to invite me, was it not for a diffidence and fear of coming unopportunely: and therefore shall take it as a very particular favour, if you would be pleased any time when you are most at leisure to let me know it; as the distance from hence will easily allow me to reach you in one day, and my time always my own.

P. 160. You seem to mention Horatio Palavicini as one concerned in

---

1. 'To deliver or hand a letter, formerly used in addressing a letter'; see OED *sub* 'present,' verb, 11 (d).

the tapestry manufacture; and possibly he might be so: however the constant tradition that prevails about him at the place where he lived, and where I was born, is, that he was collector of the Pope's dues in England in Queen Mary's time, and on her death, and sister's accession, he took the liberty of keeping his master's money, and staying in a country, where, at that time, such a piece of dishonesty would have the public applause, and not be looked upon in the light it deserved. Thus much is certain, that he was owner of the estate and house at Baberham, about five or six miles from Cambridge, where in the hall, on a noble chimney-piece, adorned with the history of Mu. Scaevola, are his arms still remaining: as they were also over the portal of the door of the manor house at Little Shelford, built by him in the Italian taste, with a large piazza or gallery with pillars on the second storey: which house was pulled down about twelve years ago, and a new one erected there by Mr Finch of Cambridge who purchased the estate. The family were all buried at Baberham, as appears by the following entries in the parish register of that village:

> Toby, son of Sir Horatio Palavicini born 20 May and baptized the same day 1593.
> Baptina, dau. of Sir Horace Palavicini bapt. 22 Sept. 1594.
> Horace Palavicini son of Toby Palavicini and Jane his wife bapt. 1 Sept. 1611.
> Tobias son of Toby Palivicini bapt. July 14, 1612.
> James son of Toby Palivicini bapt. 3 Dec. 1620.
> Sir Horace Palavicini died 6 July 1600, his body was buried 17, his funeral kept Aug. 4, 1600.
> Mr Oliver Cromwell and the Lady Anne Palivicini were married July 7, 1601.

By the last entry it appears that Sir Horace's widow paid him that respect as not to marry again till a year after the death of her husband: though it was the very first day after the year was complete. When I was in Cheshire about two or three years ago with my friend Mr John Allen of Trinity College, who had in his custody all the papers of Sir John Crew of Utkinton, a great antiquary and herald, I met with the following MS epitaph upon Sir Horace in one of his books, which for the oddity of it, and as it confirms what I said before of him I will transcribe; more especially as it is not very long:

> Here lyes Horatio Palavazene,
> Who robb'd the Pope to lend the Queene.
> Hee was a Theife: A Theife! thow lyest;
> For whie? Hee robb'd but Antichrist.
> Him Death wyth Besome swept from Babram
> Into the Bosome of oulde Abraham:
> But then came Hercules wyth his Clubb
> And struck him downe to Belzebub.

If we had not the authorities of the registers for Sir Horace's living at Baberham, we were sufficiently informed of that circumstance by that ridiculous fellow, Tom Coryate, whom you have done justice to in your last volumes, and who tells us p. 255, 259, of his *Crudities*, that he met at Mezolt one John Curtabatus, a native of Chiavenna, who spoke pretty good English, having served Sir Horace Palavicini many years in Cambridgeshire. How long before 1593 he was established at Baberham, I know not; but suppose only a short time. That he was in some repute at Court about 1596 is evident, I think, from Lord Arundel of Wardour, as he was afterwards created, his referring his case (on his being clapt up into confinement by the Queen for accepting the title of Count of the Empire) to him and others, in these words in his letter to one of the principal lords of the Court: 'Neither doe I thinke England to be so unfurnished of experienced men, but that either Horatio Pallavicino, Sir Robert Sidney, Mr Dyer, or some other, can witness a truth therein.' This is printed in Peck's *Desiderata Curiosa*, vol. 2, p. 52, lib. 7.

But I have swelled this article out to an immense length: and indeed when I first sat down to write, could I have thought that I should have wrote more in the whole, than I have done in these two articles, I would not have presumed to have troubled you with so much stuff: but antiquaries, as you have observed, love the smallest details.

Vol. 2, p. 21. Sir Francis Crane. About three years ago in my parish was an excellent half-length portrait of him in tapestry, with the collar of St George over his shoulders, as worn in K. Ch.'s time. It is in the possession of a descendant of his, Mrs Markham, a Roman Catholic lady, whose maiden name was Crane: she is now removed out of this parish into Lincolnshire; and has also an exceeding good picture, if it may be so called, in tapestry, of St George slaying the dragon: I suppose them both to be capital pictures of his manufactory.

P. 29. Lady Danvers' tomb at Stow with the nine churches in Northamptonshire. Being at Chester a few years ago, and calling upon the present bishop, his Lordship, knowing my passion for old tombs etc. desired me to look into this church of Stow in my return home, as it was not a mile out of my road; and indeed it amply rewarded me for the trouble of going to see this charming piece of sculpture, which was designed for the Lady Elizabeth Neville, dau. of John Lord Latimer, by Lady Lucy Somerset, dau. of Henry Earl of Worcester: which Lady Eliz. was first married to Sir John Danvers of Dauntesey, and then to Sir Edmund Carey, 3d son of Hen. Lord Hunsdon: she died in 1630, aged 84 years. The lady lies in an half-reclining posture, with her head on a cushion, and her hands in the most natural and easy posture imaginable, with the utmost composure and serenity in her face, as though asleep: her head is dressed in a sort of veil, and she has a robe or mantle over her shoulders in as light and loose and airy a manner as possible: in short I want words to express half the beauties of this monument, so very unlike all I have ever seen; and so much out of the taste of works of this sort. I know of but one in the same style, and which I always concluded was done by the same artist, till I saw by your book, that Stone died in 1647, the same year that this which I allude to was erected in Bassingbourn Church in Cambridgeshire by the Lady Dingley for her bro. Mr Hen. Butler; which is also a most elegant and neat piece of sculpture and probably made by his son. If you should ever pass this way, I dare venture to say you would be pleased with Lady Carey's monument: it is not far from Towcester: and if I knew of any of that lady's family, a plate of that tomb for the present edition of the *Hist. of Northamptonshire* which is now publishing, would do credit to the donor and much adorn that book: though I much question whether any engraver would do it justice. Two or three years ago I wrote to the editor of it to give a particular account of it: but it was too late, that part relating to Stow having been printed off. The reason Mr Vertue calls her Davers, is, I suppose, from his not observing the dash over Dāvers, according to the custom of that age.

P. 34. Saffron Walden is in Essex. The house built by the Earl of Suffolk I suppose occasioned the oversight.

P. 63, vol. 2. It was not in the Cathedral of Salisbury, but in the parish church of St Edmund in that city, that Sherfeild the recorder broke down with his staff a window of painted glass. See Heylin's *Hist. of Archbishop Laud*, p. 217.

To the very curious anecdote in the same page relating to my Lord Grey's being concerned in rewarding the executioner of K. Charles, give me leave to add what I have put down in one of my books concerning that affair.

'At a meeting of the Society of Antiquaries in London, Febr. 6, 1745–6, Ja. West Esqr. produced a curious and authentic account of the beheading of the Royal Martyr. The executioner's name was Ric. Brandon; his attendant, a ragman of Rosemary Lane. The villain received £30 for the hellish job, and refused 20s. for the orange stuck with cloves, which he found in the King's pocket on the scaffold, but took 10s. for it in his way home. These particulars I received from Dr Morell, a member of the Society the next day.'

P. 94. There are at Mr Wright's at Gothurst in this neighbourhood, a seat formerly belonging to Sir Kenelm Digby, several full-length portraits of the Digby family, but of whom, and of what value, I am no judge: yet there is a most elegant bust in brass or copper of the Lady Venetia, with a long inscription on the pediment, which I will copy out the first opportunity. These were left here when Sir Nathan Wright made the purchase of the estate. It is probable the bust is the same with that destroyed in the fire of London.

P. 121. Dr Michael Honeywood was Dean of Lincoln and a great benefactor to the library there. In his printed epitaph it is said that his *grandmother* lived to see 367 persons descended from her. As to the number it must be accurate, as the several persons of each generation being reckoned up make all together 367: else I should not have depended upon my authority.

P. 156. Walker's picture of Oliver is still at Horseth Hall in Cambridgeshire: It was given to the late Lord Montfort by Mr Commissary Greaves, who met with it in some ordinary ale-house or inn in the country.

As you are pleased at p. 112 of your 1st vol. to lament that we have none of our ancient architects whose names are transmitted to posterity, it may probably be some satisfaction to you to meet with one, who was concerned in building the most elegant and noble gothic church in England; I mean the cathedral of Lincoln: for such it is pronounced to be, according to an original letter now by me, by the late Earl of Burlington and Mr Kent, upon their viewing it in their return from York, which they esteemed much inferior to it. The architect's name, or at least of some part of the church, was Richard de Gaynesburgh; but the exact time of his death is uncertain, as that part of the inscription is obliterated. It was lately cleared of the dirt in order to come at the inscription, by the late Mr Sympson, an industrious antiquary of Lincoln, who has collected materials for an history of that place, and was never printed: I have it in one of his letters, and is as follows:

Hic jacet Riccardus de Gaynisburgh olym Cementarius istius Ecclesie qui obiit duodecimō. Kalendarum Junij Anno Domini M.C.C.C....

This gravestone lies in the Cathedral Church of Lincoln.

At p. 146, vol. 1, you seem to say, That the tapestry hangings representing the destruction of the Armada, were put up in the House of Lords in Oliver's time, when that House was made use of for Committees of the Commons: at least I understand you so. If so, how can we account for a print by Hollar, representing Archbishop Laud's trial in the House of Lords in 1645, where those very hangings are represented by references of the *letter T* as being the hangings of '88. This print is the frontispiece of a book printed by Prynne in 1645, called *Hidden Works of Darknesse brought to publicke Light, or a necessary Introduction to the History of the Archbishop of Canterbury's Tryal*. London. Folio. 1645.

Dear Sir, I once more beg pardon for so much impertinence, and beg leave to subscribe myself, Sir,

Your most obedient and obliged humble servant,
WM COLE

Page 1, note 2, *add* For Joseph Highmore's appreciation of the *Anecdotes*, see his letter to Sir Edward Walpole in May 1762 (misdated 1764) and Sir Edward's reply of 4 May 1762, printed in GM 1816, lxxxvi pt i. 203–4.

Page 2, line 7, *on* 1591. *add note* 3a: 3a. For HW's two copies of this book, see Hazen, *Cat. of HW's Lib*. Nos 2322, 3385.

Page 3, note 11, *add* Mr Francis Russell of East Hanney Grange, Wantage, Berks, informs us that, instead of William Ingle Finch, Cole means William Finch Ingle (ca 1757–1826), son of William Ingle (d. 1767) of Shelford, Cambs; Harrow School; Queen's College, Oxon., 1774; Emmanuel College, Cantab., 1775; who on inheriting the house at Shelford changed his name by licence to William Finch Finch, 5 June 1778 (see also Venn, *Alumni Cantab.*, Part II, 1752–1900, iii. 519).

Page 4, note 14, line 4, *for* at the time of his death *read* in 1754 (see GRAY ii. 78).

Page 5, note 17, *add* For HW's copy of *Coryats Crudities*, 1611, see Hazen, *Cat. of HW's Lib.* No. 1317.

Page 5, note 19, *add* For HW's copy of Francis Peck's *Desiderata Curiosa*, 1732–5, see Hazen, *Cat. of HW's Lib.* No. 578.

Page 6, note 24, *add* The tapestry of Sir Francis Crane was formerly on loan at the Victoria and Albert Museum, where there is a photograph of it (negative 13549) with the caption, 'Photograph of a piece of tapestry, woven with the portrait of Sir Francis Crane. . . . This tapestry was made at Mortlake and it is now the property of Lord Petre' (WSL also has a photograph, described as 'Tapestry, woven in coloured worsteds on flax warp with a portrait of Sir Francis Crane, of the Mortlake factory').

Page 7, note 36, *add* William John Monson, 6th Lord Monson, in *Lincolnshire Church Notes* says that 'An account-book of Stone's, containing details of many such works, which had been purchased by Horace Walpole, was sold at the Strawberry Hill sale to Sir John Soane, and is now in the Soane museum, Lincoln's Inn Fields' (*Lincolnshire Church Notes*, ed. 9th Lord Monson, Lincoln Record Society, vol. xxxi, Hereford, 1936, p. 82). HW in *Anecdotes of Painting* (1762, ii. 24–8, 32–3) quotes from Vertue's copy of Stone's notebook and account book, but there is no evidence that HW owned the originals of these MSS. The four MS notebooks of the Stone family in the Soane Museum had been in the possession of George Vertue, then James Paine, then Paine's son, and after his death were purchased by Sir John Soane at Christie's in March 1830 (see *The Note-Book and Account Book of Nicholas Stone*, ed. W. L. Spiers from the Soane MSS, in *Walpole Society*, 1919, vii. 35).

Page 7, note 40, *add* The invitation to accompany HW is not in the manuscript letter sent to HW.

Page 8, note 49, *for* 1704? *read* 1703

Page 9, note 53, line 1, *for* Wright *read* Wrighte   *for* ca 1703 *read* ca 1706   *Line* 2, *for* Wright *read* Wrighte

Page 9, note 55, *after* Venetia *insert* Anastasia

Page 10, note 65, *for* 1695 *read* 1694

Page 10, note 68, *add* See William Richardson to Charles Lyttelton 11 March 1762 for a biographical note on Thomas Sympson the elder; and Thomas Sympson the younger to William Richardson 6 March 1762 for a later reading of the Gaynsbourgh inscription (MISC. CORR. i. 233–5).

Page 11, note 69, *add* The print is also the frontispiece to Prynne's *Canterburies Doome. Or the First Part of a Compleat History of the Commitment, Charge, Tryall, Condemnation, Execution of William Laud Late Arch-Bishop of Canterbury*, 1646 (information from the late Lindsay Fleming).

Page 12, note 4, *add* For an identification of the sheets see Hazen, *SH Bibl.* 59.

Page 12, note 5, *add* A second copy, T.4, sold SH v. 8, is now WSL (Hazen, *Cat. of HW's Lib.* Nos 2322, 3385).

Page 13, note 6, line 16, *after* 27348–50. *add* See Hazen, *Cat. of HW's Lib.* No. 3503.

Page 13, note 7, *substitute* Bishop Lyttelton with his letter of ca 12 March 1762 sent HW a packet containing letters from William Richardson and Thomas Sympson the younger. Sympson writes, 'I have sent my reading [of the inscription] corrected by my father's which was taken upwards of 20 years ago when perhaps it was more intelligible' (*Misc. Corr.* i. 234).

Page 14, From Cole 31 July 1762, headnote, *add* The manuscript of the original letter is at Nostell Priory, Wakefield, Yorks. [The MS contains many variations from Cole's draft; the text is printed here for the first time from a photostat of the MS:]

Endorsed (by HW, in pencil): Not inserted yet.

                                                    Blecheley, July 31, 1762.
Dear Sir,

The favour of yours of the 29 instant I received yesterday; and as our post goes not out till tomorrow, though I write my answer now, it won't go forward till then. I am sorry to hear Strawberry Hill is in the same state with us in this part of the country, where there is not a blade of grass to be seen, and hardly any water for the cattle: we have been daily tantalized with rain; but not a drop has fallen here; though, by accounts, other places have had very plentiful showers.

I am sorry particular business prevents my waiting on you so soon as you mention: I am detained here all next week, and am obliged to be in Cambridgeshire the beginning of the following, where I am informed that one of my tenants is going to break; which I fancy will be the case with many this year: however I propose myself the pleasure of being with you for a day or two about the 11 or 12 of August, if that time should be agreeable to you, and not interfere with any of your engagements: in case it should, a line here would find me all next week, or at Mr Newcombe's at Hackney about the 9th or 10th of August.

On a second perusal of your book, I have made a few further observations, which I am emboldened to communicate as I have your orders for it: not that I think them of any sort of consequence any further than as they serve to illustrate a subject which has received no small honour by your condescending to treat of.

Vol. 1, p. 2.—St Wolstan, the famous Bishop of Worcester in 1062, is recorded by his historian, William of Malmsbury (who wrote his life in three books) as a proficient in the art of limning, long before the Conquest: his master's name is also transmitted to us by the historian, which was Ervenius, or Erwen. This life is published by Mr Wharton in *Anglia Sacra*, vol. 2, p. 241, and as it is possible that you mayn't have the book, I will transcribe what he says on the subject.

Habebat [Wolstanus] tunc Magistrum Ervenium Nomine, in Scribendo et quidlibet Coloribus Effingendo peritum. Is Libros scriptos, Sacramentarium et Psalterium, quorum principales Literas Auro effigiaverit, Puero Wulstano delegandos curavit. Ille preciosorum Apicum captus Miraculo, dum Pulchritudinem intentis Oculis rimatur, et Scientiam Literarum internis hausit Medullis. Verum Doctor ad Sæculi spectans Commodum, Spe majoris Præmii, Sacramentarium Regi, tunc Temporis Cnutoni, Psalterium Emmæ Reginæ contribuit. Perculit puerilem Animum Facti Dispendium, et ex imo Pectore alta traxit Suspiria.

If this does not absolutely determine St Wolstan to be a proficient in limning himself; yet it is quite clear for his Saxon master Erwen. Dr Patrick in his quotation of this passage in his supplement to Mr Gunton's *History of Peterborough*, p. 259, has made two or three considerable blunders. He calls the author of this MS life of St Wolstan, Bravonius; which indeed was only the old name of the city of Worcester: he was led into this mistake by the MS, in Sir John Cotton's Library, having Senatus Bravonius wrote on it in a modern hand. Now Senatus Bravonius, or Senatus Wigorniensis as Bale calls him Cent. 3, No. X, was Prior of Worcester from 1189, to 1196. But William of Malmsbury was the true author of this MS, as Mr Wharton evidently shows in the preface to *Anglia Sacra*, vol. 2, p. xv. Neither did Eruentus, as he calls him, for Ervenius, make St Wolstan write the Sacramentary and Psalter: he only sent them to him for his perusal and curiosity; or lent them to him before he sent them to Court; Ervenius himself being the illuminator or limner of the drawings, as is evident from the quotation above.

Vol. 1, p. 45.—In the Golden Register of all the benefactors to the Abbey of St Albans, Alan Strayler, their painter or limner, is commemorated, as remitting to the Abbey 3s. 4d. owing to him for colours, in this manner

Nomen Pictoris Alanus Strayler habetur
Qui sine Fine Choris celestibus associetur.

This is recorded in Weever's *Funeral Monuments* p. 578, and I see you have mentioned him as a limner at p. 16 of your first volume, so probably you took it from the same place.

Vol. 1, p. 99.—In the archives of Caius College in Cambridge, formerly communicated to me by the present master, Sir James Burrough, is the following particular, relating to the architect of King's College Chapel:

To alle Christen People this present writyng endented seeng, redyng or heryng, John Wulrich, Maistre Mason of the Werkes of the Kyngs College Roial of our Lady & Seynt Nicholas of Cambrigge, John Bell, Mason Wardeyn in the same Werkes, Richard Adam, & Rob. Dogett, Carpenters, Arbitrours indifferently chosen by the reverent Fader in God, Edward, by the Grace of God, Bysshopp of Karlyle, Mr. or Wardeyn of the Hous or College of St. Michael of Cambr. & the Scolers of the same on the oon Part, & Maistre Henry Cossey, Warden of the College or Hall of the Annuntiation or Gonville Hall, & the Fellowes & Scolers of the same, on the other Part, Of & Upon the Evesdroppe into the Garden of Ffysshwyke Hostle, belonging to Gonville Halle &c.—Written at Cambr. 17 Aug. 1476. 16 Edw. 4.

In Hearne's preface to the *History of Glastonbury*, p. lxv, is this further account of another architect of that most stately and elegant structure:

All that see King's College Chapel in Cambridge are struck with Admiration, & most are mighty desirous of knowing the Architect's Name. Yet few can tell it. It appears, however, from their Books at King's College (as I am informed by my Friend Mr. Baker, the learned Antiquary of Cambridge) that one Mr. Cloos (Father of Nicholas Cloos, one of the first Fellows of that College, & afterwards Bishop of Lichfeild) was the Architect of this Chapel (tho' Godwin says the Bishop himself was Master of the King's Works here) as far as Henry the 6th's Share reacheth, & Contriver or Designer of the whole, afterwards finished by Henry 7th & further beautified by Henry the 8.

In a MS account of all the members of King's College, a copy of which is in my possession, Bishop Nicholas Close is mentioned as a person, in whose 'Capacity King Henry 6 (who had placed him in Fellow in 1443) had such Confidence, that he appointed him Overseer & Manager of all his intended Buildings & Designs for this College.' And in the same MS historiette of King's College, John Canterbury, a native of Tewksbury and Fellow of the College in 1451, is said to have been Clerk of the Works for the building of the same.

Vol. 1, p. 112.—In St Michael's Church at St Albans are, or were, the following inscriptions for an architect of the same age:

Hic jacet Thomas Wolvey (or Wolven) Latonius in Arte, necnon Armiger illustrissimi Principis Ric[ardi] secundi quondam Regis Anglie, qui obiit Anno Dom. M.C.C.C.C.XXX. in vigilia Sancti Thome Martyris. Cujus Anime propitietur Deus. Amen.

'This Man, as far as I understand by this Inscription (says Weever, p. 582) was the Master Mason or Surveior of the King's Stone Works: as also Esquire to the King's Person.'

Hic jacet Richardus Wolven (or Wolvey) Lathonius, Filius Johannis Wolven, cum Uxoribus suis Agnete et Agnete, et cum octo Filiis et decem Filiabus suis, qui Richardus obiit . . . An. 1490. Quorum Animabus, &c—

Vol. 2, p. 18.—It is very probable that an half-length portrait of Bishop Felton, with his arms impaled by those of the see of Ely, and ensigned by a mitre, and which I made a present of to the late Sir Thomas Gooch, Bishop of Ely to be hung up in the gallery in the Palace at Ely, is by this Edward Norgate. The head is excellently well finished, and full of life: but the lawn and drapery stiff. It formerly belonged to Sclater Bacon Esqr. Member for the town of Cambridge, and I bought it, with other pictures out of his collection, at the sale of his goods at Catley in Cambridgeshire. There is a picture of Bishop Felton in the library of Pembroke Hall, not comparable to this.

Vol. 2, p. 22. I was lately told by a friend of mine, that Sir Francis Crane was buried at a village near Norwich, and near Mr Gurdon's of Letton; but he could not recollect the name.

Vol. 2, p. 17.—The observation of Mr Edmund Chishull, B.D. Chaplain to the English factory at Smyrna is very ingenious, with regard to the art of staining glass, in his *Travels in Turkey*, p. 6, where he observes, that this art was revived in that country, in this manner:

> It seemed strange to us to observe several pieces of painted glass in the windows of our *effendi's* house, inscribed in Turkish characters, with the name of the proprietor, together with some religious sentences of Mahometan devotion. But we were much more surprized, when we were informed, that it was the manufacture of this place [Magnesia]; for it is stained with a beautiful, as well as deep and durable colour, and comes up to the perfection of the best we have seen in England. This gave us occasion to reflect on the different fortune of arts and sciences, which, like men, seem to take delight in shifting their station: for while other arts have now left these places, and travelled westward, this alone in exchange for all the rest, seems to have retired into this, and is deplored as lost in Christendom.

And at p. 8, he observes:

> The windows of their mosques are furnished with excellent painted glass, full of flower work, and religious inscriptions. But as their *religion* forbids the making of representations of men, so by that injunction, the chief beauty of that art is of no benefit to them: inasmuch as it deprives them of the use of history-painting; the most excellent of all in that art.

In 1746, being at Glocester, the then worthy Bishop Dr Martin Benson, showed me his small and elegant chapel in the Palace, the east window of which in painted glass representing our Lord's ascension very beautifully finished, cost the Bishop £150 and was probably the work of Price: but of this I am not sure.

See an account of several painted windows in the chapels of the two universities, and at Fairford, in Dr Wilson's *Ornaments of Churches Considered*, printed in 1761, 4to, Appendix No. X, p. 32, as also the Postscript printed in 1762, p. 6, where he intimates a design of publishing an account of all the painted glass windows, of any esteem, now remaining in England and Ireland.

Vol. 2, p. 133.—Query if Raphael de Rouvigny, should not be Rachael?

Dear Sir, I hope you'll excuse all this scribble: I am sure if I don't tire you, I have myself, as this hot weather disagrees much with my constitution, and therefore will put an end to it by assuring you of my most sincere and unfeigned regard, and am, Sir,

Your most faithful servant,
WM COLE

Page 16, note 8, *add* HW's copy, now WSL, is Hazen, *Cat. of HW's Lib.* No. 594.

Page 17, note 13, *add* HW's copy of John Weever's *Ancient Funerall Monuments*, 1631, is Hazen, *Cat. of HW's Lib.* No. 643.

Page 17, note 17, *add* HW's copy, now WSL, is Hazen, *Cat. of HW's Lib.* No. 658.

Page 19, note 29, right column, line 1, *for* 1664 *read* ?1664   Line 2, *after* Cambridge *insert* Jan.–May 1715,

Page 22, headnote, *delete* The whereabouts of the original is not known. *add* The manuscript of the enclosure meant for HW is at Nostell Priory, Wakefield, Yorks. [The manuscript contains many variations from the text printed in Nichols, *Lit. Anec.* iii. 482; printed here for the first time from a photostat of the MS:]

Mr Masters has perused *the Anecdotes of Painting* you was so obliging as to lend him with great pleasure, and finds he has in his possession one of those miniatures of Hen. VII described in Vol. 1, p. 46, viz. that with the Red Rose in his hand, being 14 inches by 10 1/2. This is undoubtedly a picture of that time and in its original frame, which if worth Mr Walpole's acceptance (as a collector of such curiosities) is much at his service.

In p. 145 there must surely be some mistake in the sum paid for the tapestry, since at 10*l*. 1*s*. per ell it amounts to 7115*l*. 8*s*.

In p. 164 Mr Walpole mentions a monument and bust erected to the memory of Sir Nathaniel Bacon in the Church of Culford, which if true, there must have been two monuments, since there is certainly one at Stiffkey in Norfolk; where he built the Hall and was interred as his epitaph sets forth. See Masters *Hist. of CCCC.* App. p. 85.

The Kings in Chichester Cathedral p. 102, said to be repainted by Tremayne were done at the expense of the Bishop Matt. Mawson.

In Vol. II, p. 58 mention is made of the first lecture of Geography read at Sir Balthazar Gerbier's Academy, which may indeed be the first on that subject, but not the first read there, since Mr Masters has, 'The Art of well speaking, being a lecture read gratis at Sir Balthazar Gerbier's Academy,' and which in the Dedication *to the right high and supreme power of this Nation, the Parliament of England* etc. dat. 6 Jan. 1649, he expressly styles his first lecture. He has likewise a print of him different both in person and dress from that in the book, which has the motto *Heureux qui en Dieu se confie* under it and in the oval *D. Balthazar Gerbierius Eques auratus*, with a medal hanging on his left side, but no C. R. 1653 upon it; nor does he comprehend how a person that dedicated his Works to the Parliament in 1649, could be so much in favour with the King, as to be presented with a medal in 1653, so that he suspects the date must be wrong.

Mr Masters has part of a collection of painters etc. the last number of which is 116 painted by different hands, but chiefly engraved by Pet. de Jode and printed by Meyssens, which does not seem to be either of the collections spoken of in p. 90. Amongst these Henry Van der Borcht taken notice of in p. 73 is the 89th—Corn. Poulenbourgh 84th—

In p. 116, Nic. Laniere is said to have died in 1646 and yet to have been a purchaser of pictures in the sale of the King's goods, which could not have been begun before 1648. See p. 64.

Mr Masters has a pretty good picture of the Duchess of Richmond mentioned at p. 132, with this inscription on the frame—'Frances Dutchess of Richmond and Lenox, Daughter of Thomas Lord Howard of Binden, who was second son to Thomas Duke of Norfolk, whose mother was the Lady Elizabeth Stafford eldest daughter of Edward Duke of Buckingham. Her Grace was born 27 Jul. 1577. London 1633.' She is drawn in black with a very fine lawn ruff and handkerchief and many strings of pearls about her neck. On her left side hangs a miniature of her husband probably, very well done, her right hand is supported by her fan and on a small table to the left is placed her coronet—Question whether this may not be the picture by Petitot Vertue speaks of?

Page 23, note 3, line 1, *for* (fl. 1640) *read* (1585–1627)   *Line 2, after* Bt *insert* (see Lord Grimston to HW 8 May 1761, MISC. CORR. i. 193–4) *Last line, add* HW's copy is Hazen, *Cat. of HW's Lib.* No. 632.

Page 24, headnote, line 2, *for* here. *read* here; acquired by WSL in 1949.

Page 24, note 10, line 2, *after* yr *insert* In the manuscript this sentence belongs to the previous paragraph and reads: 'Amongst these Henry Van der Borcht taken notice of in p. 73 is the 89th—Corn. Poulenbourgh 84th—'

Page 24, note 12, line 1, *for* ca 1573 *read* ca 1576   *Line 5, for* and Richmond *read*   , 1583, cr. (1613) Bn of Settrington and E. of Richmond and (1623) E. of Newcastle-upon-Tyne and D. of Richmond.

Page 25, headnote, line 1, *after* 'original' *insert* (now WSL; it was sold by Puttick and Simpson 19 March 1850, No. 403, bought then by Holloway, 21/)

Page 26, note 5, *add* The portrait was painted by Marcus Gheeraerts, and is mentioned in HW to Lord Buchan 17 June 1786 (see DALRYMPLE 191, n. 18).

Page 26, note 6, *add* See Hazen, *Cat. of HW's Lib.* No. 910.

Page 27, note 3, line 10, *for* Mary *read* Maria

Page 28, note 1, line 7, *for* f. 149 *read* f. 76; this MS has two sets of foliation numbers.

Page 28, illustration, caption, *for* 1781 or 1783 *read* 1781 or 1782

Page 30, note 3, line 1, *delete* Probably   *Line 3, add* See HW to Lord Buchan 17 June 1786, DALRYMPLE 191, n. 17.

Page 31, note 5, *add* HW's copy is Hazen, *Cat. of HW's Lib.* No. 11.

Page 32, note 2, *for first sentence substitute* Said to have been painted by Jan Gossaert, called Mabuse (see Maurice W. Brockwell, *The 'Adoration of the Magi' by Jan Mabuse*, 1911, pp. 42–3).

Page 34, note 1, line 1, *for* 1719 *read* 1718

Page 35, note 6, *add* See Hazen, *SH Bibl.* 49.

Page 36, note 9, *add* G. M. Young in a review of COLE in the *Observer* 5 Dec. 1937 (p. 4) says that 'as *vidimus* is used in late medieval Latin in the sense of opinion or view, it probably here means "a design seen and approved." '

Page 38, note 4, *add* Cole's copy, inscribed by him, 'Wm Cole, ex Donis hon. Autoris Horatii Walpole 1762' is now in the Bodleian Library (Hazen, *SH Bibl.* 37).

Page 39, note 11, line 1, *for* 1581 *read* ca 1581

Page 39, note 12, *add* See Hazen, *SH Bibl.* 31–3.

Page 40, note 14, *add* For Cole's copy see Hazen, *SH Bibl.* 46.

Page 40, note 17, *add* See Hazen, *SH Bibl.* 41.

Page 43, note 6, *add* HW's copy is Hazen, *Cat. of HW's Lib.* No. 685.

Page 44, note 1, line 3, *for* 87 *read* 86

Page 47, note 2, *add* HW's copy is Hazen, *Cat. of HW's Lib.* No. 304.

Page 50, note 8, line 1, *for* 1622 *read* 1623

Page 52, note 4, lines 4, 5, *for* Phillips *read* Philipps

Page 52, note 6, *substitute* John Shorter, Jr had died in 1746, when Arthur was still living (see CONWAY i. 224, 255, 256, 372–3); Erasmus died in 1753 (MONTAGU i. 156–7; CONWAY i. 372–3). It was not one of HW's uncles who was the Shorter who died in 1734; GM 1734, iv. 627, calls him 'a near relation of Sir Robert Walpole's Lady.'

Page 52, note 8, line 2, *for* 1727 *read* 1728

Page 52, note 9, *add* The verses were also published in the *St James's Chronicle* 3–6 Nov. 1770.

Page 53, note 1, *add* For Joseph Highmore's suggested additions for vol. iii of the *Anecdotes* see his letter to Sir Edward Walpole 28 Feb.–3 March 1764, and Sir Edward's reply of 15 March 1764, printed in GM 1816, lxxxvi pt i. 300–4.

Page 54, note 3, line 5, *add* HW's copy of *A Catalogue . . .* is Hazen, *Cat. of HW's Lib.* No. 287; HW's copies of *Typographical Antiquities*, 1749 and 1785–90 are now WSL (ibid. Nos 29, 261).

Page 56, note 1, right column, lines 6–7, *for* now in the Folger Library *read* now WSL   *Right column, line 12, for* William *read* W[illiam]   *Last line, add* For full information about the preparation and publication of Granger's work, see Hazen, *Bibl. of HW* 130–6; *Cat. of HW's Lib.* Nos 541, 3813.

Pages 57–8, note 5, line 4, *after* 104. *add* See Hazen, *Cat. of HW's Lib.* No. 1616.

Page 58, note 6, *add* HW's copy is Hazen, *Cat. of HW's Lib.* No. 3222: 5:7.

Page 59, note 5, *substitute* Cole offered one of his two copies of *A Brief and True History of Sir Robert Walpole*, 1738, to HW. It was a re-issue, with a cancel title-page, of William Musgrave's *Genuine Memoirs of the Life and Character of Sir Robert Walpole . . .* , 1732; see Hazen, *Cat. of HW's Lib.* No. 2432.

Page 59, line 21, *on* lottery *add note* 7: 7. The second stake lottery of 1763 (see C. L'Estrange Ewen, *Lotteries and Sweepstakes*, 1932, p. 158).

Page 60, note 2, *delete first sentence and substitute* HW had the first edition, 1732, entitled *Genuine Memoirs of the Life and Character of Sir Robert Walpole and of the Family of the Walpoles* (see Hazen, *Cat. of HW's Lib.* Nos 2432, 2458).

Page 60, note 4, line 6, *for* 1685 *read* 1686   *Lines 7–11, delete* 20 Feb. . . . Cottrell sale). *and substitute* 19–28 Jan. 1764 (Frits Lugt, *Répertoire des catalogues de ventes publiques*, La Haye, 1938–64; DALRYMPLE 92 and n. 5). On 9 March at the second Cottrell Dormer sale HW bought Thuanus, *Historia sui temporis*, 7 vols extended to 14, lot 2590 (CONWAY ii. 340, n. 2; Hazen, *Cat. of HW's Lib.* No. 3556).

Pages 60–1, note 5, *add* See also Hazen, *Cat. of HW's Lib.* No. 3643.

Page 62, note 3, lines 9–10, *for Forerunners of Revenge*, 1642 *read Fore-runner of Revenge*, Frankfort, 1626 and London, 1642, a MS copy of which is listed in Hazen, *Cat. of HW's Lib.* No. 2576; see also GRAY ii. 133, n. 4.

Page 62, note 5, *for* Sunday — March 1764. *read* Sunday ?18 March 1764, GRAY ii. 133 and n. 4.

Page 62, note 7, *after* 1757 *add*   , CONWAY i. 498, n. 12

Page 65, note 2, *add* See also CONWAY ii. 340, n. 2.

Pages 66–7, note 4, *add* See Hazen, *SH Bibl.* 68–72.

Page 67, note 3, *delete first sentence and substitute* Cole's copy of Gray's letter of 7 July 1764 containing the recipe is in BM Add. MS 5825, ff. 283b, 284b; the recipe was printed in 'Coliana; Consisting of Selections of the curious MSS bequeathed by the late Mr Cole to the British Museum, and lately opened,' in *Monthly Magazine*, 1804, xvii pt i. 550; pointed out by H. W. Starr, ' "Pot-pourri": A Missing Gray Letter,' TLS 30 March 1951.

Page 67, note 4, *add* See also John Pinkerton, *An Essay on Medals,* 2d edn, 1789, ii. 178.

Page 70, note 2, *add* HW's copy, 3d edn, 1656, is Hazen, *Cat. of HW's Lib.* No. 167.

Page 70, note 5, *add* In his presentation copy of the *Life,* now in the library of King's College, Cambridge, Cole wrote 'wooden' above 'woollen' (information from John B. Hoey).

Page 71, note 10, *add* See N&Q 22 March 1941, clxxx. 209.

Page 71, note 12, *add* HW's copy of the 1742 issue is Hazen, *Cat. of HW's Lib.* No. 645.

Page 73, note 3, *for* 1699 *read* 1609

Page 75, note 9, *add* See Hazen, *Cat. of HW's Lib.* No. 588.

Page 78, note 1, lines 4–9, *delete* doubtless ... *Jour. Print. Off. and substitute* probably the 2d edition of volume iii of *Anecdotes of Painting,* since HW writes to Cole 8 Nov. that 'it is printed to past the middle of the third volume' (COLE i. 83). Hazen dates the preparation of *Additional Lives* 'in the summer or autumn of 1767' (Hazen, *SH Bibl.* 61; see also p. 62).

Page 79, note 1, *delete last sentence*

Page 80, note 3, *add* See Hazen, *SH Bibl.* 191–4; *Cat. of HW's Lib.* No. 3469:6.

Page 80, note 1, *add* See Hazen, *Cat. of HW's Lib.* No. 1614.

Page 81, note 7, line 3, *for* 52 *read* 51

Page 81, note 9, line 2, *after* Torrigiano *insert or* Torrigiani (1472–1528)

Page 85, note 3, *add* See Hazen, *Bibl. of HW* 52–4.

Page 88, note 3, line 1, *for* Cary *read* Carey   *for* (d. 1633) *read* (ca 1575–1633)

Page 88, note 3, *add* See also 'Book of Materials,' 1759, i. 63–4, where HW describes a dream 1 May 1760 in which a portrait of Richard II steps from its frame (printed in *Blackwood's Magazine,* 1927, ccxxi. 454–6).

Page 89, note 8, *delete* HW's copy ... WSL. *and substitute* HW's presentation copy of this edition was not in the 1842 sale, and presumably HW gave it away. The 2d edition, 3 vols, 1767 (now WSL) was sold SH v. 240. The 4th edition, 3 vols, 1794 (now WSL) was sold SH v. 141. See Hazen, *Cat. of HW's Lib.* Nos 2919, 3455.

Page 90, note 14, *substitute* Marie-Catherine Le Jumel de Barneville (1650 *or* 1651–1705), m. (ca 1665) François de la Motte, Baron d'Aulnoy (CHUTE 49, n. 4). HW owned a translation of her book, *Tales of the Fairies,* 3 vols, 1721 (Hazen, *Cat. of HW's Lib.* No. 1776).

Page 96, note 4, line 1, *for* French Parliament *read* Parlement de Paris *Line 5, add* See also CONWAY ii. 339, n. 4.

Page 99, From Cole 31 October 1765, headnote, *for* Rue de Colombier *read* Rue du Colombier

Page 99, middle of page, *insert the following heading*:

FROM COLE, Monday 4 November 1765

Missing; mentioned in *Jour. to Paris* 157: 'I wrote to Mr Walpole to excuse my waiting upon him to the Luxemburg Palace, and stayed within all day.'

Page 99, From Cole 5 Jan. 1766, Address, *for* A *read* À

Page 101, note 4, line 3, *for* cr. (1733) Bn Hervey of Ickworth *read* styled Bn Hervey of Ickworth, 1733

Page 104, From Cole 11 Feb. 1766, headnote, line 3, *for* A *read* À

Page 105, note 4, line 2, *after* goole *add*   , Drumgold   *for* 1720 *read* 1718   *Line 6, for* Nivernois *read* Nivernais   *Line 14, add* See also Richard Hayes, *Biographical Dictionary of Irishmen in France,* Dublin, 1949, pp. 73–4; *Dictionnaire de biographie française,* 1933– , xi. 795–6.

Page 105, note 6, *add* See Cole to Father Bedingfield 2 Aug. 1767, as quoted in Sir Henry Ellis, *Original Letters of Eminent Literary Men,* 1843, p. 403.

Page 106, note 9, *for* Charles William Ferdinand *read* Karl Wilhelm Ferdinand

Page 106, note 10, *for* Charles George Augustus *read* Karl Georg August

Page 108, note 20, *add* See F. J. B. Watson, 'Walpole and the Taste for French Porcelain in Eighteenth-Century England,' in *Horace Walpole: Writer, Politician, and Connoisseur,* ed. W. H. Smith, New Haven, 1967, pp. 189–91. Cole confuses the Saint-Cloud manufactory with the Sèvres manufactory; these were entirely separate organizations (ibid. 189, n. 16).

Page 110, note 3, *substitute* George Forbes (1740–80), styled Vct Forbes 19 June 1765 upon the death of his grandfather, Lord Granard; 5th E. of Granard, 1769. He was in Paris in June 1765 (CONWAY ii. 575–6) and also in Jan. 1766, when he was courting Lady Georgiana Berkeley (see *The Beautiful Lady Craven,* ed. A. M. Broadley and L. Melville, 1914, i. 17–20; DU DEFFAND v. 294); on 22 April 1766 he and Lady Georgiana were married in London (*Daily Adv.* 23 April; GM 1766, xxxvi. 198). The race in Paris is reported in *Daily Adv.* 12 March 1766 and *Gazette de Leyde,* No. xix, 7 March 1766, Supp., and No. xx, 11 March 1766, Supp.

Page 110, note 5, *substitute* I.e., he has come to Paris to see a horse-race, when they often occur two miles from his home, and thus he may yet see a review in Lapland, when he has not troubled to see those at Hounslow—'it is one of those things one never does, because one always may,' as HW writes to Cole 21 July 1764 (see also MONTAGU i. 189).

Page 110, note 7, *add* See also CONWAY iii. 43 and nn. 10, 11.

Page 118, note 1, line 9, *for* 12–5 *read* 12–15

Page 124, note 3, *before* Selina *insert* Lady

Page 124, note 4, line 1, *for* Madam *read* Madan

Page 124, note 5, *add* See also Hazen, *Bibl. of HW* 69–74.

Page 126, note 4, line 4, *after* Notes'). *add* In HW's copy (now WSL) he added below the date, 'August 25' (Hazen, *Cat. of HW's Lib*. No. 1609: 15:6).   *Line 13, after* 1767 *add* (HW's copy is ibid. No. 1609:17:10).

Pages 127–8, note 1, *add* See Hazen, *SH Bibl*. 68.

Page 130, note 10, *add* HW's copy, now WSL, is Hazen, *Cat. of HW's Lib*. No. 999.

Page 133, note 1, *add* See also Sandwich to HW 17 Feb. 1768, in MISC. CORR. ii. 134–5.

Page 133, note 3, line 7, after tone. *insert* The English version is (1956) BM Add. MS 48,976; the later Latin version has been *penes* College of Arms since 1786. See C. E. Wright, 'The Rous Roll: the English Version,' *British Museum Quarterly*, 1955–6, xx. 77–81.

Page 134, note 8, line 8, *after* 29. *add* See Hazen, *Cat. of HW's Lib*. No. 1261.

Page 134, note 9, line 7, *for* now in the Folger Library *read* now WSL. See *post* COLE i. 137–8, 147–8, 194 for Cole's contribution.

Page 136, note 5, right column, line 2, *for* 1478–86 *read* 1479–86

Page 139, line 1, on *Françoise add note* 13a: 13a. HW had an English translation, *Royal and Ecclesiastical Antiquities of France*, 2 vols, 1750 (Hazen, *Cat. of HW's Lib*. No. 3683).

Page 140, note 20, line 2, *after* 468 *add* (Hazen, *Cat. of HW's Lib*. No. 883)

Page 140, note 22, line 4, *after* 475 *add* (Hazen, *Cat. of HW's Lib*. No. 694)

Page 141, note 30, line 3, *after* 1713). *add* HW's copy is Hazen, *Cat. of HW's Lib*. No. 585.

Page 141, note 32, *substitute* Joseph Brown (ca 1720–1800), self-taught landscape painter of Norwich (John Chambers, *General History of . . . Norfolk*, 1829, p. 1071). Presumably the man painted by Kerrich and engraved by Facins (EBP). Benjamin Stillingfleet wrote to William Windham 16 Dec. 1754 of visiting Brown at Norwich (unpublished letter at Felbrigg Hall, Norfolk, provided, with other information, by the late R. W. Ketton-Cremer).

Page 144, note 1, line 5, *after* 1767 *add*   ; Hazen, *Cat. of HW's Lib*. No. 3274

Page 145, From Cole 20 July 1768, headnote, line 1, *add* The manuscript of the original letter is at Nostell Priory, Wakefield, Yorks. [The manuscript contains many variations from Cole's draft and includes the two letters from the University of Cambridge to King Richard III; it is printed here for the first time:]

Waterbeche, July 20, 1768.

Dear Sir,

I foresee I shall tease you with a tedious long letter, and therefore take paper accordingly. I should answer your obliging kind letter of June 6 much sooner, but don't love to take up your time, nor burthen you with writing answers. I am greatly obliged to you for your kind invitation to Strawberry Hill, and am as sensible of the favour as any one can be: but my present uncertain situation makes it not convenient to go from this place: when I am fully settled I shall be more my own master: and even this summer, if I can find leisure for two or three days' excursion will embrace to pay my respects to you, on many accounts: I long to see you yourself: I long to see your Gallery, which was not finished when I was with you last: with many other things only to be seen at Strawberry Hill. I am upon the eve of fixing either at Milton or Ely: I go tomorrow, for two or three days to the last place to look at a little dwelling offered me there: but my mind is more for Milton, as it lies so convenient for Cambridge, only three miles and an half, on a fine road. Ely, at present, would afford me much amusement: for they are going to do great things there: the Bishop has offered them £1000 to ornament the Cathedral, in case the Chapter will give as much for the same purpose: this is complied with; and they are going to remove their choir from under the great lanthorn or cupola, and lay that part all open, and to place the choir beyond it, in a part of the church they call the presbytery. As this will occasion great rummaging among the tombs and antiquities there, it would occasion me constant amusement. They talk of employing Pecket in their east window, and placing their organ immediately under it, and above their altar-piece, as it is at Versailles. If you should not have already from the Bishop of Carlisle heard an account of what they have done at Exeter very lately in that way, it may be acceptable to you: Mr Betham of our College, who has lately been there, and sent me from thence the following account, which I send in his words.

> I forget whether you have ever been at Exeter. The cathedral there is greatly ornamented: the choir all paved: the stalls too all new, and the organ. The west window within these two years has been decorated with painted glass, by Mr Pecket of York, so as to be greatly admired. It contains seven of the Apostles at full length. Saints Peter, Matthew, Mark, Luke, John, Paul and St Andrew. The rest of the window is filled with the arms of the King, Abp of Cant., Bp of Exeter, Dean, City, Nobility and principal families in Devonshire. It cost a large sum of money. Though the arms were given by the several persons, it is said to have cost the Chapter little less than £400. It makes a very grand appearance, and by connoisseurs, the whole is thought to be well executed: the arms more especially. In the figures, Mr Pecket, as a painter, to me, seems not to come up to our Chapel. The colours are very bright and vivid: but occasion, I think, rather too great a glare; so as to be somewhat painful to the eye. The window, on the outside, is strongly secured with wire. Dr Mills, the Dean, a brother of yours of the Antiquary Society, has had this work much at heart, and been very zealous in the execution of it every way.

I will now send you the letters from the University to King Richard III.

To the right high & mighty Prince, Duc of Gloucestre,
Protectour of the Realme of Englonde.

Right high & mighty Prince, in whom synglerly resteth the polityke Gov-
ernaunce, Pease & Tranquillite of ye Realme of Ynglande, your humble Oratoures commende them to your good Grace: And for Alsmyche as we have felt
in Tymes passed your bountifull & gracious Charite to us your daly Bedemen,
not alonly in sendying be your true Servant & Chancesler Master Thos. Bar-
rowghe, to his Moder ye Universite, a gret & fathfull Lover, your large &
haboundante Almons, but as wele fowndyng certeyn Prestys & Fellowes, to the
grete Worship of God, & to the Encresse of Christes Fath, in ye Qwenys Col-
legge of Cambrigge: We, uppon that Coumfourth, make our Writyng to your
Grace for suche Thynges concernyng ye Wele of the Universite, Besekyng
your noble Grace to shewe your gracious & mercyfull Goodness, at this our
humble Supplicacion, to the right reverent Fader in God ye Archebisshop of
York, our Heed & Chancesler, & many yers hath been a grete Benefactour to
the Universite, & all the Colleges therein: & thrught ye Help of God, & your
gracious Favour, shall longe continue. Most christian, & victorious Prince, we
beseche youe to heer our humble Prayours: for we must nedes mowrne & sor-
rowe, desolate of Comfurth, unto we heer & understande your benygne Spyrite
of Pite to hymwarde; whiche is a grete Prelate in the Realme of Ynglonde: &
we to be ever your true & humble Oratours & Bedemen, prayng to hym that is
called the Prince of Mercy for your noble & royall Eastate, that it may longe
prosper, to the Worship of God, who ever have youe in his blessed Kepyng.

Your true & daly Oratoures
the Universite of Cambrigge.

Insignissimo Regnorum Anglie Regi Ricardo nostro
metuendissimo.

Illustrissime Princeps.

Cum vestram immaculatam Universitatem Cantabrigie illustrissimi Princi-
pes, Antecessores vestri, accumulatissimis amplexati sunt Favoribus; ejusdem
Universitatis Privilegia ratificando, roborando, et amplificando: et jam nuper
Clementia ipsa Divina ad Regiam ipsam Celsitudinem Vos quam felicissime
extulerit; nostrum esse permaxime censuimus, ut ad illam vestram Celsitudinem Votis omnibus & affectibus convolemus, quatenus non minori Benigni-
tate, quam vestri Antecessores pernobiles, vestram ipsam Universitatem am-
plexari dignetur Regia vestra Majestas: sed et pinguiori quadam Spe vestræ
penes Nos Regiæ Caritatis confovemur: ex hoc, quod cum hujus Divinæ
Sortis vestrae Regiæ Sublimacionis ignari fueramus, et Ducatu Gloucestriae
solum militaret Nobilitas vestra. Nos nosmetipsos affectuosissime, immo effec-
tuosissime vestræ Nobilitatis Amatores ostendimus, cum illud statutum apud
Nos usque ad Secli Fratres observandum edidimus, quod quociens ad Crucem
publicam Sancti Pauli Londoniis aliquis Alumpnus nostre Matris Verbum Dei
seminabit vestram ipsius Nobilitatem specialiter Precibus suis percommenda-
bit. Istud, inclitissime Princeps, Memoriale Nemini usquiam Mortalium con-
cessimus. Dignetur ergo generosus ille Regius Animus hæc Pectore nunquam
abolere, hecque Vota nostra et Scripta supplicatoria acceptare, proque felicis-

sima vestra, Regnique Prosperitate altissimum Regem Regum exorabimus fidelissimi Oratores.

E Cantebrigia vicesima Luce Julij 1483.

These two letters, though in different languages, I suppose, were sent at the same time, notwithstanding the different style in them both. I come now to a few scraps I have picked up in your way, since I wrote last.

Helias de Berham (or Derham, as in another authority) *Canon: Sarum, qui a prima Fundatione Rector fuit novæ Fabricæ Eccl. Sarum 25 annis.*

Nova Ecclia. Sarum dedicata Aº Dñi 1258.—Leland's *Itinerary* Vol. 3. p. 80, 81.

Bp John Alcock of Ely was a great favourite of King Henry VII, who appointed him comptroller of all his works and buildings, and particularly those at Richmond. Parker's *Hist: of Cambridge*, p. 119.

Pretty account of Gothic or Saracenic Architecture in *Annual Register* for 1767. p. 148.

Hearne in his Preface to Vol. 8, p. xxv. of Leland's *Itinerary*, mentions a MS of Walter de Millemet in which are the portraits of Edw. III, and his Queen Philippa: which Book belonged formerly to Dean Aldrich.

I suppose the Duke of Manchester's Roll, is the same that is mentioned in the Preface to *Johannis Rossi Historia*, published by Hearne, at p. xxx with a picture of John Rous. Qu: The Roll there said to be then in the possession of Robert Arden of Parkhall Esqr.

Scroope House over against St Andrew's Church in Holborn, belonging to Sir John Scrope Lord Scrope of Bolton. 9 Hen. VII.—*Collection of curious Discourses* published by Hearne. p. 125.

Clifford's Inne, belonged to Isabel Lady Clifford, *temp.* Edw. III.—Id. p. 111—

Furnival's Inne, to Lord Furnival, *temp.* Ric. II.—Id. p. 124.

Derby House given to the Heralds in Queen Mary's time. Id. p. 244.

Rich. Grey Earl of Kent ob. 1523, at his house in Lombard Street in London.—Brook's *Catalogue of Kings, Nobility &c*—p. 196.

Gilbert Talbot Earl of Shrewsbury ob. 1616 at his house in Broad Street London. Id. p. 293.

Barons' Coronets—

In 1666 when Dugdale published his *Origines Juridiciales* for the first time, Barons' Coronets did not seem to be settled, at least not long before: for in a painted window in the Middle Temple Hall, are several noblemen's coats with their proper coronets over them, & among the rest, Edward Hyde Earl of Clarendon, who had not long had the title: this has an Earl's coronet over it: Wm Knolles Viscount Wallingford has a Viscount's coronet over his; & close to them are several Barons' coats without any coronet at all over their shields; as Edward Lord Stafford, Edward Lord Windsor, John Lord Darcey &c—*Orig: Jur:* p. 224.

In Fern's *Blason of Gentry*, printed 1586, p. 125 is this relating to that subject: 'Barons are with us, as the Senatours were with the Romanes, being admitted into the Upper House & Secret Chamber of Parliament: when they go to that Assembly, they wear long Robes or Kirtles of scarlet Colour, with Chapeaus set on their Heads, doubled or turned up with Ermine: according to the Fashion of the Romane Senatours, who wore, when they went to the Capitol, under their Robe, a little Kirtle of Purple with Studes, which they called *Laticlavium*.'

In the same book p. 166, 167, are two coats or shields of his two patrons, as it should seem, one of Clifford Earl of Cumberland, and close to it that of Edmond Lord Sheffeild of Butterwick: the first has an Earl's coronet over it; the other has nothing above it, to distinguish it from the coats of two Knights' shields close to it.

I have a print of Bp Mountaine with *G. Y. sculpsit 1659* and *Peter Stent excudit.*

I have another in folio, with a fat clergyman in his gown and cassock and hood, with *Wm Reader pinxit, J. Collins sculpsit.*

I herewith send you the print of Jane Shore by Mr Tyson of Benet and a print of the Countess of Exeter by Vandyke: if you should have met with one since I saw you, you may return it: I value it no more than any other print: you have two reasons to value it, as an ancestress and having the original. I am Dear Sir

Yours etc.
WM COLE

Page 146, note 3, line 3, *for* p. 249 *read* pp. 214, 249.

Page 148, note 22, *add* Cole's copy, 1622, now WSL, is heavily annotated, with many references to entries in Cole's MS volumes. He bought it 4 Dec. 1742 at a sale of duplicates from the Royal Library at Cambridge. It has the armorial bookplate of the library (in a version not described in Franks), the bookplate of a later Duke of Somerset, and the signature of an earlier owner, 'G. Dury esq.' HW's copy, 1619, is Hazen, *Cat. of HW's Lib.* No. 2346.

Page 149, note 32, line 1, *before* Frances *insert* Hon.   *for* 1580 *read* ca 1580

Page 150, note 2, line 5, *for* in the possession of Lord Derby at Knowsley *read* WSL

Page 151, note 3, *add* See also Hazen, *SH Bibl.* 87–95.

Page 151, note 8, *add* See also Hazen, *SH Bibl.* 107–10.

Page 154, note 3, *add* HW's copy of Osborne's *Works*, 9th edn, 1689, is Hazen, *Cat. of HW's Lib.* No. 1715.

Page 155, note 7, *add* Hazen believes that HW bought the 1st edn, 1767, as well; the 2d edn, 1789, is now WSL (see Hazen, *Cat. of HW's Lib.* Nos 290, 3705).

Page 157, note 2, *for* now in the Princeton University Library *read* now WSL; a second copy is in the Princeton University Library

Page 157, note 4, *delete second sentence and substitute* HW's set, misdated 1796 by Kirgate in the MS Cat., was sold SH iv. 7; see Hazen, *Cat. of HW's Lib*. No. 541.

Page 158, note 6, line 1, *for* 1731? *read* ca 1733   *Line 6, add* See also Hugh Gatty, 'Dr Ewin and Dr Pennington, A Correspondence,' *The Eagle, A Magazine Supported by Members of St John's College*, 1933, xlvii. 141.

Page 161, note 14, right column, line 5, *for* Queensborough *read* Queenborough

Page 163, note 24, *add* It is now WSL.

Page 163, To Cole 14 June 1769, line 10, *on* painted glass *add note* 1a: 1a. 'His Lordship, besides this benefaction, hath engaged ... to glaze all the windows at the east end thereof with painted-glass ... under the inspection of a gentleman [HW] of the most approved taste' (Bentham, *Ely*² p. 214).

Page 165, note 6, *add* They are now WSL; see Hazen, *Cat. of HW's Lib*. No. 2029.

Page 169, illustration, caption, *for* VOLUME TWO *read* SECOND EDITION

Page 171, note 30, line 1, *for* Van Der Dort *read* Van Der Doort

Page 173, note 63, line 5, *for* Van Der Dort *read* Van Der Doort   *Last line, add* See also Hazen, *Bibl. of HW* 120–2.

Page 174, 5th paragraph, line 6, *on* Hawkins's *add note* 74a: 74a. Sir John Hawkins (1719–89), Kt, 1772, published an edition of Isaac Walton's *Complete Angler* in 1760, but there is no evidence that he published an edition of Evelyn's *Sculptura* (Geoffrey Keynes, *John Evelyn, A Study in Bibliophily with a Bibliography of his Writings*, 2d edn, Oxford, 1968, pp. 120–2). Lombart is mentioned on p. 77 of the 2d edn, 1755, of Evelyn's *Sculptura* (on p. 80 of the 1st edn, 1662). The publisher of the 1755 edn was John Payne, a member of Dr Johnson's Club. HW had the 1662 edn (Hazen, *Cat. of HW's Lib*. No. 335).

Page 176, note 86, *add* See Hazen, *Cat. of HW's Lib*. No. 577.

Page 178, 2d paragraph, line 3, *on* expectations *add note* 3a: 3a. A similar observation was attributed to Sir Robert Walpole by William Hazlitt in Lectures on the English Comic Writers, *Wit and Humour*: on the gratitude of place-expectants, 'That it is a lively sense of *future* favours'; and also to La Rochefoucauld (*Maxime* 298): 'La reconnaissance de la plupart des hommes n'est qu'une secrète envie de recevoir de plus grands bienfaits' (*Oxford Dictionary of Quotations*, 2d edn, Oxford, 1955, pp. 407, 559; pointed out by the late Leonard Bacon).

Page 178, note 5, line 8, *for* southeast *read* southwest

Page 181, note 37, line 1, *for* 1628 *read* ca 1627

Page 182, note 47, line 1, *for* 1391 *read* 1390

Page 182, note 55, *add* HW had a black and white chalk drawing of him by Thomas Chambars; sold SH xx. 112, now WSL (Misc. Corr. i. 272, n. 4).

Page 184, note 1, lines 7–8, *delete and substitute* which was in his library by 1763; two other copies were given to him by Cole and Hawkins in 1769 (Hazen, *Cat. of HW's Lib.*, Nos 736, 2690).

Page 186, note 14, line 2, *for* 1586 *read* 1585   *for* 2d E. *read* 14th E.

Page 187, line 10, *on* present *add note* 17a: 17a. See Cole to Granger 4 Aug. 1769 (original MS in the Adam Collection).

Page 188, note 18, *add* See Hazen, *Cat. of HW's Lib.* No. 3222:9:5.

Page 189, To Cole 11 Aug. 1769, headnote, line 1, *add* A copy of this letter is among Andrew Coltee Ducarel's MSS, Add. MS 23,990, f. 100 (also it is printed, incomplete, in Nichols, *Lit. Anec.* iv. 706–8).

Page 190, note 3, line 1, *for* 1511? *read* 1512

Page 191, line 13, *for* aerial or *read* aerial and

Page 192, note 14, *add* Mark A. Tierney in *The History and Antiquities of the Castle and Town of Arundel*, 1834, i. 90–2 and notes, says that this is not the same picture as the one that formed the subject of the accusations against the Earl of Surrey (information from Lindsay Fleming).

Page 195, note 1, line 6, *after* Lowndes *add* nor in Martin   *Line 10, add* See Hazen, *SH Bibl.* 199–202.

Page 198, note 1, line 2, *for* (d. 1770) *read* (1718–70)   *Line 8, after* 206–7 *add*   ; *London Magazine*, 1749, xviii. 432

Page 198, note 2, line 4, *for* 26 *read* 25

Page 199, note 3, line 3, *for* d. 19 *read* d. 18   *Line 4, for* Collins . . . 486–7 *substitute* Sedgwick ii. 241

Page 199, note 7, line 2, *for* 1833 *read* 1832   *Lines 5–6, after* Cadogan *insert*   , n.c.

Page 201, note 1, *add* HW was one of the subscribers; see Hazen, *Cat. of HW's Lib.* No. 11.

Page 202, note 3, line 2, *for* 1742 *read* 1741   *for* 1760 *read* 1758 *Line 3, for* 60 *read* 58 and add (Sedgwick ii. 178)

Page 203, note 7, *add* HW's copy is Hazen, *Cat. of HW's Lib.* No. 3223.

Page 205, note 6, lines 5–8, *delete and substitute* Mr John Saltmarsh writes (1938) that the MS of Sir Robert's resignation is No. 45 in a volume of Original Resignations of Scholarships and Fellowships in King's College Library, press mark A-B44. See also J. H. Plumb, *Sir Robert Walpole: The Making of a Statesman*, Cambridge, Mass., 1956, pp. 88–9.

Page 206, note 4, *add* See GRAY i. 28, n. 188, 47.

Page 206, note 6, line 2, *for* Dr. *read* Dr   *Line 10, add* See Hazen, *SH Bibl.* xxi, 95–6; *Bibl. of HW* 73, 75.

Page 207, note 14, line 5, *for* 1743 *read* 1743–51   *Line 8, add* It is now WSL; see Hazen, *Cat. of HW's Lib.* No. 3637.

Page 208, note 17, *add* HW wrote in his life of Vertue (*Works* iv. 125): 'The heads of Carr Earl of Somerset and Secretary Thurloe are not only not genuine, but have not the least resemblance to the persons they pretend to represent.'

Pages 212–13, note 7, *add* After Gray's death Mason found among

Gray's papers 'your printed letter to Dr Milles' (Mason to HW 28 Aug. 1771, MASON i. 19).

Page 213, note 5, *for* Pawlet or Poulet (1485? *read* Paulet *or* Powlett (ca 1483

Page 215, note 3, *delete last sentence and substitute* The original MSS are now in the Royal Library at Windsor (Hazen, *SH Bibl.* xxii, 99–101). Cole's copies are listed in the catalogue of the library of the late Lord Castletown and the Hon. Howard S. Harrington as sold by Battersby and Co., Dublin, 5 May 1938, lot 10.

Page 216, line 18, *on* Bentham's book *add note* 3a: 3a. Cole's copy 'with additional MS notes by W. Cole' was sold in the first William Beckford sale, 'A Portion of the Library of a very Distinguished collector brought from his seat in Wiltshire' (Frits Lugt, *Répertoire des catalogues de ventes publiques,* La Haye, 1938–64; Sotheby's Catalogue 11 June 1808, lot 297, £14.35). For HW's copy see Hazen, *Cat. of HW's Lib.* No. 11.

Page 220, note 1, *add* On 23 June 1771 HW wrote to Lord Ossory that he had not yet received Fuller's *History,* but apparently during the summer he acquired the book (see Hazen, *Cat. of HW's Lib.* No. 1095; OSSORY i. 45–6).

Page 220, note 4, line 1, *for* 1506?–52 *read* ca 1500–52

Page 226, note 2, *add* A water-colour drawing of the cross (artist unidentified) faces Kirgate's copy of HW's verses mounted and bound in E. V. Utterson's copy of *Fugitive Pieces,* Strawberry Hill, 1758 (copy 13). HW's MS of the verses is in his 'Book of Materials,' 1771, p. 26.

Page 227, note 4, line 3, *for* Devonshire *read* Devon

Page 230, note 5, line 1, *for* 1704 *read* ca 1709

Page 231, note 9, line 1, *for* Stonehewer *read* Stonhewer

Page 236, note 4, line 1, *for* Seymour Conway *read* Seymour-Conway

Page 243, note 1, *add* For a discussion of the history of the armour see OSSORY iii. 235–6, Appendix 1.

Page 244, note 2, left column, line 1, *for* (d. 1750) *read* (1696–?1751)

Page 244, note 4, *add* It is now restored to its former place in the church at Bexhill, through the will of G. G. M. G. Cullum, whose grandfather, '—— Whitaker, Esq.' bought the window (N&Q 10 Dec. 1938, clxxv. 421).

Page 244, note 6, line 13, *for* Cavalini's *read* Cavallini's

Page 246, note 3, line 1, *for* 1744 *read* 1745

Page 247, note 1, *add* See Hazen, *Cat. of HW's Lib.* No. 3925. Mr James M. Osborn wrote 30 June 1937, 'Internal evidence would suggest that the letters may have been written by Almon himself, but I don't have any external evidence to substantiate this.'

Page 255, 3d paragraph, lines 2–3, *on Topography add note* 6a: 6a. HW gave them to Cole; see photostat of Add. MS 5834, f. 66 and *post* COLE i. 263.

Page 255, note 8, line 4, *after* 124 *add* (Hazen, *Cat. of HW's Lib.* No. 2875)

Page 258, line 22, *on Significatione add note* 11a: 11a. By Sir John Skene, Edinburgh, 1597.

Page 260, note 3, line 2, *after* Gray *delete* HW understood ... Whibley). *and substitute* It was an etching by Mason's servant Charles Carter after the painting by Louis Vaslet (see Mason i. 37 and n. 9, 39 and nn. 8, 13; *post* Cole to HW 9 July 1772, Cole i. 267).

Page 262, note 17, line 2, *delete and substitute* although he owned a copy of Warton's *Life of Sir Thomas Pope* by 9 May 1772; see Hazen, *Cat. of HW's Lib*. No. 2981.

Page 263, note 19a, *for* 3 Feb. 1781 *read* 2 March 1779. The building called 'Pythagoras's School' now belongs to Merton College. It is on the grounds of Merton Hall, whose tenant in 1937 was Victor, Lord Rothschild (information from the late Leonard Whibley).

Page 266, note 8, left column, line 5, *for* late in this month *read* 13 July 1772 (Index, under Walpole, to the Minutes of the Society of Antiquaries; information from H. S. Kingsford).

Page 271, note 5, *add* See Hazen, *Cat. of HW's Lib*. No. 261.

Page 272, note 2, *add* See Hazen, *Cat. of HW's Lib*. No. 884.

Page 275, note 9, line 2, *for* Scarborough *read* Scarbrough

Page 282, note 11, line 1, *for* John Maurice *read* Hans Moritz   *for* Count of *read* Graf von   *At end add* See More 83, n. 9.

Page 287, note 5, line 1, *for* 1745 *read* ?1744   *Lines 4–5, delete* he was obliged to sell his books in 1784 *and substitute* Gulston's books were sold 8 May 1786 and the ten following days by Compton (see N&Q 4 July 1908, cxviii. 6, for a note on Gulston and his collection),   *Line 7, after* DNB *add*   ; Namier and Brooke ii. 561–2

Page 288, note 5, left column, line 5, *for* (1725–1806) *read* (1721–1805) *Line 6, for* 1754–80 *read* 1756–80   *Last line, add* See J. M. Pinkerton, 'Richard Bull of Ongar, Essex,' *Book Collector*, 1978, xxvii. 41–59.

Page 289, note 1, line 6, *for* vol. v). *read* vol. v, possibly by his daughter, Eliza. Gulston. HW's copy of her print of Gulston is in his portfolio of etchings by amateurs).

Page 290, note 1, *add* A reprint (of 20 pages) from *Archæologia* ii. 198–215, issued by W. Bowyer and J. Nichols, 1772.

Page 293, 2d paragraph, lines 2–3, *for* Whittingtonion *read* Whittingtonian

Page 293, note 3, line 5, *for* MDCCLXII *read* MDCCLXXII   *Line 12, add* See Hazen, *SH Bibl*. 96.

Page 294, note 10, *add* HW's copy is Hazen, *Cat. of HW's Lib*. No. 632. HW later acquired Masters's *Memoirs of the Life and Writings of Thomas Baker*, 1784, which, HW wrote, 'proved how insufficient his materials or he himself were' (Hazen, op. cit. No. 3820).

Page 297, note 1, *add* Cole's copy of the *Miscellaneous Antiquities*, inscribed 'E. Libris Gulmi. Cole ex Donis Hon. Editoris Jan. 17, 1773' is now WSL.

Page 298, note 2, *delete* Lort's reply is dated 4 Feb. 1773. *and substitute* Lort wrote to Cole, Whitehall, 6 Feb. 1773, 'I had a card this day from Mr Walpole, to desire I would call on him, which I intend doing next week' (Cole's copy, Add. MS 5831, f. 126v; see CHATTERTON 164).

Page 298, note 2a, *add* At West's sale 'Mr Bull told me he had Mr Walpole's commissions, but said he could execute few of them' (Lort to Cole 6 Feb. 1773, Add. MS 5993, f. 10v).

Page 298, note 5, *delete last sentence and substitute* In a letter to Sir Edward Walpole 25 April 1777 HW refers to Dr Battie's earlier opinion of Lord Orford's sanity (see FAMILY 123–4; OSSORY i. 175).

Page 298, note 7, *add* See *London Evening Post* 5–7 Jan. 1768: 'Lewellin Nash, Esq. late Lieutenant in the Fourteenth Regiment of Dragoons in Ireland, is cured of an inveterate scorbutic humour (by the use of Maredant's Drops, prepared by Mr Norton, Surgeon, in Golden Square) . . . these drops are sold in bottles of 6s. each'; and also *Public Advertiser* 9 March 1779: 'Maredant's Antiscorbutic Drops, prepared solely by Mr Norton, Surgeon in Golden Square, near Piccadilly, London, where they are sold in square bottles at half a guinea and six shillings each.'

Page 299, note 9, *add* See Hazen, *Cat. of HW's Lib.* No. 2932.

Page 301, note 5, line 10, *after* WSL *add* Hazen, *Cat. of HW's Lib.* No. 1810:19:5.

Page 303, note 9, *add* HW in his copy (now WSL) has corrected 'butter' to 'batter' and notes, 'I am told, and believe, that the true reading is Batter the rooks nests. HW.' Cole's copy, p. 19, (now WSL) is also corrected.

Page 304, note 1, line 1, *before* Lady *insert* Lady Eleanor Butler was sometimes identified as   *Lines 4–5, after* Sudeley *add*   ; but this identification is apparently mistaken. See CHUTE 609, n. 7; *Complete Works of St Thomas More*, New Haven, Conn., 1963– , vol. ii, ed. R. Sylvester, p. 243.

Page 304, note 2, *add* HW's copy of *Archæologia* is now WSL, with his many notes on Masters's essay unfortunately erased (Hazen, *Cat. of HW's Lib.* No. 3223).

Pages 304–5, note 6, line 5, *for* (d. 1797) *read* (ca 1736–96), M.P.   *Line 10, after* 140 *add*   ; Namier and Brooke ii. 129

Page 305, note 9, line 6, *after West insert* (HW's copy is now WSL; see Hazen, *Cat. of HW's Lib.* No. 2050)   *Last line, add* See also Vertue's description in *Walpole Society*, 1935–6, xxiv. 167.

Page 305, note 10, line 8, *after* More. *add* In his priced copy of the *Description of SH*, 1774, HW wrote £80, forgetting that he had paid 80 guineas.   *Line 11, for* J. P. Bevan *read* John Dent   *Line 12, add* Now at Sudeley Castle, Glos, *penes* Mark Dent-Brocklehurst.

Page 305, note 13, line 6, *for* illustration and Appendix *read Anecdotes*[1] i. 50.

Page 307, note 2, line 5, *after* 1772 *add* (now WSL; see Hazen, *Cat. of HW's Lib.* No. 4001 and also No. 3917)

Page 307, From Cole 24 April 1773, 1st paragraph, line 1, *on* City *add note a: a.* On this day Cole apparently bought a copy of [Edward Neville,] *The Life of the Lady Warner of Parham in Suffolk,* 2d edn, 1692 (Wing C. 575). Cole's copy is inscribed on the fly-leaf: 'E Libris Guli: Cole A:M: de Milton juxta Cantabř Apr: 24, 1773'; and on the title-page: 'Wm Cole 1773' and 'Edwd Hanmer Decr 29th 1783.' It was bought from the Hanmer family by Lord Kenyon, Gredington, Whitchurch, Salop, in 1971 (Lord Kenyon to WSL 12 May 1971).

Page 308, note 2a, *substitute* I.e., before he knew that he was president of the Society of Antiquaries.

Page 308, note 3, line 1, *for Chronicle read Pastyme of People   for* sold *read* bought   Line 2, *after* George III *insert* (see *ante* COLE i. 306, n. 16)   *Last line, add* See DALRYMPLE 176, n. 2.

Page 309, note 3, line 3, *for Short Remarks read Some Remarks on Mr Walpole's Historic Doubts,* reprinted from *Archæologia,* ii. 198–215, *Line 4, after* 1773 *add* pp. 290, 292–3

Page 310, note 8, line 8, *for* 1772 *read* ?1772

Page 313, note 20, line 27, *for* 1744 *read* 1742

Page 325, note 4, *add* See William Coxe, *Memoirs of . . . Sir Robert Walpole,* 1798, i. 757; OSSORY ii. 277, n. 12.

Page 325, note 11, *add* Miss D. M. Stuart wrote to WSL 19 May 1936 that the terms of Lady Hervey's will 'suggest, even if it cannot be proved, that HW had no lot or part in influencing her original intention to leave her London house to her sailor son.' See D. M. Stuart, *Molly Lepell, Lady Hervey,* 1936, pp. 190–4, 342; MORE 137.

Page 326, note 12, *add* Gen. William Hervey sold the house in St James's Place in 1781; see *Journals of the Hon. William Hervey,* ed. Rev. S. H. A. Hervey, Bury St Edmunds, 1906 (Suffolk Green Book Series, no. xiv), pp. 213–14, 245, 303.

Page 328, line 5, *on* July *add note* 4: 4. Cole's presentation was on 6 June 1774, according to the *Eton College Register Books* (M. R. James, 'Presentation to Eton College Livings 1457–1880,' *Etoniana,* 1923, p. 526).

Page 329, note 5, line 1, *for* 1743 *read* 1744

Page 329, note 11, *add* From the minutes of the Society of Antiquaries, 2 vols, 1717–51, formerly HW's, now BM: '3 May 1744, Mr West showed the Society an old picture painted by Levintz of the Old Countess of Desmond, mentioned for her great age by my Ld. Bacon.' HW has noted on this, 'It is the same as that at Windsor, and is not of her, but Rembrandt's mother' (Egerton MS 1042, f. 78). In his copy of Joseph Pote's *History and Antiquities of Windsor Castle,* 1749, p. 418, HW noted on the statement that there was a portrait of the Countess of Desmond in the Queen's Dressing Room: 'This is not the Cs of Desmond, but an old woman by Rembrandt, given to K. Charles 1st by Rbt Kerr Earl of Ancram' (Hazen, *Cat.*

of HW's Lib. No. 637). See also HW to Lord Buchan 2 June 1782 (MISC. CORR. iii. 12–13).

Page 329, note 12, lines 5–6, *for* an unidentified correspondent *read* James Granger   *Last line, for* 48). *read* 48; Granger, *Correspondence* 157). *and add* In a letter to Richard Bull 13 June 1773 Pennant wrote, 'I again surveyed Lady Desmond's picture last year and plainly saw it was no Rembrandt. Which I knew was impossible when I looked into his life . . .' (National Library of Wales, MS 5500C; information from Cecil Price to WSL 3 Feb. 1956).

Page 330, note 13, *add* In a Manuscript Diary of 1817–19 (now WSL) David Pennant, the elder son of Thomas Pennant, wrote *sub* 26 June 1819 that he 'was hurt by reading the variety of acrimonious and illiterate remarks on the character and works of my father in Horace Walpole's Letters to Mr Cole, extracted without judgment from the deposit in the British Museum.'

Page 330, note 17, *substitute* Henry Herbert (ca 1689–1750), 9th E. of Pembroke, whom HW would more likely call 'the old Lord Pembroke' in 1774 (information from Sir Anthony R. Wagner, Richmond Herald).

Page 330, note 18, *substitute* John Anstis (ca 1709–54), joint Garter King of Arms 1727–44 (MANN iv. 96, n. 1), who, Sir Anthony R. Wagner points out, 'was a much sillier man than his father who, indeed, whatever his other weaknesses was not silly at all' (to WSL 1 April 1958). See Nichols's biographies of both father and son in *Literary Anecdotes* v. 269–72.

Page 334, note 8, lines 2–3, *for* in this year *read* 21 March 1774 (*London Chronicle* 5–8, 19–22 March 1774, xxxv. 226, 275)

Page 335, line 6, *on* Mount-Steward *add note* 10: 10. John Stuart (1744–1814), styled Vct Mount Stuart; 4th E. of Bute, 1792; cr. (1776) Bn Cardiff and (1796) M. of Bute; M.P. (see DALRYMPLE 161 and n. 13; OSSORY i. 19 and n. 13).

Page 338, note 4, lines 4–5, *for* in Lord Waldegrave's collection at Chewton Priory *read* now WSL

Page 338, note 5, line 2, *for* 33 *read* 27

Page 340, note 1, lines 1–2, *for* a mile *read* 2 miles   *Lines 2–3, for* Robin Wood's Hill *read* Robins Wood Hill (see SELWYN 120, n. 3)

Page 341, note 4, line 7, *after* Wheatley, *add* 1884,

Page 342, line 9, *on* crowns *add note* 11a: 11a. The painted glass was purchased by Pilgrim Trust (193?) and given to Gloucester Cathedral, where it now is in the Cloisters.

Page 343, note 23, line 1, *for* 1720 *read* ca 1720

Page 346, note 3, line 1, *for* 1720 *read* ?1720

Page 346, note 4, *add* See also Namier and Brooke ii. 167, 170, 681.

Page 348, To Cole 11 Oct. 1774, last paragraph, line 1, *on* Have *add note* 1a: 1a. This paragraph, misdated, was printed in *Blackwood's Magazine*, 1818–19, iv. 149, with two additional sentences: 'Have you seen Granger's Supplement? Methinks it grows too diffuse. I have hinted to him that fewer panegyrics from funeral sermons would not hurt it. There are few copies printed but on one side of the leaf. To my mortification, though I have four thousand heads, I find, upon a rough calculation, that I still want three or four hundred.'

Page 348, To Cole 11 Oct. 1774, note 2, *add* Published 20 Sept., according to the *London Chronicle* 13–15, 15–17 Sept. 1774, xxxvi. 263, 271. See Hazen, *Bibl. of HW* 133–5.

Page 348, From Cole 18 Nov. 1774, headnote, line 1, *after* 234–5. *insert* Collated with a photocopy of the manuscript, now in the King's College Library, Cambridge; the variations in text and punctuation are recorded here.   *Line 2, for* Its present whereabouts is not known. *read* Offered Maggs Cat. No. 433 (Christmas, 1922), lot 3099; resold Sotheby's 16 Dec. 1929, lot 634, to Dobell, £10; offered by Sotheby's 22 June 1976, lot 39, £80–120; now in the King's College Library, Cambridge.

Page 348, From Cole 18 Nov. 1774, 1st paragraph, line 3, *after* lame *add*   ,   *Line 4, for* you, *read* you: *Line 5, for* tedious. However *read* tedious: however   *Line 8, for* usual, *read* usual:

Page 349, 1st paragraph, line 2, *after* character *add*   ,   *after* court *add*   ,   *Line 5, after* paper *add*   ,   *Line 9, after* done me *add*   , *Line 10, after* letter *delete*   ,   *Line 11, after* haste *delete*   ,

Page 349, Enclosure, 1st paragraph, line 1, *after* Letter *delete*   ,

Page 349, note 6, *add* In his copy of the *Description of SH*, 1774, p. 3, on the footnote, 'In the winding cloysters on the right hand are some ancient bas-reliefs,' Cole wrote: 'The ancient bas-reliefs I gave to Mr Walpole some 10 years ago. W. C. 1774.' Cole's copy is now WSL; see Hazen, *SH Bibl.* 1973, pp. xxiii, 110.

Page 350, 1st paragraph, line 1, *for* yᵉ *read* the   *for* Trant; *read* Trant: *Line 3, for* yᵉ *read* the   *for* them; *read* them: *Line 5, for* yᵉ *read* the   *after* Potvin *add*   ,   *Line 7, after* afraid *add*   ,   *Line 11, for* pleasd *read* pleased   *Line 13, after* tell him *add*   ,   *Line 15, for* with him: *read* with him,   *Line 16, for* here *read* here: *Line 18, for* Diamonds; *read* Diamonds,   *Line 19, after* Lumley *delete*   ,   *Line 21, after* Grafton *add*   ,

Page 351, 1st paragraph, line 1, *for* shee *read* she

Page 351, 2d paragraph, line 2, *for* ill-pay-Masters *read* ill Pay-Masters

Page 351, 3d paragraph, line 1, for yʳ [their] *read* their   *Line 2, after* Leaves *add*   ,   *Line 3, begin new paragraph with* Mrs. Jennings *after* Jennings *add*   ,

Page 351, note 1, *add* See Hazen, *Cat. of HW's Lib.* Nos 3846, 3485:8.

Page 353, line 15, *on* music *add note* 1a: 1a. Ten volumes of Neapolitan operas, into which Gray inserted many of the words, are now WSL.

Page 353, note 1, line 4, *for* the end of March *read* 30 March   *Line 8, for* early in June *read* 5 May (MASON i. 184, n. 1; 216, n. 10; *Daily Adv.* 5 May 1775; *London Chronicle* 6–9 May 1775, xxxvii. 439)

Page 354, note 6, line 1, *after* Crawford *add* (b. 1752)   *Line 6, after*

218 *add* ; Venn, *Alumni Cantab.*). When Wilkes visited Cambridge 11 Feb. 1771, Crawford escorted him (*London Chronicle* 16–19 Feb. 1771, xxix. 170).

Page 354, note 7, line 8, *after* 1773; *add Public Advertiser* 6, 7, 14 Oct. 1773;

Page 354, note 8, *delete first sentence and substitute* This drawing was inserted after 1842 in HW's copy of the *Description of SH*, now WSL. *Line 10, after* fecit 1771.' *add* See illustration, *post* COLE i. 365.

Page 357, note 5, line 1, *for* (d. 1766) *read* (ca 1694–1766)   *Line 2, for* Tregoney *read* Tregony   *for* 1741–66 *read* 1741–65 (Namier and Brooke ii. 560–1)

Page 357, note 6, *add* See also Namier and Brooke ii. 561–2.

Page 357, note 8, line 5, *for* had two copies of the work *substitute* owned a copy of this two-volume edition, but only two sets of the 1779 edition remained in his library.   *Last line, after* 286. *add* See Hazen, *Cat. of HW's Lib.* Nos 411, 3814.

Page 358, note 11, *add* The lady was presumably Elizabeth Stapleton (1740–1825), who m. (1767) Watkin Williams, of Penbedw, Flintshire, in whose house the miniatures were found; see HW to Thomas Pennant 25 May 1773, MISC. CORR. ii. 252–3 and nn. 22, 23.

Page 361, note 9, *add* It was advertised as 'in the press, and will be published in a few days' in the *London Chronicle* 27–29 Dec. 1774, xxxvi. 624; and as 'This day was published' ibid. 7–10 Jan. 1775, xxxvii. 31.

Page 361, note 11, line 2, *for* Villiers's *read* the Duke of Buckingham's

Page 362, note 16, line 1, *for* 1753 *read* ?1753   *Line 5, after 1753–90 add* ; Namier and Brooke iii. 473

Page 364, note 30, *add* J. Nichols in *Biographical Anecdotes of Mr Hogarth*, 1781, p. 13, mentions a family portrait of 'Mr Western' of Rivenhall, Essex, in which appears 'the Rev. Mr Cole of Milton near Cambridge ... 1736.' See also Helen Waddell's introduction, pp. xv–xvi, to Cole's *Journal of my Journey to Paris*, 1931.

Page 365, note 41, *substitute* Possibly the Rev. Julius Hutchinson (ca 1743–71), son of Thomas Hutchinson of Hatfield Woodhall, Herts; admitted Fellow-Commoner at Sidney Sussex College, Cambridge 20 Oct. 1760; B. A. 1765, M. A. 1768. GM 1771, xli. 475 records the death of a Rev. Julius Hutchinson 29 Sept 1771 'at Hartfield, in Hertfordshire' (see also *London Magazine* 1771, xl. 524); Venn, *Alumni Cantab., 1752–1900,* iii. 504, reports the death of the above member of Sidney Sussex as 9 May 1811 and refers to GM 1811, lxxxi pt i. 601 (this entry reads: 'At Layer Bretton Parsonage, near Colchester, in his 61st year, Rev. Julius Hutchinson'). The one who died in 1811 is the Rev. Julius Hutchinson, son of Norton Hutchinson, of St George's, Bloomsbury, London; matriculated, aged 17, at New College, Oxford, 22 Jan. 1768; described as 'of Hatfield Woodhall, which he sold' (Foster, *Alumni Oxon., 1715–1886,* ii. 46). According to *Vict. Co. Hist., Herts,* iii. 107, Hatfield Woodhall passed by will to Isabel Boteler, wife of Charles Hutchinson (d. 1728); 'Their son Julius Hutchinson succeeded and was followed by his son Thomas, who died in 1774. Woodhall then passed to his nephew, the Rev. Julius Hutchinson, son of his brother Norton, and in 1792 was sold to the Earl of Salisbury, and thus became merged in the manor of Hatfield.'

Page 365, note 43, lines 2–3, *for* in the Spencer Collection, New York Public Library, *read* now WSL

Page 367, note 4, *delete second sentence* HW . . . former. *and substitute* HW's copies, probably given to him by Mrs Pye, are Hazen, *Cat. of HW's Lib.* Nos 2387:3, 2457. HW's copy of *A Short View* was bound with Mrs Pye's *Poems,* 1767.

Page 367, line 26, *on* vendible book *add note* 4a: 4a. 'Price 1s. 6d. Elegantly printed on fine writing paper, and covered with marble' (*London Chronicle* 27–29 Dec. 1774, xxxvi. 624).

Page 367, note 5, *add* She d. 12 Nov. 1782 at her house in South Audley Street (N&Q, 1944, clxxxvi. 254–5; see also *British Magazine and Review,* 1782, i. 299, 377–8).

Page 368, note 9, *add* See Hazen, *Cat. of HW's Lib.* No. 3217.

Page 368, note 10, line 1, *for or Analysis read or, an Analysis*   *Line 4, after* v. 39 *add* (Hazen, *Cat. of HW's Lib.* No. 3161)

Page 370, line 29, *on Cantabrigienses add note* 5: 5. Cole's MS 'Collections for an Athenæ Cantabrigienses' in the British Museum (see *ante* COLE i. p. xxvi).

Page 372, note 5, *add* HW's copy, containing numerous pencil markings, is now WSL (Hazen, *Cat. of HW's Lib.* No. 3355).

Page 374, line 15, *on* Edmondson *add note* 5a: 5a. Joseph Edmondson (d. 1786), herald and genealogist.

Page 375, note 9, line 21, *for* mother *read* wife   *Line 22, for* Cordell Allington, granddaughter of *read* Catherine Hastings, descended from the Poles and Dukes of York. HW's father was descended from   *Line 33, add* The Darcys were likewise descended from the Allingtons, but from an older generation of the family.

Page 377, note 9, line 1, *for* 1709 *read* ca 1709

Page 379, note 2, *add* HW's copies are Hazen, *Cat. of HW's Lib.* Nos 3222:14:7, 3892.

Page 379, note 7, line 9, *after* presents.' *add* See Hazen, *Cat. of HW's Lib.* Nos 3166, 3310.   *Line 10, for* 1573 *read* 1574

Page 385, note 6, *add* See Hazen, *Cat. of HW's Lib.* No. 3572.

Page 387, note 12, *add* Cole's copy, now WSL, is cited *ante* COLE i. 148, n. 22.

VOLUME 2

Page vii, List of Illustrations, *sub* Walpole's Letter of 9 Sept. 1776, *for* 24 *read* 25

Page 1, headnote, 1st paragraph, line 2, *add* This letter is dated by Cole's answer.

Page 1, headnote, *Address*, line 2, *for* (d. 1802) *read* (ca 1733–1802)

Page 1, note 1, line 2, *after* 1775 *add* OSSORY i. 289; he had returned to Arlington Street by 22 Jan. 1776, ibid. i. 290

Page 2, note 6, line 7, *after* Warwick *add* which is now BM Add. MS 48976   *Line 8, after* [1768]). *add* See also HW to Astle 22 April 1768 in MISC. CORR. ii. 144. HW later agreed that the document was a wardrobe account and not a coronation roll (MASON i. 238, n. 13).

Page 8, note 9, line 3, *for* 1712–75 *read* 1712–73   *Lines 4–5, for* in two parliaments *read* 1747–54, Dec. 1754–61

Page 9, note 11, line 4, *after* 1775 *add* OSSORY i. 282 and nn. 10, 11

Page 16, note 2, *add* See BERRY ii. 207–8; Hazen, *SH Bibl.*, 1973, pp. xxxi, 194–8

Page 17, note 1, line 2, *for* 1721 *read* 1719   *At end add* On 13 July 1776 he had 'a slight paralytic stroke in his face' (CONWAY iii. 278, n. 1).

Page 18, line 10, *for* that *read* than

Page 19, From Cole 28 July 1776, 2d paragraph, line 1, *on* prints *add note* 1: 1. One of them was Archbishop Philippoleos (now WSL).

Page 21, note 5, line 5, *for* 1749 *read* 1748

Page 23, note 5, *add* HW owned two of Kenrick Prescot's publications: *Letters concerning Homer the Sleeper*, Cambridge, 1773, and *Mildenhall, a Poem*, Cambridge, 1771 (Hazen, *Cat. of HW's Lib.* Nos 2932, 2968:6), both of which are listed in Lowndes, *Bibliographical Manual of English Literature*.

Page 24, note 1, *add* Perhaps a varvel for a hawk: 'a metal ring (frequently of silver with the owner's name engraved on it) attached to the end of a hawk's jess and serving to connect this with the leash' (OED; information from George Eland, Esq., F.S.A.).

Page 25, caption, *for* COLE'S COPY *read* HW'S LETTER

Page 26, note 3, *add* HW's copy is Hazen, *Cat. of HW's Lib.* No. 527.

Page 28, note 2, *add* William Bewley wrote to Charles Burney 11 June 1777, 'Did I tell you of the unlucky scrape I unwittingly got into with Mr H. Walpole?—the Knight's [Sir John Hawkins's] *friend*—as I found to my utter dismay, when it was too late.—I begged him not to *peach*, however,—and have since received assurances from him that he will keep my secret.—The case was so strangely circumstanced that, had I even known that he had written half the Knight's book, *Prudence* would have given me a jog, and whispered to me to own the two *Musical Articles*.—If I have not told you already the whole story, this will be all *Arabic* to you. . . . surely no two works, even on different subjects, can be so perfectly *alien* as the two English Historys of Music! The Knight cannot possibly hurt *you*; but you have hurt *him* most confoundedly with your first Volume. You have given us a little *Tidbit* in *Quarto*—and after relishing (*getting a say*, we say in Norfolk) this dainty, the Knight's tough bull beef, and bullock's liver can never more go down' (MS in the Osborn Collection, Beinecke Library,

Yale University; see also Roger Lonsdale, *Dr Charles Burney*, Oxford, 1965, pp. 189, 196, 198; MASON i. 248).

Page 29, note 1, line 3, *for* Cook (d. 1593?), herald. *read* Cooke (*or* Cook) (d. ca 1593), Clarencieux King of Arms, 1567 (MISC. CORR. i. 227 and n. 35). *Line 4, add* HW owned a MS copy of the *Visitation of Norfolk by Robert Cook in 1589* (Hazen, *Cat. of HW's Lib*. No. 2583).

Page 30, note 2, *add* In the *Catalogue* (a copy of which is now WSL) the shutters are described as, 'Two ancient pictures on boards, being the shutters to the altar of the Abbey of St Edmund's Bury, with the portrait of Cardinal Beaufort, Humphrey Duke of Gloster, and Abbott Babbington'; they are also described in Ives's letter to Granger 28 Feb. 1774 (now WSL).

Page 30, note 5, line 1, *for* —— Bonus *read* Richard Bonus   *Lines 2–6, delete* A 'Mr George . . . (1798). 70–1. *and substitute* See OSSORY i. 140, n. 14.

Page 32, note 14, *add* See Hazen, *Cat. of HW's Lib*. No. 3476:2.

Page 32, note 15, *add* The letter is printed in CHATTERTON 183–6.

Page 39, 4th paragraph, line 5, *for* Scots-Hibernic *read* Scoto-Hibernic

Page 40, 1st paragraph, line 4, *on* Edmondson *add note a*: a. Edmondson's *Complete Body of Heraldry* was published in 1780; HW's copy is Hazen, *Cat. of HW's Lib*. No. 528.

Page 46, 2d paragraph, line 25, *on* beautiful *add note* 2a: 2a. The passage, 'the beauty of King's College Chapel . . . innocence is beautiful,' was printed in *Blackwood's Magazine*, 1818–19, iv. 151, followed by two sentences taken from HW to Cole 5 Nov. 1782 and a last sentence taken from HW to Cole 22 May 1777: 'Were my course to recommence, and could one think in youth as one does at 65, I have no notion that I should have courage to appear as an author. Do you know, too, that I look on fame now, as the idlest of all visions? but this theme would lead me too far. I have always lived *post*, and shall now die before I can bait' (COLE ii. 46, 337).

Page 47, note 2, *add* Francis Douce left all his books to the Bodleian Library but all his carvings in ivory were bequeathed to Sir Samuel Rush Meyrick of Goodrich Court, Herefordshire. Sir Samuel published in the *Gentleman's Magazine* 1836 (new ser. v. 245–53, 378–84, 585–90; vi. 158–60, 378–84, 492–4, 598–601) a list of the Doucean Museum which included the ivories, and upon his death his property went to his second cousin Lt-Col. Augustus Meyrick. About 1871 this gentleman's son and heir sold the art treasures at Goodrich Court, mostly to M. Spitzer of Paris, and in 1893 the Spitzer collection which contained a large number of carvings in ivory, was disposed of by sale' (information from E. J. S. Parsons, Bodley Librarian).

Page 51, To Cole 19 June 1777, headnote, line 1, *add* A facsimile of the latter part of this letter, 'If any man . . . is of yesterday' (lacking the last sentence and salutation, and signed Hor. Walpole instead of H. W.), is in the State Library of Melbourne, Australia.

Page 54, note 8, *add* HW's copy is Hazen, *Cat. of HW's Lib*. No. 3383.

Page 55, note 2, line 9, *for* 1785 *read* 1786

Page 57–8, note 7, line 1, *for* 1746 *read* 1745　　*Lines 3–4, for* Redgrave, *Dict. of Artists read* Thieme and Becker xxiii. 364

Page 59, note 1, line 8, *after* 37 *add* (Hazen, *Cat. of HW's Lib.* No 3887)

Page 60, note 9, line 1, *after* 83), *insert* styled

Page 61, note 11, line 1, *for* 1459 *read* 1469　　*Line 4, add* See A. H. Lloyd, *Early History of Christ's College, Cambridge,* Cambridge, 1934, p. 391.

Page 62, To Cole 2 Oct. 1777, line 8, *for* be out out of *read* be out of

Page 63, note 1, *add* HW's copy of Masters's *Memoirs* is Hazen, *Cat. of HW's Lib.* No. 3820.

Page 66, note 1, line 4, *after* Bt *insert* (Hazen, *Cat. of HW's Lib.* Nos 3186, 4002　　*Line 6, for* Hannover *read* Hanover　　*Line 8, after* Ossian *insert* (Hazen, op. cit. No. 3198)

Page 67, note 2, line 1, *for* 24 *read* 23　　*Line 3, after* 1777 *add*　; see FAMILY 155

Page 75, note 4, line 3, *for* Shukburgh *read* Shuckburgh

Page 76, note 4, right column, line 5, *after* ii. 103 *insert* (Hazen, *Cat. of HW's Lib.* No. 568)　　*Lines 10–11, for* now Folger Library *read* now WSL

Page 78, note 9, *add* HW's copy is Hazen, *Cat. of HW's Lib.* No. 3168.

Pages 78–9, note 10, line 17, *after* 218. *add* HW's epitaph was reprinted in the *London Museum of Politics, Miscellanies, and Literature,* 1770, ii. 389–90 (see also MANN v. 132 and n. 27), and in the *Mémoires du Maréchal Duc de Richelieu,* 1793, viii. 337. For Benedict's letter about the inscription see MANN v. 124, 125–7, 204.

Page 79, 2d paragraph, line 4, *on* pottle *add note* 2a: 2a. OED *sub* 'pottle³' lists two instances of the usage, finding a needle in a pottle of hay.

Page 80, note 5, *add* HW's copy is Hazen, *Cat of HW's Lib.* No. 3347.

Page 80, note 10, *add* HW's copies are Hazen, *Cat. of HW's Lib.* Nos 217, 2041.

Page 85, note 7, line 4, *delete* [Jan. —]　　*Line 6, after* 63 *add*　; Hazen, *SH Bibl.* 116–19

Page 90, line 18, *on* mine *add note* 2a: 2a. But HW did acquire the 2d edn of *Biographia Britannica,* 5 vols, 1778–93; see Hazen, *Cat. of HW's Lib.* No. 217.

Pages 90–1, note 3, line 9, *for* 1780 *read* 1780, p. 189　　*Line 14, after* 51 *add* (Hazen, *Cat. of HW's Lib.* No. 3197).

Page 91, note 1, *delete first sentence and substitute* Although Cole noted that he never sent his letter of 28 May 1778 to HW, it seems probable that Cole enclosed the letter in his packet of materials about Thomas Baker.

Page 96, note 9, line 3, *after* that *insert* in Jan. 1603–4

Page 97, note 3, line 7, *for* J. Crouch *read* Isaac Crouch　　*Line 9, after* 796 *add*　; MASON ii. 41, n. 13

Page 99, line 18, *on* Indian summer *add note* 3a: 3a. The late Leonard Bacon suggested that HW means 'torrid summer'; see *post* Cole ii. 111; Ossory ii. 29 and n. 11; Mason i. 413.

Page 101, note 3, line 3, *for* Stonehewer *read* Stonhewer   *Line 11, for* rapture from *read* rapture in   *Last line, add* See also Mason i. 279–80, n. 8, 439, illustration.

Page 102, note 1, *add* See Hazen, *Cat. of HW's Lib.* No. 3408.

Page 105, note 10, *add* The original brass was in 1955 *penes* Anthony R. Wagner, Richmond Herald.

Page 105, note 2, *substitute* The manuscript of the *Letter to the Editor of the Miscellanies of Thomas Chatterton*, in Kirgate's hand, with HW's corrections and MS notes, is now in the Beinecke Library, Yale University.

Page 108, 4th paragraph, line 3, *for* Kerrick *read* Kerrich

Page 111, note 6, right column, line 8, *for* Anspach *read* Ansbach   *Last line, add* Cole noted on the verso of the title-page in his copy, 'Sent to me by the Hon. Horace Walpole, 27 August 1778, there being only 75 printed. Wm Cole'; see Hazen, *SH Bibl.* 114–16.

Page 111, note 8, *substitute* (ca 1722–Aug. 1778) was buried at St Chad's, Shrewsbury 11 Nov. 1778, aged 56 (*Shropshire Parish Registers. Diocese of Lichfield*, vols xv–xvii, *St Chad's, Shrewsbury*, ed. W. G. D. Fletcher, 1913–18, ii. 1381). Lord Herbert's 'account of the court of France' to which Scott refers is the 'letter book, whilst ambassador at Paris, 1619, 1620,' now in the British Museum, Add. MS 7082. The MS descended to Scott's third son, Jonathan Scott (1753–1829), the orientalist, and thence to his only child, Ann Dorothea Scott, wife of William Richard Stokes of Shrewsbury, her cousin. On the death of Jonathan Scott the younger, Stokes presented this MS and that of Lord Herbert's *Tractatus De Veritate* (now Add. MS 7081) to the British Museum. 'It appears that among the records of the Secretary's Office [of the British Museum] is a report which was made on the 14th March, 1829, of the donation of "a box of papers which belonged to the late Jonathan Scott, Esq., from his son-in-law, Mr W. R. Stokes, of Brunswick Row, Queen's Square" ' (H. F. J. Vaughan, 'Lord Herbert of Chirbury's MSS,' in *Transactions of the Shropshire Archæological and Natural History Society*, 1880, iii. 376; see also *Index to the Additional Manuscripts . . . in the British Museum, and acquired in the Years 1783–1835*, 1849). Lord Herbert's letters have been printed in *Old Herbert Papers at Powis Castle and in the British Museum*, privately printed, 1886, pp. 213–80; also in *Collections Historical and Archæological relating to Montgomeryshire . . .* , vol. xx (extra volume). The correspondence between HW and the elder Jonathan Scott is missing. H. F. J. Vaughan states that Scott 'appears to have been a friend of Walpole' (op. cit. 374).

Page 112, note 9, lines 2–3, *for* Barbara Antonia *read* Barbara   *Last line, add* See Hazen, *SH Bibl.* 68–70.

Page 112, note 10, *add* HW's presentation copy to him of *The Life of Edward Lord Herbert of Cherbury* is now WSL (Hazen, *SH Bibl.* 1973, p. xviii).

Page 112, note 11, line 1, *after* Folliott *insert* (b. 1758, d. before 1829) *Line 2, after* Henry *insert* (1762–ca 1845)   *Last line, add* See *Shropshire Parish Registers* (vols xv–xvii), St Chad's, Shrewsbury, ii. 1122–3, 1239.

Page 112, note 12, line 4, *for* (d. before 1829) *read* (b. 1750, d. before 1829)   *Line 5, for* 1754 *read* 1753   *Last line, add* See *Shropshire Parish Registers* (vols xv–xvii), St Chad's, Shrewsbury, ii. 1134, 1161.

Page 119, note 4, line 12, *for* 1720? *read* 1709

Page 120, note 5, line 8, *for* but *read* and   *Lines 9–12, delete* among the ... Gardiner's mother. *and substitute* there is 'no evidence to prove that Lord Walpole indulged in a liaison with his chaplain's wife' (*Norfolk Portraits*, 1944, pp. 110–11).

Page 124, 2d paragraph, line 16, *on* transacted *add note* 11: 11. For Sir Robert Walpole. The sum involved was said by Lord Hervey to be £100,000 (Lord Hervey, *Memoirs of the Reign of King George II*, ed. Romney Sedgwick, 1931, i. 28).

Page 125, note 11, line 1, *for* 1681? *read* ca 1688   *Line 3, after* Suffolk *add*   ; m. 2 (1735) Hon. George Berkeley.

Page 135, note 3, lines 1–4, *delete* Anna ... Pomfret. *and substitute* Hon. Henrietta Louisa Jeffreys (d. 1761), m. (1720) Thomas Fermor, 2d Bn Leominster, 1711, cr. (1721) E. of Pomfret.   *Line 10, for* backwards.' *read* backwards' (Ossory ii. 82 and n. 9).

Page 135, 3d paragraph, line 3, *on* ancestry *add note* 7a: 7a. In 'Mem. 1783–91,' *sub* 20 April 1784, HW says that Leicester was 'mad about pedigree, and called himself heir to the title [Earl of Leicester], because, as an hundred others were, he was descended from a female Sidney.' See also Ossory ii. 465 and n. 1.

Page 146, note 1, *add* It is now WSL (see Hazen, *Cat. of HW's Lib.* No. 3).

Page 147, note 1, *add* See Hazen, *SH Bibl.* 119.

Page 149, To Cole 28 March 1779, 2d paragraph, line 8, *on* fandangos *add note* 2a: 2a. HW makes a similar comment to William Robertson 30 May 1777; see DALRYMPLE 137 and nn. 11, 12.

Page 149, note 1, *add* See Hazen, *Cat. of HW's Lib.* No. 2960.

Page 150, note 3, *add* See Hazen, *Cat. of HW's Lib.* No. 1810:30.

Page 153, note 11, *add* (Hazen, *Cat. of HW's Lib.* No. 611).

Page 153, note 12, *add* It is now in the British Museum (Hazen, *Cat. of HW's Lib.* No. 475).

Page 154, note 18, *add* See Hazen, *Cat. of HW's Lib.* No. 6.

Page 154, note 21, line 1, *for* 1710 *read* 1711   *Last line, after* 280b *add*   ; Namier and Brooke iii. 304

Page 158, To Cole 23 April 1779, 3d paragraph, line 5, *on* Czarina *add note* 1: 1. 'We are credibly informed that the Empress of Russia has purchased 25 pictures from the collection of the late Earl of Orford at Houghton, at £40,000, and that a man of war is to be sent to Yarmouth to convoy them from thence to Russia' (*London Chronicle* 24–27 April 1779, xlv. 398).

Page 159, left column, note 2, line 2, *for* is possible *read* seems   *Line 3, add* See *post* COLE ii. 166, 168; MANN viii. 441 and n. 15.

Page 159, To Cole 21 May 1779, note 1, line 6, *after* 1779 *insert* (HW's copy is Hazen, *Cat. of HW's Lib.* No. 2806)

Page 160, note 5, *add* HW's copy of vol. ii. is listed in Hazen, *Cat. of HW's Lib.* No. 1568.

Page 161, 1st paragraph, line 7, *on* MS *add note* 7a: 7a. Mrs Elizabeth Carter wrote to Mrs Montagu 18 Oct. 1779, 'Have you read Mr Keate's Sketches? It was our evening amusement at Mill Hill; and I think it a very pretty book for such kind of reading. I am told Mr Walpole was caught by the story of the sisters (as the author designed he should be) and made an enquiry after the Louvain manuscript' (*Letters . . . to Mrs Montagu*, ed. Montagu Pennington, 1817, iii. 113–14).

Page 162, note 5, *add* See Nichols, *Lit. Anec.* vi. 226–58.

Page 164, note 5, *add* In *The Antiquary*, 1880, i. 17, 63, she is said to have been buried 27 Dec. 1777, although the monument to her memory gives the date of her death as 1778.

Page 164, note 8, *add* John Hillaby in the *New York Times* 7 Aug. 1959 described the archæological excavation which uncovered the basic plan of Nonsuch palace and its precise site, as well as evidence that the south wall was faced with gilded tiles.

Page 165, note 10, *add* The sale was completed in July; see MANN viii. 502 and n. 8.

Page 165, note 13, line 5, *after* 163 *add* and is now WSL (Hazen, *Cat. of HW's Lib.* No. 1840).

Page 167, note 17, line 9, *after* Plates. *insert* Since the print is inscribed 'B. 1733 D. 1793,' it could not possibly have been in the 1778 edition. The fact that it was engraved and sold separately for 5s. each print, seems to prove that it was not published in any edition of the *Tour in Wales*.

Page 168, note 2, *substitute The Catalogue of the Manuscript Library of the Late Dawson Turner*, 6 June 1859, lists as lot 383 a 2-vol. catalogue of picture sales circa 1760, which includes 171 catalogues of collections sold with the prices and names of the purchasers. Among these is 'Lord Orford (3 sales 1741–48–53)' (p. 164). The date 1741 is probably a mistake for 1751, since there was certainly a sale on 13–14 June 1751 OS; for a discussion of these sales see MANN viii. 441, n. 13.

Page 168, note 3, *add* HW wrote to Mann 11 Feb. 1779 that Giovanni Battista Cipriani and Benjamin West made an itemized list of the values of the Houghton pictures (totalling £40,555); see MANN viii. 441 and n. 15, 502 and n. 8.

Page 170, note 17, *add* The figures of Faith, Hope, and Charity were in the Royal Academy Exhibition of 1779, where HW saw the portions of Jervais's window on exhibition; see Ossory ii. 417–18 and nn. 20–3.

Page 171, 1st paragraph, line 7, *on* from *add note* 1a: 1a. For HW's explanation see Mann viii. 440–1.

Page 173, note 2, line 1, *after* 1779 *add* (Mason i. 453–5, 457; see also Mann viii. 506)

Page 178, note 7, *add* HW's copy is Hazen, *Cat. of HW's Lib.* No. 530.

Page 182, note 13, *for* 8th E. of Kinnoul *read* 9th E. of Kinnoull

Page 184, note 22, *add* See the fanciful water-colour 'Wreck of the Houghton Pictures,' 1838, by J. S. Cotman in Sydney D. Kitson, *The Life of John Sell Cotman*, 1937, plate 134 and pp. 343–4.

Page 185, note 6, *add* See Hazen, *Cat. of HW's Lib.* No. 581.

Page 188, note 13, *add* See Hazen, *SH Bibl.* 46–8.

Page 189, note 20, *add* Cunningham's note is ambiguous, but in the letter to Mason HW wrote that it was Barry's 'Venus Rising from the Sea' at which he laughed (Mason ii. 298). HW's MS reply to Barry (now WSL) is printed in Ossory iii. 243–4, Appendix 4.

Page 191, note 4, *add* Cole received a presentation copy and HW later bought the new edition (*post* Cole ii. 215, 237–40).

Page 191, note 5a, *substitute* HW had two copies, one of which is now WSL; see Hazen, *Cat. of HW's Lib.* Nos 2902, 3200.

Page 195, note 4, *add* HW's copy, 1780 edn, is Hazen, *Cat. of HW's Lib.* No. 358.

Page 195, note 5, line 1, *for* (ca 1363–ca 1431) *read* (1364–ca 1430) *Last line, add* See Marie-Josèphe Pinet, *Christine de Pisan, 1364–1430, étude biographique et littéraire*, 1927, pp. 1, 200.

Page 197, 1st paragraph, line 8, *on ferentes add note* 13a: 13a. Virgil, *Æneid*, ii. 48: 'Equo ne credite Teucri./ Quidquid id est, timeo Danaos et dona ferentis' ('Do not trust the horse, Trojans. Whatever it is, I fear the Danaans even though bearing gifts').

Page 197, 2d paragraph, line 1, *on Authors add note* 14a: 14a. This is the copy now in the Bodleian Library; HW gave Cole another copy. See *post* Cole ii. 199, 206–7, n. 1; Hazen, *SH Bibl.* 37.

Page 199, note 4, line 5, *for* Seymour-Conway *read* Seymour Conway *add* See Conway i. 484, 489.

Page 200, note 5, line 8, *after* 1780 *add*   , Mason ii. 45 and n. 21 for a complete history of this picture.   *Line 9, for* —— Smith *read* J. M. Smith   *Line 13, for* ibid. *read Works*

Page 200, note 10, line 1, *for* 1758 *read* 1738

Page 203, note 9, *add* See Mason ii. 6–7 and nn. 24, 25; HW's copy is Hazen, *Cat. of HW's Lib.* No. 2364.

Page 204, line 25, *on* history *add note* 3a: 3a. That is, the 'ideas of art and history' are the avowed ends of 'antiquities.'

Page 204, note 2, *for last sentence substitute* HW's copies are Hazen, *Cat. of HW's Lib.* Nos 2880, 3170.

Pages 204–5, note 4, line 12, *after* DNB). *add* HW's copy is now WSL (Hazen, *Cat. of HW's Lib.* No. 2366).

Page 205, line 26, *on* Academy *add note* 6a: 6a. On 23 April 1771; see HW to William Bewley 23 May 1778, CHATTERTON 129 and n. 77.

Page 206, middle of page, *insert the following heading*:

To COLE, Sunday 26 March 1780

Not sent; printed *post* COLE ii. 363–6, Appendix 3.

Pages 206–7, note 1, line 5, *for* 1759 *read* 1758   *Last line, add* See Hazen, *SH Bibl.* 37.

Page 209, To Cole 30 March 1780, 2d paragraph, line 5, *on* Constitution *add note* 1: 1. See also MASON ii. 17–18.

Page 212, note 5, *add* HW's copy is Hazen, *Cat. of HW's Lib.* No. 1609: 41:2.

Page 214, note 14, *add* See Hazen, *Cat. of HW's Lib.* No. 1101.

Page 216, note 1, *add* HW's copy of Cooke's *Civil Liberty, a Sermon* is Hazen, *Cat. of HW's Lib.* No. 3410.

Page 217, note 4, *add* See *post* COLE ii. 237–40; Hazen, *Cat. of HW's Lib.* No. 33.

Page 220, note 3, *after* 12 *add* (Hazen, *Cat. of HW's Lib.* No. 528).

Page 222, note 6, line 1, *for* 1680 *read* 1682

Page 223, note 8, line 3, *for master-cook read master-cooks   Line 6, for* G. Brander *read* Gustavus Brander, Esq.   *Line 8, for last sentence substitute* HW's copy is now WSL; it is bound in Vol. 41 of 'Tracts of George III' and bears a presentation from Gustavus Brander (Hazen, *Cat. of HW's Lib.* No. 1609:41:8).

Page 223, note 9, line 5, *after* 1780 *insert*   ; MASON ii. 18 and n. 10 *Line 12, after* 58 *add* (Hazen, *Cat. of HW's Lib.* No. 3688).

Pages 223–4, note 10, *add* It is now in the library of Brodick Castle, Isle of Arran (Hazen, *Cat. of HW's Lib.* No. 2380).

Page 224, note 3, *add* Mrs Elizabeth Carter wrote 22 June 1780, 'My brother saw the first assembling of the rioters at Bath, and immediately went to acquaint the magistrates, and did all he could to persuade them to exert themselves. The mischief might have been prevented with the greatest ease, for the rioters were half an hour in forcing open the door of the chapel. A constable, frightened out of his wits, asked what could be done against six hundred men? My brother told him he had been in the place and that there was not in the lower room above six or seven, and that he was positively sure that those above did not amount to one hundred. But the constable was not to be persuaded, he afterwards took two gentlemen whom he met, and convinced them by their own eyes, that his statement was just, but it was all of no effect' (*Letters . . . to Mrs Montagu,* ed. Montagu Pennington, 1817, iii. 132).

Page 232, note 6, line 2, *after* Masters *add* in his *Athenæ Cantabrigien-ses*

Page 233, note 4, *substitute* She died two days before her eighty-fourth birthday (DU DEFFAND v. 368, n. 23).

Page 233, note 5, *add* See FAMILY 175, 176, 178.

Page 235, note 7, line 3, *after* m. *insert* (1750)

Page 237, note 4, line 2, *for* Barrett *read* Barret   *for* 1744 *read* ?1743

Page 237, note 1, *add* HW did acquire this edition (see Hazen, *Cat. of HW's Lib*. No. 33), for which Cole had sent Gough HW's notes made in his copy of the 1st edition. For HW's further comments see *post* COLE ii. 249; OSSORY ii. 576.

Page 238, note 2, *add* The passage is on p. xi (not p. xl) of vol. i.

Page 238, note 4, *substitute* HW noted in his copy of Gough, 'This account is totally erroneous. Mr Walpole did by Bp Lyttelton's intervention purchase of Mr Lethieullier's sister for £60 the three volumes of drawings' (*British Topography*, 1780, i. p. x, now in the Huntington Library).

Page 239, line 13, *on* books *add note* 5a: 5a. They were sold London 1260, and are now BM Add. MSS 27348–50; for a complete history see Hazen, *Cat. of HW's Lib*. No. 3503.

Page 239, note 9, *delete last sentence*

Page 245, note 2, *add* HW uses this quotation in letters to Mann 6 Nov. 1769, 6 Oct. 1774 (MANN vii. 151, viii. 48).

Page 248, note 2, *add* Hazen believes that the 1st edition of volumes i, ii, iii of the *Anecdotes*, and of the *Engravers*, consisted of 300 copies, that the 2d edition of these volumes was also of 300 copies, and that the entries in *Jour. Print. Off.* and in *Description of SH* included both the 1st and 2d editions of these volumes (see *SH Bibl.* 55–6). Therefore HW's letter to Cole is accurate.

Page 248, note 3a, *add* For descriptions of further copies see Hazen, *SH Bibl.* 1973, pp. xvi–xvii, 66–8.

Page 249, note 8, *add* HW noted in his copy that only one drawing was by Marlow, the others were by Sandby and Pars, and the chimney-pieces by Bentley (OSSORY ii. 576, n. 20).

Page 251, note 6, line 5, *for* Du *read* du   *Last line, after* 1780 *add*   , DU DEFFAND iii. 28, v. 201; see also i. pp. xliii–xlvi

Page 255, note 6, *add* HW's copy, containing some notes by HW, is now WSL (Hazen, *Cat. of HW's Lib*. No. 3850).

Page 257, note 3, *for* Italian savant *read* Giulio Giuseppe Mozzi (1730–1813), cavaliere; mathematician.

Page 262, note 1, right column, line 4, *after* Walpole *add* who in 1938 gave it to the King's School, Canterbury (see Hazen, *Cat. of HW's Lib*. No. 3924)

Page 262, From Cole 4 March 1781, 2d paragraph, line 5, *on* anvil *add note* 5: 5. Possibly *A Collection of all the Wills, now known to be extant, of the Kings and Queens of England . . .*, ed. John Nichols, 1780, which

HW acquired (see Hazen, *Cat. of HW's Lib*. No. 3350) and occasionally referred to (e.g., CONWAY iii. 473).

Page 263, note 1, last line, *after* 135 *add* and is now WSL (Hazen, *Cat. of HW's Lib*. No. 999)

Page 264, note 4a, *add* Cole wrote to Gough 15 March 1781, 'You have heard, no doubt, of Mr Walpole's being chosen an Honorary Member of the new Antiquarian Society at Edinburgh. The admission of a few things into our *Archæologia*, I fear, has estranged forever one of the most lively, learned, and entertaining members on our list [i.e., the London Society of Antiquaries]. The thing is unfortunately done, and he irrecoverable' (LA i. 690).

Page 270, note 7, lines 1–2, *for* published *read* reprinted   *after* 1781. *insert* 'After the announcement of the intended publication had prevented the spurious edition, HW decided not to publish his edition' but privately presented copies to his friends (Hazen, *SH Bibl*. 82–3; see also MASON ii. 139 and nn. 16–20, 148).

Page 272, note 7, line 2, *after* 1780–90 *add* (Hazen, *Cat. of HW's Lib*. No. 3348)

Page 273, note 1, *add* HW's copy, now WSL, is Hazen, *Cat. of HW's Lib*. No. 3220.

Page 273, note 3, *add* For the 2d edition, 1782, HW sent his corrections to Nichols in a long letter, 31 Oct. 1781. HW's copies of both editions are Hazen, *Cat. of HW's Lib*. Nos 2435, 3860.

Page 273, note 4, *add* Steevens's collection of Hogarth's prints is now WSL.

Page 274, note 8, line 1, *for* 1736 *read* 1738

Page 274, note 10, *substitute* In 1781 HW printed an 'Appendix' to the 1774 edition of *Description of SH*; in the summer of 1784 he printed 'Additions since the Appendix'; in the summer of 1786 he printed more additions (see Hazen, *SH Bibl*. 109). During 1784 HW printed a new edition of the *Description*, to which he added an 'Appendix' printed in 1786, and further additions printed in 1789 and 1791 (ibid. 125).

Page 275, note 16, line 2, *for* 1673 *read* 1674   *Line 8, after* DNB *add* ; Edward Walford, *Tales of our Great Families*, 2d series, 1880, i. 180–1

Page 275, note 17, line 1, *for* over *read* Over   *Lines 17–30, delete* The head . . . Lord Lilford. *and substitute* A drawing of the head by John Carter (see illustration) was sent to HW by Lort and was pasted into HW's extra-illustrated *Description of SH*, 1784 (now WSL), opposite p. 32; another sketch, showing where the head originally hung in the church, was pasted beneath the drawing (see Lort to HW 23 Dec. 1780, 2 April 1781, CHATTERTON 192–3 and nn. 2, 3). The later history of the head is ibid. 192–3, n. 3.

Pages 277–8, note 13, *add* HW comments on this book to Mason 3 Jan. and 10 Jan. 1782 (see MASON ii. 173, 175).

Page 278, note 1, *add* HW's copy was the London, 1686, folio edition (Hazen, *Cat. of HW's Lib.* No. 607).

Page 280, note 3, line 1, *after* additions *insert* (vol. iv, 2d edn)   *Line 2, for* 4 vols *read* 5 vols (Hazen, *SH Bibl.* 65)

Page 281, note 5, *add* See Goldsmith's 'Where Calvert's butt, and Parsons' black champagne,/ Regale the drabs and bloods of Drury Lane' ('Description of an Author's Bedchamber,' ll. 3–4; pointed out by the late Leonard Bacon).

Page 287, note 1, *add* HW and Cole contributed to Gough's work, and HW lent many drawings; Gough acknowledged HW's help in his preface and on p. *36 (Hazen, *Bibl. of HW* 143 and *Cat. of HW's Lib.* No. 3644).

Page 287, note 2, *add* See Hazen, *Cat. of HW's Lib.* No. 3690:5, 6; Chatterton 351–7.

Page 287, note 3, line 3, *after* Museum *add* (Hazen, *Cat. of HW's Lib.* No. 3690:1)   *Line 5, after* correspondence *add*   , Chatterton 331–43

Pages 287–8, note 5, line 6, *after* WSL *add*   ; Hazen, *Cat. of HW's Lib.* No. 3690:10

Page 288, note 6, line 6, *after* WSL *add*   ; Hazen, *Cat. of HW's Lib.* No. 3690:9

Page 288, note 9, *substitute* The *Public Advertiser* 28, 29 Dec. 1781 printed a summary of arguments and extracts from Milles's edition. HW probably refers to 28 Dec.: '... the Dean draws certain inferences: That there did exist *Parchments*; that Chatterton early discovered a taste for preeminence; that he could not be charged with venality; that he was a lover of truth—that all these militate against the idea of forgery in these poems ... That he who was above venality, and so great a lover of truth, should make himself a living lie, and impose on the world a forgery which tempted him with no honour or advantage, unless any could be supposed to rise from the reputed antiquity of these poems.' This passage is summarized and loosely quoted from Milles's edition, pp. 12–13.

Page 289, note 14, *add* For its later history see Hazen, *Cat. of HW's Lib.* No. 258.

Page 292, note 8, left column, line 6, *after* second edition *insert*   , sent 4 Feb. 1782 by Malone to HW,   *Line 8, after* correspondence *add* , Chatterton 363

Page 292, note 9, line 7, *for* 1721? *read* ca 1720   *Lines 10–19, delete* The original ... ii. 227. *and substitute* The MS and a copy (of which there seem to have been many) are now WSL. The letter was printed in the *London Magazine* Sept. 1743, xii. 456. See Selwyn 42 and n. 11.

Pages 296–7, note 8, *for last sentence substitute* The copy presumably presented by Jephson to HW, sold SH vi. 21, is now WSL (Hazen, *Cat. of HW's Lib.* No. 2402). Another copy bound in Vol. 36 of HW's collection of plays is in the Merritt Collection of the Harvard University Library (ibid. No. 1810:33:6, 36).

Page 299, note 7, line 1, *for* 1714 *read* 1717   *Line 15, add* Whaley's letters to HW are in Misc. Corr. i. 3–6, 8–17, 21–3, 42–4, 48–50

Page 299, note 8, line 2, *for* Kings *read* King's   *Line 12, for* Varrane's *read* Varranes'   *Line 20, for* Whalley's *read* Whaley's

Page 300, To Cole 15 Feb. 1782, 1st paragraph, line 11, *on* pleasant *add note* 1a: 1a. Steevens wrote to Michael Lort 17 March 1783, 'I have had a very long and obliging letter from Mr Walpole, with an invitation to call on him. I shall show you somewhat touching the *Goth's* politeness when I see you next. He complains loudly of my monopoly, as he calls it, of the only book in which he could be supposed to have an interest; but by this time he has learned he is more deeply concerned as to others, not one of which he shall ever see' (MS in the Folger Library; photostat in the Osborn Collection, Beinecke Library, Yale University).

Page 301, note 2, *add* HW's copies of Sherlock's *Lettres d'un voyageur anglois*, 1779, and *Nouvelles lettres d'un voyageur anglois*, 1780, are Hazen, *Cat. of HW's Lib.* Nos 3050, 3051.

Page 302, note 6, *add* The *Gazetteer and New Daily Advertiser* reported 16 March 1791: 'The note left by Mr Wilkes in the album of the Grande Chartreuse says he was edified by the conversation of the fathers. If his edification is to be judged by his works, is not this note a libel upon the society?'

Page 306, note 3, last line, *after* 145 *add* ; GM 1750, xx. 188

Page 309, To Cole 9 March 1782, 2d paragraph, line 1, *on* Farmer *add note* a: a. Cole wrote to George Steevens 10 March 1782 (MS now wsl): 'By a letter today from Mr Walpole ['this day' inserted here] I am informed, that Dr Farmer has called at Berkeley Square but neither he nor you mention whether it was before or since his being at Canterbury. I have since heard, that he is expected in College tomorrow.' Farmer was installed Prebendary of Canterbury on 5 March (Cole ii. 304, 308).

Page 311, 2d paragraph, line 5, *on* inscription *add note* 7a: 7a. The *Cambridge Review* 29 Oct. 1937, lix. 48–9, prints a letter from F. A. Keynes which states that a MS containing a 'Latin inscription for the New Town Hall, Cambridge, 1782' (said to be in Cole's handwriting) had been found in the University Library, and that the stone with the lettering perfectly clear 'was discovered by the excavators, lying on its face in what was apparently its original position. . . . It is now safe in the completed portion of the present Town Hall.'

Page 315, note 5, *add* HW's copy is bound in Vol. 18 of his 'Poems of George III' now in the Harvard University Library (see Mason ii. 199 and n. 1; Hazen, *Cat. of HW's Lib.* No. 3222:18:1).

Page 319, note 3, right column, line 3, *after* wsl *add* (Hazen, *Cat. of HW's Lib.* No. 3690:17)

Page 319, note 4, line 3, *after* 1788 *insert* , Chatterton 214–15 and n. 8

Page 320, 1st paragraph, line 6, *on* garden *add note a*: a. See *Country Life* 26 Jan. 1961, cxxvii pt i. 186.

Page 320, note 3, lines 4–8, *delete* From him . . . loc. cit.). *and substitute* The picture was bought at the sale of his uncle, Hon. Felton Hervey, who died 16 Aug. 1773 (see *ante* Cole ii. 8, n. 9; Namier and Brooke ii. 619).

Page 320, note 5, *add* For his death 22 Dec. 1779 and will, see Ossory ii. 148–9.

Page 320, note 6, line 2, *after* 1776 *add*   , which is correct   *Lines 2–6, delete* The earlier account . . . the present.'

Pages 321–2, note 13, *add* HW severely criticized Cumberland's book in his letter to Mason 13 April 1782, and referred to an adverse review in *Public Advertiser* 13 April 1782 (see Mason ii. 232 and n. 14). HW's copy is Hazen, *Cat. of HW's Lib.* No. 3411.

Page 323, note 3, *add* Vertue's original water-colour copy, the basis for this engraving, is in the Royal Library (information from the late Sir Owen F. Morshead).

Page 323, 2d paragraph, line 4, *on* see it *add note 3a*: 3a. HW saw the account of Newton's life in Henry Maty's *New Review* May 1782, i. 272–84; see Mason ii. 254 and n. 10; Chute 514.

Page 323, note 7, line 2, *for* 3d E. *read* 2d E.   *Line 3, for* 2d E. *read* 3d E.

Page 324, line 1, *on* Melmoth *add note 8a*: 8a. HW's copy has not been located; see Hazen, *Cat. of HW's Lib.* No. 1810:34:2.

Page 327, note 1, *after* 138 *add*   , and is now WSL (Hazen, *Cat. of HW's Lib.* No. 997)

Page 327, note 2, *add* See Hazen, *Cat. of HW's Lib.* No. 1228.

Page 327, note 3, last line, *after* 131 *add* (Hazen, *Cat. of HW's Lib.* No. 1026)

Page 328, note 9, *add* See Hazen, *Cat. of HW's Lib.* No. 348.

Page 328, note 10, line 1, *for* 1667 *read* 1666

Page 331, note 20, lines 2–3, *for* (1760–ca 1825) *read* (ca 1758–ca 1822) *Lines 4–9, substitute* (ca 1765–1849), m. Joseph Garrow, contralto (*The New Grove Dictionary of Music and Musicians*, ed. Stanley Sadie, 1980, i. 23; Berry i. 109, n. 16).

Page 332, note 1, *add* HW's copy is now WSL (Hazen, *Cat. of HW's Lib.* No. 3349).

Page 332, note 5, line 4, *after* 1782. *insert* HW's copy is Hazen, *Cat. of HW's Lib.* No. 3225.   *Line 7, add* John Pinkerton wrote of the *Catalogue*, 'not to be named without praise, as the best digested ever yet offered to the public' (*An Essay on Medals*, 2d edn, 1789, ii. 276).

Page 333, note 2, last line, *after* 47 *add* (Hazen, *Cat. of HW's Lib.* No. 1173); HW's copy of the *Essai sur l'histoire générale* is ibid. No. 1172

Page 337, line 3, *on* genuine *add note 1a*: 1a. 'The present scarcity of the true Peruvian bark, . . . has tempted these people to vend the bark of a tree (the growth of Jamaica), called the bullen-tree. This powder . . . is always given in treble the quantity, to attain the desired effect' (*London Chronicle* 29–31 Oct. 1782, lii. 424).

Page 337, note 2, *after* v. 4 *add* (Hazen, *Cat. of HW's Lib.* No. 3338:3)

Page 341, headnote, *add* Cole may have written this note during the time (28 May to ca 7 July) when he had not found a person to deliver his letter and notes on Thomas Baker to HW, but it seems probable that Cole eventually enclosed the letter in his packet of materials about Thomas Baker. Cole writes 7 June (COLE ii. 87), 'I have all my materials together' and regrets a falsehood in the account in the new *Biographia Britannica* about Prior's allowing the profits of his fellowship to go to Baker. HW answers 10 June (ii. 90), 'Pray send me your paper on Mr Prior's generosity to Mr Baker.' Then Cole writes on 14 June (ii. 91), 'I have sent Dr Heberden<'s> letter, with some others and my own, which I meant to have sent to you on May 28.' On 4 July Cole says Lort will deliver 'my packet' (ii. 97). HW on 12 July replies (ii. 98) on the problem of Prior's support of Baker and on other topics discussed in Cole's letter of 28 May. HW returned Cole's materials 15 Jan. 1779 (ii. 138).

Page 347, line 24, *on* writer *add note* 11a: 11a. Gough (see LA vi. 4n).

Page 363, headnote, lines 1–2, *substitute* Formerly in the possession of the Earl of Derby, now WSL. Now first published.

Page 363, note 2, line 3, *for* 3d D. *read* cr. (1485) D.

Page 364, note 11, line 1, *for* (ca 1430–85), 8th D. *read* (d. 1485), cr. (1470) Lord Howard and (1483) D.

Page 364, note 13, line 1, *for* 1474 *read* 1473   *Line* 2, *for* 1494 *read* ca 1491

Page 364, note 15, line 1, *for* 18th *read* 17th

Page 365, note 16, *substitute* Mary Fitzlewis (ca 1465–after 1483), dau. of Sir Henry Fitzlewis, of Horndon, Essex, and Lady Elizabeth Beaufort, m. 1 (before Oct. 1480, as his 2d wife) Anthony Wydevill, 2d E. Rivers, 1469, who d. 1483; m. 2 Sir George Neville.

Page 365, note 18, line 1, *for* 1535 *read* ca 1540

Page 366, note 25, line 1, *for* of Lancaster *read* (Plantagenet)   *for* d. 1426 *read* d. 1425   *Lines* 2–3, *for* John Holland, D. of Exeter *read* (1386) John de Holand, cr. (1388) E. of Huntingdon, (1397) D. of Exeter *Line 3, after* (2) *add* (before 12 Dec. 1400)   *after* Cornwall *add* (*or* Cornewaille)

Page 368, note 5, *substitute* (d. Aug. 1762), lived at Cross Deep House, Twickenham (MISC. CORR. iii. Appendix 1, map and p. 487 n. 1).

Page 371, line 22, *on* her *add note* 11a: 11a. Sir Robert Walpole in his will made a bequest to Catherine Daye, who lived with her mother, Carey Daye, in Chichester. HW did know of Catherine Daye's existence, and he and Sir Edward Walpole were called upon to assist her in financial matters; but HW may not have been aware of her two sisters at this time. See MANN iv. 346–7; FAMILY 53, 59; BERRY i. 281–2 and n. 14, 306–7; OSSORY iii. 186–7.

Page 371, note 14, lines 2–3, *delete* in October . . . Oct. 1775). *and substitute* 21 Aug. 1775, aged 51 (OSSORY i. 245, 271; DU DEFFAND v. 398).

Page 373, note 23, *before* Moses *insert* Probably Aaron Franks (ca 1685 or 1692–1777), jeweller and money-lender of London, who had a house in Isleworth, where HW attended a concert 11 Nov. 1774 (CHUTE 350 and n. 5). Aaron Franks's son-in-law,

Page 373, note 24, *substitute* Phila Franks, dau. of Aaron Franks, m. her cousin Moses Franks (Hilda F. Finberg, 'Jewish Residents in Eighteenth-Century Twickenham,' Jewish Historical Society of England, *Transactions Sessions 1945–1951*, xvi. 130; Brown's *Chancery Cases* iv. 83). Their only daughter, Isabella Ball Franks (ca 1770–1855) would have been only four years old in 1774 (see GEC, *Baronetage*, ii. 447).

Page 373, note 25, line 5, *after* 107 *add* ; for further identification see MISC. CORR. iii. Appendix 1, map and p. 351; OSSORY i. 207–8 and n. 12. *Line 7, after* 1785 *add* , MORE 238, n. 7, where she is identified as the 'Mrs Salvador' who m. (1751) Abraham Prado, and who d. in 1788.

Page 375, *add to Appendix 6*

During Cole's visit at Strawberry Hill, on 29 Oct. 1774, HW gave Cole one of the six large-paper copies of the *Des. of SH*, 1774; this copy is now WSL (Hazen, *SH Bibl.* 110). Cole copied into it the notes from HW's copy, including (on the verso of p. 119) a 'List of the Books [18 items] printed at Strawberry Hill,' at the end of which Cole noted, 'Copied this at Strawberry Hill from a paper in Mr Walpole's own writing. Wm Cole. 1774.' After Cole's death in 1782 'it was sold to a bookseller,' according to HW's letter to Lady Ossory 15 Sept. 1787 (OSSORY ii. 575). But this book does not appear in Benjamin White's *Catalogue of the Entire Libraries of Charles Hedges, Esq. . . . and of the Rev. William Cole, the Eminent Antiquary . . .*' (the sale beginning on 3 Feb. 1784). Cole's copy of *Des. of SH* was acquired by Thomas Barret of Lee Priory, Kent, and remained in the possession of his descendants until 1859 (sold Sotheby's 12 July 1859, Barrett Sale, lot 523, to Boone). It was later acquired by Lord Waldegrave, whose descendant sold it to WSL in 1948.

The *Public Advertiser* 5 Sept. 1787 printed a list of books printed at Strawberry Hill which HW disclaims sending to the newspaper (to Lady Ossory 15 Sept. 1787, OSSORY ii. 574, 576): 'I am sorry too on many accounts that this idle list has been printed . . . The list of my editions was procured by some of these *liberal* artifices—and yet is not complete'; (and to Lady Ossory 4 Oct. 1787, ibid. 578) 'I told you that the list was an imperfect one, and not such as I avow—but I let newspapers and magazines say what they please of me without setting them right.' The first eighteen items of the list are said to be taken from a paper in HW's handwriting.

From the *Public Advertiser* 5 September 1787

As the Strawberry Hill editions of the following books are sold at most exorbitant prices, I have sent you a list of the number of copies which were printed.

As their value, in a great measure, depends upon their scarcity, this list (which I believe was never published before) will be of some use to the collectors:

Catalogue of books printed at Strawberry Hill.

		Copies.
1757.	Two *Odes*, by Mr Gray, 4to.	1000
	Translation of part of Hentzner's *Travels*, twelves,	220
1758.	*Royal and Noble Authors*, 2 vols, 12mo.	300
	Walpole's *Fugitive Pieces*, 12mo.	200
	Whitworth's *Account of Russia*, 12mo.	700
	Spence's *Parallel* between Magliabertie [*sic*] and Hill, 12 mo.	700
1759.	Bentley's *Lucan*, quarto,	500
1762.	*Anecdotes of Painting*, 5 vols, quarto,	600
1765.	Second edition of the same	
1764.	*Life of Lord Herbert, of Cherbury*, quarto,	200
	Lady Temple's *Poems*, 4to.	100
1768.	*Corneli Trag. par le P. Henault*, 12mo.	200
	One hundred and fifty of these were sent to Paris.	
	Mysterious Mother, a tragedy, by Mr Walpole,	50
1769.	Hoyland's *Poems*, 12mo.	300
1770.	*Mémoires de Gramont*, small 4to.	100
	Letters of Edward the Sixth, small quarto,	200
1772.	*Miscellaneous Antiquities*, 2 vols, small quarto,	500
1774.	*Description of Strawberry Hill*, small quarto,	100
	Six were printed on large paper.	

The foregoing list is copied from a paper in the handwriting of Mr Walpole.

1781.	*Muse Recalled.*
1779.	*Letters to the Editor of Chatterton's Poems.*
1778.	*Sleep Walker.*
1766.	*Castle of Otranto*, London.
1768.	*Historic Doubts*, London.
1752.	*Ædes Walpolianae*, London.

This cutting from the *Public Advertiser* was found in the following book, now WSL: [George Baker (1747–1811)] *A catalogue of books, poems, tracts, and small detached pieces, printed at the press at Strawberry-Hill, belonging to the late Horace Walpole, Earl of Orford*, [London] J. Barker, printer [1811]. Introduction signed by G. B., Dec. 31, 1810. One of 20 copies, published shortly after the author's death and distributed by his brother, Richard; J. Haslewood's copy, with note of R. Baker, portrait of G. Baker, and a life of Baker from Sotheby's catalogue of 16 June 1825. Gift of Miss A. B. Jennings to WSL, Jan. 1929.

Page 379, 3d paragraph, *at end add* A lozenge upon the street frontage of the town is inscribed with the punning rebus, Deum Cole (information from the late Sir Owen F. Morshead). Cole left HW a mourning ring, sold SH xv. 119. It was bought by William Strong of Bristol and was offered by him in his 'SH Catalogue' 1843, lot 3448 for £251.

VOLUME 3

Page xxv, note 4, *for* Remusat *read* Rémusat

Page xxxvii, (A) (I), line 8, *after* 12 March 1920, *add* lot 387,   *after* given to the Bodleian *add* in October 1920

Page xxxvii, (A) (II) at end, *for* The originals are missing. *read* The MSS are now WSL.

Page xxxvii, (A) (V) last line, *for* bequeathed by him to Miss Berry *read* left at Strawberry Hill with the Waldegraves (see FAMILY 315–16).

Page xl, line 5, *add* The letter of 26 Dec. 1770 was found after World War II 'during a . . . rearrangement of manuscripts evacuated from Holland House,' and was printed by the 6th Earl of Ilchester in an article, 'Madame du Deffand to Walpole,' in TLS 19 June 1948, xlvii. 348. The whereabouts of the MS is not known.

Page xl, *at end of 2d paragraph add* Letters in unknown hands: Hand A: 18 June 1780, 11 April 1779; Hand B: 4 March 1780.

Page xlii, lines 7–8 from bottom, *for* have been equally fruitless. *read* have resulted in the acquisition by WSL of some of Sainte-Aulaire's papers.

Page xlv, line 6, *on* receive.' *add note* 3:   3. See HW to the Hon. Thomas Walpole 30 April, 11 Nov. 1781 (FAMILY 196, 204).

Page xlv, 2d paragraph, line 8, *for* Œuvres *read* Lettres

Page xlvii, X, *at end add* ?Malesherbes MS now in the possession of the American Philosophical Society

Page xlvii, 387, last line, *for* Hobbs. Now at *read* Hobbs for Paget Toynbee and given by him to

Page xlviii, 389, *delete* probably . . . ca 1926 *and substitute* sold by J. Pearson, 23 June 1924; now in the Bibliothèque Nationale (*Voltaire's Correspondence*, ed. Theodore Besterman, Geneva, 1953–65, xvii, Appendix 54)

Page xlviii, 393, line 6, *for* Now *read* Formerly   *Line 7, after* D.C. *add* ; now WSL.

Page lvii, first item, *add* Mrs Thrale's copy was in her sale, 1823 (information from A. T. Hazen).

Page lix, *below* Hamel *insert* Hardinge, George, 'Expostulatory Remarks on "Letters by Madame du Deffand to the late Earl of Orford" in a series of letters to the editor,' *Miscellaneous Works*, 1818, iii. 159–310.

Page lxv, *sub* C-D, *for* Chesnaye-Desbois *read* Chenaye-Desbois

Page lxvii, *sub* NBG, *for* 1853–66 *read* 1852–66

Page lxvii, *sub* Rép. de la Gazette, *after* et biographique de *insert* la Gazette de

Page lxvii, *sub* 'Short Notes,' at end, *for* xxiv–lvi *read* xxxiv–lvi

Page 1, From Mme du Deffand Wednesday ?April 1766, headnote, *add* HW wrote to Conway 6 April 1766, 'This is Sunday, and Thursday is fixed for my departure; unless the Clairon should return to the stage on Tuesday sennight, as is said, and I do not know whether I should not be tempted to borrow two or three days more, having never seen her' (Conway iii. 62).

Page 3, note 3, line 12, *for* HW to Conway 6 Oct. 1765 *read* Conway iii. 12 and n. 9

Page 4, note 8, line 4, *for* Pierre Louis de Lévis de Lomagne (d. 1757) *read* Gaston-Charles-Pierre de Lévis de Lomagne (1699–1757)   *Line 6, after* France *add* (Henri Jougla de Morenas, *Grand Armorial de France*, 1934–49, iv. 456).

Page 4, note 11, *add* See also Conway ii. 516 and n. 5.

Page 4, note 12, *add* Her family name should presumably be Guillaume de Fontaine, rather than merely Fontaine. See the references to her and to her sisters in Conway ii. 480, as modified by H. H. Hawley, 'Meissonnier's Silver for the Duke of Kingston,' *Bulletin of the Cleveland Museum of Art*, Dec. 1978, pp. 320, 327, 340.

Pages 4–5, note 13, line 4, *for* d'Antin, *read* d'Antin;

Page 6, note 21, line 1, *for* (d. 1814) *read* (1742–1814) (Namier and Brooke ii. 269; *Matriculation Albums of the University of Glasgow from 1728 to 1858*, ed. W. I. Addison, Glasgow, 1913, p. 56)   *Line 2, for* Auchinames *read* Auchenames   *Line 3, after* 1768 *add* –74, Renfrewshire 1774–80, Glasgow Burghs 1780–4, Feb.–June 1790

Page 12, note 14, line 1, *for* 1706 *read* 1700   *Line 2, after* John *substitute* Hervey (1696–1743), styled Bn Hervey of Ickworth, 1733.

Page 18, note 39, *delete 1st sentence and substitute* Marie-Charlotte-Justine, Comtesse de Messey (after 1735–?after 1773), Chanoinesse de Mons, m. (by contract of 2 June 1765, as his second wife) Charles-Joseph Patissier de Bussy (1720–85), a commander of French forces in India who had made a fortune there but was publicly blamed by Lally-Tollendal for military reverses in India and lived in retirement in Paris from 1766 to 1781 (*Dictionnaire de biographie française*, 1933– , vii. 721–2; Conway iii. 50, n. 27).

Page 21, note 7, line 1, *for* 1719 *read* 1718   *Line 5, add* See François Cornou, *Élie Fréron*, 1922, p. 13.

Page 26, note 4, line 2, *for* (d. 1778) *read* (1731–78)   *Line 3, for* (d. 1777) *read* (1722–77)   *after* 1766 *insert* (DNB *sub* Elliot, Gilbert, 1st E. of Minto; *Scots Peerage*, ed. Sir James Balfour Paul, Edinburgh, 1904–14, viii. 146)

Page 41, note 5, line 3, *for* 1776 *read* 1766

Page 42, note 9, line 8, *for* 14 Sept. *read* 15 Sept.   *Line 9, for* 6 Dec. *read* 5 Dec.

Page 44, note 10, last line, *for* 1699 *read* 1669

Page 45, note 1, line 1, *for* Eleonora *read* Eleanora

Page 47, note 4, line 2, *for* ca 1732 *read* ca 1731   *Line 3, after* for *insert* Wareham 1768–74, Ludgershall Jan.–Sept. 1774,   *Line 4, after* 278 *add*   ; Namier and Brooke iii. 3–4

Page 51, headnote, line 1, *after* WSL *add* The letter was sold with the snuff-box SH xv. 25 to Strong of Bristol; resold without the snuff-box by James Robins.   *Line 3, after* bottom. *add* Lady Frances Hanbury Williams's letter to Charlotte Williams 17 June 1766 contains an extensive comment on the snuff-box, etc. (MS in the Public Record Office of Ireland, photostat WSL).   *Line 10, for* in the Waller collection *read* now WSL

Page 61, note 4, line 2, *after* (1757) *delete*   ,

Page 70, note 13, line 2, *for* François Adhémar *read* François de Castellane-Adhémar

Page 89, note 9, *for* Marie *read* Mary

Page 94, note 1, line 2, *for* General *read* Genuine   *at end add* and Margaret Hill Peoples, *La Querelle Rousseau-Hume,* in *Annales de la Société Jean-Jacques Rousseau,* xviii, Génève, 1927–8; F. A. Pottle, 'The Part Played by Horace Walpole and James Boswell in the Quarrel between Rousseau and Hume: A Reconsideration,' in *Horace Walpole: Writer, Politician, and Connoisseur,* ed. W. H. Smith, New Haven, 1967, pp. 255–91.

Page 99, note 2, line 1, *for* Molin-Dumesnil *read* Morin-Dumesnil

Page 104, note 5, line 2, *for* 1727 *read* 1729

Page 104, note 9, line 3, *for* (d. 1800) *read* (?1719–1800), M.P.   *Line 5, after* 1904–14 *add*   ; Namier and Brooke iii. 503–7

Page 106, From Mme du Deffand 5 Aug. 1766, headnote, *add* The MS, in Wiart's hand with HW's notes, was acquired by WSL in the Sainte-Aulaire collection of papers. The text has been collated and variants in words are recorded below; the differences in punctuation are not included here.

Page 107, 1st paragraph, line 5, *on* souhaiter *add note a: a.* 'souhaiter' written by HW over Wiart's indecipherable word.

Page 107, 1st paragraph, line 7, *for* de le leur laisser *read* de leur laisser

Page 107, 2d paragraph, line 4, *for* qui vinrent me prendre *read* qui me vinrent prendre

Page 107, 3d paragraph, line 2, *after* politique, *insert* et mise si peu au fait du caractère de vos ministres,   *after* m'avaient *insert* un peu   *Line 3, for* moins intelligible *read* aussi peu intelligible   *Line 4, for* du *read* <du>

Page 108, 1st paragraph, line 1, *after* ami *insert* ['ami' in HW's hand; MS torn]   *Line 3, for* je ne le suis *read* je ne la suis   *Line 7, for* Milord *read* Milord R.   *Line 11, for* tout m'est *read* tout m'en est   *Line 14, after* mettez-vous *insert* bien

Page 108, 2d paragraph, line 1, *after* du *insert* ['du' in HW's hand; MS torn]   *Line 2, after* fils de *insert* Sir [in HW's hand]   *Lines 10–11, for* car qui est-ce qui *read* car qu'est-ce qui

Page 108, 3d paragraph, lines 1–2, *for* Jean-Jacques *read* J.-Jacques

Page 108, note 2, *for* (S-A) *read* (HW)

Page 108, note 4, *for* (S-A) *read* (HW)

Page 109, 1st paragraph, line 5, *for* veut le lui faire *read* veut lui faire
Line 8, for Luxembourg *read* L.   *Line 10, for* elle me sera *read* elle sera

Page 109, 4th paragraph, line 2, *for* un génie *read* un grand génie
Line 3, after Geoffrin *insert* [HW's note: le roi de Pologne que Mme
Geoffrin appellait son fils]   *Line 4, for* je ne puis *read* je ne puis pas

Page 109, 5th paragraph, line 2, *for* Luxembourg *read* L.

Page 110, 2d paragraph, line 3, *for* M. de Secondat *read* M. Secondat

Page 110, 3d paragraph, line 1, *for* à l'avenir vous apprendre *read* vous
apprendre à l'avenir   *Lines 2–3, after* connaissance *insert* [HW's note:
Jenkinson]

Page 110, 4th paragraph, *after* semaine. *add* Vos deux dernières lettres
ne sont point numérotées; celles du 31 de juillet qui est la dernière devoit
être numéro 16. Partez de là je vous prie pour les numéroter à l'avenir et
soyez y plus exact.

Page 110, 5th paragraph, line 1, *after* Mandez-moi *insert* je vous prie
Line 3, after Macdonald *insert* [HW's note: Sir James Macdonald]

Page 110, note 18, line 1, *for* Zulestein *read* Zuylestein

Page 110, note 19, line 1, *for* ca 1742 *read* 1742   *Last line, for* 83).
read 83; CONWAY iii. 13 and n. 16).

Page 123, note 18, lines 2–3, *for* Mary Bruce (d. 1796) *read* Lady Mary
Bruce (1740–96)

Page 124, note 20, line 1, *after* m. *add* (1748)   *Line 2, after* Greville
add (1717–ca 1805) (Lodge, *Irish Peerage*, 1789, vii. 91; *Harleian Society
Register*, xi. 39; Mme d'Arblay, *Memoirs of Dr Burney*, 1833, iii. 342–5)

Page 128, note 33, *add* This and five other French tracts concerning the
quarrel were apparently sent to HW by Mme du Deffand (see Hazen, *Cat.
of HW's Lib*. No. 1680).

Page 138, note 4, *add* This may be the 'Traité de la Goutte' entered in
the SH sale catalogue, v. 193; see Hazen, *Cat. of HW's Lib*. No. 3133.

Page 156, note 3, line 4, *for* Marsh Dickenson *read* Marshe Dickinson
Line 5, after 1771 *add* (see Namier and Brooke ii. 321, *sub* Marshe Dickinson)

Page 169, note 6, line 4, *after* m. *add* (1652)   *Line 10, for* 200 *read*
199–200; see also CONWAY iii. 11

Page 171, note 3, line 1, *for* preface to *read* 'Déclaration . . . aux éditeurs'
in   *Line 4, after* 1766 *add*   ; Hume to HW 4 Nov. 1766, MISC. CORR. ii.
49 and n. 3

Page 172, note 6, line 2, *for* 1701 *read* 1706

Page 172, note 8, line 2, *for* 1722 *read* ca 1723   *Line 3, for* Zulestein
read Zuylestein

Page 173, note 12, *add* HW's copy of the French translation is Hazen,
Cat. of HW's Lib. No. 3066.

Page 178, note 2, *add* HW's copy is Hazen, *Cat. of HW's Lib*. No. 1680:2.

Page 183, note 17, line 2, *for* 1690 *read* 1694

Page 183, note 20, HW's copy is Hazen, *Cat. of HW's Lib*. No. 1680:3.

Page 184, note 1, line 4, *for* (b. 1729) *read* (1729–1801)   *Line 6, for* 1718 *read* 1717   *Line 7, after* 207 *add* ; Howard M. Jenkins, *The Family of William Penn*, Philadelphia, Penn., 1899, pp. 150ff.

Page 188, note 3, lines 3–4, *for* (1618–89) *read* (1618–99)   *Line 6, after* Belle-Isle *add* (see HW to Hardwicke 10 Aug. 1773, MISC. CORR. ii. 259, n. 27)

Page 191, From Mme du Deffand 5 Dec. 1766, 1st line, *for* A *read* LA

Page 193, note 5, line 5, *for 1761 read 1756* (see Hazen, *Cat. of HW's Lib*. No. 2597)   *Last line, add* The fourteen letters on Fouquet's trial are dated from 17 Nov. 1664 to 27 Jan. 1665 (see HW to Hardwicke 10 Aug. 1773, MISC. CORR. ii. 259, n. 27).

Page 200, note 8, *add* HW's copy of the *Testament politique*, Amsterdam and Paris, 1767, is Hazen, *Cat. of HW's Lib*. No. 2323.

Page 212, note 29, *add* It was sold SH vi. 123 (see also Hazen, *Bibl. of HW* 69).

Page 237, note 8, line 1, *for* (1727–94) *read* (1727–93)   *Line 6, after* 1770 *add* ; Henri-Alexandre Wallon, *Histoire du tribunal révolutionnaire*, 1880–2, ii. 246

Page 240, note 1, *for* Buyrette *read* Buirette   *At end add* See *Dictionnaire de biographie française*, 1933– , vii. 641–2.

Page 243, note 12, lines 2–20, *delete* Lady Charlotte Stanley . . . niece, Miss Warburton). *and substitute* Lady Charlotte Stanley (1728–76), m. (ca 1751) Gen. John Burgoyne. They went to France probably in late 1751 and soon after became acquainted with the Choiseuls (James Lunt, *John Burgoyne of Saratoga*, New York 1975, pp. 12–14).

Page 249, line 21, on fausseté *add note* 1b: 1b. G. Hall points out that this is an allusion to Jacques Esprit, *La fausseté des vertus humaines*, 1709 (HW's copy is Hazen, *Cat. of HW's Lib*. No. 730).

Page 253, note 3, *delete* Probably . . . (unidentified) *and substitute* Pierre-Chrysostome d'Usson de Bonac (1724–82), Comte d'Usson, French ambassador to Sweden 1774–82, m. (1754) Margarethe Cornelia van de Poll (1726–93), who had previously m. (1743) Cornelis Munter (MORE 102, n. 5)

Page 254, note 1a, *add* See MANN vi. 487–9.

Page 256, note 7, *add* Apparently this was the first edition with HW's name on the title-page; see Hazen, *Bibl. of HW* 55–6.

Page 262, note 8, line 4, *for* 1776 *read* 1766   *Lines 6–8, for* Fifteen volumes of the Strawberry Hill imprint are in the Bibliothèque Nationale. *substitute* HW's gift consisted of thirteen volumes of the Strawberry Hill imprint and two volumes which were printed in London (*Ædes Walpolianæ*, 2d edn, 1752, and *Castle of Otranto*, 1765); they were bound in fifteen volumes in red morocco with Walpole's arms (L. Auvray, 'Horace Walpole et la Bibliothèque du Roi (1766–1792),' *Bibliothèque de l'École des Chartes,* 1929, xc. 229–32).   *Line 9, after* 1766 *insert* (MISC. CORR. ii. 58, n. 6)

Page 262, note 9, *delete* probably

Page 270, note 7, *substitute Les Quatre Facardins* by Anthony Hamilton (ca 1645–1719) (Ruth Clark, *Anthony Hamilton . . . His Life and Works and his Family,* 1921, pp. 165 and n. 1, 244–54).

Page 274, note 1, line 2, *for* 1749 *read* 1748

Page 275, note 3, *substitute* HW invited Selwyn to dine with them at SH, probably in April; see SELWYN 244, 245, n. 2.

Page 279, From Mme du Deffand 4 April 1767, headnote, *add* The MS, in Wiart's hand, was acquired by WSL in the Sainte-Aulaire collection of papers. The text has been collated and variants in words are recorded below; the differences in punctuation are not included here.

Page 279, date-line, *for* ce 4 avril *read* ce dimanche 4 avril

Page 279, 1st paragraph, line 5, *for* n'en avez pas *read* n'en avez point *Line 6, for* une destinée *read* ma destinée   *Line 7, for* qui ne soit *read* qu'il ne soit   *Line 13, for* à juste valeur *read* à ma juste valeur   *Line 17, for* choquent ou *read* choquent et   *Line 24, for* avoir revu *read* avoir vu   *Line 34, for* effusions, etc. *read* effusions.

Page 280, 1st paragraph, line 2, *for* qualifiez pas *read* qualifiez point

Page 280, 2d paragraph, line 4, *for* huit à dix *read* huit ou dix   *Line 11, for* maintenant *read* véritablement

Page 280, 3d paragraph, line 1, *for* je vous ai *read* je ne vous ai   *Line 2, for* il y a eu *read* il y eut   *Line 4, for* On parla *read* L'on parla *Line 10, for* Je lui ai dit *read* Je dis

Page 280, 4th paragraph, line 8, *for* mettrai pas *read* mettrai point

Page 281, 2d paragraph, line 1, *after* cinq *insert* ['cinq' written in HW's hand over blotted word]   *Line 2, for* dois aller *read* devois aller   *Line 3, for* divertirait *read* divertira   *Line 4, for* bonne enfant *read* assez bonne enfant   *Lines 8 and 12, for* Jean-Jacques *read* J.-Jacques   *Line 18, for* fit pas *read* fit point   *Line 19, for* va pas *read* va point   *Line 21, delete* avoir

Page 281, 3d paragraph, line 2, *for* personnages *read* des personnages *Line 3, for* on vient d'en donner *read* on en vient de donner   *Line 4, after* l'enverrai *insert* cependant

Page 286, note 10, line 4, *for* (d. 1789) *read* (1718–89)   *Line 6, for* (d. 1785) *read* (1717–87)   *Line 7, before* GM *insert* Journal de Paris, 1789, i. 662, 680; Richard Hayes, *Biographical Dictionary of Irishmen in France,* Dublin, 1949, p. 285;

Page 288, note 2, *add* See MANN vi. 541–3.

Page 293, From Mme du Deffand 17 May 1767, note 2, *for* de Chauvelin *read* Chauvelin

Page 294, note 2, line 5, *for 1769 read 1767*

Page 295, line 17, *on* Chabrillan *add note* 8a: 8a. Jacques-Aimar-Henri de Moreton, Comte de Chabrillan; see Selwyn 245, n. 3.

Page 298, line 6, *in Voltaire's text* quelques bagatelles *reads* quelque bagatelle

Page 298, line 7, *in Voltaire's text* point *reads* pas

Page 299, note 4, lines 1–2, *for* ca 1720 *read* 1727 *for* ca 1752 *read* 1751 *Last line, after* 1938 *add* ; Dorothy H. Eshleman, *Elizabeth Griffith*, Philadelphia, Penn., 1949, pp. 9–10

Page 302, note 14, line 5, *delete* HW to Selwyn 31 Jan. 1766

Page 303, note 19, *add* For HW's copy of the Abbé Coyer's *Essais* see Hazen, *Cat. of HW's Lib.* No. 3085.

Page 318, note 2, line 5, *for* prime minister *read* secretary of state and minister of marine

Page 322, To Mme du Deffand 11 July 1767, note 1, *add* See also David Hume, *Letters*, ed. J. Y. T. Greig, Oxford, 1932, ii. 40, 45, 48, 146.

Page 322, note 3, line 1, *for* 1727 *read* 1725

Page 335, note 1, *add* See Hazen, *Cat. of HW's Lib.* No. 2285.

Page 335, To Mme du Deffand 7 Aug. 1767, line 3, *on* Londres *add note* 1a: 1a. *Lettres de Monsieur de Montesquieu à divers amis d'Italie, avec des notes de l'éditeur.* À Londres, au dépens de l'éditeur, MDCCLXVII, 12mo. It contains the full text and notes of the letters offensive to Mme Geoffrin, viz. Nos LV, LVI, LVII (pp. 221–32).

Page 347, note 8a, line 2, *for* 1752 *read* 1735

Page 349, note 14, line 1, *for* 1724 *read* 1725 *Line 3, for* 7th D. *read* 4th D.

Page 363, note 5, line 1, *for* Amelot, *read* Amelot de Chaillou (b. ca 1734, living 1809), *Line 2, for* Claude-Thomas-Sibille *read* Claude-Sibylle-Thomas *Line 4, after* Gazette *add* ; Woelmont de Brumagne i. 666

Page 376, note 19, line 6, *after* 50). *insert* Nine copies are now WSL (Hazen, *SH Bibl.*, 1973, pp. xix–xx, 78–9).

Page 392, note 4, 2d line from end, *for* portrait *read* water-colour, which hung in the Breakfast Room at Strawberry Hill, *and after* 111 *insert* to W. Smith for 7 guineas

Page 400, note 3, *add* See Mann vi. 571.

Page 405, note 4, line 12, *for* Weymiss *read* Wemyss *Line 15, after* 8 *add* ; also in Mann iii. 66

VOLUME 4

Page 2, note 4, *substitute* 'Assuredly "procès" refers to his reproaches to her. D. does not insert a different and remote subject into a closely knit paragraph. For "procès" see p. 34' (Thornton Wilder).

Page 2, note 5, *add* See David Hume, *Letters,* ed. J. Y. T. Greig, Oxford, 1932, ii. 174, 188, 208.

Page 4, note 6, *add* HW's copy of the 3d edn, 1749, is Hazen, *Cat. of HW's Lib.,* No. 964.

Page 9, note 1, *add* See also FAMILY 62, 64, 66–7.

Page 13, note *a, add* See *ante* DU DEFFAND i. 392, n. 4.

Page 15, note 1, *add* See also MANN vi. 570–2.

Page 19, note 9, *add* G. Hall points out that this phrase is from Racine's *Phèdre,* I. 41.

Page 19, note 12, line 1, *for* Hugues *read* Hughes   *Line 3, after* 465 *add*   ; see MONTAGU ii. 282, n. 1

Page 22, note 6, line 4, *for* 1764 *read* 1764–7   *and after* 156 *insert* (Hazen, *Cat. of HW's Lib.* No. 932); probably HW wanted only vol. iii since he apparently had vols i and ii, as he wrote to Joseph Warton 16 March 1765, 'Let me recommend to you also the perusal of the life of Petrarch, of which two large volumes in quarto are already published by the Abbé de Sade, with the promise of a third.'

Page 26, note 13, line 3, *after* 163 *add* (Hazen, *Cat. of HW's Lib.* No. 3023)

Page 30, note 13, *add* from which passages are quoted in the life of Queen Elizabeth, *Dictionnaire des portraits historiques,* 1768, i. 525–7, 529–30.

Page 37, note 1b, *for* was *read* was included with other works

Page 44, note 1a, *add* HW's copy is Hazen, *Cat. of HW's Lib.* No. 939.

Page 53, 2d paragraph, line 1, *for* recu *read* reçu

Page 60, note 25, line 1, *for* 1726 *read* 1725

Page 71, note 8, line 1, *delete* Charles-   *Line 2, for* 1733 *read* 1730 *after* Breteuil *add* (*Dictionnaire de biographie française,* 1933– , vii. 239–40)

Page 72, note 14, line 1, *delete* of 2 March 1689   *Line 2, after* Grave *delete* from *and insert* has not been identified; Mme de Sévigné's letter of 2 March 1689 was one of the 33 remaining letters in the possession of the Mlles Girard,   *Line 4, after* 1768 *add* and Appendix 19

Page 72, note 15, line 2, *for* 1768 *read* 1767, n. 4

Page 73, note 21, line 1, *for* (d. 1818), *read* (1738–1818), M.P.;   *Line 3, after* Selwyn *add* He was on his way to Minorca to take up a lieutenant-colonelcy there   *Line 5, after* 258 *add*   ; Namier and Brooke iii. 399–400

Page 74, note 5, *for* (d. 1779) *read* (ca 1720–79)

Page 77, note 5, line 3, *for* Mlle de Sanadon *read* Mlle Sanadon

Page 85, note 17, line 1, *for* weeks *read* months   *Line 2, add* In May the Marquis was imprisoned in the Pierre-Encise fortress near Lyon; on 10 June he was transferred from Pierre-Encise to the Conciergerie du

Palais in Paris so that he could appear before the High Court of Paris; then on 11 or 12 June he was conducted back to Pierre-Encise, where he was imprisoned until 16 Nov. 1768 (Gilbert Lély, *Vie du Marquis de Sade*, 1952–7, i. 245–53).

Page 93, note 6, line 1, *for* 1728 *read* ca 1728   *Line 2, for* later K.B. *read* K.B., 1775; M.P. East Grinstead 1762–83; Maj.-Gen., 1762; commander-in-chief in Ireland 1775–82; Gen., 1783 (Namier and Brooke ii. 667–8).

Page 94, note 12, *substitute* See HW's Postscript to the *Mysterious Mother*, p. 3; CONWAY iii. 102–3.

Page 94, note 14, *add* HW's copy, the 1766 edn, is now WSL (Hazen, *Cat. of HW's Lib.* No. 3002).

Page 100, note 6, *add* One of Hénault's copies is now WSL (Hazen, *SH Bibl.*, 1973, p. xix).

Page 114, note 10, *add* HW had the 1752 (now WSL) and 1755 editions; see Hazen, *Cat. of HW's Lib.* Nos 401, 1608:42:4.

Page 117, note 9, *for first line read* Probably James Dunn (b. 1714, d. *post* 1789), called Comte Jacques-Bernard O'Dunne,   *Last line, add* See also MANN iv. 9 and n. 7; Richard Hayes, *Biographical Dictionary of Irishmen in France*, Dublin, 1949, pp. 77–8.

Page 122, note 8, line 1, *before* Anne *insert* Hon.   *for* 1738 *read* ca 1738

Page 122, note 2, line 1, *for* translation *read* transcription of HW's translation

Page 128, note 6, *substitute* Of the Order of the Elephant; see J. H. F. Berlien, *Der Elephanten-Orden*, Kopenhagen, 1846, pp. 33, 99.

Page 132, note 13, line 2, *before* Elizabeth *insert* Lady   *Line 3, after* Russell, *insert* styled

Page 139, note 7, *substitute Recueil de lettres de diverses personnes amies de Mme de Sévigné*, the 8th volume of the 'Nouvelle édition augmentée' of the *Recueil des lettres de Mme la marquise de Sévigné à Mme la comtesse de Grignan, sa fille*, published in Paris in 1754. It is probable that HW owned the 6-volume edition of her letters published in 1734–7 (and reprinted in 1738 and 1754); he probably also had the *Recueil des lettres choisies, pour servir de suite aux lettres de Mme de Sévigné à Mme de Grignan, sa fille*, 1 vol., 1751, and also *Lettres nouvelles de Mme la marquise de Sévigné à Mme la comtesse de Grignan, sa fille*, described as 'Extraites de l'édition de 1754 en 8 vol. in -12, pour servir de supplément à l'édition en 6 vol.,' 2 vols, Paris, 1754. Another 8-volume edition of her letters was published in Amsterdam in 1756, which 'réunit en huit volumes les lettres de l'édition de 1754 et du Recueil de lettres choisies de 1751.' For descriptions of these editions see Mme de Sévigné, *Lettres*, ed. Monmerqué, 1862–6, xi. 443–6; see also Hazen, *Cat. of HW's Lib.* Nos 949, 950, 951.

Page 140, note 2, *substitute* Lady Hervey bequeathed to HW a drawing of Fontenelle, which hung in the Breakfast Room at SH, and 'a small table with a landscape of Seve porcelain, mounted in old japan,' which stood in the Great North Bedchamber at SH (see MORE 137 and Appendix 1).

Page 141, note 3, left column, line 3, *for* d'Adhémar *read* de Castellane-Adhémar

Page 141, note 3, right column, *add* See CHUTE 329–30 and n. 40.

Page 163, lines 17–18, *on empereurs add note* 1a: 1a. See Comte du Châtelet to HW 7 Feb. 1768, MISC. CORR. ii. 125 and n. 2.

Pages 166–7, note 6, line 4, *after* 2). *insert* HW's copy, 1747 edn, is Hazen, *Cat. of HW's Lib.* No. 2394.

Page 173, note 3, lines 1–2, *for* (d. 1801) *read* (ca 1725–1801)   *Line 5, for* pt i. 481 *read* pt ii. 861; Daniel Lysons, *Environs of London*, 1810, i. pt ii. 567

Page 197, note 11, line 1, *for* Dumesnil *read* Marchand   *for* 1711 *read* 1713   *Line 2, after* 1803), *insert* called Mlle du Mesnil   *after* actress *add* (CONWAY ii. 524, n. 18)

Page 198, To Mme du Deffand 9 Feb. 1769, headnote, *add* See FAMILY 48–9.

Page 207, note 7, *substitute* According to the evidence of Sir Charles Bunbury's steward at the divorce proceedings, 'Lady Bunbury came down to Great Barton on or about the 31st of January 1769, and that she used frequently in a morning to walk out alone: That on Sunday the 19th of February 1769, her Ladyship walked out as usual, but not returning home at her usual time the family were alarmed, and that he and the servants went out in search of her, but without effect; and that she never has returned since that day' (*Journals of the House of Lords*, xxxiv. 673; see also ibid. 597, 608, 659, 677, 678, 724). On 21 February 1769 Lady Mary Coke wrote that they had eloped to Knole, the Duke of Dorset's seat, that Lady Louisa Conolly had followed them and had persuaded Lady Sarah to return temporarily to Holland House (*Letters and Journals*, ed. James A. Home, Edinburgh, 1889–96, iii. 28–9). Further testimony in the divorce trial stated that Lady Sarah and Lord William were living together at Redbridge near Southampton in March 1769 (*Journals of the House of Lords*, xxxiv. 673). The first sentence of divorce in the Consistory Court was dated 17 June 1769; the bill of divorce was passed by the House of Lords 14 May 1776 (ibid. 673, 724). (Information from Richard W. Hale.)

Page 210, note 2, line 3, *after* Cholmondeley, *insert* cr. (1815) M. of Cholmondeley,

Page 212, line 18, *on* Cholmondeley *add note* a: a. See Mrs Robert Cholmondeley to HW 15 March 1769 (FAMILY 49–50) where she describes this visit with Mme du Deffand.

Page 214, note 3, *before Fables insert* St-Lambert's

Page 221, note 4, *add* The 'example' of Sir Charles Bunbury was his immediate initiating of suits for divorce: the writ of crim. con. was served on Lord William 17 March 1769, and the citation from the ecclesiastical court was served on Lady Sarah 22 April 1769 (*Trials for Adultery: or, the History of Divorces*, London, S. Bladon, 1779, vol. iii, deposition of John Swale, the process server).

Page 230, note 3, line 3, *after* Abbess *insert* 1743–89   *Line 4, for* (d. 1794) *read* (ca 1714–94)   *Line 9, after* 12 *add*   ; M. Fosseyeux, 'Une Abbesse de Panthémont,' *Revue du dix-huitième siècle*, 1918, v. 1–16

Page 234, note 5, *for* (1719–92) *read* (1720–92)

Page 237, note 7, *for* p. 134 *read* pp. 134–43

Page 238, note 11, line 2, *after* Sarum *insert* 1751–4, Grampound 1754–68

Page 248, line 13, *for* il *read* ils

Page 254, note 17, line 1, *for* 1559 *read* 1559 *or* 1560

Page 288, To Mme du Deffand 20 Oct. 1769, headnote, *add* Mentioned in HW to Mrs Robert Cholmondeley 15 Oct. 1769, FAMILY 56 and n. 27.

Page 288, note 4, *add* See also CONWAY ii. 298.

Page 292, note 17, *substitute* See HW to Mrs Robert Cholmondeley 15 Oct. 1769, FAMILY 54–5.

Page 292, note 20, *for* 11 Nov. 1769 *read* 12 Nov. 1769 (see *post* 15 Nov. 1769, DU DEFFAND ii. 306)

Page 293, note 21, line 1, *for* 1720 *read* ca 1720

Page 297, note 4, *add* See also CONWAY iii. 119.

Page 299, note 10, lines 2, 4, *for* Keroualle *read* Kéroualle   *Line 5, for* ca 1647 *read* 1649

Page 304, note 6, *before* Anne *insert* Hon.

Page 307, note 15, *substitute* Probably François Paulmier, *Traité methodique et dogmatique de la goutte*, Angers and Paris, 1769; see Hazen, *Cat. of HW's Lib.* No. 3133.

Page 313, note 5, line 1, *for* 1695 *read* ca 1695

Page 328, note 14, line 1, *for* Mello *read* Melo   *Lines 2–3, for* Marquès *read* Marquês   *Line 5, add* See also MANN vii. 100, 166; *Grenville Papers* iv. 490.

Page 329, note 16, *add* See also *Grenville Papers* iv. 488–9.

Page 329, note 17, lines 1–2, *for* Mello *read* Melo   *for* (d. 1795) *read* (1716–95)   *Line 4, after* 1769 *insert*   , MORE 144, n. 13

Page 329, note 18, *substitute* Henry Lyte (1727–91) (John Fleming, 'Lord Brudenell and his Bear-Leader,' *English Miscellany*, 1958, ix. 127–41).

Page 329, note 19, line 4, *after* Cat. *add*   ; Hazen, *Cat. of HW's Lib.* No. 3017

Page 331, note 9, line 1, *for* Mme *read* Simon-Philippe   *Line 3, after* Jour. *add*   ; P. Verlet, 'Le commerce des objets d'art,' *Annales*, 1958, xiii. 25

Page 333, note 4, line 2, *for* ibid *read* ante 2 Jan. 1770

Page 336, note 19, line 2, *after* Montval *insert* (1731–1821)   *Line 5,*
after see *insert* H. S. Vade-Walpole, 'Notes on the Walpoles,' *Genealogi-*
cal Magazine, 1898–9, ii. 433;

Page 340, note 11, *for* Louis-Charles *read* Charles-Louis

Page 356, note 28, *before* George *insert* Hon.

Page 369, note 3, line 4, *for* in 31 vols *read* included in 31 vols

Page 392, line 3, *for* n'êtes vous *read* n'êtes-vous

Page 405–6, note 4, *add* See Hazen, *Cat. of HW's Lib.* Nos 3152, 3556.

Page 409, note 5, line 4, *after* Prince *insert* (later Duc)

Page 410, note 18, line 2, *for* (d. 1793) *read* (ca 1749–93)   *Line 3, after*
Comte *insert* and (1780) Duc   *Line 5, after* 132 *add*   ; Lalanne; Frances Burney, Mme d'Arblay, *Diary and Letters*, ed. A. Dobson, 1905, iii.
262n; Ossory ii. 309, n. 10

Page 411, note 25, *add* For the music and R. A. Feuillet's notation for La
Mariée see Louis Pécour, *Recueil de Danses* AND *La Nouvelle Galliarde*,
facsimile reprint of Paris, 1700 edn by Gregg International Publishers
Limited, Farnborough, Hants, and Dance Horizons, New York, 1970, pp.
12–21.

Page 414, From Mme du Deffand 29 May 1770, 2d paragraph, line 1, *on*
grand'maman *add note* 1a: 1a. D to Mme de Choiseul 26 May and Mme
de Choiseul to D 28 May and 31 May were sold 21 Dec. 1956 at Paris at
the Hôtel Drouot to Unknown for 34,000 francs (the first two letters were
printed by Sainte-Aulaire).

Page 416, note 16, *substitute* The Counts of Montezuma (Moctezuma)
in Spain were descendants of Montezuma II (1477 *or* 1479–1520), last of
the Aztec rulers. See Alberto and Arturo Garcia Carraffa, *Diccionario
Heraldico y Genealogico de Apellidos Españoles y Americanos*, Madrid,
1952–61, lx. 248–9. The Counts of Montezuma are mentioned in William
H. Prescott's *Conquest of Mexico*, Bk v, ch. ii (Everyman's Library edn,
1931, ii. 89–90).

Page 419, note 2, *add* See Mann vii. 217.

Page 420, note 5, *add* See also Norman H. Hansen, *Caroline Mathilde,
Dronning af Danmark og Norge, 1751–1775*, Copenhagen, 1947.

Page 432, note 4, line 3, *for* 1709 *read* ca 1709

Page 432, note 5, line 1, *for* 1704 *read* ca 1704

Page 432, note 7, line 1, *for* Ann *read* Anne

Page 440, line 5, *for* Cotterets *read* Cotterêts

Page 479, To Mme du Deffand 13 Nov. 1770, note 1, line 6, *after* wsl
add (Hazen, *Cat. of HW's Lib.* No. 3055)   *Line 8, after* apparently *in-*
sert included with other works

Page 479, note 2, last line, *after* BM Cat. *insert*   ; Hazen, *Cat. of HW's
Lib.*, Nos 1661, 1662, 1663

Page 483, note 10, line 1, *for* Catherine *read* Ekaterina   *for* Voronzov
read Vorontsova   *Line 2, for* 1744 *read* 1743

Page 497, From Mme du Deffand 26 Dec. 1770, headnote, *for* Missing. *read* The MS, in Jean-François Wiart's hand, was printed by the Earl of Ilchester in the *Times Literary Supplement* 19 June 1948, xlvii. 348; reprinted in MISC. CORR. ii. 192–200. The MS, found by the 6th Earl of Ilchester while rearranging papers evacuated from Holland House during World War II, is not listed among the Holland House papers acquired by the BM in 1963.

VOLUME 5

Page 1, note 1, *for* (missing) *read* , printed in MISC. CORR. ii. 192–200.

Page 2, note 9, line 1, *for* 1747 *read* 1748   *Line 2, after* Ossory *add* (*Old Westminsters,* i. 335)

Page 46, note 1a, *for* 1717 *read* 1719   *after* Vergennes *add* Louis Bonneville de Marsangy, *Le Chevalier de Vergennes,* 1894, i. 4.

Page 68, note 8, line 2, *after* Angleterre. *add* HW's copies, 3 vols, 1771 and 4 vols, 1774 are Hazen, *Cat. of HW's Lib.* Nos 3013, 3096.   *Line 3, after* was *insert* included

Page 75, note 2, line 3, *for* Worlidge *read* Bretherton

Page 75, note 7, line 1, *for* 1802 *read* 1801   *Line 4, after* 36 *insert* , Parte I, 1935, p. 284; *Dizionario biografico degli Italiani,* 1960– , vi. 211–13

Page 75, note 9, *substitute* John Crewe (1742–1829), cr. (1806) Bn Crewe; M.P.; m. (1766) Frances Anne Greville (d. 1818) (see Namier and Brooke ii. 276; CONWAY ii. 394, n. 19; MANN vii. 499, n. 21).

Page 87, note 4, line 3, *for* Blaquière *read* Blaquiere

Page 88, note 7, line 1, *for* the Mr Croft or Croftes *read* Richard Croft (d. 1793), banker,

Page 90, To Mme du Deffand 5 July 1771, headnote, *add* See D to Mme de Choiseul 13 Aug. 1771 (now WSL): 'Je perdrai M. Walpole bien plutôt et j'aurai le chagrin de rester à Paris après qu'il n'y sera plus, c'est ce que je désirais d'éviter.'

Page 91, line 11, *for* Blaquière *read* Blaquiere

Page 91, note 7, line 9, *after* Gazette *insert* 23 Aug. 1771

Page 92, From Mme du Deffand 3 Sept. 1771, line 7, *after* Waldegrave *add note a*: a. *Gazette de France* 23 Aug. 1771 (FAMILY 67, n. 10).

Page 92, same letter, line 10, *after* Angleterre. *delete apostrophe*

Page 92, same letter, line 13, *after* Gazette. *insert apostrophe*

Page 94, note 1a, *delete lines 3–5 and substitute* rine Margaret Walpole (1756–1816) and Elizabeth Walpole (1759–1842) (GM 1816 lxxxvi pt 1. 635; *Annual Register,* 1842, p. 275; Collins, *Peerage,* 1812, v. 673; H.S. Vade-Walpole, 'Notes on the Walpoles,' *Genealogical Magazine,* 1898–9, ii. 435).

Page 97, note 14, line 1, *for* 1717 *read* 1715   *Line 4, after* 178 *add*

; *Enciclopedia italiana*, Milan and Rome, 1929–39, viii. 927–8

Page 99, note 23, line 3, *for* verité *read* vérité

Page 106, note 16, line 2, *for* (b. 1742–d. after 1800) *read* (1742–1808)
Line 4, after Cossé *add*   , Duc de Brissac, 1784   *Line 7, after* 238 *add*
; M. Blampignon, *Le Duc de Nivernais*, n. d., p. 375)

Page 109, note 28, line 2, *after* 243 *insert semicolon*   *Lines 5–8, delete*
The upper . . . discredited. *and substitute* For a discussion of the history
of the armour see OSSORY iii. 235–6, Appendix 1.

Page 117, note 8, *add* HW's Epilogue (*Works* iv. 402–3) to an adaptation
of this play by Mrs Elizabeth Griffith (called *The Times*) was first performed 2 Dec. 1779 (*London Stage* Part V, i. 301).

Page 118, date-line, *on* midi *add note* 9a: 9a. The MS of this postscript
was acquired by WSL in the collection of Sainte-Aulaire papers. The text
has been collated and the variants in words are recorded below; the differences in punctuation are not included here.

Page 118, 1st paragraph, line 1, *for* Quelle nuit *read* Jugez quelle nuit
delete three periods   *Line 4, for* n'aurais *read* n'en aurais   *Line 5,*
for racontait *read* raconta   *Line 15, for* près *read* prête   *Line 23,*
after Beauvau *insert* ['P. de B.' expanded by HW]   *Lines 23–4, for* je
pensais *read* et je pensais

Page 118, 2d paragraph, line 6, *for* je dois *read* je vais

Page 131, note 8, *before* Henry *insert* Hon.

Page 132, note 10, line 1, *for* (1753–1809) *read* (1743–1808)   *Line 2,*
before Christopher *insert* (1765)   *after* Horton *insert*   ; m. (2) (1771)
Henry Frederick, D. of Cumberland

Page 132, note 11, line 8, *for* Mrs. *read* Mrs

Page 153, note 12, line 2, *for* Auchinames *read* Auchenames

Page 154, note 13, line 2, *for* 1752 *read* 1753   *delete* later   *after*
m. *insert* (1792)   *Line 5, before* NBG *insert* OSSORY i. 66, n. 15;

Page 175, note 8, line 1, *delete* Probably   *Line 3, add* See NBG.

Page 190, note 19, line 4, *after* was *insert* included   *Last line, add*
HW's copy is now WSL (Hazen, *Cat. of HW's Lib.* No. 1255).

Page 191, note 25, last line, *after* 166 *add* (Hazen, *Cat. of HW's Lib.* No.
3003)

Page 193, note 36, line 1, *for* 1701 *read* ca 1701

Page 195, note 10, line 2, *for* viii *read* vii

Page 199, note 6, line 2, *for* Catherine *read* Catharine

Page 209, note 8, *add* For d'Alembert's relationship with Duclos see
Paul Meister, *Charles Duclos*, Genève, 1956, pp. 74–6.

Page 211, note 24, *substitute* The Bibl. Nat. Cat. lists two editions, Amsterdam, 1770 and 1772, both 6 vols in octavo. See also CONWAY iii. 167–8
and n. 7.

Page 216, note 3, line 4, *after* 101 *add* (Hazen, *Cat. of HW's Lib.* No.
2742)

Page 218, note 3, line 3, *for* 1681 *read* 1682   *after* Tencin *insert* (P.

M. Masson, *Madame de Tencin*, 3d edn, 1910, pp. 132–3; Hazen, *Cat. of HW's Lib*. Nos 2295, 3149)

Page 218, note 5, line 6, *for* Prince *read* Duque

Page 218, note 7, line 2, *for* Sienna *read* Siena

Page 220, note 14, line 3, *for* 1747 *read* 1745 *Line 5, after* 1776 *add* (A. Révérend, *Titres ... de la Restauration*, 1901–6, v. 391–2)

Page 222, note 26, line 1, *for* ca 1650 *read* ca 1649 *Line 2, for* 1665 *read* ca 1666 *Line 3, for* 1679 *read* 1681 *for* titular *read* cr. (1685) E. and (1689)

Page 232, note 15, lines 5–10, *after* and of his *substitute Description sommaire des desseins du cabinet de feu M. Crozat*, 1741 (Hazen, *Cat. of HW's Lib*. Nos 303, 3592); see also ibid. Nos 3562, 3765.

Page 245, 1st paragraph, line 7, *for* souleurs *read* douleurs

Page 262, To Mme du Deffand 3 July 1772, second fragment, *on* esclaves *add note 2:* 2. L. R. Duisit suggests that HW must have written, 'Vous ne voulez que faire des esclaves, vous n'aimez que vous et comme moi aussi, je n'aime que moi, nous ne pouvons jamais nous accorder' (see also DU DEFFAND iii. 332, n. 2); and that HW was more likely, in both cases, to have laid the blame on D than to have made such a cynical statement about himself.

Page 264, From Mme du Deffand 25 July 1772, note 4, line 1, *for* 1687 *read* ca 1687

Page 266, note 9, *for* 1706 *read* 1708

Page 269, note 7, line 1, *for* (1722–92) *read* (1723–92) *Lines 2–3, delete* and had lived near them at Chanteloup *and substitute* who had acquired their country seat at Chanteloup in 1761 (see Henri Verdier, *Le Duc de Choiseul*, 1969, p. 117; James Lunt, *John Burgoyne of Saratoga*, New York, 1975, pp. 12–14).

Page 282, note 4, *for* Cain *read* Caïn *or* Kaïn *for* 1728 *read* 1729 *for* Lekain *read* LeKain *or* Le Kain *at end add* See *Enciclopedia dello spettacolo*, Rome, 1954–62, vi. 1364–7.

Page 283, note 9, line 2, *for* the Hon. *read* Capt.

Page 286, note 16, line 1, *for* (1722–90) *read* (1721–86) *Last line, add* The découpure which D enclosed may be the silhouette of Voltaire mounted by HW with silhouettes of the Duke and Duchess of Grafton (see Samuel Taylor, 'The Duke and Duchess of Grafton with Voltaire: notes on unrecorded silhouettes by Jean Huber,' *Studies on Voltaire and the Eighteenth Century*, 1975, cxxxv. 160–2).

Page 307, note 2, line 1, *for* Peter Fector *read* James Peter Fector (1723–1814) *Line 4, add* Minet and Fector dissolved partnership in ?1778 (*Public Advertiser* 5 July 1778; MONTAGU ii. 282, n. 1; see also H. Blackstone, *Cases ... in Court of Common Pleas*, i. 569).

Page 312, note 7, lines 2–3, *for* Françoise Clairien called Mlle Raucourt (1753–1815). *read* Françoise-Marie-Antoinette-Joseph Saucerotte (1756–

1815), called Mlle Raucourt; actress, who made her debut at the Comédie-Française 23 Dec. 1772 (*Enciclopedia dello spettacolo*, Rome, 1954–62, viii. 744–6).

Page 335, note 2, *add* (Hazen, *Cat. of HW's Lib.* No. 1168)

Page 337, note 7, *after* III *insert* (b. 1701)

Page 357, note 7, line 3, *for* storica-nobiliaire *read* storico-nobiliare *italiana*   *Line 4, after* 1928–36 *add*   , vi. 924; OSSORY i. 256, n. 42; MANN viii. 328, n. 14

Page 358, note 9, line 4, *for* in 1780 *read* ca 1783   *Line 5, for* Christian *read* Christian Friedrich Karl Alexander   *Line 6, for* Anspach *read* Ansbach

Page 358, note 10, *add* Mentioned in HW's memoranda on *ante* 21 May 1771.

Page 360, note 11, *add* See OSSORY i. 254, n. 17.

Page 360, note 14, line 2, *for* 1727 *read* 1724

Page 361, note 15, line 2, *for* 14th D. *read* 9th D.

Page 361, note 16, line 1, *for* 14th *read* 9th

Page 361, note 17, line 1, *for* 15th D. *read* 10th D.

Page 361, note 18, line 1, *for* 16th *read* 11th

Page 361, note 19, line 2, *for* 17th *read* 12th   *Line 5, for* 15th *read* 10th

Page 366, note 1, line 3, *after* 1743 *add*   , MANN ii. 245; HW to Lincoln 22 June 1743, SELWYN 37 and n. 3

Page 366, note 2, line 1, *for* Anne *read* Ann   *Lines 1–2, delete* known as the 'Kitten,' *and substitute* (d. 1790)   *Line 2, after* m. *insert* (1762) *Line 5, add* See GRAY i. 36 and n. 242; SELWYN 109; *London Chronicle* 29–31 July 1762, xii. 106; *The Times* 19 Sept. 1790, p. 2.

Page 366, note 4, *add* Another daughter, 'Nancy Edgcumbe' m. (25 June 1775) 'Mons. de Fitte, at Languedoc, lieutenant of the marshals of France' (*Lady's Magazine*, 1775, 1st ser., vi. 391).

Page 367, note 3, line 4, for d'Aremberg *read* d'Arenberg   *Last line, add* See also OSSORY i. 264, n. 9.

Page 387, note 14, line 3, *for* William *read* Charles

Page 397, note 4, line 2, *for* la *read* La

Page 405, note 11, line 2, *for* (1718–99) *read* (1719–98)   *Line 3, after* France *add* 1773–88; president of the Council of Castile 1766–73   *Last line, after* 172 *add*   ; *Enciclopedia de la Cultura Española*, Madrid, 1963, i. 431–2)

Page 417, note 5, line 1, *for* 1766 *read* 1765

Page 419, From Mme du Deffand 13 Nov. 1773, line 1, *on* Sévigné *add note a: a. Lettres nouvelles ou nouvellement recouvrées de la Marquise de Sévigné, et de la Marquise de Simiane,* 1773; HW's copy is Hazen, *Cat. of HW's Lib.* No. 952. See also CHUTE 466.

Page 430, note 3, right column, lines 1–4, *delete* probably . . . 569). *and substitute* presumably Jacoba Johanna Bouwers (1741–93), m. (1758) Willem August Sirtema van Grovestins (Ossory i. 92–3, n. 5).

Page 435, note 6, line 1, *for* 1720 *read* 1718

Page 436, note 9, line 1, *before* 'Patty' *insert* Martha,   *for* (d. 1791) *read* (ca 1737–91)   *Last line, add* See also FAMILY 118, n. 9; MISC. CORR. iii. 333, n. 11.

Page 437, note 3, line 6, *after* 90 *add*   ; Hazen, *Cat. of HW's Lib.* No. 367   *Line 8, after* 37 *add* (Hazen, op. cit. No. 1224). Conway speaks of HW's love of romances, including *Cléopatre* and *Cassandre*, in letters of 25 Oct. 1743, 18 April and 10 Aug. 1745 (CONWAY i. 151, 189, 203).

Page 438, To Mme du Deffand 14 Dec. 1772, headnote, lines 2–3, *delete* Now (November 1939) in the possession of the Parke-Bernet Galleries, New York. *and substitute* The framed fragments are now WSL.

Page 439, note 4, last line, *for* 1772). *read* 1772), and by Lady Hamilton in the manner of Huber (Samuel Taylor, 'The Duke and Duchess of Grafton with Voltaire: notes on unrecorded silhouettes by Jean Huber,' *Studies on Voltaire and the Eighteenth Century*, 1975, cxxxv. 160–5).

Page 439, note 18, *add* Allen T. Hazen suggests that in December 1772 HW was considering corrections in the lives of La Mottraye and Liotard in *Anecdotes of Painting*, vol. iv (*SH Bibl.* 64).

VOLUME 6

Page 17, note 1, *at end add* See also Hazen, *Cat. of HW's Lib.* Nos 3009, 3068, 3075, 3088, 3124.

Page 18, note 3, line 1, *after* m. *insert* (5 Feb. 1774)   *Line 3, for* in 1775 *read* 6 Jan. 1775   *Last line, add* See *Colonel Saint Paul of Ewart, Soldier and Diplomat*, ed. George G. Butler, 1911, i. pp. xciv–xcv, clxxxiv.

Page 19, note 1, line 11, *after* 14 *insert* (Hazen, *Cat. of HW's Lib.* No. 2335)

Page 20, note 3, line 7, *after* 188 *add* (Hazen, *Cat. of HW's Lib.* No. 3068)   *Line 9, after* 167 *add* (Hazen, op. cit. No. 902)

Page 28, note 6, line 5, *for* 17 April *read* 25 April   *after* 16 July 1774 *add*   , FAMILY 105 and n. 2

Page 36, note 1, line 3, *after* Bentley *add*   , and is now WSL (see Hazen, *Cat. of HW's Lib.* No. 436; MASON i. 146, n. 25).

Page 37, note 10, line 1, *for* Keppel *read* van Keppel

Page 41, note 3, lines 2–5, *delete* (Edmund Burke . . . pp. 173, 176). *and substitute* (see Edmund Burke to Rockingham 7, 10 Jan. 1773, to Jane Burke 12 Jan. 1773, to Richard Burke, Jr and Thomas King 4 Feb. 1773, and other family letters at this time in Edmund Burke, *Correspondence*, ed. T. W. Copeland, Cambridge and Chicago, Ill., 1958–65, vol. ii, ed. L. S. Sutherland, pp. 409, 411–22, 537, n. 1).

Page 42, note 7, *for* 1615 *read* 1620   *at end add* See *Correspondance authentique de Ninon de Lenclos*, ed. Émile Colombey, 1886, pp. 1, 276–87, 289, 293.

Page 45, note 1, *add* See Hazen, *Cat. of HW's Lib.* No. 3143.

Page 47, note 1, line 7, *after* BM Cat. *add* Hazen, *Cat. of HW's Lib.* Nos 2207:34, 3140   *Last line, add* See MASON i. 159–61; CHUTE 419, n. 30.

Page 50, note 12, line 6, *delete* in 25 vols.

Page 53, note 8, *add* HW mentions reading this book in his letter to Mann 8 June 1774, but his copy is not listed in the SH records; see MANN viii. 16 and n. 29.

Page 55, note 2, *add* See FAMILY 106–7.

Page 56, note 7, *add* She also blamed him for her poor reception in Italy (see MORE 175–8).

Page 58, note 1, line 1, *for* Jean-Louis *read* Georges-Louis   *Line 3, after* 121 *insert* (Hazen, *Cat. of HW's Lib.* No. 2152)   *Line 6, after* was *insert* included with other works

Page 61, note 1, line 2, *for* Mme Garville *read* Mme de Garville

Page 70, note 2, last line, *after* 45 *add*   ; Hazen, *Cat. of HW's Lib.* Nos 54, 518, 1446, 2220

Page 72, line 21, *on* eux.' *add note* 13a: 13a. HW refers to this anecdote in his letter to Mary Berry 25 June 1796 *bis*, BERRY ii. 193.

Page 79, note 4, *for* Not explained. *read* Probably a reference to Lady Holland's taking laudanum; see OSSORY i. 198.

Page 84, note 3, line 2, *after* copy *insert* included

Page 87, note 7, *delete* ca   *after* 1774 *add*   , which corrects the text of the last sentence of Mme du Deffand's letter (OSSORY i. 205): 'M. de Miromenil, ci-devant Premier Président de Rouen, est garde des sceaux et Vice-chancelier,'

Page 96, line 3, *on* d'Olonne *add note* 6a: 6a. See OSSORY i. 282, n. 6.

Page 109, top of page, *insert the following heading*:

To MADAME DU DEFFAND, ca Saturday 29 October 1774
Missing. Probably written at Strawberry Hill. It was brought over by Lord Cholmondeley with HW's letter to Conway of 29 Oct. 1774; but presumably was delivered to her by Conway (see CONWAY iii. 204, 219; DU DEFFAND iv. 114).

Page 114, note 1, *add* HW's copies are Hazen, *Cat. of HW's Lib.* No. 2050:25; see also CONWAY iii. 220 and n. 3.

Page 121, note 3, *delete* reprinted ... 1775 *and substitute* bound with *Mémoires et lettres pour servir à l'histoire de la vie de mademoiselle de L'Enclos*, ed. —— Douxménil (d. 1777), Rotterdam, 1751 (copy in the University of Kansas Library [1971]; *Dictionnaire de biographie française*, 1933– , xi, 710).

Page 121, last line at bottom, *on* soixante-quatre *add note* 3a: 3a. The Bret *Mémoires*, which come first, are 164 pages long.

Page 122, note 4, line 1, *for* le *read* de　　*Line 2, for* 1616 *read* 1613 *after* 1703). *add* The letters are pp. 169–243 of the Douxménil *Mémoires*.

Page 127, note 2, *for* 1732 *read* 1733　　*after* 1816) *add* of the Comédie Italienne (*Enciclopedia dello spettacolo* ii. 1476; *Dictionnaire de biographie française*, 1933– , vii. 867–8)

Page 129, line 2, *on* véritable *add note* 3a: 3a. Mme du Deffand is presumably referring to the account of Gédoyn in the Douxménil *Mémoires*, pp. 49–55.

Page 129, line 4, *on* suit. *add note* 3b: 3b. See DU DEFFAND iv. 121, n. 3a.

Page 129, 3d paragraph, line 4, *on* Guines *add note* 4a: 4a. 'Mozart composed a concerto for the Duc (flute) and his daughter (harp), K. 299, in 1778. Mozart disliked both instruments but spoke *very* highly of the Duc's accomplishment' (Thornton Wilder).

Page 130, note 6, *add* HW is probably mistaken about Mme de la Touche. One of her sisters was mistress to the Prince de Conti, and may have been confused with Mme de Prie, mistress to the Duc de Bourbon. See CONWAY ii. 480, and H. H. Hawley, 'Meissonnier's Silver for the Duke of Kingston,' *Bulletin of the Cleveland Museum of Art*, Dec. 1978, pp. 320, 327, 340.

Page 131, note 11, *add* Conway had not sent it (see CONWAY iii. 243).

Page 131, To Mme du Deffand 4 Jan. 1775, headnote, *for* 11 Dec. *read* 11 Jan.

Page 133, note 1, line 2, *after* HW *insert* (or Mary Berry)

Page 136, note 5a, *substitute* HW is referring to the Douxménil *Mémoires*; his copy is Hazen, *Cat. of HW's Lib.* No. 988:2 (see also CONWAY iii. 242, n. 33).

Page 142, note 4, *for* 1750 *read* 1751

Page 152, note 11, *add* These lines were contributed by Mason (see MASON i. 176 and also 175–6, n. 2).

Page 159, line 21, *on* le 22 *add note* 4a: 4a. According to the *Daily Adv.* 23 Feb., Conway arrived back in London 21 Feb. and attended the King's levee 22 Feb.

Page 160, note 9, *add* See FAMILY 106–7; *Paris Jour.*, DU DEFFAND v. 344.

Page 160, note 10, *add* See MANN viii. 90, n. 4.

Page 175, note 6, *add* This paragraph in the text was inserted into the following letter of 4 April 1775 by Miss Berry.

Page 181, note 7, *add* See MANN viii. 90, n. 5.

Page 185, note 9, *add* For HW's copy of the *Éloge* see Hazen, *Cat. of HW's Lib.* No. 3151.

Page 185, note 10, *add* HW's copy is Hazen, *Cat. of HW's Lib.* No. 3036.

Page 186, From Mme du Deffand 9 May 1775, 3d paragraph, line 1, *on* Izard *add note* b: b. See MANN viii. 102 and n. 6.

Page 189, note 6, line 1, *for* 1743 *read* 1736　　*Last line, after* 145 *add* (Hazen, *Cat. of HW's Lib.* No. 2810)

Page 196, note 3, *add* HW's copies are Hazen, *Cat. of HW's Lib.* Nos 3060, 3082.

Page 202, note 1, line 1, *for* Ann *read* Ann Skottowe (1732–1803) *Line 5, delete* evidently   *Line 6, after* letter *insert* 7 July   *Line 7, at end add* HW's presentation copy is now in the Huntington Library (see Hazen, *Cat. of HW's Lib.* No. 37).

Page 207, note 4, *for* foreign affairs *read* the King's household.

Page 213, note 1, lines 1–2, *for* Eleonora . . . widow of *read* Eleanor Oglethorpe (1684–1775), m. (5 March 1707)   *for* Béthizy *read* Béthisy *Line 4, after* Gazette *add*   ; Amos A. Ettinger, *James Edward Oglethorpe Imperial Idealist,* Oxford, 1936 (reprint, 1968), pp. 19, 56 and n. 2, 305

Page 225, note 2, line 2, *before* Henry *insert* Hon.

Page 230, 1st paragraph, line 6, *on* shérif *add note* 1

Page 230, note 1, line 1, *after* Sayre *insert* (1736–1818)   *Line 11, after* 1775 *insert*   , MANN viii. 138–9 and nn. 3, 5

Page 231, note 2, line 3, *delete* perhaps   *Line 6, after* cvi *add*   ; OSSORY i. 282–3, n. 15

Page 234, note 1, right column, line 1, *for* Day *read* Daye   *Line 3, add* See OSSORY i. 245 and nn. 18, 19, 271.

Page 241, note 9, line 1, *for* ca 1697 *read* 1695   *Line 2, after* Godolphin, *insert* styled   *Last line, add* See ADD. AND CORR. for vol. 33, p. 121, n. 5.

Page 245, line 8, *on* mains *add note a*: a. See OSSORY i. 282 and nn. 6, 7.

Page 252, note 8, line 1, *for* ca 1737 *read* 1736

Page 263, 1st paragraph, line 8, *for* excusez *read* Excusez   *for* a la sienne *read* à la sienne

Page 265, note 4, line 2, *for* Louis *read* Vincent-Louis

Page 269, line 11, *on* buste *add note* 8: 8. The bust of Mme Nicolas Poussin, by Fiammingo, purchased by HW at Mariette's sale. See HW to Lady Ossory 20 Dec. 1775, OSSORY i. 282 and nn. 8, 9.

Page 273, note 1, line 2, *for*   , 1776 *read* [i.e., Paris], 1775   *Line 6, add* HW's copy is Hazen, *Cat. of HW's Lib.* No. 3125.

Page 283, note 13, line 3, *for* London *read* Paris, 1775, and Nouvelle édition rev. et cor., 1776, although the title-pages of both editions have a Londres imprint

Page 284, note 10, *add* HW's copy is Hazen, *Cat. of HW's Lib.* No. 3010.

Page 286, note 22, line 2, *for* in *read* listed as   *Line 5, after* ones *add* : *Recueil de Lettres choisies,* Paris, 1751; and also *Lettres nouvelles . . . Pour servir de supplément à l'édition de Paris en six volumes,* Paris, 1754 (see Hazen, *Cat. of HW's Lib.* Nos 949, 950, 951).

Page 287, note 4, line 3, *after* 88) *insert* Jacques de Merdy, Comte de Catuelan (*post* DU DEFFAND vi. 289, n. 8),   *Line 7, at end add* (Hazen, *Cat. of HW's Lib.* No. 3147).

Page 289, note 7, *add* HW quotes D's sentence in his letter to Mason 8 April (MASON i. 259).

Page 294, note 11, *add* See ADD. AND CORR. for vol. 1, p. 221.

Page 300, note 7a, *for* St Paul *read* St Paul's visit (see DU DEFFAND iii. 305, n. 2; MONTAGU i. 113, n. 3; MORE 182).

Page 308, note 10, line 4, *after* 116 *add* (Hazen, *Cat. of HW's Lib.* No. 2801)

Page 316, note 4, *add* HW's copy of the English edition, 3 vols, 1771–88, was sold SH v. 62. When vol. ii was published 24 Feb. 1773, HW apparently bought an extra copy of that volume to send to Mason (see MASON i. 66–7 and nn. 2, 6; Hazen, *Cat. of HW's Lib.* Nos 3186, 4002).

Page 329, note 9, *add* From a fragment, probably in Lord Sheffield's hand, among the Sheffield Papers in the Yale University Library, written on part of the back of a letter, being an extract from a memorandum book of Gibbon:

Mr Gibbin's Memorandum Book 12th May 1776—
Mr Gibbon dined and slept at Strawberry Hill—Mr Walpole his unpublished chapter on modern gardening, pleasant.
14th July 1776 to H. Walpole for gold snuff box from Paris—£37. 5. 6.

Page 333, note 2, right column, line 9, *for* (b. 1775) *read* (1775–1824) *Line 13, after* 196–7 *add* ; Vittoria Colonna Caetani, Duchessa di Sermoneta, *The Locks of Norbury*, 1940, pp. 91–2.

Page 337, note 6, *substitute* Elizabeth Whitwell (1717–76), sister of Sir John Griffin Griffin and Lady Welderen; her house was in Great Maddox Street (Collins, *Peerage*, 1812, vi. 754). Lady Mary Coke wrote in 'MS Journals' 30 June 1776, 'Mrs. Whitwell, sister to Madame de Welderen, was burnt on Saturday night [29 June 1776] ... Mrs Whittwell's maid opened the door of her Mistress's room and said, "For God's sake, Madam, come out, the house is in flames" ... but unfortunate Mrs Whitwel was looking for her dog, and by that delay lost the opportunity of saving her own life'; and again on 1 July 1776, 'I've just heard that the body of Mrs Whitwell, not entirely consumed, was found the day after the fire with her dog by her, burnt only on one side.' The *London Chronicle* 29 June–2 July 1776, xl. 3, 7, reported, 'The Lady had got downstairs in her shift but unfortunately went up again to put some clothes on.'

Page 339, note 7b, line 4, *for* 1733–1816 *read* 1733–1817

Page 341, note 1, line 3, *for* 1780 *read* 1781 (FAMILY 192, 196)

Page 352, note 5, line 3, *for* Townshend *read* Townsend   *for* (d. 1787) *read* (1737–87)   *Last line, add* See also Namier and Brooke iii. 537–8.

Page 357, note 7, line 1, *for* (d. 1830) *read* (ca 1755–1830)   *Line 6, after Life insert and Writings*

Page 357, note 11, line 4, *for* 5za *read* 5aa

Page 376, note 1, line 1, *for* Don Jerónimo Grimaldi *read* Pablo Jeronimo Grimaldi Palavicini y Spinola   *Line 2, before* minister *add* Spanish minister to Sweden 1749–53; ambassador to Holland 1755–7, to France 1761–3, to Rome, 1776;   *Line 2, after* Spain *add* 1763–76   *Line 4, after* 1776 *add*   , MANN v. 560 and n. 20

Page 377, note 5, *add* See also *Mémoires de la société de l'histoire de Paris*, 1925, pp. 153–63.

Page 383, note 6, *at beginning insert* Pierre Penet (d. ca 1827), merchant *Last line, add* See also T. Wood Clarke, *Émigrés in the Wilderness*, New York, 1941, pp. 167–9; Jacob M. Price, *France and the Chesapeake*, Ann Arbor, Michigan, 1973, ii. 702–5.

Page 383, note 8, *substitute* Hôtel d'Entragues (information from Professor William Willcox).

Page 396, note 13, *add* Fernand Baldensperger, in the *Virginia Quarterly Review*, Spring, 1940, xvi. 309, says it is certainly Suard's *Journal étranger*.

Pages 399–400, note 1, *add* See Hazen, *Cat. of HW's Lib*. No. 2801.

Page 403, note 3, line 1, *after* Charpentier *add* (b. 1732)   *Line 2, for* died in Dec. 1776 *read* died at Port au Prince 13 Dec. 1776   *Line 3, after* 197–8 *add*   ; *Mémoires de la société historique . . . de Pontoise*, 1896, xviii. p. ix; *Dictionnaire de biographie française*, 1933– , xii. 313–14

Page 412, note 8, *add* HW's copy is Hazen, *Cat. of HW's Lib*. No. 3130; see also MASON i. 295–7, DALRYMPLE 137.

Page 412, note 9, line 1, *after* Xavier *insert* Millot

Page 414, note *a, add* HW's copy, Amsterdam, 1744, is Hazen, *Cat. of HW's Lib*. No. 978.

Page 451, From Mme du Deffand 15 June 1777, headnote, *add* The MS, in Wiart's hand with notes in HW's hand, was acquired by WSL in the Sainte-Aulaire collection of papers. The text has been collated and variants in words as well as two omitted passages are recorded below; the differences in punctuation are not included here.

Page 451, From Mme du Deffand 15 June 1777, date-line, *before* 15 juin *insert* Ce dimanche   *1st paragraph, line 3, for* je n'en ai *read* j'en ai

Page 451, From Mme du Deffand 15 June 1777, *after 2d paragraph insert* Votre Duc [HW's note: (*de Richmond*)] est beaucoup moins triste qu'il ne l'était, je le trouve un peu moins occupé, il vous écrira sur votre prisonnier, il doit consulter M. Élie de Beaumont sur ce qu'il conviendra de faire. Je lui dirai les dix guinées que vous avez de plus.

Page 452, 1st paragraph, line 1, *for* encore ici *read* ici encore   *Line 2, begin new paragraph with* Mme de Luxembourg

Page 452, 2d paragraph, line 5, *for* des pièces de théâtre *read* des théâtres   *Lines 12–13*, toujours plus approfondies et plus justes *crossed out and* plus justes et plus approfondies *written above*   *Line 16, for* songer *read* penser

Page 452, 3d paragraph, lines 3–4, *for* elles seraient *read* sont

Page 452, 4th paragraph, line 1, *for* vous aviez *read* vous nous aviez

Page 452, *after 5th paragraph insert* Votre parente [HW's note: Madame Meynell] que vous m'aviez marqué dans vos précédentes lettres d'avoir venir à Paris, n'y vient point parce qu'elle est malade. Quand elle y viendra Wiart sera à son service pour ce qu'elle vous voudra lui ordonner.

Page 452, note 4, line 1, *for* Her *read* Mme de Beauvau's   *Line 2,* *after* Vicomte de *insert* Chabot, later Comte de

Page 453, note 3, *substitute* One catalogue is in the Bibliothèque Nationale, Nantes (a photostat of it is now WSL).

Page 455, note 4, line 1, *for* Scrimshire *read* Skrymsher   *Line 2, for* 1727 *read* 1737   *Line 4, after* 101 *add* , iv. pt i. 178   *Line 5, add* The passage of *ante* 15 June 1777 which was omitted in Sainte-Aulaire's printed text refers to her as 'votre parente,' identified in the MS by HW. She was HW's third cousin (see OSSORY i. 114, n. 4).

Page 461, note 3, line 3, *for* Drosménil *read* Dromesnil

Page 469, note 2, line 6, *for* 1767 *read* 1777

Page 469, note 5, line 2, *for* 1848 *read* 1847

Page 470, note 10, lines 5–6, *delete* there . . . so *and substitute* Lady Mary Coke wrote in her 'MS Journals' 31 Aug. 1777, 'Lady Browne came in and Mr Walpole (who did not go to Good-Wood) and I believe is again flattering himself with the Duke of Gloucester's recovery, from the Friday's post having brought an account of his having slept two hours without laudanum.'

Page 474, note 6, line 15, *add* See also MANN viii. 328 and nn. 14, 15; *Harcourt Papers*, ed. Edward William Harcourt, Oxford, n.d., viii. 3.

Page 475, note 1, *add* For the Duchess of Gloucester's letter of 14 Sept. 1777 see FAMILY 141–3.

Page 478, note 3, *add* HW had at least nine volumes of the set; see Hazen, *Cat. of HW's Lib.* Nos 3030, 3128; OSSORY ii. 377, n. 18.

Page 480, note *b*, line 1, *after* m. *insert* 8 Aug. 1777   *Line 3, at end add* See FAMILY 127–8, 137.

Page 486, note 1, line 1, *for* Catherine *read* Catharine

Page 490, From Mme du Deffand 12 Nov. 1777, headnote, *add* The MS, in Wiart's hand, was acquired by WSL in the Sainte-Aulaire collection of papers. The text has been collated and variants in words are recorded below; differences in punctuation are not included here.

Page 490, From Mme du Deffand 12 Nov. 1777, date-line, *after* Paris *insert* ce   *1st paragraph, line 3, for* Craufurd *read* Craufurt   *Line 6, for* après *read* d'après

Page 491, 3d paragraph, line 3, *for* vous n'avez pas *read* vous n'avez point   *Lines 11–12, for* réchauffait *read* échauffait

Page 491, 4th paragraph, lines 1–2, *for* de Luxembourg et de Mirepoix *read* [de Luxembourg et de Mirepoix]   *Line 7, for* de caractère *read* son caractère   *Line 8, for* quelque effort *read* quelques efforts

Page 492, 2d paragraph, line 2, *after* sais *insert* pas

Page 492, 5th paragraph, line 1, *for* Schuwalof *read* Schowaloff   *for* il m'a fait *read* il me fait   *Line 7, for* de bon goût *read* du bon goût   *Line 8, for* leur palais *read* leurs palais

Page 492, 6th paragraph, lines 2–3, *for* Il paraît que depuis trois ans il *read* Il paraît depuis trois ans qu'il

Page 495, note 1, line 5, *before* Jan. *insert* ca 31   *after* 1778 *insert* , CHUTE 485 and nn. 1, 2

Page 502, note 2, *add* When Lord Ossory visited HW in early December, HW may have spoken of D (see OSSORY i. 404, 406).

VOLUME 7

Page 13, note 2, lines 2–3, *for* before 1766 *read* 1756–62   *Line 3, before* John *insert* Hon.   *Line 4, after* M. *insert* (MANN viii. 417 and n. 9).

Page 14, note 6, *add* HW wrote Mason 17 Jan. 1778 of a report of Voltaire's death, and may have written an epitaph upon receiving that news (see MASON i. 343 and n. 11).

Page 16, note 4, line 2, *after* vie *insert* (d. 1832)   *Line 4, after* 197 *add* Burke, *Peerage*, 1928, p. 2016   *At end add* She was probably born 10th or 11th May, since Lady Louisa Conolly wrote the Duchess of Leinster 22 May 1778 of 'receiving Mr Ogilvie's two letters of the 11th and 16th, the first informing me of your safe delivery, in so few hours' illness, and the 2nd telling me that you continued well' (Duchess of Leinster, *Correspondence*, ed. Brian Fitzgerald, Dublin, 1949–57, iii. 286).

Page 18, note 3, *substitute* Jean-Claude-Gilles Colson (1725–78), called Bellecour, of the Comédie-Française 1750–78 (*Enciclopedia dello spettacolo*, Rome, 1954–62, ii. 193; *Dictionnaire de biographie française*, 1933– , v. 1322–3; CONWAY iii. 217 and n. 10).

Page 19, note 7, *add* She visited her sister in March and wrote from Dieppe 6 April 1778 on her return journey to England: 'I have thought of you all ever since I left you, and shall reflect back with satisfaction on the little time I spent with you, though it was so damped by your being so ill' (Duchess of Leinster, *Correspondence*, ed. Brian Fitzgerald, Dublin, 1949–57, iii. 265).

Page 24, note 1, *add* HW's copy is Hazen, *Cat. of HW's Lib.* No. 2999.

Page 28, note 2, *add* HW had La Rochefoucauld's *Réflexions, ou sentences et maximes morales*, Amsterdam, 1705 (Hazen, *Cat. of HW's Lib.* No. 992).

Page 30, note 4, *for* The Duchesse de Chartres *read* Louise-Adélaïde de Bourbon-Condé (DU DEFFAND iii. 84)

Page 32, note 12, line 1, *for* Mériadec *read* Marie   *Line 2, for* 1802 *read* 1808 *and for* Prince *read* styled Prince   *Line 4, after* 237n *insert* ; see also MANN ix. 513, n. 13

Page 41, *delete note 12*

Page 43, note 2, line 2, *for* ca 1716 *read* ca 1717

Page 43, note 3, line 2, *for* 1755 *read* 1756   *Last line, add* See also CONWAY iii. 266, n. 35, 391, n. 9.

Page 46, note 2, *add* HW sent this news to Mason 4 July (MASON i. 410).

Page 52, note 5, line 1, *before* Chadeau *insert* Jean-Isaac-Timothée *for* Clochetterie *read* Clocheterie (d. 1782)   *Line 2, after* Aug. *add*   ; *Dictionnaire de biographie française*, 1933– , viii. 161

Page 52, note 6, *add* See also OSSORY ii. 23 and nn. 1, 3.

Page 53, note 2, line 6, *after* 1797 *insert*   ; and Charlotte Augusta Keppel (1771–1852), m. (1802) Robert Foote

Page 53, note 5, line 2, *for* Souastre *read* Guines   *Line 7, after* 127 *add*   ; CHUTE 369–70

Page 60, note 1, *add* See also CONWAY iii. 306–7.

Page 61, note 3, *add* See also CONWAY iii. 305 and n. 3, 308 and n. 2.

Page 75, note 2, *add* See Hazen, *Cat. of HW's Lib.* No. 3586.

Page 79, note 7, *after* House *add* (GEC; Lady Sarah Lennox, *Life and Letters*, ed. Countess of Ilchester and Lord Stavordale, 1902, i. 280, 282); before her death she was living at Windsor, as Mary Townshend wrote to George Selwyn 16 Oct. 1778: 'Your friend Lady Sarah was gone to town, to go on to Old Windsor to visit poor Lady Holland, and was stopped by an account of her death' (J. H. Jesse, *George Selwyn and his Contemporaries*, 1882, iii. 330–1; see also Ilchester and Stavordale, op. cit. i. 260–1, 266; OSSORY iii. 248–9, Appendix 6)

Page 80, 2d paragraph, line 8, *on* appartenu *add note* 2a: 2a. Selwyn subsequently gave the cabinet to HW, or allowed him to keep it for a time (HW to Lady Ossory 23 Dec. 1779, OSSORY ii. 150–1).

Page 82, note 5, lines 5–6, *delete* The deed . . . March 1779 *and substitute* HW's agreement with the auctioneer was dated 2 Nov. 1778; it was contested and the final decree in HW's favour was dated 21 July 1779 (OSSORY iii. 250–2, Appendix 7)   *Line 8, after* 1779 *add*   , ibid. ii. 125

Page 109, note 1, line 4, *for* 335 *read* 336

Page 110, note 1, line 3, *for* [1791] *read* [?1791]

Page 118, From Madame du Deffand 13 March 1779, line 6, *on* dire. *add note* a: a. See HW to Mary Berry 19 July 1789, BERRY i. 38; [John Pinkerton,] *Walpoliana* [1799], i. 4. *Les Lettres Françaises* No. 1364, 16–22 Dec. 1970, attributes this bon mot to the Président des Brosses (Thornton Wilder).

Page 119, note 1, line 2, *for* 1774 *read* 1775

Page 121, note 4a, *add* HW perhaps gave his set away (see Hazen, *Cat. of HW's Lib.* No. 2801).

Page 125, note 4, line 2, *after* 1779, *insert* sold Sotheby's 27 April 1927, lot 246, 'Other properties,'

Page 142, note 5, line 1, *delete* Hon.   *for* (d. 1816) *read* (ca 1738–1816)

Page 142, note 10, line 2, *for* —— Abington *read* James Abington

Page 158, note 3, *for* ca 1716 *read* ca 1714

Page 160, note 1, line 1, *for Frederic read Prince Frederic*   *Line 5, after* 1779, *insert* OSSORY ii. 113, nn. 3, 6; MANN viii. 504, n. 1;

Page 166, note 2, line 3, *for* a *read* à

Page 175, To Mme du Deffand 23 Sept. 1779, headnote, *add* HW asked her to mediate in Macartney's favour (HW to Lady Ossory 11 Sept. 1779, OSSORY ii. 123).

Page 177, note *a, add* HW tells this anecdote of her in his letter to Lady Ossory 14 Oct. 1779 *bis,* OSSORY ii. 127.

Page 177, note 7, line 1, *for* Pelham Clinton *read* Fiennes Clinton (later Pelham Clinton)

Page 181, To Mme du Deffand, ca Thursday 14 Oct. 1779, *delete* ca

Page 198, note 4, line 4, *after* 1780 *add*   , MASON ii. 18 and n. 8.

Page 201, note 6, *add* See illustration in MASON ii. 145.

Page 201, note 8, line 1, *for* ca 1720 *read* 1721

Page 237, note 3, line 1, *for* Guydot *read* Guyot   *At end add* A 'presentation copy to Horace Walpole from the Abbé Desfontaines' was sold Sotheby's 18 June 1934, but this presumably refers to a copy presented to HW's uncle who was ambassador at Paris 1724–30 (see Hazen, *Cat. of HW's Lib.* No. 1456).

Page 257, 1st paragraph, line 9, *after* printed *insert* by Paget Toynbee

Page 258, 4th paragraph, line 5, *on* drawn *add note* 4a: 4a. It was, in Richard Gough's *Sepulchral Monuments in Great Britain,* 1786–96, Part II, vol. ii, facing p. 31.

Page 258, note 2, line 5, *for* Phillips *read* Philipps

Page 260, 2d paragraph, line 5, *on* bronze *add note* 12a: 12a. Described in Antoine Joseph Dezallier d'Argenville, *Voyage pittoresque des environs de Paris,* 1768, pp. 419–20; see also MORE 46 and n. 16.

Page 260, note 21, line 2, *for* ca 14 Sept. *read* 15 Sept.   *after* 1765 *add* (MORE 45–6)

Page 262, note 33, *add* HW probably owned the first French edition of *Le Siège de Calais,* sent to him by Hertford (see CONWAY ii. 521, and also ibid. 515 and n. 7, 519 and n. 19; MONTAGU ii. 150). HW's copy of Denis's translation is Hazen, *Cat. of HW's Lib.* No. 1810:7:11.

Page 263, line 2 from bottom, *for humano read humanæ*

Page 264, 4th paragraph, line 2, *on* Guido *add note* 47a: 47a. The 'Salutation,' i.e. the 'Annunciation' (see HW to Lady Ossory 9 Sept. 1775, OSSORY i. 261 and n. 32).

Page 264, note 48, *substitute* 'La Madeleine Repentante,' painted by Charles Le Brun (1619–90) ca 1656–7 for the Carmelites in the Rue d'Enfer, is now in the Louvre (see CONWAY iii. 202, n. 33). The tradition that the painting is of Mlle de la Vallière *en Madeleine* is incorrect.

Page 265, 2d paragraph, line 4, *on* Hays's; *add note* 55a: 55a. See HW to Lady Suffolk 16 Oct. 1765 (MORE 65).

Page 266, note 72, line 2, *after* 52–3 *add*   : 'This Rue de Colombier, and the Rue Jacob make one long street from the Rue du Seine quite down to the river'   *Line 5, add* The Rue du Colombier is now Rue Jacob.

Page 267, note 74, line 1, *for* Beaupréon *read* Beaupréau

Page 268, line 9, *on* Geoffrin *add note* 82a: 82a. On 27 Oct. there were also Lord William Gordon, Lord Ossory and William Cole (see Cole, *Journal of my Journey to Paris*, 1931, pp. 80, 82, 91–2); Cole was present throughout these visits, which he describes vividly.

Page 268, note 81, *delete second sentence and substitute* Amelia Ramsay (1755–1813), m. (1779) Gen. (later Sir) Archibald Campbell (1739–91) (MORE 59, n. 3).

Page 270, note 89, *add* See also *Genealog. hist. Nachrichten*, 3d ser., vi. 19–20.

Page 271, note 97, line 1, *after* Saurin *insert* (the later title was *L'Anglomane*, not *L'Anglomanie*)   *Line 2, after* Nov. *add* and to Conway 29 Nov.

Page 271, note 99, *for* Georgina *read* Georgiana

Page 271, note 103, *add* For HW's purchases see HW to Conway 29 Nov. 1765, CONWAY iii. 32 and n. 18.

Page 272, note 106, line 1, *after* (HW). *insert* This was probably Françoise-Jeanne-Élisabeth Gaultier (1720–1803), m. 1 (1744) Charles Martel, actor; m. 2 Jean-Jacques-François Drouin, dancer; of the Comédie-Française 1742–80 (CONWAY iii. 213, n. 32).

Page 275, line 13, *on* sale *add note* 125a: 125a. See *ante Paris Jour.* 14 Nov. 1765.

Page 280, line 5 from bottom, *for* 20,000 *read* 28,000

Page 281, note 159, *substitute* Probably Conte Ugolino Palazzi (b. ca 1715), with whom she was associated from 1746 to 1756 in Italy (see Robert Halsband, *Life of Lady Mary Wortley Montagu*, Oxford, 1956, pp. 236–61; MANN iv. 235, n. 6). The younger Crébillon married Lady Henrietta Maria Stafford Howard in 1748 (MANN iv. 325, n. 27).

Page 283, note 172, *add* An album of sixty-eight engraved portraits of ladies of the court at Versailles, most of them published by Henri Bonnart, Paris, 1695, and several by A. Trouvain, Paris, 1696, is now WSL. On the fly-leaf appears the signature of Michael Lort (1725–90), with Lort's note, 'Mr. H.W. has added the names to several'; on the endpaper is the bookplate of James Bindley (1737–1818). Nineteen of the portraits have been identified in HW's handwriting, and on the Princesse de Soubise he wrote, 'Madᵉ la Princ. de Soubise. Mistress of Louis XIV. She used to wear emerald earrings as a Token to him that her Husband was gone from Versailles.'

Page 289, note 201, right column, line 6, *after* 1876 *insert*   ; it is now WSL.

Page 302, bottom line, *on* Matta *add note* 258a: 258a. Probably Charles de Bourdeille (1614–74), Comte de Mastas, or Matta (N&Q, 1854, 1st ser. x. 138–9, 157–8; SELWYN 220 and n. 6).

Page 303, note 261, line 1, *for* 6 March *read* 7 March

Page 305, note 269, *add* James Anderson's *Royal Genealogies*, 2d edn, 1735, p. 631 *sub* 'Mary Teresia,' wife of Louis XIV, says: 'She bore once a BLACK *Princess* that soon died and is not usually reckoned among LEWIS'S Offspring.'

Page 307, note 276, line 3, *for* guineas *read* pounds (see Hazen, *Cat. of HW's Lib.* No. 2357).

Page 308, 3d paragraph, line 4, *on* Temple *add note* 277a: 277a. Ollivier's painting 'Thé à l'anglaise au Temple' (see illustration) must have been done in May 1766 when Mozart made a short visit to Paris, and therefore it does not represent a musicale which HW himself attended. HW may have been present, however, at the supper at the Prince de Conti's in January of 1766, when Mlle Fel sang; Ollivier's painting of this supper is at Versailles.

Page 312, note 293, *add* (CONWAY iii. 60 and n. 6, 63–4; MANN vi. 414–15 and nn. 9–12)

Page 312, note 294, line 5, *after* n. *insert* 7 (MANN vii. 106)

Page 321, note 33, line 2, *for* 1736–94 *read* 1736–93

Page 333, 9th paragraph, line 2, *on* nine. *add note* 37: 37. 'On Thursday [12 Oct.] arrived in town from Paris, the Right Hon. Horatio Walpole' (*London Chronicle* 12–14 Oct. 1769, xxvi. 366).

Page 335, line 7 from bottom, *on* marriage. *add note* 7b: 7b. This hung in the Great North Bedchamber at Strawberry Hill ('Des. of SH,' *Works* ii. 497).

Page 336, note 10, last line, *for* 22 July *read* 28 July

Page 337, note 17, line 1, *after* Janssen *add* (Cornelis Jonson van Ceulen, 1593–ca 1662)

Page 338, line 8 from bottom, *on* Thiers. *add note* 21a: 21a. See F. W. Hilles, 'Sir Joshua at the Hôtel de Thiers,' *Gazette des Beaux-Arts*, Oct. 1969, 202–3.

Page 345, note 10b, line 4, *for des read der*

Page 349, note 27b, line 2, *for Félicie. read Félicie,*

Page 354, note 5, *add* See *Mem. Geo. III* ii. 169.

Page 355, note 1, line 4, *for* HW's copy *read* The copy seen by HW *Lines 6–7, for* he must have bought other volumes because *read* he received from Mann in 1771 a six-volume set (HW to Mann 15 Jan. 1771);   *Line 11, add* See Hazen, *Cat. of HW's Lib.* No. 2342.

Page 357, note 13, *substitute* See Conway to HW 28 Sept. 1758 and HW to Conway 17 Oct. 1758 (CONWAY i. 574 and n. 4, 582 and n. 15), and Jenkinson to Grenville 29 Oct. 1757 (*Grenville Papers* i. 229).

Page 358, note 19, *add* See also Dalrymple to HW 26 Sept. 1764, DALRYMPLE 103, n. 4.

Page 361, note 24, *add* See Hazen, *Cat. of HW's Lib.* No. 1261.

Page 368, note 22, *for* Paris *read* London

Page 369, 2d paragraph, line 5, *on* footman.' *add note* 25a: 25a. See *Mem. Geo. III* ii. 126.

Page 372, note 6, line 1, *for* Marsh Dickenson *read* Marshe Dickinson *Line 2, for* Marsh Dickenson *read* Marshe Dickinson   *Line 4, after* 335 *add*   ; Namier and Brooke ii. 321

Page 376, note *a*, line 5, *for* 'my servant,' *read* 4 to 'my servant' [?Mary],

Page 376, line 22, *for* †Mr Conway   Oct. 3. by Joly. *read* Mr Conway Oct. 3. by Joly [i.e. 2 Oct., printed in CONWAY iii. 11–17].

Page 376, line 25, *for* Mr Conway *read* †Mr Conway

Page 377, line 10, *for* †Mr Conway *read* Mr Conway

Page 379, line 5, *for* †Mr Conway *read* Mr Conway

Page 381, note 1, *delete last sentence*

Page 383, line 25, *under* Ditto. 41. *add* 33 to others than D

Page 385, line 6, *under* 80. *add* 14 to others than D

Page 388, line 18, *under* Ditto 70 *add* 21 to others than D

Page 396, line 10, *on* Mrs D. *add note a*: *a*. Letter from Mme de Cambis to Mrs Damer, which HW encloses in his letter to Conway 8 Sept. 1775 (CONWAY iii. 260 and n. 28).

Page 399, Expenses at Paris, line 11, *on* head *add note a*: *a*. See HW to Mann 11 Jan. 1758, MANN v. 168.

Page 401, bottom line, *on* Ch[ute]. *add note* 4: 4. Cole wrote in his *Journal of my Journey to Paris* (ed. Stokes, 1931, p. 245), 'Mr Walpole, among other things, bought 3 most beautiful vases for a chimney, of blew enamel, set in gilt copper, for Mr Chute of the Vine in Hampshire.' They were still at the Vyne in 1964 (F. J. B. Watson, 'Walpole and the Taste for French Porcelain in Eighteenth-Century England,' in *Horace Walpole: Writer, Politician, and Connoisseur*, ed. W. H. Smith, New Haven, Conn., 1967, p. 329).

Page 402, line 22 of left column, *on* birds *add note* 5: 5. Now (1958) in the possession of J. H. Plumb.

Page 403, line 22 of left column, *for* hankerchiefs *read* handkerchiefs

Page 407, A fourth case, line 5, *for* Calera St *read* Calcraft [John (1726–72), M.P.]

Page 413, **Money laid out, 1775,** line 13, *after* Louis *add* [? a slip for Philip]

VOLUME 8

Page 32, line 3, *after* légué *add* [in this list 'dont' means 'in which is included']

Page 32, note 13b, at beginning *insert* I.e., 28 volumes of which 9 volumes are Montyon.

Page 35, note 14, lines 7–9, *delete* obviously she must have had innumerable books which were in one or two volumes. *and substitute* most lots in the inventory included many volumes which are not mentioned by name (the word 'dont' means 'including' or 'one title of which is').

Page 48, note 1, lines 4–6, *for* now in the possession of Dr James Strachey, which was sold at the Waller Sale 5 Dec. 1921, Sotheby's, lot 83. *read* which was sold Sotheby's 5 Dec. 1921 (first Waller Sale), lot 83, to Lytton Strachey; subsequently in the possession of Dr James Strachey; resold Sotheby's 27 Feb. 1973, lot 440.

Page 58, note 3a, *after* 1766 *add* now wsl

Page 84, line 5, *for* pas *read* très

Page 84, note 1, lines 3–4, *for* now in the possession of Dr James Strachey *read* which was sold Sotheby's 5 Dec. 1921 (first Waller Sale), lot 83, to Lytton Strachey; subsequently in the possession of Dr James Strachey; resold Sotheby's 27 Feb. 1973, lot 440. Sotheby's catalogue points out that HW did not write 'pas ressemblant' but the opposite 'très ressemblant.'

Page 117, bottom line, *on s'évanouit add note* 2: 2. Quoted from Rousseau, *Odes*, vi. 12th strophe.

Page 117, note 1, lines 1–2, *after lettres add*   , p. 404

Page 155, note 1, *for* x. 404 *read* x. 402–5

Page 162, note 1a, *for* dealer *read* cleaner

Page 162, note 4, *for* ibid. *read* Voltaire, *Œuvres* xxviii. 365.

Page 194, note 1, *add* See HW to Gray 25 Jan. 1766, Gray ii. 153.

Page 216, 2d paragraph, line 4, *for* Brill's *read* Bull's

VOLUME 9

Page xx, The Cabinet at Strawberry Hill, *for* ii. 72 *read* ii. 71

Page xxi, line 3, *after* This *insert* popularity

Page xxiii, line 24, *for* in the Parliaments of 1741 and 1747 *read* from 13 April 1744 to 1754 (Sedgwick ii. 268)

Page xxvii, line 2, *for* 449 *read* 450

Page xxvii, line 3, *for* 187 *read* 188

Page xxvii, note 2, line 3, *after* 20 *add*   ; ed. L. Owen Pike, 1946; see Introduction, pp. 15–16. See also Hist. MSS Comm., 1st Report, App., 1870, p. 13

Page xxviii, line 10, *for* are *read* were

Page xxviii, line 11, *after* Waller, Bt *insert* these three are now wsl (2d Waller Sale, 1947, lots 37, 53)

Page xxviii, end of 1st paragraph, *add* The MSS of the 7th Duke of Manchester (1874) are now in the Public Record Office: Gifts and Deposits 15 (Hist. MSS Comm., 22d Report, 1946, p. 54).

Page xxviii, 2d paragraph, line 5, *for* see above *read* now wsl

Page xxix, at bottom *insert the following paragraph:*

Extracts from this first edition of 1818 were printed in *Blackwood's Magazine*, 1818:

2 Aug. 1746 (most of 1st paragraph)	iii. 163
5 Aug. 1746 (most of 4th paragraph, 6th paragraph, 1st sentence of 7th paragraph)	iii. 163
11 Aug. 1746 (extract from 1st paragraph)	iii. 163
16 Aug. 1746 (2nd and 3d paragraphs)	iii. 163–4
20 Aug. 1758	iii. 164–5
28 Jan. 1760 (part of 1st paragraph)	iii. 165
19 April 1760 (most of 1st paragraph)	iii. 165–6
6 May 1760 (most of 1st paragraph)	iii. 166
13 Nov. 1760 (mid-1st paragraph to end)	iii. 166–7
25–30 March 1761 (misdated)	iii. 167–8
16 April 1761 (3d paragraph)	iii. 168

Page xxx, line 9, *for* London, 1820 *read* 2d edn, 4to, London, 1819 *Lines 10–11, for* in four octavo volumes *read* (copies in the British Museum, Bodleian Library, and University of Edinburgh Library)

Page xxxvi, 3d line from bottom, *for* E. A. Parr *read* A. E. Parr

Page xxxvii, line 4, *for* Turberbille *read* Turberville

Page xl, right column, 3d line from bottom, *for* V. R. Fox *read* R. V. Fox

Page xliii, Toynbee column, line 11, *after* Supp. *delete* I.

Page xliv, Toynbee column, line 13, *after* Supp. *delete* I.

Page liii, left column, *sub* 1766, *insert* ?15 Feb.

Page 2, note 2, line 4, *after* Chatham *insert* (see Gov. Thomas Pitt's account in Hist. MSS Comm., 13th Rep., App., pt iii, *Fortescue MSS*, 1892, i. 48–9)   *Line 7, for* £125,000 *read* £135,000

Page 8, note 8, last line, *after* 164 *add* ; see also *Two Gentlemen of Verona* IV. ii. 28

Page 9, top of page, *insert the following heading*:

To MONTAGU, ca Thursday 3 February 1737 OS

Missing; mentioned in Conway to HW 8 Feb. 1737 OS: 'I have sent the letters forward as you desired, the one to my brother, and the other to George Montague' (CONWAY i. 6).

Page 9, note 3, *delete 2d sentence and substitute* Conway wrote HW 8 Feb. 1737 OS, 'He is now carrying on an intrigue with a lady, as he says, of the first rank in Rheims' (CONWAY i. 7).

Page 10, note 7, line 2, *for* Jaime Miguel (d. 1756) *read* Don Jaime Miguel de Guzmán (1690–1767)   *Line 3, after* Mina *insert* , Duque de La Plata and Principe de Masa   *Line 4, after* 30, *insert* xxvii. 404;

Page 11, note 2, line 2, *for* next eldest brother, Edward *read* two brothers, Edward and Christopher   *At end add* Christopher Montagu (ca 1717–45) was army chaplain to the Hull garrison. Charles Montagu (d.

1777), Maj. in the 11th (Sowle's) Regiment, was wounded in the battle (see CONWAY i. 192 and nn. 18, 19; FAMILY 11 and n. 23; *Daily Adv.* 17 May 1745 OS).

Page 12, note 3, *add* For Douglas see CONWAY i. 192, n. 11; MANN iii. 43, n. 6; Sedgwick i. 618.

Page 13, note 2, lines 3–4, *delete* for some . . . 1745). *and substitute* at this time because the vacancy for the borough of Castle Rising was filled by HW's, and not Sir Edward's, candidate (see FAMILY 14–21).

Page 13, note 3, *add* Lady Mary Wortley Montagu wrote to her daughter 24 June 1759, 'I am not surprised at Lady Waldegrave's good fortune; Beauty has a large prerogative. Her Mother's was the most remarkable I have ever heard of. Being taken notice of by Mrs Seckar (who told it me) when she was in the humble position of sitting on a dust cart before the Bishop's door, that lady had the curiosity to call her in, merely to see her nearer, and assured me that, in all her rags and dirt, she never saw a more lovely creature. Some time after, she heard she was in the hands of a Covent Garden milliner, who transferred her to Neddy W[alpole], who doted on her till the day of her death' (Lady Mary Wortley Montagu, *Complete Letters*, ed. R. Halsband, Oxford, 1965–7, iii. 213).

Pages 14–15, note 1, line 3, *after* Bedford *add*   ; he was HW's candidate for the borough of Castle Rising, for which he was returned 24 Oct. 1745 (see FAMILY 14, n. 2, 16; SELWYN 87).

Page 15, note 6, line 3, *for* Mr *read* John   *Line 4, after* of *insert* Letton,   *Line 5, after* 653 *add*   ; GM 1735, v. 681

Page 15, note 11, line 1, *for* 1698 *read* 1696   *Last line, add* See also SELWYN 84; MANN ii. 166; R. Rigby to C. H. Williams 27 June 1745, Williams MSS lxviii, f. 70.

Page 16, note 17, line 1, *after* Frasi *insert* (fl. 1742–72)   *Line 2, for* 1743 *read* 1742   *Lines 5–6, for* Sir George Grove, *Dictionary of Music read The New Grove Dictionary of Music and Musicians*, ed. Stanley Sadie, 1980, vi. 808.

Page 16, note 18, lines 1–2, *for* ca 1703 *read* ca 1708

Page 16, note 23, lines 1–2, *for* Keroualle *read* Kéroualle   *for* ca 1647 *read* 1649

Page 16, note 24, line 1, *for* Amalie Sophie *read* Amalie-Sophie   *Line* 2, *for* ca 1709 *read* 1704   *Lines 2–3, for* Adam Gottlieb, Oberhauptman *read* Oberhauptmann Gottlieb Adam

Page 17, note 4, line 1, *for* 1706 *read* 1700   *Line 3, for* cr. (1733) Bn Hervey of Ickworth; *read* summoned to the House of Lords in his father's Barony as Lord Hervey of Ickworth, 1733;

Page 18, note 8, line 1, *for* 1683 *read* ca 1693

Page 19, note 17, *add* (CONWAY i. 166–7 and n. 5, 169, 173)

Page 20, headnote, *for* In the possession *read* Formerly in the possession *at end add* The MS is now WSL (2d Waller Sale, 15 Dec. 1947, lot 53).

Page 22, note 7, *add* According to GM 1745, xv. 387, the dinner was on 30 July; see SELWYN 91 and n. 5.

Page 25, note 2, *substitute* Part of the vow of chastity taken by the wife of Guy de Beauchamp, son of the 11th E. of Warwick, on her husband's death; see CONWAY i. 242 and n. 9.

Page 27, note 6, line 2, *for* 1720 *read* 1721

Page 27, note 12, line 1, *for* Elena Albrizzi, m. (1728) Pier Andrea Cappello *read* Eleonora (fl. 1742–58), Contessa di Colalto, m. (1742) Pietro Andrea Capello   *Lines 3–4, delete* (G. Catalani in N&Q 1940, clxxviii. 46). *and substitute* (MANN ii. 431, n. 9).

Page 28, note 19, line 1, *for* ca 1721 *read* 1724

Page 28, note 21, line 1, *for* ca 1722 *read* 1714   *Line 3, after* 1749 *add* ; *Miscellanea genealogica et heraldica*, 1890, 2d ser., iii. 58

Page 28, note 22, line 1, *for* Violette *read* Veigel   *for* 1725 *read* 1724

Page 30, note 11, line 1, *after* Franks *insert* (d. 1790)   *Line 4, after* married *insert* (1762)

Page 30, note 13, *for* n. 12 *read* n. 12a

Page 31, note 14, line 4, *for* 1756 *read* 1755

Page 32, note 5, line 1, *for* (d. 1776) *read* (ca 1720–76)   *after* m. *insert* (1753)   *Line 3, for* 472 *read* 554 *and add*   ; CONWAY i. 115, n. 23, 179

Page 32, note 14, line 1, *for* (?) Mary Roussel (d. 1755) *read* Elizabeth Deard   *Lines 4–6, delete last sentence and substitute* See *post* 18 May 1749; MANN ii. 366, n. 12

Page 33, note 3, line 1, *for* ca 1700 *read* 1695

Page 33, note 4, line 1, *for* 1704 *read* ca 1704

Page 35, note 19, line 3, *delete* for SH

Page 36, note 4, *add* The son, George Greville (1746–1816), was styled Lord Greville; M.P. for Warwick 1768–6 July 1773, when he succeeded his father as Earl Brooke of Warwick Castle and Earl of Warwick.

Page 39, line 19, *on windows*; *add note* 18a: 18a. Doubtless an expression of Montagu's.

Page 39, note 15, lines 1–2, *for* ca 1690 *read* 1693   *Line 2, for* (1733) *read* (1734)   *Line 3, for* Rockingham. *read* Rockingham; M.P. (Sedgwick ii. 525).

Page 41, note 12, *for* Unidentified. *read* Possibly Priscilla (b. 1690) or Bridget (b. 1692) Bethell, sisters of Hugh and Slingsby Bethell (see SELWYN 105, n. 5; Sedgwick i. 460–1).

Page 41, note 15, *add* For her letters see CONWAY i. 217–18 and n. 13.

Page 42, note 18, line 2, *for* Zulestein *read* Zuylestein

Page 44, note 1, *substitute* Patrick Jordan, of Conduit Street, parish of St George, Hanover Square, held a lease from the Dean and Canons of a tenement in Priest Street, Windsor, in 1741 (information from the late Sir Owen F. Morshead).

Page 44, note 2, lines 2–11, *delete* It was . . . Windsor). *and substitute* A lease dated 11 Nov. 1741 to Patrick Jordan describes the house as 'in

Priest Street, between a tenement belonging to the Provost and Fellows of
Eton on the South, and the way leading into the Little Park of Windsor
on the North, and a garden in the occupation of the Hon. Lt-General
Charles Wills on the East. Rent, 53s. 9d. and a couple of capons or 5/-.'
The lease was renewed 4 July 1754 'to Jane Jordan widow of Patrick Jordan, and Elizabeth Arrow, "widow sister" of the said Patrick' (information from the late Sir Owen F. Morshead).

Page 46, note 6, line 2, *for* McLeod *read* Macleod

Page 47, note 12a, line 6, *for* (d. 1751) *read* (1688–1751) *and insert* (E. A.
Webb, *et al.*, *History of Chislehurst*, 1899, pedigree; Sedgwick ii. 416)

Page 48, note 1, lines 3–4, *for* Drury Lane *read* Covent Garden ('Short
Notes,' GRAY i. 16 and nn. 105, 106)

Page 48, note 2, line 12, *for* Drury Lane *read* Covent Garden *and add*
See Hazen, *Bibl. of HW*, 24–6.

Page 49, note 4, *for* Zulestein *read* Zuylestein

Page 50, note 5, *substitute* There is a similar account of Conway in
Whitehall Evening Post 30 June–2 July 1747 OS quoted in CONWAY i.
273–4, n. 1. HW was informed of Conway's return to Maestricht in a
letter from Stephen Poyntz 1 July 1747 OS (ibid. i. 274, n. 2).

Page 50, note 13, *substitute* A letter from Col. York to Col. Barrington
30 June–11 July 1747 OS reports, 'The only disgraces of the battle are
young Cholmondley of the third regiment of Guards, who is broke and
sent from the army, and it is thought it will go hard with the deputy-
brigadier of that corps. . . . You know the Guards, unfortunately for them,
were posted between the Hessians and Bavarians, which was a bad neighbourhood' (Hist. MSS Comm., *Frankland-Russell-Astley MSS*, 1900, p.
372). The *Whitehall Evening Post* 30 June–2 July 1747 OS reported, 'Letters from the army in Flanders say the Duke was much dissatisfied with
the behaviour of the Guards in the late action, and that some officers of
considerable rank have had their commissions taken from them for cow-
ardice'; see also ibid. 2–4 July 1747 OS.

Page 51, note 19, line 1, *for* 2d *read* 3d

Page 51, note 21, *add* For a full account see HW's note in SELWYN 331–
2, n. 6.

Page 52, note 2, *substitute* Conway's letter of 5 Oct. 1747 NS; see especially CONWAY i. 279–80.

Page 52, note 3, *add* See also CONWAY i. 280, n. 13.

Page 52, note 8, lines 2–4, *delete* the siege . . . *passim*). *and substitute*
which the French had captured 16 Sept. 1747 NS (MANN iii. 440, n. 10;
CONWAY i. 278 and n. 3).

Page 53, note 1, line 1, *for* 1686? *read* 1686

Page 53, note 7, line 1, *after* eld. *insert* unmarried   *Line* 2, *after* Pelham *insert* (her older sister had married Lord Lincoln in 1744, *ante* MON-
TAGU i. 16, n. 14)

Page 54, note 9, *substitute* Lt-Col. Charles Montagu may have been technically a prisoner after the battle of Roucour (11 Oct. 1746 NS) and Montagu may have inquired whether the lapsed cartel extended to prisoners of that battle (see SELWYN 106 and n. 4). For the cartel see CONWAY i. 276, n. 2, 279, n. 9.

Page 55, note 9, *add* HW's copy, 1st edn, 1748, 4to, is now WSL (see Hazen, *Cat. of HW's Lib.* No. 458).

Page 57, note 3, *add* She apparently had a miscarriage later in the summer (see CONWAY i. 288 and n. 6).

Page 59, note 4, lines 2–3, *delete* ; Lt-Col. 3d Dragoon Guards   *Line 4, for* brother *read* first cousin once removed

Page 62, note 27, line 1, *for* 1693 *read* 1686   *Line 2, for* Leneve *read* Le Neve

Page 63, note 1, line 1, *for* ca 1702 *read* 1709

Page 65, note 17, line 4, *for* (1736) *read* (1737)

Page 65, note 20, line 8, *for* James *read* John

Page 66, note 28, line 1, *for* ca 1689 *read* 1688   *for* 3d son *read* 4th son *Line 3, for* 1726–7 *read* 1726–8   *Line 5, for* 1728–37 *read* 1729–37 *Lines 12–17, delete* He is the same person . . . West 28 Sept. 1739).   *Last line, add* See also Sedgwick ii. 125; C. R. Grundy, 'Documents Relating to an Action Brought Against Joseph Goupy in 1738,' *Walpole Society 1920– 1921,* ix. 81–4.

Page 67, note 31, *add* According to F. H. Fairweather, 'Colne Priory, Essex, and the Burials of the Earls of Oxford,'*Archæologia,* 1937, lxxxvii. 290, the effigies are those of Richard de Vere (ca 1385–1417), 11th E. of Oxford and his second wife Alice Sergaux (d. 1452), m. 1 Guy de St Aubyn; m. 2 (1406 *or* 1407) Richard, 11th E. of Oxford; m. 3 (before 1421) Nicholas Thorley.

Page 67, note 32, line 3, *for* n. 9 *read* n. 10

Page 68, note 1, line 1, *for* (d. 1669) *read* (ca 1611–69)

Page 68, note 9, lines 3–4, *for* Thomas de Montacute *read* Thomas de Montagu

Page 69, note 14, lines 1–2, *delete* a strip of heavy linen, 19″ x 87″ *and substitute* two sheets of paper joined, 19″ x 52″

Page 69, note 16, *substitute* Cadwaladr (d. 664), King of Gwynedd (see Sir John E. Lloyd, *A History of Wales,* 3d edn, 1939, i. 230 and n. 9).

Page 69, note 18, *add* For the Philipps's descent from Maximus, see Burke, *Peerage,* 1928, *sub* St David's.

Page 70, note 23, *for* n. 52 *read* nn. 52, 53

Page 70, note 25, *substitute* Possibly a playful name for Mrs Mestivyer, Mrs Clive's sister who lived with her; she may have been fond of spiced mead (H. F. Finberg, 'Mrs Metheglin,' N&Q 4 May 1946, cxc. 193; CHUTE 306, n. 16, 505, n. 20, 509; OSSORY ii. 57).

Page 71, note 30, lines 7–8, *delete* and it was probably the same at this time.   *Line 7, for* 1755), *read* 1755, CHUTE 233 and n. 6).

Page 73, note 2, line 1, *for* (d. 1763) *read* (ca 1698–1763)   *Line 3, after* Bath *add* ; M.P. Hedon 1746–7 (Sedgwick ii. 91).

Page 77, note 4, line 14, *after* Waller, Bt, 1939 *add*   , now WSL

Page 78, note 6, line 3, *for* ca 1706 *read* 1705   *Line 4, after* Chol-mondeley *add* (R. W. Ketton-Cremer, *Horace Walpole*, New York, 1940, p. 27; FAMILY 12, n. 34, 42, n. 1).

Page 81, note 3, line 1, *for* 1745 *read* 1744   *Line 3, for* 1708 *read* ca 1709

Page 82, note 19, line 2, *after* dau. of *insert* Daniel,

Page 83, note 23, lines 12–13, *delete*   , not Roussel (ibid.; *ante* 17 June 1746). *and substitute* (ibid.; MANN ii. 366, n. 12).

Page 83, note 25, line 1, *for* avoit *read* avait   *Line 2, for* appliquoit *read* appliquait   *Line 4, for* faudroit *read* faudrait   *Line 10, add* HW mentions this book in his *MS Commonplace Book of Verses* (p. 52); see MANN iii. 486, n. 1; Hazen, *Cat. of HW's Lib*. No. 907.

Page 83, note 26, *substitute A Brief History of the Life of Mary Queen of Scots*, 1681, p. 35, describes her as 'a very tall and big woman, being lame.' HW's copy is in the Pierpont Morgan Library, New York (Hazen, *Cat. of HW's Lib*. No. 2146:4).

Page 84, note 35, *add* HW's copy is Hazen, *Cat. of HW's Lib*. No. 1622.

Page 84, line 18, *on* Pindar *add note* 35a: 35a. See HW's extracts from Bayle's *Dictionary*, p. 27 (Hazen, *Cat. of HW's Lib*. No. 2039).

Page 92, note 14, line 1, *for* ca 1718 *read* 1717

Page 92, note 15, line 10, *after* p. 102 *add*   ; K. A. Esdaile, 'Changes at St Margaret's Westminster, 1761,' *Church Quarterly Review*, July–Sept. 1950.

Page 93, note 17, line 1, *for* 1673 *read* 1678

Page 94, note 25, line 1, *for* 1689 *read* 1690

Page 95, note 36, line 1, *for* Charles-Pierre-Gaston-François *read* Gaston-Charles-Pierre

Page 96, *under heading insert* Notes for this letter, written on a six of spades, are in HW's *MS Commonplace Book of Verses*.

Page 97, note 9, lines 1–2, *for* (ca 1722–72) *read* (ca 1722–62)

Page 99, line 2, *on* fountain, *add note* 26a: 26a. When Cowdray was burned down, the fountain was defaced and neglected in the ruins of the courtyard. Lord Robert Spencer (brother of Lady Diana Beauclerk) removed the fountain and set it up at his seat Woolbeding, three miles away, which he had bought in 1793 with the £40,000 won from keeping the faro bank at Brooks's (information from Mrs Michael Huxley of Longmore, Bosham, Sussex; see Thomas Creevey, *The Creevey Papers*, rev. edn, ed. John Gore, New York, 1963, pp. 241, 244).

Page 100, headnote, *for* In the possession *read* Formerly in the possession   *after* Warwick. *insert* The MS is now WSL (2d Waller Sale, 15 Dec. 1947, lot 53).

Page 100, headnote, *Memoranda by HW, substitute*

Helmet
Million of Ancest.
Stoke Pogis.

The three notes were used by HW in his reply *post* 28 Sept.

Page 100, note 6, *add* For a description see the Countess of Hertford to the Countess of Pomfret 25 June 1740 OS (Frances, Countess of Hertford and Henrietta Louisa, Countess of Pomfret, *Correspondence*, 1805, ii. 17–18).

Page 101, note 7, line 2, *for* ibid. *read Vict. Co. Hist. Berks* iii. 139–45

Page 102, note 6, *add* For HW's comments see CONWAY i. 299 and n. 7; CHUTE 233.

Page 102, note 7, line 3, *after* 15. *add* Conway called it 'cotemporary with Queen Elizabeth's grandfather' (CONWAY i. 300). *Line 4, for Buckinghamshire read Buckingham   Line 5, for* Latimer's *read* Latimers   *Lines 6–8, delete* but it is not clear . . . alterations. *and substitute* and in Bryant Burgess, 'Latimers or Latimer,' *Records of Buckinghamshire* [1887], vi. 27, is a sketch of the house ca 1786 (CONWAY i. 299, n. 7).

Page 102, line 22, *on* helmet *add note* 7a: 7a. There are four funeral helms hanging in the Bedford chapel (*Vict. Co. Hist. Bucks* iii. 201).

Page 103, note 1, line 1, *after* Leigh *insert* (1712–59)   *Lines 3–4, for* not further identified. *read* '4th son of Peter Leigh, late of Whitchurch, Salop, clerk, deceased,' admitted to Middle Temple, 27 April 1732, called to the bar, 21 Nov. 1734; Chief Justice of South Carolina 1753–9 (*Record of Admissions to the . . . Middle Temple*, 1949, iii. 312; MANN iv. 108, n. 12, 122–3, 131, 156). Leigh's copy of the Westminster poll book for 1749 was acquired by HW and is now WSL (Hazen, *Cat. of HW's Lib.* No. 1726).

Page 103–4, note 4, line 4 from end, *after passim add* especially MANN iv. 156 and n. 12.

Page 104, note 6, *add* See MANN iv. 107, n. 10.

Page 104, note 7, line 1, *delete* Probably   *after* Churchill *insert* (b. April 1750)   *Line 7, add* See GM 1750, xx. 188; FAMILY 112–13, n. 1, 127–8 and n. 2.

Page 104, note 8, line 1, *for* ca 1691 *read* ca 1690   *Line 4, after* Caroline *add* (MANN i. 339, n. 33; SELWYN 63, n. 36)

Page 104, note 9, line 3, *after* m. *insert* (1702)   *Line 5, after* 539 *add Miscellanea Genealogica et Heraldica*, 3d ser., ii. 46

Page 107, note 16, *substitute* Hon. Henry Vane (1726–92), styled Vct Barnard 1754–8, 2d E. of Darlington, 1758; at this time Lt-Col. in the Coldstream Guards (see CONWAY i. 359, n. 10)

Page 109, note 28, *add* See also Alfred Rubens, *Anglo-Jewish Portraits*, 1935, pp. 88–9.

Page 111, note 1, line 3, *after* 380 *insert*   ; see also *Penny London Post* 15–17 Aug. 1750

Page 111, note 2, *add* For references to her see Rigby's letters to C. H. Williams in Williams's MSS (now WSL), vol. lii, f. 68.

Page 113, note 5, line 1, *for* (d. 1754) *read* (ca 1701–54)   *Line 5, after* v. 91 *add*   ; Sedgwick ii. 54–5

Page 114, note 9, line 4, *for* Her father *read* Her grandfather   *Line 7, for* 2d Earl *read* 21st or 14th Earl   *Line 8, after* n. 16). *add* Her father was Edward Harley (1689–1741), styled Lord Harley, 2d E. of Oxford, 1724; M.P.   *Last line, add* See MANN i. 357, 373–4.

Page 115, note 2, line 3, *for* (d. 1784) *read* (1724–84) (Burke, *Peerage*, 1928, p. 2217)

Page 115, note 4, line 1, *for* 1720 *read* ca 1720   *Line 2, after* Hartington *insert* 1729–55   *for* cr. Bn Cavendish *read* summoned to the House of Lords, 1751, in his father's barony as Lord Cavendish of Hardwicke *Line 3, for* 1755. *read* 1755 (Sedgwick i. 538–9).

Page 117, note 16, *for* cr. (1733) Bn Hervey of Ickworth *read* styled Lord Hervey, 1723; summoned to the House of Lords, 1733, in his father's barony as Lord Hervey of Ickworth (Robert Halsband, *Lord Hervey Eighteenth-Century Courtier*, Oxford, 1974, p. 148)

Page 117, note 18, line 10, *after* copy *add*   , containing his MS notes, *Last line, for* ii. 54. *read* ii. 154 and is now WSL (Hazen, *Cat. of HW's Lib*. No. 913).

Page 117, note 20, line 2, *for* —— Langlois *read* Nicolas Langlois

Page 118, note 5, line 4, *after* n. 3 *insert*   ; DALRYMPLE 97   *Line 12, after* WSL *insert*   ; Hazen, *Cat. of HW's Lib*. No. 2511

Page 118, note 6, lines 9–13, *delete* HW's only edition . . . catalogues. *and substitute* HW had an English translation of the *Memoirs*, London, 1714, and a French edition, Paris, 1746 (now WSL), the latter containing extensive notes and a MS index by HW (see Hazen, *Cat. of HW's Lib*. Nos 1479, 2389).

Page 119, note 10, line 1, *for* 1677 *read* 1667

Page 119, note 16a, *for* (1693–1757) *read* (ca 1689–1750)

Page 120, note 25, line 2, *after* E. *insert* of

Page 120, line 18, *on* 1680 *add note* 25a: 25a. On Ragley see H. Avray Tipping, 'Ragley Hall,' *Country Life* 22 and 29 March 1924, lv. 438–44, 476–81, where other letters confirm the date 1680.

Page 121, note 26, line 6, *after* Office. *add* See DALRYMPLE 73, n. 3, 339; CONWAY i. 563 and n. 9.

Page 123, note 4, line 1, *for* Janssen *read* Jonson   *Line 3, after* 149 *add*   ; see Thieme and Becker; CHUTE 73, n. 33

Page 124, note 8, line 12, *for* not in SH Sale Cat. *read* sold SH xi. 58 *Line 15, for* Frances Knevit *read* Catharine Knyvett

Page 124, note 11, lines 3–4, *for* Edward, Lord Russell (d. 1572) *read* Edward, styled Lord Russell (d. ?1572)   *Line 5, for* Lord Francis Russell *read* Francis, styled Lord Russell

Page 125, note 16, line 4, *for* ca 1584 *read* 1584

Page 126, note 4, line 1, *after* Taaffe *insert* (ca 1708–80), M.P.   *Line 5, after* xiv *add*   ; Sedgwick ii. 460–1   *Lines 17–18, delete* Taaffe's later history has not been discovered.

Page 126, note 9, line 1, *for* Marie *read* Mary

Page 129, note 30, lines 8–11, *for* HW thought one of the sharpers was imprisoned; apparently, however, only Montagu was jailed, and in the Châtelet (ibid. 632); *substitute* Taaffe was imprisoned 31 Oct. 1751 NS; see his letter of 2 Nov. 1751 NS to Albemarle written at 'Paris, La Fort l'Éveque,' imploring Albemarle's assistance (BM Add. MS 32,831, ff. 66–7). Montagu was jailed in the Châtelet (Nichols, op. cit. 632);

Page 130, note 3, *for* 1686 *read* 1683

Page 132, note 11, line 1, *for* 1702 *read* ?1702

Page 132, To Montagu 6 June 1752, note 5, line 1, *for* 1720 *read* ca 1721

Page 134, note 10, *add* See also Richard Briggs, *The English Art of Cookery*, 3d edn, 1794, p. 402.

Page 134, note 14, *add* Cosby is referred to as Gov. of the Leeward Islands and Gov. of New York 10 June 1731 (Lord Chamberlain's Warrant Books 5.75, p. 60; 5.73, p. 66). Mrs Grace Cosby was appointed housekeeper of the Garden House at Windsor by warrant dated 31 Dec. 1719 (ibid. 3.63, p. 219) (information from the late Sir Owen F. Morshead).

Page 135, note 20, *add* In HW's original draft of the 'Parish Register of Twickenham' these lines occur after line 32 of the text as printed in *Works* iv. 382–3; they do not occur in the MS version in HW's *Description of SH*, 1774.

Page 144, To Montagu 14 Dec. 1752, line 5, *on* Vandals *add note* 2a: 2a. HW uses 'virtu' as meaning Roman or Italian works of art, but not including Gothic antiquities; this distinction does not appear in OED.

Page 146, note 3, *substitute* This is certainly a joke.

Page 154, note 18, *add* See also HW's 'Book of Materials, 1759,' p. 42; HW to Mann 20 Sept. 1772, MANN vii. 435.

Page 156, line 9, *on* chimney-piece *add note* 3a: 3a. See J. S. W. Gibson, 'A Chimney-piece at Banbury?' in *Cake and Cockhorse*, Banbury Hist. Soc., 1972, v. 43–4.

Page 164, note 1, line 1, *for* Humphrey *read* Humphry

Page 167, middle of page, *insert the following headings*:

FROM MONTAGU, ca Wednesday 5 February 1755
Missing; mentioned by HW to Bentley 8 Feb. 1755: 'George Montagu has intercepted the description I promised you of the Russian masquerade: he wrote to beg it, and I cannot transcribe from myself' (CHUTE 206).

To MONTAGU, ca Friday 7 February 1755
Missing; summarized by HW to Bentley 8 Feb. 1755 (see CHUTE 206).

Page 168, note 4, *substitute* Louise-Anne de Bourbon-Condé (1695–1758), called Mlle de Charolais, Lady Hervey's great friend (see MORE 416 and n. 11).

Page 171, note 4, lines 1–2, *delete* (or James)   *for* (d. 27 June 1755) *read* (ca 1730–22 July 1755)   *Last line, add* See Namier and Brooke ii. 321–2.

Page 171, note 5, lines 7, 21, *for* Dickenson *read* Dickinson   *Line 27,* *add* See also Namier and Brooke ii. 321–2.

Page 172, note 10, *add* Or possibly Miss Vavassor (or Vavasour) who was apparently pursuing Bentley in the ecclesiastical courts and raising 'impediments' to his return to England (see CHUTE 181 and n. 2, 219). Bentley's wife seems to have been with him in Jersey (ibid. 241).

Page 174, line 4, *after* even *insert* [sic]

Page 176, To Montagu 8 Nov. 1755, line 3, *on* Hiram *add note* 1aa: 1aa. Hiram, who supplied Solomon with men and materials for the building of the House of the Lord: 'So Hiram gave Solomon cedar trees and fir trees according to all his desire' (1 Kings 5: 10).

Page 181, note 17, line 1, *for* (d. 1787) *read* (ca 1706–87)   *Line 2, for* 1734–51 *read* 1734–50   *Line 4, for* 1745–55 *read* 1744–55   *Last line,* *add* See Sedgwick ii. 350–1.

Page 182, note 1, line 1, *for* (d. Dec. 1756; see *read* (1706–20 Dec. 1756; see MANN i. pp. xxx, 24, n. 4;

Page 183, line 6, *on* Montagu. *add note* 4: 4. Charles Montagu was appointed 30 Dec. 1755 Col. of the 61st Foot, which became the 59th Foot ca 1757 (see CHUTE 265 and n. 4).

Page 184, note 11, line 1, *after* George *insert* Augustus   *for* (d. 1794) *read* (?1727–94)   *Line 3, after* mouth *insert* and Melcombe Regis   *for* Derby 1754–94 *read* Derbyshire 1754–80, 1781–94   *Line 5, after* 358 *add*   ; Namier and Brooke ii. 201

Page 186, note 28, *add* See FAMILY 27–32, 295–304.

Page 195, note 2, line 2, *for* print *read* prints

Page 199, note 10, *add* In a letter to Bentley 4 Aug. 1755 HW says that he offered this motto to Garrick, but does not include the verse translation (see CHUTE 242). There is no evidence that Garrick used the motto or the verses to 'adorn the outside' of his temple to Shakespeare.

Page 199, To Montagu 28 Oct. 1756, 1st paragraph, line 3, *on* vails *add note* 1a: 1a. I.e., gratuities, tips (OED).

Page 199, note 1, lines 1–2, *for* tendered his resignation 26 Oct. *read* announced his intention of resigning 26 Oct., but did not surrender his office until 11 Nov.   *Line 2, after* 4 *add*   , 13   *Line 3, after* 1756 *insert*   , MANN v. 11, 17

Page 201, line 21, *on* Cliquetis *add note* 6b: 6b. Bentley (*ante* MONTAGU i. 172, n. 9).

Page 201, note 7, line 1, *for* (d. 1758) *read* (1695–1758)   *Line 2, for* 1756 *read* 1755–6   *after* see *add* Sedgwick i. 460–1;

Page 204, note 3, line 3, *for* (d. 1775) *read* (1702–75)

Page 207, note 9, line 2, *for* (d. 1759) *read* (1735–59)

Page 208, note 5, line 2, *for* 61st *read* 59th   *delete* probably   *Line 3, for* elsewhere in Ireland *read* at Cork (see HW to D. of Bedford 1 Jan. 1757; *Army Lists* 1757, p. 141).

Page 208, note 6, line 1, *after* Denton) *insert* (?1703–57)   *Last line, after* iii. 18 *add*   ; Sedgwick i. 540–1

Page 209, note 9, line 1, *for* (d. 1776) *read* (ca 1717–76)   *Line 5, for* 1750 *read* 1753   *Line 6, for* 1774 *read* 1775   *Last line, after* seq. *add* ; Namier and Brooke ii. 235.

Page 209, note 10, *add* See also Sedgwick i. 610–11.

Page 210, line 19, *on* trifle *add note* 5a: 5a. HW had requested leave of absence for the Rev. James Miller, chaplain of the 59th Foot, which was on duty in Ireland: the request was denied (see HW to Bedford 1 Jan. 1757 and Bedford to HW 3 Jan. 1757, MISC. CORR. i. 90–1). See also CHUTE 265 and n. 5.

Page 215, note 1, line 1, *delete* apparently   *Line 3, for* Charles Montagu *read* the Rev. James Miller, chaplain of the 59th Foot, Charles Montagu's regiment   *Line 4, after* buffed *add* (HW to Bedford 1 Jan. 1757 and Bedford's reply 3 Jan., MISC. CORR. i. 90–1).

Page 215, note 6, *for* ca 1720 *read* 1721

Page 215, note 8, *add* See also Hazen, *SH Bibl.* 152–3.

Page 216, note 11a, lines 2–4, *delete* Allen . . . 1942 *and substitute* Hazen, *SH Bibl.* 154–5.

Page 216, note 12, line 1, *for* ibid. *read Journal of the Printing Office   Line 3, add* 152–8.

Page 216, note 14, last line, *add* 158–60.

Page 217, To Montagu 8 Sept. 1757, note 1, lines 2–3, *for* ca 1740 *read* 1743   *Line 7, after* Hare *add*   ; HW to Mann 11 July 1743 OS, MANN ii. 268, n. 13

Page 217, note 2, line 3, *for* 19 Aug. *read* 25 Aug.   *Line 4, after* text *add* (Hazen, *SH Bibl.* 160–2, where WSL's copy dated in HW's hand is reproduced)

Page 217, To Montagu 18 Oct. 1757, note 1, at end *for* HW-Conway Corr. *read* CONWAY i. 513–21.

Page 218, To Montagu 18 Oct. 1757, note 2, *add* See SELWYN 142 and nn. 7, 10; CONWAY i. 514 and n. 8, 518–19 and n. 11.

Page 218, note 5, line 3, *for* copy *read* copyright   *Last line, add* See also Hazen, *SH Bibl.* 1973, 33–7 and also pp. xi–xii.

Page 219, note 14, lines 1–2, *for* (1728–1807), *née* Valentini *read* (1722–1808), *née* Valentin   *Lines 2–3, for* Sir George Grove, *Dictionary of Music read The New Grove Dictionary of Music and Musicians*, 6th edn, ed. Stanley Sadie, 1980, xii. 333–4; *Enciclopedia dello spettacolo*, Rome, 1954–62, vii. 615

Page 223, line 5, *on* it *add note* 5a: 5a. Christopher Hussey writes that James Gibbs's 'note that "he gave directions for the repair of Ragley," for Lord Conway, in Warwickshire, justifies assigning to Gibbs the great hall in that mansion, begun in 1680 from the design of Robert Hooke; though further rococo decoration . . . had been "just new modell'd" when Pococke saw it in 1756, possibly by Vassali' (*English Country Houses, Early Georgian, 1715–1760*, 1955, p. 18 and illustration p. 8).

Page 223, note 6, *add* In 1758 HW and Conway left together for Ragley on 11 Aug. (see CONWAY i. 551, 552, 558; MANN v. 228).

Page 223, note 8, *add* See CHUTE 104, n. 13.

Page 224, note 13, line 2, *for* Carlton *read* Carleton

Page 224, note 16, line 2, *after* 26 *add* ; CHUTE 104

Page 226, note 8, line 12, *after* terpart' *insert* (HW's copies are printed in DALRYMPLE 339–42, Appendix 4)

Page 230, note 1, line 3, *for* HW to Conway 19 Jan. 1759 *read* CONWAY i. 584 and n. 1, ii. 1, 5 and n. 13, 11 and n. 6.

Page 235, note 7, line 1, *for* ca 1712 *read* 1713   *Line 4, after* 253 *add* ; see BERRY i. 56, n. 8

Page 235, note 9, *for* n. 5 *read* n. 6

Page 236, note 23, line 1, *for* ca 1704 *read* ca 1703   *Line 4, after* 391 *add* ; ix. 104; OSSORY i. 174–5, n. 4

Page 242, note 8, line 1, *for* 1712 *read* 1711

Page 243, note 3, line 2, *after* 1759 *add* ; CONWAY ii. 16, 18, 20.

Page 244, note 6, line 1, *for* Catherine *read* Katherine

Page 248, note 9, line 1, *for* Jeffery *read* Jeffrey

Page 248, note 10, line 2, *after* 477 *add* ; CHUTE 294 and n. 5

Page 251, note 1, line 6, *for* [1773] *read* [?1774], MISC. CORR. ii. 276; OSSORY ii. 170, n. 1

Page 252, From Montagu ca 25 Oct. 1759, line 12, *after* excuse you me *add* [*sic*]

Page 253, note 9, right column, line 2, *for* 1610 *read* 1613

Page 253, note 10, *add* See also OED, *sub* 'jumble,' 3a and 3b.

Page 254, note 6, lines 4–5, *delete* The incident . . . discovered. *and substitute* HW's note to his poem 'Patapan' concerning Hanmer reads: 'afterwards espousing a young lady [Elizabeth Folkes, d. 1741], the first night he made some faint efforts towards consummation, and then begged her pardon for her disappointment' (printed in SELWYN, Appendix 1, p. 302, n. 48).

Page 255, note 12a, right column, line 3, *for* W. *read* Mary Wortley *Last two lines, delete* remains a puzzle. *and substitute* is apparently an error of Edward Jeffrey, editor of Williams's *Works* (see SELWYN 10, n. 1 and 159, n. 5).

Page 260, note 10, line 1, *after* Anne *insert* Hussey Delaval   *and for* 1811 *read* 1812   *Line 5, after* 392 *add* ; CHUTE 298, n. 15

Page 261, note 3, line 1, *for* 1710 *read* ca 1702

Page 263, note 9, lines 3–4, *for* Harriot *read* Harriet   *Lines 6–13, delete* Her mother, according . . . died 1762 *and substitute* Her mother was Sophia Bugden (d. 1762), m. 1 (before 1729, in India) George Drake, 5th son of Sir Francis Drake, 3d Bt of Buckland, Devon; m. 2 (1743)

George Morton Pitt (1693–1756), M.P., her husband's executor (Lady Eliott Drake, *The Family and Heirs of Sir Francis Drake*, 1911, ii. 224, 248; Sedgwick ii. 349–50).

Page 264, note 10a, lines 1–3, *delete* Nothing further . . . implies *and substitute* Her first husband, George Drake, in the service of the East India Company, died at sea on his way home from India in 1741 (Lady Eliott Drake, *The Family and Heirs of Sir Francis Drake*, 1911, ii. 114, 248, *et passim*); her second husband, George Morton Pitt, died 9 Feb. 1756 (GM 1756, xxvi. 91; Sedgwick ii. 350).

Page 264, line 8, *on* Pembroke *add note* 11a: 11a. See MONTAGU i. 181 and n. 19. The young Lady Pembroke was 22 and Lady Coventry was 27; both were noted for their beauty.

Page 265, note 22, *substitute* Possibly John Shelley (?1730–83), M.P., who in 1760 proposed to Miss Mary Pelham, the D. of Newcastle's niece, but was rejected (Namier and Brooke iii. 429–30).

Page 270, note 17, *at beginning insert* See *Daily Adv.* 17, 18, 20 Dec. 1759; GM 1759, xxix. 585; *Grenville Papers* i. 334.

Page 272, note 4, line 1, *after* Lavinia *insert* Beswick, called

Page 273, note 10, line 6, *after* see *insert* especially H. F. B. Compston, *The Magdalen Hospital*, 1917;

Page 273, line 9, *on* Bowman *add note* 12a: 12a. Walter Bowman (d. 1782), antiquary, travelling tutor to Lord Hertford and later to Lord Beauchamp (CONWAY i. 30–1, n. 1, 39, ii. 77).

Page 276, note 4, *add* Sloper's father, William (1709–89), was a friend of Sir Edward Walpole, and his mother, Catherine Hunter, was Col. Edward Walpole's godmother (Sir Edward Walpole to William Sloper, ca 1737, now WSL).

Page 276, note 5, *add* See also N&Q, 1942, clxxxii. 65.

Pages 278–9, note 2, *substitute* Anna Maria Falkner (fl. ?1745–84), singer and dancer; m. 1 (1748) William Donaldson; m. 2 (1784) Col. Charles Lumm; Lord Halifax's mistress (P. H. Highfill, Jr, K. A. Burnim, and E. A. Langhans, *A Biographical Dictionary of Actors, Actresses . . . 1660–1800*, Carbondale Illinois, 1973– , v. 141–4).

Page 278, To Montagu 19 April 1760, line 2, *on* ended *add note* a: a. By proclamation 5 April (MANN v. 384, n. 4, 387).

Page 279, note 4, line 1, *delete* Hon.   *Line 2, after* DNB *add*   ; MANN v. 388 and n. 6

Page 281, note 23, line 1, *for* (d. 1779) *read* (ca 1721–79)   *Line 2, for* Maudit *read* Mauditt   *after* 1761 *add*   ; M.P. (Namier and Brooke i. 293, iii. 503)

Page 283, note 4, line 4, *for* he d. 1770 *read* Rev. Cornelius Humphreys (?ca 1711–?1770)   *Line 5, add* See MANN iii. 301, n. 23.

Page 285, left column of notes, line 5, *for* Delaney *read* Delany

Page 285, note 2, *add* More likely this was a miscarriage; HW's 'Pedigree of Walpole,' 1776, in his 'Des. of SH,' 1784, credits Lady Mary with having two daughters and five sons, and HW to Mann 4 March 1759 says she has already had two daughters and five sons (MANN v. 279).

Page 288, To Montagu 19 July 1760, line 1, *on* Oxford *add note a: a.* See CONWAY ii. 59, 62.

Page 289, note 4, *substitute* The 'Holbeins' were cleaned in 1937, and attributed to Jan Scorel (W. G. Hiscock, *Christ Church Miscellany*, Oxford, 1946, pp. 80–1).

Page 289, note 10, *at end for* Boswell, *Johnson* iii. *read* Boswell, *Johnson* ii.

Page 294, note 3, *for* Probably *read* The knave of clubs, the highest trump in five-card loo (*ante* 2 June 1759, n. 5); possibly also an allusion to
Page 294, note 5, *before* Whichnor *insert* Wichnor *or*
Page 295, note 15, line 2, *after* tration) *insert* and also HW to Strafford 28 Aug. 1756, CHUTE 267, 279 and n. 12

Page 295, note 16a, line 1, *for* ca 1715 *read* ca 1720
Page 296, line 1, *delete footnote number* 22a *and also note* 22a
Page 298, note 32, *substitute* Elizabeth Hardwick (ca 1520–1608), m. 1 (1532) Robert Barlow (*or* Barley) (d. 1533); m. 2 (1547) Sir William Cavendish (d. 1557); m. 3 (ca 1559) Sir William St Loe (d. 1564 *or* 1565); m. 4 (1568) George Talbot, 6th E. of Shrewsbury (ca 1522–90) (E. C. Williams, *Bess of Hardwick*, 1959, pp. 1, 5–8, 14, 36, 39–40, 57, 62, 194; GEC).

Page 305, note 11, *add* See Hertford to HW 25 Sept. 1760, CONWAY ii. 75–6.

Page 307, note 25, *add* See CONWAY ii. 76–7.

Page 307, note 26, line 1, *for* (d. 1769) *read* (ca 1698–1769)   *Line 3, for references substitute* DNB

Pages 308–9, note 2, *add* In 'Des. of SH,' *Works* ii. 438, HW lists a landscape painting of Jersey by Bentley and notes: 'In this piece Mr Bentley has represented himself and his second wife on the sea shore.'

Page 312, note 7, *add* For HW's 'Lennox jewel' see HW to Buchan 2 June 1782 and 29 Nov. 1792 (MISC. CORR. iii. 12; DALRYMPLE 233–4).

Page 312, To Montagu 28 Oct. 1760, line 3, *after* of *insert* [into]

Page 317, note 2, line 6, *after* 609). *insert* HW received his information from Hertford in a letter of 1 Nov. 1760 (CONWAY ii. 79–80); Mrs Delany's report is essentially that in the postscript to the *London Chronicle* 4–6 Nov. 1766, vii. 448.

Page 318, note 4, line 1, *for* (d. 1765) *read* (1710–65)   *Line 2, for* (DNB) *read* M.P. (see Sedgwick ii. 13–14; Namier and Brooke ii. 402–5)

Page 320, To Montagu 13 Nov. 1760, note 2, line 5, *for* Henry *read* Charles   *Line 8, after* 357); *insert* John Brooke informs us that the more probable date for Charles Jenkinson's letter is April 1763 and therefore that the reference to Lord George Sackville does not apply to the situation in Nov. 1760;

Page 321, note 3, line 1, *for* ca 1745 *read* ca 1731

Page 324, 1st line of letter, *on* Bedchamber *add note a: a.* See HW to Mann 5 Dec. 1760, MANN v. 460.

Page 338, 2d paragraph, line 2, *for* center *read* centre

Page 338, note 3, line 14, *for* (1756) *read* (1756 in a civil, and 1760 in a religious, ceremony)   *Line 15, for* Ignacia *read* Ignacía   *for* 1745 *read* ca 1745

Page 338, note 10, line 3, *for* 2d *read* 1st   *after* WSL *insert* (Hazen, *Cat. of HW's Lib.* No. 1609:2:3)   *At end delete*   , and is in HW's copy of the *Letter. and substitute*   ; the print appears as frontispiece to the 2d edn of the *Letter from Miss F——d,* but not in the 1st edn. A copy of this 2d edn (with print) is now WSL, and also a separate coloured copy of the print.

Page 341, note 7, *add* See also SELWYN 162 and nn. 4, 5.

Page 343, note 2, line 1, *for* (ca 1719–87) *read* (d. 1787)   *Line 2, for* (1748) *read* (1734)

Page 348, note 3b, *add* 'Bathsheba bringing Abishag to David; an exceedingly high-finished picture in varnish, by Vanderwerffe; a present to Lord Orford from the Duke of Chandos' (*Ædes Walpolianæ, Works* ii. 261).

Page 350, line 19, *on* dances *add note* 11a: 11a. Printed 'dancing' in earlier editions.

Page 351, note 14, line 1, *for* 1681 *read* 1687   *Last line, after* 18 *add* ; Burke, *Landed Gentry,* 1855, i. 515; Collins, *Peerage,* 1812, v. 652

Page 353, To Montagu 7 April 1761, bottom line, *on* army *add note* 4a: 4a. Conway's colonelcy 'worth on the present establishment . . . about £1200 or £1300 per annum' (*The Question on some Late Dismissions Truly Stated,* 1764, p. 17).

Page 354, note 7, line 1, *for* (ca 1717–ca 1806) *read* (1717–ca 1805) *Line 4, for* 1745–52 *read* 1747–54

Page 356, note 3, lines 7–8, *for* now Folger Library *read* now WSL

Page 356, note 3, last line, *for* Arthur.' *read* Arthur' (printed in *Notes by Horace Walpole on Several Characters of Shakespeare,* ed. W. S. Lewis Farmington, Connecticut, privately printed, 1940, pp. 13–14).

Page 363, line 16, *for* tranquility *read* tranquillity

Page 364, bottom line of text, *on* œstrus *add note* 5a: 5a. 'Something that stings or goads one on, a stimulus; vehement impulse; passion, frenzy' (OED).

Page 365, note 7, 3d line from end, *for* 1785 edition *read* 1782 and 1785 editions   *Last line, add* HW's copies of the 1st and 2d editions of Nichols are now WSL; see Hazen, *Cat. of HW's Lib.* Nos 2435, 3860, and also HW's letter to Nichols 31 Oct. 1781, suggesting corrections.

Page 367, note 3, *add* See also L. F. Powell, 'Edmund Southwell, his Sisters, and Dr Johnson,' TLS 30 Dec. 1960.

Page 367, note 4, *substitute* Probably Anne ——, m. (before 1725) Francis Prujean (d. 1780) of Sutton Gate, Hornchurch, Essex (John Orlebar Payne, *Records of English Catholics*, 1889, p. 70).

Page 379, note 5, line 1, *for* Muhammed 'Ali Walajah (ca 1717–95). *read* Muhammad Alī K̲h̲ān (1717–95), Nawab of Arcot (1749–95) and of the Carnatic (1754); Wālājah, 1765 (MANN ix. 117, n. 15). He was

Page 379, note 10, line 3, *for* Wilhelmtahl *read* Wilhelmsthal

Page 380, note 17, *add* 'He [Burke] acquired great reputation by his Vindication of Natural Society, in which he copied the style of the late Lord Bolingbroke with so much exactness that it was by many taken for a posthumous work of that nobleman' ([William Rider], *An Historical and Critical Account of the Lives and Writings of the Living Authors of Great Britain*, 1762). HW's copy in 'Tracts of Geo. 3d' is now WSL (Hazen, *Cat. of HW's Lib.* No. 1609:5:5).

Page 381, note 1, right column, line 14, *after* Priory *insert* ; see CHUTE 644–5

Page 382, note 4, *substitute* The representation of Harlequin being hanged on stage caused a near riot in the audience; see *London Stage*, Part IV, ii, 809, 872, 876–7.

Page 383, note 1, line 1, *delete* Possibly   *Line 6, add* He was appointed chaplain of the 61st Foot (which became the 59th Foot) 15 Jan. 1756 (see CHUTE 265 and n. 5; HW to Bedford 1 Jan. 1757, in MISC. CORR. i. 90, n. 3).

Page 387, note 8, line 5, *delete* perhaps

Page 388, note 20, line 1, *for* Tyrrel *read* Tyrrell   *Line 3, delete* or 1754

Page 388, note 25, line 6, *after* John *add* ; Dymoke's own account of his performance in Samuel Lodge, *Scrivelsby*, 1893, pp. 188–92

Page 390, note 2, 2d line from end, *after* legacy *insert* , a self-portrait by Liotard, now WSL   *Last line, after* 489 *add* ; MASON i. 197, n. 19

Page 393, note 4, *substitute* Hertford wrote HW 10 Dec. 1761, 'I do not propose to go yet into Ireland; I intend seeing whether we are to have a Spanish War or a perpetual militia to defend us before I settle there' (CONWAY ii. 145).

Page 396, note 2, line 2, *for* Leightin *read* Leighlin

Page 397, note 8, *add* See Hazen, *Cat. of HW's Lib.* No. 1609:3:1, 2.

Page 398, note 9, *add* HW's copy is Hazen, *Cat. of HW's Lib.* No. 3222:1:8.

Page 398, note 12, line 2, *for* Brocklebank *read* C. M. Cracherode   *At end add* See Hazen, *SH Bibl.* 52–3.

Page 398, note 13, line 1, *for* ca 1708 *read* 1707   *Line 4, for* 67–8. *read* 67–8; Namier and Brooke iii. 336–7.

Page 401, To Montagu 7 Nov. 1761, note 6, *add* See BM, *Satiric Prints* iv. 14 for the 'Advertisement' engraved below the design.

Page 402, note 2, *substitute* The Money Bill to be presented to the Irish Parliament had been carried over from the previous year, and Halifax, the Lord-Lieutenant, warned the English Privy Council that there might be opposition in the session of 1761 (*Calendar of Home Office Papers,* 1760–1765, ed. Joseph Redington, 1878, p. 69). The E. of Egremont answered 20 Oct. 1761, 'With regard to the Money Bill, the expediency, and indeed necessity, of a Supply Bill, to be certified as the cause of calling a new Parliament, was fully debated and unanimously determined in Council. The King is therefore surprised that a possibility of resistance should exist; the more so, as His Majesty had, in order to remove all difficulties, graciously condescended to accept the Bill in the form proposed by the late Lords Justices' (ibid. p. 71). With the help of John Hely Hutchinson and the Lords Justices the first reading of the Money Bill on 14 Nov. was carried by a vote of 170 to 42 (according to Halifax, 172 to 44), and the third reading on 19 Nov. by 147 to 37 (ibid. pp. 78, 79; *Journals of the House of Commons . . . Ireland,* xii. 503, 520). See Hertford to HW 24 Oct., 14 Dec. 1761, CONWAY ii. 138 and n. 2, 147–8 and nn. 9, 10.

Page 405, note 7, *substitute* This refers presumably to Burke's unfinished *Essay towards an Abridgement of English History,* commissioned by Robert Dodsley in 1757; see Burke, *Correspondence,* vol. i, ed. T. W. Copeland, 1958, p. 164, n. 1, and also p. 124, n. 5; GRAY ii. 122, n. 5.

Page 405, note 8, *add* She died 1 May 1775 (see MANN viii. 99 and n. 8).

Page 405, To Montagu 28 Nov. 1761, note 1, *add* The account of this campaign in the *London Gazette* No. 10158, 17–21 Nov., is quoted in MANN v. 549, n. 22; HW wrote Mann 14 Nov., 'Lord Granby and Mr Conway have been successful in some fresh skirmishes.'

Page 407, 2d paragraph, line 1, *on* England *add note* 2a: 2a. Burke's *Essay towards an Abridgement of English History,* of which Dodsley printed at least six sheets; a copy of these in the Yale Library has the following note, in an unknown hand: 'This fragment given to me by Mr Nichol the Kings book seller was written by Edmund Burke and discontinued on the publication of Hume's History—' (see Burke, *Correspondence,* vol. i, ed. T. W. Copeland, 1958, p. 164, n. 1).

Page 407, note 3, *add* HW's copy is Hazen, *Cat. of HW's Lib.* No. 3328.

Page 408, note 1, *substitute* Probably for HW's collection of shells; see MANN vii. 285. Bentley sent HW some shells from Jersey in 1755 (CHUTE 207).

Page 408, note 2, *add* See also CHUTE 645.

Page 409, line 5, *on* cousin *add note* 5a: 5a. Used by Mrs Honour in *Tom Jones,* Book iv, chapter 14 (information from the late R. W. Ketton-Cremer).

Page 409, note 10, line 2, *after* 1761. *insert* HW's copies, 1767 and 1782, are Hazen, *Cat. of HW's Lib.* Nos 3222:8:3 and 3222:19:1.

Page 411, note 7, *add* See Hazen, *SH Bibl.* 58–60 for a full account.

Page 417, note 7, *for* (d. 27 Dec. 1761) *read* (ca 1683–27 Dec. 1761) *Last line, add* See also Sedgwick ii. 332.

Page 417, note 12, line 9, *after* reproduced by *insert* Wright iii, frontispiece,   *Line 10, after* i. 1 *insert*   ; also in W. B. Boulton, *The History of White's*, 1892, ii, frontispiece   *Last line, after* 276 *add*   , where Tom Taylor is quoted assigning the picture to 1761   *At end add* In 1959 it was in the City Art Gallery, Bristol.

Page 417, note 13, *add* See also *Biographical Catalogue of the Pictures at Woburn Abbey*, compiled by Adeline Marie Bedford and Ela M. S. Russell, 1892, ii. 81–3, and illustration (information from Lindsay Fleming).

VOLUME 10

Page 1, note 1, line 1, *after* Masterton *insert* (1715–77)   *Lines 3–4, for* Inverkeithing, etc. (Fifeshire) *read* Stirling Burghs   *Lines 5–8, delete* reported . . . correct   *after* cf. *insert* Namier and Brooke iii. 118–19

Page 13, From Montagu 20 Feb. 1762, line 4, *on* painting *add note* 1a: 1a. The first two volumes of the *Anecdotes*, 1762 which Montagu had bound in one volume; these copies are now WSL (see *post* 22 Feb. 1762, MONTAGU ii. 15, n. 15; 17 April 1763, ibid. ii. 66, n. 5).

Page 13, From Montagu 20 Feb. 1762, note 2, *substitute* Apparently Montagu intended to have Bentley's *The Wishes* bound in vellum for HW, but since he thought the play would not be acted and therefore not be published this season, he proposes to have the two volumes of the *Anecdotes* bound in vellum instead (see *ante* 30 Dec. 1761, 2 Jan. 1762, MONTAGU i. 418, ii. 1; *post* 25, 27 Feb. 1762, ibid. ii. 16 and n. 5, 18).

Page 15, note 12, *add* The daughter, Lady Charlotte Herbert, died in 1784, aged 10; see MANN ix. 493, 497 and n. 5.

Page 16, note 5, line 5, *after* H.W.' *add* See Hazen, *Cat. of HW's Lib.* No. 2263   *Line 15, add* See also Hazen, *Cat. of HW's Lib.* No. 313.

Page 16, note 6, *add* See Hazen, *Cat. of HW's Lib.* No. 595.

Page 18, note 6, *add* See *Journals of the House of Commons . . . Ireland*, xii (Dublin, 1782). 9–15, which lists Thomas Butler, Hon. Brinsley Butler, styled Lord Vct Newtown, Hon. Capt. Robert Butler, and Hon. John Butler as members. For the Address on 26 Feb. see ibid. xii. 237.

Page 22, note 6, line 1, *for* ca 1728 *read* 1727   *Lines 4–6, for* Dictionary . . . 36 *read* S. W. Patterson, *Horatio Gates*, New York, 1941, pp. 4, 398, *et passim*

Page 23, note 10, *delete second sentence and add* See D. M. Low's explanation in *Review of English Studies*, 1944, xx. 243; see also CONWAY ii. 89.

Page 26, note 11, line 2, *for* 1708 *read* 1710   *after* Bn Vernon *add* (GEC; Sedgwick ii. 494)

Page 29, note 1, line 3, *for* in April 1763 *read* 22 Nov. 1762 by the E. of Northumberland, who served until 20 April 1763, when he became Lord Lieutenant of Ireland and was replaced by

Page 30, note 9, last line, *after* 76 *add*   ; Richard Griffin, Lord Braybrooke, *The History of Audley End, to which are appended Notices of the Town and Parish of Saffron Walden*, 1836

Page 32, note 5, *add* See also N&Q 1930, clix. 260, 300, 341.

Page 32, note 6, line 3, *for* ?21 Oct. *read* 21 Oct.   *Last line, add* See also Namier and Brooke ii. 101; Sedgwick i. 597; *The East Anglian*, 1869, iii. 97, iv. 171.

Page 36, note 3, *for* 1763 *read* 1762 (see R. Halsband, *The Life of Lady Mary Wortley Montagu*, Oxford, 1956, pp. 286–7)

Page 38, note 7, line 1, *for* Catherine *read* Ekaterina   *for* Vorontsov *read* Vorontsova

Page 40, note 22, line 10, *after* 105–6. *insert* She died 24 March 1799, and according to the *European Magazine* 1799 (xxxv. 285–6), was Reddish's common-law wife; he had at least three women who assumed his name, and probably he was not married to any of them (information from C. Beecher Hogan).

Page 41, middle of page, *insert the following heading*:

To MONTAGU, Thursday 26 August 1762

Missing; listed in HW's memoranda on Lady Hertford's letter of 14 August 1762, CONWAY ii. 167.

Page 47, From Montagu, ca 17 Dec. 1762, note 1, *after* Italy *add* but was considering a journey there in March for his health (see MANN vi. 110)

Page 49, note 6, *add* See also SELWYN 341; MANN vi. 102, 109–10; J. W. Croker, in the *Quarterly Review*, Dec. 1845–March 1846, lxxvii. 265–6, mistakenly says that HW voted *for* the preliminary treaty.

Page 49, note 7, line 1, *for* (d. 1784) *read* (1697–1784)   *Line 3, for* 1765–?78 *read* 1765–78   *Last line, after* Cantab. *add* ; Namier and Brooke iii. 640–1

Page 49, note 8, line 1, *for* (ca 1728–91), *read* (?1727–91), cr.   *Line 3, for* 1761–74 *read* 1761–68, 25 Jan. 1769–74

Page 52, note 1, *for* 1727 *read* 1725

Page 52, note 3, lines 2–3, *for* Mountford's *read* Mountfort's   *Line 6, after* catalogues). *insert* HW's copy, the 4th edn, 1763, is now WSL (Hazen, *Cat. of HW's Lib.* No. 1810:4:8).

Page 52, note 5, line 1, *for* (d. 1769) *read* (ca 1716–69)   *Line 2, for* Croyland Abbey *read* Crowland   *Last line, add* See also Namier and Brooke ii. 656–7.

Page 53, note 12, *add* See illustration in GRAY i. 26.

Page 53, note 16, line 1, *for* 1496 *read* 1495

Page 54, note 17, line 4, *for* Capello *read* Cappello

Page 54, note 21, line 1, *for* Capello *read* Cappello   *At end add* What Phillips bought from Christie's in 1921 was not Vasari's large portrait of Bianca Cappello but Bronzino's medallion in oil, of her (information from Dr James H. Hustin).

Page 54, note 22, line 1, *for* 1615 *read* 1620   *Line 7, for* 498 *read* 496   *Line 9, before* Lord *insert* Fuller apparently acting for   *Last line, add* See MORE 6, n. 2 and illustration in CONWAY i. 531.

Page 54, note 23, *add* A transcript of these verses in HW's hand is in the

Scottish Record Office among letters of HW to Lady Mary Coke; apparently he enclosed a copy of these verses in a letter (missing) to Lady Mary. The variants from the text above are:

> *title* The Advice, to Miss P. a Song
> *stanza 1, line 7, for* hate, *read* hate;
> *stanza 2, line 6, for* kinder *read* kinder,

See also *Horace Walpole's Fugitive Verses*, ed. W. S. Lewis, New York, 1931, p. 53.

Page 65, note 13, line 1, *for* (d. 1788) *read* (1714–88)   *Line 3, for* 1758–63, *read* 1756–7, 1758–63   *Line 13, after* 1126 *insert* (portrait in GM 1805, lxxv pt i. 113)

Page 65, note 14, line 3, *for* 1766 *read* 1776

Page 68, 4th paragraph, line 6, *on* recover *add note* 4a: 4a. HW wrote a note to this effect on a playing card (six of spades) formerly Bentley, now WSL; and in HW's *MS Commonplace Book of Verses*, p. 70, Brown is included under 'Instances of extraordinary avarice and economy.'

Page 69, note 9, line 1, *for* ca 1706 *read* ca 1708

Page 70, note 4, *substitute* Margarethe Cornelia van de Poll (1726–93), m. 1 (1743) Cornelis Munter, m. 2 (1754) Pierre-Chrysostôme d'Usson de Bonac (1724–82), Comte d'Usson (MORE 102, n. 5).

Page 70, note 7, *add* HW's copy is Hazen, *Cat. of HW's Lib*. No. 960. See also DU DEFFAND iii. 209; v. 267.

Page 72, 3d paragraph, line 9, *for* Mrs. Pitt *read* Mrs Pitt

Page 72, note 13, line 1, *for* 1728 *read* ca 1731

Page 73, note 21, *substitute* Hazen doubts 'whether the French versions were ever printed, at SH or elsewhere' (see *SH Bibl*. 181).

Page 76, To Montagu 30 May 1763, *add to headnote* The MS is now WSL (2d Waller Sale, 15 Dec. 1947, lot 37).

Page 77, note 2, line 1, *for* Hallet *read* Hallett   *for* (d. 1781) *read* (1707–81)   *Line 8, add* See also Ralph Edwards, *Dictionary of English Furniture*, rev. edn, 1954, ii. 252–3.

Page 78, note 11, *add* It is now (1942) in the Walraff Richartz museum at Cologne.

Page 81, note 5, *substitute* Probably Catherine Mildmay, unmarried daughter of Humphrey Mildmay, close friend of Chute's sister Ann (H. A. St John Mildmay, *Brief Memoir of the Mildmay Family*, 1913, p. 193; Warren H. Smith, *Originals Abroad*, New Haven, 1952, pp. 158, 168; see also MANN iv. 96, n. 3).

Page 83, note 3, last line, *for* 1765 *read* the summer of 1763 (see SELWYN Appendix 7, especially p. 341, and also pp. 170–1).

Page 85, note 2, *substitute* The source of these lines appears to be Edward Benlowes, *Theophila; or love's sacrifice*, 1652:

> So fragrant Vi'lets, blushing Strawberries
> Close shrouded lurk from lofty Eyes,
> The Emblem of sweet Blisse, which low and hidden lies.

HW's copy is Hazen, *Cat. of HW's Lib.* No. 2643. Presumably HW associated these lines with Spenser because they are quoted in a note to the article on Spenser in the *Biographia Britannica*, 1747–66, vol. vi (1763), p. 3811; see Hazen, op. cit. No. 2041 (information from the late R. W. Ketton-Cremer).

Page 88, date-line, *on* Stanford *add note a*: a. Stamford, as Cole says *post* MONTAGU Appendix 4, ii. 343, 344: 'Saturday. From Drayton to Stamford is 24 post miles, which we went with ease after dinner and coffee. . . . We were in such an hurry to get to Stamford, that evening.' See also John Sargeaunt in TLS 1920, p. 302.

Page 88, note 1, *add* Also quoted in HW to Mason 23 March 1782, MASON ii. 205.

Page 92, note 35, line 4, *for* Richard *read* Jenison   *Line 5, after* 230–1 *add*   ; HW to Hertford 29 Dec. 1763, CONWAY ii. 272, n. 1.

Page 94, note 4, line 1, *for* ca 1697 *read* 1695

Page 94, note 5, *add* HW must mean the dowager.

Page 98, note 5a, line 1, *for* 1701 *read* 1706

Page 102, note 1, line 7, *delete* no doubt   *Lines 8–9, delete* Bathoe . . . him *and substitute*   , who had disappeared because of debts, and HW expected Bathoe to come to SH to examine the printing-shop to see whether Pratt had stolen any copies of *Anecdotes* (see HW to Selwyn 28 Sept. 1763, SELWYN 171–2;   *Line 10, delete parenthesis   Lines 12–15, delete* the Walker . . . DNB). *and substitute* Anthony Walker (1726–65), since the four engravings in *Anecdotes*, vol. iii are signed A. Walker (see also Hazen, *SH Bibl.* 58).

Page 102, note 4, line 1, *delete hyphen in* Knatchbull Wyndham

Page 103, note 9, *at end add* See also SELWYN 172.

Page 104, note 4, line 1, *after* Trevor *insert* (after 1754, Hampden) *Line 3, add* HW to Selwyn 28 Sept. 1763 calls her 'Miss Hambden.'

Page 105, line 5, *on* year *add note* 9a: 9a. Reeve to HW 4 March 1762, printed in MISC. CORR. i. 230–1.

Page 105, line 6, *on* himself *add note* 9b: 9b. HW preserved half a dozen drawings and etchings by Reeve in his *Etchings by Amateurs* (sold SH viii. 56).

Page 105, note 9, *delete last line*

Page 106, 1st paragraph, line 6, *on* house *add note* 12a: 12a. Reeve had given his address as 'at Holliport near Maidenhead, Berks.'

Page 108, note 1, *substitute* The Kew bridge from Kew to Brentford was built at the expense of Robert Tunstall; the first stone was laid 29 April 1758, and the bridge was opened in 1759. It was rebuilt between 1783 and 1787 (E. Beresford Chancellor, *The History and Antiquities of Richmond, Kew, Petersham, Ham, etc.*, Richmond, 1894, pp. 327–9; GM 1758, xxviii. 239). A contemporary map showing the river and some of the surrounding estates on both sides is bound into GM 1764, xxxiv. Index. There was no Twickenham bridge over the Thames river at this time (pointed out by Derek Jones, Chief Librarian and Curator, Richmond upon Thames); for the bridge built at Richmond 1774–7, and a description of the old road between Richmond and Kew, see CONWAY iii. 176 and n. 12, 187; and Richard Crisp, *Richmond and its Inhabitants from the Olden Time*, Richmond, 1866, pp. 311–19, 325–7, 333–4).

Page 108, note 4, *add* The correspondence between Northumberland and Halifax in *Calendar of Home Office Papers . . . 1760–1765*, ed. Joseph Redington, 1878 (repr. 1967), pp. 314–24, does not corroborate HW's assertion. Northumberland wrote 13 Oct. 1763, 'The Session, which commenced on the 11th of this month, opened with appearances as favourable as possible. The addresses were voted *nem. con.*, and with great cheerfulness. No difficulty whatever arose after the resolutions were brought into Parliament. Some, indeed, occurred before they were prepared for that stage, from circumstances which will readily strike his Lordship' (ibid. 314).

Page 110, From Montagu 15 Nov. 1763, note 1, line 3, *for* 1747 *read* 1746

Page 113, note 2, line 1, *for* Maclean *read* Maclaine

Page 113, note 4, line 1, *for* (1674–1722) *read* (b. 1674, d. 1737–9)   At end *add* See also N&Q 1944, clxxxvii. 125, 241; N&Q 1945, clxxxix. 107.

Page 119, note 11, lines 8–10, *delete* William . . . same, *and substitute* He   *Line 10, for* Bosinney *read* Bossiney   *after* 1746–7 *add* (Sedgwick i. 485–6)

Page 120–1, note 1, last line, *after* 1764 *add* and HW to Hertford 20 April 1764, CONWAY ii. 375, 376, 380–2

Page 122, note 12, line 1, *for* 1741 *read* 1742   *Line 3, for* 23 *read* 14 *Line 6, after* 383 *add*   ; Namier and Brooke iii. 14

Page 122, note 10, *substitute* Possibly HW's prefatory verses to the Strawberry Hill edition of *Poems by Anna Chamber, Countess Temple*, which was being printed between 9 April and 23 April 1764; HW's prefatory verses were printed soon after (Hazen, *SH Bibl.* 72–5). Also at this time HW had been writing his 'Verses sent to Lady Charles Spencer,' printed at SH between 23 April and the end of May (ibid. 181–4).

Page 122, note 13, line 4, *for* ibid. *read* Baker, op. cit.

Page 123, note 3, line 1, *for* ca 1641 *read* 1641

Page 126, last line, *for* banquetted *read* banqueted

Page 127, note 10, *add* See also Hazen, *SH Bibl.* 189–91.

Page 128, note 12, line 8, *after* Halifax; *insert* Newcastle,   *Last line, after* WSL *add* (Hazen, *Cat. of HW's Lib.* No. 1810:59:2); HW identifies Pride as Temple, Faction as Beckford, North-Briton as Wilkes, Blackbird as Churchill, Folly as Newcastle, Ambition as Pitt, and also fills in other blanks.

Page 129, note 1, lines 2–3, *after* attainted *add*   , 1738   *Last line, add* See Isenburg, *Stammtafeln*, 2d edn, Marburg, 1957–60, iv. taf. 56; MANN vii. 402, n. 15.

Page 129, note 3, *substitute* Charles-Bernard-Pascal-Janvier Fitzjames

(1751–87), Marquis de la Jamaïque; 4th D. of Berwick, attainted, 1785; 4th D. of Liria and Xerica, 1785 (Isenburg, *Stammtafeln*, 2d edn, Marburg, 1957–60, iv. taf. 56; MANN vii. 402, n. 14).

Page 129, note 6, *at end add* Montagu's copy is now WSL (see Hazen, *SH Bibl.* 1973, p. xviii).

Page 130, note 13, *add* See Hazen, *SH Bibl.* 70–1.

Page 133, note 1, right column, line 4, *for* original *read* miniature *for* James *read* Isaac　　　*after* Oliver *add* (which belongs to Earl Powis)

Page 136, note 1, *add* Lady Mary had been sworn housekeeper at Kensington 9 Feb. 1762 (Lord Steward's Warrant Books 13.203, p. 30). This post she surrendered to Mrs Rachel Lloyd who was sworn 31 Oct. 1764 (ibid. 13.203, p. 40). Lady Mary remained housekeeper at Windsor from that date until her death in 1801, when the Hon. Georgina Townshend was sworn as her successor 31 Aug. 1801 (Lord Chamberlain's Warrant Books 3.68, p. 68). As to the salaries of the two posts, they were in 1770 Windsor (Lady Mary Churchill) £320, Kensington (Mrs Rachel Lloyd) £100 (Bodleian Library MS, North B.58). There were probably board wages and perquisites in addition to these figures. The official residence of the housekeeper at Windsor then was in the circular tower forming the South flank of Norman Gate (information from the late Sir Owen F. Morshead).

Page 138, note 2, *at beginning insert Ezio*, by Johann Adolph Hasse, was performed at the King's Theatre, Haymarket, from 24 Nov. to 22 Dec. (*London Stage* Part IV, ii. 1085–89).

Page 138, note 4, *substitute* At Covent Garden *The Guardian Outwitted*, by Dr Thomas Arne, from 12–18 Dec.; at Drury Lane *The Capricious Lovers*, by Robert Lloyd, from 28 Nov. to 7 Dec. (*London Stage* Part IV, ii. 1085–89).

Page 138, note 6, *add* A caricature of her is reproduced in J. H. Cardwell, H. B. Freeman, and G. C. Wilton, *Two Centuries of Soho*, 1898, p. 38 (*sub* St Patrick's Roman Catholic Church).

Page 139, note 8, line 2, *delete* ca　　　*At end add* Seilern presented his credentials in Dec. 1763, having arrived in England 28 Oct. (GM 1763, xxxiii. 615; *London Chronicle* 25–27 Oct. 1763, xiv. 401).

Page 139, note 9, line 2, *for* 3d Bn *read* 2d Bn　　　*Line 4, after* m. *insert* (1759)　　*Line 5, for* von *read* van

Page 142, note 8, line 2, *after Anecdotes insert* 1762–3, the 'authorized reprint' described by Hazen, *SH Bibl.* 60. These two volumes HW sent to Montagu 24 Dec. 1764 (*post* MONTAGU ii. 145).　　　*Line 2, for* and *read* HW　　*Line 4, after* Office 12 *add*　; Hazen, *SH Bibl.* 55. Montagu's copy of these four volumes is now WSL (see Hazen, *SH Bibl.* 1973, p. xvii)

Page 143, note 2, *add* Possibly sent with HW to Lady Hertford 7 Jan. 1765 or HW to Lord Hertford 10 Jan. 1765 (CONWAY ii. 486, 490).

Page 148, note 6, right column, line 3, *after* 6 vols *insert* 8vo, Geneva, 1763　　*Line 4, after* 170 *insert* (see Hazen, *Cat. of HW's Lib.* No. 3028)

Page 150, note 3, *add* Hertford announced the new play 20 Feb. and sent it (probably the first French edition) to HW 22 March; see Conway ii. 515, 521; Hazen, *Cat. of HW's Lib.* No. 1810:7:11.

Page 151, note 3, *add* See also Hazen, *Bibl. of HW* 54–5.

Page 151–2, note 5, *add* See also Namier and Brooke i. 310–12, iii. 155.

Page 152, note 1, lines 2–3, *for* letters . . . time *read* HW to Hertford 20 May 1765, Conway ii. 557–66.

Page 153, note 8, *add* See Mann vi. 302–3.

Page 153–4, note 11, 5th line from end, *after* 1764 *insert*   , Conway ii. 333, n. 5; Hazen, *Cat. of HW's Lib.* No. 1609:7:2

Page 154, note 12, *add* See Add. and Corr. for vol. 10, p. 128, n. 12.

Page 156, note 2, line 1, *for* Margaret —— *read* Marguerite de Ligonier du Buisson (d. 1793)   *Lines 2–3, for* and remarried to *read* m. 1 —— de Panne; m. 2 (ca 1740)   *Last line, after* 864 *add*   ; Vittoria Colonna Caetani, Duchessa di Sermoneta, *The Locks of Norbury*, 1940, pp. 6, 8–14; Ossory i. 49, n. 31

Page 156, note 3, *substitute* Perhaps Catherine-Zélie Morin, m. (1758) Cosme de Picquet de Juillac de Vignolles (1701–69); see HW to Lady Hervey 11 June 1765, More 36 and n. 8.

Page 157, 3d paragraph, line 3, *on* fortnight *add note* 8a: 8a. Hertford to HW 21 May 1765, Conway ii. 569–70.

Page 157, note 9, *add* See Conway iii. 1, n. 2, 2, n. 7, and Appendix 7.

Page 158, note 1, *add* It has been suggested that the reference to 'Sussex man' is a specific reference to the epilogue to Congreve's *The Mourning Bride* (information from Sylvia Townsend Warner).

Page 161, note 3, *add* See also Conway iii. 1, n. 2, 2, n. 7.

Page 161, note 4, *for* ibid. *read Mem. Geo. III*

Page 161, note 5, *add* See Mann vi. 309.

Page 162, To Montagu 28 July 1765, note 1, *add* See Conway Appendix 7.

Page 163, line 3, *on* me, *add note* 1a: 1a. See Hertford to HW 27 July 1765, Conway iii. 5.

Page 165, 2d paragraph, line 5, *on* innocency, *add note* 2a: 2a. Psalms xxvi. 6.

Page 166, note 2, line 3, *for* Jefferies *read* Jeffreys

Page 168, 1st paragraph, line 11, *on* treillage *add note* 14a: 14a. HW wrote to Lady Hervey 15 Sept. 1765, 'I am in love with treillage and fountains' (More 46 and n. 10; see also Conway iii. 316).

Page 168, note 15, line 1, *delete* perhaps   *for* his *read* Lord Temple's *Line 3, after* 132–3 *add* and Mann vi. 307–8 and n. 6, 310 and n. 3.

Page 171, note 1, *after* 258 *add*   ; Conway iii. 7.

Page 172, note 5, *add* For HW's arrival 13 Sept. at the Hertfords' residence in Paris see Conway iii. 9 and n. 19; the Duke and Duchess of Richmond arrived there 6 Nov. (ibid. 17, n. 58). See also Mann vi. 341.

Page 175, note 2, *for* Cain *read* Caïn or Kaïn   *for* 1728 *read* 1729 *for* Lekain *read* LeKain or Le Kain   *after* ibid. 263 *add*   ; *Enciclopedia dello spettacolo* vi. 1364–7

Page 175, note 4, line 1, *for* Dumesnil *read* Marchand, called Mlle du Mesnil   *for* 1711 *read* 1713   *Line 3, after* 265 *add*   ; CONWAY ii. 524, n. 18

Page 175, note 5, lines 1–2, *for* -Hippolyte Legris de Latude *read* Léris *Line 11, for* DU DEFFAND i. 146, n. 5 *read* CONWAY ii. 517, n. 14

Page 181, note 11, 3d line from end, *after* mistresses. *insert* For Mrs Boothby see MORE 298, n. 37; MANN i. 173, n. 8.

Page 182, bottom line, *on* Windsor *add note* 2a: 2a. Bishop Keppel succeeded 15 Oct. Peniston Booth, Dean of Windsor, who had died 21 Sept. (GM 1765, xxxv. 443, 492).

Page 190, note 4, lines 1–2, *for* (d. 1770) *read* (ca 1715–70)   *after* GEC *add*   ; Namier and Brooke ii. 254

Page 199, From Montagu 19 Feb. 1766, 2d paragraph, line 5, *for* accomodate *read* accommodate

Page 203, note 4, line 1, *for* Virginia Kingdon *read* Jane Kingdon *Line 2, for* Anne; *read* Anne, sworn in 4 June 1702 (Lord Chamberlain's Warrant Books 5. 166, p. 73);

Page 205, note 2, *add* Fanny is mentioned in HW to Lady George Lennox 8 Sept. 1766, MORE 126, and Mme du Deffand to HW 1 Nov. 1767 and 12 Jan. 1768, DU DEFFAND i. 365, ii. 6.

Page 210, note 7, line 1, *for* (buried 4 Jan. 1813) *read* (d. 29 Dec. 1813) *Line 3, for* Bt. *read* Bt (GM 1814, n.s. vii. 97; *Hertfordshire Families,* ed. Duncan Warrand, 1907, pp. 216–17).

Page 218, note 5, *add* The 1st edn, 4to, 1766, dated 'May' by HW, is Hazen, *Cat. of HW's Lib.* No. 3222:7:3; the 2d edn, 8vo, 1766, is ibid. No. 1810:59:4.

Page 218, note 6, *add* See Hazen, *Cat. of HW's Lib.* No. 3380.

Page 219, note 14, *for* to shoe a horse *read* 'appliquer sur une plaie les remèdes nécessaires, étriller, soigner un animal' (*Petit Larousse*).

Page 222, note 2, *add* See HW to Mann 11 July 1766, MANN vi. 432–3.

Page 222, note 3, last line, *after* 243–5 *add*   ; MANN vi. 433

Page 223, To Montagu 21 July 1766, line 2, *on* not. *add note* a: a. For a full account see MANN vi. 435–6.

Page 223, note 3, *after* 1766 *add* (MANN vi. 439–44)

Page 224, note 1, line 2, *for* (d. 1801) *read* (ca 1728–1801)   *Last line, after* 116 *add* CONWAY i. 434, n. 8; Namier and Brooke ii. 284

Page 224, note 3, line 2, *after* 1771 *add* and to Selwyn 11 March 1767

Page 228, To Montagu 5 Oct. 1766, line 6, *on* Tuesday. *add note* b: b. See HW to Chute 10 Oct. 1766, CHUTE 118–20.

Page 228, note 5, line 2, *for* ca 1727 *read* 1737   *Last line, add* See also Benjamin Boyce, *The Benevolent Man: A Life of Ralph Allen of Bath,* Cambridge, Mass., 1967, pp. 71, 165, 295.

Page 228, note 6, last line, *for* 1763 *read* 1762   *add*   ; John Hawkins to HW 1 March 1762, MISC. CORR. i. 228.

Page 228, note 7, *after* Park *add*   , Bath, designed by John Wood (?1705–54) in Palladian style with a 1300-foot frontage. A view of the house and the Palladian bridge is in Christopher Hussey, *English Gardens and Landscapes 1700–1750*, 1967, plate 36 and p. 52.

Page 229, note 2, last line, *after* 45 *add*   ; Christopher Hussey, *English Country Houses, Mid-Georgian 1760–1800*, 1956, pp. 70–8 for illustrations.

Page 230, note 3, line 5, *for* 1725 *read* ca 1716   *Line 6, after* loc. cit. *add*   ; see HW to 4th D. of Devonshire 2 Sept. 1760, MISC. CORR. i. 183, n. 8; GM 1789, lix pt ii. 1153

Page 230, note 4, *for* Spalatro *read* Spalato

Page 233, note 6, line 2, *for* 1745 *read* 1747   *Line 5, after* 96 *add*   ; Sedgwick ii. 239

Page 233, note 8, line 1, *for* 1780 *read* ca 1765   *Line 2, after* 1778; *insert* M.P.;   *and for* Anne *read* Anna   *Last line, after* visit *add* (CONWAY iii. 240–2)

Page 234, note 5, *add* A 'Miss Melvil' was appointed 'Rocker' to the new-born Princess in Aug. 1737 (GM 1737, vii. [515]).

Page 235, note 6, *add* See also David Hume, *Letters*, ed. J. Y. T. Grieg, Oxford, 1932, ii. 45–6, 402.

Page 235, note 8, *add* See Namier and Brooke iii. 235.

Page 236, note 1, line 1, *after* was on *insert* the question of adjournment of the debate on   *Line 6, after* see *insert* MANN vi. 473 and nn. 20, 21

Page 236, To Montagu 12 Dec. 1766, note 2, *add* See also MANN vi. 472–3.

Page 237, note 11, line 9, *after* etc. *insert* HW pasted a cutting from the *Public Advertiser* 10 Dec. 1766 into Vol. 16 of his 'Tracts of Geo. 3d' that seems to be an early example of the cross-readings (see Hazen, *Cat. of HW's Lib.* No. 1610:16).

Page 244, note 5, *add* HW's copy is Hazen, *Cat. of HW's Lib.* No. 3173.

Page 252, note 2, *substitute* Mrs Bramston, Lady Frances Elliot's companion; see MANN vii. 416 and n. 17.

Page 252, note 4, line 1, *for* (d. 1790) *read* (1714–90)   *Line 3, after* Oxon *add* (*Records of the English Province of the Society of Jesus*, ed. Henry Foley, 1875–83, v. 850).

Page 256, note 6, *add* See also Namier and Brooke i. 344–5.

Page 256, note 9, *after* sat *add* (Namier and Brooke i. 356).

Page 259, note 7, *add* See Hazen, *SH Bibl.* 79–85.

Page 259, note 9, line 1, *for* 24 April *read* 25 April   *Lines 2–3, for* ([John Genest], *Some Account of the English Stage*, Bath, 1832, v. 170). *read* as Lady Macbeth: 'Benefit for Mrs Pritchard, being her last time of appearing on the stage' (*London Stage* Part IV, iii. 1326).

Page 261, note 4, *add* See also MANN vii. 28–30.

Page 264, note 2, *add* See also Chute 325–8.

Page 265, note 4, line 2, *for* 1768n *read* 1768, Mann vii. 43, n. 13.

Page 269, 5th line from bottom, *on* Bristol *add note* 2a: 2a. For her letter to Lord Bristol, see D. M. Stuart, *Molly Lepell, Lady Hervey*, 1936, pp. 341, 343.

Page 270, note 3, line 1, *for* frequently *read* sometimes　　*Line 2, for* center *read* centre

Page 272, note 5, *add* See also Mann vii. 74–5.

Page 272, note 10, *add* See also Mann vii. 73.

Page 273, note 2, line 9, *after* see *insert* Mann vii. 98–9.

Page 273, note 3, *substitute* Possibly Thomas Boehm (d. 1770), merchant; see Mann vii. 99, n. 11. Edmund Boehm (d. 1787) was elected a director of the East India Co. in 1784 on the City interest, but was not in the list of directors elected April 1769 (see C. H. Philips, *The East India Company 1784–1834*, Manchester, repr. 1968, pp. 29, 336; Mann ix. 490–1, n. 29; GM 1769, xxxix. 211).

Page 274, note 8, *add* For a fuller account see Mann vii. 104–5; Namier and Brooke i. 331–3, iii. 65.

Page 276, To Montagu 15 April 1769, *add to headnote* The MS of this letter was offered in the catalogue of Lowe Brothers, Birmingham, April 1954, lot 99, £18.

Page 276, note 2, lines 2–3, *delete* ?1741 . . . O.S.). *and substitute* by warrant dated 1 May 1738 (Lord Chamberlain's Warrant Books 3.65, p. 77); she was advanced to housekeeper of Somerset House in July, 1739 (GM 1739, ix. 384); she held this post until her death, when Mrs Catherine Brietzcke, *or* Britzeke, was appointed to succeed her by warrant dated 17 Nov. 1750 (Lord Chamberlain's Warrant Books 3.65, p. 244; *Court and City Register, passim*) (information from the late Sir Owen F. Morshead).

Page 277, note 4, line 3, *after* 237 *add* ; Mann vii. 105 and n. 6

Page 278, note 8, *add* There is an illustration of it in H. Avray Tipping, 'English Late Renaissance Woodwork,' *Country Life*, 4 Oct. 1913, xxxiv. 462.

Page 278, note 9, *add* Sold Christie's (different properties) 10 July 1905 for £9. 19. 6; now in Robert Spence's collection (see Eugenie Gibson, 'Some Gloves from Mr Robert Spence's Collection,' *Connoisseur*, Sept. 1920, lviii. 23, illustration).

Page 281, line 17, *on* commission *add note* 3a: 3a. I.e., the sun, like the King, is holding his levee in person, and is passing his bills in person instead of through a committee of five lords (in the House of Lords); Montagu, being a courtier, has restored the sun to his proper position over the heads of the committee who were acting as proxies (explanation from Ralph T. Catterall).

Page 282, note 1, line 7, *before* Peter *insert* James　　*Last line, after* passim add ; H. Blackstone, *Cases . . . in Court of Common Pleas*, i. 569

Page 283, note 7, *add* See Ossory i. 84, 330.

Page 285, note 12, line 1, *for* ca 1505 *read* ca 1508   *Line 3, for* third *read* fourth

Page 287, note 14, line 1, *for* 15 *read* 14

Page 288, note 19, line 6, *after* see *insert* Namier and Brooke iii. 235;

Page 290, note 9, *add* The physician was Dr Pierre Pomme (1735–1812), as HW wrote to Chute 30 Aug. 1769 (CHUTE 121 and n. 4).

Page 290, note 11, line 2, *for* (d. 1794) *read* (ca 1714–94)

Page 291, note 12, *substitute* Eleanor Oglethorpe (1684–1775), m. (1707) Eugène-Marie de Béthisy, Marquis de Mézières (see CONWAY i. 353 and n. 9).

Page 295, note 3, line 6, *after* Lists *insert* , especially 1773, p. 19, 1775, p. 19   *Line 8, for* Trevallyn *read* Trevalyn

Page 301, note 2, last line, *after* WSL *add* (Hazen, *Cat. of HW's Lib.* No. 1810:15:8)

Page 301, note 4, line 2, *after* London *insert* 1660–1; M.P.   *after* DNB *add* ; A. B. Beaven, *The Aldermen of the City of London*, 1908–13, i. 40, ii. 90, 187, 232   *Last line, add* See *post* 31 March 1770.

Page 305, note 6, line 1, *for* Scrimshire *read* Skrymsher   *for* 1727 *read* 1737

Page 305, note 8, line 3, *after* Palace *insert* 31 Oct. 1764   *before* Coke *insert* see ADD. AND CORR. for vol. 10, p. 136, n. 1;

Page 306, 2d paragraph, line 3, *for* center *read* centre

Page 306, note 1, line 2, *for* Mrs Charles Montagu *read* Anne Calladon *after* 1780) *insert* , m. Charles Montagu (N&Q 1942, clxxxii. 334)

Page 307, note 8, *substitute* 'Oft too on Stanemore's wintry waste' (David Mallet, *Edwin and Emma*, stanza 14, quoted also in OSSORY ii. 540).

Page 309, note 5, line 1, *for* Townshend *read* Townsend   *Last line, add* See also Namier and Brooke iii. 537–8.

Page 310, To Montagu 29 June 1770, line 13, *on* Atterbury *add note* 2a: 2a. I.e., Adderbury.

Page 313, note 2, line 3, *after* Amelia *insert* 1767–86

Page 313, note 3, line 4, *after* Amelia *insert* 1761–84

Page 315, note 13, last line, *after* 1762 *add* , and HW to Chute 4 Aug. 1753, CHUTE 75.

Page 319, note 2, *substitute* Montagu wrote to Lord Guilford from Prince's Street, London, on Saturday, 20 Nov. [?1773]: 'Mr Walpole and Lord Trevor found me out and have been here. They told me nothing of London and knew no more of it than I did at Sawsey' (Bodleian Library, MS North d. 15, f. 92r). After Montagu left Adderbury, his country house from ca 1773 to 1779 was Salcey Lawn, the lodge of the Ranger of Salcey Forest, Northants. (Information kindly supplied by J. S. W. Gibson, F.S.A., of 11 Westgate, Chichester.) See also MASON ii. 83–4, n. 1; COLE ii. 211, n. 3.

Page 325, note 1, left column, last line, *after* 111 *add* and in Cunningham ix. 517–19

Page 325, note 1, right column, line 3, *after* 1744 *insert* Conway to HW 18 July and 5 Aug. 1744 NS, CONWAY i. 166–7, 168–9, 173   *Same line, for* doubtless *read* possibly   *Line 4, after* composed *add*   ; for an early ballad in the same vein by HW, see CONWAY iii. 521–2

Page 329, note 1, *add* This copy was sold Christie's 15 Dec. 1947 (2d Waller Sale), lot 52, to Maggs for WSL.

Page 333, 3d line from bottom, *on* young, *add note* 1a: 1a. (ca 1717–45), as an army chaplain (*Daily Adv.* 17 May 1745; *Eton College Register, 1698–1752*, ed. R. A. Austen-Leigh, Eton, 1927, p. 238).

Page 346, line 31, *for* comprending *read* compre[he]nding

Page 352, Table II, *for* Christopher Montagu *read* Rev. Christopher Montagu (ca 1717–45)

Page 352, Table II, *beside* Charles Montagu (d. 1759) of Papplewick *add* -Anne Calladon (d. 1780)

VOLUME 11

Page xix, for line 1, *read* Misses Sandby by P. Sandby (*see* A. P. Oppé, *Sandby Drawings*, 1947, pp. 69–70).

Page xix, Anne Seymour Damer, by Richard Cosway, *add* 'Cosway is finishing, in his beautiful manner, two small whole lengths of Mrs Damer and Miss Farren for Mr Walpole's collection at Strawberry Hill' (*World* 27 Aug. 1789, No. 826).

Page xxiii, end of 1st paragraph, *add* Walpole settled Little Strawberry Hill on them in 1790.

Page xxiii, 2d paragraph, line 9, *on* rumour *add note* 1aa: 1aa. *Walpoliana* i. p. xxxviii.

Page xxvii, line 17, *for* di *read* de'

Page xxviii, end of 2d paragraph, *add* According to C. H. Timperley, *Dictionary of Printers and Printing*, 1839, p. 797, the *Works* produced £3000.

Page xxix, 2d paragraph, line 10, *on* Smith, *add note* 2a: 2a. 'I am settled at last into liking the Miss Berrys, and shall never change any more. They have both better understandings, and much more sense than from their unquiet manner they seem to have, which manner is not unlike that of seafowl before a storm' (Sydney Smith, *Letters*, ed. N. C. Smith, Oxford, 1953, i. 324). Again, he mentions 'the Berrys, whom I may call fully ripe at present' (ibid. ii. 603); and on their eagerness to meet Dickens, he says, 'The Miss Berrys, now at Richmond, live only to become acquainted with you' (ibid. ii. 687).

Page xxx, 3d paragraph, line 5, *after* began *insert* with Chatterton; it continued

Page xxxiii, 2d line from bottom, *on* (p. 3). *add note* 1a: 1a. Probably Algernon Holt White, who bought some of HW's books in the SH sale, 1842; see Hazen, *Bibl. of HW* 72; *Cat. of HW's Lib.*, 'Index of Owners,' iii. 327.

Page xxxiv, lines 1–2, *for* manuscripts . . . publisher *substitute* manuscripts which Lord Euston (later 5th D. of Grafton) as executor for the 6th Lord Waldegrave had sold to the first Richard Bentley, her publisher; see our accounts of this transaction in MANN x, Appendix 12, pp. 40–4; FAMILY, Appendix 3, pp. 313–16; MASON i. p. xxxi.

Page xxxiv, lines 6–8, *delete* (These . . . publication.)

Page xxxv, 3d paragraph, *after* British Museum *add* , unless otherwise noted in the headnotes to individual letters. The letter of 14 Oct. 1788, formerly in the Waldegrave collection, is now WSL.

Page xli, *sub* 'Berry-Damer,' *delete last sentence* They . . . edition. *and substitute* They were formerly in the possession of Sir Wathen Waller, Bt, and are now WSL.

Page liii, at bottom *add* Mary Berry's MS of her verses, formerly in the Waldegrave collection, is now WSL. For an account of HW's verses, see Hazen, *SH Bibl.* 231–4. HW's own collection of the Detached Pieces, formerly in the possession of Lady Crewe, is now WSL; it contains a MS note by HW on the Berrys, followed by twelve lines heavily crossed out, then some lines of correction in Mary Berry's hand, including, 'In the winter of 1787 they met Walpole at Strawberry Hill.'

Page 1, To Mary Berry 14 Oct. 1788, at beginning of headnote *insert* The MS, formerly in the possession of Lord Waldegrave at Chewton Priory, is now WSL.

Page 3, note 4, last line, *after* 323 *add* ; John Pinkerton, *An Essay on Medals*, 1784, p. 153.

Page 4, note 2, right column, line 8, *after* journal, *insert* formerly *Line 10, after* Warwickshire, *insert* is now WSL; it

Page 4, note 3, line 4, *for* Saint-Remy *read* Saint-Rémy

Page 10, note 2, last line, *after* 1066 *add* (Hazen, *Cat. of HW's Lib.* No. 3809)

Page 14, note 18, *add* For a detailed study, based on MS records, see Francis W. Steer, *The History of the Dunmow Flitch Ceremony*, Chelmsford, 1951.

Page 17, note 25, right column, line 3, *for* ca 1775 *read* 1774 *Last line, after* 1791 *add* ; *London Chronicle* 1–3 Dec. 1774, xxxvi. 531. HW bequeathed him ('of the Adelphi') a copy of the *Des. of SH* (now WSL; Hazen, *SH Bibl.* 1973, p. xxvi).

Page 20, note 11, line 2, *after* iii. 15 *add* ; Hazen, *Cat. of HW's Lib.* No. 1552

Page 20, note 13, left column, 4th line from bottom, *after* WSL *insert* (Hazen, *Cat. of HW's Lib.* No. 2791)

Page 21, note 21, last line, *after* 186 *add* ; Hazen, *Cat. of HW's Lib.* No. 3138

Page 23, note 32, line 3, *for* (ca 1718–75) *read* (1717–75) *Line 4, after* iv. 207 *add* ; Sedgwick i. 572–3

Page 23, note 35, line 4, *for* Catharine *read* Catherine

Page 23, note 38, line 13, *for* 1773–80 *read* 1774–80   *before* Collins *insert* Namier and Brooke ii. 22;

Page 24, note 40, line 3, *for* Clements *read* Clement

Page 25, note 7, line 17, *after* judgment *insert* (see CONWAY iii. 466) *2d line from bottom, after* 668; *insert* Hist. MSS Comm., *Report on the Manuscripts of Earl Bathurst,* 1923, p. 699;

Page 28, note 26, line 1, *for* Mary *read* Margaret   *Line 5, for* Collins, *Peerage,* 1812, v. 673 *substitute* H. S. Vade-Walpole, 'Notes on the Walpoles,' *Genealogical Magazine,* 1898–9, ii. 435

Page 32, note 20, line 1, *for* Duval d'Esprémesnil *read* Du Val d'Eprémesnil   *Last line, after pédie add*   ; *Dictionnaire de biographie française,* 1933– , xii. 996–1000

Page 32, note 22, lines 2–3, *for* Duval d'Esprémesnil *read* Du Val d'Eprémesnil

Page 33, note 27, line 4, *for* 1725 *read* 1724

Page 33, note 30, *after SH Bibliography add* 137–40

Page 34, note 35, right column, line 6, *after* 4to *add*   , Hazen, *Cat. of HW's Lib.* No. 3222:22:12

Page 35, note 40, right column, line 1, *for* 1742–84 *read* 1742–80

Page 35, note 41, last line, *after* 191 *add* (Hazen, *Cat. of HW's Lib.* No. 3093)

Page 36, note 44, line 1, *for* Louis-Charles-Auguste Le Tonnelier *read* Louis-Auguste le Tonnelier   *Line 2, for* 1733 *read* 1730

Page 36, note 45, *substitute* This report came from the D. of Dorset's messenger, as W. W. Grenville wrote to the Marquess of Buckingham 14 July 1789: 'A messenger is arrived from the Duke of Dorset with an account of the dismission of Necker and Montmorin, and the appointment of Monsieur de Breteuil to be *Chef du Conseil des Finances. . . .* The accounts which Bernard sends you of cannonades depend on the report of the messenger who brought this despatch. The violence of the mob at Paris has been hourly increasing for many days, and has proceeded to several acts of savage fury' (Hist. MSS Comm., 13th Report, App., pt iii, *Fortescue MSS,* 1892, i. 483–4).

Page 37, note 51, line 1, *for* (d. 862) *read* (ca 800–62)

Page 37, note 52, *add* See OSSORY i. 155 and n. 32; MANN viii. 417, 475.

Page 39, note 6, lines 1, 9, 11, *for* Sigismund *read* Sigismond

Page 41, note 19, line 1, *after* Charlotte *insert* Hanbury   *for* (d. 1790) *read* (1738–90)   *Line 5, after* 2085 *add*   ; Earl of Ilchester and Mrs Langford-Brooke, *Life of Sir Charles Hanbury Williams,* 1929, pp. 40–1, 430; CONWAY iii. 416 and n. 4

Page 42, note 4, line 2, *for* legitimated *read* illegitimate

Page 48, note 10, line 2, *for* ca 1721 *read* 1724

Page 56, note 10, line 3, *for* Clements *read* Clement

Page 57, note 17, line 6, *for* , sometime *read* (ca 1701–54)   *Line 8, after* 113 *add*   ; Sedgwick ii. 54–5

Page 59, note 4, line 1, *for* Barrett *read* Barret   *for* 1744 *read* ?1743

Page 59, note 5, lines 11–18, *delete* In Neale . . . 174). *and substitute* In HW's copy of Hasted's *Kent* (now WSL), vol. iii, p. 665, HW wrote the following note: 'This description of Lee was written by Mr Horace Walpole' (Hazen, *Cat. of HW's Lib*. No. 3). The account of Lee is attributed to HW in Neale, op. cit. vol. ii, *sub* Lee Priory, and in GM 1803, lxxiii pt i. 91 (see *post* 27 Sept. 1794, n. 31). See also HW to George Hardinge ca Aug. 1785, CHUTE 635.

Page 60–1, note 20, line 6, *delete* Augustus   *Last line, add* See A. H. Burne, *The Noble Duke of York*, 1949, p. 17; GEC.

Page 62, note 4, 4th line from end, *after* 163 *add* and is now WSL (Hazen, *Cat. of HW's Lib*. No. 1840)

Page 63, note 6, line 4, *for* (1765) *read* (1766)

Page 64, note 18, line 5, *before* of Putney *insert* curate   *Lines 6–8, delete* but DNB apparently is incorrect in saying he was curate of either place *and substitute* and in his 'Extracts from Diary, 1789–1800' Lysons speaks of himself as curate of Putney: '1789, July 1. Took possession of Lodgings as Curate of Putney' . . . '1800, July 14. quitted the Curacy of Putney'   *Line 12, after* 310 *add* DALRYMPLE 199, n. 4   *Last line, add* Lysons noted in his 'Extracts from Diary, 1789–1800': '1789, Sept. 2. dined at Horace Walpole's with J. Kemble and Raftor' (information from Lindsay Fleming).

Page 64, note 20, last line, *after* 1755 *add* OSSORY i. 243–4, 283

Page 65, note 27, line 10, *after* 1055 *insert*   ; Hazen, *Cat. of HW's Lib*. No. 3896   *8th line from end, after passim add* and OSSORY i. 244, n. 10

Page 66, note 29, *add* Lady Luxborough wrote to Shenstone 18 Dec. 1748, 'I eat heartily, grow too fat, and have not tasted wine, beer, nor cyder, these two months or more' (*Letters written by . . . Lady Luxborough, to William Shenstone, Esq*., 1775, p. 77).

Page 67, note 41, last line, *after* 607–8 *add*   ; CONWAY iii. 471

Page 67, note 44, *add* (see also OSSORY iii. 61, 63; CONWAY iii. 470).

Page 68, note 47, *at end add* See Hazen, *Cat. of HW's Lib*. No. 2374.

Page 69, 3d paragraph, line 6, *on* lines *add note* 2a: 2a. See also FAMILY 255, where HW sends the epitaph to the Duchess of Gloucester.

Page 71, note 13, *delete* Not identified.

Page 73, after letter of 30 Sept. 1789 *insert the following headings*:

TO MARY BERRY, December 1789

Verses by HW on Mary Berry's health; first printed in MBJ i. 155–6; reprinted in *Horace Walpole's Fugitive Verses*, ed. W. S. Lewis, New York, 1931, p. 185.

To Miss Mary Berry
Thine beauty, learning, eloquence,
With every grace of social sense,
And all with unaffected ease,
Without pretensions sure to please;
With every virtue that endears,
Why raise my wishes less than fears?
'Tis nought that heaven denied thee wealth;
Ah, why withhold its dearer blessing—health?

FROM MARY BERRY, December 1789

Verses by Mary Berry in response to the above verses of HW's. Printed from the MS, now WSL (2d Waller Sale, 15 Dec. 1947, lot 53, £9); first printed in MBJ i. 156.

Inscribed by Mary Berry: 'December 1789 wrote when I was very ill in answer to some complimentary lines from the Honourable H. Walpole.'

Though pain with unrelenting Sway
  My languid frame subdues
Can I with common thanks repay
  The wishes of thy Muse?

Ah no! my *heart* no languor knows,
  In every feeling strong
Dwells with delight on all it owes
  Thy friendship, converse, song.

The voice of praise still charms my Ear
  Yet not deceived, I see
Thy verse but tells in language clear
  What I should strive to be—

To MARY BERRY, December 1789

Verses by HW in response to Mary Berry's verses; first printed in MBJ i. 156; reprinted in *Horace Walpole's Fugitive Verses*, ed. W. S. Lewis, New York, 1931, p. 185.

An Apology for Miss Berry's Paleness,
  in Imitation of Waller. By H. W.

True on her cheek the Damask rose
Too seldom or too faintly blows;
Less does the venal mimic art
To that fair cheek its dyes impart,
E'en Hebe's bloom would ill replace
The sensibility and grace
That sweetly beams from Mary's face:
As the white lily would but lose
If tinged by Flora's brightest hues.
              Dec. 1789.

Page 76, note 20, *add* He was hanged by accident. The hangman was looking for another victim, but took d'Aulan to satisfy the mob (*Dictionnaire de biographie française*, 1933–, iv. 580–1).

Page 78, note 9, line 2, *for* 1753 *read* 1761

Page 81, note 27, line 5, *for* 1804–9 *read* 1805–9 (GM 1817, lxxxvii pt i. 376)

Page 81, note 28, line 3, *for* 1741 *read* 1740   *Line 8, for* Possibly he *read* He   *Line 9, for* —— Boydell *read* Mary Boydell (d. 1820)

Page 81, note 31, line 9, *for* (d. 1815) *read* (1730–1815)   *Line 12, before* Toynbee *insert* Namier and Brooke ii. 615–16;

Page 87, note 20, *for* Francesco Giuseppe Sallier della *read* Vittorio Amadeo Sallier de la   *Line 6, before* Domenico *insert* MORE 194–5, n. 16;

Page 90, note 1, last line, *after* 368 *add*   ; James Fergusson, *Lowland Lairds*, 1949, p. 74.

Page 93, note 13, *add* See Hazen, *Cat. of HW's Lib.* No. 3928.

Page 93, note 15, last 2 lines, *for* in the Folger Library *read* WSL

Page 94, note 17, line 3, *for* ?1666 *read* ca 1666   *Line 4, for* ?1681 *read* 1681

Page 95, note 23, *add* HW gave her a copy (now WSL) of his *Essay on Modern Gardening*, 1785; see *post* BERRY ii. 260; Hazen, *SH Bibl.* 1973, p. xxviii.

Page 96, note 29, line 2, *after* val *insert* (1731–1821)   *Line 6, after* passim *add*   ; H. S. Vade-Walpole, 'Notes on the Walpoles,' *Genealogical Magazine*, 1898–9, ii. 433

Page 96, note 35, line 1, *for* ca 1727 *read* ca 1725   *Line 4, for* Stratfield Saye *read* Stratfield-Say   *Line 5, for* Sudley *read* Sudeley

Page 98, note 8, *add* It has been suggested that the allusion to Price is a reference to his theory that the population of England was declining steadily.

Page 100, note 26, line 1, *after* 1806. *insert* Christian Friedrich   *Line 3, for* Anspach *read* Ansbach   *Line 5, after* 27 *add*   ; *Almanach de Gotha*, 1778.

Page 101, note 27, last line, *for* Anspach *read* Ansbach

Page 101, note 33, *delete last sentence and substitute* In Jan. 1790 the room was used as a puppet theatre by Pietro Carnivalli (or Carnevale) who sold it to Lord Barrymore in March 1790 (*World* 26 Dec. 1789–March 1790).

Page 104, note 16, line 3, *for* 4th D. *read* 4th [5th] D.

Page 106, note 26, line 2, *for* 1719 *read* 1717–19   *Line 3, after* WSL *insert* (Hazen, *Cat. of HW's Lib.* No. 695)

Page 107, headnote, *Address, on* Somerset Street *add note a: a.* A printed card inscribed 'Miss Berrys, Somerset Street' was in the possession of the late R. W. Ketton-Cremer.

Page 108, note 3, *add* See CONWAY iii. 479.

Page 109, note 16, line 2, *for* (1760–ca 1825) *read* (ca 1758–ca 1822)
Line 4, for 1766 *read* ca 1765   *Right column, line 1, after* Eliza *insert*
[ca 1772–ca 1830]   *Line 11, after* 1927–8 *insert* corrected by *The New
Grove Dictionary of Music and Musicians*, ed. Stanley Sadie, 1980, i. 23

Page 111, note 5, *add* See also *Lord Fife and His Factor ... 1729–1809*,
ed. Alistair and Henrietta Tayler, 1925, p. 220.

Page 125, line 8, *delete footnote number 25 and also note 25*

Page 130, note 6, *add* See also Fitzherbert's dispatches to Leeds, Oct.
1790, in *Cambridge History of British Foreign Policy*, ed. Ward and
Gooch, 1970, i. 200–1; Cobbett, *Parl. Hist.* xxviii. 916–18.

Page 132, note 16, *delete last sentence and substitute* See also HW to
Burke 4 Nov. 1790; Hazen, *Cat. of HW's Lib.* No. 1609:46:9.

Page 132, note 19, lines 2–3, *for* (b. 1730, d. after 1800) *read* (1730–
1803)   *Lines 7–8, for* 1937, p. 371 *read* 1953, p. 269   *Last line, add*
See also OSSORY iii. 86, n. 3; CONWAY iii. 470, n. 3.

Page 137, headnote, line 1, *delete* Miss Seton was doubtless visiting the
Lovedays. *and substitute* Barbara Seton lived with her mother, Mrs
George Seton, in a cottage at Caversham. Miss Seton refers to her home
in some verses addressed to the 'Tea-Caddy' (dated 23 Feb. 1788):

> Since from these scenes I must retire
> To humble Causham's cottage fire,
> Where dog, and cat, and I, and mother,
> Sit and make much of one another (MJB i. 157)

Caversham was often called Causham at that time. Another reference to
the Setons' cottage appears in Penelope Loveday's diary, where she wrote
on 25 April 1792 on leaving Caversham: 'We took leave of all our Reading acquaintances, and Sarah and I concluded the day at Park Farm, and
made our last call on the Setons in their elegant little cottage in our return home in the evening' (information from Mrs Sarah Markham, Wotton-under-Edge, Glos, who inherited the papers of the Loveday family
from her father, Dr Thomas Loveday).

Page 137, headnote, last 3 lines, *delete* who sold it (DNB, *sub* Loveday,
John), but presumably the elder Loveday's widow and children were living there in 1790, and possibly until Mrs Loveday's death in 1801. *and
substitute* who sold it in 1799. His step-mother and her daughters were
living at Caversham until 1792, when they moved to Chepstow, and later
to Milton in Wiltshire (information from Mrs Sarah Markham).

Page 147, note 29, last line, *after* 1755 *add* and HW to Conway 12 Feb.
1756

Page 148, note 8, line 2, *for* E. Onslow *read* E. of Onslow

Page 148, note 10, line 7, *after* 1774 *insert* (*London Chronicle* 20–22
Jan. 1774, xxxv. 78).   *Line 8, for* 1779 *read* 1778 (*London Chronicle*
24–26 Dec. 1778, xliv. 610)

Page 150, note 19, last line, *after* Oct. 1741 *add* OS   *for* 15 Dec. 1743 *read* 11 Dec. 1743 OS   *at end add* (MANN i. 167, ii. 355, vii. 350).

Page 150, note 23, *add* See also Hazen, *Bibl. of HW* 56–62; James Edwards to HW 21 Oct. 1791.

Page 154, note 48, *for* ca 1706 *read* 1706

Page 154, note 49, lines 1–13, *delete* The Casa Mannetti . . . 148). *and substitute* Mann's Casa Manetti is the palace now numbered Borgo S. Spirito 23/25. It was leased by Mann 1 Aug. 1740 from Giuseppe Manetti and his four brothers, the heirs of the senator Giovanni Manetti. The terms of the lease are to be found in the tythe-books in the Florentine state archives: *Decime Granducali, Giustificasioni di città dell' anno 1740*, No. 210, and *Decime Granducali, Arroti del Quarteriere di Santo Spirito dell' anno 1740*, No. 75 (information from Dott. Ferdinando Sartini, Director of the Archivio di Stato di Firenze). See also HW to West 4 Dec. 1740 NS (GRAY i. 237).   *Last 4 lines, delete* Part of the . . . 1740, N.S.

Page 157, note 3, line 1, *for* 1733 *read* ca 1732   *Line 4, add* See *Proceedings of the Suffolk Institute of Archæology*, 1891, vii. 359.

Page 160, note 2, *add* De Visme is probably the 'De Vyme' who dined in company with Edmond Malone 6 Aug. 1791; he had been in Lisbon for forty years and returned to England for his health (Sir James Prior, *Life of Edmond Malone*, 1860, pp. 409–12). A Mr Devisme is listed in HW's 'Book of Visitors,' *sub* 8 Sept. 1791 and 21 July 1796 (*post* BERRY ii. 239, 251).

Page 163, note 9, line 2, *for* 1750 *read* 1751   *Line 6, for* sister *read* friend

Page 167, note 6, *add* See also OSSORY ii. 360, 474–5, 569, n. 10; DALRYMPLE 167–8, n. 13.

Page 169, note 19, last line, *for Laetitia read Lætitia*

Page 170, note 22, *substitute* 'The bibliographical evidence . . . makes it clear that HW ordered such extensive corrections, that the publication was delayed to enable Bodoni to prepare cancels' (Hazen, *Bibl. of HW* 56). The Bodoni *Castle of Otranto* was not published until Oct. 1791, but there are extant copies bearing an uncancelled 1790 title-page; see ibid. 57–63.

Page 174, 1st paragraph, line 1, *for* lask *read* last

Page 174, 1st paragraph, line 6, *on* Clivden *add note* 1a: 1a. See HW to Jane Pope 30 Dec. 1790, MISC. CORR. iii. 306–7.

Page 177, note 5, line 1, *for* (fl. 1785–1807) *read* (ca 1764–1828)   *Last line, add* See MISC. CORR. iii. 263 and n. 1.

Page 179, note 3, *add* The Queen's actual birthday was 19 May; it was celebrated 18 Jan. (see *post* BERRY i. 272).

Page 184, note 11, line 6, *for* ca 1769 *read* 1768   *Last line, after* 1818 *add*   ; Lady Mary Coke, *Journals* ii. 366–7, 369, *et passim*

Page 185, last line of 1st paragraph, *on* two. *add note* 13a: 13a. Lady Mary Coke has a slightly different version of this anecdote in 'MS Journals' 8 Jan. 1791. An analogue appeared in *London Chronicle* 20–22 Oct. 1778, xliv. 391: 'The King of Prussia having conceived a disgust at one of his Pages, sent him with a letter to a General Officer, directing that the bearer should receive a certain number of lashes. The Page, inspecting the contents, and meeting a Jew, pretended particular business, and begged he would deliver the letter: the Jew did so, and received the lashes. The King, hearing of the affair, sent for the Page, and forgave him.'

Page 186, note 22, lines 1–2, *for* Tippoo Sahib (1753–99), Sultan of Mysore 1782–99. *read* Tipu Sultan (1750–99), ruler of Mysore, 1782 (as Nawab Tipu Sultan Bahadur); Padshah, 1787; known as Tipu Saheb (Mohibbul Hasan, *History of Tipu Sultan*, Calcutta, 1971, pp. 6, 24, 110).

Page 187, note 28, line 2, *for* 1768 *read* 1784

Page 191, note 12, line 5, *after* 1802 *add* ; Barnstables 1806–12

Page 191, note 13, line 9, *after* pages *insert* HW's copy is Hazen, *Cat. of HW's Lib.* No. 1810:50:1

Page 193, note 3, *add* 'Le comte de Coigny . . . composa d'agréables historiettes en prose et en vers. Il a aussi laissé en manuscrit la relation de la campagne d'Italie de 1733 à 1734' (NBG).

Page 195, note 11, line 4, *for* 1770–83 *read* 1770–82   *Last line, after* 77 *add* ; *London Chronicle* 19–21 Nov. 1782, lii. 493; *Dizionario biografico degli Italiani*, 1960– , vi. 211–13

Page 201, note 6, line 3, *after* M. P. *insert* Wigtown Burghs 1775–80, New

Page 207, note 12, line 6, *for* 1764 *read* ca 1765–8   *Last line, after* passim *add* ; J. J. Cotton, 'The Second Mrs Hastings and her Sons,' *Bengal Past and Present*, 1925, xxx. 11–13

Page 208, note 20, *for* 1727 *read* 1725

Page 210, illustration, in caption *for* Mrs. *read* Mrs

Page 212, note 2, line 1, *for* 1682 *read* ca 1682

Page 214, 3d paragraph, line 11, *on* dickybirds *add note* 15a: 15a. The earliest use of the word 'dicky-bird' recorded in OED is ca 1845.

Page 214, note 8, *add* See MORE 365.

Page 215, note 17, lines 2–5, *delete* There . . . Gluck's. *and substitute* The pantomime by Lewis Theobald, produced by John Rich, apparently first acted at Covent Garden 12 Feb. 1740 (see MASON ii. 4, n. 2; *London Stage* Part III, ii. 819–20, 924).

Page 215, note 18, *after* 1780 *add* , MASON ii. 4, n. 3

Page 216, note 27, line 1, *delete* Possibly   *Last line, add* Carnivalli was acting manager at the King's Opera House in 1786–7 (*London Stage* Part V, ii. 828, 920; advertisements in the *Morning Chronicle* 1787). In January 1790 he opened a very select, expensive and fashionable puppet theatre in Savile Row, presenting French light operas, under the then common Fantoccini. After three months, in March 1790, he sold out to Lord Barrymore, and his season ended on April 9. Lord Barrymore ran the theatre for his own private theatricals, and the next year it reverted to puppets (advertisements in the *World* from 26 Dec. 1789; information from G. V. Speaight). Carnivalli's wife was a singer at the King's theatre 7 Jan.–21 June 1783 and 18 March–8 June 1784, and an actress at Covent Garden 17 April–3 May 1792 (*London Stage* op. cit. i. 552, ii. 643, 1385).

Page 218, line 2, *for* Mrs. *read* Mrs

Page 218, note 14, line 1, *for* Marie-Auguste Vestris-Allard *read* Marie-Jean-Augustin Vestris, called Vestr'Allard   *Line 4, after* encyclopédie *add*   ; *Enciclopedia dello spettacolo*, Rome, 1954–66, ix. 1626–7

Page 218, note 15, *add* She died in August 1803, at Calais, according to Michael Kelly, *Reminiscences*, 2d edn, 1826, ii. 365.

Page 219, note 24, line 3, *before* Karl *insert* Christian Friedrich   *Line 4, for* Anspach *read* Ansbach

Pages 229–30, note 20, *add* See also Namier and Brooke ii. 182–3.

Page 233, line 2, *on* Bastile *add note* 10a: 10a. Actually seven; see Ossory iii. 158 and n. 13.

Page 238, note 18, line 9, *for* license *read* licence

Page 239, note 23, line 8, *after* skepticism *insert* (see CONWAY iii. 475–7).

Page 241, note 6, right column, line 1, *after* 16 Oct. 1791 *add*   ; see also Ossory iii. 110

Pages 242–3, note 17, *add* An advertisement of 'Joseph Merlin,' 'No. 42, Little Queen Anne Street, Marylebone' appears in the *Public Advertiser* 3 Sept. 1773.

Page 243, note 27, line 2, *for* (d. 1840) *read* (1767–1840)   *Line 4, after* Lucan *add*   ; E. K. Waterhouse, *Sir Joshua Reynolds*, 1941, plate 260.

Page 247, note 4, *add* Six of these drawings are now WSL; for one of them see *Fables*, 1797, p. 165.

Page 254, note 18, line 1, *for* 1756 *read* 1752   *Line 8, delete and substitute* 1785; HW's copy, dated 'June' by HW on the title-page, is now at Harvard (see Hazen, *Cat. of HW's Lib.* No. 3222:20:12; Ossory ii. 462, n. 5).

Page 255, note 23, line 3, *after* Sussex *insert*   , 1787

Page 258, note 10, *add* Her English relationships are given in the *London Chronicle* 15–18 Aug. 1772, xxxii. 162.

Page 263, note 12, line 4, *for* about 1755 *read* ca 1754   *Lines 5–6, after passim add*   ; CHUTE 185

Page 264, note 23, line 1, *for* (d. 1817) *read* (1759–1817)   *Last line, add* See HW to Mann 4 March 1759 where he is called 5th son; also the 5th son in HW's MS pedigree is 'Horatio' (MANN v. 279, n. 10).

Page 265, note 30, line 2, *for* 58 *read* 57

Page 268, note 5, *add* In HW's copy of *Description of SH*, 1774 (now WSL), the MS 'More Additions' on the last fly-leaf lists 'Sketches of Italian Peasants, 1790 by ditto [M. B.] in a small book.'

Page 268, note 8, right column, line 4, *delete* de Belle-Isle   *for* Duc *read* Comte   *Line 5, after* battle *add* (see MANN v. 221, n. 9)

Pages 268–9, note 10, *add* For Benjamin Franklin's talk with Georgiana's younger sister see *Mr Franklin, a Selection from his Personal Letters*, ed. L. W. Labaree and W. J. Bell, Jr, 1956, p. 23.

Page 272, line 1, *on* birthday *add note* 35a: 35a. This was the Queen's actual birthday, 19 May; it was celebrated on 18 Jan. (see *ante* 15 Jan. 1791, BERRY i. 179).

Page 272, note 38, *add* Mrs Damer's copy, containing her bookplate (designed by Agnes Berry) and her signature on both title-pages, was sold Sotheby's 25 March 1974, lot 66, to Dawsons of Pall Mall.

Page 274, note 20, last line, *after* 1789 *add*   , when HW sent it to the Berrys (*ante* 28 April 1789; Hazen, *Cat. of HW's Lib.* No. 3809).

Page 276, note 30, *substitute* Probably 23 April 1771, when HW, Goldsmith, and Johnson were present at the annual dinner of the Royal Academy; see HW to Bewley 23 May 1778, CHATTERTON 129 and n. 77. It is possible that HW met Goldsmith and Johnson at the Royal Academy Exhibition of 1770, when Reynolds exhibited portraits of Goldsmith and Johnson. HW in his copy of the catalogue of the exhibition (now *penes* Lord Rosebery) identified No. 151, 'A portrait of a gentleman,' as 'Dr Goldsmith,' and No. 152, similarly described, as 'Dr Johnson.'

Page 277, note 34, at beginning *insert* 'Did you hear that H. W. sent back with disdain the letter he received from Johnson's committee?' (Michael Lort to George Steevens, Brighton, 19 Feb. 1790, MS in Adam Collection, University of Rochester).

Page 278, note 46, lines 14–18, *delete* HW had heard . . . Lodge himself; *and substitute* HW was asked to be a subscriber by George Nicol, through whom HW communicated with Lodge (HW to Nicol 6 July 1790, 13 March 1791, MISC. CORR. iii. 285–6, 312–15   *Line 21, after* i. 166 *add* (Hazen, *Cat. of HW's Lib.* No. 455)   *Last line, add* Lodge included a memoir of HW in *Portraits of Illustrious Personages of Great Britain . . . with Biographical and Historical Memoirs*, begun in 1814 and completed in 40 parts in 1834, reprinted in 12 vols in 1835. Of this memoir Lodge wrote to Sir Samuel Egerton Brydges ca 18 April 1831: 'I would ask of you a memoir of H. Walpole. Such a character, both as a man and as an author, demands a higher order of criticism than I ever had to devote to him; and now, feeling as I do, I am very unwilling to treat him, as I should, with injustice. Even were I sufficiently capable, I could scarcely trust myself with the task, for I was personally acquainted with him, and such was the the [*sic*] fascination of his society that I could scarcely allow myself to believe that he had faults, even in spite of certain charges which amounted almost to evidence. The simple truth however is that I tremble at the thought of undertaking a subject which, in your hands, it would be but a relaxation from severer studies to touch with those graces that flow without effort from your pen. Should you be charitably inclined to pity my weakness, and pardon my impudence, I will go so far as to say, in addition, that if it were in my hands by the 1st of June, it would be in abundant good time' (MS in the Osborn Collection, Beinecke Library, Yale University).

Page 278, note 51, line 2, *for* ca 1528 *read* ca 1522

Page 282, note 14, left column, lines 3–4, *delete* nieces; but it is possible that they were her   *Last line, add* They were in a 'private madhouse' in 1793; see *post* 4 July 1791, BERRY i. 306; OSSORY iii. 187; FAMILY 53, n. 3.

Page 286, note 22, line 2, *after* 1791). *insert* HW's letter of invitation 27 May 1791 is printed in MISC. CORR. iii. 326   *after* Sir John *delete* Saunders

Page 286, note 24, *substitute* Two drawings by Miss Sebright, 1789 (playing cards, the Ace of Hearts and Ace of Diamonds) are in HW's *Description of SH*, 1774, now WSL, which contains over 50 drawings bound in at the end; see Hazen, *Cat. of HW's Lib.* No. 3641.

Page 291, note 11, last line, *after* 285–6 *add*   ; CONWAY iii. 492

Page 291, note 12, line 4, *after* Cambridge *insert*   ; it is now WSL *Last line, add* See Hazen, *Cat. of HW's Lib.* No. 1360.

Page 292, note 18, last line, *after* 55 *add* (Hazen, *Cat. of HW's Lib.* No. 1138)

Page 294, note 5, *substitute* Pitt proposed to the King 29 Jan. 1791 'that Lord Hawkesbury might in that case be induced to take the office of Master of the Mint, especially if your Majesty should see no objection to the farther suggestion of his being summoned to the Cabinet as President of the Committee of Council for Trade'; to which the King agreed on the same day (*The Later Correspondence of George III*, ed. A. Aspinall, 1962–70, i. 516–17). On 29 April Pitt suggested 'admitting Lord Hawkesbury, as President of the Committee of Trade, to a seat in the Cabinet' (ibid. i. 530); the King answered 30 April, 'Lord Hawkesbury should certainly be called to the Cabinet when the arrangement takes place' (J. H. Rose, *Pitt and Napoleon*, 1912, p. 222). Hawkesbury was present at a Cabinet meeting on 10 Nov. 1791 (Aspinall, op. cit. i. 575). He is listed in the Cabinets from April–June 1791 to Nov. 1803 in the chart at the end of *English Historical Documents 1783–1832*, vol. xi, ed. A. Aspinall and E. Anthony Smith, New York, 1959.

Page 294, note 6, line 8, *after* v. 155 *add*   ; Hazen, *Cat. of HW's Lib.* No. 2941

Page 302, note 27, line 5, *after* WSL *insert* (Hazen, *Cat. of HW's Lib.* No. 1810:49:6)

Page 306, note 17, *add* Mr Brown of Egham, Surrey, was taking care of the two Misses Daye in 1793 (see OSSORY iii. 186–7).

Page 307, note 27, line 1, *for* Gaspare Pacchierotti *read* Gasparo Pacchiarotti (Pacchierotti)   *for* 1744 *read* 1740   *Line 4, after* Enciclopedia italiana; insert The New Grove Dictionary of Music and Musicians, 6th edn, ed. Stanley Sadie, 1980, xiv. 42–3;

Page 312, note 16, right column, line 2, *after* 90 *insert* (Hazen, *Cat. of HW's Lib*. No. 367)

Page 320, note 12, *add* HW's copy of her *Poems*, 1786, is Hazen, *Cat. of HW's Lib*. No. 2989.

Page 322, note 21, *for* Comb *read* Combe

Page 326, note 6, line 8, *before* Collins *insert Leinster Corr*. iii. 142, 144, 147;

Page 332, note 11, *for* 1496 *read* 1495

Page 333, note 12, last line, *after* 173 *insert*   ; Hazen, *Cat. of HW's Lib*. No. 3084

Page 333, note 14, right column, line 5, *for* John *read* Frederick

Page 340, line 4, *for* Mrs. *read* Mrs

Page 341, 2d paragraph, line 1, *on* boat-race *add note* 11a: 11a. There is a printed programme of the race, with MS notes by HW, in one of Daniel Lysons's volumes of *Collectanea* in the BM ('Public Exhibitions and Places of Amusement,' iv. 281): *on* Richmond/ Boat Race HW notes, 'for a silver cup given by Lord Robert Spencer'; *on* Monday, August, 22, 1791 HW notes, 'the Birthday of the Duke of Clarence.' Lysons has pasted a cutting from the *Morning Chronicle* 26 Aug. 1791 headed 'The Duke of Clarence's Birthday' which reports: 'The accounts of the festivities at Richmond, in honour of his Royal Highness's Birthday, on Monday last, having been imperfect, or erroneous, we are favoured by a correspondent with the following: A boat race, in the morning, collected a vast concourse of people of all ranks, desirous of testifying their joy on the occasion. A silver cup, given by the Right Hon. Lord R[obert] Spencer, was rowed for and won by R[ichard] Love. Two inferior prizes, given by the Hon. Edward Bouverie, were adjudged to [Robert] Fisher and [John] Mitchell. Lord R. Spencer, delivering the cup to the winner, his Royal Highness's health was drank, with three times three, and the health of Lord R. Spencer, Lady D. Beauclerk, and the Hon. E. Bouverie, were drank with three cheers. His Royal Highness then retired to the house of Lady D. Beauclerk, with a select party, where an elegant breakfast was prepared, and a dinner at her Ladyship's expense was prepared for the rowers at the Three Pigeons.'

Page 341, note 12, *for* Richmond Castle *read* The Castle Inn at Richmond (see the *Morning Chronicle* 26 Aug. 1791)

Page 342, note 18, *at beginning insert* 'In the evening the company went to a ball and supper at the Castle Inn. His Royal Highness appeared at nine o'clock; the dance began and continued with great animation till past twelve, when the company retired to supper . . . the company then returned to the ball-room, and continued dancing till four in the morning' (*Morning Chronicle* 26 Aug. 1791).

Page 342, note 24, line 1, *for* 13 Oct. *read* 30 Oct.

Page 345, 2d paragraph, line 3, *on* Presbytyrants *add note* 4a: 4a. See

also HW to Lady Ossory 8 Aug. and to Hannah More 29 Sept. 1791 (Os-
SORY iii. 116; MORE 361).

Page 348, 1st paragraph, line 16, *on* century *add note* 4a: 4a. This was
discussed in the National Assembly 30 Aug.; see *Journal de Paris* 31 Aug.,
3, 4 Sept. (CONWAY iii. 486 and n. 9).

Page 349, note 10, line 1, *for* ca 1745 *read* ca 1731

Page 355, note 18, line 2, *for* 13 Sept. *read* 14 Sept.   *Last line, after*
1791 *add*   ; OSSORY iii. 124, n. 17

Page 361, note 16, line 1, *for* 13 *read* 30   *Lines 2–3, delete* (erroneous-
ly under the date of 30 Oct.)   *3d line from end, after* lxxvi *add*   ; Os-
SORY iii. 132–3, n. 22

Page 375, note 1, *add* This may have had some connection with the long
and eulogistic article on HW and his 'intentions' towards the Berrys which
appeared in the *General Magazine and Impartial Review*, Dec. 1791, v. 6,
29–31.

Page 376, note 3, *add* The *World* 13 Dec. 1791 reported: 'Earl Orford.—
The sensibility which occasioned the death of this Nobleman does honour
to his memory. The attentions of Mrs Turk had, at one period of his life,
called him back to reason. Never had he forgotten this circumstance. On
her death, he relapsed into phrenzy, from which medical aid for a time
relieved him; but the wound he had sustained at his heart, was not to be
so cured. He lingered for a time on a bed of sorrow more than sickness—
which at length proved too powerful for his constitution. It may be
doubted whether Horace Walpole will leave the sweets of Strawberry Hill
even for Houghton, grand and impressive as it may be. For him the game,
so nourished by Lord Orford, will perhaps have no charms. The Swaffham
Coursing Meeting will lose a great supporter by Lord Orford's death. His
dogs were reckoned amongst the best there.'

VOLUME 12

Page 5, note 2, line 8, *for* eld. dau. *read* 2d dau.

Page 5, 2d paragraph, line 3, *on* Richmondists *add note* 2a: 2a. See
MORE 392.

Page 10, To Mary Berry 25 Sept. 1793, *Address, on* Free Orford *add
note a*: a. For this style of franking see DALRYMPLE 240, n. 1.

Page 20, note 2, line 5, *for* 2d E. Mansfield *read* 2d E. of Mansfield

Page 26, note 22, line 2, *after* 1766 *add* and also to Mann 23 Dec. 1742 OS

Page 27, 1st paragraph, line 16, *on* dozen *add note* 7a: 7a. For seventeen
visitors grown to seventeen dozen, see Falstaff's account of his fight at
Gadshill, *I Henry IV*. ii. iv. 29 (pointed out by Lindsay Fleming).

Page 29, note 19, line 1, *for* 1746 *read* ?1746

Page 29, note 20, *add* His son refers to him in 1826 as 'very lame' (Sir

Daniel Lysons, *Early Reminiscences*, 1896) (information from Lindsay Fleming).

Page 32, note 18, line 5, *for* (d. 1705, aged 82, 93, or 97) *read* (ca 1623–1705)

Page 33, note 21, *add* Namier and Brooke iii. 463 lists her as Elizabeth Falconer or Faulkner.

Page 33, note 22, *add* The British bands played it at Yorktown (information from the late Leonard Bacon).

Page 36, illustration, *add to legend* 'The original [of Lawrence's drawing], which was made for Samuel Lysons Esq., is at his chambers in the Temple' (Daniel Lysons, *Supplement to . . . the Environs of London*, 1811, p. 316, n. 14).

Page 37, To Mary Berry 19 Oct. 1793, line 10, *on* disorder *add note* 1a:
1a. Mrs Damer wrote Mary Berry 8 Oct. 1793 (*Berry Papers*, ed. Lewis Melville, 1914, p. 106), quoted in headnote to HW to Lady Ailesbury 30 Sept. or 1 Oct. 1793, CONWAY iii. 507.

Page 37, note 2, *add* See CONWAY iii. 505 and n. 30.

Page 40, note 11, line 8, *for* 1785–96 *read* 1783–96

Page 42, note 3, line 9, *for* contemporaries *read* cotemporaries

Page 43, note 4, line 1, *for* ca 1716 *read* 1715   *Line 14, for* of the Princess of Wales, in 1772, *read* of the Prince of Wales, in 1751,   *Line 22, after* Castle), *insert* From 1752 to 1768 she was Housekeeper to the Princess Dowager of Wales, and from 1768 to 1772 she was also Bedchamber Woman in the household of the Princess Dowager (*Court and City Register* 1749–68 lists her as Housekeeper; 1769 as Bedchamber Woman; 1770–72 as both Housekeeper and Bedchamber Woman; see also MANN ix. 516, n. 5).   *Lines 25–31, delete* Both HW . . . not so listed in any of the available lists.   *Last 2 lines, for* Scott, loc. cit. *read* Scott, *Familiar Letters*, Boston, 1894, ii. 208–9

Page 48, note 1, line 3, *for* Claud *read* Claude

Page 50, note 8, *add* HW's copy is Hazen, *Cat. of HW's Lib.* No. 1810: 56:1.

Page 52, note 8, line 14, *after* 217–20 *insert* The Military Panorama, or Officer's Companion, Aug. 1813, ii. 395–404, with portrait facing p. 395;

Page 54, note 8, *add* See also CONWAY iii. 496, n. 7.

Page 55, note 16, last line, *after* annotated *add* (Hazen, *Cat. of HW's Lib.* No. 1609:39:7)

Page 55, note 18, last line, *after* 287 *add*   ; *Betsy Sheridan's Journal*, ed. William Le Fanu, New Brunswick, New Jersey, 1960, p. 184

Page 59, note 35, *add* For HW's copy see Hazen, *Cat. of HW's Lib.* No. 3435; see also HW to Samuel Lysons 17 Sept. 1789, 28 June 1790, DALRYMPLE 203–4.

Page 59, note 36, *add* HW's copy is Hazen, *Cat. of HW's Lib.* No. 3434.

Page 59, note 38, *add* HW's copy is Hazen, *Cat. of HW's Lib.* No. 3254.

Page 63, note 22, line 1, *for* 1726 *read* 1725

Page 74, note 44, line 5, *for* (1704–76) *read* (1703–76)

Page 76, note 5, line 1, *for* Not identified; *read* I. P. Huitson, who is identified by his nephew, J. Deere, as 'surgeon to the late Lord Orford' in a MS now WSL (quoted in ADD. AND CORR. on vol. 30, p. 377; see also OSSORY iii. 193 and n. 1).   *Lines 5–6, for last sentence substitute* HW spells the name 'Hewetson' or 'Huitson' (*post* 25 June, 24 Aug. 1796; 'Book of Visitors,' BERRY ii. 235, 241, 248, 250).

Page 78, note 3, *add* See also *London Stage* Part V, iii. 1586, 1602.

Page 79, note 6, *add* See *London Stage* Part V, iii. 1592–4, 1596, 1597, 1599, 1602–4.

Page 81, note 17, line 9, *after* Pellew *insert* [Capt. R.N.; Kt, 29 June 1793; cr. (1796) Bt, (1814) Bn Exmouth, and (1816) Vct Exmouth; M.P.]

Page 92, note 13, last line, *after* 70 *add* (Hazen, *Cat. of HW's Lib.* No. 3254)

Page 93, note 15, *add* This anecdote, applied to Sir William Temple when 'ambassador to the States of Holland, in the reign of Charles the Second,' appears in *The Town and Country Jester* [1780], pp. 36–7. The same anecdote, applied to the Earl of Stair, ambassador to The Hague 1742–3, appears in *Lord Chesterfield's Witticisms; or, the Grand Pantheon of Genius, Sentiment, and Taste* . . . [1773], pp. 33–4 (WSL's copy); *The Museum of Entertainment; or, Magazine of Wit* [1780], p. 99; and there is an abbreviated version of the story in *Thraliana,* ed. Katharine C. Balderston, Oxford, 1942, ii. 855–6, under date of 27 Feb. 1793.

Page 94, note 20, line 1, *for* 1741 *read* 1738   *Line 2, for* William Courtenay by Lady Jane Stuart *read* Henry Courtenay, a revenue officer in Ireland, by Mary Major   *Line 3, after* poetaster *add* (Namier and Brooke ii. 261–2)

Page 94, note 25, *add* In *Hasty Productions,* Norwich, 1791, this essay and another dated from Eriswell 28 Sept. 1789 are printed pp. 52–81 (WSL's copy).

Page 99, note 13, line 1, *for* ca 1759 *read* 1756   *Line 12, after* 3 May *add* (*London Stage* Part V, iii. 1640–1, 1644)

Page 101, note 7, line 4, *after* 1787 *add* (CHUTE 539 and n. 8)   *Last line, add* See also *Country Seats* 62.

Page 103, note 11, *add* Mary Berry and her father were at Park Place in July, while Agnes was at Cheltenham (*ante* 31 July 1794); HW was at Park Place 4–13 Sept. 1794 (OSSORY iii. 202, 204; DALRYMPLE 251).

Page 104, note 13, last line, *after* WSL *add*   ; the fourth volume, in boards in 1842, now in matching red morocco, is also WSL (Hazen, *Cat. of HW's Lib.* No. 3859)

Page 107, note 7, line 3, *for* (d. 1783) *read* (ca 1730–83)   *Last line, after* 1818 *add*   ; Namier and Brooke ii. 385–6

Page 107, note 10, lines 2–3, *for* 11th E. of Pembroke and Montgomery *read* 11th E. of Pembroke and 8th E. of Montgomery

Page 108, note 14, line 6, *after* iv. 95; *insert* another edition of the

Carmina was sold SH vii. 118 (see Hazen, *Cat. of HW's Lib.* Nos 2232, 3802); *Line 8, after* iii. 161 *add* (Hazen, op. cit. No. 1823; see also Nos 3917, 4001)

Page 111, note 25, left column, line 10, *after* 75 *insert* It was printed in the *European Magazine* Aug. 1788, xii. 96

Page 111, note 29, right column, line 14, *after* Cleves). *add* For an illustration of it and other details of its history ('offered for sale at auction in 1757–8 but bought in; subsequently in the collection of Francis Douce, by whom it was bequeathed, 1834, to Sir Samuel Rush Meyrick, from whose heir it passed to Miss Davies, from whom it was acquired by the present owner,' George Salting), see Burlington Fine Arts Club, *Exhibition Illustrative of Early English Portraiture*, 1909, pp. 115–16 and Plate XXXII, No. 4. On p. 116 is a reference to *Archæologia*, xl, p. 77, and a notation that the picture was in the Exhibition of Art Treasures, Manchester, 1857, No. 58. See also GM 1836, new ser. v. 251.

Page 112, note 31, *add* In HW's copy of Hasted's *Kent* (iii. 665) is HW's note on this passage: 'This description of Lee was written by Mr Horace Walpole' (see Hazen, *Cat. of HW's Lib.* No. 3).

Page 120, note 9, *add* It was Guatemotzin (or Guatemoc) (d. 1525), Aztec emperor, nephew and son-in-law of Montezuma, who being tortured by the Spaniards to make him reveal hidden treasures, answered a companion in torture, 'Am I upon a bed of roses?' See NBG, *sub* 'Quauhtemotzin'; Edmund and William Burke, *An Account of the European Settlements in America*, 5th edn, 1770, i. 125; Arthur Murphy, *Alzuma, A Tragedy*, 1773, 'Advertisement,' pp. ii–iii, where the names of Atabalipa and Guatimozin are brought together; William Robertson, *The History of America*, 1777, ii. 126–7; MASON ii. 102, n. 19.

Page 120, note 10, *substitute* Edward Jerningham, *The Fall of Mexico. A Poem*, 1775, has prefixed an Advertisement: 'Guatimozino, the last Emperor of Mexico . . . was at length . . . taken prisoner. In order to extort from him a discovery of the principal mines, he was laid on burning coals. The second in command was also condemned to the same torture, and amidst his sufferings called upon his royal master to be released from the vow of secrecy, which drew from Guatimozino these memorable words: "Am I on a bed of roses?" Dryden has put these words into the mouth of Montezuma, contrary to the testimony of the historians' (*London Chronicle* 7–9 Nov. 1775, xxxviii. 449). HW's copy of Jerningham's poem is Hazen, *Cat. of HW's Lib.* No. 3222:14:8.

Page 129, note 9, *add* See also *London Stage* Part V, iii. 1692.

Page 136, note 5, lines 4–5, *for* ca 1472–1533) *read* 1478–between 1533 and 1536)

Page 137, note 5, left column, lines 18–19, *for* Lord Derby, Knowsley Hall *read* WSL

Page 139, note 1, *add* Misdated 19 Aug. by Mrs Toynbee.

Page 140, note 4, *add* HW had also come across the Scythian lamb in

Bayle's *Dictionary,* as is shown by an extract he made in his *MS Commonplace Book,* 1750, p. 31, now WSL.

Page 141, note 12, line 2, *for* Lansdowne *read* Lansdown

Page 141, note 13, line 1, *for* Lansdowne's *read* Lansdown's

Page 141, note 14, *add* See also HW to Daniel Lysons 15 Aug. 1795, DALRYMPLE 267.

Page 143, line 2, *on* settlement *add note* 23a: 23a. That is, his alleged settlement.

Page 143, note 24, *substitute* HW wrote the Rev. Mark Noble 29 Aug. 1795: 'I am rather surprised, Sir, that you gave any credit to that most unfounded article of my settlement of this place on Lord H. It is very rarely indeed that newspapers deserve any faith at all . . .' (see MISC. CORR. iii. 320).

Page 143, note 1, left column, last line, *after* 40). *insert* For a lawsuit which Davenport brought vs [?Edward] Chapman for making bricks in the common field at Teddington, see *Daily Adv.* 4 March, 16 July 1772.

Page 144, note 4, *substitute* The bust of Mary Berry, in terra-cotta, executed by Mrs Damer, is listed by HW in a note in his extra-illustrated *Des. of SH,* 1784 (now WSL), p. 96: 'In Lord Orford's closet next to his bedchamber in the attic, a bust in terra cotta of Miss Mary Berry by Mrs Damer 1794.' This note and two others on the page were not printed in 'Des. of SH,' *Works* ii. See illustration. See also 'Book of Visitors,' BERRY ii. 274.

Page 148, 2d paragraph, line 8, *on Aunt add note* 11a: 11a. 'This must have been Merrial Paton [Patton on the genealogical chart, pp. viii–ix], née Docksey,' dau. of Elizabeth Merrial Garrick (sister of David Garrick) by Thomas Docksey (Carola Oman Lenanton, *David Garrick,* 1958, p. 380). Since her mother was born 19 Dec. 1724 (d. 20 April 1799), Mrs Paton would hardly have been elderly in 1795, but might have looked so, since she had 13 children.

Page 149, note 1, line 1, *before* Volumes *insert* See HW's letters to him 27 Sept., 29 Oct. 1795, DALRYMPLE 270, 272.   *Lines 4–5, delete last sentence and substitute* Four volumes were sold SH vii. 135 and are now WSL; see Hazen, *Cat. of HW's Lib.* No. 3859.

Page 154, note 38, last line, *after* 528–9 *add*   , ix. 31

Page 155, note 43, line 1, *for* a mile *read* 2 miles   *Line 2, for* Robbins *read* Robins   *Line 4, after* 1753 *add*   , CHUTE 152; SELWYN 120, n. 3

Page 156, note 10, line 11, *after* 97 *add*   , Hazen, *Cat. of HW's Lib.* No. 558

Page 159, note 30, line 2, *for* 1777 *read* 1779   *Line 8, after* 263 *add* Lady Mary Coke, 'MS Journals' 10 Jan., 19 July, 21 Aug. 1779; HW to Lady Browne 18 Dec. 1778, MORE 194 and n. 14

Page 165, note 17, line 1, *for* ca 1512 *read* 1512

Page 165, note 18, line 1, *for* ca 1505 *read* ca 1508

Page 169, note 8, *add* See MORE 286.

Page 178, note 6, *add* See Hazen, *Cat. of HW's Lib.* Nos 2910, 3247, 3650.

Page 179, note 7, lines 5–10, *delete* This paragraph . . . superannuated. *and substitute* In 1787 HW wrote Lady Ossory that he had offered Cowie an annuity, which was refused, 'so I have been forced to keep him' (OS-SORY ii. 567; see also CONWAY iii. 416 and n. 2). Before 1793 Christopher Vickers became HW's gardener (see *ante* BERRY i. 369, n. 3).

Page 180, note 11, *add* Robert Blake was HW's attorney in the settlement of George, Lord Orford's will; see MISC. CORR. iii. 348, n. 2.

Page 180, note 12, *add* A copy of these volumes was apparently sent to SH by the author or publisher (see Hazen, *Cat. of HW's Lib.* No. 3304).

Page 181, note 16, line 3, *after* Walpole *add* (FAMILY 27–32, 295–304)

Page 184, From Mary Berry 19 May 1796, note 1, line 4, *after* O'Hara *add* 'at the end of April 1796'

Page 185, note 4, line 5, *for* 1794 *read* 1794–6   *Line 7, after* £3 *insert* (in the SH catalogue the volumes are described as 'elegantly bound in russia'; see Hazen, *Cat. of HW's Lib.* No. 3566)   *Lines 7–8, for* The frontispiece to the second volume *read* In Vol. II, facing p. 2,

Page 189, note 1, *after* surgeon *add* I. P. Huitson, identified by his nephew J. Deere: 'My uncle I. P. Huitson was surgeon to the late Lord Orford and in conformity to the above order opened his Lordship's body' (MS now WSL, quoted ADD. AND CORR. on vol. 30, p. 377).

Page 190, To Mary Berry 25 June 1796, *bis*, headnote, *add* Sold Southgate 25 [26] Nov. 1847 (Charles Hamilton Sale), lot 426; sold Christie and Manson 23 [26] July 1856 (H. B. Ray Sale), lot 946; sold Sotheby's 23 April 1894 (Collection of Autograph Letters Sale), lot 146, to Pearson and Co. for £1. 2s.; sold Sotheby's 15 April 1918 (Morrison Sale II), lot 896, to Maggs for £1. 11s.

Page 196, note 5, line 6, *for* 1797–1806 *read* 1797–1805   *for* 1806–16 *read* 1805–16

Page 196, note 9, lines 8–10, *delete* vicar of Great Finborough, Suffolk, 1764–98; vicar of Haughley 1771–98   *Line 11, add* Venn seems to have confused this Thomas Hutchinson (b. ca 1726) with another Thomas Hutchinson (ca 1734–98) who is also described as vicar of Great Finborough 1764–98 and vicar of Haughley 1771–98; see GM 1798, lxviii pt i. 539

Page 198, note 4, last line, *after* George *add*   ; CHUTE 590–3

Page 198, note 8, *substitute* Probably Hon. Cecilia Byng (b. 1771), 3d child of John Byng, 5th Vct Torrington; m. (1805) J. Robert Gregge Hopwood (1773–1854), of Hopwood Hall, Lancashire (Collins, *Peerage*, 1812, vi. 98). 'She was a first cousin once removed of the Loveday sisters, and her sister, Bridget Augusta Herbert, was a close friend of Mary Loveday. . . . Moreover it is clear from letters here that Agnes was always particularly fond of Mrs Hopwood and that this friendship was recognized by the others as being special. Incidentally Agnes refers more than once to "Barbara" Seton in her letters' (Mrs Sarah Markham to WSL 28 March 1977, based on letters of the Loveday family in her possession).

Page 200, note 1, *for* 8 Nov. 1796 *read* 7 Nov. 1796; see OSSORY iii. 221–2 and n. 1

Page 200, note 7, line 5, *after* Dorset *insert* (*Public Advertiser* 14 Sept. 1773)

Page 201, note 16, last line, *after* 41 *add* ; Joseph Cradock, *Literary and Miscellaneous Memoirs*, 1828, iv. 276–8

Page 201, note 17, *add* See OSSORY ii. 284, n. 16.

Page 202, note 24, at beginning *insert* Presumably George James ('Gilly') Williams (*ante* BERRY i. 93, n. 11).   *Line 1, for* Daniel Lysons *read* Samuel Lysons   *Line 3, after* mother *insert* [brother]   *Last line, add* See also *ante* BERRY ii. 194; DALRYMPLE 327.

Page 204, note 5, line 1, *for* Daniel *read* Samuel

Page 204, note 9, *add* HW also quotes this line to Conway 10 April 1761 (CONWAY ii. 83).

Page 205, note 15, line 2, *for* 4th E. of Arundel *read* known as E. of Arundel after his marriage in 1138 or 1139

Page 208, To Mary Berry 24 Aug. 1796, *add headnote*: Printed in part in Wright vi. 531–2; Cunningham ix. 468–9; first printed in full in Toynbee xv. 418–20. The MS was in 1905 in the possession of Messrs Pearson and Co.

Page 210, To Mary Berry 7 Sept. 1796, *Address, after* Chichister *insert* [*sic*]

Page 210, note 13, *substitute* Probably Hon. Cecilia Byng (see ADD. AND CORR. on vol. 12, p. 198, n. 8).

Page 212, note 6, *add* See also OSSORY iii. 218.

Page 213, note 2, line 1, *for* 1717 *read* 1719

Page 215, note 10, *add* See Mary Berry to Penelope Benwell, Sunday 12 March 1797:

MARY BERRY TO PENELOPE BENWELL, Sunday 12 March 1797

Printed from a photostat of the MS in the possession of Mrs Sarah Markham, Wotton-under-Edge, Glos; first printed in N&Q 1978, new ser. xxv. 65–7. Penelope Benwell[1] was the eldest daughter of John Loveday (1711–89), of Caversham by his third wife, and the MS has remained in the possession of the Loveday family (see Mary Berry to Barbara Cecilia Seton 13 Nov. 1790, headnote, BERRY i. 137).

1. Penelope Loveday (ca 1759–1846), m. 1 (20 June 1796) Rev. William Benwell (ca 1765–96), fellow of Trinity College, Oxford, vicar of Hale Magna, co. Lincoln, 1794, rector of Chilton, Suffolk; m. 2 (18 March 1808) Rev. Dr John Hind (ca 1758–1832), fellow of Magdalen College, Oxford 1784–1808, vicar of Findon, Sussex 1807–32 (BERRY i. 137; GM 1796, lxvi pt i. 524, lxvi pt ii. 797; Foster, *Alumni Oxon. 1715–1886*, i. 98, ii. 665).

N. Audley St, Sunday 12 March.

Dearest Pen,

You would have heard from Agnes before this time on the subject of
your last kind and affectionate letter, had not I begged and promised to
write to you myself, which till today has been out of my power, for though
we were in the country from Wednesday last till yesterday, I found my
time much more occupied there than it had been in town, for in the necessary search which the executors made for papers etc. etc. at Strawberry
Hill, I was the best and indeed only person who could tell them where to
look, and from knowing what most of the cabinets etc. etc. contained
could spare them much trouble.

The state in which our poor friend had lived for this last twelve months
and the situation to which he was reduced during the last six weeks, made
his longer life, that is to say a prolongation of his suffering not to be desired by those who best loved him, and who had dreaded still more than
his death, seeing him long linger, alive only to the animal functions of
nature, and to a sense of the miseries of his own situation— As it is, we
have the satisfaction of thinking that his last moments were composed,
and without any great pain, and that our attentions and seeing us was
one of the last things of which he was sensible— Of the disposition of his
affairs you have probably heard before this time— To each of us two he
has left £4000—to my father the care of publishing such of his papers as
he has left for publication and the house at Twickenham to us, for both
our lives provided we either of us continue unmarried— To Mrs Damer
he has left Strawberry Hill for her life, and afterwards to go to his niece
Lady Waldegrave and her children. This last legacy essentially concerns
our comfort for had he left Strawberry Hill in present to Lady Waldegrave or indeed to anybody but an intimate friend of ours, such near
neighbours are we and the two places so open to one another, that it
would have been impossible for us to have continued to live there—as it
is, his Will will be completely fulfilled in everything there continuing to
be made as comfortable to us as possible— The enclosed paper will show
you the principal part of his other legacies: the sum of £59,155.0.0 is
made up by other smaller bequests to servants etc. etc. Mrs Damer and
Lord Frederick Campbell are executors and Mrs Damer residuary legatee,
but unfortunately such is at present the misera[ble] state of the Funds and
public credit, that the sum he has left (which is all in the stocks) is not
nearly equal to pay the sum of his legacies, so that except a peace or some
very favourable turn in public affairs, considerably raises the stocks within
this twelve months all our legacies must (in proportion) suffer a material
diminution, and Mrs Damer's office of residuary legatee be one of much
trouble, and no profit— In the meantime the looking over his papers, in
which I can materially assist Mrs Damer is an arduous undertaking which
is hardly begun yet, and this and the arrangement of such as are left to

my father for publication (which as yet we have not touched) and the doing honour and justice to the memory of our friend you may easily suppose will sufficiently occupy my time for many months to come.

The newspapers you will perhaps see full of his name and perhaps of ours— I have desired two or three of my friends to transcribe or cut me out all such paragraphs whatsoever, that I may know at least everything that is said, and in proper time and occasion answer or contradict what may require it—the disappointed expectations of many of his numerous family will probably make much ill nature upon the occasion— We, thank heaven, have the satisfaction of reflecting that had he not left us a farthing we should have done everything we did, and had he intended to have left us his fortune, we neither *could* nor *would* have done more.

So much for a subject, which nothing but the intimate persuasion I have of the sincere and lively interest you still my dearest Pen can take in our affairs and welfare could have induced to obtrude so long upon your notice.

In your last letter but one to Agnes you mention a subject which I assure you I had already thought of, and guessing what would be your wishes was going to propose sending you the bust[2] which was indeed long ago given to your other and dearer self[3]— Most of the world would call this recalling melancholy ideas, but I know your mind better than not to suppose it will be rather a soothing recollection to you and that the countenance of a being honoured by the esteem of the saint you have lost will never be an unpleasant companion to you— As soon as ever I have a moment's leisure, I will get the cast of the bust which was intended for you from Mrs D. and send it you carefully put upon in sawdust by the Marlborough wagon.

Farewell my dear Pen, for I am writing to you in no inconsiderable degree of pain from one of my accustomed dreadful stomach aches which never fail confining me to my room for three and often four days together—and fearing I might be worse tomorrow I was resolved to write today while it was at all in my power—which is now hardly the case— farewell and heaven protect and support you

M. B.

2. In April 1798 Mrs Benwell wrote in her diary: 'I have received a present from my dear friend Mary Berry of a beautiful cast of her head taken from a bust done by Mrs Damer. She had promised it to Mr Benwell when she saw him not long before our marriage and he had expressed much pleasure at the prospect of having so valued an ornament for our expected parsonage house' (N&Q 1978, new ser. xxv. 66–7). In March 1797 Mrs Benwell was living with her mother and sisters at Milton in Wiltshire. By the time the cast arrived they had moved to Hungerford. After her marriage to the Rev. Dr John Hind in 1808, Mrs Benwell lived at Findon in Sussex.

3. The Rev. William Benwell (who had died of a fever after only eleven weeks of marriage (see above, n. 1, and *London Chronicle* 23–25 June 1796, lxxix. 603, 10–13 Sept. 1796, lxxx. 251). A letter from Benwell to Mary Berry 27 Nov. 1794 is in MBJ i. 458–60.

[Enclosure]

To the Duchess of Gloucester	10,000. o. o.
To Lady Mary Churchill	2,000. o. o.
To Mr Churchill in trust for	
Mrs Dayes and then to Mr Churchill	3,500. o. o.
To Sir Horace Mann	5,000. o. o.
To Lady Waldegrave	5,000. o. o.
To Mrs Damer to keep up Strawberry Hill	2,000. o. o.
To Mrs Damer	4,000. o. o.
To Lady Ailesbury	4,000. o. o.
To Miss Berry	4,000. o. o.
To Miss A. Berry	4,000. o. o.
To Nephews and Nieces in legacies	
of £500 apiece	9,500. o. o.
To his deputy Mr Bedford	2,000. o. o.
To his clerk Mr Harris	1,500. o. o.
To Philip Colomb	1,500. o. o.
To the poor of Twickenham	300. o. o.
Total sum of legacies	59,155. o. o.

Page 219, 1st paragraph, line 17, *on* printed *add note* 1: 1. R. W. Ketton-Cremer, *Horace Walpole*, 1940, p. 311, prints entries for July 1788.

Page 221, title, *on* Strawberry Hill *add note a: a.* Tickets for seeing SH [Cat. of Mrs Damer's Sale, p. 16] 22 Aug. 1774–Capt. Kelly; 26 Aug. 1774–Col. Salive; Sept. 13, 1774–Lady Parry.

Page 226, *sub* 21 July, *on* Mr Hewett and 3 *add note* 3a: 3a. On the visitors for this week see HW to Lady Ossory 2 Aug. 1786, OSSORY ii. 522–3.

Page 226, *sub* 7 Aug., *on* Mr Brand *add note* 3b: 3b. John Brand (ca 1744–1806), rector of St-Mary-at-Hill and St Mary Hubbard, London, 1784; chaplain to the D. of Northumberland; F. S. A., 1777; secretary of S. A. 1784–1806 (Foster, *Alumni Oxon. 1715–1886*, i. 153). He wrote to Ralph Beilby from Sion House 14 Aug. 1786: 'Last Monday [7 Aug.], and not before, by favour of a letter from the honourable owner, I saw the famous villa and most valuable collection of pictures at Strawberry Hill' (*Letters of the Rev. John Brand . . . to Mr Ralph Beilby of Newcastle upon Tyne*, Newcastle upon Tyne, 1825, p. 18).

Page 226, *sub* 1 Sept., *on* Mr Ireland and 3 *add note* 5a: 5a. See DALRYMPLE 338.

Page 228, note 2a, *substitute* Semen Romanovich Vorontsov (1744–1832), Count, Russian ambassador to England 1785–1806 (see OSSORY iii. 68, n. 13).

Page 230, *sub* 20 June, *on* Mrs Soame *add note* 1: 1. Probably Susan Bunbury, sister of Sir Thomas Charles Bunbury, 6th Bt, 1764, m. (ca 1764–5) Henry Soame of Thurlow Hall, Suffolk (Burke, *Peerage and Baronetage*, 1926, p. 392; Countess of Ilchester and Lord Stavordale, *Life and Letters of Lady Sarah Lennox*, 1902, i. 153, 211).

Page 230, note 2, right column, lines 1–3, *delete* most of the tickets . . . but cf. *and substitute* Mr Railton deliberately broke the rule limiting each party to four people. Hazen, op. cit. 226–7, reproduces a copy of the 'printed ticket' before 1791 (beginning 'Mr Walpole is very ready to oblige . . .'; see also

Page 231, *sub* 28 August, *on* Mr Fisher *add note* 2a: 2a. John Fisher, secretary to the Board of Excise, 1784. The '3' are members of his family; see Welbore Ellis to HW ?23 Aug. 1788 (Misc. Corr. iii. 224–5).

Page 232, *sub* 20 Sept. 1788, *on* Lock *add note* 4a: 4a. William Lock (1732–1810), of Norbury Park, of whom there is a fine portrait by Sir Thomas Lawrence in the Museum of Fine Arts, Boston. He married (1767) Frederica Augusta Schaub (1750–1832); their eldest son was William (1767–1847). For other portraits by Lawrence of the Lock family see Vittoria Colonna Caetani, Duchessa di Sermoneta, *The Locks of Norbury*, 1940, pp. 220, 276, and *passim*.

Page 232, note 1, *at end add* The Bishop of London's visit must have been before 20 July 1789 (see HW to Hannah More 20 July 1789, More 312).

Page 234, *sub* 16 Aug. 1789, *on* Mr Crank *add note* 2a: 2a. John Cranch (1751–1821), painter (see Misc. Corr. iii. 257–8).

Page 234, *sub* 1 Sept. 1789, *on* Mr Simco *add note* 2b: 2b. John Simco (ca 1750–1824), bookseller of No. 11 Great Queen Street, Lincoln's Inn Fields, later of No. 2 Air Street Piccadilly (GM 1824, xciv pt 1. 186). See Simco to HW 17 Aug. 1778 and HW to Simco 20 Aug. 1789 in Misc. Corr. ii. 388–9, iii. 258.

Page 234, *sub* 2 Sept. 1789, *for footnote number* 2a *read* 2c   *At bottom of page, for* 2a *read* 2c

Page 235, *sub* 16 June 1790, *on* Mr Jerningham and 3 *add note* 3a: 3a. One of the three was Veronica Boswell (b. 1773), James Boswell's eldest daughter. She wrote to her brother, Alexander Boswell, at Eton College, 'London June 18th 1790': 'On the 16th we went to see Mr Horace Walpole's house, Strawberry Hill. It is built in the old Gothic manner, but has nothing grand about it, as it [is] built of brick and is not large, and very low. The battlements appear as if they were made of wood; the windows are painted glass, some of which render the rooms very dark. There is a room full of curiosities; the window at the top is yellow, which gives a yellow colour to everything; however there are many very curious things which would please you. In one of the rooms is a red hat which belonged to Cardinal Wolsey, which I had in my hand. The Gallery is a very pretty room; all the Gothic ornaments are gilded, which has a good effect. On the whole, though it was very well to see once in one's life, I can't say I should like to live at it. From Strawberry we proceeded to Hampton Court. . . . there are a great many fine pictures, particularly Erasmus and Charles the First by Vandyke. After we had seen Hampton Court we returned to Richmond Hill to dinner. . . . Mr Jerningham, the poet, was of our party, and we were very happy. At six we took a boat, and sailed down the river Thames to Mr Pope's house at Twickenham, and landed in the garden, where are some weeping willows planted by his own hand' (MS Boswell Papers C 548.2, Yale University Library).

Page 236, *sub* 16 Aug. 1790, *on* Myself *add note* 3b: 3b. J[acob] Schnebellie wrote to Richard Gough at Enfield, Middlesex: 'Your favour of the 16th instant I duly received. . . . Last Monday I accompanied Lord and Lady Leicester and Lady L's mother and two sisters to Mr Walpole at Strawberry Hill and was much entertained; it was a charming place. The day following, I dined with Mr Astle at Battersea Rise' (MS in the possession of Lord Waldegrave at Chewton). See also OSSORY iii. 28.

Page 237, *sub* 6 May 1791, *on* Mr Raikes *add note a: a.* Probably Thomas Raikes, merchant in London, governor of the Bank of England, 1797; m. (1774) Charlotte Finch, dau. of Hon. Henry Finch (DNB, *sub* Thomas Raikes, 1777–1848; Joseph Farington, *Diary*, ed. James Greig, 1922–8, i. 203).

Page 239, *sub* 25 Aug. 1791, *on* Mrs Berwick. *add note* 4a: 4a. Probably Mrs Joseph Berwick (DALRYMPLE 321).

Page 239, *sub* 8 Sept. 1791, *on* Mr Devisme *add note* 5a: 5a. Probably the 'De Vyme' who dined in company with Edmond Malone on 6 Aug. 1791, and whose firm served Mrs Damer as agent in Lisbon in 1790; see ADD. AND CORR. for vol. 11, p. 160, n. 2.

Page 240, *sub* 8 May 1792, *on* Mr Norford junior *add note a: a.* A printed ticket to visit SH with a note dated 2 May 1792 admitting Mr Norford and three on Tuesday next is printed in ADD. AND CORR. for vol. 12, p. 252.

Page 244, *sub* 13 Aug. 1793, *on* Mr Knight *add note* 3a: 3a. Possibly Samuel Knight (1755–1829), Auditor of Trinity College, Cambridge, 1791–1811; friend and correspondent of John Pinkerton; see HW to Pinkerton 26 June 1785 (CHATTERTON 267 and n. 2; Appendix 3, p. 372).

Page 246, *sub* 31 July 1794, *on* 31 *add note* 1a: 1a. Also on 31 July HW had Farington and Samuel Lysons for dinner (Farington's unpublished diary at Windsor Castle; Farington's 'Anecdotes of Walpole 1793–1797' in DALRYMPLE 319).

Page 248, note 1, *after* 1795 *add* (CONWAY iii. 510–12); *Harcourt Papers*, ed. E. W. Harcourt, Oxford, [1880?–1905], vi. 46–7, 246–8

Page 252, middle of page, *before* Anecdotes Written 1784–1796 *insert the following*:

TICKETS FOR ADMISSION TO STRAWBERRY HILL

Visitors were admitted to Strawberry Hill only on presentation of a ticket, which before 1784 was usually in the form of a written note to HW's housekeeper (for an example see COLE i. 316). In 1774 HW used printed cards on which he inserted the date of the proposed visit and his signature (illustrated in Hazen, *SH Bibl.* 211). In 1784 he printed 'a page of rules for admission to see my House' (ibid. 225–7); he usually wrote a note addressed to his housekeeper at the bottom of the printed rules, mentioning the name of the applicant and the number of accompanying visitors as well as the date of the visit. The previous printed versions of the rules were in italic type and printed at Strawberry Hill, but in 1788 or 1789 the rules were reprinted in roman type in London; again in 1792 the rules, beginning 'Lord Orford is very ready to oblige,' were printed in roman type in London (ibid., 1973, pp. xxxii, 275).

To JOHN HATSELL,[1] Wednesday 5 June 1782

Printed for the first time from the MS now WSL; the MS is an autograph note, probably sent with a covering letter which is missing. The MS was sold by Parke-Bernet 22 Jan. 1941 (John Gribbell Sale), lot 45, to W.J. Benjamin, who resold it to WSL, 1941.

June 5, 1782.

To Mr Walpole's Housekeeper[2] at Strawberry Hill.

Any morning between twelve and three you may show my house to Mr Hatsell and five more, on their delivering this ticket to you.

HOR. WALPOLE

To CHARLES BEDFORD,[1] Saturday 15 September 1787

Printed from the MS, now WSL; the note is written at the bottom of a copy of HW's printed rules (1784) for visitors to Strawberry Hill. This page was pasted in a bound volume consisting of seven publications from the Strawberry Hill Press, with a handwritten title-page, 'Miscellanies by Horace Earl of Orford printed at Strawberry Hill.' This volume contains the bookplates of Charles Bedford and of William Frederick, 9th E. Waldegrave; it remained in the Waldegrave family until sold by Lord Waldegrave to WSL in 1948.

Sept. 15, 1787.

You may show my house on Wednesday morning next[2] to Mr Bedford and three more, on their delivering this order to you.

HOR. WALPOLE

1. (1743–1820), senior bencher of the Middle Temple; chief clerk of the House of Commons (1768–97) (MANN ix. 572 n. 15). HW's 'Book of Visitors' records a later visit to SH by 'Mr Hatsell and 3' on 3 July 1788 (BERRY ii. 230).
2. Margaret Young (fl. 1760–85).

---

1. (ca 1742–1814), HW's deputy usher of the Exchequer 1774–97 (MISC. CORR. iii. 491–2).
2. HW's 'Book of Visitors' lists for Wednesday, 19 Sept. 1787: 'Mr Bedford and 2 sons. Miss Norths, myself' (BERRY ii. 229). Charles Bedford's sons were Grosvenor Charles Bedford (1773–1839), Horace Walpole Bedford (ca 1776–1807), and Henry Bedford (ca 1782–1844).

To PAUL PANTON,[1] Wednesday 24 June 1789

Printed from the MS now WSL; the note is written at the bottom of a copy of
HW's printed rules (1788–9) for visitors to Strawberry Hill (Hazen, *SH Bibl.*,
1973, p. xxxii). A photographic copy of the MS was printed by Major H. Lloyd-
Johnes in *Country Life*, 17 Dec. 1959, cxxvi pt iii. 1217. The MS was pasted in
volume I of Paul Panton's copy of the first edition of HW's *Anecdotes of Painting*, 1762–3; sold by Major Lloyd-Johnes, through Maggs, Feb. 1960, to WSL
(lacking the 4th vol.) (see Hazen, *SH Bibl.*, 1973, p. xvii, copy 27). The MS was
removed from the volume of *Anecdotes* by WSL.

June 24, 1789.

To Mr Walpole's Housekeeper.[2]

You may show my house on Friday morning next[3] to Mr Panton, and
three more, on their delivering this to you.

HOR. WALPOLE

To ?CUTHBERT POTTS, JR,[1] Monday 29 August 1791

Printed from GM 1803, lxxiii pt i. 224–5, where it was first printed. HW's note
to his housekeeper was written at the bottom of a copy of the printed rules (1784)
for visitors to Strawberry Hill. Preserved with the 'ticket' were some notes by two
ladies who attended on the prescribed date, 5 Sept., and commented on the
apartments shown to them (printed in GM loc. cit.).

August 29, 1791.

To Mr Walpole's Housekeeper.[2]

You may show my house to Mr [Potts] and three more[3] on Monday
next,[4] on their delivering this to you.

HOR. WALPOLE

To MR NORFORD, JR,[1] Wednesday 2 May 1792

Printed for the first time from a photostat of the MS in the Fitzwilliam Museum; the note is written at the bottom of a copy of HW's printed rules (1792)
for visitors to Strawberry Hill (Hazen, *SH Bibl.*, 1973, pp. xxxii, 275). Damer-
Waller; the MS was sold Sotheby's 5 Dec. 1921 (1st Waller Sale), lot 56, bought
in; resold Christie's 15 Dec. 1947 (2d Waller Sale), lot 50, to the Fitzwilliam
Museum.

1. (1727–97), of Plas Gwyn, Anglesey, North Wales; barrister and antiquary. See his
letter to HW of 8 Aug. 1768, MISC. CORR. ii. 160 and n. 1.
2. Ann Bransom, HW's housekeeper at SH.
3. 26 June. There is no record of a visit by Mr Panton in HW's 'Book of Visitors.'

1. Probably Cuthbert Potts, of Pall Mall, London; surgeon; who m. Ethelinda Margaret Thorpe, dau. of John Thorpe, F. S. A., the antiquary (see DNB, *sub* Laurence
Holker Potts; Nichols, *Lit. Anec.* iii. 520; *Old Westminsters* ii. 755). The entry for 5
Sept. 1791 in HW's 'Book of Visitors' is 'Mr Potts, junior, surgeon' (BERRY ii. 239).
2. Ann Bransom, HW's housekeeper at SH.
3. The 'gentleman was prevented from being of the party,' and 'two ladies' only
came to see SH on that day (GM 1803, lxxiii pt i. 225).
4. 5 Sept.

Endorsed by HW: Curiosity
        No Paradise prom. to liberty.
        destr. the Country by Scots seaboard
        Community of govts must be divided ag. every yr.
        Cowardly cannibals. La Fayette.[2]

May 2d 1792.

To Lord Orford's Housekeeper.[3]

You may show my house on Tuesday morning next[4] to Mr Norford and three more on their delivering <this to you.>[5]

To THE REV. JAMES HURDIS,[1] Sunday 21 July 1793

Printed from a transcript of the MS, made by Professor Allen T. Hazen, in the possession of the Stoke Newington Public Library, London; the note was written at the bottom of a copy of HW's rules (1792) for visitors to Strawberry Hill. The MS is bound in Samuel or Daniel Lysons's copy of the *Description of SH*, 1784; this volume is in the Stoke Newington Public Library (Edward J. Sage bequest, 1906).

July 21, 1793.

To Lord Orford's Housekeeper.[2]

You may show my house on Friday next[3] to Mr Hurdis and three more, on their delivering this to you.

ORFORD

Page 253, 1st paragraph, line 8, *on* eyes *add note* 3a: 3a. HW's conjecture is confirmed by Dr Carl P. Bausch, M.D., who points out: 'Aniseikonia (retinal disparity) is the condition wherein the images presented from the two eyes are unequal in size or shape. The difference in size is relative and the disparity becomes apparent only in binocular vision. "It would appear that the threshold for the discrimination of size-differences between the ocular images is of the order of 0.25%. The difference which

1. Not identified. Possibly the son of Dr William Norford; see MISC. CORR. iii. 333, n. 7.

2. HW discusses this subject in his letters to Lady Ossory 29 May 1792 (OSSORY iii. 141), and to Sir William Hamilton 30 Sept. 1792 (CHUTE 445). Lafayette used this phrase in his letter to the Minister of War 2 May 1792 after the murder of Gen. Theobald Dillon and some captured Austrian soldiers on 29 April by French soldiers at Lille (ibid. 445, n. 15).

3. Ann Bransom, HW's housekeeper at SH.

4. 8 May; in HW's 'Book of Visitors' the entry for 8 May 1792 is 'Mr Norford junior' (BERRY ii. 240).

5. The corner of the MS is torn off.

———

1. (1763–1801), D.D., 1797; poet. In April 1793 he was living at Temple Cowley, near Oxford, and in Nov. 1793 was appointed professor of poetry at Oxford; he was vicar of Bishopstone, Sussex, 1791–1801.

2. Ann Bransom, HW's housekeeper at SH.

3. 26 July; HW's 'Book of Visitors' records for Saturday, 27 July: 'Mr Hurdis and sister from Mr Daniel Lysons' (BERRY ii. 244). Hurdis's sister was Jane Elizabeth Hurdis (d. 1809).

gives rise to symptoms as occurs with refractive errors and heterophoria, varies greatly with the *sensitivity, the state of health and the occupation* of the patient, and it is generally stated that a difference of 1% is potentially significant" (Duke-Elder). . . . I think it is probable that in 1784, Walpole, aet. 67, was developing lens sclerosis. "An incidental feature which is not often remarked is the change in color values. The sclerosing lens absorbs the shorter wave-lengths of the spectrum, first the violet and blue, and eventually continues up to the yellow, so that the resultant effect is as if looking through a color filter with the blue and violet excluded" (Duke-Elder).'

Page 255, note 9, left column, line 14, *after* xv. 90 *add* ; for W. H. Ainsworth's transcript of HW's notes in this missal, see the SH Sale Catalogue, p. xviii

Page 256, 4th paragraph, line 3, *on* Out-I-go Jones *add note* 14a: 14a. HW gives a slightly different version of this anecdote in a marginal note on Chesterfield's *Miscellaneous Works*, with 'Memoirs' by Dr Matthew Maty, 1777; see HW's marginalia, p. 73, in *Miscellanies of the Philobiblon Society*, 1867–8, vol. xi (see also Mason i. 289 and nn. 12, 13; Hazen, *Cat. of HW's Lib.* No. 3915).

Page 258, note 28, *add* In HW's 'Book of Materials,' 1786, p. 7, he wrote: 'Dr Calder [John Calder (1733–1815)] said of Dr Johnston [*sic*] on the publications of Boswell and Mrs Piozzi, that he was like Acteon, torn to pieces by his own *pack*.'

Page 258, note 30, line 9, *after* 423). *insert* There is a photograph of the painting (then in the possession of Sir Philip Sassoon) in *The Connoisseur*, 1934, xciv. 318.

Page 258, note 31, *add* See HW to Lady Ossory 9 Aug. 1773 (Ossory i. 137), where the translation is attributed to Lord Edgcumbe.

Page 259, left column of names, line 4, *after* Fitzwilliam *add* (this copy now wsl)   *left column, line 9, after* Anderson *add* (now wsl)   *right column, last line, after* Bull *add* (now wsl)

Page 259, note 36, line 4, *for* 129–30 *read* 1973, pp. xxvii–xxviii, 129–32.

Page 260, left column, 2d line from bottom, *after* Wheeler *add* (now wsl)

Page 260, right column, line 1, *after* Dacre *add* (now wsl)

Page 260, right column, line 20, *after* Carter *add* (now wsl)

Page 260, right column, line 21, *for* Parsons.[36a] *read* Parsons.[36b] (now wsl)

Page 260, footnote 36a, *substitute* 36b. William Parsons (ca 1764–1828), poet (see Misc. Corr. iii. 263 and n. 1).

Page 262, note 46, last line, *after* 78 *add* and is now wsl (Hazen, *Cat. of HW's Lib.* No. 3223). See also HW to Lady Ossory 6 Sept. 1787, Ossory ii. 569.

Page 263, note 48, lines 2–4, *delete Catalogue . . . ix–xv. and substitute*

The Drawings of Leonardo da Vinci in the Collection of Her Majesty the Queen at Windsor Castle, 2d edn, 1968–9, i. pp. ix–xv.

Page 263, note 49, *substitute* Sir Kenneth Clark in the 2d edition of his *Drawings of Leonardo da Vinci* concludes that the mutilation of the volume of Leonardo drawings did not take place: 'As there is a discrepancy between the number of drawings recorded by Rogers, precisely 779, and that of the drawings to be seen at Windsor to-day, i.e. about 600, it was previously assumed that a considerable number of drawings had been lost. Miss Scott-Elliot has shown this is not the case. The missing pages of the Leoni volume have now been accounted for by a reconsideration of the inventories which prove that the apparent discrepancy in the number of the drawings is due to the separate reckoning of the versos' (ibid. i. p. xiv).

Page 264, note 51, line 3, *for* 1786–9 *read* 1786–8; HW owned six volumes (Hazen, *Cat. of HW's Lib.* No. 3021). HW praises Mlle Keralio's *Collection* in an 'Appendix to Royal and Noble Authors' (*Works* i. 563) and in a letter to Hannah More 12 July 1788 (MORE 270–1).

Page 265, note 61, line 4, *delete* in *and substitute* now WSL;   *Line 5, after* 69 *add*   ; Hazen, *Cat. of HW's Lib.* No. 3   *Last line, add* See MASON i. 24, n. 5.

Page 266, note 62, line 3, *after* 110 *add*   ; Hazen, *Cat. of HW's Lib.* No. 570

Page 267, note 70, line 7, *after* 1724 *add*   ; see Hazen, *Cat. of HW's Lib.* No. 1773   *Delete last 8 lines from* and his uncle John . . . her brother). *and substitute* his three sons were John, Jr (d. 1746), Arthur (d. between 1746 and 1753), Erasmus (d. 1753). See J. B. Whitmore and A. W. Hughes Clarke, *London Visitation Pedigrees, 1664,* 1940, p. 124; MASON i. 24, n. 5; CONWAY i. 224.

Page 267, note 71, *add* See Hazen, *Cat. of HW's Lib.* No. 919.

Page 269, note 78, lines 4–5, *for* 92. *read* 92   *for* The reading here *substitute* where the reading

Page 274, line 10, *on* in 1790 *add note* 15a: 15a. The *World* 2 Feb. 1790 mentions the statue as 'far advanced.'

Page 274, note 14, line 4, *after* 256 *add*   ; see also *World* 9 Feb. 1790

VOLUME 13

Page xxi, Gray's Rooms in Peterhouse, 1734–9, *to description add* The inscription in Walpole's hand does not appear in our reproduction of the print.

Page xxi, Thomas Gray, by John Giles Eccardt, *to description add* Adapted from a portrait of a musician by Van Dyck ('Des. of SH,' *Works* ii. 436).

Page xxii, final paragraph, line 3, *after* College, Cambridge, *insert* Harvard University Library,

Page xxix, section 2, 2d paragraph, line 7, *for* Miss Berry *substitute* Lord Euston (later 5th D. of Grafton) as executor for the 6th Lord Waldegrave

Page xxxiv, 2d paragraph, lines 13–14, *for* The manuscripts of sixteen . . . are missing. *read* The manuscripts of fifteen . . . are missing; the manuscript of 28 May 1752 was acquired by W. S. Lewis in 1948.

Page xxxiv, 2d paragraph, last line, *on* Eton *add note* 1: 1. Thomas Gray to HW, Cambridge, n.d., was sold Evans 13 [14] Feb. 1833 ('Collection of autograph letters formed by an eminent collector' Sale), lot 383, to Thorpe for £3.9s.

Page xxxiv, 3d paragraph, last line, *on* each letter *add note* 2: 2. Among the Gray MSS, sold Sotheby 28 April 1851 (Thomas Gray Sale), lot 53, are two volumes of correspondence, 1736–71, with letters of HW, and Gray's own copy of the *Odes*, 1757. These were sold to 'J' for £500.

Page xxxv, 3d paragraph, line 5, *on* West's letters to Walpole *add note* 3: 3. HW wrote to Mason 8 Dec. 1773, 'I have added an epitaph on West . . . and nine of his letters to me, that you may use if you have room' (MASON i. 119–20).

Page xxxv, 3d paragraph, line 13, *on* Add. MS 32,562 *add note* 4: 4. BM Add. MS 32,560, ff. 175–212, contains MS letters of Gray, West, HW and Ashton 'copied by me Mitford from the originals lent by Mrs Frankland Lewis to me, February 1853' (Vols iii and iv of Commonplace Books and Recollections of the Rev. John Mitford, 1847–56, BM Add. MSS 32,559–32,575).

Page xxxvi, 1st paragraph, line 4, *after* above. *insert* The MS of the letter from Walpole and Gray in July, 1739 was sold Sotheby's 20–21 July 1981 ('Valuable Autograph Letters, Literary Manuscripts, and Historical Documents Sale'), lot 501, reproduced on p. 305.

Page xli, 2d paragraph, line 1, *for* Deputy Keeper of Rare Books *read* Deputy Keeper of Manuscripts

Page xliii, *BM Cat. of Engraved British Portraits*, right column, line 3, *after* 25 *add* , 6 vols

Page xliii, BM, *Satiric Prints*, right column, line 5, *for* 1870–1942, 7 vols. *read* 1870–1954, 11 vols.

Page xliv, Cobbett, *Parl. Hist.*, right column, line 2, *for* William Cobbett and John Wright *read* William Cobbett, John Wright, and T. C. Hansard,

Page xlv, Grove's *Dictionary of Music*, right column, *for* Grove's *Dictionary of Music . . . 1927–8. read The New Grove Dictionary of Music and Musicians*, 6th edn, ed. Stanley Sadie, 1980, 20 vols.

Page xlvii, MONTAGU, right column, line 3, *after* 1941 *add* , 2 vols

Page xlviii, Sold London, right column, line 3, *for* June, *read* June

Page 2, 2d paragraph, line 7, *for* Mary Berry *read* Lord Euston (later 5th D. of Grafton) as executor for the 6th Lord Waldegrave

Page 2, 2d paragraph, line 8, *on* possession *add note* 1: 1. The MS was sold, with the other Walpole MSS in 'the Bentley cache,' Sotheby's 22 July 1870, lot 76. The sale was an anonymous sale, but from the invoice in Richard Bentley's copy of the catalogue (now wsl) it is clear that the property was his and that he bought in lot 76 for £23.

Page 2, 3d paragraph, line 6, *on* conjecture *add note* 2: 2. A better guess I now think for the earliest portion is 1746 (wsl).

Page 3, note 5, lines 5–12, *delete* HW was . . . p. 13). *and substitute* HW was inoculated by Dr Charles Maitland 30 Sept. 1724 (Royal Society, *Classified Papers 1660–1740*, vol. xxiii; information from Robert Halsband)

Page 4, note 7, lines 10–21, *delete* Although . . . by Junius. *and substitute* See also HW to Lady Walpole, 1725 *bis* and to Sir Edward Walpole 28 April 1769, FAMILY 2, 52.

Page 4, note 11, line 11, *before* George *add* the Hon.   *before* Augustus *add* Hon.

Page 5, note 16a, *add* The *Daily Adv.* 26 Sept. 1734 reported, 'The Hon. Mr Walpole, youngest son of Sir Robert Walpole, has been dangerously ill of a fever at Eton School, but by the care of Dr Broxholm is now on the mending hand. The Right Hon. the Lady Walpole has resided for several days with the Earl of Cholmondely's sisters, at his Lordship's apartment in Windsor Castle, in order to be near at hand to visit her son during his illness' (also reported in *Read's Weekly Journal or British Gazetteer* 28 Sept. 1734; information from Robert Halsband). HW had also been ill in Sept. 1733; see his letters to Lady Walpole 28, 30 Sept. 1733 OS, FAMILY 3, 4.

Page 8, note 37, line 4, *after* 634). *add Common Sense* 11 Nov. 1738 reported, 'Yesterday sevennight [3 Nov.] Horace Walpole, Esq., Usher of the Exchequer, youngest son of Sir Robert, was called to the bar on his being made Comptroller of the Pipe in the Exchequer and Clerk of the Estreats on which occasion a handsome entertainment was given at Lincoln's Inn Hall to the gentlemen of that society, a bottle of burgundy, a bottle of champagne, and a bottle of claret being ordered for each mess.'

Page 8, note 40, line 1, *for* (d. 1777) *read* (1703–77)   *Last line, after* 1742 *add* and Namier and Brooke ii. 412–13

Page 9, note 53, line 1, *for* ca 1706 *read* 1706

Pages 9–10, note 59, *add* See Hazen, *Cat. of HW's Lib.* No. 3841; MASON i. 69.

Page 10, note 60, line 2, *for* friend *read* cousin   *Line 4, after* n. 31 *add*   ; CHUTE 4, n. 9. Chute, Whithed, and George Hervey left Florence at the same time as HW and rejoined him at Reggio (SELWYN 16).

Page 10, note 61, line 4, *after* 182 *add*   ; SELWYN 16 and n. 2

Page 10, note 62, *add* Lady Sophia Fermor en route to Venice wrote to her brother 5 June 1741: 'Mr Walpole has been extreme ill at Reggio and sent an express from thence to Florence to fetch Doctor Cocchi, but the Princess of Modena told me that when she left Reggio he was quite out of danger, and he is to set out today from thence for Venice. Mr Gray is already there, and Cecchino Suarez travels with Mr Walpole' (Joseph Spence, *Letters from the Grand Tour*, ed. Slava Klima, Montreal and London, 1975, p. 390). See also T. B. Layton, 'Horace Walpole's Quinsy,' *Guy's Hospital Gazette*, 12 Oct. 1957, pp. 399–403.

Page 10, note 64, next to last line, *after* n. 62 *insert* (printed in Joseph Spence, *Letters from the Grand Tour*, ed. Slava Klima, 1975, pp. 387–8) *Last line, add* See also SELWYN 14, 16–17.

Page 11, note 66, line 2, *for* Aix *read* Aix-en-Provence

Page 11, note 68, *add* See also SELWYN 18–19

Page 11, note 71, last line, *after* 305 *add*   ; Sedgwick i. 207

Page 11, note 73, lines 4–5, *delete* Why Sir Robert . . . is unknown *and substitute* He took the title of Orford from his favourite residence 'Orford House' in Chelsea (J. H. Plumb, *Sir Robert Walpole: The Making of a Statesman*, Cambridge, Mass., 1956, p. 206).

Page 12, note 74, last line, *after* 29 July 1742 *add*   ; to Lincoln 23 Aug., 18 Sept. 1742

Page 13, note 85, *add* Possibly Ashton; see *post* i. 249, n. 12.

Page 14, note 90, line 3, *after* printed *insert* (now printed in SELWYN 287–306)   *Line 15, after* Grifoni. *add* HW had his portrait painted by John Wootton ('Des. of SH,' *Works* ii. 452; CHUTE 38, 44).

Page 14, note 91, right column, line 2, *after* Waldegrave MSS 2. 112–18 *add*   ; see Hazen, *Bibliography of Walpole* 154

Page 15, note 95, line 5, *after* (GEC). *add* Sir Robert's last words are printed in MANN App. 4, x. 12.

Page 15, note 96, 4th line from end, *for* legitimatized *read* illegitimate

Page 15, note 97, line 1, *after* £400 *add* because of Mrs Le Neve's death (see HW to Newcastle 12 Nov. 1758)   *Last line, add* See MANN App. 16, x. 52–4.

Page 16, note 103, line 3, *for* a Mr Jordan *read* Patrick Jordan (see ADD. AND CORR. for vol. 9, p. 44, nn. 1 and 2)   *Line 4, for* 21 August *read* 19 August   *Line 6, for* i. 44 *read* i. 44–6

Page 16, note 105, *at end add* See Hazen, *Bibliography of Walpole* 24–6.

Page 17, note 112, line 1, *after* house *add*   , SH,

Page 18, note 116, line 10, *after* p. 48). *add* See also Hazen, *Bibliography of Walpole* 154.

Page 19, note 121, left column, lines 4–5, *for* has not been elsewhere noted *substitute* was made by James Ralph, editor of *The Remembrancer* 1747–51, 'In a long Note upon [David Mallet's] *A Congratulatory Letter to Selim*, in defence of Sir George Lyttelton against one of the Libels publish'd against him on the Supposition of his being the Author of Dr Thirlby's *Letter to the Tories*, of which Ralph acquits Sir George' (Rev. Thomas Birch to Philip Yorke, 2d E. of Hardwicke, 15 April 1762, BM Add. MS 35,399, f. 274v; pointed out by John B. Shipley in N&Q Nov. 1957, ccii. 475–7).

Page 19, note 126, *delete 1st three lines and substitute Three Letters to the Whigs* (including the 3d edn of the first *Letter to the Whigs* and the 2d edn of the *Second and Third Letter to the Whigs*)

Page 20, note 132, line 2, *after* March *add* 1748

Page 20, note 133, line 1, *for* 1718 *read* ?1718

Pages 20–1, note 135, *add* But see HW to Mann 1 April 1742 OS, where HW calls Onslow 'the most notorious affecter of popularity' (MANN i. 386).

Page 21, note 141, *for last sentence substitute* Two copies of the original pamphlet have been traced: one in the University of Illinois Library and one now WSL (from P. Murray Hill, Dec. 1951).

Page 22, note 143, *add* See also HW to Middleton 22 Nov. 1741, DAL-RYMPLE 8–9.

Page 22, note 144, line 12, *for* ?Owen *read* Owen   *Line 19, for* note, *read* note to the 4th, unpublished *Remembrancer,*

Page 22, note 146, lines 3–4 from bottom, *delete* but he does not seem to have been a printer *and substitute* beginning with No. 26, 4 June 1748, the colophon of the *Remembrancer* (p. 4) reads: 'Printed by W. Owen . . .'; and at the end of a list of books noted in the *Remembrancer* No. 87, 5 Aug. 1749 (p. 4, column 1), is the following: 'The said *W. Owen* under-takes the business of *printing* and *publishing* with care and regularity . . .' (information from John B. Shipley).

Page 24, note 155, line 10, *after* House. *add* HW was one of fifty original trustees of the Sloane collection, named in a codicil of the *Will of Sir Hans Sloane, Bart. deceased,* 1753, p. 18 (HW's copies now WSL)   *Line 11, after* 1753 *add*   , MANN iv. 358, n. 3

Page 24, note 159, line 4, *for* ? Dec. *read* ca 22 Dec.   *Line 9, after* 1748.' *add* (Printed in SELWYN App. 6, pp. 333–5.)

Page 25, note 164, line 1, *after* John Shorter *add* (d. 1746)   *Line 2, for* (d. ?1753) *substitute* (d. between 1746 and 1753) (see CONWAY i. 224) *Lines 2–3, delete* whose obituary has not been found

Page 25, note 169, *add* See HW to Bentley 9 July 1754, where he says that the monument is at last erected, but he has not had the courage to venture alone to see it (CHUTE 178).

Page 26, note 170, line 18, *for* 1693 *read* 1697   *Line 6 from end, after* N. S.). *add* HW had the model, bronzed, in the Tribune at SH ('Des. of SH,' *Works* ii. 470–1).

Page 27, note 176, *add* Now printed as Appendix 1 in FAMILY 295–304; see also 24–32.

Page 27, note 177, line 9, *for* Feb. 1757 *read* 7 Feb. 1757, FAMILY 33–4 *Last line, add* An itemized bill of expenses for the election dinner at Lynn 24 Feb. 1757, amounting to £183, is now WSL; the bill was apparently paid by Lord Orford, and HW did not attend the dinner (FAMILY 33–4).

Page 27, note 178, *add* Among HW's 'utmost endeavours' were his 'Queries Addressed to Every Englishman's Own Feeling,' printed in the *London Chronicle* 8–10 Feb. 1757, i. 137–8, apparently sent by Augustus John Hervey, 3d E. of Bristol, who wrote on his MS copy of the 'Queries':

'These are not mine but Mr Horace Walpole's, lent to me which I printed' (information from Hon. David Erskine).

Page 28, note 183, line 3, *after* 240–1 *add*   ; Hazen, *Bibliography of Walpole* 125

Page 28, note 186, line 1, *for* 1690 *read* 1694

Page 28, note 187, *add* The dedication is 'To the Right Honourable Hugh, Lord Willoughby of Parham, President to the Council and Fellows of the Society of Antiquaries, This Edition and Translation, of Part of the Itinerary of Hentznerus, Is offered with great Respect by the Editor, Horace Walpole, F. S. A. and F. R. S.'

Page 29, note 193, *add* One copy containing HW's MS notes is now WSL (listed in Hazen, *Cat. of HW's Lib*. No. 2362).

Page 29, note 194, *add* HW's copy is now WSL (Hazen, *Cat. of HW's Lib*. No. 1881). On the dedication see CONWAY i. 539–40, 544, 546–7.

Page 30, note 198, last line, *after* 128–30 *add*   ; 'Walpole's Account of Richard Bentley,' CHUTE App. 2, p. 644.

Page 32, note 219, line 10, *after* 209–19 *add* in 1783 in the *Epistolary Correspondence . . . of . . . Francis Atterbury*, ii. 181–92 (HW's copy is now WSL),

Page 33, note 226, line 17, *for* five *read* six   *Line 20, after* (1938) *add* , xxix (1942, Index to previous 5 vols), xxx (1952)   *Lines 20–2, delete last sentence*

Page 34, note 227, line 1, *for* ca 1703 *read* ca 1708

Page 34, note 228, line 6, *after* Westminster Abbey *add*   : 'A monument is now erecting in the south aisle of Westminster Abbey, to the memory of the Hon. Roger Townshend' (*London Chronicle* 2–4 Nov. 1762, xii. 438)

Page 34, note 234, 6th line from end, *after* SH Bibliography 143 *add* and *Cat. of HW's Lib*. No. 347.   *Last line, add* A landscape painted in encaustic is listed in the SH Sale Catalogue xxi. 83.

Page 35, note 237, *add* See Hazen, *Bibliography of Walpole* 43–5, and *Cat. of HW's Lib*. No. 2050:21.

Page 35, note 240, line 5, *for* ?28 April *read* ?5 May   *Lines 7–8, after* tutors *add* (CONWAY ii. 50–1)

Page 36, note 242, lines 6–7, *for* Shortly afterwards *read* In 1762   *Last line, after* 366 *add*   ; *London Chronicle* 29–31 July 1762, xii. 106; *The Times* 19 Sept. 1790, p. 2

Page 36, note 243, line 3, *for* The 'sermon' *read* The MS of the 'sermon' is in the Scottish Record Office; it   *Line 11, after* Hill.' *add* It is also printed as Appendix 3 in MORE 423–6.

Page 36, note 245, *add* See CONWAY ii. 89 and n. 25.

Page 37, note 248, line 2, *after* original MS *insert*   , now in the Scottish Record Office,

Page 37, note 250, *add* His name appears as 'contributory member' in the Society's *Transactions*, 1783, i. 306.

Page 38, note 258, *add* John Hawkins in a letter of 1 March 1762 may have been the one who first told HW of Warburton's objections (see MISC. CORR. i. 228–9). Warburton had also written to Mason of his resentment (Add. MS 32,563, ff. 12–14).

Page 38, note 260, line 3, *after* K.3.17 *add*   ; Hazen, *Cat. of HW's Lib.* No. 1819

Page 39, note 262, line 5, *after* WSL *add*   , Hazen, *Cat. of HW's Lib.* No. 1806   *Line 7, after* H.3.17 *add*   ; Hazen, op. cit. No. 1425

Pages 40–1, note 268, last line, *after* 50–2 *add*   ; CONWAY ii. 395–6

Page 41, note 272, line 1, *for* ca 1681 *read* ca 1688

Page 41, note 273, last line, *after* 105 *add* (Hazen, *Cat. of HW's Lib.* No. 1614)

Page 41, note 277, last line, *after* 160–2 *add*   ; CONWAY iii. 43 and nn. 10, 11

Page 42, note 280, line 12, *after* (1770) *add*   ; the *Testament* has also been attributed to Jean-Henri Maubert de Gouvest   *Last line, add* For HW's copy see Hazen, *Cat. of HW's Lib.* No. 2323.

Page 43, note 288, *add* In his copy (now WSL) HW noted on the title-page, 'begun to be printed Dec. 23, finished Jan. 27.'

Page 44, note 298, line 7, *for* brother *read* half-brother

Page 44, note 299, line 1, *after* 400 *add*   ; Hazen, *Bibliography of Walpole* 163   *Last line, after* 226 *add*   ; *London Stage* Part IV, iii. 1400–1

Page 44, note 300, line 4, *after* 156 *add*   ; HW's copy is Hazen, *Cat. of HW's Lib.* No. 2943

Page 45, note 315, line 1, *after* MS *add* of the 'foul copy' of the *Mem. Geo. III*

Page 46, note 321, line 1, *after* MS *add* of the 'foul copy' of the *Mem. Geo. III*

Page 47, note 326, last line, *after* i. 49 *add*   ; Hazen, *Cat. of HW's Lib.* No. 3223

Page 47, note 331, *substitute* HW's resignation 13 July 1772 is noted in the Index, under Walpole, to the Minutes of the Society of Antiquaries; but there is no entry to this effect in the Minutes, the Society having finished its session on 9 July (information from H. S. Kingsford). See also OSSORY i. 84 and n. 11.

Page 48, note 336, line 3, *after* iv. 387 *add*   ; OSSORY i. 87–8   *Line 3, for* ca 1769 *read* 23 Aug. 1768   *Line 8, after* father *add* (OSSORY i. 33–4, 202, n. 2)   *Lines 8–16, delete* She was . . . 'about five.'

Page 49, note 343, line 6, *after* MS *add* of HW's parody   *Line 7, add* See also OSSORY i. 203.

Page 49, note 345, right column, line 5, *for* 1762 *read* 1761   *Line 7, for* d. 1830 *read* 1762–1830

Page 49, note 346, line 3, *after* about it *add* MASON i. 175–6 and n. 2; OSSORY i. 233 and n. 10   *Last line, add* See *London Stage* Part IV, iii. 1869–70. For HW's copy see Hazen, *Cat. of HW's Lib.* No. 1810:23:9.

Page 50, note 353, line 2, *after* times *add* that season   *Line 3, before* Genest *insert London Stage* Part V, i. 111, 180–2;   *after* 31–2). *add* It was performed several times in subsequent years through the 1786 season; the last performance was at Drury Lane in 1788.

Page 50, note 354, line 3, *after* 206–20 *add* The MS, in Kirgate's hand with HW's MS notes and corrections, is now in the Beinecke Library, Yale University. Endorsed by Thomas Percy: 'After Mr Walpole had printed these pages, which he had previously shown to me, he made me a present of his autograph.' Described in *Yale Library Gazette*, 1951, xxv. 36.

Page 50, note 355, line 2, *for* ca 1697 *read* 1695   *Line 3, for* S. C. de Jong *read* Haeck de Jong   *Lines 7–12, delete and substitute* She was baptized 12 Sept. 1695 in the Jacobikerk in Utrecht (information from J. E. A. L. Struick, town-archivist, Utrecht); therefore HW was correct in saying that she was 84 when she died in 1779 (OSSORY ii. 121).

Page 56, headnote, 3d paragraph, line 2, *for* invariably *read* usually

Page 63, note 18, line 1, *for* ca 1765 *read* 1764   *Line 3, after* 1736 *add* ; James T. Kirkman, *Memoirs of the Life of Charles Macklin*, 1799, i. 332; *London Stage* Part III, i. p. cxxx; information from C. B. Hogan

Page 64, note 21, lines 1–2, *for* (d. 1746) *read* (ca 1683–1746)   *Line 11, for* Grove's *Dictionary of Music; read The New Grove Dictionary of Music and Musicians*, 6th edn, ed. Stanley Sadie, 1980, x. 682–3;

Page 64, note 20, line 1, *for* —— Lewis *read* Sarah Lewis   *Line 3, after* dancer *add* (BM Add. Chart. 9308: Register of Actors at Drury Lane in 1722; information from C. B. Hogan)

Page 65, note 2, line 6, *after* through *insert* presumably

Page 66, line 15, *on* Mall *add note* 8a: 8a. See Horace, *Odes* IV. i and Pope's imitation (1737), lines 45–6 (pointed out by Robert Halsband).

Page 69, note 1, line 1, *for* HW *read* Mason

Page 75, note 13, *after* through *insert* possibly

Page 77, note 6, *add* The word 'Crimini' is not clear, except for the final 'i'.

Page 81, note 1, line 1, *for* (d. 682) *read* (d. 664)   *Line 3, after* p. 8) *insert* ; historically, he was King of Gwynedd, in North Wales. Sir John E. Lloyd in *A History of Wales* (3d edn, 1939, i. 230, n. 9) declares that 'The plague in the reign of Oswy which, according to the *Saxon Genealogies*, carried off Cadwaladr, can hardly be any other than the famous pestilence of 664. . . . The chronicle in Harl. MS. 3859 gives the year of the king's death as 682, but it is of inferior authority to the *Sax. Gen.*'; see also Gwynfor Evans, *Land of my Fathers*, Swansea, 1974, p. 119.

Page 84, note 7, *add* The *Daily Adv.* 8 July 1735 reported: 'On Friday next [11 July] the Right Hon. Sir Robert Walpole and several other persons of distinction, will set out for his seat at Houghton Hall in the county of Norfolk for three weeks, during which time he will keep open house, and the Treasury will be adjourned till his return.'

Page 95, note 6, lines 3–4, *for* (1685–1750). *read* (1690–1768) (*The New Grove Dictionary of Music and Musicians*, 6th edn, ed. Stanley Sadie, 1980, xix. 627–9).   *Line 4, for* 25 Nov. *read* 26 Nov.

Page 95, note 7, line 3, *for* Broschi (1700–56) and others. *read* Broschi (Brosca) (ca 1698–1756) and others (*The New Grove Dictionary of Music*, 6th edn, iii. 335).

Page 96, note 11, line 2, *for* (fl. 1677–1704) *read* (ca 1653–1706)

Page 97, note 22, lines 1–2, *delete* —— Chambers (fl. 1733–52), probably the Miss Chambers *and substitute* Possibly the Isabella Chambers who came out at Lincoln's Inn Fields in 1723 (*Daily Post* 11 Oct. 1723) and   *Line 5, after* iv. 656 *add*   ; *London Stage* Part III, i. 276, 537, 540   *Lines 5–9, delete* She is remembered . . . *Portraits* iii. 99).

Page 100, note 10, line 2, *for* 1740–1 *read* 17 Feb.–27 April 1741   *Last line, after* n. 7 *add*   ; Sedgwick i. 614

Page 102, note 3, line 3, *for* (fl. 1732–9) *read* (fl. 1732–59)   *Line 4, for* Thomas Reinhold (ca 1690–1751) *read* Henry Theodore Reinhold (d. 1751)   *Lines 7–8, for* Grove's *Dictionary of Music*). *read* *The New Grove Dictionary of Music and Musicians*, 6th edn, ed. Stanley Sadie, 1980, ii. 319–20, xv. 724, xx. 206).

Page 102, note 5, last line, *for* Grove's *Dictionary of Music*). *read* *The New Grove Dictionary of Music*, 6th edn, iv. 682–3).

Page 102, note 7, line 1, *for* Anna Strada del Pò (fl. 1729–38) *read* Anna Maria Strada del Pò (fl. 1720–40)   *Line 3, after* company *insert* (*The New Grove Dictionary of Music*, 6th edn, xviii. 187–8)

Page 103, note 11, last line, *after* n. 23 *add*   ; see also MANN ii. 366, n. 12

Page 104, note 1, *substitute* Presumably the 'confusion of wine and bawdy and hunting and tobacco' at Houghton, which HW found distasteful (see MANN ii. 498).

Page 106, note 11, *add* For R. G. Howarth's comment on Gray's lines, and W. S. Lewis's reply, see *Notes and Queries* Jan. and May 1956, cci. 29–30, 228.

Page 113, note 9, line 1, *for* (d. ?1736) *read* (d. 28 Nov. 1736)   *Line 2, before* Genest *insert* *London Daily Post* 30 Nov. 1736 [as C. B. Hogan points out];

Page 116, note 7, line 3, *for* proctors, meet in the vestry at St *read* latter were authorized to assist the

Page 118, note 16, line 2, *for* two *read* three

Page 118, note 18, *add* See also DALRYMPLE 4, n. 1. The *Daily Adv.* 31 March 1746 reported, 'To be sold, the Right Hon. the Earl of Orford's house, gardens, etc. at Chelsea. For further particulars inquire at John Ellis, Esq. in Cowley Street, Westminster.'

Page 120, From West ca Dec. 1736, headnote, *for* 3 Jan. 1736 *read* 3 Jan. 1737

Page 128, note 7, *add* See Gray to West 23 March 1737, now WSL (sold

American Art Association, April 1957, George A. Armour Sale, lot 294, to G. Wells for WSL).

Page 131, note 32, lines 2–3, *for* hero ('piddling Tibbald') of *The Dunciad. read* hero of *The Dunciad* and 'piddling Tibbald' in the *Epistle to Dr Arbuthnot*, line 164.

Page 133, note 45, *add* HW had apparently given a musical performance in Jan. 1737; see CONWAY i. 4.

Page 136, From Gray ca 16 July 1737, headnote, line 1, *after* Collection. *add* First printed (in a garbled text) by Mason; reprinted *Elegant Epistles*, Book III, Section II, p. 586.

Page 138, note 2, line 1, *for* 1685 *read* ca 1685   *Line 3, for* 1736–7 *read* 1737–8 (Sedgwick i. 435)

Page 140, note 1, line 5, *for* ca 1682 *read* 1682

Page 142, note 6, line 4, *for* ca 1766 *read* 1766   *Line 6, for* Grove's *Dictionary of Music read The New Grove Dictionary of Music and Musicians*, 6th edn, ed. Stanley Sadie, 1980, xiv. 570

Page 142, note 9, line 1, *for* (1703–83) *read* (1710–83)   *Last line, for* Grove's *Dictionary of Music read The New Grove Dictionary of Music*, 6th edn, iii. 595–7; *Enciclopedia dello spettacolo*, Rome, 1954–62, ii. 1461–2

Page 143, note 11, lines 1–2, *for* (b. 1692) *read* (1692–1748)

Page 145, note 3, *add* Francis Grose, *A Provincial Glossary, with a Collection of Local Proverbs, and Popular Superstitions*, 1787, *sub* London: 'He will follow him like St Anthony's pig' (Sig. P3v and P4).

Page 146, note 10, *add* Conway was in Ireland at this time; see his letters to HW ca 28 Sept., ca 20 Nov. 1737 OS (CONWAY i. 34 and n. 12, 35–8).

Page 146, note 13, line 1, *delete* Seymour   *Line 2, for* (1716–49) *read* (1714–49)   *Line 5, after* Harris *add*   ; or possibly Hon. Henrietta Seymour Conway (ca 1711–71), Lord Conway's dau. by his 1st wife   *Last line, after* 2–3 *add*   , 58; MANN i. 274, n. 32; CONWAY i. 5, n. 3, 63, n. 5, 254, n. 3

Page 150, lines 15–16, *on* Wantley *add note* 12a: 12a. HW wrote, 'Edward Wortley Montagu, husband of the famous Lady Mary, had a lodge where he often lived, at Wharncliffe in Yorkshire, a wild romantic spot, corruptly called Wantley. There is a terrace with clefts in the rock, one of which is supposed to have been the residence of the Dragon of Wantley. If Pope was ever there . . . I should conclude that he had copied thence these lines in his Messiah . . .' (*A Note Book of Horace Walpole*, ed. W. S. Lewis, New York, 1927, pp. 34–5; see also MASON ii. 15 and n. 17).

Page 151, note 1, *add* In 'Instructions for the Answer of Charles Churchill and Lady Maria his Wife and their Trustees under their Marriage Settlement Defendants to the Bills of Complaints of the Creditors of Robert Earl of Orford formerly Sir Robert Walpole and Robert Earl of Orford formerly Lord Walpole' the first sentences read as follows: 'You'll observe that Sir Robert Walpole by Articles of Agreement herewith left made previous to his marriage with Mrs Skerrett dated 13th September 1737 did for the consideration of £12,000 then vested in 3 1/2 percent annuities at the Exchequer the sole property of the said Mrs Skerrett which was to be received by Sir Robert in part of her portion as also £2000 South Sea Annuity Stock covenant with the said Mrs Skerrett that he would secure to her an annuity of £1000 per annum as part of her jointure issuing out of lands she <renounced> in pursuance of a power reserved to him by his son Lord Walpole's marriage settlement on a 2d or other wife and that the interest of the said £12,000 annuities should be made to her as a further jointure for her life and after her decease the principal and interest should descend to the child or children of the said marriage lawfully to be begotten. And in default of such issue to the said Sir Robert his sons and assigns forever with a power to Sir Robert to dispose of the said £12,000 in the purchase of lands upon condition that the profits thereof should go and be settled to the same uses as the said £12,000 and interest. And it was thereby further agreed between them that as and concerning all other the estates real or personal of the said Mrs Skerrett which she then enjoyed or should be entitled unto whether freehold, leasehold, or copyhold lands or held in trust for her she the said Mrs Skerrett was after the said marriage to receive the rents and profits thereof to her sole and separate use and to be disposed of as she should think . . .' (MS now WSL; in the agreement mentioned, Maria Skerrett's money was set aside by Sir Robert for their daughter, and was left to Lady Mary in his will; but it was expected that the creditors of the Orford estate would try to seize it, as being part of Sir Robert's property).

Page 151, note 2, last line, *for* Hazen, *SH Bibliography* 31 *read* Hazen, *Bibliography of Walpole* 147

Page 160, note 4, line 2, *for* ca 1681 *read* ca 1688

Page 166, note 37, line 1, *for* (d. 1770) *read* (1718–70)

Page 166, note 39, *add* He is also mentioned in Conway to HW ca 25 Feb. 1740 NS, CONWAY i. 47 and n. 17.

Page 166, note 40, *add* Frampton, Bonfoy, and Vernon appear in the subscription list to Middleton's *History of the Life of Marcus Tullius Cicero*, 1741; HW wrote to Middleton ca 1 Sept. 1739 NS that Lord Waldegrave had solicited the English at Paris for subscriptions, and that HW had added Lord Holdernesse, Lord Conway, Mr Conway, and Mr Brand (DALRYMPLE 6–7).

Page 166, note 43, line 2, *for* 1753–61 *read* Jan.–April 1754, Jan. 1755–1761

Page 167, note 3, *add* Gray also wrote West ca 15 and 22 May 1739 NS, 'We are making you a little bundle of petites pieces . . .' (*Gray's Corr.* i. 109).

Page 169, note 16, line 1, *for* 1616 *read* 1617

Page 183, note 17, lines 6–7, *delete* May 1741 (Mann to HW 9 May

1741, N.S.) *and substitute* April 1741 (MANN i. 31, 34 and n. 17) and left there 25 April

Page 183, note 19, line 1, *for* ca 1689 *read* 1688   *Line 3, for* 1728 *read* 1729   *Line 4, before* MONTAGU *insert* Sedgwick ii. 125;

Page 183–4, note 20, line 4, *for* or before June *read* March   *delete* (HW to Conway 5 July 1740, N.S.). *and substitute* (Conway to HW 6 March 1740 OS, CONWAY i. 48–50).

Page 184, From West 24 Sept. 1739 OS, 1st paragraph, line 11, *on* espagnole *add note 2*: 2. The phrase 'à la mode espagnole' is a punning reference to (a) the precarious state of peace between Spain and England, and (b) the formality associated with Spanish court decorum. The whole letter, indeed, is a parody of a diplomatic dispatch, and points a parallel between the friendly 'alliance' of West and Walpole with their political archetype. The postscript in English shows West's fear that letter-openers may misunderstand his humour (information from Robert Halsband).

Page 184, note 1, lines 6–11, *delete* In 1741 he went . . . it in 1751 *Lines 12–13, delete* 1746 . . . p. 334

Page 191, note 22, *add* See SELWYN 1–2.

Page 191, note 24, *substitute* Mr Blythe and Mr Chetwyn are in Spence's MS list of persons met at Turin (BM Egerton MSS 2235, f. 94). 'Mr Chetwyn' is mentioned in HW to Lincoln 21 Nov. 1739 NS (SELWYN 2 and n. 8); probably Walter Chetwynd (1710–86), at Eton 1722–7, fellow of King's College, Cambridge 1730–86.

Page 197, note 7, line 1, *for* 1696 *read* 1695   *Line 2, for* Sir Robert Walpole *read* the Earl of Wilmington

Page 200, note 6, line 1, *for* There is a similar episode *read* HW's summary of this tale combines two separate episodes   *Line 3, for* Contes de fées *read* Contes des fées   *after* 242) *add* , to which he frequently refers; see CHUTE 49, n. 4

Page 201, note 8, line 1, *for* (ca 1635–91) *read* (?1636–?1692) (see Sir George Etherege, *Letters*, ed. F. Bracher, Berkeley, California, 1974, pp. xiv, xxiii–xxiv)   *Last line, after* 162 *add* (Hazen, *Cat. of HW's Lib.* No. 1826)

Page 202, note 12, *substitute* Probably Charles Martin, 'our Tuscan Raphael in the crayon way' (James Tyrell to Ralph Howard, 1752, cited by Brinsley Ford to Hugh Honour, 1965). See John Fleming and Hugh Honour, 'Francis Harwood,' in *Festschrift Ulrich Middeldorf*, ed. A. Kosegarten and P. Tigler, Berlin, 1968, p. 515; see also MANN i. 6, 81.

Page 209, note 13, lines 10–11, *delete* , but Tencin had not yet arrived *Line 12, after* N.S. *add* , MANN i. 12, n. 52; CONWAY i. 57

Pages 210–11, note 18, *add* See also HW's 'The Dear Witches' (printed in *Old England, or the Constitutional Journal* 18 June 1743), where in his note on Mrs Smith he mentions 'one Williams, a vile fellow, who had been gallant to Mrs West.'

Page 211, note 19, line 10, *for* no news *read* no official news   *Line 15,*
after lation *insert* (Unofficial reports appeared in *Daily Adv.* 12 March
OS)

Page 212, note 4, line 2, *for* 18 Feb. *read* 19 Feb.

Page 214, To Ashton 14 May 1740, N.S., headnote, line 1, *after* MS *in-*
sert formerly   *after* New York City *add* now (Dec. 1939) WSL

Page 214, note 20, line 4, *for* [?1861] *read* 1861

Page 219, headnote, *add* The original letter is owned (1960) by Sir John
Molesworth-St Aubyn, Bt, of Pencarrow, Washaway, Bodmin, Cornwall
(information from H. M. Colvin, St John's College, Oxford).

Page 220, note 17, *add* HW's letters to her are mentioned by Conway
in his letter of 14 May 1740 OS (CONWAY i. 62).

Page 227, note 19, lines 6–7, *delete* In 1734 she had eloped with Thomas
Sturges *and substitute* In 1734 she had gone abroad ostensibly for her
health (see Dr George Cheyne to Selina, Countess of Huntingdon 18 Jan.
1734, in Hist. MSS Comm., *Hastings MSS*, ed. Bickley, 1928–47, iii. 19),
but had been joined by the Rev. Samuel Sturgis (ca 1701–43)   *Line 9,*
after Florence *add* (see MANN i. 70–1, n. 14)

Page 229, To West 2 Oct. 1740 N.S., 1st paragraph, line 2, *on* assembly
add note a: *a.* At the Casa Giraldi. In her diary Lady Pomfret wrote, *sub*
Thursday 29 Sept., 'I went to the public conversation on the wedding at
the Casa Girardi [*sic*]'; and in another diary, 'My lady Mary Wortley,
Sophia, Charlotte and myself went to the public conversation on the wedding at Casa Giraldi' (Finch MSS; information from Robert Halsband).

Page 231, note 9, line 17, *after* 1743; *add* see Hazen, *Cat. of HW's Lib.*
No. 1608:52:1, 2.   *Lines 17–21, delete Le Lodi . . .* Florence, 1741.
Line 21, for His *read* Cocchi's   *Line 22, after* L.3.1 *add*   ; Hazen, *Cat.*
of HW's Lib. No. 2074   *Line 23, after* 62 *add*   ; Terence Hodgkinson,
'Joseph Wilton and Dr Cocchi,' *Victoria and Albert Bulletin*, April 1967,
pp. 73–80, on the bust of Cocchi by Wilton.

Page 231, note 10, lines 1 and 4, *for* Buondelmonte *read* Buondelmonti
Line 4, after wore *add* (*Dizionario biografico degli Italiani*, Rome, 1961– ,
xv. 212–15)

Page 233, note 19, last line, *after* 1772 *add* (MANN vii. 383)

Page 235, note 4, *delete 1st sentence and substitute* Probably the Hon.
Jane Conway (see *ante* 29 Dec. 1737). By 'Miss Conway' HW sometimes
meant Anne, sometimes Henrietta (CONWAY i. 71, 110); he usually called
Jane 'Miss Jenny,' as Conway called her 'Jenny.' But Jane was the one
most often referred to among their intimate friends at this time (ibid. i.
5, 19, 21, 23, 26, 29; MANN i. 274 and n. 32, iv. 58–9; SELWYN 82).   *Lines*
16–17, for Collection of Poems *read* Collection of Original Poems and
Translations   Line 19, after Conway.' *add* See Hazen, *Cat. of HW's*
Lib. No. 1841

Page 237, note 4, line 5, *for* Via *read* Borgo

180   VOLUME 14 (GRAY ii)

Page 239, note 12, line 9, *after* place' *add* (see CONWAY i. 99).

Page 240, note 5, line 2, *delete* evidently   *Last line, add* See also CHUTE 3, n. 1; SELWYN 16.

Page 241, To West 10 May 1741, headnote, *add* West was in Paris at this time (West to Ashton, Paris, 8 May 1741 NS, MS now WSL, Maggs Cat. 513, Dec. 1928, lot 2891).

Page 241, note 8, *delete* George Augustus Selwyn *and substitute* John Selwyn (ca 1709–51), the younger, M. P. Whitchurch 1734–51; he had been ill since February (see CONWAY i. 6, 56 and n. 3, 88, 89, 93).

Page 241, note 1, right column, line 10, *after* May *insert* (see HW to Lincoln 29 April 1741 NS, SELWYN 16).

Page 243, note 14, *substitute* HW wrote to Lincoln 29 April NS, from Bologna, 'I go tomorrow to Modena, and thence to Reggio, but fear I cannot be at Venice by the Ascension [11 May NS]' (SELWYN 16). HW met Lincoln and Spence at Reggio, where HW became seriously ill and stayed behind when Lincoln and Spence went on to Venice; HW joined them there 9 June (MANN i. 54, n. 1), and they set out for Paris together 12 July (ibid. i. 91, 94; SELWYN 17). For their route to Paris see MANN i. 58, n. 1. See also Joseph Spence, *Letters from the Grand Tour*, ed. Slava Klima, Montreal and London, 1975, pp. 386–98.

Page 245, To Ashton July 1741, headnote, lines 2–3, *delete* or Saturday 25 July *and substitute*   , since Conway writes ca 23 July OS that he saw HW's letter to Mrs Grosvenor 'the very morning after she had received your letter' (CONWAY i. 100), and Ashton writes 25 July OS that Mrs Grosvenor 'enclosed your letter to me the moment she received it' (*post* i. 246);   *Line 3, for* it *read* the letter to Ashton   *Lines 3–4, for* 19 or 22 *read* 11   *Line 4, for* Genoa, bound for England *read* Venice

Page 246, note 3, *add* But West to Ashton 8 May NS is addressed 'at Mrs Lewis's in Hanover Square London' (MS now WSL; *Gray-HW-West-Ashton Corr.* ii. 8).

Page 246, note 5, *add* HW did write a letter to Mrs Grosvenor ca 11 July NS, with a letter to Ashton enclosed, which reached London probably 22 July OS since Conway in his letter postmarked 23 July OS mentions seeing HW's letter to Mrs Grosvenor (CONWAY i. 100).

Page 247, 3d paragraph, line 1, *on* Paris *add note* 6a: 6a. West wrote to Ashton from Paris 8 May 1741 NS (MS now WSL; printed in *Gray-HW-West-Ashton Corr.* ii. 8).

VOLUME 14

Page 2, note 7, line 1, *for* (d. 1746) *read* (ca 1687–1746)

Page 3, note 13, right column, lines 7–10, *delete* the forthcoming . . . Mack). *and substitute Pope's Epistles to Several Persons (Moral Essays)*, ed. F. W. Bateson, 1951, pp. 155–64.

Page 5, From Gray 7 July ?1746, headnote, line 2, *after* 1902. *insert* Previously printed by Thomas Thorpe, Catalogue 1833 (Autograph Correspondence of Distinguished Persons), lot 307, p. 33.

Page 10, note 9, line 6, *after* 246 *insert* ; see CONWAY i. 234, n. 1 for variations in dating of the commission   *Line 7, after* 1746 *insert* (for Conway's account see his letter of 18 April 1746 OS in ibid. i. 238–41) *Line 9, delete* apparently   *Last line, after* resistance *add* , and came back to London in November for the opening of Parliament (see ibid. i. 243, 247, 249–50, 263).

Page 10, note 11, line 9, *for* 1711 *read* 1713   *Line 10, after* time *add* (*The New Grove Dictionary of Music and Musicians*, 6th edn, ed. Stanley Sadie, 1980, xviii. 696–7)   *Last line, add* The *London Stage* (Part III, ii. 1268) *sub* 2 Dec. 1746 notes: 'The subscribers to the second subscription for operas, are desired to take notice, that on Thursday morning next [4 Dec.] will be a general rehearsal of the new opera called *Mitridate* upon the stage. . . . No persons to be admitted without a subscriber's ticket.' Performances are listed on 6, 9, 13, 16, 20, 22, 27, 30 Dec. 1746 (ibid. 1270–8, 1311, 1313, 1314).

Page 11, note 2, *add* Lady Mary Oldboy, wife of Col. Oldboy, is a loquacious character in Isaac Bickerstaffe's comic opera, *Lionel and Clarissa*, first performed at Covent Garden 25 Feb. 1768 (*London Stage* Part IV, iii. 1313–17).

Page 13, From Gray 8 Feb. 1747, headnote, line 3, *add* HW's pencilled (half-erased) note on the MS reads: 'You may [?see] the date of this by Cibber's book. I think him much too severe on the Author of the Careless Husband and of his own life.'

Page 14, note 8, line 8, *after* copies' *add* One of HW's copies is now WSL; see Hazen, *Cat. of HW's Lib.* No. 1101.

Page 18, note 31, line 4, *after* friends *add* and cousins (Peter Le Neve, *Pedigrees of the Knights*, ed. G. W. Marshall, 1873, p. 418; *Vict. Co. Hist. Hants* iii. 464; Sedgwick ii. 534–5)

Page 21, note 21, *add* See Hazen, *Cat. of HW's Lib.* No. 3168.

Page 21, note 22, lines 1–2, *for* cr. (1733) Bn Hervey of Ickworth *read* summoned to the House of Lords in his father's Barony as Lord Hervey of Ickworth, 1733

Page 26, note 2, *add* HW had a copy of Goldwin's *Scotch Adventure*, 1746 (now WSL); see Hazen, *Cat. of HW's Lib.* No. 3363.

Page 31, headnote, line 3, *for* ram *read* rams

Page 33, note 9, line 1, *for* had evidently *read* with his letter of 22 Nov. 1741 OS   *Line 2, for* perhaps from Italy *substitute* and explained that it was influenced by Middleton's *Letter from Rome*; see DALRYMPLE 8–9 and nn. 1a, 3, 4.

Page 34, note 1, last line, *after* Museum *add* (Hazen, *Cat. of HW's Lib.* No. 2370)

Page 36, note 14, *add* HW's copy of the 1st edn of 'The Art of Politics', 1729, is bound in a volume of Tracts, now WSL; HW's copy of the 2d edn, 1729, is also WSL (Hazen, *Cat. of HW's Lib*. Nos 1886, 2474:1).

Page 36, note 18, line 1, *for* ca 1702 *read* 1709　　*Line 2, for* (1767) Bn *read* (1767) Vct Clare

Page 37, note 31, line 9, *before* met *insert* probably　　*Line 11, after* 1774 *add*　, CONWAY iii. 233 and n. 38

Page 38, note 40, line 2, *after* 274–98). *add* HW's copy, with MS corrections and identifications, is now WSL (Hazen, *Cat. of HW's Lib*. No. 3363:2).

Page 42, note 58, line 5, *for* 1737 *read* 1738

Page 43, *before* From Gray 12 June 1750 *insert the following heading*:

To ASHTON, ca Wednesday 11 February 1750

Missing. Mentioned by HW to Duke of Bedford 11 Feb. 1750: 'I dispatched the messenger to Eton . . . with a letter to Mr Ashton. . . .'

Page 43, note 4, line 5, *after* 1724 *add* (For HW's copies see Hazen, *Cat. of HW's Lib*. Nos 1379:10:2 and 1402)

Page 43, note 5, *add* For HW's copies of tracts in this controversy see Hazen, *Cat. of HW's Lib*. No. 1379.

Page 44, From Gray ?10 Feb. 1751, headnote, line 2, *for* by Mason *read* in HW's hand, crossed through by Mason

Page 47, 1st paragraph, line 1, *on* author *add note a: a*. HW may have first met Mason at this time.

Page 49, note 1, line 1, *for* 29 *read* 30　　*Line 4, after* O.S. *add*　, MANN iv. 238, where HW says 'he expired on Friday night'; Friday was 29 March. See also MANN iv. 237, n. 1; CHUTE 66–7, which should be dated Saturday, 30 March OS.

Page 50, note 8, line 3, *for* Thorverton *read* Raddon Court　　*Line 6, after* Harris *insert* (?1690–1767)

Page 51, headnote, line 2, *delete* or Mason

Page 54, note 10, last line, *for* 52ff *read* 52–97

Page 55, line 7, *on* aside *add note* 12a: 12a. This note is at the top of folio 53, which is the first page of the letter (folio 52 is a title-page).

Page 55, note 13, line 2, *for* 21ff *read* 21–5. This passage is near the beginning of the draft in Add. MS 32,459, fol. 21–5; but there are so many variants that Gray must have seen another version. The discrepancy is probably explained by a note by (?)Heberden at the end of Add. MS 32,459, on two pieces 'Mrs Middleton probably burned'; the summary of one of them, 'a Latin dissertation in folio contained in 14 pages,' shows it to be the same in substance as this draft.

Page 58, line 4, *on* your letter *add note* 7a: 7a. Of 12 Oct. 1751 OS.

Page 58, From Gray 28 May 1752, headnote, line 1, *after* col. 7 *insert* ; now collated with the MS (now WSL)　　*Lines 4–5, for* Toynbee in *SH Accounts*, p. 62, says that *substitute* Resold Sotheby's 20 Dec. 1948 (property of the late W. Marchbank of Newcastle-upon-Tyne), lot 226, to Maggs for WSL, £22.   *for* on *read* On *and delete* (which the editors have not seen)   *Below Address insert Postmarks*: SAFFRON WALDEN 29 MA

Page 58, From Gray 28 May 1752, 1st paragraph, line 1, *for* you *read* you,   *Line 3, after* remember) *delete* ,   *after* mine *delete* ,   *Line 4, for* years; *read* years: *Line 5, for* place *read* place,   *2d paragraph, line 3, for* Chute *read* Chute,   *Line 4, for* Yours ever, *read* Yours ever

Page 59, note 5, line 2, *after* WSL. *add* HW bound it opposite Bentley's drawing.

Page 60, To Gray July–August 1752, headnote, *after* Missing. *add* This may be the letter to 'Mr Gr' 29 Aug. 1752 which is listed in *memoranda* on Conway to HW 23 Aug. 1752 (see CONWAY i. 344).

Page 62, note 12, *add* See Hazen, *Bibliography of Walpole* 113–20.

Page 63, note 1, line 13, *after* York *add* (See Hazen, *Bibliography of Walpole* 115, 119–20)

Page 68, note 12, line 6, *for* John Mabuse *read* Jan Gossaert (called Mabuse) (1478–between 1533 and 1536)   *Last line, add* HW's identification is supported by Mr Lawrence Jack of Enfield, Middlesex, who points out the likeness between the portrait of Queen Margaret formerly in the collection of the E. of Oxford and an engraving similar to HW's painting, both illustrated in John J. Bagley, *Margaret of Anjou, Queen of England,* 1948, frontispiece, and facing p. 44.

Page 69, note 3, line 1, *for* 1429 *read* ca 1430   *Last line, add* For her birth date see Philippe Ërlanger, *Margaret of Anjou Queen of England,* 1970, p. 35.

Page 69, note 5, right column, line 2, *for* King of Sicily 1435–42 *read* titular King of Sicily 1435–80 and effective King of Naples 1438–42   *Line 4, add* HW's 'Life of René of Anjou, King of Naples' is printed in MORE Appendix 10, pp. 438–9.

Page 70, note 10, *delete first sentence and substitute* The title of the English translation is *Royal and Ecclesiastical Antiquities of France,* London, 1750.

Page 70, note 11, line 3, *for* Possibly HW had the five *substitute* HW had the English edition, London, 1750, two   *Line 4, after* three *add* (Hazen, *Cat. of HW's Lib.* No. 3683)

Page 70, note 16, line 3, *for* newe *read* Newe

Page 72, note 32, *add* For HW's account of him see *Works* i. 562–7.

Pages 72–3, note 43, line 1, *for* 1390 *read* ca 1384   *Line 2, for* E. of Shrewsbury *read* E. of Salop, known as E. of Shrewsbury

Page 73, note 50, line 2, *for* 7th *read* 6th

Page 73, note 55, line 1, *for* (d. 1467) *read* (1404–67)   *Lines 2–3, for* after 1433 *read* 1425   *Line 4, for* E. of Shrewsbury *read* E. of Salop, known as E. of Shrewsbury

Page 73, note 56, lines 1–2, *for* Lady Alice de Montacute (d. before 1463) *read* Lady Alice de Montagu (ca 1406–62)

Page 75, note 68, *add* But the marriage ceremony was performed 22

April 1445 by William Ayscough, Bishop of Salisbury and Confessor to the King, at St Mary's Abbey, Titchfield (John J. Bagley, *Margaret of Anjou, Queen of England*, 1948, pp. 45, 47).

Page 82, note 1, last line, *after* 161 *add*   ; Sedgwick i. 553

Page 83, note 4, *add* See also CONWAY i. 400 and n. 16.

Page 86, To Gray 25 Dec. 1755, headnote, last line, *after* lot 1274; *add* No. 554 (Spring, 1931);

Page 87, note 1, line 1, *for* 1754 *read* 1764

Page 87, note 4, *substitute* Probably Molly Shadwell, youngest daughter of Sir John Shadwell, who was a physician (MANN i. 185, n. 18).

Page 89, note 1, line 4, *for* 1766 *read* 1768   *Line 6, add* See SELWYN 127 and n. 1.

Page 89, note 7, *add* See also SELWYN 129 and n. 3, 131 and n. 2.

Page 91, note 18, line 1, *for* ca 1721 *read* 1721

Page 92, note 4, *after* 1756 *add*   ; CHUTE 95–6

Page 93, note 1, line 1, *for* (ca 1710–80) *read* (ca 1710–1780 *or* 1786) *Line 5, after* 178 *add*   ; CHUTE 108–9 and n. 1

Page 99, note 2, *add* See also CHUTE 100.

Page 99, note 10, line 2, *for* Violette *read* Veigel   *for* 1725 *read* 1724

Page 102, note 3, *add* HW and Gray apparently did make this visit to the Vyne (see MONTAGU i. 222; CONWAY i. 556 and n. 25).

Page 104, note 3, last line, *after* n. 2 *add*   ; now printed in MISC. CORR. i. 158–60

Page 106, To Gray August 1760, headnote, line 1, *after* Maggs, *insert* Cat. No. 433 (Christmas, 1922), lot 3806, Cat. No. 471 (1925), lot 3165, Cat. No. 501 (Spring, 1928), lot 703,

Page 106, note 1, line 6, *for* 20 *read* 28

Page 117, note 6, line 1, *after* Torrigiani *insert or* Torrigiano

Page 118, note 1, line 3, *for* La *read* la   *Line 4, after* ii. 15 *add*   ; Hazen, *Cat. of HW's Lib.* No. 819; see also MASON i. 186 and n. 7

Page 120, *memoranda*, left column, *below line 8 insert* Mr Zouch books[6a]

Page 120, note 5, lines 2–3, *for* cr. (1733) Bn Hervey of Ickworth *read* styled Bn Hervey of Ickworth, 1733

Page 120, note 6, line 3, *for* publisher *read* who sold   *after Anecdotes add* but whether as HW's agent or as publisher is not clear; see Hazen, *SH Bibliography* 56; SELWYN 171–2

Page 120, *add note* 6a: 6a. Zouch's set of *Anecdotes* vols i–iii and the *Catalogue of Engravers*, bound in 2 vols, is now WSL.

Page 120, note 7, lines 4–5, *delete* of which only a few letters can be made out *and substitute* which may read, 'Print pote'; the reference is possibly to Hogarth's print of Morell, engraved by Basire, 'A Cynic Philosopher,' 1762.

Page 120, note 11, line 1, *for* 1698 *read* 1696   *Lines 2–3, delete* HW's neighbour and correspondent (MONTAGU i. 15) *and substitute* see MORE 418 and n. 33

Page 120, note 12, line 1, *for* ca 1691 *read* ca 1690

Page 120, note 14, lines 4–7, *delete* 'Wedn.' may be a contraction . . . Feb. 1762 *and substitute* 'Wedn. Mr F.' may mean Wednesday 17 Feb. on which day Bunbury intended to make a motion in the House of Commons for the recall of English troops from Germany; 'Mr F.' is probably Fox, who discouraged Bunbury's motion (see Namier and Brooke ii. 136–7; MANN vi. 8 and nn. 12, 13; *Leinster Corr.* i. 314–15, 317).

Page 120, note 15, *add* Her engagement to Bunbury was being arranged by her family at this time; see *Leinster Corr.* i. 311–14, 316, 320–1, 326–7.

Page 121, note 22, *for* Unexplained. *read* Possibly a group described by Lady Caroline Fox to Lady Kildare 27 Feb. 1762, 'It consists of my brother and the Duchess, Lord and Lady George [Lennox], the Fitzroys, Mr and Mrs Merril, Lord Essex, Lord Errol, Lord Cavendish and Lord Orford, they play and sit up at one of their houses every night till four or five in the morning; then instead of their own equipages, come home six or seven together in hackney coaches. During these elections in the House the four ladies attended as constantly as the men, come out to eat their dinner and returned to the House. The Duchess [of Richmond] goes everywhere with Mr Merril in his chariot; they are as you may suppose finely abused. . . . My brother Richmond I think don't quite enjoy it' (*Leinster Corr.* i. 317–18).

Page 121, note 23, lines 1–4, *delete* Unexplained . . . or on *and substitute* Probably 'a ridiculous epigram made on poor Sal, I believe by C. Townshend' quoted in Lady Caroline Fox to Lady Kildare 16 Feb. 1762 (*Leinster Corr.* i. 317); it related to   *Line 5, after* Bunbury *add* and to his proposed motion in the House of Commons   *At end add* Quoted also in MANN vi. 8, n. 15.

Page 122, note 2, at end, *for* now Folger Shakespeare Library *read* now WSL

Page 123, line 3, *on* materials *add note* 5a: 5a. See HW to Cole 11 Aug. 1769 (COLE i. 190–2).

Page 123, note 8, *add* See OSSORY i. 254, n. 17; MANN viii. 328, n. 14.

Page 125, From Gray 12 Sept. 1763, headnote, on last line *add note* a: a. The 'Chronological Table' of Gray's life (*Gray's Corr.* ii. p. xxix), compiled from the Pembroke College buttery books, shows Gray to have been at Cambridge in April 1763, and in London 6 May–16 June. Also, Gray wrote Wharton 5 Aug. 1763 that 'except six weeks that I pass'd in Town towards the end of spring, & a little jaunt to Epsom & Box-Hill, I have been here time out of mind' (ibid. ii. 805). Since Lady Waldegrave was living in Ragman's Castle in Twickenham from ca 22 April 1763, it is possible that the occasion when she and Gray were at SH took place in May or early June (MONTAGU ii. 69; MANN vi. 136).

Page 127, note 19, line 1, *for* 1559 *read* 1559 *or* 1560

Page 130, middle of page, transfer from page 131 heading and headnote for To Gray, January 1764

Pages 130–1, note 2, lines 13–17, *delete* public indignation . . . pamphlet war. *and substitute* although he had been summoned as witness to the House of Lords, he was not examined during the proceedings on 24 Jan. (see CONWAY ii. 294 and n. 96).

Page 131, transfer To Gray, January 1764 and headnote to middle of p. 130

Page 131, note 5, *add* Sandwich to Unknown 29 Nov. 1763 (MS WSL) begins, 'I have canvassed most of the principal people of the University of Cambridge, and have great reason to think I must meet with success on a vacancy of the office of High Steward,' and asks a recommendation to Dr Dale of Trinity Hall through Mr Hooper of the Custom House.

Page 133, note 4, *add* In a MS list, 'University Library, among the Pamphlets, Class B,' (now WSL), Gray includes 'Dr Eglisham's Petition to Charles 1st on the Death of his Father and the Marq. of Hamilton. 1642. 10.15.'

Page 133, note 10, last line, *after* 4098 *add* ; CONWAY ii. 341, 355, 362–3

Page 133, note 12, last line, *after* 871 *add* ; MANN vi. 219, n. 22

Page 134, note 13, *for* Unexplained *read* Presumably in connection with the *Life of Lord Herbert of Cherbury*, which Gray mentions in his next letter 25 April (see Hazen, *SH Bibliography* 70–1).

Page 134, note 15, *add* HW's copy of the 1st edn is Hazen, *Cat. of HW's Lib.* No. 3222:5:1 (now at Harvard), and of the 2d edn is ibid. No. 1810: 59:2 (now WSL).

Page 137, note 1, line 13, *for* first *read* last   *Line 15, after* 1765 *add* , CONWAY ii. 525

Page 138, note 11, *add* For HW's copy see Hazen, *Cat. of HW's Lib.* No. 818.

Page 139, note 11, line 1, *for* orginal *read* original

Page 142, headnote, line 2, *delete* present location of the   *Line 3, delete* is unknown *and substitute* was advertised in Maggs Cats No. 433 (Christmas 1922), lot 3805, No. 471 (1925), lot 3165, No. 501 (Spring 1928), lot 702, No. 530 (Christmas 1929), lot 2448; now in the Berg collection at the New York Public Library; reproduced in the exhibition catalogue of letters by famous men, *Other People's Mail*, ed. Lola L. Szladits, New York, 1973, pp. 14–16.

Page 142, 1st paragraph, line 16, *on* able *add note a: a.* After 'able—' Mary Berry omits the next eight sentences, through 'ten times a day.'

Page 143, 2d paragraph, line 4, *on* forever *add note* 5a: 5a. See CONWAY iii. 31, 529–32.

Page 144, 1st paragraph, last line, *on* bag *add note* 10a: 10a. This sentence was omitted by Mary Berry.

Page 144, 2d paragraph, last line, *for* lady devotees *read* Lady-Devotés

Page 145, note 14, lines 1–2, *delete* -Hippolyte   *for* Legris *read* Leris *delete* de Latude   Lines 3–4, *for* DU DEFFAND i. 146 *substitute* CONWAY ii. 517, n. 14

Page 145, note 21, lines 1–2, *for* Diepenbeek (ca 1607–75) *read* Diepenbeeck or Diepenbeke (1596–1675)

Page 150, note 6, line 1, *for* 1681 *read* 1682

Page 153, note 26, *add* Printed in DU DEFFAND vi. 194–5.

Page 154, note 35, line 3, *for* Duc *read* Comte   At end add See Lucien Perey [C.A.L. Herpin], *Un Petit-Neveu de Mazarin*, 1899, pp. 567, 571, where both his marriage contract and memorial tablet are given, and both refer to him only as Comte de Gisors.

Page 157, note 51, *add* See HW to Anne Pitt 19 Jan. 1766, where he says that 'I am the fashion' and that his letter from the King of Prussia has been 'pronounced *the fashion*' (MORE 99, 101).

Page 159, From Gray 24 Dec. 1767, headnote, *add* Another memorandum book, entitled *The Norwich Memorandum-Book, for Gentlemen and Tradesmen, for the Year 1767*, which contains MS entries by Thomas Gray, is now in the Beinecke Library, Yale University. An item *sub* 14 Nov. 1767, 'coach to Twickenham two places 5–0,' may indicate a visit by Gray to Walpole at Strawberry Hill (see W. H. Smith, 'A Memorandum Book of Thomas Gray,' *The Yale University Library Gazette*, 1974, xlviii. 41–3).

Page 162, note 5, line 6, *for* 1459–86). *read* 1459–86.   Lines 9–15, *delete* An argument . . . published. *and substitute* The author may have been John Russell (see *ante* 24 Dec. 1767).

Page 165, note 29, *add* See also *post* ii. 245; Robert Halsband, *The Life of Lady Mary Wortley Montagu*, Oxford, 1956, pp. 153–62.

Page 166, note 40, lines 2–5, *delete* Philip Yorke . . . in 1765. *and substitute* Philip Yorke (1690–1764), Earl of Hardwicke, Lord Chancellor 1737–56; Hon. Philip Yorke (1720–90), 2d Earl of Hardwicke; and Hon. Charles Yorke (1722–1770), offered the chancellorship in 1765, Lord Chancellor 17–20 Jan. 1770 (see MANN vii. 175, 178–9; Namier and Brooke iii. 676–7, 681). Two younger sons were Hon. Joseph Yorke (1724–92), ambassador at The Hague 1761–80, M.P., and Hon. John Yorke (1728–1801), M.P. (ibid. iii. 678–80).

Page 167, note 3, right column, line 2, *for* sold SH i. 25 *read* Hazen, *Cat. of HW's Lib.* Nos 70, 109   Last line, after year add (Hazen, op. cit. No. 151)

Page 168, note 11, last line, *after* i. 66 *add* (Hazen, *Cat. of HW's Lib.* No. 3229)

Page 168, note 12, add See also HW to Dalrymple 2 Feb. 1768, DALRYMPLE 119.

Page 170, note 23, line 5, *for* 28 *read* 23   *delete last sentence and substitute* See Hazen, *Cat. of HW's Lib.* No. 3069.

Page 170, note 27, line 1, *for* 1690 *read* 1694

Page 171, note 28, left column, lines 8–9, *delete*   ; the style however is Boswellian   *Lines 11–14, delete*   ,' in *Philological* . . . reprinted. *substitute*   : a Reconsideration,' in *Horace Walpole: Writer, Politician, and Connoisseur*, ed. W. H. Smith, New Haven, 1967, pp. 255–91, where Mr Pottle argues that it was probably *not* by Boswell.

Page 175, note 25, *substitute* The enclosures are now WSL; they were preserved with HW's portfolio relating to the *Historic Doubts*, formerly in the possession of Lord Derby.

Page 175, note 26, line 1, *for* (1445–1509) *read* (1447–1511)

Page 177, line 4, *on* sent me *add note* 13a: 13a. See Sandwich to HW 17 Feb. 1768, in MISC. CORR. ii. 134–5.

Page 177, line 6, *for* Lytteltons *read* Lyttelton's

Page 177, note 15, line 3, *for* 7 July *read* 16 June   *Last line, after* See *add* St James's Chronicle 6–9, 9–11, 13–16 June 1767;   *At end add* For HW's copy see Hazen, *Cat. of HW's Lib*. No. 3173.

Page 177, note 17, at beginning *insert* The English version of the roll is BM Add. MS 48,976; the later Latin version has been *penes* College of Arms since 1786.

Page 177, note 21, *for* 18th *read* 17th

Page 178, note 24, *after* COLE *add* ii. 2; HW to Astle 22 April 1768, in MISC. CORR. ii. 144

Page 181, note 23, lines 1–4, *delete* Talbot . . . notes 43, 81). *and substitute* Butler.   *Last line, after* 304 *add*   ; CHUTE 609

Page 182, note 4, *add* See also Sandwich to HW 17 Feb. 1768, in MISC. CORR. ii. 134–5.

Page 182, note 5, line 12, *for* Dr. *read* Dr

Page 182, note 7, *for* 7 Alexander *read* 7. Alexander Stewart

Page 183, note 10, *add* See also Alison Hanham, *Richard III and his Early Historians 1483–1535*, Oxford, 1975.

Page 183, note 11, last line, *after* WSL *add* (Hazen, *Cat. of HW's Lib*. Nos 3379, 3380)

Page 184, note 18, *add* See also MANN vi. 587–8.

Page 186, note 5, line 5, *after* i. 150 *add* and is now in the British Museum; see Hazen, *Cat. of HW's Lib*. No. 475

Page 187, middle of page, *insert the following heading*:

To GRAY, ?January 1771

Possibly implied in HW to Cole 10 Jan. 1771; see COLE i. 212 and n. 7, and Hazen, *Bibliography of Walpole* 73.

Pages 187–8, note 2, *add* HW's copy is Hazen, *Cat. of HW's Lib*. No. 3058.

Page 188, note 2, line 2, *for* 32 *read* 34

Page 189, note 5, line 1, *for* ca 1725 *read* 1725

Page 189, note 10, *add* HW inserted an engraving of it in the account of Essex in *Royal and Noble Authors* (see *Works* i. 321).

Page 193, note 1, *add* There is a portrait of her by Rosalba at the Vyne (C. W. Chute, *History of the Vyne*, 1888, p. 101).

Page 194, note 7, *for* Presumably 'Myrtila,' *read* Francesco Martelli,

Page 195, note 12, line 1, *for* (d. 1745) *read* (ca 1696–1745)   *Last line, after* 241–2 *add*   ; Sedgwick i. 553–4

Page 195, note 13, last line, *after* O.S. *add*   ; Chute to HW 13 Feb., 24 June 1742 NS.

Page 196, note 17, line 1, *for* (living 1775) *read* (d. 1775)   *Last line, after* 93 *add*   ; CONWAY iii. 89, n. 14

Page 197, note 19, last line, *after* 103 *add*   ; Sedgwick ii. 465; Namier and Brooke iii. 521

Page 197, note 20, line 1, *for* ca 1720 *read* 1721   *Line 2, for* see DU DEFFAND and MONTAGU *read* Sedgwick ii. 439; Namier and Brooke iii. 468

Page 199, note 28, last line, *after* n. 1 *add*   ; CHUTE 85

Page 199, note 29, last line, *after* DNB *add*   ; CHUTE 84, n. 9

Page 201, note 37, *add* In the will of Ann Chute (d. 1748), John Chute's unmarried sister, probated 17 Jan. 1748, 'my dear niece Travelt's eldest daughter' is named as a legatee.

Page 205, note 51, line 3, *for* F. L. Holland *read* Francis Caldwell Holland

Page 207, note 53, *for* Mary Magdalen (d. 1783) *read* Mary Magdelaine Lombard (ca 1695–1783)

Page 214, Supplementary Documents, headnote, *for* F. L. Holland *read* Francis Caldwell Holland

Page 225, note 2, *add* There were apparently some quite harmless books with similar titles; Hannah More presented 'Mother Bunch's Tales' to a child of three, and wrote some verses on the book (William Roberts, *Memoirs of the Life and Correspondence of Mrs Hannah More*, 1834, i. 176, 204). See also the advertisement in the *Public Adv.* 5 Jan. 1773.

Page 227, note 1, *substitute* HW's copy of 'The Bawdy Guardian; or, Miss Gi——t's Advice to the Lasses of London,' on which HW has noted 'By Mr Chute,' is now WSL.

Page 234, headnote, *after* 87 *add*   , now WSL

Page 234, note 1, *for* But *read* In 1742;   *after* n. 12. *add* Ashton wrote 3 Feb. 1747 to Newcastle, 'I am encouraged by Mr Pelham, whose name I have the honour to use on this occasion, to apply to your Grace with respect to the living of Aldingham, Lancashire, to which I was presented on your Grace's recommendation by the King, who is the patron; and which I should now be glad to resign in favour of my brother, a Fellow of Trinity College, Cambridge, who resides upon it as curate, as I have one in view more agreeable to my present situation' (BM Add. MS 32,710, f. 154).

Page 235, note 10, *add* West's verses are mentioned in *Gray-HW-West-Ashton Corr.* ii. 29–30.

Page 235, note 10a, *add* Presumably the English verses in HW to Mann 24 June 1742 OS, MANN i. 468–9.

Page 239, headnote, line 3, *add* See also Gray's 'Proposals' for printing his 'Travels' sent to Wharton 12 March 1740 NS, in *Gray's Corr.* i. 138–43.

Page 243, note 7, at end, *for* Leslie Stephen in DNB *substitute* George W. Sherburn, *The Early Career of Alexander Pope*, Oxford, 1934, chapters vi–vii; see also Robert Halsband, *The Life of Lady Mary Wortley Montagu*, Oxford, 1956, pp. 113–14, 129–32.

Page 245, note 15, line 14, *after* n. 40 *add* ; HW's copy is now WSL *Lines 14–15, for* it is further supported by *substitute* on HW's authority in   *Line 16, after Collection delete*   , where

Page 245, note 18, *add* See Robert Halsband, *The Life of Lady Mary Wortley Montagu*, Oxford, 1956, pp. 185–6, 191, 192. Mr Halsband has suggested that the 'noble Venetian' might be Count Algarotti, since HW describes him in these words in his MS commonplace book (*ante* ii. 165, n. 29), but Algarotti was in England or Berlin while Lady Mary was in Venice and her pursuit of him was by letter (Halsband, op. cit. 176–7, 187–8, 191–2

Page 246, note 21, *add* See also Robert Halsband, *The Life of Lady Mary Wortley Montagu*, Oxford, 1956, pp. 205, 207, 211–12.

Page 247, note 23, *for* 35 *read* 36

Page 259, 3d line from end, *after* traced. *insert* Conyers Middleton wrote 16 Jan. 1748–9, 'Manby has sent me down four small pamphlets proposed to come out weekly, called *The Mitre and Crown*, etc. in which I find myself and my work abused. . . . I should guess the writer to be some non-juring divine, who writes partly for bread, and partly for the orthodox cause of that ancient and hereditary right, which would give us both our kings and bishops from Rome' (*Miscellaneous Works*, 1752, ii. 495).

Page 259, *add* APPENDIX 9

WALPOLE'S MEMOIR OF GRAY

Printed from HW's 'MS Commonplace Book of Verses,' (pp. 65–6), formerly in the Waldegrave Collection, now WSL.

He was son of a money-scrivener, by Mary [Dorothy] Antrobus a milliner in Cornhill, and sister to two Antrobus's who were ushers of Eton School. He was born in 1716, and educated at Eton College, chiefly under the direction of one of his uncles, who took prodigious pains with him, which answered exceedingly: He particularly instructed him in the virtues of Simples.[1] He had a great genius for music, and poetry. From Eton,

---

1. 'A medicine or medicament composed or concocted of only one constituent, *esp.* of one herb or plant (*obs.*); hence, a plant or herb employed for medical purposes' (OED, *sub.* 'simple,' B.6).

he went to Peterhouse in Cambridge, and in 1739 accompanied Mr H.W. in travels to France and Italy. He returned in 1741, and retired to Cambridge again. His letters were the best I ever saw and had more novelty and wit. One of his first pieces of poetry was an answer in English verse to an epistle from H.W. At Naples he wrote a fragment describing an earthquake and the [ori]gin of Monte Nuovo in the style of Virgil, and at Rome an Alcaic Ode in imitation of Horace to Richard West Esq. After his return he wrote that inimitable Ode on a Distant Prospect of Eton College; another Moral Ode, and that beautiful one on a cat of Mr H.W.'s drowned in a tub of goldfishes. These three last have been published in Dodsley's Miscellanies. He began a poem on the reformation of learning, but soon dropped it, on finding his plan had too much resemblance to the Dunciad. It had this admirable line in it, *And Gospel-light first flash'd from Bullen's Eyes*. He began too a philosophical poem in Latin, and an English tragedy of Agrippina, and some other odes, one of which a very beautiful one, entitled *Stanzas written in a Country Churchyard*, he finished in 1750. He was a very slow but very correct writer. Being at Stoke in the summer of 1750, he wrote a kind of tale, addressed to Lady Schaub and Miss Speed, who had made him a visit from Lady Cobham's. The Elegy written in the Churchyard was published by Dodsley Feb. 16, 1751 with a short Advertisement, by Mr H.W. and immediately went through four editions. He had some thoughts of taking his Doctor's degree, but would not, for fear of being confounded with Dr Grey, who published the foolish edition of Hudibras. In March 1753 was published a fine edition of six of his poems, with frontispieces, head- and tail-pieces, and initial letters, engraved by Grignion and Müller, after designs of Richard Bentley Esq. He lost his mother a little before this, and about the same time finished an extreme fine poem, in imitation of Pindar, on the power of musical poetry, which he had begun two or three years before.

In the winter of 1755, George Hervey Earl of Bristol, who was soon afterwards sent Envoy to Turin, was designed for Minister to Lisbon; he offered to carry Mr Gray as his secretary, but he refused it.

In August 1757 were published two Odes by Mr Gray, one on the power and progress of poetry, the other on the destruction of the Welsh bards by Edward I. They were printed at the new press at Strawberry Hill, being the first productions of that printing house.

In Oct. 1761, he made words for an old tune of Geminiani, at the request of Mrs Speed; it begins, 'Thyrsis, when we parted, swore' etc. two stanzas;[2] the thought from the French.

VOLUME 15

Page xxvi, 3d paragraph, line 5, *for* 'a clerk *read* a 'clerk
Page xxvii, line 1, *after* reply *insert* (in two letters, 8 and 14 April)

2. HW sent these stanzas to Lady Ailesbury 28 Nov. 1761; see CONWAY ii. 144–5 and notes.

Line 2, after months *insert* Chatterton wrote again (24 July), and shortly afterwards   *Line 3, on* him *add note* 9a: 9a. See HW to Bewley 23 May 1778, CHATTERTON 127–9. In his explanation Walpole refers only to Chatterton's letter of 24 July, which Walpole should have received three weeks before his expected departure for Paris (16 Aug.).

Page xxxi, 4th paragraph, line 2, *for* his *Catalogue read* Walpole's *Catalogue*

Page xxxv, 1st paragraph, line 8, *after* full. *add* Six more letters and one extract are printed in MISC. CORR. i. 320–1, iii. 6–8, 11–14, 74–5, 399–400, 439–40, 465.

Page xxxv, lines 14–16, *delete* Mary Berry . . . or gave *and substitute* The manuscripts remained at Strawberry Hill and were inherited by the Waldegraves; Lord Euston (later 5th Duke of Grafton) as executor for the 6th Earl Waldegrave sold   *Line 16, on* Richard Bentley the publisher *add note* 1: 1. ' "The Earl of Euston [D. of Grafton, 1844], surviving executor of the late Earl of Waldegrave, has placed the whole of Walpole's unpublished manuscripts, including his letters, memoirs, private journals, etc., in the hands of Mr Bentley" . . . June 26th, 1843' (Preface to *Letters of . . . Walpole . . . to . . . Mann . . . Concluding Series*, Philadelphia, 1844). Mitford's preface to the Walpole-Mason correspondence, 1851, published by Bentley, refers to 'the collection of manuscripts purchased of the Duke of Grafton, as executor of the late Earl of Waldegrave.'

Page xxxv, line 22, *for* one in the Dreer Collection *read* two in the Dreer Collection

Page xxxv, lines 23–4, *for* in the possession of the Earl of Derby *read* formerly in the possession of the Earl of Derby, now in the collection of W. S. Lewis.

Page xxxvi, 3d paragraph, line 1, *for* Fifteen *read* Seventeen   *Line 2, delete*   , wholly or in part   *Line 4, for* thirteen *read* sixteen   *Line 5, after* scattered. *add* Dawson Turner bought at the Upcott Sale (Evans) 22 July 1846, lot 448, four of HW's letters, and lot 551, one of HW's letters. *Line 8, for* Six *read* Ten   *Lines 9–10, for* one in the possession of the Hon. Mrs Rosalind Lyell *read* one (extract) in the University of Glasgow Library

Page xxxvi, 4th paragraph, lines 2–5, *delete* five letters . . . present Earl *and substitute* six letters, of which two are from Henry, three are in Kirgate's hand (but Walpole's drafts in his hand survive), and one is in Walpole's hand. The manuscripts of Henry's letters and of Walpole's drafts, bought for the Earl of Derby in the Strawberry Hill sale in 1842, are now owned by W. S. Lewis. The manuscripts of the three letters in Kirgate's hand and one in Walpole's hand, are among the Moncreiff of Tulliebole MSS in the Scottish Record Office.

Page xxxvi, 5th paragraph, line 1, *for* eleven *read* twelve   *Line 7, for* thirteen *read* eighteen   *Line 8, for* seven *read* eleven   *Line 9, for* one in the Pierpont Morgan *read* two in the Pierpont Morgan

Page xxxvii, 1st paragraph, line 1, *for* Mr Lindsay Fleming *read* Mr Roger Barrett

Page xxxvii, 2d paragraph, line 1, *for* Two *read* Three   *Line 3, after* manuscripts of *add* two of   *Line 4, after* Libraries *add*   , one in the Bodleian Library

Page xxxvii, 4th paragraph, lines 2–4, *delete* We have found none of the original manuscripts . . . Farmington. *and substitute* All of the original manuscripts, as well as Kirgate's transcript of the letter of 12 Oct. 1794, are now at Farmington.

Page xxxvii, 5th paragraph, lines 2–3, *delete*   , except for one letter known only in an extract from a catalogue   *Line 4, for* five and the extract *read* six   *Line 5, for* Ten *read* Eleven   *Line 6, for* one of Walpole's *read* three of Walpole's   *Lines 8–9, delete* One of the manuscripts . . . Colin Davy; *and substitute* The manuscripts of two of Walpole's letters and one of Roscoe's are now at Farmington;

Page xxxix, 2d paragraph, lines 5–6, *for* 13th Earl of Derby *read* 17th Earl of Derby

Page xliv, Cobbett, *Parl. Hist.*, right column, *for* William Cobbett and John Wright *read* William Cobbett, John Wright, and T. C. Hansard

Page xlvi, MS Cat., right column, 2d line from end, *for* Norwich *read* Norfolk

Page xlvii, *MS Commonplace Book*, right column, lines 1–3, *for* Walpole's manuscript . . . in 1740 *substitute* Horace Walpole, 'A Common Place Book of Verses, Stories, Characters, Letters, &c. &c. with some Particular Memoirs of a Certain Parcel of People,' 1740–53

Page xlix, Letters between Walpole and Buchan, *sub* 1782, *insert* 2 June (extract)

Page l, *sub* 1783, *below* 12 May *insert* 2 Oct.

Page li, *sub* 1764, *for 17 April* read 17 April*

Page lii, Letters between Walpole and James Edwards, *sub* 1794 *insert* 21 March

Page lii, Letters between Walpole and Henry, *insert* 1782   16 March††

Page liii, line 3, *for* 1795   2 Aug. *read* 1795   22 Aug.

Page liii, line 13, *under* 1796 1 Dec.† *add* undated card printed MISC. CORR. iii. 465

Page liii, Letters between Walpole and Samuel Lysons, *under* 1794 *add* undated card, printed MISC. CORR. iii. 465

Page liv, Letters between Walpole and Roscoe, *sub* 1796, *for* July (fragment) *read* ca 12 July

Page 3, note 2, line 2, *for* Parliament *read* the House of Lords

Page 5, note 3, line 6, *after Polly add* (R. Sedgwick in *English Historical Review*, Oct. 1953, lxviii. 616, says there is no evidence for this.)   *Line*

8, add See also J. H. Plumb, *Sir Robert Walpole: The King's Minister,* 1960, pp. 113–14; R. W. Ketton-Cremer, *Horace Walpole,* New York, 1940, p. 30.

Page 7, note 10, line 1, *for* (d. 1770) *read* (ca 1717–70)

Page 7, note 11, last line, *after* i. 104 *add* (Hazen, *Cat. of HW's Lib.* No. 315)

Page 8, note 1a, *add* See also Hazen, *Cat. of HW's Lib.* No. 1574.

Page 8, note 2, next to last line, *after* 121 *add*   ; Hazen, *Cat. of HW's Lib.* No. 2797

Page 11, note 2, line 3, *after* removed *add* in July   *Line 5, after* 12 *add*   ; MANN i. 494–5

Page 12, note 11, line 1, *for* 1704 *read* ca 1704

Page 14, note 27, lines 5, 9, *for* Morell *read* Morel   *Last line, add* See also Hazen, *Cat. of HW's Lib.* No. 226

Page 14, note 29, line 1, *for* Morell *read* Morel

Page 19, note 1, *add* See also HW to Mann 18 June 1744 OS, MANN ii. 465.

Page 19, note 6, *after line 1 insert line 4* scholar and critic, and master of Trinity

Page 22, note 5, *for* 'Des. of SH.' *read Des. of SH.*

Page 23, note 1, *add* Probably the same visit is mentioned in HW's letter to Sir Edward Walpole of ca 16 May 1745 OS: 'Your writing against Dr Middleton who came to make me a visit at Houghton of two days' (FAMILY 19).

Page 26, note 5, line 1, *delete hyphen in* Bubb-Dodington

Page 30, note 19, last line, *after* 154 *add* (Hazen, *Cat. of HW's Lib.* No. 913).

Page 32, note 2, line 1, *before* HW's *insert* HW's copy of *A Vindication of Robert III, King of Scotland,* Edinburgh, 1695, was sold SH i. 27 (Hazen, *Cat. of HW's Lib.* No. 76); and   *Line 1, after* copy *insert* of   *Line 2, after* 24 *add* (Hazen, op. cit. No. 116)

Page 32, note 3, last line, *after* 32 *add* (Hazen, *Cat. of HW's Lib.* No. 77)

Page 33, note 10, last line, *after* 173 *add* (Hazen, *Cat. of HW's Lib.* No. 444)

Page 36, note 3, line 1, *after* (1720) *insert* John Hervey, styled

Page 39, note 3, line 2, *after* WSL *add* (Hazen, *Cat. of HW's Lib.* No. 321)

Page 47, note 5, *add* Both Reynolds and Ramsay painted HW's portrait.

Page 48, note 7, line 4, *for* Edinburgh, 1755 *read* Edinburgh, ?1757   *Last line, after* records *add* (Hazen, *Cat. of HW's Lib.* No. 1609:56:22)

Page 52, note 10, last line, *after* 152 *add* (a presentation copy of the 1759 edition; see Hazen, *Cat. of HW's Lib.* No. 1883)

Page 52, note 11, last line, *after* 35 *add* (Hazen, *Cat. of HW's Lib.* No. 1453)

Page 53, note 1, last line, *after* 156 *add* (Hazen, *Cat. of HW's Lib.* No.

464). HW wrote to Zouch 14 May 1759 that the *History* was 'sadly written, yet very amusing from the matter.'

Page 54, note 11, *add* William Beckford's MS note in his copy of D'Israeli's *Calamities of Authors*, 1812: 'H. Walpole delighted to ridicule authors as well as to starve the miserable artists he so grudgingly paid. . . . Royal & Noble Authors (Splendid Scribblers) are for the greater part no authors at all . . .' (Christie's Catalogue, 2 April 1975, 'Property of the Lord Margadale of Islay,' lot 226).

Page 57, note 5, last line, *after* 70 *add* (Hazen, *Cat. of HW's Lib.* No. 2)

Page 64, note 18, line 3, *for* copy *read* copies, 1734 and 1763 editions, *Line 4, for* was *read* were   *after* 109 *add*   , i. 25 (Hazen, *Cat. of HW's Lib.* Nos 137, 2745)

Page 66, note 6, *add* See Hazen, *Cat. of HW's Lib.* No. 356.

Page 68, note 3, last line, *after* 21 *add* (Hazen, *Cat. of HW's Lib.* No. 131)

Page 70, note 9, last line, *after* 36 *add* (Hazen, *Cat. of HW's Lib.* No. 2494)

Page 71, note 1, *add* HW's copy is Hazen, *Cat. of HW's Lib.* No. 3222: 2:5.

Page 73, note 4, last line, *after* 153 *add* (Hazen, *Cat. of HW's Lib.* No. 2535:10, 11).

Page 74, note 10, line 1, *for* Katherine Leighton (d. 1637) *read* Catherine Clifton (ca 1592–1637)

Page 75, note 11, line 2, *delete* and   *Last line, after* 27 *add* (Hazen, *Cat. of HW's Lib.* No. 3328)

Page 75, note 14, line 1, *for* ca 1588 *read* ca 1589

Page 75, note 15, line 1, *for* By Alexander Jamesone, 1728: *read* The print is by John Alexander (fl. 1715–52), sometimes called Alexander Jamesone, after a painting by George Jamesone himself (MISC. CORR. i. 260–1 and n. 6);

Page 78, note 17, *add* Advertisement to J. Boswell, A. Erskine, and G. Dempster, *Critical Strictures on the New Tragedy of Elvira*, 1763: 'We have followed the authority of Sir David Dalrymple, and Mr Samuel Johnson, in the orthography of Mr Malloch's name, as we imagine the decision of these gentlemen will have more weight in the world of letters, than even that of the said Malloch himself.'

Page 83, note 5, *add* See Hazen, *Cat. of HW's Lib.* Nos 887, 910.

Page 86, note 2, line 9, *for* returned to Dalrymple (see next note) *substitute* sold SH vi. 36, listed as 'Dalrymple's Memorials and Letters . . . a present from the author,' without specifying whether this is the James I or the Charles I volume;   *Line 10, for* another copy of it *read* another copy of volume I   *Line 11, after* 181, *insert* now in the British Museum, *At end add* HW also had the 2-volume edition of 1766; see Hazen, *Cat. of HW's Lib.* Nos 2368, 2675.

196   VOLUME 15 (DALRYMPLE)

Page 87, note 7, right column, line 3, *for* 1734–61 *read* 1734–41   *Line 5, after* SH iii. 194 *add*   , Hazen, *Cat. of HW's Lib.* No. 2039

Page 88, note 1, last line, *after* ferers' *add* (CONWAY ii. 205)

Page 91, note 3, *for* anser *read* answer

Page 94, note 4, *add* HW had two copies of Ubaldini's *Le vite delle donne illustri del regno d'Inghilterra* and also of *Descrittione del regno di Scotia* (Hazen, *Cat. of HW's Lib.* Nos 2322, 3385, 523, 3384).

Page 96, note 14, lines 1–2, *for* (ca 1478–ca 1533) *read* (1478–between 1533 and 1536)

Page 99, note 37, *at end add* But Sedgwick maintains that they were not enemies (see *English Historical Review*, Oct. 1953, lxviii. 617).

Pages 100–1, note 12, line 4, *for* Marischal *read* King's   *Last line, after* iii. 14 *add*   ; Hazen, *Cat. of HW's Lib.* No. 1602

Page 101, From Dalrymple 17 April 1764, headnote, *for* Missing. *substitute* The manuscript is in the Ferdinand J. Dreer Collection in the library of the Historical Society of Pennsylvania. Printed by Robert Hay Carnie, 'A Missing Hailes-Walpole Letter,' N&Q, 1957, ccii. 75–6; reprinted in MISC. CORR. i. 320–1.

Page 107, note 3, *add* HW's copy is Hazen, *Cat. of HW's Lib.* No. 1303.

Page 108, note 1, lines 2–3, *for* and had returned to SH by 22 Oct. (MONTAGU ii. 232) *substitute*   ; he left Bath 22 Oct. and wrote to Montagu from SH on that day (MONTAGU ii. 232); he returned to London 25 Oct., and by 3 Nov. he had gone back to SH (CONWAY iii. 76, 79; MANN vi. 461).

Pages 108–9, note 2, last 5 lines, *delete* A copy of Dalrymple's . . . volume. *and substitute* HW apparently had both volumes of the 1766 edition (the 2d edn of vol. i, the 1st edn of vol. ii), sold SH v. 103 (see Hazen, *Cat. of HW's Lib.* No. 2675).

Page 111, note 7, line 1, *for* Leveson-Gower *read* Leveson Gower   *for* ca 1704 *read* ?1703

Page 111, note 12, line 5, *after* vols *add*   , 1775   *after* 193 *add*   ; Hazen, *Cat. of HW's Lib.* No. 3143

Page 117, line 2, *on* Session *add note* 3a: 3a. Now WSL (HW had two copies: Hazen, *Cat. of HW's Lib.* Nos 1609:56:22 and 1609:57:12).

Page 118, note 3, *at beginning insert* HW's copy is dated 'May 28th' by HW (now WSL; Hazen, *Cat. of HW's Lib.* No. 1609:57:2).

Page 119, From Dalrymple 9 Feb. 1768, headnote, line 1, *after* MS *insert* formerly   *Line 2, after first* Derby *add*   ; now WSL   *after second* Derby *add*   ; acquired by WSL in 1954

Page 123, note 8, last line, *after* v. 83 *add* (Hazen, *Cat. of HW's Lib.* No. 3274).

Page 124, note 14, line 4, *after* English *add* (now BM Add. MS 48,976) *Line 6, after* Latin *add* (*penes* College of Arms since 1786)   *Line 11, after* DNB) *add*   ; see C. E. Wright, 'The Rous Roll: the English Version,' *British Museum Quarterly*, 1955–6, xx. 77–81

Page 124, note 15, *add* See also Sandwich to HW 17 Feb. 1768, in MISC. CORR. ii. 134–5.

Page 124, note 1, last line, *after* 155 *add* (Hazen, *Cat. of HW's Lib*. No. 2943).

Page 128, note 5, last line, *after* WSL *add* (Hazen, *Cat. of HW's Lib*. No. 1609:57:9)

Page 130, note 2, line 2, *for* 1765–7 *read* 1765–6

Page 134, note 12, at beginning *insert* HW repeats this story in his Notes on Dr Maty's Memoirs of the Earl of Chesterfield, pp. 31–2, in *Miscellanies of the Philobiblon Society*, 1867–8, vol. xi.

Page 135, note 1, last line, *after* WSL *add* (Hazen, *Cat. of HW's Lib*. No. 3333)

Page 136, note 1, last line, *after* Museum *add* (Hazen, *Cat. of HW's Lib*. No. 2942).

Page 136, note 3, *add* HW's copy is Hazen, *Cat. of HW's Lib*. No. 3188.

Page 136, note 4, lines 4–5, *for* in April 1777 *read* 21 Dec. 1776, although dated 1777 (*Public Advertiser* 4, 5, 17, 21 Dec. 1776; *Line 5, delete* parenthesis *before* London *Line 6, add* See also Hazen, *Cat. of HW's Lib*. No. 3216.

Page 137, note 7, *add* HW's copy, a present from the younger Duc de Noailles, is Hazen, *Cat. of HW's Lib*. No. 3130.

Page 137, note 11, line 1, *for* Sanna *read* Saña *for* 1669 *read* ca 1669 *Line 5, after* 1725 *add* ; see CHUTE 283, n. 28; Hazen, *Cat. of HW's Lib*. No. 1266

Page 137, note 12, line 9, *after* v. 153 *add* ; Hazen, *Cat. of HW's Lib*. No. 2972

Page 139, note 11, align last two lines at bottom of column

Page 140, note 2, last line, *after* 62 *add* , and are now WSL (Hazen, *Cat. of HW's Lib*. No. 3185)

Page 143, note 9, *add* R. Sedgwick argues that contemporary opinion supports HW (*English Historical Review*, Oct. 1953, lxviii. 617).

Page 143, note 11, right column, line 6, *for* (ca 1709–65), Bns von Wallmoden *read* (1704–65), m. (1727) Oberhauptmann Gottlieb Adam von Wallmoden

Page 147, note 2, *add* For HW's copy see Hazen, *Cat. of HW's Lib*. No. 217.

Page 148, note 10, line 1, *for* Barrington *read* Barrington Shute

Page 148, note 13, last line, *after* 116 *add* ; Hazen, *Cat. of HW's Lib*. No. 1060

Page 149, note 21, last line, *after* 186 *add* ; Hazen, *Cat. of HW's Lib*. No. 3108

Page 150, To Buchan 10 Feb. 1781, headnote, line 1, *after* Wright and *The Bee. insert* Collated with the MS, now WSL. *Line 2, after* xiv. 145–6; *add European Magazine* Sept. 1793, xxiv. 163–4; *Lines 3–4, for* MS not traced *substitute* MS acquired by WSL, 1962, from Goodspeed's Book

Shop, Boston, Mass.   *Under headnote add Endorsed*: Elegant letter from Horace Walpole to the E. of B.

Page 150, To Buchan 10 Feb. 1781, 1st paragraph, line 1, *after* card *delete ,   Line 5, for* distinction; *read* distinction,

Page 150, note 2, *add* See also *London Chronicle* 26–28 Dec. 1780, xlviii. 616.

Page 151, 1st paragraph, line 1, *after* who *delete ,   Line 2, after* partiality *delete ,   Line 4, after* on *delete ,   Line 8, after* course *delete ,   Line 11, for* I am, etc. *substitute* I have the honour to be with the greatest respect, my Lord,/ Your Lordship's most obedient and most obliged humble servant/ HOR. WALPOLE

Page 152, note 7, line 1, *for* ca 1697 *read* 1695

Page 156, To Buchan 1 Dec. 1781, headnote, line 5, *after* lot 1110, *add* to Walter Hill; Hill

Page 159, note 1, line 1, *for* There were *read* They were

Page 161, note 14, line 1, *for* (1725–1806) *read* (1721–1805)   *Last line, add* See J. M. Pinkerton, 'Richard Bull of Ongar, Essex,' *Book Collector*, 1978, xxvii. 41–59.

Page 161, after letter of 26 Jan. 1782 *insert the following heading*:

To HENRY, Saturday 16 March 1782

The MS, in HW's hand, is among the Moncreiff of Tulliebole MSS in the Scottish Record Office. Printed by R. S. Woof, 'Some Horace Walpole Letters,' N&Q, 1965, ccx. 24–5 (dated 15 March); reprinted in MISC. CORR. iii. 6–8.

Page 161, after letter of ca 22 April 1782 *insert the following heading*:

To BUCHAN, Sunday 2 June 1782

An extract, in Buchan's hand, now in the library of the University of Glasgow. Printed in MISC. CORR. iii. 11–14.

Page 164, note 6, *add* HW's copy is Hazen, *Cat. of HW's Lib.* No. 3225.

Page 165, note 8, *add* See also Hazen, *Cat. of HW's Lib.* No. 3690:9.

Page 165, note 9, *add* HW's copy is Hazen, *Cat. of HW's Lib.* No. 2812.

Page 166, note 5, last line, *after* WSL *add* ; see Hazen, *Cat. of HW's Lib.* Nos 1111, 1893, 2839

Page 168, From Henry 3 March 1783, headnote, line 1, *before* owned *insert* formerly   *after* Derby *add* ; now WSL   *Line 2, after* Derby *add* ; acquired by WSL in 1954

Page 168, note 15, *add* See also CONWAY i. 550–1, iii. 424–5.

Page 169, note 2, last line, *after* iv. 4 *add* (Hazen, *Cat. of HW's Lib.* No. 543)

Page 169, note 5, line 11, *for* Laing's *read* Sir Henry Moncreiff Wellwood's   *Line 13, after* xiv *add* ; see also R. S. Woof, N&Q, 1965, ccx. 24, n. 1, who points out that the 'Life of Robert Henry' in the posthumously published vol. vi of Henry's *History* is not by Laing but by Sir Henry Moncreiff Wellwood.

Page 170, headnote, line 1, *before* owned *insert* formerly   *Line 2, after first* Derby *add*   , now WSL   *At end of line add* The MS of the letter actually sent, in Thomas Kirgate's hand, (which differs from HW's draft in punctuation but not in substance) is among the Moncreiff of Tulliebole MSS in the Scottish Record Office; there is no address with the MS (see R. S. Woof, 'Some Horace Walpole Letters,' N&Q, 1965, ccx. 25).

Page 170, 2d paragraph, line 1, *the Moncreiff MS reads* ever have *for* have ever

Page 170, note 1, line 3, *for* 25 March *read* ca 23 March

Page 172, 4th line from bottom, *in the Moncreiff MS* because *is underlined*

Page 172, last line, *the Moncreiff MS reads* simpleton, without *for* simpleton, but without

Page 173, note 31, *add* See *post* 28 March 1783.

Page 174, 1st paragraph, line 5, *for* upmost *read* utmost

Page 174, From Henry ca 23 March 1783, headnote, line 1, *before* owned *insert* formerly   *after* Derby *add*   , now WSL

Page 176, headnote, line 1, *before* owned *insert* formerly   *Line 2, after first* Derby *add*   , now WSL   *At end of line add* The MS of the letter actually sent, in Thomas Kirgate's hand, (which differs from HW's draft in punctuation but not in substance) is among the Moncreiff of Tulliebole MSS in the Scottish Record Office (see R. S. Woof, 'Some Horace Walpole Letters,' N&Q, 1965, ccx. 24–5).

Page 176, headnote, *add Address* (in HW's hand): To the Reverend Dr Henry at Edinburgh   *Postmarks*: 28 MR   GC

Page 176, 1st paragraph, line 4, *in the Moncreiff MS* act . . . attainder *reads* Act . . . Attainder

Page 176, 2d paragraph, 2d line from bottom, *in the Moncreiff MS* Chronicle *reads Chronicle*

Page 177, 1st paragraph, lines 4–5, *in the Moncreiff MS* Chronicle *reads Chronicle*   Rastall *reads* Rastal

Page 177, note 6, *delete last sentence and substitute* More was born in 1478; he began to compose the *History* between 1514 and 1518, and continued to work on it until the 1530s (*Complete Works of St Thomas More*, New Haven, 1963– , vol. ii, ed. R. S. Sylvester, pp. lxiii–lxv). On the historical validity of More's *History* see Alison Hanham, *Richard III and his Early Historians 1483–1535*, Oxford, 1975; see also Unknown to HW 29 Dec. 1767, Camden to HW 8 Feb. 1768, MISC. CORR. ii. 111–15, 126.

Page 178, To Buchan 12 May 1783, headnote, line 1, *after* now WSL. *insert* Lord Buchan's transcript of this letter is now in the University of Glasgow Library (MS Murray 502/70).

Page 182, after letter of 12 May 1783, *insert the following heading*:

To BUCHAN, Thursday 2 October 1783

The MS, laid in a scrapbook collection of SH Press proofs, is now WSL. Printed in MISC. CORR. iii. 74–5.

Page 183, headnote, line 1, *before* owned *insert* formerly   *Line 2,* *after first* Derby *add*   , now WSL   *At end add* The MS of the letter actually sent, in Thomas Kirgate's hand, (which differs from HW's draft in punctuation but not in substance) is among the Moncreiff of Tulliebole MSS in the Scottish Record Office (see R. S. Woof, 'Some Horace Walpole Letters,' N&Q, 1965, ccx. 25).

Address (in HW's hand): To the Reverend Dr Henry at Edinburgh. *Postmarks*: 1 FE FE[?5].

Endorsed: From H. Walpole 1785.

Page 183, headnote, line 3, *for* Headed by HW *read* Draft headed by HW

Page 183, note 2, *add* For HW's copy see Hazen, *Cat. of HW's Lib*. No. 543.

Page 184, line 2, *for* light *read* slight

Page 184, note 9, *after* draft *add*   , and is not included in the MS letter which was sent.

Page 184, note 10, *add* Robert Henry wrote to Bishop Percy 2 May 1787: 'I am much obliged to your Lordship for your hint about Perkin Warbeck, and the two leaves from Vincent, which I shall return by some safe hand. The argument from it, that both King Richard and Lord Howard believed the young prince to be dead, is perfectly decisive. It will convince Mr Walpole. I shall use it, but not without acknowledgment' (Nichols, *Lit. Illus*. viii. 233).

Page 185, line 8, *for* Your obliged and obedient *the Moncreiff MS reads* Your obedient

Page 185, To Buchan 23 Sept. 1785, headnote, last line, *for* not further traced. *read* sold Sotheby's 27 Oct. 1959 to Maggs for WSL. [The MS contains many variations from the printed text; the text is printed here from the MS:]

Endorsed: Horace Walpole to the E. of Buchan. [on verso] Hor. Walpole to the Earl of Buchan.

Strawberry Hill
Sept. 23d 1785.

Your Lordship is too condescending when you incline to keep up a correspondence with one who can expect to maintain it but a short time, and whose intervals of health are resigned to idleness, not dedicated, as I have sometimes been, to literary pursuits—for what could I pursue with any prospect of accomplishment? or what avails it to store a memory, that must lose faster than it acquires? Your Lordship's zeal for illustrating your country and countrymen is laudable; and you are young enough to make a progress; but a man, who touches the verge of his 68th year, ought to know that he is unfit to contribute to the amusement of more active minds. This consideration, my Lord, makes me much decline correspondence: having nothing new to communicate, I perceive that I fill my letters with apologies for having nothing to say.

If you can tap the secret stores of the Vatican, your Lordship will probably much enrich the treasury of letters. Rome may have preserved many valuable documents, as for ages intelligence from all parts of Europe centered there; but I conclude that they have hoarded little that might at any period lay open the share they had in most important transactions. History indeed is fortunate when even incidentally and collaterally it lights on authentic information.

Perhaps, my Lord, there is another repository, and nearer, which it would be worth while to endeavour to penetrate; I mean, the Scottish College at Paris. I have heard formerly that numbers of papers of various sorts were transported at the Reformation to Spain and Portugal—but, if preserved there, they probably are not accessible *yet*. If they were, how puny, how diminutive would all such discoveries, and others which we might call of far greater magnitude, be to those of Herschel, who puts up millions of coveys of worlds at a beat! My conception is not ample enough to take in even a sketch of his glimpses—and lest I should lose myself in attempting to follow his investigations, I recall my mind home, and apply it to reflect on what we thought we knew, when we imagined we knew something (which we deemed a vast deal) pretty correctly. Segrais, I think it was, who said with much contempt to a lady who talked of her star— '*your* star! there are but two thousand stars in all, and do you imagine, Madam, that you have a whole one to yourself?' The foolish dame, it seems, was not more ignorant than Segrais himself. If our system includes twenty millions of worlds, the lady had as much right to pretend to a whole ticket, as the philosopher had to treat her like a servant-maid who buys a chance for a day in a state lottery.

Stupendous as Mr Herschel's investigations are, and admirable as his talents, his expression of *our retired corner* seems a little improper. When a little emmet standing on its ant-hill could get a peep into infinity, how could he think he saw *a corner* in it? *a retired corner*? Is there a bounded side to infinitude? if there are twenty millions of worlds, why not as many, and as many, and as many more?—Oh! one's imagination cracks! I long to bait within distance of home, and rest at the moon. Mr Herschel will content me if he can discover thirteen provinces there well inhabited by men and women, and by the law of nations (that law which was enacted by Europe for its own emolument, to the prejudice of the other three parts of the globe and) which bestows the property of whole realms on the first person who happens to espy them, can annex them to the crown of Great Britain in lieu of those it has lost beyond the Atlantic.

As I am very ignorant in Astronomy, as ignorant as Segrais or the lady, I could wish to ask many questions; as whether our celestial globes must not be infinitely magnified? Our orreries too, must not they be given to children, and new ones constructed, that will at least take in *our retired corner* and all its outlying constellations. Must not that host of worlds be christened? Mr Herschel himself has stood godfather for his Majesty to the new Sidus. His Majesty, thank God, has a numerous issue; but they and all the princes and princesses in Europe cannot supply appellations enough to twenty millions of new-born stars, no, though the royal progenies of Austria, Naples and Spain, who have each two dozen saints for sponsors, should consent to split their bede-roll of names among the foundlings—but I find I talk like an old nurse, and your Lordship I believe will at last be convinced that it is not worth your while to keep up a correspondence with a man in his dotage, merely because he has the honour of being

> Your Lordship's
> Most obedient humble servant
> HOR. WALPOLE

Page 191, note 16, line 8, *for* Green Room *read* Green Closet

Page 193, To Buchan 11 Feb. 1787, headnote, line 2, *after* Chelsea *add* ; the MS is now WSL   *Line 5, after* 1928 *add*   ; acquired by WSL in 1953. The cover of the letter is in the possession of Mr D. R. Bentham of Loughborough, Leicester, England. *At end of headnote add*

> *Address*: To the Earl of Buchan at Edinburgh. *Postmark*: 12 FE.
> *Endorsed*: Horace Walpole
>   Camden's Britannia—
>   Cun[n]ingham's history

Page 194, note 3, line 1, *after* appeared in *add* the *Morning Chronicle* 1 Feb. 1787 and in   *Line 2, for* 28 *read* 23   *Line 3, for* 27–29 *read* 22–24   *for* 301 *read* 285

Page 194, note 6, line 2, *after* ii. 95 *add* (Hazen, *Cat. of HW's Lib.* No. 563). Gough gave HW a presentation copy of his translation of the *Britannia*, 3 vols, 1789 (see ibid. No. 424).

Page 195, note 3, *add* HW in his copy of *Archæologia* (now WSL) noted that 'Mr Tutet's cards wanted the four aces; and instead of four queens had four knights' (p. 139). See also *A Catalogue of . . . Printed Books and Manuscripts of the late Mark Cephas Tutet, Esq.*, 1786, lot 55.

Page 196, note 2, last line, *after* v. 4 *add* (Hazen, *Cat. of HW's Lib.* No. 3338:3)

Page 196, note 4, *add* See Hazen, *Cat. of HW's Lib.* Nos 128, 2308.

Page 197, note 1, lines 2–3, *delete*   ; an early student of HW's bibliography   *Line 5, after* 1785 *add*   ; he also revised David Erskine Baker's *Biographia Dramatica, or, a Companion to the Playhouse*, new edn, 1782, which contains an article on HW's *Mysterious Mother* (ii. 247–9). See Hazen, *Cat. of HW's Lib.* No. 3912.

Page 197, note 2, line 5, *after* plays *insert* (Hazen, *Cat. of HW's Lib.* No. 3922)   *Lines 10–11, for* probably from *read* of Drayton,

Page 198, note 2, line 4, *after* 1785 *add* (Hazen, *Cat. of HW's Lib.* No. 3891:3   *Lines 9–10, delete* It is barely possible that   *for* he *read* He

Page 198, note 3, *for* Sic *read* Sic

Page 198, note 8, line 1, *for* ca 1736 *read* ?1740

Page 201, note 3, *add* For HW's copy see Hazen, *Cat. of HW's Lib.* No. 539.

Page 201, note 4, *add* See More 326 and n. 22.

Page 202, note 10, line 2, *after* 1773 *add* (Hazen, *Cat. of HW's Lib.* No. 3222:12:10)

Page 202, note 11, *add* See Hazen, *Cat. of HW's Lib.* Nos 2050, 2318.

Page 202, note 12, *add* For HW's copy see Hazen, *Cat. of HW's Lib.* No. 3222:22:12.

Page 203, To Samuel Lysons 28 June 1790, headnote, line 1, *after* 526. *insert* Collated with the MS, now WSL.   *Lines 2–3, for* not further traced *read* sold Sotheby's 16 May 1972, lot 519, to Seven Gables Bookshop for WSL.

Page 203, To Samuel Lysons 28 June 1790, *below Address add Postmarks*: 29 JU 90 ISLEWORTH

Page 203, To Samuel Lysons 28 June 1790, date-line, *for* 28th *read* 28   *Line 1, after* Cross *delete* ,   *Line 2, before and after* too *delete* ,

Page 203, note 18, *add* HW's copy is Hazen, *Cat. of HW's Lib.* No. 3435.

Page 204, line 3, *after* may *delete* ,   *after* besides *delete* ,   *for* Berkeley; *read* Berkeley—

Page 204, line 6, *for* Yours, etc., *read* Yours etc.

Page 204, line 7, *for* Horace *read* H.

Page 205, note 13, line 1, *for* 1496 *read* 1495   *Last line, add* See GEC, *sub* Suffolk

Page 206, note 21, last line, *after* WSL *add* (Hazen, *Cat. of HW's Lib.* No. 64)

Page 208, To Buchan 7 April 1791, headnote, line 2, *delete* MS offered by Langham and Co., Cat. No. 666, Nov. 1900 *and substitute* MS sold Evans 22 June 1846 (William Upcott Sale), lot 448, £2.8.0 to Lamb; sold Sotheby's 28 Nov. 1890 (Manners Sale), lot 446, to Scobell, £3; offered by S. J. Davey, 47 Great Russell Street, Cat. No. 40, 1895, lot 69, £3.5.5; re-offered by him Cat. No. 42, n.d., lot 789; offered by Langham & Co., Cat. No. 11, May 1901; sold Anderson Galleries 30 Oct. 1916 (McCurdy Sale), lot 587, $40.

Page 209, note 6, last line, *after* 45–6 *add* ; Hazen, *Cat. of HW's Lib.* No. 455

Page 210, note 1, last line, *after* 155 *add* (Hazen, *Cat. of HW's Lib.* No. 2941)

Page 214, To (?) Dalrymple 3 July 1792, headnote, *add* R. Sedgwick in *English Historical Review*, Oct. 1953, lxviii. 617, argues that this letter may not be to Dalrymple because HW had never called him 'Dear Sir'; as in HW to Dalrymple 21 Sept. 1790 HW begins, 'I should have thanked you sooner, Sir . . .' (DALRYMPLE 204).

Page 214, note 2, *add* See also *ante* 1 Dec. 1781, postscript; MASON ii. 294 and n. 13.

Page 214–15, To Samuel Lysons 17 July 1792, headnote, *add* The MS is (Jan. 1954) *penes* Roger Barrett of 222 Leicester Road, Kenilworth, Illinois. [The text is printed here from a photostat of the MS:]

Strawberry Hill
July 17th 1792.

Dear Sir,

I am sorry I cannot accept your visit on Friday, as tomorrow I expect General Conway and his family and shall have my house full till Sunday or Monday, but shall be glad to see you on the latter day or Tuesday.

Pray tell me if you have not got my two folio volumes of Edmondson's Catalogue of Coats of Arms, for which I have been in great distress, and cannot find in any of my libraries here; and be so good as to name what books of mine you have, or if any, for I am going to new-arrange all.

Yours etc.
ORFORD

Page 215, To Samuel Lysons 17 July 1792, note 1, last line, *after* 12 *add* (Hazen, *Cat. of HW's Lib.* No. 528)

Page 217, note 1, line 1, *for* 1741 *read* 1742   *At end add* For HW's low opinion of Combe see HW to Mason 18 April 1777, MASON i. 303 and n. 14.

Page 218, note 2, line 4, *after* diarist *add* (Hazen, *Cat. of HW's Lib.* No. 3566)

Page 218, To Nares 12 Sept. 1792, headnote, line 1, *after* 143–5. *add* Collated with the MS, now WSL.   *Line 3, for* not further traced *read* sold Sotheby's 28–9 Oct. 1968, lot 429 (property of Miss A. M. Smith) to WSL. [The variants in the MS are recorded below:]

Page 218, To Nares 12 Sept. 1792, under headnote *insert Address*: Isleworth September the twelfth 1792. To the Reverend Mr Nares near the Queen's house in James Street Westminster. Free Orford. *Postmark*: FREE SE 13 92 [See DALRYMPLE 240, n. 1].

Page 218, To Nares 12 Sept. 1792, line 1, *for* Oh, *read* Oh!

Page 218, To Nares 12 Sept. 1792, line 3, *for* second *read* second,

Page 219, line 5, *for* this *read* this,

Page 221, line 9, *for* you to do *read* you to do,

Page 221, line 10, *for* Sir, *read* Sir

Page 221, line 11, *for* servant, *read* servant

Page 222, To Beloe 24 Sept. 1792, headnote, line 3, *after* Pearson; *add* offered by Pearson (Cat. ?1902), lot 407 (p. 125) for £13;

Page 228, note 8, *add* For HW's copy see Hazen, *Cat. of HW's Lib.* No. 2798.

Page 231, To Nares 14 Nov. 1792, headnote, line 1, *after* 161–3. *insert* Collated with the MS, now WSL.   *Line 2, after* 1792. *add* Sold Sotheby's 28–9 Oct. 1968, lot 429 (property of Miss A. M. Smith) to WSL. [The variants in the MS are recorded below:]

Page 231, To Nares 14 Nov. 1792, under headnote *insert Address*: Isleworth November the fourteenth 1792. To the Reverend Mr Nares in James Street Westminster. Free Orford. *Postmark*: FREE 13 NO 92 [*sic*].

Page 231, To Nares 14 Nov. 1792, 1st paragraph, line 5, *for* consequently *read* consequently,   *Line 13, for* throat *read* throat,

Page 232, note 5, *for his read His*

Page 234, To Nares 14 Dec. 1792, headnote, *add* Sold Sotheby's 28–9 Oct. 1968, lot 429 (property of Miss A. M. Smith) to WSL. [The text is printed here from the MS:]

Strawberry Hill
Dec. 14, 1792.

Dear Sir,

I am very glad that your anxiety about your brother and your mother too, is relieved, and that the care of both is rewarded by success.

It is great satisfaction to me too, Sir, to hear that the Association has adopted your co-operation. I applauded and honoured their zeal, and now admire their good sense in the choice of a gentleman of such abilities and activity; and I am sure that I am one of the last men in England that would try or wish to seduce you for a single day from the service of our country. I shall be in town myself the beginning of next week, and happy to see you any morning or evening when you have half an hour's leisure.

The spirit of the Association, I see, catches rapidly round the capital: I hope it will spread as warmly into the counties, and dishearten at least, if it does not convert Scotland and Ireland, whence I fear more is to be apprehended than even was attempted and threatened here.

I do like this blaze of zeal—but then it must be nourished and kept up, till it has quashed the danger. You and I, Sir (for though you are so much younger, you too have seen and) know how easily addresses, subscriptions, associations, are obtained backwards and forwards; and some popular cry, grounded on any public misfortune, or artfully contrived by the enemy, may turn the torrent, and direct it the contrary way. The enemy is at this moment disappointed and provoked—consequently, neither convinced nor softened—and therefore must be carefully watched. The people too must be made sensible that *the enemy* is so of the public, and that the success of their schemes would produce the same inundation of miseries as has fallen on France—and the teachers of such doctrines must be made odious, or will still gain proselytes. But proper measures to be taken for defence, and to keep *watch and ward* (with attention being kept awake as is necessary) would be much too long for a letter, and I am persuaded will be suggested and pursued. We shall have time, I trust, to talk on them, and observe their institution.

On the French I cannot speak with a grain of charity or patience. If all Mr Bruce's hyenas had met in three National Assemblies, they could not have produced similar horrors, for hyenas tear both men and women to pieces at once, but do not torture and keep them in constant alarms for three years together—they do not butcher hundreds and thousands more than they can devour. They do not terrify men to flight, and then persecute the wives and children of those they have terrified. Hyenas do not promise bribes to tigers to massacre men of certain descriptions, viz. kings, when tigers are neither hungry nor provoked—no, Sir, hyenas are not French philosophers, nor claim a mission from hell to overturn all justice, laws, governments, morality, humanity and religion, and then call themselves the most august senate in the world! From their known vanity and insolence, which grew from Europe aping their trifling fashions, manners and language, they have strided at once to being proud of being the legislators of assassination—will it be believed that one could write that last sentence, and be speaking strict truth!—alas! alas! that there should be Englishmen capable of applauding such unparalleled monsters!

That the French government was bad, nobody will dispute—but at what moment did they overset it?—exactly when they had the most innocent and gentle King, that ever sat on their throne! and who have been his persecutors and tormentors? Philosophers, geometricians, astronomers, reformers, united with the bloodiest of all murderers, Marats, Robertspierres and such execrable wretches as Dr Priestly thinks it an honour to be incorporated with!

If the royal personages are actually massacred, their woes are at an end—a chance of comfort I see none for them in this world! If spared, a doleful prison must be their lot, for how could they escape through provinces sown with daggers—a manufacture our reformers were ambitious of introducing here—can Englishmen hear the sound and not quiver with indignation!

I check myself, or such scenes and unexampled ideas would hurry me into a volume. Tacitus could couch a single Nero in a few sentences—but a nation of Neroes, with prætorian guards of Marseillais; patricians disguised like women and mixed with *poissardes*, insulting a young beautiful Queen; a Princess hewed into pieces for fidelity to that Queen, an hundred and fifty priests stabbed for disdaining perjury; a Condorcet panegyricizing an Ankerström who refined on murder by loading a pistol with crooked nails, and two more massacres of Paris in the compass of six weeks—History must be very penurious of its words, if it hoards them on such details; and consider that I have but hinted at a small number of the tragedies that have been acted, nor named the 4000 butcheries in the prison at Paris, nor the 54 prisoners dragged from Orléans to have their throats cut in the Thuilleries, nor any of the massacres at Avignon, Nismes, Lyons etc. etc. etc.

I am not sorry to recapitulate these atrocious crimes diffused through a vast country, because you hear *reformers* pronounce coolly, that *no revolution can be brought about without some blood being shed*—and has man, wretched man, a right for speculative opinions on government, to doom, to dispatch thousands and thousands of his fellow creatures to destruction? Who gave that authority, that decision to man? no God certainly: the Great Creator never inspired us to make experiments on the lives of our own species for the benefit of posterity. I should shudder to cut open a poor animal to trace the circulation of the blood—the French philosophic anti-legislators have given a new sense to the term, and pretended to discover equality and the rights of mankind in sluicing the veins of their countrymen and of any nation whom they can reach.

Adieu, Sir—I probably shall not live to see this anarchy terminate—you, I hope, will, and will contribute to stave it off from this happy country, where true liberty is preserved—but it will not be one of the least demerits of the French innovators, that when the chaos they have produced shall be dispelled, for anarchy is not a lasting existence, mankind will dread the most wholesome and necessary corrections, and acquiescence will be preferred to alterations.

I am dear Sir,

> Your sincerely obedient humble servant
> ORFORD

Page 235, note 5, *add* Although HW read at least part of Bruce's volumes, he did not keep the set in his library (Hazen, *Cat. of HW's Lib.* No. 4018).

Page 237, note 11, line 2, *delete* Adolphus

Page 237, note 12, last line, *for* edn. *read* edn,

Page 238, To Beloe 26 June 1793, headnote, line 3, *after* Pearson; *add* offered by Pearson (Cat. ?1902) lot 406 (p. 124), £13;

Page 240, To Nares 5 Oct. 1793, headnote, *after* 211–4. *add* Collated with the MS, now WSL.   *after* 1792 *add* Sold Sotheby's 29–30 Oct. 1968, lot 430, (property of Miss A. M. Smith) to WSL. [The variants in the MS are recorded below:]

Page 241, date-line, *for* 5, *read* 5th

Page 241, 2d paragraph, line 5, *for* alibi *read* Alibi   *Line 7, after* works *add* ,   *after* them.' *add* —   *Line 8, for* Oh, *read* Oh!

Page 242, 1st paragraph, line 2, *on* it *add note* 5a: 5a. '—I certainly have not seen it,' is omitted at this place in the MS, and is added on last page of MS as a note.

Page 242, 2d paragraph, line 1, *after* Henry's *insert* own

Page 242, 3d paragraph, line 2, *after* tenement; *insert* and

Page 242, note 5, line 4, *after* Laing, *add* and a memoir by Sir Henry Moncreiff Wellwood   *At end add* See also Hazen, *Cat. of HW's Lib.* No. 543.

Page 243, 2d paragraph, line 5, *after* Milles *delete*   ,

Page 243, 3d paragraph, line 1, *after* engagements *add*   ,   *after* saying *add*   ,   *Line 10, after* fomented *delete*   ,

Page 244, 2d paragraph, line 2, *for* tired you, and *read* tired you, as

Page 244, PS., line 2, *for* interlineations *read* interlineation

Page 244, To Nares 20 Oct. 1793, headnote, *after* 229–30. *add* Collated with the MS, now WSL.   *After* 1792. *add* Sold Sotheby's 29–30 Oct. 1968, lot 431 (property of Miss A. M. Smith) to WSL.

Page 244, To Nares 20 Oct. 1793, after headnote *add Address*: Isleworth October the twentieth 1793. To the Reverend Mr Nares in James Street Westminster. Free Orford. *Postmark*: FREE OC 21 93. *Endorsed*: today The Reverend A. Robertson Ch. Ch. Oxford.

Page 245, line 15, *for* endeavoring *read* endeavouring

Page 245, 2d paragraph, line 2, *after* regard *delete*   ,

Page 249, To Samuel Lysons 19 March 1794, headnote, *add* The MS is now WSL.

Page 249, note 1, *add* The book is now WSL (Hazen, *Cat. of HW's Lib.* No. 3692).

Page 250, note 3, *substitute* The duplicate plates do not appear in HW's copy.

Page 250, after letter To Samuel Lysons 19 March 1794 *insert the following heading*:

To JAMES EDWARDS, Friday 21 March 1794

Printed from a photostat of the MS, now in the Bodleian Library, in MISC. CORR. iii. 399–400. Previously printed in Toynbee xv. 108 (mistakenly assigned to Joseph Cooper Walker and misdated 1792); date corrected in Toynbee, *Supp.* iii. 324. The letter refers to *ante* HW to James Edwards 12 March 1794.

Page 251, note 4, line 7, *after* WSL *insert*   ; also vol. iv and a fifth supplementary volume are now WSL (Hazen, *Cat. of HW's Lib.* No. 3859).

Page 251, note 5, right column, line 10, *after* Gloucester, 1797 *add* (Hazen, *Cat. of HW's Lib.* No. 3434)

Page 252, To Daniel Lysons 2 Oct. 1794, headnote, line 3, *for* not further traced *substitute* now (1960) in the Pierpont Morgan Library, New York City

Page 252, To (?) Nares 12 Oct. 1794, headnote, line 4, *delete* has not been found; it   *Last line, add*   ; it was offered by Bernard Quaritch, Ltd, 27 April 1960 and was then sold to WSL. [The text is printed here from the MS:]

Strawberry Hill
Oct. 12th 1794.

Dear Sir,

There has been published this a [*sic*] year a book with so uncaptivating a title, that it may not have attracted your notice; yet in some parts I think it would please and amuse you, and from one chapter I can confidently say it deserves to be highly commended and recommended, for the effect it may have on others, though not perhaps on those readers for whom it was principally calculated, and on whom good sense is not apt to make much impression—I mean Antiquaries—Lord help them!

The book is called, *The History and Antiquities of the Abbey and Borough of Evesham*, a quarto printed there; the author, W. Tindal M.A. late Fellow of Trinity Coll. Oxon. I know nothing at all of the gentleman, nor whether he is a clergyman or a laic. I am fond of English local history, a study, if it may be called so, that requires little but patience and a memory for trifles, and which to be sure from the general manner in which it is executed, produces as little satisfaction as any kind of reading can do. Thus you see I prove I am one of those insipid beings, at whom I hinted, who demand nothing but to be told facts and circumstances of no importance, that commonly are obsolete and little worth reviving.

To my great surprise—for I never set out in such tasks with sanguine hopes of entertainment, I found the work in question written with the utmost impartiality and liberality, as you will judge if you will please to turn to a few lines at the close of the fourth chapter p. 125; and still better, if you look at the conclusion of the fifth chapter beginning in p. 144, with these words 'But these poor abbots,' etc.

I think, Sir, you will discern excellent and rational reflections, and an admirable contrast between just seriousness and superstition, with an amiable picture of melancholy contemplation on the vicissitude of human affairs.

But what I chiefly mean to recommend to your observation and wish to see specified with proper encomium (the real object of this letter) are the severe but merited strictures on the French Revolution, on their insolent philosophers, and on all those monsters that have been, and are still their disciples. Those strictures extend to the end of the fifth chapter, and in my humble opinion no reprobation of the conduct of the French for the last five years has been so well expressed in the compass of six pages. How concisely has the author towards the bottom of p. 146, painted the apish and pedantic affectation of their writers in imitation of the classics!

I beg your pardon, good Sir, for giving you this trouble, though I trust

I have introduced to you an author worthy of your acquaintance. I beg
too not to have this letter shown, as I write to you most confidentially, and
should be very sorry to offend those very inoffensive personages, our antiquaries, for a few of whom I have great esteem. I am with sincere respect,
Sir,

Your most obedient humble servant
ORFORD

PS. Pray read the account of the battle of Evesham; it is a fine piece of
history.

Page 253, note 1, last line, *after* v. 58 *add* (Hazen, *Cat. of HW's Lib.*
No. 3210)

Page 255, note 4, right column, line 5, *after* v. 35 *add* (Hazen, *Cat. of
HW's Lib.* No. 3177)

Page 256, note 1, line 5, *after* vii. 77 *add*   ; see Hazen, *Cat. of HW's
Lib.* No. 3706

Page 258, note 3, line 4, *after* 1796 *add*   ; Hazen, *Cat. of HW's Lib.*
No. 3703

Page 259, line 3, *for* principles *read* promotion   *on* promotion *add*
note 4: 4. In one draft Roscoe abbreviates this word 'prom^n', and in another draft spells it out 'promotion' (Roscoe Papers, No. 2832; information from D. H. Weinglass, Univ. of Missouri, Kansas City, Missouri).

Page 261, note 6, last line, *after* iii. 13 *add* (Hazen, *Cat. of HW's Lib.*
No. 1604)

Page 263, note 3, line 4, *after* 1791 *add* (see *post* To Roscoe 27 April
1795, n. 1)

Page 264, line 4, *after* library *add* as your neighbour the Marquis of
Lansdown to whose kindness I am greatly indebted has already done in
his,   *on* neighbour *add note* 3a: 3a. 'Your neighbour' is crossed out in
the MS, Roscoe Papers, No. 2834; for this addition to the text we are indebted to D. H. Weinglass.

Page 264, note 1, line 2, *after* vii. 123 *add*   ; Hazen, *Cat. of HW's Lib.*
No. 3821

Page 265, running head, *for* 2 August *read* 22 August

Page 265, heading of letter, *for* Sunday 2 August 1795 *read* Saturday 22
August 1795 [and transfer whole letter to p. 267, after letter of 15 August
1795]

Page 265, headnote, lines 1–2, *for* with transcript made (1905) for Mrs
Toynbee *read* with the MS, now WSL   *Line 5, for* not further traced
read offered Maggs Cat. No. 388 (Spring 1920), lot 908; sold Sotheby's 17
Dec. 1973 (Misc. Sale), lot 251, to Seven Gables for WSL.

Page 265, date-line, *for* Aug. 2d, 1795. *read* Aug. 22d 1795.

Page 265, 1st paragraph, line 1, *after* moment *add*   ,   *Line 2, for*
out of order. *read* out [of] order—

Page 265, note 3, last line, *after* 120) *add* , which remained in his library; see Hazen, *Cat. of HW's Lib.* Nos 411, 3814. But HW apparently also owned the 2-volume edition of 1769–1775, which he may have given away; see MASON i. 191 and n. 7.

Page 266, To Daniel Lysons 15 Aug. 1795, headnote, line 5, *for* not further traced *read* (1954) *penes* John Holbrook, New York City; offered (1963) by Seven Gables Book Shop; sold by them to Robert H. Taylor, Princeton, New Jersey.

Page 266, note 2, lines 3–4, *for* HW's copy was sold SH ii. 41 *read* HW's copies were sold SH ii. 41, v. 106 (Hazen, *Cat. of HW's Lib.* Nos 687, 2694).

Page 267, 1st paragraph, line 5, *after* Nevilles *delete* ,

Page 267, after letter of 15 August 1795 insert letter To Daniel Lysons Saturday 22 August 1795 [from *ante* p. 265]

Page 267, To Daniel Lysons 13 Sept. 1795, headnote, line 3, *after* Maggs Cat. *insert* No. 388 (Spring 1920), lot 906; No. 427 (Autumn 1922), lot 2867; No. 449 (1923), lot 444;   *after* lot 2611 *add* ; No. 525 (Autumn 1929), lot 1902

Page 267, note 3, last line, *after* v. 148 *add* (Hazen, *Cat. of HW's Lib.* No. 2867)

Page 269, To Daniel Lysons 27 Sept. 1795, headnote, line 2, *after* Supp. iii. 77–9. *add* Sold Sotheby's 9 June 1921, lot 214, probably to Maggs (property of the late Henry William Bruton of Bewick House, Glos). *Line 3, after* p. 95; *add* re-offered, 'A Catalogue of Shakespeareana,' (Dec. 1927), lot 695;   *Line 5, after* Edwards; *add* offered by Edwards, Cat. No. 4 (n. s.), 1929 (Autograph Letters of Celebrated Authors), lot 314;

Page 271, To Daniel Lysons 29 Oct. 1795, headnote, last line, *after* Maggs; *insert* offered Maggs Cat. No. 388 (Spring 1920), lot 907;

Page 273, From Roscoe 9 Feb. 1796, headnote, line 1, *after* MS *insert* formerly   *Line 4, after* Pall Mall' *add* ; sold Christie's 17 Dec. 1957 (Mrs Davy's Sale), lot 69, to Maggs for WSL (Hazen, *Cat. of HW's Lib.* No. 3703).

Page 274, To Roscoe 15 Feb. 1796, headnote, line 3, *after* 80–1 *add* ; Henry Roscoe, *Life of William Roscoe*, 1833, i. 159–61.

Page 275, note 3, *delete* Mrs Colin Davy kindly informs us that   *Line 2, for* the *read* The

Page 276, note 1, line 5, *after* ibid. *add* 25–27 Aug.,   *Line 6, after* lxxx. *add* 196,

Page 283, note 14, *add* See Hazen, *Cat. of HW's Lib.* No. 237.

Page 285, *for heading* To Roscoe, July 1796 *read* To Roscoe, ca Tuesday 12 July 1796   *At beginning of headnote insert* Printed in full from the MS now WSL, in MISC. CORR. iii. 439–40.

Page 286, line 1, *on* medals *add note* 1a: 1a. See HW's letter of ca 12 July 1796, printed in MISC. CORR. iii. 439–40.

Page 286, To Daniel Lysons 7 Aug. 1796, headnote, last line, *after* Maggs; *add* offered Maggs Cat. No. 388 (Spring 1920), lot 909;

Page 287, To Daniel Lysons 1 Dec. 1796, line 1, *after* Sir *delete period*
Page 287, bottom of page, *insert the following heading*:

TO DANIEL OR SAMUEL LYSONS, n.d.

MS card in Kirgate's hand, now WSL, printed in MISC. CORR. iii. 465.

Page 291, headnote, 2d paragraph, line 3, *after* eleven volumes *add* (now in the Bodleian Library)   *Line 5, for* 11, 45 *read* 45, 46   *add* ; there was also an additional 4to volume sold SH iii. 54 (see Hazen, *Cat. of HW's Lib.* Nos 1379, 1337).

Page 293, note 22, line 1, *for* 1689 *read* 1690   *Last line, add* See Sedgwick i. 464–5.

Page 295, note 37, *for* n. 1 *read* n. 1a

Page 295, note 41, lines 2–3, *for* by Waterland *read* anon.

Page 296, note 45, line 2, *for* 1720 *read* 1723

Page 296, note 48, lines 4–5, *for* probably in the third day's sale *read* vi. 27   *Line 6, for* Dr A. S. W. Rosenbach *read* WSL (Hazen, *Cat. of HW's Lib.* No. 2474:6).

Page 296, note 48a, *add* HW's copy is Hazen, *Cat. of HW's Lib.* No. 451.

Page 297, line 6, *on* controversy *add note* 52a: 52a. For these tracts see Hazen, *Cat. of HW's Lib.* No. 1337.

Page 298, note 60, *for* see *ante*, prefatory note *read* see Hazen, *Cat. of HW's Lib.* No. 1370

Page 299, note 67, *add* By Philo-Christus, probably Richard Moseley (see DALRYMPLE 304, n. 88; Hazen, *Cat. of HW's Lib.* No. 1379:6:3).

Page 300, line 10, *for* Letter *read* Epistle

Page 302, line 28, *on* 1751 *add note* 81a: 81a. See Hazen, *Cat. of HW's Lib.* No. 1372.

Page 302, note 82, *at beginning insert* Hazen, *Cat. of HW's Lib.* No. 1337:6.

Page 303, note 87, line 1, *for* Samual *read* Samuel

Page 303, last line, *on* (Mr Ashton). *add note* 87a: 87a. See Hazen, *Cat. of HW's Lib.* No. 1379:10:4.

Page 304, line 4, *on* 1752 *add note* 87b: 87b. HW's copy is Hazen, *Cat. of HW's Lib.* No. 832.

Page 304, note 89, *add* HW's copy of the 1st edition is Hazen, *Cat. of HW's Lib.* No. 1379:9:1.

Page 304, note 91, *add* HW's copy is Hazen, *Cat. of HW's Lib.* No. 1379:9:6.

Page 304, note 92, *substitute* HW's copy is Hazen, *Cat. of HW's Lib.* No. 1379:9:7.

Page 304, note 93, *add* HW's copy is Hazen, *Cat. of HW's Lib.* No. 1432.

Page 310, line 5, *on* music *add note* 26a: 26a. Middleton's zeal for music and learning is commented on in *Lloyd's Evening Post* 8–10 Sept. 1773, xxxiii. 241.

Page 319, note 20, line 4, *after* vi. 76 *add* and is now WSL (Hazen, *Cat.*

of HW's Lib. No. 2404).   *Lines 4–5, for* contributed *read* permitted his Ceres to be copied for use as

Page 319, note 21, last line, *for* n. 2. *read* n. 2; CHUTE 542 and n. 3.

Page 319, note 24a, *add* See also BERRY ii. 241, 243.

Page 320, note 30, *add* When he eloped with her in 1789, she had already borne two children by him; see *Betsy Sheridan's Journal*, ed. William Le Fanu [1960], pp. 176–7.

Page 321, 2d paragraph, line 7, *for* Dramore *read* Dromore

Page 323, note 50, last line, *add* It is printed as Appendix 1 in FAMILY 295–304.

Page 325, note 60, *add* See SELWYN 370–1.

Page 325, note 63, line 1, *for* Fitzroy had been made a colonel *read* Lt-Col. Fitzroy had been made Brevet Colonel

Page 327, note 75, *after* 1797 *add* , p. 335

Page 330, note 97, line 3, *for* 1811 *read* 1807

Page 330, note 101, *add* HW's copy is Hazen, *Cat. of HW's Lib*. No. 3394.

Page 331, note 102, line 4, *for* 31 March *read* 30 March   *before* J. E. *insert* see OSSORY iii. 216, n. 13; Hazen, *Cat. of HW's Lib*. No. 3189;

Page 331, 2d line from bottom, *on* Campbells *add note* 103a: 103a. HW tells this anecdote to Lady Ossory 23 July 1775 (OSSORY i. 242); see also BERRY i. 181.

Page 333, note 108, *add* See also HW's Marginal Notes written in Dr Maty's Memoirs of the Earl of Chesterfield, p. 10, printed in *Miscellanies of the Philobiblon Society*, vol. xi.

Page 334, note 111, line 1, *for* (b. 1771) *read* (1771–1850)   *Lines 2, 3, for* Delaney's *read* Delany's   *Line 6, after* 275 *add* ; OSSORY ii. 498, n. 17

Page 337, 6th line from bottom, *for* Mrs. *read* Mrs

Page 338, 2d paragraph, line 2, *on* Ireland *add note* 126a: 126a. See 'Book of Visitors,' BERRY ii. 226.

Page 338, 4th paragraph, line 1, *for* Mr. *read* Mr   *Line 3, after* daughters *delete note number* 128

Page 338, *delete note 128*

Page 340, note 9, *for* joiefull. *read* joiefull.'

Page 343, note 4, last line, *after* n. 3 *add* , and HW to Thomas Walpole the younger 26 June 1792, FAMILY 281–2.

VOLUME 16

Page vii, List of Illustrations, *sub* Michael Lort, by John Downman, 1777, *add* Downman's sketch for this is in the 'Burleigh Court' Sketch Book, 2d series, in the Fitzwilliam Museum, Cambridge.

Page vii, *sub* John Fenn, by Henry Walton, 1775, *add* Walton's original painting is now (1952) in the possession of Mr John H. Frere.

Page x, 3d paragraph, line 1, *for* fifty *read* fifty-one   *Line 2, for* eleven *read* twelve

Page x, 3d paragraph, *at end add* Another letter to Lort, of 24 Jan. 1760, is bound in Lort's copy of *Royal and Noble Authors*, 2d edition, 1759, and is now in the Bodleian Library; it is printed in MISC. CORR. i. 175–6.

Page x, 4th paragraph, lines 4–5, *for* , except for one (from Walpole) which was owned by the late Mr Roy Coventry. *substitute* ; the one which was owned by the late Mr Roy Coventry has now been acquired by W. S. Lewis.   *Last line, add* Seven further letters between Walpole and the Fenns, from the library of J. J. Colman and his son, Russell J. Colman, are now in the Norwich Central Library, Norfolk, and were printed by Mr R. W. Ketton-Cremer in *Times Literary Supplement* 15 March 1957, lvi. 164; they are now reprinted in MISC. CORR. iii. 95, 97–8, 100–1, 105–6, 142, 188, 191–3.

Page xi, 1st paragraph, line 1, *for* thirty-two *read* thirty-nine   *for* twenty-three *read* twenty-six   *Line 6, delete* James Tregaskis and Son (1936),   *Line 9, after* Charnwood (1930). *add* Three 'missing' letters and one extract have been discovered: 5 Sept. 1784, now Lloyd W. Smith Collection, Morristown National Historical Park, Morristown, New Jersey; 29 Oct. 1788, University of Delaware Library; 10 Aug. 1790, Manchester Central Library; 30 July 1787, extract quoted in Waller Catalogue. The manuscripts of 6 Oct. 1784, 29 June 1787, and 14 Aug. 1789 have been acquired by W. S. Lewis. Other manuscripts which have come to light are: 30 Sept. 1785, sold Christie's 2 April 1975 by the Mildmay-White Family Trust; and 4 Oct. 1786, in the library of Occidental College, Los Angeles, California.

Page xv, *Anecdotes*, ed. Wornum, right column, transpose 1st two lines

Page xxi, Letters between Walpole and Fenn, *sub* 1784, *delete* ca July* *and substitute* 7 May   *14 June*   29 June   *3 July*   *sub* 1787 *add* 1 Feb. 31 March

Page xxii, Letters between Walpole and Mrs Fenn, *for ca 5 July** *read* *3 July* [with Mr Fenn]

Page xxii, Letters between Walpole and Lort, *sub* 1760 *add* 24 Jan.

Page xxiv, Letters between Walpole and Pinkerton, *sub* 1784, *for* 5 Sept.* *read* 5 Sept.   *sub* 1787 *add* 30 July, extract   *sub* 1788 *add* 29 Oct.

Page xxv, Letters between Walpole and Pinkerton, *sub* 1790 *add* 10 Aug.

Page 3, note 2, right column, line 2, *after* ii. 88 *add* ; Hazen, *Cat. of HW's Lib.* No. 612   *Last line, after* WSL *add* (Hazen, op. cit. No. 162)

Page 4, note 5, last line, *after* i. 5 *add* (Hazen, *Cat. of HW's Lib.* No. 201)

Page 4, note 8, last line, *after* ii. 171 *add* (Hazen, *Cat. of HW's Lib.* Nos 3450, 884)

Page 4, note 9, last line, *after* ii. 84 *add* ; Hazen, *Cat. of HW's Lib.* No. 588

Page 5, note 14, line 6, *after* i. 10) *add*   ; see Hazen, *Cat. of HW's Lib.* Nos 30, 149

Page 5, note 16, line 1, *for* 1st Bn *read* cr. (1629) Bn

Page 6, note 23, line 6, *after* i. 16 *add*   ; Hazen, *Cat. of HW's Lib.* No. 145

Page 6, note 29, line 4, *for* Tower hamlets *read* Tower Hamlets

Page 7, note 32, line 2, *after* i. 14 *add*   ; Hazen, *Cat. of HW's Lib.* No. 183   *Line 7, after* i. 46 *add*   ; Hazen, op. cit. No. 60

Page 7, note 35, last line, *after* i. 43 *add*   ; Hazen, *Cat. of HW's Lib.* No. 41

Page 7, note 37, right column, line 3, *after* iii. 80 *add*   ; Hazen, *Cat. of HW's Lib.* No. 1770

Page 7, note 38, line 8, *after* 1739–46 *add* (Hazen, *Cat. of HW's Lib.* No. 614)

Page 7, note 42, last line, *after* i. 16 *add*   ; Hazen, *Cat. of HW's Lib.* No. 171

Page 8, note 43, line 5, *for* 1668 *read* 1666   *delete last sentence and substitute* Both the 1st edition, 1666, and the 2d edition, 1670, were in HW's library; but he apparently acquired the 1666 edition after he had published his R&NA[2], since in that work he cited the 1670 edition (see Hazen, *Cat. of HW's Lib.* Nos 187, 2338).

Page 10, note 5, right column, line 3, *after* ii. 164 *add* (Hazen, *Cat. of HW's Lib.* No. 892)

Page 11, note 2, last line, *after* WSL *add* (Hazen, *Cat. of HW's Lib.* No. 906)

Page 11, note 4, last line, *after* 1616 *add* (Hazen, *Cat. of HW's Lib.* No. 20)

Page 12, note 12, last line, *after* iii. 102 *add*   ; Hazen, *Cat. of HW's Lib.* No. 1628

Page 12, note 14, last line, *after* iii. 31 *add* (Hazen, *Cat. of HW's Lib.* No. 1428)

Page 12, note 15, line 1, *for* Cary *read* Carey   *for* Vct Falkland *read* Vct of Falkland

Page 13, note 17, last line, *after* vi. 65 *add* and v. 11 (Hazen, *Cat. of HW's Lib.* Nos 2498, 3392

Page 14, note 1, last line, *after* WSL *add* (Hazen, *Cat. of HW's Lib.* No. 1608:9:10)

Page 14, note 3, last line, *after* i. 12 *add* (Hazen, *Cat. of HW's Lib.* No. 148)

Page 14, note 5, line 3, *after* 229–31 *add* and Hazen, *Cat. of HW's Lib.* Nos 76, 77

Page 15, note 10, line 3, *after* i. 35 *add*   ; Hazen, *Cat. of HW's Lib.* No. 83   *Last line, after* edn *add*   ; see Hazen, op. cit. Nos 2010, 47

Page 16, note 19, last line, *after* Oxford *add*   ; see Hazen, *Cat. of HW's Lib.* No. 40

Page 16, note 21, last line, *after* i. 70 *add*   ; Hazen, *Cat. of HW's Lib.* No. 2

Page 16, note 22, line 7, *after* iii. 30 *add*   ; Hazen, *Cat. of HW's Lib.* No. 1490

Page 16, note 24, *add* See Hazen, *SH Bibl.* 42.

Page 16, note 25, last line, *after* iv. 2 *add*   ; Hazen, *Cat. of HW's Lib.* No. 554

Page 18, note 2, last line, *after* Museum *add* (see Hazen, *Cat. of HW's Lib.* No. 1918)

Page 19, note 8, line 1, *for* recovered *read* tried to recover   *Last sentence, delete* The present whereabouts of these papers is unknown *and substitute* The papers that have survived are now among the Cholmondeley MSS at Houghton; see G. A. Chinnery, *A Handlist of the Cholmondeley (Houghton) MSS, Sir Robert Walpole's Archive*, Cambridge, 1953, p. 5.

Page 20, note 14, last line, after iv. 80 *add*   ; Hazen, *Cat. of HW's Lib.* No. 1092

Page 21, note 20, last line, *for* is not in the SH records *read* was bound in vol. i of 'Plays'; see Hazen, *Cat. of HW's Lib.* No. 1623:1:7.

Page 22, 2d paragraph, line 10, *on* Virgil *add note* 7a: 7a. HW had 14 editions of Virgil and only 7, including the SH edition, of Lucan.

Page 23, note 8, *add* See Hazen, *Cat. of HW's Lib.* No. 552.

Page 23, note 9, last line, *after* iv. 45 *add* (see Hazen, *Cat. of HW's Lib.* No. 1163)

Page 25, note 8, line 4, *for the read* or an   *Line 6, after* ii. 100 *add* (Hazen, *Cat. of HW's Lib.* No. 562)

Page 27, note 2, line 4, *before* sold *insert* the English translation, *Royal and Ecclesiastical Antiquities of France*, London, 1750, 2 vols in 3   *after* viii. 142 *add* (see Hazen, *Cat. of HW's Lib.* No. 3683; GRAY ii. 69–70)

Page 27, note 5, last line, *after* catalogue *add*   ; Hazen, *Cat. of HW's Lib.* No. 2040

Page 28, note 10, last line, *after* v. 27 *add* (Hazen, *Cat. of HW's Lib.* No. 3328)

Page 30, note 3, line 3, *after* Shrewsbury *add* (Hazen, *Cat. of HW's Lib.* No. 2050:13)

Page 31, note 8, line 3, *after* i. 156 *add* (Hazen, *Cat. of HW's Lib.* No. 464)

Page 34, note 5, last line, *after* iii. 34 *add* (Hazen, *Cat. of HW's Lib.* No. 1439)

Page 36, note 20, last line, *after* 242 *add* and refers to it in his *Essay on Modern Gardening* (*Works* ii. 522)

Page 37, note 3, last line, *after* iii. 75 *add*   ; Hazen, *Cat. of HW's Lib.* No. 1791

Page 38, note 5, left column, line 8, *after* WSL *add* (Hazen, *Cat. of HW's Lib.* No. 1608:66:1)

Page 38, note 6, last line, *after* iii. 40 *add* (Hazen, *Cat. of HW's Lib.* No. 1425)

Page 38, note 7, last line, *after* iii. 37 *add*   ; Hazen, *Cat. of HW's Lib.* No. 1426

Page 38, note 9, last line, *after* iii. 165 *add*   ; Hazen, *Cat. of HW's Lib.* No. 1819; see also No. 1912

Page 39, note 3, line 13, *after* WSL *add* (see Hazen, *Cat. of HW's Lib.* Nos 1608:26:3, 1608:28:2, 1608:30:6)

Page 42, note 3, *add* See also MASON i. 199, n. 6.

Page 43, note 7, line 10, *after* 170 *add*   ; Hazen, *Cat. of HW's Lib.* No. 1810:2:1

Page 44, note 9, line 4, *after* University *add* (Hazen, *Cat. of HW's Lib.* No. 3222:3:2)

Page 44, note 11, last line, *after* i. 81 *add* (Hazen, *Cat. of HW's Lib.* No. 356)

Page 45, From Zouch 15 March 1762, 1st paragraph, line 2, *on Anecdotes add note a: a.* Zouch's set of *Anecdotes* vols i–iii, and the *Catalogue of Engravers*, bound in 2 vols, with Lowther arms on sides and Lowther bookplate, is now WSL (Hazen, *SH Bibl.* 1973, p. xvii).

Page 46, note 2, line 1, *for* ca 1561–1641 *read* ?1564–1641

Page 53, note 2, line 4, *after* 55). *insert* Zouch had vol. iii of *Anecdotes* bound with the *Catalogue of Engravers*, to go with vols i–ii of *Anecdotes* which HW had given him in 1762. The set is now WSL.

Page 55, note 1, *add* See also Hazen, *SH Bibl.* 72.

Pages 63–4, note 3, *delete 1st two lines and substitute Anecdotes*[1] iii was printed by 8 Oct. 1762; *Engravers*[1] was printed by 9 May 1763   *Last line, after* but *insert* they   *after* 1764 *add* (Hazen, *SH Bibl.* 55)

Page 67, note 57, line 2, *transfer to end of note 56.*

Page 70, note 6, line 1, *for* ca 1796 *read* 1779   *Line 5, after* Exchange. *insert* 'On Sunday [3 Oct.] died at his house at Lower Tooting, in Surrey, Mr Kentish, silversmith, in Cornhill' (*London Chronicle* 2–5 Oct. 1779, xlvi. 327). 'Kentish, John, Cornhill, jeweler' was a member of the Glovers Company (*List of the Livery of London*, 1776, p. 143).

Page 71, note 2, line 2, *for* license *read* licence

Page 76, note 24, line 1, *for* (ca 1478–ca 1533) *read* (1478–between 1533 and 1536)

Page 78, note 3, line 1, *after* London *insert* vi.

Page 92, note 1, *add* For Henry Seymour Conway's use of this quotation in the House of Commons on 2 Dec. 1777, see *Last Journals* ii. 80.

Page 121, note 1, *add* See also Frances Burney, Mme d'Arblay, *Memoirs of Doctor Burney*, 1832, i. 265–7, ii. 347–53.

Pages 121–2, To Bewley 23 May 1778, headnote, 1st paragraph, last line, *after* 57–62, *insert* in the *European Magazine*, 1797, xxxi. 380–1, *3d paragraph, lines 3–4, delete* it probably contained at least part of the extract of the letter to Bewley. *and substitute* this MS, in Kirgate's hand, with HW's MS notes, is in the Beinecke Library, Yale University; it is endorsed 'After Mr Walpole had printed these pages, which he had previously shown to me, he made me a present of his autograph. Thos Percy' (gift of Mr and Mrs Edmund A. Prentis, 1949, from the Russell G. Pruden estate; see *Yale University Library Gazette*, 1951, xxv. 36).

Page 122, headnote, lines 6–7, *delete* apparently not among Sir Ernest's papers, and it has not yet been found. *and substitute* in the Russell G. Pruden collection.

Page 122, To Bewley 23 May 1778, line 1, *on* Chatterton *add note* 1a: 1a. On 29 March 1779 Bewley wrote Dr Charles Burney, 'Have you seen a Letter which Mr H. Walpole wrote to me last year, on the subject of his connections with Chatterton, and which he has found himself obliged to print; though, to avoid controversy, he does not publish it, but gives copies away to his friends?—He has, *to my knowledge*, as well as that of Mr Thom, been very *unjustly* calumniated on this head. The very same story that he *now* tells, he told *us* and some others, some years ago, at a time when he could have no suspicion of being attacked as a murderer of genius etc.' (MS in the Osborn Collection, Beinecke Library, Yale University).

Page 129, 2d paragraph, last line, *on* when *add note* 76a: 76a. So in HW's printed text; he apparently intends that this sentence should run on into the next paragraph.

Page 130, note 81, lines 2–3, *for* two months before his eighteenth birthday *substitute* 25 Aug. 1770; he would have been eighteen the following 20 Nov.

Page 134, after letter of 23 May 1778 *insert the following heading*:

To BEWLEY, n.d.

Printed for the first time from the MS, now WSL, in MISC. CORR. iii. 457.

Page 137, top of page, *insert the following heading*:

To LORT, Thursday 24 January 1760

The MS is bound into Lort's copy of HW's *Catalogue of the Royal and Noble Authors*, 2d edn, 1759, now in the Bodleian Library. It is now printed in MISC. CORR. i. 175–6.

Page 137, note 1, line 7, *after* 1780; *add* librarian at Lambeth, 1785;

Page 137, note 5, line 2, *after* (1619–81). *add* HW's copies are Hazen, *Cat. of HW's Lib.* Nos 867, 1389.

Page 139, note 14, *delete line 2 and substitute* Arthur Capell (1604–49), cr. (1641) Bn Capell

Page 139, note 15, lines 3–4, *for* HW's copy was sold SH i. 25 *read* HW's copies were sold SH i. 25, 37 (see Hazen, *Cat. of HW's Lib.* Nos 70, 109)

Page 139, note 17, right column, line 5, *after* i. 16 *add* and is now WSL (Hazen, *Cat. of HW's Lib.* No. 151).

Page 140, note 1, line 7, *after* i. 7 *add* (Hazen, *Cat. of HW's Lib.* No. 190)

Page 140, note 3, last line, *after* iii. 88 *add* (Hazen, *Cat. of HW's Lib.* No. 1666)

Page 141, note 9, line 2, *for* 1720 *read* 1723

Page 142, note 11, left column, line 3, *after* 1754 *add* (HW's copy is Hazen, *Cat. of HW's Lib.* No. 1608:71:2)

Page 142, note 2, line 9, *for* Van Der Dort's *read* Van Der Doort's

Page 143, note 5, lines 3–4, *for* King of Sicily 1435–42 (GRAY ii. 69); *read* titular King of Sicily 1435–80 and effective King of Naples 1438–42 (Jacques Levron, *La vie et les mœurs du bon roi René*, 1953, pp. 74, 81, 84, 94–5);

Page 143, note 7, last line, *after* 78 *add* (Hazen, *Cat. of HW's Lib.* No. 591)

Page 144, note 10, line 11, *after* ii. 91 *add* (Hazen, *Cat. of HW's Lib.* No. 611)

Page 145, note 22, *add* A letter of Vertue to Maurice Johnson 29 July 1732 about antiquarian studies is printed in GM 1810, lxxx. 313–14.

Page 146, note 28, line 2, *for* (1606–83) *read* (1606–88)

Page 147, note 33, *add* HW's copies are Hazen, *Cat. of HW's Lib.* Nos 487, 2440, 2737.

Page 148, note 39, *add* A Latin epigram, said to be over 100 years old and taken from *Les trois siècles de littérature*, is quoted in GM 1807, lxxvii pt ii. 999:

> Quae Dea sublimi vehitur per compita curru,
> An Juno? an Pallas? an Venus ipsa venit?
> Si Genus aspicies, Juno; si Dicta, Minerva!
> Si spectes Oculos, Mater Amoris erit!
>
> What Goddess rides triumphant in her car!
> Juno? or Venus? or the Maid of War?
> In Speech 'tis Pallas! Juno in her Race!
> But Love's sweet Mother when we view her Face!
>   (translation by William Thomas Fitzgerald)

Page 148, note 46, line 1, *for* 1537 *read* ca 1547

Page 149, note 53, line 1, *for* Cornelius *read* Cornelis   *Line 3, after* see *add* Thieme and Becker;

Page 151, note 65, left column, line 13, *after* vi. 19 *add* (Hazen, *Cat. of HW's Lib.* No. 2331)

Page 151, note 67, *add* HW's copies of Sir Francis Kynaston's *Corona Minervæ, or a masque*, 1635, and *The Constitutions of the Musæum Minervæ*, 1636, are Hazen, *Cat. of HW's Lib.* Nos 2405, 3817.

Page 153, note 85, left column, lines 4–6, *delete* (MS Cat. . . . the editors.

and substitute ; HW's copy was sold SH i. 97, and is Hazen, *Cat. of HW's Lib*. No. 360.

Page 158, note 22, line 3, *after* vi. 17 *add* (Hazen, *Cat. of HW's Lib.* No. 2497)

Page 163, note 1, right column, line 6, *after* lot 3572 *add* , and is now (1953) *penes* C. H. Wilkenson, Worcester College

Page 165, note 5, *add* See also MASON i. 363.

Page 168, note 1, line 2, *after* 1791–1828 *insert* (see GM 1829, xcix pt i. 90–1; *Old Westminsters* ii. 954; Venn, *Alumni Cantab*. vi. 300)

Page 172, note 5, line 5, *after* i. 89 *add* and another copy sold SH v. 111; see Hazen, *Cat. of HW's Lib*. Nos 395, 2759

Page 173, note 4, *add* HW's copy of the frontispiece of *L'Avare* is now WSL.

Page 178, note 2, *add* The MS is now WSL, gift of St Mary's College, Strawberry Hill; see also Hazen, *SH Bibl*. 114–16.

Page 180, note 6, last line, *after* v. 134 *add* (Hazen, *Cat. of HW's Lib*. No. 2960)

Page 184, note 9, *for* A picture-cleaner *read* Richard Bonus (fl. 1765–80), picture-cleaner (see OSSORY i. 140, n. 14).

Page 185, note 13, line 5, *after* iv. 12 *add* (Hazen, *Cat. of HW's Lib*. No. 528)

Page 185, note 14, line 6, *after* Robert *add* [John]

Page 187, note 2, line 4, *after* 1773. *add* HW's copy is Hazen, *Cat. of HW's Lib*. No. 3847. 'The Original Drawings made by Joseph Strutt for Regal and Ecclesiastical Antiquities copied from Illuminated MSS in the British Museum,' which were formerly *penes* Richard Bull, are now WSL.

Page 197, note 9, line 10, *after* Sept. *add* , 29 Sept.–2 Oct.   *Line 11*, *after* 247 *add* , 315

Page 198, To Lort 2 Nov. 1781, headnote, line 4, *after* 3808; *add* Maggs Cat. No. 486 (Christmas 1926), lot 2436;

Page 200, note 3, right column, line 4, *after* BM. *add* Hazen, *Cat. of HW's Lib*. No. 3920, places this among 'five others' in the London sale 1034 (SH vii. 47).

Page 202, note 4, line 1, *for* 1743 *read* 1744

Page 204, note 4, line 6, *after* WSL *add* ; see Hazen, *Cat. of HW's Lib*. No. 29

Page 206, To Lort 26 July 1788, headnote, line 5, *after* 94; *add* re-offered, 'A Catalogue of Shakespeareana,' [Dec. 1927], lot 695;

Page 206, note 2, last line, *after* iv. 40 *add* (Hazen, *Cat. of HW's Lib*. Nos 1176, 1177)

Page 212, note 1, *add* HW's copy is bound with his 'Collection of pieces relative to Rowley and Chatterton' (see *post* Appendix 1, p. 331; Hazen, *Cat. of HW's Lib*. No. 3690).

Page 213, To Lort 12 Nov. 1788, headnote, line 5, *after* 839; *add* Maggs Cat. No. 436 (1923), lot 282; Maggs Cat. No. 449 (1924), lot 441;

Page 219, note 1, right column, line 6, *after* iv. 3 *add* (Hazen, *Cat. of HW's Lib.* No. 539)

Page 222, From Lort 4 Aug. 1789, 1st paragraph, line 1, *for* Barret's *read* Barrett's

Page 223, 1st paragraph, line 7, *on* wit *add note* 4a: 4a. '... the women of the middle order, either through fear or wit, do not follow them [i.e., the fashionable ladies, in using great amounts of rouge]' ([Rev. William Jones,] *Observations in a Journey to Paris ... 1776*, 1777, i. 124–5).

Page 227, note 6, line 4, *for* 1773–85 *read* 1771–85

Page 228, note 3, line 4, *for* Saville *read* Savile

Page 231, To Fenn 30 March 1774, headnote, lines 2–3, *for* to his wife's nephew, William Frere, *read* to his brother-in-law, John Frere (1740–1807), then to John Frere's sons, William and Edward,

Page 232, To Fenn, 17 Sept. 1774, headnote, line 3, *for* July 1932 *read* Oct. 1932

Page 232, note 1, *delete last sentence and substitute* Mr Charles Kingsley Adams identified the painting as 'a portrait which was acquired by the late Duke of Bedford and which was sold from his collection at Christie's 19 Jan. 1951. We examined it carefully when it was at Woburn and believed it to be a portrait of Henry VII which perhaps remained on the painter's hands and which he overpainted to make it into a passable likeness of Henry VIII' (Adams to W. S. Lewis 2 Jan. 1952).

Page 234, note 16, lines 7–13, *delete* It had not been published ... the book was *and substitute* In the *Daily Adv.* 16 Sept. it was advertised: 'To-morrow will be published ...'; but in the *London Chronicle* 13–15, 15–17 Sept. (xxxvi. 263, 271) it was advertised: 'September 20, will be published, Price Eighteen Shillings in Boards'; it was

Page 235, note 16, left column, line 2, *after* annotated *add* (Hazen, *Cat. of HW's Lib.* Nos 541, 3813)

Page 235, note 1, *add* See also MASON Appendix 4, ii. 371–2.

Page 239, note 6, lines 3–4, *for* Edward IV himself was murdered in 1483; *read* Edward IV died probably of cerebral haemorrhage caused by immoderate habits, but contemporary chroniclers believed that his final illness was caused by melancholy after the disgraceful Treaty of Arras (23 Dec. 1482), which violated the agreement for the marriage of Edward's daughter to the Dauphin; *Line 6, after* 1483 *insert* (see Charles Ross, *Edward IV*, Berkeley and Los Angeles, 1974, pp. 33, 36–8, 292, 414–16)

Page 243, headnote, line 1, *after* 249–50. *insert* An extract was printed in *Paston Letters and Papers of the Fifteenth Century*, ed. Norman Davis, Oxford, 1971, p. xxiv.

Page 244, *delete* To FENN, ca July 1784 Missing. FROM MRS FENN, ca Monday 5 July 1784 Missing. *and substitute the following headings*:

To FENN, Friday 7 May 1784

The MS is in the Norwich Central Library, Norfolk; now printed in

MISC. CORR. iii. 95; previously printed, R. W. Ketton-Cremer, 'Some New Letters of Horace Walpole,' TLS 15 March 1957, lvi. 164.

FROM FENN, Monday 14 June 1784

The MS draft of the letter is in the Norwich Central Library, Norfolk; now printed in MISC. CORR. iii. 97–8; previously printed, R. W. Ketton-Cremer, 'Some New Letters of Horace Walpole,' TLS 15 March 1957, lvi. 164. The letter actually sent to HW is missing.

To FENN, Tuesday 29 June 1784

The MS is in the Norwich Central Library, Norfolk; now printed in MISC. CORR. iii. 100–1; previously printed, R. W. Ketton-Cremer, 'Some New Letters of Horace Walpole,' TLS 15 March 1957, lvi. 164.

FROM FENN AND MRS FENN, Saturday 3 July 1784

The MS draft of the letter is in the Norwich Central Library, Norfolk; now printed in MISC. CORR. iii. 105–6; previously printed, R. W. Ketton-Cremer, 'Some New Letters of Horace Walpole,' TLS 15 March 1957, lvi. 164. The letter actually sent to HW is missing.

Page 244, From Mrs Fenn 3 July 1784, note 1, line 1, *for* 1743 *read* 1744 *Line 2, for* Suffolk *read* Norfolk

Page 244, To Mrs Fenn 7 July 1784, 1st paragraph, line 2, *on* apology *add note a: a.* In his letter of 29 June 1784 HW apologizes for not thanking Mrs Fenn when she was at SH for the gift of her 2 volumes of *Cobwebs to Catch Flies*; her answer of 3 July thanks him for his approbation.

Page 244, To Mrs Fenn 7 July 1784, note 1, right column, lines 3–4, *for* Apparently her *read* Her   *Line 9, after* lvii. 399. *add* HW's copy is Hazen, *Cat. of HW's Lib.* No. 2414.

Page 245, note 2, *add* See Fenn and Mrs Fenn to HW 3 July 1784 (in MISC. CORR. iii. 105–6) and Hazen, *Cat. of HW's Lib.* No. 2414. Fenn's copy of the 2d edn of the *Castle of Otranto*, with his signature and date, 1766, and a copy in his hand of HW to Cole 9 March 1765, is now WSL.

Page 245, note 3, *add* In Fenn's letter of 3 July 1784 he asks about HW's *Description* and says that he has been unable to obtain a copy.

Page 245, note 4, line 5, *for* 1761 *read* 1781   *At end add* See also HW to Thomas Pennant 15 Oct. 1782, where he mentions printing 'a few copies of part [of the *Description*], some years ago, for the use of the housekeeper and those who come to see the house.'

Page 246, at top of page *insert the following headings:*

To FENN, Thursday 1 February 1787

The MS is in the Norwich Central Library, Norfolk; now printed in MISC. CORR. iii. 188; previously printed, R. W. Ketton-Cremer, 'Some New Letters of Horace Walpole,' TLS 15 March 1957, lvi. 164.

To Fenn, Saturday 31 March 1787

The MS is in the Norwich Central Library, Norfolk; now printed in
Misc. Corr. iii. 191–3; previously printed, R. W. Ketton-Cremer, 'Some
New Letters of Horace Walpole,' tls 15 March 1957, lvi. 164.

Page 247, To Fenn 13 Dec. 1791, headnote, *add* It was sold to wsl Oct.
1963 by Katherine McClure-Smith acting for a friend.

Page 251, headnote, line 9, *after* sale. *add* Sold, Paris, 15–20 July 1878,
from the Benjamin Fillon Collection (Catalogue now wsl). This letter is
listed in the collection of Sir Herbert H. Raphael, *Horace Walpole, a
Descriptive Catalogue*, 1909; sold Sotheby's 4 Feb. 1919 (Raphael Sale),
lot 311, to Bumpus for Lord Cowdray, the father of the Hon. Clive Pearson; bequeathed by his widow, the Hon. Mrs Pearson, to her daughter,
Mrs P. A. Tritton, of Parham Park, in 1974.

Page 252, To Pinkerton 5 Sept. 1784, headnote, line 1, *delete* Missing.
MS untraced until *and substitute* The MS is in the Lloyd W. Smith Col-
lection of Morristown National Historical Park, Morristown, New Jersey;
Line 3, for not further traced. Described as 1 p. 4to. *substitute* later *penes*
Lloyd W. Smith, whose collection of MSS was acquired by Morristown
National Historical Park in 1955. Printed in Misc. Corr. iii. 111–12.

Page 252, note 3, line 2, *after* plate in *add* the 2d edn of   *Line 3, after*
vol. 1 *add*   , published by R. Phillips, No. 71, St Paul's Church Yard, 1
Oct. 1799

Page 253, note 3, line 9, *after* iii. 77 *add* (Hazen, *Cat. of HW's Lib.* No.
1729)

Page 254, note 5, lines 8–10, *delete* HW's copy . . . British Museum. *and
substitute* HW's copy of the 1st edn, 1784, is owned by Mr Basil Carew
Hunt, Wimbledon, England; HW's two copies of the 2d edn, 1789, one
containing MS notes, are in the British Museum (see Hazen, *Cat. of HW's
Lib.* Nos 278, 279, 3823).   *Line 11, after* vol. 1 *add* of the 2d edn

Page 255, To Pinkerton 6 Oct. 1784, headnote, line 3, *after* 38–43 *add*
Collated with the original MS which is now wsl.   *Lines 8–9, for* not
further traced *substitute* sold Sotheby's 27 Oct. 1959, lot 501, to Maggs for
wsl. [The variants in the MS are listed below:]

Page 255, To Pinkerton 6 Oct. 1784, date-line, *for* 6th *read* 6

Page 255, To Pinkerton 6 Oct. 1784, line 1, *for* Sir; *read* Sir:

Page 256, 1st paragraph, line 7, *after* just *delete*   ,   *Line 9, for speaking harlequins read* speaking harlequins   *Line 11, for* O'Keeffe *read*
Okeeffe   *Line 14, for* nonsense; *read* nonsense—   *Line 17, after* produce *insert* it

Page 256, 2d paragraph, line 5, *after* whereas *delete*   ,

Page 256, 3d paragraph, line 2, *after* Winter *delete*   ,   *Line 3, for*
much. *read* much; and

Page 257, 1st paragraph, line 5, *after* song *add*   ,   *Line 7, after*
genius *add*   ,   *Line 9, after* succeeded *delete*   ,   *Line 19, after* sing-

ers *delete* ,   *Line 21, for* ill. *read* ill—   *Line 28, for* them— *read* them.

Page 257, 3d line from bottom, *under* HOR. WALPOLE *insert* Oct. 7th.

Page 258, 1st paragraph, line 2, *for* publication; *read* publication— *Line 3, after* man *delete* ,

Page 258, 2d paragraph, line 5, *after* audience) *delete* ,   *Line 7, for* taste, *read* taste—   *Line 9, after* correcting *add* ,   *Line 11, for* reproofs: ladies *read* reproofs. Ladies   *Line 13, after* Probably *delete* , *Line 14, after* reprimand *add* ,   *Line 16, for* patches, *read* patches— *Line 17, after* fortunately *delete* ,

Page 262, running head, *for* 1784 *read* 1785

Page 263, note 1, line 3, *after* Esq.' *add* For HW's copy see Hazen, *Cat. of HW's Lib.* No. 3825.

Page 263, note 1, right column, lines 9–10, transpose to bottom of right column

Page 266, note 15, line 6, *after* marginalia *add* (see Hazen, *Cat. of HW's Lib.* No. 814)   *Last line, after* 178–80 *add* ; OSSORY iii. 255–61, Appendix 9

Page 268, note 3, last two lines, *for* does not appear in the SH records. *read* is bound in 'Poems of Geo. 3,' vol. xx; see Hazen, *Cat. of HW's Lib.* No. 3222:20:6.

Page 271, note 21, last line, *after* 146 *add* ; see Hazen, *Cat. of HW's Lib.* No. 935

Page 272, note 24, last line, *after* i. 90 *add* (Hazen, *Cat. of HW's Lib.* No. 371); a copy of *The Dispensary*, 1741, with HW's notes, was in Kirgate's sale (ibid. No. 4005).

Page 272, note 25, lines 2–3, *for* HW apparently had no separate edition *read* HW's copy, 1756, is Hazen, *Cat. of HW's Lib.* No. 1263;   *Last line, add* See Hazen, op. cit. Nos 1172, 3057.

Page 272, note 26, last line, *after* Œuvres *add* (Hazen, *Cat. of HW's Lib.* Nos 1148, 1172)

Page 274, headnote, 1st paragraph, lines 8–10, *delete* later untraced . . . WSL. *and substitute* offered in George D. Smith's Cat., 1914, lot 991 (Thomas Park's 1806 edition of R&NA containing two autograph letters of HW); sold by E. Weyhe of New York April 1937 to WSL.

Page 278, headnote, last line, *after* lot 399 *insert* and Cat. No. 4 (new series, 1929), lot 313

Page 281, To Pinkerton 30 Sept. 1785, headnote, last line, *for* not further traced. *read* MS sold Christie's 2 April 1975 ('Property of the Mildmay-White Family Trust'), lot 188; now in the possession of Mr Robert H. Taylor, Princeton, New Jersey. [The text is printed here from a photostat of the MS:]

Address: To John Pinkerton, Esq. at Knightsbridge. *Postmark*: 1 OC. *Endorsed*: Mr Walpole 30 Sep[tembe]r 1785.

Strawberry Hill, Sept. 30th 1785.

As soon, Sir, as I can see the lady my friend, who is much acquainted with the Archbishop, I will try if she will ask his leave for you to see the books you mention in his library, of which I will give her the list. I did ask Mr Cambridge where Dr Lort is; he told me, with the Bishop [of] Chester and on an intended tour to the lakes.

I do not possess nor ever looked into one of the books you specify, nor Mabillon's *Acta sanctorum*, nor O'Flaherty's *Ogygia*. My reading has been very idle and trifling and desultory—not that perhaps it has not been employed on authors as respectable as those you want to consult, nor that I had not rather read the Deeds of Sinners than *Acta sanctorum*. I have no reverence but for sensible books, and consequently not for a great number; and had rather have read fewer than I have than more. The rest may be useful on certain points, as they happen now to be to you, who I am sure would not read them for general use and pleasure, and are a very different kind of author. I shall like, I dare to say, anything you do write, but I am not overjoyed at your wading into the history of dark ages, unless you use it as a canvas to be embroidered with your own opinions, and episodes, and comparisons with more recent times. That is a most entertaining kind of writing. In general I have seldom wasted time on the origin of nations, unless for an opportunity of smiling at the gravity of the author, or at the absurdity of the manners of those ages, for absurdity and bravery compose almost all the anecdotes we have of them—except the accounts of what they never did nor thought of doing.

I have a real affection for Bishop Hoadley. He stands with me in lieu of what are called *the Fathers*; and I am much obliged to you for offering to lend me a book of his—but as my faith in him and his doctrines has long been settled, I shall not return to such grave studies, when I have so little time left, and desire only to pass it tranquilly, and without thinking of what I can neither propagate nor correct. When youth made me sanguine, I hoped mankind might be set right. Now that I am very old, I set down with this lazy maxim, that unless one could cure men of being fools, it is to no purpose to cure them of any folly, as it is only making room for some other. Self-interest is thought to govern every man—yet is it possible to be less governed by self-interest than men are in the aggregate? Do not thousands sacrifice even their lives for single men? Is not it an established rule in France that every person in that kingdom should love every king they have in his turn? What government is formed for general happiness? Where is not it thought heresy by the majority to insinuate that the felicity of one man ought not to be preferred to that of millions? Had not I better at 68 leave men to these preposterous notions, than return to Bishop Hoadley, and sigh?

Not but I have a heartfelt satisfaction when I hear that a mind as liberal as his, and who has dared to utter sacred truths, meets with approbation and purchasers of his work. You must not however flatter yourself, Sir, that all your purchasers are admirers. Some will buy your book, because they have heard of opinions in it that offend them, and because they want to find matter in it for abusing you. Let them; the more it is discussed, the more strongly will your fame be established. I commend you for scorning any artifice to puff your book but you must allow me to hope it will be attacked.

I have another satisfaction in the sale of your book: it will occasion a second edition. What if, as you do not approve of confuting misquoters, you simply printed a list of their false quotations, referring to the identic sentences, at the end of your second edition? That will be preserving their infamy, which else would perish where it was born; and perhaps would deter others from similar forgeries. If any rational opponent staggers you on any opinion of yours, I would retract it—and that would be a second triumph.

I am perhaps too impertinent and forward with advice—it is at least a proof of zeal; and you are under no obligation to follow my counsel. It is the weakness of old age to be apt to give advice—but I will fairly arm you against myself, by confessing, that when I was young, I was not apt to take any.

Yours most sincerely
H. WALPOLE

Page 285, note 5, right column, align top line
Page 287, note 1, line 7, *after* 1785. *add* For HW's copy see Hazen, *Cat. of HW's Lib.* No. 2925.   *for post* 7 Jan. *read post* 6 Jan.
Page 288, To Pinkerton 6 Jan. 1786, headnote, line 3, *after* untraced until *insert* offered by John Waller, 'Catalogue of Holograph and Autograph Letters . . . and Important Unpublished Correspondence,' n.d. [ca 1850], *sub* Walpole, p. 120;
Page 289, To Pinkerton 4 Oct. 1786, headnote, line 3, *after* Hill *add* ; sold to William Zimmerman, who gave it to Mrs Phelps; she left it to her son, Austin Phelps, and it is now in the Occidental College Library, Los Angeles, California.
Page 289, To Pinkerton 4 Oct. 1786, *for Endorsed in unknown hand read Endorsed* (by Lady Pinkerton)
Pages 289–90, note 1, *substitute* One of four extant MS Catalogues of King Charles I's Collections made by Abraham Van der Doort is in the Royal Library at Windsor: a 'Catalogue of the contents of the Cabinet Room at Whitehall . . . by Abraham Van der Doort, being a fair copy of *MS Ashmole 1514*, ff. 96–161, incorporating Van der Doort's corrections and emendations to that MS' (*Walpole Society*, 1958–60, xxxvii, p. xviii). The MS Catalogue which HW bought is the one now at Windsor; it was sold SH vii. 21 (London 1116) to the Rev. Henry Wellesley; sold Sotheby's 3 Aug. 1866 (Wellesley Sale), lot 48, to Sir William Tite; purchased from

the Tite Collection 4 June 1874 for the Royal Library at Windsor (ibid.; Hazen, *Cat. of HW's Lib.* Nos 3526, 3704; HW to Richard Gough 15 March 1792, MISC. CORR. iii. 354). An inscription by HW in the MS Catalogue at Windsor states: 'This is the fair Copy made for King Charles the first of Vanderdort's Catalogue of his Majesty's pictures which were placed in his new Cabinet-room. The blank leaves have been stuffed with nonsense by some late possessor, who seems to have used it as a common-place-book. I bought it in November 1786, for two guineas. Horace Walpole' (*Walpole Society*, 1958–60, xxxvii, pp. xviii, xxi, n. 3).

Page 290, To Pinkerton, 29 Nov. 1786, headnote, lines 2–3, *for* not further traced until *substitute* offered by Ferdinand J. Dreer Collection (Catalogue, Philadelphia, Pennsylvania, 1893, ii. 192), No. 78, Nov. 1905, lot 231;

Page 291, To Pinkerton 29 June 1787, headnote, line 2, *after* London *add*   ; now WSL

Page 292, headnote, line 4, *for* lot 487 *read* lot 478   *Line 5, after* lot 245 *add*   ; sold to Mrs Robert C. Dexter, Belmont, Mass.; sold by Goodspeed to WSL, May 1957.

Page 292, note 6, lines 2–5, *delete* probably . . . was begun. *and substitute* on 30 July 1787 HW wrote again, 'Bring me a sufficient account of Lord Elibank's publications, as now my printer waits for them' (MISC. CORR. iii. 197).

Page 293, note 12, *add* HW invited Pinkerton to 'dine, and take a bed here, on Sunday,' 5 Aug. (MISC. CORR. iii. 197).

Page 294, after letter of 29 June 1787 *insert the following heading*:

To PINKERTON, Monday 30 July 1787

Missing. Offered by John Waller, *A Catalogue of Holograph and Autograph Letters . . . and Important Unpublished Correspondence*, n.d. [ca 1850], p. 120, which quotes an extract now printed in MISC. CORR. iii. 197.

Page 296, headnote, line 10, *after* Charnwood *add*   ; placed on deposit in the British Museum, 1972 (BM loan 60, vol. 2, no. 9 [1]).

Page 297, notes 8, 9, transpose bottom line so that it precedes note 9

Page 298, 1st paragraph, line 1, *on* Pindar *add note* 9a: 9a. Pindar's second Pythian ode honoured the winner of a chariot-race and contained a passage giving the lineage of the Centaurs (see MASON ii. 146–7, n. 5).

Page 298, To Pinkerton 15 Oct. 1788, headnote, last line, *after* vol. i *add* ; sold in Frank Dillon Sale, London, 8 Nov. 1909, lot 171, to Maggs.

Page 299, note 1, line 4, *after* WSL *add*   ; Hazen, *Cat. of HW's Lib.* No. 3702

Page 302, after letter of 15 Oct. 1788 *insert the following heading*:

To PINKERTON, Wednesday 29 October 1788

The MS, bound in a copy of Pinkerton's *Walpoliana*, [1799], Vol. I, is

in the University of Delaware Library; now printed from a photostat in
Misc. Corr. iii. 225.

Page 302, note 2, right column, line 8, *after* volume *add* , but there are
marginal markings in both volumes   *Line 10, for* 1848 *read* 1849
Line 12, after Dobell *add* ; sold Goodspeed, Dec. 1956, to wsl (Hazen,
Cat. of HW's Lib. No. 3253).

Page 305, To Pinkerton 14 Aug. 1789, headnote, *substitute* Printed
from the MS now wsl. Previously printed, *Walpoliana* ii. 79–83; Pinkerton, *Literary Correspondence*, 1830, i. 225–8; Wright vi. 335–6; Cunningham ix. 208–9; Toynbee xiv. 189–91. The history of the MS is the same as
ante 18 Aug. 1785; offered by Goodspeed in 1928, Cat. No. 174 (Supp. to
No. 169), p. 57; sold Parke-Bernet 3 Dec. 1957 (Thomas Henry Foster
Sale), lot 246, to Michael Papantonio (Seven Gables) for wsl. [The text is
printed here from the MS:]

Address: To John Pinkerton Esq. at Mansfield Place, Kentish Town.
Postmarks: AU 15 89   2 O'CLOCK T.

Endorsed (in an unknown hand): Mr Walpole 1789 Aug. 14.

Strawberry Hill, Aug. 14, 1789.

I must certainly have expressed myself very awkwardly, dear Sir, if you
conceived that I meant the slightest censure on your book; much less on
your manner of treating it, which is able and clear, and demonstrative as
possible. No, it was myself, my age, my want of apprehension and memory, and my total ignorance of the subject, which I intended to blame. I
never did taste or study the very ancient histories of nations—I never had
a good memory for names of persons, regions, places, which no specific
circumstances concurred to make me remember—and now at 72 when, as
is common, I forget numbers of names most familiar to me, is it possible
I should read with pleasure any work that consists of a vocabulary totally
new to me? Many years ago, when my faculties were much less impaired,
I was forced to quit Dow's *History of Indostan*, because the Indian names
made so little impression on me, that I went backward instead of forward,
and was every minute reverting to the former page, to find about whom
I was reading.

Your book was a still more laborious work to me, for it contains such a
series of argumentation, that it demanded a double effort from a weak
old head—and when I had made myself master of a deduction, I forgot it
the next day, and had my pains to renew.

These defects have for some time been so obvious to me, that I never
read now but the most trifling books, having often said that at the very
end of life it is very useless to be improving one's stock of knowledge, great
or small, for the next world.

Thus, Sir, all I have said in my last letter, or in this, is an *encomium* on your work, not a censure or criticism. It would be hard on you indeed, if my incapacity detracted from your merit.

Your arguments in defence of works of science and deep disquisition are most just; and I am sure I have neither power nor disposition to answer them. You have treated your matter as it ought to be treated. Profound men, or conversant in the subject, like Mr Dempster, will be pleased with it for the very reasons that made it difficult to me. If Sir Isaac Newton had written a fairy tale, I should have swallowed it eagerly—but do you imagine Sir, that, idle as I am, I am idiot enough to think that Sir Isaac had better have amused me for half an hour, than enlightened mankind and all ages?

I was so fair as to confess to you that your work was above me, and did not divert me. You was too candid to take that ill, and must have been content with silently thinking me very silly—and I am too candid to condemn any man for thinking of me as I deserve—I am only sorry when I do deserve a disadvantage[ous] character.

Nay, Sir, you condescend after all to ask my opinion of the best way of treating antiquities; and by the context, I suppose, I mean, how to make them entertaining. I cannot answer you in one word, because there are two ways, as there are two sorts of readers. I should therefore say; to please antiquaries of judgment, as you have treated them, with arguments and proofs—but if you would adapt antiquities to the taste of those who read only to be diverted, not to be instructed, the nostrum is very easy and short. You must *divert* them in the true sense of the word *diverto*; you must turn them out of the way; you must treat them with digressions nothing or very little to the purpose—Yet easy as I call this recipe, *you*, I believe would find it more difficult to execute, than the indefatigable industry you have employed to penetrate Chaos, and extract Truth. There have been professors who have engaged to adapt all kinds of knowledge to the meanest capacities—I doubt their success—at least on me—however, you need not despair; all readers are not as dull and superannuated as

Dear Sir
Your very humble servant
and sincere admirer
HOR. WALPOLE

Page 306, note 2, last line, *after* v. 135 *add* (Hazen, *Cat. of HW's Lib.* No. 2838)

Page 306, note 4, line 1, *for* 1816 *read* 1818

Page 310, note 3, line 2, *for* daughter *read* daughter, Charlotte   *Line 3, for* 6 Dec. 1789 *read* 9 Dec. 1789, OSSORY iii. 72 and n. 12

Page 312, after letter of 26 May 1790 *insert the following headings*:

FROM PINKERTON, ca Saturday 7 August 1790
Missing. Answered *post* 10 Aug. 1790.

To PINKERTON, Tuesday 10 August 1790
The MS is in the Stanley Withers Collection, Manchester Central Library; now printed in MISC. CORR. iii. 288; previously printed by R. S. Woof, 'Some Horace Walpole Letters,' N&Q 1965, ccx. 26.

Page 314, note 5, line 4, *for* 1715 *read* ca 1721

Page 315, To Pinkerton [?1792], headnote, line 1, *after* plate in *insert* the 2d edition of

Page 321, under headnote *insert Address* (cut-out MS, now WSL, bought by Maggs at Sotheby's Nov. 1959): To John Pinkerton Esq. at Hampstead. Free Orford.

Page 321, note 1, line 5, *after* subscriber *add*   ; Hazen, *Cat. of HW's Lib.* No. 3824

Page 321, note 3, last line, *after* 1758 *add* (Hazen, *Cat. of HW's Lib.* No. 2479)

Page 322, note 5, left column, line 15, *after Collection insert* (Hazen, *Cat. of HW's Lib.* No. 2479)

Page 322, note 9, line 7, *for* WSL *read* Royal Library, Windsor

Page 323, note 14, line 4, *for* 1720 *read* 1719

Pages 324–5, note 23, last line, *for* 595 *read* 595, now WSL; see Hazen, *Cat. of HW's Lib.* No. 3637

Page 325, note 1, line 8, *for* of the BM; see GRAY i. 24 *read* of the collection of Sir Hans Sloane, which became part of the British Museum; see MANN iv. 358, nn. 3, 5.

Page 325, note 3, transpose bottom line of right column to end of note 3.

Page 326, note 4, line 2, *for* Walpole.' *read* Walpole' (Hazen, *Cat. of HW's Lib.* No. 279).

Page 331, 1st paragraph, last line, *after* WSL *add* (Hazen, *Cat. of HW's Lib.* No. 3690)

Page 344, line 7, on *Poetry*). *add note* 3a: 3a. For a different enumeration of these pieces, omitting the Senhouse copy, see Hazen, *Cat. of HW's Lib.* No. 3690.

Page 349, left column, between pages 22 and 27 *insert* 24, l. 14   *middle column, insert* . . . a propensity to forgery, which is not the talent most wanting culture in the present age.   *far right column, insert* Some months after this vindication was printed in the Gentleman's Magazine, Mr W. received a long anonymous letter telling him that *though* he had cleared himself of being accessory to Ch.' death, *yet* the writer could believe him guilty of it from that barbarous sentence, *All of the House of Forgery are Relations.* The sentence is hypothetic, and is expressly followed by an acquittal of Chatterton on that head—yet so passionately blind was the letter-writer, that he forgot Mr W.'s defence was not written till *after* Chatterton's death; and consequently an ex post facto murder was a charge only worthy of an Irishman to make (HW's note in the presentation copy inscribed 'For Miss Berry,' now WSL).

Page 349, left column, *below* 32, l. 1 *insert* 33   *middle column, insert* . . . whereas it is ascertained that the gentleman at Bristol who possesses the fund of Rowley's poems, received them from Chatterton   *far right column, insert* Mr Barrett (HW's note in the copy presented to Miss Berry, now WSL).

Page 350, left column, *below* 44, l. 13 *insert* 47   *middle column, insert* Let them be either printed, or deposited where every man may have recourse to them.   *far right column, insert* Nothing of this sort has been done to this moment Jan. 1789, yet within this month has been printed in a magazine a new Elegy on Chatterton indirectly reflecting on Mr W. though not one syllable of this defence has ever been disproved— so that poets must believe Truth as little as they write it. H.W. (HW's note in the copy presented to Miss Berry, now WSL; the Elegy may be 'Suicide; a poem. Inscribed, by permission, to Richard Cosway,' by Mary Dawes Blackett, London, 1789).

Page 350, note 11, right column, lines 2–3, *for* Sir William Chambers *read* Sir Robert Chambers

Page 363, 3d paragraph, last line, *after* contains no *insert* other

Page 365, note 6, lines 2–4, *delete* or his brother, Richard Puttenham (ca 1520–ca 1601)

Page 366, note 19, line 1, align to the right

Page 366, note 20, lines 4–5, *for* ca 1510–ca 1556 *read* 1509–56

Page 368, note 38, *add* 'It is said that the Duchess kept several young ladies about her person, who, occasionally, wrote what she dictated. Some of them, we are told, slept in a room joining to that in which her Grace lay, and were ready at the call of her bell, to rise at any hour of the night, to put down her conceptions upon paper, lest they should have escaped her memory. It may be easily imagined that those young ladies often dreaded her Grace's nocturnal flights, which were chiefly poetical and philosophical' ('Memoir of Margaret Duchess of Newcastle,' *Lady's Magazine* 1775, vi. 37).

Page 368, note 39, line 3, *for* later Bp of Gloucester *read* Bp of Gloucester, 1759

Page 368, note 40, last line, *after* guineas *add* (Hazen, *Cat. of HW's Lib.* No. 2039)

Page 368, note 41, *delete* (1671–1713), 3d E. of Shaftesbury *and substitute* (1621–83), cr. (1672) E. of Shaftesbury

Page 369, note 46, last line, *after* vii. 527 *add* ; Sir John Hawkins, *A General History of . . . Music,* 1776, iv. 525–6, v. 151

Page 373, note 1, *for* history *read* philosophy

VOLUME 17

Page xxi, List of Illustrations, *for* HORACE WALPOLE, BY ROSALBA CARRIERA *read* LORD BOYNE, BY ROSALBA CARRIERA   *after* Lord Walpole. *add* See C. Kingsley Adams and W. S. Lewis, 'The Portraits of Horace Walpole,' *Walpole Society*, 1968–70, xlii. 27–8 and Plate 28a.

Page xxiv, 2d paragraph, line 15, *for* Patch *read* Patch,

Page xxxix, Section III, 2d paragraph, line 8, *after* no *insert* surviving

Page xli, bottom paragraph, line 5, *for* 1754.² *read* 1754² and continued until 1768.   *Line 7, for* of 22 April *read* dated 22 April   *Line 8, on* Kirgate *add note* 2a: 2a. For a complete discussion of the transcription of Walpole's letters to Mann see *post* Appendix 12, MANN x. 36–44, which corrects and supplements this history.

Page xlii, note 4, *add* Mrs Toynbee's note is as follows: 'This evidence is contained in the following memorandum (kindly communicated by Mr J. F. Rotton, who is in possession of the original document). The paper is endorsed (apparently in Mrs Damer's handwriting):

> "Dec. 12, 1810. Memorandum concerning the Destruction of Extracts from Letters of Lord Orford, &c., by T. Kirgate."

'The contents are as follows:—

> "Dec. 11, 1810.
> "To Mr George P. Harding,
>   Understanding that the Collection of Extracts of Letters from Lord Orford to Sir Horace Mann at Florence (which Extracts were in the Possession of my Father the late Mr Thomas Kirgate at his Death) were not intended by his Lordship to be either transcribed or printed I hereby authorize and desire you will destroy the same Extracts in the Presence of the Honourable Mrs Damer the Executrix of His Lordship.
> Eleanor Thomas.

'Below is added, in the same handwriting as the endorsement:—

> "December 12, 1810. The Extracts above referred to were destroyed in the Presence of us
>   ANNE SEYMOUR DAMER,
>   GEORGE PERFECT HARDING.
> Witness, M. HOPER." ' (Toynbee, i. p. xvi)

Page xlvii, lines 3–6, *delete* Possibly the . . . Sir H. Mann.'

Page xlvii, lines 7–8, *for* may have . . . discretion *read* felt the need

Page xlvii, line 11, *for* Twenty *read* Thirty

Page xlvii, last line of long quotation, *for* them?' *read* them?

Page xlviii, bottom line, *delete* who stated in his

Page xlviii, note 10, line 2, *delete* to 1758   *for* transcript is now owned *read* transcript, now wSL, was formerly owned   *Last line, add* The MS was sold Sotheby's (Holland House Sale), with transcripts of letters to Lady Ossory 27 June 1771–26 Dec. 1791, on 10 Feb. 1964, lot 289, to Maggs for wSL.

Page xlix, *delete lines 1–7 and substitute* who bought all of Walpole's unpublished manuscripts from Lord Euston (later Duke of Grafton), the executor of the late Lord Waldegrave. In 1867 Bentley offered to sell to Frances, Lady Waldegrave, the manuscripts of Mann's letters to Walpole which Bentley described thus: 'They consist of six or seven volumes . . . chiefly half bound in russia. They have never been published and are in the same state in which they were left by the Earl of Orford' (Bentley to Chichester Fortescue 26 July 1867). Lady Waldegrave apparently did not accept this offer and the manuscripts remained in the possession of the Bentley family.[11]

Page xlix, 2d paragraph, line 2, *for* W. S. Lewis. *read* W. S. Lewis, except for 27 April and 12 Dec. 1780, acquired in 1937 from Mrs Bentley, widow of the grandson Richard Bentley.

Page xlix, note 11, *substitute* For a full discussion of the manuscripts of Mann's letters to Walpole see *post* Appendix 12, MANN x. 41–2.

Page lviii, 2d paragraph, line 6, *for* Brooks *read* Brooke

Page lviii, 4th paragraph, line 7, *for* M. Kearns *read* W. Kearns

Page lxii, Cobbett, *Parl. Hist.*, right column, *for* William Cobbett and John Wright *read* William Cobbett, John Wright, and T. C. Hansard

Page lxii, DNB, right column, line 2, *for* 1908–9. *read* 1908–9,

Page lxiii, GEC, right column, line 3, *for* 1900–9. *read* 1900–9,

Page lxiv, line 5 from bottom, *for* ins *read* ins.

Page 1, note 1, *add* The first volume of HW's transcripts opens with a title-page in HW's hand: 'A / Collection / of / Letters / from / Horace Walpole / Youngest Son of Sir Robert Walpole / Earl of Orford / to / Horace Mann / Resident at Florence / from / King George the Second: / transcribed from the Originals. / Vol. 1st. / *Posteris an aliqua cura, nescio*! / Plin. epist.'

Page 1, note 5, lines 5–8, *delete* HW in copying . . . 1748 OS).

Page 2, note 5, *delete last sentence*

Page 2, note 2, line 3 from end, *after* NS). *insert* 'Old' Horace Walpole in a letter to Newcastle of 13 April 1740 OS (BM Add. MSS 32,693, ff. 203–4), accused Newcastle of obstructing Mann's appointment out of spite.

Page 2, note 4, lines 3–4, *delete* to two . . . Conway, and

Page 4, note 14, line 2, *for* Buoncompagni *read* Boncompagni

Page 4, note 18, line 9, *for* 277 *read* 277; GEC vii. 84, n. *e*

Page 4, note 22, line 2, *for* 18 Feb. *read* 19 Feb.

Page 5, note 25, *add* There were unofficial reports of the victory in the *Daily Adv.* 12 March

Page 6, note 1, last line, *for* 300). *read* 300), but he may have been Charles Martin, 'our Tuscan Raphael in the crayon way' (James Tyrell to Ralph Howard, 1752). See John Fleming and Hugh Honour, 'Francis Harwood,' in *Festschrift Ulrich Middeldorf*, ed. A. Kosegarten and P. Tigler, Berlin, 1968, p. 515, n. 4.

Page 6, note 6, line 6, *for* (1756–61) *read* (1756–60)

Page 7, note 18, line 1, *for* (1720–64) *read* (ca 1720–64)

Page 8, line 3, *on* ourselves. *add note* 20a: 20a. HW tells this same anecdote to Conway 23 April 1740 NS (CONWAY i. 56–7).

Page 8, note 19, lines 1–2, *for* Buondelmonte *read* Buondelmonti

Page 12, note 52, line 2, *for* 1686 *read* 1684   *right column, line 1, for* 767–8 *read* 767–8; *Dictionnaire de biographie française,* 1933– , v. 1220–1

Page 14, note 10, line 2, *for* 1689 *read* 1690

Page 15, note 11, *add* See *post* MANN v. 381, n. 5.

Page 17, note 14, line 2, *for* 1608 *read* 1690

Page 20, note 14, line 4 from bottom, *for* ed. J. B. *read* ed. E. J. B.

Page 23, line 3, *for* Now *read* now

Page 27, note 9, line 4, *for* ca 1722–52 *read* 1721–52   *right column, line 1, after* cit. *add*   ; see also *post* MANN x. 52

Page 27, note 2, lines 1–2, *for* the Palazzo Manetti, Via S. Spirito 23/25 *read* the Casa Ambrogi, Via de' Bardi

Page 29, note 14, *add* 'Corpus Domini' is an Italianism (Bagnani).

Page 30, line 2 from bottom, *for* command *read* command.

Page 30, last line of letter, *drop one space and indent*

Page 30, note 1, line 5, *for* Diretto *read* Diritto

Page 31, headnote, *add* 'Mr Harvey' was the Hon. George William Hervey (1721–75), 2d E. of Bristol, 1751; see *post* MANN i. 34, n. 17.

Page 31, note 4, *add* He was in England 24 March 1723–June/July 1726, having left Florence 17 April 1722 and returned there 31 Oct. 1726 (his diary, in the Bibliotèca Medica of the Università di Studi, Florence, cited by George E. Dorris to WSL, June 1962).

Page 32, note 2, *add* In Feb. 1749 the clocks were changed to French time (*post* MANN iv. 26).

Page 33, note 5, line 2, *for* Seragli *read* Serragli

Page 34, note 19, lines 2–3, *for* D[ominem] *read* D[ominum]

Page 35, line 5, *delete* <bringing their troops into Italy>

Page 35, note 23, *after* 23. *insert* Mann originally wrote 'bringing their troops into Italy.'

Page 36, note 34, *add* See also *Connoisseur,* 1955, cxxxvi. 106, 107.

Page 40, 2d paragraph, line 2 from bottom, *on* now *add note* 35a: 35a. The Queen could not appoint *Imperial* councillors and so they could not be called 'Excellency.' In her father's day they were, because he was Emperor.

Page 40, 3d paragraph, line 2, *for note* 35a *read* 35b

Page 40, 3d paragraph, line 3, *for note* 35b *read* 35c

Page 40, note 28, line 2, *for called* 'Tramontini,' *read* m. (ca 1743) Giacomo Tramontini;   *Line 5, after* 30; *insert The New Grove Dictionary of Music and Musicians,* 6th edn, ed. Stanley Sadie, 1980, xviii. 702–3; *Enciclopedia dello spettacolo,* Rome, 1954–62, ix. 855–6;

Page 41, note 42, line 2, *for* Becker). *read* Becker; John Fleming, 'The Hugfords of Florence (Part I),' *Connoisseur,* 1955, cxxxvi. 106–10).

Page 42, note 49, lines 3–4, *for* Florence . . . Reggio *read* Florence with HW and Gray and had accompanied them to Reggio   *Line 6, for* 157–76). *read* 157–76; SELWYN 16).

Page 46, note 31, *for* Milady *read* ma'am

Page 49, line 5, *for* Flo[rentinum] *read* Flo[rentinum],

Page 49, 2d paragraph, line 3, *for* Tommy *read* Tommy,

Page 49, note 14, line 1, *for* Museum florentinum *read* Museum Florentinum

Page 50, 2d paragraph, line 9, *on* think you *add note* 21a: 21a. *Sic in* MS, but apparently a slip for 'think he.'

Page 50, 2d paragraph, line 12, *on* mention and *add note* 23: 23. *Sic in* MS, but presumably a slip for 'mention at.'

Page 51, line 7 from bottom, *for* yet *read* yet,   *for* much, *read* much

Page 51, note 1, line 3, *for* n. 62. *read* n. 62; Joseph Spence, *Letters from the Grand Tour*, ed. Slava Klima, Montreal and London, 1975, pp. 386–99.

Page 53, line 9 from bottom, *for* Bartolini *read* Bartolini,

Page 55, note 5, line 6, *for* ibid. i, 181 *read* ibid. i. 181

Page 56, note 15, line 2, *after* Gizziello *insert* or Egizziello   *Lines* 2–4, for Sir George Grove . . . ii. 389 *read The New Grove Dictionary of Music and Musicians*, 6th edn, ed. Stanley Sadie, 1980, iv. 682–3; *Enciclopedia dello spettacolo*, Rome, 1954–62, iii. 1346–7

Page 57, 2d paragraph, line 11, *for* another)[21] *read* another[21])

Page 57, note 25, line 6, *for* 1743 *read* 1744   *Last sentence, substitute* HW's copy of the *Scelta* is Hazen, *Cat. of HW's Lib.* No. 3583; he also had Zocchi's *Vedute delle ville e d'altri luoghi della Toscana*, Florence, 1744 (ibid. No. 3530), bound in vellum.

Page 58, note 26, line 4, *delete* apparently   *Last line, add* See Hazen, op. cit. No. 3570.

Page 58, note 27, *add* According to Torello Sala and Federigo Tarani, *Dizionario storico biografico dell' ordine di Vallombrosa*, Florence, 1929, i. 306, his parents were of 'specchiatissime famiglie Inglesi Cattoliche' (quoted by John Fleming, 'The Hugfords of Florence (Part I),' *Connoisseur*, 1955, cxxxvi. 106).

Pages 58–9, note 2, line 1, *for* 1682 *read* ca 1675   *Last line, for* 169). *read* 169; H. F. Brown, 'Consul Smith and His Will,' N&Q, 1905, 10th ser. iv. 221–2; CHUTE 4, n. 10).

Page 63, note 38, *add* He was also with Mansell on the latter's return to England from the Continent the previous summer (Lord Mansell to Lady Mary Wortley Montagu 7 July [1740] OS, Wortley MSS iv. 181–2; information from Robert Halsband).

Page 64, note 40, line 4, *for* BM Cat. *read* Hazen, *Cat. of HW's Lib.* No. 2110.

Page 65, note 8, *for* Household *read* Pantry

Page 65, note 14, *add* See *Enciclopedia dello spettacolo*, Rome, 1954–62, vii. 494, 502.

Page 67, note 25, line 1, *for* ca 1700 *read* 1699   *Line 3, for* second *read* first

Page 68, note 33, line 2, *for* 100 *read* 107   *Line 3, add* See Hazen, *Cat. of HW's Lib.* No. 3569.

Page 69, note 45, *for* 'Demand.' *read* 'To do' (Bagnani).

Page 71, note 14, line 2, *for* 39 *read* 36   *Line 8, after* 1743 NS *add* ; Sturgis to Snape 10 May 1739, King's College MS Collection 1. 34, transcript supplied by A. N. L. Munby   *Last line, add* Lord Hervey also assumed that elopement with Sturgis was the reason for Lady Walpole's going abroad in 1734 (see *Lord Hervey and His Friends 1726–38*, ed. E. of Ilchester, 1950, p. 187), but Dr George Sheyne wrote to Selina, Countess of Huntingdon, 18 Jan. 1734: 'There is such an universal malice against me here for sending people abroad (as I did my Lady Walpole lately)' (Hist. MSS Comm., *Hastings MSS*, 1928–47, iii. 19).

Page 73, note 30, *add* See R. J. Charleston, 'Souvenirs of the Grand Tour,' *Journal of Glass Studies*, 1959, i. 63–82.

Page 75, note 11, *add* See SELWYN 8–9.

Page 77, illustration, *for* HORACE WALPOLE *read* LORD BOYNE

Page 78, note 7, line 1, *for* Collins *read* Collins,

Page 79, line 7, *for* popolo *read* Popolo   *for* ajutatemi *read* ajuta-temi!

Page 80, note 16, line 1, *after* Angelo *insert* Maria   *Lines 2–3, for* Sir George Grove . . . i. 83). *read The New Grove Dictionary of Music and Musicians*, 6th edn, ed. Stanley Sadie, 1980, i. 332; *Enciclopedia dello spettacolo*, Rome, 1954–62, i. 500–1).

Page 80, note 17, last line, *for* p. 48). *read* p. 48; *Enciclopedia* viii. 1569).

Page 81, 3d paragraph, line 7, *after* six years *insert* [but]

Page 81, 3d paragraph, line 4 from bottom, *for* course *read* course,

Page 82, 2d paragraph, line 2, *for* me *read* me,

Page 83, note 37, *add* HW's copy (2 vols, 1738–9) is listed in Hazen, *Cat. of HW's Lib.* No. 2360.

Page 88, last 2 lines, *transpose*

Page 91, note 3, right column, lines 6–7, *for* in Latin . . . translation *read* based on an ode by Horace

Page 93, note 9, line 1, *for* (d. 1754) *read* (d. ?1759)   *Line 3, for* Florence (Thieme *read* Florence; director of the Opificio delle Pietre Dure at Florence 1749–59 (Antonio Zobi, *Notizie storiche, sull' origine e progressi dei lavori di commesso in pietre dure*, Florence, 1853, pp. 347–8; Thieme

Page 103, note 2, *substitute* François Regny (d. 1779), French consul at Genoa 1756–75; directeur de la poste ca 1740–51 (René Boudard, *Gênes et la France*, 1962, pp. 89–97). See *post* 4 Nov. 1765.

Page 105, note 18, right column, line 3, *delete* vast

Page 106, note 24, line 1, *for* Tuffnell *read* Tufnell   *Lines 1–2, for*
(d. 1794) *read* (1720–94)

Page 107, note 6, right column, line 2, *for* the same Abbé Niccoli *read*
Raimondo Niccoli (d. 1780)

Page 108, note 9, line 2, *for* 59 *read* 63   *Line 5, after* 469 *insert* ;
Court and City Register, passim

Page 110, note 21, line 1, *for* the great *read* many

Page 110, note 25, last 2 lines, *for* take good aim at their target *read*
shoot straight

Page 113, note 8, line 4, *for* 1730–42. *read* 1730–42, 1744–6.

Page 114, note 14, line 4, *for* sermovente *read* semovente

Page 115, note 1, line 7, *after* dernier *insert* [1741 NS]

Page 122, 2d paragraph, line 2, *for Pupilli read pupilli*

Page 124, note 4, line 4, *for* (d. 1745) *read* (ca 1696–1745)

Page 126, note 16, lines 1–2, *for* (ca 1717–ca 1806) *read* (1717–ca 1805)
for 1745–52 *read* 1747–54

Page 126, note 17, line 2, *for* 1753–61 *read* 1754, 1755–61   *Line 4, for*
excise, who *read* excise. He

Page 130, 2d paragraph, line 2 from bottom, *for faccia read faccia,*

Page 132, note 2, *for* an occasion *read* a matter

Page 136, 2d paragraph, line 11, *on* Gondi *add note* 36a: 36a. Perhaps
Signora Maria Porzia Gondi (d. 1783) (*Gazzetta toscana*, 1783, p. 3).

Page 139, note 3, line 2, *before* Windsor *insert* New

Page 139, note 6, line 1, *for* 1710 *read* 1709

Page 139, note 8, line 1, *for* (d. 1745) *read* (ca 1679–1745)

Page 140, note 3, line 4, *for* 1759 *read* 1749

Page 141, note 7, line 1, *for* (ca 1710–64) *read* (b. 1710–15, d. 1764)
Lines 2–3, for Sir George Grove . . . iii. 507 *read The New Grove Dictionary of Music and Musicians*, 6th edn, ed. Stanley Sadie, 1980, xii. 538

Page 141, note 8, line 1, *for* Barbara *read* Barbarina   *Line 2, for* the
'Barbarina' *read* 'La Barbarina'   *Line 3, for* (ca 1748) *read* (1750)
Line 5, for was divorced *read* separated   *Line 6, for* (1789) *read* (1787)
after Gräfin *insert* von   *Line 8, for* 1740 *read* 1739   *for* 1742–3 *read*
1740–3   *Lines 14–17, for* The year of her death . . . nine Lutheran girls
of noble birth *read* In her last years she directed a home for poor girls of
noble birth   *Right column, last line, after* pp. 235–7 *insert* ; P. H.
Highfill, Jr, K. A. Burnim and E. A. Langhans, *A Biographical Dictionary of Actors, Actresses, Musicians, Dancers, Managers* [etc.] . . . *in London, 1660–1800*, Carbondale, Illinois, 1973– , iii. 25–8.

Page 141, note 9, line 4, *for* 1732–56 *read* 1732–59   *for* 855). *read*
855; CONWAY ii. 2, n. 11).

Page 144, note 4, *add* See also SELWYN 73, n. 8; CONWAY i. 141–2.

Page 146, note 17, *add* However, HW may have meant Lady Yarmouth,
whom the Duke of Newcastle describes as Pitt's supporter in a letter to
Lord Hardwicke 26 July 1756 (BM Add. MSS 32,866, f. 275).

Page 147, note 29, *substitute* 'That I had not the slightest idea that you were having a party' (Bagnani).

Page 149, note 11, *add* For the expression 'to take post' see OED, *sub* Post *sb*.2, 8.i.

Page 150, 1st paragraph, line 2 from end, *for gridere read gridare*

Page 152, note 38, right column, line 3, *for 33 read* 32

Page 153, note 3, line 2, *after* M.P. *insert* Great　　*Line 3, for* 1754 *read* 1755　　*for* Penrhyn *read* Penryn

Page 161, note 11, line 2, *for* Minerbetta *read* Minerbetti

Page 163, note 19, line 2, *for* Cucumero *read* Cocomero

Page 164, date-line, *on* Oct. 8 *add note a*: *a. Sic* in MS, but this letter may have been written on the 9th; see below, nn. 5, 36.

Page 165, note 8, line 1, *for* ca 1702 *read* 1709

Page 165, note 9, *substitute* Probably James Newsham (afterwards Newsham Craggs) (1715–69), M.P. (Namier and Brooke iii. 201).

Page 169, note 46, *add* HW wrote of him in his 'Book of Materials,' 1771, p. 48, that he was 'the greatest practical philosopher I ever knew. He ruined himself by his extravagance and had borrowed money of everybody that would lend him a farthing, even of his own servants. He had built two fine houses in Arlington Street and at Richmond, and made a noble collection of pictures at both, which were seized and sold to pay his debts. While his pictures in town were exposed to public sale, he appeared every night at the auction [in 1747] of [Jonathan] Richardson's collection buying drawings. While his goods were exposed to sale at Richmond, I saw a painter at work there painting a ceiling. . . . When that house was likewise seized and sold, Lord Cholmondeley took another at Richmond near it, would walk on the terrace of the former, which he had made, and boast that it was called the Cholmondeley Terrace.'

Page 174, note 15, lines 1–2, *for* ca 1703 *read* ?1702

Page 175, note 26, lines 1–3, *for* Some of the information . . . 28 Oct. 1741 OS *read* Reports of these conquests were printed in the *Daily Adv.* 8 Oct. 1741 and in the *Craftsman* and *Common Sense* 10 Oct. (see SELWYN 29, n. 6)

Page 175, note 27, *for* (d. 1747) *read* (?1693–1747), M.P.　　*after* 592 *add* ; Sedgwick ii. 528

Page 176, note 32, line 1, *for* ca 1714 *read* ca 1718　　*Line 2, after* 60) *insert* (*Enciclopedia dello spettacolo*, Rome, 1954–62, ix. 1993)　　*Right column, line 1, after* for *insert* most of　　*Line 2, delete* probably　　*Line 3, for* 8 Sept. *read* 22 Sept.　　*after* ibid. *add* ; *London Stage* Part III, ii. 861, 925–6, 929

Page 180, note 15, line 1, *after* Gruenemberg *insert* (ca 1693–1771)　　*Last line, after* 44 *add* ; *Gazzetta toscana*, 1771, No. 16, v. 64

Page 182, 2d paragraph, line 1, *for* before *read* before,　　*Line 4, for* Gorgona *read* Gorgona　　*Lines 11–12, for* 'You'll certainly have notice *soon that* the *peace* is *made* with *Spain.*' *read* 'You'll certainly have notice soon that the peace is made with Spain.'

Page 184, note 3, last 3 lines, *for* Sir George Grove . . . ii. 345). *read The New Grove Dictionary of Music and Musicians,* 6th edn, ed. Stanley Sadie, 1980, vii. 134–8). See also *London Stage* Part III, ii. 939.

Page 184, note 9, line 3, *for* Wake *read* Wake, apothecary of Bath   *before* GM *insert London Chronicle* 9–12 Oct. 1779, xlvi. 345;

Page 185, note 18, line 8, *for* elder daughter *read* eldest daughter, Catherine,   *Line 10, for* younger *read* youngest   *Last line, after* 215 *add* ; Thomas Shadwell, *Works,* ed. Montague Summers, 1927, i. p. ccliv

Page 186, note 21, *substitute* Probably Alice Macartney (SELWYN 45, nn. 4, 5).

Page 186, note 24, *for* Ossorio *read* Osorio

Page 188, note 43, line 1, *for* Amalie Sophie *read* Amalie-Sophie   *Line 2, for* (ca 1709–65) *read* (1704–65)   *Line 3, for* Adam Gottlieb, Oberhauptman *read* Oberhauptmann Gottlieb Adam

Page 190, 3d paragraph, line 4, *for* Monticello *read* Monticelli

Page 190, note 3a, *add* See *London Stage* Part III, ii. 939–42.

Page 190, note 4, *for* NBG *read The New Grove Dictionary of Music and Musicians,* 6th edn, ed. Stanley Sadie, 1980, vi. 397–8; *Enciclopedia dello spettacolo,* Rome. 1954–62, v. 22–8

Page 191, note 8, line 2, *for* Shoreham *read* New Shoreham

Page 191, note 12, line 1, *for* (d. 1770) *read* (1718–70)   *Last line, after* p. 44 *add*   ; John Brooke, *Chatham Administration,* 1956, pp. 256–8, 389

Page 191, note 13, line 3, *for* ca 1727–47 (NBG) *read* 1715–44 (Tarquinio Vallese, *Paolo Rolli in Inghilterra,* Milan, 1938)   *Line 4, for* Canzonette was sold SH iii. 179. *read Canzonette,* now in the Rutgers University Library, is Hazen, *Cat. of HW's Lib.* No. 2113.

Page 193, line 10, *for* replied *Eh via Monsu read* replied, *Eh via, Monsu,*

Page 193, note 9, *for* beastliness *read* stupidity

Page 195, note 21, line 10, *for* fever. *read* fever; see also SELWYN 26.

Page 198, line 15, *for* made *read* made,   *Line 20, for* men *read* men,

Page 199, note 13, *substitute* Not identified.

Page 199, note 14, *for Bibliotechina Grassoccia read* Bibliotechina Grassoccia

Page 199, note 17, *substitute* Probably Edward Penny (see *post* 17 Dec. 1741 NS).

Page 201, 3d paragraph, line 2, *on* quiet *add note* 26a: 26a. *Sic* in MS, but probably a slip for 'quite.'

Page 202, line 2, *for* welcome *read* welcome,

Page 202, line 11, *for* it *read* it,

Page 202, line 21, *for* him *read* him,

Page 202, note 3, *for* Grey'), *read* Grey');

Page 202, note 7, line 2, *for* (ibid.): *read* (ibid.),

Page 203, line 5, *for* pole] *read* pole],

Page 209, note 2, line 4, *for* ca 1706 *read* 1706

Page 209, note 6, line 1, *for* 1718 *read* 1716   *Line 4, for* 394 *read* 394; **GEC**

Page 210, note 11, *for* (d. 1734) *read* (ca 1706–34)   *after* iv. 384 *add* ; see also Sedgwick ii. 102–3

Page 211, 4th paragraph, line 1, *for* guardships *read* guard-ships

Page 211, note 18, *add* It was a Jacobite headquarters until 1748 (*post* MANN iv. 50, n. 34).

Page 212, note 6, line 3, *after* (HW). *substitute* HW's note is incorrect. William Ponsonby (ca 1704–93), styled Vct Duncannon 1739–58; 2d E. of Bessborough, 1758, did help Stosch to procure his arrears, but despite this Stosch made him pay 100 zecchini (about £50) for the ring in 1750; before Stosch bought it, the ring had been offered to Duncannon for only 30 zecchini (about £15). Its subsequent history is unknown. See *post* MANN iv. 159, v. 151.

Page 215, note 10, *substitute* José Joaquín Guzmann (d. 1771), cr. (1740) Duca di Montallegre and Marchese di Salas; Neapolitan prime minister 1735–46; Spanish ambassador to Venice 1749–71 (*post* MANN vii. 325, n. 7).

Page 217, 1st paragraph, line 11, *on* my Lady *add note* 18a: 18a. Baroness Walpole.

Page 217, note 19, *substitute* Antonio Conti (1677–1749), Italian scholar and wit; friend of Lady Mary Wortley Montagu (see GRAY ii. 246, n. 20).

Page 219, note 5, line 2, *for* 1728 *read* 1727

Page 219, note 6, line 1, *for* 1696 *read* 1695

Page 219, note 7, line 1, *for* ca 1671 *read* 1697

Page 220, note 9, line 1, *for* 1700 *read* ca 1700

Page 221, note 16, line 1, *for* 1692 *read* ?1692

Page 221, note 19, line 2, *for* 1734–42 *read* 1734–41   *Right column, line 7, for* 1760 *read* 1759

Page 222, note 30, last line, *for* Bruce *read* Brute   *add* See *London Stage* Part III, ii. 947.

Page 225, note 14, *add* His first visit was ca 18 Dec. 1739 NS (*Gray's Corr.* i. 136).

Page 226, note 16, *substitute* 'He would put him and all his servants to the sword.'

Page 231, note 12, line 9, *for* discontended *read* discontented

Page 232, note 19, line 2, *for* ca 1697 *read* 1686

Page 232, note 19a, line 2, *for* election *read* petition

Page 233, note 22, line 5, *for* 1746–54 *read* 1746–55

Page 237, note 12, *substitute* 'Gentlemen, please come in; there's trouble here.'

Page 239, 3d paragraph, line 9, *for* replying, you shall *read* replying, 'You shall

Page 239, 3d paragraph, line 10, *for* pins soon. *read* pins soon.'

Page 240, note 28, *substitute* 'Full dress rehearsal' (Bagnani).

Page 243, note 6, line 2, *after* M.P. *insert* Lostwithiel 1710,   *Line 3, for* 1713–15 *read* 1710–15   *for* Beeralston *read* Bere Alston   *Line 6, for* 1724–8 *read* 1724–30   *Line 7, after* 114 *add*   ; Sedgwick ii. 509–10

Page 243, note 7, line 1, *for* 1672 *read* ca 1672

Page 243, note 8, line 3, *after* 1716–41, *insert* Montgomeryshire 1741–2, Denbighshire

Page 244, note 9, line 1, *for* 1699 *read* ca 1699

Page 244, note 13, right column, line 18, *after* Hervey *insert* (Hazen, *Cat. of HW's Lib.* Nos 1608:28, 90; 1609:3, 6, 9, 14, 18; 4007)

Page 246, note 3, line 2, *delete* New

Page 247, note 12, line 5, *for* 4th *read* 3d   *Line 7, for* 3d *read* 2d

Page 248, note 15, lines 1–2, *for* (d. 1749) *read* (1683–1749)   *Line 5, for* (d. 1773) *read* (1714–73)   *after* 1741–54 *insert*   , Lancashire 1761–8 *Last line, add* See also Sedgwick ii. 424; Namier and Brooke iii. 438.

Page 248, note 16, *for* 1703 *read* 1707

Page 249, note 1, line 1, *for* Worseley *read* Worsley   *Line 2, for* 1745–60 *read* 1743–60   *Line 3, for* 1760–77 *read* 1760–78

Page 250, note 5, last line, *for* wsl *read* wsl,

Page 250, note 11, *add* HW's MS 'Portrait of Lord Mansfield' is now wsl.

Page 250, note 12, line 5, *for* Michael *read* Mitchell   *Lines 5–6, for* Malden *read* Maldon

Page 251, note 15, right column, line 1, *for* Edward *read* Edmund *Lines 1–2, for* (d. 1755) *read* (1703–55)   *Line 2, after* 1734–41, *insert* Weymouth 1747–54,   *Last line, add* See also Sedgwick i. 370, ii. 404.

Page 252, note 19, line 1, *for* 1685 *read* ca 1685

Page 252, note 20, line 1, *for* Whithed. *read* Whithed,

Page 252, note 21, *substitute* Esquire Carey (d. 1756), surgeon in Pall Mall; surgeon, 1738, to Frederick, P. of Wales (information from John B. Shipley, University of Colorado).

Page 253, note 22, line 8, *for* (d. 1754) *read* (ca 1695–1754)   *Last line, for* 1747–51 *read* 1743–51

Page 256, note 47, last line, *after* 345 *add*   ; *London Stage Part* III, ii. 951

Page 257, note 8, line 4, *for* Doddington *read* Dodington   *Line 5, for* 1691 *read* ?1691

Page 258, note 9, line 7, *before* E. Granville *insert* 1st

Page 262, 2d paragraph, line 10, *for* dinner *read* dinner,   *Line 11, for* account *read* account,

Page 265, line 12, *for* to him *read* to him,

Page 265, note 5a, last line, *before* end-paper *insert* front

Page 266, note 7, line 5, *for* HW *read* Mann

Page 270, note 1, *substitute* Romney Sedgwick suggests that HW is referring to Arthur Stert (d. 1755), M.P. Plymouth 1727–54, and William

Steuart (1686–1768), M.P. Inverness Burghs 1713–22, Ayr Burghs 1722–34, Elgin Burghs 1734–41 (*English Historical Review* April 1956, lxxi. 301).

Page 272, note 15, last 2 lines, *after* copy, *substitute* now WSL, is Hazen, *Cat. of HW's Lib.* No. 2328.

Page 274, note 32, line 3, *for* ca 1715 *read* 1714   *Line 10, for* iii. 2–3 *read* iii. 2–3, 58

Page 275, note 35, *substitute* Hervey was a steady supporter of Sir Robert during his administration. In 1729 Pulteney attempted unsuccessfully to win Hervey over to the Opposition, and his subsequent attacks on him in *A Proper Reply to a late Scurrilous Libel; Entitled, Sedition and Defamation Displayed*, 1731, led to a duel. See Robert Halsband, *Lord Hervey: Eighteenth-Century Courtier*, New York, 1974, pp. 87, 109–19.

Page 275, note 36, right column, line 3, *for* 1741 *read* 1733–42

Page 276, note 39, *substitute* On 16 Dec. over the choice of a chairman of the committee of elections (*ante* MANN i. 242).

Page 278, 1st paragraph, last line, *on* got rid of. *add note* 55a: 55a. Sir Robert was in the habit of calling Gibson 'my Pope,' but as a joking reference to his ambition; see J. H. Plumb, *Sir Robert Walpole: The King's Minister*, London, 1960, p. 96 and n. 1.

Page 278, note 55, line 2, *for* 1716–20 *read* 1716–23   *for* 1720–48 *read* 1723–48

Page 279, note 60, line 7, *delete* Aylesbury 1727–34,   *Line 8, for* 1734–41 *read* 1727–41

Page 284, note 28, *for* knowledge *read* understanding (Bagnani)

Page 290, note 19, line 3, *for* (d. 1769) *read* (ca 1695–1769)

Page 294, note 3, line 3, *for* 1741 *read* 1741–46   *Right column, line 1, for* 1756 *read* 1756–60

Page 295, note 8, line 3, *for* 1712 *read* ?1712

Page 295, note 12, right column, line 6, *for* 1702 *read* 1703

Page 295, note 13, line 5, *for* Philips *read* Philipps

Page 296, note 15, line 5, *for* 1765 *read* 1770

Page 296, note 15a, line 2, *for* OS, *read* OS; there were   *Line 3, for* Commons *read* Commons, a few of whom

Page 297, note 23, line 3, *for* Oak- *read* Oke-   *Line 5, after* state *insert* 1756–7,

Page 299, note 35, line 1, *for* 1696 *read* ca 1696   *Line 2, for* 1736 *read* 1737

Page 299, note 36, line 4, *for* Kirkcaldy, Burntisland, etc. *read* Dysart Burghs

Page 301, note 44, *add* See Hazen, *Cat. of HW's Lib.* No. 3556.

Page 302, note 58, lines 3–6, *after* OS). *substitute* It was first performed 19 Jan. (*London Stage* Part III, ii. 960).

Page 302, note 59, lines 1–2, *for* (ca 1704–ca 1766) *read* (1704–66) *Line 4, after* p. 88 *add*   ; *Enciclopedia dello spettacolo*, Rome, 1954–62, viii. 40

Page 304, line 11, *for* town *read* town,

Page 315, line 13, *for* garrison *read* garrison,

Page 318, note 5, line 1, *for* ca 1710 *read* 1710   *Line 5, for* 1746 *read* 1745–6

Page 319, note 16, *add* See *post* MANN i. 330.

Page 320, note 19, line 5, *for* Skerret *read* Skerrett

Page 325, note 26, *substitute* To the Prince of Wales, to whom he had offered, 5 Jan., to give an additional £50,000 a year, to pay his debts, and to receive and reward his friends at Court. The Prince refused as long as Sir Robert Walpole continued about the King. See CHUTE 20, n. 13.

Page 330, note 9, line 11, *for* 1715–22 *read* 1715–21

Page 332, note 22, line 1, *for* (d. 1762) *read* (1678–1762)

Page 332, note 23, line 1, *for* ca 1685 *read* 1685

Page 332, note 25, line 1, *for* (d. 1771) *read* (ca 1699–1771)

Page 333, note 33, last sentence, *substitute* Sir Robert took the title of Orford from his residence, Orford House, Chelsea.

Page 334, note 40, *add* See Hazen, *Cat. of HW's Lib.* No. 943:2.

Page 335, note 1, line 6, *for* now WSL, *read* now WSL (see Hazen, *Cat. of HW's Lib.* No. 119),

Page 336, note 9, line 7, *for* (now WSL), *read* (now WSL; see Hazen, *Cat. of HW's Lib.* No. 1609:9:2),

Page 336, note 10, line 1, *for* 1680 *read* ?1680

Page 336, note 13, line 1, *for* (fl. 1677–96) *read* (ca 1653–1706)   *Line* 2, *for* 1682 *read* 1681   *Line 4, for* 1576. *read* 1576 (see *Enciclopedia dello spettacolo*, Rome, 1954–62, i. 1429).   *Last line, add* See *London Stage* Part III, ii. 968.

Page 339, note 31, last line, *for* MS Cat. *read* Hazen, *Cat. of HW's Lib.* No. 1583

Page 344, note 13, lines 2–3, *for* Denbighshire 1733–42 *read* Denbigh Boroughs 1733–41, Denbighshire 1741–2

Page 346, note 26, line 2, from end, *for* are *read* is

Page 346, note 28, line 8, *for* 1705 *read* ca 1705

Page 347, note 28, lines 2–7, *for* He held the pocket boroughs . . . pp. 80, 138–9). *read* Falmouth's conversion to the Administration resulted in the Opposition's relative failure in Cornwall in the general election of 1747 (Sedgwick i. 204–5, 477).

Page 355, note 19, line 3, *for* 1735 *read* 1736

Page 355, note 20, line 2, *for* Ormistoun *read* Ormiston   *Lines 2–3,* *for* M.P. Haddingtonshire 1707–41 *read* M.P. Scotland 1707–8, Haddingtonshire 1708–41   *Line 3, after* Admiralty *insert* 1717–32,

Page 356, note 22, line 1, *delete* Hon.

Page 356, note 28, line 1, *for* (d. 1770) *read* (1718–70)

Page 356, note 31, line 2 from end, *after* SH i. 18 *add* (Hazen, *Cat. of HW's Lib.* No. 126)

Page 357, note 32, line 3, *after* SH iii. 55 *add* (Hazen, *Cat. of HW's Lib.* No. 1328)

Page 357, note 35, line 8, *for* (now WSL) *read* (now WSL; see Hazen, *Cat. of HW's Lib.* No. 2359)

Page 358, note 39, last line, *for* WSL. *read* WSL (Hazen, *Cat. of HW's Lib.* No. 472).

Page 358, note 41, last two lines, *after* April *substitute* and was revived for two nights in May and June (*London Stage* Part III, ii. 973–83, 997).

Page 364, note 7, line 1, *for* 1696 *read* ?1702

Page 366, note 15, line 2, *after* M.P. *insert* Bere Alston 1721,

Page 374, note 17, line 8, *for* WSL. *read* WSL (Hazen, *Cat. of HW's Lib.* No. 2359).

Page 376, note 12, line 3, *after* Magazine *insert* 1742, xi. 657–60, 1743, xii. 1–2,

Page 380, note 8, *add* The first motto was originally Cesare Borgia's (Bagnani).

Page 383, note 5, *for* ca 1696 *read* ?1697

Page 384, note 9, line 2, *for* ca 1691 *read* 1691

Page 384, note 10, line 2, *for* Edinburgh *read* Edinburghshire

Page 384, note 12, line 3, *for* (1748) *read* (1748),

Page 384, note 18, line 1, *for* (d. 1756) *read* (after 1688–1756)

Page 384, note 22, line 2 from end, *for* 1744–6 *read* 1744–5

Page 385, note 24, line 3, *for* (d. 1756) *read* (ca 1712–56)

Page 385, note 26, line 2, *for* ca 1704 *read* 1703

Page 385, note 27, line 1, *for* (d. 1767) *read* (1707–67)

Page 388, note 3, last line, *for* WSL. *read* WSL (Hazen, *Cat. of HW's Lib.* No. 2077).

Page 401, note 10, last line, *after* i. 205 *add*   ; *London Stage* Part III, ii. 984

Page 408, note 27, last four lines, *after* 1740 *substitute* but a Col. Moyser, accompanied by Hugh Bethell, left for the Continent in Aug. 1741 (information from the late George Sherburn; *Daily Adv.* 14 Aug. 1741 OS).

Page 411, note 11, line 1, *for* (ca 1701–1768 or 1770) *read* (1701–68) *Line 3, for* Beeralston *read* Bere Alston

Page 416, note 18, *add* (see Hazen, *Cat. of HW's Lib.* No. 536).

Page 420, note 11, lines 2–3, *for* ca 1692 *read* 1691   *Line 3, after* m. (2) *insert* (ca 1734)   *Right column, line 1, for* Macguire *read* Maguire *Line 2, for* 1764 *read* 1766   *Line 4, after* 230 *add*   ; OSSORY ii. 540, n. 24   *Lines 4–5, for* Macguire *read* Maguire

Page 429, note 7, last line, *after* iv. 51 *add* (Hazen, *Cat. of HW's Lib.* No. 1149)

Page 434, note 8, line 1, *for* second *read* third   *Last line, after* i. 205) *add*   ; *London Stage* Part III, ii. 995–6

Page 435, note 9, line 1, *for* 'farce with songs' *read* farce with songs

Line 2, for 19 May *read* 6 May   *Lines 2–4, after* Drury Lane as *substitute* an afterpiece to *Othello* (*London Stage* Part III, ii. 991).

Page 437, note 42, line 2, *for* 1742 *read* 1731

Page 438, note 44, line 2, *after* Anstruther *insert* Easter Burghs

Page 438, note 47, line 5, *delete*   , perhaps in 1771   *Lines 12–13, delete London Magazine,* 1771, xlv. 472;

Page 439, note 49, *add* HW's copies of the *Irish Register* and the *English Register* are listed in Hazen, *Cat. of HW's Lib.* No. 98:1.

Page 441, note 4, last 2 lines, *for* ii. 150–1. HW's copy of *The Art of Politics* is now WSL. *read* ii. 150–1; copies of a print (1741) illustrating an earlier version of this poem and entitled 'Scotch Tast in Vista's' are now WSL and in the British Museum (BM *Satiric Prints* No. 2510, iii. 403). For HW's copies of *The Art of Politics* (now WSL) and *The Man of Taste* (in the British Museum) see Hazen, *Cat. of HW's Lib.* Nos 881:2, 1886, 2474:1.

Page 448, note 3, line 1, *for* 1703 *read* 1710   *Lines 2–4, for* Sir George Grove . . . i. 532–3 *read The New Grove Dictionary of Music and Musicians,* 6th edn, ed. Stanley Sadie, 1980, iii. 595–6; *Enciclopedia dello spettacolo,* Rome, 1954–62, ii. 1461

Page 449, note 8, line 1, *for* Guzman *read* Guzmán   *for* 1689 *read* 1690   *Right column, line 2, for* Lecara y *read* La Plata and   *for* Massa *read* Masa   *Last line, after* pp. 260–9 *add* ; *Enciclopedia universal ilustrada,* Barcelona, 1905–33, xxvii. 404

Page 451, note 16, 1st sentence, *substitute* The Opposition Whigs (Romney Sedgwick in *English Historical Review,* April 1956, lxxi. 301).

Page 452, note 22, right column, line 7, *for* ca 1707 *read* ?1713

Page 453, 1st paragraph, lines 1–2, *on* reading *add note* 24a: 24a. The rest of this paragraph was omitted in previous editions.

Page 453, 2d paragraph, line 3, *on* robbery, *add note* 27: 27. The following phrase was omitted in previous editions.

Page 453, note 26, *substitute* An echo of Jeremiah 2. 20, 3. 6, 3. 13.

Page 462, note 15, *for* 'paist.' *read* 'paist,' but Mann must have intended to write 'pair'—i.e., an ensign's commission (OED).

Page 463, note 24, line 1, *for* 1705–?58 *read* ca 1705–ca 1760   *Lines 3–4, for* Sir George Grove . . . i. 557 *read The New Grove Dictionary of Music and Musicians,* 6th edn, ed. Stanley Sadie, 1980, iii. 778–9; *Enciclopedia dello spettacolo,* Rome, 1954–62, iii. 33

Page 469, note 20, line 9, *for* (d. 1726) *read* (ca 1691–1726)   *Right column, line 5, delete* first

Page 471, note 1, line 1, *for* (d. 1761) *read* (ca 1709–61)   *Line 7, after* ii. 449; *insert Historical Description of the Church in Bath . . . Commonly Called the Abbey,* Bath, 1778, p. 42;

Page 474, note 24, *add* John Fowle, who m. Elizabeth Turner, Sir Robert Walpole's niece, lived in Golden Square (information from J. H. Plumb).

Page 475, note 1, *add* The *Corn-Cutter's Journal* was a government periodical which ran for 18 months in 1733–4; a copy of No. 56, dated 22 Oct. 1734, is in the British Museum (BM Cat.; Laurence Hanson, *Government and the Press 1695–1763*, 1936, p. 114).

Page 485, note 6, last line, *for* ii. 49–67. *read* ii. 49–67, and in *Catalogues of the Collections of Pictures of the Duke of Devonshire, General Guise, and the Late Sir Paul Methuen*, printed by HW at SH in 1760 (see Hazen, *SH Bibl.* 52–3).

Page 485, note 9, line 2, *after* Chloé *insert* (*or* Cloiié *or* Cloué *or* Clouet) *Last line, add* See also Romney Sedgwick, 'The Duke of Newcastle's Cook,' *History Today*, 1955, v. 308–16; BM Add. MSS 32,734, ff. 138–40, 150–1.

Page 486, note 18, line 5, *for* ca 1747–67 *read* 1741–67
Page 487, note 22, line 3, *for* 1741–6 *read* 1741–5
Page 488, note 4, line 2, *for* respects *read* regards
Page 493, note 17, line 2 from end, *for* until ca 1757 *read* 1742–56
Page 494, note 20, line 2, *after* Newport *insert* I.o.W.   *Lines 5–7, for* appointed commissary-general of musters ca 1725 *read* commissioner of victualling 1725–9 and muster-master general 1729–42   *Last line, after* 50 *add*   ; Sedgwick ii. 164
Page 494, note 21, line 1, *for* Jeffries *read* Jeffreys   *Last line, after* p. 217 *add*   ; Sedgwick ii. 147
Page 504, note 23, *add* See BM *Satiric Prints* iii. 604 and n. 3.
Page 505, note 30, last sentence, *substitute* See Hazen, *Cat. of HW's Lib.* No. 2622.

VOLUME 18

Page 9, note 7, last line, *after* 1744 *add* (Hazen, *Cat. of HW's Lib.* No. 1608:90)

Page 12, note 10, line 1, *for* (ca 1708–ca 1743) *read* (1697–1744)   *Lines 2–6, for* (NBG . . . i. 76). *read* (*The New Grove Dictionary of Music and Musicians*, 6th edn, ed. Stanley Sadie, 1980, i. 636–7).

Page 13, note 18, lines 2–4, *for* at Rome in 1712 . . . i. 725). *read* at Amsterdam in 1714 (*The New Grove Dictionary of Music and Musicians*, 6th edn, ed. Stanley Sadie, 1980, iv. 772, 774).

Page 20, note 8, line 7, *for* 1736 *read* 1750   *Line 8, after* Congress *add*   ; Laurence Hanson, *Government and the Press 1695–1763*, 1936, p. 125).

Page 24, note 15, last line, *for* p. 3. *read* p. 3, or in the 7-pp. folio edition of the *Country Girl*, published by Webb, 1742, now WSL.

Page 24, note 18, line 1, *for* (d. 1753) *read* (ca 1690–1753)   *Line 3, for* ca 1725–ca 1747 *read* 1723–47

Page 25, note 24, right column, line 2, *for* 1722–6 *read* 1724–6

Page 28, note 11, lines 1 and 3, *for* Buoncompagni *read* Boncompagni
Line 3, for Soras *read* Sora

Page 31, To Mann 28 Aug. 1742 OS, 2d paragraph, line 1, *for* impresarri *read* impresarii

Page 33, note 9, *add* HW's copy is Hazen, *Cat. of HW's Lib.* No. 1506.

Page 34, note 22, line 1, *for* ca 1642 *read* 1642

Page 35, note 28, line 5, *for* Cornelius *read* Conradus   *Lines 7–9, for* (Pope's *Works* . . . x. 306–7). *read* (ed. C. Kerby-Miller, New Haven, 1950, p. 118).

Page 36, note 35, lines 1–2, *for* (1720–before 13 March 1759) *read* (1720–?1754)

Page 40, note 15, line 2, *for* Bibliothecina *read* Bibliotechina

Page 41, note 31, line 1, *for* gentlemen *read* sir (Bagnani)

Page 42, note 33, *for* shall *read* would (Bagnani)

Page 42, note 35, *substitute* An unintentional *double entendre*; the girl meant, 'Yes, milady; it is certainly *Chiaverei*,' but could be construed as saying, 'Yes, milady; I would certainly f-ck' (Bagnani).

Page 45, note 7, *add* See also Don Modesto Lafuente, *Historia general de España*, Madrid, 1850–69, xix. 200.

Page 47, note 1a, *substitute* Turnip-growing on a large scale had been introduced in Norfolk the preceding century; see J. H. Plumb, 'The Walpoles: Father and Son,' in *Studies in Social History: A Tribute to G. M. Trevelyan*, ed. J. H. Plumb, 1955, pp. 184–5.

Page 53, note 31, lines 1–3, *for* Charles (1679–1746), Comte de Gyllenborg, Swedish statesman and author (NBG). *read* Count Carl Gyllenborg (1679–1746), Swedish statesman and author (*Svenska Män och Kvinnor*, Stockholm, 1942–55, iii. 179–81).

Page 63, note 24, *add* He had been in Florence with HW in Dec. 1739 (*Hertford Corr.* i. 201).

Page 64, note 27, line 4, *for* 25 May 1698. *read* 19 May 1698 (see J. H. Plumb, *Sir Robert Walpole: The Making of a Statesman*, Boston, 1956, pp. 88–9; COLE i. 205).

Page 65, note 4, *substitute* Probably Henrietta Brookes (ca 1676–1769), widow of John Pratt, who was at Turin in Sept. 1741; she was a companion to the Duchess of Buckingham, from whom she inherited a large fortune (Lady Mary Wortley Montagu, *Complete Letters*, ed. R. Halsband, Oxford, 1965–7, ii. 255; GM 1769, xxxix. 461–2).

Page 65, note 5, line 1, *substitute* Hugh Bethell (1689–1747), M.P. (Sedgwick i. 460).   *Line 2, after* John Bethel Esq. *insert* [sic]   *Line 3, for* [?Moyzer] *read* [Moyser]   *Line 6, for* Bethel's *read* Bethell's

Page 79, note 3, line 4, *delete* NBG

Page 81, note 7, line 3, *for* (ca 1701–62) *read* (1702–62)   *Right column, line 1, for* ca 1737 *read* 1737   *delete* extra   *Line 2, for* 1740–3 *read* 1741–7

Page 82, note 9, *add* The reference is to her being mistress of George II and her later folly; see HW's 'Anecdotes of Lady Suffolk, ?1752,' MORE 421–2 and n. 23.

Page 85, note 5, *substitute* 'What do you expect? In the country one must be merry' (Bagnani).

Page 87, note 16, *substitute* Perhaps 'Signor Thomas Tyrrel of Florence' (Francesco Guarnieri to the Duke of Beaufort June 1728; Sir Osbert Sitwell, *Sing High! Sing Low!*, 1944, p. 50); he was alive in 1765, when he treated Boswell at Florence (see Frederick A. Pottle, *James Boswell: The Earlier Years 1740–1769*, New York, 1966, p. 238).

Page 91, note 9, last line, *after* Becker *add* ; John Fleming, 'The Hugfords of Florence (Part II),' *Connoisseur*, 1955, cxxxvi. 197–206

Page 94, note 12, line 7, *after* iii. 184 *add* (Hazen, *Cat. of HW's Lib.* No. 2082

Page 95, note 2, line 2, *for* (d. 1768) *read* (1700–68)

Page 96, note 10, lines 7–16, *substitute* the arias have been ascribed to Hasse, Lampugnani, Rinaldo da Capua, and Giuseppe Ferdinando Brivio (?1699–?1758), a Milanese composer (*The New Grove Dictionary of Music and Musicians*, 6th edn, ed. Stanley Sadie, 1980, iii. 308–9; *Enciclopedia dello spettacolo*, Rome, 1954–62, ii. 1134; *London Stage* Part III, ii. 1010–12).

Page 105, note 28, line 1 and last line, *for* Behan *read* Beaghan   *Last line, add* See Sedgwick i. 500.

Page 105, note 30, *add* See Hazen, *Cat. of HW's Lib.* Nos 3402, 3621.

Page 110, note 2, line 5, *for* Bothenar *read* Bothmar

Page 121, note 10, *substitute* 'When they have done their duty'; Professor Gilbert Bagnani points out that this was the idiom regularly applied to soldiers in citations, and that it is probably derived from the Latin *bene se gerere*.

Page 121, note 17, line 7, *for* Sermonetta-Gaetano *read* Sermoneta-Gaetani

Page 123, note 5, line 4, *for* 1742. *read* 1742 (imprint 1743).   *Right column, lines 4–5, for* copy of the 1743 edition is *read* copies of the 1st and 2d editions are   *Last line, add* See Hazen, *Cat. of HW's Lib.* Nos 1608:43, 46.

Page 128, note 20, lines 1–2, *for* (b. ca 1685) *read* (1691–1761)   *Lines 3–5, for* Sir George Grove . . . ii. 216). *read The New Grove Dictionary of Music and Musicians*, 6th edn, ed. Stanley Sadie, 1980, vi. 465–8; *Enciclopedia dello spettacolo*, Rome, 1954–62, v. 150–1).

Page 130, note 16, line 1, *for* Signora *read* Catherine Rinni   *for* 1723 *read* 1724   *Line 4, after* 80 *add* ; OSSORY ii. 100, n. 7

Page 135, note 5, line 1, *delete* Probably   *for* (d. 1754) *read* (ca 1701–54)   *Line 3, for* 1754. His wife has not been identified *read* 1754; m. (before 1743) Katherine Lloyd (d. 1791). The couple were reconciled, but in 1751 separated again   *Last line, after* 111 *add* ; MONTAGU i. 113

Page 141, note 6, *add* See Hazen, *Cat. of HW's Lib.* No. 1608:43.

Page 144, note 32, line 1, *for* 1678 *read* 1680   *Line 2, for* Ardrie, Scotland *read* Airdrie, Fife   *Lines 2–3, for* Lt-Col. of the Foot Guards before 1715 *read* Capt. and Lt-Col. 1st Foot Guards, 1710   *Line 4, for* Foot; *read* Foot, 1720–60;

Page 145, note 3, *for* boy *read* clerk

Page 149, note 2, *for* Federighi *read* Federigo

Page 154, note 35, lines 1–2, *for* (1718–99) *read* (1719–98)   *Line 5, after* 354 *add* ; *Enciclopedia de la cultura española*, Madrid, 1963– , i. 431–2

Page 178, note 14, line 2, *for* finally wanted *read* even decided (Bagnani).

Page 180, note 7, line 6, *after* i. 23 *add* (Hazen, *Cat. of HW's Lib.* No. 123)   *Lines 7–14, for* the *Memoirs* of . . . They contain *read* Capt. George Carleton, *A True and Genuine History of the Two Last Wars against France and Spain*, 1741 (Hazen, *Cat. of HW's Lib.* No. 1352). This work contains

Page 180, note 8, line 2, *after* pp. 114–15 *add* ; Paul Henry Lang, *George Frideric Handel*, New York, 1966, pp. 397–407

Page 180, note 9, *add* See also *London Stage* Part III, ii. illustration 5 between pp. 966–7.

Page 180, note 12, last line, *substitute* Christina Maria Avoglio and Miss Edwards also sang (Lang, op. cit. 339, 406; *London Stage* Part III, ii. 1035).

Page 180, note 13, line 2, *substitute* by Nicola Antonio Porpora (1686–1768),   *Lines 5–6, for* Sir George Grove . . . 230–2). *read* *The New Grove Dictionary of Music and Musicians*, 6th edn, ed. Stanley Sadie, 1980, xv. 123–7; *Enciclopedia dello spettacolo*, Rome, 1954–62, viii. 342–3).

Page 181, note 4, *substitute* Probably Joseph-Antoine Crozat, *Recueil d'estampes d'après les plus beaux tableaux . . . en France dans le cabinet du roi, dans celui [du] duc d'Orléans* [etc.], 1729–42, 2 vols, folio (Bibl. Nat. Cat.; HW's copy is listed Hazen, *Cat. of HW's Lib.* No. 3550).

Page 186, note 7, *substitute* 'The Honble Board of Loyal Brother-hood' was meeting in 1747 at the Bedford Head, Covent Garden, from 8 Dec. 1748 at the St Alban's Tavern, and from 14 Dec. 1756 at the Cocoa Tree, St James's Street (minutes of the Board *penes* [1957] A. N. L. Munby, King's College, Cambridge; information from J. H. Plumb).

Page 188, note 10, line 7, *after* iii. 19 *add* (Hazen, *Cat. of HW's Lib.* No. 1553)

Page 198, note 5, *substitute* I.e., *basso buffo* (Bagnani).

Page 203, note 1, line 1, *for* 58 *read* 57

Page 219, note 14, line 3, *for* 12th *read* 3d

Page 219, note 15, line 1, *for* (d. 1734) *read* (1680–1734)   *Last line, add* See Richard Hayes, *Biographical Dictionary of Irishmen in France*, Dublin, 1949, p. 25.

Page 220, note 21, line 1, *for* (b. 1711) *read* (1711–?72)   *Line 4, after* p. 456 *add* ; GM 1772, xlii. 598   *Last line, add* In 1759 Belfield (now

Lord Belvidere) won a case of crim. con. against him, obtaining a judgment of £20,000 (*London Chronicle* 24–6 May 1759, v. 402).

Page 220, note 25, line 1, *for* (ca 1678–1765) *read* (ca 1682–1764) *Line 2, after* painter *add* (see G. E. Kendall, 'Notes on the Life of John Wootton With a List of Engravings after his Pictures,' *Walpole Society 1932–1933*, xxi. 24–5, 31–3)

Page 224, note 1, *add* An anonymous satirical ballad about the King's being windbound, entitled 'The Wind in the East: or, Pri'thee Friend Keep Back. An Ominous Warning,' 8 pp. folio, was published by W. Webb, 1743; WSL's copy is endorsed 'Tom's Coffee House, May 4, 1743.'

Page 231, note 6, line 2, *for* Schulenberg *read* Schulenburg

Page 231, note 7, line 4, *for* Schulenberg *read* Schulenburg

Page 235, note 17, line 3 from end, *after* WSL *add* (Hazen, *Cat. of HW's Lib.* No. 1608:5:10)

Page 236, note 1, line 6, *after* Newport *insert* (I.o.W.) *Line 9, for* 1741–50 *read* 1741–49

Page 237, note 8, line 1, *for* ca 1684 *read* 1684 *Line 2, for* Wick *read* Tain *Lines 3–4, for* of the 'Earl of Crawford's regiment of foot,' *read* 42d Foot

Page 240, note 14, right column, line 5 from end, *after* Taylor,' *insert* in R. R. James, *Lines 3–4 from end, delete* ed. R. R. James,

Page 242, note 6, *substitute* 'The same hand holds even more sceptres' (Bagnani).

Page 243, note 15, lines 2–4, *for* (see *ante* i. 77) . . . Lord Walpole. *read* now (1976) at Houghton in the possession of the Marquess of Cholmondeley. *and delete last sentence*

Page 245, note 5, *add* Newcastle was chagrined at Lincoln's marriage and the marriage settlement (Newcastle to Hardwicke 14 Oct. 1744, BM Add. MSS 32, 703, ff. 363–8).

Page 249, note 17, line 3, *for* the loss of two *read* a loss of about two

Page 255, note 2, line 3, *for* *Works read Work*

Page 260, note 17, last 2 lines, *for* all WSL. *read* Hazen, *Cat. of HW's Lib.* Nos 1608:51, 2050:12, 2492:3, 2493:1, 6.

Page 260, note 21, line 3, *for* NS *read* OS

Page 261, note 25, left column, line 3 from bottom, *for* NS *read* OS

Page 266, note 14, last line, *after* i. 49 *add* (Hazen, *Cat. of HW's Lib.* No. 46)

Page 269, note 1, *substitute* According to Professor Gilbert Bagnani, this is the Deus Sabaoth of the *Te Deum* (in English 'Lord God of Hosts').

Page 272, note 3, right column, line 1, *for* Taylor.' *Studies read* Taylor,' in R. R. James, *Studies* *Line 2, delete* ed. R. R. James,

Page 291, note 7, last 2 lines, *substitute* the 6-vol. *Recueil des lettres* printed at Paris in 1738 (Hazen, *Cat. of HW's Lib.* No. 949).

Page 293, note 16, *add* The English passed the Rhine on 22 Aug. NS (CONWAY i. 143).

Page 303, note 18, right column, line 2, *delete* probably

Page 304, note 2, *substitute* See CONWAY i. 146 and nn.

Page 304, note 3, line 3 from end, *after* 29 Sept. OS *add*   ; HW's copies, now WSL, are Hazen, *Cat. of HW's Lib.* Nos 1608:26, 44

Page 305, note 8, *add* Reports of the resignation were current in London 6 Sept. OS (*Daily Adv.* 6 Sept.).

Page 305, note 9, line 4, *after* China *add* (Hazen, *Cat. of HW's Lib.* No. 874)

Page 308, line 3 from bottom, *on potence add note* 9a: 9a. Professor Gilbert Bagnani points out that *potence* (Fr. 'gallows') is due to the attraction of the Italian *potenza* and is a blunder still common with those who know Italian better than French.

Page 310, note 1, line 5, *for* NS *read* OS   *Right column, line 2, for* NS *read* OS   *Last line, add* See *ante* MANN ii. 305, n. 8.

Page 311, note 3, line 2, *for* in 1744 *read* with the imprint 1744   *for* quarto. *read* quarto; a copy, now WSL, is endorsed in MS 'Tom's Coffee House, Nov. 9, 1743.'

Page 311, note 5, line 7, *for* Ossorio *read* Osorio

Page 313, note 8, line 2, *for* Gabburi *read* Gabburri

Page 313, note 10, *substitute* F. Cicciaporci (see Frits Lugt, *Répertoire des catalogues de ventes publiques*, The Hague, 1938, No. 2662; BM, Department of Prints and Drawings, *Italian Drawings in the Department of Prints and Drawings in the British Museum*, vol. iii, *Michelangelo and his Studio*, by Johannes Wilde, tr. J. A. Gere and T. H. Scrutton, 1953, Nos 29, 60).

Page 319, note 21, *add* Pulteney recommended Pearce for the bishopric of Peterborough on his resigning the deanery of Winchester (Earl of Bath to Newcastle 21 July 1747 OS, BM Add. MSS 32,712, f. 181).

Page 320, note 28, line 2, *for* ca 1700 *read* 1700   *Line 3, for* Michael *read* Mitchell   *Right column, line 1, for* 1755 *read* 1755–75

Page 321, note 29, *substitute* Secretary to the Treasury (HW). John Jeffreys (1706–66), M.P. Breconshire 1734–47, Dartmouth 1747–66; joint secretary of the Treasury 1742–6; warden of the mint 1754–66 (Sedgwick ii. 173).

Page 335, verses, line 2, *for* Brevi *read* Brevi,   *Line 8, for* poi *read* noi

Page 335, note 24, *substitute* 'But —! holy Father! with every courier new vexations, new perils are heard of, and meanwhile you, laying down your backside, are scratching your most holy testicles? Other things are wanted than to add briefs, glosses, paragraphs, and articles to the Bullarium, and to study the reform of the Breviary to make saints great, middling and small! This, by God! it isn't worth a cabbage, and in other times perhaps you would have called them nonsense and sent them to the devil. And while we go to the brink you mock us and leave us to fry, by God, you who have brought us to such a pass!' (new translation incorporating suggestions of Professor Gilbert Bagnani).

Page 341, line 2, *on* Princess *insert note* 4

Page 342, note 14, last 3 lines, *for* 1903; Sir George Grove . . . Lampugnani). *substitute* 1903). *The New Grove Dictionary of Music and Musicians*, 6th edn, ed. Stanley Sadie, 1980, x. 421, says that 'Some commentators have accepted the opera as an original work by Lampugnani, but it was probably a pasticcio with music by Handel included' (see also *Enciclopedia dello spettacolo*, Rome, 1954–62, vi. 1187).

Page 342, note 19, line 1, *for* Hinde *read* Hynde

Page 342, note 22, line 1, *for* Ossorio *read* Osorio

Page 346, note 19, *substitute* 'I formerly had the honour of being very warmly recommended to your Grace by the late Duke of Richmond and Sir Charles Wager to succeed Mr Fane as his Majesty's minister at Florence when he went to England, and I had the satisfaction of hearing from them both how much inclined your Grace was to serve me at that time, and though I was afterwards disappointed in the affair, yet it was no small alleviation to me to learn from them how hard your Grace thought my case, and that you had promised to continue me your protection' (Goldsworthy to D. of Newcastle, Leghorn 23 Nov. 1752 NS, BM Add. MSS 32,841, ff. 219–20).

Page 349, note 4, line 1, *for* 1742 *read* 1732

Page 349, note 5, line 1, *for* (d. 1756) *read* (1698–1756)   *Line 7, after* 595 *add*   ; Sedgwick ii. 345

Page 350, note 12, line 1, *for* ca 1683 *read* ?1682   *Last line, after* 171 *add*   ; Sedgwick ii. 357

Page 353, note 13, *add* 'Parure' (Bagnani).

Page 355, date-line, *on* 1743. *add note a: a.* Misdated 15 Dec. by Mrs Toynbee.

Page 355, note 1, line 7, *after* 2780). *insert* HW's copy of Bragge's catalogue of pictures, 1757, now in the British Museum, identifies a Giorgione (SH Sale Cat. xxi. 92) as 'Bought by Mr H. Walpole' (note opposite p. 87).

Page 366, note 12, lines 2–3, *for* she was the occupant of SH before HW took it *read* she held the lease of SH before HW sublet it   *Line 4, after* n. 23 *add*   ; see also CONWAY i. 269–70 and nn. 2, 7; W. S. Lewis, 'The Genesis of Strawberry Hill,' *Metropolitan Museum Studies*, 1934, v pt i. 58–60

Page 367, note 1, *substitute* John Selwyn (ca 1709–51) the younger; M.P. Whitchurch 1734–51 (Sedgwick ii. 416).

Page 367, note 2, lines 2–3, *for* George Selwyn's brother John *read* George Selwyn's   *Line 3, after* 1744 OS *add* SELWYN 88, n. 14

Page 371, note 1, *for* 1744 OS *read* 1743 OS

Page 371, note 2, line 2, *delete* Craon   *Line 4, after* Levis *insert* de

Page 373, note 9, line 1, *for* ca 1697 *read* 1698   *Last line, after* 260 *add*   ; Namier and Brooke ii. 241

Page 374, note 1, line 1, *for* ca 1711 *read* ca 1710   *Line 2, for* 1791 *read* 1751–60   *Line 3, for* 1760 *read* 1760–3, 1765–86   *Last line, after* 102 *add*   ; Sedgwick ii. 252

Page 374, note 2, line 1, *for* ca 1694 *read* ?1693   *Last line, after* *Cantab. add*   ; Sedgwick i. 621–2

Page 377, note 14, lines 1 and 3, *for* Caetani *read* Gaetani

Page 378, note 16, *add* See also Alistair and Henrietta Tayler, *1745 and After*, 1938, p. 15.

Page 379, note 26, line 24, *after* 1901, xv. 591); *insert* Lady Waldegrave suggests that the *Projet de réhabilitation* was 'much more likely . . . written by Thomas Carte [*post* MANN ii. 480, n. 5]. I have photostats here of several of these "projets" in the Archives, Quai d'Orsai some of them in Thomas Carte's writing throughout, some autographed, and some with these initials, which he always used. He took a far more active part in Jacobite councils than is realized' (Lady Waldegrave to WSL, from Chewton House, Chewton Mendip, Bath, Somerset, March, 1969).   *Line 26, after* MS *insert* (see 'Cardinal Tencin's Plan, presented to the French King, for settling the Pretender's Family upon the British Throne, and completing the long-concerted Scheme of Universal Monarchy in the House of Bourbon' in *London Chronicle* 27–9 Sept. 1759, vi. 308–9)

Page 391, note 11, *substitute* 'Disfigure' (Bagnani).

Page 406, note 16, lines 3 and 8, *for* Buondelmonte *read* Buondelmonti

Page 406, note 20, line 12, *for Memoires read Memoirs*

Page 414, note 28, line 1, *for* (d. 1770) *read* (ca 1715–70)   *Line 3, for* 1741 *read* 1742   *Line 5, after* p. 34 *add*   ; Namier and Brooke ii. 254

Page 431, note 9, line 1, *for* Eleanor *read* Eleonora   *Line 2, for* ff. 1742–51 *read* fl. 1742–58   *Last line, add* He signs his name 'Capello' in letters to Pelham 9 Feb. 1748, BM Add. MSS 32,811, f. 206, and to Newcastle 9 Feb. 1748, ibid. f. 203.

Page 433, note 1, line 4, *for* Hinde *read* Hynde

Page 442, note 17, line 1, *for* ca 1679 *read* 1679

Page 448, note 1, *substitute* Conway to HW 3 June 1744 NS gives all this news; see CONWAY i. 152–4.

Page 449, note 11, *add* Pope was at Chiswick on 30 March (see *Correspondence of Alexander Pope*, ed. George Sherburn, Oxford, 1956, iv. 514).

Page 451, note 27, line 2, *for* ca 1697 *read* ?1696   *Last line, add* See Sedgwick ii. 273–4.

Page 451, note 28, line 1, *after* Dashwood *insert* (?1717–93)   *Line 3, for* Canterbury *read* Canterbury   *Lines 4–7, delete* He may have been . . . 1741 OS. *and substitute* See R. C. Dudding, *History of . . . Alford*, [Horncastle], 1930, p. 44; SELWYN 7, n. 32.

Page 451, note 29, *after* Bateman *insert* (d. 1802), m. (1744) Samuel Dashwood   *after* loc. cit. *add*   ; Dudding, loc. cit.

Page 451, note 30, line 1, *for* (b. ca 1679) *read* (b. 7 March 1681), son of

Sir Samuel Dashwood, Kt   *Line 2, after* Bateman *insert* (d. 1758) *for* ibid. *read Registers of St Botolph, Bishopsgate, London,* ed. A. W. Cornelius Haller, 1889–95, iii. 285; Dudding, loc. cit.

Page 451, 3d paragraph, line 3, *on* Selwyn *add note* 32   *on* brother's *for* 32 *read* 32a   *and add note* 32a: 32a. George Augustus Selwyn (1719–91), M.P.; HW's friend and correspondent (Sedgwick ii. 415; SELWYN 88, n. 14).

Page 452, note 34, last line, *for last sentence substitute* HW's copy of the first edition is Hazen, *Cat. of HW's Lib.* No. 1465; HW's copy of the second edition is now WSL (ibid. No. 1608:48:1).

Page 453, note 3a, line 1, *for* Montealegre *read* Montallegre

Page 455, note 21, line 6, *for* 23 Feb. *read* 17 Feb.   *Line 8, before Daily Adv. insert Register Book of Marriages . . . Parish of St George, Hanover Square,* ed. J. H. Chapman and G. J. Armitage, 1886–97, i. 36 (Harleian Society Publications, vol. xi).

Page 458, note 18, line 2, *for* 1640 *read* 1641

Page 463, 1st paragraph, line 5, *for* channel *read* Channel

Page 464, note 7, line 11, *after* iii. 83 *insert* (Hazen, *Cat. of HW's Lib.* No. 1721)   *Lines 11–12, for* derived from Algernon Sidney *read* said to be by Algernon Sidney, but is by T. Rymer

Page 464, note 9, last line, *after* WSL *add* (Hazen, *Cat. of HW's Lib.* No. 1608:41:3)

Page 465, note 20, line 1, *for* Col *read* Col.

Page 466, note 3, *add* See Conway's account of Prince Charles's crossing in his letter of 6 July 1744 NS, CONWAY i. 158–9.

Page 467, note 14, *add* Knapton had drawn HW in crayon before 1736 (HW's MS list of pictures in Sir Robert Walpole's possession, 1736, in the Pierpont Morgan Library, New York). See C. K. Adams and W. S. Lewis, 'The Portraits of Horace Walpole,' *Walpole Society,* 1968–70, xlii. 9.

Page 468, Italian poem, line 2, *on* Uno de' lumi *add note* 19a: 19a. Professor Gilbert Bagnani suggests that Rolli wrote 'Un dei lumi.'

Page 468, note 19, *add* See Hazen, *Cat. of HW's Lib.* Nos 2113, 2115, and also No. 306.

Page 477, note 10, last line, *after* WSL *add* (Hazen, *Cat. of HW's Lib.* No. 1608:52:2)

Page 480, note 1, line 4, *for* 1738 *read* 1738–40   *after* 179 *add* (Hazen, *Cat. of HW's Lib.* No. 877)

Page 480, note 2, line 4, *for* 1707 *read* 1707–17   *Last line, add* See Hazen, *Cat. of HW's Lib.* Nos 14, 40, 41.

Page 480, note 4, last line, *after* 179 *add* (Hazen, *Cat. of HW's Lib.* No. 2098; see also No. 3293)

Page 480, note 5, *add* See Hazen, *Cat. of HW's Lib.* No. 1696.

Page 480, note 5a, *add* Photostats of some MSS in Thomas Carte's handwriting, from the Archives, Quai d'Orsai, are in the Waldegrave collection at Chewton House, Chewton Mendip (see ADD. AND CORR. for *ante* vol. 18, p. 379, n. 26).

Page 480, note 6, *add* See Hazen, *Cat. of HW's Lib.* No. 611.

Page 481, note 15, *delete* Nothing is known of this opera singer except that she was *and substitute* Giulia Frasi (fl. 1742–72), who sang in many operas, oratorios, and concerts in London between 1742 and 1770, was Line 3, *after* 255 *add*   ; *The New Grove Dictionary of Music and Musicians*, 6th edn, ed. Stanley Sadie, 1980, vi. 808

Page 496, note 12, *add* See CONWAY i. 175–6.

Page 498, note 1, lines 5–6, *delete* Fox and Winnington were apparently also asked: *and substitute* See HW to Williams 14 Aug. 1744 OS (SELWYN 67–8); HW finally left for Houghton 20 Aug. (DALRYMPLE 23). Fox wrote,

Page 498, note 6, last line, *after* 147 *add* (Hazen, *Cat. of HW's Lib.* No. 948). HW quotes a similar idea from Saint-Évremond in CONWAY i. 201 and n. 12.

Page 501, note 17, *add* Lady Carteret went to Tunbridge to visit her parents and sister; Lady Townshend wrote to Lady Denbigh 25 Aug. 1744 OS, 'Lord and Lady Pomfrett and Lady Charlot Fermer are at Tunbridge, where Lady Carterete is gone for ten days to make them a visit, and Lord Carterete is to set out this week to fetch her back from that place' (Hist. MSS Comm., *Denbigh MSS*, 1911, p. 254).

Page 510, note 12, line 1, *for* Επιδαλάμιον *read* Επιθαλάμιον

Page 518, note 5, line 3, *for* xxvi. 1 *read* lib. xxvi. cap. 50

Page 522, note 6, line 1, *for* —— Turner, m. *read* Hannah Turner (d. 1759), m. (1722)   *Line 2, after* Gardiner *insert* (ca 1702–70)

Page 522, note 11, *add* See genealogical table in GEC xii pt i. 84.

Page 523, note 22, *for* Lincoln *read* Lord Middlesex   *after* Arlington St. *add* See MANN ii. 481, 527.

Page 524, note 31, last line, *after* 1744 NS *add*   , where he referred to Great Britain and Holland (MANN ii. 513)

Page 538, note 23, lines 1–2, *for* (fl. 1733–45) *read* (d. 1747)   *Line 3, for* 1744 *read* 1745   *Last line, add* See also GRAY i. 143, n. 18; GM 1779, xxix. 171

Page 538, note 24, *add* See also *London Stage* Part III, ii. 1130.

Page 544, note 25, line 1, *delete* Perhaps   *Line 2, after* 46). *insert* Sturrock to Lady Hertford, Bologna, 27 Sept. 1744 NS is printed in H. S. Hughes, *The Gentle Hertford*, New York, 1940, pp. 345–8;

Page 548, note 7, line 1, *for* Fl. 1708–44 *read* Fl. 1708–61   *Last line, add* See Mann's Letter-Books 5 Sept. 1761, S.P. 105/293, f. 117.

Page 551, note 15, line 1, *for* ca 1695 *read* 1693   *Last line, after* 1744–56 *add* (Sedgwick ii. 142)

Page 551, note 16, line 2, *for* 1734–51 *read* 1734–50   *Line 4, for* 1745–55 *read* 1744–55   *Last line, add* See also Sedgwick ii. 350–1.

Page 551, note 18, line 1, *for* (d. 1777) *read* (ca 1700–77)   *Last line, after* 1744–51 *add* (Sedgwick ii. 303)

Page 553, note 4, *substitute* 'What a lot of accidents!' (Bagnani)

Page 553, 2d paragraph, 3d line from bottom, *for bassoio read vassoio* (Bagnani).

Page 561, note 6, line 1, *for* (1693–1770), *read* (1694–1770), baptized in St George's, Antwerp, on 27 June 1694; *Line 2, for* (Thieme and Becker). *read* (M. I. Webb, *Michael Rysbrack Sculptor*, 1954, pp. 15, 47–8; see also *post* MANN iii. 63).

Page 567, note 23, left column, line 1, *for* 1744 *read* 1743–4 *Line 2, after* WSL *add* (Hazen, *Cat. of HW's Lib.* No. 64)

VOLUME 19

Page 3, note 18, *for* 'Thing for printing' *read* 'Something to be printed' (Bagnani).

Page 4, note 6, line 1, *for* 23 Feb. *read* 23 Jan.

Page 5, note 7, *add* 'Lord Strange was the only one that put a negative against it, so that this may be looked upon like a perfect unanimity: the House was very full, there being above 400 Members,' according to the report of P. H. Cornabé in a letter of 25 Jan. 1745 to Sir Thomas Robinson (Philip Henry Stanhope, Lord Mahon, *History of England*, 2d edn, 1839–44, iii. Appendix, pp. lviii–lx).

Page 5, note 13, line 2, *after* 1775 *add* ; groom of the Bedchamber to the P. of Wales, 1742 *Line 4, add* Henry Oxenden was still in Italy in Oct. 1746, to be joined by his younger brother (George Oxenden to Newcastle 2 Nov. 1746, BM Add. MSS 32,709, ff. 150–1). Henry wrote to Mann 25 March 1749 NS (S.P. 105/309, f. 81).

Page 5, note 14, lines 4–5, *delete* ; groom of the Bedchamber to the P. of Wales, 1742 *Last line, add* See Sedgwick ii. 317–18; OSSORY ii. 222 and n. 11.

Page 8, note 15, *for* 'One shall never laugh.' *read* 'They never made us laugh' (Bagnani).

Page 15, note 35, *add* Mann is transcribing the Italian (and French) 'quartier generale' (Bagnani).

Page 23, note 7, line 4, *for* Constantine *read* Constantin

Page 25, note 7, line 1, *for* (d. 1749) *read* (1689–1749) *Line 3, for* Michael *read* Mitchell *Last line, add* See Sedgwick ii. 415.

Page 26, note 14, line 2, *after* Eyles *add* (1683–1745) *Line 5, for* 1739–44 *read* 1739–45 (Sedgwick ii. 21)

Page 26, note 15, line 1, *for* (d. 1758) *read* (1682–1758) *Line 2, for* (d. 1752) *read* (1687–1752) *Line 5, after* 651 *add* ; *The Genealogist*, n. s., 1884, i. pedigree facing p. 129

Page 27, note 25, *add* See also Douglas Grant, *James Thomson*, 1951, pp. 234–8.

Page 27, note 26, *for* ca 1653 *read* ca 1648

Page 29, note 39, right column, line 3, *after* 234, n. 4 *add*   ; Hazen, *Cat. of HW's Lib.* No. 2492:2

Page 33, note 9, *substitute* Sir Charles Kemys Tynte (1710–85), 5th Bt, 1735; M. P.; the candidate for the Tory interest, who was narrowly defeated (688 to 641) by Mathews at the by-election for Glamorgan in Jan. 1745. In March 1745 Sir Charles was brought in for Monmouth, hence HW's calling him 'one of their friends in Monmouthshire' (see Sedgwick i. 377, ii. 186, 247).

Page 34, note 14, line 1, *for* 15 April NS *read* 15 April OS   *Line 4, after* April *add* NS

Page 34, From Mann 4 May 1745 NS, headnote, line 2, *for* 4 May 1745 NS *read* 1 May 1745 NS (MS now WSL)

Page 38, note 15, *for* 4 May 1745 NS *read* 1 May 1745 NS (MS now WSL, printed in MISC. CORR. i. 53).

Page 41, note 9, line 2, *after* Bernklau *add* (or Bärnklau)

Page 42, note 1, right column, line 3, *for* four miles *read* five miles

Page 43, note 6, line 1, *for* (d. 1745) *read* (ca 1703–45)   *Line 3, for* 1730–41 *read* 1730–45

Page 43, note 13, lines 8–9, *for* of the 7th Dragoon Guards *read* who was Col. of the 48th Foot   *Last line, after* 235 *add*   ; see also CONWAY i. 209, n. 4

Page 44, line 4, *for* his morning *read* this morning

Page 44, note 20, *substitute* On Saturday 4 May, the day when the news came, *Henry VIII* was performed at Covent Garden, with Quin as Henry VIII and Mrs Horton as Anne Bullen, 'By command of their Royal Highnesses the Prince and Princess of Wales, Prince George, Prince Edward, and the Lady Augusta' (*London Stage* Part III, ii. 1173).

Page 49, note 3, line 3, *for* William V of Orange *read* William IV of Orange (*post* 25 Dec. 1746 OS, n. 7)

Page 52, note 2, *add* HW's news may be based on Conway's letter of 26 May 1745 NS (CONWAY i. 194).

Page 53, note 8, *for* 4 May 1745 NS *read* 1 May 1745 NS (see MISC. CORR. i. 53).

Page 56, note 16, *at end add* Sir John Norris wrote Sept. 1747 to George II of being 'sensible of the unhappy circumstances relating to his sons' (BM Add. MSS 32,713, f. 183).

Page 58, note 12, line 1, *for* —— Shadwell *read* Catherine Shadwell *Line 2, delete* ca.   *Line 5, after* 1737 *add*   ; *ante* 2 Nov. 1741 OS, n. 18)

Page 59, note 19a, *delete* An echo of   *for* vi. 3 *read* ii. 3

Page 61, note 3, line 2, *for* James, D. of Monmouth *read* Charles, 3d Baron Cornwallis, and Anne Scott, Duchess of Monmouth and Buccleuch *Line 3, after* 239 *add* Collins, *Peerage*, 1812, ii. 552

Page 61, note 4, *add* See George Villiers, D. of Buckingham, *The Rehearsal*, Act II, scene v; wet brown paper was the 18th century adhesive tape.

Page 61, note 5, line 10, *for* pp. 219–23 *read* p. 223

Page 66, note 10, line 12, *after* 210. *add* Adolf Michaelis (*Ancient Marbles in Great Britain*, Cambridge, 1882, p. 486) denies that it was ever owned by Lord Leicester and states that it was then (1882) in London at Lord Wemyss's. Salomon Reinach in an article in *Monuments Piot* iii (1896). 40–50, states that the eagle and base were then at Gosford House, and that Lord Wemyss had told him that the statue was bought by his father at the Strawberry Hill sale and was taken direct to Gosford House, Longniddry, East Lothian (information from Gilbert Bagnani).

Page 72, note 19, line 2, *for* 1726–64 *read* 1726–66   *Line 6, after* xxxiv. 302 *add* ; *Daily Adv.* 10 June 1766

Page 77, line 7, *on* formerly *add note* 20a: 20a. What the Parliament did to Belloni formerly was to have his letter of 4 May 1732 (printed in GM 1732, ii. 768) 'burnt before the Royal Exchange by the Common Hangman; pursuant to an express order of both Houses of Parliament who unanimously voted it an insolent and audacious libel' (ibid. ii. 773, 785). In the letter Belloni volunteered information, and laid down conditions on which the relevant papers of John Thompson would be produced, in connection with the scandal of the Charitable Corporation, a financial fraud parallel to the South Sea Company failure (ibid. ii. 782–6; information from Lady Waldegrave based on correspondence in the Waldegrave collection; A. McF. Davis, 'The Charitable Corporation of London,' Massachusetts Historical Society, *Proceedings*, 1910–11, xliv. 653–5).

Page 77, note 18, *substitute* Giovannangelo Belloni, a banker in Rome (*Dizionario biografico degli Italiani*, Rome, 1960– , vii. 773–6).

Page 87, note 12, line 7, *after* 125) *add* , or 'Carret de Gorzegne' (BM Add. MS 32,809, f. 155)

Page 91, note 10, line 1, *for* Peircy *read* Piercy   *for* (1709–81) *read* (ca 1710–81)   *Last line, after* 1754–74 *add* (Namier and Brooke ii. 115)

Page 102, note 2, line 1, *for* (d. 1760) *read* (1690–1760)   *Last line, after* 1738–41 *add* (Sedgwick i. 576)

Page 103, note 13, line 4, *for* James *read* John

Page 104, note 18, lines 13–14, *for* Skerret's *read* Skerrett's   *Last line, add* See also GM 1739, ix. 304.

Page 106, note 18, *for* groom of the Chamber *read* groom of the Bedchamber to Frederick, Prince of Wales, July 1748–51, to George III as Prince of Wales 1751–60, and as King 1760–73   *Line 3, delete* perhaps   *Last line, add* See Sedgwick i. 485–6.

Page 107, note 23, line 1, *for* (d. 1768) *read* (1700–68)   *Line 2, after* M. P. *insert* Hindon 1727–34, Southwark 1734–41,   *Last line, add* See Sedgwick ii. 121–2.

Page 109, note 13, line 4, *for* Burlington Bay *read* Bridlington Bay

Page 110, note 20, *add* This number of ships seems to be an exaggeration; only four ships of the line and two smaller ships apparently were sent from the Mediterranean at this time (see SELWYN 98 and n. 27).

Page 110, note 27, *add* For additional references on the private regiments see HW to C. H. Williams 21 Sept. 1745 OS, SELWYN 98, n. 22.

Page 110, note 31, line 2, *for* cr. (1728) E. of Malton *read* cr. (1728) Baron Malton and (1734) E. of Malton   *Last line, add* See Sedgwick ii. 525.

Page 116, note 7, line 8, *for* Maqkay *read* Mackay

Page 127, note 15, *add* For the distribution of the battalions see C. T. Atkinson, 'Jenkins' Ear, the Austrian Succession War, and the Forty-Five,' *Journal of the Society for Army Historical Research*, 1943–4, xxii. 294–5.

Page 135, 1st paragraph, line 12, *for pergno read perno* (Bagnani)

Page 139, note 17, line 6, *after* 1742 *insert* (see Hazen, *Cat. of HW's Lib.* No. 2146:5:1)

Page 145, note 1, line 1, *for* fl. 1740–50 *read* fl. 1697–1750

Page 159, note 6, line 1, *for* ca 1675 *read* ca 1684   *Right column, line 6, after* 879–80 *add*   ; Sedgwick ii. 106–7

Page 167, note 20, line 1, *for* 20 *read* 20.

Page 171, note 7, *reverse order of lines 10, 11, 12 to read* house. It is not certain that these ceremonies were performed by the Pope's order' (Mann to Newcastle 14 Dec. NS,

Page 175, note 23, line 1, *for* Jane Leighton *read* Jane Thorold   *Line 2, for* [?afterwards Gen. Francis] *read* [Daniel]   *Last line, add* see William Betham, *Baronetage*, 1801–5, iii. 99–100.

Page 175, note 26, line 1, *for* (d. 1780) *read* (1697–1780)   *Last line, add* See Sedgwick ii. 447.

Page 177, note 37, line 6, *for* governor of Nova Scotia *read* lieutenant-governor of Nova Scotia   *Lines 6–7, before* of Gibraltar *insert* governor *Line 8, after* i. 145 *add*   ; Sedgwick i. 581–2; CONWAY i. 215 and n. 14

Page 182, note 35, right column, line 8, *for* ca 1720 *read* 1721

Page 184, note 9, line 1, *for* Ilarionovich *read* Illarionovich   *Last line, add* See also D. A. Rovinskii, *Podrobryĭ slovar russkikh gravirovannysh porhetov*, St Petersburg, 1886–9, i. 132; *Arkhiv kniagia Voronstova*, 1870–98, xxxi. 83–404.

Page 204, 1st paragraph, line 14, *on* gone with him *add note* 14a: 14a. See Conway to HW 7 Feb. 1746 OS, CONWAY i. 216–17.

Pages 211, note 2, lines 1–2, *for* Sir James Gray seems to have witnessed the transaction (his letter *read* Sir James Gray's letter   *Line 4, for* 290–2). *read* 290–2, repeats this.

Page 213, line 15, *on* Odd man! *add note* 10a   *Line 16, on* partner *delete note* 10a

Page 213, note 10a, at beginning *insert* See 'Oddities, 1757' which is No. 69 in a series of prints entitled *A Political and Satyrical History of the Years 1756 and 1757*, [?1759] (BM, *Satiric Prints*, No. 3576; for HW's copy see Hazen, *Cat. of HW's Lib.* No. 361:3).

Page 214, note 12, at beginning *insert* Reports to this effect were in the

London Gazette Extraordinary 10 and 13 Feb. 1746; see Conway to HW 7 Feb. 1746 OS, CONWAY i. 218 and n. 19.

Page 220, note 19, lines 2–3, *for* Ulysses Maximilian (1705–57), Graf von Brown *read* Ulysses Maximilian Brown (1705–57), Graf von Camus   *Line 4, for hist read* hist.   *Line 5, after richten insert* 1747–8 1st ser. x. 9,

Page 221, note 2, last line, *after* OS *add*   , 17 Feb. OS according to the *Register Book of Marriages . . . Parish of St George, Hanover Square*, ed. J. H. Chapman and G. J. Armitage, 1886–97, i. 36 (Harleian Society Publications, vol. xi)

Page 226, note 14, *substitute* 'Whom Satan hath bound' (Luke 13. 16).

Page 233, 2d paragraph, line 2, *on* Conway *add note* 2a: 2a. HW is following the account in Conway to HW 19 March 1746 OS, CONWAY i. 229–30.

Page 235, note 3, *for Seaforth read Seaford*

Page 239, note 5, *add* HW's account seems to be following Conway's letter of 6 April 1746 OS, CONWAY i. 235–7.

Page 240, note 6, *add* See CONWAY i. 234, n. 1.

Page 241, note 16, line 4, *after* 1734–41 *insert*   , 1747–52   *for* 1741–52 *read* 1741–7

Page 243, note 30, line 8, *after* iii. 35 *add* (now in the Bodleian Library; see Hazen, *Cat. of HW's Lib*. No. 1441)

Page 244, note 2, line 3, *for Nachricten read Nachrichten*

Page 248, note 13, *add* Conway's letter of 18 April 1746 OS on the battle of Culloden does not mention that the Young Pretender was wounded (CONWAY i. 238–41).

Page 249, note 24, *add* These are among eight pamphlets about Winnington's death in a volume of HW's miscellaneous tracts, listed in Hazen, *Cat. of HW's Lib*. No. 1608:89.

Page 250, note 29, line 6, *for Winington read Winnington   Last line, after* above *add*   , and Hazen, *Cat. of HW's Lib*. No. 1608:89

Page 262, note 11, *add* There was a closer relation by marriage: the Princesse de Beauvau's half-brother (the Duc de Bouillon, 1706–71) was married (1724, as 2d husband) to the sister (Maria Carlotta Sobieska, 1697–1740) of the Old Pretender's wife (Maria Clementina Sobieska, 1702–35).

Page 265, note 12, line 1, *for Antigono read Antigone   Last line, add* See *London Stage* Part III, ii. 1242.

Page 275, line 2, *for* Placentia,[7] *read* Placentia,[6]

Page 275, line 3, *for* taken.[8] *read* taken.[7]

Page 277, note 1, line 1, *after Lowestoffe insert* [*Lowestoft*]   *Line 5, for privisions read* provisions

Page 279, note 13, *add* See also CONWAY i. 251–3.

Page 280, note 4, *add* For a discussion of trial by peers conducted by the Lord High Steward, see Sir William Holdsworth, *A History of English*

Law, rev. edn, 1966–72, i. 388–90; *Trial of Simon, Lord Lovat of the '45*, ed. D. N. Mackay, Edinburgh and Glasgow, 1911, pp. 307–8.

Page 287, note 58, *delete* perhaps Walter Forrester . . . (GM 1752, xxii. 93). *and substitute* probably Alexander Forrester (?1711–87), barrister of Lincoln's Inn, 1731; M.P. 1758–74 (see HW to Hertford 6 Feb. 1764, CONWAY ii. 309, n. 26; Namier and Brooke ii. 451–3).

Page 287, note 59, line 1, *for* ca 1695 *read* ?1695   *Last line, add* See also Sedgwick ii. 538.

Page 292, 2d paragraph, line 1, *for* endeavoring *read* endeavouring

Page 292, note 19, *add* See *post* 30 Aug. 1746 NS (MANN iii. 297).

Page 293, note 3, right column, line 4, *for* xxv. 71 *read* l. 71

Page 298, note 5, line 1, *for* Han *read* Han-

Page 299, note 5a, *add* Slingsby Bethell (1695–1758), M.P. London 1747–58 (Sedgwick i. 460–1).

Page 309, note 15, right column, line 4, *for* 1078 *read* 1081   *Line 5, for* Cleveland *read* Cleaveland   *Line 14, after* ii. 157) *add*   ; both of these books are now WSL (see Hazen, *Cat. of HW's Lib.* Nos 589, 895)

Page 313, note 26, lines 3–4, *for* under Captain Strange *read*   ; the squadron was commanded by Captain Edmund Strange (d. 1756)

Page 318, note 5, line 3, *for* 43d Foot *read* 11th Foot   *Last line, add* For Brig.-Gen. William Graham see Richard Cannon, *Historical Record of the Eleventh . . . Foot*, 1845, pp. 34–5; *Court and City Register*, 1748, p. 142; Graham resigned the 43d Foot in Feb. 1746 (Robert Beatson, *Political Index to the Histories of Great Britain and Ireland . . .* , 1806, ii. 237).

Page 324, note 31, line 1, *for* (d. 1751) *read* (ca 1687–1751)   *Last line, add* See Sedgwick i. 578.

Page 330, 2d paragraph, line 1, *for* orange flower *read* orange-flower

Page 340, note 2, line 7, *after* Fontenoy *insert* [Laeffeld]   *Last line, add* See also Hist. MSS Comm., *Frankland-Russell-Astley MSS*, 1900, p. 372; CONWAY i. 277, n. 5.

Page 342, note 16, *add* See Sedgwick i. 358–9.

Page 342, note 19, line 2, *for* (d. 1763) *read* (ca 1698–1763)   *Last line, after* p. 248 *add*   ; Sedgwick ii. 91

Page 342, note 21, line 1, *before* John *insert* London Stage Part III, ii. 1269;

Page 342, note 25, *for* ibid. *substitute* London Stage Part III, ii. 1269; Genest, op. cit.

Page 342, note 26, line 3, *after* ibid. *add*   ; *London Stage* Part III, ii. 1253, 1263–6

Page 351, note 26, line 8, *for* MSS. *read* MSS

Page 355, note 13, line 2, *for* 1703 *read* 1704   *Last line, add* See also *Enciclopedia dello spettacolo*, Rome, 1954–62, vi. 1372.

Page 358, note 31, line 1, *for* (d. 1747) *read* (1699–1747)   *Last line, add* See also J. C. Strodtman, *Neue Gelehrte Europa*, 1754, v. 6.

Page 361, note 5, line 5, *after* year *add*   , but had been raised to £100,000 in 1742   *Last line, add* See also Romney Sedgwick in *English Historical Review*, April 1956, lxxi. 301.

Page 362, note 13, line 4, *for* (ca 1718–75) *read* (1717–75)   *Last line, add* See also Sedgwick i. 572–3.

Page 366, note 3, *after* Langlois *insert*   , possibly of Clifford Street, Burlington Gardens, who d. 19 Jan. 1790 (GM 1790, lx pt i. 90)

Page 370, note 7, *add* He is probably the one who d. 1751 (see Sir Charles Hanbury Williams to his daughters 28 March 1751 NS, Williams's MSS, lxxxi. f. 83: 'I hear (but I hope tis not true) that Reginelli died as soon as he came to England').

Page 371, note 18, line 1, *for* b. 10 Feb. *read* b. 13 Feb.   *Line 4, for* annotated *read* extra-illustrated   *after* WSL; *insert Registers of St George, Hanover Square*, photo-copy of transcript sent by the vicar;

Page 379, note 2, *add* See also *Trial of Simon, Lord Lovat of the '45*, ed. David N. Mackay, Edinburgh and Glasgow, 1911.

Pages 387–8, note 14, *add* See BM, *Satiric Prints*, No. 2857, 'The Spy.'

Page 388, note 18, *add* See also Sedgwick i. 528–9, 574.

Page 397, note 19, *add* See Fox to Sir Charles Hanbury Williams 1 May 1747 OS, Williams's MSS, lii. f. 3: 'The ball is to be at Holland House tonight. 54 people to set down to supper.'

Page 397, note 23, line 2, *for* E. of Holland *read* E. Holland

Page 402, note 2, lines 3–4, *for* 10 of which *read* of which 10

Page 404, note 14, *for* Teissoniére *read* Teissonière

Page 410, note 16, line 1, *for* (1703–52) *read* (ca 1703–52)   *Last line, add* See also Sedgwick ii. 522–3.

Page 413, note 9, lines 4–5 from end, *for* Wortley Montagu jun. defeated Sandwich's brother, William *read* Wortley Montagu jun. was returned unopposed   *Last line, add* See also Sedgwick i. 263–4, ii. 554–5.

Page 413, note 10, *add* See also Sedgwick ii. 510–13.

Page 414, note 11, last line, *after* 114 *add*   ; Sedgwick i. 290

Page 414, note 12, last line, *add* See also Sedgwick i. 207.

Page 419, line 3, *on* Mrs Horton *add note* 7a: 7a. Christiana Horton (*London Stage* Part III, i. p. ccxiii).

Page 419, line 3, *on* Rich *add note* 8a: 8a. John Rich (1691 *or* 92–1761) (*Enciclopedia dello spettacolo*, Rome, 1954–62, viii. 949–51).

Page 419, note 11, *add* See also Fox to Sir Charles Hanbury Williams 19 June 1747 OS, Williams's MSS, lii. ff. 5–7.

Page 420, note 21, *add* See also Sedgwick i. 248, ii. 534–5.

Page 420, note 23, line 3, *after* 103 *add*   ; Sedgwick i. 314, 500–3

Page 420, note 24, line 2, *for* ibid. *read* GRAY   *Line 3, after* 232) *insert* for '23.0.0. It is worth four times the money' (HW's annotated *Des. of SH*, 1774, p. 69).

Page 421, note 2, *add* See also Sedgwick i. 291, ii. 142.

Page 425, note 16, 4th line from end, *for* 3d Bt *read* 4th Bt   *Last line,* *after* 101 *add*   ; Sedgwick i. 284–7, 448, ii. 211, 428–9

Page 425, note 17, last line, *for* ibid. *read* Sedgwick i. 280, 283

Page 425, note 1, *for* NS *read* OS

Page 428, note 21, *substitute* Giulio Cesare Barberini Colonna di Sciarra (1702–87), Principe di Palestrina e di Carbognano, whose wife was heiress to the last Barberini prince (Litta, *sub* Colonna di Roma, tav. x).

Page 428, note 22, *substitute* Marcantonio (1724–96), Principe Colonna, Principe di Stigliano e d'Aliano (Litta, *sub* Colonna di Roma, tav. xv).

Page 437, note 10, *add* See also Alden Murray, 'The Court and the Cuccagna,' *The Metropolitan Museum of Art Bulletin*, 1959–60, xviii. 157–67, which reproduces some engravings showing the festival decorations by Vincenzo Re from *Narrazione delle solenni reali feste fatte celebrare in Napoli da Sua Maesta il Re delle Due Sicilie Carlo Infante di Spagna Duca di Parma, Piacenza &c. &c. per la Nascita del suo primogenito Filippo Real Principe delle Due Sicilie*, 1748.

Page 438, note 13, *substitute* Giovanna Astrua (1730–57), Italian soprano, sang at the principal Italian theatres (Venice, 1739, Naples 1741–6, also Milan) until she went to sing at the court of Berlin 1747–56; see *Dizionario biografico degli italiani*, Rome, 1962– , iv. 494; *Enciclopedia dello spettacolo*, Rome, 1954–62, i. 1040. Sir Charles Hanbury Williams in a letter to his daughter Fanny 29 Dec. 1750 NS mentions hearing her sing in Berlin in 1750 (Williams's MSS, lxxxi, f. 67): 'Signora Austrua is the best woman I ever heard upon any stage. She has a fine clear strong voice with the greatest volubility in her throat. And is besides a good actress.'

Page 438, note 13a, *add* Professor Gilbert Bagnani points out that 'picirillo' is Neapolitan dialect.

Page 438, note 15, *substitute* 'I advise you, daughter, to suck up to the first, because from the second you can have little to hope for' (Bagnani).

Page 440, note 10, lines 4–5, *for Museum, Political read Museum, . . . Political*   *Line 5, for* 1870– *read* 1870–1954

Page 450, note 13, lines 6–7, *for* (b. before 1705, d. after 1777) *read* (ca 1708–80)   *Line 8, before Members insert* Sedgwick ii. 460–1;   *Last 8 lines, delete* HW thought that they were imprisoned . . . DEFFAND iv. 134, n. 3) *and substitute* They were arrested 31 Oct. 1751 NS; Montagu was imprisoned at the Châtelet and Taaffe at the Fort l'Évêque, (*Daily Adv.* 12 Nov. 1751 OS; Taaffe to Albemarle 2 Nov. 1751 NS, dated from Fort l'Évêque, BM Add. MSS 32,831, ff. 667). See HW to Mann 22 Nov. 1751 OS, MANN iv. 287–8 and nn. 13–20.

Page 450, note 14, next to last line, *after* did not *insert* again   *Last line, add* See also Sedgwick ii. 269–70.

Page 456, note 8, line 1, *for* Sinclair (d. 1762) *read* Sinclair (*or* St Clair) (1688–1762)   *Last line, add* See Sedgwick i. 394–5, 398, ii. 402–3.

Page 459, note 11, *add* See Hazen, *Cat. of HW's Lib.* No. 1497.

Page 465, note 13, last line, *after* WSL *add* (Hazen, *Cat. of HW's Lib.* No. 1818:9:3)

Page 465, note 17, *add* See *London Stage* Part IV, i. 30.

Page 465, note 18, line 1, *after* Churchill *insert* , b. 15 Feb. (*Registers of St George, Hanover Square*, photo-copy of transcript sent by the vicar)

Page 466, note 5, *add* Professor Gilbert Bagnani suggests the translation, 'To draw up or engross despatches.'

Page 467, note 9, lines 4, 5, *delete* -Craon

Page 468, note 13, *add* The words must relate to Lady Henrietta's second marriage to Beard, the singer and actor; see HW to Mann 8 April 1785, MANN ix. 571, n. 6.

Page 469, note 20, line 1, *before* His *insert* See *London Stage* Part IV, i. 30, 34.

Page 469, note 23, *add* The peerage was not secured.

Page 471, note 33, line 2, *for* 1754–60 *read* 1754–61   *Line 3, add* See also Sedgwick ii. 540.

Pages 472–3, note 5, last line, *for* 1763–72 *read* 1763–75 (Namier and Brooke ii. 616)

Page 475, note 9, line 1, *for* (b. ca 1718) *read* (1717–92)

Page 475, note 10, lines 1–2, *for* b. ca 1727 *read* 1726–97   *Line 3, add* See also *Europaïsches genealogisches Handbuch*, ed. C. F. Jacobi, Leipzig, 1800, pt i. 557, 565–6.

Page 476, note 13, *for* 'Stink of nobility.' *read* 'She stinks of nobility' (Bagnani).

Page 477, note 4, line 3, *after* 501) *add* ; or possibly Anne Richbell, m. Samuel Strode of Ponsbourne, 'a Leadenhall Street broker, who acted for the South Sea Company'; she was mother of William Strode (ca 1712–55), M.P. (Sedgwick ii. 454).

Page 486, note 1, last line, *after* Paris, 1665 *add* ; see Hazen, *Cat. of HW's Lib.* No. 907

Page 487, note 3, line 2, *after* (NBG). *insert* For HW's copy see Hazen, *Cat. of HW's Lib.* No. 2074.

Page 493, note 11, *for* 'Behold your bishop' *read* 'Here's your bishop' (Bagnani)

Page 493, note 16, *for* 'financieri' *read* 'finanzieri' (Bagnani)

Page 494, note 6, *add* See also HW to Conway 12 Feb. 1756, CONWAY i. 439.

Page 500, note 2, *substitute* Not identified.

Page 506, note 4, line 2, *for* Torrigiani *read* Torreggiani *or* Torrigiani

Page 506, note 5, lines 1, 2, *for* Torrigiani *read* Torreggiani *or* Torrigiani

Page 507, note 9, line 1, *for* Robert Wolters *read* Dirk ('Richard') Wolters (1713–71)   *Right column, line 2, after* passim). *insert* See Frank

Spencer, *The Fourth Earl of Sandwich*, Manchester, 1961, pp. 105–6 and sources cited.

Page 510, note 3, last line, *after* WSL *add* (Hazen, *Cat. of HW's Lib*. No. 1608:42:4; HW also had a copy of the 2d edn, 1755, ibid. No. 401)

Page 511, note 11, lines 6–7, *for* 1730–2 *read* 1714–31   *Line 8, for* 1732–48 *read* 1731–48   *Last line, add* See Sedgwick ii. 505.

VOLUME 20

Page 4, note 10, *add* See *London Stage* Part IV, i. 73, 78.

Page 4, note 15, *add* The *London Stage* Part IV, i. 73, lists Angelica Saiz, Anna Laschi, Caterina Pertici, Signora Giustina Amoretti.

Page 5, note 20, *add* See Sedgwick ii. 159–60.

Page 5, note 23, line 3, *for* 1746–8 *read* 1745–8   *Line 4, for* the Prince *read* Frederick, Prince   *Line 6, for* the dowager Princess *read* George, Prince   *Last line, after* 1771–8 *add* (Sedgwick i. 446)

Page 7, 2d paragraph, line 4, *for* likly *read* likely

Page 9, note 7, line 2, *after* O'Dunne *add* (b. 1714, d. *post* 1789)   *Line 5, after* n. 9; *add* Richard Hayes, *Biographical Dictionary of Irishmen in France*, Dublin, 1949, pp. 77–8;

Page 10, note 15, line 1, *after* Finch *add* [1693–1773]   *Line 7, after* (HW). *add* See Pearl Finch, *History of Burley-on-the-Hill, Rutland*, 1901, i. 240.

Page 11, note 23, right column, lines 1–2, *for* (ca 1667–1772) *read* (1667–1722)

Page 13, note 33, line 1, *for* Levis *read* Lévis   *Line 2, for* ca 1699 *read* 1699   *Line 6, for* 1749–52 *read* 1749–55

Page 19, note 20, *add* See Sedgwick i. 224, ii. 384.

Page 20, note 33, line 1, *for* 1718 *read* 1719   *Line 3, for* Vice-Adm., 1763 *read* Vice-Adm., 1762   *Line 5, for* 1762–8 *read* 1761–8   *Last line, add* See Sedgwick ii. 389–90.

Page 22, note 3, *substitute* Maria Teresa Francesca Vestris (1726–1808), called Teresina; dancer. Of Florentine origin, she was banished from Vienna by Maria Theresa for her liaison with Comte Eszterházy and for flirting with the Emperor. Before settling in Paris in 1746, she spent eighteen months at Florence, where she became the mistress of the Marchese Riccardi. Her meagre income as a danseuse, and from occasional allowances from Comte Eszterházy, was supplemented by 'un sieur de Walpole' (Gaston Capon, *Les Vestris*, 1908, pp. 6–11, *passim*; *Enciclopedia dello spettacolo*, Rome, 1954–62, ix. 1626).

Page 22, note 4, *add* The Vestris family had spent some time at Venice (Capon, op. cit. 8).

Page 31, note 10, *add* See Sedgwick i. 260, ii. 339–40.

Page 32, note 13, line 1, *for* Smith-Stanley *read* Smith Stanley   *Lines*

3–5, for M.P. Lancaster . . . of the county of Lancaster. *read* M.P. Lancashire 1741–71, lord lieutenant of Lancaster county 1757–71, and chancellor of the duchy of Lancaster 1762–71.

Page 33, note 16, line 6, *for* (d. 1751) *read* (1686–1751)   *Last line, add* See Sedgwick ii. 233–4.

Page 38, note 4, line 1, *for* 1710 *read* ca 1702

Page 39, note 11, *add* See Sedgwick i. 502.

Page 39, note 16, *add* See Sedgwick ii. 491.

Page 39, note 17, line 1, *for* (d. 1765) *read* (ca 1696–1765)

Page 40, note 17, *add* See Sedgwick ii. 152–3.

Page 40, note 18, line 4, *for* Shoreham *read* New Shoreham   *after* loc. cit. *add*   ; Sedgwick ii. 409

Page 41, note 32, lines 2–4, *for* (Sir George Grove . . . iii. 832). *read* (*The New Grove Dictionary of Music and Musicians*, 6th edn, ed. Stanley Sadie, 1980, vii. 764–5).

Page 49, note 18, last line, *after* 486, n. 1 *add*   ; Hazen, *Cat. of HW's Lib*. No. 907

Page 49, note 19, *add* See *London Stage* Part IV, i. 116.

Page 57, note 6, *add* See *London Stage* Part IV, i. 120.

Page 63, note 51, line 4, *for* 1708–12 *read* 1708–13, 1714–17, 1728–65 (GM 1765, xxxv. 491; Collins, *Peerage*, 1812, ii. 175; DNB).

Page 65, note 16, *substitute* This seems to be an allusion to the passage on Dodington's 'patriot sentiments' in Mann's letter of 23 May 1749 NS (*ante* MANN iv. 54–5); see also HW to Mann 27 Oct. 1749 OS (*post* MANN iv. 96).

Page 72, note 9, lines 2 and 3, *for* Anspach *read* Ansbach

Page 73, note 18, *substitute* There were two ceremonies of investiture. On Thursday 22 June 'His Majesty held a chapter of the most noble order of the Garter, in his palace at Kensington, when he was pleased to present the 6 vacant blue garters' (GM 1749, xix. 284). In a letter dated 'Whitehall Sunday 4 o'clock' (25 June 1749 OS) Abp Stone wrote to Newcastle, 'I believe, that you will be very glad to know, that Prince George was this morning invested with the Ensigns of The Order by his Majesty Himself in his Closet' (BM Add. MSS 32,719, f. 357). See *Daily Adv.* 23, 30 June OS.

Page 78, note 19, *for* ca 1718 *read* 1718

Page 80, note 13, line 1, *for* 1689 *read* ca 1689

Page 86, note 1, line 3, *for* Thienne *read* Thieme

Page 86, note 6, *for last sentence read* He was the first male singer at the opera in London for the 1760–1 and 1761–2 seasons (*London Stage* Part IV, ii. 810, 884; CONWAY ii. 87, 466).

Page 88, note 8, line 1, *for* 1681 *read* 1688

Page 90, note 6, line 1, *after* Nay *add* (d. 1789)   *Line 2, after* xiv. 881 *add*   ; *Gazzetta Toscana*, 1789, xxiv. 146–7

Page 92, note 5, line 1, *for* 1798 *read* 1698

Page 103, note 15, line 1, *for* Ann *read* Anne   *Line 2, for* 1744 *read* 1745   *Last line, add* See also Sedgwick ii. 135.

Page 108, note 12, line 1, *for* 1710 *read* 1712

Page 108, note 17, line 1, *for* ca 1673 *read* 1673

Page 108, note 19, line 5, *for* (d. 1758) *read* (ca 1696–1758)   *Line 7, for* 1745 *read* 1744

Page 109, note 19, line 2, *after* 119 *add*   ; Sedgwick i. 421

Page 110, 2d paragraph, line 3, *on* snuff-box *add note* 30a: 30a. 'An amber snuff-box studded and mounted with gold' (GM 1804, lxxiv pt i. 84); the anecdote is related in full in ibid. 1771, xli. 119.

Page 113, note 12, last line, *after* 99 *add*   ; Sedgwick i. 213, ii. 277–8

Page 120, note 11, line 2, *for* breech *read* breach

Page 121, line 2, *for* practicing *read* practising

Page 121, note 20, line 1, *for* Leveson-Gower *read* Leveson Gower   *for* 1723 *read* 1724   *Last line, after* 1763 *add* (Ossory i. 275, n. 1)

Page 124, note 35, line 1, *for* Leveson-Gower *read* Leveson Gower *Last line, after* 256 *add*   ; Sedgwick ii. 212

Page 126, note 51, *add* See also Mason i. 315.

Page 127, note 54, *add* For another definition of this word see Chute 359, n. 6.

Page 136, note 31, *substitute* Perhaps John Lloyd (?1717–55), M.P. Cardiganshire 1747–55 (Conway i. 397); he was not made K.B.

Page 138, 3d paragraph, line 7, *delete* [the]

Page 139, note 51, *add* Two copies of HW's note quoting from Vincent's Baronage, in HW's hand, are now wsl.

Page 140, 1st paragraph, line 6, *on* Vane *add note* 62a: 62a. I.e., the 2d Earl of Darlington, not his father; see Conway i. 359 and n. 10.

Page 141, note 69, line 2, *for* Hon *read* Hon.

Page 145, note 14, line 1, *for* Garney *read* Garnier (1703–63)   *Line 2, for* Daily *Adv.* 24 April 1741 OS *read* see Selwyn 321, n. 122

Page 145, note 15, line 1, *for* 1722 *read* ?1721   *Lines 5–6, for* Sir Lewis Namier's Parliamentary List *read* Namier and Brooke iii. 443

Page 156, note 13, line 2, *after* Col. *add*   , 1748   *Last line, after* 367 *add* Sedgwick ii. 505.

Page 156, note 15, line 1, *for* ca 1718 *read* ?1717   *Last line, add* See also Namier and Brooke iii. 223.

Page 166, note 8, line 2, *for* 1604 *read* 1603

Page 172, note 7, line 2, *for* 1727 *read* 1722   *Line 3 after* 41; *add* Hastings 1741–61;   *Line 4, for* ?1721 *read* ca 1720   *Line 6, for* ?1729 *read* 1728   *Last line, after* p. 257 *add*   ; Sedgwick ii. 332

Page 172, note 9, line 1, *for* (ca 1726–49) *read* (ca 1726–8 Aug. 1749)

Page 174, note 20, line 4, *before* DNB *insert* see John Fleming, 'Lord Brudenell and his Bear-Leader,' *English Miscellany*, ed. Mario Praz, Rome, 1958, p. 134;

Page 182, note 23, line 4, *for* E. of Holland *read* E. Holland

Page 182, note 24, last line, *for* Earls of Holland *read* Earls Holland

Page 187, note 11, *substitute* Doll houses (G. B. Hughes, 'Two Centuries of Dolls' Houses,' *Country Life* 1 Dec. 1960, cxxviii. 1288–94; OED *sub* Baby).

Page 194, note 2, lines 1–2, *for* ca 1715 *read* ?1714   *Line 3, for* 1762 *read* 1761   *Last line, add* These were probably scagliola tables (see John Fleming, 'The Hugfords of Florence (Part I),' *Connoisseur*, 1955, cxxxvi. 106–10).

Page 203, note 35, line 3, *for* m. 1 —— *read* m. 1 Alessandro

Page 209, note 20, line 2, *for* Belleisle *read* Bellisle

Page 209, note 23, *add* See also *London Stage* Part IV, i. 215.

Page 209, note 25, line 7, *for* 1742–7 *read* 1742–6   *Last line, after* 108 *add*   ; Namier and Brooke iii. 143–4

Page 212, note 6, *add* Her mother, Mrs James Marriot, was also named Anne (information from Miss Hedley at Windsor).

Page 212, note 8, lines 10–14, *delete* Verrio must have painted . . . at Windsor Castle *and substitute* Verrio may have painted a Mrs Marriot (d. ?1714) who was pensioned from 1697, but who had no connection with Windsor; she had a minor job at Hampton Court (Establishment Book 13, in the Royal Library, Windsor; Warrant, 28 April 1724, L.C.3.63, p. 338, in the Public Record Office

Page 221, note 20, line 9, *for* anta *read* ants

Page 223, note 15, line 1, *for* ca 1709 *read* ca 1705   *Last line, after* 158 *add*   ; Namier and Brooke ii. 249

Page 224, note 21, line 1, *after* Crowle *insert* (1699–1757)   *Line 2, delete* presumably ca 1700–57,   *Line 3, after* 165 *add* Namier and Brooke ii. 279–80

Page 224, note 26, line 1, *for* ca 1696 *read* ca 1695   *Line 3, after* 220 *add*   ; Sedgwick ii. 103–4

Page 226, note 40, line 5, *for* 1716–17 *read* 1716–18   *Last line, after* Wortley *add*   ; Sedgwick ii. 554–6

Page 227, note 7, line 3, *for* d'Étioles *read* d'Étiolles

Page 229, note 4, line 1, *for* (d. 1765) *read* (1710–65)   *Line 6, after* 135 *add*   ; see also Sedgwick ii. 13–14, 402–3   *Last line, add* Cunningham's note on Erskine (ii. 242) says: 'Sir Harry Erskine, called by Walpole a military poet, and a creature of Bute's.' Following this note, H. M. Chichester in the DNB article on Erskine says: 'Horace Walpole sneers at him as a military poet and a creature of Bute's.' These comments refer to the passage in *Mem. Geo. II* i. 41–3.

Page 230, note 6, *add* There is a brief account of Porteous's death in BM Add. MSS 33,049, ff. 17–19.

Page 230, note 7, *add* See also Sedgwick i. 418.

Page 230, note 9, *add* See also *London Stage* Part IV, i. 240–1.

Page 232, note 7, *add* Pennell Hawkins was appointed 'one of his Majesty's principal and sergeant surgeons' and his son, George Edward, 'surgeon of his Majesty's household in ordinary' (*London Gazette* No. 11632, 16–20 Jan. 1776).

Page 245, note 5, *add* See also *Mem. Geo. II* i. 96–7.

Page 245, note 6, line 2, *for* 1735–41 *read* 1731–43   Line 3, *for* ?1741– 51 *read* 1743–51   Line 5, *delete* apparently   Line 12, *after* 124 *add* ; Sedgwick i. 469

Page 245, note 7, last line, *after* 101 *add* ; from 1760–72 he is listed as commissioner of the Horse

Page 246, note 9, *substitute* Harcourt became governor to the Prince, and the Bishop of Norwich preceptor; see HW's *Mem. Geo. II* i. 86–7; John Brooke, *King George III*, 1972, pp. 28–9.

Page 246, note 12, *for* Louis *read* Lewis

Page 247, note 20, last line, *for* 1792 *read* 1791

Page 247, note 25, line 1, *for* Cressett *read* Cresset   Line 3, *for* 1751– 72 *read* 1746–8, joint secretary 1748–51, and again sole secretary 1751–72 *before Court insert* Household records in the Royal Archives, information from John Brooke;

Page 261, note 31, *add* 'We hear that Samson Gideon, Esq. has purchased all the pictures at Houghton Hall, to furnish his new-purchased seat, late Lord Baltimore's, in Kent' (*Daily Adv.* 13 March 1752).

Page 265, note 2, *add* See Conway i. 307, n. 2, 316, n. 1, 324.

Page 265, note 3, line 2, *after* 7 Feb. *add* 1750

Page 271, note 3, *add* Kilmorey returned in late June 1753 (Mann to Holdernesse 29 June 1753, S.P. 98/59, f. 61).

Page 273, note 9, line 3, *delete post*   Line 4, *after passim add* ; Conway iii. 89, n. 14

Page 274, note 3, line 1, *for* Thomas *read* George

Page 274, note 6, line 4, *after* 1751 NS *add* , Conway i. 310–12

Page 280, note 6, last line, *for* perhaps the *Triton read* the *Nightingale*

Page 283, note 28, *add* wsl has a copy of the *Letters of Lady Rachel Russell*, 1773, containing a MS note by George Onslow, 1st E. of Onslow (1731–1814). On p. 189 the text of the footnote reads: 'In 1670, John Lord Roos, (or Ross, afterwards Earl and Duke of Rutland) who had married Lady Anne Pierpoint, . . . by whom he had two sons, having brought proofs of adultery against her, and obtained a sentence of divorce in the spiritual court. . . .' The MS note reads: 'See the Account of this affair in Clarendon's Continuation—Page 736 (Octavo Edition). *He* mentions only *one* Son.—He lived many years and Mr H. Walpole lately told me (and said he had it from my Father) that he, my Father, was once accidentally put into a room with this son (who was called Mr Manners) and took him for the Duke of Rutland; so strong was the resemblance between them. G. O. 1773.' For HW's copies of Clarendon's *Life* see Hazen, *Cat. of HW's Lib.* Nos 2, 4000; in the copy now wsl HW made no annotation on the passage about Lady Anne Pierrepont (pp. 386–9). In HW's MS notes on Lord Clarendon's *Life* and *Continuation* (BM Add. MSS 37,728) there is no reference to the story HW told George Onslow. See also MASON i. 85–6.

Page 284, note 2, *add* It is more likely to have been Marchese Orazio Roberto Pucci (1730–1802), nephew of HW's friend Mme Pucci (Litta, *sub* Pucci, table viii; CONWAY i. 323–4 and n. 13).

Page 284–5, note 7, *add* He was removed from the *Triton* to the *Nightingale* between 18 June and 18 Nov. 1749 and remained in command of it until 27 Sept. 1750 (see CONWAY i. 314, n. 4).

Page 288, note 15, line 1, *after* Payba *insert* (d. ?1776),   *Line 2, after* broker *add* (GM 1776, xlvi. 580; *Lady's Magazine*, 1777, viii. 55)

Page 293, note 5, last line, *for* 3 Dec. *read* 30 Dec.

Page 294, note 9, line 2, *for* 1754–81 *read* 1746–81   *Line 4, after* 1136–7 *add*   ; P. B. Gams, *Series episcoporum*, Ratisbon, 1873, p. 597; Gaetano Moroni, *Dizionario di erudizione storico-ecclesiastica*, Venice, 1840–79, li. 206

Page 302, note 3, last line, *for* must *read* may   *after* earlier. *add* His will was presented (and the handwriting of the codicil verified) on 13 March, and was proved on 18 March.

Page 302, note 8, last line, *after* 14 *add*   ; *Metropolitan Museum of Art Bulletin*, Feb. 1963, xxi. 202–13

Page 307, note 3, last line, *for* Feb. 1752 NS *read* Feb. 1752 OS

Page 311, note 14, line 4, *for* 1754–67 *read* 1741–68   *Line 5, after* 169 *add*   ; Namier and Brooke iii. 163–4

Page 313, 1st paragraph, line 7, *for* it is much *read* it as much

Page 313, note 3, *add* Mann recommended 'le sieur Astley' to Cardinal Albani 21 Feb. 1750, S.P. 105/309, f. 190.

Page 315, note 1, line 2, *for* 1752 *read* 1759

Page 315, note 8, line 1, *for* Cunninghame *read* Cuninghame   *for* (d. 1801) *read* (ca 1728–1801)   *Line 7, after* England) *add* (Namier and Brooke ii. 284–5)

Page 316, note 11, line 1, *for* 1686 *read* 1683

Page 317, note 20, line 1, *for* 1749 *read* 1748

Page 321, note 3, line 2, *after* 68 *add*   ; Cambridge University 1768–70

Page 327, note 5, *substitute* Probably Capt. Marriot Arbuthnot's wife, who was in Italy in Sept. 1751; see Conway to HW 26 Sept. 1751 NS, CONWAY i. 314 and n. 4.

Page 328, note 11, lines 2–3, *for* paymaster of the forces *read* commissary general of musters   *Last line, after* 126 *add*   ; Namier and Brooke ii. 108

Page 328, note 19, *substitute* Another name for Raphael's 'Council of the Gods' at the Villa Farnesina, Rome.

Page 328, note 20, *substitute* Another name for Raphael's 'Supper of the Gods' at the Villa Farnesina, Rome.

Page 331, note 11, line 5, *for* 2d D. *read* 7th D.

Page 333, note 21, *add* For the Young Pretender's visit to England in 1750, see Edward King, *Political and Literary Anecdotes of his Own Time*,

2d edn, 1819, pp. 196–202; Lady Shelburne's diary, 28 Feb. 1766, in Fitz-maurice, *Life of . . . Shelburne*, 2d edn, 1912, i. 272 and n. 1.

Page 338, line 16, *on* fête *add note* 8a: 8a. This is the earliest use of 'fête' listed in OED.

Page 338, note 8, line 1, *for* ca 1722 *read* 1722   *Line 2, after* Calais *add* (MONTAGU i. 172–3 and n. 3; CHUTE 208–9 and n. 10)

Page 344, note 9, line 1, *for* 1644 *read* 1641   *Line 3, for* 1692–4 *read* 1689–94 *and add* (*Dictionnaire de biographie française*, 1933– , xi. 591). HW's copy of his *Histoire des révolutions d'Espagne*, 1734, is Hazen, *Cat. of HW's Lib*. No. 3358.

Page 349, note 2, lines 1–2, *for* Esterházy *read* Eszterházy

Page 352, line 24, *on* crowns *add note* 17a: 17a. Mann wrote to Hoare the banker 6 Sept. 1754 that he had drawn upon him for £200 for North-umberland (S.P. 105/291, f. 44).

Page 358, 2d paragraph, line 5, *for* acadamies *read* academies

Page 359, note 14, line 2, *for* Reusz *read* Reuss

Page 359, note 14, line 7, *after* Adolph *add* [Nikolaus Ludwig (1700–60)]

Page 360, note 3, *add* The Council met 15–26 Feb. according to the 'Minutes of the Committee of Council,' 15–26 Feb. 1753, BM Add. MSS 33,050, ff. 200–360. A copy of Walpole's anonymous 'Memorial of Several Noblemen and Gentlemen of the First Rank and Fortunes' (Dec. 1752) was submitted to the Council (ibid. f. 363).

Page 369, note 6, *for* 'A—saunter.' *read* 'A-saunter.'

Page 370, note 12, line 1, *before* Karl *insert* Christian Friedrich   *Lines 2–3, for* Anspach *read* Ansbach

Page 375, note 7, line 1, *for* a letter of *read* letters of 8 and   *Line 2, delete* which

Page 376, note 12, line 1, *before* Karl *insert* Christian Friedrich   *Line 2, for* Anspach *read* Ansbach

Page 376, note 17, line 2, *for* (d. 1760) *read* (ca 1724–60)   *Line 3, for* (d. 1785) *read* (1719–85)   *Line 8, after* 156 *add* H. Owen and J. B. Blakeway, *History of Shrewsbury*, 1825, ii. 141

Page 378, 1st paragraph, line 14, *on* woman *add note* 3a: 3a. Lady Howe (*post* 31 May 1775).

Page 378, note 2, line 4, *for* 53–6 *read* 154–5

Page 381, note 12, *add* See OSSORY i. 294, ii. 273.

Page 381, note 13, *add* Since the *Des. of SH* (*Works* ii. 436) describes the Red Bedchamber as 'Hung with crimson paper,' it seems that the prints here mentioned were covered over in 1771, when HW '. . . paid Bromwich for papering some rooms' (*SH Accounts*, ed. Paget Toynbee, Oxford, 1927, pp. 12, 66).

Page 385, note 5, *add* (*ante* MANN iv. 274)

Page 393, 1st paragraph, line 3, *on* Uguccioni *add note* 14a: 14a. He had been her lover (Conti, *Firenze dopo i Medici* 457; see *ante* 20 June 1742 NS, MANN i. 448).

Page 406, note 12, line 2, *for* Urban I's *read* Urban II's
Page 407, note 2, line 1, *for isegne read insegne*
Page 408, note 11, line 6, *for* 255–6 *read* 265–6
Page 410, note 23, *after* 1753 *add*   , CHUTE 160; *London Stage* Part IV, i. 397–8
Page 410, note 24, line 2, *for* Niccotina or Nicolina *read* Nicolina Giordani   *Line 3, for* an Italian burletta (Henry *read Gli amanti gelosi* by Giuseppe Giordani and Gioacchino Cocchi (ca 1715–1804) (*Enciclopedia dello spettacolo*, Rome, 1954–62, iii. 1006–7, v. 1309; *The New Grove Dictionary of Music and Musicians*, 6th edn, ed. Stanley Sadie, 1980, vii. 393; Henry
Page 418, note 10, lines 3–4, *for* left several *read* had seven   *Line 5, after* 483, n. *add*   ; Sedgwick ii. 241–2
Page 418, note 11, *for* An *read* 'An
Page 441, note 1, line 1, *for* ca 1721 *read* ca 1720   *Line 5, for* 61 *read* 68   *Line 6, after* 274 *add*   ; Namier and Brooke iii. 123
Page 442, note 9, *for* del Monti *read* del Monte
Page 443, note 1, line 4, *for* Hagley *read* Ragley
Page 449, note 7, line 4, *after* p. 112 *add* (now printed in CHUTE Appendix 1 and 2, pp. 639–42)
Page 451, note 3, line 1, *for* Louise-Charlotte *read* —— *delete* (1729–57)   *Lines 6–7, delete Archivio storico italiano* 1877, 3d ser. xxv. 243;
Page 454, note 11, line 2, *for* ed *read* ed.
Page 466, note 8, *add* See also Giuseppe Bencivenni Pelli, *Saggio istorico della Real Galleria di Firenze*, Florence, 1779.
Page 470, note 12, *add* Poulett applied for Essex's offices in a letter to Newcastle 9 Feb. 1748 (BM Add. MSS 32,714, f. 198).
Page 476, lines 21–2, *on* daughter *add note* 3a: 3a. Louise-Charlotte de Nay (1729–57), m. Conte Francesco di Thurn (*Archivio storico italiano,* 1877, 3d ser., xxv. 243n).
Page 480, note 2, line 1, *for* Macnemara *read* MacNamara   *Line 5, after post add* 15 July 1755, n. 8;
Page 483, note 8, *add* See also CHUTE 230, n. 16.
Page 483, note 9, line 9, *for* Macnemara *read* MacNamara
Page 490, To Mann 21 Aug. 1755, 1st paragraph, line 2, *for* Lady O[ford] *read* Lady O[rford]
Page 493, note 23, *add* Probably what Legge refused to sign was not the treaty in June but the Treasury warrants in July; see *post* 29 Sept. 1755, MANN iv. 501 and n. 11; *Mem. Geo. II* ii. 35.
Page 494, note 3, line 1, *for* (1721–87) *read* (1719 or 20–87)   *Last line, after* 211–13 *add*   ; J. R. Alden, *General Gage in America*, Baton Rouge, Louisiana, 1948, p. 11, n. 17 and pp. 22–7
Page 497, note 3, right column, lines 3–4, *for* war (and for the navy) *read* war, 1761–70, for the navy   *Line 6, before Repertorium insert Almanach Royal* 1766, p. 144, 1767, p. 144, 1769, p. 144, 1770, p. 148;

Page 502, note 19, line 8, *for* Cumberland] *read* Cumberland]'

Page 503, note 28, line 2, *after* (HW). *add* For Hartington's indecision and Fox's advice see their correspondence in Earl of Ilchester, *Henry Fox, First Lord Holland*, 1920, ii. 74–7.

Page 517, note 3, line 3, *after* Hastings 1761–8, *add* Great Bedwyn March–Nov. 1768,

Page 517, note 4, *add* But Lyttelton was appointed governor of South Carolina in Jan. 1755, and was captured by the French in Aug. 1755 on the *Blandford* man of war bound for South Carolina (see HW to Bentley 18 Sept. 1755, CHUTE 251 and n. 22; *Mem. Geo. II* ii. 33).

Page 527, note 7, line 2, *for* 1738 *read* 1739

Page 529, note 7, lines 1–2, *for* ca 1769 *read* 1768   *Line 3, after* Becker *add Gazzetta toscana*, 1768, p. 150

Page 542, note 14, line 9, *for* pp. iii *read* pp. 111

Page 555, note 9, *add* See also CONWAY i. 461.

Page 555, note 10, *for* St Francis de Sales *read* St Francis of Assisi

Page 557, note 5, line 1, *after* m. *insert* (1747)   *Line 5, after* 784–5 *add*   ; *Enciclopedia dello spettacolo*, Rome, 1954–62, vii. 615

Page 557, note 6, *add* See also CONWAY i. 396, n. 4.

Page 562, 2d paragraph, line 1, *for* quandry *read* quandary

Page 562, note 17, line 1, *for* (d. 1768) *read* (ca 1699–1768)   *Last line, after* 164 *add*   ; Namier and Brooke iii. 480

VOLUME 21

Page 13, note 15, *add* According to Lord Waldegrave, Pitt's reception at Leicester House was gracious (*Memoirs*, ed. Lord Holland, 1821, pp. 49–50, 61–3, 157, 160–2; see also Hardwicke's letter of 31 Oct. 1756 to his son, Col. Joseph Yorke in *Hardwicke Corr.* ii. 333).

Page 18, note 8, lines 5–7, *delete* but he was not made . . . 1806, i. 325). *and substitute* June 1757–Jan. 1761, and lord chancellor Jan. 1761–July 1766 (Namier and Brooke ii. 605).

Page 23, note 12, line 4, *for* loc. cit.). *read* loc. cit.);   *for* He d. 1768, and was *read* (ca 1699–1768),   *Last line, after passim add*   ; Namier and Brooke iii. 480

Page 25, note 26, line 1, *for* ca 1705 *read* 1705   *Last line, after* 1747– 50 *add* (Sedgwick ii. 430)

Page 25, note 29, line 1, *for* (d. 1769) *read* (ca 1716–69)   *Last line, after* 238 *add*   ; Namier and Brooke ii. 656

Page 39, note 12, line 2, *for* mother's family estates *read* maternal uncle's estates

Page 45, note 18, line 1, *for* Mello *read* Melo

Page 52, line 2, *on* effect *add note* 14a: 14a. See *London Magazine*, May 1822, v. 412, where this anecdote is repeated concerning the taking and losing of Minorca by Lord Stanhope and Lord Blakeney.

Page 52, note 15, *add* Actually it was James, 1st Earl Stanhope, 1718; Byng's peerage, 1721, came after a naval victory over the Spanish fleet off Cape Passaro.

Page 53, note 26, *add* For Hanbury Williams in Russia see George Rinking to Newcastle 6 Nov. 1759 (BM Add. MSS 32,898, ff. 124–31).

Page 53, note 29, line 2, *for* ca 1721 *read* 1721   *Line 4, after* 1758–62 *add* (Namier and Brooke ii. 664)

Page 70, note 10, right column, line 3, *delete* in   *right column, line 6, for* part *read* peace

Page 73, note 5, right column, line 4, *for* Wolfenbuttel *read* Wolfen-büttel

Page 74, note 11, line 12, *for* 1768–74. *read* 1768–74,

Page 77, note 9, lines 1–2, *after* Brittanniais *add* [*sic*]

Page 79, note 19, *delete* Sir

Page 89, note 2, line 4, *for* Cary *read* Carey

Page 95, note 2, line 2, *for* Browne *read* Brown

Page 97, note 2a, *for* Leicester House *read* 'Lord Lincoln, Lady Catherine Pelham, and Lord Ashburnham' (*Mem. Geo. II* iii. 21)

Page 105, note 19, line 3, *for* Edward Thomas *read* Edmund Thomas *Line 4, after* 101 *insert*   ; Namier and Brooke iii. 522

Page 110, note 14, line 6, *for* 1761–6 *read* 1762–6

Page 120, note 15, last line, *for* post 22 June 1759 *read* see Chatterton 27, 33 n. 6

Page 127, note 15, lines 1–2, *for* (ca 1715–87) *read* (1706–87)

Page 128, note 15, last line, *after* 14–15 *add*   ; *Enciclopedia dello spettacolo*, Rome, 1954–62, ii. 1460–1

Page 129, note 11, line 3, *for* 1750–61 *read* 1751–61

Page 131, note 22, line 1, *for* (ca 1704–71) *read* (1704–71)   *Line 2, for* Adm., 1767 *read* Adm., 1768

Page 140, note 19, *add* The inscription is reprinted in the *London Chronicle* 1–4 Oct. 1757 and in the *London Evening Post* 7 Nov. 1787.

Page 143, note 1, last line, *after* way *add* (Conway i. 506–9, 513–21)

Page 143, note 2, line 1, *for* ca 1697 *read* 1697   *Line 6, after* i. 169 *add*   ; Namier and Brooke iii. 163–4

Page 149, note 14, *add* Mann wrote 17 May 1754 'to Monsieur Muzell at Lille' ('Letter-Books,' S.P. 105/291, f. 23).

Page 156, note 26, line 4, *after* Richard I *add*   , a translation of Jean de Notredame's *Les vies des plus célèbres et anciens poètes provençaux*, Lyon, 1575,   *Last line, add* See Spence to HW 27 Oct. 1757, Bowle to HW 6 Feb. 1764, in Misc. Corr. i. 115–16, 298–9.

Page 157, note 28, *add* See however John Bowle to HW 6 Feb. 1764, defending Crescimbeni. HW replied 11 Feb., but did not correct the passage on Crescimbeni in *Royal and Noble Authors*, 1787 (Misc. Corr. i. 298–301).

Page 158, note 2, right column, line 2, *for* Zelle *read* Celle

Page 164, line 1, *on* disorder *add note* 2a: 2a. An autopsy report on Cocchi is in his *Discorsi Toscani*, Florence, 1761–2, i. pp. li–lix.

Page 173, note 21, line 3, *delete* probably   *Last line, add* See HW to Benjamin Ibbot 24 Sept. 1773, MISC. CORR. ii. 263–4; BERRY ii. 270.

Page 186, note 1, line 4, *after* français *add* which was based on Sainte-Palaye's unfinished *Glossaire de l'ancienne langue française   Last line, add* See also John Drumgold to HW 15 Feb. 1764, MISC. CORR. i. 302–3.

Page 220, note 4, *add* The *London Chronicle* 21–3 Sept. 1780, xlviii. 86, also mentions Anchin and St-Amand.

Page 223, note 2, *add* See also CONWAY i. 554–5 and n. 15.

Page 226, note 5, line 5, *for* Drury *read* Dury

Page 231, note 15a, line 1, *before* Dalton *insert* Domenichino's 'St Agnes,' Carracci's 'Virgin with St Francis and Infant Christ,' Barroccio's 'Reposo,' Raphael's 'St Luke Painting the Virgin,' Guido Reni's 'Fortune' (John Young, *Catalogue of the Pictures at Grosvenor House*, 1821, pp. 9, 10, 14, 17, 21).

Page 231, note 18, line 1, *for* Nathanial *read* Nathaniel

Page 248, note 17, line 1, *for* Carlovna *read* Karlovna

Page 250, note 2, *add* The assassin was said to be Joseph Polycarpe (GM 1772, xlii. 433).

Page 252, From Mann 18 Nov. 1758, headnote, line 2, *for* 25 Dce. *read* 25 Dec.

Page 258, note 13, line 10, *for* Güstow *read* Güstrow

Page 261, note 12, line 2, *for* cr *read* cr.

Page 279, note 11, *for* later 2d E. of Orford *read* (1752–1822), 2d E. of Orford, n.c., 1809

Page 286, note 8, *for* Lord Hardwicke *read* Pitt

Page 293, note 12, line 2, *for* Paolini *read* Paolino

Page 297, note 2, *add* According to the *Daily Adv.* 5 Jan. 1760, he was condemned by court martial 'for not destroying Commodore Moore's fleet in the West Indies.'

Page 300, note 7, *substitute* Benjamin Williams left on 25 May; James Lister came on 19 June, and 'stayed but a week' (HW's *Journal of the Printing-Office*, ed. Paget Toynbee, 1923, p. 8).

Page 310, note 8, line 1, *for* (1721–75) *read* (1721–83)

Page 311, note 4, line 1, *for* (d. 1764) *read* (ca 1725–64)   *Last line, after* 545 *add*   ; Namier and Brooke ii. 269

Pages 315–16, note 9, *substitute* Jost Henrich (Just Henry) Alt (1698–1768), Hesse-Cassel's minister to England 1741–68 (information from Ronald Wells C.B.E., Rosebery Cottage, The Parade, Epsom, Surrey, a descendant).

Page 316, note 11, *add* See also CONWAY ii. 20 and n. 1.

Page 330, note 6, lines 1–2, *for* Marchese *read* Marqués

Page 348, note 2, *substitute* Probably Jeremiah Sisson or Sissons of Beaufort Buildings, Strand, successor to Jonathan Sisson (d. 1747), scientific instrument maker (Thomas Mortimer, *Universal Director*, 1763; Sir Ambrose Heal, *Signboards of Old London Shops*, 1947; information from Mr F. P. White, librarian of St John's College, Cambridge, with the aid of Mr A. H. Hall, librarian of the Guildhall Library, London).

Page 362, note 5, *add* According to Charles Creighton, *A History of Epidemics in Britain*, with additional material by D. E. C. Eversley *et al.*, 1965, ii. 702–3, the disease was probably scarlet fever or diphtheria.

Page 367, line 8, *for* attenion *read* attention

Page 373, note 14, line 2, *for* 1765 *read* 1761   *Last line, after* 320 *add* ; Namier and Brooke ii. 437

Page 376, note 8, line 7, *for* 1795 *read* 1799   *Line 8, after* 185 *add* ; Namier and Brooke ii. 397

Page 389, note 19, line 1, *for* 1723 *read* ?1723   *Line 3, for* 1757–60 *read* 1757–61   *Line 4, for* 1761 *read* 1762–3   *Line 8, after* f. 70 *add* ; Namier and Brooke iii. 166–8

Page 404, note 52, line 1, *for* 1694 *read* ca 1693   *Line 3, after* 154 *add* ; Namier and Brooke ii. 224

Page 417, note 12, line 3, *after* Fuentes *add*   ,

Page 419, note 3, line 1, *for* Saltykov's *read* Soltykov's

Page 441, note 3, line 1, *for* ca 1726 *read* 1726   *Line 2, for* 1771 *read* 1770

Page 441, note 6, lines 2, 8, *for* Saltykov *read* Soltykov

Page 457, note 11, line 4, *for* Lancaster *read* Lancashire

Page 458, To Mann 5 Dec. 1760, 2d paragraph, line 2, *on* set *add note* 3a: 3a. Mann's copy of *A Catalogue of the Royal and Noble Authors*, 2d edn, is now WSL.

Page 460, note 26, *for* Worseley *read* Worsley

Page 460, note 27, *after* Stole *add* (see *Mem. Geo. III* i. 10)

Page 473, note 12, line 8, *for* 1803 *read* 1800   *Last line, after* 348 *add* ; Namier and Brooke iii. 501, 503–7

Page 481, line 1, *on* Hervey *add note* 23a: 23a. He was in Italy ca 1728; see Robert Halsband, *Lord Hervey*, Oxford and New York, 1974, p. 83.

Page 484, note 1, *substitute* Francis Blake Delaval, one of the candidates, wrote to Newcastle 12 Sept. 1760, 'Having been at Andover and with my usual luck on these occasions having made some way there, tho I found the names of seven candidates in array against me, and having seen my Lord Portsmouth to whom I mentioned the honour of a conversation with your Grace on the subject of a coalition between his Lordship and me, I found his Lordship totally disengaged from any one but his nephew General Griffin,' (BM Add. MSS 32,911, f. 229). Newcastle wrote to Lord Portsmouth 23 Sept. on behalf of Delaval, but Lord Portsmouth replied 28 Sept. that he 'would not interfere farther in their election so that your Grace sees the impossibility of my serving Mr Delavall' (BM Add. MSS 32,912, ff. 55, 193; Namier and Brooke i. 293, ii. 309).

Page 484, note 2, *for* ibid. 159 *read* Namier, *Structure*, 2d edn, 159). *and add* For the number of new members in each Parliament, see Sedgwick i. 155 and Namier and Brooke i. 98.

Page 484, note 3, line 5, *for* op. cit. *read Structure*, 2d edn,

Page 484, note 4, *add* For a discussion of the candidates in this election, see Namier and Brooke i. 383, ii. 608, iii. 598–9.

Page 486, note 18, *add* See also Namier and Brooke i. 65, ii. 31.

Page 486, note 21, line 3, *delete* apparently

Page 486, note 23, line 2, *after comédie insert*   , one of the *Lettres sur les Anglais*

Page 489, note 20, line 1, *for* (ca 1724–91) *read* (?1724–79)   *Line 3, after* 85 *add*   ; Namier and Brooke iii. 351–2

Page 490, note 36, *for* Edward-Turnour Garth-Turnour *read* Edward Turnour Garth Turnour   *Line 2, for* ca 1734 *read* 1734   *Last line, add* (Namier and Brooke ii. 485–6)

Page 499, line 2, *on* Pitt *add note* 12a: 12a. In a list of Bute's, Chatham's, and George III's friends, HW is listed among Chatham's (Newcastle's undated memoranda, BM Add. MSS 33,002, f. 472).

Page 515, note 12, last line, *for* Beverly *read* Beverley

Page 515, note 3, lines 9–10, *for* Villinghausen *read* Vellinghausen

Page 517, note 15, *add* Romney Sedgwick points out that this account is misleading, since the King's marriage was arranged through Münchhausen and Bute over a period of seven months and the King's communication with Lady Sarah Lennox was an inquiry whether she would like a place in the new Queen's household ('The Marriage of George III,' *History Today*, 1960, x. 371–7; see also John Brooke, *King George III*, 1972, pp. 71–2, 95–7).

Page 531, note 34, line 1, *after* m. *add* (1736)   *Line 6, after* p. 101 *add* ; William Betham, *Baronetage*, 1801–5, i. 419–20

Page 538, note 5, line 5, *for* Eleven letters *read* Thirteen letters   *Right column, line 2, for* (from 1772 to 1777) *read* (from 1772 to 1777; printed in MISC. CORR. ii. 234, 237, 239–42, 257–9, 265–6, 270–2, 283–6, 352, 364–5)   *Right column, line 6, after* Royston *add*   , dated ?April 1758,

Page 540, note 10, line 3, *for* Oct *read* Oct.

Page 540, note 12, line 1, *for* (d. 1778) *read* (1717–78)   *Line 3, for* Bt. *read* Bt, 1732 (Burke, *Peerage*, 1928, *sub* Sutherland, D. of, p. 2217).

Page 543, note 5, line 5, *for* Venice *read* Padua   *Right column, line 3, after* Florence *add* See *The Complete Letters of Lady Mary Wortley Montagu*, ed. R. Halsband, Oxford, 1967, iii. 214.

Page 546, note 3, line 3, *for* ca 1712 *read* 1711

Page 547, note 10, last line, *after* WSL *add* (Farmington MSS 2305)

Page 548, note 17, line 4, *for* (1722–90) *read* (1721–86)

Page 561, note 10, line 4, *for* 1706–78 *read* 1716–78   *Last line, after* Becker *add*   ; Julius Hübner, *Catalogue of the Royal Picture Gallery in Dresden*, Dresden, 1876, p. 10

VOLUME 22

Page vii, List of Illustrations, *sub* Pencil Drawing of a Gothic Arch, *for* sketch by Thomas Pitt *read* sketch by Chute or Thomas Pitt

Page 11, note 8, line 1, *for* Vorontosov *read* Vorontsov

Page 13, From Mann 13 March 1762, 1st paragraph, line 7, *for* occassions *read* occasions

Page 31, note 5, line 1, *for* 5th Bt *read* 6th Bt   *Line 2, for* 8th Bn *read* 9th Bn

Page 31, note 10, line 2, *for* 1708–80 *read* 1710–80   *Line 4, after* Vernon *add* (Namier and Brooke iii. 579–80; GEC)

Page 37, note 2, *add* Cornwallis, 6 Jan. 1750, thanked Newcastle for his promotion; his brother, Earl Cornwallis, wrote to Newcastle 7 Jan. 1750: 'I am sure my brother will always remember that his obligation is solely to your Grace for this bishopric' (BM Add. MSS 32,720, ff. 17, 19).

Page 40, note 4, line 1, *for* ca 1742 *read* 1742

Page 45, note 9, line 4, *for* Capt. 1757 *read* Commander, 1757; Capt., 1759   *Line 6, after* Manvers *add*   ; Namier and Brooke iii. 128–9

Page 45, note 16, *add* See also James Boswell to John Johnston of Grange, Parma, 31 Jan. 1765 (*The Correspondence of James Boswell and John Johnston of Grange*, ed. R. S. Walker [1966], pp. 155–6).

Page 46, note 1, last line, *after* 1762 *add* (CONWAY ii. 161)

Page 53, note 8, line 1, *for* 1430 *read* ca 1430

Page 54, note 21, line 6, *for* Mem. *read* (Mem.

Page 56, note 31, *add* Conway to D. of Devonshire 21 July 1762 (Chatsworth MSS, 416/78) describes this victory; see CONWAY ii. 163, n. 1.

Page 64, note 12, line 1, *for* Alexei Grigori'evich *read* Alexeï Grigor-'evich   *Line 3, for* Grigori Grigori'evich *read* Grigorii Grigor'evich

Page 72, note 28, line 2, *after* m. *add* (1776)

Page 85, note 25, right column, *align first line*

Page 99, note 1, line 1, *for* Marquès *read* Marqués   *Line 2, after* below *add*   , n. 3

Page 100, note 3, line 2, *for* Marquès *read* Marqués

Page 122, note 19, *add* A tureen with stand and a pair of soup plates from this service are described in the Campbell Museum Catalogue, Feb. 1974, Camden, New Jersey, No. 76.

Page 131, note 34, line 3, *for* Lord High Steward *read* Lord Steward

Page 135, note 9, line 7, *for* Margaretha *read* Margarethe

Page 136, note 18, line 1, *for* 1727 *read* 1725

Page 139, note 19, line 4, *delete* 101st edn,

Page 148, 2d paragraph, line 2, *on* House *add note* 19a: 19a. HW's memoranda on a letter from John Jamisone of 14 May 1763 refer to HW's preparations for this masquerade (MISC. CORR. i. 284).

Page 149, From Mann 11 June 1763, date-line, *for* June 14 *read* June 11

Page 149, note 29, *before* Karl *insert* Christian Friedrich

Page 153, 1st paragraph, line 10, *on* daughter's *add note* 1a: 1a. Perhaps Luisa Elisabetta [? Roland de] Lorenzi, m. Senatore Conte Cavaliere Balì Federigo Barbolani (*Gazzetta toscana*, 1780, xv. 172).

Page 184, note 16, line 3, *for* 241–3 *read* 241–2

Page 189, note 25, next to last line, *for* ca 1726 *read* 1726   *for* Wycombe *read* Chipping Wycombe   *Last line, after* 1774–90 *add* (Namier and Brooke ii. 50)

Page 210, note 3, *add* He was recalled from Ireland by Lord Northumberland at Grenville's request; see Grenville's letters of 26 Feb. and 10 March 1764 to Northumberland (*Additional Grenville Papers 1763–1765*, ed. J. R. G. Tomlinson, Manchester, 1962, pp. 94, 100).

Page 219, note 22, lines 10, 20, *for* Foster *read* Forster   *Last line, after* 139 *add*   ; Venn, *Alumni Cantab.* Pt I, ii. 162

Page 220, note 3, line 1, *for* ca 1738 *read* 1738   *Line 5, after* 297 *add* ; Namier and Brooke iii. 399

Page 224, note 3, *add* Another Mme Bulgarini was Sir Henry Oxenden's cicisbea in 1749 (Oxenden to Mann 25 March 1749, S.P. 105/309, f. 81).

Page 233, note 13, line 12, *for* 1776 *read* 1776 [?1766]

Page 238, note 4, right column, line 7, *after* 19 April *add* and to Hertford 20 April, Conway ii. 375–6

Page 240, note 9, right column, line 4–5, *for* (b. ca 1761) *read* (ca 1761–1838)   *Last line, after* Bellas *add*   ; M.A.D. Heddle de la Caillemotte de Massue de Ruvigny, Marquis of Ruvigny and Raineval, *Plantagenet Roll . . . Essex Vol.*, 1908, p. 615

Page 242, note 3, lines 1, 4, *for* Gilmore *read* Filmore

Page 242, note 5, *for* (ibid.) *read* (ibid., n. 9; *post* 27 July 1764)

Page 256, note 1, *add* See HW to Newcastle 2 Oct. 1764 (Misc. Corr. i. 363–4).

Page 263, note 19, line 1, *for* ca 1703 *read* 1703   *Line 2, for* St Michael *read* Mitchell   *Line 4, after* 152 *add*   ; Namier and Brooke ii. 217

Page 269, 1st paragraph, line 4, *on* money *add note* 3a: 3a. Fox wrote to Bute in 1763 that Hardwicke got £20,000 a year for his family from the King (Lord Fitzmaurice, *Life of William Earl of Shelburne*, 2d edn, 1912, i. 146).

Page 270, note 13, line 1, *for* 1763 (*Dictionnaire* . . . vi. 1282). *substitute* 1764 (Lady Hertford to HW 18 Dec. 1764, Conway ii. 480).

Page 270, note 14, line 8, *for* ?1719 *read* 1732   *Line 11, for* (*La Grande encyclopédie*, [1886–1902]; NBG) *substitute* (*Dictionnaire de biographie française*, 1933– , viii. 1190)

Page 271, note 17, line 3, *for* Molin-Dumesnil *read* Morin-Dumesnil

Page 276, note 22, line 13, *for* ca 1681 *read* ca 1679   *for* ca 1719 *read* 1719   *Last line, after* 146 *add*   ; Sedgwick ii. 377

Pages 278–9, note 1, *substitute* Richard Croft (d. 1793), partner in the Messrs Backwell's bank, Pall Mall, and executor of Edward Louisa Mann's will (see *post* MANN viii. 27 and n. 23, 154 and n. 22; *European Magazine*, 1793, xxiii. 480; F. G. Hilton Price, *Handbook of London Bankers*, 1876, p. 48).

Page 288, note 4, *add* See *post* 12 Feb. 1789, n. 2; Dr Ida Macalpine and Dr Richard Hunter, *George III and the Mad-Business*, 1969.

Page 289, 2d paragraph, next to last line, *for* then a second *read* than a second

Page 291, note 5, lines 2–3, *for* P. of Nassau-Usingen, 1806 *read* D. of Nassau-Usingen, 1806

Page 296, note 22, *substitute* The next day, 1 May, by a vote of 89 to 31 (*Mem. Geo. III* ii. 85; *Journals of the House of Lords* xxxi. 171).

Page 299, note 39, *add* See also HW to Hertford 12 May 1765, CONWAY ii. 551.

Page 310, note 7, line 1, *for* ca 1721 *read* 1721

Page 327, note 1a, *substitute* Stanley had rejected the Grenville ministry's offer of a seat at the Treasury in 1763, but had remained at the Admiralty. On the formation of the Rockingham administration in July 1765, he lost his place at the Admiralty, but kept the governorship of the Isle of Wight (*Grenville Papers* ii. 43; Namier and Brooke iii. 469–70).

Page 336, note 11, line 2, *for* half-brother *read* step-brother

Page 340, To Mann 26 Sept. 1765, line 3, *after* sum of *insert* [*sic*]

Page 342, note 13, *add* For Rigby's account of their arrival see his letter to the D. of Bedford 8 Sept. 1765, *Bedford Corr.* iii. 318–19.

Page 350, note 8, *add* Wallmoden was at Court 17 Oct., according to the *Gazzetta toscana*, 1766, p. xxi, n.

Page 354, note 5, line 1, *for* Missing. *read* Hamilton to HW 15 Oct. 1765, MS now WSL, printed in MISC. CORR. i. 383–4.

Page 356, note 5, line 1, *for* Barbentane *read* Barbantane

Page 362, note 10, line 4, *for* to admission to the simple antechamber *read* to the entrée to the antechamber only   *Last line, add* See D. M. Low in *Review of English Studies*, 1962, n.s., xiii. 220.

Page 371, To Mann 30 Nov. 1765, headnote, *for* Sent, 3 Nov. *read* Sent, 3 Dec.

Page 389, note 6, *after* Pretender *add*   , who had been at Bouillon since 1758 (BM Add. MSS 32,890, f. 409, enclosure of 1 May 1759 in Yorke to Newcastle 1 May 1759); see also *post* MANN x. 46–7

Page 401, note 5, line 1, *for* Despencer *read* Despenser

Page 402, note 13, *add* Mann probably gave him the message when he returned to Florence (see *post* 7 March 1766, MANN vi. 407).

Page 411, note 2, lines 1–2, *delete* did not go to SH until 19 May *and substitute* went to SH 8 May (HW to John Hutchins 10 May 1766, MISC. CORR. ii. 17) but returned to Arlington Street by the 10th,

Page 417, note 6, line 6, *for* Francis III *read* Francis I

Page 424, note 7, line 6, *for* Felice *read* Felicità

Page 424, note 4, *add* Gloucester and Cumberland (not York) were to receive £3000 per annum on the Irish estate, beginning 1 May 1767 ('List of all the Civil and French Pensions,' *Journals of the House of Commons ... Ireland*, Dublin, xvi [1782]. 179).

Page 425, note 6, right column, line 4, *for* conster'ed *read* conster'd [*sic*]

Page 434, note 20, line 3, *for* Barbentane *read* Barbantane

Page 434, note 23, last line, *for* 90–3 *read* 94–8

Page 444, note 10, *add* 'I guess I am to have the department of Scotland but with what powers or under what appellation I know not nor am I indeed at all anxious about it' (Mackenzie to Mann, Turin, 1 July 1761, S.P. 105/313, f. 527).

Page 453, note 7, line 1, *for* ca 1700–72 *read* ca 1699–1772   *Last line, add* See also Albemarle to Sir Everard Fawkener 27 Feb. 1748, BM Add. MSS 32,714, f. 276; and CONWAY i. 217, n. 12.

Page 455, note 2, Laura Keppel's letter to Nancy Clement, Sunday 21 Sept. [?1766] mentions a visit to Strawberry Hill planned for 'Thursday' (MS now WSL).

Page 462, note 5, *add* See also CHUTE 120.

Page 464, note 11, line 1, *for* ca 1711 *read* ca 1710   *Last line, add* See also Namier and Brooke iii. 422.

Page 473, note 21, last line, *for* ibid. *read Journals of the House of Commons*

Page 474, note 26, *add* See also *London Stage* Part IV, ii. 1199, 1201, 1203, 1256.

Page 474, note 27, *add* See also *London Stage* Part IV, ii. 1182.

Page 474, note 28, *for* (1720–before 1790) *read* (ca 1720–after 1770) *for* 1771 *read* 1770   *for* 5th edn . . . 833–4 *read* 6th edn, 1980, vii. 770

Page 476, From Mann 10 Jan. 1767, 1st paragraph, line 2, *for* 8th November *read* 8th December

Page 482, note 6, *substitute* Hon. Paul or Hon. Richard Gore.

Page 518, note 8, lines 1, 4, *for* Barbentane *read* Barbantane

Page 526, note 7, lines 3–4, *for* Barbentane *read* Barbantane

Page 527, note 10, *add* He had been at Cortona 15 Oct. 1766 and at Florence 24 Oct. (*Gazzetta toscana*, 1766, i. 177–8).

Page 548, To Mann 18 Aug. 1767, 2d paragraph, line 3, *for* as Irish baron *read* an Irish baron

Page 549, note 7, line 1, *for* ca 1729 *read* 1729

Page 554, note 28, line 4, *for* Barbentane *read* Barbantane

Page 560, note 2, *add* See also CONWAY iii. 83–4.

Page 586, note 20, *add* See also Namier and Brooke iii. 78–9.

VOLUME 23

Page vii, List of Illustrations, 4th item, *for* Zeca *read* Zecca

Page vii, List of Illustrations, *sub* Patch's Conversation Piece, *delete* From the painting in the possession . . . *Apollo*, 1967, lxxxv. 353). *and substitute* From the painting formerly in the possession of Lord Talbot de Malahide, at Malahide Castle, Ireland; sold Christie's 26 March 1976 (property of the Hon. Rose Talbot), lot 34, to John Baskett for Paul Mellon; now in the Mellon Collection at the Yale Center for British Art. The figure seated at the left is Lord Tylney.

Page 5, note 3, line 9, *for* 23 *read* 25   *Line 10, after* 140 *add*   ; Namier and Brooke i. 329

Page 47, note 1, *add* The King did so in a letter of 12 Feb. 1767 (S.P. 105/284, f. 83).

Page 48, note 3, lines 5–6, *for* Its descent and present whereabouts have not been traced. *substitute* It is now (1968) in the possession of Lord Cornwallis, Ashurst Park, Tunbridge Wells, Kent; illustrated *post* MANN ix. 432.

Page 57, note 4, line 1, *for* Vanbrugh. *read* Vanbrugh,
Page 59, middle of page, *insert the following heading*:

FROM MANN, Saturday 1 October 1768

Missing; mentioned *post* 14 Nov. 1768. This letter may have been in a separate packet sent by courier to Lord Shelburne and then to Mr Larpent, although Mann seems to confuse this with the packet mentioned in his letters of 18 Oct. and 25 Oct. 1768.

Page 65, note 5, *substitute* Barré resigned as joint vice-treasurer of Ireland on 31 Oct. 1768. His letter of resignation is in the Grafton MSS; see Namier and Brooke ii. 52.

Page 82, note 7, *add* See also *London Stage* Part IV, iii. 1374–80, 1382, 1438.

Page 82, note 8, line 4, *after* Jan.) *add*   ; described upon its first performance as 'a very complete, pretty piece,—the music very striking' (*London Stage* Part IV, iii. 1356, 1379).

Page 86, note 2, *add* See also Namier and Brooke i. 331–4.

Page 98, last line of text, *for* beseiged *read* besieged

Page 116, note 13, line 4, *for* Rumiantsov's *read* Rumiantsev's

Page 123, note 8, line 4, *for* Benedict XII *read* Benedict XIII

Page 130, note 3, line 1, *after* arrived *insert* at Leghorn 16 June (Mann to Lord Bute 17 June 1769, Cardiff Public Library), at Florence

Page 132, note 4, line 7, *after* xxxviii–ix *insert*   ; also printed in Augustus Henry, 3d Duke of Grafton, *Autobiography and Political Correspondence*, ed. Sir W. R. Anson, 1898, p. 237

Page 146, note 32, line 11, *for* Rumiantsov *read* Rumiantsev

Page 175, note 16, last line, *add* (Namier and Brooke ii. 290–1).

Page 175, note 17, last line, *for* ibid. *read* HW's MS *Journal*, loc. cit.

Page 179, note 6, *add* See Namier and Brooke iii. 677–8.

Page 179, note 9, *add* See CONWAY iii. 123–4.

Page 180, note 12, lines 1–2, *for* Lord John Sackville *read* Lord George Sackville

Page 182, note 6, *add* See also CONWAY iii. 122.

Page 182, note 7, line 5, *for* ibid. *read* HW's MS *Journal*

Page 192, To Mann 27 Feb. 1770, 1st paragraph, line 5, *on* observation *add note a*: *a*. Edward Bensley ('The Ape and Tiger,' N&Q, 25 July 1925, cxlix. 67–8) suggests that HW's observation is original with Voltaire (*Candide*, ch. 22) and not with HW.

Page 198, note 17, line 1, *for* (1719–74) *read* (1719–94)   *Line 3, after* 1768–90 *add* (Namier and Brooke ii. 217–18)

Page 199, note 1, *add* See also CONWAY iii. 125–6.

Page 226, note 9, line 3, *for* S.G. Goodall's *read* S.C. Goodall's

Page 248, 4th paragraph, line 1, *on* Daschioff *add note* 21a: 21a. At Lord Hertford's, 15 Nov. See *memoranda* on Hertford to HW 15 Nov. 1770, CONWAY iii. 132.

Page 261, note 3, *add* The shocks in Florence and Leghorn are recorded by Robert Mallet, 'Catalogue of Recorded Earthquakes from 1606 B.C. to A.D. 1850,' British Association for the Advancement of Science, *Report ... 1853*, 1854, xxiii. 168–9.

Page 267, note 3, line 3, *for* 1771 *read* 1772

Page 267, note 7, line 4, *after* from *insert* descendants of

Page 271, note 8, *add* In Jesse's *Selwyn* (ii. 69) the Zamperini is said to have been born 'about the year 1745' but Lord March in a letter to Selwyn apparently dated 6 Jan. 1767, says, 'She is but fifteen' (ibid. ii. 125). In the *London Stage* Part IV, ii. 1182 and iii. 1422, she is listed as one of the principal singers at the King's Opera House for the 1766–7 and 1769–70 seasons. Lord March mentions her father, mother, and sister (Jesse, op. cit. ii. 115), who were probably the Giandomenico, Antonia, and Maria Zamperini listed in the *London Stage* Part IV, ii. 1182.

Page 272, note 17, *add* See also J. H. Cardwell, H. B. Freeman, and G. C. Wilton, *Two Centuries of Soho*, 1898, pp. 39–41.

Page 280, note 13, line 2, *for* 1770–3 *read* 1770–8   *Line 4, for* 1772–8 *read* 1772–3 (see Namier and Brooke iii. 224–5)

Page 280, note 14, line 4, *delete* vii. 629,

Page 300, note 19, *add* See also DU DEFFAND iii. 57 and n. 1.

Page 302, To Mann 8 May 1771, note 3, *add* See FAMILY 62–75, 305–9 (Appendix 2); Hist. MSS Comm., *Stopford-Sackville MSS*, i. 344–55.

Page 311, note 7, *for* Seilern *read* Belgioioso.

Page 338, note 4, line 2, *for* (1717–89) *read* (1715–89)

Page 339, note 10, lines 1–2, *for* Marie-Madeleine-Josèphe de Cusack (b. ca 1730), known as 'La Sabatin,' m. *read* Marie-Madeleine-Joséphine de Cusack (1725–78), m. 1 —— Sabatin; m. 2   *Last line, add* See also BERRY i. 43–4, n. 17.

Page 340, note 19, *add* HW did answer on 28 July the earlier 'provoking letter' but wrote that certain matters 'require a much fuller answer than I have time to give now, as the post goes out tomorrow morning'; the 'fuller answer' is apparently the one HW was 'prevented' from making. See MISC. CORR. ii. 210–11.

Page 343, note 10, line 6, *after* Mancinforte *add or* Marcinforte   *Last line, after* 195 *add*   ; Conte Francesco Cristofori, *Storia dei Cardinali di Santa Romana Chiesa*, Rome, 1888, i. 59, 446.

Page 349, note 3, *add* It is now (1972) in the possession of Sir Horace Seymour, Bratton House, Wilts (John Cornforth, 'Bratton House, Wiltshire,' *Country Life* 5 Aug. 1971, cl. 329).

Page 373, note 21, last line, *for* de *read* der

Page 413, note 2, line 1, *for* 1809 *read* 1808   *Line 6, for* NBG *read Enciclopedia universal ilustrada*, Barcelona, etc. [1905–30], xxxvi. 837–8

Page 432, note 2, lines 1–2, *for* (1480–ca 1534) *read* (ca 1480–between 1527 and 1534)

Page 451, note 6, line 3, *for* (b. 1749) *read* (1749–1827)   *Line 5, after* Capt. Smith *insert* (M. A. H. D. Heddle de la Caillemotte de Massue de Ruvigny, Marquis of Ruvigny and Raineval, *Plantagenet Roll . . . Exeter Vol.*, 1907, pp. 39, 448)

Page 460, note 4, line 2, *for* 12 Feb. *read* 14 Feb.

Page 461, note 9, line 13, *for* 1704 *read* 1703   *Line 18, after* morning' *add*   ; 'Short Notes,' GRAY i. 6, n. 25

Page 468, 2d paragraph, line 11, *on* her *add note* 6a: 6a. When she made her will 3 Nov. 1773, she was in the Via dell' Orto in the parish of San Frediano.

Page 519, note 7, line 1, *after* See illustration *insert* (*post* MANN viii. facing p. 540)

Page 524, note 5, line 11, *for* Oct. 1776 *read* Oct. 1773

Page 547, note 7, *add Bolshaia sovetskaia entsiklopedia*, 2d edn, ed. B. A. Vvedenskii, xxxv. 280, gives his dates as ca 1742–75.

Page 560, note 2, lines 1, 2, *for* Coney *read* Cony   *Line 2, for* 81 *read* 91   *Line 4, for* 1776 *read* 1777   *after* n. 1 *add*   ; FAMILY 118 and n. 4

Page 565, note 9, lines 3–4, *delete* The fate of Maron's portrait of Mann is not known;   *Last line, add* The portrait is now in the possession of Lord Cornwallis, Ashurst Park, Kent (see illustration, *post* MANN ix. facing p. 432);

VOLUME 24

Page 3, note 18, *add* See *ante* 23 Feb., 23 April 1774, MANN vii. 558, 567; MORE 1, n. 1.

Page 15, note 19, *add* 'I saw this very tomb or shrine [of St Simplicius and St Faustina] at Strawberry Hill, July 7, 1769. The church of Santa Maria Maggiore, being new ornamented, the part of the shrine which contained the pillars studded with gold, marble, etc. were sent in large cases by Sir Horace Man[n] to Mr Walpole, who designs them for a chapel in his delightful Gothic castle, at Strawberry Hill' (Quoted from Cole's MSS in the BM, in *Monthly Magazine*, 1804, xvii pt i 550).

Page 84, note 5, line 3, *for* consecrated *read* crowned

Page 96, From Mann 2 May 1775, headnote, *for* Part of the first paragraph *read* Part of the letter

Page 104, note 16, *add* Dr Ida Macalpine and Dr Richard Hunter in *George III and the Mad-Business*, 1969, pp. 223–8, diagnose her illness as porphyria.

Page 121, note 11, *add* See also CONWAY iii. 252; MASON i. 218.

Page 132, note 2, *add* See HW to Conway 6 Oct. 1775, CONWAY iii. 270 and n. 8.

Page 135, note 2, left column, line 1, *after* 13 *add*   , *post* MANN x. 48,

Page 138, note 2, *add* See also R. B. Morris, *The Peacemakers; the Great Powers and American Independence*, New York, 1965, p. 159, supported by *Sbornik* xix. 463–4, 489, 509.

Page 145, note 3, line 1, *for* 1734 *read* 1733

Page 152, note 15, line 1, *for* Youngson *read* Young (*or* Youngson) *Line 2, for* 1745–79 *read* 1745–97

Page 154, note 21, *add* Since GM 1775, xlv. 607, confirms what HW says, that Edward Louisa Mann died on Saturday 16 Dec., this is probably the correct date.

Page 164, note 8, line 1, *before* Karl *insert* Christian Friedrich

Page 172, 1st paragraph, line 6, *on* family *add note* 3a: 3a. The Duke of Gloucester wrote to HW 17 Jan. 1776; see FAMILY 115–16 and *post* 15 Feb. 1776, MANN viii. 178.

Page 172, note 3, lines 3–8, *delete* but Mann may have . . . 1777, nn. 2, 5). *and substitute*   ; he was also a banker (Brinsley Ford, 'Thomas Jenkins,' *Apollo*, June 1974, xcix, 416–25).

Page 174, note 7, line 2, *for* Nov. *read* Jan.   *Line 3, after* n. 2 *add* ; see also MISC. CORR. ii. 332–3

Page 197, note 16, line 2, *for* ca 1780 *read* ca 1765

Page 217, note 16, *add* Jackson was replaced as sub-preceptor by the Rev. William Arnold (d. 1802), Bp Hurd's chaplain, canon of Windsor, precentor of Lichfield, who later became mentally deranged (see *The Correspondence of George, Prince of Wales 1770–1812*, ed. A. Aspinall, 1963, i. 24, n. 1, 27 and n. 4; GM 1802, lxxii pt 2. 884).

Page 217, note 18, *add* Smelt was replaced as sub-governor by Lt-Col. George Hotham (1741–1806), 5th son of Sir Beaumont Hotham, Bt; treasurer and secretary to the Prince of Wales, Dec. 1780 (*The Correspondence of George, Prince of Wales 1770–1812*, ed. A. Aspinall, 1963, i. 24, n. 1, 27 and n. 3; *Old Westminsters* i. 484).

Page 222, note 2, line 5, *for* Batoni's *read* a

Page 223, note 3, lines 16–17, *for* mentioned by HW *read* mentioned by Mann

Page 224, note 8, right column, line 4, *for* Chaffaut's *read* Chaffault's

Page 227, note 8, line 1, *for* (d. 1744) *read* (?1695–1744)   *Last line, after* i. 23 *add*   ; Sedgwick i. 443, 444

Page 228, 2d paragraph, line 1, *for* Newcastle[10] *read* Newcastle[11]

Page 228, note 10, *for* 10 *read* 11

Page 230, note 12, *add* See also CONWAY iii. 282–3.

Page 243, note 1, last line, *after* below *add*   ; OSSORY ii. 182, n. 16; MISC. CORR. Appendix 1, map of Twickenham

Page 251, note 3, line 8, *for* third *read* second   *Line 9, before* Collins *insert* Namier and Brooke iii. 260–1;

Page 293, note 8, line 2, *after* n. 5 *add*   ; FAMILY 120–1

Page 293, note 11, *after* Presumably *insert* Carlos Cony (fl. 1774–91) (FAMILY 118 and n. 4),

Page 296, 1st paragraph, line 9, *for* dependents *read* dependants

Page 304, note 2, *add* Wilkes's speech was printed in the *Public Adv.* 3 May 1777 and the *Sentimental Magazine*, May 1777, v. 193–6.

Page 310, note 11, *for* Coney *read* Cony

Pages 318–19, note 3, lines 2–3, *after* Collection *delete period and close space; run-in* Collection of Etruscan, Greek, and Roman Antiquities

Page 323, note 5, line 3, *after* n. 9 *add*   ; printed FAMILY 130

Page 358, note 3, right column, line 7, *for* 1781–3 *read* 1780–3

Page 375, note 1, line 2, *for* [Billeraye] *read* [Billerey]

Page 411, 3d paragraph, line 4, *for* his kness *read* his knees

Page 411, note 11, lines 3–4, *delete*   ; another illustration of HW's un-reliability about age *and substitute*   ; he died 26 Feb. 1784, aged 90 (Namier and Brooke iii. 642).

Page 412, note 14, last sentence, *delete* She was daughter (not niece) to the Duchess of Kendal (GEC *sub* Kendal). *and substitute* She was reputed to be the daughter of George I by the Duchess of Kendal.

Page 417, note 4, line 2, *for* Udny Weymouth *read* Udny to Weymouth

Page 417, note 9, line 4, *for* M. of Camden *read* M. Camden

Page 428, note 6, line 4, *for* improvements).' *read* improvements)' (FAMI-LY 163–4).

Page 441, note 13, line 19, *for* Pierpoint *read* Pierpont

Page 441, note 15, *add* A letter from James Christie to Carlos Cony 6 April 1779 describes an interview with the Russian ambassador in which the price of £40,000 was mentioned: '. . . he showed me the Emp[r]ess's letter which translated to me the contents were that as £40,000 was equal to 240,000 rubles it was such a sum as she thought herself at liberty to lay out on objects of fancy at this critical time' (quoted in Sotheby's Catalogue 22 June 1976, lot 38). Michael Tyson also discusses the valuation of the Houghton collection in his letter to Richard Gough 3 May 1779 (Gough MSS, f. 366 verso and f. 367).

Page 463, note 2, line 2, *after* ante *insert* To Mann

Page 470, note 10, lines 5–6, *for* but made him send it back (*post* 25 Sept., 16 Oct. 1779). *read* (see *post* 25 Sept. 1779).

Page 473, note 16, *delete* Presumably from one of the evening papers of 5–7 May. *and substitute* HW learned of the retreat from Hertford's letter of 8 May 1779 with an enclosure from Lord Weymouth; see Conway iii. 319–20.

Page 488, note 2, right column, line 5, *for* 1784–9 *read* 1788–96

Page 505, note 9, last line, *for* Austrian *read* French   *after* Vienna *add* (*ante* 23 June 1778, n. 6)

Page 517, note 2, *add* Mann's copy of *The Mysterious Mother*, 1768, 'with his device stamped on the title-page' is offered in Quaritch's Cat. No. 1008, lot 402. The same catalogue, lot 403, offers a manuscript copy made 'in 1785 during residence at Pisa' from the printed copy given by HW to Mann.

Page 537, note 28, line 2, *for* Wigton *read* Wigtown

VOLUME 25

Page 81, note 13, *substitute* James Sutherland (ca 1731–91), Judge of the Vice-Admiralty Court at Minorca. In August 1780, after various disagreements, Sutherland was suspended (and later dismissed) by the Governor, General James Murray, and immediately left Minorca. Shortly afterwards he issued, from Leghorn, a challenge to General Murray to face him in an English civil court. After Murray's return to London in 1782 Sutherland brought an action against him for unlawful dismissal, and in 1783 was awarded £5,000 against Murray for having acted 'arbitrarily and unreasonably.' On 17 Aug. 1791 in the Green Park, as the King was passing from the Queen's house to the levee at St James's, Sutherland shot himself. (Information kindly provided by K. E. Hinrichsen, Esq., of London; see GM 1791, lxi pt ii. 782, 868–70; *Daily Adv.* 18, 20 Aug. 1791; DNB, *sub* James Murray; James Sutherland, 'A Letter to the Electors of Great Britain,' 1791).

Page 81, note 15, *add* In 1778 when travelling from London to Minorca, Sutherland was arrested and imprisoned by the French as he was found to be carrying Government mail for General Murray. He therefore could not travel through France and had to take the longer route through Germany. (Information from K. E. Hinrichsen, Esq., of London.)

Page 111, note 5, line 13, *for* of *read* on

Page 114, note 3, *delete last sentence* The transcript . . . n. *b. and substitute* A transcript of her will in English, dated 3 Nov. 1773, including the probate 18 Jan. 1781 before the Lord Conservator of the Laws, the certificate of death 16 Jan. 1781, the receipt of the tax or duty paid to the work of Santa Maria di Fiore 18 Jan. 1781, the Instrument of passing the before-mentioned Will 4 Nov. 1773, the attestation 19 Jan. 1781 of Nicholas Tassa who made the copy of the will, and further attestations of witnesses (including Horace Mann)—this transcript is among the Blathwayt Papers, Osborn Collection, Beinecke Library, Yale University.

Page 114, note 5, *substitute* Probably Mozzi's lawyer, Clemente de Pace, who appeared 18 Jan. 1781 with the will and death certificate before the Conservator of the Laws (Osborn Collection transcript of Lady Orford's will).

Page 114, 1st paragraph, line 10, *on* certificate of her death *add note* 5a: 5a. The certificate of death, 'On the sixteenth day of January one thousand seven hundred and eighty-one at Pisa,' signed by Dr Caesar Studiati, Dr Lorenzo Pignotti, Dr Baniere Sandrini (Lady Orford's attending physician), and notaries, states that Lady Orford died 'in the house of the illustrious Sir Frederick Lanfranchi, hired of Signor Francisco Jermy [or Jerny, *post* 20 Nov. 1781, n. 12] situated Longarno in the parish of Saint Matthew' and 'was carried to Leghorn to be there interred, she being a Protestant' (included with the Osborn Collection transcript of Lady Orford's will).

Page 114, note 6, *for* (ibid.) *read* (Lady Orford's will)

Page 120, note 1, *substitute* Perhaps Nicholas Tassa (Nicolli Tassi), who made the copy of the will in English, or Alexander Ricovere (de Recuperis), Doctor of Laws and Minister of the General Archives of Florence, who signed the 'Instrument' on 19 Jan. 1781 (Osborn Collection transcript of Lady Orford's will).

Page 120, note 2, *substitute* It is called 'Instrument of Passing the Before-Mentioned Will,' dated 4 Nov. 1773, and signed by the following witnesses: Giuseppe Barini, son of Antonio Barini of Milan; Gaetano Colesso, son of Giovanni Colesso of Venice; Pietro Mazzoni, son of Pietro Mazzoni of Florence; Dominico Ortolani, son of Gio Dominico Ortolani of Montereggi; Santi Serrati, son of Pietro Serrati of Florence; Giuseppe Cecconi, son of Giuseppe Cecconi of Florence; Giovanni Galli, son of Dominico Galli of Florence (included with the Osborn Collection transcript of Lady Orford's will). In the 'Instrument' Lady Orford reaffirms her will and revokes any other testaments, codicils, etc.

Page 120, note 3, *substitute* Antonio Filippo Montelatici, 'Doctor of both Laws and Florentine notary public and Judge Ordinary' (ibid.).

Page 120, note 4, *for* Missing. *substitute* The 'proof' begins: 'On the eighteenth day of January one thousand seven hundred and eighty one before me the most illustrious Lord Conservator of the Laws, and Lieutenant Fiscale Domenico Betti and before me his Chancellor underwritten [Bernardino Sciarelli] appeared the most excellent Doctor Clemente Son of the late Doctor John Francis de Pace, Doctor of Law and a citizen of Florence as attorney and representative of the most illustrious Knight Sir Giulio de Mozzi a noble Florentine patrician who in the name of the said Sir Giulio as being interested in the last will and testament unopened and sealed up of her Excellency the Lady Countess Margaret Orford or

Lady Walpole of the English nation passed before Anthony Philip di Ferdinando Montelatici on the fourth day of November one thousand seven hundred and seventy three, and deposited in the public general office for keeping the Archives of Florence on the twentieth day of November of the said year one thousand seven hundred and seventy three as appears by the Memorandum made in the margin thereof by the hands of the said Notary, has made application and solicited and does make and solicits that the said Will be opened and published in the usual and accustomed manner and form' (ibid.).

Page 121, note 3, *add* The 'Instrument of passing the before-mentioned Will' included Lady Orford's signature and a sample of her handwriting, but the copyist did not misspell her name (ibid.).

Page 122, 2d paragraph, line 8, *on* want of feeling *add note* 6a: 6a. When she made the 'Instrument of passing the before-mentioned Will,' the notary reminded her that it was customary to give a donation to the poor of the parish, but she declined to do so (Osborn Collection transcript of Lady Orford's will).

Page 122, note 9, *delete*   , if he sent one,   *after* missing *add* (see *post* 11 Feb. 1781)

Page 123, note 1, line 2, *for* 'paper' *read* 'proof'   *Lines 4–8, delete* it is perhaps . . . Jan. 1781. *and substitute* it testifies to the presentation of the will and other papers on 18 Jan. 1781 before the Lord Conservator of the Laws and his Chancellor Bernardino Sciarelli, and to the application by Mozzi's lawyer that the will be opened and published in the usual form. It continues: 'The private bureau in which said Instruments are locked up and preserved being opened and the said last Will and Testament having been taken out and shown to the witnesses hereinafter mentioned they saw that the seals were yet whole and untouched and that the same was and consisted in an Instrument of Last Will and Testament as aforesaid passed by and before Anthony Philip di Ferdinando Montelatici within which was found a sheet of stamp't paper of the largest size, sewed round and round with a thread of white silk and sealed with red wax in several parts and particularly in the first paper which encloses the cover on the outside whereof which is blank there did appear three seals similar to that in the Testament and three others at the foot of the page with the impression of the arms of the Lady Testatrix and opposite thereto there did also appear her signature as follows I Countess Margaret of Orford do declare that the enclosed is my Will and there follow the signatures of the witnesses who were present at the act of delivery of the said Will' (Osborn Collection transcript of Lady Orford's will).

Page 131, note 2, *for* It is missing. *substitute* It is the 'Instrument of passing the before-mentioned Will' (included in the Osborn Collection transcript of Lady Orford's will).

Page 131, To Mann 26 Feb. 1781, 1st paragraph, line 5, *on* person' *add note* 2a: 2a. 'And if it does not avail as a Testament then it shall avail and obtain as a Codicil or Deed of Gift from the cause of death or as any other subsisting last will or testamentary disposition . . .' (ibid.).

Page 132, note 6, last line, *after* WSL *add* (FAMILY Appendix 1, pp. 295–304)

Page 134, note 19, line 1, *for* Appolino *read* Apolline

Page 136, note 2, *add* Charles Brietzcke (ca 1738–95) was senior clerk in the secretary of state's office (GM 1795, lxv pt i. 533).

Page 138, note 1, left column, line 7, *for* factions *read* factious

Page 150, note 4, *for* Socket *read* Sochet

Page 154, note 14, line 5, *for* is pencil *read* in pencil

Page 159, note 3, line 1, *for* 1559 *read* 1559 *or* 1560   *at end add* See HW to Richard Gem 4 April 1776, MISC. CORR. ii. 346, n. 9.

Page 169, note 2, *substitute* The 'Instrument of passing the before-mentioned Will,' signed by Lady Orford and seven witnesses before the notary Antonio Filippo Montelatici on 4 Nov. 1773, declares and affirms that the attached is her final will and that her 'universal heir' is mentioned therein (included in the Osborn Collection transcript of Lady Orford's will).

Page 183, note 5, line 6, *for* pt v *read* pt vi

Page 201, 4th line from bottom, *for* ouselves *read* ourselves

Page 234, line 3, *for* prefectly *read* perfectly

Page 252, note 6, *add* A poetical tribute to Conway, entitled 'The Triumph of Liberty, And Peace With America: A Poem. Inscribed to General Conway,' published by J. Walker, Pater-Noster-Row, 1782, contains the following lines:

> 'To thee, brave CONWAY, be an altar rais'd,
> Thou honest veteran, godlike mercy's friend,
> Thy noble efforts be for ever prais'd,
> For virtuous fame like thine can never end
> May'st thou still live to scourge intestine foes,
> To drag each t———r from th' insulted throne,
> To trace their arts, their foul designs disclose,
> While grateful Britons shall their guardian own,
> To thee they trust, their anxious bosoms wait,
> Hope, doubt, and dread speak in each eager eye;
> And from thy lips expect their country's fate,
> Resolv'd in Freedom's arms to live—or die. . . .
> But let the Muse prophane her plume no more
> With themes like these, but raise her silver wing,
> In Freedom's cause the righteous Gods implore
> And gentle Peace, and CONWAY's praises sing. . . .' (pp. 24–5)

Another panegyric on Conway and Liberty appeared in the *Public Advertiser* 2 March 1782 with the signature 'CAUSIDICUS' from Cirencester; it began,

'When Conway speaks, what Energy divine?
Bold Freedom breathes in every glowing Line.
No Cato ever soar'd a loftier Flight,
No Chatham ever blaz'd more Patriot Light.
On every Word the wond'ring Senate hung,
And Truths divine came mended from his Tongue.
Envy was dumb, in Admiration lost,
And Parties strove, which should applaud him most.
Like Noah's Dove he brings the Olive Wand,
And shows Redemption to the War-worn Land.
With Conway's Zeal may every Briton glow,
Britons, tho' late, lo! now their Interest know.
America and Britain shall unite,
And one brave Spirit urge the rival Fight....'

Page 392, note 16, last line, *for* April–Dec. 1782 *read* April–Dec. 1783 (Namier and Brooke ii. 250–1)

Page 409, note 21, line 5, *for* Augustin-Gabriel *read* Ange-Augustin-Gabriel

Page 412, 2d paragraph, third line from end, *after* Lord Offord's *insert* [*sic*]

Page 431, note 9, line 5, *after* daughter *add* (Lady Elizabeth Bertie)

Page 438, note 10, *substitute* Giuseppe Giusto Scaliger (1540–1609), Italian scholar and polemicist.

Page 450, note 9, line 1, *for* Rozier *read* Rosier

Page 456, From Mann 13 Dec. 1783, 1st paragraph, line 6, *on* lawyer *add note a*: a. Clemente de Pace, 'Doctor of Law' (Transcript of Lady Orford's will in the Osborn Collection, Beinecke Library, Yale University).

Page 463, note 5, lines 7–8, *for* his copy of *Walpoliana*, 1781, *read* his copy of the 1st edition of *Walpoliana*, 1781 (Hazen, *Cat. of HW's Lib.* No. 3924),

Page 494, heading, *for* From Horace Mann, the Younger, *read* From Horace Mann the Younger,

Page 497, note 7, line 5, *after* letters. *insert* Mrs Piozzi identifies the 'dancer' as the Baccelli (MONTAGU ii. 15, n. 12; see also MORE 268, n. 8; MASON ii. 78, n. 5), and Boswell notes after dining with Pembroke in Aug. 1792: 'I felt it strange, and regretted it, that so amiable a man should have contracted such dissolute habits, and at this very time, instead of living respectably with his charming Countess, had Baccelli, the superannuated dancing Courtesan, in a *Cassino* in the neighbourhood' (*Private Papers of James Boswell*, ed. G. Scott and F. A. Pottle, 1928–34, xviii. 136).

Page 513, note 12, *add* See also the review of A. C. Addington, *The Royal House of Stuart*, 1972, in TLS 15 Sept. 1972 (lxxi. 1053).

Page 516, note 4, line 3, *for* ca 1716 *read* ca 1717

Page 527, note 1a, right column, line 6, *for* Rozier's *read* **Rosier's**

Page 577, note 13, line 5, *for* m *read* m.

Page 590, note 9, line 1, *for* Rozier *read* Rosier

Page 604, note 8, last line, *for* livres *read livres*

Page 625, note 7, line 5, *for* Louis *read* Vincent-Louis   *Line 10, after* 125 *add*   ; *Dictionnaire de biographie française*, 1933– , xii. 893–4

Page 633, note 31, right column, line 4, *for* Ambrozy *read* Ambroźy

Page 634, note 36, lines 6–14, *delete* The letter is not listed . . . written and sent together with *and substitute* Mrs Piozzi writes concerning 'this extraordinary stroke of Mr Boswell's' to Samuel Lysons 1 March 1786: 'I have written to Mr Lucas Pepys, to Dr Lort, to Mrs Montagu herself, and to Cadell about it—and I have not yet half expressed the degree of pain it has given me' (MS in the possession of Mrs Donald F. Hyde, the Hyde Collection, Sommerville, New Jersey; printed in *Bentley's Miscellany*, 1850, xxviii. 442).   *Line 15, delete* which

Page 640, note 8, *add* See also Mrs Thrale to Boswell 18 May 1775 (MS in the Beinecke Library, Yale University); this is the letter which Boswell was citing as proof that she had read his journal.

Page 644, note 5, last line, *after* Mainwaring 'Piozziana' *add*   , now in the Houghton Library, Harvard University

Page 655, line 1, *on* answered none *add note* 14a: 14a. He wrote a reply, written ca July 1786, did not send it, but kept an extract in his 'Miscellany,' 1786–95; the extract is now printed in Misc. Corr. Appendix 5, iii. 507.

Page 661, running head, *for* To Mann *read* From Mann

Page 665, note 4, line 18, *after* usuage *add* [*sic*]

Page 682, note 16, right column, line 1, *after* King *add*   , with the advice and consent of Parliament,

VOLUME 26

Page xliii, left column, *sub* 1768, below 22 Sept. *insert* 1 Oct.*

Page 5, note 20, *add* But Chute's sketches for the bookcases at Strawberry Hill are in the final pages of a copy of Scamozzi's *Les Cinq Ordres de l'Architecture*, Paris, 1585, now at the Vyne, Hants.

Page 45, Extract I, line 17, *on* others *add note a*: a. This painting is now WSL.

Page 52, 3d line from bottom, *on* Hare *add note* 1: 1. Henry Hare died in 1733 (GM 1733, iii. 550).

Page 53, 2d paragraph, line 3, *for* 1752–76 *read* 1752–75

VOLUME 28

Page xxi, *sub* Bentley's Sketch for *The Bard, delete* From the original . . . hand. *and substitute* From a sketch by Bentley in Walpole's copy of Mason's *Gray*, now in the Houghton Library, Harvard University. The inscription is in Walpole's hand. Three other drawings by Bentley for *The Bard* are in Walpole's volume, *Drawings and Designs by Richard Bentley*, now WSL.

Page xlii, Grove's *Dictionary of Music*, right column, *for* Sir George Grove . . . 1927–8, 5 vols. *read The New Grove Dictionary of Music and Musicians*, 6th edn, ed. Stanley Sadie, 1980, 20 vols.

Page 7, line 1, *on* modern *add note* 2: 2. See HW to Joseph Warton 16 March 1765, MISC. CORR. i. 376–7

Page 7, note 3, *add* See Hazen, *Cat. of HW's Lib.* No. 938.

Page 7, note 4, line 3, *for* Molin-Dumesnil *read* Morin-Dumesnil

Page 7, note 6, *add* Hertford apparently sent HW a copy of the first French edition (CONWAY ii. 521 and n. 3).

Page 9, From Mason 8 May 1769, headnote, line 1, *for* MS untraced until *read* MS offered in Maggs Cat. No. 196 (1903), lot 976, ' "Alterations proposed in the Mysterious Mother"; 4 pages folio, in the autograph of Rev. Wm Mason; also autograph letter signed by Mason . . . with note below it in the autograph and signed by Horace Walpole May 8, 1769. £3 7s 6d. 5 line extract';

Page 17, note 6, right column, line 5, *for* 1762 *read* 1763   *Last line, after* half-title *add* (Hazen, *Cat. of HW's Lib.* No. 1609:22:9)

Page 20, note 6, line 1, *for* ca 1727 *read* 1727   *Line 2, after* M.P. *add* Hindon 1751–4,   *Line 4, after* n. 2 *add* ; Namier and Brooke ii. 309–10

Page 24, note 7, line 2, *after* burn *add* , 'Sawney'   *Last line, add* See also Namier and Brooke iii. 618–20.

Page 27, note 1, line 8, *for* i. 147 *read* i. 47

Page 30, note 25, *add* HW's copy is Hazen, *Cat. of HW's Lib.* No. 2981.

Page 30, note 26, last line, *after* 88 *add* (Hazen, *Cat. of HW's Lib.* Nos 1667, 1684)

Page 31, line 10, *on* Sir Thomas *add note* 30: 30. HW wrote Wyatt 26 July 1772 asking if he were descended from Sir Thomas, and Wyatt answered 1 Aug. saying that his great-grandfather was a Staffordshire farmer and beyond that his ancestry was unknown to him (see MISC. CORR. ii. 231–2).

Page 34, note 2, lines 3–4, *delete* HW evidently saw a private printing of his *Poems*, which were *and substitute* HW refers to separate printings of all four poems, which were later, in 1773, published by J. Ridley. There are copies of three of the poems at Farmington although Hazen refers only to two of them in the Appendix to his *SH Bibl.* 272–3. All three are printed on the same paper, but are not identical with the published versions in typographical arrangement. Each is signature A. The collected four *Poems* were   *Line 6, add* HW's copy of the 3d edn, 1773, is Hazen, *Cat. of HW's Lib.* No. 3222:12:1.

Page 35, note 8, line 8, *after* v. 125 *add* (Hazen, *Cat. of HW's Lib.* No. 2953)

Page 36, note 15, last line, *after* 15th' *add* (Hazen, *Cat. of HW's Lib.* No. 3222:12:2)

Page 37, note 5, line 1, *for* (ca 1700–81) *read* (?1699–1781)   *Line 3, after* 243 *add*   ; Namier and Brooke ii. 14

Page 37, note 8, last line, *after* WSL *add* (Hazen, *Cat. of HW's Lib.* No. 578)

Page 39, note 12, line 1, *for* 1720 *read* 1719

Page 40, note 21, last line, *after* n. 8 *add*   ; Hazen, *Cat. of HW's Lib.* No. 1810:28:6

Page 40, note 24, lines 1–2, *for* before 28 July *read* 13 July 1772   *Line 4, after Doubts add*   ; a note in the Index to the Minutes of the Society of Antiquaries, under Walpole, records HW's resignation (information from H. S. Kingsford; see also OSSORY i. 84 and n. 11)

Page 40, note 25, last line, *after* v. 124 *add* (Hazen, *Cat. of HW's Lib.* No. 2875)

Page 41, note 29, last line, *after* v. 36 *add* (Hazen, *Cat. of HW's Lib.* No. 3173)

Page 41, note 31, line 9, *for Humphrey read Humphry*

Page 47, note 9, last line, *after* 1046 *add* (Hazen, *Cat. of HW's Lib.* No. 3906)

Page 48, note 17, line 1, *for* 1685 *read* ca 1685   *Line 3, for* 1736–7 *read* 1737–8   *Line 4, after* Walpole *add* (Sedgwick i. 435–7)

Page 49, note 1, line 1, *delete* ca   *Line 4, for* 1802–7 *read* 1801–7   *Line 5, after* n. 10 *add*   ; Namier and Brooke ii. 446–7

Page 52, note 1, line 1, *for* ca 1715 *read* ca 1720

Page 56, note 15, line 3, *for* 1753 *read* 1754   *Line 4, for* 1781–3 *read* 1779–83

Page 56, note 19, *add* See *post* 19 July 1774, when HW sent to Mason a copy of Gray's *Catalogue* with HW's MS notes; this copy has not been traced (Hazen, *Cat. of HW's Lib.* No. 3892).

Page 58, note 4, last line, *after* 75 *add* (Hazen, *Cat. of HW's Lib.* No. 632)

Page 58, note 9, line 11, *after* actor.' *add* See Hazen, *Cat. of HW's Lib.* No. 1810:19:4.

Page 61, note 5, line 3, *for* (d. 1801) *read* (1725–1801)   *Line 6, after* 1773 *add*   ; Namier and Brooke iii. 495   *Line 7, after* vi. 52 *add* (Hazen, *Cat. of HW's Lib.* No. 2471)

Page 65, note 2, line 5, *after* WSL *add* (Hazen, *Cat. of HW's Lib.* No. 1810:19:9)

Page 67, note 6, *add* See Hazen, *Cat. of HW's Lib.* Nos 3186, 4002.

Page 71, note 19, line 3, *after* Treasury *add* 1756–7,

Page 74, note 14, line 5, *after Advertiser add*   ; Hazen, *Cat. of HW's Lib.* No. 3222:12:10

Page 76, note 24, *add* There is a commendation of Carter by Michael Tyson in his letter to Richard Gough 3 May 1779 (Gough MSS, f. 367):

'Mason in his return from Cambridge called and dined with me yester-day—His man Charles has painted a portrait of Old Pegge [Samuel Pegge, 1704–96], and it is a most striking likeness.—I have persuaded Mason to let the said Charles etch it.'

Page 77, note 4, line 1, *for* ca 1739 *read* ?1738

Page 78, note 13, *add* HW's copy of the *Dispensary* with MS notes appeared in the sale of Kirgate's library (Hazen, *Cat. of HW's Lib.* No. 4005).

Page 79, note 21, last line, *after* George III' *add* ; Hazen, *Cat. of HW's Lib.* No. 1810:19:10

Page 80, note 26, *add* Mason's letter to Nicholls 31 Jan. 1775, in which he confesses that Nicholls 'will find that much liberty has been taken in transposing parts of them, &c. for the press, and will see the reason for it; it were however to be wished that the originals might be so disposed of as not to impeach the Editor's fidelity,' is now WSL (printed by Mitford in *The Works of Thomas Gray*, 1835–43, v. 163–4).

Page 80, note 27, line 1, *for* Barrett (1744–1803) *read* Barret (?1743–1803)

Page 85, 2d paragraph, line 1, *on* letters *add note* 4a: 4a. An edition of the 'Letters of Lady Rachel Russel, from the Originals in the Library at Woburn Abbey,' with an 'Introduction vindicating the Character of Lord Russel against Sir John Dalrymple, etc. . . . Printed for Edward and Charles Dilly,' was advertised in the *Public Adv.* 15 May 1773 as 'Tuesday next [18 May] will be published.' The first advertisement for 'This day is published . . . one volume quarto (price 8s in boards)' appears in the 21 May issue.

Page 85, note 5, last line, *after* 74 *add* (Hazen, *Cat. of HW's Lib.* No. 3258)

Page 86, note 12, left column, line 1, *for* 1728 *read* 1727   *Line 3, for* 1760–83 *read* 1760–84 (Namier and Brooke iii. 226, 227–30)

Page 86, note 17, last line, *after* v. 136 *add* (Hazen, *Cat. of HW's Lib.* No. 2869)

Page 89, note 31, last line, *for* v. 141 *read* i. 47 (Hazen, *Cat. of HW's Lib.* No. 42)

Page 89, note 33, line 4, *after* life *add* (HW's copy is Hazen, *Cat. of HW's Lib.* No. 54)

Page 93, note 10, last line, *after* WSL *add* (Hazen, *Cat. of HW's Lib.* No. 581)

Page 99, note 5, line 5, *after* Walpole *add* (see Hazen, *Cat. of HW's Lib.* No. 1161)

Page 101, note 18, line 7, *after* v. 31 *add* (Hazen, *Cat. of HW's Lib.* No. 3291)

Page 102, 2d paragraph, line 2, *on* verses *add note* 26a: 26a. A variant copy of these verses, in Garrick's hand, is in the Beinecke Library, Yale University.

Page 102, note 20, last line, *after* 73 *add*   ; Hazen, *Cat. of HW's Lib.* No. 3597

Page 103, note 27, *add* Another suggestion is hand-kerchief box.

Page 105, note 12, *add* See also CHUTE 460 and n. 12, 461.

Page 109, note 10, line 3, *for* Day *read* Daye

Page 109, note 2, *add* The characters are listed in *London Stage* Part IV, iii. 1753; the performance on 16 Nov., ibid. iii. 1761.

Page 110, note 11, line 7, *after* cit.). *add* Six performances of *Alfred* and a repetition of the 'Grand Naval Review' are listed in *London Stage* Part IV, iii. 1750–3, 1758, 1760, 1774.

Page 110, note 12, line 3, *after* 397 *add*   ; *London Stage* Part IV, iii. 1760   *Last line, after* November' *add* (Hazen, *Cat. of HW's Lib.* No. 1810:20:10)

Page 118, note 7, last line, *after* WSL *add* (Hazen, *Cat. of HW's Lib.* No. 1810:21:3)

Page 119, note 2, line 2, *for* 27 *read* 23

Page 131, note 8, *add* For HW's copy see Hazen, *Cat. of HW's Lib.* No. 3173.

Page 135, note 8, last line, *after* WSL *add* (Hazen, *Cat. of HW's Lib.* No. 637). Several of those commemorated were not the King's veterans, but Cromwell's: 'An Ordinance now [1655] came out, for setling the Revenue of the poor Knights of *Windsor*; and several of *Cromwel's* old Trojans were now Tituladoed with this Pensionary Honour, and none else to be admitted' (James Heath, *A Chronicle of the Late Intestine War in the Three Kingdoms*, 2d edn, 1676, p. 372; HW's copy, 1678 edn, is Hazen, op. cit. No. 1118).

Page 135, note 10, line 13, *for* 1730 *read* 1739

Page 136, note 14, right column, line 8, *after* Library *add* (Hazen, *Cat. of HW's Lib.* No. 3222:13:6)

Page 140, note 1, last line, *after* v. 39 *add* (Hazen, *Cat. of HW's Lib.* No. 3161)

Page 140, note 5, *add* See Hazen, *Cat. of HW's Lib.* No. 3214.

Page 141, note 13, right column, line 7, *for* copy *read* copies   *Line 8, after* WSL *add* (Hazen, *Cat. of HW's Lib.* Nos 1609:31:9, 1609:34:2)

Page 142, note 17, last line, *after* WSL *add*   ; Hazen, *Cat. of HW's Lib.* No. 1609:58:9

Page 145, note 21, line 2, *for* Sackville-Germain *read* Germain

Page 146, note 25, right column, line 6, *after* hand *add* (Hazen, *Cat. of HW's Lib.* No. 436)

Page 150, note 16, line 3, *for* The author has not been identified. *substitute* The *Familiar Epistle* is attributed to R. B. Sheridan and is printed in his *Plays and Poems*, ed. R. Crompton Rhodes, Oxford, 1928, iii. 169–96; but Cecil Price in his edition of *The Letters of Richard Brinsley Sheridan*, Oxford, 1966, i. 85, n. 2 questions this attribution.

Page 154, note 25, last line, *after* iii. 39 *add* (Hazen, *Cat. of HW's Lib.* No. 1389)

Page 155, note 29, line 3, *for* 1774–84 *read* 1774–80   *for* 1784–9 *read* 1780–9

Page 159, note 1, *add* See Hazen, *Cat. of HW's Lib.* No. 3140.

Page 161, note 2, line 4, *for* 1773 *read* 1772   *Line 5, before* C. S. Northup *insert* see *ante* 1 Dec. 1772;

Page 163, note 1, line 8, *for* 1773 *read* 1772

Page 173, note 6, line 2, *for* 1726 *read* ?1725   *Last line, add* See Namier and Brooke iii. 89–90.

Page 176, note 2, left column, line 7, *after* pole' *add* (Hazen, *Cat. of HW's Lib.* No. 1810:23:9)

Page 177, note 8, *for* (d. 1803) *read* (ca 1735–1803) (P. H. Highfill, Jr, K. A. Burnim and E. A. Langhans, *A Biographical Dictionary of Actors, Actresses . . . in London, 1660–1800,* Carbondale, Illinois, 1973– , i. 47–52)

Page 180, note 11, lines 4–6, *delete* from a descendant of Watkin Williams, who was 'probably descended from Sir Kenelm. . . . *and substitute* probably from three daughters (Penelope, Catherine, Frances) of Col. James Russell Stapleton (HW to Thomas Pennant 25 May 1773, Misc. Corr. ii. 253, n. 22).   *Line 7, for* This set *read* 'This set   *Lines 12–14, delete* The names of these heirs . . . the second set. *and substitute* The lady was presumably Elizabeth Stapleton (1740–1825), who m. (1767) Watkin Williams, of Penbedw, Flintshire, in whose house the miniatures were found; see Misc. Corr. ii. 253, nn. 22, 23.

Page 187, note 14, line 2, *after* Library *insert* ; see Hazen, *Cat. of HW's Lib.* No. 3841

Page 189, 2d paragraph, line 9, *on* its age.' *add note* 37: 37. A variant of this anecdote is in William Cooke, *Memoirs of Samuel Foote, Esq.,* 1805, ii. 59.

Page 189, note 32, *add* See Hazen, *Cat. of HW's Lib.* Nos 1609:33:6,7; 1609:35:1.

Page 191, note 2, line 5, *after* v. 153 *add* (Hazen, *Cat. of HW's Lib.* No. 2972)

Page 191, note 3, last line, *after* v. 145 *add* (Hazen, *Cat. of HW's Lib.* No. 2792)

Page 191, note 4, last line, *after* iii. 36 *add* (Hazen, *Cat. of HW's Lib.* No. 1431)

Page 191, note 7, last line, *add* See Hazen, *Cat. of HW's Lib.* Nos 411, 3814.

Page 192, note 10, last line, *after* v. 65 *add* (Hazen, *Cat. of HW's Lib.* Nos 3198, 3199)

Page 192, note 13, last line, *after* WSL *add* (Hazen, *Cat. of HW's Lib.* Nos 1609:35:2,3)

Page 194, note 4, line 8, *after Music insert* 6th edn, 1980, i. 115–17;

Page 195, note 5, *add* See also Hazen, *Cat. of HW's Lib.* No. 3588.

Page 200, note 17, *add* For HW's copy see Hazen, *Cat. of HW's Lib.* No. 3060.

Page 200, note 18, *add* For HW's copy see Hazen, *Cat. of HW's Lib.* No. 3082.

Page 203, note 12, *add* See Hazen, *Cat. of HW's Lib.* No. 1609:58:16.

Page 203, note 13, *add* See Hazen, *Cat. of HW's Lib.* No. 1609:58:12.

Page 204, line 2, *on* Pindar *add note* 15a: 15a. Mason and Mrs Montagu are the subject of a print, 'Abelard and Eloisa,' by Carrington Bowles, 1778; see BM, *Satiric Prints* No. 4557.

Page 204, note 21, line 3, *delete* doubtless   *Line 5, for* WH's *read* HW's   *Line 6, add* See Hazen, *Cat. of HW's Lib.* No. 4; COLE i. 374.

Page 205, note 4, last line, *after* v. 169 *add*   ; see Hazen, *Cat. of HW's Lib.* No. 3060.

Page 207, note 16, right column, line 3, *after* WSL *add* (Hazen, *Cat. of HW's Lib.* No. 1609:58:18)

Page 233, note 8, *add* But Lady Luxborough wrote to Shenstone 13 March 1751: 'Vous avez vu sans doute ces vers écrits dans une cimetière, dont notre Duchesse [the Duchess of Somerset] m'avait parlé; ils me plaisent beaucoup' (Lady Luxborough, op. cit. 248). She also praises 'four very moving lines' in the Epitaph (ibid. 251); and after the passage HW comments on she adds, 'and think all the first part of the Elegy very beautiful. I cannot see why it did not end at the most beautiful line in it' (ibid. 266).

Page 234, note 12, last line, *after* iii. 160 *add* (Hazen, *Cat. of HW's Lib.* No. 1838)

Page 238, note 12, *add* See HW to Astle 22 April 1768, in MISC. CORR. ii. 144.

Page 238, note 15, line 3, *for* vi *read* vi.

Page 239, note 20, line 2, *for* Nicholas *read* Nathaniel

Page 242, note 4, line 2, *after* admired *add* (see Hazen, *Cat. of HW's Lib.* Nos 1810:59:4, 3222:7:3)

Page 242, note 5, last line, *after* Library *add* (Hazen, *Cat. of HW's Lib.* No. 3222:15:2)

Page 242, note 7, last line, *after* 'April 8' *add* (Hazen, *Cat. of HW's Lib.* No. 3222:15:16)

Page 243, note 10, last line, *after* WSL *add* (Hazen, *Cat. of HW's Lib.* No. 1609:14:1)

Page 243, note 12, last line, *after* Harvard *add* (Hazen, *Cat. of HW's Lib.* No. 3222:14:23)

Page 243, note 14, *add* HW's copies are Hazen, *Cat. of HW's Lib.* Nos 321, 2943.

Page 243, note 15, last line, *add* See Hazen, *Cat. of HW's Lib.* No. 3188.

Page 243, note 16, line 4, *after* 'foolish.' *add* As M.P. for Petersfield

1734–41 and for Southampton 1741–7, the elder Gibbon joined the Opposition which engineered the fall of Sir Robert Walpole (see Sedgwick ii. 62).

Page 244, note 18, line 5, *after* WSL *add* ; see Hazen, *Cat. of HW's Lib.* Nos 1786, 3015

Page 244, note 21, line 4, *after* Beauclerk. *insert* She lived at Muswell Hill, Middlesex, in 1775, near Highgate (Topham Beauclerk to HW 19 Aug. 1775). *Last line, after* Hill *add* 1780–9

Page 244, note 22, *substitute* Bistre (see OED).

Page 244, note 23, *delete last sentence* Their present whereabouts is unknown. *and substitute* Six of them are now WSL (see OSSORY i. 289, n. 18).

Page 244, note 29, lines 3–5, *delete last sentence* HW owned . . . now WSL. *and substitute* HW's copy of Hanmer's edition, 1744–5, is now WSL, but 'apparently HW never owned any of the editions derived immediately from Johnson' (see Hazen, *Cat. of HW's Lib.* Nos 64, 1360).

Page 245, note 35, line 1, *for* A.-A. *read* Antoine-A. *for* (d. ca 1814) *read* (ca 1737–1814)

Page 247, last line of verses, *on* I am *add note* 52: 52. 'I'm' in HW's MS copy of Lady Craven to HW 17 Feb. 1776, now WSL (MISC. CORR. ii. 339).

Page 247, note 50, line 3, *for* in 1780 *read* ca 1783 *Line 4, for* Christian Karl Alexander Friedrich *read* Christian Friedrich Karl Alexander *Line 5, for* Anspach *read* Ansbach (see *The Beautiful Lady Craven*, ed. A. M. Broadley and Lewis Melville, 1914, i. 45, 48)

Page 248, note 1, line 11, *after* 32 *add* (Hazen, *Cat. of HW's Lib.* No. 3163)

Page 248, note 2, last line, *after* WSL *add* (Hazen, *Cat. of HW's Lib.* No. 34)

Page 249, note 8, *add* See also CONWAY iii. 476 and n. 8.

Page 249, note 14, last line, *after* iv. 72 *add* (Hazen, *Cat. of HW's Lib.* No. 1099)

Page 252, note 6, last line, *after* Library *add* (Hazen, *Cat. of HW's Lib.* No. 3222:14:1)

Page 257, note 2, line 7, *after* v. 134 *add* (Hazen, *Cat. of HW's Lib.* No. 2822)

Page 257, note 6, *add* See Hazen, *Cat. of HW's Lib.* No. 3222:14:20.

Page 258, note 12, *add* HW's copies of the first two volumes are Hazen, *Cat. of HW's Lib.* No. 3147.

Page 269, note 6, *add* See Hazen, *Cat. of HW's Lib.* No. 2893.

Page 269, note 7, last line, *after* 20 *add* (Hazen, *Cat. of HW's Lib.* No. 1527)

Page 269, note 10, last line, *after* iv. 92 *add* (Hazen, *Cat. of HW's Lib.* No. 2274)

Page 271, note 5, *add* See also Hazen, *Cat. of HW's Lib.* No. 3222:14:10.

Page 275, note 7, line 3, *for* Billingham *read* Bellingham *Last line, add* See Hazen, *Cat. of HW's Lib.* Nos 2928, 3793, and HW's bibliography of Plat in his 'Book of Materials,' 1786–95 (*Horace Walpole's Miscellany 1786–1795*, ed. Lars E. Troide, New Haven, Conn., 1978, pp. 9–10).

Page 277, note 9, *add* See *London Stage* Part V, i. 42–3. HW's copy, with his note, 'Acted for the first time Dec. 6, 1776,' is now WSL (Hazen, *Cat. of HW's Lib.* No. 1810:26:10).

Page 278, note 3, line 1, *for* Cain *read* Caïn *or* Kaïn   *for* Lekain *read* LeKain *or* Le Kain   *Line 2, for* 1728 *read* 1729   *after* actor *insert* of the Comédie-Française 1750–78   *Line 3, after* tragedian *add* (*Enciclopedia dello spettacolo*, Rome, 1954–62, vi. 1364–7)

Page 279, note 7, *add* For HW's copy see Hazen, *Cat. of HW's Lib.* No. 3363:3.

Page 280, note 9, line 2, *after* iii. 181 *add* ; Hazen, *Cat. of HW's Lib.* No. 2090

Page 281, note 1, last line, *after* Harvard *add* (Hazen, *Cat. of HW's Lib.* No. 3222:15:26)

Page 281, note 4, last line, *after* 344–5 *add* ; Hazen, *Cat. of HW's Lib.* No. 3690

Page 285, note 2, line 1, *for* 1732 *read* 1733   *Lines 2–3, for* Opéra-Comique *read* Comédie-Italienne 1760–72 (*Enciclopedia dello spettacolo*, Rome, 1954–62, ii. 1476; *Dictionnaire de biographie française*, 1933– , vii. 867–8; CONWAY iii. 213, n. 36)

Page 285, note 4, line 2, *after* 609 *add* ; *London Stage* Part III, ii. 831

Page 288, note 24, line 1, *for* (d. 1786) *read* (1709–86)

Page 289, note 12, last line, *after* BM *add* (Hazen, *Cat. of HW's Lib.* No. 3915)

Page 291, note 37, *add* See also Hazen, *Cat. of HW's Lib.* Nos 2295, 3149.

Page 291, note 38, last line, *after* ii. 134 *add* (Hazen, *Cat. of HW's Lib.* No. 1011)

Page 295, note 2, last line, *after* 420 *add* ; Hazen, *Cat. of HW's Lib.* No. 3130

Page 301, To Mason 18 April 1777, 1st paragraph, line 7, *on* book *add note* 1a: 1a. See Hazen, *Cat. of HW's Lib.* No. 4011.

Page 302, note 5, line 1, *for* 1686 *read* ca 1686   *Last line, add* See also Sedgwick ii. 561–2.

Page 303, note 14, line 6, *after* Library *add* (Hazen, *Cat. of HW's Lib.* No. 3222:15:11)

Page 303, note 15, last line, *after* Library *add* (Hazen, *Cat. of HW's Lib.* No. 3222:15:6)

Page 304, note 21, last line, *after* Library *add* (Hazen, *Cat. of HW's Lib.* No. 3222:15:6, 7, 8, 9, 14)

Page 305, note 27, right column, line 4, *for* 1775 *read* 1772

Page 309, note 11, *add* See also *London Stage* Part V, i. 81.

Page 309, note 12, last line, *after* 1774 *add* ; *London Stage* Part II, ii. 931, 954

Page 310, note 13, last line, *after* WSL *add* (Hazen, *Cat. of HW's Lib.* No. 1609:38:1)

Page 313, note 2, right column, line 4, *after* Nov. *insert* [Jan.]   *Line 5, after* 1776 *insert* (for dating of this letter see MISC. CORR. ii. 332–3)

Page 313, note 4, line 13, *after* 1777). *add* For HW's copies see Hazen, *Cat. of HW's Lib.* No. 3222:15:10, 12.

Page 314, note 12, *add* See also Hazen, *Cat. of HW's Lib.* No. 2942.

Page 317, note 10, *add* According to Mary and Robert Brian Wagg ('Two Houses by Carr of York,' *Country Life*, 12 April 1956, cxix. 752–5), the architect was John Carr (1723–1807).

Page 320, note 24, line 2, *for* a few *read* two or three

Page 323, note 1, line 1, *for* Coney *read* Cony   *for* 1774–81 *read* 1774–91   *Line 2, for* Coney *read* Cony   *Last line, add* See also FAMILY 118 and n. 4.

Page 324, note 17, line 8, *for* Anderson *read* Adamson

Page 325, note 17, last line, *add* See Hazen, *Cat. of HW's Lib.* No. 3128.

Page 328, note 8, line 1, *for* 1722 *read* 1723

Page 326, note 23, *add* See also *Enciclopedia dello spettacolo*, Rome, 1954–62, vi. 271.

Page 329, note 5, line 2, *for*   -Jumelle de Berneville *read* Le Jumel de Barneville   *Line 3, for* (d. 1705), Comtesse d'Aulnoy *read* (1650 or 1651–1705), m. (ca 1665) François de la Motte, Baron d'Aulnoy (*Dictionnaire de biographie française*, 1933– , iv. 592–4)   *Last line, after* 73 *add* (Hazen, *Cat. of HW's Lib.* No. 1776)

Page 330, note 8, line 7, *after* 1777' *add* (see Hazen, *Cat. of HW's Lib.* No. 1609:38:8, No. 1609:40:6)

Page 336, note 6, line 2, *for* Bn of Bingley *read* Bn Bingley

Page 336, note 8, line 1, *for* (d. 1776) *read* (1728–76)   *Line 3, for* (1743) *read* (ca 1751)

Page 337, note 11, last line, *after* WSL *add* (Hazen, *Cat. of HW's Lib.* No. 1609:38:9)

Page 338, heading at bottom of page, *for* To Mason, Wednesday 24 October 1777 *read* To Mason, Friday 24 October 1777

Page 339, line 1, *on* here *add* note 1aa: 1aa. Sir Edward wrote to HW at SH on 23 Oct. (postmarked 23 Oct., FAMILY 155), telling him that the Duke and Duchess had arrived at Dover on 22 Oct. and would be at Gloucester House by 3 o'clock on 24 Oct. HW presumably went to town in the morning of the 24th. According to Lady Mary Coke, 'MS Journals' 10 Oct., HW 'was invited to be at Lady George Germain's on Tuesday next; he said if the Duchess of Gloucester was not come he would go, if she was he must go to town; to this some of the company answered, "Do you expect them that day?" "One day this week they must be in town" was his reply.'

Page 339, note 2, *substitute* The Duke and Duchess arrived at Gloucester House about 3 P.M. on 24 Oct. (FAMILY 155); HW, Sir Edward, and

Conway waited on them in the early evening of 24 Oct., and then HW
and Conway went to a loo party at which HW arrived about 10:30 P.M.
He must have been writing this letter to Mason in the middle of the
night, possibly after midnight, and therefore might write 'yesterday' meaning Friday, 24 Oct. (Lady Mary Coke in 'MS Journals' 24 Oct. wrote, 'The
Gloucesters arrived this evening: two of our party at loo came from waiting upon them, General Conway and Mr Walpole: the latter did not
arrive till half an hour after ten o'clock'; for Sir Edward's visit see *Last
Journals* ii. 59). See also MANN viii. 332, n. 5.

Page 340, note 9, *substitute* 'General Sir George Howard, who at first
had gone to Gloucester House, then abstained, and lately had opposed
the increase of the allowance of the Royal Dukes, thinking the reconcilia-
tion [between George III and the D. of Gloucester] made, went the very
next morning after the Duke's arrival to pay his duty to him' (*Last Journals* ii. 68).

Page 342, note 7, line 3, *for* 1778 *read* 1777

Page 343, note 12, *for* (d. 1780) *read* (fl. 1739–80)   *Line 3, after* vi. 5
add   ; *London Stage* Part V, i. 104, 135

Page 347, note 17, line 4, *after* vi. 18 *add*   ; *London Stage* Part V, i.
108, 142–3   *Last line, add* See Hazen, *Cat. of HW's Lib.* No. 1810:27:11.

Page 347, note 18, line 2, *after* vi. 7 *add*   ; *London Stage* Part V, i. 105,
143   *Last line, after* WSL *add* (Hazen, *Cat. of HW's Lib.* No. 1810:27:6)

Page 348, note 23, last line, *after* v. 45 *add* (Hazen, *Cat. of HW's Lib.*
No. 3156)

Page 352, note 5, line 7, *after* 360–1 *add*   ; *London Stage* Part IV, iii.
1673   *Last line, add* The new version was first performed 23 Feb. 1779;
see *London Stage* Part V, i. 196, 236.

Page 355, note 11, line 4, *after* 247 *add*   ; *London Stage* Part II, ii. 987,
1023

Page 356, note 15, last line, *for* 1784–7 *read* 1786–7 (Namier and Brooke
ii. 683–5)

Page 361, note 29, *add* 'The character of Alfred is so very ill drawn that
a line in this play would be a proper motto to it "I shall surprise you
much—my name is Alfred" ' (HW's note in his copy, now WSL, of David
Erskine Baker, *Biographia Dramatica*, rev. Isaac Reed, 1782, i. 8, which
is Hazen, *Cat. of HW's Lib.* No. 3912).

Page 362, note 7, line 3, *after* 361 *add*   ; *London Stage* Part IV, iii.
1753, 1761

Page 362, note 9, line 2, *after* 95 *add*   ; *London Stage* Part V, i. 196, 236
Page 371, note 3, *add* Or 'not' may have been omitted.
Page 372, note 14, *add* See Hazen, *Cat. of HW's Lib.* No. 3197.
Page 374, note 28, right column, line 5, *after* v. 24 *add*   ; see also Ha-
zen, *Cat. of HW's Lib.* No. 2999
Page 374, note 29, line 5, *after Music add* 6th edn, 1980, vii. 465–6, xiv.
724,

Page 381, note 23, line 3, *after* vi. 56 *add* (Hazen ,*Cat. of HW's Lib*. No. 2461)

Page 383, note 5, line 5, *after* 1778). *add* See also B. F. Stevens, *Facsimiles of Manuscripts in European Archives Relating to America 1773–1778*, 1889–98, xi. No. 1109, where the embarkation is dated 15 April.

Page 383, note 6, line 2, *for* 1796 *read* 1797

Page 383, note 12, last line, *after* 133–4 *add*   ; Namier and Brooke ii. 446

Page 384, note 14, line 6, *after* Library *add*   ; Hazen, *Cat. of HW's Lib*. No. 3222:16:25

Page 384, note 18, line 5, *after* Library *add*   ; Hazen, *Cat. of HW's Lib*. No. 3222:16:24

Page 384, note 19, line 3, *after* Library *add* (Hazen, *Cat. of HW's Lib*. No. 3222:8:1)

Page 386, note 34, lines 8–10, *delete* The original drawing . . . Wayland Wells Williams. *and substitute* A second version is in the Royal Collection at Windsor and has been reproduced in the *Connoisseur*, May 1922, frontispiece; a third version was in 1957 in the possession of Mrs D. V. Garstin, New Haven, Connecticut, who inherited it from her brother, Wayland Wells Williams.

Page 387, note 2, last line, *after* 1776 *add*   ; Hazen, *Cat. of HW's Lib*. No. 3216

Page 387, note 8, line 3, *for* ca 1681 *read* 1681

Page 388, note 8, line 2, *for* Tyrconnell *read* Tyrconnel

Page 402, note 23, last line, *after* 1776 *add* and to Lady Ossory 23 Jan. 1783

Page 405, note 15, *add* See also Namier and Brooke iii. 573–4.

Page 408, note 3, line 2, *for* 1725 *read* 1723   *after* M.P. *insert* Liskeard 1759–68   *Line 4, after* Bt *add* (Namier and Brooke iii. 475)

Page 413, 4th paragraph, line 1, *on* week *add note* 10a: 10a. 11 July; see HW to Lady Ossory 12 July 1778, OSSORY ii. 26.

Page 417, From Mason 19 July 1778, 1st paragraph, line 3, *on* book *add note* 1a: 1a. HW's copy of the third book, 4to, 1779, is Hazen, *Cat. of HW's Lib*. No. 3222:16:13.

Page 420, note 4, right column, line 16, *after* 351–63 *add* (revised version in *Horace Walpole: Writer, Politician, and Connoisseur*, ed. W. H. Smith, 1967, pp. 255–91)

Page 421, note 7, *add* See *ante* 18 April 1778.

Page 423, note 19, next to last line, *after* etc. *add* (Hazen, *Cat. of HW's Lib*. No. 3408)

Page 423, note 26, *add* Despite HW's statement that he wrote the pamphlet on 23 July ('last night'), the surviving MS in Kirgate's hand has at the top (crossed out, but still legible): 'Begun July 26, 1778, finished

28th' (MS, with HW's corrections and Thomas Percy's endorsement, is in the Beinecke Library, Yale University), but this date may have been added later.

Page 443, note 13, line 2, *for* 1787 *read* 1786

Page 445, note 8, *add* See also OSSORY ii. 62 and n. 5.

Page 445, note 9, lines 4–6, *delete* and there is no reason to believe that he ever received any more of it. *and substitute* and £4000 without interest in 1786 (see MANN ix. 637; OSSORY ii. 62 and n. 7).

Page 445, note 10, *add* For a quotation from Lady Horatia's letter to Anne Clement 10 Oct., see OSSORY ii. 61, n. 3.

Page 446, note 14, line 7, *after* 19 *add* and 20

Page 447, note 21, line 1, *for* (d. 1788) *read* (1716–88)   *Line 2, for* ca 1720 *read* 1727

Page 448, note 30, line 1, *for* Pedro Jiménez de Góngora (d. 1794) *read* Pedro Francisco Luján Silva y Góngora (1727–94), 6th Marqués de Almodóvar, cr. (1780)   *Line 2, delete* del Rio   *Line 5, after* Jiménez *add* Luján

Page 453, note 3, line 2, *for* ca 1716 *read* ca 1714

Page 454, note 7, line 2, *for* 1748–65 *read* 1745–65

Page 458, note 10, *add* See also CONWAY iii. 319–20 and nn. 1, 4, 343.

Page 470, 2d paragraph, line 2, *on* Sion Hill *add note* 14a: 14a. HW dined with Lady Holdernesse at Syon Hill on 19 Oct., the other guests being Lord and Lady Hertford, Lady Margaret Compton, Lady Harriet Vernon, Lord Beauchamp, 'Mr Potenger,' and Lady Mary Coke (Coke, 'MS Journals' 19 Oct. 1779).

Page 470, note 21, *add* See Hazen, *Cat. of HW's Lib.* No. 3222:16:3.

Page 477, note 11, line 4, *after* v. 116 *add* (Hazen, *Cat. of HW's Lib.* No. 2801)

Page 481, note 12, lines 5–6, *for* solicitor-general, 1802; attorney-general, 1805; *read* solicitor-general 1802–5 and attorney-general 1805–6 to the Prince of Wales;

Page 483, note 2, *add* Peers in fact were active, particularly Rockingham, in the organization of the meeting. Wyvill had early come to an agreement with the committee, of whom Mason was one, that no members of either house of Parliament should be included on the advertisement. Seven peers attended the meeting. See Wyvill, op. cit. i and iii. *passim*; Wentworth-Woodhouse MSS, Rockingham R1–1867–1876 (information from E. C. Black).

Page 486, note 8, *add* Sir Owen F. Morshead says that the insecurity of the foundations of the castle in the 1770's was the reason for filling in the medieval ditch, but the south terrace was never removed (*Windsor Castle*, 1951, p. 40).

Page 487, note 9, *add* See Hazen, *Cat. of HW's Lib.* No. 1609:40:5.

Page 487, note 10, last line, *after* George III' *add* (Hazen, *Cat. of HW's Lib.* No. 3222:16:23)

Page 487, note 11, *add* HW's copy of the 1st edn, now WSL, is Hazen, *Cat. of HW's Lib.* No. 1810:33:5.

Page 487, note 12, line 2, *for* 29 Oct. *read* 30 Oct.   *Line 3, after* Tilburina *add* (*London Stage* Part V, i. 292)

Page 488, note 17, lines 2–3, *for* 1774–84 *read* 1774–9, 1780–4   *Line 3, for* Newton 1790–3 and 1796–1802 *read* Newtown 1790–1, 1791–3, 1796–1801   *Line 4, for* 1779 *read* 1780   *Last line, after* ii. 147 *add*   ; Namier and Brooke i. 293, iii. 659

Page 492, note 9, line 1, *for* 1749–1821 *read* 1749–1822   *Line 3, for* Kingston *read* Kingston-upon-Hull   *Line 6, for* 259. *read* 259; Namier and Brooke iii. 465–6.

VOLUME 29

Page 2, note 12, lines 1–2, *for* (b. between 1738 and 1743, d. 1783) *read* (1740–83)   *Last line, before* 1783 *insert* 1740, x. 316;   *at end add* See also CONWAY iii. 345–7.

Pages 2–3, note 19, *add* See Hazen, *Cat. of HW's Lib.* No. 3222:17:11.

Page 4, note 2, line 4, *after* 618 *add*   ; *London Stage* Part III, ii. 819

Page 4, note 4, next to last line, *after* April 1762 *add*   , to Sir William Hamilton 23 Oct. 1775,

Page 5, note 9, line 1, *for* (ca 1720–80) *read* (1721–13 Jan. 1780)   *Lines 5–6, for* envoy to Russia, 1766 *read* ambassador designate to Russia 1766–7   *Last line, add* (For his birth date, see Namier and Brooke iii. 468; but for his death date, see Lady Mary Coke, 'MS Journals' 13 Jan. 1780.)

Page 6, note 20, last line, *after* iii. 29 *add* (Hazen, *Cat. of HW's Lib.* No. 1494)

Page 6, note 23, *add* HW's copy is Hazen, *Cat. of HW's Lib.* No. 2459.

Page 7, note 24, left column, line 3, *after* Craven. *add* HW's copy is Hazen, *Cat. of HW's Lib.* No. 2364.

Page 9, note 5, line 3, *after* vi. 265–6 *add*   ; *London Stage* Part V, i. 578

Page 11, note 20, line 2, *after* vi. 146 *add*   ; *London Stage* Part V, i. 315

Page 16, note 23, line 7, *after* 426). *add* Cheshire sent a deputy to one session of the Convention (ibid.); but Portland, who helped organize the original meeting in Cheshire, was rather suspicious of Cheshire Whigs 'who, I fear, have forgot the substance though they are very attentive to the shadow of their principles' (Portland to Lady Rockingham 17 Jan. 1780, Wentworth-Woodhouse MSS, R 140/57; information from E. C. Black).

Page 18, note 8, last line, *after* 197–8 *add* Hazen, *Cat. of HW's Lib.* No. 3026

Page 18, note 10, line 7, *after* 58 *add*   ; Hazen, *Cat. of HW's Lib.* No. 3688

Page 19, note 12, last line, *after* iii. 21 *add*   ; one copy is now WSL (see Hazen, *Cat. of HW's Lib.* Nos 1501, 360:1)

Page 29, note 3, line 2, *for* 1741–7 *read* 1742–7   *Line 3, for* 1750–80 *read* 1751–80   *Last line, after* name *add* (Namier and Brooke iii. 196–9)

Page 31, note 9, last line, *after* v. 126 *add* (Hazen, *Cat. of HW's Lib.* No. 2969)

Page 36, note 34, *add* See also Namier and Brooke i. 360.

Page 36, note 40, last line, *after* Harvard *add* (Hazen, *Cat. of HW's Lib.* No. 3222:17:5)

Page 37, note 43, *add* See Hazen, *Cat. of HW's Lib.* No. 540.

Page 37, note 48, line 1, *for* (d. 1799) *read* (ca 1715–99)   *Last line, add* See also Namier and Brooke ii. 114–15.

Page 40, note 7, last line, *after* Library *add* (Hazen, *Cat. of HW's Lib.* No. 3222:17:15)

Page 43, note 1, line 7, *after* Newbury *insert* [6 April]   *Last line, after* ii. 146 *add*   ; *London Stage* Part V, i. 344

Page 43, note 2, right column, line 3, *after* Harvard *add* (Hazen, *Cat. of HW's Lib.* No. 1810:33:2; another copy is No. 2364)

Page 44, note 10, line 9, *after* vi. 137 *add*   ; *London Stage* Part V, i. 347

Page 44, note 12, *add* See also *London Stage* Part V, i. 344–5.

Page 44, note 15, line 2, *for* (ca 1759) *read* (1759)   *Last line, add* See also P. H. Highfill, Jr, K. A. Burnim, and E. A. Langhans, *A Biographical Dictionary of Actors, Actresses . . . in London, 1660–1800*, Carbondale, Ill., 1973– , i. 10–20.

Page 44, note 16, line 1, *for* ca 1753 *read* 1754   *Line 4, for* 1795 *read* 1805   *Last line, after* 1805 *add* (Namier and Brooke ii. 673–4)

Page 47, note 34, line 1, *for* 1741 *read* 1738   *Line 3, after* 1796–1807 *add*   , Oct.–Dec. 1812 (Namier and Brooke ii. 261)

Page 48, note 44, line 8, *after* Rousseau. *insert* For HW's copy see Hazen, *Cat. of HW's Lib.* No. 3369.

Page 50, note 2, *add* See also Namier and Brooke iii. 495.

Page 53, note 12, line 6, *for* Perth 1773–80, 1784–94 *read* Perthshire 1773–94   *Line 7, after* i. 484 *add*   ; Namier and Brooke iii. 184

Page 55, note 4, line 2, *for* Fleet Street *read* Surrey (OSSORY ii. 187 and n. 4)

Page 56, note 16, lines 3–4, *delete* reputed to be

Page 59, note 35, line 1, *for* ca 1740 *read* 1739   *Line 2, for* d'Aguilar *read* d'Aquilar   *Last line, add* A satirical print of him, 'Baron d'Aguilar of Starvation Farm,' published by J. Robins and Co., Albion Press, 1 Aug. 1821, appeared in *Fifty Wonderful Portraits*, 1822 (Alfred Rubens, *Anglo-Jewry Portraits*, 1935, pp. 4–5; *BM Cat. of Engraved British Portraits* vi. 117). The portrait was taken from life a few months before his death, and the coat of arms engraved beneath it was copied from his once magnificent coach (Alfred Rubens, *Portrait of Anglo-Jewry 1656–1836*, 1959, pp. 12–13, repr. from *Transactions of the Jewish Historical Society of England*, xix).

Page 60, note 38, *add* See OSSORY ii. 179 and n. 43.

Page 61, note 46, line 1, *after* 1772, *add* 'above twenty years ago,'   *Line 3, after* 1792 *add*   , or ca 1760, 'thirty years ago,' as appears in HW to Lady Ossory 9 Dec. 1790

Page 70, note 17, line 2, *after* 155–6 *add*   ; *London Stage* Part V, i. 347 *Last line, after* WSL *add* (Hazen, *Cat. of HW's Lib.* No. 1810:31:12)

Page 71, note 22, right column, line 6, *for* Montgomery *read* 8th E. of Montgomery

Page 73, note 8, *substitute* In April 1780, after her husband died, Lady Diana took a house at Richmond, apparently until 1781 or 1782; see OSSORY ii. 195, n. 5. From 1782–9 she lived at Little Marble Hill, Twickenham (MISC. CORR. iii. 484).

Page 73, note 9, line 1, *for* 1708 *read* 1710   *Last line, add* See HW to Harcourt 2 Sept. 1780 (CHUTE 506–7).

Page 77, note 14, right column, line 8, *after* 178) *add*   , which gives the number as 600,

Page 77, note 16, line 1, *for* Barrett (1744–1803) *read* Barret (?1743–1803)

Page 78, note 5, line 1, *for* Bacelli *read* Baccelli   *2d line from end, after* 1788 *insert*   , CONWAY iii. 330–1, n. 18; MORE 268, n. 8

Page 79, note 2, line 2, *for* Bn of Harewood *read* Bn Harewood   *Last line, add* See also Namier and Brooke iii. 22–3

Page 80, note 13, line 1, *for* ca 1728 *read* 1728   *Last line, after* 149 *add*   ; Namier and Brooke ii. 352–3

Page 86, note 8, *delete 1st sentence* No text or account . . . 1780–1. *and substitute* On Monday 23 October at the Royal Academy, Somerset House, 'Dr Hunter gave his introductory lecture, in which he enlarged on the taste, munificence, and virtues of the Royal Founder' (*London Chronicle* 24–26 Oct. 1780, xlviii. 394).

Page 89, note 27, line 8, *after* WSL *add* (Hazen, *Cat. of HW's Lib.* No. 3043)

Page 95, note 3, line 3, *for* 1732 *read* ca 1730   *Line 5, for* Hull *read* Kingston-upon-Hull   *after* 1782–4 *add* (Namier and Brooke ii. 592–3)

Page 96, note 6, last line, *after* 23d' *add* (Hazen, *Cat. of HW's Lib.* No. 1609:42:7); see also CONWAY iii. 353 and n. 10

Page 97, note 9, last line, *after* WSL *add* (Hazen, *Cat. of HW's Lib.* No. 2384)

Page 98, note 15, *add* See Hazen, *Cat. of HW's Lib.* No. 3188.

Page 102, note 15, line 3, *for the* Revolution *read* that of the Brunswick Line   *Line 8, after* v. 51 *add* (Hazen, *Cat. of HW's Lib.* No. 3197) *Last line, for* Mrs Macaulay *read* Mrs Macauley

Page 102, note 19, line 8, *for* Atahualpa (d. 1533), *read* Atahuallpa (or Atabalipa) (ca 1502–33),   *Line 14, for* Atahualpa *read* Atahuallpa *Line 16, for* 125–6 *read* 126–7

Page 104, note 7, *add* For one of his witticisms in the House of Commons, 20 Nov. 1780, see the *London Chronicle* 18–21 Nov. 1780, xlviii. 487.

Page 109, note 6, line 1, *for* ca 1745 *read* 1745

Page 111, note 22, *add* HW's copy of *La doctrine curieuse des beaux esprits de ce temps* is now WSL (listed in Hazen, *Cat. of HW's Lib.* No. 924).

Page 116, note 14, *add* See Namier and Brooke iii. 2.

Page 116, note 16, *add* See Namier and Brooke ii. 261–2.

Page 117, note 17, line 6, *for* 1766–94 *read* 1766–82   *Last line, add* ; Namier and Brooke ii. 201.

Page 129, note 5, line 2, *for* governor *read* preceptor

Page 129, note 11, line 3, *for* 1753 *read* 1755   *Line 5, for* 1759–60 *read* 1760 (did not take up post)   *Line 6, after* correspondent *add* (Namier and Brooke iii. 316–18)

Page 138, note 8, lines 8–9, *for* former *read* latter   *Line 10, after* No. 182 *add* (Ellis K. Waterhouse, *Reynolds*, 1941, p. 72 and plate 225)

Page 144, note 7, last line, *after* fourth *add* (Hazen, *Cat. of HW's Lib.* No. 1810:53:3)

Page 147, note 7, line 4, *after* v. 54 *add* (Hazen, *Cat. of HW's Lib.* No. 3220)

Page 147, note 10, last line, *after* WSL *add* (Hazen, *Cat. of HW's Lib.* No. 2796)

Page 148, note 2, *add* HW wrote to Joseph Cooper Walker 4 April 1791 thanking him for overseeing the publication of the Dublin edition. The presentation copy sent by Walker to HW, with HW's corrections, was sold SH iv. 162 (Hazen, *Cat. of HW's Lib.* No. 2490).

Page 162, note 7, line 3, *after* 221 *add*   ; *London Stage* Part V, i. 476–80   *Line 6, after* WSL *add* (see Hazen, *Cat. of HW's Lib.* Nos 1810:33:6; 2402)

Page 166, note 6, line 2, *after* 551 *add*   ; *London Stage* Part II, i. 344

Page 167, note 8, line 2, *after* acted *add* a total of   *Last line, add* See HW to Jephson 18 Nov. 1781, MISC. CORR. ii. 460, n. 10; *London Stage* Part V, i. 476–80, 483, 486, 487, 489, 491, 493, 518–19, 522.

Page 169, note 1, line 1, *for* is unexplained *read* apparently refers to the simile used in HW's letter to Lady Ossory 18 Dec. 1781; see OSSORY ii. 313

Page 169, note 6, *substitute* Pope and Bolingbroke to Swift 15 Sept. 1734: ' 'Tis just what my Lord Bolingbroke is doing with Metaphysicks. I hope, you will live to see and stare at the learned figure he will make, on the same shelf with Locke and Malbranche' (Jonathan Swift, *Correspondence*, ed. Harold Williams, Oxford, 1965, iv. 254).

Page 174, note 4, line 2, *after* soprano *add* (OSSORY ii. 322, n. 9)   *Line 6, after Music add*   , 6th edn, 1980, i. 265

Page 174, note 7, line 2, *for* 1954, vi. 476) *read* 6th edn, 1980, xii. 42–3) *Last line, add* See also MANN ix. 243, n. 17.

Page 176, note 3, last line, *after* 363 *add*   ; also Hazen, *Cat. of HW's Lib.* No. 3690:16

Page 178, note 20, last line, *after* BM *add* (Hazen, *Cat. of HW's Lib*. No. 3267)

Page 178, note 22, next to last line, *after* WSL *add* ; Hazen, *Cat. of HW's Lib*. No. 2453

Page 192, note 3, line 2, *for* (d. 1797) *read* (?1725–97)   *Last line, after* 180 *add*   ; Namier and Brooke iii. 556–7

Page 192, note 5, line 1, *for* (d. 1785) *read* (1738–85)

Page 198, note 8, last line, *after* 141 *add* (Hazen, *Cat. of HW's Lib*. No. 2892)

Page 199, note 1, last line, *after* title-page *add* (Hazen, *Cat. of HW's Lib*. No. 3222:18:1)

Page 206, note 11, last line, *after* 21st' *add* (Hazen, *Cat. of HW's Lib*. No. 3690:10)

Page 212, note 7, 3d line from end, *after* Locke *add*   , v. 353

Page 213, note 15, last line, *after* WSL *add* (Hazen, *Cat. of HW's Lib*. No. 1609:42:10)

Page 218, note 12, *add* It is discussed in Walpole's account of Richard Bentley, CHUTE Appendix 2, pp. 644–5.

Page 219, note 14, line 3, *after* vi. 262 *add*   ; *London Stage* Part V, i. 558

Page 223, note 1, line 5, *after* vi. 303 *add*   ; *London Stage* Part V, ii. 722–4

Page 225, note 21, last line, *after* v. 244 *add* (Hazen, *Cat. of HW's Lib*. No. 3411)

Page 225, note 22, left column, bottom line, *after* WSL *add* (Hazen, *Cat. of HW's Lib*. No. 1810:30:5)

Page 234, note 4, line 10, *after* November' *add* (Hazen, *Cat. of HW's Lib*. No. 3222:18:14)

Page 238, note 5, *add* But HW had a later edition: *Essays, Historical and Critical, on English Church Music*, York, 1795 (Hazen, *Cat. of HW's Lib*. No. 3442).

Page 239, note 15, *add* Percy was Lord Algernon's tutor for a while; Percy wrote 1 July 1765 to Evan Evans, 'My Lord Northumberland has desired me to go down with him into the North, and while I am there to superintend the education of his younger son, the Honourable Mr Percy: This will occasion an absence of two or three months' (*The Correspondence of Thomas Percy and Evan Evans*, ed. Aneirin Lewis, Baton Rouge, Louisiana, 1957, p. 111). Percy wrote 8 Sept. 1765 to Richard Farmer, 'After spending 6 weeks very agreeably at Alnwick Castle, I am come here with Mr [Algernon] Percy to the seat of Lord Warkworth, which I shall leave in a few days; setting out on a tour of six weeks thro' Cumberland and all the Southern parts of Scotland, travelling from Carlisle, thro' Dumfries, Glasgow and Stirling to Edinburgh, whence after a short stay I return to the South, and then my care of the young gentleman ends; but not my connection with the family; for Lord Northumberland has retained me in his service as his domestic chaplain and secretary' (*Corre-spondence of Thomas Percy and Richard Farmer*, ed. Cleanth Brooks, Baton Rouge, Louisiana, 1946, pp. 93–4). See also *Correspondence of Thomas Percy and Thomas Warton*, ed. M. G. Robinson and L. Dennis, Baton Rouge, Louisiana, 1951, p. 120 and n. 7.

Page 241, note 3, *add* HW dated his copy 'May' and made some identifications (Hazen, *Cat. of HW's Lib.* No. 3222:18:7).

Page 246, note 4, line 2, *after* 1782 *insert* (*London Stage* Part V, i. 513, 517)

Page 247, note 9, *add* HW's copy is Hazen, *Cat. of HW's Lib.* No. 3222:16:15.

Page 249, note 1, line 4, *for* 1853 *read* 1852

Page 252, note 4, last line, *after* WSL *add* (Hazen, *Cat. of HW's Lib.* No. 3912)

Page 252, note 1, *add* HW's copy, dated 'May 28th,' is Hazen, *Cat. of HW's Lib.* No. 3222:18:9.

Page 254, note 9, *add* HW did not purchase Newton's *Works*; see COLE ii. 323, Hazen, *Cat. of HW's Lib.* No. 317.

Page 255, note 1, last line, *after* Library *add* (Hazen, *Cat. of HW's Lib.* No. 3222:18:4)

Page 271, note 8, line 1, *for* 1725 *read* 1724

Page 279, note 1, line 2, *for* fifty *read* forty

Page 281, note 4, last line, *after* ber' *add* (Hazen, *Cat. of HW's Lib.* Nos 1609:42:13 and 1609:43:3)

Page 282, note 5, *add* For HW's copies of Bishop Berkeley's work see Hazen, *Cat. of HW's Lib.* Nos 1608:48:1 and 1465.

Page 284, note 1, *add* See Hazen, *Cat. of HW's Lib.* No. 3890.

Page 284, note 3, *delete* It does not appear in the SH library records. *and substitute* See Hazen, *Cat. of HW's Lib.* No. 3885.

Page 286, line 6, *on* unsullied *add note* 18a: 18a. 'Immortal' in HW's 'Book of Materials,' 1771, p. 84, where the epitaph, signed 'H.W.', appears.

Page 286, note 20, line 3, *for* 'about 13 times' *read* 13 times   *before* Genest *insert London Stage* Part V, i. 548, 588;

Page 291, note 3, *add* HW's copy, now WSL, is Hazen, *Cat. of HW's Lib.* No. 1810:35:8

Page 292, note 11, *delete last two lines and substitute* and Gray are shown in the top row of the illustration, fifth and sixth from the left (see illustration).

Page 293, note 2, *add* See Hazen, *Cat. of HW's Lib.* No. 2791.

Page 293, note 3, *add* HW's copy is now WSL (Hazen, *Cat. of HW's Lib.* No. 1512).

Page 293, note 11, line 5, *after* 1768 *add* (HW's copy is Hazen, *Cat. of HW's Lib.* No. 1609:57:2)

Page 298, note 6, line 9, *after* 205). *add* For HW's copy see Hazen, *Cat.*

of HW's Lib. No. 2793.   *Last line, after* WSL *add* (printed in OSSORY Appendix 4, iii. 243–4)

Page 301, note 16, *add* See Hazen, *Cat. of HW's Lib*. No. 325.

Page 302, note 24, line 2, *for* 1848 *read* 1847

Page 307, 2d paragraph, line 11, *on* Friday *add note* 17a: 17a. See HW to Alderson 1 June 1783 (MISC. CORR. iii. 54–5).

Page 308, note 2, last line, *after* WSL *add* (Hazen, *Cat. of HW's Lib*. No. 1609:45:4)

Page 309, note 8, last line, *after* v. 13 *add* (Hazen, *Cat. of HW's Lib*. No. 3289)

Page 310, note 14, last line, *after* Library *add* (Hazen, *Cat. of HW's Lib*. No. 3222:19:5)

Page 310, note 15, line 6, *for* 24 April *read* 23 April   *Line 7, after* engagement *add* (see MANN ix. 278 and n. 14)

Page 324, note 13, *add* HW's copy is Hazen, *Cat. of HW's Lib*. No. 1818:12:1. See also *London Stage* Part V, ii. 660.

Page 327, note 4, right column, 2d line from bottom, *for* 366–7). *read* 366–7; HW to Newcastle 12 Nov. 1758 (MISC. CORR. i. 145–7).

Page 331, note 40, *add* HW's copy is Hazen, *Cat. of HW's Lib*. No. 3222:19:9.

Page 334, note 2, *add* HW's copy is Hazen, *Cat. of HW's Lib*. No. 3432.

Page 334, note 4, line 2, *after* 1795 *add* (see Hazen, *Cat. of HW's Lib*. No. 3245)

Page 339, note 10, *substitute* HW permitted his bronze of Ceres to be copied for Knight's *An Account of the Remains of the Worship of Priapus*, 1786. HW wrote Sir Joseph Banks 31 March 1787, 'I return you the book, with many thanks. It is a most curious one; and as I readily lent my Ceres to be drawn for it, I confess I should have been much pleased if it had been thought fit to give me one. I should still be very glad at least, if I could obtain one or two impressions of my Ceres' (MISC. CORR. iii. 193–4); and on 3 May 1787 HW wrote Banks to thank him 'for your very obliging compliance with my request . . . allow me to beg you to present my most respectful thanks and gratitude to Mr Knight, and to the gentlemen of the Society of Dilettanti, for the honour of their very valuable present' (ibid. iii. 194).

Page 340, note 12, line 13, *after* Society). *add* See Hazen, *Cat. of HW's Lib*. No. 2404, where HW's note on the fly-leaf is quoted; and also HW to Banks 31 March, 3 May 1787, MISC. CORR. iii. 193–5.

Page 340, note 13, *add* This is a reference to the indecent buttons worn by the Duc de Chartres, mentioned *ante* 11 May 1783.

Page 354, note 9, line 1, *for* (ca 1700–69) *read* (1699–1769)   *Last line, add* See also Namier and Brooke iii. 630–1.

Page 359, note 24, *add* See CHATTERTON 254 and n. 5; Hazen, *Cat. of HW's Lib*. Nos 278–9, 3823.

Page 360, note 29, *add* HW's companion might have been Gen. John Fitzwilliam, who lived at Richmond (see Ossory iii. 59 and n. 11; Berry i. 48, n. 16).

Page 365, note 51, line 3, *for* Anspach *read* Ansbach

Page 377, 3d paragraph, line 4, *for* Richard *read* Robert

VOLUME 30

Page xxiii, List of Illustrations, *sub* Henry Fox, line 2, *for* Reynolds *read* Müntz

Page xxvi, note 3, *for* unpublished; MS in private hands in Ceylon. *read* Conway i. 157.

Page xxvi, note 4, *after* 1744 *add* , Conway i. 170

Page xxviii, 4th paragraph, line 3, *for* House of Lords *read* House of Commons

Page xxix, line 13, *for* Cole *read* Cole

Page xxxii, 1st paragraph, line 9, *after* scattered. *add* The manuscripts of 25 letters from Walpole to Fox, 4 from Fox to Walpole, and 2 from Walpole to Lady Holland are now in the British Museum (Add. MS 51,404); three from Walpole to Fox, one from Fox, and two from Walpole to Lady Holland are now printed in Misc. Corr. i. 76, 87, 205, ii. 67, 272, 274. Three letters from Walpole to Lord Ilchester (BM Add. MSS 51,349 and 51,350) are now printed in Misc. Corr. i. 249, 251, ii. 22.

Page xxxii, 2d paragraph, line 10, *after* collection (10). *add* The ten letters in the Murray Collection were sold in 1971, four of them to wsl; two previously missing letters and one undated note have also been acquired by wsl.

Page xxxvi, 3d paragraph, lines 9–10, *for* Royal Company of Surgeons *read* Royal College of Surgeons

Page xliv, Letters between Walpole and Fox, *below* 1752 *insert* 1753 20 Aug.† 120   *sub* 1756 *insert*   ?late Oct.   128   *below* 1760 *insert* 1761 ?19 Sept.   165

Page xlv, *sub* 1766   *delete* 19 July   225   *below* 14 Nov. *insert* late Nov.† 238

Page xlv, middle of page, *insert*

LETTERS BETWEEN WALPOLE AND LADY HOLLAND

| 1774 | 19 Feb. | 260 |
| | 26 Feb. | 260 |

Page xlv, Letters between Walpole and Selwyn, line 7, *on* 2 Oct. *change asterisk to dagger*

Page xlvii, line 14, *for* n.d. *read*   ?July–Aug. 1782

Page 1, note 7, line 1, *for* 1703 *read* ca 1706

Page 4, note 11, line 1, *for* Gioachimo *read* Gioacchino

Page 6, note 29, line 1, *for* 1720 *read* ca 1720

Page 11, note 7, lines 1–2, *for* ca 1703 *read* ca 1708

Page 14, note 12, line 1, *for* (ca 1743) *read* (before 1735)   *Line 2, for*
—— Tramontini *read* Giacomo Tramontini   *Line 3, after* 401–2 *add*
; *Enciclopedia dello spettacolo*, Rome, 1954–62, ix. 855–6; Wiel, op. cit.
117

Page 15, note 14, line 1, *before* Camilla *insert* Maria   *Lines 2–3, for*
i. 473, n. 14 *read* iii. 349, n. 4

Page 19, note 3, line 1, *for* Barbara *read* Barbarina   *Line 3, for* (ca
1748) *read* (1750)   *Line 4, for* was divorced *read* separated   *Line 5,*
for (1789) *read* (1787)

Page 20, note 8, line 2, *for* 1709–13 *read* 1709–14   *Line 3, for* 1713–17
read 1715–17   *Last line, after* 276 *add*   ; Sedgwick i. 551–2

Page 20, note 9, last 3 lines, *delete* in a forthcoming essay by . . . Eighteenth Century.' *and substitute* in L. P. Curtis, *Chichester Towers*, New
Haven, 1966, pp. 51–8, 83–4, 94.

Page 22, note 3, line 1, *for* ?1695 *read* 1695   *Last line, after* 1743–54
add (Sedgwick ii. 329–31)

Page 25, note 26, line 2, *for* Parliament *read* the House of Lords

Page 26, note 6, line 3, *for* 1740 *read* 1741   *Last line, after* Whaley
add   ; Sedgwick i. 614–15

Page 27, note 7, line 1, *for* (1719–44) *read* (1719–41)   *Line 4, after*
p. 230 *add*   ; Namier and Brooke ii. 326

Page 27, note 16, line 11, *delete* falsely   *Line 17, after* p. 285 *add*
; Robert Halsband, *Lord Hervey Eighteenth-Century Courtier*, New York
and Oxford, 1974, p. 304

Page 29, note 10, line 4, *for* ca 11 Nov. *read* ca 15 Nov.   *after* NS *add*
(Chute 11)

Page 31, note 20, right column, line 4, *for* Luggershall *read* Ludgershall
Last line, add See also Sedgwick i. 472.

Page 36, middle of page, *after now* WSL *delete*   ; *its conclusion is illu-*
strated here

Page 37, note 4, lines 1–2, *for* before 13 March 1759 *read* ?1754   *Last*
line, for ibid. ii. 36 n. 35 *read* Conway i. 115, n. 18, 381, n. 1

Page 45, note 6, line 4, *for* Dumbartonshire *read* Dunbartonshire

Page 48, note 3, line 1, *for* Coldbrook House *read* Coldbrook Park

Page 50, note 25, line 1, *for* 1705 *read* ?1705   *Last line, add* See also
Sedgwick ii. 195–6.

Page 52, note 42, line 1, *for* 1714 *read* 1718

Page 53, note 7, line 1, *for* 1689 *read* ca 1689   *Line 3, after* 41 *add*
(Sedgwick ii. 123–4)

Page 58, note 3, line 1, *for* Stuart-Mackenzie *read* Stuart Mackenzie
for 1719 *read* ?1719   *Last line, after* 1800 *add* (Sedgwick ii. 454–5)

Page 71, note 23, line 1, *for* ca 1720 *read* 1721   *Line 3, add* He was
with Conway in July; see Conway i. 167.

Page 78, note 1, *add* See also Sedgwick i. 204–5, 533.

Page 80, note 6, line 5, *for* pewet *read* pewit

Page 84, note 11, line 5, *for* 1792– *read* 1791–

Page 84, note 12, line 1, *for* 1698 *read* 1696   *Line 3, add* See MORE 418 and n. 33.

Page 94, note 2, line 4, *for* Cherokee *read* Yamacraw   *Last line, add* See also HW to Thomas Pennant 30 March 1789, MISC. CORR. iii. 236 and nn. 18, 19.

Page 94, note 3, lines 2–3, *for* Cherokee *read* Yamacraw

Page 94, note 7, line 3, *delete* perhaps   *Line 5, after* 18 *add*   ; Sedgwick i. 485–6

Page 95, note 8, last line, *add* See also Sedgwick i. 473–4.

Page 97, note 13, line 1, *for* (d. 1760) *read* (1690–1760)   *Lines 3–4, for* Queensborough *read* Queenborough   *Last line, after* 1738–41 *insert* (Sedgwick i. 576)

Page 105, note 5, lines 2 and 4, *for* Bethel *read* Bethell   *Line 8, for* passim). *read* passim; Sedgwick i. 460–1).

Page 106, To Fox 9 Oct. 1746, headnote, line 1, *after* i. 59. *insert* Collated with a photostat of the MS, now BM Add. MS 51,404, f. 174 [the variants are recorded below].   *Line 2, delete* all   *Lines 2–3, for* are in the possession of the Earl of Ilchester. *read* are now in the British Museum.

Page 106, To Fox 9 Oct. 1746, 1st paragraph, line 3, *for* here. Poor *read* here; poor

Page 107, 1st paragraph, line 2, *for* you; *read* you,

Page 109, note 23, line 2, *for* ca 1761 *read* 1762

Page 110, note 1, *add* The *Daily Adv.* 1 Oct. 1747 reported: 'We hear that Lieutenant-Colonel Montagu will have one of the vacant regiments of Foot'; Charles Montagu became Lt-Col. 11th Foot 15 Aug. 1745, Col. 59th Foot 30 Dec. 1755 (*Army Lists*, 1755, p. 40; 1757, p. 141).

Page 112, note 10, last line, *for* harbor *read* harbour

Page 115, note 17, last line, *after* 173 *add*   ; Sedgwick ii. 132–3

Page 115, note 18, *add* See also Sedgwick ii. 135–6.

Page 116, note 19, line 1, *for* Ann *read* Anne   *Line 3, for* 1744 *read* 1745   *Line 4, after* n. 15 *add*   ; Sedgwick ii. 135–6

Page 119, note 2, lines 10–11, *for* HW misdates this application 1751 in his 'Account *read* HW in 1751, before the death of his brother Robert, made an earlier application which is described in his 'Account

Page 119, after letter of 23 Sept. 1749 *insert the following heading*:

To Fox, ca July 1752

Missing; mentioned in HW to Montagu ca July 1752: 'I cannot flatter myself with having so much interest with Mr Fox as you think. However I have wrote to him as pressingly as I could, and wish most heartily it may have any effect. Your brother I imagine will call upon him again, and Mr Fox will naturally tell him whether he can do it or not at my request' (MONTAGU i. 136). Perhaps a request for a vacant regiment of Foot, which Lt-Col. Montagu received in 1755 (see ADD. AND CORR. on *ante* p. 110, n. 1).

Page 120, middle of page, *insert the following heading*:

To Fox, Monday 20 August 1753

Printed for the first time from a photostat of the MS in the British Museum (Add. MS 51,404, f. 180), in MISC. CORR. i. 76–7.

Page 125, To Fox ca June–July 1756, headnote, line 2, *add* The MS is now BM Add. MS 51,404, ff. 184–5.

Page 127, To Fox 27 Oct. 1756, headnote, line 1, *add* Collated with a photostat of the MS now BM Add. MS 51,404, ff. 186–7 [the variants are recorded below].

Page 128, 2d paragraph, line 2, *for* heard. *read* heard: *Line 3, after* K[ing] *delete* ,   *Line 4, after* Y[armouth] *delete* ,   *Line 5, for* Treasury.[3] *read* Treasury—[3]

Page 128, 3d paragraph, line 3, *for* will give *read* give

Page 128, after letter To Fox 27 Oct. 1756 *insert the following heading*:

To Fox, ?late October 1756

Printed for the first time from a photostat of the MS in the British Museum (Add. MS 51,404, f. 182), in MISC. CORR. i. 87–8.

Page 132, To Fox ca 22 Dec. 1756, headnote, line 1, *add* Collated with a photostat of the MS now BM Add. MS 51,404, f. 188 [the variants are recorded below].   *2d paragraph, delete* The text of this letter . . . of 20 Dec. 1756.

Page 132, To Fox ca 22 Dec. 1756, 1st paragraph, line 1, *after* home *delete* ,   *Line 7, for* mend it, *read* mend it;   *Lines 8–9, after* genuine *delete* ,   *for* letter. *read* letter: *after* better *delete* ,   *Line 13, for* consequence. *read* consequence—

Page 136, To Selwyn 6 Sept. 1757, headnote, line 2, *after* Murray *add* ; sold Sotheby's 29 June 1971, lot 376, to E. Walsh.

Page 137, note 4, line 7, *for* Sterlingshire *read* Stirlingshire

Page 138, To Selwyn 2 Oct. 1757, *delete* Missing; mentioned in the following letter. *and substitute* Printed for the first time from the MS, now WSL, in MISC. CORR. i. 113. The MS was sold Sotheby's 29 April 1969 (property of a Lady), lot 384, to Seven Gables for WSL.

Page 139, To Selwyn 6 Oct. 1757, headnote, line 2, *add* The MS was sold Sotheby's 29 June 1971, lot 377, to J. Wilson; offered Sept. 1971, Cat. 69, lot 126, by Paul Richards, Brookline, Mass.; offered by Sotheby's 3 Dec. 1974, lot 199, and again 22 June 1976, lot 257; bought by Alan G. Thomas and offered by him, Cat. 36 (1977), lot 36, and again Cat. 40 (1980), lot 1.

Line 3, for Dated in another hand *read* Dated originally by HW but written over in another hand

Page 139, note 2, *add* See Lady Ailesbury to HW 6 Oct., 7 Oct. 1757 (CONWAY i. 510–11).

Page 140, To Selwyn 8 Oct. 1757, headnote, line 2, *add* The MS was sold Sotheby's 29 June 1971, lot 378, to Seven Gables for WSL.

Page 141, To Selwyn 11 Oct. 1757, headnote, line 2, *add* The MS was sold Sotheby's 29 June 1971, lot 379, to Seven Gables for WSL.

Page 142, note 7, line 3, *for* Kloster-Zevern *read* Klosterzeven

Page 142, note 8, last line, *for* Kloster-Zevern *read* Klosterzeven

Page 142, note 10, line 3, *for* Kloster-Zevern *read* Klosterzeven

Page 143, To Selwyn 13 Oct. 1757, headnote, line 2, *add* The MS was sold Sotheby's 29 June 1971, lot 380, to E. Walsh.

Page 144, note 5, line 4, *for* Kloster-Zevern *read* Klosterzeven

Page 145, To Selwyn 18 Oct. 1757, headnote, line 2, *add* The MS was sold Sotheby's 29 June 1971, lot 381, to C. Faber.

Page 151, To Fox 11 March 1759, headnote, *add* Collated with a photostat of the MS now BM Add. MS 51,404, ff. 189–90 [the variants are recorded below].

Page 152, 1st paragraph, line 2, *for* race, *read* race—   *for* authors' *read* author's   *Line 5, for* these *read* the   *for* Berkeley.³ *read* Berkeley—³   *Line 6, for* you; *read* you.   *Line 10, for* well, *read* well—   *Line 11, for* better. *read* better—

Page 152 2d paragraph, last line, *for* way. *read* way—

Page 152, To Fox 8 May 1759, headnote, *add* Collated with a photostat of the MS now BM Add. MS 51,404, ff. 191–2 [the variants are recorded below].

Page 152, To Fox 8 May 1759, 1st paragraph, line 2, *after* trifle *delete*   ,

Page 153, 1st paragraph, line 1, *after* see him *add*   ,   *Line 3, for* MSS. *read* MSS   *Line 5, after* one *delete*   ,

Page 153, 2d paragraph, line 2, *for* pedigrees. *read* pedigrees: *Line 3, for* 27 *read* 27   *Line 4, for* Fox *read* Fox   *after* family *delete*   ,

Page 153, To Selwyn 5 June 1759, headnote, line 1, *after* 271–2 *insert* ; now collated with a photostat of the MS [the variants are recorded below]   *Line 3, after* Maggs *add*   ; resold Sotheby's 17 Dec. 1973, lot 250, to Maggs; offered by Maggs, Cat. No. 959 (summer 1974), lot 143; sold by them to Robert H. Taylor, Princeton, New Jersey, 1974

Page 154, 1st paragraph, line 2, *after* world *delete*   ,   *Line 6, for* apologies: one *read* apologies; and one   *Line 11, for* you. *read* you,

Page 154, after To Selwyn 5 June 1759 *insert the following heading*:

To SELWYN, ca Saturday 9 June 1759

Printed for the first time from the MS, now WSL, in MISC. CORR. i. 163. The MS was acquired from Goodspeed's in 1968.

Page 155, note 3, line 1, *for* 19 *read* 17 or 19   *Line 2, after* 1759 *insert* ; Mann v. 316, n. 11; Conway ii. 20 and n. 1

Page 156, note 3, line 5, *for* 1750–61 *read* 1751–61   *Line 6, after* 1774–80 *add* (Namier and Brooke iii. 679)

Page 159, To Fox 6 Feb. 1760, headnote, *add* Collated with a photostat of the MS now BM Add. MS 51,404, ff. 193–4 [the variants are recorded below].

Page 159, To Fox 6 Feb. 1760, 1st paragraph, line 4, *for* seen, *read* seen; *after* necessary *add* ,   *Line 3 of verses, for* inspirations *read* inspiration   *Line 6 of verses, for* wished *read* wish'd   *Line 2 after verses, after* House *delete* ,

Page 160, To Selwyn 19 Oct. ?1760, headnote, line 2, *add* The MS was sold Sotheby's 29 June 1971, lot 382, to J. Wilson; offered by Paul C. Richards, High Acres, Templeton, Mass., 1978, lot 76.

Page 161, To Selwyn 21 Oct. ?1760, headnote, line 2, *add* The MS was sold Sotheby's 29 June 1971, lot 383, to Maggs; offered Maggs Cat. No. 938, lot 94, and sold to wsl, 1971.

Page 161, To Selwyn 13 March 1761, headnote, line 2, *add* The MS was sold Sotheby's 29 June 1971, lot 384, to E. Walsh.

Page 163, To Selwyn 21 March 1761, headnote, line 2, *add* The MS was sold Sotheby's 29 June 1971, lot 385, to Seven Gables for wsl.

Page 164, note 11, line 1, *for* ca 1696 *read* ?1697   *Line 3, after* 160 *insert* ; Namier and Brooke ii. 254

Page 165, after To Selwyn 21 March 1761 *insert the following heading*:

To Fox, Saturday ?19 September 1761

Printed from a photostat of the MS, in the Bodleian Library, in Misc. Corr. i. 205.

Page 167, From Fox 21 Nov. 1762, headnote, line 3, *after* Waldegrave. *insert* Collated with a photostat of the MS (in Fox's hand), now BM Add. MS 51,404, f. 195 [the variants are recorded below].

Page 167, From Fox 21 Nov. 1762, 1st paragraph, line 3, *on* procrastinate *add note* 2a: 2a. In the MS 'procrastinate' written over 'protract.'

Page 167, note 6, line 6, *for* ca 1730 *read* ?1729

Page 168, 1st paragraph, line 1, *after* you *delete* ,   *after* too *delete* ,   *Line 3, on* offence *add note* 6a: 6a. In MS 'without offence' is written over 'well'

Page 168, note 6, last line, *after* n. 1 *add* ; Namier and Brooke ii. 101

Page 169, note 3, line 7, *before* of the East *insert* and deputy chairman *after* 1758–64, *add* 1772–3,   *for* 1780 *read* 1780–2   *Last line, after* 183 *add* ; Namier and Brooke iii. 508–10

Page 169, note 7, *add* Orford held the Rangership of St James's and Hyde Parks 1763–83, 1784–91 (see Mann ix. 266 and n. 11).

Page 172, note 9, line 1, *for* ca 1736 *read* ca 1735   *Line 3, after* n. 9 *add* ; Namier and Brooke ii. 212

Page 175, note 1, *add* The copy given to Lord Lincoln is now WSL (Hazen, *SH Bibl.*, 1973, p. xviii, no. 11).

Page 180, To Holland 21 May 1765, headnote, line 1, *after* 106–7. *add* Collated with a photostat of the MS now BM Add. MS 51,404, ff. 196–7 [the variants are recorded below].

Page 180, 2d paragraph, line 3, *after* (today) *delete* ,

Page 181, 1st paragraph, line 1, *for* much. The *read* much: the   *Line* 2, *for* adjourn. *read* adjourn:

Page 181, 2d paragraph, line 4, *after* Richmond *delete* .   *Line 5, after* Waldegrave *delete* ,   *after* Upon this *delete* ,   *Line 7, after* today *add* ,   *for* done.[14] But *read* done;[14] but   *Line 10, after* Court *add* ,

Page 182, 2d paragraph, line 2, *after* yesterday *add* ,   *Line 3, for* mob, *read* mob;

Page 182, 3d paragraph, line 2, *after* morning *add* ,

Page 182, 4th paragraph, line 1, *for* Lord. *read* Lord;   *for* a *read* [a]

Page 183, To Holland 29 May 1765, headnote, line 1, *after* 108–12. *add* Collated with a photostat of the MS now BM Add. MS 51,404, ff. 198–9 [the variants are recorded below].

Page 183, To Holland 29 May 1765, 1st paragraph, line 2, *after* know *add* ,   *Line 3, after* wearied *add* ,   *Line 4, after* divine *add* ,   *Line 5, after* insolence *delete* ,   *Line 6, for* detail. At *read* detail: at

Page 184, 1st paragraph, line 2, *after* spite *delete* ,   *Line 4, after* open *delete* ,   *begin new paragraph with* Lord Bute, you know

Page 185, 1st paragraph, line 3, *for* himself; *read* himself,

Page 185, 2d paragraph, line 1, *after* the Opposition *delete* ,   *after* late Opposition *delete* ,

Page 185, 4th paragraph, line 1, *after* to him *delete* ,

Page 186, 2d paragraph, line 6, *for* means: *read* means,   *Line 14, for* easily. But *read* easily; but

Page 187, 1st paragraph, line 1, *for* spirit, *read* spirit—   *Line 6, after* popularity *delete* ,   *Line 7, for* Bedford; *read* Bedford—   *Line 10, for* softened.[34] *read* softened:[34]

Page 187, 2d paragraph, line 3, *for* places; *read* places: *Line 4, for* Birthday.[40] *read* Birthday;[40]   *Line 5, for* He *read* he   *Line 6, after* brother *delete* ,

Page 188, 3d paragraph, line 1, *after* tell you *add* ,   *Line 2, after* thinks *add* ,

Page 189, 2d paragraph, line 3, *after* is *add* ,   *Line 4, for* more? *read* more—   *Line 5, for* word'; *read* word'—   *after* then *delete* ,   *Line* 7, *after* great *add* ,

Page 192, To Holland 15 July 1765, headnote, *add* Collated with a photostat of the MS now BM Add. MS 51,404, ff. 200–1 [the variants are recorded below].

Page 192, To Holland 15 July 1765, 1st paragraph, line 2, *for* transactions; *read* transactions,   *Line 4, after* stomach *delete* ,   *Line 5, after* havoc *delete* ,   *Line 6, for* a *read* [a]   *Line 7, after* couch *add* ,

Page 192, To Holland 15 July 1765, 2d paragraph, line 7, *for* King instead *read* King, instead   *Line 8, after* take it *delete* ,

Page 192, note 5, line 2, *for* 1761–90, 1796–1801 *read* 1761–1801   *Line 3, for* 1762–5 *read* 1763–5 (Namier and Brooke iii. 458–9)

Page 193, line 4, *after* Villiers *add* ,   *Line 5, after* Tamworth) *delete* ,   *Line 7, for* mouth. Now *read* mouth—now

Page 193, note 8, lines 1–2, *for* Major-Gen., 1762 *read* Major-Gen., 1765 (ante-dated to 1762)

Page 194, note 22, *add* See also CONWAY Appendix 7, iii. 529–32.

Page 195, 1st paragraph, line 1, *after* late *delete* ,   *Line 6, after* difficulty *add* ,

Page 195, To Holland 19 July 1765, headnote, *add* Collated with a photostat of the MS now BM Add. MS 51,404, ff. 202–3 [the variants are recorded below].

Page 195, To Holland 19 July 1765, 1st paragraph, line 7, *after* possessed *add* ,

Page 196, 1st paragraph, line 1, *for* not. *read* not;   *Lines 6–7, for* Commons; *read* Commons,   *Line 8, after* myself *add* ,   *Line 9, for* discourse of it. *read* discourse of it—   *Line 10, for* across *read* cross *for* resolutions; *read* resolutions,   *Line 11, for* may I not *read* may not I   *Lines 12–13, run in (no paragraph)*

Page 196, 3d paragraph, line 3, *for* Bolingbroke *read* Bolinbroke

Page 197, 1st paragraph, line 3, *for* about it. When *read* about it: when

Page 197, 2d paragraph, line 2, *after* makes it *add* ,   *for* of [it] *read* of it   *Line 3, for* walk. But *read* walk—but

Page 197, 4th paragraph, line 2, *after* who is *delete* ,

Page 198, To Holland 21 July 1765, headnote, *add* Collated with a photostat of the MS now BM Add. MS 51,404, ff. 204–5 [the variants are recorded below].

Page 199, 2d paragraph, line 4, *after* Lord *delete* ,

Page 199, 3d paragraph, line 4, *for* air. *read* air—   *Line 5, for* them; *read* them,   *Line 7, after* and *delete* ,

Page 199, To Holland 2 Aug. 1765, headnote, *add* Collated with a photostat of the MS now BM Add. MS 51,404, ff. 206–7 [the variants are recorded below].

Page 199, note 1, line 1, *for* Cunninghame (d. 1788) *read* Cuninghame (ca 1731–88)   *Line 2, for* Cunninghame *read* Cuninghame   *Line 3, for* 54th Foot *read* 45th Foot   *Last line, after* 166 *add* ; Namier and Brooke ii. 283–4

Page 200, 1st paragraph, line 2, *after* sixth *delete* ,   *Line 7, after*

you *delete*   ,   *after* think *delete*   ,   *Line 8, for* army.[6] *read* army:[6]
Line 13, after Cooper *add*   ,

Page 200, 2d paragraph, line 2, *for* Paris; *read* Paris,

Page 200, 3d paragraph, line 1, *after* room *delete*   ,   *Line 3, after*
Lord *delete*   ,   *Line 5, signature, for* H. WALPOLE *read* HOR. WALPOLE

Page 201, note 10, *add* It appears in the MS.

Page 202, To Holland 7 Sept. 1765, headnote, *add* Collated with a
photostat of the MS now BM Add. MS 51,404, ff. 208–9 [the variants are
recorded below].

Page 202, To Holland 7 Sept. 1765, 1st paragraph, line 5, *after* 14th
delete   ,   *after* for me *delete*   ,   *Line 7, after* years *add*   ,

Page 202, To Holland 7 Sept. 1765, 3d paragraph, line 1, *after* recover
add   ,   *for* further *read* farther   *on* than *add* *note* 2a: 2a. In the
MS 'than' is written over 'at.'   *Line 3, for* command *read* commands
Line 4, for me; *read* me,

Page 202, note 3, *add* She and the Duke arrived in Paris 6 Nov. (CON-
WAY iii. 24, 30).

Page 203, 1st paragraph, line 1, *after* books *add*   ,   *Line 3, after*
geometry *delete*   ,   *Line 4, after* things *delete*   ,   *Line 6, after* do
not think *delete* that   *for* ever *read* even

Page 203, 2d paragraph, line 2, *for* gout; *read* gout: *Line 3, for* as
bad as *read* so bad as

Page 208, note 37, line 1, *for* ca 1716 *read* ca 1717

Page 210, note 1, left column, line 1, *for* 1790–96 *read* 1792–96

Page 217, note 8, line 1, *for* 1681 *read* 1679.

Page 220, note 7, line 3, *for* 1720 *read* 1719

Page 221, To Holland 17 July 1766, headnote, line 1, *add* Collated with
a photostat of the MS now BM Add. MS 51,404, ff. 210–11 [the variants
are recorded below].

Page 221, To Holland 17 July 1766, 1st paragraph, line 4, *after* Hampstead *delete*   ,

Page 222, 2d paragraph, line 2, *after* accept *delete*   ,   *Line 4, after*
yesterday *delete*   ,

Page 223, 1st paragraph, line 4, *for* son; *read* son,   *Line 5 for* son;
read son,   *Line 6, for* legacies. *read* legacies:

Page 223, 2d paragraph, line 5, *for* him; that *read* him. That

Page 223, note 12, *before* An estate *insert* 'Twickenham part' in MS.

Page 224, line 1, *for* own, *read* own—

Page 224, 2d paragraph, line 4, *after* banknotes *delete*   ,   *Line 5, for*
do not *read* don't

Page 224, 4th paragraph, line 2, *after* yesterday *add*   ,

Page 225, line 1, *after* positively *add*   ,

Page 225, To Holland, Saturday 19 July 1766, *delete heading and substitute* To Ilchester, Saturday 19 July 1766   *delete headnote* Printed
from *Letters to Henry Fox* 260; reprinted, Toynbee *Supp.* i. 136. *and*

substitute This letter was mistakenly printed as a letter from HW to Lord Holland in *Letters to Henry Fox* (p. 260); the text was taken from a copy, presumably in Lord Ilchester's hand (BM Add. MS 51,404, f. 212), which Lord Ilchester sent to Lord Holland. This copy is endorsed (in Lord Holland's hand): 'Copy of H. Walpole's letter July 19. recd July 21. 1766 The original sent to Ld Ilchester.' HW's original letter was written and sent to Lord Ilchester; the MS is BM Add. MS 51,350 f. 30. This MS is now printed for the first time in MISC. CORR. ii. 22–3.

Page 226, note 7, *substitute* 'Ciceronian' in HW's MS.

Page 226, note 10, line 1, *delete* Apparently a slip for   *Line 2, after* Cartney' *add* in HW's MS.

Page 227, To Holland 22 July 1766, headnote, *add* Collated with a photostat of the MS now BM Add. MS 51,404, ff. 214–15 [the variants are recorded below].

Page 227, To Holland 22 July 1766, 1st paragraph, line 1, *for* health, *read* health;   *Line 3, after* general *delete* ,

Page 227, To Holland 22 July 1766, 2d paragraph, line 2, *after* opposition *delete* ,

Page 228, To Holland 29 July 1766, headnote, *add* Collated with a photostat of the MS now BM Add. MS 51,404, ff. 216–17 [the variants are recorded below].

Page 228, To Holland 29 July 1766, 1st paragraph, line 5, *for* farther; *read* farther,   *Line 7, for* successor; *read* successor,

Page 228, note 6, *add* See MANN vi. 442–3 and n. 1.

Page 231, To Holland 2 Aug. 1766, headnote, *add* Collated with a photostat of the MS now BM Add. MS 51,404, ff. 218–19 [the variants are recorded below].

Page 231, To Holland 2 Aug. 1766, 1st paragraph, line 3, *for* evening, *read* evening;

Page 232, 1st paragraph, line 8, *after* time *add* ,   *Line 12, after* Rigby *delete* ,   *Line 15, for* them; *read* them: *Line 17, after* resort to *add* ,

Page 232, 2d paragraph, line 7, *for* mischief; *read* mischief:

Page 233, 2d paragraph, line 2, *for* tomorrow; *read* tomorrow,   *Line 4, after* Stanley *delete* ,   *after* Hertford *delete* ,   *Line 10, after* pension *delete* ,

Page 233, 3d paragraph, line 3, *for* [in] *read* in   *after* himself *delete* ,

Page 233, note 13, line 1, *for* protonotary *read* prothonotary

Page 234, 1st paragraph, line 1, *for* earldom.14 *read* earldom:14

Page 234, 2d paragraph, line 2, *after* Portland *delete* ,   *after* believe *delete* ,   *Line 3, after* happens *add* ,   *Line 5, for* not *read* not *Line 8, for* dignity; *read* dignity,

Page 234, 3d paragraph, line 7, *for* liberty; *read* liberty,

Page 234, note 14, *add* Pitt kissed hands 30 July (*Mem. Geo. III* ii. 253); his earldom was announced in the *London Gazette* 29 July–2 Aug., *sub*

'St James's, 30 July'; the letters patent were dated 4 Aug. (*Journals of the House of Lords* xxxi. 426). See MANN vi. 442–3 and n. 1.

Page 234, note 15, line 2, *for* advisor *read* adviser

Page 234, note 17, line 1, *for* 1704 *read* ca 1704

Page 235, top of page, *insert the following heading*:

FROM HOLLAND, ca 4 August 1766

Missing; mentioned by Charles James Fox to HW 6 Aug. 1766: 'I received the enclosed [apparently a letter from Holland to HW] yesterday ... by express' (MISC. CORR. ii. 27).

Page 235, To Holland 14 Nov. 1766, headnote, *add* Collated with a photostat of the MS now BM Add. MS, 51,404, ff. 220–1 [the variants are recorded below].

Page 235, To Holland 14 Nov. 1766, date-line, *for* November *read* Nov.

Page 235, To Holland 14 Nov. 1766, 1st paragraph, line 1, *after* hands *delete* ,   *Line 4, after* sister *delete* ,   *Line 5, for* appearance *read* appearances   *Line 6, for* sea, *read* sea;   *Line 8, after* well *add* ,

Page 235, To Holland 14 Nov. 1766, 2d paragraph, line 1, *for* of Parliament *read* of the Parliament

Page 236, line 2, *after* feast *add* ,   *Line 4, after* there) *delete* ,   *Line 6, for* this. At *read* this: at   *after* Bath *delete* ,   *Line 14, after* content you *delete* ,   *Line 16, after* person *add* ,   *Line 17, after* come in *add* ,   *Lines 17–18, after* nothing *add* ,   *Line 21, after* hostilities *delete* ,

Page 236, note 9, line 1, *for* ca 1702 *read* 1709

Page 236, note 16, *for* Not identified. *read* Undoubtedly Richard Rigby (see Namier and Brooke iii. 357).

Page 237, 1st paragraph, line 3, *after* days *delete* ,

Page 237, 3d paragraph, line 1, *after* public *delete* ,   *Line 3, after* window *delete* ,   *Line 4, after* fly *add* ,

Page 238, after To Holland 14 Nov. 1766 *insert the following heading*:

FROM HOLLAND, late November 1766

Printed for the first time from a photostat of Holland's MS fragment, now in the British Museum (Add. MS 51,404, f. 222), in MISC. CORR. ii. 67–9.

Page 239, To Holland 10 Feb. 1767, headnote, *add* Collated with a photostat of the MS now BM Add. MS 51,404, ff. 223–4 [the variants are recorded below].

Page 239, To Holland 10 Feb. 1767, 1st paragraph, line 1, *after* me *add* ,

Page 240, 1st paragraph, line 5, *for* inconveniences *read* inconveniencies

Page 240, 2d paragraph, line 4, *after* House *delete* ,   *Line 5, after* divided *add* ,

Page 241, 1st paragraph, line 1, *after* ago *add* , *Line 2, after* hope *add* ,

Page 241, 2d paragraph, line 1, *for* Bladen; *read* Bladen: *Line 3, after* to *delete* , *after* refused by *add* ,

Page 241, 3d paragraph, line 2, *for* as *read* [as]

Page 241, note 21, lines 2–3, *for* cr. (1733) Bn Hervey of Ickworth *read* summoned to the House of Lords in his father's Barony as Lord Hervey of Ickworth, 1733

Page 242, To Selwyn 12 March 1767, headnote, line 3, *after* Maggs; *add* offered in Maggs Cat. No. 196 (1903), lot 975; *Line 6, for* Pearson. *read* Pearson; bequeathed by his widow, the Hon. Mrs Pearson, to her daughter, Mrs P. A. Tritton, of Parham Park, in 1974.

Page 242, To Selwyn 12 March 1767, date-line, *on* [12] *add note a: a.* A recent (1963) reading by Mrs Pearson herself supports 'March 11th' as the date on the MS.

Page 245, To Holland 7 Aug. 1767, headnote, *add* Collated with a photostat of the MS now BM Add. MS 51,404, ff. 225–6 [the variants are recorded below].

Page 245, To Holland 7 Aug. 1767, 1st paragraph, line 7, *for* deserve; *read* deserve, *Line 8, for* answer:— *read* answer. *Line 10, for* inconveniences *read* inconveniencies

Page 245, To Holland 7 Aug. 1767, 2d paragraph, line 4, *after* Duke *delete* , *Line 7, after* has said *add* , *Line 8, for* promise for *read* promise from

Page 246, 3d paragraph, line 1, *after* Woburn *delete* , *Line 3, after* October *delete* ,

Page 247, To Holland 15 Aug. 1767, headnote, *add* Collated with a photostat of the MS now BM Add. MS 51,404, f. 227.

Page 247, To Holland 15 Aug. 1767, 1st paragraph, line 5, *on* content him.' *add note a: a.* See also MANN vi. 554.

Page 248, From Holland 16 Aug. 1767, headnote, *add* A draft of this letter, in Holland's hand, is in BM Add. MS 51,404, f. 228; the variants in the text are recorded below, except for the following abbreviations: 'K.' for 'King', 'D.' for 'Duke', 'Dss' for 'Duchess', 'Bedf.' for 'Bedford', 'Gr.' for 'Grafton', 'Gr.' for 'Grenville'.

Page 248, From Holland 16 Aug. 1767, date-line omitted in the MS draft.

Page 248, From Holland 16 Aug. 1767, 1st paragraph, line 2, *for* feel *MS draft reads* very sensible of *Lines 2–3, for* he gets *MS draft reads* is got *Line 11, for* My *MS draft reads* Ly (*crossed out*) *Line 13,* Instead of *written over* Without *in MS draft* *Line 15, for* sensible *MS draft reads* and sensible

Page 249, 1st paragraph, line 2, *MS draft omits* in this matter *Line 3, MS draft omits* may *Line 5, for* sessions *MS draft reads* session

Page 249, 2d paragraph, line 4, *in MS draft* do what I now ask *written over* grace me (*crossed out*)

Page 249, 3d paragraph, *MS draft omits* Adieu, my dear Sir. Adieu! Yours, H—

Page 249, From Holland ca 17 Aug. 1767, headnote, line 2, *add* Collated with a photostat of the MS, in Holland's hand, now BM Add. MS 51,404, ff. 229–30 [the variants are recorded below].

Page 249, From Holland ca 17 Aug. 1767, salutation, *for* Hory *read* Horry

Page 249, From Holland ca 17 Aug. 1767, line 3, *after* well *add* ;   on as *add note* 1: 1. In MS 'as' written over 'which.'   *Line 4, after* go *delete* ,   *Line 5, for* a *certain read* a certain

Page 249, note 5, *for* 28 May *read* 29 May

Page 253, To Holland 30 Aug. 1768, headnote, *add* Collated with a photostat of the MS now BM Add. MS 51,404, ff. 231–2 [the variants are recorded below].

Page 253, To Holland 30 Aug. 1768, 1st paragraph, line 6, *after* looked *delete* ,   *Line 7, after* thought *delete* ,   on lighted *add note* 1a: 1a. MS reads 'lighted it upon it.'   *Line 8, after* box *add* ,   *Line 9, after* today *add* ,   *Line 10, after* fortnight *delete* ,

Page 257, note 5, line 1, *for* ca 1700 *read* ?1702   *Line 4, after* Carlisle *insert* (Sedgwick ii. 388–9)

Page 260, top of page, *insert the following headings*:

To LADY HOLLAND, Saturday 19 February 1774

Printed for the first time from a photostat of the MS, now in the British Museum (Add. MS 51,404, f. 233), in MISC. CORR. ii. 272–3.

To LADY HOLLAND, Saturday 26 February 1774

Printed for the first time from a photostat of the MS, now in the British Museum (Add. MS 51, 404, f. 234), in MISC. CORR. ii. 274.

Page 262, To Selwyn 16 Sept. 1775, headnote, line 4, *after* 545; *add* offered by Maggs, Cat. No. 494 (autumn 1927), lot 1931;

Page 270, note 7, line 2, *after* 204–5 *add* [2d edn, 1748, pp. 249–50, 286–7]   *Last line, add* HW's copy, now WSL, is Hazen, *Cat. of HW's Lib.* No. 458. HW also refers to Anson and Scipio in MONTAGU i. 55 and n. 7, 90 and nn. 22–3.

Page 272, note 2, line 1, *for* ca 1697 *read* 1695

Page 275, note 17, line 6, *for* and Montgomery *read* and 8th E. of Montgomery

Page 278, To Selwyn 5 July 1786, headnote, lines 1–2, *for* in the possession (1956) of Robert H. Taylor, Yonkers, N.Y. *read* now in the possession of Robert H. Taylor, Princeton, New Jersey   *Lines 4–5, for* R. N. Carew Hunt; it passed to Mr Taylor before Feb. 1953. *read* R. N.

Carew Hunt, a great-grandson of John Wild; sold by Mr Hunt to Seven Gables, from whom it was purchased by Mr Taylor in 1953.

Page 278, note 3, *add* Selwyn is in HW's list of recipients; see BERRY ii. 260.

Page 279, note 4, *substitute* In the *Morning Herald* 30 June, quoted in OSSORY ii. 516, n. 1.

Page 280, middle of page, *for* To Selwyn, n.d. *read* To Selwyn, Sunday *Same letter, headnote, add* Collated with the MS by WSL, at Chewton 20 April 1968. *Under headnote add Address*: To Mr G. Selwyn *On date-line add* Sunday. *Signature, for* H. WALPOLE *read* HOR. WALPOLE

Page 282, top of page, *for* To Selwyn, n.d. *read* To Selwyn, ?July–August 1782 *Same letter, headnote, line 2, for* First printed, Toynbee xv. 448. *read* First printed, J. H. Jesse, *Selwyn and his Contemporaries*, 1882, iii. 157–8 (with minor differences of spelling and punctuation); re-printed Toynbee xv. 448. Placed in 1776 by Jesse after a letter from Carlisle to Selwyn 3 Sept. 1776, which discusses the Fagnanis' giving their consent to leave Mie Mie with Selwyn for a year (Jesse, op. cit. 154). But the summer of 1782 seems a more likely date because Selwyn took a villa at Richmond in 1782, and thenceforth spent much time there (S. Parnell Kerr, *George Selwyn and the Wits*, 1909, pp. 308–9; HW to Selwyn 7 July 1779, n. 4). Also, in 1782 both Mie Mie and Lady Caroline Howard would have been eleven years old (*ante* SELWYN 255, n. 3, 263, n. 7), and on 4 Aug. 1782 HW wrote to Lady Ossory, 'George and La Mimie called on me half an hour ago' (OSSORY ii. 347).

Page 282, note 2, last line, *after* Toynbee *add* ; pointed out previously by J. H. Jesse, *Selwyn and his Contemporaries*, 1882, iii. 157

Page 283, To Selwyn, n.d., headnote, line 1, *after* xv. 452. *add* Collated with the MS, now WSL. *Line 3, after* printed it *add* ; sold at the Charles Hamilton Sale, 21 Feb. 1974, lot 383, to Seven Gables for WSL

Page 283, To Selwyn, n.d., after headnote *add Address*: To Mr Selwyn.

Page 289, note 13, right column, line 1, *for* 1678 *read* 1680 *Last line, add* See Sedgwick i. 417–18.

Page 304, note 61, line 1, *for* d. 1758 *read* ca 1691–1758 *Last line, add* See Sedgwick ii. 101–2.

Page 314, note 39, line 4, *for* 'Queen virum *read* 'Quem virum

Page 321, note 118, *add* See CONWAY i. 353–4 and n. 16.

Page 326, note 9, align first line

Page 326, note 10, line 5, *for* 1688–1723 *read* 1668–1723

Page 327, note 18, line 1, *for* ca 1715 *read* ca 1720

Page 330, HW's title, *on* Late King of the Mohocks *add note a: a.* 'One of a class of aristocratic ruffians who infested the streets of London at night in the early years of the 18th century' (OED, which cites Swift's *Journal to Stella* 8 March 1711–12 and *Spectator* No. 324, 1712; Mohocks are also mentioned in John Gay's 'Trivia,' 1716, iii. 326); see also MONTAGU ii. 219.

Page 331, note 6, right column, line 7, *for* Malden *read* Maldon

Page 332, note 6, left column, line 5, *for* 1728 *read* 1727   *right column, line 1, for* ca 1731 *read* 1731   *Last line, add* See Namier and Brooke iii. 218, 562–3.

Page 333, headnote, line 2, *after* WSL *add* Previously printed in the *London Chronicle* 8–11 Jan. 1757, i. 34–5.

Page 350, note 9, line 1, *delete* James

Page 354, note 21, line 2, *for* Sloan *read* Sloane

Page 354, note 26, lines 1–2, *for* post 1828 *read* 1852   *Last line, after* p. 27 *add*   ; GM 1852, n.s. xxxviii. 663

Page 357, note 30, line 4, *for* 1760 *read* 1761

Page 370, note 53, line 1, *for* (1632–97) *read* (1633–99)   *for* m. *read* m. (1651)   *Line 2, add* See Elizabeth Walsh, 'Mary Beale,' *Burlington Magazine*, July 1948, xc. 209.

Page 371, note 63, lines 5–9, *delete* He was probably George . . . of Surgeons). *and substitute* Identified as I. P. Huitson by his nephew J. Deere (see ADD. AND CORR. for vol. 30, p. 377).

Page 371, note 66, *add* Edmund Lodge, who wrote the biographies, acknowledges 'the late admirable Earl of Orford, who, in the course of his perusal of the proof-sheets (for he so far honoured me), did supply two or three facts, which, I think, I have already acknowledged in the proper place' (GM 1800, lxx pt ii. 916). For HW's copy of the *Imitations*, Nos 1–9, see Hazen, *Cat. of HW's Lib.* No. 3500.

Page 373, line 10, *for* sum or twenty-five pounds *read* sum of twenty-five pounds

Page 377, line 8, *on* death *add note* 70: 70. The following MS order in HW's hand is now WSL (from Mrs Hallam Murray's Collection, 1937): 'I order that on my death my body may be opened. Orford   June 6th 1796.' Endorsed: 'My uncle I. P. Huitson was surgeon to the late Lord Orford and in conformity to the above order opened his Lordship's body. The lock of hair accompanying this was secured from his Lordship's head after death as my uncle has often assured me. I give this to my friend J. T. Smith of the British Museum. J. Deere' The lock of hair is not with the MS. Another MS order in HW's hand is Stowe MS 755, f. 83, and Lord Walpole has still another copy in HW's hand (information from Robin Flower, Esq., of the British Museum).

VOLUME 31

Page vii, Bishop and Mrs Porteus, by John Downman, *for* 1784 *read* 1790

Page xi, 2d paragraph, line 17, *for* Victorians *read* Victorian

Page xiii, 1st paragraph, line 8, *for* the correspondence *read* the correspondences

Page xiii, 2d paragraph, lines 3–4, *for* are now in the possession of George Fortescue, Esq., Boconnoc, Lostwithiel, Cornwall. *read* formerly in the possession of George Fortescue, Esq., Boconnoc, Lostwithiel, Cornwall, were sold by the executors of Mr Fortescue to the British Museum in 1970.

Page xiii, 3d paragraph, lines 1–2, *for* None of the manuscripts of Walpole's twenty-six letters to Lady Mary Coke has been recovered. *read* Twenty-four of the manuscripts of Walpole's twenty-six letters to Lady Mary Coke are now in the Scottish Record Office.

Page xiv, 1st paragraph, line 3, *on* first printed *add note* 1: 1. See Lady Mary Coke, *Letters and Journals*, Edinburgh, 1889–96, i. p. cxxxii; iii. pp. vii–xxiv.

Page xiv, 1st paragraph, line 4, *for* manuscripts have disappeared *read* manuscripts have been deposited in the Scottish Record Office (we have collated the texts with photostats of the manuscripts, and the variants are recorded in ADD. AND CORR.).

Page xvi, line 11, *for* descendents *read* descendants

Page xvi, line 18, *for* eleven *read* thirteen

Page xvi, lines 19–20, *delete* two are in the Penzance Library, Cornwall,

Page xvii, line 8, *for* only four *read* only five

Page xvii, line 9, *for* one original *read* two originals

Page xvii, line 12, *for* fourteen letters *read* fifteen letters

Page xvii, lines 14–16, *delete* and one in the possession of Mr C. B. Pigot, of Woodrising, Valley Road, Ipswich, Suffolk. *and substitute* one in the Massachusetts Historical Society, one in the British Museum, and one in the possession of Dr H. Spencer Glidden.

Page xvii, line 17, *for* the original owned by Mr Pigot *read* the original acquired by W. S. Lewis from Mr C. B. Pigot

Page xvii, line 22, *for* fourteen *read* eleven

Page xix, 2d paragraph, line 10, *for* None *read* Only one (now in the British Museum) *Line 11, for* have yet *read* has yet

Page xxi, 2d paragraph, last line, *after* abridged. *add* One manuscript missing since publication of Walpole's *Works* is now in the Massachusetts Historical Society, another in the British Museum.

Page xxi, 3d paragraph, line 3, *after* vanished. *add* One of these five letters is now in the possession of Dr H. Spencer Glidden, of Tufts University. *Line 4, for* Fourteen and the draft of another *read* Fifteen and the draft of one of them

Page xxx, *sub* GEC, *for* 12 vols. *read* 12 vols

Page xxxiv, Letters between Walpole and Lady Mary Coke, *below* 1762 *insert* 1763 ca 25 March

Page xxxviii, *sub* 1789, *for* ca 25 June *read* 27 June

Page 1, To Anne Pitt 19 June 1751, headnote, line 2, *after* Cornwall. *add* The MS was sold by the executors of Mr Fortescue to the British Museum.

Page 1, note 3, lines 1–2, *for* ca 1703 *read* ca 1708
Page 2, after letter of 19 June 1751 *insert the following heading*:

To LADY HERVEY, ca Monday 20 August 1753
Missing; mentioned by HW to Henry Fox 20 Aug. 1753: 'I take the liberty you gave me of troubling you with the enclosed for my Lady Hervey' (MISC. CORR. i. 76).
Page 2, To Anne Pitt 10 Feb. 1754, headnote, line 1, *after* MS *insert* formerly   *Line 2, after* Cornwall *add*   , now in the British Museum
Page 6, note 1, lines 3–4, *for* cr. (1733) Bn Hervey of Ickworth *read* styled Bn Hervey of Ickworth, 1733
Page 6, note 2, *add* For her birth-date see *Correspondance authentique de Ninon de Lenclos*, ed. Émile Colombey, 1886, p. 1; Annie Brierre, *Ninon de Lenclos, courtisane et grande dame de Paris*, Lausanne, 1967, p. 24.
Page 6, note 3, lines 7–8, *for* Colombey, op. cit. *read Correspondance authentique de Ninon de Lenclos*, ed. Émile Colombey, 1886, pp.
Page 7, note 10, line 7, *after* Farnham *add* and (1763) E. of Farnham
Page 8, headnote, line 1, *after* iv. 116. *insert* Collated with a photostat of the MS in the Scottish Record Office [the variants are recorded below].
Page 8, 1st paragraph, line 1, *for* solicitor? You *read* solicitor?—you *Line 4, for* Legonier; *read* Legonier: *Line 5, after* young man *add*   , *Line 7, for* earth. Yet *read* earth—yet   *for* him, the *read* him, though *Line 8, for* help, *read* help;   *Line 10, after* However *delete*   ,   *Line 12, after* people *delete*   ,   *Line 14, for* be; *read* be—   *Line 17, after* halfway *add*   ,   *after* slave *delete*   ,
Page 11, note 13, line 1, *for* ca 1720 *read* 1721
Page 11, note 17, line 11, *after* Erskine). *add* Another copy with Lady Hervey's autograph in two places is in the Watkinson Library, Trinity College, Hartford, Connecticut.
Page 14, headnote, line 1, *add* Collated with a photostat of the MS in the Scottish Record Office [the variants are recorded below].
Page 14, To Lady Mary Coke 27 Dec. 1759, 1st paragraph, line 4, *after* Perhaps *delete*   ,   *Line 5, after* indeed *delete*   ,   *Line 6, for* one-self *read* one's self   *for* arms: *read* arms;   *Line 10, for* charms: *read* charms;   *Line 11, after* him *add*   ,   *Line 14, after* disdain *add*   ,
Page 15, 1st paragraph, line 2, *for* is written *read* was written
Page 15, line 7, *for* Mr. *read* Mr
Page 15, line 10, *after* Tory *add*   ,   *Line 12, for* asked *read* ask'd *Line 13, after* I *delete*   ,   *Line 16, for* kinds *read* kind
Page 15, headnote at middle of page, line 2, *after* pp. viii–ix. *insert* A manuscript copy of the verses, in an unidentified hand, survives with a batch of HW's letters to Lady Mary in the Scottish Record Office.   *Last line of headnote, for* them. *read* them, but the verses in this manuscript are not in Lady Temple's hand.

Page 15, Lady M. to Mr W., line 1, *after* on *delete* ,   *Line 2, for* on, *read* on;   *Line 5, for* motion; *read* motion,   *Line 7, after* carving *delete* ,   *Line 8, for* then when *read* there where   *for* starving, *read* starving: *Line 10, for* the *read* their   *for* face: *read* face;

Page 16, line 1, *after* spouse *delete* ,   *Line 4, for* more; *read* more: *Line 5, after* great *delete* ,   *Line 11, after* delay *delete* ,   *Line 12, for* should *read* shou'd

Page 17, To Lady Mary Coke 19 Feb. 1760, headnote, *add* Collated with a photostat of the MS in the Scottish Record Office [the variants are recorded below].

Page 17, To Lady Mary Coke 19 Feb. 1760, 1st paragraph, line 1, *for* letter; *read* letter: *Line 3, after* asked *delete* ,   *Line 4, after* but *delete* ,   *after* indeed *delete* ,   *Line 5, for* me. Did *read* me—did *Line 7, after* wit *add* ,   *Line 8, for* oneself *read* one's self

Page 18, line 1, *after* fancy *add* ,   *Line 2, after* virtues *add* , *Line 4, for* established. *read* established;   *after* spread *add* ,   *Line 5, for* children. *read* children: *Line 7, for* devoted, humble servant, *read* devoted humble servant

Page 19, note 5, *add* See also Namier and Brooke i. 342–3.

Page 19, note 7, lines 18–19 *for* Fitzpatrick *read* Fitzwilliam   *right column, line 8, for* Fitzpatrick *read* Fitzwilliam   *Last line, add* See also Namier and Brooke i. 210–11, ii. 437.

Page 20, headnote, *add* Collated with a photostat of the MS in the Scottish Record Office [the variants are recorded below].

Page 20, 1st paragraph, line 5, *for* London; *read* London—   *after* perhaps *add* ,   *Line 6, for* saw; *read* saw,   *Line 11, for* himself. Come *read* himself—come   *Line 13, after* lover *add* ,   *Line 15, for* you! *read* you!—   *Line 16, begin new paragraph with* I am lamenting *Line 18, for* voking that, *read* voking, that   *Line 19, for* so long *read* as long   *for* live? *read* live.

Page 21, 1st paragraph, line 2, *after* world *add* ,   *Line 5, for* you— *read* you,   *Line 6, after* and *delete* ,   *Line 10, after* drudges *delete* ,   *Line 14, after* Saragossa *add* ,   *Line 15, after* knew it *add* ,   *Line 16, after* born *add* ,   *Line 17, after* is *add* ,   *Line 18, for* on him *read* for him   *Line 20, after* Rhine *add* ,

Page 21, 2d paragraph, line 3, *after* heaven *add* ,   *Line 7, after* death *add* ,   *Line 8, for* Pitt, *read* Pitt;   *Line 9, after* But *delete* ,   *after* unluckily *delete* ,

Page 22, 1st paragraph, line 1, *for* prose. *read* prose;   *for* poet, and, *read* poet; and   *Line 4, for* truth. *read* truth:

Page 22, 2d paragraph, line 1, *for* you. You *read* you—you   *Line 3, for* House *read* Houses   *Line 9, for* poem. *read* poem—   *Line 10, after* forgotten *add* ,   *Line 12, after* slave *delete* ,

Page 22, after letter of 12 Feb. 1761 *insert the following heading*:

To LADY MARY COKE, ca Sunday 31 May 1761

Missing. A transcript of HW's mock sermon, in HW's hand, is in the Scottish Record Office among letters of HW to Lady Mary; apparently an enclosure in a missing letter to Lady Mary (printed *post* Appendix 3).

Page 23, headnote, *add* Collated with a photostat of the MS in the Scottish Record Office [the variants are recorded below].

Page 23, 1st paragraph, line 1, *after* vocation *add* , *for* my *read* my *for* you *read* you   *Line 4, after* moment *add* ,   *Line 5, for* looks; *read* looks: *Line 9, for* of— *read* of,   *Line 15, after* passion *add* ,   *Line 20, for* yourself, *read* yourself;   *Line 21, after* to me *delete* ,

Page 23, 2d paragraph, line 3, *for* drowned. *read* drowned—

Page 23, note 1, line 2, *after* Lady Mary *insert* written on   *for* 1762 *read* 1761

Page 24, line 3, *after* servant *delete* ,

Page 24, after letter of 5 Oct. 1761 *insert the following heading*:

To LADY MARY COKE, ca Sunday 20 December 1761

Missing. The manuscript of the verses, 'No rouge you wear,' headed 'To Lady Mary Coke,' in HW's hand, is in the Scottish Record Office among letters of HW to Lady Mary; presumably an enclosure in a missing letter to Lady Mary. The verses were sent to Montagu 23 Dec. 1761 (MONTAGU i. 413). Reproduced in facsimile in Lady Mary's *Letters and Journals*, vol. iii, facing p. xxiv.

Page 25, headnote, *add* Collated with a photostat of the MS in the Scottish Record Office [the variants are recorded below].

Page 25, 1st paragraph, line 5, *after* John *delete* ,   *after* Argyle *delete* ,   *Line 11, for* will, *read* will;   *Line 13, after* Pray *delete* ,

Page 26, line 3, *begin new paragraph with* As to peace   *after* peace *delete* ,   *Line 4, for* of war *read* of the war   *Line 6, for* break. *read* break;   *Line 7, for* killed. *read* killed,   *Line 11, for* profession, yet *read* profession. Yet   *Line 15, after* Coombe *delete* ,   *Line 16, for* Warwick; *read* Warwick—   *Line 17, after* forgot *add* ,   *Line 19, for* quiver, *read* quivers   *for* arrows, *read* arrow;   *Line 23, for* garment? *read* garment—

Page 26, note 19, line 2, *for* Liége *read* Liège

Page 27, 1st paragraph, line 1, *for* him; *read* him,   *for* another. *read* another—   *Line 2, for* warfare. *read* warfare—   *Line 4, begin new paragraph with* I can give   *Line 5, for* family. *read* family;

Page 27, 2d paragraph, line 2, *for* vain. *read* vain;   *Line 3, after* Spa *delete* ,   *Line 6, for* Madam. Whether *read* Madam; whether   *Line 8, after* yours *delete* ,

Page 30, after letter of 31 Oct. 1762 *insert the following heading*:

To LADY MARY COKE, ca Friday 25 March 1763

Missing. A transcript of 'The Advice, to Miss P[elham], a Song,' in

HW's hand is in the Scottish Record Office among letters of HW to Lady Mary Coke; apparently an enclosure in a missing letter to Lady Mary. HW also sent the verses to Montagu in a letter of 25 March 1763 (MONTAGU ii. 54–5).

Page 31, To Anne Pitt 10 Dec. 1763, headnote, line 1, *after* MS *insert* formerly   *Line 2, after* Cornwall *add*   , now in the British Museum

Page 33, To Anne Pitt 21 Feb. 1764, headnote, line 1, *after* MS *insert* formerly   *Line 2, after* Cornwall *add*   , now in the British Museum

Page 37, note 3, line 1, *for* ca 1697 *read* 1695

Page 40, To Anne Pitt 9 Aug. 1765, headnote, line 1, *after* MS *insert* formerly   *Line 2, after* Cornwall *add*   , now in the British Museum

Page 52, note 12, line 5, *for* 6 Oct. *read* 2 Oct.   *Last line, after* letters *add*   , but it does appear in letters *to* her from her cousin, the Comte de Bussy, and he attributes the sentiment to her, in an ancedote similar to Mary Berry's, in his *Histoire amoureuse des Gaules*; see CONWAY iii. 13, n. 15.

Page 53, To Anne Pitt 8 Oct. 1765, headnote, line 1, *after* MS *insert* formerly   *Line 2, after* Cornwall *add*   , now in the British Museum

Page 53, note 18, line 8, *for* Brotherton *read* Bretherton

Page 60, note 10, line 2, *for* Dumesnil *read* Mlle du Mesnil   *Line 3, after* 12 *add* CONWAY ii. 524, n. 18

Page 61, headnote, *add* Collated with a photostat of the MS in the Scottish Record Office [the variants are recorded below].

Page 61, 1st paragraph, line 3, *for* this: *read* this,   *Line 4, after* podagram *add* ,   *after* mutant *add* ,

Page 61, 2d paragraph, line 1, align with left margin, i.e. no paragraphing   *Line 2, for* gout; *read* gout: *for* Is it not *read* is not it   *Line 4, for* For *read* for   *Line 11, for* invalids *read* invalids,   *Line 12, after* charms *delete* ,   *after* own *delete* ,

Page 61, 3d paragraph, line 2, *for* have. *read* have: *Line 3, for* the sight *read* a sight

Page 62, 1st paragraph, line 3, *after* blood-thirstiness *add* ,

Page 62, 2d paragraph, line 6, *after* Indeed *delete* ,   *Line 9, after* door *delete* ,   *Line 11, for* bedside; *read* bedside: *Line 16, begin new paragraph with* Of you islanders   *for* your islanders *read* you islanders   *Line 18, after* ignorance *delete* ,

Page 63, 1st paragraph, line 3, *after* so *add* ,   *Line 7, after* gout *delete* ,   *Line 10, begin new paragraph with* When you see   *Line 16, begin new paragraph with* My letter   *after* letter *delete* ,   *Line 17, after* perceive *delete* ,   *for* legible, *read* legible;   *Line 18, after* zeal *delete* ,   *Line 21, after* servant *delete* ,

Page 63, note 16, line 1, *for* ca 1715 *read* ca 1720

Page 64, note 3, line 2, *after* 1740. *insert* In 1763 she was rumoured to be marrying Count Vorontsov (Hist. MSS Comm., *Lothian MSS*, 1905, pp. 177–8).

Page 66, To Anne Pitt 4 Nov. 1765, headnote, line 1, *after* MS *insert* formerly   *after* Fortescue, Esq. *add*   , now in the British Museum.

Page 66, note 18, line 1, *for* 1683 *read* ca 1693

Page 70, headnote, *add* Collated with a photostat of the MS in the Scottish Record Office [the variants are listed below].

Page 70, 1st paragraph, line 5, *after* other *delete*   ,   *Line 9, after* because *insert* where   *for* grief; *read* grief,   *Line 10, for* in it, *read* in it—   *Line 11, for* separation; *read* separation: *Line 14, for* Madam, *read* Madam;   *Line 15, for* miserable; *read* miserable: *Line 16, for* deserves *read* deserve[s]   *begin new paragraph with* I am got   *Line 17, after* illness *delete*   ,

Page 71, line 3, *after* forty *delete*   ,   *Line 4, after* hard *add*   ,   *Line 7, for* Vallière's *read* Valière's   *Line 9, for* self-love. *read* self-love—   *Line 10, after* head *delete*   ,   *after* indeed *delete*   ,   *Line 11, begin new paragraph with* Paris is still   *Line 17, for* have none *read* know none   *for* ever tell *read* even tell   *Line 24, begin new paragraph with* You will soon see

Page 72, line 2, *for* yours; *read* yours: *after* good-humoured *add*   ,   *Line 3, begin new paragraph with* Though I have   *Line 6, for* at least *read* at best   *Line 7, for* Fontainebleau. *read* Fontainebleau: *Line 8, for* across *read* on this side of   *Line 15, for* singularity which, *read* singularity, which   *Line 18, after* hence *add*   ,   *Line 20, for* ennuierais—in *read* ennuierais. In   *Line 22, for* the day *read* a day   *Line 23, after* but *delete*   ,   *Line 24, for* again. *read* again: *Line 28, after* them *add*   ,   *Line 32, after* Valière *delete*   ,   *Line 33, for* will ever be *read* ever will be   *Line 34, after* pastor fido *delete*   ,

Page 74, note 7, line 4, *for* cimes *read* crimes

Page 77, note 7, line 2, *for* Dumesnil *read* Mlle du Mesnil

Page 87, To Anne Pitt 25 Dec. 1765, headnote, line 1, *after* MS *insert* formerly   *Line 2, after* Cornwall *add*   , now in the British Museum.

Page 91, note 5, line 1, *for* ca 1742 *read* 1742   *Last line, add* See also Namier and Brooke ii. 269.

Page 92, To Lady Mary Coke 4 Jan. 1766, headnote, *add* Collated with a photostat of the MS in the Scottish Record Office [the variants are recorded below].

Page 93, 1st paragraph, line 4, *for* less than *read* less then than

Page 93, 2d paragraph, line 1, *after* French *add*   ,   *Line 3, for* two; *read* two—   *Lines 4–5, for* charming; *read* charming—   *for* Commons; *read* Commons,   *Line 6, after* which *delete*   ,   *after* however *delete*   ,   *Line 7, after* hours *delete*   ,   *after* manners *delete*   ,   *Line 10, after* more *delete*   ,   *after* Strawberry *delete*   ,   *Line 13, after* happy *add*   ,   *Line 15, for* Eve: *read* Eve,   *Line 16, after* who *delete*   ,   *Line 18, after* country *add*   ,   *after* where *delete*   ,   *Line 19, after* nobody *delete*   ,   *Line 20, after* nonsense *add*   ,

Page 93, 3d paragraph, line 1, *after* supposition *add*   ,   *Line 3 after* hot *add*   ,   *Line 5, after* however *delete*   ,   *Line 6, after* operas *delete*   ,   *after* told *delete*   ,

Page 94, 1st paragraph, lines 2–3, *for* amusement; they *read* amusement. They   *Line 4, after* formed *add*   ,   *Line 5, for* Lord *read* my Lord *for* thither; *read* thither—   *Line 6, for* England; *read* England— *Line 8, after* Stowe *delete*   ,   *after* ministry *add*   ,   *Line 12, for* England.[6] As *read* England:[6] as

Page 94, 2d paragraph, line 1, *for* Adieu. *read* Adieu!   *for* Mary. You *read* Mary—you   *for* levities, *read* levities—   *Line 4, after* faithful *delete*   ,   *after* servant *delete*   ,

Page 95, note 1, line 2, *for* 1773 *read* 1772

Page 98, To Anne Pitt 19 Jan. 1766, headnote, line 1, *after* MS *insert* formerly   *Line 2, after* Cornwall *add*   , now in the British Museum.

Page 103, note 7, line 2, *for* 1735 *read* 1736   *Line 3, for* 1803 *read* 1798   *right column, line 1, after* i. 91 *insert*   ; Namier and Brooke ii. 518–19

Page 105, note 5, *for* Dumesnil *read* Du Mesnil

Page 106, To Anne Pitt 1 March 1766, headnote, line 1, *after* MS *insert* formerly   *Line 2, after* Cornwall *add*   , now in the British Museum.

Page 107, note 6, *substitute* Probably George Forbes (1740–80), styled Vct Forbes 19 June 1765 upon the death of his grandfather, Lord Granard; 5th E. of Granard, 1769; he was also in Paris in June, 1765 (see CONWAY ii. 575–6).

Page 108, To Lady Mary Coke 3 March 1766, headnote, *add* Collated with a photostat of the MS in the Scottish Record Office [the variants are recorded below].

Page 108, To Lady Mary Coke 3 March 1766, 1st paragraph, line 9, *after* passion *delete*   ,

Page 109, 1st paragraph, line 4, *begin new paragraph with* Your nephews,   *Lines 5–6, for* mate as *read* make us   *Line 6, for* companions; but, *read* companions, but   *Line 8, after* nature *delete*   ,   *Line 11, begin new paragraph with* The King has

Page 109, 2d paragraph, line 3, *after* servant *add*   ,   *Line 4, begin new paragraph with* Of Lady Suffolk   *Line 6, for* my *read* my own *Line 7, for* would *read* could

Page 110, line 4, *after* servant *delete*   ,

Page 110, line 6, *for* PS.— *read* PS.

Page 110, To Anne Pitt 7 March 1766, headnote, line 1, *after* MS *insert* formerly   *Line 2, after* Cornwall *add*   , now in the British Museum

Page 128, headnote, line 1, *after* 38–9. *add* Collated with a photostat of the MS in the Scottish Record Office [the variants are recorded below].

Page 128, To Lady Mary Coke 17 Sept. 1766, date-line, *after* Wednesday *delete*   ,

Page 128, To Lady Mary Coke 17 Sept. 1766, 1st paragraph, line 7, *for* enough, *read* enough;   *Line 10, for* gold colour *read* gold-colour *Line 11, after* this *add*   ,

Page 128, note 3, line 1, *before* Coke *insert* The MS reads 'bed.'

Page 128, note 4, line 1, *before* The text *insert* The MS reads 'Bathgilt.'

Page 129, To Lady Mary Coke 17 Sept. 1766 *bis*, headnote, line 1, *add* Collated with a photostat of the MS in the Scottish Record Office [the variants are recorded below].

Page 129, To Lady Mary Coke 17 Sept. 1766 *bis*, 1st paragraph, line 2, *after* town *delete*   ,   *Line 5, after* nights *add*   ,

Page 132, To Lady Mary Coke ca 4 Nov. 1766, headnote, line 1, *add* Collated with a photostat of the MS in the Scottish Record Office [the variants are recorded below].

Page 132, To Lady Mary Coke ca 4 Nov. 1766, 1st paragraph, line 2, *for* loss. *read* loss: *after* will *delete*   ,   *after* however *delete*   ,   *Line 4, after* reason *add*   ,

Page 135, To Lady Mary Coke 20 Sept. 1767, headnote, line 1, *add* Collated with a photostat of the MS in the Scottish Record Office [the variants are recorded below].

Page 135, To Lady Mary Coke 20 Sept. 1767, date-line, *for* Sept. 20th *read* Sept. 20,   *Line 2, after* request *add*   ,   *Lines 4–5, after* fatigue *delete*   ,   *Line 8, after* beg *delete*   ,   *Line 9, for* Dalkeith, *read* Dalkeith;   *after* Townshend *delete*   ,

Page 136, 1st paragraph, line 1, *begin new paragraph with* I am very glad   *Line 3, after* Chabot's *add*   ,

Page 136, 2d paragraph, line 2, *begin new paragraph with* Nothing else *Line 3, after* nor *delete*   ,   *after* indeed *delete*   ,   *after* does *delete*   ,   *Line 4, after* marriages *delete*   ,   *after* joy *delete*   ,   *Line 7, for* Duchesse *read* Duchess   *Line 8, for* verdure, *read* verdure;

Page 137, 2d paragraph, line 4, *after* executed *add*   ,

Page 137, 3d paragraph, line 3, *after* know *delete*   ,   *Line 4, after* faithful *delete*   ,   *after* servant *delete*   ,

Page 139, To Anne Pitt 28 Oct. 1768, headnote, line 1, *after* MS *insert* formerly   *Line 2, after* Cornwall *add*   , now in the British Museum

Page 142, To Lady Mary Coke 14 Dec. 1769, headnote, *add* Collated with a photostat of the MS in the Scottish Record Office [the variants are recorded below].

Page 142, To Lady Mary Coke 14 Dec. 1769, 1st paragraph, line 2, *after* of me *delete*   ,

Page 143, line 1, *for* not, *read* not;   *Line 5, for* rights *read* right *Line 8, for* considerable return of *read* return of considerable   *Line 9, for* Voltaire[2] *read* Voltaire,[2]   *Line 11, for* impart *read* import   *Line 12, for* Avignon[5] *read* Avignon,[5]   *Line 14, after* portrait *add*   ,

Page 143, note 6, lines 1–2, *for* K. of Sicily 1435–43 *read* titular King of Sicily 1435–80 and effective King of Naples 1438–42

Page 143, note 7, line 1, *for* 1430 *read* ca 1430

Page 144, line 3, *after intendantes delete* , *Line 4, begin new paragraph with* I do not attempt *Line 6, for* Ailesbury I think *read* Ailesbury, I think, *Line 7, after* arrived *add* , *Line 8, for* deserted. *read* deserted; *after* desert *add* , *Line 9, begin new paragraph with* Lady Betty Germain *Line 12, for* Oyras's *read* Oeyras's *Line 13, for* he I believe *read* he, I believe, *Line 15, begin new paragraph with* Such a scanty *Line 20, for* folly: one *read* folly. One

Page 145, 1st paragraph, line 1, *begin new paragraph with* Poor Mrs Harris *Line 4, begin new paragraph with* When I have *Line 6, for* for me, *read* of me: *Line 8, after* servant *delete* ,

Page 145, To Lady Mary Coke, ?April ?1770, headnote, line 1, *add* Collated with a photostat of the MS in the Scottish Record Office [the variants are recorded below].

Page 145, To Lady Mary Coke, ?April ?1770, line 1, *after* nor *delete* , *Line 4, for* masquerade, *read* masquerade;

Page 146, 1st paragraph, line 1, *after* obliged *insert* to you *Line 2, for* tonight; *read* tonight:

Page 148, To Lady Mary Coke 13 Sept. 1770, headnote, *add* Collated with a photostat of the MS in the Scottish Record Office [the variants are recorded below].

Page 148, To Lady Mary Coke 13 Sept. 1770, date-line, *for* Sept. 13th *read* Sept. 13, *Line 10, after* goodness *add* , *after* Townshend *add* , *Line 12, for* more. *read* more, *Line 14, after* yours *delete* ,

Page 149, To Lady Mary Coke 24 Sept. 1770, headnote, *add* Collated with a photostat of the MS in the Scottish Record Office [the variants are recorded below].

Page 149, To Lady Mary Coke 24 Sept. 1770, 1st paragraph, line 2, *for* good to call; *read* good as to call, *Line 5, for* weather.[2] However *read* weather;[2] however *after* much *add* , *Line 6, after* commands *add* , *Line 7, begin new paragraph with* If it is possible *after* possible *add* , *Line 8, for* out: *read* out; *after* happiness *delete* , *Line 9, after* and *delete* , *Line 10, for* Emperor[4] *read* Emperor,[4] *Line 15, for* Madam; *read* Madam, *for* back: *read* back, *Line 16, for* old; *read* old, *Line 17, for* watch. Yet *read* watch—yet *Line 20, after* slave *delete* ,

Page 150, To Lady Mary Coke 27 Jan. 1771, headnote, line 1, *add* Collated with a photostat of the MS in the Scottish Record Office [the variants are recorded below].

Page 150, To Lady Mary Coke 27 Jan. 1771, 1st paragraph, line 3, *after* of *add* , *Line 6, after* epistle *add* , *Line 7, for* altitudes, *read* altitudes; *Line 11, for* Ladyship; *read* Ladyship, *after* but *delete* ,

Line 12, for Archduchess, *read* Archduchess;   *Line 13, for* pities, *read* pities;   *Line 17, for* with *read* within   *Line 18, for* However pray *read* However, pray,   *Line 21, begin new paragraph with* I do not pretend

Page 151, line 1, *for* years! *read* years.   *after* daily *add* ,   *Line 2, for* conversation; *read* conversation—   *Line 5, after* part *add* ,   *after* say *add* ,   *Line 8, begin new paragraph with* Loo begins   *for* forgotten: *read* forgotten;   *Line 10, for* yesterday for a *read* yesterday for an   *Line 12, for* brought. All *read* brought—all   *after* know is *add* ,   *Line 13, for* Castille *read* Castile   *after* Granada *delete* ,   *Line 14, for* starving, *read* starving—   *after* place *add* ,

Page 152, line 1, *begin new paragraph with* The Ladies' Club   *after* profane *add* ,   *Line 2, for* mysteries, yet *read* mysteries. Yet   *after* them *add* ,   *Line 11, begin new paragraph with* Plays, at least   *Line 14, for* King Arthur[24] *read* King Arthur,[24]   *for* scenery: *read* scenery;   *Line 15, after* temple *delete* ,   *Line 16, for* performer, *read* performer: *Line 19, after* too *delete* ,

Page 153, line 5, *after* reads *add* ,   *Line 6, begin new paragraph with* Lord Huntingdon   *Line 9, for* Shelburne *read* Shelburn   *for* wife, *read* wife;   *Line 10, for* Spain. *read* Spain: *Line 11, begin new paragraph with* The worst and   *Line 15, after* deafness *delete* ,   *Line 16, begin new paragraph with* This sketch of   *after* will *delete* ,   *after* hope *delete* ,

Page 154, line 1, *for* omissions, *read* omissions—   *Line 11, begin new paragraph with* May I trouble   *Line 16, for* I am, Madam, *read* I am Madam   *Line 18, after* knight *delete* ,

Page 155, To Lady Mary Coke 9 June 1771, headnote, line 1, *add* Collated with a photostat of the MS in the Scottish Record Office [the variants are recorded below].

Page 155, 1st paragraph, line 4, *after* true *add* ,   *for* Courtenay *read* Courtnay   *on* Courtnay *add note a: a.* For the Courtenay family see MANN iii. 309, n. 15.   *Line 13, for* once; *read* once,   *Line 17, for* or *read* Or   *after* come *add* ,   *Line 22, after* ill-bred *delete* ,   *Line 24, after* Europe *add* ,   *Line 25, for* there, *read* there;

Page 156, 1st paragraph, line 3, *for* Borgia: *read* Borgia.   *Line 4, for* part. *read* part: *Line 6, after* Nay *add* ,   *Line 10, after* adorer *delete* ,

Page 156, To Lady Mary Coke 22 Aug. 1771, headnote, line 1, *add* Collated with a photostat of the MS in the Scottish Record Office [the variants are recorded below].

Page 157, To Lady Mary Coke 22 Aug. 1771, 1st paragraph, line 8, *after* ascertain you *delete* ,   *Line 10, after* islands *delete* ,   *Line 11, after* where *delete* ,   *Line 13, begin new paragraph with* The discovery   *Line 14, for* too: it *read* too. It   *Line 17, for* Quality.[5] *read*

Quality—[5] *Line 18, for* at that *read* at the *Lines 19–20, for* vapour! No *read* vapour!—no *Line 20, for* angels. They *read* angels—*They*

Page 157, note 2, *add* HW had a print of a caricature of Solander (now in the Pierpont Morgan Library, New York), entitled 'The Simpling Macaroni,' identified in HW's hand (see also BM *Satiric Prints* No. 4696).

Page 158, line 6, *for* had ruby *read* has ruby *for* diamond, *read* diamond— *Line 8, begin new paragraph with* As this memorable *Line 11, for* here; *read* here, *Line 13, for* annihilated. No *read* annihilated—no *Line 16, after* furnace *add* , *Line 17, for* Shadrac *read* Shadrach *for* Meshac, *read* Meshach *Line 18, for* diamond: *read* diamond, *Line 19, begin new paragraph with* Nobody can tell *Line 20, after* part *add* , *Line 23, for* with. *read* with— *Line 24, for* piece *read* pair *after* weight, *delete* and

Page 159, line 2, *for* strong beer *read* strong-beer *Line 4, begin new paragraph with* The reflections one *Line 6, for* time—nor *read* time. Nor *for* with you *read* with *you* *for* Madam; *read* Madam. *Line 7, after* consideration *delete* , *Line 10, after* merit *delete* , on assail *add note* 14: 14. MS reads 'assoil.' *Line 13, for* I am, Madam, *read* I am Madam *Line 14, after* faithful *delete* , *after* servant *delete* ,

Page 160, note 4, line 5, *for* iv. 19–20 *read* iv. 28–30

Page 162, note 11, line 5, *after* 105). *insert* See also OSSORY i. 127, n. 36.

Page 163, To Lady Mary Coke 11 Dec. 1771, headnote, line 1, *add* Collated with a photostat of the MS in the Scottish Record Office [the variants are recorded below].

Page 163, To Lady Mary Coke 11 Dec. 1771, 1st paragraph, line 2, *after* obey *add* ,

Page 164, 1st paragraph, line 5, *after* their *insert* own *Line 8, after* therefore *delete* , *Line 18, for* for it; *read* for it, *Line 20, for* subject: *read* subject; *Line 23, for* friendship: *read* friendship; *Line 25, for* know *read* know of *Line 26, after* everybody *delete* ,

Page 164, 2d paragraph, line 1, *after* is *add* , *Line 2, for* desert: *read* desert; *Line 3, for* opera. The *read* opera; the *for* Brunswick *read* Brunswic *for* coming: *read* coming, *Line 4, for* going. There *read* going; there

Page 165, 1st paragraph, line 1, *for* peace. *read* peace, *Line 2, for* hubbub.[5] *read* hubbub—[5] *for* is indeed *read* indeed is *after* news *delete* to you *Line 5, after* servant *delete* ,

Page 165, To Lady Mary Coke 29 Jan. 1772, headnote, line 1, *add* Collated with a photostat of the MS in the Scottish Record Office [the variants are recorded below].

Page 165, To Lady Mary Coke 29 Jan. 1772, 1st paragraph, line 1, *delete* my *Line 4, for* myself: *read* myself; *Line 5, for* differently; what *read* differently. What

Page 166, 1st paragraph, line 1, *after* yourself *add* , *Line 2, after* another *delete* ,   *for* Madam *read* medium   *Line 3, begin new paragraph with* Your Ladyship says   *Line 6, after* grateful *add* ,   *Line 11, for* know of you *read* know in you   *after* them *add* ,   *Lines 13–14, run in, no paragraph*

Page 166, 2d paragraph, line 2, *begin new paragraph with* For what your Ladyship   *Line 10, after* truth *add* ,   *Line 17, for* she is, *read* she is!   *Line 20, after* conferred *add* ,   *for* superior, *read* superior;   *Line 21, after* favours *add* ,   *after* themselves *add* ,   *Line 22, for* seem *read* are sure   *for* honour. *read* honour—

Page 167, 1st paragraph, line 1, *after* weapons *add* ,   *Line 7, for* upon *read* of   *Line 8, after* them *insert* all   *Line 9, for* bear *read* hear   *after* nay *add* ,   *Line 14, for* message *read message*   *begin new paragraph with* I condole with you   *before* Madam *insert* dear   *Line 15, for* Amelia *read* Amelie   *Line 19, begin new paragraph with* I acknowledge   *Line 20, after* friendship *add* ,   *Line 22, for* duration: *read* duration;   *Line 24, after* servant *delete* ,

Page 170, note 1, lines 1–3, *delete* possibly the same miniatures discussed in HW to Lady Temple 20 Dec. 1773.   *Line 7, add* HW to Lady Temple 20 Dec. 1773 concerns the remaining seven Digby miniatures, which HW bought in 1775; see MASON i. 180 and HW to Thomas Pennant 25 May 1773, MISC. CORR. ii. 252–3.

Page 170, note 2, line 1, *for* ca 1733 *read* 1734   *Last line, add* For the Stapleton sisters (Penelope, Catherine, Frances, and Elizabeth) and their connection with the Digby miniatures, see HW to Thomas Pennant 25 May 1773, MISC. CORR. ii. 252–4, nn. 22, 23.

Page 173, note 8, *add* The *Public Adv.* 31 Aug. 1770 printed the following verses 'On Lord Chesterfield visiting Mr Walpole at Strawberry Hill':

> 'The tuneful Lyre that happily convey'd
> To ravish'd Ears the Notes that Orpheus play'd,
> Would prove an Instrument of less Delight
> Than Walpole's Press—if Chesterfield would write.'

Page 203, To Lady Browne ca 19 July 1781, note 1, line 2, *after* n. 17 *insert* ; Sedgwick ii. 54–5

Page 204, To Lady Browne, ? Sept. or Oct. 1783, headnote, line 2, *after* Cornwall *add* ; sold Sotheby's 25 May 1964, lot 465, to WSL   *Line 8, after* Endorsed *add* (in an unknown hand)

Page 205, From Mary Hamilton ca 6 Oct. 1783, note 1, right column, line 2, *delete* M.P.,

Page 211, note 1, line 2, *for* 1725 *read* 1724

Page 215, To Mary Hamilton ca 18 June 1784, headnote, *add* Probably HW's note to Mrs Vesey 18 June 1784, which was forwarded to Mary Hamilton by Mrs Vesey, as is shown by the second address, 'To Miss Hamilton,' in Mrs Vesey's hand on the verso of the MS, now WSL; printed in MISC. CORR. iii. 99.

Page 223, From Hannah More ca 4 April 1785, headnote, line 6, *for* one exception (*post* 20 July 1788) *read* two exceptions (*post* 20 July 1788 and 27 June 1789)

Page 234, note 3, *add* For later evidence on the armour see OSSORY iii. 235–6, Appendix 1.

Page 237, note 2, *add* See also CONWAY i. 348 and n. 11.

Page 237, note 3, *add* See also MISC. CORR. ii. 437, n. 1, iii. 392, n. 1.

Page 240, To Hannah More 9 Feb. 1786, headnote, line 2, *after* Ipswich; *add* the MS is now (1967) WSL;   *Line 9, for* the present owner *read* C. B. Pigot, Esq., the former owner,

Page 243, To Hannah More 1 Jan. 1787, headnote, last line, *for* not further traced. *read* offered by Francis Edwards, 83, Marylebone High Street, London, Cat. 976 (1973), lot 681; re-offered by Edwards Cat. 980 (1974), lot 783 and Cat. 987 (1974), lot 426.

Page 243, To Hannah More 1 Jan. 1787, 1st paragraph, line 4, *on* compliments *add note a: a.* 'Praise and compliments' crossed out and 'kindness and friendship' written above in the MS (Toynbee, *Supp.* ii. 14, n. 2).

Page 244, 2d paragraph, line 7, *on* Lactilla *add note* 3a: 3a. 'Lactilla' crossed out in MS, and a pencil note 'Anne Yearsley' written at bottom of page (Toynbee, *Supp.* ii. 14, n. 7).

Page 244, 3d paragraph, line 4, *on* milkman *add note* 4a: 4a. The words 'as I am no milkman but' crossed out; 'flatterer' written above 'milkman' in MS (Toynbee, *Supp.* ii. 15, n. 8).

Page 245, To Hannah More 23 Feb. 1787, headnote, line 1, *after* v. 586; *add* now collated with a photostat of the MS   *Last line, for* not further traced *read* the MS is now Massachusetts Historical Society (1938, from Grenville H. Norcross)

Page 245, To Hannah More 23 Feb. 1787, date-line, *for* February 23, *read* Feb. 23d   *1st paragraph, line 2, for* Charles V² *read* Charles V,² *Line 4, after* lately *delete* ,   *Lines 5–6, for* three-and-twenty *read* three and twenty   *Line 10, for* voyage:— *read* voyage;   *Line 11, after* cabin *delete* ,

Page 245, To Hannah More 23 Feb. 1787, 2d paragraph, line 2, *for* piece. Yet *read* piece—yet

Page 246, line 2, *for* town; *read* town,

Page 246, line 4, *for* HOR. *read* H.

Page 247, note 3, line 7, *for* [apparently a mistake] *read* [apparently from Berkeley Square]

Page 262, To Mrs Dickenson 13 April 1788, note 1, line 1, *for* Louisa Dickenson *read* Louisa Frances Mary Dickenson   *Line 2, for* 1814 *read* 1815   *Line 3, before* Anson *insert* Burke, *Peerage*, 1928, p. 118;

Page 263, To Mrs Dickenson 11 June 1788, note 1, last line, *after* 1788 *add* ; *London Stage* Part V, iv. 1147

Page 276, To Hannah More 17 Aug. 1788, headnote, line 1, *after* 52–4 *add* , who restored the deleted passages. Collated with a photostat of

the MS.   *Lines 4–5, for* Its present whereabouts is unknown to the editors. *read* It was sold Sotheby's 15 Oct. 1963, lot 489; in May 1964, *penes* Dr H. Spencer Glidden, Tufts University, Boston, Massachusetts.
Line 6, under Address add
Postmark: AU 18 88
Endorsed (in unknown hand): From Mr Walpole to Mrs H. More
Notes (in Hannah More's hand, crossed out):

> Not in Ld Orford's Letters
> I saw person about to exorcise a spirit.
> Lukins man exorcised.
> To be transcribed

Page 276, note 2, line 1, *before* 'On the *insert* This sentence is heavily blacked out in the MS.

Page 277, 1st paragraph, line 2, *on* crimes *add note* 3a: 3a. 'Crimes' crossed out and 'injustice' written above in the MS.   *Line 5, on* Bristol. *add note* 3b: 3b. The passage, 'so the air of Bristol . . . credit of Bristol,' is crossed out in the MS; omitted from the letter until restored in Toynbee, *Supp*. iii. 52–3.

Page 277, 2d paragraph, line 1, *on* Clarke *add note* 3c: 3c. 'Clarke' and 'the Dickensons at' are crossed out in the MS; omitted until restored in Toynbee, *Supp*. iii. 53.   *Line 3, after* believe *insert* very   *Line 4, for* enjoyment *read* enjoyments

Page 277, note 5, *after* Vesey *add* (Note in Hannah More's hand)

Page 278, note 11, *add* See HW to Strafford 2 Aug. 1788 (CHUTE 393 and n. 7).

Page 279, 1st paragraph, line 4, *for* is it not *read* is not it   *Line 10, on* s'entend. *add note* 17a: 17a. The passage, 'but for the sake of . . . s'entend,' is crossed out lightly; 'in *sheets*' is heavily blacked out in the MS; omitted until restored in Toynbee, *Supp*. iii. 54.

Page 281, note 16, line 2, *for* Occurences *read* Occurrences

Page 286, running head, *for* To Mrs Dickenson *read* From Mrs Dickenson

Page 288, note 20, line 2, *for* E. Onslow *read* E. of Onslow

Page 293, note 9, *add* See also *London Stage* Part V, ii. 1088, 1146–7, 1150, 1154, 1155.

Page 297, 4th paragraph, line 6, *for* Lady Die *read* Lady Di

Page 303, running head, *for* ca 25 June *read* 27 June

Page 303, heading, *for* From Hannah More, ca Thursday 25 June 1789 *read* From Hannah More, Saturday 27 June 1789

Page 303, headnote, *substitute* Printed from a photostat of the MS, now BM Add. MS 54,225, f. 174 (see Paul J. Korshin, 'New B.M. MSS,' *Times Literary Supplement* 9 July 1970, p. 750). [There are so many variants in the MS that the text is reprinted below.]

Address: Hon. Horace Walpole Strawberry Hill Twickenham.
London.—June Thirty—B London.

Postmark: JU [3]o 89.

Endorsed (in an unidentified hand): Bonners Ghost just come out.
Transcribed.

Cowslip Green
27 June 1789.

How you do scold me! but I don't care for your scolding, nor I don't
care for your wit neither, that I don't, half as much, as I care for a blow
which I hear you have given yourself against a table, though you were
above mentioning it yourself. I have known such very serious consequences arise from such accidents, that I beg of you to drown yourself in
the Veritable Arquebusade, which Mrs Garrick will tell you is amongst
the best gifts that Providence has given[2a] to man.

Now to exculpate myself of the heavy charges you bring against me. I
had left Fulham before the Bishop had finished the *Botanic Garden*, so it
was *he* returned you the poem without a scrap of a letter and not *I*, or
you would not have been let off so cheaply I can tell you.

As to the other charge of not sending you *Bonner's Ghost*, I declare it
is one of the most creditable things I know of myself, for I protest with
singleness of heart, that it proceeded from no worse a motive than my
very humble opinion of it. It was struck off at a heat, and I will honestly
confess, that the day it was[4] written, I had some such presumptuous design, but when that first ardour of vanity, (which I am ashamed to own
too often attends the moment of composition) was cooled, I had not the
courage to send[5] it to you. But now, that you write so encouragingly,
(though you do abuse me) I cannot bear that you should have them
copied by any other hand than mine.—I send this under cover to the Bp
of London to whom I write your emendations, and desire they may be
considered as the true reading. What is odd enough, I *did* write both the
lines so at first, but must go *a-tinkering* them after. My first thoughts are
often best; I spoil them afterwards.

I don't pretend that I am not flattered by your obliging[6] proposal of
printing these slight verses at the Strawberry Press—But what shall I say?
I gave the most unequivocal proof that I thought them good for little,
when I did not send you a copy—and to *multiply* copies! Yet don't fancy
that I am not aware of the distinction[7] you offer to bestow on this trifle.
You must do as you please I believe. What business have I to think mean-
ly of verses you have commended? Only this, *I* should never have printed
them. If you are resolved to do them so much honour, I think I would

2a. After 'that,' 'the gods ever' crossed out and 'Providence has' written above; 'gave'
altered to 'given.'

4. 'They were' crossed out and 'it was' written above.

5. After 'send' 'them' crossed out and 'it' written above.

6. Before 'obliging' 'very' crossed out.

7. Before 'distinction' 'very great' crossed out.

condition for a smaller number. Twenty or thirty I am sure are more than I shall ever give away and who knows but you would have the goodness to send a few to the Bishop to save[8] the poor lame verses the fatigue of travelling backwards and forwards in mail coaches.

I have not time to be half as pert as I intended but I live ten miles from the post, and that you should think I neglected to obey you[9] for one post would not sit so easy upon me.—I hope you have lost all remains of that tedious gout; there is never any such thing as knowing from your letters whether you are sick or well, because you never complain, when I have afterwards found you have written in great pain.

Adieu! dear Sir, I can't help being, for all you use me so ill, your obliged and faithful

H. MORE

Page 313, note 3, *add* For additional copies see Hazen, *SH Bibl.*, 1973, pp. xxviii–xxix, 140. The Rev. Charles Sturges, Vicar of Ealing wrote to Dr John Loveday, D.C.L., of Williamscote, 21 Aug. 1789, 'On Tuesday I rode over to Fulham and called upon the Bishop [of London], Vicar and Curate. During the course of the day I saw a good deal of his Lordship, and dined with him, and his amiable wife only we three—a private party. I was much pleased with them both. I found him very easy and agreeable in conversation. I wish I had thought among other subjects, of conversing with him about the good Archdeacon of Richmond. I should have been proud to have acknowledged that I knew him. We walked about before dinner, and his Lordship carried me to the "*Monk's Walk*," as it is now named, and showed me Bishop Bonner's Chair. I recollected having seen it in Bishop Terrick's time. It is now celebrated by Hannah Moore [*sic*] in an elegant little poem, printed at Strawberry Hill under Mr Walpole's direction, but not published, entitled "Bonner's Ghost." The Bishop was so kind to give me a copy. It is very ingenious irony and sarcasm upon popery, with a very pleasing compliment to the present Bishop. His Lordship wishes much to know the tradition about Bishop Bonner's Chair. I told him that possibly some months ago I could have furnished him with some traces. If among your worthy father's papers you should happen to light upon anything relative to it, or to Fulham Palace, I should esteem it a favour, if you would send it to me, copied out' (MS in the Loveday family papers, in the possession of Mrs Sarah Markham, Wotton-under-Edge, Glos).

Page 335, To Mrs Dickenson 22 Dec. 1789, headnote, line 3, *after* lot 1275; *add   idem* No. 570 (Spring 1932), lot 462;

Page 338, note 2, line 12, *after* 1762 *add* , to Sir William Hamilton 23 Oct. 1775,

8. After 'save' 'them' crossed out.
9. The MS reads 'your.'

Page 342, note 5, line 1, *for* Barrett *read* Barret   *for* ca 1744 *read* ?1743   *Line 4, after* 90–1 *add*   ; Namier and Brooke ii. 54

Page 345, note 4, line 1, *for* (d. 1828) *read* (1740–1828)   *Line 2, after* DNB *add*   ; *Enciclopedia dello spettacolo*, Rome, 1954–62, iv. 429

Page 355, To Lady George Lennox 10 Nov. 1790, headnote, *add* Offered by Sotheby's 20 Feb. 1978 (Autograph Letters and Historical Documents Sale), lot 138.

Page 357, note 3, *add* See also *Dictionnaire de biographie française*, 1933– , iv. 580–1.

Page 357, From Hannah More Sept. 1791, note 2, line 1, *for* Aiken *read* Aikin

Page 359, illustration of Bishop and Mrs Porteus, by John Downman, *for* 1784 *read* 1790

Page 373, note 19, line 2, *for* Man *read* Men

Page 383, note 1, line 4, *for* the Hospice *read* L'Hôpital

Page 395, 1st paragraph, line 1, *before* returned *insert* has

Page 397, 3d paragraph, line 2, *on* petticoats *add note* 10a: 10a. But Mrs Wollstonecraft is described in John G. Alger, *Englishmen in the French Revolution*, 1889, p. 75: 'Yet tears fell from her eyes when she saw Louis pass on his way to trial, displaying more dignity than she had expected.'

Page 401, To Hannah More 29 Aug. 1796, headnote, line 2, *after* Library. *insert* Printed now from a photostat of the MS (in Kirgate's hand) of the letter actually sent, now BM Add. MS 54,226, f. 213 [There are so many variants in the MS that the text is reprinted below].   *Line 5, for* The MS of the letter is untraced; *read* The MS of the letter is now BM Add. MS 54,226, f. 213; see Paul J. Korshin, 'New B.M. MSS,' *Times Literary Supplement* 9 July 1970, p. 750.

Strawberry-hill,
August 29, 1796.

You are not only the most beneficent, but the most benevolent of human beings: not content with being a perfect saint yourself, which (forgive me for saying) does not always imply prodigious compassion for others; not satisfied with being the most disinterested, nay, the reverse of all patriots, for you sacrifice your very slender fortune, not to improve it, but to keep the poor honest instead of corrupting them; and you write politics[a] as simply, intelligibly and unartfully, not as cunningly as you can to mislead—well, with all these giant virtues you can find room and time in your heart and occupations for harbouring and exercising what those monkeys of pretensions the French invented and called *les petites morales*, which were to supply society with filigrane duties in the room of all virtues which they abolished on their road to the adoption of philosophy and atheism—Yes, though forever busied in exercising services and charities for individuals, or for whole bodies of people, you do not

a. After 'politics' 'as ill, that is,' crossed out in the MS, probably by Mary Berry.

leave a cranny empty into which you can slip a kindness—Your inquiry
after me to Miss Berry is so friendly that I cannot trust solely to her
thanking you for your letter, as I am sure she will, having sent it to her as
she is bathing in the sea at Bognor Rocks, as Lord Chesterfield directed to
Lord Pembroke (who was always swimming) *to the Earl of Pembroke in
the Thames over-against Whitehall*—but I must with infinite gratitude
give you a brief account of myself—a very poor one indeed must I give—
Condemned as a cripple to my couch for the rest of my days I doubt I
am—though perfectly healed, and even without a scar, my leg is so weak-
ened that I have not recovered the least use of it, nor can move cross my
chamber unless lifted up and held by two servants. This constitutes me
totally a prisoner—but why should not I be so? What business had I to
live to the brink of seventy-nine? And why should one litter the world
at that age? Then, I thank God, I have vast blessings; I have preserved
my eyes, ears and teeth; I have no pain left, and I would bet with any
dormouse that it cannot outsleep me—and when one can afford to pay
for every relief, comfort or assistance, that can be procured at fourscore,
dares one complain! Must not one reflect on the thousands of old poor,
who are suffering martyrdom and have none of those alleviations!—O my
good friend, I must consider myself as at my best, for if I drag on a little
longer, can I expect to remain even so tolerably!—nay, does the world
present a pleasing scene! Are not the devils escaped out of the swine, and
overrunning the earth headlong! What a theme for meditation, that the
excellent, humane Louis Seize should have been prevented from saving
himself by that monster Drouais and that that execrable wretch should
be saved even by those, some of whom one may suppose he meditated to
massacre, for at what does a Frenchman stop?—but I will quit this shock-
ing subject, and for another reason too; I omitted one of my losses, almost
the use of my fingers; they are so lame that I cannot write a dozen lines
legibly but am forced to have recourse to my secretary—I will only reply
by a word or two to^b a question you seem to ask; how I like *Camilla*^c—I do
not care to say how little—alas, she has reversed experience which I have
long thought reverses its own utility by coming at the wrong end of our
life when we do not want it. Miss B.^d knew the world and penetrated
characters before she had stepped over the threshold; and now she has
seen so much of it she has little or no insight at all—perhaps—she apprehended having seen too much—and kept the bags of foul air that she
brought from the Cave of Tempests too closely tied—Well, however, I
am sincerely glad that the work has turned out so very profitable and
proof doubtless of my opinion to a friend of yours and mine who assisted

b. After 'two' 'by' is crossed out and 'to' written above in the MS.
c. '*Camilla*' is crossed out in the MS.
d. 'Miss B.' is crossed out and 'This Author' written above, apparently by Mary
Berry.

her so largely in her subscriptions.^e Adieu, thou who mightest be one of the cleverest of women if thou didst not prefer being *one* of the best; and when I say *one* of the best I have not engaged my vote for the second.

Yours most gratefully,
ORFORD

Page 404, To Lady Mary Coke, n.d., headnote, *add* Collated with a photostat of the MS in the Scottish Record Office [the variants are recorded below].

Page 404, To Lady Mary Coke, n.d., 1st paragraph, line 1, *for* enclosed.[1] There *read* enclosed;[1] there   *Lines 2–3, for* imitated, *read* imitated— *Line 5, for* harsh. 'Zenith-height' *read* harsh: *Zenith-height   Lines 5– 6, for* inharmonious, *read* unharmonious;

Page 405, line 1, *for* not. Your *read* not—your

Page 405, To Lady Mary Coke, n.d., headnote, *add* Collated with a photostat of the MS in the Scottish Record Office [the variants are recorded below].

Page 405, To Lady Mary Coke, n.d., line 3, *after* notice *add* ,   *Line 5, for* that gives *read* that can give

Page 406, bottom of page, To Lady Browne, n.d., headnote, 2d paragraph, *add* A possible date in Dec. 1775 is indicated by HW's letter to Mrs Grey 9 Dec. 1775 (MISC. CORR. ii. 319–20) on Lady Blandford's illness, and by Lady Mary Coke's 'MS Journals,' *sub* 1, 6 Dec. 1775.

Page 408, middle of page, To Lady Browne, n.d., headnote, *after* Penzance Library. *insert* The MS was sold Sotheby's 25 May 1964, lot 464, to WSL.

Page 410, note 2, *add* They were at Hampton Court in 1773 (see OSSORY i. 122).

Page 423, headnote, line 1, *add* Collated with a photostat of the MS in HW's hand in the Scottish Record Office; apparently an enclosure in a missing letter to Lady Mary Coke [The variants in the MS are recorded below].

Page 423, A Sermon, line 2, *after* Coke *delete* ,   *after* Sunday *delete* ,   *Line 3, after* 31st *delete* ,   *after* H.W. *delete* ,   *after* D.D. *delete* ,   *Line 6, after Camelinthians delete* ,   *for* 3, *read* 3. *Line 9, for* things: *read* things;   *Line 10, after* settled *add* ,   *Line 11, for* place *read* lay   *Line 12, begin new paragraph with* Some overweening men   *Line 14, after* text *add* ,   *after* women *delete* , *Line 15, after* followers *delete* ,   *Line 17, after* duty *add* ,   *Line 21, after* virgin *delete* ,   *after* Lubrica *delete* ,

Page 424, 1st paragraph, line 9, *after* practice *add* ,   *Line 11, for* angels; *read* angels: *Line 12, after* out *add* ,   *Line 19, after* be-

---

e. 'Well, however, . . . subscriptions.' is crossed out in the MS.

ings *add* , *Line 25, for* generality. Now, *read* generality: now *Line 26, after* construction *add* , *Line 29, for* deformed; *read* deformed, *after* suppose *add* , *Line 32, after* hags *add* , *after* This *delete* , *Line 33, after* therefore *delete* , *for* text. *read* text: I shall endeavour

Page 424, 2d paragraph, line 1, *delete* I shall endeavour, *for* secondly, *read* Secondly

Page 425, 1st paragraph, line 5, *after* rendered *add* ,

Page 425, 2d paragraph, line 6, *after* informs us *add* , *Line 15, for* Eusebius, and *read* Eusebius. And *Line 17, for* Greek, *read* Greek; *after* was *delete* , *after* moreover *delete* , *for* physician: it *read* physician. It *Line 18, for* eye, *read* eye; *Line 20, after* instruction *add* ; *after* that *delete* , *Line 21, after* physician *delete* , *Line 23, for* physicians, *read* physicians; *Lines 24–5, after* ceremonies *add* , *after* health *add* , *Line 26, after* presume *add* , *after* inference *add* , *after* say *add* ,

Page 426, line 4, *after* and *delete* , *begin new paragraph with* Having thus *Line 5, after* you *delete* , *for is not read* is not *Line 6, for* what is, *read* what is; *delete* now *Line 7, begin new paragraph with* The Apostle *Line 11, for* the Evangelist *read* the same Evangelist *Line 12, for* cries out, *read* cries out— *Line 14, for* Again, *read* Again; *Lines 15–16, for* effect: *read* effect; *Line 20, after* natural *add* , *Line 21, after* contrary *delete* , *Line 26, after* occasions *delete* , *Line 28, after* sink *add* , *Line 30, for* hither! *read* hither? *Line 31, after* do *delete* ,

Page 438, headnote, line 1, *add* See also HW to Thomas Walpole 3 Jan. 1784, FAMILY 216–17; and *Horace Walpole's Miscellany 1786–1795*, ed. Lars E. Troide, New Haven, Connecticut, 1978, pp. 10–11, 69–70.

VOLUME 32

Page v, Advisory Committee, line 3, *after* Honourable *add* Hervey

Page v, Advisory Committee, line 20, *for* K.C.V.O. *read* G.C.V.O.

Page v, Advisory Committee, 2d line from bottom, *after* Waldegrave, *add* K.G.

Page xxix, 1st paragraph, line 5, *for* of Montagu *read* to Montagu

Page xxix, 2d paragraph, line 10, *for* Seven *read* Ten

Page xxxvii, 1st paragraph, last line, *on* understandable *add note* 1a: 1a. Part of a cover to a letter from her in 1769 has since come to light at Farmington. HW used its verso for a note to his 1769 Journal.

Page xxxviii, 1st paragraph, last line, *on* omitted *add note* 5: 5. Another transcript was made at Holland House for Lord Holland by Dr John Allen, who also skipped the letters of 1778. This transcript was sold Sotheby's (Holland House Sale), lot 289, to Maggs for WSL; the lot included 4 volumes of transcripts of HW's letters to Mann.

Page xlvi, Cobbett, *Parl. Hist., for* William Cobbett and John Wright *read* William Cobbett, John Wright, and T. C. Hansard,

Page 1, note 2, last line, after illustration *add*   , which HW mistakenly dates 1762.

Page 11, note 11, lines 10–11, *delete* We have not been able to identify his house in HW's neighbourhood. *and substitute* Presumably his house in HW's neighbourhood was the villa in Petersham which Sir Henry Bellenden bequeathed to Lord Frederick in 1761 (see MONTAGU i. 359–60 and n. 15).

Page 12, note 16, line 5, *for* 7 July *read* 14 July

Pages 14–15, note 19, *add* See also CONWAY iii. 18–20, 25–6.

Page 18, note 7, line 1, *for* 1681 *read* 1679

Page 25, note 37, line 5, *for* 1720 *read* 1719

Page 30, note 12, line 1, *for* Apparently he did not. *read* He let it to John Halliday for 1768–69 (MISC. CORR. iii. Appendix 1, map and p. 483; M. P. G. Draper, *Marble Hill House and its Owners*, 1970, p. 48).   *Line 3, for* 244–5 *read* 243–4

Page 36, note 12, line 2, *delete* and only surviving

Page 39, note 16, *substitute* Lavinia Maria Guadagni (1735–ca 1790), m. (before 1767) Felice Alessandri (*Enciclopedia dello spettacolo*, Rome, 1954–62, v. 1829; *The New Grove Dictionary of Music and Musicians*, 6th edn, ed. Stanley Sadie, 1980, i. 244). Signora Guadagni and Signora Zamperini are listed as principal singers at the King's Opera House for the 1769–70 season (*London Stage* Part IV, iii. 1422).

Page 51, note 5, *add* See also a description of Ampthill in the *Transactions of the Society . . . of Arts, Manufactures, and Commerce*, vol. iii, 1785, pp. 6–12 (mentioned OSSORY ii. 480 and nn. 21–4).

Page 56, running head, *for* To Lady Ossory 27 June 1771 *read* To Lady Ossory 11 August 1771

Page 67, note 2, line 14, *for* Albermarle *read* Albemarle

Page 84, note 10, line 1, *for* 19. *read* 10.

Page 92, note 3, *add* See also *London Stage* Part IV, iii. 1688–91.

Page 96, note 11, line 2, *for* Ambrozy *read* Ambroży   *Lines 3 and 4, for* Fleming *read* Flemming

Page 98, note 20, line 18, *after* ended *add* (see *London Stage* Part IV, iii. 1496, 1568, 1655–6, 1743, 1830).

Page 103, note 27, line 1, *for* (d. 1778) *read* (ca 1746–78)

Page 106, note 15, *add* See also *London Stage* Part IV, iii. 1702.

Page 106, note 16, *add* See *London Stage* Part IV, iii. 1569, 1655.

Page 121, note 1, line 3, *for* Smith *read* Smyth   *Line 4, after Parliament add*   ; Namier and Brooke iii. 106–7

Page 121, note 2, *add* See also Sedgwick ii. 241–2.

Page 133, note 22, *add* GEC lists Orford's Rangership as stated in this note, but *Royal Kalendar* 1785–91 (p. 91) lists him as Ranger of both St James's and Hyde Parks until 1791. See MISC. CORR. ii. 378 and n. 5.

Page 134, note 3, line 1, *for* 1786 *read* 1788   *Lines 1–3, delete* attorney, d. in Bartlett's Buildings 26 April 1786 (GM 1786, lvi pt i. 441); *Line 4, after* 1782 *add*   , MANN iv. 547, n. 5; see also CONWAY iii. 171

Page 135, note 8, lines 4–7, *delete* deputy to Lord Orford . . . letter, n. 22). *and substitute* acted on behalf of Lord Orford in regard to the Rangership of St James's and Hyde Parks during Orford's illness in 1777–8 (see HW to Sir Edward Walpole 11 Feb. 1778 and to Lord North 11 Feb. 1778).   *Lines 5–6 from end, delete Royal Kalendar; Court and City Register and substitute* where Moone is mistakenly called Deputy Ranger of St James's and Hyde Parks. The official Deputy Ranger of the two parks was Hon. Thomas Shirley ca 1769–78, and then Lord William Gordon 1778–1823

Page 150, note 41, line 4, *for* ca 1761 *read* 1762

Page 155, note 30, line 1, *after* Vct *add* of

Page 163, note 14, *add* See also *London Stage* Part IV, iii. 1753, 1761–2.

Page 165, note 13, line 3, *after* Treasury *add* 1756–7,   *Line 4, for* 1762 *read* 1757   *Line 5, after* 72 *add* (Namier and Brooke iii. 114–17)

Page 170, 2d paragraph, line 4, *on* sense *add note* 30a: 30a. HW notes on the first leaf of his copy of Goldsmith's *An Enquiry into the Present State of Polite Learning in Europe,* 1759 (now WSL; Hazen, *Cat. of HW's Lib.* No. 1787): 'There are some hits in this book, few truths, little reasoning. The age has many faults, but the author has not found them; not knowing his own meaning, no wonder his remedies are ridiculous.' See also MASON i. 41, 277.

Page 170, note 30, line 2, *for* 1725 *read* 1724

Page 172, note 2, line 6, *for* 1862–6 *read* 1862–8

Page 188, 3d paragraph, line 1, *on* Holland *add note* 2a: 2a. See HW to Lady Holland 19 Feb. 1774, in MISC. CORR. ii. 272–3.

Page 200, note 16, *add* For Conway's itinerary, based on Scott's Journal, see CONWAY Appendix 9, iii. 536–9. See also ibid. iii. 184.

Page 202, note 1, line 2, *delete* Conway and   *Last line, add* See HW to Conway 18 Aug. 1774 (CONWAY iii. 179); Conway left London 8 June for his military tour, which lasted until 19 Oct., when he met Lady Ailesbury in Paris (ibid. Appendix 9).

Pages 209–10, note 7, *add* See also Namier and Brooke i. 335–6, iii. 270; CONWAY iii. 196.

Page 212, note 2, last line, *after* 449–50 *add*   ; CONWAY iii. 188, 194 and Appendix 10; Namier and Brooke ii. 246

Page 215, note 6, line 2, *after* Bedfordshire *add*   ; for an account of this contest see Namier and Brooke i. 205–6, ii. 607.

Page 216, note 12, line 2, *for* ca 1759 *read* 1759   *Last line, add* See P. H. Highfill, Jr, K. A. Burnim, and E. A. Langhans, *A Biographical Dictionary of Actors, Actresses . . . in London, 1660–1800,* Carbondale, Illinois, 1973– , i. 10–20.

Page 225, note 9, *add* See also *A Journey to the Western Islands of Scot-*

land, ed. Mary Lascelles, New Haven, 1971, p. xxx, n. 8, for a reference to this.

Page 231, running head, *for* To Lady Ossory 24 January 1775 *read* To Lord Ossory 24 January 1775

Page 231, note 1, line 4, *for* despaired . . . *read* despaired. . . .

Page 231, note 6, last line, *after* p. 206) *add*   ; 18 Jan. (Sedgwick ii. 136)

Page 231, note 7, line 1, *for* Ann *read* Anne   *for* 1744 *read* 1745 *Last line, add* A manuscript in the Osborn Collection (Beinecke Library, Yale University) quotes HW's sentence and attaches a cutting from the *Public Advertiser* about Hervey's affidavit of 15 Jan. 1771 swearing that he was not married, and another cutting declaring that Hervey will not be responsible for Mrs Hervey's debts.

Page 239, note 8, line 1, *for* 1721 *read* 1719 *or* 20   *Line 3, for* commander-in-chief *read* acting commander-in-chief   *Line 4, for* 1763–72, Aug.–Oct. 1775 *read* Nov. 1763–June 1773, May 1774–Oct. 1775   *Line 7, after* Howe *add* (J. R. Alden, *General Gage in America*, Baton Rouge, Louisiana, 1948, pp. 61, 192–3, 202–4, 283).

Page 240, note 12, *add* Joseph Highmore in a letter to Sir Edward Walpole 28 Feb.–3 March 1764 sent further anecdotes about Kneller for HW's *Anecdotes of Painting* (see GM 1816, lxxxvi pt i. 300–3), and HW included some of them in the 2d edition of volume iii of the *Anecdotes* (see *Anecdotes* 1765, iii. 121–2).

Page 248, note 38, line 2, *for* 1747 *read* 1748   *Line 3, delete* Lt-Col., 1762; Col. (on half-pay), 1763; *and substitute* Maj., 1761; retired on half-pay, 1762; promoted to Lt-Col. on half-pay, 1772;   *Line 12, for*   , and sources cited there *read*   ; J. R. Alden, *General Charles Lee*, Baton Rouge, Louisiana, 1951, pp. 3–4, 19, 21–3, 47

Page 254, note 22, *for* That is, Lady Ossory. *read* Elizabeth Wrottesley (1745–1822), m. (1769) as 2d wife, Augustus Henry Fitzroy, 3d D. of Grafton, 1757. HW mentions the resemblance between 'the present Duchess of Grafton' and the Queen in a letter to Hardwicke 12 Jan. 1775 (MISC. CORR. ii. 284).   *Last line, for* ibid. *read* 'MS Journals' 22 Aug. 1775

Page 261, note 35, line 2, *for* (ca 1745–79) *read* (ca 1745–97)

Page 264, note 10, line 1, *for* Louis-Engelbert *read* Louis-Engelbert-Marie-Joseph-Augustin   *Line 2, after* 1778 *insert* (*Dictionnaire de biographie française*, 1933– , iii. 471)

Page 270, note 7, *substitute* The Act of 15 Geo. III (1775), c. 37, first of all repealed the existing duty on imported earthenware of 10 *d.* per pound weight. Then, it provided that earthenware 'shall be liable to and pay . . . ten pounds ten shillings for every one hundred Pounds, according to the true Value and Price of such Earthen Ware.' It then continued, 'and the several further Subsidies, additional Duties, and all other Imposts and Duties whatsoever, to which such Earthen Ware was subject and liable to, at the Rate of Ten-pence per Pound Weight, before the making of this Act, shall in like Manner be paid proportionably according to such Value and

Price, and not according to any other Rate or Value.' This means that the total duty payable on imported earthenware under this Act was £10. 10s. per £100 value. See *Statutes at Large*, ed. Owen Ruffhead, 1763–1800, xii. 317–18; *Journals of the House of Commons* xxxv. 387.

Page 277, note 14, line 1, *for* A.-A. *read* Antoine-A.   *for* (d. ca 1814) *read* (ca 1737–1814)

Page 278, note 15, *at beginning insert* That is, 80; she was born 12 Sept. 1695.

Page 282, note 9, line 9, *for* 1646 *read* 1643

Page 284, note 23, left column, line 15, *for* Robert Hare *read* Henry Hare (d. 1733)   *Last line, after* i. 27 *add*   ; x. 52–3

Page 288, note 13, line 12, *for* 'Friday evening,' *read* 'Friday evening' [5 Jan. 1776],

Page 288, note 14, *at beginning insert* A MS copy in Barnard's hand is now in the Beinecke Library, Yale University; for a facsimile and discussion of this MS copy see F. W. Hilles, 'A Copy of Pleasant Verses Addressed to Sir Joshua Reynolds & Co.,' privately printed, 1970.

Page 289, note 18, *add* See Lady Diana Beauclerk to HW ?16 Dec. 1775, MISC. CORR. ii. 321–2.

Page 291, note 8, line 1, *for* ca 1743 *read* ca 1731

Page 295, note 2, line 2, *for* license *read* licence

Page 296, note 6, line 5, *for* Windsor *read* New Windsor

Page 299, note 31, lines 3–4, run in

Page 299, note 32, last line, *after* 402) *add*   , or 25 April (*Public Adv.* 27 April)

Page 300, 1st paragraph, line 7, *for* ma faite *read* m'a faite

Page 304, note 10, line 10, *for* 192 *read* 187

Page 306, note 32, *add* See CHUTE pp. xv–xvi.

Page 307, note 4, *add* For Hardinge's request for this letter of recommendation see CHUTE 580–1.

Page 312, note 7, line 2, *for* 1751 *read* 1750   *Last line, add* See also *Dictionnaire de biographie française*, 1933– , xi. 359–60.

Page 318, note 19, line 1, *for* (1782) *read* (1783)   *Last line, add* See Namier and Brooke iii. 250.

Page 342, note 7, *add* See *London Stage* Part V, i. 44.

Page 346, note 5, line 1, *for* ca 1735 *read* 1735   *Last line, after* p. 13 *add*   ; Namier and Brooke iii. 607–8

Page 346, note 7, line 6, *after* Bullock *add* [Archibald Bulloch, 1730–77]

Page 347, note 4, line 2, *for* 2d son *read* 2d surviving son

Page 363, note 6, line 3, *for* Laura Elizabeth *read* Elizabeth Laura *Last line, add* See also FAMILY 131, 149

Page 364, note 11, left column, line 3, *before* Genest *insert London Stage* Part V, i. 90–1;

Page 390, note 12, line 1, *for* Sept *read* Sept.

Page 392, note 8, line 3, *for* Col. 1780 *read* Lt-Col. 73d Foot 1780–3

Line 4, for 1770–94 *read* 1766–94   *Line 7, after* 1811 *add*   ; Namier and Brooke ii. 268–9

Page 393, note 4, line 5, *for* Baum *read* Baume   *Line 6, add* See also MANN viii. 340, nn. 16, 17

Page 393, note 6, *add* See MANN viii. 339–40 and n. 14.

Page 404, note 5, *add* See *London Stage* Part V, i. 133.

Page 407, note 6, line 1, *for* (b. before 1705) *read* (ca 1708–80)   *Line 5, after* i. 233 *add*   ; Sedgwick ii. 460–1

Page 409, note 3, line 4, *after* vi. 5 *add*   ; *London Stage* Part V, i. 104, 135

VOLUME 33

Page vii, List of Illustrations, Lady Gertrude Fitzpatrick, after Reynolds, *after* Glenconner, London *add*   ; now in the Art Gallery at Columbus, Ohio

Page 2, note 2, *add* See also MANN viii. 349, n. 9.

Page 41, 2d paragraph, line 5, *on* musicians *add note* 15a: 15a. An anecdote about HW and music appears in a letter of William Bewley to Dr Burney ca *post* Sept. 1778: 'Nay at one time (in September) I lamented the difficulties that presented themselves to me in my design of communicating to you the earliest tidings of the musical exploits of the *gifted* babe at Norwich; and which, merely to unburthen my mind of a load of *wonderment* much too heavy for me to bear alone, I remember I divided between Mr Hor. Walpole and Dr Priestley.—The former, by the bye, gave me the satisfaction the other day of authenticating a part of my narrative, by a short detail of what he and others felt and observed, on this child's performing at the Duke of Gloucester's. . . . I assure you I was so much astonished at his performance on the organ at Lynn . . . that . . . I had almost become incredulous of what I had just heard and seen. . . . I know not what you think of *this Carpenter's son*; but I think he certainly deserves a niche in your *history*; . . . I have omitted the quickness with which he catches a melody that strikes him. Playing with Mr S. Browne's children, he became at once attentive to "Slingsby's Allemande," which Miss Case was playing. He heard it repeated twice or thrice, and then played it, with a bass of his own.—This, however, I have only from hearsay—but Mr Walpole relates to me a similar incident at the Duke of Gloucester's.— "I see all this," says Mr Walpole, standing behind his chair, "but I don't believe it" ' (MS in the Osborn Collection, Beinecke Library, Yale University).

Page 47, 1st paragraph, line 3, *on* Talmache *add note* 15a. 15a. HW describes this occasion in a letter to Conway 21 Aug. 1778 (CONWAY iii. 311).

Page 78, note 12, right column, line 1, *for* Dr Batty's *read* Dr William Battie's

Page 87, note 9, line 1, *for* Dumesnil (1711– *read* Marchand, called Mlle du Mesnil (1713–

Page 87, note 10, line 3, *for* 1722 *read* 1721   *Last line, add* See *London Stage* Part II, ii. 596, 644, Part IV, i. 358.

Page 87, note 11, *add* See *London Stage* Part IV, ii. 1153.

Page 87, note 12, line 2, *after* 1717 *add* (*London Stage* Part II, ii. 472)

Page 87, note 13, line 5, *after* 480 *add*   ; *London Stage* Part IV, ii. 580

Page 98, note 14, *add* See also MANN viii. 459.

Page 99, note 18, *add* See also MANN viii. 460 and n. 12.

Page 101, note 10, line 2, *for* 1822 *read* 1832

Pages 101–2, note 1, line 4, *after* 100–102; *add London Stage* Part V, i. 254–5;

Page 102, To Lady Ossory 6 May 1779, note 2, *add* See also CONWAY iii. 319–20.

Page 105, note 19, line 2, *after* m. *insert* (before 1754)   *Line 3, after* Roberts) *insert* (ca 1717–76)   *Line 6, after* table *add*   ; Namier and Brooke ii. 235

Page 112, note 34, line 1, *for* 1672 *read* ?1671

Page 113, note 3, *add* See also CONWAY iii. 335–6.

Page 118, note 3, line 3, *for* 1771–9 *read* 1770–9

Page 121, note 5, *substitute* She was baptized 12 Sept. 1695 in the Jacobikerk in Utrecht, dau. of Peter Haeck de Jong and Anna Maria van Weede (information from J. E. A. L. Struick, town-archivist, Utrecht). GM 1779, xlix. 471, mistakenly lists her as 'aged 96.'

Page 121, note 6, line 1, *for* ca 1733 *read* 1734

Page 122, note 2, line 8, *for* D'Estaing *read* d'Estaing

Page 144, note 1, lines 3–4, *for* Aberdeen *read* Elgin

Page 149, note 1, left column, line 2, *for* 1763–72 *read* 1763–75

Page 154, note 2, line 3, *for* n. 12 *read* n. 13

Page 161, note 2, line 1, *for* ca 1721 *read* 1721

Page 161, note 3, line 1, *for* 'Mr Stanley *read* 'Thursday Mr Stanley *Line 12, for* 10 Jan. *read* 13 Jan.   *Last line, add* See also MASON ii. 5.

Page 161, note 4, right column, line 2, *for* (*ante* 1774) *read* (2 Dec. 1765) *Last line, after passim add*   ; Namier and Brooke ii. 336–7

Page 162, 1st paragraph, line 1, *on* Wales *add note* 7a: 7a. The estate was Cadoxton-juxta-Neath, Glamorganshire, South Wales (see Hans Stanley to HW 11 Jan. 1768, MISC. CORR. ii. 117 and n. 9).

Page 162, note 9, line 1, *for* ca 1724–3 Aug. 1779 *read* ?1724–2 Aug. 1779   *Last line, after* Dynevor *add*   ; Namier and Brooke iii. 351–2

Page 169, note 8, line 3, *for* Henry *read* Harry

Page 181, note 9, right column, line 2, *for* ca 1758 *read* ca 1754   *Line 5, after* in 1774 *add* (MANN viii. 15, n. 24)

Page 182, note 11, *add* See *London Stage* Part V, i. 344.

Page 197, note 19, *delete* the proverb has not been found. *and substitute*

'More know Jack-Pudding than Jack-Pudding knows' is a variation of the proverb about Tom-Fool (Apperson's *Dictionary of English Proverbs and Proverbial Phrases*, New York, 1929, p. 427; information from Raymond Mortimer, London).

Page 203, note 4, lines 1–2, *for* (1748–94) *read* (1748–95)

Page 205, note 6, line 1, *for* ca 1687 *read* ?1688   *Line 3, after* Bolingbroke *add* (Sedgwick ii. 562–4)

Page 216, note 1, *add* See also MANN ix. 78, n. 3.

Page 216, note 2, line 2, *for* 1795 *read* 1796   *Line 5, for* 1773–4 *read* 1772–4   *Line 6, after passim add*   ; Namier and Brooke iii. 346

Page 220, note 28, line 2, *for* 1709 *read* 1710   *Last line, after* Derbyshire *add* (GEC; Sedgwick ii. 494)

Page 220, note 29, line 1, *for* Barrett *read* Barret

Page 222, note 10, lines 4–5, *delete*   ; groom of the Bedchamber to the P. of Wales, 1742   *Line 4, after* 37 *add* (Sedgwick ii. 317–18).

Page 225, note 5, line 3, *for* Penyston *read* Peniston   *Line 6, after* xlviii. 242 *add*   ; see Namier and Brooke i. 210–11, iii. 10

Page 226, note 1, *add* See also Namier and Brooke i. 205–6.

Page 227, note 5, line 7, *after* 287 *add*   ; see Namier and Brooke i. 335–7

Page 230, note 8, *add* For his death date and Burke's withdrawal see the *Correspondence of Edmund Burke*, Vol. IV, ed. John A. Woods, Cambridge, England, and Chicago, Illinois, 1963, pp. 278–81.

Page 241, note 3, line 2, *for* twenty *read* thirty

Page 241, note 4, line 5, *after* vi. 201 *add*   ; *London Stage* Part V, i. 442–3

Page 243, note 17, line 5, *for* seven *read* six   *Line 6, after* 177–8 *add* ; *London Stage* Part V, i. 389, 392, 393, 395

Page 245, note 26, line 2, *for* Adolphus Friedrich III *read* Adolf Friedrich IV

Page 245, note 27, line 4, *for* Feb.–April *read* Feb.–March   *Line 6, for* 1768 *read* 1784   *Line 8, after* 471–3 *add*   ; Namier and Brooke iii. 483

Page 247, note 13, line 1, *for* 1672 *read* ca 1672   *Line 3, after* 52 *add* ; Sedgwick ii. 254

Page 248, note 18, line 1, *for* ca 1563 *read* ca 1565   *Lines 1–2, for* a surveyor rather than an architect *read* surveyor and architect   *Line 4, after* land-surveyor *add* (*Walpole Society*, 1964–6, xl. 2–12)   *Last line, after* Museum *add* The folio is described and the plates reproduced in *The Book of Architecture of John Thorpe in Sir John Soane's Museum*, ed. John Summerson, *Walpole Society*, 1964–6, vol. xl.

Page 249, note 20, lines 9–14, *delete* According to Campbell Dodgson . . . building. *and substitute* The plans of Ampthill are reproduced in *Walpole Society*, 1964–6, xl, plates 120, 121; 'Thorpe's plans probably represent a project of c. 1605–6 for remodelling and greatly enlarging the old house'; but this was not carried out (ibid. p. 108; see also pp. 8, 30, 40).

Page 249, note 22, *add* Thorpe's book was sold by Christie 3 April 1810, lot 291 (see *Walpole Society*, 1964–6, xl. 15).

Page 249, note 23, line 1, *after* Elizabeth *add* (Plantagenet)

Page 250, note 4a, *add* See *London Stage* Part V, i. 392, 394.

Page 252, note 5, *add* See also Conway iii. 348.

Page 256, note 3, *add* See also *Walpole Society* 1964–6, xl. 108 and plates 120, 121.

Page 265, 1st paragraph, line 5, *on* proceed *add note* 3a: 3a. His ship was blown back to Plymouth, and he returned to Park Place (see Conway iii. 361, n. 5, 363, n. 2).

Page 265, note 4a, *transpose to below note 4*

Page 267, note 3, last line, *after* 288–94 *add*   ; Mann ix. 31, n. 11

Page 267, note 4, line 5, *for* perferment *read* preferment

Page 268, note 9, line 3, *for* (Hants) *read* (Isle of Wight)

Page 269, note 11, line 5, *for* 1784–5 *read* 1783–5   *after* Rolliad *add* (Namier and Brooke ii. 32)

Page 269, note 14, *add* See also Conway iii. 361–2 and n. 6.

Pages 269–70, note 17, *add* See also Conway iii. 361–2, n. 5.

Page 272, note 1, *add* See Conway iii. 367, n. 4.

Page 281, To Lady Ossory 17 July 1781, 1st paragraph, line 9, *on* to-morrow *add note* 3a: 3a. See More 202.

Page 283, line 3, *on* air *add note* 2a: 2a. That is, the dancing posture; see Giovanni Andrea Battista Gallini, *Critical Observations on the Art of Dancing* [?1773].

Page 284, note 14, *add* 'The London Gentlewoman or the Hemp-Dresser,' also entitled 'The Hemp-dresser, or The London Maid,' appears in all editions of *The Dancing Master* (1651, p. 58); see Claude M. Simpson, *The British Broadside Ballad and its Music*, New Brunswick, New Jersey, 1966, pp. 302–4 (pointed out by Mrs Frank Van Cleef, Manchester, Connecticut). See also the facsimile edition of *John Playford's English Dancing Master*, ed. Margaret Dean-Smith, 1957.

Page 285, note 1, line 1, *for* Sterling *read* Stirling

Page 285, note 3, line 4, *for* , sometime M.P. *read* (ca 1701–54), M.P. (Sedgwick ii. 54–5).

Page 302, note 29, line 1, *for* 1753 *read* 1754   *Line 2, for* —— Dancer *read* William Dancer   *for* ca 1768 *read* 1767 or 1768   *Line 4, for* ca 1778 *read* 1778   *for* ca 1750–94 *read* 1750–94   *Line 5, for* (C. B. Hogan, op. cit. 5) *read* (P. H. Highfill, Jr, K. A. Burnim, and E. A. Langhans, *A Biographical Dictionary of Actors, Actresses . . . in London, 1660–1800*, Carbondale, Illinois, 1973– , i. 339–51)

Page 306, note 7, line 3, *for* Broderick *read* Brodrick

Page 308, note 4, line 4, *after* 1779 *add* (GM 1781, li. 595)   *Line 6, for* GM 1781, li. 595 *read* GM 1782, lii. 38

Page 309, note 6, *for* Not identified. *read* Possibly Thomas Walpole the younger; HW's letter to Hon. Thomas Walpole the elder 11 Nov. 1781 mentions 'a visit from your son' 'on Wednesday last' (7 Nov.) (FAMILY 203).

Page 314, note 10, *add* See Namier and Brooke ii. 307.

Page 314, note 11, *add* See Namier and Brooke iii. 486–7.

Page 319, note 3, line 6, *after* 1782 *add*   , April–July (GM 1782, lii. 189–95, 247–50, 300, 347–8)   *Last line, for* [Sept. 1782] *read* [April 1782], in MISC. CORR. iii. 9; see also Hazen, *SH Bibl.* 118

Page 321, note 3, *add* See *London Stage* Part V, i. 485, 487.

Page 321, note 6, *add* See also *London Stage* Part V, i. 460, 553.

Page 322, note 12, lines 1–2, *for* Hieronymus Custodis *read* Hieronimo Custodis (d. 1593)   *Line 5, for* 43.' *read* 43' (Hazen, *Bibl. of HW* 85–7). *Last line, for* Thieme-Becker. *read* HW to Thomas Pennant 25 May 1773, MISC. CORR. ii. 252, n. 14.

Page 324, note 9, *delete* It now (1963) belongs to Sir Osbert Sitwell, Bt. *and substitute* It is now in the British Museum; for a history of its provenance see Hugh Tait, ' "The Devil's Looking-Glass"; the Magical Speculum of Dr John Dee,' in *Horace Walpole: Writer, Politician, and Connoisseur*, ed. Warren H. Smith, New Haven, 1967, pp. 201–3, 337–8.

Page 334, note 11, line 3, *for* finally (1756) admiral. *read* rear-adm., 1755, vice-adm., 1759, adm. 1770.

Page 335, note 13, line 2, *for* Anne *read* Anna

Page 351, note 11, line 6, *for* Bridgewater's *read* Bridgwater's

Page 354, note 11, line 7, *for* officer in 1st Foot Guards 1734–48 *read* Capt. 5th Foot, 1735; Capt. and Lt-Col. 1st Foot Guards, 1740; Second Maj., 1747; ret. 1748   *Last line, after* Westminsters *add*   ; Namier and Brooke ii. 436

Page 356, note 4, line 3, *after* 303 *add*   ; *London Stage* Part V, ii. 722–4

Page 357, note 10, lines 1 and 5, *for* Cunningham *read* Cuninghame

Page 359, note 3, line 9, *after* below; *add London Stage* Part V, i. 559–60, 563–4

Page 360, note 8, *add* See *London Stage* Part II, i. 455, ii. 482, Part III, ii. 975

Page 362, note 26, line 1, *for* ca 1725 *read* 1721

Page 365, note 3, line 2, *for* DALRYMPLE *read* DALRYMPLE

Page 366, note 5, line 1, *for* Henri-Louis-Mériadec *read* Henri-Louis-Marie   *Line 2, for* 1802 *read* 1808   *delete* (Jacob-Nicolas Moreau, *Mes souvenirs*, 1906–7, ii. 237) *and substitute* (MANN ix. 604, n. 7)

Page 370, note 32, *add* See Hertford to HW 10 Nov. 1782, CONWAY iii. 397–8.

Page 377, note 17, line 7, *after* 342). *add* See also *London Stage* Part V, i. p. xcvii, ii. 769–82.

Page 391, note 2, lines 1 and 8, *for* Cunninghame *read* Cuninghame

Page 396, note 3, line 2, *after* printed account *add* from Florence, entitled *Relazione dell' orribile terramoto del di 5 febbraio 1783, seguito nella città di Messina,* and an 'abstract' of a letter about the earthquake, in a clerk's hand,   *Line 3, after* 17 Feb. *add* (see MANN ix. 374–6).

Page 396, note 5, *delete* Not mentioned in Mann's account. *and substitute* Mentioned in Mann's (missing) printed enclosure (MANN ix. 374, n. 2, 375, n. 4).   *Line 5, for* ibid. *read London Chronicle*

Page 400, note 4, line 1, *for* Grosset *read* Grosett   *Line 2, for* Grosset *read* Grosett   *Line 4, after* p. 2161; *add* Collins, *Peerage,* 1812, v. 674

Page 412, note 17, line 3, *for* 1768–95 *read* 1768–94 (Namier and Brooke ii. 499–501)

Page 420, note 10, right column, line 1, *for* [William Everard] *read* [William Augustus]

Page 422, note 8, line 1, *for* 1747 *read* 1742   *At end add* See Margaret Ashmun, *The Singing Swan,* New Haven, Connecticut, 1931, pp. 6–7.

Page 440, note 1, line 2, *for* 2 July 1784 *read* 28 June 1784   *Line 7, after* 8 July 1784 *add*   , MANN ix. 508 and n. 15; see also FAMILY 225

Page 441, note 7, line 2, *for* 2 July *read* 28 June

Page 442, note 11, line 1, *for* ca 1716 *read* 1715

Page 443, note 19, line 14, *for* Diana *read* Dinah

Page 446, note 5, *add* In a volume of Lady Louisa Stuart's writings (Clarke Papers, Bodleian Library, LS 2), she gives an account of Mrs Montagu and her circle and says: 'And in this scene, amongst these people, solely occupied with themselves, did I form a lasting friendship with the late Mrs Alison, then Miss Gregory, whom Mrs Montagu had almost adopted as a daughter. The perfection of strict truth, blunt honesty, and clear understanding. She verified the old Scotch proverb—"An ounce of mother wit is worth a pound of clergy." "That is a *natural*" said Mr Walpole, and the expression exactly suited her' (information from John Brooke).

Page 450, note 16, lines 3–4, *for* Charles (1748–1818), D. of Sudermania *read* Karl (1746–1818), D. of Södermanland   *Lines 6–7, for* Frederick Adolf (1750–1803), D. of Ostrogothia, 1772 *read* Fredrik Adolf (1750–1803), D. of Östergötland, 1772 (MANN viii. 238 and nn. 2, 4)

Page 454, note 9, lines 1–2, *delete* (d. 682), 'last king of the Britons' (GRAY i. 81 n. 1). *and substitute* (d. 664), King of Gwynedd, North Wales; see Sir John E. Lloyd, *A History of Wales,* 3d edn, 1939, i. 230 and n. 9; Gwynfor Evans, *Land of my Fathers,* Swansea, 1974, p. 119.

Page 455, note 17, line 3, *after* Matilda *add* (*London Stage* Part V, ii. 755)

Page 456, note 18, *add* See *London Stage* Part V, ii. 746, 751, 756.

Page 458, note 8, line 1, *for* 1753 *read* 1750   *Last line, add* See *Dictionnaire de biographie française,* 1933– , vi. 604–5; MANN ix. 543, n. 6.

Page 465, note 2, line 3, *after* 1784–90; *add* Stockbridge 1790–3;

Page 466, note 13, *add* See *London Stage* Part V, ii. 805–7.

Page 467, note 15, line 1, *for* Rozier *read* Rosier   *Line 2, for* 1756
read 1754

Page 469, note 5, *add* See also Sedgwick i. 437–8.

Page 471, note 15, line 12, *for* Jules *read* Jules-Hercule-Mériadec de
Rohan (1726–1800)

Page 475, note 11, *add* See Hazen, *Cat. of HW's Lib.* No. 3690:3, 14.

Page 475, note 12, last line, *for Miscellanies read Supplement to the
Miscellanies*, 1784, p. 36, 'The Defence,' 2d stanza, line 14

Page 492, note 8, lines 2–3, *for* (ca 1634–ca 1691) *read* (?1636–?1692) (see
Sir George Etherege, *Letters*, ed. F. Bracher, Berkeley, California, 1974,
pp. xiv, xxiii–xxiv)

Page 494, note 21, line 1, *for* Réné *read* René   *Last line, after* lace
add (MANN ix. 603 and nn. 3, 6).

Page 500, note 33, *add* See also CONWAY iii. 433–4.

Page 500, note 35, *add* See also CONWAY iii. 432–3.

Page 503, note 10, lines 1–2, *for* an unknown correspondent *read* Sir
John Elliott   *after* 27 Oct. 1785 *add* (MISC. CORR. iii. 151–2).

Page 503, note 11, line 3, *for* the unknown correspondent *read* Sir John
Elliott

Page 507, note 2, line 9, *after* n. 10 *add*   ; *London Stage* Part V, ii.
836   *Last line, after* 374–81 *add*   ; in December 1785 she played in
*Philaster, The Country Girl, The Romp, The Strangers at Home, Twelfth
Night, The Jubilee*, and on 9 Jan. 1786 in *A Trip to Scarborough (London Stage* Part V, ii. 846–55)

Page 508, note 12, *add* The prologue was by the Hon. Richard Fitzpatrick.

Page 509, note 13, *add* See *London Stage* Part V, ii. 855–6.

Page 511, note 14, line 3, *for* On the Characters *read* Of the Characters

Page 511, note 15, line 1, *for* Bethel *read* Bethell   *for* (d. 1748) *read*
(1689–1747)   *Line 2, for* 1715–22 *read* 1716–22 (Sedgwick i. 460)

Page 517, line 15, *on* trifle *add* note 4a: 4a. The MS of the verses, dated
16 June 1786, is now in the possession of Mr Robert H. Taylor, Princeton,
New Jersey; printed in MISC. CORR. iii. 166.

Page 519, note 11, left column, line 5, *for* SH xv. oo *read* SH xv. 90

Page 533, note 5, line 5, *for* 6 Nov. *read* 16 Nov.

Page 539, note 21, line 2, *for* Coldpig *read* Cold Pike   *Line 5, after*
lists *add*   ; Namier and Brooke ii. 106–8

Page 544, note 8, line 8, *after* pp. vii–viii *add*   ; see also *London Stage*
Part V, ii. 934, 937

Page 544, note 10, *add* John Zoffany's portrait of Miss Farren as Her-
mione in *The Winter's Tale* is reproduced in Christie's Catalogue 24
March 1961, frontispiece (lot 41).

Page 546, note 7, line 7, *before* Allardyce *insert London Stage* Part V,
ii. 929, 937   *Last line, after* cit. 285 *add*   ; *London Stage* Part V, ii.
927

Page 556, note 2, line 2, *for* Budd *read* Bubb

Page 556, note 6, line 1, *for* Behan *read* Beaghan   *Line 2, for* Budd *read* Bubb

Page 558, note 17, line 5, *for* 1 Feb. *read* 3 Feb.   *Line 6, after Chroni-cle insert* 2, 3 Feb.

Page 563, note 14, line 16, *for* Cambell *read* Campbell   *Last line, after* etc. *add* See also CONWAY iii. 448.

Page 566, note 2, *add* In his 'Book of Visitors' on 17 June, 'Major Derby, by Mr Seward' HW notes 'Neither came nor returned the ticket. Letter had miscarried' (BERRY ii. 228, n. 2).

Page 572, note 21, lines 3–4, *for* 27 April 1788. *read* 8 May 1788 (J. E. Norton, *A Bibliography of the Works of Edward Gibbon*, Oxford, 1940, p. 61; MORE 255, n. 7).

Page 573, note 27, left column, line 3, *for* license *read* licence

Page 574, note 5, line 2, *for* The list has not been found. *read* The list was printed in the *Public Adv.* 5 Sept. 1787. See ADD. AND CORR. for vol. 2, p. 375.

Page 574, note 7, line 1, *for* (ca 1363–ca 1431) *read* (1364–ca 1430) *Last line, for* m. Stephen Castel *read* m. (ca 1379) Étienne de Castel (see Marie-Josèphe Pinet, *Christine de Pisan 1364–1430, étude biographique et littéraire*, 1927, pp. 1, 13, 200).

Page 576, note 16, line 3, *for* Barrett *read* Barret

Page 587, note 25, *add* See also FAMILY 248.

VOLUME 34

Page 2, note 10, *add* See also *London Stage* Part V, ii. 1031.

Page 2, note 11, *add* See also *London Stage* Part V, ii. 1022, 1032, 1033.

Page 2, note 13, line 3, *before* Genest *insert London Stage* Part V, iii. 1932;

Page 2, note 14, line 2, *after King Lear add* (*London Stage* Part V, ii. 1036)

Page 4, note 33, line 7, *after* 363–4 *add* ; Cecil Price, *The English Theatre in Wales*, Cardiff, 1948, pp. 61–7; Cecil Price, 'Eighteenth Century Playbills of the English Theatre in Wales,' *National Library of Wales Journal*, vi (1950) 260–7.

Page 11, note 3, *add* See also Namier and Brooke i. 336–7.

Page 34, note 1, right column, line 6, *for* now WSL *read* now in the Houghton Library, Harvard University; see Hazen, *Cat. of HW's Lib.* No. 3222:22:2

Page 37, note 18, *add* See also *London Stage* Part V, ii. 1203, 1204, 1206.

Page 39, note 9, line 2, *for* 27 April *read* 8 May

Page 40, note 15, line 12, *for* Pauwe. *read* Pauw's

Pages 51–2, note 9, *add* See also *London Stage* Part V, ii. 821, 844–9, 851.

Page 64, note 7, line 1, *for* Coombe *read* Combe

Page 68, note 18, *add* See FAMILY 257–8.

Page 72, note 11, *after* Gloucester *add* , 8 Oct. (FAMILY 260–1)

Page 72, note 15, transpose 1st two lines of right column

Page 75, note 9, *add* Mentioned also in HW to Anne Clement 30 Oct. 1789; see FAMILY 268.

Page 81, note 13, line 2, *for* Julie *read* Julie-Françoise

Page 85, note 5, line 2, *for* St-Gineis *read* St-Giniez

Page 91, note 1, right column, line 2, *for Baviad*, 1794, *read Baviad*, 1791,

Page 110, note 2, lines 2–3, *delete* , HW's grand-niece

Page 130, note 11, line 2, *after* 1791 *add* in which HW thanks the Duke for his favourable acceptance of the *Notes to the Portraits.*

Page 131, note 13, line 7, *after* i. 432 *add* (HW thanks the D. of Bedford 8 Dec. 1791 for sending the portrait of the Countess of Devonshire, MISC. CORR. iii. 341).

Page 135, note 1, *add* See also *London Stage* Part V, ii. 1417–19.

Page 136, note 2, right column, line 7, *for* Macreth *read* Mackreth

Page 141, note 2, line 4, *for* Tournay *read* Tournai

Page 145, note 14, right column, line 5, *before* John Mitford *insert* Sir *Last line, after* Hamond *add* ; Mitford was solicitor-general 1793–9; see Namier and Brooke iii. 144

Page 155, note 20, line 1, *for* Duval d'Esprémesnil *read* Du Val d'Eprémesnil   *Line 2, for* 1746 *read* 1745   *Line 10, after* n. 20 *add* ; *Dictionnaire de biographie française*, 1933– , xii. 996–1000

Page 170, note 1, line 3, *for* (1719–44) *read* (1719–41)   *Line 8, after* 27 n. 7 *add* ; Namier and Brooke ii. 326

Page 182, headnote, *add* The MS was offered by Francis Edwards (83, Marylebone High Street, London), Cat. 976 (1973), lot 682, and re-offered Cat. 980 (1974) and Cat. 987 (1974) lot 427; re-offered by Kenneth W. Rendell, Inc., Newton, Massachusetts, Cat. 113, 19 Jan. 1976.

Page 193, note 2, line 1, *for* Possibly Hewetson or Huitson *read* I. P. Huitson, identified by his nephew J. Deere in a MS note: 'My uncle I. P. Huitson was surgeon to the late Lord Orford and in conformity to the above order opened his Lordship's body' (MS now WSL, quoted in ADD. AND CORR. on vol. 30, p. 377).

Page 204, note 10, *add* See also CONWAY iii. 550; BERRY ii. 37.

Page 208, note 10, line 2, *for* Vct Fielding *read* Vct Feilding

Page 214, note 14, left column, line 6, *for Shakespeare read Shakspeare*

Page 230, To Lady Ossory 15 Jan. 1797, headnote, line 2, *after* No. 46; *add* offered Maggs Cat. No. 433 (Christmas 1922), lot 3804, and Cat. No. 449 (1924), lot 445;

Page 240, headnote, line 1, *after* Written *add* (between April and July 1771)

Page 240, 1st paragraph of text, line 1, *on* Princess Louisa *add note* 1:
1. Who died 14 May 1768 (MANN vii. 22, n. 19).

Page 248, 1st paragraph, line 1, *after* 4th Oct. *add* [6th Oct.]

VOLUME 35

Page xii, 3d paragraph, line 8, *for* On Appendix 4 *read* In Appendix 4

Page xvi, 5th paragraph, *add* One unpublished letter from Hamilton, 15 Oct. 1765, was acquired by W. S. Lewis from Seven Gables Bookshop, New York City, in Nov. 1976. Another letter from Hamilton, 10 Dec. 1771, is in the Fitzwilliam Museum, Cambridge.

Page xxii, *sub* Cobbett, *Parl. Hist.*, *for* William Cobbett and John Wright *read* William Cobbett, John Wright, and T. C. Hansard

Page xxii, *sub* Coke, *Journals*, *for* Edinburgh, ed. James A. Home, 1889, *read* ed. James A. Home, Edinburgh, 1889–96,

Page xxx, *sub* 1765, *for* ca 15 Oct.* *read* 15 Oct.†, MISC. CORR. i. 383–4

Page xxx, *sub* 1771, *insert* 10 Dec.‡, MISC. CORR. iii. 460

Page 59, note 16, lines 1–2, for Rogier de Beaufort-Montboissier de Canilliac *read* de Montboissier-Beaufort   *Line 3, for* abbé *read* Abbé de Canillac   *Line 7, after* 199 n. 1 *insert* ; *Rép. de la Gazette*; La Chenaye-Desbois xiv. 123; Jougla de Morenas

Page 66, *for heading* To Chute, Tuesday 30 March 1751 *substitute* To Chute, Saturday 30 March 1751 OS

Page 73, note 33, line 1, *for* Jonson *read* Cornelis Jonson   *Line 2, for* ca 1664 *read* ca 1662   *Line 3, before* A. J. *insert* Thieme and Becker;

Page 73, note 36, line 1, *for* cr *read* cr.

Page 75, note 53, *add* See also CONWAY i. 430.

Page 75, note 57, last line, *for* Scheemakers *read* Peter Scheemakers (1691–1770)

Page 80, note 17, lines 9–10, *for Regalo* ... Niccolò Jomelli *read Regolo* ... Nicolò Jommelli   *Lines 13–14, for* 5th ... 654 *read* 6th edn, 1980, ix. 689–93

Page 98, note 3, line 1, *for* d. (1769) *read* (d. 1769)

Page 100, 2d paragraph, line 8, *on* chimney-boards *add note* 7a: 7a. For illustrations of 18th-century 'chimneyboards' or 'fireboards' see N. F. Little, 'Pictures on the Hearth: Painted Fireboards in Early American Homes,' *Country Life*, 4 Jan. 1973, cliii pt i. 39–41: 'Boards decorated with prints and cut-out coloured paper figures were made for several rooms at Bulstrode by both Mrs Delany and Miss Hamilton, as a pleasant pastime in 1772 and 1773, although impressive examples were designed and made to complement Adam's schemes of decoration both at Osterley Park and Audley End' (ibid. 39).

Page 100, note 5, line 7, *after* 1886 *add* ; it is also reproduced in CON-WAY i. 531

Page 103, note 1, *add* See CONWAY i. 551, 552, 559.

Page 118, note 4, line 1, *for* Huntington's *read* Huntingdon's

Page 121, note 12, line 2, *for* 1816 *read* 1817

Page 122, note 15, line 1, *for* Dumesnil *read* Marchand, called Mlle du Mesnil

Page 126, note 8, line 2, *for* 1616 *read* 1617

Page 151, note 35, line 2, *for* Jourdain *read* Jourdain

Page 151, note 37, right column, line 1, *for* Scheemaker *read* Peter Scheemakers

Page 153, note 53, *for* ca 1530 *read* ca 1532

Page 157, note 4, *substitute* The 'cascade scene' is in 'Drawings and Designs by Richard Bentley,' now WSL, p. 6 (*not* the drawings in soot water in the Green Closet).

Page 158, note 12, 3d line from end, *for* 'Old Horace *read* 'Old' Horace

Page 163, note 23, lines 3–4, *for* K. of Sicily 1435–42 *read* titular King of Sicily 1435–80 and effective King of Naples 1438–42

Page 163, note 24, lines 3–4, *for* King of Sicily 1435–42 (GRAY ii. 69, n. 5). *read* titular King of Sicily 1435–80 and effective King of Naples 1438–42 (Jacques Levron, *La vie et les mœurs du bon roi René*, 1953, pp. 74, 81, 84, 94–5).

Page 165, note 9, *add* Perhaps Meliora Boden, daughter of Althemea Boden and apparently sister of Bn Conway's 2d wife (see HW to Hardwicke ?March 1773 *bis*, MISC. CORR. ii. 241 and n. 2; G. Steinman Steinman, *Some Particulars Contributed towards a Memoir of Mrs Myddelton*, [Oxford] privately printed, 1864, pp. 56, 58).

Page 165, note 10, line 1, *for* 1725 *read* 1724

Page 171, note 29, right column, line 1, *for* at Petersfield *read* and Petersfield

Page 174, note 11, *add* See G. E. Kendall, 'Notes on the Life of John Wootton With a List of Engravings after his Pictures,' *Walpole Society 1932–1933*, xxi. 32.

Page 174, note 21, last line, *after* Johnston *add*   ; illustrated in CONWAY i. 330

Page 179, note 25, line 1, *for* Gardens *read* Yard

Page 188, note 40, *for* Lettres nouvelles . . . Pour servir de supplément à l'édition de Paris en six volumes, 1754. *read* Lettres nouvelles de Mme la marquise de Sévigné à Mme la comtesse de Grignan, sa fille. Extraites de l'édition de 1754 en huit volumes Pour servir de supplément à l'édition de Paris en six volumes, 1754, 2 vols.

Page 197, note 26, line 4, *for* Thomas Barrett *read* Thomas Barret (d. 1757)   *Last line, before* Hazen *insert* GM 1757, xxvii. 92;

Page 198, note 2, line 2, *for* 1648 *read* 1646

Page 202, note 14, line 1, *for* Francis *read* Frances

Page 206, note 11, line 1, *for* Ruben's *read* Rubens's

Page 211, note 25, *for* only child *read* only legitimate child

Page 216, note 18, line 3, *delete* 10–14).

Page 217, note 28, *add* See CONWAY i. 390.

Page 233, note 17, line 1, *for* Hallet *read* Hallett

Page 234, note 23, line 1, *for* ca 1710 *read* ca 1702   *Last line, add* See *An Exhibition of Paintings and Drawings by Samuel Scott c. 1702–1772,* Guildhall Art Gallery Cat., 1955; *Samuel Scott Bicentenary,* Guildhall Art Gallery Cat., 1972.

Page 238, note 27, line 1, *after* (1720–99), *insert* Marquis de Sandricourt, also called

Page 250, note 5, line 14, *for* Chalres *read* Charles

Page 256, note 5, line 1, *for* (1445–1509) *read* (1447–1511)   *At end add* See *Dictionnaire de biographie française,* 1933– , ix. 386–7.

Page 267, running head, *for* To Bentley August 1766 *read* To Bentley August 1756

Page 270, note 34, line 1, *for* ca 1521 *read* ca 1520   *Line 2, for* Barley *read* Barlow (*or* Barley)   *for* (1549) *read* (1547)   *Line 3, for* m. 3 *read* m. 3 (ca 1559)

Page 271, note 40, line 1, *after* Cavendish *add* Holles

Page 278, headnote, line 3, *add* The MS was sold Sotheby's 28 March 1972, lot 349 (property of Dr James Strachey), to Seven Gables for WSL.

Page 280, note 18, *add* Reproduced in CONWAY i. 474.

Page 285, note 4, *after* [8 Oct.] *add* (CONWAY i. 513)

Page 288, note 14, line 1, *for* 1727–80 *read* 1727–60

Page 289, note 22, line 7, *for* 3–17 *read* 13–17

Page 291, note 11, line 3, *for* Chester, and *read* Chester, also

Page 296, To Strafford 30 Oct. 1759, headnote, line 2, *for* 315–47 *read* 315–17

Page 300, note 14, line 2, *for* d'Aranda *read* de Aranda   *for* (1760) *read* (1756 in a civil, 1760, in a religious, ceremony)

Page 302, note 30, right column, line 2, *after* Donaldson *insert* ; m. 2 (1784) Col. Charles Lumm (P. H. Highfill, Jr, K. A. Burnim, and E. A. Langhans, *A Biographical Dictionary of Actors, Actresses . . . 1660–1800,* Carbondale, Illinois, 1973– , v. 141–4)

Page 305, note 12, line 2, *for* ca 1721 *read* 1724

Page 309, note 1, line 3, *for* Kirch Denkern *read* Kirch Denckern

Page 310, note 6, line 6, *for* Kirch Denkern *read* Kirch Denckern

Page 312, note 8, line 3, *for* (1748) *read* (1784)

Page 316, To Strafford 3 Sept. 1765, date-line, *on* 1765. *add note a: a.* The *Public Adv.* 4 Sept. 1765 reports, 'Yesterday the Hon. Horatio Walpole, Esq. set out from his house in Arlington Street, St James's, for his seat in Middlesex.' He wrote to Cole and Grosvenor Bedford 5 Sept. from SH.

Page 318, To Strafford 23 Jan. 1766, headnote, *add* Mentioned in HW to Lady Mary Coke 3 March 1766 (MORE 109).

Page 318, *after letter to Strafford 23 Jan. 1766 insert the following heading:*

FROM STRAFFORD, February 1766

Missing. Mentioned in HW to Lady Mary Coke 3 March 1766: 'I have this moment received a letter from Lord Strafford' (MORE 110).

Page 320, note 12, *substitute* Lord Chatham.

Page 320, To Strafford 29 July 1767, headnote, line 1, *for* 57–7 *read* 56–7

Page 328, note 26, line 4, *for* Piccini *read* Piccinni

Page 337, note 11, line 2, *after* Arras *add* , inherited by Richmond through his great-grandmother, the Duchess of Portsmouth (DU DEFFAND ii. 287, n. 23, 298–9; DALRYMPLE 158, n. 12; CONWAY iii. 119–20, n. 7)

Page 341, note 3, line 2, *for* 1756 *read* 1796

Page 342, note 12, line 2, *for* d'Arenburg *read* d'Arenberg,

Page 349, note 1, line 1, *for* ca 1697 *read* 1695

Page 350, note 5, line 6, *for* of *read* in

Page 350, note 12, line 4, *after* 56 *add* ; CONWAY iii. 210, n. 4

Page 351, 1st paragraph, line 2, *for* Chudeigh *read* Chudleigh

Page 351, note 17, *add* See also HW to Conway 12 Nov. 1774.

Page 351, note 18, last line, *for* ibid. *read* OSSORY i. 200, n. 16; CONWAY iii. 195, n. 2, 247 and n. 20.

Page 353, after letter of 2 Nov. 1776 *insert the following heading*:

To STRAFFORD, October 1777

Missing; mentioned in Lady Mary Coke, 'MS Journals' 23 Oct. 1777: 'Mr Walpole has confirmed to Lord Strafford the news that was sent to me relating to him [the Duke of Gloucester].'

Page 358, note 14, line 8, *for* ii. 237–40 *read* ii. 237 *At end add* John Blake's house was Cross Deep Lodge; Shirley's house was Heath Lane Lodge, of which Cobbett says, 'Its gardens were most extensive, reaching to the Teddington Road, and possessing a river frontage between Poulett Lodge and Cross Deep Villa, the terrace being on the upper side of the road. Old prints depict the "handsome summer-house of brick with ornaments and a dome top"—as Ironside describes it' (*Memorials of Twickenham*, 1872, pp. 261–2, 354). See also the map of Twickenham in MISC. CORR. iii. Appendix 1 and p. 481.

Page 388, note 3, line 3, *for* Book *read* Book

Page 400, note 7, *add* 'Jack Pudding' is an English dance included in John Playford's *English Dancing Master*, 1651, p. 56.

Page 405, running head and heading, From Hamilton, ca Tuesday 15 October 1765, *delete* ca *Headnote, for* Missing *read* Printed from the MS, now WSL, in MISC. CORR. i. 383–4; acquired from Seven Gables Bookshop, Inc., New York City, in Nov. 1976.

Page 412, after letter of 15 Sept. 1771 *insert the following heading*:

FROM HAMILTON, Tuesday 10 December 1771

Printed from a photostat of the MS in the Fitzwilliam Museum, Cambridge, in MISC. CORR. iii. 460.

Page 412, note 11, line 1, *for* ca 1563 *read* ca 1565   *Line 4, after* Museum *insert* (see *The Book of Architecture of John Thorpe*, ed. John Summerson, *Walpole Society*, 1964–6, xl. 14–15)

Page 417, note 10, line 1, *for* 1786 *read* 1788

Page 418, note 25, line 9, *for* France *read* Florence

Page 422, note 26, line 3, *for* Elliot *read* Elliott

Page 430, To Hamilton 23 May 1777, headnote, line 1, *for* Yonkers, N.Y., *read* Princeton, New Jersey,

Page 437, note 17, lines 6–7, *after* patent' *insert*   ; CONWAY iii. 392 and n. 6

Page 438, note 17, left column, line 3, *for* Appendix 15 *read* Appendix 16

Page 464, line 18, *on* imitation *add note* 5a: 5a. An imitation of Pope's *Essay on Man* I. 99–112.

Page 467, note 11, left column, line 9, *for* Nov *read* Nov.

Page 468, note 31, *add* See also HW to Lady Cecilia Johnston 19 Aug. 1777 (MISC. CORR. ii. 365–6).

Page 472, To Nuneham 7 July 1777, note 2, line 1, *for* [August] *read* [July]

Page 487, note 3, line 4, *for* Sandby *read* Thomas's brother, Paul Sandby *Last line, after* WSL *add*   ; ante CHUTE 451, n. 2

Page 505, note 20, line 2, *for* n. 17 *read* n. 16

Page 506, note 3, *substitute* In April 1780, after her husband died, Lady Diana took a house at Richmond, apparently until 1781 or 1782, when she moved to Little Marble Hill, Twickenham (see OSSORY ii. 195, n. 5; MISC. CORR. iii. Appendix 1, map and p. 484).

Page 516, note 7, line 2, *for* practiced *read* practised

Page 522, note 14, left column, line 7, *for* suffered, *read* suffered.

Page 560, 1st paragraph, line 4, *for* Mr. *read* Mr

Page 584, note 5, line 1, *for* 1720 *read* 1719

Page 603, note 1, *substitute* 'Set down to profit or gain,' adapted from Horace, *Odes* I. ix. 14–15 (information from Alton H. Chase, Berwick, Maine).

Page 606, note 3, line 1, *after* it *insert* (now BM Add. MS 48,976) *Line 3, after* 1768 *add* (see Sandwich to HW 17 Feb. 1768, in MISC. CORR. ii. 134–5)

Page 608, note 2, line 1, *for* (1445–1509) *read* (1447–1511)

Page 609, note 3, *add* On the historical validity of More's *History* see Alison Hanham, *Richard III and his Early Historians 1483–1535*, Oxford, 1975.

VOLUME 36

Page ix, List of Illustrations, *for* Sir Edward Walpole, by Joseph Highmore *read* Lord Malpas, later (1733) 3d Earl of Cholmondeley

Page xxi, 2d paragraph, line 8, *for* Jock *read* Jack

Page xxv, *sub* Cobbett, *Parl. Hist.*, *for* William Cobbett and John Wright *read* William Cobbett, John Wright, and T. C. Hansard,

Page xxix, Letters between Walpole and Sir Robert Walpole, 1741, *for* March *read* March*

Page 7, note 5, *add* See CONWAY i. 153 and n. 8.

Page 7, note 6, lines 1–2, *for* (d. 1788) *read* (ca 1708–88)

Page 8, note 5, lines 5–6, *for* Sir George Grove . . . iii. 488). *read The New Grove Dictionary of Music and Musicians*, 6th edn, ed. Stanley Sadie, 1980, vi. 808).

Page 15, note 9, *add* Sir Edward's worry about the illegitimacy of his children is suggested in his letter to William Sloper, ca 1737, thanking Mrs Sloper for being godmother to his son Edward: 'The manner in which my children have been christened, and in which this boy is now to be, will in a great degree wipe off the sully of their birth. And I hope, when they grow up and are well educated, the notice that Mrs Sloper and other people of fashion are pleased to take of them, will make their mother be forgot. They shall always appear in the world as mine and bear my name. And I am in hopes, as many natural children have come to be received and live in the best company, Mrs Sloper will one dare [daye] or another not be ashamed of her godson . . .' (MS WSL).

Page 19, note 17, line 17, *before* 1741 *insert* 1744, when HW wrote to Middleton 18 Aug. inviting him to come (DALRYMPLE 23), although Cole remembered the date as

Page 22, middle of page, after letter from Sir Edward Walpole 29 May 1749 OS *insert the following headings*:

TO SIR EDWARD WALPOLE, 1751

Missing. Mentioned in *The Whole Proceedings on the Wicked Conspiracy Carried on against the Hon. Edward Walpole, Esq., by John Cather, Adam Nixon, Daniel Alexander, Patrick Cane alias Kane, and Others*, 1751, p. 7: 'Mr Horace Walpole being sworn, deposed, That on hearing the report of a prosecution being carried on against his brother Edward, he wrote to him about it, and was informed by his answer, that such a prosecution was intended against him; that on receipt of his brother's letter, he came to London, to his brother's house in Pall Mall.'

FROM SIR EDWARD WALPOLE, 1751

Missing. Mentioned in the pamphlet quoted above.

Page 23, note 1, line 1, *after* December *insert* [23 Nov.]   *Last line, for* n. 8. *read* n. 8; CONWAY i. 372–3 and n. 2.

Page 26, note 5, line 10, *for* (ca 1747–85) *read* (1747–83 or 85)

Page 27, 2d paragraph, line 4, *on* Townshend *add note* 12a: 12a. George Townshend satirized Lord Orford in a caricature in the collection at the National Portrait Gallery; see Eileen Harris, *The Townshend Album*, 1974, pp. 24–5 and pl. 66.

Page 33, note 11, *add* See GRAY i. 27, n. 177.

Page 34, 2d paragraph, line 3, *on* expense *add note* 15a: 15a. An itemized bill of expenses for the 'Election Dinner of the Honble Horatio Walpole Esqr. the 24th Febry 1757,' amounting to £183, is now WSL; it was apparently paid by Lord Orford.

Page 34, note 1, *after* 1745 OS *add*   ; SELWYN 132

Page 37, after letter of 22 Nov. 1762 *insert the following heading*:

FROM CHARLES CHURCHILL, early August 1763

Missing. Mentioned in HW to Dr Andrew Coltee Ducarel 8 Aug. 1763: 'I have since had a letter from Mr Churchill' (MISC. CORR. i. 290). See *post* HW to Charles Churchill 27 March 1764.

Page 37, note 6, *add* Orford held the Rangership of St James's and Hyde Parks 1763–83, 1784–91 (see MANN ix. 266 and n. 11).

Page 41, note 22, line 3, *for* postmaster *read* paymaster

Page 42, note 3, line 1, *for* 1704 *read* ca 1704

Page 43, note 1, *add* See also CONWAY i. 277, n. 5.

Page 49, note 1, line 1, *for* ca 1724 *read* ca 1729

Page 51, note 3, line 7, *for* Toynbee *Supp.* i. 179, n. 3 *read* MISC. CORR. ii. 169

Page 52, note 4, line 1, *for* Catherine *read* Catharine

Page 56, note 19, line 1, *for* Catherine *read* Catharine

Page 56, note 24, line 7, *for* General *read* Général

Page 57, note 1, *add* See COLE i. 195 and n. 1.

Page 62, middle of page, after letter to Sir Edward Walpole 22 Aug. 1771 *insert the following heading*:

To THOMAS WALPOLE the Elder, ca Thursday 30 April 1772

Missing; mentioned in HW to Henry Sampson Woodfall 30 April 1772, MISC. CORR. ii. 226.

Facing Page 62, illustration, *for* Sir Edward Walpole, by Joseph Highmore *read* Lord Malpas, later (1733) 3d Earl of Cholmondeley

[Dr Alison S. Lewis in *Joseph Highmore: 1692–1780*, Harvard University Ph.D. dissertation, 1975, pp. 620–1, lists two versions of this painting under 'wrong attributions,' Nos 47 and 48, one of which is in the possession of the present Lady Cholmondeley, the other now WSL. Apparently there is no record of a portrait of Viscount Malpas among Highmore's portraits of Knights of the Bath of the 1725 creation.]

Page 92, last line of headnote, *on* born *add note* 1: 1. For her baptism 26 June, see OSSORY i. 129–30 and n. 52, 132; CHUTE 456, n. 2.

Page 99, To Lady Orford 4 Nov. 1773, headnote, line 5, *for* will now know *read* will not know

Page 105, note 4, line 1, *for* 1788 *read* 1778

Page 110, note 16, next to last line, *for* ed. Wheatley, i. 326, *read* ed. R. Latham and W. Matthews, Berkeley, California, 1970–4, ii. 40–1

Page 114, after letter to the Duchess of Gloucester 11 Sept. 1775 *insert the following heading*:

?TO THE DUCHESS OF GLOUCESTER, November 1775
Missing; mentioned by Mme du Deffand 10 Nov. 1775: 'Je n'ai point reçu la lettre pour votre nièce, à qui l'avait-vous confiée?' (DU DEFFAND iv. 235).

Page 115, note 4, line 1, *before* Karl *insert* Christian Friedrich

Page 118, note 3, *add* Bewley wrote to Dr Charles Burney 25 April 1777, "You have probably before this time heard of the situation of our worthy friend, Lord Orford. I was suddenly called to him, at Eriswel, on Wednesday gone a week; and at first hoped that his disorder might be only a common fever: on Friday however it declared itself; and in twelve hours afterwards it was no longer doubtful that it had too much affinity to his former complaint. The heartache I have suffered during my almost constant attendance on him till within these two days is not to be expressed. I left him, however, not without hopes that his disorder is milder in degree, and likely to terminate in perfect *sanity* in much less time, than his former. If I receive any account relating to him by tomorrow morning's post, I will subjoin it. I left Mr Horace Walpole with him' (MS in the Osborn Collection, Beinecke Library, Yale University).

Page 118, note 4, line 7, *after* 1778, n. 1 *add* and MANN x. 55

Page 121, note 2, *for* Lord Orford's deputy as Ranger of St James and Hyde Parks 1763–91 (ibid. i. 135, n. 8). *read* he acted on Lord Orford's behalf during this attack of insanity in regard to the Rangership of St James's and Hyde Parks (see HW to Sir Edward Walpole 11 Feb. 1778 and to Lord North 11 Feb. 1778). Also, HW consulted Moone concerning a candidate to replace John Acland as M.P. for Callington in Dec. 1777 (see HW to Edmund Burke 3 Dec. 1777).

Page 123, note 5, line 1, *for* Batty *read* Battie

Page 150, note 7, line 3, *after* 1777 *add*   ; HW's correspondent

Page 157, note 1, *add* Lord William succeeded Shirley as Deputy Ranger of St James's and Hyde Parks in 1778 and retained the post until his death. See *Last Journals* ii. 105, 113.

Page 157, note 2, lines 5–13, *delete* Gordon had obtained . . . in possession of the deputyship. *and substitute* Gordon had obtained the King's consent through Lord North and needed Lord Orford's authorization (as Ranger of St James's and Hyde Parks). North, thinking that HW was in charge of Orford's affairs during his attack of insanity, wrote to HW; there was an enclosure from North to Orford (see MISC. CORR. ii. 378–80).

Page 157, note 3, *add* HW apparently expected a request, not a *fait accompli*; he wrote in *Last Journals* ii. 113, that 'the King had nothing to do with it, for the Ranger not only appoints his Deputy, but pays him his salary. The King ordered Lord William should have it.'

Page 157, note 5, line 1, *delete* The   *Line 2, for* naval officer *read*

Capt. R. N., 1759; Deputy Ranger of St James's and Hyde Parks ca 1769–78   *Line 4, for* 1777, p. 75 *read* 1770, p. 75, 1777, p. 75, 1778, p. 76

Page 158, note 6, *substitute* The letter to Moone is missing. William Moone, Lord Orford's steward, was apparently acting on Orford's behalf during his attack of insanity. HW explains to Lord North 11 Feb. 1778 that he and Sir Edward had been excluded from the care of Orford's affairs (MISC. CORR. ii. 380).

Page 158, PS., *on* letter to Lord Orford *add note* 8: 8. The enclosure, missing, in North to HW 9 Feb. 1778.

Page 165, note 1, next to last line, *after* viii. 310–11 *add* and Appendix 17, x. 55

Page 172, note 6, last line, *after* n. 2 *add*   ; H. S. Vade-Walpole, 'Notes on the Walpoles . . .,' *Genealogical Magazine*, 1898–9, ii. 393–5

Page 177, note 6, line 4, *for* Redford *read* Retford   *Line 8, for* declined to poll *read* withdrew from the contest

Page 182, note 9, *add* See also Hazen, *Cat. of HW's Lib*. No. 2545.

Page 187, 3d paragraph, line 6, *on* Bedlam *add note* 12a: 12a. In a notebook containing transcripts of Lady Louisa Stuart's poems, made in the nineteenth century, there is the following entry: 'At one of the old Duchess of Montrose's evening circles a person whose actions the company happened to be canvassing was pronounced "quite out of his senses," and Mr Walpole (afterwards Lord Orford) appealed to, with—"Now, don't you think him mad?" "To be sure, Madam" (he answered) "quite—and so is everybody else. Why, we all say it of each other every day of our lives. For my part, I have long thought it so absurd for the few to attempt confining the many, that I would have those who are without any madness in their composition, seize upon Bedlam, turn out the patients, and shut themselves up in it, as a place of security." I was a silent listener to this conversation, and Horace Walpole never saw or heard of the following: [then follows a transcript of Lady Louisa's poem 'Address to Bedlam']. HW expressed this opinion to Strafford 29 Aug. 1786, to Lady Ossory 29 Jan. 1780, to Cole 12 April 1779 (CHUTE 386–7; OSSORY ii. 163; COLE ii. 156).

Page 195, note 15, right column, line 1, *for* 8 *read* 18   *Lines 2–3, for* obtained four of them for him *read* and his son sent new numbers to him from time to time   *Last line, for* 3 Jan. 1784 *read* 6 Sept. 1782, 3 Jan., 1 Feb. 1784, 25 Oct. 1786; Hazen, *Cat. of HW's Lib*. No. 2801

Page 198, note 12, line 2, *for* lord *read* first lord

Page 200, From Sir Edward Walpole, ca June 1781, headnote, *for* answered *read* mentioned

Page 200, note 1, *add* She had been staying at SH from late June until 3 July (OSSORY ii. 275, 279).

Page 201, 1st paragraph, line 6, *on* request *add note* 5: 5. See also OSSORY ii. 281–2.

Page 205, note 13, line 2, *after* William Henry Cavendish *insert* Bentinck

Page 208, note 1, lines 4–5, *for* foreign secretary *read* home secretary

Page 210, note 16, line 5, *for* on Newgate Street *read* in Newgate Street

Page 216, note 13, line 2, *for* K. of Sicily 1435–42 *read* titular King of Sicily 1435–80 and effective King of Naples 1438–42

Page 216, note 14, line 1, *for* 1429 *read* ca 1430

Page 223, note 15, lines 5–6, *for* passing to Sir Edward, and expiring on his death *read* which expired on the death of Sir Edward   *Last line,* *add* See also HW to Pelham 25 Nov. 1752, MISC. CORR. i. 73–4 and n. 1.

Page 229, To Lady Waldegrave 1 Feb. 1785, headnote, *add* Listed in HW's memoranda on the draft of his letter to Dr Henry on 1 Feb. 1785 (DALRYMPLE 183).

Page 235, note 1, *add* The marriage took place on Monday 3 April 1786 (GM 1786, lvi pt i. 351). A four-page document entitled 'Heads of a proposed Marriage Settlement,' drawn up by Joshua Sharpe, is among the Seymour of Ragley papers in the Warwickshire County Record Office. The document states 'that the marriage between the said Hugh Seymour Conway and Lady Anne Horatia his now wife was had and solemnized on the 3d day of April last by and with the consent of the said Earl of Hertford and the said Duchess of Gloucester'; at the end two memoranda state that on 7 April 1786 two fair copies were sent to the Earl of Hertford, and on 14 Aug. 1786 three copies 'as altered' were sent to 'Mr Conway, Ld Hertford, and Mr Hor. Walpole.' See also HW to Joshua Sharpe 21 Aug. 1786, MISC. CORR. iii. 173–4.

Page 237, 1st paragraph, line 11, *on* drawings *add note* 11a: 11a. The prints and drawings of Giovanni Battista Cipriani (1727–85) were sold 14–17 March 1786 at Hutchins's (DNB); see also MANN ix. 247, 316, 418.

Page 241, note 6, lines 2–3, *for* Heysley and Great Boreham *read* Harpley and Great Bircham

Page 242, note 9, line 5, *for* No. 3226 *read* No. 3026

Page 249, note 7, *add* See also BERRY i. 43–4.

Page 267, To Hon. William Waldegrave 22 Oct. 1789, headnote, *for* Missing; *read* Printed in ADD. AND CORR. *sub* vol. 42;

Page 268, From the Duchess of Gloucester ca 28 Oct. 1789, headnote, *after* iii. 75 *add* where a sentence of her letter is quoted: 'The Duchess stays till her delivery, and is so charmed with her melancholy submission to her fate, and with her piety, and with the enchanting goodness of Lord and Lady Aylesford, that in one of her letters to me she says in her usual expressive style, "In short, to learn to live, or to learn to die, one must come to Packington." '

Page 270, note 1, line 3, *after* n. 12) *add*   ; she died before HW made his will 15 May 1793

Page 274, running head, *for* To George, 5th Earl Waldegrave ?21 March 1790 *read* To George, 4th Earl Waldegrave ca 1785

Page 274, heading, *for* To George, 5th Earl Waldegrave, ?Sunday 21 March 1790 *read* To George, 4th Earl Waldegrave, ca 1785

Page 274, headnote, line 4, *for* Waldegrave; see n. 1. *read* Waldegrave.

The present Lady Waldegrave suggests that this letter seems from its content to have been addressed to George, 4th Earl Waldegrave, and therefore must have been written before his death on 17 Oct. 1789. Fanny Burney in describing a visit to SH with her father in 1786, says that HW 'pointed to a peculiar caravan, or strong box, that he meant to leave to his great nephew, Lord Waldegrave; with an injunction that it should not be unlocked for a certain number of years, perhaps thirty, after the death of Mr Walpole' (*Memoirs of Doctor Burney*, 1832, iii. 68, reprinted in her *Diary*, ii. 483–8). It is possible that this visit took place in Sept. 1785, for a visit of Dr Burney and his daughter is mentioned in HW's letters to Dr Burney 6 Sept. 1785 and to Lady Ossory 17 Sept. 1785 (MISC. CORR. iii. 149–50; OSSORY ii. 498). Also in 1785 William Mason expressed anxiety about his letters to HW in case of HW's death, and Lord Harcourt wrote Mason ca Feb. 1785 that 'should his house and fortune be left as he has told both you and I [*sic*] in the days of our favour he intended to do, you may be assured of every line of your writing being returned to you; for there are not two more honourable or strictly conscientious persons existing than Lord and Lady W[aldegrave]' (MASON ii. 356). Presumably HW's letter to Lord Waldegrave, when written ca 1785, was attached to the box of papers and was meant to be read when Chest A was inherited by the Earl Waldegrave. After the 4th Earl's untimely death in his 38th year, HW may have detached this letter from Chest A and written the memorandum dated 21 March 1790 (see n. 1). At that time the 4th Earl's son, George, 5th Earl Waldegrave, had inherited the title, and according to HW's directions Chest A would not be opened until the Earl Waldegrave reached the age of 25. For the contents of Chest A see FAMILY 312–13 and n. 13.

Page 274, note 1, lines 13–17, *delete* It appears that HW's letter . . . became E. of Orford.

Page 277, From Lord Cadogan ca 19 Nov. 1791, headnote, line 5, *for* knew it but not from me *read* knew it not but from me

Page 280, note 2, lines 1–2, *for* Fifteen volumes bearing the SH imprint *read* Fifteen volumes bound in red morocco with Walpole's arms, including eleven works bearing the SH imprint (the *Odes by Mr Gray*, 1757, and *Poems by Anna Chamber, Countess Temple*, 1764, were bound in one volume) and two works which were published in London (*Ædes Walpolianæ*, 2d edn, 1752, and *The Castle of Otranto*, 1765),   *Line 3, after* i. 262, n. 8 *add* ; Lucian Auvray, 'Horace Walpole et la Bibliothèque du Roi (1766–1792),' *Bibliothèque de l'École des Chartes*, 1929, xc. 230–1

Page 280, note 3, *substitute* Abbé Pierre-Jean Boudot (1689–1771), assistant to Jean Capperonnier who was keeper of the Bibliothèque du Roi; the letter of thanks is missing (DU DEFFAND i. 262, n. 5).

Page 281, note 6, line 1, *for* Ignace *read* Ignacy

Page 283, note 16, *for* ?1653 *read* ca 1648

Page 288, line 11, *on* catch it *add note* 6a: 6a. Lady Horatia died 12 July 1801 at Bristol (GM 1801, lxxi pt ii. 678); Lord Hugh died two months later, 11 Sept. 1801, on board ship off Jamaica (ibid. 1053–4; Namier and Brooke iii. 425). Both were buried in 'Ragley Old Vault,' Arrow Church, Warwickshire (*Miscellanea genealogica et heraldica*, 2d ser. iii [1890]. 1, 56).

Page 290, 2d paragraph, line 14, *on* forbear *add note* 6: 6. *King's Classical and Foreign Quotations*, 3d edn (London, 1904), p. 16, calls 'Ανέχου καὶ ἀπέχου (bear and forbear) 'the two words which summed up Epictetus's Golden Rule of Life,' but cites them from Aulus Gellius (grammarian, d. 175 A.D.), pp. 17, 19.

Page 291, To the Hon. William Waldegrave 2 Oct. 1795, headnote, line 5, *for* Free Oxford *read* Free Orford

Page 313, line 1, *on* memoirs *add note* 13a: 13a. Lady Louisa Stuart wrote to Lady Montagu, no date, 'Oh—I have now learned from Miss Berry the meaning of the Memoirs of George the 3rd's reign by Lord Orford. It is genuine, part of the contents of the box one heard of. Lord Holland was the editor of the first part, the reign of George 2nd but finding his grandfather much attacked in that following, he said, though it was matter of history, and he did not object to its publication, yet he could not be the Editor. So it lay by till this Lord Waldegrave, I suppose wants to make money out of everything. Lady Charlotte and I have agreed to sit quiet, and let our fathers be abused, without burning to answer the authors, dead or alive. And so, you know, whether or not, read Lord Orford somehow one must' (Clarke Papers, Bodleian Library, LS 2; information from John Brooke).

Page 331, *sub* First attack, line 1, *for* 12 Feb. *read* 14 Feb.

VOLUME 37

Page iii, Advisory Committee, 4th line from bottom, *for* Davis *read* David

Page viii, *sub* Ninon de Lenclos, *for* Engraving *read* Copy of an engraving

Page ix, *sub* Bust of Lady Ailesbury by the Hon. Anne Seymour Damer, *for* Bul's *read* Bull's

Page xiii, Introduction, line 2, *on* Seymour Conway *add note* a: a. According to HW, Conway was born in July 1719 at Beaufort House, Chelsea (see *post* Appendix 18, iii. 555); he was baptized 12 Aug. 1719 at Ragley, co. Warwick (*Miscellanea genealogica et heraldica*, 2d ser., iii. 58); he died at Park Place 9 July 1795 (*post* iii. 513, n. 12). The correct dates are in *Eton College Register 1698–1752*, p. 80, and in Namier and Brooke ii. 244.

Page xiii, Introduction, line 2, *on* Hertford *add note* b: b. See *post* i. 6, n. 1; Hertford was born 5 July 1718 at Lindsey House, Chelsea, and was baptized at Chelsea 2 Aug. 1718 (*Miscellanea genealogica et heraldica*, 2d ser., iii. 58; *Eton College Register 1698–1752*, p. 80; GEC); he died 14 June 1794 (*post* iii. 509, n. 7).

Page xvii, 3d paragraph, line 4, *for* of twelve *read* of thirteen

Page xxi, 2d paragraph, line 4, *on* Ceylon. *add note a*: *a*. On Conway's death in 1795 HW's letters were returned to him; see BERRY ii. 140, 141, 146.

Page xxii, 2d paragraph, last line, *on* Library *add note* 1a: 1a. Mr Lewis also has the red morocco covers from which the letters have been cut. The title-page of the first volume, written in HW's hand, reads: 'Letters from the Honourable Henry Conway to Horatio Walpole Youngest Son to Sir Robert Walpole Earl of Orford. Vol. 1.' HW's footnote on Conway: 'Mr Conway was only brother of Francis Seymour-Conway, 2d Lord Conway, and [Earl of] Hertford, and son of Francis Seymour Conway Lord Conway, by Charlotte Shorter sister of Catherine, first wife of Sir R. Walpole. He was member of Parliament for Higham Ferrers, aide-de-camp to His R. H. William D. of Cumberland, and Colonel of a regiment, Major General, and Secretary to Wm D. of Devonshire, Lord Lieutenant of Ireland; Groom of the Bedchamber to George II.'

Page xxii, note 1, *add* These red morocco covers are now WSL.

Page xxviii, *sub* Cobbett, *Parl. Hist.*, *for* William Cobbett and John Wright *read* William Cobbett, John Wright, and T. C. Hansard,

Page xxxiii, *sub* S. P., lines 3–4, *for* (78 or 105) *read* (98 or 105)

Page xlvi, left column *sub* 1759, line 2, *for* 21 Jan. *read* 21 *Jan.*

Page 11, note 2, *substitute* James Sutherland, (TLS 25 April 1975) points out that Conway is quoting *The Dunciad* (B), 2. 127–8:

> 'Curll stretches after Gay, but Gay is gone,
> He grasps an empty Joseph for a John.'

Page 15, 2d paragraph, line 4, *on longum est add note* 13: 13. '*Cum multis aliis, quæ nunc perscribere longum est.* Eton Latin Grammar (Genders of Nouns).—With many other things which it would now be too long to recount at length' (W. Francis H. King, *Classical and Foreign Quotations*, 3d edn, London, 1904, p. 53, item 404).

Page 46, note 9, *for* Not further identified. *read* Youngest daughter of Sir John Shadwell by his first wife (DNB).

Page 46, note 10, *for* Not identified. *read* Probably 'Miss Molly's' older unmarried sister, whom HW calls an ugly Queen of Scots at a masquerade in 1742 (see MANN i. 338).

Page 50, line 12, *for* Duchess of Norforlk *read* Duchesse of Norforlk [*sic*]

Page 50, note 3, at beginning *insert* Possibly Conway is imitating French pronunciation of the name.

Page 51, note 10, line 1, *for* ca 1697 *read* 1695

Page 51, note 21, line 4, *for* Daily *read Daily*

Page 56, note 7, lines 1–2, *for* Buondelmonte *read* Buondelmonti

Page 62, note 20, *add* HW speaks of her letters to him in his letter of 20 May 1740 NS to Ashton; see GRAY i. 220–1 and n. 17.

Page 88, note 1, *for* Parliament *read* the House of Lords

Page 100, note 11, *add* This letter, with one to Ashton enclosed, probably reached London 22 July OS, and allowing three weeks for passage might be dated ca 11 July NS, when HW was in Venice.

Page 113, To Conway 31 Oct. 1741 OS, headnote, lines 1–2, *after* First printed *insert* in *Extracts from the Journals and Correspondence of Miss Berry*, ed. Lady Theresa Lewis, 2d edn, 1866, ii. 26–8; reprinted

Page 113, note 14, line 2, *for* 1714–60 *read* 1718–60

Page 183, note 5, line 2, *after* Gardiner *insert* (ca 1702–70)   *Last line, add* See also HW to Lady Townshend 25 Aug. 1744 OS, MISC. CORR. i. 46, n. 2.

Page 218, note 17, line 2, *for* 22 Feb. *read* 17 Feb.   *Line 3, after* 26 Feb. OS *add*   ; *Register Book of Marriages . . . Parish of St George, Hanover Square*, ed. J. H. Chapman and G. J. Armitage, 1886–97, i. 36, Harleian Soc. Pub. vol. xi

Page 293, note 6, line 1, *for* ca 1689 *read* 1688   *Line 2, add* His country house was at Finchley, Middlesex, where the painter, Joseph Goupy, was in residence for a time and kept his fishing rod and tackle (see C. R. Grundy, 'Documents Relating to an Action Brought Against Joseph Goupy in 1738,' *Walpole Society 1920–1921*, ix. 81–3; Sedgwick ii. 125). Charles Hedges (d. 1756) was his brother's heir, and might be the 'Mr Hedges' referred to in the text.

Page 325, note 4, line 1, *for* 1704 *read* ca 1704

Page 326, note 25, line 1, *delete* Saunders

Page 361, note 2, line 2, *for* ca 1721 *read* 1721

Page 371, note 4, right column, line 16, *for* Robson. *read* Robson,

Page 372, note 2, right column, line 2, *delete* equally

Page 400, note 16, *add* See CHUTE 235.

Page 404, note 2, *add* See also Hartington's correspondence with Fox in E. of Ilchester, *Henry Fox, First Lord Holland*, 1920, ii. 76–7.

Page 422, note 6, line 6, *for* 1704 *read* ca 1704

Page 433, note 13, line 1, *after* Henri, *insert* Marquis de Sandricourt, also called

Page 444, note 9, lines 8–10, *delete* is in the possession of the National Trust at Felbrigg Hall *and substitute* was bequeathed by R. W. Ketton-Cremer to the National Portrait Gallery in 1971   *Last line, after* Farmington *add* and the McCord National Museum, McGill University.

Page 487, date-line of letter, *for* 16 June *read* 12 June

Page 531, note 33, right column, line 4, *for* 1755 *read* 1705

Page 539, From Conway 4 July 1758, headnote, line 4, *for* below *read* below.

Page 550, note 21, lines 3–7, *for* An appendix . . . himself (DALRYMPLE 168). *substitute* In his *Discovery of a World in the Moone*, 1638, p. 183, he suggested the possibility of applying wings to a man's body, and in an appendix entitled 'Discourse Concerning the Possibility of a Passage Thither' (added to the 1640 edn) he proposed a flying chariot (p. 238). See Pope, *Dunciad* iv. 451–2:

'The head that turns at super-lunar things,
Poiz'd with a tail, may steer on Wilkins' wings.'

Page 563, note 9, line 3, *for* in August *read* in July 1751 and more recently in August 1758   *Lines 4–5, for* 20 Aug. *read* 22 July 1751 and 20 Aug. 1758   *after* MONTAGU i. *insert* 120,

VOLUME 38

Page 4, note 7, line 1, *after* there *insert* [Ostend]

Page 57, note 9, line 2, *for* Fuzée *read* Fusée

Page 57, note 12, *delete first sentence and substitute* Anna Maria Falkner (fl. ?1745–84), singer and dancer; m. 1 (1748) William Donaldson; m. 2 (1784) Col. Charles Lumm; Lord Halifax's mistress (P. H. Highfill, Jr, K. A. Burnim, and E. A. Langhans, *A Biographical Dictionary of Actors, Actresses . . . 1660–1800*, Carbondale, Illinois, 1973– , v. 141–4).

Page 60, note 16, *substitute* 'And lest the Countess should become too pleased with herself, ma'amselle is carried in the same chariot,' after '. . . et sibi Consul/ Ne placeat, curru servus portatur eodem' (Juvenal, *Sat.* x. 41–2). See also OSSORY i. 129.

Page 70, note 1, *for* correctly *read* now spelled

Page 74, note 4, line 1, *for* ca 1721 *read* 1724

Page 77, note 8, *add* HW presumably about this time gave Bowman the presentation copy (now WSL) of the SH Lucan's *Pharsalia*, which HW had finished printing 4 Oct. (Hazen, *SH Bibl.* 46). The inscription (not in HW's hand) reads: 'Walter Bowman, Dono dedit Honorati Horatius Walpole.'

Page 78, note 1, *add* See also HW to Lord Bute 20 Oct. 1760 (MISC. CORR. i. 184–5).

Page 83, note 6, line 2, *delete* presumably   *Line 6, after* 213 *add*   ; see also BERRY ii. 204

Page 95, note 10, line 2, *for* 1738 *read* 1735

Page 97, note 35, lines 1–2, *for* (d. 1767) *read* (d. 1797)

Page 115, running head, *for* To Conway 9 September 1761 *read* From Hertford 3 September 1761

Page 146, note 7, line 3, *for* made Ranger *read* offered the Rangership *Line 4, after* Parks *insert* which he held 1763–83, 1784–91

Page 149, note 15, *for* Sexton *read* Sexten

Page 205, note 18, *before* Karl *insert* Christian Friedrich

Page 209, note 16, *substitute* See *ante* HW to Lady Ailesbury 13 June 1761, n. 15.

Page 214, note 9, line 1, *for* Margaretha *read* Margarethe

Page 272, note 1, right column, line 8, *for* 56); *read* 56;

Page 310, note 41, line 1, *for* ca 1724 *read* 1724

Page 341, note 6, line 1, *for* Queensbury *read* Queensberry

Page 342, note 18, line 5 from bottom, *for* Queensbury's *read* Queensberry's

Page 348, note 24, line 3, *for* Mongul *read* Mogul

Page 348, note 27, line 1, *for* Levinia *read* Levina   *Last line, add* See also John M. Pinkerton, 'Richard Bull of Ongar, Essex,' *Book Collector* 1978, xxvii. 42.

Page 367, note 2, line 1, *for* (d. 1778) *read* (1723–78)   *Line 2, after* painter *add* (Thieme and Becker; see also Lady Victoria Manners' articles on her in *Connoisseur*, 1931, lxxxviii. 376–86, 1932, lxxxix. 35–40, 171–8) *Line 3, for* ibid. ii. *read* in Ilchester and Stavordale, op. cit., i.

Page 372, note 3, right column, line 1, *for* Pomadour *read* Pompadour

Page 383, running head, *for* From Henrietta Seymour Conway 27 April 1764 *read* To Conway 24 April 1764

Page 399, To Hertford 8 June 1764, headnote, *add* HW's memoranda for this letter are written on Mann's letter of 19 May 1764 (MANN vi. 239).

Page 405, To Conway 2 July 1764, headnote, lines 1–2, *after* first printed *insert* in *Extracts from the Journals and Correspondence of Miss Berry*, ed. Lady Theresa Lewis, 2d edn, 1866, ii. 29–30; reprinted

Page 410, note 5, line 1, *for* (ca 1747–85) *read* (1747–83 or 85)

Page 435, note 44, *add* Lady Louisa Stuart notes on this passage: 'If Nancy Parsons was *"rather out of date"*—when with the Duke of Grafton in 1764, her history almost rivals that of Ninon l'Enclos. I do not know whether she possessed any of her talents. Some years afterwards she became the mistress of the (then young) duke of Dorset and by the name of *Mrs Horton* lived with him several more. I recollect seeing a whole length picture of her by Reynolds at Knowle, which the old servant who showed the house was so ashamed of, that when asked her name he answered gruffly, "A lady in a Grecian dress" and turned a deaf ear to any farther questions. But after a few more years had passed, there came a still younger Lord Maynard, who not only carried her off from the duke of Dorset, but was sufficiently bewitched to marry her, and, taking her abroad, wanted to fight our minister at Naples for declining to present her at court. The spell gave way at last however; they quarrelled and parted before she died of old age' (*Notes by Lady Louisa Stuart on George Selwyn and his Contemporaries*, ed. W. S. Lewis, New York and London, 1928, pp. 14–15). For further comments see MANN vii. 344, n. 6; OSSORY i. 293, n. 2.

Page 480, note 4, lines 1–2, *for* Marie-Anne-Guillaume (or Marie-Louise) de Fontaine *read* Marie-Anne (or Marie-Louise) Guillaume de Fontaine *Line 5, before* Dictionnaire *insert* H. H. Hawley, 'Meissonnier's Silver for the Duke of Kingston,' *Bulletin of the Cleveland Museum of Art*, Dec. 1978, p. 320;

Page 480, note 5, lines 1–2, *for* Françoise-Thérèse (or Françoise Guillaume) de Fontaine (b. 1712) *read* Françoise-Thérèse Guillaume de Fontaine (1712–65)   *Line 4, before* Clermont *insert* Hawley, op. cit. 320, 327, 338, 340;

Page 502, note 43, line 1, *for* ca 1720 *read* 1727   *Last line, after* 21 *add*   ; Dorothy H. Eshleman, *Elizabeth Griffith. A Biographical and Critical Study*, Philadelphia, Penn., 1949, pp. 9–10

Page 519, note 20, line 5, *for* Danican *read* Philidor   *Lines 5–6, for* Philidor *read* Danican

Page 553, note 47, line 2, *for* Molin *read* Morin

VOLUME 39

Page 3, 3d paragraph, line 2, *on* nightingale *add note* 3a: 3a. Mr James Sutherland (TLS 25 April 1975) suggests that HW is comparing a real nightingale with an artificial nightingale on a music box, which would play a tune when wound up. HW describes a snuff-box with an enamelled bird which sang the notes of a nightingale and other birds, to Mary Berry 5 March 1791 (BERRY i. 214).

Page 13, note 16, line 7, *for* 1742 *read* ca 1742

Page 38, note 13, *add* See also SELWYN 207 and n. 33.

Page 50, note 27, line 9, *for* Dictionnare *read* Dictionnaire

Page 54, headnote, line 4, *for* Lot *read* lot

Page 57, note 33, *add* The horse-race took place on the same day as his brother's wedding, and Lauraguais' absence was considered an affront to the family (see *Gazette de Leyde*, No. xix, 7 March 1766, Supp.).

Page 75, bottom of page, *insert the following heading*:

To CONWAY 9 ?September ?1766
Missing. 'Mr Conway 9th' appears in a list of memoranda on HW to Henry S. Woodfall ?Sept. 1766 (MISC. CORR. ii. 30).

Page 76, note 5, line 2, *for* later in the month *read* on 9 Oct.   *Line 3, after* n. 4 *add* and CHUTE 120

Page 78, note 4, line 2, *for* 261–2. *read* 261–2; CHUTE 120.

Page 83, From Hertford ca ? July 1767, line 1, *on* scheme *add note* a: a. A MS draft (now WSL) of Grafton's letter to Rockingham 15 July 1767, written in Hertford's hand with HW's corrections, states: 'After having delivered to his M[ajesty] the answer which your Lordship communicated to G[eneral] Conway and myself *this morning*, I was commanded to acquaint your Lordship that the K[ing] will expect *to receive from your Lordship the plan* on which you and your friends would propose to come in, in order to extend and strengthen his administration.' This letter was delivered to Rockingham on Thursday, 16 July (John Brooke, *The Chatham Administration 1766–1768*, 1956, p. 191, n. 3). A MS draft (now WSL) of Grafton's letter to Rockingham 17 July 1767, in HW's hand, says: 'I have laid your Lordship's letter before his Majesty, and have the satisfaction of acquainting your Lordship that . . . his Majesty, desirous of uniting the hearts of all his subjects, is most ready and willing to *appoint* such a comprehensive administration as may exclude no denomination of men attached to his person and government. . . . When your Lordship is ready to offer to his Majesty a plan of administration according to the views of his Majesty and your Lordship, his Majesty will be willing to receive it from your Lordship's hands.'

Page 103, note 45, *for* However, her husband did not divorce her until 1776. *substitute* Her husband instituted divorce proceedings in March. The first sentence of divorce in the Consistory Court was dated 17 June 1769; the bill of divorce was passed by the House of Lords 14 May 1776 (*Journals of the House of Lords*, xxxiv. 673, 724).

Page 167, note 7, line 7, *before* volumes *insert* 6

Page 172, note 1, line 3, *for* Aug *read* Aug.

Page 196, note 19, line 1, *for* 1752– *read* (1752–

Page 212, note 18, right column, line 1, *for* MANN *read* MANN,

Page 240, note 5, left column, line 13, *after* 14 Jan.). *add* HW's use of the words 'minute men' is among the earliest instances; see citations in OED, *sub* 'minute-man.'

Page 242, note 29, line 3, *for* Quatre-vingt-six *read* Quatre-vingt-dix

Page 253, note 20, lines 11–12, *for* ca 1735 *read* ?1734

Page 288, note 6, *add* Benjamin Franklin wrote to Thomas Wharton 20 Feb. 1768 of an interview with Conway at a court held on 12 Jan. 1768, when Conway said 'That as long as his Majesty continued to honour him with a share in his councils, America should find in him a friend' (see *The Papers of Benjamin Franklin*, vol. 15, ed. W. B. Willcox *et al.*, New Haven, Connecticut, 1972, p. 55).

Page 291, note 3, right column, line 2, *after* 1823 *add* , in which he describes his visit to SH

Page 293, note 2, *add* HW wrote a description of the 'Delineator' which he sent to William Storer in 1777 and which was later printed in Storer's *Syllabus to a Course of Optical Experiments . . .*, 1782 (see MASON ii. 371–2, Appendix 4; MISC. CORR. ii. 366).

Page 300, note 11, *add* HW is probably alluding to Virgil, *Æneid* vi. 784–7, and to Pope, *Dunciad* (A) iii. 123–6.

Page 313, note 4, *delete* Presumably Calais, though

Page 323, note 20, lines 1–2, *for* ca 1759 *read* 1759

Page 353, note 10, line 12, *after* WSL *add* , Hazen, *Cat. of HW's Lib.* No. 1609:42:7

Page 372, note 9, *add* See also HW to Lord Charlemont 17 Feb. 1791, Joseph Cooper Walker to HW 23 March 1791 (MISC. CORR. iii. 308–10, 318–19 and n. 2). The presentation copy sent by Walker to HW, with HW's corrections, sold SH iv. 162 is Hazen, *Cat. of HW's Lib.* No. 2490.

Page 385, note 11, *add* See also Hazen, *Cat. of HW's Lib.* No. 2545.

Page 390, note 1, line 2, *after* 1782 *add* and continued in that position under Shelburne   *after* ix. 262 *add*   ; CHUTE 518

Page 414, note 4, line 3, *for* is Hazen *read* is discussed in Hazen

Page 430, note 15, last two lines, *delete* MS formerly in the Waller Collection, printed in Toynbee *Supp.* ii. 8n *and substitute Horace Walpole's Miscellany 1786–1795*, ed. Lars E. Troide, New Haven and London, 1978, pp. 24–5

Page 438, note 1, line 5, *for* 2 April *read* 3 April

Page 441, line 14, *on* stanzas *add note* 7a: 7a. The MS of the verses, dated 16 June 1786, is now in the possession of Mr Robert H. Taylor, Princeton, New Jersey; printed in MISC. CORR. iii. 166.

Page 442, note 10, lines 2–6, *delete* John Udny . . . MANN viii. 233, n. 10). *and substitute* Robert Fullarton Udny (1722–1802), West India merchant of London and (1792) of Udny Castle, Aberdeenshire; F.R.S., 1785; HW's neighbour at Teddington (see BERRY i. 89–90, n. 37).

Page 443, note 13, *for* the so-called 'Beauclerk Closet.' *read* see 'Des. of SH,' *Works*, ii. 505. In 1776–7 HW built a room called the Beauclerk Closet to house Lady Diana's drawings of seven scenes from *The Mysterious Mother* (MASON i. 318–19; MANN viii. 524). Not to be confused with the 'ebony cabinet, ornamented with . . . nine capital drawings of a gipsy girl and beautiful children by lady Diana Beauclerc' which was in the Great North Bedchamber ('Des. of SH,' *Works* ii. 502).

Page 443, From Hertford 23 Oct. 1786, note 2, right column, line 1, *for* 2 April *read* 3 April

Page 451, note 22, line 3, *for* 1720 *read* 1719

Page 464, From Conway 26 May 1789, headnote, *sub Memoranda, for* D of Clar[ence] *read* D. of Clar[ence]

Page 467, note 6, line 1, *delete* Charles   *Line* 2, *for* 1733 *read* 1730

Page 473, note 6, *substitute* Mrs Damer's illness has not been identified. Apparently later in the summer she injured her leg in a fall, as HW wrote to Richard French 20 Oct. 1790, 'She has had a fall, slipping from her pedestal and cutting her leg badly. It is almost healed, and Sir W. Fordyce allowed her for the [first] time to dine here yesterday' (MISC. CORR. iii. 291–2; Mrs Damer to Mary Berry 11 Oct. 1790, *Berry Papers*, ed. Lewis Melville, 1914, p. 26).

Pages 481–2, note 6, line 1, *for* Apparently *read* Possibly   *delete last sentence and substitute* See also Vittoria Colonna Caetani, Duchessa di Sermoneta, *The Locks of Norbury*, 1940, pp. 19, 218–19, 220–1.

Page 482, note 7, line 12, *for* given *read* even

Page 489, note 1, *substitute* Probably Robert Blake, attorney in the firm of John Blake, John Norris, and Robert Blake, Essex Street, the Strand (BERRY ii. 180 n. 11), who represented HW in the settlement of Lord Orford's will (MISC. CORR. iii. 348, n. 2). HW wrote to Lady Bristol 3 April 1792, 'Fortunately, Madam, my agent goes to Houghton tomorrow, to meet the executors' (ibid. iii. 356). The correspondence of Anthony Hamond, one of Lord Orford's executors, contains letters from Robert Blake about the disposition of the estate (Hamond MSS in the possession of Capt. Anthony Hamond).

Page 496, note 8, line 1, *after* numerus *delete* ,

Page 502, note 7, *add* Lord Hugh was promoted to be Vice-Admiral of the Blue on 14 Feb. 1799 (GM 1799, lxix pt i. 537).

Page 517, note 3, line 2, *for* (d. 1771) *read* (ca 1711–71)   *Line 3, for* 1707 *read* 1709

Page 540, headnote, *for* See *ante* iii. 682 *read* See *ante* iii. 193

Page 545, 1st paragraph, line 6, *for* Catterell *read* Catterall

Page 549, headnote, *add* For a less favourable description of the gardens at Park Place, see William Gilpin's MS *Tour of the Lakes* (i. 3–10), quoted in C. P. Barbier, *William Gilpin*, Oxford, 1963, pp. 42–3. Lord Malmesbury purchased Park Place in 1796 (see BERRY ii. 176 and n. 9; DALRYMPLE 334).

Page 553, headnote, line 4, *for* now WSL *read* now in the Harvard University Library

Page 555, 1st paragraph, line 1, *on* July 1719 *add note* 1: 1. He was baptized at Ragley, co. Warwick, 12 Aug. 1719 (*Eton College Register 1698–1752*, p. 80; *Miscellanea genealogica et heraldica*, 2d ser., iii. 58). The birth-date '1721' given in DNB is wrong.

VOLUME 40

Page xi, *sub* The Gallery at Strawberry Hill, *delete* begun by Thomas Sandby and finished

Page xxxi, 2d paragraph, lines 3–4, *for* Mrs H. A. Jestin *read* Mrs H. B. Jestin

Page 187, note 6, *add* The appendix to the 2d edn (1772) of this biography includes, on pp. 518–34, seventeen of Cromwell's letters, printed from transcripts made by HW at Pusey, the seat of the Dunch family, in Berkshire.

Page 366, *before* From Lord and Lady Temple, mid-Oct. 1764 *insert the following letter*:

To LORD BESSBOROUGH,[1] Friday 12 October 1764

Printed for the first time from a photostat of the MS (Bessborough MS 305) in the possession of the Rt Hon. the Earl of Bessborough, Stansted Park, Rowlands Castle, Hants. The photostat was kindly provided by Miss Patricia Gill, West Sussex County Archivist. The MS has always remained in the possession of the Earls of Bessborough.

1. William Ponsonby (1704–93), styled Vct Duncannon; 2d E. of Bessborough, 1758; brother-in-law of the D. of Devon-shire, having married his sister, Lady Caroline Cavendish (1719–60), in 1739.

Strawberry Hill
Oct. 12, 1764.

My Lord,

I did not thank you, as I ought to have done, for the kind note[2] you was so good as to send me. The suspense and anxiety I was under, made me not know what to say to your Lordship. I am heartily grieved that the question is so sadly determined.[3] There cannot be a greater loss either public or private. The latter cannot be made up, and I have but small hopes the former will! I feel exceedingly for poor Lord John,[4] and the melancholy part he has had to act—but I will not break in upon your Lordship too long—I could not help saying thus much, which you will be so good as to excuse, as it proceeds from my great regard for your Lordship and that most estimable family with which you are connected. I am my Lord

Your Lordship's
most obedient
humble servant
HOR. WALPOLE

VOLUME 41

Page vii, *sub* The Gallery at Strawberry Hill, *delete* begun by Thomas Sandby and finished

Page 17, transpose note 1 below rule.

Page 30, *before* To Henry Sampson Woodfall ?Sept. 1766 *insert the following letters*:

To LORD BESSBOROUGH, Sunday ?31 August 1766

Printed for the first time from a photostat of the MS (Bessborough MS 305) in the possession of the Rt Hon. the Earl of Bessborough, Stansted Park, Rowlands Castle, Hants. The photostat was kindly provided by Miss Patricia Gill, West Sussex County Archivist. The MS has always remained in the possession of the Earls of Bessborough.

2. Missing.

3. William Cavendish (ca 1720–2 Oct. 1764), styled M. of Hartington 1729–55, 4th D. of Devonshire, 1755; died at Spa, in Germany, where he had gone for his health (MONTAGU ii. 133; MANN vi. 247). Charles Townshend wrote to Lord Temple 4 Oct. 1764, 'The Duke of Devonshire . . . has suffered another stroke of the palsy, by which he has entirely lost the use of one hand and one side' (*The Grenville Papers*, ed. W. J. Smith, 1852–3, ii. 441; see also CONWAY ii. 419 and n. 20, 444–5, 447, 450 and n. 4; MISC. CORR. i. 361–4).

4. Lord John Cavendish (1732–96), M.P., the Duke's youngest brother (Namier and Brooke ii. 203–5), who was with him at Spa. Lord Frederick Cavendish wrote to Lord Bessborough 5 Oct. 1764, 'I have a letter from John, the last telling me, "It is all over." Partridge thought he would not have lived the preceding night through; but blisters had raised him a little, and he was then in a doze, that he probably never would wake from . . . . John says, he shall probably be here soon after I got his letter' (BM Add. MS 32,962, f. 209). Lord John returned to London from Spa on Tuesday, 9 Oct., bringing the news of the Duke's death (*Daily Adv.* 11 Oct.; *London Chronicle* 13–16, 16–18 Oct., xvi. 363, 369–70).

Endorsed by the 2d E. of Bessborough, noting the receipt of the letter on 1 Sept. 1766; there is also a modern pencilled date of 31 Aug. 1766 (information from Miss Patricia Gill).

Strawberry Hill
Sunday night.

My Lord,

When I did myself the honour of calling upon your Lordship this morning,[1] I intended, if I had been so lucky as to find you at home, to say a few words on the behalf of that unhappy young man Haynes.[2] His father is so honest and good a man, and so heartbroken with this calamity, that I cannot help interesting myself for him. If your Lordship should think the case deserving your pity, I would willingly hope that the indictment might be softened, so as to subject the young man only to transportation. I dare not take the liberty to ask this, but I know your Lordship's good nature will dictate it if you think it proper. It would save a very reputable family from the last misfortune and disgrace, and as a young wife,[3] not bad principles, have been the real, though innocent, cause of this crime, the man may be retrieved by banishment, from proceeding in guilt, without undergoing the last punishment for what is past. But I am pleading to one who will not need intercession, if the case deserves compassion. Forgive me my Lord, who am

Your Lordship's
most obedient
humble servant
HOR. WALPOLE

To Lord BESSBOROUGH, Saturday 6 September 1766

Printed for the first time from a photostat of the MS (Bessborough MS 305) in the possession of the Rt Hon. the Earl of Bessborough, Stansted Park, Rowlands Castle, Hants. The photostat was kindly provided by Miss Patricia Gill, West Sussex County Archivist. The MS has always remained in the possession of the Earls of Bessborough.

Sept. 6, 1766.

My Lord,

I am very sensibly touched with your Lordship's great good nature and give you a thousand thanks for it. It will redeem a good and worthy fami-

1. Probably at his house at Roehampton, Surrey, near SH.

2. Possibly a member of the family of John Haynes (d. before 1789), of Heath House, Twickenham (R. S. Cobbett, *Memorials of Twickenham*, 1872, p. 355), whose first wife, Elizabeth, (ca 1690–1744) had three daughters who appear in the Twickenham records (Edward Ironside, *The History and Antiquities of Twickenham*, 1797, pp. 17, 66). His second wife, Mary, (ca 1723–1816) had five daughters and three sons; the sons were William (baptized 1751), James (baptized 1754, d. 1778), and Samuel (baptized 1757, d. 1846) (GM 1816, lxxxvi pt ii 381; Ironside, op. cit. 18–19).

3. Not identified.

ly[1] from the depth of affliction, though I know I must not let them understand how much they are indebted to your Lordship. It will live in my memory, my Lord, and as it must give you satisfaction, I hope you will never forget yourself how humane you have been in this instance.

I am my Lord

> Your much obliged
> and most obedient
> humble servant
> HOR. WALPOLE

Page 172, *after* From Duchesse de Choiseul 7 Feb. 1769 *insert the following letter*:

To UNKNOWN,[1] Friday 17 February 1769

Printed for the first time from a photostat of the MS kindly provided by Mr Clifford Maggs. The MS is untraced until sold Sotheby's 22 July 1980 (property of a gentleman), lot 587, to Maggs Bros. Ltd., who offered it as Item 184 in their Catalogue 1021, in 1981.

Enclosures: Two engravings, one of Louis XVI, the other of Emperor Joseph II, both signed 'T. F. B. f[ecit] 1780,' presumably from the collection of the person to whom the letter is addressed, but not connected with HW's letter.

> Arlington Street
> Feb. 17, 1769.

Sir,

I have looked over your collection of prints twice very carefully. The collection of Princes of Orange[2] are very fine and valuable. In the great book there are a great many good impressions, and scarce any bad. I have selected and placed in a separate leaf at one end those that are most uncommon; and have tied them up in separate parcels with labels. The print cut by Switzer[3] is as valuable as things of that nature can be to col-

1. The Haynes family; see HW to Bessborough ?31 Aug. 1766.

---

1. Possibly Richard Bull (1721–1806), who began collecting prints about 1768; he described himself to James Granger 12 June 1769 as a young and inexperienced collector (J. M. Pinkerton, 'Richard Bull of Ongar, Essex,' *Book Collector* 1978, xxvii. 46–7; N&Q 1913, 11th ser., vii. 170–1). Bull was very generous and later sent HW prints and books as gifts (MISC. CORR. ii. 414 and n. 1; iii. 53–4, 237, 282, 458). Another possible candidate is Joseph Gulston (?1744–86), who 'began in 1768 the magnificent collection of books and prints which he lived to complete unrivalled' (Nichols, *Lit. Illus.* v. 27–8; Namier and Brooke ii. 561–2). But this identification seems unlikely in view of Cole's and HW's unfavourable comments on Gulston in 1772 (COLE i. 287–9). For HW's notes on both Bull and Gulston in 1771 see ibid. i. 287–8, n. 5.

2. These prints have not been identified.

3. Possibly Christoph Switzer, German engraver on wood, who was working in England ca 1614; he made the wood engravings for John Speed's *The History of Great Britaine . . .*, 1611 (E. Bénézit, *Dictionnaire . . . des Peintres, Sculpteurs, Dessinateurs et Graveurs*, new edn, Paris, 1976, x. 32).

lectors, though of no real merit in itself. The print of Thanet house,[4] I likewise never saw, no more than two or three of the Faithornes.[5]

I am extremely obliged to you, Sir, for the obliging offer you make me, but would by no means rob a gentleman who is going to make a collection himself. You would find it very difficult to meet again with several prints in your book, especially such good impressions.

I am Sir
Your obedient humble servant
HOR. WALPOLE

Page 189, note 3, line 7, *for* HW pasted the drawing *read* Edwards made a replica of the drawing in 1781 which HW pasted   *At end add* The original by Sandby and Edwards, dated 1781 and inscribed with both artists' names, is in the Victoria and Albert Museum.

VOLUME 42

Page 37, *after* From Giuseppe Cardini 30 Aug. 1782 *insert the following letter:*

To TREADWAY RUSSELL NASH,[1] Saturday 7 September 1782

Printed for the first time from a transcript of the manuscript; the owner of the manuscript wishes to remain anonymous. The MS was in the possession of Nash's great-great-granddaughter, Lady Henry Somerset [Isabella Caroline Somers (d. 1921), dau. of 3d Earl Somers, m. (1872) Lord Henry Richard Charles Somerset, 2d son of 8th D. of Beaufort], in 1901; offered in Sotheby's Catalogue of Valuable Books, 1–4 July 1901, lots 449 and 453; bought by James Rimell & Son.

Strawberry Hill
Sept. 7, 1782.

I have this moment, Sir, received the favour of your letter[2] and the box of prints[3]—but I am quite ashamed of such a treasure and of my own im-

---

4. Thanet House, Aldersgate Street, London, was built in the 1640s by the 2d E. of Thanet (GEC xii pt i. 692 and n. h; H. B. Wheatley, *London Past and Present*, 1891, i. 23). The print has not been identified.

5. Engravings by William Faithorne (1616–91), the elder; in a letter to Cole 15 July 1769 HW sent a list of prints by Faithorne the elder or his son which HW lacked (COLE i. 179–81). HW's later collection of 246 engravings by Faithorne the elder is listed in the London Sale Catalogue vi. 737–805 (see also Hazen, *Cat. of HW's Lib.* No. 3643). Lot 806 in the London Sale Catalogue includes 39 mezzotints by William Faithorne (1656–?1701), the younger. HW's account of Faithorne the elder's life and a list of his and his son's works are in *Catalogue of Engravers, Works* iv. 49–60.

———

1. (1725–1811), D.D., 1758; F.S.A., 1773; historian of Worcestershire. Besides these four letters, the only other surviving letter of HW's correspondence with Nash is that of 1 May 1789, printed in MISC. CORR. iii. 241–2.

2. Missing.

3. Presumably copies of the engraved portraits in Nash's *Collections for the His-*

pertinence in begging it. I wish I knew how to return it in any manner that would be agreeable to you, and that would best mark my gratitude. I did receive the heads of Sir John Perrott[4] and Lady Packington,[5] but thought they came directly from Mr Pennant,[6] whom I begged to thank you for them.[7]

It would be an additional favour, Sir, if you would command me in any instance in which I could please you. If there were any of the Strawberry Editions that you would like to have, and that I still have, (for of the Hentzner,[8] Grammont[9] and Lord Herbert's life,[10] I have been able to keep but one copy of each) I should have great satisfaction in sending them to you, begging to know the proper conveyance. Pray excuse my taking this liberty, Sir—it is merely to show my sensibility of your generosity, and with how much regard I have the honour of being Dr Nash's

Most obliged

and obedient humble servant

HO. WALPOLE

Page 185, *after* To Richard Bull 10 Jan. 1787 *insert the following letter*:

tory of Worcestershire, 2 vols, folio, 1781–2. HW wrote Thomas Pennant 13 June 1782, 'I think you flattered me with hopes that Dr Nash would give me the portraits in his *Worcestershire* [Vol. I]' and expressed the desire to have those in Nash's recently published 2d volume as well (MISC. CORR. iii. 17, 19). HW's copy (untraced) of Nash's volumes is Hazen, *Cat. of HW's Lib.*, No. 6.

4. Sir John Perrot (ca 1527–92), Kt, lord deputy of Ireland, reputed to be the son of Henry VIII (MISC. CORR. i. 271, n. 3). The portrait, a mezzotint by Valentine Green, after the painting by George Powle, appeared in Nash's *Collections for the History of Worcestershire*, 1781–2, i. 350; HW's copy was sold London i. 25. The portrait is mentioned in Vertue Note Books, *Walpole Society*, 1937–8, xxvi. 62, with HW's marginal note, 'a Drawing from it in Mr Walpole's collection by Chamber [Thomas Chambars]' (see also MISC. CORR. i. 272, n. 4; *BM Cat. of Engraved British Portraits* iii. 453).

5. Dorothy Coventry (d. 1679), dau. of Thomas, 1st Bn Coventry of Aylesborough, m. (ca 1648) Sir John Pakington, 2d Bt, 1624. Her portrait, a mezzotint by Valentine Green, after the painting by George Powle, appeared on the same plate as the portrait of Sir John Perrot in Nash's *Collections for the History of Worcestershire*, 1781–2, i. 350. See also *BM Cat. of Engraved British Portraits* iii. 399; Nichols, *Lit. Anec.* ii. 597–604n.

6. Thomas Pennant (1726–98), traveller, naturalist, and writer, with whom HW had corresponded about the portraits in Nash's *Worcestershire* (above, n. 3). In *The Literary Life of the late Thomas Pennant, Esq.*, By Himself, 1793, he mentions a tour in 1774: 'From Bulstrode I took the common road to Worcester, passed a day or two, as usual, at Beverey [Bevere], with my old and constant friend the Reverend Doctor Nash' (p. 23); and another tour in 1783 with Dr Nash, Mrs and Miss Nash, down the Severn (p. 28).

7. HW's letter asking Pennant to thank Nash for the portraits is missing.

8. Paul Hentzner, *A Journey into England . . . In the Year M.D.XC.VIII*, Strawberry Hill, 1757 (Hazen, *SH Bibl.* 31–3).

9. Anthony Hamilton, *Mémoires du Comte de Grammont*, Strawberry Hill, 1772 (ibid. 96–9).

10. *The Life of Edward Lord Herbert of Cherbury*, Written by Himself, Strawberry Hill, 1764 (ibid. 68–72).

To TREADWAY RUSSELL NASH, Friday 19 January 1787
Printed for the first time from a transcript of the manuscript; the owner of the manuscript wishes to remain anonymous. For the history of the MS see *ante* To Treadway Russell Nash 7 Sept. 1782.
Address: To the Reverend Dr Nash at Benere [Bevere] Worcestershire.

Berkeley Square
Jan. 19th, 1787.

Sir,
I should not have delayed, even for two days, to thank you for your obliging present of the print of Q. Catherine's corpse,[1] if I had not been prevented by unavoidable accidents[2] from writing yesterday. The print is not only very curious and welcome to me, but gave me the agreeable satisfaction of knowing you have not forgotten me; the still more agreeable promise of renewing our acquaintance. I assure you, Sir, I lamented not knowing where to find you after you had quitted your lodgings in Charles Street,[3] where I inquired for you in vain. The two last winters I was confined entirely at home by the gout; but as I have already had a fit and a very short one,[4] I flatter myself I shall be at liberty to profit of your stay in London, and assure you in person that I have long been

Sir
your much obliged
humble servant
HO. WALPOLE

Page 262, *after* To Richard Bull ca Sept. 1789 *insert the following letters*:

To the HON. WILLIAM WALDEGRAVE,[1] Thursday 22 October 1789
Printed for the first time from a photostat of the manuscript in the possession of Lord Waldegrave. The manuscript was sold Sotheby's 21 July 1981 (Valuable Autograph Letters, Literary Manuscripts, and Historical Documents Sale), lot 602, to Pickering and Chatto, from whom Lord Waldegrave acquired it. The cover is now in the Osborn Collection, Beinecke Library, Yale University (MS d 64, f. 71).

1. The print, 'The Body of Queen Katherine Parr, found at Sudely Castle in Gloucestershire 1782,' engraved (ca 1782–7) by James Ross (1745–1821), prefaces Nash's paper, 'Observations on the Time of the Death and Place of Burial of Queen Katharine Parr,' in *Archæologia*, 1789, ix. 1–9. On 14 October 1786 Nash had visited Sudeley Castle where he and two others disinterred the Queen's body. An account of his findings is incorporated in his paper read before the Society of Antiquaries on 14 June 1787. For an account of an earlier disinterment in 1782, see MISC. CORR. iii. 112–14.
2. Unexplained.
3. Possibly the Charles Street located at the southwest angle of Berkeley Square.
4. On 9 January HW wrote Lady Ossory: 'I am recovered of my gout . . . the shortest fit I have had these twenty years (only for a fortnight)' (OSSORY ii. 551).

1. (1753–1825), 2d son of the 3d Earl Waldegrave; cr. (1800) Bn Radstock.

Address: To the Honourable Captain Waldegrave at the Earl of Aylesford's at Packington near Coventry. *Postmark*: OC 22 89.
Endorsed (in an unidentified hand): Horace Walpole.

Strawberry Hill
Oct. 22d 1789.

Even in the midst of my grief for the loss of your dear brother,[2] and of my anxiety about my poor unfortunate niece,[3] I cannot but feel extreme gratitude, dear Sir, for your kind and informing letter,[4] written in the heighth of your own affliction, which could not prevent your feeling great good nature for others—you call your account *confused*; I see nothing but the most eloquent and pathetic sorrow in it.

I am quite persuaded that nothing could have saved Lord Waldegrave;[5] and it must be a comfort to know that a longer protraction of his life would but have added to his sufferings. This certitude satisfies reason— but alas! Sir, reflections, though they silence complaints, leave the weight of affliction as heavy as it was. I did most sincerely love your brother as much as I esteemed him: I never saw anything in him that was not perfectly amiable: with all the firmness of his spirit, he was humane, gentle, reasonable and discreet; and from all ranks and descriptions of men he had the same uniform character of goodness. Lady Waldegrave knows that I have often told her that I loved her Lord as well as her. His death I certainly did not expect but as I observed him much, I have been uneasy about his health for these two years, and frequently pressed him to care and attention to it—I little suspected how vainly I urged them!

Poor dear Lady Waldegrave! I know her sincere piety—but I am almost as much alarmed at her composure[6] as I should be at her transports. She is stunned, and cannot know yet what she feels—nor shall I be at all easy about her till she is not only delivered,[7] but pronounced entirely safe. Happy she never will be again; she is naturally low-spirited, and so tender, that all her thoughts are wrapped up in her family. I hope her fondness for her children,[8] while it engrosses her, will take off her mind in part from her loss.

2. George Waldegrave (1751–17 Oct. 1789), styled Vct Chewton 1763–84; 4th Earl Waldegrave, 1784; M.P. He died at Packington Hall, Worcestershire, where he had been visiting his friends, Lord and Lady Aylesford. He was buried at Packington 23 Oct.

3. Lady Elizabeth Laura Waldegrave (1760–1816), m. (1782) George Waldegrave, styled Vct Chewton, 4th Earl Waldegrave, 1784.

4. Of 20 Oct. 1789, informing HW of the 4th Earl Waldegrave's death; printed in FAMILY 264–7.

5. He had been ill since mid-September of a 'violent bilious complaint' with symptoms of jaundice, and the post mortem examination (described by William Waldegrave) also showed an enlarged heart; see ibid. 258, 259, 264–5.

6. Lady Elizabeth Laura's piety and composure are mentioned in other letters; see ibid. 268, 271–2, 273; MORE 334.

7. Her daughter, Lady Charlotte, was born 2 Dec. 1789 (OSSORY iii. 84, 86; FAMILY 270, 271).

8. At this time she had five: Maria Wilhelmina (1783–1805), George (1784–94),

The Duchess[9] and Lady Elizabeth[10] will undoubtedly be great comfort to her. Indeed, Sir, it is most kind and compassionate in your sister, who has had so great a loss herself, to conquer her own affliction so much as to go into that house of mourning! Indeed I know how to pity you all from what I feel myself.

But while I talk of our misfortune, I should be most unjust if I did not at least try to express my admiration of the unparalleled goodness and noble behaviour of Lord and Lady Aylesford.[11] I am of too little consequence for my praise to be of any value to them—yet long as I have lived I never knew an instance of such unwearied friendship, generosity, attention, humanity and great sense; and all so properly and benevolently applied!

Lord Ossory,[12] dear Sir, will, I am sure, as you rightly judge, be one of the most concerned for the loss of Lord Waldegrave. I shall send him your letter by this post. It is so full, and whatever you please to say of it, so clear and judicious an account, and does your heart and head so much honour, Sir, that I could add nothing to it, if I had time, but as I am here confined to my room by the gout,[13] I did not receive it till this morning, and our post goes out within an hour and half after it comes in; and as my first duty was to thank you, dear Sir, for so extraordinary a mark of kindness, so I trust you will excuse my saying no more, as I could not bear to let the first post go away without telling you how exceedingly grateful I am, and how very much, dear Sir, your ever obliged and most obedient humble servant

HOR. WALPOLE

To the HON. WILLIAM WALDEGRAVE, Saturday 26 December 1789
Printed for the first time from a photostat of the MS in the possession of Lord Waldegrave. The MS was sold Sotheby's 21 July 1981 (Valuable Autograph Letters, Literary Manuscripts, and Historical Documents Sale), lot 603, to Pickering and Chatto, from whom Lord Waldegrave acquired it.
Address: To the Honble Captain Waldegrave at Claremont, Waltham Cross.
Postmark: DE 26.

John James (1785–1835), Edward William (1787–1809), and William (1788–1859) (ibid. 229, n. 1, 233, n. 1, 289, n. 2).

9. Of Gloucester, Lady Waldegrave's mother, who joined her daughter at Packington Hall about 21 Oct. and stayed with her for a few weeks (OSSORY iii. 75, 83; FAMILY 266, 268).

10. Lady Elizabeth Waldegrave (1758–1823), sister of William Waldegrave, m. (1791) as his second wife, James Brudenell, 5th E. of Cardigan, 1790 (ibid. 266).

11. Heneage Finch (1751–1812), 4th E. of Aylesford, 1777; m. (1781) Lady Louisa Thynne (1760–1832). They took care of

Lord Waldegrave during his illness at Packington Hall, and attended the burial there; later Lord Aylesford accepted the guardianship of Lady Waldegrave's children (OSSORY iii. 75; FAMILY 260, 265, 270).

12. William Waldegrave in his letter of 20 Oct. declared that Lord Ossory 'possessed the strongest regard for my brother' and asked HW to send his letter on to the Ossorys (ibid. 267).

13. HW's fit of the gout lasted intermittently from late September until mid-November (see BERRY ii. 72; OSSORY iii. 70, 79, 83).

Berkeley Square
Dec. 26, 1789.

Dear Sir,

I was abroad when the post came in, and returned home so late that I have scarce a moment to seal your letter and write a line myself, which I can scarce do as my poor lame fingers are so numbed by cold, that I can hardly direct my pen.

I am very sorry I cannot second your wishes, as I have said over and over to the Duchess,[1] that I thought the sooner Lady Waldegrave went to Navestock[2] the better, as I would always advise persons in her distress to plunge as soon as they can into everything that must be done, as the longer delayed, the greater impression is made by revived objects of grief—and I should contradict myself, if I changed so suddenly.

I own besides that I am delicate about advising Lady W.[3] I am zealous to serve her, but do not love to advise—and the more affection my nieces may have for me, the more averse I am to interfere, unless I am consulted.

You will excuse me, I am sure, dear Sir, for not obeying you,[4] and for stating my reasons so briefly, but I fear being too late for the post, and should be very sorry to seem wanting in any respect for you, when I have so much, and when I am with the greatest regard

Your most obedient
humble servant
HOR. WALPOLE

Page 354, *after* To Richard Gough 15 March 1792 *insert the following letter*:

To TREADWAY RUSSELL NASH, Wednesday 16 March 1792

Printed for the first time from a transcript of the manuscript; the owner of the manuscript wishes to remain anonymous. For the history of the MS see *ante* To Treadway Russell Nash 7 Sept. 1782.

Address: To the Revd Dr Nash at Benere [Bevere] near Worcester.

Berkeley Square
March 16, 1792.

Lord Orford having the gout in his right hand,[1] is not able to write himself, but is very sensible of Dr Nash's kindness and attention in sending

1. The Duchess of Gloucester, Lady Waldegrave's mother.

2. Navestock Park, Essex, Earl Waldegrave's seat.

3. Lady Waldegrave, HW's great-niece.

4. Captain Waldegrave apparently had suggested that HW advise Lady Waldegrave not to return to her home at Navestock Park. She 'determined to let Navestock, and till all her necessary business is finished, will take some house not far from London' (FAMILY 273).

———

1. On 15 March 1792 HW dictated a letter to Richard Gough which begins, 'Lord Orford is confined by the gout in his arm'; the letter is in Thomas Kirgate's hand (MISC. CORR. iii. 354).

him the proof sheet of his *Hudibras*,[2] in which Dr Dee's[3] black stone[4] is mentioned as being at Strawberry-Hill,[5] to which Lord Orford cannot possibly have any objection. Dr Dee's own account[6] is rather exaggerated, for the stone is not larger than the concave part of a dinner-plate, is highly polished, but being fixed in a strong leathern case, whence it cannot be taken without damage, he cannot say positively that it is not transparent,[7] but has not the least appearance of being so. It was specified in the Catalogue of the Earls of Peterborough[8] at Drayton, thence fell to Lady Betty Germaine,[9] who gave it to the Duke of Argyle,[10] and his son Lord Frederic Campbell[11] to Lord O. so there can be no doubt of its authenticity.[12]

Lord O. is very glad to see Dr Nash's *Hudibras* so far advanced, and shall be very impatient for its appearance.[13]

2. Samuel Butler, *Hudibras*, ed. Treadway Russell Nash, 3 vols, quarto, two of text one of notes, 1793; 200 copies were printed. HW's copy (untraced) was sold SH v. 59 (Hazen, *Cat. of HW's Lib.*, No. 3179). In the spring of 1789 Nash had sent his notes for HW's criticism (MISC. CORR. iii. 241).

3. Dr John Dee (1527–1608), mathematician and astrologer.

4. An obsidian mirror of Aztec origin, now in the British Museum. HW acquired it in 1771 from Lord Frederick Campbell (MANN vii. 286–7 and n. 51).

5. Nash's note on *Hudibras*, part 2, canto 3, l. 631, describes the stone and says, 'This stone is now in the possession of the very learned and ingenious Earl of Orford, at Strawberry Hill' (*Hudibras*, 1793, iii. 273). In a footnote on this sentence Nash repeats HW's account of the provenance of the stone (ibid.).

6. Dr Dee wrote *A True and Faithful Relation of what passed for many years between Dr John Dee . . . and Some Spirits*, ed. Meric Casaubon, 1659. HW's copy is Hazen, *Cat. of HW's Lib.*, No. 1109.

7. HW described it as 'a round piece of shining black marble in a leathern case, as big as the crown of a hat' (MANN vii. 286), and as 'a speculum of kennel-coal, in a leathern case' ('Des. of SH,' *Works*, ii. 501). It is a semi-transparent, extremely hard volcanic rock, found in Mexico by the Aztecs.

8. In the *Description of SH*, 1784 (p. 77; in *Works*, ii. 501) HW wrote: 'It was in the collection of the Mordaunts earls of Peterborough, in whose catalogue it is called *the black stone into which Dr Dee used to call his Spirits*. From the Mordaunts it passed to Lady Elizabeth Germaine, and from her to John last Duke of Argyll, whose son, Lord Frederic Campbell, gave it to Mr Walpole.' The catalogues of the collection of the Earls of Peterborough, and of Lady Elizabeth Germaine, at Drayton, Northants, have not been traced. See Hugh Tait, ' "The Devil's Looking-Glass": the Magical Speculum of Dr John Dee,' in *Horace Walpole: Writer, Politician, and Connoisseur*, ed. W. H. Smith, New Haven, Conn., 1967, pp. 195–212.

9. Lady Elizabeth Berkeley (1680–1769), m. (1706) Sir John Germain, Bt, who left to her the property he had inherited from his first wife, Lady Mary Mordaunt, daughter and heiress of Henry Mordaunt (1623–97), 2d E. of Peterborough.

10. John Campbell (ca 1693–1770), 4th D. of Argyll, 1761, apparently bought the stone at auction (MANN vii. 286).

11. Lord Frederick Campbell (1729–1816).

12. The stone in its leather case with HW's MS label on it was sold SH xvi. 84 to Strong, a Bristol dealer, for J. H. Smyth-Pigott, who sold it in 1849 to Lord Londesborough. In 1888 it was bought by H. Magniac, in 1892 by Romer Williams for Prince Saltykov, and before 1896 by the father of Bishop Stannard, from whom it was acquired by the British Museum in 1966.

13. It was published before Sept. 1793, and reviewed in the *British Critic*, Sept. 1793, ii. 51–61; later reviewed in the *Monthly Review*, Oct. 1794, 2d ser., xv. 170–7.

PS. March 19th. The printer[14] not having sent again for the proof sheet, as he promised, Lord Orford chooses to send this letter, which has been written three days, to Dr Nash, to show that Lord O. had not neglected to acknowledge the Doctor's civility.

Page 422, note 13, right column, line 2, *for* 1st E. of Arundel *read* cr. (1139) E. of Lincoln and (1141) E. of Sussex; known as E. of Arundel from 1138, and that title confirmed by Henry II in 1155.

Page 426, note 2, line 4, *for* Shakespeare *read* Shakspeare

Page 445, To Margaret Planta, date-line, *for* Dec. *read* Decr.

Page 446, line 6, *for* material *read* many material   *Line 15, for* feet *read* feet,   *for* gratitude, *read* gratitude;   *Line 18, for* obliged *read* obliged,

Page 468, *after* From Elizabeth Montagu 19 Jan. 1782 *insert the following letter*:

To Treadway Russell Nash, n.d.[1]

Printed for the first time from a transcript of the manuscript; the owner of the manuscript wishes to remain anonymous. For the history of the MS see *ante* To Treadway Russell Nash 7 Sept. 1782.

Address: Bond Street, No. 107.

Mr Walpole is much obliged to Dr Nash for his kind present,[2] and is very sorry he could not have the pleasure of seeing him, as Mr W. is very much out of order with the gout, but hopes to be able to wait on Dr Nash before he leaves London.

Page 477, 3d paragraph, line 1, *for* Mrs Warren G. Creamer *read* Mrs Warren M. Creamer

---

14. Thomas Rickaby (ca 1753–1802), printer at 15, Duke's Court, Drury Lane, 1785; at Bow Street, 1788; at Peterborough Court, Fleet Street, 1794; printer of the *British Critic* (Ian Maxted, *The London Book Trades 1775–1800*, 1977, p. 188; Nichols, *Lit. Anec.* iii. 737). On 2 March 1791 Nash wrote Bp Percy, 'As our friend Nichols declined printing my Hudibras, I put it into the hands of one Rickaby, who prints well but slowly, not having finished the second part, or begun the notes: so that it cannot be published till Spring twelve month, by which time I hope it will be ready to deliver' (John Amphlett, *An Index to Dr Nash's Collections for a*

History of Worcestershire, Oxford, 1894–5, p. xxxviii; Nichols, *Lit. Illus.* viii. 280).

———

1. Possibly after 19 January 1787, when HW learned that Nash was no longer living in Charles Street, and before 5 December 1791, when HW became 4th Earl of Orford upon the death of his nephew. In letters to Bp Percy 23 Nov. 1790 and 2 March 1791 Nash mentions visits to London in regard to his edition of *Hudibras* (Nichols, *Lit. Illus.*, viii. 278, 281).

2. Possibly a print. Nash had given HW several prints of illustrations used in his writings.

Note on Early English Painters

Mary Edmond, 'Limners and Picturemakers,' *Walpole Society 1978–1980*, xlvii. 60–224, gives new documentary information on the following artists (listed with revised birth and death dates): Samuel Cooper (?1608–72); William Dobson (1611–46); Marcus Gheeraerts (1561–2 – 1636); Richard Gibson (?1605–90); Anne Harding (1593–1672), m. (before May 1626) Peter Oliver; Nicholas Hilliard (ca 1547–1619); John Hoskins (ca ?1595–1665); Rowland Lockey (ca 1565–7 – 1616); Isaac Oliver (d. 1617); Peter Oliver (ca ?1589–1647); and Anne Sheppard (d. 1707), m. (1641) Richard Gibson.

John Murdoch et al., *The English Miniature*, 1981, pp. 41–5 is a new source for Levina Benninck (?1483–1576), m. George Teerlinc.

Addition to Volume 10

Page 139, note 12, *add* HW's silver subscription ticket, in the shape of a strawberry with 'Mr Horatio Walpole' engraved on one side and the opera box number on the other, is now (1982) in the possession of Kenneth Snowman, Esq.

Addition to Volume 13

Page 176, To Ashton, July 1739, headnote, *add* The manuscript was sold Sotheby's 20–21 July 1981 (Valuable Autograph Letters, Literary Manuscripts, and Historical Documents Sale, Property of Miss Avril Wood), lot 501. A photostat of the manuscript appears in Sotheby's Catalogue, p. 305. Most of the letter is in Gray's hand, written apparently with HW's pen. The passage, 'He insists that it is not him . . . forcing it into the Third,' is in HW's hand. The letter is signed by both of them: 'HW: TG:'

The variants from our printed text (not including capitalization) are recorded below.

Page 176, 1st paragraph, line 1, *for* slowness *read* slowness,   *Line 2, for* abundance *read* abundance,   *Line 3, for* matter. *read* matter: *Lines 4–5, for* borrowed *read* borrow'd   *Line 7, for* desired *read* desir'd   *for* his tongue *read* my tongue   *Line 8, for* him, *read* him   *for* used *read* us'd   *Line 9, for* screwed *read* screw'd

Page 177, 1st paragraph, line 1, *for* satire *read* satyr   *Line 2, for I,* and *me, read* I and me,   *Line 3, for* happened *read* happen'd   *Line 4, for* Selwyn and Montague *read* Selwin and Mountague   *Line 7, for* slipped *read* slip'd   *for* least, *read* least   *Line 8, for* it, *read* it;

Page 177, 2d paragraph, line 3, *for* one *read* one,   *for* fools, *read* fools; *for* so *read* so,   *Line 4, for* glory; *read* glory.   *Line 5, for* first *read* first,   *for* signify, *read* signify: *for* secondly *read* 2dly,   *Line 6, for* already: *read* already;   *for* Sir T. G. *read* Sir J: T: *for* your friend Mr Fenton, *read* your friend, Mr Fenton.   *Line 7, for* neither, *read* neither;   *Line 9, for* might [let] *read* may let   *Line 10, for* Yours, *read* Yours

Addition to Volume 36

Page 292, *add* In Thomas Kirgate's copy of the *Description of Strawberry Hill*, 1784, now in the possession of Lord Walpole of Wolterton Park, Norfolk, is the following MS obituary in Kirgate's hand:

> Yesterday died, at the very advanced age of between eighty and ninety, at his house in Berkeley Square, Horace Walpole, fourth Earl of Orford, after a severe fit of the gout all over him.
> *Endorsed*: Dictated by himself, Feb. 18, 1797, in a deranged state. He died March 2d a fortnight after.

Additions to Volume 40

Page xii, *sub* Reveley's Drawing of the Castle of Otranto, *add* A larger version in watercolour of Reveley's Southwest View of the Castle of Otranto is also in the British Museum, the gift of Mrs Fuller-Maitland (accession no. 1927–7–12–8).

Page 197, To Lord Dacre 9 June 1761, headnote, *for* not further traced. *read* The MS was offered Sotheby's 6 April 1982, lot 141.

Page 330, To Thomas Pitt 5 June 1764, headnote, line 8, *for* not further traced. *read* now in the Richards Collection, Mugar Memorial Library, Boston University.

Addition to Volume 42

Page 351, To Sylvester Douglas, 15 Feb. 1792, headnote, *for* not further traced. *read* the MS and the presentation copy of *The Mysterious Mother* were offered by Christie's 5 May 1982, lot 131.

SUBJECT INDEX TO ILLUSTRATIONS

SUBJECT INDEX TO ILLUSTRATIONS

There are 324 illustrations to the Yale Edition of Walpole's correspondence, including end-paper maps, genealogical charts, and some small line-cuts imbedded in the text of correspondence or journals.

This is not an index to the titles of the illustrations but to the artists and scribes, and to their subject matter—persons, books, MSS, buildings, objects, etc.—arranged alphabetically (within various categories) with their respective volume and page references. The volume where each illustration appears has, at its beginning, a List of Illustrations for that volume, giving the description and provenance of most items. The reader who seeks such information about a picture must turn to the list at the front of the volume where the picture occurs.

Two illustrations were mis-labelled. The pastel by Rosalba Carriera opposite **17.** 77 is not Horace Walpole but Lord Boyne. The portrait ascribed to Highmore opposite **36.** 62 is not Sir Edward Walpole but his brother-in-law Lord Malpas, later 3d Earl of Cholmondeley. Horace Walpole was mistaken about some of his works of art: the Madonna and Child, opposite **17.** 167, is now thought to be by Sassoferrato, not Domenichino, and the silver bell attributed to Cellini (**23.** 383) is now deemed to be 'School of Jamnitzer.' Walpole's letter of 9 Sept. 1776 is not 'Cole's copy' as the caption (**2.** 24) calls it, but is in Walpole's own hand.

ANIMALS AND BIRDS

Cat, (?) Mme du Deffand's, by Carmontelle	**6.** 479
Cats, Mme du Deffand's, engraved by Cochin	**6.** 360
Cats, Mme du Deffand's, stamped on spine of book	**5.** 190
Cats, 'Mandarin,' drawn by Bentley	**9.** 134
Cattle, Walpole's, by Müntz and Pars	**9.** 53, **24.** 135
Dog, Dodd's, in his portrait by Vanderbank	**40.** 3
Dog, Hertford's, by Dandridge	**37.** 54
Dog, Hertford's, by Morland	**39.** 171
Dog, Mme du Deffand's 'Tonton' on snuff-box cover	**29.** 145
Dog, Mme du Deffand's 'Tulipe' in Carmontelle's group	**4.** 13

ARTISTS (including draughtsmen, engravers, and sculptors)

BOOKS

BOOK-PLATES

EVENTS, HISTORIC

MAPS

PORTRAITS

SATIRIC PRINTS AND DRAWINGS

STRAWBERRY HILL (exterior and interior views, furnishings and outbuildings)

STRUCTURES, LANDSCAPES, AND CITY-SCAPES (other than at Strawberry Hill)

INDEX OF HORACE WALPOLE'S
CORRESPONDENTS

INDEX OF HORACE WALPOLE'S
CORRESPONDENTS

This index lists the names of all people to whom Walpole wrote letters now extant, or from whom he received letters still in existence. We give the volume numbers (in bold-face type) and page references where the letters are to be found in this edition. For single letters, the number of the opening page is given; for groups of letters inclusive page numbers are used, though there may be an occasional letter, to or from a different person, between those numbers. For major correspondences, volume numbers alone are sufficient. When textual corrections to letters have been recorded in our Vol. 43, we have added those page references here.

Missing letters are not included, even though headings for many of them are to be found in our volumes, sometimes with information about their contents. We know that Walpole corresponded with several other people though no letters in such correspondences survive—the names of these people are not listed here.

The correspondences are here arranged under the names by which the correspondents are best known, with cross-references from other names or titles. Under 'Unknown' we list letters to or from unidentified persons.

CHRONOLOGICAL LIST OF LETTERS

CHRONOLOGICAL LIST OF LETTERS

This is a list, by dates, of all existing letters to or from Horace Walpole, including fragmentary letters (or extracts from letters now lost), but *not* including letters which are completely missing, even though some information about them may have been printed from time to time in our volumes.

The letters preceding the change of calendar in 1752 are arranged in the sequence in which they were actually written, allowing eleven days' difference between 'new style' letters from the Continent, and 'old style' letters from England.

If more than one letter was written on any given day, the headings for the letters of that day are arranged alphabetically by names of correspondents.

If a letter can merely be assigned to a certain year or month, it is listed at the beginning of the letters for that year or month.

Later information has sometimes caused us to change the dating of certain letters which were printed in our earlier volumes. In the present list, we assign such letters to the corrected dates, even though the reader may yet be referred to the places originally assigned to those letters. When a letter has been completely reprinted in more correct form in one of the later volumes, the present list gives only the location of the correct text, but when mere corrections or additions are printed in the later volumes, the page numbers of both the original printings and the corrections or additions are included.

Certain letters cannot be given even approximate dates, and are therefore grouped at the end, alphabetically arranged according to correspondents' names.

1725	1725			to Lady Walpole	**36.**	1
	1725 *bis*			to Lady Walpole	**36.**	2
1733	28	Sept.	OS	to Lady Walpole	**36.**	3
	30	Sept.	OS	to Lady Walpole	**36.**	4
1734	ca 16	April	OS	from Gray	**13.**	56
	28	Aug.	OS	to Charles Lyttelton	**40.**	1

	31	Oct.	OS	from Gray	13.	57
	17	Nov.	OS	from Gray	13.	61
	8	Dec.	OS	from Gray	13.	65
	23	Dec.	OS	from Gray	13.	67
	ca 29	Dec.	OS	from Gray	13.	68
1735	6	Jan.	OS	from Gray	13.	70
	12	Jan.	OS	from Gray	13.	72
	14	Jan.	OS	from Gray	13.	73
	19	Jan.	OS	from Gray	13.	75
	21	Jan.	OS	from Gray	13.	76
	27	Jan.	OS	from Gray	13.	77
	4	Feb.	OS	from Gray	13.	79
	25	Feb.	OS	from Gray	13.	81
	5	March	OS	from Gray	13.	82
	3	July	OS	from Gray	13.	83
	7	Aug.	OS	to Charles Lyttelton	40.	2
	10	Aug.	OS	from John Whaley	40.	3
	18	Aug.	OS	to Charles Lyttelton	40.	7
	27	Aug.	OS	from John Whaley	40.	8
	19	Sept.	OS	from John Whaley	40.	10
	3	Oct.	OS	from John Whaley	40.	13
	3	Oct.	OS	from John Dodd	40.	15
	11	Oct.	OS	from John Whaley	40.	15
	ca 15	Oct.	OS	to Gray	13.	85
	21	Oct.	OS	from Lord Hervey	40.	18
	29	Oct.	OS	from West	13.	90
	9	Nov.	OS	to West	13.	93
1736	3	Jan.	OS	from Gray	13.	95
	11	March	OS	from Gray	13.	98
	2	May	OS	to Montagu	9.	1
	6	May	OS	to Montagu	9.	2
	20	May	OS	to Montagu	9.	4
	22	May	OS	to Charles Lyttelton	40.	19
	30	May	OS	to Montagu	9.	6
	1	June	OS	from West	13.	99
	11	June	OS	from Gray	13.	101
	15	July	OS	from Gray	13.	103
	27	July	OS	to Charles Lyttelton	40.	21
	27	July	OS	to Sir Robert Walpole	36.	5
		Aug.		from Gray	13.	105
	17	Aug.	OS	to West	13.	107
	ca 20	Aug.	OS	from West	13.	109
	19	Sept.	OS	from John Whaley	40.	21
	26	Sept.	OS	from Gray	13.	111

	6	Oct.	OS	from Gray	13.	113
	13	Oct.	OS	from Gray	13.	114
	27	Oct.	OS	from Gray	13.	115
	31	Oct.	OS	from West	13.	116
	25	Dec.	OS	from Middleton	15.	1
	29	Dec.	OS	from Gray	13.	119
	30	Dec.	OS	to Middleton	15.	3
1737	3	Jan.	OS	to West	13.	120
	12	Jan.	OS	from West	13.	123
	16	Jan.	OS	from Gray	13.	125
	25	Jan.	OS	from Conway	37.	1
	1	Feb.	OS	from Conway	37.	4
	8	Feb.	OS	from Conway	37.	6
	15	Feb.	OS	from Conway	37.	10
	26	Feb.	OS	from Conway	37.	12
	27	Feb.	OS	from West	13.	127
ca	8	March	OS	from Conway	37.	13
	20	March	OS	to Montagu	9.	9
	22	March	OS	from Conway	37.	15
	7	April	OS	from Conway	37.	18
	18	April	OS	from West	13.	128
?1737	5	[? May ?1737]	OS	from Conway	37.	20
1737	10	May	OS	from Conway	37.	23
ca 20–4		May	OS	from Conway	37.	24
	31	May	OS	from Conway	37.	26
	11	June	OS	from Conway	37.	27
	23	June	OS	from Conway	37.	29
	2	July	OS	from Conway	37.	30
	12	July	OS	from West	13.	133
ca 16		July	OS	from Gray	13.	136
	7	Aug.	OS	from Ashton	13.	138
ca 22		Aug.	OS	from Gray	13.	140
	25	Aug.	OS	from Middleton	15.	4
	10	Sept.	OS	from Conway	37.	33
	18	Sept.	OS	to Charles Lyttelton	40.	23
ca 28		Sept.	OS	from Conway	37.	35
	2	Nov.	OS	from James Anstey	40.	24
ca 12		Nov.	OS	from Gray	13.	141
ca 20		Nov.	OS	from Conway	37.	36
	1	Dec.	OS	from West	13.	144
?1738	[?1738]			from Mrs Porter	40.	26
1737	29	Dec. 1737	OS	from Gray	13.	145
1738	10	Jan.	OS	from Gray	13.	146
	15	Jan.	OS	from Gray	13.	148
	23	Feb.	OS	from Gray	13.	151

	7	March	OS	from Gray	**13.** 152
	20	March	OS	from Gray	**13.** 154
	28	March	OS	from Gray	**13.** 155
	7	Sept.	OS	from West	**13.** 157
	19	Sept.	OS	from Gray	**13.** 161
1739	24	March	NS	from Conway	**37.** 38
	21	April	NS	to West	**13.** 162
	ca May			from John Selwyn	
				the Younger	**40.** 27
ca 15		May	NS	to West	**13.** 167
	18	June	NS	to West	**13.** 170
	21	June	OS	from West	**13.** 172
		July		to Ashton	**13.** 176,
					43. 391
	20	July	NS	to West	**13.** 177
ca	1	Sept.	NS	to Middleton	**15.** 6
	28	Sept.	NS	to West	**13.** 180
	24	Sept.	OS	from West	**13.** 184
	15	Oct.	OS	from West	**13.** 185
	11	Nov.	NS	to West	**13.** 188
	18	Nov.	NS	from Conway	**37.** 43
	21	Nov.	NS	to Lincoln	**30.** 1
	14	Dec.	NS	to West	**13.** 192
	13	Dec.	OS	from West	**13.** 195
ca 1740	ca 1740			to Unknown	**40.** 29
1740	24	Jan.	NS	to West	**13.** 199
	23	Jan.	OS	from West	**13.** 197
ca 25		Feb.	NS	from Conway	**37.** 45
	27	Feb.	NS	to West	**13.** 200
	6	March	NS	to Conway	**37.** 48
	6	March	OS	from Conway	**37.** 49,
					43. 372
	22	March	NS	to West	**13.** 203
	24	March	OS	from Conway	**37.** 52
	16	April	NS	to Mann	**17.** 2
	16	April	NS	to West	**13.** 206
	23	April	NS	to Conway	**37.** 56
	23	April	NS	to Mann	**17.** 6
	26	April	NS	to Mann	**17.** 13
	30	April	NS	to Mann	**17.** 15
	2	May	NS	to Mann	**17.** 18
	7	May	NS	to West	**13.** 211
	14	May	NS	to Ashton	**13.** 214
	14	May	NS	to Mann	**17.** 21
	14	May	NS *bis*	to Mann	**17.** 23

	21	May	NS	to Mann	17. 26
	14	May	OS	from Conway	37. 59
	28	May	NS	to Ashton	13. 219
	4	June	NS	to Mann	17. 27
	14	June	NS	to West	13. 222
	9	June	OS	from Conway	37. 63
	3	July	NS	from Cardinal Albani	40. 29
	5	July	NS	to Conway	37. 66
	31	July	NS	to West	13. 225
before	23	Aug.	OS	from Conway	37. 72
	24	Sept.	NS	from Mark Parker	26. 3
	25	Sept.	NS	to Conway	37. 77
	2	Oct.	NS	to West	13. 229
	19	Oct.	NS	from the Prince de Beauvau	40. 30
	10	Nov.	OS	from West	13. 234
	3	Dec.	NS	from Giovanni Battista Maria Uguccioni	40. 32
	4	Dec.	NS	to West	13. 236
ca	30	Nov.	OS	from Conway	37. 80
	13	Dec.	NS	from Vittoria Tesi	40. 33
	27	Dec.	NS	to Lincoln	30. 3
1741	3	Jan.	NS	to Lincoln	30. 7
	19	Jan.	OS	from Conway	37. 85
	31	Jan.	NS	to Lincoln	30. 9
	21	Feb.	NS	to the Rev. Joseph Spence	40. 34
	12	Feb.	OS	from Conway	37. 88
	16	Feb.	OS	from Conway	37. 89
ca	21	Feb.	OS	from Conway	37. 94
	25	March	NS	to Conway	37. 95
	?	April		from Mann	17. 30
	29	March	OS	from West	13. 239
	18	April	NS	to Lincoln	30. 13
	25	April	NS	from Mann	17. 31
	29	April	NS	to Lincoln	30. 16
	2	May	NS	from Mann	17. 32, 43. 234
	9	May	NS	from Mann	17. 36
	10	May	NS	to West	13. 241
	18	May	NS	to Mann	17. 42
	23	May	NS	from Mann	17. 47, 43. 235

	30	May	NS	from Mann	**17.** 51,
					43. 235
	3	June	NS	from Mann	**17.** 54
	10	June	NS	from Mann	**17.** 58
	17	June	NS	from Mann	**17.** 64
	24	June	NS	from Mann	**17.** 69
	29	June	NS	to Mann	**17.** 74
	1	July	NS	from Mann	**17.** 77,
					43. 236
	22	June	OS	from West	**13.** 243
ca	5	July	NS	to Mann	**17.** 84
	8	July	NS	from Mann	**17.** 86
	15	July	NS	from Mann	**17.** 88,
					43. 236
	18	July	NS	from Mann	**17.** 89
	18	July	NS	from Cocchi	**17.** 90
	19	July	NS	to Mann	**17.** 91
	23	July	NS	from Mann	**17.** 93
	30	July	NS	from Mann	**17.** 96
ca	23	July	OS	from Conway	**37.** 99
	25	July	OS	from Ashton	**13.** 246
	6	Aug.	NS	from Mann	**17.** 99
	12	Aug.	NS	from Mann	**17.** 103
	6	Aug.	OS	from Conway	**37.** 101
	21	Aug.	NS	from Mann	**17.** 106
	22	Aug.	NS	from Chute	**35.** 3
	22	Aug.	NS	from Mann	**17.** 113
	27	Aug.	NS	from Mann	**17.** 115
	2	Sept.	NS	from Mann	**17.** 118
	5	Sept.	NS	to Mann	**17.** 124
	10	Sept.	NS	from Mann	**17.** 127
	16	Sept.	NS	to Lincoln	**30.** 18
	17	Sept.	NS	from Mann	**17.** 131
ca	9	Sept.	OS	from Conway	**37.** 105
	11	Sept.	OS	to Mann	**17.** 140
	13	Sept.	OS	to Lincoln	**30.** 19
	24	Sept.	NS	from Mann	**17.** 143
	18	Sept.	OS	to Lincoln	**30.** 22
?19		Sept.	OS	from Conway	**37.** 107
ca	1	Oct.	NS	from Chute	**35.** 7
	1	Oct.	NS	from Mann	**17.** 148,
					43. 238
ca	21	Sept.	OS	to Conway	**37.** 109
	8	Oct.	NS	from Mann	**17.** 153
	1	Oct.	OS	to Lincoln	**30.** 26

		15	Oct.	NS	from Mann	17. 160
	ca	5	Oct.	OS	to Mann	17. 163
		8	Oct.	OS	to Mann	17. 164
		13	Oct.	OS	to Lincoln	30. 28
		13	Oct.	OS	to Mann	17. 169
		19	Oct.	OS	to Mann	17. 170
		22	Oct.	OS	to Mann	17. 172
		26	Oct.	OS	from Conway	37. 111
		31	Oct.	OS	to Conway	37. 113
		11	Nov.	NS	from Mann	17. 178, 43. 238
		2	Nov.	OS	to Mann	17. 183
	ca	15	Nov.	NS	from Chute	35. 10
		5	Nov.	OS	to Mann	17. 190, 43. 239
		19	Nov.	NS	from Mann	17. 192
		12	Nov.	OS	to Mann	17. 196
		26	Nov.	NS	from Mann	17. 197, 43. 239
		2	Dec.	NS	from Mann	17. 201, 43. 239
		22	Nov.	OS	to Middleton	15. 8
		23	Nov.	OS	to Mann	17. 208
		26	Nov.	OS	to Mann	17. 212
		10	Dec.	NS	from Mann	17. 213
		3	Dec.	OS	to Mann	17. 219
		17	Dec.	NS	from Mann	17. 222
		19	Dec.	NS	from Mann	17. 227
		10	Dec.	OS	to Mann	17. 230
		24	Dec.	NS	from Mann	17. 235
		25	Dec.	NS	from Chute	35. 13
		16	Dec.	OS	to Mann	17. 242
		17	Dec.	OS	to Mann	17. 246
1742		1	Jan.	NS	from Chute	35. 16
1741		24	Dec. 1741	OS	to Mann	17. 249
1741		29	Dec. 1741	OS	to Mann	17. 256
1741		29	Dec. 1741	OS	to Chute	17. 257
1742		10	Jan.	NS	from Mann	17. 258
		16	Jan.	NS	from Mann	17. 264
		7	Jan.	OS	to Mann	17. 270
		21	Jan.	NS	from Mann	17. 280
		28	Jan.	NS	from Mann	17. 286
		22	Jan.	OS	to Mann	17. 294
		3	Feb.	NS	from Mann	17. 303
		6	Feb.	NS	from Mann	17. 311

11	Feb.	NS	from Mann	**17.** 313
13	Feb.	NS	from Chute	**35.** 18
4	Feb.	OS	to Mann	**17.** 318
18	Feb.	NS	from Mann	**17.** 321
9	Feb.	OS	to Mann	**17.** 328
18	Feb.	OS	to Mann	**17.** 335
5	March	NS	from Mann	**17.** 340
5	March	NS	from Chute	**35.** 22
25	Feb.	OS	to Mann	**17.** 343
11	March	NS	from Mann	**17.** 348
3	March	OS	to Mann	**17.** 352
18	March	NS	from Mann	**17.** 360
10	March	OS	to Mann	**17.** 362
10	March	OS	to Chute	**17.** 365
25	March	NS	from Mann	**17.** 367
1	April	NS	from Mann	**17.** 369
22	March	OS	to Mann	**17.** 372
24	March	OS	to Mann	**17.** 375
8	April	NS	from Mann	**17.** 379
1	April	OS	to Mann	**17.** 382
17	April	NS	from Chute	**35.** 24
17	April	NS	from Mann	**17.** 387
8	April	OS	to Mann	**17.** 389
22	April	NS	from Mann	**17.** 393
15	April	OS	to Mann	**17.** 396
22	April	OS	to Mann	**17.** 399
7	May	NS	from Mann	**17.** 402
29	April	OS	to Mann	**17.** 409
15	May	NS	from Mann	**17.** 412
4	May	OS	to West	**13.** 247
6	May	OS	to Mann	**17.** 418
20	May	NS	from Mann	**17.** 421
13	May	OS	to Mann	**17.** 425
27	May	NS	from Mann	**17.** 426
17	May	OS	to Henry Pelham	**40.** 36
20	May	OS	to Mann	**17.** 428
3	June	NS	from Mann	**17.** 432
26	May	OS	to Mann	**17.** 434
3	June	OS	to Mann	**17.** 441
17	June	NS	from Mann	**17.** 442
20	June	NS	from Mann	**17.** 447
10	June	OS	to Mann	**17.** 450
24	June	NS	from Chute	**35.** 27
24	June	NS	from Mann	**17.** 453
17	June	OS	to Mann	**17.** 456

1	July	NS	from Mann	**17.** 460,	
				43. 245	
24	June	OS	to Mann	**17.** 466	
8	July	NS	from Mann	**17.** 470	
9	July	NS	from the Princesse de Craon	**40.** 37	
9	July	NS	from the Prince de Craon	**40.** 38	
30	June	OS	to Mann	**17.** 475	
15	July	NS	from Mann	**17.** 480	
7	July	OS	to Mann	**17.** 484	
22	July	NS	from Mann	**17.** 488	
14	July	OS	to Mann	**17.** 491	
16	July	OS	from Henry Pelham	**40.** 39	
29	July	NS	from Chute	**35.** 31	
29	July	NS	from Mann	**17.** 497	
31	July	NS	from Conway	**37.** 117	
ca 21	July	OS	to Mann	**17.** 502	
5	Aug.	NS	from Mann	**18.** 1	
29	July	OS	to Mann	**18.** 7	
12	Aug.	NS	from Mann	**18.** 9	
19	Aug.	NS	from Mann	**18.** 14	
ca 9	Aug.	OS	to Mann	**18.** 18	
26	Aug.	NS	from Mann	**18.** 26	
29	Aug.	NS	from Conway	**37.** 120	
20	Aug.	OS	to Mann	**18.** 29	
23	Aug.	OS	to Lincoln	**30.** 32	
28	Aug.	OS	to Mann	**18.** 31,	
				43. 247	
10	Sept.	NS	from Mann	**18.** 37	
15	Sept.	NS	from Conway	**37.** 123	
16	Sept.	NS	from Mann	**18.** 44	
11	Sept.	OS	to Mann	**18.** 47	
23	Sept.	NS	from Mann	**18.** 54	
26	Sept.	NS	from Conway	**37.** 126	
18	Sept.	OS	to Lincoln	**30.** 34	
30	Sept.	NS	from Mann	**18.** 57	
25	Sept.	OS	to Mann	**18.** 60	
29	Sept.	OS	from Conway	**37.** 128	
15	Oct.	NS	from Mann	**18.** 64	
8	Oct.	OS	to Mann	**18.** 68	
23	Oct.	NS	from Mann	**18.** 75	
24	Oct.	NS	from Conway	**37.** 131	
16	Oct.	OS	to Mann	**18.** 79	
30	Oct.	NS	from Mann	**18.** 84	

	23	Oct.	OS	to Mann	**18.** 88
	6	Nov.	NS	from Mann	**18.** 92
	1	Nov.	OS	to Mann	**18.** 94
	13	Nov.	NS	from Mann	**18.** 97
	20	Nov.	NS	from Mann	**18.** 99
	15	Nov.	OS	to Mann	**18.** 102
	27	Nov.	NS	from Mann	**18.** 105
	23	Nov.	OS	to Middleton	**15.** 10
	11	Dec.	NS	from Mann	**18.** 109
	2	Dec.	OS	to Mann	**18.** 117
	18	Dec.	NS	from Mann	**18.** 119
	9	Dec.	OS	to Mann	**18.** 122
?1743–1744	?1743–1744			to Lincoln	**30.** 43
1743	1	Jan.	NS	from Mann	**18.** 125
1742	23	Dec. 1742	OS	to Mann	**18.** 129
1743	7	Jan.	NS	from Mann	**18.** 132
	6	Jan.	OS	to Mann	**18.** 135
	22	Jan.	NS	from Mann	**18.** 138
	13	Jan.	OS	to Mann	**18.** 140
	29	Jan.	NS	from Mann	**18.** 144
	27	Jan.	OS	to Mann	**18.** 147
	12	Feb.	NS	from Mann	**18.** 149
	2	Feb.	OS	to Mann	**18.** 158
	18	Feb.	NS	from Mann	**18.** 159
	13	Feb.	OS	to Mann	**18.** 166
	26	Feb.	NS	from Mann	**18.** 168
	5	March	NS	from Mann	**18.** 176
	24	Feb.	OS	to Mann	**18.** 179
	12	March	NS	from Mann	**18.** 181
	3	March	OS	to Mann	**18.** 184
	19	March	NS	from Mann	**18.** 186
	14	March	OS	to Mann	**18.** 190
	26	March	NS	from Mann	**18.** 194
	2	April	NS	from Mann	**18.** 197
	25	March	OS	to Mann	**18.** 200
	4	April	OS	to Mann	**18.** 202
	15 or 22	April	NS	from Mann	**18.** 204
	9	April	OS	to Middleton	**15.** 11
	14	April	OS	to Mann	**18.** 208
	15	April	OS	from Middleton	**15.** 14
	30	April	NS	from Mann	**18.** 211
		May–Sept.		to Charles [? Lyttelton]	**40.** 40
	21	April	OS	to Middleton	**15.** 18
	25	April	OS	to Mann	**18.** 217

7	May	NS	from Chute	35.	34
7	May	NS	from Mann	18.	221
4	May	OS	to Mann	18.	224
21	May	NS	from Conway	37.	133
21	May	NS	from Mann	18.	226
12	May	OS	to Mann	18.	230
28	May	NS	from Mann	18.	233
19	May	OS	to Mann	18.	236
4	June	NS	from Chute	35.	37
4	June	NS	from Mann	18.	238
9	June	NS	from Conway	37.	135
11	June	NS	from Mann	18.	241
4	June	OS	to Mann	18.	244
10	June	OS	to Mann	18.	247
25	June	NS	from Mann	18.	251
20	June	OS	to Mann	18.	254
2	July	NS	from Mann	18.	256
22	June	OS	to Lincoln	30.	36
24	June	OS	to Mann	18.	258
25	June	OS	to Chute	35.	39
8	July	NS	from Conway	37.	139
9	July	NS	from Mann	18.	261
2	July	OS	to Lincoln	30.	38
4	July	OS	to Mann	18.	264
11	July	OS	to Mann	18.	267
23	July	NS	from Mann	18.	269
27	July	NS	from Conway	37.	141
27	July	NS	from Mann	18.	272
16	July	OS	from Sir Robert Walpole	36.	6
29	July	NS	from Chute	35.	40
29	July	NS	from Mann	18.	275
19	July	OS	to Mann	18.	275
6	Aug.	NS	from Mann	18.	278
28	July	OS	to Middleton	15.	20
31	July	OS	to Mann	18.	282
13	Aug.	NS	from Mann	18.	284
20	Aug.	NS	from Mann	18.	287
21	Aug.	NS	from Conway	37.	143
14	Aug.	OS	to Mann	18.	291
20	Aug.	OS	to Chute	35.	42
3	Sept.	NS	from Mann	18.	294
25	Aug.	OS	to Lincoln	30.	39
29	Aug.	OS	to Grosvenor Bedford	40.	41

	29	Aug.	OS	to Mann	**18.** 297
	11	Sept.	NS	from Conway	**37.** 145
	17	Sept.	NS	from Mann	**18.** 299
	7	Sept.	OS	to Mann	**18.** 304
	12	Sept.	OS	from John Whaley	**40.** 42
	24	Sept.	NS	from Mann	**18.** 307
	25	Sept.	NS	from Conway	**37.** 147
	17	Sept.	OS	to Mann	**18.** 310
	1	Oct.	NS	from Chute	**35.** 44
	1	Oct.	NS	from Mann	**18.** 312
	30	Sept.	OS	from the Hon. Mary Townshend	**40.** 44
	3	Oct.	OS	to Mann	**18.** 315
	15	Oct.	NS	from Mann	**18.** 321
	22	Oct.	NS	from Mann	**18.** 324
	12	Oct.	OS	to Chute	**35.** 48
	12	Oct.	OS	to Mann	**18.** 326
	25	Oct.	NS	from Conway	**37.** 149
	27	Oct.	NS	from Mann	**18.** 328
	12	Nov.	NS	from Mann	**18.** 331, **43.** 251
	19	Nov.	NS	from Mann	**18.** 337
	17	Nov.	OS	to Mann	**18.** 340
	19	Nov.	OS	to Middleton	**15.** 21
	ca Dec.			to Mann	**18.** 367
	3	Dec.	NS	from Mann	**18.** 343
	10	Dec.	NS	from Mann	**18.** 347
	30	Nov.	OS	to Mann	**18.** 349
	17	Dec.	NS	from Mann	**18.** 352
	11	Dec.	OS	to Mann	**18.** 355
	31	Dec.	NS	from Mann	**18.** 358
1744	5	Jan.	NS	from Mann	**18.** 362
1743	26	Dec. 1743	OS	to Mann	**18.** 365
1743	27	Dec. 1743	OS	to Lincoln	**30.** 40
1744	14	Jan.	NS	from Mann	**18.** 368
	21	Jan.	NS	from Mann	**18.** 371
	22	Jan.	NS	from Mann	**18.** 374
	28	Jan.	NS	from Mann	**18.** 376
	24	Jan.	OS	to Mann	**18.** 381
	4	Feb.	NS	from Mann	**18.** 384
	18	Feb.	NS	from Mann	**18.** 389
	9	Feb.	OS	to Mann	**18.** 392
	25	Feb.	NS	from Mann	**18.** 394
	16	Feb.	OS	to Mann	**18.** 398
	23	Feb.	OS	to Mann	**18.** 401

10	March	NS	from Mann	**18.** 403
1	March	OS	to Mann	**18.** 407
5	March	OS	to Mann	**18.** 410
17	March	NS	from Mann	**18.** 411
15	March	OS	to Mann	**18.** 416
31	March	NS	from Mann	**18.** 417
22	March	OS	to Mann	**18.** 422
7	April	NS	from Mann	**18.** 425
2	April	OS	to Mann	**18.** 428
15	April	OS	to Mann	**18.** 430
28	April	NS	from Mann	**18.** 433
6	May	NS	from Mann	**18.** 437
8	May	OS	to Mann	**18.** 440
19	May	NS	from Mann	**18.** 442
2	June	NS	from Mann	**18.** 445
3	June	NS	from Conway	**37.** 152
29	May	OS	to Mann	**18.** 448
16	June	NS	from Mann	**18.** 452
11	June	OS	to Mann	**18.** 456
23	June	NS	from Mann	**18.** 459
18	June	OS	to Mann	**18.** 463
1	July	NS	from Conway	**37.** 155
6	July	NS	from Conway	**37.** 158
26	June	OS	to C. H. Williams	**30.** 48
29	June	OS	to Conway	**37.** 161
29	June	OS	to Mann	**18.** 466
17	July	NS	from Mann	**18.** 469
18	July	NS	from Conway	**37.** 165
7	July	OS	to C. H. Williams	**30.** 52
21	July	NS	from Mann	**18.** 476
14	July	OS	from Sir Robert Walpole	**36.** 8
17	July	OS	to C. H. Williams	**30.** 58
20	July	OS	to Conway	**37.** 168
22	July	OS	to Mann	**18.** 479
4	Aug.	NS	from Mann	**18.** 483
5	Aug.	NS	from Conway	**37.** 171
26	July	OS	to C. H. Williams	**30.** 63
15	Aug.	NS	from Chute	**35.** 51
16	Aug.	NS	from Mann	**18.** 486
6	Aug.	OS	to Mann	**18.** 494
7	Aug.	OS	to C. H. Williams	**30.** 64
10	Aug.	OS	from Edgcumbe	**30.** 65
14	Aug.	OS	to C. H. Williams	**30.** 67
16	Aug.	OS	to Mann	**18.** 498

	18	Aug.	OS	to Middleton	15. 23
	1	Sept.	NS	from Mann	18. 502
	2	Sept.	NS	from Conway	37. 175
	25	Aug.	OS	to Lincoln	30. 72
	25	Aug.	OS	to Lady Townshend	40. 46
	1	Sept.	OS	to Mann	18. 504
	5	Sept.	OS	to Lincoln	30. 75
	10	Sept.	OS	from Edgcumbe	30. 78
	22	Sept.	NS	from Mann	18. 506
	29	Sept.	NS	from Mann	18. 508
	19	Sept.	OS	to C. H. Williams	30. 80
	6	Oct.	NS	from Mann	18. 511
	7	Oct.	NS	from Conway	37. 178
	13	Oct.	NS	from Mann	18. 514
	6	Oct.	OS	to Conway	37. 180
	6	Oct.	OS	to Mann	18. 517
	19	Oct.	NS	from Conway	37. 182
	27	Oct.	NS	from Mann	18. 519
	28	Oct.	NS	from Conway	37. 184
	19	Oct.	OS	to Mann	18. 521
	31	Oct.	NS	from Conway	37. 186
	10	Nov.	NS	from Mann	18. 525
	9	Nov.	OS	to Mann	18. 527
	24	Nov.	NS	from Mann	18. 529
	22	Nov.	OS	to Middleton	15. 24
	26	Nov.	OS	to Mann	18. 535
	8	Dec.	NS	from Mann	18. 541
	4	Dec.	OS	from John Whaley	40. 48
	22	Dec.	NS	from Mann	18. 546
	24	Dec.	OS	to Mann	18. 549
1745	5	Jan.	NS	from Chute	35. 54
	5	Jan.	NS	from Mann	18. 553, 43. 256
	12	Jan.	NS	from Mann	18. 557
	4	Jan.	OS	to Mann	18. 560
	14	Jan.	OS	to Mann	18. 563
	26	Jan.	NS	from Mann	19. 1
	27	Jan.	OS	from Thomas Copleston	40. 50
	1	Feb.	OS	to Mann	19. 4
	16	Feb.	NS	from Mann	19. 6, 43. 256
	ca	March		to Lady Townshend	40. 51
	9	March	NS	from Mann	19. 9
	28	Feb.	OS	to Mann	19. 16

23	March	NS	from Mann	19.	21
6	April	NS	from Mann	19.	21
29	March	OS	to Mann	19.	24
20	April	NS	from Mann	19.	29
15	April	OS	to Mann	19.	31
18	April	OS	from Conway	37.	187
1	May	NS	from the Prince de Craon	40.	53
4	May	NS	from Mann	19.	34
29	April	OS	to Mann	19.	38
14	May	NS	from Conway	37.	190
18	May	NS	from Mann	19.	40
7	May	OS	to Horatio Walpole, Sr	36.	10
ca 11	May	OS	to Montagu	9.	11
11	May	OS	to Mann	19.	42,
				43.	257
25	May	NS	from Mann	19.	46
26	May	NS	from Conway	37.	193
15	May	OS	from Sir Edward Walpole	36.	14
ca 16	May	OS	to Sir Edward Walpole	36.	16
17	May	OS	to Sir Edward Walpole	36.	21
18	May	OS	to Montagu	9.	12
	June		to Mann	19.	60
1	June	NS	from Mann	19.	48
24	May	OS	to Mann	19.	52
25	May	OS	to Montagu	9.	13
27	May	OS	to Conway	37.	195
30	May	OS	to C. H. Williams	30.	83
15	June	NS	from Mann	19.	54
21	June	NS	from Conway	37.	197
26	June	NS	from Chute	35.	57
29	June	NS	from Mann	19.	56
24	June	OS	to Mann	19.	60
25	June	OS	to Montagu	9.	14
25	June	OS	to C. H. Williams	30.	86
1	July	OS	to Conway	37.	200
13	July	NS	from Mann	19.	64
5	July	OS	to Mann	19.	67
12	July	OS	to Mann	19.	70
13	July	OS	to Montagu	9.	17
15	July	OS	to Mann	19.	73

27	July	NS	from Mann	19.	75
26	July	OS	to Mann	19.	77
28	July	OS	from Montagu	9.	20
10	Aug.	NS	from Conway	37.	203
10	Aug.	NS	from Mann	19.	79
1	Aug.	OS	to Montagu	9.	21
17	Aug.	NS	from Mann	19.	86
6	Aug.	OS	to C. H. Williams	30.	90
7	Aug.	OS	to Mann	19.	90
24	Aug.	NS	from Mann	19.	93
28	Aug.	NS	from Chute	35.	60
30	Aug.	NS	from Conway	37.	206
31	Aug.	NS	from Mann	19.	95
7	Sept.	NS	from Mann	19.	98
6	Sept.	OS	to Mann	19.	101
7	Sept.	OS	to C. H. Williams	30.	94
13	Sept.	OS	to Mann	19.	104
17	Sept.	OS	to Montagu	9.	23
20	Sept.	OS	to Mann	19.	108
21	Sept.	OS	to C. H. Williams	30.	96
5	Oct.	NS	from Mann	19.	112
26	Sept.	OS	from Lord Edgcumbe	40.	53
27	Sept.	OS	to Mann	19.	116
12	Oct.	NS	from Mann	19.	119
4	Oct.	OS	to Mann	19.	125
19	Oct.	NS	from Mann	19.	130
11	Oct.	OS	to Mann	19.	133
25	Oct.	NS	from Conway	37.	208
26	Oct.	NS	from Mann	19. 135, 43.	259
21	Oct.	OS	to Mann	19.	137
9	Nov.	NS	from Mann	19.	140
10	Nov.	NS	from Mann	19.	145
4	Nov.	OS	to Mann	19.	152
23	Nov.	NS	from Mann	19.	155
15	Nov.	OS	to Mann	19.	158
30	Nov.	NS	from Mann	19.	162
22	Nov.	OS	to Mann	19.	165
7	Dec.	NS	from Mann	19.	169
29	Nov.	OS	to Mann	19.	172
30	Nov.	OS	from Conway	37.	210
9	Dec.	OS	to Mann	19.	178
21	Dec.	NS	from Mann	19.	182
13	Dec.	OS	from Conway	37.	213

	18	Dec.	OS	from the Hon. Ed- ward Cornwallis	40.	55
	20	Dec.	OS	to Mann	19.	182
1746	4	Jan.	NS	from Mann	19.	190
	3	Jan.	OS	to Mann	19.	193
	18	Jan.	NS	from Mann	19.	196
	25	Jan.	NS	from Mann	19.	197
	17	Jan.	OS	to Mann	19.	201
	28	Jan.	OS	to Mann	19.	203
	3	Feb.	OS	from Gray	14.	1
	15	Feb.	NS	from Mann	19.	205
	7	Feb.	OS	from Conway	37.	216
	7	Feb.	OS	to Mann	19.	207
	14	Feb.	OS	to Mann	19.	210
	1	March	NS	from Mann	19.	214
	19	Feb.	OS	from Conway	37.	220
	3	March	OS	from Conway	37.	223
	15	March	NS	from Mann	19.	217
	6	March	OS	to Conway	37.	225
	6	March	OS	to Mann	19.	221
	22	March	NS	from Mann	19.	225
	19	March	OS	from Conway	37.	227
	21	March	OS	to Mann	19.	228
	5	April	NS	from Mann	19.	230
	28	March	OS	from Gray	14.	4
	28	March	OS	to Mann	19.	233
	30	March	OS	from Conway	37.	231
	6	April	OS	from Conway	37.	233
	19	April	NS	from Mann	19.	235
	15	April	OS	to Mann	19.	239
	26	April	NS	from Mann	19.	244
	18	April	OS	from Conway	37.	238
	25	April	OS	to Mann	19.	246
	7	May	NS	from Mann	19.	251
	7	May	OS	from Conway	37.	242
	24	May	NS	from Mann	19.	252
	16	May	OS	to Mann	19.	254
	31	May	NS	from Mann	19.	256
	21	May	OS	from Conway	37.	248
	22	May	OS	to Montagu	9.	25
	14	June	NS	from Mann	19.	260
	5	June	OS	to Montagu	9.	26
	6	June	OS	to Mann	19.	263
	21	June	NS	from John Hobart	40.	56
	21	June	NS	from Mann	19.	265

	12	June	OS	to Montagu	**9.** 29
	28	June	NS	from Mann	**19.** 268
	17	June	OS	to Montagu	**9.** 31
	20	June	OS	to Mann	**19.** 271
	24	June	OS	to Montagu	**9.** 33
	3	July	OS	to Montagu	**9.** 36
?1746	7	July [?1746]	OS	from Gray	**14.** 5
1746	7	July	OS	to Mann	**19.** 273
	19	July	NS	from Mann	**19.** 275
	19	July	OS	to Fox	**30.** 99
	22	July	OS	from Fox	**30.** 102
	24	July	OS	to Fox	**30.** 104
	9	Aug.	NS	from Mann	**19.** 277
	1	Aug.	OS	to Mann	**19.** 280
	2	Aug.	OS	to Montagu	**9.** 38
	5	Aug.	OS	to Montagu	**9.** 40
ca 8		Aug.	OS	to Montagu	**9.** 43
	11	Aug.	OS	to Montagu	**9.** 44
	12	Aug.	OS	from Conway	**37.** 250
	23	Aug.	NS	from Mann	**19.** 290
	12	Aug.	OS	to Mann	**19.** 293
	16	Aug.	OS	to Montagu	**9.** 45
	30	Aug.	NS	from Mann	**19.** 297
	21	Aug.	OS	to Mann	**19.** 298
	6	Sept.	NS	from Mann	**19.** 303
	29	Aug.	OS	from Conway	**37.** 254
	13	Sept.	NS	from Mann	**19.** 305
	15	Sept.	OS	to Mann	**19.** 307
	27	Sept.	NS	from Mann	**19.** 310
	24	Sept.	OS	from Conway	**37.** 256
	2	Oct.	OS	to Mann	**19.** 316
	3	Oct.	OS	to Conway	**37.** 258
	9	Oct.	OS	to Fox	**30.** 106, **43.** 314
	9	Oct.	OS	from Fox	**30.** 107
	14	Oct.	OS	to Mann	**19.** 318
	25	Oct.	NS	from Mann	**19.** 321
	18	Oct.	OS	from Conway	**37.** 259
	20	Oct.	OS	from Gray	**14.** 6
	24	Oct.	OS	to Conway	**37.** 260
	3	Nov.	OS	to Montagu	**9.** 48
	4	Nov.	OS	to Mann	**19.** 326
	5	Nov.	OS	from Conway	**37.** 263
	22	Nov.	NS	from Mann	**19.** 329
	12	Nov.	OS	to Mann	**19.** 331

		6	Dec.	NS	from Mann	**19.** 333
		13	Dec.	NS	from Mann	**19.** 335
		5	Dec.	OS	to Mann	**19.** 339
		20	Dec.	NS	from Mann	**19.** 343
		15	Dec.	OS	from Gray	**14.** 9
1747			Jan.		from Gray	**14.** 11
1746		25	Dec. 1746	OS	to Mann	**19.** 346
1747		10	Jan.	NS	from Mann	**19.** 348
		31	Jan.	NS	from Mann	**19.** 354
		27	Jan.	OS	to Mann	**19.** 360
		14	Feb.	NS	from Mann	**19.** 362
		8	Feb.	OS	from Gray	**14.** 13
		28	Feb.	NS	from Mann	**19.** 365
	ca	19	Feb.	OS	from Gray	**14.** 18
		21	Feb.	OS	to Middleton	**15.** 25
	ca	22	Feb.	OS	from Gray	**14.** 21
		23	Feb.	OS	to Mann	**19.** 369
		7	March	NS	from Mann	**19.** 372
		1	March	OS	from Gray	**14.** 22
		14	March	NS	from Mann	**19.** 375
		21	March	NS	from Mann	**19.** 377
		20	March	OS	to Mann	**19.** 379
		11	April	NS	from Mann	**19.** 382
		15	April	NS	from Conway	**37.** 264
		10	April	OS	to Mann	**19.** 386
		25	April	NS	from Mann	**19.** 391
		16	April	OS	to Conway	**37.** 266
		5	May	OS	to Mann	**19.** 394
		16	May	NS	from Mann	**19.** 399
		12	May	OS	from Gray	**14.** 25
		19	May	OS	to Mann	**19.** 402
		6	June	NS	from Mann	**19.** 405
		12	June	NS	from Conway	**37.** 272
		13	June	NS	from Mann	**19.** 408
		5	June	OS	to Mann	**19.** 412
		8	June	OS	to Conway	**37.** 269
	ca	15	June	OS	from Gray	**14.** 26
		27	June	NS	from Mann	**19.** 415
		26	June	OS	to Mann	**19.** 418
		8	July	NS	from Lord Hobart	**40.** 57
		9	July	NS	from Conway	**37.** 273
		11	July	NS	from Mann	**19.** 421
		1	July	OS	from Stephen Poyntz	**40.** 58
		2	July	OS	to Montagu	**9.** 49
		3	July	OS	to Mann	**19.** 423

	1	Aug.	NS	from Mann	**19.** 425
	28	July	OS	to Mann	**19.** 428
	14	Aug.	NS	from Conway	**37.** 275
	22	Aug.	NS	from Mann	**19.** 430
	19 or 26	Aug.	OS	from Gray	**14.** 30
	1	Sept.	OS	to Mann	**19.** 434
	19	Sept.	NS	from Mann	**19.** 436
	9	Sept.	OS	from Gray	**14.** 31
	5	Oct.	NS	from Conway	**37.** 277
	10	Oct.	NS	from Mann	**19.** 439
	1	Oct.	OS	to Montagu	**9.** 51
	2	Oct.	OS	to Mann	**19.** 442
ca	5	Oct.	OS	to Montagu	**9.** 53
	7	Nov.	NS	from Mann	**19.** 443
	30	Oct.	OS	from Fox	**30.** 110
	?10	Nov.	OS	from Gray	**14.** 32
	10	Nov.	OS	to Mann	**19.** 445
	24	Nov.	OS	to Mann	**19.** 447
	19	Dec.	NS	from Mann	**19.** 450
1748	ca	Jan.		from Gray	**14.** 34
	9	Jan.	NS	from Mann	**19.** 453
	12	Jan.	OS	to Mann	**19.** 455
	26	Jan.	OS	to Mann	**19.** 457
	6	Feb.	NS	from Mann	**19.** 460
	16	Feb.	OS	to Mann	**19.** 463
	27	Feb.	NS	from Mann	**19.** 465
	11	March	OS	to Mann	**19.** 467
	26	March	NS	from Mann	**19.** 471
	28	March	OS	from Fox	**30.** 112
	9	April	NS	from Mann	**19.** 474
	29	April	NS	from Conway	**37.** 281
	7	May	NS	from Mann	**19.** 476
	29	April	OS	to Mann	**19.** 479
	18	May	OS	to Montagu	**9.** 54
	26	May	OS	to Montagu	**9.** 57
	7	June	OS	to Mann	**19.** 484
	24	June	NS	from Conway	**37.** 284
	2	July	NS	from Mann	**19.** 486
	27	June	OS	to Conway	**37.** 287
	27	June	OS	to C. H. Williams	**30.** 113
	23	July	NS	from Mann	**19.** 489
	14	July	OS	to Mann	**19.** 494
	14	July	OS	to Montagu	**9.** 59
	25	July	OS	to Montagu	**9.** 63
	ca	Aug.		to Mann	**19.** 495

	13	Aug.	NS	from Mann	**19.**	497
	11	Aug.	OS	to Montagu	**9.**	67
	1	Sept.	NS	from Conway	**37.**	290
	3	Sept.	NS	from Mann	**19.**	500
	29	Aug.	OS	to Conway	**37.**	292
	3	Sept.	OS	to Montagu	**9.**	73
	18	Sept.	OS	to Mann	**19.**	502
	23	Sept.	OS	from Lord Chedworth	**40.**	59
	25	Sept.	OS	to Montagu	**9.**	77
	9	Oct.	NS	from Conway	**37.**	295
	11	Oct.	NS	from Mann	**19.**	504
	6	Oct.	OS	to Conway	**37.**	296
	25	Oct.	NS	from Mann	**19.**	507
	20	Oct.	OS	to Fox	**30.**	116
	20	Oct.	OS	to Montagu	**9.**	79
	24	Oct.	OS	to Mann	**19.**	510
	3	Nov.	OS	from Chute	**35.**	65
	15	Nov.	NS	from Mann	**20.**	1
	2	Dec.	OS	to Mann	**20.**	3
	13	Dec.	NS	from Mann	**20.** 6, **43.**	265
?1748	3	Dec. [?1748]	OS	from Mrs Clive	**40.**	61
1748	15	Dec.	OS	to Mann	**20.**	8
1749	1749			to the Rev. Joseph Spence	**40.**	62
	3	Jan.	NS	from Mann	**20.**	14
1748	26	Dec. 1748	OS	to Mann	**20.**	16
1749	31	Jan.	NS	from Mann	**20.**	22
	7	Feb.	NS	from Mann	**20.**	24
	8	March	NS	from Mann	**20.**	26
	4	March	OS	to Mann	**20.**	30
	21	March	NS	from Mann	**20.**	34
	25	March	NS	from Mann	**20.**	37
	23	March	OS	to Mann	**20.**	38
	18	April	NS	from Mann	**20.**	42
	3	May	OS	to Mann	**20.**	46
	23	May	NS	from Mann	**20.**	54
	17	May	OS	to Mann	**20.**	56
	18	May	OS	to Montagu	**9.**	80
	29	May	OS	from Sir Edward Walpole	**36.**	22
	4	June	OS	to Mann	**20.**	63
	19	June	NS	from Mann	**20.**	67
	20	June	NS	from Mann	**20.**	68

25	June	OS	to Mann	**20.**	71
5	July	OS	to Montagu	**9.**	87
25	July	NS	from Mann	**20.**	75
20	July	OS	to Montagu	**9.**	91
24	July	OS	to Mann	**20.**	79
15	Aug.	NS	from Mann	**20.**	82
26	Aug.	NS	from Mann	**20.**	85
17	Aug.	OS	to Mann	**20.**	87
26	Aug.	OS	to Montagu	**9.**	96
12	Sept.	OS	to Mann	**20.**	89
14	Sept.	OS	from Conway	**37.**	298
22	Sept.	OS	to ? Selwyn	**30.**	117
23	Sept.	OS	to C. H. Williams	**30.**	118
ca 25	Sept.	OS	from Montagu	**9.**	100,
				43.	115
28	Sept.	OS	to Montagu	**9.**	101
10	Oct.	NS	from Mann	**20.**	91
7	Nov.	NS	from Mann	**20.**	94
27	Oct.	OS	to Mann	**20.**	96
10	Nov.	OS	from James Maclaine	**40.**	63
12	Nov.	OS	from Gray	**14.**	42
28	Nov.	NS	from Mann	**20.**	97
17	Nov.	OS	to Mann	**20.**	99
ca 12	Dec.	NS	from Mann	**20.**	101
1750	2	Jan.	NS	from Mann	**20.**	103
10	Jan.	OS	to Mann	**20.**	106
31	Jan.	OS	to Mann	**20.**	111
13	Feb.	NS	from Mann	**20.**	114
11	Feb.	OS	to the Duke of Bedford	**40.**	65
25	Feb.	OS	to Mann	**20.**	119
13	March	NS	from Mann	**20.**	127
11	March	OS	to Mann	**20.**	130
2	April	OS	to Mann	**20.**	133
17	April	NS	from Mann	**20.**	143
8	May	NS	from Mann	**20.**	146
22	May	NS	from Mann	**20.**	149
15	May	OS	to Montagu	**9.**	103
19	May	OS	to Mann	**20.**	154
12	June	OS	from Gray	**14.**	43
26	June	NS	from Mann	**20.**	158
23	June	OS	to Montagu	**9.**	105
28	June	OS	from Conway	**37.**	300
18	July	NS	from Mann	**20.**	160

	17	July	OS	from Conway	**37.** 302
	25	July	OS	to Mann	**20.** 162
	2	Aug.	OS	to Mann	**20.** 165
	21	Aug.	NS	from Mann	**20.** 171
	31	Aug.	NS	from Mann	**20.** 174
	4	Sept.	NS	from Mann	**20.** 176
	1	Sept.	OS	to Mann	**20.** 179
	10	Sept.	OS	to Montagu	**9.** 111
	20	Sept.	OS	to Mann	**20.** 185
	2	Oct.	NS	from Mann	**20.** 189
	9	Oct.	NS	from Mann	**20.** 193
	18	Oct.	OS	to Mann	**20.** 196
	29	Oct.	OS	from Conway	**37.** 304
	19	Nov.	OS	to Mann	**20.** 200
	4	Dec.	NS	from Mann	**20.** 204
	19	Dec.	OS	to Mann	**20.** 207
1751	1	Jan.	NS	from Mann	**20.** 210
1750	22	Dec. 1750	OS	to Mann	**20.** 212
1751	29	Jan.	NS	from Mann	**20.** 216
	19	Feb.	NS	from Mann	**20.** 218
	9	Feb.	OS	to Mann	**20.** 221
	?10	Feb.	OS	from Gray	**14.** 44
	20	Feb.	OS	from Gray	**14.** 46
	12	March	NS	from Mann	**20.** 227
	3	March	OS	from Gray	**14.** 47
	13	March	OS	to Mann	**20.** 229
	21	March	OS	to Mann	**20.** 231
	2	April	NS	from Mann	**20.** 234
	23	March	OS	to George Lee	**40.** 66
	30	March	OS	to Chute	**35.** 66, **43.** 360
	1	April	OS	to Mann	**20.** 237
	3	April	OS	to the Duke of Bedford	**40.** 67
	23	April	NS	from Mann	**20.** 241
	16	April	OS	from Gray	**14.** 49
	30	April	NS	from Mann	**20.** 242
	22	April	OS	to Mann	**20.** 244
	14	May	NS	from Mann	**20.** 251
	4	June	NS	from Mann	**20.** 252
	30	May	OS	to Mann	**20.** 256
	30	May	OS	to Montagu	**9.** 112
	3	June	OS	to the Rev. Joseph Spence	**40.** 68
	13	June	OS	to Montagu	**9.** 115

	18	June		OS	to Mann	20. 258
	19	June		OS	to Anne Pitt	31. 1
	20	June		OS	from Horatio Walpole, Sr	14. 214
	2	July		NS	from Mann	20. 262
	21	June		OS	to Horatio Walpole, Sr	14. 215
	21	June		OS	from Horatio Walpole, Sr	14. 216
	22	June		OS	to Horatio Walpole, Sr	14. 205
	24	June		OS	to Francis Capper	14. 206
	28	June		OS	to Margaret Nicoll	14. 210
	14	July		NS	from Conway	37. 307
	16	July		OS	to Mann	20. 264
	30	July		NS	from Mann	20. 265
	22	July		OS	to Montagu	9. 117
	7	Aug.		OS	to Mrs Harris	14. 193
	20	Aug.		NS	from Mann	20. 269
	4	Sept.		NS	from Conway	37. 310
	10	Sept.		NS	from Mann	20. 273
	31	Aug.		OS	to Mann	20. 271
	26	Sept.		NS	from Conway	37. 313
	8	Oct.		NS	from Mann	20. 276
	29	Sept.		OS	from Gray	14. 51
	8	Oct.		OS	from Gray	14. 52
	8	Oct.		OS	to Montagu	9. 122
	12	Oct.		OS	to the Rev. Henry Etough	40. 69
	14	Oct.		OS	to Mann	20. 279
	3	Nov.		OS	from Lady Ailesbury	37. 316
	26	Nov.		NS	from Mann	20. 283
	3	Dec.		NS	from Conway	37. 317
	22	Nov.		OS	to Mann	20. 286
	3	Dec.		NS	from Mann	20. 290
	26	Nov.		OS	from Gray	14. 56
	12	Dec.		OS	to Mann	20. 291
	24	Dec.		NS	from Mann	20. 292
?1752	?1752				from Bentley	35. 131
1752	7	Jan.		NS	from Mann	20. 295
1751	31	Dec.	1751	OS	from Gray	14. 57
1752	9	Jan.		OS	to Montagu	9. 125
	23	Jan.		NS	from Conway	37. 322
	28	Jan.		NS	from Mann	20. 296

	22	Jan.	OS	to the Duke of Bedford	40.	71,
					42.	493
	2	Feb.	OS	to Mann	20.	299
	ca 15	Feb.	OS	from Lady Ailesbury	37.	325
?1752		[? March ?1752]		from Conway	37.	328
1752	27	Feb.	OS	to Mann	20.	301
	10	March	NS	from Mann	20.	304
	31	March	NS	from Mann	20.	306
	23	March	OS	to Mann	20.	309
	2	April	OS	from Lord Chesterfield	40.	72
	5	May	NS	from Mann	20.	312,
					43.	270
	ca 30	April	OS	from Conway	37.	329
	2	May	OS	from Conway	37.	330
	5	May	OS	to Conway	37.	332
	12	May	OS	to Montagu	9.	130
	13	May	OS	to Mann	20.	315
	22	May	OS	from Conway	37.	335
	28	May	OS	from Gray	14.	58,
					43.	182
	6	June	OS	to Montagu	9.	132
	9	June	OS	from Lady Ailesbury	37.	337
	30	June	NS	from Mann	20.	318
	ca July			to Montagu	9.	136
	23	June	OS	to Conway	37.	339
	8	July	OS	from Gray	14.	59
	14	July	OS	from Conway	37.	342
	ca Aug.			from Gray	14.	60
	27	July	OS	to Mann	20.	321
	30	July	OS	to Montagu	9.	137
	11	Aug.	NS	from Mann	20.	326
	5	Aug.	OS	to Bentley	35.	131
	31	Aug.	NS	from Mann	20.	330
	23	Aug.	OS	from Conway	37.	344
	28	Aug.	OS	to Montagu	9.	141
?1752	22	Sept. [?1752]		from Lady Lyttelton	42.	466
?1752	22	Sept. [?1752]		from Sir George Lyttelton	42.	467
1752	4	Oct.		from Conway	37.	346
	20	Oct.		from Mann	20.	334
	28	Oct.		to Mann	20.	337
	8	Nov.		to Conway	37.	347

	1	Sept.	to Selwyn	**30.** 120
	7	Sept.	from Mann	**20.** 391
	6	Oct.	to Mann	**20.** 395
	23	Oct.	from Conway	**37.** 370
	4	Nov.	to Robert Dodsley	**40.** 78
	9	Nov.	from Mann	**20.** 397
	6	Dec.	to Mann	**20.** 401
	6	Dec.	to Montagu	**9.** 156
	18	Dec.	from Conway	**37.** 372
	19	Dec.	to Bentley	**35.** 157
?1754–8	[?1754–8]		from Conway	**37.** 374
1754	18	Jan.	from Mann	**20.** 404
	28	Jan.	to Mann	**20.** 407
	2	Feb.	from Charles Pratt	**40.** 78
	10	Feb.	to Anne Pitt	**31.** 2
	15	Feb.	from Gray	**14.** 67
	? ca March		to C. H. Williams	**30.** 124
	2	March	to Bentley	**35.** 161
	3	March	from Gray	**14.** 69
	6	March	to Bentley	**35.** 164
	7	March	to Mann	**20.** 411
	8	March	from Mann	**20.** 414
	13	March	from Fox	**30.** 122
	17	March	to Bentley	**35.** 168
	17	March	from Gray	**14.** 80
	19	March	to Montagu	**9.** 159
	28	March	to Mann	**20.** 416
	29	March	from Mann	**20.** 419
	ca April		from Montagu	**9.** 160
	11	April	from Gray	**14.** 81
	19	April	from Mann	**20.** 421
	24	April	to Mann	**20.** 425
	30	April	to Chute	**35.** 78
	3	May	from Mann	**20.** 427
	14	May	to Chute	**35.** 81
	15	May	from Conway	**37.** 375
	17	May	from Mann	**20.** 430
	18	May	to Bentley	**35.** 172
	21	May	to Chute	**35.** 83
	21	May	to Montagu	**9.** 161
	23	May	from Gray	**14.** 82
	23	May	to Mann	**20.** 432
	5	June	to Mann	**20.** 434
	8	June	to Montagu	**9.** 162

	14	June	from Mann	20. 436
	26	June	from John Michael Rysbrack	40. 80
	29	June	to Montagu	9. 162
	3	July	from Conway	37. 377
	5	July	to Mann	20. 438
	5	July	from Mann	20. 441
	6	July	to Conway	37. 378
	7	July	from Conway	37. 379
	9	July	to Bentley	35. 177
	?23	July	from Conway	37. 380
	27	July	to Bentley	35. 180
	30	July	from Conway	37. 381
	4	Aug.	from Conway	37. 382
	6	Aug.	to Conway	37. 383
?1754	9	Aug. [?1754]	from Conway	37. 384
1754	9	Aug.	from Mann	20. 443
	29	Aug.	to Montagu	9. 163
	13	Sept.	from Mann	20. 445
	30	Sept.	from the Hon. Anne Seymour Conway (later Mrs Harris)	37. 385
	30	Sept.	from Sir George Lyttelton	40. 81
	6	Oct.	to Mann	20. 447
	15	Oct.	from Montagu	9. 164
	17	Oct.	to Montagu	9. 165
	20	Oct.	from Conway	37. 385
	24	Oct.	to Conway	37. 387
	3	Nov.	to Bentley	35. 183
	8	Nov.	from Mann	20. 450
	11	Nov.	to Bentley	35. 188
	16	Nov.	to Montagu	9. 165
	20	Nov.	to Bentley	35. 190
	1	Dec.	to Mann	20. 453
	13	Dec.	to Bentley	35. 194
	13	Dec.	from Mann	20. 456
	24	Dec.	to Bentley	35. 197
	29	Dec.	from Conway	37. 389
ca 1755	ca 1755		to Selwyn	30. 124
1755	7	Jan.	to Montagu	9. 166
	9	Jan.	to Bentley	35. 200
	9	Jan.	from Conway	37. 391
	9	Jan.	to Mann	20. 458
	17	Jan.	from Mann	20. 462

8	Feb.	to Bentley	**35.** 205
23	Feb.	to Bentley	**35.** 207
5	March	from Mann	**20.** 464
6	March	to Bentley	**35.** 212
10	March	to Mann	**20.** 468
27	March	to Bentley	**35.** 214
12	April	from Mann	**20.** 471
13	April	to Bentley	**35.** 218
22	April	to Mann	**20.** 474
24	April	to Bentley	**35.** 221
6	May	to Bentley	**35.** 223
8	May	from Conway	**37.** 392
ca 9	May	from Lady Ailesbury	**37.** 395
10	May	from Mann	**20.** 475
13	May	to Montagu	**9.** 167
30	May	from Mann	**20.** 479
10	June	to Bentley	**35.** 226
15	June	to Mann	**20.** 481
18	June	from Conway	**37.** 397
5	July	to Bentley	**35.** 231
16	July	to Mann	**20.** 484
17	July	to Bentley	**35.** 235
17	July	to Montagu	**9.** 168
19	July	from Mann	**20.** 486
19	July	from the Marquis de Saint-Simon	**40.** 82
22	July	from Gray	**14.** 83
26	July	to Montagu	**9.** 170
4	Aug.	to Bentley	**35.** 239
8	Aug.	from Gray	**14.** 84
10	Aug.	from Gray	**14.** 84
14	Aug.	from Gray	**14.** 85
15	Aug.	to Bentley	**35.** 242
16	Aug.	from Mann	**20.** 488
21	Aug.	to Grosvenor Bedford	**40.** 84
21	Aug.	to Mann	**20.** 490, **43.** 272
28	Aug.	to Bentley	**35.** 245
28	Aug.	to Mann	**20.** 494
1	Sept.	from Hertford	**37.** 402
2	Sept.	to Lady Essex	**40.** 85
16	Sept.	from Conway	**37.** 403
18	Sept.	to Bentley	**35.** 249
20	Sept.	from Mann	**20.** 496

20	Sept.	to Montagu	**9.** 172
22	Sept.	from Montagu	**9.** 173
23	Sept.	to Conway	**37.** 405
29	Sept.	to Chute	**35.** 87
29	Sept.	to Mann	**20.** 500
30	Sept.	to Bentley	**35.** 253
7	Oct.	from Conway	**37.** 409
7	Oct.	to Montagu	**9.** 174
14	Oct.	from Gray	**14.** 86
15	Oct.	from Montagu	**9.** 175
16	Oct.	to Grosvenor Bedford	**40.** 86
19	Oct.	to Bentley	**35.** 254
20	Oct.	to Chute	**35.** 90
25	Oct.	from Mann	**20.** 504
27	Oct.	to Mann	**20.** 505
31	Oct.	to Bentley	**35.** 257
8	Nov.	to Montagu	**9.** 176
14	Nov.	from Mann	**20.** 507
15	Nov.	to Conway	**37.** 413
16	Nov.	to Bentley	**35.** 259
16	Nov.	to Mann	**20.** 509
25	Nov.	to Montagu	**9.** 178
27	Nov.	from Conway	**37.** 418
4	Dec.	to Mann	**20.** 511
6	Dec.	from Mann	**20.** 513
11	Dec.	from Conway	**37.** 421
17	Dec.	to Bentley	**35.** 261
20	Dec.	to Montgau	**9.** 180
21	Dec.	to Mann	**20.** 516
25	Dec.	to Gray	**14.** 86
25	Dec.	from Mann	**20.** 519
30	Dec.	to Montagu	**9.** 182
1756 5	Jan.	from Conway	**37.** 425
6	Jan.	to Bentley	**35.** 264
11	Jan.	from Mann	**20.** 521
22	Jan.	to Conway	**37.** 428
24	Jan.	to Conway	**37.** 431
25	Jan.	to Mann	**20.** 522
31	Jan.	from Lady Ailesbury	**37.** 433
5	Feb.	to Mann	**20.** 525
12	Feb.	to Conway	**37.** 436
20	Feb.	from Conway	**37.** 440
21	Feb.	from Mann	**20.** 527
23	Feb.	to Mann	**20.** 529

		28	Feb.	from Mann	20. 535
		4	March	to Conway	37. 443
		6	March	from Conway	37. 448
		18	March	to Mann	20. 537
		25	March	to Conway	37. 451
		27	March	from Mann	20. 540
?1756			[? April ?1756]	from Hertford	37. 464
1756		2	April	from Mann	20. 543
		5	April	from Conway	37. 455
		10	April	from Mann	20. 544
		10	April	from Lord Orford	36. 24
		10	April	to Lord Orford	36. 25
		13	April	to Horatio Walpole, Sr	36. 27
		13	April	from Horatio Walpole, Sr	36. 29
		14	April	from Horatio Walpole, Sr	36. 29
		14	April	to Horatio Walpole, Sr	36. 31
		16	April	to Conway	37. 457
		16	April	from Mann	20. 547
		18	April	to Mann	20. 549
		20	April	to Montagu	9. 183
		29	April	from Conway	37. 461
		4	May	to Montagu	9. 187
		15	May	from Mann	20. 551
		16	May	to Mann	20. 554
		19	May	to Montagu	9. 188
		26	May	from Montagu	9. 190
		27	May	to Mann	20. 556
		28	May	from Mann	20. 558
			ca June–July	to Fox	30. 125
	ca	6	June	to Montagu	9. 190
		6	June	to Strafford	35. 275
		8	June	to Chute	35. 92
		14	June	to Mann	20. 559, 43. 273
		15	June	from Lady Ailesbury	37. 465
		19	June	from Mann	20. 563
	ca	21	June	from Montagu	9. 191
		24	June	to Grosvenor Bedford	40. 86
		29	June	from Conway	37. 467
		3	July	from Mann	20. 565

6	July	from Conway	**37.** 470
11	July	to Mann	**20.** 569
12	July	to Montagu	**9.** 192
ca 13	July	from Montagu	**9.** 193
16	July	from Mann	**20.** 571
21	July	from Mann	**20.** 574
23	? July	to Chute	**35.** 95
24	July	to Mann	**20.** 577
25	July	from Conway	**37.** 472
?29	July	from Chute	**35.** 96
30	July	from Gray	**14.** 89
31	July	to Fox	**30.** 127
	Aug.	to Bentley	**35.** 266
1	Aug.	from Mason	**28.** 1
4	Aug.	from Gray	**14.** 91
7	Aug.	from Mann	**20.** 580
21	Aug.	from Mann	**20.** 582
28	Aug.	to Montagu	**9.** 195
28	Aug.	to Strafford	**35.** 278
29	Aug.	from Gray	**14.** 92
29	Aug.	to Mann	**20.** 585
2	Sept.	to Conway	**37.** 473
8	Sept.	from Gray	**14.** 93
12	Sept.	from Conway	**37.** 475
12	Sept.	from Gray	**14.** 94
18	Sept.	from Mann	**20.** 587
19	Sept.	from Gray	**14.** 95
19	Sept.	to Mann	**21.** 1
21	Sept.	from Gray	**14.** 96
	? late Oct.	to Henry Fox	**40.** 87
7	Oct.	from Montagu	**9.** 196
14	Oct.	to Montagu	**9.** 197
17	Oct.	to Mann	**21.** 4
21	Oct.	from Lady Ailesbury	**37.** 476
23	Oct.	from Mann	**21.** 8
24	Oct.	from Conway	**37.** 478
27	Oct.	to Fox	**30.** 127, **43.** 315
28	Oct.	from Conway	**37.** 479
28	Oct.	to Montagu	**9.** 199
3	Nov.	from Montagu	**9.** 200
4	Nov.	to Mann	**21.** 10
6	Nov.	to Montagu	**9.** 202
13	Nov.	from Mann	**21.** 14
13	Nov.	to Mann	**21.** 17

	15	Nov.	from Hertford	37. 480
	25	Nov.	to Montagu	9. 203
	27	Nov.	from Mann	21. 19
	28	Nov.	from Lady Brown	40. 89
	29	Nov.	to Mann	21. 22
	3	Dec.	from Mann	21. 27
	4	Dec.	to Fox	30. 129
	5	Dec.	from Fox	30. 130
	8	Dec.	to Mann	21. 30
	16	Dec.	to Mann	21. 32
	20	Dec.	to Fox	30. 131
	ca 22	Dec.	to Fox	30. 132, 43. 315
	23	Dec.	to Mann	21. 34
	23	Dec.	to Montagu	9. 204
ca 1757	ca 1757		to Selwyn	30. 133
1757	1	Jan.	to the Duke of Bedford	40. 90
	1	Jan.	from Mann	21. 35
	3	Jan.	from the Duke of Bedford	40. 91
	6	Jan.	to Mann	21. 38
	8	Jan.	from Mann	21. 40
	15	Jan.	from Mann	21. 42
	17	Jan.	to Mann	21. 43
	29	Jan.	from Mann	21. 47
	30	Jan.	to Mann	21. 49
	7	Feb.	from Lord Orford	36. 33
	13	Feb.	to Mann	21. 54
	19	Feb.	from Mann	21. 58
	27	Feb.	to Chute	35. 97
	27	Feb.	from William Pitt	40. 92
	2	March	from Mann	21. 60
	3	March	to Mann	21. 62
	[?7	? March]	from Lady Hertford	37. 482
	11	March	from Gray	14. 97
	17	March	to Mann	21. 66
	25	March	from Mann	21. 68
	2	April	from Mann	21. 71
	7	April	to Mann	21. 72
	18	April	to Lord Holdernesse	40. 92
	20	April	to Mann	21. 75
	23	April	from Mann	21. 80
	30	April	from Mann	21. 83
	5	May	to Mann	21. 85

12	May	to Montagu	**9.** 205
13	May	from Fox	**30.** 133
13	May	to the Hon. George Grenville	**40.** 93
14	May	from Mann	**21.** 89
19	May	to Mann	**21.** 91
19	May	to Montagu	**9.** 206
27	May	to Montagu	**9.** 206
ca 29	May	from Montagu	**9.** 208
29	May	from Conway	**37.** 483
1	June	to Mann	**21.** 92
2	June	to Montagu	**9.** 209
3	June	from Lady Ailesbury	**37.** 484
4	June	from Mann	**21.** 94
9	June	from Conway	**37.** 485
9	June	to Mann	**21.** 97
ca 10	June	from Montagu	**9.** 211
12	June	from Conway	**37.** 487, **43.** 373
14	June	to Mann	**21.** 99
16	June	from Conway	**37.** 488
18	June	to Fox	**30.** 134
18	June	from Mann	**21.** 101
18	June	to Montagu	**9.** 212
ca 20	June	from Montagu	**9.** 212
20	June	to Mann	**21.** 103
2	July	from Mann	**21.** 106
3	July	to Mann	**21.** 108
4	July	to Strafford	**35.** 281
5	July	from Conway	**37.** 490
7	July	from Lady Ailesbury	**37.** 492
9	July	from Mann	**21.** 111
11	July	from Gray	**14.** 97
12	July	to Chute	**35.** 98
16	July	to Montagu	**9.** 213
22	July	from Mann	**21.** 113
22	July	from Lord Sandwich	**40.** 94
25	July	to Mann	**21.** 117
26	July	to Chute	**35.** 99
3	Aug.	from David Garrick	**40.** 95
4	Aug.	from Conway	**37.** 493
4	Aug.	to Charles Lyttelton	**40.** 96
4	Aug.	to Mann	**21.** 118
4	Aug.	to Montagu	**9.** 214
5	Aug.	from David Garrick	**40.** 97

	13	Oct.	from Gray	14. 100
	13	Oct.	to Selwyn	30. 143
	18	Oct.	to Montagu	9. 217
	18	Oct.	to Selwyn	30. 145
	21	Oct.	from Gray	14. 101
	24	Oct.	to Mann	21. 145
	27	Oct.	from the Rev. Joseph Spence	40. 115
	9	Nov.	to Grosvenor Bedford	40. 117
	12	Nov.	from Mann	21. 146
	19	Nov.	from Mann	21. 150
	20	Nov.	to Mann	21. 152
	24	Nov.	from Conway	37. 520
	ca 25	Nov.	to Conway	37. 522
	26	Nov.	to Grosvenor Bedford	40. 118
	3	Dec.	from Mann	21. 158
	17	Dec.	from Mann	21. 160
	25	Dec.	to Andrew Coltee Ducarel	40. 119
	31	Dec.	from Mann	21. 162
?1758	?1758		to Lady Mary Coke	31. 8, 43. 328
1758	11	Jan.	to Mann	21. 164
	12	Jan.	to Andrew Coltee Ducarel	40. 120
	17	Jan.	from Gray	14. 101
	21	Jan.	from Mann	21. 168
	23	Jan.	from David Garrick	40. 121
	ca 24	Jan.	to David Garrick	40. 122
	9	Feb.	to Mann	21. 171
	11	Feb.	from Mann	21. 174
	23	Feb.	to Mann	21. 177
		March	from Sir John Fielding	40. 123
	4	March	from Mann	21. 179
	[?16 or ?23 ? March]		from Conway	37. 523
	21	March	to Mann	21. 181
	23	March	to Charles Lyttelton	40. 124
?1758	[?24 or ?31 ? March ?1758]		from Lady Ailesbury	37. 525
1758	25	March	from Mann	21. 185
		? late April	from Lord Royston	40. 125
	14	April	to Mann	21. 188
	15	April	from Mann	21. 191

	1	Aug.		from Conway	**37.** 553
	2	Aug.		from David Hume	**40.** 140
	3	Aug.		to Zouch	**16.** 3
	11	Aug.		from Conway	**37.** 557
	11	Aug. *bis*		from Conway	**37.** 559
	12	Aug.		to Mann	**21.** 225
	12	Aug.		to Selwyn	**30.** 145
	12	Aug.		to Zouch	**16.** 8
	15	Aug.		from C. H. Williams	**30.** 146
	19	Aug.		from Mann	**21.** 228
	20	Aug.		to Montagu	**9.** 222
	22	Aug.		to Chute	**35.** 103
	22	Aug.		to Selwyn	**30.** 148
	24	Aug.		to Mann	**21.** 232
	27	Aug.		from Conway	**37.** 559
	29	Aug.		to Grosvenor Bedford	**40.** 142
	29	Aug.		to Selwyn	**30.** 149
	2	Sept.		to Conway	**37.** 562
	5	Sept.		to Dalrymple	**15.** 36
	8	Sept.		to David Mallet	**40.** 143
	9	Sept.		from Mann	**21.** 234
	9	Sept.		to Mann	**21.** 237
	14	Sept.		to Zouch	**16.** 10
	16	Sept.		from Mann	**21.** 241
	17	Sept.		from Conway	**37.** 564
	19	Sept.		to Conway	**37.** 568
	22	Sept.		to Mann	**21.** 243
	28	Sept.		from Conway	**37.** 573
	3	Oct.		to Montagu	**9.** 225
	5	Oct.		to Zouch	**16.** 13
	15	Oct.		from Conway	**37.** 576
	17	Oct.		to Conway	**37.** 579
	17	Oct.		to Lady Hervey	**31.** 9
	21	Oct.		from Mann	**21.** 245
	21	Oct.		from Lady Townshend	**40.** 144
	21	Oct.		to Zouch	**16.** 18
	24	Oct.		to Mann	**21.** 249
	24	Oct.		to Montagu	**9.** 227
ca 1758–61		[ca Nov. 1758–May 1761]		to Selwyn	**30.** 151
1758	12	Nov.		to the Duke of Newcastle	**40.** 145
	18	Nov.		from Mann	**21.** 252
	20	Nov.		to Robert Dodsley	**40.** 148

	26	Nov.	to Montagu	**9.** 229
	27	Nov.	to Mann	**21.** 256
	7	Dec.	to Dalrymple	**15.** 38
	9	Dec.	to Zouch	**16.** 22
	10	Dec.	from Conway	**37.** 583
	25	Dec.	to Mann	**21.** 259
	26	Dec.	to Montagu	**9.** 230
1759	1759		from Allan Ramsay	**40.** 150
ca 1759	ca 1759		to George Selwyn	**40.** 151
ca 1759	ca 1759		from David Mallet	**40.** 151
ca 1759	ca 1759 *bis*		from David Mallet	**40.** 152
?1759	[? Jan. ?1759]		from Lady North-umberland	**40.** 153
1759	9	Jan.	from Robertson	**15.** 39
	12	Jan.	to Zouch	**16.** 24
	18	Jan.	to Robertson	**15.** 40
	19	Jan.	to Conway	**38.** 1
	20	Jan.	from Mann	**21.** 263
	21	Jan.	from Conway	**38.** 3
	28	Jan.	to Conway	**38.** 7
	28	Jan.	from Conway	**38.** 9
	1	Feb.	to Chute	**35.** 105
	2	Feb.	to Chute	**35.** 106
	3	Feb.	to the Hon. Henry Bilson Legge	**40.** 153
	3	Feb.	to Grosvenor Bedford	**40.** 155
	4	Feb.	to Robertson	**15.** 41
	6	Feb.	to Chute	**35.** 108
	7	Feb.	from the Rev. William Harris	**40.** 156
	9	Feb.	to Mann	**21.** 266
	9	Feb.	from John Sharp	**40.** 158
	10	Feb.	from Mann	**21.** 268
	14	Feb.	from Lord Corke	**40.** 161
	14	Feb.	from Gray	**14.** 103
	15	Feb.	to Gray	**14.** 103
	20	Feb.	to Lady Hervey	**31.** 12
	20	Feb.	from Robertson	**15.** 45
	25	Feb.	to Dalrymple	**15.** 46
	3	March	from Mann	**21.** 272
	4	March	to Mann	**21.** 277
	4	March	to Robertson	**15.** 48
	11	March	to Fox	**30.** 151, **43.** 316

1	Aug.	to Mann	21. 311
3	Aug.	from Hertford	38. 18
7	Aug.	from Hertford	38. 19
8	Aug.	to Mann	21. 313
9	Aug.	to Montagu	9. 245
9	Aug.	to Strafford	35. 292
14	Aug.	to Conway	38. 20
14	Aug.	to Selwyn	30. 154
23	Aug.	to Selwyn	30. 155
24	Aug.	from Henrietta Seymour Conway	38. 24
25	Aug.	from Mann	21. 317
27	Aug.	from Thomas Farmer	40. 164
29	Aug.	to Mann	21. 319
29	Aug.	to Selwyn	30. 157
1	Sept.	from Hertford	38. 25
8	Sept.	from Mann	21. 322
12	Sept.	to Lady Townshend	40. 165
13	Sept.	to Conway	38. 27
13	Sept.	to Mann	21. 326
13	Sept.	to Strafford	35. 294
15	Sept.	from Mann	21. 329
21	Sept.	to Lady Townshend	40. 166
27	Sept.	from Hertford	38. 29
29	Sept.	from Mann	21. 331
9	Oct.	from Montagu	9. 247
11	Oct.	from Conway	38. 30
11	Oct.	to Montagu	9. 248
12	Oct.	from Mann	21. 334
14	Oct.	to Conway	38. 34
15	Oct.	to Dalrymple	15. 58
16	Oct.	to Mann	21. 335
17	Oct.	from Lady Townshend	40. 168
18	Oct.	to Conway	38. 37
19	Oct.	to Mann	21. 337
21	Oct.	to Montagu	9. 250
ca 25	Oct.	from Montagu	9. 251
30	Oct.	to Strafford	35. 296
ca 1	Nov.	to Lady Hervey	31. 13
3	Nov.	from Mann	21. 339
4	Nov.	to Chute	35. 110
8	Nov.	to Montagu	9. 253
10	Nov.	from Mann	21. 342

	12	Nov.		from Johann	
				Heinrich Müntz	**40.** 169
	ca 15	Nov.		from Montagu	**9.** 257
	16	Nov.		to Mann	**21.** 344
	17	Nov.		from Mann	**21.** 347
	17	Nov.		to Montagu	**9.** 258
	17	Nov.		from William Pitt	
				(later Lord	
				Chatham)	**40.** 170
	19	Nov.		to William Pitt (later	
				Lord Chatham)	**40.** 171
	ca 20	Nov.		from Montagu	**9.** 260
	20	Nov.		from William Pitt	
				(later Lord	
				Chatham)	**40.** 172
?1759	20	Nov. [?1759]		to Lord Cardigan	**40.** 173
1759	30	Nov.		to Mann	**21.** 350
	4	Dec.		from Montagu	**9.** 261
	13	Dec.		to Mann	**21.** 352
	15	Dec.		from Mann	**21.** 356
	23	Dec.		to Montagu	**9.** 262
	23	Dec.		to Zouch	**16.** 31
	27	Dec.		to Lady Mary Coke	**31.** 14,
					43. 328
	29	Dec.		to Lady Ailesbury	**38.** 40
	29	Dec.		from Montagu	**9.** 266
ca 1760	ca 1760			to ? Henry Reade	**40.** 174
1760	9	Jan.		from Zouch	**16.** 33
	12	Jan.		to Lady Hervey	**31.** 16
	12	Jan.		from Mann	**21.** 358
	14	Jan.		to Montagu	**9.** 267
	ca 17	Jan.		to Grosvenor	
				Bedford	**42.** 453
	20	Jan.		to Mann	**21.** 361
	24	Jan.		to Lort	**40.** 175
	28	Jan.		to Montagu	**9.** 271
	3	Feb.		to Dalrymple	**15.** 61
	3	Feb.		to Mann	**21.** 363,
					43. 276
	3	Feb.		from Montagu	**9.** 275
	4	Feb.		to Zouch	**16.** 36
	6	Feb.		to Fox	**30.** 159,
					43. 317
	7	Feb.		from Lort	**16.** 137
	16	Feb.		from Mann	**21.** 369

		18	Feb.	to the 4th Duke of Devonshire	**40.** 176
		19	Feb.	to Lady Mary Coke	**31.** 17, **43.** 329
		25	Feb.	from Lort	**16.** 140
		28	Feb.	to Mann	**21.** 371
		3	March	from Beauchamp	**38.** 43
		4	March	from Mann	**21.** 375
		4	March	to Mann	**21.** 376
		8	March	from Mann	**21.** 378
		17	March	from Beauchamp	**38.** 45
		22	March	from Mann	**21.** 381
		26	March	to Mann	**21.** 384
		27	March	to Montagu	**9.** 276
		29	March	from Mann	**21.** 385
			ca April	from Gray	**14.** 105
		2	April	to Lady Northumberland	**40.** 178
		4	April	to Dalrymple	**15.** 64
	ca	9	April	from Montagu	**9.** 277
		11	April	from Henrietta Seymour Conway	**38.** 46
?1760	[?14	? April ?1760]		from Lincoln	**30.** 160
1760		19	April	to Montagu	**9.** 278
		20	April	to Mann	**21.** 387
	ca	25	April	from Montagu	**9.** 281
		26	April	from Mann	**21.** 390
		29	April	to ? the Rev. Christopher Wilson	**40.** 179
		3	May	from Mann	**21.** 392
		3	May	to Zouch	**16.** 38
		?5	May	to Conway	**38.** 48
		?5	May	from Beauchamp	**38.** 50
		5	May	from Montagu	**9.** 282
		6	May	from Henrietta Seymour Conway	**38.** 51
		6	May	to Montagu	**9.** 283
		7	May	to Mann	**21.** 394
		9	May	from Beauchamp	**38.** 52
		15	May	to Dalrymple	**15.** 67
		17	May	from Mann	**21.** 405
		24	May	to Mann	**21.** 407
		31	May	from Mann	**21.** 410
		5	June	from Hertford	**38.** 53
		7	June	to Strafford	**35.** 299

	14	June	from Mann	**21.** 414
	20	June	to Mann	**21.** 416
	21	June	from Hertford	**38.** 54
	21	June	to Conway	**38.** 55
	28	June	to Conway	**38.** 59
	28	June	to Dalrymple	**15.** 69
	28	June	from Lady Hertford	**38.** 61
	3	July	from Lord Holdernesse	**40.** 180
	4	July	to Montagu	**9.** 284
	7	July	to Mann	**21.** 418
	8	July	from Montagu	**9.** 286
	9	July	from Beauchamp	**38.** 62
	10	July	to Montagu	**9.** 287
	11	July	from Montagu	**9.** 287
	12	July	from Mann	**21.** 421
	15	July	from Mann	**21.** 425
	19	July	from Hertford	**38.** 62
	19	July	to Montagu	**9.** 288
	20	July	from Montagu	**9.** 290
	24	July	from Hertford	**38.** 63
	27	July	from Lort	**16.** 141
		Aug.	to Gray	**14.** 106
	1	Aug.	to Mann	**21.** 426
	7	Aug.	to Conway	**38.** 65
	7	Aug.	to Strafford	**35.** 303
	9	Aug.	from Mann	**21.** 429
	10	Aug.	from Hertford	**38.** 67
	12	Aug.	to Hertford	**38.** 68
	12	Aug.	to Montagu	**9.** 291
	14	Aug.	from Hertford	**38.** 69
	ca 15	Aug.	to Unknown	**40.** 181
	23	Aug.	to Lady Ailesbury	**38.** 70
	23	Aug.	from Montagu	**9.** 292
	28	Aug.	to Mann	**21.** 432
	1	Sept.	to Montagu	**9.** 293
	2	Sept.	to the 4th Duke of Devonshire	**40.** 181
	2	Sept.	from Gray	**14.** 107
	4	Sept.	to Strafford	**35.** 304
?1760	[?8	? Sept. ?1760]	to Conway	**38.** 72
1760	13	Sept.	from Mann	**21.** 433
	16	Sept.	from Montagu	**9.** 300
	19	Sept.	to Conway	**38.** 74
	25	**Sept.**	from Hertford	**38.** 75

		2	Oct.	to Montagu	**9.**	301
		5	Oct.	to Mann	**21.**	437
		5	Oct.	from Montagu	**9.**	302
		11	Oct.	from Hertford	**38.**	76
		14	Oct.	to Montagu	**9.**	303
		19	Oct.	from Montagu	**9.**	308
?1760		19	Oct. [?1760]	to Selwyn	**30.**	160
1760		20	Oct.	to Lord Bute	**40.**	184
		20	Oct.	from Mann	**21.**	440
?1760		21	Oct. [?1760]	to Selwyn	**30.**	161
1760		22	Oct.	from Lord Bute	**40.**	185
		22	Oct.	from Lady Hertford	**38.**	78
		25	Oct.	to Thomas Brand	**40.**	186
		25	Oct.	from the Rev. William Harris	**40.**	186
		25	Oct.	to Montagu	**9.**	310
		25	Oct.	to Strafford	**35.**	307
	ca	28	Oct.	from Gray	**14.**	116
		28	Oct.	to Mann	**21.**	442
		28	Oct.	to Montagu	**9.**	312
	ca	30	Oct.	from Montagu	**9.**	315
		31	Oct.	to Montagu	**9.**	315
		1	Nov.	from Hertford	**38.**	79
		1	Nov.	from Mann	**21.**	445
		1	Nov.	to Mann	**21.**	448
		4	Nov.	to Montagu	**9.**	317
	ca	9	Nov.	from Montagu	**9.**	319
		13	Nov.	to Montagu	**9.**	320
		13	Nov. *bis*	to Montagu	**9.**	323
		14	Nov.	to Mann	**21.**	451
		16	Nov.	from Mann	**21.**	453
		22	Nov.	from Mann	**21.**	455
		24	Nov.	to Montagu	**9.**	325
		27	Nov.	to Zouch	**16.**	40
	ca	30	Nov.	from Montagu	**9.**	328
		5	Dec.	to Mann	**21.**	458
		6	Dec.	from Mann	**21.**	461
		11	Dec.	to Montagu	**9.**	328
		13	Dec.	from Hertford	**38.**	80
		13	Dec.	from Mann	**21.**	463
		?15	Dec.	from Lady Hertford	**38.**	81
		15	Dec.	to Lord Bute	**40.**	187
		17	Dec.	from Lord Bute	**40.**	189
1761	ca	2	Jan.	from Gray	**14.**	118
		2	Jan.	to Mann	**21.**	465

	3	Jan.	to Zouch	**16.** 41
	7	Jan.	to Montagu	**9.** 330
	7	Jan.	from William Pitt (later Lord Chatham	**40.** 190
	10	Jan.	from Mann	**21.** 468
	11	Jan.	from Montagu	**9.** 332
	17	Jan.	from Montagu	**9.** 333
	22	Jan.	to Montagu	**9.** 334
	27	Jan.	to Mann	**21.** 471
		[ca Feb.–March]	to Lady Suffolk	**31.** 18
ca 1761	3	Feb. [ca 1761]	from Montagu	**9.** 336
1761	7	Feb.	from Mann	**21.** 474
	7	Feb.	to Montagu	**9.** 337
	12	Feb.	to Lady Mary Coke	**31.** 20, **43.** 329
	17	Feb.	from Mann	**21.** 477
	ca 25	Feb.	from Montagu	**9.** 339
	28	Feb.	from Mann	**21.** 481
	3	March	to Mann	**21.** 483
	7	March	to Zouch	**16.** 43
	13	March	to Montagu	**9.** 340
	13	March	to Selwyn	**30.** 161
	ca 15	March	from Montagu	**9.** 342
	17	March	to Mann	**21.** 487
	17	March	to Montagu	**9.** 343
	ca 17	March	from Montagu	**9.** 345
	21	March	from Mann	**21.** 492
	21	March	to Montagu	**9.** 346
	21	March	to Selwyn	**30.** 163
	28	March	from Mann	**21.** 492
	ca 29	March	from Montagu	**9.** 347
	25–30	March	to Montagu	**9.** 347
	ca 4	April	from Montagu	**9.** 351
	ca 6	April	from Montagu	**9.** 352
	7	April	to Montagu	**9.** 353
	ca 9	April	from Montagu	**9.** 354
	10	April	to Conway	**38.** 82
	10	April	to Mann	**21.** 497
	ca 14	April	from Montagu	**9.** 356
	14	April	to Dalrymple	**15.** 71
	16	April	to Montagu	**9.** 358
	ca 21	April	from Montagu	**9.** 360
	25	April	from Mann	**21.** 499
	ca 26	April	from Montagu	**9.** 361

	26	Oct.	to Conway	38.	139
	31	Oct.	from Mann	21.	543
	4	Nov.	from Montagu	9.	399
	7	Nov.	to Montagu	9.	401
	14	Nov.	to Mann	21.	545
	17	Nov.	from Montagu	9.	402
	19	Nov.	from Montagu	9.	403
	21	Nov.	from Mann	21.	550
	23	Nov.	from Montagu	9.	404
	27	Nov.	from Montagu	9.	404
	28	Nov.	to Lady Ailesbury	38.	142
	28	Nov.	to Montagu	9.	405
	30	Nov.	to Dalrymple	15.	73
	8	Dec.	to Montagu	9.	407
	10	Dec.	from Hertford	38.	145
	12	Dec.	to Mann	21.	551
	12	Dec.	from Mann	21.	555
	14	Dec.	from Hertford	38.	147
ca	15	Dec.	from Montagu	9.	408
	21	Dec.	to Dalrymple	15.	76
	23	Dec.	to Montagu	9.	410
ca	24	Dec.	from Montagu	9.	414
	28	Dec.	to Mann	21.	557
	30	Dec.	to Montagu	9.	416
?1762	?1762		from Unknown	40.	207
ca 1762	ca 1762		to Unknown	40.	208
1762	2	Jan.	from Montagu	10.	1
	4	Jan.	to Mann	21.	560
	5	Jan.	from Dalrymple	15.	78
	9	Jan.	from Mann	21.	563
	18	Jan.	to Dalrymple	15.	82
	23	Jan.	from Montagu	10.	2
	26	Jan.	to Montagu	10.	3
	29	Jan.	to Mann	22.	1
	2	Feb.	to Montagu	10.	5
	6	Feb.	from Mann	22.	4
	6	Feb.	from Montagu	10.	7
	6	Feb.	to Montagu	10.	9
	11	Feb.	from Gray	14.	119
	13	Feb.	from Lord Bute	40.	209
	13	Feb.	to Dalrymple	15.	84
	13	Feb.	to Zouch	16.	44
	15	Feb.	to Lord Bute	40.	210
	15	Feb.	from Lincoln	30.	165
	18	Feb.	from Montagu	10.	10

20	Feb.	from Montagu	10. 13
22	Feb.	to Montagu	10. 13
23	Feb.	from Andrew Coltee Ducarel	40. 212
24	Feb.	to Andrew Coltee Ducarel	40. 218
25	Feb.	to Mann	22. 6
25	Feb.	to Montagu	10. 15
27	Feb.	from Andrew Coltee Ducarel	40. 220
27	Feb.	from Mann	22. 10
27	Feb.	from Montagu	10. 17
27	Feb. *bis*	from Montagu	10. 19
28	Feb.	from Gray	14. 121
ca March		from the Rev. Charles Parkin	40. 222
? mid-March		to John Ratcliffe	40. 235
mid-March		from Lady Northumberland	40. 237
1	March	from John Hawkins	40. 227
ca 2	March	from Montagu	10. 19
2	March	to Lord Kames	40. 229
4	March	from Sir Thomas Reeve	40. 230
ca 6	March	from Lord Kames	40. 232
9	March	to Montagu	10. 20
10	March	from Beauchamp	38. 150
ca 12	March	from Bishop Lyttelton	40. 233
13	March	to Beauchamp	38. 152
13	March	from Mann	22. 13, 43. 278
14	March	from Lort	16. 142
15	March	to Lady Ailesbury	38. 153
15	March	from Zouch	16. 45
16	March	to Lort	16. 155
20	March	to Zouch	16. 51
22	March	from Lort	16. 159
22	March	to Mann	22. 15
22	March	to Montagu	10. 21
27	March	from Mann	22. 18
10	April	from Mann	22. 21
12	April	from Montagu	10. 23
13	April	to Mann	22. 23
17	April	from Mann	22. 27

19	April	from Unknown	40.	237
20	April	to Lord Bute	40.	239
24	April	from Mann	22.	29
26	April	from Montagu	10.	25
29	April	to Montagu	10.	25
30	April	to Mann	22.	30
before 4	May	to Lady Henrietta Cecilia West	40.	241
before 4	May	from Lady Henrietta Cecilia West	40.	245
? mid-May		from Lady North- umberland	40.	246
5	May	from Montagu	10.	27
ca 10	May	from Montagu	10.	28
14	May	to Montagu	10.	29
15	May	from Mann	22.	33
16	May	from Cole	1.	1,
			43.	32
17	May	from Montagu	10.	30
20	May	to Cole	1.	11
20	May	to Dalrymple	15.	85
20	May	from Andrew Coltee Ducarel	40.	247
20	May	from Hertford	38.	156
20	May	from Montagu	10.	31
25	May	to Montagu	10.	31
26	May	to Mann	22.	36
27	May	from Beauchamp	38.	157
27	May	from Montagu	10.	33
ca June		from William Pratt	40.	249
1	June	to the Duchess of Grafton	32.	5
8	June	from Henrietta Seymour Conway	38.	159
8	June	to Montagu	10.	34
10	June	to Lord Ilchester	40.	249
12	June	from Mann	22.	39
20	June	to Mann	22.	41
26	June	from Mann	22.	43
30	June	to Lady Mary Coke	31.	25,
			43.	330
30	June	from Hertford	38.	161
1	July	to Mann	22.	46
23	July	from John Davidson	40.	250
28	July	to Montagu	10.	35

29	July		to Cole	**1.** 14
29	July		from Hertford	**38.** 162
29	July		to Lord Ilchester	**40.** 251
31	July		to Lady Ailesbury	**38.** 163
31	July		from Cole	**1.** 14,
				43. 39
31	July		from Mann	**22.** 50
31	July		to Mann	**22.** 52
	Aug.		from the Rev.	
			Robert Masters	**1.** 22
5	Aug.		to Cole	**1.** 21
5	Aug.		to Strafford	**35.** 314
7	Aug.		from Hertford	**38.** 166
7	Aug.		from Mann	**22.** 61
9	Aug.		from Montagu	**10.** 37
10	Aug.		to Montagu	**10.** 38
12	Aug.		to Mann	**22.** 64
13	Aug.		from John Sharp	**40.** 253
14	Aug.		from Lady Hertford	**38.** 167
14	Aug.		from Mann	**22.** 67
18	Aug.		from Hertford	**38.** 169
18	Aug.		from Montagu	**10.** 41
19	Aug.		to Cole	**1.** 24
21	Aug.		to Thomas Warton	**40.** 253
29	Aug.		to Mann	**22.** 69
31	Aug.		to Selwyn	**30.** 165
	Sept.		to the Printer of	
			the *Gazetteer*	**40.** 256
4	Sept.		from Mann	**22.** 74
9	Sept.		to Grosvenor	
			Bedford	**40.** 258
9	Sept.		to Conway	**38.** 172
9	Sept.		from Andrew Coltee	
			Ducarel	**40.** 259
10	Sept.		from Hertford	**38.** 176
11	Sept.		from John Jamisone	**40.** 260
11	Sept. *bis*		from John Jamisone	**40.** 263
19	Sept.		from Montagu	**10.** 41
21	Sept.		from Hertford	**38.** 177
23	Sept.		from John Jamisone	**40.** 269
24	Sept.		to Grosvenor	
			Bedford	**40.** 270
24	Sept.		to Montagu	**10.** 43
ca 25	Sept.		from Cole	**1.** 26
25	Sept.		to Bishop Lyttelton	**40.** 271

	26	Sept.	to Mann	22.	77
	28	Sept.	to Conway	38.	178
	30	Sept.	to Cole	1.	28
	1	Oct.	to Lady Hervey	31.	27
	3	Oct.	to Mann	22.	82
	4	Oct.	to Conway	38.	182
	9	Oct.	from Mann	22.	86
	13	Oct.	from Hertford	38.	184
	14	Oct.	to Montagu	10.	45
	16	Oct.	to Bishop Lyttelton	40.	272
	19	Oct.	from Cole	1.	29
	23	Oct.	from Mann	22.	88
	28	Oct.	to Mann	22.	91
	29	Oct.	to Conway	38.	185
	30	Oct.	from Hertford	38.	190
	31	Oct.	to Lady Hervey	31.	29
		? Nov.	from Montagu	10.	46
	2	Nov.	from John Baskerville	40.	274
	3	Nov.	from Cole	1.	30
	4	Nov.	to Montagu	10.	45
	9	Nov.	to Mann	22.	95
	13	Nov.	to Cole	1.	32
	13	Nov.	from Mann	22.	98
	21	Nov.	from Fox	30.	167,
				43.	317
	21	Nov.	to Fox	30.	168
	22	Nov.	to Lord Orford	36.	36
	30	Nov.	to Mann	22.	101
	4	Dec.	from Mann	22.	105
ca	17	Dec.	from Montagu	10.	47
	20	Dec.	to Mann	22.	109
	20	Dec.	to Montagu	10.	48
	23	Dec.	to Cole	1.	32
	25	Dec.	from Mann	22.	111
1763		? Jan.	from Montagu	10.	51
ca	3	Jan.	to Gray	14.	123
ca	5	Jan.	from Gray	14.	124
	20	Jan.	from Fox	30.	170
	22	Jan.	from Mann	22.	114
	28	Jan.	to Mann	22.	116
	26	Feb.	from Mann	22.	117
	28	Feb.	to Conway	38.	191
	4	March	to Mann	22.	119
	14	March	to Lord Bute	40.	277

15	March	from Samuel Martin	40.	277
16	March	to Lord Bute	40.	278
16	March	to Nuneham	35.	451
25	March	to Montagu	10.	51
26	March	from Mann	22.	122
6	April	to Montagu	10.	55
ca 8	April	to Unknown	40.	279
8	April	to Montagu	10.	58
ca 9	April	to the Contessa Rena	40.	280
9	April	from Hertford	38.	194
9	April	from Mann	22.	124
ca 10	April	from Montagu	10.	60
10	April	to Mann	22.	126
11	April	from Montagu	10.	61
14	April	to Montagu	10.	62
17	April	from Montagu	10.	65
20	April	to Lord Egremont	40.	280
21	April	from Lord Egremont	40.	281
21	April	to Lord Egremont	40.	282
21	April	from Montagu	10.	67
22	April	to Montagu	10.	67
30	April	from Mann	22.	131
30	April	to Mann	22.	133
1	May	to Conway	38.	196
2	May	to Dalrymple	15.	88
6	May	to Conway	38.	200
10	May	to Mann	22.	137
14	May	from John Jamisone	40.	283
16	May	to Cole	1.	33
17	May	to Montagu	10.	69
19	May	from Cole	1.	34
21	May	to Conway	38.	203
21	May	from Mann	22.	141
21	May	from Montagu	10.	74
ca 25	May	from Montagu	10.	76
28	May	to Conway	38.	206
28	May	from Mann	22.	143
30	May	to Montagu	10.	76
	ca June	to the Hon. Robert Hampden	40.	286
4	June	from Montagu	10.	80
5	June	to Mann	22.	145
11	June	from Mann	22.	149,
			43.	278
14	June	from Montagu	10.	81

16	June	to Montagu	10. 82
23	June	from Montagu	10. 83
30	June	to Mann	22. 151
1	July	to Cole	1. 36
1	July	to Dalrymple	15. 90
1	July	to Montagu	10. 84
3	July	from Cole	1. 37
5	July	from Montagu	10. 85
10	July	to Bishop Lyttelton	40. 287
ca 12	July	from Montagu	10. 86
12	July	to Cole	1. 41
14	July	from William Pratt	40. 289
16	July	to Cole	1. 41
23	July	from Mann	22. 152
23	July	to Montagu	10. 88
31	July	from Cole	1. 42
8	Aug.	to Cole	1. 43
8	Aug.	to Andrew Coltee Ducarel	40. 289
9	Aug.	to Conway	38. 207
10	Aug.	to Strafford	35. 316
11	Aug.	to Mann	22. 154
15	Aug.	to Montagu	10. 92
20	Aug.	from Hertford	38. 209
20	Aug.	from Mann	22. 156
23	Aug.	from Montagu	10. 95
27	Aug.	from William Bathoe	40. 290
27	Aug.	from Cole	1. 44
27	Aug.	from Hertford	38. 210
28	Aug.	from Montagu	10. 97
29	Aug.	from Hillier	16. 63
30	Aug.	from Hertford	38. 210
31	Aug.	from Lady Hervey	31. 30
1	Sept.	to Mann	22. 158
3	Sept.	to Montagu	10. 98
5	Sept.	from Montagu	10. 99
7	Sept.	to the Hon. George Grenville	40. 291
7	Sept.	to Montagu	10. 100
8	Sept.	from the Hon. George Grenville	40. 292
9	Sept.	from Montagu	10. 101
10	Sept.	from Mann	22. 165
12	Sept.	from Gray	14. 125
13	Sept.	to Mann	22. 167

	19	Sept.	from Gray	14. 129
	27	Sept.	from Montagu	10. 102
	28	Sept.	to Selwyn	30. 171
	30	Sept.	from Cole	1. 45
	1	Oct.	from Mann	22. 169
	3	Oct.	to Montagu	10. 103
	8	Oct.	to Cole	1. 46
	8	Oct.	from Mann	22. 172
	13	Oct.	from Cole	1. 47
	15	Oct.	from Hertford	38. 211
	17	Oct.	to Mann	22. 174
	18	Oct.	to Hertford	38. 213
	19	Oct.	from Montagu	10. 107
	28	Oct.	from Hertford	38. 216
	11	Nov.	from Hertford	38. 220
	12	Nov.	from Mann	22. 178
	12	Nov.	to Montagu	10. 108
	15	Nov.	from Montagu	10. 109
	17	Nov.	to Hertford	38. 223
	17	Nov.	to Mann	22. 181
	19	Nov.	from Hertford	38. 236
	20	Nov.	to Montagu	10. 110
	25	Nov.	to Hertford	38. 239
	26	Nov.	from Montagu	10. 112
	30	Nov.	from Hertford	38. 244
	1	Dec.	from Cole	1. 48
	2	Dec.	to Hertford	38. 246
	6	Dec.	to Cole	1. 51
	7	Dec.	from Hertford	38. 252
	9	Dec.	to Hertford	38. 253
	10	Dec.	to Anne Pitt	31. 31
	12	Dec.	to Mann	22. 186
	15	Dec.	from Mann	22. 192
	16	Dec.	from Hertford	38. 260
	16	Dec.	to Hertford	38. 262
	21	Dec.	from Hertford	38. 267
	28	Dec.	from Hertford	38. 270
	29	Dec.	to Hertford	38. 272
	29	Dec.	to Mason	28. 2
?1764	?1764		to Lincoln	30. 172
?1764	?1764	*bis*	to Lincoln	30. 173
1764	6	Jan.	from Hertford	38. 278
	6	Jan.	from Mason	28. 4
	8	Jan.	to Mann	22. 194
	11	Jan.	to Montagu	10. 113

14	Jan.	from Montagu	10. 119
18	Jan.	to Mann	22. 197
ca 20	Jan.	to Lady Temple	40. 294
21	Jan.	from Mann	22. 200
22	Jan.	to Hertford	38. 282
23	Jan.	from Hertford	38. 297
27	Jan.	from Gray	14. 130
28	Jan.	to Lady Temple	40. 295
29	Jan.	from Hertford	38. 304
31	Jan.	to Cole	1. 53
31	Jan.	to Dalrymple	15. 91
31	Jan.	from Gray	14. 132
2	Feb.	from Cole	1. 53
6	Feb.	from John Bowle	40. 296
6	Feb.	to Hertford	38. 306
7	Feb.	to Cole	1. 56
11	Feb.	to John Bowle	40. 300
11	Feb.	from Cole	1. 57
13	Feb.	from Hertford	38. 313
15	Feb.	from John Drumgold	40. 302
15	Feb.	to Hertford	38. 315
16	Feb.	from John Bowle	40. 305
17	Feb.	to Lincoln	30. 174
18	Feb.	from Hertford	38. 328
18	Feb.	from Mann	22. 203
20	Feb.	to Mann	22. 206
21	Feb.	to Anne Pitt	31. 33
21	Feb.	to Zouch	16. 53
23	Feb.	to Cole	1. 60
23	Feb.	to Dalrymple	15. 94
24	Feb.	to Hertford	38. 332
25	Feb.	to John Bowle	40. 307
25	Feb.	from Hertford	38. 336
29	Feb.	to Grosvenor Bedford	40. 308
3	March	to Cole	1. 61
4	March	from Cole	1. 63
8	March	from Hertford	38. 338
11	March	to Hertford	38. 340
?18	March	from Gray	14. 132
18	March	to Hertford	38. 345
18	March	to Mann	22. 210
ca 20	March	from Beauchamp	38. 349
22	March	from Hertford	38. 350
25	March	from Hertford	38. 352

14	May	to Mann	22. 237
16	May	from John Bromfield	40. 324
17	May	from Hertford	38. 388
19	May	from Mann	22. 239
25	May	from Thomas Pitt	40. 328
27	May	to Hertford	38. 390
27	May	from Montagu	10. 125
	mid-June	to Lord March	40. 342
5	June	to Conway	38. 395
5	June	to Thomas Pitt	40. 330
6	June	from Hertford	38. 397
8	June	to Hertford	38. 399
8	June	to Mann	22. 241
10	June	from Thomas Pitt	40. 338
18	June	to Montagu	10. 126
22	June	from Hertford	38. 403
27	June	from Montagu	10. 128
	July	to Zouch	16. 55
2	July	to Conway	38. 405
4	July	from Hertford	38. 408
7	July	from Mann	22. 244
10	July	from Gray	14. 135
16	July	to Cole	1. 66
16	July	to Montagu	10. 128
17	July	from Hertford	38. 409
18	July	from Cole	1. 66
ca 21	July	from Montagu	10. 131
21	July	to Cole	1. 68
23	July	from Montagu	10. 132
27	July	to Mann	22. 247
28	July	from Hertford	38. 411
28	July	to the Duke of Newcastle	40. 343
28	July	from the Duke of Newcastle	40. 343
30	July	to Grosvenor Bedford	40. 344
2	Aug.	from Cole	1. 69
3	Aug.	to Hertford	38. 414
3	Aug.	from Christopher Wren	40. 345
6	Aug.	to Lincoln	30. 175
9	Aug.	to Christopher Wren	40. 351
11	Aug.	from Mann	22. 249
16	Aug.	to Montagu	10. 133

17	Aug.	from Gray	14. 136
21	Aug.	from Hertford	38. 424
21	Aug.	to Nuneham	35. 452
27	Aug.	to Hertford	38. 428
29	Aug.	to Cole	1. 72
29	Aug.	to William Pitt (later Lord Chatham)	40. 355
30	Aug.	from Montagu	10. 133
30	Aug.	from William Pitt (later Lord Chatham)	40. 356
30	Aug.	from the Rev. Thomas Birch	40. 356
ca 31	Aug.	to William Pitt (later Lord Chatham)	40. 359
	Sept.	to Dalrymple	15. 101
1	Sept.	to Conway	38. 437
2	Sept.	from Cole	1. 73
3	Sept.	to the Rev. Thomas Birch	40. 360
13	Sept.	to Mann	22. 251
20	Sept.	from Hertford	38. 439
22	Sept.	from Mann	22. 254
23	Sept.	from Cole	1. 75
25	Sept.	to Cole	1. 76
26	Sept.	from Dalrymple	15. 102
29	Sept.	from the Duke of Newcastle	40. 361
29	Sept.	to the Duke of Newcastle	40. 362
	mid-Oct.	from Lady Temple	40. 366
	mid-Oct.	from Lord Temple	40. 367
2	Oct.	to the Duke of Newcastle	40. 363
5	Oct.	to Hertford	38. 442
5	Oct.	to Conway	38. 445
5	Oct.	from Montagu	10. 134
9	Oct.	to Thomas Warton	40. 365
12	Oct.	to Lord Bessborough	43. 379
12	Oct.	from Hertford	38. 447
13	Oct.	to Conway	38. 449
14	Oct.	from Montagu	10. 135
18	Oct.	from Cole	1. 76
20	Oct.	to Cole	1. 77
21	Oct.	from Hertford	38. 450

	21	Oct.	to Mann	**22.** 256	
	25	Oct.	from Montagu	**10.** 136	
	26	Oct.	from Montagu	**10.** 137	
	27	Oct.	to Cole	**1.** 77	
	28	Oct.	from Cole	**1.** 78	
	29	Oct.	to Conway	**38.** 452	
	30	Oct.	to Cole	**1.** 79	
	30	Oct.	to Thomas Warton	**40.** 367	
	1	Nov.	to Hertford	**38.** 454	
	4	Nov.	from Cole	**1.** 80	
	8	Nov.	to Cole	**1.** 82	
	9	Nov.	to Hertford	**38.** 460	
	10	Nov.	from Hertford	**38.** 464	
	10	Nov.	to Lady Hervey	**31.** 34	
	10	Nov.	from Mann	**22.** 258	
	15	Nov.	to Mann	**22.** 260	
	18	Nov.	from Cole	**1.** 83	
	24	Nov.	from Mann	**22.** 265	
	25	Nov.	to Hertford	**38.** 466	
	1	Dec.	to the Rev. James Merrick	**40.** 368	
	3	Dec.	to Hertford	**38.** 471	
	7	Dec.	from Hertford	**38.** 477	
	16	Dec.	to Montagu	**10.** 137	
	18	Dec.	from Lady Hertford	**38.** 479	
ca	19	Dec.	from Montagu	**10.** 141	
	20	Dec.	from Hertford	**38.** 483	
	20	Dec.	to Mann	**22.** 268	
	23	Dec.	from Montagu	**10.** 143	
	24	Dec.	to Montagu	**10.** 144	
	28	Dec.	from Hertford	**38.** 485	
	30	Dec.	from Gray	**14.** 136	
1765	1765		from Allan Ramsay	**40.** 370	
	ca 3	Jan.	from Montagu	**10.** 146	
	5	Jan.	from Mann	**22.** 271	
	10	Jan.	to Hertford	**38.** 486	
	13	Jan.	to Mann	**22.** 274	
	18	Jan.	from Hertford	**38.** 491	
	19	Jan.	from Mann	**22.** 278	
	20	Jan.	to Hertford	**38.** 493	
	27	Jan.	to Hertford	**38.** 498	
?1765		[? Feb. ?1765]	from Lady Townshend	**40.** 371	
1765	5	Feb.	to the Rev. Thomas Percy	**40.** 372	

	9	Feb.	from Hertford	38. 504
	9	Feb.	from Mann	22. 280
	11	Feb.	to Mann	22. 283
	12	Feb.	to Hertford	38. 508
	19	Feb.	to Montagu	10. 147
	20	Feb.	from Hertford	38. 513
	24	Feb.	from Montagu	10. 148
	28	Feb.	to Cole	1. 84
	3	March	from Cole	1. 86
	9	March	to Cole	1. 88
	9	March	from Hertford	38. 516
	16	March	to the Rev. Joseph Warton	40. 376
	17	March	from Cole	1. 91
	18	March	to Jean-Baptiste-Jacques Élie de Beaumont	40. 378
	22	March	from Hertford	38. 520
	23	March	from Mann	22. 285
	26	March	to Hertford	38. 522
	26	March	to Lincoln	30. 177
	26	March	to Mann	22. 287, 43. 280
?1765		[? April ?1765]	to Selwyn	30. 179
1765	5	April	to Montagu	10. 149
	7	April	to Hertford	38. 526
	10	April	from Hertford	38. 531
	14	April	from Gray	14. 138
	14	April	from Mason	28. 5
	ca 15	April	from Montagu	10. 151
	17	April	to Mason	28. 6
	18	April	to Hertford	38. 533
	21	April	to Dalrymple	15. 105
	26	April	to Lady Hervey	31. 35
	29	April	from Hertford	38. 537
	4	May	from Mann	22. 290
	5	May	to Hertford	38. 540
	10	May	from Lort	16. 160
	11	May	to Mann	22. 292
	12	May	to Hertford	38. 547
	14	May	to Mann	22. 293
	16	May	from Hertford	38. 555
	17	May	from Hertford	38. 556
	20	May	to Hertford	38. 557
	21	May	from Hertford	38. 568

	20	Dec.	from Mann	**22.** 375
	24	Dec.	from Montagu	**10.** 188
	25	Dec.	to Anne Pitt	**31.** 87
	30	Dec.	from Montagu	**10.** 189
?1766	?1766		to Unknown	**41.** 1
1766	2	Jan.	to Lady Hervey	**31.** 90
	3	Jan.	from Mann	**22.** 377
	4	Jan.	to Lady Mary Coke	**31.** 92,
				43. 332
	5	Jan.	from Cole	**1.** 99
	5	Jan.	to Mann	**22.** 380
	5	Jan.	to Montagu	**10.** 191
	7	Jan.	to Chute	**35.** 115
	8	Jan.	from Montagu	**10.** 193
	10	Jan.	from Mann	**22.** 383
	11	Jan.	to Lady Hervey	**31.** 95
	12	Jan.	to Conway	**39.** 42
	12	Jan.	to Selwyn	**30.** 209
	13	Jan.	from Hertford	**39.** 44
	17	Jan.	from Mann	**22.** 386
	18	Jan.	to Cole	**1.** 102
	19	Jan.	to Anne Pitt	**31.** 98
	ca 20	Jan.	to James Boswell	**41.** 1
	20	Jan.	from Lady Hertford	**39.** 47
	20	Jan.	from Montagu	**10.** 195
	24	Jan.	from Mann	**22.** 387
	25	Jan.	to Gray	**14.** 148
	31	Jan.	to the Duchess of	
			Grafton	**32.** 26
	31	Jan.	to Selwyn	**30.** 212
	3	Feb.	to Lady Hervey	**31.** 101
	4	Feb.	from Hertford	**39.** 51
	5	Feb.	to Montagu	**10.** 197
	6	Feb.	from the Comtesse	
			de Boufflers	**41.** 2
	7	Feb.	from Mann	**22.** 391
	9	Feb.	to Mann	**22.** 394
	11	Feb.	from Cole	**1.** 104
	11	Feb.	from Montagu	**10.** 198
	15	Feb.	from Mann	**22.** 397
	19	Feb.	from Montagu	**10.** 199
	23	Feb.	to Montagu	**10.** 200
	25	Feb.	to Cole	**1.** 109
	28	Feb.	from Mann	**22.** 399
	1	March	to Lady Hervey	**31.** 104

26	June	from Montagu	**10.** 221
28	June	from Madame du Deffand	**3.** 85
28	June	to Lady Hervey	**31.** 118
5	July	from Mann	**22.** 428
9	July	from Madame du Deffand	**3.** 88
10	July	to Montagu	**10.** 221
10	July	to Lady Suffolk	**31.** 121
11	July	to Mann	**22.** 431
11	July *bis*	to Mann	**22.** 435
12	July	from Montagu	**10.** 222
16	July	from Madame du Deffand	**3.** 90
16	July	to Madame du Deffand	**3.** 94
17	July	to Lord Holland	**30.** 221, **43.** 320
17	July	to Lady Suffolk	**31.** 122
18	July	to Mann	**22.** 435
18	July	to the Hon. Thomas Walpole	**36.** 45
19	July	from Madame du Deffand	**3.** 98
19	July	to Lord Ilchester	**41.** 22
19	July	from Mann	**22.** 437
21	July	to Montagu	**10.** 223
22	July	to Lord Holland	**30.** 227, **43.** 321
23	July	to Mann	**22.** 439
24	July	from Madame du Deffand	**3.** 99
26	July	from David Hume	**41.** 24
26	July	to David Hume	**41.** 25
28	July	from Montagu	**10.** 224
29	July	to Lord Holland	**30.** 228, **43.** 321
30	July	from Madame du Deffand	**3.** 103
31	July	from Lord Holland	**30.** 229
1	Aug.	to Mann	**22.** 442
2	Aug.	to Lord Holland	**30.** 231, **43.** 321
2	Aug.	from Mann	**22.** 445
ca 3	Aug.	from Montagu	**10.** 225

5	Aug.	from Madame du Deffand	**3.** 106, **43.** 82
6	Aug.	from Charles James Fox	**41.** 27
12	Aug.	from Madame du Deffand	**3.** 111
17	Aug.	to Président Hénault	**41.** 28
19	Aug.	from Madame du Deffand	**3.** 115
23	Aug.	from Mann	**22.** 447
ca 27	Aug.	from Madame du Deffand	**3.** 119
?31	Aug.	to Lord Bessborough	**43.** 380
	? Sept.	from Madame du Deffand	**3.** 148
	? Sept.	to Henry Sampson Woodfall	**41.** 30
4	Sept.	from Madame du Deffand	**3.** 121
ca 5	Sept.	from Montagu	**10.** 226
6	Sept.	to Lord Bessborough	**43.** 381
6	Sept.	from the Comtesse de Boufflers	**41.** 32
7	Sept.	from Madame du Deffand	**3.** 131
8	Sept.	to Madame de Forcalquier	**41.** 33
8	Sept.	to Lady George Lennox	**31.** 124
9	Sept.	to Mann	**22.** 449
10	Sept.	from the Duke of Newcastle	**41.** 35
11	Sept.	from Madame du Deffand	**3.** 132
12	Sept.	from the Duke of Newcastle	**41.** 36
16	Sept.	from Cole	**1.** 118
17	Sept.	to Lady Mary Coke	**31.** 128, **43.** 333
17	Sept. *bis*	to Lady Mary Coke	**31.** 129, **43.** 334
17	Sept.	from Président Hénault	**41.** 37
18	Sept.	to Cole	**1.** 118

20	Sept.	from Mann	**22.** 452
21	Sept.	from Cole	**1.** 119
21	Sept.	from Madame du Deffand	**3.** 135
23	Sept.	to Montagu	**10.** 226
24	Sept.	from Madame du Deffand	**3.** 137
24	Sept.	from Gray	**14.** 158
24	Sept.	from Wiart	**3.** 140
25	Sept.	to Mann	**22.** 454
25	Sept.	to the Duke and Duchess of Newcastle	**41.** 38
ca 26	Sept.	to Robert Adam	**41.** 39
ca 26	Sept.	to Gray	**14.** 159
27	Sept.	from Montagu	**10.** 227
28	Sept.	from Madame du Deffand	**3.** 141
30	Sept.	from Madame du Deffand	**3.** 143
2	Oct.	to Conway	**39.** 76
4	Oct.	to Strafford	**35.** 319
5	Oct.	from Madame du Deffand	**3.** 149
5	Oct.	to Montagu	**10.** 228
6	Oct.	to Lady Suffolk	**31.** 130
8	Oct.	from Hertford	**39.** 77
10	Oct.	to Chute	**35.** 118
10	Oct.	to Madame du Deffand	**3.** 150
12	Oct.	from Madame du Deffand	**3.** 151
12	Oct.	from Montagu	**10.** 229
14	Oct.	from Mann	**22.** 456
18	Oct.	to Conway	**39.** 78
18	Oct.	to Madame du Deffand	**3.** 153
18	Oct.	to Montagu	**10.** 230
19	Oct.	from Madame du Deffand	**3.** 153
20	Oct.	from Madame du Deffand	**3.** 156
21	Oct.	from Mann	**22.** 459
22	Oct.	to Madame du Deffand	**3.** 161

	2	Dec.	from Madame du Deffand	3. 387
	2	Dec.	to Mann	22. 565
	6	Dec.	from Wiart	3. 389
	8	Dec.	to the Duchesse de Choiseul	41. 108
	9	Dec.	from Madame du Deffand	3. 390
	11	Dec.	from Madame du Deffand	3. 394
	14	Dec.	to Mann	22. 568
	19	Dec.	from the Duchesse de Choiseul	41. 108
	19	Dec.	to Cole	1. 123
	20	Dec.	from Madame du Deffand	3. 398
	21	Dec.	from Madame du Deffand	3. 400
	24	Dec.	from Gray	14. 159
	25	Dec.	to Mann	22. 571
	26	Dec.	from Madame du Deffand	3. 403
	27	Dec.	from Cole	1. 125
	27	Dec.	from Mann	22. 573
	29	Dec.	from Unknown	41. 111
?1768	?1768		to Selwyn	30. 252
ca 1768–9	ca 1768–9		to Dr Henry Harington	42. 461
1768	3	Jan.	from Madame du Deffand	4. 1
	9	Jan.	from Mann	22. 575
	10	Jan.	from Madame du Deffand	4. 3
	11	Jan.	from Hans Stanley	41. 116
	12	Jan.	from Madame du Deffand	4. 5
	16	Jan.	to Thomas Astle	41. 119
	17	Jan.	to Dalrymple	15. 115
	17	Jan.	to Mann	22. 577
	22	Jan.	to Madame du Deffand	4. 9
	24	Jan.	from Madame du Deffand	4. 9
	26	Jan.	from Thomas Astle	41. 121
	26	Jan.	from Madame du Deffand	4. 13

	3	Nov.	to Mann	**23.** 65
	7	Nov.	from Montagu	**10.** 265
	10	Nov.	to Montagu	**10.** 266
	11	Nov.	from David Hume	**41.** 166
	12	Nov.	from Montagu	**10.** 267
	13	Nov.	from Madame du Deffand	**4.** 157
ca	14	Nov.	from Hertford	**39.** 113
	14	Nov.	from Mann	**23.** 67
	15	Nov.	to Montagu	**10.** 268
	18	Nov.	to Mann	**23.** 69
	19	Nov.	from Madame du Deffand	**4.** 160
	20	Nov.	from the Duchess of Norfolk	**41.** 167
	25	Nov.	to Mann	**23.** 70
	27	Nov.	from Montagu	**10.** 270
	28	Nov.	from Mann	**23.** 71
	30	Nov.	from Madame du Deffand	**4.** 162
	1	Dec.	to Montagu	**10.** 271
	2	Dec.	to Mann	**23.** 73
	7	Dec.	from Madame du Deffand	**4.** 165
	13	Dec.	to the Duchesse de Choiseul	**41.** 168
	15	Dec.	from Madame du Deffand	**4.** 167
	18	Dec.	from Lord Bristol	**41.** 169
	20	Dec.	to Mann	**23.** 76
	27	Dec.	from Madame du Deffand	**4.** 172
1769	1769		from 'F. W.'	**41.** 170
	5	Jan.	from Madame du Deffand	**4.** 176
	9	Jan.	from Madame du Deffand	**4.** 180
	12	Jan.	from Madame du Deffand	**4.** 183
	13	Jan.	from Mann	**23.** 79
	14	Jan.	from Madame du Deffand	**4.** 185
	14	Jan.	to Mann	**23.** 81
	25	Jan.	from Madame du Deffand	**4.** 187

29	Jan.	from Madame du Deffand	**4.** 190
31	Jan.	to Mann	**23.** 84
5	Feb.	to Madame du Deffand	**4.** 194
6	Feb.	from Madame du Deffand	**4.** 194
6	Feb.	to Mann	**23.** 86
7	Feb.	from the Duchesse de Choiseul	**41.** 171
13	Feb.	from Madame du Deffand	**4.** 198
15	Feb.	from the Hon. Robert Walpole	**36.** 48
17	Feb.	to Madame du Deffand	**4.** 204
17	Feb.	to Unknown	**43.** 382
20	Feb.	from Hertford	**39.** 113
22	Feb.	from Madame du Deffand	**4.** 204
24	Feb.	from Mann	**23.** 88
28	Feb.	to Mann	**23.** 92
1	March	from Madame du Deffand	**4.** 206
7	March	to Robertson	**15.** 124
11	March	from Mann	**23.** 94
12	March	from Madame du Deffand	**4.** 208
14	March	from Madame du Deffand	**4.** 209
15	March	from Mrs Robert Cholmondeley	**36.** 49
16	March	from Madame du Deffand	**4.** 211
21	March	to Madame du Deffand	**4.** 213
23	March	to Mann	**23.** 97, **43.** 282
24	March	to Grosvenor Bedford	**41.** 172
25	March	from Chatterton	**16.** 101
25	March	from Mann	**23.** 102
26	March	from Madame du Deffand	**4.** 215
26	March	to Montagu	**10.** 273

28	March	to Chatterton	**16.** 105
30	March	from Chatterton	**16.** 107
	ca April	from Gray	**14.** 184
1	April	from Madame du Deffand	**4.** 216
5	April	to Mason	**28.** 7
6	April	to Madame du Deffand	**4.** 220
7	April	from Madame du Deffand	**4.** 221
8	April	from Chatterton	**16.** 112
11	April	from Montagu	**10.** 275
12	April	from Madame du Deffand	**4.** 224
13	April	from Hertford	**39.** 114
14	April (1,2,3)	from Chatterton	**16.** 113–6
14	April	to Mann	**23.** 104
15	April	from Madame du Deffand	**4.** 226
15	April	from Mann	**23.** 108
15	April	to Montagu	**10.** 276
23	April	from Madame du Deffand	**4.** 229
26	April	from Madame du Deffand	**4.** 230
26	April	from Madame Élie de Beaumont	**41.** 173
28	April	to Sir Edward Walpole	**36.** 51
29	April	from Mann	**23.** 110
3	May	from Madame du Deffand	**4.** 232
8	May	from Mason	**28.** 9
10	May	from Madame du Deffand	**4.** 233
11	May	to Mann	**23.** 114
11	May	to Mason	**28.** 16
11	May	to Montagu	**10.** 277
14	May	from Montagu	**10.** 280
16	May	from Madame du Deffand	**4.** 236
22	May	from Sir Edward Walpole	**36.** 53
23	May	from Mann	**23.** 117

24	May	from Madame du Deffand	**4.** 239
25	**May**	to Mann	**23.** 120
26	May	from Gray	**14.** 185
27	May	to Cole	**1.** 156
29	May	from Cole	**1.** 157
30	May	from Madame du Deffand	**4.** 241
3	June	from Mann	**23.** 122
6	June	from Cole	**1.** 159
6	June	to Madame du Deffand	**4.** 244
11	June	from Madame du Deffand	**4.** 245
14	June	to Cole	**1.** 163
14	June	to Mann	**23.** 125
17	June	from Cole	**1.** 166
18	June	from Madame du Deffand	**4.** 247
25	June	from Madame du Deffand	**4.** 249
26	June	to Cole	**1.** 176
27	June	from Mann	**23.** 129
30	June	from Hertford	**39.** 114
1	July	from Madame du Deffand	**4.** 252
3	July	to Strafford	**35.** 332
4	July	from Madame du Deffand	**4.** 254
7	July	to Conway	**39.** 115
11	July	from Madame du Deffand	**4.** 260
15	July	to Cole	**1.** 178
15	July	from Hertford	**39.** 116
18	July	from Madame du Deffand	**4.** 263
19	July	to Mann	**23.** 131
22	July	from Mann	**23.** 135
24	July	from Chatterton	**16.** 116
26	July	from Madame du Deffand	**4.** 266
ca 27	July–4 Aug.	to Chatterton	**16.** 116
2	Aug.	from Madame du Deffand	**4.** 268

23	Nov.	to Robert Wood	**41.** 176
25	Nov.	from Madame du Deffand	**4.** 311
27	Nov.	from Madame du Deffand	**4.** 312
28	Nov.	from Mann	**23.** 153
30	Nov.	from the Duchesse de Choiseul	**41.** 179
30	Nov.	to Mann	**23.** 155
4	Dec.	from Madame du Deffand	**4.** 314
5	Dec.	to Lady Ossory	**32.** 37
10	Dec.	from Madame du Deffand	**4.** 316
14	Dec.	to Lady Mary Coke	**31.** 142, **43.** 334
14	Dec.	to Cole	**1.** 192
14	Dec.	to Dalrymple	**15.** 127
14	Dec.	to Montagu	**10.** 300
ca 18	Dec.	from Montagu	**10.** 302
18	Dec.	from Cole	**1.** 192
18	Dec.	from Mann	**23.** 159
20	Dec.	from Madame du Deffand	**4.** 320
21	Dec.	to Cole	**1.** 195
24	Dec.	from Madame du Deffand	**4.** 323
26	Dec.	from Madame du Deffand	**4.** 325
26	Dec.	from David Garrick	**41.** 181
31	Dec.	to Mann	**23.** 163
1770	1770	to the Rev. Thomas Percy	**41.** 181
1	Jan.	to Dalrymple	**15.** 127
2	Jan.	from Madame du Deffand	**4.** 330
5	Jan.	from Cole	**1.** 197
8	Jan.	from Madame du Deffand	**4.** 332
10	Jan.	to Mann	**23.** 167
12	Jan.	from Madame du Deffand	**4.** 336
13	Jan.	from Mrs Robert Cholmondeley	**36.** 57
14	Jan.	from Mann	**23.** 171

	16	March	to Madame du Deffand	**4.** 387
	20	March	from Conway	**39.** 125
	21	March	from Madame du Deffand	**4.** 387
	23	March	to Mann	**23.** 199
	23	March	to Lady Ossory	**32.** 41
	24	March	from Mann	**23.** 201
after	26	March	to Lady Jersey	**41.** 184
	27	March	from Montagu	**10.** 303
	28	March	from Madame du Deffand	**4.** 390
	31	March	to Montagu	**10.** 303
?1770		[? April ?1770]	to Lady Mary Coke	**31.** 145, **43.** 335
1770	4	April	from Madame du Deffand	**4.** 394
	11	April	from Madame du Deffand	**4.** 397
	?12	April	to Selwyn	**30.** 253
	14	April	from Madame du Deffand	**4.** 399
	14	April	from Mann	**23.** 203
	16	April	from Hardinge	**35.** 549
	19	April	to Mann	**23.** 205
	20	April	from Hardinge	**35.** 550
	22	April	from Madame du Deffand	**4.** 401
	30	April	from Lord Dacre	**41.** 185
		ca May	from the Rev. James Granger	**41.** 186
	1	May	from Madame du Deffand	**4.** 403
	5	May	from Sir Edward Walpole	**36.** 59
	6	May	to Mann	**23.** 208
	6	May	to Montagu	**10.** 304
	12	May	from Mann	**23.** 213
	13	May	from Madame du Deffand	**4.** 405
	19	May	from Madame du Deffand	**4.** 408
	19	May	from the Rev. James Granger	**41.** 187

23	May	from Madame du Deffand	**4.** 413
24	May	to Mann	**23.** 215
29	May	from Madame du Deffand	**4.** 414
6	June	from Madame du Deffand	**4.** 417
7	June	to Madame du Deffand	**4.** 419
ca 8	June	to Mary Dewes	**41.** 188
11	June	from the Hon. Robert Cholmondeley	**36.** 60
11	June	to Montagu	**10.** 306
13	June	from Madame du Deffand	**4.** 420
15	June	to Mann	**23.** 217
18	June	from Montagu	**10.** 308
19	June	from Madame du Deffand	**4.** 423
20	June	to Madame du Deffand	**4.** 426
20	June	from Mann	**23.** 219
24	June	to Paul Sandby	**41.** 189
27	June	from Madame du Deffand	**4.** 426
29	June	to Montagu	**10.** 310
1	July	to Montagu	**10.** 311
4	July	from Madame du Deffand	**4.** 429
7	July	to Montagu	**10.** 313
8	July	to Madame du Deffand	**4.** 431
9	July	to Strafford	**35.** 338
12	July	to Conway	**39.** 127
14	July	from Mann	**23.** 221
14	July	to Montagu	**10.** 316
15	July	from Madame du Deffand	**4.** 433
15	July	to Montagu	**10.** 317
17	July	from Montagu	**10.** 318
22	July	from Madame du Deffand	**4.** 436
23	July	from Hertford	**39.** 129
25	July	from Hertford	**39.** 129
26	July	to Mann	**23.** 223

9	Oct.	from Madame du Deffand	4. 473
16	Oct.	to Montagu	10. 322
16	Oct.	to Strafford	35. 340
20	Oct.	to Lord Charlemont	41. 190
21	Oct.	from Madame du Deffand	4. 475
27	Oct.	from Mann	23. 243
5	Nov.	from Madame du Deffand	4. 476
12	Nov.	to Mann	23. 245
13	Nov.	to Madame du Deffand	4. 478
14	Nov.	from Madame du Deffand	4. 479
15	Nov.	to Cole	1. 198
15	Nov.	from Cole	1. 199
15	Nov.	from Hertford	39. 132
20	Nov.	to Cole	1. 200
21	Nov.	from Madame du Deffand	4. 481
23	Nov.	from Madame du Deffand	4. 483
25	Nov.	from Madame du Deffand	4. 485
26	Nov.	to Mann	23. 250
27	Nov.	to Madame du Deffand	4. 487
27	Nov.	from Mann	23. 252
28	Nov.	from Cole	1. 201
2	Dec.	from Madame du Deffand	4. 488
11	Dec.	to Madame du Deffand	4. 489
12	Dec.	from Madame du Deffand	4. 490
14	Dec.	from Madame du Deffand	4. 493
15	Dec.	from Cole	1. 203
17	Dec.	from Madame du Deffand	4. 494
18	Dec.	to Mann	23. 255
20	Dec.	to Cole	1. 205
25	Dec.	to Conway	39. 133

24	June	to Cole	**1.** 227
26	June	from Madame du Deffand	**5.** 86
27	June	to Grosvenor Bedford	**41.** 209
27	June	from Madame du Deffand	**5.** 88
27	June	to Lady Ossory	**32.** 51
30	June	from Madame du Deffand	**5.** 89
6	July	to Mann	**23.** 316
9	July	to Chute	**35.** 123
ca 23	July	from Hertford	**39.** 141
28	July	to Edward Louisa Mann	**41.** 210
28	July	from the Prince de Monaco	**41.** 213
30	July	to Conway	**39.** 143
5	Aug.	to Chute	**35.** 125
11	Aug.	to Conway	**39.** 148
11	Aug.	to Lady Ossory	**32.** 53
12	Aug.	to Cole	**1.** 228
21	Aug.	from Cole	**1.** 230
22	Aug.	to Lady Mary Coke	**31.** 156, **43.** 336
22	Aug.	from the Duc de Nivernais	**41.** 214
24	Aug.	from Cole	**1.** 232
24	Aug.	from Mann	**23.** 317
25	Aug.	to Strafford	**35.** 343
28	Aug.	from Mason	**28.** 18
31	Aug.	from Mrs Abington	**41.** 215
1	Sept.	to Mrs Abington	**41.** 215
3	Sept.	from Madame du Deffand	**5.** 90
3	Sept. *bis*	from Madame du Deffand	**5.** 92
5	Sept.	from Madame du Deffand	**5.** 94
7	Sept.	to Conway	**39.** 150
9	Sept.	to Mann	**23.** 320
9	Sept.	to Mason	**28.** 19
9	Sept.	to Selwyn	**30.** 254
10	Sept.	to Cole	**1.** 235

10	Sept.	from Madame du Deffand	**5.** 99
15	Sept.	from Madame du Deffand	**5.** 101
15	Sept.	from Hamilton	**35.** 411
16	Sept.	from Cole	**1.** 237
16	Sept.	to Richard Stonhewer	**41.** 216
17	Sept.	from Mann	**23.** 324
21	Sept.	from Mason	**28.** 21
22	Sept.	from Madame du Deffand	**5.** 102
23	Sept.	from Madame du Deffand	**5.** 103
24	Sept.	from Mann	**23.** 326
25	Sept.	to Mason	**28.** 23
26	Sept.	to Mann	**23.** 328
29	Sept.	from Madame du Deffand	**5.** 112
1	Oct.	from Madame du Deffand	**5.** 114
8	Oct.	to Madame du Deffand	**5.** 115
9	Oct.	from Madame du Deffand	**5.** 115, **43.** 93
11	Oct.	from Madame du Deffand	**5.** 119
12	Oct.	to Cole	**1.** 240
15	Oct.	from Mann	**23.** 330
18	Oct.	from Mann	**23.** 333
19	Oct.	from Cole	**1.** 241
20	Oct.	from Madame du Deffand	**5.** 121
21	Oct.	from Mann	**23.** 336
22	Oct.	to Mann	**23.** 337
23	Oct.	to Cole	**1.** 243
23	Oct.	from Madame du Deffand	**5.** 123
27	Oct.	from Madame du Deffand	**5.** 124
29	Oct.	from Mann	**23.** 341
30	Oct.	from Madame du Deffand	**5.** 126

	? ca Nov.		to Lady Mary Coke	**31.** 159
3	Nov.		from Cole	**1.** 245
6	Nov.		from Madame du Deffand	**5.** 129
7	Nov.		to Madame du Deffand	**5.** 130
7	Nov.		to Mann	**23.** 343
13	Nov.		from Madame du Deffand	**5.** 133
15	Nov.		from Madame du Deffand	**5.** 135
15	Nov.		from Mann	**23.** 347
18	Nov.		to Mann	**23.** 349
20	Nov.		from Madame du Deffand	**5.** 140
21	Nov.		to Madame du Deffand	**5.** 143
27	Nov.		from Madame du Deffand	**5.** 144
29	Nov.		from Mann	**23.** 351
30	Nov.		to Lady Ossory	**32.** 57
2	Dec.		from Madame du Deffand	**5.** 147
4	Dec.		to Lord Ossory	**32.** 58
4	Dec.		to Lady Ossory	**32.** 64
9	Dec.		from Mann	**23.** 355
10	Dec.		from Madame du Deffand	**5.** 151
10	Dec.		from William Hamilton	**42.** 460
11	Dec.		to Lady Mary Coke	**31.** 163, **43.** 337
13	Dec.		from Madame du Deffand	**5.** 155
13	Dec.		from Mann	**23.** 356
14	Dec.		to Lady Ossory	**32.** 67
15	Dec.		to Mann	**23.** 358
17	Dec.		from Madame du Deffand	**5.** 157
28	Dec.		to Mann	**23.** 361
29	Dec.		from Madame du Deffand	**5.** 161
1772	5	Jan.	from Madame du Deffand	**5.** 163

22	June	to Conway	**39.** 156
23	June	from Madame du Deffand	**5.** 258
27	June	from the Duchesse de Mirepoix	**41.** 230
28	June	to Cole	**1.** 264
28	June	from Madame du Deffand	**5.** 261
1	July	to Mann	**23.** 418
3	July	to Madame du Deffand	**5.** 262
6	July	to Mason	**28.** 36
7	July	to Cole	**1.** 264
8	July	from Madame du Deffand	**5.** 262
9	July	from Cole	**1.** 266
ca 16	July	from Hardinge	**35.** 564
18	July	to Lady Ossory	**32.** 83
21	July	to Mason	**28.** 38
23	July	to Mann	**23.** 421
25	July	from Madame du Deffand	**5.** 264
26	July	to James Wyatt	**41.** 231
27	July	from Hardinge	**35.** 565
28	July	to Cole	**1.** 270
30	July	from Cole	**1.** 272
31	July	from Lady Hertford	**39.** 159
1	Aug.	from James Wyatt	**41.** 232
3	Aug.	to Mann	**23.** 425
6	Aug.	from Cole	**1.** 274
11	Aug.	from Mann	**23.** 426
12	Aug.	to Selwyn	**30.** 256
24	Aug.	to Mason	**28.** 42
25	Aug.	from Dr James Brown	**41.** 233
25	Aug.	to Cole	**1.** 274
25	Aug.	from Cole	**1.** 276
25	Aug.	from Mann	**23.** 429
27	Aug.	from Hertford	**39.** 160
28	Aug.	to Cole	**1.** 279
29	Aug.	to Mann	**23.** 431
30	Aug.	from Madame du Deffand	**5.** 265
3	Sept.	from Madame du Deffand	**5.** 265

ca 1773	ca 1773		to Sir Thomas Cave	**41.** 236
1773		? Jan.	to Lord Hardwicke	**41.** 237
		? Jan.	to Nuneham	**35.** 455
	3	Jan.	from Madame du Deffand	**5.** 305
	5	Jan.	from Madame du Deffand	**5.** 306
	6	Jan.	from Cole	**1.** 289
	8	Jan.	to Cole	**1.** 292
	9	Jan.	to Mason	**28.** 57
	9	Jan.	to Lord Sandwich	**41.** 237
	10	Jan.	from Madame Geoffrin	**41.** 238
	11	Jan.	from Madame du Deffand	**5.** 310
	13	Jan.	from Cole	**1.** 295
	14	Jan.	from Mason	**28.** 59
ca	17	Jan.	to Madame du Deffand	**5.** 316
	20	Jan.	from Madame du Deffand	**5.** 316
	21	Jan.	to Lord Hardwicke	**41.** 239
	21	Jan.	to Mann	**23.** 454
	25	Jan.	from Madame du Deffand	**5.** 318
	25	Jan.	to Lady Ossory	**32.** 88
	30	Jan.	from Mann	**23.** 456
	1	Feb.	to Madame du Deffand	**5.** 321
	1	Feb.	from Madame du Deffand	**5.** 321
	1	Feb.	to Mason	**28.** 61
	4	Feb.	from Lort	**16.** 163
	4	Feb.	to Lady Ossory	**32.** 92
	7	Feb.	from Madame du Deffand	**5.** 324
	11	Feb.	from Madame du Deffand	**5.** 328
	11	Feb.	to Lady Ossory	**32.** 94
	12	Feb.	from Cole	**1.** 297
	13	Feb.	from Mann	**23.** 458
	17	Feb.	from Madame du Deffand	**5.** 329
	17	Feb.	to Mann	**23.** 459
	18	Feb.	to Cole	**1.** 300

11	June	to Lady Ossory	**32.** 120
12	June	from Madame du Deffand	**5.** 367
13	June	from Cole	**1.** 319
15	June	to Mann	**23.** 487
16	June	from Madame du Deffand	**5.** 371
19	June	from Mann	**23.** 492
20	June	from Madame du Deffand	**5.** 372
21	June	from Hertford	**39.** 171
21	June	to Lady Ossory	**32.** 124
26	June	to Lady Ossory	**32.** 131
27	June	from Madame du Deffand	**5.** 375
28	June	from Mason	**28.** 89
28	June	to Mason	**28.** 92
30	June	from Madame du Deffand	**5.** 376
1	July	to Madame du Deffand	**5.** 379
1	July	to the Hon. Thomas Walpole	**36.** 93
5	July	to Mason	**28.** 94
6	July	to Dr John Berkenhout	**41.** 255
7	July	from Madame du Deffand	**5.** 380
7	July	to Lord Ossory	**32.** 134
13	July	from Mann	**23.** 493
13	July	to Mann	**23.** 495
14	July	from Madame du Deffand	**5.** 381
16	July	from Mason	**28.** 96
17	July	to Nuneham	**35.** 456
25	July	from Madame du Deffand	**5.** 383
27	July	from Madame du Deffand	**5.** 384
27	July	to Nuneham	**35.** 458
29	July	from David Garrick	**41.** 256
29	July	to Mason	**28.** 99
1	Aug.	from Madame du Deffand	**5.** 387

26	Sept.	from Madame du Deffand	5. 402
28	Sept.	from Mann	23. 517
ca 29	Sept.	from Lady Fenouilhet	32. 150–1, 41. 264
	mid-Oct.	to Lord Hardwicke	41. 265
1	Oct.	to Lady Ossory	32. 145
3	Oct.	to Lady Ailesbury	39. 173
3	Oct.	from Madame du Deffand	5. 403
4	Oct.	to Mann	23. 519
ca 5	Oct.	to Madame du Deffand	5. 406
7	Oct.	to Dr William Hunter	41. 264
7	Oct.	to Lady Ossory	32. 151
9	Oct.	from Madame du Deffand	5. 408
12	Oct.	to Lord Ossory	32. 157
14	Oct.	to Lady George Lennox	31. 172
24	Oct.	from Madame du Deffand	5. 409
ca 26	Oct.	to Madame du Deffand	5. 411
26	Oct.	to Lady Ossory	32. 157
30	Oct.	from Madame du Deffand	5. 411
1	Nov.	from Madame du Deffand	5. 414
2	Nov.	from Madame du Deffand	5. 414
4	Nov.	to Mann	23. 522
6	Nov.	to Nuneham	35. 463
7	Nov.	from Madame du Deffand	5. 416
9	Nov.	from Mann	23. 525
13	Nov.	from Madame du Deffand	5. 419
15	Nov.	to Strafford	35. 347
17	Nov.	from Madame du Deffand	5. 420
ca 18	Nov.	to Madame du Deffand	5. 422

5	March	from Madame du Deffand	**6.** 25
12	March	from Mann	**23.** 558
13	March	from Madame du Deffand	**6.** 28
14	March	from Madame du Deffand	**6.** 29
19	March	to Mason	**28.** 138
ca 22	March	to Madame du Deffand	**6.** 31
23	March	to Mason	**28.** 139
27	March	from Madame du Deffand	**6.** 31
28	March	to Mann	**23.** 560
29	March	from Mann	**23.** 563
30	March	to Fenn	**16.** 231
3	April	from Madame du Deffand	**6.** 34
6	April	to Lady Ossory	**32.** 192
7	April	to Mason	**28.** 143
after 7	April	to Mrs Delany	**41.** 275
12	April	to Madame du Deffand	**6.** 36
ca 13	April	from Mason	**28.** 147
13	April	from Madame du Deffand	**6.** 39
17	April	from Madame du Deffand	**6.** 40
17	April	to Mason	**28.** 151
23	April	from Mann	**23.** 565
23	April	from Mason	**28.** 157
24	April	from Madame du Deffand	**6.** 42
ca 25	April	to Madame du Deffand	**6.** 43
25	April	from Sir Edward Walpole	**36.** 105
27	April	from Madame du Deffand	**6.** 45
30	April	from Madame du Deffand	**6.** 45
	ca May	to Mason	**28.** 159
1	May	to Madame du Deffand	**6.** 47
1	May	to Mann	**23.** 567

ca	7	July		from Hardinge	35. 573
	9	July		from Madame du Deffand	6. 70
	10	July		to Mann	24. 19
	11	July		from Hardinge	35. 573
	16	July		from Sir Edward Walpole	36. 106
	17	July		from Madame du Deffand	6. 74
	18	July		from Cole	1. 335
ca	19	July		to Madame du Deffand	6. 76
	19	July		to Mason	28. 161
	21	July		to Cole	1. 336
after	21	July		from Beauchamp	39. 177
	24	July		from Madame du Deffand	6. 77
	25	July		from Cole	1. 338
	25	July		from Madame du Deffand	6. 78
	26	July		from Mann	24. 22
	30	July		to Lady Ossory	32. 197
	31	July		from Madame du Deffand	6. 79
	3	Aug.		to Mann	24. 24
	6	Aug.		from Mann	24. 28
	7	Aug.		from Madame du Deffand	6. 80
ca	9	Aug.		to Madame du Deffand	6. 82
	9	Aug.		from Mason	28. 163
	10	Aug.		to Selwyn	30. 260
	11	Aug.		to Lady Ossory	32. 202
	14	Aug.		from Madame du Deffand	6. 83
	15	Aug.		to Cole	1. 340
	18	Aug.		to Conway	39. 178
	23	Aug.		from Mann	24. 31
	23	Aug.		to Mason	28. 165
	24	Aug.		from Madame du Deffand	6. 86, 43. 97
	29	Aug.		to Lady Ossory	32. 203

	1	Sept.	from Madame du Deffand	6. 88
	2	Sept.	from Madame du Deffand	6. 89
	2	Sept.	to Mann	24. 34
	4	Sept.	from Madame du Deffand	6. 90
	7	Sept.	to Conway	39. 181
	11	Sept.	from Madame du Deffand	6. 92
	14	Sept.	to Lady Ossory	32. 205
?1774	16	Sept. [?1774]	to John Cowslade	41. 276
1774	16	Sept.	to Mason	28. 167
	17	Sept.	to Fenn	16. 232
	18	Sept.	to Mann	24. 36
	20	Sept.	from Madame du Deffand	6. 94
	20	Sept.	from Mann	24. 39
	24	Sept.	from Mann	24. 41
	26	Sept.	to John Craufurd	41. 277
	27	Sept.	to Conway	39. 185
	28	Sept.	to Conway	39. 188
		Oct.	to Mason	28. 173
	1	Oct.	from Hertford	39. 192
	1	Oct.	to Hertford	39. 193
	1	Oct.	from Mann	24. 42
	2	Oct.	from Madame du Deffand	6. 96
	2	Oct.	from Mason	28. 170
	5	Oct.	from Cole	1. 346
	6	Oct.	to Mann	24. 44
	8	Oct.	from Mann	24. 49
	10	Oct.	from Madame du Deffand	6. 99
	11	Oct.	to Cole	1. 347
	12	Oct.	from Madame du Deffand	6. 99
	15	Oct.	to Lady Ossory	32. 209
	16	Oct.	to Conway	39. 195
	16	Oct.	from Madame du Deffand	6. 101
	22	Oct.	to Mann	24. 51
	23	Oct.	from Madame du Deffand	6. 104

26	Oct.	from Madame du Deffand	6. 105
27	Oct.	to Lady Ossory	32. 211
28	Oct.	from Madame du Deffand	6. 107
29	Oct.	to Conway	39. 200
30	Oct.	from Madame du Deffand	6. 109
ca 4	Nov.	from Conway	39. 205
6	Nov.	from Madame du Deffand	6. 111
7	Nov.	to Lady Ailesbury	39. 206
11	Nov.	to Mann	24. 54
11	Nov.	to Isaac Reed	41. 280
11	Nov.	to Strafford	35. 349, 43. 363
12	Nov.	to Conway	39. 210
14	Nov.	to Lady Ossory	32. 214
15	Nov.	from Madame du Deffand	6. 112
18	Nov.	from Cole	1. 348
18	Nov.	from Mann	24. 57
22	Nov.	from Mann	24. 58
23	Nov.	from Lady Ailesbury	39. 216
23	Nov.	to Lady Ossory	32. 217
24	Nov.	to Mann	24. 59
25	Nov.	to Madame du Deffand	6. 114
27	Nov.	to Conway	39. 220
? Dec.		to Selwyn	30. 261
4	Dec.	from Madame du Deffand	6. 114
11	Dec.	from Madame du Deffand	6. 117
13	Dec.	from Mann	24. 64
15	Dec.	to Conway	39. 225
17	Dec.	from Madame du Deffand	6. 119
23	Dec.	from Madame du Deffand	6. 122
23	Dec.	to Mann	24. 66
26	Dec.	to Conway	39. 229
26	Dec.	to Madame du Deffand	6. 124

13	April	from Hardinge	35. 576
14	April	to Mason	28. 190
17	April	to Mann	24. 89
ca 18	April	from Madame du Deffand	6. 180
[20]	April	from Cole	1. 358
22	April	from Mann	24. 94
25	April	to Cole	1. 366
29	April	from Cole	1. 369
30	April	from Madame du Deffand	6. 182
2	May	from Mann	24. 96
7	May	from Madame du Deffand	6. 184
7	May	to Mann	24. 97
7	May	to Mason	28. 194
9	May	from Madame du Deffand	6. 186
9	May	from the Duke of Richmond	41. 299
17	May	from Madame du Deffand	6. 188
17	May	to Mann	24. 101
18	May	from Mason	28. 198
20	May	from Madame du Deffand	6. 190
20	May	from Mann	24. 104
27	May	to Mason	28. 201
28	May	from Madame du Deffand	6. 194
31	May	from Mann	24. 106
2	June	from Cole	1. 371
4	June	from Madame du Deffand	6. 196
5	June	to Cole	1. 373
5	June	to Mann	24. 109
9	June	from Beauchamp	39. 249
9	June	from Cole	1. 376
11	June	from Madame du Deffand	6. 198
ca 12	June	to Lord Camden	41. 302
12	June	to Mason	28. 205
14	June	to Nuneham	35. 469
17	June	from Mason	28. 207

	23	Dec.	from John Robinson	41. 325
	24	Dec.	from Cole	1. 385
	25	Dec.	to John Robinson	41. 327
	26	Dec.	from Madame du Deffand	6. 248
	26	Dec.	to Mann	24. 160
	27	Dec.	to Lady Ossory	32. 286
	30	Dec.	from Mann	24. 163
?1776	?1776		from Mason	28. 273
?1776	?1776		to Elizabeth Ryves	41. 329
1776	3	Jan.	from Madame du Deffand	6. 252
	9	Jan.	from Mann	24. 165
	10	Jan.	from Madame du Deffand	6. 254
	13	Jan.	from Madame du Deffand	6. 256
	13	Jan.	from Mann	24. 167
	16	Jan.	from Madame du Deffand	6. 258
	17	Jan.	from the Duke of Gloucester	36. 115
	19	Jan.	from Hertford	39. 273
	22	Jan.	to Lady Ossory	32. 290
	23	Jan.	from Mann	24. 171
	24	Jan.	from Madame du Deffand	6. 261
	26	Jan.	to Cole	2. 1
	27	Jan.	from the Prince de Beauvau	41. 330
	28	Jan.	from Lady Albemarle	41. 332
	28	Jan.	to Mann	24. 173
	30	Jan.	from Cole	2. 3
	1	Feb.	from Madame du Deffand	6. 262
	5	Feb.	from Madame du Deffand	6. 263
	6	Feb.	to Mason	28. 240
	?10	Feb.	from Lady Hertford	39. 274
	10	Feb.	from Madame du Deffand	6. 264
	ca 12	Feb.	to Edward Gibbon	41. 333
	14	Feb.	to Edward Gibbon	41. 334
	15	Feb.	to Mann	24. 176

8	April	from Madame du Deffand	**6.** 297
8	April	to Mason	**28.** 257
10	April	from Mason	**28.** 259
13	April	from Mann	**24.** 189
14	April	to Mason	**28.** 260
16	April	to Cole	**2.** 9
17	April	to Mann	**24.** 191
19	April	from Madame du Deffand	**6.** 303
20	April	to Mason	**28.** 262
21	April	to Mason	**28.** 264
23	April	to Mason	**28.** 266
24	April	from Madame du Deffand	**6.** 306
24	April	to Mann	**24.** 195
27	April	from Madame du Deffand	**6.** 307
1	May	from Mason	**28.** 266
4	May	from Mann	**24.** 198
4	May	to Mason	**28.** 268
5	May	from Madame du Deffand	**6.** 309
12	May	from Madame du Deffand	**6.** 311
14	May	from Mann	**24.** 202
14	May	to Mason	**28.** 270
15	May	from Madame du Deffand	**6.** 312
17	May	to Mann	**24.** 204
19	May	from Madame du Deffand	**6.** 315
20	May	from Hardinge	**35.** 578
20	May	to Mason	**28.** 271
22	May	from Madame du Deffand	**6.** 317
25	May	from Lady Charlotte Maria Waldegrave	**36.** 116
27	May	to Mann	**24.** 209
ca 28	May	to Nuneham	**35.** 471
28	May	from Mann	**24.** 213
28	May	from Mason	**28.** 272
30	May	from Cole	**2.** 10
ca 1	June	to Lady Ossory	**32.** 291

15	Sept.	from Madame du Deffand	6. 356
17	Sept.	from Madame du Deffand	6. 359
17	Sept.	to Mason	28. 274
18	Sept.	from Mann	24. 239
19	Sept.	from Cole	2. 26
20	Sept.	to Mann	24. 241
22	Sept.	from Madame du Deffand	6. 360
22	Sept.	to Lady Ossory	32. 320
29	Sept.	from Madame du Deffand	6. 362
3	Oct.	from Lady Hertford	39. 287
7	Oct.	from Madame du Deffand	6. 364
8	Oct.	to Mason	28. 276
9	Oct.	to Lady Ossory	32. 322
12	Oct.	from Mann	24. 243
12	Oct. *bis*	from Mann	24. 247
13	Oct.	from Madame du Deffand	6. 367
13	Oct.	to Mann	24. 248
13	Oct.	to Lady Ossory	32. 326
19	Oct.	from Mann	24. 250
20	Oct.	from Madame du Deffand	6. 368
23	Oct.	from Madame du Deffand	6. 369
27	Oct.	from Madame du Deffand	6. 370
31	Oct.	to Conway	39. 288
31	Oct.	from Hertford	39. 290
	? Nov.	to Mason	28. 278
	ca Nov.–Dec.	from Hardinge	35. 582
1	Nov.	to Mann	24. 252
1	Nov.	from Mann	24. 256
2	Nov.	to Strafford	35. 351
3	Nov.	from Madame du Deffand	6. 372
9	Nov.	to James Bindley	41. 350
13	Nov.	to Lady Ossory	32. 330
16	Nov.	from Mann	24. 259
24	Nov.	to Mann	24. 260

	26	Nov.	from Mann	**24.** 264
	27	Nov.	from Madame du Deffand	**6.** 374
	1	Dec.	from Madame du Deffand	**6.** 376
	1	Dec.	to Mann	**24.** 265
	3	Dec.	to Lady Ossory	**32.** 333
	9	Dec.	to George Allan	**41.** 350
	9	Dec.	to Cole	**2.** 27
	9	Dec.	from Madame du Deffand	**6.** 377
	15	Dec.	from Cole	**2.** 29
	17	Dec.	to Lady Ossory	**32.** 336
	18	Dec.	from Madame du Deffand	**6.** 380
	20	Dec.	to Mann	**24.** 268
	22	Dec.	from Madame du Deffand	**6.** 382
	23	Dec.	to Lady Ossory	**32.** 338
	28	Dec.	to George Colman	**41.** 351
	29	Dec.	from Madame du Deffand	**6.** 384
	31	Dec.	from Madame du Deffand	**6.** 385
1777	1	Jan.	to Lady Ossory	**32.** 340
	5	Jan.	from Madame du Deffand	**6.** 387
	7	Jan.	from Mann	**24.** 270
	7	Jan.	to Lady Ossory	**32.** 341
	8	Jan.	from Madame du Deffand	**6.** 388
	13	Jan.	from Madame du Deffand	**6.** 389
	15	Jan.	from Madame du Deffand	**6.** 392
	15	Jan.	to Lady Ossory	**32.** 343
	19	Jan.	to Lady Ossory	**32.** 344
	22	Jan.	from Madame du Deffand	**6.** 394
	24	Jan.	to Mann	**24.** 272
	25	Jan.	from Madame du Deffand	**6.** 396
	25	Jan.	from Mann	**24.** 274
	26	Jan.	from Madame du Deffand	**6.** 398

ca 20	May	to Madame du Deffand	6.	444
22	May	to Cole	2.	45
23	May	to Hamilton	35.	430
25	May	from Madame du Deffand	6.	444
26	May	from Mason	28.	310
27	May	from Madame du Deffand	6.	445
28	May	to Cole	2.	47
30	May	to Robertson	15.	135
1	June	from Cole	2.	48
1	June	from Madame du Deffand	6.	448
3	June	from Mann	24.	305
8	June	from Madame du Deffand	6.	450
9	June	to John Robinson	41.	358
10	June	to Mason	28.	312
10	June	to Lady Ossory	32.	351
15	June	from Cole	2.	50
15	June	from Madame du Deffand	6. 43.	451, 101
15	June	to Lady Ossory	32.	356
18	June	to Mann	24.	307
19	June	to Cole	2.	51
21	June	from Mason	28.	316
22	June	from Madame du Deffand	6.	453
28	June	from Mann	24.	311
29	June	from Madame du Deffand	6.	454
29	June	to Lady Ossory	32.	359
	July	from Hardinge	35.	594
2	July	from Madame du Deffand	6.	455
6	July	from Hardinge	35.	590
6	July	to Mason	28.	318
6	July	to Lady Ossory	32.	362
7	July	to Nuneham	35.	472
9	July	from Madame du Deffand	6.	456
9	July	to Hardinge	35.	591
10	July	to Conway	39.	291

28	Sept.	to Harcourt	35. 476
29	Sept.	to Lady Ossory	32. 382
1	Oct.	from Lady Cadogan	36. 152
1	Oct.	to Robert Jephson	41. 367
2	Oct.	to Cole	2. 62
4	Oct.	from Cole	2. 63
5	Oct.	to Conway	39. 295
5	Oct.	to Mason	28. 335
6	Oct.	from Madame du Deffand	6. 481
6	Oct. *bis*	from Madame du Deffand	6. 481
7	Oct.	from Cole	2. 65
8	Oct.	to Harcourt	35. 477
8	Oct.	to Lady Ossory	32. 385
12	Oct.	from Madame du Deffand	6. 483
15	Oct.	to Cole	2. 66
17	Oct.	to Robert Jephson	41. 368
18	Oct.	to Harcourt	35. 479
18	Oct.	from Sir Edward Walpole	36. 153
ca 22	Oct.	from Madame du Deffand	6. 485
22	Oct.	from Mason	28. 337
23	Oct.	from Sir Edward Walpole	36. 155
24	Oct.	to Mason	28. 338, 43. 301
26	Oct.	from Madame du Deffand	6. 486
26	Oct. *bis*	from Madame du Deffand	6. 487
26	Oct.	to Mann	24. 331
26	Oct.	from Mason	28. 340
28	Oct.	to Lady Ossory	32. 389
29	Oct.	from Hardinge	35. 595
30	Oct.	from Cole	2. 68
30	Oct.	to Lady Ossory	32. 391
2	Nov.	from Madame du Deffand	6. 488
3	Nov.	to Lady Ossory	32. 393
6	Nov.	to Lady Ossory	32. 395
7	Nov.	to Mann	24. 334
8	Nov.	to Robert Jephson	41. 371

9	Nov.	from Madame du Deffand	**6.** 489
11	Nov.	from Mann	**24.** 336
12	Nov.	from Madame du Deffand	**6.** 490, **43.** 102
13	Nov.	to Lady Ossory	**32.** 397
19	Nov.	from Madame du Deffand	**6.** 493
23	Nov.	from Madame du Deffand	**6.** 494
26	Nov.	to Harcourt	**35.** 481
1	Dec.	from Madame du Deffand	**6.** 495
3	Dec.	to Edmund Burke	**41.** 375
4	Dec.	to Mann	**24.** 338
5	Dec.	from Madame du Deffand	**6.** 496
5	Dec.	to Lady Ossory	**32.** 399
7	Dec.	from Madame du Deffand	**6.** 497
10	Dec.	from Madame du Deffand	**6.** 498
10	Dec.	from Mann	**24.** 343
11	Dec.	to Lady Ossory	**32.** 404
14	Dec.	from Madame du Deffand	**6.** 500
17	Dec.	to Lady Ossory	**32.** 406
?22	Dec.	to Anne Clement	**36.** 156
22	Dec.	from Hardinge	**35.** 597
23	Dec.	to Lady Ossory	**32.** 408
24	Dec.	from Madame du Deffand	**6.** 501
26	Dec.	from Hardinge	**35.** 597
27	Dec.	to Harcourt	**35.** 482
27	Dec.	to Lady Ossory	**32.** 410
29	Dec.	from Madame du Deffand	**6.** 502
29	Dec.	to Lady Ossory	**32.** 411
ca 1778	ca 1778	from Hardinge	**35.** 599
ca 1778	ca 1778	to Lady Ossory	**33.** 1
1778	1778	to Harcourt	**35.** 483
	1778 *bis*	to Harcourt	**35.** 484
	1778	to Sir William Musgrave	**41.** 376

	ca spring		from Hardinge	**35.** 598
1	Jan.		to Lady Ossory	**33.** 1
3	Jan.		from Mann	**24.** 345
4	Jan.		to Mann	**24.** 347
6	Jan.		from Madame du Deffand	**7.** 1
8	Jan.		from Madame du Deffand	**7.** 3
8	Jan.		to Lord Ossory	**33.** 3
12	Jan.		from Madame du Deffand	**7.** 4
17	Jan.		to Mason	**28.** 341
17	Jan.		to Lady Ossory	**33.** 5
19	Jan.		from Madame du Deffand	**7.** 7
20	Jan.		from Mason	**28.** 343
21	Jan.		from Madame du Deffand	**7.** 8
24	Jan.		to Mason	**28.** 345
27	Jan.		to Charles Rogers	**41.** 377
28	Jan.		from Madame du Deffand	**7.** 10
ca 31	Jan.		to Harcourt	**35.** 485
	? Feb.		from Madame du Deffand	**7.** 18
1	Feb.		from Madame du Deffand	**7.** 12
3	Feb.		from Madame du Deffand	**7.** 14
4	Feb.		to Mason	**28.** 348
4	Feb.		to Strafford	**35.** 353
6	Feb.		to Mann	**24.** 349
6	Feb.		from Mason	**28.** 351
7	Feb.		from Mann	**24.** 351
8	Feb.		from Madame du Deffand	**7.** 15
8	Feb.		from Mason	**28.** 352
9	Feb.		from Lord North	**41.** 378
10	Feb.		from Madame du Deffand	**7.** 16
11	Feb.		to Lord North	**41.** 379
11	Feb.		to Sir Edward Walpole	**36.** 157
12	Feb.		from Madame du Deffand	**7.** 18

12	April	from Madame du Deffand	**7.** 39
14	April	from Mann	**24.** 373
15	April	from Madame du Deffand	**7.** 41
16	April	from Cole	**2.** 73
16	April	to Harcourt	**35.** 486
18	April	to Mason	**28.** 382
23	April	to Charles Bedford	**41.** 384
23	April	to Cole	**2.** 74
28	April	from Mann	**24.** 375
	? May	to Edward Gibbon	**41.** 385
6	May	to Harcourt	**35.** 487
9	May	to Mann	**24.** 376
10	May	from Cole	**2.** 76
10	May	from Madame du Deffand	**7.** 43
10	May	to the Duchess of Gloucester	**36.** 159
12	May	to Mason	**28.** 390
15	May	to Mason	**28.** 394
17	May	to Lady Ossory	**33.** 7
19	May	to Lady Ossory	**33.** 11
21	May	to Cole	**2.** 79
23	May	to Bewley	**16.** 121
23	May	from Cole	**2.** 81
24	May	from Madame du Deffand	**7.** 44
24	May	from Mason	**28.** 397
26	May	to Harcourt	**35.** 488
28	May	unsent letter from Cole	**2.** 341
30	May	from Mann	**24.** 380
31	May	from Madame du Deffand	**7.** 45
31	May	to Mann	**24.** 382
31	May	to Mason	**28.** 399
31	May	to Lady Ossory	**33.** 15
3	June	to Cole	**2.** 83
3	June	to Lady Ossory	**33.** 17
7	June	from Cole	**2.** 85
7	June	from Madame du Deffand	**7.** 46
9	June	to Lady Ossory	**33.** 18
10	June	to Cole	**2.** 88

22	July	to Lady Ossory	33. 27
24	July	to Cole	2. 102
24	July	to Mason	28. 419
29	July	from Madame du Deffand	7. 60
29	July	from Lort	16. 177
1	Aug.	from Mann	24. 396
2	Aug.	from Madame du Deffand	7. 62
4	Aug.	from Cole	2. 103
4	Aug.	to Mann	24. 399
4	Aug.	to Lady Ossory	33. 31
7	Aug.	to Lady Ossory	33. 33
9	Aug.	from Madame du Deffand	7. 64
10	Aug.	to Mason	28. 425
11	Aug.	to Lady Ossory	33. 38
14	Aug.	from Mason	28. 427
15	Aug.	to Cole	2. 105
16	Aug.	from Madame du Deffand	7. 65
17	Aug.	from Cole	2. 106
17	Aug.	from John Simco	41. 388
21	Aug.	to Conway	39. 309
ca 22	Aug.	from Mason	28. 430
22	Aug.	to Cole	2. 109
22	Aug.	from Mann	24. 402
23	Aug.	from Madame du Deffand	7. 66
25	Aug.	to Mann	24. 405
25	Aug.	to Mason	28. 432
ca 25	Aug.	from Mason	28. 435
28	Aug.	to Mason	28. 439
29	Aug.	from Cole	2. 112
29	Aug.	from Hertford	39. 312
29	Aug.	to Lady Ossory	33. 43
30	Aug.	from Madame du Deffand	7. 67
1	Sept.	to Cole	2. 115
3	Sept.	from Cole	2. 118
3	Sept.	from Lort	16. 178
6	Sept.	from Madame du Deffand	7. 69
6	Sept.	from Hertford	39. 313

6	Sept.	to Lady Ossory	**33.** 47
10	Sept.	to Cole	**2.** 120
13	Sept.	from Madame du Deffand	**7.** 70
15	Sept.	from Mann	**24.** 408
16	Sept.	to Lady Ossory	**33.** 49
17	Sept.	to Harcourt	**35.** 489
17	Sept.	to Mann	**24.** 410, **43.** 286
17	Sept.	to Mason	**28.** 442
20	Sept.	from Madame du Deffand	**7.** 71
27	Sept.	from Madame du Deffand	**7.** 73
27	Sept.	to Harcourt	**35.** 490
27	Sept.	to Lady Ossory	**33.** 53
1	Oct.	from Lord Orford	**36.** 163
2	Oct.	from Hertford	**39.** 314
5	Oct.	to Lord Orford	**36.** 164
7	Oct.	from Madame du Deffand	**7.** 74
7	Oct.	from Mason	**28.** 444
8	Oct.	to Mann	**24.** 413
9	Oct.	to Harcourt	**35.** 492
9	Oct.	to Lady Ossory	**33.** 58
10	Oct.	from Hertford	**39.** 315
11	Oct.	to Mason	**28.** 444
12	Oct.	from Madame du Deffand	**7.** 75
14	Oct.	to Cole	**2.** 123
15	Oct.	from Madame du Deffand	**7.** 76
17	Oct.	from Madame du Deffand	**7.** 77
18	Oct.	from Cole	**2.** 126
21	Oct.	to Lady Ossory	**33.** 61
23	Oct.	to Conway	**39.** 316
24	Oct.	from Madame du Deffand	**7.** 79
26	Oct.	to Cole	**2.** 129
26	Oct.	to the Hon. Thomas Walpole	**36.** 166
27	Oct.	from Mann	**24.** 416
28	Oct.	to Lady Browne	**31.** 188

28	Oct.	to Lady Ossory	33. 65
30	Oct.	from Madame du Deffand	7. 81
30	Oct.	to Mann	24. 418
1	Nov.	from Cole	2. 131
4	Nov.	to Cole	2. 132
5	Nov.	to Lady Browne	31. 190
8	Nov.	from Cole	2. 133
8	Nov.	from Madame du Deffand	7. 83
9	Nov.	to Lady Ossory	33. 69
11	Nov.	from Madame du Deffand	7. 84
15	Nov.	from Madame du Deffand	7. 85
16	Nov.	to Mann	24. 421
18	Nov.	from Madame du Deffand	7. 86
18	Nov.	to Lord and Lady Ossory	33. 70
20	Nov.	to Lady Ossory	33. 70
24	Nov.	to Lady Ossory	33. 72
27	Nov.	to Mann	24. 422
29	Nov.	from Madame du Deffand	7. 87
3	Dec.	from Madame du Deffand	7. 89
5	Dec.	to Lady Ossory	33. 74
6	Dec.	from Madame du Deffand	7. 90
8	Dec.	from Madame du Deffand	7. 91
8	Dec.	from Mann	24. 425
8	Dec.	to Charles Rogers	41. 389
10	Dec.	from Charles Rogers	41. 390
10	Dec.	to Charles Rogers	41. 391
12	Dec.	to Lady Ossory	33. 75
15	Dec.	to Lord Dacre	41. 392
18	Dec.	to Lady Browne	31. 192
18	Dec.	to Mann	24. 425
19	Dec.	from Mann	24. 428
19	Dec.	to Lady Ossory	33. 76
20	Dec.	from Madame du Deffand	7. 93
24	Dec.	to Buchan	15. 138

15	June	from Madame du Deffand	**7.** 151
16	June	to Conway	**39.** 328
16	June	to Mann	**24.** 482
19	June	from Mann	**24.** 486
19	June	to Mann	**24.** 488
20	June	from Madame du Deffand	**7.** 152
21	June	from Hardinge	**35.** 600
22	June	from Mann	**24.** 489
22	June	to Lady Ossory	**33.** 102
27	June	from Madame du Deffand	**7.** 154
30	June	to Mann	**24.** 490
1	July	from Hardinge	**35.** 600
3	July	from Mann	**24.** 495
4	July	to Hardinge	**35.** 601
5	July	from Madame du Deffand	**7.** 156
5	July	to Selwyn	**30.** 266
ca 6	July	from Hardinge	**35.** 603
6	July	to Lady Ossory	**33.** 106
7	July	to Mann	**24.** 496
7	July	to Selwyn	**30.** 268
10	July	to Lady Ailesbury	**39.** 331
11	July	from Madame du Deffand	**7.** 157
12	July	to Cole	**2.** 168
12	July	from Madame du Deffand	**7.** 159
14	July	to Lady Ossory	**33.** 108
20	July	to Lady Ossory	**33.** 113
20	July	to Selwyn	**30.** 269
22	July	from Madame du Deffand	**7.** 160
23	July	to Lady Ailesbury	**39.** 335
24	July	from Cole	**2.** 171
24	July	from Madame du Deffand	**7.** 161
24	July	to Lady Ossory	**33.** 115
30	July	from Madame du Deffand	**7.** 162
	Aug.–Sept.	to Lady Browne	**31.** 197
	Aug.–Sept. *bis*	to Lady Browne	**31.** 197
1	Aug.	from Mason	**28.** 452

2	Aug.		from Hertford	**39.** 337
4	Aug.		to Mann	**24.** 501
6	Aug.		from Madame du Deffand	**7.** 163
7	Aug.		from Mann	**24.** 504
7	Aug.		to Lady Ossory	**33.** 118
9	Aug.		to Mason	**28.** 453
12	Aug.		to Cole	**2.** 173
17	Aug.		from Madame du Deffand	**7.** 165
ca 18	Aug.		to Lady Browne	**31.** 195
18	Aug.		to Mason	**28.** 457
19	Aug.		to Mann	**24.** 506
20	Aug.		from Madame du Deffand	**7.** 167
21	Aug.		from Mason	**28.** 459
22	Aug.		to Charles Rogers	**41.** 402
23	Aug.		to Lady Browne	**31.** 196
23	Aug.		to Mason	**28.** 460
27	Aug.		from Mann	**24.** 508
30	Aug.		from Madame du Deffand	**7.** 168
31	Aug.		to Lady Browne	**31.** 196
31	Aug.		from Lort	**16.** 188
	? ca Sept.–Oct.		to Lady Browne	**31.** 198
3	Sept.		from Madame du Deffand	**7.** 170
3	Sept.		from Hertford	**39.** 338
5	Sept.		to Mann	**24.** 511
5	Sept.		to Mason	**28.** 462
5	Sept.		to Lady Ossory	**33.** 120
8	Sept.		from Lort	**16.** 189
10	Sept.		from Madame du Deffand	**7.** 172
11	Sept.		from Mann	**24.** 513
11	Sept.		to Lady Ossory	**33.** 122
13	Sept.		to Conway	**39.** 338
14	Sept.		to Mason	**28.** 463
16	Sept.		to Mann	**24.** 515
18	Sept.		from Madame du Deffand	**7.** 174
18	Sept.		from Mason	**28.** 464
21	Sept.		to Selwyn	**30.** 271
23	Sept.		from Madame du Deffand	**7.** 175

24	Sept.	to Lady Ossory	**33.** 123
25	Sept.	from Mann	**24.** 517
28	Sept.	to Mason	**28.** 466
	Oct.	to Harcourt	**35.** 495
1	Oct.	from Madame du Deffand	**7.** 177
4	Oct.	to Selwyn	**30.** 273
8	Oct.	from Madame du Deffand	**7.** 180
11	Oct.	to Mann	**24.** 518
14	Oct.	from Madame du Deffand	**7.** 182
14	Oct.	to Mann	**24.** 521
14	Oct.	to Lady Ossory	**33.** 124
14	Oct. *bis*	to Lady Ossory	**33.** 125
16	Oct.	from Mann	**24.** 522
21	Oct.	to Mason	**28.** 468
24	Oct.	from Madame du Deffand	**7.** 183
27	Oct.	from Hertford	**39.** 340
27	Oct.	to Lady Ossory	**33.** 128
28	Oct.	to Lady Ailesbury	**39.** 341
30	Oct.	from Madame du Deffand	**7.** 184
30	Oct.	from Hertford	**39.** 343
31	Oct.	to Mann	**24.** 524
?1779	[? Nov. or ? Dec. ?1779]	from Hertford	**39.** 344
1779	Nov.	to Lady Craven	**41.** 403
1	Nov.	to Lady Ossory	**33.** 130
5	Nov.	from Madame du Deffand	**7.** 186
6	Nov.	to Lady Ossory	**33.** 133
12	Nov.	to Mann	**24.** 526
12	Nov.	from Mason	**28.** 471
13	Nov.	from Mann	**24.** 530
14	Nov.	from Cole	**2.** 173
14	Nov.	to Lady Ossory	**33.** 135
15	Nov.	to Lady Ossory	**33.** 139
16	Nov.	to Cole	**2.** 176
16	Nov.	to Mason	**28.** 473
ca 19	Nov.	to Mason	**28.** 475
19	Nov.	from Madame du Deffand	**7.** 187
21	Nov.	to Lady Ossory	**33.** 140
21	Nov.	to [? Oliver] Tilson	**41.** 405

	24	Nov.	from Madame du Deffand	7. 188
	28	Nov.	to Mann	24. 532
ca	29	Nov.	to Harcourt	35. 499
	29	Nov.	to Mason	28. 479
	29	Nov.	to Lady Ossory	33. 143
	2	Dec.	to Lady Ossory	33. 144
	3	Dec.	from Madame du Deffand	7. 191
	6	Dec.	to Lady Ossory	33. 145
	7	Dec.	from Mason	28. 483
	9	Dec.	from Madame du Deffand	7. 192
	10	Dec.	from Mann	24. 539
	11	Dec.	to Mason	28. 485
	14	Dec.	to Lady Ossory	33. 146
	20	Dec.	from Madame du Deffand	7. 193
	20	Dec.	to Mann	24. 542
	23	Dec.	from Madame du Deffand	7. 194
	23	Dec.	to Lady Ossory	33. 148
	25	Dec.	from Hertford	39. 344
	25	Dec.	to Mason	28. 488
	27	Dec.	to Cole	2. 178
	28	Dec.	from Mason	28. 489
	30	Dec.	from Cole	2. 179
	31	Dec.	from Mason	28. 490
ca 1780	ca 1780		to Selwyn	30. 276
1780	1	Jan.	to Lady Ossory	33. 151
	3	Jan.	from Hertford	39. 345
	3	Jan.	from Mann	25. 1
	3	Jan.	to Lady Ossory	33. 154
	4	Jan.	from Hertford	39. 346
	4	Jan.	to Mann	25. 3
	4	Jan.	to Mason	29. 1
	5	Jan.	to Cole	2. 183
	?7	Jan.	to Harcourt	35. 500
	7	Jan.	from Madame du Deffand	7. 196
	8	Jan.	to Lady Ossory	33. 157
ca	9	Jan.	from Madame du Deffand	7. 197
	13	Jan.	to Mann	25. 5
	13	Jan.	to Lady Ossory	33. 159

4	July	to Cole	**2.** 229
6	July	to Mann	**25.** 65
7	July	to Richard Bull	**41.** 414
7	July	from Madame du Deffand	**7.** 235
8	July	from Cole	**2.** 230
8	July	from Mann	**25.** 69
ca 12	July	to Lady Ossory	**33.** 204
12	July	from Mason	**29.** 66
15	July	from Madame du Deffand	**7.** 237
15	July	to Mason	**29.** 68
15	July	to the Hon. Thomas Walpole	**36.** 169
17	July	from Hardinge	**35.** 606
23	July	from Madame du Deffand	**7.** 239
24	July	from Hardinge	**35.** 608
24	July	to Mann	**25.** 73
29	July	from Mann	**25.** 76
1	Aug.	to Lady Ossory	**33.** 209
3	Aug.	from Madame du Deffand	**7.** 240
5	Aug.	from the Prince de Bauffremont	**41.** 415
8	Aug.	to Mason	**29.** 72
16	Aug.	to Lady Ossory	**33.** 211
17	Aug.	from Madame du Deffand	**7.** 241
17	Aug.	from Hardinge	**35.** 611
20	Aug.	from Mason	**29.** 73
22	Aug.	from Madame du Deffand	**7.** 242
23	Aug.	to Lady Ossory	**33.** 216
24	Aug.	to Mann	**25.** 77
24	Aug.	to Mason	**29.** 75
26	Aug.	from Mann	**25.** 80
27	Aug.	from Wiart	**7.** 243
30	Aug.	from Wiart	**7.** 244
31	Aug.	to Mason	**29.** 78
31	Aug.	to Lord Ossory	**33.** 220
1	Sept.	to Lady Ossory	**33.** 221
2	Sept.	to Harcourt	**35.** 506
3	Sept.	from Wiart	**7.** 245

ca	5	Sept.	from Mann	25.	83
	6	Sept.	to the Hon. Thomas Walpole	36.	170
	6	Sept.	from Wiart	7.	245
	9	Sept.	to Strafford	35.	356
	10	Sept.	from Hardinge	35.	612
	10	Sept.	from Wiart	7.	246
	12	Sept.	to Lady Ossory	33.	225
	13	Sept.	from Wiart	7.	247
	15	Sept.	to Lady Browne	31.	198
	17	Sept.	from Wiart	7.	248
	19	Sept.	to Mann	25.	85
	19	Sept.	to the Hon. Thomas Walpole	36.	173
	20	Sept.	from Mason	29.	79
	20	Sept.	from Wiart	7.	249
	23	Sept.	to Lady Ossory	33.	226
	24	Sept.	to Mason	29.	81
	27	Sept.	to Cole	2.	233
	27	Sept.	to Lady Ossory	33.	229
	27	Sept.	from Wiart	7.	250
	28	Sept.	to the Hon. Thomas Walpole	36.	176
	30	Sept.	from Cole	2.	234
	3	Oct.	to Cole	2.	236
	3	Oct.	to Harcourt	35.	507
	4	Oct.	to Mrs Hogarth	41.	416
	4	Oct.	to Mann	25.	87
	5	Oct.	from Lady Lucan	41.	418
	7	Oct.	to Mann	25.	89
	8	Oct.	to the Hon. Thomas Walpole	36.	178
	10	Oct.	to Lady Ossory	33.	231
?1780	13	Oct. [?1780]	from John Cowslade	41.	419
1780	13	Oct.	to Mason	29.	83
	18	Oct.	to Charles Bedford	41.	421
	19	Oct.	from Hillier	16.	92
	22	Oct.	from Wiart	7.	251
	24	Oct.	from Mann	25.	93
	26	Oct.	to the Hon. Thomas Walpole	36.	181
		? Nov.	to Dr William Hunter	41.	422
	1	Nov.	to Mason	29.	85
	1	Nov.	to Lady Ossory	33.	234

	2	Nov.	to Mann	25. 95
	11	Nov.	to Cole	2. 237
	ca 12	Nov.	from the Prince de Beauvau	41. 423
	13	Nov.	from Cole	2. 241
	16	Nov.	to Lady Ossory	33. 237
	20	Nov.	to Mann	25. 98
	24	Nov.	to Cole	2. 244
	24	Nov.	to the Hon. Thomas Walpole	36. 185
	26	Nov.	to Lady Ossory	33. 241
	27	Nov.	from Cole	2. 246
	30	Nov.	to Cole	2. 248
	5	Dec.	to Lady Ossory	33. 246
?1780	7	[? Dec. ?1780]	from Lady Hertford	39. 351
1780	11	Dec.	to Dalrymple	15. 141
	11	Dec.	to Lady Ossory	33. 249
	12	Dec.	from Mann	25. 100
	12	Dec.	to Mann	25. 103
	17	Dec.	from Cole	2. 250
	17	Dec.	to Lady Ossory	33. 251
	19	Dec.	to Cole	2. 253
	21	Dec.	to Mann	25. 104
	23	Dec.	from Lort	16. 192
	25	Dec.	to Lady Ossory	33. 255
	29	Dec.	from Sir Edward Walpole	36. 188
	29	Dec.	to the Hon. Thomas Walpole	36. 188
	30	Dec.	from Mann	25. 106
	31	Dec.	to Mann	25. 108
1781	1	Jan.	to Dalrymple	15. 146
	2	Jan.	to Lady Ossory	33. 258
	3	Jan.	to Conway	39. 352
	4	Jan.	to Mason	29. 89
	4	Jan.	to Lady Ossory	33. 261
	8	Jan.	from Hertford	39. 357
	9	Jan.	from Hertford	39. 358
	9	Jan.	to Mann	25. 110
	9	Jan.	to Lady Ossory	33. 264
	11	Jan.	from Hertford	39. 359
	13	Jan.	from Mann	25. 112
	14	Jan.	from Hertford	39. 361
	14	Jan.	to Lady Ossory	33. 266
	16	Jan.	from Mann	25. 113

30	March	from Cole	2. 266
30	March	to Mann	25. 140
30	March	to Mason	29. 122
1	April	to Mason	29. 126
2	April	from Lort	16. 193
3	April	to Cole	2. 267
14	April	to Mason	29. 128
16	April	to John Henderson	41. 427
21	April	from Mann	25. 143
21	April	from Mason	29. 131
25	April	to Mason	29. 134
27	April	to Mann	25. 145
28	April	to Henry William Bunbury	41. 429
30	April	to the Hon. Thomas Walpole	36. 195
	May	to Harcourt	35. 508
4	May	to Cole	2. 268
6	May	to Conway	39. 368
6	May	to Mann	25. 147
6	May	to Mason	29. 137
7	May	from Cole	2. 270
12	May	from Mann	25. 149
14	May	to the Hon. Thomas Walpole	36. 197
15	May	from Mason	29. 140
16	May	to Mann	25. 151
18	May	to Harcourt	35. 509
22	May	to Mason	29. 143
26	May	from Mann	25. 155
28	May	to Conway	39. 372
	ca June	from Hardinge	35. 613
3	June	to Conway	39. 378
8	June	to Lord Bagot	41. 430
8	June	to Mann	25. 157
9	June	from Mann	25. 159
12	June	to Charles Bedford	41. 432
13	June	to Lady Ossory	33. 273
13	June	to Strafford	35. 358
14	June	to Mason	29. 145
16	June	to Cole	2. 272
18	June	to Charles Bedford	41. 433
20	June	to Lady Ossory	33. 275
30	June	from Cole	2. 276
1	July	to Lord Charlemont	41. 433

3	July	from Mann	**25.** 161
3	July	to Mason	**29.** 148
4	July	to Lady Ossory	**33.** 278
4	July	from Sir Edward Walpole	**36.** 200
5	July	to Mann	**25.** 163
6	July	to John Nichols	**41.** 435
ca 9	July	to Lady Browne	**31.** 201
13	July	to Mann	**25.** 166
17	July	to Lady Ossory	**33.** 281
ca 18	July	to Lady Browne	**31.** 202
18	July	to John Henderson	**41.** 436
ca 19	July	to Lady Browne	**31.** 202
23	July	from Cole	**2.** 278
24	July	from Mann	**25.** 168
25	July	to Lady Ossory	**33.** 282
26	July	to Cole	**2.** 279
31	July	to the Hon. Thomas Walpole	**36.** 201
	? Aug.	to Mrs Gostling	**41.** 437
	? Aug.	from Mrs Gostling	**41.** 438
1	Aug.	to Mann	**25.** 171
5	Aug.	from Cole	**2.** 280
7	Aug.	to Cole	**2.** 282
7	Aug.	to Lady Ossory	**33.** 285
13	Aug.	to Thomas Cadell	**41.** 439
13	Aug.	from Lort	**16.** 195
16	Aug.	to Mason	**29.** 149
18	Aug.	from Mann	**25.** 173
23	Aug.	to Mann	**25.** 176
26	Aug.	to John Henderson	**41.** 439
31	Aug.	to Strafford	**35.** 360
1	Sept.	from Mann	**25.** 178
4	Sept.	from Mann	**25.** 179
4	Sept.	to Lady Ossory	**33.** 287
7	Sept.	to James Bindley	**41.** 440
7	Sept.	to Mann	**25.** 182
9	Sept.	to Mason	**29.** 151
11	Sept.	to Mann	**25.** 185
12	Sept.	to Lady Ossory	**33.** 289
16	Sept.	to Conway	**39.** 384
17	Sept.	from Lort	**16.** 196
19	Sept.	to Mann	**25.** 185
19	Sept.	from Mason	**29.** 153
22	Sept.	from Mann	**25.** 188

25	Sept.	to Mason	**29.** 155	
ca 1	Oct.	to Lady Browne	**31.** 203	
	? Oct.	to Lady Browne	**31.** 203	
1	Oct.	from Mason	**29.** 157	
3	Oct.	to Mann	**25.** 190	
7	Oct.	to Lady Ossory	**33.** 293	
9	Oct.	from Mann	**25.** 192	
9	Oct.	to Mason	**29.** 160	
15	Oct.	to John Henderson	**41.** 441	
15	Oct.	to Thomas Pennant	**41.** 442	
17	Oct.	to Lady Ossory	**33.** 297	
18	Oct.	to Mann	**25.** 193	
18	Oct.	from Horatio Mann the Younger	**25.** 196	
22	Oct.	to Elizabeth Younge	**41.** 446	
25	Oct.	from Mann	**25.** 198	
26	Oct.	to Lady Ossory	**33.** 299	
29	Oct.	to Mann	**25.** 200, **43.** 290	
31	Oct.	to John Nichols	**41.** 448	
2	Nov.	to Lort	**16.** 198	
6	Nov.	to Lady Ossory	**33.** 305	
7	Nov.	to Robert Jephson	**41.** 453	
7	Nov.	to Mason	**29.** 161	
8	Nov.	from Lort	**16.** 200	
9	Nov.	from Mason	**29.** 163	
10	Nov.	to Robert Jephson	**41.** 456	
10	Nov.	from Mann	**25.** 203	
11	Nov.	to the Hon. Thomas Walpole	**36.** 203	
13	Nov.	to Robert Jephson	**41.** 457	
13	Nov.	to Mason	**29.** 165	
15	Nov.	to Lady Ossory	**33.** 308	
18	Nov.	to Conway	**39.** 386	
18	Nov.	to Robert Jephson	**41.** 459	
20	Nov.	from Mann	**25.** 204	
21	Nov.	to Robert Jephson	**41.** 460	
22	Nov.	to Lady Ossory	**33.** 311	
23	Nov.	to Edmond Malone	**41.** 463	
26	Nov.	to Mann	**25.** 208	
26	Nov.	to Mason	**29.** 166	
27	Nov.	to Strafford	**35.** 362	
28	Nov.	to Mason	**29.** 168	
29	Nov.	to Mann	**25.** 210	
	ca Dec.	to Edmond Malone	**41.** 465	

		late Dec.	to Richard Bull	**41.** 469
	1	Dec.	to Buchan	**15.** 156
	3	Dec.	to Robert Jephson	**41.** 466
	4	Dec.	to Mann	**25.** 215
	13	Dec.	from Mann	**25.** 219
	16	Dec.	from Mason	**29.** 168
	18	Dec.	to Lady Ossory	**33.** 313
	19	Dec.	to Lady Ossory	**33.** 315
	20	Dec.	to Richard Bull	**41.** 467
	20	Dec.	to Mason	**29.** 170
	21	Dec.	to Mann	**25.** 219
	22	Dec.	from Cole	**2.** 284
	22	Dec.	to Edmond Malone	**41.** 468
	22	Dec.	to Lady Ossory	**33.** 316
	23	Dec.	from Horatio Mann the Younger	**25.** 222
	25	Dec.	to Lady Ossory	**33.** 318
	28	Dec.	to Mann	**25.** 223
	29	Dec.	from Mann	**25.** 228
	30	Dec.	to Cole	**2.** 286
	31	Dec.	to Fenn	**16.** 236
[?1782–3]	[?1782–3]		from Horatio Mann the Younger	**25.** 353
1782	2	Jan.	from Fenn	**16.** 238
	3	Jan.	to Mason	**29.** 173
	4	Jan.	from Cole	**2.** 290
	7	Jan.	to Lady Ossory	**33.** 320
	10	Jan.	to Mason	**29.** 174
	12	Jan.	from Mann	**25.** 233, **43.** 290
	12	Jan.	to Lady Ossory	**33.** 323
	15	Jan.	from Horatio Mann the Younger	**25.** 234
	17	Jan.	to Mann	**25.** 235
	19	Jan.	from Elizabeth Montagu	**42.** 468
	19	Jan.	to Lady Ossory	**33.** 324
	26	Jan.	to Buchan	**15.** 159
	27	Jan.	to Cole	**2.** 292
		? Feb.–March	to Harcourt	**35.** 510
	2	Feb.	from Mann	**25.** 238
	4	Feb.	from Edmond Malone	**42.** 1
	4	Feb.	to Edmond Malone	**42.** 1
	7	Feb.	from Cole	**2.** 293

7	Feb.	to Mann	25. 240
7	Feb.	to Mason	29. 176
9	Feb.	from Mason	29. 181
9	Feb.	to Lady Ossory	33. 325
11	Feb.	from Cole	2. 295
14	Feb.	to Cole	2. 297
14	Feb.	to Mason	29. 183
15	Feb.	to Cole	2. 300
17	Feb.	from Cole	2. 303
22	Feb.	to Cole	2. 305
23	Feb.	to Mason	29. 186
23	Feb.	to Lady Ossory	33. 328
24	Feb.	from Cole	2. 306
24	Feb.	from Mason	29. 189
25	Feb.	to Mann	25. 244
26	Feb.	from Mann	25. 248
28	Feb.	to Mason	29. 191
28	Feb.	to Lady Ossory	33. 330
1	March	to Mann	25. 251
4	March	to John Henderson	42. 4
5	March	from Cole	2. 308
6	March	from Hardinge	35. 615
8	March	to Hardinge	35. 616
9	March	to Cole	2. 309
10	March	from Mason	29. 194
11	March	to Mann	25. 253
14	March	to John Henderson	42. 5
14	March	to Mason	29. 196
15	March	from Hardinge	35. 617
15	March	to Hardinge	35. 619
15	March	to Mason	29. 199
16	March	from Hardinge	35. 620
16	March	to Robert Henry	42. 6
17	March	to Harcourt	35. 511
ca 21	March	from Lady Ossory	33. 331
21	March	to Mann	25. 258
21	March	to Mason	29. 201
21	March	to Lady Ossory	33. 333
23	March	from Mason	29. 203
23	March	to Mason	29. 205
26	March	to Mann	25. 260
26	March	to Mason	29. 208
27	March	to Lady Harcourt	35. 511
30	March	from Mason	29. 211
? April		from Hardinge	35. 622

	April		42.	9
	April	to John Nichols	42.	9
1	April	to Mason	29.	214
2	April	to Mason	29.	217
6	April	from Mason	29.	220
6	April	to Mason	29.	222
7	April	to Mann	25.	263
10	April	from Hertford	39.	389
10	April	from Mason	29.	226
11	April	from Mason	29.	229
12	April	from Cole	2.	310
13	April	to Cole	2.	313
13	April	from Mann	25.	268
13	April	to Mason	29.	230
14	April	to Mason	29.	233
18	April	to Hardinge	35.	621
18	April	to Charles Rogers	42.	9
22	April	to Mason	29.	236
24	April	from Mason	29.	240
25	April	from Mason	29.	240
26	April	from Mann	25.	270
27	April	to Mason	29.	242
30	April	from Mann	25.	271
4	May	from Fenn	16.	240
5	May	to Mann	25.	272
7	May	to Mason	29.	243
8	May	from Mason	29.	246
13	May	from Cole	2.	315
14	May	to Cole	2.	317
15	May	to Fenn	16.	243
16	May	from Cole	2.	317
18	May	to Mann	25.	277
18	May	from Mason	29.	247
24	May	to John Baynes	42.	10
24	May	to Cole	2.	318
25	May	to Mason	29.	249
27	May	from Cole	2.	320
28	May	from Hamilton	35.	432
1	June	to Cole	2.	322
2	June	to the Earl of Buchan	42.	11
2	June	to Benjamin Ibbot	42.	14
2	June	from Mason	29.	251
3	June	to Harcourt	35.	514
4	June	to Mason	29.	252
5	June	to John Hatsell	43.	163

12	Aug.	to Charles Bedford	42.	29
15	Aug.	to Lady Ossory	33.	349
16	Aug.	from George Rose	42.	31
16	Aug.	to Strafford	35.	365
17	Aug.	from Mann	25.	302
18	Aug.	to George Rose	42.	32
18	Aug.	to John Nichols	42.	33
19	Aug.	from Mann	25.	305
20	Aug.	to Conway	39.	390
20	Aug.	to Mann	25.	306
23	Aug.	to Charles Bedford	42.	34
27	Aug.	to Edward King	42.	35
30	Aug.	from Giuseppe Cardini	42.	36
30	Aug.	to Mann	25.	309
31	Aug.	from Mann	25.	313
31	Aug.	to Lady Ossory	33.	352
6	Sept.	to Thomas Walpole the Younger	36.	206
7	Sept.	to Harcourt	35.	520
7	Sept.	to Treadway Russell Nash	43.	383
8	Sept.	to Mann	25.	315
15	Sept.	to Buchan	15.	163
15	Sept.	from Mann	25.	317
17	Sept.	to Conway	39.	391
20	Sept.	to Mason	29.	273
25	Sept.	to Mann	25.	319
26	Sept.	from Mason	29.	274
28	Sept.	from Mann	25.	322
ca 30	Sept.	from Conway	39.	393
1	Oct.	to Lady Ossory	33.	355
3	Oct.	to Strafford	35.	366
5	Oct.	from Mann	25.	323
8	Oct.	from Mann	25.	325
12	Oct.	to Mann	25.	326
12	Oct.	from Mann	25.	329
15	Oct.	to Thomas Pennant	42.	37
23	Oct.	to Harcourt	35.	524
23	Oct.	to Mann	25.	330
29	Oct.	to Harcourt	35.	526
29	Oct.	from Mann	25.	332
30	Oct.	from Cole	2.	334
30	Oct.	to Hertford	39.	394
	Nov.	to Mrs Garrick	42.	40

	31	Jan.	to William Suckling	42. 46
	1	Feb.	from William Suckling	42. 47
	3	Feb.	to Mann	25. 360
	8	Feb.	to Lady Ossory	33. 385
	10	Feb.	to Mason	29. 284
	16	Feb.	from Mann	25. 366
	18	Feb.	to Mann	25. 367
	18	Feb.	to Lady Ossory	33. 388
	24	Feb.	to Mann	25. 371
	25	Feb.	from Mann	25. 374
?1783	1	March [?1783]	to Harcourt	35. 530
1783	2	March	to Mann	25. 377
	3	March	from Henry	15. 168
	5	March	from Mason	29. 286
?1783	7	March [?1783]	from Lort	16. 201
1783	7	March	to Mason	29. 289
	8	March	from Mann	25. 382
	10	March	to Mann	25. 385
	11	March	to Lady Ossory	33. 390
	13	March	to the Duchess of Gloucester	36. 208
	13	March	to Mann	25. 387
	13	March	to Lady Ossory	33. 393
	15	March	to Henry	15. 170, 43. 199
	18	March	from Mann	25. 388
	18	March	to Lady Ossory	33. 395
	19	March	to Benjamin Ibbot	42. 48
	ca 23	March	from Henry	15. 174
	26	March	to Richard Bull	42. 49
	28	March	to Henry	15. 176, 43. 199
	3	April	to Mann	25. 390
	5	April	from Mann	25. 393
	5	April	to Lady Ossory	33. 397
	17	April	to Lady Ossory	33. 398
	25	April	to Lady Ossory	33. 400
	26	April	from Mann	25. 395
	30	April	to Mann	25. 397
	1	May	from Hardinge	35. 623
	4	May	from Mason	29. 290
	5	May	to Mason	29. 292
	7	May	to Mason	29. 297
	8	May	to Mann	25. 401

	10	May	to George Colman	42.	50
	11	May	to Mason	29.	299
	12	May	to Buchan	15.	178
	16	May	to the Hon. Thomas Fitzwilliam	42.	52
	17	May	to Hardinge	35.	623
	19	May	from Mason	29.	302
	27	May	from Mann	25.	404
	29	May	to Mann	25.	406
	30	May	from Richard Bull	42.	53
	31	May	to Mason	29.	304
	1	June	to the Rev. Christopher Alderson	42.	54
	5	June	from Mann	25.	411, 43. 291
	9	June	to Mason	29.	308
	11	June	to ? Thomas Cadell	42.	56
?1783	11	June [?1783]	to George Colman	42.	56
1783	11	June	to Mann	25.	412
	19	June	to Lord Shelburne	42.	57
	20	June	to Lady Ossory	33.	401
	24	June	to Strafford	35.	368
	25	June	from Richard Gough	42.	59
	25	June	from Mrs John Duncombe	42.	60
	28	June	to Anthony Highmore	42.	61
	28	June	from Mann	25.	414
	5	July	to Richard Gough	42.	62
	8	July	to Mann	25.	417
	12	July	from Mann	25.	420
	15	July	to Lady Ossory	33.	404
	16	July	to Unknown	42.	62
ca	20	July	from Hardinge	35.	624
	20	July	from Jean-Baptiste-Louis-Georges Seroux d'Agincourt	42.	63
	23	July	to Lady Browne	31.	204
	23	July	to Lady Ossory	33.	407
	23	July	to the Hon. Thomas Walpole	36.	211
	26	July	from Hardinge	35.	625
	27	July	to Conway	39.	402
	30	July	to Mann	25.	421

	? Aug.		from Charles James Fox	**42.** 70
1	Aug.		to Strafford	**35.** 371
2	Aug.		from Hardinge	**35.** 626
2	Aug.		from Mann	**25.** 425
4	Aug.		to Lady Ossory	**33.** 409
5	Aug.		to Harcourt	**35.** 531
13	Aug.		to Edward Edwards	**42.** 71
15	Aug.		to Conway	**39.** 405
27	Aug.		to Mann	**25.** 426
27	Aug.		to Lady Ossory	**33.** 412
30	Aug.		to Harcourt	**35.** 534
31	Aug.		to Lord Dacre	**42.** 72
	? Sept. or **Oct.**		to Lady Browne	**31.** 204, **43.** 338
	? Sept. or **Oct.** *bis*		to Lady Browne	**31.** 205
6	Sept.		from Mann	**25.** 429
9	Sept.		to Lady Ossory	**33.** 415
10	Sept.		from Charles James Fox	**42.** 73
10	Sept.		to Mann	**25.** 432
12	Sept.		to Strafford	**35.** 374
22	Sept.		to Mason	**29.** 311
27	Sept.		to Mann	**25.** 432
27	Sept.		to Lady Ossory	**33.** 419
2	Oct.		to Lord Buchan	**42.** 74
7	Oct.		to Mary Hamilton	**31.** 206
9	Oct.		to Lady Ossory	**33.** 421
10	Oct.		from Mann	**25.** 434
11	Oct.		to Strafford	**35.** 376
17	Oct.		to Lady Browne	**31.** 209
18	Oct.		to Lady Ossory	**33.** 425
?21	Oct.		to Lady Browne	**31.** 210
ca 25	Oct.		from Thomas Pownall	**42.** 76
27	Oct.		to Thomas Pownall	**42.** 77
?30	Oct.		to Elizabeth Montagu	**42.** 83
7	Nov.		to Thomas Pownall	**42.** 84
8	Nov.		to Mason	**29.** 313
8	Nov.		to Lady Ossory	**33.** 427
8	Nov.		to Henry Sampson Woodfall	**42.** 85
10	Nov.		to Strafford	**35.** 378
12	Nov.		to Mann	**25.** 437

	18	Nov.	from Mann	25. 441
	21	Nov.	to Mann	25. 444
	2	Dec.	to Mann	25. 448
ca	6	Dec.	to Mann	25. 452
	11	Dec.	to Strafford	35. 380
	13	Dec.	from Mann	25. 456
	15	Dec.	to Mann	25. 458
	19	Dec.	to Mann	25. 460
	25	Dec.	from Mason	29. 320
	29	Dec.	from Horatio Mann the Younger	25. 461
	30	Dec.	to Mason	29. 322
	30	Dec.	to Lady Ossory	33. 430
before 1784	before 1784		to Edward Jerningham	42. 86
?1784	?1784		to John Nichols	42. 87
ca 1784	ca 1784		to Hardinge	35. 632
ca 1784	ca 1784		from Hardinge	35. 633
1784	1784		to Ozias Humphry	42. 463
	3	Jan.	to the Hon. Thomas Walpole	36. 214
	6	Jan.	to the Hon. Thomas Walpole	36. 217
	8	Jan.	to Mann	25. 462
	10	Jan.	from Mann	25. 464
	13	Jan.	to Mann	25. 466
	16	Jan.	from the Hon. Thomas Walpole	36. 218
	19	Jan.	to Lady Ossory	33. 432
	24	Jan.	from Mann	25. 467
	28	Jan.	from Mason	29. 324
	31	Jan.	from the Hon. Charles Hamilton	42. 88
	31	Jan.	from Mann	25. 469
ca	1	Feb.	unsent letter to Mason	29. 349
	1	Feb.	to the Hon. Thomas Walpole	36. 220
	2	Feb.	to Mann	25. 470
	2	Feb.	to Mason	29. 326
	4	Feb.	from the Duke of Gloucester	36. 224
	6	Feb.	to Lady Ossory	33. 433
	14	Feb.	from Mann	25. 473
	6	March	to Hannah More	31. 211

8	March	to Benjamin Ibbot	**42.**	91
8	March *bis*	to Benjamin Ibbot	**42.**	92
11	March	from Joseph White	**42.**	93
12	March	to Benjamin Ibbot	**42.**	94
12	March	to Mann	**25.**	475
13	March	from Mann	**25.**	478
23	March	from Hardinge	**35.**	628
23	March	to Hardinge	**35.**	630
26	March	to Mann	**25.**	481
30	March	to Mann	**25.**	484
	ca April	to Lady Ossory	**33.**	434
9	April	from Mann	**25.**	492
14	April	from Horatio Mann the Younger	**25.**	494
20	April	to Harcourt	**35.**	536
29	April	to Mann	**25.**	495
5	May	to Conway	**39.**	407
7	May	to John Fenn	**42.**	95
10	May	to Mary Hamilton	**31.**	214
13	May	to Edmond Malone	**42.**	96
21	May	to Conway	**39.**	411
22	May	from Mann	**25.**	498
3	June	to Mann	**25.**	500
8	June	to Lady Ailesbury	**39.**	413
14	June	from John Fenn	**42.**	97
18	June	to Elizabeth Vesey	**42.**	99
19	June	to Lady Ossory	**33.**	435
25	June	to Conway	**39.**	415
26	June	from Mann	**25.**	504
29	June	to John Fenn	**42.**	100
29	June	from Jean-Baptiste-Louis-Georges Seroux d'Agincourt	**42.**	101
30	June	to Conway	**39.**	417
ca 3	July	from Lady Chewton	**36.**	225
3	July	from John Fenn	**42.**	105
3	July	from Mrs Fenn	**42.**	106
7	July	to Mrs Fenn	**16.**	244
8	July	to Mann	**25.**	505
10	July	to Mann	**25.**	509
14	July	to Richard Bull	**42.**	107
24	July	from Mann	**25.**	511
31	July	from Mann	**25.**	514
4	Aug.	to Benjamin Ibbot	**42.**	108

6	Aug.	to Edward Jerningham	42.	109
6	Aug.	to Strafford	35.	382
8	Aug.	to James Dodsley	42.	110
9	Aug.	to Mann	25.	515
14	Aug.	to Conway	39.	420
19	Aug.	to Lady Ossory	33.	437
24	Aug.	to Pinkerton	16.	251
25	Aug.	to Mann	25.	519
26	Aug.	to Lady Ossory	33.	440
5	Sept.	to Pinkerton	42.	111
7	Sept.	to Strafford	35.	384
8	Sept.	from William Fermor	42.	112
11	Sept.	from Mann	25.	521
16	Sept.	to Lady Browne	31.	217
16	Sept.	to William Fermor	42.	114
18	Sept.	from Mann	25.	524
26	Sept.	from William Fermor	42.	115
27	Sept.	to Pinkerton	16.	252
30	Sept.	to Mann	25.	527
6	Oct.	to Pinkerton	16.	255,
			43.	223
8	Oct.	from Mann	25.	533
10	Oct.	from Hertford	39.	422
16	Oct.	to Conway	39.	423
16	Oct.	from Hardinge	35.	630
16	Oct.	to Hardinge	35.	631
23	Oct.	to Lady Ossory	33.	445
ca 26	Oct.	from Hardinge	35.	633
27	Oct.	to Pinkerton	16.	258
28	Oct.	to Frederick Montagu	9.	1
1	Nov.	to Mann	25.	537
8	Nov.	to Mann	25.	540
12	Nov.	to Lady Ossory	33.	447
13	Nov.	to Hannah More	31.	219
16	Nov.	from Hertford	39.	426
17	Nov.	to Lady Ossory	33.	451
20	Nov.	from Hertford	39.	427
20	Nov.	to Lady Ossory	33.	453
27	Nov.	to Lady Lyttelton	42.	117
28	Nov.	to Conway	39.	428
28	Nov.	from Lady Lyttelton	42.	118
2	Dec.	to Lady Lyttelton	42.	119

	2	Dec.	to Samuel Ireland	**42.** 120
	2	Dec.	to Mann	**25.** 542
	2	Dec.	to Thomas Walpole the Younger	**36.** 227
	9	Dec.	to Lady Ossory	**33.** 453
	9	Dec.	to the Rev. Joseph Warton	**42.** 121
	13	Dec.	from Horatio Mann the Younger	**25.** 546
	18	Dec.	from Mann	**25.** 548
	26	Dec.	to Edmond Malone	**42.** 124
	26	Dec.	from Horatio Mann the Younger	**25.** 550
	27	Dec.	to Lady Ossory	**33.** 456
ca 1785	ca 1785		to George, 4th Earl Waldegrave	**36.** 274, **43.** 369
1785	1785		to Sir William Musgrave	**42.** 124
? early 1785	? early 1785		to Edmond Malone	**42.** 125
1785		? ca Jan.–March	from Harcourt	**35.** 537
	1	Jan.	to Lord Sandwich	**42.** 127
	3	Jan.	to Lady Ossory	**33.** 456
	4	Jan.	to Mann	**25.** 551
	4	Jan.	from Mann	**25.** 553
	6	Jan.	to the Duc de Nivernais	**42.** 128
	11	Jan.	to the Rev. Mark Noble	**42.** 133
	13	Jan.	to Lady Ossory	**33.** 457
	ca 26	Jan.	to Lord Sandwich	**42.** 134
	?27	Jan.	to Selwyn	**30.** 277
	1	Feb.	to Henry	**15.** 183, **43.** 200
	1	Feb.	to the Duc de Nivernais	**42.** 135
	2	Feb.	to Mann	**25.** 555
	5	Feb.	to Lady Ossory	**33.** 459
	7	Feb.	from Lady Waldegrave	**36.** 229
	8	Feb.	from Mann	**25.** 559
	ca 10	Feb.	to Pinkerton	**16.** 262
	11	Feb.	to Edmond Malone	**42.** 137
	19	Feb.	to Thomas Walpole the Younger	**36.** 231

5	July	to Lady Ossory	**33.** 516
5	July	to Selwyn	**30.** 278
6	July	to Dr Charles Burney	**42.** 170
7	July	from Lady Waldegrave	**36.** 239
8	July	from Mann	**25.** 656
20	July	from Dr Charles Burney	**42.** 171
22	July	to Lady Ossory	**33.** 519
2	Aug.	to Lady Ossory	**33.** 521
11	Aug.	from Mann	**25.** 658
20	Aug.	from Horatio Mann the Younger	**25.** 659
21	Aug.	to Joshua Sharpe	**42.** 173
27	Aug.	to Samuel Ireland	**42.** 175
29	Aug.	to Strafford	**35.** 386
30	Aug.	to Lady Ossory	**33.** 523
5	Sept.	from Mann	**25.** 660
25	Sept.	from Horatio Mann the Younger	**25.** 662
28	Sept.	to Lady Ossory	**33.** 526
	Oct.	to Horatio Mann the Younger	**25.** 663
4	Oct.	to Pinkerton	**16.** 289, **43.** 226
13	Oct.	to Lady Ossory	**33.** 532
18	Oct.	to Pinkerton	**16.** 289
23	Oct.	from Hertford	**39.** 443
25	Oct.	to Thomas Walpole the Younger	**36.** 240
29	Oct.	to Conway	**39.** 444
4	Nov.	to Lady Ossory	**33.** 532
6	Nov.	from Horatio Mann the Younger	**25.** 663
12	Nov.	to the Hon. Thomas Walpole	**36.** 243
17	Nov.	from Horatio Mann the Younger	**25.** 664
27	Nov.	to Lady Craven	**42.** 176
28	Nov.	to Mrs Delany	**42.** 179
29	Nov.	to Lord Duncannon	**42.** 180
29	Nov.	to Pinkerton	**16.** 290
30	Nov.	from Mrs Delany	**42.** 181
1	Dec.	to Lady Ossory	**33.** 536

3	May	to Sir Joseph Banks	42. 194
18	May	from Horatio Mann	
		the Younger	25. 675
28	May	to the Hon. Thomas	
		Fitzwilliam	42. 195
	June	from Hannah More	31. 248
?7	June	from Hertford	29. 446
14	June	to Lady Ossory	33. 561
15	June	to Hannah More	31. 246
17	June	to Conway	39. 447
24	June	to Conway	39. 448
28	June	to Lady Ossory	33. 566
29	June	to Pinkerton	16. 291
30	June	from Hertford	39. 452
? ca	July	to Hannah More	31. 250
9	July	to the Duchess of	
		Gloucester	36. 244
20	July	to Conway	39. 453
26	July	to the Hon. Mrs	
		Boyle Walsingham	42. 196
28	July	to Strafford	35. 388
29	July	to Samuel Lysons	15. 195
30	July	to Pinkerton	42. 197
9	Aug.	to Charles Bedford	42. 198
1	Sept.	to Harcourt	35. 538
6	Sept.	to Lady Ossory	33. 567
15	Sept.	to Charles Bedford	43. 163
15	Sept.	to Lady Ossory	33. 573
22	Sept.	from George, 4th Earl	
		Waldegrave	36. 247
24	Sept.	from Hertford	39. 457
	Oct.	from Hannah More	31. 251
4	Oct.	to Lady Ossory	33. 577
10	Oct.	to Thomas Pennant	42. 198
14	Oct.	to Hannah More	31. 254
28	Oct.	to Lady Lyttelton	42. 199
11	Nov.	to Conway	39. 459
3	Dec.	to Lady Ossory	33. 581
9	Dec.	to the Hon. Thomas	
		Walpole	36. 248
15	Dec.	to Lady Ossory	33. 583
19	Dec.	to Dr Charles Burney	42. 202
22	Dec.	to Mrs Dickenson	31. 256
28	Dec.	to the Hon. Mrs	
		Boyle Walsingham	42. 203

29	July	to Thomas Astle	42. 223
2	Aug.	to Strafford	35. 393
14	Aug.	to Pinkerton	16. 295
16	Aug.	to Lady Ossory	34. 11
17	Aug.	to Hannah More	31. 276,
			43. 339
?23	Aug.	from Welbore Ellis	42. 224
	Sept.	from Hannah More	31. 279
6	Sept.	to Lady Ossory	34. 14
12	Sept.	to Strafford	35. 395
22	Sept.	to Hannah More	31. 282
22	Sept.	to Mrs Dickenson	31. 285
22	Sept.	from Mrs Dickenson	31. 285
24	Sept.	to Lady Ossory	34. 19
27	Sept.	to Lady Browne	31. 286
11	Oct.	to Lady Ossory	34. 22
13	Oct.	from Hertford	39. 463
14	Oct.	to Mary Berry	11. 1
15	Oct.	to Pinkerton	16. 298
19	Oct.	to Lady Ossory	34. 26
27	Oct.	from George, 4th Earl	
		Waldegrave	36. 252
29	Oct.	to Pinkerton	42. 225
	Nov.	from Hannah More	31. 289
late Nov.		from Thomas	
		Holcroft	42. 226
1	Nov.	from Mary Berry	11. 1
10	Nov.	from Lort	16. 212
12	Nov.	to Lort	16. 213
21	Nov.	to Lort	16. 215
28	Nov.	to Thomas Holcroft	42. 227
3	Dec.	to Lady Ossory	34. 30
4	Dec.	to Thomas Holcroft	42. 228
11	Dec.	to Lady Craven	42. 228
14	Dec.	to Lord	
		Buckinghamshire	42. 232
26	Dec.	to Lady Ossory	34. 33
ca 1789	ca 1789	to Hardinge	35. 636
1789	1789	to Richard Cosway	42. 233
2	Feb.	to Mary Berry	11. 3
4	Feb.	from Mary Berry	11. 4
6	Feb.	to Lady Ossory	34. 34
10	Feb.	to Lady Ossory	34. 38
11	Feb.	to Mrs Horatio	
		Churchill	36. 253

	12	Feb.	to Horatio Mann	
			the Younger	25. 679
	24	Feb.	to Lady Ossory	34. 41
	28	Feb.	to Lady Ossory	34. 46
	11	March	to Lord Charlemont	42. 234
?1789	11	March [?1789]	to Hannah More	31. 291
1789	20	March	to Mary and Agnes	
			Berry	11. 4
	25	March	to Mary Berry	11. 6
	30	March	to Thomas Pennant	42. 234
	30	March	to Richard Bull	42. 237
		April	from Hannah More	31. 294
		April	to Mrs Yorke and	
			Miss Yorke	42. 238
	10	April	to Thomas Pennant	42. 238
	?11	April	to Mary and Agnes	
			Berry	11. 7
	12	April	from Mary Berry	11. 7
	14	April	to Mary Berry	11. 8
	18	April	from Mary Berry	11. 9
	22	April	to Hannah More	31. 292
	28	April	to Mary and Agnes	
			Berry	11. 10
	29	April	from Mary Berry	11. 12
	1	May	to Treadway Russell	
			Nash	42. 241
	15	May	to Fenn	16. 246
	16	May	to Fenn	16. 246
	26	May	from Conway	39. 464
	27	May	to Fenn	16. 246
	27	May	from Richard Gough	42. 242
	28	May	to Richard Gough	42. 243
	1	June	to Fenn	16. 247
	13	June	to Elizabeth Carter	42. 244
ca	15	June	to Lady Ossory	34. 49
	22	June	to Lady Ossory	34. 49
	23	June	to Mary and Agnes	
			Berry	11. 13
	23	June	to Hannah More	31. 300
	24	June	to Paul Panton	43. 164
	27	June	to Richard Gough	42. 246
	27	June	from Hannah More	31. 303,
				43. 340
	30	June	to Mary Berry	11. 18
	1	July	to Lady Ossory	34. 50

2	July	to Hannah More	**31.** 304
5	July	to Lort	**16.** 216
6	July	from Lort	**16.** 218
7	July	to Lort	**16.** 219
ca 8	July	from Hannah More	**31.** 307
9	July	to Mary Berry	**11.** 24
10	July	to Mary Berry	**11.** 30
10	July	to Hannah More	**31.** 308
ca 13	July	from Hannah More	**31.** 310
15	July	to Conway	**39.** 467
16	July	to Lady Ossory	**34.** 52
ca 18	July	from Hannah More	**31.** 311
19	July	to Mary Berry	**11.** 38
19	July	to the Rev. Joseph Warton	**42.** 248
20	July	to Hannah More	**31.** 312
22	July	to Lady Ossory	**34.** 54
25	July	to Elizabeth Carter	**42.** 250
27	July	to Lort	**16.** 219
27	July	from Hannah More	**31.** 315
28	July	from the Duchess of Gloucester	**36.** 254
29	July	to Mary Berry	**11.** 41
30	July	to Edward Jerningham	**42.** 252
31	July	to Pinkerton	**16.** 302
4	Aug.	from Lort	**16.** 222
4	Aug.	to Lady Ossory	**34.** 57
5	Aug.	to Joseph Cooper Walker	**42.** 253
6	Aug.	to Mary Berry	**11.** 47
7	Aug.	from Lort	**16.** 224
9	Aug.	to Edward Jerningham	**42.** 256
9	Aug.	to Lort	**16.** 226
9	Aug.	to Hannah More	**31.** 318
13	Aug.	to Agnes Berry	**11.** 51
14	Aug.	to Lady Ossory	**34.** 60
14	Aug.	to Pinkerton	**16.** 305, **43.** 228
17	Aug.	from John Cranch	**42.** 257
19	Aug.	to Pinkerton	**16.** 308
20	Aug.	to Mary Berry	**11.** 55
20	Aug.	to John Simco	**42.** 258
23	Aug.	to Lady Ossory	**34.** 61

	8	Nov.	to Lady Ossory	**34.**	75
	23	Nov.	from Lady Waldegrave	**36.**	269
	26	Nov.	to Lady Ossory	**34.**	80
		Dec.	to Mary Berry	**43.**	141
		Dec.	from Mary Berry	**43.**	142
		Dec.	to Mary Berry	**43.**	142
	6	Dec.	to Lady Ossory	**34.**	84
	12	Dec.	to Lady Ossory	**34.**	86
	15	Dec.	to Pinkerton	**16.**	310
	22	Dec.	to Mrs Dickenson	**31.**	335
	26	Dec.	to Lady Ossory	**34.**	88
	26	Dec.	to the Hon. William Waldegrave	**43.**	387
	30	Dec.	to Lady Ossory	**34.**	91
?1790	?1790		to William Parsons	**42.**	263
1790	1790		to John Wilkes	**42.**	263
	1790		to Sir William Musgrave	**42.**	264
	16	Jan.	to Mrs Archibald Alison	**42.**	264
	30	Jan.	to Thomas Astle	**42.**	266
	3	Feb.	from the Hon. William Waldegrave	**36.**	271
	6	Feb.	to the Hon. William Waldegrave	**36.**	272
	14	Feb.	from Richard French	**42.**	267
ca	18	Feb.	from Hannah More	**31.**	336
	18	Feb.	to Mrs Archibald Alison	**42.**	272
	20	Feb.	to Hannah More	**31.**	338
	21	Feb.	to William Parsons	**42.**	275
	22	March	to William Fermor	**42.**	276
	9	April	to the Hon. Thomas Walpole	**36.**	275
	10	April	to Lord Carlisle	**42.**	277
	19	April	to Thomas Pennant	**42.**	278
	30	April	to ? Thomas Astle	**42.**	279
	17	May	to Richard Gough	**42.**	281
	26	May	to Pinkerton	**16.**	311
	28	May	from Richard Bull	**42.**	282
	?5	June	to Harcourt	**35.**	541
	5	June	to Lort	**16.**	227
	25	June	to Conway	**39.**	472
	26	June	to Strafford	**35.**	398

12	July	to Mary Berry	**11.** 309
17	July	to Mary Berry	**11.** 312
20	July	to Mary Berry	**11.** 316
26	July	to Mary Berry	**11.** 319
3	Aug.	to Mary and Agnes Berry	**11.** 324
8	Aug.	to Mary Berry	**11.** 327
8	Aug.	to Lady Ossory	**34.** 115
10	Aug.	to Mary Berry	**11.** 330
15	Aug.	to Barbara Cecilia Seton	**11.** 333
17	Aug.	to Mary Berry	**11.** 335
22	Aug.	to Lady Ossory	**34.** 117
23	Aug.	to Mary Berry	**11.** 339
29	Aug.	to ? Cuthbert Potts, Jr	**43.** 164
	Sept.	from Hannah More	**31.** 357
5	Sept.	to Mary Berry	**11.** 343
8	Sept.	to Lady Ossory	**34.** 121
11	Sept.	to Mary Berry	**11.** 348
16	Sept.	to Mary and Agnes Berry	**11.** 351
25	Sept.	to Mary Berry	**11.** 356
27	Sept.	to Conway	**39.** 485
29	Sept.	to Hannah More	**31.** 358
30	Sept.	to Lady Ossory	**34.** 125
3	Oct.	to Mary Berry	**11.** 359
9	Oct.	to Mary Berry	**11.** 361
12	Oct.	to Thomas Walpole the Younger	**36.** 276
16	Oct.	to Mary Berry	**11.** 367
20	Oct.	to Mary Berry	**11.** 368
21	Oct.	from James Edwards	**15.** 212
26	Oct.	to Lady Ossory	**34.** 127
27	Oct.	to Mary Berry	**11.** 371
11	Nov.	to Barbara Cecilia Seton	**11.** 373
12	Nov.	to Barbara Cecilia Seton	**11.** 374
23	Nov.	to Lady Ossory	**34.** 129
30	Nov.	from Lord Townshend	**42.** 332
	Dec.	to Mary Berry	**11.** 377
2	Dec.	to Lord Townshend	**42.** 335
after 5	Dec.	to Unknown	**42.** 337

	6	Dec.	to ? Carlos Cony	42. 338
	7	Dec.	to Thomas Coutts	42. 340
	8	Dec.	to the Duke of Bedford	42. 340
	?9	Dec.	from Mary Berry	11. 374
	10	Dec.	to Jane Clement	36. 278
	10	Dec.	to Anne Clement	36. 279
	10	Dec.	to Lady Ossory	34. 133
	?11	Dec.	to Mary Berry	11. 376
	13	Dec.	to Mary Berry	11. 376
	13	Dec.	to Fenn	16. 247
	18	Dec.	to Lady Bristol	42. 342
	26	Dec.	to Lady Ossory	34. 134
	26	Dec.	to Pinkerton	16. 312
	29	Dec.	to Lord Townshend	42. 343
?1792	?1792		to Pinkerton	16. 315
ca 1792	ca 1792		from Richard Gough	42. 346
1792	1	Jan.	to Hannah More	31. 363
	3	Jan.	to J. R. Dashwood	42. 348
	13	Jan.	to the Hon. Hugh Seymour-Conway (later Lord Hugh Seymour)	39. 489
	14	Jan.	to Lady Ossory	34. 135
	17	Jan.	to Lady George Lennox	31. 366
	18	Jan.	to Lady Ossory	34. 136
	21	Jan.	to Sir Isaac Heard	42. 349
	23	Jan.	to Buchan	15. 213
	30	Jan.	to ? Charles Lucas	42. 350
	4	Feb.	to Lady Ossory	34. 138
	15	Feb.	to Sylvester Douglas	42. 351
	29	Feb.	from the Duc de Nivernais	42. 352
	15	March	to Richard Gough	42. 354
	16	March	to Treadway Russell Nash	43. 388
	28	March	to Mrs Dickenson	31. 367
	30	March	to Mrs Dickenson	31. 368
	3	April	to Lady Bristol	42. 355
	5	April	to Mrs Dickenson	31. 368
	5	April	from Le Fèvre d'Ormesson	42. 357
	5	April	to Lady Bristol	42. 358
	9	April	to Lady Bristol	42. 360

after 9	April	to Lady Bristol	**42.** 361
10	April	to Lady Ossory	**34.** 139
17	April	from Hamilton	**35.** 440
30	April	to Lady Ossory	**34.** 140
2	May	to Mr Norford, Jr	**43.** 164
8	May	to Mrs Dickenson	**31.** 369
14	May	to Thomas Barret	**42.** 362
22	May	to Lady Ossory	**34.** 140
29	May	to Lady Ossory	**34.** 141
26	June	to Thomas Walpole the Younger	**36.** 280
27	June	to Lady Ossory	**34.** 142
1	July	to Unknown	**42.** 364
3	July	to ? Dalrymple	**15.** 214
4	July	from Lady Waldegrave	**36.** 283
7	July	to Lady Ossory	**34.** 146
17	July	to Samuel Lysons	**15.** 214, **43.** 204
17	July	to Lady Ossory	**34.** 147
4	Aug.	to Joseph Cooper Walker	**42.** 365
5	Aug.	to Beloe	**15.** 215
7	Aug.	to Pinkerton	**16.** 315
9	Aug.	to ? Daniel Lysons	**15.** 217
11	Aug.	from Bishop Percy	**42.** 366
ca 18	Aug.	from Hannah More	**31.** 369
18	Aug.	to Lady Ossory	**34.** 151
20	Aug.	to Bishop Percy	**42.** 369
21	Aug.	to Hannah More	**31.** 371
27	Aug.	to Pinkerton	**16.** 316
30	Aug.	to George Nicol	**42.** 371
31	Aug.	to Conway	**39.** 491
4	Sept.	to Lady Ossory	**34.** 156
10	Sept.	to Lady Ossory	**34.** 160
12	Sept.	to Nares	**15.** 218, **43.** 204
12	Sept.	to George Nicol	**42.** 375
13	Sept.	to Samuel Lysons	**15.** 221
17	Sept.	to the Earl of Lisburne	**42.** 376
18	Sept.	to Bishop Percy	**42.** 378
20	Sept.	to Joseph Cooper Walker	**42.** 384
24	Sept.	to Beloe	**15.** 222

18	Sept.	to Hannah More	**31.** 391
22	Sept.	to Conway	**39.** 501
24	Sept.	to Mary Berry	**12.** 6
25	Sept.	to Mary Berry	**12.** 10
25	Sept.	to Pinkerton	**16.** 317
25	Sept.	to Unknown	**42.** 393
26	Sept.	to Mary Berry	**12.** 13
29	Sept.	to Mary Berry	**12.** 17
2	Oct.	to Mary Berry	**12.** 20
5	Oct.	to Nares	**15.** 240, **43.** 207
6	Oct.	to Mary Berry	**12.** 23
10	Oct.	to Mary Berry	**12.** 26
15	Oct.	to Mary Berry	**12.** 30
15	Oct.	to Bishop Percy	**42.** 394
17	Oct.	to Agnes Berry	**12.** 35
19	Oct.	to Mary Berry	**12.** 37
20	Oct.	to Nares	**15.** 244, **43.** 208
22	Oct.	to Mary Berry	**12.** 39
24	Oct.	to Mary Berry	**12.** 42
25	Oct.	to Mary Berry	**12.** 45
28	Oct.	to Beloe	**15.** 245
29	Oct.	to Mary Berry	**12.** 47
2	Nov.	to Lady Ossory	**34.** 190
5	Nov.	to Mary Berry	**12.** 50
7	Nov.	to Mary Berry	**12.** 53
8	Nov.	to Samuel Lysons	**15.** 247
10	Nov.	to Lady Ossory	**34.** 191
14	Nov.	to Mary Berry	**12.** 60
17	Nov.	to Beloe	**15.** 248
19	Nov.	to Mary Berry	**12.** 64
23	Nov.	to Mary Berry	**12.** 68
30	Nov.	to Mary Berry	**12.** 75
30	Nov.	to Lady Anne North	**42.** 396
2	Dec.	to Lady Diana Beauclerk	**42.** 397
4	Dec.	to Mary Berry	**12.** 78
6	Dec.	to Mary Berry	**12.** 82
9	Dec.	to Lady Ossory	**34.** 193
13	Dec.	to Mary Berry	**12.** 85
26	Dec.	to Lady Ossory	**34.** 195
1794 7	Jan.	to Harcourt	**35.** 543
10	Jan.	to Conway	**39.** 508

30	Jan.	to Lady Ossory	34. 196
6	Feb.	to William Seward	42. 399
1	March	to Hannah More	31. 393
2	March	to Pinkerton	16. 318
12	March	to James Edwards	15. 248
19	March	to Samuel Lysons	15. 249
21	March	to James Edwards	42. 399
4	April	to Pinkerton	16. 383
11	April	to Pinkerton	16. 319
17	April	to Mary Berry	12. 91
21	April	to Mary Berry	12. 95
27	April	to Hannah More	31. 394
1	May	to Mary Berry	12. 97
8	May	to George Nicol	42. 401
15	May	to Pinkerton	16. 319
27	May	to Unknown	42. 402
3	June	from Mary Carter	42. 405
15	June	to Lady Ossory	34. 197
16	July	to Lady Douglas	42. 407
22	July	to Lady Ossory	34. 199
28	July	to Edmond Malone	42. 409
29	July	to Lady Ossory	34. 200
31	July	to Agnes Berry	12. 99
3	Aug.	to Lady Ossory	34. 201
4	Sept.	to Lady Ossory	34. 202
12	Sept.	from Lady Waldegrave	36. 285
16	Sept.	to Daniel Lysons	15. 250
19	Sept.	to Daniel Lysons	15. 251
21	Sept.	to Mary Berry	12. 101
24	Sept.	to Mary Berry	12. 104
27	Sept.	to Mary Berry	12. 106
28	Sept.	from Mary Berry	12. 112
29	Sept.	to Mary Berry	12. 114
1	Oct.	to Mary Berry	12. 119
1	Oct.	from Mary Berry	12. 122
2	Oct.	to Daniel Lysons	15. 252
4	Oct.	to Mary Berry	12. 125
5	Oct.	from Mary Berry	12. 126
6	Oct.	from Mary Berry	12. 127
6	Oct.	to Lady Ossory	34. 204
7	Oct.	to Mary Berry	12. 129
12	Oct.	to ? Nares	15. 252, 43. 208
14	Oct.	to Mary Berry	12. 133

15	Oct.	to Mary Berry	**12.** 135
17	Oct.	to Mary Berry	**12.** 136
19	Oct.	to Beloe	**15.** 254
25	Oct.	to Mrs Garrick	**42.** 410
29	Nov.	to Lady Mount Edgcumbe	**42.** 410
	ca Dec.	to Beloe	**15.** 257
2	Dec.	to Beloe	**15.** 256
7	Dec.	from Lady Waldegrave	**36.** 287
8	Dec.	to Lady Ossory	**34.** 207
ca 1795	ca 1795	to Richard Bull	**42.** 413
1795	1795	to Mrs Dickenson	**31.** 400
24	Jan.	to Hannah More	**31.** 395
25	Jan.	to Pinkerton	**16.** 320, **43.** 230
3	Feb.	from Pinkerton	**16.** 325
5	Feb.	to Pinkerton	**16.** 327
13	Feb.	to Hannah More	**31.** 398
	March	from Roscoe	**15.** 258, **43.** 210
16	March	to Unknown	**42.** 414
20	March	from Lady Anne Conolly	**42.** 416
22	March	to James Edwards	**15.** 259
4	April	to Roscoe	**15.** 259
7	April	to Mary Berry	**12.** 138
15	April	from Roscoe	**15.** 262, **43.** 210
17	April	from William Harrison	**42.** 417
27	April	to Roscoe	**15.** 264
	ca June	from Harcourt	**35.** 544
1	June	to Mrs Dickenson	**31.** 400
18	June	to Edward Jerningham	**42.** 419
19	June	to Edmund Lodge	**42.** 420
2	July	to Conway	**39.** 510
7	July	to Conway	**39.** 511
26	July	to Bishop Percy	**42.** 423
15	Aug.	to Daniel Lysons	**15.** 266, **43.** 211
18	Aug.	to Mary Berry	**12.** 139
22	Aug.	to Mary Berry	**12.** 143

22	Aug.	to Daniel Lysons	**15.** 265,
			43. 210
22	Aug.	to the Rev. Mark Noble	**42.** 423
23	Aug.	to Mary Berry	**12.** 144
25	Aug.	to Mary Berry	**12.** 146
26	Aug.	to Mary Berry	**12.** 149
29	Aug.	to the Rev. Mark Noble	**42.** 424
1	Sept.	to Mary Berry	**12.** 155
6	Sept.	to Mary Berry	**12.** 159
8	Sept.	to Mary Berry	**12.** 162
10	Sept.	to Mary Berry	**12.** 163
13	Sept.	to Daniel Lysons	**15.** 267
15	Sept.	to Mary Berry	**12.** 166
18	Sept.	to Mary Berry	**12.** 168
22	Sept.	from Lady Waldegrave	**36.** 289
27	Sept.	to Daniel Lysons	**15.** 269
29	Oct.	to Daniel Lysons	**15.** 271
4	Nov.	to Mary Berry	**12.** 173
6	Nov.	to Mary Berry	**12.** 174
22	Nov.	to Mary Berry	**12.** 177
24	Nov.	to Mary Berry	**12.** 178
25	Nov.	to Mary Berry	**12.** 181
26	Nov.	to Agnes Berry	**12.** 182
1	Dec.	to Mary Berry	**12.** 182
3	Dec.	to Mary Berry	**12.** 183
6	Dec.	to Mary Berry	**12.** 183
11	Dec.	to Lady Ossory	**34.** 209
26	Dec.	to Lord Ossory	**34.** 211
1796 5	Jan.	to Dr Charles Burney	**42.** 425
11	Jan.	to Mrs Garrick	**42.** 426
9	Feb.	from Roscoe	**15.** 273
14	Feb.	to Lady Ossory	**34.** 211
15	Feb.	to Roscoe	**15.** 274
20	Feb.	to Dr Charles Burney	**42.** 427
?22	Feb.	from Dr Charles Burney	**42.** 428
22	Feb.	to Bertie Greatheed	**42.** 429
	March	from Roscoe	**15.** 276
4	March	to Lady Ossory	**34.** 214
15	March	from Mason	**29.** 334
17	March	to Roscoe	**15.** 277

19	March	to Mason	**29.** 337
22	March	to Mason	**29.** 338
24	March	from Mason	**29.** 341
27	March	from Roscoe	**15.** 279
31	March	from Sir James Colquhoun	**42.** 431
1	April	to Mrs Garrick	**42.** 434
2	May	from A. Gomes	**42.** 435
3	May	to Sir James Colquhoun	**42.** 436
19	May	from Mary Berry	**12.** 184
19	May	from Roscoe	**15.** 281
27	May	to Roscoe	**15.** 283
30	May	to Mary Berry	**12.** 184
	? June	to Rachel, Lady Walpole of Wolterton	**36.** 291
2	June	to Mary Berry	**12.** 186
7	June	to Thomas William Coke	**42.** 436
20	June	to Sir James Colquhoun	**42.** 437
25	June	to Mary Berry	**12.** 189
25	June *bis*	to Mary Berry	**12.** 190
27	June	to Robert Blake	**42.** 438
ca 12	July	to Roscoe	**15.** 285, **42.** 439
12	July	from Mrs Anna Aufrere	**42.** 441
12	July	to Lady Ossory	**34.** 216
25	July	to Mary Berry	**12.** 194
26	July	to Mary Berry	**12.** 195
29	July	to Mary Berry	**12.** 197
4	Aug.	to the Rev. John Elderton	**42.** 442
5	Aug.	to Mary Berry	**12.** 199
6	Aug.	from Roscoe	**15.** 285
7	Aug.	to Daniel Lysons	**15.** 286
9	Aug.	to Mary Berry	**12.** 199
16	Aug.	to Mary Berry	**12.** 203
24	Aug.	to Mary Berry	**12.** 208
29	Aug.	to Hannah More	**31.** 401, **43.** 343
2	Sept.	to Lady Ossory	**34.** 217
7	Sept.	to Mary Berry	**12.** 210

17	Sept.	to Lady Ossory	**34.** 219
30	Sept.	to Lady Ossory	**34.** 220
13	Nov.	to Lady Ossory	**34.** 221
20	Nov.	to Lady Ossory	**34.** 224
early Dec.		to Lady Anne Conolly	**42.** 443
1	Dec.	to Daniel Lysons	**15.** 287
1	Dec.	to Lady Ossory	**34.** 225
5	Dec.	to Richard Gough	**42.** 444
6	Dec.	to Lady Ossory	**34.** 227
13	Dec.	to Margaret Planta	**42.** 445, **43.** 390
14	Dec.	to Mary Berry	**12.** 212
15	Dec.	to Mary Berry	**12.** 213
1797 4	Jan.	to Lady Ossory	**34.** 228
12	Jan.	to the Rev. Mark Noble	**42.** 446
15	Jan.	to Lady Ossory	**34.** 230
16	Jan.	from the Rev. Mark Noble	**42.** 447
	Feb.	from Richard Clarke	**42.** 448
6	Feb.	to the Duchess of Gloucester	**36.** 292

UNDATED LETTERS

to Lady Diana Beauclerk [1782–90]	**42.** 450
from the Duchess of Bedford	**42.** 452
to Grosvenor Bedford	**42.** 454
to Grosvenor Bedford	**42.** 454
to Grosvenor Bedford	**42.** 455
to Grosvenor Bedford	**42.** 455
to Grosvenor Bedford	**42.** 456
to William Bewley	**42.** 457
to Lady Browne	**31.** 405
to Lady Browne	**31.** 406
to Lady Browne	**31.** 406, **43.** 345
to Lady Browne	**31.** 407
to Lady Browne	**31.** 407
to Lady Browne	**31.** 407
to Lady Browne	**31.** 408
to Lady Browne	**31.** 408
to Lady Browne	**31.** 409
to Lady Browne	**31.** 409
to Lady Browne	**31.** 410

APPENDIX
LETTER FROM GEORGE KEATE 17 JUNE 1788

Printed from a facsimile of the MS in *The Turnbull Library Record*, May 1982, xv. 6. The MS and the presentation copy of Keate's *An Account of the Pelew Islands,* 1788, are in the Turnbull Library, Wellington, New Zealand.

Tuesday morning 17th June.

Dear Sir

Allow me before its publication to request you will do me the honour of accepting the Account of the Pelew Islands which accompanies this in which I flatter myself you will find some scenes to engage your attention. I am sorry that the necessary attendance on this publication hath deprived [me] of the pleasure of meeting you but I hope I shall see you before I leave town or you fix for the summer.

I beg leave to present the compliments of Mrs Keate and my daughter and to assure you that I am with great respect Dear Sir

Your obliged and most
obedient humble servant
GEO. KEATE

Neil Jespersen
Department of Chemistry
University of Texas

D. O. Jones
David O. Jones Company
Chelan, Washington

Charles H. Lochmüller
Department of Chemistry
Duke University

J. West Loveland
Applied Physics Laboratory
Sun Oil Company

Ronald E. Majors
Instrument Division
Varian

Harry B. Mark, Jr.
Department of Chemistry
University of Cincinnati

S. P. Perone
Department of Chemistry
Purdue University

J. W. Prather II
Department of Chemistry
University of Missouri—Kansas City

George H. Schenk
Department of Chemistry
Wayne State University

S. Sternhell
Department of Organic Chemistry
University of Sydney

John R. Wasson
Department of Chemistry
University of North Carolina

Lo I Yin
Astrochemistry Branch
Laboratory for Extraterrestrial Physics
NASA Goddard Space Flight Center

Instrumental Analysis

This book is part of

The Allyn and Bacon Chemistry Series

and was developed under the co-consulting editorship of

DARYLE H. BUSCH AND HARRISON SHULL

Instrumental Analysis

Editors

HENRY H. BAUER
University of Kentucky

GARY D. CHRISTIAN
University of Washington

JAMES E. O'REILLY
University of Kentucky

Allyn and Bacon, Inc.
Boston,   London,   Sydney,   Toronto

Second printing . . . August, 1978
Copyright © 1978 by Allyn and Bacon, Inc.
470 Atlantic Avenue, Boston, Massachusetts 02210.

Library of Congress Cataloging in Publication Data

Main entry under title:
Instrumental analysis.

    (Allyn and Bacon chemistry series)
    Includes index.
    1. Instrumental analysis. I. Bauer, Henry H.
II. Christian, Gary D. III. O'Reilly, James E., 1945–
QD79.I5I5   543'.08   77–12051

ISBN 0-205-06556-2 (*International*)

Contents

Preface

The editors embarked on the venture of editing a textbook dealing with instrumental methods in chemical analysis for several reasons. None of the available texts seemed to us to be as well suited to the types of courses generally given in this area as we would like: coverage of the various types of techniques was uneven in depth, emphasis, and modernity; and in particular there seemed to be insufficient attention to applications of the techniques in practice. We felt that these shortcomings might be minimized if we could have each method discussed by people active in that particular field.

The individual authors were asked to make the theoretical background of each method as brief and qualitative as possible consistent with clarity and accuracy, to limit discussion of instrumentation to general principles as far as possible (i.e., no details of the operation of commercially available apparatus), and to emphasize the utility and actual applications of each method.

Some cynics, particularly in academia, maintain that the last thing ever successfully accomplished by committee was the King James version of the Bible. In a sense, this text has also been composed by a committee. As editors, we have tried to keep the depth of presentation more or less even, consistent with our feelings as to the importance of a particular method for quantitative applications; and to provide the continuity of thought and mode of expression so important in a text. We happily allot to the authors whatever credit may accrue for the quality of the individual parts and, as editors, assume responsibility for the shortcomings of the whole.

We thank the authors for their efforts, for the quality of their presentations, for their patience with the various changes and requests made during several drafts of the manuscript, and in particular for their benign attitude to the liberties we have taken with their style and mode of expression.

It is appropriate at this point to elaborate a few of the things we have chosen to do and not do. We have chosen to concentrate particularly on those applications and methods that are, in our opinion, most useful for quantitative analytical measurements—not because these are intrinsically more important than measurements that are more physically oriented, but simply because of the limitations of space. Thus, for example, we have no discussion of optical rotatory dispersion, certainly an important instrumental technique, because it presently has no practical usage as a quantitative method.

The text does not have a description of basic and advanced electronics, except for some discussion of digital electronics in the chapter on computers. There are perhaps two distinct approaches to instrumental analysis: one is in terms of *instrumentation* and instrument design, the second in terms of *instrumental methods* of analysis. We have chosen the latter approach because, first, we believe this to be the more profitable approach for the majority of students in a course of this nature, and second, because there is simply too much material in modern scientific electronics and instrumental methods to cover both comfortably in one semester and do justice to either. There are several excellent texts devoted to scientific electronics and several packages of electronics experiments on the market today; and many universities and colleges now offer separate courses in this area. We have chosen to leave the subject of electronics to these, and to the discretion of the individual instructor.

We have also not included an accompanying set of laboratory experiments. There are several excellent compendia of instrumental analysis experiments available, and a number of quantitative analytical experiments, particularly those involving analysis of "real" samples, appear in the *Journal of Chemical Education* monthly. Moreover, because of the cost and complexity of modern instrumentation, many instructors face a very limited array of instruments, and are forced to drastically redesign experiments for their particular instrument or model anyway. We have chosen to leave the instrumental laboratory to the ingenuity of the individual instructor.

A number of people have helped us in various ways, and we wish to thank them all, while mentioning specifically only a few—Petr Zuman for sharing with us his unmatched experience in the practice of polarographic techniques; Stan Smith for a complete set of NMR problems; Regina Palomo and Ellen Swank for patiently typing, retyping, and reretyping the entire manuscript; and our colleagues for putting up with us through the entire production stage. One of us (JEO) makes Acknowledgement to the Donors of The Petroleum Research Fund, administered by the American Chemical Society, for partial support of this research.

We genuinely hope that instructors will find this book a useful pedagogical aid, and we would appreciate comments concerning shortcomings and errors that we could attempt to rectify should there be the occasion for a later edition.

It is our fondest hope that students will read this text, and feel good about it. We have tried to express things as though we were talking to students, and not with an eye toward impressing an instructor with the depth of coverage or sophistication of the discussion. We hope that, at the end of a semester, the student can emerge with an idea of what the various instrumental methods are capable of doing in order to solve a problem or make a measurement. We hope to impart the overview of the true analytical chemist—selecting the right tool for the job at hand. Perhaps this can be expressed with a quotation from the Bible:

Thou shalt not have in thine bag divers weights, a great and a small.
Thou shalt not have in thine house divers measures, a great and a small. But
thou shalt have a perfect and just weight, a perfect and just measure shalt
thou have . . .

—DEUTERONOMY 25: 13–15

Instrumental Analysis

1

Introduction to Electrochemical Methods

HENRY H. BAUER
JAMES E. O'REILLY

Electrochemistry is a scientific discipline with a well developed system of theories and quantitative relationships. It has many applications and uses in both fundamental and applied areas of chemistry—in the study of corrosion phenomena, for example, for the study of the mechanisms and kinetics of electrochemical reactions, as a tool for the electrosynthesis of organic and inorganic compounds, and in the solution of quantitative analytical problems. This last area will be emphasized in the next four chapters.

1.1 GENERALITIES OF ELECTROCHEMICAL METHODS

It can be said with some degree of accuracy that, with the exception of the nearly universal use of the potentiometric pH-meter, electrochemical methods in general are not as widely used as are spectrochemical or chromatographic methods for quantitative analytical applications. A recent informal readers' survey conducted by *Research/Development* [1] indicated that about 75% of the laboratories responding used pH meters, ranking them approximately fifth in usage behind analytical balances, hot plates, fume hoods, and laboratory ovens. Yet where about half of the respondents used visible, ultraviolet, and infrared spectrophotometers and about 30% used atomic absorption spectrophotometers, only about 12% used what were termed polarographic analyzers and 30% used ion-selective electrodes. In general, there is a more widespread usage of electrochemical methods in Europe and Japan than in the United States.

There are probably several reasons why electrochemical methods are not as "popular" as chromatographic or optical methods. One is that electrochemistry and electrochemical methods are not emphasized in typical college curricula. One can cite the nearly universal disappearance of fundamental electrochemistry from beginning general and physical-chemistry courses, whereas the interaction of electromagnetic radiation with matter and the energy levels concerned is covered in many first-year courses. Electrochemical theory is really no more complex or abstruse, but probably not so well unified at present, as spectrochemical theory.

A second reason is that spectrochemical methods appear somewhat more amenable to automation or mechanization than electrochemical methods. An extreme example of this can be seen in the clinical analysis laboratory. In 1971, for instance, one particular hospital performed nearly a half-million chemical tests, 91% of which were done with spectrochemical methods and instruments [2]. This, of course, was due to its use of automated clinical analyzers, which are primarily optical in approach.

There are, however, many times when electrochemical methods can provide essentially the same information as other methods, thus offering an alternative approach, and other times when only electrochemistry will provide the answer or will provide the best answer to the problem at hand.

Advantages of Electrochemical Methods

Although it is very difficult to consider electrochemical methods *in general* versus other methods *in general*, electrochemical methods do have certain advantages. First of all, electrochemical instrumentation is comparatively inexpensive. The most expensive piece of routine electrochemical instrumentation costs about $15,000, with most commercial instrumentation under about $3000. By contrast, some sophisticated nonelectrochemical equipment, such as nuclear-magnetic-resonance or mass spectrometers, may run over a quarter of a million dollars.

Secondly, elemental electrochemical analysis is generally *specific for a particular chemical form* of an element. For example, with a mixture of Fe^{2+} and Fe^{3+}, electrochemical analysis can reveal the amount of each form present, where most elemental spectrochemical or radiochemical methods simply give the total amount of iron present almost regardless of its chemical form. Depending on the analytical problem at hand or the question to be answered, one particular method may be "better." For example, mercury is a serious environmental pollutant. Elemental or inorganic forms of mercury [Hg^0, Hg^{2+}, Hg_2Cl_2, $\cdots$] are bad, but organic mercury [CH_3Hg^+, $(CH_3)_2Hg$, $\cdots$] is much worse. Perhaps, in a given situation, it is important to know both the total mercury level and the forms it takes.

Another advantage (or disadvantage, depending on the problem at hand) of many electrochemical methods is that they respond to the *activity* of a chemical species rather than to the *concentration*. An example where this may be of importance is the calcium level in serum. Ion-selective electrodes respond to free, aquated Ca^{2+} ions, whereas the usual clinical method for serum calcium is flame photometry, which measures the total calcium present including a large amount tied up as protein-bound calcium. The more important physiological parameter, the measure of the *effective* level of calcium actually available for participation in various enzymatic reactions, may be the free Ca^{2+} level. For another example, lead is a cumulatively toxic substance; plants grown in lead-laden soils can accumulate high levels of lead. If these plants are then eaten by humans, toxic levels of lead may be reached. Lead in heavy clay soils is, however, much less available for absorption by plants than is lead in more sandy soil. Perhaps the more useful measure of the arability of trace-metal-contaminated land is the metal-ion activity, rather than the total metal concentration.

It can be safely said that in recent years there has been a renaissance of interest in quantitative electrochemical methods. This has been brought about primarily by two factors: the development of ion-selective potentiometric electrodes, which can quantitatively monitor most of the common ionic species in solution (Chap. 2); and the introduction of a new generation of inexpensive commercial voltammetric instrumentation based on pulse methods (Chap. 3), which has increased the sensitivity of electrochemical methods by several orders of magnitude.

Classification of Electrochemical Methods

For the present purpose, an electrochemical method can be defined as one in which the electrical response of a chemical system or sample is measured. The experimental system can be divided as follows: the electrolyte, a chemical system capable of conducting current; the measuring or external circuit, used to apply and to measure electrical signals (currents, voltages); and the electrodes, conductors that serve as contacts between the measuring system and the electrolyte.

Electrodes are classed as *anodes* and *cathodes*. At the anode, *oxidation* occurs—electrons are abstracted from the electrolyte and pass into the measuring circuit; at the cathode, *reduction* occurs—electrons flow from the cathode into the electrolyte. Furthermore, one speaks of *working* or *indicator electrodes*—those at which a reaction being studied is taking place; of *reference electrodes*, which maintain a constant potential irrespective of changes in current; and of *counter electrodes*, which serve to allow current to flow through the electrolyte but whose characteristics do not influence the measured behavior—the latter depends on what happens at the working electrode.

When current flows in an electrochemical system, the current is determined by the total resistance of the whole circuit. Good experimental design ensures that the magnitude of the current is not influenced by the measuring circuit. That done, one can distinguish two types of methods: those in which the resistance of the electrodes is made negligible, so that one measures the conductance of the electrolyte (see Chap. 5); and those in which the resistance of the electrolyte is made negligible, and one studies phenomena occurring at the electrodes (Chaps. 3 and 4).

A multitude of electrochemical techniques based on electrode processes exist; however, only a comparatively small number are of real importance to the analytical chemist. Some of the chief features of these techniques are shown in Table 1.1.

Electrochemical methods can be divided into two classes: those involving no net current flow ("potentiometric"), and all others. In potentiometry, one measures the equilibrium thermodynamic potential of a system essentially without causing electrolysis or current drain on the system—because this would affect the existing equilibrium. In all other methods, a voltage or current is applied to an electrode

TABLE 1.1. *Analytically Useful Electrochemical Techniques*

Technique	Controlled Electrical Variable	Response Measured	Relative Time-Scale for Analysis
Potentiometry	$i(=0)$	E	short
Potentiometric titration	$i(=0)$	E vs. volume of reagent	long
Voltammetry	E	i vs. E	
Polarography			medium
Linear-sweep or			
cyclic voltammetry			short
Pulse methods			medium
Stripping analysis	E	i vs. E	medium
Electrogravimetry	i or E	weight of deposit	long
Coulometry	i or E	charge consumed (integrated current)	long
Coulometric titration	i	time	medium
Conductivity	V (AC)	i (AC)	short

and the resultant current flow through, or voltage change of, the system is monitored. The applied waveform is often quite complex. Although this approach may be more complicated than is the case in potentiometry, there are advantages in that we are not forced to deal with the particular equilibrium characteristics of the system. By forcing the system to respond electrochemically to a stimulus, we can gain a good deal of analytical control over it.

1.2 ELECTROCHEMICAL DEFINITIONS AND TERMINOLOGY

As in all other disciplines, electrochemistry has its own terminology with which one needs to be familiar before studying specific electrochemical methods.

Faradaic and Nonfaradaic Processes

Two types of processes occur at electrodes. One kind includes those in which charge (e.g., electrons) is transferred across the electrode-solution interface. In these processes, actual *oxidation or reduction occurs*; they are governed by Faraday's laws, and are called *faradaic* processes.

Under some conditions an electrode may be in a potential region where charge-transfer reactions do not occur because they are either thermodynamically or kinetically unfavorable. However, such processes as adsorption can occur, and the structure of the electrode-solution interface can change, causing transitory changes in current and/or potential. These processes are called *nonfaradaic* processes.

Charging Current. An important example of a nonfaradaic process is that of the *charging* of an electrode (see Fig. 1.1). At some potential E_A (Fig. 1.1A) there is a

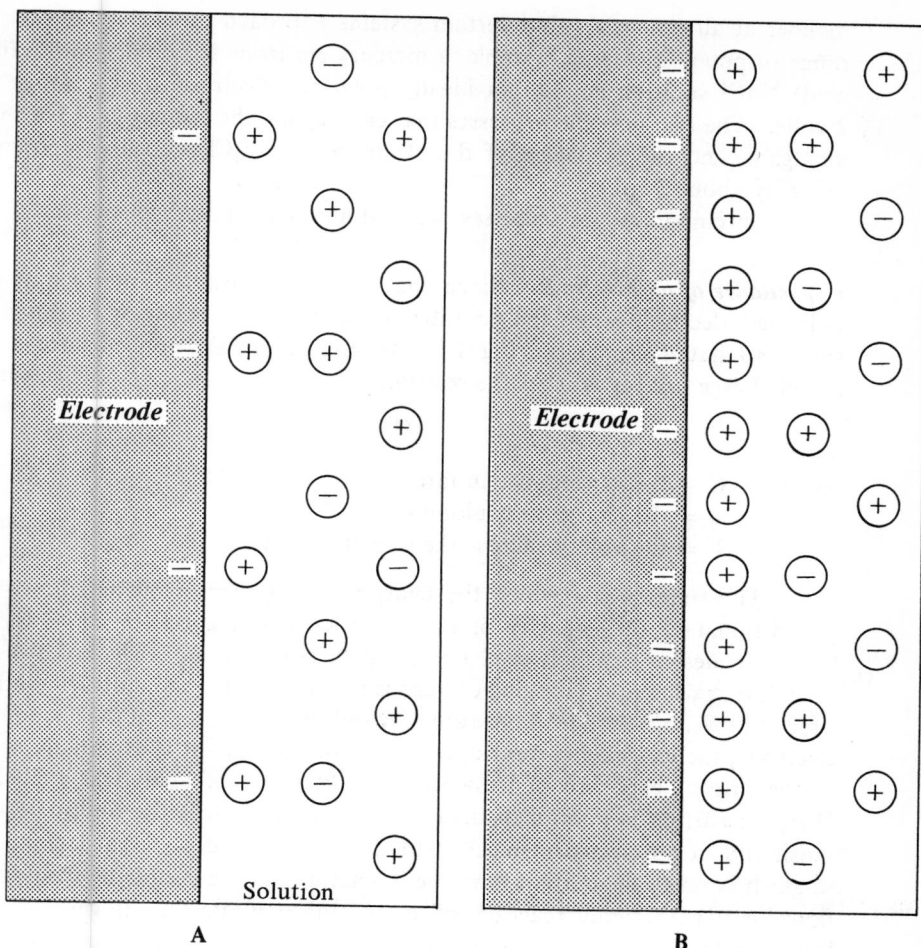

Electrode

Solution

A

Electrode

B

FIGURE 1.1. *Arrangement of charge at the electrode-solution interface.*
In case B, the electrode is at a more negative potential than in A; hence
the greater amount of negative charge at the electrode surface in B.

certain charge per unit area in the metal electrode, with an equal amount of charge
of opposite sign present in the solution immediately adjacent to the electrode (forming
what is called the *electrical double-layer*). If the potential is now changed to E_B,
where the charge per unit area is greater, current must flow to bring these extra charges
to the interface. This is the *charging current*, and it is a transient current, flowing
only until the new charge equilibrium is attained. Then the current stops, since there
is no mechanism to cause current to flow *across* the interface, in the absence of redox
reactions. So the charging process is nonfaradaic, and the charging current is a
nonfaradaic current.

An electrode at which no charge-transfer occurs across the electrode-solution
interface, regardless of the potential imposed from an outside source of voltage, is
called an *ideally polarized electrode*. No real electrode, of course, can behave in this

manner at all potentials; but certain systems approach this behavior over a limited range of potentials. For example, a mercury electrode in contact with a (deoxygenated) NaCl solution acts as an ideally polarized electrode over a range of nearly 2 volts. The two *faradaic* processes that can occur—the reduction of Na^+ to sodium amalgam, and the oxidation of the electrode to Hg_2Cl_2—occur at potentials that differ by about 2 volts.

Only nonfaradaic processes occur at an ideally polarized electrode.

Capacitance of an Electrode. Since charge cannot cross the interface at an ideally polarized electrode when the potential is changed, the behavior of this interface is similar to that of a capacitor (Fig. 1.1). When a potential is applied across a capacitor, it will charge until it satisfies the relation

$$C = q/V \qquad (1.1)$$

where $C = $ the capacitance in farads
$q = $ the charge in coulombs
$V = $ the voltage across the capacitor in volts

The time during which the charging or condenser current flows is directly proportional to the capacity of the electrode and the resistance of the solution; for electrodes of constant area immersed in solutions of fairly low resistance, the time during which the charging current is appreciable is very short, small fractions of a second. With electrodes whose area expands with time, e.g., at the dropping mercury electrode, the charging current dies down more slowly—it is essentially proportional to the rate of exposure of fresh surface. In terms of analytical applications, the charging current is often a distinct liability, as it often is the limiting factor in the sensitivity of an electrochemical method. One must use special techniques to distinguish between the current flow due to charging of the double layer and the current flow due to the faradaic reactions of the substance of interest. In general, this is done by using the fact that charging current decreases rapidly with time, whereas faradaic current changes with time much more slowly in typical experiments.

Faradaic Processes. Consider an ideally polarized electrode; only nonfaradaic processes occur, no charges cross the interface, and no continuous current can flow. Upon addition of a substance that can be oxidized or reduced at the particular potential difference, current now flows—the electrode is *depolarized*, and the substance responsible is called a *depolarizer*.

The faradaic process may proceed at various rates, within a wide range of possible rates. If the process is so rapid that the oxidized and reduced species are in equilibrium, then the reaction is termed *reversible* and the Nernst equation (1.3) applies.

Reversibility, so defined, actually depends on the relative rates of the electrode process and of the rapidity of the electrochemical measurement: a particular system may behave reversibly when measurements are made slowly, but irreversibly if the measurement involves short times (pulses of current or voltage, or high frequencies of an alternating electrical signal). Consequently, in modern usage, one prefers to talk about electrode processes as *being* fast or slow, and as *behaving* reversibly or irreversibly (rather than the classical usage in which systems were talked of as *being* reversible or irreversible).

Once faradaic current flows, the equilibrium between oxidized and reduced species is disturbed, and can be continually reestablished only if all the steps involved in the electrode process are rapid enough. (These steps include charge transfer, movement of depolarizer to the electrode and of product away from it (mass transport), and possibly adsorption or chemical reactions.) If there is a lag, then the electrode potential changes from its equilibrium value, the magnitude of the change being the *overpotential* or *overvoltage*.

Most systems can show overvoltages; i.e., they can become *polarized*. At a polarized electrode, current flows—but the magnitude of the current is less than if the system were behaving reversibly. The current is limited by the rate of one (or more) of the steps in the electrode process. If charge transfer is the slow (limiting) step, the effect is called *activation polarization*; if slow movement of depolarizer or product is responsible, one speaks of *concentration polarization*.

If the electrode process were infinitely fast, then current could be drawn without producing an overvoltage; this would be a *nonpolarizable electrode*. In practice, there are some electrode systems that permit appreciable currents to flow with negligible overpotentials, and such systems are used in reference electrodes.

Sign Conventions and the Nernst Equation

The sign conventions of electrochemistry have caused students and researchers a great deal of difficulty and misunderstanding over the years. All electrochemical cells are considered as a combination of two half-cells—one for the reduction reaction, one for the oxidation reaction. To have current flow in *any* electrochemical system, both an oxidation and a reduction reaction must occur; electrons must have someplace to go, they simply do not appear and disappear.

Any half-cell reaction can be written as either an oxidation or a reduction; by convention, they are written as reductions.

$$\text{Ox} + ne^- \rightleftharpoons \text{Red} \tag{1.2}$$

where   Ox = general symbol for the *ox*idized form of the balanced half-reaction
Red = general symbol for the *red*uced form of the balanced half-reaction
n = the number of electrons involved in the half-reaction.

By use of a table of electromotive forces or standard reduction potentials (E^0 values) for half-reactions, the potential of each half-cell can be calculated by means of the Nernst equation

$$E = E^0 - \frac{RT}{nF} \ln \frac{(\text{Red})}{(\text{Ox})} \tag{1.3}$$

where R = the molar gas constant (8.314 J/mole-K)
T = the absolute temperature in K
F = the faraday constant (96,487 coulombs/mole)
(Red) = *activity* of the reduced chemical species
(Ox) = *activity* of the oxidized chemical species

If the ln term is converted to $\log_{10}$ basis, the value of the constant term $2.303\,RT/nF$ becomes $0.05916/n$ V at 25°C. The logarithmic term (Red)/(Ox) is simply the thermodynamic equilibrium expression for the electrochemical reaction, *written as a reduction*, and will be affected by changes in concentration of the various chemical species in the same manner as any other equilibrium expression. Further details on the Nernst equation and its use are contained in Chapter 2.

Modes of Electrochemical Mass Transport

In general, chemical species are transported in solution by one or more, conceptually distinct, processes: *migration*, *convection*, and *diffusion*.

Migration. Electrical migration is the movement of charged substances in an *electrical gradient*, a result of the force exerted on charged particles by an electric field; this can be viewed as a result of simple coulombic attraction of, for example, a positively charged ion to a negatively charged electrode surface or, alternatively, repulsion from a positively charged electrode. In almost all electrochemical methods of analysis, migration effects serve no useful purpose; they are usually swamped out by the addition of a relatively large amount (perhaps 0.1 or 1 M) of "background" (or "inert" or "indifferent") electrolyte such as KCl or HNO_3. Current can then flow as a result of migration of, for instance, K^+ or Cl^- ions, with negligible migration of the electroactive species, which then moves as a result of concentration differences only (diffusion, see below).

Convection. Convection means, essentially, the mass transport of electroactive material to the electrode by *gross physical movement*—fluid or hydrodynamic flow—of the solution. Generally, fluid flow occurs because of natural convection (caused by density gradients) or forced convection (usually caused by *stirring* of some sort).

Diffusion. Mass transfer by diffusion is the natural transport or movement of a substance under the influence of a *gradient of chemical potential*, that is, due to the *concentration gradient*; substances move from regions of high concentration to regions of low concentration in order to minimize or eliminate concentration differences. Diffusion is perhaps the most widely studied means of mass transport.

The rate of diffusion is given by

$$\text{Rate} = D\,\frac{dc}{dx} \qquad (1.4)$$

where D = the *diffusion coefficient* (in cm^2/sec) of the substance
dc/dx = the concentration gradient

This expression is often approximated by

$$D\,\frac{\Delta c}{\delta} \qquad (1.5)$$

where Δc = the difference in concentration across the region where diffusion occurs (the *diffusion layer*)
δ = the thickness of the diffusion layer (Fig. 1.2)

The diffusion coefficient, D, is a constant for a given substance under a specified set of solution conditions (temperature, electrolyte nature, and concentration). Since a concentration gradient is established as soon as any electrolysis is begun, diffusion is a part of every practical electrode reaction.

Faradaic current reflects the rate of the electrode process. If the latter is a

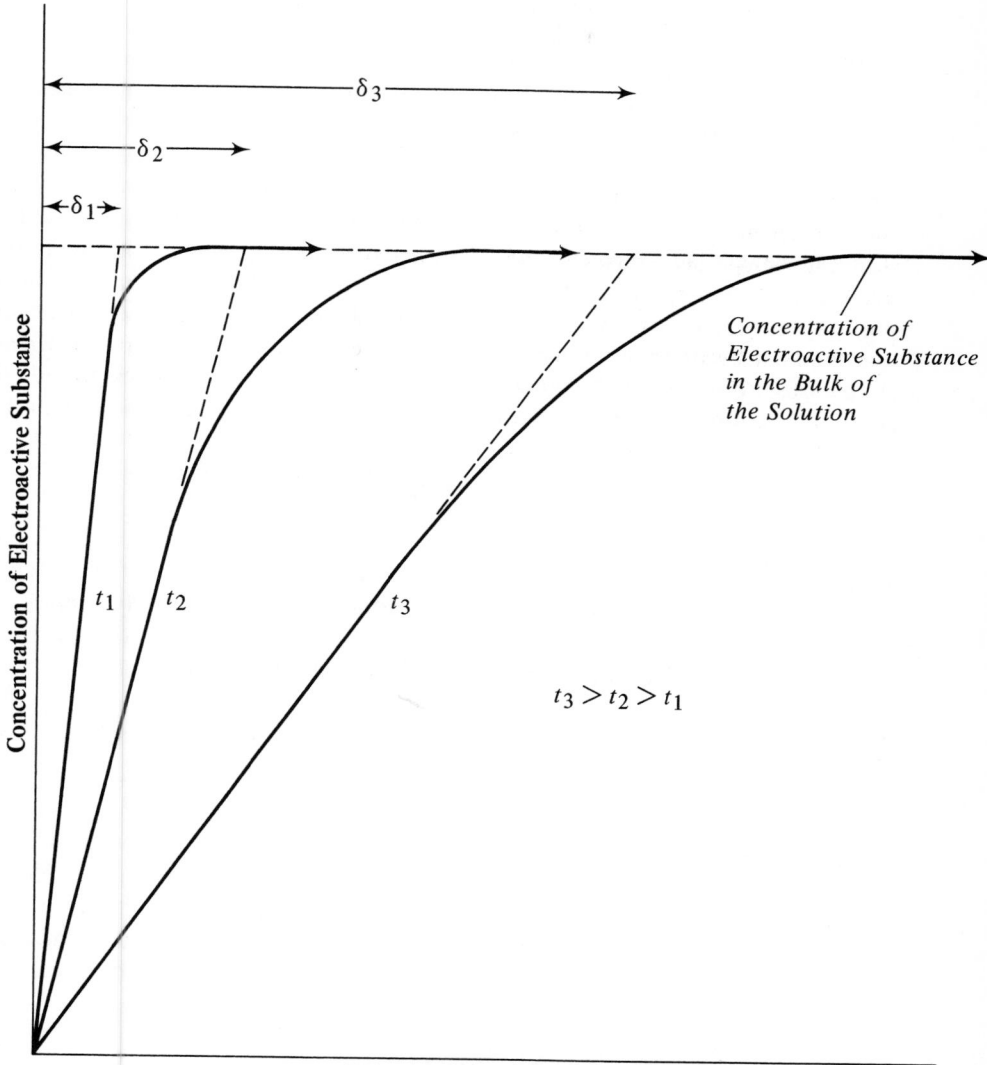

FIGURE 1.2.   *Concentration-distance profiles for diffusion of an electro-active substance to an electrode surface at different times.   At zero time, a voltage large enough to cause the electrode reaction to occur is suddenly applied to the electrode.   Note that with increasing time ($t_3 > t_2 > t_1$), the concentration gradient—the slope of the concentration-distance curve—becomes less steep, and the diffusion layer thickness, δ, becomes larger.*

multi-step reaction, then each step has its own inherent rate and the faradaic current reflects the rate of the slowest process in the sequence of steps. That might be an adsorption process, or some chemical reaction in solution involving the oxidant or the reductant, or the charge-transfer process itself, or the rate at which the electroactive species diffuses to the electrode from the bulk of the solution. When a supporting electrolyte is present, in the simplest cases, the movement of the electroactive species is limited by diffusion; therefore, the solution of the equations governing diffusion is relevant to many electrochemical techniques.

Consider an electrode of fixed area immersed in a solution containing an electroactive species and a supporting electrolyte. Initially, the composition of the solution is uniform throughout. When a potential large enough to cause a faradaic reaction to occur is applied, those particles of the electroactive species in the immediate vicinity of the electrode undergo reaction. Then the rate of the reaction, and consequently the magnitude of the current, depends on the rate at which the electroactive species diffuses to the electrode surface. The concentration gradient is steep at first, and the layer of depleted solution (the diffusion layer δ) is thin (see Fig. 1.2); as time goes by, the thickness of the diffusion layer increases, the concentration gradient becomes less steep, and the rate of diffusion decreases. As a result, a large current flows when the potential is first applied, and then the magnitude of the current decreases with time. Solution of the equations for diffusion leads to the relation

$$i(t) = \frac{nFAD^{1/2}c}{\pi^{1/2}t^{1/2}} \qquad (1.6)$$

where
$i(t)$ = current at time t
n = number of electrons involved in the electrochemical process
A = area of the electrode
c = the concentration of the electroactive species

That is to say, the current decreases in proportion to the square root of time from the instant at which electrolysis starts.

We can now proceed, in the following chapters, to consider details of the analytical applications of four classes of electrochemical techniques: in Chapter 2, measurements of electrode potentials in the absence of current flow; in Chapter 3, measurements of current flow as potential is varied; in Chapter 4, measurements of the amount of charge required for complete electrolysis (or deposition) of the substance concerned; and in Chapter 5, measurements of the conductances of solutions under conditions where processes at the electrodes themselves are not of concern.

SELECTED BIBLIOGRAPHY

BAUER, H. H. *Electronics: Modern Ideas Concerning Electrode Reactions.* Stuttgart: Thieme, 1972.

BOCKRIS, J. O'M., and REDDY, A. K. N. *Modern Electrochemistry*, vols. 1 and 2. New York: Plenum Press, 1970. *A*

thorough treatment of electrochemical fundamentals.

MURRAY, R. W., and REILLEY, C. N. In *Treatise on Analytical Chemistry*, I. M. Kolthoff and P. J. Elving, eds., part I, vol. 4. New York: John Wiley, 1963, pp 2109–

2232. *Fundamentals of electrode processes and introduction to electrochemical techniques.*

SAWYER, D. T., and ROBERTS, J. L., JR. *Experimental Electrochemistry for Chemists.* New York: John Wiley, 1974. *A good introduction to the more popular electrochemical methods; details of cell constructions, instrumentation, purification of solvents and electrolytes.*

REFERENCES

1. "Trends in Analytical Instruments and Equipment," *Res./Dev.*, *26*(*2*), 20 (1975).
2. G. N. BOWERS, JR., in *Analytical Chemistry: Key to Progress on National Problems,* W. W. Meinke and J. K. Taylor, eds., NBS Special Publication 351, U.S. Government Printing Office, Washington, D.C., 1972, pp 77–157.

2

Potentiometry

JAMES E. O'REILLY

Potentiometry—the measurement of electric potentials in electrochemical cells—is probably one of the oldest methods of chemical analysis still in wide use. The early, essentially qualitative, work of Luigi Galvani (1737–1798) and Count Alessandro Volta (1745–1827) had its first fruit in the work of J. Willard Gibbs (1839–1903) and Walther Nernst (1864–1941), who laid the foundations for the treatment of electro-chemical equilibria and electrode potentials. The early analytical applications of potentiometry were essentially to detect the endpoints of titrations. More extensive use of direct potentiometric methods came after Haber developed the glass electrode for pH measurements in 1909. In recent years, several new classes of ion-selective sensors have been introduced, beginning with glass electrodes more or less selectively responsive to other univalent cations (Na^+, NH_4^+, etc.). Now, solid-state crystalline electrodes for ions such as F^-, Ag^+, and sulfide, and liquid ion-exchange membrane electrodes responsive to many simple and complex ions—Ca^{2+}, BF_4^-, ClO_4^-—provide the chemist with electrochemical probes responsive to a wide variety of ionic species.

2.1 ELECTROCHEMICAL CELLS

An electrochemical cell can be defined as two conductors or electrodes, usually metallic, immersed in the same electrolyte solution, or in two different electrolyte solutions which are in electrical contact. Electrochemical cells are classed into two groups. A *galvanic* (sometimes, *voltaic*) cell is one in which electrochemical reactions occur spontaneously when the two electrodes are connected by a conductor. These cells are often employed to convert chemical energy into electrical energy. Many types are of commercial importance, such as the lead-acid battery, flashlight batteries, and various fuel cells. An *electrolytic* cell is one in which chemical reactions are caused to occur by the imposition of an external voltage greater than the reversible (galvanic) voltage of the cell. Essentially, these cells are used to carry out chemical reactions at the expense of electrical energy. Some important commercial uses of electrolytic cells involve synthesizing processes, such as the preparation of chlorine gas and caustic soda from brines, and electroplating procedures.

A simple galvanic electrochemical cell (shown in Fig. 2.1) consists of a strip of zinc and a strip of copper immersed in solutions of a zinc and a copper salt, respec-

FIGURE 2.1. *Schematic diagram of a simple galvanic electrochemical cell. V is a voltmeter or other voltage-measuring device. The arrows indicate the direction of the spontaneous flow of electrons. The + and − indicate the* polarity *of the cell as measured by a voltmeter.*

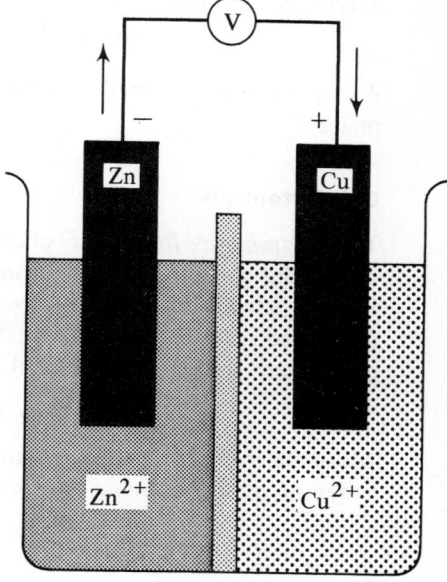

tively. If the Zn^{2+} and Cu^{2+} concentrations are approximately equal, the spontaneous reactions correspond to the *oxidation* of zinc metal (at the anode) and the *reduction* of copper ions (at the cathode):

$$Zn \rightleftharpoons Zn^{2+} + 2e^- \tag{2.1}$$

$$Cu^{2+} + 2e^- \rightleftharpoons Cu \tag{2.2}$$

Both reaction 2.1 and reaction 2.2 represent a *half-cell* reaction. If the strips of copper and zinc are connected by a wire so that electrolysis proceeds, the solution in the zinc compartment shows an increase in zinc-ion concentration, while the solution in the copper compartment is depleted in cupric ions. It is the purpose of the porous barrier separating the two compartments to allow the migration of ions between the two compartments so that there is no buildup of charge inhomogeneity, but without the gross mixing of solutions.

Schematic Representation of Cells

In order to simplify the description of cells, a type of electrochemical shorthand has evolved, which allows an easier depiction of cells and cell components. For example, for the cell in Figure 2.1, one would write

$$- \quad Zn/Zn^{2+}(c_{Zn^{2+}})//Cu^{2+}(c_{Cu^{2+}})/Cu \quad + \tag{2.3}$$

Slant lines, vertical lines, or sometimes a semicolon, indicate phase boundaries across which there arise potential differences that are included in the measured potential of the entire cell. Conventionally, a double slant or vertical line signifies a liquid junction—the zone of contact between two electrolyte solutions. Physically, this may be a porous membrane as in Figure 2.1, or a salt bridge of some sort. The anode is written to the left, the cathode on the right. If there are several components in one electrolyte solution, the components are separated by a comma. For example, for a cell (without liquid junction) composed of a silver/silver-chloride half-cell and a hydrogen gas electrode, one could write for one set of conditions

$$- \quad Pt, H_2 \ (0.5 \ atm)/HCl \ (0.1 \ M), AgCl/Ag \quad + \tag{2.4}$$

A comma is usually used to separate different chemical species occurring in the same phase.

Cell Potentials

The *electromotive force* (emf) of cell 2.3 is the algebraic sum of the potentials developed across the two electrode-solution interfaces, and the liquid-junction potential, E_{lj}. If the electrode reactions are *written* as reductions, and the electrode potentials are calculated according to the Nernst equation using *reduction potentials*, as in the present convention [1], the cell potential can be written as

$$E_{cell} = E_{Cu^{2+}, Cu} + E_{lj} - E_{Zn^{2+}, Zn} \tag{2.5}$$

More generally, E_{cell} is the potential of the right-hand electrode (cathode) minus the potential of the left-hand electrode (anode)

$$E_{cell} = E_{cathode} + E_{lj} - E_{anode} \tag{2.6}$$

If all the substances participating in the *reversible* operation of a cell are in their standard states (unit activities), the potential of an individual electrode is simply its respective *standard potential*, E^0. The free energy change for the cell reaction is therefore

$$\Delta G^0_{cell} = -nFE^0_{cell} \tag{2.7}$$

where n = number of electrons transferred in the cell reaction
                   F = the faraday (96,487 coulombs/mole)

No valid method exists for determining the *absolute* potential of an electrode. All potential measurements require a second electrode, and are therefore *relative* potentials. It is then necessary to choose one particular electrode to be arbitrarily assigned the zero position on the potential scale. By convention, the standard hydrogen electrode (SHE) is defined to have a potential of exactly 0 V, and is the reference point from which the potentials of all other electrodes are stated (Sec. 2.3). The electromotive force of a cell is the potential difference between two electrodes and is independent of the particular reference-electrode scale used.

Liquid-Junction Potentials. At the boundary between two dissimilar solutions, a junction potential is always set up. The solvents, the nature of the electrolytes, and the concentration of a given electrolyte can all differ, and therefore the mobilities of positive and negative ions diffusing across the boundary will not be equal. Thus a slight charge separation arises, which results in the junction potential. Junction potentials can become rather large (50 mV or more), particularly when one of the electrolyte ions, such as H^+ or OH^-, has a very high mobility.

Almost all electrochemical cells contain at least a small liquid-junction potential, generally of unknown magnitude. Only in a few special cases can it be calculated or measured. Experimentally, the usual approach is to minimize the junction potential by use of a concentrated *salt bridge* between dissimilar solutions. Because the mobilities of potassium and chloride ions are nearly equal, the usual choice for the electrolyte in a salt bridge is saturated KCl. When potassium or chloride ions are undesirable for chemical reasons, such as in trace Cl^- determinations, saturated KNO_3 or K_2SO_4 or 5 M lithium trichloroacetate can be used. Various styles of electrolyte junctions or salt bridges have been designed such as a ground glass joint or a wick of asbestos sealed into glass (Fig. 2.3), an agar gelatin bridge containing an electrolyte (Fig. 3.9), a porous glass or ceramic plug, or a fine capillary drip.

2.2 THE NERNST EQUATION

For the generalized half-cell reaction, *written as a reduction*

$$Ox + ne^- \rightleftharpoons Red \qquad (2.8)$$

the potential is given by the generalized form of the Nernst equation

$$E = E^0 - \frac{RT}{nF} \ln \frac{(Red)}{(Ox)} = E^0 - \frac{RT}{nF} \ln \frac{a_{Red}}{a_{Ox}} = E^0 - \frac{2.303\,RT}{nF} \log \frac{a_{Red}}{a_{Ox}} \qquad (2.9)$$

where E^0 = *standard* electrode potential
R = molar gas constant (8.314 joule/K-mole)
T = absolute temperature
(Red) or a_{Red} = *activity* of reduced form
(Ox) or a_{Ox} = *activity* of the oxidized form

If numerical values are inserted for the constants and the temperature is 25°C, the Nernst equation becomes

$$E = E^0 - \frac{0.05916}{n} \log \frac{a_{Red}}{a_{Ox}} \qquad (2.10)$$

A change of one unit in the logarithmic term changes the value of the electrode potential by $59.16/n$ mV. If the copper electrode of cell 2.3 is dipped into a solution of copper ion at $a = 0.001$ M, the electrode potential is

$$E_{Cu^{2+},\,Cu} = E^0_{Cu^{2+},\,Cu} - \frac{0.05916}{2} \log \frac{(Cu)}{(Cu^{2+})} \qquad (2.11)$$

Since the activity of a solid-phase, such as the copper metal, is unity,

$$E_{Cu^{2+},\,Cu} = E^0_{Cu^{2+},\,Cu} + \frac{0.05916}{2} \log (Cu^{2+}) \qquad (2.12)$$

$$= +0.337 + \frac{0.05916}{2} \log (0.001\ M)$$

$$= +0.248\ \text{V}$$

relative to the standard hydrogen electrode.

Effect of Concentration—Activity Coefficients

If the Nernst equation (2.9) is written in terms of *concentrations* and *activity coefficients*, it becomes

$$E = E^0 - \frac{RT}{nF} \ln \frac{f_{Red}[Red]}{f_{Ox}[Ox]} = E^0 - \frac{RT}{nF} \ln \frac{f_{Red}}{f_{Ox}} - \frac{RT}{nF} \ln \frac{[Red]}{[Ox]}$$

$$= E^{0\prime} - \frac{RT}{nF} \ln \frac{c_{Red}}{c_{Ox}} \tag{2.13}$$

where $E^{0\prime}$ = *formal electrode potential*
f_{Red} = the activity coefficient of the reduced species
f_{Ox} = activity coefficient of the oxidized species
c (or brackets) stand for *concentration* units

The formal potential, which is somewhat like a standard potential under a given set of experimental conditions, lacks the fundamental thermodynamic significance of the standard potential; but it is often experimentally useful, and can often be directly measured.

There are several ways in which activity coefficients can be calculated or estimated [2]; the simplest of these is known as the Debye-Hückel Limiting Law. The *ionic strength, I*, of any electrolyte medium is given by

$$I = \frac{1}{2} \sum c_i z_i^2 \tag{2.14}$$

where c_i = concentration of ionic species i
z_i = charge on that ion

For aqueous solution at 25°C, the activity coefficient of an ion, f_i, is then given approximately by

$$-\log f_i = 0.5 z_i^2 I^{1/2} \tag{2.15}$$

This illustrates the fact that as the total electrolyte concentration increases, the *activity* coefficients decrease. For example, the activity of Ca^{2+} in a solution containing only 0.01 *M* $CaCl_2$ is 0.0045 *M*; whereas if 0.1 *M* NaCl is also present, the Ca^{2+} activity is only 0.0019 *M*.

Effect of Complexation on Electrode Potentials

As mentioned previously, electrodes respond directly to the activity of ionic species, the "free" or "effective" concentration. For example, if a complexing reagent is also present that reacts with a metal ion, the metal ion is then no longer as free to react with the electrode; its "effective concentration" has been decreased. The simplest case that can be considered is that of a single ionic species formed over a range of concentrations of complexing agent. For example, let us again consider the copper electrode of cell 2.3, where EDTA (ethylenediaminetetraacetic acid) has also been added to the Cu^{2+} solution. The formation of the copper-EDTA complex can be represented by the equilibrium

$$Cu^{2+} + EDTA^{4-} \rightleftharpoons CuEDTA^{2-} \tag{2.16}$$

(where EDTA^{4-} is the basic form of the tetra-acid) for which the formation constant is written as

$$K_f = \frac{(CuEDTA^{2-})}{(Cu^{2+})(EDTA^{4-})} = 6.17 \times 10^{18} \tag{2.17}$$

For the half-reaction involving copper ions and copper, Equation 2.2, the Nernst equation is expressed by Equation 2.12. Combining Equation 2.17 with 2.12 yields the potential of a copper electrode in aqueous EDTA^{4-} systems

$$E_{Cu^{2+}, Cu} = E^0_{Cu^{2+}, Cu} + \frac{RT}{nF} \ln \frac{1}{K_f(EDTA^{4-})} + \frac{RT}{nF} \ln (CuEDTA^{2-}) \tag{2.18}$$

At 25°C, for 0.001 M Cu^{2+} and 0.10 M EDTA^{4-}, the potential would then be −0.278 V (neglecting activity coefficients), since for a strong complexing agent like EDTA it can be assumed that nearly 100% of the copper is present as CuEDTA^{2-}; that is, (CuEDTA^{2-}) ≈ 0.001 M and (EDTA^{4-}) ≈ 0.10 M.

The shift in electrode potential caused by the complexing agent is contained in the second term of Equation 2.18. In this case, it amounts to a shift of −0.526 V. The important practical consequences of chelation and complexation will be discussed in more detail later. For example, one can determine copper ion by direct potentiometry using a copper-ion-selective electrode, or via a potentiometric titration with EDTA using the electrode as an endpoint detector.

2.3 REFERENCE ELECTRODES

In most practical situations involving potentiometry, one uses a reference electrode (in conjunction with a sensing or indicator electrode) whose potential is invariant with respect to solution composition, and unchanging with the passage of the small amount of current (10^{-9} A or less) required to "drive" the measuring instrument— an electrometer, pH meter, or high-impedance voltmeter. Furthermore, one strives to make all liquid-junction potentials either constant or negligible. Ideally, therefore, the reference electrode is of known and constant potential, with negligible variation in the liquid-junction potential from one test or standard solution to another. In this case, the cell potential of the overall system, Equation 2.6, can be expressed as

$$E_{cell} = E_{constant} + E_{ind} \tag{2.19}$$

where $E_{constant}$ = some constant potential
        E_{ind} = the potential (varying with the solution composition) of the indicator or sensing electrode

Under these conditions, the indicator electrode can provide unambiguous information about ionic activities in the cell solution. In most analytical work, it is not necessary to know the actual value of the reference electrode potential—as long as it is constant—because $E_{constant}$ is determined using known standard solutions.

Hydrogen Gas Electrode

The hydrogen electrode is the ultimate standard electrode not only for the determination of (relative) potentials, but also for the determination of pH values. Owing to the experimental difficulties associated with it, however, it is seldom used for routine measurements, but rather for the evaluation of secondary reference and pH electrodes such as the calomel reference electrode and the glass pH electrode.

The hydrogen electrode consists essentially of a piece of platinum foil, electroplated ("platinized") with a thin layer of finely divided platinum. This provides a catalytic surface on which the half-cell reaction

$$2H^+ + 2e^- \rightleftharpoons H_2 \tag{2.20}$$

can proceed reversibly. The electrode is immersed in the test solution, and high-purity hydrogen gas is bubbled through the solution and over the electrode surface so that both will be saturated with hydrogen gas. The construction of a typical hydrogen electrode is illustrated in Figure 2.2.

FIGURE 2.2. *Typical hydrogen-gas electrode assembly.*

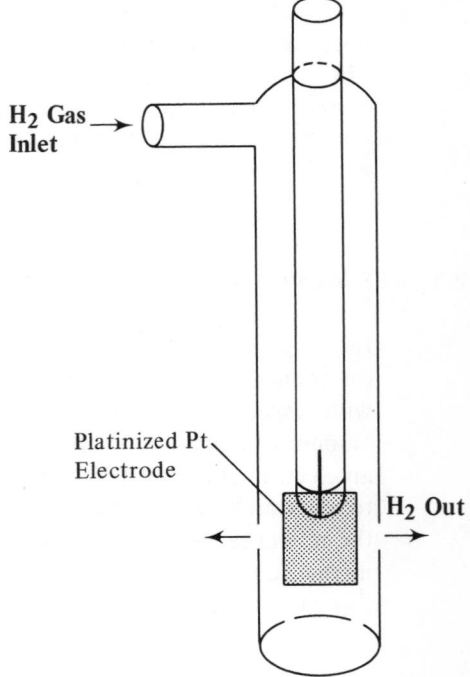

The primary disadvantage of the hydrogen gas electrode is that it is rather difficult to prepare properly and inconvenient to use. Another disadvantage is that its potential is sensitive to oxidants and reductants in solution—anything that will oxidize H_2 or reduce H^+. Also, the catalytic Pt surface is poisoned by a variety of substances including As, CN^-, H_2S, and Hg, and is coated by high-molecular-weight substances, such as proteins, and other surface-active compounds. Nevertheless, the hydrogen gas electrode, at least the hypothetical [3] standard hydrogen electrode (SHE), is used as the ultimate standard for potential and pH.

Calomel Electrodes

Perhaps the most widely used reference electrode for electrochemical measurements is one form or other of the calomel electrode. This electrode consists of mercury, mercurous chloride (calomel), and a chloride-ion solution:

$$Hg/Hg_2Cl_2 \text{ (satd.), } Cl^- \text{ (X } M) \tag{2.21}$$

The half-cell reaction is

$$Hg_2Cl_2 + 2e^- \rightleftharpoons 2Hg + 2Cl^- \qquad E^0 = +0.2676 \text{ V} \tag{2.22}$$

Since the activities of solid Hg_2Cl_2 and Hg are unity, the potential of this electrode is governed entirely by the activity of the chloride ion. The most common type of calomel electrode is the saturated (with KCl) calomel electrode (SCE). It is easily made and maintained, and its potential is quite reproducible. A great variety of commercial calomel electrodes is available; two of these are illustrated in Figure 2.3.

Perhaps the major disadvantages of the SCE are that its potential varies strongly with temperature, owing to the change in solubility of KCl; that there is a perceptible hysteresis effect following temperature changes, partly owing to the time required for solubility equilibrium to be established; and that it can only be used at temperatures less than about 80°C, probably owing to the disproportionation of mercurous ion to form mercury and mercuric ion.

For accurate work, 0.1 M or 1 M KCl calomel electrodes may be used because they reach their equilibrium potential more rapidly, and have less temperature-dependence. Calomel electrodes with NaCl electrolyte have also found use. Table 2.1 gives the potentials of several common reference electrodes at selected temperatures.

Silver/Silver-Chloride Electrodes

A silver/silver-chloride reference electrode is prepared by plating a layer of silver chloride onto a metallic silver wire or sheet. The electrode is immersed in a chloride solution (usually KCl) of known concentration, which is also saturated with AgCl.

TABLE 2.1. *Potentials of Some Reference Electrodes in Volts versus the Standard Hydrogen Electrode as a Function of Temperature*

Temperature °C	Calomel[a] (0.1 M KCl)	Calomel[a] (Satd. KCl)	Ag/AgCl[a] (Satd. KCl)
10	0.3362	0.2543	0.2138
20	0.3359	0.2479	0.2040
25	0.3356	0.2444	0.1989
30	0.3351	0.2411	0.1939
40	0.3336	0.2340	0.1835

Source: Reprinted from R. G. Bates, *Determination of pH*, 2nd ed., pp 325–35, by permission of the author and John Wiley and Sons. Copyright © 1973 by John Wiley and Sons.
a. Liquid-junction potential included.

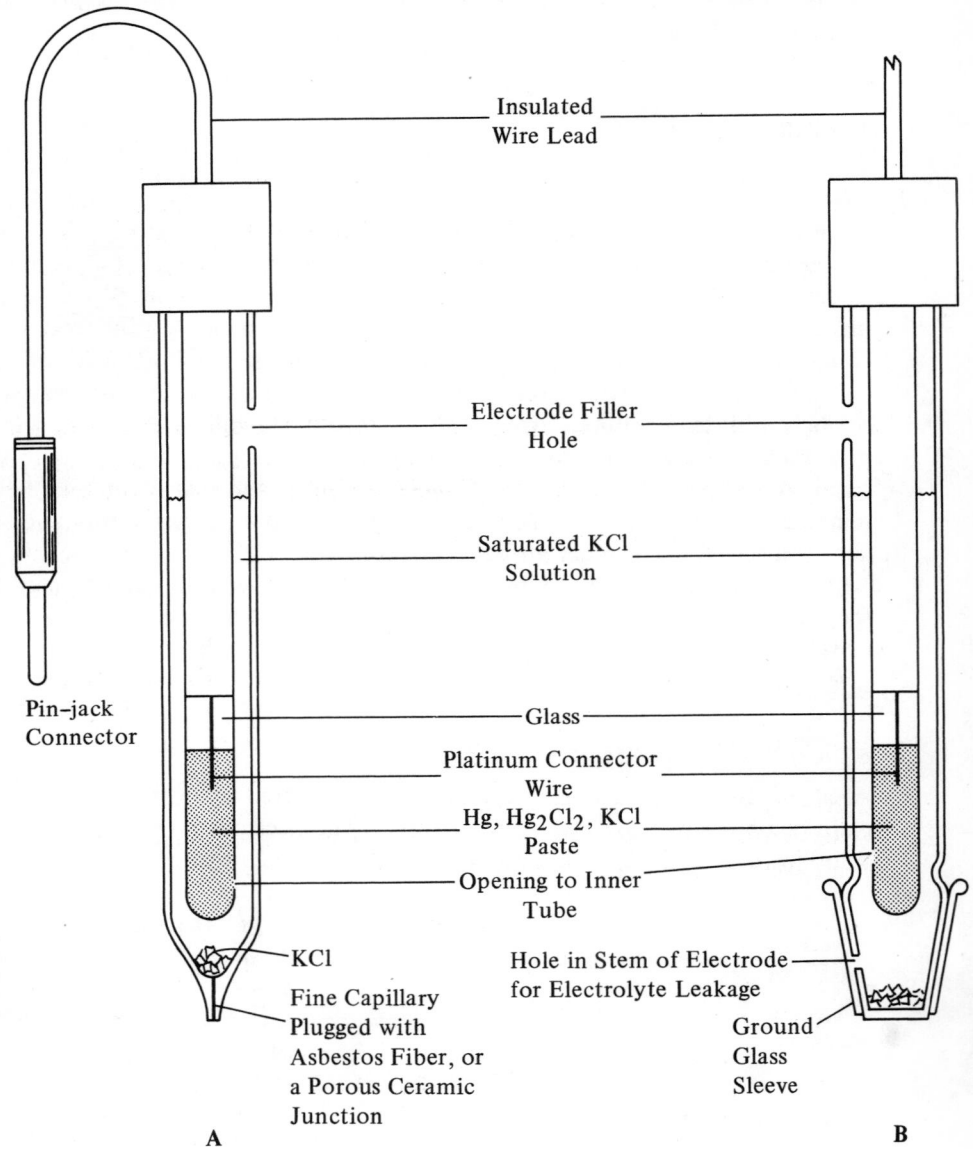

Insulated
Wire Lead

Electrode Filler
Hole

Saturated KCl
Solution

Pin–jack
Connector

Glass

Platinum Connector
Wire

Hg, Hg$_2$Cl$_2$, KCl
Paste

Opening to Inner
Tube

KCl

Fine Capillary
Plugged with
Asbestos Fiber, or
a Porous Ceramic
Junction

Hole in Stem of Electrode
for Electrolyte Leakage

Ground
Glass
Sleeve

A

B

FIGURE 2.3.   *Schematic cross-section representation of the construction of some typical commercial calomel electrodes: (A) fiber or porous-ceramic junction type and (B) ground glass–sleeve type.   The electrolyte leak rate of the fiber or porous-ceramic junction type is quite low, typically 1–10 μl/hr; that for the sleeve type around 100 μl/hr.*

Since AgCl is appreciably soluble in concentrated chloride media, solid AgCl is usually added to the solution to insure saturation and prevent dissolution of AgCl from the electrode surface. The half-cell thus constructed may be represented as

$$\text{Ag/AgCl (satd.), Cl}^- \text{ (X } M) \tag{2.23}$$

for which the half-reaction is

$$\text{AgCl} + e^- \rightleftharpoons \text{Ag} + \text{Cl}^- \qquad E^0 = +0.2223 \text{ V} \tag{2.24}$$

As in the calomel electrode, the potential is governed by the chloride ion activity. Useful silver-chloride electrodes can be prepared by simply anodizing a silver wire in chloride media, but the apparent equilibrium potential of these electrodes may differ by several millivolts from one electrode to another. More care is necessary for the preparation of highly stable and reproducible electrodes [4].

Commercial silver/silver-chloride reference electrodes are available in a variety of styles and sizes. They are often used as the internal reference electrodes in glass pH and other ion-selective electrodes. Ag/AgCl microelectrodes formed from very thin silver wire have found extensive use, for example, in biomedical applications such as *in vivo* studies of biological fluids and intracellular measurements, because of the miniaturization possible with these electrodes.

The Ag/AgCl electrode is also sufficiently stable for use at temperatures up to about 275°C, making it a useful alternative to calomel electrodes at elevated temperatures.

Mercury/Mercurous-Sulfate Electrodes

When leakage of chloride ion through the reference electrode into the test solution is not permissible (as in titrations involving Ag^+), a mercury/mercurous-sulfate reference electrode may be used instead of calomel or silver-chloride electrodes. This consists of a mercury electrode in contact with a sulfate electrolyte saturated with excess mercurous sulfate:

$$\text{Hg/Hg}_2\text{SO}_4 \text{ (satd.), SO}_4^{2-} \text{ (X } M) \tag{2.25}$$

Electrolytes commonly used are saturated K_2SO_4 ($E = +0.64$ V vs. SHE) or 0.5 M H_2SO_4 ($E = +0.68$ V vs. SHE). The electrode potential is quite stable and reproducible.

Thallium-Amalgam/Thallous-Chloride Electrodes

The $Tl(Hg)/Tl^+$ reference electrode (Thalamid®) is said to be superior to either calomel or silver-chloride electrodes when measurements are made over a range of temperatures, because it attains its equilibrium potential very rapidly after changes in temperature. The half-cell can be written as

$$\text{Tl (40\% amalgam)/TlCl (satd.), KCl (satd.)}$$

Some commercial glass pH electrodes use Thalamid® electrodes as internal reference electrodes.

2.4 pH—DEFINITION AND MEASUREMENT

Perhaps the earliest definition of pH was given by Sørensen [5], who defined it as the negative logarithm of hydrogen-ion concentration,

$$pH \equiv pcH = -\log [H^+] \qquad (2.26)$$

Because of deficiencies in the theoretical assumptions made, this early definition was a measure of neither concentration nor activity. When the concept of thermodynamic activity became established, primarily through the efforts of Lewis and Randall, Sørensen and Linderstrøm-Lang defined pH as the negative logarithm of the hydrogen-ion activity

$$pH \equiv paH = -\log a_{H^+} = -\log [H^+] f_{H^+} \qquad (2.27)$$

Unfortunately, since individual ionic activity coefficients cannot be evaluated without extrathermodynamic assumptions, the theoretical thermodynamic elegance and desirability of this pH definition cannot be rigorously related to experimental quantities. For this reason, the modern *operational* NBS (National Bureau of Standards) scale of acidity has been developed.

Operational Definition of pH

For the analytical chemist, an experimentally useful scale of acidity should allow the interpretation of the most important and common measurements as, for example, those with a glass electrode and saturated calomel reference electrode. The operational definition of pH of an aqueous solution is

$$pH = pH_s + \frac{(E - E_s)F}{RT \ln 10} \qquad (2.28)$$

where E = the electromotive force of a cell containing the unknown solution
 E_s = the electromotive force of a cell containing a standard reference buffer solution of known or defined pH, that is, pH_s

This definition has been endorsed by standardizing groups in many countries and has been recommended by the International Union of Pure and Applied Chemistry.

In actual practice, the NBS pH standards were assigned pH_s values from measurements of a hydrogen gas–silver/silver-chloride cell without liquid junction,

$$\text{Pt/H}_2, \text{Buffer Solution}, \text{Cl}^-, \text{AgCl/Ag} \qquad (2.29)$$

while making reasonable assumptions about activity coefficients in such a way as to make pH_s represent as nearly as possible $-\log a_{H^+}$.

Since every practical pH electrode can be regarded only as a somewhat imperfect tool that functions more or less unevenly over the whole pH range, and every practical pH reading involves a (possibly variable) liquid-junction potential, the NBS has adopted a series of six primary standard pH buffer solutions (Table 2.2). The pH of the standards is temperature dependent, primarily because of the variation of the K_a of the buffer system with temperature.

The primary standards cover the pH range from about 3.5 to 10.5, and were chosen for their reproducibility, stability, buffer capacity, and ease of preparation.

TABLE 2.2. *pH$_s$ Values of NBS Primary Standards*

Temp. °C	KH Tartrate[a]	KH Phthalate[b]	Phosphate[c] (Equimolal)	Phosphate[d] (3.5:1)	Borax[e]	Carbonate[f]
0	——	4.003	6.982	7.534	9.460	10.321
10	——	3.996	6.921	7.472	9.331	10.181
20	——	3.999	6.878	7.430	9.227	10.064
25	3.557	4.004	6.863	7.415	9.183	10.014
30	3.552	4.011	6.851	7.403	9.143	9.968
40	3.547	4.030	6.836	7.388	9.074	9.891
50	3.549	4.055	6.831	7.384	9.017	9.831

a. Saturated at 25°C; NBS Certificate 188
b. 0.05 m $KHC_8H_4O_4$; NBS Certificate 185e; m = molality (mole/kg)
c. 0.025 m KH_2PO_4, 0.025 m Na_2HPO_4; NBS Certificates 186-I-c and 186-II-c
d. 0.008695 m KH_2PO_4, 0.03043 m Na_2HPO_4; NBS Certificates 186-I-c and 186-II-c
e. 0.01 m $Na_2B_4O_7 \cdot 10H_2O$; NBS Certificate 187b
f. 0.025 m $NaHCO_3$, 0.025 m Na_2CO_3; NBS Certificates 191 and 192

From studies of the internal consistency of the six primary standards, it appears that the total uncertainty of the pH$_s$ values is within ±0.006 pH. This means that the pH determined by a practical cell like

$$Pt/H_2, \text{Solution/Saturated KCl/Reference Electrode} \qquad (2.30)$$

with properly designed liquid junction will be the same regardless of which of the six buffers is chosen as a standard. The same is true if a glass electrode with perfect pH response is substituted for the hydrogen electrode.

With regard to the significance of pH values, it can be said that they are at best an *estimate* of $-\log a_{H^+}$, depending on how accurately the liquid-junction potential remains constant for the measurement of standard and unknown. For many dilute solutions (less than 0.1 M) between pH 2 and 12, the pH may be considered to correspond to the true hydrogen-ion activity to within about ±0.02 pH. This is equivalent to ±1.2 mV in the potential reading, and about a ±5% uncertainty in a_{H^+}.

Secondary Standards. In addition to the six primary standards, the NBS has designated two secondary standards, one on the acidic and one on the basic end of the intermediate pH region, in order to affirm the proper functioning of the glass electrode (Table 2.3). Furthermore, a great number and variety of "secondary" pH standard solutions have been collected in various treatises and compendia [4, 6, 7]. A secondary standard may often prove convenient because it may be more easily prepared or more stable than the primary standards, or matches more closely the composition and pH of a group of unknowns on which many measurements are to be made over a period of time. Particularly in process-control applications with, for example, very concentrated electrolyte solutions, reproducibility may be the most important concern.

TABLE 2.3. *pH of NBS Secondary Standards*

Temp. °C	K Tetroxalate[a]	Ca(OH)$_2$[b]
0	1.666	13.423
10	1.670	13.003
20	1.675	12.627
25	1.679	12.454
30	1.683	12.289
40	1.694	11.984

Source: V. E. Bower, R. G. Bates, and E. R. Smith, *J. Res. Natl. Bur. Stand.*, *51*, 189 (1953); R. G. Bates, V. E. Bower, and E. R. Smith, *J. Res. Natl. Bur. Stand.*, *56*, 305 (1956).
a. 0.05 *m* $KH_3(C_2O_4)_2 \cdot 2H_2O$; NBS Certificate 189
b. Saturated at 25°C

pH Electrodes

The premier pH electrode, from both a historical and a fundamental point of view, is the H_2 gas electrode. As was mentioned in Section 2.3, however, this electrode is difficult to prepare and use, and has been replaced almost universally by the modern glass electrode except for specialized applications.

Glass Electrode. The glass pH electrode is composed of (a), a thin, H^+-ion-responsive glass membrane sealed to a stem of high-resistance, nonresponsive glass, and (b), an internal reference electrode with a constant internal hydrogen-ion concentration. The internal electrode may be either $Ag/AgCl$ in HCl or Hg/Hg_2Cl_2 in HCl. The entire cell requires an external reference electrode for operation. The complete cell may be diagrammed schematically as

$$
\left.
\begin{array}{l}
\text{Internal} \\
\text{Reference} \\
\text{Electrode}
\end{array}
\right/
\left.
\begin{array}{l}
\text{Internal} \\
\text{Electrolyte}
\end{array}
\right/
\left.
\begin{array}{l}
\text{H}^+\text{-responsive} \\
\text{Glass} \\
\text{Membrane}
\end{array}
\right/
\left.
\begin{array}{l}
\text{External} \\
\text{Solution}
\end{array}
\right/\!\!\left/
\begin{array}{l}
\text{External} \\
\text{Reference} \\
\text{Electrode}
\end{array}
\right. \qquad \textbf{(2.31)}
$$

Glass is an irregular three-dimensional arrangement of silicate tetrahedra in which each oxygen atom is shared by two silicate groups. With one type of pH-responsive glass, Na^+ and Ca^{2+} cations are located in this array. Modern glass pH electrodes contain Li^+ and Ba^{2+} to varying degrees, in place of Na^+ and Ca^{2+}, to make the electrode more selective to H^+. When immersed in aqueous solution, cations from the surface of the glass are leached out and replaced by protons to form a hydrated silica-rich layer about 500 Å thick, depending on the hygroscopic nature of the glass. The external part of this hydrated gel layer can act as a cation exchange membrane which has a particularly high degree of selectivity among the various cations. By variation of the glass composition, glass electrodes can be made responsive to a variety of monovalent cations (Sec. 2.5). When a thin membrane of glass is interposed between two solutions, an electrical potential difference is developed across the membrane that depends on the activities and nature of the ions present in the two solutions, the composition of the glass, and other factors. Although the mechanism by which cations affect the potential developed across the glass membrane is not completely understood, the most generally accepted theory is based on an ion-exchange equilibrium occurring at the solution-glass boundary [8].

It is a fact that glass electrodes give a Nernstian response to hydrogen-ion activity, at least over a large portion of the pH range.

Because of their convenience and wide use, a great variety of glass pH electrodes is commercially available in various sizes, shapes, temperature ranges, and so forth. Figure 2.4 illustrates the construction of a common type of glass electrode.

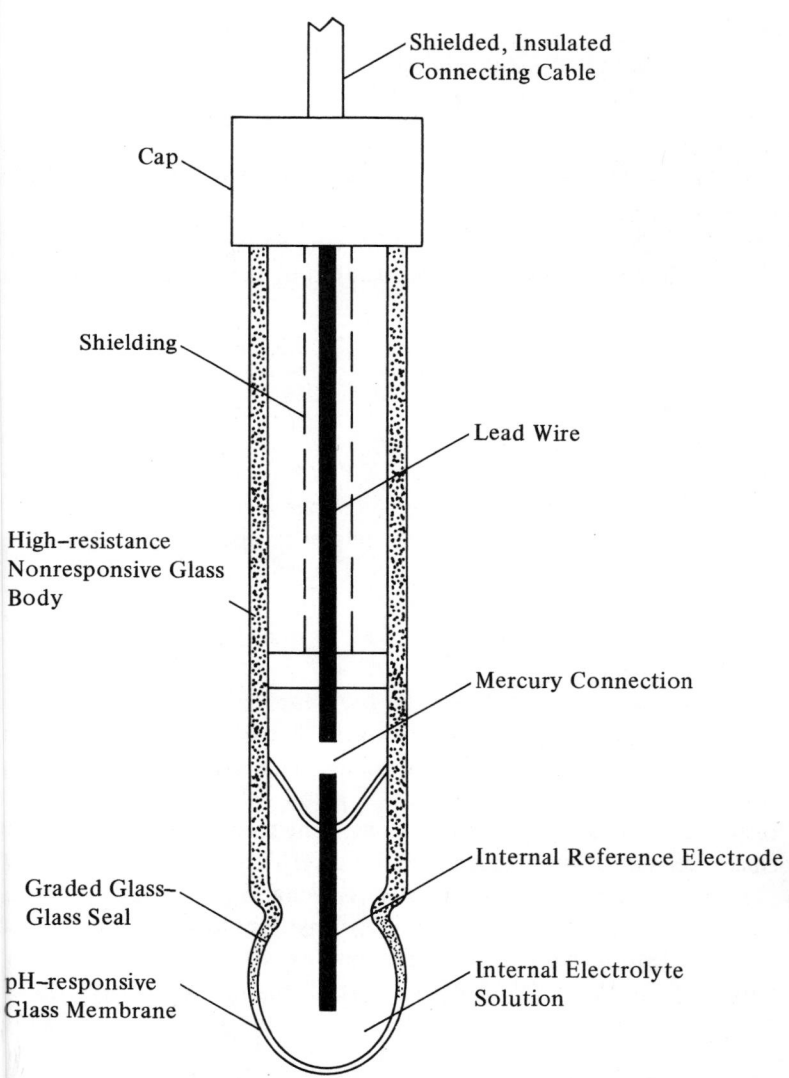

FIGURE 2.4. *Schematic representation of the construction of a typical glass pH electrode.*

A major advantage of glass electrodes is that there is no formal *electron* exchange involved in their functioning; thus they are completely uninfluenced by oxidizing and reducing agents in solution, unlike all other pH electrodes. Their major disadvantage is that they have a very high impedance (1 to 500 megohms, typically) thus necessitating the use of a voltmeter with very high input impedance or an electrometer. Glass electrodes must also be calibrated fairly often, preferably with buffers within about a pH unit of the pH to be measured; they also cannot be used in acidic fluoride media, and exhibit "acid" and "alkaline" errors. In highly acidic media, glass electrodes exhibit a negative "acid" error which is thought to be due to the migration of the anions of the acid into the gel layer and/or a change in activity of water in the gel layer, thereby affecting the hydrogen-ion activity. In highly basic media, glass electrodes exhibit a positive "alkaline" error owing to the partial exchange of cations other than H^+ (notably Na^+) between the pH-sensitive surface layer and the basic solution.

Quinhydrone Electrode. The quinhydrone electrode is an important hydrogen-ion electrode, and is perhaps typical of a whole class of such electrodes which function as pH sensors owing to a reversible organic oxidation-reduction pair involving protons. Quinhydrone (an equimolar compound of benzoquinone and hydroquinone) is only slightly soluble in water. The reversible oxidation-reduction couple

$$\text{(Quinone, Q)} + 2e^- + 2H^+ \rightleftharpoons \text{(Hydroquinone, } H_2Q\text{)} \tag{2.32}$$

Quinone, Q   *Hydroquinone*, H_2Q

involving H^+ will fix the potential of an "inert" electrode, usually gold or platinum, immersed in a solution, as given by

$$E_{Q, H_2Q} = E^0_{Q, H_2Q} + \frac{RT}{2F} \ln \frac{(Q)(H^+)^2}{(H_2Q)} \tag{2.33}$$

The quinhydrone electrode, therefore, responds directly to hydrogen-ion activity in a Nernstian manner as long as the ratio of activities of Q and H_2Q remains constant. The electrode is simple to construct, reaches equilibrium fairly rapidly, and is less disturbed by poisons and by oxidizing and reducing agents than is the hydrogen-gas electrode. It functions well in many nonaqueous and partially aqueous media, and has a relatively low impedance. Its chief disadvantage is that it cannot be used in solutions of pH greater than about 8 owing to the air oxidation of hydroquinone to quinone and the acidic dissociation of hydroquinone, both of which cause the ratio $(Q)/(H_2Q)$ to increase and the apparent pH to be too low.

Antimony Electrode. The antimony electrode is perhaps the best representative of a whole class of metal/metal-oxide redox electrodes that respond to pH. The potential is probably developed as a result of an oxidation-reduction reaction involving antimony and a skin of antimony(III) oxide which forms on the surface of the metal:

$$Sb_2O_3 + 6H^+ + 6e^- \rightleftharpoons 2Sb + 3H_2O \tag{2.34}$$

Since antimony and the oxide are both solids, and can be regarded as being in their standard states of unit activity, the potential of the electrode can be expressed as

$$E_{Sb_2O_3, Sb} = E^0_{Sb_2O_3, Sb} + \frac{RT}{F} \ln (H^+) \qquad (2.35)$$

if the activity of liquid water is unity, as would be expected for dilute solutions.

In actual practice, the antimony electrode does not give highly accurate results. The previous history, preparation, and surface characteristics of each antimony billet used affect the response. Each electrode must be carefully calibrated over the pH range to be used; and factors such as dissolved oxygen and the composition of the buffer solution affect response. Nevertheless, the ruggedness, simplicity, very low resistance, and low cost of the antimony electrode have made it useful, for example, in continuous industrial-process monitoring when high precision and accuracy is not required.

2.5 ION-SELECTIVE ELECTRODES

Within about the last 10 years a wide variety of commercial and homemade ion-selective electrodes (ISEs) has become available; they respond more or less selectively to a wide range of ions in solution.

Properties of Ion-Selective Electrodes

One of the more interesting intrinsic properties of ion-selective electrodes is that they respond *logarithmically* to the *activity* of an ion of interest; that is, in the case where the reference-electrode and liquid-junction potentials are constant, for a cation electrode

$$E_{cell} = E_{constant} + E_{ISE} = E'_{constant} + \frac{RT}{nF} \ln a_1 \qquad (2.36)$$

One interesting result of this property is that the relative concentration error for direct potentiometric measurements is theoretically independent of the actual concentration. Unfortunately, the error is rather large—approximately $\pm 4n\%$ per mV uncertainty in measurement, perhaps the most serious limitation of ISEs. Since potential measurements are seldom better than ± 0.1 mV total uncertainty, the best measurements for monovalent ions under near-ideal conditions are limited to about $\pm 0.5\%$ relative concentration error. For divalent ions, this error would be doubled; and in particularly bad cases where, for example, liquid-junction potentials may vary by ± 5 to 10 mV (as in high or variable ionic-strength solutions), the relative concentration error may be as high as 50%. This limitation may be overcome, however, by using ISEs as endpoint indicators in potentiometric titrations (Sec. 2.6). At the cost of some extra time, accuracies and precisions on the order of 0.1% or better are possible.

Another intrinsic property of ISEs is that they measure activities—the thermodynamic "free" concentration of an ion—although they can be made to determine concentrations by appropriate calibration procedures. Activity measurements may be more valuable in certain cases because activities or "free" concentrations determine rates of reactions and equilibria. Therefore, ISEs can be used to study such phenomena as complexation or chelation, activity coefficients, and so forth.

Interferences. Broadly speaking, interferences may be classed into two general categories: chemical interferences in solution, such as complexation, and electrode interferences due to less than perfect electrode specificity. An ion-selective electrode will respond, more or less strongly, to ions other than the one for which it is nominally designed.

Consider Figure 2.5, for example, which shows a typical calibration curve that might be obtained with a calcium ion–selective electrode. Note that the elec-

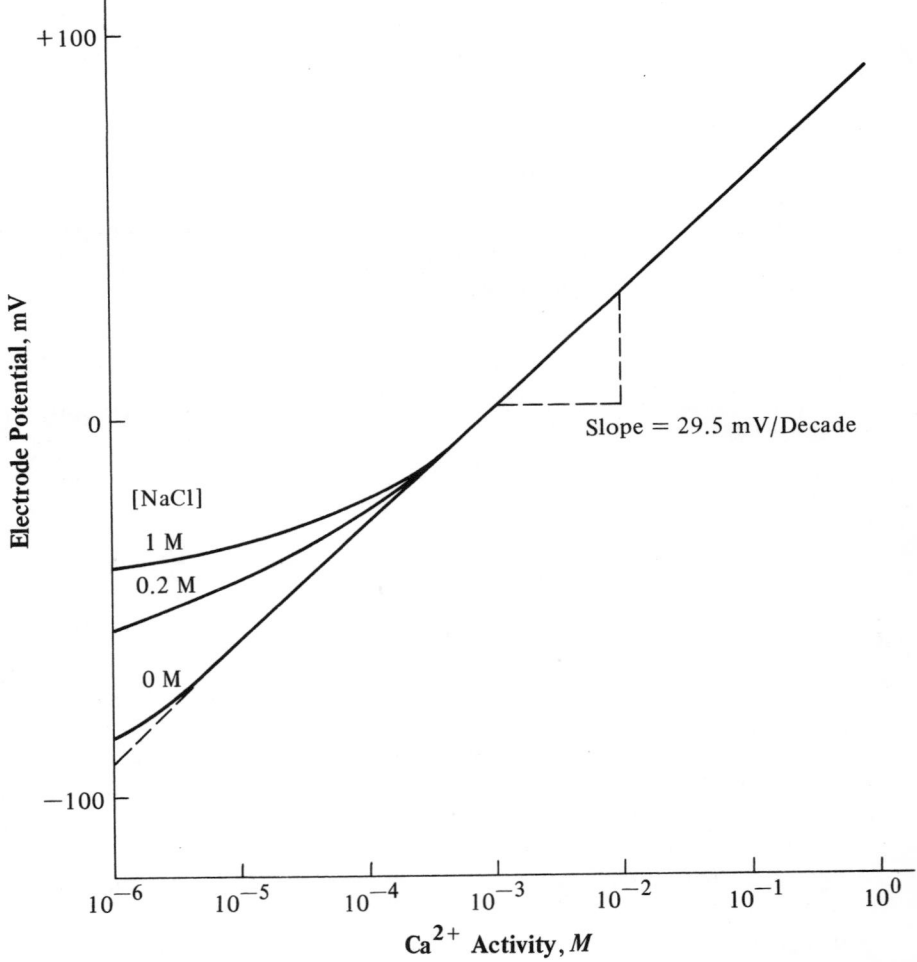

FIGURE 2.5. *The response of a calcium ion–selective electrode to pure CaCl₂ solutions, and to CaCl₂ solutions with 0.2 or 1 M NaCl also present. Redrawn from J. W. Ross, Jr., in* Ion-Selective Electrodes, *R. A. Durst, ed., N.B.S. Special Publication 314, chap. 2, Washington, D.C.: U.S. Government Printing Office, 1969, by permission of the author and the National Bureau of Standards.*

trode response is linear with the logarithm of the calcium activity and has a Nernstian slope. In pure Ca^{2+} solutions, there is departure from the theoretically linear slope at about 6×10^{-6} M, as the electrode nears its detection limit—that concentration below which the electrode output is constant, regardless of the Ca^{2+} activity. The calcium electrode, however, also responds somewhat to Na^+ ion. The curve obtained with Ca^{2+} solutions of varying activity, but also containing 1 M NaCl, exhibits a departure from the theoretical linear portion at about 3×10^{-4} M Ca^{2+} activity— a much higher concentration than with the pure Ca^{2+} solutions. In this region, the calcium electrode is responding appreciably to the Na^+ ion present.

In the case where an electrode is responding to more than one ion, the response can be approximated by a modification of Equation 2.36 above, namely

$$E_{cell} = E'_{constant} + \frac{RT}{nF} \ln (a_1 + k_{1j}a_j^{n/z}) \qquad (2.37)$$

where a_j = the activity of the interferent ion of charge z
k_{1j} = the *selectivity coefficient*

Selectivity coefficients can vary from about zero for no interference to about 10^3 for different electrodes and different interfering ions. For example, the sodium-ion glass electrode actually responds about 350 times more strongly to Ag^+ ($k_{1j} = 350$) and about 10^4 times less strongly to Cs^+ ($k_{1j} = 0.0001$) than to Na^+. As the selectivity coefficient is written in Equation 2.37, *small* values of k_{1j} mean a more selective electrode, one less affected by interferences. Selectivity coefficients can really be regarded as only approximations, perhaps accurate to within an order of magnitude depending on experimental conditions and solution composition. Most selectivity coefficients, for example, show a dependence on total concentration as well as on the ratio of the interfering ion to the ion of interest.

Types of Ion-Selective Electrodes

In recent years, most of the significant electrode discoveries have involved materials for electrodes of the membrane type—that is, electrodes whose potential originates at two interfaces and the intervening bulk membrane. At present, ion-selective electrodes, including the pH glass electrode, imply membrane electrodes.

There are various ways of classifying ion-selective electrodes; for example, by the type of mechanism that produces the electrode response. The approach taken here will be to subdivide the description of electrodes according to the composition of the membrane sensor.

Glass Electrodes. By varying the chemical composition of the thin, ion-sensitive glass membrane, glass electrodes can be prepared that are differentially responsive to (primarily monovalent) cations. The pH glass electrode already discussed is one member of this class; its general construction and mechanism of operation also holds for other glass electrodes. Table 2.4 shows the typical properties of some commercial glass electrodes. These electrodes show very little response to divalent cations.

TABLE 2.4. *Typical Properties of Commercial Glass Ion-Selective Electrodes*

Type of Electrode	Concentration Range M	Glass Composition	Relative Electrode Response
H^+	10^0–10^{-13} (with corrections)	Li_2O–BaO–La_2O_3–SiO_2 or Na_2O–CaO–SiO_2 (21%) (6%) (72%)	$H^+ \gg Li^+, Na^+ > K^+$
Na^+	10^0–10^{-6}	Li_2O–Al_2O_3–SiO_2 or Na_2O–Al_2O_3–SiO_2 (11%) (18%) (71%)	Ag^+ (350) > H^+ (100) > Na^+ (1) $\gg Li^+, K^+,$ Cs^+ (0.001) > NR_4^+, Tl^+ (0.0003) > Rb^+, NH_4^+ (0.00003)
General Cation (monovalent)	10^0–10^{-5}	Na_2O–Al_2O_3–SiO_2 (27%) (4%) (69%)	K^+ (33), Rb^+ (17), NH_4^+ (11), Na^+ (4), H^+ (3), Li^+ (2), Cs (1), Tl^+, Cu^+, R_4N^+

Solid-State Crystalline and Pressed-Pellet Electrodes. There are two basic types of crystalline-based electrodes. The first is exemplified by the fluoride electrode, with a europium-doped LaF_3 single crystal as the sensor. The LaF_3 crystal is sealed into the end of a rigid, cylindrical electrode body made of plastic; an internal electrolyte solution, typically NaF and NaCl, and an internal reference electrode complete the construction (Fig. 2.6). At room temperature, LaF_3 is a pure F^--ion conductor,

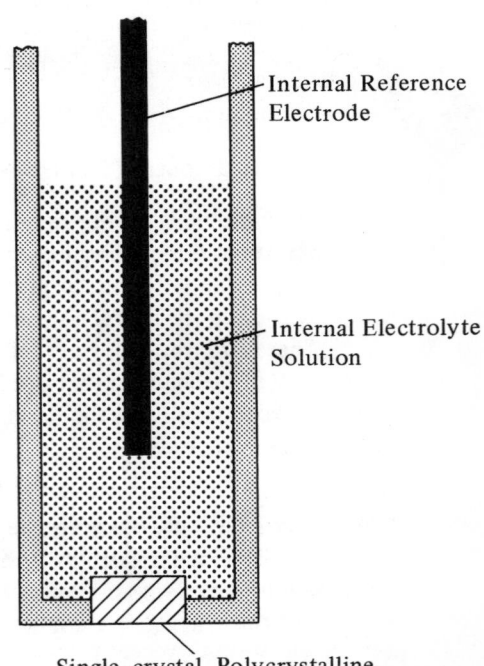

FIGURE 2.6. *Schematic representation of the construction of a crystal-sensor ion-selective electrode.*

Internal Reference Electrode

Internal Electrolyte Solution

Single–crystal, Polycrystalline, or Pressed–pellet Sensor

thus remarkably free from interferences, an almost "specific" electrode. Virtually the only interferences encountered with the electrode are at low pH, where fluoride ion forms HF ($pK_a \approx 3$), and at pHs greater than about 8, where OH^- interferes— probably by some chemical modification of the LaF_3 crystal. The fluoride electrode was the first to really capture the minds of chemists; and there are probably several hundred publications dealing with the analytical determination of fluoride in such samples as municipal drinking and waste waters, seawater, air particulates, bone, minerals, organic materials, plant tissues, biological fluids, soils, toothpastes, and so forth.

The second class of crystalline sensors is based on the easily fabricated, low-resistance, selectively permeable cast-disk and pressed-pellet membranes based on Ag_2S. Silver sulfide is an ionic conductor in which silver ions are the mobile species. By itself, it can be used to detect silver ions or to measure sulfide-ion levels. The potential-determining mechanism in an Ag_2S electrode is due to the very low solubility product of Ag_2S [$K_{sp} = 10^{-51}$]. The silver-ion activity

$$Ag_2S \; \rightleftharpoons \; 2Ag^+ + S^{2-} \tag{2.38}$$

of the test solution on one side of the membrane and the (constant) silver-ion activity of the inner filling solution (Fig. 2.6) establish an electrochemical half-cell that responds to the Ag^+ activity of the test solution.

$$E = E_{constant} + \frac{RT}{F} \ln (Ag^+) \tag{2.39}$$

($E_{constant}$ contains such factors as E^0 for the electrode and a term containing the silver-ion activity of the inner solution.)

By making mixed pellets containing AgX-Ag_2S, where X = Cl, Br, I, or SCN, one has an electrode responsive to one of these particular anions. The silver-ion activity at the surface of the electrode is controlled by the activity of X^- in solution via its solubility equilibrium

$$AgX \; \rightleftharpoons \; Ag^+ + X^- \tag{2.40}$$

This in turn controls the electrode potential by being coupled with the Ag_2S solubility equilibrium. By substituting into Equation 2.39,

$$E = E_{constant} + \frac{RT}{F} \ln (Ag^+) = E_{constant} + \frac{RT}{F} \ln \frac{K_{sp}}{(X^-)} = E'_{constant} - \frac{RT}{F} \ln (X^-) \tag{2.41}$$

These electrodes, of course, are also responsive to Ag^+ or S^{2-} ions.

In an entirely similar manner, electrodes responsive to Cu^{2+}, Cd^{2+}, and Pb^{2+} cations (M^{2+}), which form insoluble metal sulfides, can be made by mixing the appropriate metal sulfide with Ag_2S. In this case, the M^{2+} activity controls the sulfide-ion activity in solution, which in turn controls the Ag^+ activity and the electrode response.

The selectivity and properties of these various electrodes are basically a function of the solubility products involved. Anything with a lower solubility product than the ion being determined will interfere. For this reason, AgCl membranes are subject to greater interference than AgBr, and so on. Iodide and bromide must be reduced to levels less than 5×10^{-7} and 2×10^{-3} times the lowest chloride activity anticipated when using an AgCl membrane.

Cast pellets of silver halides alone can also serve as membranes for the respective halide-selective electrode, but function less well than the mixed crystalline sensors. A CN^- electrode can be made with an AgI/Ag_2S membrane. The typical properties of some commercial crystalline-sensor ion-selective electrodes are listed in Table 2.5. Although most of the electrodes cannot be used at total concentrations below about 10^{-6} to 10^{-7} M, this lower limit is generally too high to be caused by the solubility of the membrane, and reflects instead the experimental difficulty of accurately preparing very dilute solutions. With solutions of higher concentrations, it is quite possible to obtain accurate measurements of very low activities of the free ions—for example, free sulfide ion activities can be measured in acid solutions down to about 10^{-19} M. In such equilibrium systems, the parent compound is at high enough total concentration that losses of the free ion by adsorption on the container walls, and so forth, are negligible and are compensated by equilibrium shifts.

The Ag_2S-based electrodes can be fabricated with a solid-state internal connection—a silver wire attached directly to the membrane. This eliminates the problems associated with internal filling solutions.

Another variation of the polycrystalline-type electrode is the Pungor design [9], which involves incorporation of the membrane material in a matrix such as sili-

TABLE 2.5. *Typical Properties of Commercial Crystalline Solid-State Electrodes*

Electrode	Concentration Range (M)	Activity Limit $C > 10^{-6}\ M$	Interferences
F^-	10^0–10^{-6}		$OH^- < 0.1\ F^-$
Ag^+ or S^{2-}	10^0–10^{-7}	10^{-20}	$Hg^{2+} < 10^{-7}\ M$
Cl^-	10^0–5×10^{-5}	10^{-6}	$S^{2-} < 10^{-7}\ M$; trace Br^-, I^-, CN^- permitted
Br^-	10^0–5×10^{-6}	10^{-7}	$S^{2-} < 10^{-7}\ M$; $I^- < 2 \times 10^{-4}\ Br^-$
I^-	10^0–2×10^{-7}	10^{-10}	$S^{2-} < 10^{-7}\ M$
CN^-	10^{-2}–10^{-6}		$S^{2-} < 10^{-7}\ M$; $I^- < 0.1\ CN^-$; $Br^- < 5 \times 10^3\ CN^-$
SCN^-	10^0–5×10^{-6}		I^-, $S^{2-} < 10^{-7}\ M$; $Br^- < 3 \times 10^{-3}\ SCN^-$; CN^-, $S_2O_3^{2-} < 10^{-2}\ SCN^-$; $NH_3 < 0.1\ SCN^-$; $OH^- < SCN^-$; $Cl^- < 20\ SCN^-$
Cd^{2+}	10^0–10^{-7}	10^{-10}	Ag^+, Hg^{2+}, $Cu^{2+} < 10^{-7}\ M$
Cu^{2+}	10^0–10^{-8}	10^{-10}	S^{2-}, Ag^+, $Hg^{2+} < 10^{-7}\ M$
Pb^{2+}	10^0–10^{-7}	10^{-10}	Ag^+, Hg^{2+}, $Cu^{2+} < 10^{-7}\ M$

Source: Selected values have been taken from data supplied through the courtesy of Orion Research, Incorporated.

cone rubber. The proportion of material imbedded in the matrix must be high enough to produce physical contact between particles.

Liquid-Membrane Ion-Exchange Electrodes. One design of a liquid-membrane ion-exchange electrode consists of two concentric cylindrical tubes constructed of inert plastic (Fig. 2.7). The inner tube holds the internal reference electrode and an aqueous

FIGURE 2.7. *Schematic representation of the construction of a liquid-liquid ion-exchange electrode.*

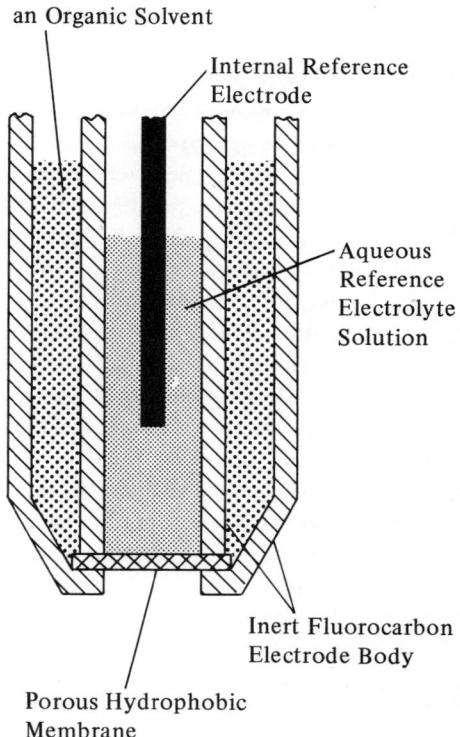

Ion–exchanger in an Organic Solvent

Internal Reference Electrode

Aqueous Reference Electrolyte Solution

Inert Fluorocarbon Electrode Body

Porous Hydrophobic Membrane

electrolyte solution containing the ion of interest. The outer compartment contains a charged or neutral organic ion-exchanger dissolved in an organic solvent that wicks into a thin hydrophobic membrane; this now forms a thin organic-membrane phase separating two aqueous solutions. The membrane may be, for example, a cellulose-acetate Millipore® filter. An ion-exchange equilibrium is set up at both the inner and outer surfaces of the membrane, and the difference in activity of the ion of interest in the inner electrolyte and outer test solutions gives rise to the potential response of the electrode.

The selectivity and sensitivity of these electrodes is determined primarily by the selectivity of the particular organic ion-exchanger for the ion of interest and, secondarily, by the organic solvent used to dissolve the exchanger. The extent of interference is related to the stability of the complex formed between the ion and the ion-exchanger in the membrane, and the mobility of the complexes within the membrane. One of the consequences of this selectivity is that the electrodes are occasionally more sensitive to an interferant ion than to the ion for which the electrode was nominally designed. Thus, by soaking a Ca^{2+} electrode in Zn^{2+} or Fe^{2+} solution, or better, by preparing the electrode with zinc or ferrous ion in the internal solution instead of calcium, an electrode for Zn^{2+} or Fe^{2+} is obtained.

Phosphate diesters ($(RO)_2PO_2^{-}$, with R groups in the $C_8–C_{16}$ range) dissolved in a relatively polar solvent such as dioctylphenylphosphonate show good selectivity for Ca^{2+} in the presence of Na^+, as well as for Ca^{2+} in the presence of other alkaline-earth ions. Less polar solvents such as decanol produce electrodes that give virtually identical response to all the alkaline-earth ions; electrodes of this type are useful for the determination of water hardness.

Ion-exchangers of the form $R–S–CH_2COO^{-}$ (in which the sulfur and carboxylate groups can readily form a 5-member chelate ring with a heavy-metal ion) show good selectivity for Cu^{2+} and for Pb^{2+}.

Certain positively charged ion-exchangers can be used for anion-selective electrodes. Charged metal salts of appropriately substituted orthophenanthrolines—$M(o\text{-phen})_3^{2+}$—result in good electrodes for nitrate, fluoroborate, or perchlorate by forming ion-association complexes with these anions. The ClO_4^{-} electrode, in particular, has few interferences; and perchlorate is a difficult ion to measure by almost any other method. A dimethyl-distearyl-ammonium ion, R_4N^+, can be used as an ion-exchanger in an electrode that has fair selectivity for chloride.

The organic ion-exchanger used need not be charged. Neutral organic ligands, typically dissolved in a low-dielectric liquid such as decane, can show good selectivity for certain cations. These lipid-soluble molecules usually contain a ring-arrangement of oxygen atoms that can replace the aqueous hydration shell around cations and thus extract them into organic solvents. This provides a mechanism for transport of the cations across the membrane and, thereby, an electrode response to the cation. The antibiotics valinomycin and the macrotetrolides such as nonactin and monactin are highly selective natural products that can be used for the measurement of K^+ or NH_4^+. The valinomycin electrode, in particular, shows excellent selectivity for K^+ over Na^+ (4000:1), H^+ (20,000:1), and divalent metal ions (ca. 5000:1), which is much better than the best potassium-sensitive glass electrode. The actin-based membranes are about four times more responsive to NH_4^+ than to K^+. Synthetic cyclic polyethers ("crown" compounds) can be used as ion exchangers for univalent and for some alkaline-earth cations, although they generally show much less specificity than the above natural compounds.

The lower limit of detection for liquid ion-exchange electrodes is determined primarily by the solubility of the ion exchanger in aqueous media. As with crystalline solid-state electrodes, Nernstian response is obtained until the activity of the solution is within a factor of about 100 of the solubility of the membrane salt. Then the response deviates and levels off at a constant potential reflecting this solubility.

Typical characteristics of some commercially available liquid ion-exchange electrodes are presented in Table 2.6.

Liquid-membrane electrodes are more sensitive to the solution environment than are solid-state electrodes. Their usable temperature range, generally 0–50°C, is more restricted than that of solid-state electrodes so that water will not permeate the membrane, nor membrane liquids bleed excessively into the aqueous solution. Normally, it is best to restrict use of the electrodes to purely aqueous media so the

TABLE 2.6. *Typical Properties of Selected Commercial Liquid-Liquid Ion-Exchange Electrodes*

Electrode	Concentration Range (M)	Interferences (approximate k_{ij})
Ca^{2+}	10^0–10^{-5}	Zn^{2+} (50); Pb^{2+} (20); Fe^{2+}, Cu^{2+} (1); Mg^{2+}, Sr^{2+} (0.01); Ba^{2+} (0.003); Ni^{2+} (0.002); Na^+ (0.001)
Cl^-	10^0–10^{-5}	ClO_4^- (20); I^- (10); NO_3^-, Br^- (3); OH^- (1); HCO_3^-, OAc^- (0.3); F^- (0.1); SO_4^{2-} (0.02)
Divalent Cation	10^0–10^{-5}	Zn^{2+}, Cu^{2+} (3); Fe^{2+} (2); Ni^{2+}, Ca^{2+}, Mg^{2+} (1); Sr^{2+} (0.25); Ba^{2+} (0.2); Na^+ (0.1)
BF_4^-	10^{-1}–10^{-5}	NO_3^- (0.005); Br^-, OAc^-, HCO_3^-, OH^-, Cl^- (0.0005); SO_4^{2-} (0.0002)
NO_3^-	10^{-1}–10^{-5}	ClO_4^- (1000); I^- (10); ClO_3^- (1); Br^- (0.1); NO_2^- (0.05); HS^-, CN^- (0.02); Cl^-, HCO_3^- (0.002); OAc^- (0.001)
ClO_4^-	10^{-1}–10^{-5}	I^- (0.05); NO_3^-, OH^-, Br^- (0.002)
K^+	10^0–10^{-5}	Cs^+ (1); NH_4^+ (0.03); Tl^+, H^+ (0.01); Ag^+ (0.001); Na^+ (0.0002)

Source: Selected values have been taken from data supplied through the courtesy of Orion Research, Incorporated.

membrane or ion exchanger will not dissolve in the test solution. The electrodes must be recharged every few weeks with new ion exchanger and internal electrolyte. Otherwise they are handled much as glass or solid-state electrodes are.

Enzyme-Substrate Electrodes. Electrodes that can respond to a variety of organic and biological compounds are constructed by coating the surface of an appropriate ion-selective electrode with an enzyme immobilized in some matrix. Perhaps the most well-known of these is the urea electrode [10], which makes use of the enzyme urease to hydrolyze urea (the "substrate"):

$$\text{urea} + H_2O \xrightarrow{\text{urease}} HCO_3^- + NH_4^+ \qquad (2.42)$$

In this case, the urease is physically entrapped in a polyacrylamide matrix polymerized on the surface of an ammonium-ion glass electrode. The enzyme-gel matrix is supported on the electrode by a sheer dacron or nylon gauze, about the thickness of a nylon stocking, or it is held by a thin semipermeable cellophane sheet. The urea diffuses to the urease-gel membrane, where it is hydrolyzed to produce ammonium ion. Some of the ammonium ion diffuses through the thin membrane to the electrode surface, where it is monitored by the ammonium-sensitive electrode. The urea electrode is fairly stable, sensitive, specific for urea, has a usable lifetime of 2–3 weeks before a new gel layer must be prepared, and has a fairly fast response time (< 120 sec). The output of the electrode is linear from about 10^{-4} to 10^{-2} M urea.

There are literally thousands of enzyme-substrate combinations that yield products which could theoretically be measured with ion-selective electrodes. The high sensitivity of the electrodes and the specificity of enzymes can thus be coupled to produce sensors of value in many biomedical applications. Electrodes responsive to the following substrates have already been described in the literature: urea,

L-amino acids, D-amino acids, asparagine, glutamine, amygdalin, creatinine, penicillin, and others.

With some modifications, an electrode system can be made responsive to *enzyme* levels in test solution by surrounding the ion-sensitive membrane with *substrate* molecules. For example, an electrode that will measure the enzyme activity of cholinesterases in blood fractions has been described. Generally, such electrodes must be designed to replenish the substrate since it is consumed in the reaction.

Gas-Sensing Electrodes. There are several gas-sensing electrodes available, which function by interposing a thin, highly gas-permeable membrane between the test solution and an appropriate sensing element. The dissolved gas passes through the membrane into a small volume of internal filling solution, where a chemical equilibrium is established between the gas dissolved in the test solution and the internal electrolyte. The internal sensor monitors the changes in this equilibrium, and thus produces an output proportional to this concentration of dissolved gas. Potentiometric electrodes for ammonia (ammonium), sulfur dioxide (sulfite), nitrogen oxide (nitrite), and carbon dioxide (carbonate) are available.

The operation of gas-sensing electrodes can be illustrated by considering the sulfur-dioxide electrode, which responds directly to dissolved SO_2. Sulfite (SO_3^{2-}) and bisulfite (HSO_3^-) are measured by acidifying the sample to convert these species to SO_2. Dissolved SO_2 diffuses through the gas-permeable membrane until an equilibrium is established in the internal filling solution by the reaction of SO_2 with water

$$SO_2 + H_2O \rightleftharpoons HSO_3^- + H^+ \qquad (2.43)$$

The hydrogen-ion level is then sensed by the internal sensing element (a conventional glass pH electrode), and is directly proportional to the level of SO_2 in the sample. The electrode has a usable range of 10^{-6} to 10^{-2} M SO_2, and has very few interferences, essentially only volatile weak acids such as acetic acid and HF.

The SO_2 level of stack gases can be measured by drawing a known volume of gas through an absorbing solution, acidifying an aliquot, and measuring SO_2 directly. The sulfite level of pulping liquors can be determined directly after acidification.

Ion-Selective Microelectrodes. Ion-selective electrodes can be fabricated in microassemblies for use in such applications as measuring ion activities in microsamples (10^{-3} ml) and as direct probes in tissues, tubules, capillaries, or even within individual cells. Microelectrodes can be fabricated with sensors made of glass, liquid ion-exchanger, or solid-state crystals [11, 13].

Closed-tip glass microelectrodes are fabricated by fusing a very small active tip onto a body of insulating glass or by coating the electrode stem with insulation, leaving only the tip exposed. Tip diameters of less than 1.5 μm exposed to a length of 3 to 5 μm can be achieved. Electrodes of this type have been used successfully to measure alkali-metal-ion activities in frog skeletal muscle. On a somewhat larger scale, miniaturized glass electrodes have been built within a small hypodermic syringe needle, intended for continuous monitoring of fetal blood pH during birth.

Open-tip liquid ion-exchange microelectrodes can be fabricated by pulling borosilicate glass capillary tubing to an appropriate tip diameter (0.5 to 1 μm), rendering the interior of the tip hydrophobic by coating the surface with an organic silicone compound, and filling the tip with an ion exchanger appropriate for the ion of interest (K^+, Cl^-, Ca^{2+}, and so on). The internal circuit is completed with an electrolyte solution and an Ag/AgCl reference electrode. Such electrodes can measure ion activities in single *aplasia* neurons (0.5 μl total volume).

An interesting approach to miniature electrodes is the coating of a fine platinum wire with a mixture of a liquid ion-exchanger and poly(vinyl chloride) or poly(methyl methacrylate) [14]. Although the mechanism by which these electrodes function is not known (there is no internal reference electrode), they do appear to function almost as well as the larger commercial varieties.

pH Meters

Other than the appropriate electrodes, the only major piece of instrumentation needed to perform pH and ion-electrode measurements is a pH meter. This is a very-high-impedance electronic voltmeter that draws negligible current from the reference-indicator electrode pair; thus no error arises from the voltage drop across the inherent (usually high) resistance of the electrochemical cell. A great variety of pH meters is commercially available, with an even greater variety of features. In general, pH meters can be divided into four classes based on price and "accuracy," although there is considerable overlap between classes: *utility* (portable), *general-purpose*, *expanded-scale*, and *research* grades.

Utility-grade pH meters usually cost about $100–300. Most are battery operated, and thus portable; generally they offer enough sensitivity to be used in many quality-control applications and out in the field. Their relative accuracy is about ±0.1 pH unit, and they have taut-band meter movements. General-purpose pH meters are more often line operated, and cost about $300–700. For the extra cost, they usually offer better stability and accuracy (±0.05 pH or ±3 mV), larger taut-band scales, and extra features such as a recorder output, mV scales, and a constant-current jack for performing polarized electrode measurements or dead-stop titrations such as the Karl Fischer titration for water determination.

For increased accuracy, expanded-scale pH meters (retailing for about $400–900, depending on features) generally offer accuracy of about ±0.01 pH unit. Usually any 1.0 pH unit or 100 mV range is expandable to full scale; many types that fall into this class have digital (4-digit) displays. For the most demanding applications, research-grade pH meters offer a relative accuracy of about 0.002 pH or ±0.1 mV (readability to 0.001 pH) for about $700–1200. Most of these have digital (5-digit) displays, full-range expanded-scale operation, recorder outputs, and highly adaptable slope and calibration controls.

Since there is such a wide variety of specialized features available on specific pH meters, manufacturers' literature must be consulted to select the best possible unit for the intended use.

Applications of Ion-Selective Electrodes

Ion-selective electrodes are used extensively as quantitative analytical probes in such diverse areas as air and water pollution, fundamental biomedical research, oceanography, geology, agriculture, and clinical analysis. Only a few representative examples of specific applications will be considered in detail.

Direct Potentiometry: Determination of Hydrogen Chloride Gas. A system has been described for the continuous monitoring of the HCl levels in gases or aerosols using a chloride-ion–selective electrode [15]. This arose from a study on the loss of volatile decomposition products from poly(vinyl chloride) (PVC) and other chlorocarbon polymers in simulated fires. The method works well because of the excellent solubility of HCl in water, and the fact that the chloride electrode senses only free Cl^- ion. Thus, other volatile chloride compounds will not be sensed.

The detection limit is about 20 ppm HCl in the original gaseous sample, and the accuracy of the method is within 5% from 20–6000 ppm HCl, as determined from analyses of standard gaseous samples.

The use of direct potentiometry for determination of ionic activities is quite popular, probably owing to its simplicity. The nitrate content of potatoes, for example, can be determined directly in the slurry resulting from peeling, dicing, and blending potatoes with water. The Ca^{2+} content of soils can be determined directly by diluting the supernatant from a pH 8.2 sodium-acetate extraction of dry soil. Orion Research, Incorporated, manufactures a complete system, incorporating a flow-through calcium electrode, for anaerobic ionized-calcium measurements on serum and other biological fluids. The sample volume is quite small, about 200 μl, and results are available in about two minutes. Bromide, chloride, and fluoride in rain and snow samples can be determined directly with the appropriate ion-selective electrode. Cupric ion in acid-plating baths can be determined directly after 100:1 dilution.

Ionic-Strength Buffering: Fluoride in Natural Waters. The fluoride electrode has found many uses in the determination of fluoride in various materials, primarily because of its applicability to a wide concentration range (10^0–10^{-6} M) and its simplicity and ease of use—particularly when compared with other methods for fluoride, which usually involve a time-consuming distillation step.

Because the ionic strength of natural waters may vary markedly, and thus affect activity coefficients, both samples and standards are usually diluted 1:1 with a Total Ionic Strength Adjustment Buffer (TISAB). By treating the unknown and standards in the same manner, and swamping out the ionic strength of the test solution, one calibration curve serves to determine the *concentration* of a given ion regardless of its original environment. The fluoride TISAB contains a 1 M acetic-acid/sodium-acetate buffer of pH 5.0 to buffer the solution in the middle of the electrode's pH range—thus avoiding erroneous results from HF formation or OH^- interference; about 10^{-3} M sodium citrate to preferentially complex metal ions such as iron and aluminum, which have some affinity for F^-; and 1 M NaCl to further increase the ionic strength.

A calibration curve for the determination of F^- in municipal waters is illustrated in Figure 2.8. The 40 mV difference in electrode response to two different water supplies, one with and the other without added fluoride, is easily measured. This measurement system can be readily automated for continuous monitoring of fluoride levels.

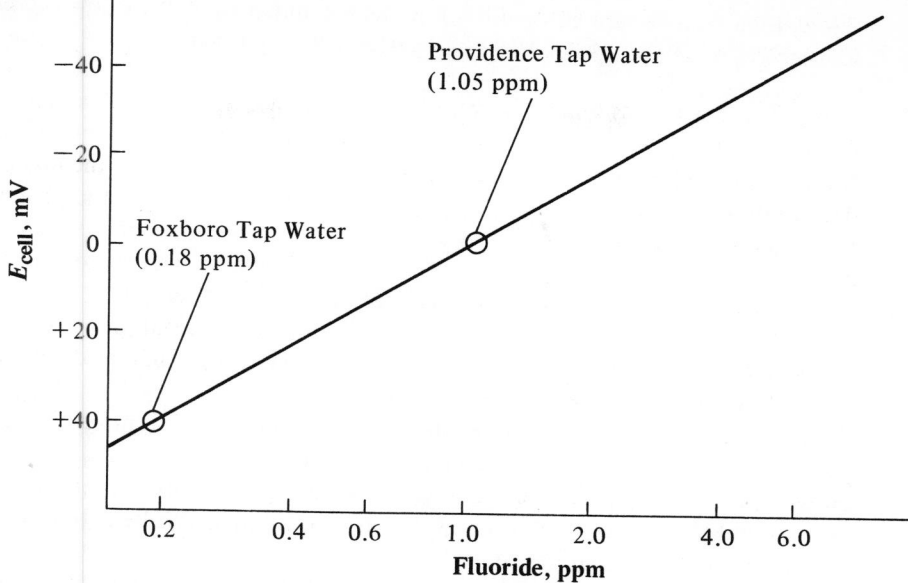

FIGURE 2.8.   *Determination of fluoride in municipal water supplies by the calibration curve method using ionic-strength buffering. Redrawn from* T. S. Light, *in* Ion-Selective Electrodes, *R. A. Durst, ed., N.B.S. Special Publication 314, chap. 10, Washington, D.C.: U.S. Government Printing Office, 1969, by permission of the author and the National Bureau of Standards.*

The fluoride content of fluoridated toothpastes (typically about 0.09%) can be determined in an analogous manner [16].

The practice of ionic-strength buffering to fix activity coefficients (with possible use of a pH buffer and complexing agents to minimize interferences) is a fairly common practice when using ion-selective electrodes. Low levels (10–150 ppb) of Ag^+ can be determined accurately after ionic-strength adjustment with solid $NaNO_3$ [17].

Running standards and samples through the same digestion and separation procedures, for example, is another way of insuring that solution compositions and ionic strengths are similar in all test solutions.

Method of Standard Additions: Determination of Ammonia in Aquaria and Sea Water.
The method of standard addition, or the known increment (or decrement) method, is a way of measuring analyte concentration, particularly for samples with high but unknown total ionic strength or for samples with highly variable solution components. This approach does not require the preparation of a calibration curve, although it is necessary to know the experimental electrode response slope (theoretically RT/nF) in the region of interest.

The initial potential reading is taken on a sample of concentration c

$$E_1 = E_{const} + \frac{RT}{nF} \ln fc \tag{2.44}$$

where f = the activity coefficient

Next, a known amount of the ion of interest is added to the test solution so that the concentration is changed by a known amount Δc, and the potential is read again.

$$E_2 = E_{\text{const}} + \frac{RT}{nF} \ln f(c + \Delta c) \qquad (2.45)$$

Usually, the standard addition is a small volume of a concentrated solution, so that the total solution volume and ionic strength does not change appreciably. The above two equations can be combined to give

$$\Delta E = E_2 - E_1 = \frac{RT}{nF} \ln \left(\frac{c + \Delta c}{c} \right) \qquad (2.46)$$

Equation 2.46 is solved for c by rearranging and taking antilogs.

Usually, the most accurate determinations are made when Δc is such that the total concentration is approximately doubled. The only requirement is that the electrode be in a linear portion of its calibration curve over the concentration range of interest. The slope of the calibration need not be precisely equal to the Nernst factor, RT/nF; if it is not, the empirically determined slope S of the calibration curve can be substituted.

By the technique of adding several small increments and measuring the potential after each addition, concentrations can be determined with better precision than by a single standard-addition measurement. Potential is plotted against concentration on special graph paper (semi-antilogarithmic) to yield a Gran's plot [18]. The straight line obtained is extrapolated back to the horizontal axis, and the concentration corresponding to this intercept value is the sought-for concentration.

An example of the use of the standard-addition method is the determination of ammonia in aquaria and sea water [19] using an ammonia-gas electrode. To a 100 ml sample is added a sufficient number of NaOH pellets to raise the pH above 11 (to convert all ammonium ion to ammonia). The equilibrium potential is read, then a sufficient volume of standard NH_4Cl solution to approximately double the concentration is added, and the new equilibrium potential is read. The effective detection limit for this method is approximately 1 ppb NH_3; but below about 10 ppb considerable time is required for the electrode to stabilize, making the method somewhat impractical at the 1–10 ppb level. Results compare favorably with the phenol-hypochlorite spectrophotometric method for ammonia.

Calcium in beer can be determined by filtering the sample, adjusting the pH to 6, and employing a known addition of Ca^{2+}. The copper-ion content of tap water can be determined with a solid-state crystalline copper electrode using a multiple standard-addition procedure [20]. Tap water is mixed 1:1 with a complexing anti-oxidant buffer (sodium acetate, acetic acid, sodium fluoride, and formaldehyde) to buffer the pH at 4.8, to complex the Cu^{2+} uniformly with acetate, and to complex the Fe^{3+} interferant with fluoride. Copper in tap water can be determined down to about 9 ppm with a standard deviation of about $\pm 8\%$. The recovery of Cu^{2+} added to natural waters, an indication of the accuracy of the method, averaged 103% for samples in the range of 3 to 60 ppm Cu.

Only a few specific applications have been mentioned above. A great many more are contained in the scientific literature and manufacturers' literature, particularly Orion Research's *Analytical Methods Guide* [21].

Advantages and Disadvantages of Ion-Selective Electrodes

After this discussion of the types and applications of ion-selective electrodes, it is well to consider and review the general advantages and disadvantages of ion-selective electrodes as analytical tools. As mentioned previously, a unique characteristic of these electrodes is that they measure activity directly, not concentration. Another uncommon characteristic is their logarithmic response, which results in a constant, albeit rather large, error over the concentration range where the Nernst relation holds. The linear working range of many electrodes is quite large, generally from 4 to 6 orders of magnitude or more. Electrodes will function well in colored or turbid samples, where spectral methods generally will not.

In most cases, electrode measurements are reasonably rapid—equilibrium being reached in less than a minute; but in some cases, usually in very dilute solutions, slow electrode response may require fifteen minutes to an hour for equilibrium. The normally rapid response of ion-selective electrodes make them suitable in kinetic studies and for monitoring changes in flowing process streams. The equipment used is simple, quite inexpensive, and can be made portable for field operations. The method is virtually nondestructive of the sample (once it is in the liquid state), and can be used with very small samples (< 1 ml).

Perhaps the most decided disadvantage of ion-selective electrodes is that they are subject to a rather large number of interferences. The electrodes themselves respond more or less strongly to several ions; and various chemical interferences are possible, including chelation, complexation, and ionic-strength effects. Generally, fairly frequent calibration is necessary. Ion-selective electrodes are not ultra-trace level sensors; some electrodes, for example, are good only down to about 10^{-4} M and most are not usable below about 10^{-6} M concentration level—although this does correspond to perhaps 0.1 ppm.

An advantage or disadvantage, depending on the situation, is that ion-selective electrodes are responsive to a particular chemical form of an element. For example, an iodide electrode responds only to I^-, not to the total iodine content which could include IO_3^- or organically bound iodine.

2.6 POTENTIOMETRIC TITRATIONS

Many different types of ion-selective electrodes can be used as endpoint indicators in potentiometric titrations. For example, an acid-base titration can be performed with a glass pH electrode as an endpoint detector, rather than with a phenolphthalein indicator; or calcium can be titrated with EDTA using a calcium ion–selective electrode. During such a titration, the *change* in potential of a suitable indicator electrode is observed as a function of the volume added of a titrant of precisely known concentration. Since it is the change in potential rather than the absolute potential that is of interest, liquid-junction potentials and activity coefficients have little or no effect. Perhaps the primary advantage of potentiometric titrations is that (with the addition of classical titration procedures) they generally offer a large increase in accuracy and precision; $\pm 0.1\%$ levels are not uncommon. (We should note, however, certain disadvantages: the increase in analysis time and operator attention required, and the difficulties associated with the preparation, standardization, and storage of standard titrant solutions.)

Another advantage of potentiometric titrations is that substances to which the electrode does not respond can be determined, if the electrode responds to the titrant or to some low level of an indicator substance that has been added to the solution. For example, low levels of Al^{3+} can be determined by titration with standard fluoride solution, using a fluoride electrode [22]. EDTA and other chelates can be determined by titration with standard calcium or copper solution. Manganese(II), vanadium(II), or cobalt(II) can be determined via EDTA titration if a small amount of CuEDTA indicator is added to the solution and a copper electrode is used. The electrode responds directly to the Cu^{2+} activity which, however, is dependent on the activities of the EDTA and the other metal ion in solution.

The experimental apparatus for a potentiometric titration can be quite simple: only a pH or millivolt meter, a beaker and magnetic stirrer, reference and indicator electrodes, and a burette for titrant delivery are really needed for manual titrations and point-by-point plotting. Automatic titrators are available that can deliver the titrant at a constant rate or in small incremental steps and stop delivery at a preset endpoint. The instrument delivers titrant until the potential difference between the reference and indicator electrodes reaches a value predetermined by the analyst to be at, or very near, the equivalence point of the reaction. Alternatively, titrant can be delivered beyond the endpoint and the entire titration curve traced. Another approach to automatic potentiometric titration is to measure the amount of titrant required to maintain the indicator electrode at a constant potential. The titration curve is then a plot of volume of standard titrant added versus time, and is very useful, for example, for kinetic studies. The most extensive use of this approach has been in the biochemical area with so-called *pH-stats*—a combination of pH meter, electrodes, and automatic titrating equipment designed to maintain a constant pH. Many enzymes consume or release protons during an enzymatic reaction; therefore, a plot of the volume of standard base (or acid) required to maintain a constant pH is a measure of the *enzyme activity*, the amount of enzyme present.

Since potentiometric titrations are an old and well-known technique, particularly in regard to acid-base and oxidation-reduction titrations, only a few selected examples will be presented here. For more detailed treatments, the student is urged to consult the bibliography at the end of the chapter. It will be assumed that the student is already familiar with titration curves and their calculation from ionic equilibria and other pertinent data.

Acid-Base Titrations

Acid-base titrations can be performed with a glass indicator electrode and a suitable reference electrode. Titrations of strong acids and bases with suitable strong titrants are relatively simple, since there is a relatively large and abrupt change in pH at the endpoint. Calculated titration curves for the titration of various acids (0.1 M concentration) with 0.1 M sodium hydroxide are shown in Figure 2.9. Note that as the acid titrated becomes weaker, pK_a increases, and the sharpness and magnitude of the endpoint break decreases. A somewhat similar situation occurs when the concentration of the substance titrated (and the titrant) is decreased. As a rough rule of thumb, for the titration of a strong acid (or base) with strong titrant, the

FIGURE 2.9. *Theoretical potentiometric titration curves for the neutralization titration of 0.1 M solutions of various acids with 0.1 M NaOH. The number beside each curve is the pK_a value for that acid.*

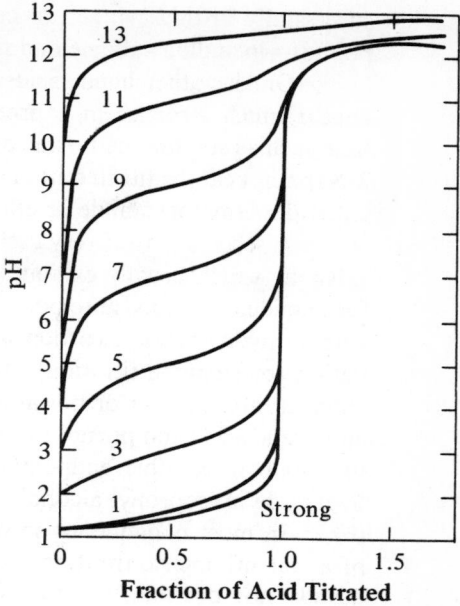

concentration of the substance titrated should be greater than about $3 \times 10^{-4}\ M$ for a 0.1% accuracy. If a 1% accuracy is sufficient, the concentration can be decreased an order of magnitude. For titration of a weak acid with strong base, the product of the acid concentration and its dissociation constant, K_a, should be greater than about 10^{-7} for a 0.1% accuracy, 10^{-9} for a 1% accuracy.

The acetic-acid content of household vinegar can be determined by potentiometric titration with sodium hydroxide. Mixtures of carbonate and bicarbonate can be analyzed by titration with HCl.

Acid-Base Titrations in Nonaqueous Solvents.

It is a fact that the apparent acidity or basicity of a compound is strongly dependent on the acid-base properties of the solvent. For example, very strong acids such as HCl and HNO_3 cannot be individually titrated in water because water is sufficiently basic that these acids appear to be totally ionized. Very weak bases, such as amines, cannot be successfully titrated with strong acid in water. Many acids or bases that are too weak for titration in an aqueous medium, however, become amenable to titration in appropriate nonaqueous solvents. As a consequence, there are now many neutralization methods that call for solvents other than water [23–25].

The earliest advantages recognized arose from the use of *amphiprotic* solvents, those that have both acidic and basic properties. The prototype is water. Significant differences in acid-base properties are seen in the case of either protogenic solvents (more acidic than water), for example acetic acid, or protophilic solvents (more basic than water), for example ethylenediamine. In the protogenic cases it was found that bases too weak to be titrated in water could be successfully titrated with a strong acid dissolved in the same solvent. For example, primary, secondary, and tertiary amines can be titrated in acetic acid with perchloric acid in acetic acid as titrant. Medicinal sulfonamides, which have a primary amino group, can be titrated successfully in this manner, as can most of the common alkaloids, and purine compounds—including caffeine and theobromine.

On the other hand, acids too weak to be titrated with strong base in water appear much stronger in a protophilic solvent and can be titrated with a strong base such as sodium methoxide dissolved in the basic solvent or a compatible solvent. 2-Naphthol can be titrated in this manner. Many enols and imides can be titrated in either dimethylformamide or ethylenediamine.

A second type of very useful behavior occurs in *aprotic* (or sometimes "inert") solvents, which usually exhibit very weak acid properties. Examples are dimethylformamide, dimethylsulfoxide, dioxane, ether, various nitriles, methyl isobutyl ketone, hydrocarbons, carbon tetrachloride. These solvents often permit differentiation (or stepwise titration) of a series of acidic or basic species which, in water, either titrate together or not at all. For example, perchloric, hydrochloric, salicylic, and acetic acids and phenol can be titrated stepwise in methyl isobutyl ketone solvent to obtain discernible endpoints for each compound, using tetrabutyl ammonium hydroxide in isopropyl alcohol as titrant.

In most nonaqueous solvents, precise explanation or prediction of the shape of a potentiometric titration curve, or the possible utility of a specific titration, is usually not possible because of the lack of complete thermodynamic equilibrium constants for the numerous possible processes. In general, the shapes of curves must be determined experimentally, and the behavior of substances in diverse solvents must be considered empirically.

Oxidation-Reduction Reactions

Potentiometric titrations of oxidizing or reducing agents can be performed by making the titrated sample one-half of an electrochemical cell. Typically, the indicator electrode is an "inert" electrode such as a platinum foil or wire which is used to monitor the solution potential; the cell is completed with the addition of a suitable reference electrode such as an SCE.

Thus, in titrating a reducing substance such as Fe^{2+} with a standard solution of an oxidizing substance such as MnO_4^- or Ce^{4+}, the solution potential at equilibrium is given *either* by the formal potential of the titrant couple and the ratio of activities of its oxidized and reduced forms, *or* by the formal potential of the substance titrated and the ratio of its oxidized and reduced forms. For an analytically useful titration, the system of titrant and substance titrated reacts rapidly, and at least one of the electrode couples is reversible at the indicator electrode.

Typical examples of applications include the titration of ferrous ion with permanganate; the titration of arsenic(III) with bromate; the determination of ascorbic acid with iodine; and the determination of organic compounds such as azo, nitro, and nitroso compounds and quinones with chromous ion.

Precipitation and Complexation Reactions

Given the wide variety of ion-selective electrodes already commercially available and the many more specialized ones that can be fabricated, titrations involving the precipitation or complexation of ions are widely used. Halides, cyanide, thiocyanate, sulfide, chromate, and thiols can be titrated with silver nitrate, using the appropriate silver sulfide–based electrode; silver ion can be titrated with sodium iodide. Many metal ions can be titrated with standard EDTA, using the appropriate electrode, and possibly with the addition of an indicator reagent. Molybdate, selenide, sulfate, telluride, and tungstate can be titrated with lead perchlorate and a lead electrode. Aluminum, lithium, phosphate, various rare earths, and zirconate can be titrated with fluoride.

Generally, the sensitivity for determination is between 10^{-3} and 10^{-4} M.

SELECTED BIBLIOGRAPHY

BATES, R. G. *Determination of pH: Theory and Practice*, 2nd ed. New York: John Wiley, 1973. *Probably the definitive monograph on the fundamentals of pH.*

DURST, R. A. "Ion-Selective Electrodes in Science, Medicine, and Technology," *Amer. Sci.*, *59*, 353 (1971). *A short, easily readable article on the theory, functioning, and applications of ion-selective electrodes.*

DURST, R. A., ed. *Ion-Selective Electrodes*, N.B.S. Special Publication 314, Washington, D.C.: U.S. Government Printing Office, 1969.

IVES, D. J. G., and JANZ, G. J. *Reference Electrodes.* New York: Academic Press, 1961.

LINGANE, J. J. *Electroanalytical Chemistry*, 2nd ed., chaps. 2–8. New York: Interscience, 1958. *The fundamentals of potentiometry and many applications of potentiometric titrations.*

WEISSBERGER, A., and ROSSITER, B. W., eds. *Physical Methods of Chemistry*, vol. 1, part IIA. New York: Interscience, 1971.

REFERENCES

1. T. S. LICHT and A. J. DEBÉTHUNE, *J. Chem. Educ.*, *34*, 433 (1957).

2. H. A. LAITINEN and W. E. HARRIS, *Chemical Analysis*, 2nd ed. New York: McGraw-Hill Book Company, 1975, pp 5–17.

3. T. BIEGLER and R. WOODS, *J. Chem. Educ.*, *50*, 604 (1974).

4. R. G. BATES, *Determination of pH*, 2nd ed. New York: John Wiley, 1973, pp 328–35.

5. S. P. L. SØRENSEN, *Biochem. Z.*, *21*, 131 (1909); ibid., p 201.

6. R. A. ROBINSON and R. H. STOKES, *Electrolyte Solutions*, 2nd ed. New York: Academic Press, Inc., 1959.

7. D. D. PERRIN and B. DEMPSEY, *Buffers for pH and Metal Ion Control.* New York: Halsted Press, 1974.

8. R. A. DURST, *J. Chem. Educ.*, *44*, 175 (1967).

9. E. PUNGOR, *Anal. Chem.*, *39*(13), 28A (1967).

10. G. G. GUILBAULT, *Pure. Appl. Chem.*, *25*, 727 (1971).

11. G. A. RECHNITZ, *Chem. Eng. News*, January 27, 1975, p 29.

12. J. L. WALKER, JR., *Anal. Chem.*, *43*(3), 89A (1971).

13. G. A. RECHNITZ, *Res./Dev.*, *25*(8), 18, August, 1973.

14. R. W. CATTRALL and H. FREISER, *Anal. Chem.*, *43*, 1905 (1971).

15. T. G. LEE, *Anal. Chem.*, *41*, 391 (1969).

16. T. S. LIGHT and C. C. CAPPUCCINO, *J. Chem. Educ.*, *52*, 247 (1975).

17. D. C. MÜLLER, P. W. WEST, and R. H. MÜLLER, *Anal. Chem.*, *41*, 2038 (1969).

18. G. GRAN, *Analyst*, 77, 661 (1952); F. J. C. ROSSOTTI and H. ROSSOTTI, *J. Chem. Educ.*, *42*, 375 (1965).

19. T. R. GILBERT and A. M. CLAY, *Anal. Chem.*, *45*, 1757 (1973); R. F. THOMAS and R. L. BOOTH, *Environ. Sci. Technol.*, 7, 523 (1973).

20. M. J. SMITH and S. E. MANAHAN, *Anal. Chem.*, *45*, 836 (1973).

21. *Analytical Methods Guide*, Orion Research, Incorporated, Cambridge, Mass., 7th ed., May, 1975.

22. B. JASELKIS and M. K. BANDEMER, *Anal. Chem.*, *41*, 855 (1969); E. W. BAUMANN, *Anal. Chem.*, *42*, 110 (1970).

23. A. H. BECKETT and E. H. TINLEY, *Titra-tions in Non-Aqueous Solvents*, 3rd ed. Pook, England: British Drug Houses, Ltd., 1962.

24. J. S. FRITZ, *Acid-Base Titrations in Non-aqueous Solvents*. Boston, Mass.: Allyn and Bacon, 1973.

25. J. J. LAGOWSKI, *Anal. Chem.*, *42*, 305R (1970).

PROBLEMS

1. Beginning with the Nernst equation for a cation electrode

$$E = E_{\text{constant}} + \frac{RT}{nF} \ln a_1$$

and differentiating, show that the *relative* concentration error incurred in the measurement of a_1 by *direct potentiometry* ($\Delta a_1/a_1$) is about $\pm 4n \%$ per mV uncertainty in the measurement of E.

2. Why should one always calibrate a pH meter with a standard solution that is within 2 pH units of that of the test solution(s) to be measured?

3. Calculate the ionic strength of the following electrolyte solutions, assuming complete dissociation into ions: (a) 0.01 M $CaCl_2$, (b) 0.05 M KCl, (c) 0.1 M Na_2SO_4, (d) 0.001 M $AlCl_3$.

4. Using the simple form of the Debye-Hückel limiting law, calculate the individual activity coefficients for the ions in the following electrolyte solutions: (a) 0.002 M $MgCl_2$, (b) 0.002 M $MgCl_2$ + 0.01 M KCl, (c) 0.002 M $MgCl_2$ + 0.1 M KCl.

5. Using the simple form of the Debye-Hückel law, calculate the pH of a solution which is 0.03 M in the acid, 0.02 M in its conjugate base, and 0.1 M in KCl for the systems: (a) CH_3COOH + CH_3COONa ($K_a = 1.75 \times 10^{-5}$), (b) $CH_3NH_3^+Cl^-$ + CH_3NH_2 ($K_a = 2.0 \times 10^{-11}$).

6. Calculate the theoretical potential of a half-cell composed of a silver wire dipped into a solution of $10^{-3} M$ $AgNO_3$ versus the standard hydrogen electrode (SHE) and versus the saturated calomel electrode (SCE). Assume activity coefficients are unity and the temperature is 25°C.

7. Calculate the theoretical potential of the following cell at 25°C. Assume activity coefficients are unity; K_{sp} (AgI) = 8.3 × 10^{-17}.

$$Ag/AgNO_3 \ (1 \ M)//KI \ (1 \ M),$$
$$AgI \ (\text{satd.})/Ag$$

8. A 0.6079 g sample of a purified organic acid was dissolved in 45.67 ml of a NaOH solution, and the excess base was titrated with 3.25 ml of 0.1200 N HCl. In a second titration, it was established that 39.33 ml of the base was equivalent to 31.69 ml of the HCl. Calculate the equivalent weight of the unknown acid.

9. Suppose that you are considering the application of a previously unreported potentiometric titration to a routine analysis involving hundreds of titrations daily by several analysts under one skilled supervisor. Outline the steps you would take, as a research chemist, to develop the method (a) under conditions of minimum expenditure for equipment, and (b) under conditions of minimum analyst time per sample.

10. Calculate the relative error incurred in the direct potentiometric determination of the calcium concentration of sea water due to magnesium ion interference. A typical magnesium level is 1300 parts per million (ppm), and calcium level is 400 ppm. The selectivity coefficient of the calcium electrode for magnesium is 0.014.

11. What is the maximum concentration of interfering ions that can be tolerated for a 1% interference level when measuring $10^{-4} M$ Ca^{2+} with a calcium-sensitive liquid ion-exchange electrode? For a 10% interference level? The interfering ions and

their selectivity coefficients are: Zn^{2+}, 3.2; Fe^{2+}, 0.80; Pb^{2+}, 0.63; Mg^{2+}, 0.014; Na^{+}, 0.003.

12. A 0.200 g sample of toothpaste was suspended in 50 ml of fluoride ionic-strength buffering medium (TISAB), and boiled briefly to extract the fluoride. The mixture was cooled, transferred quantitatively to a 100 ml volumetric flask, and diluted to volume with deionized water. A 25.00 ml aliquot was transferred to a beaker, a fluoride ISE and reference electrode inserted, and a potential of -155.3 mV was obtained after equilibration. A 0.10 ml spike of 0.5 mg/ml fluoride stock solution was added after which the potential was -176.2 mV. Calculate the percentage of F^- by weight in the original toothpaste sample.

13. A sample of skim milk is to be analyzed for its iodide content by the method of multiple standard additions. A 50.0-ml aliquot of milk is pipetted into a 100-ml beaker, 1.0 ml of 5 M $NaNO_3$ is added to increase the ionic strength, and the resultant solution is allowed to equilibrate to room temperature (25°C). A double-junction reference electrode and an iodide ion-selective electrode are inserted, and the solution is magnetically stirred. After equilibrium is reached, the voltage reading, E, is -50.3 mV. Then 100-, 100-, 200-, and 200-μl aliquots of 2.00 mM KI are added sequentially. After each addition, the equilibrium potential is measured: -64.9, -74.1, -86.0, and -94.2 mV respectively. Given that the slope, S, of the iodide calibration curve in this concentration range is 59.2 mV/decade, calculate the original I^- concentration of the milk in μg/ml. [Hint: Plot $10^{\Delta E/S}$ as a function of the total μg of I^- added, and extrapolate the straight line back to the x-axis.]

14. One way to estimate selectivity coefficients for ion-selective electrodes is to first equilibrate the electrode in a pure solution of the test ion and measure the potential

$$E_1 = E_{constant} + \frac{RT}{nF}\ln a_1$$

(for a cation-selective electrode). Then, small aliquots of an interferant ion are added, and the potential is measured each time

$$E_2 = E_{constant} + \frac{RT}{nF}\ln(a_1 + k_{1J}a_J).$$

Solve and rearrange these two equations to obtain a single linear equation of the form $y = mx + b$ which can then be used to determine k_{1J}. [Hint: Review the derivation of Equation 2.46, and the suggestion for taking antilogs.]

15. The selectivity coefficient of an iodide ion-selective electrode for bromide ion is to be determined using the equation derived in problem 14, above. An iodide ion-selective electrode and an appropriate reference electrode are equilibrated in 50.0 ml of 1.00×10^{-4} M KI at 25°C. The equilibrium potential is -130.2 mV. Then, 0.50-, 1.00-, 2.00-, and 2.00-ml aliquots of 1.00 M KBr are added sequentially. After each addition, the equilibrium potential is measured: -131.5, -133.9, -137.5, and -140.8 mV, respectively. Determine the selectivity coefficient for bromide ion if the slope of the calibration curve for iodide is 59.2 mV/decade. What assumptions have been made in this approach?

16. More precise location of the endpoint (i.e., inflection point) of a potentiometric titration curve can frequently be obtained from a first ($\Delta E/\Delta$ml vs. ml) or second ($\Delta^2 E/\Delta$ml^2 vs. ml) derivative plot. The following data were collected near the endpoint of a titration. Plot the first and second derivatives of the titration curve near the endpoint and compare the endpoint values.

Ml	Potential, mV
47.60	372
47.70	384
47.80	401
47.90	512
48.00	732
48.10	748
48.20	756

17. One way of experimentally estimating selectivity coefficients for ion-selective electrodes is to record the equilibrium potential of the

electrode for a series of solutions of interferant ions of (constant) known concentration. The equilibrium potentials at 25°C for a calcium ion–selective electrode in 10^{-2} M Ca^{2+} solution and in 10^{-2} M solutions of various ions were measured below. Neglecting activity coefficients, calculate selectivity coefficients for the interferant ions, assuming that the Nernst equation is valid, that the E^0 for the electrode does not change, and that liquid-junction potentials are constant.

Ion	E	Ion	E
Ca^{2+}	+63.3 mV	H^+	+92.9 mV
Zn^{2+}	+113.6	Na^+	−70.4
Pb^{2+}	+101.8	K^+	−84.6
Mg^{2+}	+4.2		

3

Polarography and Voltammetry

HENRY H. BAUER
JAMES E. O'REILLY

In Chapter 2, the one electrochemical method involving no net current flow—potentiometry—was discussed. In Chapter 3, two methods will be studied—voltammetry and polarography—in which a voltage is applied to an electrode and the resulting current flow is measured.

For various reasons, classical polarographic techniques became less widely used for routine analytical purposes for some years. Particularly with the advent of flame spectroscopic methods (Chap. 10) for the analysis of metals and metalloids, polarography became primarily a tool for more fundamental studies: corrosion processes, electrode mechanisms, and kinetics. However, with the advent of low-cost commercial instrumentation and the introduction of some modern variants of the polarographic method—pulse polarography, stripping analysis, and so forth—the use of voltammetric methods for quantitative analytical measurements is again increasing. The newer variations of the method can permit selective, parts-per-billion, analyses of a variety of organic and inorganic species. The areas of application include environmental and toxicological studies, biochemistry and pharmacy, geology, and routine industrial quality control.

3.1 INTRODUCTION AND THEORETICAL BASIS

Principles

In *voltammetry*, current-versus-voltage curves are recorded when a gradually changing voltage is applied to a cell containing (a) the solution of interest, (b) a stable reference electrode, and (c) a small-area working or indicator electrode (Fig. 3.1). Usually, the voltage is increased linearly with time. Such curves are generically called *voltammo-*

49

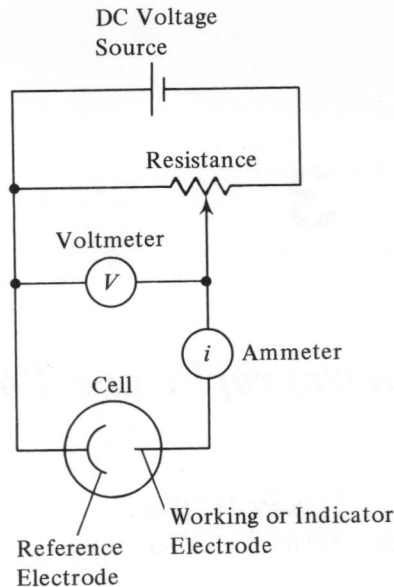

DC Voltage Source

Resistance

Voltmeter

V

i) Ammeter

Cell

Working or Indicator Electrode

Reference Electrode

grams. In the special case where the indicator electrode is the *dropping mercury electrode* (DME), introduced by J. Heyrovský in 1922, the technique is known as *polarography,* and the current-versus-voltage curves are called *polarograms.*

The DME consists of a glass capillary attached to a mercury reservoir. Drops of mercury fall from the orifice of this capillary at a constant rate, usually between 5 and 30 drops per minute (Fig. 3.2). Each drop is the electrode while attached to the column of mercury in the capillary. At the slow rate of voltage scanning generally used in polarography—about 50–200 mV/min—the change of potential of the DME during the life (usually between 2 and 12 sec) of a single drop can be neglected; thus, the current measured on each drop can be considered to be obtained under practically potentiostatic conditions (i.e., at constant potential). To distinguish this method from modern variants, it is sometimes called "conventional" or "DC" (direct-current) polarography.

The current-versus-voltage curves obtained with the DME are very reproducible, since the surface of every new mercury drop is fresh, clean, and practically unaffected by electrolysis at earlier drops. The total amount of electrolysis is very small because of the small area of the electrode and the small currents involved; for example, with 20 ml of a typical solution, 100 polarograms can be recorded without noticeable change in the curve. The small size of the DME permits the analysis of small volumes of solutions; if necessary, less than 0.01 ml can be used.

Mercury is chemically inert in most aqueous solutions, and hydrogen is evolved on it only at quite negative potentials; consequently, the reduction of many chemical species can be studied at mercury electrodes, but not at electrodes made of most other materials. However, the anodic dissolution of mercury makes it impossible to study reactions at potentials more positive than about +0.4 V versus the saturated calomel electrode (SCE).

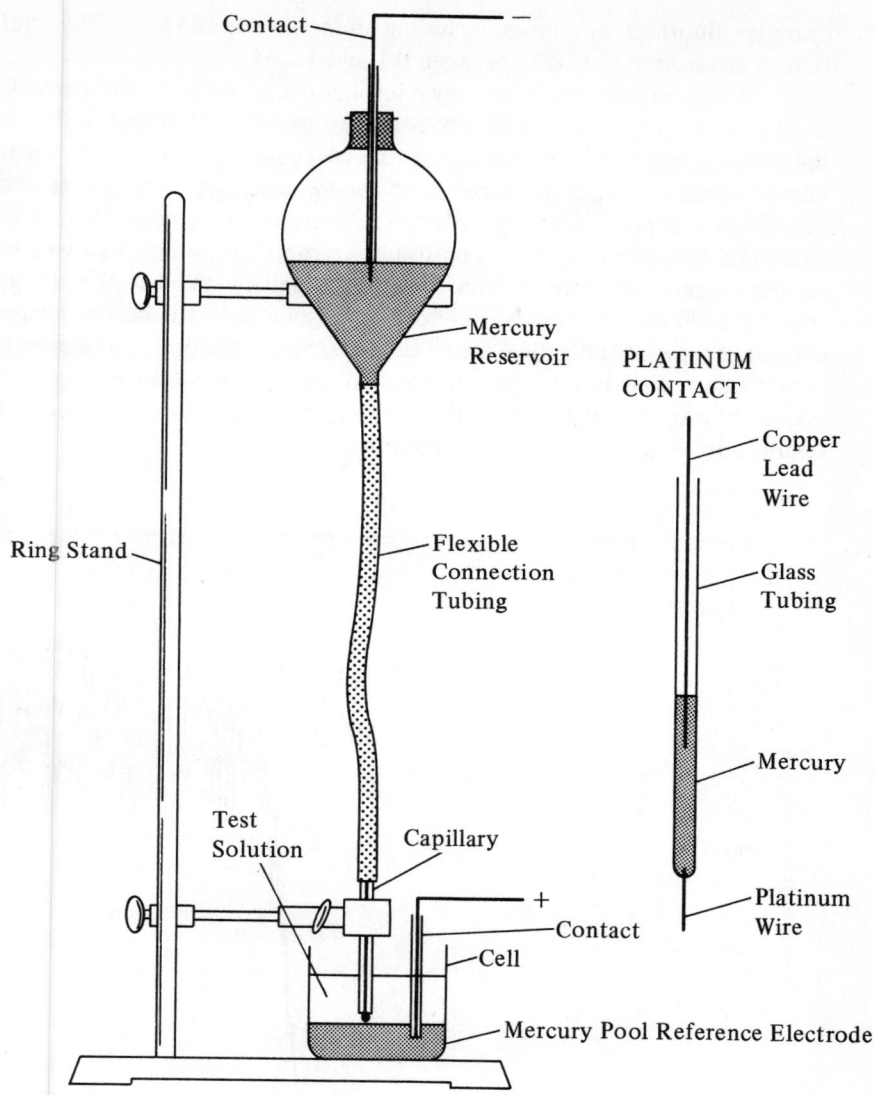

FIGURE 3.2. *Illustration of a dropping mercury electrode (DME) and a simple polarographic cell for reductions.*

Supporting electrolytes are commonly used in polarography to decrease the resistance of the solution and to ensure that the electroactive species moves by diffusion and not by electrical migration in the voltage field across the cell. The supporting electrolyte is often chosen also to provide optimum conditions for the particular analysis: e.g., buffering at a preferred pH value and elimination of interferences by selective complexation of some species. Solutions of strong acids (e.g., hydrochloric, sulfuric), strong bases (sodium or lithium hydroxide), or neutral salts (e.g., chlorides, perchlorates, sulfates of alkali metals, or tetraalkylammonium ions) are frequently used, as are buffer solutions or solutions of complexing agents (e.g., tartrates, citrates, cyanides, fluorides, or amines, including ammonia and EDTA).   The total concentration of electrolyte is usually between 0.1 and 1.0 M.

A typical polarogram is shown in Figure 3.3.   Only a small current flows at the most positive potentials.   This nonfaradaic current is often practically identical with the current obtained in the same potential range with the supporting electrolyte alone and is called the *residual, charging,* or *condenser current*.   This part of the curve is followed by a potential range where the current increases steeply: this is called a *polarographic wave* or *step*.   Then follows a range of potential in which the current remains practically constant, and is often virtually parallel to the charging current; this is the plateau of the wave.   The difference between the charging current and the current at the plateau is the *limiting current* (i_l in Figure 3.3) or the *wave height*.   The limiting current is usually proportional to the concentration of a polarographically active substance in the examined solution, and its measurement forms the basis of quantitative applications of polarography.

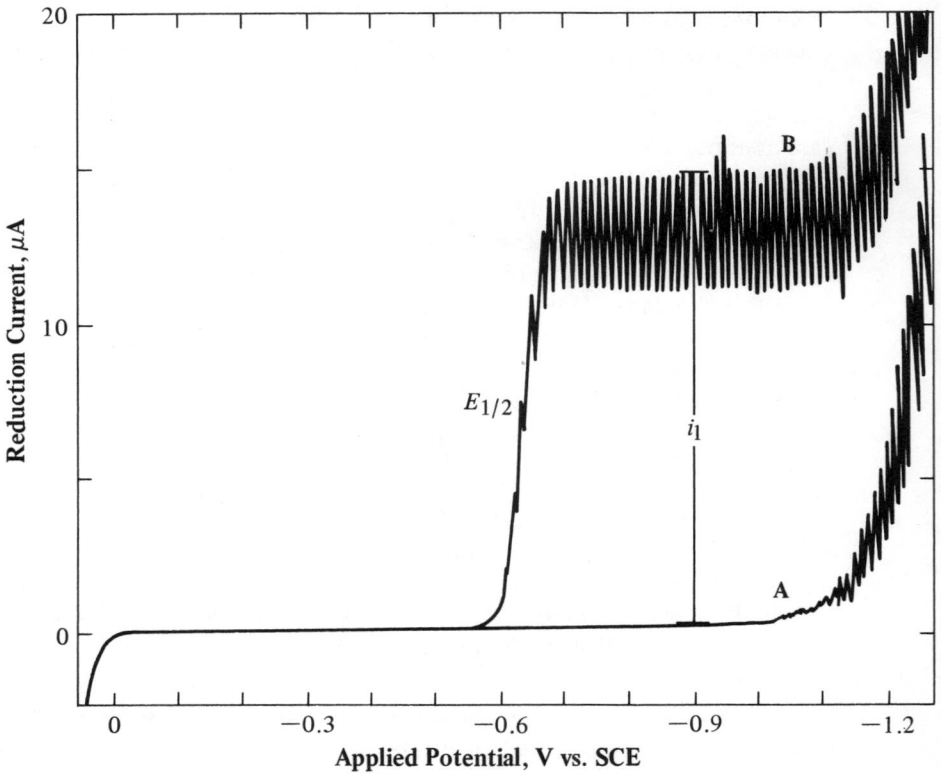

FIGURE 3.3.   *Typical polarogram.   Curve A: Background, residual current, or supporting electrolyte curve (1 M HCl).   Curve B: Polarogram of 0.5 mM Cd^{2+} in 1 M HCl. $E_{1/2}$ is the half-wave potential and i_l is the limiting current of the polarogram.   Adapted from D. T. Sawyer and J. L. Roberts, Jr.,* Experimental Electrochemistry for Electrochemists, *New York: Wiley-Interscience, 1974, by permission of John Wiley and Sons. Copyright © 1974 by John Wiley and Sons.*

Note the oscillations in current as the mercury drop grows and falls. As the current increases, the magnitude of the oscillations increases in direct proportion. The recorded current does not fall to zero at the instant the drop falls because of the slow response of the current-recording device.

When one polarographic wave is preceded by another, the limiting current is measured as the difference between the two plateaus, which are usually parallel to one another; the wave heights are almost always additive.

The potential at which the current reaches half the magnitude of the limiting current is called the *half-wave potential* (denoted as $E_{1/2}$ in Figure 3.3). In most instances, the half-wave potential is practically independent of the concentration of the particular compound; it characterizes the oxidation-reduction properties of the studied substance and can be used as a qualitative identification of the electroactive species present. The $E_{1/2}$ is of fundamental importance and can be related to the standard oxidation-reduction potential (E^0) of the electrochemical reaction involved.

Removal of Oxygen. One difficulty encountered in voltammetric or polarographic analyses is that dissolved oxygen interferes severely and must be removed from test solutions before analysis. This is because oxygen is electrochemically reducible, producing large reduction currents, and it or its oxidation-reduction products react chemically with many solutions. Oxygen is reduced in two steps: a two-electron reduction to H_2O_2, and then a second two-electron reduction to H_2O. The $E_{1/2}$'s are at about 0 and -1 V versus SCE at pH 7. Air-saturated aqueous solutions have about a 4 mM O_2 level, and produce a total of about 5 μA diffusion current at the DME. The usual procedure for removing O_2 from solutions is to bubble them for 5 to 20 min with high-purity nitrogen or argon, or with electrolytically generated hydrogen. Compressed nitrogen in tanks often contains enough residual oxygen to be detected polarographically; it is usually further purified before use by first bubbling it through acidic V^{2+} or Cr^{2+} or passing it over hot copper turnings, to remove O_2; and then passing it through a bubbler filled with background electrolyte to further wash the gas and presaturate it with water vapor. The length of time required for complete deaeration may be greatly reduced by using a medium- or coarse-porosity fritted-glass dispersion tube in the test-solution compartment.

The Ilkovic Equation. The current that flows through the polarographic cell depends on the rate of the electrode reaction and on the rate of transport of the electroactive species to the electrode surface. At sufficiently negative potentials (that is, where the limiting current is observed) the rate of the electrode process is so fast that the rate of transport of the species to the surface becomes the limiting factor.

In the absence of migration (eliminated by addition of supporting electrolyte) and convection (prevented by keeping the electrolyzed solution unstirred), diffusion is the only mode of transport involved. Therefore, the limiting current is proportional to the rate of diffusion, and

$$i_l = nFAD\left(\frac{\partial c}{\partial x}\right)_{x=0} \tag{3.1}$$

where A = the area of the electrode
D = the diffusion coefficient of the electroactive species
$(\partial c/\partial x)_{x=0}$ = the concentration gradient of the latter at the electrode surface

The DME is virtually spherical; its volume can be calculated from the rate of flow of mercury m (mg/sec), the time t (sec) measured from the beginning of drop growth, and the density of mercury. This gives the radius of the drop, from which the surface area, A in mm², is

$$A = 0.851(mt)^{2/3} \tag{3.2}$$

Solution of the equations for diffusion to a spherical drop then gives the Ilkovic equation

$$i_d = 708ncD^{1/2}m^{2/3}t^{1/6} \tag{3.3}$$

where i_d = diffusion current in microamperes
c = concentration in millimoles per liter of solution (mM)
D = diffusion coefficient in cm² sec^{-1}

The subscript "d" signifies that a current limited by the rate of diffusion is considered.

When $t = t_d$, the lifetime of each drop, Equation 3.3 becomes the expression for the maximum current observed at the end of each drop, i.e., the highest value of the current recorded on the oscillating curve (Fig. 3.3). Modern strip-chart and x-y recorders have a sufficiently fast response to ensure that the recorded maximum current can be equated to the theoretical one. In the earlier literature, when fast-response recorders were not common, average currents rather than maximum currents were frequently measured; the theoretical average current is 6/7 of the maximum current, that is, the value of the constant in Equation 3.3 equals 607. Even today, many people prefer to use heavy damping when recording polarographic curves, and thus measure average currents.

It is evident from Equation 3.3 that the measured maximum current on the plateau of the wave can serve for quantitative analysis, since it is linearly proportional to the concentration of the substance being reduced. Moreover, when c is known and when the electrode reaction is known (i.e., the value of n), measurements of i_d can be used to obtain the diffusion coefficient. In other cases, where the electrochemical reaction is not yet known, one can postulate a plausible value for D and use i_d to calculate n; since the latter must be an integer, it is not necessary that D be known with accuracy.

Currents Controlled by Factors other than Diffusion

The electrochemical reaction may involve, in addition to diffusion and charge transfer, chemical reactions in which the oxidant or reductant is involved and/or adsorption of the electroactive species. Sometimes the magnitude of the current is limited by the rate of a chemical reaction or an adsorption process.

Kinetic Currents. Polarographic currents whose magnitudes are controlled by the rates of chemical reactions are called *kinetic* currents. For instance, one may have a reaction sequence

$$A + B \xrightarrow{k_1} Ox + ne^- \rightleftharpoons Red \tag{3.4}$$

in which k_1 limits the overall rate. A is the species to be determined, and it reacts with another substance B to form the reducible species Ox. It can be shown that the magnitude of the limiting current is linearly proportional to the concentration of A provided that the concentration of B is constant (or B is present in large excess). Thus, polarography can be used to determine substances that are not reducible or oxidizable but which can be reacted in situ to give an electroactive species. In some cases when dealing with kinetic currents, the conditions for polarographic electrolysis (e.g., pH of the solution and temperature) need to be closely controlled.

Catalytic Currents. Another type of polarographic current is governed by catalytic processes. Such *catalytic currents* are of two types: either the substance undergoing electrolysis is regenerated in the vicinity of the electrode by a chemical reaction, or the electroreduction of a species is shifted to more positive potentials than would occur in the absence of the catalyst. An example of the former case is the reduction of Fe(III) to Fe(II)—the electrogenerated ferrous ion can be reoxidized back to ferric ion if hydrogen peroxide is present in solution. An example of the second case is the catalytic reduction of hydrogen ions—many substances, proteins for example, catalyze this reduction and shift the corresponding wave to more positive potential.

In both cases, the current is a nonlinear function of concentration (or a linear function only over a certain concentration range) and a calibration curve must be used for analytical determinations.

Adsorption Currents. If either the oxidized or the reduced species is adsorbed at the electrode, the magnitude of the current may be limited by the available surface area of the electrode: surface covered by the adsorbed species may not be available for charge-transfer at that particular electrode potential. A system in which adsorption is significant often has a polarogram like that shown in Figure 3.4.

FIGURE 3.4. *Polarographic curve of methylene blue (0.4 mM), showing the adsorption prewave.*

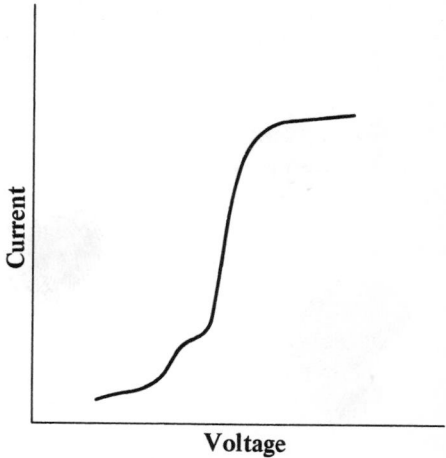

The reduced species remains adsorbed at the electrode surface, "inactivating" the surface, and current flows only at the rate at which fresh surface is exposed to the solution. The height of the *adsorption prewave* increases with increasing concentration of the depolarizer up to a particular concentration and thereafter remains constant. However, a second wave then appears, at a potential where the reduced species is no longer adsorbed, and this second wave is usually diffusion-controlled. The combined wave heights are often linearly related to concentration and quantitative analysis can be carried out.

If it is the oxidized, rather than the reduced, species that is strongly adsorbed, the adsorption wave typically appears as a "postwave" on the plateau of the diffusion-controlled "main" wave.

In general, it is preferable to deal with diffusion-controlled currents because they are generally much less affected by experimental variables and usually result in linear current-versus-concentration calibration curves.

Polarographic Maxima

Sometimes polarograms show currents that are, over certain ranges of potential, considerably higher than diffusion currents—higher by as much as 2 orders of magnitude. These *polarographic maxima* may be sharp or rounded, and may cover only small regions of potential or quite wide ones (Fig. 3.5). These large currents arise because of spontaneous stirring of the solution near the mercury electrode (maxima are observed at hanging mercury drops and at mercury-pool electrodes as well as at dropping mercury electrodes).

There are several mechanisms that can lead to movement of the solution and the appearance of maxima. The subject is too complicated to be satisfactorily discussed here; the origins of maxima are discussed fully in Reference [1], and methods of dealing with them to permit quantitative analysis are given in the general texts on polarography listed at the end of the chapter. One can, however, make the following generalizations:

Maxima are least likely to be encountered if one uses a low rate of mercury flow ($m < 0.5$ mg/sec), a concentrated supporting electrolyte, and a low concentration of the electroactive species ($< 10^{-3} M$). Maxima can sometimes be avoided by altering the chemical nature of the supporting electrolyte. If need be, the maxima can usually be suppressed by adding to the solution a small amount of a surface-active substance, such as Triton X-100. One should add just enough to eliminate the maximum (determining the amount by trial and error), since even a moderate excess can distort the polarographic wave.

For quantitative analytical purposes, it is almost invariably desirable to eliminate maxima because of the distortion of the polarographic wave involved, and the resultant difficulty in measuring wave heights.

Tests for Current-Limiting Processes

Criteria used to distinguish among diffusion, kinetic, adsorption, and catalytic currents include changes in the wave height (limiting current) with (1) concentration of the electroactive species, (2) mercury pressure, (3) pH, (4) buffer concentration, and (5) temperature. (Peak-shaped current maxima (Fig. 3.5A) caused by increased transport of electroactive species by convection in the vicinity of the electrode can usually be easily recognized.)

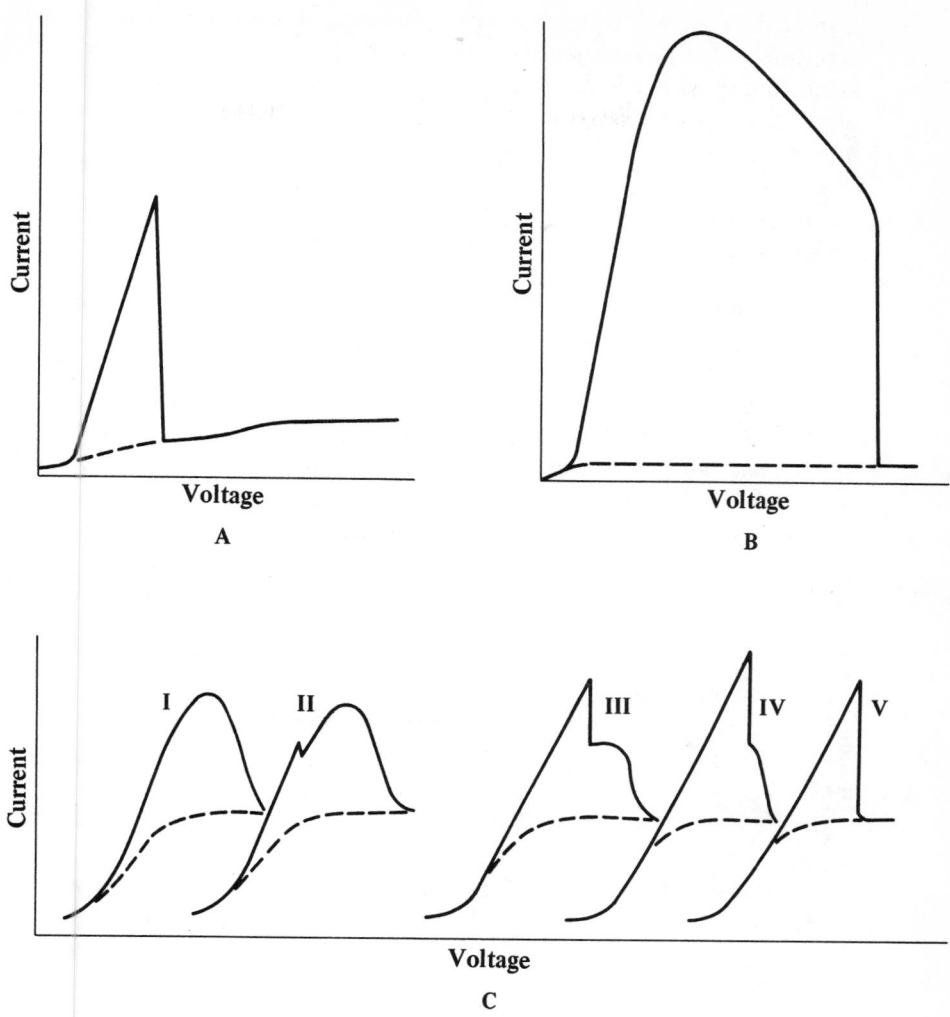

FIGURE 3.5. *Various types of observed polarographic maxima, showing actual currents (solid lines) and diffusion currents (dashed lines). A: Oxygen in 10^{-3} M KCl. B: 8 mM Cu^{2+} in 0.1 M Na_2SO_4. C: Oxygen in 0.01 M KCl; the mercury-column height is decreasing from I through V.*

Linear dependence of the limiting current on concentration as illustrated in Figure 3.6A is observed for diffusion currents, for the majority of kinetic currents, and for some catalytic currents (e.g., those involving regeneration of a reducible metal ion). Limiting dependences (Fig. 3.6, curves B, C) are observed for adsorption currents and for some catalytic currents.

Varying the height of the mercury column (h) above the orifice of the capillary provides a useful criterion for distinguishing among the various possible current-limiting processes. Diffusion currents are linearly proportional to $h^{1/2}$; kinetic currents are independent of h; and adsorption currents are linearly proportional to h (Fig. 3.7). The dependence of adsorption currents (i_a) on h should be measured at

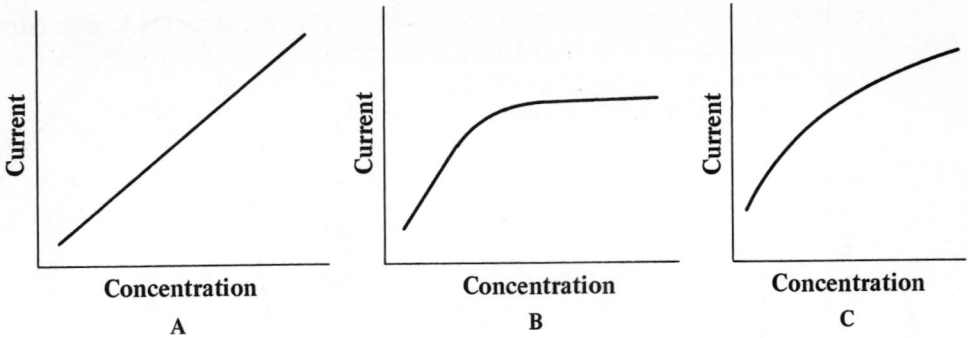

FIGURE 3.6. *Relation of limiting current to concentration. Curve A: Linear dependence observed for diffusion currents and for some kinetic and catalytic currents. Curves B and C: Limiting dependencies observed for adsorption and some catalytic currents.*

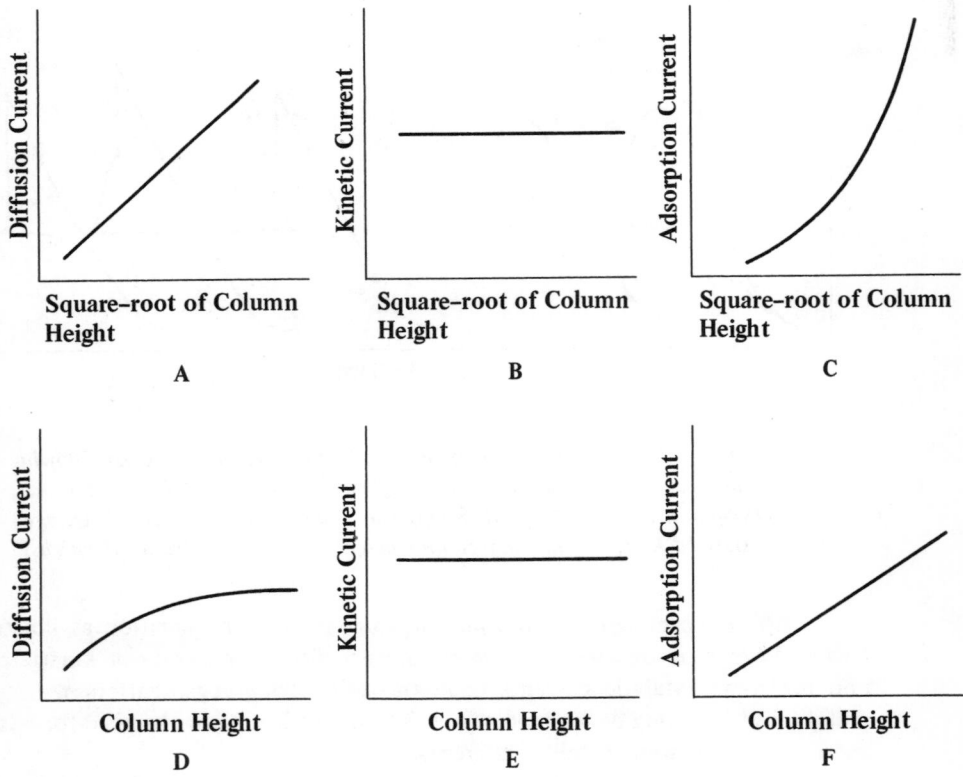

FIGURE 3.7. *The variation of the limiting current with mercury-column height for various types of polarographic currents. Curves A and D: Variation of diffusion current, i_d. Curves B and E: Variation of kinetic current, i_k. Curves C and F: Variation of adsorption current, i_a.*

concentrations where the current is concentration-independent; kinetic currents (i_k) are independent of h provided that measurements are carried out under conditions (e.g., pH) where i_k is less than $0.2\, i_d$.

The variation of current with time during the life of a single drop can be a most valuable criterion for determining the current-limiting process. With fast pen-recorders, one can obtain a moderately accurate measure of current-versus-time behavior by expansion of the time axis, but oscilloscopic observations are much to be preferred.

Equation 3.3 showed that diffusion-limited currents vary with time as $t^{1/6}$. This dependence is understandable from the combined effects of the increase in thickness of the diffusion layer with time, and the increase in area of the mercury drop. The first factor leads to a current proportional to $t^{-1/2}$ (Eqn. 1.6), the second to a current proportional to $t^{2/3}$ (Eqn. 3.2), and the combined effect ($t^{-1/2} \times t^{2/3}$) is $t^{1/6}$.

The rates of the homogeneous reactions responsible for kinetic and catalytic currents depend on the volume of solution in which the reactions occur. Since the reactions of interest occur near the electrode, the relevant volume is proportional to the area of the electrode, i.e., to $(mt)^{2/3}$, and thus kinetic and catalytic currents usually are proportional to $t^{2/3}$.

Adsorption-limited currents are proportional to the rate at which fresh mercury surface appears, that is, to the rate of change of the area of the electrode:

$$i_a \propto \frac{d}{dt}(mt)^{2/3} \propto t^{-1/3} \qquad (3.5)$$

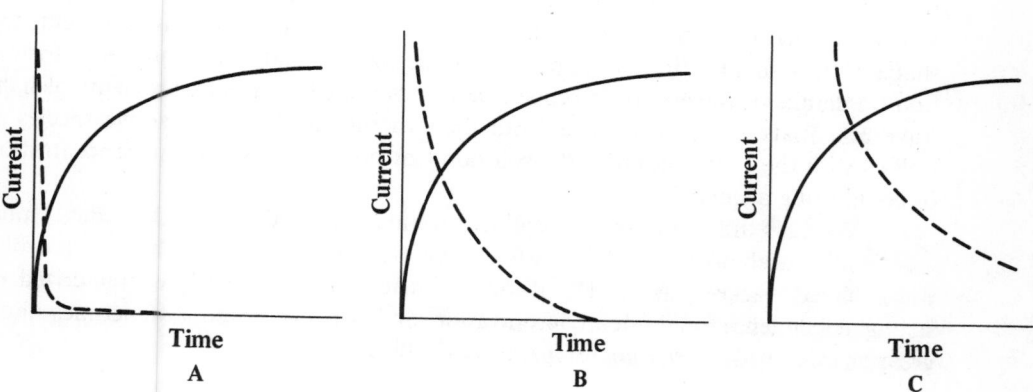

FIGURE 3.8. *Illustration of the relative importance of faradaic and charging current as the concentration of the electroactive species is reduced during the life of a single mercury drop. Solid lines: faradaic current; dashed lines: charging current. Curve A: for a 1 mM solution the contribution of the charging current is small and can be neglected. Curve B: for a 0.2 mM solution the contribution of the charging current is still small but not negligible and should be corrected for. Curve C: for 0.03 mM solution the charging current becomes larger than the faradaic and the separation of the two currents becomes necessary. The y-axes on the three curves have been normalized so that the faradaic current curves (solid lines) are the same size.*

TABLE 3.1. *Characteristics of Polarographic Currents*

Nature of Current	Symbol	Variation with					
		c	h	pH	Buffer Concentration	Temperature	Time
Diffusion	i_d	kc	$kh^{1/2}$	independent	independent	$+1.3\%/°C$	$t^{1/6}$
Kinetic	i_k	kc	independent	dependent	dependent	$+5\text{--}20\%/°C$	$t^{2/3}$
Adsorption	i_a	lim	kh	usually independent	independent	different	$t^{-1/3}$
Catalytic	i_c	lim	varies	strongly dependent	strongly dependent	——	$t^{2/3}$

The residual or charging current is also limited by the rate at which fresh electrode surface is formed, and hence is proportional to $t^{-1/3}$. This fact is of considerable significance in understanding variations of polarographic methods aimed at increasing sensitivity. Since diffusion currents increase with time (as $t^{1/6}$), and charging current decreases (as $t^{-1/3}$), measurement of the current late in the life of the drop gives a better sensitivity ("signal/noise") than measurements of average currents, or of currents early in the drop-life (see Fig. 3.8).

Here, only the currents (or wave heights) have been discussed, since these are the important measure for the quantitative analytical applications of polarography. When information concerning mechanisms and kinetics of reactions is sought, the shape of the rising portion of the polarographic wave is analyzed. Further, information on details of the electrode process can be obtained from measurements of half-wave potentials and their changes with the structure of the electroactive species as well as with the composition of the solution (for instance, pH and the concentration of complexing agents).

Whereas diffusion and adsorption currents are usually pH-independent, most kinetic and catalytic currents (in particular catalytic currents due to hydrogen evolution) change markedly with pH. Catalytic currents are frequently characterized by strong dependence on buffer concentration and kinetic currents sometimes show great changes with increasing temperature (Table 3.1).

3.2 INSTRUMENTATION AND APPARATUS

The apparatus for voltammetric analysis consists of a suitable cell, electrodes, a potentiostat or polarograph, and a system for removing oxygen from the solution.

Cells

Frequently, a stoppered lipless beaker is quite suitable as a polarographic cell; the stopper should have holes to accommodate the DME, reference electrode, counter electrode (when used), and gas-inlet and -outlet tubes for bubbling gas (usually purified nitrogen) through the solution to remove dissolved oxygen.

A "remote" or "isolated" reference electrode, separated from the cell by means of salt bridges, is sometimes used to prevent contamination of the sample solution by ions from the reference electrode.

Usually the gas used to remove oxygen is purified with a gas-washing train. It may be necessary (with volatile solvents or solutes) to pass the gas through a solution identical to that of the sample to avoid changes of concentration during deaeration. There may also be provision for passing gas *over* the sample solution after deaeration, if the analysis takes an appreciable time.

The cell may be immersed in a constant-temperature bath, or may have a jacket through which water from such a bath is circulated (diffusion-controlled currents increase by about 1.3% for each degree Celsius of rise in temperature).

Perhaps the most commonly used polarographic cell is the H-cell (Fig. 3.9), which has one compartment for the solution to be analyzed and a second compartment containing the reference electrode. Mixing of the solutions in the two compartments is prevented by the use of a porous glass frit (plug) and an agar-KCl salt bridge. Often, as illustrated in the figure, the reference electrode is a saturated calomel electrode constructed directly in the second compartment.

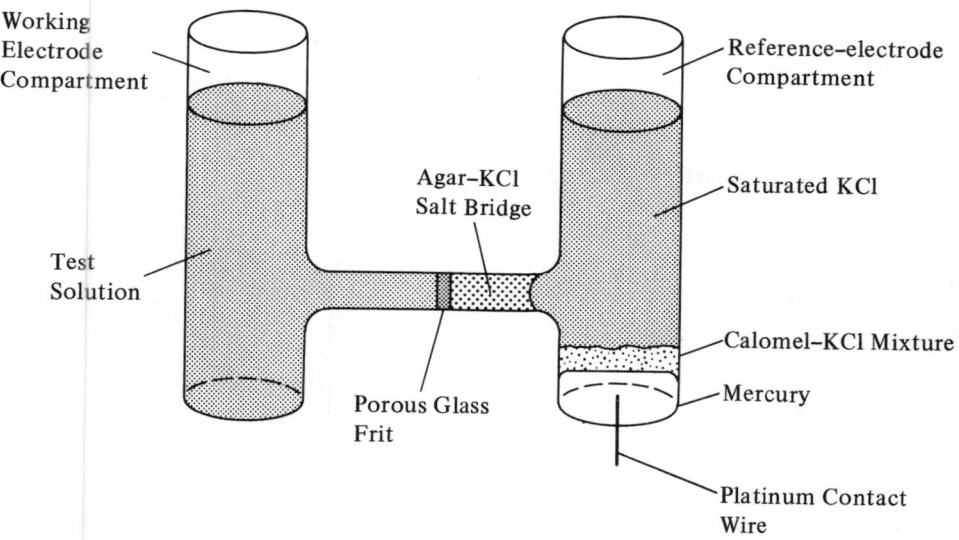

FIGURE 3.9. *Diagram of a common H-cell for polarographic analysis.*

A very large number of designs for polarographic cells have been described in the literature as being suitable for particular applications. For example, cells with reproducible liquid junctions that eliminate the use of glass frits or agar salt bridges (Fig. 3.10); very simple, easily assembled, and easily cleaned cells for routine analysis of large numbers of samples; microcells for use with test-solution volumes of a milliliter or less; and many others.

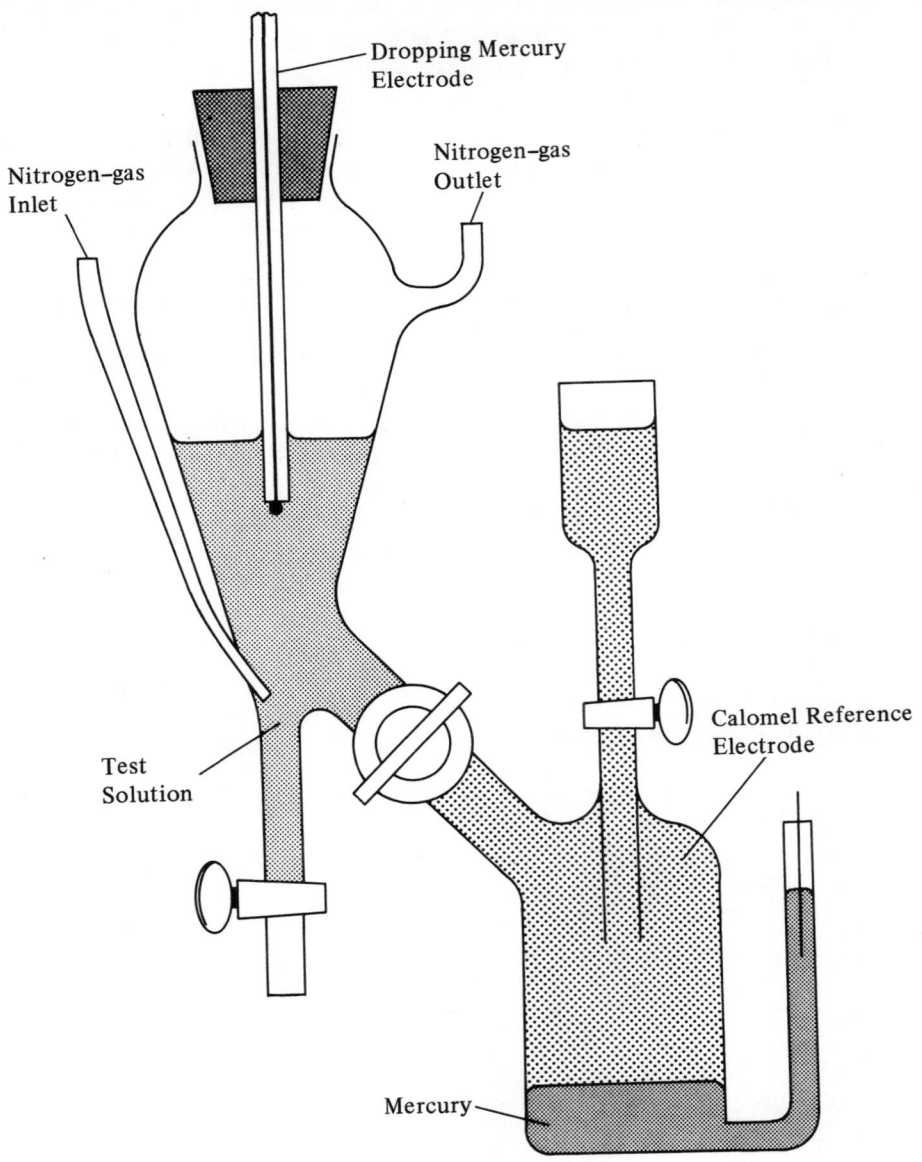

Nitrogen–gas Inlet

Dropping Mercury Electrode

Nitrogen–gas Outlet

Test Solution

Calomel Reference Electrode

Mercury

FIGURE 3.10. *Diagram of a polarographic cell designed for maintenance of a reproducible liquid junction.*

Electrodes

The DME can be made most economically by using suitable lengths (8 to 30 cm) of marine-barometer tubing (available from Corning Glass Works; 0.05 to 0.07 mm i.d.). The capillary is joined by plastic tubing to a mercury reservoir whose level can be adjusted to produce a suitable drop-time. (The drop-time is inversely proportional to the height of the mercury column, and directly proportional to the length of the capillary.) Mechanical devices to obtain a constant drop-life (drop-time) by tapping the capillary have been described in the literature, and are commercially available (Metrohm, Princeton Applied Research Corporation).

The reference electrode most commonly used is a saturated calomel, a mercurous sulfate, or silver/silver-chloride electrode. When accurate measurement of the potential is not required, a mercury pool or a platinum wire, foil, or gauze can be used. In nonaqueous solutions, various other reference electrodes may be more suitable.

Instrumentation

A simple polarograph can be constructed from a potentiometer and a sensitive current-measuring instrument according to the scheme in Figure 3.1. Manual recording of polarographic curves with such an apparatus is, however, very time consuming and cannot be recommended for practical analyses.

A number of reliable, low-cost ($2000–5000), recording DC polarographs are commercially available such as the Princeton Applied Research Model 174, Sargent XVI, Tacussel PRGS, and Beckman Electroscan.

Some of these instruments offer other applications in addition to recording DC polarographic curves. These polarographs principally consist of a source of gradually increasing voltage, a voltage-range selector, and a current-range selector. Some instruments permit a partial compensation of the charging current by a counter current linearly proportional to the applied voltage; some allow large shifts of the position for zero current, to shift unwanted waves outside the recording zone.

A wide variety of recording polarographs or potentiostats capable of simple DC polarography and linear-sweep voltammetry can be built from modern operational amplifiers for as little as about $100, depending on the number of extra features and the quality of the amplifiers desired. All that is needed in addition is a suitable x-y or strip-chart recorder.

Potentiostats. Most modern voltammetric instrumentation involves the use of the three-electrode potentiostatic polarograph as shown in Figure 3.11. Although simple DC polarography and slow-scan linear-sweep voltammetry can be performed with a two-electrode system in high-conductivity (low-resistance) systems, a three-electrode system (which automatically compensates for solution resistance) is necessary for investigation of nonaqueous systems of low conductivity and for investigations involving pulse-polarographic or rapid-scan techniques.

A potentiostat functions in the following manner: The reference electrode, used to measure the potential of the working electrode, is isolated by the voltage-follower amplifier so that very little current is drained from it. The output of the voltage follower (that is, the working-electrode potential measured by the reference electrode) is fed into the control or scan amplifier along with the various input voltages. If the potential measured by the reference electrode is different from the sum of the other input voltages (implying that the potential of the working electrode differs from the desired value), the control amplifier will supply a corrective voltage at the counter electrode to compensate for this. The current flow in the cell is essentially

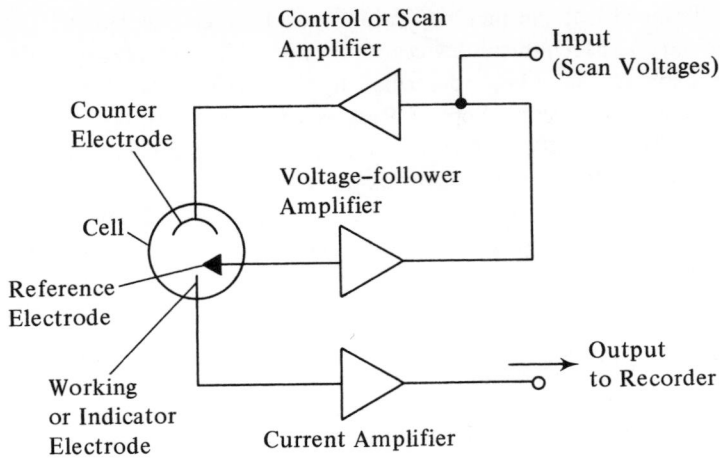

FIGURE 3.11. *Schematic diagram of a modern, three-electrode potentiostat.*

between the counter and working electrodes. Finally, the current amplifier takes the current flowing to (or from) the working electrode, converts it to a voltage that is proportional to the magnitude of the current, and amplifies the voltage for presentation to a recorder.

3.3 APPLICATIONS

Measurement of Voltammetric and Polarographic Curves

Although polarography may be occasionally used for qualitative analysis, the typical application is in quantitative analysis. To determine concentrations, the polarographic limiting current is measured.

Numerous methods of measuring the wave height are described in the literature and a choice amongst these might seem to be a difficult task. However, most of the methods used give essentially equivalent results, provided that the measurements are carried out with sufficient care and accuracy and that the wave height is measured in the same way for all waves to be compared—that is, for the samples themselves and for the standards used in calibration.

In the measurement of wave heights, corrections for the residual or capacity current must be made. This can be done either by recording the residual current separately in a solution containing all the components with the exception of the electroactive species under study, or by extrapolation. The graphical subtraction of residual current is generally considered more reliable, particularly for inorganic species and at lower concentrations. For larger organic compounds the basic assumption involved—i.e., identity of the residual current in the sample solution and in the blank—is not generally fulfilled: adsorption of the organic compound results in a change in the capacity current. In such cases, the extrapolation of portions of the polarographic curves, as shown in Figure 3.12, seems to be the most accurate approach.

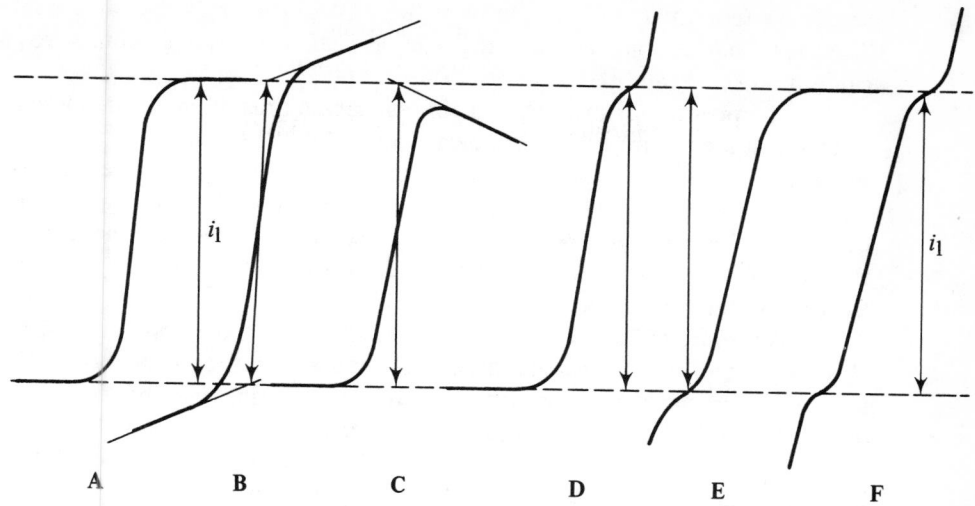

FIGURE 3.12. *Illustration of several methods for measuring the wave height of variously shaped polarographic waves. Curves A–C illustrate the technique of extrapolating the linear portions of the waves before and after the current rise. Curves D–F illustrate the technique of estimating current magnitudes for ill shaped waves.*

The exact method of measurement depends on the shape of the polarographic wave. Some examples are shown in Figure 3.12.

The maximum value of the oscillating current is the magnitude commonly measured and used in calculations. In the earlier literature, when fast-response recorders were not available, measurement of the average of the oscillations was recommended.

Determination of Concentration

Once the height of the wave has been obtained, it remains to relate this to the concentration of the studied solution. As with the majority of physical methods used in analytical chemistry, such evaluation is based on comparison with a standard.

The two methods of comparison most frequently used are that of employing a calibration curve and that of standard addition.

Calibration Curves. The calibration curve is constructed by successively adding increasing amounts of the substance to be studied to a solution of supporting electrolyte, which is prepared using all the other components present in the sample solution. The polarographic curves are recorded and measured, and the wave height is plotted as a function of concentration.

Next, curves are recorded for solutions containing samples to be analyzed in the same supporting electrolyte as was used for the construction of the calibration curve. It is essential that the curves for the sample analysis be recorded under *exactly* the same conditions as those used in the construction of the calibration curve. In particular, one uses the same capillary, the same pressure of mercury, the same sensitivity (current range) of the recording instrument, and the same temperature. The wave height obtained with the sample is then measured, compared with the calibration curve, and the concentration read off.

The pressure of mercury is kept constant by maintaining the mercury in the reservoir at a constant level. Somewhat more difficult to guarantee is the use of the same capillary. This implies that when a capillary is broken, or behaves erratically (commonly, as a result of penetration of impurities into the bore), a new calibration curve must be constructed. If the highest accuracy is aimed at, the temperature of the electrolytic cell must also be controlled by using a water-jacket or by immersing the cell in a thermostatted bath.

The most difficult condition to meet is making the solutions used for constructing calibration curves identical to those used for sample analysis. Frequently the calibration curves are recorded in solutions containing only the studied compound and supporting electrolyte; however, the preparation of the sample solution often introduces other substances. It can usually be assumed that these substances will have a negligible effect on the waves of the compound to be determined, but sometimes such electro-inactive components of the sample can affect the height of the measured wave.

If such an effect of electro-inactive components cannot be neglected, an attempt can be made to prepare synthetic sample solutions that would contain all components with the exception of the studied substance. Such synthetic samples are then added to all solutions used in the preparation of the calibration curve.

Serious difficulty with this approach can result from insufficient knowledge of the sample composition. Alternatively, it is sometimes impossible to obtain or prepare samples that would not contain any of the component to be determined. For example, in the analysis of biological material for a common trace metal or widely distributed organic compound (e.g., pyruvic acid), it is practically impossible to obtain biological material that contains a negligible concentration of the substance to be determined.

One possible solution is to use a sample with a small concentration of the investigated compound as the starting point instead of pure supporting electrolyte. Curves recorded for solutions containing successively increasing concentrations of the compound added are then corrected for the small wave in the original sample before the wave height is plotted.

Standard-Addition Method. An alternative possibility is the use of the standard-addition method. When this method is used, the condition of identical composition of compared solutions is most closely fulfilled. Moreover, because the curve of the sample and the curve obtained after addition of the standard are usually recorded within a short time interval, the temperature of the two solutions is sufficiently similar even without thermostatic control. This method assumes a direct linearity between the wave height and concentration, $i = kc$.

In the method of standard addition, a curve of the sample solution is recorded first. Then a known amount of a standard stock solution is added to the sample solution and another curve recorded. The principle of evaluation of these curves is best demonstrated with an example (Fig. 3.13). In this case, a sample of steel was dissolved in acidic solution and two aliquots taken. To one, a known volume of a standard dichromate solution was added; then a solution of hydrogen peroxide and an excess of sodium hydroxide was added to both. After removing the unreacted hydrogen peroxide by boiling, cooling, and adjusting the volume to a known value, oxygen was removed and both curves recorded (Fig. 3.13). The height, i, of the wave obtained with the steel sample was measured similarly as the height, i', of the wave obtained after addition of amount a of chromium (as metal) to the steel sample. Calculation of the weight of chromium present in the aliquot (x) is possible by means of

$$x = a \frac{i}{i' - i} \tag{3.6}$$

Knowing the weight of steel sample originally taken and the fraction of the total sample contained in the aliquot analyzed, the percentage of chromium in the steel sample can be determined.

FIGURE 3.13. *Illustration of the determination of concentration by the method of standard additions. Curve A: Polarogram of chromate ion reduction from the chromium in an aliquot of a digested steel sample. Curve B: A polarogram of a similar aliquot to which has been added a known volume of a standard chromium solution.*

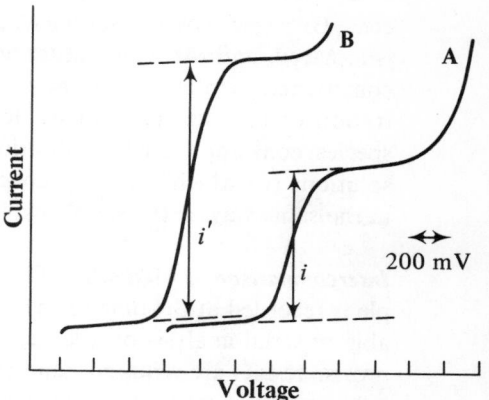

This approach, based on addition of the standard prior to any chemical operation and sample handling, is usually the most reliable, since it can be assumed that all losses affecting the determined component in the sample are proportional to losses in the added standard. However, it is necessary to handle two solutions in all operations.

To simplify the handling and thus to gain time, it is possible to modify the proposed procedure in cases where the dissolution of the sample is complete, the resulting solution is homogeneous, and no source of losses is known. In this modification, only one solution of the sample is prepared and handled. All separations and chemical reactions are carried out with this solution and supporting electrolyte is added. An aliquot (of volume V) of the final solution (c_{unk}) is transferred into the polarographic cell and the polarographic curve recorded (the height of which is denoted i). Then volume v of a standard stock solution of concentration c_{std} is added and a second curve (height i') is recorded. The concentration of the sample solution can then be calculated using

$$c_{unk} = c_{std} \frac{i}{i' + (i' - i) \dfrac{V}{v}} \tag{3.7}$$

If the volume of the standard addition or "spike," v, is very much smaller than the original solution volume V (1% or less), then any volume change can be ignored and Equation 3.7 simplifies somewhat to

$$c_{\text{unk}} = c_{\text{std}} \frac{iv}{(i' - i)V} \qquad (3.8)$$

Pilot-Ion Method. Another method, known as the "quotient of two waves" or "pilot-ion" method, is less frequently used, but offers some advantages. (This is known more generally as an "internal standard" method.) A known quantity of a standard "pilot" substance is added to each investigated solution. This pilot substance must be polarographically active and give a wave or waves in a potential region (preferably at more positive potentials) sufficiently different from that of the compound to be determined.

The ratio of the wave height of the unknown to that of the pilot can be assumed to be independent of capillary characteristics, viscosity of the solution, temperature, etc. Hence, a new measurement of this ratio is not needed whenever the capillary is replaced, and the temperature need not be controlled. The calibration curves are constructed by plotting the ratio of the heights of the two waves against the concentration of the substance to be determined, keeping the concentration of the pilot species constant. Such calibration curves can be used for evaluation of sample solutions (to which the same concentration of the pilot substance has been added) in the same way as the simple calibration curves mentioned above.

Intercomparison of Methods. The speed of analysis where only one curve of the sample is recorded at the time of the analysis makes the calibration-curve method preferable in serial analysis of a large number of samples of similar composition. When precise results are required, temperature control is necessary, and when the capillary is blocked or broken, additional work for construction of a new calibration curve is necessary. The calibration-curve method is always used when the relation between the measured current and concentration is nonlinear (e.g., when catalytic or adsorption currents are dealt with).

The method of "quotient of two waves" can be applied in cases similar to those in which the simple calibration curve is used. Temperature control is unnecessary, but construction of several calibration curves for different concentrations of the "pilot" substance is usually necessary.

The method of standard addition is useful when analysis of only a limited number of samples is required. In such instances the construction of a calibration curve would be too time consuming. The apparatus is simplified by the fact that temperature control is unnecessary. On the other hand, because two curves (with and without addition of the standard) have to be recorded for each sample, the time spent on a single analysis is somewhat longer.

The accuracy of the standard-addition method is somewhat lower than the procedure based on the use of calibration curves. This is because, in calculating concentrations using Equations 3.6 to 3.8, a direct proportionality is assumed between the measured current and concentration. This corresponds to a linear calibration curve passing through the origin where current and concentration equal zero. This assumption may be approximately valid at concentrations larger than about

10^{-4} *M*, but is rarely fulfilled in trace analysis. Nevertheless, the method of standard addition remains a first choice in cases where sample components might affect the wave height of the component analyzed, and yet it is difficult to obtain a sample with zero content of this component (e.g., biological material).

The relative methods mentioned above, based on comparison with standards, are to be preferred over so-called "absolute methods" where concentrations are calculated using predetermined and tabulated "diffusion-current constants" or diffusion coefficients, both known to be dependent on experimental conditions.

Scope of Applications

Electroactive Species. Inorganic cations, anions, and molecules can be determined polarographically. Among cations, the transition metals are most profitably determined polarographically, but some alkaline-earth and rare-earth ions also offer useful analytic curves. Strongly hydrolyzed metals (e.g., aluminum, thorium, zirconium) present difficulties (which can be circumvented by using nonaqueous solvents); so do some elements that form predominantly covalent bonds (e.g., silicon; however, some germanium complexes are reducible). Typical ions frequently determined are those of $Cu(II)$, $Cu(I)$, $Tl(I)$, $Pb(II)$, $Cd(II)$, $Zn(II)$, $Fe(II)$, $Fe(III)$, $Ni(II)$, $Co(II)$, $Bi(III)$, $Sb(III)$, $Sb(V)$, $Sn(II)$, $Sn(IV)$, and $Eu(III)$; and Mo, W, V, Mn, Cr, Ti, N, and Pt in a number of oxidation states. Even when it is possible to determine alkali metals polarographically, flame photometry or some other spectral technique is usually superior.

Anions of the halides, as well as sulfides, selenides, and tellurides, can be determined by means of anodic waves due to mercury-salt formation. Among the oxygen-containing anions—in addition to those of the metals mentioned above—cathodic reduction waves can be used for determination of bromates, iodates, periodates, sulfites, polythionates, etc.

Finally, among inorganic molecules, polarography can be used to determine oxygen, hydrogen peroxide, elemental sulfur, some sulfur oxides, and oxides of nitrogen, as well as some undissociated acids.

A great number and variety of organic compounds can be quantitatively determined by reduction at the DME. Only highly polarizable single bonds between carbon and heteroatoms are reducible in the available potential range, e.g., C–Cl, C–Br, or C–I bonds. Other single bonds, e.g., C–O, C–S, or C–N, require the presence of an adjacent activating group such as a carbonyl group or a pyridine ring.

Some single bonds between heteroatoms, such as those in peroxides and disulfides, as well as N–N, N–O, S–O, and similar bonds are also easily reducible.

Double and triple bonds are frequently reducible, in particular when the reduced bond is a part of a conjugated system; for example, unsaturated conjugated or aromatic hydrocarbons, carbonyl compounds and their nitrogen analogues, and nitro-, nitroso- and azo-compounds.

Because of the relatively easy oxidation of mercury, anodic waves are observed with the DME only for the strongest reducing agents such as hydroquinones, enediols (e.g., ascorbic acid), phenylhydroxylamine derivatives, and certain aldehydes. Numerous organic substances nevertheless yield anodic waves corresponding to mercury-salt formation, e.g., thiols and other derivatives of bivalent sulfur, amines, and some heterocycles. The organic compounds, in these cases, are not oxidized, but only make the oxidation of mercury easier (the amount being directly related to the concentration of the compound). The more stable the mercury salt, the more easily the oxidation occurs, i.e., the more negative the wave appears on the potential axis.

Nature of the Sample. Since electrolysis is almost invariably carried out in solution, it is necessary first to convert any sample into a solution. The sample itself can be a solid, liquid, or gas. In the last two cases the dissolution is usually straightforward; for solid samples, procedures used in other wet analytical procedures are followed, with the exception that the use of nitric acid is usually avoided because of the possibility of generating electroactive nitrogen oxides.

Typical examples of samples range from metals, alloys, slags, ores, minerals, and fertilizers to a variety of organic materials such as polymers, petroleum and its products, fibres and textile materials, pesticides, insecticides, herbicides, food and food products, including beverages (beer and wine), biological materials, pharmaceuticals, plants, and soils. Examples of liquid samples subjected to polarographic analysis are body fluids such as blood and urine, natural and industrial water, and seawater. Polluted atmosphere and industrial gases represent samples of gaseous nature. In particular, the ability to determine oxygen in the presence of practically all other gases is often utilized.

Detection Limits, Accuracy and Precision, Selectivity. The detection limit in DC polarography is usually between 1 and $5 \times 10^{-6} M$. Other polarographic techniques (see Sec. 3.4) offer lower detection limits: $10^{-8} M$ with differential-pulse polarography, and even lower when preconcentration is used, as in stripping voltammetry. In the last case, metals that form amalgams and anions that form insoluble mercury salts can be determined down to $10^{-9} M$ and even $10^{-10} M$. The typical range for stripping analysis, however, is 10^{-6} to $10^{-9} M$, with an absolute sample size of about 0.1 ng of the element analyzed. With care, the precision is about ± 10–20% at the $10^{-10} M$ level, and about ± 2–5% for concentrations greater than about $10^{-9} M$.

Considerably lower detection limits (than $10^{-6} M$) in DC polarography are observed for some catalytic currents. For example, cobalamine in buffers and iron in sodium hydroxide can be detected even with DC polarography down to about $10^{-8} M$.

The final volume of the solution for polarographic analysis is usually of the order of 5 to 20 ml; decrease of the volume down to 0.1 ml does not present any difficulties apart from the need to use special cells. If necessary, polarographic electrolysis can be carried out in as little as 0.01 ml. However, the handling of small volumes requires considerable skill and is much more time consuming than operation on the milliliter level (as is usually the case with microchemical operations, regardless of the particular analytical method used).

The accuracy and reproducibility of the results depend considerably on the shape of the wave under study. For well developed waves or well separated peaks, the limiting current (wave height) can be measured with an error of ± 1–2%. Considering the required constancy of the various experimental factors controlling the limiting current and inaccuracies in the preparation of the sample, an overall error of about $\pm 3\%$ can be said to be typical for polarographic determinations. In high-precision serial analyses, the error can be improved to 1% when all factors are strictly controlled.

The accuracy and precision decrease for ill-shaped waves. If, moreover, the composition of the sample with respect to electro-inactive materials that affect the shape of polarographic curves varies from sample to sample (e.g., in samples of biological materials), the error may increase to $\pm 5\%$ or even to $\pm 20\%$. However, even this level is often sufficient for clinical analysis, studies of natural products, or other biochemical applications.

For the whole concentration range from 10^{-3} M to about one order of magnitude above the detection limit of the particular polarographic technique, the *relative* error of polarographic determinations usually remains practically unchanged. This means that, from an absolute point of view, the accuracy is good or sufficient at low concentration levels but poorer at higher concentrations. This in turn means that polarography is relatively well suited for trace analysis, is suitable for determination of samples containing 30% or more of the active component only when high precision is not required, and is unsuitable for *accurate* determination of the main component when the sample consists of 90% or more of this component.

In addition to sensitivity, the main advantage of polarographic methods is their selectivity. Current-versus-voltage curves often reveal the presence of interfering substances—not the case in optical methods, especially when measurements are carried out at only one wavelength. The selectivity of polarographic methods is particularly great when the analysis is carried out in more than one supporting electrolyte.

All the characteristics of polarographic methods as analytical tools indicate that they are particularly useful for trace analysis. Components can be determined in the ppm to ppb range with accuracy sufficient for most practical analyses. The amount of sample needed for analysis varies between a few micrograms and about 50 mg. Larger samples are used only when an average composition is aimed at.

Interferences. Two types of interference may be encountered in polarographic analysis. The first is identical with problems encountered with other analytical methods in the presence of two or more species that give signals too similar to be distinguished. When two species give waves whose potentials differ by less than about 100 mV in DC polarography (and by less than about 50 mV in single-sweep voltammetry and differential-pulse polarography, Sec. 3.4), such waves or peaks overlap and prevent the determination of the individual components.

In addition, DC polarography has a more specific limitation. Measurement of a more positive wave in the presence of an excess of material reduced at more negative potentials (wave A in Fig. 3.14) can be carried out with maximum accuracy; but when the trace material to be determined is reduced at more negative potentials (wave B' in Fig. 3.14)—that is, when a small wave follows a large one—measurement of the small, more negative, wave can be carried out only when the concentration ratio between the excess component and the analyzed species is less than about 10:1. At larger excess the accuracy of the determination of the trace component decreases considerably.

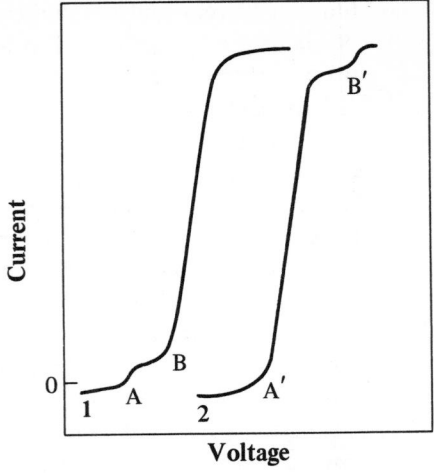

FIGURE 3.14. *Polarograms of mixtures of electroactive substances in different ratios. Curve 1: Reduction of a small amount of a more easily reduced substance in the presence of a larger amount of a substance reduced at a more negative potential. Curve 2: Reduction of a small amount of a substance in the presence of a large amount of a substance reduced at more positive potential.*

Separation of overlapping waves or peaks is frequently possible by changing the composition of the supporting electrolyte. Differences in complexing properties are made use of primarily in inorganic analysis, while differences in acid-base properties are used in organic analysis. Alternatively, a change in solvent may result in separation of overlapping curves, owing to differences in solvation of the electroactive species.

An example of separation of overlapping waves is the analysis of mixtures of lead(II) and thallium(I). A mixture of these two ions in neutral media gives a wave that cannot be resolved into the individual waves of Pb^{2+} and Tl^+; the half-wave potentials differ by only about 60 mV. When excess sodium hydroxide is added, the wave for thallium(I) remains at virtually the same potential as in neutral media (as thallium does not form hydroxo complexes), whereas the wave of lead(II) is shifted to more negative potential by about 300 mV, due to formation of plumbate (Fig. 3.15). Generally, when a metal cation forms a complex, its reduction potential is made more negative—it is more difficult to reduce.

Selectivity depends very much on the system studied, and may be either better or worse than in ultraviolet spectrophotometry. This can be illustrated for the simple alkaline cleavage of α,β-unsaturated carbonyl compounds. When cleavage of chalcone ($C_6H_5COCH{=}CHC_6H_5$) is followed, polarography permits determination of the parent compound, of benzaldehyde, and of the sum of acetophenone and the intermediate ketol $C_6H_5COCH_2CH(OH)C_6H_5$ in the mixture. Because the concentrations of benzaldehyde and acetophenone as final products must be equal, the concentrations of all four components in the mixture can be determined polarographically. Ultraviolet spectra of the intermediates and products overlap, however, and only the concentration of the starting material can be determined spectrophotometrically without interference.

On the other hand, when the products of the alkaline cleavage of cinnamaldehyde ($C_6H_5CH{=}CHCHO$) are investigated, the polarographic waves of the aldol intermediate and of benzaldehyde overlap, and the acetaldehyde waves are ill-developed. Ultraviolet spectra, on the other hand, allow the determination of cinnamaldehyde and of the aldol [$C_6H_5CH(OH)CH_2CHO$] in the presence of benzaldehyde.

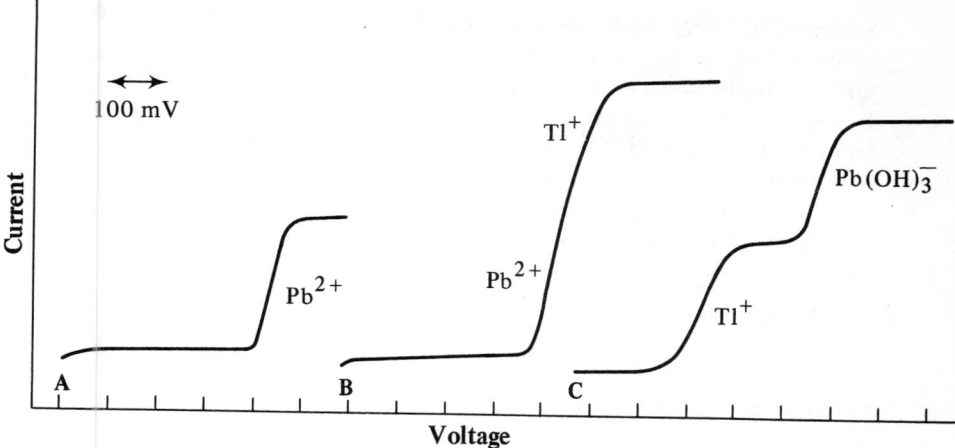

FIGURE 3.15. *Polarographic waves of Pb^{2+} and Tl^+, illustrating the shift of waves with change in background electrolyte. Curve A: Lead reduction in neutral media. Curve B: Merged waves for the reduction of lead and thallium in neutral media. Curve C: Separate waves for the reduction of lead and thallium in excess hydroxide.*

Polarographic and optical methods are thus frequently complementary rather than competitive.

Examples of Practical Applications

Since the invention of polarography in 1922, more than 30,000 papers dealing with this technique have been published. Since more than 90% of those papers deal with practical applications, any choice of examples cannot be more than an indication of the possibilities the method offers. The following selection, which is necessarily subjective, was made with the aim of showing applications in a variety of fields.

Manganese and Iron in Ores. In alkaline triethanolamine solution, manganese(III) gives a reduction wave at -0.3 V whereas the iron(III) wave is at -1.0 V. Since copper, lead, and nickel interfere, the ore is dissolved in hydrochloric acid and the resulting solution is first reduced with powdered zinc. After addition of triethanolamine and concentrated sodium hydroxide solutions, the mixture is vigorously shaken for about half a minute to ensure oxidation of the manganese and iron complexes to the trivalent state by atmospheric oxygen. The current-versus-voltage curves are recorded after removal of oxygen.

Iron in iron ores can, of course, also be analyzed by the classical redox titration with standard dichromate solution using a diphenylamine sulfonate indicator. Trace manganese in ores can also be determined using colorimetric methods or atomic absorption spectroscopy. An atomic absorption spectrophotometer, however, will cost a minimum of about $4500 and requires the periodic replacement of expensive hollow-cathode lamps. The point is that one usually has some choice of analytical methods, each with its particular advantages and disadvantages for the problem at hand.

Copper and Other Impurities in Lead. Lead (that used in storage batteries, for instance) is dissolved in nitric acid and the greater part of the lead precipitated by adding sulfuric acid. The supernatant is treated with citric acid and the pH adjusted to about 6 with ammonia. The polarograms show waves of copper at -0.2 V, bismuth at -0.5 V, and lead (the unprecipitated remainder) at -0.4 V. The wave of iron(III), if present, coincides with that of copper(II).

To another portion of the supernatant, evaporated to a small volume, ammonia–ammonium chloride buffer is added. The curve recorded in this solution shows waves of copper at -0.25 and -0.5 V, nickel at -1.1 V, zinc at -1.3 V, and manganese at -1.6 V. Cobalt, if present, gives a wave that overlaps that of zinc.

If antimony is present, it can be detected by recording the current-versus-voltage curve in the original acidic solution, where its wave follows a combined wave of copper, iron, and bismuth.

Lead in Tinned Food. The sample, digested with sulfuric and nitric acids, is treated with hydrogen peroxide to remove the oxides of nitrogen. Treating the sample with sodium thiosulfate and nitric acid precipitates stannic acid. Any iron present is reduced by metallic magnesium, and the polarogram of lead is recorded after adding tartaric acid and adjusting the pH to about 5 with base.

Morphine. Morphine can be determined in pharmaceutical preparations after reacting it with nitrite to form a nitro compound. The procedure can also be used to analyze blood or other biological fluids for morphine after separating the fluid into its constituents by paper or thin-layer chromatography. The sample is dissolved in hydrochloric acid, potassium nitrite is added, and the sample is allowed to stand for 5 min at 20°C. After adding an excess of potassium hydroxide and removing oxygen, the polarogram is recorded.

When nitration is carried out under the described conditions, the presence of narcotine, papaverine, or codeine does not interfere. Heroin can be determined after acid hydrolysis of the acetyl group.

DDT. The insecticide DDT (p,p'-dichlorodiphenyltrichloroethane) gives a well developed wave at -0.9 V in 96% ethanol containing lithium and tetraalkylammonium salts.

A mixture of the biologically active p,p'-dichlorodiphenyl derivative and the inactive o,p'-isomer can be analyzed. Polarography is useful for residue analysis of a number of insecticides, both chlorinated (e.g., hexachlorocyclohexane) and non-chlorinated (e.g., dithiocarbamates, pyrethrins, rotenone, etc.).

Ascorbic Acid in Fruit and Vegetables. Anodic waves corresponding to the oxidation of ascorbic acid (vitamin C) can be used for analysis of fruit and vegetables. Soft and juicy fruits (e.g., citrus fruit, currants, melons, gooseberries) and vegetables (e.g., tomatoes) can simply be squeezed, the collected juice mixed with deoxygenated (to prevent oxidation of ascorbic acid) pH 4.7 acetate buffer and the anodic waves recorded. For hard fruit and vegetables, prior homogenization is necessary.

Biological thiols such as glutathione, which interfere with or complicate titrimetric methods, do not interfere with the polarographic determination.

Carbon Disulfide in the Atmosphere. The pulp and paper industry often causes pollution of the atmosphere with carbon disulfide. To determine CS_2 in the atmosphere, a gaseous sample from a chimney, for instance, is drawn into a vessel containing diethylamine solution in 96% ethanol which converts the carbon disulfide into diethyldithiocarbamate while still at the site. The solution does not deteriorate with time, so the sample vessel can be left in place for several days to enrich the sample in CS_2. In the laboratory, the sample is diluted with a lithium-chloride solution and a polarogram recorded.

The method is unaffected by a fivefold excess of hydrogen sulfide and of most mercaptans (phenylmercaptan, however, interferes). If carbon oxysulfide is present, the method must be modified.

Dissolved Oxygen: The "Oxygen Electrode." Compact portable units are available for the determination of dissolved O_2 gas in aqueous solutions. The "oxygen electrode" or sensor probe is really an electrochemical cell composed of a gold or platinum cathode and a suitable reference anode—usually some type of silver electrode. A constant potential of about 0.8 V is applied between the two electrodes. The cell is separated from the test solution by a gas-permeable membrane, typically cellophane, polyethylene, or Teflon. Oxygen diffuses from the test solution through the membrane and is reduced at the cathode; the resulting current is proportional to the oxygen level of the test solution. The entire system must be calibrated with one or more solutions of known oxygen content.

Complete benchtop units are used routinely for monitoring dissolved oxygen in biological fluids and systems. Portable pressure- and temperature-compensated oxygen-electrode systems are available for monitoring oxygen levels in oceans, lakes, and rivers and in effluents and wastewaters at depths down to about 30 m.

3.4 VARIATIONS OF THE CONVENTIONAL POLAROGRAPHIC METHOD

Many modifications of polarography have been proposed for a number of specific purposes: to investigate mechanisms of electrode reactions, to decrease the time needed for examination of a given sample, to increase sensitivity (usually by decreasing the residual or charging current), and so on. Here, those modifications that have found significant applications in analytical work will be briefly described.

Pulse Polarography

One approach that minimizes the effect of charging current is *pulse polarography*. In this technique, instead of applying a continuously increasing voltage, a single rectangular voltage pulse is applied to the electrode during the last portion of its life. In this way, the period at the beginning of the drop-life, when changes in charging current are greatest, is avoided. Moreover, the current is measured over a very short time, and appreciably later than the sudden change in voltage, so that the charging current has decreased more than the faradaic current has at the time the current is measured.

In pulse polarography, two main variants can be distinguished: techniques using gradually increasing amplitude of the voltage pulse (pulse polarography) and those in which the voltage pulse used has a constant amplitude, superimposed on a slowly increasing voltage (differential-pulse polarography).

In *pulse polarography*, a square-wave voltage pulse of about 40 msec duration is applied to the electrode during the last quarter of the drop-life (Fig. 3.16A). At the instant the voltage pulse is applied, the charging current is very large, but it decays rather rapidly (exponentially). The current is then measured during the 20 msec of the second half of the pulse (Fig. 3.16B) when the charging current is quite small. The amplitude of the applied voltage pulses increases linearly with time. When the current response is recorded as a function of voltage, the shape of the resulting curve resembles waves in DC polarography (Fig. 3.16C), except that it has a "staircase" appearance because the current is sampled once during each drop-life and stored until the next sample period.

In *differential-pulse polarography* the duration of pulses is similar to that used in the previous technique (i.e., 40–60 msec), the pulses are also applied during the last quarter of the drop-life (when the surface area of the dropping electrode changes little with the time), but the pulses used have a constant amplitude (usually 5 to 100 mV) and are superimposed on a slowly increasing linear voltage ramp (Fig. 3.16D). Two measuring periods are used, one immediately preceding the pulse, the other very near the end of the pulse. The overall response plotted is the difference in the two currents sampled: one at point *b* in Figure 3.16E, corresponding to the polarographic current that would be measured at the given potential in the absence of a voltage pulse, and one at point *d* in Figure 3.16E, which is the sum of the current at *b* and the current resulting from the application of the additional voltage. The plot of this difference (Δi) as a function of potential is peak-shaped (Fig. 3.16F).

By measuring the difference in current before the application of the voltage pulse and towards the end of the pulse, the charging current contribution is further reduced in magnitude.

The peak shape of differential-pulse polarograms results from the relation

FIGURE 3.16. *Waveforms for pulse and differential-pulse polarography. Curves A and D: Excitation signal applied to the working electrode. Curves B and E: Instantaneous current observed at a single drop as a function of time. Curves C and F: The resulting current-versus-voltage curves. In pulse polarography, square-wave voltage pulses of 40-msec duration are applied to the mercury drop, of drop-life mechanically controlled at 2.5 sec (A); $t_d, t'_d, t''_d, \ldots$ represent successive drops. The overall rate of increase of the amplitude of the voltage pulses is about 0.1 V/min. The instantaneous current at a single drop (B) shows the decay of current, primarily capacitive, during the first 20 msec after the application of the pulse, and the amount of the current flowing during the latter 20 msec of the pulse duration. The response (C) of the system has the familiar sigmoidal shape of an ordinary polarogram. In differential-pulse polarography, constant-amplitude pulses between about 5 and 100 mV are superimposed on a linearly increasing DC voltage ramp (D). The instantaneous current response at a single drop is similar to that for pulse polarography, except that the current is sampled at two places (E). The response is now peak shaped (F).*

POLAROGRAPHY

1

2

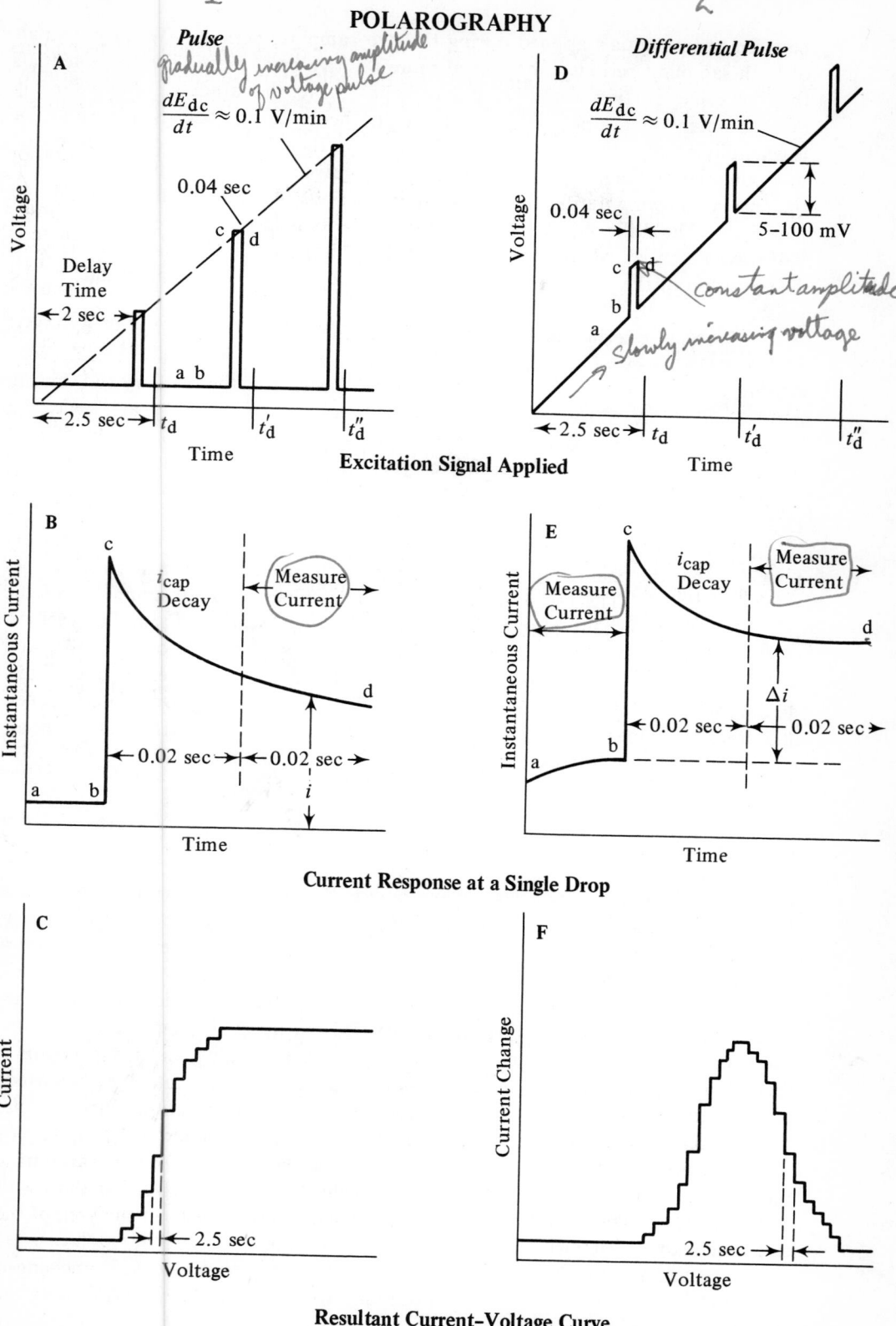

A — Pulse

gradually increasing amplitude of voltage pulse

$\dfrac{dE_{dc}}{dt} \approx 0.1$ V/min

0.04 sec

c d

Delay Time
← 2 sec →

a b

← 2.5 sec → t_d t'_d t''_d

Voltage / Time

D — Differential Pulse

$\dfrac{dE_{dc}}{dt} \approx 0.1$ V/min

0.04 sec

5–100 mV

c d

constant amplitude

b

a

slowly increasing voltage

← 2.5 sec → t_d t'_d t''_d

Voltage / Time

Excitation Signal Applied

B

Instantaneous Current

c

i_{cap} Decay

Measure Current

d

a b

← 0.02 sec → ← 0.02 sec →

i

Time

E

Instantaneous Current

c

i_{cap} Decay

Measure Current

Measure Current

d

Δi

a

b

← 0.02 sec → ← 0.02 sec →

Time

Current Response at a Single Drop

C

Current

→ ← 2.5 sec

Voltage

F

Current Change

2.5 sec → ←

Voltage

Resultant Current–Voltage Curve

between the potentials applied during the two sampling periods. When potentials of both sampling periods are either at more positive or at more negative potentials than the rising portion of the DC polarographic wave, the faradaic currents flowing at both potentials are practically the same and hence Δi approaches zero value (or is generally small). However, when at least one of the sampling periods corresponds to a potential on the rising portion of the polarographic wave, the difference between the currents flowing during the two sampling periods is different from zero, and Δi increases. The difference between the two currents is largest in the vicinity of the half-wave potential, where the slope of the DC polarographic wave is usually largest. The position of the peak on the Δi-versus-E curve depends on the amplitude of the pulse.

Both pulse techniques involve synchronization of the drop-time of the DME with the frequency of the applied pulses. This is achieved by mechanical drop-control using a magnetically controlled "hammer" knocking the capillary and causing detachment of drops from the capillary. The frequency of knocking, and hence the drop-time, can be electronically controlled and synchronized with the application of voltage pulses. It has proven useful to synchronize the detachment of the mercury drop with the power-line frequency to minimize electrical noise picked up by the electrodes and metal supporting stands from the surroundings.

Both techniques produce signals that are a linear function of concentration provided that the characteristics of the capillary electrode and the pattern of pulses remain constant. The use of differential pulse assumes constant amplitude of the pulse as well as constant frequency, pulse duration, and location of sampling periods.

The detection limit for pulse polarography is typically about 10^{-7} M, and about 10^{-8} M for the differential-pulse method—although, of course, detection limits do depend on the electrochemical properties of the substance analyzed, interferences, and other experimental variables. The detection limit for arsenic(III) by differential-pulse polarography, for example, has been reported to be 4×10^{-9} M (0.3 ppb), with a linear calibration curve up to 8×10^{-4} M.

Linear-Sweep Voltammetry

Principles. Instead of working under essentially potentiostatic conditions with a DME as in DC and pulse polarography, it is possible to carry out the whole potential scan (e.g., from 0 V to -2.0 V or over any other similar potential range) on a more or less constant electrode surface.

This can be achieved in two different ways. In the first, a slow scan, comparable to that used in DC polarography, is carried out using an electrode with a constant, unchanging surface such as a mercury pool, a hanging mercury drop, or a solid electrode. The electrode can be stationary and the solution stationary or stirred; or the electrode can be periodically displaced in the solution by rotation, vibration, etc.

Alternatively, an electrode with a periodically renewed surface (dropping or streaming mercury electrodes) can be used. To accomplish the voltage scan during the life of a single drop, the rate of scanning must then be much faster than with stationary electrodes, and the scanning speed must be even greater if the area of the electrode is to remain virtually constant during the scan.

Recording of current-versus-voltage curves using electrodes with unchanged surface and slow rate of scanning has not found wide analytical application, with the

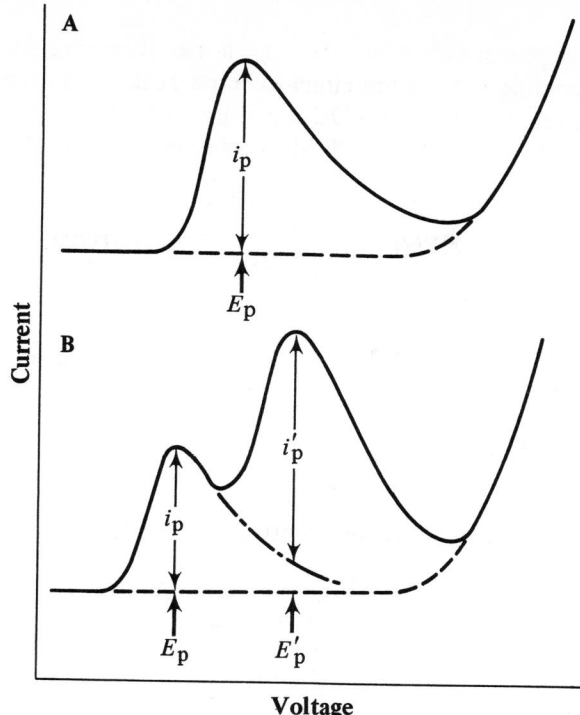

FIGURE 3.17. *Typical linear-scan voltammograms for reductions. Curve A: Reduction of a single species. The peak potential (E_p), and the magnitude of the peak current (i_p) are marked. The dashed line represents the "background" current obtained in the absence of the electroactive species. Curve B: Reduction of two species, with some overlap of peaks. Note that the peak current for the second wave, i'_p, is measured from the (extrapolated) current due to the first peak.*

exception of some uses of graphite and platinum electrodes, and those are generally used in oxidations. On the other hand, the use of fast voltage scanning for analytical purposes seems promising for some applications. The current-versus-voltage curves obtained under such conditions show a peak (Fig. 3.17A).

For qualitative interpretation of the shape of such curves, it is useful to consider two potential regions. At potentials more positive than that of the peak, the increase in current with increasing voltage is caused by the same factors as the rise of the wave in DC polarography, namely, the increased rate of the electrolytic process with increasing potential. On the other hand, at potentials more negative than that of the maximum current (E_p), the depletion of the electroactive species in the vicinity of the electrode surface becomes of importance. At the high voltage-scan rates employed, diffusion of the electroactive species from the bulk of the solution is not fast enough to replenish that removed at the electrode surface; hence, the concentration at the surface, and thus the current, decreases with time. This appears also as a decrease with increasing potential, since the voltage is linearly proportional to time.

Theory. For a reversible oxidation-reduction system where both oxidized and reduced forms are soluble, it can be shown that the current under these conditions depends on potential in such a way as to pass through a maximum. For the potential of a peak obtained with a planar electrode it can be shown that

$$(E_p)_{planar} = E_{1/2} - 1.1 \frac{RT}{nF} \qquad (3.9)$$

The potential of the peak corresponding to a reduction process is thus more negative than the half-wave potential by $28/n$ mV. Similarly, it is possible to show that for anodic peaks corresponding to the reversible oxidation of the reduced form of the couple, the potential of the peak is more positive than the half-wave potential by $28/n$ mV.

The current (with both spherical and planar electrodes) is a linear function of concentration and can be used for analytical purposes. For reversible systems the peak current (i_p) obtained with a linear sweep at a planar electrode of area A is given by

$$i_p = kn^{3/2}AD^{1/2}cv^{1/2} \qquad (3.10)$$

where k = the Randles-Sevcik constant
v = the scanning rate

The current thus depends on the area of the electrode, on the concentration of the electroactive species, and on its diffusion coefficient. Apart from the difference in the value of the proportionality constant k, the peak current i_p shows a dependence on the number of electrons transferred (n) different from that observed in polarography: in DC polarography, the diffusion current is directly proportional to n, whereas in linear-sweep voltammetry the peak current is proportional to $n^{3/2}$. Finally, the essential difference between the currents obtained by the two techniques is in the dependence of the peak currents on the rate of scanning, v, which becomes an important variable, whereas polarographic diffusion currents are not dependent on v.

For irreversible electrode processes, the peak current is often lower than that for a reversible one. Peaks for irreversible processes are also less sharp, and the whole curve is more drawn out; but the peak potential E_p is independent of the concentration of the oxidized form and the current is a linear function of concentration.

Measurement of Peak Current. Measurement of the peak current is usually carried out by extrapolating the current before the peak and measuring the difference between this extrapolated baseline and the peak (Fig. 3.17A). This presents no problems provided that there is only one peak on the current-versus-voltage curve or, if there is more than one peak, that the individual peaks are separated by several hundred mV.

In the presence of several peaks that differ by 100–200 mV or less, measuring the most positive peak (in reductions) is still relatively simple. Measuring peak currents corresponding to successive processes is more difficult, since extrapolating the decreasing current of the more positive peak is always somewhat arbitrary (see Fig. 3.17B).

Stripping Voltammetry

For cations of amalgam-forming metals and for anions forming slightly soluble compounds with mercury, the sensitivity of polarographic techniques can be increased by accumulating the material within the electrode (as an amalgam) or at the surface

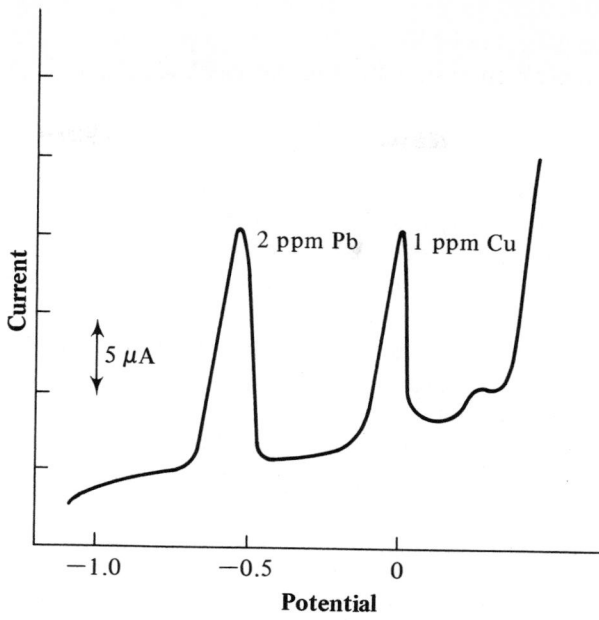

FIGURE 3.18. *Linear-sweep anodic-stripping voltammogram, 2 ppm Pb and 1 ppm Cu in 0.1 M HNO$_3$. Conditions: 5-min plating time at -1.10 V; 15-sec rest time; a thin-mercury-film electrode on glassy carbon; and a voltage scan rate of 1 V/min for the stripping step.*

of the electrode by preelectrolysis. This electrolysis, carried out at a controlled potential usually corresponding to the limiting current of the investigated species, is essentially an electrochemical preconcentration step wherein the electroactive material is concentrated from the relatively large solution volume, perhaps 5 to 20 cm^3, into the much smaller electrode "volume," perhaps 10^{-3} to 10^{-4} cm^3. Typical increases in concentration are of the order of 10- to 500-fold. This is followed by a voltage sweep from negative to positive potentials (when metal amalgam was formed by reduction) or from positive to negative potential (when mercury salts were anodically formed). Resulting curves (Fig. 3.18) correspond to the anodic dissolution of the amalgam or to the cathodic reduction of mercury from the mercury salts, the current signals being a measure of the amount of amalgam or mercury salt formed.

Mercury electrodes, particularly the hanging mercury drop electrode (HMDE) and mercury-coated platinum or graphite electrodes, are frequently used. A HMDE can be made by collecting two or three drops from a DME in a small glass or teflon spoon and attaching the resulting drop to the tip of a platinum wire that has been sealed into soft glass tubing. Another method is to use a capillary attached to a small mercury reservoir into which extends a micrometer-driven plunger. The micrometer is turned an appropriate number of divisions, and a mercury drop is extruded at the capillary orifice. Electrical contact is made to the mercury reservoir and, thus, to the mercury drop. Mercury film electrodes can be prepared by plating a thin (10–100 μm) mercury film onto a small platinum wire or onto the surface of a carbon or graphite rod, the sides of which have been suitably insulated. A recent innovation involves the simultaneous plating of mercury and metal ion during the preelectrolysis step: all solutions are made about 10^{-4} M in mercuric ion, the mercury film is formed and the amalgam generated during preelectrolysis at negative potential, and then the trace metal and mercury film are sequentially stripped off during the anodic reoxidation step. The mercury, since it is present in much larger concentration, gives a very large peak at about $+0.1$ V.

The types of elements that can be determined by cathodic deposition at mercury electrodes are the amalgam-formers—Cu, Pb, Cd, Bi, Sn, Zn, Tl, and so forth. Using anodic deposition, halides and various sulfides can be determined at mercury electrodes, iodide at silver electrodes, and lead (as PbO_2) and iron (as Fe_2O_3) at various solid electrodes.

The overall sensitivity of the stripping technique depends on the amount formed in preelectrolysis, which in turn depends on (a) the concentration of the substance in the solution; (b) the geometry of the electrode and the current density in the course of the preelectrolysis; (c) transport from the bulk of the solution (diffusion in unstirred solutions, convection and diffusion in stirred solutions); (d) the duration of electrolysis; and (e) the particular electrochemical technique used in the stripping step. Usually either linear-sweep voltammetry or differential-pulse voltammetry is used for the stripping of the accumulated material. Sensitivities can be truly spectacular, rivalling even those of neutron activation analysis. In fact, sensitivities are usually limited by the trace contaminants in the reagents used for digestions or for background electrolytes. For example, 0.1 M analytical reagent KCl with 0.0002% Pb (approximately the maximum impurity limit) has about 10^{-7} M Pb; and stripping analysis is normally used for the 10^{-6} to 10^{-9} M level. One way around this is to purify large volumes of the reagent solutions to be used by long-term controlled-potential electrolysis over large mercury-pool cathodes.

Signals obtained with linear-sweep voltammetry are less sensitive than those obtained with the differential-pulse technique. Therefore, the time needed for accumulating a sufficient amount of the preelectrolysis product is typically 10–60 min for the linear-sweep technique as opposed to 30 sec to 5 min for the differential-pulse mode. Since it is more difficult to control the conditions of the electrolysis over a prolonged period of time, the results obtained with differential-pulse voltammetry are usually more reproducible than those obtained with linear-sweep stripping voltammetry.

Instrumentation

Instrumentation for pulse polarography is quite complex. For differential-pulse polarography, the instrumentation requires various timing and sampling circuits, low-drift analog memories to allow storage and subtraction of two sampled currents, and good differential amplifiers to allow the amplification of Δi, etc. Early instruments used tube circuits of limited reliability. Recent instruments (Princeton Applied Research 170, 171, and 174, and the Tacussel PRG4), employing stable integrated-circuit amplifiers and high-impedance field-effect transistors, are reliable and not overly expensive ($2500–15,000).

For stripping analysis, only a special electrode (HMDE, mercury-coated carbon electrode, or another solid electrode) is needed. Any instrument generating a slow linear voltage sweep and recording the resulting current-versus-voltage curves can be used for linear-sweep stripping voltammetry. Preferably the instrument allows curve-recording both from positive to negative potentials and vice versa. For differential-pulse stripping voltammetry, any pulse polarograph can be used.

The measurement of peaks in linear-sweep voltammetry and pulse polarography is usually done by measuring the current at a chosen potential (usually that of the peak) and comparing it to the current at the same potential obtained with a blank. Such measurements are sufficiently accurate when the measured peak is not preceded by any other peak. Measuring a second peak at more negative potentials presents all the problems encountered with overlapping spectrophotometric absorption bands or chromatographic elution peaks. An empirical extrapolation of the tailing of the first peak is often used; computer-based analysis of such curves is possible.

Separation of adjacent peaks in differential-pulse polarography, where the symmetry of the peak can also be made use of, is usually easier than that of consecutive peaks in linear-sweep voltammetry. As is the case in conventional polarography, more positive peaks that interfere can sometimes be shifted to more negative potentials and the sequence of peaks inverted by change in supporting electrolyte.

In linear-sweep voltammetry and differential-pulse polarography, the problem of an excess of a species reduced at more positive potentials is of considerably smaller consequence than in conventional polarography. When the current peaks of the species present in excess and that of the components to be determined are separated by more than about 0.3 V in the former and about 0.2 V in the latter technique, the presence of the more positive peak has almost no influence.

Applications

Once again, only a few examples are presented from a very large number of actual reported analyses.

Differential-Pulse Stripping Analysis of Water. The water to be analyzed is deaerated and a voltage of -1.2 V is applied to a hanging mercury drop electrode and a platinum counter electrode for 60 sec while the solution is gently stirred by a magnetic stirrer. The stirring must be constant and reproducible. After 60 sec the stirrer is turned off, and after 15 sec the stripping curve is recorded using a differential-pulse technique. The peak for zinc appears at -1.0 V, that for lead at -0.5 V, and that for copper at -0.1 V. Typical concentrations in tapwater might be 2 ppb for Pb and 10–600 ppb for Zn and Cu [2].

This method was devised for tapwater analysis. When lower metal-ion concentrations are to be determined (e.g., in distilled or deionized water) the pre-electrolysis period can be prolonged.

Cu, Pb, Cd, and Zn have been determined in seawater by pulsed stripping analysis. A similar analysis of the metallic content of fish, seaweed, and oysters inhabiting this water indicates that there are biological concentration factors of 10^2 to 10^5 for these trace metals.

Stripping analysis has been used to determine 10^{-9} M Ag levels in rain and snow samples from clouds seeded with AgI. Precisions are about $\pm 20\%$ at the 0.2 nM level, and $\pm 4\%$ at concentrations above 1 nM.

Differential-Pulse Stripping Determination of Lead in Blood. The blood sample (typically 50 μl) is digested with a mixture of sulfuric and perchloric acids, transferred into the electrolytic cell and, after removal of oxygen, preelectrolyzed at -0.7 V for about 5 min using a hanging mercury drop electrode in a stirred solution (the period of deposition chosen depends on the electrode used). The differential-pulse stripping curve shows a peak for lead at -0.4 V. A typical "normal" level of 200–300 ppb of lead in blood will give a large signal, well above background, unless the acids are contaminated [3].

Barbital, Phenobarbital, Pentothal. Barbital can be determined in a borate buffer of pH 9.3 by means of an anodic wave that corresponds to mercury-salt formation. Since the wave height is governed by adsorption at higher concentrations, it is necessary to keep the concentration of barbital below 1×10^{-4} M.

When DC polarography is applied to phenobarbital, the wave is indistinct. However, when differential-pulse polarography is used, easily measurable peaks corresponding to mercury-salt formation are obtained, the total height of which is a linear function of concentration. This procedure has been successfully applied to the determination of phenobarbital in the presence of a number of other drugs in studies of drug metabolism.

Pentothal [ethyl(1-methylbutyl)thiobarbiturate] can be easily determined by simply dissolving the sample in 0.1 M sodium hydroxide and recording the well developed anodic wave.

Linear-Sweep Voltammetry of Tocopherols and Antioxidants in Oils and Fats. Phenolic antioxidants are added to many food products to enhance their stability. In addition, certain foods, particularly vegetable oils, contain significant quantities of natural phenolic materials, the most prominent of which are the various tocopherols (vitamin E group). Linear-sweep voltammetric oxidation of vegetable oils dissolved in 2:1 ethanol/benzene solvent (0.12 M sulfuric acid) is a rapid method for estimating the tocopherol content of oils and fats. (Almost all other methods involve considerable sample preparation, such as saponification and extraction, before chromatographic separation and measurement.) The reproducibility of the voltammetric method is good; for a typical α-tocopherol content of 0.3 mg/g of oil, the standard deviation is ± 0.02 mg/g. Quantitation is achieved by the method of standard additions, and a glassy carbon electrode is used [4].

Differential-Pulse Polarography of Arsenic. The determination of metallic elements by polarographic methods generally faces stiff competition from atomic absorption spectroscopy (Chap. 11), which is often the method of choice. Atomic absorption, however, is comparatively insensitive to arsenic. In acidic media, As(III) gives two well developed polarographic peaks; the first (-0.5 V) is due to its three-electron reduction to As, and the second (-0.8 V) to its further reduction to AsH_3. In 1 M HCl, the detection limit for arsenic determination is about 0.3 ppb (4×10^{-9} M), with a linear current-versus-concentration response up to 60 ppm [5], a linear range of five decades of concentration. The relative standard deviation is about $\pm 16\%$ at 2 ppb and $\pm 2\%$ at 20 ppb. The inorganic ions that interfere seriously are Pb^{2+}, Sn^{2+}, Sn^{4+}, Tl^+, and Tl^{3+}. One interesting aspect of the pulse-polarographic method is that As(V) is polarographically inactive, so that this method can be used to study the oxidation state of arsenic in various samples. Total arsenic can be determined by prior chemical reduction of As(V) with suitable reducing agents such as hydrazine salts or acidic KI. With the possible exception of neutron-activation analysis (Chap. 19), differential-pulse polarography is probably the most sensitive method presently available for arsenic assay.

3.5 AMPEROMETRIC TITRATIONS

A titration in which measurement of the current flowing at a voltammetric indicator electrode is used for detection of the equivalence point is termed an *amperometric titration*. The current measured is almost always a limiting current which is proportional to concentration, and can be due to the substance titrated, to the titrant itself, to a product of the reaction, or to any two of these—depending on the potential of the electrode and the electrochemical characteristics of the chemical substances involved. The titration curve is a plot of the limiting current, corrected for dilution by the reagent and, if necessary, for any residual current, as a function of the volume of titrant. Ideally, the titration curve consists of two linear segments which intersect at the equivalence point.

Amperometric titrations can be classified into two groups: those using one polarized (indicator) electrode plus a reference electrode, and those using two polarized or indicator electrodes.

One Polarized or Indicator Electrode

Many of the principles of amperometric titrations can be understood by considering an example: the titration of Pb^{2+} with standard sodium sulfate solution. Figure 3.19 illustrates the current-versus-voltage curves for lead ion that could be obtained during the course of an amperometric titration, and the resulting amperometric titration. Under the experimental conditions employed, lead ion is reducible, with an $E_{1/2}$ at about -0.4 V, and the sulfate ion is nonreducible. A constant voltage which may have any value on the diffusion-current plateau is applied to the indicator electrode; in this case, -1.0 V is applied to a dropping mercury electrode.

At the start of the titration, a polarogram of the test solution would have the appearance of curve a in Figure 3.19A (after sufficient deaeration to remove the dissolved oxygen). Therefore, the current measured at -1.0 V would have the value i_0. Increments of titrant precipitate $PbSO_4$ and remove some of the Pb^{2+} from solution; since the titrant does not produce a reduction current at the applied voltage, the current decreases with successive additions to i_1, i_2, and so on. When the lead ions have been completely removed from solution, the only current flowing is the residual current, i_R, caused by the supporting electrolyte. A plot of current as a function of titrant volume will have the L-shaped appearance shown in Figure 3.19B.

Normally, there will be some rounding in the vicinity of the equivalence point because of equilibrium effects—the more dilute the solutions employed and the more the position of equilibrium favors the reactants, the more pronounced

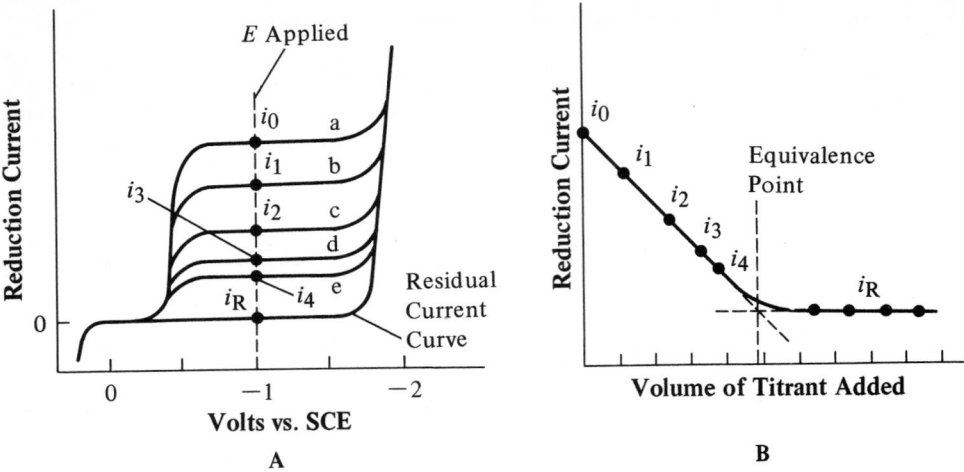

FIGURE 3.19. *Current-versus-voltage curves and amperometric titration curve for the titration of Pb^{2+} with Na_2SO_4 solution. A: Successive current-versus-voltage curves for the reduction of Pb^{2+} ion at a mercury electrode, made after increments of SO_4^{2-} were added. B: The resulting amperometric titration curve for currents ($i_0, i_1, i_2, \ldots$) measured at an applied potential of -1 V versus SCE.*

the rounding. In the example, the finite solubility of $PbSO_4$ will result in some Pb^{2+} ions being still in solution at the equivalence point, and an excess of titrant is necessary to drive the lead-ion concentration to a sufficiently low level that the lead-ion diffusion current is insignificant compared to the residual current.

One advantage of amperometric titrations is that the substance titrated does not have to be electroactive if an appropriate titrant with electrolytic properties is used. For example, sulfate ion can be determined by titration with Pb^{2+}. In this case, an essentially constant residual current flows until there is *excess* titrant in the test solution. After the endpoint a linearly increasing current appears which is proportional to the concentration of the excess titrant. The amperometric titration curve will have a shape the reverse of that shown in Figure 3.19B: ⟋-shaped, or "reverse L-shaped."

When both the substance titrated and the titrant undergo electrochemical reactions at the voltage selected, the current will decrease (linearly) up to the equivalence point, then increase again with addition of excess titrant, resulting in a V-shaped titration curve. An example of this is the titration of Pb^{2+} with potassium dichromate in a weakly acidic supporting electrolyte. Dichromate ion is reduced to Cr^{3+} at the DME with $E_{1/2} \approx 0$ V versus SCE. If -1.0 V is applied to the indicator electrode, both Pb^{2+} and $Cr_2O_7^{2-}$ are reducible, and a V-shaped titration curve will result. If, on the other hand, the applied voltage is -0.2 V, only dichromate ion is reducible, and a reverse L-shaped titration curve results.

In general, the best way to predict the shape of amperometric titration curves is to look at or construct the current-versus-voltage curves of the test solution during the course of the electrolysis.

Two Polarized or Indicator Electrodes

The apparatus used for titrations with one polarized electrode, described above, includes a reference electrode whose potential remains fixed during the course of the titration. A second approach involves applying a small, fixed, potential difference (20–250 mV) across two identical indicator electrodes; this is often called a *bi-amperometric* titration.

Again the principles underlying this type of titration can best be understood by considering an example, in this case the titration of ferrous ion (Fe^{2+}) in acidic medium with standard cerate (Ce^{4+}) solution—two reversible redox couples. Figure 3.20 illustrates the current-versus-voltage curves expected during the titration. At the start (Fig. 3.20A), the only electrochemical processes that occur are the oxidation of Fe^{2+} to Fe^{3+} at about $+0.5$ V and the two background processes—reduction of protons to hydrogen gas and oxidation of water to oxygen. The small, fixed, potential difference (ΔE) applied to the indicator electrodes shifts along the potential axis until it stops at that place on the current-versus-voltage curve where the current due to the reduction taking place at the cathode is equal to the current due to the oxidation taking place at the anode. This is at the voltage where the residual current curve crosses the $i = 0$ axis; and the actual current flowing is very close to zero.

Once some Ce^{4+} is added, Fe^{3+} and Ce^{3+} are generated by the chemical redox reaction, and the current-versus-voltage curves for the test solution now have components reflecting the reduction of Fe^{3+} and oxidation of Ce^{3+}, as shown in Figure 3.20B. The ΔE shifts along the current-versus-voltage curve to the point where the

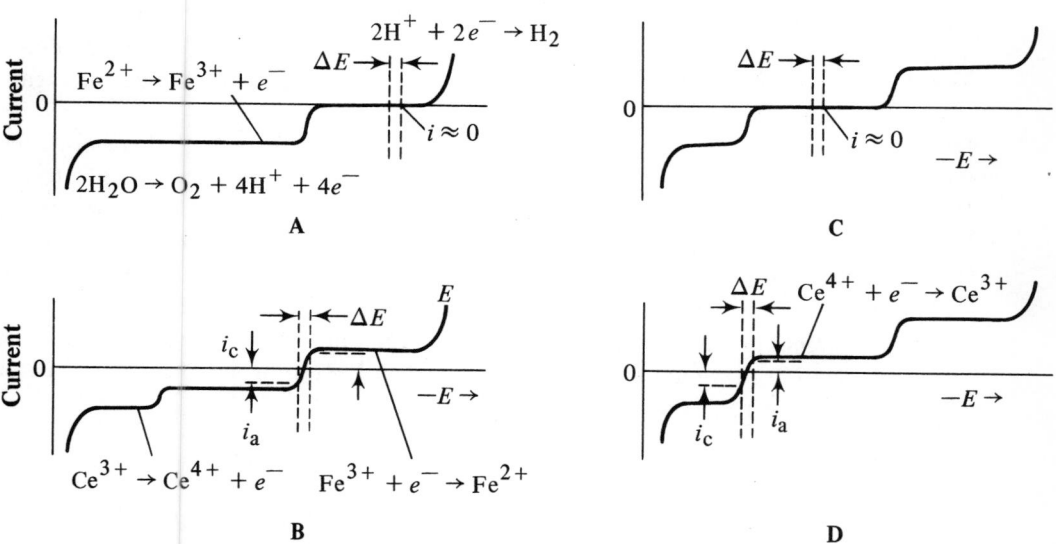

FIGURE 3.20. *Theoretical current-versus-voltage curves at a platinum electrode during an amperometric titration of Fe^{2+} with Ce^{4+} with two polarized or indicator electrodes. ΔE is the constant voltage applied to the two indicator electrodes. A: At the start of the titration. B: At the midpoint of the titration. C: At the equivalence point. D: After the equivalence point.*

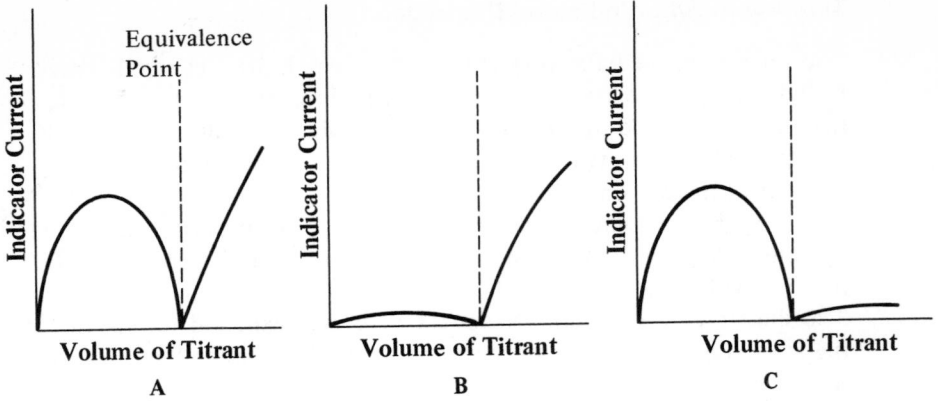

anodic and cathodic indicator currents, i_a and i_c, are equal; they are due to the reversible Fe^{2+}/Fe^{3+} oxidation-reduction couple. Prior to the equivalence point, the indicator current, $i = i_a = i_c$, increases until about halfway to the equivalence point and then decreases back to 0 at the equivalence point—Figure 3.20C—where the current is once again due to only the small residual current. The voltage applied is insufficient to cause appreciable oxidation of Ce^{3+} and reduction of Fe^{3+}. After the equivalence point, there is some excess Ce^{4+} in solution, ΔE shifts to the potential of the reversible Ce^{3+}/Ce^{4+} couple at about $+1.4$ V, and the indicator current again begins to increase.

The shape of the amperometric titration curve in this case, where both the titrant and the substance titrated undergo reversible redox reactions, is illustrated in Figure 3.21A. In the case where the substance titrated does not have a reversible voltammetric wave, the titration curve will have the shape illustrated in Figure 3.21B. Prior to the equivalence point, the applied voltage is too small to cause both oxidation and reduction of the redox couple of the substance titrated. If the titrant has an irreversible wave, the titration curve will look like that in Figure 3.21C. This type of titration is commonly called a "dead-stop" titration, because the indicator current falls to zero at the equivalence point.

Applications of Amperometric Titrations

If the stoichiometry of the titration reaction is known and reproducible, ampero-metric titrations are intrinsically more accurate and precise than direct voltammetric analyses. Precision and accuracy of a few tenths of a percent are commonly attain-able with sufficiently concentrated solutions, about 10^{-4} M or greater. Precision and accuracy are limited primarily by the errors involved in standardizing the titrant and measuring the volume delivered, and by the abruptness of change in indicator current at the equivalence point. High accuracies require, of course, minimization of or correction for any volume change during the titration. The apparatus for amperometric titrations is quite simple, and requires no prior calibration. Their primary disadvantages, as with potentiometric titrations, are the time required to perform a titration as opposed to a single measurement, and the effort involved in the preparation and storage of standard solutions.

There are numerous examples of the application of amperometric titrations in the literature [6, 7]. One popular titrant is the silver ion, in the form of a silver-nitrate solution, coupled with a rotating platinum indicator electrode. Ions such as cyanide, tetraphenylborate, various sulfides, and (singly or mixed) chloride, bromide and iodide can be titrated. For example, anywhere from 8 μM to 0.1 M cyanide in 0.1 M sodium hydroxide can be titrated amperometrically with silver-nitrate solution with good accuracy and precision. Again, the total chlorine in insecticides decomposed with sodium and xylene has been titrated at silver electrodes using biamperometric endpoint detection. A very important application is the determination of sulfhydryl groups, especially in proteins and other natural materials. The method is based on the reaction of silver ion—and some other heavy-metal ions such as Hg^{2+}—with sulfhydryl compounds to form highly undissociated mercaptides. For example, SH groups in cysteine, glutathione, certain proteins, and dialyzed human sera can be determined. Under appropriate conditions, as little as about 10 nmoles of protein can be titrated reproducibly.

Another important amperometric titrant is bromine solution, which undergoes stoichiometric oxidation-reduction reactions with many substances such as As(III), Sb(III), ammonium salts, and others. Often the titration involves adding an excess of KBr to an acidified solution of the substance to be oxidized and then titrating it with potassium bromate solution. Bromine is thereby generated in situ.

$$BrO_3^- + 5Br^- + 6H^+ \rightleftharpoons 3H_2O + 3Br_2 \qquad (3.11)$$

This avoids the problems involved in storing unstable Br_2 solutions. Bromine can be used to titrate a wide variety of oxidizible organic compounds such as phenols, hydrazines, and anilines. The "bromine numbers" of olefinic hydrocarbons—a measure of the total unsaturation present—are often determined by titrating the hydrocarbon with acidified potassium bromate, or by generating Br_2 electrolytically from an acetic-acid/methanol/water solvent containing KBr. Olefinic hydrocarbons generally display no electrochemical properties under the experimental conditions employed; however, at the equivalence point, the presence of a small excess of bromine increases the current through the indicator electrode pair. Chapter 4 discusses a number of other reagents that can be electrolytically generated in situ in order to perform an amperometric titration.

SELECTED BIBLIOGRAPHY

ADAMS, R. N. *Electrochemistry at Solid Electrodes.* New York: Marcel Dekker, 1969.

BARD, A. J., ed. *Electroanalytical Chemistry,* vols. I–VII. New York: Marcel Dekker, 1966–1974.

BREYER, B., and BAUER, H. H. *Alternating Current Polarography and Tensammetry.* New York: John Wiley, 1963.

BREZINA, M., and ZUMAN, P. *Polarography in Medicine, Biochemistry, and Pharmacy.* New York: Interscience, 1958.

HEYROVSKY, J., and KUTA, J. *Principles of*

Polarography. New York: Academic Press, 1965.

KOLTHOFF, I. M., and LINGANE, J. *Polarography*, 2nd ed, vols. I and II. New York: Interscience, 1952.

MEITES, L. *Polarographic Techniques*, 2nd ed. New York: John Wiley, 1965.

SCHMIDT, H., and VON STACKELBERG, M. *Modern Polarographic Methods.* New York: Academic Press, 1963.

SCHMITZ, C. L.; EWEN, E. F.; and DODD, S. P. *Bibliography of Polarographic Literature 1922–1967.* Skokie, Ill.: Sargent-Welch Scientific Co., 1969.

ZUMAN, P. *Organic Polarographic Analysis.* Oxford: Pergamon Press, 1964.

REFERENCES

1. H. H. BAUER, in *Electroanalytical Chemistry*, A. J. Bard, ed., vol. 8, New York: Marcel Dekker, 1965, pp 169–279.

2. H. SIEGERMAN and G. O'DOM, *Amer. Lab.*, 5(6), 48 (1972).

3. Application Note AN-16, Princeton Applied Research Corporation, Princeton, New Jersey, 1972.

4. H. D. MCBRIDE and D. H. EVANS, *Anal. Chem.*, 45, 446 (1973).

5. D. J. MYERS and J. OSTERYOUNG, *Anal. Chem.*, 45, 267 (1973).

6. J. T. STOCK, *Amperometric Titrations*, New York: Interscience Publishers, 1965.

7. J. T. STOCK, *Anal. Chem.*, 48, 1R (1976).

PROBLEMS

1. Brass contains about 65% copper and 30% zinc. Would you suggest polarography as a method for determining the main components? When and why? The alloy contains also 1% or less of lead and cadmium. Is polarography useful for those metals? Explain why or why not.

2. Deionized water contains ppb levels of heavy metals, mostly zinc, copper, and lead. Which method would you suggest for determining these levels? All common chemicals contain metal ions at the same concentration level or greater. How would you choose your supporting electrolyte? (Suggestion: Gases usually do not contain metal ions as impurities.)

3. Reaction of *p*-cyanoacetophenone with hydroxylamine is being investigated. An analytical method is needed to follow concentration changes in *p*-cyanoacetophenone. Assuming that *p*-cyanoacetophenone has not been studied polarographically before, how would you carry out preliminary experiments to elucidate the electrode process? Find a description of the electroreduction in the literature and propose conditions for the kinetic study, keeping in mind that only the unprotonated form of hydroxylamine ($pK_a = 6.0$) reacts.

4. You have to determine: (a) formaldehyde and acetaldehyde in 50 samples of white wine per day; (b) 2,4,6-trinitrotoluene in white powder samples which might be potential material in making bombs—3 to 5 samples per month; (c) copper content in a rare Etruscan vase; (d) a toxic keto compound in an antibiotic, the analysis being done in a production-line quality-control laboratory in a pharmaceutical company. In which cases and why would you use a standard-addition method and when would you use a calibration curve for evaluating current-versus-voltage curves?

5. Explain differences (with the help of the literature) between pulse polarography, differential-pulse polarography, and AC polarography.

6. List advantages and limitations of linear-sweep voltammetry. Suggest examples of when this technique can be used in practical analysis.

7. Why do we speak about "diffusion current"? Describe how you would check equations for diffusion currents. What can cause a difference between theoretical values and experimental data?

8. The *diffusion current constant* I_d is used to correct polarographic diffusion currents for differences in capillary characteristics. For average currents

$$I_d = \frac{i_d}{cm^{2/3}t^{1/6}} = 607nD^{1/2}$$

For a given electroactive substance under a given set of experimental conditions (temperature, supporting electrolyte, potential of the DME, etc.), I_d should actually be a constant according to the Ilkovic equation; it should be independent of the capillary characteristics and reproducible in different laboratories or in the same laboratory with different capillaries. Cadmium ion exhibits a reversible two-electron reduction wave at -0.64 V in 1 M HCl. A 0.50 mM Cd²⁺ solution gave a wave with average $i_d = 3.96$ μA at the $E_{1/2}$; the capillary characteristics were $m = 2.50$ mg/sec, $t = 3.02$ sec. (a) Calculate I_d for Cd²⁺. (b) Calculate the diffusion coefficient for Cd²⁺ in 1 M HCl.

9. A typical value for the mercury flow-rate m for a DME is 2.5 mg/sec and a typical drop-time is 3.0 sec. What is the maximum area of the mercury drop under these conditions?

10. The oxygen content of aqueous solutions can be estimated by simply measuring the height of its polarographic reduction wave, and inserting a known value of the diffusion coefficient D (2.12×10^{-5} cm²/sec) into the Ilkovic equation. A sample of tap water was taken, sufficient solid KCl was added to make a 0.10 M solution, and the solution was analyzed polarographically. The average current for the first two-electron oxygen-reduction wave at $E_{1/2} = -0.05$ V was 1.81 μA. If the capillary used had $m = 2.00$ mg/sec and $t = 5.00$ sec at -0.05 V, what was the oxygen level of the tap water in mM? In ppm?

11. With the experimental system described in problem 8 above, the average residual (charging) current was 0.32 μA at the plateau of the wave due to the reduction of Cd²⁺ ions. Assuming that the limit of detectability corresponds to a diffusion current whose magnitude is one-half of the residual current, what is the lowest concentration of Cd²⁺ that could be detected?

12. It is often said that one can run polarograms many times with the same solution because the amount of material electrolyzed under polarographic conditions is so small. With the system described in problem 8, for how long could one electrolyze at the plateau of the wave before the diffusion current changes by 1%? Assume that the volume of solution in the polarographic cell is 50 ml.

13. In studying the mechanisms of reduction of organic compounds, one vital parameter is the number of electrons transferred per molecule. An estimate of this parameter can be obtained by assuming a value for the diffusion coefficient. (a) For a particular ketone, we wish to decide whether n is 1 or 2. A millimolar solution yields a (maximum) diffusion current of 7.2 μA at a DME with $m = 2$ mg/sec at $t = 5$ sec. A reasonable value for the diffusion coefficient is 5×10^{-6} cm²/sec. What is the value of n? (b) Suggest another way of determining n with the polarograph—a way that does not depend on knowledge of the diffusion coefficient and does not presuppose that the reduction is reversible.

14. The following voltammograms were recorded in a suitable supporting electrolyte at a silver electrode versus the SCE: (a) Solution of silver ion; (b) Solution of chloride ion.

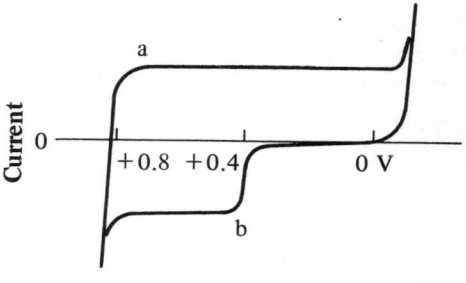

A titration of 10 ml of 0.001 M silver

nitrate with 0.001 M sodium chloride was performed, and the endpoint was detected biamperometrically with two silver-wire electrodes. Sketch the biamperometric titration curve for the titration with (a) an applied potential difference of 100 mV, and (b) with an applied potential difference of 600 mV. Assume no Ag^+ nor Cl^- can be detected in a saturated AgCl solution. (c) Specify the anodic and the cathodic reaction occurring in each segment of the titration curves.

4

Electrogravimetry and Coulometry

Donald G. Davis

In this chapter, we shall consider those electroanalytical methods characterized by the fact that some reaction goes to completion in an electrochemical cell. The amount of the material analyzed is found either by weighing an insoluble compound (usually a metal) deposited on an electrode, or by measuring the number of coulombs necessary to complete the reaction. In the latter type of experiment, use is made of Faraday's law, which states that the quantity of chemical change produced at the electrodes of a cell is directly proportional to the quantity of electricity passed through the cell. To produce one equivalent of chemical change, one *faraday* is required. Very accurate determinations of a variety of substances can be made by these methods because of the relative ease with which electrical quantities (and weights) can be measured. The value of the faraday (96484.56 ± 0.27 coulombs) is known to within about 3 ppm at present; and atomic weights are often known to the same accuracy or better. Many coulometric methods are more time consuming than polarography, direct potentiometry, or other methods, but the high accuracy and precision attainable (often 0.1% or better) may well be worth the extra time and effort.

4.1 ELECTROGRAVIMETRY

The technique of electrogravimetry consists of electroplating a metal (usually) onto a previously weighed electrode, and then reweighing to determine the amount of metal initially present in solution. Sufficient voltage is applied to the electrochemical cell for long enough to remove the metal quantitatively from solution.

Many of the principles involved in electrogravimetry can be illustrated by considering the determination of copper. A simplified version of the apparatus used for electrogravimetry is shown in Figure 4.1. Instruments using 60 Hz line voltage (rectified to DC) rather than batteries and incorporating all components in a single case are commercially available. Before the experiment starts, the platinum gauze is cleaned with nitric acid, rinsed, dried, and carefully weighed. It is then immersed in the copper solution. The potential across the cell is increased until appreciable current flows, as indicated by ammeter A. At this point the copper will start to plate on the cathode and oxygen will be liberated at the anode.

The total voltage, E_{app}, applied across the cell is given by

$$E_{app} = (E_a + \eta_a) - (E_c + \eta_c) + iR \tag{4.1}$$

where

E_a = the reversible anode potential
η_a = the anodic overpotential
E_c = the reversible cathode potential
η_c = the cathodic overpotential
i = the current through the cell
R = the resistance of the cell

The reversible potentials can be calculated from the appropriate Nernst equation. For instance, for copper at 25°C

$$E_c = E^0_{Cu^{2+}, Cu} + \frac{0.059}{2} \log [Cu^{2+}] \tag{4.2}$$

This equation neglects activity coefficients—not a very good approximation under normal experimental conditions—but this is usually compensated for by simply applying a greater voltage than calculated. Equation 4.2 can be used to decide what potential the cathode must attain to eventually reduce the concentration of copper remaining in solution to an acceptable value. For instance, if the initial solution was 10^{-2} M in Cu^{2+} and it was desired to plate 99.9% of the copper, the following calculation would pertain: At the start of the electrolysis the cathode potential would be

$$E_c = 0.34 + \frac{0.059}{2} \log [10^{-2}] = 0.28 \text{ V} \tag{4.3}$$

To achieve the 1 ppt accuracy, the copper concentration must be reduced to 10^{-5} M. Thus,

$$E_c = 0.34 + \frac{0.059}{2} \log [10^{-5}] = 0.19 \text{ V} \tag{4.4}$$

Therefore, a cathode potential of 0.15 V more reducing than E^0 would have to be attained to achieve the required analysis.

The overpotentials (ηs) are composed of two parts. One is termed the *concentration overpotential* and results from the fact that the concentration of, for instance, copper ions *at the electrode surface* is depleted relative to the rest of the solution during the passage of any appreciable current. Efficient stirring helps to keep this term to a minimum, but nevertheless, extra voltage must be applied to compensate. At the anode, concentration overpotential is caused by the accumulation of hydrogen ion as oxygen is evolved.

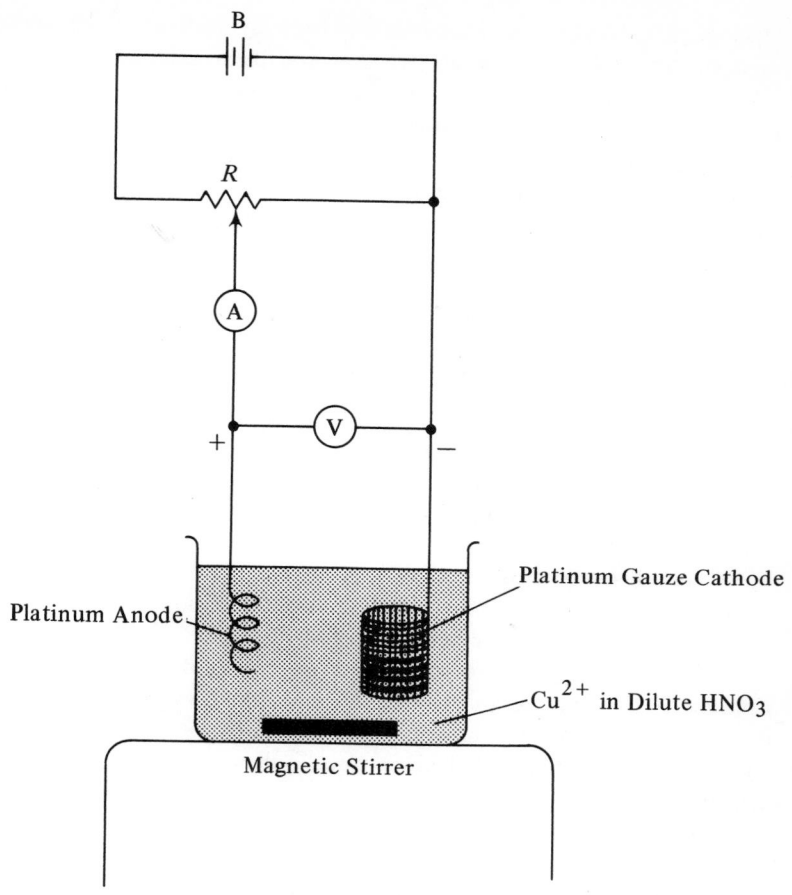

FIGURE 4.1. *Apparatus for electrogravimetry. B is a battery or other source of stable DC voltage, R is a resistor with a sliding contact used to vary the voltage applied to the cell, A is an ammeter that measures the current passing through the cell, and V is a voltmeter which measures the voltage applied to the cell.*

The other part of the overpotential term is the *activation overpotential.* The magnitude of the activation overpotential depends on the inherent rate of the electrode reaction. The activation overpotential is always such that it discourages reactions—that is, it is negative for a reduction. The activation overpotential is characteristic of the reaction under consideration, and is also influenced by the electrode material. For example, the activation overpotential for the generation of hydrogen approaches one volt on mercury, but is negligible on platinum. In our present example, however, the overpotential for O_2 generation on platinum can be as much as 1 V at fairly high current densities.

The last term in Equation 4.1 is the iR drop that develops when a current passes through the cell. The magnitude of this, in volts, is the product of the current in amperes and the resistance in ohms. Most of the iR drop occurs between the electrodes in the cell and can be minimized by adding a high concentration of an inert electrolyte to decrease the resistance of the solution.

It is not possible to calculate all of the terms in Equation 4.1 exactly, so in practice enough voltage is applied to cause considerable current (a few amperes) to flow, and electrolysis is allowed to continue with occasional adjustment of the voltage until deposition is complete. However, it is clear from the discussion that a potential larger than two volts will be required. Completeness can be tested with an appropriate spot test on a small drop of solution, or by lowering the cathode to expose more platinum to the solution and seeing if more metal plates.

Frequently, a "depolarizer" of one sort or another is added that undergoes a particular (neutral) electrode reaction more easily than an unwanted one, thus "preempting" the latter. For instance, the deposition of copper is usually carried out in nitric acid media because nitrate ion is reduced to ammonium ion at a copper surface:

$$NO_3^- + 10H^+ + 8e^- = NH_4^+ + 3H_2O \qquad (4.5)$$

Thus, hydrogen is not evolved as copper is deposited. (Hydrogen evolution should be avoided because it makes the copper deposit spongy and of poor quality.) Also, metals more difficult to reduce, such as nickel, cannot deposit along with the copper because of the excess nitric acid.

Again, difficulties sometimes arise in chloride media because chlorine is generated at the anode and some platinum may dissolve. Both cause difficulties at the cathode, the first by reoxidizing copper and the second by depositing platinum; so hydrazine is often added as an anodic depolarizer since it is easily oxidized to nitrogen:

$$N_2H_4 \longrightarrow N_2 + 4H^+ + 4e^- \qquad (4.6)$$

In any case, once the deposition is complete the cathode is removed from solution *with the voltage still on* and washed at the same time. It is important that the voltage not be turned off before the electrode is removed from solution, because the spontaneous cell reaction is the reverse of what we have forced to occur by applying an appropriate potential. In the copper example, the *electrolytic cell* reaction is

$$Cu^{2+} + H_2O \longrightarrow Cu + 1/2\,O_2 + 2H^+ \qquad (4.7)$$

But if we look at the relative potentials of the two half-reactions involved ($Cu^{2+} + 2e^- = Cu$ at the cathode and $1/2\,O_2 + 2H^+ + 2e^- = H_2O$ at the anode), we note that Cu is a better reducing agent than H_2O; or conversely, O_2 is a better oxidizing agent than Cu^{2+}. In other words, in a *galvanic cell* (battery), the above reaction (4.7) will spontaneously go in the opposite direction. We make it go as written by supplying the appropriate energy or back emf, plus overvoltages and iR drop, as calculated from Equation 4.1.

Washing is usually accomplished by directing a gentle stream of distilled water from a wash bottle over the electrode as it is being removed from the solution. The electrode may then be dipped in alcohol (to speed drying), dried for a short time in a drying oven, cooled, and weighed. The drying time should be short in order to minimize oxide formation. Hopefully, the deposit will not flake off in the process.

The probability of obtaining good deposits is enhanced by efficient stirring, low current-density, and proper depolarizers. For some determinations (e.g., silver), adding complexing agents such as cyanide will improve the deposit, as will adding small amounts of surface-active agents.

Electrogravimetric procedures have been devised for a large number of elements. Relatively noble metals such as copper and silver are frequently determined this way since there are few interferences. The more electronegative metals like cadmium, cobalt, iron, nickel, tin, and zinc can be electrodeposited from alkaline solutions. Under these conditions the potential for hydrogen evolution is more negative because of the decreased hydrogen ion concentration. Often, complexing agents such as ammonia or cyanide are added to prevent the metal hydroxide from precipitating and to improve the nature of the deposit. Lead is often determined at the anode in nitric acid solution as PbO_2. This can be done simultaneously with the cathodic deposition of copper. Procedures exist for most common metals and a number of nonmetals [1]. Mixtures of metals can sometimes be analyzed by changing solution conditions, but most mixtures are better handled by controlled-potential electrolysis.

4.2 ELECTROLYSIS AT CONTROLLED POTENTIAL

In order to achieve separation of metals, or to assure that one and only one electrode reaction occurs, it is usually necessary to maintain the potential of the cathode (or anode) working electrode at some prescribed value. Thus, if copper is to be determined gravimetrically in the presence of tin, the cathode potential must be held at a value reducing enough to deposit copper but not reducing enough to plate out tin. In addition to gravimetric determinations of this type, controlled-potential electrolysis can be effectively used for coulometric determinations (Sec. 4.4), for separating easily reduced metals from ones reduced with more difficulty, and in synthesizing organic and inorganic chemicals. In the last case, side reactions may be avoided by careful potential control.

Figure 4.2 shows the main features of apparatus for controlled-potential electrolysis. The potential of the working electrode (cathode in the case shown) is measured versus a reference electrode, such as a saturated calomel electrode, by a potential-measuring device. The desired potential, found by calculation (Equations 4.3 and 4.4) can be set on the potentiostat. If the cathode potential varies from the desired one, a mechanical or electronic linkage is activated that causes more or less voltage to be applied to the cell by the voltage source. In its simplest form, the potential-measuring device is a pH meter, the linkage a human being, and the voltage source a variable power-supply. Because many adjustments are necessary over a period of time because of changes in concentration and iR-drop as the electrolysis proceeds, the job is tedious. Thus, amplifier-servomotor combinations and, finally, completely electronic devices were designed. Potentiostats, as these instruments are called, are now often based on operational amplifiers and resemble the three-electrode polarograph (see Chap. 3), except that a certain potential is set and maintained throughout the experiment. Potentiostats are now available that can control an electrode potential to ± 1 mV or better, which is sufficient for most analytical

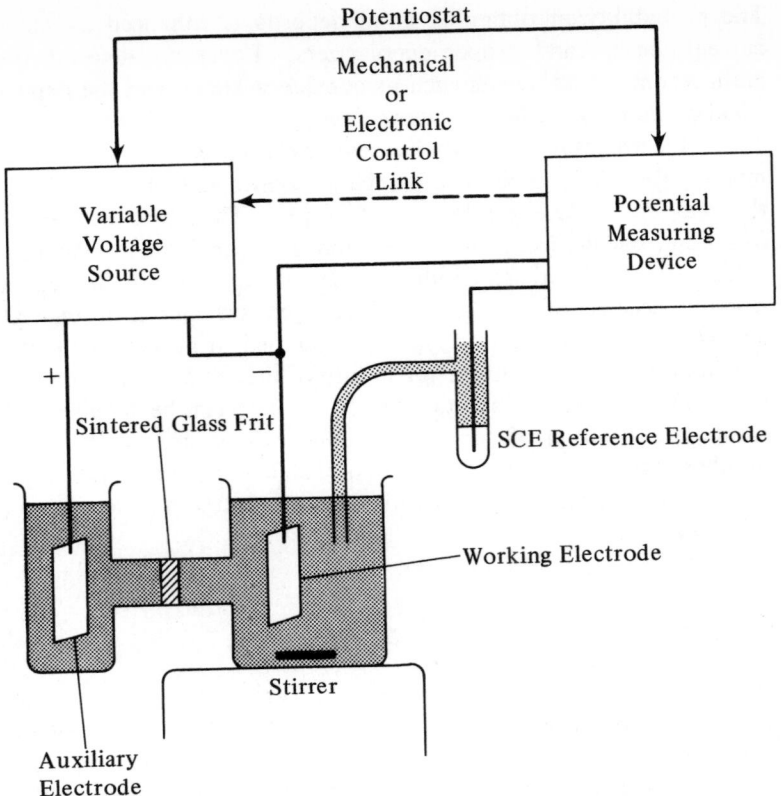

Potentiostat

Mechanical
or
Electronic
Control
Link

Variable
Voltage
Source

Potential
Measuring
Device

+

−

Sintered Glass Frit

SCE Reference Electrode

Working Electrode

Stirrer

Auxiliary
Electrode

FIGURE 4.2. *Basic apparatus for controlled-potential electrolysis.*

purposes. Some of these are designed with very short rise times (a few nanoseconds) for kinetic studies, and some have current capacities up to 25 A for preparative-scale experiments.

The potential at which the electrode is energized is often selected by examining a voltammogram of the sample solution, made using an electrode of the material to be used for the controlled-potential electrolysis—a rotating platinum electrode if platinum is to be used, or a dropping mercury electrode if a mercury-pool cathode* is to be used. The desired potential is usually set just at the top of the limiting-current plateau. Here the reaction will be relatively rapid and complete, but a minimum danger of plating other metals will be encountered.

In the simplest case, the current flowing during a controlled-potential electrolysis is limited by the amount of the reducible species arriving at the electrode, and is proportional to its concentration; both the concentration and the current will decrease exponentially as the electrolysis proceeds [2]:

$$\frac{c_t}{c_0} = \frac{i_t}{i_0} = e^{-(DA/V\delta)t} = 10^{-0.43(DA/V\delta)t} \qquad (4.8)$$

---

* Because of the large hydrogen overvoltage on mercury, mercury-pool cathodes are especially useful for electrodeposition of metals that are difficult to reduce. They are not used for gravimetry, however, owing to their high weight and liquid form.

where c_t = concentration at time t
$\qquad$ i_t = current at time t
$\qquad$ c_0 = the concentration at time zero (the start of the electrolysis)
$\qquad$ i_0 = the current at time zero
$\qquad$ V = the volume of the solution

The diffusion-layer thickness, δ, depends primarily on the rate of stirring. Usually, Equation 4.8 is written more simply as

$$\frac{c_t}{c_0} = e^{-kt} \qquad k = \frac{mA}{V} \tag{4.9}$$

where m = a *mass-transfer coefficient* equal to D/δ

In this form, it is obvious that the expression is simply that for a first-order chemical reaction.

Equation 4.8 indicates that, provided the electrode reaction is mass-transfer limited and uncomplicated by coupled chemical reactions, the electrolysis time may be reduced by making the electrode large and the volume small, and by stirring the solution as fast as possible to decrease the diffusion-layer thickness. In a well designed cell it is possible to carry an electrolysis to 99.9% completion in about 10 to 20 min, although times down to 1 min can be achieved by proper cell design.

In cases where a metal plated on a platinum cathode is to be quantitatively determined by weighing, the deposit may not adhere well to the cathode because of the high initial current-densities. Hence, it may be desirable to begin the electrolysis at a potential less negative than that required to reach the limiting-current plateau. The potential is later shifted to a more negative value to complete the electrolysis.

4.3 ELECTROLYTIC SEPARATIONS

Controlled-potential electrolysis can at times be useful for separating large amounts of easily reduced metals from small amounts of less easily reduced materials. This method has the advantage over precipitation in that, with adequate potential control, no coprecipitation occurs and no extraneous reagents need to be added to the solution. For example, it is possible to remove copper from solutions of copper alloys using a platinum cathode, leaving behind tin, lead, nickel, and zinc. Bismuth and antimony will be removed with the copper at a controlled potential of -0.35 V versus SCE from hydrochloric-acid solution. The minor elements can now be subjected to polarographic analysis, which would have failed before because of the large current from copper reduction preceding the smaller currents from the metals of interest. Mercury cathodes can also be successfully applied to a variety of separations. In one application, copper, lead, and cadmium have been concentrated from uranium solutions into a mercury electrode. The mercury is subsequently distilled, leaving behind the concentrated metals.

Controlled-potential electrolysis at a mercury-pool cathode to remove traces of metallic impurities is useful in preparing very pure electrolytes for use in polarography or for such applications as the "total" removal of heavy-metal ions from

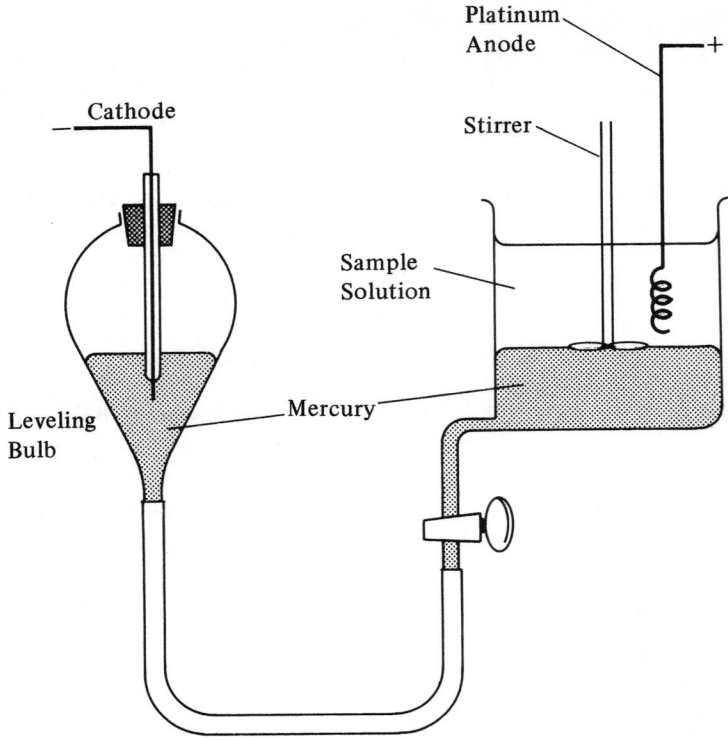

FIGURE 4.3. *Apparatus for electrolysis at a mercury-pool cathode.*

solutions to be used in enzyme work (even traces of certain metal ions will deactivate some enzymes). The apparatus shown in Figure 4.3 is suitable for accomplishing this. Furthermore, there are several commercially available units designed specifically for the purification of electrolyte solutions.

4.4 CONTROLLED-POTENTIAL COULOMETRY

Faraday's law of electrolysis states that a given amount of chemical change caused by electrolysis is directly proportional to the amount of electricity passed through the cell:

$$w = \frac{QM}{nF} \tag{4.10}$$

where w = the weight of substance oxidized or reduced
   M = the formula weight of the substance
   Q = the number of coulombs passing through the cell

This law may be applied to the quantitative analysis of a variety of substances, provided conditions are such that the reaction proceeds with 100% current efficiency (no side reactions). One approach to 100% current efficiency is to hold the potential of the working electrode at such a value that only one reaction will occur, as can be done with the apparatus shown in Figure 4.2. The auxiliary electrode must be isolated for 100% current efficiency, otherwise its electrolysis products will migrate to the working electrode and be electrolyzed. This done, a way of measuring Q is all that is needed. Actually the integral $\int idt$, where i is the current at any instant and t is the time in seconds, is what is generally measured. The integration can be done graphically by measuring the area under a current-versus-time curve recorded on a strip-chart recorder that monitors the current passing through the cell. However, various electrochemical, mechanical, or electronic integrators are usually used.

Coulometers

Some of the first methods of measuring quantities of electricity involved the use of chemical coulometers. To do this, an electrolytic cell is placed in series with the sample electrolysis cell so that the same current passes through both. A typical coulometer cell consists of a platinum crucible containing a silver-nitrate solution and a silver anode. Silver metal is deposited on the preweighed platinum crucible and the latter reweighed to determine the amount of electricity passed; Q is calculated from Equation 4.10.

Another, more convenient, coulometer is the hydrogen-oxygen coulometer, which consists of a gas burette into the bottom of which are sealed two platinum electrodes. The burette is initially filled with an electrolyte solution. Again, this device is connected in series with the cell of interest. The volume of the gas mixture generated by the passage of current is measured, and after correcting this figure for temperature, pressure, and the partial pressure of water vapor, the quantity of electricity passed may be calculated (see Prob. 6). Accuracies of 0.1% have been obtained with this device. For best results, the electrolyte must be presaturated with hydrogen and oxygen. Oxidizable and reducible impurities may cause considerable errors.

A similar gas coulometer that uses hydrazine sulfate as an electrolyte is more accurate at low currents. In this case the hydrazine is oxidized to nitrogen at the anode (see Eqn. 4.6) so the gas mixture consists of nitrogen and hydrogen.

Several electromechanical integrators have been described. The ball-and-disk integrator, often attached to recorders on gas chromatographs, can be used; but the accuracy of these devices is about 1%, which is not really good enough for most electrochemical work. A fixed-field DC motor attached to a counter can be used as an integrator, since the speed of such motors is proportional to the voltage applied to the armature. The current to be integrated is passed through a resistor and the iR drop across this resistor is applied to the motor terminals. If compensated for electrical and mechanical losses, these motor integrators are capable of 0.1% accuracy over a 200 to 1 range [3].

In most present-day work, integrations are performed electronically. One of the best electronic integrators makes use of an operational amplifier fitted with a feedback capacitor. Another popular type of electronic integrator is a voltage-to-frequency converter, which measures the voltage drop across a standard resistor and feeds the output to a scaler, from which the current-time integral is obtained as a number of counts. Electronic integrators can be extremely accurate (to $\pm 0.01\%$) and can measure even very small amounts of charge.

Applications

Controlled-potential coulometry may be applied to the analysis of a wide variety of substances. Clearly, metals like copper could be deposited and determined without the necessity of weighing the electrode. More importantly, mercury electrodes can be used and thus most of the metals more difficult to reduce can be determined. Also, it is possible to apply coulometry to systems in which both oxidized and reduced forms are soluble, such as determining iron by reducing iron(III) to iron(II). Anions such as chloride or bromide may be converted to AgCl or AgBr by deposition on a silver anode.

Controlled-potential coulometric analysis is most often used to determine quantities from about 10 meq to about 1 μeq. The detection limit for coulometry using electronic integrators is about 0.1 μeq under normal conditions, which corresponds to the passage of about 10 μA for 15 min. This lower limit depends primarily on the precision with which the steady, final, background current can be subtracted from the total current flowing during the electrolysis. A special case occurs in surface or "stripping" analysis—for example, in determining the thickness of a metal plating on a conductive substrate. In this case, the absolute lower detection limit is of the order of about 10 μA-sec, which is as little as a few nanograms of material. Here, the limit is determined primarily by the precision with which the quantity of electricity consumed in charging the electrical double-layer can be measured.

Controlled-potential coulometry has also found some use in the study of basic electrochemistry. It is not always obvious how many electrons are involved in a newly studied electrochemical reaction, e.g., in polarography. Thus, coulometry at controlled potential, in which a known quantity of the substance is electrolyzed and Q is measured, is often used to determine values for n and thereby help elucidate electrode mechanisms for a wide variety of compounds, both organic and inorganic. Very slow chemical reactions coupled with the electrochemical reaction may also be studied by controlled-potential coulometry [4]; other electrochemical techniques usually are suitable only for much faster chemical reactions, with time scales of μsec to sec.

4.5 COULOMETRIC TITRATIONS

Coulometric titrations make use of an electrically generated titrant rather than a previously standardized solution. Usually, though not always, the reagent is generated by passing a known and constant current through a cell containing the unknown and an appropriate generating electrolyte. Since the current is constant, the number of coulombs passed can be measured by carefully measuring the length of time that the current flows (the time of generation required to reach the endpoint of the titration). Both current and time can be measured easily and accurately, so this approach has a distinct advantage over the integrators described in the previous section.

Suppose it is desired to titrate ceric ion with ferrous ion according to the reaction

$$Ce^{4+} + Fe^{2+} = Ce^{3+} + Fe^{3+} \tag{4.11}$$

by coulometric titration. This can be done in an electrochemical cell using a platinum cathode as a generator electrode, and an isolated anode. The original solution consists of the Ce^{4+} sample and 0.6 M ferric ammonium sulfate in 2 M sulfuric acid. If a current-versus-potential curve of this solution were taken (analogous to a polarogram but using the platinum generator electrode and a stirred solution instead of a DME), the solid curve in Figure 4.4 would result. The first plateau (A) is the limiting current for the reduction of Ce^{4+} to Ce^{3+} and the second plateau (B) is the limiting current for the reduction of Fe^{3+} to Fe^{2+}. Beyond this plateau, the current rises again owing to the production of hydrogen gas.

FIGURE 4.4. *Current-versus-potential working curves for the coulometric titration of ferrous ion with cerate.*

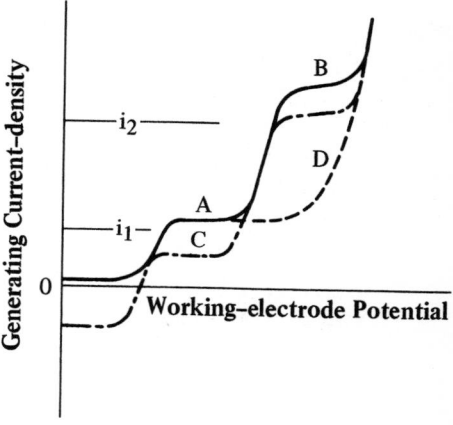

Exactly what happens in the cell depends on the magnitude of the constant current selected. Suppose that current at level i_1 was chosen. When the current is first turned on, all of the current would go to the reduction of Ce^{4+} to Ce^{3+}. As this reaction lowers the concentration of Ce^{4+}, the limiting current also goes down, eventually to the point where it is less than i_1. When this occurs, the current-versus-potential curve looks like curve C. Now part of the current i_1 must be used for another reaction, since not enough Ce^{4+} remains in solution to carry this amount of current. In other words, the potential of the generating electrode shifts to a more reducing value. This is analogous to what happens in controlled-current electrogravimetry as the electrolysis proceeds, and is one of the primary reasons a depolarizer is added in electrogravimetry to prevent the potential from shifting to a point at which undesired reactions may occur, such as deposition of another metal.

The next most easily reduced material is Fe^{3+}, which is reduced to Fe^{2+}. The Fe^{2+} is stirred out into the bulk of the solution where it reacts with the remaining Ce^{4+}. If a higher current (i_2) were originally selected, then the current divides from the beginning between the reduction of Ce^{4+} and Fe^{3+}. The net result is the same, however, since all of the Ce^{4+} eventually is reduced, either directly at the electrode or indirectly by Fe^{2+}. If the ferric ammonium sulfate were not added, the current-versus-potential curve would have the original plateau (A) but then would follow the dashed curve D. In this case, either at the start of the titration (level i_2), or sometime during the titration (level i_1), hydrogen would be produced and be lost from solution. Under these conditions the titration efficiency would be less than

100% and the results would be greatly in error; the error would be positive since current would have to be passed for a longer period of time to reduce all the Ce^{4+}.

It is obvious from the above discussion and Figure 4.4 that there will be a limiting current-density which must be exceeded for 100% current efficiency. Although it will vary from case to case (and should be checked empirically), the current density as a rule of thumb should not exceed about 0.05 mA/(cm²-mN). For example, with an electrode area of 2 cm² and a 0.1 N concentration of generating electrolyte (100 mN), the current should not exceed 10 mA. A high concentration of generating electrolyte is generally used to increase the current-density range. Obviously, the current can also be increased if the electrode area is increased. For the generation of acids and bases from electrolysis of water, a very large current density can theoretically be used, since essentially an infinite supply of water is available.

A major contribution to decreased current efficiency is the presence of electroactive impurities in the sample. This can be a particular problem with acid-base titrations. In such cases, it may be necessary to generate the titrant *externally* (in the absence of sample), and then add it to the sample in increments. A suitable arrangement is illustrated in Figure 4.5. By the use of stopcocks the titrant can be generated and flushed into the cell in increments.

FIGURE 4.5. *Apparatus for the external generation of titrant for coulometric titrations.*

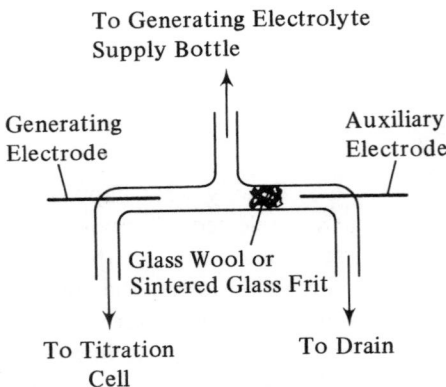

The apparatus for coulometric titrations is shown in Figure 4.6. The counter electrode is isolated in a tube terminating with a sintered glass disk to prevent products from this electrode from reacting with components of the sample solution. Provision is often made for removing air with a stream of nitrogen, if oxygen-sensitive reagents are to be generated.

The constant-current supply could be high-voltage batteries connected through a large resistance or, more likely, an electronic device. Various types of the latter are available from a number of manufacturers. Typical generating currents might be in the range of 1–200 mA. The current supply includes an on-off switch or push button which may be manipulated by the operator in an analogous way to a burette stopcock. Current supplies also have counters or timers that run only when the current is turned on. Currents are usually known to 0.1% or better and time is measured to the nearest 0.1 sec. Therefore, four-significant-figure accuracy is achieved if titrations exceed 100 seconds; this is for typical microequivalent samples.

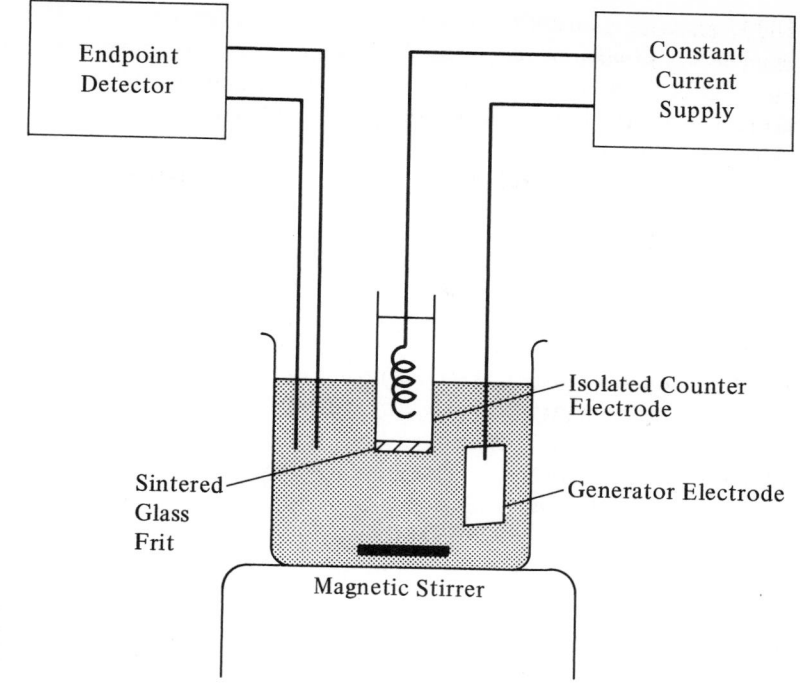

FIGURE 4.6. *Coulometric titration apparatus.*

Commercially available instruments usually read directly in microequivalents. This is accomplished by setting the current in some multiple of the Faraday constant so that the microequivalents are simply equal to some decimal fraction or multiple of the seconds of generation (see Prob. 4).

Suppose the solution of unknown Ce^{4+} was coulometrically titrated with a constant current of 75.00 mA and required 650.0 sec to complete. Then,

$$650.0 \text{ sec} \times 75.00 \text{ mA} = 48{,}750 \text{ millicoulombs}$$
$$\text{or } 48.75 \text{ coulombs}$$

were used. From Faraday's law it is known that there are 96,485 coulombs per equivalent and it is also known that the cerium underwent a one-electron change. Thus

$$\frac{48.75 \text{ coulombs}}{96{,}485 \text{ coulombs/mole}} \times 140.12 \text{ g/mole} = 0.07080 \text{ g}$$

of Ce were present in the original sample.

Naturally, some means of detecting the endpoint of the titration must be available. Indicators can be used (although their sensitivity is not good at the low levels usually investigated), as well as essentially any other method available for regular titrations. Potentiometry (Chap. 2) or amperometry with two similar electrodes is often used because of increased sensitivity over visual indicators.

Table 4.1 lists a number of titrants that have been successfully used, along with the appropriate electrodes and generating solutions. It should be noted that

TABLE 4.1. *Methods for Coulometric Generation of Titrant*

Substance Generated	Typical Solution Conditions	Working Electrode	Typical Substances Titrated
Br_2	0.1 M H_2SO_4 0.2 M NaBr	Pt	Sb(III), I^-, Tl(I), U(IV), various organic compounds
I_2	0.1 M KI 0.1 M phosphate buffer pH = 8	Pt	As(III), Sb(III), $S_2O_3^{2-}$, S^{2-}
Cl_2	2 M HCl	Pt	I^-, As(III), fatty acids
Ce(IV)	0.1 M cerous sulfate 1.5 M H_2SO_4	Pt	Fe(II), $Fe(CN)_6^{4-}$
Mn(III)	0.45 M $MnSO_4$ 1.8 M H_2SO_4	Pt	Oxalic acid, Fe(II), As(III)
Ag(II)	0.1 M $AgNO_3$ 5 M HNO_3	Au	As(III), V(IV), Ce(III), oxalic acid
$Fe(CN)_6^{4-}$	0.2 M potassium ferricyanide pH = 2	Pt	Zn(II)
Cu(I)	0.02 M $CuSO_4$	Pt	Cr(VI), V(V), IO_3^-
Fe(II)	0.6 M ferric ammonium sulfate 2 M H_2SO_4	Pt	Cr(VI), V(V), MnO_4^-
Ti(III)	0.6 M titanic sulfate 6 M H_2SO_4	Pt (Hg also used)	Fe(III), V, U(VI), Ce(IV)
Ag(I)	0.5 M $HClO_4$	Ag anode	Cl^-, Br^-, I^-
EDTA (Y^{4-})	0.02 M $HgNH_3Y^{2-}$ 0.1 M NH_4NO_3 pH = 8.3; O_2 removed	Hg	Ca(II), Zn(II), Pb(II), etc.
H^+ or OH^-	Various electrolytes	Pt	OH^- or H^+ Organic acids or bases

certain unstable titrants such as Br_2, Cl_2, and Ag(II) can be generated with 100% current efficiency, even though standard solutions of these compounds cannot be made. This is one of the important advantages of coulometric titrations, and results from the fact that the titrant reacts with the sample as it is formed.

Under proper conditions, coulometric titrations can be performed with typical accuracies of 0.1% or better, even with small quantities of compounds. (Work in the microgram range may, however, have errors on the order of 1%.) If special precautions are taken, accuracies can be obtained that are difficult to achieve by any other method. Taylor and coworkers, for example, have titrated milligram quantities of substances with precisions of 0.005% or better [5, 6]. For these titrations, series resistors in a constant-temperature oil bath are used to control and measure the current from a 48 V storage battery; the oil bath dissipates heat and thus stabilizes the resistance. The current is determined by measuring the iR drop across a precision resistor with a very sensitive potentiometer and comparing it with a standard Weston cell maintained at 1.017875 V $\pm$ 0.8 μV by careful thermostatic control. The titration time is measured with a quartz-crystal-controlled time-interval meter capable of an accuracy of 1 ppm. The meter is compared with NBS standard time signals to check its performance.

One difficulty often encountered, especially with small amounts of sample, is the effect of impurities in the supporting electrolyte. Even small percentages of impurities in the relatively large concentrations of electrolytes used may cause spurious results. These must be corrected for by performing a blank titration on a separate aliquot of the generating solution. Another way of circumventing this problem is by a pretitration during which reagent is generated until the endpoint potential, current, or whatever, has been reached or exceeded. The sample is then added and reagent generated until the endpoint detection device is in the same state as when the sample was added.

Assuming impurities can be satisfactorily pretitrated, the lower limit of the amount of sample that can be titrated is governed primarily by the sensitivity of the available endpoint detection system. Very small currents, such as 0.1 μA, can be measured accurately (actually, currents smaller than 60 electrons per second have been measured!) and the time of electrogeneration can be measured accurately. With conventional amperometric and potentiometric endpoint indication, coulometric titrations in typical solution volumes cannot be accurately made at generating currents of less than about 100 μA.

A few highly sensitive endpoint detection systems have been described. A zero-current potentiometric method using an extremely sensitive galvanometer allows the titration of 3 ng of manganese as permanganate (2.5×10^{-10} eq) with electrogenerated iron(II) in a volume of 7 ml [7]; actually, the measurement is done in an amperometric mode by setting the endpoint potential and generating titrant until the off-null galvanometer returns to zero current. The error is only 9%. A constant-current potentiometric method has been used to titrate as little as 0.8 ng of bromide in a volume of 0.5 ml (20 nM) with silver ion electrogenerated at 0.1 μA [8]; sub-micromole quantities of acids have also been titrated with precisions of $\pm 2\%$ [9]. An indirect procedure for amperometric [10] and biamperometric [11] titration using a very sensitive current-recorder has been used to titrate as little as 9 ng of arsenic(III) (0.24 neq) in a volume of 35 ml with generated bromine. A sufficient excess of bromine is electrogenerated, the sample is then added and the decrease in the detector current is measured. The "titration time" is calculated to the nearest 0.01 sec from the slope of the detector current-versus-time curve. An accuracy of better than 4% is obtained.

Coulometric titrations are easily automated—more easily, in fact, than titrations using a standard solution. This is because the addition of titrant (in effect, the electron) is so easily controlled and its rate of addition is so constant. Generally, the endpoint potential or current of the indicating electrode activates a relay which shuts off the generating current and timer at the end of the titration.

Also, there are a number of continuous coulometric analyzers that record the current magnitude required to maintain a constant solution composition while a chemical reaction removing the electrogenerated reagent is occurring. For instance, chlorinated hydrocarbons can be detected coming off a gas chromatography column (see Chap. 22) with a coulometric detector which generates Ag^+. The chlorinated compounds are burnt in a small furnace at the end of the gas chromatography column, producing HCl among the products. The HCl is carried into an electrolytic cell where it precipitates as AgCl. A potentiometric indicator electrode senses the loss of Ag^+ and causes more to be generated. The generating current is proportional to the amount of silver that has reacted, and its magnitude is recorded as a function of time to give the characteristic chromatographic peaks.

This general approach, which requires the combustion of the sample and the introduction of its gaseous products into a microcoulometric cell, has now been applied to the analysis of nitrogen, halogens, sulfur, carbon, hydrogen, phosphorus, and water. These determinations may or may not involve previous gas chromatographic separation. Sulfur is converted to H_2S which precipitates Ag_2S, while phosphorus gives PH_3 which reacts with silver to give Ag_2PH. Nitrogen-containing compounds are determined by passing them over a nickel catalyst to convert the nitrogen to NH_3, which is absorbed in an acid solution and titrated with coulometrically generated H^+ at a platinum anode. Sulfur can be determined in the presence of halides by burning it in oxygen, producing SO_2 which is absorbed in an iodine solution and titrated with electrogenerated iodine.

A wide variety of samples can be handled, including petroleum, minerals, and air and water (pollution analysis). Amounts of materials approaching the nanogram range can be handled, although, of course, the accuracy drops into the percent range rather than the ppt range usual for coulometric work.

Coulometers for this type of work typically cost about $3000, which is roughly the price of a good potentiostat and integrator. Sampling systems, however, may double the price. These costs may be contrasted with the few hundred dollars needed for a constant-current supply for simple coulometric titrations (although some sort of endpoint detecting device is also usually needed).

One final advantage not yet mentioned is that coulometry is an *absolute* technique needing no calibration with standard solutions—the electron is the standard. This minimizes error and eliminates the preparation and storage—and problems—of standard solutions; in fact, the electron has been proposed as a permanent, nondestructible standard for the analysis of materials.

All in all, with their simplicity, accuracy, relative low cost, and wide applicability, coulometric techniques deserve serious consideration by the analyst.

SELECTED BIBLIOGRAPHY

DAVIS, D. G. *Anal. Chem.*, *44*(5), 79R (1972); *46*(5), 21R (1974).

LINGANE, J. J. *Electroanalytical Chemistry*, 2nd ed. New York: Wiley-Interscience, 1958.

MILNER, G. W. C. *Coulometry in Analytical Chemistry*. Oxford: Pergamon Press, 1967.

RECHNITZ, G. A. *Controlled Potential Analysis*. Oxford: Pergamon Press, 1963.

REFERENCES

1. J. A. PAGE, in *Handbook of Analytical Chemistry*, L. Meites, ed., New York: McGraw-Hill Book Co., 1963, pp 5–170 to 5–186.

2. J. J. LINGANE, *Electroanalytical Chemistry*, 2nd ed., New York: Wiley-Interscience, 1958, pp 222–28.

3. J. J. LINGANE, *Anal. Chim. Acta*, **44**, 199 (1969).

4. A. J. BARD and K. S. V. SANTHANAM, in *Electroanalytical Chemistry*, A. J. Bard, ed., vol. 4, New York: Marcel Dekker, Inc., 1970, pp 215–315.

5. J. K. TAYLOR and S. W. SMITH, *J. Res. Natl. Bur. Stand.*, **63A**, 153 (1959).

6. G. MARIENKO and J. K. TAYLOR, *J. Res. Natl. Bur. Stand.*, **67A**, 31 (1963).

7. W. D. COOKE, C. N. REILLEY, and N. H. FURMAN, *Anal. Chem.*, **24**, 205 (1952).

8. E. BISHOP and R. G. DHANESHWAR, *Anal. Chem.*, **36**, 726 (1964).

9. E. BISHOP and G. D. SHORT, *Analyst*, **89**, 587 (1964).

10. G. D. CHRISTIAN and F. D. FELDMAN, *Anal. Chim. Acta*, **34**, 115 (1966).

11. G. D. CHRISTIAN, *Microchem. J.*, **9**, 484 (1964).

PROBLEMS

1. In order to deposit 99.99% of a 10^{-2} M lead solution as PbO_2, what would be the required anode potential, neglecting overvoltage?

2. A sample (100 ml) of a 1.00×10^{-3} M solution of lead ion is electrolyzed at a mercury cathode of 5.0 cm^2 at a potential of -0.68 V versus SCE. The solution is also 0.1 M in $HClO_4$. Stirring is such that the diffusion layer is 0.02 mm thick. The diffusion coefficient of lead is about 1×10^{-5} cm^2/sec. Plot the current-versus-time curve for this electrolysis and calculate the time necessary to reduce the lead concentration to 0.1% of its original value.

3. The iron in a 0.1000 g sample was converted to Fe^{3+} and titrated coulometrically with electrogenerated titanous ion (Ti^{3+}). A current of 1.567 mA was used and the time to reach the endpoint was found to be 123.0 seconds. Calculate the percentage of iron in the sample.

4. In constant-current coulometry, what current would be required so that the time in seconds would be equal to the number of microequivalents?

5. An air sample, polluted with SO_2, is passed through a continuous coulometric cell which automatically maintains a small concentration of I_2 by electrogenerating it from acidic potassium iodide. The SO_2 is oxidized to SO_3 by the iodine. If the air sample flow rate is 5 l/min, and the coulometer averaged an output of 1.40 mA to maintain the I_2 concentration for 10 min, what is the concentration of SO_2 in ppm? The density of air may be taken as 1.2 g/l.

6. A constant-potential coulometric determination of copper is being done using a mercury-pool cathode and a water coulometer. A volume of 32.14 ml of hydrogen-oxygen mixture is obtained. The temperature of the gas is 24.0°C and the barometric pressure in the room is 752.0 mm of mercury. The water vapor pressure above the 0.1 M sodium sulfate solution in the coulometer is as follows:

T (°C)	P_{H_2O}, mm Hg
20	17.5
21	18.6
22	19.2
23	21.0
24	22.3
25	23.7

Using the experimental value of 0.1739 ml of hydrogen-oxygen mixture per coulomb for standard conditions, calculate the quantity of copper in the cell. Compare the 0.1739 ml/coul with the theoretical value.

7. The thickness of a pure silver plate on a base metal is to be determined by controlled-potential coulometry. The metal sheet is masked except for a circular area 0.50 cm in diameter; electrical connection is made to the metal, the sheet is clamped in a cell so that the unmasked area is covered with electrolyte, and the silver plate is anodically stripped. Calculate the average thickness of the silver

plating in μm, if the stripping required 0.600 coulombs and if the density of silver is 10.50 g/cm^3.

8. What is the minimum working electrode potential versus SCE required for quantitative (99.9%) electrodeposition of silver from 0.001 M solution?

9. A protein sample is analyzed by digesting it with sulfuric acid to convert protein nitrogen to ammonium sulfate (Kjeldahl digestion). The digested sample is diluted to 100.0 ml, a 1.00-ml aliquot is adjusted to pH 8.6, and the ammonia produced is titrated coulometrically with electrogenerated hypobromite:

$$Br^- + 2OH^- \longrightarrow OBr^- + H_2O + 2e^-$$
$$2NH_3 + 3OBr^- \longrightarrow N_2 + 3Br^- + 3H_2O.$$

The titration is performed at 10.00 mA current and the endpoint occurs at 159.2 sec. How many milligrams of nitrogen was present in the sample?

5

Conductance and Oscillometry

J. West Loveland

Electrical conductance occurs in many different materials—either by the flow of electrons (as in metals) or by the movement of other charged species (as in electrolytes or semiconductors). Electrolytic conductance involves the transport of anions to the anode and cations to the cathode while electrons are transferred to and from the ions at the electrode surfaces to complete the current path. Fused salts and colloidal charged particles behave in a similar fashion. Solid semiconductors carry current by the movement of positive or negative ions into vacated "hole" structures in the lattice network. Increasing the temperature of electrolytic solutions or solids improves the mobility of the charged species and hence increases the conductance; on the other hand, metallic conduction decreases with increasing temperature because of the increased vibrational-energy barriers created and a consequent loss of mobility or free energy bands of the electrons. A specialized form of conductance is that observed in the gaseous state (often called a "plasma"), where both ions and electrons conduct electricity when a potential is applied between two electrodes. A simple example of this is a fluorescent light or bunsen burner flame.

For electrolytic solutions of ions, the magnitude of the electric current depends on the number and types of ions present, their mobility, the type of solvent, and the voltage applied. The number of ions depends on the concentration, but for weak electrolytes it also depends on the degree of ionization, as well as on the temperature.

Ohm's law applies to both metallic conductors and electrolyte solutions. However, anomalies occur under special conditions such as high voltages or very high frequencies. Our emphasis will be to explore electrolytic conductance for analytical uses under the more ideal conditions of low voltage (1 to 100 V) and low frequencies (0 to 5000 Hz). We will also introduce the technique of oscillometry, which is an

111

electrodeless method (using high frequencies) that gives results similar to conductance but is influenced to a large degree by the capacitative and dielectric properties of the system.

5.1 DEFINITIONS AND UNITS

Ohm's law states that the current i (in amperes) flowing in a conductor is directly proportional to the applied voltage E (in volts) and inversely proportional to the resistance R (in ohms, Ω) of the conductor. The familiar equation results:

$$i = E/R, \quad \text{or} \quad R = E/i \tag{5.1}$$

For a conductor of uniform composition and cross-section, the resistance is proportional to the length, l, and inversely proportional to the area, A. The standard unit of resistance for both metallic and electrolytic conductors is called the *specific resistance* ρ (in ohm-cm) which is the resistance of a 1-centimeter cube of the material. The resistance expressed in ohms is

$$R = \rho \times l/A \tag{5.2}$$

The reciprocal of Equation 5.2 is the *conductance* and $1/\rho$ is generally called the specific conductance, κ, with units of $\text{ohm}^{-1}\,\text{cm}^{-1}$ or mho/cm. Conductance G now can be written as

$$1/R = G = \kappa \times A/l \,(\text{mho or ohm}^{-1}) \tag{5.3}$$

The specific conductances of several different types of materials are given in Table 5.1.

Equivalent Conductance

The specific conductance of electrolytic solutions depends on the concentration of the ionic species present. It becomes useful, therefore, to define the conductance of electrolytes on a basis that takes into account the concentration. This is chosen as the conductance of a hypothetical solution containing one gram-equivalent of solute between two parallel electrodes 1 cm apart. The gram-equivalent weight is equal to the gram-formula (or atomic) weight divided by the charge on the ion. Hence, the number of gram equivalents is the number of gram-formula weights (moles) multiplied by the charge, and the normality is the molarity multiplied by the charge. A 1 N solution requires 1000 cm^3, and by reference to Equation 5.3, the *equivalent conductance* Λ becomes

$$\Lambda = \kappa \frac{1000}{N} \, \text{cm}^2/(\text{eq-ohm}) \tag{5.4}$$

As a hypothetical example, a 0.1 N solution requires 10^4 cm^3 of solution for one gram-equivalent, or by Equation 5.3, 10^4 cm^2 of area for each of two electrodes spaced 1 cm apart.

TABLE 5.1. *Specific Conductance of Various Materials*

Material	Temp. °C	Specific Conductance[a] κ, mho/cm
Silver	20°	(6.18×10^5)
Copper	20°	(5.81×10^5)
Aluminum	20°	(3.55×10^5)
Iron	20°	(1.03×10^5)
Mercury	0°	(1.06×10^4)
Fused NaCl	850°	3.5
1 N HCl	25°	3.33×10^{-1}
0.1 N NaCl	25°	1.07×10^{-2}
Conc. H_2SO_4	25°	1×10^{-2}
1 N Acetic Acid	18°	1.32×10^{-3}
0.001 N HCl	25°	4.21×10^{-4}
0.001 N Acetic Acid	18°	4.10×10^{-5}
Bunsen Flame	1725°	(2.5×10^{-6})
Water[b]	18°	0.8×10^{-6}
Acetone	25°	6×10^{-8}
Acetic Acid	25°	1.12×10^{-8}
Ethyl Alcohol	25°	1.35×10^{-9}
Hexane	18°	$(\sim 1 \times 10^{-18})$

a. Values in parentheses calculated from ρ when κ not available from critical tables or handbooks.
b. "Equilibrium water" resulting from dissolution of the CO_2 present in air.

Cell Constant

Obviously, the use of very large platinum electrodes to make conductance measurements is both awkward and expensive. In actual practice, it is not necessary to fabricate a cell where two platinum electrodes are spaced exactly 1 cm apart to obtain either the specific conductance or the equivalent conductance. Moreover, the potential field between such large electrodes so far apart usually arches outward between them, and errors will occur in measuring the specific conductance. It is more feasible, therefore, to approximate the cell configuration with smaller electrodes and to determine a *cell factor* using solutions of known specific conductance. KCl solutions are generally used, since their specific conductances have been determined with high precision. Table 5.2 gives values of κ for several solutions of KCl. More generally, the specific conductance of any aqueous solution of KCl at 25°C can be calculated from the data of Lind, Zwolenik, and Fuoss [1].

The cell factor or cell constant, K, is related to the measured resistance, R, and κ of the solution by the relationship

$$K = \kappa R \text{ cm}^{-1} \tag{5.5}$$

Thus if $K = 1$, the observed resistance is equal numerically to the reciprocal of the specific conductance of the solution used. Once K has been determined for a

TABLE 5.2. *Specific Conductances of Potassium Chloride Solutions for the Determination of Cell Constants*

Normality	Specific Conductance, κ, mho/cm		
	18°C	20°C	25°C
1.000[a]	0.09822	0.1021	0.1118
0.1000	0.01119	0.01167	0.01288
0.01000	0.001225	0.001278	0.001413
0.001000	0.0001271	0.0001326	0.0001469

a. Dissolve 74.555 g KCl (weighed in air) and dilute to 1 liter.

cell, then the measurement of the resistance of any other solution will provide values of Λ or κ using Equations 5.4 and 5.5 respectively.

> *Example 5.1.* A conductance cell was filled with a KCl solution that has a specific conductance of 0.01288 mho/cm. The measured resistance at 25°C was 48.3 ohms. (a) What is the cell factor, K? When the same cell was filled with 0.100 N CdCl$_2$, a resistance of 123.7 ohms was obtained. (b) What is the equivalent conductance of the CdCl$_2$ solution?

> *Solution:* (a) $K = \kappa R = (0.01288 \text{ ohm}^{-1} \text{ cm}^{-1} \times 48.3 \text{ ohm}) = 0.622 \text{ cm}^{-1}$
>
> (b) $\Lambda = \dfrac{1000}{N} \left(\dfrac{K}{R}\right) = \dfrac{1000}{0.100} \times \dfrac{0.622}{123.7} = 50.3 \text{ cm}^2/\text{(eq-ohm)}$

5.2 THEORY

The conductivity of electrolyte solutions is equal to the sum of the conductivities of each type of ion present. For a single dissolved salt, the equivalent conductance can be expressed as

$$\Lambda = \lambda_+ + \lambda_- \tag{5.6}$$

where λ_+ = the equivalent conductance of the cation
λ_- = the equivalent conductance of the anion

For mixtures, Λ would be equal to the sum of all the individual ionic λ_+'s and λ_-'s.

The equivalent conductance of salts or ions increases as the concentration decreases. This phenomenon is directly related to the interionic forces present in solution; a given cation, for example, will have more anions in its vicinity than expected from a purely random distribution. This "ionic atmosphere" has two effects, *electrophoretic* and *time of relaxation*, both of which tend to decrease the ion's mobility. In the former effect, the solvent molecules associated with the ionic atmosphere are moving in a direction opposite to that of the central ion. In the latter, the ionic atmosphere moves slower than the central ion, causing a charge separation (electrostatic retarding force) on the central ion.

As solutions become more dilute, the ionic atmosphere becomes weaker, with the result that both the electrophoretic and time-of-relaxation influences decrease approximately with the square root of the ionic strength of the solution. At infinite dilution there are no disturbing effects on the mobilities of the ions other than variations in solvent and temperature, and the equivalent conductance reaches its maximum value. Equation 5.6 may be written

$$\Lambda^0 = \lambda_+^{\ 0} + \lambda_-^{\ 0} \tag{5.7}$$

where $\Lambda^0 =$ the equivalent conductance of the electrolyte at infinite dilution

$\lambda_+^{\ 0} =$ the limiting ionic equivalent conductances of the cation at infinite dilution

$\lambda_-^{\ 0} =$ the limiting ionic equivalent conductance of the anion at infinite dilution

Onsager [2] has shown that Λ (at finite concentrations) and Λ^0 can be related to the equation

$$\Lambda = \Lambda^0 - (A + B\Lambda^0)\sqrt{c} \tag{5.8}$$

where $A =$ a factor accounting for the electrophoretic effect

$B =$ a factor accounting for the time-of-relaxation effect

Table 5.3 gives the limiting equivalent conductances for several ions. Figure 5.1 shows graphically the equivalent conductance of several electrolytes in water at 25°C over the concentration range of 0 to 0.1 N.

TABLE 5.3. *Limiting Equivalent Conductance of Ions in Water at 25°C*

Cations	$\lambda_+^{\ 0}$	Anions	$\lambda_-^{\ 0}$
H^+	349.8	OH^-	198.6
Li^+	38.6	F^-	55.4
Na^+	50.1	Cl^-	76.4
K^+	73.5	Br^-	78.1
Rb^+	77.8	I^-	76.8
Ag^+	61.9	NO_3^-	71.5
NH_4^+	73.3	ClO_3^-	64.6
$(CH_3)_2NH_2^+$	51.8	ClO_4^-	67.4
Hg^{2+}	53.0	IO_4^-	54.5
Mg^{2+}	53.1	——	——
Ca^{2+}	59.5	Formate	54.6
Ba^{2+}	63.6	Acetate	40.9
Cu^{2+}	53.6	Benzoate	32.4
Zn^{2+}	52.8	SO_4^{2-}	80.0
La^{3+}	69.7	CO_3^{2-}	69.3
Ce^{3+}	69.8	$Fe(CN)_6^{4-}$	111.0

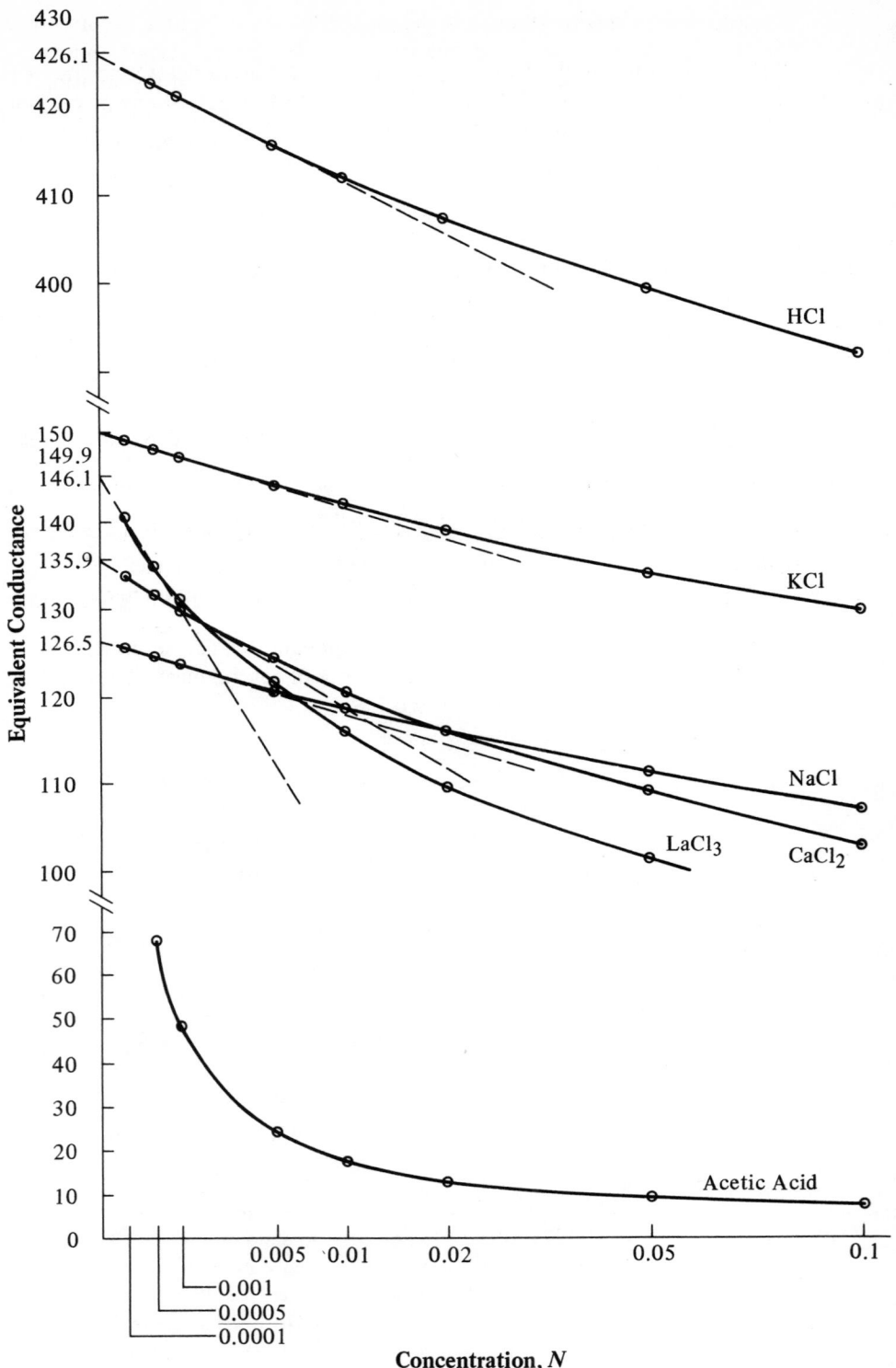

FIGURE 5.1. *Equivalent conductance versus concentration for several electrolytes at 25°C.*

Conductance Ratio: Weak Electrolytes

One of the early uses of limiting conductances was to determine the degree of dissociation of weak electrolytes. Arrhenius suggested that, at any given concentration, the measured equivalent conductance (when compared to the limiting equivalent conductance where all ions are dissociated) should be a measure of the degree of dissociation, α. This can be expressed as

$$\alpha = \Lambda/\Lambda^0 \qquad (5.9)$$

To a first approximation, this equation gives values that vary only slightly from the true values. Any variation is due mainly to the fact that activity coefficients and the effect of concentration on the ionic conductances have been neglected. Acetic acid, HOAc, dissociates according to the reaction

$$HOAc \rightleftharpoons H^+ + OAc^-$$

The ionization constant K_i is expressed as

$$K_i = \frac{[H^+][OAc^-]}{[HOAc]} = \frac{\alpha[HOAc] \times \alpha[HOAc]}{[HOAc](1 - \alpha)} = \frac{\alpha^2[HOAc]}{(1 - \alpha)} \qquad (5.10)$$

Using the data from Table 5.3, the limiting equivalent conductance of acetic acid is $\Lambda^0_{HOAc} = \lambda_{H^+}{}^0 + \lambda^0_{OAc^-} = 349.8 + 40.9 = 390.7 \ cm^2/(eq\text{-}ohm)$.

> *Example 5.2.* The equivalent conductance of a 0.0125 N acetic-acid solution was determined at 25°C to be 14.4. Calculate both the degree of dissociation and the ionization constant.

> *Solution:* $\alpha = \Lambda/\Lambda^0 = 14.4/390.7 = 0.0369$

> $$K_i = \frac{\alpha^2 c}{(1 - \alpha)} = \frac{(0.0369)^2 \times 0.0125}{0.9631} = 1.77 \times 10^{-5}$$

5.3 CONDUCTOMETRIC INSTRUMENTATION

The apparatus required for making conductance measurements and performing conductance titrations is generally inexpensive and basically simple in detail. For these reasons, the measurement of conductance finds wide acceptance in industry as an analytical tool, both in the laboratory and in process control.

Conductivity Cells

Various types of conductance cells are used depending upon the application. The most popular type uses platinum electrodes about 1 cm^2 in area, preferably oriented in a vertical position so that solids do not collect on the surface. The electrodes, welded to heavy platinum wire, must be sealed rigidly in Pyrex or some other rigid nonconducting medium so that no movement of the electrodes takes place during stirring. Figure 5.2 depicts three cells: (a) a cell used for exact conductance

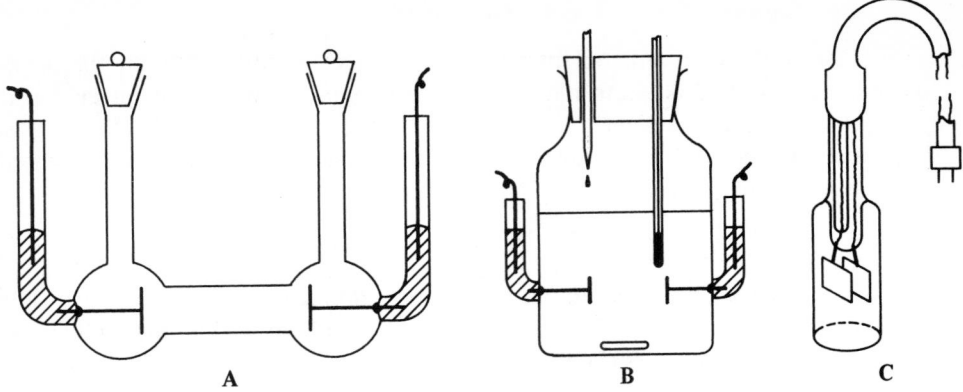

FIGURE 5.2. *Three types of conductance cells, A: Precision conductance cell. B: Conductometric titration cell. C: Concentration dip cell.*

measurement, (b) one used for conductometric titration, and (c) a concentration dip-cell for process or laboratory application.

Preparation of the electrode surfaces is very important. The electrodes should be cleaned in an acid cleaning solution, rinsed thoroughly with distilled water, and immersed in a platinizing solution. DC voltage is adjusted to give a moderate evolution of gas for about 20 seconds, after which the polarity is reversed. The reversal process is repeated until a gray (not black) deposit of platinum has formed on the surface. Too heavy a deposit should be avoided because spongy platinum will absorb unwanted chemical species.

The electrodes are washed with distilled water, immersed in 1 N H_2SO_4, electrolyzed with DC voltage using repeated polarity reversal to remove impurities, and finally washed and stored in distilled water. Platinizing solutions as well as cells may be purchased from a number of supply houses. More detailed discussion and exact procedures of platinization are available in an article by Jones and Bollinger [3].

Measuring Circuitry

AC Circuits. The Wheatstone bridge is used most often for determining the resistance or conductivity of an electrolyte solution. In Figure 5.3, R_c is the resistance of the electrolyte solution and R_1 is the resistance of an adjustable resistance box containing 3 or 4 decades of resistances. R_2 and R_3 may be fixed known resistors, two halves of a resistance slide-wire, or two separate decade-boxes of resistors.

The signal generator may be a 60-Hz transformer, a 1000-Hz oscillator, or a variable-frequency oscillator. If earphones are used as a null, the 1000-Hz oscillator is preferred. The null indicator can also be a sensitive microammeter or more elaborate null-point indicators.

Alternating currents are preferred to direct current because little or no polarization of platinized electrodes takes place. During electrolysis the platinum black

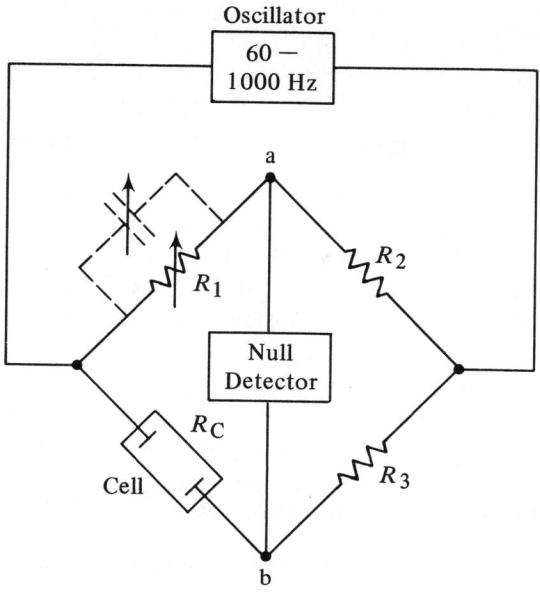

FIGURE 5.3. *Basic Wheatstone AC bridge circuit for measuring conductance.*

adsorbs gases and catalyzes their electrochemical reaction. The alternating current prevents any buildup of material on a given electrode.

In practice, one should attempt to keep R_2 and R_3 in the same range of values. If this is done, then R_1 will have to be adjusted to a range near that of the cell resistance, R_c. This requires that the size and spacing of the electrode be considered in selecting a cell to use in making the conductance measurement. For concentrated electrolyte solutions, small electrodes and long path-lengths (high cell-constant) are used, while for dilute or weak electrolytes, cells with large electrodes and short spacing (low cell-constant) should be employed.

When making the measurement, the resistance R_1 is adjusted until a null is observed. (For maximum accuracy, R_2 and R_3 may also be altered—but see previous paragraph.) Under this condition, there is no potential difference between points a and b of Figure 5.3 and therefore $E_c = E_1$ and $E_2 = E_3$, where the various Es are the voltage drops across the appropriate resistors; from Ohm's law

$$i_c R_c = i_1 R_1 \quad \text{and} \quad i_2 R_2 = i_3 R_3 \tag{5.11}$$

and

$$\frac{R_c i_c}{R_3 i_3} = \frac{R_1 i_1}{R_2 i_2} \tag{5.12}$$

Since the current passing through resistances R_1 and R_2 is the same and the current passing through the cell and R_3 is the same (there is no net current flow through the detector at null), the currents cancel and Equation 5.12 can be solved for R_c:

$$R_c = \frac{R_1 R_3}{R_2} \qquad (5.13)$$

This is the basic relationship for Wheatstone bridges at balance.

Note that in Figure 5.3 a variable capacitor shunts R_1. This is to balance out any phase shifts in the alternating signal caused by the capacity effects present at the electrode surfaces. It is adjusted to give the sharpest minimum in the null signal. For conductometric titrations it is generally not needed.

DC Circuits. Measurements of conductance can also be made with direct current, and in some respects this is simpler than with the AC Wheatstone bridge arrangement. Figure 5.4 shows a simplified DC circuit for measuring conductance. With switch A closed, the current flowing through the solution is determined by the 500-V

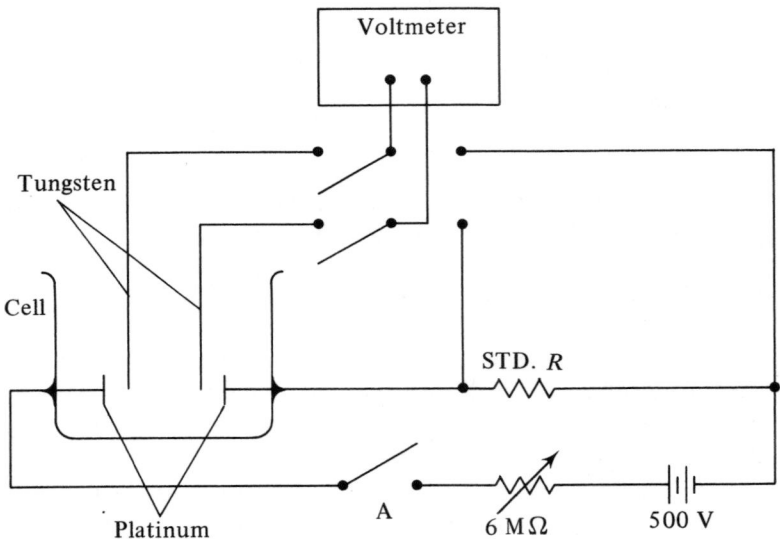

FIGURE 5.4. *Direct-current circuit for measuring conductance.*

source and the 6-MΩ variable resistor, and is measured across the standard resistor. This assumes that the resistance of the solution between the platinum electrodes is several orders of magnitude less than that of 6 MΩ plus the standard resistor. The two immersed tungsten electrodes will be at potentials that depend on the iR drop across the solution. Knowing the current and measuring the voltage between the tungsten electrodes, the resistance of the solution can be calculated from Ohm's law. The meter used to measure the voltage should be of high impedance to prevent polarization of the probe electrodes.

In order to minimize the consumption of electrodes or the introduction of new ions, small currents are employed and only for a short length of time to measure the potential drop. If the working electrodes show signs of polarization from too much current flow, then reversible working electrodes, such as Ag/AgCl should be used.

In low-conductance nonaqueous solutions, where resistances of the order of 10^8 to 10^{10} Ω are observed, a single pair of electrodes may be used with a large known external resistance of about 10^8 Ω and a 1.5 V battery; iR drops across the external resistor are measured with an electrometer. Nonaqueous conductometric titrations can be followed in solvents of low dielectric constant by this arrangement.

5.4 CONDUCTANCE TITRATIONS AND OTHER APPLICATIONS

One of the most frequent uses of conductance is in quantitative titrations of systems in which the conductance of the solution varies in such a manner (prior to and after the endpoint) that two intersecting lines can be drawn to indicate the endpoint. The actual shape of the curve depends on the sample, the titrant, and the reactions occurring. To maximize accuracy in all titration work, corrections to the measured resistance may have to be made for dilution by the titrant. To minimize this correction, titrants should be at least 10, and preferably 100, times stronger than the solute. While the term conductance implies that titrations require that conductance be measured, it should be pointed out that the reciprocal of resistance can be plotted and values need only be relative and not absolute.

Volume corrections for the added titrant are made according to the equation

$$R_s = \frac{V}{V + v} R_0 \qquad (5.14)$$

where
R_0 = the measured resistance
R_s = the corrected solution resistance
V = the original volume of solution
v = the amount of titrant added at the time of reading R_0

In general, four to six points are taken prior to the end point and a similar number of points after the end point.

Acid-Base Titrations

Many applications of conductance titrations involve acid-base titrations.

Strong Acids and Bases. Because of the high mobilities of H^+ and OH^-, the sharpest and most accurate endpoints are obtained when strong acids are titrated with strong bases and vice versa. Referring to Table 5.3, it is seen that the equivalent conductance (or mobility) of H^+ is about 5 times that of the other cations, and that of OH^- is about 3 times greater than that of other anions.

A typical example is the titration of 100 ml of 0.001 N HCl with 0.1 N NaOH:

$$(H^+ + Cl^-) + (Na^+ + OH^-) \longrightarrow (Na^+ + Cl^-) + H_2O \qquad (5.15)$$

The relative or even exact resistance values during the titration can be calculated and the shape of the curve predetermined. We will make a calculation for this

TABLE 5.4. *Specific Conductances of Ions During the Titration of 100 ml of 0.001 N HCl with 0.1 N NaOH*

Ml Titrant	Specific Conductance $\times$ 10^4, mho/cm (25°C)					
	H^+	Cl^-	Na^+	OH^-	NaCl	Total
0.00	3.50	0.76	0.00	0.00	0.00	4.26
0.20	2.80	0.76	0.10	0.00	0.25	3.66
0.50	1.75	0.76	0.25	0.00	0.63	2.76
0.75	0.87	0.76	0.38	0.00	0.95	2.01
1.00	0.00	0.76	0.50	0.00	1.26	1.26
1.25	0.00	0.76	0.63	0.50	1.26	1.89
1.50	0.00	0.76	0.75	0.99	1.26	2.50
1.75	0.00	0.76	0.88	1.49	1.26	3.13
2.00	0.00	0.76	1.00	1.99	1.26	3.75

Note: Specific conductances have not been corrected for volume dilution.

simple titration as an example to use in approaching the more complicated titrations discussed later.

For the reaction of Equation 5.15, the total conductance is the sum of the conductances due to each of the four types of ions present:

$$G = \frac{1}{R} = \frac{1}{R_{H^+}} + \frac{1}{R_{Cl^-}} + \frac{1}{R_{Na^+}} + \frac{1}{R_{OH^-}} = \frac{\lambda_{H^+}{}^0 c_{H^+}}{1000\,K} + \cdots \tag{5.16}$$

To simplify the calculations, it will be assumed that the cell constant K is unity and that the λ^0's of the four ions are sufficiently close to those of the 0.001 N solutions to be used without affecting the result. Under these conditions, the specific conductances of each ion and the total specific conductance of the titrated solution are given in Table 5.4.

When these data are plotted, as shown in Figure 5.5, it is seen that the conductance at first decreases rapidly owing to neutralization of H^+ and then, after the endpoint, increases rapidly as excess OH^- ions are added. The dashed line represents the conductance contribution of the salt (NaCl) formed during the neutralization. This dashed line is significant in the titration of weak and very weak acids or bases—up to the endpoint the conductance generally follows this line closely. If salts are already present in solution, the curve of Figure 5.5 is pushed upward and the relative change (as measured by the conductance bridge) decreases. When salt concentrations are very high, the relatively small change in conductance produces inaccuracy, and better results would be obtained by potentiometric titration.

In the absence of excess salts, accurate measurements can be made equally well on both very dilute and very concentrated solutions. Very dilute solutions, of course, must be protected from contamination by acidic or basic gases in the atmosphere.

Weak Acids and Bases. The titration of weak acids and bases does not result in as sharp an endpoint as is obtained with strong acids and bases.

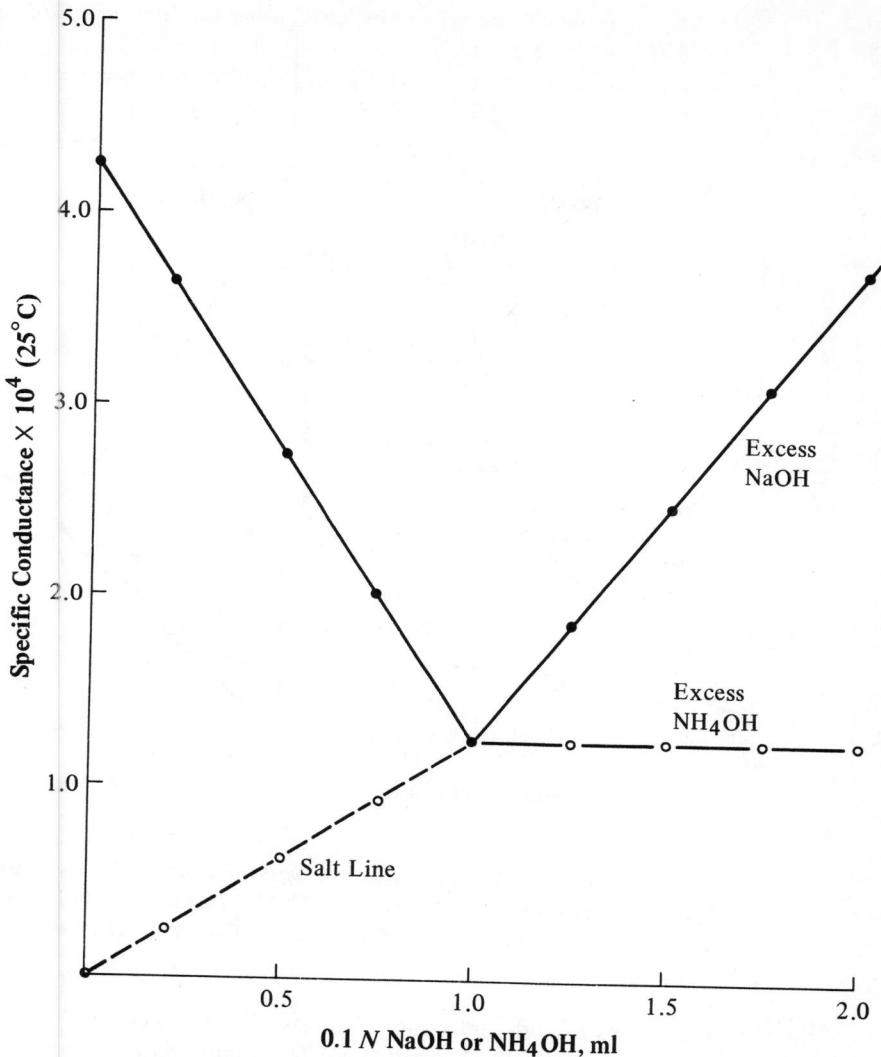

FIGURE 5.5. *Titration curve for the neutralization of* 0.001 *N HCl with* (a) 0.1 *N NaOH and* (b) 0.1 *N NH₄OH (the actual salt line and excess NH₄OH line have slightly higher values than shown).*

During the titration of weak acids, the law of mass action applies and, in the case of acetic acid titrated with NaOH, the common ion OAc^- causes a decrease in the hydrogen-ion concentration over and above that due to stoichiometric neutralization. Since the increase in conductance due to the production of Na^+ and OAc^- is less than the decrease due to the loss of hydrogen ions, the net conductance decreases during the early stages of the titration. At some point, depending on the concentration of the weak acid being titrated and its pK_a value, the concentration of H^+ becomes negligible and the conductance of Na^+ and the weak-acid anions follows the salt line indicated in Figure 5.5. However, owing to hydrolysis of the sodium acetate, near the endpoint a very slight rounding will take place. Figure 5.6A shows

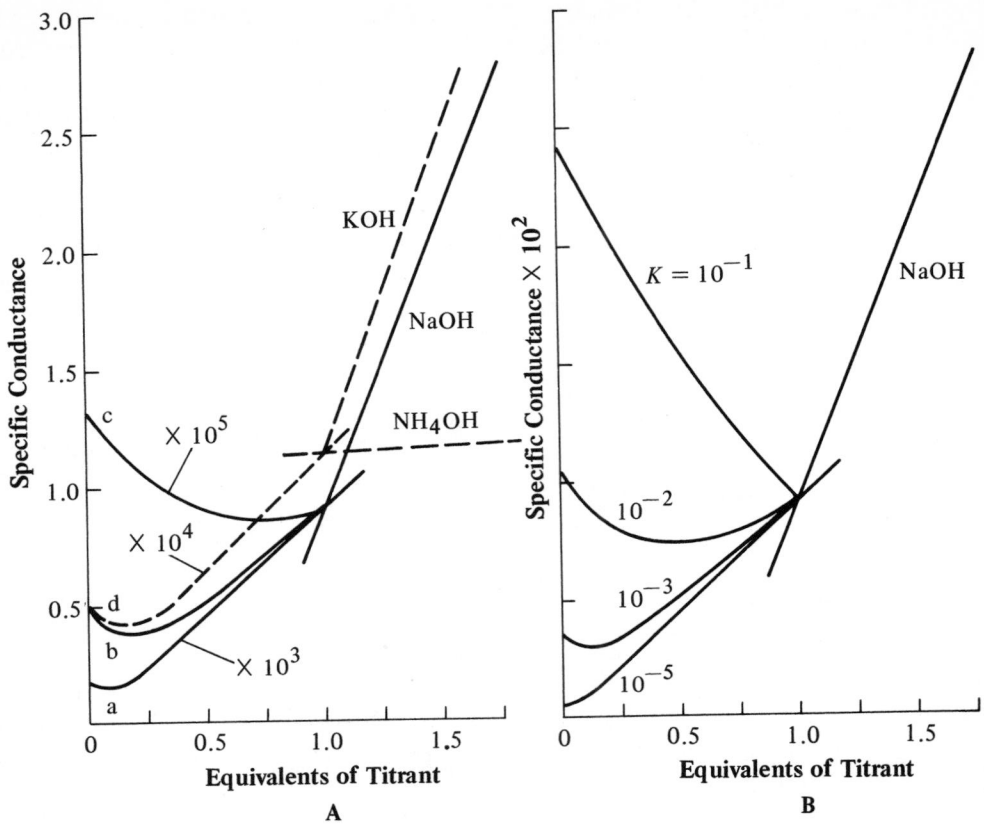

FIGURE 5.6. *A: Titration of various strengths of acetic acid—(a) 0.01 N;*
(b) 0.001 N; and (c) 0.0001 N (titrated with NaOH) and (d) 0.001 N acetic
acid (titrated with NH₄OH or KOH). B: Various moderately weak acids
with NaOH.

the titration curves of different concentrations of acetic acid with NaOH and also
with the weak base NH₄OH at about 0.001 N. Figure 5.6B shows the effect of the
ionization constant of acids at concentrations of 0.1 N on the shape of the titration
curves.

Curve c of Figure 5.6A indicates that the very dilute solution of 0.0001 N
acetic acid is dissociated to such an extent that no straight-line portion can be obtained—as in curve a—to provide a useful endpoint calculation. Even for the 0.001 N
solution (curve b), only about the last 20% of the neutralization is linear and some
care must be taken if one is to obtain accurate endpoints.

When NH₄OH is the base (curve d), a slightly sharper endpoint is obtained.
In this particular case, the titration up to the endpoint will proceed as if a strong
base were being used. However, after the endpoint, owing to the common-ion effect
of NH_4^+ on the ionization of NH₄OH, the conductance remains essentially constant
since NH₄OH remains mostly in the un-ionized state. Also, since the conductance
of NH_4^+ ($\lambda^0 = 73$) is greater than that of Na^+ ($\lambda^0 = 50$), the conductance prior to
the endpoint increases slightly faster, thereby enhancing the angle at the endpoint.

Figure 5.6B indicates that a moderately strong acid ($K_a = 10^{-1}$) at a concentration of 0.1 N can be titrated if several points are taken between the 50 and 100% neutralization points; a nearly V-shaped curve is obtained, although there is a slight curvature. The situation deteriorates rapidly, however, as slightly weaker acids are titrated; for example, for an acid with a pK_a of 2, no linear portion is available during the neutralization to obtain an endpoint.

Dilution of moderately strong acids will often provide better titration curves. For example, the 0.1 N solution of an acid with a pK_a of 2 will ionize to a much greater extent ($\sim 62\%$ vs. 27%) when diluted 10-fold, resulting in a titration curve similar to that of an acid with a pK_a of 1 at 0.1 N. Further dilution will provide still better V-shaped curves, at least up to a point.

A general rule for obtaining useful curves is that moderately strong acids (and bases) can be titrated as strong acids if their concentration is about 100 times smaller than their ionization constant. Alternatively, they may be titrated as weak acids when their concentration is at least 150 times larger than the ionization constant. For example, the last 25% of the salt line will be followed for an acid with a pK_a of 3 if its concentration is 0.15 N or greater.

A technique for obtaining good endpoints when single titrations give poorly defined curves is to titrate equal portions of the unknown weak acid with equal concentrations of KOH and NH_4OH on two equal aliquots. The curves obtained prior to the endpoint should be identical, but after the endpoint will diverge along the weak- and strong-base lines. The intersection of the two lines formed by the excess bases gives the endpoint. The important point to observe in this technique is that the cations of the two base titrants have essentially identical equivalent conductances (NH_4^+, $\lambda^0 = 73$ and K^+, $\lambda^0 = 74$). If NaOH were the strong base, an incorrect endpoint would be determined, as can be deduced from a comparison of the three base curves of Figure 5.6A.

When no linear region prior to the endpoint can be easily obtained, one can add alcohol or some other water-soluble organic compound to reduce the dissociation of the acid so that it behaves more like a very weak acid. This often may be the easiest approach for titrating weak and moderately weak acids. If these techniques fail, then potentiometric methods should be tried.

Very Weak Acids and Bases. These compounds may be considered to have pK_a's or pK_b's in the range of 7 to 10. Since they are very weakly ionized, the initial conductance is very low. With a strong base as titrant, the curve follows the salt line from the start of the titration. Rounding of the curve in the vicinity of the endpoint takes place because of the release of OH^- ions by the hydrolysis of the anion formed. The weaker the acid, the more pronounced this effect. After the endpoint, the conductance increases rapidly because of the excess OH^- ions. The endpoint is determined by extrapolating the first straight portion of the neutralization curve and the latter portion of the excess hydroxide curve.

A marked improvement with very weak acids can be accomplished by adding an excess amount of weak base such as NH_4OH, pyridine, or ethylamine. Addition of such bases causes an increase in the dissociation of the very weak acids according to the equation

$$HA + B \longrightarrow HB^+ + A^- \qquad (5.17)$$

Therefore, the following reaction occurs during titration:

$$HB^+ + Na^+ + OH^- \longrightarrow Na^+ + B + H_2O \qquad (5.18)$$

In effect, the titration becomes one of replacing the HB^+ cation by the Na^+ of the titrant up to the endpoint. After the endpoint, the excess OH^- causes the conductance to rise rapidly. An additional advantage of the use of a weak base is its ability to solubilize many slightly soluble weak acids that otherwise require nonaqueous solvents, in which generally poorer endpoints are obtained. Figure 5.7 compares titrations of a very weak acid, such as phenol, with and without the addition of NH_4OH.

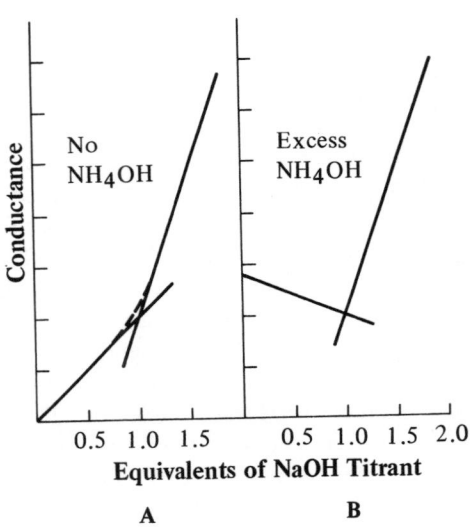

FIGURE 5.7. *Titration of a very weak acid with (A) NaOH only, and (B) excess NH_4OH and NaOH titrant.*

By referring to the ionic-equivalent conductances (Table 5.3), it can be deduced that LiOH should give a more acute angle for endpoint determination than NaOH or KOH. In many cases, titrations of alkaloids and their salts are more accurately followed by conductometry than by potentiometry or by using phenolphthalein as indicator.

A general guideline is that, if it is desired to have 50% of the neutralization follow the initial salt line, the K_a value should be greater than $5 \times 10^{-12}/c$, where c is the molar concentration of the weak acid.

Mixtures of Strong and Weak Acids. Where mixtures of strong and weak acids are titrated, the conductance method often may be preferred to other techniques such as potentiometry. Figure 5.8 shows the relative conductivity changes occurring when a mixture of hydrochloric and acetic acids is titrated with either (*a*) NaOH or (*b*) NH_4OH.

When a mixture of a very weak acid and a strong acid is titrated, a strong base must be used. The use of a weak base leads to large hydrolysis effects and indistinct curves at the weak-acid endpoint, although the first endpoint will give the amount of strong acid.

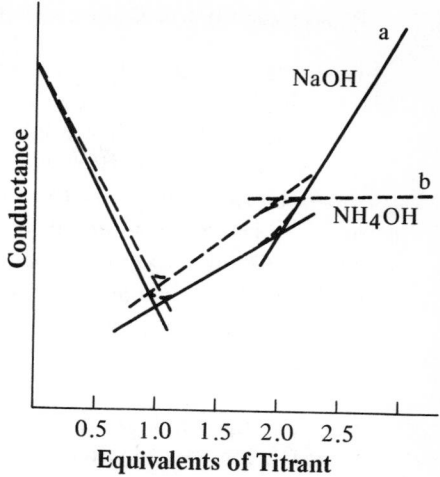

FIGURE 5.8. *Titration of a mixture of a strong and a weak acid with (a) NaOH and (b) NH$_4$OH.*

Salts of Weak Acids or Bases. Salts of weak acids can be titrated with a strong acid, since they are themselves Bronsted bases—that is, proton acceptors. A typical example is the titration of sodium acetate with hydrochloric acid:

$$H^+ + Cl^- + Na^+ + OAc^- \longrightarrow Na^+ + Cl^- + HOAc \qquad (5.19)$$

As sodium acetate is titrated, the acetate ion is replaced by the chloride ion, which, owing to its slightly higher ionic-equivalent conductance, causes a slight increase in conductivity up to the endpoint. Beyond the endpoint, excess hydrochloric acid causes large increases. Such titrations are useful where the ionization constant of the liberated weak acid or base, when divided by the salt's concentration, does not exceed 5×10^{-3}. If a difunctional acid is formed, then the two ionization constants should differ by about 10^{-5} if two endpoints are to be observed; Na$_2$S is an example of this type. Figure 5.9 shows typical replacement titration curves.

FIGURE 5.9. *Replacement reactions: Titration of (a) Na₂S with HCl and (b) NH₄Cl with NaOH titrants.*

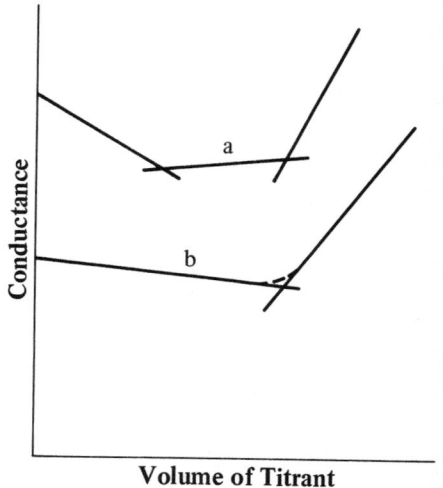

Replacement titrations are useful for titrating such salts as oxalates, phosphates, benzoates, etc.

Precipitation and Complexation Reactions

Whenever a reaction between two compounds or salts produces a change in the conductivities of the ions present before and after the endpoint, conductometry can be considered as a possible analytical method. Precipitation reactions, for instance, involve replacing one ion with another. Silver in $AgNO_3$ solution may be determined by titrating it with the chlorides of sodium, potassium, or lithium. From the ionic-equivalent conductances of the cations involved ($\lambda^0_{Li^+} = 39$, $\lambda^0_{Na^+} = 50$, $\lambda^0_{Ag^+} = 62$, and $\lambda_{K^+}^0 = 74$), lithium will give the sharpest endpoint. Since Li^+ is replacing Ag^+, the conductance decreases during the precipitation of silver chloride, but since the amount of NO_3^- remains constant, the conductivity will increase again after the endpoint because of the excess Cl^-.

The concentrations of the salts and the solubility product of the precipitate play an important role in determining whether satisfactory linear portions are obtained prior to and after the endpoint. High solubility of the precipitate causes rounding of the conductance curve at the endpoint; good curves will be obtained if no more than 1% of the precipitate exists in the ionized form. A few typical precipitation-titration curves are shown in Figure 5.10. A general rule is that the solubility product, when divided by the concentration of the titrant, should not be greater than about 5×10^{-6}. For example, the concentration of $AgNO_3$ with Cl^- titrant should be at least $0.3 \times 10^{-4} N$, since AgCl has a K_{sp} of 1.7×10^{-10}.

FIGURE 5.10. *Precipitation reactions: Titration of $AgNO_3$ with (a) KCl and (b) LiCl titrant.*

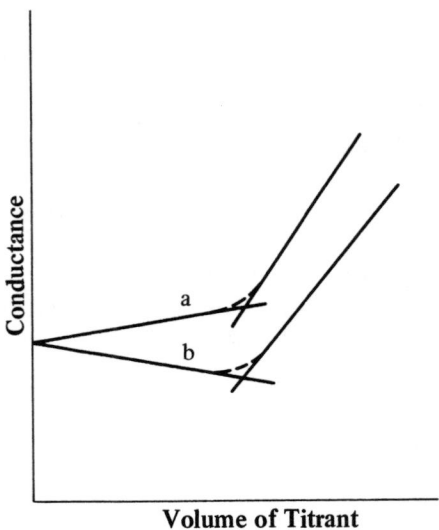

Errors in locating true endpoints during precipitation reactions can be caused by several factors: contamination of the electrodes by the adhering precipitate, occlusion of ions by the precipitate, and incomplete or slow precipitation reaction.

Complexometric reactions require that stable complexes be formed. A typical example is the formation of the cyanide complex of Hg^{2+} according to the reaction

$$Hg^{2+} + 2NO_3^- + 2K^+ + 2CN^- \longrightarrow Hg(CN)_2 + 2K^+ + 2NO_3^- \quad (5.20)$$

A number of metal ions, M^{2+}, can be titrated conductometrically with the disodium salt of ethylenediaminetetraacetic acid, Na_2H_2EDTA, in buffered solutions [4].

Titrations in Nonaqueous Solutions

In nonaqueous media such as alcohols, not only Arrhenius acids and bases but also Lewis acids and bases can be titrated. (Lewis acids and bases cannot be titrated in aqueous solutions.) Interpreting the curves obtained, however, is more complex than in aqueous solution. One factor that needs to be considered is the suppression or enhancement of the ionization of the acids or bases by the solvent; another is the viscosity of the solvent (as viscosity increases, the ionic mobility decreases). In Lewis acid-base reactions, factors such as ion-pair formation, hydrogen bonding, and solute-solvent and solute-solute interactions must also be taken into account.

A few examples showing the versatility of nonaqueous titrations are the following:

1. In glacial acetic acid, sulfuric acid gives two endpoints when titrated with a strong base or sodium acetate, since the ionization of the second hydrogen is sufficiently reduced that HSO_4^- acts as a weak acid. When hydrochloric acid is present, three endpoints are observed and both acids may be determined.
2. Phenols in low-dielectric solvents often give sharper endpoints than in aqueous solutions; for instance, when 2,3,5-trimethylphenol is titrated with tetrabutyl-ammonium hydroxide in toluene solvent [Fig. 5.11A], as opposed to water. Simi-

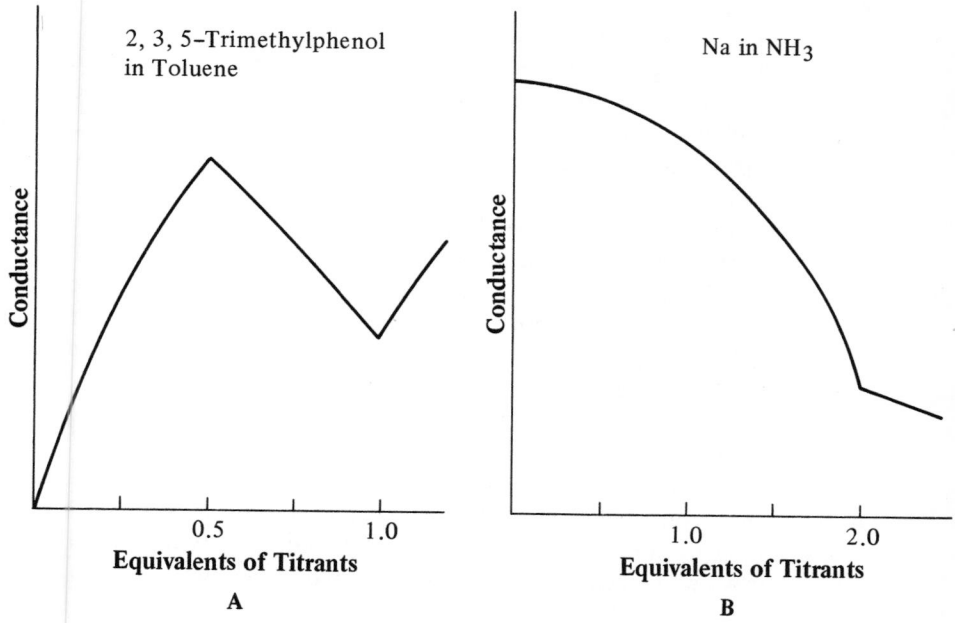

FIGURE 5.11. *Titration curves in nonaqueous solvents: A: Titration of 2,3,5-trimethylphenol with tetrabutylammonium hydroxide in toluene. B: Titration of Na in NH3 with dimethyl sulfide.*

lar results are observed in pyridine solvent when sodium isopropoxide is the titrant.

3. New molecular species can be deduced or at least the molar ratios of complexes can be ascertained. In liquid ammonia ($-33°C$), elemental sodium titrated with dimethyl sulfide indicates that 2 moles of sodium react with the dialkyl sulfide (Fig. 5.11B).

In general, nonaqueous conductance titration is superior to other electrochemical methods for analyzing difficult systems. The major difficulty is the developmental work needed to establish suitable endpoints for the particular solvents and titrants required.

Single (Batch) and Continuous Measurements of Conductance

Determination of Solubilities. We have mentioned the use of single measurements of conductance in determining the ionization constants of weak acids and bases. In addition, the solubilities of many weakly soluble salts and oxides have been determined by conductance measurements. When the solubility product is less than 10^{-8}, a correction must be made for the specific conductance of water.

Water Purity: Salt Content and Moisture Content. Pure water has a specific conductance of slightly less than 1×10^{-6} mho/cm. Water purity is, of course, important in the laboratory where a few parts per million of dissolved salts may mask the component being looked for. It is also important in industry, particularly in power plants (where dissolved salts left behind in flash-boiler pipes may clog them) and in plants where water rinsing is employed. In most cases, it is the total salt content that is of importance. Compact and inexpensive instruments are available with special cells in which direct readout in specific conductance, or parts per million, or grams per gallon is provided. Sensors are of the insertion, flow, and submission variety. Automated continuous devices are used to control the flow of raw and treated water in demineralizers (ion-exchange beds), to reroute off-test condensate, to control blowdown of boiler water, and for similar operations.

Extensive use of conductometry is now made for controlling pollution in our streams, rivers, and lakes, and for detecting sources of contaminants. Work in oceanography uses portable batch or continuous conductivity analyzers which quite often are scaled to read directly in percent salinity.

In the metal industry, the acid strength of pickling, caustic degreasing, anodizing, and rinse baths are monitored by conductance measurements.

Some automatic analyzers use conductance to indicate the concentration of some specific component. For example, ambient concentrations of SO_2 in air as low as 0.01 ppm can be recorded continuously. Sulfur dioxide is oxidized to sulfuric acid, after which the increase in conductance due to the hydrogen and sulfate ions is directly proportional to the SO_2 concentration. The moisture content of wood and soil has been measured with special electrodes.

Other analytical uses will undoubtedly be made of conductance instruments in the future because of their simplicity, ease of operation, inexpensiveness, and portability and because they can be used for both single (batch) measurement and continuous measurement.

5.5 OSCILLOMETRY OR HIGH-FREQUENCY TITRATIONS

Oscillometry differs from conductometry in several respects.

1. Electrodes are not in direct contact with the solution, but are usually separated from it by the glass walls of the container.
2. Frequencies used are of the order of 10^6 to 10^7 Hz compared with 10^3 Hz for conductance.
3. Instrument response is generally to a combination of resistance and capacitance.

In conductance, the ions absorb energy which is translated into heat and motion. In oscillometry, we have not only this aspect, but also the capacitance effect in which molecules absorb and return energy each frequency cycle owing to the induced polarization and alignment of electrically unsymmetrical molecules.

Generally, if one is working with solutions of high dielectric constant but low conductivity, the response will be primarily capacitive in nature; where the solution has a low dielectric constant and contains salts, the response will be mainly due to the conductance of the ions present.

The end result is that high-frequency titrations give a variety of responses, including the usual V-shaped curves, nonlinear intersecting curves, and inverted V-shaped curves. The shape of a curve may vary with frequency, or at a given frequency a change in dielectric constant or salt content can change the response.

Equivalent Circuit

Cells. Figure 5.12A, a drawing of a high-frequency cell, shows the essential parts affecting cell response in high-frequency titrations. Figure 5.12B is the equivalent circuit, where C_s and C_g are the capacitances and R_s and R_g the resistances of the solution and the glass walls, respectively. Figure 5.12C is a reasonable approximation, since R_g is much larger than R_s, and R_s controls the response due to resistance changes.

Oscillators. The parallel-tuned oscillator circuit is the most commonly used in high-frequency titration work; its circuit is shown in Figure 5.13. The resonance frequency, f_r, of an oscillator is given by

$$f_r = \frac{1}{2\pi\sqrt{LC}} \tag{5.21}$$

where L = the inductance in henries
C = the capacitance in farads

Both L and C display *reactance*: they resist changes in the alternating signal. The capacitive reactance X_C is equal to $1/(2\pi f C)$ and the inductive reactance X_L is $2\pi f L$

FIGURE 5.12. *Physical and equivalent circuit of high-frequency titration cell. A: High-frequency cell: solution, glass cell, and metal electrode arrangement. B: Equivalent electrical circuit of cell. C: Simplified equivalent circuit.*

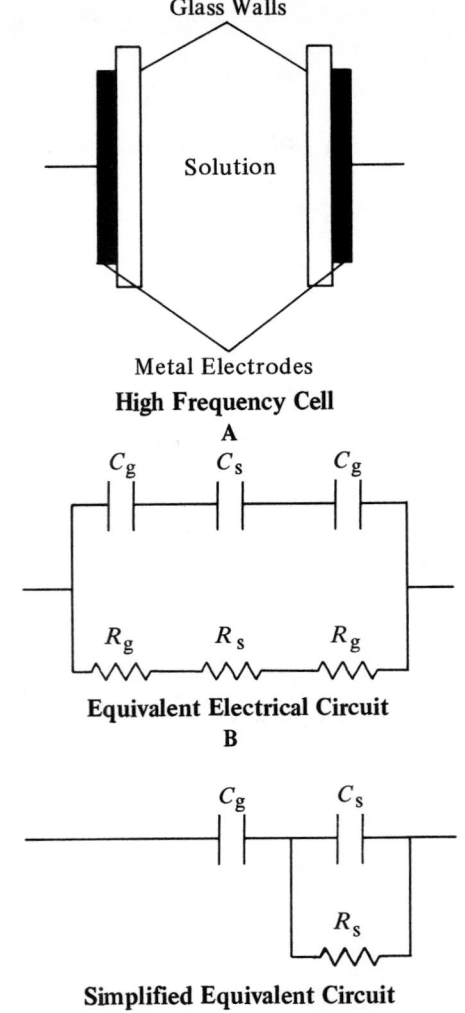

Glass Walls

Solution

Metal Electrodes

High Frequency Cell

A

C_g C_s C_g

R_g R_s R_g

Equivalent Electrical Circuit

B

C_g C_s

R_s

Simplified Equivalent Circuit

C

where f is the frequency. Both are 90° out of phase with ohmic resistance, and at the resonance frequency are equal in magnitude and opposite in sign.

Assume for the moment that all the resistance is due to the coil resistance, R_L. The total impedance, Z, across the oscillator circuit is

$$Z = \frac{L}{C\sqrt{R_L^2 + (X_L - X_C)^2}} \tag{5.22}$$

and at resonance $Z = L/CR_L$. When the oscillator is at resonance, the current i_L is at a minimum since Z is at its maximum. The current i_0 in the LC oscillator is larger than i_L, by a factor of X_L/R_L. The latter is referred to as the Q of the circuit and is a measure of the power-loss factor.

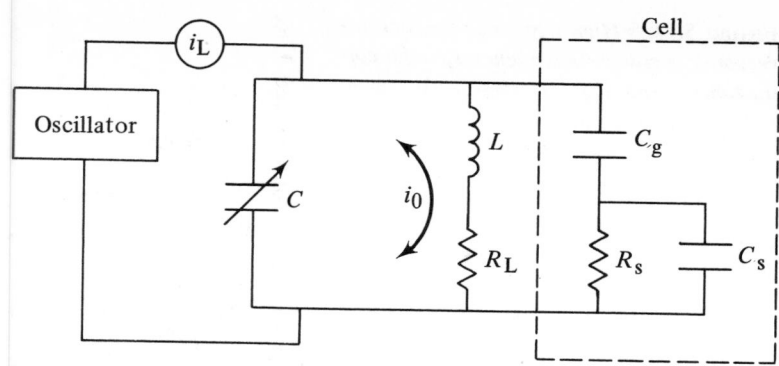

FIGURE 5.13. *Parallel-tuned oscillator circuit for high-frequency titrations (with cell addition in dashed-line section).*

Relationship Between Low- and High-Frequency Conductance

When the parallel-oscillator circuit is loaded by the cell, the predominant factors affecting response are (a) capacitors C_g and C_s (Fig. 5.13), which change the total C in Equation 5.21, and hence the resonance frequency; and (b) R_s, which changes the resistive load in parallel with R_L and reduces the Q of the circuit. As a result, i_0 is reduced while i_L is increased. Reilley [5] has determined that the conductance term $1/R_s$ in the high-frequency method as related to the low-frequency specific conductance κ is:

$$1/R_s = \frac{\kappa 2\pi f C_g{}^2}{\kappa^2 + (2\pi f)^2(C_g + C_s)^2} \tag{5.23}$$

This implies the following points:

1. When the cell capacitance C_g increases due to larger areas or thinner walls, $1/R_s$ increases.
2. As the frequency increases, $1/R_s$ increases, and as the frequency approaches zero, $1/R_s$ approaches zero.
3. When κ is either very large or very small, $1/R_s$ approaches zero, and at some intermediate value of κ, $1/R_s$ shows a peak response.

Figure 5.14 shows how the high-frequency conductance varies with the low-frequency conductance at several different frequencies.

Instruments. A few instruments are commercially available. Response detection generally takes one of three forms: (a) a calibrated dial to increase or decrease capacity to maintain f_r; (b) a meter to record the change in current i_L (Fig. 5.13) or some other related parameter; and (c) a beat-frequency oscillator where the difference between reference frequency and the working frequency is measured using a frequency-discriminator output signal. One requirement is that the oscillator have good frequency stability.

Cells should be made of glass or some other nonconducting material, and the electrodes should be affixed firmly to the walls either mechanically or with an

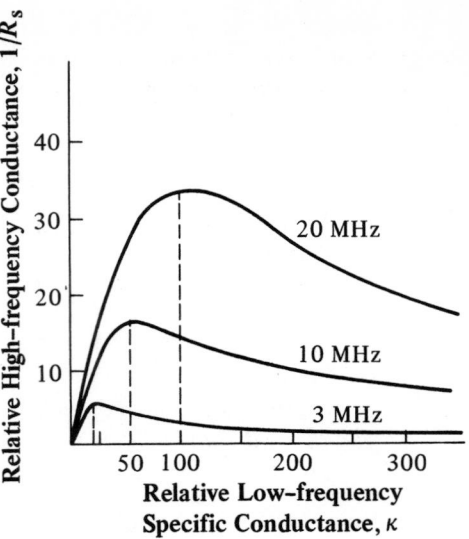

FIGURE 5.14. *High-frequency conductance response versus low-frequency specific conductance response.*

adhesive. The electrode material should be a metal to which leads can be easily soldered. The diameter of the cell and the salt concentration of the solution will determine the loading of the oscillator. If the oscillator cannot sustain oscillations, then smaller diameter cells and lower salt concentrations should be used.

Analytical Use

Titration Curves. Generally it can be expected that if a low-frequency conductance titration can be performed, a high-frequency one can also. However, the cell size, ionic strength of the solution, and frequency needed to give a good endpoint are variables that must be determined by trial and error. Even after the best conditions are found, the curves obtained may be nonlinear and show little response. However, if an endpoint *can* be found, there is a definite advantage to a method in which no

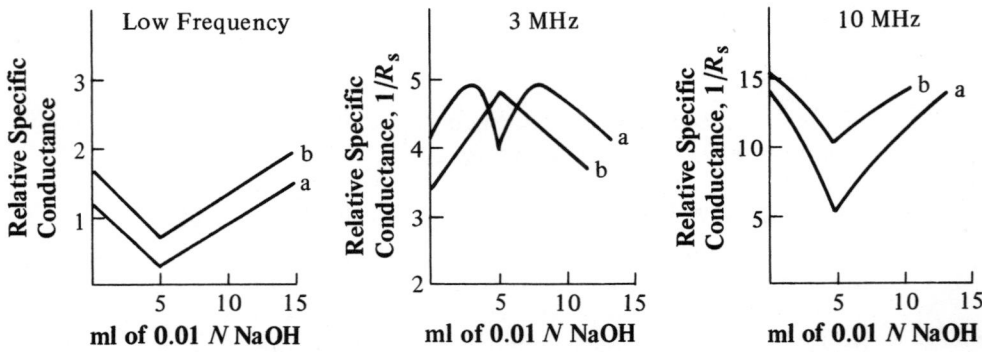

FIGURE 5.15. *Comparison of low- and high-frequency titration curves: A: Low frequency ~1000 Hz; B: 3 MHz; and C: 10 MHz. (a) 5 ml of 0.01 N HCl + 55 ml of water. (b) 5 ml of 0.01 N HCl + 55 ml of 0.001 N KCl.*

direct contact is necessary between solution and electrodes, particularly with precipitation titrations, since the electrodes will not be contaminated (for example, by adsorption of precipitates) or affected by electrolysis that could produce polarization.

Figure 5.15 shows a comparison of a low-frequency acid-base titration at two different ionic strengths with high-frequency titrations conducted at 3 and 10 MHz. In each case, 50 milliequivalents of HCl is titrated with 0.01 N NaOH. Obviously 10 MHz is the best frequency to use, but because of the curvature several additional titration points need to be taken to increase the precision of the endpoint determination. The M-shaped curve resulting at 3 MHz could lead to misinterpretation and an incorrect endpoint.

Dielectric Constant: Measurement of Binary Mixtures. When the conductance term κ of Equation 5.23 becomes very small, the response of the oscillator depends primarily on the values of C_g and C_s. The parallel equivalent capacity, C_p, is given by

$$C_p = \frac{C_g C_s}{C_g + C_s} \tag{5.24}$$

If C_g is relatively large compared to C_s, then the response of C_p will be dependent mainly on C_s. C_g can be increased by decreasing wall thickness and C_s decreased by increasing the distance between the walls of the cell. Since the dielectric constant of the sample will alter C_s, the instrument response will follow the dielectric constant. Figure 5.16 indicates the type of nonlinear, but smooth, response obtained with a commercially available oscillometer for compounds of varying dielectric constant.

Table 5.5 gives the dielectric constants for several of the more common liquids. The very large value for water compared to benzene, for example, makes it possible to detect trace amounts of water or some other highly polar material in benzene.

FIGURE 5.16. *Response of high-frequency readings to dielectric constant of some liquids.*

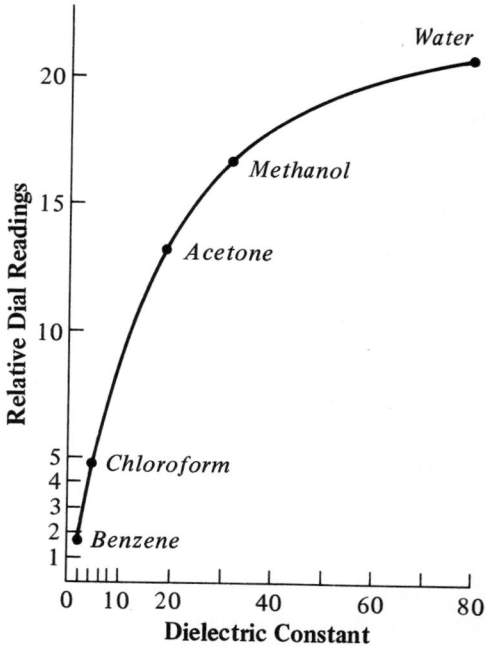

TABLE 5.5.   *Dielectric Constants of Several Common Liquids*

Formamide	109 (20°C)	Phenol	9.78 (60°C)
Water	78.5	Acetic acid	6.15 (20°C)
Formic acid	58.5 (16°C)	Ethyl acetate	6.02
Methanol	32.6	Chloroform	4.81 (20°C)
Ethanol	24.3	Benzene	2.27
Acetone	20.7	Carbon tetrachloride	2.23
Isopropanol	18.3	*n*-Octane	1.95 (20°C)

Note: Values at 25°C unless otherwise specified.

Standard curves for each binary mixture have to be prepared at a given temperature. Some examples of binary systems that can be analyzed are hexane–benzene and acetone–water, as well as various lower-molecular-weight alcohols in water.

Moisture in solids such as wood, foods, and textiles can be measured. However, such determinations are more often made by instruments designed to directly measure the dielectric changes between two parallel plates of a condenser.

Reaction Rates.   A fascinating application of high-frequency conductance is determining rates of reactions.   The response must be related directly to the change in the composition of the solution.   Thus, for example, the rapid rates of hydrolysis of esters have been determined, as well as the rates of some polymerization reactions.

Liquid Chromatograph Detector.   By placing the electrodes on the outside of chromatographic columns, changes in the composition of the eluates can be followed; or by moving these electrodes up and down the column, zones or chromatographic bands can be located.

SELECTED BIBLIOGRAPHY

Conductance

FUOSS, R. M., and ACCASCINA, F. *Electrolytic Conductance.* New York: Interscience Publishers, 1959.

GLASSTONE, S. *Introduction to Electrochemistry.* New York: Van Nostrand, 1942.

KOLTHOFF, I. M., and ELVING, P. J. *Treatise on Analytical Chemistry*, part I, vol. 4, chap. 51. New York: Interscience Publishers, 1963.

ROBINSON, R. A., and STOKES, R. H. *Electrolyte Solutions.* New York: Academic Press, 1959.

WEISSBERGER, A. *Physical Methods of Organic Chemistry*, volume 1, part IV, 3rd ed., chap. XLV. New York: Interscience Publishers, 1960.

Oscillometry

BLAEDEL, W. J., and PETITJEAN, D. L. "High-Frequency Method of Chemical Analysis." In W. C. Berl, ed., *Physical Methods in Chemical Analysis*, vol. III, pp 108–34. New York: Academic Press Inc., 1956.

REILLEY, C. N., "High-Frequency Methods." In P. Delahay, ed., *New Instrumental Methods in Electrochemistry*, pp 319–45. New York: Interscience Publishers, 1954.

REFERENCES

1. J. E. LIND, JR., J. J. ZWOLENIK, and R. M. FUOSS, *J. Amer. Chem. Soc.*, *81*, 1557 (1959).
2. L. ONSAGER, *Phys. Z.*, *28*, 277 (1927).
3. G. JONES and D. M. BOLLINGER, *J. Amer. Chem. Soc.*, *57*, 280 (1935).
4. J. L. HALL, J. A. GIBSON, JR., P. R. WILKINSON, and H. O. PHILLIPS, *Anal. Chem.*, *26*, 1484 (1954).
5. C. N. REILLEY and W. H. McCURDY, JR., *Anal. Chem.*, *25*, 86 (1953).

PROBLEMS

1. The concentrations of three dilute solutions of sodium acetate were measured in a conductance cell in which the parallel electrodes were 1 cm^2 in area and 0.25 cm apart. Resistances of 274,700, 91,000 and 18,320 ohms were determined for the three solutions. Calculate the normality of each solution. $T = 25°C$.

2. A conductance measurement was made of brackish water containing equimolar concentrations of $MgCl_2$ and NaCl, with traces of other salts that can be ignored. What is the concentration of chloride ion in ppm when a cell with a cell constant of 5.0 gives a resistance of 1549 ohms? Use the limiting equivalent conductances for the calculation.

3. In a chemical process, an aqueous solution of sodium hydroxide is to be maintained in the range 9 to 14% by weight. This corresponds to roughly 2.5 and 4.0 N solutions with equivalent conductances of 117 and 85, respectively. The commercial conductivity bridge available covers conductance ranges of 0 to 100, 0 to 10,000, and 0 to 100,000 micromhos. The midpoint of each range on the logarithmic scale is a factor of 10 lower in micromhos. (a) Should the cell constant of the conductivity cell be 0.01, 1.0, or 25 cm^{-1}, and (b) what range is most suitable for monitoring the solution?

4. A special conductance bridge reads directly over the range of 1 to 12% H_2SO_4. The recommended cell constant is 50. Extrapolating from data in handbooks and critical tables, calculate the approximate resistance and micromho range involved at 18°C.

5. 2.4425 grams of benzoic acid is dissolved in one liter of pure water at 25°C. When placed in a conductance cell having a constant of 0.150, a resistance value of 1114 ohms is obtained. Calculate the equivalent conductance of the solution, the degree of ionization, and the ionization constant.

6. The solubility product of calcium fluoride at 25°C is 3.9×10^{-11}. What was the resistance reading when the cell constant was 0.100 cm^{-1}? Ignore the conductance contribution of the water.

7. In the titration of 100 ml of acetic acid with 1.0 N NaOH, the following relative conductance readings were observed for the corresponding burette readings. What is the concentration of the acid?

0.00 ml = 0.22	1.60 ml = 1.47
0.10 ml = 0.19	1.80 ml = 1.73
0.20 ml = 0.23	2.00 ml = 2.21
0.40 ml = 0.39	2.20 ml = 2.71
0.60 ml = 0.56	2.40 ml = 3.21
0.80 ml = 0.74	2.60 ml = 3.70
1.00 ml = 0.92	3.00 ml = 4.70
1.20 ml = 1.10	3.40 ml = 5.69
1.40 ml = 1.28	

8. Using the conductance values of Table 5.3, draw the shape of the relative conductance curves for the following titrations: (a) sodium benzoate with hydrochloric acid; (b) silver acetate with lithium chloride; (c) sulfuric acid in glacial acetic acid with sodium hydroxide; (d) mercuric nitrate with potassium chloride; (e) mixture of hydrochloric acid and acetic acid with ammonium hydroxide and with sodium hydroxide; (f) ammonium chloride with potassium hydroxide; and (g) sodium carbonate with calcium nitrate (check the effect of intermediate product formation).

9. In an experiment to determine the solubility of silver chloride, the specific conductance of the demineralized water used

was 0.81×10^{-6} mho/cm at 25°C. When solid silver chloride was equilibrated in the same water at 25°C, the specific conductance was 2.62×10^{-6} mho/cm. Determine the solubility product, assuming that the limiting equivalent conductance of silver chloride is 138.3 mho/cm.

10. An oscillometer was used to determine the amount of ethylene glycol in a hydrocarbon layer and of hydrocarbon in the glycol layer. The following calibration curves were established.

0% Glycol	115	95% Glycol	1298
1% Glycol	300	96% Glycol	1324
2% Glycol	436	97% Glycol	1348
3% Glycol	551	98% Glycol	1369
4% Glycol	652	99% Glycol	1386
5% Glycol	743	100% Glycol	1399

The reading observed for the hydrocarbon layer was 371 and for the glycol layer, 1361. Draw the curves and determine the percentage of hydrocarbon in glycol and the percentage of glycol in hydrocarbon.

6

Introduction to Spectroscopic Methods

Eugene B. Bradley

The word spectroscopy is widely used to mean the separation, detection, and recording of energy changes (resonance peaks) involving nuclei, atoms, or molecules. These changes are due to the emission, absorption, or scattering of electromagnetic radiation or particles. Spectrometry is that branch of physical science that treats the measurement of spectra.

The experimental applications of spectroscopic methods in chemical problems are diverse, but all have in common the interaction of electromagnetic radiation with the quantized energy states of matter. A chemist may wish to determine a molecular structure or the value of an electric dipole moment. He may wish to make an elemental analysis or to verify the presence of a chemical bond. In order to solve such problems, the chemist chooses a particular spectroscopic method, using his knowledge of the possible energy states of matter in particular configurations and the particular wavelengths of electromagnetic radiation that interact with these states.

This chapter is meant to serve as a very general overview of spectroscopic methods; many of the topics will be covered later in greater detail, particularly in Chapters 7–9.

6.1 THEORY

The theoretical basis for the interaction between radiation and the energy states of matter is the quantized nature of energy transfer from the radiation field to matter and vice versa. Matter, composed of "particles" like protons, neutrons, and electrons, sometimes behaves like a wave; radiation, a self-propagating "wave" of crossed

...ric and magnetic fields, sometimes behaves like a particle. This seeming paradox is reconciled in quantum theory, which is used to calculate quantized energy states. The wavelike properties of matter are illustrated in the double-slit experiment [1], in which the wave property of *diffraction* is exhibited by an electron beam passing through a double slit. The quantized, particle-like nature of electromagnetic radiation is shown by the photoelectric effect [2], in which the number of electrons emitted by an electrode is shown to be dependent on the number of incoming "packets" of radiation at a certain minimum energy, or frequency—one electron per packet. (This particular effect is useful for some types of detectors discussed later.)

The wavelike character of radiation can be described by its *wavelength*, λ; by the *wavenumber* $\bar{\nu}$, which represents the number of waves per unit of distance (the reciprocal of the wavelength); by the speed at which the wave front advances, the *velocity*, V; and by the number of waves passing a given point in unit time, the frequency, ν. The relationship among these properties is given by

$$\bar{\nu} = \frac{1}{\lambda} = \frac{\nu}{V} \tag{6.1}$$

The velocity of electromagnetic waves in a vacuum is c (the speed of light), which is about 3×10^{10} cm/sec; the velocity in any other medium is lower.

The following units are in common use for measurement of electromagnetic spectra:

$$\mu\text{m (micrometer)} = 10^{-6} \text{ meters} = 10^{-4} \text{ centimeters}$$
$$\text{nm (nanometer)} = 10^{-9} \text{ meters} = 10^{-7} \text{ centimeters}$$
$$\text{Å (angstrom)} = 10^{-10} \text{ meters} = 10^{-8} \text{ centimeters}$$

In recent years, the nanometer (nm) unit has replaced the older unit, millimicron (mμ), and micrometer (μm) has replaced micron (μ).

The terms for wavelength that are customarily used depend on the spectral region being described. The Å is commonly used to describe x-ray radiation, nm for ultraviolet and visible wavelength, and μm for infrared wavelengths.

Electromagnetic radiation is an alternating electrical and magnetic field in space. Its wave properties can be explained in terms of mutually perpendicular electric and magnetic vectors, both perpendicular to the direction of wave propagation and each maintaining the other. A continuously propagating wave motion does not appear subdivisible into discrete units having an independent existence, and could be considered a continuous stream of energy; but when radiation interacts with matter, its properties are those of particles, not waves. A quantitative description of many interactions between radiation and matter is possible by considering radiation as discrete quanta of energy called *photons*. The energy of a photon is proportional to the frequency of radiation. These dual views of radiation as waves and particles are not mutually exclusive. Indeed this duality is useful for the quantitative description of other phenomena, such as the behavior of electrons or other elementary particles.

The wave nature of radiation is familiarly illustrated by refraction effects in material media, diffraction, and interference phenomena. Discrete and band spectra are evidences of quantized energy states in matter and of quantized energy transfer between radiation and matter. The amount of energy transferred per photon is given by the Einstein-Planck relation

$$E = h\nu = \frac{hc}{\lambda} = hc\bar{\nu} \tag{6.2}$$

where
E = the energy in joules
h = Planck's constant (6.62×10^{-34} joule-sec)
ν = the frequency of the radiation in hertz

Although it may seem strange at first, wavenumbers are easier for most spectroscopists to use. (Frequencies are a factor of 10^{10} greater.) Note that $1 \mu m = 10^{-4}$ cm $= 10^{-6}$ m. Thus

$$\lambda(\mu m) = \frac{10^4}{\nu(cm^{-1})}$$

To convert wavenumbers to electron volts

$$E(eV) = \frac{12399}{\lambda(\text{Å})}$$

Table 6.1 presents some conversion factors useful in spectroscopy.

The Einstein-Planck relation indicates that the energy of a photon of *monochromatic* (single-frequency) radiation depends only on its wavelength or frequency. A beam of radiation is more or less intense depending on the quantity of photons per unit time and per unit area, but the quantum energy (E) per photon is always the same for a given frequency of the radiation.

Planck explained correctly the energy *distribution with frequency* of a black body by assuming the atomic oscillators in the body to be quantized according to Equation 6.2. Bohr, in 1914, laid the foundation for the correct interpretation of spectra of atoms and molecules with these postulates:

1. Atomic systems exist in stable states without radiating electromagnetic energy.
2. Absorption or emission of electromagnetic energy occurs when an atomic system changes from one energy state to another.
3. The absorption or emission process corresponds to a photon of radiant energy $h\nu = E' - E''$, where $E' - E''$ is the difference in energy between two states of an atomic system.

TABLE 6.1. *Conversion Factors Useful in Spectroscopy*

Unit	ergs/molecule	cm^{-1}	cal/mole	eV/molecule
1 eV/molecule =	1.602×10^{-12}	8065.5	23,060	1
1 cal/mole =	6.948×10^{-17}	0.34975	1	4.336×10^{-5}
1 cm^{-1} =	1.986×10^{-16}	1	2.8591	1.240×10^{-4}
1 erg/molecule =	1	5.034×10^{15}	1.439×10^{16}	6.241×10^{11}

Source: Adapted from C. E. Meloan, *Elementary Infrared Spectroscopy*, New York: Macmillan, 1963, p 5.

TABLE 6.2. *Interaction of Radiation with Matter*

Radiation Absorbed	Energy Changes Involved
Visible, ultraviolet, or x-ray	Electronic transitions, vibrational or rotational changes
Infrared	Molecular vibrational changes with superimposed rotational changes
Far-infrared; microwave	Rotational changes
Radio-frequency	Too weak to be observed except under an intense magnetic field (see Chaps. 12 and 13).

The absorption or emission of radiant energy by matter is one of the most important fingerprints furnished by nature. When a beam of radiation is passed through an absorbing substance, the intensity of the incident radiation (I_0) will be greater than that (I) of the emergent radiation. (I_0 and I are sometimes symbolized by P_0 and P, since the intensity to which we refer has units of energy per unit time, or power.) Part of the radiation that passes into a substance, instead of being absorbed, may be scattered or reflected when emerging from the substance, or re-emitted at the same wavelength or at a different wavelength. In other cases, the radiation may undergo changes in orientation or polarization. The absorption of radiation at various wavelengths is summarized in Table 6.2.

Those portions of the electromagnetic spectrum useful to chemists are shown in Figure 6.1. The spectrum is divided according to frequency (energy), and corresponding spectroscopic methods are shown in the appropriate frequency ranges. For clarity, these methods and the corresponding energy states of matter are listed in Table 6.3. Notice that the various energy states and basic phenomena are diverse, and so there are different methods and techniques. These methods and techniques are not difficult to learn, however, and one need not be an expert to obtain many extremely important and useful results.

TABLE 6.3. *Spectroscopic Methods and Corresponding Energy States of Matter or Basis of Phenomenon*

Nuclear Magnetic Resonance	Nuclear spin coupling with an applied magnetic field
Microwave Spectroscopy	Rotation of molecules
Electron Spin Resonance	Spin coupling of unpaired electrons with an applied magnetic field
Infrared and Raman Spectroscopy	Rotation of molecules
	Vibration of molecules
	Rotation/vibration of molecules
	Electronic transitions (some large molecules only)
Ultraviolet-visible Spectroscopy	Electronic energy
	Impinging monoenergetic electrons causing valence-electron excitations
x-Ray Spectroscopy	Electronic transitions
	Diffraction and reflection of x-ray radiation from atomic layers

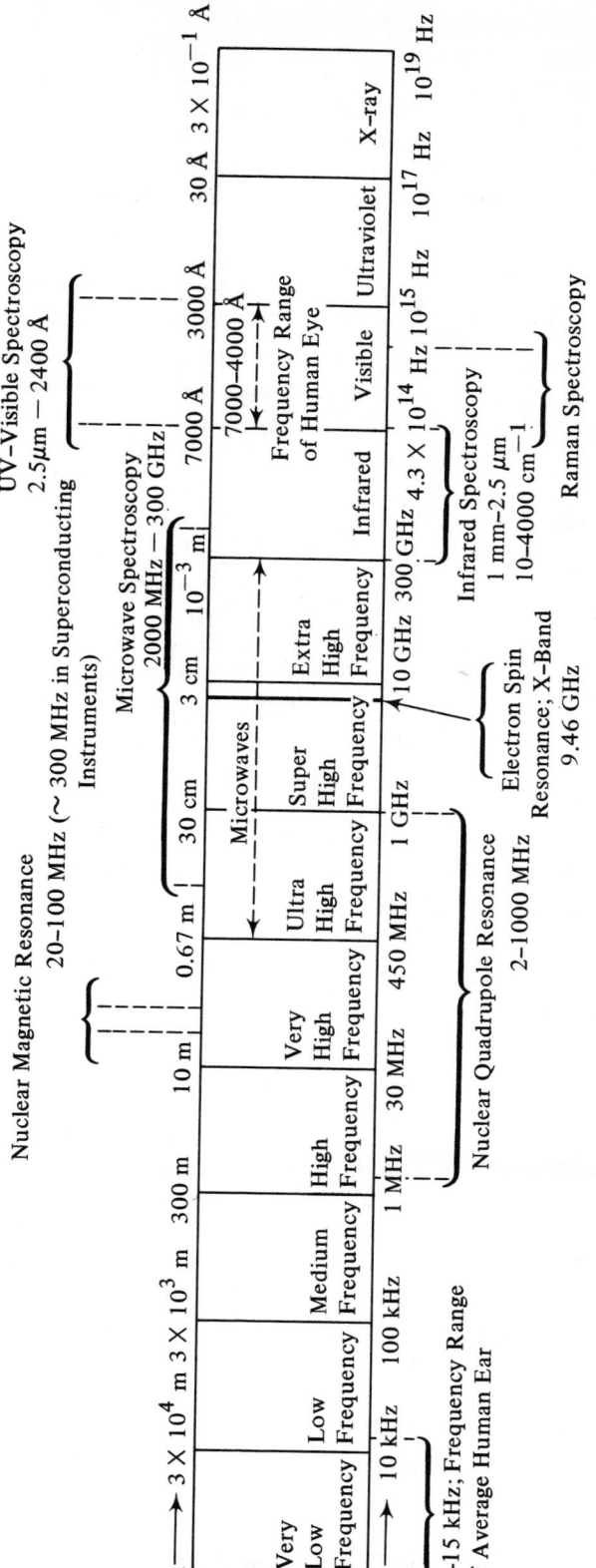

FIGURE 6.1. *The electromagnetic spectrum from DC to x-ray; frequency ranges are shown for different spectroscopic methods.*

6.2 APPLICATION OF QUANTUM THEORY TO SPECTROSCOPY

The laws of classical mechanics, which apply to the energies of objects of ordinary size, such as Ping-Pong balls, cannot be used to understand the behavior of microscopic bodies such as atoms, electrons, and molecules. For example, a Ping-Pong ball can spin (rotate) and bounce with any speed depending on how it is hit; that is, the rotational energy and the bouncing velocity of a Ping-Pong ball can assume any value on a continuous scale. However, a molecule cannot rotate or vibrate freely with any particular energy; it is subject to what are called quantum restrictions, and is limited to only certain discrete values of velocities and energies. The significance of quantum restrictions on a particular motion of a microscopic body depends on the space available for such a motion: if there is a large space for a motion, that motion is less subject to quantum restrictions on its energy.

We learn from quantum mechanics that allowed energy states exist in which a molecule or an atom may spend long or short periods of time. A molecule or atom can exist in intermediate energy states for only a transient time when it is ascending or descending from one level (or state) to another.

Monoatomic substances normally exist in the gaseous state and absorb radiation only through an increase in their electronic energy. It should be remembered that electrons in a given atom occupy discrete energy levels and are thus quantized. These quantized levels take the form of the various subshells illustrated in Figure 6.2. Therefore electronic absorption of radiation can take place only if the impinging photon has an energy that is equal to the energy difference, ΔE, between two quantized energy levels.

FIGURE 6.2. *Energy levels for the electrons in a polyelectron atom.*

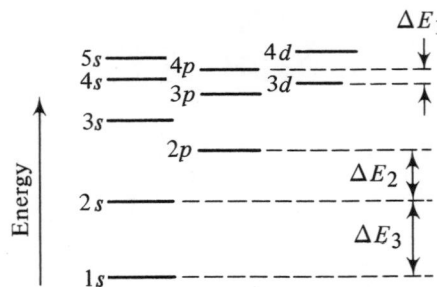

For a polyelectron atom, a multiplicity of absorptions is permissible. The energy required to produce a $3d \rightarrow 4p$ transition (ΔE_1) corresponds to visible radiation; $2s \rightarrow 2p$ (ΔE_2) requires far-ultraviolet radiation; and $1s \rightarrow 2s$ (ΔE_3) requires x-ray radiation.

For polyatomic molecules, electronic transitions involve molecular orbitals; such transitions require energy in the ultraviolet region and are of vital importance in ultraviolet spectroscopy.

Effect of Structure on Absorption

The spectrum is a function of the whole structure of a molecule rather than of specific bonds. Photons of low energy (far infrared, microwave) can produce changes of rotational energy. More energetic photons change the energy of molecular vibration as well as rotation (near-infrared). With visible and ultraviolet light, valence-shell electrons are excited, and these electronic transitions are usually accompanied by changes in vibration and rotation. In the far ultraviolet, the energies of the photons may even break bonds.

6.3 INSTRUMENTATION

A *spectrograph* is an "instrument with an entrance slit and a dispersing device that uses photography to obtain a record of spectral range. The radiant power passing through the optical system is integrated over time, and the quantity recorded is a function of radiant energy." An *optical spectrometer* has "an entrance slit, a dispersing device, and one or more slit exits, with which measurements are made at selected wavelengths within the spectral range, or by scanning over the range. The quantity detected is a function of radiant power." A *spectrophotometer* "furnishes the ratio, or a function of the ratio, of the radiant power of two beams as a function of spectral wavelength. These two beams may be separated in time, space, or both." [3]

Figure 6.3 shows the block diagram of a basic spectrometer which may be used for the study of various energy states of matter; typical components are listed in each block.

Commercial spectroscopic instruments are readily available; some of these are very sophisticated, for use in exacting research studies that require high precision. Many studies do not require such precision; for these, simple, less expensive, models are also available. In some cases, part or all of such instruments may be built by the investigator at a considerable saving.

Usually the building blocks are the same for any spectrometer, i.e., a source of electromagnetic energy, a sample to be investigated, an analyzer to sort out energies that are modified by the sample in some manner, a detector of these energies, and a recorder (which may include an electronic amplifier to boost the power level of the detected energy).

One of the simplest "spectroscopic"—more properly "optical"—methods is termed "colorimetric." In this technique, white light is passed through a sample and the percentage of energy absorbed is recorded and related to sample properties. If some type of dispersing device such as a prism or grating is used to restrict the white light to a narrow band of frequencies, the method resembles the monochromatic method in which only a single frequency, or very narrow band of frequencies, is viewed at any instant of time.

However, monochromatic methods are used more extensively because of the frequent need to extract more detailed information from a sample. The method may involve emission, absorption, or scattering of electromagnetic energy, or *fluorescence* (radiation is absorbed and reemitted).

Source

The source of electromagnetic radiation is chosen according to the spectral range to be studied, i.e., according to energy requirements (source intensity is usually less important than source energy). The typical sources listed in Figure 6.3 span the

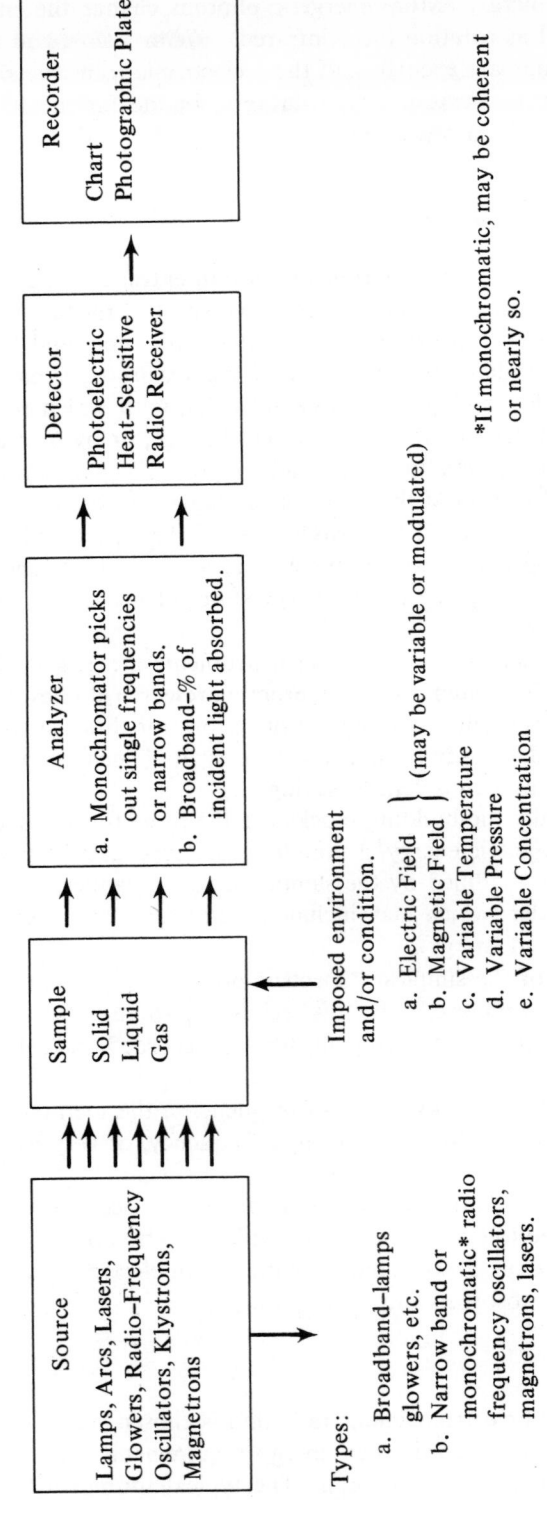

FIGURE 6.3. *Block diagram of a basic spectrometer, including some typical devices and conditions.*

electromagnetic spectrum from radio frequencies to x-rays. Some sources such as lasers and klystrons emit nearly monochromatic, nearly phase-coherent radiation, while other sources such as lamps and glowers emit a broad spectrum of phase-incoherent frequencies.

Sample

The sample may be a solid, a liquid, or a gas. A certain physical arrangement or enclosure of a sample is usually necessary for successful spectroscopic results; often, environmental conditions are imposed upon the sample to create either a necessary set of conditions for a recordable effect, or a perturbation of some type that produces additional energy states for study. Standard sampling techniques and apparatus suffice for the majority of compounds, but occasionally the chemical nature of the sample is troublesome and the usual techniques fail. A troublesome sample may be a highly corrosive gas, an easily decomposed compound, or a hygroscopic compound; it may be explosive, highly toxic, deeply colored, radioactive, or viscous. In cases like these, the chemist must develop a new sampling technique for his particular problem, and the integrity of the data may depend upon his ingenuity and finesse in developing it.

Experiments require that energy be absorbed or transmitted by a sample, while at the same time gases, liquids, hygroscopic materials, and other sensitive or dangerous compounds must be contained. Therefore, it is often necessary to enclose the sample in a cell of some sort. Each cell must have windows that transmit a particular band of wavelengths and resist particular forms of chemical degradation. As an example, suppose one wished to obtain the pure-rotational energies of the HF molecule (see the application section of this chapter for some reasons for wanting such information). Hydrogen fluoride is highly corrosive, and the temperature of the sample must be above room temperature to avoid dimerization. The pure-rotation energy absorption of HF occurs in the far infrared (50 μm–1000 μm wavelength) region, so one must choose a window for a low-pressure gas cell that will withstand atmospheric pressure from the outside, be highly resistant to chemical attack, transmit the desired wavelengths, and not decompose when the sample cell is heated. Polyethylene satisfies these requirements.

Monochromators

Monochromators are frequency (energy) analyzers. The analysis is usually accomplished by varying the incidence angle of prism(s) or grating(s) with respect to the incident radiation. The spectral range scanned is determined by the apex angle of the prism or by the spacing of grating lines. Filters may also be used to pass or reject specific frequencies.

Prisms. A prism is constructed to take advantage of Snell's law. Recall that for a light ray this law relates angle of incidence to angle of refraction by

$$n \sin \phi = n' \sin \phi' \tag{6.3}$$

where ϕ = the angle of incidence
ϕ' = the angle of refraction
n = the refractive index of the medium of incidence
n' = the refractive index of the medium in which refraction occurs

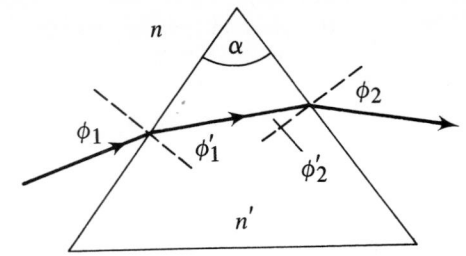

FIGURE 6.4. *Refraction of a light ray by
a prism.*

In a prism, two plane surfaces are inclined at some apex angle, α, such that the deviation produced by the first surface is increased by the second surface (see Fig. 6.4). The refraction obeys Snell's law, so that

$$\frac{\sin \phi_1}{\sin \phi_1'} = \frac{n'}{n} = \frac{\sin \phi_2}{\sin \phi_2'} \qquad (6.4)$$

The refractive index of the prism material depends upon the wavelength of the incident light, so the angle of deviation ϕ becomes a function of wavelength

$$\frac{d\phi}{d\lambda} = \frac{d\phi}{dn}\frac{dn}{d\lambda} \qquad (6.5)$$

The factor $d\phi/dn$ is determined by geometrical considerations, but the factor $dn/d\lambda$ is characteristic of the prism material and it is called the *dispersion*. Typical prism materials are quartz glass, NaCl, KBr, or CsI. Quartz is used in the ultraviolet region, glass is used in the visible region, and the other three materials are used in the medium infrared region.

   If many wavelengths strike the prism simultaneously, each wavelength emerges from the prism at a different angle. In practice, the prism is rotated about an axis perpendicular to the triangular cross-section. A radiation detector is placed at a fixed distance from the prism, so that as the prism rotates, successive wavelengths fall upon the detector.

Diffraction Gratings. The diffraction grating was invented by Joseph von Fraunhofer (1787–1826). The word *diffraction* implies effects produced by cutting off portions of wave fronts. A diffraction grating may be used either in transmission or reflection, but the dispersion of incident wavelengths depends upon the geometry of the grating.

   A grating is a parallel array of equidistant grooves, closely spaced. The spacing between these grooves is called d. A transmission grating is made by ruling parallel grooves on glass with a diamond edge. Reflection gratings are made by ruling parallel grooves on a metal mirror. The great majority of spectroscopic applications of gratings use reflecting optics. In these applications, the reflection gratings are replicated from a master grating.

   The reflection of incident light by a grating is shown in Figure 6.5. A portion of the collimated light beam incident at angle i is reflected at angle θ. The angle i does not have to equal the angle θ as in reflection. The path difference for incoming rays 1 and 2 is AB $= d \sin i$, and the path difference for outgoing rays 3 and 4 is

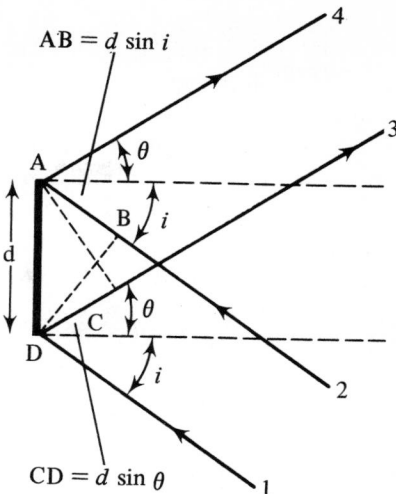

FIGURE 6.5. *Diffraction of incident light by a reflection grating having a groove spacing of d.*

AB = $d \sin i$

CD = $d \sin \theta$

CD = $d \sin \theta$. The total path difference for an incident and reflected ray is $d \sin i -d \sin \theta$. When this difference is equal to one or more wavelengths, no interference occurs and a bright image is seen. In general

$$n\lambda = d(\sin i \pm \sin \theta),\qquad (6.6)$$

where n (an integer) = the *order* of the grating

The path differences are added when both light rays are on the same side of the normal to the grating surface.

Assume that angles i and θ remain constant, and that values of n (> 1) and smaller values of λ are chosen so that the product, $n\lambda$, remains constant. It is seen that shorter wavelengths may be reflected at the same angle, θ, as were the longer wavelengths corresponding to $n = 1$. These shorter wavelengths are called *higher orders*. To disperse incident light of many wavelengths, the grating is rotated so that the angle i changes. Assuming $n = 1$, different wavelengths will be reflected at the same angle, θ. Higher-order wavelengths will also be reflected at this same angle and these wavelengths will have to be filtered out before they reach the detector.

The dispersion of the grating, $d\theta/d\lambda$, may be calculated by assuming the angle i is a constant. Then

$$\frac{d\theta}{d\lambda} = \frac{n}{d \cos \theta} \qquad (6.7)$$

The dispersion equals the order divided by the product of the grating spacing and the cosine of the angle of reflection. The *resolving power* of a grating is the product of the number of rulings and the order. Hence the resolving power of a large grating (more area) is greater than that of one with smaller area.

Filters. Optical filters are used extensively in spectroscopy to pass or reject certain frequencies or bands of frequencies. These filters are of three main types: (a) cut-in (or cut-off), (b) bandpass, and (c) band-rejection. The nomenclature is illustrated by the graph in Figure 6.6. Filter A is a cut-in filter if one reads from left to right along the frequency axis. The cut-in frequency is usually defined as f_0, the frequency at which the transmission begins to be approximately constant. Notice that the rate of cut-in (% T vs. f) may vary depending upon the construction of the filter. Filter **B** (a bandpass filter) rejects all frequencies except those between f_1 and f_2. Practically speaking, the useful frequency range of the filter is between those frequencies where the transmission is greater than 30%. Filter C (a band-rejection filter) passes all frequencies except those in the range f_3 to f_4. This filter is most useful in the region of high attenuation (small-percentage transmission). The shapes and widths of the transmission regions of these various filters may be varied considerably, depending upon the application.

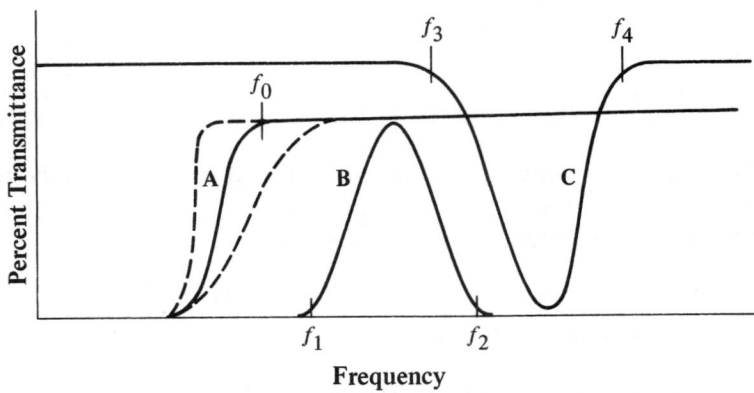

FIGURE 6.6. *Frequency versus percentage transmission for three types of optical filters. A: cut-in or cut-off. B: bandpass. C: band-rejection.*

A fourth type of filter, not shown in Figure 6.6, is called a *restrahlen* filter. This type of filter is used in reflection only, and it reflects a relatively narrow range of frequencies—all other frequencies are absorbed. Restrahlen filters are useful, for example, in suppressing unwanted orders from a grating.

It is also possible to use a prism or a grating as a selective filter. The selective transmission or reflection of electromagnetic energy is a function of the incidence angle. For example, a prism may be used in transmission to restrict the number of frequencies incident upon a grating, making it unnecessary to use additional filters to eliminate higher orders of the grating. Such a prism is called a *fore-prism*.

Resolution

The resolution (ability to separate frequencies) of a spectrometer is determined by various factors such as the dimensions of the dispersing element, the arrangement of the associated optics, and the spectral limits imposed by a mechanical slit of some sort.

The mechanical slit is placed before the detector to limit further the number of frequencies that impinge simultaneously upon it. Transfer optics may differ from one type of monochromator to another and yield different spatial spreads of the frequencies that arrive at the mechanical slit. An adjustment of the slit width effects a mechanical control of the bandwidth of radiation seen by the detector. The real measure of the radiation seen by the detector is called the *spectral slit width* (in cm^{-1}) which is a measure of the frequency spread seen by the detector. The spectral slit width is a function of the optical geometry, the instrument's dispersion, and the mechanical width of the slit.

If the source is monochromatic or nearly so, or if the source is monochromatic and tunable, then very high resolution is possible, providing the frequency stability of the source is good. Tunable sources have been available for some time in the radio-frequency and microwave regions of the spectrum, but it is only recently that tunable lasers have become available in the infrared and visible regions.

An important criterion for a monochromator is the amount of stray radiation reflected and transmitted through the system to the detector. Such extraneous radiation produces signal errors at the detector. Roughly speaking, stray light decreases as the resolution improves. Two monochromators may be coupled optically into a double monochromator to decrease stray light markedly. Also, a monochromator may be a double-pass or a single-pass type, depending upon the number of times the radiation is dispersed.

Detectors

Research has continued over the years to develop sensitive, noise-free detectors. There are inherent quantum-imposed limits on detectors, which we do not expect to exceed, but in recent years many significant breakthroughs in detector technology have occurred. Detectors are classified into two general groups, selective and nonselective. The response of a selective detector varies with the frequency of the incident radiation whereas the response of a nonselective detector does not. A listing of typical detectors is shown in Figure 6.3, but each spectroscopic method imposes its special requirements for a detector. Photoelectric detectors, photographic plates, and photoconductive cells are selective detectors, whereas thermocouples, bolometers, pneumatic cells, and square-law crystals have responses (at infrared and microwave frequencies) that are *relatively* insensitive to wavelength and thus can be classified as nonselective.

Photoelectric detectors are useful in the ultraviolet-visible region of the spectrum. When coupled with the appropriate electronic circuitry, these detectors are capable of counting as little as one photon per second. Specific types of photoelectric detectors have frequency (energy) responses that peak in different subregions of the ultraviolet-visible region. Photoelectric detectors are often cooled to reduce random tube noise ("shot" noise).

Photographic plates are extremely sensitive photon detectors in this same region. The speed of data acquisition is, of course, much lower owing to the processing time required for the plate. Most photographic plates are insensitive in the infrared region, but infrared phosphors extend their range somewhat into the infrared.

A photoconductive cell is an important selective detector. Such cells show an increase in conductivity when illuminated with infrared light, and they have high sensitivity with fast response. These cells are used extensively in the spectral region 0.5–3.5 μm (5000 Å–35,000 Å). The range may be extended slightly by cooling the cell with liquid hydrogen.

In a thermocouple—used for measuring infrared radiation—a junction of two dissimilar metals is blackened to increase absorption of incident radiation. The temperature rise at the junction relative to a "cold junction" on which infrared radiation does not fall increases the potential across the junction; this potential is amplified to a usable voltage. Thermocouples have a relatively slow response (thermal lag) and if the infrared radiation is time-varying, it must not vary too rapidly.

Bolometers have a faster response than do thermocouples, and they are useful in the infrared and microwave regions. Metal bolometers have a small thermal capacity that permits a quicker response than thermistor bolometers. Incident radiation falls upon an element that forms one arm of a Wheatstone bridge. The resistance of the arm changes with temperature and the bridge goes unbalanced, producing an error signal which is amplified. Some types of bolometers are useful in the microwave region at frequencies up to about 60 GHz. Commercial thermistor bolometers are matched pairs of "flakes" that have similar electrical and thermal properties. One of the flakes serves as a compensatory element to eliminate the effect of background radiation.

Pneumatic cells are very sensitive devices, useful from the near-infrared region to the 300–150 GHz microwave range (1 GHz = 1 Gigahertz = 10^9 Hertz). In a pneumatic cell, incident radiation heats a confined gas, which expands, moving a curved diaphragm with a mirror surface. A light beam reflected from this surface to a photocell varies in intensity with the movement of the diaphragm.

6.4 APPLICATIONS

The applications of modern spectroscopic methods are legion! They are used in such widely diverse fields as controlling pollution and detecting art forgeries. A few general applications will be discussed here for each spectroscopic method listed in Table 6.3.

Nuclear magnetic resonance (NMR) is the spectroscopic method used to study proton resonances. Electromagnetic radiation causes the magnetic moment of protons to "flip" in the presence of an external applied magnetic field. Proton chemical shifts are usually measured with respect to an arbitrary reference compound such as tetramethysilane. Proton resonances of different functional groupings occur at characteristic values called "τ-values," which depend upon the chemical and magnetic environment in which the group occurs. NMR of fluorine, phosphorus, boron, and some other elements with a nuclear magnetic moment is also used extensively. Undoubtedly, the single most important application of NMR has been in the qualitative identification of organic compounds and the elucidation of their structure. NMR, gas-liquid chromatography, and infrared spectroscopy are probably the three most important tools available today for the organic chemist.

Microwave spectroscopy is used to measure dipole moments and moments of inertia of simple molecules in the gas phase. The chemical composition of the molecule and the masses of its atoms are usually known, so one uses moments of inertia to help determine the structure of a molecule, perhaps the most important application of microwave spectroscopy. Sometimes it is necessary to use x-ray data also to supplement the microwave data. From the pattern of the rotational spectrum it is possible to determine the symmetry of the molecular configuration, i.e., whether planar, linear, or polar. The technique is very sensitive to sample concentration and pressure, and it is used in some important air-pollution measurements.

Electron-spin resonance is used to map unpaired-electron distributions in molecules and molecular fragments. The method is versatile and may be used to detect free radicals in cancer tissue, for example, or for routine monitoring of vanadium in crude petroleum. Because the effect depends simply upon the presence of unpaired electrons, there are many other analytical and practical applications.

Infrared and Raman spectroscopy are complementary methods used, for instance, to study molecular structure, identify compounds and functional groups, determine interatomic forces and bond-stretching distances, perform quantitative and qualitative analyses, and determine thermodynamic properties. The three states of matter may be studied by these methods over wide ranges of temperature and pressure. Selection rules for different molecular structures determine which spectral lines are allowed, and these rules differ for the infrared and Raman methods. This difference is used to advantage in studies of molecular structure, because two types of information are brought to bear on the same problem.

The ultraviolet-visible method is useful for the study of electronic transitions in molecules and atoms. Although various forms of ultraviolet-visible spectroscopy can be used to study a myriad of important chemical and physical properties, we will be most concerned with its use in quantitative analysis. It is probably the single most frequently used analytical method, with the possible exception of the analytical balance. For example, a single clinical analysis laboratory in a major hospital may perform a million chemical analyses a year, primarily on serum and urine, and about 70% of these tests are done by ultraviolet-visible absorption spectroscopy. Atomic absorption and emission spectroscopy (Chaps. 10 and 11) is used primarily to analyze for metallic elements in a variety of matrices—serum, natural waters, tissues, and so forth.

X-ray spectroscopy rivals visible spectroscopy as a tool for elemental analysis. Because the energies of x-rays are much higher than those of visible radiation, however, x-rays usually cause transitions of inner-shell electrons rather than of valence-shell electrons. There are many advantages of this method in spectrochemical analysis. A quantitative analysis of a mixture of rare-earth oxides may be performed or a crystal structure may be determined. A specimen that contains two elements widely separated in atomic number may be studied, or the thickness of a very thin layer of tin plating may be measured. The most widespread use of x-rays has been in the field of metallurgy, but x-rays may also be used to analyze metals, minerals, liquids, glasses, ceramics, or plastics.

REFERENCES

1. R. B. LEIGHTON, *Principles of Modern Physics*, New York: McGraw-Hill, 1959, p 81.

2. R. B. LEIGHTON, *Principles of Modern Physics*, New York: McGraw-Hill, 1959, p 67.

3. "Spectrometry Nomenclature," *Anal. Chem.*, 46, 2257 (1974).

7

Ultraviolet and Visible Absorption Spectroscopy

K. L. Cheng
J. W. Prather II

Photometric methods are perhaps the most frequently used of all spectroscopic methods, and are important in quantitative analysis. The amount of visible light or other radiant energy absorbed by a solution is measured; since it depends on the concentration of the absorbing substance, it is possible to determine quantitatively the amount present.

Colorimetry refers to the determination of a substance from its ability to absorb visible light. Visual colorimetric methods are based on the comparison of a colored solution of unknown concentration with one or more colored solutions of known concentration. In spectrophotometric methods, the ratio of the intensities of the incident and the transmitted beams of light is measured at a specific wavelength by means of a detector such as a photocell.

The absorption spectrum also provides a "fingerprint" for qualitatively identifying the absorbing substance.

7.1 MOLECULAR ABSORPTION OF RADIATION: ELECTRONIC SPECTRA

Molecular absorption in the ultraviolet and visible region depends on the electronic structure of the molecule. Energy is absorbed in quanta, elevating electrons from orbitals in a lower-energy (ground) state to orbitals in a higher-energy (excited) state. Since (for quantum-mechanical reasons) only certain states are possible in any mole-

TABLE 7.1. *Absorption of Visible Light and Color*

Wavelength nm	Color (Absorbed)	Color Observed (Transmitted) or Complementary Hue
< 380	Ultraviolet	
380–435	Violet	Yellowish-Green
435–480	Blue	Yellow
480–490	Greenish-Blue	Orange
490–560	Bluish-Green	Red
500–560	Green	Purple
560–580	Yellowish-Green	Violet
580–595	Yellow	Blue
595–650	Orange	Greenish-Blue
650–780	Red	Bluish-Green
> 780	Near Infrared	

cule and the energy difference between any ground and excited state must equal the energy added by the quantum, only certain frequencies can be absorbed. In many electronic structures, absorption does not occur in the readily accessible part of the ultraviolet region, so that, in practice, ultraviolet spectrophotometry is mostly confined to conjugated systems.

When a beam of radiation is passed through an absorbing substance, the intensity of the incident radiation (I_0) will be greater than that of the emergent radiation (I). The absorption of visible (Table 7.1), ultraviolet, and x-ray radiation usually results in electronic transitions in matter, with accompanying vibrational and rotational changes in the case of molecular substances. In general, the excited atoms and molecules resulting from absorption of radiation return to the ground state very rapidly, either by losing energy in the form of heat to the surroundings or by re-emitting electromagnetic radiation (luminescence or fluorescence).

The absorption of electromagnetic radiation by molecules is far more complex than absorption by individual atoms, which have no vibrational or rotational energy levels. The total energy may be considered as a sum of contributions from electronic, rotational, and vibrational energies:

$$E_{total} = E_{el} + E_{rot} + E_{vib} \qquad (7.1)$$

where E_{el} = the electronic energy of the molecule

E_{rot} = the energy associated with the rotation of the molecule around its center of gravity

E_{vib} = the energy of the molecule due to interatomic vibrations

For each electronic energy state of the molecule, there normally are several possible vibrational states and for each of these, in turn, numerous rotational states (Fig. 7.1). Consequently, the number of possible energy levels for a molecule is much larger than for an atomic particle.

The electronic energy is generally larger than the other two (E_{rot} and E_{vib}), and electronic transitions ordinarily involve energies corresponding to ultraviolet

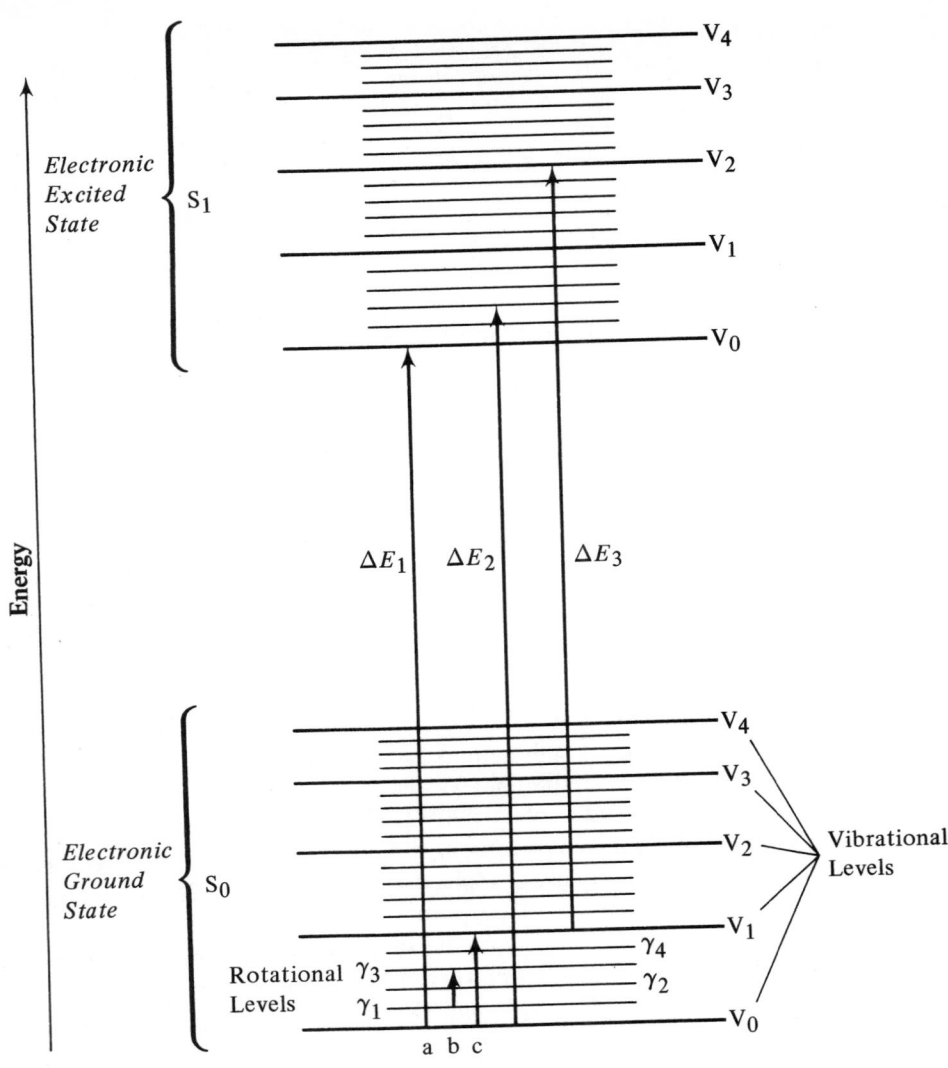

FIGURE 7.1. *Molecular energy levels and (a) electronic, (b) rotational, and (c) vibrational transitions.*

or visible radiation. Pure vibrational transitions are caused by the less energetic infrared radiation (1 to 15 μm); rotational transitions require even less energy (10 to 10,000 μm). Furthermore, changes in vibrational and rotational levels invariably accompany electronic excitation of a molecule. A molecule may jump from any of the vibrational and rotational levels in the ground state to any of a large number of possible vibrational and rotational levels in a given excited state. Because a photon of slightly different energy corresponds to each of the many possible jumps, visible and UV molecular absorption spectra consist of hundreds or thousands of lines so closely spaced that they appear as continuous absorption bands, in contrast to the sharp lines that characterize atomic spectra or rotational spectra in the far-infrared region.

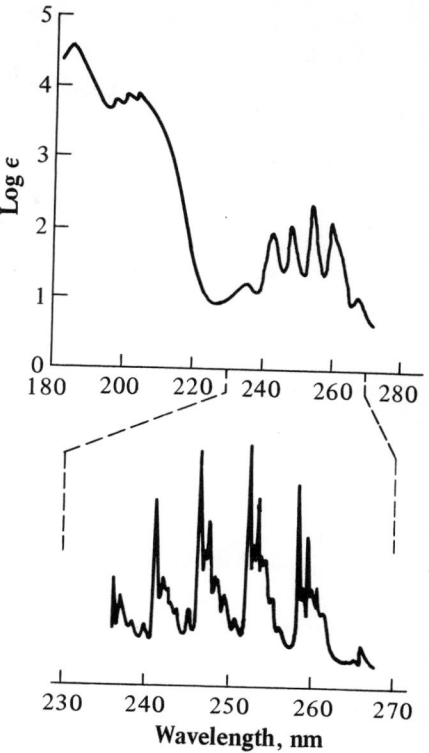

FIGURE 7.2. *Ultraviolet absorption spectra of benzene. Upper: Benzene solution in ethanol solvent. Lower: Benzene vapor. From R. E. Dodd,* Chemical Spectroscopy, *Amsterdam: Elsevier, 1962, p 227, by permission of the publisher.*

Collisions between neighboring molecules in solution cause slight modifications of the various energy levels and lead to further broadening and merging of absorption bands. A dramatic illustration of the effects due to changing from a gaseous state to a liquid state is given in Figure 7.2. The many sharp absorption peaks are an example of vibrational fine structure superimposed on the electronic absorption band; the much broader bands show that a substantial portion of the fine structure is lost because of molecular interaction and collision.

Selection Rules

In addition to matching the energy of a photon with the energy difference between two levels, a second requirement must be met for the absorption of radiation by matter: the energy transition in the molecule must be accompanied by a change in the electrical center of the molecule so that electric work can be carried out on the molecule by the electromagnetic radiation. Requirements for the absorption of radiation by matter are summarized in quantum-mechanical "selection" rules, which determine which transitions may take place. These rules, based on considerations of the symmetry of the system in the upper and lower states, point out that some transitions are more probable than others.

The first selection rule is related to all molecules with centers of symmetry and deals with the *parity-forbidden* transitions. The second rule states that singlet-triplet transitions are forbidden. The third rule applies to forbidden transitions that arise from the symmetry of states—for instance, the long-wavelength bands of C=O, C=S, some chromophores, and the 260-nm band of benzene. In addition to these three types of forbidden transitions, there are also many other *weak energy* transitions with low intensities.

However, forbidden transitions are still observed in many molecules, because intramolecular or intermolecular perturbations cause the rules to relax considerably. Singlet-triplet transitions, for instance, occur with increased intensity in the presence of paramagnetic substances such as O_2 or NO or in solvents such as C_2H_5I that contain heavy atoms.

Franck and Condon have suggested an important rule for understanding the nature of electronic transitions. Their principle states that movement of the nuclei is negligible during the time taken by an electronic transition because these transitions are so fast (about 10^{-15} sec) that the positions and velocities of nuclei have no time to change. The idea is obviously closely related to the Born-Oppenheimer approximation in which the various motions of a molecule are considered to be separable. The Franck-Condon principle indicates that electronic transitions will occur only when the internuclear distances are not significantly different in the two states and when the nuclei have little or no velocity.

Nomenclature

Unfortunately, the terms used in spectrophotometry and spectroscopy are confusing. The recommendation of the American Society for Testing Material, endorsed by *Analytical Chemistry* [1], is now widely accepted. The recommended terms, symbols, and definitions used in this chapter are given in Table 7.2. The Commission

TABLE 7.2. *Spectrophotometry Nomenclature*

Name	Symbol	Definition	Name Not Recommended
Absorbance	A	$-\log T$	Optical density (O.D.), extinction, absorbancy
Absorptivity	a	$= A/bc$*	Absorbancy index, absorbing index
Path length	b	Internal cell or sample length, in cm	l or d
Molar absorptivity	ε	$= A/bc$†	Molar absorbancy index, molar extinction coefficient, molar absorption coefficient
Transmittance	T	I/I_0‡	Transmittancy
Wavelength unit	nm	10^{-9} meter	$m\mu$ (millimicron)
	μm	10^{-6} meter	μ (micron)
Absorption maximum	$\lambda_{\max}$	Wavelength at which a maximum absorption occurs	——

* The concentration is in grams per liter.
† The concentration is in moles per liter.
‡ The ratio of radiant power transmitted to radiant power incident.

on Nomenclature, Division of Analytical Chemistry of the International Pure and Applied Chemistry (IUPAC), has made recommendations to stan the terms used in spectrometry. The following guidelines are suggested:

1. Single words are preferred, e.g., "wavelength" instead of "wave length" an "absorbance" instead of "optical density."
2. The commonly accepted metric system is preferred. The IUPAC has recommended the SI system and the U.S. National Bureau of Standards has strongly recommended the SI system.
3. The expression of absorption spectra by plotting the molar absorptivity as a function of wavelength, instead of simply plotting absorbance versus wavelength, is preferred. In addition to showing the maximum absorptions, it also gives information about sensitivity for analysis.

7.2 EFFECT OF STRUCTURE ON ABSORPTION

Spectroscopic characteristics are held in common by molecules with some of the same chemical features. It may then be reasonable to expect that the correlation can be extended, and that the presence of a certain chemical feature may be implied by the presence of a certain spectral characteristic.

Determination of molecular structure and the identification of specific functional groups are extremely important to modern chemistry. Since the interaction of ultraviolet and visible radiation with molecules is governed by the electronic structure of the molecule, these regions of the spectrum are of particular interest to the chemist. At present, most of the reported work has been on the absorption spectra (from 200 to 1000 nm) of organic molecules in dilute solutions [2–4]. In the future the trend may be to employ greater dispersion and to extend the range of wavelengths investigated.

Electronic Transitions

Electronic transitions in organic molecules are characterized by the promotion of electrons in ground-state bonding or nonbonding molecular orbitals to excited-state antibonding molecular orbitals. If molecular structure is the dominant factor in determining the electronic energies of the ground and excited states, then the photon energy required for $n \to \pi^*$, $\pi \to \pi^*$, and $n \to \sigma^*$ transitions will vary from molecule to molecule, depending on structural and environmental variations. When radiation of a frequency corresponding to one of the fundamental frequencies of a molecule interacts with that molecule, the radiant energy is absorbed to increase the energy content of the molecule by an amount equal to the energy of the quantum absorbed, in accordance with the relation

$$\Delta E = h\nu = hc/\lambda = 2.86 \times 10^5/\lambda \qquad (7.2)$$

where ν = the frequency in Hz
  h = Planck's constant (6.62×10^{-27} erg/sec)
  λ = the wavelength in cm
  c = the speed of light in vacuum (2.998×10^{10} cm/sec)

The most common types of electronic transitions are illustrated in Table 7.3.

Region of Electronic Spectra	Example
cuum ultraviolet	CH_4 at 125 nm
r ultraviolet, sometimes near ultraviolet	Acetone at 190 nm
	Methylamine at 213 nm
traviolet	Saturated aldehydes at 180 nm
$n \rightarrow \pi^*$ — Near ultraviolet and visible	Acetone at 277 nm
	Nitrobutane at 665 nm

The $\sigma \rightarrow \sigma^*$ transitions are very energetic and are found only below 200 nm, in the far-ultraviolet region. This is often termed the "vacuum ultraviolet" region because the normal constituents of air, N_2 and O_2, also absorb strongly below about 160 and 200 nm, respectively; and spectra of other substances must be obtained in a "vacuum." The $n \rightarrow \sigma^*$ transitions are also high-energy transitions and generally appear at the shorter ultraviolet wavelengths; for example, absorption by alkyl halides (where the nonbonding electrons are supplied by the halogen) shows a λ_{max} that increases in the order Cl < Br < I, as the electrons are successively easier to excite. The most common examples of $\pi \rightarrow \pi^*$ transitions are found in conjugated polyenes, in which the energy required for the transition decreases with increasing length of the conjugated systems and correspondingly, λ_{max} increases. The $\pi \rightarrow \pi^*$ transitions are usually the least energetic, which results in their appearance at longer wavelengths.

The molar absorptivity (ε) of a compound is a function of the cross-sectional area (θ) of the absorbing species and of the transition probability (P):

$$\varepsilon = 9 \times 10^{19} \, P\theta \tag{7.3}$$

Using this relation, a molar absorptivity of the order of 10^5 has been calculated for the average organic molecule with an assumed cross-section of about 10^{-15} cm^2 and a unit transition probability. The highest values known for ε are a few hundred thousand; any value above 10,000 is considered high, and one under 1000 low.

By examining the locations, distribution patterns, and intensities of absorption spectra, one can gain information helpful in the identification of compounds. Unfortunately, interpretation of electronic (ultraviolet-visible) spectra is usually less certain than that of vibrational (infrared) spectra because of the broad overlapping bands that characterize electronic absorption. Even so, a great deal of research effort has been expended in hopes that the structural changes of a molecule and the shifts observed in their electronic absorption spectra can be correlated. On the other hand, absorptivities in the infrared are much lower than at shorter wavelengths, rarely exceeding 1000. As a consequence, electronic (ultraviolet-visible) spectrophotometry is sensitive to a much smaller amount of sample and is quite useful for dilute solutions.

Chromophores

It is a long-recognized fact that colored substances owe their color to absorption of light by one or more unsaturated linkages. Such linkages or groups were named

TABLE 7.4. *Representative Chromophores and Their Approximate ε_{max} and λ_{max} Values*

Chromophore	λ_{max} (nm)	ε_{max}
$\diagdown C = C \diagdown$	185	8000
$-C \equiv C-$	175	6000
$\diagdown C = O$	188	900
$-NH_2$	195	2500
$-CHO$	210	20
$-COOR$	205	50
$-COOH$	205	60
$-N = N-$	252	8000
	371	14
$-N = O$	300	100
	665	20
$-NO_2$	270	14
$-Br$	205	400

chromophores by Witt in 1876. Certain groups which by themselves do not confer color to a substance but which increase the coloring power of a chromophore were called auxochromes.

Ultraviolet radiation is usually absorbed by a chromophore rather than by the molecule as a whole. Chromophores are, in most cases, covalent unsaturated groups such as those given in Table 7.4; they are functional groups that usually absorb in the near ultraviolet or visible region when they are bonded to a non-absorbing, saturated, residue that possesses no unshared or nonbonded electrons (e.g., a hydrocarbon chain). Auxochromes contain functional groups that have nonbonded valence electrons and exhibit no absorption at wavelengths above 220 nm. They do, however, absorb strongly in the far-ultraviolet region ($n \rightarrow \sigma^*$). If an auxochrome and a chromophore are combined in the same molecule, the chromophore absorption will typically shift to a longer wavelength and show an increase in intensity. Shifts to longer wavelengths are called bathochromic shifts; changes to shorter wavelengths, hypsochromic shifts. Increases in intensity of an absorption band are called hyperchromic effects, while a decrease in intensity is termed a hypochromic effect.

In general, molecules containing two or more chromophores show absorption that is the sum of all the chromophores present, provided they are separated by two or more single bonds. If two chromophores are conjugated, they exhibit a much enhanced absorption with an increase in both λ_{max} and ε_{max}; three conjugated chromophores result in a still further increase in λ_{max} and ε_{max}. Such bathochromic shifts are attributed to the formation of a new chromophore from the conjugated systems; the π electrons associated with each chromophore of the conjugated system are able to move with increased freedom throughout the new structure. Systems that show bathochromic shifts with an increase in ε_{max} are shown in Table 7.5. This

TABLE 7.5. *Effect of Structure on the Sensitivity of Reagent for Iron(II)*

Compound	Structure	$\lambda_{max, (nm)}$	ε_{max} ($\times 10^{-3}$)
A. *Pyridines*			
2,2'-Pyridyl		522	8.0
2,2',2'' Terpyridyl		522	11.1
2,6-Bis(4-phenyl-2-pyridyl)-4-phenylpyridine		583	30.2
B. *Phenanthrolines*			
1,10-Phenanthroline		508	11.1
Bathophenanthroline		533	22.3
C. *Triazines*			
2,4,6-Tripyridyl-*S*-triazine		595	24.1
3-(4-Phenyl-2-pyridyl)-5,6-diphenyl-1,2,4-triazine		561	28.7
3-(2-Pyridyl)-5,6-diphenyl-1,2,4-triazine-*p,p'*-disulfonic acid disodium salt		562	27.8

Source: From K. L. Cheng in J. D. Winefordner, ed., *Spectrochemical Methods of Analysis*, New York: John Wiley, 1971, p 358, by permission of the editor and John Wiley and Sons.

demonstrates an excellent application of chromophoric principles to the synthesis of new, selective, and sensitive analytical reagents.

Single Bonds and Saturated Compounds

Saturated hydrocarbons contain only single bonds with σ electrons; thus the only transitions available to these compounds are transitions of $\sigma \rightarrow \sigma^*$ type, which occur at the very short wavelengths of the vacuum ultraviolet. For example, methane and ethane are saturated hydrocarbons with all electrons involved in σ bonds. Electronic transitions are accordingly of the same type as those in the hydrogen molecule, and the separation of the levels is of the same order. Therefore, the first electronic absorption bands for methane and ethane are at 125 nm and 135 nm, respectively; this band continues to move to longer wavelengths in the larger hydrocarbons, suggesting that the C–C bond is involved.

Because of the excitation of electrons in nonbonded orbitals, saturated molecules that contain atoms with lone pairs of electrons exhibit electronic transitions at longer wavelengths than the corresponding saturated hydrocarbons. Thus, alkyl iodides and monosulfides containing the C–S–C linkage give $n \rightarrow \sigma^*$ transitions near 260 and 215 nm, respectively.

The $n \rightarrow \pi^*$ transitions associated with carbonyl groups are observed in the 270–290 nm region and are quite useful in the identification of aldehydes and ketones. For example, acetone exhibits three bands—a weak band at 280 nm ($n \rightarrow \pi^*$), a more intense band near 190 nm ($n \rightarrow \sigma^*$), and a still more intense band near 150 nm ($\pi \rightarrow \pi^*$). For these compounds, the $n \rightarrow \pi^*$ transition of the carbonyl group varies with the substituents R_1 and R_2 in the molecule:

$$\begin{matrix} R_1 \\ \diagdown \\ \text{C==O} \\ \diagup \\ R_2 \end{matrix}$$

Substituting a hydroxyl, amino, or halogen group (auxochromes) for hydrogen shifts the transition to higher energy, because these groups donate electron density by a resonance interaction and raise the energy of the excited state with respect to the ground state. In addition, these groups give rise to an inductive effect that withdraws electron density from the carbonyl group, thus lowering the ground state relative to the excited state.

Conjugated Chromophores

As stated above, a molecule that contains more than one chromophore has an absorption band that may be the sum of the separate chromophores, or it may be the result of an interaction between the chromophores. If the two chromophores are separated by a single bond, however, conjugation occurs and the electronic absorption spectra show dramatic changes from the bands due only to the isolated chromophores. One of the simplest examples is 1,3-butadiene, $CH_2{=}CH{-}CH{=}CH_2$, where the two C==C double bonds separated by a single bond give rise to an absorption spectrum that is shifted to lower energy by conjugation. In conjugated systems, the π electrons are delocalized over a minimum of four atoms; this causes a decrease in the $\pi \rightarrow \pi^*$ transition energy and the molar absorptivity increases as the result of a higher probability for the transition. The effect of conjugation on $\pi \rightarrow \pi^*$ transitions is considerable. Thus, for the series: ethylene (193 nm), 1,3-butadiene (217 nm), hexatriene (258 nm), octatetraene (300 nm), a bathochromic shift accompanied by an increase in molar absorptivity is observed as an additional $C{=}C$ double bond is added to each compound in progressing along the series.

Electronic absorption bands for conjugated alkynes are also shifted to lower energy; however, the molar absorptivity is much lower than for the conjugated alkenes. As an example, vinylacetylene, $CH_2{=}CH{-}C{\equiv}CH$, exhibits an absorption band near that of 1,3-butadiene ($\lambda_{max} = 219$ nm); however, its molar absorptivity is only 6500 compared to 21,000 for 1,3-butadiene.

An important feature of ultraviolet absorption spectra is that chromophores that are not conjugated give, not $\pi \rightarrow \pi^*$ bands, but a summation of n $\rightarrow \pi^*$ bands. A $-CH_2-$ group is sufficient to isolate two chromophores, but $-O-$, $-S-$, or $-NH-$ is not. An example of this effect is seen for hexacene, a green compound, and 6,15-dihydrohexacene, a colorless compound whose absorption spectrum is essentially the sum of the spectra of anthracene and naphthalene:

Hexacene   6,15-Dihydrohexacene

Aromatic Hydrocarbons

Benzene, a cyclic conjugated polyene, absorbs at 260, 200, and 180 nm. All of these bands are associated with the π-electron system of benzene. The intense bands at 200 and 180 nm are assigned to transitions to dipolar excited states, and the weak band at 260 nm is ascribed to a forbidden transition to a homopolar excited state.

Electronic transitions in "linear" polycyclic aromatics, such as benzene, naphthalene, and anthracene, exhibit a regular shift toward lower energy with increasing size of the molecule. Figure 7.3 shows that the larger compounds absorb in the same region as benzene, but the bands are more intense. Other compounds in this class, such as phenanthrene, benzanthracene, and pyrene, show absorption spectra similar to those of the "linear" ring system but with a more complex pattern.

Resolution of the fine structure of the bands in the spectrum of benzene is highly dependent on two parameters: solvent polarity and ring substitution. Polar solvents tend to merge the bands into a broad hump while nonpolar solvents give very good resolution into narrow, separate, peaks. Electronic spectra of benzene in the vapor state exhibit excellent resolution (Fig. 7.2). Upon substitution on the benzene ring, fine structure is diminished considerably and all three bands in benzene are affected markedly.

The effects of substitution on aromatic nuclei have been studied and detailed in the literature [5–7]. Usually, but not always, the absorption maxima shift to

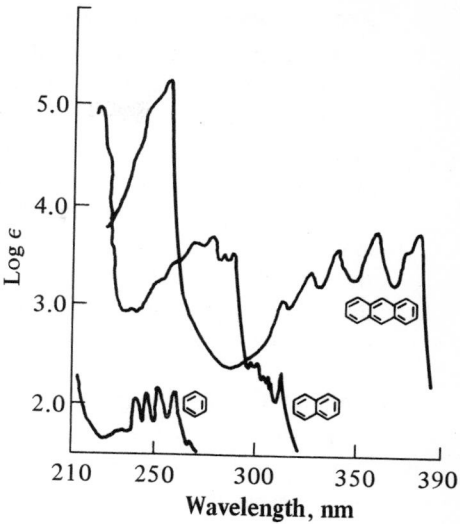

FIGURE 7.3. *Ultraviolet absorption spectra of benzene, naphthalene, and anthracene in ethanol. From K. L. Cheng, "Absorptiometry," in J. D. Winefordner, ed.,* Spectrochemical Methods of Analysis, *New York: Wiley-Interscience, 1971, chap. 6, by permission of the editor and John Wiley and Sons.*

longer wavelengths and the intensity of the absorption changes. The effects of substitution on the 200-nm band in benzene have been studied in great detail by Doub and Vanderbelt [8]. The authors found that the ratio of the wavelength of the 260-nm band to that of the 200-nm band is about 1.25 for most homo-substituted benzenes.

It is well known that resonance and induction have a marked effect on orientation in aromatic substitution. A correlation between orientation in substitution and electronic absorption spectra of benzene derivatives would be expected. Table 7.6 shows data for the position of the 200-nm benzene band [8, 9] as compared with the percentage of the meta isomer produced in nitration.

TABLE 7.6. *Variation in Position of the 200-nm Benzene Band with Percentage of the Meta Isomer Produced in Nitration*

Substituent	Meta in Nitration (percent)	λ_{max} (nm) of 200-nm benzene band
OH	2	210
Cl	0.2	210
Br	0.2	210
CH_3	4	207
CH_2Cl	16	207
$CHCl_2$	34	207
$COCH_3$	55	246
COOH	80	230
CN	81	224
NO_2	93	260

Sources: L. Doub and J. M. Vanderbelt, *J. Amer. Chem. Soc., 69,* 2714 (1947); *71,* 2414 (1949). J. R. Platt, *J. Chem. Phys., 19,* 263 (1951).

Azo Compounds

Straight-chain compounds that contain the –N=N– linkage give rise to low-intensity bands in the near-ultraviolet and visible regions. The long-wavelength bands are thought to arise from n → π^* transitions. For aliphatic azides, the low-energy band at 285 nm is assigned to a π → π^* electronic transition, whereas the 215-nm band is considered to arise from a s-p → π^* transition.

For aromatic azides, the –N=N– linkage may be conjugated with the ring π system. In azobenzene, the azo linkage is conjugated with two benzene rings and the π orbitals extend over the whole molecule. The levels are brought closer together and the π → π^* transition occurs at 445 nm. This absorption is responsible for the orange-red color of azobenzene.

Solvent Effects

Since there is electrostatic interaction between polar solvents and polar chromophores, such as the carbonyl group, these solvents tend to stabilize both the nonbonding electronic ground states and the π^* excited states. This interaction causes the n → π^* transitions, which usually occur at lower energy than the π → π^* transitions, to move to higher energy and π → π^* transitions to move to lower energy. Thus the π → π^* and n → π^* absorptions of polar chromophores move closer to each other with increasing polarity of the solvent. An example of this phenomenon is the solvent shift of the n → π^* transition to lower energy in the ultraviolet spectrum of N-nitroso-dimethylamine. For various solvents, the order for decreasing n → π^* energy is given by cyclohexane > dioxane > ethanol > water. For a series of hydrocarbon solvents, the effect on λ_{max} and ε_{max} is slight and can usually be neglected.

Steric Effects

Electronic interactions may be increased or decreased by steric effects and in certain cases totally new interactions may result. Extended conjugation of π orbitals requires coplanarity of the atoms involved in the π-cloud delocalization for maximal resonance interaction. If large bulky groups are in positions that cause perturbation of the coplanarity of the π system, λ_{max} is usually shifted to shorter wavelengths and ε_{max} also decreases. For example, diphenyl (λ_{max} = 246 nm, ε_{max} = 20,000) has coplanar rings and shows higher molar absorptivity than its derivative, o,o'-dialkyl-diphenyl which has nonplanar rings (λ_{max} = 250 nm, ε_{max} = 2000).

Molar absorptivity increases with conjugation as a result of increased transition-moment length, and reaches its maximum for a displacement of 0.1–0.3 nm, corresponding to ε_{max} = 10^5. This length is very sensitive to structural changes; in most cases this effect is more noticeable in the *trans*- rather than the *cis*-isomers. If conjugation is in an open-chain system rather than a constrained ring system, the effect is also greater. The isomeric absorption difference is clearly demonstrated by comparing the ultraviolet absorption spectra of *cis*- and *trans*-azobenzene [2].

Qualitative Identification

In principle, any organic molecule that contains a chromophore will probably give rise to a characteristic electronic spectrum. This provides a method for identifying structural components in such molecules. In addition to characteristic λ_{max} values, the molar absorptivities are also important in both qualitative and structural applications because this information can sometimes differentiate two chromophores that absorb at the same wavelength. Great care must be taken in suggesting relations from an observed electronic absorption spectrum without fully exploring all possibilities. It can usually be assumed that absorption at a particular wavelength is indicative of a given group, and intensity measurements may lend support to this assumption; however, a small amount of impurity from a substance with high molar absorptivity may result in misleading conclusions.

Studies of electronic absorption in the ultraviolet and visible regions find many applications. For a better appreciation of the variety of problems studied, the book by Gillam and Stern [10] should be consulted.

7.3 MAGNITUDE OF ABSORPTION OF RADIATION

Radiant power (P) is defined as the radiant energy impinging on unit area in unit time. Since the color of a solution is due to the partial absorption of visible light, the power of a beam of light will be reduced as it passes through a colored solution. The changes in radiant power that occur as monochromatic radiation passes through an absorption cell are illustrated in Figure 7.4. P_1 is the radiant power of incident radiation, P_0 is the radiant power after passing through one cell wall, P is the radiant power after passing through the absorbing solution or medium, and P_2 is the radiant power after the beam has traversed the last cell wall. An important quantity (see Table 7.2) is the transmittance, T, defined as

$$T = \frac{I}{I_0} = \frac{P_2}{P_1} \qquad (7.4)$$

which is the quantity that is usually measured in spectrophotometers. T_i is the *internal* transmittance of the system,

$$T_i = \frac{P}{P_0} \qquad (7.5)$$

FIGURE 7.4. *Radiation impinging on an absorption cell whose optical path length is b. From K. L. Cheng, "Absorptiometry,"* in J. D. Winefordner, ed., Spectrochemical Methods of Analysis, *New York: Wiley-Interscience, 1971, chap. 6, by permission of the editor and John Wiley and Sons.*

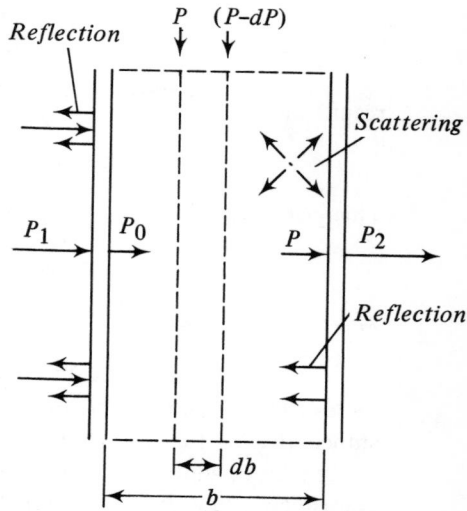

Usually, the quantities T and T_1 are nearly the same because cells are made of materials that will not appreciably absorb or scatter the radiation used. Any slight difference can be minimized by using matched cells, one containing the sample and the other the reagent blank (a solution containing all the components except the compound of interest). If T is set at 100% for the blank, a measurement of T for the sample gives T_1.

Beer's Law

Bouguer, and later Lambert, observed that the fraction of the energy, or intensity, of radiation absorbed in a thin layer of material depends on the absorbing substance and on the frequency of the incident radiation, and is proportional to the thickness of the layer. At a given concentration of the absorbing substance, summation over a series of thin layers, or integration over a finite thickness, leads to an exponential relationship between transmitted intensity and thickness. This is generally called Lambert's law. Beer showed that, at a given thickness, the absorption coefficient introduced by Lambert was directly proportional to the concentration of the absorbing substance in a solution. Combination of these results gives the relationship now commonly known as Beer's law. This law states that the amount of radiation absorbed or transmitted by a solution or medium is an exponential function of the concentration of absorbing substance present and of the length of the path of the radiation through the sample.

Beer's law can be derived as follows (see Fig. 7.4). For a layer of infinitesimal thickness, db, the decrease in radiant power $(-dP)$ is given by

$$-\frac{dP}{P} = kcdb \tag{7.6}$$

where $k =$ a proportionality constant

Integration over the entire absorbing cell length, b,

$$\int_{P_0}^{P} \frac{dP}{P} = -k \int_{0}^{b} cdb \tag{7.7}$$

results in

$$\ln(P/P_0) = -kbc = 2.303 \log(P/P_0) \tag{7.8}$$

This gives (Table 7.2)

$$-\log(P/P_0) = -\log T = A = \varepsilon bc \tag{7.9}$$

where $\varepsilon = k/2.303$

The constant ε is called the *molar absorptivity* when the concentration c is in moles per liter and b is in cm. The value of ε is characteristic of the absorbing substance at a particular wavelength in a particular solvent and is independent of the concentration and of the path length, b. Equation 7.9 is a fundamental law on which colorimetric and spectrophotometric methods are based. It is known variously as the Bouguer-Beer, Lambert-Beer, or more simply, Beer's law. When other concentration units are used, such as grams per liter, the symbol a (for absorptivity, Table 7.3) instead of ε is used.

Example 7.1. Palladium reacts with Thio-Michler's ketone, forming a colored 1:4 complex. A 0.20 ppm Pd sample gave an absorbance of 0.390 at 520 nm using a 1.00-cm cell. Calculate the molar absorptivity (ε) for the palladium Thio-Michler's ketone complex.

Solution: $\quad 0.20 \text{ ppm Pd} = \dfrac{2.0 \times 10^{-4} \text{ g/l}}{106.4} = 1.9 \times 10^{-6} M$

In a 1.00-cm cell for $A = 0.390$, the molar absorptivity is calculated from Beer's law:

$$A = \varepsilon bc$$
$$0.390 = (\varepsilon)(1.00)(1.9 \times 10^{-6})$$
$$\varepsilon = \frac{0.390}{1.9 \times 10^{-6}} = 2.1 \times 10^5 \text{ l/mole-cm}$$

Beer's law assumes that (a) the incident radiation is monochromatic, (b) the absorption occurs in a volume of uniform cross-section, and (c) the absorbing substances behave independently of each other in the absorption process. Thus, when Beer's law applies to a multicomponent system in which there is no interaction among the various species, the total absorbance may be expressed as

$$A_{\text{total}} = \varepsilon_1 bc_1 + \varepsilon_2 bc_2 + \cdots + \varepsilon_i bc_i \tag{7.10}$$

where $\quad \varepsilon_i$ = the molar absorptivity for the i-th absorbing species
$\qquad\quad c_i$ = its molar concentration

This equation is the basis of quantitative methods for determining mixtures of absorbing substances.

Deviation from Beer's Law

Beer's law states that a plot of absorbance versus concentration should give a straight line passing through the origin with a slope equal to εb. However, deviations from direct proportionality between absorbance and concentration are sometimes encountered. In these cases, a nonlinear working curve may be prepared with solutions of known concentration, and the concentration of the unknown solution found from the absorbance obtained under the same experimental conditions.

Deviations from Beer's law may be due to instrumental factors or to chemical factors. These deviations may result in an upward curvature (positive deviation) or in a downward curvature (negative deviation), as shown in Figure 7.5. A check on instrumental factors can be made by plotting absorbance versus cell length at a constant concentration; this plot will be linear if the instrument is performing satisfactorily. Deviations arising from chemical factors are observed only when concentrations are changed.

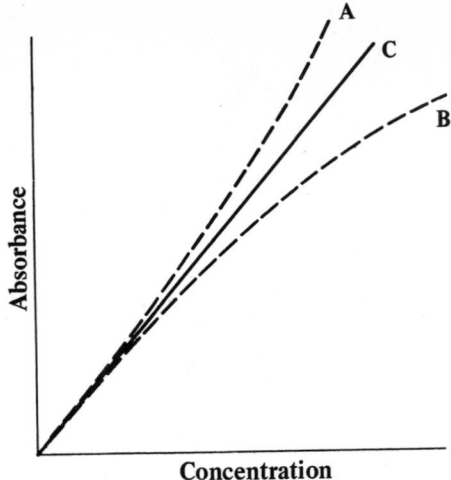

FIGURE 7.5. *Deviations from Beer's law. A: positive deviation; B: negative deviation; C: no deviation.*

Instrumental Factors. Unsatisfactory performance of an instrument may be caused by fluctuations in the power-supply voltage, an unstable light-source, or a nonlinear response of the detector-amplifier system. A double-beam system helps to minimize deviations due to these factors. In addition, the following instrumental sources of possible deviations should be understood:

1. *Polychromatic radiation.* Strict conformity of an absorbing system to Beer's law requires that the radiation be monochromatic. However, one always works with a band of wavelengths and not with a single sharp line (laser light sources are available, but there is as yet no tunable laser incorporated into a spectrophotometer).

Let us consider the effect of polychromatic radiation on the relationship between concentration and absorbance. When the radiation consists of two wavelengths, λ and λ', and assuming that Beer's law applies at each of these individually, the absorbance at λ is given by

$$\log (P_0/P) = A = \varepsilon bc \tag{7.11}$$

or

$$P_0/P = 10^{\varepsilon bc} \tag{7.12}$$

Similarly, at λ',

$$P_0'/P' = 10^{\varepsilon' bc} \tag{7.13}$$

The radiant power of two wavelengths passing through the solvent is given by $P_0 + P_0'$, and that passing through the solution containing absorbing species by $P + P'$. The combined absorbance is

$$A_c = \log \frac{(P_0 + P_0')}{P + P'} \tag{7.14}$$

Substituting for P and P', we obtain

$$A_c = \log \frac{(P_0 + P_0')}{P_0 10^{-\varepsilon bc} + P_0' 10^{-\varepsilon' bc}} \tag{7.15}$$

In the very special case where $\varepsilon = \varepsilon'$, Equation 7.15 simply reduces to Beer's law.

However, in the general case where $\varepsilon \neq \varepsilon'$, the relationship between A_c and c will be nonlinear; therefore, departures from linearity will be greater as the difference between ε and ε' becomes greater. Further, when $\varepsilon > \varepsilon'$, the measured absorbance A_c is lower than the true "monochromatic" absorbance at wavelength λ, resulting in negative deviation, and when $\varepsilon < \varepsilon'$, the measured absorbance A_c is higher, resulting in a positive deviation (Fig. 7.5).

When a broader bandwidth (see below) is used, the lower absorbances toward the edges of the finite band contribute greater total intensities of transmitted light than the higher absorbances at the center of the band, and the summed, "average," absorbance includes those over the bandwidth. It is further noted that the steeper the absorption curve included within the bandwidth, the greater the error. From the same principle, as the concentration is increased the absorption peak becomes narrower, so the error is greater.

2. *Slit width.* The ability of a spectrophotometer to distinguish between two frequencies differing only slightly from each other depends upon the widths of the images produced (relative to the separation of two images). The width of the image produced is thus an important measure of the quality of performance of a spectrophotometer. The spread of the image along the frequency, wave number, or wavelength scale is defined as the "spectral slit width" or "spectral bandwidth." It is very closely proportional to the actual width of the slit (the mechanical slit width). The effect of slit width on absorbance is illustrated in Figure 7.6.

FIGURE 7.6. *Effect of slit width on absorbance. From K. L. Cheng, "Absorptiometry," in J. D. Winefordner, ed.,* Spectrochemical Methods of Analysis, *New York: Wiley-Interscience, 1971, chap. 6, by permission of the editor and John Wiley and Sons.*

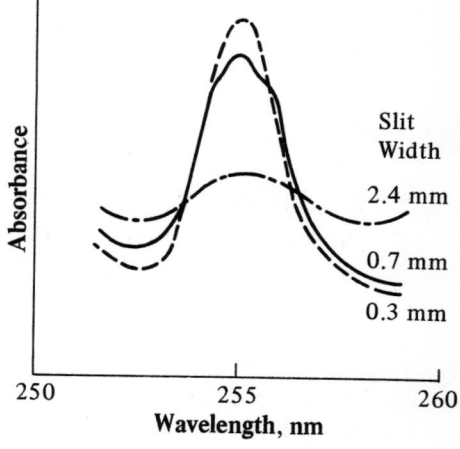

The spectral bandwidth of an ultraviolet spectrophotometer is typically of the order of 1 nm. In general, molecular absorption bands are smooth and much broader than 1 nm, so that the effect of spectral bandwidth is practically negligible, especially when the absorbance is measured at the maximum absorption. If the absorption band is sharp, or if measurements are made on a steep slope of the spectral band, the absorptivity may be different over the spectral bandwidth, and deviations from the Beer's law will be noticed. Figure 7.7 shows the effect of spectral bandwidth: with increasing slit width (also increasing spectral bandwidth), the recorded bands gradually merge together.

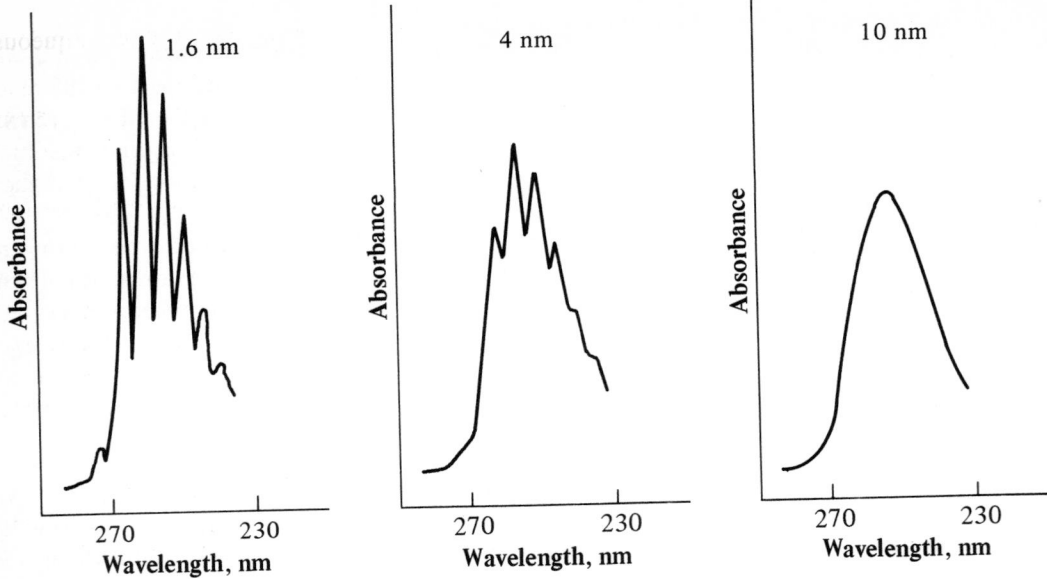

FIGURE 7.7. *Effect of spectral bandwidth on the absorption spectrum of benzene in cyclohexane.*

3. *Stray light.* Stray light that strikes the detector is a potential source of error; the apparent absorbance is decreased as a result:

$$A_m = \log \left(\frac{P_0 + P_s}{P + P_s} \right) \qquad (7.16)$$

where P_s = the radiant power of the stray light
            A_m = the measured absorbance

When P diminishes owing to increasing concentration and becomes small in comparison with P_s, $P + P_s \approx P_s$; and Equation 7.16 becomes

$$A_m = \log \frac{P_0 + P_s}{P_s} \qquad (7.17)$$

Thus, there is a negative deviation from Beer's law. Errors due to stray light are more commonly found near the wavelength limits of the instrument components. Many reports of spectra in the UV region below 220 nm should be carefully checked, since false peaks have been reported. Visible radiation usually presents the most serious stray-light problem for ultraviolet-visible spectrophotometers, because both the spectral radiance of most visible sources and the spectral response of most detectors to visible radiation are high.

Chemical Factors. Apparent deviations from Beer's law are often due to chemical effects such as dissociation, association, complex formation, polymerization, or solvolysis.

Association and polymerization are examples of the process of self-interaction, and their effects are important in both ultraviolet and visible spectroscopy. Benzoic acid exists as a mixture of the ionized and un-ionized forms, and in dilute aqueous solution it dissociates

$$C_6H_5COOH + H_2O \rightleftharpoons C_6H_5COO^- + H_3O^+ \qquad (7.18)$$
$$(\lambda_{max} = 273 \text{ nm}, \varepsilon = 970) \qquad (\lambda_{max} = 268 \text{ nm}, \varepsilon = 560)$$

The effective molar absorptivity at 273 nm will thus decrease with increased dilution or at high pH.

Another example is observed with unbuffered $K_2Cr_2O_7$ solutions. In pure water, the dichromate and chromate ions are in equilibrium

$$Cr_2O_7^{2-} + H_2O \rightleftharpoons 2CrO_4^{2-} + 2H^+ \qquad (7.19)$$
$$(\lambda_{max} = 350, 450 \text{ nm}) \qquad (\lambda_{max} = 372 \text{ nm})$$

The equilibrium constant may be expressed as

$$\frac{[CrO_4^{2-}]^2[H^+]^2}{[Cr_2O_7^{2-}]} = K \qquad (7.20)$$

Obviously, there are deviations from Beer's law when aqueous solutions of chromate or dichromate are diluted with water, and the pH will affect the concentrations of $Cr_2O_7^{2-}$ and CrO_4^{2-}. The effect can be controlled by buffering dichromate with a strong acid or chromate with a strong base.

Occasionally, the absorbance is measured at an isosbestic point (or isoabsorptive wavelength)—that is, a wavelength at which the two absorbing species in equilibrium have a common value of ε; then, Beer's law holds even though there is a shift of equilibrium. Isosbestic points are often taken as criteria for the existence of two interconvertible absorbing species of a compound, the total quantity of which is constant, though points of common ε value occur also in some irreversible decomposition reactions giving two products.

1. *Solvent.* Dissolution may shift the spectrum of an absorbing substance to longer wavelength (with respect to the spectrum of the gas). This so-called "red shift" or bathochromic effect is greater in solvents of high dielectric constant because the charge displacement for the upper energy state requires less energy in a dielectric solvent than in a vacuum. A "blue shift" (to shorter wavelengths) is generally believed to be associated with a $n \rightarrow \pi^*$ transition involving a nonbonding orbital in the ground state. Dissolution generally causes larger effects on infrared spectra than on ultraviolet spectra, but may cause significant errors even in ultraviolet quantitative work. The greatest effect occurs after mixing dipolar solvated molecules (dissolved in nonpolar solvents) with polar solvents or additives. Many carbonyl compounds are sensitive to changes in solvent media.

2. *Temperature.* Changes in temperature may shift ionic equilibria. In addition, an increase in temperature exerts a bathochromic effect on ions in solution—for instance, the color of a hydrochloric acid solution of ferric chloride changes from yellow to reddish brown on heating. However, temperature is ordinarily not considered an important factor in simple systems, within limits of say $\pm 5°$.

3. *Photo effects.* Fluorescence resulting from frequencies of ultraviolet radiation in a certain range may cause an apparent increase in transmittance with

fluorescing substances. Light scattering is found in colloidal systems, the extent depending upon the particle size and shape and the wavelength region used. Photo effects in many organic compounds or indicator solutions may cause dichroism—different colors are produced by thick and thin layers. For a polymer or crystal, pleochroism may be observed; unpolarized radiation becomes partially polarized on passing through an ordered absorbing substance. Photochemical reactions or photodecomposition, of course, cause a deviation from Beer's law. The effect is usually of little significance unless high-intensity radiation is used close to the sample solution or the sample is highly photosensitive, such as the silver thio-Michler's ketone complex.

7.4 QUANTITATIVE ABSORPTION SPECTROSCOPY

Methods based on the absorption of radiation are powerful and useful tools for the analytical chemist. The ultraviolet region is particularly important for the qualitative and quantitative determination of many organic compounds. In the visible region, spectrophotometric methods are widely used for the quantitative determination of many trace substances, especially inorganic elements.

The basic principle of quantitative absorption spectroscopy lies in comparing the extent of absorption of a sample solution with that of a set of standards under radiation at a selected wavelength.

Visual Colorimetric Methods

In its simplest form, colorimetry consists of visual matching of the color of the sample with that of a series of standards. A colored compound is first formed by suitably reacting the constituent to be determined, then the colored solutions are racked side-by-side in Nessler tubes* for viewing from the top. The approximate concentration of the unknown is estimated by finding which standard most closely matches the unknown in color. Visual colorimetry suffers from poor precision since the eye is not as sensitive to small differences in absorbance as is a photoelectric device. The use of a Duboscq colorimeter constitutes a more refined method of analysis for color comparison. This is equipped with an eyepiece with a split field that permits the ready comparison of beams passing through sample and standard.

Photometric Methods

Photometers equipped with filters are suitable for many routine methods that do not involve complex spectra. Spectrophotometers can provide narrow bandwidths of radiation for accurate work and can handle absorption spectra in the ultraviolet region.

Choice of Wavelength. When filter photometers are employed, a suitable filter is selected in preparing an analytical curve for the unknown substance. With a spectrophotometer, the spectrum of the absorbing substance is determined, and a suitable

---

* Nessler tubes are essentially large, uniform, flat-bottomed test tubes, about 30 cm in length and perhaps 2.5 cm in diameter.

wavelength is chosen. Generally, a wavelength close to that of maximum absorption is chosen, for maximum sensitivity; but the wavelength chosen should also fall in a region where the absorbance does not change rapidly with change in wavelength.

Unfortunately, use of the wavelength of maximum absorption is not always feasible because the color-forming reagents often also absorb significantly at the wavelength of maximum absorption of the species being measured. The spectra of 3,3'-diaminobenzidine (DAB) and its monoselenium compound, shown in Figure 7.8, both have absorption maxima at 340 and 420 nm. At 340 nm, the reagent also absorbs strongly. Although it is possible to select 340 nm and subtract the absorbance contributed by the excess reagent, it is difficult to know the amount of excess reagent precisely, and errors increase with increasing absorption by the reagent itself. A better approach is to use a wavelength at which the absorbing substance absorbs rather strongly but at which the absorbance contribution by the excess reagent is minimal, 420 nm in this case.

FIGURE 7.8. *Absorbance curves of toluene solution of 3,3'-diaminobenzidine and its monoselenium compound with* λ_{max} *at 340 and 420 nm. A: 25 mg Se in 10 ml of toluene. B: 5 mg Se in 10 ml of toluene. C: Diaminobenzidine in toluene. Toluene as blank. From K. L. Cheng,* Anal. Chem., *28, 1738 (1956), by permission of the publishers. Copyright © 1956 by the American Chemical Society.*

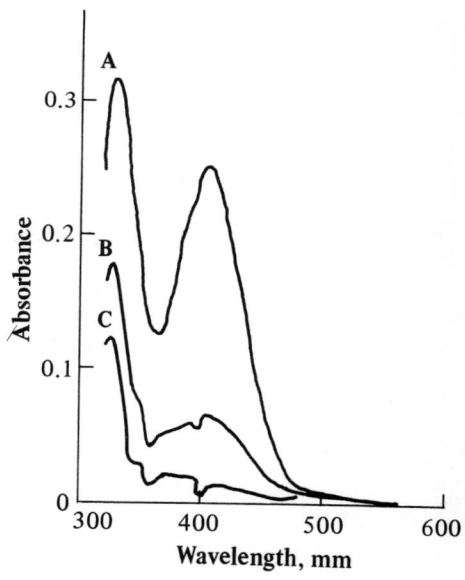

For systems that are sensitive to pH, and for which an isosbestic point can be located, measurements at the wavelength of the latter are preferred if the pH cannot be readily controlled.

Separation and Formation of Absorbing Compounds. In general, more than one method is available for the spectrophotometric determination of a given substance, and selecting a suitable method plays an important role in successfully analyzing the sample. It is often necessary to separate the absorbing substance before the absorbance measurement; for instance, chromatographic separation of vitamins in natural products is made before the actual spectrophotometric determination. In many instances, the sample compound does not absorb radiation appreciably in the wavelength regions provided; it is then necessary to form an absorbing substance by reacting the compound in question with other reagents. The reagents should be selective in their reactions and should not form interfering absorbing species with foreign substances likely to be present.

Some common and important factors involved in the formation of absorbing compounds are:

1. *pH.* Since pH plays a very important role in complex formation, proper adjustment of pH or the use of a buffer often eliminates certain interfering reactions. For instance, methylthymol blue and xylenol orange (analogues of EDTA) react with many metal ions. Their selectivity for certain metals is much improved in highly acidic media. For example, zirconium may be determined in the presence of hafnium in 1 *N* perchloric acid [11].

2. *Reagent concentration.* The amount of reagent required is dictated by the composition of the absorbing complex formed. An optimum concentration of reagents should be determined, since either not enough reagent or too much reagent can cause deviation from Beer's law.

3. *Time.* Formation of the absorbing complex may be slow, in some cases requiring several minutes or a few hours. For example, the phosphomolybdate blue method—a very common analytical method for phosphate determinations—requires about fifteen minutes standing time for full color development after addition of the reagents.

4. *Temperature.* The optimum temperature should be established in the procedure. Certain reactions require elevated temperature to decrease the time necessary for complete color development.

5. *Order of mixing reagents.* Frequently it is important to add the reagents in a specified sequence, otherwise full color development will not be possible or interfering reactions may occur. For instance, the highly selective color reaction of cobaltic NTA (nitrilotriacetate) in the presence of hydrogen peroxide must be preceded by the formation of the cobaltous NTA complex [12].

6. *Stability.* If the absorbing complex formed is not very stable, the absorbance measurement should be made as soon as possible. If the absorbing complex is photosensitive, precautions should be taken in order to avoid its photodecomposition. Certain reagents may sometimes be added to help stabilize the absorbing complex.

7. *Masking.* Very few reactions are truly specific. However, highly selective reactions may be developed through the sophisticated use of *masking*. The term masking refers to the addition of a complexing agent to form a metal complex of such stability that, in this case, color-forming reactions with another reagent do not occur to any appreciable extent. For example, in the presence of excess EDTA, ferric ion does not form the colored $FeSCN^{2+}$ complex with thiocyanate ion.

8. *Organic solvent.* Many organic reagents or complexes are only slightly soluble in water. In such cases, it is necessary to add a water-miscible organic solvent to avoid precipitation or to aid color development. In other cases, solvent extraction might be employed, for example, to separate the colored compound from excess reagent or from interfering substances.

9. *Salt concentration.* High concentrations of electrolyte often influence the absorption spectrum of a compound. This effect may be due to the formation of

ion-association complexes that cause a shift in the maxim... type of masking effect and usually causes a decrease in the ab...

Photometric Errors. Because of the logarithmic relationship betwe... and concentration, small errors in measuring the transmittance cause... errors in the calculated concentration at low and at high transmittances... centration of a sample solution or the path length or both should be so... that the absorbance will be within the range of approximately 0.2 to 0.7 (i.e., mittance in the range of 20 to 60%). As shown in Figure 7.9, an absorbance 0.434 (36.8% transmittance) is considered optimum, but in practice there is littl... difference in relative error between 0.2 and 0.7 absorbance. The relative error curve shown in Figure 7.9 is approximately correct, in practice, only for relatively simple instruments with phototube detectors. With photomultiplier detectors, and in most of the more sophisticated commercial spectrophotometers, the usable transmittance range of "minimum" error is extended to improve the electronic signal-to-noise ratio.

FIGURE 7.9. *Relative concentration error as a function of transmittance. From K. L. Cheng, "Absorptiometry," in J. D. Wine-fordner, ed.,* Spectrochemical Methods of Analysis, *New York: Wiley-Interscience, 1971, chap. 6, by permission of the editor and John Wiley and Sons.*

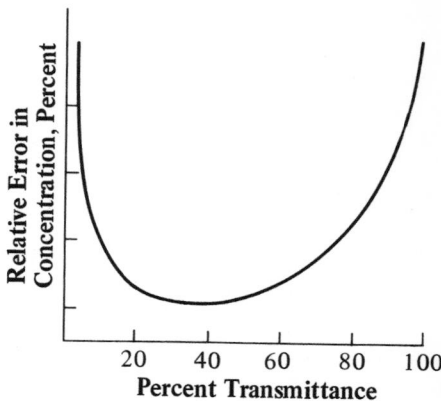

7.5 SPECTROPHOTOMETRIC APPLICATIONS

Analysis of Mixtures

Beer's law states that absorbance is an additive property of all the absorbing molecules present in a mixture (see Eqn. 7.10). In principle, n absorbance measurements at n different wavelengths are needed to determine the concentrations of n components in a mixture; this procedure gives n independent simultaneous equations in n unknowns. The molar absorptivities must be known or determined for each individual absorbing species, 1, 2, etc., at each wavelength. If, in a two-component mixture, the values are ε_1, ε_2 at wavelength λ, and ε_1', ε_2' at a second wavelength, λ', and the absorbance of the mixture is A at λ and A' at λ', for a path length b and unknown concentrations c_1, c_2, then Equation 7.10 becomes

$$A = A_1 + A_2 = \varepsilon_1 b c_1 + \varepsilon_2 b c_2 \tag{7.21}$$

$$A' = A_1' + A_2' = \varepsilon_1' b c_1 + \varepsilon_2' b c_2 \tag{7.22}$$

concentrations are calculated by solving these two simul-
are obtained by measuring the absorbance of the mixture
ns. Since these equations depend upon the use of correct
errors may occur in systems where there are deviations
n.

vo-component system where the two components are in
r and contribute all the absorption, it can be shown that
n the spectrum at which the absorbance is independent of
ons of the two components. If the bands overlap, there is
two absorbing species in equilibrium have the same ε
which the absorbance depends only on the total number
wo absorbing species) is called the isosbestic point, or
isobestic point, or isoabsorptive wavelength. All curves intersect at this point. The existence of such a point is not proof of the presence of only two components; there may be a third component with $\varepsilon = 0$ at this particular wavelength. The absence of an isosbestic point, however, is definite proof of the presence of a third component, providing the possibility of a deviation from Beer's law in the two-component system can be discounted. In one respect, then, the isosbestic point is a unique wavelength for quantitative determination of the total amount of two absorbing substances in mutual equilibrium.

Determination of Stoichiometry

The spectrophotometric method is particularly valuable for studying complexes of low stability. Consider the formation of a complex M_nL_p, where M is a metal ion and L is a ligand:

$$n\text{M} + p\text{L} \rightleftharpoons M_nL_p \tag{7.23}$$

The molar ratio of the two components of a complex is important. In a quantitative determination, an excess of ligand should be added in order to force the equilibrium toward completion.

Molar-Ratio Method. In this method, the concentration of one component is kept fixed and that of the other varied to give a series of [L]/[M] ratios. The absorbances of these solutions, measured at an absorption maximum for the complex M_nL_p, increase linearly up to the molar ratio of the complex, at which virtually the whole amount of both components is complexed (assuming little dissociation). Further addition of component L cannot increase the absorbance, and the line becomes horizontal, or shows a break if component L absorbs at the same wavelength (Fig. 7.10). In rare cases, an excess component L may cause a decrease in absorbance owing to the stepwise formation of higher-order complexes that have smaller ε values at this wavelength. The composition of molybdogermanic acid has been studied by the molar-ratio method [13] showing a ratio of 36 molybdate:1 germanate.

Continuous-Variation Method. The molar ratios may also be varied by changing the concentrations of both components while the total number of moles of both com-

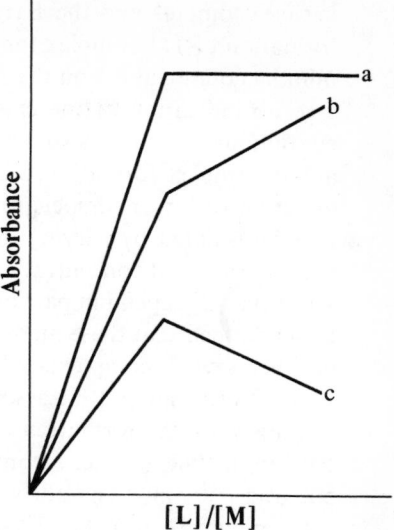

FIGURE 7.10. *Molar-ratio method, showing different curves. (a) Component L does not absorb at the wavelength of maximum absorption for the complex, e.g., Fe(III)-Tiron. (b) Component L absorbs slightly at the wavelength of maximum absorption for the complex, e.g., Zn-Pan. (c) An excess of component L causes a decrease in absorbance of the complex, e.g., Bi-xylenol orange. From K. L. Cheng, "Absorptiometry," in J. D. Winefordner, ed.*, Spectrochemical Methods of Analysis, *New York: Wiley-Interscience, 1971, chap. 6, by permission of the editor and John Wiley and Sons.*

ponents are kept constant; this is termed the method of continuous variation, or Job's method [14, 15]. The mole fraction of one of the components is plotted on the abscissa scale; the ordinate scale is usually a difference in absorbance, ΔA, representing the difference between the observed absorbance and the summed absorbances of the independent (noncomplexed) components. When the curvature is pronounced and the maximum is not apparent, the apex may be obtained by drawing tangents. The results may be verified by repeating the process at other wavelengths or total concentrations, since the position of the maximum is independent of wavelength and concentration.

These methods are also applicable at the absorption wavelengths of one of the components—that is, when breaks occur at minimum instead of maximum values of ΔA. The results in Figure 7.11 show the predominant 1 Pd:4 TMK (thio-Michler's

FIGURE 7.11. *Job curves of thio-Michler's ketone (TMK) complexes of mercury (○) and of palladium (●). From K. L. Cheng, "Absorptiometry," in J. D. Winefordner, ed.*, Spectrochemical Methods of Analysis, *New York: Wiley-Interscience, 1971, chap. 6, by permission of the editor and John Wiley and Sons.*

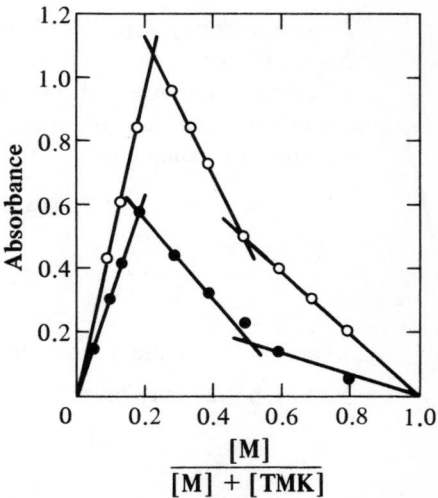

ketone) complex and the 1 Hg:3 TMK complex maxima, but they also indicate the formation of 1:1 complex for both Pd and Hg when TMK is not in large excess (the minima coming at 0.5 on the x-axis). The molar-ratio curves for the same complexes give no indication of the existence of a 1:1 complex; in general, Job's method of continuous variation is somewhat more accurate and may provide more information about complex formation. Deviations from Beer's law will result in errors in the direction of larger dissociation constants with either of these methods. The effects may be isolated by varying the path length and concentrations independently or by varying the total concentration of reactants for a given ratio of concentrations. The selection will depend in part on the nature of the deviation from Beer's law. It should be mentioned that these methods are, however, not reliable if the complexes are weak or when several complexes are simultaneously formed in solution.

Vosburgh and his associates [14] have extended Job's method, particularly in dealing with the formation of more than one complex. They investigated the o-phenanthroline (o-phen) complexes of Ni(II) in a range of wavelengths between 500 and 650 nm. The absorption by $[Ni(o\text{-phen})]^{2+}$ at 620 nm, $[Ni(o\text{-phen})_2]^{2+}$ at 580 nm, and $[Ni(o\text{-phen})_3]^{2+}$ at 528 nm were shown with three linear plots.

Bjerrum Method. In the method of Bjerrum, one plots $\varepsilon/[M]_t$ versus $[L]_t$ for various constant values of $[M]_t$, where t denotes *total* concentration of the designated form. A line drawn horizontally on the graph intersects the experimental curves at points whose coordinates show the composition of the so-called "corresponding solutions" which have a given value of $\varepsilon/[M]_t$. For complexes of the type ML_n ($n = 1, 2, 3, \ldots$), the solutions also have the same value of $\bar{n}$. The value of $\bar{n}$ (an average number of ligands bonded to the central group) may be obtained at various concentrations of L when the total concentrations of such solutions are known. For detailed description, see references [16, 17].

Studies of Chemical Equilibria

Spectrophotometry can be used to assess chemical equilibria, provided the participating species absorb at markedly different wavelengths.

Determination of Acid-Base Equilibria. Since the absorption spectra of organic molecules with acidic or basic functional groups depend upon the pH of the medium, the absorption maxima and intensities vary with the hydrogen-ion concentration. The dissociation constant of an acid or a base may be determined spectrophotometrically as a result of such changes. For a weak acid in water

$$HA + H_2O \rightleftharpoons H_3O^+ + A^- \tag{7.24}$$

$$K_a = \frac{[H_3O^+][A^-]}{[HA]}$$

where K_a = the dissociation constant of acid HA

Equation 7.24 may be expressed as

$$-\log K_a = -\log [H_3O^+] - \log [A^-]/[HA]$$
$$pK_a = pH + \log [HA]/[A^-] \tag{7.25}$$

If the pH and the concentrations of HA (acid form) and A⁻ (basic form) are known, pK_a can be easily calculated. The ratio of [HA] to [A⁻] may be found spectrophotometrically if ε_{HA} and ε_{A^-} are known. These latter values can be determined after converting completely to A⁻ or HA by adding excess acid or base. As an example, the dissociation constants of several weak acids and bases have been determined photometrically [18]; the base strengths of pyridine derivatives have been determined using a similar procedure [19].

According to Equation 7.25, when [HA] = [A⁻], pK_a = pH. The pH at this point may be called $pH_{1/2}$, as it occurs at the midpoint of a photometric titration curve, namely, 50% of the titration of acid HA.

This point can be used to calculate K_a: one plots the absorbance at a particular wavelength, say λ_{max}, against the pH of the solution and obtains the midpoint graphically to find $pH_{1/2}$.

King and Hirt [20] have described an instrument called a Spectrotitrimeter, which offers a rapid and accurate determination of dissociation constants. A titration flask combined with a pH meter and a spectrometer with an automatic pump as described by Rehm et al. [21] will serve the same purpose.

The pK_a of bromophenol blue has been determined spectrophotometrically [22]. The color change may be followed spectrophotometrically as in Figure 7.12, which shows the absorption spectrum of bromophenol blue in solutions of pH from 3.0 to 5.4. Usually photometric titration gives a sigmoid curve; if the curve fails to flatten out at the ends, the midpoint is determined by a graphic method commonly used in polarography for locating $E_{1/2}$ (see Chap. 3). The spectra in Figure 7.12 suggest that the peak at 590 nm is due solely to the conjugate base, A⁻, of bromophenol blue (since the peak intensity is reduced by decreasing the pH) and the HA absorption evidently occurs somewhere below 450 nm. There is no problem of overlap in this example. Hence, we may write the equation

$$[A^-] = A/\varepsilon b \qquad (7.26)$$

where A = the absorbance at the maximum
ε = the absorptivity at the maximum

For a total concentration of bromophenol blue of c, [HA] = c − [A⁻] and

$$[H_3O^+] = K_a\left(\frac{c}{[A^-]} - 1\right) = K_a\left(\frac{c \cdot \varepsilon b}{A} - 1\right) \qquad (7.27)$$

$$pH = pK_a - \log\left(\frac{c \cdot \varepsilon b}{A} - 1\right) \qquad (7.28)$$

This gives the sigmoid curve shown in Figure 7.12. Such a curve can be obtained experimentally without prior knowledge of K_a or ε by measuring the absorbance of HA in various buffer solutions.

Conversely, this experiment offers information about the nature of the indicator conjugate pair itself. Equation 7.27 can be fitted to the plot of A against pH to obtain ε and K_a. In that equation $A \neq \varepsilon bc$, because c refers to the total concentration, [HA] + [A⁻]. If the pH is made sufficiently large so that practically all the indicator exists as A⁻, then c = [A⁻] and $A = \varepsilon bc$, and hence ε is obtained. At the value of A corresponding to $(\varepsilon bc)/2$, pH = pK_a.

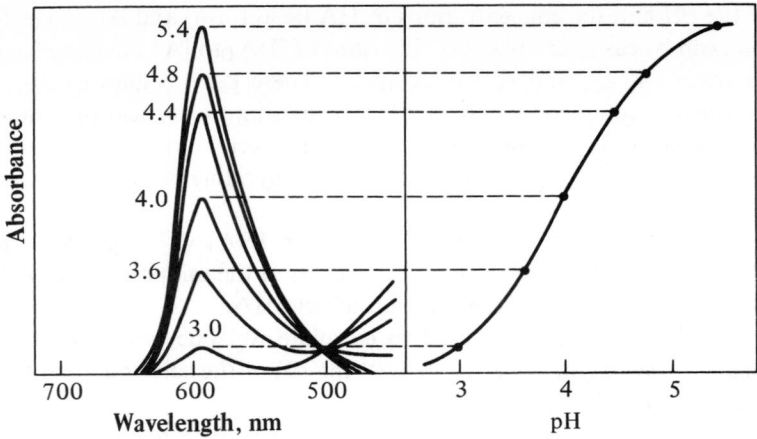

FIGURE 7.12. *The absorption spectrum of bromophenol blue at various pH values (left). The variation of A_{max} with pH (right).*

Kambe et al. [23] determined the dissociation constants of some furfurylidene-*p*-nitrophenylhydrazones by plotting appropriate absorbance values versus pH. The pK_1 and pK_2 of *p*-hydroxybenzoic acid have been found to be 4.61 and 9.31 by a spectrophotometric method [24]. Since the equations employ concentration instead of activity, the experimental results for pK values are approximate unless corrected for activity.

Equilibrium Constants. Job [15] has pointed out that, when the formula is known for a complex in solution, its equilibrium constant can be calculated through a relation between concentration and absorptivity. As a part of his continuous-variation studies, Job determined spectrophotometrically the equilibrium constants of many complexes.

Cheng [25] applied Job's method to the determination of the apparent formation constant of the Hf-xylenol orange (XO) complex using the method of mixtures of equimolar solutions. This is a rapid, though probably not too accurate, method of estimating the formation constant of a colored complex with the mole ratio 1 to 1. Application of this method gave a value of $K = 1.6 \times 10^4$ for the Hf-XO complex formational constant in 0.8 N $HClO_4$. The formation constants of the cerium, titanium, cadmium, and UO_2^{2+} [26] complexes have also been reported.

The determination of formation constants may involve the photometric measurement of the complex formed in the presence of a large excess of one of the reagents, so that the formation of the complex may be considered to be essentially complete; this is known as the method of mixtures of nonequimolar solutions. This method is based on Job's general equation [27, 28] for systems involving mixtures. The method has been applied to the determination of the dissociation constant of Fe(III)-sulfosalicyclic acid mixtures in a pH 5.3 buffer, using sulfosalicyclic acid solutions 3, 5, and 8 times as concentrated as the ferric perchlorate. The best results were obtained by assuming that a 1:1 complex is formed, and K_d was calculated to be 2×10^{-5}.

Spectrophotometric methods of determining stability constants are generally unreliable when the complexes are rather weak, or when several complexes are formed in solution. These methods are most suitable for a situation where only one or two complexes are concerned in the equilibrium and when absorption by the free ligand is negligible at the wavelength used. Reviews of spectrophotometric methods for determining equilibrium constants are available [17, 29].

Molecular-Weight Determinations

If an unknown compound can be treated to form a derivative in which a chromophore of known ε value is incorporated, the molar concentration of the chromophore may be obtained spectrophotometrically. This provides a simple method for determining molecular weights. Although the molar absorptivity of the absorption band remains constant in all the derivatives, the absorbance (A) will depend upon the molar concentration and hence on the molecular weight of the molecule of interest. The molecular weight (M) may be determined spectrophotometrically from the relation

$$M = \varepsilon w b / A \qquad (7.29)$$

where w = the weight of the compound in grams per liter
b = the thickness of the medium

It is assumed in this method that ε is not affected by intra- or intermolecular forces, and that no interfering bands exist.

Picric acid and the picrate salts of amines absorb at 380 nm with a molar absorptivity of 13,400. An accuracy of $\pm 2\%$ was obtained for the spectrophotometric determination of molecular weights of amines [30]. Molecular-weight determinations have been reported of sugars from the absorption spectra of their osazones [31], of aldehydes and ketones from the absorption spectra of their 2,4-dinitrophenylhydrazones [21, 32, 33], and of saturated alcohols from the absorption of their β-2,4-dinitrophenylpropionyl esters [34].

Reaction-Rate Determinations

The concentration dependence of absorbance has an obvious analytical application in the study of reaction rates. If the absorption spectra of the reactants and products are quite different, we may follow spectrophotometrically changes in concentration of either the reactants or the products during the reaction. For slow reactions, samples can be withdrawn and analyzed at leisure. Absorption spectrometry may play its part in such analysis, but no new features are involved. For fast reactions, spectrophotometry offers advantages, particularly in following the concentration changes of the reactants in situ. Chapter 18 discusses the determination of reaction rates in detail.

Purification and Trace Analysis

Trace impurities in a "pure" organic compound may be easily detected or estimated if they have fairly intense absorption bands. As when carrying out a crystallization of a solid compound to a constant (maximum) melting point, the purification should be continued until the molar absorptivity reaches a constant (minimum) value. For example, commercial absolute ethanol commonly contains benzene as an impurity, and the latter is easily detected by spectrophotometric means. The presence of CS_2 in CCl_4 can be detected spectrophotometrically at 318 nm. The absorption data can be taken as truly characteristic of a compound only when its purity has been verified by attainment of constant minimum absorption intensity after repeated fractional purifications. Absorption data have been commonly cited for the purity specifications of some therapeutic solutions of vitamins A, C, and D. Absorption spectra are often used to indicate the purity of unstable biological compounds such as nucleotides or enzymes, because this is often the most convenient, or perhaps the only, way to do so.

7.6 APPARATUS AND INSTRUMENTS

The instruments used in the ultraviolet-visible region of the electromagnetic spectrum fall into three categories, distinguished by complexity of design. Colorimeters generally are the simple visual and photoelectric devices used in the visible region. Photometers include colorimeters, but are more flexible in design so as to include ultraviolet and infrared as well as the visible region. Spectrophotometers are more complex and versatile than either of the others in that they include a monochromator, which provides a narrow band of continuously variable wavelength. A wide variety of spectrophotometers are commercially available.

The choice of source, optical materials, monochromator, and detector depends on the spectral region of interest. This usually imposes a limit on the range of a given instrument. The four ranges for which instruments are presently available are: (1) the visible region (400 to 700 nm); (2) the near ultraviolet, visible, and very near infrared (190 to 1,000 nm), using quartz optics; (3) the vacuum ultraviolet (below 190 nm), requiring an evacuated instrument; and (4) the nitrogen ultraviolet region (200 to 160 nm) requiring instruments purged with N_2.

The Components of a Spectrophotometer

There are several light sources available for use in the ultraviolet-visible region. *Mercury-vapor* lamps have been used but, owing to the heat evolved by these lamps, thermal insulation or cooling is required. More commonly used for the visible and near-infrared region are *tungsten-filament* "incandescent" lamps. These are thermal or "blackbody" sources in which the radiation is the result of high temperature of the solid filament material, with only a small dependence on its actual chemical nature. These sources provide continuous radiation from about 320 to 3000 nm—most of it, unfortunately, in the near-infrared. At the usual operating temperature of about 3000 K, only about 15% of the total radiant energy falls in the visible region, and at 2000 K, only 1%. Increasing the operating temperature above 3000 K greatly increases the total energy output and shifts the wavelength of maximum intensity to shorter wavelengths, but the lifetime of the lamp is drastically shortened. Inconveniently high temperatures are required for the production of much radiation in the ultraviolet. The lifetime of a tungsten filament lamp can be greatly increased by the presence of a low pressure of iodine or bromine vapor within the lamp; with the addition of a fused silica lamp envelope, these are now called *quartz-halogen* lamps— a popular source at present. Most work in the ultraviolet region is done with *hydrogen* or *deuterium* electrical-discharge lamps typically operated under low-pressure DC conditions (about 40 V with 5 mm gas pressure). These lamps provide a continuum emission down to about 160 nm, but the window material generally limits the

FIGURE 7.13. *Schematic diagram of three common detectors used in the ultraviolet-visible region. A: The barrier-layer or photovoltaic cell. B: A vacuum phototube. C: The vacuum photomultiplier.*

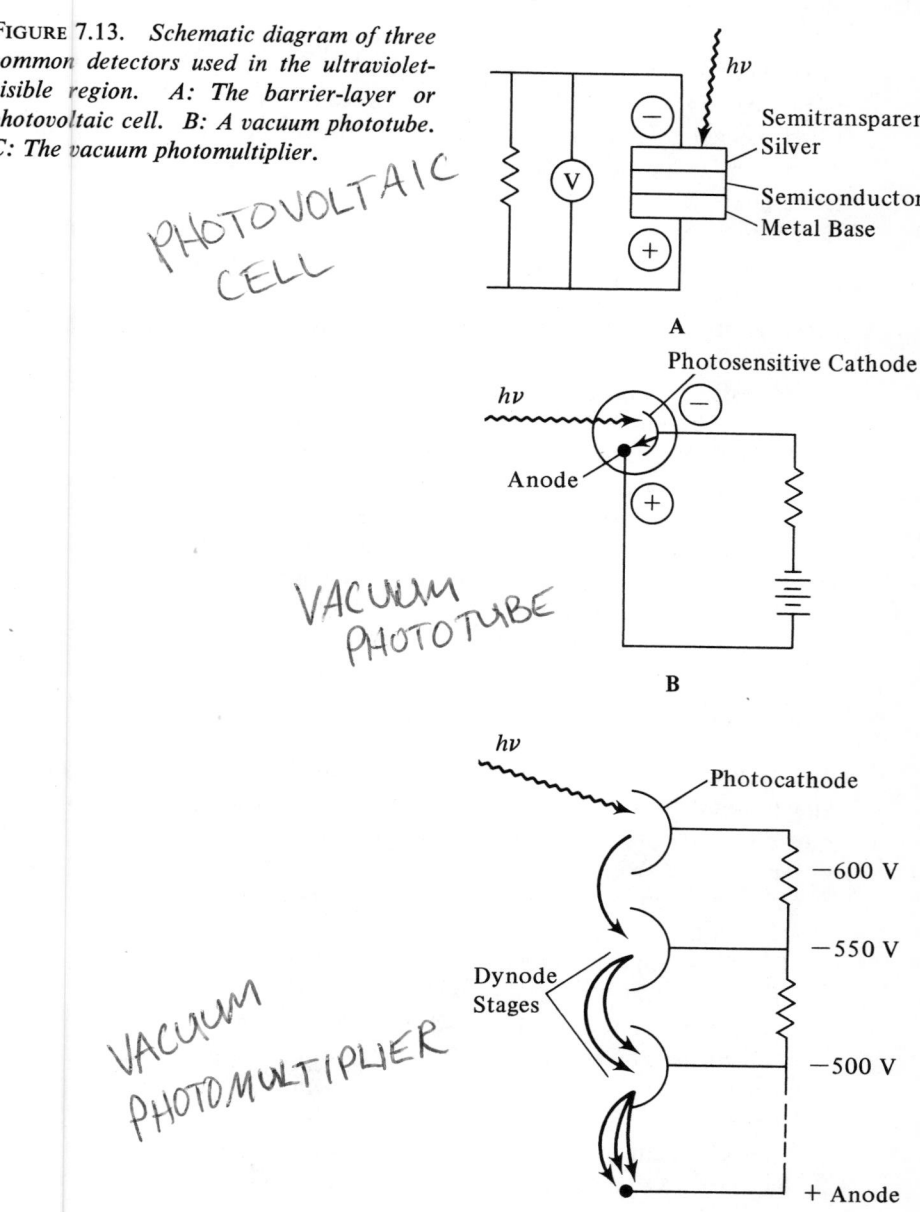

transmission at short wavelengths (about 200 nm with quartz and 185 nm with fused silica). Above about 360 nm, hydrogen emission lines are superimposed on the continuum, so incandescent sources are generally used for measurements at longer wavelengths. Deuterium lamps are more expensive, but have about 2 to 5 times greater spectral intensity and lifetime than a hydrogen lamp of comparable design and wattage.

The continuous radiation from the sources listed above is dispersed by means of monochromators (see Chap. 6).

There are three main types of detectors presently in use. The *barrier-layer* or *photovoltaic* type is illustrated in Figure 7.13A. This device measures the intensity of photons by means of the voltage developed across the semiconductor layer. Electrons, ejected by photons from the semiconductor, are collected by the silver layer. The potential depends on the number of photons hitting the detector. A second type is the photodetector or *phototube* shown in Figure 7.13B. This detector is a vacuum tube with a cesium-coated photocathode. Photons of sufficiently high energy hitting the cathode can dislodge electrons which are collected at the anode. Photon flux is measured by the current flow in the system. The vacuum-phototube type of detector needs further (external) amplification to function properly. The last type of commonly used detector is schematically illustrated in Figure 7.13C. This detector consists of a photoemissive cathode coupled with a series of electron-multiplying dynode stages, and is usually called a *photomultiplier*. The primary electrons ejected from the photocathode are accelerated by an electric field so as to strike a small area on the first dynode. The impinging electrons strike with enough energy to eject two to five *secondary electrons*, which are accelerated to the second dynode to eject still more electrons. This cascading effect takes place until the electrons are collected at the anode. Typically, a photomultiplier may have 9 to 16 stages, and an overall gain of 10^6 to perhaps 10^9 electrons per incident photon.

Single- and Double-Beam Spectrometers

The measurement of absorption of ultraviolet-visible radiation is of a relative nature. One must continually compare the absorption of the sample with that of an analytical reference or blank to insure the reliability of the measurement. The rate at which the sample and reference are compared depends on the design of the instrument. In *single-beam* instruments there is only one light beam or optical path from the source through to the detector. This usually means that one must remove the sample from the light beam and replace it with the reference after each reading. Thus, there is usually an interval of several seconds between measurements.

Alternatively, the sample and reference may be compared many times a second, as in *double-beam* instruments. The light from the source, after passing through the monochromator, is split into two separate beams—one for the sample and the other for the reference. Figure 7.14 shows two types of double-beam spectrophotometers. The measurement of sample and reference absorption may be separated in space, as in Figure 7.14A; this, however, requires two detectors which must be perfectly matched. Alternatively, the sample and reference measurement may be separated in time as in Figure 7.14B; this technique makes use of a rapidly rotating mirror or

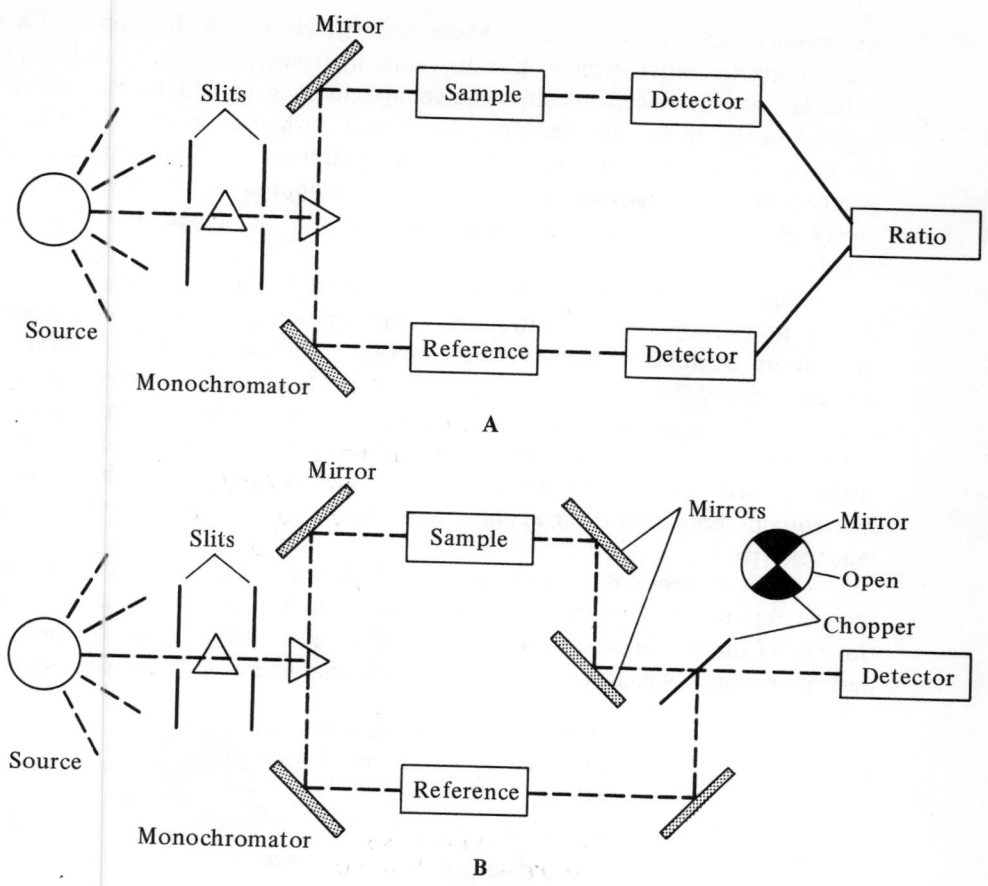

FIGURE 7.14. *Schematic diagram of two types of double-beam spectro-photometers. A: The double-beam-in-space configuration. B: The double-beam-in-time configuration.*

"chopper" to switch the beam that comes from sample and reference very rapidly. The latter method requires only one detector and is probably the better of the two methods.

There are two main advantages of double-beam operation over single-beam operation. Very rapid monitoring of sample and reference helps to eliminate errors due to drift in source intensity, electronic instability, and any changes in the optical system. Also, double-beam operation lends itself to automation—the spectra can be recorded by a strip-chart recorder.

Derivative Spectrophotometers

Derivative spectroscopy was introduced by Griese and French [35] in 1955. These authors achieved better resolution by electronically obtaining first and second derivatives of absorption spectra. More recently, Hager [36] has reported a means of obtaining derivative spectra optically rather than electronically. This is important, as derivatives taken electronically sense changes in intensity with time as well as wavelength, whereas those obtained optically do not. Changes in intensity with respect to time are considered noise; thus, by taking derivatives of these fluctuations the spectrum actually becomes "noisier." If the technique senses only changes of intensity with wavelength, time fluctuations will not be sensed and noise is minimized.

One important feature of derivative spectra is that peak heights are usually directly proportional to concentration. This is more desirable than the logarithmic relationship in direct absorption spectroscopy. Another important feature is that the sensitivity to concentration depends on the rate of change in molar absorptivity at a particular wavelength, $d\varepsilon/d\lambda$, rather than on the absolute magnitude of ε itself. Thus, very sensitive analyses are possible for compounds that have sharp absorption peaks. Since absorption spectra are broadened in condensed phases, derivative spectroscopy finds particular application in gas analysis where absorption peaks are much sharper.

Typical second-derivative spectra are shown in Figure 7.15. The derivative spectra obtained for a given sample can be analyzed for both composition and concentration. Component gases may be identified from the location of their second-derivative peaks, which occur at wavelengths characteristic of the compound. The

TABLE 7.7. *Detection Limits of Some Compounds by Use of a Second-Derivative Gas Analyzer*

Compound	Concentration (ppb)
Ammonia	1
Nitric oxide	5
Nitrogen dioxide	40
Ozone	40
Sulfur dioxide	1
Mercury vapor	0.5
Benzene	25
Toluene	50
Xylene	100
Styrene	100
Formaldehyde	200
Benzaldehyde	100
Acetaldehyde	400

Source: From R. N. Hager, Jr., *Anal. Chem.*, *45*, 1131A (1973), by permission of the author and publisher. Copyright © 1973 by the American Chemical Society.
Note: Signal-to-noise ratio of two.

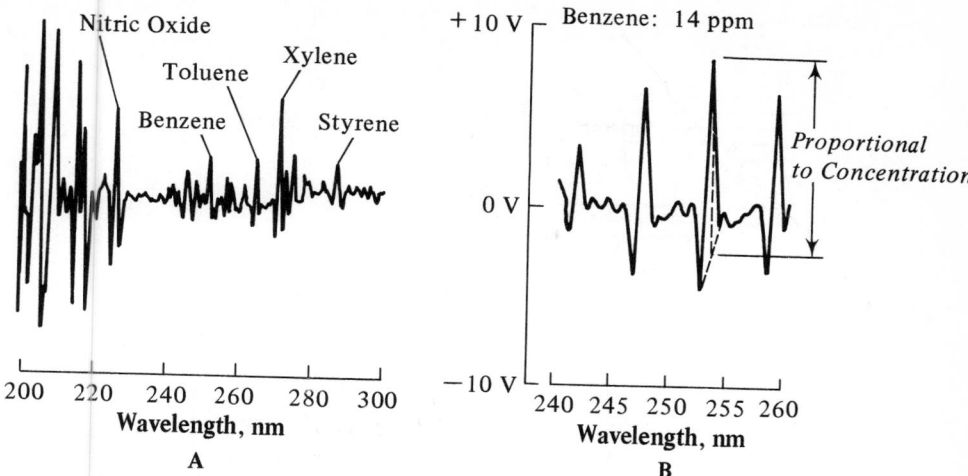

FIGURE 7.15. *Typical second-derivative absorption spectra of gaseous samples. A: Spectrum of an automobile exhaust. B: Spectrum of 14 ppm benzene. Spectra courtesy of Lear Siegler Inc., Environmental Technology Division, Englewood, Colorado.*

concentration of each species is determined directly from the peak height. Table 7.7 shows the sensitivity of the technique to various gases.

Rapid-Scan Spectrophotometers

Rapid-scanning spectroscopy (RSS) is a method in which a selected portion of the ultraviolet, visible, or near-infrared spectrum is scanned on a time scale ranging from several sec to a few μsec. The applications of this technique to systems in which short-lived transient species exist or large reaction rates are encountered are numerous [37]. Examples include studies of enzyme-substrate complexes [38], mixed complexes in ligand exchange reactions [39], and flash photolysis [40] or electrochemical reactions [41].

The instrumentation for rapid-scanning spectroscopy is divided into two groups: dispersion or multiplex. The more common is the *dispersion* method in which the light emerging from the sample is dispersed by a prism or grating into narrow bands of wavelength which are monitored independently. *Multiplex* methods use mathematical techniques, Fourier or Hadamard transforms, to resolve the spectral bands. Dispersion methods are the faster of the two groups, but have lower signal-to-noise ratios. Multiplex methods have their best application in the infrared region.

Several detectors are used in RSS. At present the one that most closely approaches the ideal is the Vidicon camera tube, Figure 7.16. This detector consists of an array of photodiodes spaced about 15 μm apart. The diodes are biased in sequence by an electron beam that repetitively scans the array in the Vidicon tube. Once the

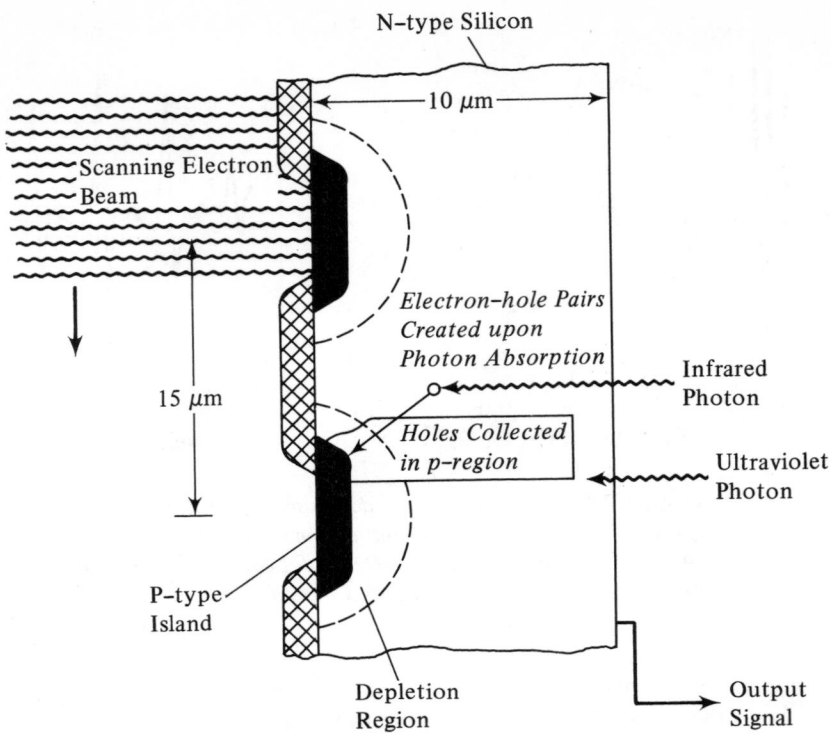

N-type Silicon

10 μm

Scanning Electron
Beam

*Electron–hole Pairs
Created upon
Photon Absorption*

Infrared
Photon

15 μm

*Holes Collected
in p–region*

Ultraviolet
Photon

P-type
Island

Depletion
Region

Output
Signal

FIGURE 7.16. *Schematic diagram of a silicon Vidicon camera tube. An array of photosensitive diodes are grown on a silicon wafer about 15 μm apart. From P. Burke,* Research/Development, *24(4), 24 (1973), by permission of the publisher. Copyright © 1973 by Technical Publishing Company.*

diodes are biased they are nonconducting and no signal is recovered from the array. The diodes are discharged by photon-generated electron-hole pairs or by leakage. Once discharged, the diodes are conducting, and current flows through the diode. This current is the Vidicon signal and is directly proportional to the number of photons hitting the array. Other high-speed detectors are being refined. Two that show promise are the electrooptic type, which have the fastest scan times, 5 μsec, and the charged coupled devices (CCD) which give the best resolution.

Figure 7.17 shows time-resolved spectra of the reaction of $CuCyDTA^{2-}$ (copper cyclohexanediaminetetraacetate) with ethylenediamine (en). This reaction involves a mixed complex [39] as represented in the following equations:

$$Cu(CyDTA)^{2-} + en \longrightarrow Cu(CyDTA)en^{2-} \tag{7.30}$$

$$Cu(CyDTA)en^{2-} + en \longrightarrow Cuen_2^{2+} + CyDTA^{4-} \tag{7.31}$$

This example shows the value of RSS for the study of intermediates in relatively slow reactions. Faster reactions may be studied by using stopped-flow techniques.

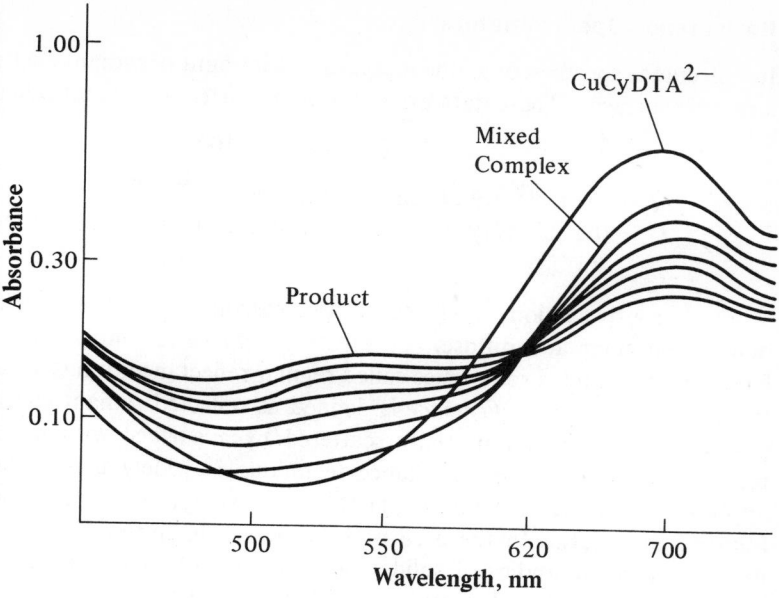

FIGURE 7.17. *Time-resolved spectra of the reaction of CuCyDTA with ethylenediamine. The scan time for one spectrum was 20 msec; spectra were taken every 2 sec.* (*CyDTA = cyclohexanediaminetetraacetate*). *Reprinted with permission from R. E. Santini, M. J. Milano, and H. L. Pardue*, Anal. Chem., *45, 915A (1973), by permission of the authors and publisher. Copyright © 1973 by the American Chemical Society.*

Tuned Lasers in Spectrophotometry

Laser light sources have both a high degree of monochromaticity and very high intensity. For molecular absorption measurements, it is desirable to be able to scan the spectrum, and an ideal source for such absorption measurements would be a tunable laser, one whose wavelength could be varied continuously over the spectral range of interest.

A digital scanning, tunable, dye laser has been constructed for use in the 358–641 nm range [42]. The range can be extended to both longer and shorter wavelengths by selecting other dyes, and the tunable range of laser radiation now available is from about 265 to 800 nm. Spectrophotometers using laser radiation as the source routinely exhibit resolution of about 1 nm.

The tuning action of the laser is accomplished by exciting various organic dyes with a pulsed nitrogen laser. The dyes presently available are only tunable over a 60–70 nm range (essentially, the width of their absorption bands), and thus one must use several dyes to cover a wide wavelength range. The major limitation at present is the 15% deviation in quantitative studies, owing mainly to instabilities in the laser. A further limitation is that the calibration of a particular laser is dependent upon operating conditions.

Reflectance Spectrometers

In reflectance spectroscopy, one measures the amount of radiant energy reflected from a sample surface. These data are generally reported as percent reflectance

$$\%R = I/I_0 \times 100 \qquad (7.32)$$

where I = the intensity of reflected radiation
I_0 = the intensity of radiation reflected from some "standard" reflecting surface.

For a discussion of reflectance spectroscopy, two types of reflectance must be defined, specular and diffuse. *Specular reflectance* is simply mirrorlike reflectance from a surface and is sometimes called regular reflectance; it has a well-defined reflectance angle. *Diffuse reflectance* is defined as reflected radiant energy that has been partially absorbed and partially scattered by a surface with no defined angle of reflectance. The diffuse reflectance technique is widely used today for industrial applications involving textiles, plastics, paints, dyestuffs, inks, paper, food, and building materials. In the area of basic research, diffuse reflectance spectroscopy has been used in studies of solid-solid reactions, of species absorbed on metal surfaces, of radiation transfer, and of slightly soluble species.

A common design feature of all commercial diffuse-reflectance instruments is the integrating sphere, which permits the collection of reflected light. Many of the

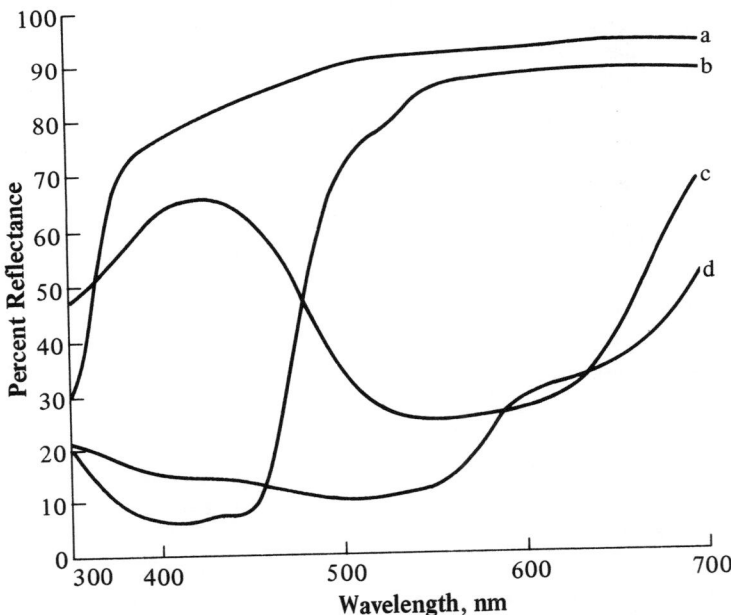

FIGURE 7.18.   *Diffuse reflectance spectra of colored papers: (a) off-white, (b) yellow, (c) purple, and (d) maroon.   The reference material was* $MgCO_3$. *From T. Surles, J. O. Erickson, and D. Priesner,* Amer. Lab., 7(3), 55 (1975), *by permission of International Scientific Communications, Inc., copyright holder.*

commercial ultraviolet-visible spectrophotometers offer this mode of operation as an accessory. The integrating sphere is usually coated with barium sulfate, which is a highly diffuse-reflecting material and serves to "homogenize" the energy being reflected from the sample surface. The intensity of reflected light at any given point in the sphere should be independent of spatial distribution and therefore directly proportional to the diffuse reflectance of the sample. A design feature of some instruments, for example, the Cary 1711, allows for exclusion of specular reflectance or, alternatively, inclusion of both types of reflectance to give total reflectance.

An example of an industrial application of reflectance is presented in Figure 7.18. This figure shows spectra taken from various colored papers. In the paper industry, diffuse reflectance is often used to monitor color, whiteness, brightness, and gloss of papers. The degree of whiteness is an important parameter that requires a system capable of detecting small variations in reflectance. As little as 0.05% R in the paper's reflectance has a perceptible effect on the whiteness observed by the human eye.

In the area of basic research, the surface properties of plastics are of continuing interest. Figure 7.19 shows the total reflectance of a clear piece of plastic on an expanded scale. An interference pattern is observed (the ripples on the curve) and the thickness of the surface film can be calculated from these data.

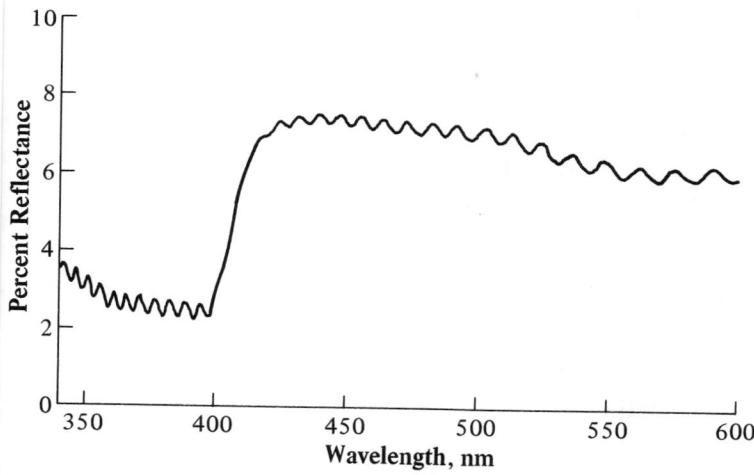

FIGURE 7.19. *A total reflectance spectrum of clear plastic. The reference material is $MgCO_3$. From T. Surles, J. O. Erickson, and D. Priesner, Amer. Lab., 7(3), 55 (1975), by permission of International Scientific Communications, Inc., copyright holder.*

Accessories

Matched Absorption Cells. For routine investigations in the ultraviolet and visible regions, absorption cells of silica or glass are commercially available. Commercial products offered are (1) quartz cells usable in the ultraviolet, visible, and near-infrared range between 220 and 2400 nm; and (2) fused-silica cells with extremely high ultraviolet transmission in the region from 160 nm to 2400 nm. Cells used in quantitative ultraviolet work must be matched with respect to cell width and transmission properties. Silica cells must also be fluorescence-free if accurate quantitative data are needed.

Volumetric Absorption Cells. Often the amount of sample available for trace analysis is rather limited; also, it is often desirable to make the final volume as small as possible, so that absorbance is maximized. This may be accomplished by calibrating an absorption cell to a definite volume by putting a mark on the side and using it as a "volumetric flask." Color development may be carried out in the cell, in order to keep the final volume at a minimum. If pH adjustment is required, a glass microelectrode may be used. For an ordinary 1-cm cell, volumes of about 3 ml may be used.

Long-Path and Multiple-Path Absorption Cells. For sensitive trace analysis, reactions catalyzed by the trace component are often used (see Chap. 18). One thus can resort to rate measurements for quantitative analysis of trace materials or materials that have low molar absorptivities. Another solution to this problem is to use long path length cells. According to the Beer-Lambert law, absorbance is proportional to the length of the light path. Thus, absorbance cells with long path length—5–10 cm—are commercially available for measuring solutions of low concentration or weakly absorbing species. Another approach to this problem is to use, instead of a long cell, a small cell through which the light beam may be passed many times. This should produce the same effect as cells of longer path length. Two simple designs are shown in Figure 7.20. Example A shows a cell to which two mirrors with good reflection characteristics have been attached (or deposited); the radiation beam is adjusted at an angle that will bounce it out to the detector after several passes through the sample. The number of passes is controlled by the incident angle of the light beam. If a light beam perpendicular to the wall is desired, the more complicated design shown in Figure 7.20B may be used. These designs offer increased absorption without the increased cell dimensions needed for single-pass experiments.

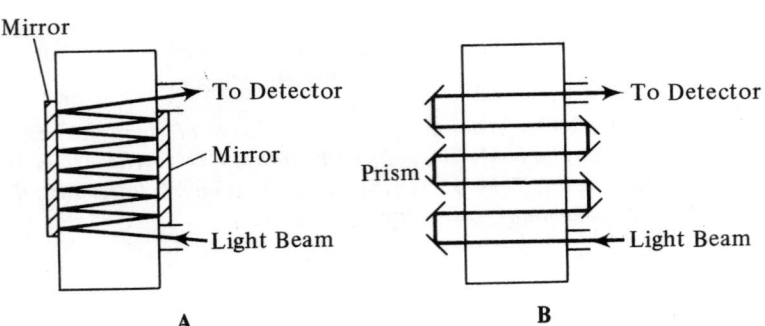

FIGURE 7.20. *Multiple-path absorption cells. From K. L. Cheng, "Absorptiometry," in J. D. Winefordner, ed.,* Spectrochemical Methods of Analysis, *New York: Wiley-Interscience, 1971, chap. 6, by permission of the editor and John Wiley and Sons.*

Curve Resolvers. Many
electrophoresis, and spec
lapping) peaks or distrib
the experimental curve
possible. One commer
complex overlapped cur
function-generator chan
ian, exponential, or ot
horizontal position of
summation curve exact
presented separately or
ment also integrates th

7.7 OTHER DEVELOPMEN

Charge-Transfer Spe

The classical molecul
charge-transfer spectr
to an antibonding or
(or $\sigma \to \sigma^*$ and $\pi \to$
rather than the energy state of the entire mol....

that a definite transfer of electric charge
tion, because neither I_2 nor the arom
Spectrophotometric methods have
between various aromatic compo

Precision Spectrophoto

Precision spectrophoto
volves comparing a
at zero using a s
a reagent blan
measured a

R

that i
of t

Many systems exhibit spectra generally considered to be charge-transfer spectra. Absorptions of this type are characterized by high intensity (large ε_{max}), and are fully allowed transitions. Charge-transfer transitions involve an intramolecular or an interionic redistribution of charge whereby an electron or a fraction of an electron is transferred from one ion or molecule to another ion or molecule in the same species. A complex, DA, is formed between a donor species, D, and an acceptor species, A. This type of complex can exist in two energy states, the difference in energy between these two states being equal to the energy of a quantum at the maximum of the electronic absorption band.

One of the earliest examples classified as a charge transfer is in the spectra of alkali halides [43, 44]. Frequently, a definite (and sometimes pronounced) color change is produced on mixing two compounds which would not be expected to react chemically. For example, aromatic nitro compounds mixed with aromatic hydrocarbons yield intense colors, and, in addition, stable complexes that can be isolated. In solution, however, the complexes are usually considerably dissociated. The electronic-absorption maxima of these complexes are often shifted some hundreds of nanometers to the long-wavelength side of the nearest absorption band of either component. Absorptions of this type usually result in very broad bands that lack fine structure. Charge-transfer complexes are normally formed between one member with a low ionization potential and a partner with a high electron affinity. Sensitive methods of determining amino acids with chloranil base from the charge-transfer reactions have been reported.

Charge-transfer complex formation is not limited to organic species. Mixing I_2 with benzene, naphthalene, or diphenyl produces complexes with electric dipole moments of 1.8, 2.6, and 2.9 debyes, respectively. This observation demonstrates

must be taking place upon complex forma-
tic hydrocarbon alone has a dipole moment.
established charge-transfer complex formation
nds and the halogens.

metry

ometry (differential spectrophotometry) is a technique that in-
unknown solution with a reference. The reference scale is set
olution of a highly colored (radiation-adsorbing) species in place of
k. Concentrations of the unknown higher than the reference are then
gainst this zero in the usual way.

illey and Crawford [45] described a precision spectrophotometric method
volves the use of two standard solutions to set the 0% and 100% T readings
he photometer. By this means, the full scale can be used for a concentration range
uch narrower than usual, and precision is thus increased. This method generally
requires two standard solutions and several other standard solutions of intermediate
concentration to construct a calibration curve, since the measured absorbance is
often not a linear function of concentration (deviation from Beer's law at higher
concentrations).

A method described by Ramaley and Enke [46] replaces the two-standard and
calibration-curve procedure with one standard and isomation. This method involves
a titration in which the absorbance of the unknown determines the endpoint. A
known amount of solvent is placed in an absorption cell. A standard solution of
the sample substance is then added to the cell until the absorbance, and hence the
concentration, is identical to that of the unknown solution. To obtain the maximum
accuracy, the cell lengths are calibrated as follows: at the endpoint

$$\frac{c_u}{c_s} = \frac{b_s}{b_u} \tag{7.33}$$

where c_s = the concentration of the standard
c_u = the concentration of the sample
b_s = the standard cell length
b_u = the sample cell length

The ratio of the cell lengths may be obtained by using standard solution in both cells
and adjusting their concentration until the absorbance is the same for both. The
ratio is calculated from Equation 7.33. With knowledge of the cell-length ratio and
the concentration of the standard solution, the unknown concentration may be readily
determined. With this method, species with molar absorptivity of 10^4 may be determined in the 10^{-6} M concentration range with ± 2 ppt accuracy.

Photon Counting in Spectrophotometry

Light is a source of discrete photons. When light is measured with a detector such
as a photomultiplier, the photons are converted to current pulses which may not be
completely resolved in time from each other. Usually these pulses are smoothed to

a continuous or continuously varying signal and recorded by a readout device such as a meter. However, the number of photons per unit time reaching the detector can be decreased to a point where the individual current pulses from the photomultiplier tube become resolvable. This can be done by decreasing the light intensity, by isolating a particular wavelength region with a monochromator, and by stopping down the optical aperture of the light beam. If the rate of photoelectron ejection and the frequency response of the measurement system are such that individual current pulses can be resolved, then the number of pulses per unit time can be counted. Because the count rate is a measure of the rate at which photons are striking the photocathode, the measurement technique is appropriately called *photon counting*. In both single- and double-beam instruments, a number proportional to the radiant power of the sample beam is obtained by counting the photoelectric pulses of the sample beam during a precisely controlled time interval [47].

Recently, photon counting has become an important technique in spectrophotometric methods where the radiation is so low in intensity that it is difficult to obtain measurements by conventional means. The ability to deal with low radiation levels with a satisfactory signal-to-noise ratio is of course one of the important factors in the photon-counting method. Improvements in precision, resolution, signal-to-noise ratio, and readout are obtainable by photon counting, and this method should be applicable to all spectrophotometric procedures (absorption, emission, reflection, fluorescence, and light scattering) in which a photomultiplier is used.

SELECTED BIBLIOGRAPHY

BAUMAN, R. P. *Absorption Spectroscopy.* New York: Wiley, 1962.

BOLTZ, D. F., and SCHENK, G. H. "Visible and Ultraviolet Spectroscopy." In L. Meites, ed., *Handbook of Analytical Chemistry.* New York: McGraw-Hill, 1963.

DODD, R. E. *Chemical Spectroscopy.* Amsterdam: Elsevier, 1962.

DONHROW, M. *Instrumental Methods in Analytical Chemistry: Their Principles and Practices*, vol. II, *Optical Methods.* New York: Pitman, 1967.

KOLTHOFF, I. M., and ELVING, P. J., eds. *Treatise on Analytical Chemistry*, part I, vol. 5. New York: Interscience, 1964.

WALKER, S., and STRAW, H. *Spectroscopy*, vol. II. London: Chapman and Hall, 1967.

REFERENCES

1. H. K. HUGHES, *Anal. Chem.*, 24, 1349 (1952); 40, 2271 (1968).

2. H. H. JAFFE and M. ORCHIN, *Theory and Applications of Ultraviolet Spectroscopy*, New York: Wiley, 1962.

3. J. R. DYER, *Applications of Absorption Spectroscopy of Organic Compounds*, Englewood Cliffs, N.J.: Prentice-Hall, 1965.

4. R. M. SILVERSTEIN and G. C. BASSLER, *Spectrometric Identification of Organic Compounds*, 2nd ed., New York: Wiley, 1967.

5. E. A. BRAUDE, *Determination of Organic Structures by Physical Methods*, New York: Academic Press, 1955.

6. C. N. R. RAO, *Ultraviolet and Visible Spectroscopy*, 2nd ed., London: Plenum, 1967.

7. S. F. Mason, *Quart. Rev.* (London), *287* (1961).

8. L. Doub and J. M. Vanderbelt, *J. Amer. Chem. Soc.*, *69*, 2714 (1947); *71*, 2414 (1949).

9. J. R. Platt, *J. Chem. Phys.*, *19*, 263 (1951).

10. A. E. Gillam and E. S. Stern, *An Introduction to Electronic Absorption Spectroscopy in Organic Chemistry*, London: Edward Arnold, 1954.

11. K. L. Cheng, *Anal. Chim. Acta*, *28*, 41 (1963).

12. K. L. Cheng, *Anal. Chem.*, *30*, 1035 (1958).

13. R. Jakubiec and D. F. Boltz, *Anal. Chem.*, *41*, 78 (1969).

14. W. C. Vosburgh and G. R. Cooper, *J. Amer. Chem. Soc.*, *53*, 435 (1941).

15. P. Job, *Anal. Chim.*, *9*, 113 (1928).

16. J. Bjerrum, *Kgl. Danske Videnskab. Selskab, Mat-Fys. Medd.*, *21*(4) (1944); H. Olerup, Thesis, "Jarn Kloridernas Komplexitet," Lund, 1944.

17. F. J. C. Rossotti and H. Rossotti, *The Determination of Stability Constants*, McGraw-Hill, New York, 1961; S. D. Christian, *J. Chem. Educ.*, *45*, 713 (1968).

18. L. A. Flexser, L. P. Hammet, and A. Dingwall, *J. Amer. Chem. Soc.*, *57*, 2103 (1935).

19. H. C. Brown and D. H. McDaniel, *J. Amer. Chem. Soc.*, *77*, 3752 (1955).

20. F. T. King and R. C. Hirt, *Appl. Spectrosc.*, *7*, 164 (1953).

21. C. Rehm, J. I. Bodin, K. A. Connors, and T. Higuchi, *Anal. Chem.*, *31*, 483 (1959).

22. W. R. Brode, *J. Amer. Chem. Soc.*, *46*, 581 (1924).

23. M. Kambe, E. Shindo, and M. Marito, *Japan Analyst*, *16*, 1017 (1967).

24. B. N. Mattoo, *Trans. Faraday Soc.*, *52*, 1462 (1956).

25. K. L. Cheng, *Talanta*, *2*, 266 (1959); *5*, 254 (1960).

26. M. Otomo, *Bull. Chem. Soc. Jap.*, *36*, 146 (1962).

27. B. Ricca and G. Fraone, *Gazz. Chim. Ital.*, *79*, 340 (1949); *Chem. Abstr.*, *43*, 8935b (1949).

28. R. T. Foley and R. C. Anderson, *J. Amer. Chem. Soc.*, *72*, 5609 (1950).

29. R. W. Ramette, *J. Chem. Educ.*, *44*, 647 (1967).

30. K. G. Cunningham, W. Dawson, and F. S. Spring, *J. Chem. Soc.*, 2305 (1954).

31. V. C. Barry, J. E. McCormick, and P. W. D. Mitchell, *J. Chem. Soc.*, 222 (1955).

32. E. A. Braude and E. R. H. Jones, *J. Chem. Soc.*, 498 (1945).

33. C. Djerassi and E. Ryan, *J. Amer. Chem. Soc.*, *71*, 1000 (1949).

34. J. P. Riley, *J. Chem. Soc.*, 2108 (1952).

35. A. Griese and C. French, *Appl. Spectrosc.*, *9*, 78 (1955).

36. R. N. Hager, Jr., *Anal. Chem.*, *45*, 1131A (1973).

37. R. E. Santini, M. J. Milano, and H. L. Pardue, *Anal. Chem.*, *45*, 915A (1973).

38. V. Massey and G. H. Gibson, *Fed. Proc.*, *23*, 18 (1964).

39. J. D. Carr, R. A. Libby, and D. W. Margerum, *Inorg. Chem.*, *6*, 1083 (1967).

40. J. I. H. Patterson and S. P. Perone, *Anal. Chem.*, *44*, 1978 (1972).

41. J. W. Strojek, G. A. Gruver, and T. Kuwana, *Anal. Chem.*, *41*, 481 (1969).

42. D. Harrington and H. V. Malmstadt, *Amer. Lab.*, *6*(3), 33 (1974).

43. J. Frank, H. Kuhn, and G. Rollefson, *Z. Physik*, *43*, 155 (1927).

44. R. Hilsch and R. W. Pohl, *Z. Physik*, *64*, 606 (1930).

45. C. N. Reilley and C. M. Crawford, *Anal. Chem.*, *27*, 716 (1955).

46. L. Ramaley and C. G. Enke, *Anal. Chem.*, *37*, 1073 (1965).

47. E. H. Piepmeier, D. E. Braun, and R. R. Rhodes, *Anal. Chem.*, *40*, 1667 (1968); M. L. Franklin, G. Horlick, and H. V. Malmstadt, *Anal. Chem.*, *41*, 2 (1969); K. C. Ash and E. H. Piepmeier, *Anal. Chem.*, *43*, 26 (1971).

PROBLEMS

1. A sodium-vapor lamp emits radiation with a wavelength of 5889.97 Å. Express the wavelength in nm and calculate its frequency. The speed of light in vacuum is 2.99776×10^{10} cm/sec.

2. The energy of the electronic transition for $\text{D-A} \xrightarrow{h\nu} \text{D}^+ + \text{A}^-$ may be estimated by the equation $h\nu = I_D$ (ionization potential of donor) $- E_A$ (electron affinity of acceptor) $- C$ (mutual electrostatic energy of D^+ and A^-). Gaseous NaCl will absorb in the UV due to a charge-transfer transition. Estimate the energy and wavelength at which absorption may be expected. $I_{Na^+} = 5.14$ eV, $E_{Cl^-} = 3.82$ eV, $C \approx 6.2$ eV.

3. The Pd 4,4'-bis(dimethylamino)thiobenzophenone complexation has been reported to be one of the most sensitive color reactions, with a molar absorptivity of 2.12×10^5. Assuming that the minimum measurable absorbance is 0.001 and that a cell with a 10-cm light path is available, what is the lowest possible molar concentration of Pd that can be determined spectrophotometrically? If the volume of the cell is 10 ml, what is the smallest quantity of Pd that can be determined?

4. In 25.0 ml of 0.8 N $HClO_4$, 5.0×10^{-7} mole of Zr forms a 1:1 complex with xylenol orange (XO) giving an absorbance of 0.484 at 535 nm in a 1.00-cm cell. Calculate the molar absorptivity of the Zr-XO complex.

5. A mixture of *ortho* and *para* nitroanilines is analyzed by ultraviolet spectrophotometry, measuring absorbances of the mixture at two different wavelengths. Using the data given below, calculate the molar concentrations of the *ortho* and *para* isomers.

6. A conjugate base of a weak acid, HA, has an absorption maximum at 520 nm. The following data were obtained by measuring the absorbances of solutions of the weak acid having the same concentration but different pH buffers.

pH	Absorbance
2.0	0.00
4.0	0.00
5.0	0.030
6.0	0.180
7.0	0.475
8.0	0.565
9.0	0.590
10.0	0.590
11.0	0.590
12.0	0.590

What is the approximate pK_a of this weak acid?

7. A colored substance X has an absorption maximum at 400 nm. A solution containing 2.00 mg X per liter had an absorbance of 0.840 using a 2.00-cm cell. The formula weight of X is 150. (a) Calculate the absorptivity of X at 400 nm. (b) Calculate the molar absorptivity of X at 400 nm. (c) How many mg of X is contained in 25.0 ml of a solution giving an absorbance of 0.250 at 400 nm when measured with a 1.00-cm cell? (d) How many ppm of X are in the solution in (c)?

8. A 0.200 g sample containing Cu is dissolved, and a diethyldithiocarbamate colored complex is formed in the presence of EDTA. The solution is then diluted to 50.0 ml and the absorbance measured as 0.260. A 0.500 g sample containing 0.240% Cu is treated in the same manner, and the result-

	Absorbance		Molar absorptivity	
	285 nm	347 nm	285 nm	347 nm
o-nitroaniline	——	——	5260	1280
p-nitroaniline	——	——	1400	9200
mixture	0.520	0.458	——	——

ing solution has an absorbance of 0.600. Calculate the percentage of Cu in the sample.

9. A 0.5000 g steel sample is dissolved and the Mn in the sample is oxidized to permanganate by periodate using Ag^+ as a catalyst. After the sample is diluted to 250.0 ml, the absorbance is 0.393 at 540 nm in a 1.00-cm cell. Calculate the percentage of Mn in the steel. The molar absorptivity for permanganate at 540 nm is 2025.

10. ERIO X forms a 1:1 colored complex with Mg^{2+} at pH 10.00. The ERIO X solution was titrated with Mg^{2+} photometrically. This titration showed that, at the equivalence point, [Mg-ERIO X] = [ERIO X] = 5×10^{-7} M. Calculate the formation constant of the Mg complex.

11. A solution containing 0.1500 g of pure weak acid, HA, was titrated with 0.0500 N NaOH. Only the anion, A^-, in the solution absorbed at 350 nm. The following titration data were obtained at 350 nm. What is the molecular weight of this acid?

NaOH, ml	Absorbance
0.0	0.000
0.50	0.185
1.00	0.370
1.50	0.555
2.00	0.680
2.50	0.750
3.00	0.800
3.50	0.842
4.00	0.870
4.50	0.890
5.00	0.900
5.50	0.910
6.00	0.910
7.00	0.910

12. Plot two Job's curves for the Bi-xylenol orange (XO) complex from the following data obtained in 0.1 N H_2SO_4 at 545 nm. (a) What is the molar ratio of Bi to XO? (b) Estimate the formation constant of the Bi-XO complex.

	Corrected absorbance	
$[Bi^{3+}]/([Bi^{3+}] + [XO])$	I	II
0.0	0.00	0.00
0.1	0.049	0.070
0.2	0.095	0.145
0.3	0.145	0.208
0.4	0.180	0.260
0.5	0.198	0.278
0.6	0.190	0.270
0.7	0.160	0.226
0.8	0.108	0.158
0.9	0.058	0.075
1.0	0.00	0.00

13. The following absorbance values were obtained in preparing a spectrophotometric calibration curve: "blank", 0.03 A; 1.00 mM standard, 0.11 A; 2.00 mM standard, 0.19 A; 4.00 mM standard, 0.35 A. Plot the calibration curve. What is the most probable reason for the noncompliance of the data to Beer's law?

14. Literature values for the molar absorptivities of nucleotides are often used to determine the concentration of nucleotide solutions, since even highly purified nucleotides may contain variable waters of hydration or a variable salt content. A sample of the disodium salt of cytidine 5'-monophosphate (5'-CMP, $C_9H_{12}N_3O_8PNa_2$) was weighed out (0.0814 g), dissolved, and diluted to 25.00 ml in a volumetric flask with distilled water. 5'-CMP has $\varepsilon = 13.0 \times 10^3$ at $\lambda_{max} = 280$ nm in 0.01 M HCl. An aliquot of the CMP stock solution (0.100 ml) was diluted to 10.0 ml with 0.01 M HCl. The absorbance of this solution was 0.831 in a calibrated cuvette of 0.992-cm path length. (a) Calculate the "nominal" or expected concentration of 5'-CMP, assuming it to be a pure anhydrous salt. (b) Calculate the concentration based on spectrophotometric data. (c) Assuming the difference in concentration is due only to absorbed and bound water molecules, what is the average number of water molecules per 5'-CMP molecule?

8

Infrared and Raman Spectroscopy

Eugene B. Bradley

Infrared and Raman spectroscopy are important analytical tools used to investigate a wide variety of molecules in the solid, liquid, and gas states, and yielding complementary information about molecular structure and molecular bonds. Both methods supply information about resonances caused by vibration, vibration-rotation, or rotation of the molecular framework, but because the interaction mechanism between radiation and the molecule differs in the two types, the quantum-mechanical selection rules differ as well. Therefore, not all of the molecular motions recorded by one type of spectroscopy will necessarily be recorded by the other. The geometrical configuration of the molecule and the distribution of electrical charge within that configuration determine which molecular motions may appear in each type of spectrum.

8.1 THEORY AND BACKGROUND

Infrared spectroscopy is used to investigate quantized molecular resonances that absorb electromagnetic energy selectively from a broadband infrared source. Thus, it requires the spectral analysis of infrared energy transmitted through the sample. The spectral analysis is done with a prism or grating monochromator or by auto-correlation (Fourier transform) techniques. The resulting signals are amplified, detected, and recorded in some form.

A molecule will absorb infrared radiation if it vibrates in such a way that its electric dipole moment changes during vibration. The electric dipole moment $\bar{\mu}$ is a vector quantity

$$\bar{\mu} = q\bar{d} \tag{8.1}$$

ic charge

ted distance of that charge from some defined origin of co-
; for the molecule

its charge distribution with respect to that origin may or may
upon the structure of the molecule. Thus not all vibrations
lar structure will necessarily absorb infrared radiation, but
hat cause the electric dipole moment to change.

scopy is used to investigate quantized molecular resonances
nt point of view. The Raman effect is the inelastic scattering
es. If a photon is scattered inelastically by a molecule it may
gain energy and be scattered at a frequency higher than the original frequency, or it
may lose energy and be scattered at a frequency lower than the original frequency.
This process is shown in Figure 8.1. The exciting photon $h\nu_L$ may impinge upon a
molecule in its ground vibrational state ($n = 0$) or upon a molecule in the first excited
vibrational state ($n = 1$) and raise the molecule to a virtual state (sometimes called
a pseudo-excited state). If the molecule loses energy and decays back to $n = 1$, a
frequency $h(\nu_L - \nu_1)$ is produced if the scattering originated from $n = 0$. If the
molecule loses energy and decays back to $n = 0$, a frequency $h(\nu_L + \nu_1)$ is produced
if the scattering originated from $n = 1$.

For historical reasons, the shifted frequencies that appear below the exciting
frequency are called Stokes frequencies, and those that appear above the exciting
frequency are called anti-Stokes frequencies. Notice that the frequency displacement
(the Raman shift) of either Stokes or anti-Stokes lines from the exciting line is ν_1,
a frequency that is characteristic of a particular molecular mode of vibration. The
Stokes lines are more intense because the population of the molecular-energy levels
as a function of temperature follows a Boltzmann distribution (most molecules are
in the ground vibrational level at room temperature); thus the Stokes lines are
recorded with a higher signal-to-noise ratio.

Most collisions of the exciting radiation with molecules are elastic; only about
one in 10^6 collisions is inelastic. The incident energy that is scattered with no change
in frequency (*elastically* scattered) is called the Rayleigh line and it is much more
intense than either Stokes or anti-Stokes lines.

The scattering efficiency of the molecules is proportional to the fourth power
of the incident frequency, so visible light, usually from a laser, is used to excite the
Raman spectrum. It is important to note that the Raman shift is *independent* of the
exciting frequency over a wide range of visible wavelengths, so, for example, one obtains the same lines whether a He-Ne laser (6328 Å) or an Argon-ion laser (4880 Å)
is used. Certain molecules photodissociate more easily than others, however, so the
laser frequency should be chosen with care. It is a good idea to obtain a spectrum of
the sample in the visible region and avoid choosing a laser frequency in a region
of strong absorption. (One may use a laser frequency corresponding to a region of
strong absorption if resonance Raman scattering is to be studied, but the reader is
referred to advanced reading for applications and information on this subject.)

Usually one records the right-angle scattering of intense, monochromatic
laser-light incident upon the sample. The vibrating molecules scatter the light at
frequencies that are shifted up or down with respect to the exciting frequency, and

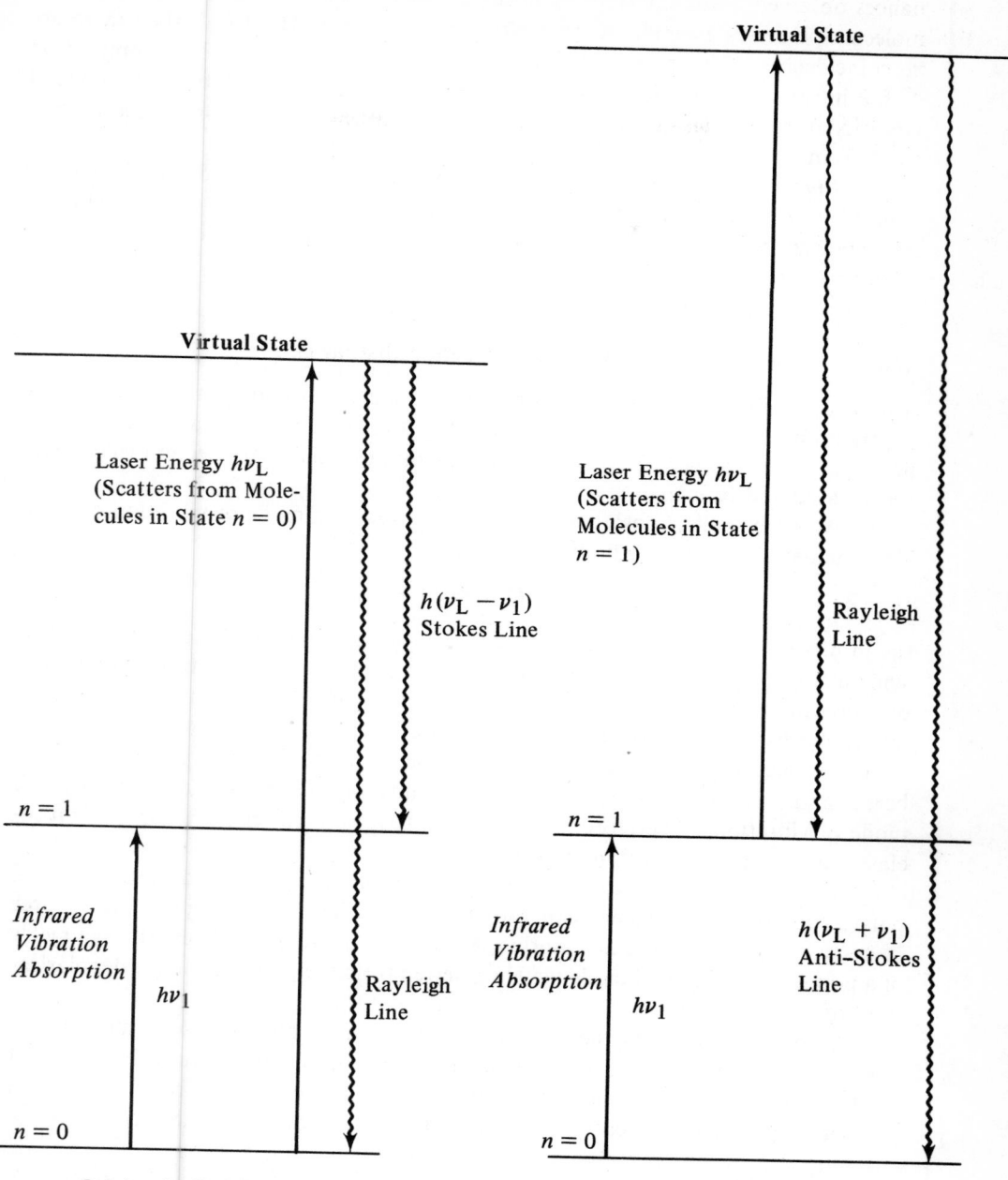

Virtual State

Laser Energy $h\nu_L$
(Scatters from Mole-
cules in State $n = 0$)

$h(\nu_L - \nu_1)$
Stokes Line

$n = 1$

*Infrared
Vibration
Absorption*

$h\nu_1$

Rayleigh
Line

$n = 0$

Origin of a Stokes Line

Virtual State

Laser Energy $h\nu_L$
(Scatters from
Molecules in State
$n = 1$)

Rayleigh
Line

$n = 1$

*Infrared
Vibration
Absorption*

$h\nu_1$

$h(\nu_L + \nu_1)$
Anti–Stokes
Line

$n = 0$

Origin of an Anti-Stokes Line

FIGURE 8.1.   *Origins of Stokes and anti-Stokes Raman lines.*

these *shifts* (Raman lines) correspond to all, some, or none of the molecular resonances observed in the infrared. The correspondences are called *coincidences*. If a molecule possesses a center of symmetry (for example, C_2H_4, CO_2), then there are *no* coincidences. This case is, of course, particularly easy to spot by a comparison of the infrared and Raman spectra. For example, CO_2 exhibits two fundamental vibrational frequencies in the infrared, at 667 and 2349 cm^{-1}, and one in the Raman at 1340 cm^{-1}.

A molecule will scatter monochromatic radiation and produce Raman lines if the molecule vibrates in such a way that its polarizability is changed during the vibration. As a molecule vibrates, its electric dipole moment $\bar{\mu}$ or its polarizability α may change, or both $\bar{\mu}$ and α may change:

$$\bar{\mu} = \alpha\bar{E} \tag{8.2}$$

where $\bar{E}$ = the electric field of the incident radiation

The polarizability α is usually a function of the molecular coordinates. The charge distribution of the molecule may be such that $\bar{\mu}$ changes with vibration and α does not change, or vice versa; this is why the quantum-mechanical selection rules differ for infrared and Raman.

As an example, consider the symmetric stretching mode of vibration of CO_2. The symmetrical stretching motion is

$$\longleftrightarrow \quad O{=}C{=}O \quad \longleftrightarrow$$

the in-phase motion of the two oxygen atoms (in and out). With respect to C, this symmetrical motion involves motions of atoms with the same electronegativity and produces no *net* change in $\bar{\mu}$. For this reason, this mode of vibration does not absorb infrared radiation. The polarizability of a molecule, however, is almost entirely due to the displacements of electrons by the alternating electric field of an incident light beam, and analysis shows that the polarizability of CO_2 does change during this mode of vibration. Therefore this motion in CO_2 will scatter a photon of light inelastically and produce a Raman line.

The electric-field vector of a Raman line may correspond to partial or total polarization of the electromagnetic radiation in that line, depending upon the degree of symmetry of the molecular motion(s) that spawn the line. Thus, the symmetry of a particular vibrational mode may be inferred from the polarization (or depolarization) of a Raman band.

The polarization of the light in a Raman line is obtained experimentally by measuring a quantity called the "depolarization ratio," ρ. It is defined by a ratio of the band areas observed when the light is passed through a polarizer turned first perpendicular, then parallel to the scattered light. The expression that results is

$$\rho = \frac{3\bar{\beta}^2}{45\bar{\alpha}^2 + 4\bar{\beta}^2} = \frac{I_\perp}{I_\parallel} \tag{8.3}$$

where $\bar{\alpha}$ = the isotropic part of the polarizability
$\bar{\beta}$ = the anisotropic part of the polarizability

The quantity ρ has no infrared counterpart, and it is usually reported along with the Raman shift. If $\rho = 0$ ($\bar{\beta} = 0$), then polarized radiation is scattered by a totally symmetric mode of vibration. If $\rho = 3/4$ ($\bar{\alpha} = 0$), then depolarized radiation is scattered by the vibration. When the value of the depolarization ratio is less than 0.2, the $\bar{\alpha}$ term is dominating, but if ρ is greater than 0.2, the $\bar{\beta}$ term is becoming more important and there is some degree of asymmetry in the vibrational mode.

The depolarization ratio is measured by first placing a polarization analyzer between the sample and the entrance slit of the monochromator; ρ is obtained by finding the ratio of the band peak-heights when the polarizer is rotated perpendicular ($\perp$) and parallel ($\parallel$) to the scattered radiation coming from the sample. The Raman spectrometer should be standardized first by measuring the polarized 459 cm^{-1} bands of carbon tetrachloride ($\rho = 0.005 \pm 0.002$) and the depolarized band of carbon tetrachloride at 218 cm^{-1} ($\rho = 0.75$).

Depolarization ratios are not obtainable directly on finely ground crystals or powders because refractions and reflections scramble the polarization, but one may measure depolarization ratios of polymer films, liquids, and gases.

The analytical spectroscopist is usually more concerned with "peak intensity" measurement, i.e., I and I_0, whereas the theoretical spectroscopist is often concerned with band areas and band-shape parameters (bandwidth, band contour, etc.). However, before attempting any serious work with areas or shapes, the reader is advised to consult a paper on this subject by Seshadri and Jones [1].

Spectral Region

Chemists work most often in the medium infrared region (2.5–50 μm or 4000–200 cm^{-1}) where most molecular vibrations (in liquids and gases) and vibration-rotations (in gases) occur; purely rotational resonances usually occur in the far infrared between 50 and 1000 μm (or 200–10 cm^{-1}). There are molecules, however, whose motions give rise to (a) vibration or vibration-rotation spectra at wavelengths longer than 50 μm or (b) pure rotation spectra at wavelengths less than 50 μm.

The state of the sample and the environment imposed upon it are clues to the type(s) of spectral frequencies one will observe. Table 8.1 is not complete, but it is representative of what one observes for each of the three states of matter. In

TABLE 8.1. *States of a Sample and Types of Spectra that may Occur for Each*

State of Sample	Types of Spectra
Gas	Fundamental modes of vibration ν_1, ν_2, ν_3, etc. Vibration-rotation Pure rotation Overtones (multiples) of fundamental (for example, 2ν, 3ν, etc.) Combinations of fundamentals (for example, $\nu_1 + \nu_2$, etc.)
Liquid	Fundamental modes of vibration Overtones Combination
Solid	Lattice modes Impurity modes Absorption edges (semiconductors)

TABLE 8.2. *Information Obtainable from Molecular Infrared Spectra*

1. Far Infrared, 50–1000 μm (200–10 cm^{-1})
    A. rotational constants, internuclear distances, possible geometrical arrangements of atoms
    B. rotational contributions to specific heats
    C. effects of isotopes
    D. molecular symmetry
    E. nuclear spins (from intensities)
    F. fundamental vibrational modes of heavy molecules

2. Medium Infrared, 2.5–50 μm (4000–200 cm^{-1})
    A. fundamental vibrations
    B. vibration-rotation
    C. vibrational contributions to specific heats
    D. force fields inside molecules
    E. characteristic bond frequencies
    F. force constants of potential function
    G. heats of dissociation
    H. structure
    I. effects of isotopes
    J. vibrational amplitudes

3. Near Infrared, 0.7–2.5 μm (14,285–4000 cm^{-1})
    A. fundamental vibrations of X-H (stretching vibrations)
    B. overtone or combination bands of X-H stretching

the infrared, gas spectra usually have well defined lines of absorption; these lines are rather narrow because the number density of molecules is relatively small and the pressure is usually low ($\sim$5–10 cm Hg). When a gas is cooled to its liquid state, the sharp, well defined absorption lines in the spectrum of the gas become reduced in number and broaden somewhat. This reduction and broadening occurs because the number density is much larger in the liquid and free rotation of the molecules is no longer possible (with few exceptions).

Considerable experience is required to interpret the spectra of solids and gases; usually, less is needed for those of a liquid, because most of the spectral bands are relatively strong and broad.

Listed in Table 8.2 is some of the information available from molecular spectra in each region of the infrared.

8.2 INSTRUMENTATION

As in almost all spectroscopic methods, the instrumentation for infrared or Raman spectroscopy consists of a radiation source, a monochromator or wavelength-selection device of some type, a sample holder, and a detector.

Infrared Spectrometers

Infrared spectroscopy produces a spectrum by analyzing the frequency of the radiation that passes through the sample. The frequency analysis is done by a prism or grating monochromator that sorts out the various frequencies contained in the radiation and passes them to a detector, connected to an amplifier system, for recording. Infrared spectrometers are either single-beam or double-beam. The double-beam type is a ratio recording system which, when properly used, cancels background absorption caused by atmospheric gases, particularly CO_2 and H_2O. These are recording instruments in which the ratio is taken automatically and continuously over the entire spectrum. A schematic diagram of a double-beam infrared spectrophotometer is shown in Figure 8.2.

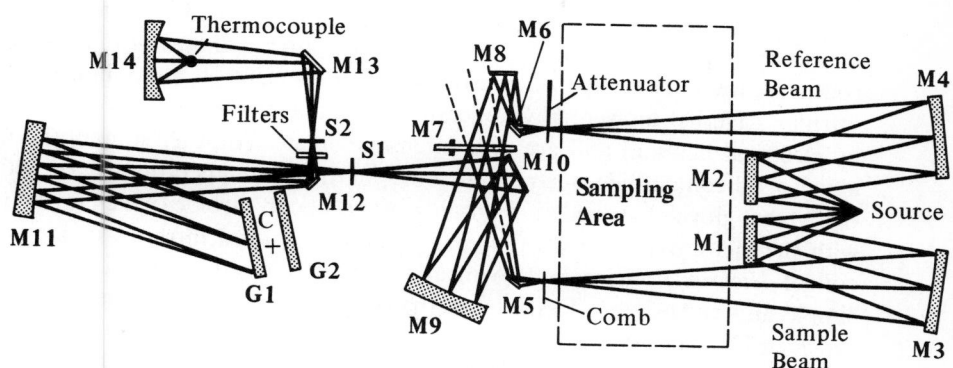

FIGURE 8.2. *A schematic diagram of a typical double-beam infrared spectrometer. The symbols* $M1, M2, \ldots$ *indicate mirrors;* $S1$ *and* $S2$ *indicate slits; and* $G1$ *and* $G2$ *indicate gratings. Courtesy of the Perkin-Elmer Corporation.*

The source radiation is split into sample and reference beams that are recombined by the rotating sector mirror M7 after passing through the sampling area. The sample beam and the reference beam travel through the monochromator in alternate pulses. Each pulse is dispersed by grating G1 or G2, depending upon the spectral range desired, and focused on the detector (a thermocouple). No alternating signal is developed by the thermocouple if the intensities of the sample and reference beams are equal at the frequency emerging from the exit slit. If they differ, an alternating voltage is developed by the thermocouple. This alternating signal is amplified and its phase compared with the angular position of the rotating mirror; then it is used to move the attenuator in or out of the reference beam. The attenuator subtracts from the reference beam the same amount of energy as the sample absorbs in the sample beam. What the instrument actually records is the position of the attenuator, which is related to the absorption spectrum of the compound.

One fundamental difference between infrared and ultraviolet-visible spectrophotometers is the position of the sample with respect to the monochromator. In ultraviolet-visible spectrophotometers, the sample is placed after the monochromator to minimize the exposure of the sample to the high-energy radiation. In infrared instruments, the sample is placed before the monochromator to minimize the amount of stray radiation (emanating from the sample and the cell) reaching the detector. Stray light is a particularly serious problem in most of the infrared region, more so than in the ultraviolet-visible region. Chopping the light from the source and measuring the alternating signal from the detector helps to alleviate this problem.

Single-beam systems require a background spectrum and a spectrum of the sample plus background. The ratio of the two spectra is found by dividing the two ordinates (that is, the two intensities) at small frequency increments over the entire range scanned. A plot of these ratios against the frequencies at which each ratio was obtained is the spectrum of the sample. Almost all quantitative and qualitative analysis today is done on double-beam instruments.

Infrared Radiation Sources. In the infrared region, blackbody radiation sources are used. These sources have characteristics not unlike those of a tungsten incandescent lamp. Perhaps the most widely used infrared source is the *Nernst glower*, a sintered rod or hollow tube composed of oxides of such elements as zirconium, thorium, and yttrium. Nernst glowers have operating temperatures as high as 1500°C (attained by electrical heating) and are very intense sources. Another source, the *Globar*, is a rod of silicon carbide operated at somewhat lower temperatures (ca. 1300°C) than the Nernst glower to avoid air oxidation of the silicon carbide (which is not a problem with the metal oxides used in Nernst glowers). A third infrared source is a simple coil of *Nichrome* wire raised to incandescence by electrical heating; this source is simple and rugged, but less intense than the other two. For the near infrared, a tungsten filament lamp is often used.

A major problem in mid-infrared spectroscopy is the generally low intensity of the radiation sources at the wavelengths being used. Most of the radiation emitted by these sources is in the near-infrared and visible regions, and a small, but significant, fraction of this shorter radiation will be present as stray light, a particularly serious problem for long-wavelength measurements.

Infrared Detectors. There are two general classes of infrared detectors: (1) *photon* or *quantum detectors* which detect photons of infrared light via the photoconductive effect that occurs in certain semiconductor materials, and (2) *thermal detectors*, in which absorbed infrared radiation heats the detector and alters one of its physical properties, such as resistance. In general, quantum detectors have a much faster response and a greater sensitivity to infrared radiation than do thermal detectors; but the former can operate only over a very restricted range of wavelengths because there is a limited range of photon energies that will excite electrons in bound states to the conduction band of a semiconductor. Thermal detectors, on the other hand, are usable over a very wide wavelength range: essentially, all that is necessary is that the detector *absorb* a photon; no specific electronic transitions have to occur.

Photon detectors consist of a thin film of semiconductor material, such as lead sulfide, lead telluride, indium antimonide, or germanium doped with copper or mercury, deposited on a nonconducting glass and sealed into an evacuated envelope. Photon flux impinging on the semiconductor increases its conductivity. Lead-sulfide detectors are sensitive to radiation below about 3 μm in wavelength and have a response time of about 10 μsec. Doped germanium detectors cooled to liquid-helium temperatures are sensitive to radiation up to about 120 μm in wavelength, and have a response time of approximately 1 nsec.

There are three types of thermal detectors: the *thermocouple*, the *bolometer*, and the *Golay detector*. The thermocouple, the most widely used infrared detector, is usually composed of a small piece of blackened gold foil, welded to two fine wires made of dissimilar metals, chosen to produce a large thermoelectric emf change on heating and cooling. To minimize conductive heat loss, the entire assembly is sealed in an evacuated housing having an infrared-transmitting window. The cold junction of the thermocouple actually consists of the heavy copper wires attached to the thermocouple wires. Since the incident radiation is chopped and the AC output of the detector is amplified, only the temperature *change* of the thermocouple is important, not the absolute temperature.

A bolometer is a miniature resistance thermometer, usually using a fine platinum wire or a semiconductor thermistor as the sensing element. The resistance of platinum increases by about 0.4% per °C, while that of a typical thermistor decreases by between about 4 and 7% per °C. Two matched sensing elements are used as two arms of a Wheatstone bridge, one of which is shielded from the infrared radiation. A temperature difference between the shielded and nonshielded detectors is thus manifested as a voltage difference which can then be amplified.

The Golay or "pneumatic" detector is based on the increase in pressure of a confined inert gas with temperature. Infrared radiation is absorbed by a rigid blackened metal plate sealed to one end of a small metallic cylinder. The heat is transmitted to the gas, which expands and causes a flexible silvered diaphragm affixed to the other end of the tube to bulge outward. The distortion of the thin diaphragm can be measured either by making it part of an optical system in which a light beam reflects from it to a phototube, or by making it one plate of a dynamic parallel-plate capacitor: the distortion of the flexible diaphragm relative to a fixed plate changes the average plate separation and thus the capacitance.

Raman Spectrometers

Recall that Raman spectroscopy produces a spectrum of a sample by frequency analysis of the light *scattered* from a sample. The sample is "excited" by an intense, monochromatic light-source such as a laser, and the frequency is analyzed with a grating monochromator. Table 8.3 lists some lasers and their characteristics.

TABLE 8.3. *Characteristics of Some Lasers*

Laser	Emission Wavelength (Å)	Typical Power Level (watts)[a]
He-Ne	6328	0.08
Ruby	6943	1–10 MW[c]
Cadmium	4416	0.2
Ar-Kr	4880 (Ar)[b]	0.5
	5145 (Ar)	0.5
	5682 (Kr)	0.5
	6471 (Kr)	0.5

a. Power levels are for *continuous* power output, except for the ruby laser which is pulsed.
b. Most commonly used wavelength.
c. The ruby laser is operated in a pulsed mode, with typical peak-power levels of a few MW and pulse widths of a few nsec.

Some Raman lines are very close to the frequency of the exciting radiation (which is very intense compared to the Raman frequencies). Therefore, it is necessary for the monochromator to have high rejection of scattered light, so those Raman frequencies separated by only a few wavenumbers from the exciting frequency can be observed. A double monochromator is often used for high rejection of scattered light; the detection system often uses a highly sensitive photon-counting technique.

Transform Spectroscopy

Infrared spectra may also be obtained by two other relatively new techniques, Fourier or Hadamard transform spectrometry. The Fourier method utilizes a Michelson

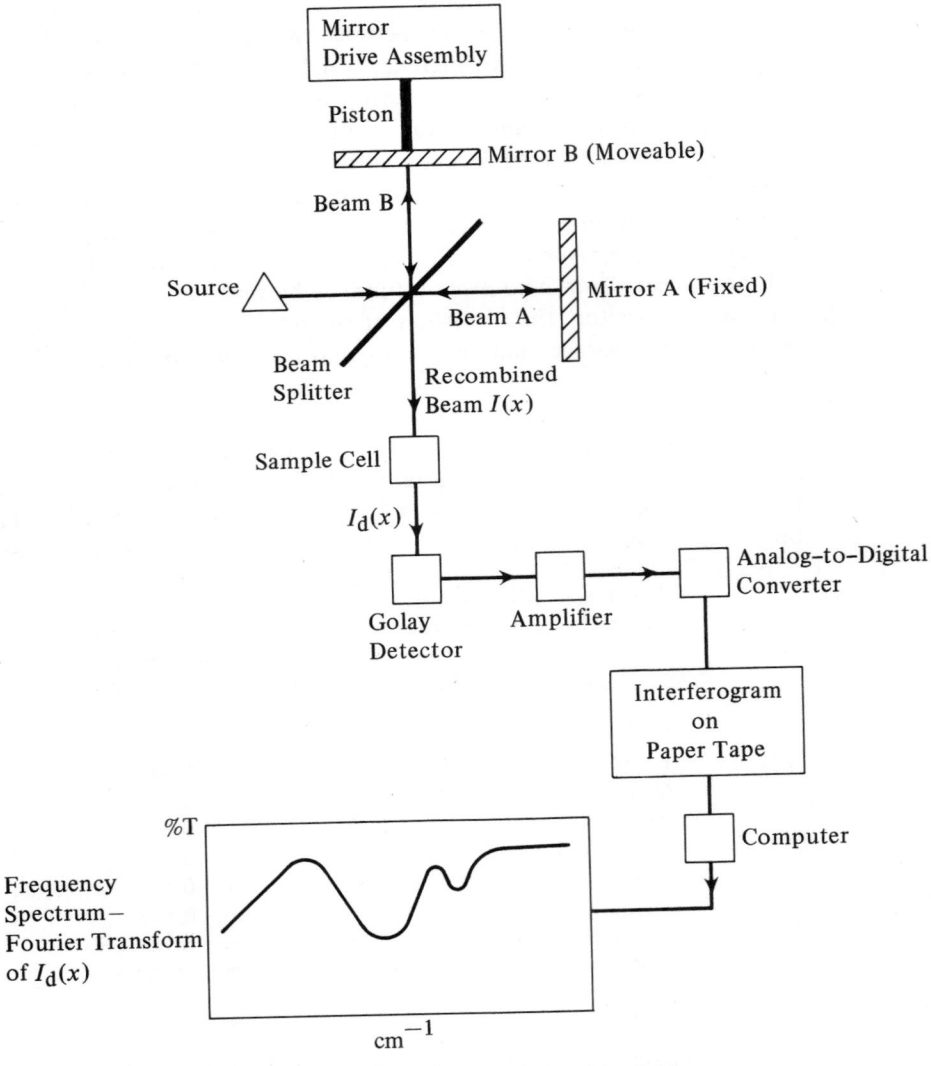

FIGURE 8.3. *An interferometer and associated electronics.*

interferometer constructed to cause interference at infrared frequencies. The interferometer and associated electronics is shown in Figure 8.3. The sample is placed in front of a detector which senses the radiation from the interferometer; that is, radiation exhibiting a variable intensity $I(x)$ as a function of the optical path difference x in the interferometer. The optical path difference is the difference in the distance the light travels in Beam A and in Beam B in Figure 8.3.

The molecules in the sample absorb at their characteristic frequencies, and hence the radiation intensity $I_a(x)$ that reaches the detector is modified by the presence of the sample. The Fourier transform of $I_a(x)$ *is* the absorption spectrum of the sample, and this transform yields percent transmission versus wavenumber (cm^{-1}). This type of spectroscopy is single-beam, so a background spectrum is required in most cases. Also it requires the use of a digital computer to calculate the Fourier transform of $I_a(x)$.

Fourier transform spectroscopy is especially useful for work in the far infrared where photon energy is low, but it may be used throughout the infrared with a typical five-fold improvement in signal-to-noise ratio. The resolution obtainable is inversely proportional to the optical path difference through which the interferometer is scanned.

Hadamard transform spectrometry achieves the performance of the Fourier method but employs the technology of the dispersive prism or grating monochromator. A Hadamard transform instrument utilizes "multiplexing"; that is, it observes all the wavelengths in a spectrum at the same time. This technique also produces a significant gain in the signal-to-noise ratio when compared to more conventional prism or grating monochromators. It is a transform technique because the multiplexing is accomplished by an optical coding so that data points are the transform of the dispersed optical spectrum.

8.3 SAMPLING SYSTEMS

Infrared and Raman techniques may be used to examine solid, liquid, or gas samples, and the samples may or may not be in some imposed environment such as low or high temperatures, applied electric field, and so forth. The state of the sample and its environment is a clue to what type of spectrum to expect.

Infrared Cells

Infrared cells are constructed to transmit infrared energy, so the windows of a cell have to pass the desired range of infrared wavelengths. A bar graph of the spectral transmission of various window materials is shown in Figure 8.4. Most analytical work is done in the range of 4000–400 cm^{-1}, but some work may require spectra extending to 200 cm^{-1}. Commonly used window materials are NaCl, KBr, CsBr, and KRS-5 (a TlBr-TlI mixture). The first three crystals are hygroscopic and must be kept in a desiccator when not in use; they tend to cloud with age and with use and must be polished periodically. The choice of a window material is dictated by cost, the spectral range desired, and the chemical reactivity of the window with the sample. If water solutions are to be analyzed, then AgCl is a good choice for a cell window.

Window thickness is not so critical except in unusual experiments with, for instance, high gas pressures.

Solids are sometimes difficult to sample because some of the incident infrared energy must be transmitted for spectral analysis through a comparatively opaque material. Only a small amount of sample is needed. The sample may be dispersed

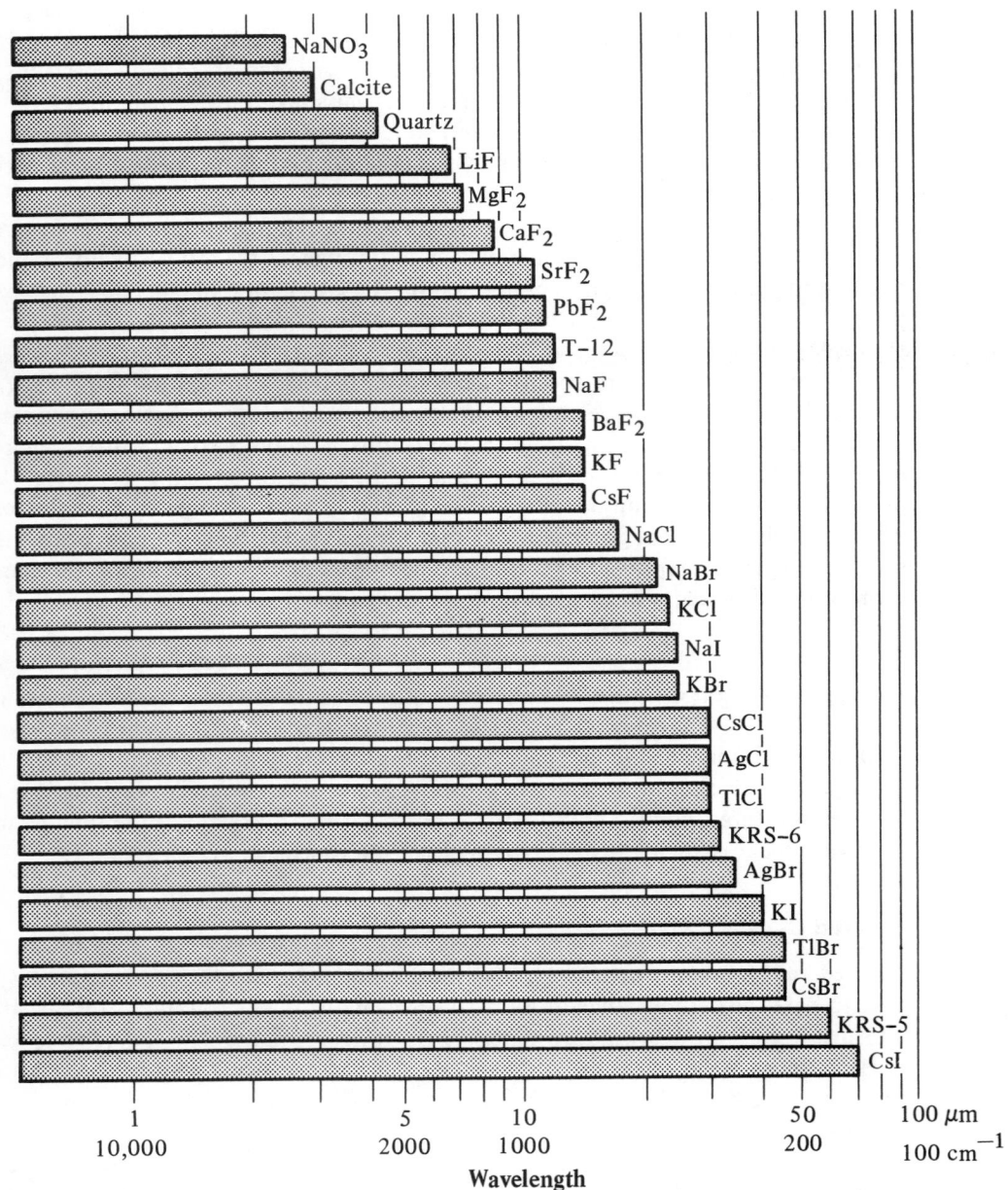

FIGURE 8.4.   *Infrared transmission of optical materials.   Courtesy of the Harshaw Chemical Company.*

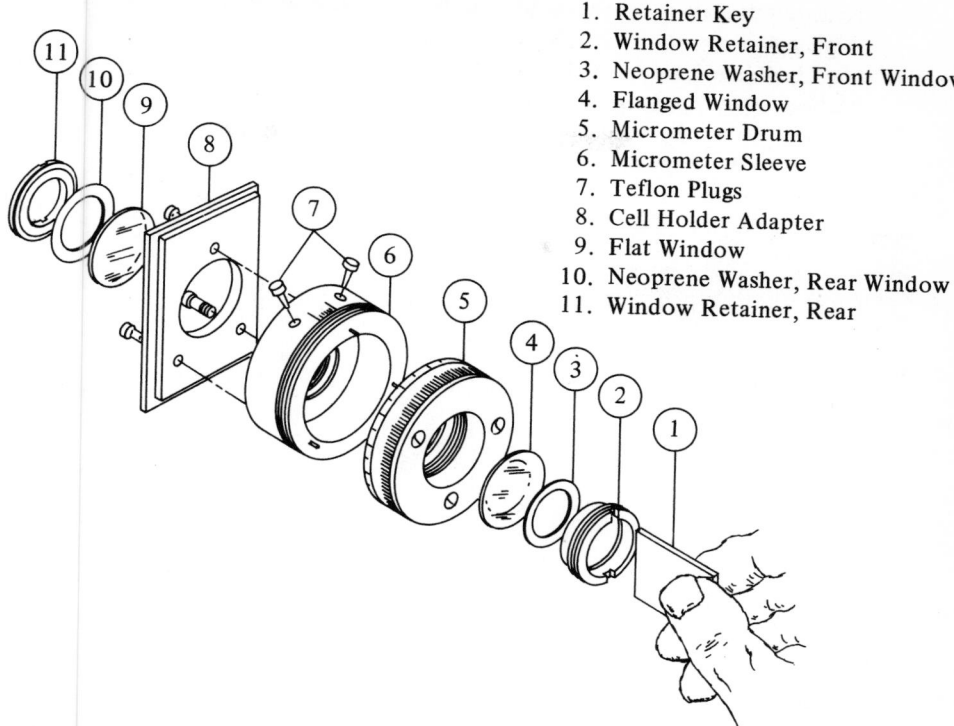

1. Retainer Key
2. Window Retainer, Front
3. Neoprene Washer, Front Window
4. Flanged Window
5. Micrometer Drum
6. Micrometer Sleeve
7. Teflon Plugs
8. Cell Holder Adapter
9. Flat Window
10. Neoprene Washer, Rear Window
11. Window Retainer, Rear

FIGURE 8.5. *Variable path-length infrared cell. Courtesy of Beckman Instruments, Inc.*

in a liquid matrix such as Nujol mineral oil (a "mull"), or in a pellet of KBr or CsBr. The pellet is made by first grinding the sample in a "Wiggle-Bug" or with a mortar and pestle; then the powdered sample (typically 10 mg or so) is thoroughly mixed with about 200 mg of the matrix and the combination pressed into a transparent disc in an evacuable die.

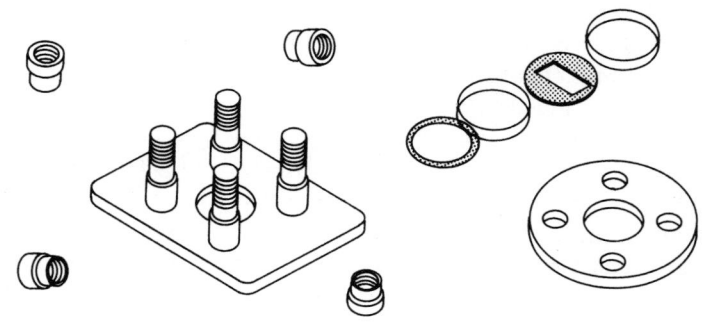

FIGURE 8.6. *A demountable-type infrared cell for liquids. Adapted from N. B. Colthup, L. H. Daly, and S. E. Wiberly,* Introduction to Infrared and Raman Spectroscopy, *New York: Academic Press, 1964, by permission of the senior author and the publisher.*

FIGURE 8.7. *A fixed path-length or sealed cell for liquids. Adapted from N. B. Colthup, L. H. Daly, and S. E. Wiberly,* Introduction to Infrared and Raman Spectroscopy, *New York: Academic Press,* 1964, *by permission of the senior author and the publisher.*

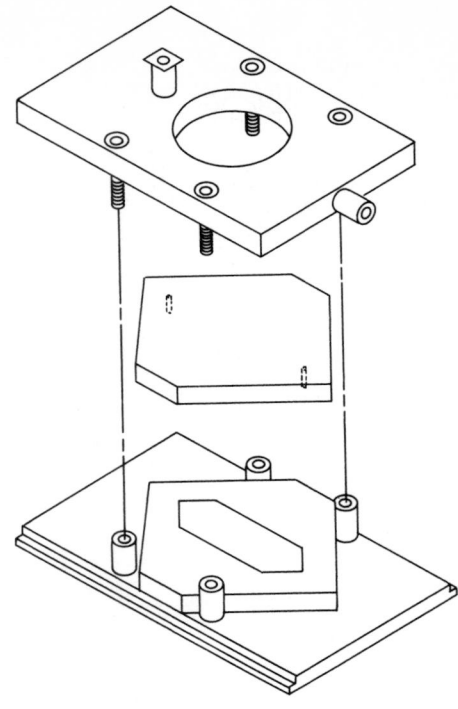

A variety of cells is available for the liquid samples. A liquid cell may be as simple as a drop of liquid sandwiched between two windows to form a capillary film, or as refined as a variable-path cell costing several hundred dollars (see Fig. 8.5). The optical path length required for a liquid is usually less than 1 mm, and spacers of different thicknesses are used to establish a suitable path, often by trial and error. Liquid cells whose path length may be altered are called "demountable" or "sandwich," cells (Fig. 8.6) while others with one fixed path length are termed "fixed-path" cells (Fig. 8.7). If a liquid has to be distilled directly into a cell, then it must be connected to the transfer system by a pipe connection.

Dilution of a liquid sample may be required to weaken the absorption of a strong band in order to observe the band shape, or in order to study solvent effects. Some solvents often used for diluting liquid samples, and the spectral ranges of their usefulness, are illustrated in Figure 8.8.

Gas cells for infrared use range from 2 to 10 cm in length. They are often constructed with a cylindrical glass body, a ground-glass joint, and a vacuum stopcock for filling from a vacuum-transfer system, as shown in Figure 8.9. If a gas absorbs weakly, a longer path length may be needed. Gas cells longer than 10 cm will not fit into most commercial instruments, so multi-pass cells are available for extended path-length. Multi-pass arrangements may also be combined with beam condensors for use with microsamples.

The windows in homemade cells may be held on each end of the cell with hot wax, epoxy cement, or pressure plates tightened against each other over the body of the cell. In the last case, the ends of the glass cell must be carefully polished in order to hold a vacuum of 10^{-5} mm. If epoxy cement is used, it may be loosened for

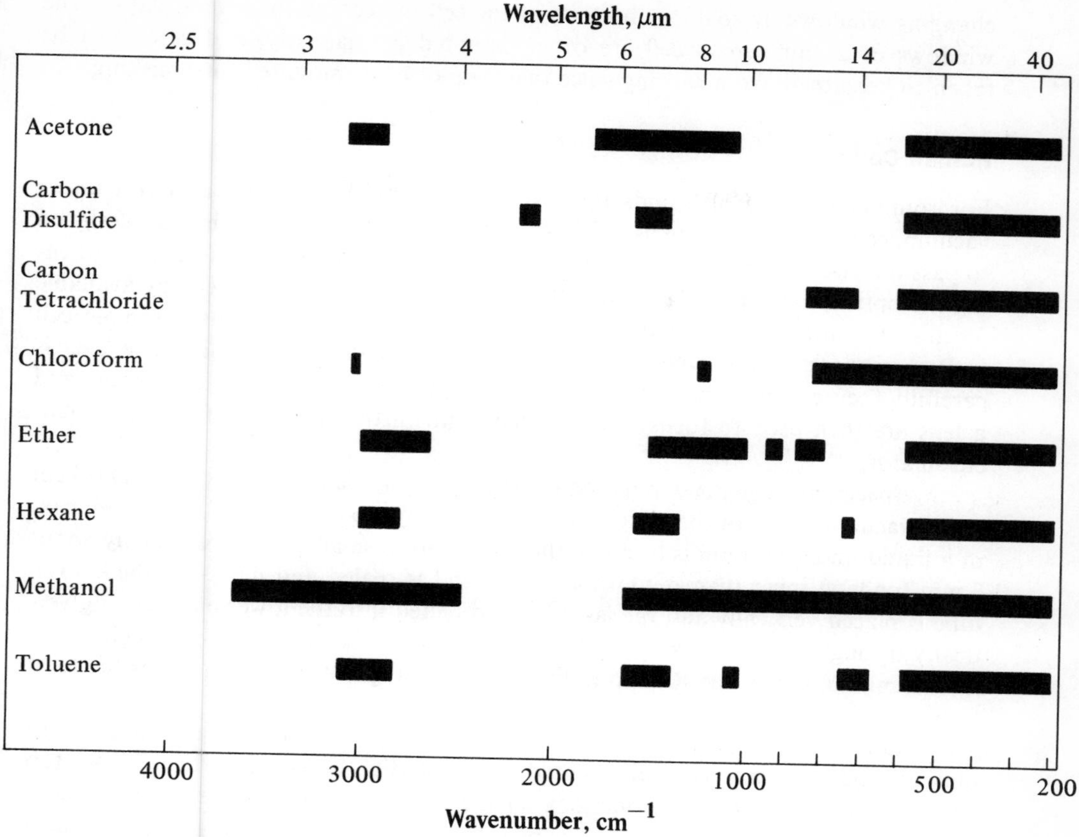

Wavelength, μm

| 2.5 | 3 | 4 | 5 | 6 | 8 | 10 | 14 | 20 | 40 |

Acetone

Carbon
Disulfide

Carbon
Tetrachloride

Chloroform

Ether

Hexane

Methanol

Toluene

| 4000 | 3000 | 2000 | 1000 | 500 | 200 |

Wavenumber, cm^{-1}

FIGURE 8.8. *Transparent regions of some common solvents used for infrared spectroscopy. The darkened regions are those in which a 0.1 mm thickness of solvent (in an NaCl cell) transmits 30% or less of the incident radiation.*

FIGURE 8.9. *A typical infrared cell for gas samples. Adapted from N. B. Colthup, L. H. Daly, and S. E. Wiberly,* Introduction to Infrared and Raman Spectroscopy, *New York: Academic Press, 1964, by permission of the senior author and the publisher.*

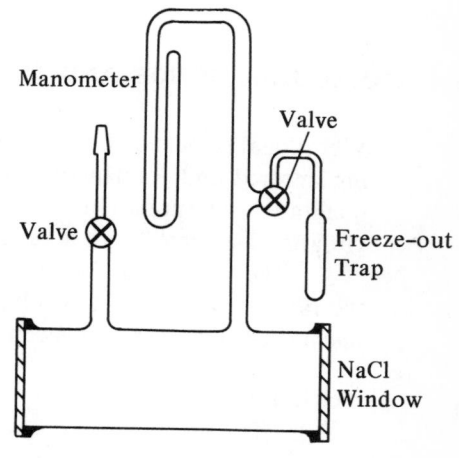

Manometer

Valve

Valve

Freeze–out
Trap

NaCl
Window

changing windows by soaking the ends of the cell in acetone for several days. The windows of a commercial cell are often mounted permanently, and care must be taken to keep them from fogging since they cannot be dismounted for polishing.

Raman Cells

For routine sampling of liquids that do not need distillation or transferral under vacuum, commercial cells are used for Raman spectroscopy because they are designed to pass the laser beam many times through the sample if necessary, thereby lengthening the optical path through the liquid and increasing the scattered energy available for transfer into the monochromator. Perhaps the most widely used sample cell in Raman work is an ordinary glass capillary tube, sealed at one end. The laser is carefully focused on a small volume of the sample; parabolic collection mirrors and a lens are then used to focus the scattered light on the entrance slit of the monochromator.

Special arrangements must be made if the liquid is to be transferred and kept under vacuum. One of the easiest and cheapest ways to obtain the Raman spectrum of a liquid under vacuum is to distill the liquid into a small glass tube, usually about 3 mm (or less) inner diameter, whose lower end is sealed and flame-polished. The tube is placed vertically and the laser beam directed into the lower end, passing vertically through the tube. A spherical mirror is placed behind the tube to collect the maximum amount of the Raman radiation. A lens system in front focuses the total Raman radiation on the entrance slit of the monochromator.

Solids may be sampled by this technique also, although it takes practice to obtain good spectra. The tube should be tilted slightly in the vertical plane, top end *back* (from the monochromator), so the laser beam grazes the *front* (towards monochromator) of the sample. It is possible, however, to obtain the Raman spectrum of the glass using this technique, so care must be taken to distinguish between sample spectra and the container spectrum.

Water, which is usually a poor infrared solvent because it dissolves most cell windows, is an excellent solvent for Raman work because it has few Raman-active frequencies, and these are relatively weak. Very symmetrical, highly Raman-active molecules such as CCl_4 are generally poor solvents for Raman spectroscopy.

8.4 MOLECULAR BONDS AND MOLECULAR STRUCTURE

Vibrational frequencies, so-called "good group frequencies," are important in applying infrared and Raman spectroscopy to many chemical problems that require the qualitative interpretation of infrared spectra. A *group frequency* is that mode of vibration associated with a particular bond or sets of bonds.

The vibrational frequency of a bond is determined by the bond strength and the masses of the atoms involved, and this frequency is often *unchanged* (or nearly unchanged) by other atoms connected to the original group. For example, the symmetrical stretching vibration of the C–H bond in the —CH, $\diagdown$CH$_2$, and –CH$_3$ groups occurs at 2890, 2853, and 2872 cm^{-1}, respectively (with further small shifts, depending on the other substituents on the carbon atom). Using the mathematical model of a harmonic oscillator, the quantized absorption of infrared radiation can be expressed as

$$\bar{\nu} = \frac{1}{2\pi c} \sqrt{\frac{k}{\mu}} \tag{8.4}$$

where $\bar{\nu}$ = the frequency of the bond vibration
c = the velocity of light
k = the force constant of the bond
μ = the reduced mass of the atoms involved

The reduced mass is defined by

$$\mu = \frac{m_1 m_2}{m_1 + m_2} \tag{8.5}$$

where m_1 = the mass of the first atom, in grams
m_2 = the mass of the second atom, in grams

The near-constant absorption frequency of a particular bond or group is used to advantage to check for the presence or absence of certain bonds in a new compound or to follow the progress of a reaction—for example, to determine the presence and type, or absence, of C–H vibrations. Later in this chapter a general procedure for the qualitative interpretation of infrared spectra will be outlined.

Molecular structure may often be inferred for simple molecules (up to 10 atoms) by correlating an assumed geometric structure with the "selection rules" for that structure. This process can be learned by a student without knowing much about the quantum mechanics or group theory that underlies it, but it does take time and practice. The selection rules tell us which modes of vibration are permitted to appear in the infrared and Raman spectrum. Thus, from the actual infrared and Raman spectral patterns and those implied by the selection rules for the *assumed* structure, the structure may be proven or disproven. The process is often like working a crossword puzzle. Bits of information are gathered from several analytical and spectroscopic methods and then fitted properly into place to obtain the structure of the molecule.

In practice, infrared spectroscopy is seldom used alone to infer the total structure of molecules. Usually, much other information is available, and infrared data identify certain molecular features that contribute to a total or final structure determination. Chemists more often need to interpret infrared spectra qualitatively in order to learn what bonds are present or what groups are present, absent, or modified. The general procedure outlined on pages 220 and 221 is useful in many qualitative problems.

FIGURE 8.10. (*Next two pages*). *Correlation chart of group frequencies. Courtesy of Dow Chemical Company.*

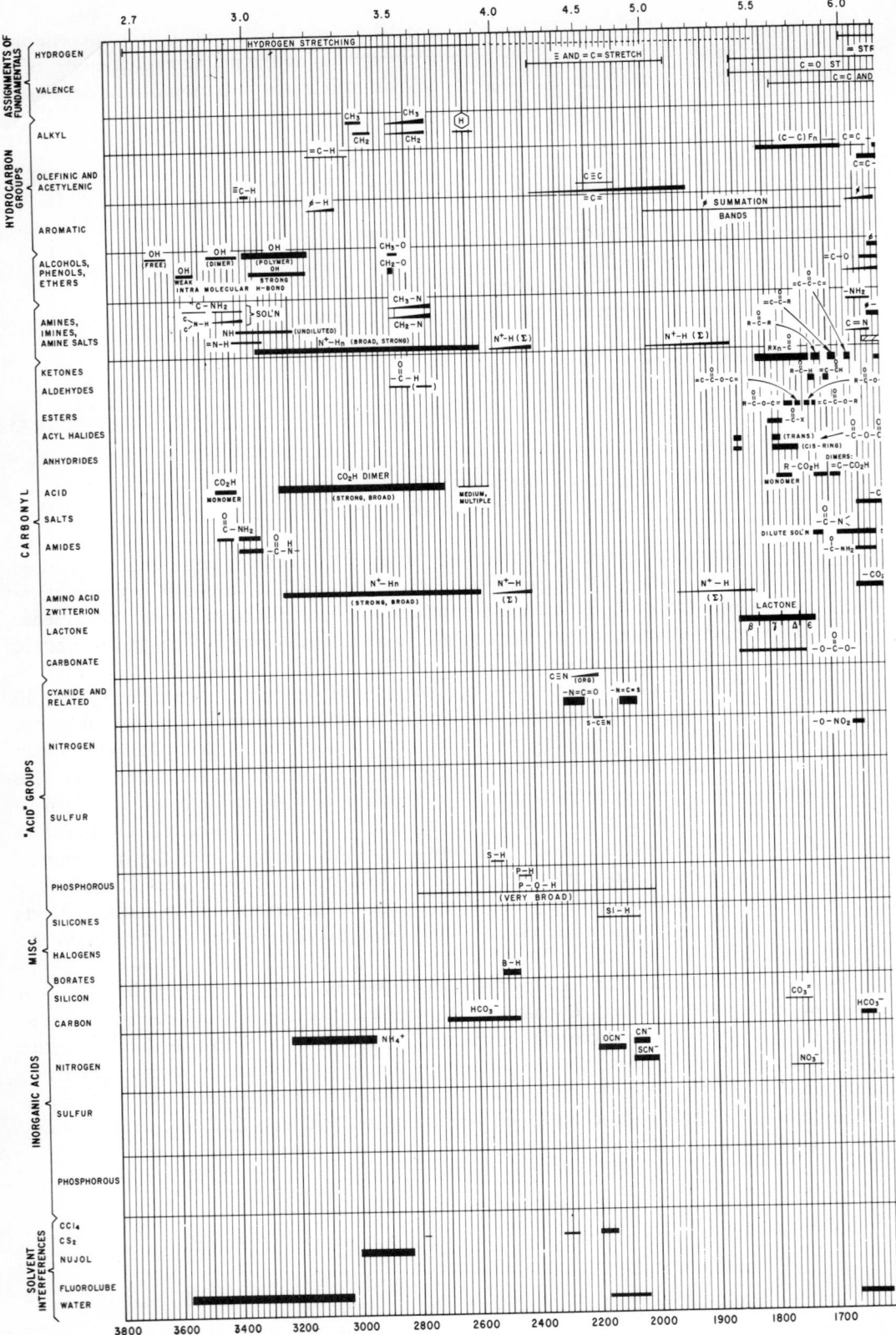

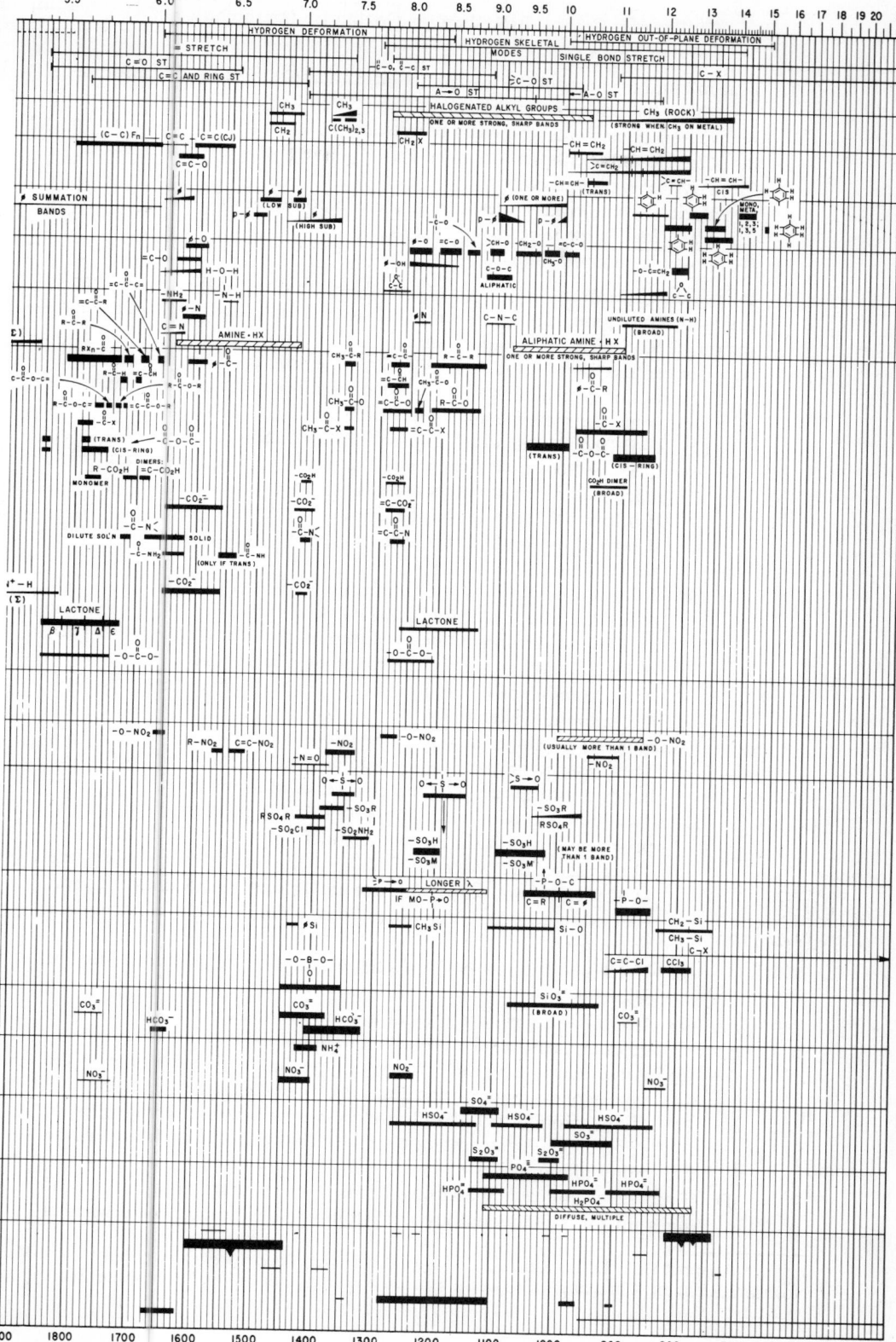

Outline of a General Procedure for Qualitative Interpretation of Infrared Spectra*

1. Bear in mind throughout the interpretation, and apply, all available information about the unknown such as:
   A. Chemical elements known to be present
   B. Chemical elements known to be absent
   C. Physical state and color
   D. Purity of unknown—whether a single compound or mixture
   E. Use which is made of the unknown
   F. Possible component(s)

2. Divide the rocksalt infrared region (2 to 15 μm) into the characteristic functional-group region, 5000–1350 cm^{-1} (2 to 7.5 μm), and the *fingerprint region*, 1350–650 cm^{-1} (7.5 to 15 μm).
   A. Concentrate first on the 5000–1350 cm^{-1} region; consider the strongest absorptions, then medium ones (weak ones only if necessary and helpful).
   B. Determine the presence and type, or absence, of C–H vibrations.
      (1) C–H frequencies occur between 3200 and 2800 cm^{-1}.
      (2) If above 3000 cm^{-1}, then the C atom is unsaturated or a highly halogenated compound is present.
      (3) If below 3000 cm^{-1}, then the C atom is saturated.
      (4) If both above and below 3000 cm^{-1}, then the C's are unsaturated and saturated.
      (5) A band at about 1455 cm^{-1} indicates CH$_3$ and/or CH$_2$.
      (6) A band at about 1375 cm^{-1} indicates C–CH$_3$.
         a. Use an assignment chart (Colthup) to determine whether this is an ethyl, *n*-propyl, isopropyl, or *t*-butyl group.
      (7) A medium-intensity band at about 725 cm^{-1} indicates a chain of 4 or more methylenes.
   C. Determine, if possible, the type of compound(s) present.
      (1) The presence or absence of medium-strength 1500 and 1600 cm^{-1} bands indicates the presence or absence of aromatics.
      (2) The presence of a medium 1650–1610 cm^{-1} band indicates the presence of olefins (in its absence, olefin may still be present).
      (3) The presence of a weak band at about 2210 cm^{-1}, or a medium one at 3250 cm^{-1} and a medium one at 2115 cm^{-1}, indicates the presence of an acetylenic derivative (in its absence, acetylenics may still be present).
      (4) If CH$_2$ is present but not CH$_3$–C, investigate the possibility of alicyclics.
      (5) If CH$_2$ and CH$_3$ are present and no aromatics, olefins, or acetylenics are, suspect the presence of aliphatic compound(s).
      (6) After determining the compound type, follow through to learn the type of olefin, number and position of aromatic substituents, etc.
      (7) If only from 3 to 10 bands are present with several broad ones, or if organic assignments of bands lead nowhere, consider the possibility of inorganics.
   D. Proceed to interpret the strong bands, then medium ones. If a band lines up for a functional group(s), follow along to determine whether

---

* Adapted from D. N. Kendall, ed., *Applied Infrared Spectroscopy*, by permission of Van Nostrand Reinhold Company. Copyright © 1966 by Litton Educational Publishing, Inc.

all absorptions of the group are present, and to classify it as closely as possible; e.g., class of ester, type of amide, class of amine, etc.

3. Concentrate next on the 1350–650 cm⁻¹ region, proceeding from strong bands to medium ones as in 2D.

4. When the interpretation reaches the stage of suggesting the presence of possible compound(s), comparison should be made with the spectra of knowns for final identification.

    A. If this comparison shows that more than a single component is present, mark off absorptions belonging to the first component identified, then proceed to interpret the remaining bands as above.

5. General considerations to bear in mind:

    A. The absence of an absorption band is more convincing evidence of a functional group's absence, than the presence of a band is evidence of its presence.

    B. All the bands in a spectrum can never be interpreted—some are absorptions characteristic of the molecule as a whole, some are combination bands, and some are overtone bands.

    C. Eight to 10 components is about the most that can be identified in a mixture (sometimes fewer, depending on the similarity and structural complexity of the components).

    D. The presence of bands about 3350 and 1645 cm⁻¹ often indicates the presence of water in a sample.

    E. Generally, polymers have fewer, broader, and often less intense bands than the monomers from which they are derived.

    F. Some unknowns we will not be able to identify. Of these, some we may identify later as new correlations are learned and the spectra of new knowns are run—the identification of others may perhaps elude us indefinitely.

The interpretation of infrared spectra requires practice, but the task is eased with the help of correlation charts of group frequencies [2, 3]. Such a chart is shown in Figure 8.10, pp. 218–19. Other charts are available that document group frequencies in the near infrared and the far infrared.

As an example, consider the relatively simple infrared spectrum of ethylene (Fig. 8.11). The sample is contained in a 10-cm cell with NaCl windows (see Fig.

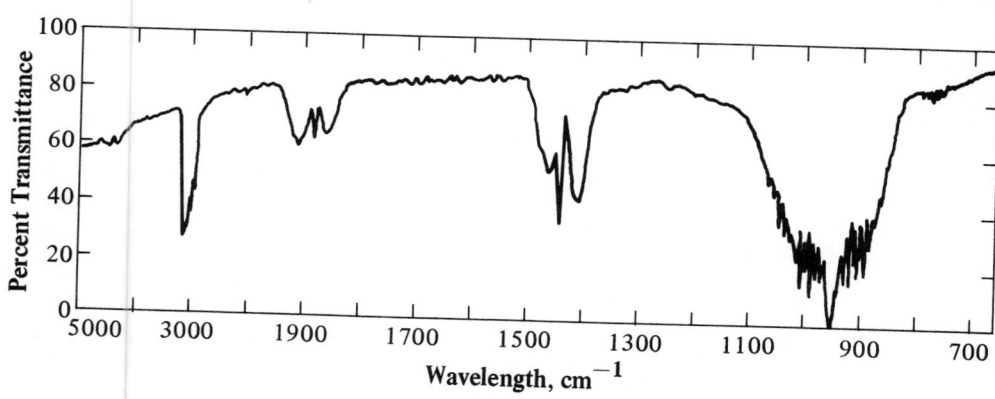

FIGURE 8.11. *Infrared spectrum of gaseous ethylene.*

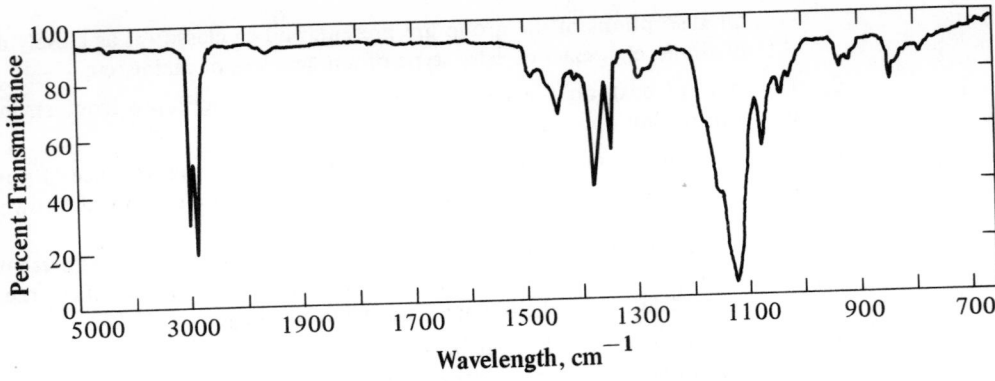

FIGURE 8.12. *Infrared spectrum of diethyl ether.*

8.4 for the spectral transmission of NaCl). The broad spectral bands with fine structure are typical of a low-molecular-weight vapor. Notice the absorption bands from olefinic CH vibrations (3100, 1440, 950 cm^{-1}). The C═C frequency is absent; this indicates that ethylene is a symmetrical molecule.

A second example is shown in Figure 8.12. The sample is diethyl ether, a pure liquid with a low boiling-point. The infrared spectrum is that of a capillary film of this sample between two salt plates. Notice the aliphatic CH bands (2900, 1460, CH_3 at 1380). There is also an aliphatic ether band at 1130 cm^{-1}.

8.5 QUANTITATIVE ANALYSIS

Quantitative analysis of a sample is essentially performed by determining its absorbance and comparing this with the infrared absorptivity a or the molar absorptivity ε (see Table 7.2 and Sec. 7.3) of pure compounds.

Ideally, the intensity (I_0) of infrared radiation incident upon a sample cell is reduced (to I) by the absorption of the samples. Actually, some of the incident energy is scattered by the sample and this scattered energy makes the Beer-Lambert law inaccurate, especially at high values of absorbance [4]. The baseline method for quantitative analysis is an empirical method used to establish a calibration curve of $\log(I_0/I)$ versus concentration. Infrared absorption bands may overlap neighboring bands or may appear on a sloping background, so transmittance is measured in practice as shown in Figure 8.13. The absorbance, A, is determined from measurements of I and I_0, then a calibration curve of absorbance versus concentration is plotted.

A corollary of the Beer-Lambert law is the law of additivity of absorbance ($\log I_0/I$), which states that the absorbance of a mixture is equal to the sum of the absorbances of its components. Stated another way, equal absorbing paths of the same material will always absorb the same fraction of the incident light. Deviations from linearity may occur in practice. The Beer-Lambert law is true for monochromatic light passing through the cell; however, all spectrometers (except those recent ones using tunable, narrowband, infrared lasers) send through the sample a band of wavelengths centered approximately at the wavelength setting of the spectrom-

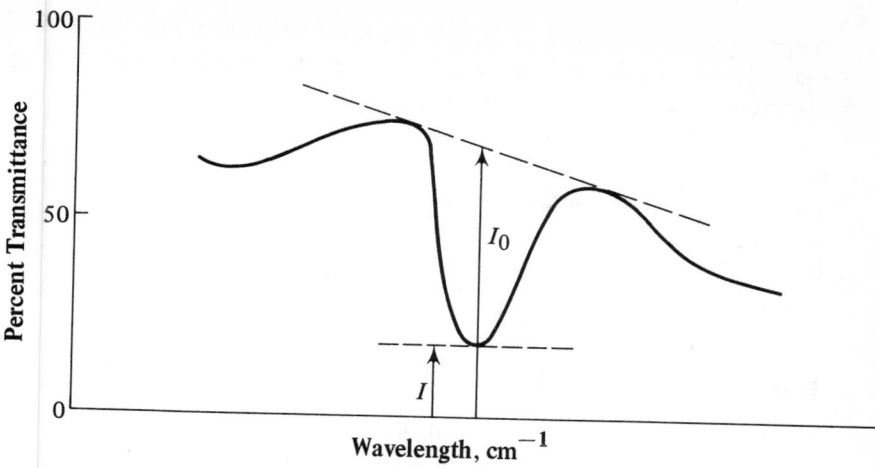

FIGURE 8.13. *Measurement of I_0 and I for an infrared absorption band with a sloping background.*

eter. If the slit width is too wide or the absorption bands too narrow, then rapid changes occur in absorptivity over the wavelength interval established by the slit, and deviations from the Beer-Lambert law will occur. For this reason, the spectral slit-width should be set at about one-tenth the width of the absorption band at one-half the peak height of the band. This is a particularly serious problem in infrared work, because sources are generally not very intense and wide slits are usually employed to compensate for this.

Thus, errors incurred in quantitative analysis by the infrared method include error in measurement of the 100% line, deviations from the Beer-Lambert law, error in the zero line and error in the measurement of %T. The effect of deviations from the Beer-Lambert law is such that one should try to work at values of %T greater than 40% for the most accurate results.

Component Cancellation

If a double-beam spectrometer is used to analyze a multicomponent mixture, then it is possible to eliminate the spectrum of one or more of the components by putting the same amount of the component in the reference beam. In principle, one may cancel the spectrum of each component separately and successively, making it possible to analyze the mixture without overlapping bands. In practice, this is usually limited to three or fewer components. This procedure is useful if small amounts of impurities are to be determined.

A danger in this approach is that strong absorbance in the reference beam can cause loss of servo power in the instrument and the production of erroneous spectra as the instrument tries to take the ratio of two very small signals.

Differential Analysis

The analysis of a mixture by directly comparing a known with an unknown sample in a double-beam spectrophotometer is called differential analysis. When two or more components absorb at or near the same frequency, differential analysis is often the only way to unravel the overlap. The technique has been used in ultraviolet-visible spectroscopy for a long time, so it is not new (see Sec. 7.5).

The Beer-Lambert law is assumed to hold for the components (solvents and solute), and the path length must be known. One of the absorbing components is placed in the reference beam and the mixture is placed in the sample beam. The double-beam spectrophotometer records the ratio of the radiant power of the two beams. The path length should be varied until the solution as a whole transmits about 40% of the incident energy, and the slit width should be *constant*.

Direct Infrared Analysis

Much in the same manner as in ultraviolet-visible absorption spectroscopy, infrared spectroscopy can be used to determine the concentration of a particular compound using the standard quantitative methods discussed in Chapter 7, provided that a sufficiently intense absorption band, relatively free from interferences, can be found. For example, isosorbide dinitrate, a coronary vasodilator, can be determined in pharmaceutical preparations after dissolving it in water, extracting it with CCl_4, and comparing its infrared absorption intensity with a calibration curve [5]. This is a highly specific, rapid, and sensitive analytical method for isosorbide dinitrate because of the strong, sharp band at 1650 cm^{-1} characteristic of nitrate esters. The ultraviolet spectrum of isosorbide dinitrate is of low intensity and noncharacteristic shape; therefore direct ultraviolet techniques cannot be used. Direct infrared analysis is applicable to most organic nitrates, as long as interfering groups such as –COOH, C=N, and ketone and amide functionalities are not present.

Infrared analysis has been used to rapidly determine trace quantities (0.1 to 1 ppm) of various volatile fluoride impurities—such as BF_3, SiF_4, MoF_6, and Freons—in UF_6 used in nuclear applications [6]. The absorption-band wavelengths present indicate the particular impurities present. The precision of the method is about ± 5–10%. Chemical methods of analysis are rather time-consuming and require a good deal of laboratory skill, and gas chromatography or mass spectral analysis cannot be used because of the extremely corrosive nature of fluorides.

One interesting example of infrared analysis is an infrared gas analyzer used to determine breath-alcohol levels of motorists [7].

Total Functional-Group Analysis

One particular advantage of infrared analysis is its ability to determine the total amount of a particular functional group present in even a very complex mixture. For example, the total ketone content of a mixture can be determined because almost all ketone carbonyl bands come at about 1720 cm^{-1}, and the intensity of absorption does not vary a great deal from one compound to another. Therefore, one can determine an "average" absorptivity for a particular functional group from known mixtures, and use this value in the analysis of real samples. The total content of a particular functional group is often an important consideration, particularly in industrial situations.

An example of total functional-group analysis is determin[ing] content of carboxyl-terminated polybutadienes (CTPB's), which are [~7000) used as elastomeric binders for solid propellants [8]. A solu[tion 2%) of the CTPB sample in CCl_4 is prepared, and the magnitude of the carboxyl-carbonyl band is measured in a 1-mm cell. Quantitation is achiev[ed] by the calibration-curve method, or by the internal-standard method usi[ng] 1435-cm^{-1} methylene band or the 1638-cm^{-1} vinyl band as standards. The re[s] for the total carboxyl content by this method agree with those of standard chemic[al] titration procedures to within a relative error of about $\pm 0.03\%$ carboxyl content, for a carboxyl-content range of about 0.5 to 2.5% in commercial CTPB samples.

High-molecular-weight aliphatic amines are used extensively in many industries. The total primary- and secondary-amine content of aliphatic amines can be determined easily and rapidly by functional-group analysis in the near infrared [9], using chloroform solvent and 5-cm fused-silica cells. Primary amines have characteristic absorption maxima at $2.02 \mu m$ and $1.55 \mu m$, whereas secondary amines absorb only at $1.55 \mu m$. Quantitation is achieved by the calibration-curve method using a series of standard solutions of primary and of secondary amines. Most other methods for the determination of total primary, secondary, or tertiary amine in a mixture are lengthy or inaccurate, or are unsuitable for small samples.

Raman Analyses

In general, Raman spectroscopy has been used very little, if at all, to perform quantitative analyses; its primary use has been in the study of molecular structure. However, one possible use of laser Raman spectroscopy for quantitative purposes is the identification and determination of trace levels of molecular pollutants in water [10]. The Raman spectrum of distilled water is weak and uncomplicated; thus it is possible to detect and distinguish Raman bands of pollutants in natural waters. For example, it is possible to detect as little as 50 ppm of benzene in distilled water using only 5 mW of laser power from a He-Ne gas laser at 6328 Å. With improved excitation techniques and 50 mW laser power, it should be possible to detect certain Raman-active pollutants at less than 5 ppm levels.

A very unusual application of Raman analysis is the remote detection of atmospheric pollutants [11, 12]. At present, over 40 atmospheric pollutants are monitored at stations across the United States. In general, most of these pollutants are in the gaseous state in concentrations of 0.01 to 10 ppm for molecules and 0.01 to 10 ppb for metal vapors. At present, detecting and quantitatively measuring these pollutants requires fixed monitoring stations using wet chemical techniques. One approach to a remote, instantaneous sensing method involves coupling a very-high-power (50 MW) pulsed laser with a 20" reflecting telescope to which is attached a monochromator and a photomultiplier tube. The apparatus can be "aimed" at a source of polluted air, such as the emission from a smokestack, up to a mile or so distant. Although quantitation is very difficult and there are many factors involved, the back-scattered laser light of unchanged frequency can be used to measure the amount of particulate matter in the air; and the various Raman lines can be used to measure the molecular species. For example, SO_2 and CO_2 can be accurately measured at the 1 ppm level.

SELECTED BIBLIOGRAPHY

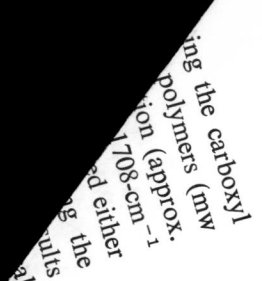

...ctra of Complex
...en; New York:

...opy. Boston:

...aser Raman
...Wiley-Inter-

... Infrared and Raman Spectra of
Polyatomic Molecules. New Jersey: Van
Nostrand, 1945.

JONES, R. N., and SANDORFY, C. Chemical
Applications of Spectroscopy. Vol. IX of

Technique of Organic Chemistry, A. Weissberger, ed. New York: Interscience
Publishers, 1956.

SZYMANSKI, H. A. A Systematic Approach to
the Interpretation of Infrared Spectra. Cambridge Springs, Pa.: Hertillon Press, 1967.

SZYMANSKI, H. A. Correlation of Infrared and
Raman Spectra of Organic Compounds.
Cambridge Springs, Pa.: Hertillon Press,
1969.

SZYMANSKI, H. A., ed. Raman Spectroscopy,
Theory and Practice. New York: Plenum
Press, 1967.

REFERENCES

1. K. S. SESHADRI and R. N. JONES, "The Shapes and Intensities of Infrared Absorption Bands—A Review," *Spectrochim. Acta*, *19*, 1013 (1963).

2. H. A. SZYMANSKI, *A Systematic Approach to the Interpretation of Infrared Spectra*, Cambridge Springs, Pa.: Hertillon Press, 1971.

3. N. B. COLTHUP, L. H. DALY, and S. E. WIBERLY, *Introduction to Infrared and Raman Spectroscopy*, New York: Academic Press, 1964, p 319.

4. D. ROBINSON, *Anal. Chem.*, *23*, 273 (1951).

5. D. WOO, J. K. C. YEN, and P. SOFRONAS, *Anal. Chem.*, *45*, 2144 (1973).

6. R. AUBEAU, G. BLANDENET, and G. BROGNIART, *Anal. Chem.*, *44*, 1628 (1972).

7. Y. FUKUI and Y. YAMAMOTO, *Med. Sci. Law*, *11*, 182 (1971); *Chem. Abstr.*, *77*, 29866n (1972).

8. A. S. TOMPA, *Anal. Chem.*, *44*, 628 (1972).

9. R. B. STAGE, J. B. STANLEY, and P. B. MOSELEY, *J. Amer. Oil Chem. Soc.*, *49*, 87 (1972); *Chem. Abstr.*, *76*, 107688b (1972).

10. E. B. BRADLEY and C. A. FRENZEL, *Water Res.*, *4*, 125 (1970).

11. H. INABA and T. KOBAYASI, *Nature*, *224*, 170 (1969).

12. H. KILDAL and R. L. BYER, *Proc. IEEE*, *59*, 1644 (1971).

PROBLEMS

1. List the upper and lower limits of the near-, mid-, and far-infrared spectral regions in (a) micrometers; (b) wavenumbers (cm^{-1}).

2. Convert 7000 Å to (a) wavenumbers (cm^{-1}); (b) micrometers (μm); (c) eV.

3. Compute the range of energy (in eV) spanned by (a) the near infrared; (b) the mid infrared; (c) the far infrared.

4. The wavelength of the fundamental frequency of vibration of $^{12}C^{16}O$ is 4.663 μm.

Express this wavelength in wavenumbers (cm^{-1}); in eV; in cal/mole.

5. In the literature find the infrared and Raman spectra of S_2Cl_2, S_2Br_2, S_2F_2, and H_2O_2. Note similarities in the number of active modes and coincidences. What fundamental frequencies are approximately constant among these molecules? What fundamental frequencies are different? Explain the similarities and differences. By

what reasoning would you assign a structure to each molecule? Do the polarization measurements support the assignments?

6. An infrared spectrophotometer is set at a wavelength of 4 μm and the transmittance of the sample is observed to be 0.50 at this wavelength. Calculate the absorbance at this wavelength if $I_0 = 100$.

7. In what spectral region does one observe (a) the pure rotation spectrum of a gas; (b) the vibration-rotation spectrum of that gas?

8. It is desired to obtain the vibration fundamentals of a gas that contains some "heavy" atoms (say, $z > 30$). In addition, it is suspected that the interatomic forces are weak. In what region(s) of the infrared should one record the spectrum in order to record all of the fundamentals?

9. It is desired to obtain the infrared spectrum of a water solution in the region 2.5–18 μm. What sampling arrangement should be used?

10. Calculate the molar absorptivity of a liquid sample in an infrared cell of thickness 0.1 μm. The absorbance reading of the spectrometer at the frequency of interest is 0.4. The concentration of the sample is 1 M.

11. A band at about 1370 cm^{-1} is indicative of a methyl group. At what frequencies would the first and second overtones be?

12. The symmetrical C–H stretch in alkanes occurs at about 2880 cm^{-1}. At what frequency should this band occur if deuterium were substituted for hydrogen? Tritium?

13. Single, double, and triple bonds have force constants that are approximately 5, 10, and 15 × 10^5 dynes/cm, respectively. (a) At what frequencies would you expect to find C–C, C=C, and C≡C stretches? (b) What force constant would you expect the carbon-carbon bond in benzene to have? At what frequency should the absorption occur? (c) Compare the calculated frequencies with the actual ones (see Fig. 8.10).

14. The fundamental vibrational frequencies of ethylene are at 3374, 3287, 1974, 729, and 612 cm^{-1}. At what wavelengths will these bands be observed for each of the exciting lines of the Ar-Kr laser—4880, 5145, 5682, and 6471 Å? Discuss the extent of spectral overlap if unfiltered laser light was used.

15. Chloroform exhibits Raman bands at 258, 357, 660, and 760 cm^{-1}. Polarized spectra were taken and peak heights measured. $I_\perp$ was determined to be 30.8, 5.8, 1.3, and 4.7 units; $I_\parallel$ was 40.9, 78.2, 83.2, and 6.0 units, for the four peaks. Calculate the depolarization ratios for these bands, and indicate whether each band is "polarized" or "depolarized."

16. Calculate the relative intensities of a Raman line when excited by each of the four lines from an Ar-Kr laser.

9

Molecular Fluorescence and Phosphorescence

GEORGE H. SCHENK

The mechanism of the absorption of ultraviolet and visible light was discussed in Chapter 7. In this chapter, two processes that involve absorption of radiation as the first step will be discussed; these are fluorescence and phosphorescence.

Both fluorescence and phosphorescence are types of *photoluminescence* (often simply referred to as *luminescence*), the emission of radiant energy (usually visible radiation, but sometimes ultraviolet or infrared radiation) by a molecule, ion, or atom that has reached the excited state by absorbing radiant energy (usually, but not always, ultraviolet radiation):

$$\text{ground state} + \text{UV} \xrightarrow[\text{(excitation)}]{\text{absorption}} \text{excited state} \xrightarrow{\text{emission}} \text{ground state} + \text{fluorescence (or phosphorescence)} \qquad (9.1)$$

$$X + h\nu \longrightarrow X^* \longrightarrow X + h\nu'$$

The energy of the fluorescence or phosphorescence ($h\nu'$) is usually much lower than that of the ultraviolet radiation used for excitation. Therefore, since wavelength is inversely proportional to energy, fluorescence or phosphorescence is located at longer wavelengths in the ultraviolet (>300 nm), in the visible region (380–750 nm), or even in the near infrared (>750 nm).

In general, fluorescence emission occurs very soon (10^{-6} to 10^{-9} sec) after a species reaches the excited state. Thus, it is impossible for the eye to perceive a fluorescent substance once the source of ultraviolet radiation has been removed. Phosphorescence emission occurs more slowly ($>10^{-4}$ sec) and with a greater variation in the lifetimes of the phosphorescence emission. Thus, while many phosphorescent substances, including most organic molecules, also cannot be perceived by the eye once the ultraviolet source has been removed, a number of inorganic minerals phosphoresce markedly after ultraviolet excitation has ceased. The longest recorded case is one particular sample of the mineral willemite ($ZnSiO_4$), which phosphoresced for 340 hours!

While the phosphorescence of solids is easily observed at room temperature, it is often impossible to observe the phosphorescence of solutions at room temperature; apparently oxygen molecules, absorbing energy in collisions with the excited species involved, quench its phosphorescence. To avoid this, solutions are cooled in liquid nitrogen (77°K) and allowed to freeze; such solutions are referred to as "rigid solutions" or "glasses." Two organic solvents commonly used to prepare such solutions are ethanol and EPA, a mixture of ethyl ether, isopentane, and ethanol.

Experimental Aspects of Excitation and Emission. Although there are many pathways for a species to reach the excited state, photoluminescence by definition must involve *photoexcitation*, which may occur by absorption of one of the following forms of radiant energy: (1) sunlight, (2) visible radiation, including room light, (3) ultraviolet radiation, or (4) x-rays.

The emission process in photoluminescence is the emission of radiant energy from an excited electronic state. Photoluminescence is called *fluorescence* when the spin of the excited electron does not change as the photoexcited species undergoes a transition from the excited state to the ground state. If there is a change in spin, then the photoluminescence is called *phosphorescence*. For organic molecules, the term fluorescence commonly means emission of radiant energy during a transition from the lowest excited singlet state, S_1, to the singlet ground state, S_0. Phosphorescence of organic molecules commonly means emission during a transition from the lowest excited triplet state, T_1, to the singlet ground state, S_0. For inorganic species, any emission involving a change in the spin of the excited electron is, by definition, phosphorescence.

In contrast to absorption spectrophotometry, fluorescence and phosphorescence spectrometry involve the recording of both an excitation and an emission spectrum; the instruments used are called spectrofluorometers or spectrophosphorimeters.

Excitation and Emission Spectra of UO_2^{2+}. The use of a spectrofluorometer for obtaining emission and excitation spectra will be illustrated with the uranyl (UO_2^{2+}) ion (see Fig. 9.1). To obtain such spectra, one starts by choosing an intense absorption band from the absorption spectrum (250 nm was chosen here). The compound is then excited at this wavelength—that is, energy at this wavelength is pumped in for the compound to absorb—using a grating that limits the incoming radiation to a narrow band about 10–15 nm wide. To obtain the fluorescence emission spectrum, one adjusts the spectrofluorometer to measure and record any radiation emitted from the solution of UO_2^{2+}, starting with a wavelength such as 300 or 400 nm and ending at a wavelength such as 700 nm. The emission spectrum is automatically "scanned" by using a second (motor-driven) grating to vary the wavelengths being measured and recorded by the spectrofluorometer.

The resulting fluorescence *emission* spectrum obtained for the uranyl ion is shown in Figure 9.1. Note that UO_2^{2+} begins to emit fluorescence at 450 nm, and that the most intense bands fall in the green region of the visible spectrum.

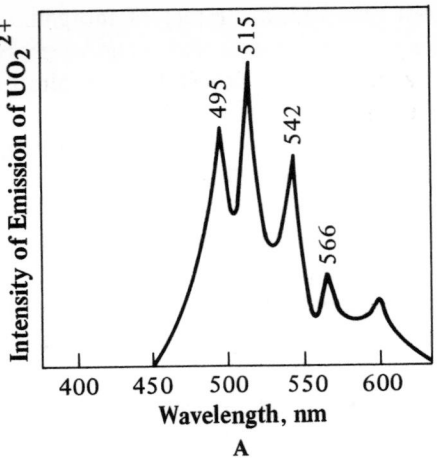
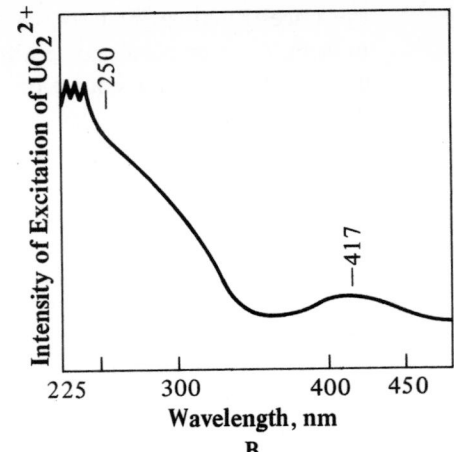

FIGURE 9.1. *Spectra of uranyl nitrate. A: The corrected emission spectrum of 10^{-4} M uranyl nitrate in 0.1 N H_2SO_4–1% H_3PO_4 solution as measured on the Turner absolute spectrofluorometer. B: The corrected excitation spectrum. (The excitation spectrum was measured by setting the emission grating at 515 nm; the emission spectrum was obtained by excitation at 250 nm. Bandwidths were 10 nm.) From G. H. Schenk,* Absorption of Light and Ultraviolet Radiation, *Boston: Allyn and Bacon, 1973, p 102, by permission of the publisher.*

To obtain the fluorescence *excitation* spectrum, the grating through which fluorescence emission passes is generally set at the wavelength of the most intense emission band (for the spectrum in Fig. 9.1, at 515 nm). Then, one adjusts the spectrofluorometer so that it automatically varies the wavelength of exciting radiation striking the solution. (The first grating, which was set at 250 nm when recording the fluorescence emission spectrum, is now driven by a motor, so that the exciting radiation from the source in the spectrofluorometer is continuously varied and measured.) The spectrofluorometer therefore records the emission at 515 nm as a function of the excitation wavelength.

9.1 THEORY OF FLUORESCENCE AND PHOSPHORESCENCE

The theory of luminescence transitions is best described by using a molecular-energy interpretation; for a molecular-orbital interpretation, the reader is referred to specialized monographs [1, 2]. The transitions of an aromatic hydrocarbon, anthracene, will be used to illustrate the molecular-energy interpretation given below.

Excitation and Emission of Anthracene

When interpreting the excitation (absorption) of anthracene, it should be noted that anthracene has two main absorption bands. The higher-energy band is centered at 255 nm; the lower-energy band extends over the 325–375 nm region. Anthracene fluoresces maximally at 380, 402, and 425 nm and phosphoresces at 680 nm. By using a *state* or *molecular-energy diagram*, these energy changes can be portrayed accurately. First the excitation and relaxation processes will be considered, then the fluorescence and phosphorescence processes.

Excitation and Relaxation Processes. For anthracene, there are at least two representative excitation processes:

$$S_0 + UV_{255 \, nm} \longrightarrow S_2 \tag{9.2}$$

$$S_0 + UV_{325-375 \, nm} \longrightarrow S_1 \tag{9.3}$$

Excitation by either process results in the same fluorescence emission spectrum, implying that only the S_1 state emits, and that anthracene in the S_2 state has to reach the S_1 state before it can emit fluorescence. The molecular-energy diagram in Figure 9.2 symbolizes the steps involved in reaching the S_1 state.

At the extreme left of Figure 9.2 are shown three representative transitions within the $S_0 \rightarrow S_2$ process. Because the S_2 state possesses many vibrational sublevels, there are actually many such transitions. All of the resulting S_2 molecules fall, or relax, to the EV_0 sublevel of the S_2 state by rapid vibrational relaxation. In this process, excess vibrational energy is transferred (within 10^{-13} to 10^{-11} sec) to solvent molecules by thermal relaxation (via collisions). This process also occurs for S_1 molecules in the various sublevels.

Once the S_2 molecule has reached its EV_0 sublevel, it is believed to undergo rapid *internal conversion* to the S_1 state:

$$S_2 \xrightarrow{\text{(10}^{-13} \text{ to 10}^{-11} \text{ sec)}} S_1 \tag{9.4}$$

By definition, this process involves no change in spin of the excited electron, only a conversion of excess electronic energy to excess vibrational energy. At the end of this process, the molecule arrives at the EV_0 sublevel of the S_1 state. The process is as rapid as vibrational relaxation; indeed, if one assumes that electronic energy and vibrational energy are instantly interconvertible, then the slowest part of this process is vibrational relaxation from the EV_n sublevel of the S_1 state to its EV_0 sublevel.

Deactivation of the S_1 State at Room Temperature. There are four important processes that can deactivate the S_1 state at room temperature; that is, allow the S_1 state to lose its excess electronic energy and return to the S_0 state. These are

1. Fluorescence emission: $S_1 \rightarrow S_0 + h\nu_f$ (1st order rate constant $= k_f$)
2. Internal conversion: $S_1 \rightsquigarrow S_0 + $ heat
3. Intersystem crossing: $S_1 \rightsquigarrow T_1$ (1st order rate constant $= k_{isc}$)
4. Collisional quenching: $S_1 + Q \rightsquigarrow S_0 + $ heat

Each process will be discussed below in terms of the molecular-energy diagram in Figure 9.2. It should be stressed that each process involves only S_1 molecules in the EV_0 sublevel.

1. *Fluorescence emission.* In this process, S_1 molecules emit photons of various energies, depending on the vibrational sublevel (of the S_0 state) involved in the

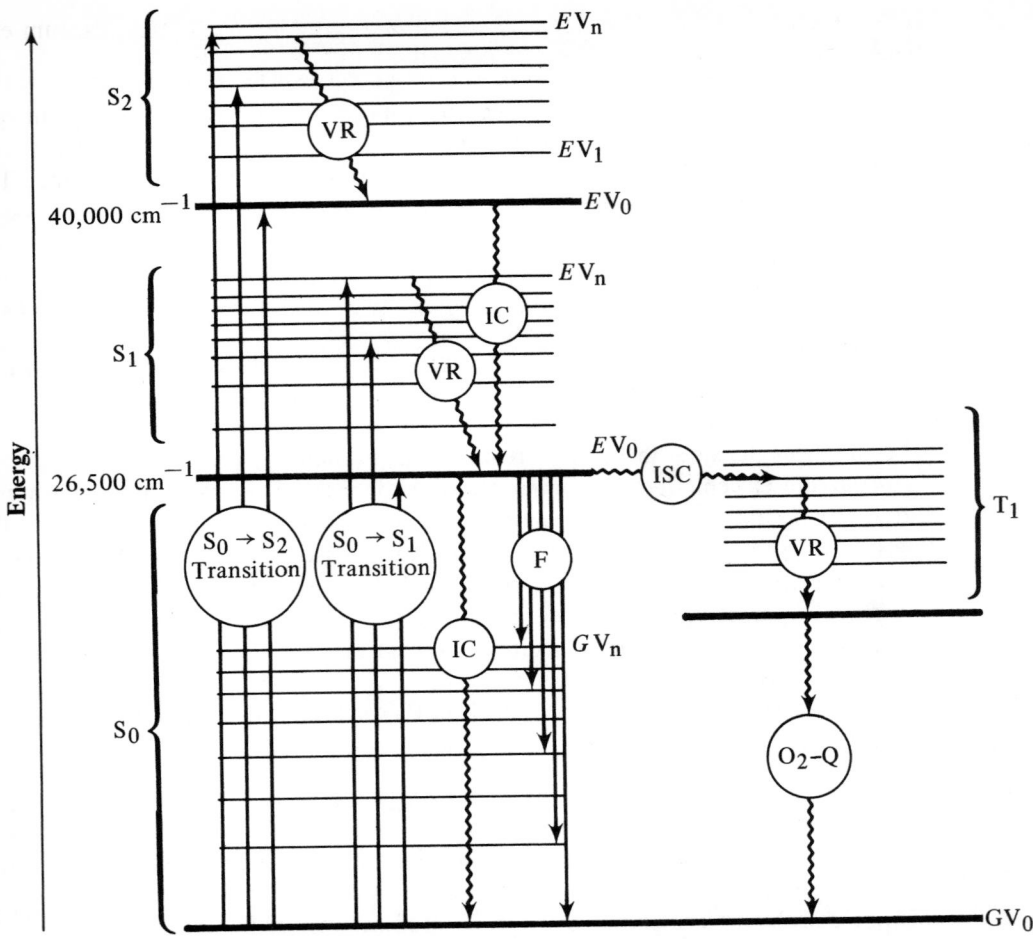

FIGURE 9.2. *A state (molecular-energy) diagram for transitions involving anthracene.* S_0 = *ground (singlet) state,* S_1 = *first excited singlet state,* S_2 = *second excited singlet state,* T_1 = *first triplet state,* VR = *vibrational relaxation,* IC = *internal conversion,* F = *fluorescence emission,* ISC = *intersystem crossing, and* O_2-Q = *quenching of* T_1 *by oxygen molecules dissolved in the solution.* EV *and* GV *refer to the various vibrational sublevels of the excited and ground states.* Straight arrows (→) refer to radiative processes—photon emission or absorption. Wavy arrows (⤳) refer to nonradiative processes.

transition. The smallest amount of energy is involved in the EV_0–GV_n transition, the largest in the EV_0–GV_0 transition. The molecules do not remain in sublevels higher than the GV_0 sublevel; they undergo further vibrational relaxation, with loss of heat, to the GV_0 sublevel.

Because it is so rapid, fluorescence emission is not generally measured after termination of excitation but during excitation. The fastest emitters have k_f values near 10^9 sec^{-1}; the slowest emitters, such as benzene, have k_f values in the range of

10^6 or even 10^5 sec^{-1}. The larger the value of k_f, the larger ϕ_f, the quantum efficiency for fluorescence, is likely to be (see Eqn. 9.8).

2. *Internal conversion.* By definition, this process involves no change in spin of the excited electron, only a conversion of excess electronic energy into excess vibrational energy, and loss of this as heat through vibrational relaxation. The kinetics of this process are presumably first order (rate constant, k_c). The $S_1 \rightsquigarrow S_0$ conversion in rigid molecules is thought to be a relatively inefficient (slow) process because of the large amount of electronic energy that must be converted into vibrational energy. According to Lim [3], internal conversion does not occur with aromatic hydrocarbons. Thus, in Figure 9.2, the $S_1 \rightsquigarrow S_0$ conversion involves the equivalent of 26,500 cm^{-1} of energy, whereas the $S_2 \rightsquigarrow S_1$ conversion involves only about half as much.

3. *Intersystem crossing.* In contrast to internal conversion, this process involves a change in the spin of the excited electron and thus a change in spin multiplicity. The details are beyond the scope of this chapter, but one should stress the kinetic competition of this process with fluorescence at room temperature. Where k_{isc} is larger than k_f, S_1 molecules will exhibit weak emission or possibly no detectable emission; further, it appears that at room temperature nearly all T_1 molecules undergo quenching after colliding and complexing with dissolved oxygen (this process is symbolized in Figure 9.2). Another possible process at room temperature, especially in the absence of oxygen, is the photochemical reaction of T_1 molecules.

4. *Collisional quenching.* This process is not shown in Figure 9.2; it can be symbolized as a collision of a quencher Q with an S_1 molecule:

$$S_1 + Q \xrightarrow{\text{(rate constant} = k_2)} \text{complex} \rightsquigarrow S_0 + Q + \text{heat} \qquad (9.5)$$

This type of reaction involves pseudo–first-order kinetics because the concentration of the quencher does not change. The first-order rate-constant is thus equal to $k_2[Q]$. A typical example of such a quencher is oxygen, which quenches a significant amount of the fluorescence of aromatic hydrocarbons. Oxygen, being paramagnetic, apparently enhances the rate of the $S_1 \rightsquigarrow T_1$ crossing, and the T_1 molecule in turn undergoes rapid $T_1 \rightsquigarrow S_0$ crossing with loss of the excess energy as heat [1].

Deactivation of the T_1 State in Solids. In frozen solutions (say, at 77 K) or in a dry solid at room temperature, T_1 molecules are not quenched; instead, they return to the S_0 state by two slower pathways: (1) phosphorescence emission, and (2) nonradiative intersystem crossing. In the latter pathway, excess electronic energy is converted to vibrational energy as the T_1 molecule crosses over to some higher vibrational level (GV$_x$) of the ground state. This is faster than the internal conversion pathway for S_1 molecules because much less electronic energy is involved.

Relation Between Concentration and Fluorescence Intensity

The intensity F of fluorescence (or phosphorescence) emission is usually directly proportional to the concentration c of the emitter. At the low concentrations

$(\leq 10^{-5}\,M)$ most often employed in fluorometric measurements, the following equation relating F and c can be derived [2, 4]:

$$F = k\phi_{\mathrm{f}}P_0(1 - e^{-\varepsilon bc}) \approx k\phi_{\mathrm{f}}P_0(2.3\,\varepsilon bc) \tag{9.6}$$

In this equation, ε and b have the same meaning as in Beer's law, Equation 7.9. Thus, $(2.3\,\varepsilon bc)$ represents the fraction of the exciting radiation that is absorbed. Because of the geometry of the fluorometer (see Sec. 9.2), only a fraction (k) of the emitted photons can be measured and recorded as F; thus,

$$k = \frac{\text{photons measured}}{\text{photons emitted}} \tag{9.7}$$

P_0 is the radiant power of the exciting radiation; note that the fluorescence intensity is directly proportional to P_0; ϕ_{f} is the *quantum efficiency* of fluorescence, i.e., the fraction of excited molecules that fluoresce:

$$\phi_{\mathrm{f}} = \frac{\text{photons emitted/sec}}{\text{photons absorbed/sec}} = \frac{\text{photons emitted}}{\text{photons absorbed}} \tag{9.8}$$

For quantitative analysis, a plot of F versus c is used as a calibration curve. In theory, such a plot should be linear; in practice, it is usually linear over one to four orders of magnitude, but typically curves downward at higher concentrations because of excessive absorption of the exciting radiation (the inner-filter effect [2]).

The relation between the intensity of phosphorescence emission and concentration is similar to that in Equation 9.6, but the full expression is more complicated [5, 6].

9.2 INSTRUMENTATION FOR FLUORESCENCE AND PHOSPHORESCENCE

The two types of fluorescence instruments are the filter fluorometer and the spectrofluorometer; the principal type of phosphorescence instrument is the spectrophosphorimeter.

The four main components of any fluorescence or phosphorescence instrument are the source of excitation, the sample cell, the detector, and the filters or gratings used to select the exciting and emitted radiation. Phosphorescence instruments must also include a Dewar flask for the liquid nitrogen used to freeze samples. Since phosphorescence instruments have the same four main components as fluorescence instruments, the common components of both will be discussed first.

Design of Instruments

Figure 9.3 shows the four essential components of any filter fluorometer or spectrofluorometer. The source is a mercury-arc or xenon-arc lamp (the latter is usually used in spectrofluorometers). The exciting radiation passes through a grating or primary filter, allowing only a certain range of wavelengths to strike the sample. Gratings are used in spectrofluorometers, filters in filter fluorometers. The major advantages of the grating are that it selects any given wavelength from 200 to 600 nm

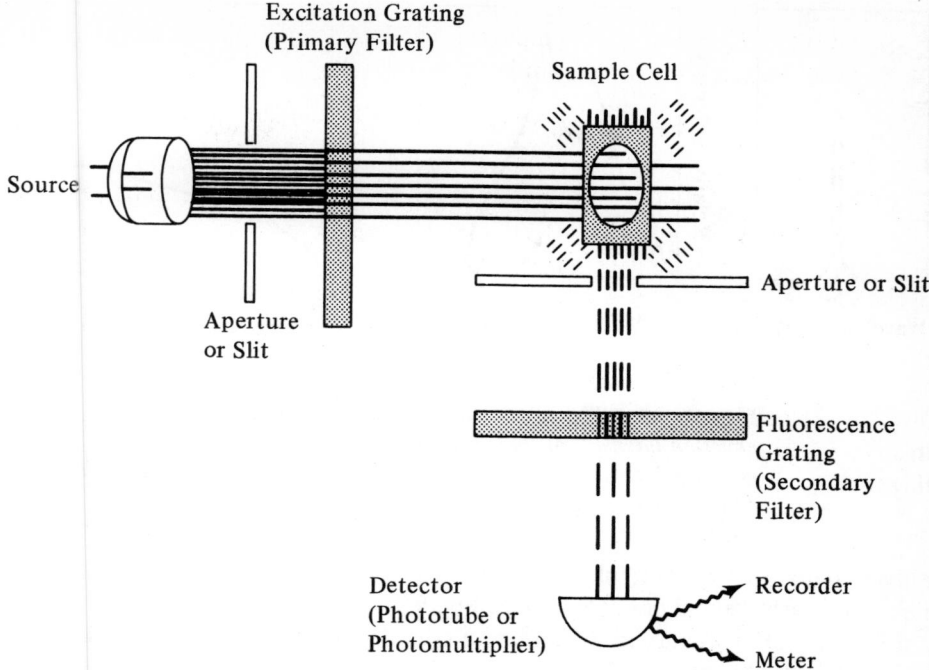

FIGURE 9.3. *Schematic diagram (top view) of the components of a fluorometer (filter fluorometer or spectrofluorometer). The source is a mercury-arc or xenon-arc lamp. The excitation grating or primary filter transmits only a portion of the radiation emitted by the source. Most of the exciting radiation passes through the sample cell without being absorbed. The radiation absorbed causes the sample to fluoresce in all directions, but only the emission that passes through the aperture or slit and through the secondary filter or fluorescence grating is measured by the phototube, or photomultiplier. The output of the detector is either measured on a meter or plotted on a recorder. From G. H. Schenk,* Absorption of Light and Ultraviolet Radiation, *Boston: Allyn and Bacon, 1973, p 260, by permission of the publisher.*

and that it passes a constant bandwidth (such as 10 nm) of radiation, no matter what the wavelength. The major advantage of most filters is that they transmit a greater fraction of the exciting radiation than do gratings, because of the wider bandwidth of the filters. This is a definite advantage for trace analysis, but a disadvantage as far as interferences are concerned—a filter may allow two substances to be excited whereas a spectrofluorometer, with its more selective grating, may be adjusted so that only one substance is excited. The disadvantage of the mercury source (plus filter) is that there are a limited number of mercury lines available with which to excite a sample.

Excitation with a Mercury Arc in a Filter Fluorometer

The usual source employed in filter fluorometers is a 4-watt mercury-arc lamp, either with a clear quartz envelope (emitting primarily 254-nm radiation) or one

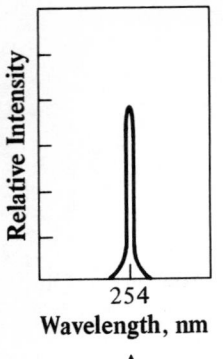
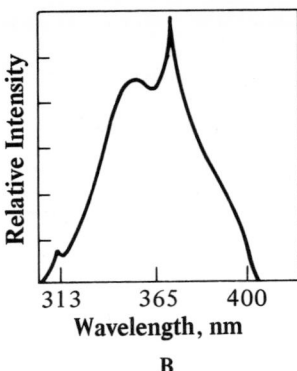
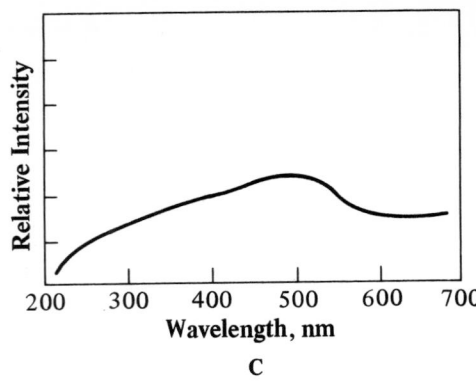

FIGURE 9.4. *The relative intensities of three different sources. A: The emission intensity of the short-wavelength (254 nm) mercury arc. B: The emission intensity of the phosphor-coated mercury arc, showing the intense emission band. C: The intensity of the xenon-arc lamp.*

coated with a white phosphor that emits a continuum from 300 to 405 nm and particularly strongly at 366 nm (see Fig. 9.4).

For excitation at 254 nm, a combination of filters is used that transmits only below 300 nm, namely a 7-54 filter plus a special plastic filter, as shown in Figure 9.5A. Alternatively, because the plastic filter gradually decomposes and must be replaced, a mercury-line interference filter may be used. This is a single, permanent filter for isolating the 254-nm line without transmitting the 313-nm, etc., lines emitted by the low-pressure mercury arc.

A filter that may be used for excitation at longer wavelengths is the 7-60 filter, whose transmittance is shown in Figure 9.5B. This transmits nearly all of the intense band of radiation emitted by the 4-watt low-pressure, phosphor-coated mercury source.

Sample Cells and the Cell Compartment. The sample cell may be made of glass, of optical-grade quartz, or synthetic silica. Glass cells transmit reasonably well down to about 320 nm, depending on the thickness of the cell wall, although there is appreciable absorption below about 360 nm. Ultraviolet grade quartz transmits well down to about 190 nm.

The cell compartment is painted a dull black and constructed so that any

FIGURE 9.5. *A plot of percent transmittance versus wavelength for several types of filters used in fluorescence. A: The 7-54 filter (solid line); a plastic filter that absorbs radiation above 300 nm (dotted line) is used in combination with the 7-54 filter to isolate the 254-nm mercury line. B: The 7-60 narrow-bandpass filter (left) and several sharp-cut filters. The nominal cut-off wavelength for the sharp-cut filters is indicated on each curve. C: Several Bausch-and-Lomb interference filters. The bandwidth at half the peak transmittance is given under each peak. From G. H. Schenk,* Absorption of Light and Ultraviolet Radiation, *Boston: Allyn and Bacon, 1973, p 265, by permission of the publisher.*

A
80
60
40
20
Percent Transmittance
230
300
420
Wavelength, nm
B
100
50
30
10
Percent Transmittance
360 mm
7–60
415
430
455
465
485
2A
PC–1
3
4
PC–9A
300
400
450
500
550
600
Wavelength, nm
C
40
30
20
10
Percent Transmittance
39%
42%
36%
24
nm
15
nm
10
nm
341
394
438
Wavelength, nm

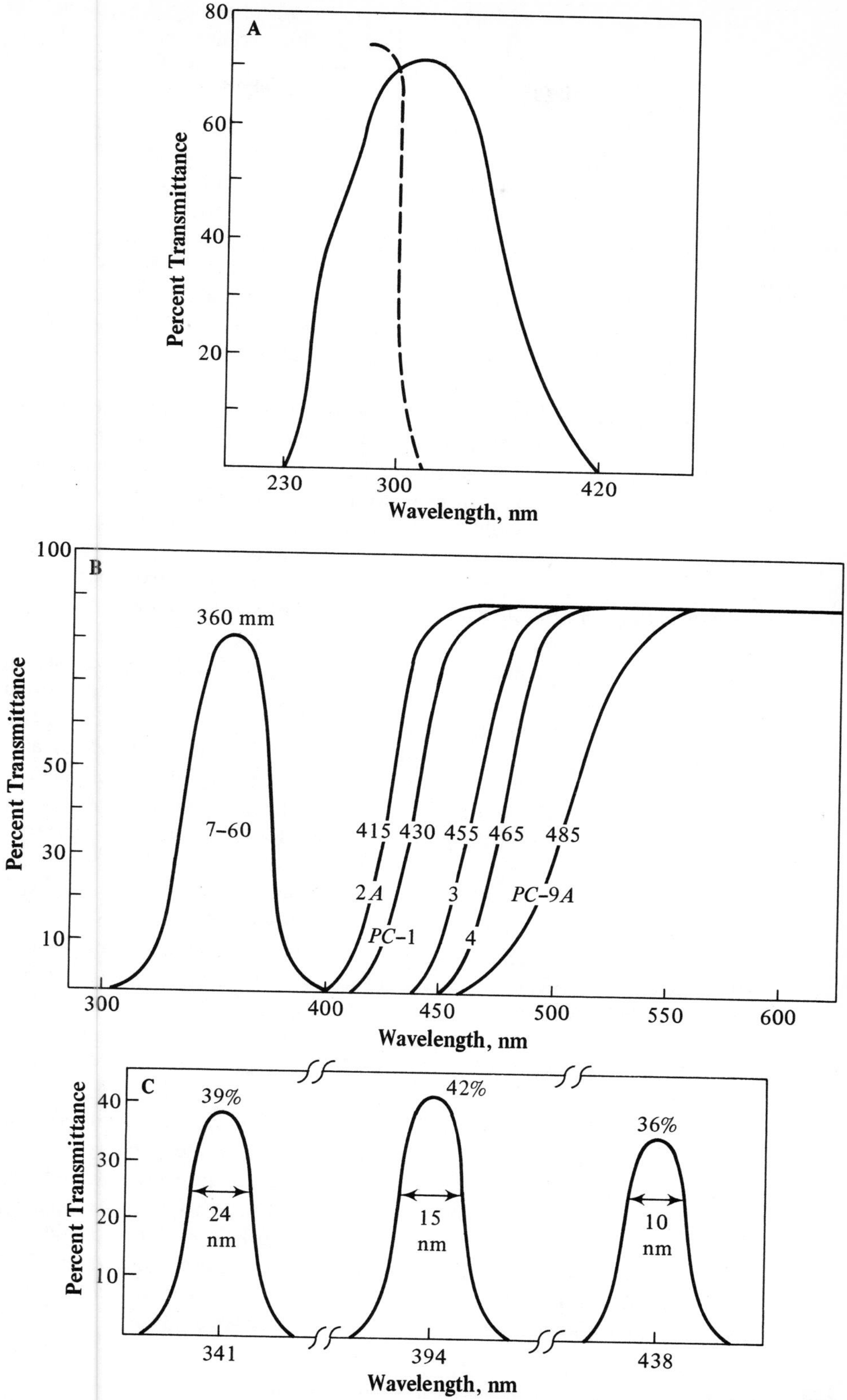

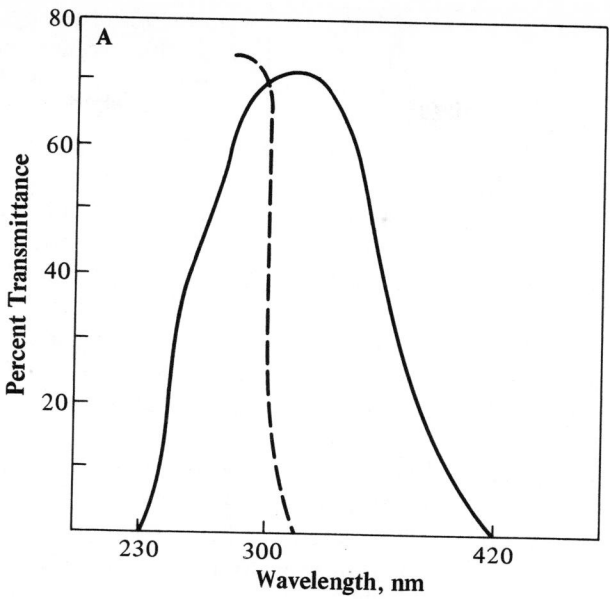

scattered radiation neither leaving the cell nor absorbed by the sample will be absorbed by the paint, not reflected through the fluorescence aperture (or slit). This is important because more than 95% of the exciting radiation is usually not absorbed by the solution, but passes through it.

There are three possible geometrical arrangements of the cell with respect to the source and the detector. The right-angle arrangement shown in Figure 9.3 is the most common, and the most advantageous for dilute solutions. The other two methods [7] are the frontal method and the in-line method.

The advantage of the right-angle arrangement is that stray exciting radiation or other stray light reflected from the cell walls is minimized. Note that in Figure 9.3, the fluorescence aperture blocks the optical path from the cell walls so that the detector cannot "see" reflected radiation from the side walls. Of course, reflection from the wall of the cell facing the detector can still occur.

Selecting a Secondary Filter and Measuring Emission. After penetrating the aperture, the emitted luminescence passes through a secondary filter or fluorescence grating that eliminates any scattered radiation. The bandwidths of the primary and secondary filters should not overlap. For example, if a 7-60 primary filter were used, then the secondary filter chosen should not transmit below about 400 nm; a good choice would be the so-called 2A secondary filter shown in Figure 9.5B.

Three types of secondary filters are available: the narrow-bandpass filter, the sharp-cut filter, and the interference filter. Typical examples of all three are shown in Figure 9.5. The most common type used in filter fluorometers is the sharp-cut filter. Sharp-cut filters are usually made of glass, as are the narrow-pass filters, but they contain chemicals that absorb all ultraviolet and visible radiation up to the wavelength specified. They have a higher transmittance (up to 85%) than do the narrow-pass filters, and have the advantage that they transmit nearly all radiation at wavelengths longer than the specified wavelength. This makes them very satisfactory for trace analysis because they allow a much more intense beam of fluorescence emission to reach the phototube than do narrow-pass or interference filters. For an extensive survey, see the article by Sill [8].

Interference filters consist of (a) two outer layers of glass on whose inner surfaces a thin semitransparent metallic film has been deposited, and (b) an inner layer of some transparent material, such as quartz, calcium fluoride, or magnesium fluoride. Most radiation striking this filter suffers destructive interference, except for the narrow band of radiation that the filter is manufactured to transmit. The bandwidth of the interference filter decreases as the wavelength it is made to transmit increases: thus the 341-nm filter (Fig. 9.5C) has a bandwidth of 24 nm, but the 438-nm filter has a bandwidth of only 10 nm.

The advantages of the fluorescence grating over the secondary filter are the same as those of the excitation grating over the primary filter. However, the secondary filter generally transmits a greater fraction of the emitted radiation than does the fluorescence grating (a possible exception would be some newer grating spectrofluorometers that have wide emission bandwidths). If the secondary filter is a sharp-cut type, then the energy that reaches the detector will be greater than if a narrow-bandpass or interference filter were used. In general, the use of secondary filter and filter fluorometers is recommended for trace analysis.

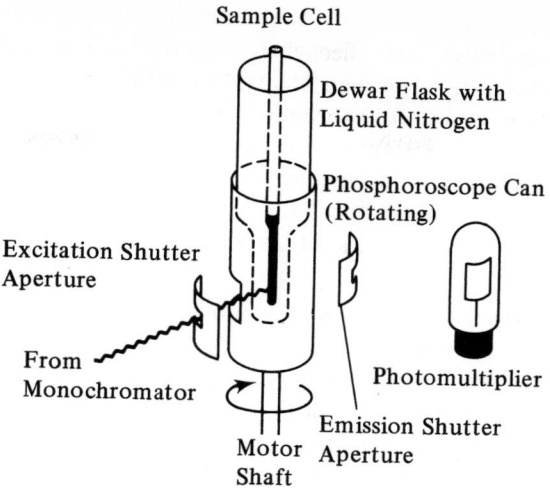

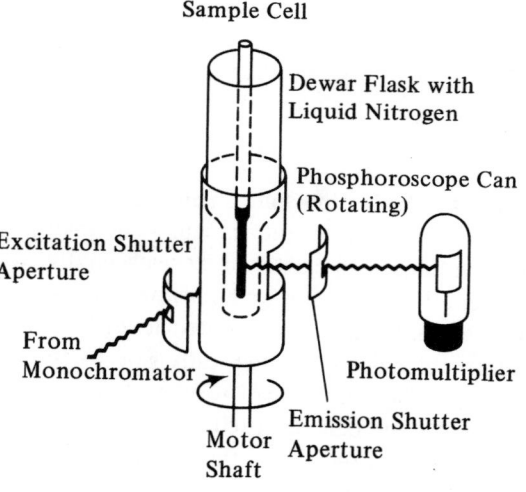

FIGURE 9.6. *Schematic diagram of rotating-can phosphoroscope used in
the phosphoroscope attachment on commercial spectrofluorometers. Top:
The slit in the can is in a position to allow exciting radiation to strike the
sample, but any fluorescence and phosphorescence emitted from the sample
is prevented from reaching the photomultiplier by the wall of the can.
Bottom: Further rotation now brings the slit in a position to allow any
long-decaying emission (phosphorescence) to pass through and reach the
photomultiplier. At the same time, exciting radiation is prevented from
striking the sample by the wall of the can, and the sample does not fluoresce. (The phosphoroscope can usually has two slits, but the second is
omitted in the diagram for clarity.) From G. H. Schenk,* Absorption of
Light and Ultraviolet Radiation, *Boston: Allyn and Bacon, 1973, p 193,
by permission of the publisher.*

The detector in some inexpensive filter fluorometers is a phototube, but in most of the better filter fluorometers and in all spectrofluorometers a high-gain photomultiplier tube is used. The photomultiplier is far more sensitive to low radiation levels and is therefore recommended for trace analysis.

In a filter fluorometer the output of the detector is usually displayed on a meter. In a spectrofluorometer, the output is displayed on a recorder to give the excitation and emission spectra. An oscilloscope may also be used, particularly when decay rates are to be measured.

Phosphorimeters. The design of a phosphorimeter is the same as that of the fluorometer, except for the use of a rotating can and Dewar flask. The sample solution is transferred into a small round quartz tube and the tube placed in a special Dewar flask filled with liquid nitrogen to freeze the solution into a glass. The lower part of the flask is smaller than the upper (see Fig. 9.6) and is also made of quartz to permit transmission of the exciting radiation and the phosphorescence emission. The Dewar is placed inside the rotating can, which has two apertures, or slits. As a slit moves into line with the monochromator beam, the sample is excited; but the speed of rotation is such that any fluorescence emission ceases before the slit moves into line with the emission detector, so that only phosphorescence is observed.

Filter Fluorometers

Commercially available filter fluorometers can be grouped into two categories. One category includes those filter fluorometers designed primarily or exclusively for glass cells and hence limited to excitation at wavelengths above 320 nm. In practice, this means wavelengths of 366 nm or higher with a medium-pressure mercury-arc lamp, or 320–400 nm with a phosphor-coated low-pressure mercury-arc lamp. This kind of filter fluorometer is usually modestly priced; the Coleman photofluorometer is a good example. The second category of filter fluorometer includes those instruments designed for mercury-arc excitation at 254 nm, as well as at longer wavelengths. Quartz cells must be used for 254-nm excitation, whereas glass cells can be used at wavelengths above 320 nm. The Turner and the Aminco instruments are examples of this kind of instrument.

Filter fluorometers can be used in automated analytical systems, for example the Technicon AutoAnalyzer®.

Spectrofluorometers

The commercially available spectrofluorometers can be grouped into three categories: (1) Medium-priced uncorrected spectrofluorometers, inexpensive enough to be used for routine analytical work. (2) Uncorrected research spectrofluorometers, more expensive and adaptable for many different types of investigation; one such instrument, for example, can be fitted with a phosphorescence attachment (including a rotating can) that converts it into a spectrophosphorimeter. (3) Corrected, or absolute, spectrofluorometers that *directly* record fluorescence excitation and emission spectra already corrected for instrumental parameters varying with wavelength. Naturally, this type of instrument is very expensive. Examples of each category of instrument will be discussed after the general principles have been introduced.

Components of an Uncorrected Spectrofluorometer. The design of filter fluorometers and spectrofluorometers has already been discussed; here, we shall describe in more detail the components of an uncorrected spectrofluorometer (see Fig. 9.7).

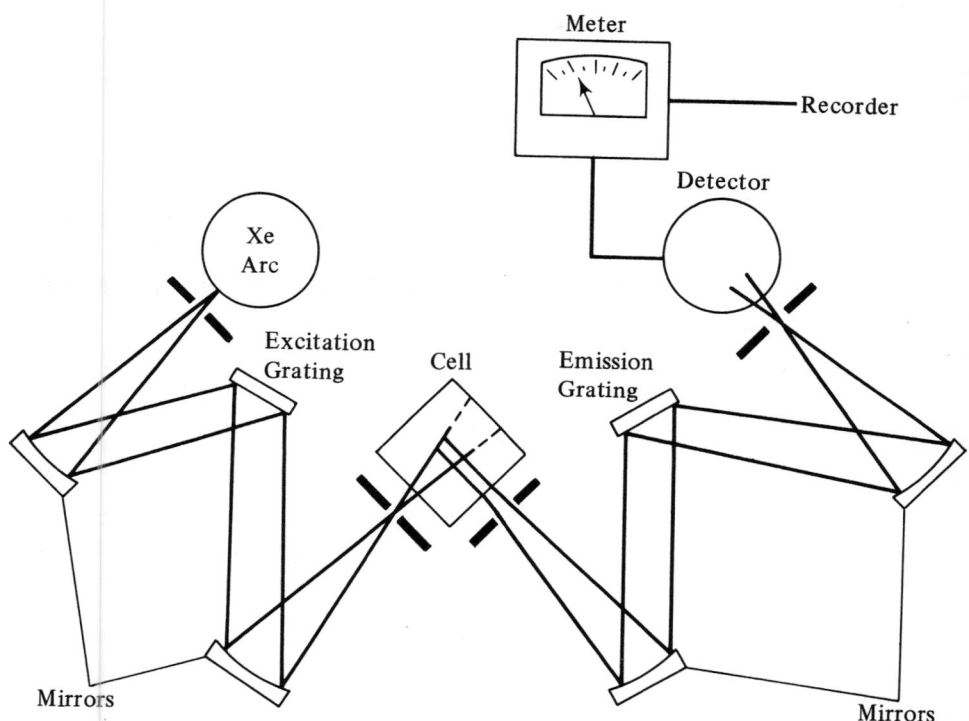

FIGURE 9.7. *Schematic diagram of an uncorrected spectrofluorometer. A high-pressure xenon arc is the usual source. The gratings can be adjusted manually, or driven by a motor for recording. The usual detector is the 1P21 photomultiplier tube. The response of the tube is displayed on a meter and is sometimes recorded.* From G. H. Schenk, Absorption of Light and Ultraviolet Radiation, *Boston: Allyn and Bacon, 1973, p 278, by permission of the publisher.*

A xenon-arc lamp is used as the source in most spectrofluorometers, since it emits continuously over the range 200–700 nm (see Fig. 9.4C) and hence can be used to obtain fluorescence excitation spectra as well as emission spectra. (Emission spectra for many substances could be obtained with a mercury-arc source, but excitation spectra could not, because the emission is discontinuous and the frequency range is so limited.) However, in uncorrected instruments using a xenon-arc lamp, no correction is made for the variation in intensity of the source with changing wavelength.

In many spectrofluorometers, the source is not directly aligned with the sample; instead (Fig. 9.7), mirrors are used to focus the radiation on the cell. The excitation grating has a fixed bandpass (such as 10 nm) on some instruments, so that the spectral bandwidth is fixed. However, on other instruments the spectral bandwidth can be varied by changing the slit-width.

As in filter fluorometers, fluorescence emission is measured at right angles to the path of the incident radiation. The emitted light passes through an exit slit and is focused by a mirror onto the emission grating. The bandwidth of the emission grating should be greater than 10 nm to achieve maximum intensity, unless a fluorescence-emission spectrum is being measured.

All spectrofluorometers are equipped with high-gain photomultipliers as detectors; this partly compensates for the smaller amount of energy that gratings transmit compared to filters. However, uncorrected spectrofluorometers do not compensate for the variable response of the photomultiplier at varying wavelengths, so the measured relative intensities of two fluorescence-emission bands of a given species are not a correct indication of the true intensities.

Medium-Priced Uncorrected Spectrofluorometers. There are now available a number of so-called "medium-priced" spectrofluorometers. Some are equipped with a mercury source for optimum trace analysis, but a xenon source is also available. The important advantage of these instruments is that the variable-slit-width emission grating allows one to measure fluorescence at the wavelength of maximum emission using as narrow or wide a bandwidth as allowed by the instrumental design.

Uncorrected Spectrofluorometers for Research. This category of instrument is adaptable to all kinds of research, and is generally much more expensive than the medium-priced spectrofluorometers. The best known example is the Aminco-Bowman SPF instrument. The latter can be used as a spectrofluorometer, but with the attachment of an Aminco-Keirs phosphoroscope, it can also be used as a spectrophosphorimeter. When used as a spectrofluorometer, it consists of essentially the same components as those shown in Figure 9.7.

Corrected Spectrofluorometers. To obtain "absolute" spectra, the spectra obtained on uncorrected spectrofluorometers must be corrected point by point for instrumental parameters that vary with wavelength. Such corrections are tedious, and it is desirable to obtain spectra on a corrected spectrofluorometer if possible. These instruments correct for variations in the intensity of the xenon source so that the sample is excited at *constant energy* at all wavelengths, and for variations with wavelength in the response of the photomultiplier; emission spectra are presented directly in quanta per unit bandwidth.

Once solvent corrections have been made, *relative* quantum efficiencies (ϕ_f) can be measured directly using fluorescence emission spectra. A standard for the determination of quantum yield, however, must also be run [9]. Typical standards whose quantum yields are known are quinine sulfate ($\phi = 0.55$), fluorescein ($\phi = 0.85$), and 5-dimethylaminonaphthalene-1-sulfonic acid, or DANS acid ($\phi = 0.36$ in 0.1 M NaHCO$_3$ [10]).

Applications to organic and inorganic substances will be discussed in separate sections. Organic applications will be discussed first since many organic compounds are used to form fluorescent chelates with inorganic cations. The applications will be restricted primarily to fluorescence, which has more analytical uses than phosphorescence at the present time.

Organic Compounds

Planar, conjugated molecules fluoresce, whereas saturated molecules and those with only one double bond do not; usually a molecule must possess at least one aromatic ring if one is to observe fluorescence or phosphorescence. Even conjugated olefins such as 1,3,5-hexatriene do not fluoresce; however, aryl-substituted olefins do. For example, *trans*-stilbene, which is planar, fluoresces; *cis*-stilbene does not, presumably because it is not planar.

The common classes of simple fluorescent organic compounds are listed in Table 9.1 according to functional groups. When a compound possesses two or more such groups, then it can also be expected to fluoresce. For example, 8-hydroxyquinoline is both a phenol (class 10) and a heterocyclic compound (class 7) and is predictably fluorescent.

Fluorescence of Selected Drugs. As an example of the use of fluorescence analysis for the determination of organic compounds, some of the recent work on drugs will be considered. Methods have been developed for the following drugs: "phenylethylamines," barbiturates, and aspirin. The "phenylethylamines" are really substituted 1-amino-2-phenylethanes; the best known phenylethylamine is amphetamine (2-amino-1-phenylpropane). Many of these compounds are excited at 260–270 nm, emit at 282–300 nm, and can be determined fluorometrically at concentrations as low as 0.2 mg/100 ml [11]. Phenylephrine and epinephrine have about the same molar absorptivities as amphetamines, and have quantum efficiencies of about 0.08, so that they can be determined at concentrations as low as 10^{-3} mg/100 ml (0.01 ppm).

Several approaches [12, 13] have been published for the fluorometric determination of barbiturates. A general structure for the "enol" tautomer of most common barbiturates is

Most barbiturates are fluorescent in 0.1 M base, but not in acid, because the base removes protons from the 4-hydroxyl group and the 1-nitrogen to form a fluorescent dianion [13]. Where a methyl or ethyl group is substituted on the 1-nitrogen, the barbiturate is not fluorescent. Most barbiturates are excited at 255 nm and emit at 405–420 nm [12].

TABLE 9.1. *Classes of Organic Compounds Exhibiting Usable Fluorescence*

Class	Best Examples (ϕ_f)	Weak or No Fluorescence	Literature Reference
Hydrocarbons			
1. Aryl-substituted olefins	*trans*-Stilbene	*cis*-Stilbene	[1]
2. Unsubstituted aromatic hydrocarbons	Anthracene (0.2), pyrene (0.3)	Benzene (0.04), biphenyl (P)	[1, 2]
3. Alkyl-substituted hydrocarbons	Toluene (0.1), mesitylene (0.2), 9-methylanthracene (0.3)		[7]
Nitrogen Compounds			
4. Aromatic amines	Aniline (0.1), 2-naphthylamine (0.5)	Nitroanilines (P)	[2, 7]
5. Amino acids	Tyrosine (0.2), tryptophan (0.2)	Phenylalanine (0.04)	[2]
6. "Phenylethyl-amines"	Amphetamine (0.02)		[9]
7. Heterocyclics	Quinine (0.55)	Pyridine	[2]
Halogen Compounds			
8. Cl-substituted aromatic hydrocarbons	1-Chloronaphthalene (0.06), *p*-chlorotoluene (0.02)	Chlorobenzene (P)	[2]
9. F-substituted aromatic hydrocarbons	Fluorobenzene (0.1), 1-fluoronaphthalene (0.06)		[1]
Oxygen Compounds			
10. Phenols	Phenol (0.2), 2-naphthol (0.3)	Nitrophenols (P)	[2]
11. Phenyl ethers	Anisole (0.3)		
12. Barbiturates	Phenobarbital (0.001)	5,5′-Dialkyl barbiturates	[9, 10]
13. Aromatic acids	Acetylsalicylic acid (0.02)	Benzoic acid (P)	[11]

Note: The quantum efficiency for fluorescence ϕ_f is indicated in parentheses. A (P) indicates useful phosphorescence properties.

For many years, acetylsalicylic acid (ASA) was thought not to fluoresce and was commonly determined by hydrolysis to salicylic acid, followed by fluorometric determination of the salicylic acid. A tedious separation of the salicylic acid from the acetyl derivative was therefore necessary for the determination of both in aspirin tablets. Recently, it was found that ASA does indeed fluoresce in a solvent of 1% acetic acid in chloroform [14]. ASA is excited at 280 nm and emits at 335 nm, whereas salicylic acid is excited mainly at 308 nm and emits mainly at 450 nm; it is therefore possible to determine each in the presence of the other. It is worth noting that ASA can also be determined in the presence of salicylic acid by measuring its phosphorescence [15].

Inorganic Compounds

Space does not permit a complete survey of all inorganic species; the reader is referred to an extensive account by Lytle [16] of luminescence over the entire periodic table, and to a recent monograph [2]. To be discussed here will be certain simple luminescent ions, chelates of non-transition-metal ions, and chelates of transition-metal ions.

Simple (Unchelated) Luminescent Ions. The most well-known simple ion that luminesces in solution is the uranyl ion, UO_2^{2+} (see spectra in Fig. 9.1); another is the aquated cerium(III) ion. The electron configuration of the latter is $[Xe]4f^1 5d^0$; the luminescence involves excitation of a $4f$ electron to a $5d$ orbital, after which luminescence occurs during a $5d \rightarrow 4f$ return transition. Cerium(III) is known to be excited at 254 nm [17]; five absorption bands in aqueous solution have been assigned to various $4f \rightarrow 5d$ transitions (those at 200, 211, 221.5, 239.5, and 252.5 nm). Cerium(III) has been determined fluorometrically in 0.4 N H_2SO_4 [17] using excitation at 254 nm and measuring the emission at 350 nm. Since cerium(IV) does not fluoresce, cerium(III) can be determined in the presence of cerium(IV).

Of the other lanthanides, europium(III) chloride, an f^6 ion, and terbium(III) chloride, an f^8 ion, have been reported to fluoresce weakly in dimethylformamide solution [16]. The chloride and sulfate salts of samarium(III), an f^5 ion, of gadolinium(III), an f^7 ion, and of dysprosium(III), an f^9 ion, are also reported to luminesce weakly in solution [16]. All five of these lanthanides give rise to weak lines which have been assigned to $f \rightarrow f$ transitions.

The other important ion that is luminescent in solution is the thallium(I) ion. The aquated Tl^+ ion can be excited at 215 nm and emits weakly at 370 nm; the $TlCl_4^{3-}$ ion is excited at 240 to 250 nm and emits strongly at 450 nm. A qualitative test [18] for thallium(I) is based on its violet luminescence following addition of 1 M potassium chloride. The fluorometric determination [19] of 10^{-7} M thallium(I) in 3.3 M HCl plus 0.8 M KCl is based on excitation at 250 nm and emission at 430 nm.

Chelates of Non-Transition-Metal Ions. This is the largest class of luminescent inorganic systems, and a full discussion is beyond the scope of this chapter; the reader is referred to the monograph of White and Argauer [20] for the many analytical applications of these systems. In general, the diamagnetic ions of the metals in Groups IA, IIA, IIB, IIIA, and IIIB, as well as Zr^{4+}, can be determined by measuring the fluorescence of their chelates with aromatic organic ligands. The major means of exciting these chelates is by using the $\pi\text{-}\pi^*$ absorption bands of the chelated ligand [16]. The ions most frequently measured by fluorescence are those in Group IIIA—aluminum(III), gallium(III), indium(III), and thallium(III)—which form metal chelates with a large number of organic ligands: 8-hydroxyquinoline, 2,2'-bipyridine, salicylaldehyde derivatives, and many compounds of the azobenzene type. These ligands are usually weakly fluorescent when uncomplexed, but intensely fluorescent when complexed by these ions.

TABLE 9.2. *Selected Fluorometric Reagents for the Determination of Aluminum*

Organic Chelate	Excitation Wavelength nm	Emission Wavelength nm	Concentration Range (Final Solution)
Morin (2′,3,4′,5,7-Pentahydroxy-flavone)	270 (440)	500	4×10^{-6} to 5×10^{-5} M[a]; 4×10^{-8} to 2×10^{-7} M[b]
Pontachrome Blue Black R (PBBR)	330	635	7×10^{-8} to 6×10^{-7} M[c]
8-Hydroxyquinoline	405 (366)	520	detection limit of 10^{-6} M[d]
Acid-Alizarin Garnet R (AAGR or 2,4,2′-Trihydroxy-azobenzene-5′-sodium sulfonate)	470	575	$\sim 4 \times 10^{-8}$ to 9×10^{-6} M[e]
N-Salicylidene-2-amino-3-hydroxyfluorene (NSAHF)	445	530	$< 3 \times 10^{-8}$ to 3×10^{-7} M[f]

a. C. E. White and C. S. Lowe, *Ind. Eng. Chem. Anal. Ed.*, *12*, 229 (1940).
b. F. Will, III, *Anal. Chem.*, *33*, 1360 (1961).
c. A. Weissler and C. E. White, *Anal. Chem.*, *18*, 530 (1946).
d. W. T. Rees, *Analyst*, *87*, 202 (1962).
e. C. E. White and R. J. Argauer, *Fluorescence Analysis*, New York: Marcel Dekker, 1970, pp 55–57.
f. C. E. White, H. C. E. McFarlane, J. Fogt, and B. Fuchs, *Anal. Chem.*, *39*, 367 (1967).

The metal ion for which the most methods are available is aluminum(III); as an example of the kinds of organic ligands that have been used in fluorescence analysis, some selected organic reagents used for the determination of aluminum(III) are shown in Table 9.2.

Chelates of Transition Metals. Although many transition-metal ions form stable chelates and complexes with aromatic ligands, relatively few such systems are fluorescent. In the case of chelated paramagnetic metal ions, this is because the rate of intersystem crossing from the S_1 state to the T_1 state of the aromatic ligand is greatly increased by the unpaired electrons of metal ions. In solution, most T_1 states lose all their electronic energy by collisional deactivation or by rapid conversion to their S_0 states without emitting a photon. Thus paramagnetic metal ions such as Fe^{3+}, Co^{2+}, Ni^{2+}, and Cu^{2+} are said to quench the fluorescence of their chelates.

Another phenomenon that operates in these chelates to prevent emission is the heavy-atom effect. Heavy diamagnetic atoms such as Hg^{2+}, Au^+, and Tl^{3+} increase spin-orbit coupling, which increases the rate of intersystem crossing [21]. This effect appears to be most effective with Hg^{2+}, for which no well-documented metal-chelate luminescence has been reported. Certain Group VIII d^6 transition-metal ions have been reported to luminesce [2]. When complexed by such strong-field ligands as 1,10-phenanthroline, 2,2-bipyridine, and 2,2,2-terpyridine, iridium(III), ruthenium(II), osmium(II), and rhodium(III) form diamagnetic metal chelates. Such chelates exhibit low-energy charge-transfer absorption $(d \rightarrow \pi^*)$ and emission

$(\pi^* \to d)$ bands [21, 22]. Iridium(III) has actually been determined [22] by measuring luminescence (which appears to be phosphorescence) at room temperature in ethanol-water solution. It is interesting that no iron(II) chelates have been observed to luminesce, although such chelates exhibit $d \to \pi^*$ absorption bands. Fink and Ohnesorge [23] have postulated that this is the result of a crossover to a $t_{2g}^3 e_g^2 \pi^*$ spin state during the lifetime of the initial excited state of the iron(II) chelates. Such a spin state is paramagnetic and undergoes rapid intersystem crossing and rapid internal conversion to the ground state before emission can occur.

Techniques Useful for Analysis of Mixtures

The analysis of simple mixtures of organic or inorganic compounds by fluorometry without any separation is often possible because of the versatility of fluorometers. In contrast to spectrophotometers, these instruments have two instrumental variables instead of one. The analysis of the following hypothetical mixture will illustrate the use of these variables.

Suppose compound A is to be determined in the presence of compound B. Using a fluorometer, three possible techniques may be investigated:

1. If A absorbs ultraviolet radiation in a spectral region where B does not, then the grating or primary filter that selects the excitation wavelength can be adjusted so that only A is excited. Then only A will emit fluorescence and the detector will measure only emission from A.

2. Suppose that B absorbs in the same spectral region as A, but that the term $\varepsilon bc\phi_f$ (see Eqn. 9.6) for B is ≤ 0.01 of that of A. It is probable that $\leq 1\%$ of the instrumental readout, F, will be emission from B, and A can still be accurately measured.

3. If A and B both absorb in the same spectral region, but A emits fluorescence in a different spectral region than B, then the fluorometer can be adjusted to measure only fluorescence from A. This is done by manipulating the grating or secondary filter that selects the fluorescence-emission wavelengths falling on the detector. Even though both A and B are emitting light, the detector "sees" only the emission from A.

As an example of the first technique, consider the determination of the aromatic hydrocarbon, anthracene, in the presence of its isomer, phenanthrene. Phenanthrene does not absorb in the ultraviolet at wavelengths longer than 360 nm. Since anthracene has an excitation band above 360 nm, it is possible to excite only anthracene. In an experimental study [24] of this type of mixture, the actual wavelength used was 365 nm. As can be seen from Figure 9.8, the best wavelength at which to measure the fluorescence of anthracene on an uncorrected spectrofluorometer would be about 400 nm. It is also possible to determine phenanthrene by use of the second technique. Phenanthrene and anthracene are excited intensely at 265 nm, but phenanthrene fluoresces at 350 nm where anthracene does not (Fig. 9.8).

It should not be assumed that all simple mixtures can be analyzed by either of the above techniques. Consider the aromatic hydrocarbon pyrene in the presence of an equal amount of anthracene. The ultraviolet absorption (and fluorescence excitation) spectrum of anthracene completely overlaps that of pyrene. It can be

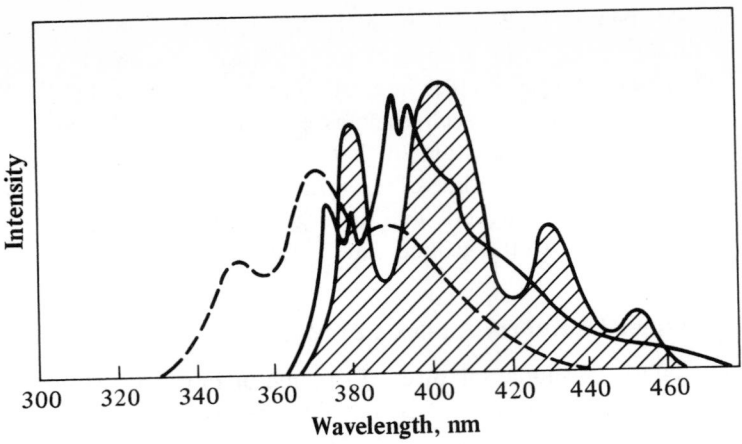

FIGURE 9.8. *The uncorrected fluorescence spectra of phenanthrene (dotted line), anthracene (shaded area), and pyrene (solid line). (Phenanthrene is excited best at 265 nm; anthracene may be excited at 365, 375, or 250 nm; and pyrene is excited at 335 nm.)* From G. H. Schenk, Absorption of Light and Ultraviolet Radiation, *Boston: Allyn and Bacon, 1973, p 175, by permission of the publisher.*

seen from Figure 9.8 that the same is true for the fluorescence emission spectra. Therefore, a separation or chemical reaction is needed before the pyrene can be measured fluorometrically.

In some cases it has been found possible to measure the concentration of each component of a two-component mixture (A and B) by measuring the total fluorescence from both components at two wavelengths. The concentration of each component is calculated by inserting the measured fluorescence intensities into two simultaneous equations, in a manner similar to that used in analyzing ultraviolet-visible absorption measurements (Sec. 7.5).

Quantitative Analysis after Chemical Reaction. A large number of fluorometric analyses have been performed after converting a nonfluorescent or weakly fluorescent compound into an intensely fluorescent species. One example, which involves only hydrolysis, is the measurement of acetylsalicylic acid as salicylic acid or the salicylate anion. Because the *total* concentration of these two acids in blood is very important in the treatment of rheumatic disease, acetylsalicylic acid is converted to salicylic acid by hydrolysis and the total measured as salicylate. First the serum protein is removed, then the acetylsalicylic acid is hydrolyzed under alkaline conditions to salicylic acid and acetic acid (in alkaline solution, an equilibrium mixture of the anions and acids is present). The alkaline solution is then excited at 310 nm and the fluorescence emission is measured at 410 nm.

Instrumental Approaches for Problem Solving

It is of interest to briefly compare the use of a spectrofluorometer and a filter fluorometer in solving analytical problems. The standard procedure is to use the spectrofluorometer to obtain the excitation and emission spectra, and then choose the proper filters so that quantitative measurements can be made on the filter fluorometer. What happens, however, if the excitation band in a routine analysis does not straddle a prominent mercury line? Should one resort to a medium-priced spectrofluorometer with a xenon arc for routine analytical work? Again, what should be done if the emission band of a desired constituent in a mixture overlaps with the band of a second constituent so that it is impossible to use a sharp-cut secondary filter? Possible approaches to these problems can be seen in the filter-fluorometric analysis of aspirin tablets for acetylsalicylic acid (ASA) and salicylic acid [25].

The corrected excitation and emission spectra of ASA and salicylic acid are shown in Figure 9.9. The first problem involved choosing the most efficient method of exciting ASA, since its excitation bands were at 235 and 278 nm. One possible approach was to use the intense 254-nm line emitted by a low-pressure mercury arc (even though this line was not straddled by either excitation band), hoping that its high intensity would compensate for the low ε of ASA at 254 nm. Using this excitation wavelength, however, meant that salicylic acid would also be excited somewhat. This in turn prevented the use of a sharp-cut secondary filter or even the 7-60 narrow-pass filter, since salicylic acid emits between 350 and 400 nm. This problem was solved by using an interference filter with a transmittance range of 329–353 nm, peaking at 341 nm. No interference was encountered from salicylic acid in this region because the emission was so weak, and because the aspirin tablets analyzed contained low levels of salicylic acid.

Obviously, a medium-priced spectrofluorometer could have been equipped with a xenon-arc source and used for the analysis, but the filter fluorometer is usually preferred for routine work. In addition, the latter is more sensitive; for example, the detection limit for ASA on the Turner spectrofluorometer is 10^{-6} M, whereas the detection limit using the Turner filter fluorometer is 10^{-7} M.

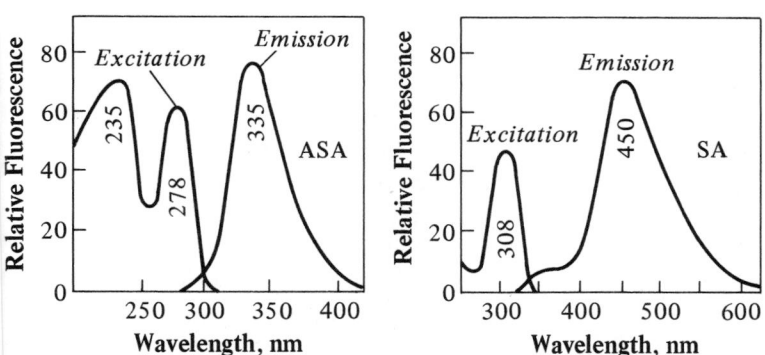

FIGURE 9.9. *Left: The corrected fluorescence excitation and emission spectra of acetylsalicylic acid (ASA). In 1% acetic acid in chloroform, only the 278-nm excitation band can be observed; in ethyl ether-isopentane-ethanol solvent, both the 235- and 278-nm excitation bands are observed. Right: The corrected fluorescence excitation and emission spectra of salicylic acid (SA) as obtained in 1% acetic acid in chloroform. From G. H. Schenk,* Absorption of Light and Ultraviolet Radiation, *Boston: Allyn and Bacon, 1973, p 285, by permission of the publisher.*

Another problem was to choose the most efficient method of exciting salicylic acid, which has only one useful excitation band (at 308 nm). One approach was to use a special phosphor-lamp source emitting between 270 and 340 nm with a peak at 306 nm; this gave good sensitivity for salicylic acid. Another approach was to use the somewhat weak 313 nm line emitted by a low-pressure mercury-arc lamp, selected with a combination primary filter consisting of the 7-54 filter along with a plastic filter used to cut out the 254-nm mercury line. This procedure essentially excited only the salicylic acid, not ASA. In both cases, a sharp-cut filter with 37% T at 465 nm was used to exclude any possible emission by ASA.

In routine analysis for salicylic acid, a medium-priced spectrofluorometer again could have been used. Since the xenon arc has a higher intensity at 308 nm than at 254, a spectrofluorometer with a xenon arc could give a lower detection limit for salicylic acid than would a filter fluorometer. In the analysis for salicylic acid in aspirin tablets, however, it did not prove necessary. The filter fluorometer thus provided a cheaper, more convenient, approach to routine analysis.

Uses of Fluorescence and Phosphorescence in Chromatography

Fluorescence and phosphorescence measurements have long been used to follow the separation of certain luminescent organic compounds in such techniques as liquid chromatography, gas-liquid chromatography, paper chromatography, and thin-layer chromatography (TLC). Such measurements are useful in many cases, but their application to the first three separation techniques is limited, since usually only organic molecules containing an aromatic ring fluoresce or phosphoresce. Thus, luminescence measurements cannot detect acyclic or nonaromatic cyclic organic molecules. In contrast, luminescence measurements find general use in TLC. Before discussing this, some applications of luminescence to the first three separation techniques will be mentioned.

An outstanding example is the separation and characterization of polynuclear aromatic hydrocarbons in polluted air reported by Sawicki and coworkers [26]. Column chromatography employing alumina was used to separate the hydrocarbons; fluorescence, ultraviolet spectrophotometry, and colorimetric tests were used to identify aromatic hydrocarbons in the various fractions.

Fluorescence and phosphorescence have been used by Drushel and Sommers [27] to identify nitrogen compounds in petroleum fractions following gas-chromatographic separations. The nitrogen-rich petroleum fractions investigated were so complex and so small in size that the greater sensitivity of luminescence techniques over other spectroscopic techniques was essential for good analysis.

In the field of paper chromatography, spots of fluorescent organic molecules have been identified on paper chromatograms by inspecting the paper under either short-wavelength (254 nm) or long-wavelength (300–400 nm) ultraviolet radiation. In most cases, the spots appear as blue or violet colors. Sawicki and Pfaff [28] have shown that phosphorescent organic molecules can also be identified on paper chromatograms.

In the more popular TLC separations, on the other hand, adsorbents or precoated TLC sheets containing certain inorganic phosphors are available that emit intense visible radiation over the entire length of the TLC chromatogram *except* where spots of the separated organic compounds are present. Most organic compounds quench the luminescence of the phosphor, and the spots appear as dark shadows against the brilliant luminescent background of unquenched phosphor.

Green (522 nm) is the most common luminescent color used on TLC sheets. Typical green phosphors are (a) pure zinc silicate and (b) calcium silicate with a manganese-lead activator. Most such green phosphors emit only under short wavelength (254 nm) ultraviolet excitation, permitting examination of the TLC sheet for fluorescent organic compounds under long-wavelength excitation. A phosphor of zinc and cadmium sulfides is available that yields an off-white luminescence under both short-wavelength and long-wavelength ultraviolet excitation.

In addition to the qualitative work described above, quantitative measurements on TLC plates are also possible. Lefar and Lewis [29] have measured organic compounds both by the amount of emission on an adsorbent without a phosphor, and by the amount of quenching of a phosphor mixed with an adsorbent. Janchen and Pataki [30] have discussed many examples of direct quantitative measurement on TLC plates of spot luminescence. Another interesting application is the phosphorimetric measurement of nicotine, nornicotine, and anabasine in tobacco after separation by TLC [31].

Applications in Studies of Pollution

Fluorescence and phosphorescence have been used to investigate the pollution of both water and air. Fluorescent compounds, especially, have been used in the study of water flow and water pollution [32]. "Fluorescent tracers" are superior to radioactive tracers because they can be used at concentrations so low (≤ 0.001 ppb) that they constitute neither a real contamination nor a health hazard. A common fluorescent dye, the first such dye to be used, is Rhodamine B; its fluorescence emission is independent of pH from pH 5 to 10 and it can be determined at concentrations above 0.01 ppb.

The use of tracers enables industries and cities to control or reduce pollution before it occurs. Measuring the "time-of-travel" (mean velocity) of rivers and streams and the mixing of those waters into lakes and oceans helps to indicate where to discharge waste, when to discharge it, and at what rate. Tracers have been used, for instance, in San Francisco Bay and in Chesapeake Bay to facilitate correct waste disposal in those waters.

Fluorescence and phosphorescence both find use in the analysis of polluted air for specific chemical pollutants. Fluorescence is especially useful because many aromatic hydrocarbons are intensely fluorescent.

Since aromatic hydrocarbons are one of the chief pollutants in air, the fluorometer has been used by the Public Health Service [33] for determining these compounds. Fluorometry is more useful than ultraviolet spectrophotometry in pollution analysis, not only because it is more versatile, but also because it can measure the very low concentrations of hydrocarbons found in samples collected from the air. Such analyses are all the more important because some aromatic hydrocarbons are carcinogenic. One of the best known carcinogenic aromatic hydrocarbons is benzo[a]pyrene, or 3,4-benzpyrene. A very specific method for determining benzo-

[a]pyrene in the aromatic-hydrocarbon fraction of polluted air samples has been developed, using sulfuric acid as a solvent in which the compound forms a cation with a strong absorption band at 520 nm [33]. A few other aromatic hydrocarbons have weak absorption bands at 520 nm, but none of these emit fluorescent light at 545 nm as does benzo[a]pyrene. To determine benzo[a]pyrene, the sample is excited at 520 nm and the fluorescence emission at 545 nm measured with the fluorometer. It has been shown that benzo[a]pyrene can be estimated in artificial mixtures of over 40 similar compounds without separation. This analysis is also unusual in that visible light, not ultraviolet light, is used to excite a molecule.

Medicine

One of the most useful applications of fluorescence is in the routine determination of certain important molecules in body fluids for diagnostic purposes. Some such molecules are naturally fluorescent, but others must be chemically treated to form fluorescent products. For example, the amino acids tyrosine, tryptophan, and phenylalanine are all measured fluorometrically. Both tyrosine and tryptophan possess aromatic rings that absorb intensely and therefore have an intense natural fluorescence. Tyrosine is excited at both 225 and 280 nm, and emits at 303 nm; tryptophan is excited at 220 and 280 nm and emits at 438 nm [34].

In contrast, phenylalanine possesses a weakly absorbing benzene ring and does not emit fluorescence intensely enough for measurement of trace quantities. The usual analytical methods involve treating it with ninhydrin, copper(II) ion, and L-leucyl-L-alanine [35] to give a highly fluorescent product. Fluorometric measurement of phenylalanine is useful in testing for phenylketonuria, a hereditary metabolic disorder that causes mental retardation. In one series of tests, adult control samples ran 1.5 mg phenylalanine per 100 ml of blood serum; in contrast, parents of phenylketonuriac children ran 1.9 mg per 100 ml, and the phenylketonuriacs themselves ran 30 mg per 100 ml. Since phenylketonuriacs cannot convert phenylalanine efficiently to tyrosine, the levels of tyrosine were about half of those in the blood of control samples.

Advantages and Disadvantages of Fluorescence Analysis

In summary, the two main advantages of fluorescence analysis are that it is capable of measuring much lower concentrations than spectrophotometric analysis (high sensitivity), and that it is potentially more selective because both the excitation and emission wavelengths can be varied. At its best, fluorometric analysis is sensitive to 10^{-8} to 10^{-9} M, depending on the intensity of the source and the quantum efficiency and molar absorptivity of the sample. Where the molar absorptivity or quantum efficiency are small, the source or monochromator can be adjusted to make analysis possible. Such an adjustment is normally not done in absorption spectrophotometry.

Another advantage (also a disadvantage) is that only certain aromatic molecules fluoresce. This excludes from fluorometry all acylic and alicyclic molecules, as well as those aromatic molecules that do not fluoresce. (This is of course an advantage when analyzing a mixture containing a fluorescent aromatic molecule and several acylic or alicyclic molecules.)

Other disadvantages to fluorescence analysis have to do with unwanted excited-state interactions. The principal and most serious disadvantage here is quenching; since many nonfluorescent molecules, even in trace quantities, can quench a fluorescent molecule in the S_1 state, the direct analysis of complex mixtures without separation is uncommon. Secondly, since many organic compounds undergo photochemical reactions when irradiated with ultraviolet light, care must be taken to avoid photodecomposition in making quantitative analytical measurements, particularly with intense sources.

Finally, another general disadvantage to fluorescence analysis is that it does not exhibit very high precision or accuracy; a typical level might be ± 2–10%. Still, the high sensitivity and selectivity of fluorescence analysis make it the method of choice in many instances.

SELECTED BIBLIOGRAPHY

For further reading in the area of recent developments in fluorescence, the reader is referred to the following monographs:

GUILBAULT, G. G., ed. *Fluorescence: Theory, Instrumentation, and Practice.* New York: Marcel Dekker, 1967.

GUILBAULT, G. G. *Practical Fluorescence: Theory, Methods, and Techniques.* New York: Marcel Dekker, 1973.

SCHENK, G. H. *Absorption of Light and Ultraviolet Radiation: Fluorescence and Phosphorescence Emission.* Boston: Allyn and Bacon, 1973.

UDENFRIEND, S. *Fluorescence Assay in Biology and Medicine.* New York: Academic Press, 1962.

WHITE, C. E., and ARGAUER, R. J. *Fluorescence Analysis.* New York: Marcel Dekker, 1970.

For further reading in the area of recent luminescence work in general, the reader is referred to the following monographs:

PARKER, C. A. *Photoluminescence of Solutions.* New York: Elsevier, 1968.

WINEFORDNER, J. D., SCHULMAN, S. G., and O'HAVER, T. C. *Luminescence Spectrometry in Analytical Chemistry.* New York: Wiley-Interscience, 1972.

ZANDER, M. *Phosphorimetry.* New York: Academic Press, 1968.

REFERENCES

1. D. N. HERCULES, ed., *Fluorescence and Phosphorescence Analysis.* New York: Wiley-Interscience, 1966, chap. 1.

2. G. H. SCHENK, *Absorption of Light and Ultraviolet Radiation: Fluorescence and Phosphorescence Emission.* Boston: Allyn and Bacon, 1973, chap. 4.

3. E. LIM, quoted in *J. Chem. Phys., 41,* 3042 (1964).

4. A. L. CONRAD, *Treatise on Analytical Chemistry,* part I, vol. 5. New York: Wiley-Interscience, 1964, pp 3057–78.

5. J. D. WINEFORDNER, in D. M. Hercules, ed., *Fluorescence and Phosphorescence Analysis.* New York: Wiley-Interscience, 1966, pp 169–84.

6. W. J. McCARTHY and J. D. WINEFORDNER, *J. Chem. Educ., 44,* 136 (1967).

7. C. A. PARKER, *Photoluminescence of Solutions.* New York: Elsevier, 1968, pp 220–34.

8. C. W. SILL, *Anal. Chem., 33,* 1584 (1961).

9. G. K. TURNER, *Science, 146,* 183 (1964).

10. C. M. HIMEL and R. T. MAYER, *Anal. Chem., 42,* 130 (1970).

11. C. I. MILES and G. H. SCHENK, *Anal. Chem., 45,* 130 (1973).

12. C. I. MILES and G. H. SCHENK, *Anal. Lett.*, *4*, 71 (1971); and *Anal. Chem.*, *45*, 130 (1973).

13. L. A. GIFFORD, W. P. HAYES, L. A. KING, J. N. MILLER, D. T. BURNS, and J. W. BRIDES, *Anal. Chim. Acta*, *62*, 214 (1972); *Anal. Chem.*, *46*, 94 (1974).

14. C. I. MILES and G. H. SCHENK, *Anal. Chem.*, *42*, 656 (1970).

15. J. D. WINEFORDNER and H. W. LATZ, *Anal. Chem.*, *35*, 1517 (1963).

16. F. E. LYTLE, *Appl. Spec.*, *24*, 319 (1970).

17. W. A. ARMSTRONG, D. W. GRANT, and W. G. HUMPHREYS, *Anal. Chem.*, *35*, 1300 (1963).

18. C. W. SILL and H. E. PETERSON, *Anal. Chem.*, *21*, 1266 (1949).

19. G. F. KIRKBRIGHT, T. S. WEST and C. WOODWARD, *Talanta*, *12*, 517 (1965).

20. C. E. WHITE and R. J. ARGAUER, *Fluorescence Analysis*. New York: Marcel Dekker, 1970.

21. W. E. OHNESORGE, in D. M. Hercules, ed., *Fluorescence and Phosphorescence Analysis*. New York: Wiley-Interscience, 1966, chap. 4.

22. D. W. FINK and W. E. OHNESORGE, *Anal. Chem.*, *41*, 39 (1969).

23. D. W. FINK and W. E. OHNESORGE, *J. Amer. Chem. Soc.*, *91*, 4995 (1969).

24. G. A. THOMMES and E. LEININGER, *Talanta*, *7*, 181 (1961).

25. G. H. SCHENK, F. BOYER, C. I. MILES, and D. R. WIRZ, *Anal. Chem.*, *44*, 1593 (1972).

26. E. SAWICKI, W. ELBERT, T. W. STANLEY, T. R. HAUSER, and F. T. FOX, *Anal. Chem.*, *32*, 810 (1960).

27. H. V. DRUSHEL and A. L. SOMMERS, *Anal. Chem.*, *38*, 10, 19 (1966).

28. E. SAWICKI and J. D. PFAFF, *Anal. Chim. Acta*, *32*, 521 (1965).

29. M. S. LEFAR and A. D. LEWIS, *Anal. Chem.*, *42*(3), 79A (1970).

30. D. JANCHEN and G. PATAKI, *J. Chromatogr.*, *33*, 391 (1968).

31. J. D. WINEFORDNER and H. A. MOYE, *Anal. Chim. Acta*, *32*, 278 (1965).

32. G. K. TURNER, *Fluorometry Reviews Bulletin on Fluorescent Tracers*, Feb. 1968, Acc. No. 9941.

33. E. SAWICKI, W. ELBERT, T. W. STANLEY, T. R. HAUSER, and F. T. FOX, *Int. J. Air Poll.*, *2*, 273 (1960).

34. F. W. J. TEAL and G. WEBER, *Biochem. J.*, *65*, 476 (1957).

35. P. K. WONG, *Clin. Chem.*, *10*, 1098 (1964).

PROBLEMS

1. (a) Draw a molecular-energy diagram similar to Figure 9.2 for the uranyl (UO_2^{2+}) ion, assuming that the transition in the 225–250 nm region is S_0-S_2 and the transition in the 417 nm region is S_0-S_1. (b) Repeat part (a), assuming instead that the transition in the 225–250 nm region is S_0-S_1 and the transition in the 417-nm region is S_0-T_1. Will the emission be fluorescence or phosphorescence?

2. Draw a molecular-energy diagram showing the transitions involved in the phosphorescence of anthracene, which occurs at 680 nm.

3. Show that each side of Equation 9.8 has the proper units.

4. Compare the slope of a calibration curve for a molecule with a molar absorptivity of 10^5 and a quantum efficiency of 0.01 with that for a molecule having a molar absorptivity of 10^3 and a quantum efficiency of 0.10.

5. Propose two different spectrofluorometric schemes of analysis for the determination of anthracene in phenanthrene, giving all wavelengths. (Only one scheme should use selective excitation of anthracene.)

6. Propose two different filter-fluorometric schemes of analysis for the determination of anthracene in the presence of naphthalene; the schemes must involve two different mercury sources. Assume that $\varepsilon c \phi_f$ for naphthalene is less than 1% that of anthracene at any excitation wavelength employed.

7. Explain what instrumental difficulties might be involved in the filter-fluorometric analysis of acetylsalicylic acid in the presence of a large excess of salicylic acid. Would a spectrofluorometer be superior? Why or why not?

8. A bottle of tonic water is to be analyzed for its quinine content by fluorescence spectrometry, with excitation at 350 nm and emission intensity measured at 450 nm. One milliliter of tonic water is diluted to 100 ml with 0.05 M H_2SO_4; its emission intensity is 8.44 (arbitrary units). A series of quinine standards, in 0.05 M H_2SO_4, is prepared and the emission intensities measured (in parentheses): 100 ppm (293 units), 10.0 ppm (52.3), 1.00 ppm (12.0), 0.100 ppm (1.26), 10 ppb (0.158), and 1.0 ppb (0.015). The emission intensity of 0.05 M H_2SO_4 is negligible. Plot the calibration curve for quinine fluorescence, and determine the quinine content of the original tonic-water sample.

9. Two urine specimens from patients undergoing quinine therapy for malaria are to be analyzed for their quinine level. The following samples are run through the analytical procedure: A. a distilled water blank; B. a standard containing 2.00 μg quinine/ml in distilled water; C. a "blank" urine, which contains no quinine; D. urine specimen #1; and E. urine specimen #2. Two milliliters are taken from each sample, their pH is raised to 9 with concentrated ammonium hydroxide, and they are extracted with 4.00 ml of chloroform. Two milliliters of the chloroform extract is extracted with 2.00 ml of 0.05 M H_2SO_4, which is then placed in a fluorescence cuvette and the fluorescence intensity at 450 nm is determined. The relative emission intensities for the five samples are: A. 1.7; B. 50.2; C. 14.3; D. 82.8; and E. 58.7. Assuming that the emission intensity is directly proportional to the quinine concentration (once allowance has been made for the two "blank" emissions), determine the quinine level in the urine specimens.

10. An organic compound is to be determined by fluorescence spectrometry, with a choice of excitation at 250 nm (with emission at 350 nm) or at 500 nm (600-nm emission). A xenon-arc lamp is to be used as the excitation source of a spectrofluorometer (see Fig. 9.4C, p 236), with an S-5 photomultiplier tube as the detector (see Fig. 10.8, p 267). The compound has a molar absorptivity of 15,000 at 250 nm and of 4,000 at 500 nm. Assume that the quantum efficiencies for fluorescence are the same at the two wavelengths. (a) From this information and that in Figures 9.4C and 10.8, estimate the ratio of the signal obtained with excitation at 250 nm to that with excitation at 500 nm. (b) What other assumptions have to be made?

11. Describe the principles of phosphorescence. Why are phosphorescence measurements frequently made at liquid nitrogen temperatures?

10

Flame Spectroscopy

GARY D. CHRISTIAN

In this chapter, the spectroscopy of atoms will be discussed. Since free atoms cannot undergo rotational or vibrational transitions as do molecules, only electronic transitions can take place when energy is absorbed or emitted. Because the transitions are discrete (quantized), line spectra are observed.

There are various ways of obtaining free atoms and measuring the radiation they absorb or emit. This chapter will deal with flame spectroscopic and related techniques. The next chapter will describe emission spectroscopic methods using electrical excitation.

In flame spectroscopy, a solution is aspirated into a flame and the inorganic compounds thermally dissociated into atomic vapor. There are three types of flame spectroscopy: atomic absorption, atomic emission, and atomic fluorescence. The first two techniques will be emphasized because commercial instruments are widely available for these, whereas atomic fluorescence is used more for specific applications and as a research tool. Many of the points made with respect to flame chemistry, interferences, and so forth apply also to atomic fluorescence. Various types of atomic fluorescence and the specific instrumentation required are considered at the end of the chapter.

10.1 PRINCIPLES

When a solution is aspirated into a flame, the heat of the flame first causes the solvent to evaporate. The microcrystals remaining are partially or wholly dissociated into elements in the gaseous form (atomization). Some of these atoms can absorb radiant energy of a characteristic wavelength and become excited to a higher electronic state; or, they may absorb energy from the flame and become thermally excited.

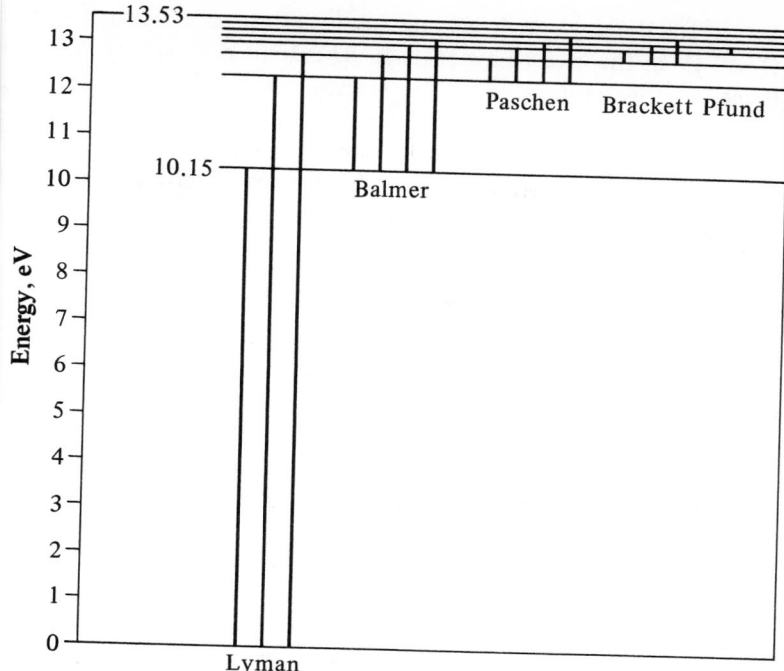

FIGURE 10.1.   *Energy-level diagram for hydrogen.*

The atoms lose their excitation energy either as heat by collision with other atoms, or as radiation of a characteristic wavelength as the electron returns to a lower excited state or to the ground state.   The absorption of thermal energy from a flame with subsequent emission of some or all of the energy as a spectral line is called *atomic emission*.   Measurement of this emitted radiation is known as *atomic emission spectroscopy* or *flame emission spectroscopy* [1]; we will use the first term.

The term *atomic absorption* refers to the absorption of energy from a light source, with a consequent decrease in the radiant power transmitted through the flame. Measurement of this absorption corresponds to *atomic absorption spectroscopy.*

In order to better understand the physical basis of atomic absorption, let us consider the hydrogen atom.   In the hydrogen atom, the electron can exist in several well defined and quantized energy states, as shown on the energy-level diagram in Figure 10.1.*   The lowest energy state is arbitrarily put at zero on the energy scale.   The other energy levels, calibrated relative to this ground state, are represented by the horizontal bars on the diagram.

---

* The names on the series of lines refer to the discoverers of the different series.   The series are described accurately by Balmer's law:

$$\frac{1}{\lambda} = R\left(\frac{1}{n^2} - \frac{1}{m^2}\right)$$

where R is a constant (109,677.58 cm^{-1}), and n and m are integers ($m > n$).   The Balmer series, for example, corresponds to $n = 2$, and $m = 1, 2, 3, \ldots$.   The Lyman series is $n = 1$, the Paschen series is $n = 3$, the Brackett series is $n = 4$, and the Pfund series is $n = 5$.

The diagram indicates that states do not occur beyond a definite energy level (13.53 eV in the case of hydrogen). This limit is called the *ionization potential* and is the "energy level" at which the electron has left the influence of the nucleus.

The vertical lines on the diagram indicate some of the possible transitions the electron can make from one energy level to another. Each transition requires either a gain or a loss of energy equal to the difference between the two energy levels. If this energy is in the form of radiation, it is given by

$$E_u - E_l = h\nu = h\frac{c}{\lambda} \qquad (10.1)$$

where E_u = the energy of the upper energy state
 E_l = the energy of the lower energy state

The majority of atoms in a flame are in the ground state (E_0); therefore, many electronic transitions originate from this state. Such transitions are limited in number, since by quantum-mechanical selection rules some energy levels are not directly accessible from the ground state.

Usually, a *resonance wavelength* is defined as the wavelength corresponding to a transition between the ground state and the next accessible level. Here, the term will be used more broadly to include all transitions originating from the ground state. These are the transitions of most interest for the present purpose, because they represent the wavelengths at which absorption or emission is strongest and is usually measured.

The partial energy-level diagrams for lithium, sodium, and potassium are illustrated (in a slightly different form) in Figure 10.2. The dashed lines represent the respective ionization potentials of the elements. Only the major resonance transitions are shown. (Sodium, for example, has over twenty allowed transitions.) The primary resonance lines for these elements are the 671-nm red lithium doublet, the 590-nm sodium doublet, and the 767/769-nm potassium doublet.* Absorption is strongest at these three wavelengths and is followed in intensity by the lines originating in the ground state and ending in a higher excited state. Absorption lines are also observed that arise from transitions involving two excited states. Analytical advantage can be taken of these different absorption intensities for measuring different concentration ranges of a metal, because each absorption line has a different sensitivity.

Figure 10.3 illustrates energy changes in a simple system. The electron has been excited from the ground state to an excited state by the absorption of a quantum of light whose energy is equal to the energy difference between the two states. Within a short time, about 10^{-14} to 10^{-7} sec, the electron is *deactivated* by one of several processes. For instance, it may spontaneously revert to the ground state by emitting a quantum of radiation of the same wavelength as was absorbed (i.e., it fluoresces— cf. Chap. 9). Since this radiation is emitted in all directions, the amount entering

---

* Doublets and higher-order multiplets arise owing to spin (of the valence electrons involved in spectral transitions) which is associated with orbital motion. That is, the spin quantum number, s, may have the value of $+1/2$ or $-1/2$, and so there exist two energy levels for the electron. The occurrence of doublets and multiplets is limited by selection rules (i.e., there are certain forbidden transitions) and by the number of valence electrons.

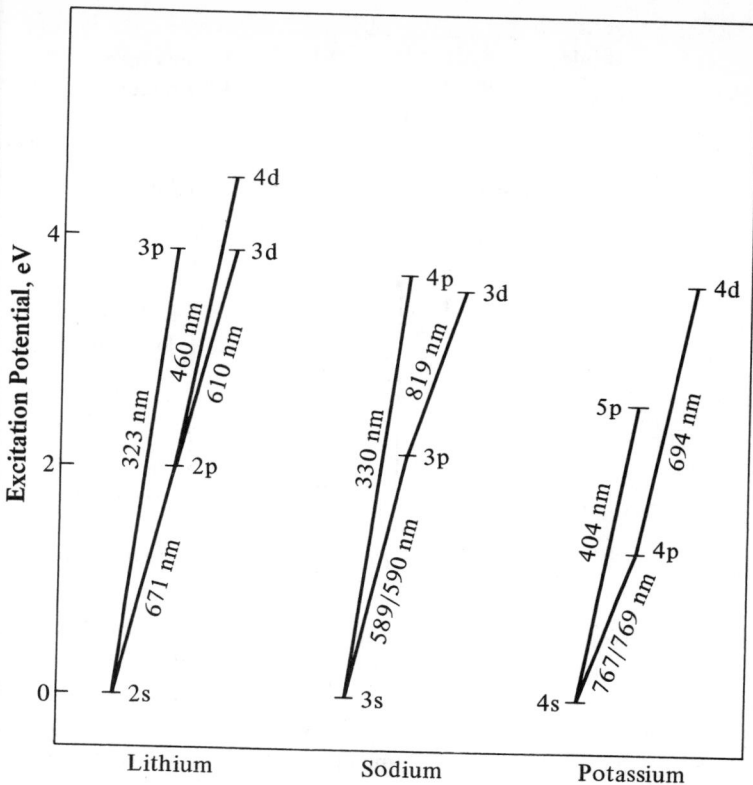

FIGURE 10.2. *Partial energy-level diagrams for lithium, sodium, and potassium. Adapted from G. D. Christian and F. J. Feldman,* Atomic Absorption Spectroscopy: Applications in Agriculture, Biology, and Medicine, *New York: Wiley-Interscience, 1970, p 8, by permission of John Wiley and Sons.*

the monochromator-detector stage of the instrument being used is generally negligible compared to the amount absorbed, and usually does not interfere with the absorption measurement.

Of the other possible methods of deactivation or "energy relaxation," the most common is *quenching*, or radiationless deactivation. This occurs when another atom interacts with the excited atom. The energy of the excited electron is converted into an increase in the kinetic energy of the two atoms; that is, it is usually lost as heat.

A combination of radiation deactivation and radiationless deactivation may occur with a given atomic species if there is another state between the excited state and the ground state. The electron may revert to this intermediate state by emitting radiation of a different wavelength; the wavelength will be longer than that of the radiation absorbed since it corresponds to a smaller amount of energy. The electron may then proceed to the ground state by radiationless deactivation.

The energy required to excite an electron from the ground state may also be acquired thermally, i.e., from collision with other atoms, or with molecules, ions,

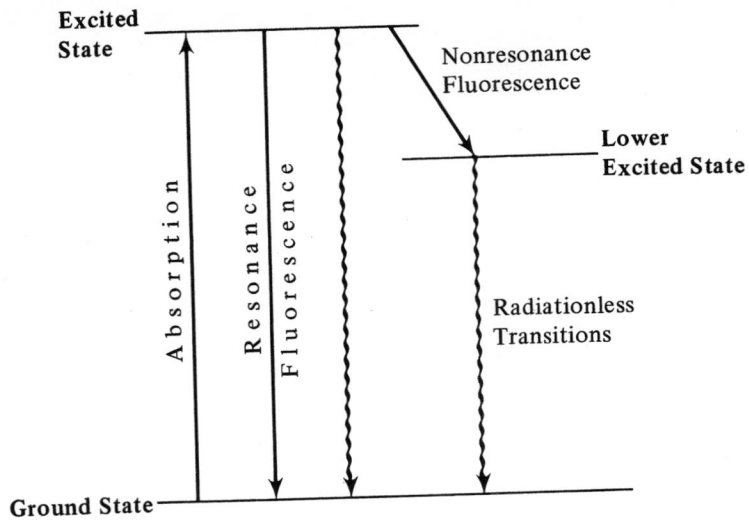

FIGURE 10.3. *Energy changes in a simple system.*

or free electrons present in the flame. Deactivation by emitting a photon following thermal excitation is termed *atomic emission*. For excitation to occur, the flame temperature must be sufficiently high to produce the electronic transition; for this reason, only those elements with long-wavelength (low-energy) emission resonance lines generally exhibit intense flame emission in a relatively cool flame.

10.2 THEORY

It is of interest to know the number of thermally excited atoms relative to the number of ground state atoms at a given flame temperature. In a quantity of atoms, under the same external conditions, the electrons are not all in the same energy level but are statistically distributed among the levels. At a flame temperature T (in K), the ratio of the number of atoms N_u in an excited (upper) state u to the number of atoms N_0 in the ground state is given by the Maxwell-Boltzmann expression

$$\frac{N_u}{N_0} = \frac{g_u}{g_0} e^{-(E_u - E_0)/kT} \tag{10.2}$$

The excited state has energy E_u and the ground state has energy E_0; g_u and g_0 are the *statistical weights* of the excited and ground states, respectively, and k is the Boltzmann constant. The statistical weights can be regarded as the probability that an electron will reside in a given energy level, and can be obtained from quantum-mechanical calculations. Equation 10.2 permits calculation of the ratio (N_u/N_0) at a given flame temperature when the frequency or wavelength for the transition is known. Some typical values are given in Table 10.1.

The statistical weights, g, can be calculated from the equation $g = 2J + 1$, where J is the Russel-Saunders coupling and is equal to $L + S$ or $L - S$. L is the total orbital angular momentum quantum number, represented by the sharp (S),

TABLE 10.1.   *Values of N_u/N_0 for Different Resonance Lines*

Resonance lines (nm)	Excitation energy (eV)	g_u/g_0	N_u/N_0		
			2000 K	3000 K	4000 K
Cs 852.1	1.46	2	4.44×10^{-4}	7.24×10^{-3}	2.98×10^{-2}
Na 589.0	2.11	2	9.86×10^{-6}	5.88×10^{-4}	4.44×10^{-3}
Ca 422.7	2.93	3	1.21×10^{-7}	3.69×10^{-5}	6.04×10^{-4}
Zn 213.8	5.80	3	7.29×10^{-15}	5.38×10^{-10}	1.48×10^{-6}

principal (P), diffuse (D), and fundamental (F) series ($L = 0, 1, 2$, and 3, respectively); S is spin, $\pm 1/2$. The information is generally supplied in the form of *term symbols*, which have the general form $N^M L_J$, where N is the principal quantum number and M is the multiplicity. Hence, the transition for the cesium 852.1-nm line, omitting the principal quantum number N is $^2 S_{1/2} - {}^2 P_{3/2}$, and $g_u/g_0 = [2(3/2) + 1]/[2(1/2) + 1] = 4/2 = 2$.

Example 10.1.   The 228.8-nm cadmium line corresponds to a $^1 S_0 - {}^1 S_1$ transition. Calculate the ratio of N_u/N_0 in an air-acetylene flame.

Solution: The temperature (Table 10.2, p 271) is 2250°C or 2523 K.

$$g_u/g_0 = [2(1) + 1]/[2(0) + 1] = 3/1.$$

$$\nu = \frac{c}{\lambda} = \frac{2.998 \times 10^{10} \text{ cm/sec}}{2.288 \times 10^{-5} \text{ cm}} = 1.310 \times 10^{15} \text{ sec}^{-1}$$

$$E_u - E_0 = h\nu = (6.626 \times 10^{-27} \text{ erg-sec})(1.310 \times 10^{15} \text{ sec}^{-1})$$
$$= 8.682 \times 10^{-12} \text{ erg}$$

$$\frac{N_u}{N_0} = \frac{g_u}{g_0} e^{-(E_u - E_0)/kT}$$

$$= \frac{3}{1} \exp \left[-\frac{8.682 \times 10^{-12} \text{ erg}}{(1.3805 \times 10^{-16} \text{ erg K}^{-1})(2523 \text{ K})} \right]$$

$$= 3e^{-24.93} = 4.5 \times 10^{-11}$$

The hottest flames generally used in atomic absorption and emission spectroscopy rarely reach temperatures of 4000 K. It is apparent from the data in Table 10.1 that even at the highest temperature, the excited-state population is very small in comparison to the ground-state population. This is true even for the relatively easily excited alkali metals, which are readily determined by atomic emission spectroscopy. Elements such as zinc show poor sensitivity by atomic emission because an extremely small number of the atoms is thermally excited.

Why, then, do the alkali metals exhibit good sensitivity by atomic emission spectroscopy? The answer is that one measures the difference between a theoretically zero signal in the absence of the sample and a finite signal in the presence of the sample. Therefore, the small signal arising from the sample can be readily amplified and measured. The limit of detection is governed by the noise level of the photomultiplier detector, primarily the "shot-noise" (the random fluctuation of the electron current from any electron-emitting surface in a phototube), and by the fact that the atomic emission signal may be superimposed on an intense and noisy flame spectrum.

In absorption methods, as distinguished from emission methods, one measures the difference between two finite signals with similar noise levels, and so the measurable signal decrease is governed by the noise level of these two signals. In absorption methods, the flame spectrum (a DC signal) can be effectively removed by modulating the radiation source and using an AC-sensitive detection system.

Some other conclusions can be drawn from the data in Table 10.1. First, note that the relative fraction of atoms in the excited state is very dependent on temperature: a small temperature variation can be expected to have a marked effect on the emission signal. Fortunately, flame temperatures can be adequately controlled so that precise atomic-emission measurements can be made. On the other hand, the total number of ground-state atoms (neglecting ionization and compound-formation effects discussed below) is in principle independent of the temperature. Many elements partially react with flame gases to form molecular oxide and hydroxide species (which do not absorb the resonance lines), the extent of the reaction being temperature-dependent; so atomic absorption in practice is essentially as temperature-dependent as atomic emission. A second conclusion is that since most atoms reside in the ground state, absorption is greatest for lines resulting from transitions originating in the ground state—that is, for the resonance lines.

The strongest absorption line does not necessarily correspond to the most sensitive emission line. The strength of either an absorption or an emission signal is governed by the number of absorbing atoms or emitting atoms plus a quantity known as the *oscillator strength*.* In addition, emission intensity is influenced by the spectral region involved—electrons require more thermal energy for shorter-wavelength emission than for longer. In practice, the strongest absorption line is always at a shorter wavelength than the strongest emission line, when the two do not coincide.

A third conclusion to draw from the data in Table 10.1 is that the intensity of emission will vary markedly from one element to another because the relative number of thermally excited atoms varies significantly for the different elements. Atomic absorption, on the other hand, should exhibit more uniform sensitivity for a large number of elements, except for large differences in oscillator strengths. This is true, provided that all the elements can be efficiently converted to atomic vapor.

Relationship Between Atomic Absorption and Concentration

Atomic absorption follows an exponential law for the intensity of transmitted light as a function of the path length b, similar to Lambert's law in molecular spectrophotometry:

$$P = P_0 e^{-k_v b} \tag{10.3}$$

The absorption coefficient k_v characterizes the intensity of an absorption line. It is

---

* The oscillator strength f is an expression of the intensity of a spectral line and represents the probability that an atom will undergo an electronic transition in unit time and absorb or emit a photon.

proportional to the number of absorbing atoms and hence to the solution concentration. It is also proportional to the oscillator strength.

For analytical purposes, the *absorbance A* is the parameter measured.

$$A = \log(P_0/P) = k_\nu b \log e = 0.434 k_\nu b \qquad (10.4)$$

In other words, the absorbance is directly proportional to the absorption coefficient, and therefore to the solution concentration.

One needs to distinguish between the terms *sensitivity* and *detection limit* as used in the atomic absorption literature. Sensitivity is defined as the concentration that gives an *absorption* of 1% (or an *absorbance A* of 0.0044); it is a measure of the absolute signal expected under a given set of conditions, but says nothing about the noise level. Nevertheless, sensitivity is frequently within an order of magnitude of the detection limit, which is typically defined as the concentration that gives a signal twice the root-mean-square (rms) noise level, or twice the standard deviation of the noise.

Broadening of Spectral Lines

Spectral lines are not truly monochromatic or infinitely narrow. Line widths are usually described in terms of half-width, the width of the line profile at half-height (see Fig. 10.6 for a typical line profile). Lines can be broadened by a number of factors. In a flame, an absorption- or emission-line profile is governed almost entirely by the combined effect of *natural broadening, Doppler broadening,* and *collisional broadening.* The first is the result of the finite amount of time that atoms spend in the energy levels between which transitions take place; the second is due to the random thermal motion of the atoms relative to the observer (the detector); and the last is due to interaction or collision of the absorbing or emitting atoms with other molecules or atoms, for example, those of the flame gases.

Natural broadening is generally very small compared to Doppler and collisional broadening, Doppler broadening dominating at the center of the line and collisional broadening dominating at the wings (edges) of the line. Broadening can have a small effect on the sensitivity of atomic-absorption measurements in which the absorption of the center of the line is measured. For most elements at 2000–3000 K, the total half-width of the resonance lines is on the order of 0.002 nm (0.02 Å), although some may be an order of magnitude wider.

10.3 INSTRUMENTATION

Atomic-absorption and atomic-emission spectrophotometers both require an atomizer, a monochromator, and a detector. Atomic absorption requires, in addition, a radiation source.

Radiation Sources

The two principal means of making atomic-absorption measurements are those employing a continuum source and those employing a line radiation-source. A continuum

FIGURE 10.4. *Schematic diagram of a hollow-cathode lamp.*

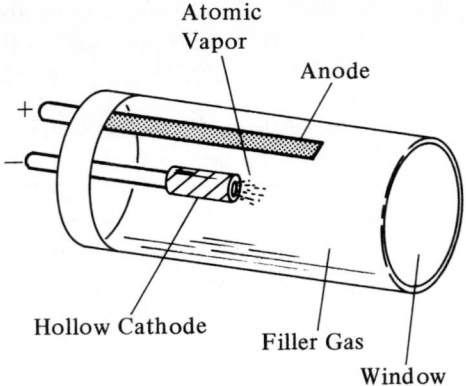

Atomic Vapor

Anode

+

−

Hollow Cathode

Filler Gas

Window

source such as a xenon-arc lamp is rather limited in application because of factors to be considered below; in practice, line sources are used almost exclusively.

The most commonly used (line) source in atomic absorption is the *hollow-cathode lamp.* Figure 10.4 is a schematic representation of such a lamp. In the back of the lamp is a hollow cathode made out of the element to be analyzed or an alloy containing that element. The open end of the cathode faces the anode (generally a tungsten wire, ring, or disc) and the window of the lamp, which is constructed of borosilicate glass or, if ultraviolet radiation is measured, quartz. The lamp is filled under reduced pressure with an inert gas, usually argon or neon, and a sufficient potential is applied across the electrodes to cause a current of from 1 to 50 mA to flow. The potential ionizes the inert gas at the anode and accelerates it at a high velocity to the cathode, where it hits and causes metal atoms to "sputter" out of the cathode. Further collisions with the free atoms then produce excited metal atoms which, upon deactivation, emit the spectrum of the cathode material. (The spectrum of the filler gas is also emitted by gas atoms struck by the accelerated ions.)

The intensity of the radiation emitted will increase with increased current—

FIGURE 10.5. *Intensity of two copper spectral lines as a function of hollow-cathode lamp current. Courtesy of Westinghouse Electric Corporation.*

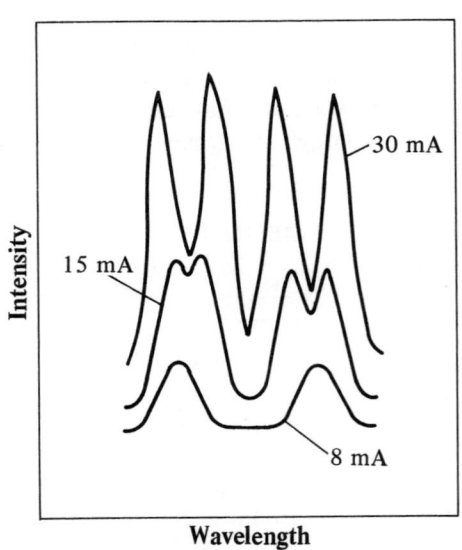

Intensity

30 mA

15 mA

8 mA

Wavelength

up to a point. At too high a current, Doppler broadening and self-absorption (absorption of part of the emitted radiation by the dense cloud of atoms in the source itself) will occur, with the result that the center of the line (the portion absorbed by the test element) will be decreased in intensity while the wings broaden out (see Fig. 10.5). Although, in principle, line intensity will not affect the absorbance measured, line broadening will. Therefore, an operating current should be chosen that, while avoiding broadening, is high enough to give good lamp stability and signal-to-noise ratio.

A sharp-line source and a continuum source are compared in Figure 10.6. Figure 10.6A illustrates the absorption of light from a line source. The source line and the absorption line are at the same wavelength, but the half-width of the source $(\Delta\lambda_s)$ is narrower than that of the absorption line $(\Delta\lambda_a)$ because temperatures and pressures are lower in the source than in the flame. Therefore, the entire center of the source line is absorbed in accordance with Beer's law.

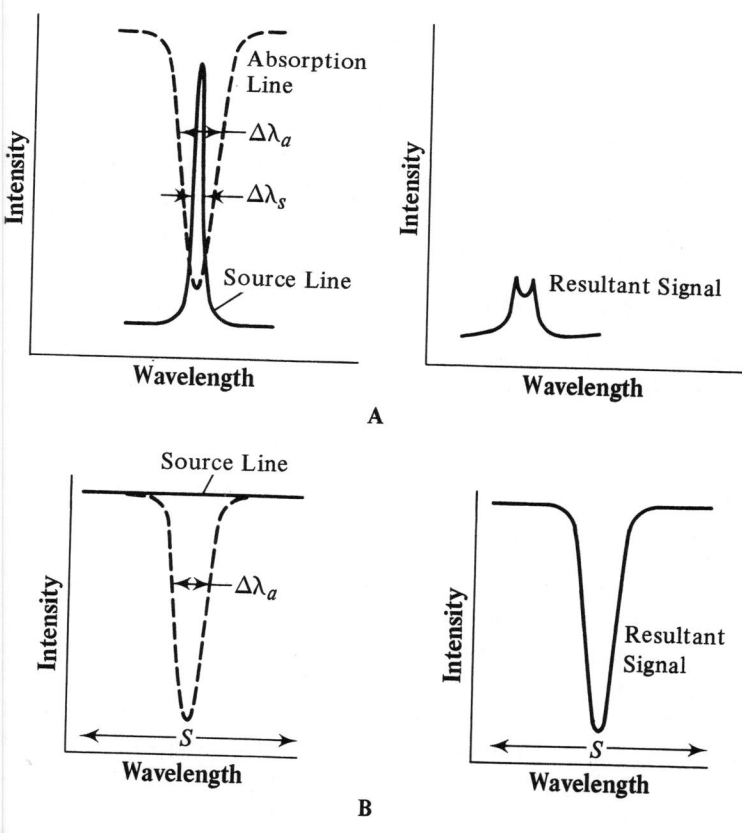

FIGURE 10.6. *Atomic absorption with (A) a sharp-line source and (B) a spectral-continuum source.* $\Delta\lambda_a$ = *absorption line half-width;* $\Delta\lambda_s$ = *source line half-width; S = spectral bandwidth of monochromator. Adapted from G. D. Christian and F. J. Feldman,* Atomic Absorption Spectroscopy: Applications in Agriculture, Biology, and Medicine, *New York: Wiley-Interscience, 1970, p 58, by permission of John Wiley and Sons.*

Figure 10.6B shows the situation for a continuum source. In this case, only a small fraction of the band of radiation passed by the monochromator is absorbed (even very good monochromators pass a band of radiation on the order of 0.1 Å wide), and a large portion of unabsorbed light falls on the detector. This results in decreased sensitivity (absorbance) and a nonlinear plot of absorbance versus concentration. Figure 10.7 illustrates the difference between calibration curves for line and continuum sources.

FIGURE 10.7. *Comparison of absorption from continuum and sharp-line sources.*

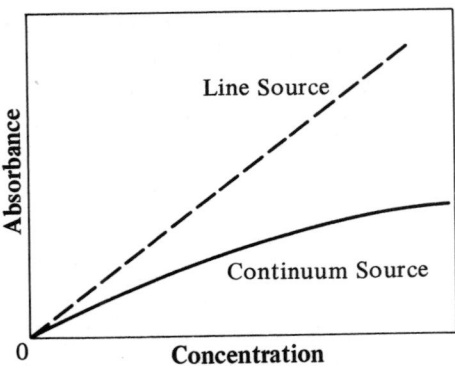

Linearity and sensitivity using a continuum source will of course be improved as the bandpass of the monochromator (and hence the band of unabsorbed radiation) is narrowed; however, this results in a loss of source intensity and an increased noise level as more gain is required on the detector. In order to approach the sensitivity of a line source, resolution beyond the capabilities of ordinary spectrophotometers would be required.

Monochromators and Detectors

In atomic absorption, the *ratio* of signals is measured with and without absorption. In flame emission, however, the signal intensity is measured directly superimposed on a flame background. For these reasons, the exit-slit adjustment, radiation-detector quality, and so forth are generally less critical in absorption methods than in emission methods.

The major requirement for a monochromator in atomic-absorption measurements is that it has the ability to separate the selected resonance-absorption line from other lines emitted by the source. Although overlap of absorption lines (that is, between two different elements) can occur, this is relatively rare.

Atomic-absorption and emission lines occur in the ultraviolet and visible regions, so a monochromator for either technique should be a general-purpose ultraviolet-visible instrument. Detectors are generally photomultiplier tubes. The most commonly used photomultiplier is the RCA 1P28 tube or the equivalent with an S-5 response curve (Fig. 10.8). This functions well over a broad range of the ultraviolet-visible region (approximately 200–650 nm). For the short-wavelength ultraviolet region below about 200 nm, it may be necessary to use an R106 PM tube which gives about 10-fold better response, whereas in the red region of the visible spectrum, a tube with an S-1 response is preferred.

Atomic-absorption instruments may be either single or double beam. Mono-

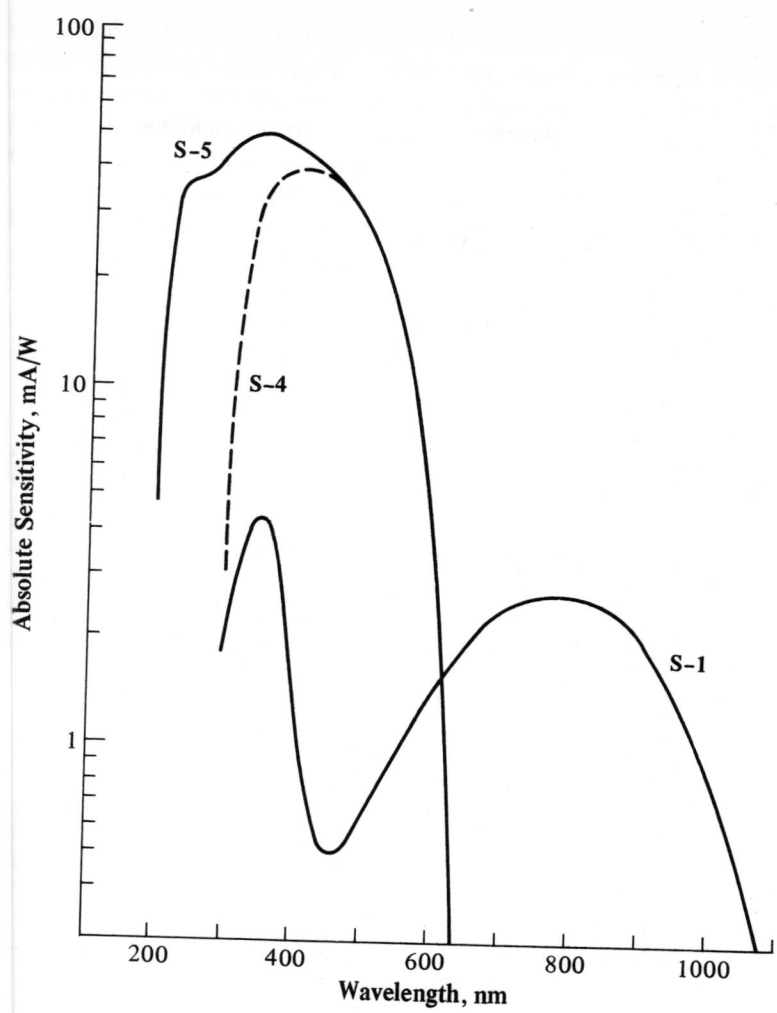

FIGURE 10.8. *Some spectral responses of photomultipliers.* *S-5* = *RCA* 1P28, *S-1* = *RCA* 7102, *S-4* = *RCA* 1P21.

chromator slit-width and photomultiplier-tube voltage will have little effect on most atomic-absorption signals, since a ratio of P/P_0 is recorded; but increasing either one will result in increased emission signals, since either more light enters the mono-chromator, or what light passes it is amplified more in the photomultiplier. However, the noise level will also be increased and an increased signal-to-noise ratio may not result. With some atomic-absorption light sources, such as nickel or cobalt, a non-absorbed line falls close to the resonance absorption line, causing decreased sensi-tivity and nonlinearity of calibration curves. In these cases, decreased slit width will increase the resolution of the absorbed line from the nonabsorbed line, improving sensitivity and linearity.

Instruments designed specifically for the atomic-emission determination of alkali metals (commonly found in clinical chemistry laboratories) may contain simply a single interference filter as the monochromator and a vacuum phototube as the detector. These instruments employ low-temperature flames in which only the most prominent lines of the elements appear. Frequently, a two-filter, two-detector arrangement is employed for making internal-standard measurements; lithium, for example, may be used as an internal standard for sodium measurements. A constant amount of lithium is added to all samples and standards, and the ratio of the intensities of the sodium line and the lithium line is recorded. Such a measurement minimizes the effects of fluctuations in the aspiration rate, flame temperature, and so forth, since the test element and the internal-standard element (if similar enough chemically) should be influenced in the same way, causing the ratio of their spectral intensities to be constant at given concentrations [2].

Burners

The nebulizer and burner system is probably the most important component of the atomic-absorption or emission spectrophotometer, because it is imperative that neutral (un-ionized) atoms of the test element be presented to the optical system. When the sample solution passes into the flame, it must be in the form of small droplets. The process of breaking down a solution into a fine spray is known as *nebulization*. Nebulization is generally carried out with the support or oxidant gas.

There are two major types of nebulizer burners, illustrated in Figures 10.9

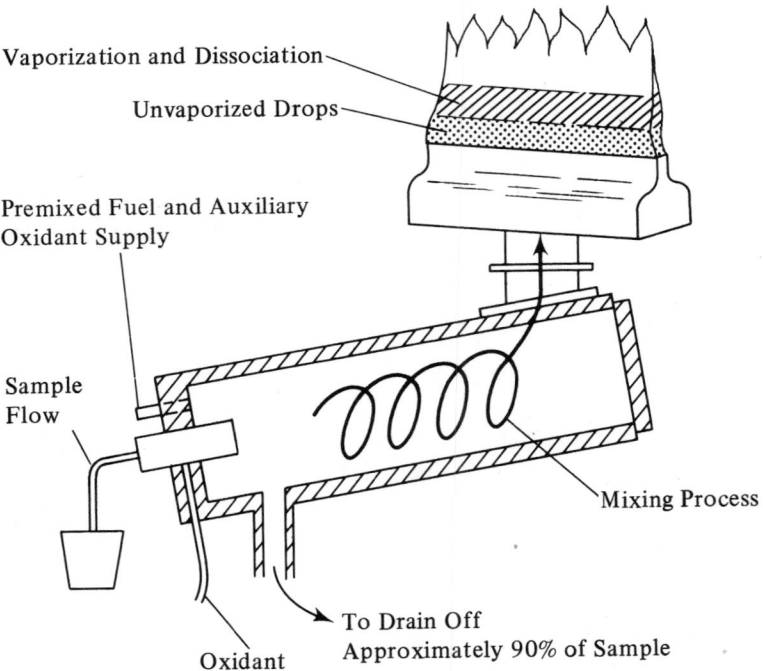

FIGURE 10.9. *Premix nebulizer-burner system. Adapted from G. D. Christian and F. J. Feldman,* Atomic Absorption Spectroscopy: Applications in Agriculture, Biology, and Medicine, *New York: Wiley-Interscience,* 1970, p 80, *by permission of John Wiley and Sons.*

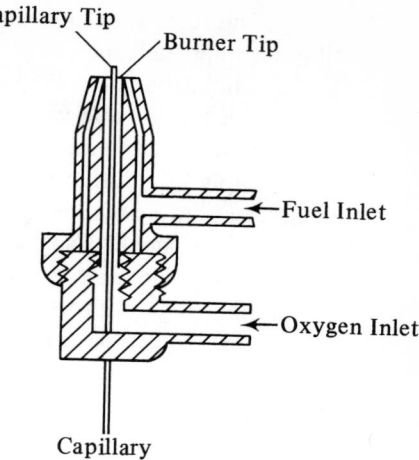

FIGURE 10.10. *Total-consumption burner.*
Courtesy of Beckman Instruments, Inc.

and 10.10. In the first, liquid is sprayed into a mixing chamber where the droplets are mixed with the combustion gas. This process is called indirect nebulization, and the arrangement is known as the premixed chamber or laminar-flow burner system. In the second type of arrangement, the nebulizer and burner are combined. Nebulization takes place at the burner tip where the combustion gas is mixed with the support gas. The sample aerosol passes directly into the flame. These units are called direct-sprayer burners, total-consumption burners, or turbulent-flow burners.

In the premix burner, the sample is drawn up through the capillary by the decreased pressure created by the expanding oxidant gas at the end of the capillary (the Venturi effect), and is broken into fine droplets. The drops are turbulently mixed with additional oxidant and fuel and then pass into a burner head and out into the flame. Larger droplets condense out and go down the drain.

The total-consumption burner operates essentially as an ordinary pneumatic nebulizer. The oxidizing gas enters the burner through the aspirating gas inlet at a fairly high pressure, about 20–35 psi. It is directed around the capillary aspirator tip where the velocity of the gas produces a Venturi effect, drawing the sample into the stream. The fuel gas, in turn, is directed around the oxidizing stream and mixed with the oxidant and sample, and aids in breaking up the sample. The flame burns at the top of the burner.

In a typical nebulizer, liquid droplets will be produced with particle sizes ranging from a few micrometers in diameter to several hundred micrometers. The majority of droplets have a diameter of 5 to 10 μm, but most of the sample volume is contained in droplets 20 μm or greater in diameter. Whereas in a turbulent burner all droplets will enter the flame, in a premix burner the larger droplets may never reach the flame at all. Particles larger than 10 to 20 μm are either used inefficiently in the flame or are deposited on the premix chamber walls and flow out the drain tube. From 85 to 90% of the sample literally goes down the drain. However, the 10 or 15% that does reach the flame is of fairly small and uniform particle size and is quite efficiently atomized (converted to atomic vapor). The larger particles in a turbulent burner are less efficiently atomized and may never even have time to be desolvated. These particles will scatter the source radiation in atomic-absorption measurements, thus increasing the noise level.

The surface tension and, to a lesser extent, the viscosity of the sample solution are important factors in nebulization efficiency, since work must be performed in the nebulization step to overcome these properties of the liquid. For this reason, the surface tension and viscosity should be maintained as nearly identical as possible in samples and standards. With reasonably concentrated solutions, this can be done quite simply by diluting the test solution. With less concentrated solutions, it may be necessary to match the matrix composition of samples and standards. Concentrated solutions should also be diluted to avoid encrustation of salts on the nebulizer and burner. The same is true when handling heterogeneous systems such as colloids or solutions high in protein content.

One danger in using a premix burner is that certain gas mixtures may detonate (explode) in the chamber, especially when oxygen is used as the support gas. This occurs when the flame front propagates with a speed greater than normal gas-rise speeds. The burning velocity of the O_2-H_2 flame, for example, is 2180 cm/sec and that of the O_2-C_2H_2 flame is 2920 cm/sec. (These compare with speeds of a few tens or hundreds of cm/sec for the commonly used air-supported premix flames!) In the case of detonating flames, the gases obviously cannot be mixed before they are fed into the burner, so a turbulent-flow burner must be used. The turbulent-flow burner is inherently safer than premix burners because flashback is impossible. (The flame will, however, "pop" if it is extinguished by turning off the fuel gas first. This creates a very fuel-lean flame condition when the fuel in the line is used up.)

To summarize the major advantages and disadvantages of the nonpremix and premix burners, the advantages of the turbulent-flow burner are:

1. The entire sample is aspirated into the flame.
2. There is no explosive hazard from a mixture of unburned gases, so high-burning-velocity flames can be used.
3. Solutions containing large amounts of solid solutes can be aspirated, although encrustation of salts can be troublesome.
4. The burner is easy to clean and maintain.

Disadvantages are:

1. Even though the entire sample is aspirated, vaporization and desolvation efficiency is poor, with drop size varying over a broad range, and larger droplets failing to desolvate in the short time spent in the flame.
2. Disburbances such as condensed-phase interferences are more severe because of the desolvation and vaporization problems.
3. The flame temperature is seriously affected by loss of heat used for desolvation.
4. The flame is noisy, both to the ear and to the detector, because of turbulence.
5. The flame geometry is poor (short path-length) for atomic absorption.

The advantages of the premix burner are:

1. Nebulization can be controlled separately, and nearly uniform small droplets are fed to the flame. This leads to less light scattering.
2. Less solvent reaches the flame with less disturbance of the flame.
3. The flame is more homogeneous, and the height dependence for observation is not so critical.

4. Encrustations are reduced because large drops are eliminated.
5. There is low turbulence with less effect on the noise level, and the flame is quiet.
6. There is an elongated absorption path.

Some of the disadvantages of the premix burner are:

1. The relatively large volumes of fuel-oxidant mixture used can be explosive and only low-burning-velocity flames can be used, except under special conditions.
2. There can be a memory effect if large amounts of solids are aspirated.
3. The burner and chamber are harder to clean.
4. Several seconds are required between the initiation of nebulization and the attainment of a steady state within the chamber and in the flame gases.
5. With mixed solvents, the more volatile ones are selectively evaporated.
6. More than 90% of the sample goes down the drain, although that portion reaching the flame is efficiently atomized.

Thus, several factors are involved in the choice of a burner. Generally speaking, a premix burner is preferred for atomic-absorption work, except when a high-burning-velocity flame must be used. Turbulent-flow burners are widely used for atomic-emission measurements, but in recent years premix burners have also found more use, particularly with the high-temperature nitrous oxide–acetylene flame.

Flames

Table 10.2 lists the most commonly used flames in absorption and emission measurements, together with their maximum temperatures. All these flames can be used with a premix burner *except* the two oxygen-supported flames.

Flame Structure. The structure of a typical flame in a premix burner (such as a Bunsen burner) is illustrated in Figure 10.11. The fuel-air mixture emerging from the burner tube is heated in the *preheating zone* by conduction from the *combustion zone*; this heating initiates combustion (oxidation of the fuel). The main combustion reactions take place in the *primary reaction* or *combustion zone* (*inner cone*). This zone, about 0.1 mm thick, is recognized by its bright luminescence (with hydrocarbon fuels, a strong blue-green light due to C_2 and CH radicals). In this zone, thermal

TABLE 10.2. *Flames Used in Atomic Absorption and Emission*

Gas Mixture	Maximum Temperature, °C
Air–Coal Gas	1825
Air-Propane	1725
Air-Hydrogen	2045
Air-Acetylene	2250
Oxygen-Hydrogen	2677
Oxygen-Acetylene	3060
Nitrous oxide–Acetylene	2955
Argon-Hydrogen-Entrained air	1577

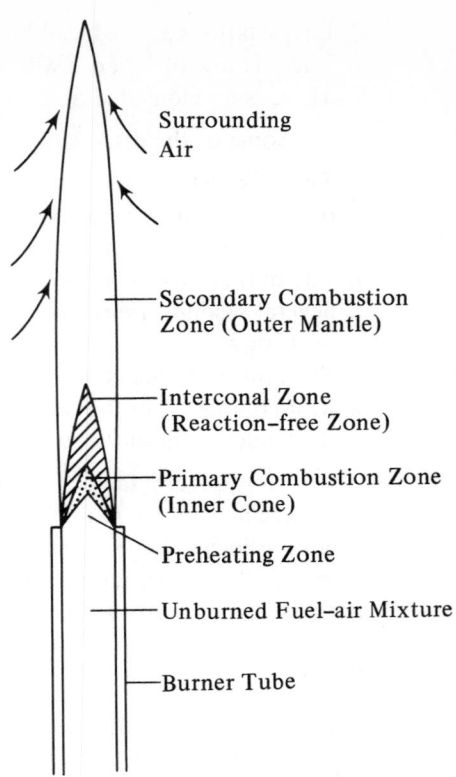

FIGURE 10.11. *Structure of a flame.*

Surrounding
Air

Secondary Combustion
Zone (Outer Mantle)

Interconal Zone
(Reaction–free Zone)

Primary Combustion Zone
(Inner Cone)

Preheating Zone

Unburned Fuel–air Mixture

Burner Tube

equilibrium is not achieved, so it is rarely used for atomic emission or absorption measurements. Gases emerging from the reaction zone of a hydrocarbon flame consist mainly of CO, CO_2, H_2, H_2O and N_2 (if air is the oxidant), with smaller amounts of H, O, and OH radicals.

The *interconal* or *reaction-free zone* is the part usually employed for atomic emission and absorption measurements. It exhibits nearly complete thermal equilibrium, is not very luminous, and can extend to several millimeters in height. Under conditions of thermal equilibrium, knowledge of only the temperature suffices to account for atomic emission or absorption phenomena, with no need to consider the manner in which the temperature is generated (for example, the particular fuel and oxidant gases used or their ratio). The gas mixture expands appreciably after passing from the reaction zone to the interconal zone because of thermal expansion, and sometimes because of an increase after combustion in the total number of moles of gas.

The major part of the flame, the *secondary combustion zone*, consists of the burned gas mixture, which extends around and above the intercone. By molecular or turbulent diffusion, oxygen and nitrogen from the surrounding air penetrate into the flame, oxidizing carbon monoxide from the interconal gases to carbon dioxide, with weak emission of blue-violet light. This outer cone is more distinct when the primary combustion is incomplete (that is, in a fuel-rich flame). Under these conditions, the edge of the outer cone may actually be hotter than the interior of the flame, but because it also emits background radiation, it is not usually sampled for analytical measurements.

The structure of the flame produced by a turbulent burner is more difficult to describe than that of a premix (laminar) burner, because it is obscured by the strong turbulence. The inner cone, while recognizable, is vague, thickened by turbulence. The combustion process in a turbulent burner is somewhat different; the turbulence aids in the ignition of the gases, making the burning velocity higher, but incomplete mixing of the gases above the burner port can cause considerable local variation within the flame. The turbulent flame entrains more air from the surroundings than does a laminar flame, and its temperature, for a given gas composition, is generally higher. Where aspiration of an aqueous solution into a premix flame usually results in a slight decrease in the flame temperature (e.g., 40°C), the drop in a turbulent flame can be much larger (for example, several hundred degrees), depending on the aspiration rate. Hence, substitution of organic solvents can result in striking enhancements in atomic-emission intensities in the turbulent flame.

Selection of Flames. The alkali metals are best determined in the lower-temperature flames (air–coal gas or air–propane) because of their ease of ionization in higher-temperature flames. The neutral atoms are readily excited in these two flames for atomic-emission determination. In many instruments designed specifically for the atomic-emission measurement of these elements, a simple Meker-type burner is suitable.

For the atomic-emission determination of the majority of elements, however, a high-temperature flame is required for excitation. Either an oxyacetylene or a nitrous oxide–acetylene flame can be used. The latter can be used with a premix burner. In order to prevent the burner from overheating, it must be more massive than usual; generally, a thick stainless-steel head is used (sometimes with cooling wings) with a narrower and shorter slot than usual. Under these conditions, the flame is quite safe from flashback unless it is operated in too lean a condition (i.e., with too high an oxidant/fuel flow-rate ratio). Some manufacturers have safety features built into their instruments to prevent igniting a nitrous oxide–acetylene flame using the wrong burner.

When using the nitrous oxide–acetylene flame, an air-acetylene flame is first ignited and adjusted to a fuel-rich condition. Then nitrous oxide is introduced to replace the air. In this manner, one can avoid igniting the flame under lean conditions. The reverse sequence is used to extinguish the flame.

The most commonly used flame for atomic-absorption measurements is the air-acetylene flame combined with a premix burner. Although its advantages are many, certain limitations affect its use for some elements. Metals such as molybdenum, tin, and some alkaline earths are only partially atomized in this flame. Elements that form refractory compounds, including silicon, aluminum, and vanadium, are not appreciably atomized at all. In general, this can be attributed to the tendency of these elements, when heated in the flame, to form refractory oxides that are not decomposed at the temperatures available.

The development of high-temperature, reducing flames has allowed the routine determination of elements that tend to form refractory compounds. Measurements in the nitrous oxide–acetylene flame are generally made in the red secondary zone, which is practically devoid of oxygen. (This red zone has been attributed to long-lived CN and NH species which form a strongly reducing atmosphere.) So, the flame apparently inhibits formation of refractory oxides by its nonoxidizing atmosphere and high temperature.

The high-temperature flames also remove many chemical interferences that occur in the air-acetylene flame for several of the other elements. Chemical interferences may occur, for example, when anions in solution combine with the test element to form thermally stable compounds. These are discussed in more detail below.

A disadvantage of high-temperature flames is that there is a marked increase in the ionization of many elements. Thermal ionization of an element—for example, $Na \rightleftharpoons Na^+ + e^-$—is undesirable because it decreases the number of neutral atoms in the flame; thus, sensitivity is lost. This can be circumvented by adding about 200 ppm of an easily ionized element, such as potassium, to suppress the ionization of the other elements. This should be done routinely with all elements with ionization potentials less than about 7.5 eV. This includes the elements Li, Ca, Sr, Ba, Al, Ga, In, Tl, Pb, Sc, Ti, V, Cr, Mn, Y, Zn, Nb, Mo, Ta, and the rare earths.

The air-hydrogen flame is more transparent than hydrocarbon-based flames, and sometimes offers advantages in atomic absorption when working at short wavelengths. This flame has been demonstrated superior to the air-acetylene and nitrous oxide–acetylene flames for the determination of low concentrations of tin, for instance.

An interesting flame useful for atomic-absorption measurements in specific cases is the argon-hydrogen-entrained air flame. The support (oxidant) gas entering the burner is replaced by argon, and combustion is supported by the influx of entrained air from the surrounding atmosphere. This flame can be used with either a turbulent burner or a premix burner. The advantage of this flame is that it is much more transparent at short wavelengths than even the air-hydrogen flame. It exhibits very little emission in the visible region of the spectrum and is nearly colorless to the eye. One can better observe the flame by aspirating tap water and noting the sodium emission. Because of its transparency, this flame offers superior detection limits for elements that absorb below 200 nm. Two specific examples are arsenic at 193.7 and selenium at 196.0 nm. A primary limitation of this flame, however, is its low temperature and the severe chemical interferences allowed by that temperature. For this reason, the nitrous oxide–acetylene flame is preferred for the measurement of arsenic and selenium in most applications. It turns out that this flame also exhibits good transparency below 200 nm, although this is not true at wavelengths around 300 nm. The argon-hydrogen-entrained air flame does find use in newer techniques in which arsenic, antimony, or selenium is converted to a volatile hydride and enters the flame as a gas separated from the sample solution.

Summarizing, then, most atomic-absorption determinations are routinely made with a premix burner using either the air-acetylene flame or the nitrous oxide–acetylene flame. A few specific examples require different conditions, depending on the test element and the sample.

Adjusting Flame Conditions. The optimum ratio of fuel-to-oxidant flows will depend on the types of gases used, the burner, the element determined, and whether absorption or emission is measured. Usually the oxidant is used to aspirate and nebulize the sample solution, so control of the oxidant flow-rate is important in determining the rate at which the sample is introduced. Fuel flow is not usually so critical except under fuel-rich conditions or in emission measurements where flame temperature is important. When optimizing the flows, it is important to keep in mind that the signal-to-noise ratio is as important as, if not more so than, the magnitude of the signal.

One procedure to select the best flow is to set a given oxidant flow-rate and then to vary the fuel flow over a range. The signal and noise levels are measured at each setting while aspirating a solution of the test element. After the initial measurements, the oxidant flow is changed and the process repeated until the conditions for maximum signal-to-noise ratio are found.

Increasing the oxidant flow-rate will increase the rate of uptake of the sample up to a point, while decreasing the efficiency of production of atoms in the flame; usually, a net increase in atom production will result. It should be pointed out that interferences may be reduced under conditions that are not optimum for maximum sensitivity.

To obtain a stoichiometric flame, the flow rate of the gases should be close to the ratio in the chemical reaction. For example, in the oxyacetylene flame, 2.5 moles of O_2 react with each mole of C_2H_2. The flow rate of O_2 should then be about 2.5 times that of C_2H_2; actually, it should be slightly less since atmospheric oxygen is entrained. For a stoichiometric air-acetylene flame, the air flow would be 5×2.5 or 12.5 times the C_2H_2 flow, since air contains only 20% O_2.

A strongly reducing flame is best for elements that form refractory compounds, in order to prevent or minimize the formation of refractory oxides. By making a flame very fuel-rich and perhaps also aspirating an organic solvent, highly reducing species such as free carbon atoms and carbon monoxide are produced in the interior of the flame. (Incandescent unburned carbon particles, in fact, are what make a fuel-rich flame appear yellow.) A stoichiometric flame usually occurs near the point at which yellow incandescence just appears. A fuel-rich oxyhydrogen flame will not usually be as effective as either a fuel-rich oxyacetylene or nitrous oxide–acetylene flame for elements that form refractory compounds; this is because no very strongly reducing species are formed in the oxyhydrogen flame. However, when organic solvents are aspirated, this flame can be quite effective since it is a high-temperature flame.

The position of measurement in the flame is important, particularly in flame emission where the signal is very dependent on the flame temperature. In the typical flame, the maximum-temperature region occurs slightly above the inner cone. Positioning is not as critical in atomic absorption, particularly with the slot burners, although the lateral position is important. Nevertheless, standard practice is to adjust the height of the burner relative to the path of the light beam through the flame to obtain the maximum signal-to-noise ratio for a given element under given conditions of flame stoichiometry and aspiration rate.

The aspiration rate can also affect signals because of the influence of the solvent on flame temperature as well as on droplet size and nebulization losses. An optimum flow will generally be achieved that will represent a compromise between increased introduction of sample atoms and lowering of the temperature by the solvent (usually water). Typical aspiration rates are 1 ml/min for total consumption burners and 3–10 ml/min for premix burners.

We showed previously that, barring formation of molecules, the number of ground-state atoms is essentially independent of the flame temperature. Limits of detection in atomic absorption can, however, be somewhat affected by temperature changes owing to the line-broadening factors and their dependence on temperature. Increased temperatures result in Doppler broadening at the center of the absorption line where absorbance is being measured, which causes a decrease in the peak height of the absorption line. Fortunately, the effect is quite small over small temperature changes, since Doppler broadening is proportional to the square root of the temperature. In practice, temperature control is more necessary for controlling atomization than for controlling Doppler broadening.

A problem encountered in atomic absorption is that of emission from the flame. Emission from the flame gases is normally broadband over a large portion of the spectrum; the instrument can be "zeroed" in the presence of the flame (solvent aspirated) to negate this. In some cases, however, the sample element emits strongly at precisely the same wavelength at which it absorbs; a small fraction of this emission will enter the monochromator, fall on the detector, and be registered as "negative" absorption. Both these emission problems can be overcome by modulating the radiation source, either mechanically with a rotating or vibrating chopper in front of the source, or electronically in the power supply. The detector electronics (amplifier) are tuned to the frequency of modulation of the light source and will record only light modulated at that frequency. High intensity DC emission, however, may "overload" the detector, causing increased noise. When such an AC source and detector are used, flame-emission measurements can be made (with the source turned off) by placing a chopper between the flame and the detector to modulate the emitted radiation at the same frequency.

Furnace Atomizers

Although aspiration into a flame is the most convenient and reproducible means of obtaining atomic vapor, it is one of the least efficient in terms of converting all the sample elements to atomic vapor and presenting this to the optical path. The overall efficiency of atomic conversion and measurement of atoms present in aspirated solutions has been estimated at as little as 0.1%. Also, aspiration methods usually require several milliliters of solution for analysis.

Furnace atomizers have conversion efficiencies much higher than do flame atomizers; absolute detection limits are typically 100 to 1000 times improved over flame-aspiration methods. Our discussion will center on atomizers heated by electrical resistance. Although these are not generally useful for emission measurements, they are well suited for atomic-absorption and atomic-fluorescence measurements [3].

In most of the furnace techniques, a few microliters of sample is placed in a horizontal graphite tube or on a carbon rod or tantalum ribbon; it is dried and (usually) submitted to an ashing step to destroy organic material, using resistive heating of the tube, rod, or ribbon. Finally, it is thermally atomized by resistive heating to produce a transient cloud of atomic vapor above the atomizer. The light path passes through the tube or over the rod or ribbon; a sharp peak of absorbance versus time is recorded. Either the height of the observed peak or its area is directly related to the quantity of metal vaporized. The heating is done in an inert atmo-

TABLE 10.3. *Representative Detection Limits for Furnace Atomic-Absorption Spectroscopy*

Element	Perkin-Elmer HGA[a]	Detection Limit, g Varian CRA-90[b]	IL CTF[c,d]
Ag	2×10^{-13}	2×10^{-13}	5×10^{-13}
Al	3×10^{-12}	5×10^{-12}	4×10^{-13}
Cd	1×10^{-13}	1×10^{-13}	4×10^{-13}
Cr	5×10^{-12}	2×10^{-12}	5×10^{-13}
Cu	1×10^{-12}	3×10^{-13}	8×10^{-13}
Mn	1×10^{-12}	2×10^{-13}	4×10^{-13}
Ni	1×10^{-11}	5×10^{-12}	2.5×10^{-12}
Tl	1×10^{-11}	2×10^{-12}	
Zn	6×10^{-14}	1×10^{-13}	

a. "Perkin-Elmer High Sensitivity Sampling Systems for Atomic Absorption," Brochure L-332A. Courtesy of the Perkin-Elmer Corporation.
b. Varian Carbon Rod Atomizer, Model CRA-90. Courtesy of Varian Associates.
c. "Sensitivities for IL 155 CTF (Controlled-Temperature Furnace) Atomizer." Courtesy of Instrumentation Laboratory, Inc.
d. These numbers represent sensitivities rather than detection limits.

sphere to prevent oxidation of the graphite or tantalum at the high temperatures involved, and also to prevent formation of refractory oxides.

Detection limits quoted by the manufacturers of flameless atomizers are typically in the range of 10^{-10} to 10^{-12} g. Table 10.3 lists representative detection limits for some typical elements. The concentrational detection limit will, of course, depend on the sample volume. The volume will in turn depend on the composition of the sample matrix and on the concentration of the test element. Assuming that a 10-μl sample is analyzed for an element with a detection limit of 10^{-11} g, the concentration detection limit would be 10^{-9} g/ml; this is equal to 1 ng/ml or 1 part per billion. The extreme sensitivity of these techniques is therefore quite apparent, even when dealing with very small samples.

A major difficulty with furnace atomic-absorption methods is that interelement effects or interferences are much more pronounced than in flames, and precision is generally poorer. The interferences can sometimes be minimized by using a standard-addition method for calibration. Often, when the matrix concentration is changed, there is a change in the height as well as in the shape of the analytical peak. In such instances, better accuracy with less influence by the matrix can sometimes be achieved by integrating the signal (measuring its area) rather than by measuring its maximum intensity. Of course, this requires more sophisticated instrumentation.

10.4 INTERFERENCES

Several different types of interferences can occur in atomic-emission and atomic-absorption spectroscopy.

Spectral Interferences

Spectral-line interference, in which two atomic lines overlap or are unresolved, is relatively rare in atomic-absorption analysis. This type of interference is more common in atomic emission, where light is emitted not only by the test element but also by other elements in the sample. If the wavelength of the interfering radiation is close enough to the line of the element being measured, it will not be resolved and will be detected and recorded along with the signal for the element. For example, when small amounts of magnesium are being determined in the presence of large amounts of sodium, the 285.28-nm line of sodium will contribute some emission intensity along with the 285.21-nm line of magnesium. Spectral interference of this type can usually be eliminated by choosing a second resonance line for the test element (probably with a decreased sensitivity), or by removing the interferent by chemical means.

In atomic absorption, the line that is being measured is the resonance line from the source, which has a bandwidth of ~0.001 nm and ensures effective resolution. Hence, interference from absorption by another spectral line is quite rare, although some cases have been reported.

A more common type of spectral interference in either emission or absorption measurements arises from the occurrence of band emission-spectra due to molecular species in the flame. (In fact, many elements can be measured by means of the band spectra of the molecules they form in certain flames.) Calcium and strontium, for example, exist partially as molecular hydroxides and oxides in a flame and emit bands in the vicinity of both the sodium and lithium resonance lines. When the alkaline-earth/alkali-metal ratio is high, the interference can become serious, unless a high-resolution monochromator is used.

Molecular-absorption interference, although less common, does occur. For example, a CaOH absorption band occurs in the region of the barium 553.6-nm line. A 1% calcium solution has been reported to give an absorption equivalent to that expected from 75 ppm barium, well within the analytical measurement range for barium (see Table 10.4). High concentrations of alkali-metal and other salts can exhibit appreciable molecular absorption, particularly at wavelengths less than 300 nm.

If a flame contains solid particles or solvent drops that are not vaporized, these particles can scatter the light beam that impinges on them, giving rise to "false" absorption signals; this can be especially troublesome with total-consumption burners.

Molecular-spectral interferences and light-scattering interferences can be fairly easily minimized in either atomic emission or absorption measurements, provided the interferences are not dominant. Molecular-band and light-scatter spectra are approximately constant in intensity within several spectrometer bandpasses (or bandwidths) of a given spectral line. Hence, emission spectra can be corrected for background emission by making measurements at least two bandpasses away on each side of the line wavelength, averaging the two measurements, and subtracting the average from the analytical measurement at the resonance line. Measurements should be made on each side of the line in case the line is sitting on the side of a sharp band. Alternatively, if a scanning monochromator is available, the actual spectrum can be recorded in the vicinity of the resonance line and the background extrapolated to give a baseline for the peak.

Background corrections in atomic absorption are made similarly; that is, by assuming the background absorption to be constant over several bandpasses. A nonresonance line emitted by the test hollow-cathode lamp or by another lamp is selected. This line (often an emission line of the filler gas) must be at least two bandpasses from the resonance line of the test element. After checking to make certain that the test element does not absorb the chosen line, the absorbance of this line by the sample is measured and subtracted from the total absorbance at the resonance wavelength.

A correction can also be made with a hydrogen or deuterium continuum source with the monochromator set at the same wavelength as the resonance line. Sharp line-absorption of the continuum source by the test element is negligible compared to the background over the bandwidth of the monochromator, so the absorbance of the continuum source can simply be subtracted from the absorbance of the resonance line. Several commercial instruments have arrangements that allow automatic background corrections with continuum sources.

A typical setup is shown in Figure 10.12. The two light beams from the lamps are combined by a half-coated mirror (e.g., coated with small reflecting circles so that it will reflect the continuum radiation but will allow space in the mirror for the radiation from the hollow-cathode lamp to pass). Each lamp is pulsed electronically to provide an AC signal, but the two lamps are 180° out of phase. A phase-sensitive detection system then measures the difference of the two signal intensities (which are initially balanced). The sharp-line source measures both atomic absorption and

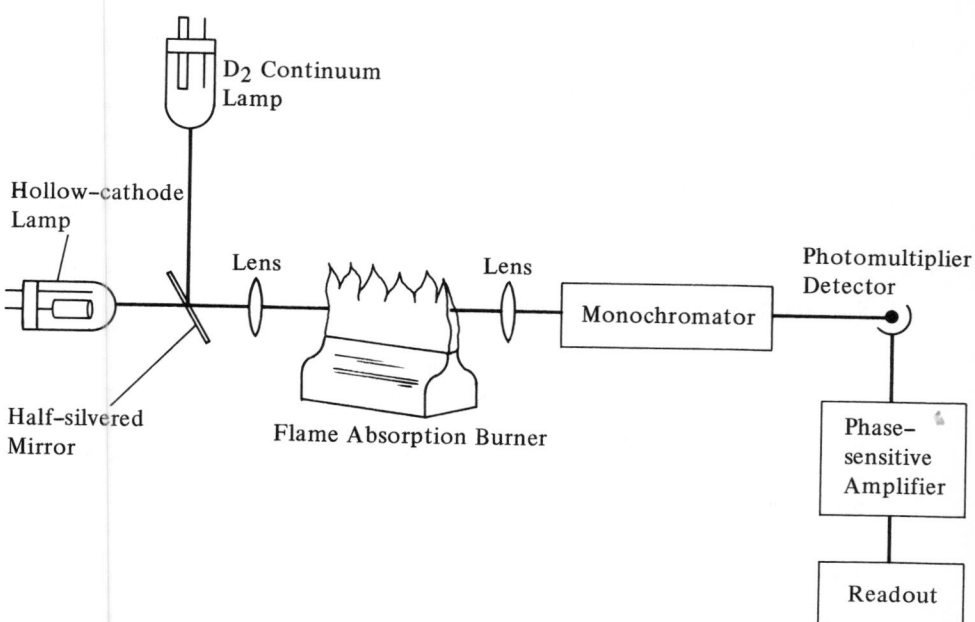

FIGURE 10.12. *Typical setup for atomic-absorption background correction with a continuum source.*

background absorption, but the continuum source measures only the background absorption since any sharp-line absorption removes a negligible portion of its band of radiation. The difference, then, represents the net sharp-line absorption.

Chemical Interferences

Chemical interference, or the chemical combination of the element of interest with other elements in the sample or the flame, is probably the most important interference in flame methods. It directly affects the efficiency of production of neutral atoms in the flame and hence affects both absorption and emission in a similar manner. One of the most common types of chemical interference is the formation of refractory compounds with the test element, usually by an anion in the aspirated solution. The result is a decreased signal. For example, phosphate will react with calcium ions to produce calcium pyrophosphate in the flame. Less frequently, the presence of another cation may result in a decreased signal. For example, aluminum causes low results in the determination of magnesium, owing to the formation of a heat-stable aluminum-magnesium compound. Occasionally, a positive interference will occur in the presence of an interfering substance. The mechanism is not clearly understood, but has to do with the formation of a compound more volatile than the test element.

Chemical interferences, fortunately, can generally be minimized by adding an appropriate *releasing agent*. These agents either compete for the interfering substance or displace it from the test element. For example, phosphate interference with calcium absorption or emission can be eliminated by adding a sufficiently high concentration (about 1%, depending on the actual phosphate levels) of strontium or lanthanum chloride to the solution. The strontium or lanthanum will preferentially combine with the phosphate and prevent its reaction with the calcium. Or, a high concentration of EDTA can be added to form a chelate with the calcium and prevent its reaction with phosphate. The calcium-EDTA chelate is readily dissociated in the flame. Because addition of an external reagent can sometimes change the test signal, the reagent should generally also be added to standards.

The use of high-temperature flames will frequently eliminate chemical interferences. Phosphate interference on calcium, for example, does not occur in the nitrous oxide–acetylene flame. In extremely difficult cases, a chemical separation of the interferent may be required.

Acids will frequently cause a depression of the signal, especially with total-consumption burners. This is particularly so for the alkali metals, probably because of the low-temperature flames used for these elements. Elements that form stable oxides are affected even more. Acids can influence the aspiration rate and nebulization efficiency, a physical interference (see below). Chemical interference by the acid anions may also be involved. For these reasons, matching the acidity in the standards and samples may be required.

Ionization Interferences

Certain elements, particularly the alkali metals and some of the alkaline-earth elements, are appreciably ionized in most flames. This causes a decrease in the number of neutral atoms and a decrease in sensitivity. It is not an interference in itself since standards would be ionized in the same manner; but if a second easily ionized element (e.g., potassium) is added to the test solution, it will contribute free electrons to the flame and cause the equilibrium for the test element (e.g., sodium) to shift toward the formation of a larger fraction of neutral atoms. The result is a positive interference.

Ionization interference can be overcome by adding a large amount (200 to 1000 ppm) of an easily ionized element such as potassium to both sample and standard solutions. This will effectively suppress ionization of the test element to a small and constant value and at the same time increase the sensitivity. Ionization can usually be detected by noting that the calibration curve has a positive deviation (upward curvature) at higher concentrations, because a smaller fraction of the atoms is ionized at higher concentrations.

Physical Interferences

Physical interferences are caused by altering some physical property of the solution, such as its viscosity, surface tension, vapor pressure, or temperature. These alterations will cause a change in aspiration, nebulization, or atomization efficiency. For these reasons, solvent temperature and composition should be maintained reasonably constant.

10.5 APPLICATIONS

More than sixty elements can be determined by atomic-absorption or flame-emission spectroscopy, many at or below about 1 ppm [4]. Only metals and metalloids can be determined by usual flame methods, because the resonance lines for nonmetals occur in the vacuum-ultraviolet region; however, a number of indirect methods for determining nonmetals have been described. For example, chloride can be determined by precipitating it with silver ion and then measuring either the excess or the reacted silver. Phosphorus (525.9 nm) and sulfur (383.7 nm) species (e.g., S_2) exhibit sharp molecular-band emission in the argon-hydrogen flame.

General Considerations

Table 10.4 lists the atomic-absorption and atomic-emission detection limits and wavelengths for the different elements, using the nitrous oxide–acetylene flame for atomic emission and either the air-acetylene or nitrous oxide–acetylene flame for atomic absorption. The detection limits are taken as the concentration required to give a signal equal to twice the standard deviation of the background reading. Generally, at wavelengths shorter than 300 nm, atomic absorption is more sensitive, while at wavelengths in the visible region, certain elements may exhibit improved sensitivity by atomic emission. Some reported detection limits for atomic fluorescence spectroscopy are also given for comparison.

Some elements exhibit maximum emission sensitivity using molecular band emission, but this is more limited in its specificity. Thus, marked improvement in

TABLE 10.4. *Comparison of Detection Limits for Atomic-Emission (AES), Atomic-Absorption (AAS), and Atomic-Fluorescence Spectroscopy (AFS)*

Element	Wavelength (nm)	Detection limit (ppm)		
		AES[a]	AAS[a,b]	AFS[c]
Ag	328.07	0.008	0.001 (A)	0.0001
Al	396.15	0.05		0.005
	309.28		0.1 (N)	
As	193.70	10	0.03[f]	0.1
Au	267.60	2		0.05
	242.80		0.02 (N)	
B	518.0[a]	0.05		
	249.68		2.5 (N)	
Ba	553.55	0.002	0.02 (N)	
Be	234.86	1	0.002 (N)	0.01
Bi	306.77	20		
	223.06		0.05 (A)	0.05
Ca	422.67	0.0002	0.002 (A)	0.000001
Cd	326.11	0.8		
	228.80		0.001 (A)	0.00001
Ce	569.92	10		0.5
Co	345.35	0.03		
	240.72		0.002 (A)	0.005
Cr	425.43	0.004		
	357.87		0.002 (A)	0.004
Cs	455.53	0.6		
	852.11		0.05 (A)	
Cu	324.75	0.01	0.004 (A)	0.001
Dy	404.60	0.05		
	410.39		0.2 (N)	
Er	400.80	0.07	0.1 (N)	0.5
Eu	459.40	0.0005	0.04 (N)	0.02
Fe	371.99	0.03		
	248.33		0.004 (A)	0.008
Ga	417.21	0.06		0.01
	287.42		0.05 (A)	
Gd	440.19	5		
	622.09[d]	0.07		
	368.41		4 (N)	
Ge	265.12	0.4	0.1 (N)	20
Hf	531.16 (II)[e]	20		
	286.64		20 (N)	
Hg	253.65	10	0.5 (A)	0.002
Ho	410.38	0.1	0.1 (N)	
In	451.13	0.003		0.002
	303.94		0.03 (A)	

Table 10.4. (*continued*)

Element	Wavelength (nm)	Detection limit (ppm)		
		AES[a]	AAS[a,b]	AFS[c]
Ir	380.01	3		
	550.0[a]	0.4		
	284.97		1 (N)	
K	766.49	0.00005	0.003 (A)	
La	550.13	6	2 (N)	
	441.82[d]	0.01		
Li	670.78	0.00002	0.001 (A)	
Lu	451.86	1		
	331.21		3 (N)	
Mg	285.21	0.07	0.003 (A)	0.001
Mn	403.31	0.008		
	279.48		0.0008 (A)	0.002
Mo	390.30	0.2		
	313.26		0.03 (N)	
Na	589.00	0.0005	0.0008 (A)	
Nb	405.89	1	3 (N)	1
Nd	492.45	0.7		
	463.42		2 (A)	
Ni	352.45	0.02		
	232.00		0.005 (A)	0.003
Os	442.05	2		
	305.87		0.4 (N)	
Pb	405.78	0.1		0.01
	283.31		0.01 (A)	
Pd	363.47	0.05		
	247.64		0.01 (A)	
Pr	495.14	0.07	4 (N)	
Pt	265.94	4	0.05 (A)	
Rb	780.02	0.008	0.005 (A)	
	794.76	3		
Re	346.05	0.2	0.6 (N)	
Rh	343.49	0.03	0.02 (A)	
Ru	372.80	0.3		
	349.89		0.06 (A)	
Sb	252.85	0.6		
	217.58		0.03 (A)	
Sc	402.37	0.8		
	391.18		0.1 (N)	
Se	196.03	100	0.1[f]	0.04
Si	251.61	3	0.1 (N)	
Sm	476.03	0.2		
	429.67		0.6 (N)	
Sn	284.00	0.1		
	235.48		0.05 (A)	

(*continued*)

TABLE 10.4. (*continued*)

Element	Wavelength (nm)	Detection limit (ppm) AES[a]	AAS[a,b]	AFS[c]
Sr	470.73	0.0005	0.005 (A)	0.01
Ta	474.02	4		
	271.47		3 (N)	
Tb	432.65	0.5	2 (N)	
	534.0[d]	0.03		
Te	486.62	2		
	214.28		0.05 (A)	0.05
Th	491.98 (II)[e]	10		
Ti	334.90	0.2		
	364.27		0.1 (N)	
Tl	535.05	0.02		
	276.79		0.02 (A)	
	377.57	0.1		0.008
Tm	371.79	0.08	0.04 (N)	0.1
U	544.8[d]	5		
	351.46		20 (N)	
V	437.92	0.1		
	318.40		0.02 (N)	
W	400.88	0.6	3 (N)	
Y	362.09	1		
	597.2[d]	0.03		
	407.74		0.3 (N)	
Yb	398.80	0.006	0.02 (N)	0.01
Zn	213.86	10	0.001 (A)	0.00002
Zr	360.12	5	4 (N)	

a. Adapted from G. D. Christian and F. J. Feldman, *Appl. Spectrosc.*, **25**, 660 (1971). Nitrous oxide–acetylene flame.
b. Fuel is acetylene. Letter in parentheses indicates the oxidant. A = air, N = nitrous oxide.
c. From V. A. Fassel and R. N. Knisely, *Anal. Chem.*, **46**, 1110A (1974).
d. Band emission.
e. Ion line.
f. Argon-hydrogen-entrained air flame.

sensitivity is found with band emission from gadolinium, iridium, lanthanum, terbium, and yttrium, in addition to boron and uranium which can only be determined by band emission. For analytical measurements, concentrations should be at least ten-fold higher than the detection limits listed in the table, since by definition the precision at the detection limit is no better than $\pm 50\%$.

The analytical application of atomic-absorption or atomic-emission spectroscopy generally involves obtaining the sample in an appropriate solution for measurement and calibrating the instrument properly. Commonly used methods for different materials are described below. Frequently, a releasing agent will have to be added, or a solvent extraction will be required to concentrate the element and increase the sensitivity. Standards should be treated in a similar manner.

Instruments can be calibrated by preparing standard solutions over the concentration range of interest and measuring the absorption or emission of these under the same conditions as sample measurement. At least one standard should be run with each set of samples to determine any correction that should be applied to the calibration curve, because the variables of flame stoichiometry, aspiration rate, and positioning of the burner are difficult to reproduce precisely.

Sometimes, the method of standard additions is used to compensate for chemical and other matrix interference. The principles of this method of calibration, in which the standard is added to an aliquot of the sample, are described in Chapter 2 and elsewhere.

Atomic-absorption and atomic-emission spectroscopy are used for the analysis of a large variety of materials, containing from trace elements (ppm concentrations) to major (>1%) inorganic constituents. Included are agricultural and biological samples, geological samples, petroleum products, glass and its raw materials, cement, ferrous metals and alloys, water, and air. Because of the general ease—or even lack—of sample preparation and because deaeration of the solution is not required, flame methods have largely replaced polarographic methods for many inorganic analyses. Anodic-stripping methods and the more sensitive pulse-polarographic techniques are becoming strong competitors, but furnace atomic-absorption methods rival the detection limits of these. This last technique can often be used for the direct analysis of small solid samples that can be decomposed or "ashed" at temperatures insufficient to vaporize the test elements present, followed by a higher temperature atomization step for the analysis itself. Examples are tissue homogenates and leaves.

The prime instrumental disadvantage of atomic-absorption techniques is that generally only a single element can be measured at a time. A different light source is required for each element. Atomic emission possesses a similar disadvantage, although it is fairly simple to change to a different wavelength for the measurement of another element. Simultaneous multi-element determinations have been made in recent years by atomic-emission spectroscopy using diode array (Vidicon camera) detectors (described in Chap. 7). The array of diodes effectively serves as multiple detectors (as many as several hundred) which can be arranged to detect several different wavelengths over a range.

Organic or biological samples will usually require destruction by dry ashing or wet digestion with oxidizing acids before flame analysis. Biological fluids (blood or urine) frequently can be aspirated after a simple dilution. For blood analysis, serum or plasma is generally preferred since this fraction of the blood generally contains clinically significant concentrations of metals. (An exception is blood-lead analysis for lead poisoning, because lead will concentrate in the red cells.) In other cases, the metal may be more concentrated in the red cells, but concentration changes in the serum or plasma are more clinically indicative; examples are potassium, zinc, iron, and magnesium. In these cases, it is critical that blood samples do not hemolyze (red cells burst) before separation of the serum or plasma is completed.

Serum is the supernatant obtained from clotted blood. Plasma, the liquid portion of circulating blood, is chemically similar to serum except that it contains in addition fibrinogen, the clotting agent in blood. Plasma is obtained by treating the blood with an anticoagulant such as heparin or oxalate, after which the red cells are separated from the plasma by centrifuging. Oxalate should generally be avoided for metal analysis since many metal oxalates are insoluble; an efficient digestion mixture for biological samples is a mixture of HNO_3, H_2SO_4, and $HClO_4$ in the ratio of 3:1:1 by volume, using about 1 ml per gram of wet material.

Metals and alloys can usually be dissolved in acids, whereas materials such as glass will require alkaline or acid fusion. An important consideration in any analysis is matching the matrix of the standards to that of the sample, or else diluting the sample enough to render the physical effects of the matrix harmless. (Chemical effects may still exist.)

One of the most common applications of atomic-emission spectroscopy is the determination of the alkali metals, particularly in the clinical laboratory. Blood-serum samples need only to be diluted with water (or an internal-standard solution) and aspirated.

Use of Organic Solvents

The overall atomization efficiency in a flame is increased by the use of organic solvents. Such increase is due to a variety of causes, including increased rate of aspiration, finer droplets, more efficient evaporation or combustion of the solvent, and so forth. Thus, increased sensitivity would be obtained by adding a miscible organic solvent such as acetone to the solution. (A three-fold increase is typical.) The problem is that adding the miscible solvent dilutes the sample solution, which more or less defeats the purpose. Therefore, the technique of solvent extraction (Chap. 20) is usually employed to obtain increased sensitivity. The dissolved metal is extracted from the aqueous solution into an immiscible organic solvent in which it is more soluble. The organic phase containing the metal is then aspirated into the flame. A number of advantages accrue. (1) The test element is separated from the bulk matrix of the sample, thereby frequently eliminating possible interferences. (2) It is obtained in a pure organic solvent, which results in maximum atomization efficiency; a ten-fold signal enhancement can be obtained for a given concentration. (3) The test element can be extracted into a smaller volume of organic solvent, with (in many cases) a ten- to hundred-fold gain in concentration. Methyl isobutyl ketone (MIBK) is one of the best materials for solvent extraction and aspiration into a flame. Ammonium 1-pyrrolidinecarbodithioate (APCD) is a commonly used extracting agent because it reacts with a large number of elements in acidic solution [this reagent is often referred to as ammonium pyrrolidine dithiocarbamate (APDC) in the literature].

When using organic solvents, the initial flame adjustment before aspirating the solvent should generally be very lean because the solvent must be burned as well as the fuel. If the flame is too rich in fuel, the solvent will not be completely burned and the flame will be very smoky. The proper flame condition can be adjusted with the solvent aspirating. Solvent should be aspirated between samples because the hot lean flame will tend to heat up the burner.

Determination of Lead in Blood

Lead in unclotted blood can be determined by atomic-absorption spectroscopy. Five ml of heparinized blood is treated with trichloroacetic acid (TCA) to precipitate proteins, which are centrifuged. The pH of the filtrate is adjusted to 3, 1 ml of aqueous ammonium-1-pyrrolidinecarbodithioate (APCD) is added, and the lead is extracted into 5 ml of methyl isobutyl ketone (MIBK) as the $Pb(APCD)_2$ chelate. The organic phase is separated and aspirated into an air-acetylene flame for atomic-absorption measurement. Standards are treated in the same manner, and water-saturated MIBK is used to zero the instrument. The detection limit for this procedure is about 0.1 ppm lead in the blood. The upper level of "normal" blood is 0.6 ppm, with most values being in the range of 0.3–0.4 ppm. Instead of precipitating proteins before solvent extraction, the blood can be hemolyzed with 1 ml of 5% Triton X-100 solution to release the lead from the red cells.

Lead in blood can be determined in microsamples using the Delves microcup sampling procedure. This is a technique similar in operation to furnace atomic-absorption. Ten milliliters of blood is placed in a small nickel crucible, dried on a hot plate at 140°C (ca. 30 sec), and then partially oxidized at 140° with 20 ml of 30% H_2O_2 until a dry yellow residue is obtained. The crucible is then mounted on a holder and thrust into a flame where the lead is vaporized into a horizontal nickel tube above the flame (through a hole in the bottom of the tube). The light path is through the tube. A transient signal results (as in furnace atomic-absorption), and the peak height of the recorded signal is related to the lead concentration. This technique generally is more precise for blood-lead microanalysis than most other atomic-absorption methods (coefficient of variation = 8% at the 0.4 ppm level). A method of standard additions is used for calibration.

Simultaneous Determination of Sodium and Potassium in Serum

Sodium and potassium in serum are determined in the clinical laboratory by atomic-emission spectroscopy, using an instrument designed specifically for this purpose [5]. Two filter monochromators isolate the sodium and potassium emission lines. A lithium internal standard is used, and the ratios of the Na/Li and K/Li signals are read out on two separate meters. The internal standard compensates for minor fluctuations in flame temperature, aspiration rate, and so forth. A cool flame, such as air-propane, is used to minimize ionization. Typically, the serum sample and standards are diluted 1:200 with a 100 ppm Li solution and aspirated directly. The instrument can be adjusted to read directly in meq/l for sodium and potassium by adjusting the gain while aspirating appropriate standards.

Determination of Zinc in Plants

Zinc is an essential trace element in plants. One gram of dried and ground plant material is dry ashed in a silica crucible overnight at 500°C. The ash is treated with 5 ml of 6 M HCl and slowly dried on a steam bath. This operation is repeated with another 5 ml of acid to hydrolyze pyrophosphate and to dehydrate any silica from the sample or the crucible. The residue is taken up in 20 ml of 0.1 M HCl and filtered. This solution can be aspirated directly into an air-acetylene flame for atomic-absorption measurement. Standards are prepared in 0.1 M HCl. As always, a blank is prepared in the same way as the sample.

Determination of Copper in Sea Water

Major constituents in sea water, such as sodium or magnesium, can be determined by appropriate (at least ten-fold) dilution with distilled water and direct aspiration. Many elements exist in sea water, however, at parts-per-billion or smaller concentrations and must be concentrated prior to analysis. Copper is one of these (1–25 ppb). Common procedures include ion-exchange chromatography, solvent extraction, or a combination of these. Copper can be determined by adjusting the pH of sea water (1 liter) to 3, adding 5 ml of 2% APCD solution and extracting the copper with 25 ml of methyl-*n*-amyl ketone, which has a low solubility in water. The separated ketone layer is aspirated into an air-acetylene flame for atomic-absorption measurement.

Determination of Beryllium in Airborne Particulate Matter

Particulate matter in a measured volume of air can be collected on a cellulose-acetate-membrane filter (e.g., Millipore®). The filter is dry ashed in a low-temperature asher. (This device uses oxygen radicals in a radio-frequency plasma for ashing at below 100°C, thus minimizing losses due to volatility of the test element and retention on crucible walls.) The ash is taken up in dilute HCl and aspirated directly, or the filter can be digested with a mixture of nitric and perchloric acids. For beryllium determination, a nitrous oxide–acetylene flame is used. Results are reported as $\mu g/m^3$ of air.

Determination of Sodium, Potassium, Magnesium, Manganese, and Calcium in Cement

A half-gram sample of cement is decomposed in 4 M HCl and evaporated to dryness, after which the residue is taken up in 4 M HCl. After filtering the solution and diluting it to 100 ml, aliquots are taken to determine each element by atomic-absorption spectroscopy using an air-acetylene flame. Standards for sodium and potassium must contain about the same concentration of calcium as the sample solutions. The presence of the high concentrations of calcium in the sample suppresses interference by aluminum or silicon on magnesium absorption. Phosphate, aluminum, and silicon interference on calcium absorption is eliminated by adding 50 ml of 25,000 ppm strontium solution to 5 ml of the stock sample solution and diluting this to 250 ml with water. Standards all contain the same concentration of acid or other reagents as the samples.

Determination of Molybdenum in Steel

A half-gram sample is dissolved in 10 ml of 1:1 HCl on a hot plate, oxidized with ten drops of concentrated HNO_3, boiled, and diluted to 100 ml when cool. The molybdenum can be determined in either an air-acetylene or nitrous oxide–acetylene flame.

10.6 ATOMIC-FLUORESCENCE SPECTROSCOPY

Although atomic fluorescence is not often used in commercial instrumentation, a good deal of research and special applications are performed with this technique. Hence, some details pertinent to atomic fluorescence are summarized here.

Types of Atomic Fluorescence

As mentioned before, atomic fluorescence involves excitation of atomic vapor by a radiation source, followed by deactivation by the emission of radiation; the emitted radiation is then measured. This process is not unlike molecular fluorescence spectroscopy, described in Chapter 9. Some of the modes of atomic fluorescence were alluded to in Section 10.1 (and in Fig. 10.3); a fluorescent line can be at a wavelength identical to the exciting wavelength, or it can be longer or (very rarely) shorter. There are two main types of fluorescence, resonance and nonresonance. A third type is sensitized fluorescence.

Resonance Fluorescence. Resonance fluorescence occurs when the atoms absorb and reemit radiation at the same wavelength. The most common examples correspond to transitions originating in the ground state (resonance transitions). For example, resonance fluorescence is observed for zinc at 213.86 nm, for nickel at 232.00 nm, and for lead at 283.31 nm. Some atoms may have an appreciable population in a low-lying metastable energy-level and exhibit resonance fluorescence originating from these levels. The intensity of emitted radiation in this case is generally less than for the more abundant ground-state atoms. Resonance fluorescence originating from ground-state atoms is often accompanied by nonresonance fluorescence having the same upper excitation level.

Nonresonance Fluorescence. Nonresonance fluorescence occurs when the exciting wavelength and the wavelength of the emitted fluorescence line are different. There are two basic types: direct-line fluorescence and stepwise-line fluorescence.

In *direct-line fluorescence*, an atom is excited (usually from the ground state) by a radiation source, and then undergoes a direct radiational transition to a metastable level above the ground state. An example is absorption at the 283.31 nm line by ground-state lead atoms, with subsequent emission at 405.78 nm. As with resonance fluorescence, direct-line fluorescence may be excited by absorption of a nonresonance line (e.g., tin fluorescence at 333.06 nm).

In *stepwise fluorescence*, the upper levels of the exciting and the emitted lines are different. In the normal case, the excited atoms lose part of their energy by collisional deactivation (by collision with flame molecules) and then return to the original (usually ground) state by radiational deactivation. Sodium, for example, is excited at the 330.3-nm line and undergoes stepwise fluorescence to emit a line at 589.0 nm. In a second type of stepwise-line fluorescence, the radiationally excited atom is further excited (thermally) to a higher electronic state and then undergoes radiational deactivation to a metastable state (that is, the emitted radiation is still longer in wavelength than the exciting radiation).

A less common type of nonresonance fluorescence is *anti-Stokes fluorescence*, or thermally assisted fluorescence, in which the emitted wavelength is shorter than the absorbed wavelength. This occurs when atoms populating an energy level lying near but above the ground state are excited to a higher energy-level and then undergo a radiational transition to the ground state; or when a ground-state atom is excited to a certain electronic state by absorbing a photon, then raised again to a slightly higher excited state by absorbing thermal energy from the flame, and finally radiationally deactivated to the ground state. The former is a special case of direct-line fluorescence, while the latter is a special case of stepwise fluorescence. Anti-Stokes fluorescence is always accompanied by resonance fluorescence.

All types of nonresonance fluorescence, particularly direct-line fluorescence, can be analytically useful; sometimes it is more intense than resonance fluorescence, and it offers the advantage that scattering of the exciting radiation can be eliminated from the fluorescence spectrum by removing it with a filter or a monochromator. Self-absorption problems (absorption of the emitted radiation by the sample atoms) can also be avoided by measuring fluorescence at a nonresonance line that is not also absorbed.

Sensitized Fluorescence. In this type of fluorescence, an atom emits radiation after collisional activation by a foreign atom that was excited previously by absorbing resonance radiation, but which has not yet been deactivated again. An example is the sensitized fluorescence of thallium atoms in a gas mixture containing a high pressure of mercury vapor and a low pressure of thallium vapor. When irradiated at the 253.65-nm mercury line, the thallium atoms emit at 377.57 and 535.05 nm. This type of fluorescence requires a higher concentration of foreign atoms than can be obtained in flame cells, but presumably it could be observed in nonflame cells.

Instrumentation

The basic instrumentation for atomic-fluorescence spectroscopy is shown in Figure 10.13. The source is placed at right angles to the monochromator so that its radiation (except for scattered radiation) does not enter the monochromator. The source is chopped to produce an AC signal and minimize flame-emission interference. As in molecular fluorescence (Chap. 9), the intensity of atomic fluorescence is directly proportional to the intensity of the light impinging on the sample from the source.

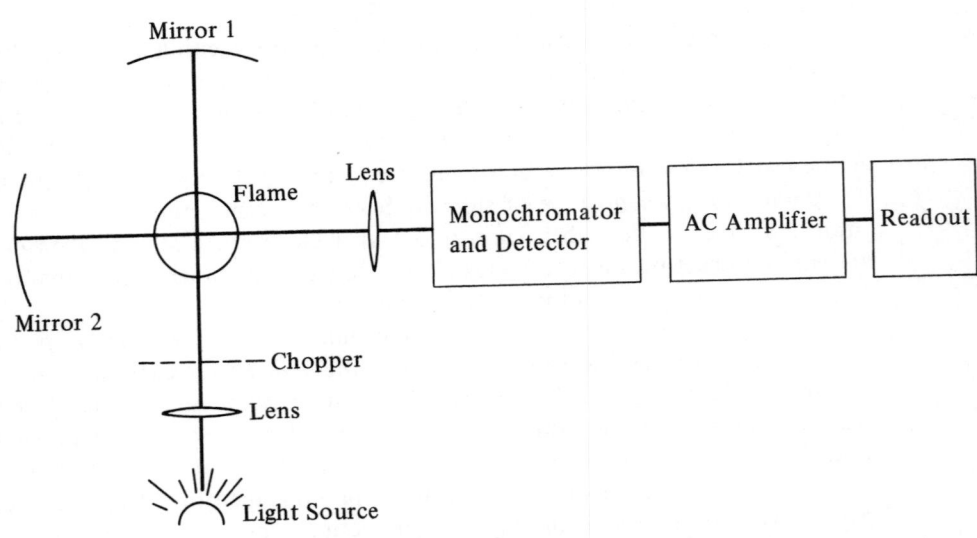

FIGURE 10.13. *Block diagram of atomic-fluorescence setup.*

It is also possible in many cases to increase the signal strength by using mirrors; in Figure 10.13, the light from the source is reflected back into the flame by mirror 1, while the fluorescence radiation that would normally be 180° from the monochromator is reflected back by mirror 2. Other suitable arrangements are possible.

The source can be a continuum source, since it is not necessary to isolate the emitted line from the source wavelengths; a 150-watt xenon lamp is commonly used. A major advantage of a continuum source, of course, is that it can be used for many elements. High-intensity sharp-line sources are also used, however, in an attempt to increase the sensitivity. Since conventional hollow-cathode lamps do not provide the desired intensity, the most widely used sharp-line source for atomic fluorescence is the *electrodeless discharge lamp*. This consists of a small quartz tube into which a small amount of metal or metal iodide is placed. The tube is evacuated, an inert gas (usually argon) at a pressure of 1–5 torr is added, and the tube is sealed. It is then placed in a resonant cavity where it is inductively coupled to a microwave radio-frequency field. The excited electrons produced by the ionization of the inert gas collide with the metal atoms, producing an intense spectrum. Detection limits one or more orders of magnitude lower than those using a continuum source are achieved with these lamps. In recent studies, high-intensity laser sources have been used for further increases in sensitivity.

Both turbulent burners and premix burners have been used for atomic fluorescence. The premix burner is usually round in shape (a modification of the Meker-type burner), since this provides better geometry for fluorescence than does a slot burner. For an optimum detection limit, the premix burner is also "shielded"; that is, an inert gas such as argon or nitrogen is directed in a sheath around the flame. This elongates the interconal zone and lifts the secondary reaction zone above the burner, separating it from the lower part of the interconal zone where the excitation beam passes. The result is less background emission and less noise, particularly in hydrocarbon flames like air-acetylene or nitrous oxide–acetylene. The premix burner, especially when shielded, appears to offer increased sensitivity over the turbulent burner.

For easily atomized elements, hydrogen flames are generally used because of their low flame-emission and flame-flicker noise. For the more refractory elements, however, a fuel-rich nitrous oxide–acetylene flame is required.

A problem with atomic-fluorescence measurements, much as in molecular fluorescence, is quenching of the signal. Quenching in an air-hydrogen flame can be decreased by replacing the nitrogen (in the air) with argon, which has less quenching effect than nitrogen. This would not help appreciably in hydrocarbon flames, however, because the CO and CO_2 present are much better quenchers than even nitrogen.

Non-flame atomizers have also been used in atomic-fluorescence spectroscopy.

Reported detection limits for determination of some elements by atomic-fluorescence spectroscopy are given in Table 10.4. A number of these were obtained using a laser source.

The same detectors are used for atomic-fluorescence measurements as are used for atomic-absorption and atomic-emission spectroscopy. By using a diode-array detector, simultaneous multi-element determinations can be made.

SELECTED BIBLIOGRAPHY

ANGINO, E. E., and BILLINGS, G. K. *Atomic Absorption Spectrometry in Geology*, 2nd ed. Amsterdam: Elsevier, 1972.

BURRIEL-MARTI, F., and RAMIREZ-MUÑOZ, J. *Flame Photometry: A Manual of Methods and Applications*. Amsterdam: Elsevier, 1957.

CHRISTIAN, G. D., and FELDMAN, F. J. *Atomic Absorption Spectroscopy: Applications in Agriculture, Biology, and Medicine*. New York: Wiley-Interscience, 1970.

DEAN, J. A. *Flame Photometry*. New York: McGraw-Hill, 1960.

DEAN, J. A., and RAINS, T. C., eds. *Flame Emission and Atomic Absorption Spectrometry*, vol. 1, *Theory* (1969); vol. 2, *Components*

and Techniques (1971); vol. 3, *Applications* (1975). New York: Marcel Dekker.

MAVRODINEANU, R., ed. *Analytical Flame Spectroscopy: Selected Topics*. New York: Springer-Verlag, 1970.

MAVRODINEANU, R., and BOITEAUX, H. *Flame Spectroscopy*. New York: John Wiley, 1965.

PARSONS, M. L., and McELFRESH, P. M. *Flame Spectroscopy: Atlas of Spectral Lines*. New York: IFI/Plenum, 1971.

PUNGOR, E. *Flame Photometry Theory*. Princeton: Van Nostrand, 1967.

SYCHRA, V., SVOBODA, V., and RUBESKA, I. *Atomic Fluorescence Spectroscopy*. London: Van Nostrand Reinhold, 1975.

REFERENCES

1. E. E. PICKETT and S. R. KOIRTYOHANN, *Anal. Chem.*, *41*(14), 28A (1969).

2. F. J. FELDMAN, *Anal. Chem.*, *42*, 719 (1970).

3. J. P. MATOUSEK, *Amer. Lab.*, *3*(6), 45 (1971).

4. G. D. CHRISTIAN, *Anal. Chem.*, *41*(1), 24A (1969).

5. P. M. HALD, "Sodium and Potassium by Flame Photometry," in D. Seligson, ed., *Standard Methods of Clinical Chemistry*, vol. 2, New York: Academic Press, 1958, pp 165–85.

PROBLEMS

1. Describe or define the following terms: (a) ground state (b) resonance wavelength (c) line half-width.

2. Describe the various ways by which an electronically excited atom may lose its excess energy.

3. For the elements listed in Table 10.1, calculate the ratios of N_u/N_0 given for the different temperatures.

4. Describe the factors that cause broadening of a spectral line.

5. Why will a nonlinear calibration curve and a loss in sensitivity generally occur in atomic-absorption spectroscopy when using a continuum light-source as compared to a sharp-line source?

6. Why is the half-width of a line emitted from a hollow-cathode lamp narrower than the absorption line half-width for an element in a flame?

7. Compare the resolution requirements of a monochromator for atomic-absorption measurement and atomic-emission measurement.

8. Compare the advantages and disadvantages of the total-consumption burner and the premix burner in atomic-absorption spectroscopy.

9. Although chemical interferences are generally more prevalent in "cool" flames, a relatively cool flame like air-propane is preferred for the alkali metals. Why?

10. Why is a high-temperature flame, for example, the nitrous oxide–acetylene flame, sometimes required in atomic-absorption spectroscopy?

11. Why is a high concentration of a potassium salt sometimes added to samples and standards in flame-spectroscopic measurements?

12. Why is it important to have a steady flame temperature in atomic-absorption as well as in atomic-emission measurements?

13. Why is the light source in atomic-absorption instruments generally modulated?

14. Why do furnace atomizers provide greatly increased sensitivity over flame atomizers in atomic-absorption measurements?

15. Identify and describe the major types of interferences encountered in flame atomic-emission and atomic-absorption measurements. Discuss how each can be minimized.

16. Why are organic solvents sometimes used in flame-spectroscopic measurements?

17. A 12-ppm solution of lead gives an atomic-absorption signal of 8.0% absorption. What is the atomic-absorption sensitivity?

18. A serum sample is analyzed for lithium by atomic-emission spectroscopy using the method of standard additions. Three 0.500-ml aliquots of sample are added to 5.00-ml portions of water. To these are added (a) 0 μl, (b) 10.0 μl, and (c) 20.0 μl of standard 0.0500 M LiCl solution. The emission signals (in arbitrary units) are 23.0, 45.3, and 68.0 for solutions (a), (b) and (c), respectively. What is the concentration of lithium in the serum sample in parts per million (wt/vol)?

19. You are asked to analyze for calcium and aluminum in a glass sample. Outline a procedure, including sample preparation, method of measurement, type of flame used, and method of calibration.

20. A sample of an unusual amino-acid analog —L-canavaninosuccinic acid, $C_9H_{16}N_4O_7$— was synthesized and converted to its barium salt to prevent a slow internal cyclization reaction during storage. A barium assay was performed by atomic-absorption spectroscopy to obtain an indication of the purity of the compound: 0.210 g of the compound was dissolved in dilute HNO_3 and diluted to 100.0 ml; 20.0 ml of the resultant solution was further diluted to 100.0 ml. Five replicate atomic-absorption readings were taken on a blank, 6 standards, and the test sample. The data are:

Sample	Average Meter Reading ± Standard Deviation (arbitrary absorbance units)
Blank	0 ± 7
1 ppm Ba	44 ± 3
4 ppm	178 ± 4
10 ppm	483 ± 12
14 ppm	684 ± 21
20 ppm	993 ± 36
30 ppm	1512 ± 88
Test Sample	762 ± 18

(a) Plot the calibration curve and determine the percentage of barium by weight in the original compound. (b) Compare this result with the expected Ba content for the "pure" compound, and comment on the purity of the synthesized sample.

21. The following atomic absorption data were obtained with solutions made up with varying amounts of methanol and a 1.00 mM aqueous stock solution of a metal ion:

Sample	Added Methanol (ml)	1 mM Stock Solution (ml)	Percent Absorption
#1	0	12.0	31.6
#2	1.0	11.0	31.8
#3	3.0	9.0	34.5
#4	4.0	8.0	28.5
#5	6.0	6.0	22.6
#6	8.0	4.0	16.3

(a) Explain the results. (b) What are the most favorable conditions for the analysis of aqueous solutions of the metal ion (that is, highest sensitivity)? (c) Calculate the concentration of the metal ion required to give 1% absorbance in the absence of added methanol, and with the optimum amount of added methanol.

22. A sodium solution is analyzed by flame emission using the 589-nm sodium-doublet line. In developing a procedure for the analysis, the analyst notes that a 1 ppm solution of sodium gives an emission reading of 112, while the same solution containing 10 ppm potassium gives a reading of 123. In view of the fact that a 10 ppm solution of potassium gives no appreciable reading at 589 nm, give a probable explanation for the enhancing effect of the potassium.

11

Emission Spectroscopy

Ramon M. Barnes

This chapter describes methods of observing the emission spectra of atoms, ions, and molecules using excitation sources powered by electrical energy. The common names *emission spectroscopy* or *optical-emission spectroscopy* are applied to these methods.

In emission spectroscopy, the excitation source transforms the sample from its initial state as solid, liquid, or gas into a plasma of atoms, ions, and molecular radicals that can be electronically excited. The radiative deactivation of these excited states produces light quanta which are sorted by wavelength in a spectrometer or spectrograph; the resulting emission spectrum is detected by either photographic or photoelectric means. Many aspects of these measurements resemble those described in Chapter 10 for flame-emission spectroscopy; but electrical arcs or sparks, glow or plasma discharges, or lasers replace the flame as the means of atomization and excitation of the sample. Most of the electrical-discharge excitation sources provide greater energies than do flame sources, and they produce more complex spectra that require spectrometers and spectrographs with better resolution.

Since every element possesses characteristic spectra, emission spectroscopy is applicable in both theory and practice to the entire periodic table. However, the emission spectra for some elements, notably halogens and the noble gases, require more energy to produce than do those for a metallic element, and special excitation conditions must be applied. Normally, the emission spectra of all metals and metalloids in a sample occur simultaneously when the sample is electrically excited.

Emission spectroscopy forms the basis for numerous practical qualitative and quantitative analyses in industrial quality-control and research applications. Quantitative analyses are very rapid once the procedure is defined and the instrument standardized, and analyses are generally simultaneous, multi-element ones; the determination of 25 to 35 metals and metalloids in steel or aluminum in a fraction of a minute is common. Furthermore, emission spectroscopy is customarily used to obtain a rapid qualitative or semiquantitative survey of elements contained in unknown materials, because of the ability of electrical excitation-sources to atomize and excite samples submitted in many forms—powders, solids, liquids, or gases. A spectrographic qualitative analysis may take no more than 20 minutes.

This chapter will describe the instrumentation required, the types of samples generally studied, and typical examples of techniques and applications of emission spectroscopy.

11.1 PRINCIPLES AND THEORY

The principles and theory described in Chapter 10 for atomic emission apply also to emission spectra produced by electrical excitation-sources. In those sources for which the Maxwell-Boltzmann expression (Eqn. 10.2) describes the distribution of energy levels for an atom or ion, the absolute temperature T represents the equilibrium temperature of the discharge. Since the temperatures of electrical sources are generally higher than those of flames, sufficient energy is available to produce ions. The concentrations of electrons and ions are uniquely related to the temperature and to the composition of the gas (all charged particles originate from thermal ionization of the gaseous form of the elements). The basic concept of thermal ionization introduced by Saha is the application of the law of mass action to ionization. The equilibrium constant can be expressed as a function of the absolute temperature in an expression known as the *Saha relationship* [1].

$$K_{nj} = \frac{n_{ij}n_e}{n_{aj}} = \frac{(2\pi mkT)^{3/2}}{h^3} \frac{2Z_{ij}}{Z_{aj}} e^{-E_{ij}/kT} \tag{11.1}$$

where n_{ij} = the density or concentration (in number per cm³) of the singly-charged ions of the component j

n_{aj} = the density of the neutral atoms

m = the mass of the electron

k = the Boltzmann constant

h = Planck's constant

Z = the partition function

E = the ionization energy

The subscripts a, i, e refer to the neutral *atom*, the *ion*, and the *electron*, respectively.

The practical version of the Saha formula (for a total pressure of one atmosphere) is given as follows:

$$\frac{n_{ij}n_e}{n_{aj}} = 4.83 \times 10^{15} T^{3/2} \frac{Z_{ij}}{Z_{aj}} 10^{(-5040V_{ij}/T)} \tag{11.2}$$

V_{ij}, the ionization potential, is expressed in electron volts. For calcium ($V_{ij} = 6.1$ eV) at T = 6000 K, the exponential factor is $10^{-5.12}$, whereas Z_{ij}/Z_{aj} for the Ca ($^1S_0$) and Ca$^+$ ($^2S_{1/2}$) ground states is ~2; so the equation gives a value of 3.4×10^{16}. For $n_e = 10^{17}/$cm³, as might be found in a high-current arc, $n_{ij} = 0.34n_{aj}$, or 25% ionization.

In an arc discharge (T = 4000 to 7000 K), at least 0.01 to 0.1 percent of all particles exist as ions. Electrical discharges require this minimum level of ionization to be conductive and remain self-supporting. The discharges, however, are essentially neutral because the negative charge carried by the free electrons is balanced by the total positive charge of the ions. Spectral lines from neutral atoms are designated with a Roman numeral I and those from singly charged ions with a Roman numeral II. The intensities of the lines depend upon the degree of ionization, the concentration of the element in the source, and the partition function, as well as the absolute temperature, the Boltzmann constant, the statistical weight, the frequency, the transition probability, and the excitation or ionization energies.

Thus, for electrical sources in thermal equilibrium, the processes of dissociation, excitation, and ionization can be treated as if the gas mixture were contained in a furnace at the same temperature. Excitation is described by the Maxwell-Boltzmann distribution law (Eqn. 10.2), ionization by the Saha relationship (Eqn. 11.1), and dissociation by the general relationships for chemical equilibrium.

Some electrical discharges, such as spark discharges, are transient in nature; others, such as glow discharges, operate at subatmospheric pressures. In both, the equilibria that characterize thermal atmospheric discharges are absent, so that the Boltzmann distribution and Saha relationship are no longer applicable. In practice, this means that one method will produce spectra with absolute intensities different from those produced by another. For instance, the emission spectrum of a spark discharge differs significantly with time from that of an arc; also, the excitation of halogens in a hollow-cathode discharge is more efficient than in an arc.

11.2 INSTRUMENTATION

The measurement of emission spectra requires a number of instrumental components, some common in principle to other spectrometric methods (Chap. 6). An excitation source powered by a suitable generator converts the sample into an emitting discharge plasma. The sample is held or contained in an excitation chamber or stand, and the radiation emitted from the electrical discharge is transferred by suitable optics to a spectrometer or spectrograph, which sorts the radiation according to wavelength. The readout translates the photoelectric (spectrometric) or photographic (spectrographic) record of the spectrum into an analog or digital display of the wavelengths and intensities. The wavelength region generally encompasses 180 to 900 nm; vacuum instrumentation permits investigation of shorter wavelengths, and many commercial systems do not operate at wavelengths longer than 500–600 nm.

Spectrometers

The components of a spectrometer include an entrance slit and at least one exit slit, a dispersive element such as a prism or grating, and optical components such as mirrors or lenses to collimate the entering light and to focus the spectrally resolved wavelengths on the exit slits. The term spectro*meter* implies that the detectors are photoelectric *measuring* devices such as photomultipliers, whereas the name spectro*graph* implies that the detector is an emulsion supported on either a glass or film backing that makes a direct photographic *representation* of a complete spectrum.

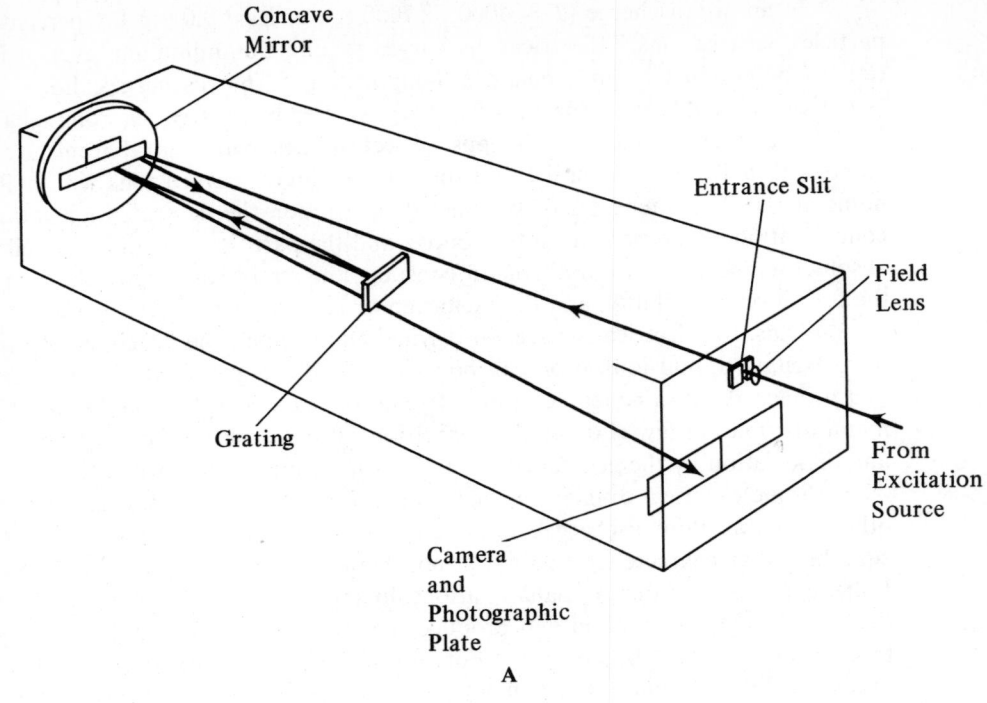

Concave
Mirror

Entrance Slit

Field
Lens

Grating

From
Excitation
Source

Camera
and
Photographic
Plate

A

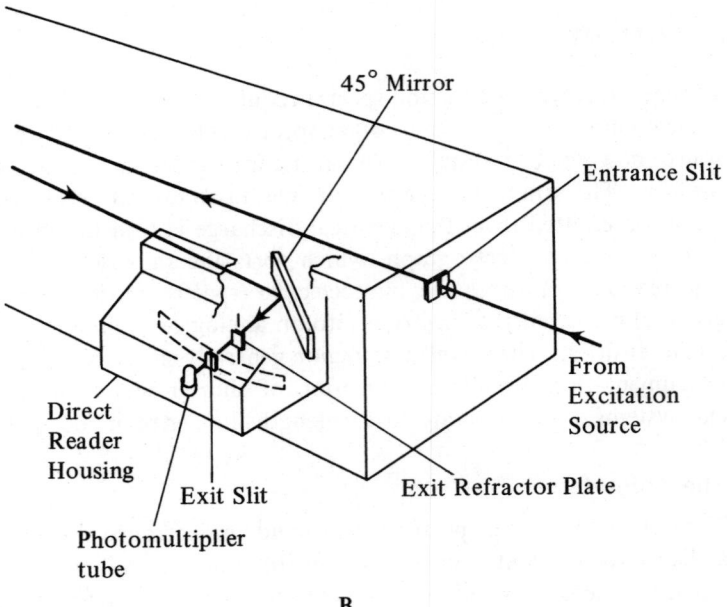

45° Mirror

Entrance Slit

Direct
Reader
Housing

From
Excitation
Source

Exit Slit

Exit Refractor Plate

Photomultiplier
tube

B

FIGURE 11.1. *Fastie-Ebert plane-grating convertible spectrograph-spectrometer. Courtesy of Jarrell Ash Division, Fisher Scientific Co.*

Figure 11.1 illustrates a Fastie-Ebert arrangement which can be used either as a spectrograph or a spectrometer by simply deflecting the spectrum with a large 45° plane mirror. One large, concave mirror is used both to collimate the entering light illuminating the grating and to focus the dispersed light onto the exit focal plane. Since its rediscovery in 1952, the Fastie-Ebert arrangement and the closely related Czerny-Turner arrangement have become the most popular monochromator-spectrometer-spectrograph instruments in atomic spectroscopy.

The use of photomultipliers in spectrometers requires the accurate positioning of exit slits along the spectrometer's focal curve, allowing the selection of individual spectral lines and groups of lines to detect many elements simultaneously. Emission spectrometers often have room for as many as 90 different exit slits, although only 20–35 separate detectors and readouts, called channels, might be used for a particular analysis. For some types of analysis, more than one spectral line from an element can be monitored to provide appropriate concentration ranges for the elements in various samples. Other channels may be used for background detectors or internal reference lines. Such instruments are sometimes called *direct-reading spectrometers* or *direct readers*.

Associated with each phototube is an electronic system in which the phototube current is converted to a voltage that is generally collected or integrated on a storage capacitor. The capacitor voltage is read during or at the end of the exposure, and analog devices or digital processors record and compute the concentration of the element detected. Many modern spectrometer readout systems operate with digital mini- or microcomputers. The computers control sample handling, excitation conditions, exposure times, and other spectrometer parameters, as well as data acquisition, computation, and presentation. Very rapid, precise readings can be obtained in this manner.

Spectrographs

Spectrographs employ a photographic emulsion to record the entire emission spectrum at one time, so exit slits or multiple detectors are not required. The record is permanent and can be inspected later for more detailed information, which cannot be done with readings obtained from spectrometers. Scanning the entire spectrum with a single-channel spectrometer (monochromator) requires approximately the same time as exposing and processing a spectrogram.

After the photographic emulsion is exposed in the spectrograph, the latent image (the spectrogram) is developed. A dark image appears for each emission line detected (Fig. 11.2). These dark images are generally in the shape of the entrance slit of the spectrograph, and the amount of darkening or blackening is directly related to the intensity of the emission signal for each emitting species in the discharge source —that is, to the number of photons striking the emulsion in unit time at each frequency.

In order to determine the positions of these darkened images or spectral lines, the plate or film is positioned in a comparator or microphotometer which projects a portion of the spectrum onto a viewing screen for direct comparison with a known or standard spectrum. The optical arrangement and photograph of a commercial microphotometer is shown in Figure 11.3. Typically, an iron spectrum will also be

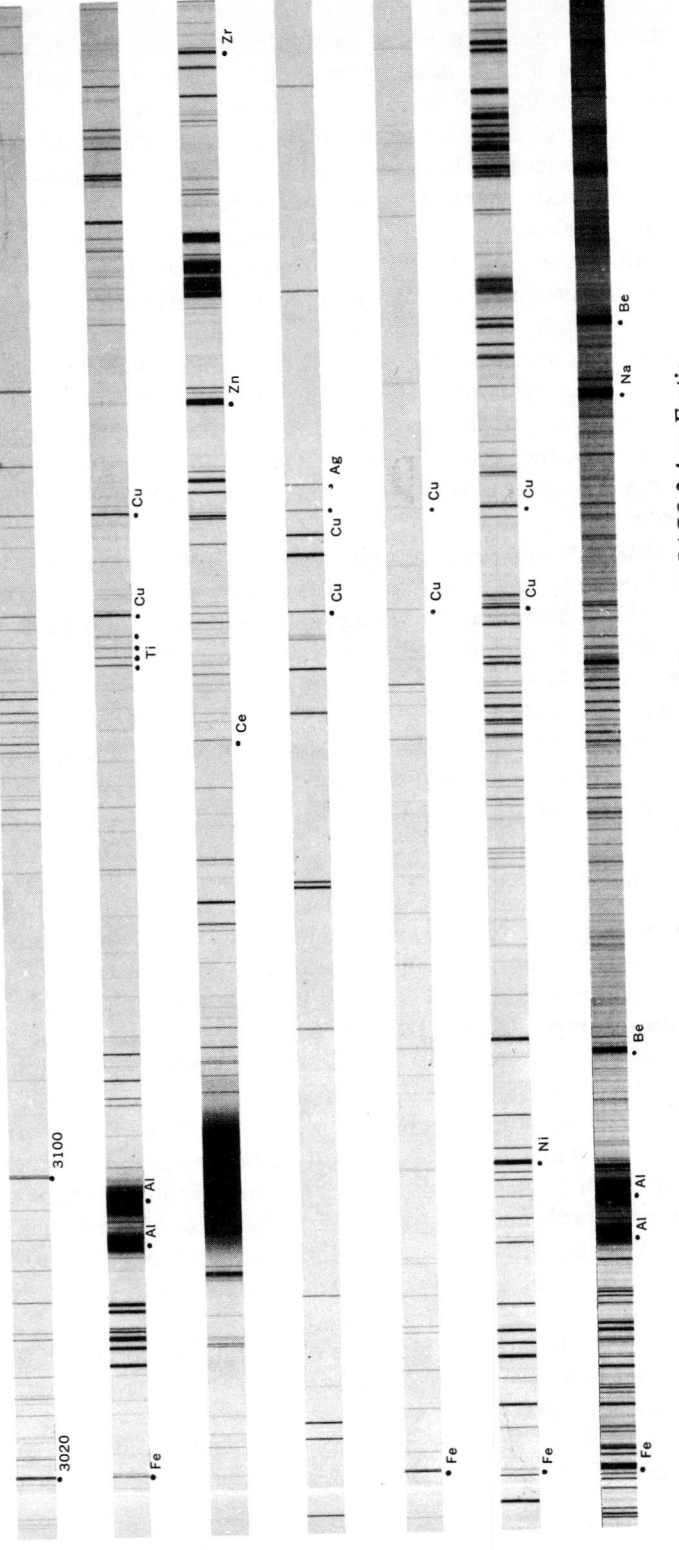

FIGURE 11.2. *Portions of typical spectra taken on a JACO 3.4-m Fastie-Ebert spectrograph employing a 15,000 line/inch grating giving a dispersion of 5 Å/mm at the focal plane. From top down, materials are: iron, aluminum, magnesium, lead, steel, nickel, and beryllium ore. Courtesy of Jarrell Ash Division, Fisher Scientific Co.*

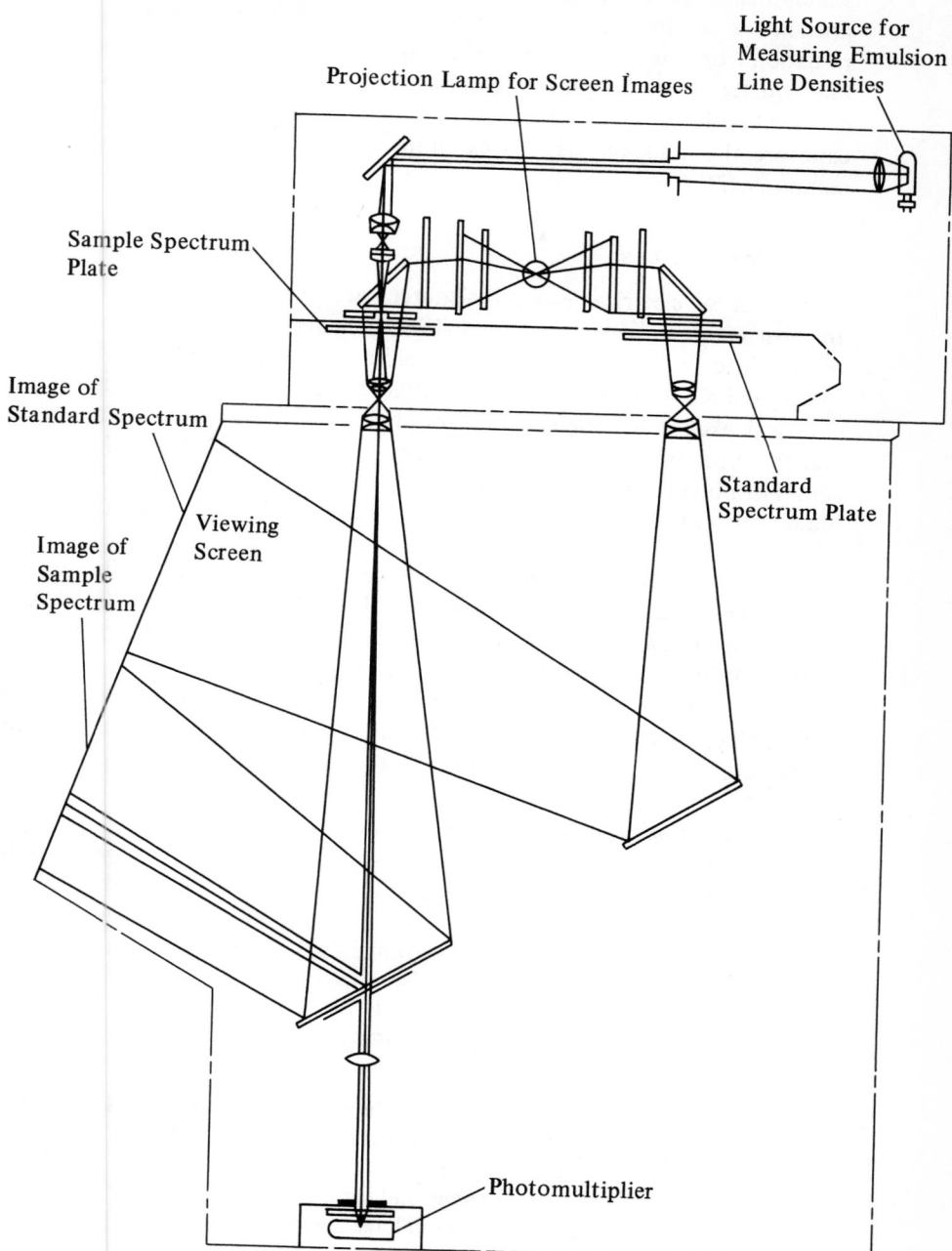

Light Source for
Measuring Emulsion
Line Densities

Projection Lamp for Screen Images

Sample Spectrum
Plate

Image of
Standard Spectrum

Standard
Spectrum Plate

Image of
Sample
Spectrum

Viewing
Screen

Photomultiplier

FIGURE 11.3. *Optical system for a microdensitometer. Courtesy of Spectrochemical Division, Baird-Atomic, Inc.*

recorded on the sample film; this allows one to align the sample spectrum with the standard spectrum. To determine the darkening of the spectral lines, the transmittance of the line is measured photometrically with the microphotometer [2]; the radiation from the light source is focused on a line, and the light passing through the line is detected by the photomultiplier tube. A galvanometer or digital readout is obtained. Since the blackening of the photoemulsion is not a linear function of the exposure, the emulsion has to be calibrated; this can be done easily using a laboratory computer [3].

Excitation Sources

A number of electrical excitation-sources are available for emission spectroscopy. In most commercial spectrochemical instruments, more than one excitation source is contained in a single power-supply cabinet; a typical combination may include a spark, a direct-current arc, and an alternating-current arc. A list of the various electrical excitation-sources, some of their characteristics, their approximate cost and the types of samples generally required is given in Table 11.1. Because of the actual or potential widespread use in emission spectroscopy, only the arc, spark, and inductively coupled plasma discharges will be described here in detail.

DC Arc. The DC arc is the least complex of the electrical excitation-sources discussed here; it consists of a low-voltage (10–50 V), high-current (1–35 A) discharge between a sample electrode and a counter electrode. The DC power supply may consist of no more than a full-wave rectifier and a filter.

The sample, most often prepared as a finely ground powder, is placed in a graphite cup electrode (see Fig. 11.4); the counter electrode is also fabricated from a graphite rod. The sample is usually (but not always) made the anode, and the

TABLE 11.1. *Some Emission Spectroscopy Sources*

Type	Characteristics	Samples Used	Price
DC Arc	Continuous, self-maintaining, direct-current discharge with low voltage and high current between sample and counter electrodes.	powders, solids, residues	$1000–6500
AC Arc	A series of separate discharges individually initiated once during each half-period of supply voltage and extinguished when voltage across the gap falls and becomes too low to sustain the discharge. Current continuous during conduction periods, similar to DC arc.	powders, solids, residues	$3000–4000

TABLE 11.1. (*continued*)

Type	Characteristics	Samples Used	Price
Spark	Transient discharge reaching high instantaneous current, produced by the discharge of a capacitor between the sample and counter electrodes with a duration of a few hundreds of microseconds and reoccurring 1–5000 times each second.	solid flats or rods, pressed pellets, liquids, residues	$3000–7000
DC Arc Plasma Jet; Gas Stabilized Arc	DC arc discharge formed between nonsample electrodes in flowing gas streams of argon or helium. Sample introduced separately.	liquids, powders	$1500–3500
Inductively Coupled Plasma Discharge	An electrodeless radio-frequency discharge produced by magnetically induced eddy currents in flowing argon confined in a quartz tube at atmospheric pressure.	liquids, powders, gases	$6000–10,000
Microwave Plasma Discharge	A discharge produced with or without electrodes by microwave fields in stationary or flowing gas streams in a microwave cavity.	liquids, gases	$1500
Glow Discharge Lamp	A low-pressure discharge in an inert gas, characterized by abnormal glow and sputtering of solid sample cathodes.	solids, residues	$10,000
Hollow Cathode Lamp	A low-pressure discharge in inert gas characterized by normal glow and sputtering of solid cathode.	solids, residues, gases	$2000–3500
Laser Microprobe	A plasma produced by the absorption of laser radiation, forming an emitting vapor cloud. Sometimes supplemented by auxiliary excitation by spark.	conducting and nonconducting solids	$19,000

counter electrode the cathode. The arc is initiated either by momentarily touching the two electrodes together or, more commonly, by applying an initial high-voltage spark. Once the discharge is formed, a bright, self-sustaining, electrically conducting path is established between the two electrodes. The electrodes heat rapidly and the sample is vaporized into the arc discharge. Graphite electrodes are generally used for routine samples, because graphite does not melt under these conditions and is a

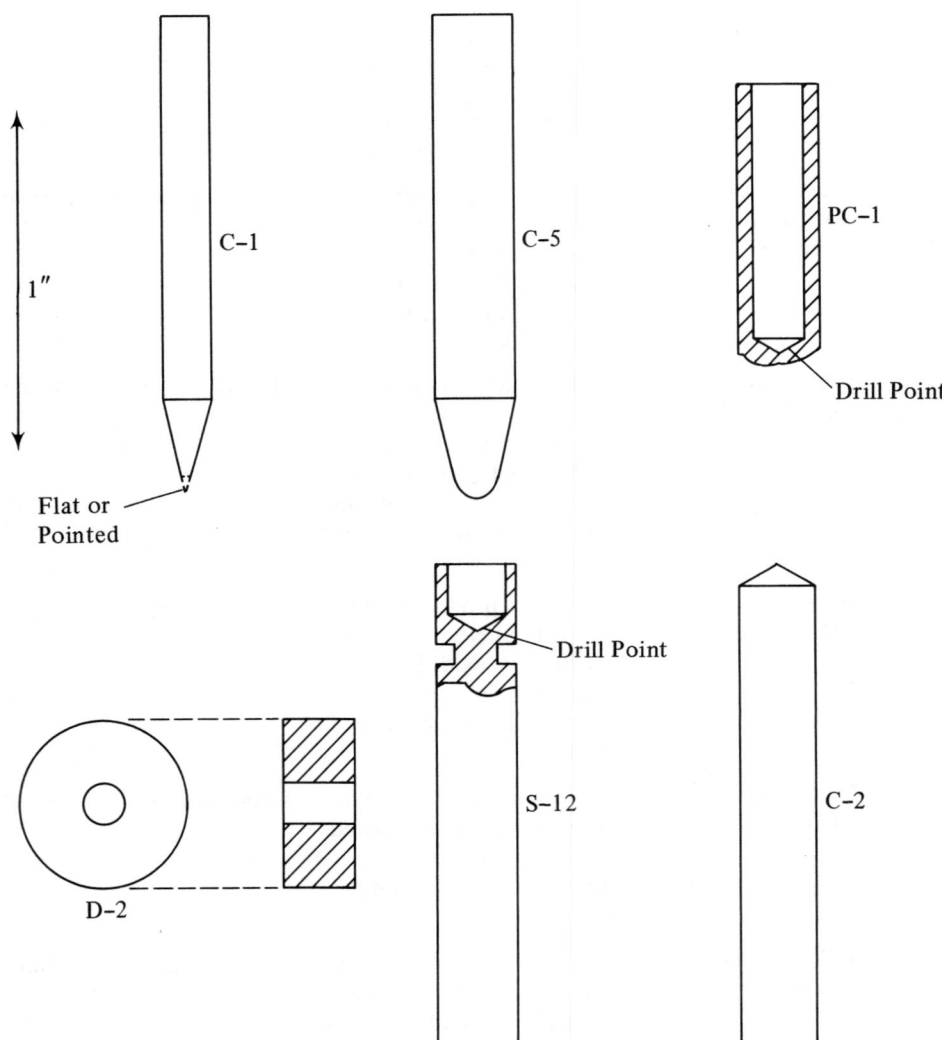

FIGURE 11.4. *Some standard forms of graphite sample and counter electrodes. Counter electrodes represented by "C", sample electrodes by "S", rotating disk by "D", and porous cup by "PC."* Adapted from Methods for Emission Spectrochemical Analysis, 6th ed., Philadelphia: *American Society for Testing and Materials, 1971, pp 105–10, by permission of the publisher. Copyright © 1971 by the American Society for Testing and Materials.*

good electrical conductor. The anode reaches a temperature of about 4200 K, whereas the cathode is at ≤ 3500 K; the conducting channel between the two electrodes ranges at equilibrium between 4000 and 7000 K, depending upon the atmosphere and the composition of the channel plasma. This conducting channel or arc is surrounded by a region of heated gas known as the mantle or envelope. The mantle reaches a temperature of approximately 3000–4000 K, but does not serve as a conducting pathway.

The sample does not simply "boil out of" the hot electrode, introducing the sample vapor into the arc region. Elements do not all vaporize at the same rate unless some additional steps are taken; the vaporization rate depends upon the chemical composition of the sample and upon the chemical and physical reactions that occur in the hot electrode. From a very simple point of view, the graphite electrode acts like a high-temperature oven in which each element is vaporized according to its thermal properties. However, factors such as the reduction of oxides, the formation of volatile compounds such as chlorides, alloying, and carbide formation alter these vaporization processes and, hence, the sequential appearance of emissions from the various elements. Refractory materials such as silicates may remain behind in the electrode cup long after other, more volatile, elements have escaped. In some applications, this separation of volatile from nonvolatile elements is deliberately enhanced by the addition of other compounds (the *carrier distillation* method). The determination of trace elements in uranium by addition of a carrier such as AgCl is an example: the trace elements rapidly volatilize along with the AgCl during the first 10–20 sec of arcing, but the uranium matrix remains mostly nonvolatilized and, thus, its complex spectrum is greatly diminished in intensity. In other situations, additional compounds are mixed with the sample to promote uniform and simultaneous vaporization. This admixture might include powdered graphite or salts with an easily ionized cation, such as Li_2CO_3, as diluents. The presence of lithium in the mixture will also provide a uniform arc temperature during vaporization of the sample. If lithium were not present, the ionization current flow and hence the arc temperature would change as each element or group of elements evaporated from the sample electrode. The arc temperature remains relatively constant in the presence of a sufficient quantity of lithium because the lithium is readily ionized and provides the arc with a constant supply of ions and electrons. In this application, Li_2CO_3 is called a *spectrochemical buffer*.

The high temperatures of electrodes and arcs result in consumption of the graphite electrodes. When the carbon from the electrode reacts with nitrogen in the ambient air, cyanogen (CN) forms, which emits an intense and complex molecular spectrum that obscures some useful atomic-emission spectra. One way to avoid cyanogen bands, and to stabilize the arc discharge at the same time, is to exclude air from the arc by operating it in a closed chamber filled with argon [4] or in a flowing stream (3–4 l/min) of mixed argon (70–80%) and oxygen (20–30%). The latter arrangement is called a *Stallwood jet*.

The evaporation of sample from the electrode and the consumption of the electrode during arcing also cause the arc column to shift its position on the electrode surface. This movement or wander of the arc relative to the optical axis of the spectrograph drastically reduces the precision of arc analysis. The Stallwood jet also aids in reducing arc wander.

The spectra of DC-arc discharges are considerably different from those observed for flames and sparks. Because of the high temperature of the arc column, sufficient energy is available to populate higher atomic states. A complex spectrum, generally composed of neutral-atom and ion emission, results.

The high efficiency of atomization and excitation shown by the DC arc, together with the line-rich spectra it produces, make the arc technique valuable for qualitative analysis and multi-element quantitative analysis. Large emission signals for relatively small amounts of sample characterize the sensitivity of the DC-arc source.

Spark. The chief characteristic of the spark discharge is its dependence upon short times and short-time processes. In routine use, the spark signal is time-integrated by a photographic emulsion or by the electronics associated with photoelectric detectors. The spark is typically produced by the discharge of a capacitor between the sample and counter electrodes; Figure 11.5 is a simplified circuit diagram of a

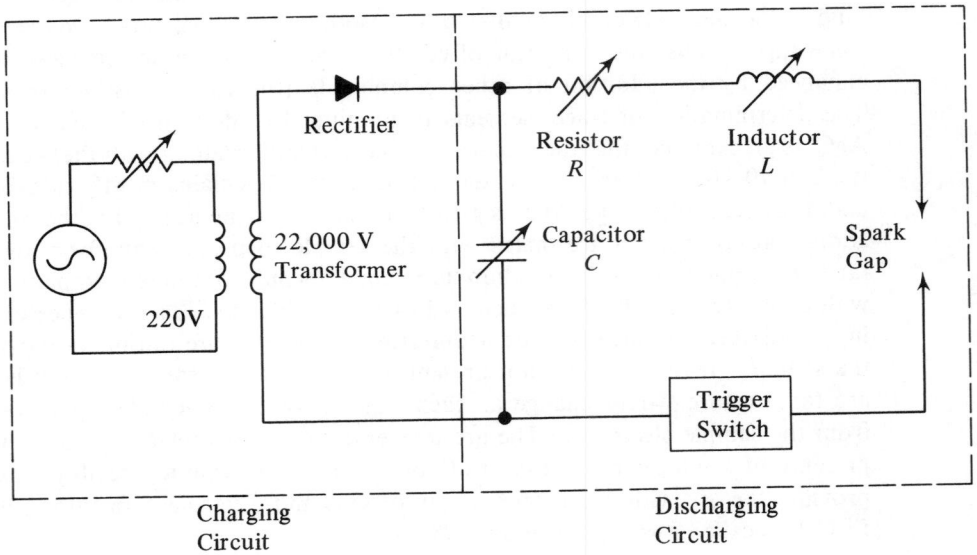

FIGURE 11.5. *Schematic diagram of a spark source for an emission spectrograph.*

typical spark source. A capacitor of 5–100 nf is charged to 1–30 kV and is then discharged (by the trigger switch) to form a conducting discharge channel or *spark* between the electrodes. There are typically 2 to 30 sparks per cycle of the line signal, or 120 to 1800 sparks per second. The amplitude of the oscillating discharge current flowing through the spark gap decays exponentially with time. The amplitude, frequency, and duration of the oscillation depend upon the discharge circuit parameters—resistance (R), capacitance (C), and inductance (L)—and on the voltage across the capacitor. For a particular analysis, these various parameters are specified after considerable trial-and-error experimentation to achieve the best quantitative results. Recently, a new design has markedly improved the operation of spark sources [5], and research into the mechanisms of the spark discharge [6] has led to ways of electronically shaping the waveform of the spark discharge for improved analytical results.

Although numerous spark-source arrangements have been developed, two types are most common: the high-voltage source (with or without a diode rectifier) shown in Figure 11.5, and a medium-voltage (1000 V) source.

Events happen very rapidly in the spark discharge, and what happens is substantially different from what happens in an arc. For example, during the first oscillation of the current, which may last only about 10 μsec, the spark-discharge channel is formed and the sample material is vaporized, atomized, ionized, excited, and propelled into the spark gap at velocities of up to 10 km/sec. As the excited atoms and ions travel away from the sample electrode, they emit their characteristic spectra. As the spark current falls, the spark-discharge channel contracts, ions recombine into excited atoms, and the sample is vapor-deposited on the counter electrode. The process is repeated in subsequent half-cycles until the capacitor voltage is insufficient to maintain the spark discharge. Clearly, the emission spectra from a spark discharge depend not only upon the part of the spark gap viewed by the spectrograph (near the anode, near the cathode, or in the middle) but on the selected time during the spark discharge. Without special equipment, spark-emission spectra are integrated over the total time of all these events.

Although the spark discharge appears complex, the quantitative application of the spark provides a very efficient means for transforming solid samples into emitting atomic vapors. The spark discharge provides fast, precise analysis; in quality-control steel analysis, for example, the time is less than 10 sec. Although the sensitivity is commonly not as high as that obtained with a DC arc, high precision can be obtained without special techniques.

The spark discharge is often applied to solid samples in the form of rods approximately a quarter-inch in diameter or cast disks or flats a half-inch thick by 1 to 3 inches in diameter. Powders are most often pressed into pellets and treated as solid samples for spark analysis. Liquid samples are also analyzed by spark discharges in many cases. Several different ways of analyzing liquid samples have been developed:

1. The porous-cup electrode (Fig. 11.4) is a quarter-inch graphite rod hollowed out by drilling, leaving a few millimeters at the end of the rod to form a bottom through which solutions can seep. The hollow electrode is filled with a few milliliters of sample solution, and the bottom is sparked against a graphite rod below it.

2. The rotating-disk electrode is a graphite disk about a half-inch in diameter held vertically; it dips into a solution and carries a thin film of the solution to the top of the electrode, where it is sparked. The disk is rotated at about 5 to 30 rpm.

3. Liquids can also be dried onto the top of quarter-inch graphite or metal rods, or on half-inch graphite disks, and the dried residue sparked. The *copper-spark* method uses a dried residue on a quarter-inch copper rod, and the *rotating-platform* method employs a half-inch graphite disk onto which the residue is dried and which is rotated horizontally during sparking. Both methods give good precision, and the copper-spark method is characterized by excellent sensitivity (cf. Table 11.2).

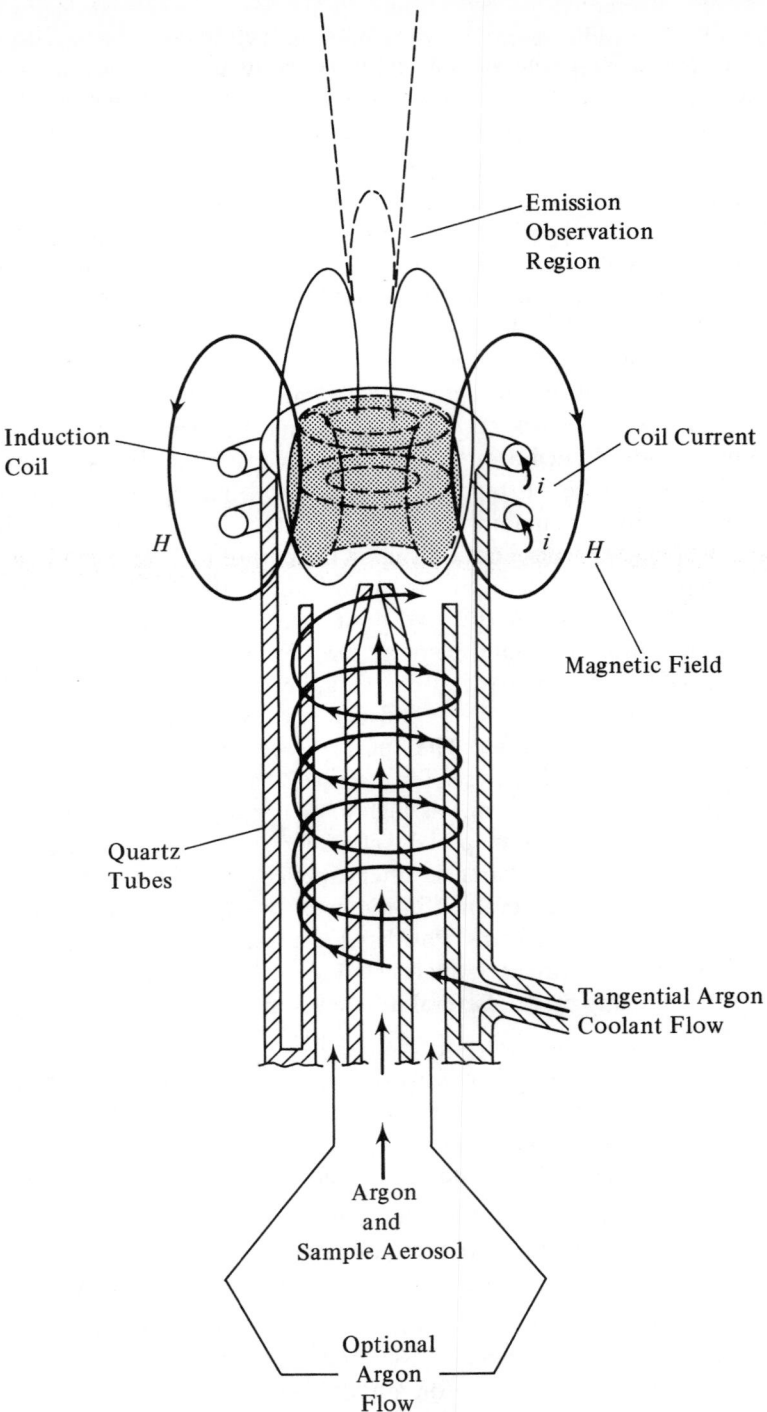

FIGURE 11.6. *Schematic representation of an inductively coupled plasma discharge. Adapted from V. A. Fassel and R. N. Kniseley,* Anal. Chem., *46,* 1110A (1974), *by permission of the publisher. Copyright © 1974 by the American Chemical Society.*

Inductively Coupled Plasma (ICP) Discharge. The arc and spark sources date to the early development of emission spectroscopy in the mid-1800s; the inductively coupled plasma (ICP) discharge is a relatively recent development, and is perhaps the most promising emission spectroscopic source today. Commercial ICP systems became available only in 1974, but research on this source has been going on since the early 1960s [7].

The ICP discharge is caused by the effect of a radio-frequency field on a flowing gas. In Figure 11.6, it is induced without electrode contact in argon flowing upward through a quartz tube inside a copper coil or solenoid. The coil is energized by a radio-frequency generator operating between about 5 to 75 MHz; a typical frequency is 27 MHz. The radio-frequency signal creates a changing magnetic field H inside the coil in the flowing argon gas.

A changing magnetic field induces a circulating (eddy) current in a conductor, which in turn heats the conductor. At room temperature, argon is not a conductor, but it can be made electrically conductive by heating it. To start the ICP discharge, a pilot spark, arc, or Tesla discharge is applied to the argon. This pilot discharge absorbs energy from the changing magnetic field and turns rapidly into a stable discharge plasma that is thermally very hot and spectrally very intense. The equilibrium temperature in the core of an ICP discharge operating at 1–2 kw input power is about 9,000–10,000 K.

More than one stream of argon is often used for spectrochemical analysis with the ICP discharge. One argon stream is confined to a volume near the tube walls to protect the quartz from the high-temperature discharge. A second argon stream carries the sample into the center of the discharge to produce an effective pathway through the discharge. If this pathway were not formed, the sample might flow around the hot discharge and be less effectively heated.

Although samples may be injected either as powders or as liquids, an arrangement similar to the spray-chamber nebulizer assembly used in flame spectroscopy (Chap. 10) is presently utilized. A complete nebulizer, spray chamber, and ICP discharge assembly is illustrated in Figure 11.7 [8]. The solvent is evaporated from the solution droplets formed in the spray chamber, so that only dried particles flow with the argon into the high-temperature discharge.

Because of the high temperatures available and the inert atmosphere of the ICP discharge, some of the difficulties found in flame, arc, and spark techniques are not present in the ICP discharge. Chemical interferences caused by the formation of stable compounds in flames (see Chap. 10) are negligible with the ICP discharge, so that releasing agents or special conditions are not needed. All compounds are likely to be atomized completely during their passage through the hot pathway in the center of the discharge. Ionization interferences occur in excitation sources with high temperatures such as the DC arc and the ICP plasma; however, adding a spectroscopic buffer such as 1000 ppm LiCl remedies any difficulty in the ICP discharge.

Spectral interferences with the ICP source are also possible, especially when the hot region of the discharge is viewed. However, the continuum background from the hot discharge does not extend appreciably beyond the end of the induction coil, and very high signal-to-background ratios are obtained just a short distance (1–3 cm) above the induction coil. Background from the argon continuum and interference from Ar(I) emission is minimal.

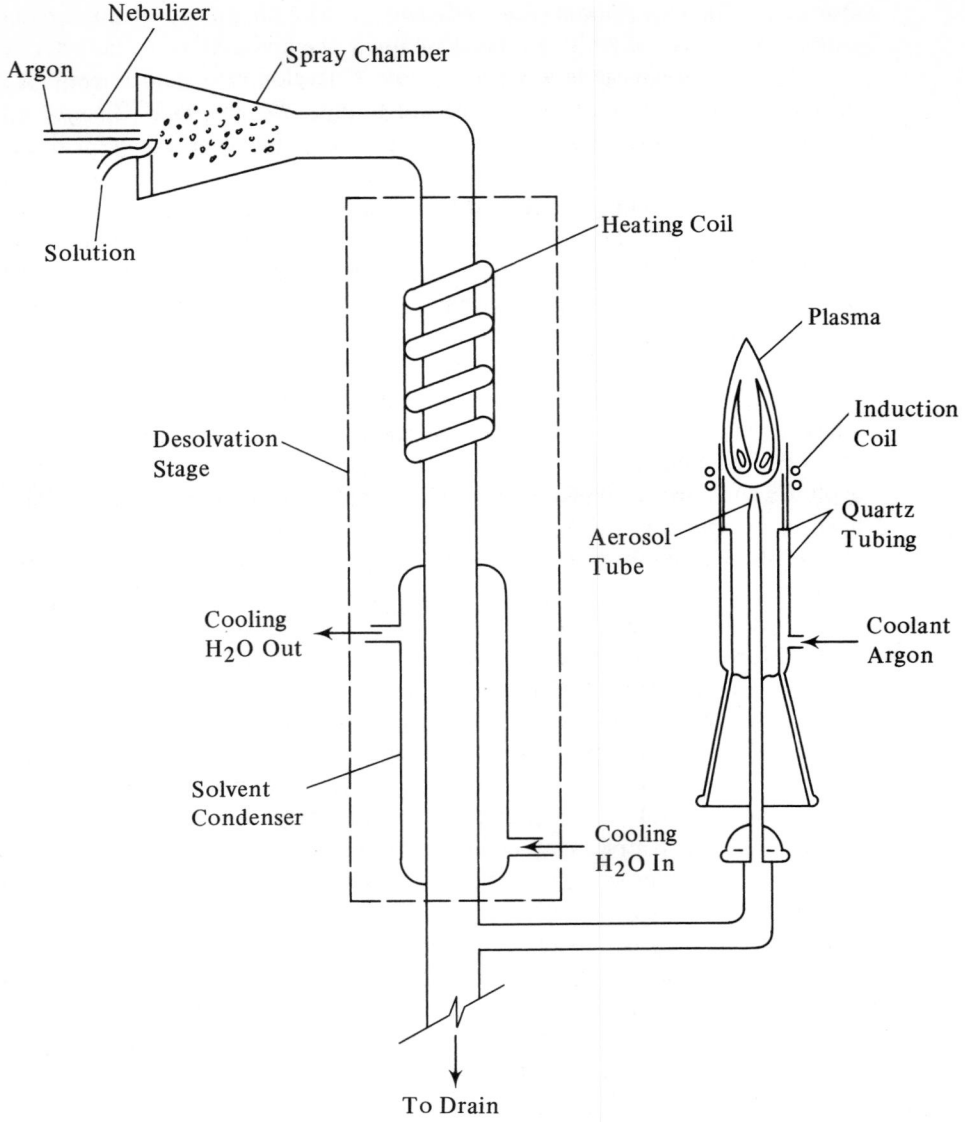

FIGURE 11.7. *Sample nebulizer, spray chamber, and desolvation apparatus for ICP discharge spectrometry. (Not to scale.) Adapted from R. N. Kniseley, V. A. Fassel, and C. C. Butler, Clin. Chem., 19, 807 (1973), by permission of the publisher.*

The spectrum of an element in the ICP discharge resembles most closely one obtained in the DC arc rather than in a spark or a flame, so that the ICP discharge provides a rich spectrum for qualitative and simultaneous multi-element quantitative analysis. Even molecular spectra such as that due to CN are minimized in the ICP discharge or are located in a separate region of the discharge. In addition, the stabilities of the signal intensities observed in the ICP discharge are comparable to those of the flame rather than the arc or spark discharges.

The temperature distribution of the ICP discharge differs from other electronic excitation-sources owing to the induction coupling effect. Instead of finding the highest temperature along the axis of the discharge, as in the DC arc, the highest temperatures of the ICP discharge are found off-axis in the induction-coil region.

All of these properties of the ICP discharge provide excellent capabilities for quantitative analysis. Flow and operating conditions can be readily selected, so that nearly optimum signal-intensities for most elements can be obtained in a single spectroscopic viewing region above the hot discharge. This allows the simultaneous determination of 35 elements, for example, in a single sample without modifying the conditions for each element.

Table 11.2 presents detection limits for emission spectroscopy with several excitation sources. (These may be compared with those given in Table 10.4 for flame methods.) Generally less than 5 ml of sample solution is required for both emission analysis and the flame methods. The ICP discharge has been found to have both the precision of flame methods and the sensitivity of arc methods [9]. (For precise determinations, concentrations should generally be 100 times the detection limits listed.)

Although quantitative analysis with the ICP discharge may be performed with a spectrograph, the ICP discharge is more efficiently used with a spectrometer. One of the major reasons is that the high signal-to-background ratio and high stability provide linear analytical curves (readout signal as a function of concentration) over ranges of 10^4 to 10^5 [10]. This linearity exceeds by orders of magnitude that ob-

TABLE 11.2. *Comparison of Some Experimentally Determined Emission Spectroscopic Detection Limits* ($\mu g/ml$)

Element	DC Arc[a]	Spark[b]	ICP[c,d]
Ag	0.0006	0.2	0.004
Al	0.05	0.05	0.00008
As	0.1	5	0.002
Au	0.05	0.1	0.04
B	0.07	0.5	0.0001
Ba	0.005	0.02	0.00001
Be	0.0006	0.0002	0.000003
Bi	0.03	0.1	0.05
Ca	0.01	0.05	0.0000001
Cd	0.02	1	0.0002
Ce	0.02	0.3	0.0004
Co	0.01	0.05	0.003
Cr	0.01	0.05	0.0008
Cu	0.0003	—	0.0006
Fe	0.01	0.5	0.00009

(*continued*)

TABLE 11.2. (*continued*)

Element	DC Arc[a]	Spark[b]	ICP[c,d]
Ga	0.02	0.02	0.0002
Ge	0.02	——	0.0005
Hf	1	0.25	0.01
Hg	0.07	1	0.01
In	0.03	0.3	0.03
La	0.03	0.02	0.0001
Mg	0.007	0.05	0.000003
Mn	0.003	0.01	0.00002
Mo	0.006	0.03	0.0001
Na	0.005	0.1	0.00002
Nb	5	0.10	0.0002
Ni	0.02	0.05	0.0001
P	0.15	4	0.015
Pb	0.005	0.1	0.001
Pd	0.02	0.02	0.0008
Pt	0.04	0.4	0.08
Rh	0.02	0.05	0.003
Sb	0.07	2	0.2
Sc	0.2	0.01	0.003
Se	——	——	0.03
Si	0.1	0.20	0.01
Sn	0.05	0.30	0.003
Sr	0.00003	0.002	0.00003
Ta	30	0.3	0.03
Te	60	4	0.08
Th	0.02	0.5	0.003
Ti	0.0001	0.01	0.00003
Tl	0.07	0.8	0.2
U	——	2	0.03
V	0.02	0.02	0.00006
W	0.3	0.4	0.0007
Yb	0.0009	0.005	0.00002
Zn	0.01	0.5	0.00001
Zr	0.004	0.01	0.00006

a. V. Svoboda and I. Kleinmann, *Anal. Chem.*, *40*, 1534 (1968).
b. J. P. Faris, *Proc. 6th Conf. Anal. Chem. Nucl. Reactor Tech.*, TID-76655, Gatlingburg, Tenn., 1962.
c. V. A. Fassel and R. N. Kniseley, *Anal. Chem.*, *46*, 1110A, 1155A (1974).
d. P. W. J. M. Boumans and F. J. de Boer, *Proc. Anal. Div. Chem. Soc.*, *12*, 140 (1975).

tained in routine spark and arc analyses, as well as in flame methods. The linearity of the photographic emulsion is insufficient to cover this range, and only photomultipliers have the capability needed.

11.3 QUALITATIVE AND QUANTITATIVE ANALYSES

Emission spectroscopy is widely used for both qualitative and quantitative analysis. The high sensitivity and the possible simultaneous excitation of as many as 72 elements, notably metals and metalloids, makes emission spectroscopy especially suited for rapid survey analysis of the elemental content in small samples at the level of 10 μg/g or less. With control over excitation conditions to maintain constant and reliable atomization and excitation, the spectral line intensities can be used for quantitatively determining concentrations. An analytical curve must be constructed with known standards, and often the ratio of analyte intensity to the intensity of a second element contained in, or added to, the sample (the internal-standard method) is used to improve the precision of quantitative analyses. Preparation of standards for arc and spark techniques requires considerable care to match chemical and physical forms to the sample; this is not commonly required for ICP discharge.

Qualitative Analysis

Emission spectroscopy is especially well suited to the identification of elements contained in a sample, because meaningful results are obtained in less than an hour in a single exposure requiring only a few mg of sample in almost any form. Conventionally, DC-arc excitation is used for qualitative analysis because of its high sensitivity for metals and metalloids. To perform a DC-arc qualitative analysis, the sample (as a powder, small chunks, chips, filings, residue, or other form) is placed in a graphite-cup electrode (Fig. 11.4), and the electrode arced until the entire sample is vaporized. The spectrum is integrated photographically, providing a permanent record over a comprehensive wavelength range. Generally, several spectra are recorded on one photographic film or plate by moving (racking) this film in the camera between each run (see, e.g., Fig. 11.2). One of the spectra is usually that of iron to allow alignment with master plates. Processing the photoplate takes about ten minutes, and the spectrum is compared on a comparator-densitometer (Fig. 11.3) with either a master plate or a series of spectra of known elements (Fig. 11.3). The master plate, available commercially, contains a standard iron-arc spectrum, a wavelength scale, and wavelength markers for the persistent or most sensitive characteristic lines for each element. A portion of a master plate is shown in Figure 11.8. After aligning the unknown spectrum with the master plate, major line coincidences are identified for characteristic lines on the master. Three lines are generally required for positive identification of an element. An additional aid is that certain elements have characteristic patterns or groupings of spectral lines, which, with a little practice, are rapidly found and used for positive identification. Reference to standard wavelength tables provides additional lines that may be found in the unknown spectrum but not on the master plate.

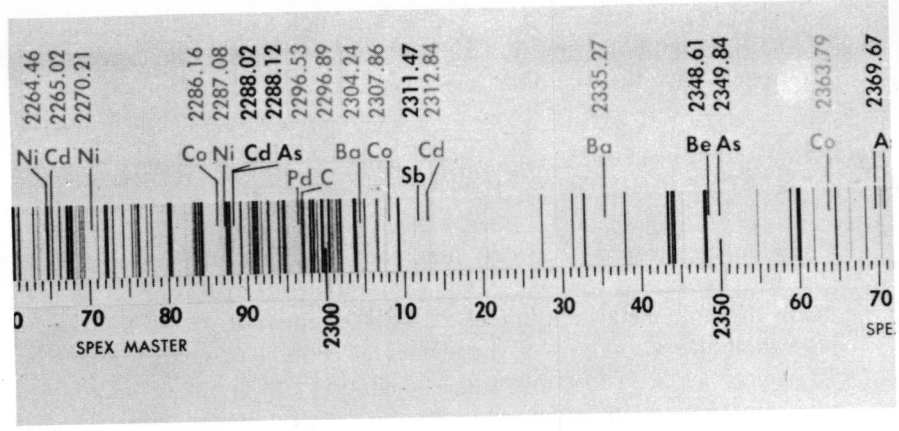

FIGURE 11.8. *Segment of Spex Master plate. In the complete plate, persistent lines of about 70 elements are given with color-coded labeling for ease of identification. Lines are superimposed on an iron spectrum. Units are angstroms. Courtesy of Spex Industries, Metuchen, N.J.*

Qualitative analysis by laser microprobe is popular for identifying small inclusions or areas in conducting and nonconducting samples. The laser can be focused to sample areas of 10 to 50 μm in diameter.

Often, qualitative analyses are performed with slightly more control over the various experimental conditions to obtain a rough estimate of the concentration range of the elements identified as major, minor, or trace. For better concentration estimates, semiquantitative or quantitative techniques, demanding greater control over parameters, are applied.

Quantitative Analysis

Emission spectroscopy is an important quantitative technique widely used in many industrial and research laboratories. In order to achieve an absolute concentration error of less than $\pm 10\%$, sample preparation and handling, experimental variables, and operating parameters must be strictly controlled. With conventional arc and spark procedures, absolute errors of ± 1–5% can be achieved. The development of a routine spectrometric analysis may take months, but once the method is optimized, high-quality quantitative results are obtained rapidly and routinely for large numbers of similar samples.

Fluctuations in electronic excitation-sources (described in Sec. 11.2), together with sample irregularities, constitute the major sources of error in emission spectroscopy. Modern spectrometers provide excellent stability and precision, and new sources like the ICP discharge and the controlled-waveform spark discharge have reduced many of the previous limitations. Photoelectric detection generally provides precision superior to that of photographic methods.

Some other critical considerations in quantitative emission spectroscopy include obtaining a representative sample, treating the sample to provide a suitable form without contamination, and matching standards with samples.

Electrodes. For arc and spark analyses, graphite electrodes are commonly used as sample and counter electrodes; some standardized electrode shapes are presented in Figure 11.4 [11]. The purity of these electrodes must be high, and most suppliers provide a quantitative DC-arc analysis for at least 15 elements with each box of electrodes. Electrodes are generally guaranteed to have a total ash content of less than 1 ppm, a maximum allowable impurity per element of 2 ppm, and total maximum impurities of 6 ppm.

High-purity graphite powder for DC-arc mixtures, or for pressed pellets for spark analysis, is also analyzed and guaranteed by manufacturers. In spark methods, the sample (if conductive) is often one of the two electrodes, and only a counter electrode is needed. Graphite electrodes are common, but metal counter electrodes, especially silver (to permit determination of carbon), are routinely employed in vacuum spark analysis.

Samples. Careful control of sampling and sample preparation is essential in quantitative emission spectroscopy. Even in the routine spark analysis of steel or aluminum, which requires only the grinding or machining of the surface of cast samples, the detailed characteristics of the sample-casting procedures had to be studied extensively during the method-development phase.

In arc analyses, the sample may require treatment before analysis; this can contribute contaminants or cause loss of some elements. For example, samples with high carbon content, like coal, require the removal of the organic portion by ashing in a muffle furnace at elevated temperatures or in a low-temperature oxygen plasma. Coal is ashed in platinum or silica crucibles at 500°C to eliminate the organic portion, but these high temperatures may cause volatilization and loss of some trace elements. Other inorganic materials such as rock, cement, slag, or chemicals need only to be dried, ground, and sieved. However, each step can also contaminate the sample. Typically, samples are ground so that known sources of contamination are eliminated. For example, in the analysis of beryllia (BeO) for other elements, samples are ground with a high-purity BeO mortar and pestle. (The use of a mortar and pestle made of tungsten carbide or of alumina will contaminate the specimen with iron and cobalt traces from the tungsten carbide or with aluminum from the alumina.) Sieving with metal screens can also contaminate the sample with traces of the screen material.

Sample contamination must also be taken into account when adding internal-reference and spectrochemical-buffer compounds. High-purity materials used for these special purposes are commercially available, since most laboratory chemicals are not pure enough.

Standards. The preparation of solid and powder standards for quantitative emission analysis is an important phase of the development and testing of new emission methods. Sometimes the lack of suitable standards hinders the analysis or limits the obtainable accuracy. Standard reference materials are being continually tested and authorized by the National Bureau of Standards, and a number of major steel and aluminum companies have developed standard disk samples for emission and x-ray spectrometry. Standards for trace metals in oil are also produced commercially.

In arc- and spark-emission spectroscopy, one of the critical aspects of quantitative analysis is the need to match the standard as closely as possible to the sample. Dilution of sample and standards by a common matrix in DC-arc methods somewhat reduces the dependence upon exact matches. Gordon and Chapman devised a common matrix-dilution technique for DC-arc analysis which is almost totally independent of the forms of the sample and the standard [4].

Internal-Standard Method. In emission spectroscopy, some of the variables in the excitation and processing of spectra can be minimized or eliminated by adopting the internal-standard technique. The technique is based upon measuring the ratio of the analyte signal-intensity and the reference-line signal-intensity. The internal standard is added to both the sample and the standards at the same concentration. The method assumes that as the excitation-source and spectrometer-readout conditions vary, the signal from the internal standard will change in the same way as those for the analyte elements. Thus, a ratio of the line intensities should minimize variations. Barnett et al. [12] has detailed the factors considered in selecting an internal standard. The technique is applied in both photographic and photoelectric detection systems; for photographic emulsions, the internal standard tends to correct for differences in processing and in emulsion properties from one plate to the next.

In routine industrial analysis, multi-channel spectrometers under computer control generally acquire, store, and update analytical curves for numerous elements simultaneously as part of a periodic check on standards. Excellent precision and accuracy can be obtained with these procedures.

In developing an emission spectroscopic method, especially arc and spark techniques, considerable effort must be devoted to the selection of internal-standard materials and spectral lines. Some arc and all ICP methods exhibit good precision without use of an internal standard.

Analytical Curves. Emission spectroscopy is not an absolute technique, and the intensity response for each analyte element must be calibrated for various known amounts of the element introduced into the excitation source. The analytical curve from the microphotometer (Fig. 11.3) represents this calibration. The transmittance of the analyte line is measured along with a nearby background, and these values are transformed into relative intensities using the emulsion calibrations. The selection of photographic emulsion depends upon the wavelength range to be covered and on the strengths of the spectral signals. Operating parameters, including exposure conditions and film-developing time and temperature, are selected in preliminary experiments to provide calibration linearity and good signal-to-noise ratio. Once determined, these conditions must then be maintained rigorously throughout the calibration and analysis stages.

Concentration is the independent variable, and the relative intensity or intensity ratio is the dependent variable. Some analytical curves are plotted on logarithmic coordinates, but computer curve-fitting procedures readily allow wide-range rectilinear calibrations, as well as calculation of the concentration values for unknown samples. For very accurate work, emulsion calibrations are repeated for each spectrum by adopting the sample spectrum as the source of the emulsion calibration.

Accuracy and Precision. The accuracy and precision required of an atomic-emission spectroscopic method affect the approach used in the analysis as well as the time involved. A qualitative analysis requires a minimum of effort, but as better accuracy and precision are demanded, increasing care is needed. Even if a representative sample has been obtained, errors inherent in the method, human errors, and random errors contribute to inaccuracies. Spectrochemical equipment is largely responsible for the random errors that influence precision, and both method and individual laboratory errors influence the accuracy. In addition, relative precision and accuracy depend upon concentration levels. The standard deviation increases with increasing concentration, but the relative standard deviation decreases; the latter may vary from a few percent to less than one percent using photographic detection, depending on the element and the concentration.

Precision is usually improved with a photoelectric detector. Electronic stabilities determined with a stable excitation source have a relative standard deviation ranging over ±0.03–0.2% (with modern instruments, using 10-sec integrations and 10 runs). Precision may range over ±0.3–3.0% for homogeneous samples with concentration levels above about 0.5% in spark analysis, or for solution samples with concentration levels about 100 times greater than the limit of detection for the ICP discharge. The precision of DC-arc techniques for determining trace elements in powdered samples at concentrations greater than 20 ppm is typically in the range ±2–12% relative standard deviation.

Evaluation of accuracy requires comparing results against standard materials or the results obtained using other independent techniques. Figure 11.9 illustrates the correlation for iron in orchard leaves determined by atomic-absorption, DC-arc, and x-ray-fluorescence spectroscopy, and ICP-emission spectrometry. The standard deviations are also indicated.

FIGURE 11.9. *Comparison of results for iron in six samples of orchard leaves. The "average value" for each sample is the average of the values obtained by a number of independent laboratories using one or more of the techniques given in parentheses. The standard deviation of these values is given for each sample by the error bars, as well as the standard deviation of the results obtained by ICP emission spectroscopy for 7 dissolutions. A recent atomic-absorption value is also given, indicated by ■. Adapted from R. H. Scott and A. Strasheim, Anal. Chim. Acta, 76, 71 (1975), by permission of the author and publisher.*

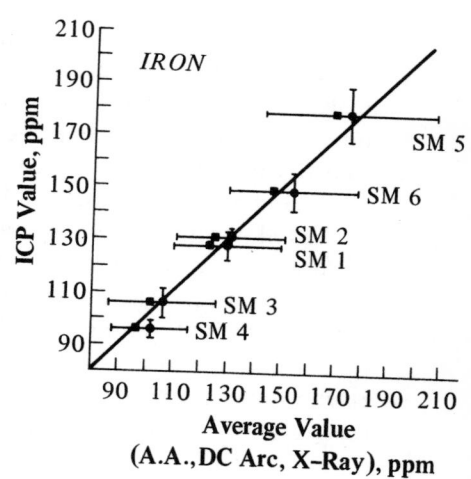

Typically, the accuracy and precision change with the composition of the sample, since the different matrices introduce errors; however, the ICP discharge is particularly free of errors caused by the sample type. For example, determination of some 16 elements in samples as varied as distilled water, steel, blood serum, whole blood, food, and soil showed the detection limits to be within a factor of 2 to 3; the detection limit is proportional to the slope of the analytical curve and the precision (or noise).

11.4 APPLICATIONS

The applications of emission spectroscopy with electrical excitation-sources are diverse and extensive. A few examples are selected in this section to illustrate typical analyses. A number of annual and biennial reviews collect and describe new applications as they are published.

Analysis of Metals by Spark Discharge

The determination of 23 elements in aluminum and its alloys by the *point-to-plane* spark technique with an emission spectrometer [13] represents an example of the type of routine quality-control analysis performed on metals and alloys in mills and foundries. Preheated sample molds designed to produce homogeneous castings free of voids or porosity in the regions to be sparked are filled from a sampling ladle containing molten metal taken from the aluminum furnace. After cooling, the disks are transported to the spectroscopy laboratory where an operator machines a smooth surface on the sample. The sample is placed on a Petrey stand that aligns the sample with the entrance slit of the spectrometer. Only predetermined locations on the disk are sparked. A freshly cut graphite counter-electrode (C-5 in Fig. 11.4) is positioned 3.0 mm from the machined surface.

A spark discharge is produced between the flat surface of a chill-cast aluminum sample and the tip of a pointed graphite counter electrode. The emission intensities for 31 different spectral lines and an aluminum internal-reference line are measured simultaneously by 32 photomultiplier tubes positioned behind exit slits. At the end of the 10–15 sec exposure period, the accumulated capacitor potentials for each analytical line relative to the potential for the aluminum internal reference line are automatically measured and recorded. The unknown values are calculated automatically in terms of percent concentration.

Secondary standards and blank standards of similar metallurgical composition as the unknown samples are used for the principal analytical curve. The averages of 20 results on standards and 20 readings from the blank standards establish the analytical curve. The 20 readings are produced by five separate spark spectra obtained on each of four different occasions.

This overall approach remains basically the same for analysis of steel, brass, zinc, or other metals, although there are specific differences in spectrometers, analyte spectral lines, sample-preparation techniques, and excitation conditions.

Metals in Lubricating Oils

The determination of wear metals in the lubricating oils used in aircraft, truck, locomotive, and other engines can provide an excellent indication of the mechanical condition of the engine. In fact, as the presence of certain metals is noticed or their concentrations begin to increase, the parts or components of the engine that are wearing out can be identified and replaced or repaired. This routine program of wear-metal analysis saves tens of millions of dollars annually, and the analysis is one of the largest analytical operations in the world. Tens of thousands of samples are run monthly. The most important wear metals are iron, aluminum, magnesium, copper, and silver. Iron appears as an indicator of more than 80 percent of all failures detected by wear-metal analysis. Aluminum usually relates to wear of oil pumps, cases, housings, pistons, and cylinder heads, and copper to wear of bronze parts such as bushings and retainers. Silicon is useful as an indicator of lubricant contamination from dust and dirt.

The spark analysis is performed with a rotating graphite disk electrode. The spectra of ten or more elements in the 0.1 to 500 ppm range are determined with a spectrometer during a 45-sec exposure after a 30-sec prespark [14]. For calibration, eight analyses of each of five standards containing the wear metals are used to establish the analytical curves. The samples are agitated in the original container until all sediment is dispersed homogeneously in the oil. The graphite electrode disk is mounted as the cathode on a graphite spindle and positioned in the spark stand. A graphite counter electrode spaced 3 mm above the top of the rotating disk is centered on the optical axis. An aluminum or porcelain boat holding the oil sample is positioned on the spark stand and raised until the disk dips into the oil. The spark is started after the turning disk is evenly coated with the oil sample. Duplicate determinations are made with new electrodes on each sample.

Trace Elements in Airborne Particulate Matter

Emission spectrography has been used extensively for the determination of trace elements in atmospheric particulates, especially in large-scale survey studies in which simultaneous multi-element analysis is important [15, 16]. Airborne particulate matter is routinely collected by drawing a measured volume of air through filter materials such as fiberglass, asbestos, cellulosic paper, porous plastic, or graphite in the form of disks or electrodes. However, for the determination of trace elements, the chemical composition of the filter is important. For example, glass filters show high concentrations of Ba, Sr, Rb, Zn, Ni, Fe, Ca, As, and other elements. The composition of the filter materials is particularly significant in sampling relatively clean atmospheres because of the low particulate levels collected in reasonable sampling times.

A membrane filter which can be dissolved in acetone, or a spectrochemically pure graphite filter which can be examined directly with a powder DC-arc technique, can provide passable results. After air has been drawn through a previously weighed filter, the membrane filter is dissolved in acetone, then centrifuged. The particulates are collected, dried, and weighed; then a spectroscopic buffer is added composed of 1 part NaF and 1 part graphite powder, with 100 ppm indium oxide and 20,000 ppm tantalum oxide as internal standards. About 35 mg of the final mixture is placed in a graphite electrode and arced at 15 A for 60 sec in a controlled (90% Ar–10% O_2) atmosphere.

Alternatively, the graphite filter can be a standard porous-cup spectrographic electrode (Fig. 11.4) through which air is drawn. An indium internal-reference solution is dried in the electrode before sampling. When excited in a 28 A DC arc for 20 sec in an argon atmosphere saturated with HCl, this technique gives absolute detection limits between 0.1 and 5 ng for 14 elements.

Trace Elements in Plant Material, Soil, and Blood

The routine determination of trace elements in agricultural, geological, and biological samples is of considerable interest. Ideally, many trace elements in each sample should be determined simultaneously using a single group of standards. Atomic-emission spectroscopy using the ICP source provides that capability.

Inorganic analysis of plant materials for certain trace elements is frequently used in agricultural studies. For example, orchard leaves can be examined for their Fe, Mn, Cu, Al, B, and Zn content [17]. The leaves are first dried and finely ground, then ashed in silica crucibles in a muffle furnace at 500°C. The ash is dissolved in HNO_3 and diluted to a known volume. Once the linearity of response for each element is established by use of standards, calibration is carried out with only one composite standard solution containing all the elements. The ICP discharge results compare well with those obtained by other methods. An example for iron is given in Figure 11.9. Agreement among alternative methods provides a good test for the accuracy of determination. The standard deviations are indicated by the horizontal and vertical lines in the figure. Better precision was obtained for the ICP discharge method.

The sampling and analysis of soils is extensively used in exploring for minerals. The application of the ICP-discharge technique for Cu, Zn, Ni, Co, and Pb is rapid and free from certain interference effects common to atomic-absorption analysis [18]. After drying and screening, weighed samples are dissolved in a 9 : 1 mixture of concentrated perchloric and nitric acids.

In health-care programs, knowledge of the concentrations of biologically essential or toxic elements in body fluids is important. Moreover, one must be able to measure accurately small changes in concentration that can be significant with respect to diseases. The ability to determine rapidly and simply several trace elements, some at the ppb level, in body fluids such as blood and urine is achieved by the ICP discharge [8]. This analytical system is able to determine many elements simultaneously, which conserves both sample and time. For biological fluids, only very small volumes (less than 1 ml) are usually available, and sample volumes of 10–25 μl can be used with the ICP discharge.

SELECTED BIBLIOGRAPHY

AHRENS, L. H., and TAYLOR, S. R. *Spectrochemical Analysis*, 2nd ed., Reading, Mass: Addison-Wesley, 1961.

BARNES, R. M. "Emission Spectroscopy," *Anal. Chem.*, *44*, 122R (1972); *46*, 150R (1974).

BARNES, R. M. *Emission Spectroscopy*. Stroudsburg, Pa.: Dowden, Hutchinson, & Ross, 1975.

GROVE, E. L., ed. *Analytical Emission Spectroscopy*, vol. 1, parts I and II. New York: Marcel Dekker, 1971 and 1972.

HARRISON, G. R. *M.I.T. Wavelength Tables,* 2nd ed., Cambridge, Mass.: MIT Press, 1969.

MIKA, J., and TOROK, T. *Analytical Emission Spectroscopy,* New York: Crane, Russak, & Co., 1974.

SLAVIN, M. *Emission Spectrochemical Analysis,* New York: Wiley, 1971.

ZEIDEL, A. N.; PROKOFEV, V. K.; RAISKII, S. M.; SLAVNYI, V. A.; and SCHREIDER, E. Y. *Table of Spectral Lines,* New York: IFI/Plenum, 1970.

REFERENCES

1. P. W. J. M. BOUMANS, *Theory of Spectrochemical Excitation,* New York: Plenum Press, 1966.

2. "Description and Performance of the Microphotometer," in *Methods for Emission Spectrochemical Analysis,* 6th ed., Philadelphia: American Society for Testing and Materials, 1971, pp 296–98, ASTM E 409-71.

3. "Photographic Photometry in Spectrochemical Analysis," in *Methods for Emission Spectrochemical Analysis,* 6th ed., Philadelphia: American Society for Testing and Materials, 1971, pp 74–96, ASTM E 116-70a.

4. W. A. GORDON and G. B. CHAPMAN, *Spectrochim. Acta, 25B,* 123 (1970).

5. J. P. WALTERS, *Appl. Spectrosc., 26,* 323 (1972).

6. J. P. WALTERS, *Appl. Spectrosc., 26,* 17 (1972).

7. V. A. FASSEL and R. N. KNISELEY, *Anal. Chem., 46,* 1110A, 1155A (1974).

8. R. N. KNISELEY, V. A. FASSEL, and C. C. BUTLER, *Clin. Chem., 19,* 807 (1973).

9. P. W. J. M. BOUMANS and F. J. DE BOER, *Spectrochim. Acta, 27B,* 391 (1972).

10. C. C. BUTLER, R. N. KNISELEY, and V. A. FASSEL, *Anal. Chem., 47,* 825 (1975).

11. "Designation of Shapes and Sizes of Graphite Electrodes," in *Methods for Emission Spectrochemical Analysis,* 6th ed., Philadelphia: American Society for Testing and Materials, 1971, pp 106–11, ASTM E 130-66.

12. W. B. BARNETT, V. A. FASSEL, and R. N. KNISELEY, *Spectrochim. Acta, 23B,* 643 (1968).

13. "Spectrochemical Analysis of Aluminum and Its Alloys by the Point-to-Plane Technique Using an Optical Emission Spectrometer," in *Methods for Emission Spectrochemical Analysis,* 6th ed., Philadelphia: American Society for Testing and Materials, 1971, pp 196–207, ASTM E 227-67.

14. "Proposed Spectrochemical Method of Test for Wear Metals in Used Diesel Lubricating Oils by a Rotating-Disk Electrode Technique Using a Direct-Reading Spectrometer," in *Methods for Emission Spectrochemical Analysis,* 6th ed., Philadelphia: American Society for Testing and Materials, 1971, pp 375–82, ASTM D-2-1968.

15. A. SUGIMAE, *Anal. Chem., 46,* 1123 (1974).

16. J. L. SEELEY and R. K. SKOGERBOE, *Anal. Chem., 46,* 415 (1974).

17. R. H. SCOTT and A. STRASHEIM, *Anal. Chim. Acta., 76,* 71 (1975).

18. R. H. SCOTT and M. L. KOKOT, *Anal. Chim. Acta., 75,* 257 (1975).

PROBLEMS

1. Explain why the simultaneous determination of several elements would be more difficult by means of atomic-absorption spectrophotometry than by atomic-emission spectrometry using either flame, arc, or ICP excitation sources.

2. Alkali and alkaline-earth metals in solution are in the ionic form and appear colorless, but in an excitation source, emission from neutral atoms and ions is observed, perceived as bright colors in the visible region. (a) To go from ions to atoms, these

species must acquire one or more electrons. From where do these electrons come? (b) How do you account for the colorful emission from these metals? (c) What color would you predict each of these metals to show in an arc or ICP discharge?

3. In Table 11.2, the halogens and gases are conspicuously absent from the lists of elements. What reasons can you give for the difficulty in determining these elements by arc or spark sources in air? Suggest one or two methods that you would try if you were required to determine halogens, permanent gases, or rare gases by emission spectrometry.

4. Would a DC arc make a very good source for production of neutral atoms for atomic absorption? Explain your answer.

5. If you were given a brass block for analysis and told that the tin and zinc distributions in the block were very heterogeneous, would you or would you not choose a spark point-to-plane technique for analysis? On what grounds do you make your selection? If you chose not to use a spark point-to-plane technique, what alternative spark techniques might you employ for the analysis of zinc and tin?

6. A sample of an unknown light-metal alloy was analyzed using the point-to-plane spark technique. By means of a projection comparator the following wavelengths were identified. What elements are present? (Hint: the CRC *Handbook of Chemistry and Physics* contains lists of wavelengths.) What is the alloy matrix?

236.706 nm	283.307	327.926
251.612	288.158	328.233
252.852	288.958	330.259
255.796	294.920	330.294
256.799	296.116	330.628
259.373	307.399←(internal	332.513
261.020	reference)	334.502
266.039	317.933	334.557
270.170	318.020	343.823
270.574	322.129	396.153
277.983	324.754	403.076
278.142	327.396	481.053

7. The accompanying figure illustrates the emission signals from Mn in 25-μl aliquots of human whole blood, and of blood to which spikes of a Mn standard solution were added. The whole blood had first been diluted tenfold with 0.1 *M* HCl, and an ICP source was used. What is the concentration of Mn in the blood sample?

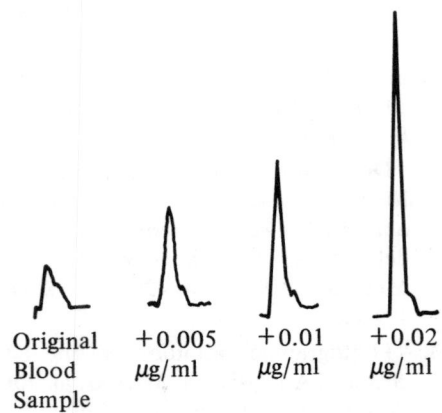

Original   +0.005   +0.01   +0.02
Blood   μg/ml   μg/ml   μg/ml
Sample

Signals obtained for Mn in human whole blood (10-fold dilution) and from addition standards. Adapted from R. N. Kniseley, V. A. Fassel, and C. C. Butler, Clin. Chem., 19, 807 (1973), by permission of the publisher.

8. The reproducibility of the signals for the Mn 403.0-nm line in problem 7 is indicated by the recordings in the following figure. What is the precision of these signals expressed as standard deviation and relative standard deviation?

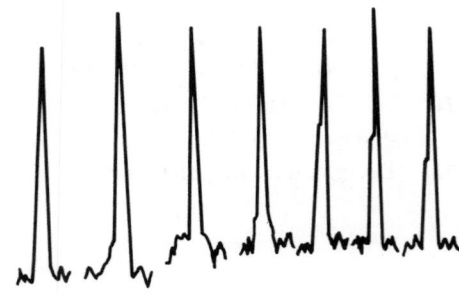

Reproducibility of signals for Mn from 25 μl samples of whole blood (undiluted). Adapted from R. N. Kniseley, V. A. Fassel, and C. C. Butler, Clin. Chem., 19, 807 (1973), by permission of the publisher.

9. Describe the considerations involve[d in] selecting (a) an internal-standard eleme[nt] and spectral line (b) a spectrochemical buffer (c) a matrix diluent.

10. Predict the change in atomic-absorption sensitivity when a flame of temperature $T = 2500\ K$ is replaced by an arc of temperature $T = 5000\ K$ for the resonance transition of calcium corresponding to a wavelength of 422.673 nm. (The transition is $3p^6 4s^2\ {}^1S_0 \leftarrow 3p^6 4s^1\ {}^1P_1{}^0$, corresponding to $E = 2.93$ eV.) Will ionization make an appreciable contribution?

ele[ment]
level, [
graphite
weight of e[ach]
dard, 0.01% o[
and so forth.
obtained from a den[
of an exposed film on t[
line and the sodium 330.2[

Arc Number	Sample	Si line (% T)	Na line (% T)
1	0.0001% standard	>99	>99
2	0.001% standard	96	92
3	0.01% standard	66	71
4	0.1% standard	<1	23
5	Pure dolomite	<1	<1
6	1 part dolomite + 9 parts graphite	58	16
7	1 part dolomite + 99 parts graphite	95	65

Plot a calibration curve (log absorbance versus log concentration), and determine the concentration of Si and Na in the dolomite sample.

in

11. A sample of dolomite was analyzed semi-
quantitatively for its Si and Na content
using a DC arc with a matrix-dilution technique. Standards are available (Spex
Industries, Inc.) which contain about 50
...ments, each at a specified concentration
...mixed with a high-purity spectroscopic
powder; for example, 0.1% by
...ch of 50 elements in one stan-
...f each in a second standard,
...The following data were
...iometer measurement
...e silicon 288.16-nm
...-nm line:

Like other forms of spectroscopy (for instance, infrared and ultraviolet), nuclear magnetic resonance spectroscopy (NMR) deals with the measurement of energy gaps between states of different energy. However, unlike most other forms of spectroscopy, the phenomenon requires the presence of an external magnetic field and concerns nuclei rather than electrons. This is the origin of the terms "nuclear" and "magnetic" in *nuclear magnetic resonance spectroscopy.*

NMR spectroscopy is of relatively recent origin and has had a spectacular rise, owing principally to its applications in organic chemistry—it is at present the most powerful technique for structural analysis available to the organic chemist, because it utilizes commonly found elements (in particular, hydrogen) as "chromophores." With the aid of NMR it is possible to define the environment of practically all commonly occurring functional groups, as well as of fragments (such as hydrogen atoms attached to carbon) which are not otherwise accessible to spectroscopic or analytical techniques. NMR may also be utilized for quantitative determination of compounds in mixtures and hence for following the progress of chemical reactions. More sophisticated applications often yield kinetic and thermodynamic parameters for certain types of chemical processes; and others, in particular spin-spin coupling, often give accurate information about the relative positions of groups of magnetic nuclei within molecules. The principal limitations of the method are its inherently low sensitivity and its virtual nonapplicability to samples in the solid state.

The phenomenon of nuclear resonance was first observed in 1946 by two teams of physicists: Purcell, Torrey, and Pound at Harvard and Bloch, Hansen, and Packard at Stanford, who shared a Nobel Prize for this discovery. The first observation of the *chemical shift,* the phenomenon on which all chemical applications are based, was made by Knight in 1949 and the first systematic applications to organic chemistry were reported in 1953 by Meyer, Saika, and Gutowsky. The first commercial instruments appeared in about 1956 and, in spite of their high cost, several thousand are now in use. Relatively inexpensive models are now available that, although not as sophisticated as the more expensive models, are easier to operate and are capable of handling many routine measurements.

12.1 THEORY AND INSTRUMENTATION

Two elementary principles of classical electromagnetism, summarized in Figures 12.1 and 12.2, should be recalled. Atomic nuclei have charge (they contain protons) and some also behave as if they spin. A spinning charge is equivalent to a current in a conductor loop; therefore, nuclei with nonzero spin will generate a magnetic field, i.e., will have a *magnetic moment* or a magnetic dipole.

FIGURE 12.1. *Right-hand rule. A current i flowing in a conductor loop generates a magnetic field H in the direction shown.*

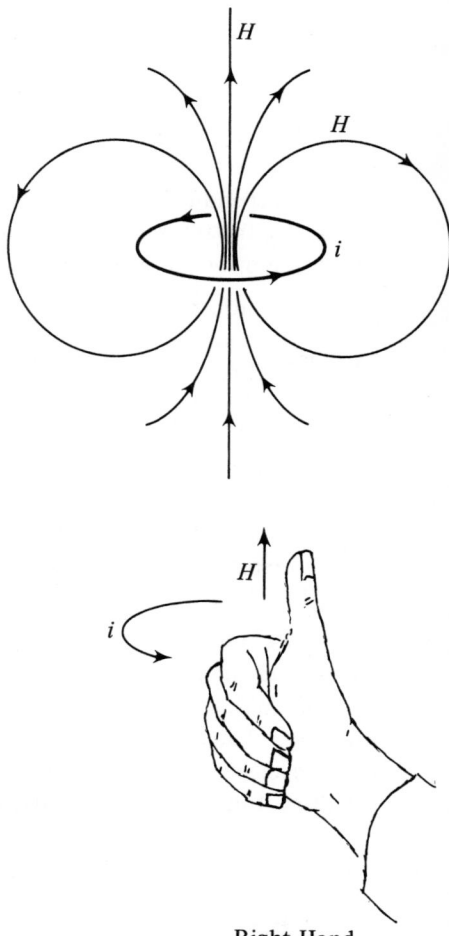

Right Hand

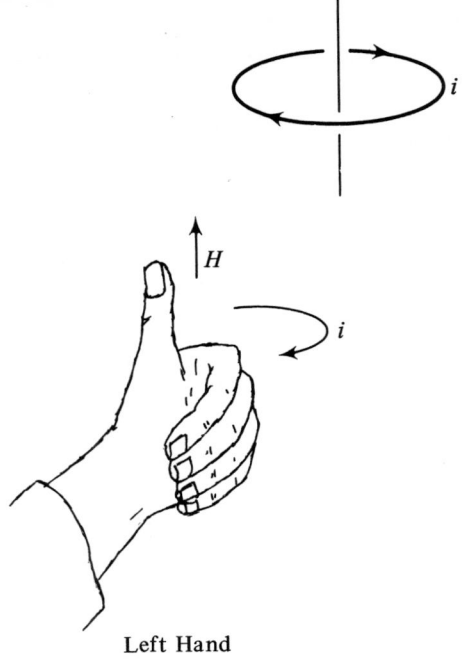

FIGURE 12.2. *Left-hand rule. A magnetic field H causes current i to flow in the conductor loop in the direction shown. As given, this rule is incomplete, since relative motion of the field and conductor is necessary in the macroscopic case, but the rule gives the correct direction of the effect in the nuclear case.*

Left Hand

Depending on the shape of the nuclear charge and the number and type of nucleons, the *spin quantum number*, I, can have values 0, 1/2, 1, 3/2, and so on. There are three principal groups of nuclei:

1. $I = 0$ (nonspinning nuclei). These have no magnetic moment and are composed of even numbers of protons and neutrons, e.g., $^{12}_{6}C$, $^{16}_{8}O$.
2. $I = 1/2$ (spherical spinning charges). These nuclei have a magnetic moment but no *electric quadrupole*. This group is by far the most important from the chemical point of view. Chemically useful nuclei in this group, in decreasing order of importance, are: $^{1}_{1}H$, $^{13}_{6}C$, $^{19}_{9}F$, $^{31}_{15}P$, $^{15}_{7}N$. Of these, the proton (^{1}H) alone accounts for well over 90% of all NMR observations made.
3. $I > 1/2$ (nonspherical spinning charges). These nuclei have both magnetic dipoles and electric quadrupoles; examples are $I = 1$: $^{2}_{1}H$, $^{14}_{7}N$; $I = 3/2$: $^{11}_{5}B$, $^{35}_{17}Cl$, $^{37}_{17}Cl$, $^{79}_{35}Br$, $^{81}_{35}Br$, $^{7}_{3}Li$; $I = 2$: $^{36}_{17}Cl$, $^{58}_{27}Co$; $I = 5/2$: $^{25}_{12}Mg$, $^{27}_{13}Al$, $^{17}_{8}O$.

A fundamental quantum law is that: *In a uniform magnetic field, a nucleus of spin I may assume 2I + 1 orientations.* Thus, for a nucleus of $I = 1/2$ (for instance, the proton), there are $2(1/2) + 1 = 2$ permissible orientations. This makes a nucleus of $I = 1/2$ analogous to a bar magnet in a magnetic field (Fig. 12.3). Since we shall deal exclusively with nuclei of spin $I = 1/2$ in this chapter, and almost exclusively with protons, the "bar-magnet analogy" will be useful.

As with the bar magnet, the two orientations of the nuclear magnet in the magnetic field (of strength* H_0) have different energies, and it is possible to induce a

---

* The units are *gauss*: 1 gauss is defined as the strength of a magnetic field that induces a voltage of 1 V in a conductor 1 cm long moving at 1 cm/sec.

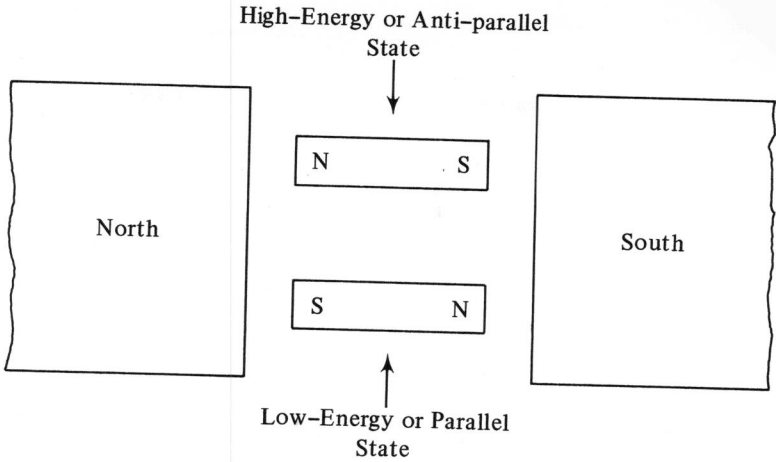

High–Energy or Anti–parallel
State

N   S

North

S   N

South

Low–Energy or Parallel
State

FIGURE 12.3. *The bar-magnet analogy for nuclei with I = 1/2.*

nuclear transition, analogous to the flipping of the bar magnet, by applying electromagnetic radiation of an appropriate frequency ν given by

$$\nu = \frac{\gamma H_0}{2\pi} \tag{12.1}$$

where γ = a fundamental constant known as the *gyromagnetic ratio* or *magneto-*
gyric ratio, and is characteristic of the particular nucleus concerned

It can be seen that Equation 12.1 can be reduced to

$$\nu = \text{constant} \times H_0 \tag{12.2}$$

Equation 12.1 is known as the *Larmor equation*; it shows that one could observe
a nuclear transition (*spin flip*) by keeping the magnetic field constant and varying the
applied frequency (or vice versa) until the combination of field strength and irradiating frequency characteristic of the nucleus concerned is reached. This condition is
often described as *resonance* and is, of course, the origin of the term "resonance" in
nuclear magnetic resonance. The term *resonance frequency* is also sometimes used,
but it must be remembered that the term would be meaningless without specifying the
field strength H_0. Thus, the resonance frequency of the proton is 60 MHz *at 14,092
gauss*. In practice, NMR spectrometers may be capable of varying (or "sweeping")
either the frequency or the magnetic field, and one often uses the terms *frequency-
sweep spectrometer, frequency-sweep spectrum, field-sweep spectrometer,* and *field-
sweep spectrum.*

The magnitudes of the various constants involved are such that the energy gap
corresponding to the spin flip, given by $\Delta E = h\nu$, is very small; 60 MHz corresponds
to only 6×10^{-6} kcal/mole. Thus, all NMR frequencies at usable field strengths
fall in the radio-frequency (RF) region of the electromagnetic spectrum; the source
of the radiation is a radio-frequency transmitter, generally a crystal oscillator.

Now consider the details of the energy transfer to a nuclear magnet placed
in an external field H_0. The magnet, in either the parallel or the antiparallel

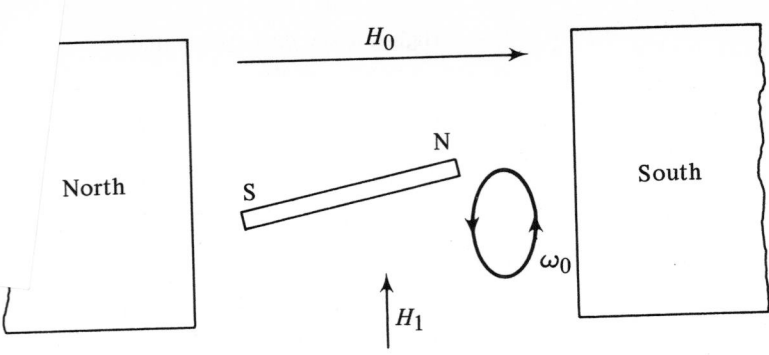

FIGURE 12.4. *The relation between precession and the exciting field H_1.*

orientation (Fig. 12.3), will not remain stationary, but will precess (Fig. 12.4) in a magnetic field H_0 with an angular velocity ω_0 given by

$$\omega_0 = \gamma H_0 \qquad \textbf{(12.3)}$$

Combining Equations 12.1 and 12.3, we get

$$\omega_0 = 2\pi\nu \qquad \textbf{(12.4)}$$

Thus, if one can get ω_0, one can also determine ν, the resonance frequency. This is done as follows: a second magnetic field (H_1) is generated at right angles to H_0 by passing a very-high-frequency alternating current supplied by an RF oscillator through a coil (the transmitter coil). When the angular component of H_1 matches ω_0, the frequency of this alternating current is equal to ν and a transition, or spin flip, can occur. The geometry of the arrangement in Figure 12.4 follows from the simple rules of electromagnetism stated at the beginning of the chapter, and the NMR experiment can be seen to amount to "nuclear induction."

We can now construct an *NMR spectrometer*. A typical arrangement is shown in Figure 12.5. This diagram represents a *field-sweep, crossed-coil spectrometer*, but the essential features are the same for other types of spectrometers. The essential parts of any high-resolution (the significance of this term will become apparent later) NMR spectrometer are:

1. The *magnet*, which may either be a permanent magnet or an electromagnet, but which must be capable of generating a very strong, very stable, and very homogeneous magnetic field. (These magnetic-field requirements are the principal reasons for the cost and complexity of NMR spectrometers.) To average out small magnetic-field inhomogeneities throughout the sample, the sample tube is rotated at several hundred rpm.
2. The *sweep generator*, which is used to vary the magnetic field over a small range by passing a variable direct current through coils that are coaxial with the direction of the main magnetic field H_0.
3. The *transmitter coil*, which is placed at right angles to the sweep coils and is used to generate the exciting field H_1.
4. The *receiver coil*, which is placed around the sample holder in the remaining orthogonal plane. A small current is generated in it when the resonance condition is achieved (see nuclear induction, above).

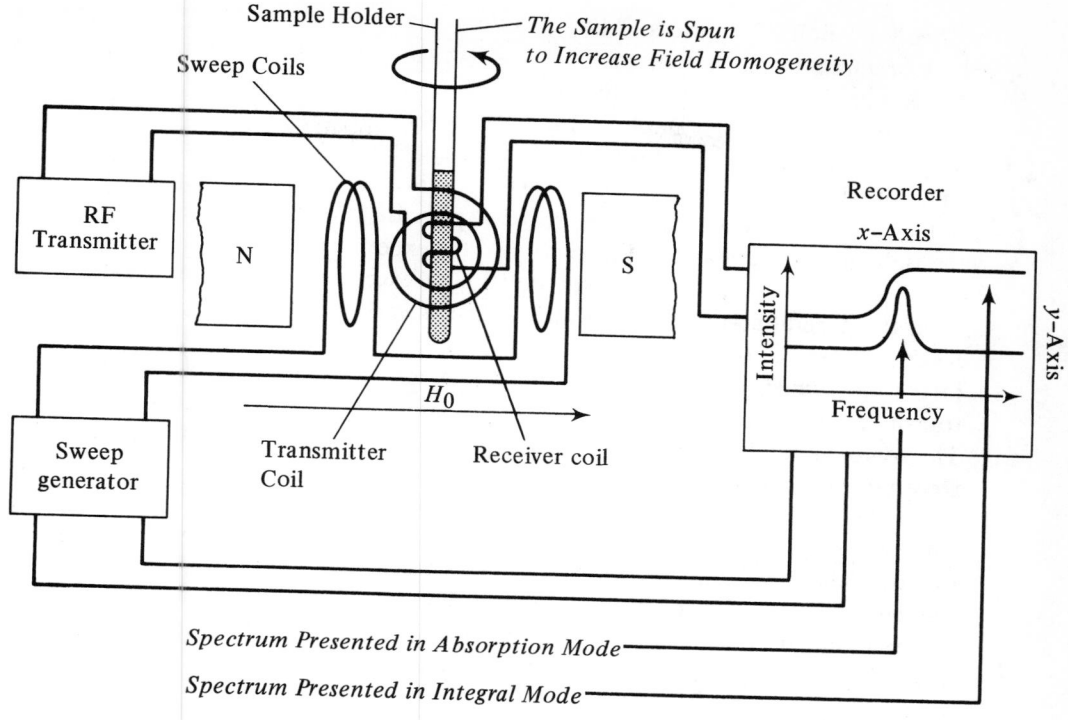

FIGURE 12.5. *Schematic diagram of an NMR spectrometer.*

The signal from the receiver coil is suitably amplified and is made to deflect the recorder pen along the y-axis while the x-axis is synchronized with the sweep generator. Thus one plots the signal from the receiver coil as a function of the field strength; the intensity of the signal is proportional to the number of nuclei undergoing the transition. This is the *field-sweep experiment*. The *frequency-sweep experiment* is analogous, except that the field is kept constant while the frequency is swept and synchronized with the x-axis of the recorder. In either case one can express the x-axis scale in terms of "signal frequency" because, by Equation 12.1, the field strength and frequency for the resonance condition are always directly connected.

The intensity of the signal is proportional to the area under the absorption curve (Fig. 12.5) and is usually obtained by electronic integration, yielding a step function whose height is a direct measure of the relative intensity of the absorption signal.

There are certain consequences of the small size of the energy gap involved in a nuclear-spin transition. The Boltzmann relation gives the populations of nuclear spins in the upper energy state (N_2) and in the lower energy state (N_1) in terms of the energy gap ΔE between them:

$$\frac{N_1}{N_2} = e^{\Delta E/RT} \tag{12.5}$$

When the energy gap is very small, as is the case here, the right-hand side approaches e^0 (unity), and the excess population in the lower energy state, given by $N_1 - N_2$ and called the "Boltzmann excess," becomes very small. Since an absorption signal can only originate from the Boltzmann excess (typically only 1 nucleus in 100,000 in an NMR experiment), it follows that the method is inherently not very sensitive and that sophisticated signal amplification must be used in an NMR spectrometer. One of the reasons for the use of very high magnetic fields becomes apparent: the Larmor equation shows that high magnetic fields require high resonance frequencies. This in turn widens the energy gap between the spin states ($\Delta E = h\nu$), thereby increasing the Boltzmann excess and the sensitivity of the experiment.

A consequence of the small Boltzmann excess in NMR experiments arises from the general spectroscopic principle that absorption cannot occur unless some mechanism exists for a radiationless transition that can restore the excess population in the lower energy state. This is related to the fact that upward and downward transitions are equally probable on collision with an appropriate energy quantum. Therefore excess absorption, that is, observable absorption signals, can only originate from unequal populations, as stated above.

The mechanisms of radiationless transitions from the upper to the lower energy states are particularly critical in NMR spectroscopy because of the small Boltzmann excess. These mechanisms are termed *relaxation* and are characterized by their *relaxation times T*, which are equal to half the time necessary to restore equilibrium by the mechanism considered. Clearly, large values of T indicate inefficient relaxation. Two relaxation mechanisms are important:

1. *Spin-spin* or *transverse relaxation* (characterized by T_2) occurs when the energy is lost by spin exchange, that is, by transmission to neighboring spins. This operates extremely efficiently in solids, where magnetic nuclei are close together. However, the positive effects of this efficiency are offset by another general spectroscopic principle, the uncertainty principle, which states that the width of a spectral line is inversely proportional to the time spent in the upper energy state,

$$\text{line width} = \frac{\text{constant}}{\text{time in upper state}} \qquad (12.6)$$

Since the spin-spin relaxation mechanism in solids is so efficient, very small values of T_2 result, producing very broad lines. Further, such spin exchanges between identical nuclei average the resonance frequencies of nuclei whose environments are not quite identical, and broaden the spectral lines further (dipolar broadening). For these reasons, solids give spectra with lines about 1000 times too broad to give information of much chemical interest (see below). Spectra of solids, or *wide-line spectra*, will therefore not be further discussed here, although they are of interest in solid-state physics.

2. *Spin-lattice* or *longitudinal relaxation* (characterized by T_1) occurs when the energy is lost to the "lattice," i.e., to any component of the sample, inter- or intramolecular. The lattice contains magnetic nuclei in rapid thermal motion in a magnetic field, generating a variety of electric currents and magnetic dipoles; energy may be lost to them by the nuclear magnets observed, thus restoring the equilibrium. This mechanism operates with gases, liquids, and solutions and is of just the right efficiency to produce narrow lines, or so called *high-resolution spectra*.

Interactions between nuclear magnetic dipoles and nuclear electric quadrupoles in nuclei where $I > 1/2$ offer another relaxation mechanism that prevents the observation of the NMR signals from some elements.

Interactions of the nuclear magnet with unpaired electrons (for example, in free radicals and in atoms of the transition metals) can also result in efficient relaxation. Since an unpaired electron has about 1000 times the strength of a nuclear magnet, line broadening often occurs in solutions containing even small amounts of paramagnetic impurities, which must therefore be rigorously excluded from NMR samples; even dissolved oxygen causes some broadening.

If for some reason the spin-lattice relaxation mechanism is not operating efficiently, as when high viscosity interferes with the thermal movement of the lattice, the signal strength will diminish with time even during the relatively short interval needed to scan the signal, thus causing the phenomenon of *saturation.* The same phenomenon will occur if the current in the transmitter coil, and therefore the strength of the RF field, is increased to too high a value, flipping the nuclei into their upper states faster than the relaxation processes can restore the equilibrium. The onset of saturation is also accompanied by some line broadening, because it is the nuclei exactly at resonance, and hence in the middle of the signal line, that are saturated first.

With most spectrometers operating under routine conditions, the line widths are controlled by the inhomogeneity of the magnetic field (line widths are generally measured as the width at half height of a single line and denoted by W_H or $W_{1/2}$). In a slightly inhomogeneous field, different parts of the sample will experience slightly different magnetic fields and hence resonate over a range of frequencies, broadening the spectral lines. Line widths of as little as 0.1 Hz are sometimes desirable; line widths in excess of about 1 Hz result in the loss of considerable information. Clearly, this imposes very stringent demands upon the magnet as regards homogeneity. A line of 1 Hz width obtained with a spectrometer operating at the equivalent of 100,000,000 Hz requires a homogeneity of better than 1 in 10^8; however, this is routinely available with modern spectrometers.

To summarize: some nuclei, notably protons, have magnetic moments. "Spin-flip" nuclear-magnetic transitions of these nuclei can be observed at frequencies predicted by the Larmor equation, using complicated and expensive apparatus. The strength of the signal is directly proportional to the number of nuclei involved.

If this were all NMR had to offer, it would not be considered particularly useful in chemical investigations, since all one achieves is a costly and inconvenient estimate of the total hydrogen, fluorine, etc., content in a sample. In practice, all applications of NMR to chemistry are from three secondary phenomena: the *chemical shift*; the *time-dependence* of NMR phenomena; and *spin-spin coupling*. These effects will now be discussed.

12.2 THE CHEMICAL SHIFT

From now on, unless otherwise indicated, we shall refer to protons and deal with PMR (*proton magnetic resonance*) rather than with NMR. However, the principles are strictly analogous for all magnetic nuclei with $I = 1/2$.

The statement that protons resonate at 60 MHz at 14,092 gauss is only an approximation. Actually, protons in organic molecules are found to resonate, at 14,092 gauss, over a frequency range of about 1000 Hz at approximately 60 MHz. The exact frequency at which a proton resonates within this range is related to its chemical environment (hence the term *chemical shift*). The resonance of ^{19}F at 56.54 MHz in the same magnetic field is the closest resonance to that of ^{1}H; this is some 3,500,000 Hz away. It is apparent that the proton chemical shift range of about 1000 Hz is actually the fine structure of a single line.* To put it pictorially, at a chart width where the chemical-shift range of protons corresponds to about 2 feet, the fluorine resonances will turn up $2\frac{1}{2}$ miles away; the ^{13}C range will be found 48 miles away.

Since the chemical shift reflects molecular structure, it can be used to determine the structures of unknown compounds; and since hydrogen is an almost universal constituent of organic compounds, the method is very widely applicable. Furthermore, as mentioned before (Fig. 12.5), the intensity of the signal caused by any group of protons (the area under the curve, generally determined by electronic integration) is directly proportional to the number of protons in it. We can therefore determine the environments of hydrogen atoms in an organic molecule and obtain the relative distribution of hydrogens between the various environments.

Measurement of the Chemical Shift

Modern NMR spectrometers can determine resonance frequencies of sharp lines to a precision of better than 0.05 Hz. It would be almost impossible to measure a frequency of (say) 60,000,000 Hz to an absolute accuracy of 0.05 Hz, as this implies an absolute accuracy of 1 part in 10^{10}. Instead, all chemical shifts are measured relative to some standard substance which is added to the sample being investigated; one can then express the chemical shift in terms of displacement in Hz from the signal caused by the standard. As the range of proton chemical shifts at 14,092 gauss is approximately 1000 Hz, measurement to a precision of 0.05 Hz implies an accuracy of 1 part in 10^4—which is realistic, but still requires high stability of the magnetic field over the time necessary to scan the spectrum, and hence an advanced magnet technology.

The standard substance almost universally used is tetramethylsilane (Me$_4$Si), commonly abbreviated as TMS. This standard was chosen because it gives rise to a single sharp line as a result of the identical environment of all the protons in the symmetrical molecule and because the chemical environment of protons in TMS is such that they resonate at a higher field than practically any other proton. Further, TMS is an inert, low-boiling liquid and can be easily removed from the sample after the spectrum has been run. Therefore, in practice, the procedure is nondestructive. The sample size required for examination by NMR, however, is relatively large, generally at least 10 mg, because of the inherently low sensitivity of the method.

The chemical shift of any proton can be expressed in terms of "Hz from TMS." By convention, the absence of a sign implies "Hz to lower field, or downfield, from TMS," remembering at all times that "field" and "frequency" can be

---

* The ability to resolve this line defines *high-resolution NMR*.

used interchangeably. The chemical shift thus expressed depends upon the operating field of the spectrometer (Eqn. 12.1) so that one would have to state: "Proton X resonates at Y Hz from TMS at Z MHz spectrometer frequency." However, if one divides this value by the spectrometer frequency, one obtains the chemical shift in terms of dimensionless units. In practice, a factor of 10^6 is also introduced to avoid handling very small numbers, so the dimensionless unit turns out to be parts per million (ppm). Chemical shifts expressed in ppm versus TMS are usually designated as δ. Thus:

$$\text{Chemical shift in ppm } (\delta) = \frac{\text{Chemical shift in Hz vs. TMS}}{\text{Spectrometer frequency in Hz}} \times 10^6 \qquad (12.7)$$

The δ scale ranges from 0 to about 12 ppm. Another system sets TMS arbitrarily at 10 and expresses the chemical shifts in terms of τ values, so that:

$$\tau = 10 - \delta \qquad (12.8)$$

The unit is still ppm, only the scale is different. In other words, with the numbers reading in ppm, we have:

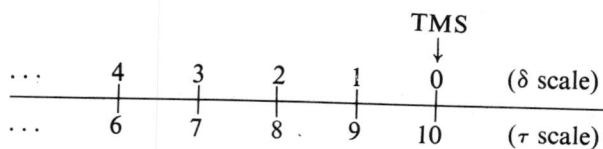

Chart paper for NMR spectrometers is marked in either, or both, scales and also (nearly always) with a grid scaled in Hz, thus ensuring maximum confusion for the beginner. (The τ-system is no longer recommended usage.)

Physical Causes of the Chemical Shift

The chemical shift occurs because the resonance frequency depends not upon the gross field (H_0) between the poles of the magnet of an NMR spectrometer, but on the actual field at the resonating nucleus. Only for the hypothetical case of an isolated proton will the field at the nucleus be equal to the gross field. For all other cases

$$H_{\text{nucl.}} = H_0(1 - \sigma) \qquad (12.9)$$

where σ = the *shielding constant* for the particular situation

The shielding constant cannot in general be predicted, but the factors governing it, and hence determining the chemical shift, are qualitatively understood.

Consider an isolated hydrogen atom—a proton with its electron. Under the influence of H_0, the $1s$ electron will circulate in the direction given by the left-hand rule, thus becoming equivalent to a current in a circular loop. This current will generate (by the right-hand rule) a small magnetic field H_e which, in the region of the nucleus, will be in such a direction as to oppose H_0 (Fig. 12.6). The electron is then said to *shield* the proton in a hydrogen atom. Therefore, for a hydrogen atom, the gross field H_0 required for resonance at a fixed frequency will be slightly larger than that required for an isolated (unshielded) proton.

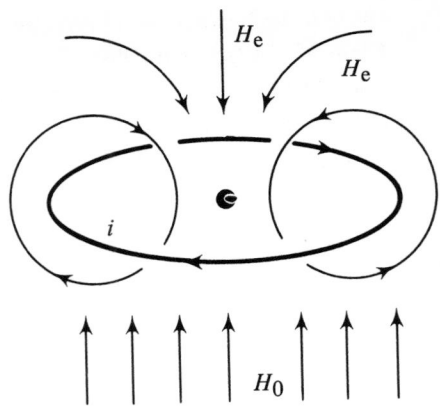

FIGURE 12.6. *Shielding of the proton by the electron in an isolated hydrogen atom.*

Now consider a hydrogen atom bonded to a carbon atom—that is, one existing as a part of a molecule. From simple bonding theory, we know that the electron density about the hydrogen will be reduced because the carbon atom is more electronegative; hence, the shielding effect of the circulating $1s$ electron (now part of a σ bond) is smaller than that in an isolated hydrogen atom. In other words, a hydrogen atom bonded to carbon is *deshielded*, compared to an isolated hydrogen atom. Clearly, the exact amount of deshielding is related to the electron distribution in the bond joining the hydrogen atom to the rest of the molecule. Thus, through the operation of the inductive mechanism in chemical bonding, one would expect the protons of methane to be more shielded than those of methyl chloride, and therefore to resonate at a higher field (closer to TMS). This is, in fact, borne out by experiment:

Compound	δ (ppm vs. TMS)
CH_4	0.23
CH_3Cl	3.05 (2.82 ppm downfield of CH_4)
CH_2Cl_2	5.33 (2.28 ppm downfield of CH_3Cl)
$CHCl_3$	7.24 (1.91 ppm downfield of CH_2Cl_2)

This series also shows that the effect of increasing electron withdrawal on the chemical shift of the remaining proton(s) is cumulative, but not strictly additive.

As is typical of all inductive effects, this type of deshielding decreases rapidly with increasing distance from the electronegative atom. Thus, the methyl group of ethyl chloride resonates at $\delta = 1.33$ ppm. In general, factors influencing electron density in the proximity of the proton are reflected in the chemical shift. Electron deficiency is associated with deshielding and therefore results in downfield shifts from TMS.

The second major effect, besides deshielding by bonding, that governs the chemical shifts of protons is the influence of *magnetically anisotropic* neighboring groups. A group (which can be a bond or the environment of an atom, but which is here considered a collection of electrons) is said to be magnetically anisotropic if the circulation of electrons within it under the influence of a magnetic field depends upon its orientation with respect to this field.

FIGURE 12.7. *Induced circulation of π-electrons in the benzene ring.*

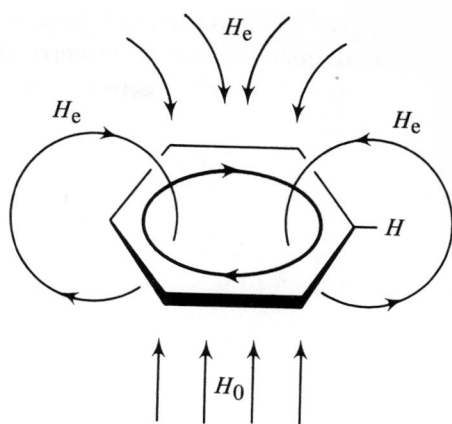

For instance, when a molecule of benzene is oriented with respect to the magnetic field H_0 as shown in Figure 12.7, a movement of the delocalized π-electrons occurs (left-hand rule) which is known as the *ring current*. This current generates (according to right-hand rule) a subsidiary magnetic field H_e whose direction is such that it reinforces H_0 at the periphery of the benzene ring while opposing H_0 above and below the plane of the benzene ring. Thus, the aromatic protons, which are at the periphery of the benzene ring, are deshielded, and are found to resonate at a field considerably lower than that expected solely on the basis of the electron-density distribution.

When the benzene ring assumes, with respect to the field H_0, an orientation orthogonal to that shown in Figure 12.7, little circulation of electrons takes place, so the net effect results only from the phenomenon shown above. It can be demonstrated, by an extension of such arguments, that magnetically *isotropic* groups will not exert any net shielding effects on neighboring magnetic nuclei, because thermal motion will average all shielding influences.

Magnetically anisotropic groups can be considered to be surrounded by volumes of space in which protons will be shielded ($+$) or deshielded ($-$), that is, moved upfield or downfield, respectively. The best-established effects are associated with the groups shown in Figure 12.8.

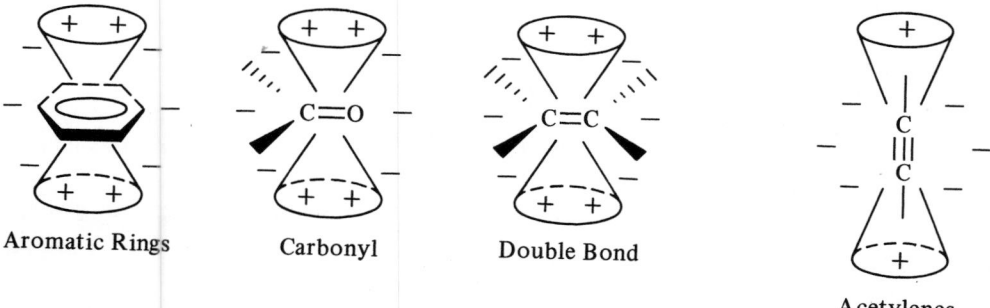

Aromatic Rings   Carbonyl   Double Bond

Acetylenes

FIGURE 12.8. *Shielding zones associated with some magnetically anisotropic groups.*

It can be seen that both of the effects discussed above depend upon the circulation of electrons in the magnetic field of the spectrometer. Their magnitude will therefore be directly proportional to the spectrometer field, H_0, or the "spectrometer frequency." This is the physical rationalization of the statement made in Section 12.2, that chemical shift expressed in Hz depends upon the spectrometer frequency.

The chemical shift of any given proton depends upon the combination of effects, which are (roughly) additive; the effects reinforce or cancel one another. Thus, acetylenic protons are deshielded by the inductive effect (acetylene is acidic) but shielded by the anisotropy of the triple bond; a value of $\delta = 1.80$ ppm results.

Because it is almost impossible to disentangle the various contributory effects, the theory of chemical shifts can be used only as a general guide. For the solution of problems, empirical correlations are almost invariably used. Some of the more fundamental of these are given in Table 12.1.

The choice of solvent is important. Since the standard (TMS) and the sample are in the same environment, one would expect negligible solvent effects. However, different solvents, which may have different degrees of magnetic anisotropy, will generally interact with various molecules in different ways, and the molecules will on the average be oriented in some preferred manner. Therefore solutions used for accurate measurements of chemical shifts should be as dilute as possible (preferably less than 10%) to avoid solute-solute interactions, and the solvent should not interact strongly with the sample (as do, for instance, hydrogen-bonding solvents). Carbon tetrachloride is a preferred solvent because it is magnetically isotropic and has no sites for strong interactions. Further, CCl_4 has no protons, so there will be no

TABLE 12.1. *Chemical Shift Data for Protons* (δ scale)

Aliphatic protons (cyclic or acyclic excluding cyclopropane derivatives):
  Methyl (with only H or alkyl substituents on both α and β carbon): 0.9
  Methylene (with only H or alkyl substituents on both α and β carbon): 1.25
  Methine (with only H or alkyl substituents on both α and β carbon): ca. 1.6

Presence of electron-withdrawing substituents on the α-carbon (e.g., halogens, –OH, –OR, –O–CO–R, –NH$_2$, –NO$_2$) shifts the proton by 2–4 ppm downfield. Carbonyl groups, C=C, and aromatic rings have a similar but less pronounced effect, the downfield shift being generally about 0.5–1.5 ppm.

Benzylic protons: 2–3 (toluene methyl: 2.34)

Acetylenic protons: 2–3

Olefinic protons: 5–7, varying regularly with substitution. Ethylene: 5.30

Aromatic and heterocyclic protons: 6–9. Benzene: 7.27

Aldehydic protons: 9–10

Hydroxylic and amino protons: Anywhere between 1 and 16 ppm, depending on the state of hydrogen bonding (strong H-bonding is deshielding). Signals due to such protons may be easily recognized by shifts with temperature, which alters the degree of hydrogen bonding, and by their facile exchange with D_2O. The latter procedure can be carried out in an NMR sample tube and the signals due to –OH, –NH$_2$, etc., simply vanish.

---

blanked-out areas in the spectrum. The most commonly used solvent is deutero-chloroform ($CDCl_3$), whose dissolving power for most compounds is greater than that of CCl_4 and which is also proton-free. Chemical shifts in CCl_4 and $CDCl_3$ are generally very similar.

In summary, the phenomenon of chemical shift enables the chemist to obtain some fundamental information about electronegativities, bond anisotropies, and so on. Above all, the ability to observe the chemical shift causes hydrogen atoms (and to some extent other nuclei) to become *functional groups* that can be qualitatively and quantitatively estimated.

12.3 TIME-DEPENDENCE OF NMR PHENOMENA

The time scale of the NMR phenomenon is best realized when it is recalled that NMR transitions occur at the low-frequency end of the electromagnetic spectrum.

Consider two protons situated in different environments. They will give rise to two separate resonances in the NMR spectrum, say $\Delta\nu$ Hz apart (Fig. 12.9C). However, if, by one of the mechanisms discussed below, the two protons exchange their environments at a rate *faster* than $\Delta\nu$ times per second, one obtains only one signal, at an intermediate frequency (Fig. 12.9A); the two nuclei are *equivalent* on the NMR time scale.

The definition of equivalence is important in NMR spectroscopy. A group of nuclei is defined as *chemically equivalent* if they possess the same chemical shift. Thus, by symmetry, the six protons of the benzene molecule are inherently chemically equivalent. However, the three protons of a methyl group are chemically equivalent only by virtue of the normally fast rotation about the bond joining the methyl group to the rest of the molecule. A group of nuclei is *magnetically equivalent* when they not only have the same chemical shift but also the same spin-spin coupling (see below) to all nuclei outside the group.

NMR spectra are characteristic of exchange rates. Thus, at slow (on the NMR time-scale) exchange-rates, one can simply observe separate signals for each of the environments and estimate the relative populations at each site. At intermediate exchange-rates, characteristically broadened spectra are observed (Fig. 12.9B) from which information about the rate of the process taking place can be extracted. At high exchange-rates, the single averaged signal occurs at a frequency determined by the relative populations at each site. Given the characteristic frequency of the individual resonances from the slow-exchange case (typically from low-temperature spectra), it is possible to determine the relative populations at two sites from the averaged (typically high-temperature) spectra.

The most common observable mechanisms for averaging the environments of protons, or of groups of equivalent protons, that can be observed on the NMR time-scale are proton exchange, conformational changes, and rotation about partial double-bonds. An example of each follows:

1. *Proton exchange.* In dilute solutions in aprotic solvents, the hydroxylic protons of mixtures of ethanol and water give rise to separate signals. However, an increase in temperature or concentration, or a change in pH, speeds up the proto-tropic exchange so that only one signal for the –OH protons is observed.

FIGURE 12.9. *The effect of exchange rates (k) on the appearance of NMR spectra.*

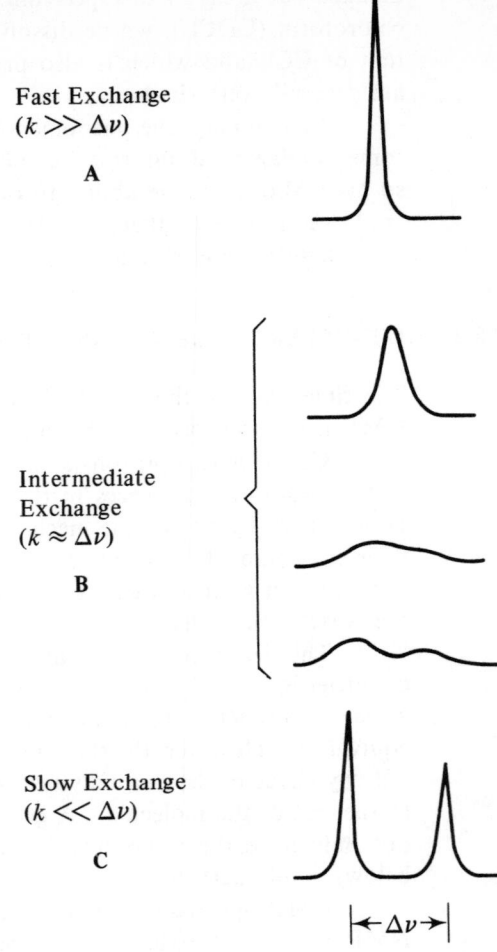

Fast Exchange
$(k \gg \Delta\nu)$

A

Intermediate
Exchange
$(k \approx \Delta\nu)$

B

Slow Exchange
$(k \ll \Delta\nu)$

C

$\leftarrow \Delta\nu \rightarrow$

The chemical shift of the –OH protons of just ethanol in an aprotic solvent will also vary with concentration and temperature, because of different degrees of hydrogen bonding. Further, at low exchange-rates, the –OH signal of ethanol shows splitting due to spin-spin coupling with the methylene protons (see below); but at high exchange-rates it gives rise to a singlet because the methylene protons "see" only the average spin-state of the –OH protons.

2. *Conformational changes.* At room temperature, the NMR spectrum of cyclohexane consists of a single sharp line, because the rate of conformational inversion between the two equivalent chair forms, which is associated with the interchange between axial and equatorial positions, is fast compared with the difference (in Hz) between the chemical shifts of axial and equatorial protons. At about $-160°C$, this inversion slows down enough to make separate signals for the axial and the equatorial protons observable.

3. *Rotation about partial double-bonds.* At low temperatures, the signals caused by the *N*-methyl groups of *N,N*-dimethylformamide appear as two bands of

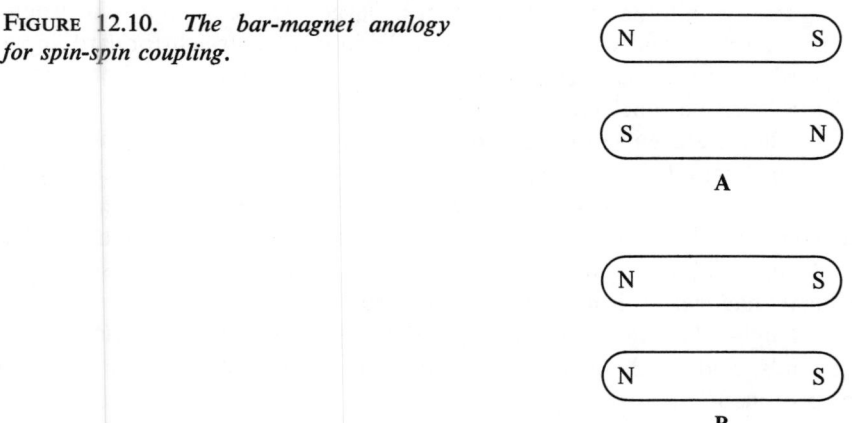

equal intensity. At higher temperatures, they coalesce to a single band midway between the original signals.

12.4 SPIN-SPIN COUPLING

Many signals in PMR spectra exhibit fine structure because of the splitting of spin-state energy levels of the protons by other magnetic nuclei in the neighborhood.

As an analogy, consider pairs of small bar magnets constrained into a specific spatial relation to each other (as nuclei are in real molecules) and which can assume just two North-South directions (as nuclei of spin $I = 1/2$ do). It is immediately obvious that, for the relative arrangements depicted in Figure 12.10, the antiparallel arrangement A has a lower energy than the parallel arrangement B.

FIGURE 12.10. *The bar-magnet analogy for spin-spin coupling.*

In the case of the nuclear magnets, the interaction does not take place through space, but through the agency of the binding electrons. The strength of this interaction is expressed by the parameter J, the *coupling constant*, which is related to the degree of splitting of resonances and which is expressed in Hz. The value of J depends only upon the electronic and steric relationship between the interacting protons, and hence does not depend on the spectrometer frequency. Thus, obtaining the NMR spectra of the same compound at two frequencies allows one to distinguish between multiple lines caused by protons of different chemical shift and those caused by the splitting of energy levels as a result of spin-spin coupling.

A detectable interaction between protons takes place only across a limited number of bonds. In general, no significant spin-spin coupling is observed between protons separated by more than four σ-bonds (or by more than four σ-bonds and one π-bond).

Two separate problems are involved in obtaining chemically useful information from spin-spin coupling; first the multiplets in question must be analyzed so as to yield the values of J and the chemical shifts of the interacting protons; and second, these values must be interpreted in terms of molecular structure.

Analysis of Spin-Spin Multiplets

In principle, any set of multiplets due to a number of interacting protons (or groups of equivalent protons) can be analyzed by computerized quantum-mechanical calculations. Such calculations are always tedious and often very difficult; fortunately, the multiplets can be analyzed by direct measurement in a large number of cases. Such spectra are known as *first-order spectra*; we shall deal with the analysis of first-order spectra and with some general features of the more complex *second-order spectra*.

The parameter that determines whether a group of protons (a *spin system*) will give rise to a first- or second-order spectrum is the ratio, $\Delta v/J$, of the chemical-shift difference between the relevant protons and the coupling constant J between them, both expressed in Hz. Large $\Delta v/J$ ratios, indicating *weakly coupled* systems, are associated with simple first-order spectra. For a true first-order spectrum, *all* $\Delta v/J$ ratios within the spin system must be large. Quite often a spin system has sets of both strongly and weakly coupled nuclei in it, and straightforward application of first-order rules to such cases will lead to errors in analysis. For most purposes, $\Delta v/J \geq 3$ can be considered "large."

Because chemical shifts, and therefore Δv, increase with increasing strength of the magnetic field while coupling constants do not, it follows that spectra taken at higher frequencies are easier to interpret. This is the principal reason why, despite the considerably greater expense, spectrometers operating at ever higher frequencies are being built. (The limits of field strengths obtainable with reasonably sized permanent magnets or iron-core electromagnets have apparently been reached. The latest high-field NMR instruments use superconducting (liquid-helium cooled) solenoids, and reach fields corresponding to an operating frequency of 360 MHz for protons.)

There are certain conventions used in naming spin systems. The letters A, B, C, D, ... are used to describe groups of protons whose chemical-shift differences are small compared with the values of their coupling constants; that is, strongly coupled sets. Subscripts are used to give the number of protons in an equivalent group. A break in the alphabetical sequence shows which groups are weakly coupled. For example, writing A_2BMXY describes a six-spin system. The two A nuclei and the B nucleus are strongly coupled to each other, but only weakly coupled to the nuclei M, X, and Y. The nucleus M is weakly coupled to all other nuclei. The nucleus X is strongly coupled to the nucleus Y, but weakly coupled to the other nuclei.

Primes are used to denote protons that are chemically equivalent but are not coupled identically to other protons and therefore are not magnetically equivalent.

The A_nX_m system will give rise to a first-order spectrum (A yielding $m + 1$ lines and X yielding $n + 1$ lines, with all spacings equal to J_{AX}), while the A_nB_m system will give a complex spectrum. Fortunately, the number of spins in a spin system, and hence its complexity, is limited by the rapid attenuation of J with the number of bonds separating the coupled nuclei.

The rules for interpreting first-order spectra are as follows:

1. When a proton (or a group of magnetically equivalent protons) is spin-spin coupled to n equivalent protons with a coupling constant of J Hz, its NMR signal is split into $n + 1$ lines* separated by J Hz. The relative intensities of the lines are in the ratio of the binomial coefficients of $(x + y)^n$. The true chemical shift of the protons concerned lies at the center of the multiplet.

Splitting by one proton therefore results in a doublet of equal intensity; splitting by two protons results in a triplet of relative component intensities of 1:2:1; splitting by three protons results in a quartet of relative component intensities 1:3:3:1; splitting by four protons results in a quintet of relative intensities 1:4:6:4:1; and splitting by six protons results in a septet of relative component intensities 1:6:15:20:15:6:1. (Compare Table 13.2, p 376.)

2. If there are more than two interacting groups of protons ($A_nM_mX_p\cdots$), the multiplicity of the signal due to the A protons is given by $(m + 1)(p + 1)\cdots$; i.e., the part of the spectrum due to nuclei A takes the form of a multiplet of sub-multiplets. Note that the number "n" does not enter into the expression. Clearly, the appropriate J values control splittings.

3. In first-order spectra, equivalent protons appear not to split one another; in other words, the transitions corresponding to such interactions are forbidden, or of zero probability. However, interactions between equivalent protons do take place and the corresponding coupling constants can be obtained from some second-order spectra.

The physical basis of the first-order rules is quite clear. Consider a system of two protons, H_A and H_X, and let the two allowed spin-states be α (high energy) and β (low energy). Then for upward transitions of the nucleus H_A we can have:

$H_A\beta$ to $H_A\alpha$ with H_X in state α and $H_A\beta$ to $H_A\alpha$ with H_X in state β

Since the populations of H_X in the α and β states are almost completely equal (recall the vanishingly small Boltzmann excess discussed previously), the two transitions are of equal probability and hence H_A will give rise to a symmetrical doublet.

Similarly, for a system of three spins, one H_A and two H_X, we can have the following upward transitions for H_A:

$H_A\beta$ to $H_A\alpha$ with the first H_X in state α and the second in state β
$H_A\beta$ to $H_A\alpha$ with the first H_X in state β and the second in state α
$H_A\beta$ to $H_A\alpha$ with both H_X nuclei in state α
$H_A\beta$ to $H_A\alpha$ with both H_X nuclei in state β

The first two transitions are equivalent (*degenerate*) and hence H_A will give rise to a triplet with the intensity ratios 1:2:1.

---

* More generally, splitting by a nucleus of spin $= I$ gives $2nI + 1$ lines.

However, this sort of reasoning is not the full theoretical treatment for the system; the full treatment merely reduces to this description for cases where $\Delta v/J$ assumes large values; in other words, for first-order spectra.

We shall now deal with the spectral characteristics of some commonly encountered spin systems.

Two-Spin Systems. This can, by definition, be either an AX spectrum (i.e., a doublet of equal-intensity lines for H_A centered on the chemical shift δ_A of H_A with a separation of J_{AX}, and an identical doublet centered on δ_X) or a second-order AB spectrum.

The AB spectrum also consists of two doublets whose separations are exactly equal to J_{AB}, but the "inner" lines are more intense than the "outer" lines. The chemical shifts of H_A and H_B are given by the following expression

$$\nu_A - \nu_B = \sqrt{(1 - 4)(2 - 3)} \tag{12.10}$$

where $\nu_A - \nu_B$ is the separation of the chemical shifts of H_A and H_B, and the numbers refer to the frequencies of the lines as marked in Figure 12.11. Once $\nu_A - \nu_B$ (in Hz) has been determined, δ_A and δ_B can be located by measuring from the center of the always perfectly symmetrical AB systems (often referred to as an "AB quartet").

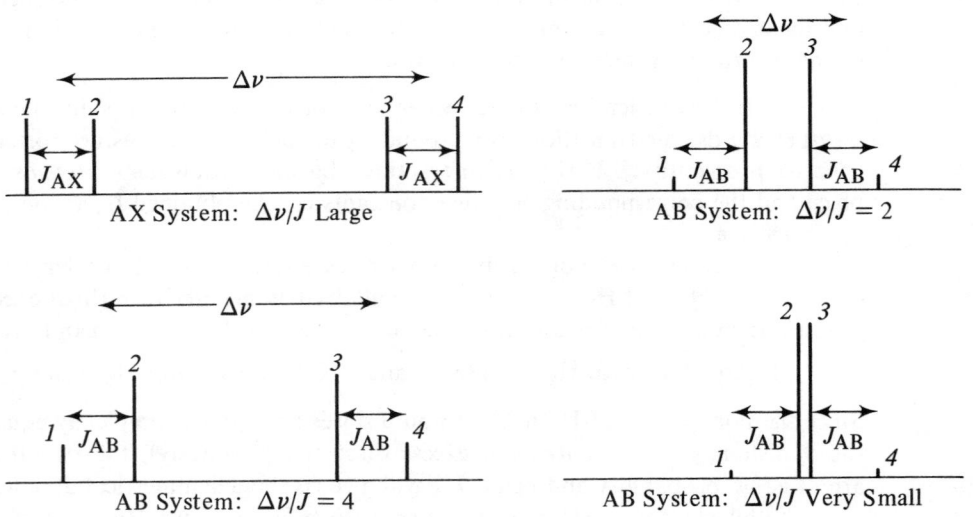

FIGURE 12.11. *Calculated spectra of two-spin systems.*

As δ_A and δ_B become more nearly identical, the intensities of the inner lines increase at the expense of the outer lines until, at the limit of $\nu_A - \nu_B = 0$, the transitions corresponding to the outer lines become forbidden and the system reduces to a singlet of two-proton intensity, i.e., the trivial A_2 case.

The characteristic of a part of the spectrum "sloping" away from the position of the other part is common to all spectra that are not strictly first order; practically speaking, this means nearly all observable spectra.

Three-Spin Systems. A system of three protons can always be described by no more than six parameters. Thus, the first-order AMX case is described by: δ_A, δ_M, δ_X, J_{AM}, J_{AX}, and J_{MX} (obviously J_{AX} and J_{XA} are the same). In this first-order case, one observes four lines for each proton (a doublet of doublets) with separations corresponding to the coupling constants with the other nuclei for a total of 12 lines. Many experimental spectra, such as the one shown in Figure 12.12, approach the ideal AMX case, i.e., the directly measured line spacings are very close to the true coupling constants, as computed by the appropriate quantum mechanics ("ABC analysis"). Note that even here the intensities depart from the first-order ideal, where all lines within each doublet-of-doublets should be equal. Thus, the lines in the H_A and H_M multiplets slope toward each other (cf. the AB case above). The lines of the H_X multiplet appear broader because of small additional unresolved coupling to the protons on the phenyl ring.

If all the protons have similar chemical shifts and are coupled—that is, in the ABC case—a spectrum of up to 15 lines results, which is so distorted that it is often not possible to recognize it as such. A very common system is the partially strongly coupled ABX case, which must not be analyzed as an AMX case. Where two of the protons are equivalent, one can get an A_2X or an A_2B system.

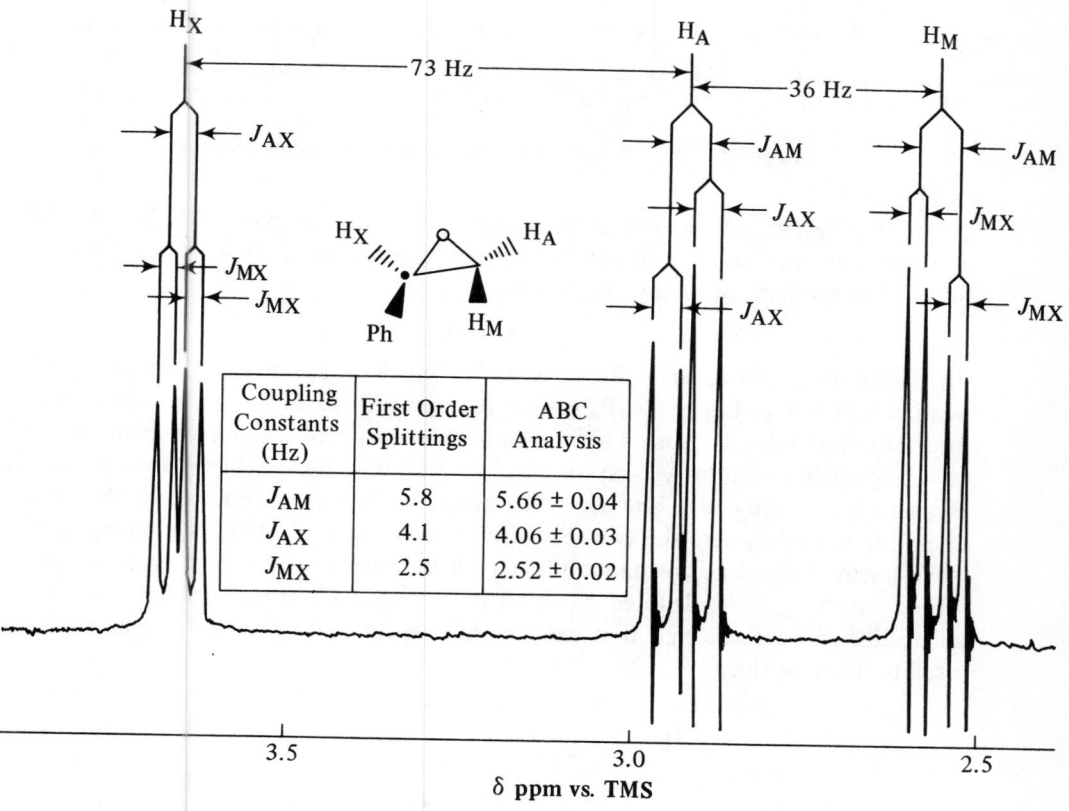

Coupling Constants (Hz)	First Order Splittings	ABC Analysis
J_{AM}	5.8	5.66 ± 0.04
J_{AX}	4.1	4.06 ± 0.03
J_{MX}	2.5	2.52 ± 0.02

FIGURE 12.12. *100-MHz spectrum of styrene oxide (25% in CCl$_4$). The part of the spectrum due to aromatic protons is not shown.*

By first-order rules, the A_2X system gives rise to a doublet of two-proton intensity and a triplet of one-proton intensity. The A_2B spectrum may have up to 9 lines and can be highly asymmetrical.

Four-Spin Systems. The system AX_3 is quite common and occurs, for example, in

the spectrum of the fragment $CH_3-C\overset{/}{\underset{\backslash}{H}}$. The X resonance is a doublet of three-

proton intensity, with spacings equal to J_{AX}, while the A resonance is a 1:3:3:1 quartet with the same spacings.

The intensity distribution in the three commonly encountered "four-line" patterns—namely, the AB quartet, the AMX doublet-of-doublets, and the AX_3 quartet—are very characteristic and can be distinguished on sight (see Fig. 12.13).

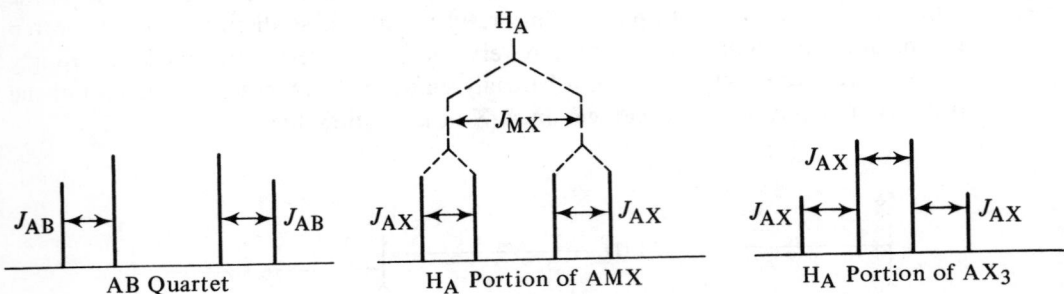

FIGURE 12.13. *The intensity distribution in four-line patterns.*

The system AB_3 is only of theoretical interest. The systems A_2X_2 and A_2B_2 are very common and are found in the spectra of compounds with freely rotating pairs of nonequivalent methylene groups:

$$R-CH_2-CH_2-R'$$

In the extreme first-order A_2X_2 case, each methylene group gives rise to a triplet with spacings J_{AX}, but the A_2B_2 system may give up to 24 lines. However, it can be easily recognized because it always consists of two identical mirror-image halves.

By definition, an A_2B_2 system can be described by the three parameters J_{AB}, δ_A, and δ_B, although J_{AA} and J_{BB} will enter into the second-order case. However, there are systems where the two sets of chemically equivalent (by symmetry) nuclei have unequal coupling constants to each other because they lack magnetic equivalence. Such systems, denoted by AA'BB' or AA'XX', are associated with *para*-disubstituted benzenes and it is easily seen that an additional parameter must be used to describe them:

$$
\begin{array}{cc}
\delta_A \\
\delta_B \\
J_{AA'} \\
J_{BB'} \\
J_{AB} \ (= J_{A'B'}) \\
J_{AB'} \ (= J_{A'B})
\end{array}
$$

Other types of four-spin systems, including the general (and quite formidable) ABCD case, have no obvious qualitatively distinguishing characteristics.

Five-Spin and Higher Systems. The asymmetrical first-order A_2X_3 case is very common since it is associated with the ethyl group attached to an electronegative center (e.g., ethyl chloride). The completely distorted A_2B_3 case is not very common, but gradual transitions can be observed in many spectra. The partially symmetrical AA'BB'C system and its first-order analogue AA'MM'X are both common, since they are observed in the spectra of pyridine and also of all monosubstituted benzenes. Complete analysis involves the placing of up to 124 lines.

The symmetrical AX_4 system, as in $R–CH_2–\overset{|}{C}H–CH_2–R'$, gives rise to a doublet and a quintet. Similarly, the AX_6 (seven-spin) system exhibited in the spectra of isopropyl derivatives gives rise to a doublet and a septet. Second-order examples of these spectra are rare.

Common Errors in Analysis of NMR Spectra

The obvious effects associated with second-order spectra (for instance, extra lines, distorted intensity patterns, and unequal spacings) generally preclude any injudicious attempts to analyze such systems by first-order rules. However, in some cases second-order spectra have features that are qualitatively indistinguishable from some features of first-order spectra, and so are often misinterpreted. It must be understood that the three cases discussed below are not physical phenomena—they are simply the result of certain combinations of the chemical-shift and spin-coupling parameters.

Partially Strongly Coupled Spectra. The X portion of an ABX spectrum gives rise to four lines, which are often regularly spaced and appear identical to the X portion of an AMX spectrum. However, the spacings *cannot* be used to obtain the values of J_{AX} and J_{BX}, although the distance between the outer lines does correspond to $J_{AX} + J_{BX}$. When the AB portion of the spectrum can be clearly resolved, no misinterpretation should result, because it is more complex than the AM portion of an AMX spectrum. However, when only the X portion is visible (for example, when the remainder is hidden by overlapping resonances) the problem is not simple and the possibility of a partially strongly coupled system must be considered.

Virtual Coupling. A resonance due to a proton may be complicated (split) because of a proton which is *not* directly coupled to it, but which is strongly coupled to a proton which *is* coupled to it. This "phenomenon" is really a special case of the trap described above. Consider, for example, a linear system of 3 protons:

$$-\overset{|}{\underset{H_A}{C}}-\overset{|}{\underset{H_B}{C}}-\overset{|}{\underset{H_C}{C}}-$$

Although protons H_A and H_C are usually not significantly coupled (they are separated by four σ-bonds), the resonance due to H_A may not be a simple doublet with spacing

J_{AB} if H_B and H_C are strongly coupled; that is, if at the spectrometer frequency employed, $(\nu_B - \nu_C)/J_{BC}$ is a small number. Clearly, mistakes are most likely to occur if the B and C portions of the spectrum cannot be discerned, as in the case discussed above.

Deceptive Simplicity. Sometimes the combination of parameters is such that a deceptively simple spectrum results. Consider the spectrum of furan,

$$J_{AB} \neq J_{AB'}$$

The 60-MHz spectrum of this compound gives rise to two triplets suggesting an A_2X_2 case, whereas symmetry considerations show that it should give rise to an AA'XX' or AA'BB' spectrum. Deceptive spectra should always be suspected when a first-order analysis appears to yield a number of apparently equal coupling constants while structural considerations suggest coupling constants of widely different magnitudes. Thus, the incorrect analysis of the spectrum of furan leads to a postulation of equal *ortho* and *meta* coupling constants. More sophisticated analysis shows that this is not the case, as should be expected on structural grounds.

Signs of Coupling Constants

Coupling constants have sign ($+$ or $-$) as well as magnitude. By convention, the sign of the coupling constant between two nuclei is taken to be positive if the state with the two spins in an antiparallel orientation is of lower energy. The relative signs of coupling constants cannot be obtained from first-order spectra but may be determined from more strongly complexed spectra and from some multiple-resonance experiments (see below). The absolute signs of coupling constants cannot be obtained from spectral analysis because the reversal of all signs leaves the spectrum unchanged. Many absolute signs have been determined from the NMR spectra of compounds in a nematic (partially oriented) phase.

Aids to Spectral Analysis

Besides first-order approximations and quantum-mechanical calculations, several other (essentially experimental) aids are available.

Examination of NMR Spectra at More than One Frequency. As mentioned before, coupling constants do not depend on the operating frequency of the NMR spectrometer, whereas the chemical shifts on the Hz scale do. It follows that what is a second-order spectrum at 60 MHz may become a first-order spectrum at 100 MHz.

Solvent Shifts. Chemical shifts are often strongly influenced by the nature of the solvent used, whereas coupling constants are essentially solvent-independent. Thus, a change of solvent may simplify a spectral pattern. Although experiments of this nature are essentially shots in the dark, the procedure is widely used; the common solvent pairs are deuterochloroform and benzene or pyridine.

Deuterium Substitution. Substitution of deuterium (D or $^2_1$H) for protium ($^1_1$H) tends to simplify NMR spectra in two ways. First, it removes that part of the spectrum due to the replaced proton(s), and second, it simplifies the remainder because, while deuterium is magnetic and will split the resonances of the remaining protons, the coupling constants between ^{1}H and ^{2}H are only about one-seventh of the corresponding coupling constants between ^{1}H and ^{1}H. For example, while the methyl resonance of ethanol is a triplet (X part of A_2X_3), the methyl resonance of CH_3CH_2OH is a slightly broadened singlet.

Spin Decoupling. It is possible to introduce one (or more) irradiating radio-frequencies into the transmitter coil of an NMR spectrometer, thus generating one or more perturbing magnetic fields in addition to H_1. Such experiments are known as *double-* (or *multiple-*) *irradiation* experiments and give rise to *double-* (or *multiple-*) *resonance spectra.* *Spin decoupling*, in which the second (and further) fields are relatively strong and are directed at the resonances of protons coupled to the protons being observed, is a special case and is the most common experiment of this type.

If the resonance from proton A (which is coupled to proton B) is observed while simultaneously proton B is strongly irradiated at its resonant frequency, the normal doublet expected of H_A (half of an AB quartet) will collapse to a singlet. This results from the fact that the second irradiating field causes rapid transitions of H_B between its two spin states, so that H_A experiences only the averaged spin state of H_B and hence no splitting in its energy levels results. Clearly, this phenomenon is related to the time dependence of NMR.

The capacity of spin decoupling in simplifying spectra is obvious. However, strongly coupled protons cannot be decoupled because the introduction of the second radio-frequency field perturbs the region near the field and hence makes the resonances impossible to observe.

There are two basically different methods of spin decoupling: *field-sweep decoupling*, in which the frequency difference between the decoupling field (H_2) and the observing field (H_1) is kept constant as the spectrum is swept, and *frequency-sweep decoupling*, in which the value of H_2 is kept constant as the value of H_1 changes. The latter is more commonly used for routine studies and the results are easier to interpret.

Shift Reagents. In 1970, Williams, elaborating on the preliminary work of Hinckley, discovered that adding *tris-β*-diketonate lanthanide complexes to solutions of substances with lone pairs of electrons available for coordination (such as oxygen- and nitrogen-containing organic compounds) resulted in vastly more dispersed NMR spectra. This phenomenon, named *lanthanide-induced shift* (LIS), arises from the

unusual combination of paramagnetic properties in most lanthanides, whereby large local changes in the magnetic fields are produced in the immediate vicinity of the lanthanide. This type of induced shift is known as *pseudo-contact shift* and is propagated through space in a normal manner, in contrast to the *contact shifts* found with other paramagnetic species where the effect is transmitted through bonds.

As lanthanide-induced shifts often have values of up to 20 ppm, the increased dispersion, and hence interpretability, of NMR spectra afforded by this method is enormous. Moreover, pseudo-contact shifts diminish regularly with the distance from the paramagnetic center, r in Figure 12.14, and since this can be approximately located (the lanthanide complex is attached to the lone pair), their magnitudes give valuable structural information.

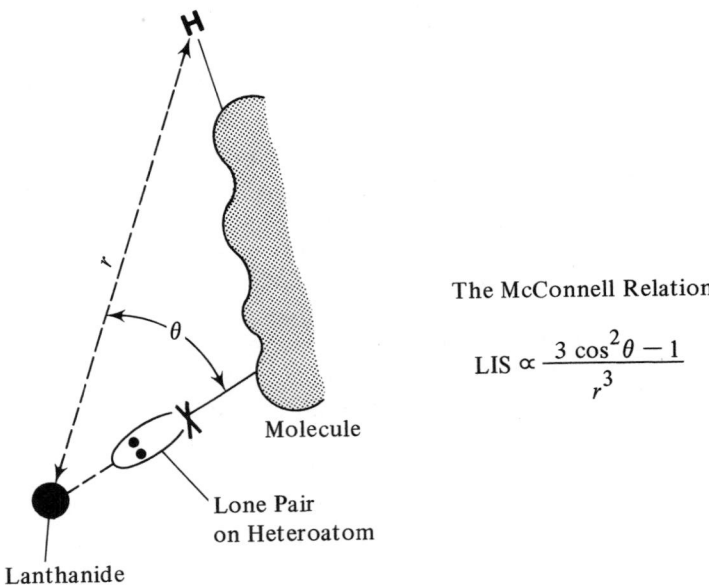

The McConnell Relation

$$\text{LIS} \propto \frac{3\cos^2\theta - 1}{r^3}$$

FIGURE 12.14. *The magnitude of the lanthanide-induced shift (LIS) as a function of molecular geometry. H is a proton on the molecule whose resonance is being shifted by the presence of the lanthanide.*

The most commonly used shift reagents are based on europium (downfield shifts) and praseodymium (upfield shifts) and contain either dipivaloyl methane ($R_1 = R_2 = t$-butyl, $R_3 = H$) or fluoroalkyl derivatives of β-diketones as ligands.

Interpretation of Spin-Spin Coupling in Terms of Structure

The magnitudes of coupling constants (J) are very characteristic of molecular environment and are especially sensitive to stereochemistry. Further, multiplicities of resonances can give information about the number of neighboring protons. The theory of spin-spin coupling is far too complex to be routinely used and empirical correlation tables are invariably resorted to. The common correlations given below are well established. All coupling constants are quoted as their absolute magnitudes only.

Geminal Coupling Across an sp³ Carbon.

$$\begin{array}{c}R_1 \quad\quad H_A\\ \diagdown\quad\diagup\\ C\\ \diagup\quad\diagdown\\ R_2 \quad\quad H_B\end{array}$$ Typical range: 12–18 Hz

The full range is 0–22.4 Hz. Double bonds adjacent to the central carbon give larger values (e.g., an aromatic ring or a carbonyl group for R_1). Smaller values are associated with R_1 = a heteroatom.

Vicinal Coupling Across Three Single Bonds.

$$H_A\text{–C–C–}H_B$$

The magnitude of J_{AB} is dominated by the size of the dihedral angle (ϕ) and is given by the Karplus equation:

$$J_{AB} = J^0(\cos^2\phi) - 0.3 \quad \text{for angles } 0\text{–}90°$$
$$J_{AB} = J^{180}(\cos^2\phi) - 0.3 \quad \text{for angles } 90\text{–}180° \tag{12.11}$$

The values of the constants J^0 and J^{180} are substituent-dependent, with the ranges $J^0 = 9\text{–}12$ and $J^{180} = 14\text{–}16$ covering most situations. Within the variations caused by substituents those due to the cases

$$H-\overset{|}{\underset{|}{C}}-\overset{|}{\underset{|}{C}}-H, \quad H-\overset{\|}{C}-\overset{|}{\underset{|}{C}}-H, \text{ and } H-\overset{\|}{C}-\overset{\|}{C}-H$$

can usually be ignored. Typical values for freely rotating methyl and methylene groups are 6–8 Hz. The Karplus relation has obvious importance in determining the stereochemistry of organic compounds and is summarized graphically in Figure 12.15.

Olefinic Systems. Typical values are:

$$J_{cis} (J_{AB}) = 6\text{–}14 \text{ Hz}$$ 10 Hz

$$\begin{array}{c}H_B \quad\quad H_A\\ \diagdown\quad\diagup\\ C=C\\ \diagup\quad\diagdown\\ H_C \quad\quad R\end{array}$$ $$J_{trans} (J_{AC}) = 11\text{–}18 \text{ Hz}$$ 6 Hz

$$J_{gem} (J_{BC}) = 0\text{–}3 \text{ Hz}$$ 4 Hz

Electronegative substituents (i.e., R = heteroatom) lead to smaller values of olefinic coupling constants.

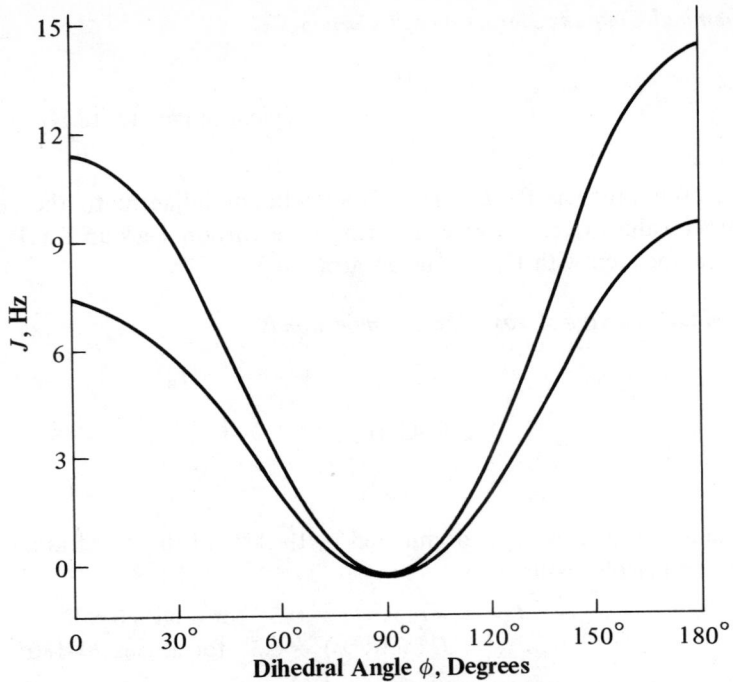

FIGURE 12.15. *The dependence of vicinal coupling constants on dihedral angles.*

Long-Range Coupling. This is defined as coupling across more than 3 bonds. Long-range coupling constants are rarely larger than 3 Hz, but may be highly characteristic of structure. The most common type of long-range interactions is *allylic coupling*, which is due to the protons in H–C–C=C–H, *cisoid* (J_{AX}) or *transoid* (J_{BX}), and which is highly dependent on stereochemistry (see Fig. 12.16).

Homoallylic coupling, i.e., the coupling across 5 bonds in the fragment H–C–C=C–C–H, takes up a slightly larger range of values and also has a characteristic stereochemical dependence. In general, coupling between two protons separated by 4 single bonds becomes significant ($J = 1$–3 Hz) only if the 5 atoms of the system H–C–C–C–H take on a planar "W" (or "M") arrangement.

Aromatic Systems. Typical values in benzenoid compounds are:

$$J_{ortho} = 7\text{–}10 \text{ Hz}$$
$$J_{meta} = 1\text{–}3 \text{ Hz}$$
$$J_{para} = 0\text{–}1 \text{ Hz}$$

Similar ranges apply for heterocyclic systems, except that the J_{ortho} involving protons on carbons α to a heteroatom takes on lower values (cf. olefinic systems) and that a

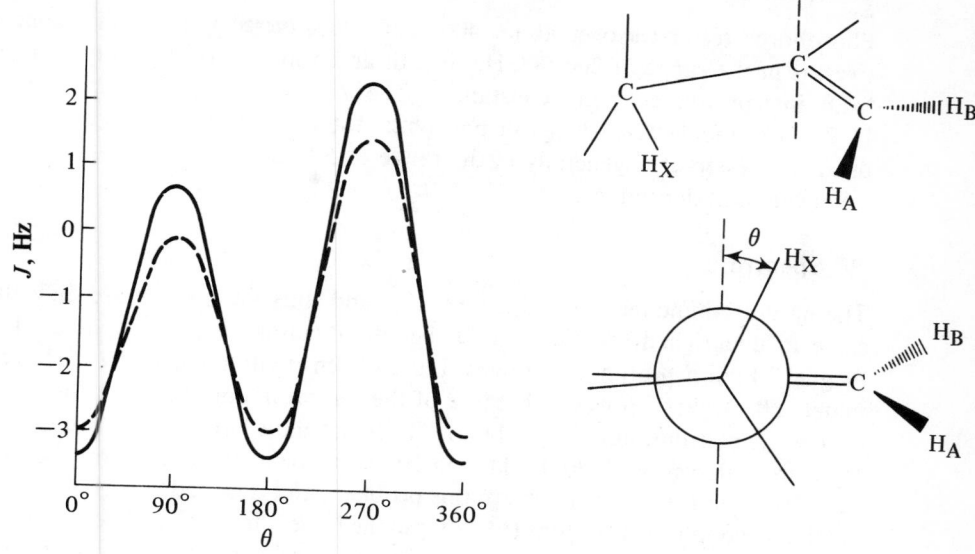

FIGURE 12.16. *Dependence of allylic coupling constants on stereochemistry. Solid lines: Transoid (J_{BX}); dashed lines: Cisoid (J_{AX}). θ is the dihedral angle formed by the C–H_X bond and the (dashed) line perpendicular to the plane formed by the C=$CH_A H_B$ moiety.*

ring-size dependence of J_{ortho} (analogous to that in cycloölefins) is also observed. Such influences are cumulative, so that $J_{\alpha,\beta}$ in furans is only 1–3 Hz.

12.5 NMR SPECTROSCOPY OF NUCLEI OTHER THAN PROTONS

By accident, almost all the nuclei of interest to the vast majority of chemists have spins $I = 1/2$ and hence do not differ at all from protons in their basic theoretical aspects. However, their usefulness does not warrant the effort of learning any empirical parameters relating to them, so the remarks below do not reflect the amount of data available.

It must be realized that the effect of spin-spin coupling of protons to other magnetic nuclei may be observed in the *proton* spectra, and hence some idea of the magnitudes of coupling between protons and some commonly occurring magnetic nuclei may be useful in interpreting proton spectra.

^{19}F Spectra

Fluorine resonates over a range of some 300 ppm, i.e., its chemical shift is more sensitive than ^{1}H to the changes of environment. In saturated systems, $J_{H–F}$ for H–C–F (geminal) ranges from 40–80 Hz and for H–C–C–F (vicinal) from 0–30 Hz. The latter has a Karplus-like dependence on stereochemistry (Eqn. 12.11).

³¹P Spectra

Phosphorus resonates over about 400 ppm. J_{P-H} (direct), as in phosphine deriva-tives, is in the range of 200–700 Hz, i.e., of an entirely different order of magnitude from interproton coupling constants. The J_{H-P} coupling constants for H–C–P, H–C–C–P, and H–C–O–P (as in phosphate esters) vary between 0 and 30 Hz. In phosphate esters it is generally in the range of 5 to 20 Hz and shows a Karplus-like stereochemical dependence.

¹³C Spectra

The natural abundance of ¹³C is only 1%, and thus ¹³C spectra are difficult to ob-serve in unenriched samples. A further disadvantage is that ¹³C is a "less good magnet" than a proton. The overall loss of sensitivity compared to ¹H is approxi-mately 6000-fold. However, because of the central importance of carbon in organic chemistry, constant efforts to obtain ¹³C NMR data have been made over the last 15 years. Recently (1970–1971) Fourier Transform NMR spectroscopy (see Sec. 12.6) has been routinely applied to this problem, and this method in conjunction with blanket decoupling of protons (to collapse the large, direct, ¹³C–H coupling constants and obtain further enhancement due to the Nuclear Overhauser Effect) affords spectra whose signal-to-noise ratio is comparable with that of proton NMR spectra.

There is little doubt that ¹³C–NMR ("CMR") will become of great im-portance in the near future as instrumentation becomes more widely available. The structural implications are considerable; the chemical shifts of ¹³C cover over 200 ppm and fall into very characteristic ranges. Further, by using the "off-resonance de-

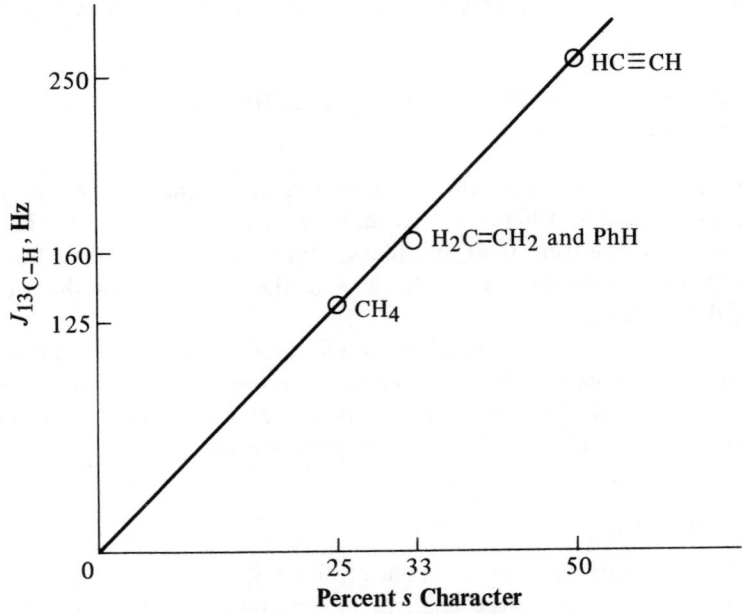

FIGURE 12.17. *The relation between direct ¹³C–H coupling constants and the hybridization of the carbon atom.*

coupling technique," the direct coupling between carbon and protons may be diminished in magnitude, but not completely eliminated, thus permitting us to distinguish methyl carbons (quartet), methylene carbons (triplet), methine carbons (doublet), and tertiary carbons (singlet), by inspection.

The effect of direct (i.e., across one bond) coupling between ^{13}C and protons can often be observed in proton spectra in the form of so-called ^{13}C satellites, from which the ^{13}C–H coupling constants can be obtained by direct measurement. To a first degree of approximation, this coupling is directly proportional to the percent s character in the carbon (Fig. 12.17).

Unfortunately, quantitative applications of CMR spectroscopy are less straightforward than those of PMR because, under the usual experimental conditions, the relative intensities of ^{13}C signals do not reflect accurately their relative abundances. This is due principally to relaxation phenomena and makes proton rather than carbon NMR the method of choice for the analysis of mixtures.

12.6 SPECIAL TOPICS

Pulse Spectroscopy

The normal method of scanning NMR spectra (or, for that matter, other spectra) consists of altering the wavelength of the electromagnetic energy supplied and observing absorption whenever the Larmor relation for a particular nucleus is met. This is known as continuous-wave (CW) spectroscopy.

By contrast, it is possible to apply electromagnetic energy effectively over the whole range of the spectrum in a short, intense burst (pulse) and to observe the spectral effect produced by the nuclei promoted to their upper energy state as they fall back to their lower energy state. The record thus obtained (*free induction decay, FID*) is not identical to the normal absorption spectrum but is related to it, and may be converted to it by performing a Fourier transformation. Consequently, spectra of this type are often called *Fourier Transform Spectra* and the apparatus is often described as a *Fourier Transform (FT)* spectrometer. The advantage of this method is that the information obtained in each pulse is equivalent to scanning the whole spectrum and thus, for equivalent acquisition time, FT spectroscopy leads to a great improvement in sensitivity.

In practice, the data from hundreds, or thousands, of such pulses are stored in a minicomputer and are then processed (Fourier transformed) into an absorption spectrum.

Spectra of Compounds Dissolved in Nematic Phases

As already stated, rapid reorientation of molecules is a necessary prerequisite for the observation of high-resolution NMR spectra; solids give rise to "wide-line" spectra of little chemical interest. However, at intermediate rates of molecular reorientation, it is possible to obtain high-resolution NMR spectra without averaging out through-space interactions between magnetic nuclei.

These rates are attainable for molecules dissolved in the nematic phases of liquid crystals; such spectra give information about molecular geometry, in particular about interproton distances, which is not easily available from other physical measurements.

Nematic-phase spectra are considerably more complicated than those obtained in liquids or gases. Thus, the spectrum of benzene in nematic phase consists of at least 50 observable lines, whereas benzene in the liquid or gas phase gives rise only to a single sharp line in its high-resolution NMR spectrum.

The Nuclear Overhauser Effect (NOE)

One of the important ways in which magnetic nuclei may relax from their upper to their lower energy levels is through a dipolar spin-spin interaction with another magnetic nucleus. This process takes place through space, and its efficiency is inversely proportional to the sixth power of the internuclear distance involved. It follows that the most efficient relaxation by that route can take place when two magnetic nuclei are in close spatial proximity in the same molecule.

This phenomenon must not be confused with spin-spin coupling, which is transmitted through bonds and which leads to the splitting of energy levels. Only relaxation times are involved.

Consider now two magnetic nuclei, A and B, which are in sufficiently close spatial proximity to influence each other's relaxation times. If the nucleus A is observed while the nucleus B is simultaneously irradiated (see Sec. 12.4 for multiple irradiation), the relaxation process in nucleus A becomes more efficient because nucleus B, which is undergoing rapid up-and-down transitions, becomes effectively a rotating magnetic field. This results in a perturbation of the usual Boltzmann distribution of nuclei A towards the lower state and increases up to 50% the intensity of the signal due to the nucleus A. This enhancement of intensity is known as the Nuclear Overhauser Effect and is diagnostic for the presence of magnetic nuclei in close spatial proximity. Structural information can thus be obtained, for example, in connection with *cis-trans* isomerism.

Commercially Available Instruments

High-resolution NMR spectrometers are complex and expensive instruments produced by a very limited number of manufacturers—Varian (USA), Perkin-Elmer (UK), Bruker (Germany), and Jeol (Japan) account for virtually all instruments. They range from proton-only routine instruments (e.g., Varian EM360 and Perkin-Elmer R24) operating at 60 MHz* and costing approximately $10,000 to flexible research spectrometers, operating usually at 90 or 100 MHz, which may cost up to $150,000 with accessories (e.g., Varian XL100-15 and Bruker HX-90). At the extreme ends of the scale Varian offers its model EM300 which can be used only to observe protons (at 30 MHz) and costs about $5,000, while several manufacturers offer high-field systems (220–360 MHz) based on helium-cooled superconducting magnets, which may cost up to $300,000.

---

* NMR spectrometers are usually described in terms of their operating frequency for protons even if they are not used to obtain proton NMR spectra, rather than in terms of the more logical parameter, the strength of the magnetic field.

The vast majority of analytical applications of NMR spectroscopy can be classified under two headings: determination of structures of pure compounds and quantitative determination of mixtures. The monitoring of the progress of reactions is, of course, only a subcategory of the latter class.

In practice, structural determination is not carried out solely by means of NMR spectroscopy, although proton NMR is probably the most important single method available in this area. For this reason, a detailed discussion of structure determination by NMR alone is generally not included even in extensive general texts on NMR spectroscopy and is best considered in conjunction with other major techniques.

Quantitative applications of NMR have, however, certain inherent strengths and limitations that are summarized below:

1. NMR spectroscopy is nondestructive—a sample may be recovered completely unchanged after being subjected to an NMR experiment because the energy changes involved are negligible compared with the strengths of chemical bonds. The solvents used are usually easily evaporated, and the cell (a glass test-tube) is easily washed out.

2. It is often possible to identify the components of a mixture and to carry out a quantitative analysis in one step—that is, it is not always necessary to carry out precalibration procedures.

3. The results of quantitative analysis by NMR, while not inherently of great accuracy, tend to be quite positive. Thus, even a small number of resonances can lead to a positive identification because chemical shifts can be determined very accurately, and the substances identified can then be quite positively estimated in a mixture. In addition, the integration of several resonance signals often leads to internal verification.

4. When applicable, quantitative analysis by NMR can be very fast (a typical spectrum takes less than 5 min to run) and convenient (simple sample preparation).

5. The principal limitation of NMR spectroscopy as an analytical tool is its inherently poor sensitivity. This is particularly important in examining mixtures, because with pure compounds one may assume that protons resonating at different frequencies are present in ratios of whole numbers whereas the corresponding ratios in mixtures can only be determined to within the accuracy of integration. It is difficult to determine a small amount of impurity, except when it gives rise to well separated signals; therefore, NMR is very rarely used for this purpose. This insensitivity is not wholly a disadvantage because, by converse reasoning, samples used for structural determination need not be highly purified. As a rule of thumb, a purity of 90% is adequate and even larger quantities of impurity can be tolerated provided they can be identified.

6. The integrated intensities of resonances in an NMR spectrum give only relative abundances of magnetic nuclei in the various environments. This limitation is not serious, since precalibrating the integrator with samples of known composition or introducing internal standards can be used to convert the relative values

into absolute numbers. Using an internal standard avoids errors arising from changes of spectrometer response with time, so it is the preferred procedure. Substances suitable for this use should give rise to easily observed resonances (preferably singlets) not overlapping with those being determined, should be chemically inert toward the other components, and should be easy to weigh accurately. The most useful internal standards for nonaqueous systems are 1,3,5-trinitrobenzene and methylene bromide, and for aqueous systems the salts of terephthalic acid.

7. It is obvious that with the aid of an internal standard it is possible to determine the total weight of hydrogen in a known weight of a pure compound and thus obtain a rapid and nondestructive analysis for this element. Furthermore, by making certain assumptions (e.g., that the resonance of lowest intensity corresponds to a single proton in a molecule or that a sharp singlet near $\delta = 4$ ppm is due to a methoxy group), it is possible to obtain the molecular weight of an unknown substance. If the assumption was wrong, it would typically result in the apparent molecular weight becoming equal to the "equivalent" weight with respect to the fragment whose resonance is considered. This must be less than the true molecular weight and therefore represents a very useful check on molecular weights determined by mass spectrometry (Chap. 16): when the molecular weight obtained by NMR is higher than the m/e ratio of the peak of highest mass in the mass spectrum, the molecular ion is not detectable in the latter. This condition is not uncommon with many compounds (for instance, with many iodo-derivatives where the molecular ion cannot be observed even at the lowest practicable electron energy).

Experimental Considerations

The operation of NMR instruments is far too complex to be discussed within the present framework, but the user should know some of the experimental variables, even if he or she does not normally operate the instrument.

Sample Preparation. As mentioned above, very high purity is not normally essential, but certain types of impurities such as paramagnetic substances must be excluded. The presence of solid impurities of any sort in the solution of a substance will degrade the homogeneity of the magnetic field and hence cause line broadening. For this reason solutions should be filtered before being placed in the NMR sample tube.

Solvent. For all practical purposes, NMR spectra are recorded in solution, although pure ("neat") liquids and even gases can, in principle, also be examined. The solvents must meet certain requirements (Sec. 12.1) and a compromise must often be employed between using concentrated solutions (for high sensitivity) and dilute solutions (for measuring chemical shifts uninfluenced by solute-solute interactions). Besides the commonly used carbon tetrachloride, deuterochloroform, and D_2O, a range of deuterated solvents (dimethyl sulfoxide, benzene, pyridine, acetone, dioxane) is commercially available. It must be emphasized that direct comparison of chemical shifts obtained in different solvents is invalid, as solvent-induced changes of up to 0.5 ppm are by no means uncommon.

Instrumental Variables. Most of these serve self-evident purposes (e.g., amplification, noise filtering, phasing of signals, width of sweep, and adjustments of field homogeneity) but two variables are of particular importance in analytical applications. As mentioned above, the strength of the irradiating field H_1 (the amplitude of the RF radiation) may cause saturation when set at too high a value, but high RF field also causes increased sensitivity. For this reason, the RF field is often set at a value that saturates *some* of the resonances over the finite range of relaxation times in a real sample. Deviations from the ideal behavior (the exact correspondence between the number of protons and the height of the integral step) caused by such settings will not lead to error when examining pure substances where the ratios between the various steps can be legitimately rounded off to whole numbers, but may become a source of serious error in quantitative work on mixtures. For this reason, such measurements should be repeated with at least two settings of the RF field strength. Also, since saturation is a function of the duration of exposure of magnetic nuclei to the RF field H_1, as well as its strength, the parameters governing the scanning velocity (*sweep time*) and RF-field strength cannot be considered independently. Furthermore, a pure absorption signal corresponds only to an infinitely slow sweep-time, while very rapid sweep-times will be associated with various distortions.

SELECTED BIBLIOGRAPHY

General Texts

BECKER, E. D. *High Resolution NMR.* New York: Academic Press, 1969.

BOVEY, F. A. *NMR Spectroscopy.* New York: Academic Press, 1969.

EMSLEY, J. W.; FEENEY, J.; and SUTCLIFFE, L. H. *High Resolution NMR Spectroscopy*, vols. I and II. Oxford: Pergamon Press, 1965.

JACKMAN, L. M., and STERNHELL, S. *Applications of NMR Spectroscopy in Organic Chemistry*, 2nd ed. Oxford: Pergamon Press, 1969.

MATHIESON, D. W., ed. *Nuclear Magnetic Resonance for Organic Chemists.* London: Academic Press, 1967.

Analysis of NMR Spectra

ABRAHAM, R. J. *Analysis of High Resolution NMR Spectra.* Amsterdam: Elsevier, 1971.

CORIO, P. L. *Structure of High-Resolution NMR Spectra.* New York: Academic Press, 1966.

DETAR, D. F., ed. *Computer Programs for Chemistry*, vol. 1. New York: W. A. Benjamin, 1968.

ROBERTS, J. D. *An Introduction to Spin-Spin Splitting in High Resolution NMR Spectra.* New York: W. A. Benjamin, 1962.

Carbon-13 NMR Spectroscopy

CLERC, J. T.: PRETSCH, E.; and STERNHELL, S. *^{13}C Kernresonanzspectroscopie.* Frankfurt: Akademische Verlagagesellschaft, 1973.

LEVY, G. C., and NELSON, G. L. *Carbon-13 NMR for Organic Chemists.* New York: Wiley-Interscience, 1972.

STOTHERS, J. B. *Carbon-13 NMR Spectroscopy.* New York: Academic Press, 1972.

Collections of NMR Data

BHACCA, N. S. et al. *High Resolution NMR Spectra Catalog*, vols. 1 and 2. Palo Alto: Varian Associates, 1963.

BOVEY, F. A. *NMR Data Tables for Organic Compounds*, vol. 1. New York: Interscience, 1967.

BRÜGEL, W. *NMR Spectra and Chemical Structure.* New York: Academic Press, 1967.

HOWELL, M. G.; KENDE, A. S.; and WEBB, J. S., eds. *Formula Index to NMR Literature Data*, vols. 1 and 2. New York: Plenum Press, 1966.

JOHNSON, L. F., and JANKOWSKI, W. C. *Carbon-13 NMR Spectra.* New York: Wiley-Interscience, 1972.

Special Topics

BOVEY, F. A. *High Resolution NMR of Macromolecules.* New York: Academic Press, 1972.

CASEY, A. F. *PMR Spectroscopy in Medicinal and Biological Chemistry.* London: Academic Press, 1971.

DWEK, R. A. *NMR in Biochemistry.* Oxford: Clarendon Press, 1973.

FARRAR, T. C., and BECKER, E. D. *Pulse and Fourier Transform NMR.* New York: Academic Press, 1971.

KASLER, F. *Quantitative Analysis by NMR Spectroscopy.* London: Academic Press, 1973.

NOGGLE, J. H., and SCHIRMER, R. E. *The Nuclear Overhauser Effect.* New York: Academic Press, 1971.

Determination of Molecular Structure by Combined Spectroscopic Methods (including NMR)

SILVERSTEIN, R. M.; BASSLER, C. G.; and MORRILL, T. C. *Spectrometric Identification of Organic Compounds*, 3rd ed. New York: Wiley-Interscience, 1974.

SIMON, W., and CLERC, T. *Structural Analysis of Organic Compounds by Spectroscopic Methods.* London: Macdonald, 1971.

WILLIAMS, D. H., and FLEMING, I. *Spectroscopic Methods in Organic Chemistry*, 2nd ed. London: McGraw-Hill, 1973.

PROBLEMS

1. The methyl protons of *n*-propyl alcohol show an absorption peak 352.3 Hz upfield from a benzene external-reference peak, using a radio-frequency field of 60 MHz. (a) If the benzene peak occurs at $\delta = 6.73$ ppm (downfield) from the TMS peak, what is the chemical shift of the sample peak relative to TMS? (b) If the applied frequency had been 50 MHz, at what equivalent frequency from the benzene peak would the absorption peak have occurred?

2. Match the following NMR spectra (pp 360–61) with the following compounds: (a) ethyl bromide; (b) 1,1-dibromoethane; (c) 1,2-dibromo-2-methylpropane; (d) 1,1,2-tribromoethane; (e) ethyl alcohol; and (f) *p*-(*t*-butyl)toluene. The number in a circle near a set of peaks refers to the relative area for those peaks.

3. Predict the relative shape of the NMR spectrum for methyl ethyl ketone, 2-butanone. Compare with that for acetone. Include the number of peaks and their relative areas.

4. Predict the relative shapes of the NMR spectra for propane and 1-nitropropane.

5. Using the Larmor equation and the fact that hydrogen resonates at 60 MHz in a field of 14,092 gauss, (a) calculate the gyromagnetic ratio for hydrogen; (b) calculate the resonance frequency for hydrogen in a spectrometer with a magnetic field strength of 23,487 gauss. (c) If the spectrometer described in (b) above is used to obtain ^{13}C spectra, resonance occurs at 25.1 MHz. What is the resonance frequency for ^{13}C in a spectrometer that obtains ^1H signals at 80 MHz?

6. Define, illustrate, or explain each of the following terms or phrases: (a) frequency-sweep spectrometer; (b) spin-lattice relaxation; (c) chemical shift; (d) TMS; (e) ring current; (f) LIS; (g) pulse FT NMR; and (h) NOE.

7. (a) What is the chemical shift of a proton whose NMR signal is observed at 320 Hz downfield from TMS in a spectrometer whose basic resonance frequency for hydro-

gen is 90 MHz? (b) What is the chemical-shift difference between two different hydrogens whose NMR signals are observed at 180 and 400 Hz from TMS in a spectrometer operating at 60 MHz? (c) An NMR signal is observed at 7.3 ppm downfield from TMS in a spectrometer operating at 100 MHz. Calculate the position in Hz of that same signal in a spectrometer operating at 60 MHz.

8. Explain why the ^{1}H-NMR spectrum of N-methylacetamide shows signals for two different N-methyl groups.

9. Sketch the first-order splitting patterns you would expect to observe for the following spin systems (your sketches should be similar to those in Figs. 12.11 and 12.13): (a) AX (b) A_3X_2 (c) A_3X (d) AMX with $J_{AM} > J_{MX} > J_{AX}$.

10. Sketch the ^{1}H-NMR spectrum you would expect to observe for each of the following compounds: (a) ethyl chloride; (b) t-butyl amine; (c) toluene; (d) methyl methacrylate; (e) 1,1,1-trifluoroethane.

11. The ^{1}H-NMR spectrum of a mixture of toluene and benzene showed two signals; one at 7.3 ppm (integral = 85) and one at 2.2 ppm (integral = 15). From the relative intensities of these signals, calculate the ratio of benzene to toluene in the mixture.

12. Propose structures for the unknown compounds whose ^{1}H-NMR spectra (60 MHz) and molecular formulas are given on pp 362–64. In each instance explain your analysis of the spectrum and how it leads to the structure you propose. The number in a circle by a set of peaks refers to the relative area under the peaks for that set.

13. A particular chlorination reaction could have yielded one of the following isomers: $CH_3(CO)CCl_2CH_2COOH$, $CH_2Cl(CO)CHClCH_2COOH$, or $CHCl_2(CO)CH_2CH_2COOH$. From the 60-MHz proton-NMR spectrum of the isolated product (p 364), determine which compound was actually formed, and explain your selection.

14. Gas chromatographic separation of a mixture of halocarbons gave two isomeric compounds whose molecular formula was found to be $C_2HCl_3F_2$. What are the structures of the two isomers whose 60-MHz NMR spectra are given on p 365? [Hint: Remember that ^{19}F has a spin of 1/2 and splits hydrogen signals as if it were another hydrogen.]

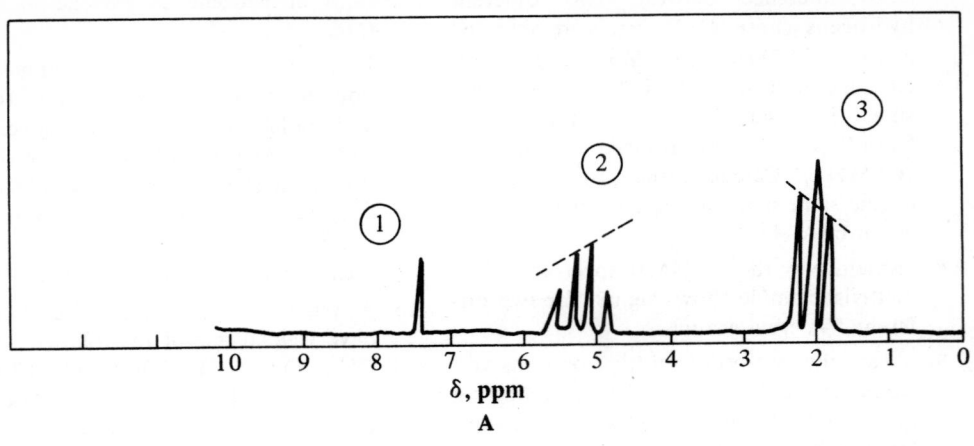

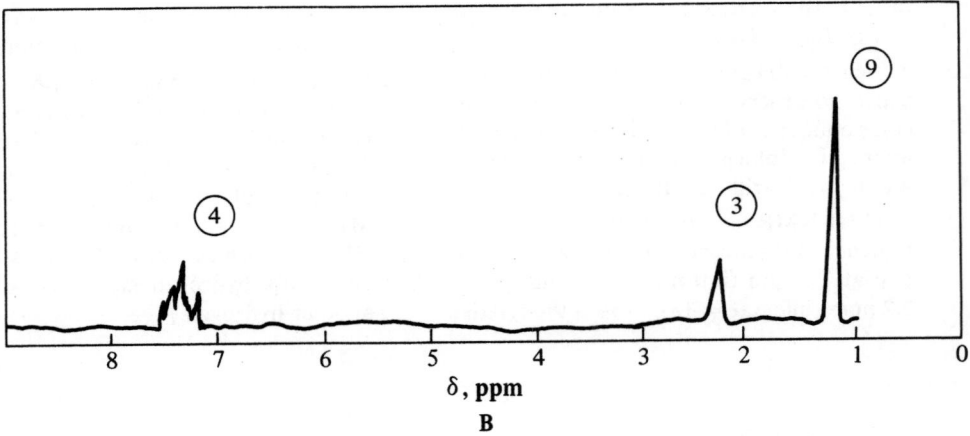

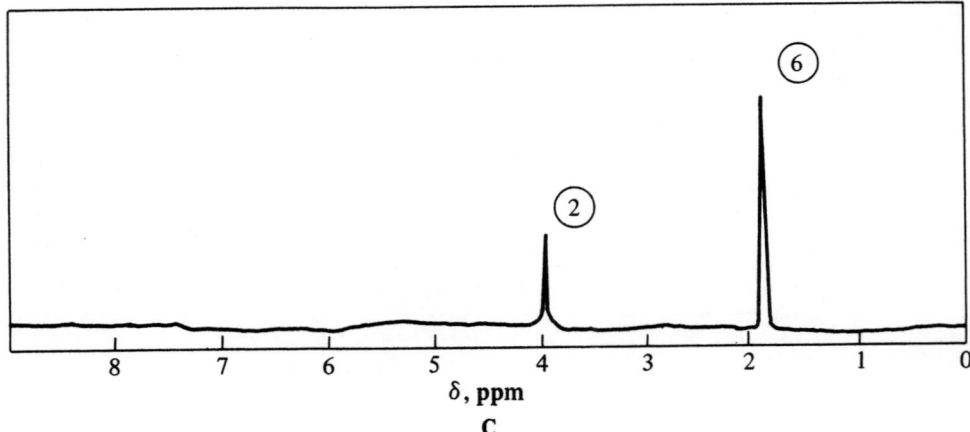

Spectra for Problem 2

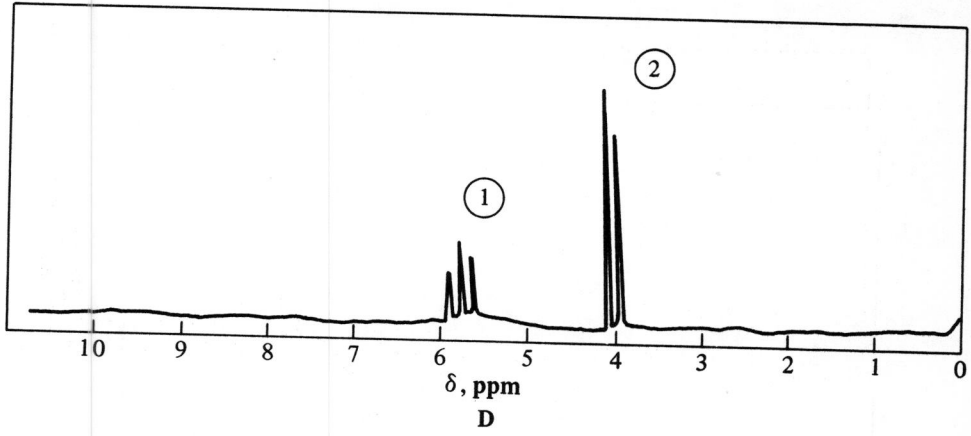

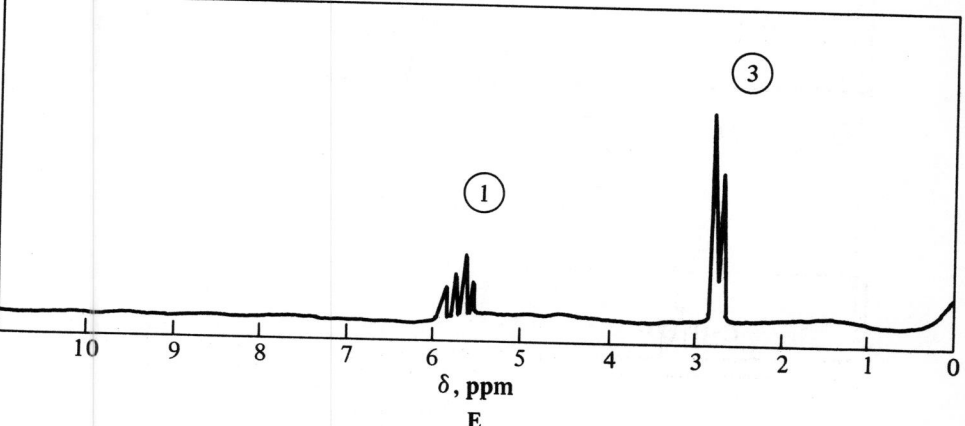

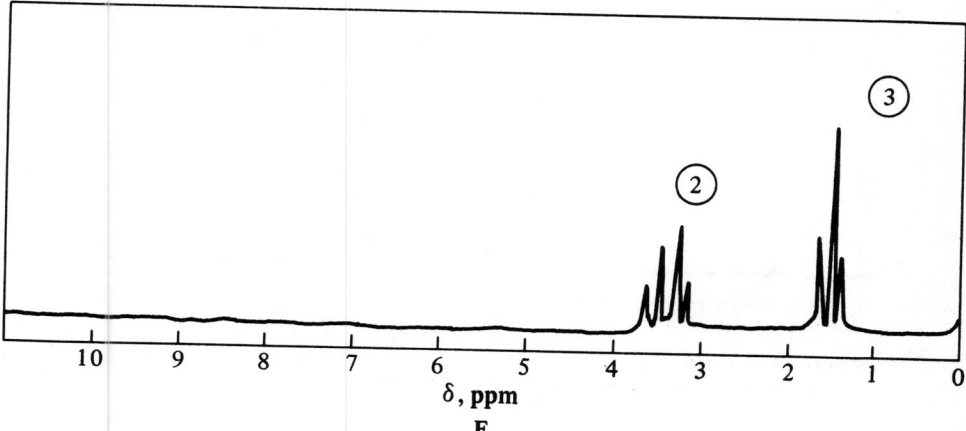

Spectra for Problem 2

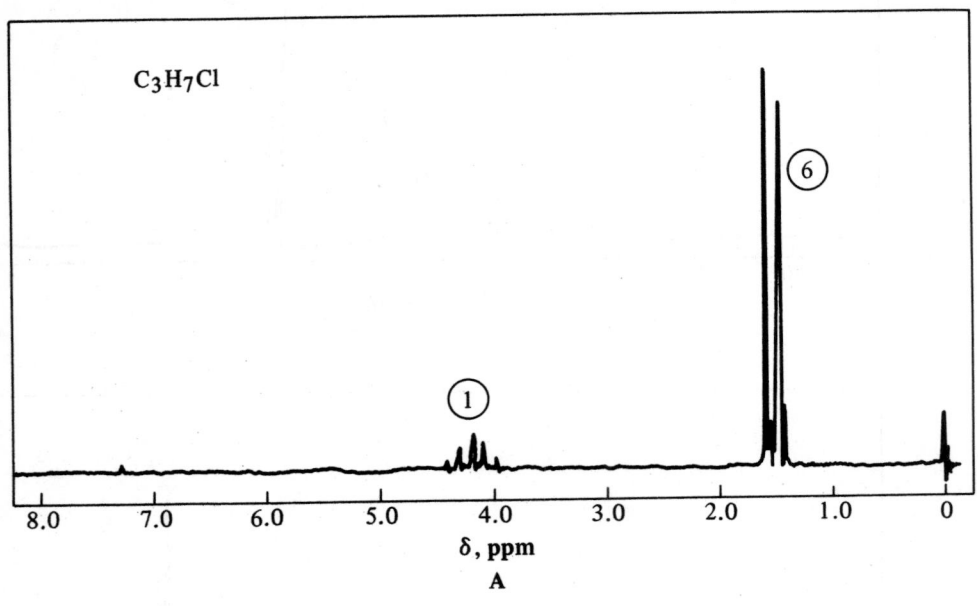

C₃H₇Cl

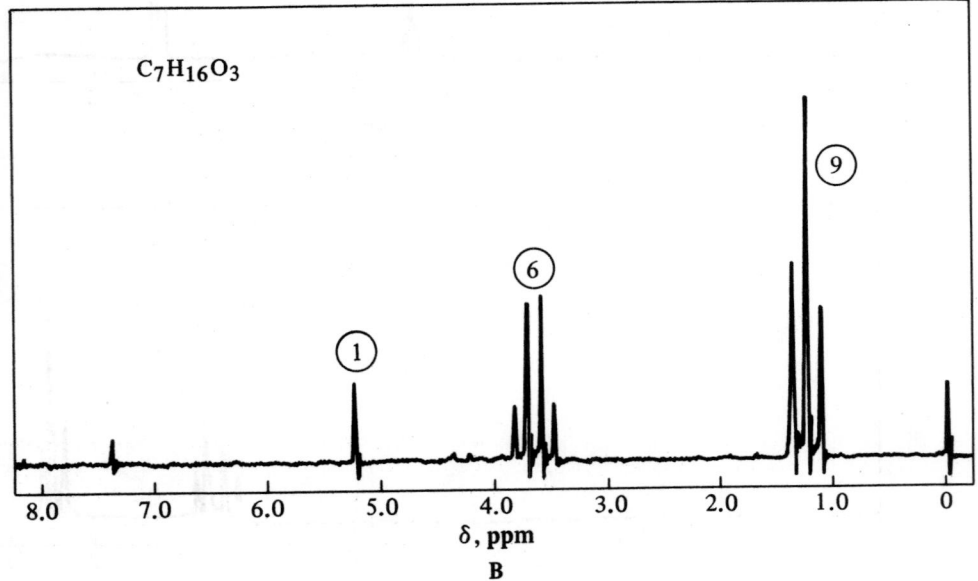

C₇H₁₆O₃

Spectra for Problem 12

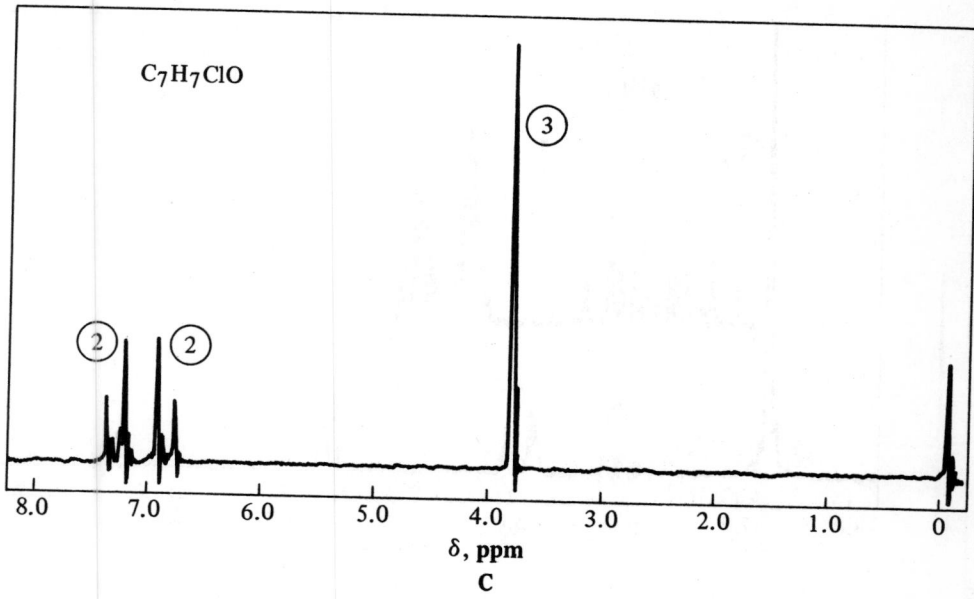

C₇H₇ClO

C

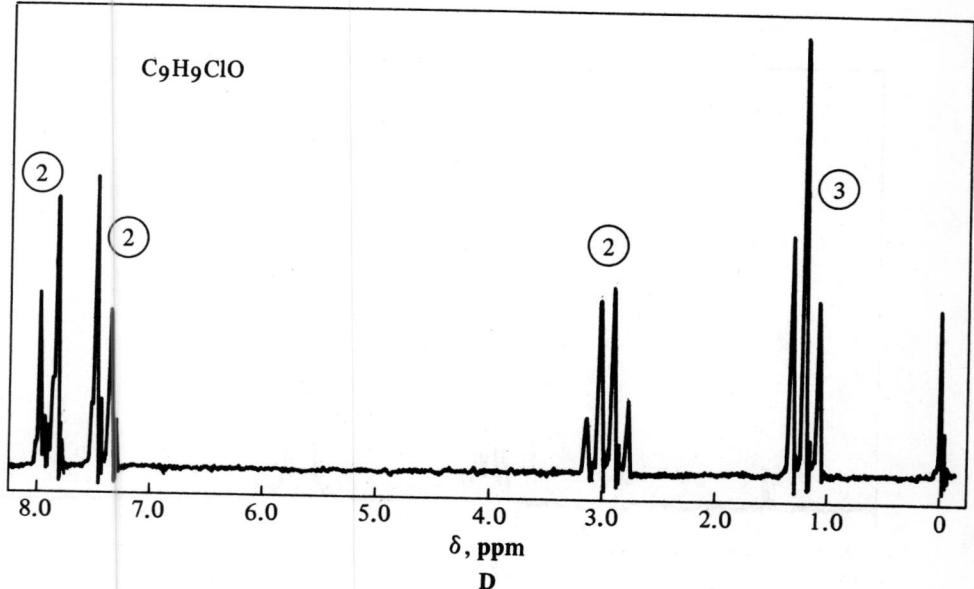

C₉H₉ClO

D

Spectra for Problem 12

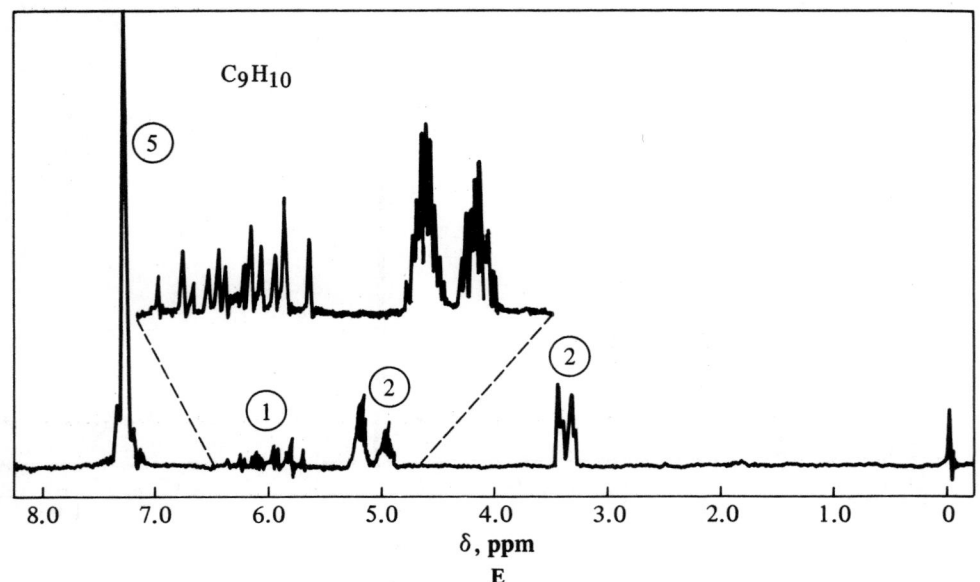

C₉H₁₀

Spectrum for Problem 12

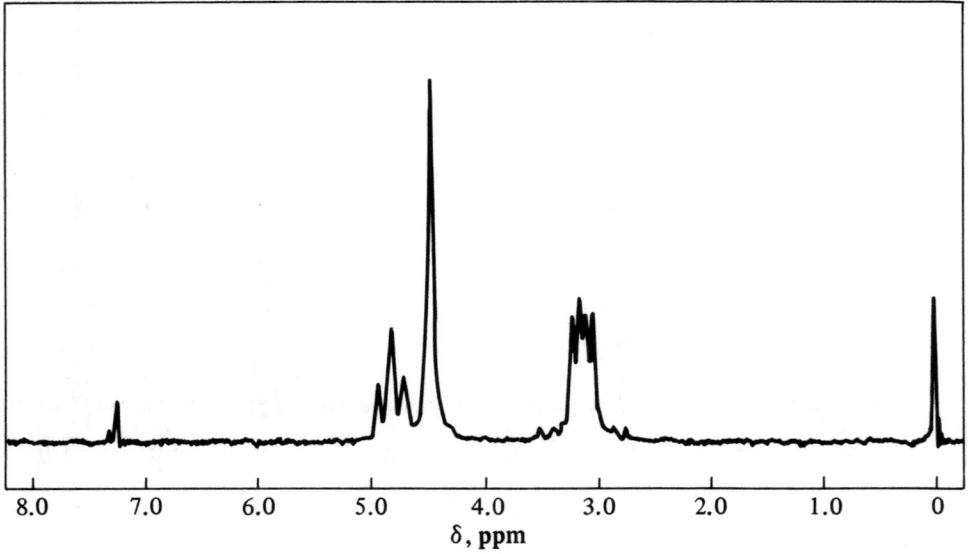

Spectrum for Problem 13

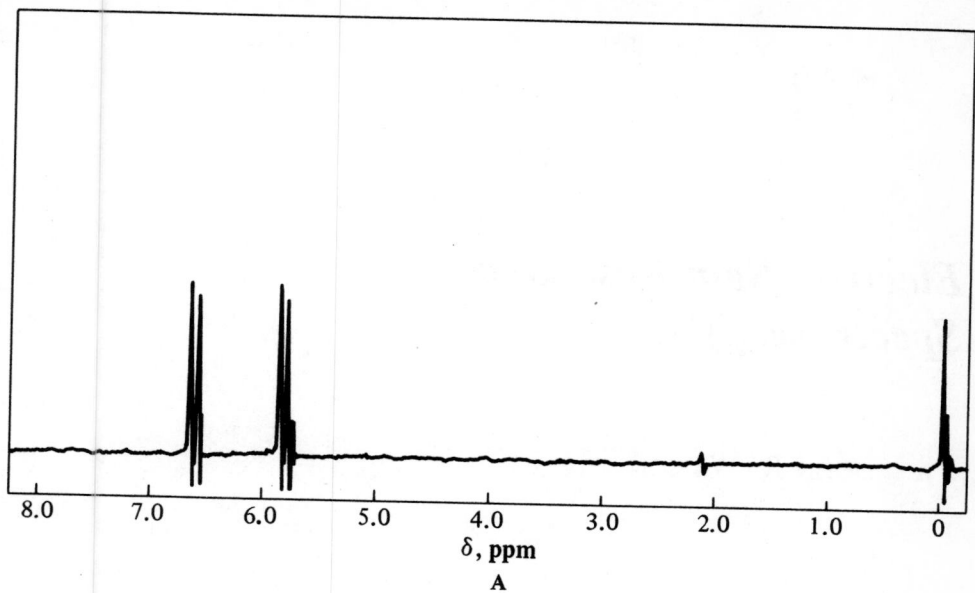

δ, ppm

A

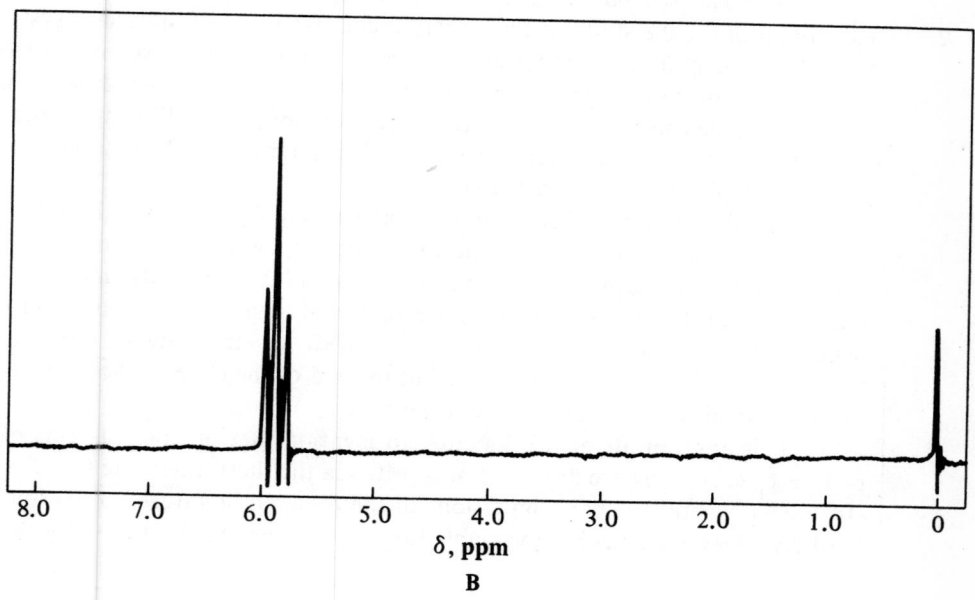

δ, ppm

B

Spectra for Problem 14

13

Electron Spin Resonance Spectroscopy

JOHN R. WASSON

Since its discovery by Zavoisky in 1944, *electron spin resonance* spectroscopy (ESR) (also called *electron paramagnetic resonance* spectroscopy [EPR]) has become an essential tool for the study of the structure and dynamics of molecular systems containing one or more unpaired electrons. Such paramagnetic systems can frequently be examined using magnetic susceptibility techniques as well, but these do not provide the detailed information that ESR spectroscopy does. ESR spectroscopy and magnetic susceptibility methods each have their strengths and limitations and often provide complementary information.

The theory of ESR spectroscopy shares much in common with that of nuclear magnetic resonance spectroscopy; however, the magnetic moment of the electron is about 1000 times as large as the nuclear moment and the constants employed in NMR theory frequently are different in magnitude and sign. Here, the concern is only with the fundamentals and applications of ESR spectroscopy to chemistry. The texts and specialized monographs cited at the end of the chapter should be consulted for more detailed treatments of the technique.

It is appropriate at this juncture to mention that practical aspects of the use of ESR spectroscopy are discussed most often in the thesis literature (see *Dissertation Abstracts*), where the space limitations of the research literature do not apply. The book by Alger is particularly valuable for descriptions of experimental techniques.

Types of Materials Studied by ESR

ESR spectroscopy is used to study a wide variety of materials, of which the following is a sample:

1. Inorganic and organic free radicals which possess an odd number of electrons, such as Fremy's radical, $ON(SO_3)_2^{2-}$, and diphenylpycrylhydrazyl (DPPH):

These radicals can be generated by a variety of methods, including pyrolysis and the irradiation of a sample with γ-rays. Free radicals are frequently encountered as intermediates in such chemical reactions as enzyme-substrate reactions. Most free radicals, being unstable, cannot be readily purchased and stored. However, Fremy's radical (obtained from Fremy's salt, $K_4[ON(SO_3)_2]_2$), DPPH, and various nitroxide radicals can be obtained from commercial sources.

2. Odd-electron molecules such as NO, NO_2, and ClO_2. Many molecules of this type have been examined by gas-phase ESR techniques.

3. Triplet-state molecules, such as O_2 and S_2. These systems have two unpaired electrons. Optical irradiation of solids and solutions can often permit investigation of photoexcited triplet states, which are important in photochemistry.

4. Transition-metal complexes, organometallic compounds, and catalysts containing metal ions with incomplete $3d$, $4d$, or $5d$ electron subshells. The detection of V(IV) (which has the $1s^2 2s^2 2p^6 3s^2 3p^6 3d^1$ configuration) in crude petroleum is one notable application of ESR spectroscopy.

5. Rare earth and actinide compounds containing incomplete $4f$, $6d$, or $5f$ subshells.

6. Impurities in solids, such as semiconductor materials. Odd electrons gained by an acceptor or lost by a donor impurity may be associated with energy bands in crystals.

7. Metals. The electrons in conduction bands of metals can be examined by ESR spectroscopy.

Although ESR spectroscopy can be utilized to probe the structure of many materials, it has certain limitations. Many materials, particularly those containing more than one unpaired electron (Ni(II) compounds, for instance) do not exhibit room-temperature ESR spectra because of large zero-field splitting (discussed later) or unusually large line-broadening. These materials are best examined using conventional magnetic susceptibility methods, although on occasion NMR studies are possible. It is also important to be aware that ESR spectroscopy is concerned with a particular electronic state, the ground state (which may be a photoexcited state), and that other electronic states of a system are important only insofar as they become "mixed in" the electronic state being studied via perturbations or structural dynamics.

The electron is a charged particle with angular momentum (orbital and spin) and, as such, it possesses a magnetic moment, μ_e, given by

$$\mu_e = -g\beta J \tag{13.1}$$

Here J (in units of $h/2\pi$, where h = Planck's constant) is the *total angular momentum vector*, g is a dimensionless constant (the *g-value, g-factor*, or *spectroscopic splitting factor*), and β is a constant, the *Bohr magneton*. The negative sign in Equation 13.1 is a consequence of negative electronic charge. Neglecting orbital angular momentum and considering only the total spin angular momentum S, Equation 13.1 can be written as

$$\mu_e = -g\beta S \tag{13.2}$$

The g-value for the free electron, g_e, is 2.0023. The approximation made in Equation 13.2 is valid for most discussions of the ESR spectra of the organic free radicals and transition-metal complexes whose orbital angular momentum can be considered to be "quenched." Treating the g-value as an experimental quantity does not harm the present discussion, since deviations of g-values from g_e can be accounted for by introduction of spin-orbit coupling.

Magnetic moments can be detected by their interactions with magnetic fields. In zero field, the magnetic moments of unpaired electrons in a sample are randomly oriented. In the presence of a magnetic field H, electron moments assume orientations with respect to the applied field, giving rise to $2S + 1$ energy states (Zeeman splitting). The measurable components of μ_e are $g\beta m_s$ where m_s is the magnetic spin quantum number, which can take the values $+S$, $+(S-1), \ldots, -(S-1), -S$. The application of a magnetic field to an $S = 1/2$ (or larger) system is said to remove the *spin degeneracy* (i.e., the equal energy values of m_s in the absence of an applied magnetic field).

The energy of an electron moment in a magnetic field is given by

$$E = -\mu_e \cdot H \tag{13.3}$$

Upon combining Equation 13.2 and 13.3, the expression

$$E = g\beta H m_s \tag{13.4}$$

results (assuming that the direction of the applied field defines the z-axis). When $S = 1/2$, there are two energy levels

$$E_{m_s = +1/2} = +\tfrac{1}{2}g\beta H \tag{13.5}$$

FIGURE 13.1. *Energy levels and spectra in ESR spectroscopy. A: Energy levels for an unpaired electron in a magnetic field. B: ESR absorption peak: RF power (P) absorbed vs. magnetic field. C: ESR first-derivative presentation—change of power absorbed per unit change in magnetic field vs. magnetic field. ΔH is the peak-to-peak line width. The first-derivative spectrum is the usual form obtained using ESR spectrometers, since phase-sensitive crystal detection of the microwave power absorbed by the sample is usually employed.*

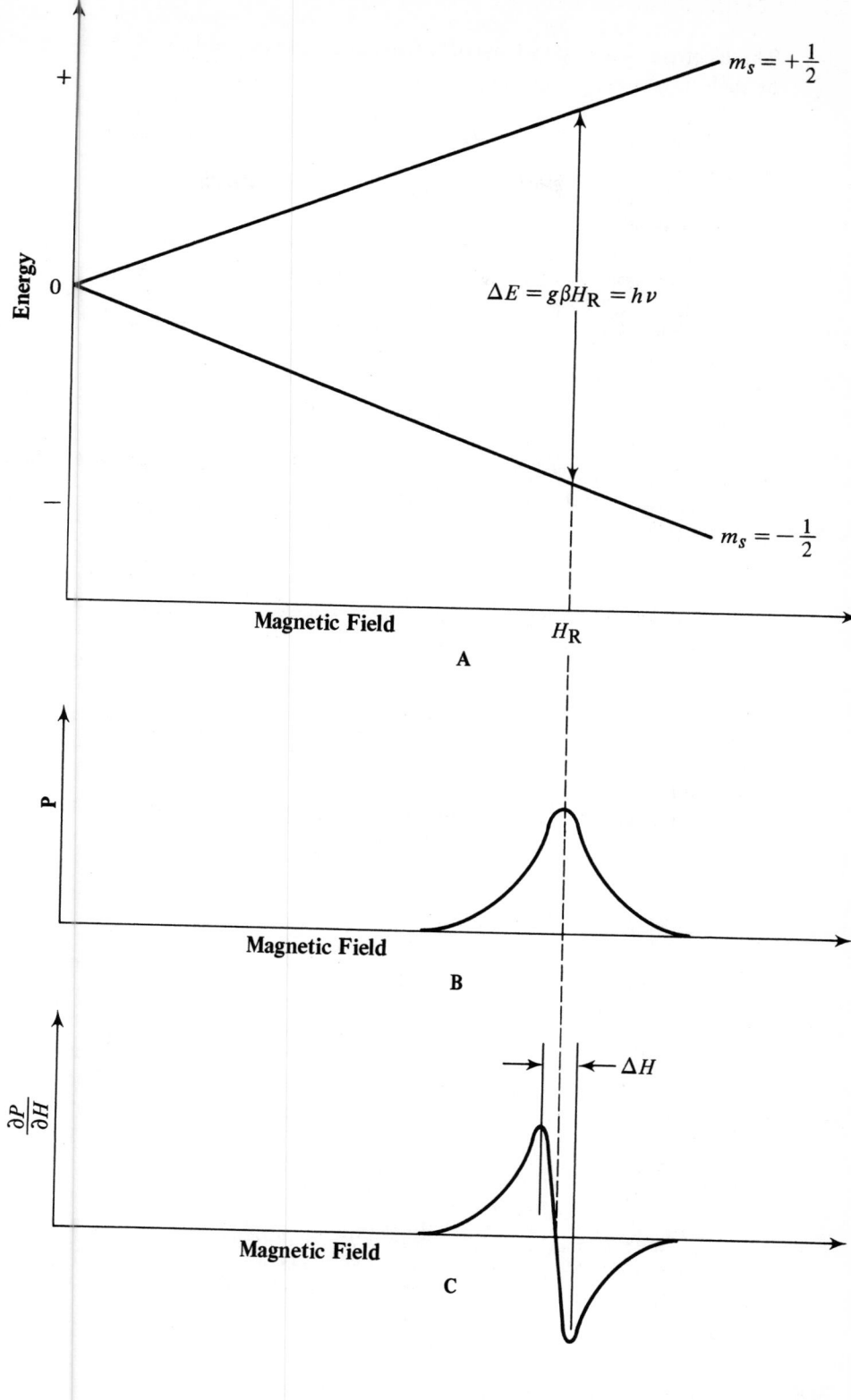

$m_s = +\dfrac{1}{2}$

$\Delta E = g\beta H_R = h\nu$

$m_s = -\dfrac{1}{2}$

Energy

0

Magnetic Field

H_R

A

P

Magnetic Field

B

$\dfrac{\partial P}{\partial H}$

ΔH

Magnetic Field

C

TABLE 13.1. *Spectrometer Frequencies and g_e, Resonance Field Strength*

| Designation | Spectrometer Frequency | | | g_e (oe)[a] |
	ν(Hz)	λ(cm)	ν(cm^{-1})	
X-band	$\sim 9.5 \times 10^9$	3.156	0.317	3390
K-band	$\sim 23 \times 10^9$	1.303	0.767	8207
Q-band	$\sim 35 \times 10^9$	0.856	1.168	12,489

a. For the purposes of magnetic resonance spectroscopy, Oersteds (oe) and Gauss (G) are effectively the same and are employed interchangeably.

and

$$E_{m_s = -1/2} = -\tfrac{1}{2}g\beta H \qquad (13.6)$$

whose energy is linearly dependent on H. The separation between these energy levels (Fig. 13.1) at a particular value of the magnetic field, H_R, is

$$\Delta E = +\tfrac{1}{2}g\beta H_R - (-\tfrac{1}{2}g\beta H_R) = g\beta H_R \qquad (13.7)$$

In an ESR experiment, an oscillating magnetic field perpendicular to H_R induces transitions between the $m_s = -1/2$ and $m_s = +1/2$ levels, provided the frequency, ν, is such that the resonance condition

$$\Delta E = h\nu = g\beta H_R \qquad (13.8)$$

is satisfied. The frequency is held constant and the magnetic field is varied. At a particular value of the magnetic field, H_R, resonance absorption of energy occurs, resulting in a peak in the spectrum (Fig. 13.1B). The frequencies commonly employed in ESR experiments are in the microwave region; these frequencies and magnetic field strengths for g_e resonance absorption signals are given in Table 13.1.

13.2 ESR INSTRUMENTATION

As in most other types of spectroscopy, the instrumentation employed in ESR spectroscopy consists of a source of electromagnetic radiation, a sample holder, and appropriate detection equipment for monitoring the amount of radiation absorbed by the sample. In ESR spectroscopy a magnetic field provided by an electromagnet is also required. Monochromatic radiation of the various frequencies employed in ESR work (Table 13.1) is obtained from klystrons, which are electronic oscillators producing microwave energy. Spectrometers operating at X-band (3-cm wavelength) are the ones most commonly employed. The microwave radiation is transmitted along hollow rectangular metal pipes called waveguides.

Figure 13.2 gives a block diagram of a simple ESR spectrometer. The sample is placed at the center of the sample cavity where the magnetic vector is at a maximum. Quartz tubes (~ 3 mm o.d.) are generally employed to contain solid and solution samples. Unlike the NMR technique, the sample tubes are not rotated. The magnetic field is slowly and linearly increased until the resonance condition (Eqn. 13.8) is satisfied, at which point power is absorbed by the sample and a change in current in the detector crystal is monitored. A pair of Helmholtz coils are mounted around the cavity to increase sensitivity. Feeding the coils from an oscillator superimposes a variable amplitude sinusoidal modulation on the slowly varying magnetic field. The signal detected by the phase-sensitive detection system is proportional to the slope of the ESR absorption as the magnetic field passes through resonance. The recorder then presents the first-derivative spectrum. Many spectrometers are also equipped to present second-derivative spectra.

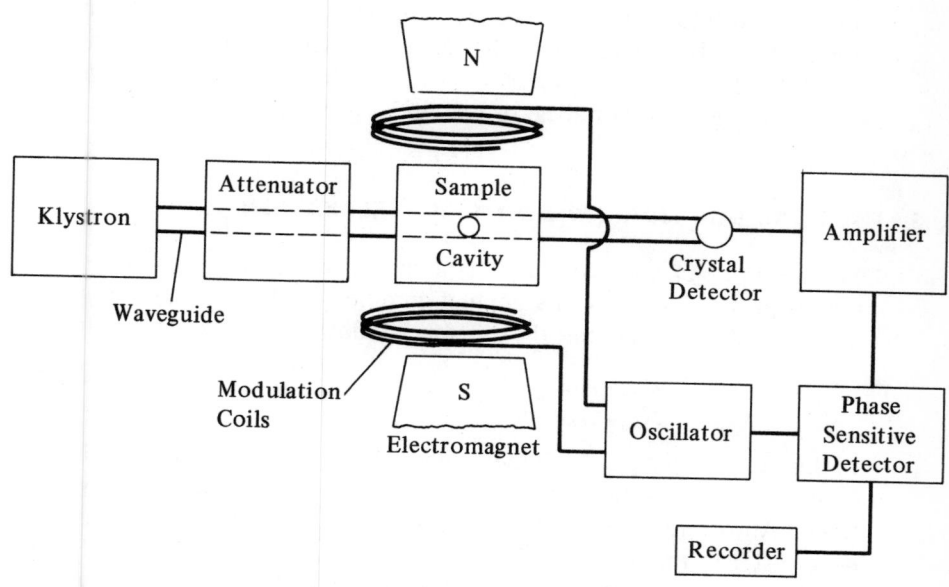

FIGURE 13.2. *Block diagram of a simple ESR spectrometer.*

The sample tube must be chosen with careful attention to the physical, chemical, and magnetic properties of each sample. For instance, when the sample is dissolved in a polar solvent with an appreciable dielectric constant, quartz sample tubes are usually not suitable and capillaries or thin rectangular cells of glass are used. Again, when studying free radicals with $g \approx g_e$, Pyrex tubing can be used, whereas only quartz can be used for triplet ($S = 1$) compounds because of paramagnetic impurities such as Fe^{3+} in most laboratory-grade glassware. Finger sized Dewar flasks (of the appropriate materials) and other cryogenic equipment permit ESR spectra to be obtained as a function of temperature.

The spectral sensitivity of ESR depends on a variety of factors, but with a response time of 1 sec, as few as 10^{11} spins ($\sim 10^{-12}$ moles) can be detected with currently available spectrometers. This sort of sensitivity suggests that ESR spectroscopy would be useful for trace analysis. A minimum detectable concentration is perhaps 10^{-9} M in samples with very small dielectric loss. For qualitative measurement in aqueous solutions, 10^{-7} M is more reasonable, while for quantitative measurements the sample concentration should be greater than about 10^{-6} M. Unfortunately, ESR spectra are more applicable to qualitative and semiquantitative than to quantitative analysis—to answering "What?" rather than "How much?"—because of the variety of instrumental variables in the method and the absence of suitable standards. Additional work in this area should markedly extend the utility of ESR techniques for quantitative analytical purposes.

In any ESR experiment it is important to monitor the microwave frequency at which the spectrometer operates and the magnetic field range swept during the experiment. Although the frequency is constant during an experiment, the frequency available from a given klystron will vary a little with tuning of the instrument. The frequency can be determined using a built-in frequency meter or appropriate transfer oscillators and frequency counters. The magnetic field can be monitored using an NMR gaussmeter or by using samples of known g-value; for instance, the DPPH free radical for which $g = 2.0036$. The magnetic field sweep can also be checked using Fremy's radical or oxobis(2,4-pentanedionato)vanadium(IV).

13.3 THERMAL EQUILIBRIUM AND SPIN RELAXATION

For a sample in thermodynamic equilibrium containing N spin systems ($S = 1/2$) in a magnetic field, there is a population difference between the two m_s levels arising from each $S = 1/2$ system; the difference follows the Boltzmann distribution.

$$\frac{N_{m_s = +1/2}}{N_{m_s = -1/2}} = e^{-h\nu/kT} \approx 1 - \frac{h\nu}{kT} \quad \text{where } kT \gg g\beta H \qquad (13.9)$$

In this expression $N_{m_s = \pm 1/2}$ is the number of spins having $m_s = +1/2$ and $m_s = -1/2$. Under normal conditions there is a slight excess population in the lower ($m_s = -1/2$) level. Absorption of microwave energy by the sample induces transitions from the $m_s = -1/2$ to the $m_s = +1/2$ level. To maintain steady-state conditions, electrons promoted to the excited state must lose energy and return to the lower level; otherwise, saturation would occur and no resonance absorption would be observed. This is similar to the situation in NMR spectroscopy.

Saturation is normally avoided by working at low RF power levels. The electrons lose energy and return to the ground state by two relaxation mechanisms, spin-lattice and spin-spin relaxation, similar to mechanisms encountered in NMR spectroscopy. In spin-lattice relaxation, nonradiative transitions from the $m_s = +1/2$ to the $m_s = -1/2$ state occur because of interactions between the electrons and their surroundings that cause the spin orientation to change. Strong spin-lattice coupling of this type enables the spin system to lose energy to the lattice (surroundings) as rapidly as the oscillating field can supply it; thermal equilibrium values of the spin-state populations are maintained and energy is continuously absorbed as long as the resonance condition is satisfied. Weak spin-lattice coupling leads to saturation at comparatively low microwave power levels, whereas strong coupling can only be overcome by increasing the microwave power. Strong interactions are characterized by short relaxation times giving rise to wide lines (recall the Heisenberg Uncertainty Principle, which can also be written $\Delta E \Delta t \geq h/2\pi$). If spin-lattice relaxation leads to an m_s-level lifetime of about the period of the microwave radiation, or less, it is impossible to observe ESR spectra, since the microwave-induced transitions are lost among those due to relaxation.

The ESR spectra of samples with short relaxation times can be sharpened just by reducing the temperature, since this stabilizes the excited state, thereby lengthening the relaxation time. Spin-lattice relaxation is enhanced (relaxation times shortened) by the presence of energy levels separated from the ground state by the order of kT. This situation is often encountered in paramagnetic ions and radicals where spin-orbit coupling (interaction of electron spin and orbital moments) is relatively large.

Unpaired electrons can interact with other magnetic dipoles in the system. Such interactions do not dissipate energy and hence do not directly contribute to returning the spin systems to equilibrium. However, the spin-lattice transition may be enhanced if the interaction with the magnetic dipoles brings the excess energy to a position for transfer to the lattice. A variety of dipoles are frequently part of an unpaired electron's environment; for example, other unpaired electrons, magnetic nuclei of the lattice, and various electronic and impurity dipoles. Since dipolar interactions decrease with the cube of the separation, i.e., $E_{di} = \mu_1 \cdot \mu_2 / r_{12}{}^3$, many of the spin-spin (spin dipolar) interactions can be eliminated by diluting the paramagnetic material of interest into a diamagnetic ($S = 0$, i.e., no unpaired electrons) and (hopefully) isomorphous lattice. The reduction of spin-spin relaxation results in the sharpening of ESR spectra and improved resolution of g-values, hyperfine structure, and so forth. This will be referred to again later in this chapter.

Energy Levels and Spectral Parameters

The energy of an ion can be considered to consist of a number of parts,

$$E_{tot} = E_C + E_{CF} + E_{SO} + E_{SS} + E_Z + E_{HF} + E_Q + E_N \qquad (13.10)$$

where
E_C = the free ion or Coulomb energy ($\sim 10^5$ cm^{-1})
E_{CF} = the Stark crystalline-field or electrostatic energy associated with the environment of the ion ($\sim 10^4$ cm^{-1})
E_{SO} = the spin-orbit interaction energy ($\sim 10^2$ cm^{-1})
E_{SS} = the electronic spin-spin interaction energy (~ 1 cm^{-1})
E_Z = the Zeeman-interaction energy of the electron with the external magnetic field (~ 1 cm^{-1})
E_{HF} = the hyperfine interaction energy—the energy of coupling between electron and nuclear magnetic moments ($\sim 10^{-2}$ cm^{-1})
E_Q = the nuclear quadrupole energy ($\sim 10^{-3}$ cm^{-1})
E_N = the Zeeman-interaction energy of the nucleus with the external field ($\sim 10^{-4}$ cm^{-1})

An additional energy term describing the effects of electron exchange between ions is sometimes added to Equation 13.10.

In Table 13.1 it is noted that the energies associated with ESR are on the order of 1 cm^{-1}. This means that electronic transitions requiring energies greater than ~ 1 cm^{-1} are not of immediate concern, so the energy levels accessible to ESR spectroscopy will primarily involve the last five terms of Equation 13.10. The calculation of these energies requires some knowledge of quantum mechanics, particularly angular-momentum theory, and cannot be effectively dealt with here.

The simplest free radical is the hydrogen atom. In freshman chemistry, the electronic configuration of the ground state is given as $1s^1$ and, at that time, the student is more or less lucidly informed that the spin quantum number m_s can take the values $+\frac{1}{2}$ or $-\frac{1}{2}$. From the preceding discussion (Eqns. 13.1 to 13.8), ESR spectroscopy requires these values and configurations. The energy levels and observed ESR spectrum of the hydrogen atom are sketched in Figure 13.3. If only electron spin is considered, the situation depicted in Figure 13.1 would result; however, the nuclear spin of hydrogen ($I = 1/2$) interacts with the electron spin and with the external magnetic field as well. The result of these two interactions (analogous to the interactions producing spin-spin splitting in a NMR spectrum) is that the ESR spectrum consists of two peaks separated by 506.8 gauss with the resonant field H_R centered between them at a strength such that $g_0 = 2.00232$. If A_0, a measure of the hyperfine coupling energy, were equal to zero, only a single derivative peak, centered at H_R, would be observed corresponding to a transition between the dashed levels in Figure 13.3. The components of m_I are shown in Figure 13.3, where it is seen that each spin level

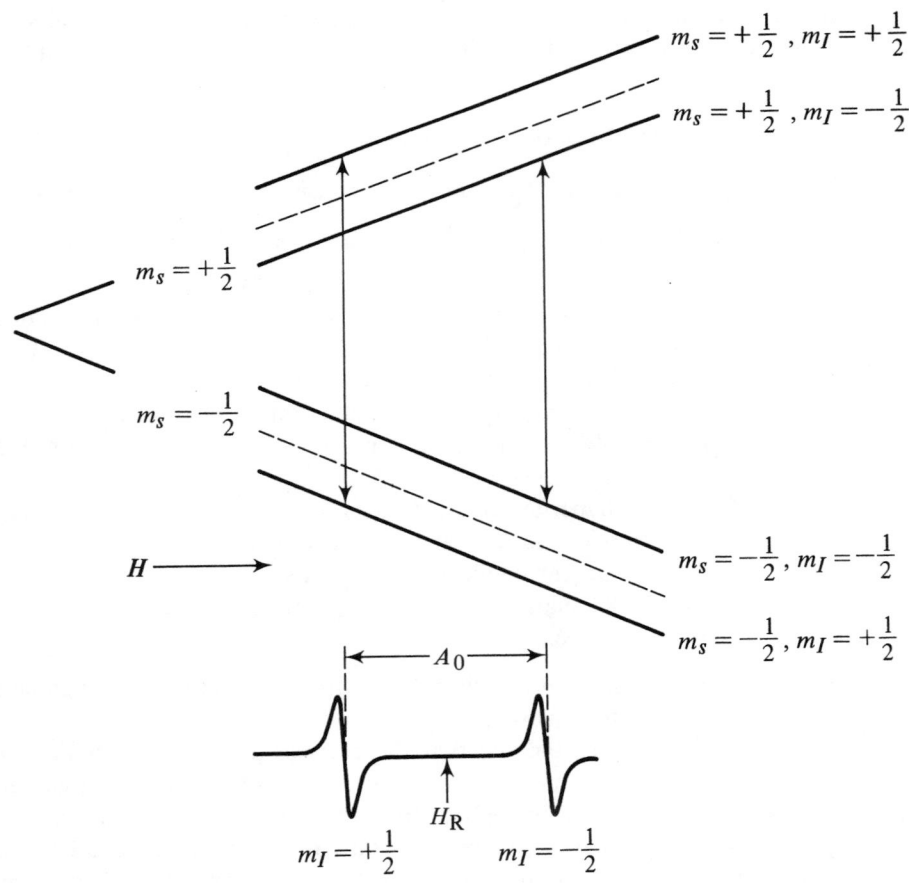

FIGURE 13.3. *The ESR spectrum and energy levels for the hydrogen atom.*

is split into two levels by the hyperfine interaction between electron and nuclear spins. The derivation of this energy level diagram is lucidly presented in the text by Wertz and Bolton.

It is to be noted that A_0, the isotropic electron-spin–nuclear-spin hyperfine coupling constant, can be qualitatively related to the amount of time the unpaired electron spins in an s-orbital on the nucleus in question; the larger A_0, the greater the probability of finding the electron at the nucleus.

For an ion with a nonzero nuclear moment I, $2I + 1$ lines can be expected centered around g_0 with a hyperfine spacing A_0 between them. For example, for $^{63}Cu(II)$ (a $3d^9$ ion), $I = 3/2$; four lines are expected and generally observed in the first-derivative spectrum (see Fig. 13.4). The A_0 value is taken as the separation between the two central ESR lines, and the g_0 value is calculated from the magnetic field halfway between those lines. For V(IV) compounds (^{51}V, $I = 7/2$), eight lines are expected for the solution ESR spectra. The selection rules for ESR spectroscopy, as implied in Figure 13.3, are $\Delta m_s = \pm 1$ and $\Delta m_I = 0$.

FIGURE 13.4. *The general shape of the ESR spectra for $^{63}Cu^{2+}$ (a $3d^9$ ion), where $I = 3/2$.*

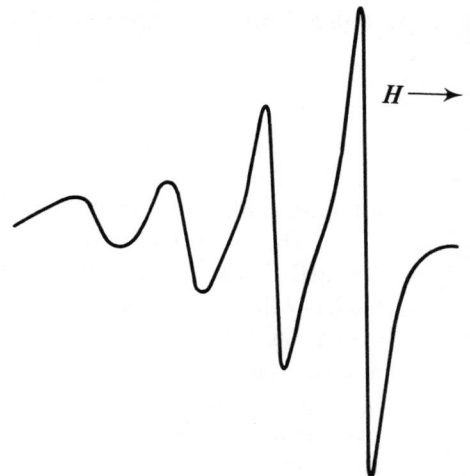

$H \longrightarrow$

Organic free radicals in solution generally exhibit hyperfine coupling with several nuclei. When the nuclei are chemically equivalent, the number of lines is given by

$$2n_i I + 1 \tag{13.11}$$

where n_i is the number of equivalent nuclei having nuclear spin I. Thus, the methyl radical, $H_3C\cdot$, exhibits a four-line spectrum from splitting by three equivalent hydrogens. The p-benzosemiquinone radical anion (A)

(A) (B)

exhibits a five-line spectrum while the benzene radical anion (B) gives a seven-line

TABLE 13.2. *Relative Intensities of ESR Lines*

Number of Equivalent Atoms with $I = 1/2$ (n)	Relative Intensities of ESR Lines	Number of Lines ($n + 1$)
1	1:1	2
2	1:2:1	3
3	1:3:3:1	4
4	1:4:6:4:1	5
5	1:5:10 : 10:5:1	6

spectrum. Note that in hydrocarbon radicals the abundance of ^{13}C (1.108%, $I = \frac{1}{2}$) is so low that satellite peaks due to interaction of the unpaired electron with the ^{13}C atoms are not readily resolved. For hydrocarbon radicals in which the unpaired electron interacts only with hydrogen atoms, Equation 13.11 reduces to $n + 1$.

When an organic radical possesses two or more sets of equivalent atoms, the total number of lines in the ESR spectrum is given by

$$\prod_{i=1}^{j} (2n_i I_i + 1) = (2n_1 I_1 + 1)(2n_2 I_2 + 1) \cdots (2n_j I_j + 1) \qquad (13.12)$$

For example, for the hypothetical $(H_2N)\dot{B}(PF_2)$ radical where $I = 3$ for ^{10}B, $I = 1$ for ^{14}N, $I = 1/2$ for ^{31}P, and $I = 1/2$ for ^{19}F, a total of 378 lines could be expected if the unpaired electron interacted appreciably with each of the nuclei.

The number of lines in the ESR spectrum of a radical is a clue to its identity. Of further assistance is the intensity pattern in the spectrum. For n equivalent nuclei with $I = 1/2$, the $n + 1$ lines have intensities proportional to the binomial expansion of order n. Table 13.2 lists the relative intensities up to $n = 5$. The intensity patterns for sets of equivalent nuclei with $I > 1/2$ are handled in a similar fashion. Figure 13.5 shows the ESR spectrum of diphenylpicrylhydrazyl (DPPH) free radical in benzene. Under low-resolution conditions, the proton hyperfine coupling is not observed and the five-line spectrum with the intensity distribution 1:2:3:2:1 results from the interaction of the unpaired electron with two (effectively equivalent) ^{14}N ($I = 1$) nuclei; for nuclei with $I > 1/2$, the intensity distribution is more complex than a simple binomial expansion, and is beyond the scope of this text.

FIGURE 13.5. *Low-resolution ESR spectrum of the diphenylpicrylhydrazyl (DPPH) radical in benzene.*

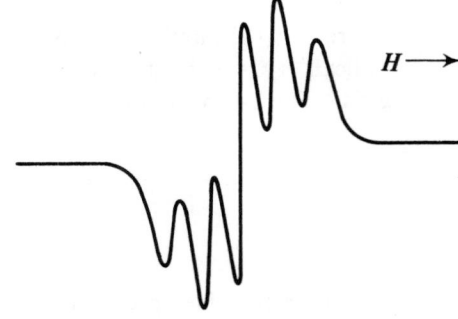

Magnetically nonequivalent protons will normally have different splitting constants, and the observed ESR spectra can be analyzed by reconstructing the spectrum from the splitting patterns and intensity distributions expected for each equivalent set of protons. Some examples should serve to illustrate this procedure. The photolysis of hydrogen peroxide in methanol produces the $\cdot CH_2OH$ free radical. The protons bound to carbon and the proton bound to the oxygen atom comprise two nonequivalent sets. For $\cdot CH_2OH$, either a doublet of triplets (Fig. 13.6A) or a triplet of doublets (Fig. 13.6B) could be expected, depending on whether the A value for the OH proton is larger or smaller than the A value for the CH_2 protons. Experiments show that a triplet of doublets appears, with a 1:2:1 intensity distribution, $A_{CH_2} = 17.4$ gauss, and $A_{OH} = 1.15$ gauss in accordance with the stick diagram given in Figure 13.6B [1]. More complicated spectra are analyzed similarly but, as can be imagined, the difficulty of interpretation increases with the increasing number of sets of equivalent protons.

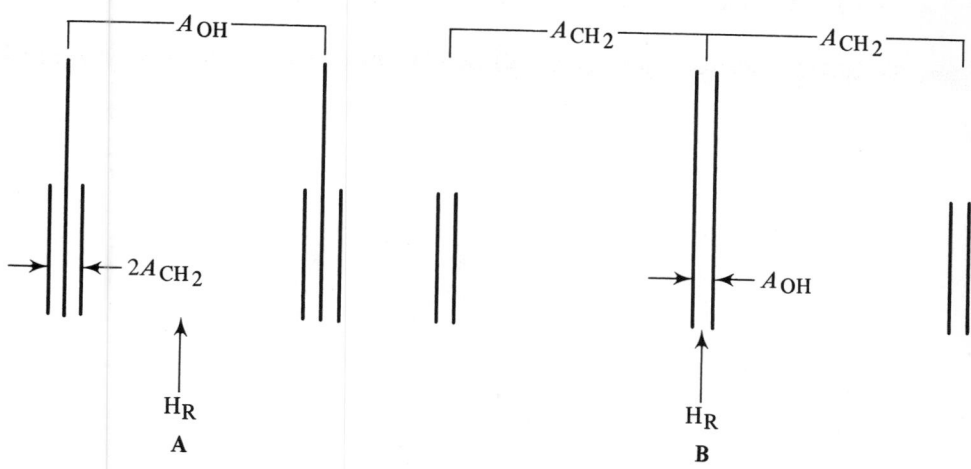

FIGURE 13.6. *Possible ESR splitting patterns for the $\cdot CH_2OH$ radical. A: The hyperfine splitting constant for the OH proton (A_{OH}) is larger than that for the CH_2 protons (A_{CH_2}). B: The hyperfine splitting constant for the OH proton is smaller.*

The origin of the proton hyperfine splitting in the ESR spectra of hydrocarbon radicals can be explained by quantum-mechanical calculations. These results give rise to the well-known McConnell relation [2]

$$A = \rho Q \qquad (13.13)$$

where A = the hyperfine coupling constant for a proton in a C–H fragment having an unpaired π-electron density of ρ
  Q = a constant having a value of 22.4 gauss

This relation permits unpaired electron distributions in π-electron radicals, such as the benzene radical anion and the *p*-benzosemiquinone radical anion, to be mapped experimentally; while at the same time, the ESR spectra of π-electron radicals can be calculated using simple Hückel-molecular-orbital theory of the type taught in sophomore-level organic-chemistry courses.

Transition-Metal Complexes

Generally, the spectra of transition-metal complexes are associated with the central metal ion. Frequently, *superhyperfine* splitting is also encountered which demonstrates that the unpaired electron of the ligand is delocalized over the metal complex. Figure 13.7 shows the ESR spectrum of $VO[S_2PC_2H_5(OCH_3)]_2$ in chloroform solution. Each of the eight vanadium hyperfine lines is split into three by interaction of the unpaired electron with two equivalent phosphorus nuclei ($I = 1/2$), each line having roughly the 1:2:1 intensity distribution expected. Line overlapping contributes to deviation from the anticipated intensity distribution.

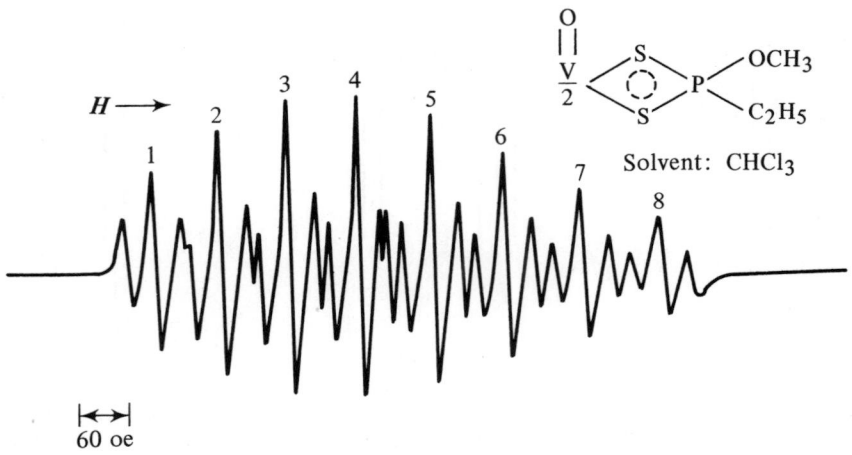

FIGURE 13.7. *ESR spectrum of $VO[S_2PC_2H_5(OCH_3)]_2$ in chloroform. The eight vanadium hyperfine lines are numbered; each of these is split into a triplet from interaction with the two equivalent phosphorus nuclei.*

In oxovanadium(IV) complexes ($3d^1$ systems) of this type, it can be shown [3] that the ^{31}P superhyperfine splitting arises from interaction of the ground-state vanadium(IV) $3d_{x^2-y^2}$ orbital with the phosphorus $3s$ orbitals. This *trans*-annular interaction can be pictorially represented as in Figure 13.8. The $d_{x^2-y^2}$ orbital is not σ-bonding with respect to the sulfur atoms, but does possess the correct symmetry to interact directly with phosphorus $3s$ and $3p$ orbitals. The essentially isotropic nature of the phosphorus superhyperfine splitting constants indicates that phosphorus $3p$ orbitals are not appreciably involved in the *trans*-annular interaction. Ligand superhyperfine splitting in the ESR spectra of metal complexes provides detailed

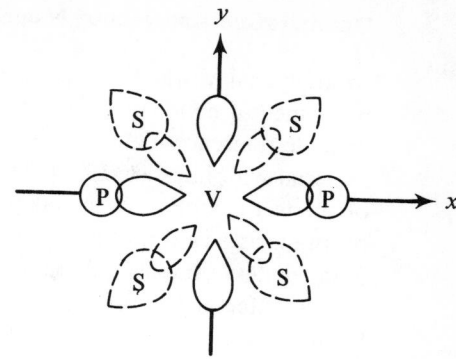

information regarding the covalency of metal-ligand bonding. The above example is only one of the many that can be cited.

13.5 ANALYTICAL APPLICATIONS

The chief application of ESR spectroscopy to chemical problems is the identification of the presence and nature of species containing unpaired electrons. Determination of concentrations of electron spins in a given sample is not very precise; in general, only order-of-magnitude estimates of spin concentrations can be obtained. Accurate quantitative analyses can seldom be performed using ESR spectroscopy.

ESR lines usually exhibit shapes very close to those of Gaussian or Lorentzian functions. The intensities of ESR lines may be obtained by integration of the full absorption curve, by two consecutive integrations of the first-derivative curve, or by the approximation

$$\text{intensity} = \text{derivative height} \times (\Delta H)^2 \qquad (13.14)$$

where ΔH is defined as in Figure 13.1, which yields the relative intensities of lines in a spectrum.

Applying first principles to measurements of the ESR signal and to all pertinent instrumental parameters, absolute numbers of spins can be determined. However, this is rarely done since the number of variables to be controlled is considerable and the labor involved is disproportionate. Relative concentrations of species with the same spectral shape and line widths can be determined simply by comparing peak heights of the normal first-derivative curve under identical conditions, i.e.,

$$\frac{N_1}{N_2} = \frac{h_1}{h_2} \qquad (13.15)$$

If the linewidths differ, Equation 13.15 can be modified to yield (cf. Eqn. 13.14)

$$\frac{N_1}{N_2} = \frac{h_1}{h_2} \frac{(\Delta H_1)^2}{(\Delta H_2)^2} \qquad (13.16)$$

Again, employing a standard sample as a reference, intensities of ESR lines obtained by one or more integrations can be compared to yield spin concentrations.

Quantitative Analysis of Metal Ions

In analytical work, the biggest problems are associated with maintaining identical instrumental conditions for both reference compounds and samples, and finding a suitable reference material. The reference sample should be a stable, easily handled material with line-shape, line-width, and power-saturation properties similar to those of the test sample. Reasonably good semiquantitative information can be obtained by preparing calibration curves using standard samples, and comparing them with data for test samples. A good example of this technique is the detection of Cu(II) in sea water at the parts-per-billion level [4]. In this example, copper is extracted from sea water with 8-hydroxyquinoline in ethyl acetate. The ESR-line intensities of the extracted solutions are then compared to those obtained for standard samples of known copper concentration similarly prepared. The curve of standard-line intensity versus copper-concentration can lead to a deviation of ± 0.2 ppb in the copper analyses; this means that the relative deviation is about $\pm 8\%$. While a deviation of this magnitude is intolerable for macroscopic methods, such as gravimetric analysis, it is more palatable with trace analyses. Since this approach to monitoring copper concentration is rather rapid and fairly reliable, its semiquantitative nature can often be tolerated.

Another representative type of analysis by ESR is that of Fe(III) [5]. Fe(III) can be extracted from 1.8 M hydrochloric acid with tributyl phosphate. The ESR intensity of the extracted iron, presumably $FeCl_4^-$, can then be determined relative to the signal from the DPPH radical employed as an external standard. The relative intensity is proportional to concentration in the range 10–200 ppm of Fe(III) in the extract.

Other metal ions that can be determined quantitatively by ESR include V(IV), Cr(III), Mn(II), and Ti(III).

Spin-Labeling of Biological Systems

Spin labels are stable, paramagnetic molecules that, by their structure, easily attach themselves to various biological macromolecular systems such as proteins or cell membranes. Examples of spin labels that can be covalently bonded to specific sites of biological systems include nitroxide derivatives of N-ethylmaleimide, which bind specifically to –SH groups, and nitroxide derivatives of iodoacetamide, which bind specifically to methionine, lysine, and arginine residues of amino acids. Noncovalently bonded spin-labels that can be incorporated into biological systems include nitroxide derivatives of stearic acid, of phospholipids, and of cholesterol.

Spin labels provide information about the static and dynamic nature of the system, including structure, relative polarity, fluidity, viscosity, conformational changes, phase transitions, and chemical reactions.

In recent years the systems most often studied by the spin-label method have been biological membranes and various models thereof. For example, using nitroxide derivatives of stearic acid, the organization of the phospholipid phase of biological membranes has been studied [6]. One interesting practical application of this type of spin-labeling is in the study of disease-state membranes. Intact erythrocyte membranes were shown to be in a more fluid state near the membrane surface in patients suffering from myotonic muscular dystrophy as compared to those from normal controls [7], thus providing an early diagnostic test for this disease.

Determination of Surface Area

Because of its specificity for molecules with unpaired electrons, ESR has been used to determine the active surface area of catalysts. The total area of the ESR signal is proportional to the number of unpaired electrons in the sample. A comparison is made of the catalyst, which has had a paramagnetic molecule adsorbed on its surface, with a standard containing a known number of unpaired electrons, usually DPPH which has 1.53×10^{21} unpaired electrons per gram.

In a study of the surface area of an MnO_2 catalyst [8], ESR measurement of the surface area based on adsorption of DPPH indicated a surface area of 46 m²/g, whereas ESR measurement of active adsorbed oxygen indicated a surface area of 42 m²/g. These two values compared favorably with the results from the usual BET method, which gave a surface area of 61 m²/g. The BET method consists of volumetric or gravimetric measurements of the quantity of gas that will completely cover the surface of the solid with an adsorbed layer.

SELECTED BIBLIOGRAPHY

ABRAGAM, A., and BLEANEY, B. *Electron Paramagnetic Resonance of Transition Ions.* Oxford: Clarendon Press, 1970.

ALGER, R. S. *Electron Paramagnetic Resonance: Techniques and Applications.* New York: Interscience Publishers, 1968.

ATHERTON, N. M. *Electron Spin Resonance.* New York: John Wiley, 1973.

GERSON, F. *High Resolution E.S.R. Spectroscopy.* New York: John Wiley, 1970.

SWARTZ, H. M.; BOLTON, J. R.; and BORG, D. C., eds. *Biological Applications of Electron Spin Resonance.* New York: Wiley-Interscience, 1972.

WERTZ, J. E., and BOLTON, J. R. *Electron Spin Resonance: Elementary Theory and Practical Applications.* New York: McGraw-Hill, 1972. *This is probably the best basic text on ESR now available.*

REFERENCES

1. R. LIVINGSTON and H. ZELDES, *J. Chem. Phys.,* 44, 1245 (1966).

2. H. M. McCONNELL, *J. Chem. Phys.,* 24, 632, 764 (1956).

3. D. R. LORENZ, D. K. JOHNSON, H. J. STOKLOSA, and J. R. WASSON, *J. Inorg. Nucl. Chem.,* 36, 1184 (1974).

4. Y. P. VIRMANI and E. J. ZELLER, *Anal. Chem.,* 46, 324 (1974).

5. T. TAKEUCHI and N. YOSHIKUNI, *Bunseki Kagaku,* 22, 679 (1973).

6. H. M. McCONNELL and B. G. McFARLAND, *Quart. Rev. Biophys.,* 3, 91 (1970).

7. D. A. BUTTERFIELD, A. D. ROSES, M. L. COOPER, S. H. APPEL, and D. B. CHESNUT, *Biochemistry,* 13, 5078 (1974).

8. A. T. T. OEI and J. L. GARNETT, *J. Catal.,* 19, 176 (1970).

PROBLEMS

1. Calculate the resonant field strengths for substances which have g-values of 2.100 and 1.989 when $\nu = 9.4$, 23, and 35 gigahertz (1 GHz $= 10^9$ Hz $= 10^9$ sec^{-1}), respectively. (Note: Planck's constant, $h = 6.6256 \times 10^{-27}$ erg-sec, and the Bohr magneton, $\beta = 0.9273 \times 10^{-20}$ erg/gauss.)

2. What are the separations between resonant field strengths for substances having g-values of 1.964 and 1.989; 2.080 and 2.073, when $\nu = 9.4$, 23, and 35 GHz, respectively?

3. What are the values of $h\nu$ (cm^{-1}/molecule) when $\nu = 9.4$, 23, and 35 GHz? (Planck's constant, $h = 33.3586 \times 10^{-12}$ cm^{-1}-sec).

4. Evaluate the ratios of populations in $m_s = +1/2$ and $m_s = -1/2$ spin states when $\nu = 9.4$, 23, and 35 GHz and $T = 298$, 77, 20, and 4 K. Boltzmann's constant, $k = 1.3804 \times 10^{-16}$ erg/K.

5. How many ESR lines can be expected for the 1,2-; 1,3-; and 1,4-difluorobenzene radical anions? ($I = 1/2$ for ^{19}F.)

6. How many ESR lines could be expected for the tetrahedral P_4^- radical? ($I = 1/2$ for ^{31}P.)

7. How many ESR lines can be expected for $Cu[S_2P(OCH_3)_2]_2$ and $VO[S_2P(OCH_3)_2]_2$ ($I = 3/2$ for Cu; $I = 7/2$ for V) if only the metal hyperfine and phosphorus hyperfine splittings are observable?

14

X-Ray Spectroscopy

William J. Campbell

Since the discovery of x-rays by Roentgen in 1896, this region of the electromagnetic spectrum has been a source of significant contributions to our fundamental knowledge of atomic structure and to our techniques for chemical analysis. By 1927, six Nobel prizes in physics had been awarded for studies on the physics of x-rays and the interaction of x-rays with matter.

The analytical importance of the x-ray technique can be judged by the growth from fewer than 50 x-ray spectrometers in use in 1953 to over 10,000 now. Following the successful development and utilization of laboratory-type instrumentation, the field has expanded to include a wide range of process-control instrumentation: probes for analyzing millimeter- and micrometer-size areas, portable analyzers using radioisotopes to excite x-rays, and ion accelerators for measuring surface concentrations and trace elements.

14.1 INTRODUCTION

X-rays are generated by bombarding matter with either high-energy particles such as electrons or alpha particles or with x-ray photons. When an atom is so bombarded, an electron is ejected from one of the inner shells of the atom. This vacancy is immediately filled by an electron from a higher energy shell, creating a vacancy in that shell that is, in turn, filled by an electron from a yet higher shell. Thus, by a series of transitions, $L \rightarrow K$, $M \rightarrow L$, $N \rightarrow M$, each new vacancy is filled until the excited atom returns to its ground state.

Each electronic transition (apart from radiationless transitions) results in the emission of a characteristic x-ray spectral line whose energy $h\nu$ is equal to the difference between the binding energies of the two electrons involved in the transition (see

Fig. 14.1). Only certain electronic transitions are permitted by quantum-mechanical selection rules, which are described in various text books on atomic physics. The x-ray spectral lines are designated by symbols such as Ni $K\alpha_1$, Fe $K\beta_2$, Sn $L\alpha_2$, and U $M\alpha_1$. The symbol of an x-ray line represents the chemical element (Ni, Fe, Sn, and U); the notations K, L, or M indicate that the lines originate by the initial removal of an electron from the K, L, or M shell, respectively; a particular line in the series is designated by the Greek letter α, β, etc. (representing the subshell of the outer electron involved in the transition), plus a numerical subscript. This numerical subscript indicates the relative strength of each line in a particular series—for example, $K\alpha_1$ is more intense than $K\alpha_2$. Because there are a limited number of possible inner-shell transitions, the x-ray spectrum is much simpler than the complex optical spectrum that results from the removal or transition of valence electrons; in addition,

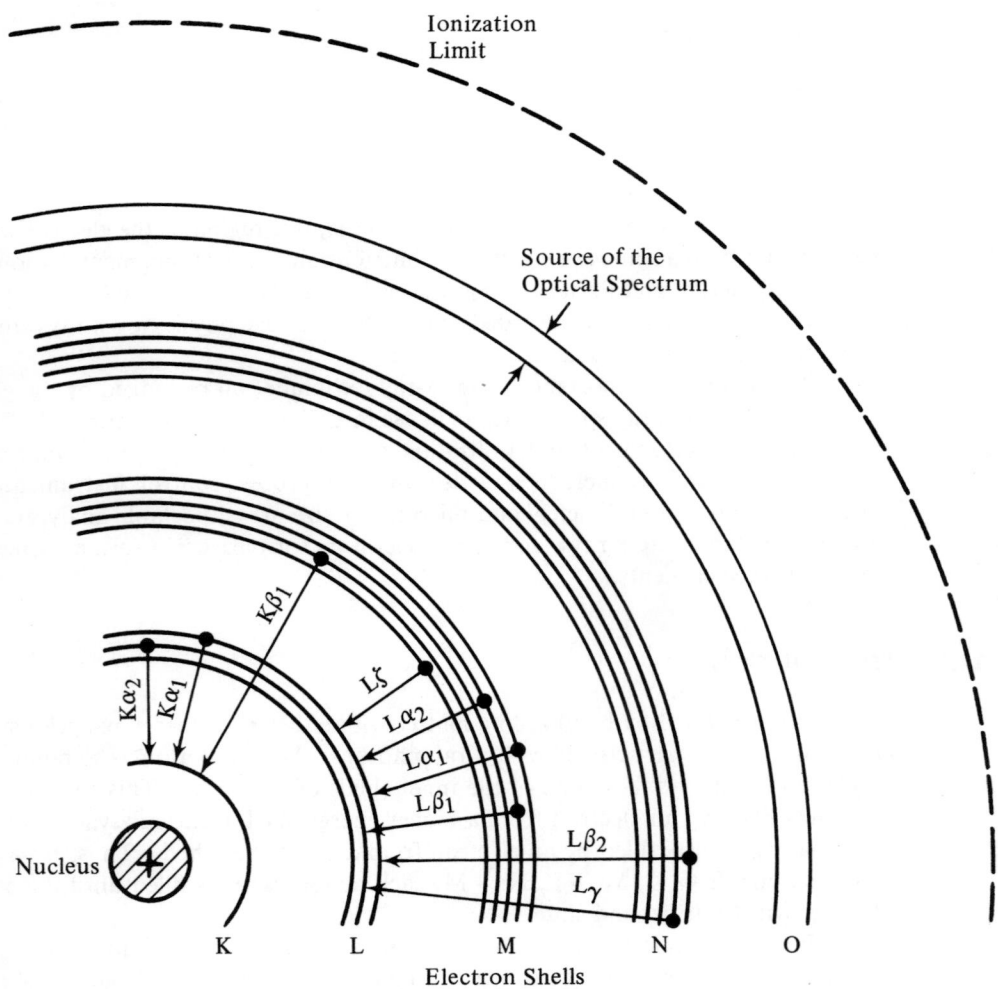

FIGURE 14.1. *Origin of characteristic x-ray lines.*

both the intensity and wavelength of x-rays are essentially independent of the chemical and physical state of the element emitting them.

There are a number of approaches to x-ray analysis. In *x-ray absorption*, the absorption of energetic x-rays that occurs when an electron is removed from its orbital is related to the concentration of the absorbing species. In *x-ray emission*, the sample is bombarded with an electron beam in an x-ray tube and the emitted x-ray photons are measured. Measurements are generally restricted to qualitative or, at best, semiquantitative determinations because of the heating and selective volatilization of different elements by the impinging electron beam. In *x-ray fluorescence*, or *secondary x-ray emission*, the sample is bombarded with an x-ray beam and the reemitted x-radiation (at a longer wavelength) is measured. The difficulties found in using x-ray emission for quantitative analysis are not experienced in x-ray fluorescence, so this technique is widely used for that purpose.

Crystalline materials, in which the atomic spacing is about the same magnitude as x-ray wavelengths, are capable of diffracting x-rays. This serves as the basis of *x-ray diffraction* analysis; qualitative identification of crystalline materials is readily made from a measurement of the angles of diffraction. X-ray diffraction also serves as a means for isolating x-rays of a particular wavelength in an x-ray spectrometer.

X-ray fluorescence spectroscopy is the most widely used x-ray technique for quantitative analysis; this chapter will be primarily concerned with this method of analysis. X-ray absorption and x-ray diffraction analysis are treated briefly at the end of the chapter.

14.2 INSTRUMENTATION

An x-ray fluorescence spectrometer needs an x-ray source, a means of dispersing the x-rays, and a detector. This is illustrated in Figure 14.2. The conventional x-ray spectrometer consists of a high-intensity x-ray tube with a stabilized, high-voltage power supply; a multi-sample chamber that can be evacuated; a goniometer (for measuring the diffraction angle) with either a parallel-plate collimator or a slit system, depending on the x-ray optics; and a proportional or scintillation-counter detector, together with its associated electronics which include a DC power supply, scaler-ratemeter, linear amplifier, single-channel analyzer, and recorder (see Chap. 19 for a detailed description of ionizing-radiation detectors). Many of the newer units have the output of the single-channel analyzer coupled to magnetic or paper-tape storage and a dedicated or time-sharing computer. Research-type, single-channel x-ray spectrometers cost on the order of $25,000 to $50,000; control instrumentation can range in cost from a few thousand dollars for a portable analyzer to $200,000 for a 15- to 20-element simultaneous analyzer with computer and automatic sample transports.

Generation of X-Rays

For most analytical applications, primary x-rays are produced by bombarding a suitable target with 10- to 100-keV electrons. This is a Coolidge-type x-ray tube and is illustrated in Figure 14.3. The spectrum resulting from electron excitation consists of a broad band of energies (the *continuum* or *Bremsstrahlung*) plus photons of dis-

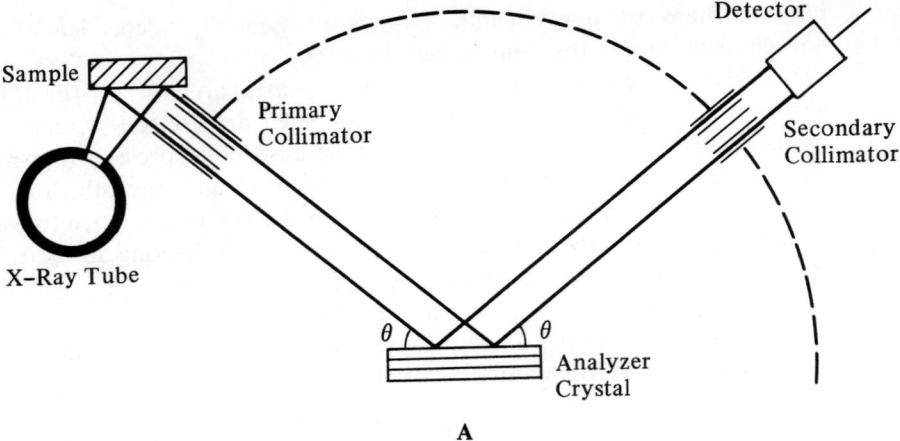

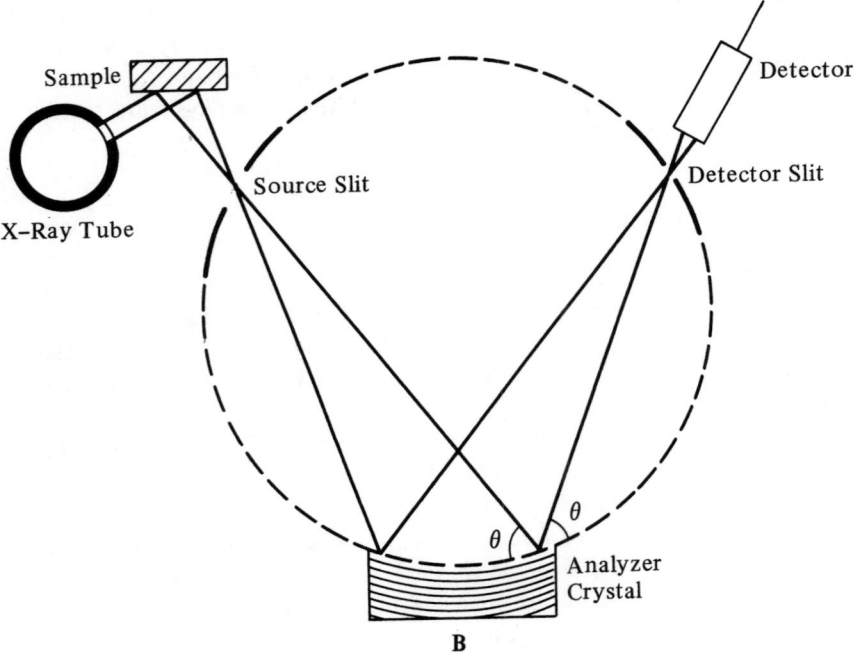

FIGURE 14.2. *Wavelength dispersion using nonfocusing (A) and focusing (B) optics.*

crete energies that are characteristic of the target element (see Fig. 14.4). The frequency of the characteristic photons is described by Moseley's law:

$$\nu = k(Z - 1)^2 \qquad \textbf{(14.1)}$$

where Z = the atomic number of the target element
          k = a constant

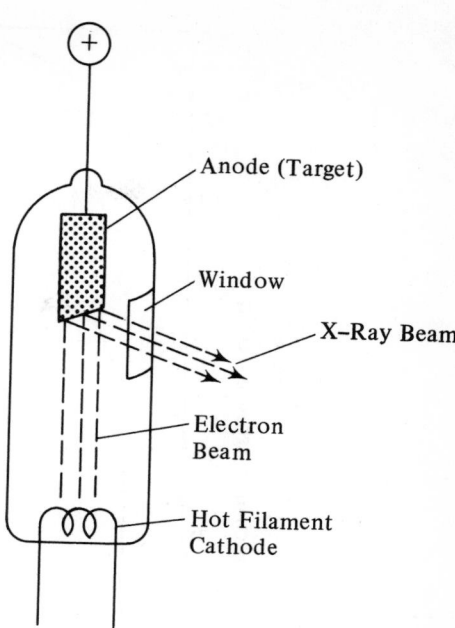

FIGURE 14.3. *Schematic diagram of a Coolidge high-vacuum x-ray tube.*

Anode (Target)

Window

X–Ray Beam

Electron Beam

Hot Filament Cathode

The integrated intensity (I) of the continuum is related to the current, voltage, and atomic number of the target by

$$I = kiZV^2 \qquad (14.2)$$

where i = the x-ray tube current in mA
V = the voltage in kV

Inspection of Equation 14.2 shows that the integrated intensity of the continuum is proportional to the atomic number; therefore, higher-atomic-number elements such as tungsten or platinum are often used as targets. Other essential properties of a target besides high atomic number are a high melting point and good thermal conductivity. The efficiency of primary x-ray production is less than one percent; the other 99+ percent of the electron energy is released into the target as heat.

As indicated in Equation 14.2, the continuum intensity is proportional to the square of the applied voltage. The distribution of the continuum from an yttrium target as a function of applied voltage is shown in Figure 14.4. Note that, as the voltage is increased, the peak of the continuum moves to a higher energy (shorter wavelength). As a first approximation, the wavelength of maximum intensity in the continuum is $3\lambda_0/2$, where λ_0 is the short-wavelength limit in Å set by the relationship

$$\frac{hc}{\lambda_0} = Ve \qquad (14.3)$$

where V = the potential in volts
h = Planck's constant
c = the speed of light in vacuum
e = the charge on the electron

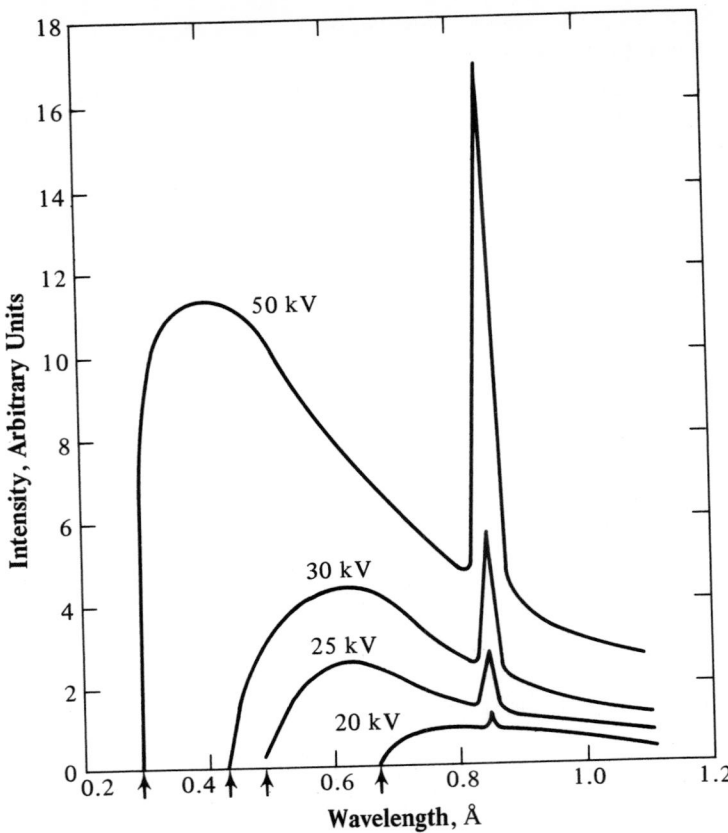

FIGURE 14.4. *Variation in x-ray distribution with voltage (yttrium target). The characteristic Y Kα line is at 0.83 Å. The short wavelength cutoff is indicated by an arrow for each voltage. From F. J. Welcher, ed.,* Standard Methods of Chemical Analysis, *6th ed., vol. IIIA, p 169, by permission of Van Nostrand Reinhold Company. Copyright © 1966 Litton Educational Publishing, Inc.*

At the short-wavelength limit, all the energy of the electron hitting the target is converted to a single photon, with none left over for heat loss or multiple emission.

The voltage required to produce the characteristic lines of each spectral series also increases with increasing atomic number. Minimum voltages, in keV, for the K, L, and M series are in the following ranges:

K series: 1.1 for ^{11}Na to 115 for ^{92}U
L series: 1.2 for ^{30}Zn to 21.7 for ^{92}U
M series: 0.41 for ^{40}Zr to 5.5 for ^{92}U

Each of these minimum (critical) voltages, corresponding to the minimum photon or electron energy that can expel an electron from a given level in the atom, is known as the *absorption edge* of that level for the particular element. Each element has as many absorption edges as it has excitation potentials—one K, three L, five M. For example, the K edge for calcium is 4.038 keV; the three L edges for lead (L_I, L_{II}, and L_{III} corresponding to the different L electrons—see Fig. 14.1) are 15.870, and 13.044 keV, respectively.

The intensity of a characteristic line excited by electrons is related to the app. voltage by the expression

$$I = ki(V - V_0)^n \tag{14.4}$$

The value of n (which ranges over the interval between 1 and 2) depends on the ratio between the applied voltage V and the critical voltage V_0; for voltages less than $4\,V_0$, the value of n is close to 2.

In x-ray fluorescence spectroscopy, the characteristic x-rays of the sample are generated (excited) by both the characteristic and continuum x-rays of the source. An important consideration is the relative excitation of secondary x-rays by the

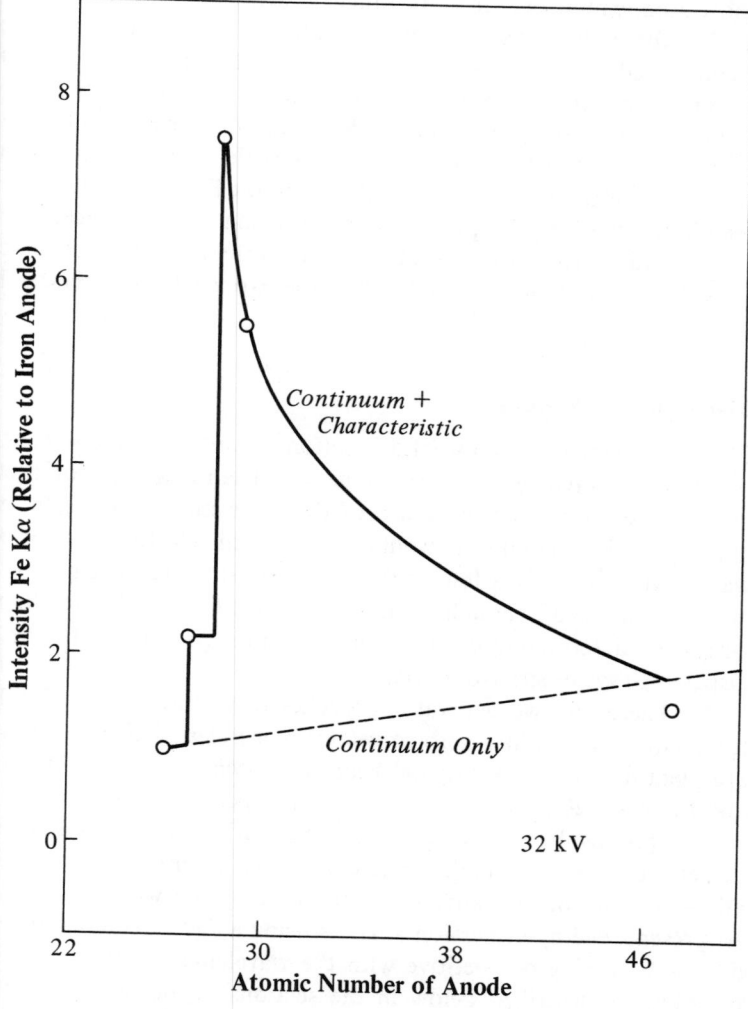

FIGURE 14.5. *Secondary excitation of iron using various x-ray tube targets.*

as compared to those generated by primary characteristic x-rays. Al-
total intensity of the characteristic primary peak or peaks is low
the continuum, the efficiency of excitation by the characteristic
cantly greater in many instances because of the higher absorption of
se to the surface. This higher excitation efficiency is a result of the
pth beyond which all secondary (fluorescence) x-rays are absorbed within
sample (the depth being related to the linear absorption coefficient of the sample
for the spectral or "analytical" line). The depth of sample analyzed will range from
less than 1 mm to 1 cm, depending on the energy of the spectral line and the composition of the sample. Because of this internal absorption, only those incident
photons absorbed close to the surface are efficient producers of fluorescence x-rays.

Figure 14.5 shows the relative intensity of the secondary Fe Kα line emitted
from an iron sample, using as primary targets in the x-ray tube some of the elements
whose atomic numbers are in the range of 26 to 47. With an iron target (atomic number 26), the only source of excitation is the continuum and, therefore, that intensity
is considered as unity. With targets of nickel and copper ($Z = 28$ and 29, respectively), the characteristic primary x-rays just exceed the critical energy of the Fe K-
absorption edge, so excitation of Fe K radiation is a maximum. When using a high-Z
target such as silver ($Z = 47$), the characteristic Ag K radiation is not absorbed near
the surface of the iron sample, so the resultant Fe Kα radiation, generated relatively
deep in the sample, is absorbed before escaping to the surface.

Radioisotopes (for instance, alpha emitters) can be used as sources for exciting
x-ray fluorescence and are used in portable x-ray spectrometers. These are discussed
later.

Dispersion of X-Rays

Chapter 6 described the use of diffraction gratings to disperse electromagnetic radiation in the ultraviolet-to-infrared regions. The radiation is diffracted if the spacings
between lines on the grating are of the same magnitude as the wavelength of the
radiation. This condition would be very difficult to meet for x-rays, since their
wavelengths are only a few angstroms at most. The spacings of atoms in crystals,
however, are small enough to diffract x-rays; this has led to the widespread use of
x-rays for determining crystal structures and, conversely, to the use of crystals to
disperse x-rays in spectrometers.

There are two general approaches to sorting x-rays of different wavelengths
(different energies) in a spectrometer: by *wavelength dispersion*, in which the x-rays
are identified after the original beam has been spread out by an analyzing crystal,
and by *energy dispersion*, in which the undispersed x-rays are sorted into 100 to 1000
energy groups by means of a high-resolution frequency-sensitive semiconductor
detector coupled to a multi-channel analyzer. Until approximately 1970, essentially
all x-ray spectrometer analyses were made by the wavelength-dispersion technique.
At present, energy-dispersion analysis using a dedicated computer for processing the
data is becoming competitive with the wavelength method. The energy-dispersion
technique is described below in the sections on detectors and radioisotope-source
portable instruments.

The condition for diffraction of x-rays can be described by considering the

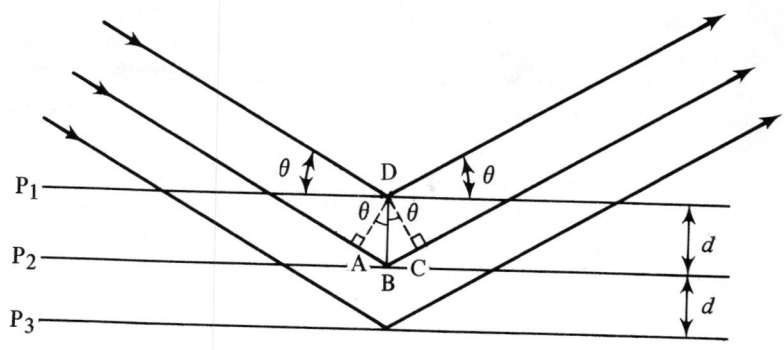

FIGURE 14.6. *Diffraction of x-rays from the planes of a crystal.*

diffraction of a monochromatic beam impinging on a row (plane) of atoms (or ions) as shown in Figure 14.6. Lines AD and CD are perpendicular to the incident and diffracted beams, respectively. The beam diffracted from plane P_2 must travel a distance $\overline{ABC}$ further than that diffracted from plane P_1. Since angles ADB and BDC are equal to the angle of incidence and diffraction θ,

$$\overline{AB} = d \sin \theta \qquad (14.5)$$

or

$$\overline{ABC} = 2d \sin \theta \qquad (14.6)$$

where d = the distance between planes in the crystal

Those waves out of phase after diffraction will interfere destructively and not be observed. Only those in phase will reinforce and be observed. This occurs when $\overline{ABC}$ is an exact multiple of the wavelength of the incident beam λ. Hence,

$$n\lambda = 2d \sin \theta \qquad (14.7)$$

where n = the *order* of the diffraction pattern

When n is unity, the diffracted radiation is called first order. Higher orders of diffracted radiation fall off in intensity. Equation 14.7 is known as *Bragg's law*, and may be compared to Equation 6.6 for the diffraction of radiation from a grating. For x-rays of a given wavelength, then, diffraction will be observed at only certain values of θ (determined by d). These θ values can be determined by rotating the crystal and measuring the angle of diffracted x-rays with respect to the angle of the incident beam. The d-spacings of a given plane can therefore be calculated. Or, if the d-spacing of a crystal is known, the angle at which a given x-ray will be diffracted (in a spectrometer, for instance) can be calculated.

Example 14.1. The first-order diffraction of the Mo Kα 0.712 Å line from a plane of calcium fluoride is observed as strong radiation at 6.48°. What is the distance between planes?

Solution:
$$n\lambda = 2d \sin \theta$$
$$1(0.712) = 2d \sin (6.48)$$
$$d = 3.16 \text{ Å}$$

Bragg originally used this relationship to determine the wavelengths of x-rays. He diffracted x-rays from a sodium-chloride crystal and used as the *d*-value that calculated from the density of the crystal and Avogadro's number. Once λ was determined, then x-ray diffraction could be used to determine *d* spacings in other crystals, and x-ray crystallography (the study of crystals) was born.

The two types of x-ray optical systems used in spectrometers are *nonfocusing* (flat-crystal) and *focusing* (curved-crystal) systems (see Fig. 14.2). In flat-crystal optics, the x-ray beam is collimated by a closely spaced series of parallel metal foils (see Fig. 14.2A), where the beam divergence is limited by the spacing between the foils and the lengths of the foils. In curved-crystal optics, either a small region of the sample is excited using a pinhole collimator to limit the size of the primary x-ray beam, or a large area is irradiated and a divergence slit serves as the "optical source" of secondary x-rays (see Fig. 14.2b). With focusing optics, a cylindrical concave crystal focuses the diffracted x-rays onto a circle having a radius equal to one-half the radius of curvature of the crystal. The crystal has been mechanically bent to a radius 2*r*, then ground to the radius *r* of the focusing circle. The x-ray source, crystal surface, and detector slit all lie on the focusing circle. Focusing and nonfocusing optics give essentially the same intensity and line-to-background ratio for large samples, whereas for small samples, focusing optics are at least an order of magnitude more efficient.

Analyzer crystals must satisfy the Bragg relationship for the analytical line without exceeding the maximum 2θ angle available with commercial instrumentation, approximately 150°. In general, the analyzing crystal should be composed of elements of low atomic number to avoid high background from fluorescence x-rays generated in the analyzing crystal itself. The dispersion of x-rays is inversely related to the *d*-spacing and to the Bragg angle, so

$$\frac{d\theta}{d\lambda} = \frac{n}{2d\cos\theta} \tag{14.8}$$

TABLE 14.1. *Properties of Analyzing Crystals*

Crystal	Reflecting Plane (hkl)	2*d*, Å	Comments
Lithium fluoride	200	4.03	Optimum crystal for all wavelengths less than 3 Å
Silicon	111	6.27	Suppresses even-ordered reflections, $n = 2, 4, 6, \ldots$
Pentaerythritol	002	8.74	Optimum for atomic numbers 13 to 17
Mica	002	19.93	Used primarily in curved-crystal optics for long-wavelength x-rays
Potassium hydrogen phthalate	002	26.63	Used for atomic numbers 6 to 12
Barium stearate	——	100	Used with curved- or flat-crystal optics for wavelengths greater than 20 Å

Therefore, crystals of low *d*-spacing (high dispersion) are used to disperse partially overlapping x-ray spectral lines. The characteristics of some of the more widely used crystals are given in Table 14.1.

Detectors

Four types of detectors are used in x-ray analysis: Geiger, proportional, scintillation, and semiconductor detectors. These are described in detail in Chapter 19. (They detect ionizing radiation, of which x-rays are an example.) Geiger tubes are simple to operate and do not require highly stabilized electronic circuitry. However, they have two principal disadvantages: first, the counting loss (nonlinear response) is significant even at moderate x-ray intensities because of the relatively long dead-time between counts; second, discrimination of x-ray energies is not possible.

The spectral sensitivity of proportional detectors is similar to that of Geiger counters, but proportional detectors can be used at relatively high counting rates (high x-ray intensities), since the dead-time is small. Also, the output voltage of this detector is proportional to the energy of the incident x-ray photon, so that direct energy-discrimination is possible without the need for a dispersing medium. For x-rays longer than 2 Å, the windows of these detectors are very thin organic films of mylar, formvar, or nitrocellulose, all of which have a high transmittance for long-wavelength x-rays. Since these windows are porous, the counting gas is passed in a continuous stream through the detector (*flow-proportional detectors*).

The most generally useful detector in conventional x-ray spectrometry is the scintillation counter, which incorporates a very low dead-time and excellent sensitivity for x-rays of wavelength less than 2 Å. Since the output voltage is proportional to the energy of the incident x-ray photon, electronic pulse-amplitude discrimination can be used to reject x-rays whose energies are sufficiently different from those of the spectral lines being measured. The resolving power of the scintillation counter is approximately one-half to one-third that of the proportional detector. However, a high degree of energy resolution is not generally required in wavelength-dispersion applications, since the discrimination is against higher-order x-rays whose energies are multiple integer values of the desired radiation.

Table 14.2 presents some guidelines for selecting the optimum detector for a specific application using wavelength discrimination or dispersion.

The excellent resolution provided by the more recently developed lithium-drifted silicon [Si(Li)] and germanium [Ge(Li)] semiconductor detectors (see Chap.

TABLE 14.2. *X-Ray Detectors and Guidelines for Use*

Detector	Application
Geiger	Routine control analysis where low counting rates and physical discrimination are adequate.
Flow-proportional	Determination of all elements of atomic number 24 or below.
Proportional	Unique applications where the maximum resolution of a detector is required.
Scintillation	Determination of all elements of atomic number 25 and above.

19) has been a significant breakthrough in x-ray analysis. To obtain optimum pulse-resolution and performance with these solid-state detectors, low-noise preamplifiers and amplifiers are required, in addition to liquid-nitrogen cooling of the detector and the first stage of the preamplifier. Because of their smaller size, greater complexity, and higher cost, the use of semiconductor detectors is generally limited to energy-dispersion applications where the increased resolution is required.

In Figure 14.7, the energy resolution of proportional, scintillation, and semiconductor detectors is compared to wavelength-diffraction resolution. The energy resolution of the three types of detectors has approximately the same slope, that is, it is proportional to the square root of the photon energy. The resolving power of

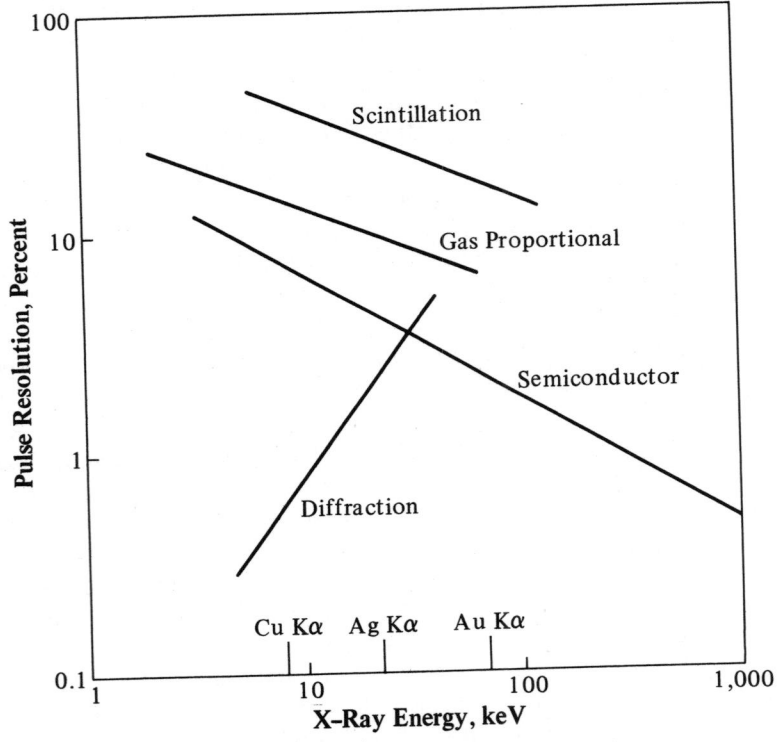

FIGURE 14.7. *Resolution of energy-proportional detectors and of crystal diffraction as a function of photon energy.*

the semiconductor detector is approximately a factor of ten better than that of the scintillation counter and a factor of three better than the gas-proportional detector. For lower energies, the resolution provided by a LiF-crystal (diffraction) spectrometer is a factor of 5 to 10 superior to the best semiconductor detector. With increasing photon energy, the semiconductor detector becomes more favorable and, at high energy, provides superior resolution since high-reflectivity crystals of very low d-spacing are not available.

The initial applications of semiconductors utilized radioisotopic sources (see below); currently the trend is toward direct excitation with low-powered x-ray tubes.

Some advantages of the energy-dispersion semiconductor approach are: simultaneous multi-element analysis, high collection efficiency, no higher-order diffraction lines, and low sensitivity to surface preparation of the sample. In comparison, wavelength dispersion offers superior resolution for most elements, higher count-rate per element, better peak-to-background ratio, and is applicable to the low-energy x-ray region where chemical effects (valence, coordination) can be measured using high-resolution x-ray spectroscopy. There is a wide variety of energy-dispersion systems commercially available, ranging from very simple and compact portable analyzers to completely computerized semiconductor systems.

Energy Dispersion With Radioisotope Sources— Portable Instruments

Until the early 1960s, the application of radioisotopes in x-ray spectroscopy was limited to the calibration of proportional or scintillation detectors. At that time, simple and compact energy-dispersion instruments using radioactive sources were developed for specific applications where resolution and sensitivity requirements are not severe. Radioisotopic sources have a flux 6 to 8 orders of magnitude lower than high-powered sealed x-ray tubes; therefore, any application based on radioisotopic sources must be limited to those energy-dispersion techniques in which there is a close coupling of the radioisotopic sources, the sample, and the detector. These portable analyzers employ the technique of balanced filters to isolate the line of analytical interest. These filters consist of two thin metallic foils with K-absorption edges on the low- and high-energy sides of the x-ray line of interest. For example, as shown in Figure 14.8, the Sn Kα line just exceeds the K edge of the palladium filter, and therefore is absorbed, whereas the Sn Kα x-rays are readily transmitted by the silver foil. The thicknesses of the two filters are carefully controlled so that their

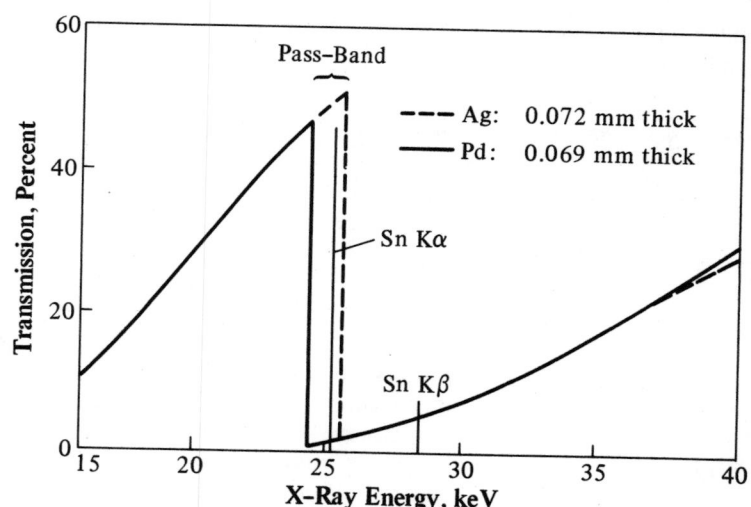

FIGURE 14.8.   *Balanced filters for isolating Sn Kα radiation. The transmission and absorption filters are made of silver and palladium, respectively. From S. H. V. Bowie, A. G. Darnby, and J. R. Rhodes, Trans. Inst. Min., Met. 74, 36 (1964–65), by kind permission of J. R. Rhodes, Columbia Scientific Industries, P.O. Box 9908, Austin, Texas.*

absorption characteristics are virtually the same for all radiation, except in the narrow pass-band. The difference in measured intensity, using first the silver and then the palladium filter, is related to the tin content of the sample. The portable analyzers complement the conventional x-ray spectrometer for process control and field applications, but are not competitive in the laboratory.

Radioactive Sources

Radioisotopes commonly used for energy-dispersion analysis are listed in Table 14.3. Sealed sources of all types are now commercially available. The price of a source depends on the cost of the radioisotope and the complexity of the instrument design.

Alpha emitters such as polonium-210 and curium-242 are used to excite emission of low-energy x-rays. They offer the advantage of large signal-to-background ratio, but the thickness of sample analyzed is extremely small. The alpha emitters are health hazards and generally have very limited application in energy-dispersion analysis.

Beta emitters are used to generate continuum plus characteristic x-rays that collectively excite the sample. These beta sources may be a thin layer of the isotope on a suitable target, or a mechanical or chemical mixture of isotope and target.

Isotopes that decay by K-electron capture emit essentially monoenergetic x-radiation; for example, ^{109}Cd and ^{55}Fe emit Ag K and Mn K x-rays, respectively. Large signal-to-background ratios can be achieved with these "monoenergetic" sources. Many analysts recommend the use of a K-capture isotope whose characteristic radiation just exceeds the absorption edge of the element being determined. This criterion is applicable to wavelength dispersion. However, for energy dispersion one must allow for the poorer resolution of the analytical system, so the criterion must be modified so as to resolve the characteristic x-ray emitted by the sample from the incoherent "Compton radiation" (see Chap. 19) and the coherent scattered incident radiation. To achieve this resolution, the primary x-rays must either be significantly higher in energy than the K or L absorption edge of the element being

TABLE 14.3.   *Radioisotopes Commonly Used in Energy-Dispersive X-Ray Analysis*

Radio-isotope	Half-life (years)	Principal Mode of Decay	Principal Radiation
^{55}Fe	2.7	electron capture	Mn K x-rays
^{109}Cd	1.3	electron capture	Ag K x-rays, 88 keV gamma
^{125}I	0.16	electron capture	Te K x-rays, 35 keV gamma
^{3}H/Zr	12.3	β emission	Bremsstrahlung 3–12 keV
^{147}Pm/Al	2.6	β emission	Bremsstrahlung 10–50 keV
^{241}Am	458.0	α emission	Np L x-rays, 26 and 60 keV gamma
^{153}Gd	0.65	electron capture	Eu K x-rays, 97 and 103 keV gamma
^{57}Co	0.74	electron capture	Fe K x-rays, 14, 122, and 136 keV gamma
^{242}Cm	17.6	electron capture	Pu L x-rays
^{238}Pu	86.4	electron capture	U L x-rays

determined, or so close to the edge tha͏̶
of the analytical line.

Two examples of source-sample-c͏̶
and x-ray emitting isotopes are shown
14.9A) is more widely used for portable
source. The important parameters of th͏̶
sample-source-detector distances and the
The x-ray filters are usually placed betwee͏̶
Using the central source, counting rates of
pure samples of the element being analyzed.
by the sample.

Gamma emitters are often used in a so͏̶
principal radiation for exciting the sample is th͏̶

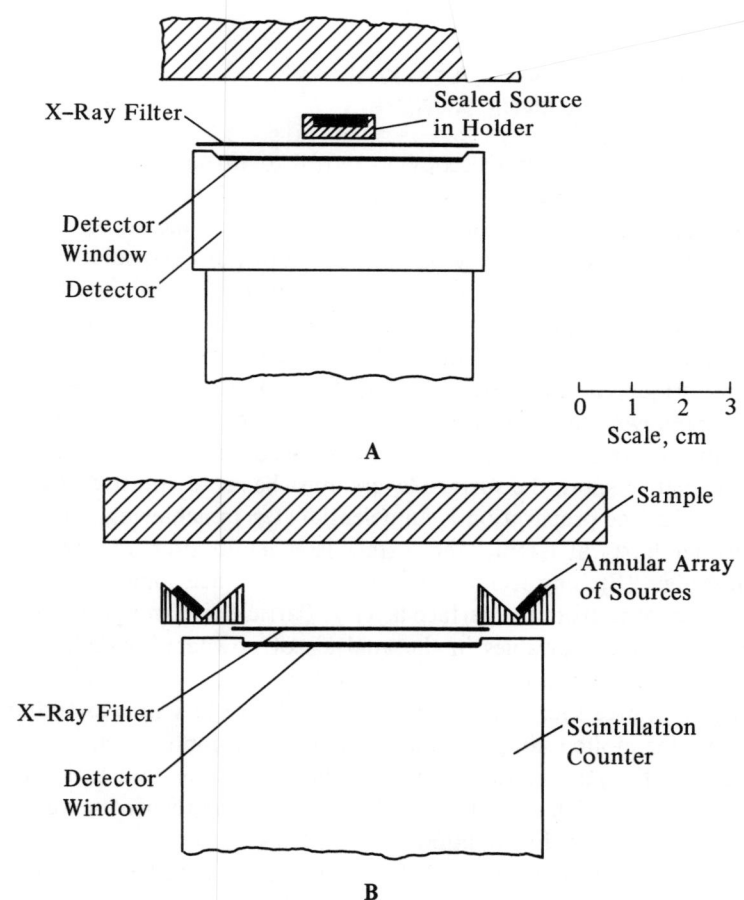

A

B

FIGURE 14.9. *Central (A) and annular (B) source geometries used with portable radioisotopic x-ray analyzers. From S. H. V. Bowie, A. G. Darnby, and J. R. Rhodes, Trans. Inst. Min., Met.* **74**, *36 (1964–65), by kind permission of J. R. Rhodes, Columbia Scientific Industries, P.O. Box 9908, Austin, Texas.*

gamma emitter and target, the analyst has available a
tion source. There are a number of commercially available
lies that allow the analyst to easily change the target material.
gh-intensity gamma emitter, is positioned in a cup formed by the
t. The high-energy gamma radiation from the source excites charac-
ays that are superimposed on a scattered gamma background. Annular
-targets are used extensively with semiconductor detectors. By removing the
get and aiming the source directly at the sample, direct excitation of the sample
may be utilized. These high-energy gamma photons increase the depth of sample
analyzed by a factor of ten or more compared to their lower-energy L lines. Increased
penetration into the sample is very important for applications such as analysis of
inhomogeneous samples and in situ analyses of ore samples. Thus, particle-size effects,
a common problem in the analysis of powdered samples, are reduced by the use of
high-atomic-number K radiation.

14.3 PREPARATION OF SAMPLES FOR
X-RAY FLUORESCENCE ANALYSIS

X-ray fluorescence spectroscopy is applied to virtually every type of elemental determination encountered by control and research laboratories. The types of samples
analyzed include ashes, ores, minerals, ceramics, metals and alloys and films and
coatings. The samples may be in the form of powders, solutions, rods, sheets, films,
or particulates. The method is, in general, nondestructive; the sample can be retained for other analyses.

Solid samples used in x-ray fluorescence analysis include metallurgical specimens, briquetted powders, and borax discs. For quantitative analysis, both standards
and unknowns must be in the same matrix and subjected to the same preparation.
Because of the limited escape depth of secondary x-rays, particularly in the long-
wavelength region, the surface layers must be representative of the entire sample.

Surface preparation is an essential step in achieving good quantitative results.
For metallurgical samples the surface is generally prepared by grinding, followed by
polishing. (Etching techniques are not used, since some elements may be preferentially removed from the surface layer.) Particle size and particle-size distribution are
very important variables in the analysis of powdered samples. Powdered samples
are either processed by adding a small amount of binder and forming into a briquet
using high pressure, or by fusing with a suitable flux such as sodium tetraborate and
casting the molten sample into a glass disk. Fusion methods are generally preferable
to briquetting, as the fused sample is homogeneous on a scale of micrometers, thus
eliminating particle-size effects. Also, the fluxing reagent serves as a diluent for the
sample, thereby reducing interelement effects.

Solution samples are held in plastic or metallic containers with thin mylar
windows transparent to x-rays. The most convenient procedure is to use cup-like
containers with 0.006- or 0.02-mm mylar windows, with the sample held in an inverted position over the x-ray tube.

Samples in the gaseous or vapor state require cells with x-ray–transparent
windows that can withstand high pressure-differentials. Some type of pressure regu-

lation must be used to maintain the number of atoms in the x-ray beam at a specified level.

Preparation of Samples for Trace Analysis

Trace analyses are conveniently classified into two types: Minor or trace constituents in large samples (e.g., gold in low-grade ores) and major constituents of very small samples (e.g., titanium in a flake of paint). Samples of the first type can be converted to the second by physical or chemical concentration of the desired elements. Limits of detectability for the first type range from 0.1 to 100 ppm, depending on the elements being determined, the overall sample composition, and the complexity of the x-ray spectra. This is a concentration detection limit. Limits of detectability with the second type of sample are expressed in micrograms (generally about 0.01 to 1 μg) and may represent ppm, ppb, or lower concentrations in the original sample, depending on the sensitivity for the element and the size of the starting sample. The minimum amount, detected is an absolute detection limit. Good examples of these sample types that are of environmental concern are aqueous discharges from industrial plants (type 1) and particulates collected on filter disks from air samples (type 2).

For the determination of trace elements in aqueous samples, the best approach is to use ion-exchange techniques to isolate and collect the elements of interest and to provide a sample that can be directly inserted in the x-ray instrument. Using papers impregnated with cation and anion resins (see Chap. 21 regarding strong exchangers), groups of elements can be quantitatively collected from dilute aqueous solutions, as shown in Table 14.4 for anions. These strong-acid and strong-base papers are not selective; therefore, the analyst has to be aware that all the ions present are competing for the available exchange sites. A very high concentration of

TABLE 14.4. *Collection Efficiency of Anions by Paper Impregnated With a Strong Anion-Exchanger*

Anion	Collection efficiency, percent	
	Resin in Cl^- form	Resin in OH^- form
IO_3^-	71	90
HPO_4^{2-}	76	99
BrO_3^-	88	98
Br^-	97	>99
VO_3^-	98	>99
$PtCl_6^{2-}$	99	>99
SO_4^{2-}, $Cr_2O_7^{2-}$	>99	>99
CrO_4^{2-}, MnO_4^-	>99	>99
MoO_4^{2-}, $Fe(CN)_6^{4-}$	>99	>99

Note: This data is for SB-2 anion exchange paper, available from H. Reeve-Angel and Company.

one particular ion may "swamp" the ion exchanger, and the particular ion of interest may not be effectively retained.

Other types of exchange media include chelate-resin–loaded paper, reagent-impregnated paper, cellulose-phosphate paper, and cellulose–sulfuric-acid paper. The chelate-resin–loaded and reagent-impregnated papers can selectively collect one or more elements; for example, there is a chelating resin that is highly selective for Hg^{2+}, CH_3Hg^+, Au^{3+}, and some of the platinum-group metals. Other approaches for collecting either groups of elements or individual elements are coprecipitation, wherein the elements of interest are collected on filter paper after treatment with a precipitation reagent, or electrochemical preconcentration by plating onto the surface of a pyrolytic-graphite electrode. Standards are prepared by treating aliquots of known solutions in the same manner as the unknowns. Standards prepared with resin-loaded papers have a very long shelf-life and are easily stored.

When the separation-collection procedure is not quantitative, a radiotracer of the element being determined can be added to the initial sample to serve as a collection monitor. For example, in the determination of gold in low-grade ores, radioactive ^{195}Au is added to the ore prior to dissolution and subsequent collection on chelate-resin–loaded paper. The intensity of the Pt K x-rays from the K-capture decay of the ^{195}Au is a linear function of the fraction of gold collected on the resin-loaded paper. Radiotracers of $^{203}Hg^{2+}$ and $CH_3{}^{203}Hg^+$ are used to determine the collection efficiency for inorganic and organic mercury in aqueous effluents. The actual chemical form in which the mercury is present, as well as the total mercury content, is an important parameter in environmental studies.

In the analysis of particulates in air, the samples are collected by passing measured volumes of air through filter paper (or some other suitable filter media). One method of standardization is to pipette small volumes of solution containing known amounts of the elements to be determined onto the same filter medium. Depending on the energy of the x-ray line and the size of the particulates, there may be systematic errors in the analysis using standards prepared from solutions. Another approach to standardization is to disperse known quantities of elements in the form of finely divided powders onto paper or glass-fiber filters. Problems with this approach include variation in particle size between standards and unknowns, and quantitative collection of the standard powders by the filter.

14.4 QUANTITATIVE X-RAY FLUORESCENCE ANALYSIS

Quantitative analysis is achieved by comparing intensities from unknowns to those from primary or secondary standards. Depending on the degree of similarity between unknown and standard, small or large correction factors may be necessary.

Because of the limited penetration of characteristic x-ray lines from the source, most samples can be assumed to be infinitely thick; that is, the intensity of the measured x-ray fluorescence line will not increase if the sample thickness is increased. For "infinitely" thick samples, the intensity of fluorescence from element x is related to concentration by the relationship

$$I_x = \frac{kW_x}{\mu_{\lambda_1} + \mu_{\lambda_2}} \tag{14.9}$$

where I_x = the measured line intensity

W_x = the weight fraction of the element being determined

μ_{λ_1} = the averaged linear-absorption coefficient of the sample as a whole for the incident radiation λ_1

μ_{λ_2} = the averaged linear-absorption coefficient of the sample as a whole for the fluorescent radiation λ_2

k = a proportionality constant

The value of the averaged linear-absorption coefficient for the sample, μ_s, for any wavelength is equal to the summation of the linear-absorption coefficient of each element x times its weight fraction

$$\mu_s = \sum \mu_i W_i \qquad (14.10)$$

Although Equation 14.9 is oversimplified, the main points are correctly indicated; the measured intensity depends on both the concentration of the element being determined and on the overall composition of the sample. For example, the intensity of the Ag Kα line from various silver ores depends on both the total silver content and the matrix composition (Fig. 14.10). These samples represent matrices containing various amounts of lead, barium, and transition elements, plus minerals

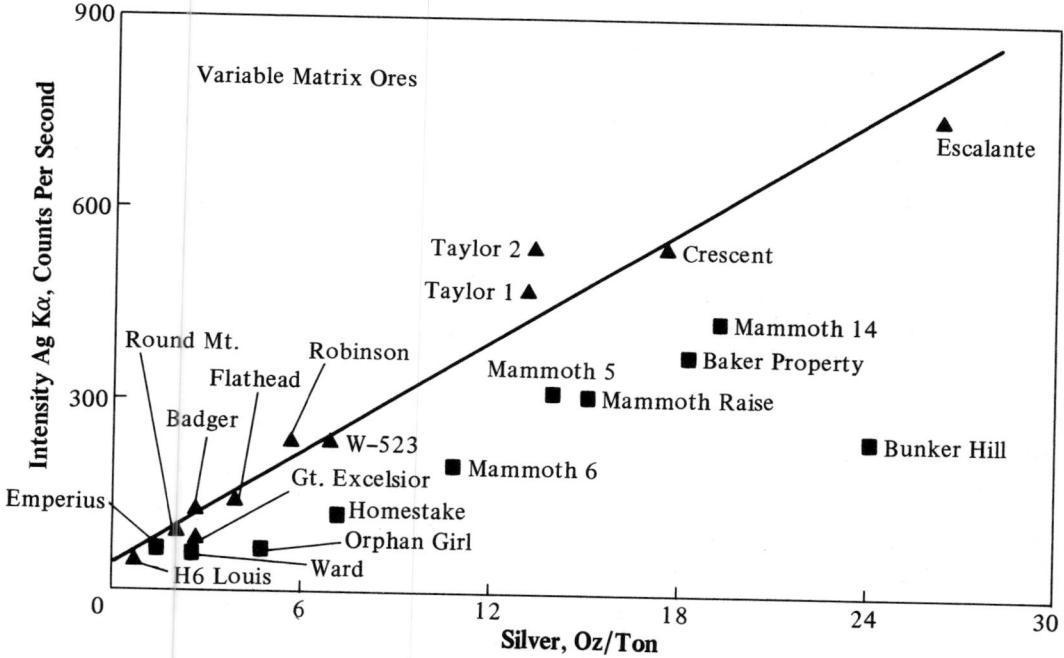

FIGURE 14.10. *Variation in Ag Kα intensity with mineralogical composition.* ▲ = *low-Z matrix;* ■ = *high-Z matrix. The line is a calibration curve derived from silver standards prepared in a silica matrix. From* P. G. Burkhalter, Anal. Chem., *43*, 10 (1971), *by permission of the publisher. Copyright © 1971 by the American Chemical Society.*

such as quartz and feldspar. Therefore, the analyst must have adequate knowledge regarding the composition of the unknowns, or employ some technique that will minimize the compositional dependence. This dependence, commonly called the matrix effect, is the principal source of systematic error in quantitative x-ray analyses.

Six general procedures are available to reduce or correct for the matrix dependence: comparison standards, internal standards, standard addition, dilution, thin films, and scatter correction. Each of these is discussed below. One essential requirement for both samples and standards in all methods (other than those using thin films) is homogeneity on a micrometer scale because of the low penetration of incident x-ray photons. Other practical factors to be considered for quantitative results include surface preparation and particle-size distribution.

Comparison Standards

The most widely used method of calibration is the comparison of intensities from unknowns with those from standards of similar composition. Obviously, this direct comparison requires knowledge regarding the probable composition of the sample (in industrial-control analyses, for example, the approximate composition of the sample is frequently known). When unknowns and standards are very close in composition, a simple ratio of intensities and composition is adequate, for example

$$\frac{I_u}{I_s} = \frac{c_u}{c_s} \qquad (14.11)$$

where the subscripts u and s refer to unknowns and standards, respectively. Applications in which the unknowns vary over a wide range of compositions require the use of graphical or mathematical correction techniques. The present trend in process control is to use simultaneous equations to derive correction factors (for absorption and for enhancement by higher-energy x-rays emitted within the sample). Then, using these correction factors, the composition of the unknown is obtained by a multiple-regression technique. Originally, the mathematical approach was limited to a few laboratories having access to large computers. Nowadays, dedicated computers are an integral part of many modern industrial-control x-ray spectrometers.

Internal Standards

In the internal standardization method, a known concentration of a reference element is added to the sample being analyzed. For x-ray spectroscopy, the reference should have a characteristic radiation that will be excited and absorbed to a similar extent as the characteristic radiation of the element being determined. Therefore, the internal standard is generally an element one atomic number higher or lower than the element being determined. In some instances, it may be necessary to use an element of much higher atomic number and to make use of its L or M radiation, for example Br Kα (11.9 keV) and Au Lβ_1 (11.4 keV).

Regardless of the reference line used, the matrix may affect the relative intensities of the reference and analytical lines in one of the following ways:

1. the matrix will have a slightly higher absorption coefficient for the longer-wavelength line;
2. another element in the matrix will have an absorption edge between the reference line and the analytical line of interest;
3. an emission line from the matrix will preferentially excite the element of lower atomic number.

Classes of samples representing each of these situations are shown graphically in Figure 14.11. The matrix M is considered to be the third element and the symbols X and R represent the element being determined (the unknown) and the reference element, respectively. If the matrix element emits lines L_1 or L_3 or has absorption edges E_1 or E_3, there is no significant preferential absorption or enhancement of either the unknown or reference emission line. In contrast, if the matrix element has an absorption edge at E_2, then X $K\alpha$ is preferentially absorbed by the matrix element so that the internal standard is not applicable. Another source of systematic error is when the matrix element emits a strong line of wavelength L_2, whereby the reference element R is preferentially excited (by absorption at RE). The original sample, of course, must not contain appreciable amounts of the reference element.

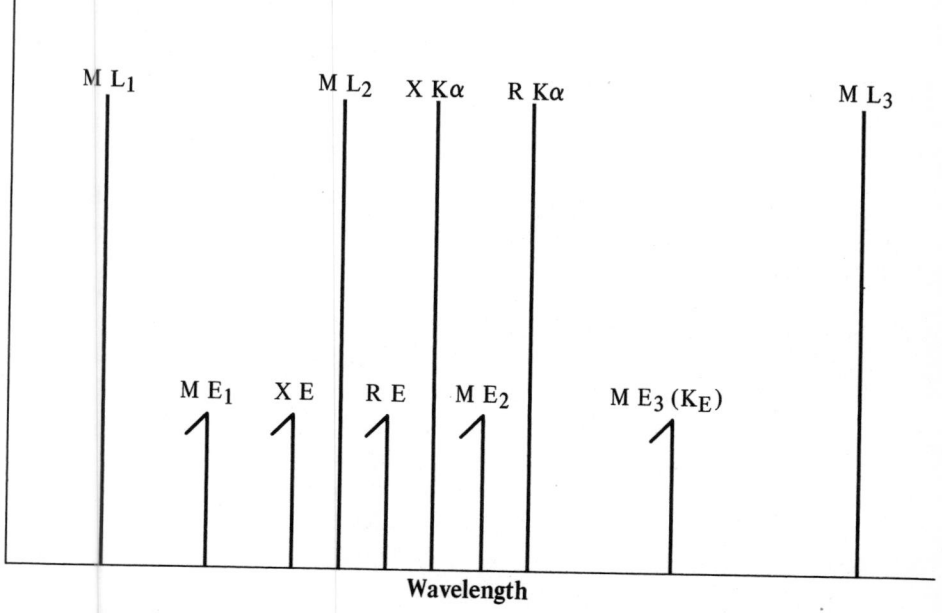

FIGURE 14.11. *Possible interfering lines and absorption edges when using internal standards. M is the matrix element, X is the element being determined, R is the reference element, E_1 represents an absorption edge, K_E is the K absorption edge, and vertical lines represent emission wavelengths.*

Within these limitations, the internal-standard method has enjoyed wide application in mineral and ore processing. It is essential that the reference element be intimately mixed with the sample on a micrometer scale. Various procedures have been used to achieve this blending, such as grinding the sample and reference with an abrasive such as silicon carbide, or by fusion using borax, carbonate, or pyrosulfate as a flux.

Standard Addition

The standard-addition method is similar to the internal-standard method, except that the element being determined serves as the reference standard itself. Analysis is accomplished by measuring the intensity of the characteristic spectral line before and after the addition of a known amount of the element being determined. It is assumed that a linear relationship exists between line intensity and concentration (over a limited concentration range), and that the matrix is not significantly altered by the addition. In general, the addition method is limited to the determination of trace and minor elements. All of the comments regarding sample preparation for internal standards apply directly to the standard-addition approach.

Dilution

One general method of reducing the matrix effect is to dilute standards and unknowns in a common "solvent." With sufficient dilution, the small weight-fraction of the solute makes its contribution to the matrix negligible:

$$\lim_{W_A \to 0} \mu_{sample} = \mu_{solvent} \tag{14.12}$$

where W_A = the weight fraction of the sample

As a result of dilution, the element or elements being determined are now present as minor constituents, so the intensity-to-concentration relationship is linear and thus minimizes the matrix effects.

Dilution may be achieved by dissolving the sample in an inorganic or organic solvent (for example, water or chloroform), or by fusing it with a flux (such as borax, carbonate, or pyrosulfate). Another approach is to add a strong absorber of x-rays, such as lanthanum oxide, to the flux to minimize the degree of dilution required to reduce matrix effects; that is, to swamp out the effects of a variable sample matrix. A typical application of the La_2O_3-flux approach is determining copper in a series of ore samples having a variable iron concentration. The dilution plus the strong absorber minimizes the absorption of Cu Kα by the iron.

Thin Films

Interelement effects are small or negligible in thin-film samples, because neither the primary nor the secondary x-rays are strongly absorbed. Thus, the intensities of the secondary x-rays are directly proportional to the amount of the element present; matrix effects are minimized by this technique. Because standards and unknowns are prepared in a similar manner, linear comparison of intensities is valid.

In order to prepare thin-film samples, the desired elements must usually be chemically or physically separated from the host compound. The elements being determined are collected in a physical form suitable for x-ray analysis using such methods as ion exchange, solvent extraction, or precipitation. Metallic ions, for example, may be collected on resin-loaded paper, which also serves as the mechanical support in the x-ray spectrometer. The absolute sensitivity for elements isolated from the host compound is 0.01 to 1 μg; analysis of elements present in trace concentrations is possible with this preconcentration approach, if the total sample size is sufficiently large.

Scatter Correction

The basic assumption in the scatter-correction approach is that both scattered source and emitted fluorescence x-rays are subject to similar losses owing to absorption. Therefore, for samples with widely varying matrices, the ratio of emitted to scattered x-ray intensities I_e/I_s is relatively constant. In general, scatter-correction methods significantly improve the reliability of the analytical results, although the ultimate accuracy is poorer than that of other, more reliable, methods such as dilution. Scatter correction is one area where considerably more research is needed.

Accuracy and Precision

The accuracy and precision of the x-ray fluorescence method is related to the care taken in sample preparation, to the stability of the instrument, and ultimately to counting statistics.* With modern instrumentation, minor or major constituents may give counting rates of 10,000 counts/sec or higher above background, so that a relative precision of 0.1% can be achieved in 100-sec counting times. The accuracy of the analyses is related to the similarity of composition between the unknowns and the standards or to the analyst's ability to apply appropriate correction factors. In routine industrial-control applications, a relative analytical accuracy of 1% is not unusual, whereas for many unknown samples the relative accuracy may be 5–10% or poorer. X-ray fluorescence methods can be applied for concentrations ranging from several ppm in favorable cases to essentially 100% by weight. Times are on the order of several minutes or less for control applications (total analytical time may be considerably longer, depending on the amount of sample preparation required).

14.5 SPECIAL TOPICS AND OTHER X-RAY METHODS

Coating and Film-Thickness Determinations

An important application of x-ray spectroscopy in the metallurgical industry is measuring the thickness of coatings or films. The thickness can be calculated by determining either the intensity I_s of the characteristic radiation emitted from the substrate (after being attenuated by the coating) or by measuring the intensity I_f of

---

* The counting error is inversely proportional to the square root of the number of photons counted for each analytical line being measured.

a characteristic line emitted from the coating (see Fig. 14.12). These measurements are correlated to data obtained with coatings of known thickness. Virtually all coating-thickness monitors used in the metallurgical industries are based on such x-ray intensity measurements. The methods are rapid, nondestructive, and can be applied to a variety of coatings and thicknesses; measurements are not affected by physical properties such as hardness or magnetism, and only to a minor or negligible extent by oils used to protect metal surfaces. Compared to wavelength dispersion, the energy-dispersion analyzers using radioisotopic sources of x-rays or gamma rays have the advantages of compactness, reduced maintenance, stability, lower price, and can be used with much lower radiation fluxes.

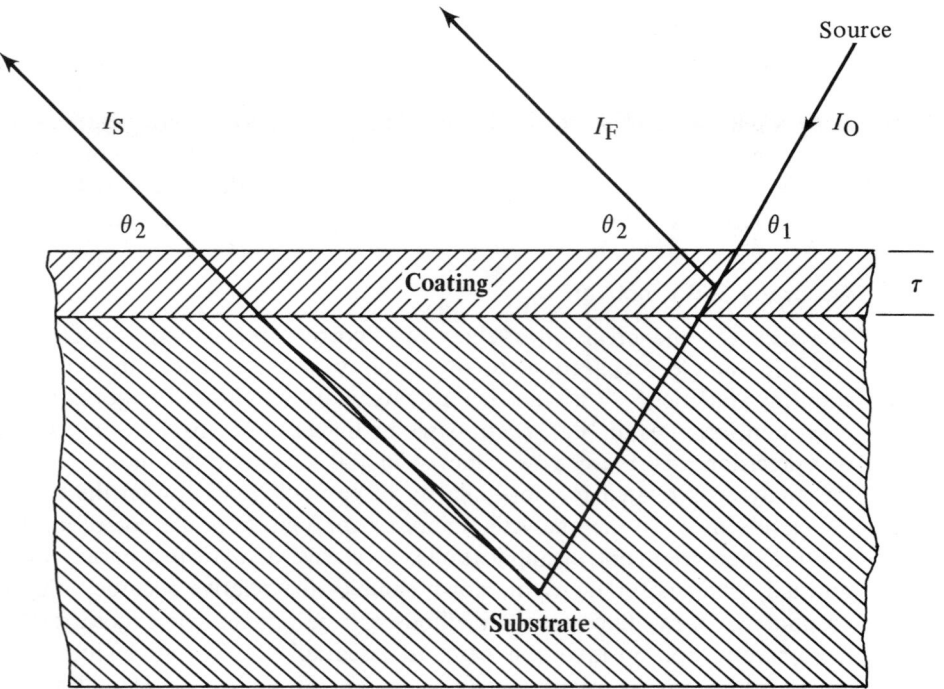

FIGURE 14.12. *Film-thickness measurements using characteristic x-rays emitted by the coating or the substrate.*

A typical "thickness gauge" of this type will measure an area of 40 cm² with a repeatability of 1%. The measurement ranges for tin and zinc gauges using different sources are given in Table 14.5. Errors due to changes in hardness, chemical composition, and thickness are less than 0.3%.

One of the first important applications of x-rays to the measurement of the thickness of coatings was in the control of tin plate on steel, using attenuation of the Fe Kα line. The incident radiation may be either polychromatic or monochromatic (the latter makes isolation of the signal from background easier). However, it is essential that the primary radiation be of sufficient energy to excite the substrate. In the example of tin on steel, x-rays or γ-rays in the 10 to 25 keV range will excite

	Electrolytic Tin	Hot-Dipped Zinc	Electrolytic Zinc
Measurement Range (One Side of Sample)	1–15 g/m²	60–450 g/m²	5–30 g/m²
Approximate Plating Thickness	0.1–2 μm	8–60 μm	0.7–4 μm
Preferred Source and Energy	^{241}Am 17 keV Secondary γ-rays	^{241}Am 60 keV γ-rays	^{241}Am 17 keV Secondary γ-rays

Source: Adapted from J. F. Cameron and C. G. Clayton, *Radioisotope Instruments*, New York: Pergamon Press, 1971, by permission of the publisher.

Fe K lines without exciting the characteristic Sn K lines. Referring to Figure 14.12, the coating thickness τ is related to the intensity I_s from the substrate by

$$\frac{I_s}{I_{s(\tau = 0)}} = e^{-(\mu_1 \, \csc \, \theta_1 + \mu_2 \, \csc \, \theta_2)\tau} \qquad (14.13)$$

where
$I_{s(\tau = 0)}$ = the intensity when coating thickness equals 0

μ_1 = the linear-absorption coefficient (in cm⁻¹) of the coating for the primary radiation

μ_2 = the linear-absorption coefficient of the coating for the secondary radiation

τ = the coating thickness in cm

Example 14.2. Calculate the thickness (τ) in μm of a tin coating ($\rho = 7.3$ g/cm³) deposited uniformly on an iron substrate, using Equation 14.13. Use the following parameters: Cu Kα (1.54 Å) as the monochromatic source; Fe Kα (1.93 Å) as the secondary radiation; $\theta_1 = \theta_2 = 45°$; and the measured value $I_s/I_{s(\tau = 0)} = 0.50$.

Solution: The magnitude of τ will depend on the values of μ_m, the *mass absorption coefficient*, $\mu_m = \mu/\rho$ where ρ is the density of the material. The following values were taken from the *Handbook of Chemistry and Physics*: (1) μ_m for tin = 247 at 1.54 Å; (2) μ_m for tin = 470 at 1.93 Å.

$$\mu_1 = \mu_{(m, \, 1.54 \, Å)}\rho = 247 \, (7.3) = 1800 \text{ cm}^{-1}$$
$$\mu_2 = \mu_{(m, \, 1.93 \, Å)}\rho = 470 \, (7.3) = 3400 \text{ cm}^{-1}$$

Substituting these values, and noting that csc 45° = 1.41:

$$0.50 = e^{-[1800 \, (1.41) + 3400 \, (1.41)]\tau} = e^{-7300\tau}$$
$$-0.69 = -7300\tau$$
$$\tau = 9.4 \times 10^{-5} \text{ cm} = 0.94 \, \mu\text{m}$$

An important point from the problem is that input parameters will vary 2–10 percent or more; therefore, the reliability of the calculated value is related proportionally. The range of thicknesses over which this method can be used is determined primarily by the average value of μ_1 and μ_2. The higher the value of μ, the smaller the range of thicknesses that can be measured. In the case of electroplated tin on steel, the usual range is 0.1–2.5 μm.

Most determinations of coating thickness are based on measurements of characteristic radiation from the coating. The thickness can be considered to fall into one of three regions: linear, exponential, and infinite thickness. In the linear region, absorption of the incident and fluorescent radiation by the very thin coating is negligible; therefore, the intensity is linearly related to the coating thickness. For films of intermediate thickness, the intensity is an exponential function of thickness. As the thickness approaches infinity, the intensity becomes constant.

A typical example of the use of characteristic radiation is measuring the thickness of nickel coatings on steel. The function of the nickel is to provide a thin, but strong, bond between an enamel or porcelain coating and the steel substrate. Current practice in the enamel-coating industry is to cut samples from the sheet and submit them to the x-ray laboratory. With a portable analyzer, however, satisfactory results can be obtained by semiskilled personnel directly on the sheets.

Energy-dispersion x-ray spectroscopy has received considerable attention for the determination of lead on interior walls of houses in the inner cities of the United States (ingestion of lead-bearing paints is a significant health hazard to young children). The highly penetrating Pb K radiation is used for these measurements, since the lower-energy Pb L lines may be absorbed in overlayers of nonlead paints, giving a false negative reading.

Positive-Ion Excitation

The use of highly energetic positive ions for the generation of low- and medium-energy characteristic x-rays from samples is receiving considerable attention for applications in surface-structure analysis and in the environmental sciences. The important features of positive-ion excitation are the high sensitivity for low-atomic-number elements, the small depth of sample analyzed, and the relatively low level of continuous radiation scattered from the sample. Generally, protons in the 100-keV to 5-MeV range are used; however, alpha particles and higher-atomic-number positive ions have some unique advantages.

In surface studies, particularly in the fields of corrosion and thin-film technology, low-energy x-ray spectra generated by 100- to 300-keV protons are used in conjunction with Auger and photoelectron spectroscopy (Chap. 15) to analyze changes in the surface caused by implantation, oxidation, diffusion, etc. Fractions of a monolayer of various elements on the surface can be determined by this new analytical technique. The sampling depth is of the order of 1–5 monolayers using protons for excitation of low-energy x-rays. Depth profiles can be obtained by sputtering successive monolayers and analyzing the new surface. The beam diameter can be reduced to approximately 1 mm if spatial resolution is required.

For trace applications, microgram amounts of sample are supported on a very thin substrate. The detection limits for most elements using a 1.5-MeV proton beam at 5 μA current is of the order of 10^{-9} to 10^{-12} g, the detection limit being a function of the thickness of the support material. Trace applications include examination of water residues, biological specimens, tissue sections, and air particulates.

Electron-Probe Microanalysis

In the early 1940s, Hillier of the Radio Corporation of America conceived the idea of using a focused electron beam for localized x-ray spectroscopic analysis. Several years later, the first practical electron-probe x-ray spectrometer was designed by Castaing at the University of Paris. This microanalyzer proved to be a major break-through, since the instrument made possible the nondestructive analysis of micrometer-sized volumes.

In *electron-probe x-ray spectroscopy* (EPXS), an electron beam of moderate energy, 10 to 50 keV, is focused on the sample at the location where elemental com-position is to be determined. The atoms in a minute volume, one-half to several μm in diameter and one or more μm in depth, are excited by the incident electrons and, upon returning to the ground state, emit x-rays characteristic of the excited elements. The actual volume of sample analyzed depends on such variables as the diameter and energy of the electron beam, the diffusion of electrons in the sample, and the path length of the scattered primary and secondary x-rays.

Until the late 1960s, commercial EPXS instruments consisted of four major components: an electron-optical system for producing a stable electron beam of $1\text{-}\mu m$ (or smaller) diameter, light optics for viewing the microscopic area under investiga-tion, a precision stage for accurately locating and translating the sample under the electron beam, and one or more focusing x-ray spectrometers for measuring the characteristic x-rays (see Fig. 14.13). More recently, EPXS has been superseded by *scanning electron microscopy* (SEM). In the scanning electron microscope, the sample image is obtained by either backscattered or transmitted electrons, and the elemental composition is determined by energy-dispersion x-ray methods.

Quantitative analysis is accomplished by the use of standards similar in com-position to the sample being analyzed, or by using pure elements as standards and applying theoretical and semiempirical corrections for differences in absorption, secondary fluorescence, and atomic number. The mathematical methods using pure-element standards have received the greatest attention because of the difficulty in obtaining multi-element standards that are homogeneous on a submicrometer scale. Computer programs are available for performing the complex corrections. Since the development of SEM, it has been realized that qualitative or semiquantitative analysis is adequate for many practical applications. Therefore, pictorial displays of concentration across the sample surface, obtained by sweeping the electron beam across the sample, are generally adequate, as contrasted to the older technique of point-by-point analysis.

For most elements, the sensitivity of the EPXS method is approximately 0.01–0.1 weight-percent with a relative accuracy of 1–5 percent, depending on the correction procedure, the availability of suitable standards, and the reliability of the parameters used in the calculations. Elements from boron, atomic number 5, to all higher-atomic-number elements can be determined. Although the EPXS method is not applicable to trace elements in a homogeneous sample, its absolute detection limit—10^{-12} to 10^{-14} g—is very impressive.

The EPXS or modified SEM methods have been applied extensively to virtually all fields of science. Applications include the qualitative identification of the com-position of small inclusions, determination of diffusion rates of elements in solids,

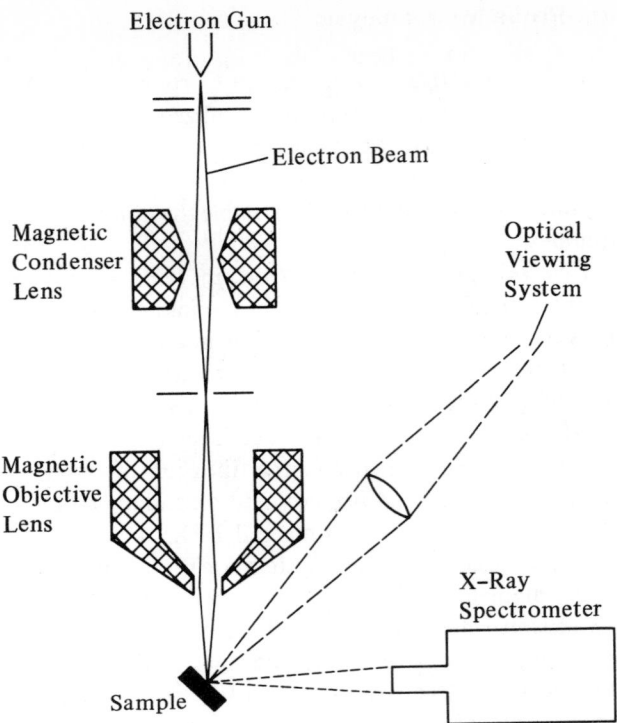

FIGURE 14.13. *Electron optics for the excitation of x-rays in a micro-meter-sized volume.*

phase-equilibria studies, the determination of the thickness and uniformity of films, and the qualitative and quantitative analysis of minute samples such as airborne particulates. Specific applications include the study of the metallic phases in meteorites, the depletion of uranium in the grain boundaries of iron alloys, the diffusion of chromium during oxidation of steels, and inorganic inclusions in oil shale.

Essentially all types of samples can be analyzed by this technique. Ideally, samples should be good electrical conductors to avoid charge buildup; however, a very thin conducting film, for example gold or carbon, can be deposited on non-conductors such as ceramics, glasses, and biological samples.

X-Ray Absorption Spectroscopy

The intensity of an x-ray beam is attenuated (decreased) during passage through matter by a dual process—*photoelectric absorption* and *x-ray scattering*. The amount of attenuation can serve as the basis of quantitative analysis in specific cases. In photoelectric absorption, virtually all of the energy of the incident x-ray quantum is converted into the kinetic energy of the photoelectron ejected; this is the process that results in the emission of characteristic (fluorescence) x-rays. The extent of attenuation is governed by the linear-absorption coefficient μ, which is similar to *absorptivity* in molecular absorption (Beer's law). For a given element, this is equal to the sum of the photoelectric-absorption coefficient τ and the scattering coefficient σ.

Photoelectric absorption predominates, except for low values of Z and high values of λ. By application of Beer's law, x-ray transmittance (P/P_0) can be used to determine either composition or thickness:

$$\frac{P}{P_0} = e^{-\mu_m \rho b} \qquad \text{(14.14)}$$

where μ_m = the mass absorption coefficient
            ρ = the density of the sample in g/cm³
            b = the thickness in cm

Values for the mass-absorption coefficient, which is equal to μ/ρ, are listed in standard reference tables. As a first approximation, μ_m is proportional to $Z^4 \lambda^3$ up to the K or L absorption edge; thus, the absorption coefficient is dependent on both the element composition and the wavelength of the x-ray (see Fig. 14.14). As mentioned before, there can be one K-absorption edge, three L edges, and five M edges.

FIGURE 14.14. *Relationship of the mass-absorption coefficient to wavelength.*

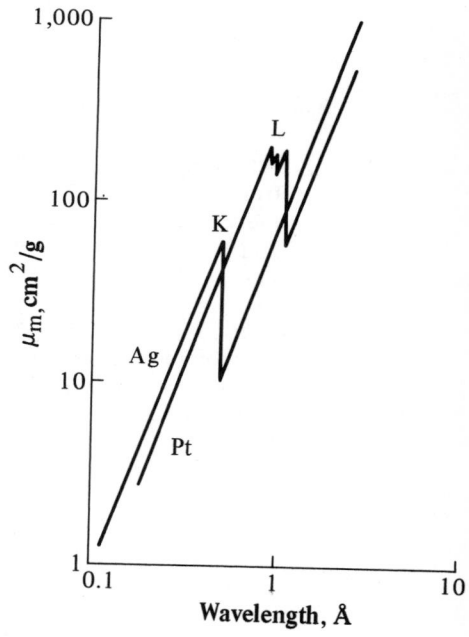

X-ray absorption measurements have been utilized for two types of analytical applications. The principal application has been for process monitoring in which the sample composition is essentially constant except for a variable amount of the element of interest. Examples are tetraethyl lead in gasoline or sulfur in fuel oil, where intense continuous radiation provides adequate signal for instantaneous process control. This approach, using a polychromatic source, has essentially no specificity, so that the sample parameters are very limited. Unknown samples can be analyzed by measurement of two monochromatic x-ray line intensities, one on each side of a characteristic absorption edge of the element being determined. This absorption-edge technique is then specific for the element being determined.

Quantitative calculations when there is more than one absorber are based on the additive absorption of different elements. The mass-absorption coefficient of a sample containing different elements is given by an equation similar to Equation 14.10.

$$\mu_{m(s)} = \sum_{i=1}^{j} \mu_{m(i)} W_i \qquad (14.15)$$

where $\mu_{m(i)}$ = the mass-absorption coefficients (in cm^2/g) of the individual elements $m(i)$ at the given wavelength
    W_i = the weight fractions of the elements

Strictly speaking, this equation holds only for monochromatic light. The sensitivity for a given element depends markedly on the sample composition. Very small concentrations of elements with large mass-absorption coefficients can be determined in samples where the bulk matrix has a low mass-absorption coefficient. Thus, for example, 10^{-10} g of phosphorus can be determined in biological tissues. Classical examples of quantitative x-ray absorption analysis are the determination of lead tetraethyl in gasoline and sulfur in petroleum.

> *Example 14.3.*   A 3.00-ml gasoline sample is placed in a cell of 0.250-cm thickness. The sample, which contains a small amount of lead tetraethyl in *n*-octane and has a density of 0.720 g/cm^3, absorbs 75.0% of the Cu Kα line from an x-ray source. If the mass-absorption coefficients ($\mu_m = \mu/\rho$) for the Cu Kα line for lead, carbon, and hydrogen are 230 cm^2/g, 4.52 cm^2/g, and 0.48 cm^2/g, respectively, what is the percent of lead tetraethyl in the sample?

Solution: We must first calculate the mass-absorption coefficients for the two compounds present and then for the sample. Then we can calculate the weight fraction of lead tetraethyl. The formula weight of lead tetraethyl, $Pb(CH_2CH_3)_4$, is 323.4, so

$$W_{Pb} = \frac{207.2}{323.4} = 0.6407$$

$$W_C = \frac{8(12.011)}{323.4} = 0.2971$$

$$W_H = \frac{20(1.0080)}{323.4} = 0.06234$$

Therefore, for lead tetraethyl

$$\mu_{m(LTE)} = 230(0.641) + 4.52(0.297) + 0.48(0.062)$$
$$= 149 \ cm^2/g.$$

The formula weight of *n*-octane, $CH_3(CH_2)_6CH_3$, is 114.23, so

$$W_C = \frac{8(12.011)}{114.23} = 0.8412$$

$$W_H = \frac{18(1.0080)}{114.23} = 0.1588$$

Therefore, for octane,

$$\mu_{m(o)} = 4.52(0.841) + 0.48(0.159) = 3.88 \text{ cm}^2/\text{g}.$$

We can calculate the mass-absorption coefficient for the sample, $\mu_{m(S)}$, from Equation 14.14,

$$\log \frac{100}{25.0} = \frac{\mu_{m(S)}(0.720)(0.250)}{2.303}$$

$$\mu_{m(S)} = 7.70 \text{ cm}^2/\text{g}.$$

Let W be the weight fraction of lead tetraethyl in the sample. Therefore,

$$\mu_{m(S)} = \mu_{m(LTE)}W + \mu_{m(o)}(1 - W)$$
$$7.70 = 149W + 3.88(1 - W)$$
$$W = 0.0264 \text{ wt. fraction of tetraethyl.}$$

Therefore, the sample contains 2.64% lead tetraethyl.

Mass-absorption coefficients at different wavelengths for the various elements are available in various handbooks such as those in the bibliography at the end of this chapter. As in conventional spectrophotometry (Chap. 7), the optimum absorbance range for x-ray absorption analysis is about 0.1 to 1.

Although specific examples like those mentioned above are well suited for x-ray absorption analysis, with good selectivity using the absorption-edge technique, in general the method does not offer significant advantages over x-ray fluorescence analysis. Since the latter technique is easier to apply, it is more widely used.

X-Ray Emission Spectroscopy

In this technique, the sample to be studied is the target of an electron beam in an x-ray tube; x-rays are emitted by the sample and are measured. Metals and alloys can be studied in this way. Measurements are generally restricted to qualitative or, at best, semiquantitative determinations. Selective volatilization of different elements by the impinging electron beam make quantitative analysis difficult.

X-Ray Powder Diffraction Analysis

Although x-ray diffraction by single crystals is a useful technique for determining crystal structure, a more useful analytical technique is *powder* diffraction; the sample crystals are ground to a powder, after which the diffraction pattern can readily be used to identify unknown substances, based on tables of known diffraction patterns.

The powdered sample (200–300 mesh) in the form of a cylinder is placed in the path of a narrow beam of essentially monochromatic x-rays. The diffraction pattern is recorded on a photographic film at right angles to the incident beam. The powder contains fine, randomly oriented crystals. Hence, the requirements of Equation 14.7 (the proper θ) are fulfilled by many of these crystal orientations. The random orientation results in a circular cone of diffracted beam for a given reflecting plane with the incident beam as the axis. Since there are planes at different angles in the crystal, several different cones are observed. The film strip is too narrow to

FIGURE 14.15. *Typical x-ray powder diffraction pattern. The numbers represent opposite arcs of the same cone. A: The instrumental arrangement. B: The developed film strip. The radius of the film is r; the S's are the distances between the arcs of a given cone.*

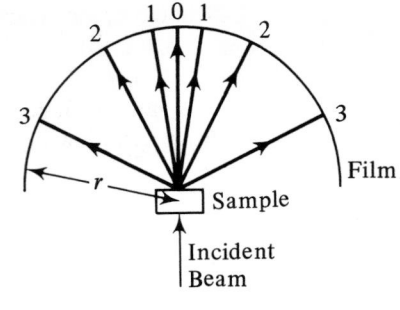

A

B

record the entire circle of the cone impinging upon it, so the developed film contains curved lines marking the intersection of the various cones with the film (see Fig. 14.15).

The film strip is placed circularly (either half or full circle) around the sample, which is at the origin. For this geometry,

$$4\theta = \frac{S}{r} \qquad (14.16)$$

where r = the radius of the film
S = the distance between the two recorded arcs of a given cone of diffracted x-rays
θ = the angle of diffraction in radians

Converting from radians to degrees (1 radian = 57.296 degrees),

$$4\theta = \frac{S}{r}(57.296) \qquad (14.17)$$

If r is set as a multiple or fraction of 57.296, measurement of θ becomes simple. For example, camera diameters are often set at 57.296 mm, so

$$S = 2\theta \qquad (14.18)$$

where S is in millimeters.

Diffraction patterns are usually identified from the three most intense lines by comparing the distances between lines and their relative intensities with standard catalogued spectra.

Example 14.4. Using a camera with a diameter of 57.296 mm and a Cu Kα 1.54-Å (first-order) source, diffraction lines are observed with the following distances between their arcs: 28.66 mm, 52.20 mm, and 82.08 mm. Comparing with the x-ray data in tables listed in the bibliography, what is the probable compound?

Solution: From Equation 14.18, we calculate

$$\theta_1 = \frac{28.66}{2} = 14.33°$$

$$\theta_2 = \frac{52.20}{2} = 26.10°$$

$$\theta_3 = \frac{82.08}{2} = 42.04°$$

Therefore, from Equation 14.7,

$$d_1 = \frac{1.54}{2 \sin (14.33)} = 3.04 \text{ Å}$$

$$d_2 = \frac{1.54}{2 \sin (26.10)} = 1.75 \text{ Å}$$

$$d_3 = \frac{1.54}{2 \sin (42.04)} = 1.15 \text{ Å}$$

From comparison of measured and tabulated *d*-values, the substance is probably cesium bromide.

Cameras are calibrated by running the spectrum of a substance (such as sodium chloride) with accurately known *d*-values. A commonly used x-ray source is the Cu Kα doublet at 1.54 Å with the Kβ line filtered out by a nickel foil. Some elements exhibit x-ray fluorescence upon irradiation by the Cu Kα line, which causes fogging of the film, so another target of longer wavelength is chosen for the x-ray source. Although resolution increases with wavelength, lines of x-rays longer than 2–3 Å tend to be scattered by air and lose their sharpness. It should be remembered that the angles 2θ are dependent upon the wavelength of the diffracted radiation. The absorption paths, and consequently the relative intensities, also vary with the wavelength of the source. The tabulated *d*-values are within 0.001 Å for *d* of 1 Å or less, but may vary by 0.01–0.05 Å for *d* up to 8 Å.

The cylindrical sample is kept as small as possible to minimize the absorption of diffracted radiation. The optimum thickness is $1/\mu_m\rho$, where ρ is the sample density. Cylinders are generally kept at 0.5-mm or less diameter. When dilution is necessary, an amorphous substance such as flour is used as the diluent. It is best that the cylindrical sample not be in a container, but in many cases this is not possible. Satisfactory container materials include lithium borate ("Lindemann" glass) or various plastics because of their low mass-absorption coefficients; the container is a tube with a wall-thickness of about 0.01-mm.

Although quantitative measurements can be made, x-ray powder diffraction is used primarily as a qualitative tool to obtain information about the actual compounds appearing in a sample. Selectivity and sensitivity will depend on the composition of the sample; identification of minor components will be rather limited because of the overlap of their diffraction patterns with weak lines of the various major constituents.

It is more convenient nowadays to use a direct-recording x-ray diffraction spectrometer for powder-diffraction measurements than to use film detection. The detector (for instance, a scintillation counter) is placed on a goniometer and slowly rotated about the sample. The intensity of diffracted radiation is recorded on chart paper as a function of the angle of rotation; the resultant spectrum is a series of peaks at different angles. These and their relative intensities are correlated with the tabulated *d*-values.

SELECTED BIBLIOGRAPHY

Books

Advances in X-Ray Analysis, Proceedings of the Annual Conference on Applications of X-Ray Analysis, University of Denver, vols. 1–16. New York: Plenum Press, 1958–1973.

BERTIN, E. P. *Principles and Practices of X-Ray Spectrometric Analysis.* New York: Plenum Press, 1970.

BIRKS, L. S. *Electron Probe Microanalysis.* New York: Interscience, 1963.

JENKINS, R., and DEVRIES, J. L. *Practical X-Ray Spectrometry.* Phillips Technical Library, New York: Springer-Verlag, 1967.

JENKINS, R. *An Introduction to X-Ray Spectrometry.* New York: Heyden, 1974.

JENKINS, R. H., and DEVRIES, B. *Worked Examples in X-Ray Spectrometry.* New York: Springer-Verlag, 1970. *An excellent set of problems for students.*

LIEBHAFSKY, H. A.; PFEIFFER, H. G.; WINSLOW, E. H.; and ZEMANY, P. D. *X-Rays, Electrons, and Analytical Chemistry.* New York: Wiley-Interscience, 1972.

Tables of Wavelengths, 2θ Angles, Photon Energies, and Mass-Absorption Coefficients

BEARDEN, J. A. *X-Ray Wavelengths.* U.S. Atomic Energy Commission Report, N.Y.O. 10586, 1964.

FINE, S., and HENDEE, C. F. "A Table of X-Ray K and L Emission and Critical-Absorption Energies for All the Elements." *Nucleonics, 13*(3), 36 (1955).

STAINER, H. M. *X-Ray Absorption Coefficients: A Literature Survey.* Bureau of Mines Information Circular 8166, 1963.

WHITE, E. W.; GIBBS, G. V.; JOHNSON, G. G., Jr., and ZECHMAN, G. A., Jr. *X-Ray Emission Line Wavelength and Two-Theta Tables.* ASTM Series 37. Philadelphia: American Society for Testing and Materials, 1965.

SWITZER, G.; AXELROD, J. M.; LINDBERG, M. L.; and LARSEN, E. S. *Tables of Spacing for Angle 2θ, Cu K_α, Cu K_{α_1}, Cu K_{α_2}, Fe K_α, Fe K_{α_1}, Fe K_{α_2}.* Circular 29, Geological Survey, Washington, D.C.: U.S. Department of the Interior, 1948.

Sources of Standards

Catalog of Standard Reference Materials. Special Publication 260. Washington, D.C.: National Bureau of Standards, 1975.

Standard Reference Materials and Meaningful Measurements. 6th Materials Research Symposium, National Bureau of Standards, Washington, D.C.

Report on Available Standard Samples and Related Materials for Spectrochemical Analysis. Special Technical Publication 58-D. Philadelphia: American Society for Testing and Materials, 1960.

PROBLEMS

1. You have been asked to determine low concentrations of tantalum and niobium in an ore concentrate in which the tantalum-to-niobium ratio is 1:50. Discuss methods to achieve maximum fluorescence signal from tantalum with minimum interference from niobium.

2. Using wavelength dispersion, which detector would you use for the x-ray fluorescence measure of Si $K\alpha$, U $M\alpha$, Cu $K\alpha$, and I $K\alpha$?

3. For the determination of 1–10 weight-percent lead in an ore concentrate, what elements and characteristic lines can be used as internal standards for x-ray fluorescence?

4. An analytical laboratory was requested to determine potassium (present as KCl) in a silica matrix. Suggest some possible approaches to the problem.

5. Discuss methods for determining the thickness of a zinc coating on a iron substrate; include discussion on the preparation of standards and on calibration.

6. Outline a method for calculating the energies of the Kα and Lα lines of plutonium ($Z = 94$).

7. Discuss methods for extending the limits of detectability of x-ray fluorescence spectroscopy down to the ppm–ppb range. Also include comments regarding possible sources of systematic errors.

8. Describe the operation of a Coolidge tube.

9. What is an absorption edge?

10. Describe the principles of x-ray emission, x-ray absorption, and x-ray fluorescence analysis. Distinguish between each technique with respect to instrumentation requirements.

11. A powder-diffraction x-ray spectrometer uses a Cu $K\alpha$ x-ray source (1.54 Å, first-order). The spectrum of an unknown pure substance gives three intense peaks at the following 2θ values: 25.70°, 40.50°, and 31.38°. The relative intensities of the three peaks are 100:40:35, respectively. What is the probable substance?

12. An analyst, using an x-ray fluorescence spectrometer with a molybdenum target source and a sodium-chloride analyzer crystal, wishes to determine nickel in a meteorite sample. At what 2θ value would he look for the nickel peak?

13. A powdered ammonium thiosulfate sample was given to a student as an unknown. The diffraction pattern was obtained using a camera with a radius of 57.3 mm and using a cobalt x-ray source with an iron filter. What would be the distances between corresponding arcs of the three strongest lines?

14. Using a tungsten x-ray tube and a LiF analyzing crystal ($d = 2.01$ Å), a very strong x-ray fluorescence peak for a pure but unknown metal was observed at $2\theta = 69.36°$. Calculate the wavelength of the fluorescence radiation and identify the metal.

15. An x-ray tube with a copper target is operated at 50 kV. What will be the cutoff wavelength for the continuous radiation?

16. Calculate the transmittance of a monochromatic x-ray beam from a copper target (Kα line) passing through a 1 cm³ sample of carbon tetrachloride in benzene (1% by weight) contained in a cell with a cross-sectional area of 9.80 cm². The density of the solution is 0.880 g/cm³.

15

Electron Spectroscopy

Lo I Yin
Isidore Adler

In recent years there has been a rapid development of instrumental techniques; one of the fastest growing areas is that of electron spectroscopy. This is a technique for studying the energy distribution of electrons ejected from a material that has been irradiated with a source of ionizing radiation such as x-rays, ultraviolet light, or electrons.

It is convenient to distinguish among the various electron spectroscopies on the basis of the excitation sources used. When x-ray radiation is employed, the technique is commonly called ESCA [1] (for *electron spectroscopy* for *chemical analysis*); it is also sometimes called *x-ray photoelectron spectroscopy* (XPS). When ultraviolet excitation is used, the method is generally called *photoelectron spectroscopy* (PES) or *ultraviolet photoelectron spectroscopy* (UPS). A third variation, in which electrons are generally used as the ionizing radiation, is commonly referred to as *Auger spectroscopy*.

Of the three types of electron spectroscopy, ESCA has perhaps been the most widely used for chemical studies. For this reason, this chapter will concentrate most heavily on ESCA. Although simple quantitative chemical analysis can be performed by ESCA, this probably represents the least effective use of this powerful tool, which provides quantitative information about such basic parameters as binding energies, charges, valence states, etc., which involve the atom as a function of its chemical environment.

We thank S. O. Grim, Professor of Chemistry at the University of Maryland, for many helpful discussions.

A unique quality of ESCA is that it permits direct probing of the valence and core electrons, where much chemical information is contained. This is achieved mainly through the photoelectric process: when any material is bombarded by photons with energy greater than the binding energy of an electron in a given atomic shell or subshell, there is a finite probability that the incident photon will be absorbed by the atom and an atomic electron either promoted to an unoccupied level or ejected as a photoelectron. Figure 15.1 illustrates schematically the process of photoelectron production by absorption of a photon. The probability of photoelectric absorption

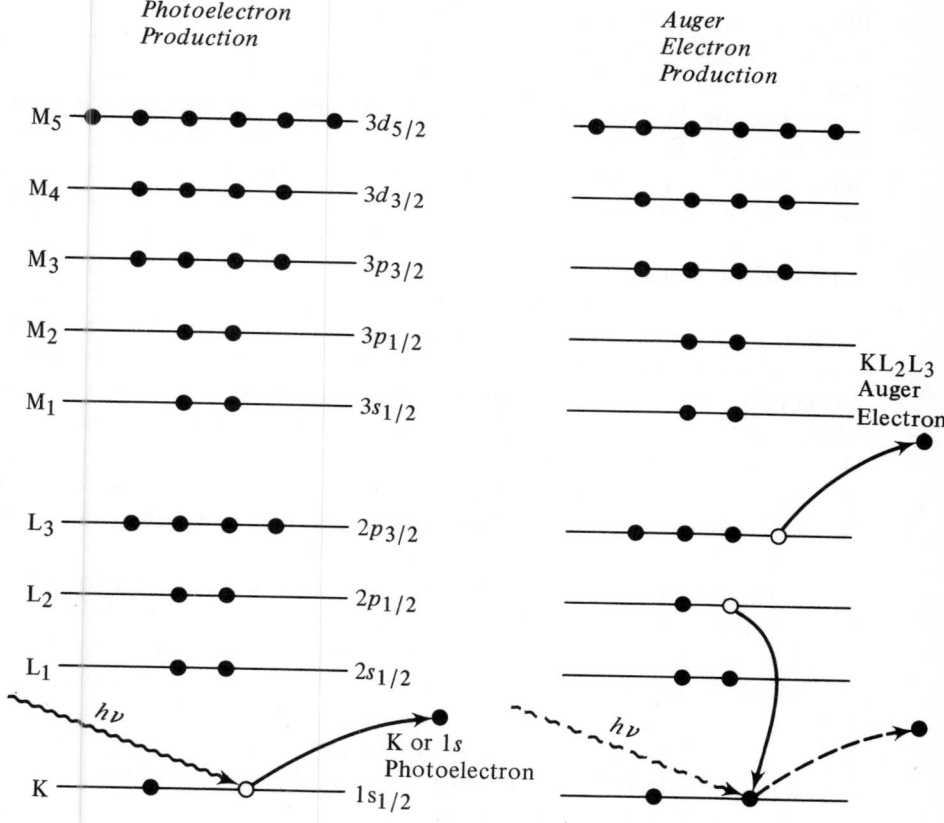

FIGURE 15.1. *Schematic diagram illustrating the production of primary photoelectrons and Auger (secondary) electrons in an atom. In primary-photoelectron production, an atom absorbs an x-ray photon that causes the ejection of a core electron (in this case, a K-shell electron). An Auger electron is produced when, after the primary photoelectron has been ejected from the inner shell (indicated by the dotted lines), an electron from a higher shell (in this case, from the L shell) fills the orbital vacancy. The excess energy, instead of being emitted as a secondary x-ray, is simultaneously transferred to another electron (the Auger electron) which is ejected from the atom; in this case the Auger electron is also from the L shell.*

depends on the energy of the incident photon and the atomic number of the element being irradiated.

The kinetic energy of the photoelectron is, to a first approximation (ignoring solid-state and relaxation effects), given by

$$E_p = h\nu - E_b \tag{15.1}$$

where E_p = the kinetic energy of the photoelectron
$h\nu$ = the energy of the incident photon
E_b = the binding energy of the electron in its particular shell

It is clear from Equation 15.1 that, if the incident photons are "monoenergetic," the photoelectrons ejected from a given shell will also be monoenergetic. Thus, at a given energy of the incident photons, the photoelectron spectrum of a material reflects the various occupied electronic levels and bands in the material.

Because the energies of the various electronic levels are usually different among different materials, photoelectron spectra are characteristic of the material. It is important to emphasize that the photoelectrons possess characteristic energies as they leave the atom, but that only a relatively small fraction of the electrons emerge from the target material with their energies undisturbed, since energy is lost by a variety of mechanisms.

Figure 15.2 illustrates the excitation of a solid sample by x-ray photons. Although the x-rays may penetrate deeply into the sample to produce photoelectrons, most of these electrons lose energy in numerous inelastic collisions; only those atoms residing in the top few monolayers give rise to undistorted photoelectron spectra. Thus, a typical spectrum resulting from a group of initially monoenergetic photo-electrons will consist of a single peak due to the "undisturbed" electrons (i.e., those that are directly ejected), plus a large continuum on the low-kinetic-energy side of the peak. Since the typical escape depth in ESCA and Auger spectroscopy is only about 3–50 Å, these are truly techniques for surface analysis.

The electron continuum, however, does not begin at the photoelectron peak but rather at a discrete distance away from the peak. This is because an electron emerging from a solid loses its kinetic energy in quantized amounts by exciting plasma oscillations (plasmons). For example, Figure 15.3A shows a wide-range scan (170–1480 eV) of a germanium sample. The x-axis is the kinetic energy of the electrons (E_p). For the purpose of display, the electron counts (intensity) are compressed into a logarithmic scale on the y-axis. We see the photoelectrons from the various L and M shells as well as the LMM Auger-electron lines.* We also note a small, broad shoulder at the same distance (~ 17 eV) from the low-energy side of each peak. This is the plasma-loss peak, which is common to all electrons (whether photo-electrons or Auger electrons) emerging from the solid sample. In Figure 15.3B, two of the more prominent electron lines are shown in detail, with electron intensity displayed linearly on the y-axis. In this case, the plasma-loss peaks are situated far enough from the main peak to allow the precise positions of the various electron

---

* An LMM Auger electron is one emitted by the following mechanism: A vacancy, initially created in the *L shell* by the photoejection of an electron, is filled by the fall of an M-shell electron, accompanied by the ejection of another *M-shell* electron from the atom. The second M-shell electron is the LMM Auger electron.

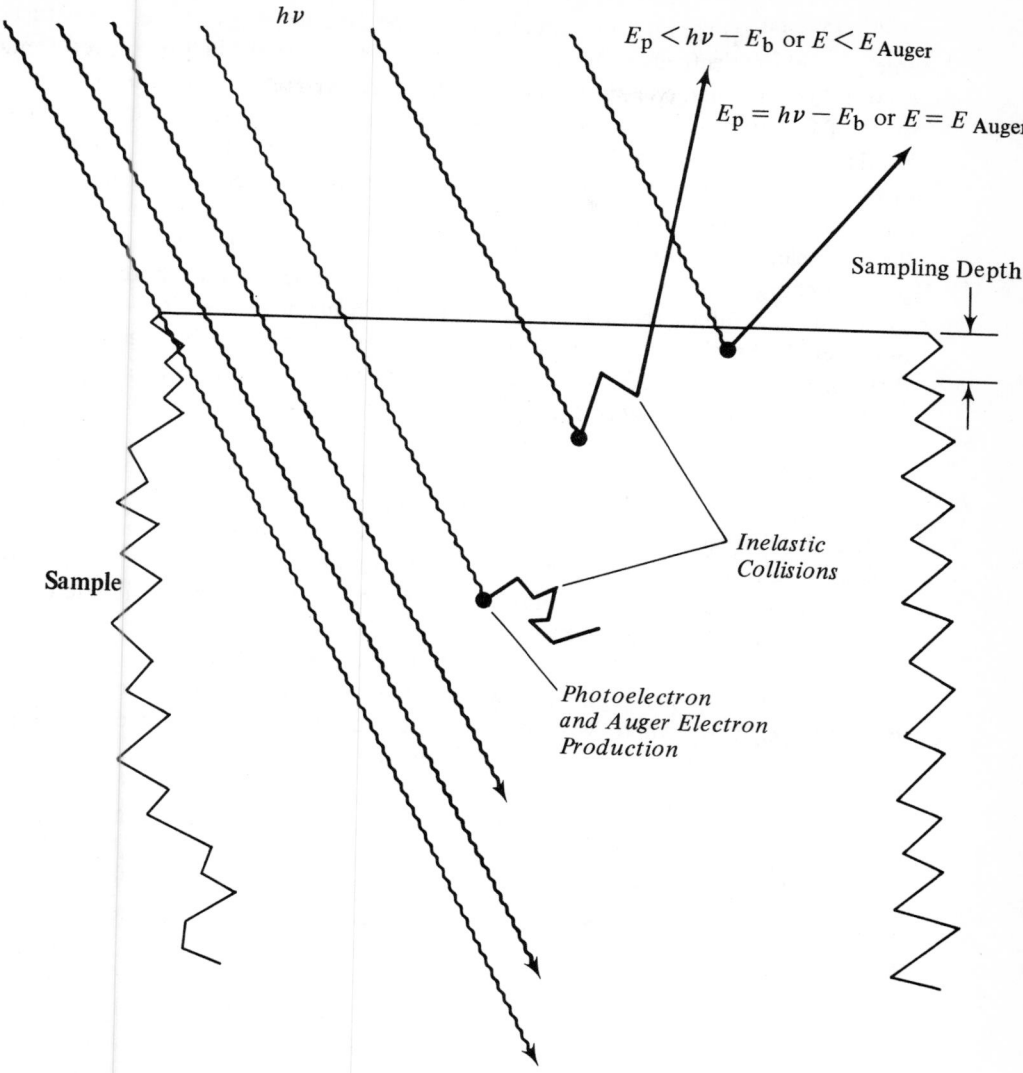

$h\nu$

$E_p < h\nu - E_b$ or $E < E_{\text{Auger}}$

$E_p = h\nu - E_b$ or $E = E_{\text{Auger}}$

Sampling Depth

Inelastic Collisions

Photoelectron and Auger Electron Production

Sample

FIGURE 15.2. *Production and escape characteristics of photoelectrons and Auger electrons in a solid sample. Because most electrons lose energy by inelastic collisions, the effective sampling depth is about 3–50 Å. E_p is the kinetic energy of the ejected photoelectron and E_b is its binding energy; $h\nu$ is the (monoenergetic) energy of the incident x-ray photon. In the case of Auger electrons, E_{Auger} is its original kinetic energy and E is that seen by the spectrometer.*

lines to be identified unambiguously. However, plasma-loss peaks can occasionally cause confusion in the identification of fine structure associated with some electron lines.

Because the positions of photoelectron lines can be precisely determined from these spectra, and the photoelectron energies are characteristic of the atomic levels of a given element, these energies can be used as the basis for elemental identification.

On closer examination, one finds that the kinetic energy of the "undisturbed" emerging photoelectrons is not entirely constant for a given shell in a given element, even for a monoenergetic photon source: there are variations as the chemical environment of the atom changes. As the outer electrons participate in forming chemical bonds, the net charge on the atom changes, which in turn affects the binding energy of the core electrons. For example, in electropositive elements (such as metals), the outer-shell electrons move away from the nucleus as bonds are formed, after which the core electrons become more strongly bound because the atom now has a net positive charge. As a consequence, the kinetic energies of the photoelectrons shift toward lower values relative to the uncombined element (see Eqn. 15.1). On the other hand, the electronegative elements show a net increase in negative charge as they form chemical bonds, so the ejected photoelectrons emerge with higher kinetic energies, reflecting the decreased binding energies the core electrons have to overcome to escape.

This is a highly simplified picture of the effects of chemical bonding on photoelectron spectra. There are a variety of other factors that affect the binding energy of the electron and the kinetic energy of the ejected photoelectron: for example, relaxation effects, stereochemistry, crystal structure, and lattice energy, to name a few. The electron senses the total of all these effects; their proportionate contributions are very difficult to assign.

An excellent discussion of the various factors involved in binding energies is given in a recent paper [2] dealing with a series of metal-dithiene compounds of the type $[M(S_2C_2R_2)_n]^z$ where M is one of a large variety of transition metals; n is generally 2 or 3; R is one of a variety of substituents such as CN, C_6H_5, CH_3; and z is 0, -1 or -2. The problem presented by these compounds is the possible oxidation states of the metal necessary to satisfy stoichiometrically the possible charges of the complex. For instance, the nickel species in both $[(C_2H_5)_4N]_2\{Ni[S_2C_2(CN)_2]_2\}$ and $[(C_2H_5)_4N]\{Ni[S_2C_2(CN)_2]_2\}$ have identical ligands, have square-planar geometry, and are diamagnetic. Tests using ESCA showed that the binding energies of the Ni electrons were identical in both. By contrast, the binding energies of the sulfur ($2p$) electrons decreased as the negative charge on the complex increased. This evidence shows clearly that the "oxidation state" of the Ni remains relatively constant and that the increased negative charge of the complex mainly resides on the anionic ligands, specifically on the sulfur atoms. Some investigators use such observations to deduce the chemical environment around an atom, whereas others use theoretical calculations to predict the binding energies.

Resolution

The resolving power needed for ESCA is defined more by binding-energy shifts caused by chemical changes than by overlaps between the binding-energy values of

---

FIGURE 15.3. *A: Al-K$\alpha_{1,2}$ x-ray excited electron spectrum of germanium. Photoelectron peaks from various atomic shells are labelled "photo." Note the presence of a plasma-loss shoulder, indicated by an arrow, about 17 eV on the low-energy side of each prominent electron line. B: Expanded display of the Auger portion of the germanium spectrum showing plasma-loss ("plasmon") peaks adjacent to the main peaks.*

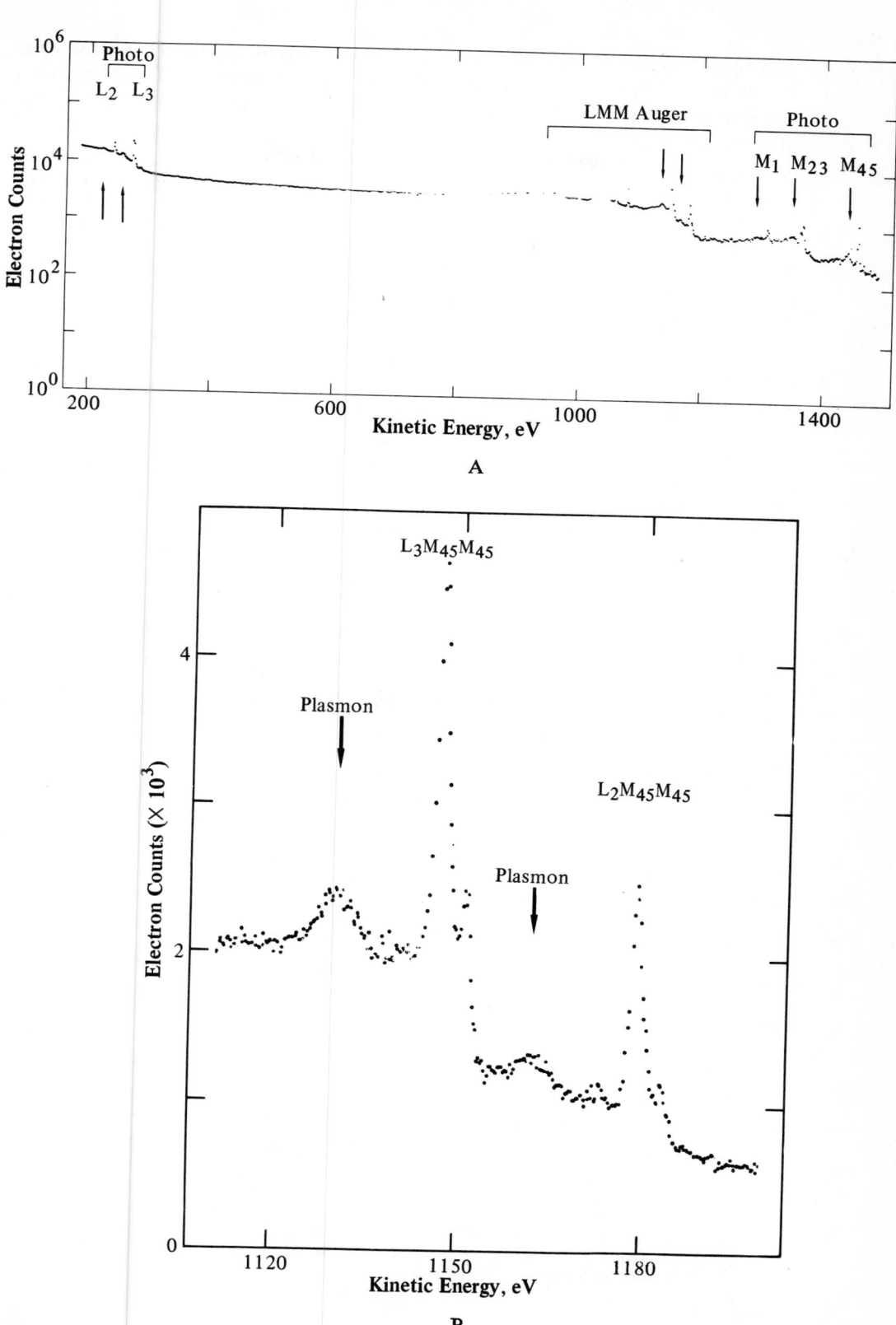

A

B

elements.   For a normal range of chemical phenomena, the binding energy for a particular photoelectron can change by about 0.1–10 eV, whereas the energy separation between corresponding electrons of different elements is considerably greater, 50–100 eV.   (The binding energies of $1s$ electrons in boron and carbon atoms, for instance, differ by 96 eV [see Table 15.1].)   There is some energy overlap between electrons in *different* orbitals of different elements—the scandium $2p$ electrons at 407 and

TABLE 15.1.   *Selected ESCA Binding Energies*

Atomic No.	Element	Binding Energy, E_b (eV)	Type of Electron
3	Li	55	$1s$
4	Be	111	
5	B	188	
6	C	284	
7	N	399	
8	O	532	
9	F	686	
10	Ne	867	$1s$
11	Na	1072; 63	$1s, 2s$
12	Mg	89	$2s$
13	Al	74; 73	$2p_{1/2}, 2p_{3/2}$
14	Si	100; 99	
15	P	136; 135	
16	S	165; 164	
17	Cl	202; 200	
19	K	297; 294	
20	Ca	350; 347	
21	Sc	407; 402	
22	Ti	461; 455	
23	V	520; 513	
24	Cr	584; 575	
25	Mn	652; 641	
26	Fe	723; 710	
27	Co	794; 779	
28	Ni	872; 855	
29	Cu	951; 931	
30	Zn	1044; 1021	$2p_{1/2}, 2p_{3/2}$
32	Ge	129; 122	$3p_{1/2}, 3p_{3/2}$
47	Ag	373; 367	$3d_{3/2}, 3d_{5/2}$
78	Pt	74; 70	$4f_{5/2}, 4f_{7/2}$
79	Au	87; 83	$4f_{5/2}, 4f_{7/2}$

Source: These values are taken from Appendix 1 of K. Siegbahn, C. Nordling, A. Fahlman, R. Nordberg, K. Hamrin, J. Hedman, G. Johansson, T. Bergmark, S. Karlsson, I. Lindgren, and B. Lindberg, *ESCA: Atomic, Molecular, and Solid-State Structure Studied by Means of Electron Spectroscopy*, Uppsala: Almquist and Wiksells, 1967, by permission of the senior authors.

402 eV are very close in energy to the nitrogen $1s$ electron at 399 eV—but these over-laps are not usually significant. The chemical changes, being relatively small (<10 eV) compared to the usual kinetic energies of photoelectrons (500–1500 eV), require resolutions of up to about $\pm 0.01\%$ for adequate measurements. These requirements will be discussed in more detail in the section on instrumentation.

Auger Spectra

The nature of atomic-deactivation processes is such that photoelectrons are accom-panied by x-ray emission or by Auger electron emission. For the lighter elements and for the outer atomic shells of the medium and heavy elements, Auger-electron emission is the predominant mode by which an atom deactivates. Moreover, when using high-energy electrons rather than x-rays to bombard a sample, Auger-electron emission predominates.

When a vacancy is produced in an inner shell by photoelectron ejection, the filling of this vacancy by an electron from a higher-energy shell is either followed by the emission of a fluorescence x-ray photon or by the simultaneous ejection of another outer-shell electron—the Auger or secondary electron (Fig. 15.1). Like the fluores-cence x-rays, these electrons have characteristic energies for each atomic shell and each element. However, the Auger spectrum is generally more complex than the x-ray spectrum. For instance, two prominent x-ray peaks, $L\alpha$ and $L\beta$, are observed with initial vacancies in the $L_3(2p_{3/2})$ and $L_2(2p_{1/2})$ shells of copper ($L\iota$ and $L\eta$ are extremely weak). In contrast, Figure 15.4 shows the corresponding Auger spectrum of Cu with vacancies in the L_2 and L_3 shells. There are many more groups of prom-inent peaks, as well as fine structures in the peaks themselves. Most of these Auger

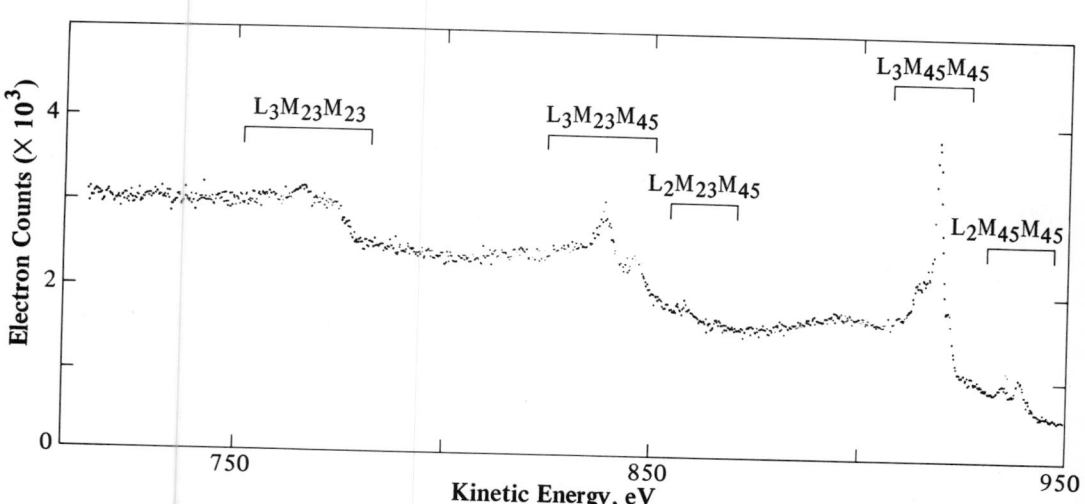

FIGURE 15.4. *Detailed $L_{2,3}MM$ Auger spectrum of copper. These lines are due only to vacancies in the L_2 and L_3 shells of copper. Note the abundant fine structure in the spectrum. The separation between a par-ticular $L_3M_iM_j$ group and the corresponding $L_2M_iM_j$ group is equal to the binding-energy difference between L_3 and L_2 shells.*

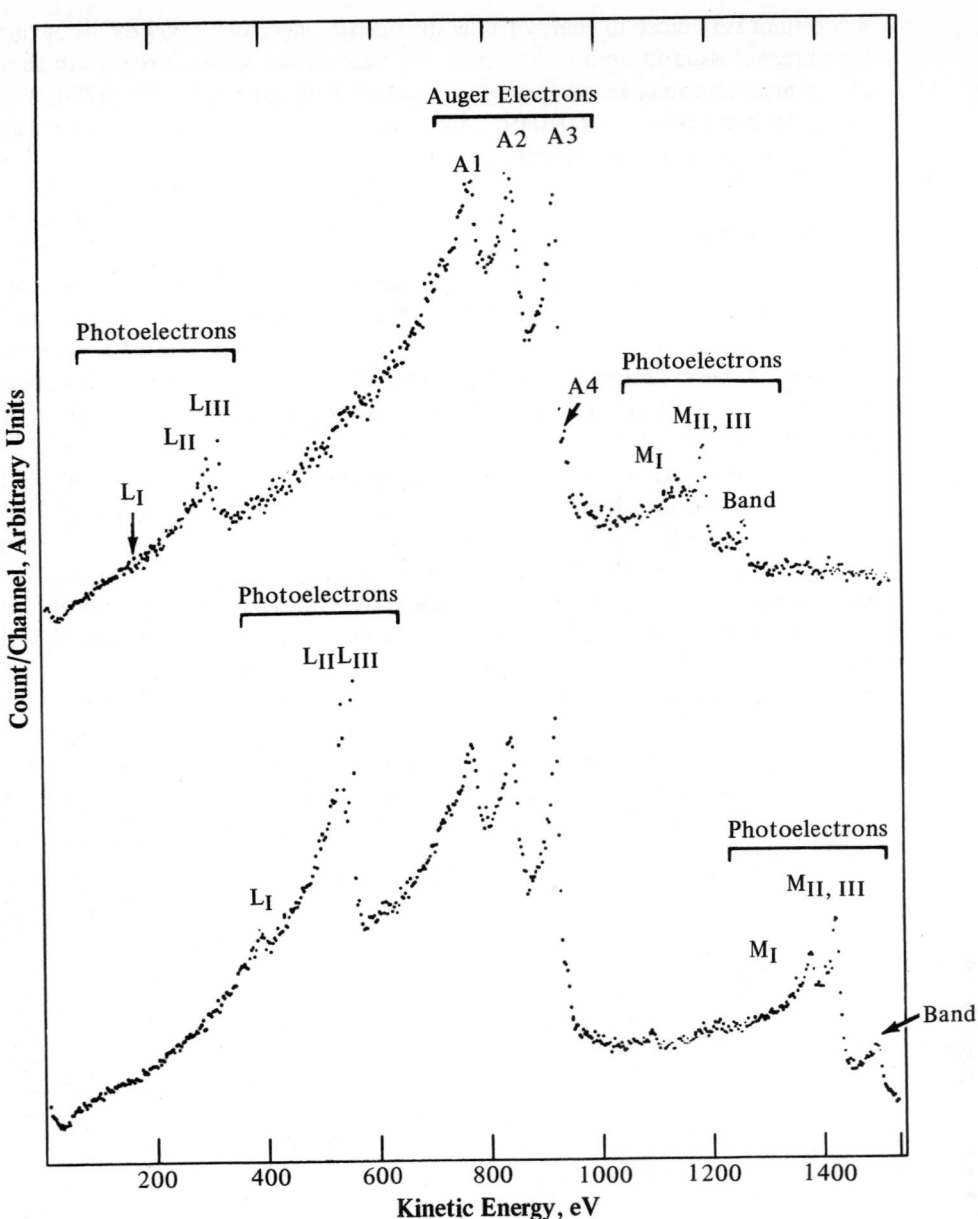

FIGURE 15.5. *Electron spectra of copper. Top: Mg Kα₁,₂ x-ray (1254 eV) excitation. Bottom: Al Kα₁,₂ x-ray (1487 eV) excitation. Note that, whereas the kinetic energies of the photoelectrons are proportional to the energies of the incident x-rays, those of the Auger electrons are independent. "Band" means the conduction band. The details of the Auger portion of the spectra are shown in Figure 15.4. From L. Yin, E. Yellin, and I. Adler*, J. Appl. Phys., **43**, 3595 (1971); *by permission of the authors and the American Institute of Physics.*

spectral lines have been catalogued for various elements and can be identified by reference to these tables. Like photoelectrons, the Auger electrons are sensitive to chemical environment, which may produce some ambiguities in identification; so the tables must be used with care.

Some characteristics of Auger lines can be used to distinguish them from photoelectron lines. This is important since photoelectron lines are so frequently accompanied by Auger lines. One useful fact is that the position (energy) of the Auger lines is always independent of the energy of the exciting photon because the Auger process occurs after the atom is ionized. A wide-range scan of the electron spectrum of copper is shown in Figure 15.5. The top spectrum was obtained by using Mg K$\alpha_{1,2}$ x-rays (1254 eV) as an excitation source, the bottom by using Al K$\alpha_{1,2}$ x-rays (1487 eV). Whereas the kinetic energies of the groups of peaks labeled "photoelectrons" increase with the incident x-ray energies (Eqn. 15.1), the energies of the group labeled "Auger electrons" remain unchanged. In practice, however, changing the energy of the incident radiation is not a trivial matter, because it generally involves changing the x-ray anode.

Fortunately, in some instances there are other methods of distinguishing Auger electrons from photoelectrons. In the case of KLL Auger electrons, there is a single group of lines which one identifies from appropriate tables, keeping in mind a possible discrepancy of a few eV caused by chemical shifts. For outer-shell Auger electrons, there are groups of lines corresponding to vacancies produced in subshells. Although these groups may contain complex features, the component lines of these groups are separated by energies corresponding to the difference in binding energies. For example, the L$_3$MM group of Auger lines is separated from a comparable group of L$_2$MM Auger lines by the difference in binding energy between the L$_3$ and L$_2$ shells (Fig. 15.4). Further, this difference is usually independent of the chemical environment.

Another practical generalization is that, for any given group of Auger lines from a major shell, the most intense group results from vacancies in the outermost subshell. This follows quite naturally, because in a given major shell the electron population is greatest in the outermost subshells. Therefore, roughly speaking, the probability of producing a vacancy by x-ray absorption is also highest for the outermost subshell. Furthermore, after photoionization, physical processes occur that reorganize the vacancy distribution among the subshells. Such reshuffling always results in increased vacancies in the outermost subshell. Thus, for example, one would predict (and actually find) that for the L-shell Auger groups, the intensities are as follows: L$_3$MM > L$_2$MM > L$_1$MM; similarly, for the M-shell groups, M$_5$NN > M$_4$NN > M$_3$NN > M$_2$NN > M$_1$NN; and so forth for higher shells.

15.2 INSTRUMENTATION

As in many fields, ESCA instrumentation was initially designed and built by pioneering investigators and thus was found in very few laboratories. Today ESCA instrumentation may be purchased commercially. There are excellent instruments available which offer relative ease of operation, high sensitivity, and good resolution.

In this section we shall review the principles underlying the instrumentation,

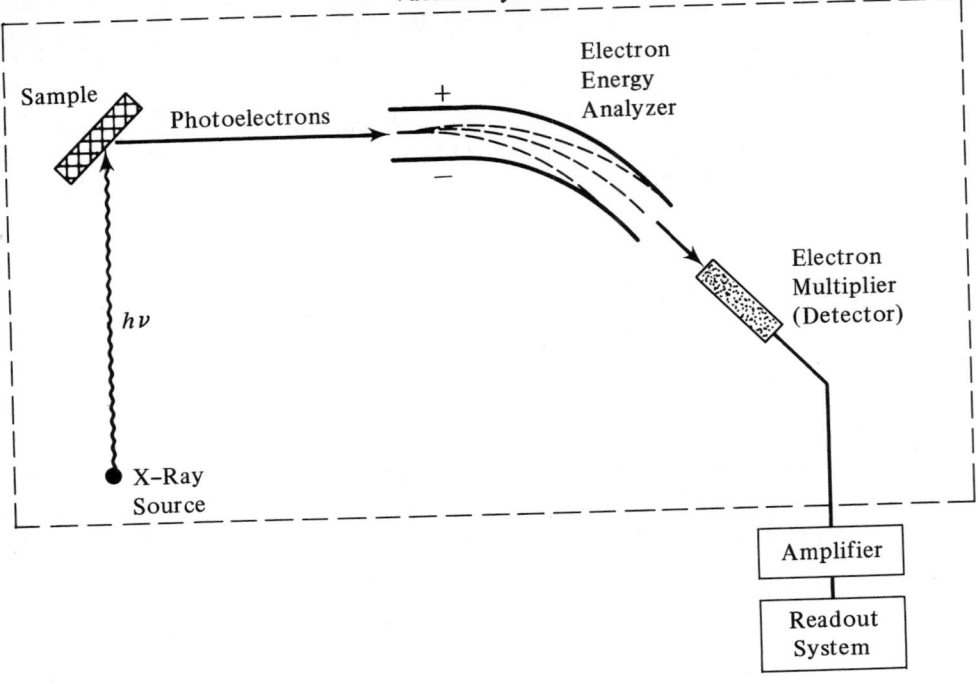

FIGURE 15.6. *Schematic diagram of an electron spectrometer. The electrostatic analyzer "sorts" or spreads out the photoelectrons, Auger electrons, and other secondary electrons of various energies so that only monoenergetic electrons reach the detector. In this, the energy analyzer serves much the same function as does a monochromator in optical spectroscopy.*

which consists of the following components: an excitation source, an electron-energy analyzer, a detector and associated electronics, and a sample-handling device. Figure 15.6 is a block diagram of an ESCA spectrometer.

Excitation Source

There are alternate methods of excitation in ESCA. We shall concentrate on photon excitation—in particular, x-ray excitation. As Equation 15.1 implies, the exciting source must be "monoenergetic." The important question in ESCA is "how monoenergetic," since this is a relative term. Because the demands of ESCA require the measurement of line shifts on the order of 0.1–1 eV, the energy spread of the exciting source must be of the same magnitude or less. ESCA systems are generally quite inefficient, which demands a high-intensity source as well.

The best way of obtaining such a source is to make use of the characteristic x-rays from an x-ray anode. However, it is a well known fact that characteristic x-ray lines have a finite width or energy spread. Such widths decrease with decreasing atomic number. It should be noted also that K x-ray lines are preferable as excitation sources because the L spectra are inherently more complex. Using these criteria (as well as the following practical considerations) the characteristic Al or Mg K lines (1487 eV or 1254 eV, respectively) were chosen for use in ESCA. The elements heavier than Al or Mg produce x-rays with higher efficiency, but the lines are inherently too broad and the $K\alpha_1$ and $K\alpha_2$ components begin to become distinct, so the radiation is no longer monoenergetic. The elements lighter than Mg or Al are either gases, or (if solid) the width of the K line begins to increase because the x-rays are now coming from transitions of electrons in the valence bands. In the case of Mg or Al, the $K\alpha_1$ and $K\alpha_2$ lines are so close in energy that for practical purposes they can be considered as a single line; the total energy spread is about 0.7 and 0.9 eV for Mg and Al, respectively. Power dissipation on the order of 1 kW or more is required to produce adequate electron intensities.

A recent development for producing monoenergetic x-rays involves a crystal monochromator in conjunction with an Al x-ray source to further reduce the energy spread of the characteristic x-rays and the background continuum. Because of the greatly reduced x-ray intensities following the use of the monochromator, it has been necessary to develop an ingenious method for processing the electron output from the spectrometer. The solution is analogous to a parallel-processing procedure that permits a band of electron energies to be measured simultaneously. The total energy spread of the exciting x-rays and the spectrometer is of the order of 0.5 eV for such instruments.

Another readily available monochromatic source uses the resonance lines of He I at 21.2 eV or He II at 40.8 eV, which have linewidths of about 0.005 eV. These are the major sources used in vacuum-ultraviolet photoelectron spectroscopy (UPS). Unfortunately, good photon sources with energies between 1000 and 40 eV are still not easily available.

Electron Spectrometer

Because of the commercial availability of very adequate electron spectrometers (the heart of the ESCA instrument), it will not be necessary to furnish here the detailed theory of operation. The discussion will concern itself only with the principles of operation.

Three types of electron spectrometers are presently in use: magnetic, electrostatic, and retarding-grid types. Of these, the first two are focusing instruments whereas the last is not. Historically, the magnetic spectrometer was the first type, used notably in the work of Siegbahn and coworkers [1]. Today the most common type of spectrometer in photoelectron spectroscopy, whether x-ray or ultraviolet, is the electrostatic type. The third variety (retarding grid) is employed mainly with electron excitation and is usually used in conjunction with the LEED (*low energy electron diffraction*) apparatus for studying Auger spectra.

The magnetic spectrometer is a momentum analyzer—the momentum of the electron is proportional to the applied magnetic field. In such instruments the percentage momentum resolution ($\Delta mv/mv$) is an instrumental constant. The momentum resolution achieved by Siegbahn et al. is about 0.01%. Instruments of this type are usually very large and very sensitive to stray magnetic fields. It is usually necessary to cancel any extraneous magnetic fields by the use of large Helmholtz coils and to place the spectrometer in iron-free rooms. These are essentially custom-built research instruments with low efficiency and are found in very few laboratories.

Electrostatic instruments come in a variety of forms: complete concentric hemispheres, hemispheric and spherical sectors, coaxial cylinders, etc. In such analyzers, the kinetic energy of the electron is proportional to the applied potential between the two conducting surfaces. Owing to the spherical or axial symmetry of such spectrometers, most have double-focusing properties. In general, the percentage energy resolution ($\Delta E/E$) is a constant of the instrument; resolutions of the order of 0.05% have been achieved. Because the percentage resolution is a constant, the absolute resolution ΔE is directly proportional to the energy E of the electron. In other words, at low electron energies the absolute resolution is better (ΔE is smaller). Consequently, there are two approaches to achieving good resolution in electrostatic analyzers: (1), building an instrument with a high enough resolution that the absolute resolution ΔE is small enough even at high kinetic energies to contribute little to the measured linewidth; and (2), reducing the energy of the electron entering the spectrometer by a constant value so that ΔE becomes small and constant. This is done by the simple expedient of applying a retarding potential, or by using a retarding lens which reduces the initial kinetic energy of the electron to the desired value prior to entering the spectrometer. At present, most commercial ESCA instruments employ the latter technique and offer resolutions of the order of 0.1 eV. Like the magnetic analyzer, the electrostatic analyzer is sensitive to stray magnetic fields, but less critically so; some form of magnetic shielding is usually required, but not the use of Helmholtz coils as in magnetic spectrometers.

The third type of spectrometer, which uses retarding grids and electronic differentiation for energy analysis, is rather uncommon in conventional photoelectron spectroscopy. The reader is referred for further details to texts on LEED and Auger spectroscopy.

Detection Systems

As a general rule, the electron energies and intensities measured in ESCA are both relatively low because of the various factors discussed above. The low electron-energies dictate the use of windowless detectors and the low intensities dictate the use of pulse-counting techniques; most of the available ESCA instruments employ both. The low counting-rates also make automated data-acquisition and analysis attractive; thus, many commercial instruments offer on-line computers as part of the entire ESCA system.

Sample Systems

Because ESCA can be applied to a great variety of problems, sample-handling capabilities should have enough flexibility that investigations can be performed on solids, liquids, or gases. These requirements are not easy to meet in practice and generally require specially engineered sample devices.

Vacuum System. It is essential to have strict control over the sample surface because the response in ESCA is entirely determined by the surface. A minimum requirement is a "very clean vacuum"; that is, a vacuum relatively free of vapors that can be adsorbed on the surface of the sample and thus distort and contaminate the observed spectra. As a rule of thumb, a vacuum of 10^{-8} torr or better is necessary for general purposes, because surface contamination is very rapid and the surface in poorer vacuums may be contaminated to an unknown extent; a vacuum in the range of 10^{-10} torr is often required. In fact, since most surfaces are already contaminated by the time the sample is introduced into the sample chamber, it is also very desirable to have auxiliary surface-cleaning capabilities in the sample chamber itself, such as sample-heating and ion-sputtering devices (an argon-ion gun, for example), to clean the samples in place so they can be quickly studied before the surface becomes contaminated again.

Surface Charging. The ESCA investigator working on nonconducting samples must be constantly aware of the problem of surface charging. Surface-charge buildup will affect the values of the observed kinetic energies of photoelectrons from which chemical information is subsequently obtained. Surface charge occurs as a consequence of the ejection of electrons from the sample by the incident x-rays. The surface of a nonconductor becomes electron-deficient (positively charged) because there are not enough charge carriers to neutralize the deficiency, as would happen in a conductor. The electrons now must leave a surface that attracts them and thus experience a retardation and consequent loss of kinetic energy. Sample charging is not a simple effect but is sensitive to the geometry and environment of the sample and its container. The amount of charging will thus vary from instrument to instrument, even for the same sample.

There are various techniques for dealing with sample charging—some instrumental, some involving special sample-preparation, and some involving both. Instrumental techniques include using an electron gun to flood the sample with low-energy electrons and designing special geometries to surround the sample with a cage that discharges it. Among sample-preparation methods are such techniques as depositing on the nonconducting sample a very thin conducting film of a noble metal (such as gold or platinum) that has strong photoelectron lines with well established energies. The deposited film must be thin enough not to obscure the sample of interest underneath, should not have electron lines with energies similar to those of the sample, and must not react with the sample. Other methods to minimize sample charging include depositing a thin film of nonconducting sample onto a conducting substrate and incorporating the nonconducting sample into a conductive wire mesh.

The phenomenon of charging is important only when absolute energy values are required; provided the degree of charging is constant or quickly reaches an equilibrium value, the relative energies are unaffected.

Another parameter that affects the measured electron energies and which must be taken into account in determining the electron binding energies is the *work function.* The kinetic energy the spectrometer sees is not necessarily the energy the electron has as it leaves the atom; every electron that escapes the surface of the sample must overcome a surface potential known as the work function, usually on the order of a few eV. Although work functions differ from sample to sample, it has been shown that only the work function of the entrance material to the spectrometer needs to be accounted for in the determination of absolute kinetic energies.

Because the work function of a particular spectrometer is an instrumental constant, it can readily be determined either by direct measurement or by reference to some standard electron energy. For example, the well known 83.8-eV binding energy of the $4f_{7/2}$ level of gold is often used to calibrate the spectrometer work-function. The work function can then be subtracted from the right side of Equation 15.1 to give

$$E_p = h\nu - E_b - E_{wf} \tag{15.2}$$

15.3 APPLICATIONS

In current applications, the somewhat limited usefulness of ESCA in the area of simple quantitative elemental analysis does not detract from its potential in a myriad of other chemical studies. In order to demonstrate the principles of the technique, we will show how to go about interpreting ESCA data in the following examples. Some of these are from our own work and were selected merely for convenience. These examples, although typical, are by no means exhaustive; they only serve to highlight some of the current applications of ESCA.

Elemental Analysis

Examination of the literature discloses very few examples of classical quantitative elemental analysis. ESCA is an extraordinarily sensitive surface technique involving the top twenty or so angstroms; in this sense, almost vanishingly small amounts of an element, about 0.001 monolayer, can be detected. To attempt an elemental analysis of a sample, however, immediately presents the analyst with the question of how representative the surface is of the rest of the sample, particularly in view of the possibility of surface contamination. Sample preparation is critical and must contend with a wide variety of surface phenomena such as adsorption and chemisorption, oxidation, and mechanical contamination, as well as more subtle phenomena that will be brought out in greater detail below. One important point is that both ESCA and Auger spectroscopy are essentially nondestructive techniques.

In summary, the use of ESCA for elemental analysis is primarily limited to the qualitative identification of surface elements, and monitoring the presence or absence of these elements. Nevertheless, progress is being made in the application of both ESCA and Auger spectroscopy to quantitative analysis.

Valence States

Studies of chemical bonding, charge distribution, and valence state are perhaps the best established applications of ESCA at present and account for the bulk of the published papers in this area. In contrast to the heretofore more classical techniques which are essentially inferential in character, ESCA is able to directly probe both the valence electrons, which actually participate in bonding, and the core electrons, which are directly influenced by the behavior of the valence electrons. It is this capability of ESCA that has led to its rapid growth; it is perhaps the most powerful and direct tool for these types of studies.

The transition metals are excellent examples of elements capable of various valence states, some of which are stable. In a systematic study of Fe_2O_3 and FeF_2 under argon-ion bombardment [3], the Fe $2p_{3/2}$ photoelectron peak was examined after various periods of ion bombardment (Fig. 15.7). With extended periods of bombardment, the peak shifts toward higher kinetic (lower binding) energy until its position coincides with that for metallic iron. In other words, Fe^{2+} and Fe^{3+}

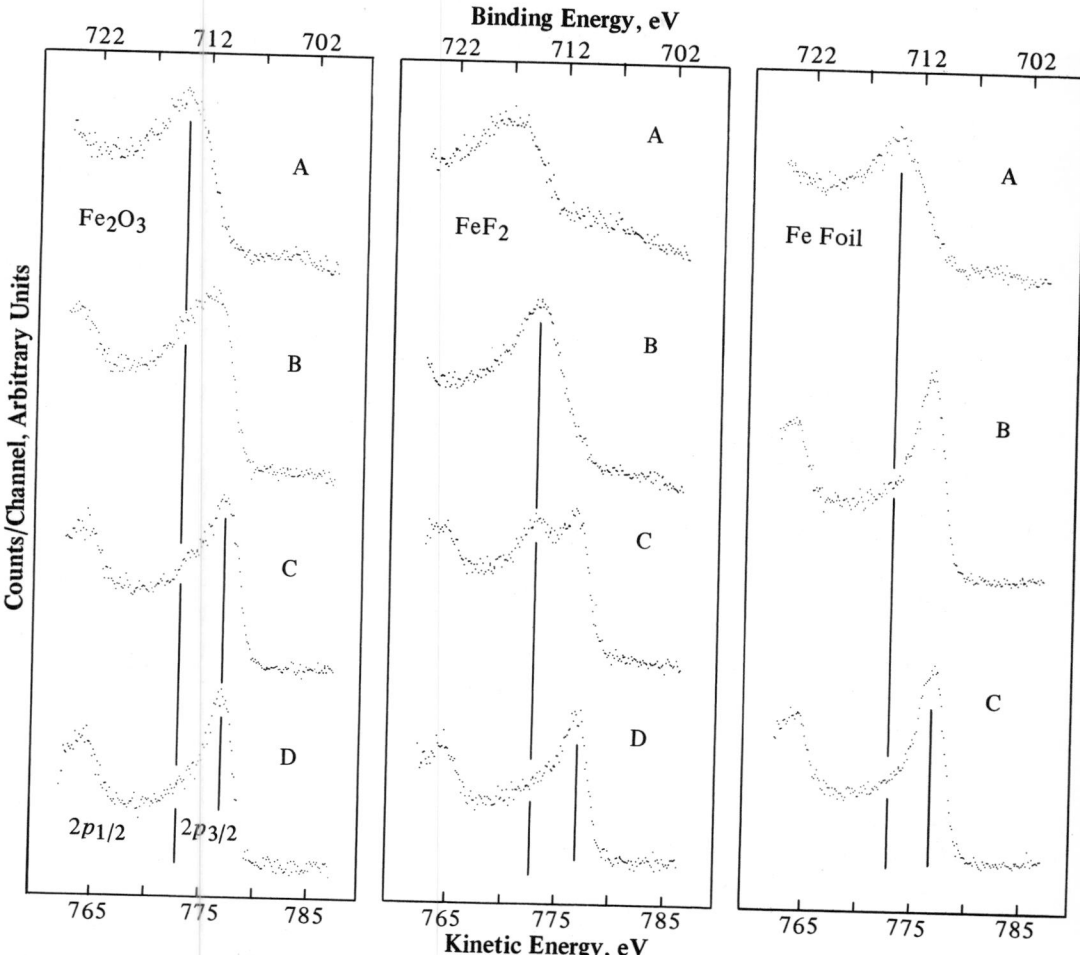

FIGURE 15.7. *Al $K\alpha_{1,2}$ x-ray excited photoelectron spectra of the Fe $2p_{3/2}$ (L_3) level in Fe_2O_3, FeF_2 and Fe foil, showing chemical reduction induced with argon-ion sputtering. Sputtering was performed at a pressure of 25 microns, a voltage of 1.5 kV, and a current density of 0.2 mA/cm². Fe_2O_3 sequence: A, prior to ion-sputtering; B, after 12 min; C, after 72 min; D, after 120 min of sputtering. FeF_2 sequence: A, prior to sputtering; B, after 15 min; C, after 120 min; D, after 210 min of sputtering. Fe foil sequence: A, prior to sputtering; B, after 60 min; C, after 160 min of sputtering. From L. Yin, S. Ghose, and I. Adler, Appl. Spectr., 26, 355 (1972); by permission of the publisher.*

are being reduced to their metallic state under argon-ion bombardment. This is a clear example of how one can study surface reactions in a dynamic or time-dependent way. The spectra also show what we assume to be FeO as an intermediate product in the case of Fe_2O_3 samples. It is well known that FeO is unstable in air and would normally be prepared only with extreme difficulty. We have no way of knowing whether the observed FeO is stoichiometric. This kind of chemical reduction under ion bombardment is fairly common among the 3d transition-metal compounds.

The effect of surface contamination is shown by the fact that initially the position of the photoelectron line from the "metallic iron" actually is indistinguishable from that for Fe_2O_3. This is caused by a surface layer of oxidized iron that is subsequently sputtered away by the ion bombardment.

The examples cited above demonstrate a need for caution in the use of ion-sputtering as a cleaning technique in the preparation of sample surfaces for ESCA analysis; the ion-sputtering process itself can produce chemical changes on the sample surface.

Stereochemistry

Because ESCA can directly probe the electronic structures of substances ranging from free atoms to solids, it is useful in a host of related fields such as stereochemistry, geochemistry, crystallography, and atomic and solid-state physics. Among the phenomena lending themselves to study are stereostructures, band structures, paramagnetism, atomic lifetimes, and Auger transitions.

An example of the use of ESCA to study the effect of steric arrangements concerns the binding energies of the core electrons of Ni in nickel compounds [4]. Some 70 compounds containing Ni in all of its known oxidation states were examined. Among other things, the results indicate that when Ni is bonded to the same ligand under different geometries, the binding energy of the Ni-ion electrons increases in the order: planar < tetrahedral < octahedral. This is not surprising because, for a given type of ligand, the nickel-to-donor distances increase in the same order; thus, since the valence electrons in the octahedral case are farthest removed from the Ni core, the binding energy of the remaining electrons is greatest. This relationship will not necessarily hold if the ligand is varied.

There is also a direct correlation between Ni $2p$ binding energy and the estimated charge on Ni for some simple Ni(II) compounds, as shown in Figure 15.8. Similar correlations have been observed recently for a large number of copper compounds [5].

Surface Studies

One of the more important practical applications of ESCA is in the study of surface phenomena. Such areas as the direct study of surface reactions, diffusion processes under preselected conditions, the study of dopants in solids, surface-catalysis phenomena, sputtering processes, and gas-surface interactions are open to investigation.

Some contributions in this area have been made by the LEED method, with the instruments modified to measure the energies of the emerging Auger electrons.

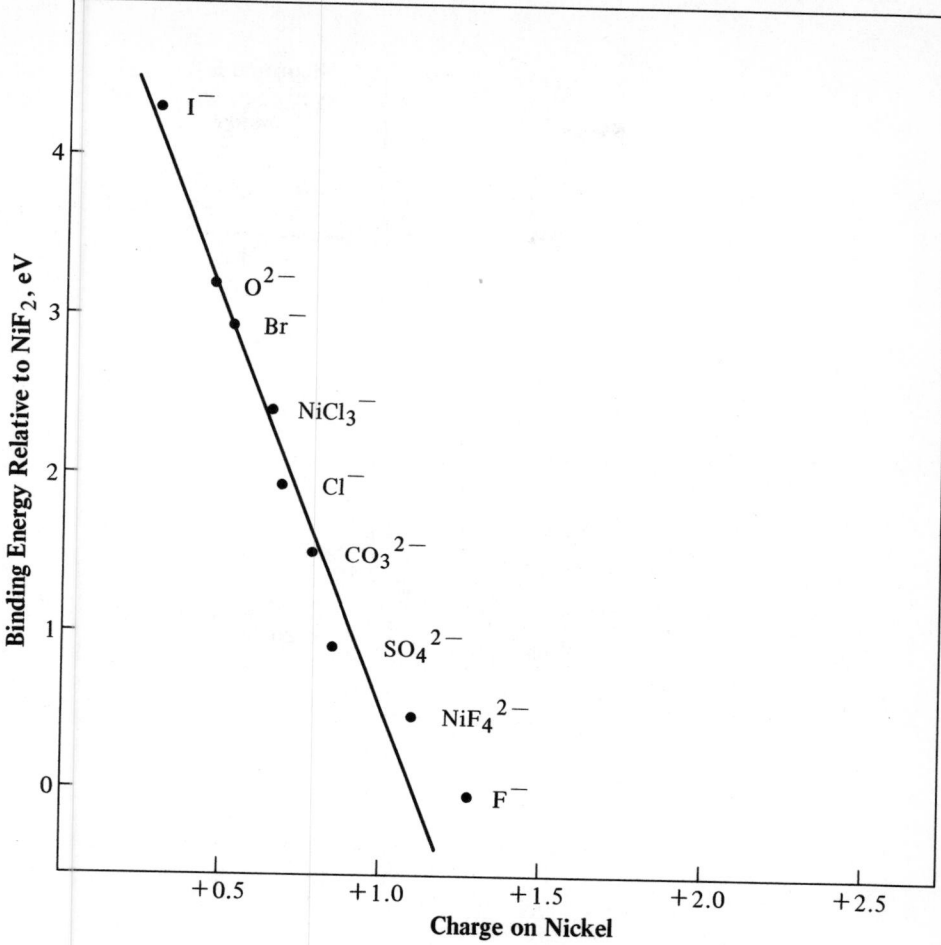

FIGURE 15.8. *Correlation between the Ni* $2p_{3/2}$ *(L_3) binding energy (relative to NiF$_2$) and the estimated charge on nickel for some simple Ni(II) compounds.*

Because LEED is based on excitation of the sample by electrons (typically, samples are bombarded with a focused beam of electrons in the energy range up to 5 keV), these studies are limited to the use of Auger spectra. Further, electron excitation requires electronic differentiation of the energy spectra to minimize the high background of scattered electrons. Therefore, Auger spectra have the shapes shown in Figure 15.9 rather than the hump-shaped peaks of ESCA spectra. The degraded resolution, the complexity of Auger spectra, and the uncertainty of Auger chemical shifts limit such surface studies to the identification of elements and the monitoring of the presence or absence of surface constituents, rather than their chemical states or activities. Nevertheless, a great deal of surface information can be extracted even from the simple elemental identification of the presence, absence, or change of surface constituents.

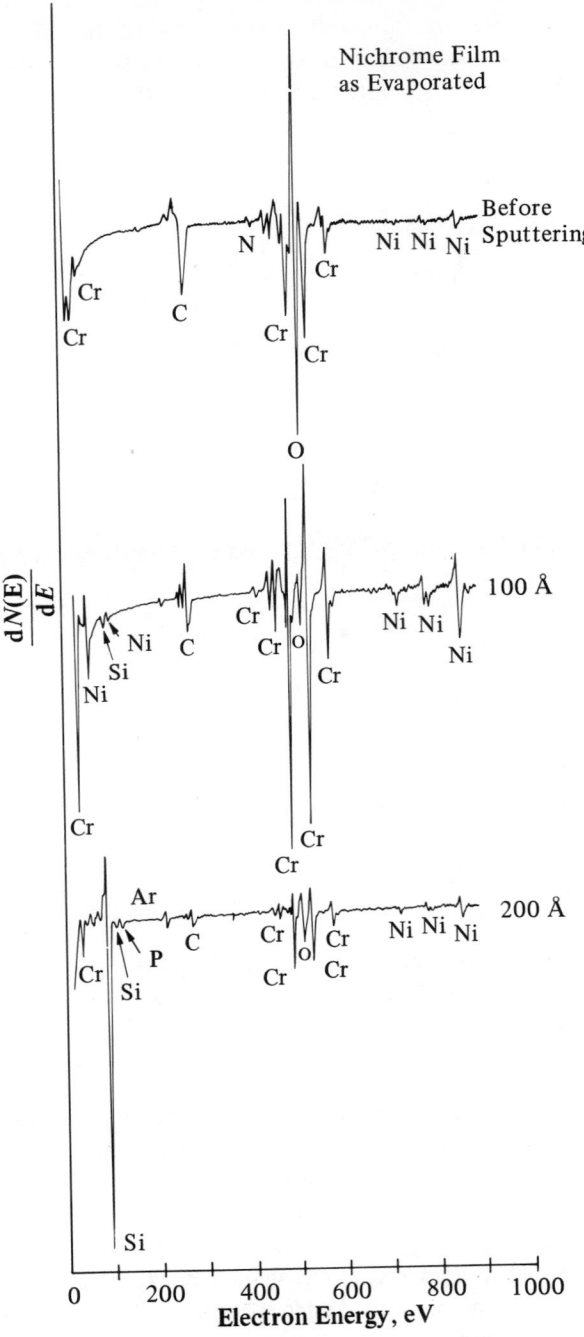

FIGURE 15.9. *Electron-excited Auger spectra from a 150-Å nichrome film deposited on a silicon substrate. The spectra represent a profile of the film from the surface down to a depth of 200 Å as various amounts of the material have been sputtered off. Note that the unit on the ordinate is the derivative of the electron intensity, dN(E)/dE, rather than the intensity N(E). From R. E. Weber,* J. Crystal Growth, *17, 342 (1972), by permission of the author and the North Holland Publishing Company.*

An excellent example of surface studies is given by Weber [6] using ion-sputtering to determine the in-depth composition of thin films on selected substrates. Figure 15.9 shows the effect of sputtering and surface thickness on sequentially observed Auger spectra. Note that the unit on the y-axis is $dN(E)/dE$, the first derivative of the number of electron counts, rather than $N(E)$. The top spectrum is that of a 150-Å nichrome film deposited on a silicon substrate. The Ni and Cr from the nichrome as well as the surface oxygen are visible, but not the substrate. In the middle spectrum, after 100 Å has been sputtered away, an Auger line from the silicon substrate appears while the oxygen-line intensity drops greatly. In the bottom spectrum, after 200 Å of material has been removed, the Si from the substrate shows very strongly, whereas the Ni and Cr peaks have almost disappeared. Auger peaks for argon from the sputtering source have also begun to appear. The amplitudes of the various Auger peaks are shown as a function of material sputtered in Figure 15.10. By contrast, these same amplitude profiles are shown for a heat-treated film in Figure 15.11. It is clear that in the latter case the first 75 Å of the surface consists

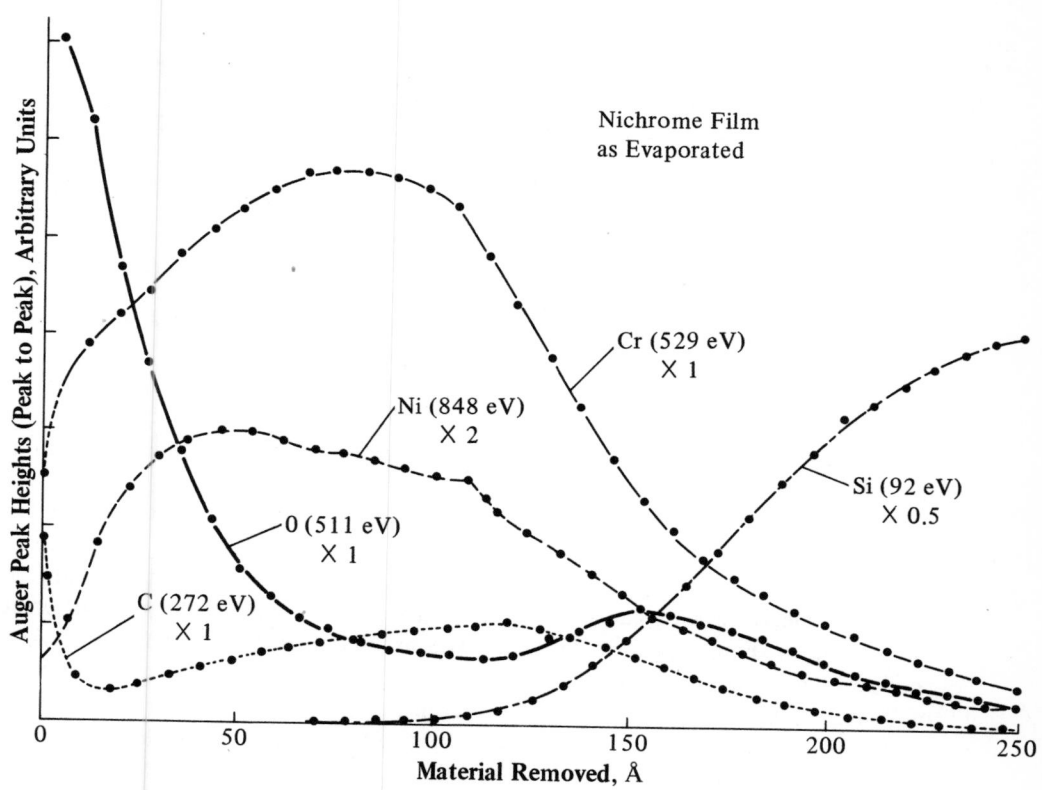

FIGURE 15.10. *Amplitudes of the various Auger peaks from a nichrome film on a silicon substrate as a function of the amount of material sputter-etched from the film. From R. E. Weber, J. Crystal Growth, 17, 342 (1972), by permission of the author and the North Holland Publishing Company.*

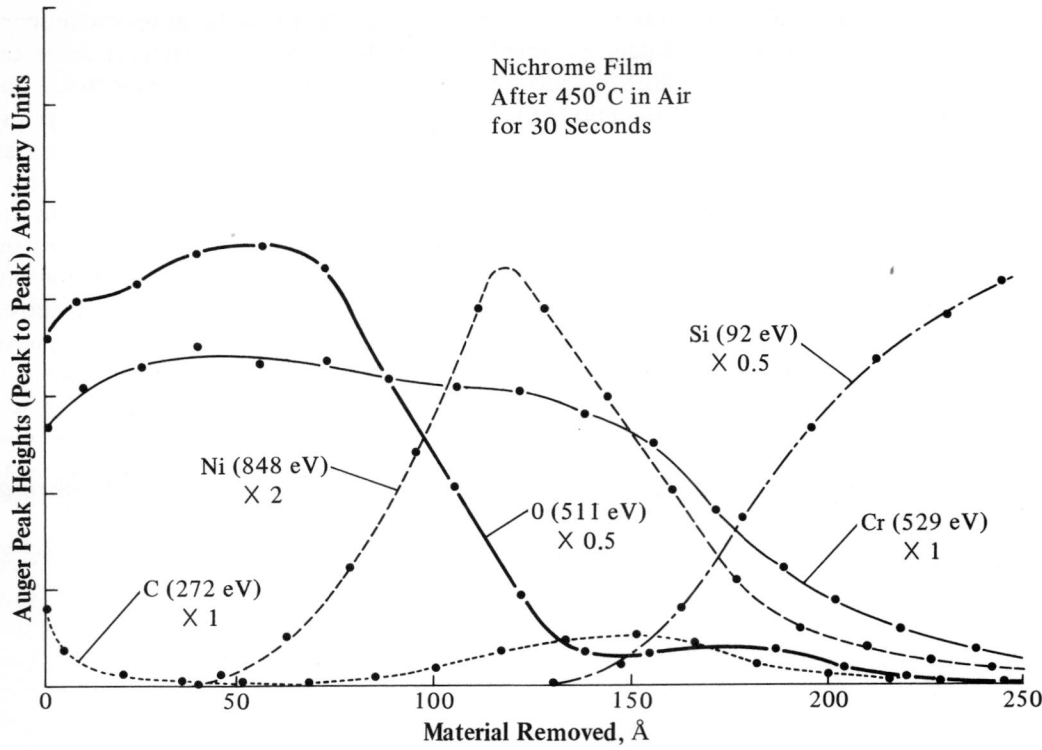

FIGURE 15.11. *Amplitudes of the Auger peaks from a heat-treated nichrome film as a function of the amount of material sputter-etched from the film. From R. E. Weber,* J. Crystal Growth, *17, 342 (1972). Reproduced with the permission of the author and the North Holland Publishing Company.*

of Cr and O, whereas the Ni has now diffused to the interface between the film and the silicon substrate.

Other examples of surface phenomena that have been studied involve grain boundaries, surface diffusion, corrosion, etc.

One significant advantage of Auger spectroscopy with electron bombardment is that the electron beam can be focused on a very small area of the sample surface. Typical beam diameters have been as little as 25 μm, although the use of Auger spectroscopy in conjunction with the scanning electron microscope allows the use of beam diameters below 5 μm. At present, ESCA photon-beam diameters are limited to about a mm or so. With scanning capability and small beam-diameters, one can now perform lateral or even two-dimensional characterization of a surface. For a two-dimensional semiquantitative analysis of a surface, the spectrometer is locked onto the energy of an Auger peak characteristic of a particular element. The electron beam is scanned systematically across the surface of the sample, and the position of the probe beam is correlated with the *x-y* position of the light beam on an oscilloscope screen. Finally, the light intensity of the oscilloscope signal is made proportional to the intensity of the Auger signal. The net result is an oscilloscope picture of the sample surface magnified perhaps $400\times$, with the bright areas on the screen corresponding to the "image" of the element analyzed on the surface. One can then "lock" on to the Auger peak of a second element, get its "picture," and so on. By this sequential multi-element capability, the presence of several elements at specific sites can be correlated.

Examples of this type of application abound in the literature. Segregation of impurities in metals and alloys often occurs at grain boundaries. A study of the embrittlement and stress-failure of a tungsten sample showed a nearly uniform distribution of phosphorus across the sample, except for certain grains that appeared to be completely free of it; this complete absence of phosphorus can be interpreted as related to cleavage failure at these points.

Surface Catalysis

For the most part, the behavior of surface catalysts have not been well understood; as a result, their development is still something of an art. ESCA offers perhaps the best potential for studying such phenomena because, since the suspected mechanisms probably involve some form of charge transfer, there should be an associated change in binding energy.

One such example is the study of the binding energy of platinum in a series of complexes [7]. The ESCA binding-energy data show that the coordination of "neutral ligands" can lead to a considerable transfer of charge from the metal to the ligands, thus confirming that the catalytic behavior of these platinum complexes is indeed related to charge transfer. Other typical examples of this sort have been given by Kelly and Tyler [8] and Larsson et al. [9].

Quantum Structure of Free Molecules

Studies of molecular structure and molecular energy-levels by ultraviolet photoelectron spectroscopy are being conducted by a large number of investigators. Such studies are fundamental in nature and to a large extent theoretical. In order to provide meaningful data free of solid-state effects, the samples are usually gaseous. Further, in order to see the closely spaced molecular orbitals and final-state vibrational structures, very high instrumental resolution (a few meV) and (usually) ultraviolet excitation are required. This subject is well covered in review articles and texts [10–13].

Valence-Band Structure

Photoelectron spectroscopy provides a useful (because direct) tool for studying the valence-band structure of solids. It is unlike soft x-ray emission spectroscopy where one must contend with transitions (to inner shells) that are constrained by selection rules and where one must take into account the character of the shell to which the transitions occur. In photoelectron spectroscopy, any of the occupied states in the band can be examined by ejecting the band photoelectrons. Thus, the photoelectron spectral shape essentially reflects the structure of the occupied band itself.

Consequently, ESCA has been widely used to study the band structures of metals, alloys, and compounds. These data in turn are compared with density-of-state or molecular-orbital calculations.

Because band structures are of interest to investigators in a wide variety of disciplines besides chemistry (such as solid-state physics, geochemistry, and crystallography), this area of application of ESCA is growing rapidly. This is especially so with the improved vacuum and resolution of second-generation instruments.

In principle, ultraviolet-excited photoelectron spectroscopy would be ideally suited for valence-band-structure studies because of its extremely high resolution. However, ultraviolet-photoelectron spectra may not truly represent the band structure being probed; because the energy of the ultraviolet source is so low, it tends to induce valence-electron transitions and thereby distort the intensity distribution of the resulting photoelectron spectrum. X-ray excitation, on the other hand, while providing poorer resolution, is essentially free of such distortions. Thus, the two types of photoelectron spectra serve to complement each other and provide a more complete picture of the valence-band structure.

REFERENCES

1. K. SIEGBAHN, C. NORDLING, A. FAHLMAN, R. NORDBERG, K. HAMRIN, J. HEDMAN, G. JOHANSSON, T. BERGMARK, S. KARLSSON, I. LINDGREN, and B. LINDBERG, *ESCA: Atomic, Molecular, and Solid-State Structure Studied by Means of Electron Spectroscopy*, Uppsala: Almquist and Wiksells, 1967.

2. S. O. GRIM, L. J. MATIENZO, and W. E. SWARTZ, Jr., *Inorg. Chem.*, *13*, 447 (1974).

3. L. YIN, S. GHOSE, and I. ADLER, *Appl. Spectrosc.*, *26*, 355 (1972).

4. L. J. MATIENZO, L. YIN, S. O. GRIM, and W. E. SWARTZ, Jr., *Inorg. Chem.*, *12*, 2762 (1973).

5. D. C. FROST, A. ISHITANI, and C. A. MCDOWELL, *Mol. Phys.*, *24*, 861 (1972).

6. R. E. WEBER, *J. Crystal Growth*, *17*, 342 (1972).

7. C. D. COOK, K. Y. WAN, U. GELIUS, K. HAMRIN, G. JOHANSSON, E. OLSON, H. SIEGBAHN, C. NORDLING, and K. SIEGBAHN, *J. Amer. Chem. Soc.*, *93*, 1904 (1971).

8. M. A. KELLY and C. E. TYLER, *Hewlett-Packard Journal*, July, 1973, pp 1–14.

9. R. LARSSON, B. FOLKESSON, and G. SCHÖN, *Chemica Scripta*, *3*, 88 (1973).

10. K. SIEGBAHN, C. NORDLING, G. JOHANSSON, J. HEDMAN, P. F. HEDÉN, K. HAMRIN, U. GELIUS, T. BERGMARK, L. O. WERME, R. MANNE, and Y. BAER, *ESCA Applied to Free Molecules*, Amsterdam: North-Holland, 1969.

11. D. W. TURNER, C. BAKER, A. D. BAKER, and C. R. BRUNDLE, *Molecular Photoelectron Spectroscopy*, London: Wiley-Interscience, 1970.

12. C. R. BRUNDLE, *Appl. Spectrosc.*, *25*, 8 (1971).

13. D. W. TURNER, *Phil. Trans. Roy. Soc. Lond.*, *A268*, 7 (1970).

PROBLEMS

1. Identify the elements present in the sample which gives the ESCA spectrum pictured at top of facing page.

2. Identify the elements present in an organic compound which has the ESCA spectrum shown at foot of facing page.

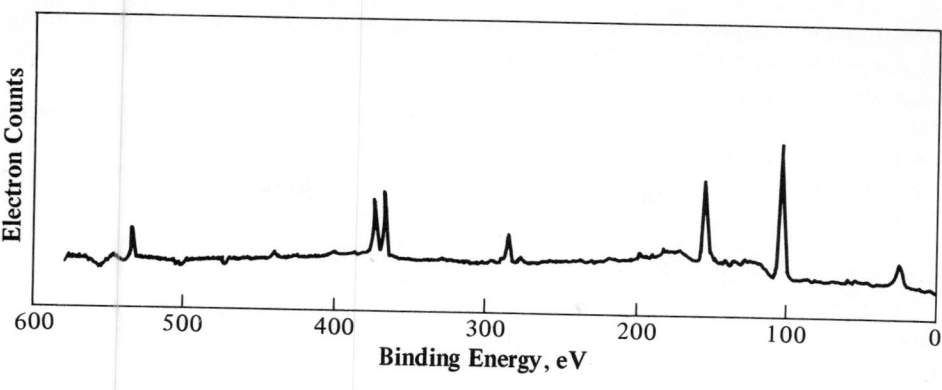

Binding Energy, eV

Problem 1

3. Determine the binding energies ($2p_{3/2}$ electrons) for iron in the compounds whose spectra are shown in Figure 15.7. Compare the shifts in binding energy caused by the differing chemical environments with the binding energy differences between elements near iron in the periodic table.

4. What are the advantages and disadvantages of ESCA as a method for analysis of surfaces? Compare ESCA with Auger spectroscopy.

5. In an attempt to solve an analytical problem in the design and production of a semiconductor device, you are trying to determine the approximate detection limit for silver vacuum-deposited on a silicon substrate. Given that the beam-probe diameter in ESCA is about one millimeter, that the analysis depth is about 20 Å, and that ESCA can detect about 0.001 of a monolayer of an element, answer the following questions: (a) What is the absolute "detection limit"

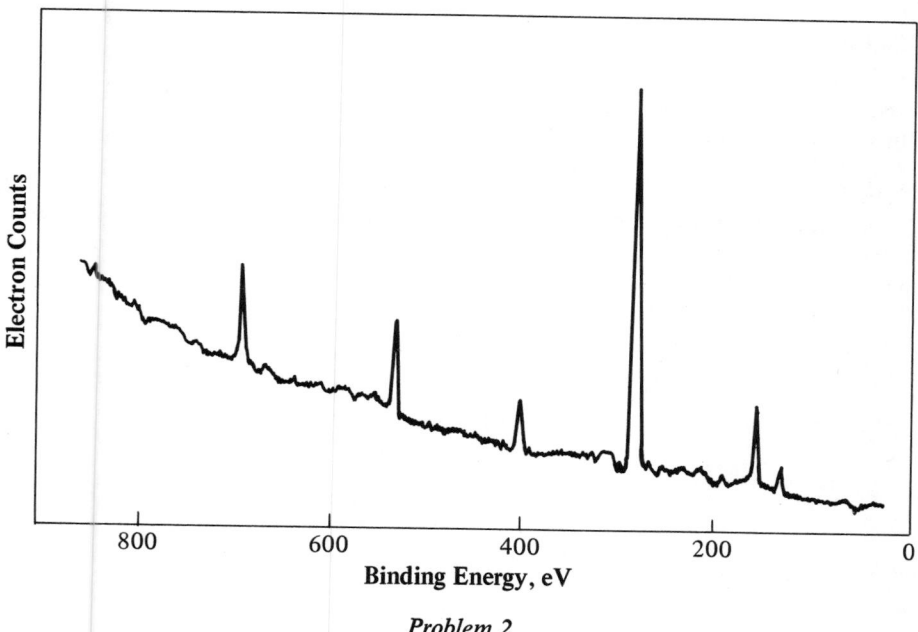

Binding Energy, eV

Problem 2

for Ag in grams? (b) How many atoms does this correspond to? (c) If the Ag were homogeneously distributed in the Si substrate, what would be the concentration detection limit in g/cm³ and in ppm? The densities of elemental Ag and Si are 10.5 and 2.33 g/cm³; the atomic radii are 1.44 and 1.32 Å; and the atomic weights are 107.87 and 28.086 g/mole, respectively.

6. The ESCA spectrum of an inorganic compound is taken using Al Kα radiation. The photoelectron energy (E_p) of the $4f_{7/2}$ level for gold, a thin layer of which has been deposited on the sample, is measured at 1353 eV. (a) At what photoelectron energy should you look for the carbon 1s photoelectron peak to determine whether the surface of the sample has been contaminated with vacuum-pump oil? (b) With the same spectrometer, at what photoelectron energy should the carbon 1s peak be if Mg Kα radiation were used?

7. An ESCA spectrum of a gaseous mixture of CO, CO_2, and CH_4 is taken. Prominent peaks are noted at binding energies of 290.1, 295.8, 297.9, 540.1, and 541.3 eV. Assign the observed peaks to the element and compound responsible.

8. The surface of an aluminum sample was thoroughly cleaned by abrasion and immediately put into the sample chamber of an ESCA spectrometer. Two prominent peaks in the spectrum occurred at binding energies of 72.3 and 75.0 eV, whose relative intensities were 15.2 and 5.1 (arbitrary) units. After a week's exposure to laboratory air, the same sample was rerun under the same conditions; the two peaks were again observed (at 72.2 and 74.5 eV), although the intensities were now 6.2 and 12.3 units. Explain.

9. ESCA can be used for the quantitative analysis of MoO_3/MoO_2 mixtures, compounds for which an instrumental method was not previously available [W. E. Swartz, Jr., and D. M. Hercules, *Anal. Chem.*, 43, 1774 (1971)]. This is done by analyzing the Mo $3d_{3/2}$–$3d_{5/2}$ region of the electron spectrum. Mo(VI) in MoO_3 has a peak at 235.6 eV for $3d_{3/2}$ and 232.5 eV for $3d_{5/2}$; Mo(IV) in MoO_2 has corresponding peaks at 233.9 and 230.9 eV. Thus, the electron counts at 235.6 eV are due primarily to MoO_3 and those at 230.9 to MoO_2. The following data were obtained on standard MoO_3/MoO_2 samples.

% MoO_2	$N_{235.6}:N_{230.9}$
100	1.30 ± 0.10
95	1.41 ± 0.20
90	1.70 ± 0.10
80	2.10 ± 0.20
75	2.30 ± 0.20
60	2.95 ± 0.05
55	2.99 ± 0.20
50	3.31 ± 0.10
45	3.46 ± 0.06
40	3.60 ± 0.17
25	4.17 ± 0.05
20	4.53 ± 0.20
10	5.00 ± 0.30
5	5.05 ± 0.20
0	5.07 ± 0.05

Three unknowns gave the following count ratios: 1.94 ± 0.15, 2.55 ± 0.15, and 4.08 ± 0.10. Determine the % MoO_2 in the three unknowns.

16

Mass Spectrometry

MICHAEL L. GROSS

The practice of mass spectrometry is carried out with rather sophisticated instruments (mass spectrometers) which produce, separate, and detect both positive and negative gas-phase ions. Since samples are typically neutral in charge, they must be first ionized in the spectrometer. Ionization of molecular substances is often followed by a series of spontaneous competitive decomposition or fragmentation reactions which produce additional ions. The ion masses (more correctly, their mass-to-charge ratios) and their relative abundances are displayed in a *mass spectrum*. Most compounds produce unique or distinctive patterns, so most substances can be identified by their mass spectra.

Mass spectrometry is noteworthy among modern structural tools because the information produced is of a chemical nature. The signals produced by a spectrometer are the direct result of chemical reactions (ionization and fragmentation) rather than energy-state changes that typify most other spectroscopic tools. To intelligently apply mass spectrometry, it is important to understand how this chemical information is produced. This chapter is intended to introduce the reader to the instrumentation necessary to carry out and identify these chemical reactions and to the procedure used in interpreting the information obtained.

Mass spectrometry is one of the oldest instrumental methods used in chemical analysis. The most important contribution of early mass spectrometry was the discovery of nonradioactive isotopes. The first study was reported by J. J. Thomson in 1913 [1] on the gaseous element neon. He showed that neon consists of two isotopes: ^{20}Ne and ^{22}Ne.

Major instrumental improvements followed closely just after World War I. F. W. Aston [2] in England constructed a more elaborate mass spectrograph which was used to verify the neon work and to identify other isotopes. The first mass spectrometer that utilized electrical rather than photographic detection was built in the United States by A. J. Dempster [3]. Whereas the mass spectrograph was better suited to measuring the exact masses of the isotopes, the spectrometer excelled in determinations of isotopic abundances. By the mid-thirties, most of the stable isotopes had been identified, and exact mass measurements established the idea that atomic masses are not whole numbers, a fact crucial to the understanding of nuclear chemistry. It was not until 1942, however, that the first commercial mass spectrometer was put into use, for petroleum analysis at the Atlantic Refining Corporation.

More general application of mass spectrometry as an analytical tool in the organic and biochemical areas was not developed until the 1960s. Within a period of a few years a number of chemists in the United States (McLafferty, Bieman, and Djerassi) and in England (Beynon) demonstrated that molecular structure could be elucidated for a wide variety of substances using mass spectrometry. Since then, the technique has become a standard addition to most research and analytical laboratories.

16.1 INSTRUMENTATION IN MASS SPECTROMETRY

To obtain a mass spectrum, the sample must be vaporized, ionized, and then (provided the substance is molecular) allowed to fragment or decompose. The various ions must then be separated according to their mass-to-charge ratios (m/e values) and finally detected. The instrumentation necessary to accomplish these requirements has four major components: (1) inlet systems for vaporization; (2) a source which serves to ionize and then detain the ions for a short period of time (usually about 1 μsec) so that fragmentation may occur; (3) a method of mass analysis; and (4) a detection scheme.

Inlet Systems

A generally useful inlet system must be able to vaporize molecules of quite low vapor pressure such as high-molecular-weight organic and organometallic compounds. Since many substances of interest to chemists do not have large equilibrium vapor pressures at room temperature, the inlet must operate at low pressure (10^{-4}–10^{-7} torr) and high temperature (up to 300°C). Actually, the full development of mass spectrometry in the organic and inorganic areas had to await the development of these inlet systems. The problems involved with leak-tight high-temperature vacuum systems with many remotely operated valves are not trivial, and these problems have only been overcome in the last 15 to 20 years.

Most analytical mass spectrometers have two inlet systems: a batch inlet for gases and liquids and for solids of moderately high vapor pressure, and a direct inlet for high-molecular-weight nonvolatile solids and for thermally unstable compounds. A typical design for a batch inlet is shown in Figure 16.1.

A small quantity of solid or liquid sample (approximately 10–100 μg) is introduced via the detachable sample tube into the reservoir. The sample is maintained in the gaseous state by the low background pressure of the inlet (10^{-5}–10^{-6} torr) and the high temperature of the surrounding oven. It should be obvious that a sample whose vapor pressure at the oven temperature is less than the background pressure

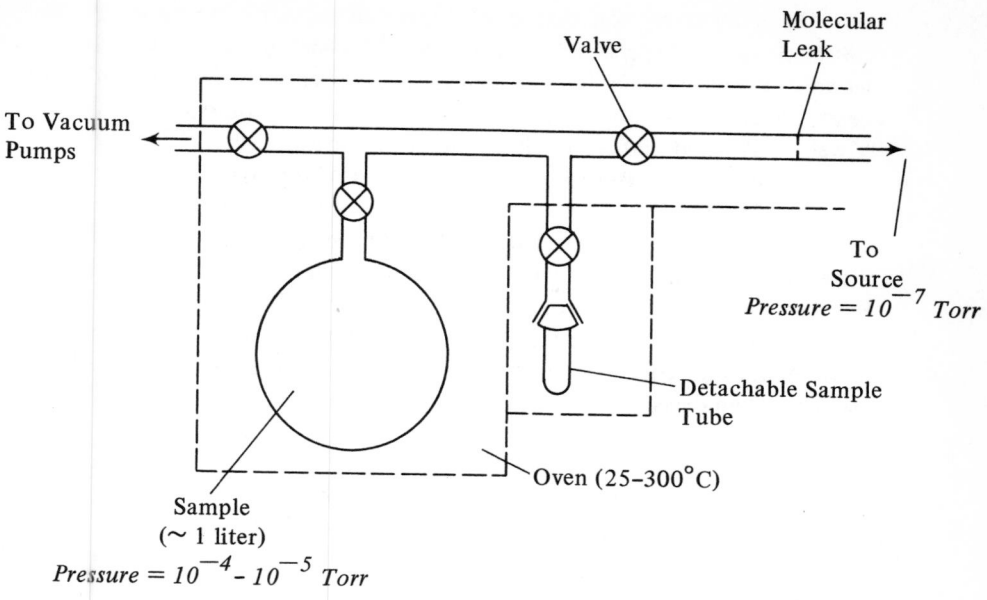

To Vacuum Pumps

Valve

Molecular Leak

To Source
Pressure = 10^{-7} Torr

Detachable Sample Tube

Oven (25–300°C)

Sample
(~ 1 liter)

Pressure = 10^{-4}- 10^{-5} Torr

FIGURE 16.1. *Schematic diagram of a typical batch-inlet system. This inlet is used for gases, volatile liquids, and volatile solids.*

of the inlet cannot be admitted to the spectrometer using this inlet. In fact, it is preferable that the sample have a vapor pressure of 10^{-2}–10^{-3} torr at the operating temperature so that a steady stream of the vapor can be admitted to the source through the leak—a glass or metal diaphragm containing a pinhole—for ionization. The flow is often molecular, which means the rate of effusion is inversely proportional to the square root of the molecular weight. This is the case when the opening is very small (ten times smaller than the mean free path of the gas particles). Since the lower-weight molecules pass more quickly through the leak, the inlet reservoir slowly becomes enriched in the higher-weight molecules. [This is not a serious problem unless very precise data are needed (e.g., in isotope-ratio work), because leak rates are usually quite slow.]

Solid samples that do not have a high enough vapor pressure to evaporate under conditions of the batch inlet, or that are thermally sensitive, are admitted directly to the source. Usually the sample is placed in a small cup and introduced into the source through a vacuum lock. The sample cup can be cooled (e.g., with liquid nitrogen) or heated by infrared radiation or by thermal contact with a hot metal block surrounding the container. Using this technique, it is no longer necessary to fill the sample reservoir with vapor and, thus, smaller sample sizes (as low as 1 ng) and lower-vapor-pressure substances can be readily admitted. The direct inlet provides a dramatic increase in the versatility of mass spectrometry. No other analytical tool can produce as much information on such small quantities of complex organic or organometallic compounds. Mass spectra can be obtained for such diverse and nonvolatile samples as steroids, carbohydrates, dinucleotides, and low-molecular-weight polymers.

In many cases, nonvolatile substances are converted into more volatile derivatives prior to mass-spectral analysis. Examples include trimethylsilyl derivatives of alcohols or molecules containing sugar groups, ester derivatives of acids, and volatile chelates of trace-metal ions. Usually, a suitable volatile derivative can be synthesized by well established and relatively simple procedures.

Another method for sample introduction is the gas chromatograph (GC), discussed in Chapter 22. Components separated by a GC can be admitted to the source of a mass spectrometer after enriching the eluent vapor (that is, separating the helium carrier-gas from the sample vapor with a molecular separator.) A common design (Fig. 16.2) uses either a porous glass or Teflon membrane through which the small, mobile helium atoms preferentially diffuse and are then pumped away. The larger sample molecules continue through the separator into the source for ionization and finally mass analysis.

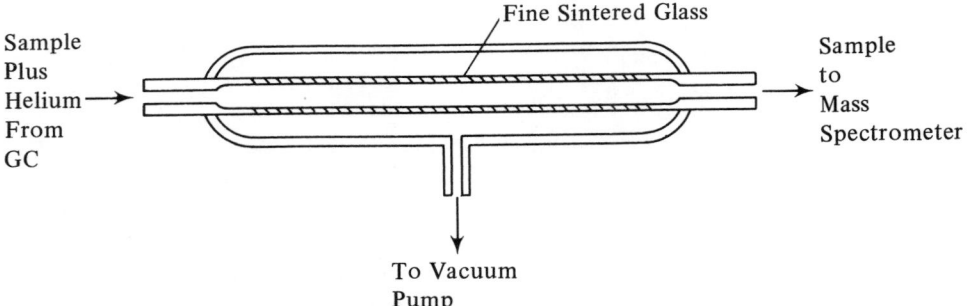

FIGURE 16.2. *A molecular separator used as an interface in GCMS. The GC and interface serve as inlet for the mass spectrometer. The carrier gas (H_2 or He) preferentially effuses through the porous glass and is pumped away.*

Since the width of GC peaks is on the order of a few seconds, a fast-scanning mass analyzer is necessary. The combination of gas chromatography and mass spectrometry (usually given the acronym GCMS) is perhaps the most versatile and sensitive tool in mixture analysis and is often used in petroleum, environmental, and biochemical research.

Electron-Impact Source

The ion source is the heart of the mass spectrometer—the region where the sample ionizes and fragments. One may look at the source as a rather sophisticated chemical reactor initiating a series of characteristic degradation reactions (fragmentation) of an ionized sample. The decompositions take place in a very short time (usually 1 μsec), so a mass spectrum can be obtained very rapidly—as will be seen, some instruments can produce up to 1000 spectra per second.

The most common method of ionization is by electron impact (EI); that is, a high-energy electron beam dislodges an electron from a sample molecule to produce a positive ion.

$$M + e^- \longrightarrow M^+ + 2e^- \tag{16.1}$$

where M = the molecule under study
                  M^+ = the *molecular* or *parent ion*

The beam produces M^+ in a variety of energy states. Some are produced with rather large amounts of internal energy (rotational, vibrational, and electronic) that is dissipated by fragmentation reactions; for instance,

$$M^+ \left\langle \begin{array}{l} M_1{}^+ \longrightarrow M_3{}^+ \\[2ex] M_2{}^+ \longrightarrow M_4{}^+, \text{ etc.} \end{array} \right. \tag{16.2}$$

where $M_1{}^+, M_2{}^+, \ldots$ are lower-mass ions. Other molecular ions resist decomposition because they are formed with insufficient energy for fragmentation. It should be noted that most fragmentation processes are endothermic, and thus low-energy molecular ions will not fragment in the source and will be detected at the molecular mass.

     A schematic of a typical electron-impact source is given in Figure 16.3. The device consists of an *electron gun* that accelerates and focuses electrons emitted by a thin, red-hot filament usually made of rhenium or tungsten. The electrons are accelerated by placing a negative bias of 70 V on the filament, producing a beam with a Gaussian distribution of kinetic energies around a maximum at 70 eV (1 eV = 23.06 kcal/mole). Since most covalent molecules have ionization potentials of around

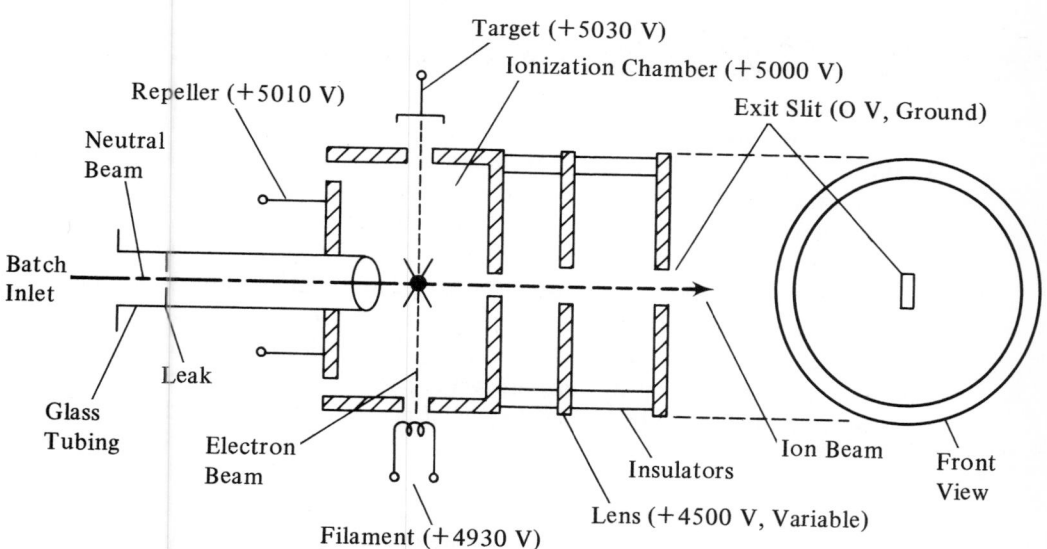

FIGURE 16.3. *Typical electron-impact source. The source is mounted on a frame and inserted into the flight tube of the mass spectrometer. The voltages in parentheses are typical values for the component parts of a spectrometer operating at 5000 V accelerating potential. Note that the target is at +100 V with respect to the filament, and the filament is at −70 V with respect to the ionization chamber.*

TABLE 16.1. *Ionization Potentials of Some Common Organic Molecules*

Compound	Ionization Potential (eV)
Methane	12.98
n-Hexane	10.17
Benzene	9.25
Naphthalene	8.12
Ethanol	10.48
Ethylamine	8.86
Acetone	9.69
Acetic Acid	10.35

Source: J. L. Franklin, J. G. Dillard, H. M. Rosenstock, J. T. Herron, K. Draxl, and F. H. Field, *Nat. Stand. Ref. Data Ser. Nat. Bur. Stand.*, 26 (1969).

10 eV (see Table 16.1), 70-eV electrons are sufficient to dislodge an electron from one of the higher-energy molecular orbitals and produce a molecular ion with a distribution of internal energies. Molecular ions in higher energy states can then decompose, producing various fragment ions. Since fragmentation patterns do not change significantly above 25–30 eV of ionizing energy, 70 eV is simply an arbitrary choice, and 50 eV or 80 eV would be equally acceptable. It is possible to vary this ionization energy by simply changing the voltage applied to the filament. A useful technique is to obtain a spectrum at a low voltage, such as 15 eV; this spectrum will be considerably simplified because of decreased fragmentation. In addition, ionization potentials of complex molecules can be measured by studying the decrease in the molecular-ion signal as a function of ionizing voltage.

The electron beam is collected on a target usually operated at a positive voltage (100 V) with respect to the filament. The target and filament are incorporated into the proper electronic circuitry to insure a constant current or flow of electrons through the ionization region. The regularity of the electron beam is important to achieve a constant number of ionizing events per unit time. (Under normal conditions, only about one neutral molecule out of every 1000 introduced into the source is ionized; the remainder are pumped away by the large-capacity diffusion pumps located outside the source.)

The second important feature of the source is the *ion gun* which accelerates all the molecular and fragment ions out of the source into a mass-analysis sector (the region in which sorting of ions occurs according to m/e value). Accelerating voltages are unique for each spectrometer and are in the 1000–10,000 V range. If a spectrometer operates with 5000 V accelerating potential, the voltages applied to the various components are shown in Figure 16.3.

The repellers are charged to a slightly higher voltage than the chamber to draw the positive ions into the ion gun. The lens plates are two semicircular discs to which is applied a variable voltage to focus the ion beam. Thus, the ions are formed in a positive field whose strength decreases in the direction of the exit slit and therefore accelerates positive sample ions in that direction. As was mentioned previously, the residence time of the ions is about 1 μsec in the ionization chamber. Since the time is short and the pressure low (10^{-6}–10^{-7} torr), each ion acts as an independent entity and will remain as a molecular ion or as a fragment, depending on the amount of internal energy imparted to it by the electron beam.

To review: A steady stream of neutral molecules is drawn into the source from an inlet system and ionized where the stream of molecules intercepts the electron beam. The positive ions created are constantly drawn out with the ion gun, while the remaining neutral molecules are steadily pumped away. Thus, the source operates on a steady-state principle: constant input of neutral molecules and output of ions (and leftover neutral molecules).

The electron-impact source is the work horse of analytical mass spectrometry. It is efficient, durable, and capable of producing a steady, intense beam of positive ions. Like all instruments, it must be periodically disassembled and cleaned, in addition to being equipped with a new filament. However, a well cared-for source may operate for 6 months or more.

Spark Source

Of course, the electron-impact source cannot be used if nonvolatile inorganic samples such as metal alloys or ionic residues are to be analyzed. These substances can be investigated using a different kind of ionization chamber called a spark source, similar to the excitation sources used in emission spectroscopy (Chap. 11). The other parts of the spectrometer can be the same as a general-purpose instrument; however, a Mattauch-Herzog double-focusing instrument is preferred (Fig. 16.7 below), because the spark source produces ions with a wide spread of kinetic energies. The entire device is known as a *spark-source mass spectrometer* (SSMS).

Ions are produced by applying a pulsed radio-frequency voltage of approximately 30 kV to a pair of electrodes mounted directly behind the ion gun; i.e., about where the electron beam is located in an electron-impact source (see Fig. 16.3). The electrodes may be made of the sample itself if it is an electrical conductor or (for a nonconducting specimen) from a mixture of graphite and sample mixed and pressed into an electrode. The high-voltage spark causes localized heating of the electrode with simple vaporization as atoms or simple ions. As in electron impact, the ions are accelerated through the ion gun and then mass analyzed.

There are a number of advantages of SSMS that recommend it as a general-purpose tool for trace elemental analysis in a variety of different samples. First, the method has uniformly high sensitivity for almost all the elements; as little as 1 ppb can be detected. Second, extremely complex samples can be submitted to elemental analysis; as many as sixty different elements have been determined simultaneously in a given sample. Third, the information is relatively simple—only the mass-to-charge ratios of the elements are observed. Complications can arise if the element has a large number of isotopes or if the probability of forming multi-charged ions is large, but nonetheless, the mass spectrum is much simpler than the spectrum obtained in emission spectroscopy. Fourth, the response of the instrument is linear over a wide range of concentrations of a given element in the sample; therefore, it is not necessary to use a wide range of standards to calibrate the measurements.

The detection systems used in SSMS are either photographic plates or electron multipliers (discussed below). The former has the advantage of being an integrating detector and is used for rapid monitoring of the elemental composition of a complex sample. If accurate data are required, electrical recording is preferred.

Thus, SSMS is an extremely powerful technique for routine elemental analysis of complex nonvolatile samples. The chief disadvantages are the high cost of the equipment and the fact that a skilled technician is needed to operate the instrument. Some specific applications will be discussed in Sec. 16.4.

Mass Analysis by Magnetic Sectors

A number of methods of mass analysis can be employed in mass spectrometry. The most common type uses a magnetic sector. Once outside the source, the ion beam moves down a straight, evacuated tube toward a curved region placed between the poles of a magnet (see Fig. 16.4). This region is called the magnetic sector and its purpose is to disperse the ions in curved trajectories that depend on the m/e of the ion. Low-mass ions (beam 1 in the figure) are deflected most, and the heavier mass ions (beam 3) the least.

The kinetic energy of the ions leaving the source is given by the product of the ion charge e and the accelerating voltage V

$$\frac{mv^2}{2} = Ve \qquad (16.3)$$

where m = the mass of the ion
            v = its velocity

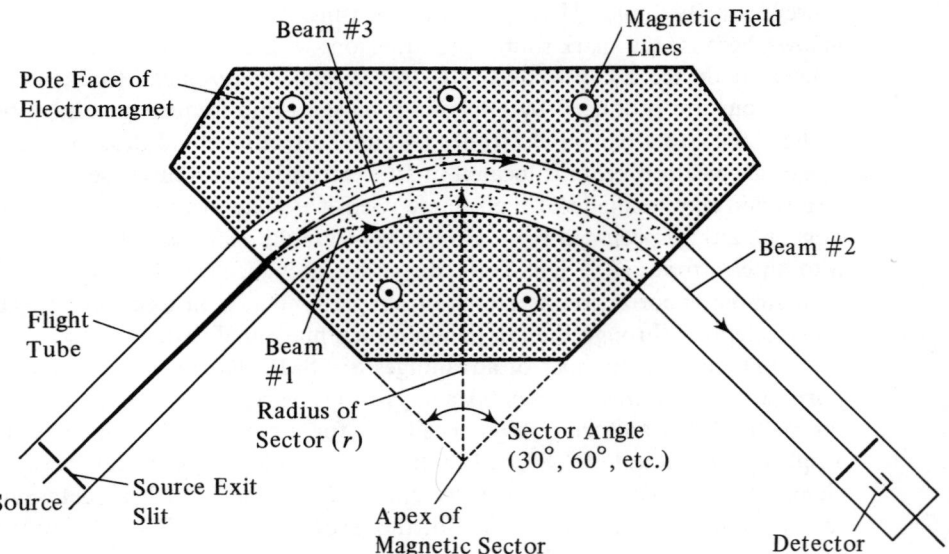

FIGURE 16.4. *Mass analysis in a sector magnetic field. Poles of the electromagnet are located above and below the plane of the page. The magnetic field H points perpendicularly out of the plane of the page. Note that the two slits and the apex of the sector are colinear.*

In the magnetic field, the ions experience a centripetal force of Hev, where H is the field strength that causes deflection. This force must be balanced by the centrifugal force of the ions, mv^2/r, where r is the radius of curvature. Therefore,

$$\frac{mv^2}{r} = Hev \tag{16.4}$$

or

$$v = \frac{Her}{m} \tag{16.5}$$

If the ion velocity is substituted into Equation 16.3, one obtains

$$\frac{m}{2}\left(\frac{Her}{m}\right)^2 = Ve \tag{16.6}$$

or

$$m/e = \frac{H^2r^2}{2V} \tag{16.7}$$

This equation may be rewritten in a form where mass is in atomic mass units, e is the number of charges ($+1$, $+2$, and so on), H is in gauss, r is in centimeters, and V is in volts:

$$m/e = \frac{H^2r^2}{20{,}740V} \tag{16.8}$$

The radius of deflection necessary for an ion to impinge on the detector is determined by the curvature built into the flight tube, and is therefore a constant. A scan of mass spectrum is accomplished either by keeping H constant and decreasing the accelerating voltage so that ever-increasing ion masses are brought to focus (that is, are given a deflection equal to the radius-of-curvature of the flight tube) or by increasing H at constant V to accomplish the same result. Older instruments that used permanent magnets were scanned by the first method; however, most modern instruments are equipped with electromagnets and are scanned by increasing the electric current in the magnet coils.

Mass spectrometers with only a sector magnetic field for mass analysis are known as single-focusing instruments. A well designed single-focusing spectrometer may have resolution as high as 5000. In mass spectrometry, resolution R is defined as

$$R = \frac{m}{\Delta m} \tag{16.9}$$

where Δm = the mass difference between two resolved or separated peaks
m = the nominal mass at which the peaks occur

A resolution of 5000 would indicate that $m/e = 5000$ would be resolved from $m/e = 5001$ (or $m/e = 50.00$ from 50.01). A resolution of 500 is sufficient for many applications in organic chemistry, and low-cost instruments offering such resolution may be adequate to solve many problems.

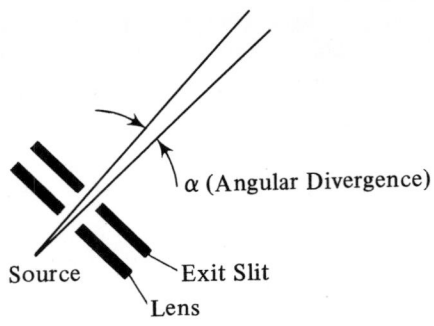

FIGURE 16.5. *An angular divergent beam at the exit of an electron-impact source.*

α (Angular Divergence)

Source

Exit Slit

Lens

Double-Focusing Mass Spectrometers. If resolution greater than about 5000 is required, a double-focusing mass spectrometer is necessary. Two factors that limit resolution in the single-focusing instruments are the angular divergence and spread in kinetic energy of the ion beam as it leaves the ion gun (see Fig. 16.5). The various ions in the beam always have a small spread of kinetic energies (on the order of a few eV) because they are formed in different regions of the ionization chamber and, therefore, experience different total accelerations. In addition, the neutral molecules enter the source with a Boltzmann distribution of thermal energies, which must be added to the ionization and acceleration energies to obtain the total kinetic energy.

To correct for these aberrations, an *electrostatic analyzer* (ESA) or sector is introduced, usually before the magnetic sector. This device consists of two cylindrical electrodes; a positive voltage is applied to the outer one and a negative voltage of equal magnitude to the inner (see Fig. 16.6). The radius of curvature of an ion beam through this sector is determined by the kinetic energy of the beam for a constant voltage—the higher the kinetic energy, the greater the radius. Ultimately, high-energy ions will be deflected so little that they will impinge on the positive electrode. Ions of low kinetic energy are discharged on the negative electrode. Thus, the ESA serves as a kinetic-energy analyzer.

More specifically, the ESA serves to sort out ions of equal kinetic energy and bring them to a common focus. Thus a beam emanating from a single point (the source) is brought to focus at many points, each representing a common kinetic energy (only two are shown in Fig. 16.6). In turn, the magnetic-field shape can be designed, by proper machining of the pole faces, to refocus the separate beams at one point for each mass-to-charge ratio.

Resolution as high as 150,000 with mass-measuring accuracy of 0.3 ppm can be achieved with one commercial double-focusing spectrometer, and a resolution of 20,000–50,000 is not uncommon. Thus, the exact weight of a compound of nominal molecular weight 600 could be measured to ca. ± 0.0002 mass units using the 150,000 resolution instrument. This accuracy allows unambiguous assignment of the elemental composition (chemical formula) of the sample ion and consequently of the neutral sample. Detailed applications will be considered in a later section.

Two designs are prevalent for double-focusing or high-resolution mass spectrometers: (1) Nier-Johnson and (2) Mattauch-Herzog (both shown in Fig. 16.7). The Nier-Johnson design operates only with an electrical detector. The Mattauch-Herzog design uses either a photographic film detector at the focal plane or an electrical detector placed at one point of the plane. The advantage of a photoplate is that it

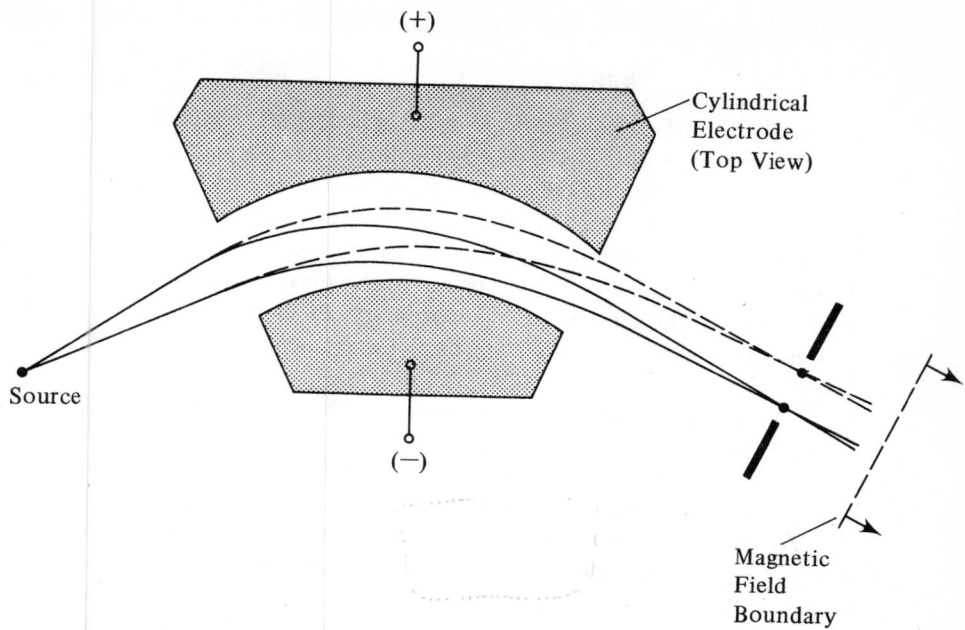

(+)

Cylindrical
Electrode
(Top View)

Source

(−)

Magnetic
Field
Boundary

FIGURE 16.6. *Focusing of a divergent beam of two slightly different kinetic energies (solid and dashed lines) by an electrostatic analyzer (ESA). The ESA is followed by a sector .magnet, see Figures 16.4 and 16.7.*

is an integrating detector and can give a reliable spectrum even when evaporation of the sample is discontinuous or sporadic. It is also useful for very small samples because the operator does not have to wait for the magnetic field to be scanned; instead, the entire spectrum is exposed at once.

The disadvantage of film detection is that the plate must be developed and the lines identified to obtain the mass spectrum. Also, intensity data suffer in accuracy (at best, ion abundances can be measured to 10% relative error). Identification of line position and intensity is done with a microdensitometer (as in x-ray crystallography or emission spectroscopy); high-resolution measurements can be made in this manner. The densitometer is usually interfaced to a computer.

Using a Nier-Johnson design, the exact (high resolution) mass measurement is obtained by peak matching. The exact mass of an unknown peak is determined by a high-precision measurement of the changes in accelerating voltage and ESA voltage that are necessary to superimpose the unknown peak on a peak of known mass produced by a mass standard introduced with the unknown sample. Typical mass standards are perfluorinated hydrocarbons or amines. Since $m/e = H^2r^2/2V$,

$$\frac{m_s}{m_{st}} = \frac{V_{st}}{V_s} \tag{16.10}$$

where V_{st} = the accelerating voltage needed to focus the standard ions at constant H and r

V_s = the voltage needed to focus the sample ions at constant H and r

These measurements are very time-consuming and are usually used to obtain exact mass measurements for only a few important peaks in an unknown spectrum.

A more convenient and expeditious means of mass measurement with either design is to interface an electronic detector with an on-line computer that acquires and stores all the data, both m/e values and intensity data, while the spectrum is being scanned. After identifying the m/e ratios of the mass standard, the computer calculates the exact masses of all the unknown peaks from the scanning time between standard and unknown and, within a few minutes, prints on a teletype the exact masses and intensities of all the peaks in the mass spectrum. This is possibly the most elegant technique in mass spectrometry, for it provides the analyst with exact masses which can be used to determine the elemental compositions of all peaks in a mass spectrum.

For example, a molecular mass of 150.0681 ± 0.003 (2 ppm accuracy) is unique for the composition $C_9H_{10}O_2$ and rules out other samples of nominal mass 150 such as $C_5H_{10}O_5$ (m/e = 150.0528), $C_7H_6N_2O_2$ (m/e = 150.0429), or $C_9H_{14}N_2$ (m/e = 150.1157). Similar arguments can be made for fragment ions as well. Certainly, sample identification using this technique is greatly facilitated compared to that using a low-resolution spectrum, which yields nominal masses only. As might be expected, the high-resolution mass spectrometer equipped with computer is quite expensive ($150,000–$200,000) and complicated to operate and maintain.

Time-of-Flight Mass Analysis

Time-of-flight (TOF) mass spectrometers are equipped with a modified electron-impact source and a long, straight flight-tube. Different masses are distinguished by their different arrival times at the detector located at the end of the tube. Since the kinetic energy of the ions after acceleration is given by Equation 16.3, we can write

$$v = \left(\frac{2Ve}{m}\right)^{1/2} \tag{16.11}$$

Every ion has its own unique velocity, inversely proportional to the square root of the mass. Now if the ions should be accelerated into a long flight-tube of length L, the time necessary for an ion to reach the end of the tube is

$$t = L/v \tag{16.12}$$

The difference in time, Δt, which separates ion 1 from another ion 2, is

$$\Delta t = L(1/v_1 - 1/v_2) \tag{16.13}$$

$$\Delta t = L\frac{\sqrt{m_1} - \sqrt{m_2}}{\sqrt{2Ve}} \tag{16.14}$$

and depends on the difference in the square roots of the masses.

FIGURE 16.7. *Schematic diagrams of the two most commonly used double-focusing mass spectrometers. The Nier-Johnson is really a modified design capable of resolution of 150,000 because of the added hexapole lenses. From S. Evans and R. Graham,* Advan. Mass Spectrom., *6, 429 (1974), by permission of Applied Science Publishers, Ripple Road, Barking, Essex, England.*

Mattauch–Herzog

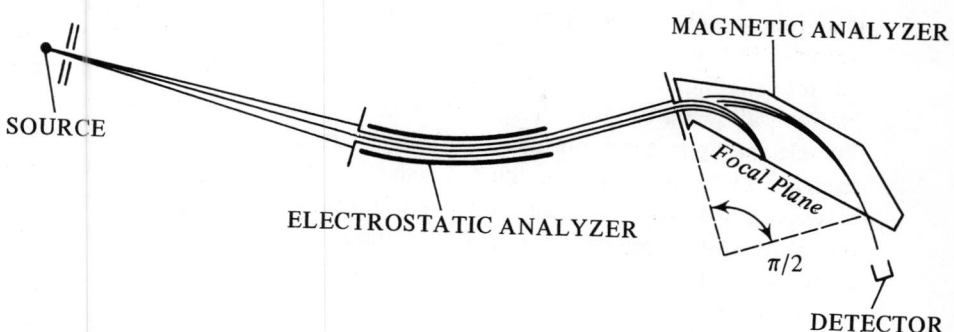

SOURCE

MAGNETIC ANALYZER

ELECTROSTATIC ANALYZER

Focal Plane

$\pi/2$

DETECTOR

Nier–Johnson

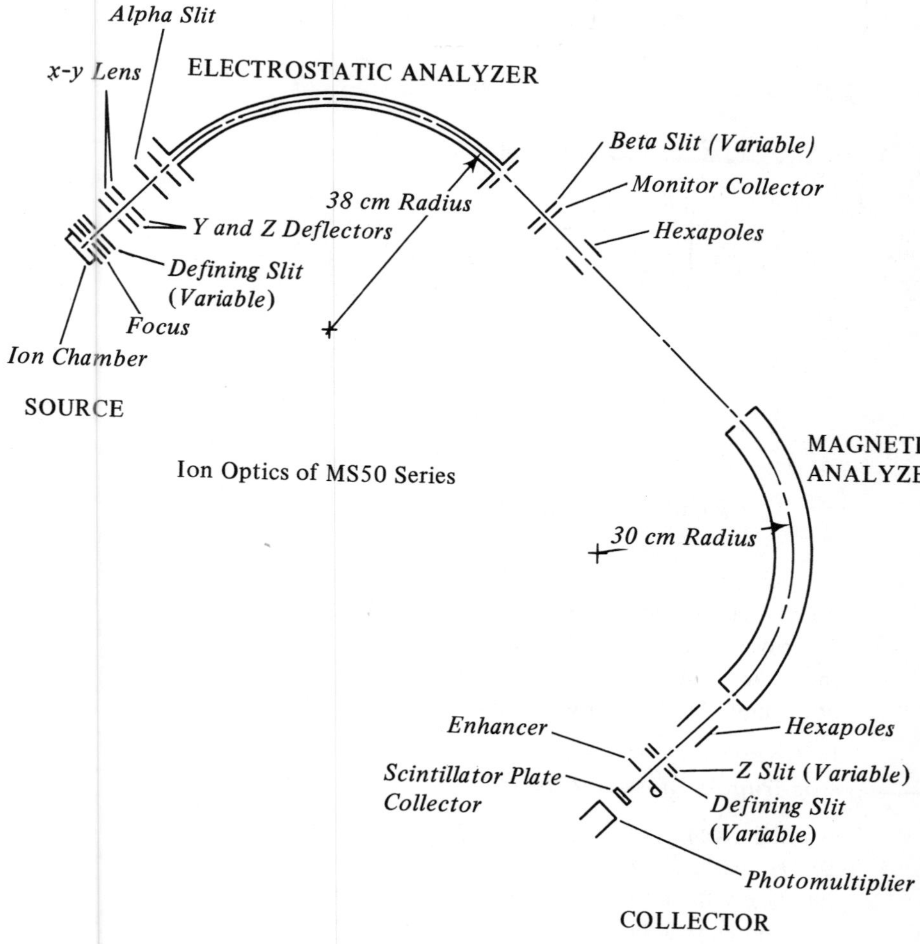

Alpha Slit

x-y Lens

ELECTROSTATIC ANALYZER

Beta Slit (Variable)

Monitor Collector

Hexapoles

38 cm Radius

Y and Z Deflectors

*Defining Slit
(Variable)*

Focus

Ion Chamber

SOURCE

Ion Optics of MS50 Series

MAGNETIC
ANALYZER

30 cm Radius

Enhancer

Hexapoles

*Scintillator Plate
Collector*

Z Slit (Variable)

*Defining Slit
(Variable)*

Photomultiplier

COLLECTOR

The instrument is operated in a pulsed mode because continuous ionization and acceleration would lead to a continuous output at the detector with intractable overlapping of various masses. A typical sequence of events for pulsed operation is as follows: (1) The electron gun is turned on for about 10^{-9} sec to form a packet of ions. (2) The accelerating voltage is turned on for about 10^{-4} sec to draw the ions out into the flight tube. (3) All power shuts off for the rest of the millisecond pulse interval, allowing the ion packet to "coast" unhindered down the flight tube. (4) The electron gun turns on again, forming a fresh packet of ions. The spectrum is recorded by bringing the amplified signals from the detector to the vertical deflection plates of a storage oscilloscope. The horizontal axis of the scope is a time base and starts when the accelerating voltage is activated (see Fig. 16.8). With this instrument, as many as 1,000 spectra per second can be obtained.

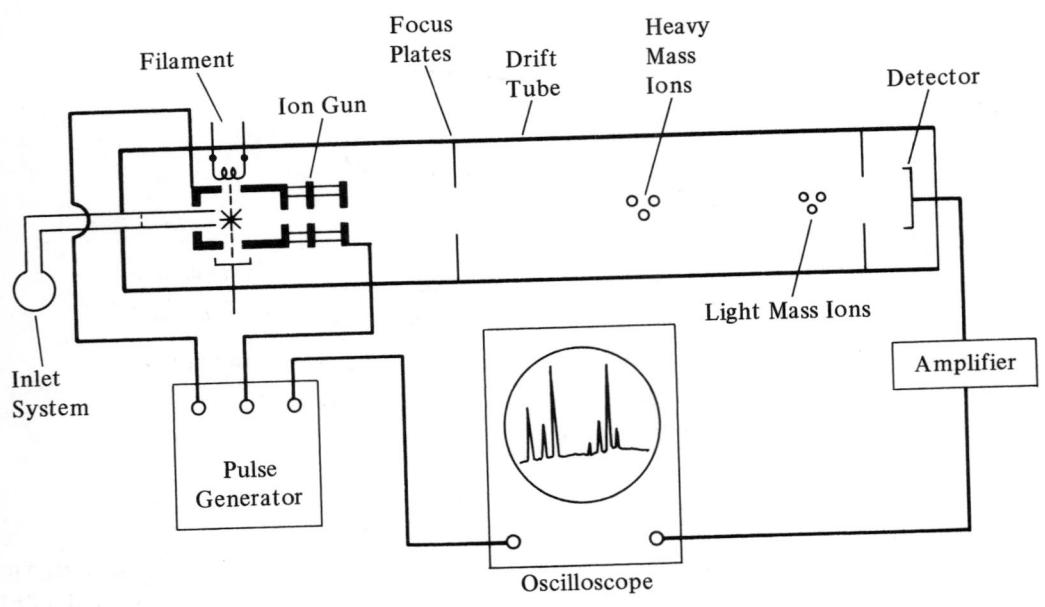

FIGURE 16.8.   *Schematic diagram of a time-of-flight mass spectrometer.*

The advantage of a TOF mass spectrometer is its rapidity in scanning a spectrum. The device is extremely useful in monitoring fast gas-phase kinetics, flash photolysis, and shock-tube experiments, and can be used in GCMS applications. It can be used in routine analytical applications, and the best designs have a resolution of around 500 with an upper mass limit of 1000.

Quadrupole Mass Analyzers

Another means of accomplishing mass analysis without the use of magnetic fields is a *path-stability mass spectrometer* (often called a *mass filter*). In these devices, an ion beam from a conventional source is injected into a dynamic arrangement of electromagnetic fields. Certain ions will take a "stable" path through the analyzer and be collected; others will describe "unstable" paths and be filtered out. The quadrupole is one example of this type of mass spectrometer and has become quite popular in recent years, especially in the area of GCMS.

The quadrupole mass analyzer consists of four poles arranged as shown in Figure 16.9. Ions are injected along the z-axis into a radio-frequency field formed by application of a DC voltage U and an RF voltage $V \cos \omega t$ to the four electrodes. The voltage of the positive electrode is $+(U + V \cos \omega t)$ and that of the negative electrode is $-(U + V \cos \omega t)$. Because V is larger than U, the opposite poles change polarity at twice the RF frequency. The polarity changes are $180°$ out of phase

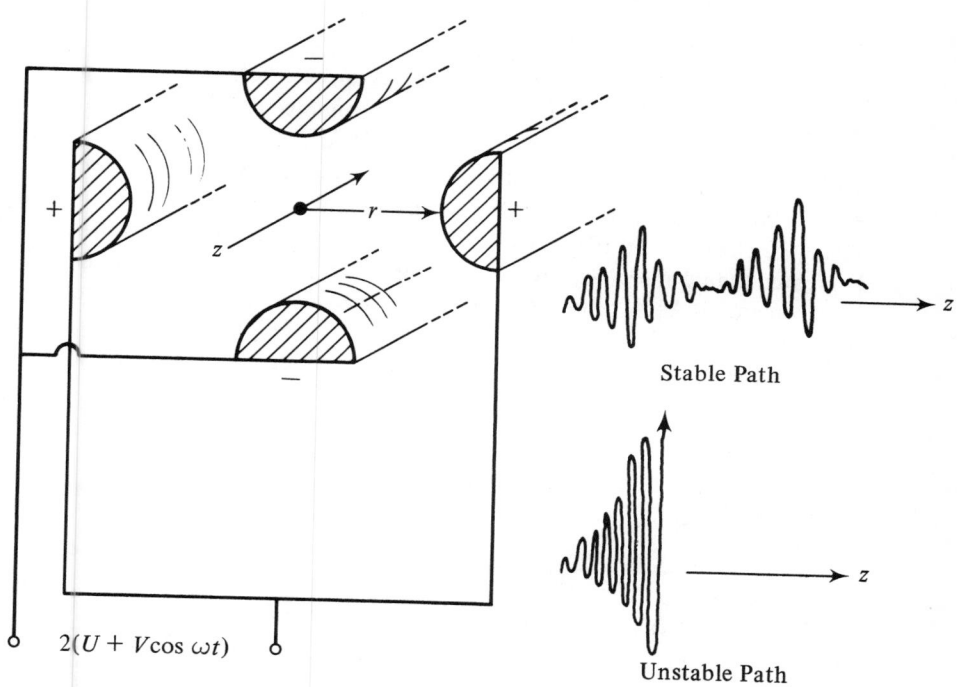

Stable Path

Unstable Path

FIGURE 16.9. *Quadrupole mass-analyzer. Ions are injected from the electron-impact source along the z-axis. Ideally, the poles are hyperbolic in cross-section; in practice, circular poles are used. Pole length is approximately 20 cm and r about 2 cm.*

(that is, when the vertical poles are positive, the horizontal poles are negative). Solution of the differential equations of motion for the ions is rather complicated; it is sufficient here to point out that two types of solution are obtained, representing either a stable path or an unstable path. Both paths involve oscillation about the z-axis because of the alternating field, but as can be seen from Figure 16.9, those ions (ideally of one mass only) in a "stable" path will pass through whereas all others will take the unstable course and be discharged on collision with the poles (they are filtered out). As U and V are varied while keeping the U/V ratio constant, ions of one mass after another will take the stable path and be collected on a detector located at the end of the mass analyzer.

Quadrupoles have a number of distinctive advantages. First, the path does not depend on the kinetic energy or the angular divergence of the incoming ions, so these instruments have high transmission. Second, they are relatively inexpensive and compact. Third, a complete scan can be achieved very rapidly since only a change in voltage is required. As a result of these advantages, such instruments are often used in the GCMS combination (where rapid scanning is a requirement) and in space or satellite work. They perform fairly well as routine analytical instruments; for some designs, an upper mass limit of ~1000 amu with resolution of 700–800 can be achieved.

Ion Cyclotron Resonance

A recent and exciting development in mass spectrometry is *ion cyclotron resonance* (ICR), a technique used for the study of ion-molecule reactions [4–6]. Here ions are formed by electron impact in crossed electric and magnetic fields. The ions then drift along the length of the cell with a velocity given by cE/H, where E is the static electric field, H is the magnetic field strength, and c the speed of light (see Fig. 16.10). Since the electric field (drift field) is quite small (~ 0.1–1.0 V/cm), the residence time is greater than 1 msec—approximately 10^3 times longer than in a conventional mass spectrometer. As a result, reactions between the ions and any neutral molecules present can take place.

Mass analysis occurs in the analyzer section using the cyclotron principle.

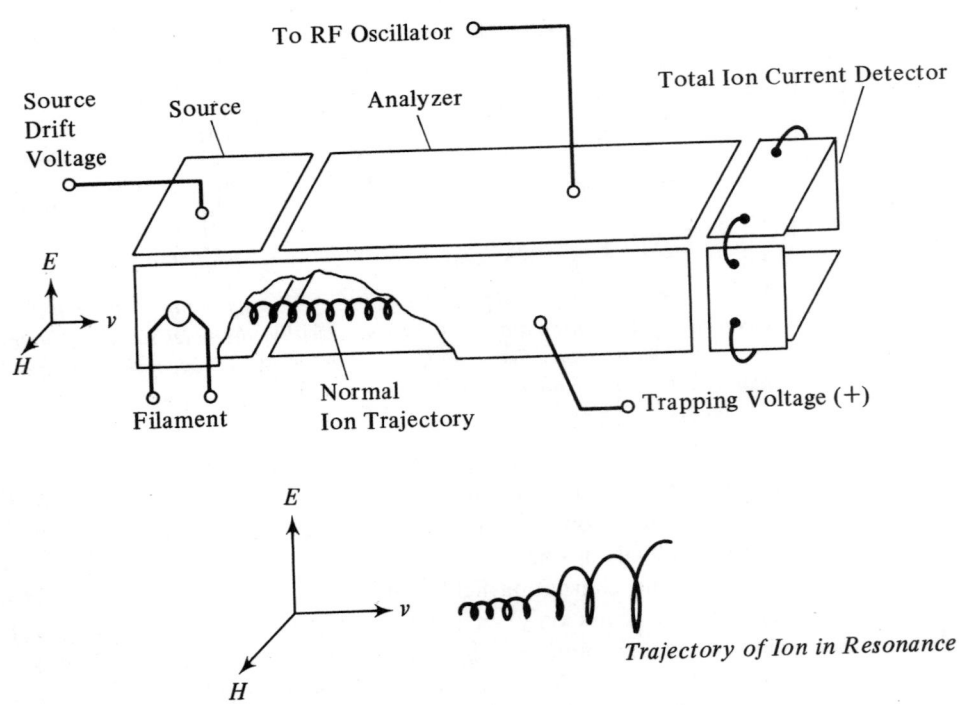

FIGURE 16.10. *The cell used in ion-cyclotron resonance spectroscopy. The cell is located in a vacuum chamber, placed between the poles of an electromagnet with the E and H fields as shown by the axes.*

Drifting ions formed in a uniform magnetic field will travel in a cycloid with a frequency given by

$$\omega = \frac{eH}{mc} \qquad\qquad (16.15)$$

where ω = the frequency in radians/sec

If an alternating electric field is applied to the plates of the analyzer, an ion with a cyclotron frequency equal to the electric-field frequency will absorb energy and begin to spiral (a resonance condition). This energy absorption is detected using a "marginal" oscillator as the source of the alternating voltage (usually in the radio-frequency region), much as in NMR. Using a constant RF input, a mass spectrum of both the primary ions and the secondaries produced in the ion-molecule reactions can be obtained by varying the magnetic field H. The final section of the cell simply collects all the ions and is used to register the total ion current in the cell.

Ion-molecule reactions add a new dimension to mass spectrometry. In addition to the unimolecular decomposition reactions (which are also observed in conventional instruments), bimolecular reactions can be observed. Investigations of these reactions are useful in increasing our understanding of the fundamentals of chemical kinetics and for studying structures and properties of ions without solvation effects (acidity, basicity, stability, etc.). The structure of neutral molecules can also be investigated by allowing them to react with reagent ions. Conventional instruments can be used for ion-molecule reaction studies, but a high pressure (0.01–1 torr) of the neutral molecules must be employed because of the short residence time, thus restricting the reaction studies to molecules with a high vapor pressure. ICR has the advantage of a long residence time and a low kinetic energy of the ions, which means that lower pressures (10^{-5} torr) are adequate.

Methods of Ion Detection

The most useful and sensitive method of detection is to focus the mass-analyzed beam of ions on an *electron multiplier*. (The design of electron multipliers is much the same as that of a photomultiplier tube in ultraviolet-visible spectroscopy [see Chap. 7].) The tube current is amplified and sent to a strip-chart recorder, which often contains, instead of a pen, a mirrored galvanometer that reflects high-intensity light onto photographic paper. The mirror method allows faster scanning than a pen trace; it also allows simultaneous recording of the spectrum at a number of different sensitivities using several galvanometers.

Another, less common, method of detection is a photographic film placed along the focal plane of a Mattauch-Herzog instrument.

16.2 INTERPRETATION OF A MASS SPECTRUM

Certainly the most important applications of mass spectrometry are the identification of complex molecules and the elucidation of their structures. It might be expected that a given molecule would give a unique fragmentation pattern that would distinguish it from all other substances. This expectation is realized often, but not always. As in other forms of spectroscopy, the analyst must be able to interpret the pattern he observes; this requires considerable skill and experience. In the following pages, we will discuss the types of ions found in a mass spectrum in order to present some rather basic procedures in interpretation. More thorough approaches can be found in specialized monographs.

Mass spectrometry is an extremely information-rich technique, producing many signals or peaks for a single substance. Its chief advantage over other information-rich tools (such as NMR, IR, and x-ray spectroscopy) is its sensitivity—useful spectra can be obtained for samples as small as one nanogram. However, a complete understanding of all the fragmentation mechanisms has not yet been achieved.

Assignment of the Molecular Ion

As previously discussed, the *molecular ion* has a mass that corresponds to the molecular mass of the neutral sample. Because one electron has been removed, it is a radical cation, symbolized by $M^{\ddagger}$ or often just M^+. Most substances produce a recognizable molecular ion, although there are important exceptions. High-molecular-weight hydrocarbons, aliphatic alcohols, ethers, and amines produce only a small number of molecular ions that may be difficult to find if the signal-to-noise ratio is small. Polyfunctional compounds such as carbohydrates and polyamines often do not yield a molecular ion upon electron impact. On the other hand, molecules possessing an aromatic ring often give abundant molecular ions, presumably because of their ability to delocalize positive charge.

The first problem in dealing with an unknown spectrum is the identification of the molecular ion. Some simple rules are helpful. First, M^+ should have the highest mass, ignoring isotopic contributions. Second, the molecular mass will be an even mass-number if it contains an even number $(0, 2, 4, \ldots)$ of nitrogen atoms, and will be an odd mass number otherwise; this is known as the "nitrogen rule." Some examples are: benzene, C_6H_6, $M^+ = 78$; ethanol, C_2H_5OH, $M^+ = 46$; cholesterol, $C_{27}H_{46}O$, $M^+ = 386$; dimethyl hydrazine, $CH_3NHNHCH_3$, $M^+ = 60$; methylamine, CH_3NH_2, $M^+ = 31$; pyridine, C_5H_5N, $M^+ = 79$. A final test of a correct M^+ assignment is that no illogical losses should be found. Seldom do organic molecules lose more than 4 hydrogen atoms, to give $(M - 4)$ fragments. The next reasonable fragmentations of molecular ions are losses of a methyl group $(M - 15)$, NH_2 or O $(M - 16)$, OH or NH_3 $(M - 17)$, H_2O $(M - 18)$, F $(M - 19)$, HF $(M - 20)$, and C_2H_2 $(M - 26)$. Thus, if a tentative molecular ion has lost 4 to 14 or 21 to 25 mass units, either the assignment of M^+ is incorrect or the spectrum is of a mixture.

Elemental Composition of the Molecular Ion

In the spectrum of methane (CH_4), a small peak located at $m/e = 17$ has an intensity 1.1% that of the M^+ peak at $m/e = 16$. The signal at $m/e = 17$ arises because carbon consists of two naturally occurring stable isotopes: ^{12}C and ^{13}C. Assigning the value 100% to the quantity of ^{12}C (an incorrect, but useful, procedure), we find that ^{13}C is 1.1%. Thus $m/e = 17$ in methane is $^{13}CH_4{}^+$. A molecule that contains six carbon atoms, such as benzene (C_6H_6), will have M^+ at $m/e = 78$ and $^{13}CC_5H_6$

TABLE 16.2. *Relative Isotopic Abundances of Some Common Elements*

Element	M Mass	M Percent	M + 1 Mass	M + 1 Percent	M + 2 Mass	M + 2 Percent
H	1	100	2	0.015	———	
C	12	100	13	1.08	———	
N	14	100	15	0.36	———	
O	16	100	17	0.04	18	0.20
S	32	100	33	0.80	34	4.4
Cl	35	100	———		37	32.5
Br	79	100	———		81	98.0

at $m/e = 79$, but now the intensity at 79 is 6.6% (1.1% × 6), since the probability of finding one ^{13}C is six times greater.

The analyst can make use of the natural abundance of ^{13}C to assign the number of carbon atoms in M^+. For example, if M^+ is 100% and $(M + 1)^+$ is 7.7%, M^+ contains 7 carbons. Often M^+ is not the largest peak in a mass spectrum and therefore is not assigned an intensity of 100% (the largest peak in a spectrum is usually arbitrarily assigned an intensity of 100% and all other peaks are measured relative to this). In that case, a useful formula is

$$\text{No. of carbon atoms} = \left(\frac{M + 1}{M}\right)\Big/0.011 \qquad \textbf{(16.16)}$$

where $M + 1$ and M are the intensities of the respective peaks. This procedure works fairly well if M^+ contains 10 or fewer carbon atoms. A relative error of 10% in the measurement of $M + 1$ or impurities in the spectrum make the number of carbon atoms a maximum rather than exact number at best. If $M^+ = 100\%$ and $M + 1 = 17.8\%$, the maximum number of C's is 16 (1.1% × 16 = 17.6%); although the molecule may contain 15 carbons, it cannot contain 17 carbon atoms.

Other elements have isotopic contributions helpful in determining how many atoms of that element are contained in M^+. Table 16.2 gives some examples. The halogens are noteworthy: an M^+ that contains one Cl must have an $M + 2$ peak with at least 1/3 the abundance of M^+, and a bromine-containing molecule will have nearly a 1:1 ratio of $M:(M + 2)$.

Using the data in the table, the chemist can predict the pattern at M, M + 1, and M + 2 for a suspected compound and compare it with experiment. For example, with 4-chloropyridine one would expect the following:

Ion		Composition	m/e	Abundance (calculated)
M^+	=	$C_5H_4N^{35}Cl$	113	100%
$M + 1$	=	$^{13}CC_4H_4N^{35}Cl$ $C_5H_4{}^{15}N^{35}Cl$ }	114	$5(1.1) + 1(0.4) = 5.9\%$
$M + 2$	=	$C_5H_4N^{37}Cl$	115	$1(32.5) = 32.5\%$
$M + 3$	=	$^{13}CC_4H_4N^{37}Cl$ $C_5H_4{}^{15}N^{37}Cl$ }	116	$0.325[5(1.1) + 1(0.4)] = 1.9\%$

If the observed pattern at $m/e = 113–116$ agrees with the calculation, the evidence is strong that M^+ is C_5H_4NCl.

Most other elements have distinctive isotopic compositions which can be obtained by referring to a handbook. These patterns are useful for confirming the presence of that element in M^+.

The procedures outlined above for estimating the elemental composition of molecular ions can be applied to fragment ions as well. For example, a common ion in hydrocarbons or molecules with large alkyl substituents is $C_3H_7^+$ ($m/e = 43$). Molecules containing acetyl groups will give a CH_3CO^+ ion, also at $m/e = 43$. The $m/e = 44$ in the former case will be 3.3% of the intensity at 43, whereas in the latter $m/e = 44$ will be 2.2%. A cautionary note must be interjected: to apply the rules, one must be certain that the $F + 1$ and $F + 2$ masses (where F is a fragment mass) consist only of isotopic contribution to F and not of other fragment ions.

Fragment Ions from Simple Cleavage Reactions

After ionization, most molecules fragment by the simple loss of a portion of the molecule in the form of a free radical. For example, isobutane can readily lose a methyl radical to form the propyl ion ($m/e = 43$).

$$\overset{\displaystyle\overset{\textstyle \overline{CH_3}}{|}}{CH_3CHCH_3} \longrightarrow CH_3\overset{+}{CH}CH_3 + \dot{C}H_3 \qquad (16.17)$$

The fragment ions formed in these reactions are often gas-phase carbonium ions, the same ions observed as intermediates in certain solution reactions of organic compounds. Many mass-spectral fragmentations produce the thermodynamically most stable carbonium ions. Notice that the propyl ion has an odd mass-number ($m/e = 43$), which is typical for all simple cleavage ions possessing an even number of nitrogen atoms. (Molecular ions with an even number of nitrogen atoms have even masses, by the nitrogen rule described above.) Although a complete treatment of simple cleavage reactions is not possible here, a brief introduction in terms of structural types will be presented [7–9].

Aliphatic Hydrocarbons. The mass spectra of two isomeric hydrocarbons are given in Figure 16.11. Straight-chain hydrocarbons and molecules containing large *n*-alkyl groups typically give a pattern similar to that shown in Figure 16.11A. The data are reported in bar-graph form with the largest peak (called the *base peak*) assigned an abundance of 100%. The right-hand axis is expressed as a percentage of all ion intensities summed together. Another common method of presenting mass-spectral data is in tabular form, a list of all m/e ratios and their relative abundances (again normalized to the most intense peak).

Various alkyl ions such as $C_3H_5^+$, $C_3H_7^+$, $C_4H_7^+$, $C_4H_9^+$ ($m/e = 41, 43, 55,$ and 57) dominate hydrocarbon spectra, but these do not come from initial simple

FIGURE 16.11. *A: Electron-impact spectrum of n-decane, $C_{10}H_{22}$, at 70 eV ionizing energy. B: Electron-impact spectrum of 3,3,5-trimethylheptane, an isomer of n-decane. Notice the change from the "normal" alkyl pattern.*

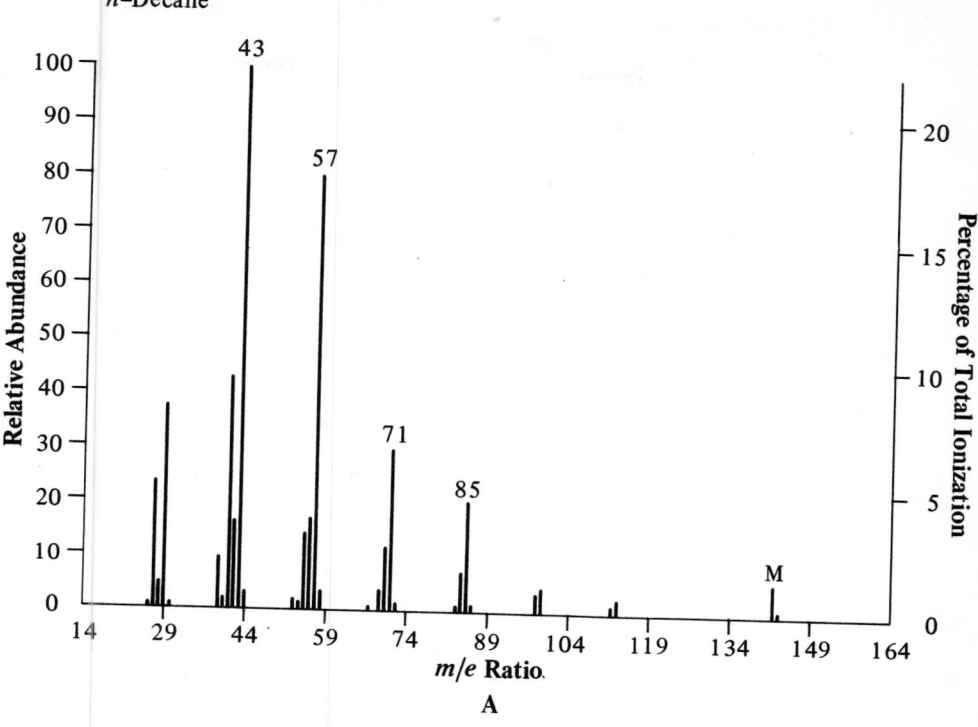

A

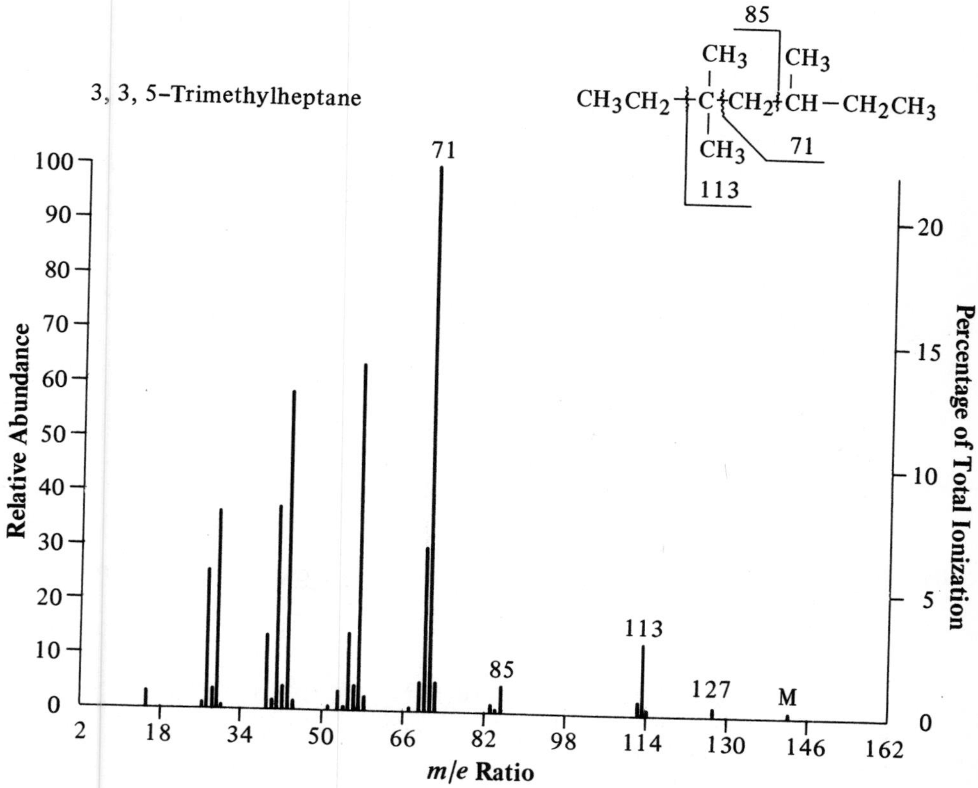

B

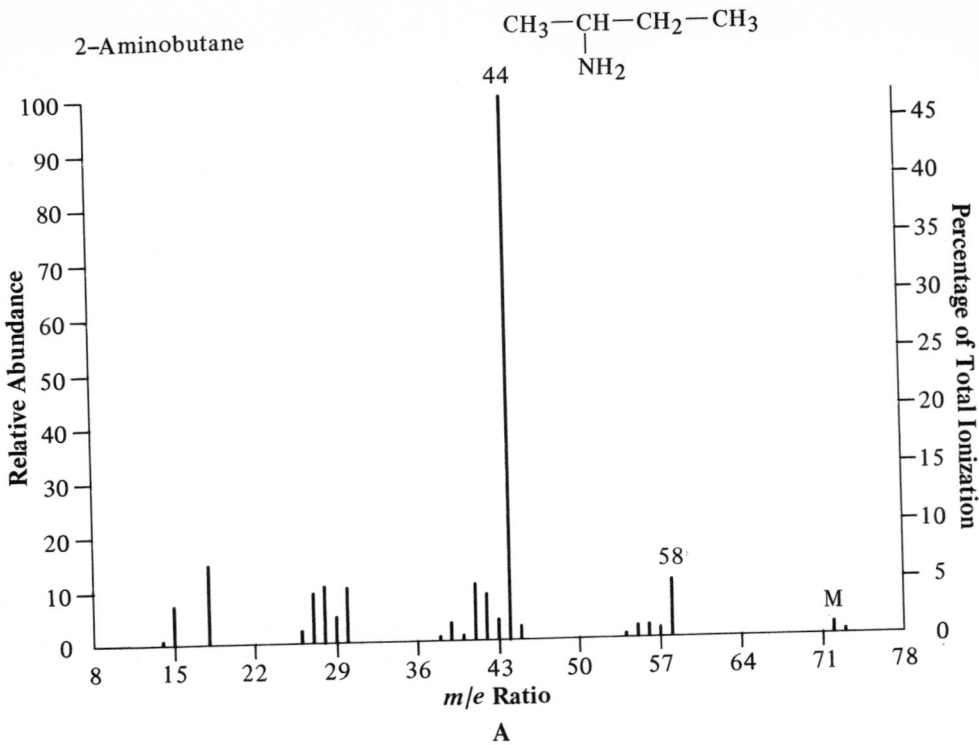

FIGURE 16.12. *Mass spectra of a series of sec-butyl compounds. Major features of the spectra can be interpreted in terms of simple initial cleavage reactions. All are at 70 eV ionizing energy.*

cleavages of M^+, but rather from subsequent decomposition of the initially formed ions. Branching in an alkyl chain can be detected by slight perturbations of the straight-chain spectrum caused by preferential cleavages at the branch points (see Fig. 16.11B). Thus, the most significant fragments are not the high-abundance ions at low mass, but rather the low-abundance high-mass ions formed by simple cleavage at branch points.

Saturated Aliphatic Compounds Containing Heteroatoms. A great variety of organic matter falls in this classification—for example, alcohols, ethers, mercaptans, amines, and halides. Two types of simple cleavage reactions may occur that are initiated or directed by the presence of the heteroatom (O, S, N, X, etc.), as exemplified by Equations 16.18 and 16.19 for ethyl ether. Heteroatoms that can stabilize the positive

$$CH_3CH_2OCH_2CH_3^{\overset{+}{\cdot}} \longrightarrow \cdot CH_3 + [CH_3CH_2O\overset{+}{C}H_2 \longleftrightarrow CH_3CH_2\overset{+}{O}{=}CH_2]$$
$$m/e = 59 \ (51\% \ \text{Rel. Abund.}) \qquad \textbf{(16.18)}$$

$$CH_3CH_2OCH_2CH_3^{\overset{+}{\cdot}} \longrightarrow CH_3CH_2O\cdot + \overset{+}{C}H_2CH_3 \qquad \textbf{(16.19)}$$
$$m/e = 29 \ (40\% \ \text{Rel. Abund.})$$

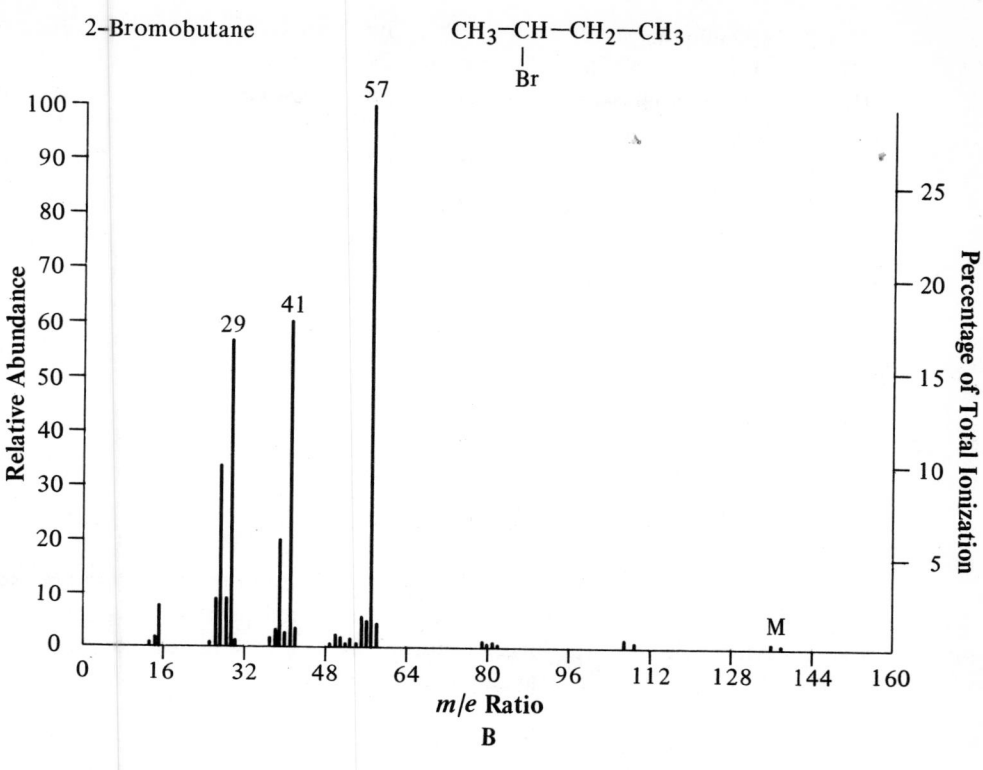

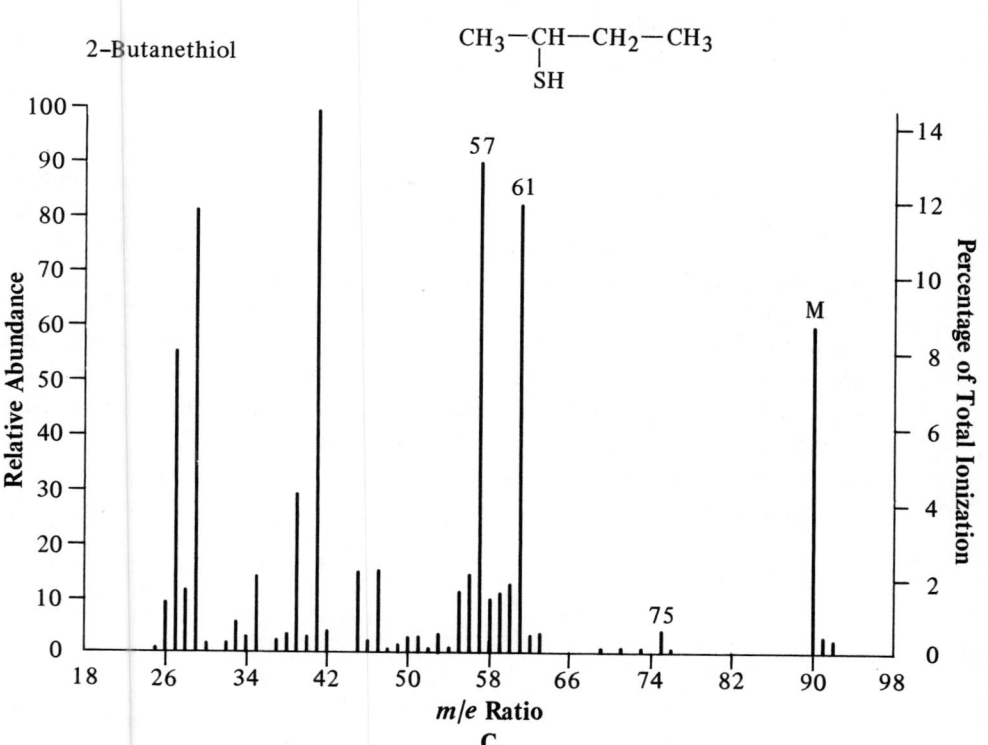

charge by resonance prefer path 16.18. Other, more electronegative, heteroatoms prefer path 16.19. Aliphatic amines fragment almost exclusively by path 16.18; alcohols, ethers, and thio compounds fragment by both pathways; and halogen compounds preferentially lose the X· (path 16.19). Thus, 2-aminopropane undergoes loss of both hydrogen and a methyl group to give $m/e = 58$ and 44, respectively; whereas 2-bromopropane loses Br almost exclusively.

$$
\begin{array}{c}
\overline{CH_3} \\
| \\
CH_3\text{-}CH\text{-}NH_2
\end{array}^{+\cdot}
\longrightarrow
\begin{cases}
CH_3\text{-}CH\text{=}\overset{+}{N}H_2 + \cdot CH_3 \\
m/e = 44\ (100\%\ \text{Rel. Abund.}) \\[2ex]
\begin{array}{c}
CH_3 \\
| \\
CH_3\text{-}C\text{=}\overset{+}{N}H_2 + \cdot H
\end{array} \\
m/e = 58\ (10\%\ \text{Rel. Abund.})
\end{cases}
\qquad (16.20)
$$

$$
\begin{array}{c}
\overline{CH_3} \\
| \\
CH_3\text{-}CH\text{-}Br
\end{array}^{+\cdot}
\longrightarrow
\begin{array}{c}
CH_3 \\
|+ \\
CH_3CH
\end{array} + Br\cdot
\qquad (16.21)
$$
$$m/e = 43\ (100\%\ \text{Rel. Abund.})$$

Try to rationalize the three spectra in Figure 16.12 using the rules just discussed!

Notice that when there is a choice between the loss of various radicals (hydrogen, methyl, ethyl, etc.), the larger group is preferred, as in reaction 16.20. This is generally true of all simple cleavage reactions at 70 eV of ionizing energy.

Alkenes and Doubly Bonded Heteroatoms. One might expect that a double bond in a long hydrocarbon chain, such as a fatty acid, could be located by mass spectrometry since formation of allyl ions would be preferred:

$$
\begin{array}{c}
R\text{-}CH_2\text{-}CH\text{=}\overline{CH} \\
|
\end{array}^{+\cdot}
\xrightarrow{-H}
R\text{=}CH\text{=}CH\text{-}\overline{CH_2}{}^{+\cdot} \longrightarrow \text{ etc.}
$$
$$
\xdownarrow{-R}\ \overset{+}{C}H_2\text{-}CH\text{=}CH + \text{other fragments}
\qquad (16.22)
$$

This possibility is not realized because the double bond rearranges or migrates after ionization but prior to fragmentation. As a result, isomeric olefins tend to give nearly identical spectra. Examples of this kind constitute a serious drawback of electron-impact ionization if complete sample identification is required.

If the molecule contains a double bond to a heteroatom, such as in a carbonyl group, the simple cleavage reaction occurs adjacent to this group and locating the functional group is often straightforward. Here, double-bond migration is not a problem. An example is 2-butanone, which gives a base peak corresponding to loss of an ethyl group, but also experiences some loss of methyl.

$$
\begin{array}{c}
O \\
\| \\
CH_3\overset{}{C}CH_2CH_3
\end{array}^{+\cdot}
\longrightarrow
\begin{cases}
\begin{array}{c}
O \\
\| \\
CH_3\overset{}{C}{}^{+} + CH_3\overset{\cdot}{C}H_2
\end{array} \\
m/e = 43\ (100\%\ \text{Rel. Abund.}) \\[3ex]
\begin{array}{c}
O \\
\| \\
CH_3CH_2\overset{}{C}{}^{+} + \cdot CH_3
\end{array} \\
m/e = 57\ (7\%\ \text{Rel. Abund.})
\end{cases}
\qquad (16.23)
$$

Note again that loss of the larger alkyl is preferred. This type of fragmentation is found in most carbonyl compounds (acids, aldehydes, esters, etc.).

Aromatic Compounds. The spectrum of benzene (Fig. 16.13) is archetypal of unsubstituted aromatic compounds. Usually one of the most intense peaks is M^+, and the fragmentation pattern is quite simple (compare with Fig. 16.11). The reason is that aromatic compounds are readily able to stabilize a positive charge by delocalization. The only possible single cleavage in benzene is loss of H to give $C_6H_5^+$ ($m/e = 77$). Ring opening and cleavage give rise to $C_4H_4^+$ ($m/e = 52$) and $C_3H_3^+$ ($m/e = 39$).

Substituted aromatics such as shown in Equation 16.24 fragment preferentially by loss of R to give the stable benzyl ion, which is known to rearrange to the symmetrical tropylium ion (*A*)

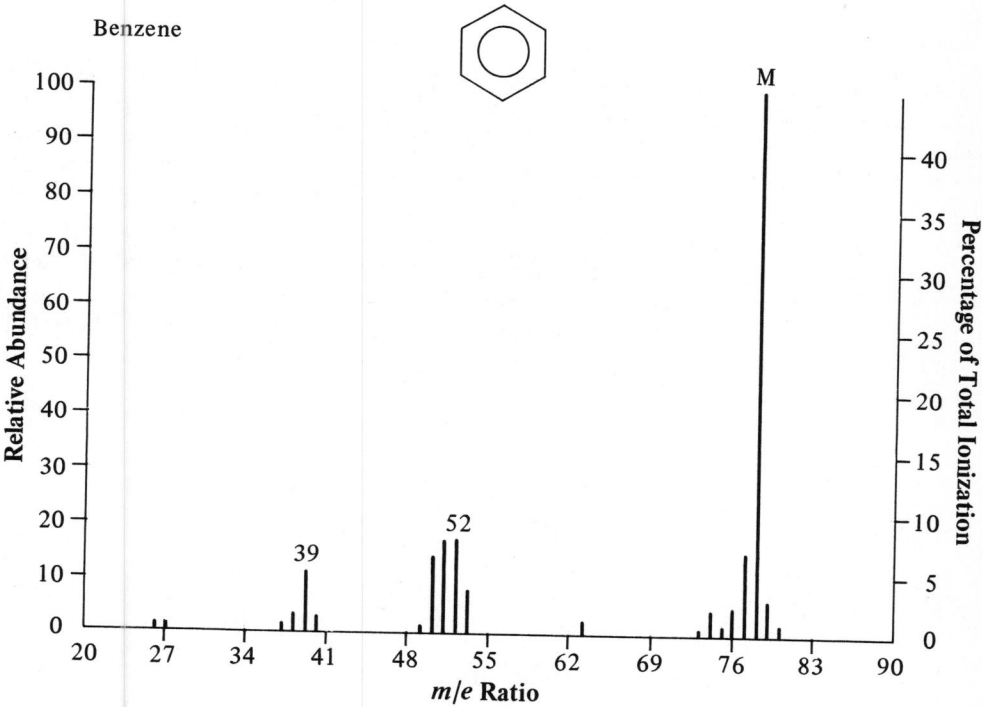

$$(16.24)$$

(*A*)

The spectra of *ortho-*, *meta-*, and *para-*substituted compounds are often identical because the substituent location is lost in the 7-membered ring ion. Except for

Benzene

FIGURE 16.13. *Electron-impact mass-spectrum of benzene at 70 eV of ionizing energy.*

specific *ortho*-disubstituted compounds, the chemist cannot use mass spectrometry for assigning ring-substituted isomers in various aromatics.

Fragment Ions from Rearrangements of M⁺

Since rearrangements may alter the original skeleton of a molecule, one might think that they are troublesome in mass-spectral interpretation. Actually, a number of fragmentations of M^+ involving rearrangement are analytically very useful. Most of these processes occur by loss of a neutral molecule, rather than a radical, and are found at even masses in a mass spectrum (if the number of nitrogen atoms is even). Thus, a rather abundant even-mass ion at the higher-mass end of the spectrum should be singled out for special attention. We will discuss only a few examples to illustrate the interpretive procedure.

The McLafferty Rearrangement. In many compounds containing a doubly bonded heteroatom (C=X), a hydrogen will transfer to X from the third carbon down the chain from C=X, with the loss of an olefin. The process is illustrated for 2-hexanone:

$$\left[\begin{array}{c} \text{H} \quad \text{CH}_3 \\ \text{O} \quad \text{CH} \\ \| \\ \text{C} \quad \text{CH}_2 \\ \text{CH}_3 \; \text{CH}_2 \end{array} \right]^{\ddagger} \longrightarrow \left[\begin{array}{c} \overline{\text{OH}} \\ | \\ \text{C} \\ \| \\ \text{CH}_3 \; \text{CH}_2 \end{array} \right]^{\ddagger} + \text{C}_3\text{H}_6 \qquad (16.25)$$

$$m/e = 58$$

The transfer is highly specific, involving only the hydrogen shown. This fragmentation is known as the *McLafferty rearrangement*. Notice the fragment ion has an even mass-number ($m/e = 58$), which is typical for rearrangements of this kind. Because most initial fragmentations are cleavage reactions that yield odd mass-numbers (unless the number of nitrogen atoms is odd), highly abundant rearrangements are easy to pick out of the spectrum. The fragmentation occurs in many other carbonyl compounds (acids, esters, amides, aldehydes, and so on), provided a hydrogen is situated 3 atoms from the carbonyl.

The analytical utility of the McLafferty rearrangement is illustrated for 3-methyl-2-pentanone, an isomer of 2-hexanone:

$$\left[\begin{array}{c} \text{H} \quad \text{CH}_2 \\ \text{O} \\ \| \\ \text{C} \quad \text{CH}_2 \\ \text{CH}_3 \quad \text{CH} \\ | \\ \text{CH}_3 \end{array} \right]^{+} \longrightarrow \left[\begin{array}{c} \overline{\text{OH}} \\ | \\ \text{C} \\ \| \\ \text{CH}_3 \quad \text{CH} \\ | \\ \text{CH}_3 \end{array} \right]^{+} + \text{C}_2\text{H}_4 \qquad (16.26)$$

$$m/e = 72$$

The molecular ion is again of the correct structure to give a McLafferty rearrangement, but this time to yield $m/e = 72$, indicating that the methyl substituent is in position 3. Rather subtle differences in molecular structure, such as the position of the branch point, can be often uncovered using information from this rearrangement.

Rearrangements in Aromatic Compounds. An important fragmentation in various substituted aromatic compounds involves the transfer of a side-chain hydrogen atom to X (where X = CH_2, O, S) or to the aromatic ring:

$$\left[\bigcirc X(CH_2)_n \overline{CH_3} \right]^{\dot{+}} \longrightarrow \left[\bigcirc \overline{XH} \right]^{\dot{+}} \quad or \quad \left[\bigcirc \underset{H}{\overset{X}{\Vert}} \underset{H}{\overset{}{}} \right]^{\dot{+}} \qquad (16.27)$$

$$[n = 1, 2, \ldots]$$

Thus, the base peak in the spectrum of phenyl ethyl ether is $m/e = 94$ (C_6H_5OH); and an important peak (55% relative abundance) in the spectrum of butyl benzene is $m/e = 92$ (C_7H_8). Isotopic labeling studies with deuterium show that H-transfer occurs from any one of the four carbon atoms in phenyl butyl ether, suggesting a nonspecific rearrangement. Nevertheless, the fragmentation is analytically useful— only phenyl ethyl ether, of the other $C_8H_{10}O$ isomers shown, gives loss of C_2H_4.

We have only discussed two types of rearrangement involving M^+ processes. Many others are highly specific and quite useful in elucidating molecular structure; others, less specific, can still yield information (for instance, the side-chain rearrangement above). Rearrangements invariably involve the loss of small neutral molecules such as olefins, H_2O (in alcohols), small alcohols (in some esters), acids, carbon monoxide, formaldehyde, etc. They are readily identified in the high-mass region of the spectrum as even-mass-number ions (for an even number of nitrogen atoms) and are usually useful in mass-spectral interpretation.

Further Fragmentation Reactions

Enough energy is often deposited in the molecular ion by the ionization process to again decompose the initially formed fragments, producing secondary, tertiary, etc., ions at lower masses. The mass spectra for complicated molecules often contain very abundant fragment ions of low mass, which are products of these consecutive decompositions. In the hydrocarbon spectra (Fig. 16.11), notice the abundant peaks around $m/e = 29$, 43, and 57. These are not initially formed fragments, but rather arise by successive rearrangement reactions. For example, $m/e = 43$ ($C_3H_7^+$) probably originates by the loss of C_2H_4 from $C_5H_{11}^+$, C_3H_6 from $C_6H_{13}^+$, or of other neutral olefins from higher-mass primary ions. These rearrangements are less useful for interpretation than the initial fragmentations and may even be misleading to the inexperienced analyst. There is a strong tendency, for instance, to incorrectly interpret abundant $C_3H_7^+$ as indicating a branched propyl group, although in some instances this may be the case. [An abundant $m/e = 43$ ($C_3H_7^+$) would be significant if the abundances at $m/e = 57$ ($C_4H_9^+$) and $m/e = 29$ ($C_2H_5^+$) were very small.]

The extensive fragmentation that often occurs in complex molecules can be attenuated so as to emphasize the initial cleavages. This is done by lowering the ionizing energy to 15–20 eV or by using other methods of ionization (e.g., chemical or field), which are discussed later.

Multiply Charged Ions

Besides the singly charged ions that dominate a mass spectrum, some doubly charged fragments can be found. For example, a weak peak at $m/e = 38.5$ (77/2) in the spectrum of benzene is $C_6H_5^{2+}$. Gas-phase metal ions from organometallic compounds or from volatile metals such as mercury are often found in +2 or even +3 states. Usually, multiply charged ions are of low abundance and not very useful in interpretation.

Metastable Ions

In all mass spectrometers, fragmentation continues to occur outside the source (that is, after full acceleration). If, in a sector instrument, an ion (M_1^+) decomposes to M_2^+ prior to entering the magnetic field [$M_1^+ \rightarrow M_2^+ + (M_1 - M_2)$], the M_2^+ will no longer have the same kinetic energy as the "normal" ions and, therefore, will not be mass analyzed at M_2. Instead, its kinetic energy is $M_2(M_2/M_1)$ because of energy conservation, and the ion will be analyzed at a lower apparent mass $m^* = M_2^2/M_1$.

Metastables are usually identified by broad low-abundance peaks occurring at fractional masses. For example, in acetophenone, one might postulate that a methyl group is lost to form the $m/e = 105$ ion, which then loses CO to form $m/e = 77$. An alternate route is the direct, one-step loss of CH_3CO. Both processes are

$$(16.28)$$

verified by the observation of two metastable peaks (designated by * in 16.28) at $77^2/105 = m/e = 56.5$ and at $77^2/120 = m/e = 49.4$. Metastable peaks, then, are invaluable aids in determining which decompositions took place to give the observed mass-spectral patterns.

Negative Ions

Negative ions can be investigated by reversing the polarity of the accelerating voltage and the magnetic field. Usually they are formed by one of two processes: (a) the neutral molecule captures an electron from the ionizing beam to form M^-, or (b) ion-pair production ($AB + e^- \rightarrow A^+ + B^- + e^-$), which yields fragmentary negative ions. The abundances of negative ions are 10–1000 times less than those of positive ions, and it is not yet clear how useful the technique of negative-ion mass spectrometry will be in identifying compounds.

16.3 ANALYTICAL APPLICATIONS OF ELECTRON-IMPACT MASS SPECTROMETRY

Identification and Structural Elucidation of Compounds

It should be clear from the last section that a mass spectrum yields a wealth of information from very small samples (10^{-6}–10^{-9} g). If the mass spectrum has been previously reported, identification of the unknown is accomplished by checking for a match. However, caution must be employed because spectra obtained with different instruments using different temperatures and source conditions will not match identically; small quantitative differences in relative abundances arise because of different residence times in the source and because certain instrument designs may discriminate against low- or high-mass ions. Checking for a match can be done rapidly using a computer with a data file of previously determined spectra. Compilations are available on magnetic tape or in book form (see bibliography). Ideally, the file spectra should be determined using the same instrument under the same conditions; proof of identity is then a peak-to-peak match of the unknown spectrum with a reference.

The use of mass spectra to identify dangerous drugs, both for diagnosis in a hospital setting and in forensics, is an important application. Applications in other fields include identifying such substances as pollutants (environmental work), natural products (biochemistry), flavor components (the food industry), or hydrocarbons (the petroleum industry). Often, the analyst begins with a complex mixture which can be separated by gas chromatography on-line with a mass spectrometer.

Proof of structure for new compounds is more difficult since the mechanisms of mass-spectral fragmentations are not well enough understood to be used to predict the entire spectrum of a postulated structure from basic principles. Using mass-spectral information together with infrared, ultraviolet-visible, and nuclear-magnetic resonance data is a powerful approach. High-resolution mass spectrometry expedites structural studies by providing the formulas (elemental compositions) of M^+ and the fragment ions.

Analysis of Mixtures

Mass spectrometry made important contributions in the analysis of petroleum mixtures during the Second World War. However, GC (gas chromatography) is now preferred because of the convenience and simplicity inherent in a chromatographic procedure. Mass spectra of different hydrocarbons contain many identical peaks, and it is difficult to find one peak characteristic of each component; the reverse is often the case in GC. Nevertheless, the percent composition of a mixture can be obtained by quantitative mass spectrometry using a series of simultaneous equations, much as is done in analyzing mixtures by ultraviolet or visible spectrophotometry (see Chap. 7).

Mass-spectral analysis of simple mixtures may be used in one-time experiments for which the set-up and calibration of a gas or liquid chromatograph are too time-consuming, even though the mass spectrometer must also be calibrated. The convenience of mass-spectral methods for gaseous mixtures recommends this approach, especially if the appropriate gas-handling apparatus is not readily available for GC. However, GC is often preferred for routine work.

With complex mixtures, it may only be necessary to know the types of compounds present. For example, it is important in the petroleum area to determine the approximate concentrations of saturated hydrocarbons, alkenes and cycloalkanes, and aromatics or substituted aromatics in some mixture. The lower-mass series of ions are useful in this pursuit. Alkanes yield abundant fragments at $C_2H_5^+$, $C_3H_7^+$, $C_4H_9^+$, . . . ; alkenes and saturated cyclic alkanes at $C_2H_3^+$, $C_3H_5^+$, $C_4H_7^+$, . . . ; and aromatics at $C_6H_5^+$, $C_7H_7^+$, $C_8H_9^+$. The sum of the intensities of the fragment peaks for any of these series is proportional to the concentration of each type of hydrocarbon.

For complex mixtures, which often occur in biochemical and environmental problems, the mass spectrometer can serve as a highly specific detector for a gas chromatograph. For example, the organic extract of polluted waters may contain hundreds of organic compounds which cannot be perfectly separated by one pass through a GC. Thus, what appears to be a single peak by GC may actually be a

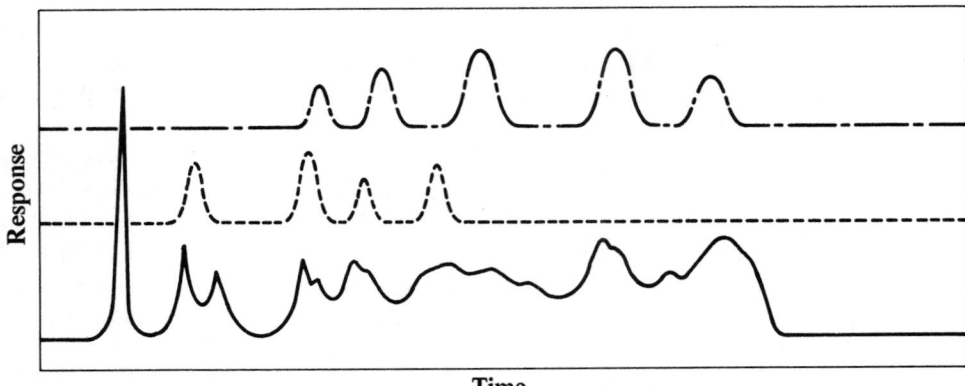

Time

FIGURE 16.14. *Comparison of a total gas-liquid chromatogram obtained from the output of the GC detector or the total ion-current monitor of the mass spectrometer, along with two hypothetical chromatograms obtained by monitoring specific peaks in the mass spectra. Solid line is the total chromatogram; dashed line is the chromatogram made by monitoring one specific ion; broken solid line is the chromatogram made by monitoring another specific ion.*

mixture of a number of components. Each component may have unique M^+ or fragment peaks. To make use of this fact, mass spectra are rapidly obtained at many points across the GC peak and the data stored in an on-line computer. The abundance of certain ions can then be plotted versus time; each ion is specific for one compound in the unresolved GC peak (see Fig. 16.14).

The procedure can be simplified by rapid switching from one peak to another over the GC profile. This is accomplished most efficiently on a sector magnetic instrument by varying the accelerating voltage at a constant magnetic-field strength, and is even more easily carried out with a quadrupole or time-of-flight instrument. The technique is known as *mass fragmentography*.

In inorganic chemistry, mixtures of metal ions in solution can be analyzed by electron-impact mass spectrometry. First the metal ions are complexed with an organic ligand (usually various substituted acetylacetonates) to form volatile metal chelates. If many metal ions are anticipated, the mixture is separated by GC and the separated fractions identified by mass spectrometry. Simple mixtures can be analyzed directly using the mass spectrometer. Because of the high sensitivity of mass spectrometry, trace analysis is possible.

Biochemical Applications

The need for sophisticated analytical tools in the biochemical and health-science areas continues to grow each year. Mass spectrometry is ideally suited for many problems because of its high sensitivity. For instance, the action of drugs in living systems can be better understood if the drug metabolites are isolated and identified. A urine or blood specimen will contain metabolites in trace quantities, and a mass spectrum can be obtained after extraction, concentration, and separation.

Many compounds of biochemical interest have been thoroughly investigated by mass spectrometry. The mechanisms of fragmentation of alkaloids, steroids, and terpenes are fairly well understood [10]. Mass-spectral studies have been reported for amino acids, carbohydrates, and various lipids [11]. However, some molecules of biochemical importance (for example, proteins and nucleic acids) are highly polar, thermally sensitive and of high molecular weight. Thus, it is impossible to vaporize these substances in the source of a mass spectrometer. Prior chemical conversion to various volatile derivatives is helpful, provided the molecular weight is not too high. In this way, small polypeptides (containing 10–12 amino acids) have been analyzed, and the amino-acid sequence determined by mass spectrometry. Spectra can also be obtained of mono- and di-nucleotides after converting the OH groups to $OSi(CH_3)_3$ to break the hydrogen bonding.

Isotope Abundance Studies

Mass spectrometry was originally developed to identify and analyze quantitatively the natural abundances of stable isotopes. The determination of isotopic abundances is still important today, but for different reasons. Isotopic labeling of molecules is quite important in studies of chemical mechanisms and kinetics, both in the organic and biochemical areas. Prior to studies of this kind, the extent of labeling must be determined, and mass spectrometry is usually the method of choice. For example, the amounts of benzene-d_5, -d_4, etc. in benzene-d_6 can be determined by measuring the abundances of $C_6D_6^+$ ($m/e = 84$), $C_6D_5H^+$ ($m/e = 83$), $C_6D_4H_2^+$ ($m/e = 82$), etc. The best procedure is to lower the ionizing energy so that no peaks corresponding to loss of H or D interfere [12].

Sometimes the position of an isotopic label (^2H, ^{13}C, ^{15}N, etc.) can also be determined. The analyst must know whether the compounds undergo prior scrambling reactions before attempting studies of this nature. It would be folly to search for the position of a deuterium in an olefin by mass spectrometry because of the tendency for double-bond migrations to occur while the compound is in the mass spectrometer. However, for compounds giving no scrambling, or only well-understood rearrangements, mass spectrometry can be utilized to locate the label.

Precise isotope ratios are also necessary in studies of kinetic isotope-effects, isotope-dilution studies, and dating work.

The isotope-dilution technique involves "spiking" the sample with the element of interest; the added element, however, has an appreciable difference in isotope-abundance ratios from the natural abundance. As an example, consider a trace analysis of organic bromide, say bromobenzene. If the sample were spiked with 1 μg of C_6H_5Br which contains only bromine-81, and the observed ratio of $^{79}Br : ^{81}Br$ changes from $1:1$ (natural abundance) to $1:2$, then the original sample must contain 2 μg of bromobenzene. The method is sensitive to trace amounts of particular elements and has been used for determination of carbon, nitrogen, oxygen, and sulfur in organic and biochemical samples and for analysis of metals in geological specimens.

As one example of dating work, the age of rocks can be determined by measuring the ratio of argon-40 to argon-36 using the mass spectrometer. Argon-40 is a product of potassium-40 decay with a half-life of 1.3×10^9 years. The exact amount of argon-40 is obtained by measuring the ratio of argon-36 to argon-40 with argon-38 added as a tracer. In this way, ages of meteorite and geological samples have been determined in the one-million to one-billion year range.

If high precision is required (1 part in ten thousand), an isotope-ratio mass spectrometer is used. These instruments are normal magnetic-sector instruments with dual inlets and dual collectors. The ion containing one isotope is focused on one collector (^{40}Ar) and an adjoining detector collects the other peak (^{36}Ar). The signals are accurately compared using precision resistors and null detection.

Another timely example is tracing the origin of nitrate in ground and surface waters. At high concentration this substance is toxic, and can only be dealt with if its source can be identified. Different sources (animal waste, fertilizers, natural rocks) have different $^{15}N/^{14}N$ ratios; however, the differences are so small that precise ratios requiring an isotope-ratio instrument are needed.

Thermodynamic Studies

An ionization-efficiency curve is a plot of the decrease in intensity of a certain peak (molecular ion or fragment) as the ionizing energy is lowered. There is usually a particular "threshold" energy below which a negligible number of ions appear; this is the ionization potential.

In one method, the energy of the electron beam is varied by changes in the voltage applied to the filament; a more elegant way is to use an intense light source

and a monochromator (photoionization). Because most molecules h‍‍
potentials around 10 eV (124 nm), a rather costly and complicated va‍
chromator is required to select the ionizing wavelength. Of course, a ma‍
eter is used to monitor ion intensities.

From ion-efficiency curves, the ionization potential of M and the '‍‍ ‍
potentials of the fragments can be obtained and in turn, bond-dissociation energies
and heats of formation of gas-phase ions can be obtained from the ionization potentials [13].

16.4 NEW DEVELOPMENTS AND SPECIALIZED APPLICATIONS

Chemical- and Field-Ionization Mass Spectrometry

Certainly, the molecular weight of the unknown is one of the most important pieces
of information to gain from a mass spectrum, but the M^+ peak for certain types of
compounds is often absent or of low intensity. Another related drawback to mass
spectrometry is consecutive ion-fragmentation in complex molecules, which results
in low-mass ions carrying a large share of the total intensity (see Fig. 16.11). Thus,
the more analytically important molecular ion and primary fragments (those formed
in the initial fragmentation of M^+) are of low abundance or even missing in the spectrum. A major advance is the development of chemical- (CIMS) [14, 15] and field-
ionization (FIMS) [16] techniques, which are gentler ionization procedures. The
result is enhancement of the abundance of ions containing molecular-weight and
initial-fragmentation information.

Instead of ionizing with an energetic electron beam, *chemical ionization* occurs
via ion-molecule reactions. The ion, often referred to as a reagent ion, reacts with a
sample molecule by transferring a proton or by abstracting an H^- or an electron,
which imparts a $+1$ charge to the sample molecule.

Typically, the source of a conventional mass spectrometer is redesigned to
operate at a higher pressure (1–10 torr). Methane is admitted and ionized to produce CH_4^+ and CH_3^+. These react to form CH_5^+ and $C_2H_5^+$ as follows:

$$CH_4^+ + CH_4 \longrightarrow CH_5^+ + CH_3\cdot \tag{16.29}$$

$$CH_3^+ + CH_4 \longrightarrow C_2H_5^+ + H_2 \tag{16.30}$$

The CH_5^+ and $C_2H_5^+$ do not react further with the neutral methane, but once a small
amount of sample (XH) is admitted to the source (1 part in 1000 parts methane), the
sample molecules are ionized by proton and hydride-ion transfers:

$$CH_5^+ + XH \longrightarrow XH_2^+ + CH_4 \tag{16.31}$$

$$C_2H_5^+ + XH \longrightarrow X^+ + C_2H_6 \tag{16.32}$$

XH_2^+ and X^+ may then fragment, giving a mass spectrum. No molecular ion per
se is observed, but the molecular weight is readily obtained from the $M + H$ or
$M - H$ peaks.

Other reagent ions, which are weaker gas-phase acids than CH_5^+, may be
employed to further simplify the spectrum. Examples include $C_4H_9^+$ (from iso-

butane), NH_4^+ (ammonia), or H_3O^+ (water). These acids also ionize by proton transfer, but the energies are somewhat less, and the fragmentation of XH_2^+ is minimized. Figure 16.15 shows the electron-impact and chemical-ionization spectra of ephedrine, a biologically important amine. Notice the striking absence of M^+ by electron impact and the abundant $M + 1$ in the CI spectra. The fragmentation is also simplified by CI.

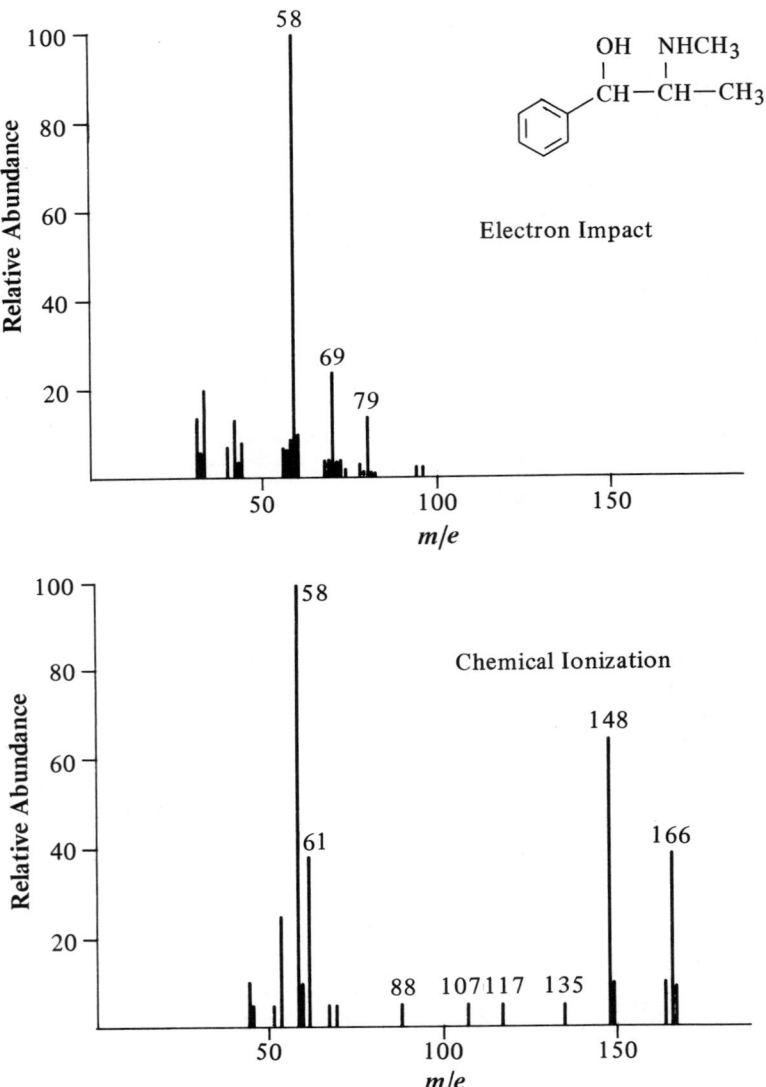

FIGURE 16.15. *Comparison of the electron-impact (EI) and chemical-ionization (CI) mass spectra of ephedrine. From H. M. Fales, H. A. Lloyd, and G. A. W. Milne,* J. Amer. Chem. Soc., 92, *1590 (1970), by permission of the publisher. Copyright © 1970 by the American Chemical Society.*

Field ionization employs a conventional mass analysis with a modified source. A small wire or sharp-edged anode is mounted at the input end of the ion gun as shown in Figure 16.16, and a very large electric field (10^5 V/cm) is applied between the anode and cathode. (The anode is first activated so that its surface contains many sharp points (whiskers) by filling the chamber with acetone at 0.04–0.1 torr and applying 10,000 V for several hours.) The electric field is then sufficient to remove an electron from gaseous molecules in the field. It is thought that the high field so distorts

FIGURE 16.16. *Schematic diagram of a typical field-ionization source. This source is simply substituted for the conventional electron-impact source. The remainder of the mass spectrometer is the same. Combined EI/FI sources have been used.*

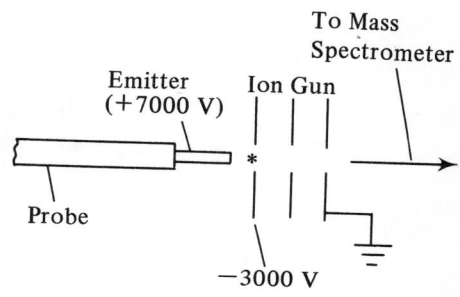

the potential-energy surfaces of the sample molecule that an electron is quantum-mechanically tunneled through the energy barrier to the anode. The practical consequence of this is that the molecular ion so formed is not excited, and very little fragmentation results. Almost every compound gives an abundant M^+ or $(M + 1)^+$ by field ionization, and considerably simplified fragmentation patterns. The electron-impact and field-ionization spectra of ribose are compared in Figure 16.17.

Chemical- and field-ionization are important complements to electron-impact mass spectrometry because they emphasize the molecular-ion region producing small numbers of primary fragmentations and almost no secondary and further fragmentations. By contrast, electron impact gives a wealth of fragmentations at the expense of the molecular ion and of primary fragments. In most cases, the analyst can combine this information to identify the sample. As a result, CI and FI are especially useful for analysis of complex molecules, and in direct analysis of mixtures because of the simple spectra that are produced. Chemical ionization is often a hundred times more sensitive than electron impact, for two reasons: First, the ionization of the sample is concentrated in only a few peaks rather than dispersed over hundreds of peaks as in the electron-impact ionization of complex molecules. Second, the efficiency of ionization by electron impact is approximately 0.1%; that is, only one out of every thousand sample molecules is ionized. The un-ionized sample molecules are lost to the vacuum pumps. Because chemical ionization takes place by ion-molecule reactions, ionization efficiency could be raised significantly by increasing the reagent gas pressure and thus the concentration of reagent ions, and by extending ion-residence times.

Spark-Source Mass Spectrometry

As mentioned previously, mass spectrometry can be applied to nonvolatile inorganic substances by using a spark source. One important analytical application is the

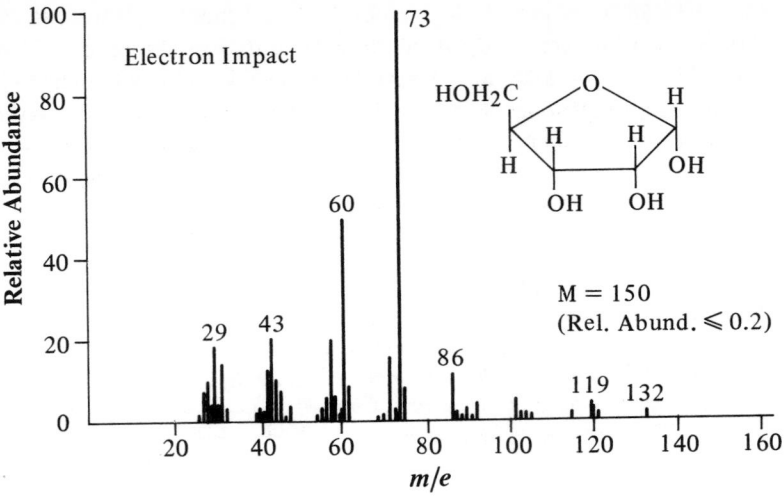

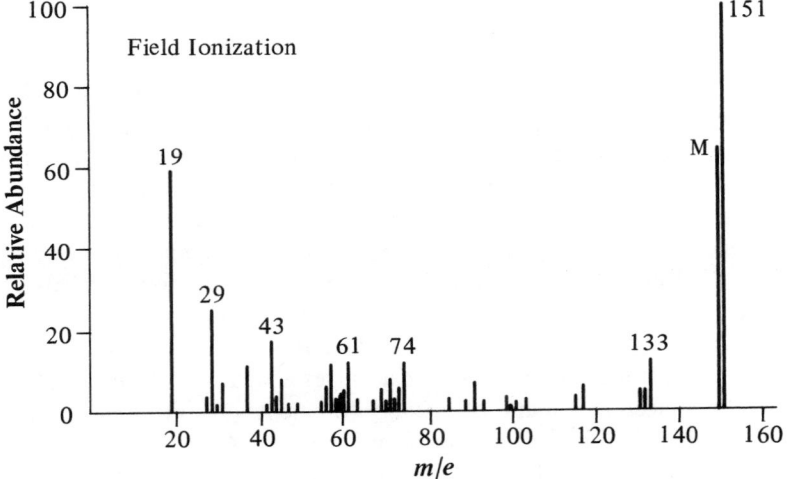

FIGURE 16.17. *Comparison of the electron-impact and field-ionization mass-spectra of d-ribose. The molecular ion is found at m/e = 150. The abundant peak at m/e = 151 is formed by a protonation ion-molecule reaction occurring in the vicinity of the emitter. From H. D. Beckey, Field Ionization Mass Spectrometry,* Braunschweig-Vieweg, *1971; New York: Pergamon Press, 1971, p 284, by permission of the publisher.*

analysis of fossil fuels, fly ash, and coal dust for trace metals. Because many metals such as mercury, cadmium, arsenic, beryllium, and lead are environmental hazards, it is important to determine their concentration in coal for evaluation of suitable fuels. Another useful application is the analysis of semiconductors for trace elements that affect the electrical properties of the material.

In the biological area, *spark source mass spectrometry* (SSMS) is an ideal tool for trace elemental analysis. First, the sample is ashed by strong heating or by a microwave discharge in oxygen to remove the organic material. The residue is then mixed with pure graphite and sparked in the spectrometer. The presence of elements at ppb levels has been verified in samples such as plant leaves, human and animal tissue, bones, and plasma. A major advantage is that multi-element analysis is possible, although the precision may be less than in other trace element techniques such as anodic stripping voltammetry or atomic absorption spectroscopy.

Surface Analysis

Analysis of solid surfaces in terms of elemental composition is an important problem in modern research. Mass spectrometry, as *secondary-ion mass spectrometry* (SIMS) or *ion-probe analysis* [17], can play a useful role.

The procedure involves bombarding the sample surface with a fast-moving (5–20 keV) ion beam. This beam is produced in a highly efficient discharge source called a duoplasmatron (see Fig. 16.18). The primary ions are focused by a series

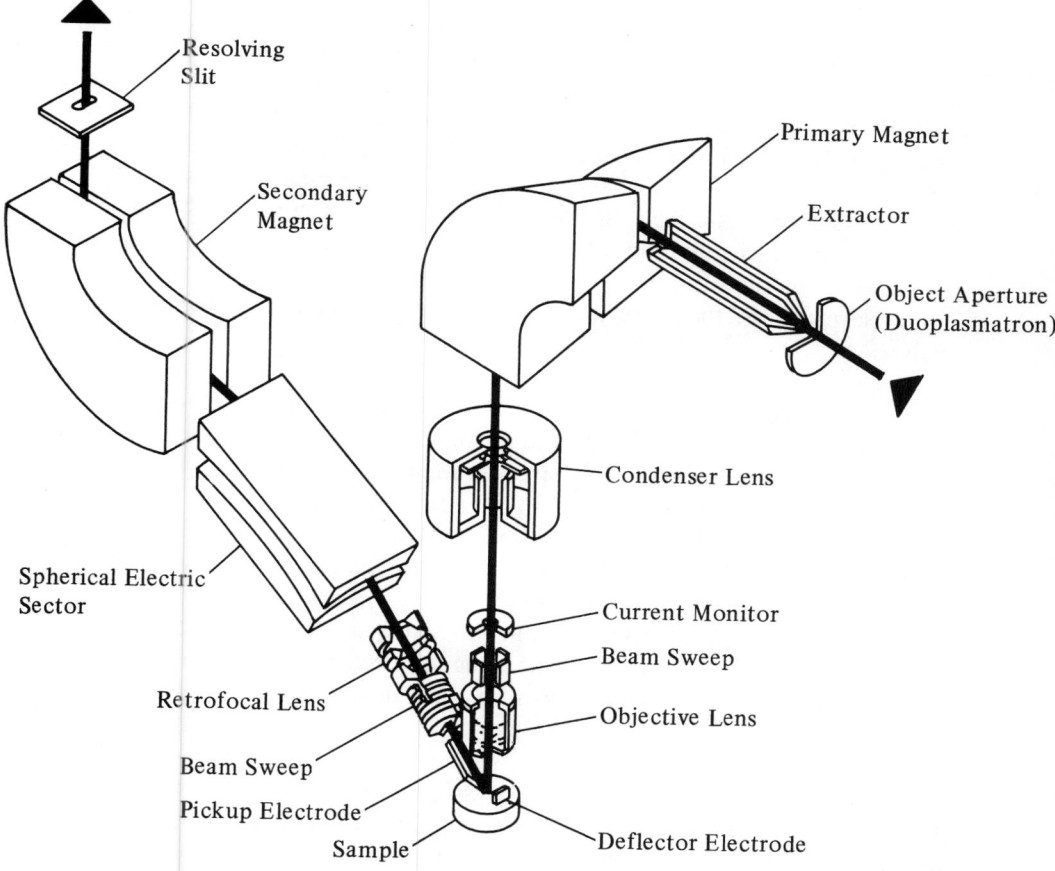

FIGURE 16.18. *Schematic diagram of a secondary-ion mass spectrometer. This particular design is called the Ion Microprobe because very small areas can be investigated with it. From* Chemical and Engineering News, *August 19, 1968, p 30, by permission of the American Chemical Society, copyright owner.*

of lenses to obtain a narrow, well defined beam. The impacting ions dislodge ("sputter") atoms and ions from the sample as gas-phase species. The secondary ions are drawn into the mass spectrometer for mass analysis. Figure 16.18 shows the use of a double-focusing spectrometer to perform an energy analysis on the secondary beam before a mass analysis. Suitable primary ions can be either inert (Ar^+ or N_2^+) or reactive (O_2^+, O^+).

When the primary ion beam impacts the surface, energy transfer occurs to break lattice bonds and vaporize ions or atoms. Some of the atoms may possess sufficient internal excitation to eject an electron, forming additional gas-phase ions. The majority of the secondary ions are singly charged and monoatomic. One mechanism for ion loss is neutralization at the surface before entering the gas phase. This can be minimized if the surface is a nonconducting matrix, such as a metal oxide, or if the primary ion beam is O_2^+, which reacts at the surface to form a less conducting oxide region. Thus, an oxide-coated metal surface bombarded with Ar^+ will release more ions than a pure metal surface.

This phenomenon brings up a disadvantage of the technique. The ion yield or ionization efficiency of a surface depends on the nature of the element and on the chemical composition at the bombardment location. The yield of an ion from one element relative to another will change as the composition and conditions vary. The results may be complicated because a change in ion output as the surface is sputtered does not necessarily mean a change in the relative elemental composition. Another problem occurs because the sputtering may be nonuniform, i.e., certain elements are removed more efficiently than others. This effect can be minimized by scanning the ion beam across the surface.

Nevertheless, there are many important advantages of secondary ion mass analysis.

1. The technique is highly sensitive, permitting detection of ppb concentrations.
2. Surface areas between 1 mm² to 1 μm² can be investigated, depending on the width of the primary-ion beam. The narrower limits are approached with instrumentation called an *ion microprobe*.
3. Like SSMS, the technique is applicable to all elements and is especially useful for light elements (H through Na), which are not amenable to techniques such as the electron microprobe (Chap. 14).
4. Changes in isotopic composition can be examined because the procedure is mass spectral in nature. Again this is not true for electron microprobes.
5. Three-dimensional analysis is possible with depth resolution of approximately 50–100 Å.

Although secondary-ion mass analysis is still relatively new in terms of applications, it is clear that it will be extremely useful for studies of metallurgical, geological, and semiconductor surfaces and for samples from corrosion and metal-catalyst studies. There may be biochemical and organic applications as well. A number of units are commercially available, including instruments with double-focusing and quadrupole mass-analyzers for the secondary beam. However, the expense is high, ranging from $100,000 to $250,000.

Another technique that permits in-depth profiling of solid surfaces is *ion-*

scattering spectrometry (ISS). A commercial instrument is available from the 3M Company at lower cost than SIMS.

In this method, a sample is mounted in a vacuum chamber and bombarded with noble-gas ions at 0.5 to 3 keV. The primary ions scattered at 90° pass into an electrostatic analyzer identical in principle with those used in double-focusing mass spectrometers. By scanning the voltage to the ESA, velocity analysis is accomplished.

It can be shown that the energy loss of the primary beam at the first monolayer of surface is determined by the mass of the surface atom responsible for the scattering. The relevant equation is

$$E_1/E_0 = (m_s - m_0)/(m_s + m_0) \tag{16.33}$$

where m_0 = the mass of the primary beam
E_0 = the kinetic energy of the primary beam
E_1 = the energy of the ions scattered at 90°
m_s = the mass of the surface atom

It is clear that if E_1 is measured and m_0 and E_0 are known, the mass of the surface atom, m_s, can be determined and the element identified. The method involves an indirect mass measurement. The number of ions scattered at a certain intensity is proportional to the amount of the element present.

This technique possesses many of the advantages of secondary-ion mass analysis, including studies of isotopic abundances. The method is not as extensively evaluated as SIMS; however, it appears to be capable of major-component analysis extending down to the 0.1 part per thousand range.

Mass-spectrometry principles and techniques have been employed in other kinds of surface studies in which sample atoms are sputtered by interaction with a laser beam or by RF glow discharges. These approaches are more highly specialized, but it should be clear that mass spectrometry is an important tool in surface chemistry. The student should compare SIMS and ISS with other surface analytical techniques such as ESCA, Auger spectroscopy, electron microprobe, and low-energy electron diffraction (see Chaps. 14 and 15).

SELECTED BIBLIOGRAPHY

Instrumentation in Mass Spectrometry

BEYNON, J. H. *Mass Spectrometry and Its Applications to Organic Chemistry.* Amsterdam: Elsevier, 1960.

BLAUTH, E. W. *Dynamic Mass Spectrometers.* Amsterdam: Elsevier, 1966.

KISER, R. W. *Introduction to Mass Spectrometry and Its Applications.* Englewood Cliffs, N.J.: Prentice-Hall, 1965.

MELTON, C. E. *Principles of Mass Spectrometry and Negative Ions.* New York: Marcel Dekker, 1970.

ROBOZ, J. *Introduction to Mass Spectrometry: Instrumentation and Techniques.* New York: Interscience, 1968.

Compilations of Standard Spectra

Catalog of Mass Spectral Data, API Research Project 44. Pittsburgh, Pa.: Carnegie Institute of Technology.

CORNU, A., and MASSOT, R. *Compilation of Mass Spectral Data.* London: Heyden, 1966.

Index of Mass Spectral Data. Philadelphia, Pa.: American Society for Testing and Materials, 1969.

STENHAGEN, E.; ABRAHAMSSON, S.; and Mc-LAFFERTY, F. W., eds. *Atlas of Mass Spectral Data*. New York: John Wiley, 1969.

STENHAGEN, E.; ABRAHAMSSON, S.; and Mc-LAFFERTY, F. W., eds. *Registry of Mass Spectral Data*. New York: John Wiley, 1974.

Interpretation of Mass Spectra

BIEMAN, K. *Mass Spectrometry: Organic Chemical Applications*. New York: McGraw-Hill, 1962.

HILL, H. C. *Introduction to Mass Spectrometry*. London: Heyden, 1966.

MCLAFFERTY, F. W. *Interpretation of Mass Spectra*. Reading, Mass.: W. A. Benjamin, 1973.

REED, R. I. *Application of Mass Spectrometry to Organic Chemistry*. London: Academic Press, 1966.

REFERENCES

1. J. J. THOMSON, *Rays of Positive Electricity and Their Application to Chemical Analyses*, London: Longmans, Green, and Co., 1913.

2. F. W. ASTON, *Phil. Mag.*, *38*, 707, 709 (1919).

3. A. J. DEMPSTER, *Phys. Rev.*, *11*, 316 (1918).

4. J. D. BALDESCHWIELER and S. S. WOODGATE, *Acc. Chem. Res.*, *4*, 114 (1971).

5. M. L. GROSS and C. L. WILKINS, *Anal. Chem.*, *43*(14), 65A (1971).

6. J. L. BEAUCHAMP, *Ann. Rev. Phys. Chem.*, *22*, 527 (1971).

7. H. BUDZIKIEWICZ, C. DJERASSI, and D. H. WILLIAMS, *Mass Spectrometry of Organic Compounds*, San Francisco: Holden-Day, 1967.

8. J. H. BEYNON, R. A. SAUNDERS, and A. E. WILLIAMS, *The Mass Spectra of Organic Molecules*, Amsterdam: Elsevier, 1968.

9. Q. N. PORTER and J. BALDAS, *Mass Spectrometry of Heterocyclic Compounds*, New York: Wiley-Interscience, 1971.

10. H. BUDZIKIEWICZ, C. DJERASSI, and D. H. WILLIAMS, *Structure Elucidation of Natural Products by Mass Spectrometry*, vol. I, *Alkaloids*; vol. II, *Steroids, Terpenoids, Sugars, and Miscellaneous Natural Products*, San Francisco: Holden-Day, 1964.

11. G. R. Waller, ed., *Biochemical Applications of Mass Spectrometry*, New York: Wiley-Interscience, 1972.

12. K. BIEMAN, *Mass Spectrometry: Organic Chemical Applications*, New York: McGraw-Hill, 1962, pp 204–50.

13. R. W. KISER, *Introduction to Mass Spectrometry and Its Applications*, Englewood Cliffs, N.J.: Prentice-Hall, 1965, pp 162–206.

14. F. H. FIELD, *Acc. Chem. Res.*, *1*, 42 (1968).

15. B. MUNSON, *Anal. Chem.* *43*(13), 28A (1971).

16. H. D. BECKEY, *Field Ionization Mass Spectrometry*, Oxford: Pergamon Press, 1971.

17. C. A. EVANS, Jr., *Anal. Chem.*, *44*(13), 67A (1972).

PROBLEMS

1. A sector instrument is designed to operate with a radius of 30.00 cm and an accelerating voltage of 3000 V. Calculate the magnetic field (in gauss) necessary to focus the M^+ of methane. What would be the radius of trajectory for CH_3^+ under these conditions?

2. Repeat the calculation for the necessary field to focus the M^+ of naphthalene ($C_{10}H_8^+$). What would be the radius of curvature for the $M - 1$ ion in naphthalene? Comment on the resolution necessary to separate M and $M - 1$ in methane and naphthalene.

3. A sector mass-spectrometer is built to scan to $m/e = 500$ with the maximum field of the electromagnet at 6000 gauss and an accelerating voltage of 3000 V. To examine the molecular ion of a compound of molecular mass 850, what modification in the accelerating-voltage power-supply is required?

4. Draw a schematic diagram of an electron-impact source showing what voltages should be applied to the various components using an accelerating voltage of 1765 V, an ionizing energy of 50 eV, a repeller voltage of 10 V, and a target voltage of 80 V.

5. An unknown compound gives a nominal molecular mass of 220. A mixture of the unknown and perfluorotributylamine $[(C_4F_9)_3N]$ is admitted to a double-focusing mass spectrometer with an accelerating voltage of 5000 V. With $C_4F_9^+$ in focus ($m/e = 218.9856$), the accelerating and ESA voltages are reduced to exactly 99.463% of the originals to bring the unknown peak to an identical focus. What is the exact mass of $m/e = 220$? From the data below, what is the elemental composition of $m/e = 220$?

Compound	m/e
$C_{17}H_{16}$	220.1251
$C_{10}H_{20}O_5$	220.1311
$C_{13}H_{20}N_2O$	220.1576
$C_{11}H_{24}O_4$	220.1674
$C_{15}H_{24}O$	220.1827

6. The exact mass of CO is 27.9949 and that of C_2H_4 is 28.0313. What resolution is necessary to just separate CO^+ and $C_2H_4^+$ found in a mixture of carbon monoxide and ethylene? Compare this requirement with that necessary to separate $C_{20}H_{40}^+$ and $C_{19}H_{36}O^+$, both nominally at $m/e = 280$.

7. The mass spectrum of benzene is obtained on a time-of-flight mass spectrometer of length 100 cm with an accelerating voltage of 3000 V. Calculate the time required for $C_2H_2^+$ (one of the low-mass ions), $C_6H_5^+$, and $C_6H_6^+$ to reach the detector. (Note: the voltage must be expressed in erg/esu,

where 300 volts = 1 erg/esu. The magnitude of the electronic charge is 4.803×10^{-10} esu.)

8. What is the residence time for M^+ of benzene in an ion-cyclotron-resonance cell of length 10 cm with a drift field in both the source and analyzer of 0.25 V/cm? The magnetic field is set at 7,800 gauss. Compare with the residence time of around 10^{-6} sec for a conventional mass-spectrometer source.

9. An electric field of what frequency (in kHz) is necessary to observe the $m/e = 78$ ion from benzene under the conditions in problem 8?

10. Calculate the M + 1, M + 2, etc., abundances for the following molecular ions. To approximate the probability of finding two ^{13}C atoms in a molecule, the following relation can be employed:

$$\frac{M + 2}{M} = \frac{(1.1n)^2}{200}$$

where $(M + 2)/M$ is expressed in percent and n is the number of carbon atoms. Consider the abundance of M^+ to be 100%. (a) C_6H_6; (b) $C_2H_4O_2$; (c) $C_2H_8N_2$; (d) C_3H_7Cl; (e) C_4H_4S; (f) $C_{16}H_{34}$.

11. Mercury as an environmental pollutant is sometimes found as dimethyl mercury. Look up the natural abundance of the mercury isotopes and calculate the pattern to be expected in the molecular-ion region.

12. The methyl group in acetophenone can be deuterated by refluxing a mixture of acetophenone and D_2O with a little base catalyst.

At 15 eV of ionizing energy, no M − 1 is detected for unlabeled acetophenone, and

M + 1 is 8.8%. Calculate the percentage of $-d_3$, $-d_2$, and $-d_1$ after one exchange, if the following abundances are found in the mass spectrum. Remember to correct for ^{13}C.

m/e	Rel. Abund.
124	8.75
123	100.00
122	7.01
121	4.42
120	——

13. Postulate a structure for the compound with the following mass spectrum. After you have settled on a structure, account for the ions found in the spectrum.

m/e	Rel. Abund.	m/e	Rel. Abund.
25	0.10	61	0.74
26	0.36	62	0.64
27	0.77	63	0.51
28	0.14	64	0.07
35	0.12	72	0.35
36	0.30	73	2.1
37	2.0	74	4.3
37.5	0.84	75	4.6
38	5.71	76	3.4
38.5	0.33	77	45.2
39	1.10	78	3.0
40	0.05	79	0.06
47	0.18	84	0.70
48	0.19	85	0.89
49	1.5	86	0.89
50	9.6	87	0.32
51	12.0	88	0.22
52	1.0	97	0.26
53	0.03	99	0.07
54	0.05	108	0.11
54.5	0.08	109	0.04
55	0.34	110	0.10
55.5	0.07	111	0.78
56	3.91	112	100.00
56.5	0.28	113	6.9
57	1.25	114	32.9
57.5	0.09	115	2.1
60	0.47	116	0.06

14. The following mass spectrum was obtained for an amine containing four carbon atoms. What is the compound?

m/e	Rel. Abund.	m/e	Rel. Abund.
15	1.9	43	3.1
27	0.75	44	100.0
28	4.2	45	2.8
29	9.1	56	2.3
30	2.9	57	1.6
31	4.1	58	10.0
32	0.39	59	0.41
33	1.1	71	0.39
39	2.0	72	2.3
40	0.75	73	1.2
41	9.4	74	0.07
42	6.0		

15. The first evidence to prove the existence of a certain inorganic compound was the mass spectrum taken on a time-of-flight mass spectrometer. The data below were measured from a photograph of the oscilloscope display, and as such the M + 1 peaks were too weak to measure. Identify the compound.

m/e	Rel. Abund.	m/e	Rel. Abund.
111	100	128	6
112	10	129	15
113	100	130	7
114	12	144	33
127	15	146	33

16. The following compounds are isomeric C-6 *ketones*. Complete identification should be possible by considering carbonyl-directed cleavages and the McLafferty rearrangement (or lack of it). Identify the compound using these processes.

	Ketone #1		Ketone #2
m/e	Rel. Abund.	m/e	Rel. Abund.
27	14.8	27	49.4
28	4.4	28	10.9
29	33.7	29	68.3
30	0.8	30	1.7
39	7.7	39	12.8
40	1.0	40	1.6
41	26.2	41	23.0
42	3.8	42	8.0
43	100	43	100
44	2.2	44	3.3
55	2.7	55	3.1

Ketone #1		Ketone #2	
m/e	Rel. Abund.	m/e	Rel. Abund.
56	9.0	56	1.9
57	27.4	57	76.1
58	1.3	58	2.5
71	0.9	71	45.6
72	17.1	72	2.5
73	0.8	73	——
85	2.4	85	2.0
100	3.5	100	19.9
101	0.2	101	1.3

17. The following spectrum is that of a compound containing C, H, and O. Also present in the molecule is an aromatic ring. Identify the material.

m/e	Rel. Intensity	m/e	Rel. Intensity
26	0.10	67	0.35
27	4.0	74	0.40
28	0.2	75	0.35
39	6.0	76	0.39
40	1.4	77	7.2
41	4.8	78	0.80
42	0.3	79	0.81
43	4.1	93	0.70
44	0.10	94	100.00
49	0.05	95	6.6
50	1.3	96	0.42
51	4.6	107	2.0
52	0.43	108	0.40
55	1.1	121	0.20
56	0.06	122	0.03
62	0.34	135	0.20
63	1.2	136	25.0
64	0.50	137	2.5
65	4.3	138	0.18
66	5.9		

18. What resolution is necessary to distinguish between molecular oxygen and sulfur in a mass spectrometer?

19. The mass spectrum of methyl alcohol has peaks at $m/e = 15, 28, 29, 30, 31$, and 32. A broad, low intensity, metastable peak was found at $m/e = 27.13$. Determine the mother and daughter ions.

20. The decomposition of ions with the elemental composition $C_2H_5O^+$ has been studied by Shannon and McLafferty [J. Amer. Chem. Soc., 88, 5021 (1966)]. A. Metastable peaks caused by the following decompositions were observed:

(a) $C_2H_5O^+ \longrightarrow H_3O^+ + C_2H_2$; and
(b) $C_2H_5O^+ \longrightarrow CHO^+ + CH_4$.

At what m/e values would the metastable peaks caused by these decompositions be found? B. Of the following structural formulas, $HOCH_2CH_2Y$, $CH_3CH(OH)Y$, CH_3OCH_2Y, CH_3CH_2OY, one was found to decompose by route (a) one hundred times less often than any of the other three structures did. Predict which structure it was.

21. The mass spectra of two different trimethylpentanes showed the following relative abundances. [H. W. Washburn et al., Ind. Eng. Chem., Anal. Ed. 17, 75 (1945).]

m/e	Relative Abundance	
	(a)	(b)
43	20	50
57	80	9
71	1	40
99	5	0.1
114	0.02	0.3

Of the two isomers, 2,2,4- and 2,3,4-trimethylpentane, which is more likely to produce the abundances given in column (a)? Write the structures of the ions most likely responsible for the m/e values found.

22. From the following table of mass spectral data deduce the probable structure of the unknown $C_xH_yN_z$.

m/e	Rel. Abund.	m/e	Rel. Abund.
15	3.7	43	2.7
27	3.3	44	0.29
28	4.1	55	2.0
29	3.6	56	2.7
30	6.2	57	5.6
31	0.10	58	100
39	4.8	59	3.6
40	1.4	60	0.05
41	18	73	0.41
42	11	74	0.02

23. The mass spectrum of an unknown compound had the following relative intensities for the M, ($m/e = 86$), M + 1, and M + 2 peaks respectively: 18.5, 1.15, and 0.074 (percentage of base peak). From the following partial list of isotopic abundance ratios, determine the molecular formula of the unknown.

Isotope Abundance
Ratios (M = 100%)

Formula	M + 1	M + 2
$C_4H_6O_2$	4.50	0.48
C_4H_8NO	4.87	0.30
$C_4H_{10}N_2$	5.25	0.11

Isotope Abundance
Ratios (M = 100%)

Formula	M + 1	M + 2
$C_5H_{10}O$	5.60	0.33
$C_5H_{12}N$	5.98	0.15
C_6H_{14}	6.71	0.19

24. Determine the m/e order in which the following gases will appear in the mass spectrum of a mixture containing them: C_2H_4, CO, N_2.

25. Compare and contrast ESCA, Auger spectroscopy, ISS, and SIMS as methods for surface analysis.

17

Thermal Methods of Analysis

NEIL JESPERSEN

In thermal methods of analysis, either temperature change is measured or the temperature is manipulated to produce the measured parameter. Thermogravimetry (TG), differential thermal analysis (DTA), and differential scanning calorimetry (DSC) are the three major methods that use temperature change as the independent variable. Thermometric titration (TT) and direct-injection enthalpimetry (DIE) use temperature as the dependent variable. These five methods will be discussed primarily from an analytical point of view. Each method has its unique characteristics and capabilities; for that reason, the major aspects of each method are considered individually.

17.1 GENERAL CHARACTERISTICS OF THERMAL METHODS

Thermogravimetry involves measuring the mass of a sample as its temperature is increased. A plot of mass versus temperature permits evaluation of thermal stabilities, rates of reaction, reaction processes, and sample composition.

Differential thermal analysis is the monitoring of the difference in temperature between a sample and a reference compound as a function of temperature. These data can be used to study heats of reaction, kinetics, phase transitions, thermal stabilities, sample composition and purity, critical points, and phase diagrams.

Measurement of the differential power (heat input) necessary to keep a sample and a reference substance isothermal as temperature is changed (scanned) linearly is the basis of *differential scanning calorimetry*. In addition to the capabilities mentioned for DTA, DSC can provide more precise values for heats of reaction; it allows quantitative measurement of effects that involve little or no heat of reaction (but do involve finite changes in heat capacity) and may be used to determine heat capacities as a function of temperature. DSC is very sensitive to heat-capacity changes, and allows for more precise measurement of these effects than does DTA.

Thermometric titrations involve monitoring of temperature change as a function of the volume of titrant added. From this, concentrations may be evaluated as in normal titrimetry; ΔH^0, ΔG^0, and ΔS^0 for the reaction may also be calculated under appropriate conditions.

Direct-injection enthalpimetry data are similar to those from TT. However, titration is replaced by a virtually instantaneous injection of reagent, and temperature is monitored as a function of time. As a result, more rapid analysis is possible. Heats of reaction can be readily deduced, and kinetics may be studied in favorable situations.

General Thermodynamic Relationships

Since thermal analyses are usually run under conditions of constant pressure, the underlying thermodynamic equation is the Gibbs-Helmholtz expression:

$$\Delta G^0 = \Delta H^0 - T\,\Delta S^0 \qquad (17.1)$$

where G = the free energy of the system
H = the enthalpy of the system
S = the entropy of the system
T = the temperature in K

The general chemical reaction

$$aA + bB \longrightarrow cC + dD \qquad (17.2)$$

is spontaneous as written if ΔG is negative, is at equilibrium if $\Delta G = 0$, and does not proceed if ΔG is positive.* Thermal analysis involves the monitoring of spontaneous reactions.

Methods involving temperature change as the independent variable (TG, DTA, and DSC) take advantage of the $T\,\Delta S$ term in Equation 17.1. Differentiating the Gibbs-Helmholtz equation with respect to temperature, one obtains†

$$\frac{d(\Delta G)}{dT} = -\Delta S \qquad (17.3)$$

This shows how to move from a stable situation (ΔG positive) to one where reaction will occur. If ΔS is positive, an increase in temperature will eventually cause ΔG to become negative, whereas if ΔS is negative, decreasing the temperature will achieve the desired spontaneous reaction.‡ Once the reaction is made to occur, each of the

---

* It is important to note that in some cases the reaction may not proceed under certain conditions even though ΔG is negative. A mixture of oxygen and hydrogen is a case in point. Such metastable states, while of considerable interest, are outside the scope of this discussion.

† Equation 17.3 is a gross oversimplification: it assumes that neither ΔS nor ΔH varies with temperature. This is not so. However, the possible variations of ΔH and ΔS will usually only affect the temperature at which ΔG becomes negative, not the fact that it will eventually do so.

‡ Once the spontaneous reaction starts, it proceeds at a rate dependent upon the kinetic characteristics of the sample.

three methods may be used to detect the process, often yielding different and complementary information.

The second group of methods (TT and DIE) involves the creation of a spontaneously reacting mixture by combining two or more chemical species. Then,

$$\Delta T = \frac{-\Delta H n_p}{C_p'} \tag{17.4}$$

where n_p = the number of moles of product formed
         C_p' = the heat capacity (cal/deg) for the entire system

Since the amount of product (n_p) may be equilibrium controlled (as in TT) or kinetically controlled (as in DIE), Equation 17.4 may be expanded in various ways in order to calculate the parameters listed previously.

These relationships have been presented in their simplest forms; later discussions will illustrate the complexities involved. For instance, the thermodynamic terms calculated are not usually standard-state terms (e.g., ΔH calculated is not ΔH°). The additional effort necessary to extrapolate to standard states (e.g., infinite dilution) is usually excessive for analytical situations, and in some cases the quality of the data does not warrant such treatment. References will be given to treatments of data or theory beyond the scope of this text that may interest those who wish to become more deeply involved with methods of thermal analysis.

17.2 THERMOGRAVIMETRY

Thermogravimetry (TG) involves continuously measuring the mass of a sample as a function of its temperature. Plots of mass versus temperature are called *thermogravimetric curves* or *TG curves*. The use of other names is discouraged.

General Considerations

Suitable samples for thermogravimetry are solids that undergo one of the two general types of reaction:

$$\text{Reactant(s)} \longrightarrow \text{Product(s)} + \text{Gas}$$
$$\text{Gas} + \text{Reactant(s)} \longrightarrow \text{Product(s)}$$

The first process involves a mass loss, whereas the second involves a mass gain. Processes occurring without change in mass obviously cannot be studied by TG (e.g., the melting of a sample).

A simple thermogram, for the dehydration of copper sulfate pentahydrate, is shown in Figure 17.1. There are two points of major interest to the analytical chemist. First is the general shape of the thermogram and the particular temperatures at which changes in mass occur. From this information, individual compounds may be identified under given conditions. Unfortunately, the reproducibility of the temperatures at which mass changes occur is severely affected by many experimental conditions, as noted later. For this reason, the obvious qualitative analytical capabilities of TG have yet to be fully realized.

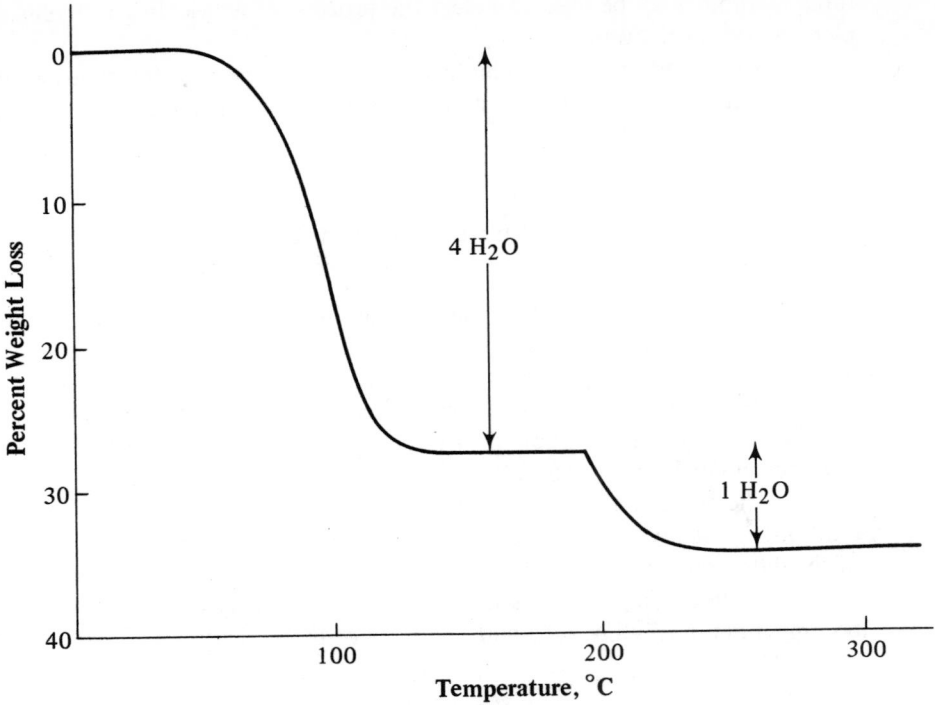

FIGURE 17.1. *A thermogravimetric curve for the dehydration of copper sulfate hydrate.*

The second major feature of the curve (the magnitudes of the mass changes observed) has found much more use, because it is independent of the many factors that affect the shape of the thermogram. Mass changes are directly related to the specific stoichiometries of the reactions occurring, independent of the temperature. As a consequence, precise quantitative analysis of samples whose qualitative composition is known can be made, or else the composition of novel compounds can be deduced.

Instrumentation

Thermogravimetric instrumentation should include several basic components in order to provide the flexibility necessary for the production of useful analytical data. These components are (a) a balance; (b) a heating device; (c) a unit for temperature measurement and control; (d) a means for automatically recording the mass and temperature changes; and (e) a system to control the atmosphere around the sample.

Balances. Balances must remain precise and accurate continuously under extreme temperature and atmospheric conditions, and should deliver a signal suitable for continuous recording. These requirements may be met in many ways: the two books by Duval and Wendlandt (see bibliography) show at least ten different commercial thermobalances that perform satisfactorily. The basic characteristics of such balances will be illustrated by describing one, the Cahn Electrobalance (Ventron Instruments

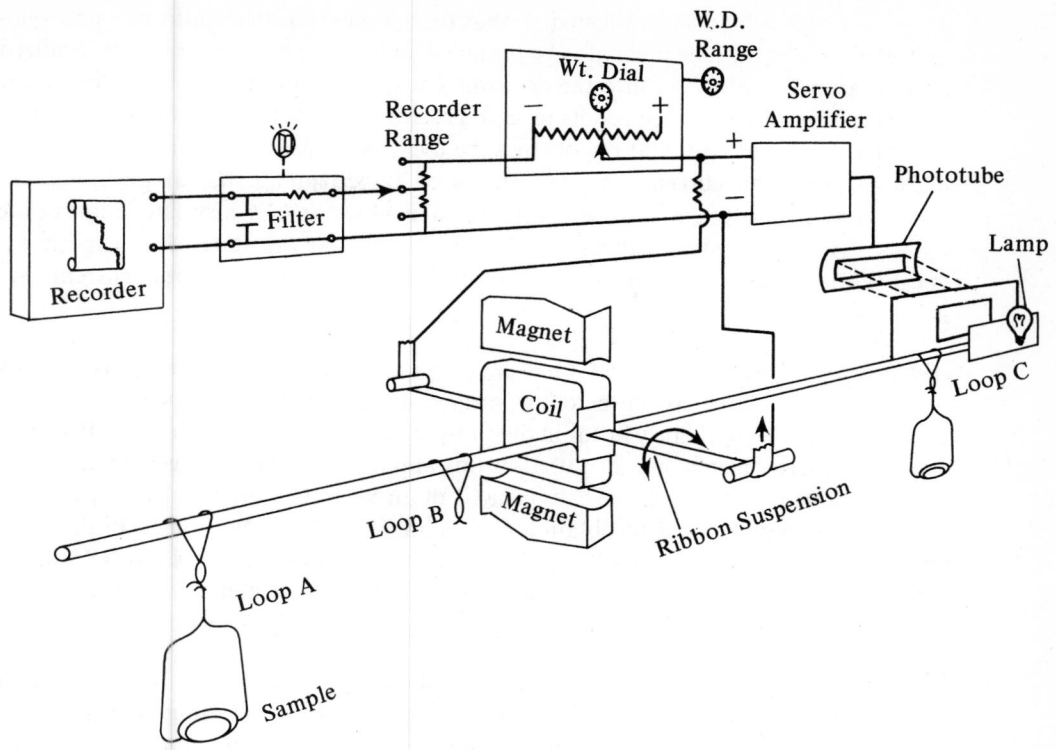

FIGURE 17.2. *Schematic diagram of the Cahn Electrobalance. Courtesy of Cahn Instruments Div., Ventron Instruments Corp.*

Corp., Cahn Div., Paramount, California. See Fig. 17.2). It operates as a null-type device by providing an electrical force to restore the beam to a predetermined position as the mass of the sample changes. As the beam is moved off balance, a shutter affixed to the beam changes the amount of light reaching a phototube, which causes a restoring force to be generated by passing a current through an electromagnet that serves as the pivot for the balance beam. ⚫A permanent magnet above and below the pivot point supplies magnetic attraction to the electromagnet. The force necessary to restore the beam is proportional to the current passed through the electromagnet, which is recorded. Additional features of the balance are two loops for hanging sample pans (loop A affording 2.5 times the sensitivity of loop B) and controls that adjust the range of the recorder and set the initial balance of the instrument (mass dials).

Null and other types of balances are available that have the capability of measuring the mass of a sample between 100 and 0.02 g to a precision of 0.01–1%. As will be shown later, the smaller the sample, the better the results often will be.

Heating Devices. The sample can be heated by resistance heaters, infrared or microwave radiation, or by heat transfer from hot liquids or gases. Resistance heaters are the most common.

Furnaces should be designed so that the sample is heated uniformly and symmetrically. The furnace must also be designed so that the heat generated is localized on the sample. Heat flow into the environment is an inconvenience to the operator, and heat flow to the balance results in serious errors. These are minimized by cooling the exterior of the oven, and by locating the oven as far as possible from the balance itself. Convection currents can be minimized by designing the sample holder so that it provides the least possible resistance to air flow, and by installing appropriate baffles. Apparent mass changes are always observed at the start of an experiment because of convection currents. Best results are obtained when these currents are held constant after start-up.

Temperature Measurement and Control. Temperature-sensing devices are usually thermocouples placed as close to the sample as possible. Thermocouples are inexpensive, rugged, and fairly linear in their response to temperature changes. Platinum resistance thermometers are also used in this application. The emf generated by the thermocouple may be used to drive one axis of an *x–y* recorder, or a feedback circuit to the heater may be used to obtain a programmed linear heating rate. In the latter case, the time axis of a strip-chart recorder is proportional to temperature. Instruments that depend upon a linear increase in power to the heater often have severely nonlinear temperature increases because of heat losses to the environment.

Recording the Signal. Electrical signals from the balance (see Fig. 17.2) and from the measuring thermocouple (after amplification) are fed into a recording potentiometer. If a strip-chart recorder is used, then the time-base axis is also the sample-temperature axis; an event marker may be used to indicate the temperature in increments of 10, 25, 50, or 100 degrees in order to monitor the linearity of heating. The *x–y* recorder is also used, but this method of recording suffers from the disadvantage that any nonlinearity in the heating rate will not be observed.

Control of the Atmosphere. The composition of the atmosphere surrounding the sample can have large and (if properly used) advantageous effects. For that reason, most thermogravimetric instruments provide some means of altering this atmosphere; in most cases, a static or flowing atmosphere of any desired composition can be provided. In addition, thermogravimetric determinations can be done in a vacuum (many systems can achieve pressures of 10^{-3} torr or less), or at elevated pressures.

TG Theory and Experimental Considerations

Figure 17.1 is a typical thermogravimetric curve. In virtually all TG analyses, the mass is monitored as the temperature is increased; accurate measurements under decreasing temperature are difficult and tend to yield little additional information. As discussed earlier, a reaction occurs when ΔG for the process becomes zero or negative, and its start is indicated when the mass deviates from the initial plateau. When the reaction stops, a new plateau is reached. The temperatures at which the reaction appears to start (T_i) and end (T_f), as well as the shape of the curve, depend upon many factors. Some of these are heating rate, heat of reaction, furnace atmosphere, amount of sample, nature of sample container, particle size, and packing of the sample.

The major use of TG is in the precise determination of mass changes for several sequential reactions. Necessarily, each reaction involving a change in mass must begin with and be followed by a plateau in order to distinguish sequential events. Two processes may occur more or less simultaneously, resulting in shoulders or complete merging of the decomposition reactions. Proper use of the variables listed above can often be used to avoid this. A rather simplified discussion of these variables is presented to illustrate the possibilities.

Heating Rate. In any heating process, there is always a difference in temperature between the sample and the oven. The magnitude of this thermal lag is roughly proportional to the rate at which the sample is heated. As a result, if a change in mass of a sample occurs always at a temperature T_i^0, then the observed T_i (measured outside the sample) will always be greater than T_i^0. Because of the thermal lag, the difference between T_i and T_i^0 will increase as the heating rate is increased. T_f is the temperature at which the end of mass change occurs. This value will depend upon the heating rate in a similar fashion. It is also found that the temperature range of mass loss $(T_f - T_i)$ tends to increase with heating rate. Figure 17.3 shows the effect of a much slower heating rate for the sample as in Figure 17.1.

Heat of Reaction. Since this is an intrinsic property of the material studied, it cannot be altered; however, its effects can be modified. An endothermic process will show a

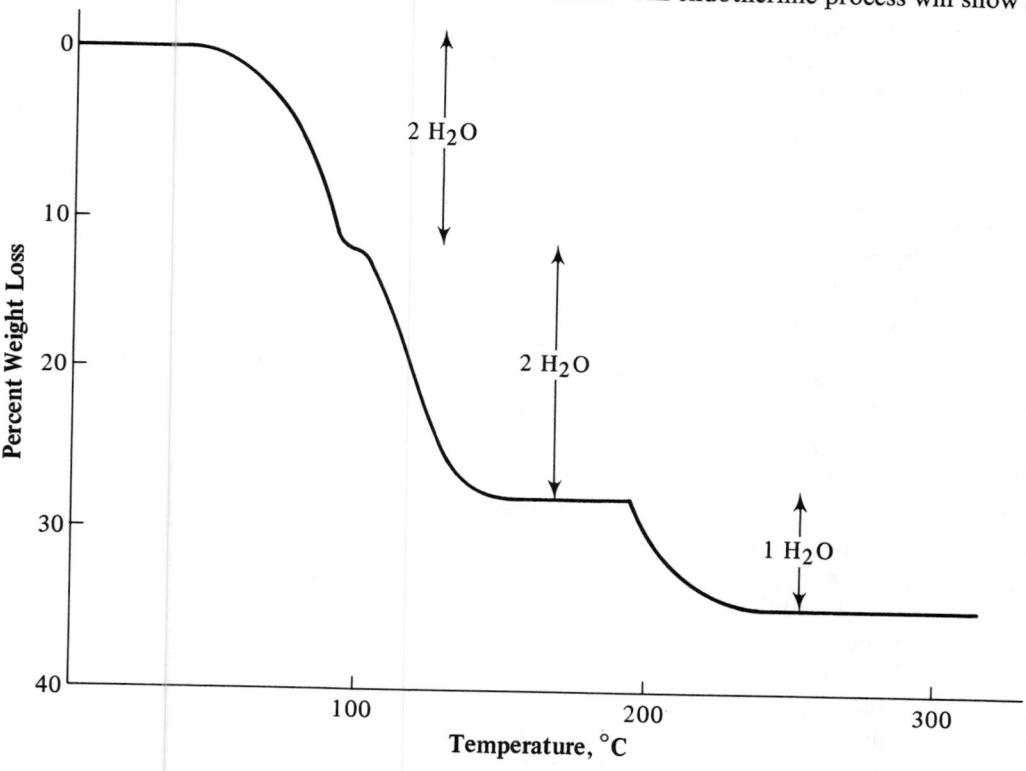

FIGURE 17.3. *Increased resolution of thermogravimetric curves by lower heating-rate (compare to Fig. 17.1).*

larger thermal lag than an exothermic one; the latter will sometimes cause the sample to be hotter than the observed temperature. Obviously, T_f is greatly affected whereas T_i is not. If T_f increases greatly, other processes may be obscured. This increase only occurs in endothermic reactions and may be minimized by heating the sample at a low rate so that the heat absorbed by the reaction can be replaced by heat flow from the oven. Decreasing the temperature range of mass loss ($T_f - T_i$) increases the probability of obtaining usable plateaus.

Furnace Atmosphere. This is perhaps the most useful variable in altering TG curves. The basic feature is that, by providing an atmosphere rich in the reaction product, decomposition is delayed to higher temperatures. Conversely, in an inert atmosphere or vacuum the reaction will proceed at lower temperature. Simultaneous reactions can be separated by the choice of atmosphere, provided that different gases are liberated.

In addition to moving the temperatures of the decompositions, it is possible to alter the reaction that occurs. A notable example of this is found in the heating of organic samples: oxidation will occur in the presence of oxygen, whereas pyrolysis will occur if oxygen is excluded.

Nature of Sample Container. The container is important in that (a) the material used to hold the sample may catalyze an entirely unexpected reaction and (b) the container may trap some of the gases generated. The former may be evaluated by analyzing the reaction products. In the latter case, irreproducible mass changes can occur because of adsorption of the gas, or the curve can be displaced by a self-generated atmosphere around the sample. Metallic sample holders reduce the chances of adsorption, and self-generated atmospheres can be removed by flowing an inert gas past the sample during analysis.

Physical Characteristics of Sample. The amount, particle size, and packing of the sample generally affect its thermal homogeneity. Large systems have large temperature-gradients whereby the outer portions may be reacting while the inner portions are still cool and stable. The result is a greater thermal lag for larger samples, with the effects noted above. Smaller particle size tends to decrease thermal lag, but tighter packing increases it. Nonuniformity of particle size and packing leads to irreproducible curves.

Depending upon the processes studied, it may be necessary to have very good control over some or all of these variables. Generally, to distinguish between reactions that occur within 50–100°C of one another, very stringent control is needed. If long plateaus separate the decompositions, control is less critical.

In addition to gravimetric analysis, TG has also been used to elucidate the kinetics of decomposition reactions. This involves analyzing the shape of the TG curve. In general, the rate of reaction at any measured temperature is proportional to the slope of the curve, but a number of uncertainties sometimes make these analyses of questionable value. Freeman and Carroll [*J. Phys. Chem.*, 62, 389 (1958)] describe the most popular of the kinetics-analysis methods, while Clarke et al. [*Chem. Comm.*, 266 (1969)] present the major objections to kinetics analysis by TG.

Analytical Calculations

Under controlled and reproducible conditions, quantitative data can be extracted from the relevant TG curves. Most commonly, the mass change observed is related to sample purity or composition.

Example 17.1. A mixture of CaO and $CaCO_3$ is analyzed. The thermogram shows one reaction between 500 and 900°C, where the mass of the sample decreases from 125.3 mg to 95.4 mg. What is the percentage of $CaCO_3$ in the sample?

Solution: mmoles CO_2 = (mg lost)/(MW CO_2) = 29.9/44.0 = 0.682

mmoles CO_2 = mmoles $CaCO_3$

mg $CaCO_3$ = mmoles $CaCO_3$ (MW $CaCO_3$) = 0.682 × 100.1 = 68.2 mg

% $CaCO_3$ = (68.2/125.3)(100%) = 54.6%

Example 17.2. A pure compound may be either MgO, $MgCO_3$, or MgC_2O_4. A thermogram of the substance shows a loss of 91.0 mg from a total of 175.0 mg used for analysis. What is the formula of the compound? The relevant possible reactions are

$$MgO \longrightarrow \text{ no reaction}$$
$$MgCO_3 \longrightarrow MgO + CO_2$$
$$MgC_2O_4 \longrightarrow MgO + CO_2 + CO$$

Solution: % mass loss sample = (91.0/175.0)(100%) = 52.0

% mass loss if $MgCO_3$ = (44.01/84.33)(100%) = 52.3

% mass loss if MgC_2O_4 = $\left(\dfrac{44.01 + 28.00}{112.3}\right)(100\%)$ = 64.3

If the preparation was pure, the compound present is $MgCO_3$.

Applications of TG

Books by Duval, Vallet, and Wendlandt (referenced at the end of this chapter) contain a good summary of TG work. A few interesting analytical applications are given below.

Mixtures of divalent-cation oxalates can be analyzed successfully with a high degree of precision. A mixture of calcium, strontium, and barium oxalate mono-hydrates will lose all its water of hydration between 100° and 250°C; the three anhydrous oxalates will decompose simultaneously to the carbonates between 360° and 500°; and the carbonates will in turn decompose to the oxides in the following order: calcium (620–860°C), strontium (860–1100°C), and barium (1100° and up). In addition to the rather common oxalates, the precipitates formed with other organic precipitating agents have been studied, including those of the very similar lanthanide metals. Examples of precipitating agents are cupferron and neocupferron, and significant differences in the decomposition curves of their chelates may be needed for analysis of mixtures.

Direct analysis of solid materials eliminates the precipitation steps referred to above. Clays and soils can be evaluated by TG to determine water content, carbonate content, and organic matter content.

Thermograms can be used to compare the stabilities of similar compounds (e.g., of metal carbonates by studying the thermal decomposition to their respective oxides). Qualitatively, the higher the decomposition temperature, the more positive is the ΔG value at room temperature and the greater the stability.* The example given earlier of the dehydration of copper sulfate pentahydrate is interesting in that one of the five water molecules is not equivalent to the other four. This is confirmed by x-ray crystallography, which shows that four water molecules surround the copper(II), whereas the more tightly bound water molecule is hydrogen-bonded to two neighboring sulfate ions.

17.3 DIFFERENTIAL THERMAL ANALYSIS

In *thermal analysis* (TA), the temperature of a sample is monitored while heat is supplied at a uniform rate. In the more sophisticated method of differential thermal analysis, the difference in temperature between a sample and a reference is measured as they are heated.

General Considerations

Differences in temperature between the sample and an inert reference substance will be observed when changes that involve a finite heat of reaction, such as chemical reactions, phase changes, or structural changes, occur in the sample. If ΔH is positive (endothermic reaction), the temperature of the sample will lag behind that of the reference. If ΔH is negative (exothermic reaction), then the temperature of the sample will exceed that of the reference. Figure 17.4 shows TA and DTA curves for these two cases. DTA is more widely applicable than TG because it is not limited to reactions in which a change in mass occurs. On the other hand, a reaction with a ΔH of zero will not be observed. However, if a measurable change in heat capacity accompanies the process, a change in the position of the baseline will be noted. Table 17.1 lists the various reaction types observable and the expected nature of ΔH.

DTA heating curves are useful both qualitatively and quantitatively. The positions and shapes of the peaks can be used to determine the composition of the sample. (Sadler publishes an index of DTA curves similar to the tabulations of optical spectra.) The area under the peak is proportional to the heat of reaction and the amount of material present, and thus permits quantitative analysis. In addition, the shape of the heating curve can be used in evaluating the kinetics of the reaction under carefully controlled conditions.

Instrumentation

Implementing differential thermal analysis requires the following components: (a) a circuit for measuring differences in temperature, (b) a heating device and temperature-control unit, (c) an amplifying and recording apparatus, and (d) an atmospheric-control device.

---

* This assumes a constant ΔS for the reactions compared, and is most valid when a homologous series of compounds is studied.

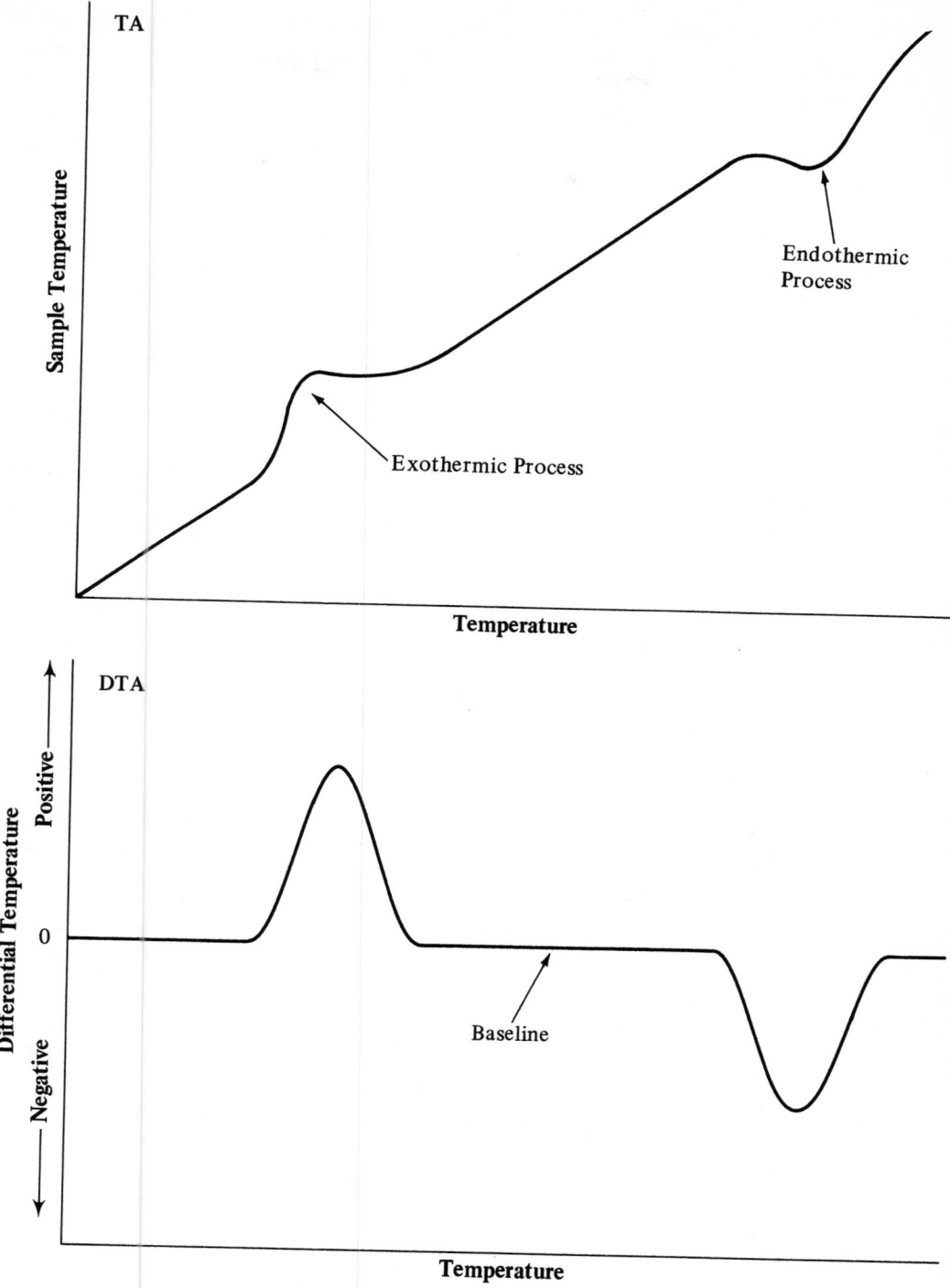

FIGURE 17.4. *A comparison of thermal analysis (TA) and differential thermal analysis (DTA) curves, illustrating exothermic and endothermic peaks.*

TABLE 17.1. *Processes Observable Using DTA, and the Heats of Reaction Typically Observed*

Phenomena	Heat of Reaction	
	Exothermic	Endothermic
Physical		
Crystalline transition	×	×
Fusion	——	×
Vaporization	——	×
Sublimation	——	×
Adsorption	×	——
Desorption	——	×
Absorption	——	×
Chemical		
Chemisorption	×	——
Desolvation	——	×
Dehydration	——	×
Decomposition	×	×
Oxidative degradation	×	——
Oxidation in gaseous atm.	×	——
Reduction in gaseous atm.	——	×
Redox reactions	×	×
Solid-State reactions	×	×

Source: Adapted from S. J. Gordon, *J. Chem. Educ., 40,* A87 (1963), by permission of the publisher.

Temperature Measurement. Thermocouples are by far the most reliable devices for monitoring temperature in DTA. A typical arrangement is shown in Figure 17.5.

One of the major considerations in DTA is obtaining valid readings of the actual temperature of the sample and reference materials conveniently and reproducibly. As in TG, thermal equilibrium is of utmost importance. There is always a definite temperature difference between the outer and inner portions of the sample; indeed, reactions often occur at the surface of the sample while the interior is still unreacted. This effect is minimized by using as small a sample as possible with uniform particle-size and packing. Depending upon the instrument used, the thermocouple may be imbedded in the sample, or at the other extreme, may simply be in direct contact with the sample holder. In any case, the thermocouple must be precisely positioned for every experiment. To obtain the best results, the reference and sample thermocouples should be matched in temperature response and the geometric arrangement of the sample and reference thermocouple should be perfectly symmetrical within the oven.

Heating and Temperature Control. The heating and temperature-control units are very similar to those used in TG. Ovens should be constructed to avoid electrical interference with the thermocouples. To reduce this possibility even further, most instruments have an inner metallic chamber for the sample and reference, to act as

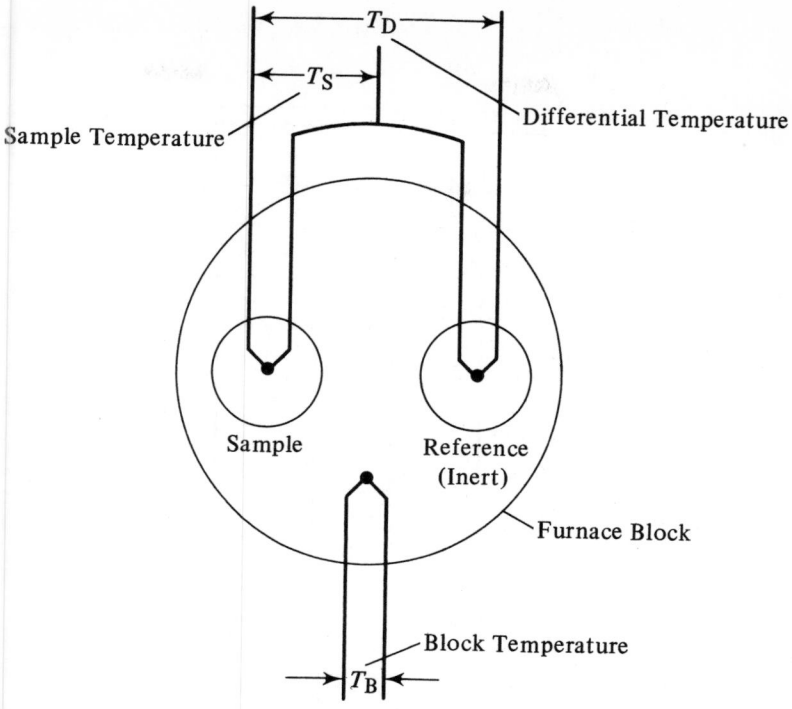

FIGURE 17.5. *Schematic of the thermocouple arrangement in the DTA cell. Adapted from S. J. Gordon,* J. Chem. Educ., 40, *A87 (1967), by permission of the journal editor.*

an electrical shield and to minimize thermal fluctuations. Needless to say, convection currents are no longer important, and atmospheric control is much more easily achieved—particularly a flowing atmosphere.

Recording the Signal. Amplifying the signal and recording the results is done in much the same way as in TG, replacing the signal for mass changes with the potential difference between the thermocouples. Figure 17.6 shows a schematic of a typical DTA apparatus.

The similarities of TG and DTA are obviously great, at least instrumentally. As a consequence, many commercial instruments are designed to perform both types of analysis; the heating device, temperature-control unit, atmospheric control, and recording device are essentially used in common and are contained in a single control unit, only the thermobalance and DTA sample compartments being separate.

Theoretical and Experimental Considerations

The equation for heat flow from the environment to the sample or vice versa is given by the Newtonian cooling equation:

$$\frac{dQ}{dt} = c(T_s - T_e) \tag{17.5}$$

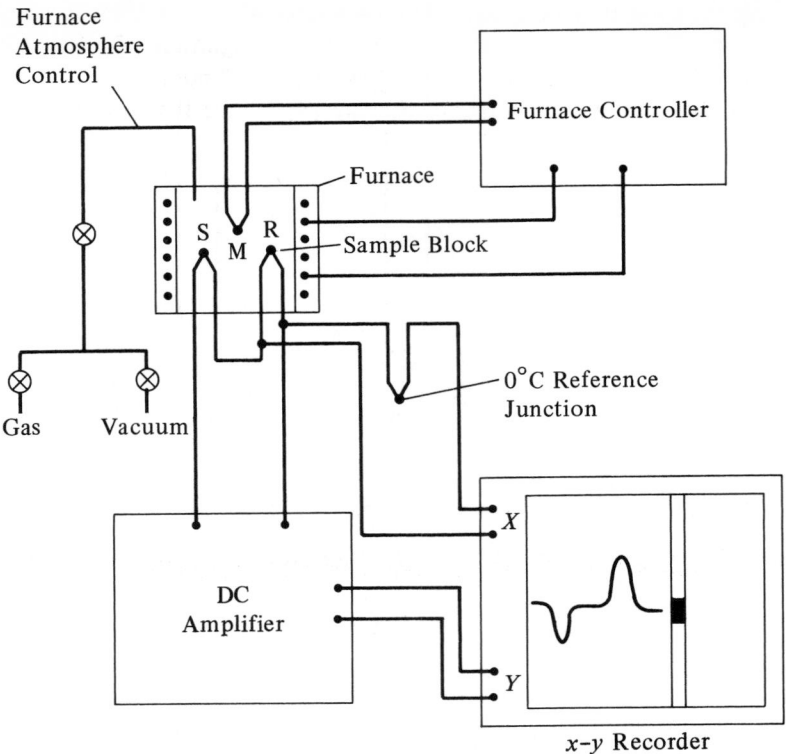

FIGURE 17.6. *Schematic of the entire differential thermal analysis setup. S, R, and M represent the sample, reference, and furnace-monitoring thermocouples, respectively. Adapted from W. W. Wendlandt,* Thermal Methods of Analysis, *New York: John Wiley, 1964, by permission of the publisher.*

where c = a constant related to the thermal conductivity of the system
T_s = temperature of the sample
T_e = the temperature of the environment

The flow of heat (Q) is from the environment to the sample if dQ/dt is negative; this is always the case in a heating curve, in the baseline regions. The equation for the rate of heat production for chemical processes is

$$\frac{dQ}{dt} = (-\Delta H)\frac{dn_p}{dt} \tag{17.6}$$

where n_p = the number of moles of product formed

The net heat-change in the sample is given by the sum of Equations 17.5 and 17.6. For an exothermic process, the start of the reaction causes an increase in the rate of gain of heat (Eqn. 17.6) but the rate of transfer of heat from the environment is decreased [in Eqn. 17.5, $(T_s - T_e)$ tends to decrease]. When Equation 17.5 is equal to Equation 17.6, the maximum (or minimum) of the DTA peak is observed.

If the constant c in Equation 17.5 is known, the exact point at which the reaction ends can be calculated. Usually, however, the magnitude of c is not known and all that can be said is that the reaction ends at some point after the maximum. This behavior may be compared to that in TG, where the reaction unambiguously ceases when a new plateau is reached.

DTA peak areas depend mainly upon the amount of material, the heat of reaction, and the thermal flow to or from the sample. These are related by the equation

$$A = \frac{-m\,\Delta H}{gc} \tag{17.7}$$

where
- g = a constant related to the geometry of the sample
- c = a constant related to the thermal conductivity
- m = the amount of reactive component in the sample (in moles)

Although the constants g and c can be evaluated experimentally, they are usually combined into a simple empirical conversion factor, c', to give:

$$A = c'm(-\Delta H) \tag{17.8}$$

The parameters discussed below also have some effect upon the observed areas, but the proportionality given by Equation 17.8 holds well under controlled experimental conditions.

As in TG, the maintenance of thermal equilibrium throughout the system becomes the overriding consideration in obtaining reproducible results. As noted previously, the placement of the thermocouple becomes critical; slight displacements in the position of the thermocouple from the center of the sample can contribute to irreproducible results. Placing the thermocouple outside the sample cell in good thermal contact with it assures consistent positioning, while simplifying the experimental procedure.

The magnitude of the difference in temperature between the exterior and the interior of the sample depends upon two factors: the rate of heating (as in TG), and the thermal conductivity of the sample and sample holder. Thus, a metal sample (which has a high thermal conductivity) is close to isothermal, even at high rates of heating. An apparent solution to the problem of thermal equilibrium is to increase the thermal conductivity of the sample appreciably (for instance, by mixing it with a diluent of high conductivity). This approach has limitations, however: Equation 17.5 shows that the heat produced or absorbed by the reaction will then be partially or completely compensated for by heat flow to or from the environment.

The best solution is to use a cell whose thermal conductivity is low relative to that of the sample. This minimizes the effect described by Equation 17.5 so that a large proportion of the effects described by Equation 17.6 can be measured. Therefore, ceramic sample-holders are used in reactions where ΔH is relatively small, and more convenient metallic sample-holders are used in reactions involving great amounts of heat. Best results are obtained with well powdered samples, and uniformity of results is enhanced by consistently using samples of the same particle-size and density of packing.

Table 17.2 summarizes the major factors that affect the shape and size of the DTA heating curve. The effects of the atmosphere around the sample are precisely

TABLE 17.2. *Some Common Factors That Influence DTA Heating Curves*

Factor	Effect	Correction or Control
Heating rate	Changes in peak size and position	Use low heating-rate
Sample size	Changes in peak size and position	Decrease size or lower the heating rate
Thermocouple placement	Irreproducible curves	Use the same location for each run
Sample particle size	Irreproducible and erratic curves	Use small, uniform particle size
Thermal conductivity of sample	Changes in peak position	Mix with thermally conductive diluent or lower the heating rate
Thermal conductivity of cell	Affects peak area	Decrease thermal conductivity to increase peak area
Reaction with atmosphere	Changes in peak size and position	Control carefully (can be used advantageously)
Sample packing	Irreproducible curves	Control carefully (affects thermal conductivity)
Diluent	Changes heat capacity and thermal conductivity	Choose carefully (can be used advantageously)

the same as those in TG and may either be a serious problem or a tool to use to analytical advantage.

Reference Materials. The subject of reference materials is important and often neglected. The major requirements are that the reference material should be inert over the temperature range of the analysis, that it should not react with the sample holder or thermocouples and that its thermal conductivity should match that of the sample. The last item is important since changes in thermal conductivity or heat capacity

TABLE 17.3. *Common Diluents and Reference Materials for DTA*

Compound	Approximate Temperature Limit, °C	Reactivity
Silicon carbide	2000	May be a catalyst
Glass beads	1500	Inert
Alumina	2000	Reacts with halogenated compounds
Iron	1500	Crystal change at ~700°C
Iron(III) oxide	1000	Crystal change at 680°C
Silicone oils	1000	Inert
Graphite	3500	Inert

with temperature result in sloping baselines. Table 17.3 lists some of the more common reference materials.

Diluents. The materials listed in Table 17.3 can also be used as diluents. Naturally, the diluent must also be inert in the presence of the sample.

One purpose of using a diluent has already been discussed: it permits the thermal conductivities of sample and reference to be matched. In addition, it may be used to maintain a constant sample-size while the amount of the reacting component is varied; this will decrease the influence of many of the factors listed in Table 17.2. A diluent can also be used where the sample is so small that weighing it out directly is inconvenient.

Analytical Calculations

Equation 17.8 predicts a direct proportionality between peak area and mass. Hence, for quantitative analysis, the peak area (A) of a sample of known mass (m_k) is compared to that for an unknown sample run under identical conditions:

$$m_{\text{unk}} = m_k \left(\frac{A_{\text{unk}}}{A_k} \right) \tag{17.9}$$

Similarly, the heat of reaction may be determined by comparison with a sample of known ΔH, although particular caution has to be exercised in determining heats of reaction: the constant in Equation 17.8 which relates peak area and ΔH varies with temperature. As a result, the known sample should react at the same temperature as the unknown, and the peak areas of the known and unknown should be roughly equal.

> **Example 17.3.** Compound A has a molecular weight of 98.4 and a heat of fusion of 1.63 kcal/mole. Compound B has a molecular weight of 64.3 and melts at approximately the same temperature as compound A. 500-mg samples of each yield DTA peak areas of 60.0 cm² and 45.0 cm² for A and B, respectively. What is the heat of fusion of B?
>
> *Solution:* From Equation 17.8,
>
> $$\Delta H_B = \Delta H_A \left(\frac{A_B}{A_A} \right) \left(\frac{m_B}{m_A} \right)$$
>
> m_A and m_B must be expressed in molar quantities to compare different compounds.
>
> $$\Delta H_B = 1.63 \text{ kcal/mole} \left(\frac{45.0 \text{ cm}^2}{60.0 \text{ cm}^2} \right) \left(\frac{500/64.3}{500/98.4} \right) = 1.87 \text{ kcal/mole}$$

Calculation of the area under the peak of the heating curve (see Fig. 17.7) can be subject to ambiguity, since, more often than not, the initial and final baselines do not coincide—the thermal conductivity or heat capacity has changed as a result of the reaction. A method for rapidly estimating the area of interest is illustrated in the figure. Both baselines are extended to a perpendicular line drawn from the maximum of the curve, and the areas under the two halves of the curve are determined and summed to give the total area.

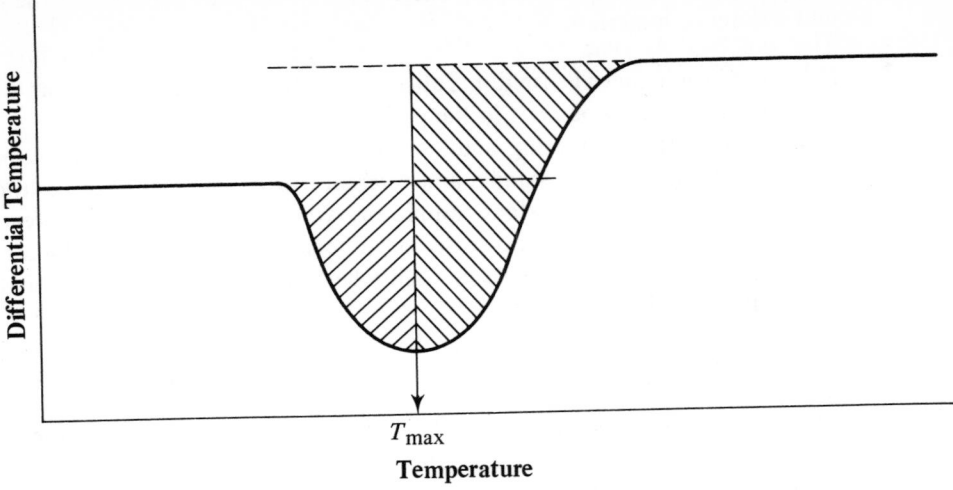

FIGURE 17.7. *Illustration depicting the calculation of DTA peak areas.
The displacement of the baseline indicates a change in heat capacity.*

The rates and activation energies of the reactions observed in DTA can be calculated from observed changes in DTA curves as the heating rate is changed; the essential data are the rate of heating b and the temperature at the curve maximum T_{max} (in K). The applicable equation is

$$d[\ln (b/T_{max}^2)]/d(1/T_{max}) = -E^*/R \tag{17.10}$$

where $E^* =$ the activation energy of the reaction
$R =$ the gas constant

A plot of $\ln (b/T_{max}^2)$ versus $1/T_{max}$ yields a line of slope $-E^*/R$ [1].

The order of the reaction process (first-order, second-order, etc.) can be determined from the asymmetry of the DTA curve [1] (see Fig. 17.8). The asymmetry of the peak is simply x/y, and the reaction order is estimated from:

$$\text{Reaction Order} = 1.26(x/y)^{1/2} \tag{17.11}$$

There are many more complete treatments, and interested readers are referred to the bibliography at the end of this chapter for more detail. The problems associated with kinetic analysis by TG are also present with DTA.

FIGURE 17.8. *Parameters used to calculate the DTA peak asymmetry. Adapted from H. E. Kissinger,* Anal. Chem., 29, 1702 (1957), *by permission of the publisher. Copyright © 1957 by the American Chemical Society.*

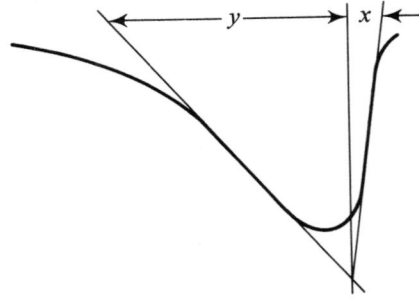

Applications of DTA

The general reference books of MacKenzie and Wendlandt summarize a large number of DTA studies and analytical applications. A few of these are outlined below.

Heat capacity estimates may be made using DTA. In the ideal system, with identical reference and sample materials, the "true" baseline of the instrument is obtained. Using a reference and sample of different heat capacities, the baseline will not be the same; and an estimate of the heat capacity of an unknown may be obtained by comparing the baseline shift with that for a sample of known heat capacity. A shift in the baseline is almost always observed after a DTA peak because of change in heat capacity of the sample. In addition, some reactions such as the glass transition of polymers yield virtually no DTA peak, but there is a rather sharp shift in the baseline after the transition temperature.

Polymer analysis is perhaps the most common application of DTA. Under carefully controlled conditions, the shape of the heating curve indicates both the type of polymer and the method used to prepare it; consequently, not only can the polymer be identified, but often (when production processes differ) the particular manufacturer as well. The "crystallinity" of a polymer determines its physical properties to a great extent. In DTA, there are commonly two peaks, one for the reaction of the crystalline part of the sample and another for that of the noncrystalline part (these two peaks often overlap). The magnitudes of these peaks can be used to evaluate the percent crystallinity. A significant advantage of DTA in this application is that the untreated polymer can be studied, thus avoiding possible changes caused by pretreatment (such as dissolution or grinding) of the sample.

Fuels (such as coal) can be evaluated rapidly to determine the source and BTU rating. As with TG, clays and soils can be analyzed using DTA.

Some of the most interesting analyses are of biological materials. Heating curves of such materials (e.g., plant leaves, cell cultures) give characteristic plots; indeed, cell cultures of the same strain of bacteria yield different heating curves, depending on the growth medium. In addition, the calorific value of organic material and foods can be evaluated using DTA.

17.4 DIFFERENTIAL SCANNING CALORIMETRY

In DTA, reactions are observed by measuring the deviation of the sample temperature from that of the reference material. This deviation causes thermal fluxes (Eqn. 17.5) which complicate the theoretical description of the curves and decrease the sensitivity. It would be advantageous to keep the sample and reference at the same temperature and to measure the rate of heat flow into each that was necessary to maintain the constant temperature. This is achieved by placing separate heating elements in the sample and reference chambers; the rate of heating by these elements can be controlled and measured as desired. This is the basis of differential scanning calorimetry (DSC).

DSC plots are graphs of the differential rate of heating (in cal/sec) versus temperature (see Fig. 17.9). The area under the peak is directly proportional to the heat evolved or absorbed by the reaction, and the height of the curve is directly

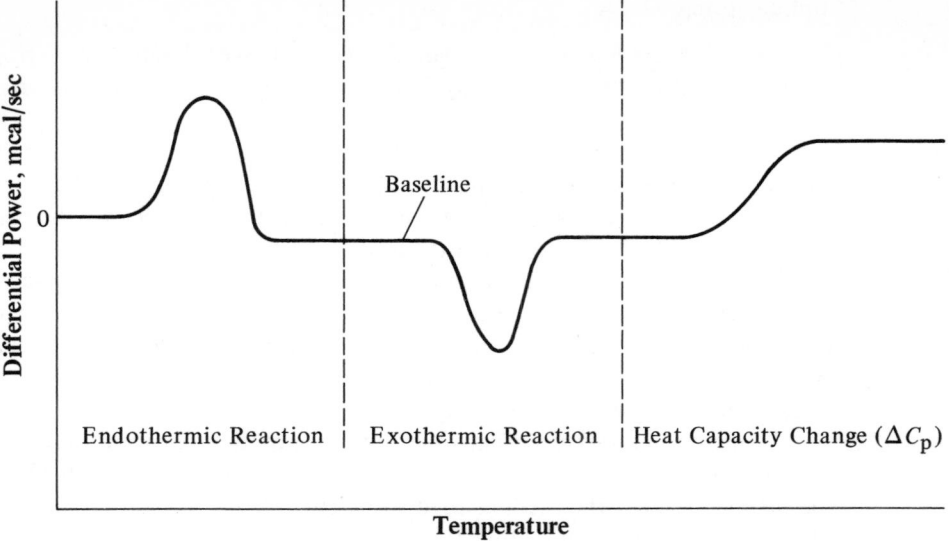

Differential Power, mcal/sec

0

Baseline

Endothermic Reaction | Exothermic Reaction | Heat Capacity Change (ΔC_p)

Temperature

FIGURE 17.9. *Ideal representation of the three processes observable via differential scanning calorimetry.*

proportional to the rate of reaction. Although a proportionality constant similar to c' in Equation 17.8 exists, it is an electrical conversion factor rather than one based on sample characteristics; that c' is now independent of temperature is a major advantage of DSC over DTA.

Instrumentation

Figure 17.10 illustrates the circuitry of a differential scanning calorimeter. There are two separate heating circuits, the average-heating controller and the differential-heating circuit. In the average-temperature controller, the temperatures of the sample and reference are measured and averaged and the heat output of the average heater is automatically adjusted so that the average temperature of the sample and reference increases at a linear rate. The differential-temperature controller monitors the difference in temperature between the sample and reference and automatically adjusts the power to either the reference or sample chambers to keep the temperatures equal. The temperature of the sample is put on the *x*-axis (time) of a strip-chart recorder and the difference in power supplied to the two differential heaters is displayed on the *y*-axis. The power difference is calibrated in terms of calories per unit time.

A simple differential scanning calorimeter can be constructed to monitor endothermic reactions, since heat can be added to the sample compartment without affecting the heating rate. If the process is exothermic, however, the mere addition of heat to the reference will, while keeping the sample and reference isothermal, make the rate of heating nonlinear. The circuit in Figure 17.10 avoids this problem: when an exothermic process occurs, the average-temperature circuit decreases the

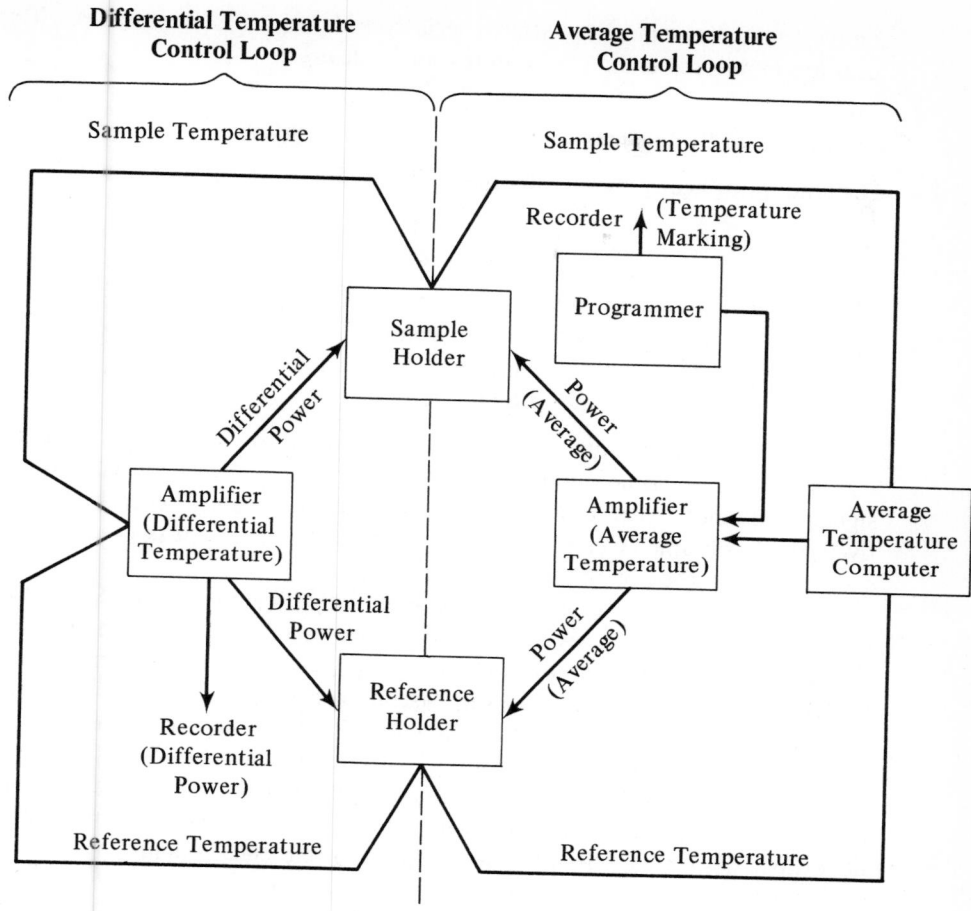

Differential Temperature Control Loop

Average Temperature Control Loop

Sample Temperature

Sample Temperature

Recorder ↑ (Temperature Marking)

Programmer

Sample Holder

Differential Power

Power (Average)

Amplifier (Differential Temperature)

Amplifier (Average Temperature)

Average Temperature Computer

Differential Power

Reference Holder

Power (Average)

Recorder (Differential Power)

Reference Temperature

Reference Temperature

FIGURE 17.10. *Schematic diagram of the DSC apparatus. Adapted from E. S. Watson, M. J. O'Neill, J. Justin, and N. Brenner,* Anal. Chem., *36, 1233 (1964), by permission of the publisher. Copyright ©️ 1964 by the American Chemical Society.*

rate of heating of both the reference and sample equally. In the sample compartment, this decrease in the rate of heating is compensated for by the heat of the reaction, while the differential heater in the reference compartment compensates for the decreased heating by the average heater.

Samples for analysis range in size from 1 to 100 mg and are sealed in a foil or metallic container for direct contact with the heaters and temperature sensors. The sample and reference compartments are well isolated to avoid flow of heat from one to the other, and heat flow to the environment is equalized by careful choice of material and geometry in the compartments. A wide range of heating rates (0.5 to 80°C/min) can be used, and instruments are generally sensitive enough to detect heat evolution or absorption at a rate of less than one millicalorie per second. Electrical signals are amplified and recorded as in TG and DTA. The use of sealed sample-containers eliminates atmospheric considerations in most cases. Temperatures are monitored using platinum resistance devices.

Experimental Considerations

The amount of heat generated by the differential heaters per unit time is

$$P = \frac{dQ}{dt} = i^2 R \qquad (17.12)$$

where
P = the power in watts
Q = the quantity of heat in joules
i = the current in amperes
R = the resistance in ohms

Chemical reactions liberate or absorb heat according to Equation 17.6. Thus, when ΔH is positive (endothermic reaction), the sample heater is energized and a positive signal is obtained; when ΔH is negative, the reference heater is energized and a negative signal is obtained (see Figure 17.9). The integral of the peak is equal to the heat evolved or absorbed by the reacting sample.

Not only is DSC sensitive to processes where there is a finite ΔH, but it is also very sensitive to differences in the heat capacities of the sample and reference. If the sample has a greater heat capacity than the reference, the sample differential heater will be operating even in the baseline region, giving a positive signal; similarly, a higher heat capacity for the reference will yield a negative baseline. A change in the heat capacity of either the sample or reference will be seen as a displacement of the baseline. The difference between the actual baseline and the zero of the instrument (in cal/sec), divided by the heating rate (°C/sec), is equal to the difference in heat capacities (cal/°C) between the sample and reference systems.

If the heat capacity of the reference is known, then the heat capacity of the sample can be determined over a wide range of temperatures. There is a great interest in this type of application; for example, changes in structure of many large polymers have a very small ΔH (virtually undetectable by DTA), but a ΔC_p quantitatively measurable by DSC.

The factors in Table 17.2, which have detrimental effects on DTA curves, have minimal effects on DSC curves. In particular, measurements obtained from the total area under the curve (calculation of ΔH and sample mass) are not affected. However, these factors still have an effect on the rate of reaction, particularly if large thermal gradients are allowed to develop in the sample or reference, that have a severe effect upon the apparent rate of reaction and any values calculated from these rates.

The rate at which heat is evolved in exothermic reactions must be taken into account in DSC; rapid exothermic reactions may cause the rate of temperature increase of the sample to be greater than the programmed rate of heating, even when both the average and differential heaters are off. A similar problem sometimes occurs with endothermic processes, where a rapid endothermic reaction may cool the sample so severely that the combined maximum heating of the two heaters cannot maintain a linear heating rate and isothermal conditions. Both these situations can be easily rectified by adjusting the heating rate or the sample size.

Analytical Calculations

Virtually every chemical process involves a change in the heat capacity of the sample. When measured by differential scanning calorimetry, such changes produce a curve similar to Figure 17.7 (except with a y-axis in cal/sec). The area under the DSC curve is determined in the same manner as in DTA. This area is proportional to the amount of heat evolved or absorbed by the reaction, and the heat of reaction is obtained by dividing this by the moles of sample used. If the heat of reaction is known, the moles of sample present can be calculated from essentially the same equation (i.e., the integral of Equation 17.6). All determinations should be preceded by an analysis of a standard sample of known mass and ΔH in order to calibrate the particular instrument used.

Processes where ΔH is zero yield no area for the curve (see Fig. 17.9C). In this case, the change in the specific heat is determined from

$$\Delta C_p (\text{cal}/{}^\circ\text{C-g}) = \frac{\Delta \text{ Baseline}}{mb} \qquad (17.13)$$

where m = the mass of the sample
         b = the heating rate

Analytical Applications of DSC

Because of the great similarity between DSC and DTA, the analyses previously described and referred to for DTA are amenable to DSC studies.

The unique feature of DSC is the determination of heat capacities (specific heats). As noted, the differential power (cal/sec) divided by the heating rate (°C/sec) yields the difference in heat capacities between the sample and the reference (in the baseline regions only). A change in heat capacity is seen by a shift in the baseline. A sharp increase in the baseline of the plot is typical of glass transitions in polymers. By comparing the heat capacity of the sample with the known heat capacity of the standard, the absolute heat capacity of the sample can be calculated.

17.5 THERMOMETRIC TITRATION AND DIRECT-INJECTION ENTHALPIMETRY

Early thermometric measurements were laborious and time consuming and not very sensitive, although many excellent thermometric studies were reported up to the early 1950s, when thermometric titration became suitably automated for routine analytical use. Around that time, the thermistor temperature-sensor, the constant-delivery pump and sophisticated thermostatic control were introduced in rapid succession.

Thermometric titrations (TT) and direct-injection enthalpimetry (DIE) are both calorimetric techniques; the heat evolved or absorbed serves as an indicator of the progress of the reaction. Nowadays, TT and DIE are used for routine analysis and in fundamental research involving the chemical equilibrium, reaction kinetics, and thermochemistry of processes not readily studied by other methods.

Thermometric titration plots are characteristically graphs of temperature change versus titrant added. Direct-injection enthalpimetry yields plots of temperature versus the time following injection of a titrant. Both are illustrated in Figure 17.11. The methods are discussed together in this section because of the many similarities between them.

In TT, temperature changes occur only when titration is in progress and when there is sample reactant present. As a consequence, the start and endpoint of a titration are readily observed, and the number of moles titrated is calculated as in regular titrimetry. By determining the heat capacity of the system under study, heats of reaction can be readily determined. In addition, equilibrium constants can be evaluated under the appropriate conditions.

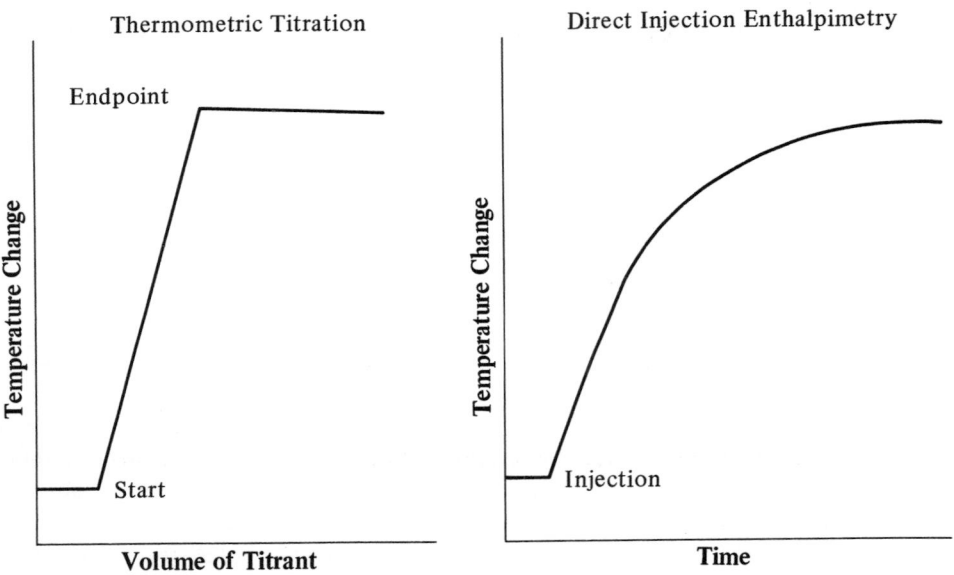

FIGURE 17.11. *Characteristic curves obtained from thermometric titration and direct-injection enthalpimetry.*

In direct-injection enthalpimetry, the titrant at the same temperature as the sample is injected rapidly into the sample and the data obtained as a temperature-versus-time curve. No endpoint is obtained, but the magnitude of the temperature change is proportional to the concentration. Also, one can generate kinetic curves to evaluate slow reactions. The speed of analysis is enhanced, and processes with equilibria unfavorable for titration are readily studied by using a large excess of one reactant.

Both DIE and TT are subject to the same restrictions as in classical calorimetry. If TT is used simply as an endpoint detection method, the restrictions also apply, but to a much lesser degree.

Instrumentation

Thermometric titrations can be implemented with a buret, a Dewar flask, and a Beckman thermometer, as in early studies. In modern instrumentation, however, automated electronic methods are used to obtain and often to evaluate the data. A typical TT setup consists of (a) a constant-delivery pump, (b) a temperature-control system, (c) an adiabatic cell, (d) a calibration unit, (e) an electronic temperature-sensing system, and (f) an amplifying and data-processing system.

Delivery Pump. A constant-delivery pump permits the time axis of a strip-chart recorder to be used as the volume-of-titrant axis (with a simple conversion factor). Typically, a syringe driven by a synchronous motor (that drives a carriage or screw) is used, and solutions can be delivered at constant rates ranging down to a few microliters per minute. Because of their variable flow rates, the more common peristaltic pumps are not often used for thermometric titrations.

In DIE, the syringe is rapidly emptied at the start of the experiment to deliver the titrant virtually instantaneously into the sample cell.

Temperature-Control Requirements. The temperature control needed in the TT apparatus depends upon the results desired. It is often possible to obtain useful endpoints in titrations simply by bringing both the sample and titrant to room temperature. However, for precise calorimetric results, the titrant and sample must be as close to the same temperature as possible. This is the main purpose of the thermostat.

Currently, using modern temperature-controllers, it is possible to maintain the temperature of the system at a wide range of set temperatures to a precision of $\pm 0.001°C$ or less. As a rule of thumb, the temperature change caused by the reaction observed must be at least as great as the temperature difference between the titrant and sample (i.e., the precision of the thermostat). Consequently, letting the random heat flows of the environment control the temperature of the apparatus is only sufficient for highly exothermic or endothermic processes.

Adiabatic Cell. The "adiabatic" cells used for TT and DIE have widely varying designs. They range from an insulated beaker to a Dewar flask to the highly elegant and efficient Dewar-type cell of Christiansen et al. [2] (Fig. 17.12). All are designed to minimize the heat transfer from the cell to the environment, thus maximizing the temperature change observed. When only titration endpoints are of interest, the simplest cell suffices; but if quantities such as heats of reaction, equilibrium constants, or kinetic parameters are sought, better cells are necessary.

These cells may be evaluated in terms of their heat-leak modulus, which is defined by the Newtonian cooling equation

$$\frac{dT}{dt} = -C(T_c - T_e) \tag{17.14}$$

where C = the heat-leak modulus
T_c = the temperature of the cell
T_e = the temperature of the environment

The Christiansen cell has the very low heat-leak modulus of $1.1 \times 10^{-3} \, min^{-1}$. Another factor is the mass of the cell and its contribution to the overall heat capacity and response; the better cells have thin walls to minimize the heat capacity and maximize the speed of response to temperature changes.

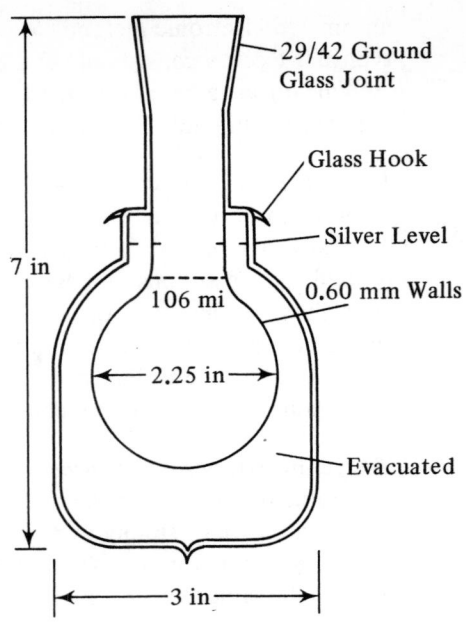

FIGURE 17.12. *An efficient adiabatic cell used for TT and DIE. Adapted from J. J. Christensen, R. M. Izatt, and L. D. Hansen, Rev. Sci. Instr., 36, 779 (1965), by permission of the senior author.*

29/42 Ground Glass Joint

Glass Hook

Silver Level

0.60 mm Walls

Evacuated

7 in

106 mi

2.25 in

3 in

Whereas it is relatively easy to maintain the titrant at any particular temperature by having it in good thermal contact with the thermostat bath, the cell temperature is not controlled easily in this manner, and an external means is usually employed to bring the cell quickly to thermal equilibrium. This is done using the calibration heater.

Calibration Unit. The calibration circuitry has two purposes: to determine the heat capacity of the system, and to control the temperature in the cell itself.

The heat evolved or absorbed is calculated from the temperature change using the relation

$$\Delta Q = \Delta T C'_p \tag{17.15}$$

C'_p is the heat capacity of the system, readily measured as the amount of heat necessary to raise the cell temperature a known amount by electrical-resistance heating.

$$C'_p(\text{joules}/°C) = i^2 R t / \Delta T \text{ (watts-sec}/°C) \tag{17.16}$$

where
$t =$ the time of heating
$i =$ the current (measured)
$R =$ the resistance (known)

Division by 4.184 joules/cal permits conversion to cal/°C. The voltages V_s and V_h across a standard resistor (R_s) and the heater (R_h) connected in series are the measurements of interest, since $i^2 R_h = V_s V_h / R_s$. The heater can be used to advantage in hastening the cell to a thermal equilibrium with the thermostat bath and titrant by heating the cell and its contents to a temperature very close to that at which the thermostat is set.

Temperature-Sensing System. Temperature sensing is the heart of the thermometric titration technique. The principal temperature-sensors used are thermistors. A thermistor is a temperature-sensitive semiconductor whose resistance obeys the equation

$$R_T = Ae^{B/T} \tag{17.17}$$

where A and B are constants whose values depend upon the nature of the thermistor. In general, thermistors decrease in resistance as the temperature increases, by 3–6%/°C. If the thermistor is incorporated into a Wheatstone bridge, the off-balance potential caused by the change in R_T can be recorded on a strip-chart recorder; when the input potential of the Wheatstone bridge is about 1 V, the output voltage changes by approximately 10 mV/°C (thermocouples produce a voltage of approximately 10 μV for a similar temperature change).

Both the thermistor response and the Wheatstone bridge readout are not linear with temperature. However, it has been found that the nonlinearity is unimportant over a small enough temperature range (less than 0.1°C). Other factors that make thermistors ideal for TT and DIE are their small size, fast response to temperature change, and (when encapsulated with glass) inertness to most chemicals.

Amplification and Recording. Although the thermistor is already as sensitive as a thousand-junction thermocouple would be, it is often advantageous to amplify the signals obtained. Using a DC amplifier, it is possible to obtain good signals for temperature changes of the order of 10^{-4} °C or less. An AC Wheatstone bridge with a lock-in amplifier can detect temperature changes of the order of 10^{-6} °C [3].

The two most popular data-acquisition systems are the strip-chart recorder and the digital data-storage system. The latter is used when a great deal of data processing is anticipated.

Experimental Considerations

Figure 17.13 represents an idealized thermometric titration curve. Region 1 is the baseline. Ideally horizontal, in practice is has a finite slope as a result of frictional heat added by stirring, resistive heat added by the thermistor (Eqn. 17.12), and the transfer of heat from the cell to the thermostat (Eqn. 17.14). If frictional and resistance heating are constant and equal to W, then the slope in Region 1 is

$$\frac{dT}{dt} = -C(T_c - T_e) + W \tag{17.18}$$

The slope in Region 2 is due to the same effects, plus the following: the temperature change generated by the reaction, the heat of dilution of the reactants (ΔH_D), and the difference in temperature between titrant and sample after the start of titration (ΔT_R). This may be expressed as

$$\frac{dT}{dt} = -C(T_c - T_e) + W + (-\Delta H/C_p')\left(\frac{dn_p}{dt}\right) + \Delta H_D/C_p' + \Delta T_R k \tag{17.19}$$

where k = a constant

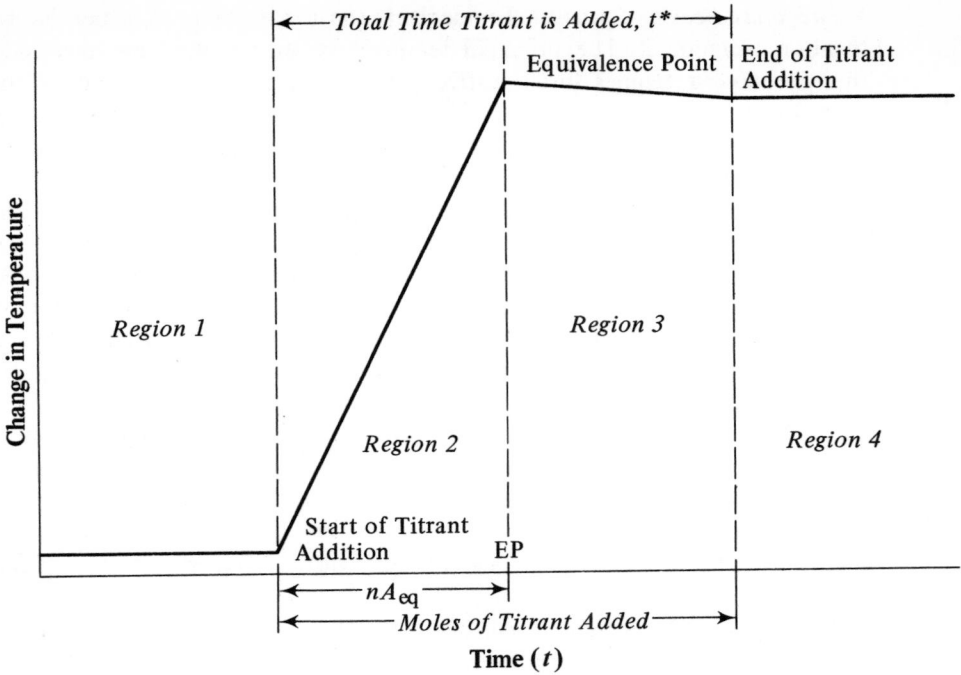

FIGURE 17.13. *Idealized representation of the four major regions of the TT curve. With a constant-delivery pump, the x-axis can be in units of time or moles of titrant.*

In Region 3, where the equivalence point has been passed, the slope of the curve is described by

$$\frac{dT}{dt} = -C(T_c - T_e) + W + \Delta H_D/C_p' + \Delta T_R \qquad (17.20)$$

When no further titrant is added (Region 4), the slope again obeys Equation 17.18. (There is usually some rounding at the equivalence point in real titrations.)

These expressions can be combined to obtain the heat of reaction ΔH and, if the production of product (n_p) is equilibrium controlled, the equilibrium constant of the reaction can also be calculated [4].

In DIE, temperature-versus-time curves indicate the progress of the reaction. Kinetic processes can be evaluated (usually for reactions having half-reaction times greater than 5 sec), and from the total temperature change, heats of reaction can be evaluated. The general equation for a DIE curve is

$$\frac{dT}{dt} = \frac{-\Delta H}{C_p'}\left(\frac{dn_p}{dt}\right) + W \qquad (17.21)$$

where dn_p/dt is governed by the appropriate rate expression. An obvious advantage of this type of kinetic analysis is that the system is not disturbed (and is continuously monitored) in obtaining the data.

Equations 17.18 to 17.21 are straightforward, but often it is not necessary to solve them rigorously to obtain useful and reliable results—see the following section.

In applying the equations, however, there are a few points to consider. First, the heat capacity of the system in TT is continuously changing in Regions 2 and 3; thus, C'_p in Equation 17.19 is not truly a constant. As the volume of the system increases during the titration, the change in temperature per unit time decreases, even though the amount of heat released remains constant; this can cause a large error if not corrected [5]. The correction is made by replotting the entire curve in terms of Q (calories of heat evolved)—instead of T—versus volume of titrant added. To obtain Q, the change in temperature at each point on the curve is multiplied by the heat capacity (C_p) at that point. The heat capacity at every point in Regions 2 and 3 can be determined by measuring C_p in Regions 1 and 4 of the curve, obtaining C_{p1} and C_{p4}. At any point t in Regions 2 and 3, the heat capacity is given by

$$C_{pt} = C_{p1} + (t/t^*)(C_{p4} - C_{p1}) \qquad (17.22)$$

where t^* is the total time interval over which titrant is added (this assumes a linear increase in heat capacity during the course of titration). The curve of heat evolved (Q) versus volume of titrant is called an *enthalpogram*. This procedure is tedious, and can be avoided by using a titrant that is 100 or more times as concentrated as the sample [6]; the term ($C_{p4} - C_{p1}$) in Equation 17.22 then approaches zero.

DIE curves are equivalent to enthalpograms, since the heat capacity does not change significantly once the reactants are mixed.

Analytical Calculations

Knowing the concentration of either the titrant or the sample, the volume added to reach the endpoint yields the concentration of the unknown. Heats of reaction are obtained from the rigorous solution of Equations 17.18 to 17.20 [4].

> *Example 17.4.* A thermometric titration of acid A with base B was performed, and a curve similar to that in Figure 17.13 was obtained. The slopes of the four regions of the curve were 1.0×10^{-5}, 8.0×10^{-4}, -1.0×10^{-5}, and -0.5×10^{-5} °C/sec, respectively. The overall temperature change was 0.100°C. Prior to the experiment, the heat capacity of the cell was determined to be 1.000 cal/°C. The titration rate was 6.0×10^{-8} moles B/sec. In addition, it was found that the titration of B into pure water gave a slope of 2.0×10^{-5} °C/sec under identical experimental conditions. Use these data to calculate the heat of reaction.
>
> *Solution:* Using Equation 17.18, the slope in Region 1 corresponds to the value W, since $T_c = T_e$. The same equation applies to Region 4, but now the constant C can be evaluated since W and ($T_c - T_e$) are known. The value of C is 1.5×10^{-4} sec^{-1}. The heat of dilution factor in Equation 17.20 is the difference between the slope of the titration of B into pure water and the slope in Region 1

$$\Delta H_D / C'_p = 2.0 \times 10^{-5} - 1.0 \times 10^{-5} = 1.0 \times 10^{-5} \text{ °C/sec}$$

Now it is possible to solve Equation 17.20 for T_R, obtaining a value of -1.5×10^{-4} sec^{-1}. Lastly, all of the above information is used in Equation 17.19 to obtain

$$8.1 \times 10^{-4} = \frac{-\Delta H}{C'_p}\left(\frac{dn_p}{dt}\right)$$

The term dn_p/dt is equal to the titration rate and C_p' was given as 1.000 cal/°C. The heat of reaction is then: $\Delta H = -8.1 \times 10^{-4}/6.0 \times 10^{-8} = -13.5 \times 10^3$ cal/mole $= -13.5$ kcal/mole.

In the above data, the terms in units of °C can be replaced by any other value proportional to the temperature (e.g., recorder deflection); similarly, the terms in units of sec can be replaced by any measure which is directly proportional to time. Equation 17.19 can also be integrated and then evaluated. This requires a knowledge of the variation of T_c and C_p' with time in Region 2.

Instead of using the equations, heats of reactions can be estimated graphically to a few percent knowing the change in temperature, the heat capacity at the midpoint of the titration curve, and the moles of product formed (not the molarity). The heat capacity at the midpoint of the curve is obtained by extrapolating the part of the curve in Region 3 back to Region 2 and measuring Q from the baseline to the extrapolated line at the midpoint of the titration.

Estimates of equilibrium constants can be made from TT curves when there is distinct curvature near the equivalence point. Taking the general reaction

$$A + B \rightleftharpoons AB$$

at the equivalence point, the analytical concentrations (A) and (B) can be calculated. The equilibrium concentrations [A] and [B] are then calculated as

$$[AB] = \frac{h}{h_t}(A) \tag{17.23}$$

$$[A] = (A) - [AB] \tag{17.24}$$

$$[B] = (B) - [AB] \tag{17.25}$$

These concentrations can then be combined to obtain the equilibrium constant. Figure 17.14 illustrates the meaning of h and h_t. As the equilibrium constant increases, the degree of curvature decreases and h approaches h_t.

Example 17.5. Figure 17.14 is a titration curve where chemical equilibrium causes curvature near the endpoint. An estimate of the equilibrium constant is made by measuring h and h_t as diagrammed. The concentration of the sample must be known. Assume that the reaction of a metal (M) with a ligand (L) takes place to form the complex ML. The sample concentration is given to be 0.0100 molar initially. Calculate the stability constant of the complex.

Solution: At the endpoint, the following relationships hold:

$$C_L = 0.0100 = [ML] + [L]$$
$$C_M = 0.0100 = [ML] + [M]$$

Then

$$[ML] = C_M\left(\frac{h}{h_t}\right) = C_L\left(\frac{h}{h_t}\right)$$

$$[L] = [M] = C_M - [ML] = C_L - [ML]$$

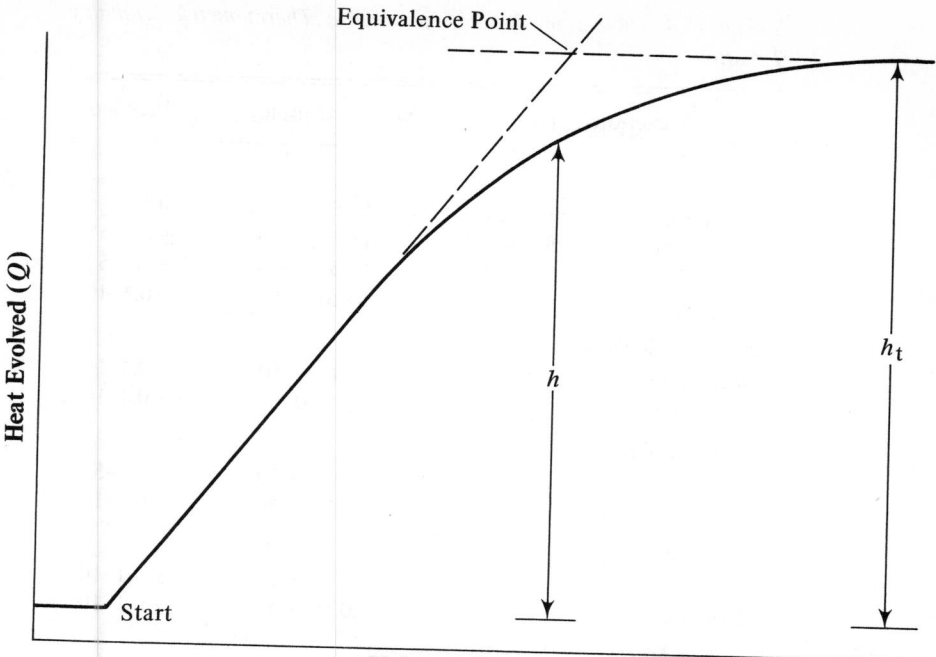

FIGURE 17.14. *Equilibrium curvature of enthalpograms, illustrating parameters h and h_t used to estimate equilibrium constants.*

The stability constant is

$$K_s = \frac{[ML]}{[M][L]} = \frac{C_M(h/h_t)}{(C_M - [ML])^2}$$

If h and h_t are measured to be 77.8 and 87.3, respectively, then

$$K_s = \frac{(0.0100)(77.8/87.3)}{[0.0100 - 0.0100(77.8/87.3)]^2} = 7.50 \times 10^3$$

The units of h and h_t cancel in the above expressions, and any appropriate and convenient measure of their relative magnitudes may be used (e.g., °C, cm, mV, etc.).

Once the heat of reaction and equilibrium constant have been determined, the entropy change, ΔS, of the reaction can be calculated from

$$-RT \ln K_{eq} = \Delta H - T \Delta S \tag{17.26}$$

Often, titrations can be done with samples of 10^{-2} M or less. When dilute solutions are used, it may be safely assumed that the measured thermodynamic parameters are essentially the same as in the standard state of infinite dilution (i.e., $\Delta H_{mean} \approx \Delta H^0$, etc.).

Analytical Applications of TT and DIE

The monograph by Tyrell and Beezer lists many of the analyses possible using these two methods; some of these analyses are listed in Table 17.4.

TABLE 17.4. *Reaction Types Amenable to Thermometric Enthalpy Titration*

Reaction Type	ΔH_r (kcal/mole) [a]	Precision
Neutralization		
Strong acid + strong base	-13.5	$\pm 0.1\%$
Weak acid + strong base	-13.5 to -4	± 0.1–5%
Weak base + strong acid	-13.5 to -4	± 0.1–5%
Polyprotic or basic systems	-14 to -4	± 0.1–10%
Oxidation-Reduction		
Inorganic [b]	-40 to -10	$\pm 0.1\%$
Organic [b]	-40 to 0	± 0.1–10%
Complexation		
EDTA [b]	-15 to $+10$	± 0.1–5%
Other [b]	-20 to $+20$	± 0.1–10%
Precipitation		
Inorganic [b]	-20 to -5	± 0.1–10%
Organic [b]	-20 to -5	± 0.1–10%
Heats of Mixing		
Dilution of inorganic ions	-15 to $+10$	——
Organic solvents	-15 to $+15$	——

a. ΔH_r is the approximate overall heat of the process; 1 cal = 4.184 joules.
b. These processes may have slow kinetics which severely affect the results.

An almost classical example of the advantages of TT is in the titration of boric acid ($K_a = 6.4 \times 10^{-10}$) with a strong base. This titration is impossible by classical methods without pretreating the sample. However, as shown in Figure 17.15, TT yields results differing little from those obtained with a strong acid such as HCl, the reason being that the ΔH for the two processes is essentially the same, whereas ΔG and ΔS are significantly different.

Analysis of mixtures is possible when the two species have different equilibrium constants and heats of reaction with the titrant. This occurs, for example, in the titration of a mixture of calcium and magnesium with EDTA. Calcium ($K_f = 10^{11}$) reacts first and exothermically ($\Delta H = -5.7$ kcal/mole); magnesium ($K_f = 10^{9.1}$) reacts second and endothermically ($\Delta H = +5.5$ kcal/mole). This titration is illustrated in Figure 17.16.

It is also possible to titrate biochemical species. Antibodies have been titrated with antigen, and enzyme-substrate mixtures have been titrated with appropriate coenzymes. Proteins are readily titrated with acid or base, or precipitated with phosphotungstic acid, yielding very informative thermometric titration curves [7, 8].

DIE permits rapid analysis. For instance, SO_2 and CO_2 in air [8] can be determined by injecting air samples into concentrated KOH. Sharp temperature changes or pulses indicate the presence of reactants, and the magnitude of the temperature change gives the concentration. Analysis time is very short (ca. 3 min)

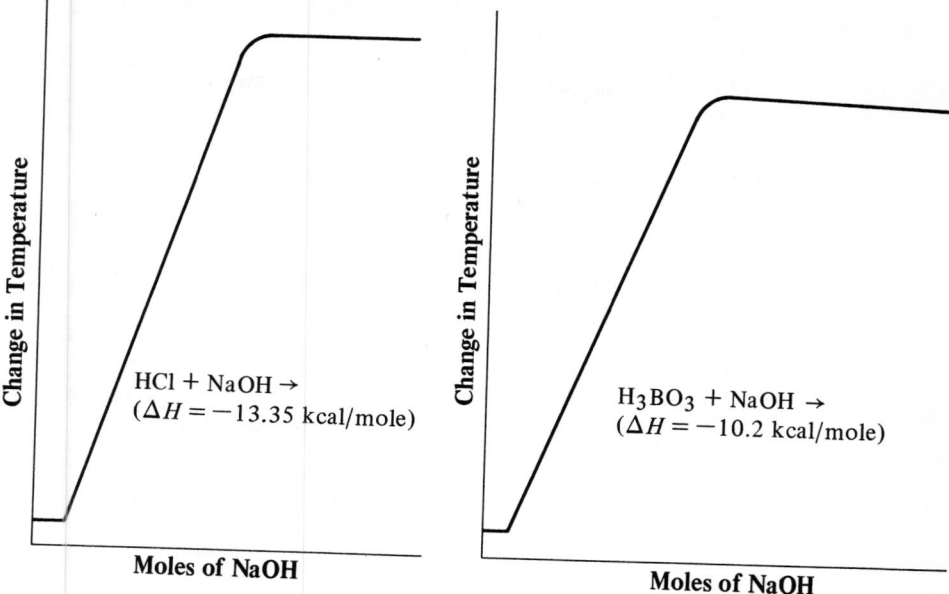

FIGURE 17.15. *Comparison of the titration of H_3BO_3 and HCl with NaOH, observed thermometrically.*

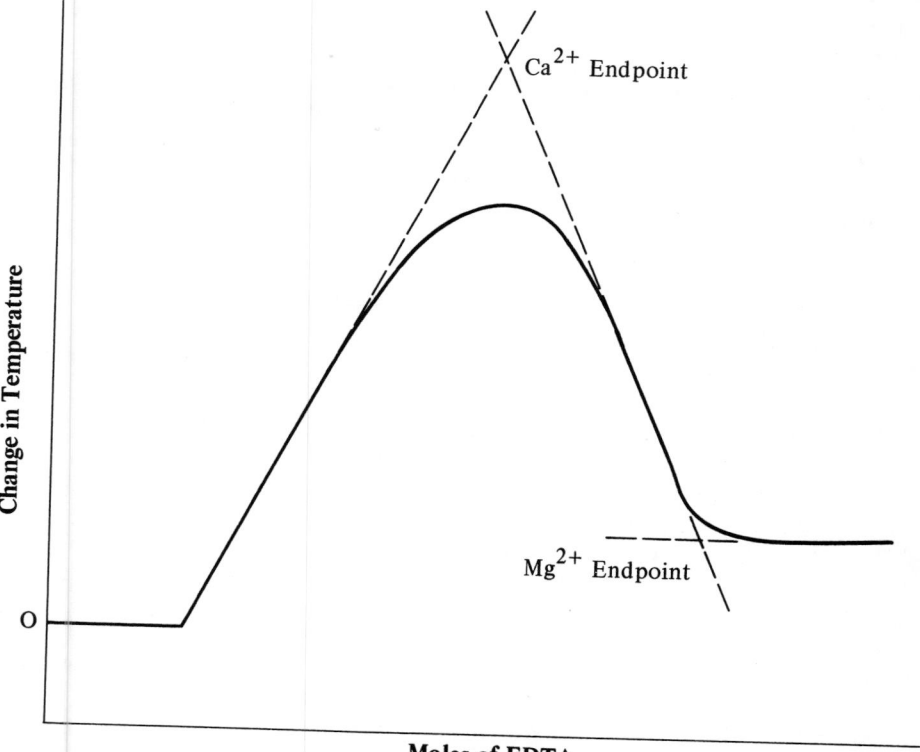

FIGURE 17.16. *Thermometric titration of a mixture of Ca^{2+} and Mg^{2+} with EDTA.*

for this type of determination, and the precision and accuracy, although not as good as with TT, are acceptable.

Kinetic studies have been made by DIE of the hydrolysis of organic nitrates and of esters. Enzyme reactions have also been studied. In all cases, a continuous recording of the process is obtained, and the system is not disturbed by sampling. This can be quite important in sensitive biochemical reactions.

SELECTED BIBLIOGRAPHY

DUVAL, C. *Inorganic Thermogravimetric Analysis*, 2nd ed. Amsterdam: Elsevier, 1963.

MACKENZIE, R. C. *Differential Thermal Analysis*, vol. 1. New York: Academic Press, 1970.

TYRRELL, H. V., and BEEZER, A. E. *Thermo-*

metric Titrimetry. London: Chapman and Hall, 1968.

VALLET, P. *Thermogravimetrie.* Paris: Gauthier-Villars, 1972.

WENDLANDT, W. W. *Thermal Methods of Analysis*. New York: Interscience, 1964.

REFERENCES

1. H. E. KISSINGER, *Anal. Chem.*, 29, 1702 (1957).

2. J. J. CHRISTENSEN, R. M. IZATT, and L. D. HANSEN, *Rev. Sci. Instr.*, 36, 779 (1965).

3. E. B. SMITH, C. S. BARNES, and P. W. CARR, *Anal. Chem.*, 44, 1663 (1972).

4. J. J. CHRISTENSEN, J. RUCKMAN, D. J. EATOUGH, and R. M. IZATT, *Thermochim. Acta*, 3, 203, 219, 233 (1972).

5. N. D. JESPERSEN and J. JORDAN, *Anal. Lett.*, 3, 323 (1970).

6. P. W. CARR, *Thermochim. Acta*, 3, 427 (1972).

7. E. B. SMITH and P. W. CARR, *Anal. Chem.*, 45, 169 (1973).

8. P. G. ZAMBONIN and J. JORDAN, *Anal. Chem.*, 41, 437 (1969).

PROBLEMS

1. List some of the factors that influence (a) thermogravimetry curves, (b) differential thermal analysis curves, and (c) differential scanning calorimetry curves, indicating which are most important for the various techniques.

2. What is a self-generated atmosphere? What effect may it have on DTA and TG?

3. A thermogravimetric curve shows that a compound will not start to decompose until the temperature reaches 150°C. However, upon storage overnight at 140°C this same compound decomposes totally. Suggest why.

4. Figure 17.1 is a typical TG curve. What

would an ideal curve look like? (Hint: See footnotes.)

5. A hydrate of Na_2HPO_4 weighing 150 mg decreases to a weight of 119 mg after heating to 150°C. Calculate the number of waters of hydration.

6. From the information in the text, draw a fully labeled diagram of the TG curve obtained by heating a mixture of 50 mg of $CaC_2O_4 \cdot H_2O$ and 50 mg of $BaC_2O_4 \cdot H_2O$ to 1200°C. Calculate the magnitude of all weight losses.

7. Sketch a DTA curve for the process in Problem 6. Assume no additional reactions.

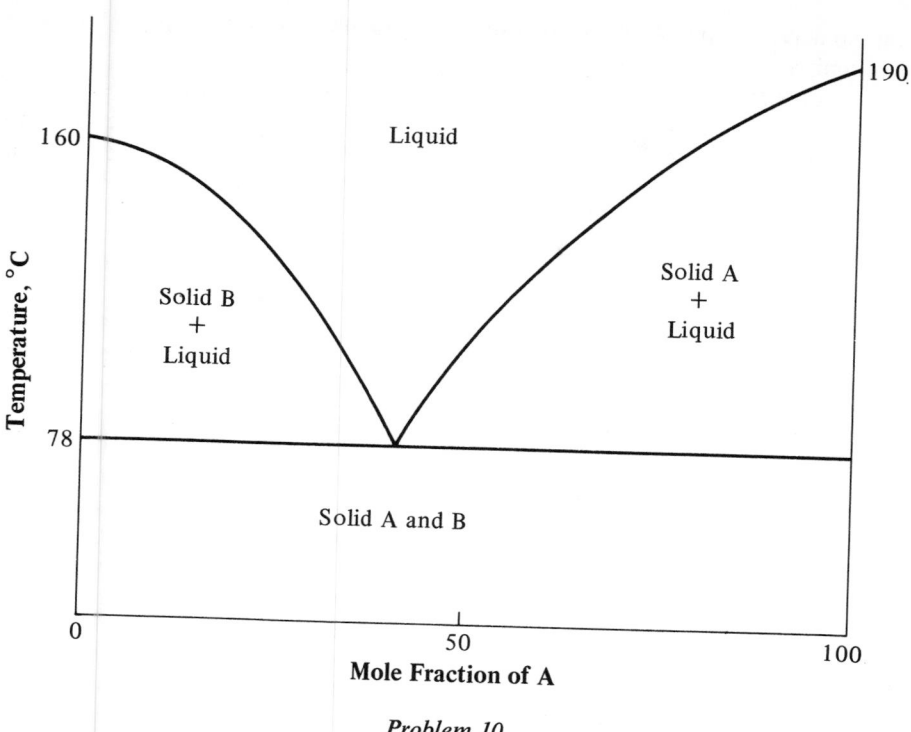

Temperature, °C

Mole Fraction of A

Problem 10

8. Calculate, from data in handbooks, the TG curve for the thermal decomposition of 100 mg of urea (see *Merck Index*). Assume all processes are quantitative.

9. A. Show mathematically the direction in which the reaction temperatures will move when (a) the atmosphere contains the gaseous product and (b) when the atmosphere contains the gaseous reactant. B. Show how the stoichiometric coefficient of the gaseous reactant can be deduced by varying the atmosphere.

10. Phase diagrams can be deduced from DTA curves. A simple phase diagram is given. Sketch the heating curves obtained when the mole percent of A is 0, 25, 50, 75, 100%. Assume that the heat of fusion of A is twice that of B and that both are endothermic.

11. Comment on the advisability of using DTA for routine melting- and boiling-point determinations.

12. On heating, a sample of bismuth gives an endothermic peak at 270°C, whereas on cooling, an exothermic peak appears at 257°C. What is occurring?

13. The heat of fusion of naphthalene is 4.63 kcal/mole at 80°C and the DTA peak observed using 100 mg of sample is 36.3 cm². Water has a heat of fusion of 1.43 kcal/mole at 0°C. What should the peak area for 100 mg of ice be under the same conditions? From experimental considerations, would it be expected to be slightly larger or smaller? Why?

14. Calculate the heat capacity of a thermometric titration system (cal/°C system) given the following data: $\Delta T = 0.0235°C$, $V_s = 1.234$; $V_h = 1.876$; $t = 64.3$ sec, and $R_s = 10.003$. What is the resistance of the heater R_h? Is the answer too high or too low if the heater leads have an appreciable resistance? Why?

15. Why is the TT curve for boric acid so sharp (Fig. 17.15), although the ionization constant indicates that it should be otherwise? (Hint: There is another chemical process occurring.)

16. Using the data in Figure 17.15, what is the heat of ionization of boric acid?

17. Calculate K, ΔG, ΔH, and ΔS at 25°C for the reaction $M + L \rightleftharpoons ML$, given the following data: Sample concentration (L) = 1.00×10^{-2} M; sample volume = 100.0 ml; titrant (M) = 1.00 M; titration rate = 0.0400 ml/sec.

Time, sec	Cal Evolved
5.0	1.95
10.0	3.87
15.0	5.73
20.0	7.42
25.0	8.68
30.0	9.30
35.0	9.56
40.0	9.69
50.0	9.89
60.0	9.97
70.0	10.0
80.0	10.0

Assume all appropriate corrections have been made. Sketch the titration curve.

18. Ignoring the heat capacity of the adiabatic cell, show that ΔT is independent of the sample volume for a given titration. What effect does the cell have?

19. If a reaction is slow, what sort of error (positive or negative) can be expected in calculating unknown concentrations?

20. The heat of ionization of *tris*-(hydroxymethyl)aminomethane (TRIS) is $+11.45$ kcal/mole. Sketch the thermometric titration curve of 50.0 ml of 0.01 M TRIS with 1 M HCl. Sketch the titration curve of the resulting cation with 1 M NaOH. Estimate the temperature change for each titration.

21. The DSC curve for an inorganic complex exhibits an endotherm at 375°C. A TG trace shows no weight loss at this temperature. What transition may be occurring?

22. Silver nitrate is thermally stable up to 473°C, at which point NO_2 and O_2 are gradually lost, leaving a residue of metallic silver at about 608°C. $Cu(NO_3)_2$, on the other hand, decomposes below 470°C in two steps to CuO, which is stable up to at least 950°C. Suggest a method for determining the percent composition of the alloy formed by heating an unknown mixture of silver and copper nitrates above 950°C.

18

Kinetic Methods

Harry B. Mark, Jr.

In chemical analysis, the species to be determined is usually accompanied by one or more substances that interfere with its analysis. Separation techniques are commonly employed to isolate the desired species prior to the actual measurement; but frequently, especially in complex biological and natural-environment systems, quantitative separations are virtually impossible or at best laborious. Obviously, performing analyses without prior separation is always more convenient.

Methods for the in situ chemical analysis of a mixture of species having closely related chemical and physical properties can be placed in two general classes, according to the technique employed to eliminate (or reduce) the interference by the other components of the system. A *thermodynamic* approach involves changing the equilibrium conditions of the system to render all reactions thermodynamically unfavorable except the one of analytical interest. A *kinetic* approach involves adjusting, or simply taking advantage of, the differences in reaction rates of the components of the mixture in order to measure the reactions of the desired species.

The concept of employing reaction-rate parameters to determine the initial analytical concentration of reactants dates back over 50 to 60 years to the early literature in biochemistry, radiochemistry, and gas-phase diffusion; furthermore, among all the analyses performed in all the laboratories around this country, the number carried out by kinetic-based methods probably exceeds that carried out by thermodynamic methods and direct instrumental measurement combined. This comes as a surprise at first, until one considers the large numbers of enzymatic and other determinations done on multi-channel autoanalyzers used in clinical laboratories. Most of these rapid automated instruments use kinetic methods.

Thus, it is somewhat surprising that it was not until the 1950s that several research groups started to point out to *chemists* the broad inherent possibilities and advantages of kinetic-based analyses. In spite of considerable activity in development of methods, there has still not been any large surge in the application of kinetic-based techniques to routine analytical problems in chemistry; and most undergraduate textbooks on analytical chemistry and instrumental analysis do not mention the subject, or at best devote a few pages to outmoded methods.

There are two main reasons for this lack of use. First, almost all commercial instruments for chemical measurement are expressly designed for steady-state or equilibrium measurement, and do not perform satisfactorily when used for quantitative time-dependent measurement. Second, the practice of analytical chemistry is conservative, and new methods are accepted slowly, particularly methods that introduce another parameter that is difficult to control—in this case, time. However, recent developments in instrumentation are likely to change the present situation, and kinetic-based analytical techniques are likely to become commonplace in the next decade. Consequently, a chapter on this subject is included in this text.

18.1 COMPARISON OF KINETIC AND THERMODYNAMIC METHODS

Kinetic techniques often have advantages over equilibrium or thermodynamic techniques despite the greater difficulty of making measurements on a dynamic system. Equilibrium differentiations (free-energy differences) for the reactions of very closely related compounds (such as homologues or isomers) are often too small to permit direct resolution of the components of a mixture. However, the kinetic differentiations obtained when these compounds are reacted with a common reagent are often quite large. The reason is that the free energy of activation for the formation of the activated complex in such reactions is much more sensitive to the small structural differences between similar compounds than is the overall free-energy change for the reaction. These differences may involve polar effects, inductive effects, steric effects, or resonance effects, among others. Table 18.1 gives values for the relative rate-constants for the reactions of several alkyl halides with a variety of reagents.

Another advantage of kinetic methods is that they permit a larger number of chemical reactions to be used analytically. Many chemical reactions cannot be employed analytically in equilibrium or thermodynamic-based techniques: the reactions attain equilibrium too slowly, side reactions or subsequent reactions of the products occur as the reaction proceeds to completion, or the reactions are not sufficiently quantitative (equilibrium constants are too small) to be applicable. However, kinetic-based techniques can be employed in many of these cases. For example, complications arising from an unfavorable equilibrium constant, slow reaction, side reactions, reverse reactions, and so forth are circumvented by measuring the reaction rate during the initial 1–2% of the overall reaction (where the mechanism is usually straightforward). Thus, virtually any chemical reaction whose initial rate can be measured can be employed in a kinetic-based method.

Kinetic-based methods employing catalytic (especially enzymatic) reactions are inherently more selective than many comparable chemical equilibrium methods. For example, of the approximately sixty oxidizable sugars and their derivatives, only two (β-D-glucose and 2-deoxy-D-glucose) are enzymatically oxidized by glucose oxidase at a significant rate. The oxidation of all others, including the isomeric

TABLE 18.1. *Relative Reaction Rates of Alkyl Halides with Various Reagents*

Reaction[a]	Relative Rate-Constants								
	R = CH₃	C₂H₅	i-C₃H₇	i-C₄H₉	n-C₃H₇	i-C₄H₉	n-C₄H₉	Allyl	Benzyl
1. $RCl + I^- \rightarrow RI + Cl^-$	——	1	0.0077	0.0092	0.53	——	0.52	41	95
2. $RI + C_6H_5O^- \rightarrow$ $C_6H_5OR + I^-$	1	0.22	0.077	——	0.086	0.032	0.080	4.7	——
3. $RI + C_6H_5CH_2O^- \rightarrow$ $C_6H_5CH_2OR + I^-$	1	0.091	0.021	——	0.035	0.033	0.025	——	——
4. $RI + N(C_2H_5)_3 \rightarrow$ $(C_2H_5)_3NR^+ + I^-$	1	0.0087	0.0017	v.sl.[b]	0.0017	0.00027	0.0012	——	——
5. $RI + C_6H_5N(CH_3)_2 \rightarrow$ $C_6H_5N(CH_3)_2R^+ + I^-$	1	0.0657	——	——	0.0208	——	——	7.55	~20
6. $RI + Ag^+ \rightarrow R^+ + AgI$	1	2.35	~90	——	1.05	0.148	0.734	——	——
7. $RBr + H_2O \rightarrow$ $ROH + HBr$	1	0.413	0.641	2700	——	——	——	——	——

Source: H. B. Mark, Jr., G. A. Rechnitz, and R. A. Grienke, *Kinetics in Analytical Chemistry*, New York: Wiley-Interscience, 1968, pp 178–79, by permission of John Wiley and Sons. Copyright © 1968 by John Wiley and Sons.

a. Notes on reactions: 1. Allyl chloride and potassium iodide in acetone at 60°C, in some cases extrapolated from data at lower temperatures. 2. Alkyl iodide and sodium phenolate in ethanol at 42.5°C. 3. Alkyl iodide and sodium benzyloxide in ethanol at 30°C. 4. Alkyl iodide and triethylamine in acetone at 100°C. 5. Alkyl iodide and dimethylaniline in ethanol at 40°C. 6. Alkyl iodide and silver nitrate in ethanol at 25.4°C. 7. Solvolytic hydrolysis of alkyl bromide in 80% ethanol at 25°C.
b. v.sl. = too slow for measurement.

aldo-D-hexoses and the anomer α-D-glucose, is catalyzed at less than a few percent of the rate at which β-D-glucose and 2-deoxy-D-glucose are oxidized. The catalytic activity of urease, which hydrolyzes urea, is even more specific. With respect to sensitivity, the enzyme-catalyzed luminescent reaction of luciferin

$$\text{Luciferin} + O_2 + \text{ATP} \xrightarrow[\text{Mg}^{2+}]{\text{Luciferase}} \text{Oxyluciferin} + \text{ADP} + h\nu \qquad (18.1)$$

the "firefly reaction," can be used to measure as little as 4×10^{-13} mole of ATP. In cases where the catalyst or enzyme itself is the species being measured, or where chemical amplification techniques have been used, it has been shown that these methods are capable of measuring such species as NAD^+ at the 10^{-16} mole level, and can determine the activity of single molecules of the enzyme. These are, of course, special reactions.

Closely similar functional groups on the same molecule can be determined by kinetic differentiation—for example, analysis of both the primary and secondary alcohol groups on the polymeric molecule, poly(propyleneglycol). This is an important problem, since the ratio of primary to secondary alcohols on the chain affects the physical properties of the material and, hence, its price. Obviously, separation is impossible and any reagent for alcohol functional groups will give only total –OH content. However, by taking advantage of the difference in the reaction rates of primary and secondary –OH groups with acetic anhydride, a kinetic technique has been developed to determine the concentrations of each. Similar techniques have been employed to measure the ratio of internal to external (terminal) double bonds in polyalkenes.

For reactions that do not attain equilibrium virtually instantaneously, kinetic methods are also more rapid than those relying on measurements made after equilibrium has been reached. The kinetic approach does imply poorer sensitivity limits for a given reaction, however, since the rate is measured when only a fraction of the reaction has been completed.

One last point in comparing kinetic and equilibrium measurements is the wide variety of techniques that can be used to control the rates (and rate constants) of reactions and thus optimize measurements. The free energy of activation of a reaction is very sensitive to temperature, to the nature of the solvent and to ionic strength, among other factors.

18.2 MEASUREMENT OF REACTION RATES

Chemical reaction rates cover a very wide range. Some reactions, such as the neutralization of a strong acid with a strong base, are so rapid that they appear to reach equilibrium instantaneously, whereas others, such as the (noncatalyzed) reaction between oxygen and hydrogen at room temperature, are so slow that no reaction can be detected at all.

In order to determine the initial concentration of a desired species by kinetic-based methods, the rate of the chemical reaction must be measured by monitoring the concentration of at least one of the reactants or products as a function of time. Chemical methods (titration) or physical methods (spectrophotometry or conductivity) can be employed. If chemical methods are used, the rates of reaction must be quite slow or, if the reaction has suitable properties, quenching methods can be utilized when some reaction occurs at a significantly fast rate. Continuous measurement of the reaction rate is possible by physical, but not by chemical, methods: the reaction rates observable are limited only by the response times of the instruments.

In Figure 18.1 is a schematic presentation of the change with time of a measured experimental parameter P. P is proportional to the concentration of product formed on reaction of a five-component mixture (A, B, C, D, and E, which have widely varying rate-constants). Thus, if A reacts faster than B, etc., the product that is formed during the early stage of the reaction results mostly from A. Likewise, if E is the slowest reacting of the five components, the product formed in the latter stages results almost entirely from the reaction of E. Reactions with half-times larger than about 10 sec are considered "slow," whereas those with half-times smaller than 10 sec are considered "fast." The methods for measuring each type and the experimental limitations for each are briefly discussed below.

Slow Reactions

The rates of slow chemical reactions in solution can generally be studied by quite simple and conventional methods. The reactants are mixed in some vessel and the progress of the reaction is followed by titrating aliquots of the mixture or by measuring, at known times, a physical property of the solution such as optical absorption or polarographic diffusion current.

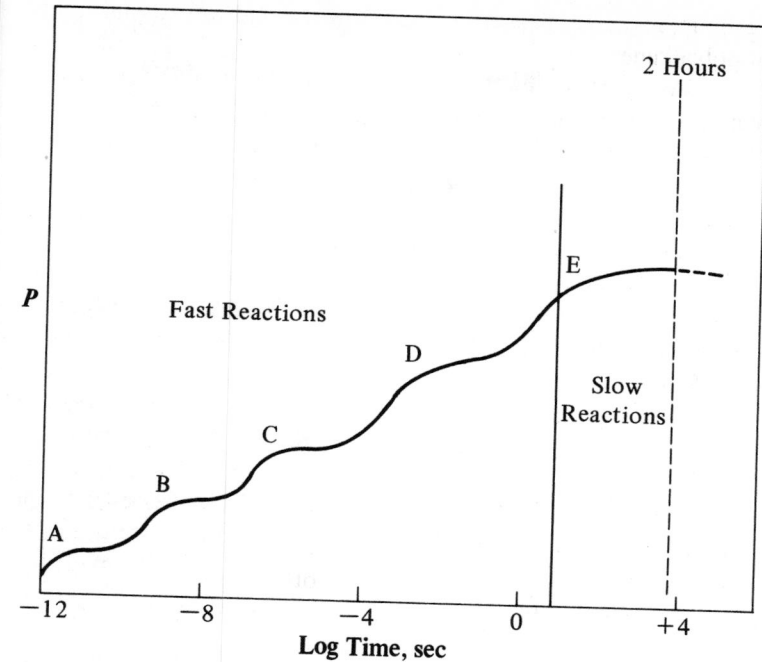

FIGURE 18.1. *Experimental parameter P (proportional to concentration) vs. time t for a five-component mixture (A, B, C, D, and E). From H. B. Mark, Jr., G. A. Rechnitz, and R. A. Grienke,* Kinetics in Analytical Chemistry, *New York: Wiley-Interscience, 1968, by permission of John Wiley and Sons. Copyright © 1968 by John Wiley and Sons.*

The speed of initial mixing of the components in the vessel places a definite limit on the minimum half-time that can be measured in this way. If the mixing is accomplished by simple stirring devices such as magnetic stirring bars, the mixing time is a few seconds, and reactions with half-times smaller than 10 sec are difficult to measure with acceptable accuracy.

On the other hand, the kinetics of reactions with long half-times can be determined, but such determinations consume considerable time and are, therefore, undesirable for analytical purposes. A 2-hr time limit (Fig. 18.1) is arbitrarily considered the longest acceptable time for routine analysis.

If the reaction rate is greater than 2 hr or less than 10 sec, several simple techniques can be employed to adjust the rate so that the half-time will lie within the desired range. These are: (1) changing the temperature of the reaction system, (2) changing the concentration of the reactants, and (3) changing the solvent medium or ionic strength of the solution.

Change in Temperature. The relationship between temperature and the rate constant k of a chemical reaction is given by the Arrhenius equation

$$\frac{d(\ln k)}{dT} = \frac{E^*}{RT^2} \tag{18.2}$$

or (in its integrated form)

$$k = Ae^{-E^*/RT} \qquad\qquad (18.3)$$

where E^* = the activation energy
R = the universal gas constant
A = the frequency factor

For a large number of homogeneous reactions, the rate constant increases 2 or 3 times for each 10°C rise in temperature.

Reactions that are fast at room temperature can be slowed by cooling to allow measurement by "convenient" or "conventional" physical or chemical methods. For example, the conductometric analysis of a mixture of certain aliphatic aldehydes by differential reaction rates can be carried out at 0–5°C, whereas, at room temperature, the reactions are too fast. On the other hand, slow reactions can be made to proceed at considerably faster rates by raising the temperature. For example, fructose reacts with anthrone at room temperature in the presence of glucose and within 10 min develops a highly colored product. Glucose does not react appreciably even over a long period of time, but by elevating the temperature of the reaction mixture to 100°C after the fructose has reacted, the glucose can be made to react to completion in a few minutes and can be determined.

Change in Concentration.   Reactions with very large rate-constants can be measured simply by using low concentrations of reactants, provided that sensitive enough methods are available to measure the small changes in concentration. For example, the bromination of N,N-diethyl-m-toluidine is extremely fast in aqueous solution, but since 10^{-8} M bromine can be estimated from the redox potential of a platinum electrode, the concentration of the free amine can be reduced to 10^{-8} M and the reaction can then be readily followed. Spectrophotometric methods can be used to measure extremely small concentrations of highly colored compounds. A reaction involving color change and a large rate-constant is that between ferrous ion and cobaltioxalate ion in aqueous solution.

$$Fe^{2+} + [Co(C_2O_4)_3]^{3-} = Fe^{3+} + [Co(C_2O_4)_3]^{4-} \qquad\qquad (18.4)$$

High concentrations of the reacting species can be employed to speed up reactions with small rate-constants, although changes in activity coefficients may hamper the calculation of initial concentration when high concentrations of reactants are used.

Change in Solvent or Ionic Strength.   The rate constant of a chemical reaction can be considerably altered by changing the solvent or by adding a salt to the reaction medium, partly as a consequence of changes in the dielectric constant of the solvent or the ionic strength of the solution. More specifically, as the dielectric constant increases, (1) the rate of a reaction between two ions of the same sign increases, (2) the rate of a reaction between two ions of the opposite sign decreases, (3) the rate of a reaction between two neutral species that form a polar product increases, and (4) the rate of reaction between an ion and a neutral molecule is not significantly changed. As the ionic strength of the medium increases, (1) the rate of reaction between two ions of the same sign increases, (2) the rate of reaction between two ions of opposite sign decreases, (3) the rate of reaction between two neutral species that form a polar product changes only slightly, and (4) the rate of reaction between an ion and a neutral molecule changes only slightly.

Fast Reactions

The kinetic methods of analysis discussed in this chapter have mostly been applied to slow reactions, but many of these methods are also applicable to fast reactions, provided that sufficient accuracy in the measurement of the reaction rate can be achieved. Special techniques to measure fast reactions have become more accurate in recent years, and practical analytical applications of them are now being devised.

For the most part, experimental methods for studying fast reactions can be classified into four groups: mixing, relaxation, periodic, and continuous methods. The approximate upper limit of reaction rates that can be measured by each of these techniques depends upon the mixing time or, in the case of relaxation and periodic methods, the displacement time, which is the time required to bring the system to a suitable nonequilibrium condition.

Mixing Methods. Mixing methods, the most common experimental method employed in kinetic studies of fast reactions, involve the actual rapid mixing of reacting species that were initially separated. They are of special interest because they are the only methods that do not rely on displacing an established equilibrium. Hence, reactions that are virtually irreversible under conditions of interest can be studied; it is for this reason that mixing methods are also the most applicable to pseudo-first-order reactions.

The most widely used fast mixing method is the *continuous-flow method.* The reactants flow in separate continuous streams that meet in a mixing chamber and then pass along an observation tube or chamber with detection devices at appropriate points along its length (see Fig. 18.2). The detection devices, which measure the composition of the flowing sample, may be optical, thermal, chemical, electrical, or any other method applicable to a rapidly moving sample. Reactions with half-times of the order of 10^{-3} sec can be observed by this method.

The *stopped-flow* method is perhaps the next most commonly used mixing method. This technique employs a pair of driven syringes to force the reactants into a mixing chamber and then into the observation cell. As soon as the mixed solution reaches the observation cell, the flow is stopped in order to observe changes in the measured parameter without interference from artifacts arising from flow and turbulence.

Other mixing methods have been employed with considerable success for monitoring reaction rates of intermediate magnitude.

Relaxation and Periodic Methods. Relaxation methods involve a single sudden alteration of one or more conditions of a system initially at equilibrium, whereas periodic methods involve a periodic alteration or disturbance of the system. These two methods can be subdivided into two classifications, based on the parameter altered: either the *equilibrium constant* is changed (ΔK methods), or the *concentration* of one or more of the species of the system is changed (Δc mthods). These methods

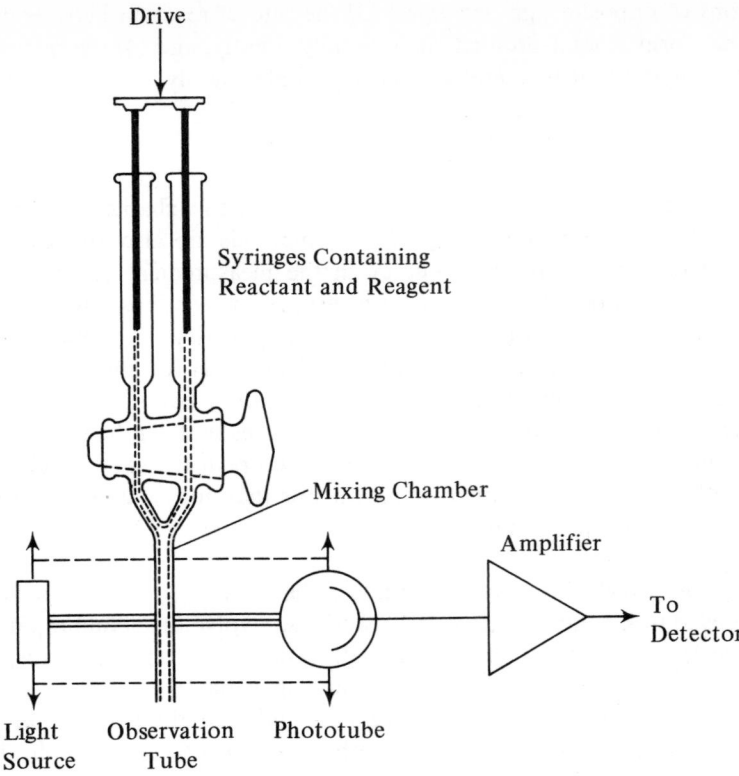

Drive

Syringes Containing
Reactant and Reagent

Mixing Chamber

Amplifier

To
Detector

Light   Observation   Phototube
Source   Tube

FIGURE 18.2.   *Schematic diagram of a continuous-flow apparatus.   From
H. B. Mark, Jr., G. A. Rechnitz, and R. A. Grienke,* Kinetics in Anal-
ytical Chemistry, *New York: Wiley-Interscience, 1968, by permission of
John Wiley and Sons.   Copyright © 1968 by John Wiley and Sons.*

can be used to measure rate constants of the order of 10^{12}/mole-min; hence, they are
applicable to fast ionic reactions such as neutralization and hydrolysis, which typically have half-times of 10^{-9} sec or less.

ΔK Methods.   After a rapid alteration of K by changing an external condition, the
solution composition readjusts at a finite rate in an attempt to reattain equilibrium;
this process of adjustment is called *relaxation.*   Several experimental techniques for
achieving the necessarily rapid alterations of K have been developed.   These include
a pressure-jump (sound-absorption) method, an electric-field (dissociation) method,
and a temperature-jump method.   A temperature jump is brought about by passing
an electrical current through the solution in a special cuvette, producing an abrupt,
nearly instantaneous, rise in the temperature of the solution.   A reaction then takes
place as the concentrations adjust to the new temperature.   Regardless of the type
of perturbation used, the treatment of the data is essentially the same.

Δc Methods.   A rapid change is made of the concentration of one or more species
in a system initially at equilibrium; changes in the concentrations of all the species

then occur as the system moves back toward equilibrium. Commonly employed methods are flash photolysis (minimum $t_{1/2} \sim 10^{-5}$ sec), which can measure first-order rate constants as large as 5×10^6 min^{-1}, and electrochemical potential-step, coulostatic, and galvanostatic methods, used for studying fast electrode reactions or the homogeneous reactions following the electron-transfer step.

18.3 MATHEMATICAL BASIS OF KINETIC METHODS OF ANALYSIS

The past few years have seen the development of many methods for calculating the initial concentration of the species of interest from reaction-rate data. These methods involve, in general, manipulating and rearranging the differential or integral forms of the classical reaction-rate equations to put them in a convenient form for calculating the initial concentrations of the unknown reactants. Such methods can be classified into two main categories: methods for a single species and methods for the simultaneous (in situ) analysis of mixtures. Within each of these two categories, the methods can be subdivided according to the kinetic order of the reactions employed: pseudo-zero-order or initial-rate methods, first-order and pseudo-first-order methods, and second-order methods.

Although most investigators classify reactions by their rate order, the actual mechanisms of the chemical reactions employed in virtually all of these methods (except those involving catalytic reactions or radiochemical decay) are bimolecular reactions of the type

$$A + R \underset{k_b}{\overset{k_f}{\rightleftharpoons}} P \qquad (18.5)$$

where A = the species of analytical interest
R = the added reagent
P = the product (or products)
k_f = the forward rate constant
k_b = the backward rate constant

The general differential rate expressions then have the form

$$-\frac{d[A]_t}{dt} = -\frac{d[R]_t}{dt} = \frac{d[P]_t}{dt} = k_f[A]_t[R]_t - k_b[P]_t \qquad (18.6)$$

($[A]_t$, $[R]_t$, and $[P]_t$ represent the concentrations of these species at any time t.) Thus, the nomenclature zero, first, and second order actually refers to the experimental conditions under which the rate measurements are made or to the relative concentrations of the reactants A and R.

If the rate data are taken only during the initial 1–2% completion of the total reaction, then the concentrations of A and R remain virtually unchanged and equal to the initial concentrations ($[A]_0$ and $[R]_0$, respectively); and the reverse reaction can be ignored, since only a negligible amount of product is formed. Thus, Equation 18.6 simplifies to a pseudo-zero-order form

$$\left(\frac{d[P]_t}{dt}\right) \approx k_f[A]_0[R]_0 \approx \text{Constant} \qquad (18.7)$$

Experimentally, only the rate of initial change of concentration of product is followed, since the change in concentration of either A or R is very small under these conditions and cannot be measured accurately.

If Reaction 18.5 is run under such conditions that the initial concentration of one of the reactants (either A or R) is very large compared to that of the other, then the concentration of that reactant will remain virtually unchanged as the reaction proceeds to equilibrium and can be considered equal to the initial concentration. Also, the reverse reaction can usually be neglected since the large excess of one of the reactants drives the reaction to virtual completion. Under these conditions, the reaction is pseudo-first-order and the rate expression takes the form (for R in excess)

$$-\frac{d[A]_t}{dt} \approx k_f[R]_0[A]_t = k_f'[A]_t \tag{18.8}$$

A completely analogous expression can be written for $-d[R]_t/dt$ for the case where A is in large excess.

If the rate of Reaction 18.5 is measured while the reaction goes to a significant degree of completion under conditions where $[A]_0$ is of the same order of magnitude as $[R]_0$, then the method is called a second-order method and the exact differential-rate expression (Eqn. 18.6) must be employed in analyzing the data. Note also that only when the reaction mechanism is virtually irreversible can the reverse reaction be ignored in Equation 18.6. Furthermore, for the special case $[R]_0 = [A]_0$, a modified form of the calculation of initial concentrations must be used.

It is obvious from the discussion above that any kinetic-based analytical procedure must take into account the degree of approximation made in the various rate equations with respect to the period of measurement, the relative initial concentrations of reactants, and, in some cases, the reversibility of the reactions. Care must be taken, for example, in using a pseudo-first-order method when the initial concentration of the unknown varies over several orders of magnitude; the error introduced in assuming the validity of the pseudo-first-order approximation of Equation 18.8 is a function of $[A]_0$. Although the reaction mechanisms and rate equations for enzymatic and other catalyzed reactions in general are somewhat more complex, similar assumptions and simplifications (and, therefore, restrictions in validity) apply to the rate-measurement techniques employed in the analytical use of these systems.

Within each of the classifications of reaction-rate methods, there are many different methods of display or mathematical manipulation of the data or equations used to calculate the initial concentration of the species being determined. The calculating technique used can have very significant effects on the accuracy of the analysis. For example, the kinetic role of the species being determined in methods employing first-order or enzymatic or other catalyzed reactions has a strong effect on the choice of measurement of the reaction rate. For the simultaneous, in situ, analysis of several components of a mixture, the choice of method is even more critical with respect to accuracy. Both the relative and absolute values of the rate constants, as well as the initial concentrations of the species to be determined, dictate the choice of method. Furthermore, within the mathematical framework of each of these calculation procedures, there are generally optimum or limited times at which rate data should be taken in order to minimize the effects of random and absolute error in measurement. The choice of procedure and optimization of the measurement is very complex and no simple rules can be given, but some of the general principles are discussed below.

18.4 RATE EQUATIONS FOR THE DETERMINATION OF A SINGLE SPECIES

Three types of reactions have been employed in kinetic techniques for determining a single species: first- (or pseudo-first-) order, enzyme-catalyzed, and other catalyzed reactions.

First- (or Pseudo-First-) Order Reactions

A first-order or pseudo-first-order irreversible reaction of a reactant A to form the product P can be written as

$$A \xrightarrow{k_A} xP \tag{18.9}$$

where k_A = the rate constant
x = a number describing the stoichiometry of the reaction

The rate of disappearance of A as a function of time is

$$-\frac{d[A]_t}{dt} = k_A[A]_t \tag{18.10}$$

where $[A]_t$ = the concentration of A at any time t

Integrating Equation 18.10 yields a relationship between $[A]_t$ and the initial concentration $[A]_0$, which is the quantity to be measured in a kinetic-based analysis:

$$[A]_t = [A]_0 e^{-k_A t} \tag{18.11}$$

Substituting Equation 18.11 into 18.10 defines the rate of the reaction in terms of $[A]_0$,

$$-\frac{d[A]_t}{dt} = k_A[A]_0 e^{-k_A t} \tag{18.12}$$

Equation 18.12 is the basis for the *derivative* approach to rate-based analysis, which involves directly measuring the reaction rate at a specific time or times and relating this to $[A]_0$. Equation 18.11 is the basis for the two different *integral* approaches to kinetic analysis. In one case, the amount of A reacted during a fixed time is measured and is directly proportional to $[A]_0$ (*fixed-time* method); in the other case, the time required for a fixed amount of A to react is measured and is also proportional to $[A]_0$ (*variable-time* method). Details of these methods will be discussed in Section 18.5. Primarily because of difficulties in reproducing mixing times, Equation 18.11 is not often applied directly. Some time t_1 ($t_1 \neq 0$), when the solution is homogeneously mixed, is used as the initial point from which Equation 18.10 is integrated. Thus, the difference in concentration ΔA over a time interval Δt ($\Delta t = t_2 - t_1$) is related to $[A]_0$ by

$$\Delta A = [A]_0(e^{-k_A t_2} - e^{-k_A t_1}) \tag{18.13}$$

In many situations, the concentration of the product P is the experimentally measured variable, rather than the concentration of A. In such cases, since $\Delta[P] = -x \Delta[A]$, Equations 18.12 and 18.13 can be rewritten as

$$\frac{d[P]_t}{dt} = x k_A [A]_0 e^{-k_A t} \tag{18.14}$$

and

$$\Delta[P] = x[A]_0 (e^{-k_A t_1} - e^{-k_A t_2}) \tag{18.15}$$

When the concentration is measured instrumentally, it is related to the magnitude of some electrical signal $\mathscr{S}$ produced in the detector or sensor portion of the instrument. When $\mathscr{S}$ is linearly related to the concentration of the product—for example, in conductance or amperometric measurements—$\Delta \mathscr{S} = \nu \Delta[P]$ and $d\mathscr{S} = \nu \, d[P]$, where ν is the proportionality constant or *transfer function* in electrical units per concentration unit. Substituting for $\Delta[P]$ and $d[P]$ in Equations 18.14 and 18.15, and replacing t_2 by the term $(t_1 + \Delta t)$, yields

$$\frac{d\mathscr{S}_t}{dt} = \nu x k_A [A]_0 e^{-k_A t} \tag{18.16}$$

and

$$\Delta \mathscr{S} = \nu x [A]_0 e^{-k_A t_1}(1 - e^{k_A \Delta t}) \tag{18.17}$$

Thus, $[A]_0$ in both cases is directly related to the signal output of the instrument.

Often an instrumental method is employed in which $\mathscr{S}$ is not a linear function of $[P]$. For example, in optical absorption or potentiometric measurements, the output of a photomultiplier or an electrode is a logarithmic function of concentration. In such cases, the direct instrumental response can be written in a general form as

$$\mathscr{S} = f([P]) \tag{18.18}$$

where $\quad f[P] =$ an arbitrary function

The mathematics becomes more complicated and, in general, nonlinear calibration curves result.

Enzyme-Catalyzed Reactions

Enzyme-catalyzed reactions are used analytically to determine both enzyme activities $[E]$ and substrate concentrations $[S]$, and are very important in clinical diagnoses. The usual Michaelis-Menten mechanism for enzymatic reactions is

$$E + S \underset{k_{-1}}{\overset{k_1}{\rightleftarrows}} E{\cdot}S \xrightarrow{k_2} P + E \tag{18.19}$$

In this equation, $E{\cdot}S$ is the intermediate enzyme-substrate complex. A steady-state treatment of this reaction mechanism gives the rate law

$$\frac{-d[S]_t}{dt} = \frac{d[P]_t}{dt} = \frac{k_2[E]_0[S]_t}{K_M + [S]_t} \tag{18.20}$$

The enzyme concentration appears only as the initial concentration in Equation

18.20, since the enzyme is cyclically regenerated during the reaction. K_M, the so-called Michaelis constant, is equal to $(k_{-1} + k_2)/k_1$. Equation 18.20 is the basis for the derivative techniques for determining both $[E]_0$ and $[S]_0$. If the concentration of product is monitored by a linear-response sensor, the resulting electrical signal at a given time is

$$\frac{d\mathcal{S}_t}{dt} = \frac{v k_2 [E]_0 [S]_t}{K_M + [S]_t} \tag{18.21}$$

If the substrate concentration is large compared to K_M, then the reaction is pseudo-zero-order and the rate of change of the signal with time is directly proportional to $[E]_0$. Under conditions where $[S]_t \ll K_M$, the rate of change of the signal is also directly proportional to $[S]_t$ and, when initial reaction rates are measured, $[S]_t \approx [S]_0$.

Integrating Equation 18.20 between two substrate concentrations $[S]_1$ and $[S]_2$ (the concentrations at times t_1 and t_2 respectively) yields

$$-K_M \ln \left(\frac{[S]_2}{[S]_1} \right) - \Delta[S] = k_2 [E]_0 (t_2 - t_1) \tag{18.22}$$

which is the basis of the integral methods.

Other Catalyzed Reactions

Homogeneous catalyzed reactions (other than enzyme-catalyzed reactions) have been used extensively in trace analysis. The general approach is to employ a reaction in which the species of analytical interest acts as a catalyst. Since the mechanisms of such reactions are varied and complex and often are not completely known, it is impractical or impossible to give exact rate equations for such mechanisms here. However, the rate expressions in terms of the rate of formation of product can usually be written in the general form

$$\frac{d[P]_t}{dt} = K[C]_0 f([X_1], [X_2], \ldots, [X_i]) \tag{18.23}$$

where $[X_i]$ = the reactant and product concentrations
          f = an arbitrary function
         K = the proportionality constant
     $[C]_0$ = the initial catalyst concentration

It can be seen from the form of Equation 18.23 that the derivative approach can be used to determine $[C]_0$. The mathematical relationships for the integral methods can be obtained by rearranging and integrating.

18.5 METHODS FOR DETERMINING A SINGLE SPECIES

Two types of techniques are employed for analyzing a single-component system. The most straightforward is the *derivative* or *slope* method in which one obtains the derivative of the electrical signal by electronically differentiating the signal from the transducer. The second approach uses the integral forms of the rate equations, and one of two possible types of measurement: the *fixed-time* or *constant-time* method in which the reaction is allowed to proceed for a fixed time, and the *variable-time* method in which the signal output varies between two fixed limits and the time Δt required for the complete sweep is measured.

The Derivative Technique

For first- and pseudo-first-order reactions monitored by an instrument with a linear response, Equation 18.16 is solved for $[A]_0$ to yield the relationship between the rate of change of the signal and the initial concentration of A:

$$[A]_0 = \left(\frac{e^{k_A t}}{\nu x k_A} \right) \left(\frac{d\mathcal{S}_t}{dt} \right) \qquad (18.24)$$

There are two modes in which Equation 18.24 is employed. If the derivative measurement is made at a specified time after the reaction is initiated, the first term is a constant and $[A]_0$ can be obtained directly from the measured value of $d\mathcal{S}_t/dt$. A more common approach is to make the derivative measurement during the initial 1% of the overall reaction, before $e^{k_A t}$ differs significantly from unity. Then the initial rate is virtually independent of time, and Equation 18.24 simplifies to

$$[A]_0 \approx \left(\frac{1}{\nu x k_A} \right) \left(\frac{d\mathcal{S}_t}{dt} \right)_{\text{initial}} \qquad (18.25)$$

During the initial portion of the reaction, the slope is approximately constant (to within 1%) and pseudo-zero-order kinetics apply.

For enzyme-catalyzed reactions used to measure enzyme activities with a linear-response instrument, solving Equation 18.21 for $[E]_0$ gives

$$[E]_0 = \left(\frac{K_M + [S]_t}{\nu k_2 [S]_t} \right) \left(\frac{d\mathcal{S}_t}{dt} \right) \qquad (18.26)$$

If the measurement is at a fixed value of $[S]_t$, $d\mathcal{S}_t/dt$ is directly proportional to $[E]_0$ since the first term is a constant. However, measurement at constant $[S]_t$ is obviously difficult, and the analysis itself can be greatly simplified by arranging experimental conditions so that $[S]_t \gg K_M$. In this case, the initial rate is obtained and

$$[E]_0 \approx \left(\frac{1}{\nu k_2} \right) \left(\frac{d\mathcal{S}_t}{dt} \right)_{\text{initial}} \qquad (18.27)$$

The determination of the substrate concentrations using enzyme-catalyzed reactions by the derivative method follows from Equation 18.20, under the following conditions: (1) a linear instrumental response, (2) reaction conditions where $[S]_t \ll K_M$, (3) a fixed value for $[E_0]$, (4) a measured initial rate ($[S]_t \approx [S]_0$).

$$[S]_0 = \left(\frac{K_M}{\nu k_2 [E]_0} \right) \left(\frac{d\mathcal{S}_t}{dt} \right)_{\text{initial}} \qquad (18.28)$$

Because of the complexity of other catalyzed reactions, initial reaction-rates are usually measured for analytical purposes. Equation 18.23 shows that, if all reactant concentrations are approximately equal to their initial concentrations, a direct proportionality is obtained between the catalyst concentration and the initial measured rate, provided the instrument has a linear response. With a nonlinear response, it is necessary to make the measurement at a fixed signal level in order to have a direct proportionality between $[C]_0$ and the derivative.

Fixed-Time Method

The fixed-time approach is an integral technique, although conditions are usually so arranged that measurement times and concentration changes are small enough to produce a good approximation to the instantaneous reaction-rate.

If the product concentration in a first- or pseudo-first-order reaction is measured by a linear-response instrument, Equation 18.17 can be solved for $[A]_0$ to give

$$[A]_0 = \left(\frac{e^{k_A t_1}}{vx(1 - e^{k_A \Delta t})} \right) \Delta \mathscr{S} \tag{18.29}$$

If all measurements are begun at the same value of t_1 after the start of the reaction and Δt is constant, the quantity in brackets will be constant for all experiments, and $[A]_0$ is directly proportional to $\Delta \mathscr{S}$. This is true for any fixed time-interval during the reaction and, thus, the fixed-time method is not restricted to measurements of initial rates. However, the analysis can be considerably simplified if the measurement is made before 1–2% of A has reacted.

$$[A]_0 \approx \left(\frac{1}{vxk_A \Delta t} \right) \Delta \mathscr{S} \tag{18.30}$$

The use of this equation in the fixed-time method is shown in Figure 18.3. It is clear from the format of the fixed-time method and Equations 18.29 and 18.30 that, if $\Delta \mathscr{S}$ is not directly proportional to $\Delta[P]$ (as is the case with nonlinear-response instruments), the fixed-time method will lead to a nonlinear relation between $\Delta \mathscr{S}$ and $[A]_0$; this virtually rules out the use of this method with such instruments.

When enzyme-catalyzed reactions are employed to measure enzyme activities, Equation 18.22 can be solved for $[E]_0$ to give

$$[E]_0 = \frac{-K_M \ln \left(\frac{[S]_2}{[S]_1} \right) - \Delta[S]}{k_2 \Delta t} \tag{18.31}$$

where $\Delta t = t_2 - t_1$. If the relation $[S]_2 = \Delta[S] + [S]_1$ is substituted into Equation 18.31 and the logarithmic term expanded in a Maclaurin series, one obtains

$$[E]_0 = \frac{-K_M \left[\frac{\Delta[S]}{[S]_1} - \frac{1}{2} \left(\frac{\Delta[S]}{[S]_1} \right)^2 + \frac{1}{3} \left(\frac{\Delta[S]}{[S]_1} \right)^3 - \cdots \right] - \Delta[S]}{k_2 \Delta t} \tag{18.32}$$

In order to use the fixed-time approach, several approximations to simplify this equation are necessary. First of all, the relative change of concentration $(\Delta[S]/[S]_1)$ must be made very small (less than 2%) during the interval Δt so that the higher-order terms of the series can be ignored, which gives

$$[E]_0 = \frac{-1}{k_2 \Delta t} \left(\frac{K_M}{[S]_1} + 1 \right) \Delta[S] \tag{18.33}$$

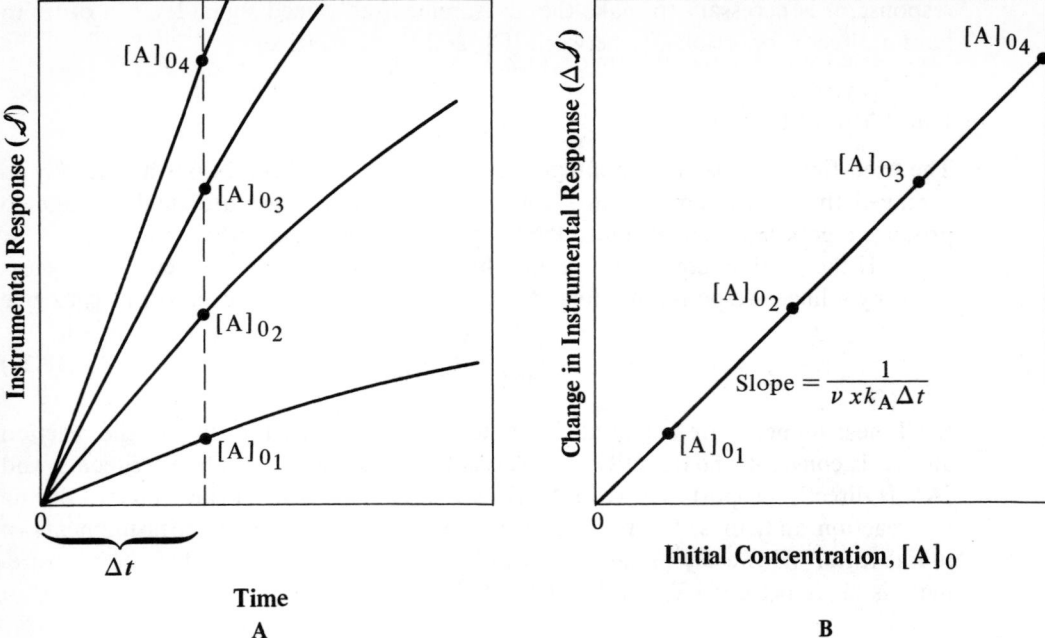

FIGURE 18.3. *The fixed-time method for uncatalyzed reactions, in the case where $t_1 = 0$ and $\mathscr{S}_{t=0} = 0$. (a) Variation of $\mathscr{S}$ as a function of time for various different initial concentrations of A. (b) Variation of $\Delta\mathscr{S}$ at a fixed time-interval Δt with change in $[A]_0$.*

This equation is further simplified if the condition $[S]_1 \gg K_M$ is employed, which yields

$$[E]_0 \approx \left(\frac{-1}{k_2\,\Delta t}\right) \Delta[S] \qquad (18.34)$$

and which, for a linear-response instrument ($\Delta S \approx \Delta\mathscr{S}$), gives a direct proportionality between $\Delta\mathscr{S}$ and $[E]_0$. Again, a nonlinear-response instrument will lead to nonlinear relations between ΔS and $[E]_0$, and the fixed-time method is not readily applicable.

The fixed-time technique for determining substrate concentrations using enzyme-catalyzed reactions follows much the same mathematical development as given above.

With respect to the use of catalyzed reactions, the catalyst concentrations can be determined using the fixed-time method, but strict adherence to pseudo-zero-order conditions (initial reaction-rate measurement) is generally necessary to obtain linear calibration curves.

The Variable-Time Method

The variable-time method, like the fixed-time method, is an integral method which, for short measurement times and small changes in concentration, also gives results approaching the instantaneous reaction-rate.

The variable-time method, as employed for first- or pseudo-first-order reactions, also uses the integral form of the first-order rate equation (Eqn. 18.15). Solving for $[A]_0$ yields

$$[A]_0 = \frac{\Delta[P]e^{k_A t_1}}{x(1 - e^{-k_A \Delta t})} \tag{18.35}$$

In the variable-time method, $\Delta[P]$ is held constant and Δt is the measured parameter that is related to $[A]_0$. If measurements are carried out during the first 1–2% of the overall reaction (initial-rate conditions), the exponential term, $e^{k_A t_1}$, is approximately equal to unity; and if the measurements are begun very near zero reaction-time, Equation 18.35 becomes

$$[A]_0 = \left(\frac{\Delta[P]}{xk_A}\right)\frac{1}{\Delta t} \tag{18.36}$$

Thus, in contrast to the fixed-time procedure, it is absolutely necessary to employ pseudo-zero-order conditions (initial-reaction conditions) in order to obtain a linear calibration curve. For a linear-response instrument, $\Delta[P]$ can be replaced by $\Delta \mathscr{S}/\nu$ to give

$$[A]_0 = \left(\frac{\Delta \mathscr{S}}{\nu xk_A}\right)\frac{1}{\Delta t} \tag{18.37}$$

The application of this equation to rate data is shown in Figure 18.4. The variable-time procedure has several advantages over the fixed-time procedure when used with instruments having a nonlinear relationship between signal output and concentration.

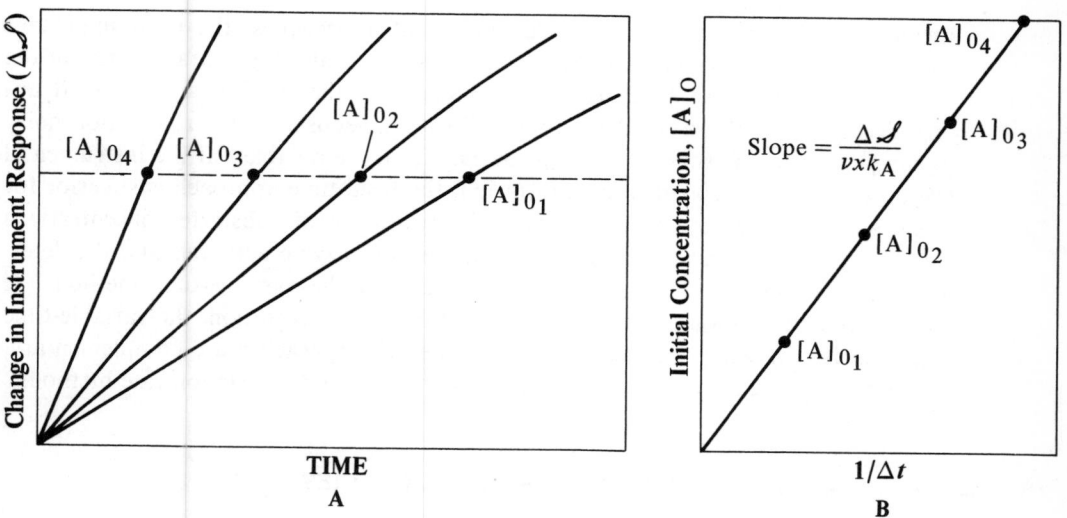

FIGURE 18.4. *Variable-time method for uncatalyzed reactions.* (a) *Variation of $\mathscr{S}$ as a function of time for various different initial concentrations of A.* (b) *Variation of $1/\Delta t$ required to reach a fixed value of $\Delta \mathscr{S}$ as a function of $[A]_0$.*

The variable-time approach is ideally suited to the determination of enzyme activities; rearrangement of the integral form of the rate law (Eqn. 18.22) yields

$$[E]_0 = \left[-K_M \ln \left(\frac{[S]_2}{[S]_1} \right) - \Delta[S] \right] \left(\frac{1}{k_2 \, \Delta t} \right) \tag{18.38}$$

Since $[S]_2$, $[S]_1$, and (thus) $\Delta[S]$, are held constant in the variable-time method, a linear relation between $[E]_0$ and $1/\Delta t$ always exists because the bracketed term is a constant. Again, if $[S] \gg K_M$ and $\Delta[S]/[S]_1$ is kept small (initial-rate conditions), Equation 18.38 can be simplified to

$$[E]_0 = - \left(\frac{\Delta[S]}{k_2} \right) \frac{1}{\Delta t} \tag{18.39}$$

If a linear-response instrument is used, the $\Delta[S]$ term in this equation simply becomes $\Delta \mathscr{S}/\nu$; with a nonlinear-response instrument $\Delta[S]$ becomes $[f(\mathscr{S}_2) - f(\mathscr{S}_1)]$. Thus, a linear relationship between $[E]_0$ and $1/\Delta t$ is independent of the linearity of the instrumental response and measurements need not be made during the initial stages of the reaction.

The variable-time method, however, is not as well suited for determining substrate concentrations as the fixed-time method; there will be a nonlinear relationship between $[S]_0$ and $1/\Delta t$ unless pseudo-zero-order conditions are used during the interval Δt and the measurements are begun very close to $t = 0$.

For other types of catalyzed reactions, the variable-time method is well suited for determining catalyst concentrations. Initial-rate procedures and linearity of instrumental response are not necessary.

Summary and Comparison of Single-Component Techniques

In choosing between the three single-component approaches, the most important factors are the type of reaction, the species sought for, and the characteristics of the instrumental response. The derivative technique is the most straightforward approach and gives the desired read-out of instantaneous reaction-rate. For noisy signals, however, the two integral approaches are more reliable. If the instrumental response is linearly related to concentration, the fixed-time approach is superior for pseudo-first-order reactions and for the determination of substrate concentrations using enzyme reactions. Reaction-rate analyses of enzyme activities and the determination of other catalysts are best carried out by the variable-time method. If the instrumental response is a nonlinear function of concentration, the variable-time approach is of great advantage. The two integral approaches are complementary, and both should be available for the maximum usefulness of reaction-rate methods.

18.6 RATE EQUATIONS AND METHODS FOR MIXTURES

Often, the reaction rates of closely related components of a mixture with a common reagent are similar, and the rates cannot be sufficiently separated by either a thermodynamic or a kinetic masking technique to permit the faster or slower reacting component to be neglected. When this specific situation occurs, *differential reaction-rate methods* can be employed for analyzing the mixtures without resorting to separation techniques.

Consider the irreversible bimolecular reactions of a binary mixture of **A** and **B** with a common reagent **R**.

$$A + R \xrightarrow{k_A} P \tag{18.40}$$

$$B + R \xrightarrow{k_B} P' \tag{18.41}$$

The range of concentrations of reactant and reagent for which general differential reaction-rate methods have been developed is illustrated in Figure 18.5. When the concentration of common reagent is very large with respect to the total concentration of A and B, the reaction proceeds by pseudo-first-order kinetics (Region I) and several general methods are available. The rates of change of the concentrations of either the product or the total reactants (total A and B) are monitored as a function of time.

As $[R]$ becomes less than 50 times the total concentration of reactants $([A] + [B])$, pseudo-first-order kinetics are no longer valid (Region II); however, as $[R]$ approaches $([A] + [B])$ in magnitude, simple second-order kinetic treatments of the rates of reaction can be used. Regions III, IV [special cases where $[R] = ([A] + [B])$], and V of Figure 18.5 represent the concentration ranges where the

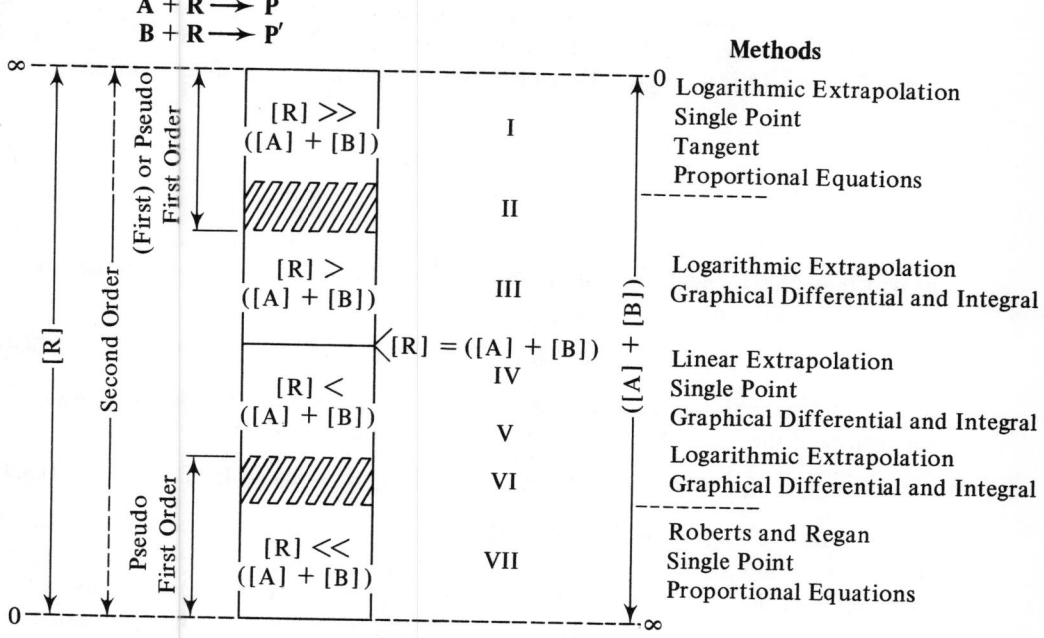

FIGURE 18.5. *General analytical techniques applicable to second-order reactions. From H. B. Mark, Jr., G. A. Rechnitz, and R. A. Grienke,* Kinetics in Analytical Chemistry, *New York: Wiley-Interscience, 1968, by permission of John Wiley and Sons. Copyright © 1968 by John Wiley and Sons.*

second-order treatment is employed. General methods based on second-order kinetics have been developed in which either [R], ([A] + [B]), or [P] can be followed.

As [R] decreases further, the kinetics again approach pseudo-first-order rates (Region VI), but now with respect to R. As [R] ≪ ([A] + [B]) (Region VII), a pseudo-first-order rate again applies, and general differential reaction-rate methods have been developed for this situation. There are also differential methods based on measurements of *initial* reaction-rates, where the kinetics become pseudo-zero-order.

Theoretical treatments for analysis based on second-order kinetics are considerably more involved than those for first-order or pseudo-first-order processes. Therefore, whenever possible, the conditions of a bimolecular reaction are adjusted so that the reaction follows pseudo-first-order kinetics; a 50-fold or greater excess of reagent (Region I) or reactants (Region VII) is necessary. There are systems, however, for which pseudo-first-order conditions cannot be employed—for example, with a large excess of either reagent or reactants, the reactions of interest may be too fast for practical measurements.

Three of the more commonly used first-order differential kinetic methods are discussed in detail in this section. These are the *logarithmic-extrapolation method*, the *method of proportional equations*, and the *method of Roberts and Regan*.

Logarithmic-Extrapolation Method

The logarithmic-extrapolation method is suitable for reactions that are first-order or pseudo-first-order with respect to the reactants; that is, in Region I of Figure 18.5, where $[R]_0 \gg ([A]_0 + [B]_0)$. Consider two competing irreversible reactions of the type

$$A \xrightarrow{k_A} P \qquad (18.42)$$

$$B \xrightarrow{k_B} P \qquad (18.43)$$

in which A and B react to form a common product P, whose concentration at any time t is given by the expression

$$[P]_\infty - [P]_t = [A]_t + [B]_t = [A]_0 e^{-k_A t} + [B]_0 e^{-k_B t} \qquad (18.44)$$

After A has reacted essentially to completion ($[A]_t \approx 0$) in the case where $k_A \gg k_B$, one can take the logarithm of both sides of Equation 18.44 and obtain:

$$\ln([P]_\infty - [P]_t) = \ln([A]_t + [B]_t) = -k_B t + \ln[B]_0 \qquad (18.45)$$

Thus, a plot of $\ln([A]_t + [B]_t)$ or $\ln([P]_\infty - [P]_t)$ versus time yields a straight line with a slope of $-k_B$ and an intercept (at $t = 0$) of $\ln[B]_0$. The value of $[A]_0$ may then be obtained by subtracting $[B]_0$ from the total initial concentration of the mixture; the latter can be determined either by independent methods or calculated from $[P]_\infty$, provided the reaction mechanism does not change during the final stages. A typical reaction-rate curve of this type is illustrated in Figure 18.6. Because of its simplicity, this method is one of the most widely used differential kinetic methods; it gives somewhat greater accuracy than do the other methods for mixtures where the ratio of rate constants is relatively large.

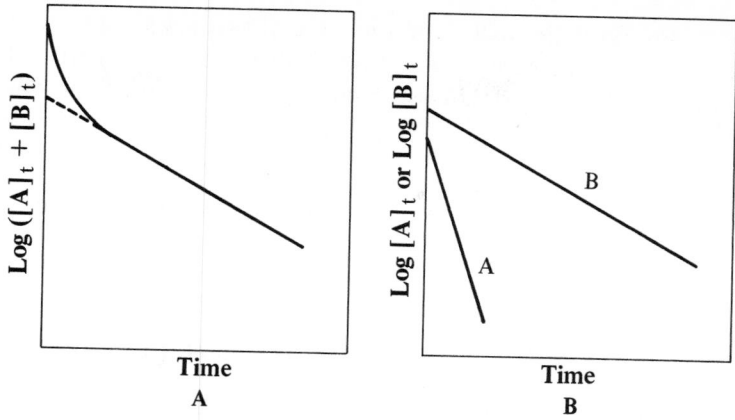

FIGURE 18.6. *Logarithmic-extrapolation method for a mixture of species A and B reacting by first-order kinetics. (a) Rate data obtained for the mixture. (b) Rate data for each component separately. From H. B. Mark, Jr., G. A. Rechnitz, and R. A. Grienke,* Kinetics in Analytical Chemistry, *New York: Wiley-Interscience, 1968, by permission of John Wiley and Sons. Copyright © 1968 by John Wiley and Sons.*

Method of Proportional Equations

This method is based on the principle of constant fractional life (usually called "half-life"), which applies to a species undergoing reaction in such a way that, after any time interval, a constant fraction of the amount left unreacted at the end of the previous interval has reacted (or a constant fraction remains unreacted), irrespective of the initial concentration. This property is associated with first-order or pseudo-first-order reactions—such as radioactive decay—for which "half-lives" are often quoted as a measure of reaction rate. This property of constant fractional life also applies to more complex reactions—such as successive and parallel reaction-sequences—involving first-order reactions. The initial concentration of a species reacting with constant fractional life is directly proportional to the amount of product formed at any given time.

For Reaction 18.9,

$$[P]_t = x([A]_0 - [A]_t) = x[A]_0[1 - e^{-k_A t}] = G_A[A]_0 \qquad (18.46)$$

Therefore, the concentration of P at any given time is directly proportional to the initial concentration of A. The proportionality constant is a function only of the stoichiometry, the reaction time, and the rate constant.

Instead of the actual concentration, any parameter directly proportional to $[P]_t$, such as absorbance of light, electrical conductivity of the solution, polarographic diffusion-current, or volume of reagent required for a titration, can be measured. Then, since $\mathscr{S} = \nu[P]$,

$$\mathscr{S}_t = K_A[A]_0 \qquad (18.47)$$

where $\quad K_A = \nu G_A$
$\qquad \nu$ = the proportionality constant

Consider the analysis of a mixture of two similar species, A and B. If B also reacts by first-order kinetics to produce P (not necessarily with the same stoichiometry as A), the same treatment given above for A can be applied. For the reaction of B alone,

$$[P]_t = G_B[B]_0 \tag{18.48}$$

where $G_B = x_B[1 - e^{-k_B t}]$ and is a constant at any specified time t

If the reactions of A and B are independent of one another,

$$[P]_{t_1} = G_{A_1}[A]_0 + G_{B_1}[B]_0 \tag{18.49}$$

$$[P]_{t_2} = G_{A_2}[A]_0 + G_{B_2}[B]_0 \tag{18.50}$$

The numerical values of constants G_A and G_B at times t_1 and t_2 are determined by measuring the amount of P produced by known amounts of pure A and pure B after times t_1 and t_2. Alternatively, the constants can be calculated by substituting known reaction-rate constants (k_A and k_B), stoichiometries, and times into the equations for G_A and G_B. Usually, the former procedure is preferred because it minimizes the influence of the numerous experimental variables.

Thus, the analysis of a two-component mixture is accomplished by measuring the concentration of P at times t_1 and t_2. These data are then substituted into Equations 18.49 and 18.50, which are then solved simultaneously to yield the concentrations $[A]_0$ and $[B]_0$. This method can also be applied to situations in which two species react to form different products,

$$A \longrightarrow nC \tag{18.51}$$

$$B \longrightarrow mD \tag{18.52}$$

provided [C] and [D] are both directly proportional to the same parameter, the instrumental signal $\mathscr{S}$. This may be the case, for instance, in analyzing a mixture of two organic compounds containing the same functional group. If the two reactions proceed independently, one can write

$$\mathscr{S}_t = K_A[A]_0 + K_B[B]_0 \tag{18.53}$$

The initial concentrations of the two species can be found by determining $\mathscr{S}_t$ at two reaction-times and solving the resulting simultaneous equations.

This method can also be used for mixtures containing more than two reacting species. For a series of compounds (A, B, ..., N) that react with constant fractional lives to yield products directly proportional to $\mathscr{S}$, a series of n equations analogous to Equation 18.53 can be written for n different reaction-times, and, in theory, can be solved for the initial concentration of each species.

Method of Roberts and Regan

The method developed by Roberts and Regan is used for reactions in which it is possible to detect and follow concentration changes of R with high sensitivity. It is applicable to reactions that are pseudo-first-order with respect to the reagent (Region VII of Fig. 18.5). For example, an excellent reagent for carboxylic acids is diphenyldiazomethane, because it is very highly colored. The reaction between these two species can be made to proceed by a pseudo-first-order reaction with respect to the reagent, and thus the reaction can be followed spectrophotometrically even though the concentration of the reagent is small compared to that of the acid.

The rate of disappearance of R, reacting with a two-component mixture of A and B, is given by

$$\frac{-d[R]}{dt} = k_A[A]_0[R] + k_B[B]_0[R] = K^*[R] \tag{18.54}$$

where $\quad K^* = k_A[A]_0 + k_B[B]_0$

The amounts of A and B consumed during the course of the reaction are negligible because the concentrations of these species are in great excess.

An analysis is accomplished by measuring K^* in the usual manner for first-order reactions, for example from

$$K^* = \frac{\ln \dfrac{[R]_0}{[R]_1}}{t_1 - t_0} \tag{18.55}$$

and by determining k_A and k_B, by reacting the pure components, A and B, with the reagent. The total initial concentration of the reactants, $[M]_0$, is found by an independent method

$$[M]_0 = [A]_0 + [B]_0 \tag{18.56}$$

Equations 18.54 and 18.56 are solved simultaneously for $[A]_0$ and $[B]_0$.

Comparison of General First-Order Methods for Mixtures

In the preceding sections, the general kinetic methods have been discussed in terms of their mathematical framework. Relatively little comparative work has been reported utilizing the various kinetic methods, so that it is difficult to compare these methods critically with respect to actual experiments. In other words, experimental verification of the theory is lacking. The following comparisons are based primarily on the mathematical framework of the methods and on the limitations of commonly employed analytical techniques.

Below is a list of practical aspects that must be considered before selecting a kinetic method for a given circumstance and system. The relative advantages and disadvantages of each method are discussed with respect to each aspect.

Ratios of $[A]_0/[B]_0$ and k_A/k_B. The limitations of the logarithmic-extrapolation method lie in the fact that A must react essentially to completion [i.e., $[A]_0 e^{-k_A t} \ll [B]_0 e^{-k_B t}$] before any significant data can be obtained. Hence, the main limitations of the method are really in the ratios k_A/k_B and $[A]_0/[B]_0$. Figure 18.7 illustrates calculated curves for cases in which $[A]_0/[B]_0 = 1$ and for several values of k_A/k_B; the curves are normalized for all values of k_B by plotting with respect to $k_B t$ as the time axis.

The accuracy of the method increases as the ratio $[A]_0/[B]_0$ grows smaller. Figure 18.8 illustrates calculated curves for the cases in which $k_A/k_B = 7.5$ for several values of $[A]_0/[B]_0$. The solid circles indicate the time at which the ratio

$k_A[A]_t/k_B[B]_t = 1/30$; this is the time at which the extrapolation becomes valid. The error will increase as the ratio $[A]_0/[B]_0$ increases, because t becomes larger. Thus, accurate experimental methods are required for determining concentration in cases where $[B]_t$ is small when the reaction of A is complete. In addition, the kinetics must be sufficiently well behaved for a lengthy extrapolation to be meaningful. The method of proportional equations is less limited with respect to $[A]_0/[B]_0$ and k_A/k_B, because it does not demand that $k_A[A]_t$ be negligible compared to $k_B[B]_t$ in order to collect analytically useful data.

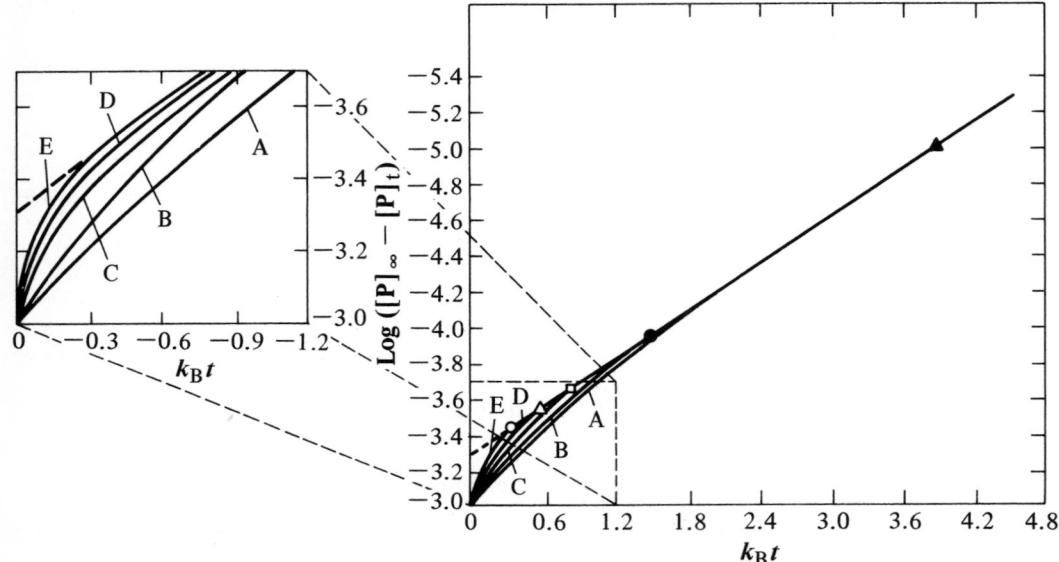

FIGURE 18.7. *Effect of rate-constant ratio in the logarithmic-extrapolation method.* $[A]_0/[B]_0 = 1$; $k_A/k_B = $ (A) 2; (B) 4; (C) 7.5; (D) 10; (E) 25. *The symbols* $\bigcirc$, $\triangle$, $\square$, $\bullet$, *and* $\blacktriangle$, *respectively, indicate the points beyond which the curves can be considered linear.* [P] *is the concentration of product. Adapted from H. B. Mark, Jr., G. A. Rechnitz, and R. A. Grienke,* Kinetics in Analytical Chemistry, *New York: Wiley-Interscience, 1968, by permission of John Wiley and Sons. Copyright © 1968 by John Wiley and Sons.*

The method of Roberts and Regan has a wider range of applicability with respect to $[A]_0/[B]_0$ and k_A/k_B than either of the other two. In fact, a useful advantage of this method is that small k_A/k_B ratios can be tolerated rather easily because this method does not depend on the manner in which the fractions of A and B remaining vary with respect to each other. This method depends on measuring a composite pseudo-first-order rate constant K^* for the mixture (Eqn. 18.55), and $[A]_0$ can be determined over a wide range of $[A]_0/[B]_0$ as long as $k_A[A]_0$ contributes significantly to the measured value of K^*. Under these conditions, as $[A]_0/[B]_0$ changes, K^* likewise changes. It is possible to determine smaller values of $[A_0]$ with this method than is possible with the others, provided that k_A/k_B is large. This is,

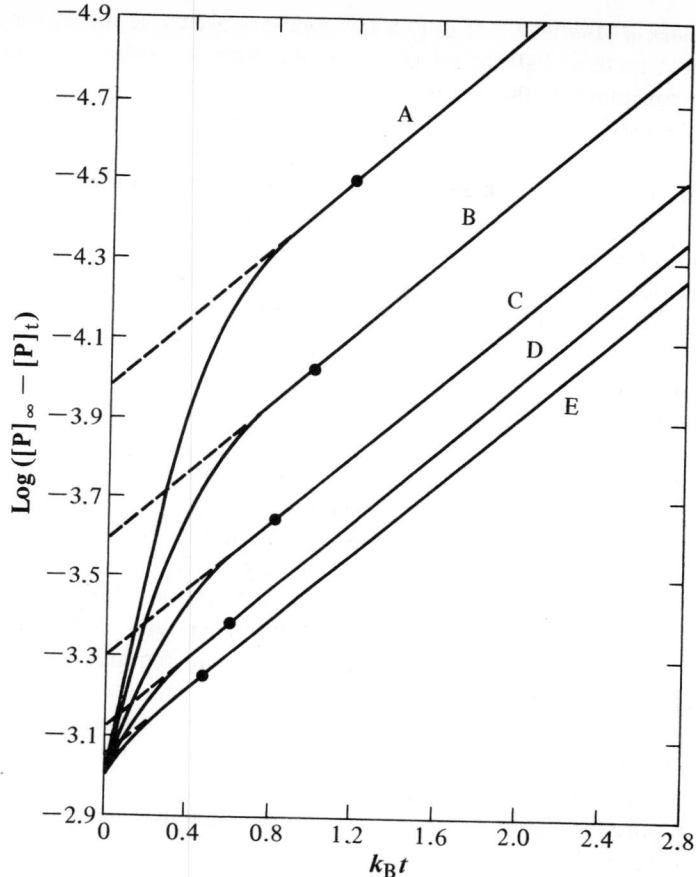

FIGURE 18.8. *Effect of the ratio of sample concentrations in the logarith-mic-extrapolation method for $k_A/k_B = 7.5$. $[A]_0/[B]_0 = (A)$ 9; (B) 3; (C) 1; (D) 0.25; (E) 0.1. $[A]_0 + [B]_0$ is constant throughout; $[P]$ is the concentration of the product. From H. B. Mark, Jr., G. A. Rechnitz, and R. A. Grienke,* Kinetics in Analytical Chemistry, *New York: Wiley-Interscience, 1968, by permission of John Wiley and Sons. Copyright © 1968 by John Wiley and Sons.*

perhaps, its chief advantage. In general, as the ratio of $[R]_0$ to $([A]_0 + [B]_0)$ decreases, the minimum amount of $[A]_0$ that can be determined decreases also, reaching a limit when the reaction becomes pseudo-first-order with respect to $[R]_0$.

Species to be Measured. The method of Roberts and Regan can only be used if the concentration of some species (reagent or product—or a parameter proportional to one of those concentrations) can be measured. The logarithmic-extrapolation method or the method of proportional equations can only be used if the total concentration of some species can be measured. These are relatively unimportant considerations, but in some instances could eliminate one or two of the potential methods at the outset.

Number of Analyses. If only a few analyses are to be made, the logarithmic-extrapolation method has a distinct advantage over the other two methods, because the rate constants of the individual species need not be determined before the method can be used.

Rigidity of Control of Reaction Conditions. The logarithmic-extrapolation method has the advantage over the other two methods with respect to control of reaction conditions, because the rate constants need not be known. It is necessary to control conditions strictly during any single determination (a complete kinetic run), but it is not necessary to reproduce these conditions exactly from one analysis to the next, as is the case with the other two methods. For the same reason, the logarithmic-extrapolation method is more applicable if varying amounts of a catalyst are to be present in the system.

Ease of Analysis. Once the rate constants for the system under study have been determined, the method of Roberts and Regan and the method of proportional equations are about equal in ease of operation and are considerably easier to use than the logarithmic-extrapolation method. The latter requires a prior determination of $([A]_0 + [B]_0)$ and numerous determinations during the kinetic run; and the reaction must be rather slow so that enough points can be taken to plot a kinetic curve. The method of Roberts and Regan requires a prior determination of $([A]_0 + [B]_0)$, but only one subsequent point is needed. Another advantage is that, after the reaction is completed, a check determination can be made by adding another aliquot of reagent because the concentrations of the reactants are still in large excess over that of the reagent. As an example, the analysis of carbonyls by the graphical-extrapolation method required the use of second-order kinetic conditions at 0°C to slow down the reactions sufficiently. However, with the Roberts and Regan method, complete duplicate analyses were obtained in less than 10 min using the same system (except that different concentrations were used). The method of proportional equations is just as simple as the method of Roberts and Regan and does not require a prior determination of $([A]_0 + [B]_0)$. It does, however, require two points to be obtained.

The nonextrapolation methods are also much easier to adapt to automated analysis than is the logarithmic-extrapolation method.

Kinetic Complications. In later stages, many reactions are complicated by side reactions, reversibility, equilibrium, complex kinetics, etc. The logarithmic-extrapolation method can be seriously affected by these phenomena, thus limiting even further the useful k_A/k_B and $[A]_0/[B]_0$ ranges, to the point where the method might not be applicable. Even worse, if the analyst is not aware of these complications, erroneous data might be obtained. The method of proportional equations is also affected by these phenomena, but to a lesser extent in some cases because measurements can be made before complications arise. The method of Roberts and Regan handles these situations best because only a negligible quantity of A and B reacts. There is no appreciable accumulation of product, and interference caused by side reactions will therefore be at a minimum. Reactions that normally become complex in the latter stages will remain pseudo-first-order throughout.

More Than Two Components. All three of the methods are alleged to be applicable to systems of three components or more! The logarithmic-extrapolation method would require tremendous rate differences to handle such a system, but in theory it could be done. The method of proportional equations should handle this somewhat more easily but also would require a greater rate difference than in the two-component case, and one more determination. The method of Roberts and Regan could only be applied to three-component systems if another determination such as density, refractive index, etc., could be made. Needless to say, experimental error will significantly increase if these methods are used to analyze three-component systems; at this stage, it is difficult to envisage using them for the simultaneous determination of four components.

Accuracy. An error-analysis study of the method of proportional equations results in the conclusion that if t_2 is any time, even t_∞, the optimum short time is always before A has reacted to completion. Thus, the method of proportional equations is inherently more accurate than the logarithmic-extrapolation method if the data points can be determined with the same amount of error in both methods. It can be argued that the logarithmic-extrapolation method avoids this by averaging the experimental data with the best straight line. However, is this line, if drawn by visual inspection, really the best straight line? Unless the data are weighted correctly (weighting varies as the reaction proceeds), the answer is no. Also, it is the author's experience that it is difficult to decide how to draw this line by visual inspection of the data. The construction of the line might well be the greatest error in the method. Furthermore, by taking duplicate measurements (still at a great saving in time) the method of proportional equations can be made even more accurate.

A theoretical comparison of the accuracy of the above two methods with that of Roberts and Regan has not been made. Some experimental studies have shown that comparable accuracies are obtained with the method of Roberts and Regan and that of logarithmic extrapolation. Perhaps the best guide to comparing the various methods lies in the many published experiments in which these methods have been employed: in these, the various methods were applied to suitable systems, producing results with comparable accuracies.

18.7 INSTRUMENTATION

The accuracy and precision of the experimental measurement is, of course, important to both kinetic-based and equilibrium-based analytical methods. However, a few special factors—instrumental and experimental—are of critical importance in kinetic-based techniques; these are discussed below. The block diagram of a typical rate-measuring system is shown in Figure 18.9.

Instrument Stability

High-frequency noise in an instrument used to measure reaction rates can generally be eliminated or minimized by simple electronic filtering, since the frequency of the noise is usually very high compared to the rate of change of the signal. However, low-frequency noise or drift, which comes mainly from the reaction monitor and

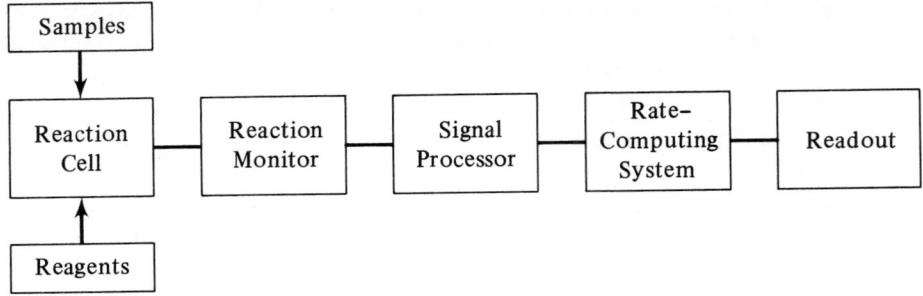

FIGURE 18.9. *Schematic diagram of typical rate-measuring instrument. Adapted from J. S. Mattson, H. B. Mark, Jr., and H. C. MacDonald, Jr., eds.,* Spectroscopy and Kinetics, *vol. 3, New York: Marcel Dekker, 1973, by permission of the publisher.*

which varies at about the same rate as the reaction rate itself, presents a much more difficult problem. In this case, it is necessary to design the instrument in such a way as to eliminate these sources of drift, because there is no way of electronically separating the reaction signal from the random drift once the data reach the rate-computation system.

Light-Source Stabilization. The effect of light-source variations can be minimized by several methods. In most conventional spectrophotometers, a double-beam system can partially cancel fluctuations by comparing reference and sample beam intensities. However, since instruments employed for kinetic methods are not often called upon for spectral scanning, most designers have discarded the double-beam approach and have developed less expensive electronic stabilization techniques for light-source regulation.

The simplest technique for stabilizing the light source against short-term fluctuations is to regulate the AC line voltage, since line-voltage fluctuations can cause changes in light intensity comparable to those caused by the measured reaction-rate. Circuits that regulate the lamp power-supply voltage or current have also been used. However, this regulation is not sufficient; a more elaborate electronic regulator has been designed that compensates for changes in light-bulb resistance and is, thus, superior to circuits that regulate only the applied voltage or the applied current.

Light-intensity variations can result from heat flow around the light bulb itself; the use of baffling to eliminate convection currents across the optical path has been reported to give satisfactory results. Such a stabilized-light-source spectrophotometer was reported to have drift stability of better than 0.003 absorbance units (AU) per hour, a noise level that produced a rate error of less than 0.001 AU per minute, and a photometric accuracy of 0.01 AU at 1.0 AU and 0.001 AU near zero absorbance.

One disadvantage of such control systems is that they control the electrical input to the lamp rather than the actual lamp intensity. Several systems have been described using optical-feedback techniques to directly control the lamp intensity. Usually in these techniques the lamp intensity is monitored with a second photodetector, and a signal from this detector is fed back to the lamp power-supply.

Detector Noise and Drift. Transducers for modern spectrophotometric systems are usually vacuum phototubes or photomultiplier tubes. Noise and drift from the transducer can be quite troublesome in kinetic methods, and special care is normally taken to ensure low-noise operation.

There is some controversy about which detector provides the highest signal-to-noise ratio—the phototube or the photomultiplier. If comparisons are made at the same light level, the photomultiplier is capable of a higher signal-to-noise ratio, because its internal amplification is so high (often about 10^6) that the Johnson noise* of the load resistor is insignificant. When a phototube, on the other hand, is used at low light-levels, Johnson noise becomes the limiting factor and external amplification does not help. If comparisons are made at the same anode current, however, the phototube has the higher signal-to-noise ratio because the light level has to be much higher to obtain an equivalent output current. Thus, in systems where the operator can control the light level, such as with absorption spectrophotometers, it is recommended that intense light-sources be used with a phototube detector. As is true in any measurement, if the input signal can be made high enough that little or no amplification is needed, higher signal-to-noise ratios can be obtained than with amplification. For systems where the light level cannot be controlled, such as in emission spectroscopy, or where the light level is very low, the photomultiplier will give superior results.

Another important consideration in detectors is power-supply stability. For phototubes, regulation is not critical because the current-versus-voltage characteristic is essentially flat in the usual operating region. For photomultipliers, however, the gain is highly dependent on the power-supply voltage. As a rule of thumb, the power-supply stability should be at least an order of magnitude better than the desired stability in gain.

Temperature Control

The rate of chemical reaction is considerably more sensitive to temperature variation than is the position of equilibrium (provided the formation constant is very large and the reaction can be considered "quantitative"). Thus, temperature control is critical in reaction-rate methods.

Two factors in temperature control must be considered. The accuracy of temperature control in the jacket of the reaction cell is the initial consideration, of course. However, since chemical reactions are either exothermic or endothermic, it has been shown that rapid temperature exchange and equilibration of the reaction solution with the cell jacket is also an extremely important consideration in obtaining good data.

Rise-Time of the Instrument

As mentioned above, high-frequency noise can often be eliminated by simple electronic filtering. However, caution is necessary and the investigator should be very familiar with the actual effective rise-time of the measuring instrument over all

---

* Johnson or thermal noise is produced by random thermal motion in resistive circuit elements.

operating ranges. Obviously, a fixed time-constant cannot be applicable over a large range of initial concentrations, since the reaction rate at any time is a function of initial concentration. Thus, it is necessary to quantitatively evaluate the rise-time of the instrument under all conditions of damping employed and to compare those results with the maximum reaction-rates measured under each setting of the filter time-constant.

Linearity of Transducer Response

Most transducers converting chemical concentration into an electrical signal have a nonlinear response; for example, electrode potential and optical transmission are not directly proportional to concentration. In general, this nonlinearity is easily and simply corrected in equilibrium analytical measurements. However, it is considerably more difficult to instrumentally correct the response-versus-concentration function in reaction-rate methods, and often the correction itself can introduce significant errors in the analytical results. For example, the simple nonlinear feedback elements employed in log-response operational-amplifier circuits are not sufficiently accurate in transforming transmittance into absorbance to be used for many analytical purposes.

As mentioned earlier, the variable-time approach can be used advantageously in the case of nonlinear response, since the measured reaction-rate in this procedure is linearly proportional to the initial concentration of the species of interest in spite of the fact that the actual transducer response is not proportional to concentration. This is because the time required to reach a fixed concentration level is the parameter measured and, thus, linearity of the overall response-versus-concentration curve is not necessary. The point here is that in some cases the instrument and not the chemical reaction can dictate the method used.

Data-Acquisition Considerations

Most reaction-rate methods utilize only a small number of actual data points (from one to about four) in the calculation of the initial concentrations. Clearly this approach throws away a considerable amount of data that could be used advantageously. Recent studies have examined parameters affecting the accuracy of mixture analysis by pseudo-first-order reaction methods, and have shown that continuous data-utilization is superior in several cases. In the early development of reaction-rate methods, the procedures used chemical reactions that were not suitable for the continuous automatic measurement of reaction-rate curves. Also, calculations at that time attempted to limit the number of data points taken and to predetermine the optimum times, concentrations, and so on for taking this minimal amount of data. However, recent advances in electronic circuitry and computer technology have had a tremendous influence on the design of kinetic-analysis instrumentation. These advances have also strongly influenced differential-rate methods in both principles and approach. Several groups have designed instruments with built-in computation systems allowing continuous analysis of the reaction-rate curve over the entire reaction; in these instruments, data are processed using both ensemble-averaging and smoothing routines in real time. Experimental results and detailed error-analysis have shown conclusively that this approach to data acquisition, reduction, and display leads to much greater accuracy and precision in the analytical results. In fact, good results can be obtained from fast differential-rate analyses in which the usual finite or minimal data-point methods fail completely.

Automation of Operations

It is obvious that automated control of solution mixing, measurement sequences, and so on, will minimize the time-measurement errors arising from manual solution

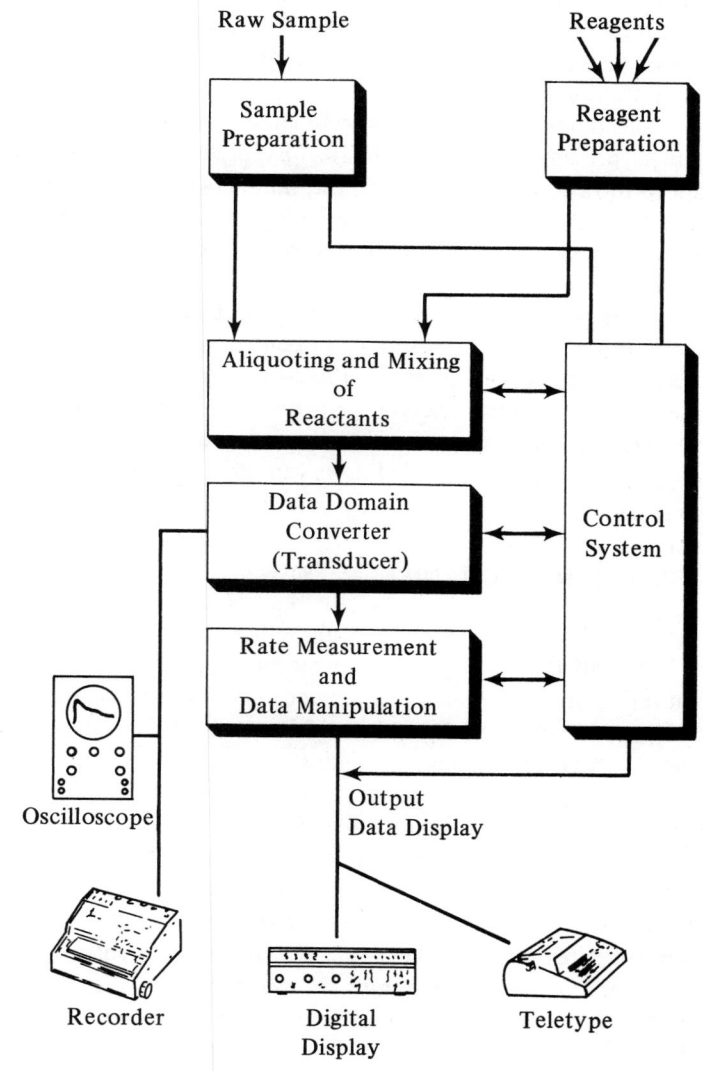

FIGURE 18.10. *Block diagram of completely automated system for reaction-rate methods. From H. V. Malmstadt, E. A. Cordos, and C. J. Delaney,* Anal. Chem., *44(12), 26A (1972), by permission of the senior author and the publisher. Copyright © 1972 by the American Chemical Society.*

handling and measurement control and, hence, will increase the accuracy of a given reaction-rate procedure.

As the expense of high-speed digital computers decreases, the applications of these small computers as built-in (on-line) units in chemical instrumentation for data reduction, system control, data acquisition, and experimental optimization in "real time" have increased sharply. Systems have been described in which the computer not only handles the data acquisition and sample manipulation, but actively takes part in all stages of the experiment by examining the data in real time and making decisions to optimize the experimental parameters and variables while the experiment is running. This is probably the most important single improvement in kinetic-based analysis; it will greatly expand both the routine and the specialized applications of the technique.

The block diagram for a completely computer-automated rate-measurement system is presented in Figure 18.10. By preliminary treatments (e.g., dissolution, dilution, filtration, ion exchange), the sample and reagent solutions are prepared as required for the specific procedure being used. Predetermined volumes of sample and reagents are then introduced, mixed, and transported to the reaction cell. The control and rate-measurement systems can be hardwired for specific applications, or they can be incorporated in a minicomputer-interfaced system that can provide, through software, much versatility in control of the measurement sequence and the processing and read-out of data. Read-out is visually displayed with digital lights or printed out on a serial teletype or a high-speed parallel printer. When desired, a servo recorder or storage oscilloscope can display the parameter-versus-time and rate curves. Totally automated units can analyze as many as 1000 samples per hour.

18.8 THE REACTION MECHANISM

In most equilibrium-based analytical methods, the success or failure of a determination is not affected by the reaction mechanism, provided that the reaction is either quantitative or the measured parameter at equilibrium is linearly proportional to the initial concentration of the species of interest. This is not the case in reaction-rate methods. Any development of a kinetic method should include, if possible, a complete study of the reaction mechanisms involved in the procedure. (Unfortunately, some reactions, such as catalytic reactions, are so complicated that complete elucidation of the mechanism is impossible.) It should also include a detailed study of the effects of typical sample-matrix components, which can act as catalysts, induce side-reactions, alter the activity of the reactants, and so on. The rates and rate constants for chemical reactions are very sensitive to low concentrations of such "spectator" species; hence, samples containing the same true initial composition of the species of interest but coming from different sources can very often give quite different apparent concentrations. Unless the experimenter is aware of the total reaction mechanism and of all possible factors that can affect either the activation energy or the reaction path, erroneous analytical results can be obtained. A detailed investigation of the simultaneous, in situ, analysis of binary amine mixtures illustrates this point. (Most systems, by the way, are less error-prone than this one.) The rate constants for the reaction of many individual organic amines with methyl iodide in acetone solvent had an ideal range and differentiation of absolute values when the reactions were conducted under pseudo-first-order conditions with respect to the methyl iodide. The Roberts and Regan data-reduction method was used along with a simple and accurate data-acquisition system employing a continuously recording conductivity instrument; almost ideal analytical results should have been attained. However, most binary mixtures gave very poor results when analyzed by this procedure.

A careful examination of the reaction mechanism of the system revealed numerous unexpected sources of error. First, it was found that the acetone used as a solvent undergoes a Schiff-base reaction with some primary amines at a rate comparable to that of the methylation reaction of the method. This results in the variation of the composite rate-constant, K^*, during the course of the reaction of mixtures

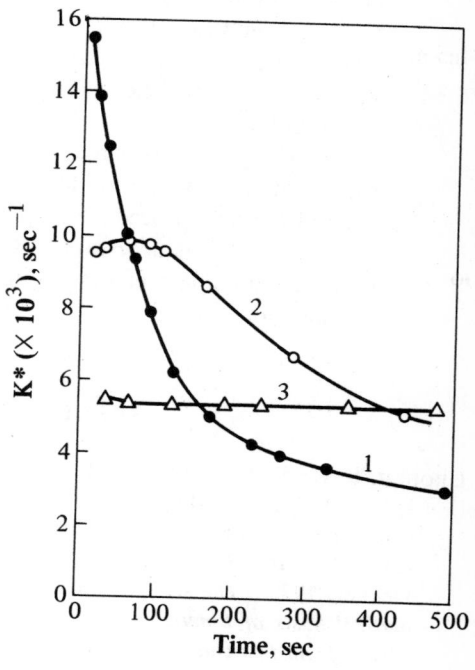

containing such primary amines, as shown in Curve 1 of Figure 18.11. As the calculation of initial concentration from K^* by the method of Roberts and Regan requires K^* to remain constant over the total reaction-time, serious errors are introduced by this side-reaction. As added water would suppress the Schiff-base reaction, acetone-water mixtures were then used as the solvent systems. Although this improved the results obtained for several amine mixtures, those containing high-molecular-weight amines still gave poor results. For example, K^* is not constant over the whole reaction for n-butylamine-tributylamine mixtures (see Curve 2 of Fig. 18.11). In this case the addition of water results in the formation of small suspended micelles of amine in the solution, which alters the reaction rates. Thus, it was necessary to use a less basic solvent system, DMSO–n-propyl alcohol, which has no significant tendency to react with primary amines and in which most amines are soluble. Curve 3 of Figure 18.11 shows that K^* for the *n*-butyl-amine-tribultylamine mixture is then constant and, thus, accurate initial concentrations are obtained.

However, certain amine mixtures, generally those containing methylamine, still gave poor analyses. It was found that such mixtures are slightly hygroscopic and samples often contain traces of water. This trace water acts as a catalyst in the methylation reaction. Thus, the rate constants obtained from the reactions of standard dry amine solutions and used in calculating the initial concentrations of unknown mixtures containing traces of water were not valid for the unknown mixture reactions. The addition of water to the solvent system (10% or more) swamped out these variations of rate constants in unknown amine mixtures; recall, however, that adding water can result in solubility complications for some amines. This investigation also revealed that a synergistic effect, probably caused by changes in the activity of the amines by the build-up of product, resulted in a variation of K^* during the reaction when the amine-mixture concentration was high. Other sources of error arose from the reaction of the reagent methyl iodide with its solvent during storage, and loss of measurement sensitivity when conducting impurities were present in the unknown.

The point here is that no simple general procedure for this method can be given that is universally applicable to all types of amine mixtures. This is probably true in general for any procedure employing a kinetic-based method. Thus, in using any such method, it is necessary to have investigated the chemistry of the reactions used so as to anticipate errors resulting from the chemical nature and composition of the samples.

SELECTED BIBLIOGRAPHY

CROUCH, S. R., in J. S. Mattson, H. B. Mark, Jr., and H. C. MacDonald, Jr., eds., *Computers in Chemistry and Instrumentation*, vol. 3, chap. 3. New York: Marcel Dekker, 1972. *The sections on the mathematical basis of kinetic methods were condensed from this chapter. It is an excellent source for instrumental and computerization consideration in rate measurement.*

GRIENKE, R. A., and MARK, H. B., JR., "Kinetic Aspects of Analytical Chemistry," *Anal. Chem.*, *46*, 413R (1974).

GUILBAULT, G. G. *Enzymatic Methods of Analysis.* Oxford: Pergamon, 1970.

MALMSTADT, H. V.; CORDOS, E. A.; and DELANEY, C. J., "Automated Reaction-Rate Methods," *Anal. Chem.*, *44*(12), 26A (1972).

MALMSTADT, H. V.; DELANEY, C. J.; and CORDOS, E. A., "Instruments for Rate Determination," *Anal. Chem.*, *44*(12), 79A (1972).

MARK, H. B., JR.; RECHNITZ, G. A.; and GREINKE, R. A. *Kinetics in Analytical Chemistry.* New York: Wiley-Interscience, 1968. *Much of the sections on methods of the analysis of mixtures was condensed from this source.*

PARDUE, H. L., in C. N. Reilley and F. W. McLafferty, eds., *Advances in Analytical Chemistry and Instrumentation*, vol. 7, pp 141–200. New York: Wiley-Interscience, 1968. *Instrumental considerations in rate measurement.*

SANTINI, R. E.; MILANO, M. J.; and PARDUE, H. L., "Rapid Scanning Spectroscopy: Prelude to a New Era in Analytical Spectroscopy," *Anal. Chem.*, *45*, 915A (1973).

YATSIMIRSKII, K. B. *Kinetic Methods of Analysis.* Oxford: Pergamon, 1966.

PROBLEMS

1. The conversion of γ-hydroxyvaleric acid to γ-valerolactone is an acid-catalyzed reaction. The reaction can be followed by taking aliquots of the reaction mixture and titrating with standardized base. The following data were obtained for the reaction, run at 25°C with 0.025 M HCl as catalyst:

Time, min	% Converted	Time, min	% Converted
48	17.3	238	61.3
76	25.7	289	68.1
124	38.9	∞	100
204	55.6		

(a) Ascertain that the overall reaction is first order (plot the appropriate graph). (b) Determine the rate constant for the reaction from the slope of the plot and from the appropriate equation for first-order kinetics using the second, fourth, and sixth points. (c) If the first-order rate constant determined above is equal to $k_2[H^+]$, where k_2 is the second-order rate constant for the forward reaction, calculate k_2. (d) How long would it require to obtain a 40% yield of the product at 25°C in 0.075 M HCl? A 90% yield?

2. The alkaline hydrolysis of an ester is a bimolecular second-order reaction. Walker [*Proc. Roy. Soc.*, *A78*, 157 (1906)] obtained the following data at 25°C for the reaction

$$CH_3COOCH_3 + OH^-$$
$$= CH_3COO^- + CH_3OH$$

The initial concentrations of sodium hydroxide and methyl acetate were both 0.0100 M.

Time, min	Amount Converted, mM	Time, min	Amount Converted, mM
3	2.60	10	5.36
4	3.17	12	5.84
5	3.66	15	6.37
6	4.11	18	6.81
7	4.50	21	7.12
8	4.81	25	7.46

Prove that the data satisfy the second-order equation $[1/[A] - 1/[A]_0 = kt]$ by plotting the appropriate graph, and determine the rate constant for the reaction.

3. At 298°C azomethane decomposes according to

$$CH_3NNCH_3 \longrightarrow C_2H_6 + N_2$$

The first-order rate constant for the reaction is 2.50×10^{-4} sec^{-1}. Determine the partial pressures of the reactant and products after 30 min if the initial azomethane pressure is 200 torr.

4. The acid-catalyzed inversion of sucrose can be monitored by measuring the angle of rotation α of plane-polarized light with time, since the rotation shifts from dextro in sucrose to levo in invert sugar. The following data were obtained on sucrose inversion at 30°C in 2.5 M formic acid.

For an initial sucrose concentration of 0.44 M:

t, hours	α	t, hours	α
0	57.90°	40	3.40°
4	48.50°	52	−2.95°
8	40.50°	85	−11.25°
15	28.90°	∞	−15.45°
27	13.50°		

For an initial sucrose concentration of 0.167 M:

t, hours	α	t, hours	α
0	22.10°	45	0.35°
5	17.85°	73	−3.20°
10	14.15°	94	−4.30°
20	8.65°	133	−5.10°
30	4.50°	∞	−5.50°

Determine the first-order rate constant at 30°C for each concentration. Does the constant vary with the sucrose concentration? Does it depend on the concentration unit chosen?

5. Kinetic data were obtained for the reaction of benzene diazonium chloride with water:

$$C_6H_5N_2Cl + H_2O = C_6H_5OH + N_2 + HCl$$

Time, min	HCl Generated, mM	Time, min	HCl Generated, mM
0	0	180	7.07
90	3.49	206	7.78
120	5.09	231	8.42
147	6.04	258	9.13
152	6.20		

The original solution was aqueous 27.37 mM $C_6H_5N_2Cl$ (25°C). Determine the order and the rate constant for the reaction, and calculate the time required for 90% and 99% reaction.

6. The reaction between methyl iodide and thiosulfate

$$CH_3I + S_2O_3{}^{2-} = CH_3S_2O_3{}^- + I^-$$

is followed by withdrawing 10.00-ml aliquots from the reaction mixture and quickly titrating the thiosulfate remaining with 0.0101 N iodine.

Time, min	Volume I_2 Solution, ml	Time, min	Volume I_2 Solution, ml
0	35.35	35.0	20.3
4.75	30.5	55.0	18.6
10.0	27.0	∞	17.1
20.0	23.2		

Determine the order and rate constant of the reaction.

7. The following exchange reaction occurs at the presence of strong acid

$$[Co(NH_3)_5H_2{}^{18}O]^{3+} + H_2O \rightleftharpoons [Co(NH_3)_5H_2O]^{3+} + H_2{}^{18}O$$

If the mole fraction of ^{18}O in the complex is initially 0.006649, after 25.1 hours is 0.004366, and at equilibrium is 0.002192, calculate the first-order rate constant for the reaction and the half-life of the cobalt complex in aqueous solution.

8. For the enzymatic conversion of fumarate to L-malate at pH 7, the Michaelis constant is 4.0×10^{-6} M and the maximum reaction rate is 1.3×10^3 [E] sec^{-1}, where [E] is the total molar concentration of the enzyme. For the reverse reaction the Michaelis constant and maximum reaction rate are 10×10^{-6} M and 0.80×10^3 [E] sec^{-1}, respectively. Calculate the equilibrium constant for the reaction.

9. Explain clearly the difference between thermodynamic- and kinetic-based analytical techniques.

10. Are kinetic methods of analysis commonly used? If so, in what applications?

11. What advantages do kinetic-based techniques have? What disadvantages?

12. Discuss the special instrumentation requirements encountered in kinetic-based methods.

13. What are the *derivative* and the *integral* approaches to kinetic analysis? Compare their applicability and their advantages (or disadvantages).

19

Radiochemical Methods of Analysis

WILLIAM D. EHMANN
MORTEZA JANGHORBANI

Radiochemical methods of analysis employ radioactivity, with or without chemical manipulations, to obtain qualitative or quantitative information about the composition of materials. This information may concern the nature and quantity of elements or the specific chemical form of the component of interest. For example, qualitative and quantitative determinations of elements present in river waters can be readily accomplished; on the other hand, radiochemical methods can be used to determine the quantity of vitamin B_{12} (which contains an atom of cobalt) in a mixture of similar organic compounds. The fundamental difference between this method of analysis and all others is that, in this method, one either induces radioactivity in the sample or adds a radioactive substance to the sample.

Radiochemical methods of analysis are used in a wide range of analytical applications. Not only can these methods be used to obtain information regarding the nature and quantities of substances present in materials of interest, but radioactive elements can also be employed as tracers to study various physicochemical processes. Radioactive substances can be used to follow the movement of elements or of specific compounds in soils and plants, the absorption of elements in the body, and the self-diffusion of lead atoms in metallic lead, among other applications. Although these tracer applications are of great practical value, the present chapter will be concerned only with applying radioactivity to determining the presence and quantity of elements and compounds in various materials—that is, the use of radioactivity in chemical analysis.

19.1 FUNDAMENTALS OF RADIOACTIVITY

In this section, we will discuss only those fundamental aspects of radioactivity directly relevant to radiochemical analysis. For a more detailed treatment, the references given at the end of the chapter should be consulted.

All atomic nuclei are made up of protons and neutrons (known collectively as *nucleons*); the only exception is the lightest hydrogen nucleus, which consists of a single proton. The *atomic number* (Z) of an atom is the number of protons present in its nucleus (also the number of electrons in the neutral atom). The sum of protons (Z) and neutrons (N) in a nucleus is referred to as the *mass number* (A). The mass number should not be confused with the atomic or nuclidic mass, which is the mass of the atom relative to that of a ^{12}C atom (which is, by definition, exactly 12.000... *atomic mass units*, amu).

All atoms whose nuclei contain the same number of protons (and are thus atoms of the same element) have virtually the same chemical properties, because these properties are determined by the structure of the orbital-electron cloud. But, atoms of the same element may have a different number of neutrons and, therefore, a different mass-number. Atoms having the same Z and a different A are referred to as *isotopes*. In nature, with few exceptions, the abundance of each isotope is in a fixed ratio to that of the other isotopes of the same element; the relative abundance of any isotope (usually expressed in units of atom percent) is called its *isotopic abundance*. Each element has two types of isotopes: (1) *stable isotopes*, and (2) *radioactive isotopes*. Stable isotopes are those whose nuclei have not been observed to undergo spontaneous radioactive disintegration. The nuclei of radioactive isotopes, on the other hand, undergo spontaneous disintegration and eventually become stable isotopes of some element. Radioactive isotopes disintegrate by emitting *electromagnetic radiation* (x- or gamma rays),* by emitting *elementary particles* (α, β, n, p, or e^-), or by undergoing *fission* (breaking up into smaller nuclei). These isotopes are either *artificial* (manmade, such as ^{60}Co) or *natural* (such as ^{40}K).

Whether or not a given isotope is stable depends on the particular number of protons and neutrons present in its nucleus and on the state of excitation of the nucleus. If one plots the atomic numbers of all stable isotopes as a function of the number of neutrons present in their nuclei, one obtains the graph shown in Figure 19.1. In order to form stable light elements, approximately equal numbers of neutrons and protons are required; however, for the heavier elements, considerably more neutrons are needed. This deviation from $Z/N = 1$ occurs because protons are charged particles and repel each other according to Coulomb's law. Since the nucleus is held together by strong, short-range binding forces between nucleons, additional forces are needed to dilute the increased Coulombic repulsion forces.

Nuclei that do not fall on this curve are unstable and disintegrate, emitting the appropriate particles or radiation until the final product nuclei are on the curve. If the unstable *nuclide*† is on the proton-rich side of the curve, it disintegrates by emitting a *positron*,‡ or by a related process known as *electron capture*. The *daughter* nuclide will then have one less proton and one more neutron than the *parent* nuclide. If, on the other hand, the radionuclide is on the neutron-rich side of the curve, it

---

* X-rays are electromagnetic radiations resulting from an orbital-electron rearrangement in the atom, whereas gamma-rays are emitted directly by the nucleus. Only their point of origin distinguishes one from the other.

† Nuclide is a general term referring to a nucleus containing Z protons and N neutrons; if the nuclide is radioactive, it is called a radionuclide.

‡ A positron is a particle having the mass of an electron, but a unit positive charge. Its symbol is β^+.

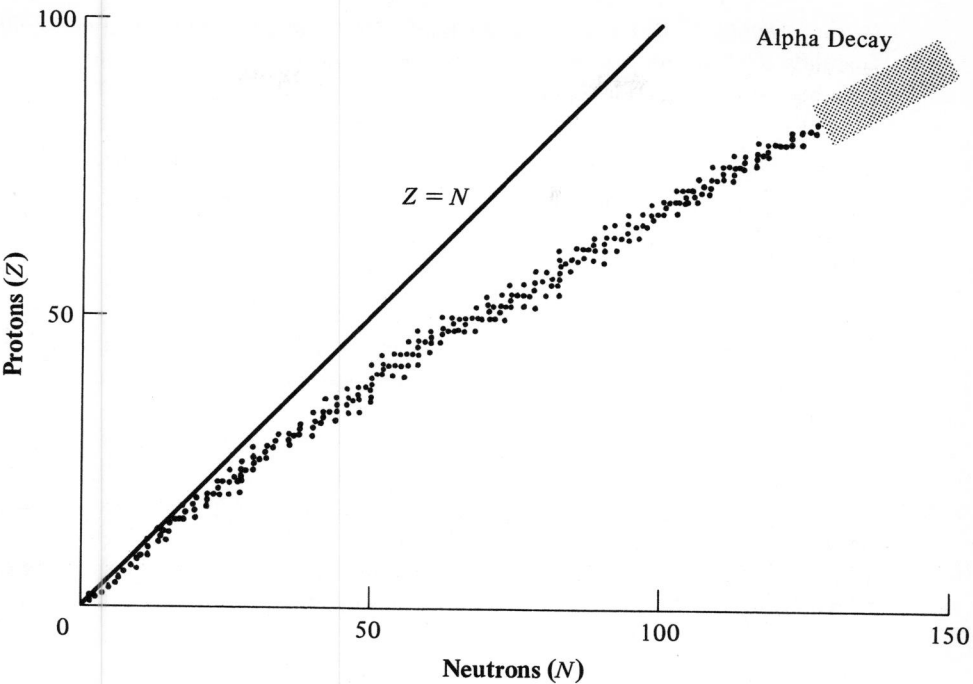

FIGURE 19.1. *The line of beta stability. Each point corresponds to a stable isotope.*

emits a *negatron** and the daughter nuclide will contain one less neutron and one more proton than the parent nuclide. For heavy nuclides, emission of an *alpha particle* (the nucleus of an ordinary helium atom) is also very common. The daughter product of an alpha decay contains two protons and two neutrons less than does the parent nuclide.

Rates of Disintegration

Not all radionuclides disintegrate at the same rate. The disintegration of any radionuclide is a first-order process and follows Equation 19.1:

$$-\frac{dN}{dt} = \lambda N \qquad (19.1)$$

where N = the number of radioactive atoms of a specific radionuclide present at time t
λ = the *nuclear-decay constant* in $\sec^{-1}$

The left-hand side of Equation 19.1, dN/dt, is the number of disintegrations taking place per unit time. Each radionuclide has its own characteristic nuclear-decay constant. The minus sign indicates that the decay results in a decrease in N. Equation 19.1 indicates that the rate of decay of any radionuclide is directly proportional

---

* A negatron is an ordinary negative electron emitted from the nucleus. Its symbol is β^-. It is also often called a β-*ray* or a β-*particle*.

to the number of those atoms present at that time. One can use this equation to calculate N, the number of radioactive atoms present at any time t, by separating variables and integrating to give

$$N = N_0 e^{-\lambda(t-t_0)} \qquad (19.2)$$

N_0 is the number of radioactive atoms present at time t_0, which is the reference point in time. For convenience, t_0 is generally taken to be zero time, in which case Equation 19.2 simplifies to

$$N = N_0 e^{-\lambda t} \qquad (19.3)$$

Equation 19.3 states that if, at time $t = 0$, there are N_0 radioactive atoms having a nuclear-decay constant λ, then at any later time t there will be N radioactive atoms remaining, and $(N_0 - N)$ radioactive atoms will have undergone radioactive decay during the time t.

A convenient measure of how fast a radionuclide disintegrates is the *half-life* (H) of the radionuclide. This parameter is defined as the length of time required for one-half of a statistically large number of radioactive atoms to undergo radioactive decay. Thus, if there are N_0 radioactive atoms at time $t = 0$, one half-life later there will be $N_0/2$ radioactive atoms of the original radionuclide remaining. From Equation 19.3, it can be shown that the relationship between the half-life and the decay constant of a radionuclide is

$$H = \frac{0.693}{\lambda} \qquad (19.4)$$

Since each radionuclide has its own characteristic decay-constant, its half-life has a definite value. Half-lives of radionuclides vary over a very large range. For instance, one radioactive isotope of boron has a half-life of about 3×10^{-19} sec, whereas the half-life of naturally occurring bismuth is greater than 2×10^{18} years.

From a knowledge of the half-life of any radionuclide, one can accurately predict the relative amount of that nuclide at any time later than or prior to some reference time. This fact is extensively employed in determining the ages of materials by methods of radioactive dating. More importantly, as far as this chapter is concerned, Equation 19.1 can be used to determine the amount of radioactive material present at any given time in a sample. If the sample contained a single radionuclide, its amount could be measured by simply measuring the absolute activity of the sample with an appropriate detection system (see Sec. 19.3). Combining Equations 19.1 and 19.3,

$$A = -\frac{dN}{dt} = \lambda N_0 e^{-\lambda t} \qquad (19.5)$$

One can measure A, the *absolute activity*,* experimentally and then calculate N_0, given knowledge of the decay constant λ and the decay time t.

---

* Activity is the measure of the number of specific particles or radiations emitted per unit time (commonly, per second). In contrast, the absolute activity (A) of a given radionuclide in units of disintegrations per second (dps) or disintegrations per minute (dpm) is the total number of disintegrations taking place per unit time without regard to the distribution of emitted particles or radiations. For example, one could measure either the positron or the negatron activity from a ^{64}Cu source (a radionuclide that decays by both modes) or the absolute activity of the source, which is independent of the mode of decay. The fraction of decays occurring by either path is described by the *branching ratio*.

If the sample contains more than one radionuclide, the method of activity measurement can still be used with the following modifications. The total (gross) activity of a sample containing several independently decaying radionuclides is

$$A_{tot} = \lambda_1 N_1 + \lambda_2 N_2 + \cdots$$

or

$$A_{tot} = \lambda_1 (N_0)_1 e^{-\lambda_1 t} + \lambda_2 (N_0)_2 e^{-\lambda_2 t} + \cdots \qquad (19.6)$$

Inspection of Equation 19.6 shows that, if one knows the nature of the radionuclides present in the sample, one should be able to calculate their abundances [$(N_0)_1$, $(N_0)_2$, and so on], by making the appropriate number of activity measurements as a function of time.

For example, if the sample contains only two independent radionuclides, two independent measurements will permit application of the two following simultaneous equations with two unknowns, $(N_0)_1$ and $(N_0)_2$:

$$(A_{tot})_{t_1} = \lambda_1 (N_0)_1 e^{-\lambda_1 t_1} + \lambda_2 (N_0)_2 e^{-\lambda_2 t_1} \qquad (19.7)$$

$$(A_{tot})_{t_2} = \lambda_1 (N_0)_1 e^{-\lambda_1 t_2} + \lambda_2 (N_0)_2 e^{-\lambda_2 t_2} \qquad (19.8)$$

In general, it should be possible to calculate the individual abundances of all radioisotopes present in the sample by making the appropriate number of activity measurements, provided that two conditions are met: (1) the half-lives of the sample constituents are sufficiently different, and (2) the half-lives are such that at least one of the components has significantly changed its activity during the time interval between consecutive measurements.

A general method for distinguishing among the radioactive constituents in a sample is to plot the logarithm of total observed activity as a function of time. First, consider a single-component system. Taking the logarithm of Equation 19.5 yields

$$\log \left(-\frac{dN}{dt} \right) = \log (\lambda N_0) - 0.43 \, \lambda t \qquad (19.9)$$

Therefore, if $\log \left(-\frac{dN}{dt} \right)$ is plotted as a function of time, one obtains a straight line whose slope is a measure of the half-life of the radionuclide and whose intercept at $t = 0$ is a measure of N_0. In practice, one plots the observed activity on the logarithmic ordinate of semilog graph paper as a function of time, which is plotted on the linear abscissa. If there were more than one radioactive component present in the sample, the observed activity at any time would be the sum of the activities of all components. A plot of total activity on semilog graph paper as a function of time would then appear as a curve. However, if the half-lives of the components are sufficiently different and if the time of experiment is long compared with at least one of the half-lives involved, one can graphically resolve this composite curve into its component straight lines. By extrapolating these straight lines to $t = 0$, one can then calculate the abundance of each of the radionuclides. Figure 19.2 shows such a plot for a two-component system.

Normally, the experiment is conducted for a sufficient length of time that all but the longest-lived component have decayed essentially completely, and the longest-lived component, therefore, produces a straight-line plot. One then fits the best

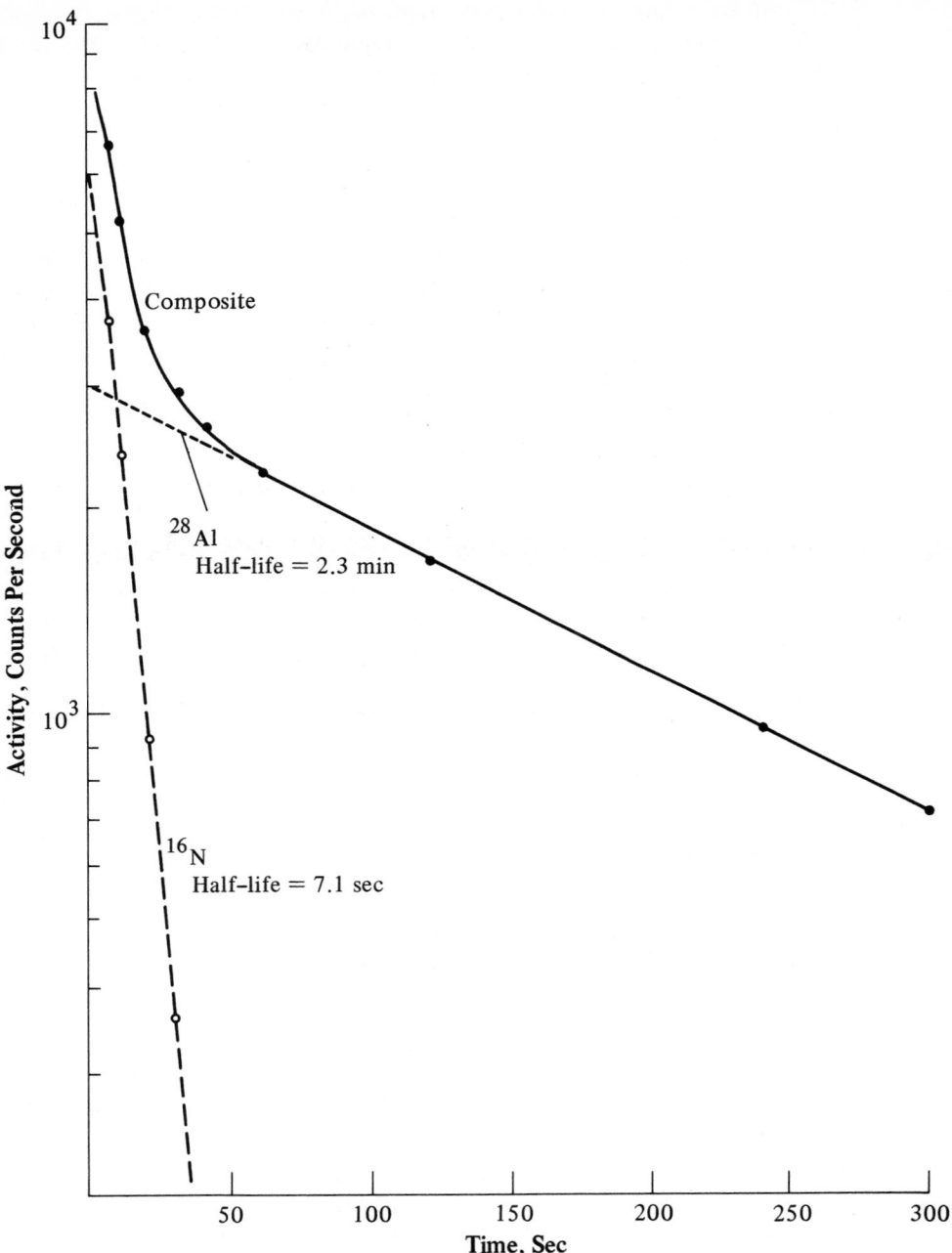

FIGURE 19.2. *Two-component decay curve for ^{28}Al and ^{16}N.*

straight line to this linear portion (computer line-fitting routines are commonly used) and extrapolates it to the origin. Point-by-point subtraction of this fitted straight line from this composite curve leaves another composite curve with one less member than the original one and whose end portion is also a straight line. Repetition of this *stripping* technique will give all component straight lines, from which one can calculate the quantities $(N_0)_1$, $(N_0)_2$, etc. Ordinarily, the stripping technique is applied to mixtures of three or fewer components.

In general, the great advantage of the decay curve and stripping method over the method of direct calculation using simultaneous equations is that these plots often reveal the presence of unsuspected contaminant radionuclides in the sample. In addition, a large number of points are used to characterize each straight line in the decay curve and stripping method. Therefore, the effect of random errors associated with single determinations is lessened. The advantage of the method of simultaneous equations lies in the simplicity of the experiment and subsequent mathematical manipulations, but the method assumes a priori knowledge of all sample components.

For the resolution of a decay curve of a two-component system whose half-lives are not greatly different, another simple method is often used. Writing Equation 19.6 for a two-component system and multiplying both sides by $e^{\lambda_1 t}$,

$$A_{\text{tot}}(e^{\lambda_1 t}) = \lambda_1(N_0)_1 + \lambda_2(N_0)_2 e^{(\lambda_1 - \lambda_2)t} \qquad (19.10)$$

If one plots $A_{\text{tot}}e^{\lambda_1 t}$ as a function of $e^{(\lambda_1 - \lambda_2)t}$, a straight line is obtained whose intercept and slope may be used to directly calculate $(N_0)_1$ and $(N_0)_2$.

19.2 NUCLEAR REACTIONS AND TYPES OF RADIOACTIVE DECAY

By convention, a nuclide is specified as $^A_Z X$, where X is the chemical symbol for the element, the superscript A denotes the mass number, and the subscript Z the atomic number of the nuclide. When particles or radiations interact with a nucleus, nuclear reactions occur. For example, a neutron may interact with the nucleus of the nuclide $^{27}_{13}$Al according to

$$^{27}_{13}\text{Al} + ^1_0\text{n} \longrightarrow ^{28}_{13}\text{Al} + Q \qquad (19.11)$$

This equation states that a neutron is added to the nucleus of $^{27}_{13}$Al to produce the nuclide $^{28}_{13}$Al and the *energy* Q, which appears largely as gamma radiation.

Q may be calculated in MeV as follows:

$$Q = 931 \left[\sum_{i=1}^{n} m_{r_i} - \sum_{i=1}^{k} m_{p_i} \right] \qquad (19.12)$$

where m_{r_i} = the mass of reactant r_i in amu
m_{p_i} = the mass of product p_i in amu

The constant 931 is the proportionality constant between mass in units of amu and energy in units of million electron volts (MeV). If the value of Q is positive, energy is produced and the reaction will proceed spontaneously; such a reaction is said to be *exoergic*. If Q is negative, energy is required for the reaction to proceed and the reaction is said to be *endoergic*. The energy required to initiate endoergic reactions is often supplied in the form of kinetic energy of the incident particle. The energy released in exoergic reactions may be in the form of electromagnetic radiation (called gamma radiation), or in the form of kinetic energy given to emitted particles.

An abbreviated form is usually used for writing nuclear reactions. The reaction given in Equation 19.11 can be written as

$$^{27}_{13}\text{Al}(n, \gamma)^{28}_{13}\text{Al} \qquad (19.13)$$

This is understood to mean that a neutron is absorbed by a nucleus of $^{27}_{13}\text{Al}$ and gamma radiation is emitted, resulting in the formation of a product nucleus $^{28}_{13}\text{Al}$. The product nucleus of a nuclear reaction can be either stable or radioactive. If the product nuclide is radioactive, it will eventually decay to a different nuclide. The most common modes of decay are emission of alpha particles, beta particles, and gamma rays; other particles or radiations can also be emitted in radioactive decay, but they are of little analytical utility and will not be discussed here. Radioactive decay may involve a single-step transformation or may proceed through a series of steps. An example of the former is

$$^{28}_{13}\text{Al} \longrightarrow {}^{28}_{14}\text{Si} + \beta^- \qquad (19.14)$$

The nuclide $^{28}_{14}\text{Si}$ is stable with respect to further nuclear decay. The latter type of decay scheme is exemplified by

$$^{47}_{20}\text{Ca} \longrightarrow {}^{47}_{21}\text{Sc} + \beta^-$$
$$\downarrow \qquad\qquad (19.15)$$
$$^{47}_{22}\text{Ti} + \beta^-$$

The final product nuclide, $^{47}_{22}\text{Ti}$, is stable.

Beta Decay

There are three forms of beta decay. One is called *negatron* (β^-) emission. Negatrons are ordinary electrons that are emitted from nuclei as the result of a nuclear transformation. Negatron decay is illustrated by the symbolic equation

$$^A_Z\text{X} \longrightarrow {}_{z+1}^A\text{Y} + \beta^- + \bar{\nu} \qquad (19.16)$$

where $\bar{\nu}$ is an antineutrino, an elusive particle of no practical analytical interest. The daughter nuclide Y formed by this transformation may initially exist in an excited state or in its ground state. If negatron emission results in an excited daughter state, deexcitation usually follows promptly, with the emission of one or several gamma rays. The radionuclides ^3H (tritium) and ^{14}C are examples of pure negatron emitters that decay directly to the ground state of their daughters without the emission of gamma radiation. Many other negatron emitters do have accompanying gamma radiations which may be detected in preference to measuring the short-ranged negatrons, which may be absorbed within the sample.

The second beta-decay process is *positron* (β^+) emission. Positron decay is illustrated by the symbolic equation

$$^A_Z\text{X} \longrightarrow {}_{z-1}^A\text{Y} + \beta^+ + \nu \qquad (19.17)$$

where ν is a *neutrino*—again of no analytical utility. The radionuclides $^{22}_{11}Na$ and $^{65}_{30}Zn$ are examples of positron emitters commonly used in radioanalytical work. Again, the daughter nuclide may be formed in an excited state or in its ground state. Hence, gamma radiation may also accompany this mode of decay.

The third beta-decay process is electron capture. In this process, the nucleus captures an orbital electron (usually a K-electron), which creates an orbital vacancy. This vacancy is then filled by electrons from higher energy levels. The energy difference between the electronic energy levels involved is released in the form of x-rays or by the emission of low energy *Auger* or *secondary electrons* (see Chap. 15) from higher electronic-energy orbitals. The symbolic equation for this process is similar to that for positron decay, but no positrons are emitted from the nucleus. Gamma radiation may also accompany this type of beta decay. The x-rays emitted in electron-capture decay are sometimes useful for analytical determinations. An example of a radionuclide decaying by electron capture is

$$^7_4Be + e^- \longrightarrow {}^7_3Li + \text{x-rays} + \nu \tag{19.18}$$

The energy distribution of beta particles emitted in negatron or positron decay is continuous (Fig. 19.3). The maximum energy associated with the distribution is called E_{max} and is characteristic of the particular nuclear transformation. At energies less than this, part of the energy resides in the neutrino or antineutrino emitted with the beta particle; the sum of the two energies is equal to the characteristic maximum energy.

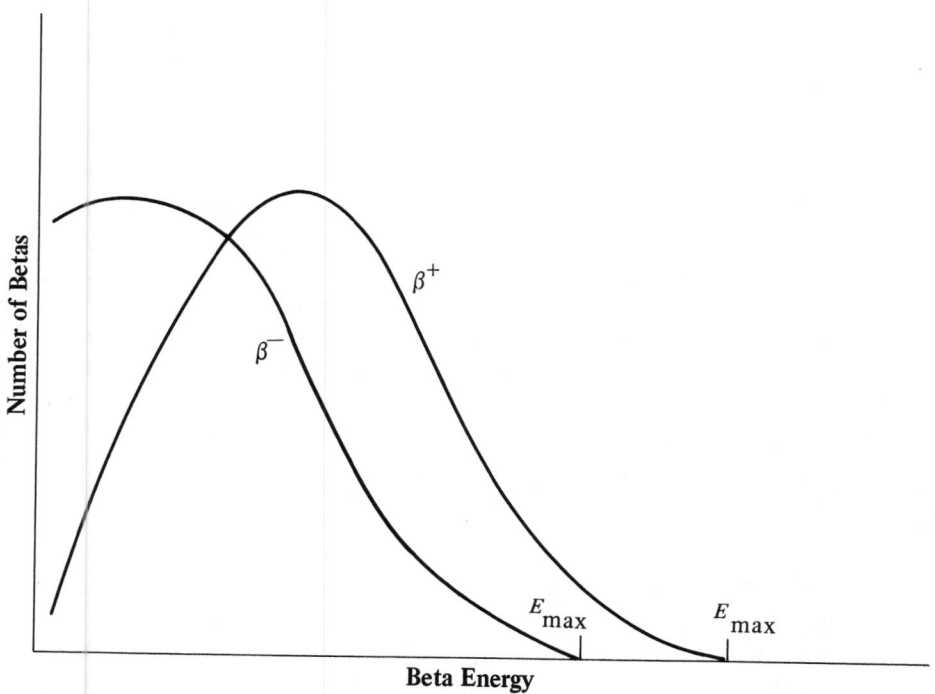

FIGURE 19.3. *Spectra of negatrons and positrons emitted during beta decay. E_{max} corresponds to the total energy of the transition.*

Beta particles generally have a short range in matter. For instance, beta particles from a transformation having $E_{max} = 1.0$ MeV are completely stopped by a 1.5 mm thickness of aluminum foil. From an analytical point of view, this is a very important observation. When counting beta rays, sample thickness becomes an extremely important parameter and must either be controlled accurately (all samples must have equal thicknesses), or appropriate corrections must be applied.

Negatrons commonly interact with matter in three ways: excitation, ionization, and bremsstrahlung. As negatrons pass through matter, they may interact with a bound electron and either eject the electron, forming an *ion pair* between the ejected electron and the ionized atom, or simply raise the electron to one of its excited levels. The incident negatron may lose part or all of its energy in each collision. On the other hand, high-energy beta particles may strike the target nucleus itself; the sudden deceleration in the strong electric field surrounding the nucleus generates an "electromagnetic shock wave," called *bremsstrahlung*, carrying away part of the kinetic energy of the electron.

Interactions of positrons with matter are similar to those encountered with negatrons. However, after dissipating most of its energy, the positron undergoes a process known as *annihilation*. The positron interacts with an electron in the vicinity of an atom and the masses of both particles are converted to energy according to Einstein's equation $E = mc^2$. Two gamma-ray photons, each having an energy equal to 0.511 MeV, are produced simultaneously. The detection of 0.511-MeV gamma rays usually indicates that a sample contains a positron-emitting radionuclide.

Alpha Decay

This type of decay is common among nuclei with high atomic number. Alpha decay is illustrated by

$$_Z^A X \longrightarrow {}_{Z-2}^{A-4}Y + {}_2^4He \tag{19.19}$$

An example of a radionuclide decaying by alpha emission is $_{84}^{210}Po$.

The emitted alpha particles have discrete energies. In passing through matter, they interact chiefly with electrons, dissociating molecules and exciting or ionizing molecules and atoms. The range of alpha particles in matter is much shorter than that of beta particles of similar energies. For example, a beam of 1.0-MeV alpha particles is stopped completely by a 3–4 μm thickness of aluminum foil (compared to about 1.5 mm for beta particles). This difference in penetrability is due to the lower velocity and greater charge of the alpha particle as compared to the beta particle. As in the case of beta decay, gamma radiation may accompany alpha decay, if the immediate product nuclide is formed in an excited state.

Electromagnetic Radiation

Electromagnetic radiation (photons) emitted from the nucleus is called gamma radiation. This radiation has neither charge nor mass, although its energy can be converted to an equivalent mass using the energy-mass equation ($E = mc^2$). Since gamma rays carry only energy, the emitting nuclide does not change in mass number or atomic number, thus preserving its chemical identity. Gamma rays emitted from any radionuclide have discrete energies characteristic of the different nuclear-energy states of that nuclide. Therefore, they can be used to "fingerprint" the materials from which they are emitted. The technique used to measure the numbers and energies of gamma rays emitted by radionuclides is called *gamma-ray spectrometry*.

The interaction of gamma radiation with matter is much more complex than the interaction of charged particles. There are three modes of interaction; the extent of each depends on the nature of the material and the energy of the radiation. In the first mode, called the *photoelectric effect*, the incoming gamma ray intersects with one of the orbital electrons in an absorber atom, ejecting that electron. The electron carries away kinetic energy equal to the energy of the gamma ray less the binding energy of the electron to the absorber atom. The ejected electron may then interact with other electrons, causing secondary ionization. The important characteristic of this process is the fact that essentially all of the energy of the gamma ray is given up in a single primary interaction. This process is most important for gamma rays of low energy (up to 1 MeV) and target materials with high atomic number.

The second process of gamma-ray interaction is called *Compton scattering*. In this process, the incoming gamma ray interacts with either a bound or free electron, losing only part of its energy in the encounter. If an electron is ejected from a bound state, its kinetic energy will be equal to the energy given up by the gamma ray less the binding energy of the electron. In this process, any one gamma ray may interact with many electrons. Of course, a gamma ray that has lost only part of its energy by this process may then undergo a photoelectric interaction, or simply escape from the absorber or detector.

The third process of gamma-ray interaction is *pair production*. This process occurs only when gamma rays have an energy equal to or greater than 1.02 MeV. In this process, the gamma-ray photon interacts with the absorber to produce an electron-positron pair. This is the reverse of the positron annihilation process discussed earlier. The reason for the minimum energy requirement is that 1.02 MeV is the energy equivalent of the two electron masses that must be created. The excess energy of the gamma ray ($E_\gamma - 1.02$ MeV) largely appears as kinetic energy given to the positron and the electron. The two particles may then interact further with other atomic electrons, causing secondary ionization.

Electromagnetic radiation penetrates much deeper into matter than do charged particles. Attenuation of gamma rays in matter follows an exponential law, similar to the Beer-Lambert law for absorption of visible light. To decrease the intensity of a 1.0-MeV parallel beam of gamma rays to one-half its original value requires a 4-cm thickness of aluminum (compared with 3–4 μm for alpha and 1.5 mm for beta radiation). In general, light materials are very ineffective for stopping gamma rays. Common shielding materials used are lead and high-density concrete.

19.3 DETECTION OF NUCLEAR RADIATION

In order to detect nuclear radiation, one ordinarily uses a transducer capable of converting the energy of the radiation into an electrical signal, usually a voltage pulse. Depending on the nature of the application, a satisfactory transducer must meet one or both of the following criteria: (1) there must be strict proportionality (preferably one-to-one) between the number of photons or particles interacting with the detector and the number of voltage pulses generated; and (2) there should be a strictly known relationship (preferably linear) between the energy that the radiation dissipates in the detector and the amplitude of the voltage pulse (called *pulse height*, PH) generated by the transducer.

Three types of radiation detectors are in common use: the *gas-ionization* detector, the *scintillation* detector, and the *solid-state* (or *semiconductor*) detector. Generally, the type used depends on the specific application. Gas-ionization detectors are commonly used for inexpensive detection of charged particles, scintillation detectors for beta- and gamma-ray detection, and solid-state detectors for x-ray and gamma-ray detection. The operation and properties of these detectors will be briefly described.

Gas-Ionization Detectors

A gas-ionization detector consists of two electrodes at different potentials and a (nonconducting) gas between them. The radiation produces ion pairs in the gas; the ions are then collected by the electrodes, yielding a voltage pulse which is measured. Figure 19.4 shows a typical cylindrical detector together with its associated measurement system. The detector proper is made of a cylindrical conducting material with an electrically isolated wire located on the central axis of the cylinder. A very thin window made of mylar, aluminum, or beryllium separates the radioactive source from the main volume of the detector (or the source can be placed directly inside the chamber). The chamber can either be permanently filled with some appropriate gas (e.g., 90% Ar + 10% CH_4), or a continuous flow of the gas can be sent through the chamber.

The detector operates as follows: as long as there is no ionizing radiation present, the filler gas acts as a very large resistor (R_2) and allows virtually no current

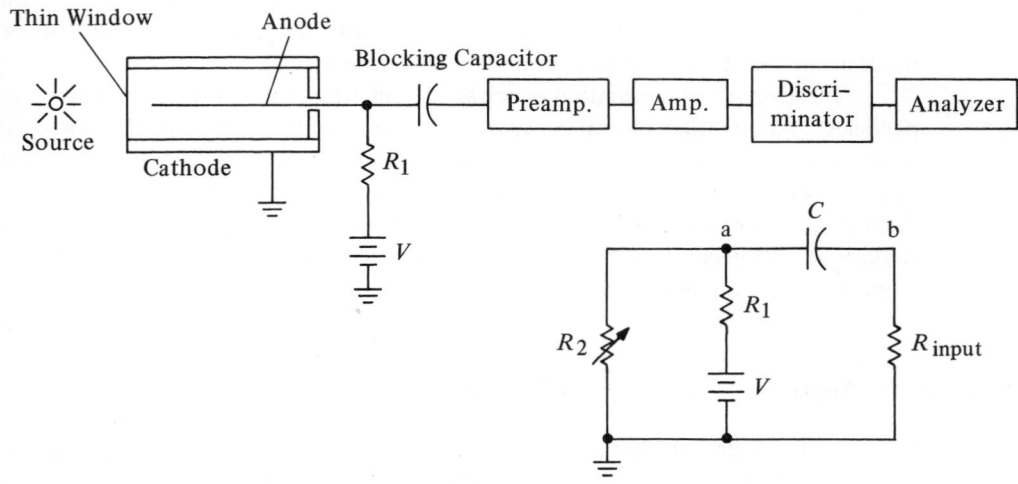

FIGURE 19.4. *A gas-ionization detector system. Top: Block diagram illustrating system components. Bottom: A simplified electrical analogue.*

to pass through the tube. The voltage appearing at point a is then equal to the bias voltage V of the battery or regulated power supply. Capacitor C acts to block this voltage from reaching point b. Therefore, the voltage seen by the input of the amplifier (R_{input}) is zero. Now, assume that a single ionizing particle enters the detector volume and produces a number of ion pairs. Since there is an electrostatic potential between the two electrodes, the positive ions are attracted towards the cathode and the electrons towards the anode. The electrons that reach the anode pass through the external circuit (made of R_1 and V), while an equal number of electrons flow from the negative terminal of the battery to the cathode to neutralize the positive ions that reach the cathode. This is analogous to a sudden drop in resistance of the filler gas (R_2 of Fig. 19.4). Thus, the voltage at point a will suddenly drop from V to v.

$$v = V \frac{R_2}{R_1 + R_2} \qquad (19.20)$$

R_2, the effective resistance of the filler gas, depends on the number of ion pairs produced. The overall effect is a sudden change in voltage at point a in the form of a sharp spike. This spike appears at the input of the preamplifier as a negative voltage pulse. The amplitude of this spike is the pulse height (PH).

Three types of ionization detectors, differing by the magnitude of the bias voltage V, are generally recognized: *ion chambers*, *proportional counters*, and *Geiger-Müller counters*. Each of these is best suited for a specific application. A plot of PH as a function of bias voltage has the general features shown in Figure 19.5. (It is important to note at this stage that PH is proportional to the number of ion pairs actually reaching the electrodes and not necessarily to how many were produced inside the detector, since some ion pairs may combine on their way and not reach the electrode—a phenomenon called ion recombination.)

Depending on their mode of production, two types of ion pairs are recognized: primary ion-pairs and secondary ion-pairs. The former are ion pairs produced from the direct interaction of radiation with the filler gas, whereas the latter are those produced by the energetic electrons of the primary ion pairs. The number of primary ion-pairs produced per incoming particle depends on the amount of energy dissipated inside the detector volume. If all of the energy of the incoming particle is dissipated inside the detector, the number of primary ion-pairs will then be directly proportional to the energy of the incoming radiation. The number of secondary ion-pairs produced depends on the kinetic energy of each primary electron and on the voltage applied to the detector.

To understand the curve in Figure 19.5, assume that a single particle of radiation enters the detector volume, dissipating all of its energy and producing 1000 primary ion-pairs. If the voltage applied is smaller than V_1, only a fraction of these primary ion-pairs will reach the electrodes. The remainder will undergo ion recombination. The higher the applied voltage (for $V < V_1$), the larger the number of primary ion-pairs reaching the electrodes and the larger the PH. This region of the curve is of limited practical value. For voltages between V_1 and V_2, the kinetic energy of the primary ion-pairs is sufficient for almost all of them to reach the electrodes, but is not enough to produce secondary ion-pairs. In this region PH is independent of applied voltage, but is directly proportional to the energy dissipated inside

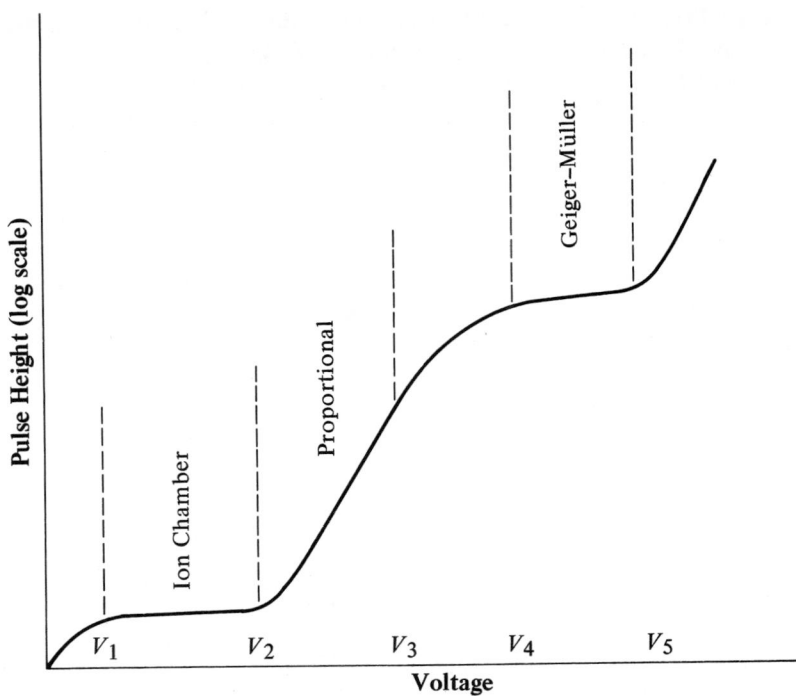

FIGURE 19.5. *Pulse height (PH) as a function of applied bias voltage for a gas-ionization detector.*

the detector. This is the region used for ion-chamber detectors. Since there are no secondary ion-pairs produced, PH is extremely small (the voltage pulse would be approximately 0.001 μV).

If the applied voltage is increased beyond V_2, the primary electrons will be subject to a relatively large electrostatic field and will acquire enough kinetic energy to, in turn, ionize the filler-gas atoms, producing secondary ion-pairs. In the region between V_2 and V_3, the total number of ion pairs reaching the electrodes, and thus PH, is proportional to both the applied voltage and the energy dissipated in the detector. This region is called the *proportional region* and is extensively used for measuring alpha and beta radiation. One important feature of this region is that PH is generally in the range of 1–100 mV and, therefore, is relatively easy to measure. Also, since PH is proportional to the energy dissipated in the detector, not only can the number of incoming particles per unit time be measured, but also their energies. Another very important feature of proportional counters is that of *detector dead-time*— only a short time (a few microseconds) passes between the entry of radiation and the time when all ion pairs are collected at the electrodes and current stops flowing. Therefore, radioactive sources with fairly high disintegration rates can be measured without correcting for detector dead-time losses.

When the applied voltage exceeds V_3, the electrostatic field becomes so large that a chain reaction results from the interaction of any ionizing particle, resulting in loss of proportionality between energy dissipated and PH. This proportionality is lost first gradually (region between V_3 and V_4) and then completely ($V_4 < V < V_5$) —the detector discharges throughout its entire volume. For the region between V_4 and V_5, PH becomes independent of the energy dissipated in the detector by the incoming particle, but may increase slightly with increasing applied voltage. This is called the *Geiger-Müller* region, and detectors operating in this region are referred to as *GM counters*. These counters produce large voltage pulses (a fraction of a volt to a few volts) and require little external amplification. Therefore, GM counting systems are often inexpensive. The basic limitations of GM counters are their large dead-time (a few hundred μsec per pulse) and their lack of energy discrimination. These counters are widely used for portable radiation monitors and for counting gross beta-activity in tracer experiments.

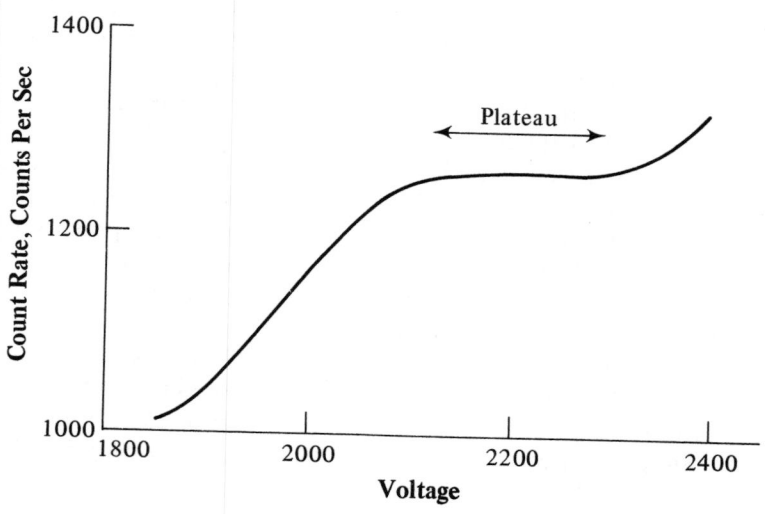

FIGURE 19.6. *The voltage plateau for a neutron proportional counter. Proper operating voltage is at the midpoint of the plateau.*

At voltages greater than V_5, the filler gas itself begins to ionize because of the large voltages involved, and produces a continuous discharge whether or not there is any ionizing radiation present. When using either proportional or GM counters, it is important to realize that the magnitude of the bias voltage may affect the observed count rate. Therefore, before using the counter, one must establish the proper bias voltage by counting an essentially constant-activity source with different bias voltages (Fig. 19.6). The proper operating voltage is that corresponding to the midpoint of the plateau. With a proportional counter, different plateaus are obtained for alpha and beta particles and, hence, discrimination is possible.

Scintillation Detectors

It was pointed out earlier that interaction of radiation with matter can result in the production of ion pairs. The electron from the ion pair can in turn produce secondary ionization, which is important in gas-ionization detectors. These secondary electrons can also electronically excite the atoms in the detection medium, which in turn can emit light quanta. *Fluors* or *phosphors* are materials in which such a sequence of events occurs. The number of light quanta emitted is proportional to the energy of the radiation absorbed, so these materials can be used as radiation detectors permitting energy discrimination. Detectors of this type are called *scintillation detectors*. Typical materials used as scintillators are thallium-doped NaI crystals, anthracene crystals, and certain organic compounds such as *p*-terphenyl dissolved in organic solvents. NaI(Tl) crystals are particularly efficient for gamma-ray detection because they contain a high-Z material (iodine) and have a relatively high density.

Liquid scintillators (organic scintillators dissolved in an appropriate solvent) are generally used for detecting beta particles. They are particularly useful for low-energy beta emitters such as ^{3}H or ^{14}C; these are used widely as tracers in biochemistry and organic chemistry. The sample is commonly dissolved in the solvent along with the scintillator. Special counters are required because the pulses generated by tritium, ^{3}H, are of nearly the same amplitude as the background pulses from thermionic emission in the photomultiplier detector at room temperature; therefore, the photo-multiplier and amplifier electronics are cooled to $-10°C$.

A scintillation detector generally consists of a fluor placed in close contact with a photomultiplier tube. The flashes of light emitted from the fluor enter the photo-multiplier, generating a large current pulse from each primary scintillation event. The current pulse is then converted to a voltage pulse, which is amplified and anal-yzed. The amplitude of this pulse is the PH, and is proportional to the energy origi-nally deposited in the fluor by the radiation.

As discussed previously, gamma rays have discrete, well defined energies. Each incoming gamma ray interacts with the detector material by one or more of the three processes discussed before, leaving part or all of its energy inside the detec-tor. Since each gamma ray (of the same energy) may deposit a different fraction of its initial energy, the output voltage pulses will not have identical PHs, although the PH distribution will be characteristic.

If the material of interest emits gamma rays having more than one charac-teristic energy, the PH distribution (gamma-ray spectrum) will be quite complex. In order to analyze such a spectrum, a multi-channel analyzer (MCA) is used with the scintillation detector. The MCA receives the voltage pulses, classifies each pulse according to its PH, and stores all the pulses of equal PH in the same memory loca-tion (channel). For example, a 400-channel analyzer can be calibrated to store a 10-V pulse in channel 400 and a 5-V pulse in channel 200. Any gamma ray giving rise to a PH of 7.5 V will be stored in channel 300, since the relationship between pulse height (gamma-ray energy) and channel number for a MCA is (generally) linear.

If one places a monoenergetic source of gamma radiation in front of a NaI(Tl) detector and uses a MCA to analyze the PH distribution of the detector, a spectrum similar to that in Figure 19.7 is obtained. Note that the total number of counts registered in each channel during the entire counting time is plotted as a function of channel number (which is proportional to energy). The actual gamma-ray spectrum is a continuum (the *Compton continuum*) with a peak (the *full-energy peak*), even if the source emits only gamma rays with a single energy. The Compton continuum, starting from low energies and ending at the point CE, is caused by incomplete de-

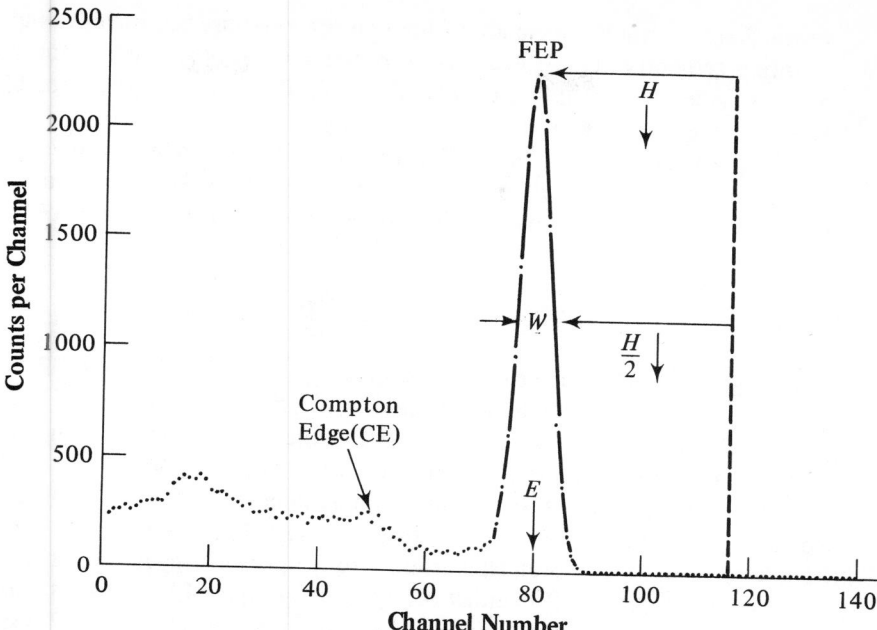

FIGURE 19.7.   *Gamma-ray spectrum of a* ^{137}Cs *source, using a 4″ × 4″ NaI(Tl) scintillation-detector.   The energy resolution of the detector is measured by the width (W) of the full-energy peak (FEP) at one-half the maximum height (H/2) of the FEP.*

position of the gamma-ray energy following a Compton interaction with the detector crystal.   The edge of the Compton continuum is called the *Compton edge* (CE) and corresponds to the maximum energy that a gamma ray can transfer to an electron following a Compton interaction.   The degraded gamma-ray produced in the Compton interaction may either escape the crystal or undergo further interaction.   If all the energy of the primary gamma ray is eventually deposited in the crystal, the event is recorded in the *full-energy peak* (FEP), together with the events from photoelectric-effect interactions.   If the degraded gamma ray escapes the crystal, the event is re-corded in the Compton continuum.

For analytical purposes, the most important feature of the spectrum is the FEP.   This peak includes all primary gamma-ray interactions that occur by the photoelectric effect, as well as those interactions caused by Compton scattering and pair production in which the energies of the secondary radiations or particles are completely dissipated in the detector crystal.   Although the gamma-ray energy is well defined, the FEP always has a certain width that is a function of both the type of detector and the energy of the FEP.   The energy corresponding to the channel at the center of the FEP is essentially the energy of the primary gamma ray that interacted with the crystal.   The area under this peak is related to the *activity* of the source at the beginning of the counting time (t_o) by

$$\text{FEP area} = \xi \int_0^{t_o} A_0 e^{-\lambda t}\, dt = \frac{\xi A_0}{\lambda}\left(1 - e^{-\lambda t_o}\right) \tag{19.21}$$

where ξ is the overall efficiency of the counting system and includes factors for the counting geometry and FEP detection probability; it is a constant for any fixed experimental set-up. A_0 is the activity of the specific gamma-ray emitted by the radioactive source at $t_c = 0$.

The width (W) of the FEP at the point corresponding to one-half its height (Fig. 19.7) is called the *full width at half maximum* (FWHM). The ratio of W to E_γ (both in units of energy) expressed in percent is called the *resolution* (R) of the detector:

$$R = \frac{W}{E_\gamma} 100\% \tag{19.22}$$

For a typical NaI(Tl) detector, R is about 8% for the 1.332-MeV FEP of ^{60}Co; for the newer Ge(Li) semiconductor detectors, R may be as low as 0.2% for ^{60}Co.

If a source emits gamma rays with different energies, a composite spectrum results. Figure 19.8 shows a composite spectrum for $^{54}_{25}$Mn, $^{60}_{27}$Co, and $^{137}_{55}$Cs. In any quantitative analysis using composite gamma-ray spectra, one needs to measure the area under each FEP. To do this, one must first select the portion of the FEP that lies above the Compton background from higher-energy peaks. This is commonly done by locating the left channel (C_1) just before the FEP appears to rise above the background and the right channel (C_2) at the point where the FEP disappears into

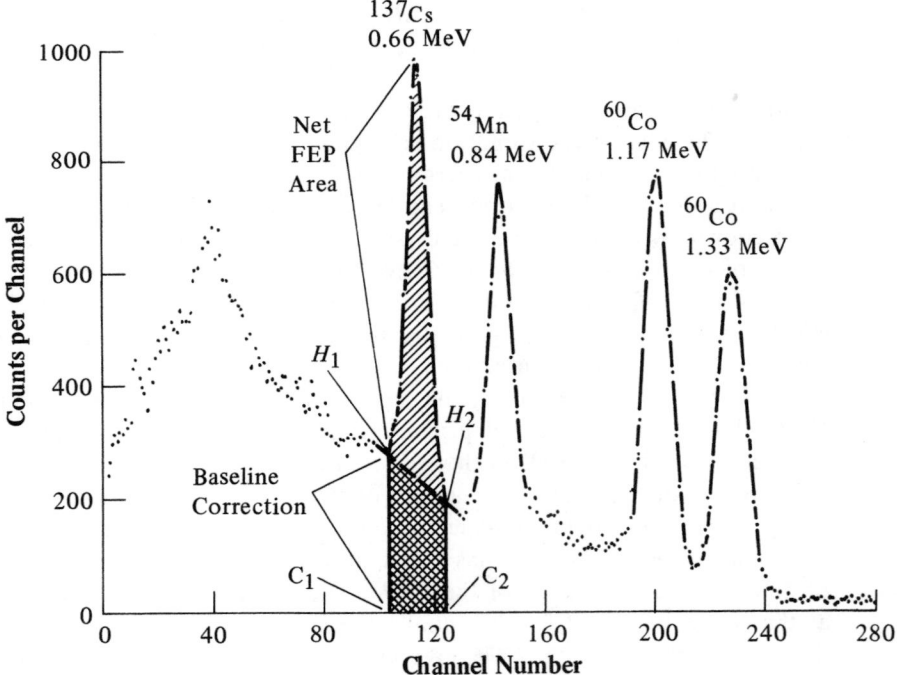

FIGURE 19.8. *A composite gamma-ray spectrum of* ^{137}Cs, ^{54}Mn, *and* ^{60}Co. *The net area of the full-energy peak (FEP), as obtained by baseline subtraction, is proportional to the activity of the radionuclide.*

the background. (This selection is sometimes difficult because of statistical variations, especially if the FEP of interest is small compared to the underlying Compton background.) One then calculates the net area of the FEP by subtracting from the total area the average background count per channel multiplied by the number of channels:

$$\text{Net area (counts)} = \left(\begin{array}{c}\text{Total area}\\ C_1 \to C_2\end{array}\right) - \left(\frac{H_1 + H_2}{2}\right)(C_2 - C_1 + 1) \quad \textbf{(19.23)}$$

It is often necessary to determine the statistical error involved in this calculation, following the procedures given in Section 19.5. If the background count distributions around C_1 and C_2 appear to be horizontal, it is often advisable to take averages of several channels preceding the FEP and several channels following the FEP in order to obtain a more representative baseline correction. There are several more sophisticated methods of baseline correction, but their discussion is beyond the scope of this chapter.

Solid-State or Semiconductor Detectors (SSD)

A SSD operates on the same principle as a gas-ionization detector, but using a solid semiconductor instead of a filler gas. A SSD is a block of some semiconductor material (commonly Ge or Si) into which has been incorporated a minute quantity of a Group IIIA element such as gallium (Fig. 19.9). The doped block, having a lower

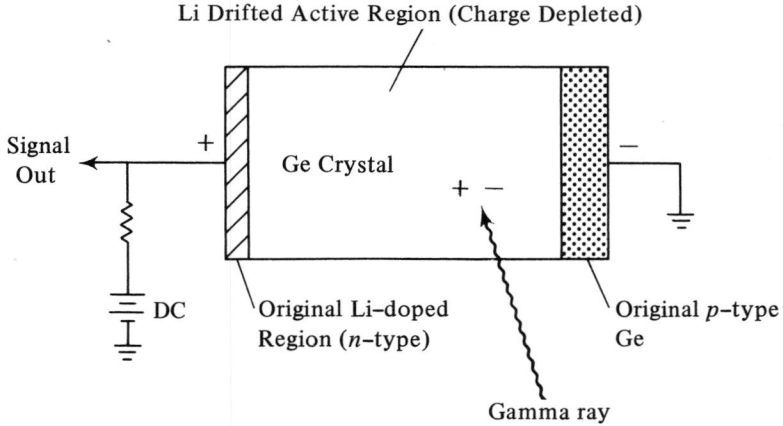

FIGURE 19.9. *Schematic diagram of a Ge(Li) detector.*

density of free electrons than the pure semiconductor, is called a p-type semiconductor. (An n-type semiconductor has a higher density of free electrons than the pure semiconductor.) A very thin layer (a few μm) of Li is then diffused into one surface of the block. If a reverse bias is applied between the p-side ($-$ bias) and the lithium side ($+$ bias) of the block, it will develop a *charge-depleted region*. This region has a very high effective resistance; by cooling the block to the temperature of liquid nitrogen, the current flow is decreased even further. The depletion region comprises the effective volume of the detector.

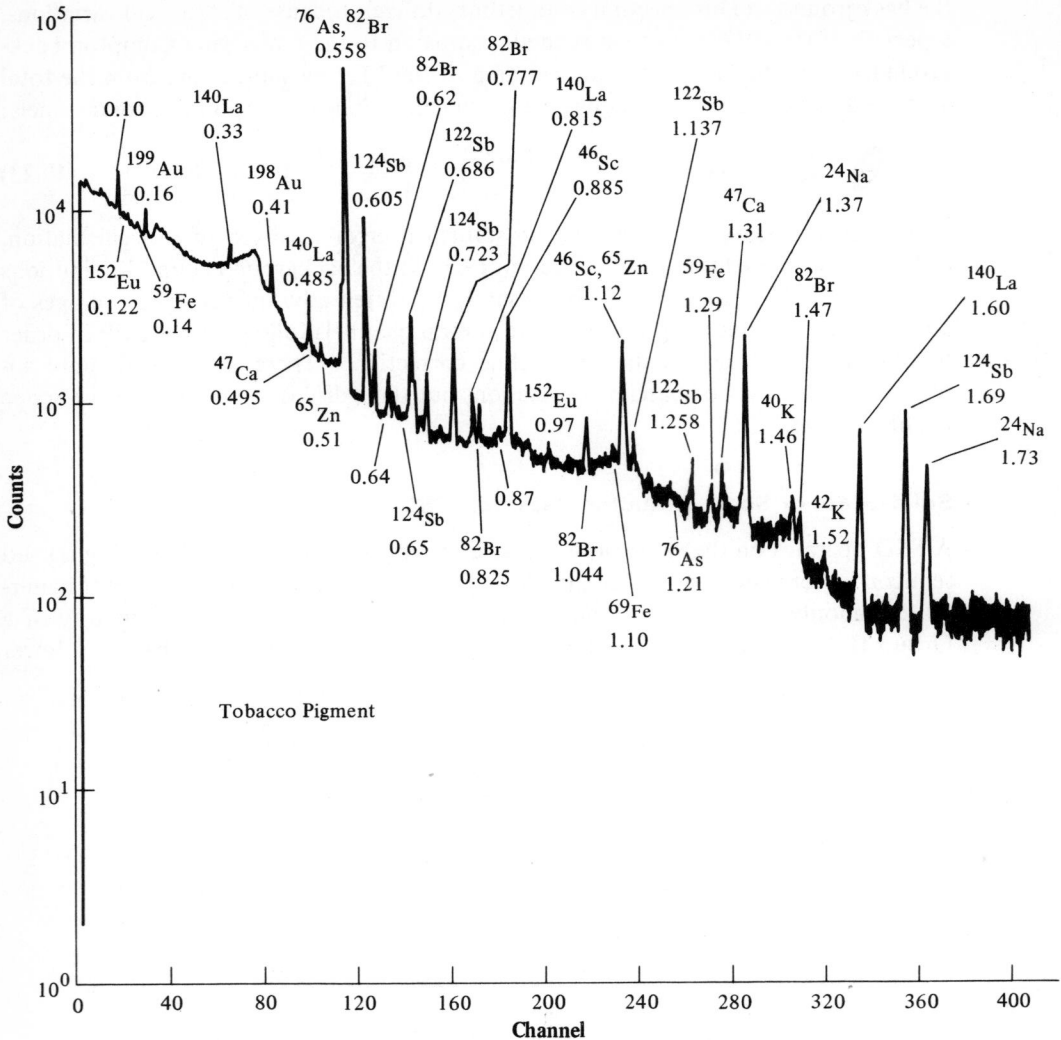

FIGURE 19.10. *A high-resolution gamma-ray spectrum obtained with a 35-cm³ Ge(Li) detector and a reactor-irradiated tobacco extract. Note that the number of counts is on a logarithmic scale.*

If a gamma ray enters the depletion region of the detector, it may interact and form an ion-electron pair, which may in turn cause secondary ionization on their way to the lithium side of the detector (the positive electrode). These electrons charge up the detector (the two electrodes of the detector separated by its dielectric form a capacitor) and produce a voltage pulse across the electrodes. The magnitude of this pulse is

$$V = \frac{Q}{C} \tag{19.24}$$

where Q = the total charge collected on the electrodes
C = the detector capacitance

This voltage pulse is very small (of the order of microvolts) and is amplified by a very sensitive preamplifier before it can be processed by conventional amplifiers and MCA's.

The two important parameters characterizing gamma-ray detectors are *resolution* and *efficiency*. The resolution of a detector measures its capability to separate (resolve) adjacent gamma rays and becomes very important when unwanted gamma rays are present near the FEP of interest. Efficiency, on the other hand, measures only the fraction of the incoming gamma rays of any given energy that contribute to the corresponding FEP. Ideally, the detector has as good a resolution (low R) and as large an efficiency (ξ) as possible. However, with present-day gamma-ray detectors these two properties are conflicting—detectors with high efficiency have poor resolving power and vice versa. Therefore, the type of detector chosen depends on the requirements of the analysis. For example, if a sample contains many gamma-emitting radionuclides, one must select a detector with good resolution and accept its lower inherent efficiency. On the other hand, if one is analyzing a region of the spectrum where there are no spectral interferences and the sample has a low activity, one would choose a detector having a high efficiency.

The fundamental advantage of a SSD over a scintillation detector is its superior resolution. The efficiency of a Ge(Li) SSD is often expressed relative to that of a $3'' \times 3''$ NaI(Tl) scintillation detector for a point source of ^{60}Co 1.332-MeV gamma rays at a distance of 25 cm from the detectors. Measured in this way, a typical Ge(Li) detector efficiency is only 10 percent. Therefore, although the resolution may be improved by a factor of 40, the efficiency is decreased by a factor of 10. The superior energy-resolution of a Ge(Li) detector is well illustrated by the spectrum in Figure 19.10. This spectrum was obtained by counting a reactor-irradiated extract from tobacco with a Ge(Li) detector. Gamma-ray peaks from at least a dozen elements can be distinguished.

19.4 NEUTRON ACTIVATION ANALYSIS

Radiochemical methods of analysis can be grouped according to whether one measures radioactivity present in the sample or employs some means of introducing radioactivity into an otherwise nonradioactive sample in order to analyze for some component. An example of the first type is the determination of radioactive ^{40}K in rock samples. The second type is exemplified by using labeled KI^*O_3 (I^* denoting a radioisotope of iodine) to determine the concentration of SO_2 in air by the radio-release method. This chapter will deal with the use of radioactivity to analyze otherwise nonradioactive substances.

Radiochemical methods discussed in this chapter are further divided into two general categories. Consider first those methods that induce radioactivity in the components of the sample to be analyzed. In all such methods, the sample is bombarded with nuclear radiations or particles (neutrons, protons, gamma rays, etc.) and the radiations emitted from the sample are measured, either simultaneously or subsequently. This general class of radiochemical methods is referred to as *activation analysis.* If the sample is bombarded with neutrons, the method is called *neutron activation analysis* (NAA), whereas if the sample is bombarded with gamma rays, the method is called *photon activation analysis.* Although the principles of the various forms of activation analysis are the same, the experimental capabilities and limitations of the method differ widely for different types of bombarding particles or radiation. Neutron activation analysis is currently the most widely employed technique and is the activation method that will be discussed in this chapter.

Principles of Neutron Activation Analysis

This method involves bombarding the sample with neutrons and measuring the radioactivity induced in the sample (commonly using gamma-ray spectrometry). In order to understand the principles of neutron activation analysis, some pertinent properties of neutrons and their interactions with matter will first be discussed.

Neutrons are nuclear particles with unit mass-number and neutral charge; they are commonly produced as a result of nuclear reactions or nuclear fission, and interact with matter almost exclusively by collisions with nuclei. A neutron interacts with the nucleus of an atom in several ways. It can undergo *elastic scattering*, whereby the neutron collides with the target nucleus and is scattered (similar to a moving billiard ball striking another (stationary) ball). Depending on the size of the target nucleus and the angle of collision, a varying amount of the kinetic energy of the neutron is lost in adding kinetic energy to the target nucleus. If the target nucleus has a low mass (hydrogen, deuterium, carbon, etc.), a considerable fraction of the energy of the incident neutron may be lost in the collision. This is why low-mass materials (H_2O, D_2O, etc.) are used to reduce the kinetic energy of fast neutrons produced by fission in nuclear reactors—a process known as *thermalization.*

A neutron also undergoes *inelastic scattering* with a target nucleus. In this case, the neutron scatters off the nucleus of a target atom, transfers part of its kinetic energy, and excites the nucleus to one of its higher energy levels. The target nucleus can then dissipate this excess energy by emitting electromagnetic radiation.

The third type of neutron interaction, the *capture reaction*, is the most important one for activation analysis. The incoming neutron is absorbed (captured) by the target nucleus, forming a new nuclide with the same atomic number as the parent nuclide, but one unit higher in mass number. An amount of energy equal to the binding energy of the neutron in that nucleus plus the kinetic energy of the incoming neutron is then available to raise the product nucleus to an excited state. The binding energy differs for different nuclides; but, for the most stable nuclides of intermediate mass, it is about 8 MeV/nucleon. Thus, even if the captured neutron had almost zero kinetic energy, the excess energy of the compound nucleus is about 8 MeV.

There are two ways in which the compound nucleus can release this excess energy: (1) it may radiate gamma rays, or (2) it may emit one or more nuclear particles (neutrons, protons, or alpha particles). Which of these two processes predominates depends on the total excitation energy of the compound nucleus. If sufficient energy is available, more than one reaction can take place.

In order to determine whether a given nuclear reaction can occur, the energy balance for the complete reaction must be calculated. If the overall reaction produces energy (Q is positive), the reaction proceeds spontaneously. Consider the nuclear reaction

$$^{27}_{13}\text{Al} + ^1_0\text{n} \longrightarrow ^{28}_{13}\text{Al} + Q \tag{19.25}$$

Using Equation 19.12,

$$\sum m_r = 26.981535 + 1.008665 = 27.990200 \text{ amu}$$

$$\sum m_p = 27.981908 = 27.981908 \text{ amu}$$

$$Q = 931\,(27.990200 - 27.981908) = +7.7 \text{ MeV}$$

The positive value of Q indicates that the reaction will proceed with neutrons having nearly zero kinetic energy ("thermal" neutrons have an energy of approximately 0.04 eV).

For the following reaction

$$^{27}_{13}\text{Al} + ^1_0\text{n} \longrightarrow ^{26}_{13}\text{Al} + 2\,^1_0\text{n} + Q \tag{19.26}$$

$Q = -13.1$ MeV. Since the value of Q is negative, this reaction cannot take place without the input of energy. The needed energy must be supplied by the kinetic energy of the incoming neutron. The minimum amount of kinetic energy that the incoming neutron must provide for the above reaction is somewhat more than the calculated 13.1 MeV, because part of the kinetic energy of the incoming neutron is merely transferred to the target nucleus ($^{27}_{13}\text{Al}$) to produce a moving product nucleus, according to the principle of conservation of momentum. The *laboratory threshold energy*, E_T, required to initiate the reaction may be calculated by means of

$$E_\text{T} = Q\left(\frac{m_\text{a} + m_\text{n}}{m_\text{a}}\right) \tag{19.27}$$

where m_a = the mass of the target nuclide
m_n = the mass of the neutron

Therefore,

$$E_\text{T} = -13.1\left(\frac{26.981535 + 1.008665}{26.981535}\right) = -13.5 \text{ MeV}$$

For the above reaction to occur, the incoming neutron must have at least 13.5 MeV kinetic energy.

Now consider the slightly more complicated case

$$^{27}_{13}\text{Al} + ^1_0\text{n} \longrightarrow ^{27}_{12}\text{Mg} + ^1_1\text{p} + Q \tag{19.28}$$

where $Q = -1.8$ MeV and $E_\text{T} = -1.9$ MeV. E_T is the minimum energy required for the reaction; but, once the proton is created, it has a low probability of leaving the nucleus because it is a charged particle. In order to increase the probability of leaving the nucleus, it must have enough energy to overcome the *coulombic barrier*. For the case of the emission of a neutron there is no coulombic barrier and, therefore, once the neutron is created it can leave the nucleus. The minimum kinetic energy that a charged particle must have in order to overcome the coulombic barrier and leave the nucleus is determined by the following equation:

$$E_c = -1.44 \frac{Z_a Z_b}{r_s} \qquad (19.29)$$

where
E_c = the coulombic barrier energy in MeV
Z_a = the atomic number of the product nuclide
Z_b = the atomic number of the emitted particle
$r_s = r_a + r_b$
r_a = the radius of the product nucleus
r_b = the radius of the emitted particle

The various radii are calculated using the empirical equation

$$r \approx 1.5 \, A^{1/3} \qquad (19.30)$$

where
A = the mass number
r = radius in Fermis (1 Fermi = 10^{-13} cm)

In this example,

$$E_c = -1.44 \left(\frac{12(1)}{1.5(27^{1/3} + 1^{1/3})} \right) = -2.9 \text{ MeV}$$

Therefore, at least 1.9 MeV is needed to create the proton and an additional 2.9 MeV for it to overcome the coulomb barrier. For the above reaction to take place with high probability, the incident neutron must have a minimum kinetic energy of 1.9 + 2.9 = 4.8 MeV. Endoergic reactions are also called *threshold reactions*.

The probability that a nuclear reaction will occur is measured by a quantity called the *reaction cross-section*. The most common unit of cross-section is the *barn* (1 barn = 1×10^{-24} cm²). If the energetics are favorable for more than one reaction, then each reaction has a specific reaction cross-section and proceeds independently of other reactions.

The rate at which a nuclear reaction proceeds depends on three parameters: the number of target atoms present, the reaction cross-section, and the number of neutrons incident per unit area of the target material per unit time. This relationship is expressed by

$$R = N\phi\sigma \qquad (19.31)$$

where
R = the reaction rate in sec^{-1}
N = the number of target nuclei present
ϕ = the neutron flux density in n/(cm²-sec)
σ = the reaction cross-section in cm²

The magnitude of the reaction cross-section depends on the nature of the target nuclide and on the energy of the incident neutrons. With thermal (low energy) neutrons, (n, γ) reactions generally have large cross-sections, although there are some exceptions. Threshold reactions, of course, cannot take place with thermal neutrons to any appreciable extent.

Sources of Neutrons

Three sources of neutrons are commonly used in activation analysis.

Nuclear Reactors. A nuclear reactor generates neutrons by the process of *fission*. Although the actual workings of nuclear reactors are quite complicated, the principles, for the present purpose, can be understood by considering a $^{235}_{92}U$-fueled nuclear reactor. Upon capturing a neutron, a $^{235}_{92}U$ nucleus breaks up into several lighter nuclei and produces more neutrons:

$$^{235}_{92}U + ^{1}_{0}n \longrightarrow ^{A_1}_{Z_1}X + ^{A_2}_{Z_2}X' + k\,^{1}_{0}n + Q \qquad (19.32)$$

where
$$A_1 + A_2 + k = 236$$
$$Z_1 + Z_2 = 92$$

The *average* value of k is 2.5. The fact that each nucleus of $^{235}_{92}U$ produces more neutrons than it requires for fission is responsible for the copious production of neutrons by nuclear reactors.

The fission neutrons produced in nuclear reactors have a continuous kinetic-energy spectrum, mostly in the range of 1–10 MeV. Since (n, γ) reactions are of more widespread analytical use, fission neutrons must be slowed to thermal energies by passing them through H_2O, D_2O, or graphite, which act as *moderators*. Depending on the type of nuclear reactor and the irradiation position in the reactor, the neutron spectrum may vary widely. Therefore, both (n, γ) and threshold reactions can occur in samples placed in nuclear reactors. Threshold reactions may produce interferences, of which the experimenter should be aware.

Isotopic Sources of Neutrons. Nuclear reactors are the only sources of copious quantities of neutrons. A typical research reactor might have a useful flux density of 10^{11}–10^{13} n/(cm²-sec). However, moderate flux densities of neutrons can be obtained from isotopic sources of neutrons at relatively low cost and with minimal space and maintenance requirements.

Isotopic neutron sources are of two general types. The first is a manmade radionuclide that undergoes spontaneous fission and produces neutrons. $^{252}_{98}Cf$ is a radionuclide commonly used for this purpose; a 1-mg $^{252}_{98}Cf$ source will produce 2.34×10^9 n/sec. The neutron spectrum of this source is similar to that of reactor neutrons, and therefore, for practical applications, the source is placed in a moderator or "thermalizer." The useful thermal-neutron flux density available in a typical facility is about 3×10^7 n/(cm²-sec).

The second type of isotopic neutron source consists of a radionuclide emitting intense alpha or gamma radiation, mixed with the element beryllium; one of the following reactions takes place:

$$^{9}_{4}Be + ^{4}_{2}He \longrightarrow ^{12}_{6}C + ^{1}_{0}n \qquad (19.33)$$

$$^{9}_{4}Be + \gamma \longrightarrow 2\,^{4}_{2}He + ^{1}_{0}n \qquad (19.34)$$

These neutrons also have a "fast," continuous spectral distribution and are usually slowed (moderated) by placing the source in a hydrogen-rich medium, such as water or paraffin.

Accelerators. The accelerator most commonly used for the production of neutrons is the Cockcroft-Walton neutron generator. A schematic diagram of this generator is given in Figure 19.11. Deuterium molecules are ionized in the ion-source bottle, accelerated in an electrostatic field of 100–200 kV, and focussed on a target containing tritium (^3_1H). The following nuclear reaction takes place:

$$^3_1H + ^2_1H \longrightarrow ^4_2He + ^1_0n + Q \tag{19.35}$$

where $Q \approx +14$ MeV. The neutrons produced are, therefore, nearly monoenergetic at 14 MeV.

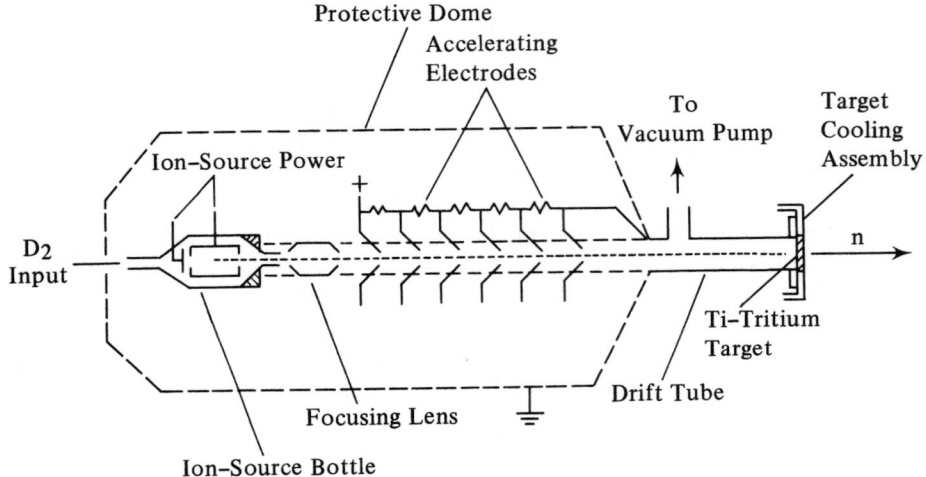

FIGURE 19.11. *Schematic diagram of a Cockcroft-Walton 14-MeV neutron generator.*

These neutrons are capable of inducing many threshold reactions. For example, consider the reaction

$$^{16}_8O + ^1_0n \longrightarrow ^{16}_7N + ^1_1H + Q \tag{19.36}$$

for which $Q = -9.6$ MeV, $E_T = -10.2$ MeV, and $E_c = -1.9$ MeV. Therefore, the minimum kinetic energy of neutrons required for the above reaction must be 12.1 MeV. This method is widely used for the determination of oxygen, an element that is difficult to determine by other analytical techniques. Benchtop-sized sealed-tube neutron generators are commonly employed.

Theory of Instrumental Neutron Activation Analysis (INAA)

The procedure in INAA is as follows:

1. the sample is exposed to neutrons for a known length of time, t_i
2. it is transported to the counting station and allowed to *cool* or decay for a definite length of time, t_d
3. the gamma-ray spectrum is acquired for counting time, t_c
4. the area under the FEP of interest is calculated

This procedure is repeated for another sample (the standard) containing a known amount of the element of interest. From the weight of the element in the standard, the relative FEP areas of the sample and standard, the relative neutron fluxes used for irradiating the sample and standard, and the times involved, the amount of the element in the sample is calculated.

Assume that the weight of the element present in the unknown sample is W_u grams and that one irradiates the sample for $t_{i(u)}$ sec, allows it to decay for $t_{d(u)}$ sec, and counts the emission for $t_{c(u)}$ sec. The activity of the radionuclide of interest at the end of the irradiation is given by

$$A_u^0 = N\phi_u\sigma(1 - e^{-\lambda t_{i(u)}})$$

$$= 6.02 \times 10^{23} \frac{I}{M} \phi_u\sigma(1 - e^{-\lambda t_{i(u)}})W_u \qquad (19.37)$$

where
I = the isotopic abundance of the element
M = the atomic mass of the element
ϕ_u = the neutron flux density in n/(cm²-sec)
N = the number of atoms of target present

Most tables list I in units of atom percent, in which case M should be the atomic mass of the element, not the mass of the individual isotope.

When acquisition of the spectrum begins, the activity will be

$$A_u = A_u^0 e^{-\lambda t_{d(u)}} \qquad (19.38)$$

The detector will, of course, detect only a fraction of this activity. Furthermore, only those events that register in the FEP are of interest. These factors are accounted for by the *detector photopeak efficiency* ξ. The *count rate* registered by the detection system in the FEP at the instant when counting starts is therefore given by

$$CR_u = \xi A_u^0 e^{-\lambda t_{d(u)}} \qquad (19.39)$$

The analyzer will integrate the count rate for the period of time, t_o. At the end of this time, *total counts* registered in the FEP, excluding any background effects, will be

$$C_u = \xi A_u^0 e^{-\lambda t_{d(u)}} \int_0^{t_{o(u)}} e^{-\lambda t}\, dt$$

$$= \frac{1}{\lambda} \xi A_u^0 e^{-\lambda t_{d(u)}}(1 - e^{-\lambda t_{o(u)}}) \qquad (19.40)$$

Combining Equations 19.37 and 19.40 results in

$$C_u = \frac{\xi}{\lambda} \frac{I}{M} \phi_u\sigma(1 - e^{-\lambda t_{i(u)}})e^{-\lambda t_{d(u)}}(1 - e^{-\lambda t_{o(u)}})W_u(6.02 \times 10^{23}) \qquad (19.41)$$

If the exact values of the parameters in the above equation were known, W_u could be calculated directly. However, because of uncertainties in the numerical values of

ξ, ϕ, and σ, it is more convenient to employ a comparative method whereby one also irradiates a sample of known content of the element of interest. Then

$$\frac{C_u}{C_s} = \frac{\xi_u \phi_u (1 - e^{-\lambda t_{i(u)}}) e^{-\lambda t_{d(u)}} (1 - e^{-\lambda t_{c(u)}}) W_u}{\xi_s \phi_s (1 - e^{-\lambda t_{i(s)}}) e^{-\lambda t_{d(s)}} (1 - e^{-\lambda t_{c(s)}}) W_s} \qquad (19.42)$$

Several parameters having the same values for the sample and standard (I, M, and σ) have been canceled out. It is quite a simple matter with present-day solid-state electronics to accurately control the various times involved. If each corresponding time is the same for both the sample and standard, and if both are counted with the same detection system, then

$$W_u = \frac{C_u}{C_s} \frac{\phi_s}{\phi_u} W_s \qquad (19.43)$$

Equation 19.43 is the working equation commonly used in neutron activation analysis. When employing nuclear reactors or an isotopic source, the value of ϕ_u and ϕ_s may also be the same, and a further simplification results. However, when using accelerator-generated neutrons, this is not easily done, and the values of ϕ_u and ϕ_s (or the ratio ϕ_s/ϕ_u) must be determined experimentally.

Capabilities and Limitations of Neutron Activation Analysis

This technique is a method for determining the elemental contents of substances. Its fundamental limitation is its inability to distinguish among different chemical forms or oxidation states of an element. Like most analytical methods, this technique also suffers from possible interferences and matrix effects. Three types of interferences may occur.

Type I Interferences. These arise from nuclear reactions in the other elements present in the sample that produce the same radionuclide as the one measured. For example, in determining Al in rocks by reactor irradiation employing the reaction $^{27}_{13}$Al (n, γ) $^{28}_{13}$Al, a possible interference is $^{28}_{14}$Si (n, p) $^{28}_{13}$Al.

Type II Interferences. These are caused by the release of secondary nuclear particles from a primary reaction. For instance, when determining nitrogen in protein products with a neutron generator, the reaction employed may be $^{14}_{7}$N (n, 2n) $^{13}_{7}$N. If the sample is packaged in polyethylene containers, the incident neutrons may collide with the hydrogen atoms present in the container material, producing energetic protons which may in turn react with carbon in the sample according to the reaction $^{13}_{6}$C (p, n) $^{13}_{7}$N. This type of interference is generally of limited significance, because the flux density of protons produced is much less than that of the primary neutrons.

Type III Interferences. These are caused by the inability of some detectors to resolve closely similar gamma-ray energies. For example, when determining the Al content of a material by the reaction $^{27}_{13}$Al (n, p) $^{27}_{12}$Mg, one employs the 0.842-MeV gamma ray emitted by $^{27}_{12}$Mg. Iron, if present in the sample, will undergo the reaction $^{56}_{26}$Fe (n, p) $^{56}_{25}$Mn, which emits 0.847-MeV gamma rays. If a NaI(Tl) detector is used to detect the 0.842-MeV gamma rays, the two gamma rays cannot be resolved. Sometimes Type III interferences involve radionuclides with half-lives different from those of the desired elements, and can be resolved by the decay-curve method discussed previously.

One of the most important advantages of INAA over many other methods of analysis is that it is essentially nondestructive. Very often a complete analysis can be performed without appreciably altering the physical or chemical nature of the sample. This is important for several reasons. First, it may be imperative to preserve the sample, such as in forensic analysis where the sample is needed as evidence in a courtroom, or in the analysis of lunar samples or works of art. Second, nondestructive analysis involves minimum sample manipulation and, therefore, a trace sample is not contaminated by reagents and containers as in conventional destructive wet-chemical techniques.

Neutron activation analysis has a high degree of sensitivity for the majority of elements. Trace-level determinations are routinely performed with reactors and can, in certain favorable cases, be performed with the other types of neutron sources. A very important advantage of neutron activation analysis over many other analytical methods is that simultaneous analyses of multi-component systems are easy to perform; many routine procedures are available to determine more than a dozen elements in a single small sample.

Practical Considerations in Neutron Activation Analysis

Figure 19.12 shows the block diagram of a complete NAA facility. As in any other analytical method, each step may introduce both random and determinate errors, degrading the overall precision and accuracy of the results. We will briefly examine each step and point out a few of the most important points that should be kept in mind.

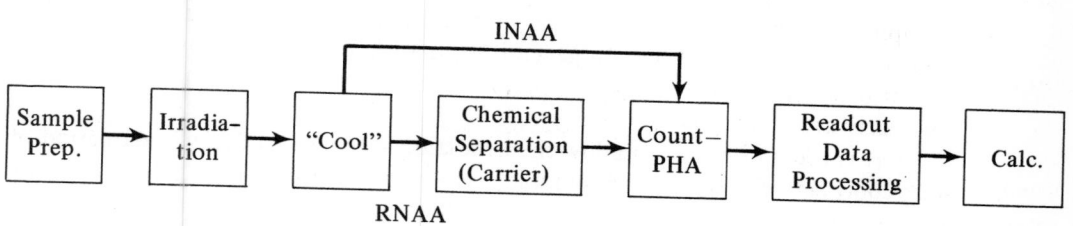

FIGURE 19.12. *Block diagram of a typical neutron-activation-analysis experiment.*

The sample may be solid, liquid, or gas, although the first two forms are most commonly used. Problems associated with sampling are the same as in any other method of analysis. Once the sample is secured, it is packaged in an appropriate container. An important point to keep in mind is that the sample and standards should be as similar as possible in matrix composition. For example, when analyzing rocks the sample is generally pulverized to a fine powder, and the standards are also preferably made from finely powdered standard rocks (such as those provided by the U.S. Geological Survey). An alternate standard could be prepared by evaporating an aliquot of a standard solution of the element on a matrix of high-purity SiO_2.

The size of the packaged samples should be as close to that of the standards as possible, so that self-absorption of the neutron flux does not introduce errors. When analyzing heterogeneous materials, complete mixing is very important. When irradiating organic materials, decomposition of the sample may occur; this is especially serious when high fluxes of neutrons are employed, since considerable heat may be generated inside the sample. The same problem occurs in the irradiation of aqueous solutions, where the build-up of pressure inside the container must be allowed for. Heat-sealed quartz vials are often used for reactor irradiations. If pressure build-ups are anticipated, the vials may be cooled to liquid-nitrogen temperatures before they are opened.

The irradiation assembly must provide the same neutron flux for both sample and standard, or appropriate correction factors must be determined. In addition to variations in the absolute magnitude of the thermal-neutron flux as a function of the position inside the nuclear reactor, the ratio of thermal-neutron and fast-neutron fluxes changes appreciably with position. This may result in serious errors caused by unwanted threshold reactions. When employing 14 MeV generators, time-dependent variations in the neutron flux may also become significant.

The optimum irradiation time is a very important factor in activation analysis. The decision is based on the specific nature of the sample and the type of information desired. Generally, two factors are considered. First, longer irradiation times increase the activity produced. However, Equation 19.37 shows that the factor $(1 - e^{-\lambda t_i})$ approaches unity as t_i becomes large with respect to the half-life of the product radionuclide. Therefore, irradiation times in excess of 3–5 half-lives of the product desired result in little additional activity. Second, the longer the irradiation time, the greater will be the induced activities due to long-lived radionuclides that may interfere with the specific determination. (Of course, the higher the overall activity of the sample, the higher the health hazard and the more care must be used in handling it.) In general, irradiation times of approximately 3 half-lives of the product, but rarely more than one week total time, are used for conventional activation analysis.

It is often desirable to allow the irradiated specimen to decay for a period of time (cool) before counting. A suitable decay-period permits short-lived interfering activities to decay and, again, lessens the health hazard.

After the cooling period, the sample is either counted directly or some chemical manipulation is performed before counting. The first procedure is known as *instrumental neutron activation analysis* (INAA), whereas the latter is referred to as *radiochemical neutron activation analysis* (RNAA). In RNAA a stable *carrier* for the element to be determined may be added to the sample after irradiation. The carrier is equilibrated with the element in the sample (often by fusing it with Na_2O_2, or treating it with strong acid). Then the element of interest is separated along with the carrier. The chemical yield of the separation is determined from the amount of carrier recovered, and this correction is applied to the measured activity.

As mentioned earlier, in selecting the proper detector, the criteria used are detector efficiency and resolution. Where sensitivity is the overriding consideration, a NaI(Tl) detector is the detector of choice. If there are interferences, RNAA must be employed to eliminate them. In multi-element analyses of complex matrices, detector resolution becomes critical and Ge(Li) detectors should be used.

The electronic components needed for processing the detector signals have evolved into standardized modular units, and are relatively simple to select. One important factor when using multi-channel analyzers is the analyzer dead-time. Typically, a multi-channel analyzer receives a pulse, digitizes that pulse, and stores

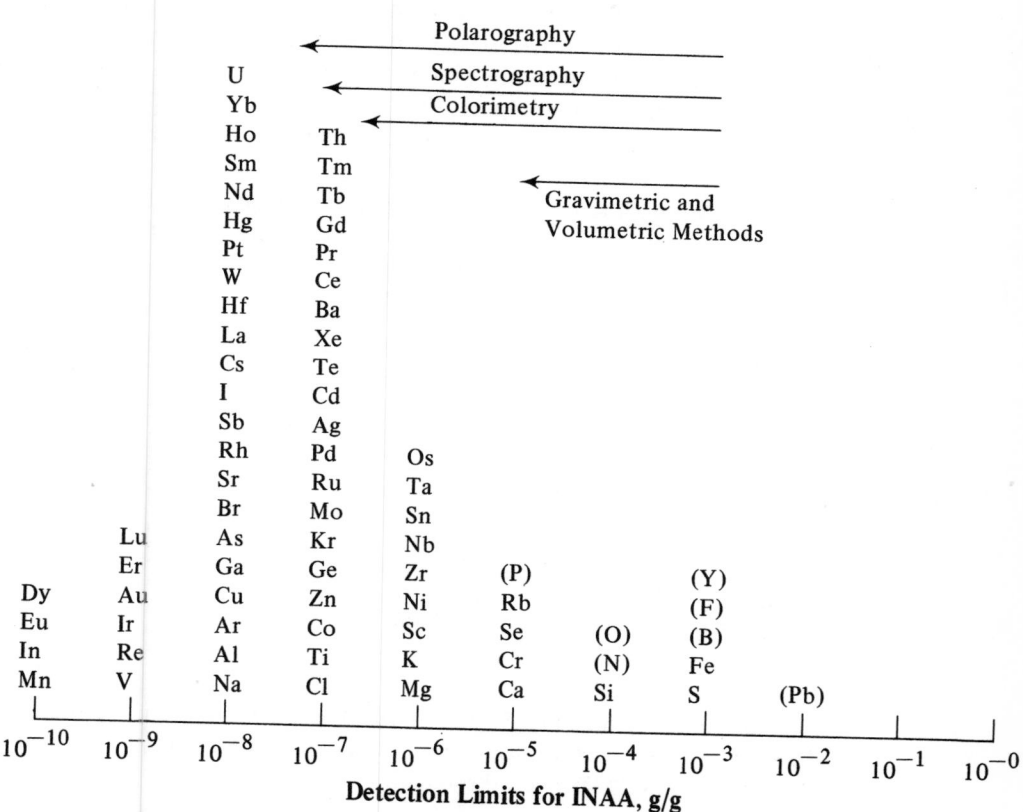

FIGURE 19.13. *Detection limits for instrumental neutron activation analysis (INAA) compared to the usual sensitivity ranges for several commonly used analytical techniques. Elements listed in parentheses are determined by 14-MeV neutron activation with a flux density of 2×10^8 n/(cm²-sec) for a maximum irradiation time of 5 min, followed by NaI(Tl) gamma-ray spectrometry. Detection limits for all other elements are based on reactor irradiations of one hour or less at a flux density of 10^{13} n/(cm²-sec), followed by gamma-ray spectrometry using a 40 cm³ Ge(Li) detector. Sensitivities for many elements could be improved by several orders of magnitude by using longer irradiation times, positions of higher flux-density, or radiochemical separations. For example, Ir has been determined in rocks at levels well below 10^{-12} g/g (0.001 ppb) by long, high-flux reactor irradiations.*

it in the proper memory channel. During this time, the analyzer is *dead* to any incoming pulses. If the sample has a high activity level, this could result in an appreciable loss of counts. Most modern analyzers keep track of this *dead time* and automatically lengthen the counting time to compensate for its effect. This internal correction works best when the counting time is short compared to the half-life of the radionuclide of interest.

Figure 19.13 compares NAA with other commonly used analytical techniques. NAA, with its important advantage of high sensitivity for many elements and its inherent freedom from problems of reagent and laboratory contamination, is often the benchmark technique against which other trace-element techniques are measured. The increasing availability of inexpensive, easily housed, isotopic neutron sources and sealed-tube neutron generators can now put a "reagent bottle" of neutrons in even the most modest analytical laboratory.

Let us consider an example of an activation-analysis calculation:

> **Example 19.1.** We wish to determine the element vanadium in a 1.00 g sample of petroleum. We anticipate the vanadium content to be about 100 ppm by weight. A ^{252}Cf neutron source with a useful flux density of 2×10^7 n/(cm²-sec) is available, along with a detector system with a total FEP efficiency of 10.0% for the ^{52}V 1.43-MeV gamma ray. The 1.43-MeV gamma rays are emitted in 100% of the ^{52}V disintegrations. Calculate the number of counts that would be obtained for ^{52}V if the sample is irradiated to saturation and "cooled" for 2.00 min prior to counting for a period of 10.0 min.
>
> NUCLEAR DATA:
>
> Atomic mass of V $\qquad$ = 50.94 amu
> Natural abundance of ^{51}V = 99.76%
> Cross section ^{51}V $\qquad$ = 4.9 barns
> Half-life of ^{52}V $\qquad$ = 3.75 min
> The nuclear reaction is ^{51}V (n, γ) ^{52}V
>
> CALCULATIONS: Combining Equations 19.37 and 19.40 and noting that if the sample is irradiated to saturation (a time long with respect to the half-life of ^{52}V) the term $(1 - e^{-\lambda t_i}) \sim 1$,
>
> $$\text{Counts} = \frac{\xi}{\lambda} \frac{W}{M} I \phi \sigma e^{-\lambda t_d}(1 - e^{-\lambda t_c})(6.02 \times 10^{23})$$
>
> $$\text{Counts} = \left(\frac{0.100}{0.693/[3.75 \text{ min } (60 \text{ sec/min})]}\right)\left(\frac{100 \times 10^{-6} \text{ g}}{50.94 \text{ g/g atom}}\right)$$
>
> $\qquad \times [6.0 \times 10^{23} \text{ atom/(g-atom)}](0.9976)[2 \times 10^7 \text{ n/(cm}^2\text{-sec)}]$
> $\qquad \times (4.9 \times 10^{-24} \text{ cm}^2)(e^{-0.693(2.00 \text{ min})/3.75 \text{ min}})$
> $\qquad \times (1 - e^{-0.693(10.0 \text{ min})/3.75 \text{ min}})$
> $\qquad = 2{,}180$ counts recorded in counting period.

Assuming no interferences, this calculation shows that one could determine V in this sample at the 100 ppm level with a relative statistical error due to counting of less than 1% (see Sec. 19.5). Indeed, this method has been commonly employed by the petrochemical industry for the determination of vanadium in petroleum and its products.

Well over 10,000 papers dealing with activation analysis have appeared in the literature. Most of these (99%) have been published since 1955. Some of the more interesting applications have been determining potentially toxic trace elements in natural waters and environmental samples, authenticating paintings and other objects of art, and studying impurities in semiconductor materials, trace elements in plant and animal metabolism, and trace-element abundances in terrestrial rocks, meteorites, and lunar samples. In the analyses of lunar samples, more than twice as many trace-element determinations have been reported by activation analysis than by any other technique. In fact, the activation-analysis determinations on these rare samples probably exceed those by all other techniques combined.

14-MeV neutron activation analysis has been widely employed in the direct determination of oxygen in rocks and of nitrogen in food grains and explosives. Charged-particle activation analysis is useful in the analysis of thin films or coatings on metals.

Activation analysis is not without its own unique problems. However, for the determination of elements at the sub-ppm level it is certainly the technique against which other methods must be compared. Accuracy and precision of the order of a few percent are readily attainable at the nanogram level for many elements. High sensitivity, multi-element capability, and freedom from reagent and laboratory contamination problems are the major advantages offered.

19.5 METHODS INVOLVING ADDITION OF RADIONUCLIDE

The second general category of radiochemical analysis involves adding a radioactive substance to the sample, manipulating the sample by chemical or physical means, measuring the radioactivity, and ultimately calculating the amount of the component of interest. This category includes *direct and inverse isotope dilution analysis, radiochemical titrations,* and *radiorelease methods of analysis.*

Direct Isotope Dilution Analysis

In the method of activation analysis, radioactivity is induced in the sample to be analyzed. In the method of *direct isotope dilution analysis* (DIDA), a radioactive form of the component of interest is added to the sample. The component is then exhaustively purified without regard to quantitative recovery and a fraction of the pure component isolated. The amount and activity of the isolated component are measured and the quantity present in the original sample is calculated using that information.

Theory of DIDA. Consider a complex sample of W grams containing W_1 grams of the component of interest. To this sample is added W_1^* grams of a radioactive form of the component with a total activity A_1. W_2 grams of the pure component is then isolated; it contains both the active and the inactive forms and has an activity of A_2.

The *specific activity* SA_1 of the radioactive ("spike") material before it is mixed with the sample is defined as

$$SA_1 = \frac{A_1}{W_1^*} \qquad (19.44)$$

and SA_2, the specific activity of the *recovered* component, as

$$SA_2 = \frac{A_2}{W_2} \qquad (19.45)$$

SA_2 will remain constant regardless of how much of the pure component was isolated since it is activity per unit weight of recovered component. One can then write the following balance sheet:

	Weight of Component	Specific Activity
Before Mixing	W_1 (inactive form)	0
	W_1^* (active form)	SA_1
After Mixing but Before Purification	$W_1 + W_1{}^*$ (mixture)	SA_2
After Purification	$f(W_1 + W_1^*) = W_2$ (isolated component)	SA_2

Note that f is the fraction of the component recovered and is unknown. Also, note that the specific activity of the component of interest remains the same before and after purification. It follows that

$$W_1^* SA_1 = (W_1 + W_1^*) SA_2 \qquad (19.46)$$

and solving this equation for W_1

$$W_1 = W_1^* \left(\frac{SA_1}{SA_2} - 1 \right) \qquad (19.47)$$

The percentage of the component of interest in the original sample is then

$$\% \text{ Unknown} = 100 \frac{W_1^*}{W_1} \left(\frac{SA_1}{SA_2} - 1 \right) \qquad (19.48)$$

Since W, W_1^*, and SA_1 are known and SA_2 can be determined experimentally, the amount of the component of interest in the original mixture can be easily calculated.

> *Example 19.2.* A dilute aqueous solution (density = 1.000 g/ml) is to be analyzed for its I^- content. A 50-ml aliquot of the solution is available for analysis.
>
> PROCEDURE: An aliquot of a standard solution of $^{129}_{53}I^-$ tracer is added to the 50.0 ml of solution. The standard solution added is known to contain 0.00500 mg of I^- and has an activity of 3120 counts per minute. To the resultant mixture is added an aliquot of a standard $AgNO_3$ solution sufficient to precipitate only 0.0100 mg of I^-. The precipitate obtained is then filtered and counted. Its activity is found to be 347 counts per minute.

CALCULATIONS:

$$SA_1 = \frac{3120 \text{ cpm}}{0.00500 \text{ mg}} = 6.24 \times 10^5 \text{ cpm/mg}$$

$$SA_2 = \frac{347 \text{ cpm}}{0.0100 \text{ mg}} = 3.47 \times 10^4 \text{ cpm/mg}$$

Therefore, using Equation 19.47,

$$W_{\text{I}^-} = 0.00500 \text{ mg}\left(\frac{6.24 \times 10^5 \text{ cpm/mg}}{3.47 \times 10^4 \text{ cpm/mg}} - 1\right)$$

$$= 0.085 \text{ mg I}^-$$

and ppm I$^-$ $= \dfrac{0.085 \text{ mg I}^- \times 10^{-3} \text{ g/mg}}{50.0 \text{ ml} \times 1.000 \text{ g/ml}} \times 10^6$

$$= 1.7 \text{ ppm}$$

In the conventional gravimetric method, it would have been necessary to quantitatively precipitate the I$^-$ present and to weigh the precipitate (less than 0.1 mg). The only precautions in the present method are that all of the Ag$^+$ added should be used to precipitate AgI, and that all of the AgI be collected. If other species are precipitated (for instance, AgCl), the precipitate should be separated and purified before measuring its activity.

Advantages and Limitations of DIDA. In wet-chemical analyses, exhaustive multistep purification procedures are often required to obtain the component in a highly pure form, and a quantitative yield is almost impossible to achieve. The main advantage of DIDA is that no quantitative separation of the component of interest is necessary. The instrumentation required is usually quite simple, since measurements of gross activity with simple counting systems are sufficient. The separated component must be in highly pure form; and once the pure component is obtained, its quantity must be accurately measured, or deduced from stoichiometric considerations. The separated component must also have a high enough level of activity to minimize statistical counting error. (This is usually not a serious limitation, since the activity of the initial labeled compound can often be adjusted to compensate for a low efficiency in the purification step.) The weight W_1^* should not be much larger than W_1, and tracer solutions of high specific activity are ordinarily used.

A very important effect, which could become either an advantage or a disadvantage, is inherent in the fundamental requirement of the method: both the active and inactive forms behave identically in the subsequent purification steps. This means either that the labeled component must be in the same chemical form as the inactive component, or that the mixture must be treated chemically to convert both forms into the same chemical compound. This situation can, of course, be of great advantage if one is trying to distinguish among different chemical forms of a given element. For instance, a solution containing both Cr^{3+} and Cr$_2$O$_7^{2-}$ can be analyzed for Cr$_2$O$_7^{2-}$ by adding ^{51}Cr$_2$O$_7^{2-}$ tracer and excess NaOH, after which Ba^{2+} is added to precipitate BaCrO$_4$.

Inverse Isotope Dilution Analysis

In DIDA, a radioactive form of the component of interest is added to the sample and the quantity of the inactive form initially present is determined. In some instances, one may wish to determine the amount of a radioactive substance in the sample. A method similar in principle to DIDA can then be used wherein a quantity of an inactive form of the component of interest is added to the sample, the sample is purified without regard to quantitative recovery, and the amount of the recovered component and its activity are measured. From this information, the quantity of the radioactive substance initially present in the sample is calculated. This method is referred to as *inverse isotope dilution analysis* (IIDA).

Theory of IIDA. Let W_1^* and SA_1 be the weight and specific activity, respectively, of the radioactive substance initially present in the sample. W_1 grams of an inactive form of the component is added, and some fraction of the pure component, having specific activity SA_2, is recovered. Writing the balance sheet for this situation:

	Weight of Component	Specific Activity
Before Mixing	W_1^* (active form)	SA_1
	W_1 (inactive form)	0
After Mixing but Before Purification	$W_1 + W_1^*$ (mixture)	SA_2
After Purification	$f(W_1 + W_1^*) = W_2$ (isolated component)	SA_2

Note that f is less than unity and that SA_2 is the same before and after purification. Then

$$SA_2(W_1 + W_1^*) = SA_1(W_1^*) \tag{19.49}$$

Although SA_1 is not known, the product $SA_1(W_1^*)$ can be measured; this is the total activity of the component in the sample before any processing. Therefore,

$$SA_2(W_1 + W_1^*) = A_1 \tag{19.50}$$

and

$$W_1^* = \left(\frac{A_1}{SA_2}\right) - W_1 \tag{19.51}$$

Since $SA_2 = A_2/W_2$, where A_2 is the total activity of the recovered pure sample and W_2 is the weight of recovered sample,

$$W_1^* = \left(\frac{A_1}{A_2}\right) W_2 - W_1 \tag{19.52}$$

Advantages and Limitations of IIDA. The main advantage of this method is that one can determine the quantity of a specific radioactive component of a sample without comparing it with a known radioactive standard. The method also avoids preparing standards with the same matrix as the sample in order to assure equivalent counting efficiencies. However, the method cannot be applied if spectral interferences prevent the specific measurement of A_1. Furthermore, the method is applicable only when W_1 does not differ greatly from W_1^*. In the case of trace analysis, the method offers the advantage of not requiring a quantitative separation of the component of interest. The method of IIDA has not been applied as widely as has DIDA.

Radiometric Titrations

All titrimetric methods of analysis require some means of detecting the equivalence point. This could be an abrupt change of color (colorimetric titrations), a sudden change in the potential difference between two electrodes (potentiometric titrations), a change in current flow through two electrodes (amperometric titrations), and so on. Similarly, the radioactivity of either the titrant or the substance titrated can be employed for detecting the equivalence point. This type of analysis is called *radiometric titration*. It should be noted that the sole purpose of the radioactivity is to signal attainment of the equivalence point and that it takes no part in the titration process. The technique can be employed in all classes of titrations, provided that a phase separation can be effected.

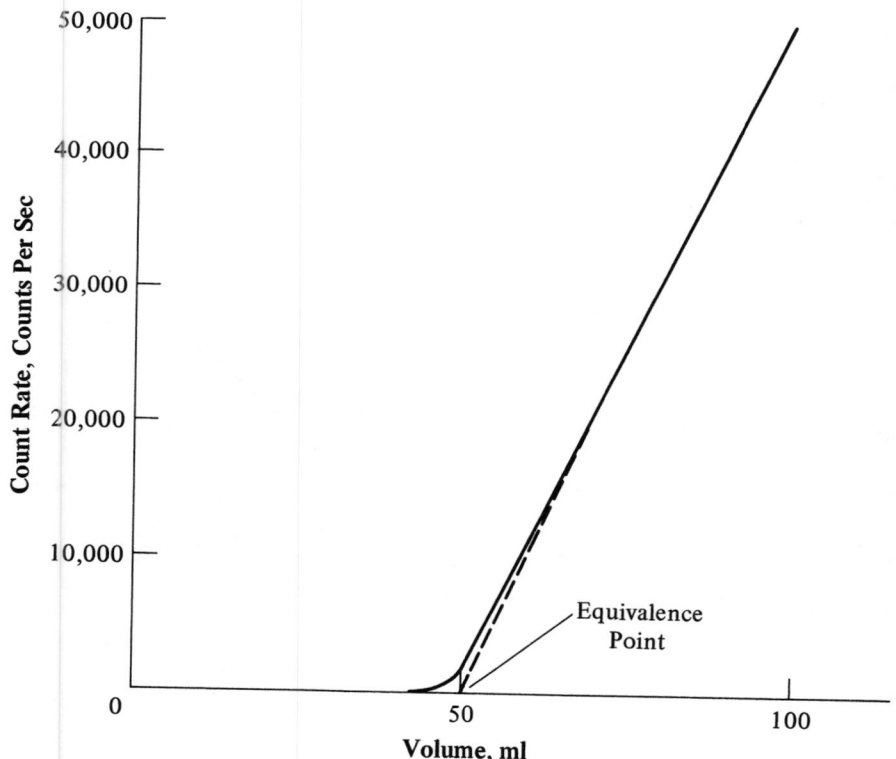

FIGURE 19.14.   *Theoretical titration curve for the radiometric titration of* 0.001 M Cl⁻ *with a solution of* 0.001 M Ag⁺ *spiked with* ¹¹⁰Ag.

The most straightforward application is in precipitation titrations, where the phase separation occurs spontaneously. In order to understand the method, consider the titration of 50 ml of a 0.001 M Cl^- solution with a 0.001 M solution of $^{110}_{47}Ag^+$, with an activity of 1×10^9 dps/mol. The reaction is

$$Ag^+ + Cl^- \rightleftharpoons AgCl \downarrow \qquad (19.53)$$

with $K_{sp} = 1.82 \times 10^{-10}$. The activity of the supernatant is monitored after equilibrium has been reached following each incremental volume of added titrant. Prior to the endpoint, the supernatant has very little activity because almost all of the radioactive silver is present as precipitated AgCl. The theoretical activity of the supernatant at any point in the titration can easily be calculated from mass-action principles and the K_{sp} for silver chloride. The data for this titration are plotted in Figure 19.14. The equivalence point is the intercept of the two straight-line portions of the curve.

A typical experimental arrangement for precipitation titrations is shown in Figure 19.15. After each addition of titrant and attainment of equilibrium, an aliquot of the supernatant is drawn into the counting chamber and its activity measured. The solution is then ejected back into the titration vessel, and the next addition of titrant is made.

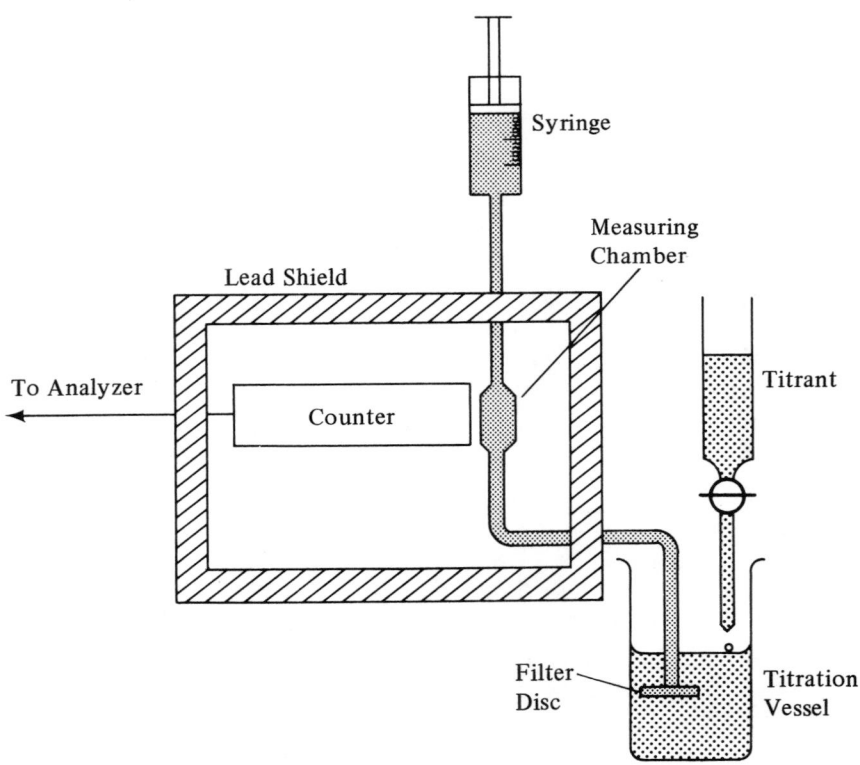

FIGURE 19.15. *A simple experimental set-up for radiometric titrations employing precipitation reactions.*

Advantages and Limitations of Radiometric Titrations. Radiometric detection of the equivalence point is a general method that does not depend on the chemical reaction employed. This contrasts with other methods of detection, which depend on specific chemical or physical transitions at the equivalence point. Amperometric titrations are applicable only to electrochemically active systems; conductometric titrations apply only to ionic solutions, and so on. In principle, any titration system in which a phase separation can be effected is amenable to radiometric detection, provided there exist suitable radioactive labels. The major limitation of the method is the requirement for phase separation. In precipitation titrations, the phase separation is automatic and the method is well suited to this class of titrations. For other classes of titrations, special phase-separation methods, such as solvent extraction, need to be applied. At the present time, the method suffers from a lack of phase-separation techniques suitable for continuous monitoring of the titration curves.

Radiorelease Methods of Analysis

This method is based on the chemical reaction of the constituent of interest with a radio-labeled reagent. The labeled component is then released either as a gas or in some readily extractable form. From a measurement of the amount of radioactivity released and the stoichiometry of the reaction, the quantity of the constituent of interest is determined. Consider the determination of SO_2 in air by this method. If air is passed through a basic solution of $KI*O_3$, the following reaction takes place:

$$5 SO_2 + 2 KI*O_3 + 4 H_2O \longrightarrow K_2SO_4 + 4 H_2SO_4 + I_2^* \qquad (19.54)$$

The solution is then acidified and the liberated I_2^* is extracted into chloroform. The chloroform phase is separated and counted for its I_2^* content. From the stoichiometry of the reaction and the quantity of liberated I_2^*, the content of SO_2 in air can be determined.

The chief advantage of this method of analysis is its sensitivity, since highly active radio-reagents are available. For instance, a micromole of I_2^* may easily have 10^7 dpm activity. However, the method is chemical in nature and suffers from all limitations inherent in the particular chemical reaction involved. In the above example, any other substance that can reduce $KI*O_3$ to I_2^* will, of course, interfere with the determination (oxides of nitrogen are potential interferences). Furthermore, at trace levels quantitative extraction of the released species becomes critical.

19.6 STATISTICAL CONSIDERATIONS IN RADIOCHEMICAL ANALYSIS

In reporting the results of any analysis, two important parameters are the accuracy and the precision of the data. Accuracy is a measure of how close the reported data are to the true values. Precision, on the other hand, is only a measure of how closely one can expect to reproduce the reported data, if the experiment is repeated. Good precision does not necessarily imply accurate results. A discussion of these factors can be found in most books on quantitative analysis. However, since radioactive counting follows a different distribution law than do most other analytical manipulations, calculations of the precision of radiochemical methods require a knowledge

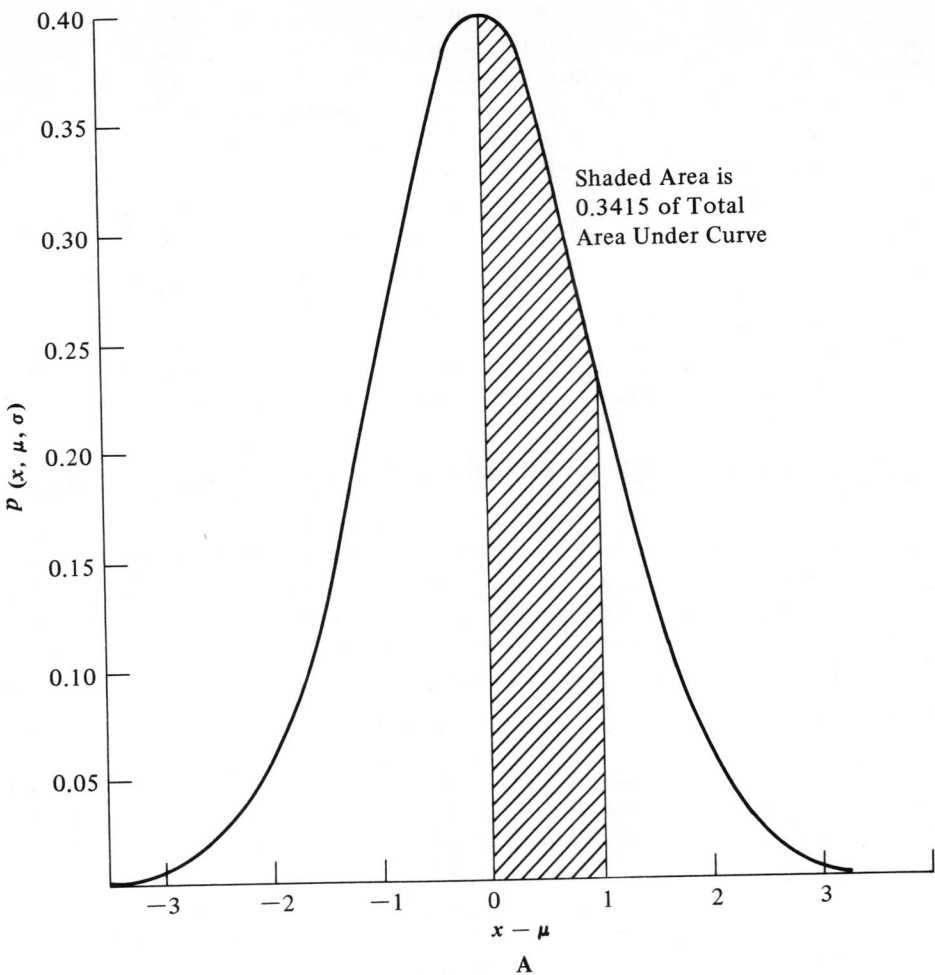

Shaded Area is
0.3415 of Total
Area Under Curve

FIGURE 19.16. *Probability curves.* (*A*) *The normal distribution curve
for σ = 1.0.* (*B, opposite*) *Poisson distribution curves for* μ = 5.0 *and*
μ = 10.0.

of this distribution. In this section the distribution law involved will be presented,
and the calculations compared with those of most other types of analysis.

It is generally accepted that random errors arising in various analytical operations, except radioactive counting, follow a normal distribution, described by the
normal distribution function (see Fig. 19.16A)

$$p_{(x,\mu,\sigma)} = \frac{1}{\sqrt{2\pi}\sigma} e^{-1/2[(x-\mu)/\sigma]^2} \tag{19.55}$$

where   μ = the true mean of the population*
        x = an individual measurement

---

    * The true mean of a population is the quantity obtained if a given measurement is repeated
an infinite number of times and the results averaged, assuming no determinate errors.

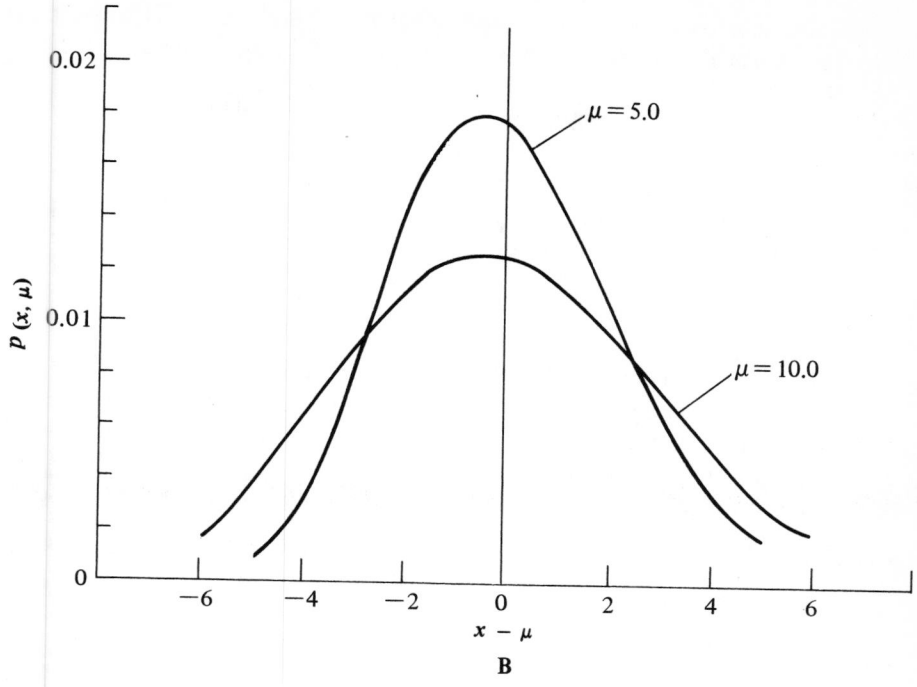

σ = the *standard deviation* of the distribution function

p = the probability of obtaining the value x in a single trial

Practically speaking, σ is a measure of the broadness of the curve in Figure 19.16A; a total of 68.3% of the entire area under the curve falls within ±1σ of the value of the mean (which, in this case, is the same as the most probable value).

In practice, a finite number (n) of measurements are made, all of which would be identical were it not for the random errors involved in each measurement. From this finite (and often small) set of measurements, one estimates the most probable value of the function by averaging the experimental results. The question is: if another single measurement were made, how close would this last measurement be to the mean of the previous measurements? The answer, of course, is that this depends on the broadness of the distribution function for these measurements, as well as on the degree of confidence to be placed on the answer. For this purpose, one calculates the *standard deviation of the individual sample determination*, using

$$s_x = \sqrt{\frac{\sum (x_1 - \bar{x})^2}{n - 1}}$$ (19.56)

where $\bar{x}$ = the *average* or *mean* of the n individual measurements, $x_1, x_2, \ldots, x_1$

One would thus expect any other individual measurement to fall within $\mu \pm 1\,s_x$ in 68.3% of the measurements and within $\mu \pm 2\,s_x$ in 95.5% of such measurements. As can be seen, the greater the degree of confidence, the wider the range of possible values.

One can now ask, how close would one come to the first mean if one makes another set of measurements and calculates a new mean? To answer this, calculate the *standard deviation of the mean* using the following formula:

$$s_{\bar{x}} = \frac{s_x}{\sqrt{n}} \tag{19.57}$$

In contrast to most analytical operations, radioactive counting does not, in general, follow the normal distribution law. It follows the *Poisson distribution law*, an asymmetric distribution function described by

$$p(x, \mu) = \frac{\mu^x}{x!} e^{-\mu} \tag{19.58}$$

Figure 19.16B shows a typical Poisson distribution function. A very important distinction between this function and the normal distribution function is that, in order to characterize the latter, we must know both μ and σ because the broadness of the normal distribution is independent of its mean. In contrast, the Poisson distribution curve is completely characterized by its mean alone. The broadness of the distribution is a function of the mean, and is given by

$$\sigma_x = \sqrt{\mu} \tag{19.59}$$

For a finite set of measurements,

$$s_x = \sqrt{\bar{x}} \tag{19.60}$$

Thus, from only a single measurement (an estimate of the mean), the standard deviation can be estimated to be

$$s_x = \sqrt{x} \tag{19.61}$$

The standard deviation of the mean is, as before, given by Equation 19.57. As the magnitude of μ (or its estimator $\bar{x}$) increases, the portion of the Poisson distribution curve close to its mean becomes more symmetrical, and resembles more closely the normal distribution curve. Therefore, only for large values of $\bar{x}$ can one assume that the statistics of radioactive counting follow the normal distribution law, and then only as an approximation.

Propagation of Errors

Most radiochemical procedures consist of a number of measurement steps. In each step, random errors can occur which will contribute in different degrees to the uncertainty of the final result. One can therefore estimate the uncertainty of the final result, given estimates of the uncertainty of each step. Assume that two measurements or two steps with numerical values $A \pm \sigma_A$ and $B \pm \sigma_B$, yield the result $C \pm \sigma_C$. If $C = A + B$, or $C = A - B$, then

$$\sigma_C = \sqrt{\sigma_A{}^2 + \sigma_B{}^2} \tag{19.62}$$

If $C = AB$ or $C = A/B$, then

$$\sigma_C = C\sqrt{\left[\frac{\sigma_A}{A}\right]^2 + \left[\frac{\sigma_B}{B}\right]^2} \tag{19.63}$$

In combining the uncertainties, each step is assumed to have the same error distribution function, so that σ_C also has the same function. This is generally true for most analytical operations. However, when combining measurements of radio-activity with measurements such as weighing that follow the normal distribution function, one cannot always obtain a meaningful error distribution in the manner indicated above (this is analogous to adding apples to oranges!). However, if the specific Poisson distribution being considered does approximate a normal distribution, it is approximately correct to pool the standard deviations in this way. In addition, if one or more steps contribute predominantly to the uncertainty of the complete analysis, one can safely calculate error based on the uncertainty of only those steps.

SELECTED BIBLIOGRAPHY

BRAUN, T., and TÖLGYESSY, J. *Radiometric Titrations.* New York: Pergamon Press, 1967. *This book is the only authoritative book on the subject of radiometric titrations. A detailed and up-to-date account of both theoretical and experimental aspects of this subject is given.*

EHMANN, W. D. "Nondestructive Techniques in Activation Analysis," *Fortsch. Chem. Forsch., 14*(1), 49 (1970). *This is a general article on the technique of nondestructive neutron activation analysis with major emphasis on 14-MeV neutrons. Practical aspects of this area as well as some advanced developments are discussed.*

FRIEDLANDER, G.; KENNEDY, J. W.; and MILLER, J. M. *Nuclear and Radiochemistry,* 2nd ed. New York: John Wiley and Sons, 1964. *This is a standard senior-level textbook on principles of nuclear chemistry and radiochemistry.*

HOLDEN, N. E., and WALKER, F. W. *Chart of the Nuclides, Physical Constants and Conversion Factors and Table of Equivalents,* General Electric Company, Atomic Power Equipment Department, 175 Curtner Avenue, San Jose, CA 95125. *An inexpensive ($1.00) compilation of nuclear data in a paperback format. The booklet is revised periodically. The most recent edition is dated October, 1970.*

KRUGER, P. *Principles of Activation Analysis.* New York: Wiley-Interscience, 1971. *A senior-level textbook covering various aspects of neutron activation analysis in fair depth.*

KRUGERS, J., ed. *Instrumentation in Applied Nuclear Chemistry.* New York: Plenum Press, 1973. *This is a comprehensive in-depth treatment of all aspects of nuclear instrumentation.*

LUTZ, G. J.; BORENI, R. J.; MADDOCK, R. S.; and WING, J. *Activation Analysis: A Bibliography Through 1971.* Technical Note 467. Washington, D.C.: U.S. Department of Commerce, National Bureau of Standards, 1972. *This document contains a thorough list of publications relating to activation analysis. It is periodically updated by NBS and is the most thorough source of activation analysis literature.*

MEINKE, W. W. "Is Radiochemistry the Ultimate in Trace Analysis?" *Pure Appl. Chem., 34,* 93 (1973). *This article points out the advantages of activation analysis, as compared to other widely used methods of analysis for trace elements. Practical experience at the National Bureau of Standards is cited.*

PROBLEMS

1. A ^{252}Cf isotopic neutron-source is available that provides a flux density of 2.0×10^7 n/(cm^2-sec) at the irradiation positions.

The aluminum content of 1.0-gram alloy samples is to be determined by the ^{27}Al (n, γ) ^{28}Al reaction; a counting rate of at least 100 counts per minute at the start of the counting period is required for these determinations. Using the following data, calculate the minimum aluminum content that could be determined in these alloys by this technique: (1) ^{28}Al is a negatron and gamma-ray emitter that emits one 1.78-MeV gamma ray per disintegration. (2) Half-life of ^{28}Al = 2.3 min. (3) Cross-section of ^{27}Al for the (n, γ) reaction = 0.24 barns. The natural isotopic abundance of ^{27}Al is 100% and its atomic mass is 26.98. (4) The overall efficiency of the counting system is 10%, based on the 1.78-MeV gamma-ray FEP. (5) The sample is irradiated to saturation (the time of irradiation is long with respect to the half-life of ^{28}Al) and "cooled" 2 min prior to the start of counting.

2. The radionuclide $^{16}_{7}$N emits a high-energy gamma ray at 6.13 MeV. A gamma-ray spectrum of a $^{16}_{7}$N source exhibits peaks at 5.62 MeV, 5.11 MeV, and 0.511 MeV in addition to the FEP at 6.13 MeV and the usual Compton distribution. Assuming these features are not due to primary gamma rays emitted in the decay of $^{16}_{7}$N, how would you explain the existence of these three extra peaks?

3. A sample containing both Mn and Fe was irradiated with neutrons in a nuclear reactor for a period of 50 hours. The radionuclides ^{56}Mn and ^{59}Fe were formed by (n, γ) reactions on 100% natural-isotopic-abundance ^{55}Mn and 0.33% natural-isotopic-abundance ^{58}Fe. At the end of the irradiation the absolute activity ratio, ^{56}Mn activity/^{59}Fe activity, was observed to be 10^5. Using the following data, calculate the weight ratio (grams Mn/grams Fe) of the elements in the sample. (1) Cross-section for (n, γ) reactions: ^{55}Mn = 13.3 barns; ^{58}Fe = 1.2 barns. (2) Atomic masses: Mn = 54.94 amu; Fe = 55.85 amu. (3) Half-lives: ^{56}Mn = 2.57 hours; ^{59}Fe = 45 days.

4. A sample of sea water (density ≈ 1.00 g/ml) is to be analyzed for its I$^-$ content. A 5-ml aliquot is placed in an electrolytic cell, to which is added 5 ml of a mixture of 0.1 M sodium acetate and 0.1 M acetic acid as supporting electrolyte, plus 1.0 ml of a solution of K^{129}I containing 1.0 μg of iodide with a specific activity of 312,000 cpm/μg I$^-$. An identical cell containing only the supporting electrolyte plus 1.0 ml of K^{129}I is also prepared. The two cells are placed in series, and a potential of -100 mV with respect to a saturated calomel electrode is imposed on two silver electrodes acting as the anodes for each cell. After ten minutes the activity of the two anodes is measured to be 20,800 and 104,000 cpm. Assuming that the current efficiency of the two cells for deposition of I$^-$ is the same, calculate the I$^-$ concentration in the sea water in ppm.

5. A sample containing N_0 atoms of $^{38}_{17}$Cl (Half-life = 37.3 min) was received at 1200 hours for beta counting. It was placed in a liquid scintillation-counter with 100% efficiency at 1230 hrs and counted for exactly 60 min. The accumulated counts were 100,000. Calculate N_0.

6. A 50-ml solution of 1.00 mM Ag$^+$ is titrated with a 1.0 mM solution of K$_2$^{51}CrO$_4$ (Half-life = 27.8 days) with an activity of 1.00×10^7 dps/mol. Plot the anticipated radiometric titration curve.

7. With reference to a *Chart of the Nuclides*, discuss the various neutron-activation-analysis techniques that might be used to determine Ni at the mg level. What neutron sources could be used? What nuclear reactions would be involved? What are the relative advantages and disadvantages of the various approaches to this determination?

8. Rapid analyses for Co in steel are often done by isotope dilution analysis. Assume that a 1.00-gram sample of steel is dissolved in acid and that exactly 2 ml of a "spike" solution of ^{60}Co is added to the solution. The spike solution has a concentration of 3 mg of Co/ml and a specific activity of 1.50×10^4 dpm/mg Co. Two electrodes are immersed in the solution and a small amount of Co$_2$O$_3$ plated out on the anode. The weight increase of the anode is determined to be 12.5 mg and its activity is 2500 dpm. Calculate the percent of Co in the steel sample.

9. A 2.00-min background count for a given counter yielded 3600 counts. A radioactive sample was counted for 2.00 min with the same counter and a total of 6400 counts were recorded. Calculate the background-corrected counting rate for the sample and its standard deviation, s_x. Express the counting rate in units of counts per minute.

10. Sample A, sample B, and background alone were each counted for 10 min with a given counter. The observed counting rates were 110, 205, and 44 counts per minute, respectively. Calculate the ratio of the activity of sample A to that of sample B and determine the standard deviation of this ratio.

11. Carbon-14, a β emitter with a half-life of 5720 years, is produced in the atmosphere by the reaction $^{14}N(n, p)^{14}C$, the neutrons coming from cosmic rays. The dating is based on the assumption that the amount of ^{14}C in the atmosphere (the ratio of $^{14}C/^{12}C$) remains constant over thousands of years. A living species incorporates this same ratio in all its carbon-containing molecules. When it dies, the incorporation of ^{14}C ceases, and the ^{14}C decays. The $^{14}C/^{12}C$ ratio determined from a wood sample taken from a dugout canoe at the bottom of a lake was found to be one-tenth the ratio determined from a wood sample less than 1 year old. How old is the dugout canoe?

12. One gram of pure radium emits 3.70×10^{10} disintegrations per second (1 curie). (a) How many atoms of radium are decaying each second? (b) How long will it take before half of the radium atoms have disintegrated?

13. Radon-222, the first decay product of ^{226}Ra, is an alpha-particle emitter with a 3.82 day half-life. A sample of ^{222}Rn gas was found to have an activity of 2.22×10^6 disintegrations per minute. (a) What is its activity in microcuries? (b) What is the decay constant in sec^{-1}? (c) How many atoms of ^{222}Rn does the sample contain? (d) How many grams? (1 curie = 3.70×10^{10} dps.)

14. Sodium-24 is a beta-particle emitter with a half-life of 14.8 hours. Calculate the activity in curies of a 20-mg sample of NaCl enriched with ^{24}Na so that it contains 1 atomic percent of ^{24}Na. (1 curie = 3.70×10^{10} dps.)

15. The neutron-activation-analysis limit of detection for arsenic is listed as 2×10^{-10} g for 1-hour irradiation in a neutron flux of 10^{13} n/(cm² sec). Using the value of 4.3×10^{-24} cm² as the cross-section of the arsenic nucleus for neutron capture, calculate the disintegrations per second expected from ^{76}As after irradiation for this period of time.

16. For any given isotope, what period of neutron irradiation is required to raise the observed activity to one-half the maximum activity?

17. Derive the relationship between the average lifetime of a radioactive atom and its half-life.

20

Fractionation Processes: Solvent Extraction

Henry Freiser

Great strides have been made in the development of highly selective analytical methods. However, the analytical chemist is called upon nowadays to deal with increasingly complex samples; as a result, separation steps can be necessary even with highly selective instrumental methods such as neutron activation or atomic absorption. Furthermore, separation of a component of interest can also concentrate it, which effectively increases the sensitivity of the analytical technique ultimately used. Although separation procedures are often not, strictly speaking, instrumental techniques, they frequently comprise an integral part of an instrumental procedure, and in fact may be incorporated into an instrumental design. Because of their importance, solvent extraction and chromatographic techniques are covered in the next three chapters.

20.1 PHASE PROCESSES

One of the most powerful approaches to separations involves pairs of phases in which the component of interest transfers from one phase to the other more readily than do interfering substances. For all phase-distribution equilibria, the classical phase rule of Gibbs is applicable and useful. The phase rule

$$P + V = C + 2 \tag{20.1}$$

relates the number of independent variables (degrees of freedom) V needed to describe a system of C components with a number of phases P that can coexist in equilibrium with one another. Note that a *component* is not the same as a *chemical species*; a two-component mixture of NaCl and H_2O contains the following species: H^+, OH^-, Na^+, Cl^-, H_2O, and NaCl.

The degrees of freedom include both temperature and pressure. Hence, in systems containing only condensed phases (liquids or solids) whose properties are only slightly affected by pressure changes, the phase rule reduces to

$$P + V = C + 1 \qquad (20.2)$$

It is useful to classify phase-separation processes according to the following criteria:

1. the states of the phases involved (solid, liquid, or gas)
2. whether the phase is in bulk or spread thin as on a surface
3. the manner in which the two phases are brought into contact (batch, multi-stage, or counter-current)

Bulk and "thin" phases can be distinguished by the fact that, in the latter, the phase involved spreads out over a relatively large area. Thus, both distillation and gas-liquid chromatography (GC) are separations involving a gas and a liquid phase, but in the latter the liquid phase is spread out as a thin layer on a largely inert solid supporting material, in the form of a column. Similarly, solvent extraction and liquid-partition chromatography (either paper or column) involve two liquid phases, but, in the latter, one of the liquid phases is present as a supported thin layer. In these examples, the mode of contacting the phases can also be different. In a simple distillation process, a batch of the mixture is heated in the boiler and the distillate consists of the more volatile components. In contrast, in GC the gas mixture moves in a *counter-current* manner to the immobilized liquid layer, insuring that the increasingly depleted, mobile gas phase encounters a fresh, clean portion of the immobilized liquid phase. In counter-current processes, a component comes—or almost comes—to equilibrium between two phases many times. It is possible to carry out separations using pairs of *bulk* phases which undergo counter-current contact. Thus, fractional distillation, in which a packed distillation column and reflux head are used, involves counter-current contact.

The focus of this chapter will be the chemistry of solvent extraction and its use as a separation process, particularly altering the chemical parameters of an extraction system in order to bring about the desired separation in a single step. The following two chapters will describe in more detail the principles and applications of chromatographic processes (in which a large number of equilibrium steps occur), in contrast to the "batch" solvent extraction processes.

20.2 GENERAL PRINCIPLES AND TERMINOLOGY OF SOLVENT EXTRACTION

Solvent extraction enjoys a favored position among separation techniques because of its ease, simplicity, speed, and wide scope. Separation by extraction can usually be accomplished in a few minutes using a simple pear-shaped separatory funnel (Fig. 20.1), and is applicable both to trace-level impurities and to major constituents. Furthermore, inorganic constituents are often separated in a form suitable for direct analysis by spectrophotometric, atomic absorption, radiochemical, or other methods.

FIGURE 20.1. *Separatory funnel.*

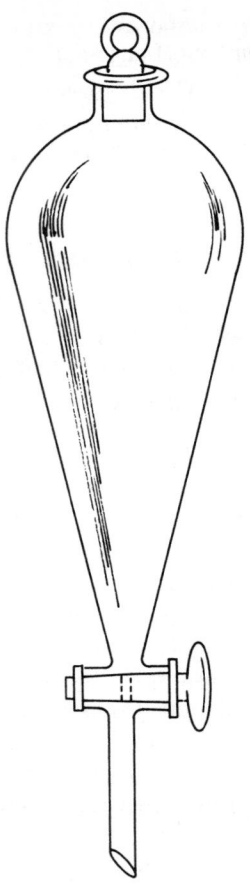

In solvent extraction, a solute of interest transfers from one solvent into a second solvent that is essentially immiscible with the first. The extent of transfer can be varied from negligible to essentially total extraction through control of the experimental conditions.

All solvent-extraction procedures can be described in terms of three aspects, or steps:

1. *The distribution of the solute,* called the extractable complex or species, *between the two immiscible solvents.* This step can be quantitatively described by Nernst's distribution law, which states that the ratio of the concentrations of a solute distributing between two essentially immiscible solvents at constant temperature is a constant, provided that the solute is not involved in chemical interactions in either solvent phase (other than solvation). That is,

$$K_D = \frac{[A]_0}{[A]} \qquad (20.3)$$

where $[A]_0$ = the molar concentration of solute A in organic solvent
    $[A]$ = the concentration of solute A in aqueous solution
    K_D = the distribution constant or distribution coefficient of A

2. *Chemical interactions in the aqueous phase or formation of the extractable complex.* Inasmuch as most of the substances of interest, particularly metal ions, are not usually encountered in a form that can be directly extracted into an organic solvent, chemical transformations to produce an extractable species are of primary importance in solvent-extraction processes.

3. *Chemical interactions in the organic phase*, such as self-association or mixed-ligand-complex formation. Such chemical interactions do not invalidate the Nernst distribution law (Eqn. 20.3), but the extraction cannot be quantitatively described by that simple equation. It becomes necessary to know how each of the contributing reactions affects the extent of extraction.

The extent of extraction is described in terms of the *distribution ratio, D*, given by

$$D_A = \frac{C_{A(0)}}{C_A} \tag{20.4}$$

where $C_{A(0)}$ = the *total analytical concentration* of component A (in whatever chemical form) in the organic phase

C_A = the total analytical concentration of A in the aqueous phase

If the substance does not undergo chemical reactions in either phase, then D_A reduces to K_D.

Another important way of expressing the extent of extraction is by the *fraction extracted F*, which is

$$F_A = \frac{C_{A(0)} V_0}{C_{A(0)} V_0 + C_A V} = \frac{D_A R_V}{D_A R_V + 1} \tag{20.5}$$

where V_0 = the volume of the organic phase

V = the volume of the aqueous phase

R_V = the *phase-volume ratio, V_0/V*

The *percentage extraction* is simply 100F. The fraction remaining in the aqueous phase, G_A, is

$$G_A = \frac{1}{D_A R_V + 1} = 1 - F_A \tag{20.6}$$

Equation 20.5 shows that for a given value of D, the extent of extraction can be increased by increasing the phase-volume ratio—that is, by increasing the volume of the organic phase. Another way of increasing the fraction extracted is to extract several times using only part of the total volume of organic solvent at a step. With $D_A R_V = 10$, the fraction extracted in a single batch-extraction is about 0.90. Two extractions with $R_V/2$ increases the fraction extracted to about 0.97; three extractions with $R_V/3$ increases it to 0.99—essentially quantitative extraction.

Consider two substances, A and B, present in a solution. Initially, the concentration ratio is C_A/C_B; after extraction, the concentration ratio in the organic phase will be $C_A F_A/C_B F_B$, where F_A and F_B are the corresponding fractions extracted. The ratio F_A/F_B (the factor by which the initial concentration ratio is changed by the separation) is a measure of the *separation* of the two substances. A corollary measure of separation is G_A/G_B, the change in the ratio of concentrations remaining in the aqueous phase.

Two substances whose distribution ratios differ by a constant factor will be most effectively separated if the product $D_A D_B$ is unity. For instance, consider a pair of substances whose distribution ratios D_A and D_B are 10^3 and 10^1, respectively. If these substances were present in equal quantity, then a single extraction would remove 99.9% of the first and 90% of the second. However, if the two distribution ratios were 10^1 and 10^{-1} (again differing by a factor of 100), the respective fractions extracted would be 90% of A and 10% of B, a much more effective separation.

Classification of Extraction Systems: Organic and Inorganic

The following classification refers essentially to inorganic systems, particularly those involving metal ions. Many organic compounds, of course, are extractable without any significant chemical reaction occurring—for instance, alcohols, ethers, carboxyl compounds, and so on. Systematic changes in the extraction of such compounds by various solvents can be related to the degree of hydrogen bonding and to other, less specific, interactions of the organic compounds, as well as to their molecular weights.

Most metal salts are soluble in water but not in organic solvents, particularly hydrocarbons and chlorinated hydrocarbons. This solubility is caused by the high dielectric constant of water and by its ability to coordinate with ions, especially metal ions, so that the hydrated salt more nearly resembles the solvent. To form a metal complex that can be extracted by an organic solvent, it is necessary to replace the coordinated water around the metal ion by groups, or ligands, that will form an uncharged species compatible with the low-dielectric-constant organic solvent.

Extractable metal species can be formed in a great variety of ways. A classification system of metal extractions is therefore very useful, particularly as a guide to understanding the hundreds of different extraction systems now in use. Methods for forming an extractable species include:

1. *Simple* (monodentate) *coordination* alone, as with $GeCl_4$.

2. *Heteropoly acids*, a class of coordination complexes in which the central ion is complex rather than monatomic, as with phosphomolybdic acid, $H_3PO_3 \cdot 12MoO_3$.

3. *Chelation* (polydentate coordination) alone, as with $Al(8\text{-quinolinate})_3$.

4. *Ion-association* alone, as with $Cs^+,(C_6H_5)_4B^-$ (the comma is used to indicate association between the two ions).

Combinations of the above can be used, such as

5. *Simple coordination and ion-association*, as with $(\text{"Onium"})^+,FeCl_4^-$. "Onium" stands for one of the following cation types: hydrated hydronium ion, $(H_2O)_3H^+$, a rather labile cation requiring stabilization by solvation with an oxygen-containing solvent; a substituted ammonium ion, $R_nNH_{(4-n)}^+$, where R is an alkyl or aralkyl group and n may vary from 1 to 3; a substituted phosphonium ion R_4P^+;

stibonium ion R_4Sb^+; sulfonium ion; and other ions of this sort, including cationic dyes such as Rhodamine B.

6. *Chelation and ion-association* with either positively or negatively charged metal chelates, such as $Cu(2,9\text{-dimethyl-1,10-phenanthroline})_2^+, ClO_4^-$ or $3(n\text{-}C_4H_9NH_3^+), Co(\text{Nitroso-R-Salt})_3^{3-}$.

7. *Simple coordination and chelation*, such as in $Zn(8\text{-quinolinol} \cdot \text{pyridine})$. This category is of significance for coordinatively unsaturated metal chelates—those with a monoprotic bidentate reagent in which the coordination number of the metal is greater than twice its valence.

The above classification is used in Table 20.1; clearly, a thorough understanding of solvent extraction of metals presupposes a deep knowledge of coordination chemistry.

Methods of Extraction

Generally, one has a choice of three methods of extraction: batch extraction, continuous extraction, and counter-current extraction. The choice is generally determined by the distribution coefficient of the substance extracted and, in the case where separation is desired, by the closeness of the various distribution coefficients involved. Because of the speed and simplicity of batch extraction, this method is preferred when applicable.

Batch Extraction. When experimental conditions can be adjusted so that the fraction extracted is 0.99 or higher ($DR_v \geqslant 100$), then a single or batch extraction will transfer the bulk of the desired substance to the organic phase. Most analytical extractions fall into this category. The usual apparatus for a batch extraction is a separatory funnel such as the Squibb pear-shaped funnel (Fig. 20.1), although many special types of funnels have been designed [1].

Even with DR_v equal to only 10, two successive batch extractions will transfer 99% of the material to the organic phase. If one chooses as a criterion of separation that substance A be at least 99% extracted and substance B no more than 1% extracted, then, from Equation 20.5, one must have $D_A R_v > 100$ and $D_B R_v < 0.01$ for a single (batch) extraction.

Continuous Extraction. For relatively small DR_v values, even multiple batch extraction cannot conveniently or economically be used—too much organic solvent is required. Continuous extraction using volatile solvents can be carried out in an apparatus in which the solvent is distilled from an extract-collection flask, condensed, contacted with the aqueous phase, and returned to the extract collection flask in a continuous fashion.

Counter-Current Distributions. A special multiple-contact extraction is needed to effect the separation of two substances whose D values are very similar. In principle, counter-current distribution (CCD) could be carried out in a series of separatory

TABLE 20.1. *Representative Metal-Extraction Systems, with Examples*

Primary Systems

  I. Simple (Monodentate) Coordination Systems

    A. Certain Halide Systems: $HgCl_2$, $GeCl_4$

    B. Certain Nitrate Systems: $(UO_2)(TBP)_2(NO_3)_2$

  II. Heteropoly Acid Systems: $H_3PO_4 \cdot 12MoO_3$

  III. Chelate Systems   Reactive Grouping

    A. Bidentate Chelating Agents

      1. 4-Membered Ring Systems

        a. Disubstituted dithiocarbamates: Na^+, $S{=}C{-}S^-$
           $(C_2H_5)_2NCSS^-$ or $(C_6H_5CH_2)_2NCSS^-$

        b. Xanthates: Na^+, $C_2H_5OCSS^-$

        c. Dithiophosphoric acids: diethyldithio- $S{-}P{-}S^-$
           phosphoric acid

        d. Arsenic and arsonic acids: benzenarsonic $^-O{-}As{-}O^-$
           acid

      2. 5-Membered Ring Systems

        a. *N*-Nitroso-*N*-arylhydroxylamines: Cup- $O{=}N{-}N{-}O^-$
           ferron (*N*-nitrosophenylhydroxylamine)

        b. α-Dioximes: Dimethylglyoxime $N{=}C{-}C{=}N^-$

        c. Diaryldithiocarbazones: Dithizone $N{-}N{=}C{-}S^-$
           (diphenylthiocarbazone)

        d. 8-Quinolinols: Oxine (8-quinolinol), $N{=}C{-}C{-}O^-$
           methyloxine (2-methyl-8-quinolinol)

      3. 6-Membered Ring Systems

        a. β-Diketones: Acetylacetone, TTA $O{=}C{-}C{=}C{-}O^-$
           (thenoyltrifluoroacetone), Morin,
           quinalizarin

        b. *o*-Nitrosophenols: 1-nitroso-2-naphthol $O{=}N{-}C{=}C{-}O^-$

    B. Polydentate Chelating Systems: Pyridylazo- $N{=}C{-}N{=}N{-}C{=}C{-}O^-$
       naphthol (PAN) and pyridylazoresorcinol
       (PAR)

  IV. Simple Ion-Association Systems

    A. Metal in Cation

      1. Inorganic anions: Cs^+,I_3^- or Cs^+,PF_6^-

      2. Tetraphenylboride anion

Mixed Systems

  V. Ion-Association and Simple Coordination Systems

    A. Metal in Cation

      1. Oxygen Solvents (alcohols, ketones, esters,
        ethers): $[(UO_2)(ROH)_6]^{2+}$,$2NO_3^-$

    B. Metal in Anion (paired with "onium" ion)

      1. Halides: $FeCl_4^-$

Continued

TABLE 20.1. *Continued*

2. Thiocyanates: $Co(CNS)_4{}^{2-}$
3. Oxyanions: $MnO_4{}^-$

VI. Ion-Association and Chelation Systems
  A. Cationic Chelates
    1. Phenanthrolines and polypyridyls: $Cu(I)$-$(2,9$-dimethylphenanthroline$)_2{}^+$
  B. Anionic chelates
    1. Sulfonated Chelating Agents
      a. 1-Nitroso-2-naphthol: $Co(III)(nitroso$ R Salt$)_3{}^{3-}$
      b. 8-Quinolinol: $Fe(III)(7$-iodo-8-quino-linol-5 sulfonate$)_3{}^{3-}$

VII. Chelation and Simple Coordination Systems: $Th(TTA)_4 \cdot TBP$, $Ca(TTA) \cdot (TOPO)_2$

funnels, each containing an identical lower phase. The mixture is introduced into the upper phase in the first funnel. After equilibration, the upper phase (containing the substance of interest) is transferred to the second funnel, and a new portion of upper phase (devoid of sample) is introduced into the first funnel. After both funnels are equilibrated, the upper phase of each is moved on to the next funnel, and a fresh portion of upper phase is again added to the first funnel. This process is repeated for as many times as there are funnels, or more, collecting the upper phases as "elution fractions." With automated CCD equipment, several hundred transfers can be conveniently accomplished, which will permit the separation of two solutes whose D_A/D_B ratio is less than two.

It can be shown that the distribution ratio D of a solute in a CCD process is related to the concentration in the various separatory funnels or stages by the binomial expansion

$$(F + G)^n = 1 \tag{20.7}$$

where n is the number of stages in the CCD process and F and G are given by Equations 20.5 and 20.6.

The fraction $T_{n(r)}$ of the solute present in the rth stage for n transfers can be calculated from

$$T_{n(r)} = \frac{n!}{r!(n-r)!} \frac{(DR_v)^r}{(1 + DR_v)^n} = \frac{n!}{r!(n-r)!} F^r G^{n-r} \tag{20.8}$$

The distribution of two solutes with differing distribution ratios in the tubes after different numbers of transfers is illustrated in Figure 20.2. As the number of transfers is increased, the solute is spread through a larger number of tubes. The separating ability, however, increases with increased number of transfers. After the run is complete, each tube is analyzed for the solute. In a preparative run, the contents of the tubes containing a particular solute are combined.

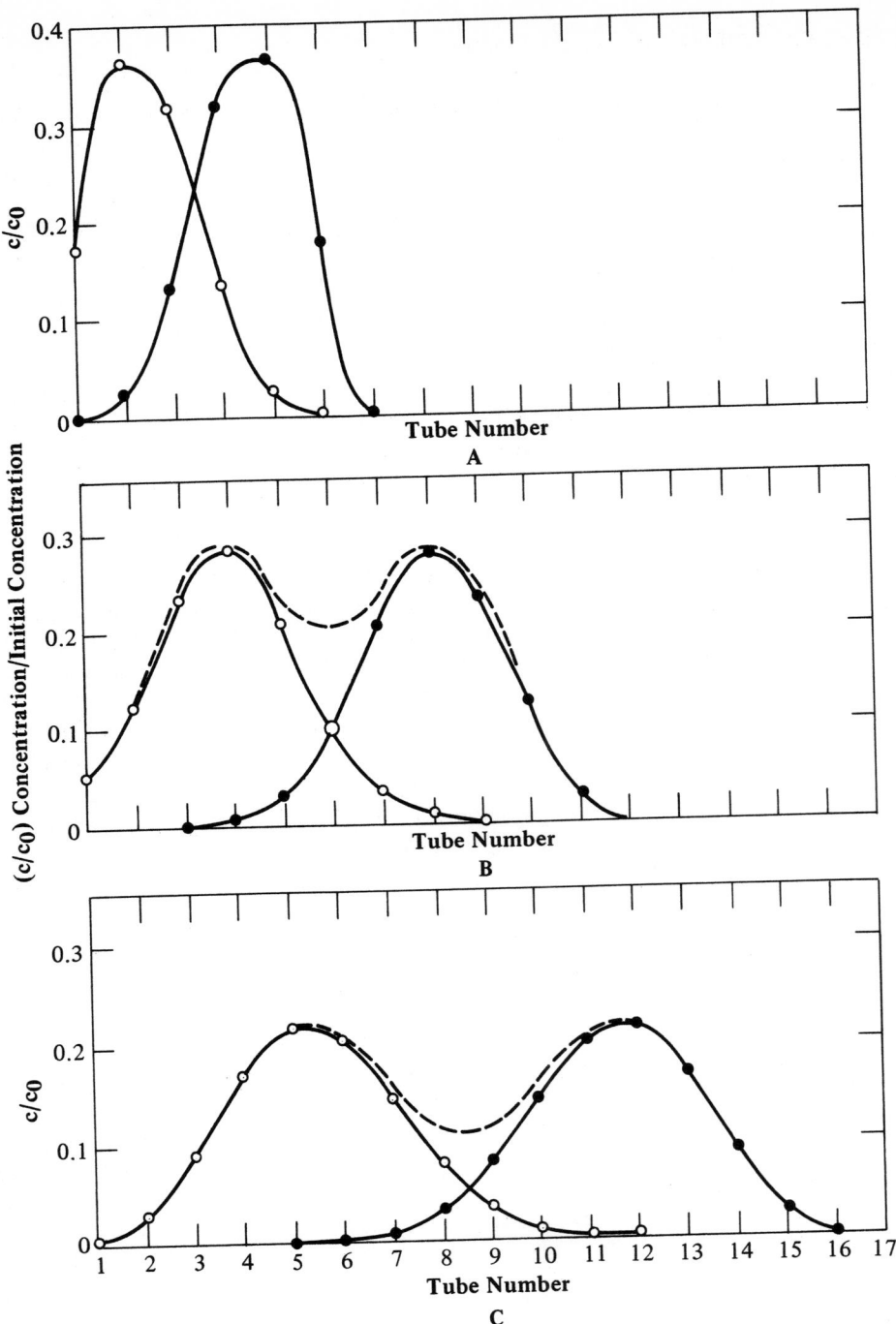

FIGURE 20.2. *Distribution of two solutes in counter-current distribution tubes after different numbers of transfers. The distribution ratio for the left peak is 7/3 and that for the right peak is 3/7. (A) After 5 transfers (n = 5); (B) After 10 transfers (n = 10); (C) After 15 transfers (n = 15). From H. Purnell,* Gas Chromatography, *New York: John Wiley, 1962, p 95, by permission of the publisher.*

20.3 EXPERIMENTAL TECHNIQUES

Selection of a particular extraction method from the large number of methods available involves considering the behavior of interfering substances that might be present, as well as that of the substance of interest. Another important factor is how the species in question is to be analytically determined after extraction. Some of the chelate systems (for instance, dithizone chelates) are strongly enough colored to provide the basis for a spectrophotometric determination. If the extract is to be aspirated into the flame of an atomic absorption apparatus, however, a dithizone solution is not as desirable as a nonbenzenoid reagent, because of its behavior in the flame.

The problem is greatly simplified by referring to the literature, from which one can choose a method on the basis of similarity or even exact matching of separation problems. One generally proceeds in a new situation by following published precedents, but a better understanding of the design of an extraction procedure can be obtained from a careful study of the *basis* of previous work.

Choice of Solvent

Solvents differ in polarity, density, and ability to participate in complex formation. Generally, it is more convenient to use a solvent denser than water when the substance of interest is being extracted and a less dense solvent when interferences are extracted away from the substance of interest. In the former case, this is because the (denser) phase containing the extracted substance of interest can be conveniently drained from a separatory funnel leaving behind the original solution; this can then be easily re-extracted if necessary. In the latter case, the (less dense) solvent containing the interferences can be left behind in the funnel. If multiple extractions are necessary to remove the interferences, however, it may be more convenient to use a solvent denser than water.

Ion-association complexes in which one of the ions is strongly solvated, such as the hydrated hydronium ion encountered in extracting chloride complexes from HCl solutions (for instance, $(H_2O)_3H^+, FeCl_4^-$), can be most effectively extracted with oxygen-containing solvents such as alcohols, esters, ketones, and ethers. Such solvents increase extractability significantly over that obtainable with hydrocarbon (or chlorinated hydrocarbon) solvents with coordinatively unsaturated chelates—that is, those in which the coordination number of the metal ion is greater than twice its oxidation state (e.g., $ZnOx_2$, where Ox refers to the 8-quinolinate (oxine) anion).

On the other hand, ion-association complexes involving quaternary ammonium, phosphonium, or arsonium ions, and coordinatively saturated chelates, can be readily extracted into hydrocarbons as well as into oxygenated solvents. In such cases, the principle of "like dissolves like," as expressed by the Hildebrand "solubility parameter" δ (defined as the heat of vaporization of one cm^3 of a liquid), offers a guide to extractability. Using this approach, the following expression can be derived:

$$2.3RT \log K_D = V_s(\delta_0 - \delta_w)(\delta_0 + \delta_w - 2\delta_s) \tag{20.9}$$

where
  V_s = the molar volume of the solute
  δ_0 = the solubility parameter of the organic solvent
  δ_w = the solubility parameter of the aqueous phase
  δ_s = the solubility parameter of the distributing solute

A plot of K_D versus δ_0 is parabolic, with a maximum K_D for an organic solvent whose δ_0 matches δ_s. Simply expressed, in the absence of specific chemical interactions, a substance will be most extractable in a solvent whose δ value most closely matches its own. Thus, 8-quinolinine ($\delta = 10$) is more extractable into benzene ($\delta = 9.2$) than into CCl_4 ($\delta = 8.6$), and more into CCl_4 than into heptane ($\delta = 7.4$). The application of this principle is limited by the lack of known δ values for many extractable species.

It must not be assumed that the best solvent to use is always the one that gives the highest extractability, because a poorer solvent is often more selective for separations.

Stripping and Backwashing

Occasionally it is of advantage to remove (*strip*) the extracted solute from the organic phase into which it has been extracted as part of the analytical procedure. This is done by shaking the organic phase with a fresh portion of aqueous solution containing acids or other reagents that will decompose the extractable complex in the organic phase. The charged metal ion will then be extracted preferentially into the new aqueous solution.

The technique of *backwashing* also involves contacting the organic extract with a fresh aqueous phase. Here, the combined organic phases from multiple extraction of the original aqueous phase, which contain almost all the desired element and some of the impurities, are shaken with small portions of a fresh aqueous phase containing the same reagent concentrations initially present. Under these conditions, most of the desired element remains in the organic phase while the bulk of the impurities are back-extracted (backwashed) into the aqueous phase because of their lower distribution ratios.

Treatment of Emulsions

After shaking two immiscible liquids, a sharp phase boundary should rapidly reappear; therefore, emulsions should not be allowed to form. The tendency to form emulsions decreases with increasing interfacial tension. In liquids of relatively high mutual solubility or that contain surfactants, the interfacial tension is low and the tendency to form emulsions is correspondingly high. Low-viscosity solvents and solvents with densities significantly different from that of water are also helpful in avoiding emulsions. With systems that tend to form emulsions, repeated inversion of the two phases rather than vigorous shaking is called for. In an extreme case, using a continuous extractor rather than a separatory funnel is often successful. The tendency to form emulsions can be reduced by adding neutral salts or an anti-emulsion agent.

20.4 IMPORTANT EXPERIMENTAL VARIABLES

In addition to such important factors as the choice of organic solvent, the avoidance of emulsions, and the actual method of extraction—batch, continuous, or countercurrent—there are other important and easily controlled experimental variables. In the extraction of metals, the most important and critical of these are the pH of the aqueous solution and the use of masking agents. These two factors are often primarily responsible for the specificity (degree of separation) of an extraction method.

Chelate Extraction Systems

As seen from Table 20.1, many chelating extractants are weak acids and can be represented as HR. For a chelate extraction process

$$M^{n+} + nHR \text{ (org)} \rightleftharpoons MR_n \text{ (org)} + nH^+ \qquad (20.10)$$

the distribution ratio, D_M, is given by

$$D_M = \frac{C_{M(0)}}{C_M} = \frac{[MR_n]_0}{[M^{n+}]/\alpha_M} = \frac{[MR_n]_0}{[M^{n+}]} \alpha_M \qquad (20.11)$$

In this equation, $C_{M(0)} = [MR_n]_0$, since there is only one metal-containing species in the organic phase. In the aqueous phase there may be many metal-containing species in addition to M^{n+}, but these can be accounted for by using α_M, the fraction of the total metal concentration actually present as M^{n+},

$$\alpha_M = [M^{n+}]/C_M \qquad (20.12)$$

The formation of the chelate MR_n is expressed by the formation constant

$$\beta_n = \frac{[MR_n]}{[M^{n+}][R^-]^n} \qquad (20.13)$$

and the formation of the anion R^- from HR is quantitatively given by the acid-dissociation constant

$$K_a = \frac{[H^+][R^-]}{[HR]} \qquad (20.14)$$

Incorporating these expressions as well as those for the distribution of the reagent HR and chelate MR_n (their distribution coefficients),

$$K_{D_R} = \frac{[HR]_0}{[HR]} \qquad (20.15)$$

$$K_{D_C} = \frac{[MR_n]_0}{[MR_n]} \qquad (20.16)$$

it can be seen that

$$D_M = \frac{[MR_n]_0}{[M^{n+}]} \alpha_M = \beta_n \frac{[MR_n]_0}{[MR_n]} [R^-]^n \alpha_M = \beta_n \frac{K_{D_C} K_a^n}{K_{D_R}^n} \frac{[HR]_0^n}{[H^+]^n} \alpha_M \qquad (20.17)$$

The combination of constants (K_{D_C}, K_a, K_{D_R}) in Equation 20.17 is called the *overall extraction constant*, K_{ex}. Representative values of K_{ex} are listed in Table 20.2. The $pH_{1/2}$ values are explained below.

Equation 20.17 shows that the value of D_M increases with increasing concentration of the reagent in the organic phase, and decreases with increasing hydrogen-ion concentration in the aqueous phase. Control of pH is therefore important in

TABLE 20.2. *Values of Extraction Constants, K_{ex} and $pH_{1/2}$, in Selected Metal-Chelate Systems*

Metal Ion	Extractant			
	8-Quinolinol (0.10 M in CHCl$_3$)		Dithizone (10^{-4} M in CCl$_4$)	
	log K_{ex}	$pH_{1/2}$	log K_{ex}	$pH_{1/2}$
Ag$^+$	——	6.5	7.18	-3.2
Al^{3+}	-5.22	2.87	Not extracted	
Ca^{2+}	-17.9	10.4	Not extracted	
Cd^{2+}	——	4.65	2.14	2.9
Cu^{2+}	1.77	1.51	10.53	-1.3
Fe^{3+}	4.11	1.00	Not extracted	
Pb^{2+}	-8.04	5.04	0.44	3.8
Zn^{2+}	——	3.30	2.3	2.8

chelate extractions. Inasmuch as the extractions of different metal ions with a given reagent are characterized by different extraction constants, the extraction curves (percent extracted versus pH) will be similar in shape, but displaced in pH. Figure 20.3 shows a typical set of extraction curves for various metal dithizonates. Note that, whereas the curves of all the divalent metal ions are parallel, those for Ag$^+$ and Tl$^+$ are less steep, because $n = 1$ in Equation 20.17. From the curve it can be

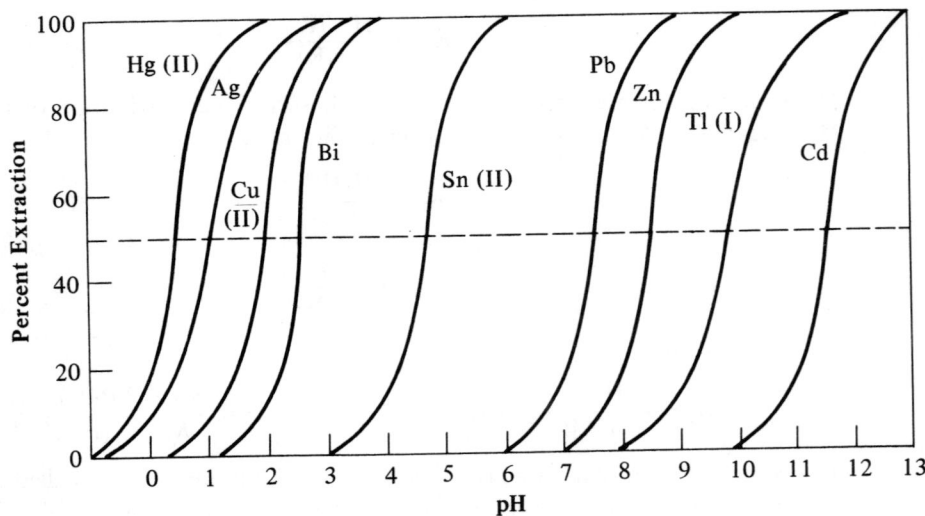

FIGURE 20.3. *Qualitative extraction curves for metal dithizonates. From G. H. Morrison and H. Freiser in C. L. Wilson and D. Wilson, eds.,* Comprehensive Analytical Chemistry, *vol. 1A, Amsterdam: Elsevier, 1959, by permission of the publisher.*

concluded that at pH = 2, Hg^{2+} is 100% extracted; Ag^+, Cu^{2+}, Bi^{3+} are fractionally extracted; and the other ions listed are not extracted at all. It would be simple to separate Hg^{2+} from Sn^{2+}, Pb^{2+}, Zn^{2+}, Tl^+, and Cd^{2+} in a mixture by extracting with dithizone at pH = 2, but difficult to separate Hg^{2+} from Ag^+, Cu^{2+}, or Bi^{3+}. Since Bi^{3+} is only 10% extracted at this pH, backwashing several times with fresh aqueous (pH = 2) portions would quantitatively remove Bi^{3+} (90% of the remaining amount each time) from the extract without appreciably affecting the extracted Hg.

One useful way to condense extraction information from curves such as in Figure 20.3 or from expressions such as Equation 20.17 is to specify the $pH_{1/2}$ value for the metal ion, obtained with a particular concentration of the reagent. The $pH_{1/2}$ is the pH value at which half the metal is extracted into the organic solvent (i.e., when $D = 1$). Thus, from Figure 20.3, the $pH_{1/2}$ values for the dithizonates are 0.3 for Hg, 1.0 for Ag, 1.9 for Cu, 2.5 for Bi, 4.7 for Sn, 7.4 for Pb, 8.5 for Zn, 9.7 for Tl, and 11.6 for Cd. For a single batch extraction, a minimum of three units difference in $pH_{1/2}$ is required to permit the quantitative separation of two metal ions; however, as mentioned above, a smaller difference suffices if backwashing is used.

Masking Agents. The factor α_M in Equation 20.17, which represents the fraction of the total metal concentration in the aqueous phase that is in the form of the simple hydrated metal ion, points to the importance of masking agents in improving the selectivity of extraction. Masking agents are competing complexing agents that form charged water-soluble complexes. Their effectiveness in preventing reaction of a metal ion with an extracting agent increases with increasing formation constant of the masking complex, increasing concentration of the masking agent, and, for the many masking agents that are bases, with increasing pH. Some representative values of α_M are listed in Table 20.3 for different masking agents.

As an illustration of masking, consider a mixture of Ag^+ and Cu^{2+} from which Ag^+ is to be selectively extracted. It can be seen from Figure 20.3 that Ag^+ can be quantitatively extracted at pH = 3; but Cu^{2+} is also appreciably extracted. In the presence of 0.1 M EDTA, the value of log $\alpha_{Cu} = -6.6$ (estimated from Table 20.3), which displaces the extraction curve of copper dithizonate to the right, increasing $pH_{1/2}$ by 3.3 units (see Eqn. 20.17). Since the value of log α_{Ag} under these conditions is about -0.2, EDTA has little effect on the extraction curve of silver dithizonate. Hence, in the presence of 0.1 M EDTA at pH = 3, Ag^+ will be selectively extracted from Cu^{2+}.

Similarly, the use of cyanide as a masking agent will permit the selective extraction of Al^{3+} by 8-quinolinol in the presence of such transition-metal ions as Cu^{2+} and Fe^{3+}, as well as Ag^+; Al^{3+} does not form a CN^- complex, whereas the other metals form strong complexes. Other examples of successful masking can be predicted with the help of Table 20.3. Masking such as this is also useful in improving the selectivity of ion-exchange separations.

Kinetics of Extraction. Kinetic factors may be important in all types of extraction, but they are most frequently observed with chelate-extraction systems. Extraction equilibrium can usually be achieved in one or two minutes of shaking because mass-transfer rates are reasonably rapid; however, the formation of an extractable complex

Metal Ion[a]	Masking Agent	pH			
		2	5	8	10
Ag^+	EDTA	0	0.5	3.7	5.5
	NH_3	0	0.1	4.6	7.2
	CN^-	4.7	10.7	16.7	19.0
Al^{3+}	EDTA	1.8	3.2	14.5	18.3
	OH^-	0	0.4	9.3	17.3
	F^-	10.0	14.5	14.5	17.3
Ca^{2+}	EDTA	0	3.2	7.1	8.9
	Citrate	0	1.8	2.5	2.5
Cd^{2+}	EDTA	1.8	7.9	12.2	14.0
	NH_3	0	0	2.3	6.7
	CN^-	0	0.7	10.1	14.5
Cu^{2+}	EDTA	4.6	10.7	15.0	16.8
	NH_3	0	0	3.6	8.2
Fe^{3+}	EDTA	10.3	17.2	22.0	26.4
	OH^-	0	3.7	9.7	13.7
	F^-	5.7	8.9	9.8	13.7
Pb^{2+}	EDTA	4.2	10.2	14.4	16.2
	OH^-	0	0	0.5	2.7
	Citrate	1.0	4.2	4.2	5.3
Zn^{2+}	EDTA	2.8	8.8	12.9	14.7
	NH_3	0	0	0.4	0.7
	CN^-	0	0	7.5	2.3

a. Al^{3+}, Ca^{2+}, and Pb^{2+} are not masked by NH_3 or CN^-. Cu^{2+} is very strongly masked by CN^-, >20. Fe^{3+} is very strongly masked by CN^-, but is not masked by NH_3.

is sometimes slow enough to affect the course of the extraction, particularly with certain metal chelates. For example, most substitution reactions of Cr^{3+} are very slow; thus, although Cr^{3+} forms stable chelates, it is rarely extracted in the usual chelate-extraction procedure. Less dramatic, but analytically useful, is the difference in the speed of formation of various metal dithizonates, which makes it possible to separate Hg^{2+} from Cu^{2+}, and Zn^{2+} from Ni^{2+}, by using shaking times of no longer than one minute.

Ion-Association Extraction Systems

As with chelate systems, ion-association extraction equilibria involve a number of reactions. An example is the extraction of Fe^{3+} from HCl solutions into ether,

$$Fe^{3+} + 4 Cl^- \rightleftharpoons FeCl_4^- \tag{20.18}$$

$$H(H_2O)_4^+ + FeCl_4^- \rightleftharpoons H_9O_4^+, FeCl_4^- \tag{20.19}$$

$$H_9O_4^+, FeCl_4^- \rightleftharpoons H_9O_4^+, FeCl_4^- \text{ (ether)} \tag{20.20}$$

The importance of chloride and of acid in the overall extraction is evident. About 6 M HCl is required for optimum extraction of iron. Ether, an oxygen-containing solvent, is needed to stabilize the $H_9O_4^+$ ion. If a $(C_4H_9)_4N^+$ salt is added, then the iron can be extracted out of a much less acidic solution, provided that the chloride concentration is about 6 M; and, more significantly, it would be possible to use benzene, CCl_4, or $CHCl_3$ for the extraction as well as oxygen-containing solvents.

In many ion-association extraction systems, high concentrations of electrolyte are effective in increasing the extent of extraction. The addition of such salts, referred to as *salting-out* agents, serves two purposes. The first, and more obvious, is to aid the direct formation of the complex by the mass-action effect—the formation of a chloro or nitrato complex, for instance, is promoted by increasing the concentration of Cl^- or NO_3^-. Second, as the salt concentration increases, the concentration of "free," (uncomplexed) water decreases because the ions require a certain amount of water for hydration. This decreases the solubility of the complex in the aqueous phase. Because Li^+ is more strongly hydrated than K^+, $LiNO_3$ is a much better salting-out agent than KNO_3 for nitrate extraction systems, even though equimolar solutions supply the same nitrate concentration.

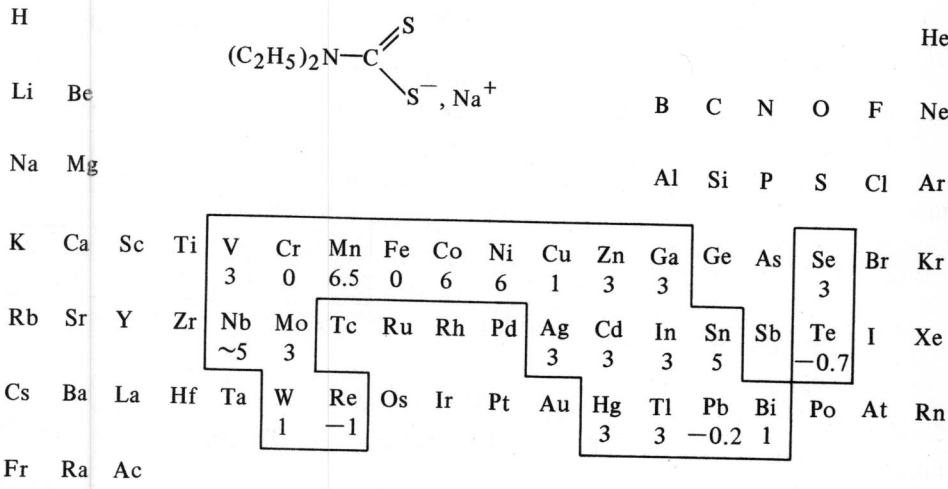

FIGURE 20.4. *Elements extractable with sodium diethyldithiocarbamate. The number under an element symbol indicates the pH value at which the element can be completely extracted. From H. Freiser and G. H. Morrison*, Ann. Rev. Nucl. Sci., *9, (1959), by permission of Annual Reviews, Inc.*

In this section, the applications of a few representative extractants are described in periodic array. Elements extractable as diethyldithiocarbamates are shown in Figure 20.4. The numbers under the element represent the lowest pH at which it will be extracted. Because the reagent is nonaromatic, its chelates are readily decomposed in a flame; consequently, this reagent is widely used in a separation or preconcentration step prior to atomic absorption spectrometry.

The application if dithizone is shown in Figure 20.5. Because of the highly conjugated double-bonds in the reagent molecule, the chelates are all highly colored, so that the metal ion can be determined with good sensitivity by absorption spectrophotometry once it has been extracted.

Dithizone

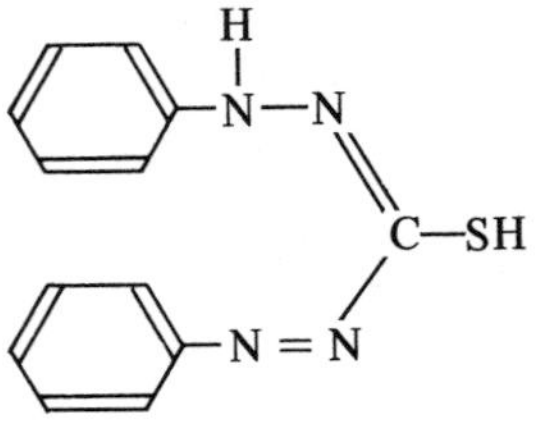

H																	He
Li	Be											B	C	N	O	F	Ne
Na	Mg											Al	Si	P	S	Cl	Ar
K	Ca	Sc	Ti	V	Cr	Mn ~11	Fe 6	Co 7	Ni 8	Cu 1	Zn 8	Ga	Ge	As	Se	Br	Kr
Rb	Sr	Y	Zr	Nb	Mo	Tc	Ru	Rh	Pd <0	Ag <0	Cd 13	In 8	Sn 6	Sb	Te	I	Xe
Cs	Ba	La	Hf	Ta	W	Re	Os	Ir	Pt 2	Au <0	Hg <0	Tl 3	Pb 8.5	Bi >2	Po <0	At	Rn
Fr	Ra	Ac															

Ce	Pr	Nd	Pm	Sm	Eu	Gd	Tb	Dy	Ho	Er	Tm	Yb	Lu
Th	Pa	U	Np	Pu	Am	Cm	Bk	Cf	E	Fm	Md	102	103

FIGURE 20.5. *Elements extractable by dithizone. The number under the element symbol indicates the pH value at which the element can be completely extracted. From H. Freiser and G. H. Morrison,* Ann. Rev. Nucl. Sci., 9, (1959), *by permission of Annual Reviews, Inc.*

Extractions with 8-quinolinol (8-hydroxyquinoline, oxine) are shown in Figure 20.6. These chelates are often used in the spectrophotometric or fluorimetric determination of the element.

The conditions for extracting metal ions from hydrochloric acid solution into ethyl ether as ion-association complexes are shown in Figure 20.7.

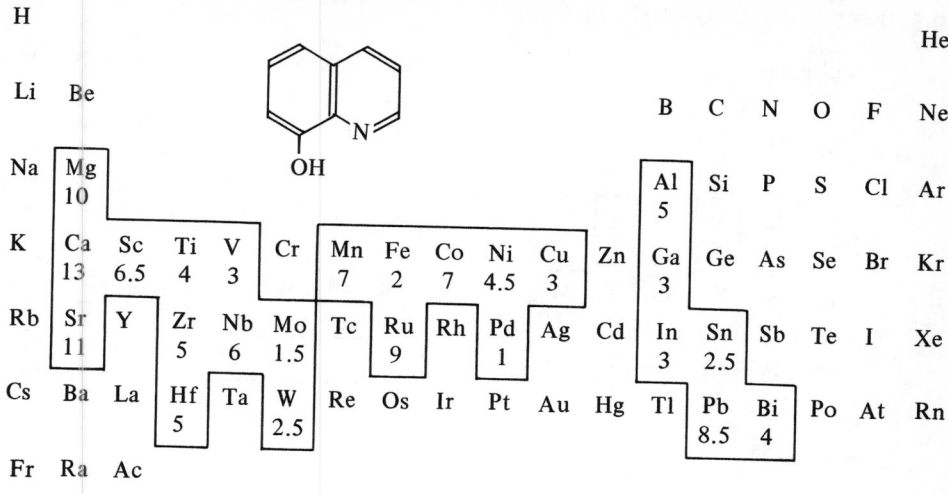

FIGURE 20.6. *Elements extractable by 8-quinolinol. The number under the element symbol indicates the pH value at which the element can be completely extracted. From H. Freiser and G. H. Morrison,* Ann. Rev. Nucl. Sci., *9, (1959), by permission of Annual Reviews, Inc.*

Outline of Illustrative Extraction Procedures

Several specific extraction procedures are outlined below to illustrate the principles discussed in previous sections. For a working method, more detailed procedures can be found in the selected bibliography at the end of the chapter. The usual precautions peculiar to trace-element determinations (for instance, impurities and solution stability) must also be carefully observed.

Extracting Cadmium with Dithizone. It is possible to separate Cd^{2+} from Pb^{2+} or Zn^{2+} by using a highly alkaline solution during extraction; and from Ag^+, Hg^{2+}, Ni^{2+}, Co^{2+}, and Cu^{2+} by stripping the Cd^{2+} at a pH of 2 where the other dithizonates are stable.

A solution containing up to 50 μg Cd^{2+} is treated with tartrate (to avoid precipitating the hydroxide), and made basic with an excess of 25% KOH. This is now shaken with successive 5-ml portions of dithizone in $CHCl_3$ until the aqueous layer remains yellowish brown (indicating excess dithizone). The combined chloroform extracts are then shaken for two minutes with an aqueous solution buffered at pH = 2, which will strip the Cd^{2+} quantitatively. To remove small amounts of Cu^{2+} and Hg^{2+} that may accompany the Cd^{2+}, re-extract the aqueous solution (pH = 2)

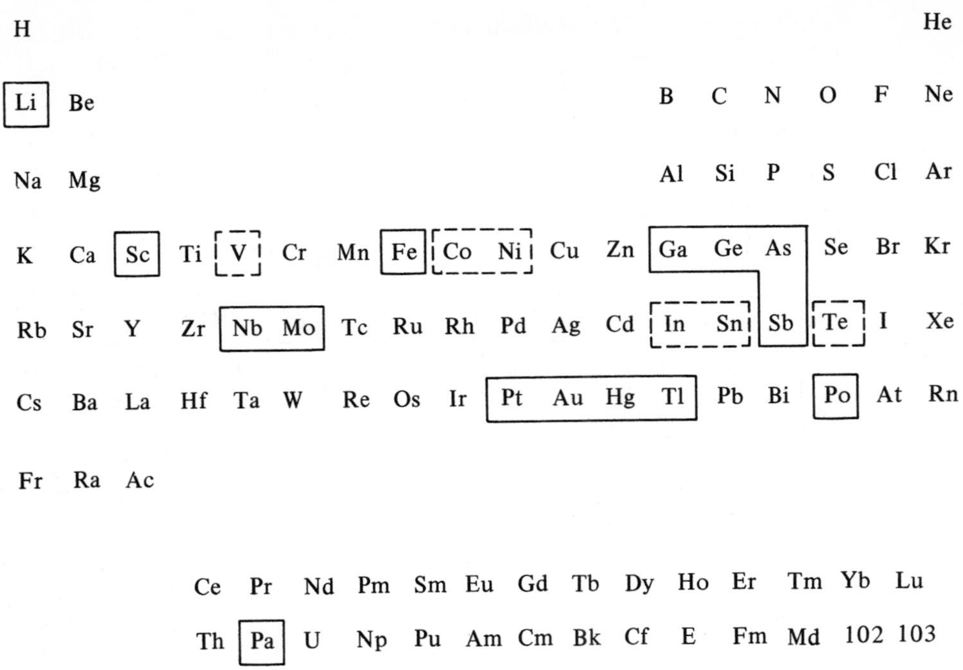

H   He

Li Be   B   C   N   O   F   Ne

Na Mg   Al Si P   S   Cl Ar

K   Ca Sc Ti V   Cr Mn Fe Co Ni Cu Zn Ga Ge As Se Br Kr

Rb Sr Y   Zr Nb Mo Tc Ru Rh Pd Ag Cd In Sn Sb Te I   Xe

Cs Ba La Hf Ta W   Re Os Ir Pt Au Hg Tl Pb Bi Po At Rn

Fr Ra Ac

        Ce Pr Nd Pm Sm Eu Gd Tb Dy Ho Er Tm Yb Lu

        Th Pa U   Np Pu Am Cm Bk Cf E   Fm Md 102 103

FIGURE 20.7. *Elements extracted in chloride system. Solid blocks: appreciably extracted; broken blocks: partially extracted. From H. Freiser and G. H. Morrison,* Ann. Rev. Nucl. Sci., *9, (1959), by permission of Annual Reviews, Inc.*

with a fresh portion of dithizone in $CHCl_3$; the Cd^{2+} will remain in the aqueous solution.

Extracting Lead with Dithizone. A slightly acid solution containing up to 100 μg Pb^{2+} is treated with aqueous NH_3 and KCN prior to extraction with dithizone in $CHCl_3$. Under these conditions, no metal other than Bi^{3+} or Tl^+ interferes.

Extracting Copper with Sodium Diethyldithiocarbamate. Adjust the pH of a solution containing up to 50 μg Cu^{2+} to 4.5–5.0 with acetate buffer, add disodium EDTA followed by sodium diethyldithiocarbamate, and shake the mixture for one minute. Add butyl acetate and shake again for one minute. Backwash the butyl acetate extract with dilute H_2SO_4. There is essentially no interference.

Extracting Iron with 4,7-Diphenylphenanthroline (Bathophenanthroline). After adding $NH_2OH \cdot HCl$ to a solution containing up to 10 μg Fe to produce Fe^{2+}, adjust the pH to 4 with sodium acetate and add bathophenanthroline dissolved in ethanol. Add *n*-hexanol and shake to extract the iron. The iron complex absorbs strongly at 533 nm.

Extracting Germanium with Hydrochloric Acid. Dissolve the sample in either H_3PO_4 or HNO_3, and add concentrated HCl. The $GeCl_4$ that forms can then be extracted with portions of CCl_4. To return Ge to an aqueous phase prior to determination, the CCl_4 extract may be stripped with an ammonium oxalate and oxalic acid solution.

Liquid Chromatography

As one proceeds from a single-stage batch separation to the multi-stage counter-current distribution process, separating two components whose D values are relatively close together becomes easier. Chromatography can be viewed as a logical extension of counter-current distribution (L. C. Craig first developed CCD as a simple form of liquid chromatography) in which discrete stages or tubes are replaced by immobilized solvent supported on granules of carrier either in a two-dimensional (paper, thin-layer chromatography) or three-dimensional (column) bed. After the mixture of solutes is added to the bed, the eluant, a solvent of constant or uniformly varying composition (the latter used in *gradient elution*), is passed over or through the bed. This *elution* may be continued just long enough to separate the components on the bed—"developing the chromatogram." (This is common practice in paper or thin-layer chromatography.) In column chromatography it is more customary to continue the flow of eluant until all of the components have appeared in the eluate flowing out of the column. The distribution of solutes along the column is similar to the distribution illustrated in Figure 20.2, where tube number represents the distance along the column. Regardless of the particular chromatographic process used (that is, adsorption, partition, etc.), the separation of components is related to differences in their distribution ratios between the immobile and mobile phases. In ordinary *elution chromatography*, the eluting solvent has a low D value, so that the components move at large and varying elution volumes. On the other hand, if a component with a very high D value is part of the eluant, it will displace the solute components. In *displacement chromatography*, therefore, the solute components appear one after the other in much more tightly spaced bands than in elution chromatography. An interesting variation involves using the sample solution itself as a developing solvent. In this case, called *frontal development*, the solutes do separate in the order of their D values, but appear in the eluate as fronts rather than bands, in which the least retained solute appears first, followed by a mixture of the first solute and the next more strongly retained component and so on, until finally all of the components of the original solution appear together, as in the original solution.

The next two chapters will treat chromatography in more detail.

SELECTED BIBLIOGRAPHY

Analytical Chemistry Fundamental Reviews. The reviews published in April of even-numbered years include comprehensive surveys of newly published extraction procedures, and many references.

MORRISON, G. H., and FREISER, H. *Solvent Extraction in Analytical Chemistry.* New York: John Wiley, 1957. *A general text covering in detail the principles of solvent extraction and its application to separation and analysis.*

STARY, J. *The Solvent Extraction of Metal Chelates.* New York: Macmillan, 1964.

DYRSSEN, D.; LILJENZIN, J.-O.; and RYDBERG, J., eds. *Solvent Extraction Chemistry.* New York: Wiley-Interscience, 1967.

DEAN, J. A. *Chemical Separation Methods.* New York: Van Nostrand Reinhold, 1969.

REFERENCES

1. G. H. MORRISON and H. FREISER, *Solvent Extraction in Analytical Chemistry*, New York: John Wiley, 1957.

PROBLEMS

1. Name the categories of extractable complexes used in metal-extraction procedures and illustrate each by specific examples.

2. How does Hildebrand's theory of regular solutions apply to the role of the organic solvent in extraction processes?

3. What are masking agents? How can one tell whether a substance that masks effectively in one situation will do so in another?

4. What are ion-association complexes? Under which conditions will they form and what properties must they have to be useful in extraction?

5. What factors affect the value of an oxygen-containing solvent used in extracting ion-association complexes?

6. Relate D, the distribution ratio, to $\%E$, percent extraction as a function of R_V (the phase-volume ratio V_0/V). For what purposes is D a more (or less) appropriate criterion than $\%E$?

7. When can the ratio of D values for two substances A and B, D_A/D_B, serve as a satisfactory means of evaluating the separation of A and B? Why is D_A/D_B not used as a "separation index"?

8. What are batch, continuous, and counter-current extraction processes and when would each be used?

9. Develop an algebraic expression with which to define the influence of each of the following factors on the extraction of metal ions using chelating extractants: (a) the reagent concentration; (b) the metal-ion concentration; (c) the pH; (d) the presence (and concentration) of masking agents; (e) the nature of the organic solvent; and (f) the ionic strength of the aqueous phase.

10. What is meant by K_{ex} (extraction constant) and pH_0 (or $pH_{1/2}$), and how can each be used to calculate the D (or $\%E$) value under various conditions? How different must the K_{ex} or pH_0 values be for a pair of metals to get a separation of 100/1? Does the amount of difference depend on the valence of the metal ions? Are other characteristics relevant as well? If so, which ones? Does the efficiency of separation depend on the value of K_{ex} or on the ratio of the two constants?

11. What are the optimal conditions for using a dithizone solution in $CHCl_3$ to separate Bi(III) from a solution containing a hundredfold excess of zinc?

21

Solid and Liquid Phase Chromatography

RONALD E. MAJORS

Chromatography is the general name given to the methods by which two or more compounds in a mixture physically separate themselves by distributing themselves between two phases: (1) a *stationary phase*, which can be a solid or a liquid supported on a solid; and (2) a *mobile phase*, either a gas or a liquid, which flows continuously around the stationary phase. The separation of individual components results primarily from differences in their affinity for the stationary phase.

In *liquid chromatography* (LC) the flowing or mobile phase is a liquid, whereas in *gas chromatography* (GC) it is a gas. *Gas-solid chromatography* (GSC) is the specific term used when the stationary phase is a solid; in *gas-liquid chromatography* (GLC), the stationary phase is a liquid spread over the surface of a solid support. The present chapter is concerned with LC; the following chapter deals with GC in its various forms.

21.1 INTRODUCTION

Chromatography was discovered and named in 1906 by Michael Tswett, a Russian botanist, when he was attempting to separate colored leaf pigments by passing a solution containing them through a column packed with adsorbent chalk particles. The individual pigments passed down the column at different rates and were separated from each other. The separated pigments were easily distinguished as colored bands—hence, chroma ("color") + graphy ("writing").

The next major development was that of *liquid-liquid (partition) chromatography* (LLC) by Martin and Synge in 1941. Instead of only a solid adsorbent they used a stationary liquid phase spread over the surface of the adsorbent and immiscible with the mobile phase. The sample components partitioned themselves between the two liquid phases according to their solubilities. For this work, Martin and Synge received the Nobel prize in chemistry in 1952.

In the early days of column chromatography, reliable identification of small quantities of separated substances was difficult, so *paper chromatography* (PC) was developed. In this "planar" technique, separations are achieved on sheets of filter paper, mainly through partition. Appreciation of the full advantages of planar chromatography then led to *thin-layer chromatography* (TLC), in which separations are carried out on thin layers of adsorbent supported on plates of glass or some other rigid material. TLC gained popularity after the classic work by Stahl in 1958 standardizing the techniques and materials used. To aid or enhance the separation of ionic compounds by PC or TLC, an electric field can be applied across the paper or plate. The resulting techniques are referred to as *paper* or *thin-layer electrophoresis*, respectively.

The most recently developed chromatographic technique, gas chromatography, was first described by Martin and James in 1952 and has become the most sophisticated and widely used of all chromatographic methods, particularly for mixtures of gases or for volatile liquids and solids. Separation times of a matter of minutes have become commonplace even for very complex mixtures. The combination of high resolution, speed of analysis, and sensitive detection have made GC a routine technique used in almost every chemical laboratory.

In the last few years, interest has renewed in closed-column LC because of new instrumentation, new column packings, and a better understanding of chromatographic theory. *High-performance liquid chromatography* (HPLC) is rapidly becoming as widely used as gas chromatography and is often the preferred technique for the rapid separation of nonvolatile or thermally unstable samples.

Basic Principles of Liquid Chromatography

To illustrate the basic principles of liquid chromatography, we shall consider a hypothetical separation of a three-component sample in a closed column. The stationary phase (*packing*) consists of solid porous particles (normally small—less than 150 μm in diameter) contained inside a long narrow tube, the *column*.

Figure 21.1 demonstrates the chromatographic process. A small volume of sample solution is injected at the column inlet (Fig. 21.1A). The mobile solvent phase moves the sample through the column packing (Fig. 21.1B). The individual components undergo sorption and desorption on the packing, thereby slowing their motion in varying amounts depending on their affinity for the packing. Each component X is distributed between the stationary phase (s) and the mobile phase (m) as it passes down the column. According to

$$X_m \rightleftharpoons X_s \qquad (21.1)$$

the corresponding *distribution coefficient* for component X is given by

$$K_X = \frac{[X]_s}{[X]_m} \qquad (21.2)$$

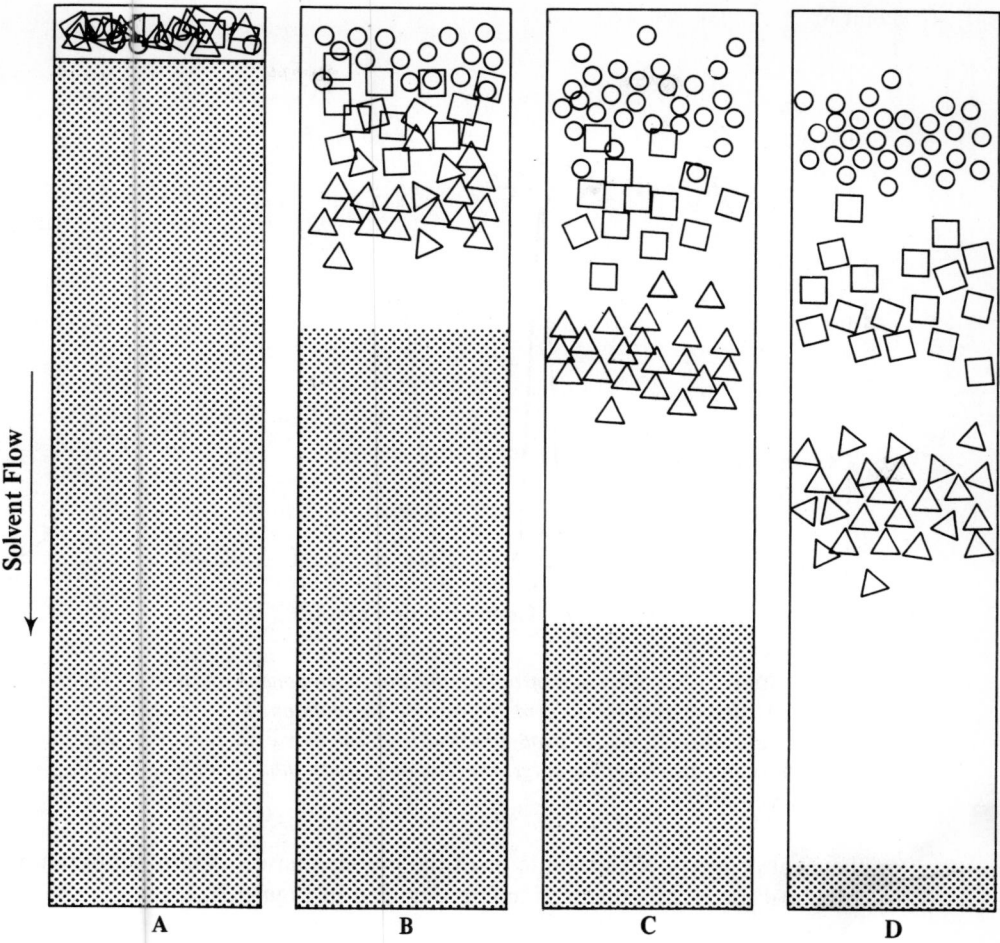

Solvent Flow

A   B   C   D

FIGURE 21.1. *Hypothetical separation of a three-component mixture: Component A:* △*; Component B:* □*; Component C:* ○*. The dotted area represents the original solvent in the column, which is being "displaced" during elution.*

A large value of K_x indicates that the component favors the stationary phase and moves slowly through the column, whereas for small values of K_x the component favors the mobile phase and moves quickly through the column.

The different speeds of the components separate them along the column (Fig. 21.1C). In elution, the separated components are moved down the entire length of the column by the mobile phase (Fig. 21.1D). If one measures the concentration of each component as it exits from the column and plots it as a function of the volume of mobile phase passed through the column, a *chromatogram* results. Individual volumes of mobile phase may be collected and the solute concentration in each measured externally (for example, spectrophotometrically), but normally the column effluent is monitored continuously by a detector that measures some physical

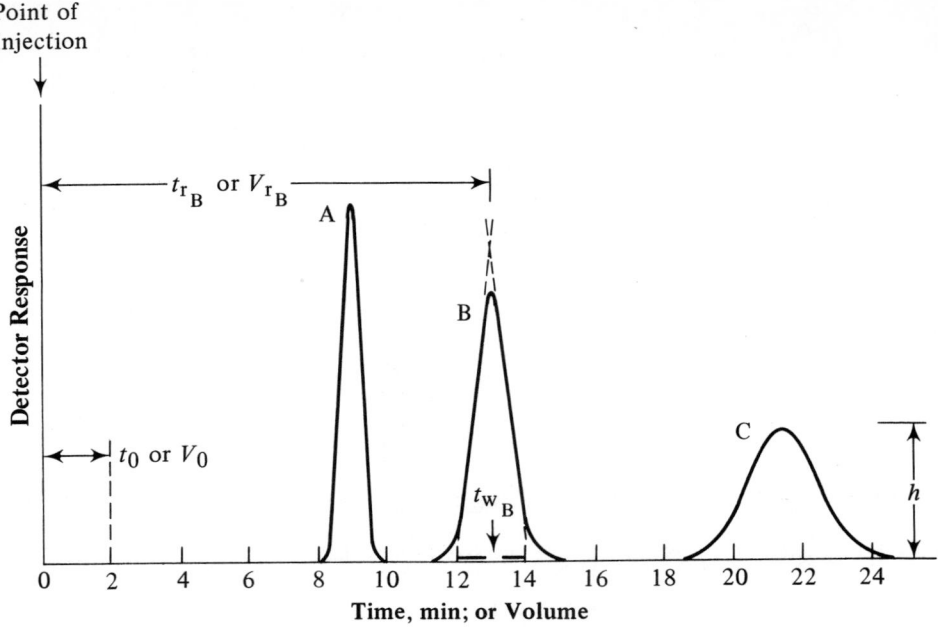

FIGURE 21.2. *Chromatogram of the three-component mixture of Figure 21.1. t_0 = time for solvent to traverse the column, t_{r_B} = retention time of substance B, t_{w_B} = peak basewidth of substance B, h = peak height. Units can also be given in terms of volume rather than time: V_0, V_{r_B}, V_{w_B}, and so forth.*

or chemical property of the solute or of the mobile phase. A chromatogram for the hypothetical three-component sample is depicted in Figure 21.2.

Types of Liquid Chromatography

Several types of LC are distinguished by their predominant mechanism of separation. The stationary phase governs the separation mode. The various modes will be briefly outlined here; each will be dealt with in somewhat greater detail in Sections 21.4 and 21.5. Since the solute molecule usually has some affinity for the stationary phase, it transfers from the mobile phase to the stationary phase, setting up the equilibrium described by Reaction 21.1. This alternating process of solute mass transfer, depicted in Figure 21.3A, eventually leads to separation.

Adsorption Chromatography. Adsorption chromatography (Fig. 21.3B), often referred to as *liquid-solid chromatography* (LSC), is based on interactions between the solute and fixed active sites on a solid adsorbent used as the stationary phase. The adsorbent may be packed in a column, spread on a plate, or impregnated into a porous paper. The adsorbent is generally an active, porous solid with a large surface area, such as silica gel, alumina, or charcoal. The active sites, such as the surface silanol groups of silica gel, generally interact with the polar functional groups of the compounds to be separated. The nonpolar (for instance, hydrocarbon) portion of a

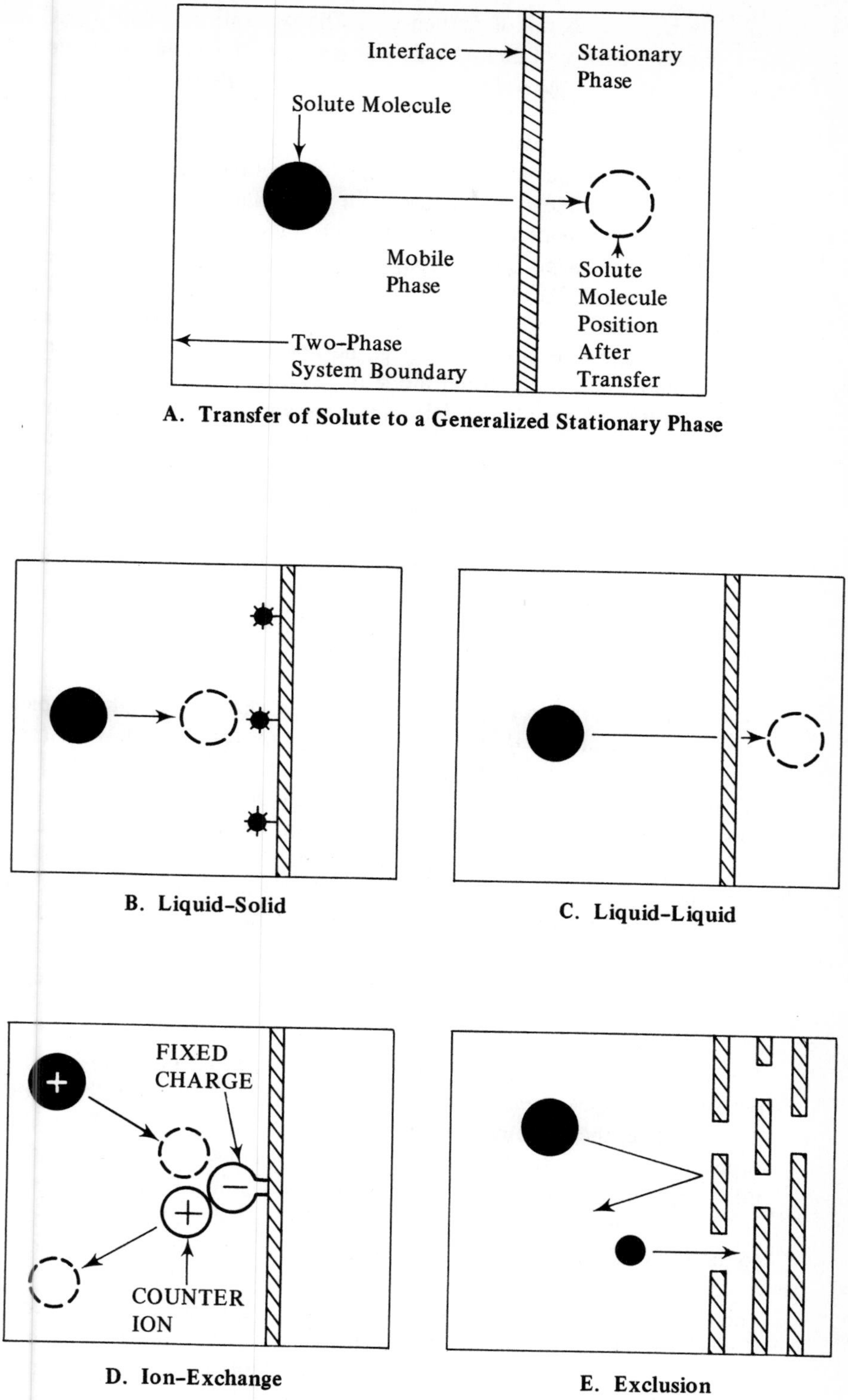

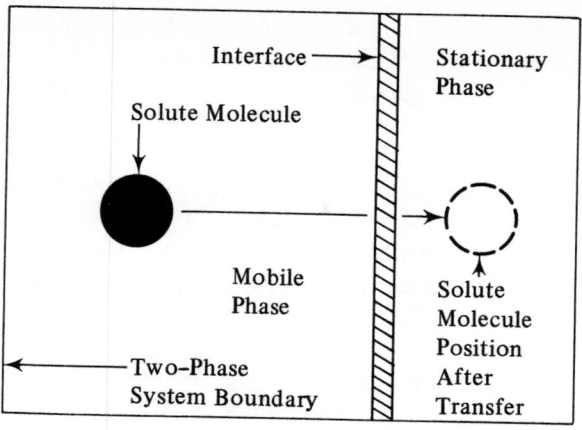

Interface
Stationary
Phase
Solute Molecule
Mobile
Phase
Solute
Molecule
Position
After
Transfer
Two-Phase
System Boundary
A. Transfer of Solute to a Generalized Stationary Phase
B. Liquid-Solid
C. Liquid-Liquid
FIXED
CHARGE
+
−
+
COUNTER
ION
D. Ion-Exchange
E. Exclusion

FIGURE 21.3. *Schematic representation of the four modes of liquid chromatography. Courtesy of Varian Associates.*

molecule has only a minor influence on the separation. Thus, LSC is well suited for separating classes of compounds (for instance, separating alcohols from aromatic hydrocarbons).

Partition Chromatography. In partition chromatography (Fig. 21.3C), also referred to as liquid-liquid chromatography, the solute molecules distribute themselves between two immiscible liquid phases, the stationary phase and the mobile phase, according to their relative solubilities. The stationary phase is uniformly spread on an inert support—a porous or nonporous particulate solid or porous paper (paper chromatography). To avoid mixing of the two phases, the two partitioning liquids must differ greatly in polarity. If the stationary liquid is polar (e.g., ethylene glycol) and the mobile phase is nonpolar (e.g., hexane), then polar components are retained more strongly; this is the usual mode of operation. On the other hand, if the stationary liquid is nonpolar (for instance, decane) and the mobile phase polar (for instance, water), polar components favor the mobile phase and elute faster. The latter technique (which has a reversed polarity) is referred to as *reverse-phase* LLC. Because of the subtle effects of solubility differences, LLC is well suited for separating homologues and isomers.

Often, the stationary phase is chemically bonded to the support material rather than mechanically applied to it. This is referred to as *bonded-phase chromatography*. The mechanism of this relatively new technique is not clear, but both partition and adsorption mechanisms may be involved.

Ion-Exchange Chromatography. Ion-exchange chromatography, depicted in Figure 21.3D, is based on the affinity of ions in solution for oppositely charged ions on the stationary phase. Ion-exchange packings consist of a porous solid phase, usually a resin, onto which ionic groups are chemically bonded. The mobile phase is usually a buffered aqueous solution containing a counter ion whose charge is opposite to that of the surface groups—that is, it has the same charge as the solute—but which is in charge equilibrium with the resin in the form of an ion pair. Competition between the solute and the counter ion for the ionic site governs chromatographic retention. Ion-exchange chromatography has found wide application in inorganic chemistry for separating metallic ions, and in biological systems for separating water-soluble ionic compounds such as proteins, nucleotides, and amino acids.

Exclusion Chromatography. The mechanism of exclusion chromatography, also referred to as *gel-permeation* or *gel-filtration chromatography*, is shown in Figure 21.3E. Here, the stationary phase should be chemically inert. Exclusion chromatography involves selectively diffusing solute molecules into and out of mobile-phase–filled pores in a three-dimensional network, which may be a gel or a porous inorganic solid. The degree of retention depends upon the size of the solvated solute relative to the size of the pore. Small molecules will permeate the smaller pores, intermediate-sized molecules will permeate only part of the pores and be excluded from others, and the very large molecules will be completely excluded. The larger molecules will travel faster through the stationary phase and elute from the column first. Thus, exclusion chromatography is especially useful in separating high-molecular-weight organic compounds and biopolymers from smaller molecules.

Uses of Liquid Chromatography

In a given chromatographic system, the volume of mobile phase at which a particular component elutes is usually constant and a characteristic of that component. Thus, the *retention volume* V_r for a chromatographic peak or spot can be used for its qualitative identification. Sometimes one or more substances may elute at the same V_r; in those cases, cross-correlation techniques may allow a more positive identification. In these techniques, a sample is run using two or more different chromatographic systems or conditions; it is unlikely, although still possible, that two substances will give the same elution behavior in more than one system. Positive identification is best accomplished by trapping the peak of interest and subjecting it to mass-spectral, infrared, NMR, or some other appropriate analysis.

Liquid chromatography can also be used for the quantitative analysis of the separated compounds. In column chromatography, the detector response is normally related to the amount of sample in the effluent. Thus, the area under a chromatographic peak is useful for quantitative analysis; in Fig. 21.2, the darkened area under peak C represents the peak area of that component. The peak height (distance h in Fig. 21.2) can also be used. In thin-layer or paper chromatography, the area of the spot is related to the amount of substance. The separated component can also be eluted from the plate or paper and measured externally by another technique (for instance, spectrophotometry).

Since many sample components are completely separated, the eluted fractions from liquid chromatography can be used for preparing pure materials in milligram to gram quantities for further use in experimentation, or for studying the molecular structure of the compounds.

21.2 THEORY RELATED TO PRACTICE

Theoretical considerations are a useful guide to the practical design and operation of the chromatographic experiment. The object of chromatography is separation— or rather, separation in a reasonable time.

Retention

In order to achieve separation, one must first have retention. Earlier, the thermodynamic distribution coefficient K_X was defined as a measure of the degree of retention for compound X. The *capacity factor* k'_X is a more practical quantity that can be determined directly from the chromatogram. It is given by

$$k'_X = \frac{\text{total moles of X in stationary phase}}{\text{total moles of X in mobile phase}} = \left(\frac{V_s}{V_m}\right)\frac{[X]_s}{[X]_m} = \left(\frac{V_s}{V_m}\right)K_X \quad (21.3)$$

where V_s = the volume of the stationary phase within the column
   V_m = the volume of the mobile phase within the column

The fundamental equation for any chromatographic process, relating the *retention volume* V_r to other quantities, is

$$V_r = V_m(1 + k'_X) = V_m + V_s K_X \quad (21.4)$$

The value of V_r can be obtained from the chromatogram, since $V_r = Ft_r$, where F

is the *flow rate* (ml/min) and t_r is the peak *retention time* (Fig. 21.2). Similarly, V_m, termed the *void volume* (also *dead volume* or *interstitial volume*) is equal to Ft_0, where t_0 is the time required for solvent molecules or any other nonretained compound to traverse the column. Note that V_m is the total volume of mobile phase in the column at any given time. Substituting V_m and V_r into Equation 21.4, and rearranging, produces

$$k'_x = \frac{t_r - t_0}{t_0} \qquad (21.5)$$

Example 21.1. (a) Using the hypothetical chromatogram in Figure 21.2, calculate the capacity factors of peaks B and C. (b) Assuming that 60% of the volume of a column 25 cm in length by 0.40 cm in internal diameter is occupied by solid packing particles, calculate the expected retention volume for peak C, Figure 21.2 (Hint: treat the column as a cylinder).

Solution:
(a) By Equation 21.5,

$$k'_B = \frac{t_r - t_0}{t_0} = \frac{13 - 2}{2.0}$$

$$= 5.5$$
$$k'_C = 9.8$$

(b) $V_m = 0.40\pi r^2 L$ is the fraction of column volume occupied by mobile phase, where r is the internal radius of the column and L its length.

$$V_m = (0.40)(3.14)(0.20 \text{ cm})^2(25 \text{ cm}) = 1.2_6 \text{ cm}^3$$
$$V_r = V_m(1 + k') = 1.2_6 \text{ cm}^3(1 + 9.8) = 13._6 \text{ cm}^3$$

In TLC or PC, the degree of retention for a compound is its R_f value, defined as the ratio of the distance the solute has moved to the distance the solvent front has moved. Figure 21.4 shows how one measures the R_f value; normally, the center of the solute spot is used for calculating the distance a.

Column Efficiency

Column efficiency describes the rate of band broadening as the solute travels through the column or across the plate or paper. As illustrated in Figure 21.1, all molecules do not move at the same speed. Dispersion of molecules generally results in a Gaussian profile. The center of the profile or elution band—that is, the k' value of each component—represents the average rate of travel of a solute molecule. Small deviations from the mean value are brought about by the finite rate of solute mass-transfer between the mobile and stationary phases, the different flow paths through the stationary phase caused by irregular packing in the bed, and axial (*longitudinal*) diffusion in the direction of flow.

The quantitative measure of efficiency is the number of *theoretical plates N* calculated from the chromatogram by using

$$N = 16\left(\frac{t_r}{t_w}\right)^2 \qquad (21.6)$$

where t_w = the peak width measured in the same units as the retention time

FIGURE 21.4. *Measuring the R_f value from a paper or thin-layer chromatogram. R_f for component 2 = a/b.*

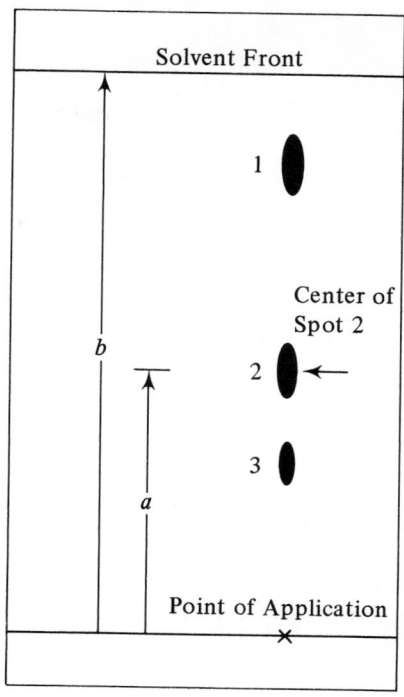

Solvent Front

1

Center of
Spot 2

b

2 ←

3

a

Point of Application

The peak width is obtained from the intersection of the baseline with the tangents drawn through the inflection points on the sides of each peak. The theoretical-plate model, a carryover from distillation theory, assumes a column to be made up of a series of plates. At each plate, one equilibrium distribution of solute between the mobile phase and stationary phase occurs. Thus, the higher the value of N, the more chance there is for separation to occur (that is, the better the separating power of the column).

Another useful parameter for column efficiency is the *height equivalent to a theoretical plate*, HETP (the H value). The following simple relationship shows that H has the units of length.

$$H = \frac{L}{N} \tag{21.7}$$

where L = the column length

Thus, a column or plate with a low H value is better than one with a high value. Values of H less than 1–3 mm are commonplace in gas chromatography and high-performance liquid chromatography.

Example 21.2. (a) From the chromatogram of Figure 21.2, determine the number of theoretical plates for peak C. (b) Assuming the same column as in Example 21.1, calculate the value of H in mm for peak C. (c) How would doubling the column length affect the peak width of peak C, keeping other parameters constant?

Solution:
(a) By Equation 21.6

$$N = 16\left(\frac{t_r}{t_w}\right)^2 = 16\left(\frac{21.5}{4.1}\right)^2 = 440 \text{ plates}$$

(b) By Equation 21.7

$$H = \frac{L}{N} = (250 \text{ mm})/440 \text{ plates} = 0.57 \text{ mm}$$

(c) By Equations 21.6 and 21.7,

$$N = 16\left(\frac{t_r}{t_w}\right)^2 \quad \text{and} \quad \frac{L}{H} = 16\left(\frac{t_r}{t_w}\right)^2$$

Therefore, $\frac{t_r}{t_w} \propto \sqrt{L}$.

Since $t_r \propto L$, then $t_w \propto L$, so t_w increases by $\sqrt{2} = 1.41$.

Band-Broadening Contributions to H

The development of the generalized nonequilibrium theory by Giddings and co-workers [1] has led to a more thorough understanding of the factors contributing to band spreading in chromatography and hence to the design of better chromatographic columns. In the nonequilibrium theory of chromatography, the movement of the solute through the column is treated as a random walk—that is, the progress of a molecule through the column is a succession of random stops and starts about a mean equilibrium concentration. In this dynamic nonequilibrium, represented in Figure 21.5, mass-transfer of the solute into the stationary phase results in a lag behind the equilibrium concentration (band center): when it desorbs and transfers into the mobile phase the solute moves more rapidly than the band center. Thus, dispersion in-

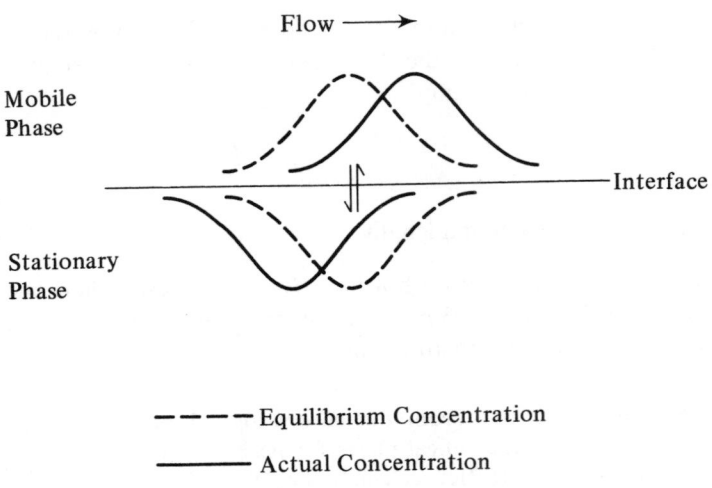

FIGURE 21.5. *Illustration of the influence of local nonequilibrium on band dispersion. Dashed lines: equilibrium concentration profile; solid lines: actual concentration profile.*

creases with the number of transfers and decreases as the velocity of the mobile phase decreases (closer approach to equilibrium).

Solute mass-transfer in the stationary phase (H_{sp}) or in the "stagnant" mobile phase contained in the pores of the column packing (H_{sm}) are a source of band broadening (Fig. 21.6). The mass-transfer rate can be increased by (a) decreasing the mean diffusion path through which the solute must pass (that is, decreasing the pore depth or the particle size); (b) increasing the rate of solute diffusion by decreasing the viscosity of the media through which it passes; (c) decreasing the thickness of the stationary phase so that the molecule can diffuse into and out of it very rapidly; or (d) lowering the k' value of the molecule so that it spends less time in the stationary phase.

Mass transfer of solute in the mobile phase (H_{mp}) also contributes to band spreading. Complex flow-patterns arise from the flow of the mobile phase through a packed bed of particles. These patterns are difficult to describe quantitatively, but this form of band dispersion is minimized by homogeneous packing of the bed with uniform particles, by small interparticle channels (less convective mixing between particles), and by the use of mobile phases of low viscosity.

Another source of band dispersion is so-called *eddy diffusion* (H_{ed}). This term arises from irregular flow through the packed particles in a column. The solute proceeds through the channels between the particles by many interconnected paths that differ in their tortuosity and degree of constriction. Because of the many possible paths, solute molecules arrive at the column exit at different times. Longitudinal molecular diffusion, H_{ld} (that is, random diffusion in and against the direction of mobile-phase flow) is minimal in liquid chromatography, although it is an important source of band broadening in gas chromatography. H_{ld} only becomes appreciable at very low flow-rates (Fig. 21.6), because the solute diffusion-coefficients in liquids are 10^5 smaller than they are in gases. Thus, these diffusional contributions to H are rarely observed.

The individual band-broadening contributions to H can be described mathematically by

$$H = \frac{1}{\left(\dfrac{1}{H_{ed}} + \dfrac{1}{H_{mp}}\right)} + H_{ld} + H_{sm} + H_{sp} \qquad (21.8)$$

where
$H_{ed} = C_e d_p$ (eddy diffusion)

$H_{mp} = \dfrac{C_m d_p^2 v}{D_m}$ (mobile-phase mass-transfer)

$H_{ld} = \dfrac{C_d D_m}{v}$ (longitudinal diffusion)

$H_{sm} = \dfrac{C_{sm} d_p^2 v}{D_m}$ (stagnant-to-mobile-phase mass-transfer)

$H_{sp} = \dfrac{C_s d_f^2 v}{D_s}$ (stationary-phase mass-transfer)

d_p = the particle diameter
D_m = the solute diffusion-coefficient in the mobile phase
D_s = the solute diffusion-coefficient in the stationary phase
v = the linear velocity of the mobile phase
d_f = the thickness of the stationary-phase film (mainly for LLC)

When the stationary phase is the same as the support or particle (as in LSC), d_t is replaced by d_p. C_e, C_m, C_d, C_{sm}, and C_s are coefficients whose characteristics are given in Reference [1].

Equation 21.8 is a slightly modified version of the Van Deemter equation, Equation 22.10, used in gas chromatography. Because of the so-called "coupling" between the A term (eddy diffusion) and the C_{llq} term of Equation 22.10, a different relationship between H and v is observed in LC than in GC. The fundamental difference between GC and LC is the great difference in sample diffusion rates in liquids and in gases: D_m is 10^4–10^6 times greater in GC. Thus, the H_{ld} contribution in LC is much smaller than in GC, whereas the H_{mp} term is larger.

A pictorial representation of the various contributions to H at different mobile-phase velocities is given in Figure 21.6. For comparison, a similar curve is presented for a typical GC column. In practice, H-versus-v relationships are determined experimentally. These curves are then used for optimizing operating conditions. For best efficiency, one prefers to use a velocity (proportional to flow rate) near the minimum of the H-versus-v plot. Although this is often done in GC, in

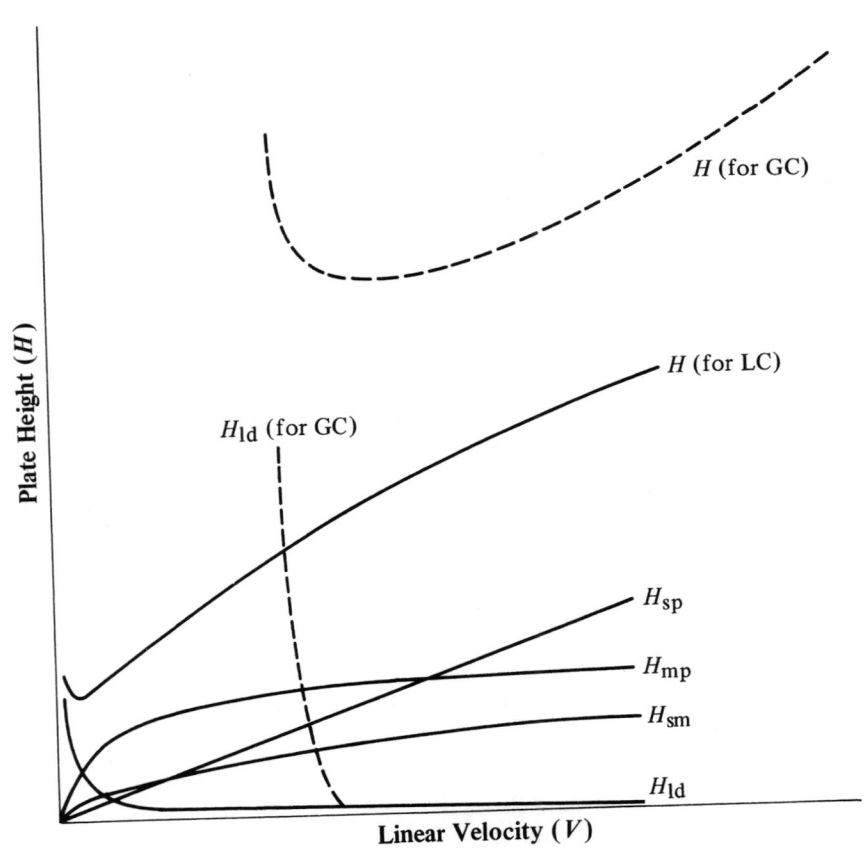

FIGURE 21.6. *Plot illustrating the flow-velocity dependence of overall plate height H and various contributions to H (Eqn. 21.8).*

LC one normally works above the minimum since the latter occurs at very low velocities and separation times would be intolerably long.

From Equation 21.8, one can deduce experimental conditions that minimize the value of H. It can be seen that H decreases with decreasing particle diameters (d_p), linear velocities (v), thickness of films of stationary phase (d_f), viscosity of the mobile phases and elevated temperatures (to increase D_m and D_s), and with uniform packing of the particles (to decrease eddy diffusion).

Care must be taken to keep additional band-broadening outside the column to a minimum. Extra-column contributions to band broadening, such as mixing or poor sample-introduction technique, will increase the H-value. Because of the slow diffusion of samples in liquid phases, extra-column volumes are more detrimental to efficiency in LC than in GC; hence, great effort should be exercised to keep those volumes between the point of injection and the top of the column to a minimum. Likewise, the volume between the column exit and the detector, and the volume of the detector itself, should be minimized. In TLC or PC, the applied spot should be kept as small as possible.

Resolution and Its Optimization

The degree of separation is referred to as *resolution, R*. Figure 21.2 and the following equation

$$R = 2 \frac{(t_{r_B} - t_{r_A})}{t_{w_A} + t_{w_B}} \tag{21.9}$$

are helpful in discussing the characteristics of chromatographic peaks that determine R. If the two components A and B of the chromatogram of Figure 21.2 are examined, resolution is determined by (a) the distance between the peak maxima and (b) the peak or bandwidths. The separation between peaks is related to the *selectivity factor* α, sometimes called relative retention, by

$$\alpha = \frac{t_{r_B} - t_0}{t_{r_A} - t_0} = \frac{k'_B}{k'_A} \tag{21.10}$$

Selectivity refers to the capability of a chromatographic system to distinguish between two components, and is a thermodynamic quantity governed by the relative solute distributions between the mobile phase and the stationary phase. Selectivity in chromatography is very difficult to predict, but one can often use possible molecular interactions between the solute and stationary phase, such as hydrogen-bonding or acid-base relationships, to roughly predict α values. As α approaches 1, separation becomes exceedingly difficult. To modify selectivity one must change the stationary phase, the mobile phase, or both.

The bandwidth is related to the efficiency of the chromatographic process, which was discussed in the previous section. Unlike selectivity, efficiency is a kinetic phenomenon and can be increased by better column design as well as by the other factors discussed previously. Figure 21.7 illustrates the influence of selectivity and efficiency on chromatographic resolution. Figure 21.7A depicts a two-component separation displaying poor resolution. By decreasing peak width (i.e., more theoretical plates), resolution can be increased without affecting selectivity (Fig. 21.7B).

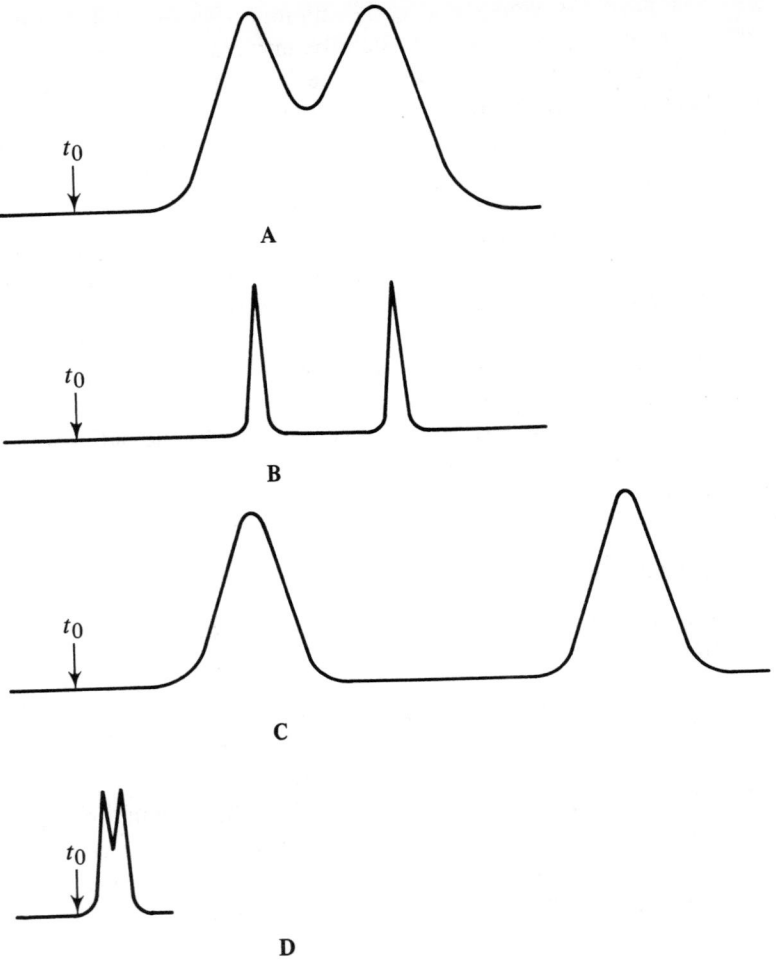

FIGURE 21.7. *Effect of selectivity, efficiency, and capacity factor on resolution. A: Poor resolution. B: Good resolution due to column efficiency. C: Good resolution due to column selectivity. D: Poor resolution due to low capacity factor despite adequate column efficiency and selectivity. Courtesy of Varian Associates.*

On the other hand, Figure 21.7C indicates that better resolution results from increasing the distance between peak maxima (that is, improving selectivity), even without increasing efficiency. Poor resolution caused by low capacity-factor (despite adequate column efficiency and selectivity) is depicted in Figure 21.7D. Better resolution can be obtained by increasing V_s (Eqn. 21.3)—for instance, by using a longer column or an adsorbent with a higher surface area.

In chromatography, a value of $R = 1$ is considered the minimum value for quantitative separation. For a two-component separation, this corresponds to a 2% contamination of each band by the other. When $R = 1.5$, the separation of the two bands is considered complete (cross-contamination less than 1%). Such a baseline separation is often required in preparative chromatography when pure substances are desired. As the value of R approaches zero, it becomes more difficult to discern separate peaks.

Example 21.3. (a) For the chromatogram shown in Figure 21.2, determine the resolution between peaks B and C. (b) Determine the value of α for the same peaks. (c) Two peaks with similar retention times generally have similar widths; for retained peaks with a width of 2 ml, what must be the difference in retention volumes to increase the resolution to 2?

Solution:

(a) $R = \dfrac{2(t_{r_C} - t_{r_B})}{t_{w_B} + t_{w_C}} = \dfrac{2(21.5 - 13)}{2.1 + 4.1} = 2.7$

(b) $\alpha = \dfrac{t_{r_C} - t_0}{t_{r_B} - t_0} = \dfrac{21.5 - 2}{13 - 2} = 1.8$

(c) $R = 2\dfrac{(t_{r_2} - t_{r_1})}{t_{w_1} + t_{w_2}} = 2\dfrac{(t_{r_2} - t_{r_1})}{2t_{w_1}} = \dfrac{t_{r_2} - t_{r_1}}{t_{w_1}}$

$2 = \dfrac{t_{r_2} - t_{r_1}}{t_{w_1}} = \dfrac{t_{r_2} - t_{r_1}}{2\ \text{ml}}$ and $t_{r_2} - t_{r_1} = 4\ \text{ml}$

An alternative equation for the resolution, which can be derived from Equation 21.10, namely

$$R = \frac{1}{4} \sqrt{N} \left(\frac{\alpha - 1}{\alpha} \right) \left(\frac{k'}{1 + k'} \right) \qquad \textbf{(21.11)}$$

$$\phantom{R = \frac{1}{4} \sqrt{N}\ } a \qquad\quad b \qquad\quad c$$

shows that resolution is a function of three separate factors: the efficiency term a, the selectivity term b, and the capacity-factor term c (see Eqn. 22.12 in the next chapter); these parameters a, b, and c can be adjusted independently. It is evident from Equation 21.11 that R approaches zero (resolution is lost) as N or k' approach zero or as α approaches one. An increase in α, N, or k' favors better resolution, but, according to Equation 21.5, a large value of k' corresponds to a long separation time. In practice, one does not optimize all factors simultaneously, but selects a column with a high plate-number, then optimizes the k' value (usually between 2 and 5) by modifying the mobile-phase composition. If resolution is not adequate, then either N or α can be increased. If α is close to one, an increase in N may give only a modest increase in R. In that case, it is better to change α by changing the mobile phase or the stationary phase. This often time-consuming trial-and-error process of selecting and optimizing mobile and stationary phases makes the practice of chromatography something of an art.

Example 21.4. On silica gel an unretained peak, benzene, gave $V_m = 2.0$ ml, and o-diaminobenzene (ODB) and m-diaminobenzene (MDB) displayed k' values of 10 and 12, respectively. For a 100-cm column, the resolution between the isomers was 1.2. (a) Determine the length of column necessary to achieve complete baseline resolution. (b) With the new column from (a), what will be the void volume for benzene? (c) If the k' value for

MDB is increased to 18 while k' for ODB remains the same, what length of column would be necessary to resolve them to baseline? Note that in Equation 21.11, the k' value generally refers to the last eluting peak.

Solution:

(a) By Equations 21.7 and 21.11,

$$\frac{R_2}{R_1} = \frac{\sqrt{N_2}}{\sqrt{N_1}} = \frac{\sqrt{L_2}}{\sqrt{L_1}} \qquad \sqrt{L_2} = \frac{R_2\sqrt{L_1}}{R_1} = \frac{1.5\sqrt{100}}{1.2}$$

$$L_2 = 160 \text{ cm}$$

(b)
$$\frac{V_{m_2}}{V_{m_1}} = \frac{L_2}{L_1} \qquad V_{m_2} = \frac{V_{m_1}L_2}{L_1} = \frac{2.0(160)}{100} = 3.2 \text{ ml}$$

(c) By Equations 21.10 and 21.11,

$$\alpha_1 = \frac{k'_{1(\text{MDB})}}{k'_{1(\text{ODB})}} = \frac{12}{10} = 1.2$$

and

$$\alpha_2 = \frac{k'_{2(\text{MDB})}}{k'_{2(\text{ODB})}} = \frac{18}{10} = 1.8$$

$$\frac{R_2}{R_1} = \frac{\sqrt{L_2}}{\sqrt{L_1}} \frac{\left(\dfrac{\alpha_2 - 1}{\alpha_2}\right)}{\left(\dfrac{\alpha_1 - 1}{\alpha_1}\right)} \frac{\left[\dfrac{k'_{2(\text{MDB})}}{1 + k'_{2(\text{MDB})}}\right]}{\left[\dfrac{k'_{1(\text{MDB})}}{1 + k'_{1(\text{MDB})}}\right]}$$

$$\frac{1.8}{1.2} = \frac{\sqrt{L_2}}{\sqrt{100}} \frac{\left(\dfrac{1.8 - 1}{1.8}\right)}{\left(\dfrac{1.2 - 1}{1.2}\right)} \frac{\left(\dfrac{18}{1 + 18}\right)}{\left(\dfrac{12}{1 + 12}\right)}$$

$$L_2 = 30 \text{ cm}$$

Sample Capacity

The earlier discussion involving the distribution coefficient was based on the assumption that the coefficient is linear with respect to sample concentration (i.e., a linear sorption isotherm). Nonlinear isotherms, however, are sometimes encountered with the sample sizes employed in practical applications of chromatography, particularly in adsorption systems. The *sample capacity* of the stationary phase is an important consideration in practical applications. The sample capacity corresponds to the amount of sample that can be sorbed onto a particular stationary phase before overloading occurs. Exceeding the sample capacity results in unsymmetrical peak shapes, change in retention times, and loss of resolution. Sample capacity is generally expressed in milligrams of sample per gram of stationary phase. It is proportional to V_s, the volume of available stationary phase (e.g., adsorbent surface area in LSC or liquid phase loading in LLC). For porous LSC adsorbents, typical sample capacities are in the range of 2–5 mg/g. Sample capacity should not be confused with the capacity factor k' defined earlier.

The Chromatographic Compromise

The relationships among sample capacity, speed, and resolution can be represented by the triangular diagram in Figure 21.8. For a particular LC system, any one of these attributes can be improved at the expense of the other two or any two can be improved at the expense of the other one. The chromatographer must always compromise. In analytical LC, speed and resolution are the desired characteristics; sample capacity is usually unimportant, provided a detectable amount of sample is separated. In preparative LC, capacity is the main objective, provided the resolution is consistent with purity requirements; speed is usually sacrificed.

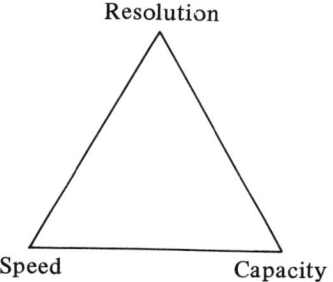

FIGURE 21.8. *Relationship of resolution, speed, and capacity. Courtesy of Varian Associates.*

21.3 APPARATUS AND TECHNIQUES OF LIQUID CHROMATOGRAPHY

Experiments in liquid chromatography can be performed with equipment ranging from simple laboratory glassware to complex and expensive automated chromatographs. The simplest technique, paper chromatography, requires a filter paper, a pipette to apply a sample, a closed jar, and the necessary solvents. On the other hand, high-performance liquid chromatography can require high-pressure pumps with electronic programmers, columns with specially prepared microparticles, and highly sensitive, flow-through, microvolume detectors.

Paper Chromatography

The basic technique is quite simple. A sheet of cellulose filter paper, such as Whatman No. 1, serves as the separation medium. For one-dimensional paper chromatography (PC), the paper is cut into strips about 5 cm wide and 20 cm long; for two-dimensional PC (below), a 20 × 20-cm sheet is commonly used. The papers come in various porosities (fine, medium, coarse); the porosity determines the rate of movement of the developing solvent. Low-porosity paper gives slow solvent movement but good resolution. Thick papers, which have increased sample capacity, are available for preparative separations.

Preparation. Prior to use, the paper strips are stored under conditions of controlled humidity. Since the predominant mechanism is partition between sorbed water and the mobile phase, the amount of water in the cellulose fibers governs its separating characteristics. The paper may also be impregnated with another stationary phase by dipping and careful drying.

The sample, dissolved in a volatile solvent, is applied to the paper as a drop or "spot" by means of a syringe or micropipette. To minimize band spreading, the spot should be restricted to about 2 mm in diameter. Sample sizes are normally 10–50 μg, and the total quantity of sample should not exceed 500 μg. Larger spots and larger sample sizes lead to poorer separations. Figure 21.9 illustrates the correct

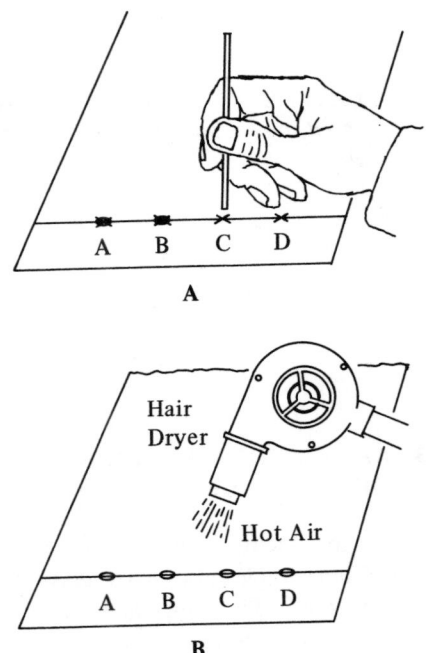

FIGURE 21.9. *Application of sample to paper in PC (or TLC). A: Applying the sample to paper. B: Drying the spots on the paper. From D. Abbott and R. S. Andrews,* An Introduction to Chromatography, *Boston: Houghton Mifflin, 1965, by permission of the publisher.*

manner of sample application. Several samples or standards can be applied as separate spots across the bottom of the paper. The solvent is removed by evaporation, often by means of a hair dryer or heat gun. If the sample is too dilute, several drops may be applied to concentrate it; the solvent should be evaporated between each application. For preparative PC, multiple spots or bands of sample are applied across the bottom of the paper. The paper is now ready to be developed.

Operation. The separation takes place inside a closed container, usually glass, as shown in Figure 21.10. Within the chamber, the paper can be supported so that the solvent flows upward (ascending PC), downward (descending PC), or horizontally. The airtight container ensures that the paper and developing solvent vapors are in equilibrium; for reproducible R_f values, the paper is usually preequilibrated with solvent vapor for 1–3 hours before development begins. For ascending PC, development begins by placing the bottom edge of the suspended paper (but not the spots) into the mobile phase, which ascends through the fibers by capillary action. In the descending method, the spotted edge of the paper strip is immersed in a trough

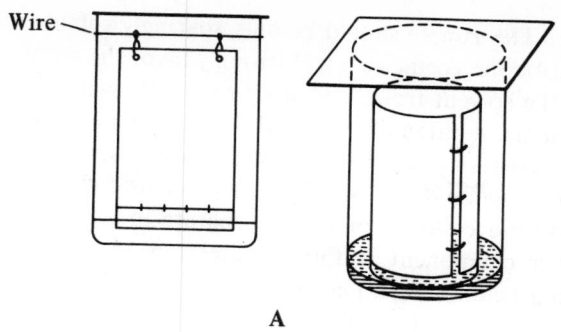

Wire

A

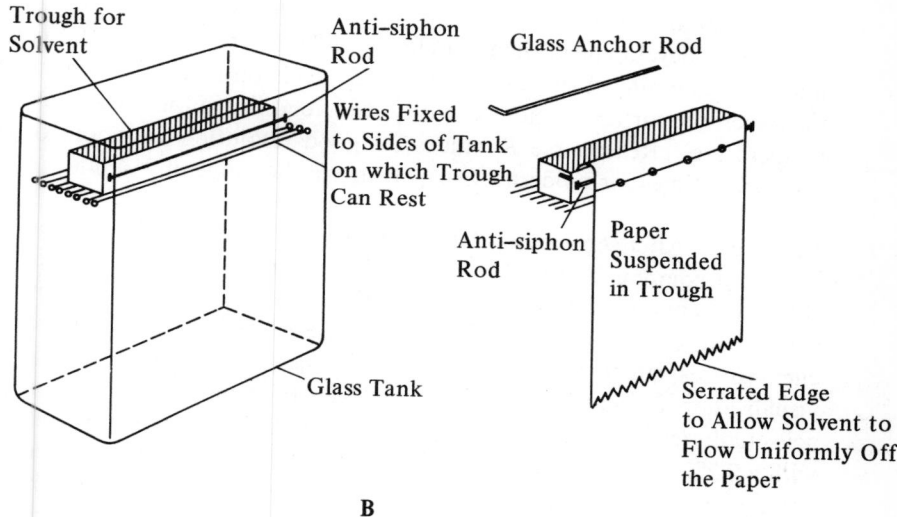

Trough for Solvent

Anti-siphon Rod

Glass Anchor Rod

Wires Fixed to Sides of Tank on which Trough Can Rest

Anti-siphon Rod

Paper Suspended in Trough

Glass Tank

Serrated Edge to Allow Solvent to Flow Uniformly Off the Paper

B

FIGURE 21.10. *Developing chambers for paper chromatography. A: Ascending development; B: Descending development. Note that similar chambers are used in TLC. From D. Abbott and R. S. Andrews,* An Introduction to Chromatography, *Boston: Houghton Mifflin, 1965, by permission of the publisher.*

near the top of the chamber, containing the solvent (Fig. 21.10A). The downward flow of solvent, caused by both capillary action and gravity, moves the solvent farther than in the ascending method. For this reason, the descending PC method is often preferred.

In ascending PC, the paper is supported by means of a clip or hook, or wrapped around a cylinder as depicted in Figure 21.10A. In descending PC, the top edge of the paper is held down by a glass rod or strip. In the horizontal (or radial) method, a circular paper is used and sample is applied in its center. After the sample dries, solvent is applied at the center and spreads out radially, carrying the sample with it. The main advantage of the radial method lies in its simplicity and its economical use of paper and solvents.

The mobile phase used for development depends on the nature of the substances to be separated. The sample should be only sparingly soluble in the solvent; if it is too soluble, distribution coefficients will strongly favor the mobile phase, components will move with the solvent front, and poor resolution will result. A single organic solvent (for example, *n*-butanol) saturated with water may serve as a mobile phase. Many popular solvents are of this type, but several useful partition solvents incorporate only small amounts of water. Very polar compounds (phenols, sugars, amino acids) will move slowly or fail to separate in these binary systems. Often, including another component in the mixtures (an acid, a base, or a complexing agent) results in a better separation of polar compounds. Organic solvent mixtures are frequently employed. One disadvantage of solvent mixtures, however, is that multi-component solvents themselves can partition along the paper, resulting in solvent "bands" which may affect component separation.

The development time should be sufficient to separate the components of interest. The rate of solvent movement depends on factors such as the porosity of the paper, the surface tension, viscosity, and volatility of the solvent, and the ambient temperature. Reasonable R_f values for good resolution are about 0.4–0.8; typical separation times for modern PC papers are in the range of 2–4 hours.

Detection. After separation, the solvent front is marked and the sheet is dried. The separated compounds are then detected in a variety of ways, chemical or physical. If they are colored, detection presents little or no problem; usually, however, the substances are colorless. In the latter case, the sheet is sprayed with or dipped in a chemical reagent to produce a colored product. There are a large variety of such visualization reagents [2] for various classes of compounds. For example, amino acids (colorless) are easily detected as a pale blue-violet product by treating the paper with a 0.2% solution of colorless ninhydrin. A number of unsaturated organic compounds fluoresce and can readily be detected under an ultraviolet lamp, and labeled (radioactive) compounds can be detected using a radiation counter.

Compounds are identified by their R_f values, as described in Section 21.2. Sometimes a reference substance, chemically similar to the sample, is run simultaneously alongside the sample and relative migration rates obtained by comparison. In this case, the R_X value defined by

$$R_X = \frac{\text{(distance moved by substance)}}{\text{(distance moved by standard substance X)}} \qquad (21.12)$$

is used. This procedure is especially useful in descending PC, in which the solvent is allowed to run off the bottom end of the paper to increase the migration distances.

In two-dimensional PC, a single sample is applied near one corner of the paper and the paper developed. The paper is then removed from the tank, dried, turned 90°, and developed in a second solvent. This procedure effectively increases the distance of migration, but more importantly, can separate the unresolved components, because the second solvent can have characteristics different from the first.

Thin-Layer Chromatography

Thin-layer chromatography (TLC), like paper chromatography, is performed on an open bed—a glass, aluminum, or plastic plate of dimensions not unlike those mentioned for PC, covered with a porous solid powder comprised of small particles about 5–40 μm in diameter. Commonly used phases include silica gel, alumina, cellulose, polyamides, and ion-exchange resins. To promote adhesion and to give better mechanical strength to the TLC plate, a binder such as calcium sulfate (5–10% by weight) is mixed with the powder.

Preparation. In preparing the plate, the powder is first usually made into a slurry with water (or other solvent) and then spread on the plate. For plate-to-plate reproducibility the layer must be very uniform. The slurry can be spread manually using a spatula or another plate, or (more reproducibly and conveniently) with a special apparatus. A "moving spreader" is shown in Figure 21.11. The cleaned plates

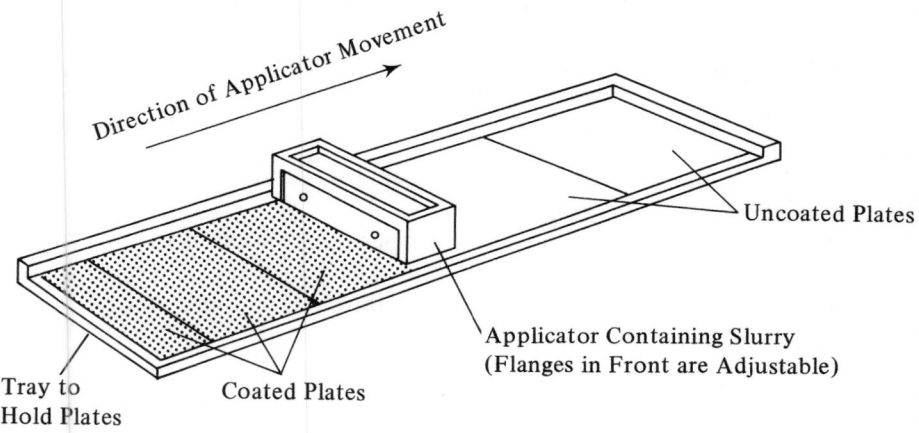

FIGURE 21.11. *Moving-spreader apparatus for preparing TLC plates. Applicator is filled with slurry.*

are held in a frame and the applicator containing the slurry is passed over them, depositing the slurry as a thin film. The thickness applied can be varied by adjusting flanges at the base of the applicator. For analytical work, the layer is 0.2–0.3 mm thick, whereas for preparative TLC, the thickness varies from 2–10 mm. After spreading, the plate is dried in air and activated by heating it at 110°C for a short period of time. Ready-made plates are available commercially; they are more expensive than homemade plates, but they are undoubtedly convenient and provide good reproducibility.

Operation. After activation, the sample application and developing procedures are carried out almost exactly as in PC. Normally, sample sizes range from 10–100 μg per spot for analytical TLC, but in preparative TLC when samples are applied as bands, up to 100 mg can be used with a 20 × 20-cm plate. Spots should be 2–5 mm in diameter. Ascending or descending development and one- or multi-dimensional techniques can be used. Because of differences in capillary action and possibly in solvent heat of adsorption, development times are usually faster in TLC than in PC. Depending on the mobile phase and the particle size of the adsorbent, a typical time is 20–30 min for a 10-cm distance, whereas for a high-porosity paper developed under similar conditions, development might take two hours. On thin layers, spots often remain compact; on filter paper, they tend to spread somewhat because of its fibrous structure. Thus, resolution is better in TLC and smaller amounts of substances can be separated and identified than in PC.

Detection. In TLC, since the supports, such as silica and alumina, are chemically more inert than paper, more strongly reactive reagents can be used to locate the separated substances. Concentrated sulfuric acid sprayed onto a silica plate makes organic substances visible as charred spots after the plate is heated in an oven. Selective color-forming reagents or iodine vapor are also used. Viewing the plate under ultraviolet radiation can reveal fluorescent substances, or an immobile fluorescent compound can be added initially to the preparation slurry. In the latter case, separated substances show up as dark spots against a fluorescing background when the plate is viewed under ultraviolet, because of their quenching effect.

R_f values are more difficult to reproduce in TLC than in PC because there are more experimental variables. R_f values are influenced by the following factors:

1. The nature of the adsorbent (its chemical nature, particle size, surface area, and binder)
2. The nature of the mobile phase (its purity, precision of mixing, moisture content, and volatility)
3. The activity of the adsorbent and its thickness and uniformity
4. The temperature of the apparatus
5. The amount of sample used
6. The vapor-pressure equilibrium between the plate and the development-chamber atmosphere

A comparison between TLC and PC for the separation of nucleotides is given in Figure 21.12. A one-dimensional development using identical conditions shows the superiority of cellulose-layer TLC over PC for separating various mixtures (a different mixture for each vertical column of spots). Note that, in the same development distance, the isomeric 2'- and 3'-nucleotides (spots 1 to 4) were only partially resolved by PC but were fully resolved by TLC, whereas spots 7 to 9 were completely resolved only by TLC. The reduced degree of spot diffusion in TLC can be readily observed. Standardization of procedure is of considerable importance. For details on TLC standardization, the reader is referred to the book by Stahl [3].

Quantitative Aspects of TLC and PC

Compared to TLC or PC, quantitation is carried out more easily in column chromatography. A good deal of care is required to obtain reproducible and accurate quantitative results in TLC or PC. It is imperative that chromatographic conditions be well standardized. Standards and samples must be applied to the paper (or plate) in spots of similar size and at similar concentrations; solvents must be prepared, the chamber brought to equilibrium, and so forth, in the same manner. The locating reagent must be applied in a reproducible way. Having obtained a developed chro-

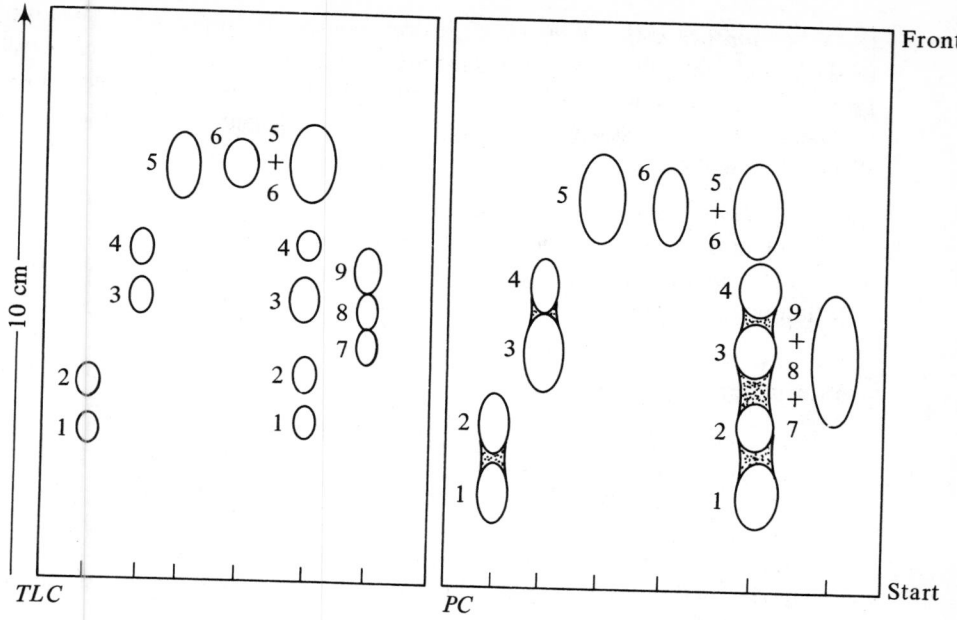

FIGURE 21.12.   *Comparative TLC and PC separation of nucleotides.*
A: Cellulose thin-layer chromatogram—development distance, 10 cm in
91 min.   B: Paper chromatogram run under identical conditions—develop-
ment distance, 10 cm in 134 min; paper Schleicher and Schull 2043b.   The
solvent used for both was saturated ammonium sulfate/1 M sodium
acetate/isopropanol (80:18:2).   Each vertical column of spots corresponds
to separate mixtures separated.   Samples: (1) 3'-AMP; (2) 2'-AMP; (3) 3'-
GMP; (4) 2'-GMP; (5) 2'- and 3'-GMP; (6) 2'- and 3'-UMP; (7) 5'-AMP;
(8) 5'-ADP; (9) 5'-ATP.   (A = adenosine, G = guanine, C = cytidine,
M = mono-, D = di-, T = tri-, P = phosphate.)   From K. Randerath,
Biochem. Biophys. Res. Comm., **6**, 452 (1961–62), *by permission of*
Academic Press.

matogram, the separated substance can be measured directly on the paper (or plate) or it can be removed from the paper and measured by some other means.

1. *Visual Comparison of Spots.*   Samples and reference solutions containing known amounts are run on the same sheet, and the relative areas of the unknown and the standards estimated by eye.

2. *Physical Measurements of Colored Spots.*   Transmission or reflectance measurements on a strip or plate are made using a spectrophotometer.   Scanning photodensitometers are devices that measure spot intensity by reflectance and display the result on a recorder.   Visual methods are accurate to 5–10%; scanning methods, to 3–5%.

3. *Radioactive Measurements.*   For radioactive substances included in the sample, one may scan the strip with an automatic scanning device.

4. *Spot-Area Measurement.* The area of a spot is proportional to the logarithm of the amount of substance. The spot area can be determined by using transparent graph paper and counting the squares covered by the spot. Standards are run under the same conditions and a calibration curve of area versus log(standard weight applied) obtained.

5. *Spot Removal.* The spot may be removed from the paper by cutting or from a plate by scraping off the adsorbent containing the spot. The substance can be eluted or extracted from the strip or plate, and then handled as any other sample solution (e.g., measured by spectrophotometry, polarography, etc.)

Column Liquid Chromatography

Earlier, the basic principles of column chromatography were outlined. Although classical open-column LC is still a widely used technique, modern high-performance liquid chromatography (HPLC)—also called high-speed liquid chromatography (HSLC)—is quickly becoming the standard technique for column separation. There is no difference in the basic mechanism involved; only the apparatus employed and the practice of the technique are different. Relative to classical LC, the main advantages of HPLC are increased speed, resolution, and sensitivity, and its convenience for quantitative analysis.

General Considerations. When particles are packed into a column, they offer a restriction to solvent flow. The longer the column and the smaller the particles, the greater the restriction. If flow is forced through the column, it generates a back pressure. The relation of this column back pressure ΔP to the other chromatographic variables is given by

$$\Delta P = \frac{\eta L v}{\theta \, d_p^{\,2}} \qquad\qquad (21.13)$$

where η = the viscosity of the mobile phase
    v = the linear velocity of the mobile phase
    L = the column length
    d_p = the average diameter of the particles
    θ = a dimensionless structural constant, ~ 600 for packed beds

If the chromatographic variables are expressed in the cgs-mks system, then ΔP has units of kg/cm² or of atmospheres. Often, the pressure is expressed in units of pounds-per-square-inch above gravity or psig.

High-Performance Liquid Chromatography. The difference between classical LC and HPLC can be explored by referring to Figures 21.13 and 21.14. For classical LC, large porous particles with d_p = 100–250 μm (Fig. 21.13A) are packed into columns with internal diameters of 1–5 cm (Fig. 21.14A). Little pressure is required to permit slow solvent flow between these large particles. Normally, a small head of liquid in the column above the surface of the packing or, in some cases, a reservoir container connected to and placed above the column acts as the constant-pressure source. Pressure drops are of the order of 0.1–1 atmosphere. Flow rates are very

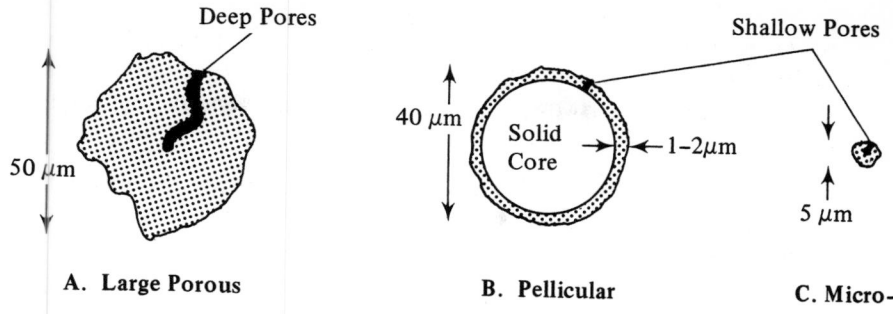

FIGURE 21.13. *Types of particles used in liquid chromatography.* A: *Large porous particle* (d_p = 50–250 μm); B: *Pellicular particle* (d_p = 37–50 μm); C: *Porous microparticle* (d_p = 5–10 μm).

slow (approximately 0.1 ml/min or less), and separation times very long. If attempts are made to speed up the solvent velocity, say by pumping, then, according to Equation 21.8, column efficiency (already low) and resolution will decrease because of mass-transfer limitations in the deep pores (that is, large values of H_{sm} or H_{sp}), and large interparticle channels (that is, large values of H_{ed} and H_{mp}). H-versus-v curves for such packings give steep slopes; hence the need for low flow-rates. Because of their large surface areas with high ion-exchange capacities, though, the large porous packings exhibit large sample capacities, important in preparative chromatography. Large porous packings are available at a nominal price and can be packed into columns by simple procedures.

Although an increase in column efficiency with a decrease in d_p was predicted very early in the development of column chromatography, only during the 1960s were column packings available that permitted application of the theory. These packing materials (in the range of $30 \leqslant d_p \leqslant 75 \,\mu$m), when packed into narrow columns, gave rise to larger back-pressures than the classical LC columns (Fig. 21.14B). Thus, to assist in mobile-phase flow through the column, high-pressure pumps were required. This was the advent of HPLC. For analytical HPLC, flow rates of 0.5–5 ml/min became typical and pressure drops up to 300 atm were obtained. On the other hand, column efficiency was increased 10–100-fold compared to classical LC, and separation times were decreased.

These improvements were caused by the development of pellicular packings in the late 1960s. These spherical packings consist of a solid, nonporous core (usually a glass bead approximately 40 μm in diameter) and a thin, porous outer shell, as depicted in Figure 21.13B. The outer shell, normally 1–3 μm thick, may be silica gel, alumina, resin, or polyamide. Because of their dense solid cores, pellicular particles are easily packed into columns. Compared to a porous particle of equivalent diameter, stationary-phase mass-transfer in this thin shell (the value of H_{sm} and/or H_{sp} of Equation 21.8) is greatly improved. However, on account of the thin shell, V_s is significantly reduced and sample capacity is 0.05–0.1 that of the totally porous packings. Therefore, pellicular packings are less useful in preparative LC.

A decrease in d_p below 30 μm for porous particles leads to further improvements in efficiency. Ion-exchange chromatographers were among the first to recognize the advantages of using very small spherical particles—in the 10-μm range.

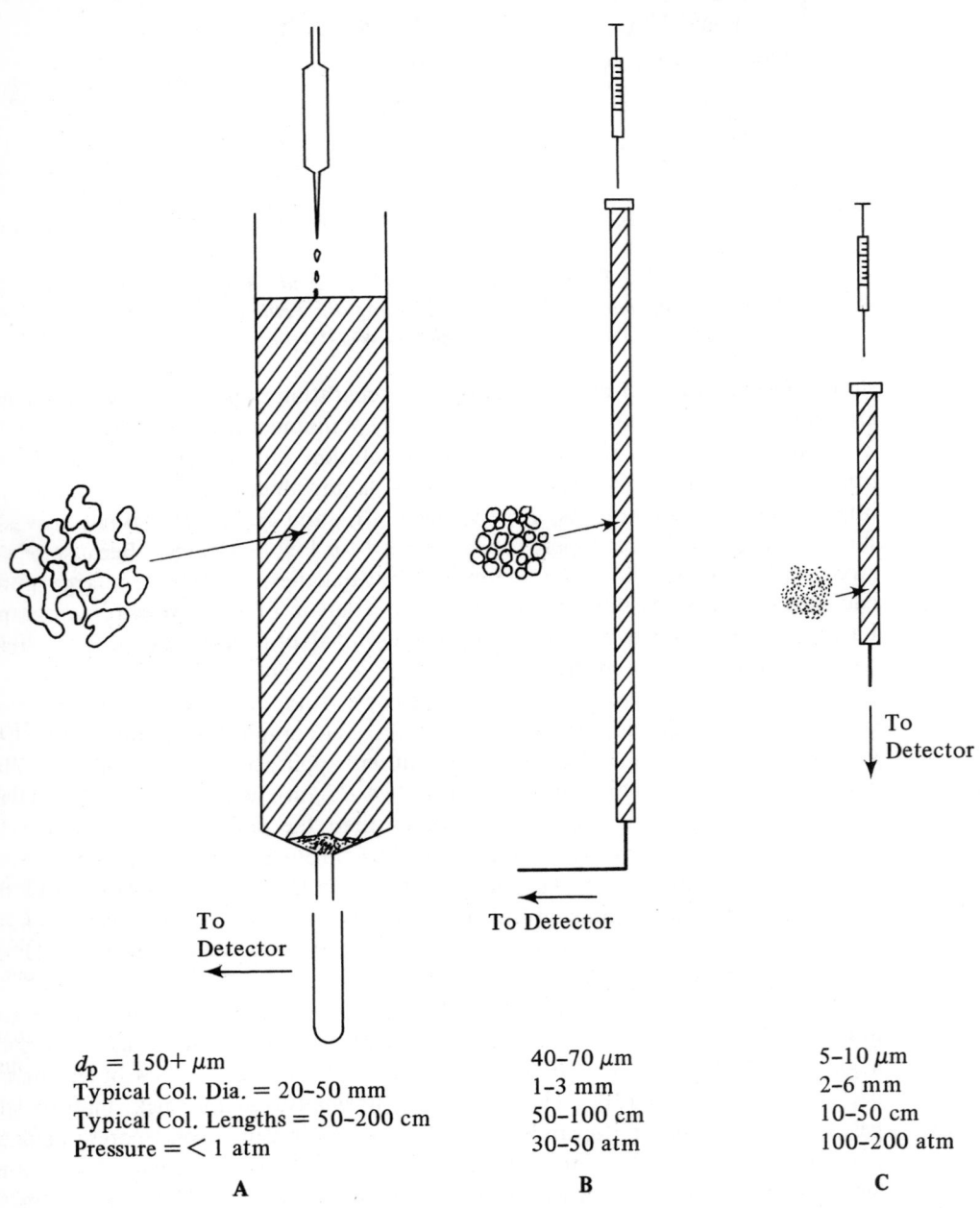

$d_p = 150+ \mu m$	40–70 μm	5–10 μm
Typical Col. Dia. = 20–50 mm	1–3 mm	2–6 mm
Typical Col. Lengths = 50–200 cm	50–100 cm	10–50 cm
Pressure = < 1 atm	30–50 atm	100–200 atm
A	**B**	**C**

FIGURE 21.14. *Comparison of columns used in liquid chromatography. A: Classical open column chromatography with large porous particle packings; B: HPLC with pellicular packings; C: HPLC with microparticulate packings.*

Ion-exchange resins were synthesized and then separated into narrow size-fractions by sedimentation or elutriation procedures. For the other modes of LC, commercial quantities of microparticles in narrow size-distributions, and the technology to pack them, were unavailable until the early 1970s. Through the use of air-centrifugal particle-classifiers, narrow size-distributions of adsorbents are now commercially available. In addition, high-pressure slurry-packing procedures have been developed. Microparticles in the 5–15 μm range (Fig. 21.13C) are commonly used for producing highly efficient HPLC columns. The increased efficiency (an extra factor of 10) is caused by improvements in the stationary-phase and mobile-phase mass-transfer terms of Equation 21.8. Thus, separation times and H values of 0.001–0.01 those of classical LC are obtained routinely. In addition, as their surface areas (or ion-exchange capacities) are the same as those of the large porous packings, the microparticles provide large sample capacity. Unfortunately, these microparticles are more expensive than large porous particles and require rather specialized packing techniques.

Since efficiencies for microparticulate columns are very high (optimum H values of 0.01–0.03 mm), only short columns (15–25 cm) are required for analytical HPLC, as can be seen in Figure 21.14C. The use of 5-μm particles implies greatly increased column back-pressures compared to those produced by the larger porous or pellicular particles, as suggested by Equation 21.13. However, these short columns exhibit moderate back-pressures (less than 200 atm) when used at flow rates of 1–2 ml/min with nonviscous mobile phases. But, for more difficult separations which may require tens of thousands of theoretical plates, long columns (50–100 cm) with the smallest available particles and high-pressure solvent feed are sometimes required. Likewise, according to Equation 21.13, high flow-rates or viscous mobile phases result in increased column back-pressure. In these cases, pressure drops of several hundred atmospheres may be encountered.

The overall influence of a reduction in particle size on the efficiency of a packed column is illustrated in Figure 21.15. Here curves of H-versus-v are plotted for 6.1 μm $\leqslant d_p \leqslant$ 44.7 μm for six different particle sizes of a porous silica gel. A standard test solute (N,N'-diethyl-p-aminoazobenzene) and the same mobile phase were used for all columns. Columns were packed by a high-pressure slurry technique. Note the significant decrease in H as the particle size is reduced to 6.1 μm. For comparison, an H-versus-v curve for Corasil®, a pellicular silica with an average d_p of 42.5 μm, is included. Porous silicas below 20 μm in d_p would be expected to give greater efficiency than 40-μm pellicular packings. Such H-versus-d_p relationships hold for all LC modes, including TLC.

Apparatus for Column Chromatography. A glass, metal, or plastic tube with a tapered outlet (Fig. 21.14A) is used as the column. To contain the packing, a wad of glass wool or a porous metal frit is placed at the bottom of the column, and the solid particles are poured into the top in increments until the column is full. It is important that the column be tightly packed with no voids. Although gravity can be used to force the liquid through the packed column, a pump is used for smaller diameter packings (less than 100 μm), as depicted in Figure 21.16. The sample can be injected by pipetting the sample, dissolved in a suitable solvent, onto the top of the packing. For the forced-flow systems in HPLC, an injection device—most commonly a syringe—is incorporated into the top of the column. The column temperature can be controlled by placing the column in an oven or by using a water jacket. Although glass columns are useful for low-pressure and classical open-column work, stainless-steel columns and compression-type fittings are required for high pressures (above 70 atm).

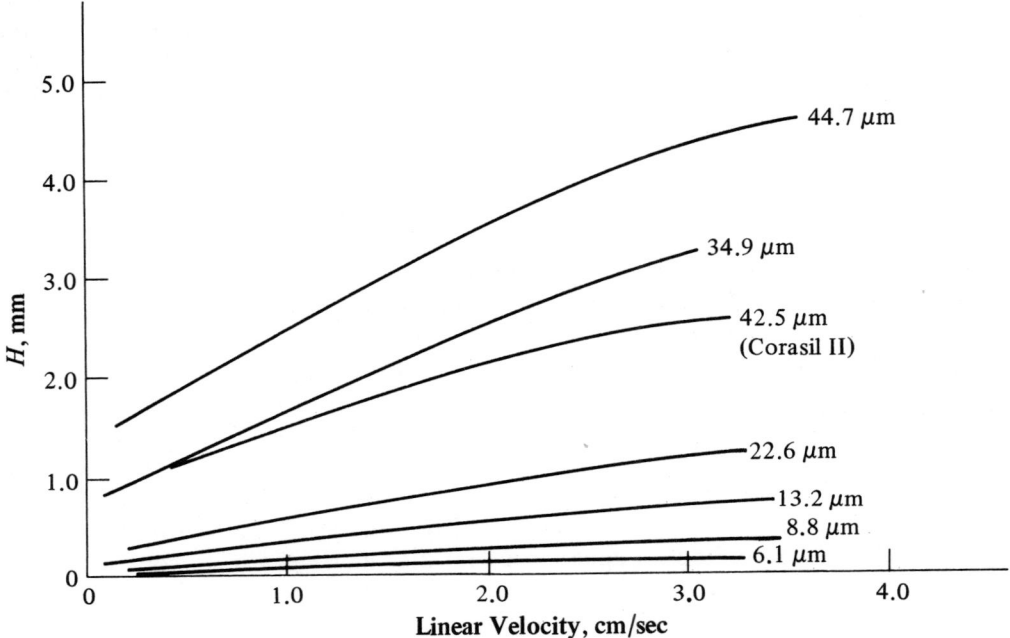

FIGURE 21.15. *Effect of velocity on plate height for porous silica gels of various particle diameters. Test solute: N,N'-diethyl-p-phenyl azoaniline (k' = 1.2). Mobile phase: 90/9.9/0.125 parts by volume of hexane/methylene chloride/isopropanol. Included for comparison is the same test solute run on Corasil II, a pellicular silica gel of d_p = 37–50 μm. From R. E. Majors,* J. Chromatogr. Sci., *11, 92 (1973), by permission of the publisher.*

To measure the substances eluting from the column, fractions of mobile phase can be collected and the concentration of the separated components measured externally—for example, in a spectrophotometer or using a pH meter. An automatic fraction-collector which collects a defined volume of column effluent in test tubes is sometimes employed. However, it is more convenient to employ a continuous-detection device at the exit of the column. The detector can be selective (for instance, it detects ultraviolet-absorbing or fluorescent compounds only) or universal (that is, it detects all components). In some cases, two detectors placed in series are used to gain additional information. The detector output is usually displayed on a strip-chart recorder or some other data-acquisition device. For quantitative analysis, an integrator or a minicomputer are useful to automatically measure peak areas.

The continuous detectors most often used in liquid chromatography are based on ultraviolet or visible absorption, fluorescence, and differential refractometry.

To minimize broadening of the narrow peaks often obtained in HPLC, modern detectors measure a small volume, usually 15 μl or less. A schematic of an ultraviolet detector with a flow-through cell is presented in Figure 21.17. The light source is a low-pressure mercury lamp with an intense emission line at 254 nm. The light is collimated by a quartz lens, passes through the reference and sample cells, is filtered to remove unwanted radiation, and is sensed by a dual photocell. Typically, a flow-through cell of this kind has a 1-mm diameter and 10-mm length with a 15-μl volume. The normal laws of spectrophotometry hold for these detectors—absorbance is linear with concentration. An ultraviolet detector can resolve absorbance differences as small as 0.00005 absorbance unit, equivalent to ppb detection limits in favorable cases.

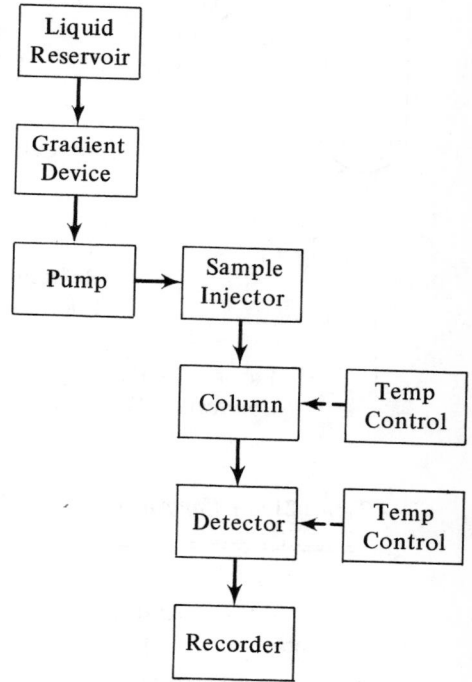

FIGURE 21.16. *Block diagram of a liquid chromatograph. Courtesy of Varian Associates.*

Table 21.1 classifies popular LC detectors according to several criteria for purposes of comparison. At the present time, LC detectors are generally less sensitive than GC detectors, which can detect picograms of material under good conditions. Most LC detectors provide only limited structural information. However, spectrophotometers fitted with micro flow-cells can be used to obtain a stop-flow ultraviolet- or visible-absorption spectrum of an LC peak trapped in the flow cell. On-line coupling of liquid chromatographs with mass or infrared spectrometers offers sophisticated, but indeed expensive, detection/identification methods. Such systems have been described in the literature, but are quite limited by the solvents that can be used in the chromatography step.

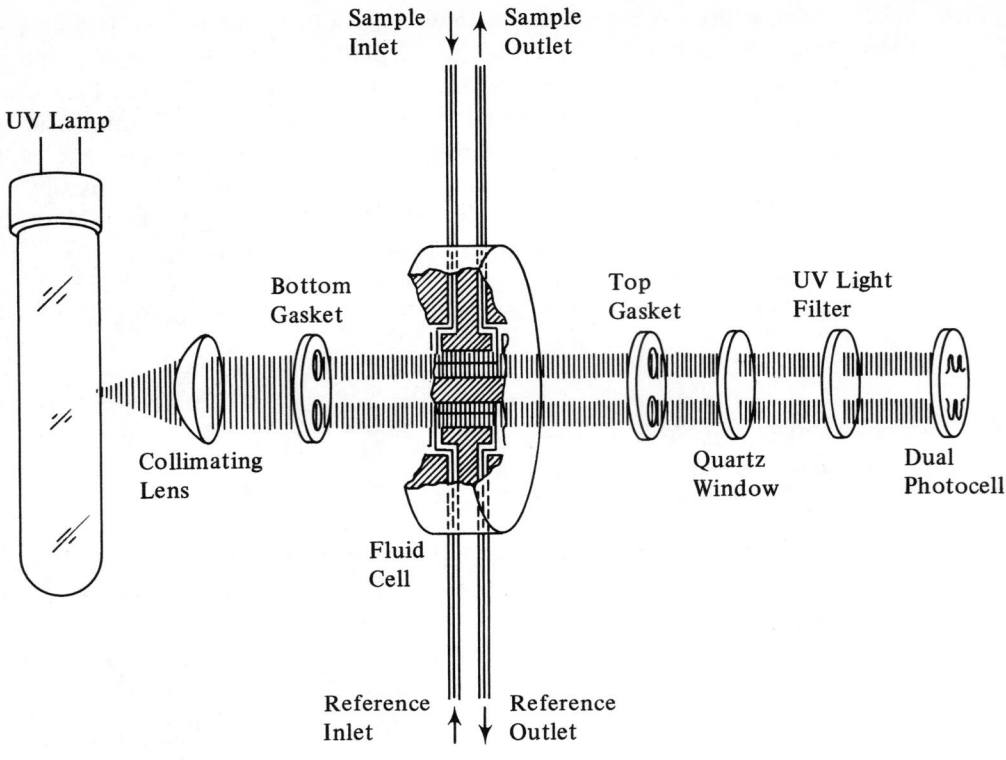

FIGURE 21.17. *Expanded optical schematic of ultraviolet detector. Courtesy of Varian Associates.*

TABLE 21.1. *Comparison of LC Detectors*

Factor	Ultraviolet (UV)	Refractive Index (RI)	Fluores-cence	Electro-chemical	Moving Wire/Flame Ionization
Specificity	Selective	Universal	Selective	Selective	Universal
Detection Limit	10^{-10} g/ml	10^{-7} g/ml	10^{-10} g/ml	10^{-9} g/ml	10^{-7} g/ml
Gradient Compatible	Yes	No	Yes	Yes	Yes
Major Limitations	Non-UV active solvents only	Low sensi-tivity, precise tempera-ture con-trol required	Limited dynamic range	Compound adsorption, no electro-active solvents	No salt buffers or volatile solutes

21.4 USES AND APPLICATIONS OF ADSORPTION CHROMATOGRAPHY

Liquid chromatography is most applicable to nonvolatile compounds such as ionic compounds or polymers, thermally unstable compounds such as explosives, and labile compounds such as many biological substances. For volatile compounds, GC is the preferred technique. However, approximately 80% of the known organic compounds are nonvolatile enough to be handled by LC. Liquid chromatography is a relatively "gentle" technique in the sense that many separations can be carried out at ambient temperature, provided the sample can be dissolved in a suitable solvent. It suffices to say that if the sample can be dissolved, it can be analyzed by LC. Sample sizes can range from nanograms to grams; the only limitation on the low end is finding a suitable detector for subnanogram quantities. As new detectors are developed, detection limits for HPLC will be lowered below the nanogram range.

Influence of the Stationary Phase in LSC

Selecting the correct chromatographic technique for a particular mixture is sometimes difficult. We will discuss those properties of the various types of stationary phases that serve to distinguish one mode of LC from another.

Adsorption or liquid-solid chromatography (LSC), the oldest chromatographic method, is the most widely used of all modes. Thin-layer or column chromatography is used by most laboratories that use liquid-chromatographic techniques, often as a screening method to select the best experimental conditions for LC. Adsorbents are porous solids with specific surface areas ranging from 50–1000 m²/g. Table 21.2 lists typical adsorbents used in several chromatographic techniques. Most adsorbents come in particle sizes to suit the needs of the various kinds of chromatography, are specially made, and can be purchased commercially. For TLC, particle sizes of 20–40 μm are frequently used, whereas for open columns the particles are larger (100–150 μm) and for HPLC they are smaller (down to 5 μm).

To illustrate the manner in which adsorbents separate compounds, consider the surface characteristics of the most widely used adsorbent, silica gel. Chromatographic-grade silica gels are prepared by reacting sodium silicate with a mineral acid, such as hydrochloric acid. Polymerization occurs and a three-dimensional array of SiO_4 tetrahedra results. This polysilicic acid, when dehydrated, forms a stable porous solid, terminated at the surface with either silanol or siloxane bonds, as illustrated in Figure 21.18. The slightly acidic silanol groups are considered to be important in separation; siloxane bonds, to have little or no influence. Silanol groups themselves are believed to have varying degrees of acidity. The most acidic ones, located on adjacent silicon atoms with intramolecular hydrogen-bonding, often lead to undesirable chromatographic effects, such as chemisorption and peak tailing. Often a polar modifier, such as water, is added to the adsorbent in order to deactivate the strongest adsorption sites.

Interactions between the adsorbent surface and the solute can vary from nonspecific ones (such as dispersion or van der Waals' forces) to specific ones (electrostatic interactions involving permanent dipoles or electron-donor-acceptor interactions, such as hydrogen bonding). Retention on silica gel or alumina is governed mainly by interactions with the polar functional groups of the solute. Thus, compounds of different chemical types (e.g., hydrocarbons and alcohols) are easily separated by LSC. Weak dispersive interactions with the hydrocarbon (especially aliphatic) portion of the solute allows little or no differentiation among homologues or other mixtures differing only in the extent of aliphatic substitution. The relative positions of the functional groups in the solute molecule, and the number and spatial arrangement of surface adsorption sites, lead to a geometric specificity that makes LSC unique in

TABLE 21.2. *Adsorbents for Adsorption Chromatography*

Adsorbent	Chemical Structure	Estimated Usage (percent)	Surface Properties	Applications
Silica	$(SiO_2)_x$	80	Slightly Acid	General-Purpose Adsorbent
Alumina	$(Al_2O_3)_x$	10	Slightly Basic [a]	General-Purpose Adsorbent
Charcoal	Carbon	1	Graphitized-nonpolar	Sample Cleanup
			Oxidized Polar (Slightly Basic)	
Florisil®	Magnesia-silica coprecipitate	2	Strongly Acidic	General-Purpose Adsorbent
Polyamides	——	3	Basic	Phenols and Aromatic Nitro Compounds
Others (clays, Kieselguhr, diatomaceous earth, Celite®, etc.)	——	5	Relatively Nonpolar	Very Polar Compounds

a. Depends on method of preparation; can also be neutral or acidic.

its ability to separate polyfunctional compounds, especially positional isomers. For instance, *cis-trans* pairs or substituted aromatic isomers can be separated. Such a separation, by HPLC, of the three isomers of nitroaniline is shown in Figure 21.19. Note that the first to elute is the *ortho* isomer, which is intramolecularly hydrogen-bonded and thus has less (intermolecular) interaction with the surface, whereas the *para-* isomer is more likely to react intermolecularly and is the most strongly retained.

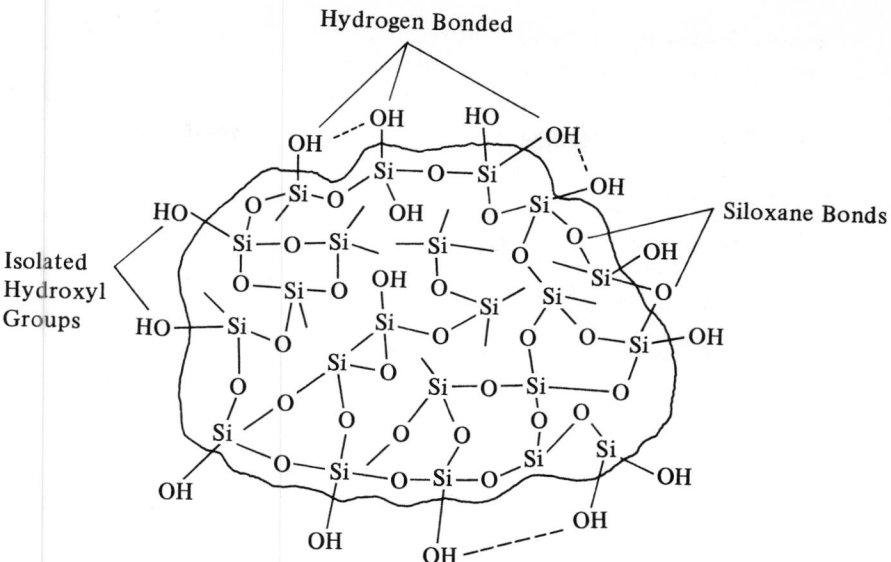

FIGURE 21.18. *Structure of silica gel depicting the various types of bonds and silanol groups present.*

Influence of the Mobile Phase in LSC

Actually, the interactions in LSC involve a competition between the solute molecules (X) and the molecules (S) of the mobile phase for the adsorption sites. This equilibrium is illustrated by

$$X_m + nS_{ads} \rightleftharpoons X_{ads} + nS_m \qquad (21.14)$$

where

X_m = the solute molecules in the mobile phase
X_{ads} = the solute molecules in the adsorbed state
S_{ads} = the mobile-phase molecules adsorbed on the surface site
S_m = the solvent molecules in the free mobile phase
n = the number of adsorbed solvent molecules displaced by the adsorption of one molecule of X

Thus, stronger adsorption of the mobile phase decreases adsorption of the solute. Solvents can be classed according to their strength of adsorption. Such a quantitative classification is referred to as an *eluotropic series*. Table 21.3 is an abbreviated eluotropic series specifically for alumina as the adsorbent, but qualitatively this series holds for other polar adsorbents as well [4].

An eluotropic series can be used to find an optimum solvent strength for a particular separation. Using a solvent of constant composition is called *isocratic elution*. If an isocratic solvent is too strong (if the k' values for the solutes are too small), a weaker solvent is substituted. On the other hand, if the initial solvent is too weak (the k' values are too large), a stronger solvent is selected. This trial-and-error approach to finding the optimum solvent can be done more rapidly by TLC than by column chromatography.

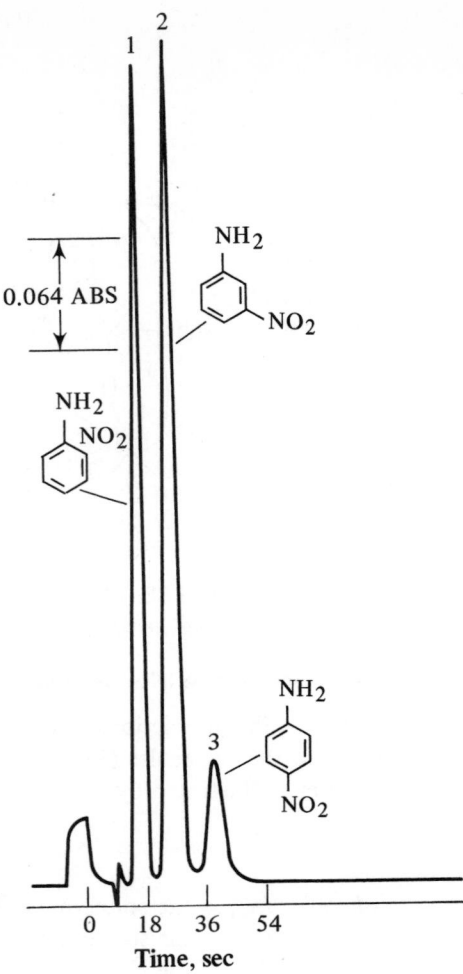

FIGURE 21.19. *LSC separation of nitro-aniline isomers on* 10-*μm alumina,* (1) *o-nitroaniline;* (2) *m-nitroaniline;* (3) *p-nitroaniline. Column: Micropak® Al-10. Packing:* 10-*μm alumina, type T. Dimensions:* 15 *cm* × 2.4 *mm. Mobile phase:* 40% CH_2Cl_2 *in hexane. Flow rate:* 100 *ml/hr. Sample size:* 1 *μg of each isomer. Detector:* 254-*nm ultraviolet absorption. From R. E. Majors,* Anal. Chem., 45, 757 (1973), *by permission of the publisher. Copyright © 1973 by the American Chemical Society.*

Binary solvent mixtures may also be used to find an optimum value of the *solvent-strength* parameter ε^0. For example, a mixture of isoöctane ($\varepsilon^0 = 0.01$) and methylene chloride ($\varepsilon^0 = 0.42$) can be found (see Table 21.3) with an isocratic solvent strength similar to that of carbon tetrachloride ($\varepsilon^0 = 0.18$). However, the relationship between binary composition and solvent strength is not necessarily linear, owing to the solvent-solvent and preferential solvent-surface interactions. Additional selectivity in LSC can be achieved through secondary solvent effects. Such effects are produced by solvent mixtures that display equivalent values of ε^0 but that, because of various solvation interactions such as hydrogen-bonding ability, basicity, and so forth, also give rise to variations in relative retention (i.e., selectivity).

In all forms of chromatography, one must be aware of the so-called general elution problem (illustrated in Fig. 21.20) when dealing with isocratic solvent systems and multi-component samples with widely differing k' values. If a strong isocratic mobile phase is selected that will adequately elute strongly retained compounds, then the weakly retained ones will be eluted too quickly and will be poorly separated

TABLE 21.3. *Eluotropic Series for Alumina*

Solvent	Solvent-Strength Parameter (ε^0)
n-Pentane	0.00
Isoöctane	0.01
Cyclohexane	0.04
Carbon Tetrachloride	0.18
Xylene	0.26
Toluene	0.29
Benzene	0.32
Ethyl Ether	0.38
Chloroform	0.40
Methylene Chloride	0.42
Tetrahydrofuran	0.45
Acetone	0.56
Methyl Acetate	0.60
Aniline	0.62
Acetonitrile	0.65
i-Propanol, *n*-Propanol	0.82
Ethanol	0.88
Methanol	0.95
Ethylene Glycol	1.11
Acetic Acid	Large

Source: L. R. Snyder, *J. Chromatog.*, *16*, 55 (1964), by permission of the author and the North Holland Publishing Company.

(Fig. 21.20A). Conversely, if a weak mobile phase is chosen, so that weakly retained sample components will be retained and separated, then very strongly retained solutes may not be eluted at all—or only very slowly (Fig. 21.20B)—and possibly with the peaks so broadened as to be undetectable. No single isocratic solvent can be found that will be effective for such a mixture of components with widely varying k' values. To handle this kind of sample, the rates of band migration must be changed during the chromatographic run.

In GC, the general elution problem is solved by temperature programming and to a lesser extent by flow programming (see Chap. 22). In LC, the most common technique is called *solvent programming* or *gradient elution*. Here, elution is begun with a weak solvent and the solvent strength is increased with time. The changes are made either stepwise or continuously. The overall effect is to elute successively the more strongly retained substances and at the same time to reduce tailing. The k' values, and hence the analysis time, can be decreased by as much as 10^6 using solvent programming. Figure 21.20C demonstrates how solvent programming provides a solution to the general elution problem for the compounds shown.

In HPLC, since columns are reusable, the stationary phase must be returned to its initial condition at the conclusion of a solvent program so that, if necessary, another sample can be run under equivalent conditions. This process is called *regeneration*. Regeneration is accomplished by an instantaneous return to the initial

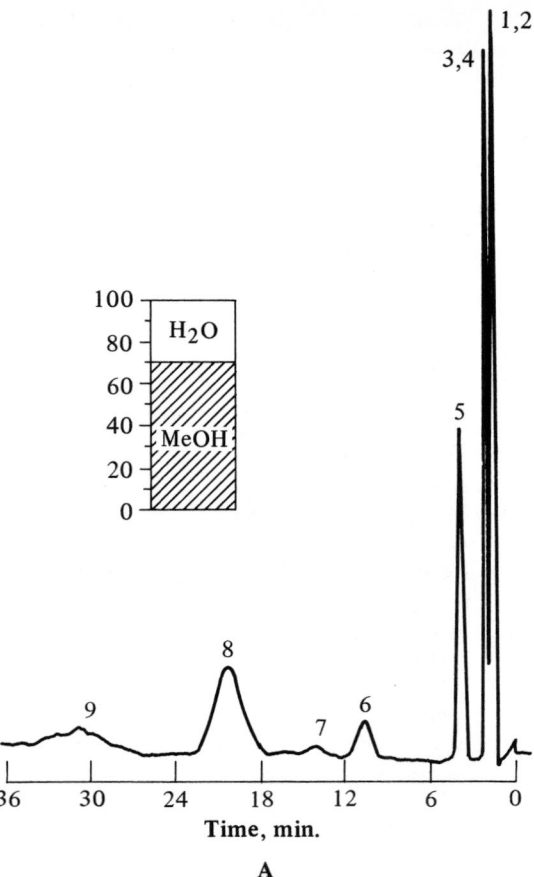

FIGURE 21.20. *Illustration of the general elution problem: separation of commercial flame retardants (brominated aromatics). Column: Permaphase®-ODS (DuPont), 1 m × 2.4 mm. Solvent flow rate: 1 ml/min. A and B are isocratic elutions. C is a solvent-programmed run: 40% methanol in water to 100% methanol at 3%/min. Compounds: (1) Bisphenol A; (2) Firemaster LV-723P; (3) Firemaster BP4A (Tetrabromobisphenol A); (4) p-Dibromobenzene; (5) 4,4′-Dibromobiphenyl; (6) Hexabromobenzene; (7) Hexabromobenzene impurity; (8) Firemaster BP-6 (Hexabromodiphenyl); (9) Firemaster BP-6 impurity (probably isomer). (Firemasters are products of the Michigan Chemical Company.) Chromatograms courtesy of Varian Associates.*

composition of the solvent, then prolonged washing to remove the stronger solvent. The time required depends on V_s, the amount of stationary phase. An alternate, and in most cases more rapid, regeneration technique is to run a "negative" solvent program to remove the stronger solvent more gradually. At the end of the negative program, the column is usually ready for another injection.

In column chromatography, solvent gradients can be formed stepwise by

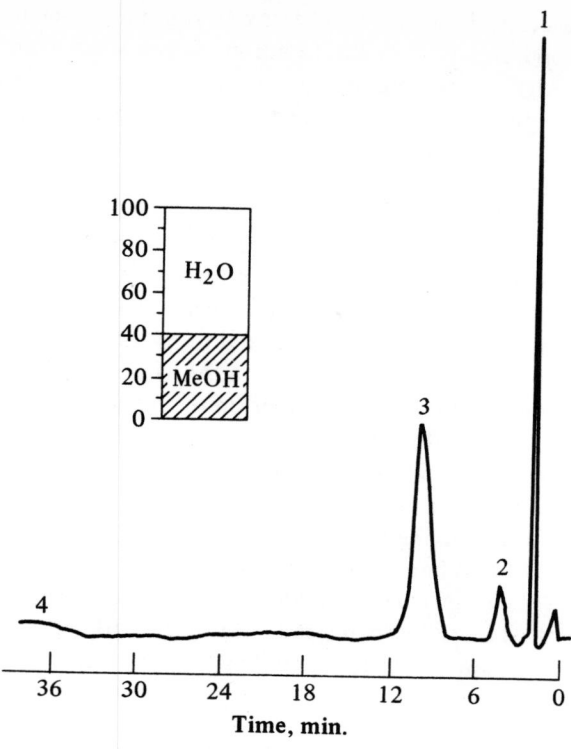

B

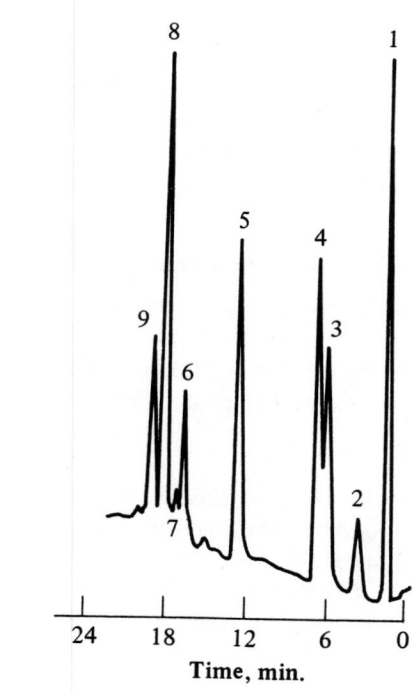

C

adding successively stronger solvents one at a time to the top of the column. A commercial apparatus is available to automatically select from two to twelve successive solvents, each at predetermined times. Continuous gradients can be formed by using a simple apparatus equipped with a magnetic stirrer (see Fig. 21.21A). The pure weaker solvent (B) is placed in the mixing flask and the stronger solvent (A) is placed in the reservoir. Solvent A is permitted to flow into the mixing flask and the mixture of A and B is delivered to the column, often by means of a reciprocating pump. Equations are available for calculating the composition of the mixture in the flask at any given time. The shape (profile) of the gradient can be varied, as shown in Figure 21.21B; both linear and nonlinear profiles are useful in LC.

Homogeneous mixing is required to provide smooth and reproducible profiles. In HPLC, gradients may be formed on the low-pressure side of the pump (analogous to the technique described above), or on the high-pressure side of the pump (depicted in Fig. 21.21C). With electronic programmers controlling the pump flows, the ratio of A to B can be varied easily and gradient profiles changed reproducibly. In addition, stepwise gradients, negative gradients, and isocratic mobile phases can be generated in the mixing chamber.

In TLC, although continuous solvent programming is feasible, it is seldom used because it is experimentally inconvenient. Stepwise development or two-dimensional TLC is used instead. More recently, programmed multiple development with the same solvent system has been introduced.

21.5 USES AND APPLICATIONS OF PARTITION CHROMATOGRAPHY

Partition or liquid-liquid chromatography is similar to solvent extraction. In fact, solvent-extraction data can be used to predict partition coefficients for LLC. The resolving power and speed of LLC are considerably greater than that of solvent extraction, however, since the equivalent of several thousand partitions takes place as the sample components move down a column. LLC is generally better suited to analytically separating complex mixtures, whereas extraction is used more for large-scale preparative separations or for separating relatively simple mixtures.

Selecting Stationary and Mobile Phases in LLC

The stationary and the mobile phases are selected so as to have little or no mutual solubility. Therefore, they generally are quite different in their solvent properties. For example, referring to Table 21.3, one might choose water as the stationary phase and pentane as the mobile phase for normal LLC. However, water does have

---

FIGURE 21.21. *Gradient devices used in liquid chromatography. A: Simple mixing device for gradient elution, gradient formed on low-pressure side of pump. R_1 is the flow rate of A into the flask. R_2 is the flow rate of A + B to column. B: Gradient profiles obtained from A. C: Schematic for two-pump gradient chromatograph. Gradient formed on high-pressure side of pump.*

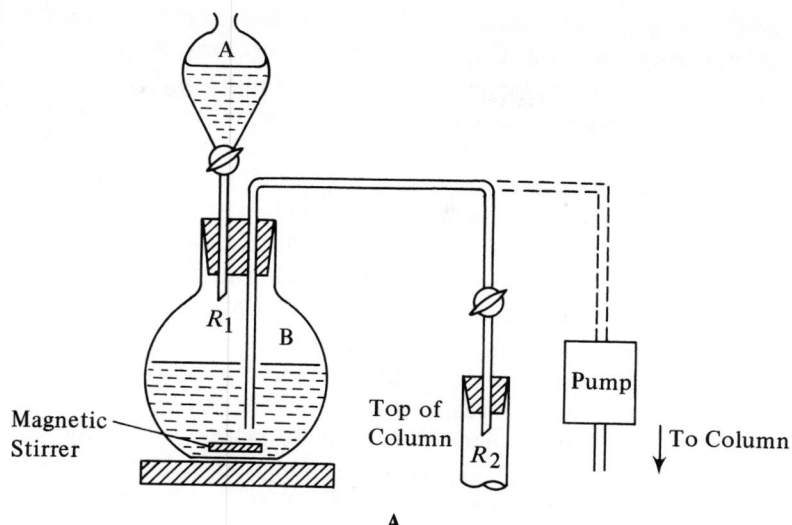

A

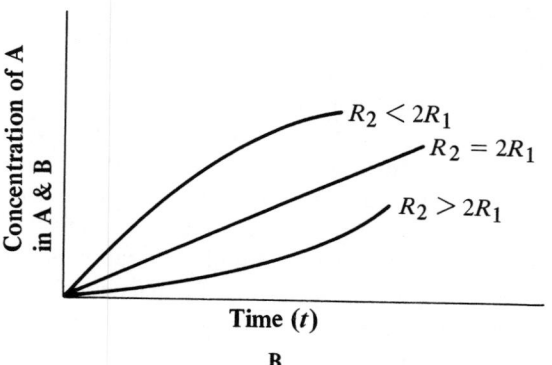

B

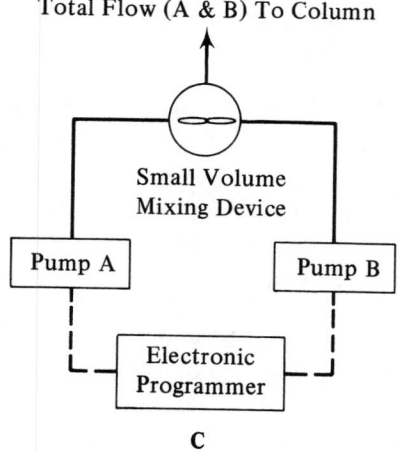

C

a finite (though very slight) solubility in pentane. If pentane, used as a mobile phase, is allowed to flow over a water-coated support long enough, it will slowly remove the water and change the nature of the separation mechanism. For this reason, the mobile phase must be presaturated with the stationary phase before it enters the column. Presaturation can be done by stirring the two phases together until equilibration takes place; but it is more conveniently done by placing a "precolumn" before the chromatographic column. The precolumn should contain a high-surface-area packing, such as silica gel, coated with a high percentage (say 30–40% by weight) of the stationary phase used in the analytical column. As the solvent passes through the highly dispersed stationary phase, the solvent becomes saturated with it and will not remove it from the analytical column.

Liquid-liquid chromatography is limited to compounds with comparatively low values of K (or k'), because the stationary phase must be a good solvent for the sample but a poor solvent for the mobile phase. In practice, increasing solvent strength in order to elute compounds with high K (or k') values will increase the solubility of the stationary phase and remove it from its support. When the solvent strength is high enough to dissolve an appreciable amount of stationary phase, presaturation is rendered difficult. Needless to say, in conventional LLC solvent programming is ruled out.

Even with its limitations, LLC is a very useful technique because it can resolve minute differences in the solubility of the solute. Many solvent pairs are available, and the choice of the proper ones allows great selectivity to be achieved. Selection of useful solvent pairs has been greatly improved by classifying solvents in terms of their ability to undergo different types of intermolecular interactions. Recently, a scheme based on the Hildebrand solubility parameter (δ) has been described [5, 6]— common chromatographic solvents are classified quantitatively in terms of parameters such as dispersion interactions, dipole interactions, and proton donor–acceptor ability. By matching the properties of the particular solute (for instance, its proton-acceptor ability) with one or more of these individual parameters, one can estimate K values and vary δ until the desired separation is obtained. The K value of a solute is related to the ratio of its concentrations (more correctly, its activities) in the two partitioning phases; selecting partitioning solvents with quite different δ values (polarity) magnifies these differences in solubility. Since the activity coefficients of members of a homologous series vary with their molecular size, members of a homologous series can be separated by LLC, whereas in LSC there is little discrimination between successive members of a homologous series.

Both PC and TLC have been carried out with coated liquid phases. The paper strip (or thin-layer plate) is impregnated with stationary phase, either neat or dissolved in a volatile solvent. In the latter case the solvent should be allowed to evaporate slowly to ensure homogeneous distribution of the stationary phase. Normal development is carried out, but some care is required to locate the separated spots since the coated liquid phase may interfere with detection.

Substances only very sparingly soluble in water are not separated by ordinary paper chromatography, since they move with the solvent front. If the paper is impregnated with silicone oil or paraffin and a highly polar solvent is used as the mobile phase, such samples are more easily separated. This technique is referred to as reverse-phase PC. In the same way, reverse-phase TLC can be carried out.

Bonded-Phase Chromatography

The limiting requirements of conventional LLC—that is, finding immiscible solvent pairs, presaturating the mobile phase to avoid removing the stationary phase, and the impossibility of using gradient elution to solve the general elution problem—have been overcome in *bonded-phase chromatography* (BPC). Although the latter is grouped here as a branch of LLC, the chromatographic behavior of bonded phases is somewhat dependent on the manner of preparation, and bonded-phase chromatography has also been classed as a form of LSC since the bonded phases may not be liquid-like, and modified adsorption may be the predominant mechanism.

Although, in principle, any number of chemical species can be bonded to the support, in practice only three general types of chemical bonding have been used with LC packings.

1. Since silica gel contains large numbers of reactive silanol groups extending from the surface, the Si–OH groups can be esterified by reaction with alcohols to yield *silicate esters*.
2. The Si–OH groups can be silanized by reaction with organochloro- or organo-alkoxysilanes.
3. Silica Si–OH groups can be converted to Si–Cl by chlorination, after which Grignard reaction, Wurtz reaction, or some other reaction typical of organo-halogen compounds yields chemically bonded species with Si–C linkages.

Because of the hydrolytic and thermal instability of the Si–O–C band, silicate esters have not proven satisfactory. Likewise, the experimental difficulty of preparing and purifying Si–C phases has discouraged their use. Therefore, most available packings for LC are of the silane (i.e., Si–O–Si–C) type. This bonded phase is stable under most conditions employed in LC and is attacked only in very basic or acidic solutions.

Siloxane phases have been prepared by reaction under anhydrous conditions to yield phases with short chain-length, or by polymerization under controlled humidity to yield polymeric phases. Polymeric phases behave like partitioning phases, whereas the short chains act like modified adsorbents. The chromatographic efficiency of polymeric phases is somewhat lower because of limitations on the mass transfer of the solute. However, both types of siloxanes can be used with solvent programming; this is a major advantage of BPC. Figure 21.20C shows a solvent-programmed separation of several brominated aromatic compounds using a water-methanol gradient and an octadecylsilane (hydrophobic) bonded phase. A conventionally-coated LLC phase could not have been used in such a solvent system; the stationary phase would have been dissolved in the mobile phase.

21.6 ION-EXCHANGE CHROMATOGRAPHY

Ion-exchange chromatography is generally applicable to ionic compounds, to ionizable compounds such as organic acids or bases, and to compounds (such as chelates or ligands) that can interact with ionic groups. Ion-exchange chromatography is carried out with stationary phases having charge-bearing functional groups. The mobile phase usually contains a counter ion, opposite in charge to the surface ionic group, in equilibrium with the resin in the form of an ion pair. The presence of a solute ion of the same ionic charge sets up an equilibrium as follows

$$\text{Cation exchange:} \quad X^+ + R^-Y^+ \rightleftharpoons Y^+ + R^-X^+ \qquad \textbf{(21.15)}$$

$$\text{Anion exchange:} \quad X^- + R^+Y^- \rightleftharpoons Y^- + R^+X^- \qquad \textbf{(21.16)}$$

where   X = the sample ion
          Y = the mobile-phase ion (counter ion)
          R = the ionic site on the exchanger

Competition between the sample ion and the counter ion for the fixed ionic site is very similar to the competition between solute and solvent for adsorption sites in LSC. In fact, sometimes ion exchange is referred to as adsorption chromatography involving electrostatic interactions. However, as the nature of the stationary and mobile phases, as well as the samples handled, are quite unlike those used for LSC, we prefer to classify ion-exchange chromatography separately.

Stationary Phases

The stationary phases used in ion exchange may be naturally occurring inorganic solids such as sodium aluminosilicate and clays such as montmorillonite, or synthetic ones such as zirconium phosphate. More often, though, they are resins prepared by the copolymerization of styrene and divinylbenzene. The amount of divinylbenzene used in the synthesis controls the extent of cross-linking in the resin. High cross-linking decreases the solubility of polystyrene and improves the structural rigidity, required for high-pressure use in HPLC. However, high cross-linking also decreases the porosity required for good mass-transfer. Low-cross-linked resins have a tendency to "swell" by absorption of mobile phase. The amount of cross-linking expressed as percent of divinylbenzene varies from 2–12%, with 8% being an average value.

The ionic groups are added by chemical reaction after preparing the cross-linked resin. Cationic or anionic resins are classified as strong or weak, depending on the acidic or basic strength of the functional group. Strong cation-exchangers normally have sulfonic ($-SO_3H$) functionality (incorporated by sulfonation of the resin) whereas weak ones have carboxyl ($-COOH$) functionality. Strong anion-exchangers have tetraalkylammonium groups—for instance, $-CH_2-N(CH_3)_3{}^+Cl^-$ (incorporated by chloromethylation followed by treatment with trimethylamine)—whereas weakly basic ones might have $-NH_3{}^+Cl^-$ or $-NHR_2{}^+Cl^-$ functional groups. Resins of intermediate strength are also available.

Exchange Capacity

The number and strength of fixed ionic groups on the solid governs its exchange capacity. Since the ion-exchange capacity affects solute retention, exchangers of high capacity are most often used for separating complex mixtures, where increased retention improves resolution. The capacities of weakly acidic and basic resins show a marked dependence on pH; generally, these resins have a small range of maximum capacity, dependent on the pK of the functional group. The strongly acidic and basic resins have a much wider range of maximum capacity and are generally more widely used. Weak ion-exchangers are most often used in separating strongly basic, strongly acidic, or multi-functional ionic substances which are often firmly retained on the strong ion-exchangers; they have been used for separating such substances as proteins, peptides, and sulfonates. For porous strong resins, capacities are of the order of 3–10 meq/g. For pellicular strong resins, the capacity is much lower (5–50 μeq/g).

Influences on Distribution Coefficients and Selectivity

Ion-exchange chromatography involves more variables than other forms of chromatography. Distribution coefficients and selectivities are functions of pH, solute charge and radius, resin porosity, ionic strength and type of buffer, type of solvent, temperature, and so forth. The number of experimental variables makes ion-exchange chromatography a very versatile technique, since each may be used to effect a better separation, but a difficult one because of the time needed to optimize a separation. When using polystyrene-divinylbenzene resins, organic ions (especially aromatic ones) are sorbed both by ionic forces with exchange groups and by interactions with the resin matrix itself. For example, because of "solvent" effects of the resin matrix, phenols are more strongly retained in anion exchange than their weak ionization would suggest. Even nonionic compounds can be separated on resins, probably by a partition mechanism. In these cases, the presence of a buffer decreases the solubility of the compound in the mobile phase, thus increasing its affinity for the resin. This form of "salting out" chromatography is used to separate alcohols in order of increasing molecular weight.

Electrically neutral species that form a complex with ions can be separated by the exchange process. A well known example is separating sugars through the adducts formed with the borate buffer used to elute them. Ligands can be separated through their interaction with metallic ions sorbed by the resin.

Cellulose powder, chemically modified to contain ion-exchange groups, is also used in both thin-layer and column chromatography. Because of its lack of rigidity, application is limited to low-pressure columns. Sheets of modified cellulose are available for use as exchangers in paper chromatography, and ion-exchange resins and inorganic ion-exchangers have been impregnated into cellulose strips. Liquid ion-exchangers, such as trioctylamine and bis-(2-ethylhexyl)-phosphoric acid (which are immiscible with aqueous solutions) can be coated onto a support, as in LLC.

Uses of Ion-Exchange Chromatography

Ion-exchange chromatography is used most often in inorganic chemistry and in biochemistry, the latter often to deal with water-soluble polar compounds such as proteins and amino acids. Metallic ions can be separated by cation exchange using the characteristic charge-to-radius ratio of the hydrated ions. Under comparable conditions, tetravalent ions are generally retained more than monovalent ions. Within a particular series of ions carrying the same charge, there is also a range of selectivity. As a rough guide, resin affinity decreases as the radius of the hydrated ion increases.

The development of ion-exchange methods for separating lanthanides and various fission products was instrumental in the development of atomic reactors. Tables of distribution coefficients as a function of pH for almost every cation in the periodic table, and for many synthetic resins, came out of this monumental work. More recently, the extension of ion-exchange methods into the biochemical field has aided in the structural elucidation of proteins and nucleic acids. Figure 21.22 depicts the separation of amino acids, one of the most used areas of ion-exchange chromatography. The amino acids are detected as they are eluted by their reaction with ninhydrin in a postcolumn reactor. The colored product is measured in a flow-through colorimetric detector.

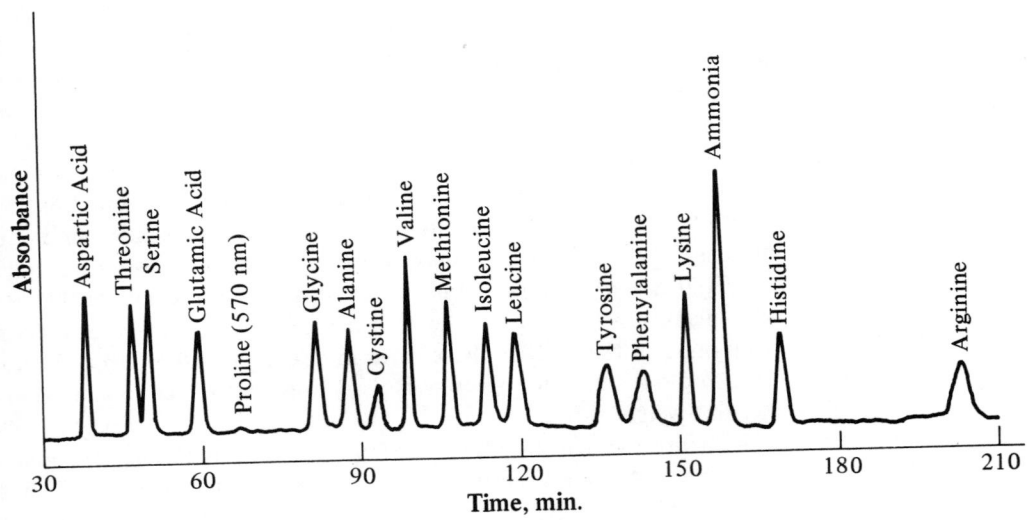

FIGURE 21.22. *Separation of amino acids by ion-exchange chromatography. Resin: Durrum® DC-1A, a sulfonated polystyrene-divinylbenzene cation exchanger of $d_p = 8$ μm. Ten nanomole calibration mixture. Flow rate: 70 ml/hr. From James R. Benson, Durrum Resin Report No. 5, April, 1973, Durrum Chemical Corp., by permission of Durrum Chemical Corp.*

21.7 EXCLUSION CHROMATOGRAPHY

Exclusion chromatography, also called gel chromatography, is the predominant method used for separating and characterizing substances of high molecular weight. The process is almost always carried out in a column, but it also has been performed on a thin layer. Column packing materials with pores of different (controlled) sizes are generally used. The materials can be soft gels, semirigid gels, or rigid materials. The soft and semirigid gels can change their pore sizes, depending on the solvent used as a mobile phase. The soft gels, of the polydextran or agarose type, can swell to many times their dry volume, whereas the semirigid gels of the polyvinylacetate or polystyrene type swell to 1.1–1.8 times their dry volume; the rigid materials, such as porous glass or porous silica beads, have fixed pore sizes and do not swell at all.

General Considerations

To understand how steric exclusion differs from the other forms of chromatography, refer to Equation 21.4. In this context, V_m and V_s are referred to as the *void volume* and the *total pore volume*, respectively. The distribution coefficient K_X depends on the molecular weight of the sample and on the pore size of the packing. The equilibrium established in exclusion chromatography is described by Equation 21.1; K_X is defined by Equation 21.2. In a true permeation process, assuming all pores to be accessible to a small solute molecule, $X_s = X_m$ and $K_X = 1$. If none of the pores is available to a large solute molecule (that is, it is excluded), then $X_s = 0$ and $K_X = 0$. Intermediate molecules have access to various portions of the pore volume; for them, $0 < K_X < 1$. Unlike other forms of LC, all sample molecules elute between the excluded volume V_m and the total permeation volume, V_t. Note that V_r of Equation 21.4 is then equal to V_t. If $K_X > 1$, another mechanism of sorption is present and the process is not strictly exclusion.

Selecting the pore size of the packing depends on the size of the solute molecules to be separated as well as on the overall geometric shape of the molecules. Often the samples have a wide variation of solute sizes (that is, molecular weights) and one pore size is insufficient to separate all molecular species. Some are completely excluded from the pores ($K_X = 0$) and elute as a single peak at V_m, whereas others may permeate all the pores and elute as a single peak at V_t. Others will selectively permeate part of the pores and elute at various values of V_r. A calibration curve (Fig. 21.23) is usually plotted as log(molecular weight) versus V_r. Each exclusion packing of a different average pore-size will have its own calibration curve. Note that neither the exclusion limit nor the molecular-weight range is sharply defined. Lack of precise definition occurs because the pores of the packings do not have a narrow distribution, and the distribution of the pores governs the slope of the calibration curve. If the pore distribution is wide, the curve will have a steep slope. Thus, the molecular weight operating range will be large, but the column will provide less discrimination (resolution) of species of close molecular sizes. If the pore distribution is narrow, the curve will be flatter, the molecular weight operating range smaller, but the resolution of closely-sized molecules will be increased.

Uses of Exclusion Chromatography

In exclusion chromatography, columns of different molecular weight operating ranges are used to separate components in a sample of wide molecular weight distribution. The columns are usually defined in terms of their molecular weight exclusion limits. As many as eight columns, each covering a different molecular weight range, are connected in series; each set of columns will have its own calibration curve. Calibration curves are determined by injecting standard samples of known molecular weight, and V_r is determined for each. With nonaqueous mobile phases, polystyrenes with known narrow molecular weight ranges are used; with aqueous mobile phases, soluble dextrans are employed.

To illustrate the results obtainable in steric exclusion chromatography, Figure 21.24 depicts an HPLC separation of polystyrene standards in a column packed with cross-linked polystyrene particles (average pore size 260 Å) of 10-μm d_p, using tetrahydrofuran as a mobile phase. Unlike mobile phases in other forms of chromatography, the mobile phase in exclusion chromatography serves only to dissolve the sample and transport it through the column; it does not interact with the column packing. Note that in Figure 21.24 the polymers elute in the order of decreasing molecular weight.

Calibration Curve For Exclusion Chromatography

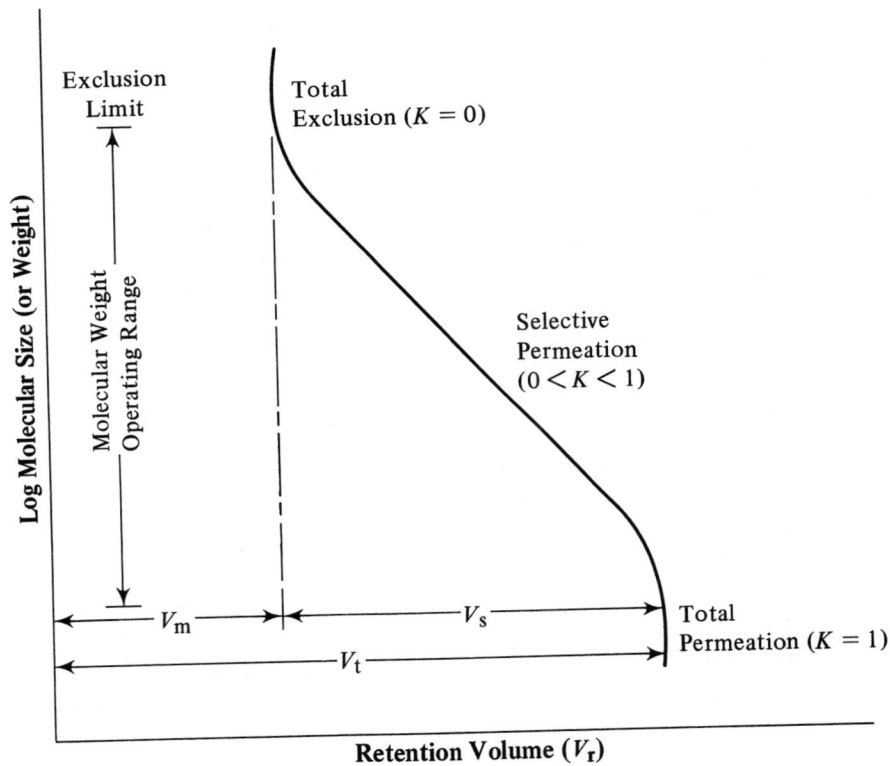

Steric Exclusion Chromatogram

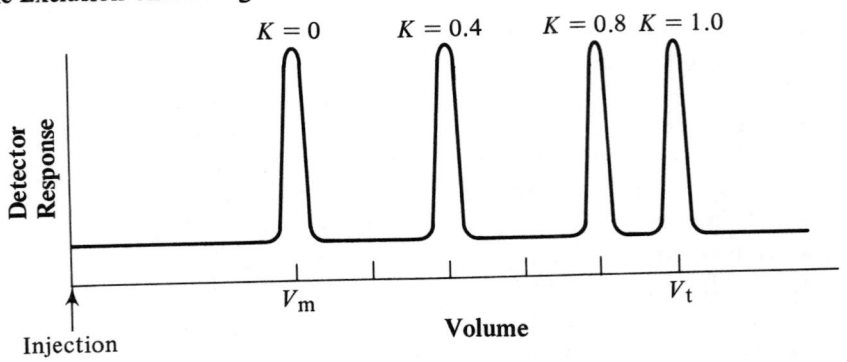

FIGURE 21.23. *Calibration curve and chromatogram for exclusion chromatography. Courtesy of Varian Associates.*

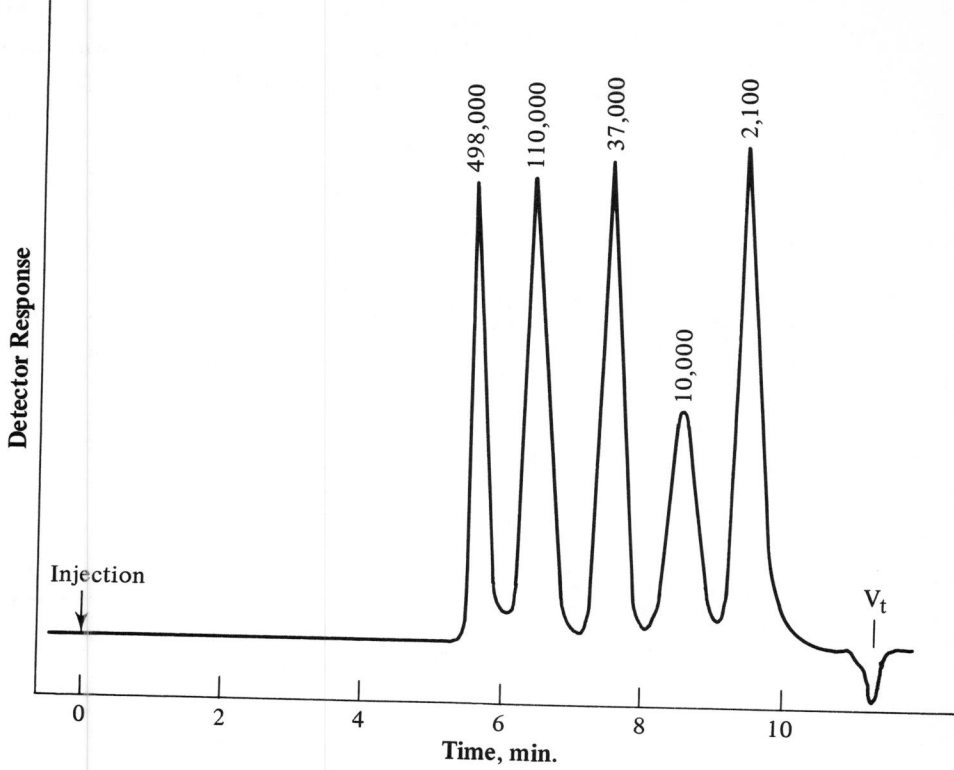

FIGURE 21.24. *High-speed exclusion chromatogram of polystyrene samples with various molecular weights. Column: Toyo Soda TSK® G 4000H8 Gel. Mobile phase: Tetrahydrofuran. Flow rate: 1.7 ml/min. Numbers on peaks represent molecular weights of fractions separated. Courtesy of Toyo Soda Manufacturing Ltd.*

Exclusion chromatography is used not only for separating sample molecules, but also (in organic chemistry) to determine the average molecular weight and the molecular weight distribution of polymers. Polymers are not separate, unique chemical entities, but are comprised of a continuous distribution of molecular weights. In these cases, the chromatogram shows a single broad peak as depicted in Figure 21.25. From such a chromatogram, the polymer chemist can obtain molecular weight and molecular weight distribution data and relate these to the physical properties of the polymeric materials (such as rigidity, tensile strength, and stability). Thus, optimum polymerization conditions can be established.

Exclusion chromatography is also widely used to separate biological compounds, which are often water soluble and of high molecular weight. Proteins, nucleic acids, enzymes, and polysaccharides are routinely examined by exclusion chromatography in aqueous solution. Most applications have been performed on soft gels of the crossed-linked polydextran variety, such as Sephadex®, in open-column chromatography. These soft gels are limited by their compressibility to low column-inlet pressures. Rigid hydrophilic gels and controlled-pore-size glasses,

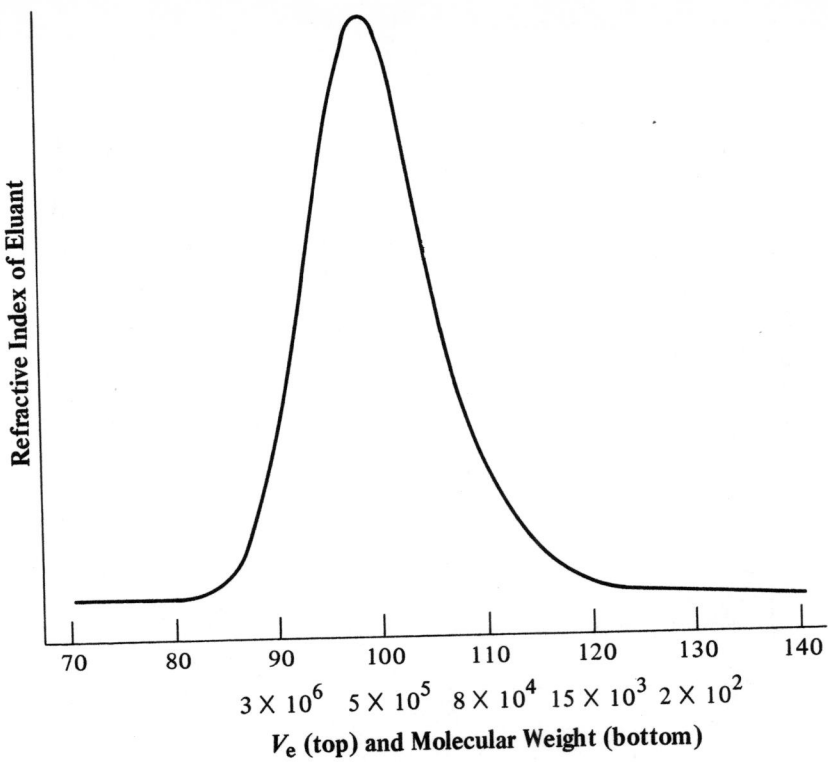

FIGURE 21.25. *Typical chromatogram of a polymer sample (polyvinyl chloride) by exclusion chromatography. From L. R. Snyder and J. J. Kirkland,* Modern Liquid Chromatography Slide Book, *Washington, D.C.: American Chemical Society, 1973, fig. 1.7, by permission of the publisher. Copyright © 1973 by the American Chemical Society.*

which can withstand high pressures, have recently become available and should soon be widely used in high-pressure systems.

21.8 TECHNIQUES RELATED TO LIQUID CHROMATOGRAPHY

A number of peripheral techniques closely allied to the basic chromatographic methods are worthy of mention.

Zone Electrophoresis

In electrophoresis, separation depends on the differences in the electrical properties of the components in a mixture. Although not, in principle, a chromatographic technique, electrophoresis is especially helpful in separating ionic compounds difficult to separate by paper chromatography alone. The principles of operation are depicted in Figure 21.26. Each end of a supported filter paper or cellulose-acetate strip is

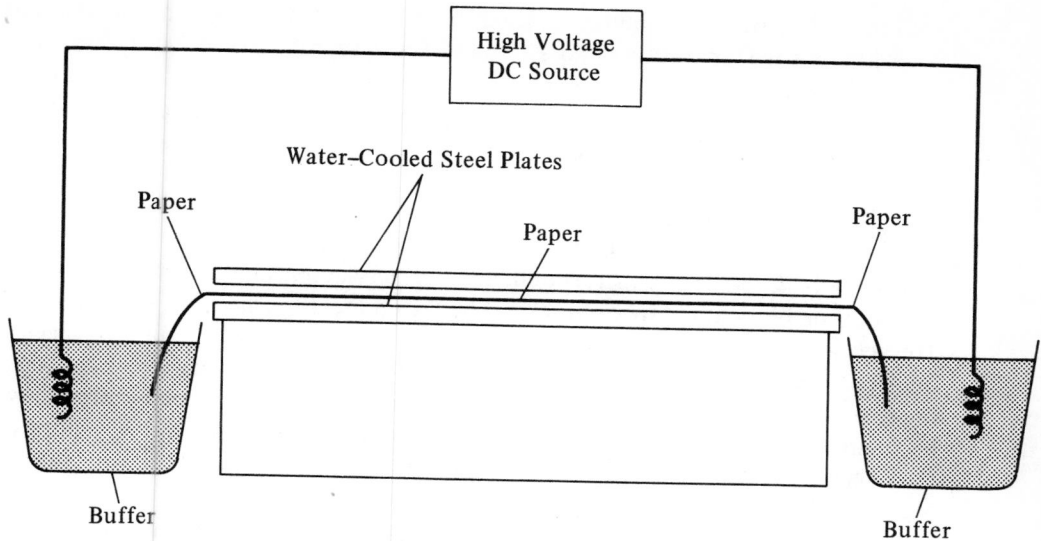

FIGURE 21.26. *Experimental setup for high-voltage electrophoresis.*

dipped into a vessel containing a buffer solution, which also acts as an electrolyte. The strip is carefully moistened with buffer solution. The sample is placed at some point on the paper strip. Then electrodes are dipped into the two vessels and connected to a high-voltage (500 V) direct-current source for a predetermined period of time, permitting a constant current to flow through the electrolyte-moistened paper. Any substance that bears an electrical charge will migrate along the paper, the direction and rate being governed by the sign and magnitude of the charge on the ion and by the mobility of the ion. The current is switched off before the substances reach the two vessels. The paper is removed, dried, and the spots or zones located in the same way as those in paper chromatograms.

The migration rate of each substance depends on several factors, such as the voltage applied, the structure and charge of the ion, and the type and pH of the buffer employed. The migration of each mixture component is independent of that of the other substances present. Since there is no solvent front, a known substance is normally used as a standard.

The primary applications of the technique are in the fields of biology and clinical chemistry, for separating amino acids and proteins. Because of the presence of acidic and basic ionic groups in amino acids, proteins, and other biological macromolecules, pH has a profound effect on migration. In acidic solution, amino acids are positively charged, whereas in basic media they are negatively charged. At a certain pH value, the net charge is zero and the amino acid exists as a zwitterion. This point is called its *isoionic* or *isoelectric point*; provided other ionic interactions are absent, there should be zero electrophoretic mobility at this point.

In some cases, compounds that bear no electrical charge themselves can be separated because they can form complexes with ions present in the buffer solution. These separations are probably based on the principle of electroosmotic buffer flow and, in that respect, are similar to separations in ordinary paper chromatography. An example is the separation of borate complexes of sugars in a sodium-borate buffer.

Voltages applied are expressed in terms of V/cm. In low-voltage electrophoresis, the applied voltage is up to about 500 V. High-voltage electrophoresis, in which voltages up to several thousand volts are used, is a technique well suited to the high-speed separation of low-molecular-weight substances; it is less suited to separating macromolecules, presumably because of their lower ionic mobilities.

In addition to filter paper and cellulose-acetate membranes, other supports can be used. Gels such as agar, starch, and polyacrylamide are supported in the form of a slab or block on a special rack. The technique is termed *gel electrophoresis*. The gels with varying pore sizes exert a slight molecular-sieve effect. In fact, specially prepared polyacrylamide-gel slabs with a continuous gradient of pore size can be used to improve resolution, since the migration of a particular macromolecule will be retarded when its pore limit is reached. *Thin-layer electrophoresis*, usually used for polar compounds such as phenols or amines, uses a thin-layer silica or alumina plate to take advantage of adsorption effects.

Two-dimensional combined techniques using electrophoresis in one direction and chromatography in the other can give better separation than either alone.

Affinity Chromatography

Affinity chromatography is a selective "filtration" technique for macromolecules utilizing highly specific, reversible biochemical reactions. A ligand with a high specificity for the component of interest is attached to a support particle, much like a chemically bonded phase. The ligand is an immobilized enzyme or an antigen, and the macromolecule of interest is an enzyme inhibitor or antibody in a complex biological sample. The immobilized enzyme (or antigen) is placed in a column and the sample introduced in a suitable buffer, the pH and ionic strength of which favors the selective interaction. Elution with the buffer removes the unwanted substances from the column, then the buffer is changed to one that reverses the enzyme-inhibitor interaction and the inhibitor is eluted. Only a small number of specific systems have been investigated thus far, but they have proved very successful. Depending on the system of interest, each ligand must be individually chemically bonded. Some intermediate packings onto which a ligand can attach are now available, and this technique should become even more useful in the future.

Desalting and Deionization

Often, isolating pure substances from biological systems requires the elimination of samples containing large amounts of inorganic salts. These can be desalted by one of several techniques. Exclusion chromatography is quite useful if the component of interest has a higher molecular weight than the salts. Most salts are of low molecular weight and, provided the correct pore-size packing is selected, are retained at the total permeation volume V_t. The higher-molecular-weight sample passes through the column and is collected before the salt elutes. This technique is commonly used for desalting proteins that have been purified by salting out.

A second technique for desalting involves the use of a hydrophobic packing, such as polystyrene-based resins like Amerlite XAD-2®. Provided the component to be collected is organic in character, the sample will pass through the column, selectively concentrating the organic species but allowing the salt to pass through unretained. Afterwards, an organic solvent is used to elute the organic compounds. Organic pollutants can be selectively concentrated from large volumes of water using this approach.

Alternatively, an ion-exchange resin can be used to adsorb ionic species, allowing uncharged organic compounds or nonelectrolytes to pass through. For example, if the contaminant is sodium chloride, a cationic resin in the hydrogen form could be used. Passing a salt sample through the column will exchange Na^+ for H^+. The hydrogen chloride can, in turn, be removed from the effluent by evaporation, or the effluent can be passed through an anion-exchange column in the OH^- form, thereby removing the Cl^- ions. Of course, this classic technique has been used for many years for deionizing water.

SELECTED BIBLIOGRAPHY

General

HEFTMANN, E. *Chromatography*, 3rd ed. New York: Van Nostrand Reinhold, 1974.

KARGER, B. L.; SNYDER, L. R.; and HORVATH, C. *An Introduction to Separation Science.* New York: John Wiley, 1973.

MORRIS, C. J. O. R., and MORRIS, P. *Separation Methods in Biochemistry.* New York: Wiley-Interscience, 1964.

MILLER, J. M. *Separation Methods in Chemical Analysis.* New York: John Wiley, 1975.

STOCK, R., and RICE, C. B. F. *Chromatographic Methods*, 3rd ed. London: Chapman and Hall, 1974.

High-Performance Liquid Chromatography

SNYDER, L. R., and KIRKLAND, J. J. *Modern Liquid Chromatography.* New York: Wiley-Interscience, 1974. *An advanced treatise on HPLC.*

BAUMANN, F., and HADDEN, N., eds. *Basic Liquid Chromatography.* Walnut Creek, Calif.: Varian Aerograph, 1971. *A paperback coverage of practical aspects of HPLC.*

Ion Exchange

HELFFERICH, F. *Ion Exchange.* New York: McGraw-Hill, 1962.

RIEMAN, W., and WALTON, H. F. *Ion Exchange in Analytical Chemistry.* New York: Pergamon Press, 1970.

Paper and Thin-Layer Chromatography

BLOCK, R. J.; DURRUM, E. L.; and ZWEIG, G. *A Manual of Paper Chromatography and Paper Electrophoresis*, 2nd ed. New York: Academic Press, 1958.

KIRCHNER, J. G. *Thin-Layer Chromatography.* New York: Wiley-Interscience, 1976.

Electrophoresis

BIER, M., ed. *Electrophoresis*, vol. 1 (1959); vol. 2 (1967). New York: Academic Press.

SHAW, D. J. *Electrophoresis.* New York: Academic Press, 1969.

REFERENCES

1. J. C. GIDDINGS, *Dynamics of Chromatography*, part 1, *Principles and Theory*, New York: Marcel Dekker, 1965. *A complete theoretical account of chromatographic principles.*

2. I. M. HAIS and K. MACEK, *Paper Chromatography*, New York: Academic Press, 1963.

3. E. STAHL, *Thin-Layer Chromatography: A*

Laboratory Handbook, 2nd ed., Heidelberg: Springer-Verlag, 1969.

4. L. R. SNYDER, *Principles of Adsorption Chromatography*, New York: Marcel Dekker, 1968.

5. L. R. SNYDER, in J. J. Kirkland, ed., *Modern Practice of Liquid Chromatography*, New York: Wiley-Interscience, 1971.

6. R. A. KELLER, B. L. KARGER, and L. R. SNYDER, in R. Stock and S. G. Perry, eds., *Gas Chromatography 1970*, Institute of Petroleum, 1971.

PROBLEMS

1. The R_f value of a solute can be expressed as the probability of finding it in the mobile phase at any given instant, expressed as the mole fraction of a solute in the mobile phase. (a) Derive a simple equation relating the solute R_f value to its k' value. (b) From this equation, determine the k' value of estradiol, a steroid whose R_f value on a silica-gel plate was 0.3. (c) Relative to estradiol, estriol showed a selectivity factor $\alpha = 1.2$ on a silica-gel column. Would you expect the two steroids to be separated on a silica-gel thin-layer plate, assuming that spots are only distinguishable if their R_f values are at least 0.02 units apart?

2. Because of refractive-index effects, an unretained solvent used to dissolve the sample—if different from the chromatographic mobile phase—often deflects the base-line when passing through an ultraviolet detector cell. This indicates the void volume or the void time. Consider the chromatogram in Figure 21.19. (a) Determine the capacity factors for each nitroaniline isomer. (b) Determine the selectivity factor for the *m*- and *p*-substituted isomers relative to the *o*-nitroaniline.

3. (a) From the TLC chromatogram of Figure 21.12, determine the R_f values for 3'-GMP and 2'-GMP. (b) Using an equation similar to that derived in Problem 1 (a) above, determine the selectivity factor α between the two nucleotides.

4. In Figure 21.15, H was found to be proportional to $d_p^{1.8}$ at constant v. (a) If the average d_p of a silica gel were reduced from 20 μm (where $H = 0.3$ mm) to 2 μm, how many theoretical plates would one obtain from a 25-cm column? (b) Would this column be able to give a baseline separation between geometric isomers whose α value is 1.05 and k' value is close to 10?

5. The polystyrene peaks in Figure 21.24 were obtained by using standards with narrow molecular-weight distributions. (a) Assuming that the polystyrene with the highest molecular weight was totally excluded, construct a calibration curve like that depicted in Figure 21.23A. (b) An unknown polybutadiene gave a peak maximum $V_r = 17$ ml; determine its average molecular weight based on polystyrene. (c) Estimate the lower molecular-weight limit of the operating range (that is, the molecular weight below which no separation will occur).

6. Porous silica has a packing density of 0.55 g/ml, whereas pellicular silica, on account of its glass-bead core, has a packing density of 3.0 g/ml. Surface areas measured by nitrogen adsorption are typically 400 m²/g for porous silica and only 10 m²/g for pellicular silica. The sample capacity for a porous silica was found to be 2 mg/g. (a) For a preparative LC column of dimensions 50 cm by 0.8 mm, determine the maximum amount of sample that can be injected into the column filled with porous silica. (b) Assuming the sample capacity is proportional to the surface area, what sample size can be injected into the same column packed with pellicular silica? (c) How long would the latter column have to be to have the same sample capacity as the porous silica from (a)?

7. Linear velocity can be determined from a chromatogram by $v = L/t_0$. For a chromatograph separation, t_r for the last eluting peak is considered to be the separation time. (a) Derive an expression relating separation time to v and k'. (b) Using the equation

from (a), calculate the total separation time on a 100-cm column exhibiting an H value of 0.4 mm for the last eluting peak ($k' = 24$). The flow rate was 2 ml/min and the column void volume was determined to be 4 ml.

8. Some HPLC systems are limited to an operating pressure of 250 atm. A 100-cm column containing 40-μm particles of ion-exchange resin had a pressure drop of 10 atm at $v = 1.0$ cm/sec. The total time required for the analysis was 30 min. The produced 300 theoretical plates, bu separation of interest required 8000 pla The number of plates can be increased (a) using a longer column, (b) using a lower linear velocity (i.e., flow rate), or (c) using a smaller particle size in the packing. Assuming that the relationship $H = A(v^{0.6})d_p^{1.8}$ holds for the above system (A is a constant), which of the three options would be the most advantageous to pursue, and why?

_∠

Gas Chromatography

CHARLES H. LOCHMÜLLER

It was noted in the previous chapter that, in 1952, A. J. P. Martin and R. L. M. Synge received the Nobel prize for the discovery of partition chromatography. In 1941, these authors had also written [1] that,

> The mobile phase need not be a liquid but may be a vapour. We show below that the efficiency of contact between the phases (theoretical plates per unit length of column) is far greater in the chromatogram than in ordinary distillation or extraction columns. Very refined separation of volatile substances should therefore be possible in a column in which a permanent gas is made to flow over a gel impregnated with a nonvolatile solvent in which the substances to be separated approximately obey Raoults' law.

Despite this clear and unequivocal prediction of gas-liquid partition chromatography, no one seized the opportunity until ten years later, when Martin and James [2] demonstrated its great potential. The growth of gas chromatography in the last quarter century has been phenomenal, and its use is now routine in many aspects of experimental chemistry, including analysis. The aim of this chapter is to give a beginning student a practical understanding and a physical model of gas chromatography, sufficient to carry out elementary experiments and to provide a basis for further reading.

Gas chromatography (GC) is one type of partition chromatography; it is similar in many ways to other techniques of this kind, such as HPLC (high-performance liquid chromatography), paper chromatography, etc. The distinguishing features are that the mobile phase is a gas and that the motion of the component bands, in the direction of "chromatographic development," involves the forced diffusion of the respective substances in their vapor phases. Many of the differences between, say, HPLC and GC are due to the physical properties of the mobile phase—for instance, its viscosity, acidity, basicity, and compressibility. The basis for differential zone-migration remains the same: two components will migrate at different rates in the same chromatographic system if their distribution constants are different. Here, the main emphasis will be on gas-liquid chromatography, but gas-solid techniques (which have some advantages) will also be mentioned.

22.1 THE THERMODYNAMICS OF GAS CHROMATOGRAPHY

Gas chromatography involves the same two types of phenomena as any chromatographic method: first, static or equilibrium processes that can be described thermodynamically; second, dynamic or flux processes (including mass-transport) that must be described kinetically. A rudimentary understanding of both statics and dynamics as they apply to gas chromatography should help the student to understand the potential and limitations of this technique and to improve his or her attack on a problem in analysis. In this section, the static aspects are considered.

Principles

The concept of retention volume in chromatography was discussed in Chapter 21. One can distinguish between the retention volume V_r (or retention time t_r) and the *adjusted retention volume* V_r' (or adjusted retention time t_r'):

$$V_r' = V_r - V_0$$

or

$$t_r' = t_r - t_0 \tag{22.1}$$

where V_0 = the elution volume of an unretained species
          t_0 = the elution time of the species

V_r' and t_r' are also called the *elution* volume or time. The relation between t_r and V_r is

$$V_r = t_r F_c \tag{22.2}$$

where F_c = the adjusted flow-rate

(See Fig. 22.1 for a simple device for measuring flow rates.)

Consider a chromatographic column. When the mobile phase is a liquid, the carrier velocity (v) is not a strong function of the axial position in the column because, in general, liquids are not very compressible. Gases are, however, quite compressible and so a correction is applied to the adjusted volume V_r' to obtain the *net volume* V_n. It can be shown that the average carrier velocity in the column $\bar{v}$ is related to the outlet velocity v_0 by a correction factor j, given by

$$j = \frac{3}{2}\left[\frac{(P_i/P_0)^2 - 1}{(P_i/P_0)^3 - 1}\right] \tag{22.3}$$

where P_i = the inlet pressure
          P_0 = the outlet pressure

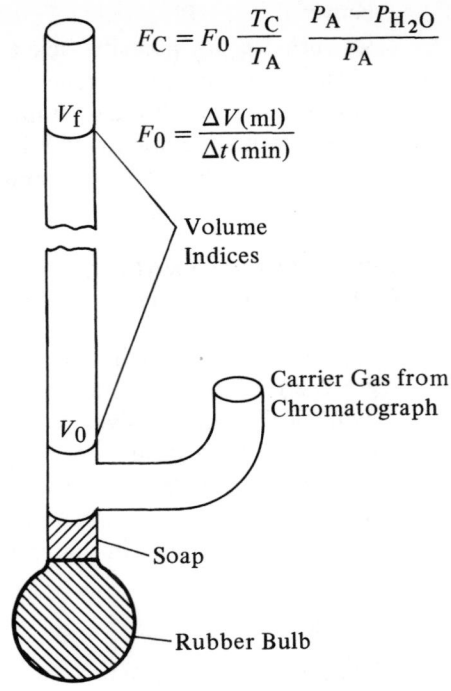

FIGURE 22.1. *A bubble-type flowmeter for volumetric flow measurements. A soap-bubble film is swept past the indices V_0 and V_f and the transit time is measured. $\Delta V =$ the volume of tube between V_0 and V_f; $\Delta t =$ the transit time; $F_0 =$ the volumetric flow-rate; $F_c =$ the adjusted flow rate; $T_c =$ the column temperature (K); $T_A =$ the ambient temperature (K); $P_A =$ the ambient pressure; $P_{H_2O} =$ the vapor pressure of water at the ambient temperature.*

$$F_C = F_0 \frac{T_C}{T_A} \frac{P_A - P_{H_2O}}{P_A}$$

$$F_0 = \frac{\Delta V(\text{ml})}{\Delta t(\text{min})}$$

V_f

Volume
Indices

V_0

Carrier Gas from
Chromatograph

Soap

Rubber Bulb

Now

$$V_n = jV'_r \qquad (22.4)$$

and $\bar{v} = jv_0$; and since v and F are related (assuming a column of constant cross-section), $\bar{F} = jF_0$. When the sample (generally a mixture of solutes) enters the column containing the stationary phase (solvent in GLC), it rapidly distributes itself between the vapor and condensed or solution phases. This is described by a distribution coefficient K, given by

$$K = \frac{c_s}{c_m} = \left(\frac{n_s}{V_s}\right)\left(\frac{n_m}{V_m}\right) \qquad (22.5)$$

where $c =$ the concentration of the solute in a phase (*stationary* or *mobile*)
$n =$ the number of moles of solute in a phase
$V =$ the total volume of a phase in the column

In conventional gas chromatographic experiments (i.e., at low pressures and with inert carrier gases such as helium), nonideal behavior of the solute in the gas phase contributes to only about 1–3% of the observed distribution coefficient.

The net retention volume increases or decreases with increasing or decreasing mass of stationary phase W_s, and the specific retention volume V_g is defined as

$$V_g = \frac{V_n}{W_s}\frac{273}{T_c} \qquad (22.6)$$

The factor $\frac{273}{T_c}$ corrects V_g to the reference temperature of 273 K. It can be shown that, for ideal behavior, the specific retention volume is given by

$$V_g = \frac{273R}{\gamma_\infty P^0 MW_s} \tag{22.7}$$

where
R = the gas constant
γ_∞ = the activity coefficient of the solute at infinite dilution in the stationary phase
P^0 = the saturation vapor pressure of pure solute at a given temperature
MW_s = the molecular weight of the stationary-phase material

Thus, the specific retention volume depends on only two factors in a given solvent (MW_s is assumed constant): the saturation vapor pressure of the solute P^0 and the activity coefficient γ_∞ of the solute.

Influence of Temperature and Volatility on Retention

Consider the practical significance of the above result. First, other things being equal, the greater P^0 is, the smaller V_g will be (Eqn. 22.7), and the shorter the retention time will be (Eqn. 22.2). P^0 increases with increasing temperature; thus, retention time decreases as the temperature is increased. One can also shorten retention times by converting the solutes of interest into more volatile derivatives, thus increasing P^0. For example, amino acids converted to the volatile ester-amides have smaller overall retention times than the amino acids themselves.

$$H_2N - \overset{\overset{\displaystyle R}{|}}{C} - \underset{\underset{\displaystyle O}{\|}}{C} - OH \longrightarrow H - \overset{\overset{\displaystyle R}{|}}{\underset{\underset{\displaystyle O=C}{|}}{N}} - \overset{\overset{\displaystyle O}{\|}}{C} - OR'$$
$$\underset{\displaystyle CF_3}{|}$$

The CF_3-amide is more volatile than the CH_3-analogue owing to the greater electronegativity of fluorine: the tendency for the $\rangle C{=}O$ group to accept hydrogen bonds is lessened.

The Separation Factor

Separation of several substances occurs when the respective values of either K or V_g are different. A measure of this difference is the selectivity factor (or separation factor) α (see Eqn. 21.10). For two substances indicated by subscripts 1 and 2:

$$\alpha = \frac{V_{g2}}{V_{g1}} \tag{22.8}$$

For instance, if solute 1 is a hydrocarbon and solute 2 an alcohol, a polar stationary phase such as the polyethylene glycols or the polar silicones (Table 22.1) will increase the retention of the alcohol because of the strong specific interactions involving the –OH group. This is an example of stationary-phase selectivity.

Extreme selectivity is required for the direct chromatographic resolution of

TABLE 22.1. *A Tabulation of Commercial Stationary Phases and Their Skeletal Structures*

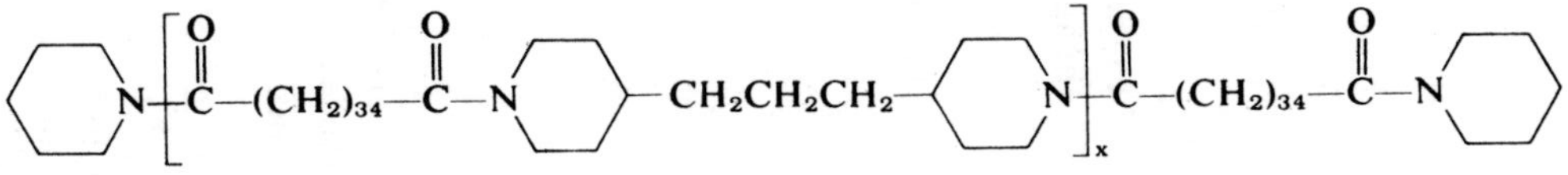

POLY-A 103 (polyamide)

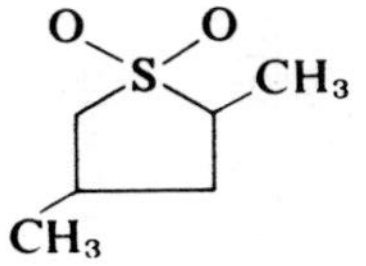

Dimethylsulfolane

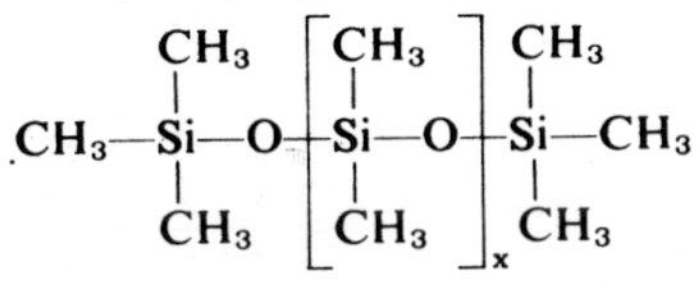

OV-225

OV-17

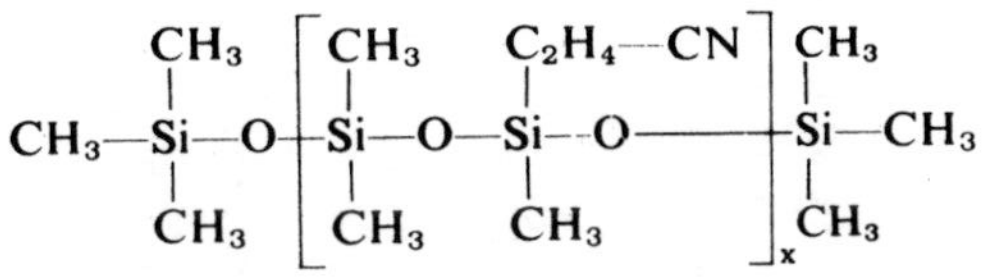

Silicone GE XE-60

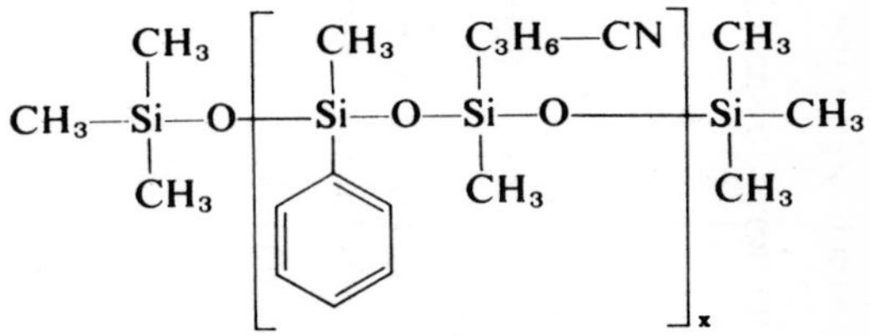

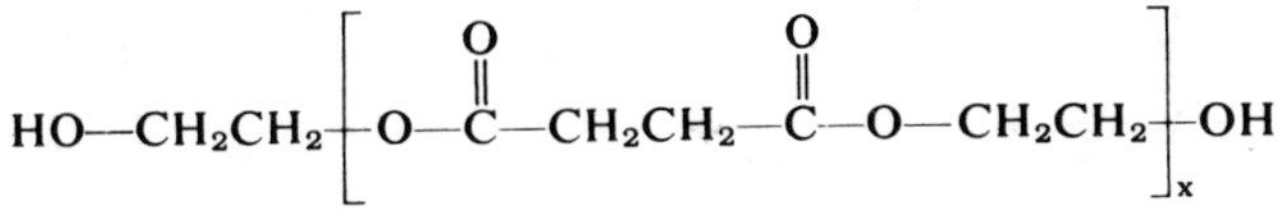

HI-EFF-2B (ethylene glycol succinate)

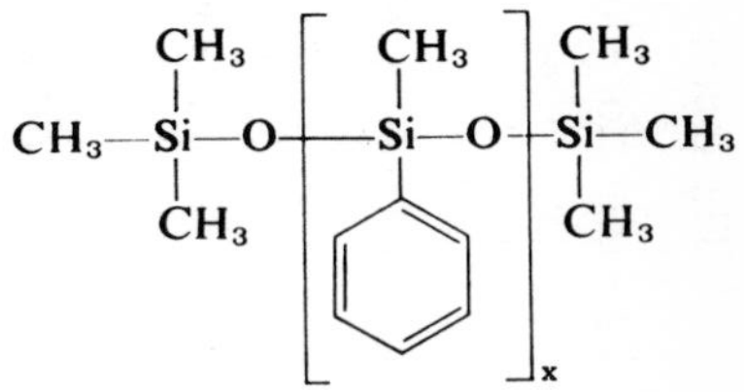

OV-101

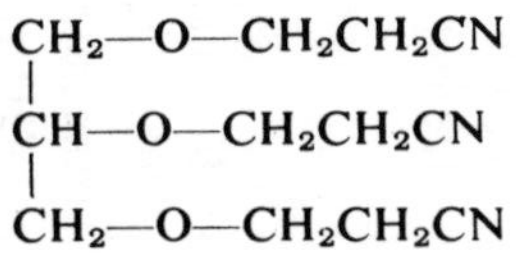

1,2,3-Tris(2-cyanoethoxy)propane

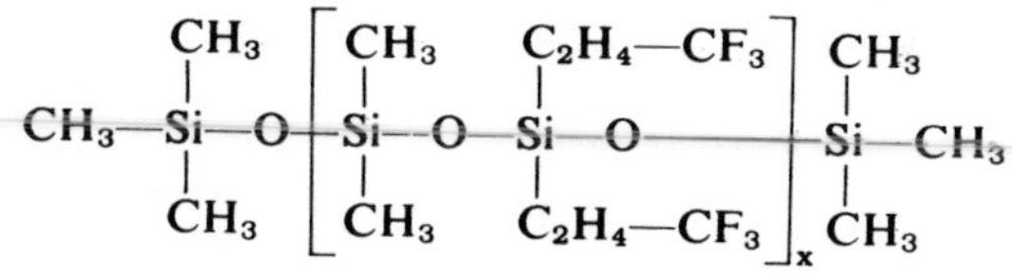

CH₂OCH₂CH₂CN → $CH_2OCH_2CH_2CN$

$NCCH_2CH_2OCH_2 - C - CH_2OCH_2CH_2CN$

$CH_2OCH_2CH_2CN$

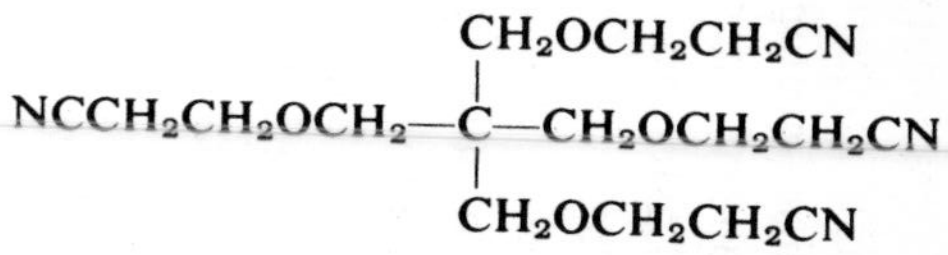

Tetracyanoethylated Pentaerythritol

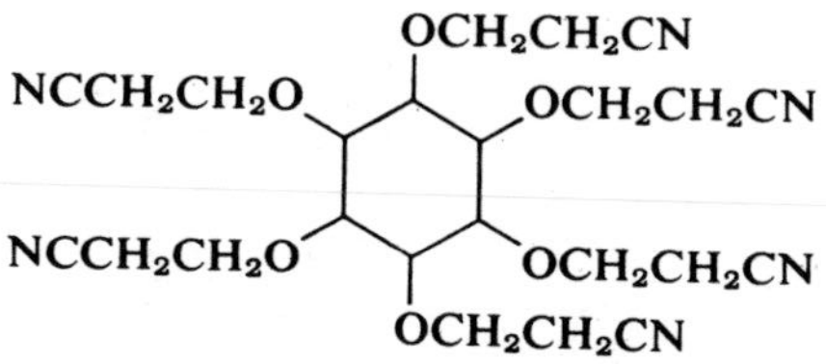

SILAR-5CP

$HO\text{---}(CH_2\text{---}CH_2\text{---}O)_x\,H$

Carbowaxes

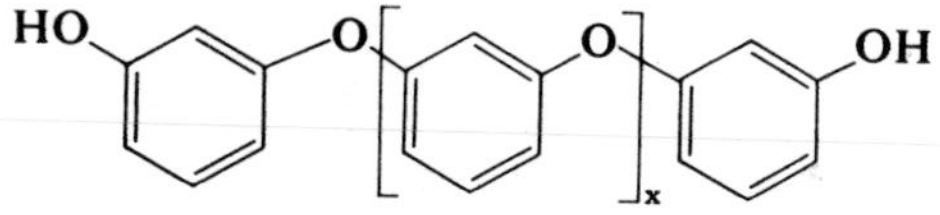

Polysev (polyphenyl ether)

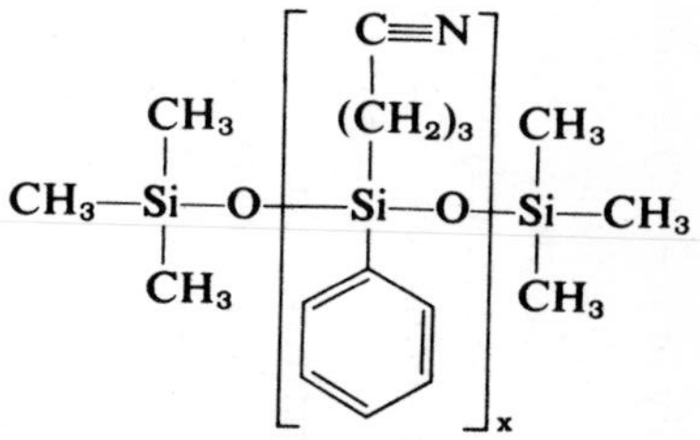

POLY-I 110

OV-210

CYCLO-N [1,2,3,4,5,6-
hexakis(2-cyanoethoxy)cyclohexane]

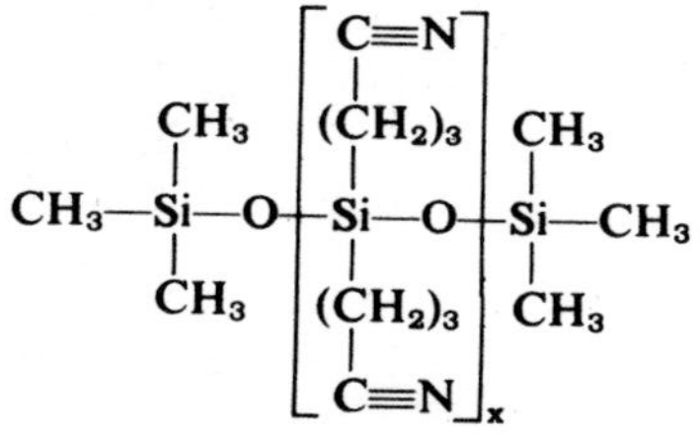

SILAR-10C

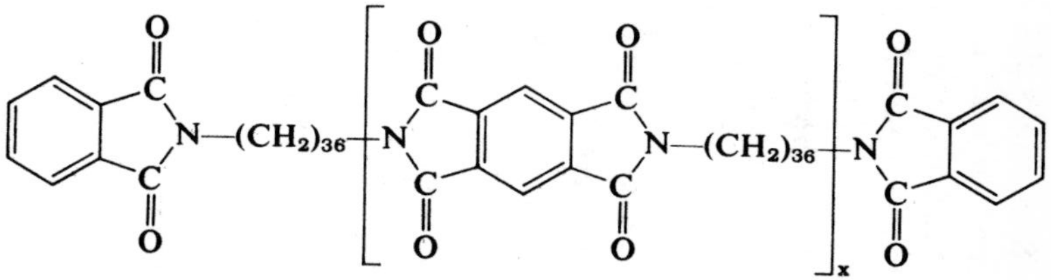

OCH_2CH_2CN
OCH_2CH_2CN
OCH_2CH_2CN
$NCCH_2CH_2O$
$NCCH_2CH_2O$

Source : Courtesy of Applied Science Laboratories, State College, Pennsylvania, Catalog 17 (1974), p 12.

enantiomers. Such molecules differ only in their "handedness"; stationary phases must be designed to take advantage of this single distinguishing property. The enantiomers of amino acids are resolved as their ester-*N*-trifluoro-acetamides by using the stationary phase *N*-trifluoroacetyl-L,L-valylvaline cyclohexyl ester. There the separation mechanism involves the formation of transient diastereomeric complexes of R–S and S–S configuration.

At an intermediate level of selectivity, adding certain metal ions, especially Ag^+, to a stationary phase significantly increases the retention of alkenes and the α values for geometrical (*cis-trans*) isomers. The mechanism probably involves π-complexes formed between Ag^+ and the unsaturated C=C double bond.

To achieve good separation, α needs to be either large or small in magnitude compared to unity. Thus, one desires a large difference in P^0 (by selective derivatiza-

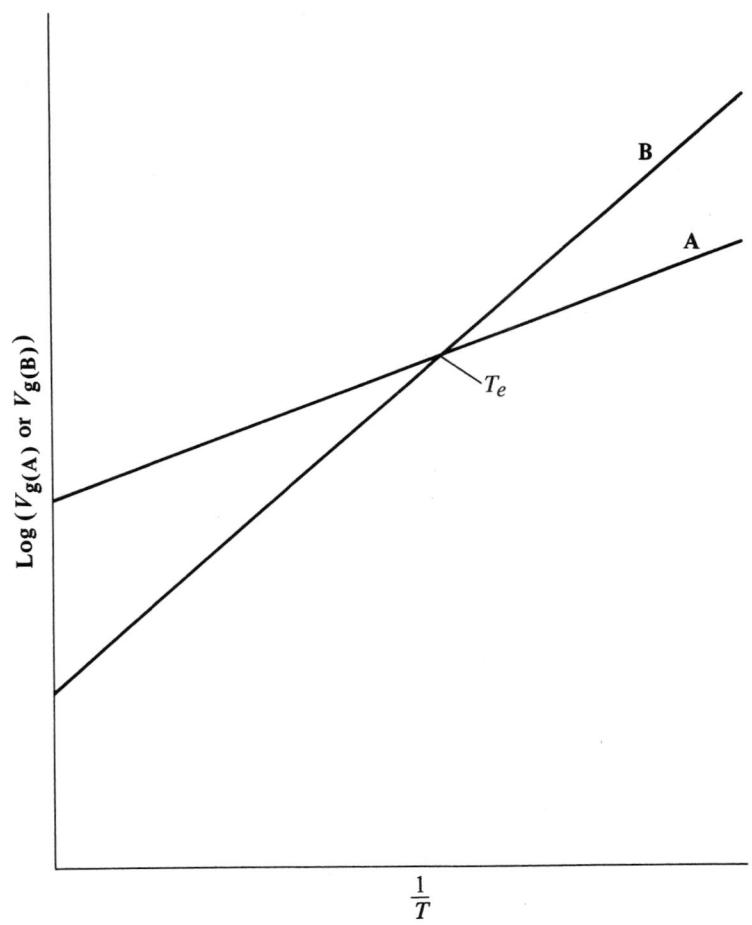

FIGURE 22.2. *A plot of log V_g for two dissimilar solutes A and B on the same stationary phase as a function of $1/T$, illustrating the possibility of resolution, no resolution, and reversal of elution order as the column temperature is varied.*

tion or varying the temperature) or a large difference in γ_∞ (Eqn. 22.7). The latter can often be achieved by invoking the rule that "like dissolves like"; but, at times, finding a suitably selective liquid stationary phase can require a great deal of experience, since there are systems whose interaction mechanisms are not known.

For dissimilar species, enthalpies of vaporization are often quite different, so α can depend strongly on temperature. Figure 22.2 shows that at low temperatures, A will elute before B ($\log V_g^A < \log V_g^B$) but as the temperature is increased, the difference in retention time decreases until at temperature T_e, $\log V_g^A = \log V_g^B$. At temperatures higher than T_e, B elutes before A, since now $\log V_g^A > \log V_g^B$. Such a reversal of elution order is not uncommon for dissimilar molecular species.

22.2 THE DYNAMICS OF GAS CHROMATOGRAPHY

The successful separation of two substances depends not only on the separation factor α but also on the quality of the column in terms of performance or efficiency. The latter is described in terms of the *height equivalent to a theoretical plate* (*HETP*) or *plate height* (*H*). The plate height (more precisely, the number of plates) for a given solute on the column is related to the variance σ^2 of the chromatographic zone. This total variance is the sum of many contributing factors, but three general areas of variance production can be identified: the inlet system, the column, and the detector; and

$$\sigma_{tot}^2 = \sigma_{in}^2 + \sigma_{col}^2 + \sigma_{det}^2 \tag{22.9}$$

The standard deviation σ of a chromatographic zone with (approximately) a Gaussian profile is related to the width of the zone at the inflection points. As in any error process, the square of the standard deviation (the variance) accumulates and hence Equation 22.9 follows. It is useful to keep in mind that in column-chromatographic methods, σ is a volume element and that increasing extra-column "dead volume" (for example) will increase σ_{tot}^2 and decrease the total number of plates.

Broadening Factors Affecting Column Performance

The analyst should understand the physical basis for zone broadening in gas chromatography in order to properly select the right column system for the job to be done. In the following discussion, the term σ_{col}^2 of Equation 22.9 will be expanded into separate factors, each factor adding to H. The broadening factors to be considered are:

1. Finite rate of diffusion of the solute vapor in the mobile (gas) phase along the length of the column.
2. Noninstantaneous equilibration of the solute vapor with the stationary solvent phase.
3. Factors that depend on the geometry of the column packing.

This is not a complete list, but it is sufficient for the present purpose.

It is important that the reader have a clear mental picture of an actual chromatographic column before proceeding in this section. Packed columns are similar to those discussed in Chapter 21. Open tubular columns are practically unique to GC, and the reader may wish to go forward to the section on columns first before continuing on here. These columns are open tubes coated on the inside with a film of stationary phase, the advantage being that very long columns (large numbers of theoretical plates) can be attained with a small pressure drop.

The overall plate height arising from the above factors is described by the *Van Deemter equation* as a function of carrier-gas velocity v.

$$H = A + \frac{B}{v} + (C_{\text{liq}} + C_{\text{gas}})v \tag{22.10}$$

The A term is the eddy diffusion contribution and has the form $2\lambda\, d_{\text{p}}$, where d_{p} is the diameter of the particles packed in the column and λ is a geometric factor indicating how uniformly the column is packed. A represents the distance a flowing stream moves before its velocity is seriously changed by the packing; A is independent of the velocity of the gas. The B term is the longitudinal or molecular-diffusion contribution, which is a function of the diffusion coefficient D_{g} of the solute vapor in the carrier gas and of the time spent in the column. If a sample could be placed on the column as a zone of infinitesimal width at a time $t_0 = 0$, diffusion would cause the zone to become wider and less concentrated as time goes by, even with no flow. Diffusion is much more important in gas chromatography than in liquid chromatography (H_{ld} in Eqn. 21.8) because the diffusion coefficients of solutes are $\sim 10^5$ greater in gases than in liquids. The C terms represent the rate of mass transfer—the finite time required to establish equilibrium between the two phases. The C_{liq} term is a function of the capacity (partition) factor k' (Chap. 21), the film thickness d_{f}, and the interdiffusion constant D_{l} of the solute in the liquid stationary phase. The C_{gas} term is related to $d_{\text{p}}^2/D_{\text{g}}$ in packed columns or r^2/D_{g} in open tubular columns. The C_{liq} and C_{gas} terms are often combined into a single C term, and represent the kinetic lag in attaining equilibrium between phases as well as transverse diffusion within the mobile phase itself. The B and C terms depend on the carrier gas velocity in opposite manners; B decreases with increased velocity while C increases.

The resulting equation and its components are shown in Figure 22.3. The sum curve is quasi-hyperbolic, exhibiting a minimum value of H (or *HETP*) at an optimum carrier velocity (v_{opt}); $H_{\text{min}} = A + 2\sqrt{BC}$ and $V_{\text{opt}} = \sqrt{BC}$. Equation 22.10 can be compared with Equation 21.8 for liquid chromatography. Also, as in Equation 21.6 used in liquid chromatography, $N = 16(t_r'/W)^2$ in gas chromatography.

The Van Deemter equation contains important information for the practical analyst planning to use gas chromatography. The A term suggests that the use of smaller-sized supporting particles will result in a smaller H. In practice, particles with a mesh-size of greater than 100–120 (i.e., smaller particles) are not used, since decreasing d_{p} increases the pressure drop in the columns.* Narrow mesh-ranges produce a more uniform packing geometry, also resulting in a smaller H. Efficiency increases with decreasing column radius, but it is difficult to pack columns less than 3 mm in inner diameter. Diffusion in the gas phase will be reduced by using carrier gases of higher molecular weight or by operating the column at increased pressure. The combined C factor suggests that the plate height depends on the partition ratio,

---

* Supports are usually sized by screening through standard ASTM screens. Mesh numbers refer to the number of openings per linear inch. Particles that will pass through 60 mesh, but not through 80 mesh, are referred to as 60/80 mesh.

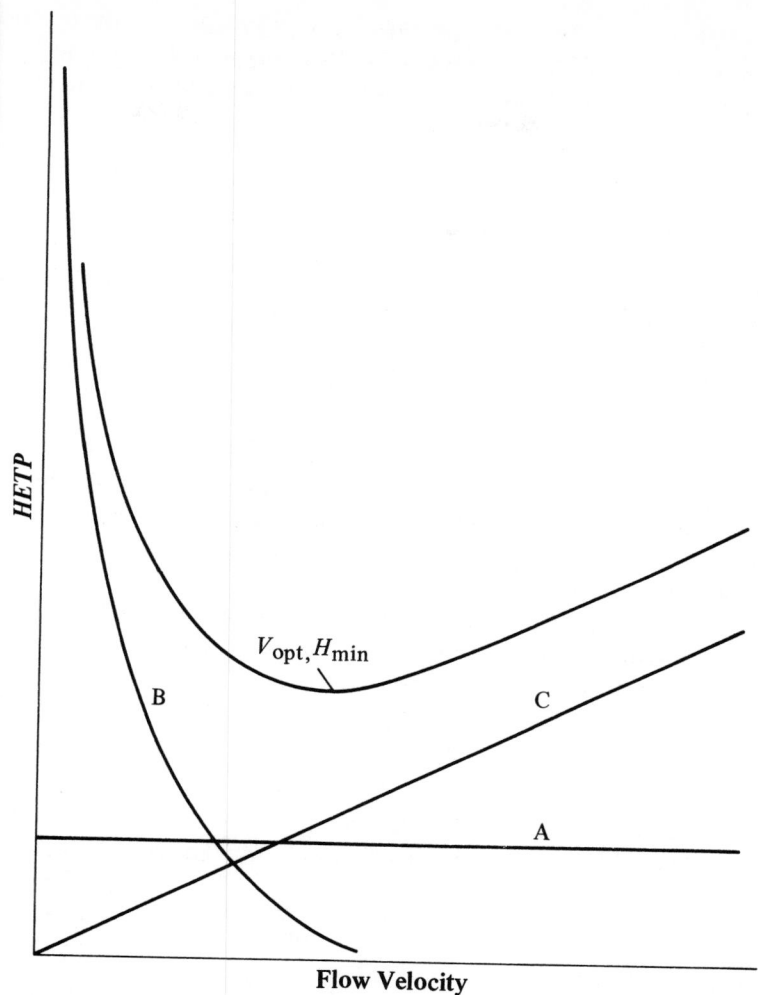

FIGURE 22.3. *A plot of HETP (height equivalent to a theoretical plate) against flow velocity, illustrating the contributions of the following factors to plate height and the position of optimum velocity for minimum HETP: (A) eddy diffusion, (B) ordinary diffusion, and (C) combined gas and liquid resistance to mass transfer.*

and therefore that the observed plate height is different for different compounds. Since small ratios between the volume of gas and the volume of liquid lead to small values of H, as much stationary phase should be used as possible. When the available surface area of the support has been covered, however, the film thickness d_f increases (and along with it H, since it is proportional to d_f^2), thus degrading column performance—an important consideration in scaling up from lightly loaded analytical columns to heavily loaded "preparative" columns. The stationary phase should not be viscous at the column temperature; high viscosity means small D_1, which increases H. A compromise must be made between capacity and sample size:

the amount of stationary phase must be large enough, and the operating temperature low enough, to produce significant retention times, but not so large or low as to broaden zones excessively by producing large mass-transfer effects.

The Resolution Factor

The separation efficiency of a particular pair of components is described by the resolution obtained, as determined by the peak-to-peak separation α and the average peak-width at the baseline V_w. A resolution factor R for substances 1 and 2 can be defined as follows:

$$R = \frac{V_{r_2} - V_{r_1}}{0.5(V_{w_1} + V_{w_2})} = \frac{V_{r_2} - V_{r_1}}{4\sigma} \qquad (22.11)$$

This equation is similar to Equation 21.9. $R = 1$ corresponds to reasonably good separation, since there are 2σ units between zone centers and thus only 2% of each zone overlaps the other. At $R = 1.5$, there is a *baseline separation* with a zone overlap of less than 1%. The effective resolution also depends on the relative concentrations of the solutes.

Equation 22.11 does not show the relationship between experimental variables and the quality of a given separation. A more fundamental equation was given in the previous chapter, Equation 21.11:

$$R = \left(\frac{\sqrt{N}}{4}\right)\left(\frac{\alpha - 1}{\alpha}\right)\left(\frac{k'}{1 + k'}\right) \qquad (22.12)$$

This shows the relation between the number of theoretical plates N, the separation factor α, and the capacity factor k' for the second solute in determining R. The analyst is often interested in R but more often in N_{req}, the number of plates required to give a certain R value. For $R = 1$, Equation 22.12 can be rearranged to yield

$$N_{req} = 16\left(\frac{\alpha}{\alpha - 1}\right)^2\left(\frac{k' + 1}{k'}\right)^2 \qquad (22.13)$$

Usually, $k' = 2$–3 is optimum. The effect of k' on resolution is important only for fast-moving peaks with packed columns where k' values range from 2–200.

The whole advantage of open tubular columns is lost if k' has a fractional value (the usual range of k' values being 0.2–20). As an example, consider the case of a vapor with $k' = 0.2$ on an open tubular column and $k' = 2$ on a packed column. The packed column would require 1/16 the number of plates to give the same resolution. Many examples of the performance of open tubular columns show capacity ratios even smaller than 0.2, so that the resolution is poorer than could be obtained on a short packed column of only a few thousand plates. Actually, it is often convenient to speak in terms of *effective* plates, N_{eff}, when comparing columns, where $N_{eff} = N(k'/1 + k)^2$. For example, open tubular columns (because of their greater length) have much larger values of N than do packed columns, but the values of N_{eff} are often comparable. In other words, the plate heights of open tubular columns are larger than those of properly prepared packed columns.

Optimizing Speed in Chromatographic Analysis

An analyst seeks to obtain chromatographic results in the minimum possible time, so he or she must compromise between larger k' values and shorter times of analysis. This is simple if the initial value of R is greater than 1.5, since increasing the carrier velocity will shorten the analysis without degrading the results. Since $v = 1/t_m$ and $H = L/N$ (where L = the total length of the column) then $t = [NH(1 + k')]/v$; combining this with the expression for the resolution yields a relation between analysis time and resolution,

$$ t = 16R^2 \left(\frac{\alpha}{\alpha - 1} \right)^2 \left(\frac{k' + 1}{k'} \right)^3 \frac{H}{v} \qquad (22.14) $$

which indicates that if double the resolution is required (k', α, H, and v being constant), then the analysis time is increased by a factor of four. If k' is either very small or very large, then t tends toward very large values. The minimum in the expression occurs at $k' = 2$. This corresponds to a retention time for the second peak that is three times that of an unretained species (*air peak* or *methane time*).

The value of R has a practical significance that depends on the relative concentrations of adjacent zones. For example, quantitative analysis is always possible for $R = 1.5$ regardless of relative concentrations; but for $R = 0.6$, it is difficult to detect two peaks at concentration ratios smaller than $1/8$. An approach that takes into account the degree of zone overlap is that of Glueckauf [3].

22.3 GAS-CHROMATOGRAPHIC INSTRUMENTATION

Gas-chromatographic instrumentation differs very little from that used for other forms of column chromatography (see Fig. 22.4). A gas chromatograph consists of (1) a source of carrier gas, the flow rate of which can be fixed at a desired magnitude within the range provided; (2) an inlet that can be heated (25–500°C); (3) a column in a thermostatted air-bath (25–400°C); and (4) a detector suitable for vapor-phase samples. The high temperatures are needed to vaporize the solutes of interest and maintain them in the gas phase. Because the distribution coefficient depends on the temperature, the latter is controlled to between ± 0.1 and ± 0.01°C (depending on the precision desired in the measured retention times). The inlet and detector are generally maintained at a temperature approximately 10% (in °C) above that of the column (in any case, above 100°C for flame-ionization detectors, see later) to insure rapid volatilization of the sample and to prevent condensation. The temperature of the column is usually set at least 25°C higher than the boiling point of the solute. (This is not, of course, an absolute requirement, since it is only necessary that a substance have a reasonably high vapor pressure at the operating temperature.)

Columns for Gas Chromatography

The most commonly used gas-chromatographic column consists of a tube filled with solid particles of fairly uniform size; the particles are coated with the liquid stationary phase. Perhaps the most commonly used support is marine diatomite (for instance, Johns-Manville Chromosorb®). The choice of tubing material depends on the experiment. Aluminum and copper are commonly used, but may have chromatographically and catalytically active oxide films that make them undesirable for sensitive compounds (for instance, steroids); in such cases, stainless steel or glass are used (the latter is more inert, but is less conveniently manipulated).

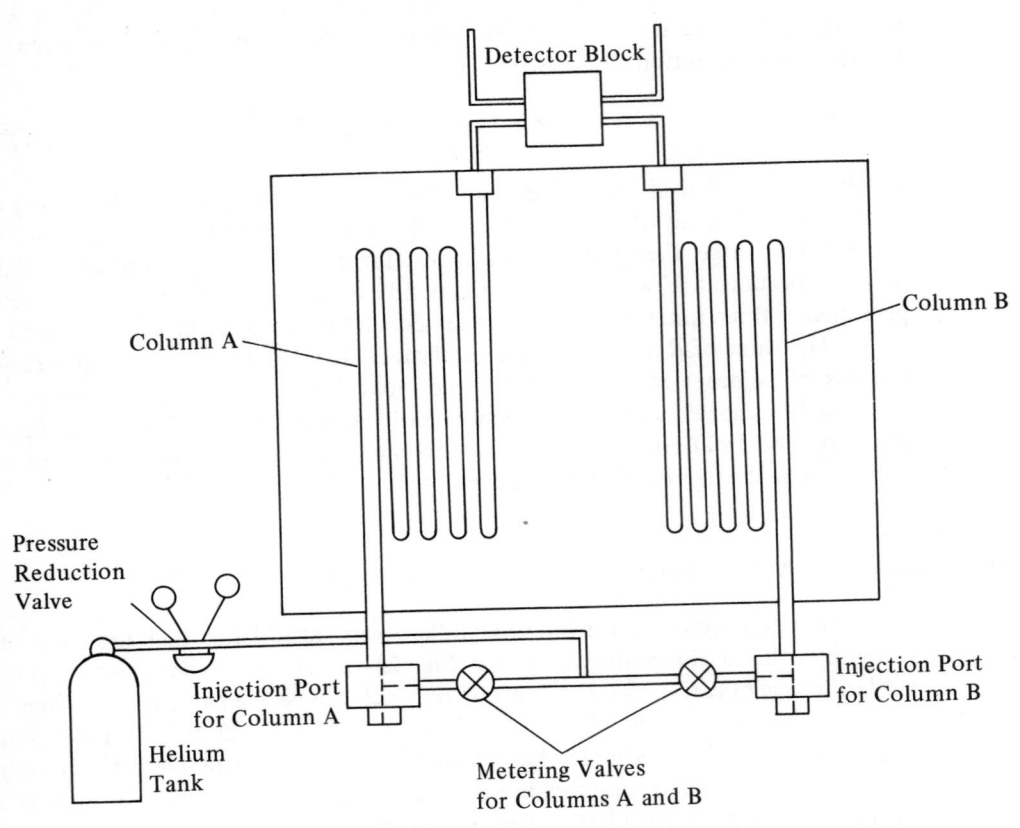

FIGURE 22.4. *Block diagram of a dual-column gas chromatograph showing essential parts. Courtesy of Gow-Mac Instrument Co., Madison, New Jersey.*

Open tubular or capillary columns consist of 50–300 m of 0.3–0.5 mm i.d. steel or glass tubing coated on the inside with a film of stationary phase. The advantage of these columns is not in plate height, which is generally larger than with well packed columns, but in the number of plates achievable with a relatively small pressure-drop. For example, if 20,000 theoretical plates is a good upper limit for packed columns, then open tubular columns can have 75,000–150,000 plates. Open tubular columns have limited capacity and, for this and other reasons, surface-coated open tubular (SCOT) columns have been introduced; these columns are internally coated with finely divided metal oxide, graphite, or alumino-silicate before the stationary phase is applied and, because of the larger surface area presented, have increased capacity.

Chromatographic Support Materials

The function of a chromatographic support is to hold the stationary phase. One useful type of support is provided by the marine diatomites, which are the skeletons of tiny unicellular algae (diatoms) and consist chiefly of amorphous hydrated silica with traces of metal-oxide impurities. This material has the advantages of high porosity and large surface-area. Some properties of a variety of diatomite supports are given in Table 22.2. Chromosorb P, for example, is prepared from one particular grade of firebrick and is a pink (hence P), calcined diatomite that is relatively hard and not easily friable. It is used mainly with solutes of low to moderate polarity (for instance, hydrocarbons). It is a relatively good adsorbent, a quality that can be an interference. If there were no liquid phase at all, the support would act as an adsorbent, and gas-solid chromatography could be carried out. The effect of placing a thin film of liquid on an active adsorbent is to moderate the gas-solid activity, but not to eliminate it. It has been shown that even 20% by weight liquid loading does not eliminate this activity. Several techniques are used to reduce the activity—for instance, acid washing, and "silanizing" the active silica sites with dimethyldichlorosilane to displace the hydrogen. The effect of these treatments on chromatograms is shown in Figure 22.5. The choice of a support for a given analysis is as important as the choice of a stationary phase; for instance, if retention is partly due to solution in the stationary phase and partly to adsorption on the support, then the retention time will vary with the size of the sample. Some compounds (such as sterols) may actually decompose on the column if a poor choice of support has been made.

Stationary Phases

The selection of the stationary phase is also important. Several guides are available in which the types of solute and of stationary phase are correlated (see Selected

TABLE 22.2. *Properties of Some Diatomite Supports*

	Chromosorb®			
Properties	A	G	P	W
Color	Pink	Oyster White	Pink	White
Type	Flux-Calcined	Flux-Calcined	Calcined	Flux-Calcined
Density, g/cm³				
(i) Loose Weight	0.40	0.47	0.38	0.18
(ii) Packed	0.48	0.58	0.47	0.24
Surface Area, m²/g	2.7	0.5	4.0	1.0
Surface Area, m²/cm³	1.3	0.29	1.88	0.29
Maximum Liquid-Phase Loading	25%	5%	30%	15%
pH	7.1	8.5	6.5	8.5
Handling Characteristics	Good	Good	Good	Slightly Friable

Source: Courtesy of Johns-Manville Corporation.

FIGURE 22.5. *Effect of treatment on support activity (Chromosorb® P). 1. Non-acid-washed; 2. acid washed; 3. acid washed, dimethyldichlorosilanized. Solutes: (A) ethanol, (B) methylethyl ketone, (C) benzene, (D) cyclohexane. Conditions: 6' × 1/4" column, 60/80 mesh support, 75 ml/min He flow, 100°C (no liquid coating). Courtesy of Johns-Manville Corporation.*

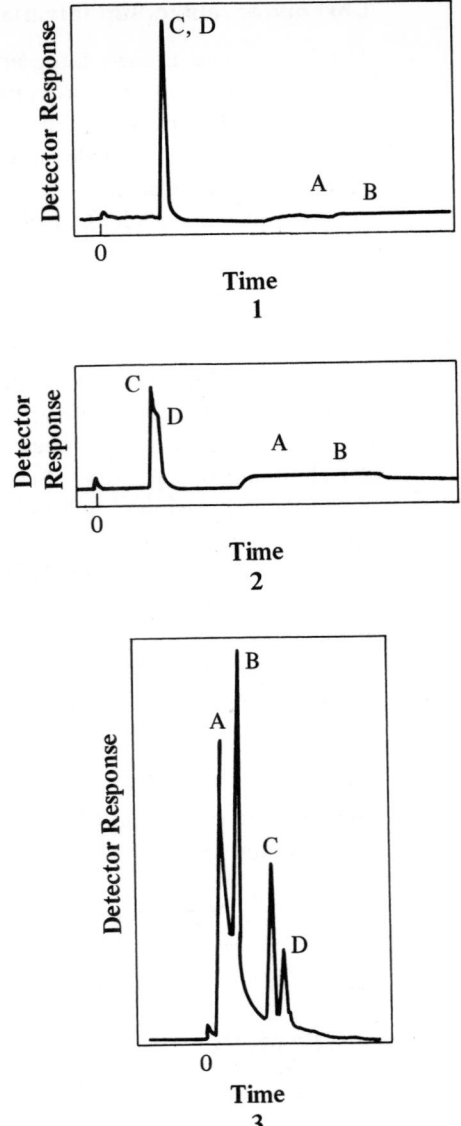

Bibliography). Although such information is useful, the phases listed are not necessarily the best ones; the lists merely indicate that a given stationary phase has been used with some success for a given class of compounds. The situation is complicated by the fact that about a thousand stationary phases have been reported in the literature. Many attempts have been made to glean a list of standard phases from these reported phase materials, many of which give substantially the same separations and possess unique stability. Many researchers have developed various retention-index methods to indicate the preferred phases for a given separation. Such studies involve investigating specific solute-solvent interactions fundamental to our understanding of stationary-phase selectivity. (Note particularly the recent work of Rohrschneider

TABLE 22.3. *A Proposed List of Standard Stationary Phases*

Preferred Phase	Structure	Temp Limit °C	Uses
Squalene	2,6,10,15,19,23-hexamethyl-tetracosane	150	Hydrocarbons, Gases
SE-30	Polydimethyl siloxane	350	Gases, Hydrocarbons, Aldehydes, Ketones (b.p. separ.)
OV-3	Polyphenyl methyl dimethyl siloxane	350	Alcohols, Fatty Acids, Esters, Aromatics
OV-7	Polyphenyl methyl dimethyl siloxane	350	Aromatics, Heterocyclics
DC-710	Polymethyl phenyl siloxane	300	Aromatics (similar to OV-17)
OV-22	Polyphenyl methyl diphenyl siloxane	350	Alcohols, Aromatics
QF-1	Polytrifluoropropyl methyl siloxane	250	Alcohols, Amino Acids, Steroids, Nitrogen Compounds
XE-30	Polycyanomethyl siloxane	275	Drugs, Alkaloids, Halogenated Ampds
Carbowax 20M	Polyethylene glycol	250	Alcohols, Esters, Pesticides, Essential Oils
DEG adipate	Diethylene glycol adipate	200	Fatty Acids, Esters, Pesticides
DEG succinate	Diethylene glycol succinate	200	Steroids, Amino Acids, Alcohols
TCEP	*Tris*-cyano ethoxy propane	175	Alcohols, Steroids, Pesticides

Source: Adapted from J. Leary, J. Justice, S. Tsuge, S. Lowry, and T. L. Isenhour, *J. Chromatog. Sci.*, *11*, 201 (1973), by permission of the senior author and the publisher.

and of McReynolds [4, 5].) Table 22.3 contains a list of twelve stationary phases and the compound classes that can be separated by each. The list was compiled [6] by applying the following criteria: phases should be (1) well tested, (2) readily available, (3) stable over a wide range of temperatures, and (4) cover a wide polarity range. Of the several hundred phases studied, this list is presented as a preliminary guide, but of course the infinite number of possible combinations of solutes will not always be separated using phases from this list. Squalene is a hydrocarbon; SE-30 is a methylsilicone rubber with hydrocarbon-like properties. These are selective for nonpolar species, but will also separate alcohols with different enough boiling points. Carbowax 20-M is moderately polar, and is selective for hydrogen-bonded species such as alcohols. Many synthesis laboratories do 90% of their work with SE-30 and Carbowax 20-M. As often as not, a significant difference of vapor pressure exists between starting material and product, and little selectivity is required. The result is that two phases of markedly different polarity may serve quite well.

Preparing the Column

The three most critical steps in the actual preparation of a gas-chromatographic column are: (1) coating the support, (2) packing the column, and (3) curing or conditioning after packing but before use. Highly efficient columns give lower limits of detection and shorter analysis times; a common goal, though rarely achieved, is a column with more than 3000 plates/meter.

There are some guidelines, however, by which columns with more than 2,000 plates per meter can be prepared consistently. Uniformity of particle size is achieved by using a narrow range of mesh size, by carefully removing any *fines* (particles of very small size), and by not producing more fines by rough handling in the coating and packing processes. For analytical columns of 2–3 mm i.d., 100–110 mesh size is desirable.

Coating the support can be carried out by many methods; the least desirable is using a rotary evaporator in the drying step, which tends to agitate the packing and produce fines. A reliable method is as follows:

1. Dissolve the liquid phase in a solvent in a flask. (A suitable solvent can be found in any of the suppliers' catalogs. Select one that does not boil under the vacuum to be used.)
2. Add the cooled solution to the support, swirling gently to insure wetting.
3. Stopper, and apply vacuum to remove air from the pores of the support. When no more air bubbles escape, seal the vacuum and hold for 5 min.
4. Release the vacuum, transfer the support to either a glass funnel with a coarse-porosity frit in the neck or to a fluidized-bed dryer, and immediately suck the solution off.
5. When the solution ceases to drip out, fluidize the bed of coated packing and dry with a gentle flow of hot nitrogen gas. (The packing is dry and ready for filling into the column when no odor of solvent remains.)

The coated packing is transferred, a little at a time, into the column with the aid of vacuum and gentle tapping. Electric vibrators are popular, but their use will degrade column performance by producing fines. The key factors are uniformity of the packing material and gentle tapping. To condition the packing, heat the column slowly to the upper working limit and maintain this temperature, along with a small flow of carrier gas, for several hours. This distributes the liquid evenly over the surface of the support. Many of the modern polysiloxanes do not require extensive conditioning. The most important consideration in obtaining good column performance and long life is to avoid overheating.

Column Inlets

As in liquid chromatography, the gas-chromatography sample is introduced to the column through a specially designed inlet, generally by injecting it in nanoliter amounts through a rubber septum with a microliter syringe. The inlet should be hot enough to flash evaporate the sample, and large enough in volume to allow the sample vapor to expand without blowing back through the septum. Two types of inlet are shown in Figures 22.6 and 22.7.

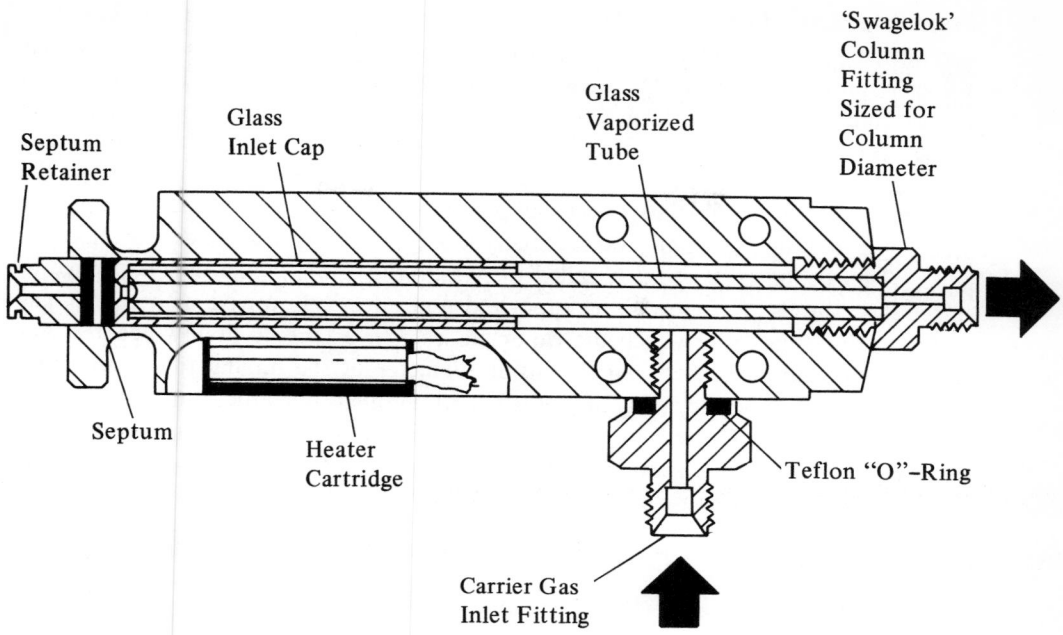

FIGURE 22.6. *Diagram of glass-lined flash-evaporation inlet. Courtesy of Hamilton Co.*

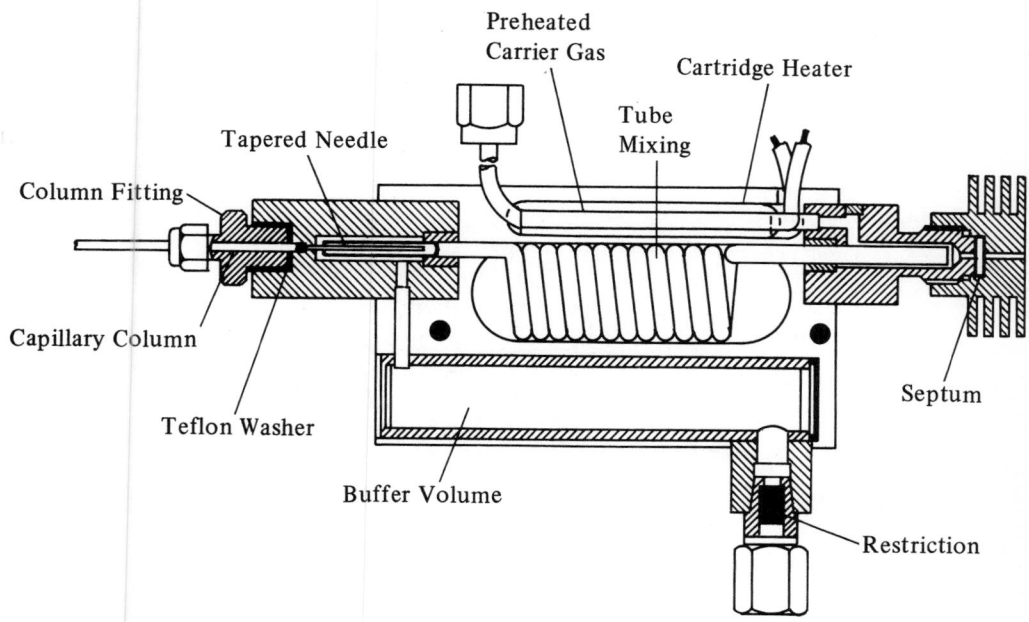

FIGURE 22.7. *Diagram of an inlet-splitter for open tubular or small-diameter packed columns. Courtesy of Hamilton Co.*

The first (most common) type is the *flash-vaporization inlet* (Fig. 22.6), an arrangement of concentric glass tubes that washes the septum area with a high-velocity, preheated carrier-gas stream, thus preventing blowback. The gas passes to the column through a 1- or 2.5-mm glass vaporizer tube heated by a cartridge heater mounted in the body of the inlet. A glass lining is preferred for samples that might decompose in an all-metal inlet. A slight modification in the position of the septum makes it possible to inject samples almost directly onto the column, for studying compounds that are too thermally labile to withstand flash evaporation.

The second type of inlet, called a *splitter* (Fig. 22.7), again uses a syringe to inject the sample. The sample is vaporized and effectively mixed with carrier gas in the mixing tube, after which the vapor passes over a tapered hollow needle. Because of the difference between the inside diameter of the mixing tube outlet and that of the tapered needle, a fraction of the total sample is introduced into the column as a narrow zone. The splitting ratio is a function of the pressure in the inlet, and can be varied. Such a sample splitter is used with capillary columns and high-resolution columns because of their relatively low capacity.

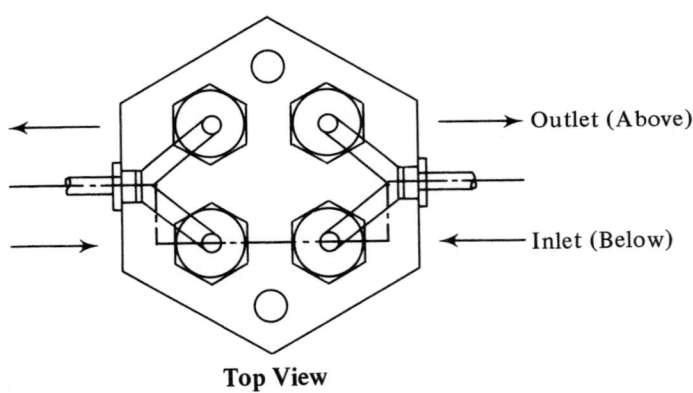

Top View

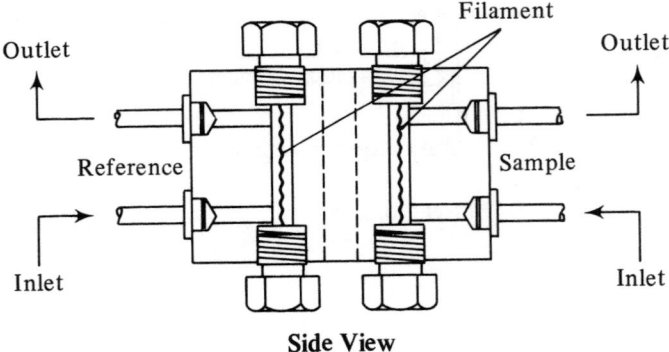

Side View

FIGURE 22.8. *Cross-section of a typical four-wire conductivity cell. Courtesy of Gow-Mac Instrument Co.*

Detectors

The three most common detectors in gas chromatography are those using thermal conductivity, flame ionization, and electron capture. The first is also the oldest; it measures heat conductivity, which is different for different gases. The second and third types respond to changes in electron currents; the electrons are produced in a flame by burning the sample, or by exposing the sample to a radioactive source.

Thermal Conductivity Detector. The thermal conductivity detector (TCD) is a simple universal detector (see Fig. 22.8) that produces a large signal requiring no amplification. The detector cell has either two or four filaments arranged in a Wheatstone bridge circuit (Fig. 22.9). In the four-filament model, two filaments in

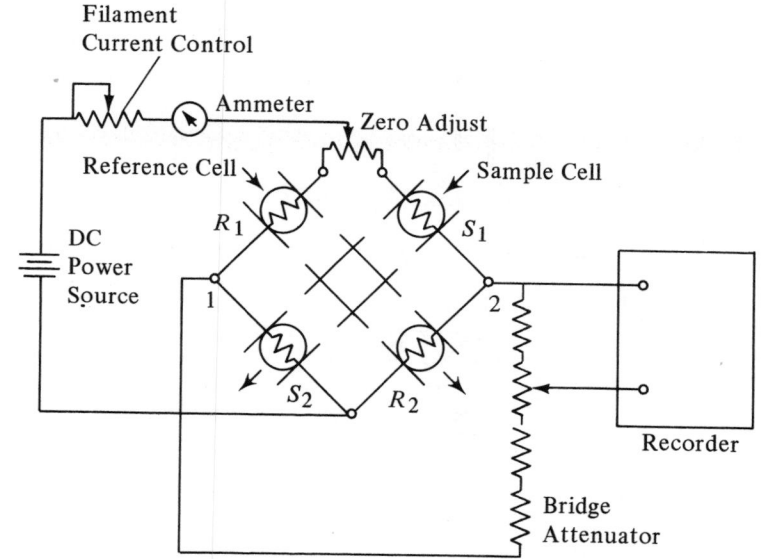

FIGURE 22.9. *Typical bridge configuration for thermal conductivity detection. Courtesy of Gow-Mac Instrument Co.*

opposite arms of the bridge are surrounded by carrier gas flowing in a reference stream, the other pair by carrier gas flowing out of the column. When the bridge is balanced, no signal appears across points 1 and 2 in Figure 22.9. Since the temperature of the filaments is proportional to the rate at which heat is transported to the cell body by the gas, and since resistance is proportional to temperature, a change in the heat conductivity of the gas will produce an output signal at points 1 and 2. Most organic vapors have low thermal conductivities (λ) compared to hydrogen or helium ($\lambda_{acetone} = 2.37 \times 10^{-5}$, $\lambda_{H_2} = 41.6 \times 10^{-5}$, $\lambda_{He} = 34.80 \times 10^{-5}$ at 0°C). For this reason, helium is widely used as a carrier gas; but if one were interested in analyzing the noble gases, nitrogen might be the carrier of choice. The TCD is reliable, simple, nondestructive, and moderately sensitive; it responds to essentially all compounds, and is widely used in preparative work. Since it is nondestructive, the solutes can be collected (for instance, in a dry ice–acetone bath) for further examination by other means, such as infrared spectroscopy. Relative responses vary widely and are frequently nonlinear with concentration, so quantitative analyses require careful calibration. The analyst is rarely justified in merely taking peak ratios as an accurate indication of relative amounts. This detector has a concentration detection limit of about $5–10 \times 10^{-6}$ g/ml of eluant gas, and a dynamic (working) range of about 10^5.

Flame-Ionization Detector. The flame-ionization detector (FID) has a wide linear range and high sensitivity, and is quite reliable. It consists of a hydrogen–air flame polarized in an electrostatic field (Fig. 22.10). The flame ignites and ionizes the

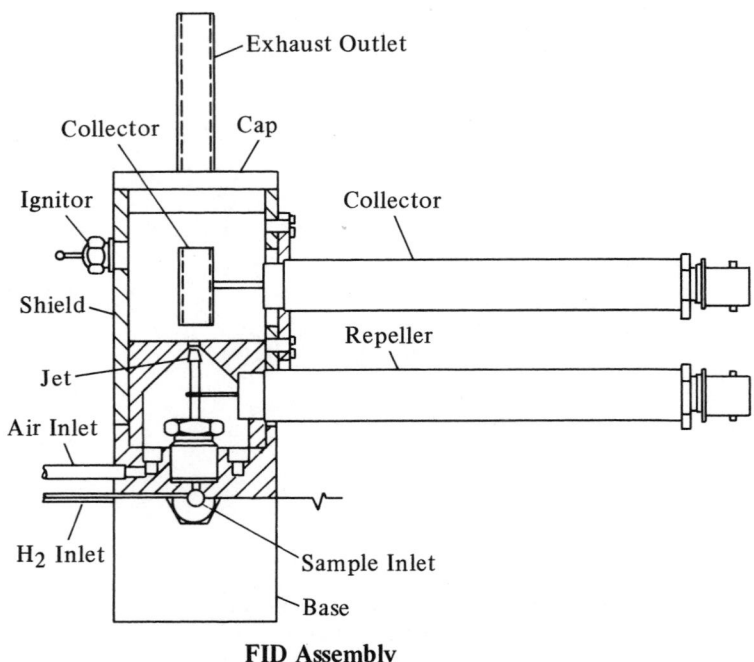

FID Assembly

FIGURE 22.10. *A flame-ionization detector. Courtesy of Gow-Mac Instrument Co.*

combustible sample components as the carrier gas passes into it, after which the ions (primarily carbon compounds) are collected at the electrodes, producing a current. The FID does not respond fully to oxygenated carbons such as carbonyls, carboxylic acids, or their sulfur analogs (for instance, cyclohexane and cyclohexanone have different response factors). However, it does not respond at all to water or to the permanent gases (N_2, O_2, CO_2, etc.), making it ideally suited for trace analysis in aqueous solutions and atmospheric samples. Response is proportional to the number of carbon atoms, but diminishes with increasing substitution by halogens, amines, hydroxyl groups or any electron-capturing species. The limit of detection is $1–5 \times$

10^{-9} g/ml of sample gas, with a dynamic range of 10^8. Sample collection is possible if the column effluent is split into two streams.

Electron-Capture Detector. The electron-capture detector (ECD) takes advantage of the affinity of certain functional groups for free electrons (the reason for loss of sensitivity in the FID). The principle is almost identical to flow-through proportional counting of a radioactive source. The carrier gas is passed through a cell containing a beta source (e^- for nuclear decay), which ionizes the carrier gas. The source can be a Pt foil saturated with $^3H_2$, but a ^{63}Ni foil is used more frequently because of its higher temperature stability. Some typical carrier gases are He-CH_4, N_2-CH_4, and Ar-CH_4. The beta particles ionize the carrier molecules and produce electrons, which migrate to the anode (Fig. 22.11) under an applied potential of

FIGURE 22.11. *A "pin-cup" design for electron-capture detection, in cross-section.*

1–100 V. An electron-capturing species eluting from the column will react with the electrons to form an ion or neutral molecule, which is swept from the cell. The net result is a reduction in the number of electrons found at steady state or a drop in the *standing current*. A "peak" in ECD detection is therefore actually a detector-current "valley," since the maximum current is found in the absence of capturing species. Response is very nonlinear, but a linear range of $0.5–1 \times 10^3$ can be achieved by pulsing the polarizing voltage. The pulse duration is long enough for electron collection, but not for ion collection. The limit of detection is about 1×10^{-12} g.

The major advantage of the electron-capture detector, however, is its selectivity. The ECD is insensitive to amines, alcohols, and hydrocarbons, but very sensitive to halogens, anhydrides, peroxides, ketenes, nitro groups, and so forth, with selectivity ratios of $10^5:1$ being not uncommon in practice. Table 22.4 lists electron-capturing compounds and relative sensitivities. It is not uncommon for FID and ECD to be combined, displaying the response of both detectors on the same chart using a two-pen recorder. The many applications of ECD include analyzing pesticides (e.g., aldrin, dieldrin, DDT, lindane) and organometallics (e.g., lead alkyls) and tracing SF_6 in flue and stack gases.

Other Specific Detectors. The most elegant of the specific detectors used for gas chromatography is the mass spectrometer. (This application of mass spectrometry was discussed in Chapter 16.) Infrared spectrometry has become a practical detection method, now that rapid-scan infrared systems have made collecting samples unnecessary. In fact, part of the impetus behind developing both these techniques was the difficulty in collecting gas chromatographic fractions; vapor samples entering cold

TABLE 22.4. *Electron Absorption Coefficients of Various Compounds and Classes of Compounds for Thermal Electrons*

Electron Absorption Coefficient [a]	Compounds and Classes	Electrophores
0.01	Aliphatic Saturated, Ethenoid, Ethinoid, and Diene Hydrocarbons; Benzene; Cyclopentadiene.	None
0.01–0.1	Aliphatic Ethers and Esters; Naphthalene.	None
0.1–1.0	Aliphatic Alcohols, Ketones, Aldehydes, Amines, Nitriles; Monofluoro- and Chloro- Compounds.	–OH –NH$_2$ $>$CO –CN Halogens
1.0–10	Enols; Oxalate Esters; Stilbene; Azobenzene; Acetophenone; Dichloro-, Hexafluoro-, and Mono-bromo- Compounds	–CH=C–OH –CO–CO– Halogens
10–100	Anthracene; Anhydrides; Benzaldehyde; Trichloro- Compounds; Acyl Chlorides.	–CO–O–CO– Phenyl–CO– Halogens
100–1,000	Azulene; Cyclooctatetrene; Cinnamaldehyde; Benzophenone; Monoiodo-, Dibromo-, Trichloro-, and Tetrachloro-Compounds; Mononitro- Compounds.	Halogens NO$_2$ Phenyl–CH=CH–CO–
1,000–10,000	Quinones; 1,2-Diketones; Fumarate Esters; Pyruvate Esters; Diiodo-, Tribromo-, Polychloro-, and Polyfluoro-Compounds; Dinitro Compounds	–CO–CO– –CO–CH=CH–CO– Quinone structure Halogens NO$_2$

Source: From J. E. Lovelock and N. L. Gregory, in N. Brenner, J. E. Callen, and M. D. Weiss, eds., *Gas Chromatography*, New York: Academic Press, 1962, by permission of the publisher.
a. Values are relative to the absorption coefficient of chlorobenzene, which is arbitrarily taken to be unity.

traps from detectors at elevated temperatures tend to form aerosol fogs that do not condense on the trap walls, but are swept out by the carrier gas instead. However, at high concentrations, enough material can be collected to run remote infrared, mass-spectral, or nuclear magnetic resonance spectra. The concentrations here are in the range of 10^{-3} g/sec, as compared to 10^{-12}–10^{-9} g/sec with the directly coupled methods.

If the detector is of the FID type, flame optical emission or absorption can also be used. Commercial detectors are available that use essentially nondispersive or filter analyzers coupled to a FID. Phosphorus, sulfur, and nitrogen are commonly detected by this method. A hollow-cathode light source makes possible the detection of many organometallic compounds by atomic absorption.

22.4 QUALITATIVE AND QUANTITATIVE ANALYSIS

Qualitative Analysis

Gas chromatographic retention times are most frequently determined from the positions of peak maxima, although the thermodynamically meaningful (and analytically preferred) value is the position of the peak center-of-gravity. Under carefully controlled conditions, values of t_r are reproducible to better than $\pm 0.1\%$; however, agreement between retention times of a standard and an unknown peak is not conclusive evidence that they arise from the same substance. To produce more conclusive evidence, the retention times can be varied by changing the operating conditions (for instance, column material, flow rate, and temperature); if the two peaks move identically, they probably represent the same material. Most analyses are carried out under isothermal conditions, but it is possible to program the temperature to change at some predictable rate (°C/min). The latter technique can be especially valuable in separating mixtures of substances with widely varying vapor pressures, but determining a suitable programming rate can be a tedious trial-and-error process. An example of temperature programming is given in Figure 22.12. By starting at a lower initial temperature, the germane (GeH_4) and arsine (AsH_3) peaks are more fully resolved, and by programming to higher temperatures, the stannane (SnH_4) and stibine (SbH_3) are eluted sooner and with less broadening.

It is a common practice for qualitative analysis to be based on measurements of t_r; this is especially true in those laboratories that run standards with each analysis. Nevertheless, t_r is not the ideal parameter for identification purposes because it is a function of temperature, flow rate, and liquid-phase volume. (Indeed, the liquid-phase volume is continuously changing with time because of evaporation; even its chemical composition can vary under the conditions of the experiment.) What is needed, then, is a parameter that is independent of all these factors. A very successful, but not perfect, solution is the Kováts index system, which relates the retention volume V_r (or the retention time t_r) of the unknown compound with that of n-hydrocarbons eluting before and after it. To each of a series of paraffins is attached an index I, given by

$$I = 100n \qquad (22.15)$$

where n = the carbon number of a given paraffin

The retention index of an unknown is calculated from the relation

$$I = 100\left[\frac{\log V_n^{u} - \log V_n^{x}}{\log V_n^{x+1} - \log V_n^{x}}\right] + 100x \qquad (22.16)$$

where x = the carbon number of the compound eluted before the unknown
       V_n^{u} = the net retention volume of the unknown
       V_n^{x} = the net retention volume of the hydrocarbon eluted before the unknown
       V_n^{x+1} = the net retention volume of the hydrocarbon eluted after the unknown
       $x + 1$ = the carbon number of the compound eluted after the unknown

(x and $x + 1$ are the bracketing hydrocarbon carbon-numbers.)

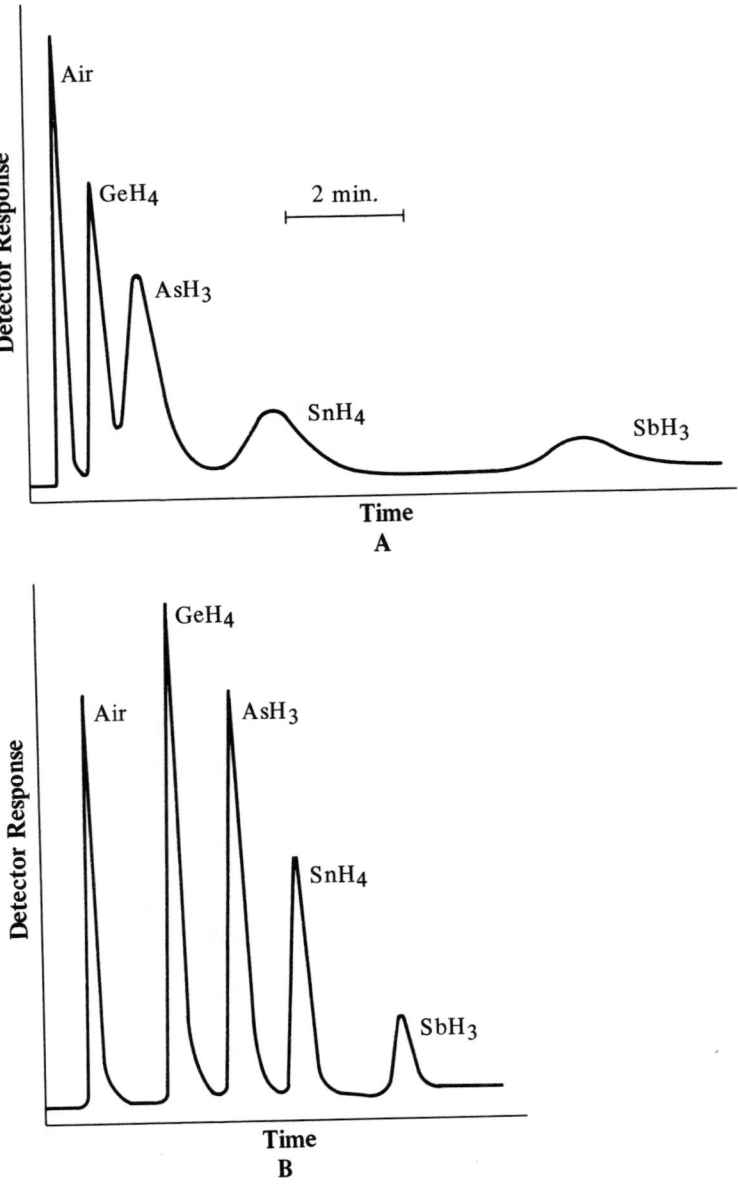

FIGURE 22.12. *Example of temperature programming to improve separations. A: Isothermal temperature, 85°C. B: Temperature programmed 8°C/min, 75°–120°C. From R. D. Kadeg and G. D. Christian,* Anal. Chim. Acta, *88, 117 (1977), by permission of the publisher.*

This method is based on a linear relation between log V_r and carbon number in a homologous series and essentially places any species on its appropriate place on the plot. The basic assumption is that variations in the retention of hydrocarbons will be reflected in the retention of all other species under isothermal conditions; hence, if the flow rate changes or if the stationary-phase volume is reduced, all observed V_r values will change, but the value of I for a given species will not. A problem arises only when the chemical composition of the phase changes with time because of polymerization or oxidation. For example, a polyglycol polymer stationary phase might change in polarity after long heating and exposure to an active catalytic support surface, so that changes in its retention of alcohols will not be mirrored by changes in its retention of paraffins. The retention of the hydrocarbons on this phase is mainly a function of vapor pressure, with almost a uniform activity coefficient contribution and no directed (that is, H-bonding) interactions, whereas the retention of alcohols depends not only on vapor-pressure differences but on directed solute-solvent interactions. A loss of H-bonding capacity will influence the retention of alcohol markedly, but may not affect that of the paraffins. Some workers use homologous series of analogous compounds—alcohols with alcohols, ketones with ketones, and so on—in an attempt to avoid this problem. The use of computers in GC is strongly encouraged, since they make the calculation of retention indices a trivial operation. Of course, just as a single t_r measurement (even with standards) does not conclusively identify a given substance, neither does a single index value. Several columns should be used and index values calculated for each as cross-references to known materials.

Quantitative Analysis

If the analyst is willing to assume that peak shape is not a function of solute concentration, he or she can carry out quantitative analyses by establishing standard curves of peak height versus concentration. The quantitative information in a gas chromatogram is found in the peak areas and not in the peak heights, since zone shape is a function of many different variables, notably injection rate. Peak areas are obtained by conventional methods, such as triangulation, mechanical or electronic integration by analog devices on the recorder, and summation in digital recorders (analog-to-digital conversion); the ease and accuracy of measurement increase in the order of the methods mentioned, as does the cost. The relative response factors for the different species are important to determine, so as to normalize the areas measured to a common base for comparison. Quantitative analysis is generally carried out with reference to standard calibration curves; in practice, an error of $\pm 2\%$ is quite reasonable. Quantitative analysis also depends on using a recording method that has the correct frequency-response for the signal observed.

22.5 APPLICATIONS OF GAS CHROMATOGRAPHY

Applications of gas chromatography are best illustrated by the actual chromatograms themselves. The examples were chosen to illustrate the utility of the technique in many areas of scientific endeavor, and because they combine many of the ideas presented in this chapter. They do not necessarily illustrate the method of choice for a given analysis.

Industrial Environmental Analysis

A good example of a gas-chromatographic analysis in the area of air quality is in the study of coke-oven emissions. By its very nature, the coke process can be expected to produce polycyclic organic matter; this is of concern because many compounds in this class are carcinogenic. Such compounds as benz[a]anthracene, benzo[a]-pyrene, and benz[c]acridine are of particular importance.

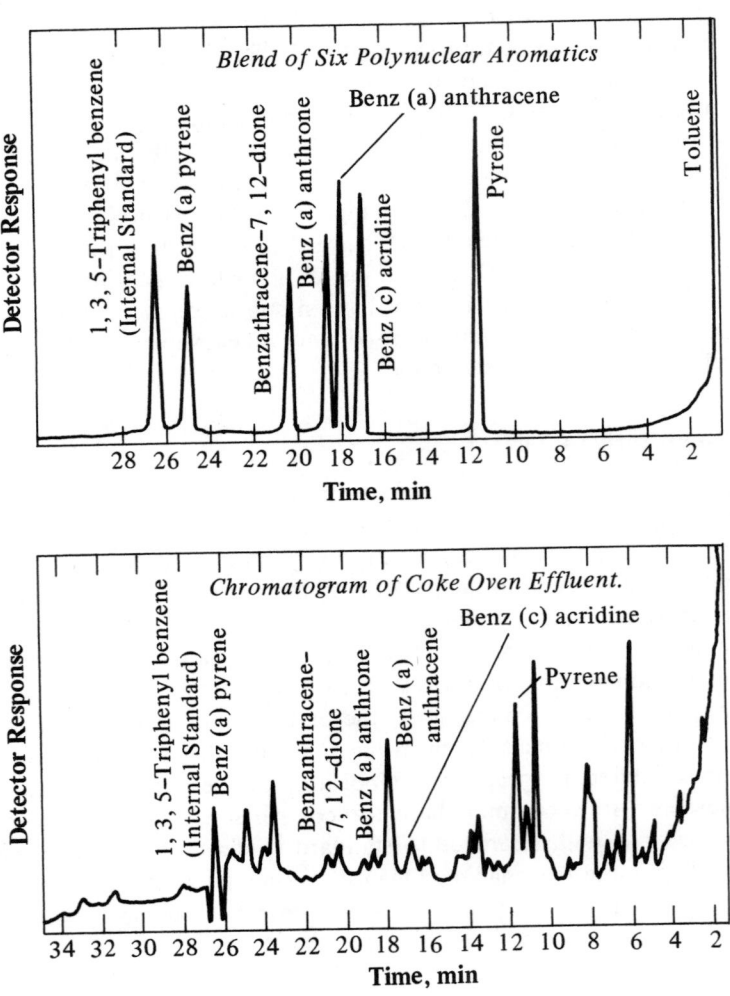

FIGURE 22.13. *Chromatograms of a standard mixture of polycyclic aromatic hydrocarbons and of a coke-furnace emission. From T. D. Searl, F. J. Cassidy, W. H. King, and R. A. Brown, Anal. Chem., 42, 954 (1970) by permission of the senior author and the publisher. Copyright © 1970 by the American Chemical Society.*

The chromatograms shown in Figure 22.13 were obtained using a 10 ft × 0.125 in (o.d.) column packed with 2% SE-30 on Chromosorb G. Temperature programming was utilized (175–275°C at 4°C/min, then held for 15 min). Pertinent fractions were trapped and analyzed remotely by ultraviolet spectrometry. Recoveries (grams found/grams present) were about 86% for benzo[a]pyrene. Actual coke-oven samples were collected by ambient-air–filter techniques and extracted with cyclohexane. Detection was by FID in a split-effluent stream.

Forensic Analysis for Drugs of Abuse

One of the major applications of gas chromatography is in finding legal evidence of the presence of illicit material. Two examples are given here. The first is the analysis of "street-quality" heroin; the second is an analysis for amphetamine and related materials in biological fluids.

Analysis for the heroin content of illicit heroin, which is often "cut" with quinine hydrochloride, can be accomplished directly using gas-liquid chromatography. In this example, an internal standard (cholesterol) is added to improve both qualitative and quantitative accuracy. The chromatogram is isothermal (235°C) with a 6 ft × $\frac{1}{4}$ in column packed with 3% OV-1 on 80/100 mesh Chromosorb W. The peak area is determined using a digital integrator. Figure 22.14 shows a typical analysis. Heroin content is calculated by the following relations:

$$c_s = \frac{A_s}{A_{std}} \left(\frac{A_{i.s./std}}{A_{i.s./s}} \right) c_{std} \tag{22.17}$$

$$\% \text{ Heroin} = \frac{c_s}{S} (100 \ \%) \tag{22.18}$$

where
A_s = the area count of sample
A_{std} = the area count of standard
$A_{i.s./std}$ = the area count of the internal standard in standard solution
$A_{i.s./s}$ = the area count of the internal standard in sample solution
c_{std} = the concentration of the standard
c_s = the concentration of the sample (heroin)
S = the weight of the sample

An analysis of amphetamine and related compounds is easily achieved in standard solutions by derivativization to the N-trifluoroacetamide. The situation is much different in the world of "real" samples. Biological fluids are very complex mixtures of materials. In urine, such materials as amphetamine can be extracted, a derivative made, and the latter analyzed without much problem; at high dilution in blood, the problem becomes more complicated. In this example, the following procedure yielded the highest recoveries (98%) at the 2.5×10^{-8} g/ml of blood level: (1) extracting the substance with benzene in coated glassware, (2) scavenging the amine with a volatile amine (diethylamine) in a HCl salt-formation step, and (3) derivativization to the N-trifluoroacetamide. Chromatographic conditions were similar to that of the previous example. A typical chromatogram is given in Figure 22.15.

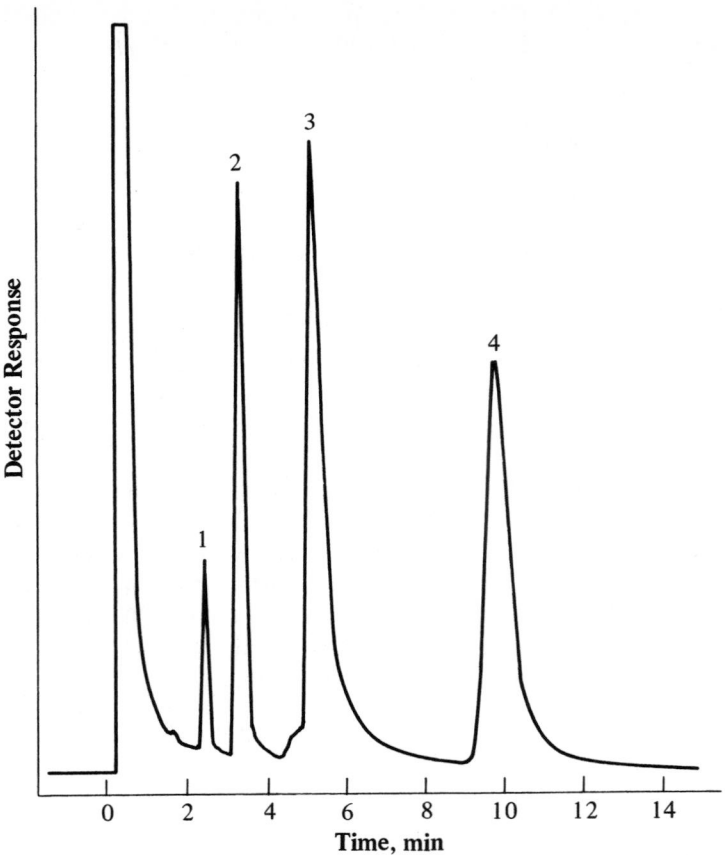

FIGURE 22.14. *Chromatogram of heroin preparation showing internal standard. Compounds:* 1. *Acetylcodeine or O⁶-monoacetylmorphine;* 2. *Heroin hydrochloride;* 3. *Quinine hydrochloride;* 4. *Cholesterol internal standard. From P. De Zan and J. Fasenello,* J. Chromatogr. Sci., *10,* 333 (1972), *by permission of the publisher.*

Pharmacological Studies

This example of the recovery of a drug and its metabolites is important because it illustrates electron-capture detection. The drug studied is 7-chloro-1,3-dihydro-5-(2'-chlorophenyl)-2H-1,4-benzodiazepin-2-one. In this study, the intent was to recover the intact drug and to recover and identify its metabolites in blood and urine. Figure 22.16 shows a typical chromatogram of a diethyl-ether extract of blood. The detection limit for the drug was 0.002 μg/ml of blood; the very low levels of the drug

FIGURE 22.15. *A typical chromatogram of amphetamine as determined in an extract of human whole blood. A: Chromatogram. B: Calibration curve illustrating linearity, sensitivity, and recovery from whole blood. From J. E. O'Brien, W. Zazulan, V. Abbey, and O. Hinsvark,* J. Chromatogr. Sci., *10,* 336 (1972), *by permission of the publisher.*

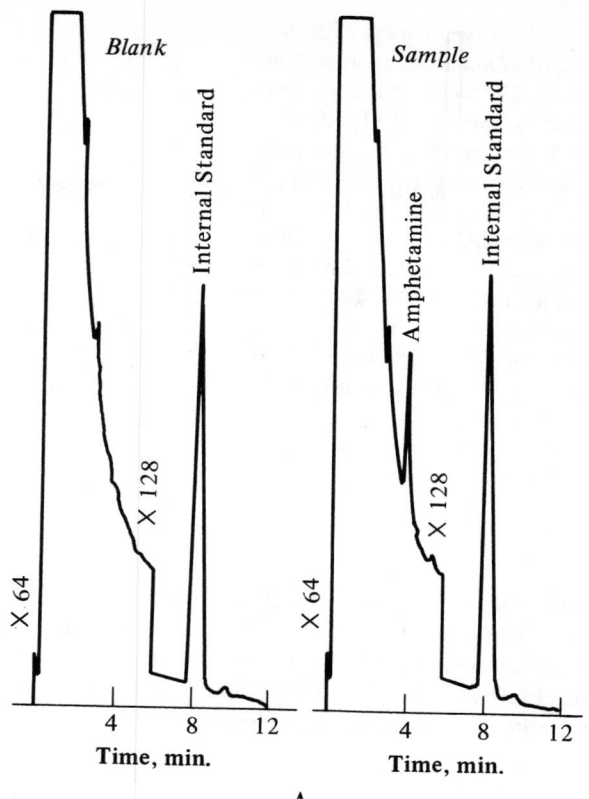

A

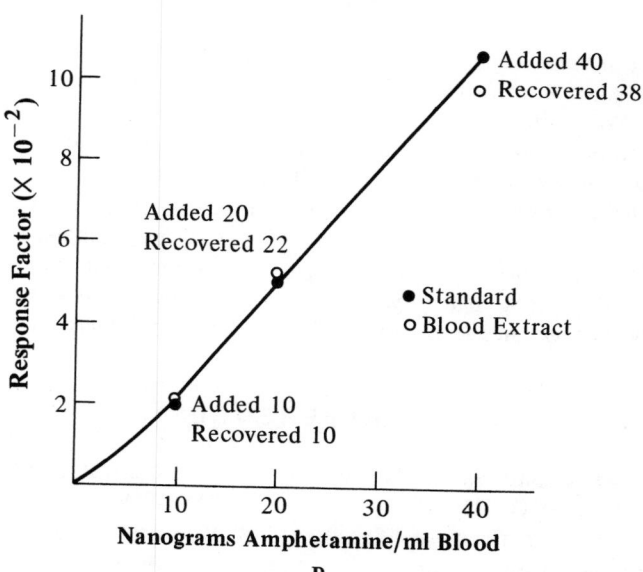

B

FIGURE 22.16. *Chromatogram of diethyl-ether extract of blood showing a drug and its metabolites. Compounds: 1. Lorazepam (an identified metabolite); 2. Unidentified metabolite; 3. Parent drug; 4. Reference standard. Column: 4 ft × 4 mm borosilicate glass, 3% OV-17 stationary phase on 60/80-mesh diatomite. Argon-methane (90:10) carrier gas. Column: Isothermal at 240°C. Injection part, 280°C; detector, 325°C. Adapted from J. A. F. de Silva, I. Bekersky, and C. V. Puglisi, J. Chromatogr. Sci., 11, 547 (1973), by permission of the publisher.*

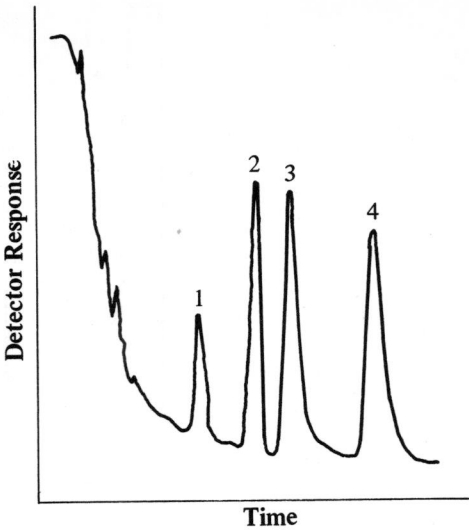

expected in human-subject studies required gas chromatography with electron-capture detection (^{63}Ni sources) as opposed to more common spectrophotometric procedures. The chromatogram is relatively simple, because of the selectivity of the detection system; the ECD is essentially responding only to the chlorinated compounds. The only metabolite positively identified was Lorazepam, the 3-hydroxy analog of the parent drug.

SELECTED BIBLIOGRAPHY

KARGER, B. A.; SNYDER, L. R.; and HORVATH, C. *An Introduction to Separation Science.* New York: Wiley-Interscience, 1973. *This text organizes the various separation techniques into a unified theme and is strongly recommended to those whose work involves separations.*

LITTLEWOOD, A. B. *Gas Chromatography: Principles, Techniques and Applications,* 2nd ed. New York: Academic Press, 1970.

McNAIR, H. M., and BONELLI, E. J. *Basic Gas Chromatography.* Varian Aerograph, 2700 Mitchell Dr., Walnut Creek, Calif. 94598. *A very good "first" book on practical aspects.*

Guide to Stationary Phases for Gas Chromatography. Analabs, Inc., North Haven, Connecticut. *A correlated listing of stationary phases and solute types, updated on a regular basis.*

REFERENCES

1. A. J. P. MARTIN and R. L. M. SYNGE, *Biochem. J., 35,* 1358 (1941).

2. A. T. JAMES and A. J. P. MARTIN, *Biochem. J. Proc., 48,* vii (1951); *Analyst, 77,* 915 (1952).

3. E. GLUECKAUF, *Trans. Faraday Soc., 51,* 34 (1955).

4. L. ROHRSCHNEIDER, *Z. Anal. Chem., 170,* 256 (1959).

5. W. O. McREYNOLDS, *J. Chromatog. Sci., 8,* 685 (1970).

6. J. LEARY, J. JUSTICE, S. TSUGE, S. LOWRY, and T. L. ISENHOUR, *J. Chromatog. Sci., 11,* 201 (1973).

PROBLEMS

1. Predict the effect of changing from He to N_2 carrier gas on (a) retention volume, and (b) HETP. What might be the effects of using a super-critical vapor such as CO_2?

2. Compare the following two methods of scaling up an analytical separation to preparative levels: (1) keeping column size (volume and length) constant and increasing the percent liquid loading; and (2) increasing column diameter, keeping the length and the percent liquid loading constant.

3. The following data were obtained on a nonpolar column for n-butylacetate (retention time in mm of chart paper): n-heptane, 174 mm; n-octane, 373.4 mm; n-butyl-acetate, 310 mm. (a) Calculate the Kováts index I for n-butylacetate. (b) Does the value of $I/100$ have any physical significance?

4. A column of support coated with an ester of low volatility is operated at 23 lb/in² and 40°C. The following results were obtained:

Compound	t_r, min
Methane + Air	1.8
Ethane	2.4
Propane	3.6
Propylene	4.3
Isobutane	5.5
Butane	7.5
Isobutylene	8.6
Trans-2-Butene	10.6
Cis-2-Butene	12.3
Isopentane	13.6
Pentane	18.2

Construct a plot of log V'_r versus carbon number, including all compounds significantly retained. What can be seen in the results?

5. Derive the expressions for optimum velocity and minimum plate-height using the simple Van Deemter expression. What are the dominant factors in each?

6. From a survey of ten articles in the literature dealing with gas-chromatographic separations, list structures of the stationary phase and the compounds separated, and your estimate of the kind of forces involved in the retention mechanism.

7. The adjusted retention times (t'_R) in min for a series of compounds were determined carefully on a nonpolar column: n-pentane, 2.8; n-hexane, 5.3; n-heptane, 13.7; n-octane, 29.3; toluene, 16.5; cyclohexane, 12.4. Calculate the Kováts index for toluene and for cyclohexane.

8. Gas-reduction valves used on helium tanks in gas chromatography commonly give the pressure in units of psig (pounds per square inch above atmospheric pressure). (a) Calculate the actual inlet pressure in mm of mercury (torr) for 20, 40, 60, and 80 psig if ambient pressure is 740 mm Hg and normal atmospheric pressure (760 mm) is 14.696 psi. (b) Calculate the compressibility factor j for each of these cases.

9. Uncorrected flow rates (F_0) measured on a bubble-type flowmeter must be corrected for temperature and pressure (see Fig. 22.1). Calculate F_c for $F_0 = 23.8$, 40.2, and 51.9 ml/min. The ambient pressure and temperature are 750 mm Hg and 25°C; the column temperature is 110°C.

10. The following data were obtained on a 1/8″ i.d. × 10′ column of 15% SE-30 (by weight) on Chromosorb W. Inlet pressure = 60.0 psig; ambient pressure = 740 mm Hg; column temperature = 116°C; ambient temperature = 24°C; uncorrected He flow rate = 26.4 ml/min on a bubble-type flowmeter. A total of 1.09 g of SE-30 was contained in the column.

Compound	t'_R (min)	Peak Width, W (min)
Ether	1.78	0.31
Hexane	6.78	0.84
Ethylbenzene	18.14	1.64

For each compound, calculate (a) the adjusted retention volume, (b) the net retention volume, and (c) the specific retention volume (at 0°C). Calculate (d) the resolution between ether and hexane, and (e) between hexane and ethylbenzene.

11. The chromatographic data shown overleaf were obtained on the column used in Problem 10 with 2-µl injections of heptane.

F_0 (ml/min)	t_0 (min) "air peak"	t_r (min)	Peak Height (Chart Divisions)	Peak Width, W (min)
121.2	1.38	4.49	50.2	0.30
91.3	1.69	5.37	60.3	0.34
72.8	1.94	6.17	64.9	0.38
63.7	2.09	6.62	67.6	0.42
51.2	2.42	7.62	69.2	0.49
40.9	2.78	8.83	79.4	0.63
32.7	3.30	10.31	78.5	0.76
27.4	3.74	11.69	76.8	0.90
18.1	5.03	15.84	72.3	1.47

Ambient temperature and pressure were 25.0°C and 740-mm Hg; inlet pressure was 60.5 psig; column temperature was 109°C. For each flow rate calculate F_c, t'_r, V'_r, V_n, N, H, and the (triangulated) area A of the peak. Plot N and H versus F_0 and estimate the optimum flow rate. Plot the peak height and peak area versus F_0 and comment on the effect of flow rate on these.

12. What number of plates would be required to effect a separation with less than 1% contamination ($R = 1.5$) for $\alpha = 1.10$ in (a) a packed column with a capacity factor of 50; (b) a packed column with $k' = 5$; (c) an open tubular column with $k' = 2$; (d) an open tubular column with $k' = 0.5$. (e) Calculate the effective number of plates in each case. (f) What column lengths would be necessary for a good packed column of $H = 0.2$ mm and an open tubular column of $H = 10$ mm?

23

Computers in Analytical Instrumentation

S. P. PERONE
D. O. JONES

Digital instruments and digital computers have become important elements in modern analytical instrumentation, for many reasons. Together with the advances in instrumentation of the 1950s and 1960s came the need to use electronic data-processing to handle the vast amounts of raw data that could be generated. As a result of space-age technological advances, digital devices became so compact and inexpensive by the late 1960s and early 1970s that laboratory-size computers became a reality. These minicomputers could be connected to instruments to automatically acquire and process digitized data, control experimental parameters, print reports, and so forth. Because of the heavy analytical load carried by gas chromatography in industrial laboratories, chromatographs were among the first types of instruments to be computerized on a wide scale. High-resolution mass spectrometry benefited greatly from the availability of laboratory computers, because of the need to handle large quantities of data for runs lasting only a few seconds. Also, such methods as Fourier-transform nuclear magnetic resonance and infrared spectroscopy became feasible only when instruments were developed that included dedicated minicomputers.

Many other areas of analytical instrumentation have benefited greatly from computerization, and the reader is referred to review articles describing various applications in detail [1]. The objective of this chapter is to introduce the fundamental principles of on-line computer instrumentation, focusing attention on the characteristics of digital devices important for interfacing laboratory instruments to digital computers. These fundamentals include a consideration of number systems,

711

digital logic, digital devices, analog/digital translation devices, sampling of raw data, interface design, and on-line computer operations. After the principles of interfacing devices and their components have been presented, the design of interface devices for some specific functions will be described (Sec. 23.4).

23.1 THE DIGITAL COMPUTER

Figure 23.1 provides a block diagram of the essential components of a typical digital-computer configuration. The *memory* is a component capable of storing many thousands of binary-coded (digital) packets of information. Each packet is com-

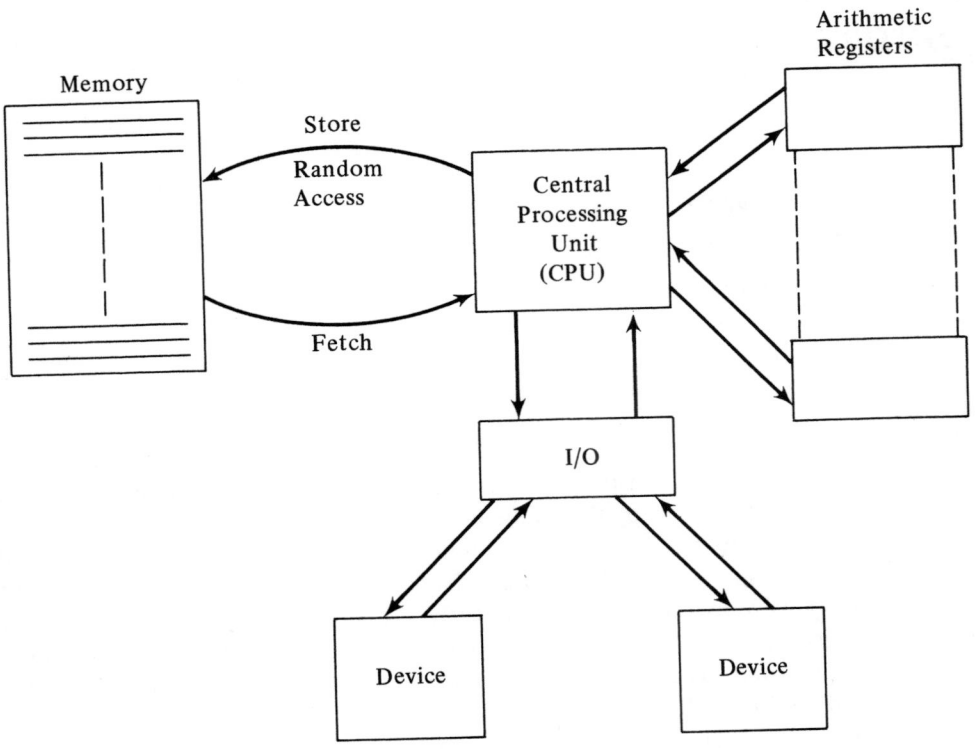

FIGURE 23.1. *Typical digital computer configuration. From S. P. Perone,* J. Chromatogr. Sci., 7, 714 (1969) *by permission of the publisher.*

posed of *n* binary digits (*bits*) and is called a *word* of information. Each of these *n*-bit words has an *address* associated with it, and the information contained within can be fetched or stored by specifying the address. The internal memory is usually either a semiconductor memory or a magnetic-ferrite-core memory [2]. Three types of information are stored in memory: *data, instruction,* or *address.* The speed with which information is fetched or stored in memory is the *memory cycle time* and is usually about 1 μsec for core memory.

The *central processing unit* (CPU) controls the overall operation of the computer. It is made up of electronic registers and logic circuits that execute the simple logical and arithmetic operations of which the computer is capable. When these operations are executed in appropriate sequences, the computer can accomplish complex mathematical or data-processing functions. Moreover, if one provides the appropriate electronic *interface*, these simple operations can be used to control experimental systems, acquire data, or print results on a teletype printer, line printer, oscilloscope, or other peripheral device.

The sequence of instructions to be executed by the computer is called a *program*. In actuality, the program is a set of binary-coded instructions stored in memory. The CPU fetches each instruction from memory, interprets and executes it, and then moves on to the next instruction. The CPU fetches instructions sequentially from memory, unless told to do otherwise by one of the instructions.

The *arithmetic registers* are high-speed electronic *accumulators* (ACs). That is, each is a set of n electronic two-state devices (like flip-flops—see Sec. 23.2), which can be used to accumulate intermediate results of binary arithmetic involving n-bit data. Nearly all the arithmetic and logical operations of the CPU are carried out in the arithmetic registers. Binary information can be transferred to or from memory and the arithmetic registers by the execution of appropriate instructions.

The *I/O* (input/output) *bus* allows transfer of binary-coded information between peripheral devices and the central processing unit. The number of peripheral devices that can be connected to the I/O bus is limited primarily by the sophistication of the hardware and software (programs).

A small digital computer (of the types currently being used for laboratory automation and experimental control)* has an instruction set of 50–100 different instructions. Each of these instructions corresponds to a specific binary coding which, when decoded by the CPU, results in the execution of a fairly simple arithmetic or logical step. Examples of some simple machine operations are binary addition of a datum in some memory location to the contents of an AC, the transfer of the contents of an AC to a memory location (and vice versa), rotation of the binary digits of the AC contents to the left or right, and the application of logical tests such as determining whether the AC is zero, nonzero, odd, even, positive, negative, etc. By developing programs composed of appropriate sequences of these elementary operations, the most sophisticated mathematical computations can be carried out. Since the computer can execute instructions so rapidly—about 10^6 instructions per second—it can complete complex computations with fantastic speed.

Thus, the digital computer is really a very simple-minded device, which must be told how to accomplish even the most fundamental computations but which can accomplish these operations with blinding speed. Moreover, it is a tireless machine, which is content to calculate endlessly and consistently. It is also very versatile, since it is programmable and capable of accomplishing an infinite variety of computational, logical, or control operations. Finally, it is a device that can (in fact, must) communicate in a variety of ways with the outside world. It is this characteristic that defines the computer as a general-purpose experimental device.

---

* Examples are the small desk-top laboratory computers manufactured by Data General Corp., Hewlett Packard Corp., Digital Equipment Corp., and others.

Programming the Digital Computer

The programming of a computer is usually accomplished with some sort of symbolic language; that is, readily recognized symbols are used to represent simple machine operations or groups of machine operations. Translating programs are supplied by the computer manufacturer to convert symbolic programs into the binary-coded machine-language programs. The simplest of these symbolic languages is the *assembly language*, where there is nearly a one-for-one conversion from symbolic statements to machine language. A program for translating these programs into machine language is called an *assembler*. The relationship between assembly and machine languages is shown in Figure 23.2. The figure shows that the assembly

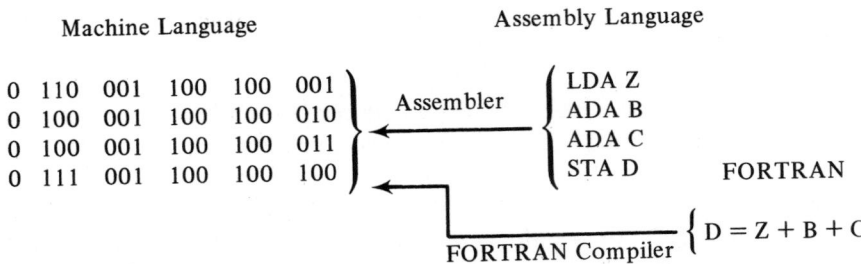

FIGURE 23.2. *Relationship of machine language to assembly language and FORTRAN. From S. P. Perone,* J. Chromatogr. Sci., 7, 714 (1969), *by permission of the publisher.*

language instructions, such as LDA Z (which may mean load the contents of memory location Z into the A register) must be translated into numerical machine language, the only language that the central processer can understand.

Because programming in assembly language can be very tedious, higher-level languages have been developed in which single statements are translated into large blocks of machine-language program segments. The translating program is called a *compiler*; one such high-level language is FORTRAN. The relationship to machine language is also shown in Figure 23.2.

Obviously, it is much simpler to prepare programs in FORTRAN than in assembly language. However, compiler-generated programs are often very inefficient in utilizing available memory space; moreover, speed of execution and synchronization of computations with outside events are relatively difficult to control with these programs. These considerations are particularly important for on-line computer applications in the laboratory; therefore, assembly-language programming must be used extensively so that the programmer can exercise the detailed control of computer operations required. Section 23.2 will deal extensively with such programming.

Off-Line Computers

The computer configuration with which most scientists are familiar is the *off-line* system (see Fig. 23.3). To use the computer in this configuration, the scientist

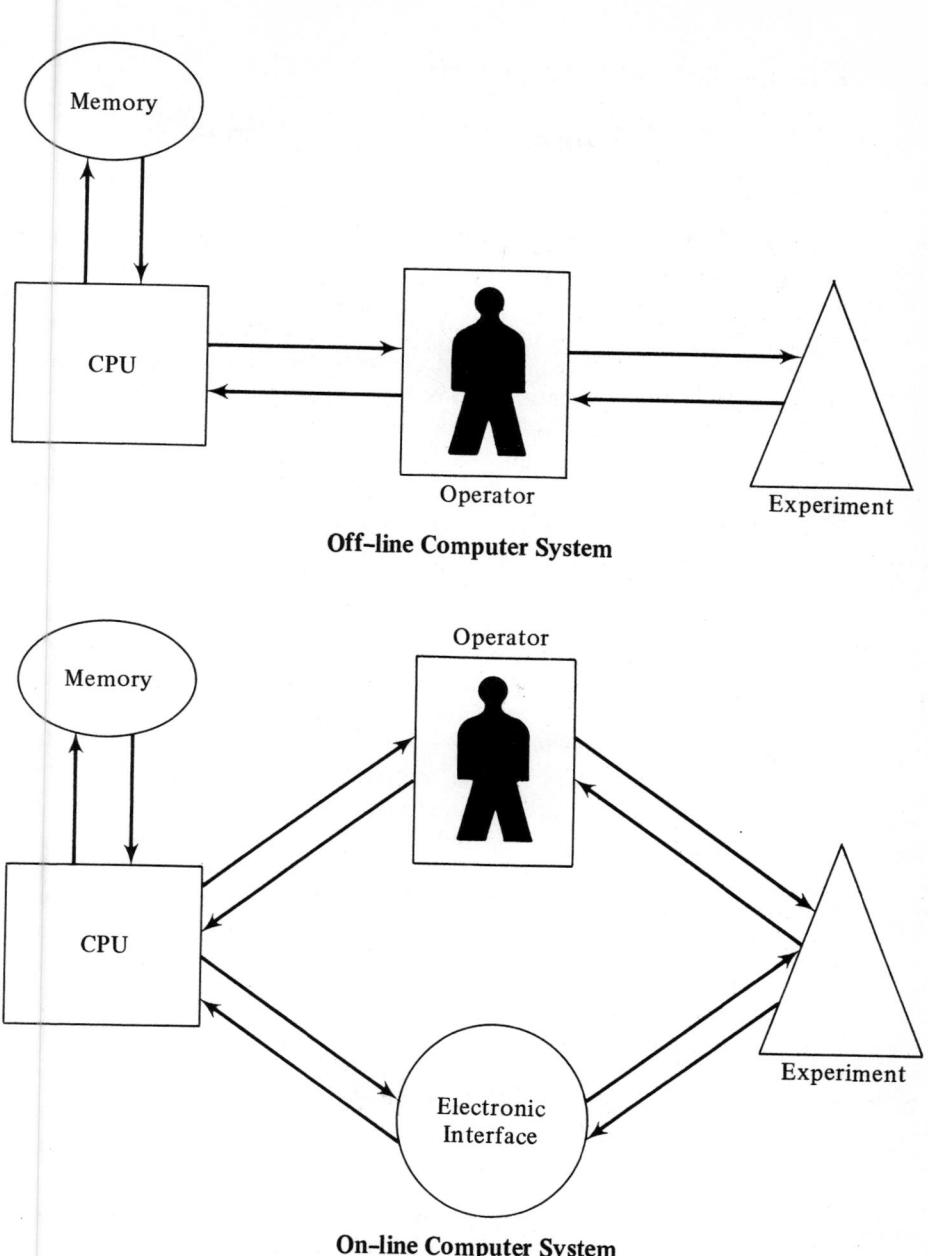

Memory

CPU

Operator

Experiment

Off–line Computer System

Operator

Memory

CPU

Electronic
Interface

Experiment

On–line Computer System

FIGURE 23.3. *Computer systems. Adapted from S. P. Perone*, J. Chem.
Educ., *47*, 105 (1970) *by permission of the publisher.*

typically writes a data-processing program in FORTRAN or some other high-level
computer language, runs the experiment, manually tabulates the data from the strip-
chart recorder or oscilloscope trace, transfers the tabulated data to punched cards,
adds the data cards to the deck of program cards, transports the combined card-deck

to the computer center for processing, and then waits until the program has been executed and the results printed. Turnaround times may vary from a few minutes to a few days, depending on the capacity of the computer facility, the number of users, and the backlog and priorities of work to be processed.

On-Line Computers

For the investigator who requires very rapid or instantaneous results from his computer system, for whatever reason, the solution may be to employ an on-line computer system. The most important distinction of this configuration is that there is a *direct* line of communication between the experiment and the computer (Fig. 23.3B). The line of communication is through an electronic *interface*. (This interface includes control logic, electronic elements to provide timing and synchronization, and conversion modules, such as digitizing devices, which translate real-world data into information that the digital computer recognizes.) Data are acquired under computer control or supervision, and the program for data processing is usually held in memory to provide for very rapid completion of the computational tasks. Results can be made available to the investigator quickly by means of teletype display, line-printer, oscilloscope, or other forms of printout. In addition, the computer can be programmed to communicate directly with the experiment by controlling electronic or electromechanical devices, such as solid-state switches, relays, stepping motors, servomotors, or other devices that can be activated by changes in voltage or current.

The advantages of on-line computer operation, then, include elimination of the middle man by substituting an electronic interface, possible direct computer control of the experiment, and possible real-time interaction between the computer and the experiment. Because the computer can make computations and decisions at speeds exceeding most ordinary data-acquisition rates, it can modify the experimental conditions during the experiment. An additional advantage, of course, is that the logistic barriers of the remote computer system are eliminated.

23.2 PRINCIPLES OF DIGITAL INSTRUMENTATION

Binary and Octal Number Systems

All information handled or generated by the central processing unit (CPU) must be binary or binary-coded machine language. This includes instructions, memory addresses, and data. Thus, the small-computer user must quickly become familiar with this number system. It would be well to review here the binary number system and binary arithmetic.

The *decimal* number 369_{10}* can be broken down into $3 \times 10^2 + 6 \times 10^1 + 9 \times 10^0$. Similarly, the *binary* number (in base 2) 10101 represents $1 \times 2^4 + 0 \times 2^3 + 1 \times 2^2 + 0 \times 2^1 + 1 \times 2^0 = 21_{10}$. Large binary numbers (for instance, 101101110010101) are conveniently represented in the *octal* (base 8) system for easy

---

* 369 to the base 10.

recall or reference. The applicability of the octal system can be seen from the binary representation of the numbers 0 to 7:

000	0	011	3	110	6
001	1	100	4	111	7
010	2	101	5		

This sequence illustrates the normal binary counting sequence, which can be extended to an infinite number of binary digits (bits). It also shows the octal digits equivalent to all three-bit combinations. To convert any large binary number to octal, group binary digits in groups of three, *starting at the rightmost digit*:

$$\underbrace{..1}_{1} \quad \underbrace{001}_{1} \quad \underbrace{101}_{5} \qquad = 115_8$$

$$\underbrace{101}_{5} \quad \underbrace{101}_{5} \quad \underbrace{110}_{6} \quad \underbrace{010}_{2} \quad \underbrace{101}_{5} \quad = 55625_8$$

$$201_8 = 010 \quad 000 \quad 001$$
$$356_8 = 011 \quad 101 \quad 110$$

Counting in octal: 0, 1, 2, 3, 4, 5, 6, 7, 10, 11, 12, 13, 14, 15, 16, 17, 20, 21, 22, 23, ... 75, 76, 77, 100, 101, 102, ..., 776, 777, 1000, 1001, ..., 7776, 7777, 10000, ...

Often it is necessary to convert numbers from one base to another. The above examples illustrate the ease of converting from octal to binary and vice versa. Consider the following examples:

Decimal-to-Binary Conversion. For example, $876_{10} = ?$ in binary?

$$876$$
$$512 = 2^9 = \text{largest power of 2 to fit in } 876_{10}$$
$$\underline{-512}$$
$$364$$
$$256 = 2^8 = \text{largest power of 2 to fit in } 364_{10}$$
$$\underline{-256}$$
$$108$$
$$64 = 2^6 = \text{largest power of 2 to fit in } 108_{10}$$
$$\underline{-64}$$
$$44$$
$$32 = 2^5$$
$$\underline{-32}$$
$$12$$
$$8 = 2^3$$
$$\underline{-8}$$
$$4$$
$$4 = 2^2$$
$$\underline{-4}$$
$$0$$

Thus, the binary representation of 876_{10} must include 2^9, 2^8, 2^6, 2^5, 2^3, and 2^2, so the binary number is

$$
\begin{array}{ccccccccc}
1 & 1 & 0 & 1 & 1 & 0 & 1 & 1 & 0 & 0 \\
\downarrow & \downarrow & & \downarrow & \downarrow & & \downarrow & \downarrow & & \\
2^9 & 2^8 & & 2^6 & 2^5 & & 2^3 & 2^2 & &
\end{array}
$$

The octal equivalent of this binary number is 1554_8.

Digital Information

The laboratory scientist is accustomed to seeing experimental information displayed as analog data. That is, data are usually made available in a continuous signal such as given by a strip-chart recorder or oscilloscope trace. Unfortunately, the digital computer cannot handle analog information directly. The computer must have information in a digital (usually binary-coded) format.

The differences between analog and digital information are illustrated graphically in Figure 23.4. Whereas analog data are continuous with an infinite number of real values between any two points on a trace, digital data are discrete, with well defined finite limits of resolution between any two points. Thus, when digitizing an analog signal that varies between 0 and 15 V, the digital resolution will be $\pm \frac{1}{2}$ V if only 4 bits can be used to encode the digital information; that is, only 16 values (2^4) can be represented by 4 bits, allowing only 1 V increments (see Fig. 23.4). If only 2 bits are used to encode the digital information, the resolution decreases even further as there are now only four digital states possible.

It should be obvious, then, that digitizing data always results in some loss of information. This is tolerated only because it is a format change required to use the powerful data-handling features of the digital computer. However, the scientist developing and using computerized instrumentation should be aware of the problems inherent in this approach, and should learn how to take maximum advantage of digital instrumentation. To this end, digital devices, digitization methods, sampling considerations, and so forth will be discussed.

Digital Logic States

Digital logic devices are the foundation upon which digital instrumentation, including computers, interfaces, and so on, are built. They consist of a set of electronic circuits that perform simple logic operations, usually represented by the binary number system. They can be connected into more complex building blocks so as to perform the necessary logic, storage, arithmetic, interface, and timing operations required by digital instrumentation.

In the simplest case, a digital logic function can be simulated with conventional switches and a battery, the output states being indicated with a light bulb. Two such simple logic circuits are shown in Figure 23.5.

The circuit in Figure 23.5A performs the basic OR digital logic function. When both switches A and B are open, no current flows to the lamp. However, when either switch A *or* B or both are closed, current flows to light the lamp. The *output* state (whether the lamp is on or off) corresponds to the numbers of the binary

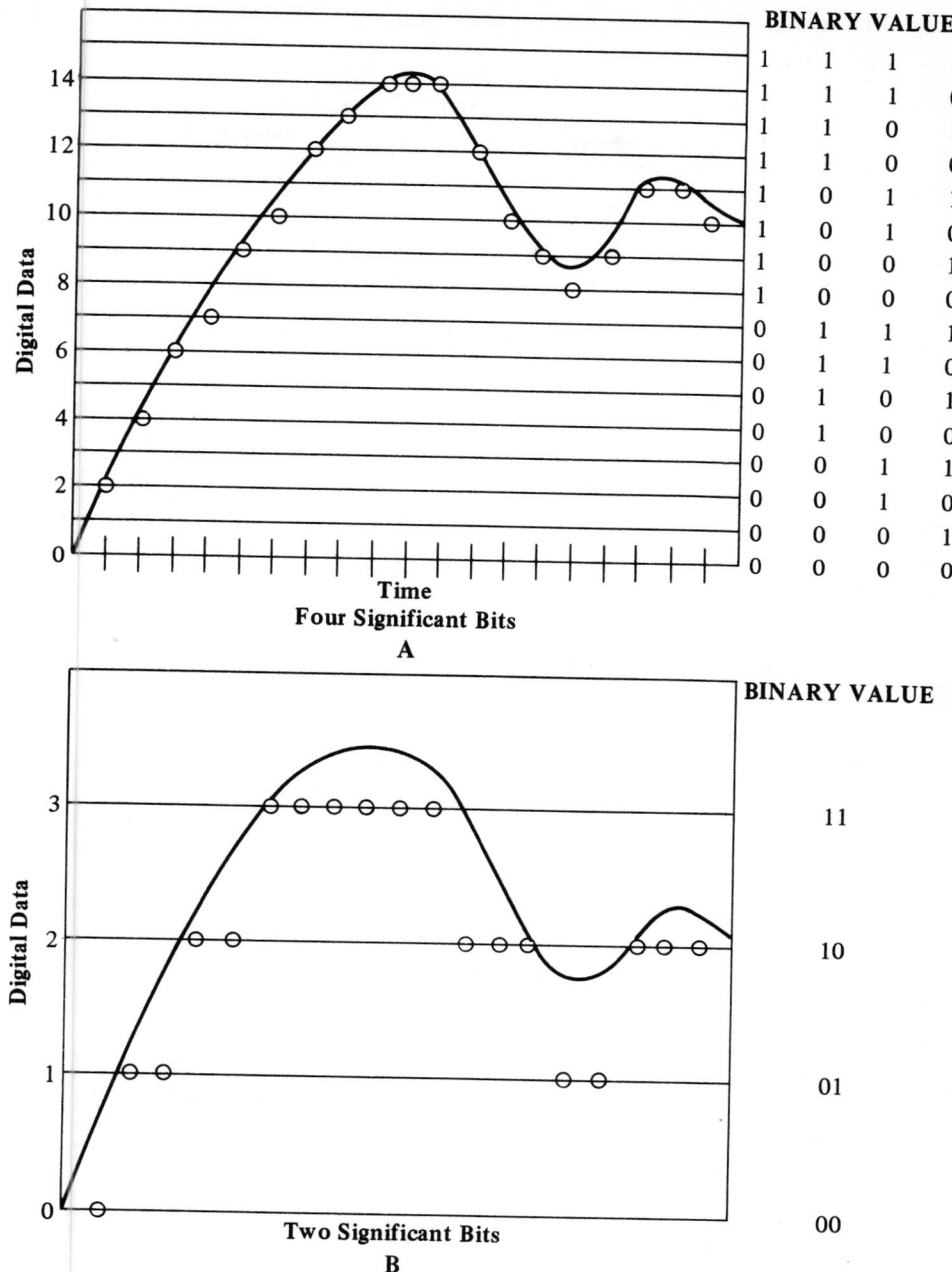

FIGURE 23.4. *Digital representation of analog data. From S. P. Perone and D. O. Jones*, Digital Computers in Scientific Instrumentation, *New York: McGraw-Hill, 1973, by permission of the publisher. Copyright © 1973 by McGraw-Hill, Inc.*

FIGURE 23.5. *Simple logic functions. From S. P. Perone and D. O. Jones,* Digital Computers in Scientific Instrumentation, *New York: McGraw-Hill, 1973, by permission of the publisher. Copyright © 1973 by McGraw-Hill, Inc.*

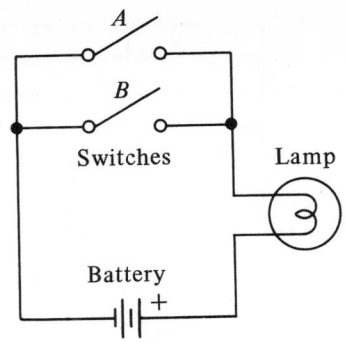

**The OR Function
A**

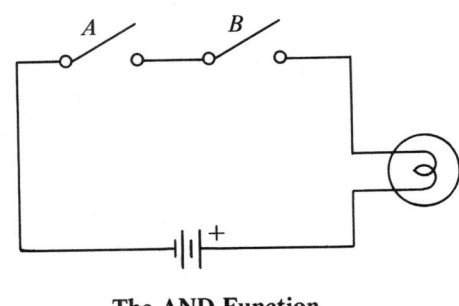

**The AND Function
B**

number system; the *on* condition is defined as the binary number 1 and the *off* condition as the binary number 0. The *input* functions or switch positions are defined in the same manner, with the open-switch condition as a binary 0 and the closed condition as a binary 1.

A circuit for performing another basic logic function is that in Figure 23.5B; here, the two switches A and B are connected in series rather than in parallel, so that both switch A *and* switch B must be closed for the lamp to light. This is a basic digital logic circuit performing the AND function.

In Table 23.1, the operation of the circuits presented in Figure 23.5 is described in terms of the binary number system. The output states are listed for all combinations of the input-switch conditions. If the circuits in Figure 23.5 are expanded with more input switches, similar, but more complex, tables can be constructed. The AND and OR circuits can also be connected together to perform more complex logic operations. A complex logic circuit performing both AND and OR logic is shown in Figure 23.6.

The "switch" circuits presented above are useful for defining digital logic; they are not, however, used in modern digital computers. Modern digital logic, available in *integrated-circuit* form, uses transistors to perform the switching opera-

TABLE 23.1. *Binary Number Representation of Logic Circuit Operation*

OR Function			AND Function		
Input Conditions		Output Condition	Input Conditions		Output Condition
Switch A	Switch B		Switch A	Switch B	
1	1	1	1	1	1
1	0	1	1	0	0
0	1	1	0	1	0
0	0	0	0	0	0

FIGURE 23.6. *Complex logic function. From S. P. Perone and D. O. Jones*, Digital Computers in Scientific Instrumentation, *New York: McGraw-Hill, 1973, by permission of the publisher. Copyright © 1973 by McGraw-Hill, Inc.*

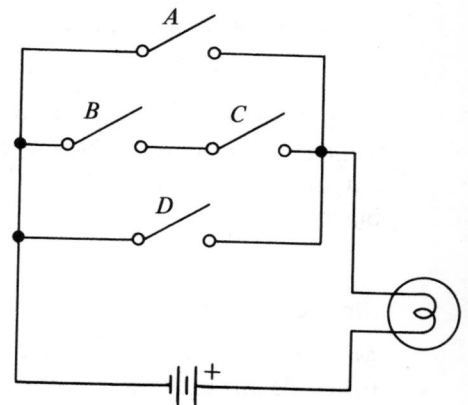

tions. Integrated circuits are miniaturized solid-state devices that may contain several complete electronic circuits; a single integrated-circuit logic package can perform extremely complex logic functions.

The logic states in integrated-circuit digital logic are usually represented by voltage levels, such as 0 and +5 V for both the inputs and outputs. For example, the basic OR logic function (Fig. 23.5) can be represented in terms of a box with two inputs and an output (Fig. 23.7). Instead of opening and closing switches as before, voltage levels are applied to the inputs and the voltage measured at the output. If

FIGURE 23.7. *Electronic logic OR function. From S. P. Perone and D. O. Jones,* Digital Computers in Scientific Instrumentation, *New York: McGraw-Hill, 1973, by permission of the publisher. Copyright © 1973 by McGraw-Hill, Inc.*

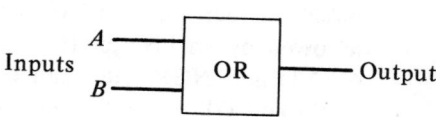

+5 V corresponds to a binary 1 and 0 V corresponds to a binary 0, the operation of the box in Figure 23.7 can be defined in the same way as the operation of the circuit in Figure 23.5A. Complex logic operations can be represented by simply connecting boxes together as in Figure 23.8, which performs the same logic function as the one represented in Figure 23.6.

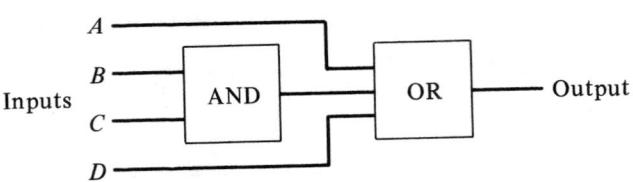

FIGURE 23.8. *Complex electronic logic function. From S. P. Perone and D. O. Jones*, Digital Computers in Scientific Instrumentation, *New York: McGraw-Hill, 1973, by permission of the publisher. Copyright © 1973 by McGraw-Hill, Inc.*

Often it is necessary to define the operation of a logic system in a *sentence* format. This can easily be done; for the circuits in Figures 23.6 and 23.8, the logic output is equal to a binary 1 when either A OR (B AND C) OR D is equal to a binary 1.

Simple Logic Elements: Introduction to Gates

Modern electronic digital logic comes in several microelectronic integrated-circuit forms, details of which are presented elsewhere [3]. Suffice it to say here that these different types of logic differ only in their electronic operating characteristics and requirements, not in the logic functions they perform.

The five basic logic functions are presented in Figure 23.9, along with their common symbols and "truth tables." The actual hardware electronic device used to perform a particular basic logic function is called a *gate*. The symbols in Figure 23.9 are often referred to as the *basic positive logic gate symbols*. Of these logic functions, the AND and OR gates have been considered above using switches and box diagrams. The symbols presented in the figure will, however, be used from now on.

The INVERT or NOT gate does exactly what its title suggests—it negates the input. When a binary 1 is placed on the input, the output is a binary 0. In like manner, when a binary 0 is placed on the input, the output is a binary 1. The inverter is a fundamental part of two more basic gates, the NAND and NOR gates. The term NAND is derived from AND and NOT and functionally refers to an AND gate followed by an inverter (Fig. 23.10). The logical operating characteristics of the NAND and NOR gates can be defined in the same manner as was done for the AND and OR functions previously described; the tabulations presented in Figure 23.9, commonly called *truth tables*, are by far the most commonly used road map to the operation of logic systems.

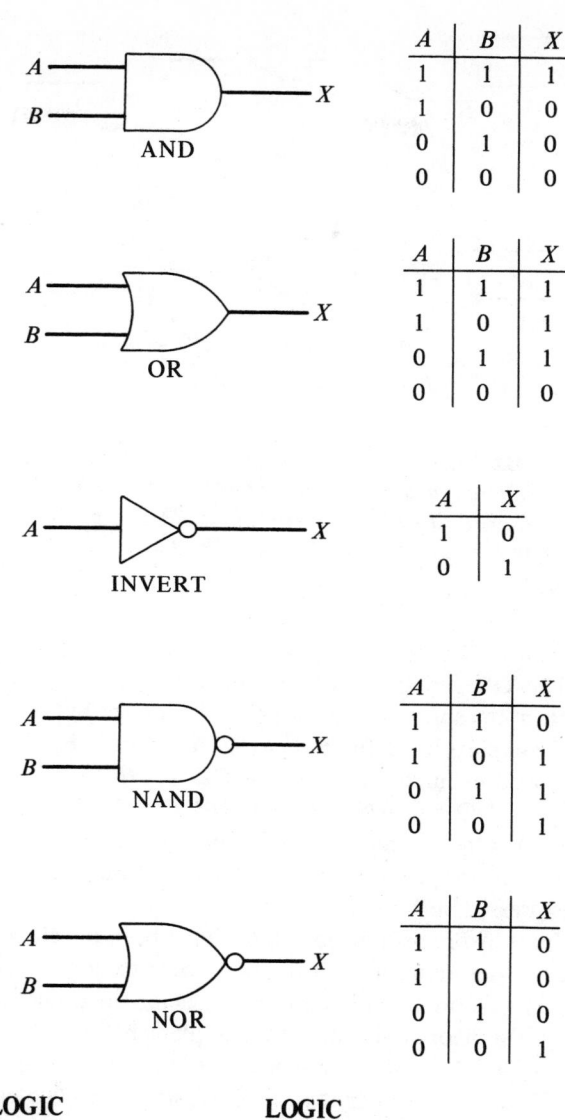

A	B	X
1	1	1
1	0	0
0	1	0
0	0	0

AND

A	B	X
1	1	1
1	0	1
0	1	1
0	0	0

OR

A	X
1	0
0	1

INVERT

A	B	X
1	1	0
1	0	1
0	1	1
0	0	1

NAND

A	B	X
1	1	0
1	0	0
0	1	0
0	0	1

NOR

LOGIC INPUTS   **LOGIC OUTPUTS**

FIGURE 23.9. *Common electronic logic symbols and truth tables. From S. P. Perone and D. O. Jones,* Digital Computers in Scientific Instrumentation, *New York: McGraw-Hill,* 1973, *by permission of the publisher. Copyright © 1973 by McGraw-Hill, Inc.*

Boolean Algebra

Boolean algebra, the algebra of logic, is a symbolic method for studying logical operations. We have previously discussed AND, OR, and NOT or INVERT functions. The Boolean algebra symbols for these functions are given in Table 23.2. The AND

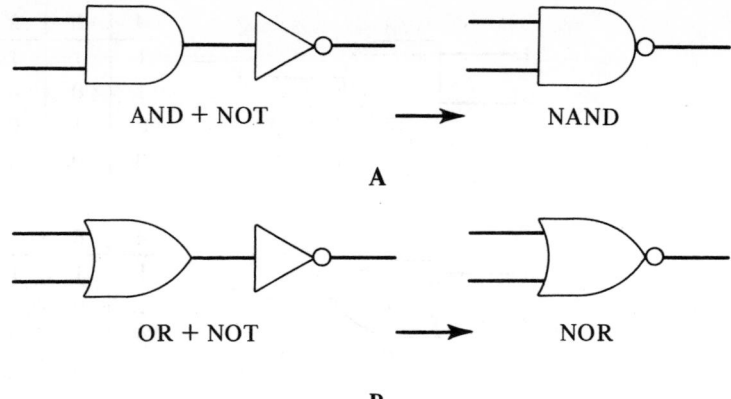

AND + NOT $\longrightarrow$ NAND

A

OR + NOT $\longrightarrow$ NOR

B

FIGURE 23.10. *Logical construction of NAND and NOR gates. From S. P. Perone and D. O. Jones,* Digital Computers in Scientific Instrumentation, *New York: McGraw-Hill, 1973, by permission of the publisher. Copyright © 1973 by McGraw-Hill, Inc.*

function can be represented by a " · " or by placing the variables adjacent to each other. The OR function can be represented by a " +." The NOT or INVERT function can be represented by a prime beside, or bar above, the variable.

A complex logic function can, of course, be written in terms of Boolean algebra. For example, $X = AB + CD + F(\bar{G} + H)$ is read, "$X = 1$ whenever A AND $B = 1$ OR C AND $D = 1$, OR $F = 1$ when $G = 0$ OR $H = 1$." Notice that $G = 0$ is a requirement rather than $G = 1$. This is because of the complement bar above it in the Boolean expression. It implies that G must be equal to 0; $\bar{G}$ is usually expressed verbally as "not G."

Many theorems and postulates have been developed for Boolean algebra and are used for designing and evaluating complex logic systems. Only one theorem, De Morgan's theorem, will be presented here; the others are presented elsewhere [4]. De Morgan's theorem is used to complement complex logic expressions such as NAND and NOR gates. A NAND gate, for instance, is equivalent to an AND gate followed by an inverter—that is, it is an *output-inverted* or *complemented* AND gate.

TABLE 23.2. *Symbols for Boolean Algebra Operations*

Function	Example	Symbol	Example
AND	$X = A$ AND B	·	$X = A \cdot B$ or $X = AB$
OR	$X = A$ OR B	+	$X = A + B$
NOT	NOT A	$^-$ or $'$	$\bar{A}$ or A'

Source: S. P. Perone and D. O. Jones, *Digital Computers in Scientific Instrumentation*, New York: McGraw-Hill, 1973, by permission of the publisher. Copyright © 1973 by McGraw-Hill, Inc.

TABLE 23.3. *Complementing Boolean Expressions*

Expression	Dual	Complement
$1 \cdot A + B$	$0 + AB$	$\overline{AB}$
$\overline{A}B + C$	$\overline{A} + BC$	$A + \overline{BC}$
$A(B + C)$	$(A + B)(A + C)$	$(\overline{A} + \overline{B})(\overline{A} + \overline{C})$

Source: S. P. Perone and D. O. Jones, *Digital Computers in Scientific Instrumentation*, New York: McGraw-Hill, 1973, by permission of the publisher. Copyright © 1973 by McGraw-Hill, Inc.

Thus, a Boolean expression can be written in the following manner for a NAND gate, saying that $X = 1$ when the complement of (A AND B) $= 1$:

$$X = (AB)' \quad \text{or} \quad X = \overline{AB} \qquad (23.1)$$

This is a correct expression, but it makes constructing a complex truth-table cumbersome because it requires first constructing the AND-gate truth-table and then complementing its output column. With the use of De Morgan's theorem, the expression can be placed in a more convenient form. De Morgan's theorem states that

$$(AB)' = \overline{A} + \overline{B} \qquad (23.2)$$

and

$$(A + B)' = \overline{A} \cdot \overline{B} \qquad (23.3)$$

The more general implications of De Morgan's theorem can be considered after defining two new terms, a *dual* and a *literal*. To obtain the dual of a Boolean expression, one must interchange all occurrences of a "+" and a "·" and of a 1 and a 0. A literal is defined as any single *variable* within the dual expression. For example, in the expression

$$\overline{A} \cdot B + C \qquad (23.4)$$

whose dual is

$$\overline{A} + B \cdot C \qquad (23.5)$$

the letters $\overline{A}$, B, and C are all literals. In order to complement a Boolean expression, one must complement all literals in the dual expression. This is illustrated in Table 23.3. The application of these rules for the NAND and NOR functions leads to the statements of De Morgan's theorem presented above.

Boolean algebra is often used to interpret and generate logic diagrams. In Figure 23.11A, there are two inputs A and B; B is inverted by the upper inverter to $\overline{B}$ and A is inverted by the lower inverter to $\overline{A}$. The inputs to the upper NOR gate are then A and B. From the Boolean expression for a NOR gate (Eqn. 23.3), the output of the upper gate is $\overline{A} \cdot B$; similarly, the output of the lower NOR gate is $A \cdot \overline{B}$. These outputs become inputs to the OR gate, resulting in the output expression

$$X = A \cdot \overline{B} + \overline{A} \cdot B \qquad (23.6)$$

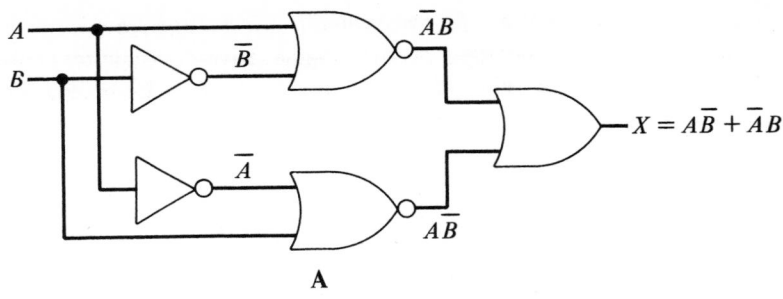

A

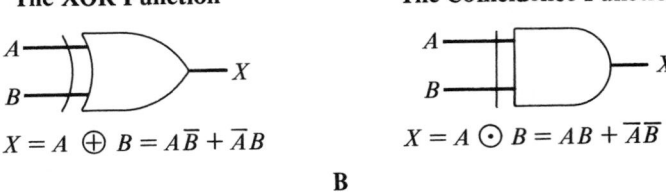

The XOR Function

$$X = A \oplus B = A\bar{B} + \bar{A}B$$

The Coincidence Function

$$X = A \odot B = AB + \bar{A}\bar{B}$$

B

FIGURE 23.11. *Exclusive OR and coincidence gates. From S. P. Perone and D. O. Jones,* Digital Computers in Scientific Instrumentation, *New York: McGraw-Hill, 1973, by permission of the publisher. Copyright © 1973 by McGraw-Hill, Inc.*

This particular function is called the *exclusive* OR function (XOR) and is the basis for binary arithmetic operations. It says that X is true if A or B, but not both, are true. It has a defining symbol "$\oplus$" and is written as

$$X = A \oplus B \equiv A \cdot \bar{B} + \bar{A} \cdot B \qquad (23.7)$$

The XOR function is available in integrated-circuit form and is designated by the symbol presented in Figure 23.11B.

One more function needs to be defined, the *coincidence* function, symbolized by "$\odot$." As the name implies, this function gives a 1 output whenever both inputs are the same, either all 0's or all 1's. Its symbol is also illustrated in Figure 23.11B. The reader should construct its logic diagram using AND, OR, NAND, NOR, and INVERT gates in a manner similar to that just presented for the XOR function.

Flip-Flops

The basic device for counting and storage operations is the *flip-flop* or *bistable multivibrator*. The flip-flop, in its many forms, can be constructed from individual gates, but it is usually purchased as a single unit in integrated-circuit form.

The most basic flip-flop is called a *reset-set* or RS flip-flop. It can be constructed from two cross-coupled NAND gates, as illustrated in Figure 23.12A. It has two inputs, labeled S for set and C for clear, and two outputs, labeled Q and $\bar{Q}$. The Q output goes to a binary 1 and remains there when the S input momentarily goes from 1 to 0. In like manner, the $\bar{Q}$ output goes to a binary 1 and remains there when the C input momentarily goes from 1 to 0. Whenever Q is a 1, $\bar{Q}$ is a 0; that is, they are always complementary. As a result, the C input will also clear the Q

output to 0.   The RS flip-flop will remain in whatever state it has been set or cleared to until its states are changed by applying negative-going pulses (pulses dropping from 1 to 0) to one or the other of the inputs.   It is thus a bistable device with two stable states that can be used for binary data storage.

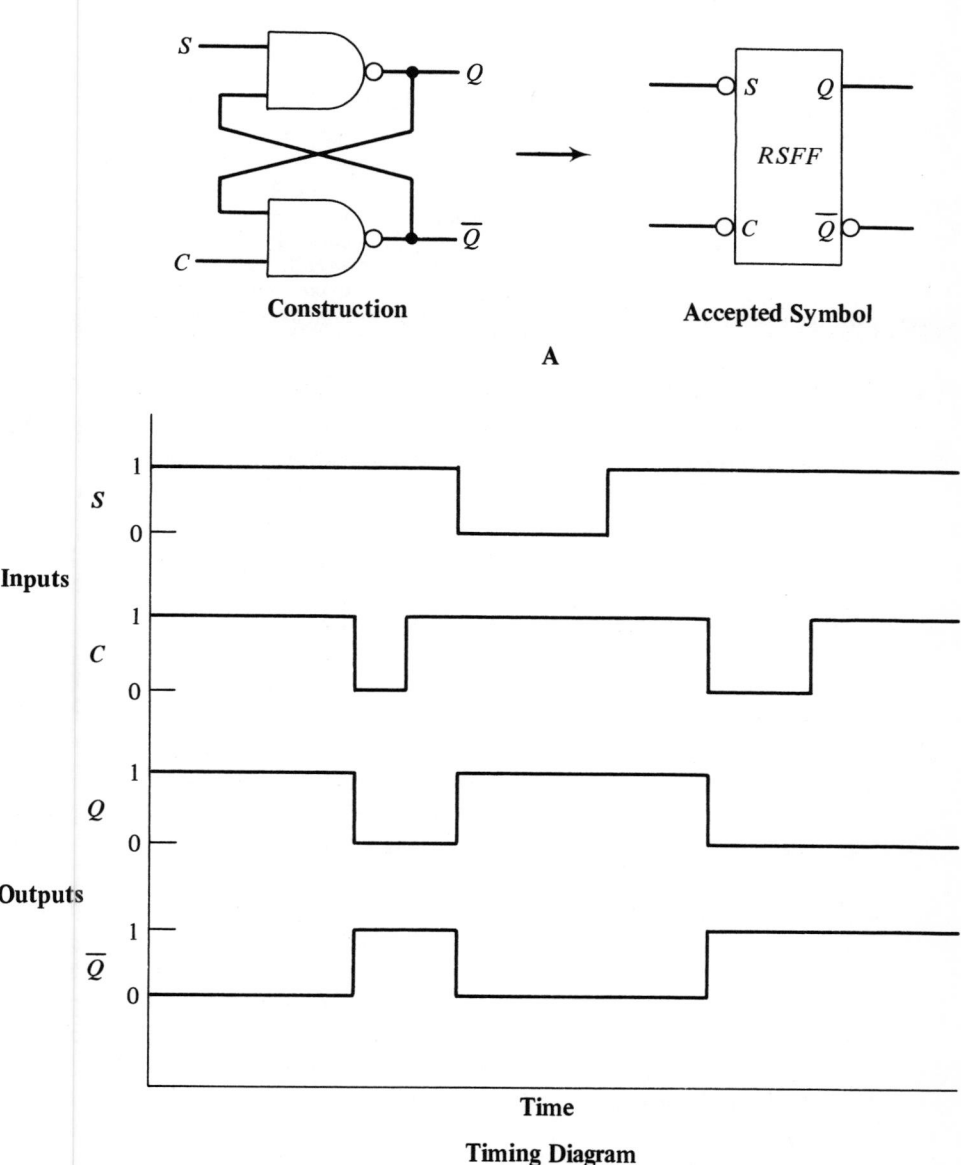

Construction

Accepted Symbol

A

Time

Timing Diagram

B

FIGURE 23.12.   *The Reset-Set* (*RS*) *flip-flop.   From S. P. Perone and D. O. Jones,* Digital Computers in Scientific Instrumentation, *New York: McGraw-Hill,* 1973, *by permission of the publisher.   Copyright © 1973 by McGraw-Hill, Inc.*

TABLE 23.4. *RS Flip-Flop Truth Table*

Case	Inputs S	C	t_n Q	t_{n+1} Q
1	1	0	X	0
2	0	1	X	1
3	1	1	X	NC
4	0	0	X	U

Source: S. P. Perone and D. O. Jones, *Digital Computers in Scientific Instrumentation*, New York: McGraw-Hill, 1973, by permission of the publisher. Copyright © 1973 by McGraw-Hill, Inc. Note: NC means the output is unchanged from its previous state; U means the output is undefined and may go to either state. X means that the inputs at t_n can be in any state.

A truth table for the operation of the RS flip-flop is presented in Table 23.4. This is a somewhat different kind of table than before, in that it has time as a variable: t_n is the time before the specified input conditions have been imposed, and t_{n+1} is the time after they have been imposed. Since Q and $\bar{Q}$ always complement each other, only Q is given in the table. NC means that the output is unchanged from its previous state. U means that the output is undefined and may go to either state. X means that the inputs at t_n can be in any state.

The RS flip-flop is commonly used for control and storage operations in cases where two input signals occur. One signal is used to set its output and allow storage of a binary 1; the other input is used to clear its output and store a binary 0. Notice in Table 23.4 that when $S = C = 0$, the output is undefined. When using the RS flip-flop as a storage element with two data inputs that always complement each other, this condition offers no hindrance to its use. However, for other operations, such as counting, where only one data input signal is provided, the RS flip-flop cannot be used directly.

A timing chart for the RS flip-flop is presented in Figure 23.12B. Notice that the Q output is initially set at 1 and remains so until the C input goes to a binary 0. Q then changes to 0 and remains there until it is again set to 1 by the S input. $\bar{Q}$ is then cleared back to 0. Notice that the $\bar{Q}$ output always complements the Q output state. Timing charts are useful for defining the dynamic operation of logic devices. Often they are used in place of, as well as with, truth tables.

A more versatile flip-flop than the RS type is called a *clocked flip-flop* (Fig. 23.13), which can be used for counting operations. The clocked flip-flop has direct set S_D and direct clear C_D inputs that operate in the same manner as the S and C inputs of the RS flip-flop. (This is commonly called *asynchronous* operation, since no timing requirements are made.) For asynchronous operation, the same truth table as presented in Table 23.4 can be used, by substituting S_D and C_D for S and C. The clocked flip-flop has, however, another mode of operation called the *synchronous* mode. In the synchronous mode, information is entered into the flip-flop through

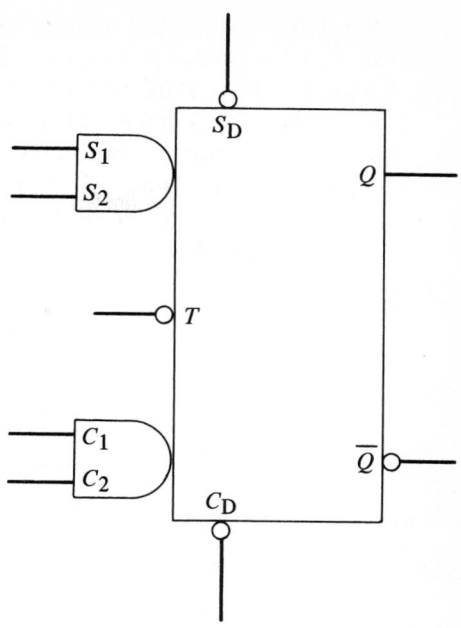

FIGURE 23.13. *The clocked flip-flop. From S. P. Perone and D. O. Jones, Digital Computers in Scientific Instrumentation, New York: McGraw-Hill, 1973, by permission of the publisher. Copyright © 1973 by McGraw-Hill, Inc.*

the AND-gated S and C inputs (S_1, S_2 and C_1, C_2). The flip-flop does not change state, however, until a transition occurs at the *clock* or T *input*. The truth table for the synchronous mode of operation is presented in Table 23.5. Again X indicates that an input can be in either logical state. In the truth table, t_n refers to the input conditions prior to a timing pulse, and t_{n+1} refers to the time after a timing pulse has been applied to the T input. Notice, however, that there is still an undefined state. It occurs when all gated synchronous inputs are 1. As a result, the clocked

TABLE 23.5. *Clocked Flip-Flop Truth Table*

Case	t_n				t_{n+1}
	S_1	S_2	C_1	C_2	Q
1	0	X	0	X	NC
2	X	0	X	0	NC
3	X	0	0	X	NC
4	0	X	X	0	NC
5	0	X	1	1	0
6	X	0	1	1	0
7	1	1	0	X	1
8	1	1	X	0	1
9	1	1	1	1	U

Source: S. P. Perone and D. O. Jones, *Digital Computers in Scientific Instrumentation*, New York: McGraw-Hill, 1973, by permission of the publisher. Copyright © 1973 by McGraw-Hill, Inc.

flip-flop still cannot be used for counting in this mode. If, however, S_1 is connected to $\bar{Q}$, C_2 is connected to Q, and S_2 and C_1 are connected to a binary 1, as shown in Figure 23.14A, a different condition exists. Since either Q or $\bar{Q}$ must always equal 0 and since Q is connected to C_2 and $\bar{Q}$ is connected to S_1, a condition where all gated inputs equal 1 can never be generated. As a result, there will never be an undefined output state. If a pulse train is applied to the T input, the flip-flop will change state on each negative-going pulse. This is called *JK operation*; a truth table is presented in Table 23.6. Since the S_1 and C_2 inputs are connected to the outputs,

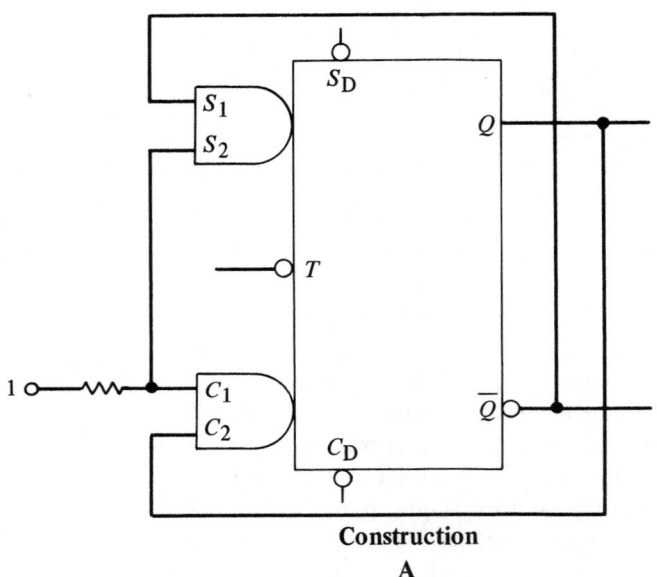

Construction

A

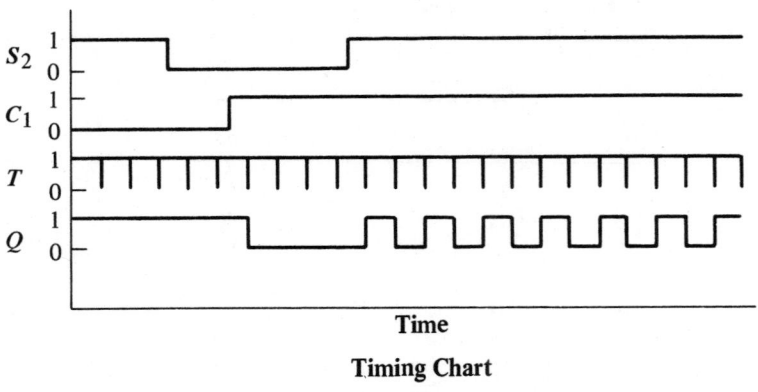

Time

Timing Chart

B

FIGURE 23.14. *JK operation of a clocked flip-flop. From S. P. Perone and D. O. Jones,* Digital Computers in Scientific Instrumentation, *New York: McGraw-Hill, 1973, by permission of the publisher. Copyright © 1973 by McGraw-Hill, Inc.*

TABLE 23.6.   *JK Flip-Flop Truth Table*

t_n		t_{n+1}
S_2	C_1	Q
0	0	NC
1	0	1
0	1	0
1	1	$\bar{Q}_n$ (complements)

they are not listed in the table.   The timing chart is shown in Figure 23.14B; notice that when S_2 and C_1 are 1, the Q output changes from 0 to 1 on every other input pulse, dividing the frequency in half.   This flip-flop will serve for counting functions.

Normally, one would not have to connect a clocked flip-flop into the JK mode since many integrated-circuit JK flip-flops are available (see Fig. 23.15).   Notice that the gated S and C inputs are renamed J and K.   The connections from J and K to $\bar{Q}$ and Q are made internally and usually do not appear on the diagram.

In addition to the RS, clocked, and JK flip-flops, there are others developed for many varied applications of input gating, including capacitor coupling for AC-only operation.

Each of the above types of flip-flops come in the *master-slave* configuration,

FIGURE 23.15.   *The JK flip-flop.   From S. P. Perone and D. O. Jones*, Digital Computers in Scientific Instrumentation, *New York: McGraw-Hill, 1973, by permission of the publisher.   Copyright © 1973 by McGraw-Hill, Inc.*

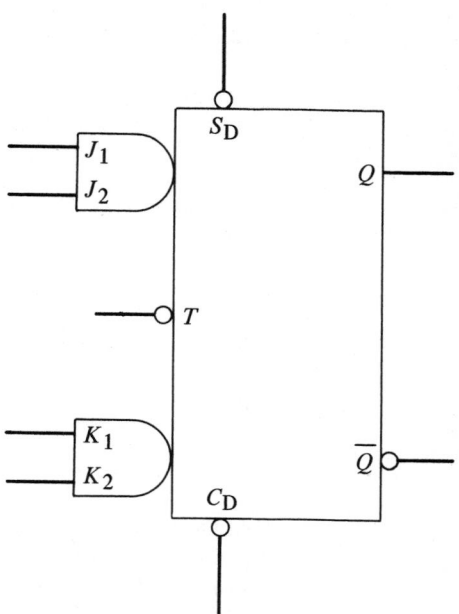

developed to overcome the timing requirements of the flip-flops already discussed. When one actually uses clocked flip-flops such as the JK units described above, one problem is that, because of the feedback required by JK operation (Fig. 23.14A), the output from a given clock pulse and set of input parameters can change the *input* information during the life of the clock pulse, thus undoing the intended result. Very critical timing requirements are often needed to ensure that the flip-flop does not settle in the wrong state. This involves very careful synchronization of clock pulses and input information, and selecting the proper clock-pulse duty cycle.

A master-slave flip-flop is actually two flip-flops in one, with a master flip-flop that feeds data to a slave flip-flop. A JK master-slave flip-flop and clock-input waveform are presented in Figure 23.16. In this figure, the various internal gates and connections are presented for the sake of illustration. In actual practice, the symbols for master-slave flip-flops are not distinguished from those already presented; almost all clocked flip-flops available in integrated-circuit form are of the master-

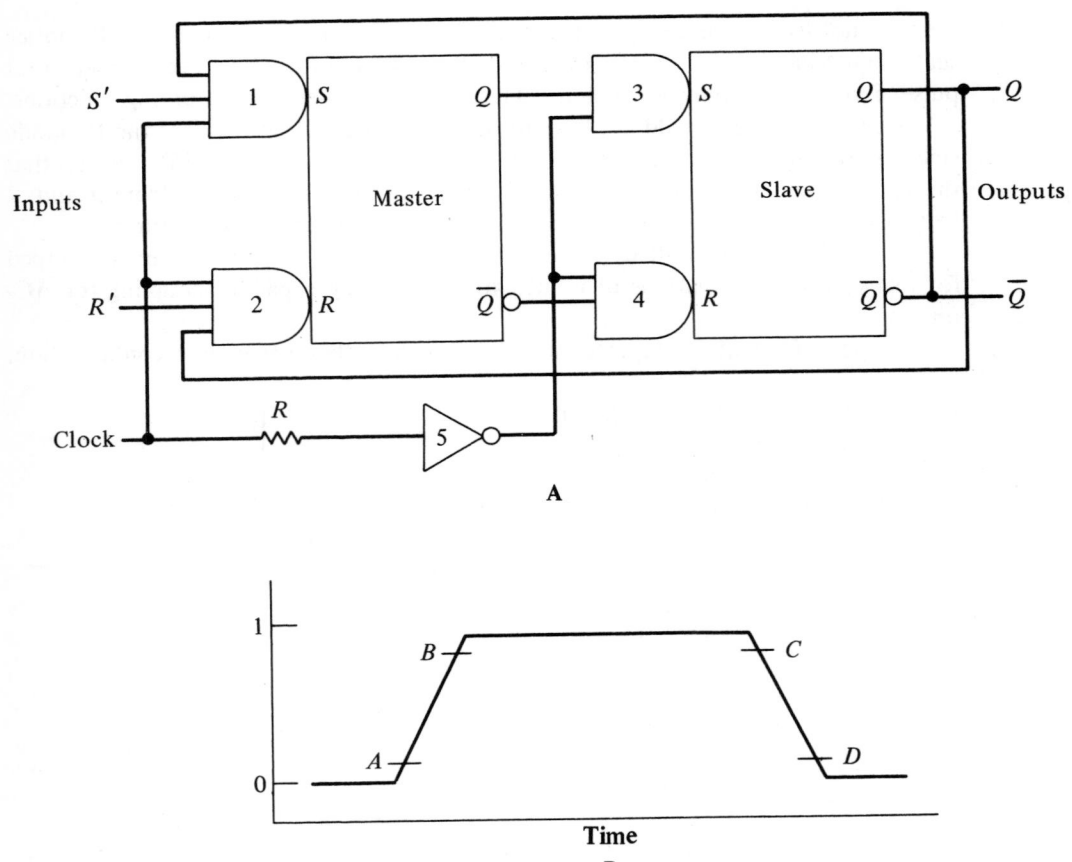

FIGURE 23.16. *The JK master-slave flip-flop. From S. P. Perone and D. O. Jones*, Digital Computers in Scientific Instrumentation, *New York: McGraw-Hill, 1973, by permission of the publisher. Copyright © 1973 by McGraw-Hill, Inc.*

slave type. All the counter and register circuits presented in the pages that follow were designed with master-slave flip-flops, so that when we say RS, clock, and JR, we mean an RS master-slave flip-flop, a clocked master-slave flip-flop, and so on.

Referring to Figure 23.16A, notice that both the master and the slave are gated RS flip-flops. The clock-pulse waveform presented in Figure 23.16B has four points on it, labeled A, B, C, and D. The master-slave JK flip-flop operates as follows: As the clock pulse goes positive from 0 to 1 past point A, the slave input gates 3 and 4 become disabled, isolating the slave from the master. The state of the master prior to A is stored on the slave outputs. As the clock pulse passes point B, input gates 1 and 2 of the master are enabled, allowing data to be transferred in through the S and R inputs. As the clock passes C, gates 1 and 2 are disabled, isolating S' and R' from the master. As the clock pulse falls past D, inverter 5 enables gates 3 and 4, allowing data transfer from the master to the slave. Notice that with master-slave operation, the outputs of the slave do not change until the clock pulse is completed, so that changes in the slave outputs cannot reach the master inputs during a clock pulse. Master-slave flip-flop configurations thus have much less critical timing requirements and much better immunity from noise.

Data-Storage Latches

One simple data-storage device is called a data *latch*, often used to temporarily store binary information. A data latch can be built either with RS or with synchronous flip-flops; the one shown in Figure 23.17A is constructed from RS flip-flops. When the timing-pulse (TP) input is high (a binary 1), the outputs of all the input OR gates are high, and no information from the data inputs D_0 and D_1 can be transferred to the latch. However, when the TP input is a binary 0, the data inputs can transfer information to the flip-flops. For example, if a binary 1 is presented at D_0, the S input of FFA will be a binary 0, which will set Q to a binary 1. (Notice that the C input will be a binary 1.) As a result, when TP is low, the Q outputs will follow the D inputs, whereas when TP is high, the Q outputs will not change regardless of what conditions occur at the D inputs. Data is thus stored in binary form until the TP input again goes momentarily to 0.

A data latch can be built using JK flip-flops, clocked flip-flops, and all varieties of synchronous master-slave flip-flops (see Figure 23.17B). The clocked flip-flop data-latch operates in much the same way as the RS flip-flop data-latch; the TP line must undergo a negative-going 1 to 0 transition each time data is transferred. However, the clocked flip-flop data-latch will operate only in a synchronous manner (that is, each time a negative-going clock pulse is present), in contrast to the RS flip-flop data-latch, in which the outputs will follow the inputs whenever the TP input is 0.

Latches can, of course, be constructed for any number of data bits. Integrated-circuit data latches are commonly available in 4-bit, 8-bit, and larger configurations.

Shift Registers

Shift registers, like data latches, are often used for data storage, but they are much more versatile. They can acquire and output data in both serial and parallel modes and also move data within the register while it is being stored.

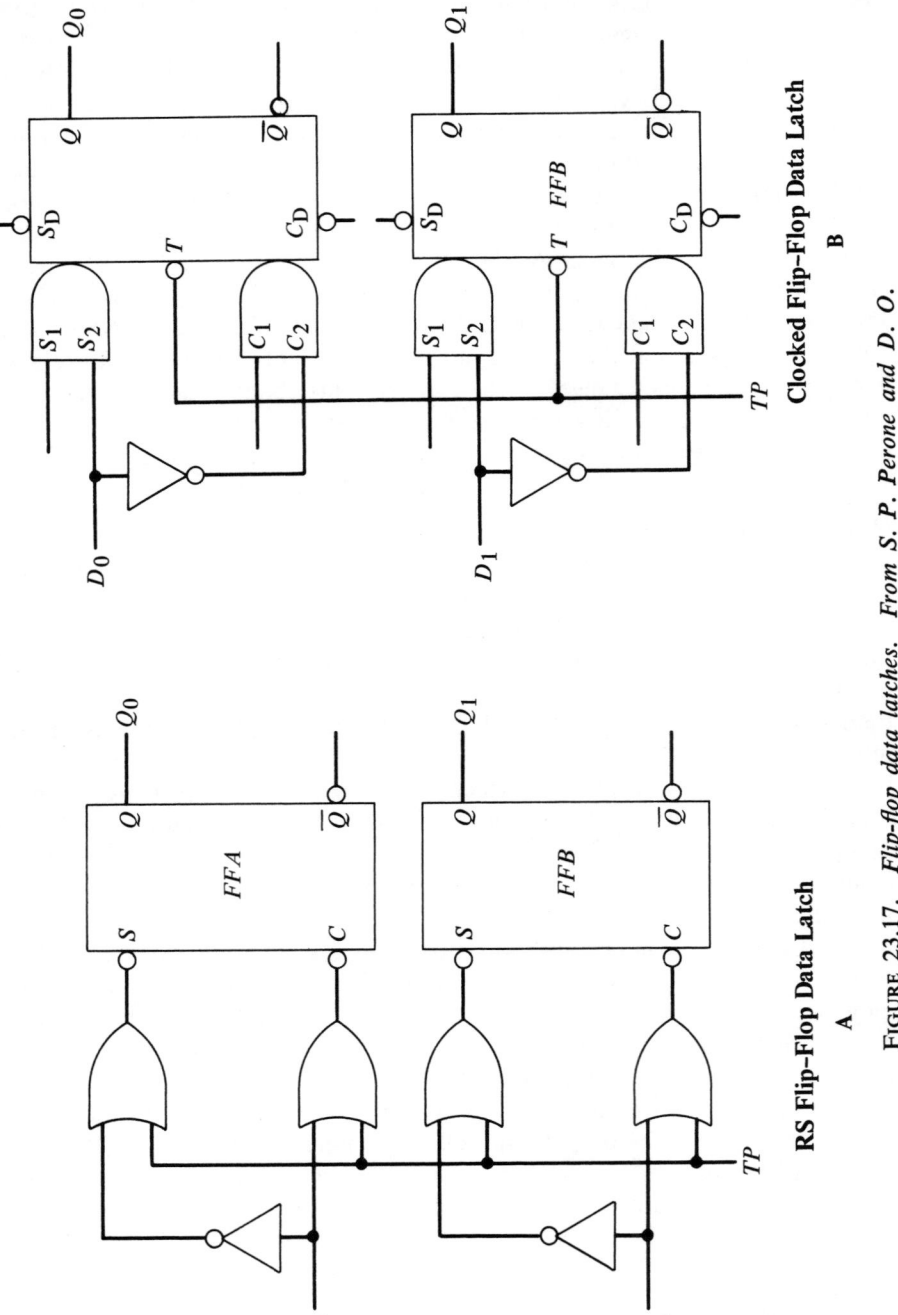

RS Flip–Flop Data Latch

A

Clocked Flip-Flop Data Latch

B

FIGURE 23.17. *Flip-flop data latches. From S. P. Perone and D. O. Jones, Digital Computers in Scientific Instrumentation, New York: McGraw-Hill, 1973, by permission of the publisher. Copyright © 1973 by McGraw-Hill, Inc.*

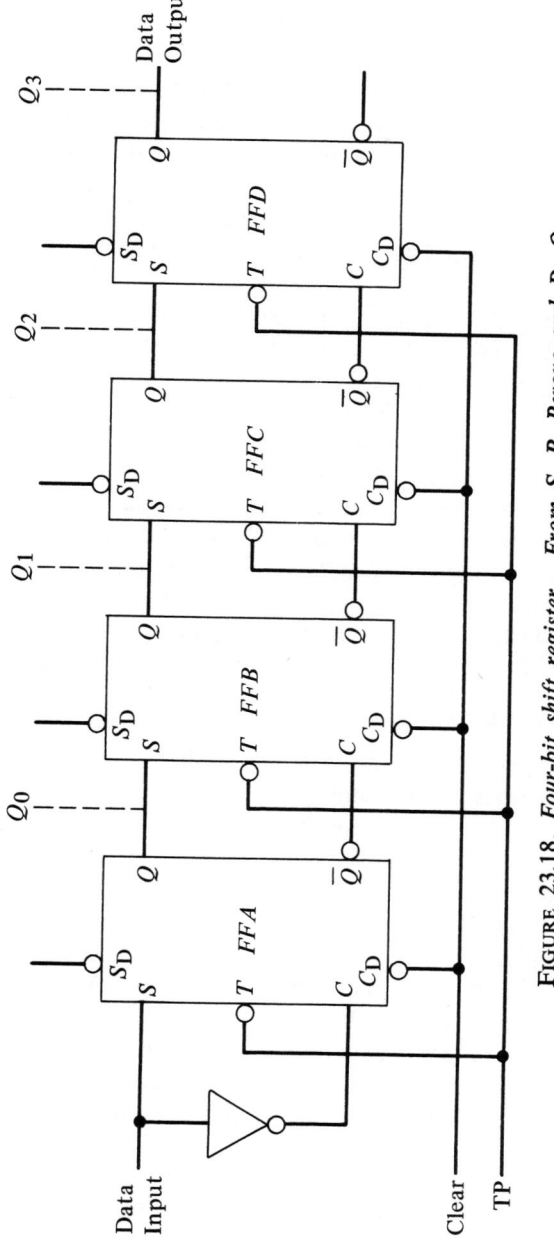

FIGURE 23.18. *Four-bit shift register. From S. P. Perone and D. O. Jones, Digital Computers in Scientific Instrumentation, New York: McGraw-Hill, 1973, by permission of the publisher. Copyright © 1973 by McGraw-Hill, Inc.*

The simplest shift-register is the *serial* I/O type, shown in Figure 23.18 (omitting the dashed-line outputs). The 4-bit register presented is constructed from master-slave clocked flip-flops. (It can also be constructed from JK flip-flops in exactly the same manner; but it cannot be constructed from RS flip-flops.) Notice that a shorthand notation, with the AND gate symbols omitted, is used for the clocked flip-flops.

The operation of the register is quite simple. The C_D inputs are all tied together to provide a common "clear" line, allowing all of the flip-flops to have their Q outputs set to 0 simultaneously. (A common "set" line could also be used.) The first-stage inputs to FFA are connected in exactly the same manner as for the synchronous data-latch previously presented. Successive stages have their outputs and inputs connected together to allow data to be transferred from one to the other in a serial manner. If, after the register is cleared, a binary 1 is presented at the data input and the clock-pulse changes from 1 to 0 on the TP input line, then the binary 1 will appear on the output of FFA. Notice that the binary 1 is now applied to the S input of FFB. The next clock-pulse will transfer the binary 1 to the output of FFB, presenting it at the input of FFC. Thus, data present at the data input will appear at the output of FFD four clock-pulses later. An n-clock-pulse data-delay can be generated by using n flip-flops.

In some applications, digital data is received in serial form, but is needed in parallel for the computer or data-acquisition system. A serial-to-parallel converter can be built by waiting through enough clock pulses to fill the serial I/O shift-register with data, then reading the outputs of each flip-flop in the register simultaneously. This is a *serial-input parallel-output* shift-register and is the configuration in Figure 23.18 with the dashed (parallel) outputs—Q_0 through Q_3—included.

Asynchronous Counters

Often one needs counters in an interface to divide down the clock frequencies and to count such events as the number of data points taken and the number of times data exceed a predetermined threshold. The flip-flop used in modern integrated-circuit counters is the master-slave JK flip-flop. It is used to construct two basic types of counters, asynchronous and synchronous, that will count up or down in a variety of counting schemes.

The simplest counter is the *asynchronous* binary up-counter, in which the Q output of each flip-flop is connected to the T (count) input of the next. The one presented in Figure 23.19 (with its timing chart) counts from 0 to 15 and resets. Initially, all flip-flops in the counter are cleared to 0. When the first negative-going transition or clock-pulse is presented at the count input, the output of FFA (Q_0) changes state from 0 to 1. When the second clock pulse occurs, it again changes the output state of FFA, returning it from 1 to 0. This negative-going output, fed into the count input of FFB, causes FFB (Q_1) to change state from a binary 0 to a binary 1. Two clock pulses later, FFB changes state back to 0, causing FFC to change state to 1; four clock pulses after that, FFC causes FFD to change state to 1, and so on. Any number of flip-flops can be connected in this way to count to larger numbers, the output of each flip-flop corresponding to a power of 2—$Q_0 = 2^0$, $Q_1 = 2^1$, $Q_2 = 2^2$, and so on. The asynchronous counter is often called a *ripple counter*

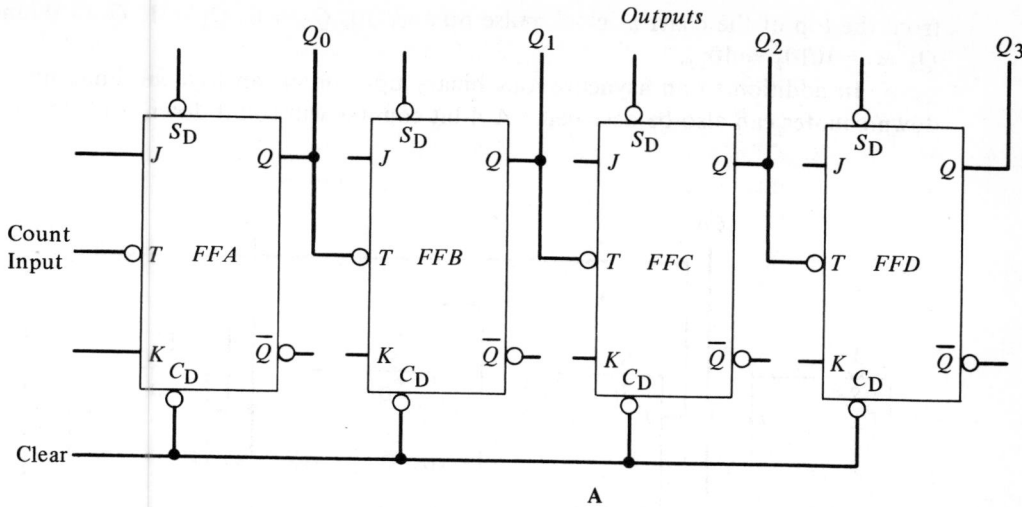

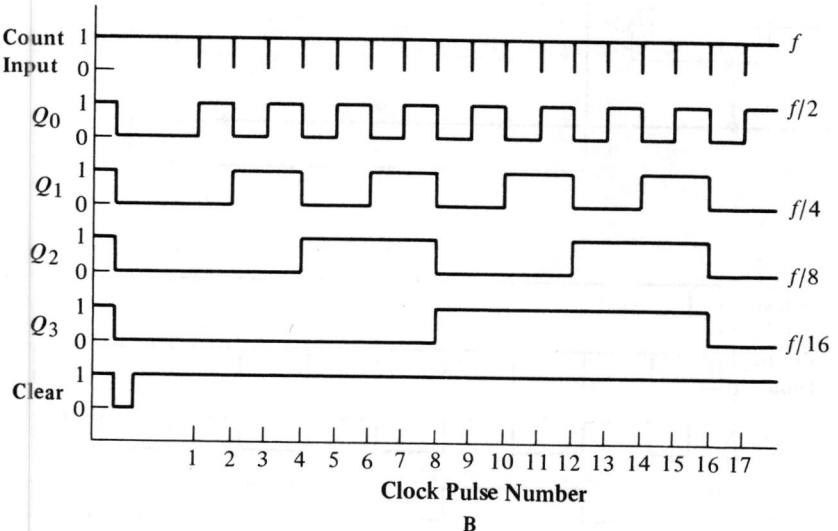

FIGURE 23.19. *Asynchronous binary counter. From S. P. Perone and D. O. Jones,* Digital Computers in Scientific Instrumentation, *New York: McGraw-Hill, 1973, by permission of the publisher. Copyright © 1973 by McGraw-Hill, Inc.*

because of the way counts ripple through or are passed along from flip-flop to flip-flop. From the timing chart, one can see that binary frequency division occurs, with $Q_0 = f/2$, $Q_1 = f/4$, $Q_3 = f/16$. This is then a convenient way to divide down clock frequencies in binary orders of magnitude. Notice also that the binary number output of the counter can be read from the timing chart after any given number of clock pulses has occurred. Consider the case after 10 clock-pulses. Reading down from the top of the chart at clock pulse number 10, $Q_0 = 0$, $Q_1 = 1$, $Q_2 = 0$, and $Q_3 = 1$; $1010_2 = 10_{10}$.

In addition to an asynchronous binary up-counter, an asynchronous binary down-counter can also be designed. A 4-bit counter will count down from 15 to 0.

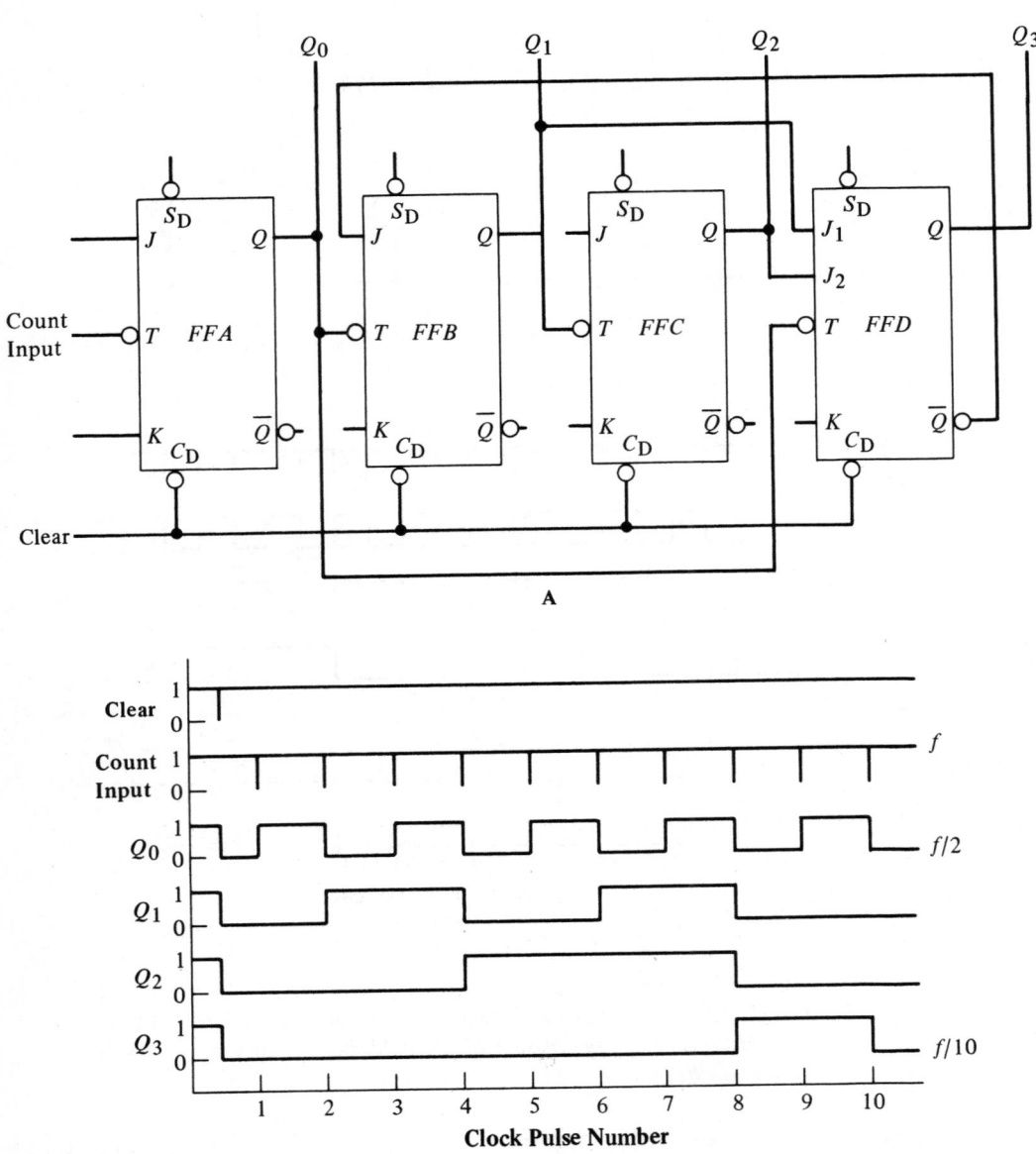

FIGURE 23.20. *Asynchronous decade counter. From S. P. Perone and D. O. Jones,* Digital Computers in Scientific Instrumentation, *New York: McGraw-Hill,* 1973, *by permission of the publisher. Copyright © 1973 by McGraw-Hill, Inc.*

This is accomplished by disconnecting each T input in the up-counter from the corresponding Q output and connecting it to the corresponding $\bar{Q}$ output, and setting all the flip-flops in the counter to 1.

Since we are accustomed to thinking in terms of the decimal (base 10) number system, decade counters are often used in interface systems. They not only count in powers of 10 but can be used to divide clock frequencies in decade rather than binary steps. The *decade counter* presented in Figure 23.20, along with its timing chart, follows the count sequence presented in Table 23.7. The BCD (*Binary Coded Decimal*) number system is a binary representation of the decimal number system.

Notice that the timing chart is the same as the binary up-counter timing-chart in Figure 23.19B up through clock-pulse number 8. From there on, however, it differs. The chief requirement for the operation of the decade counter is that it must reset to 0 after a count of 9_{10} or 1001_2. This requires some additional connections over those needed for the binary counter. Notice in Figure 23.20 that the $\bar{Q}$ output of FFD is connected to the J input of FFB. This allows FFB to change state only when the $\bar{Q}$ output of FFD $= 1$. This occurs for counts 0 to 7. However, for counts 8, 9, and above, FFB is disabled. Notice also that FFD has two J inputs, J_1 and J_2. They allow FFD to change state from 0 to 1 (Q output) only when $Q_1 = 1$, $Q_2 = 1$, and Q_0 goes from 1 to 0. These conditions are only present at a count of 7 and allow the count of 8 to occur. The count transition from 9 to 0 (clock-pulse number 10 in Fig. 23.20B) occurs in the following way: For a count of 9, FFB is disabled because of the connection from $\bar{Q}$ of FFD to its J input. It cannot change from the $Q_1 = 0$ state it is in. Inputs J_1 and J_2 of FFD are also 0. Any 1-to-0 timing signal will thus set Q_3 back to 0. This can be verified by reviewing the JK flip-flop truth-table presented in Table 23.6. Clock-pulse 10 toggles Q_0 of FFA from 1 to 0. Q_0 is connected to the T input of *FFD*, causing its Q output also to go from 1 to 0. The counter thus resets to 0 on clock-pulse 10.

Synchronous Counters

Unlike asynchronous counters, in which the output change of one flip-flop is applied to the clock input and thus changes the state of a succeeding flip-flop, *synchronous-counter* flip-flop outputs set up the J and K inputs of succeeding flip-flops so that a common clock-signal can cause the proper count sequence to occur.

A synchronous binary up-counter is illustrated in Figure 23.21A. Compare this counter with the asynchronous binary up-counter in Figure 23.19. Notice that the synchronous counter requires external gating whereas the asynchronous counter does not; this is because the count sequence is generated by the external gates which set up the J and K inputs of each flip-flop. The timing chart in Figure 23.19B for the asynchronous binary counter can also be used for the synchronous counter.

The operation of the synchronous binary counter is quite simple. If one starts with all flip-flops set to 0, the first pulse applied to the count input will change the state only of FFA. This is because the J and K inputs of all other flip-flops are at a logical 0, which disables the count input to those flip-flops. On each succeeding clock-pulse, FFA will change state. When the second clock-pulse is applied to the clock input, FFB changes state, with the Q output going to a logical 1. This occurs because its J and K inputs, which are connected to the Q output of FFA, were at a logical 1 after the first clock-pulse. Notice now that the Q output of FFA is at a logical 0, that of FFB is at a logical 1, and those of FFC and FFD are both at a logical 0. On the third clock-pulse, FFA changes state. It is now, along with FFB, at a logical 1. Since the outputs of FFA and FFB are connected to the J and K inputs of FFC through AND gate G_1, FFC now has both inputs at a logical 1. This means that the next clock-pulse will change the state of FFC. And, in fact, on the fourth clock-pulse FFA changes from 1 to 0, FFB changes from 1 to 0, and FFC changes from 0 to 1, giving a binary count of 4. In a like manner, when FFA, FFB, and FFC are all at a logical 1, FFD will change state. This occurs at a count of 8. The reader should work through the complete count-sequence from 0 to 15 in binary for the synchronous binary up-counter.

A synchronous *decade* up-counter is shown in Figure 23.21B; it should be compared to the asynchronous decade counter in Figure 23.20. (The timing chart in Figure 23.20B applies equally well to both counters.) Notice again that the synchronous counter involves more complex external gating. The operation of the synchronous decade up-counter is the same as for the binary synchronous counter, if one remembers that a flip-flop will only change state when it receives a clock pulse and when either or both of the J and K inputs are a logical 1. The reader should work through the operation of the synchronous decade counter, paying especially careful attention to what occurs between the counts of 9 and 10.

The question arises, why one would use the more complex synchronous counters rather than the simple asynchronous counters? One important reason is that in asynchronous counters the various count sequences must ripple from one flip-flop to the next. This means that an incoming count on the first flip-flop, which will

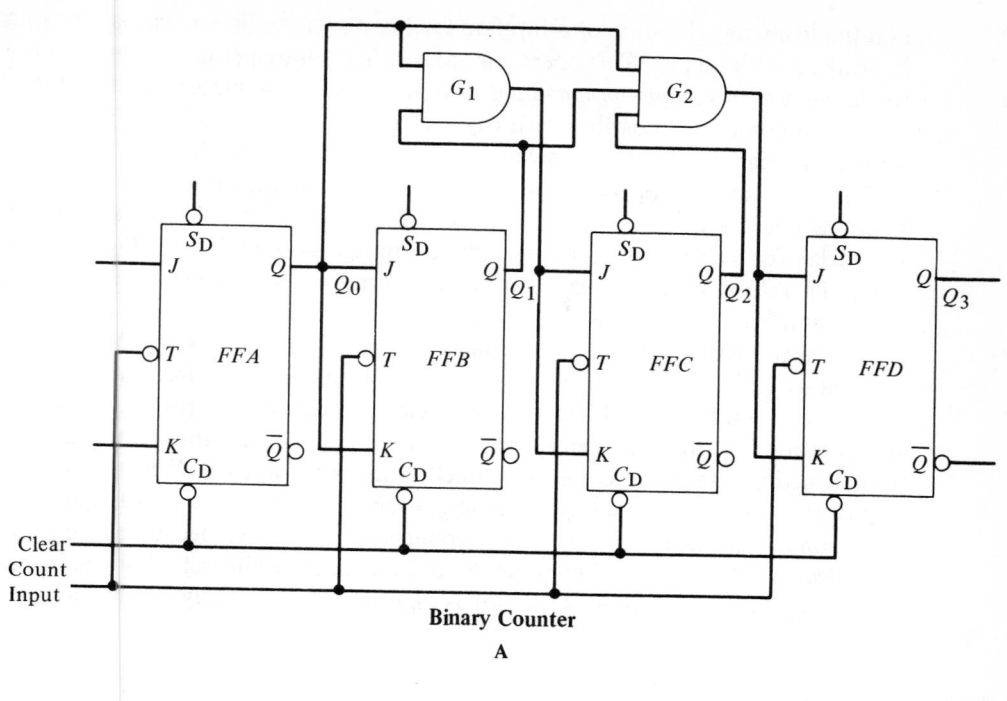

Binary Counter

A

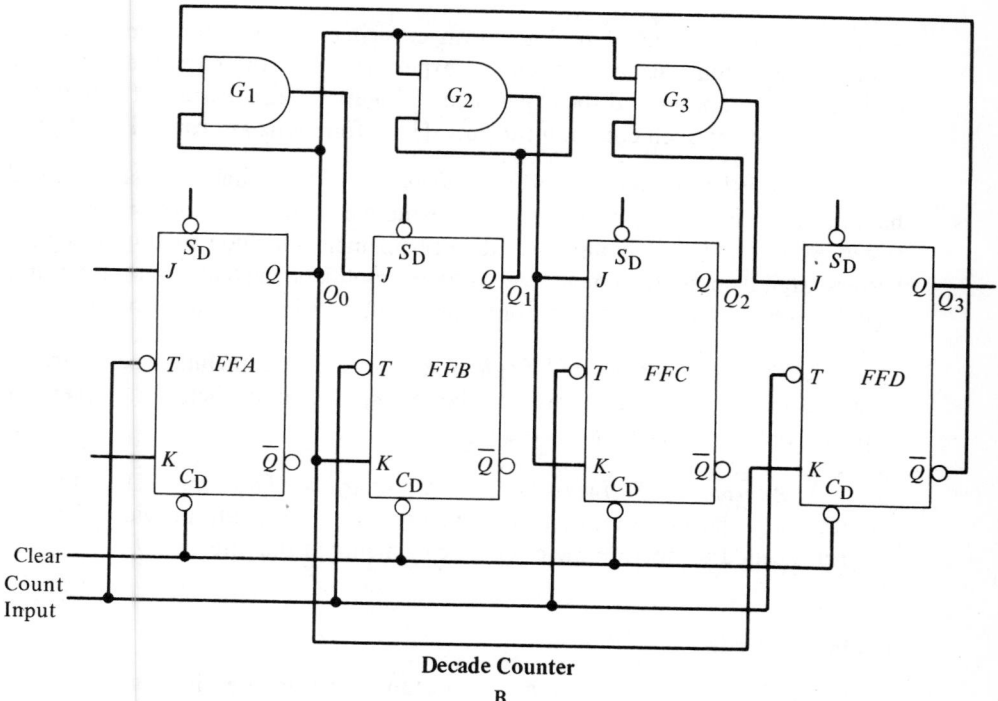

Decade Counter

B

FIGURE 23.21. *Synchronous counters. From S. P. Perone and D. O. Jones*, Digital Computers in Scientific Instrumentation, *New York: McGraw-Hill, 1973, by permission of the publisher. Copyright © 1973 by McGraw-Hill, Inc.*

eventually change the state of a flip-flop farther down the line, must pass through all intermediate flip-flops. This operation takes a fairly long period of time and is equal to the sum of the *signal-propagation delay-times* of each succeeding flip-flop. The maximum count-rate possible with asynchronous counters is determined, then, not only by the signal-propagation delay of an individual flip-flop, but by the total propagation delay of all the flip-flops in sequence. In synchronous counting systems, since the count sequences do not have to ripple down all the flip-flops, the propagation delay for a given counter is usually no more than that for one flip-flop and one gate. Therefore, synchronous counters can operate at much higher speeds. However, as the number of stages increases in synchronous counters, so does the number of inputs to the gates used between counter stages; in fact, in a synchronous binary up-counter of 15 stages, an input gate with 14 inputs is required at the last stage. One way around this problem is to use semisynchronous operation. In this mode of operation, flip-flops are run synchronously in units of perhaps eight or nine stages, and then these units are connected together asynchronously. When semisynchronous operation is used in decade counters, each decade is made up of four internally synchronous individual stages and is connected to another decade asynchronously. This decreases the cost and complexity of the counter while still allowing high-speed operation—though its speed is still not as high as that of a totally synchronous system.

23.3 INTERFACING DEVICES

A computer is considered on-line to an experimental system when there is direct electronic communication between the experiment and the computer and, perhaps, between the computer and the experiment. Figure 23.22 illustrates the various functions required for such communication. These functions are carried out by:

1. *Translation and transmission elements.* These include analog and digital hardware to convert or otherwise handle the electronic information exchanged between experiment and computer. Typical elements include analog-to-digital converters, digital-to-analog converters, voltage amplifiers, current-to-voltage converters, signal conditioners, sample-and-hold amplifiers, multiplexers, and so on.

2. *Timing, Control, and Logic Elements.* These include such hardware as digital clocks, logic gates, flip-flops, counters, one-shots, Schmitt triggers, analog switches, level converters, and so on.

3. *Appropriate Software to Drive the Interface Hardware.* The I/O programs are necessary and important parts of the interface. Software provides the necessary controls needed to operate the electronic elements in the interface.

Timing Devices

Figure 23.23 illustrates the most important experimental interface function, the generation of a stable time base. The *time-base generator*, or *digital clock*, is generally a combination of two elements: (1) a crystal-controlled, stable, fixed-frequency *oscillator* that emits a pulse train of very accurately known frequency, and (2) a *counter* or *scaler* logic section used to divide this frequency and thus generate a variety of output frequencies. The output frequency can be incrementally changed through the use of counters and can be controlled by enabling (starting) or disabling (stopping) the counter system. In subsequent discussions, the clock will be represented by the block diagram in Figure 23.23B, which shows only an enable/disable input and a series of outputs.

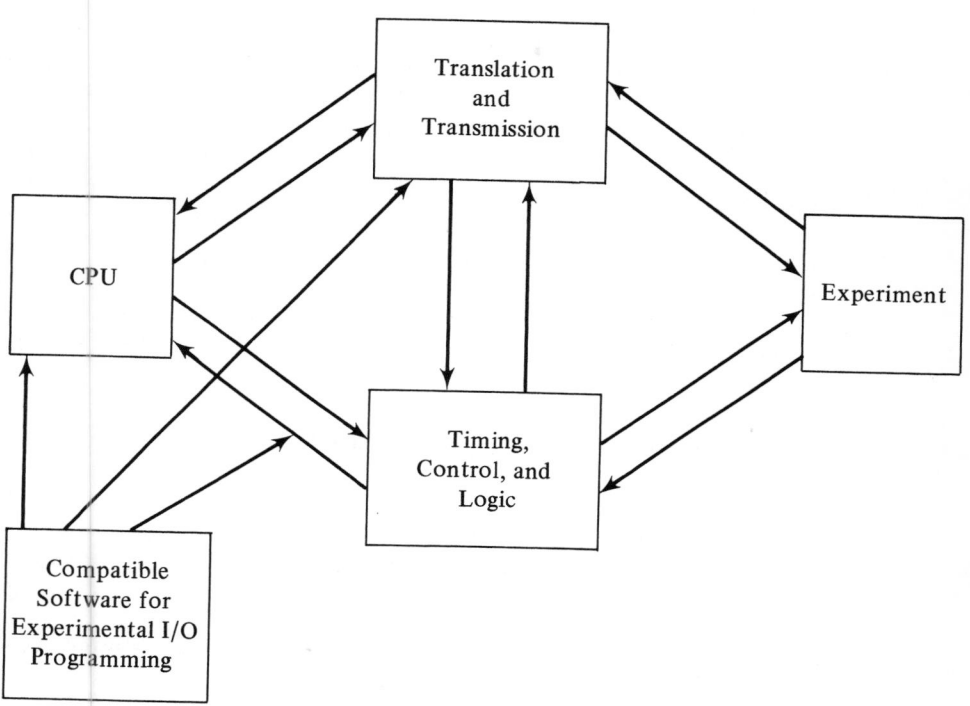

FIGURE 23.22. *On-line computer communication functions. From S. P. Perone and D. O. Jones,* Digital Computers in Scientific Instrumentation, *New York: McGraw-Hill, 1973, by permission of the publisher. Copyright © 1973 by McGraw-Hill, Inc.*

Adjustable time-delays, accurately known and reproducible, are often required in an interface system. The *monostable multivibrator* or *one-shot* is often used for generating these delays. (The diagram in Figure 23.24 is that of a gated one-shot; the series of gates allow logic to be performed at the input of the device.) The one-shot remains in a stable state until a trigger pulse is applied to the input; then the output changes state for a period of time called the *pulse width* (PW), which depends on the value of the resistance-capacitance (*RC*) timing network employed in the circuit. Generally, the one-shot device has a provision for attaching different resistances and capacitances. Delay times can generally be varied over wide ranges, from nanoseconds to many seconds or even minutes. Many integrated-circuit one-shots are commercially available.

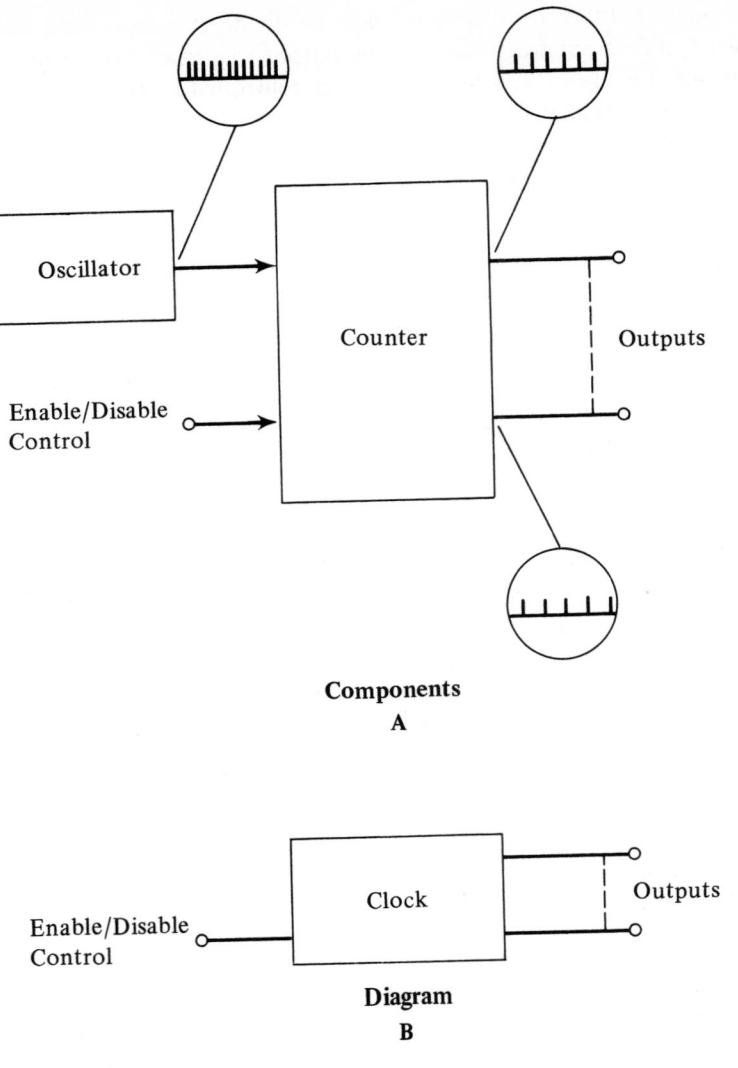

Components
A

Diagram
B

FIGURE 23.23. *Interface time-base generator. From S. P. Perone and D. O. Jones,* Digital Computers in Scientific Instrumentation, *New York: McGraw-Hill,* 1973, *by permission of the publisher. Copyright* © 1973 *by McGraw-Hill, Inc.*

Translation Elements

Digital-to-Analog Conversion. A *digital-to-analog converter* (DAC) is used to change digital numerical information into a continuously variable analog output. DACs are often used as control devices in chemical experiments. For example, in a fast-sweep polarographic experiment, a DAC can be used to provide control voltages and ramp functions for the electrochemical cell. Because the computer can generate numbers in any sequence, nonlinear ramps can be generated, allowing very precise control over the cell.

A basic DAC application is illustrated in Figure 23.25. The DAC takes a

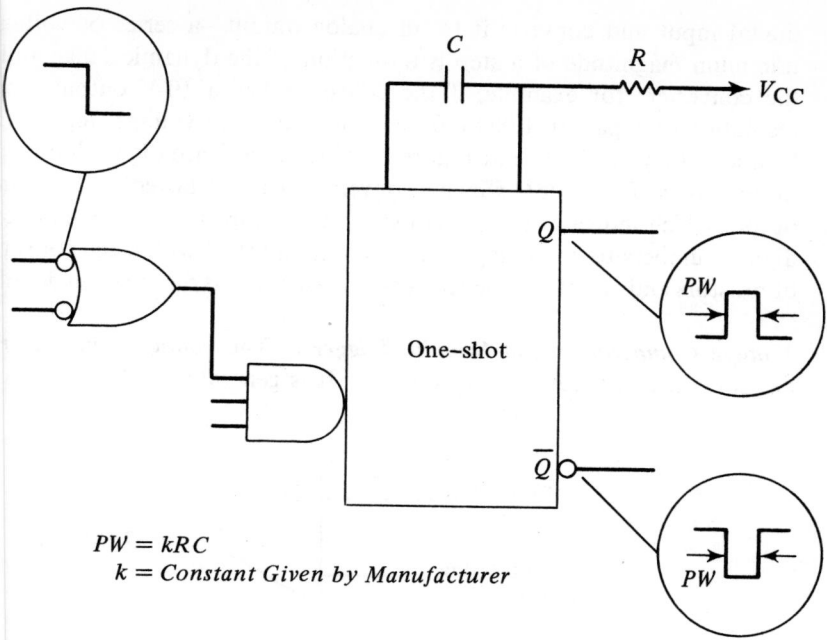

$$PW = kRC$$
$$k = Constant\ Given\ by\ Manufacturer$$

FIGURE 23.24. *Monostable multivibrator or one-shot. From S. P. Perone and D. O. Jones*, Digital Computers in Scientific Instrumentation, *New York: McGraw-Hill*, 1973, *by permission of the publisher. Copyright © 1973 by McGraw-Hill, Inc.*

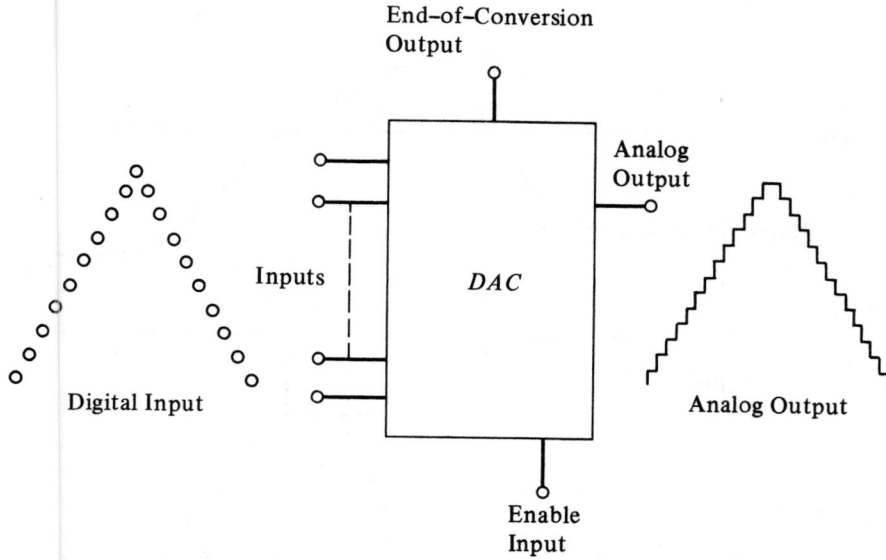

FIGURE 23.25. *Digital-to-analog conversion. From S. P. Perone and D. O. Jones*, Digital Computers in Scientific Instrumentation, *New York: McGraw-Hill*, 1973, *by permission of the publisher. Copyright © 1973 by McGraw-Hill, Inc.*

digital input and converts it to an analog output—a series of voltage steps. The minimum magnitude of a step is a function of the dynamic range and resolution of the converter; for example, if the converter has a 10-V output maximum and a resolution of 1 part in 1,024 (10 bits), the minimum voltage-step on the output will be about 10 mV. Notice in Figure 23.25 that there are digital inputs and an analog output, an *enable* input at which a conversion can be started, and an *end-of-conversion* output which indicates when a conversion is complete. The actual conversion from digital numbers to an analog output is accomplished within the converter by a series of resistors and switches called a *ladder network* and is discussed in detail elsewhere [5].

Voltage Comparators and Schmitt Triggers. The *voltage comparator* is an analog device with two inputs and an output. It is generally used to compare one voltage

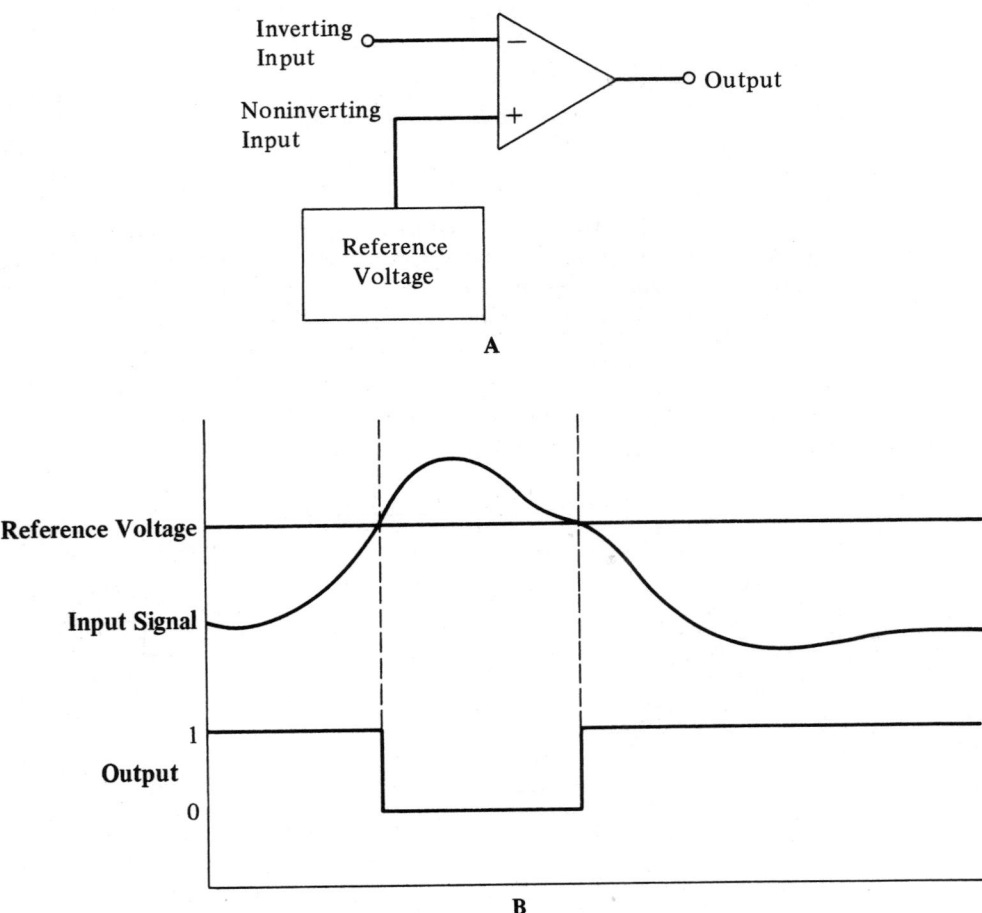

FIGURE 23.26. *Voltage comparator. From S. P. Perone and D. O. Jones*, Digital Computers in Scientific Instrumentation, *New York: McGraw-Hill*, 1973, *by permission of the publisher. Copyright* © 1973 *by McGraw-Hill, Inc.*

with another and to indicate which is larger. A voltage comparator and its resulting waveforms are shown in Figure 23.26. Notice that there are both a reference voltage and an input signal. The comparator compares the input signal with the reference voltage. When the input signal rises above the magnitude of the reference voltage, the comparator output changes state from 1 to 0; when the input signal falls below the reference voltage, the output changes back from 0 to 1.

A device somewhat similar to a comparator is the *Schmitt trigger*; Figure 23.27 shows its input, output, and upper and lower threshold terminals and also its typical waveform. The two reference levels V_{t+} and V_{t-} are the upper and lower thresholds. When the input signal goes above the *upper* threshold, the output changes from 1 to 0. However, when it goes below the upper threshold again, the output signal does not change back until it has gone below the *lower* threshold.

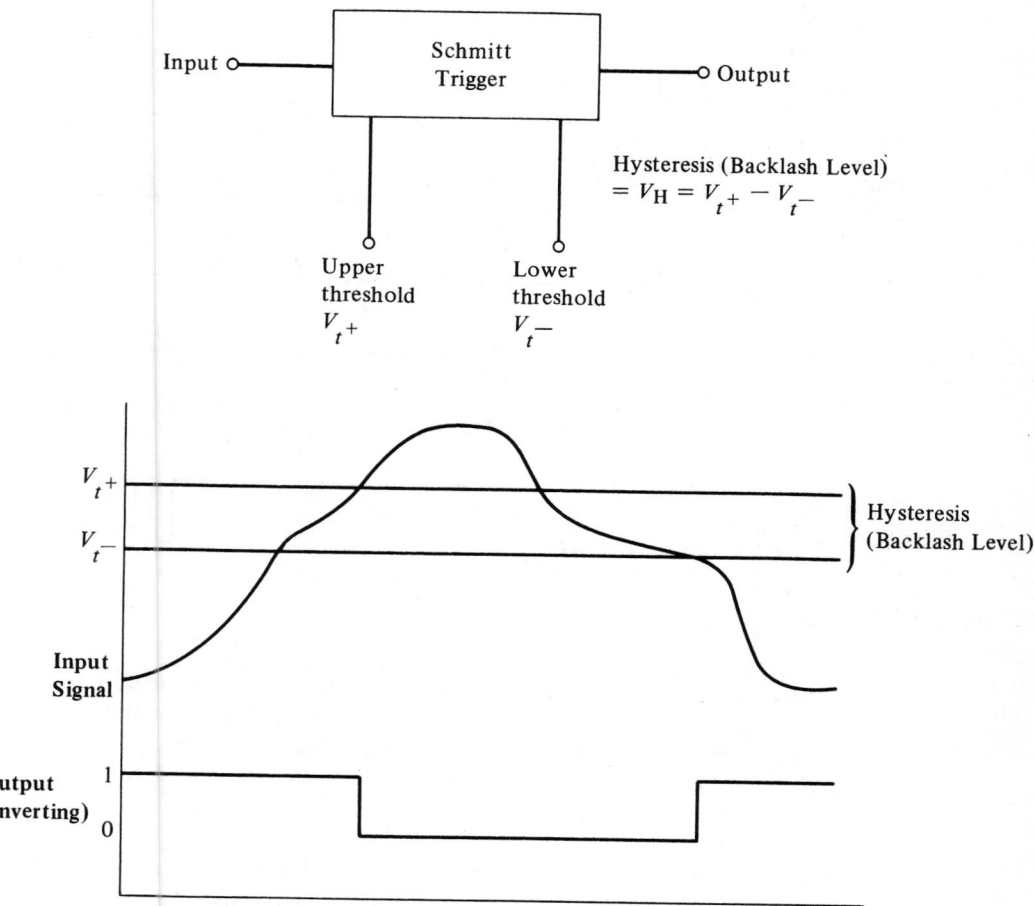

FIGURE 23.27. *Schmitt trigger. From S. P. Perone and D. O. Jones,* Digital Computers in Scientific Instrumentation, *New York: McGraw-Hill, 1973, by permission of the publisher. Copyright © 1973 by McGraw-Hill, Inc.*

The difference between the upper threshold and lower threshold is commonly called the *hysteresis* or *backlash level* of the Schmitt trigger; it provides noise immunity for the device.

In Figure 23.28, both Schmitt trigger and comparator outputs are given for a noisy input signal. Notice that, as the signal oscillates above and below the comparator reference-voltage, its output also oscillates. However, since the magnitude of the noise is less than the hysteresis of the Schmitt trigger, the output of the latter has no noise spikes. The trigger can extract control signals from noisy input signals, provided that the proper hysteresis level is selected. It is often used to convert digital signals of one voltage level to another level.

The lack of hysteresis in the comparator makes it more susceptible to noisy environments; it also makes it a more accurate switch.

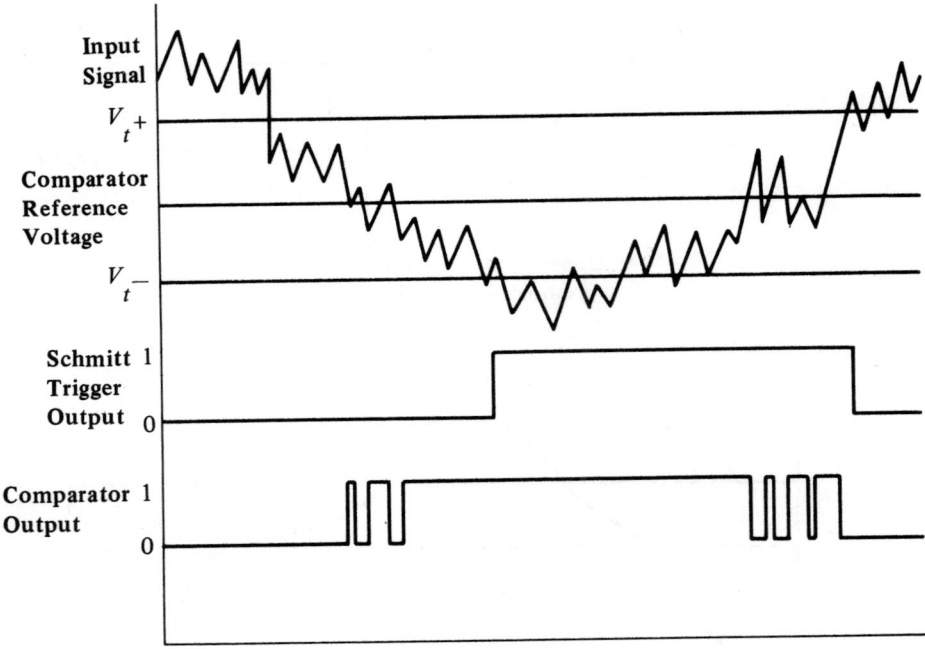

FIGURE 23.28. *Comparison of Schmitt trigger and voltage comparator for noisy signals. Source: S. P. Perone and D. O. Jones,* Digital Computers in Scientific Instrumentation, *New York: McGraw-Hill*, 1973, *by permission of the publisher. Copyright © 1973 by McGraw-Hill, Inc.*

Analog Multiplexers. When one has several signals that must be connected to the input of one ADC, a common device used is the *analog-signal multiplexer* (Fig. 23.29). With it, several input signals can be sequentially switched to one output. Often, the input signals will come from the output of sample-and-hold or track-and-hold amplifiers. Analog-signal multiplexers are a series of electronic switches with digital control inputs to allow a computer or interface to control this operation.

Analog Switches. Analog switches can generally be divided into three categories: mechanical, electromechanical, and electronic. Common toggle, slide, and rotary switches are examples of mechanical types; their contacts are opened or closed manually. Electromechanical switches are usually relays of one sort or another in which an electromagnetic coil is energized to open or close the contacts. The contacts are either dry or coated with mercury; mercury-wetted contacts usually exhibit somewhat better switching characteristics.

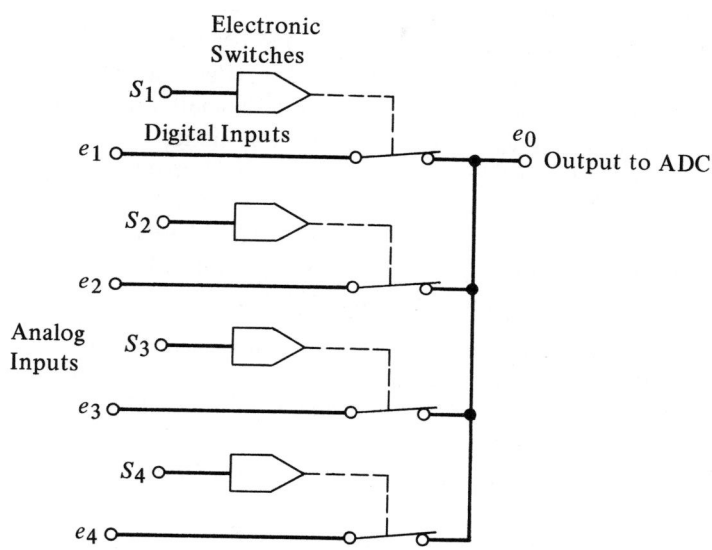

FIGURE 23.29. *Analog multiplexer. From S. P. Perone and D. O. Jones,* Digital Computers in Scientific Instrumentation, *New York: McGraw-Hill, 1973, by permission of the publisher. Copyright © 1973 by McGraw-Hill, Inc.*

Electromechanical analog switches exhibit some very desirable characteristics. They have essentially zero resistance when the contacts are closed and infinite resistance when they are open. They can handle a range of many orders of magnitude of voltage and current of either polarity. They also have, as might be expected, some undesirable characteristics. First, the contacts bounce whenever they are opened or closed. This can result in noise that must be filtered out. Mercury-wetted contacts can lessen bounce noise, but do not eliminate it. Second, electromechanical switches are rather slow in switching; the faster ones take 1 msec or so to open or close.

Electronic analog switches are usually constructed from *junction field-effect transistors* (JFETs) or *metal oxide–silicon field-effect transistors* (MOSFETs). FETs used as switches are usually activated by transistor driving circuits that open or close them. A typical FET analog switch might be closed when a logical 0 is applied. FET switches have advantages over electromechanical switches in one principal area—speed. They are orders of magnitude faster than electromechanical switches, with turn-on or turn-off times of less than 1 μsec. Since they have no contacts, they do not exhibit contact bounce noise, but they can, if not correctly designed into a circuit, generate electronic switching spikes.

Electronic analog switches also have some shortcomings. They have finite on and off resistances. JFETs usually have the smaller on or closed resistance, some types as low as 1 Ω or so. MOSFETs, on the other hand, have the higher off or open resistance, typically of the order of 10^{16} Ω. In other words, FET switches are not ideal switches, but rather electronically variable resistors.

FET switches are restricted to certain ranges of voltage and current, and have polarity restrictions. Common voltage-levels are of the order of 10 V or so, but some specialized units go as high as 100 V. Maximum currents are often no greater than 100 mA but may be greater. FET switches usually do not work well for signal levels less than a few millivolts because of a small inherent voltage drop in the transistors, which may vary with operating conditions.

Generally speaking, one should use electromechanical analog switches for low-level or high-level signals that can be switched in more than 1 msec or so, and electronic analog switches for moderate signal-levels with switching times less than 1 μsec or so. Both electromechanical and electronic types are available that can be driven directly from integrated-circuit digital logic.

Analog-to-Digital Conversion. A typical *analog-to-digital converter* (ADC) is illustrated in Figure 23.30. It consists of an analog input, digital outputs, a start-conversion input, and an end-of-conversion output. The ADC changes an analog or continuous voltage from an experimental system into a series of discrete digital values so that a computer can be presented with digital data in a format that it can handle. The most common output format is a binary digital representation of the analog input. There are many types of ADCs, some fast and some slow—some that require high-level voltage inputs in the range of from one to several volts, and some that require low-level voltage, current, or resistance inputs. In this section, several types of fast converters will be discussed.

1. *Counter Converters.* Probably the simplest ADC is the *counter converter* (Fig. 23.31A). It is usually a fast, high-level converter with a conversion time of less than 1 msec, thus capable of providing more than 1000 data-points per second. Basically, it consists of a comparator, a clock or pulse generator, a counter, and a DAC. When an analog input signal is presented to one input of the comparator and a start-of-conversion signal is presented to the counter, the counter resets to 0 and starts counting up, and presents a digital input to the DAC. The DAC in turn provides a corresponding analog output voltage to the other input of the comparator. When the counter output number reaches a magnitude that provides a voltage to the comparator (through the DAC) equal in magnitude to the analog input signal, the comparator changes state, turning off the clock and stopping the counter. The digital output representation of the analog input is read in parallel from the counter outputs. A status or end-of-conversion signal can be obtained from the output of the comparator as it changes state upon completion of a conversion. The counter converter is simple and inexpensive. The conversion time is proportional to the magnitude of the input voltage. That is, since the counter always starts counting from 0, the larger the analog input voltage, the longer it will take for the counter to count up to the value where the DAC output applied to the comparator is equal to the analog input voltage.

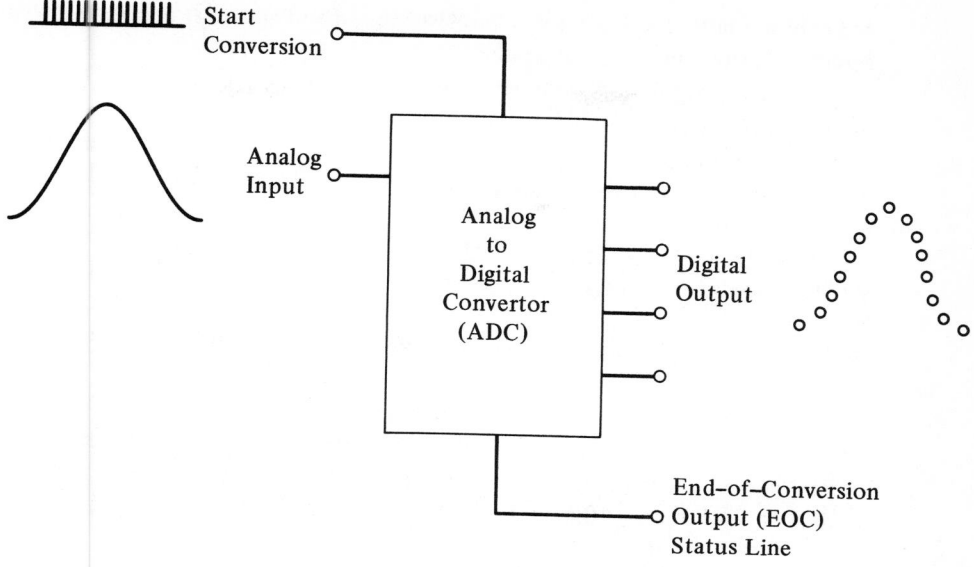

FIGURE 23.30. *Analog-to-digital conversion. From S. P. Perone and D. O. Jones*, Digital Computers in Scientific Instrumentation, *New York: McGraw-Hill*, 1973, *by permission of the publisher. Copyright* © 1973 *by McGraw-Hill, Inc.*

2. Continuous Converters. The *continuous converter* in Figure 23.31B is very similar to the counter converter. The main differences are that the counter used can count both up and down, that the comparator, instead of turning off the clock, controls the counting direction of the counter, and that the counter counts all the time. When the comparator senses that the output of the DAC exceeds the analog input voltage, it reverses the counting direction from up to down; likewise, when the DAC output falls below the analog input voltage, the counting direction is reversed from down to up. The up-down counter tracks the analog input voltage if it is not changing faster than the counter can follow. When a new signal is applied to the analog input, the continuous converter locks onto it and follows it. Digital outputs can be read at intervals from the output of the counter. After it locks on to a signal, the continuous converter is extremely fast.

3. Successive-Approximation Converters. The 4-bit *successive-approximation* ADC shown in Figure 23.32 differs from both the counter and the continuous converters in that, in place of a counter, it has a pattern generator. It consists of a comparator, a DAC, a buffer-register data-latch in which the digital output is stored, the pattern generator, and some control logic. Its operation is most easily understood with reference to Figure 23.33. The analog voltage is approximated by testing one bit at a time, beginning with the most significant (highest power of two) bit and ending with the least significant bit. All the possible number combinations generated by the pattern generator are presented for a 4-bit successive-approximation ADC. Notice that a 4-bit conversion always takes four steps to complete, so that a successive-approximation converter has a fixed conversion time.

Important Features of ADCs. In selecting high-level ADCs, several criteria are important, including:

1. the input-voltage range
2. the output format
3. the resolution of the output
4. the logic voltage-levels of the output
5. the conversion speed
6. the control signals needed
7. the power-supply requirements

Input voltages generally range from 1–10 V full scale. They may be positive, negative, or bipolar.

The most commonly used ADC output format is the binary number system, because it is directly compatible with many digital computers. Other codes, usually binary coded decimal, are sometimes used. In addition, bipolar input-converters such as the ± 1 V or ± 10 V units can have different forms of binary coding to account for the dual polarity.

The resolution and dynamic range of the converter output are determined by the number of data bits available. Common binary converters have 8-, 10-, 12-, or more output bit configurations, giving resolutions of 1 part in 256, 1024, 4096, or greater, respectively. Converters using BCD output configurations often have three or four decimal digits represented, giving resolutions in the range of 10^3–10^4. Higher-resolution converters are available if required.

By far the most common output voltage levels for logic circuits and ADCs are 0 and $+5$ V, the common integrated-circuit levels for diode-transistor (DTL) and transistor-transistor (TTL) logic [3]. Other different logic voltage-levels, including 0 and $+12$ V and 0 and -3 V, are also used. The logic voltage levels should, of course, be compatible with those used in the computer or data system. If they are not, some sort of voltage-level conversion will be necessary.

Conversion time is the time required, after a start signal, for a conversion to be completed. It determines the maximum data-rate of a given converter. High converter data-rates range from 10 kHz to about 10 MHz.

Control signals for fast ADC units usually consist of a start command and an end-of-conversion or status signal. Other control signals are possible. In units with output storage-buffers, controls may be available to load or store in the buffer.

Power-supply requirements, although they may seem trivial, are in fact very important. The presence or absence of an internal reference voltage is a good example of this. The output and stability of the general power supply are also important. ADC units with built-in voltage regulators have much less severe power-supply requirements than those with no internal regulation.

FIGURE 23.31. *Counter and continuous analog-to-digital converters. From S. P. Perone and D. O. Jones,* Digital Computers in Scientific Instrumentation, *New York: McGraw-Hill, 1973, by permission of the publisher. Copyright © 1973 by McGraw-Hill, Inc.*

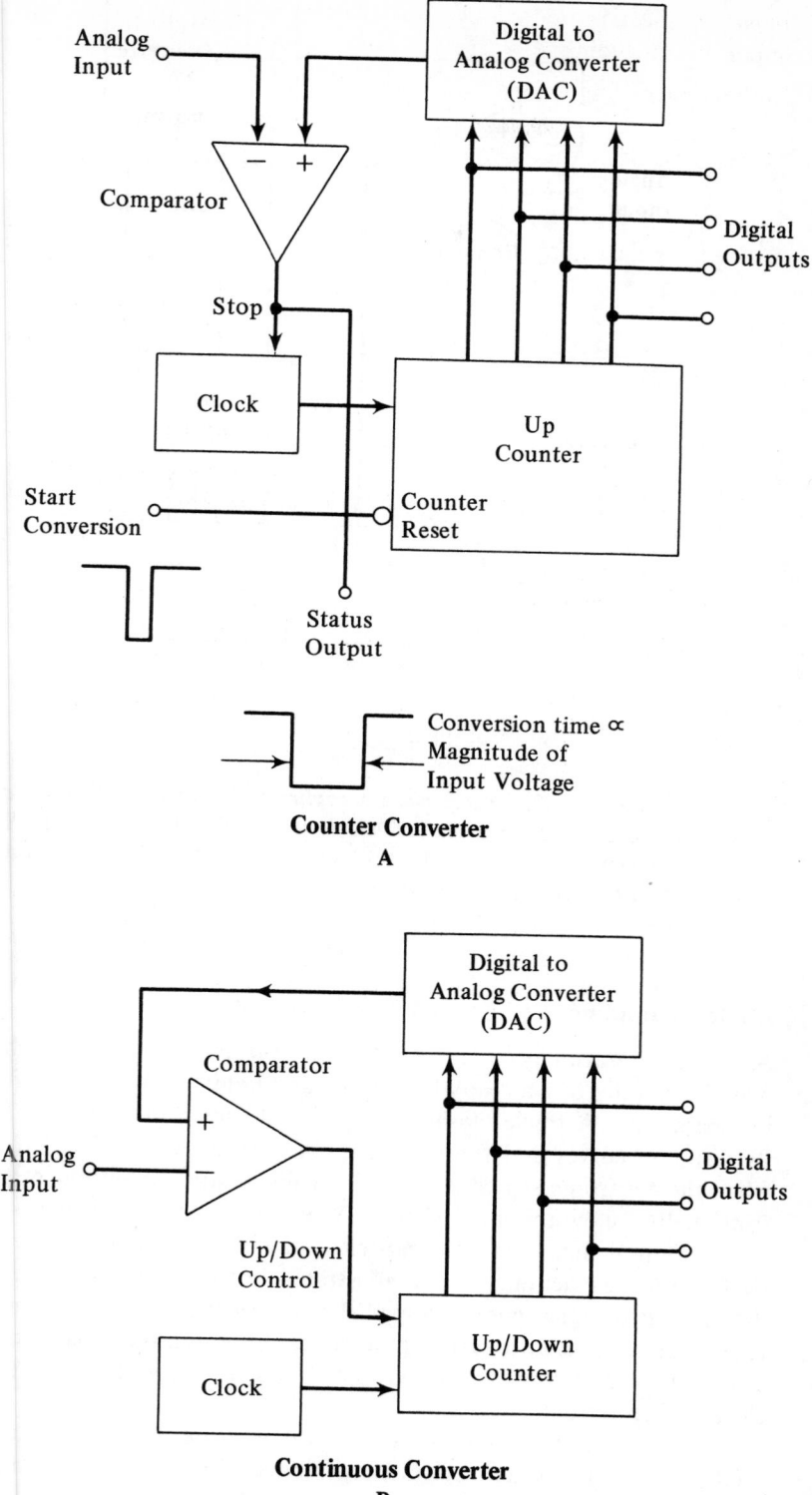

Analog Input

Digital to Analog Converter (DAC)

Comparator

− +

Stop

Clock

Up Counter

Start Conversion

Counter Reset

Status Output

Digital Outputs

Conversion time ∝ Magnitude of Input Voltage

Counter Converter
A

Digital to Analog Converter (DAC)

Comparator

+
−

Analog Input

Up/Down Control

Clock

Up/Down Counter

Digital Outputs

Continuous Converter
B

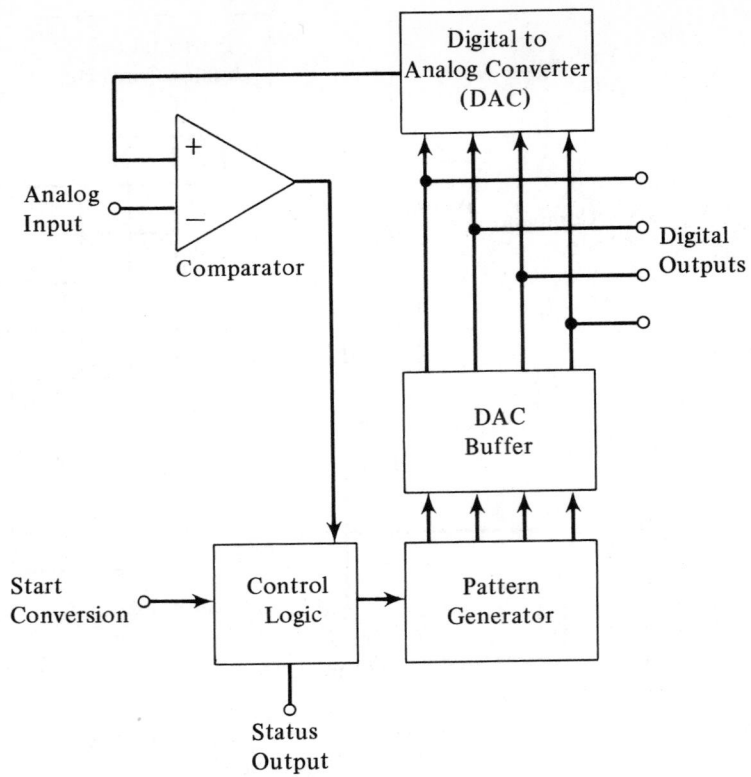

FIGURE 23.32. *Successive-approximation analog-to-digital converter. From S. P. Perone and D. O. Jones,* Digital Computers in Scientific Instrumentation, *New York: McGraw-Hill, 1973, by permission of the publisher. Copyright © 1973 by McGraw-Hill, Inc.*

Analog Sampling

A useful interface device is the *track-and-hold* amplifier. Although in practice one would generally buy a ready-built track-and-hold system, it is useful here to review its operation. A track-and-hold amplifier is shown in Figure 23.34, together with its response curves and timing chart. An incoming signal is fed to the capacitor when the electronic switch is closed. In this mode, the output of the amplifier will continually follow the input signal. When the electronic switch is opened and isolates the input signal from the capacitor, the output remains at the voltage last seen by the input capacitor. This is illustrated in Figure 23.34B, where, each time the digital control signal goes to a logical 1, the electronic switch opens and the magnitude of the voltage at that time remains (is stored) on the capacitor. Notice that the output waveform consists of a series of levels stored on the capacitor and read from the amplifier output.

      Track-and-hold amplifiers are used to store incoming signals briefly for an ADC, particularly when several signals have to be stored simultaneously and then

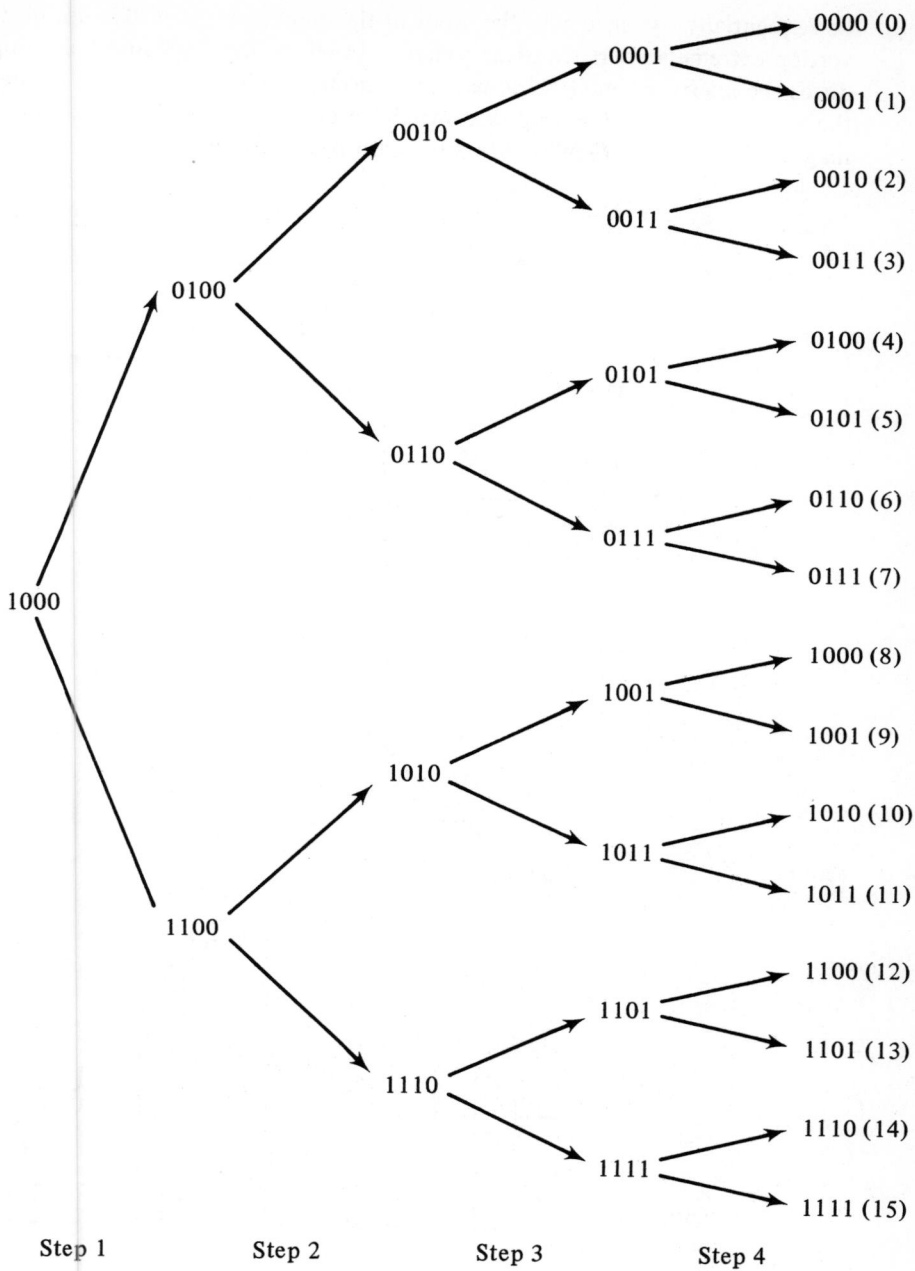

Step 1   Step 2   Step 3   Step 4

FIGURE 23.33. *Successive-approximation conversion pattern. From S. P. Perone and D. O. Jones,* Digital Computers in Scientific Instrumentation, *New York: McGraw-Hill, 1973, by permission of the publisher. Copyright © 1973 by McGraw-Hill, Inc.*

be sequentially switched into the input of the converter. It is also useful when converting extremely short transient signals. In effect, the track-and-hold amplifier reduces the aperture time (the actual time during which data is taken) of the ADC to the aperture time of the amplifier switch—a condensation of at least two orders of magnitude, usually. (See further discussion below.)

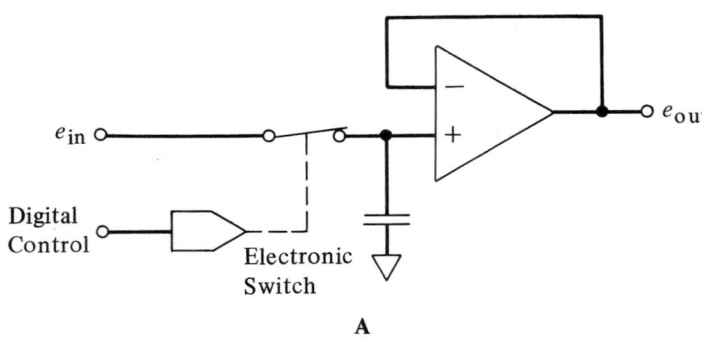

A

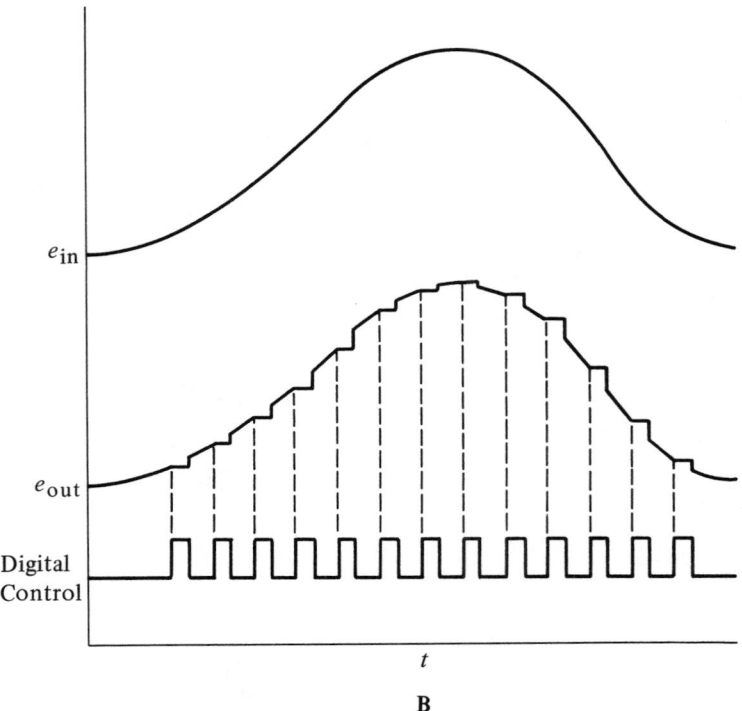

B

FIGURE 23.34. *Track-and-hold amplifier. From S. P. Perone and D. O. Jones*, Digital Computers in Scientific Instrumentation, *New York: McGraw-Hill*, 1973, *by permission of the publisher. Copyright © 1973 by McGraw-Hill, Inc.*

23.4 PRINCIPLES OF DATA ACQUISITION

Using the analog and digital devices described above, one can design the on-line communication link, or interface, between the digital computer and the experimental system. Several fundamental considerations must be kept in mind: How does the particular computer use, recognize, and interpret information from the outside world? How does the computer transmit information? What are the computer machine-language instructions available for input/output (I/O) functions?

One fundamental principle that should be emphasized here is that the computer communicates with the outside world by recognizing incoming binary voltage level changes at particular terminals at particular times, and producing other such changes at other (outgoing) terminals. Thus, the interface design is reduced to the problem of monitoring and interpreting voltage-level changes produced by the computer and ensuring that voltage-level changes produced by the experiment are detected and properly interpreted by the computer. Thus, interface design can be completed only if both the I/O hardware and software of the computer are well understood. The experimenter must also know the availability and characteristics of the hardware interface components described above.

Program-Controlled Data Acquisition

Two kinds of data-acquisition approaches can be defined. One is to operate the data-acquisition programming under *interrupt control*. That is, the computer is operated in a mode where data-acquisition devices are serviced upon demand. The other approach is called *program-controlled* data acquisition. This approach involves programming the computer to look for service requests from specific devices and to wait for these requests if necessary. The latter approach will be discussed here.

Perhaps the best way to discuss program-controlled data acquisition is to consider a specific problem. Consider the case in which an experiment of a transient nature is to be conducted and data acquired during the lifetime of the experiment— for example, monitoring the gaseous products of an explosion. The computer is to initiate the explosion and to simultaneously initiate data acquisition at a constant rate of 10 kHz. When a specified total number of data has been taken, the computer is to terminate data acquisition and reset the experimental instrumentation to the original conditions. Each data point is to be taken in from the ADC and stored in memory for later processing.

A schematic diagram of the computerized data-acquisition system is given in Figure 23.35. The computer initiates the data-acquisition cycle by executing a COMMAND instruction; this terminal goes to a "1" state and is connected to the ENABLE input of a 10-kHz clock, the output of which enables a 10-bit ADC every 0.1 msec. Simultaneous with enabling the clock and the data-acquisition process, the COMMAND output initiates the experiment. The experimental output is continuously available at the input to the ADC. Every time a conversion is completed, the ADC sets a STATUS flip-flop. When that flag goes to a 1 state, the computer determines that a conversion has been completed and that the digitized datum has been inserted into the input buffer-register.

Under program-controlled data acquisition, the computer will be programmed

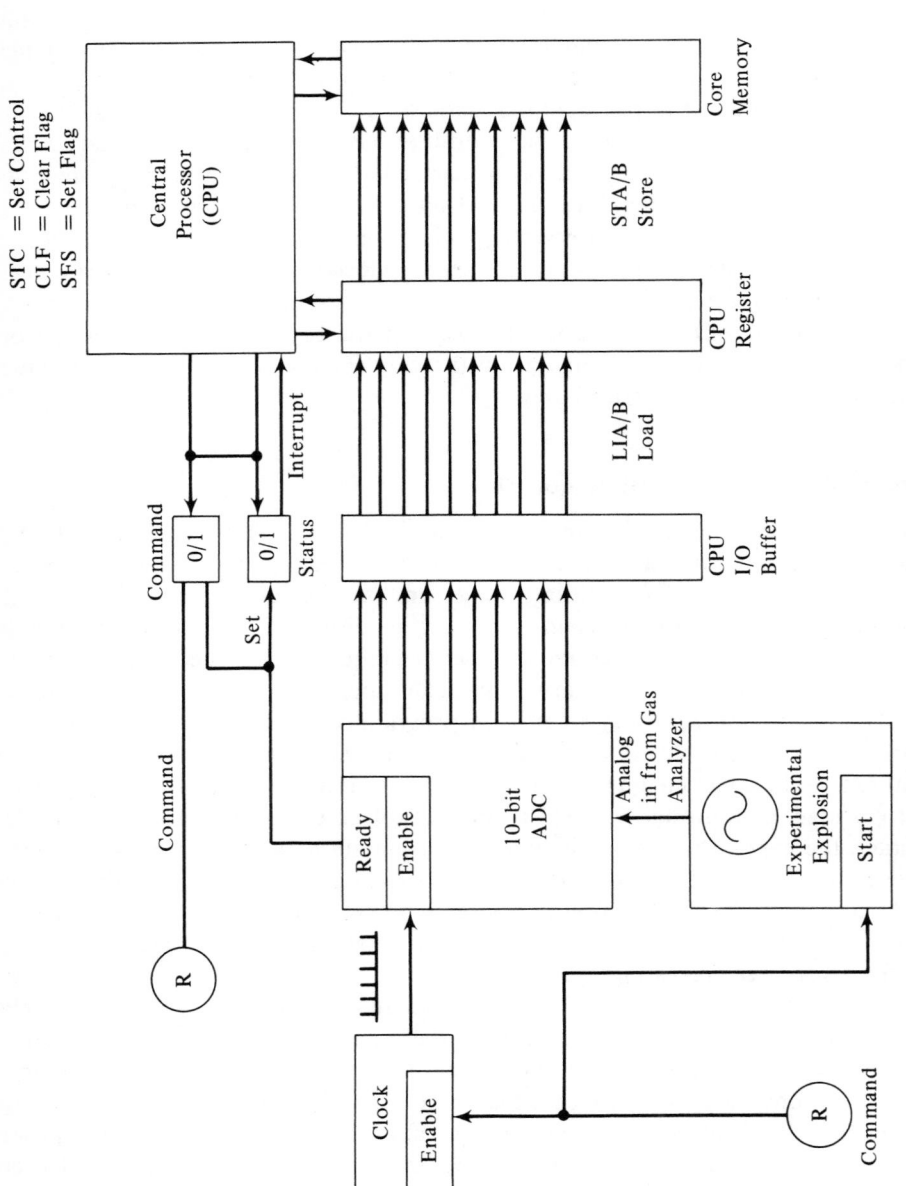

FIGURE 23.35. *Program-controlled data-acquisition system. From S. P. Perone and D. O. Jones, Digital Computers in Scientific Instrumentation, New York: McGraw-Hill, 1973, by permission of the publisher. Copyright © 1973 by McGraw-Hill, Inc.*

to test the STATUS bit to determine when each conversion has been completed. When the computer gets a "true" answer in querying this flip-flop, it goes to a data-input routine that loads the contents of the buffer register into a CPU register, clears the STATUS bit, and then stores the datum in core memory. This routine must keep track of the total number of data taken and handle sequential storage of data in a specified block of memory. When the specified total number of data has been taken, the computer terminates the data acquisition by clearing the COMMAND bit. This disables the clock and resets the experimental instrumentation to the initial conditions.

Timing and Synchronization in Data Acquisition

Although the need for synchronization between data-acquisition operations and experimental events should be obvious, the importance of this has not been illustrated. Figure 23.36 describes what can happen when a synchronization error occurs.

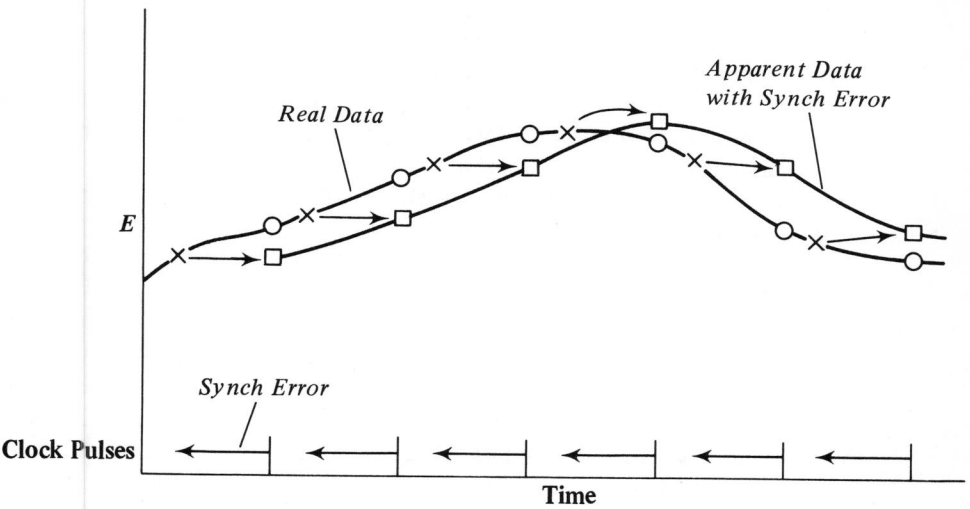

FIGURE 23.36. *Data-acquisition timing and synchronization error. From S. P. Perone and D. O. Jones*, Digital Computers in Scientific Instrumentation, *New York: McGraw-Hill, 1973, by permission of the publisher. Copyright © 1973 by McGraw-Hill, Inc.*

The trace representing the real data which starts at time zero (t_0) is presumably sampled by the data-acquisition system at time points indicated by the clock pulses on the x-axis. Because the clock can generate pulses at an accurately known frequency f, the time between pulses, $1/f$, is precisely known. The program generally will assume that the first clock-pulse is seen at exactly the fundamental time-interval $1/f$ after t_0. However, this will only be true if data acquisition has been synchronized exactly with the start of the experiment. If they are not synchronized, the first clock-pulse can come anywhere during that first time-interval. If the first clock-pulse occurs early, as shown in Figure 23.36, and the program is not aware of the synchronization error, then the program will assume that the first datum obtained really corresponds to the time assigned to the first clock-pulse on the diagram. Thus, the data points taken at the xs on the real data-trace are effectively displaced along the time axis to the points indicated by the squares on the diagram, and the digitized waveform seen by the computer has the appearance of having been translated on the time axis. For experiments where the data density is great, an error of this sort may be insignificant; however, for most experiments, this type of error causes severe difficulties in data processing. (An example of such an experiment is one involving ensemble signal-averaging, described below.)

Generally, a crystal oscillator is used for precise timing. However, this type of clock provides a continuously available pulse-train at a fixed frequency. Thus, there is no way to determine when a given clock-pulse occurs in real time. The uncertainty can be minimized if one selects a clock with a very high frequency and scales this down to the desired frequency range (see Fig. 23.23). The countdown logic can be initialized, enabled, or disabled. Thus, the output of the scaler provides a pulse train in which the uncertainty in the duration of the first time interval is no greater than the time interval $1/f_0$ of the crystal oscillator. For example, if the basic clock rate f_0 is scaled by a factor of 100, then the uncertainty in the initial scaled time-interval will be no greater than 1 percent.

The scaled clock is most valuable for establishing a time base for experiments that cannot be started at a precisely known moment by external control. If the start of a spontaneously initiated experiment can be detected electronically, this signal can be used to enable the scaler logic of the clock. Thus, a time base precisely synchronized with the experiment is obtained.

If the exact frequency of a free-running clock is to be used for data-acquisition timing, synchronization can be achieved by simple gating. This is demonstrated in Figure 23.37. The output of the free-running clock is brought to one input of an AND gate. The other input can be enabled by the command output of the computer or some other source. When this input of the AND gate is triggered, clock pulses get through the gate and are seen at the output. The first clock pulse that gets through the AND gate is used to initiate data acquisition and simultaneously start the experiment. Subsequent pulses are seen at exact multiples of the fundamental time interval $1/f_0$ of the free-running clock. Thus, data acquisition is exactly synchronized with the start of the experiment because the first available clock pulse was used to initiate the experiment. Note that this synchronization approach can be used only if the experiment can be initiated externally; for an experiment that initiates spontaneously, the alternative approach of enabling scaler logic on a high-frequency clock should be used. The scaled clock is the most generally applicable timing method and is the type implied in most illustrations here. The laboratory-computer user should be keenly aware of the synchronization limits and capabilities of the time-base generator (clock) used in his system.

Ensemble-Averaging Application

A good example of many of the principles discussed in previous sections, and a useful application of the digital computer for enhancing experimental measurements, is

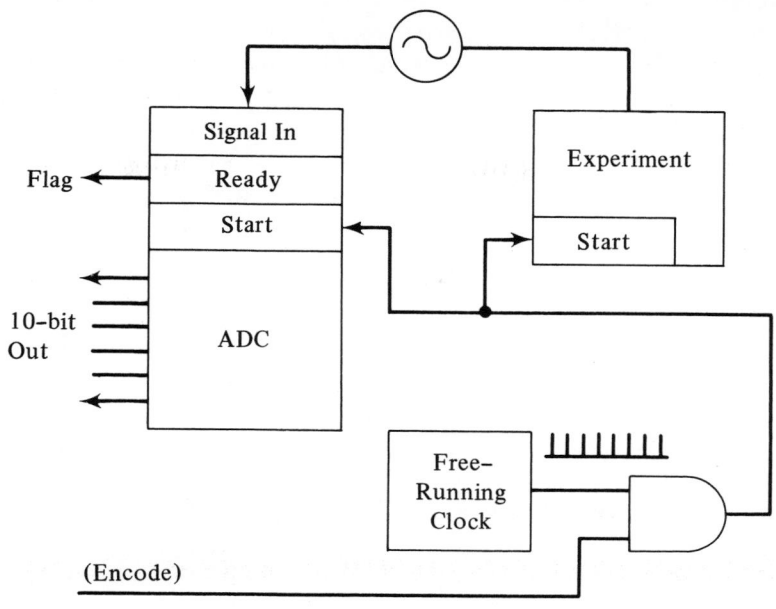

FIGURE 23.37. *Synchronization of experimental time-base generator. From S. P. Perone and D. O. Jones,* Digital Computers in Scientific Instrumentation, *New York: McGraw-Hill, 1973, by permission of the publisher. Copyright © 1973 by McGraw-Hill, Inc.*

the technique of *ensemble signal-averaging.* This technique can be applied in cases in which experimental data are obtained with large amounts of superimposed background noise. Although many approaches can be taken to handle instrumental problems leading to noisy data, it is not always possible to eliminate noise. (For example, standard noise-elimination procedures are inadequate in cases where the source of the noise is not in the electronics but is an inherent part of the experimental system.) When the frequency of the noise is similar to the frequency of the fundamental waveform of interest, conventional filtering techniques are not adequate. In such cases, some sort of signal-averaging approach must be used in order to extract the fundamental signal from the noise. However, two conditions must be met: (1) the signal must be repeatable, and (2) the noise must be random and not synchronized with the experimental output.

The ensemble signal-averaging approach involves running the experiment many times while acquiring the digitized waveform each time, and then summing the repetitive waveforms. When many such experimental outputs have been summed in this coherent fashion, the random noise-fluctuations in the individual waveforms will begin to cancel. The signal-to-noise ratio, in fact, should increase in proportion to the square root of the number of averaging cycles. This approach is illustrated in Figure 23.38.

It is extremely important in an ensemble-averaging experiment that the experimental output be synchronized exactly with the data-acquisition process. If any

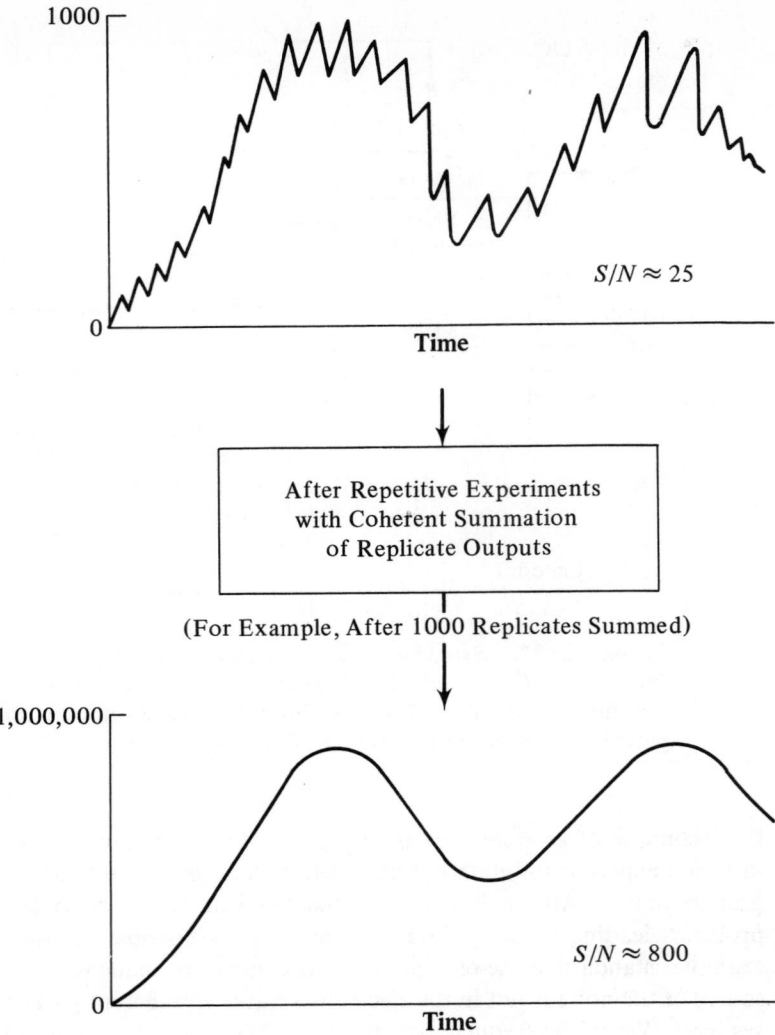

FIGURE 23.38. *Ensemble signal averaging. In this example, the signal-to-noise ratio increases from about 25 to about 800 with averaging. From S. P. Perone and D. O. Jones*, Digital Computers in Scientific Instrumentation, *New York: McGraw-Hill, 1973, by permission of the publisher. Copyright © 1973 by McGraw-Hill, Inc.*

significant fluctuation in synchronization with the time base occurs, the extracted fundamental waveform will be distorted.

Sampling of Experimental Data

Using Track-and-Hold Amplifiers. The tracking capabilities of even a high-speed ADC are relatively limited. To substantially improve the tracking features of a data-acquisition system, a track-and-hold (T/H) amplifier should precede the ADC.

During each hold period, the voltage output of the track-and-hold amplifier remains constant so that digitization may take place (see Fig. 23.34B). The digital output of the ADC will reflect the voltage level at the specific time corresponding to the beginning of each hold period, despite the fact that the conversion is completed at some later time. Thus, the T/H amplifier allows waveform sampling with time-base precision independent of the conversion rate of the ADC. The uncertainty in the timing of the sampling (the aperture time) depends on the switch-opening time and is a characteristic of the T/H amplifier. T/H amplifiers are available commercially with aperture times of the order of 10–100 nsec. Other important characteristics include *response* and *settling* times, which refer to the amplifier's ability to follow rapidly changing signals. These features actually limit the overall acquisition or sampling rate. Sampling intervals (the time from the end of one hold-period to the beginning of the next) of the order of one to several microseconds can be attained with currently available devices.

Sampling Frequency. The sampling frequency selected for data acquisition obviously should be related to the bandwidth of the sampled waveform. From information theory, the criterion for adequate sampling is that the minimum sampling frequency (*Nyquist frequency*) must be twice the bandwidth of the sampled waveform. Thus, for a 100-Hz signal, the sampling frequency must be at least 200 Hz to retain the information inherent in the waveform.

This criterion is strictly applicable in such applications as the sampling of interferograms for Fourier-transform analysis. However, sampling frequencies considerably greater than the Nyquist frequency should be used to allow faithful reproduction of the signal for straightforward data-processing algorithms. A rule-of-thumb criterion is that the sampling frequency should be at least 10 times the bandwidth of the waveform. (Of course, the previously discussed limits imposed by ADC or T/H aperture-times or amplifier response place an effective upper limit on sampling frequencies with a specific resolution.)

Oversampling of an experimental signal can cause problems, mainly because of excessive memory requirements; on the other hand, undersampling can cause even more serious problems. One of these is producing signal artifacts by *aliasing*. This phenomenon occurs when sampling frequencies lower than the Nyquist frequency are used. Figure 23.39 illustrates how a 3-kHz sine wave can be aliased to a 1-kHz signal or a 158-Hz signal by using sampling frequencies of 4 kHz and 3.16 kHz, respectively.

Multiplexing. It is sometimes necessary to sample more than one experimental waveform simultaneously during a single experiment. To accomplish this, an analog multiplexer can be used, the configurational and sampling considerations of which will be discussed here.

The primary characteristic of an analog multiplexer is that it can accommodate multiple analog inputs, any one of which can be sampled through a single output channel. The selection of the input channel to be transmitted to the digitization hardware can be accomplished by a binary-coded command from the computer or by generating an appropriate external sequencing code. The critical characteristic is the time required to switch between input channels. With solid-state analog switches, the sequential selection of analog inputs can proceed with time intervals of the order of a few microseconds or less between channels.

The reader should recognize immediately that the analog multiplexer need not provide the slow step in an overall data-acquisition process. Indeed, the slower processes will be associated with the data-acquisition hardware and software that follow the analog multiplexer. Another point is that it is impossible for the multiplexer to sample independent waveforms in a truly simultaneous fashion. Some finite time-interval must exist between samplings of different channels. The manner in which this problem is handled will depend on the need for acquiring truly simultaneous data from the different channels.

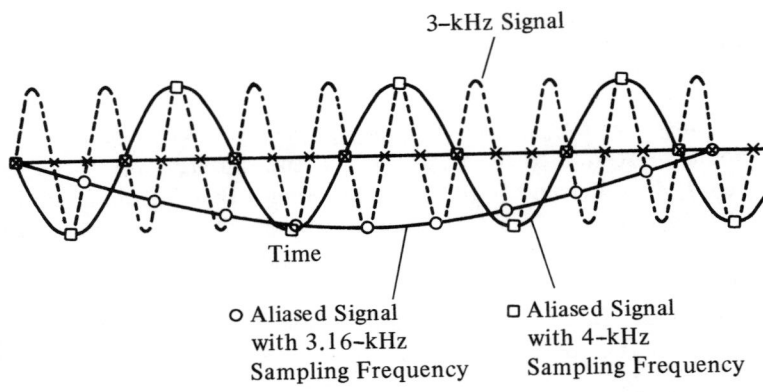

FIGURE 23.39. *Aliased signal phenomenon. From S. P. Perone and D. O. Jones*, Digital Computers in Scientific Instrumentation, *New York: McGraw-Hill, 1973, by permission of the publisher. Copyright © 1973 by McGraw-Hill, Inc.*

Figure 23.40 illustrates two alternative configurations for multiplexing analog signals from four independent sources. In Figure 23.40A, the multiplexer is followed by a T/H amplifier and ADC. This configuration is used if there is no need to achieve simultaneous sampling of the four input-channels. Moreover, if the total time required to complete data acquisition from the four channels is small compared to the time interval between samplings, this configuration can be used. For example, if an overall data-acquisition frequency of 10 Hz is employed for all four channels and the total sampling time per channel is 100 μsec, the maximum *skew* of the sample data will be 300 μsec. That is, the fourth channel will be sampled 300 μsec after the first channel. This amount of skew is negligible compared to the 100-msec time interval between samplings.

For the case in which simultaneous sampling is required and the time required to sequentially sample each of the input channels is long compared to the overall data-acquisition time base, the configuration shown in Figure 23.40B is recommended. In this case, each analog signal is funneled through a T/H amplifier. Because all the T/H amplifiers can be gated to the *hold* mode simultaneously, the time required to sample all channels through the multiplexer will be inconsequential, provided that it does not exceed the overall data-acquisition time-base interval. Another consideration is the *droop* specification on the T/H amplifier. That is, the T/H amplifier must be capable of holding the analog signal without significant decay until the particular channel is sampled and the digitization complete.

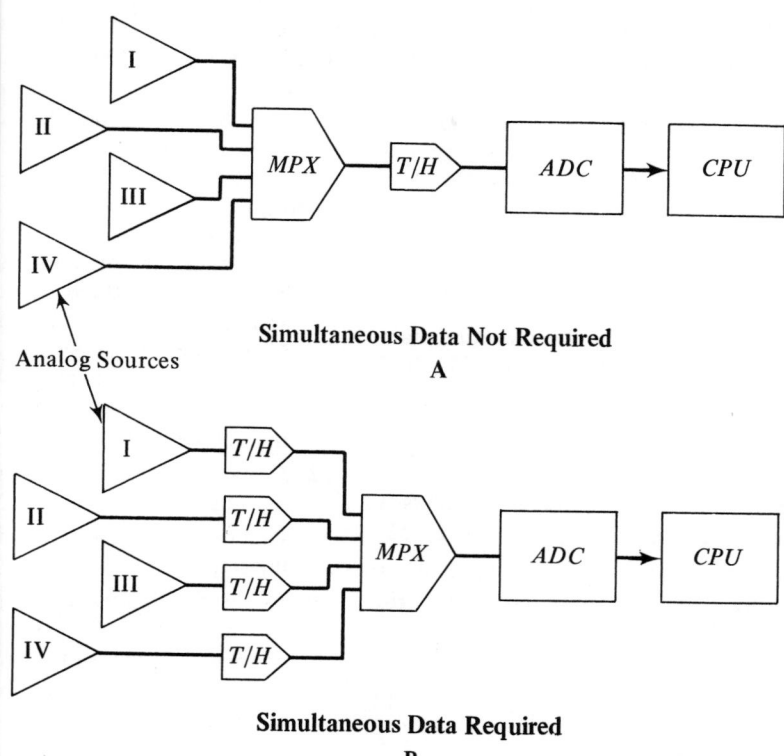

FIGURE 23.40. *Multiplexed data-acquisition system. From S. P. Perone and D. O. Jones,* Digital Computers in Scientific Instrumentation, *New York: McGraw-Hill, 1973, by permission of the publisher. Copyright © 1973 by McGraw-Hill, Inc.*

SELECTED BIBLIOGRAPHY

HOESCHELE, D. F., Jr. *Analog-To-Digital/ Digital-To-Analog Conversion Techniques.* New York: Wiley, 1968.

MALMSTADT, H. V., and ENKE, C. G. *Digital Electronics for Scientists.* New York: Benjamin, 1969.

PERONE, S. P., and JONES, D. O. *Digital Computers in Scientific Instrumentation.* New York: McGraw-Hill, 1973.

WILKINS, C. L.; KLOPFENSTEIN, C. E.; ISEN-HOUR, T. L.; and JURS, P. C.; with J. S. EVANS and R. C. WILLIAMS. *Introduction to Computer Programming for Chemists, BASIC Version.* Boston: Allyn and Bacon, 1975.

WILKINS, C. L.; PERONE, S. P.; KLOPFENSTEIN, C. E.; WILLIAMS, R. C.; and JONES, D. E. *Digital Electronics and Laboratory Computer Experiments.* New York: Plenum Press, 1975.

REFERENCES

1. S. P. PERONE and D. O. JONES, *Digital Computers in Scientific Instrumentation*, New York: McGraw-Hill, 1973, chap. 12 and references therein.

2. L. NASHELSKY, *Digital Computer Theory*, New York: Wiley-Interscience, 1966, p 238.

3. S. P. PERONE and D. O. JONES, *Digital Computers in Scientific Instrumentation*, New York: McGraw-Hill, 1973, chaps. 7 and 8, and app. B.

4. S. P. PERONE and D. O. JONES, *Digital Computers in Scientific Instrumentation*, New York: McGraw-Hill, 1973, app. C.

5. S. P. PERONE and D. O. JONES, *Digital Computers in Scientific Instrumentation*, New York: McGraw-Hill, 1973, chap. 8.

PROBLEMS

1. Convert the following decimal numbers to binary: (a) 5 (b) 52 (c) 387 (d) 10652

2. Convert the following binary numbers to decimal: (a) 1101 (b) 1000101 (c) 1010-1010 (d) 10000100001

3. Convert the following decimal numbers to octal: (a) 5 (b) 52 (c) 387 (d) 10652

4. Convert the following octal numbers to binary: (a) 5 (b) 52 (c) 307 (d) 10652

5. Convert the following binary numbers to octal: (a) 111 (b) 1101100 (c) 10101-110110 (d) 1000000101

6. Convert the following octal numbers to decimal: (a) 36 (b) 652 (c) 21237 (d) 4142437

7. Construct the four basic logic functions— AND ($X = A \cdot B$), OR ($X = A + B$), NAND ($X = \overline{A \cdot B}$), and NOR ($X = \overline{A + B}$) —using only NAND gates.

8. Construct the four basic logic functions in Problem 7 using only NOR gates.

9. Construct a truth table for $X = A \cdot B + C$.

10. Construct a truth table for $X = A \cdot \bar{B} \cdot \bar{C}$.

11. A commercial analog-to-digital converter is available in three models with 8-, 10-, and 12-bit resolution. Each model has four externally selectable full-scale input-voltage ranges: 0 to +5 V, 0 to +10 V, −5 to +5 V, −10 to +10 V. What is the theoretical resolution in mV for each case?

12. Design a divide-by-seven circuit using RS flip-flops.

13. Design a divide-by-25 circuit using JK flip-flops.

14. Define the following terms as used in relation to computers: (a) bit (b) word (c) address (d) memory cycle time (e) interface (f) assembly language (g) machine language

15. The following are common abbreviations— what do they mean? (a) CPU (b) BCD (c) I/O (d) DAC (e) FET (f) MOSFET

16. What functions are performed by the following gates? (a) AND (b) OR (c) NOT (d) NAND

17. What is meant by an *on-line* computer? What are the important implications of using a computer in this manner?

24

Automation in Analytical Chemistry

KENNETH S. FLETCHER III
NELSON L. ALPERT

Automated instruments are classed as *continuous* or *discrete* (*batch*), depending on the nature of their operation. A continuous instrument senses some physical or chemical property by directly observing the sample, yielding an output that is a smooth (continuous) function of time. A discrete instrument works upon a batch-loaded sample and supplies information only after each batch. Each derives its operating principles from conventional analytical procedures, and must include provision for continuous unattended operation: receiving samples, performing selective chemical analyses under uncontrolled environmental conditions, and communicating with monitoring or control equipment.

A clear distinction should be made between *automatic* and *automated* devices [1]. Automatic devices cause required acts to be performed at given points in an operation without human intervention. For instance, an *automatic titrator* records a titration curve or simply stops a titration at an endpoint by mechanical or electrical means (such as a relay) instead of manually. Automated devices, on the other hand, replace human manipulative effort by mechanical and instrumental devices regulated by *feedback of information*; so, the apparatus is self-monitoring or self-balancing. An *automated titrator* may be intended to maintain a sample at some preselected (set point) state—for example, at pH = 8. To do this, the pH of the solution is sensed and compared to a set point of pH = 8, and acid or base is added continuously so as to keep the sample pH at the set point. This type of automated titrator is called a *pH-stat* [2].

In the past, automated instruments were not well accepted because of their limited capability and reliability. However, because of the increased complexity and number of clinical, industrial, and other types of samples requiring analysis, classical (nonautomated) techniques, as well as automated techniques, have been improved in capability and reliability. Well established instruments such as infrared analyzers, gas chromatographs, ion-selective electrode systems, and automatic wet-chemical analyzers can now measure quite complex species and mixtures. Reliability has also increased, because the maturity of solid-state electronics has brought easier data-handling and equipment maintenance along with it.

This chapter presents some basic considerations encountered in automating analytical instruments and illustrates some of the important interactions between the instrument and the system of which it is a part. The first part of the chapter will deal with general concepts and some automated industrial applications in which continuous monitoring and feedback control is important. The second part will deal with the approaches used in the clinical laboratory, where literally billions of tests are performed annually using automatic instruments.

24.1 INSTRUMENTAL PARAMETERS FOR AUTOMATED INSTRUMENTS

Several instrumental parameters need to be evaluated when unattended operation is proposed for a particular instrument. The definitions that follow have been accepted by the Scientific Apparatus Makers Association (SAMA) [3], and endorsed by the Instrument Society of America (ISA).

Sensitivity

Sensitivity is specified by the relationship between concentration and instrument output and hence by the slope of the instrument-response curve. Sensitivity also specifies the minimum detectable change in concentration, governed by the signal-to-noise ratio of the instrument. Sensitivity is generally defined as the concentration required to give a signal equal to twice the root-mean-square of the baseline noise. The ISA has recommended that this second definition be denoted by the term *dead band*, which is the range over which an input to an instrument can be varied without detectable response. A change in the slope of the instrument-response curve will generally result in a change in the level of detectable response—that is, the signal-to-noise ratio.

Inconspicuous instrumental, environmental, or chemical effects often cause a loss of instrument response. In atomic emission spectroscopy, for example, sensitivity is affected by such instrumental factors as flame temperature, aspiration rate, and slit width. In amperometric measurements, diffusion currents vary with temperature, and a significant loss in sensitivity may occur with a drop in sample temperature. In ion-selective electrode measurements, sensitivity may be affected by chemical effects, such as changes in ionic strength or pH.

Accuracy

Accuracy indicates how close a measured value is to an accepted standard or true value. Statements of accuracy should be a percentage of the upper-range value of the reading, or (preferably) an absolute number of measured units. In each case, accuracy is measured in terms of the largest *error* occurring when the device is used under described operating conditions.

Reproducibility

Reproducibility, or precision, differs from accuracy. A poorly calibrated instrument may be inaccurate, but these inaccurate results may nonetheless be reproduced well. Although an automated instrument used primarily as a monitor may require high accuracy (and hence precision), an instrument used for control purposes may only need high reproducibility. The first kind of instrument is used, for instance, in cost control or in clinical testing where accuracy is paramount; the second kind is used in process control, where a particular factor is to be held at a stable set point. There are various measures of precision. One of the most common is the *standard deviation s*, given by

$$s = \sqrt{\frac{\sum (\bar{X} - X_i)^2}{N - 1}} \qquad (24.1)$$

where $\bar{X}$ = the mean of the individual measurements X_i
        N = the number of measurements

Defining objectives in terms of accuracy, reproducibility, and sensitivity is only part of the task. The effect of ambient environmental factors, such as temperature, pressure, humidity, and supply-voltage stability, must also be evaluated. A common problem leading to loss of accuracy and sensitivity in real-world applications is the build-up of deposits on measurement transducers, such as electrodes, which then have to be periodically cleaned, either manually or automatically.

Selectivity

The selectivity of the chemical transducer is its ability to discriminate between the species of interest and possible interferences. Since commercially available instruments are designed for the largest possible number of applications, the instrument may not operate optimally in a particular situation. Therefore, both the measuring method and the chemical system being measured should be thoroughly understood.

Range and Span

Range is defined as the interval over which a quantity is measured. The *span* is simply the width of the range, the difference between the upper- and lower-range values. Consider the following example. For a typical pH-meter, 0 mV corresponds to pH 7, and (at 30°C) each unit change in pH produces a change in potential of approximately 60 mV. In Figure 24.1A, pH is measured over the range pH 7 to 9 (0 to +120 mV); the span is 2 pH-units (120 mV) and the zero is normal. If one wishes to measure pH over the range pH 8 to 10 (Fig. 24.1B), the 2-pH span is maintained, but the zero is suppressed and the millivolt range becomes +60 to +180 mV. The official glossary of the Instrument Society of America [3] defines a suppressed-zero range as one in which the zero value of the measured variable is smaller than the lower-range value. Likewise, an elevated-zero range is one in which the zero value of the measured variable is greater than the lower-range value; in Figure 24.1C,

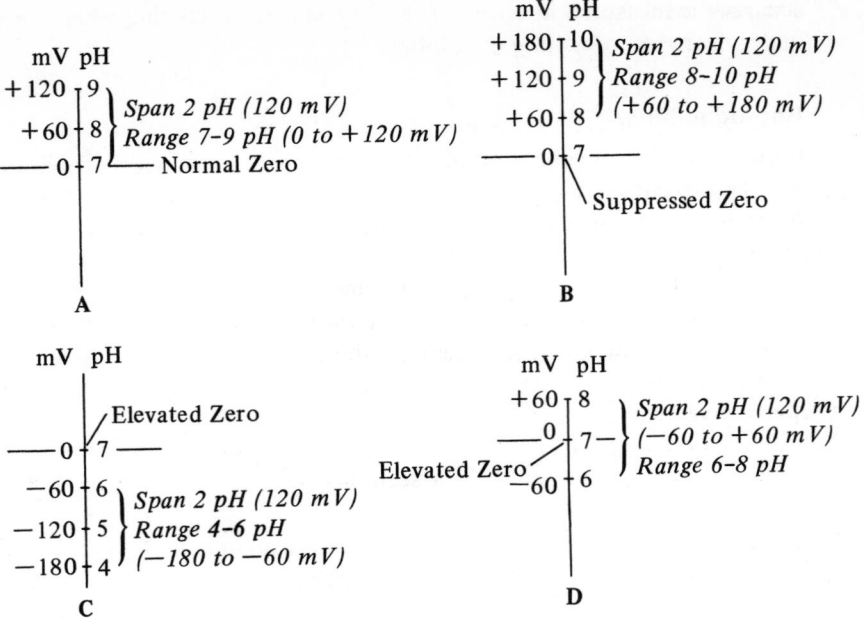

FIGURE 24.1. *Illustrative relationship between range, span, elevated-zero and suppressed-zero. Courtesy of the Foxboro Company.*

the pH range is pH 4 to 6 (-60 to -180 mV), and the span is again 2 pH-units. Note in Figure 24.1D that, if the zero value falls between the upper- and lower-range values, there is again an elevated zero.

Since a change in span requires a change in the per unit response of the instrument, it requires a change in gain; likewise, since a change in range requires a change in the zero point of the instrument, it requires a change in bias.

The dynamic (working) range of an automatic or automated instrumental technique must obviously fit the working range of concentrations to which it is being applied. In a continuous or automatic titration, for example, the dynamic range and span are governed by the sample size (the volume of the sample and the concentration of desired species in it), the size of the buret, and the concentration of the titrant. The presence of a second titratable species (interference) in the system reduces the usable span by the amount of the second species, since the titration will measure both species.

For cases in which the amount of the interference is known to be constant, a blank correction (zero elevation) may be possible if a small enough portion of the span is consumed. Unfortunately, since the concentrations of most interferences are subject to the same variations as those of the species of interest, one is usually left with three possible alternatives:

1. Find a method more selective for the species of interest
2. Find a selective measurement for the interfering species and use it to correct the primary measurement signal
3. Use chemical conditioning to remove the interference from the sample

Speed of Response

In electronic instruments, there is always some lag between the physical change being measured and the recorded signal. Speed of response is usually defined as the time required for the instrument to reach a specified percentage of the total change observed. It may be stated in terms of *rise time*, the time required for an instrument output to change from, say, 10% of the ultimate value to 90%. Another measure is the *time constant*, defined as the time required for the response to build from 0% to 63% $(100 - 100/e)$ of the ultimate value when a step-function signal is received at the detector. Approximately four time-constants are required to reach 98% of the final value; this is called the *response time*. Increasing the amplification of a system increases its noise in proportion to the square root of the amplification. This will require a larger response time to damp out the fluctuations, and so the response-time should be increased in proportion to the square root of the amplification. If the amplification is increased ten-fold, for example, the response time should be increased about three-fold. In a scanning instrument, the scan rate should be correspondingly reduced.

Dead-Time

Dead-time is often of great importance in automated systems. This is defined as the time interval, after alteration of the parameter being measured, during which no change in the parameter is observed at the detector. It can be minimized by placing transducers properly, keeping the sample lines short, and using high flow rates. It is never entirely absent. Batch-sampling analyzers introduce additional dead-time, since delay invariably exists between the time at which a sample is taken and that at which a signal is generated. The response of a gas chromatograph in an automated process-control analyzer is a good illustration of this type of delay, since the elution time of the species in the column is dead-time. In automatic batch-samplers (not used for automated process-control), times between sample injections can be much shorter than the dead-time so that after the first sample is detected, data output for subsequent samples is obtained in rapid succession.

24.2 SAMPLE CONDITIONING

Sample conditioning is the physical or chemical change needed to render samples suitable for measurement. Ignoring this basic requirement has caused many serious problems for automated instruments, particularly those designed for unattended operation.

From the physical point of view, the most important considerations are temperature, pressure, and sample cleanness. Suspended solids in liquid samples and dust in gas samples often interfere with transducers in continuous-sampling instruments and with the volumetric sampling techniques used in batch-sampling instruments. Automated systems that filter out solids should be amenable to automatic cleaning. In continuous instruments, data output must be interrupted while the filters are cleaned; in batch-sampling systems, filters can be cleaned during the dead-time after a sample has been injected for analysis.

Often the physical state of the sample (gas, liquid, or solid) is dictated by the physical principle upon which the measurement is based, and a phase conversion may be required. Some instruments (for example, gas chromatographs and infrared analyzers) utilize either gas or liquid samples; the appropriate phase may be chosen to optimize any of the instrumental parameters discussed earlier. If the measurement is temperature sensitive and the sample temperature may vary, temperature compensation or temperature control must be provided. Temperature compensation is usually supplied as part of the measuring system; the sample temperature is continuously monitored and the measurement signal electrically corrected to offset the temperature effects. When temperature control is required, a batch sample or a sample side-stream is used, and the sample temperature is adjusted prior to measurement. This procedure adds dead-time to the measurement because the sample has to be in the temperature converter long enough to come to thermal equilibrium.

The sample pressure (in a gas, for instance) may vary widely; it is often restricted by the mechanical constraints of the transducer. If a pressure drop is required in the measurement, phase changes or degassing (in liquids) may also occur and interfere severely with the measurement.

Chemical sample conditioning or reagent addition is often more difficult to apply on a practical scale than is physical conditioning, but can be invaluable in optimizing instrumental parameters. In many cases, it makes otherwise-impossible measurements feasible. Three types of reagent addition are utilized. In the first, the sample is diluted to lower the concentration of the species to be analyzed into the dynamic range of the measuring instrument. In the second, reagent addition converts a species for which no useful measurement technique exists into one amenable to measurement. In the third, reagent addition is used to suppress the effect of interfering species and thus render the measurement more selective.

The quantity of reagent added may not be critical. Frequently, only a moderate excess of reagent is required and, therefore, a 10–50% accuracy in this quantity suffices. The practical requirement in flowing systems is to maintain a constant ratio between the reagent flow and the sample flow. A simple system for accom-

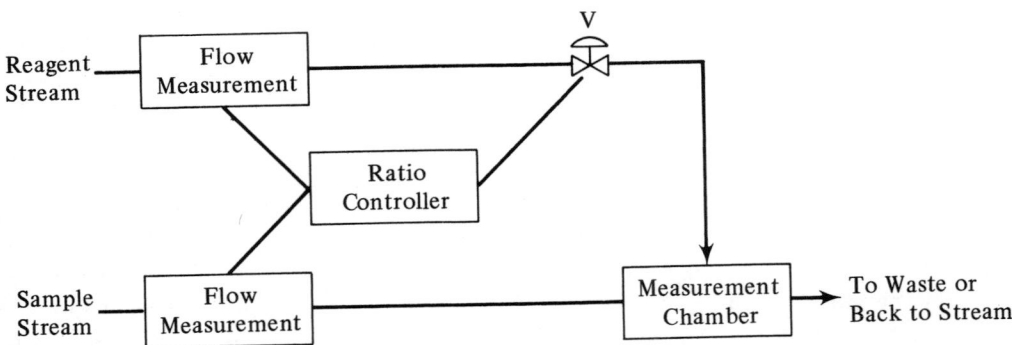

FIGURE 24.2. *Reagent addition system. The ratio controller compares reagent flow to sample flow and maintains a preset ratio by operating control valve V on the reagent stream. The streams are then mixed in (or before) the measurement chamber where the desired analytical measurement is performed. Courtesy of the Foxboro Company.*

plishing this is shown in Figure 24.2. In this system, the ratio controller maintains a flow of reagent to the sample stream at a level proportional to sample flow. This proportion is important in maintaining chemical stoichiometry as well as a known, constant dilution at the measurement point.

24.3 AUTOMATED PROCESS-CONTROL

The successful implementation of automated instruments in routine monitoring functions has led to their increased use in automated process-control. Process control is accomplished by means of the *control loop*, which contains at least three parts:

1. An instrument that senses the value of the variable being regulated
2. A controller that compares the measured variable to a reference value (set point) and produces an output proportional to the difference
3. A final operator (controlled by the output of the controller) that actuates some mechanism to reduce the difference

The two basic types of control loops applied to automated systems are termed *feedback* and *feedforward*, and are shown in Figure 24.3. The fundamental difference between these two types lies in the position of the measuring instrument. In feedback control, the measurement is performed either within or at the output of the process, and deviation from the set point causes an operation at the process input. Thus, an error must occur before corrective action can be initiated. In feedforward control, measurement is made at the input to the process, and any deviation from the set point is fed forward to initiate corrective action prior to occurrence of the error. Thus, feedforward systems are theoretically capable of perfect control.

Since a control loop is a dynamic system, its efficiency is governed by the response time of the entire system [4], which includes that of the measuring instrument, the controller, the final operator, and the process itself. Two time-response characteristics of the process are important in selecting the proper control strategy—the *dead-time* and the *resistance-capacitance (RC) time-constant*. Dead-time was discussed above; an example is the time required to initiate many polymerization reactions. The *RC* time-constant results from the ability of the process to absorb a change in input without an immediate proportionate change in output.

Process capacitance represents the ability of a process to store energy or material. An electrical capacitor, for instance, stores a quantity of electric charge determined by the potential difference. Capacitance represents the change in a quantity per unit change in a reference variable; the units depend on the particular type of system being considered. Thus, the capacitance of electrical systems is in coul/V (farads), of liquid systems is in m^3/m, of thermal systems is in cal/deg, and of pressure systems is in lbs/psi.

Resistance represents the opposition to flow of energy or material into (or out of) a process. The rate of charge flow through a conductor is determined by the applied potential difference; electrical resistance to charge flow is measured in ohms [V/(coul-sec)]. The volumetric flow-rate (m^3/sec) from a liquid-level system with a

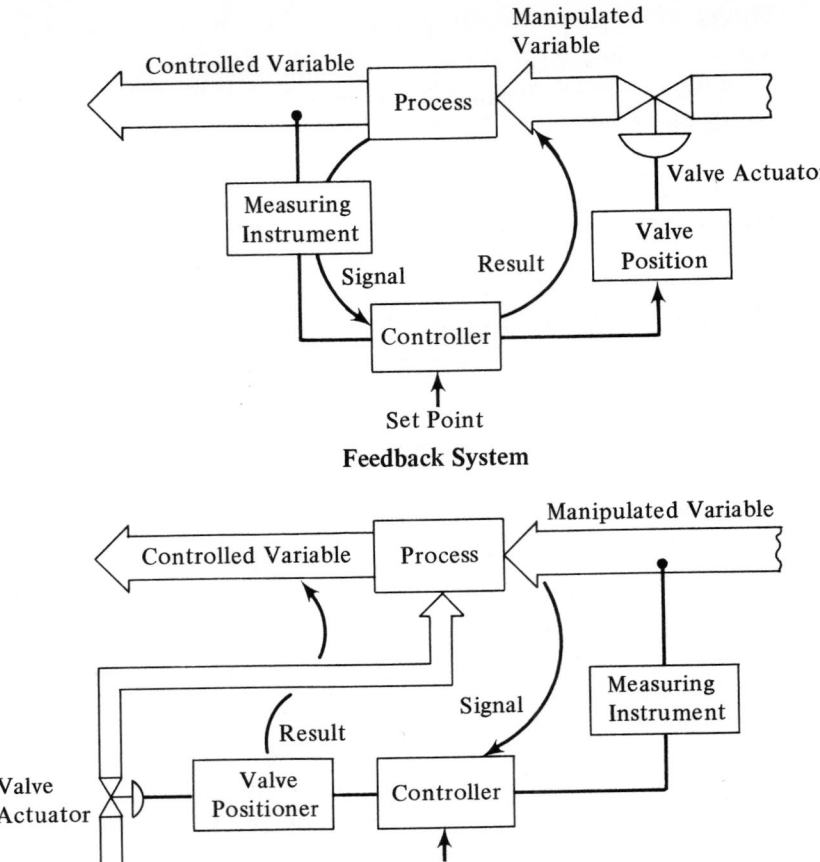

FIGURE 24.3. *Feedback and feedforward control systems. In feedback control, a measuring instrument obtains information at the output of a process, the signal obtained is compared to a set point, and the difference (or result) is applied to a final actuator. The result is ultimately detected by the measuring instrument and closed-loop control results. In feedforward control a measuring instrument obtains information at the input of a process, the signal obtained is again compared to a set point, but now the result is applied to an actuator that controls another input to the process. The result is not detected by the measuring instrument and open-loop control results. Courtesy of the Foxboro Company.*

fixed head (m) has the resistance units m/(m³-sec). Similarly, the resistance of thermal systems is expressed in °C/(cal-sec), and of pressure systems in psi/(lbs-sec).

The chemical composition of a process can also introduce *RC* time-constants. The presence of undissolved solid reactants, for example, represents chemical capacitance, and the rate of dissolution of sparingly soluble reactants represents resistance.

Modes of Process Control

Automated process control can utilize any of several modes of control, the choice being dictated by the dynamic characteristics of the process. Several of these methods are discussed below.

Two-Position Control. The simplest case is two-position (on-off) control. Here, any deviation of the measured value from a set point drives the final control-operator to either a full-on or full-off position. This forces the measured value back and forth across the set point, and the measurement signal cycles about this point. The amplitude and frequency of this cycle depend on the response characteristics of the process. As the process dead-time becomes small, the frequency of the cycle becomes high; likewise, as the process capacitance becomes high, the amplitude of the cycle becomes small. This mode of control is used only for processes in which this cycling effect can be tolerated; it is most successful with those having large capacitance.

Proportional Control. As the capacitance of the process decreases, on-off control leads to increasing amplitude of oscillation. In proportional control, a continuous linear relation between the value of the measured quantity and the position of the

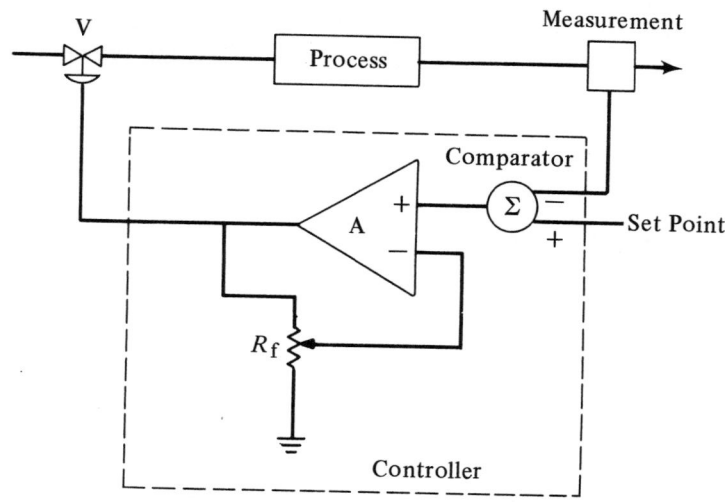

FIGURE 24.4. *The proportional controller. The feedback resistor R_f determines the gain or proportional band of the proportional controller. The symbol V means a valve, and A is an amplifier. Courtesy of the Foxboro Company.*

final control operator is established. This control scheme is shown schematically in Figure 24.4. The *proportional band* is determined by the amount of feedback around the amplifier (the value of R_f in Fig. 24.4). The proportional band is inversely proportional to the gain and is expressed as a percentage of the measurement span; it is defined as the change in the property measured that will cause the control operator to move between the fully open and fully closed positions. A narrow proportional band gives a full swing of control-operator position for a small change in the measured value, whereas a wide proportional band requires a large deviation from the set point for a full swing.

The proportional band (PB) is related to the gain by

$$\text{Gain} = \frac{100}{\% \text{ PB}} \qquad (24.2)$$

Controller gain is given by the ratio of change in output to change in input.

$$\text{Gain} = \frac{\Delta \text{ output}}{\Delta \text{ input}} = \frac{\text{output}}{e} \qquad (24.3)$$

where e = the error between set point and measurement

A bias adjustment is usually included to allow the controller output to be set at 50% of span when the measurement equals the set point. Thus,

$$\text{Output} = \frac{100}{\% \text{ PB}} e + b \qquad (24.4)$$

The bias b is equal to the output when the error is zero. From Equation 24.4, it is clear that proportional action is not capable of perfect control since, after a load upset, the controller output cannot track the error as e approaches zero. The difference between the resulting measured value and the set point is called *offset*, Δe. This is shown schematically in Figure 24.5.

Under this new operating condition,

$$\text{Gain} = \frac{\text{output}}{\Delta e} \qquad (24.5)$$

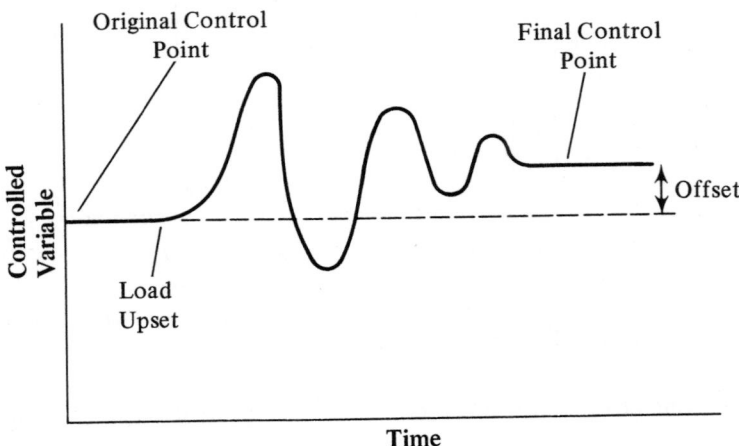

FIGURE 24.5. *Proportional control action. After a load upset, the controlled variable deviates from the set point. The new control-point may then differ from the set point by the offset. Courtesy of the Foxboro Company.*

and from Equation 24.2,

$$\Delta e = \frac{\% \text{ PB}}{100} (\text{output}) \tag{24.6}$$

Equation 24.6 shows that the offset is directly related to the proportional band. In the limit as % PB approaches zero (gain approaches infinity), the offset approaches zero. Pure proportional action is therefore adequate for processes that require proportional bands no wider than a few percent—that is, to easily controlled processes in which load changes are moderate.

Proportional-Plus-Integral Control. Addition of integral action to proportional action is necessary for processes requiring wide proportional bands. In integral control, the time integral of the offset is fed back, thereby forcing the deviation to zero. This control scheme is shown in Figure 24.6. At balance, the error signal is zero and

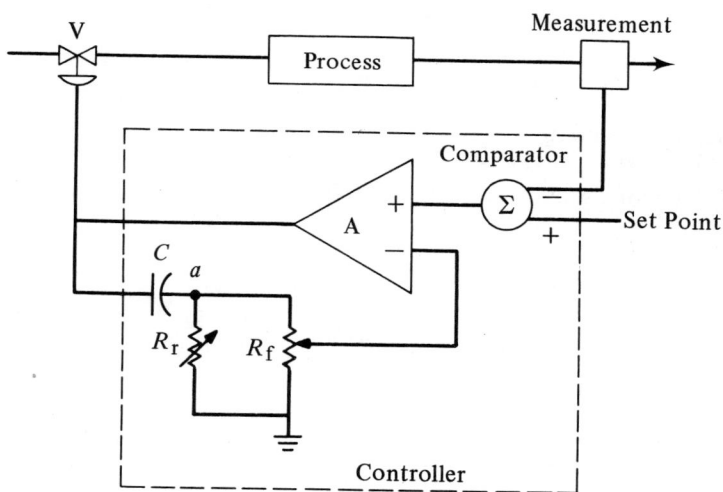

FIGURE 24.6. *The proportional-plus-integral controller. Integral action is accomplished by the series capacitor C in the feedback loop. The presence of offset causes this capacitor to charge at a rate that depends on R_rC, where R_r is the reset resistor. This forces the output to change in such a manner as to drive the offset to zero at a rate determined by the adjustment of the reset resistor. Courtesy of the Foxboro Company.*

point *a* is maintained at ground potential. If an offset is present, a voltage develops across the capacitor, which charges at a rate proportional to R_rC. This signal is fed back to the control operator to eliminate the offset and thus return point *a* to ground potential.

The response equation for the proportional-plus-integral controller may be written

$$\text{Output} = \frac{100}{\% \text{ PB}} \left(e + \frac{1}{R_rC} \int \Delta e \, dt \right) + b \tag{24.7}$$

me constant of the controller R_rC is called *reset time* and is the time interval
which the controller output changes by an amount equal to the input change or
deviation. Note that, when the offset returns to zero, Equation 24.7 reduces to that
describing pure proportional control, Equation 24.4.

Proportional-plus-integral control is the most generally useful control mode
and therefore the one usually applied to automated process-control. Its major
limitation is in processes with large dead-time and capacitance; if reset time is faster
than process dead-time, the controller-response changes are faster than the process,
and cycling results. In these cases, derivative control is beneficial.

Proportional-Plus-Derivative Control. Here, derivative action is added to proportional controllers for processes with large capacitance and appreciable dead-time.
Control action is now proportional to the rate of change (the time derivative) of the
error signal. The response equation is written as

$$\text{Output} = \frac{100}{\% \text{ PB}} \left(e + t_D \frac{de}{dt} \right) + b \qquad (24.8)$$

where $\quad t_D$ = the *derivative-action time*

Derivative-action time is defined as the amount of lead, in seconds, that the derivative
action advances the effect of pure proportional action. Figure 24.7 illustrates a
proportional-plus-derivative controller.

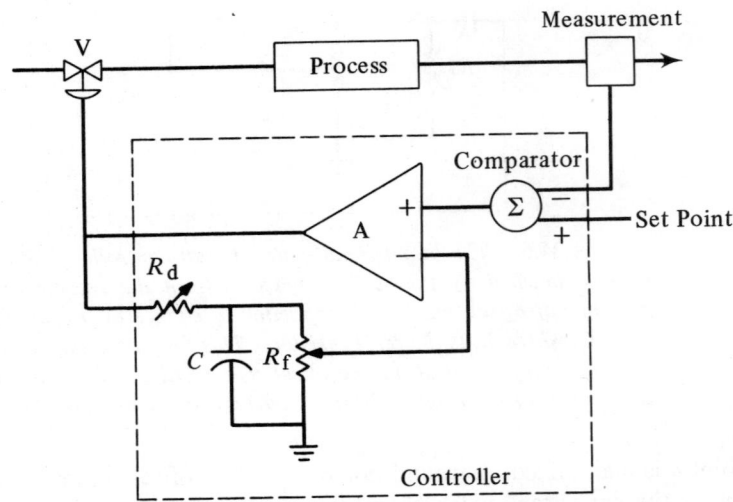

FIGURE 24.7. *The proportional-plus-derivative controller. Derivative
action is accomplished by a shunt capacitor C across R_f. When deviation
from the setpoint is rapid, the low reactance of the capacitor causes less
negative feedback—hence, greater amplifier gain. The derivative time
resistor R_d allows adjustment of the magnitude of derivative control action
to a given rate of change of the error signal. Courtesy of the Foxboro
Company.*

Derivative action is accomplished by placing a capacitor across the gain resistor. This capacitor has low reactance and reduces the feedback when the error signal is changing. Thus, a rapidly changing input-signal increases the controller gain, producing a larger corrective output. When the time rate of change of the error signal becomes zero, derivative action ceases and Equation 24.8 reduces to that for pure proportional control. Note that derivative action is anticipatory since, if the rate of change of a load upset on the process is rapid, the controller can take large corrective action even though the magnitude of the load change is small, thus overcoming the inertia of the process.

The Controller

An example of a typical commercial controller is shown in Figure 24.8. The Foxboro SPEC 200 PID Controller and Display provides proportional-plus-integral (PI) or proportional-plus-integral-plus-derivative (PID) control. The set-point dial on the

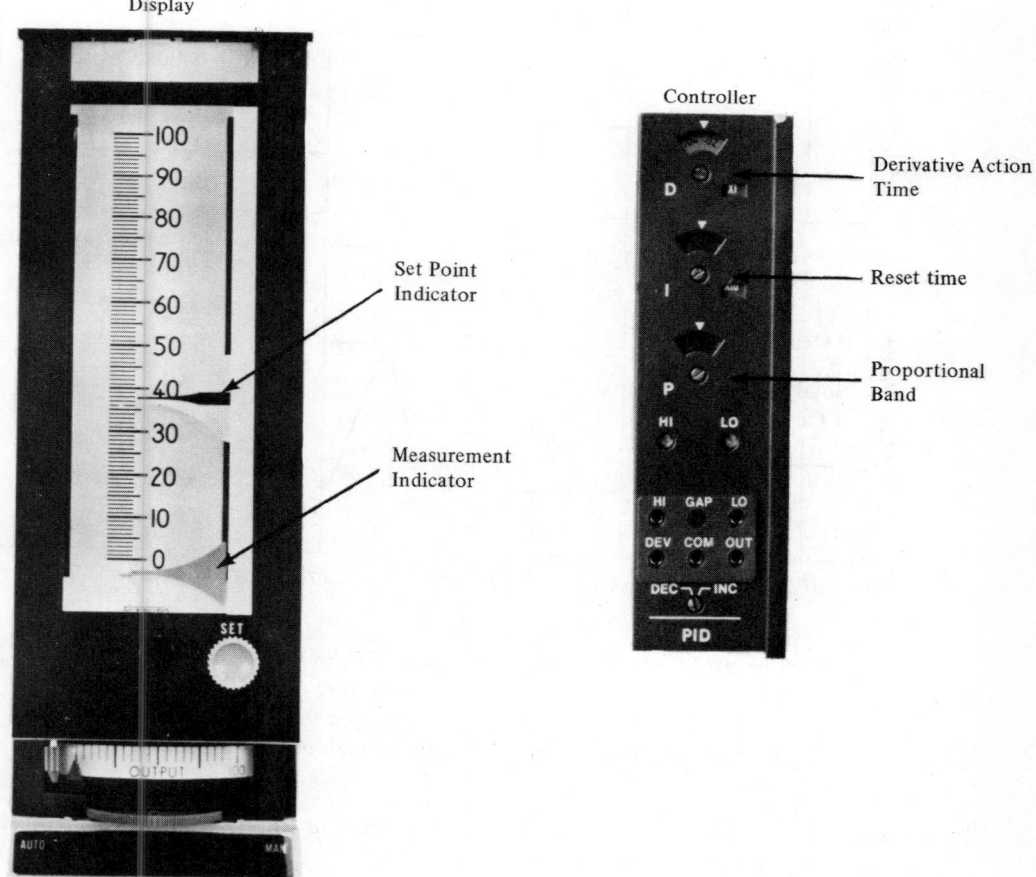

FIGURE 24.8. *The Foxboro SPEC 200 controller and display. Courtesy of the Foxboro Company.*

display unit places the set point at any level between 0 and 100% of the measurement range. A second pointer indicates the actual measurement value on the same scale. Additionally, an output meter indicates the percent of output being applied to the final control-operator. The control unit holds the adjustments for setting proportional band (R_f in Figure 24.4), reset time (R_r in Fig. 24.6), and derivative-action time (R_d in Fig. 24.7). Process controllers are also manufactured by Minneapolis Honeywell Co., General Electric Co., Leeds & Northrup Co., and others.

Discrete Instruments

Automatic instruments with discrete (batch) sample handling and analysis have special problems when used for automated process-control. These instruments consist of a sampling system, an analyzer, and a memory device that maintains the

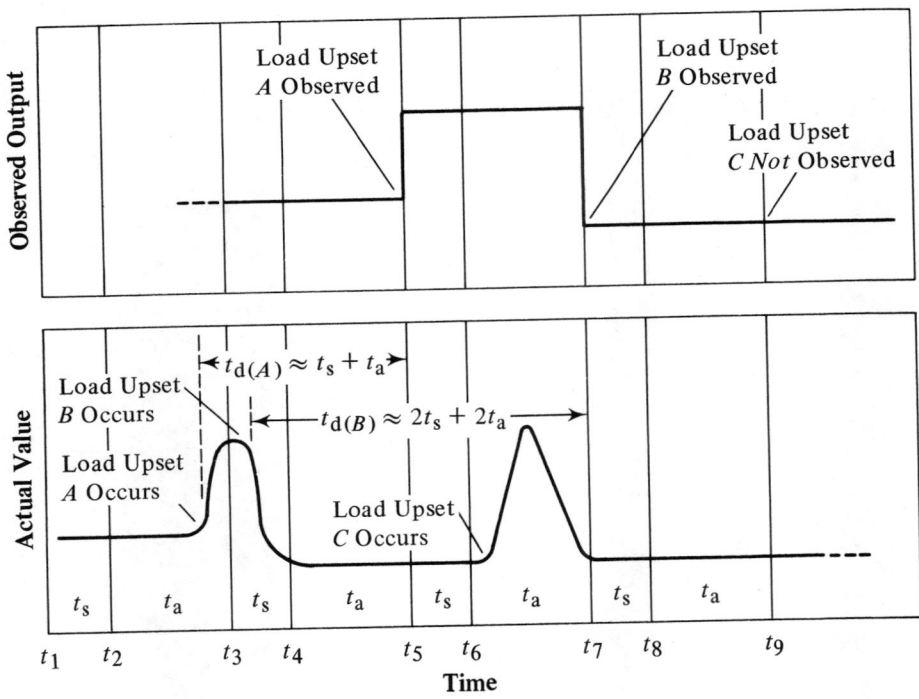

FIGURE 24.9. *Output response behavior of discrete instruments.* $t_s =$ *sampling dead-time* $= t_2 - t_1 = t_4 - t_3 = \cdots$; $t_a =$ *analytical dead-time* $= t_3 - t_2 = t_5 - t_4 = \cdots$; $t_s + t_a < t_d < 2t_s + 2t_a$, *where t_d is the total measurement dead-time. Courtesy of the Foxboro Company.*

output at a fixed level until the next signal appears (a trend output). Their output-response behavior is shown in Figure 24.9.

Two sources of dead-time are obvious. *Sampling dead-time t_s* is the time elapsed between the instant the sample is taken and the instant it enters the analyzer.

This is shortened by using short sample-lines and high flow rates. *Analytical dead-time* t_a is the time elapsed between the instant the sample enters the analyzer and the instant a new output-value is displayed.

The total measurement dead-time is not constant. In the best case, a load upset that occurs just prior to sampling (load upset A in Fig. 24.9) may be detected with the least possible dead-time—that is, $t_{d(A)} \approx t_s + t_a$. In the worst case (load upset B in Fig. 24.9) a load upset occurs just after a sampling instant, and its detection is delayed for about twice the interval observed above—that is, $t_{d(B)} \approx 2t_s + 2t_a$. Finally, a load upset that occurs entirely within an analyzer interval t_a may be completely missed (load upset C in Fig. 24.9).

Whereas derivative action is of great value in the control of continuous processes with dead-time, it is useless for batch instruments because the instrument output changes in steps. This local high rate of change produces pulsing of the manipulated variable, the effect of which cannot be seen because of the measurement dead-time.

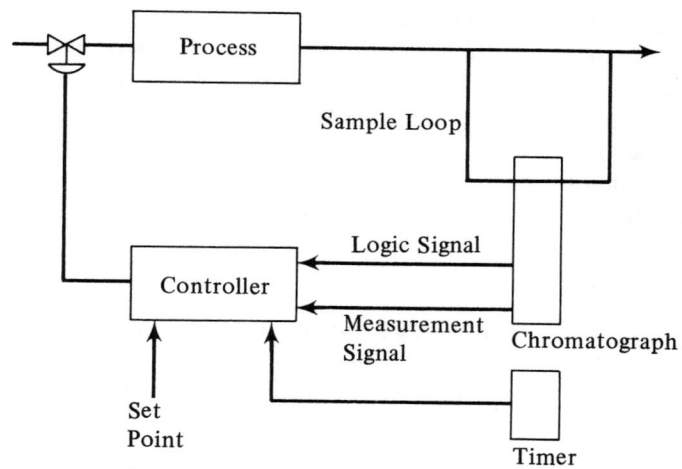

FIGURE 24.10. *The sampling controller. The sampling controller accepts a logic signal from a discrete analyzer (the chromatograph) and applies corrective action for a control interval established by a timer. Courtesy of the Foxboro Company.*

A *sampling controller* using proportional-plus-integral action is most generally useful with discrete-sampling instruments. This is illustrated for a process using a gas chromatograph in Figure 24.10. A logic signal starts a timer that allows the controller to operate for only a fraction of the analytical dead-time. After this control interval, the error signal is removed, the controller output is held, and further corrective action is prevented until the next control-interval. The time the controller waits before applying further corrective action is the total dead-time, t_d. The major limitation of this system is that it is impossible to synchronize sampling instants with changes in the variable being controlled.

24.4 AUTOMATED INSTRUMENTS IN PROCESS-CONTROL SYSTEMS

The chemical instrumentation discussed in the preceding chapters of this text can all be utilized in automated systems. The choice is largely dictated by economics and the applicability of the instrument to the proposed problem. Three groups of instruments have been widely automated: spectrometers, electrochemical instruments, and chromatographs. Some of the many techniques commonly used and a few others are listed in Table 24.1. A review of all the instruments used in automated control systems cannot be given in the space allotted here. Additional reading is found in the bibliography at the end of this chapter.

Spectroscopy

Ultraviolet-visible absorption spectrophotometry, an inherently precise and accurate measurement, is most often applied to such gaseous materials as Cl_2 (for which no other convenient method is available), SO_2, NO_2, O_3, and Hg (vapor). An interesting automated instrument in this category measures low concentrations of mercury in water streams and industrial atmospheres [5]. Mercury in any chemical form is reacted with suitable reagents to give the elemental material, the Hg is stripped with clean air as vapor, and the absorbance of the vapor is measured at the 253.7-nm resonance wavelength obtained from a Hg-vapor lamp. A pyrolysis system is used to give additional specificity when other ultraviolet absorbing materials are present. This type of instrument is capable of accurately measuring mercury at the parts-per-billion level.

TABLE 24.1. *Analytical Techniques Commonly Used in Automated Systems*

1. Spectroscopy

    A. Ultraviolet, Visible, Infrared Absorption
    B. Turbidimetry
    C. Emission Spectrometry
    D. Refractometry
    E. Chemiluminescence Measurements

2. Chromatography

    A. Gas-Liquid
    B. Liquid-Liquid

3. Electrochemistry

    A. Potentiometry
    B. Voltammetry
    C. Coulometry
    D. Conductivity
    E. Amperometry
    F. Dielectric-Constant Measurements

Applying absorption spectroscopy to liquid samples suffers from two important limitations. The spectra of two or more components may overlap, causing poor selectivity. Broad shoulders may appear on the sides of the more important absorption peaks, causing difficulty in discriminating between the components in a mixture. These problems may sometimes be avoided by using the optimum wavelength of the component sought and perhaps blank subtraction techniques (see Chaps. 6 and 7). Another approach is to use a double wavelength technique. Here one wavelength is used at which the component of interest absorbs and another at which it does not. This can compensate for the presence of an interfering substance, an indistinct shoulder on the side of a band, or even for the effects of scattering and dirty cell windows.

A second limitation of this technique arises from the high absorption and scattering of high-molecular-weight solutes and solvents between 200 and 800 nm. This causes marked loss in sensitivity and restricts the use of this technique in important applications, such as measuring high-molecular-weight polymers, colloids, or proteins. To overcome this problem, a high-intensity tungsten source is used along with low-noise photomultiplier tubes having large windows, and the sample is placed close to the detector to minimize scattering losses. Most liquid samples are measured for organic materials, such as aromatics, diolefins, ketones, and aldehydes.

This type of instrument is widely applied to measurements other than chemical composition, such as film thickness, turbidity, color, and optical rotation. The DuPont Company manufactures a versatile instrument, in modular form, that is used for all of these measurements. The same company also produces automated systems designed specifically for SO_2, NO_x, and H_2S/SO_2 ratio, all of which are useful in stack-gas pollution control. Other manufacturers are Beckman Instruments, ITT Barton Co., and GEC-Elliot Ltd. (Hallikainen Instruments).

Gas Chromatography

The chromatograph is a discrete instrument, since it operates as a batch-sampling device (see Chaps. 21 and 22) requiring that one take samples, inject them into the chromatograph, and record the chromatograms. A *process gas chromatograph* (PGC), therefore, requires an automatic sampling valve. Suitable ceramic sampling valves, electrically or pneumatically actuated, have been developed using linear and rotary sliding seals. These valves can add identical samples to the column for millions of cycles. Both liquid and gas sampling valves are available, as well as several detectors, such as thermal-conductivity and flame-ionization detectors, by which this technique can be applied over a range of concentrations from trace ppm to present levels.

Because of the complexity of many industrial fluids, the recent trend has been toward use of the PGC as a single or two-component dedicated device. In addition, *column switching* and *backflushing* techniques are essential to PGCs. Column switching allows chromatogram development using different columns during each analysis, thereby enhancing the separation of the desired components and allowing for rejection (often at an early stage of analysis) of unwanted components. Backflushing is useful for eliminating components with long elution-times. In one case, the flow of carrier gas through the column is reversed after the last component to be measured has been eluted. The slow components emerge from the beginning of the column in a single band since they leave the column at the same relative rates at which they entered. Thus, they may be used to form a composite peak on the chromatogram for "total heavies," or vented, as desired.

The operation of the chromatograph makes data utilization difficult, for two reasons. First, much effort is needed to extract information from the complex chromatographic display. Automated procedures for doing this usually employ a time-base generator that selects a predetermined portion of the chromatogram for integration. When this *window* includes only the peak of interest, the answer can be automatically presented at periodic intervals. However, the position of this window relies on the fixed time-interval between sample injection and component retention time. Since retention time is affected by column loading, temperature, and flow rate, these factors must be rigorously controlled. In one PGC system, this problem was eliminated (or at least minimized) by using programming techniques tied to a chromatogram time-base rather than an absolute time-base [6].

Second, the application of chromatography to dynamic systems is limited by the time interval between analyses. This is particularly serious when chromatography is used in automated control systems. A significant solution may be *correlation chromatography* [7]. Here, samples are repeatedly injected into the column using a predetermined switching sequence (a pseudo-random chain code), and the chromatographic output is mathematically related (correlated) with the input using a digital computer. This results in an average of the several chromatograms taken over the period of the chain code. Since many more analyses are obtained per unit time, the chromatogram is continuously updated, and the output, though still delayed by the analysis dead-time, is more nearly continuous.

Chromatography is perhaps one of the most widely applied automated instruments in process analysis, particularly in the nonaqueous chemical and petrochemical industries [8]. In petroleum refining, for example, the crude petroleum, containing hundreds of chemicals from methane to asphalt, is converted to salable cuts by distillation. Further processing by catalytic reforming, distillation, and chemical reaction yields materials used for fuels, lubricants, petrochemical feedstock, and other applications.

An illustration of the use of chromatography in this industry is in the control of distillation towers. Distillation uses the difference in composition between a liquid and the vapor formed from that liquid as the basis for separation. The efficiency of the process is affected by temperature, pressure, feed composition, and feed flow-rate. Chromatography is used to monitor the composition of the feedstock and to apply feedforward control of the heat input (temperature) to the tower, or to monitor and control the composition of the product. In this latter case, the chromatograph output is simply compared with a set point, and the controller (using feedback) manipulates the temperature, pressure, or feed flow-rate by activating the appropriate final operator. Both types of distillation control are widely employed in petroleum refining.

In the petrochemical industries, hundreds of materials are produced using catalytic reforming, isomerization, and polymerization. Tower-distillation monitoring and control using the PGC is of great importance here also. Other specific applications include (1) monitoring the purity of monomers used in manufacturing such polymers as vinyl chloride, vinyl acetate, polyethylene, and styrene; and (2) monitoring chlorinated hydrocarbons produced by chlorination and oxychlorination reactions—chlorinated solvents, weedkillers, pesticides, and many intermediates that are polymerized directly into plastics. Additional applications of PGC are found in the pharmaceutical and food industries and, to a more limited extent, in analyzing furnace flue-gas for combustion control.

Electrochemical Instruments

Several types of electrochemical techniques have been used in automated systems (see Table 24.1). At first glance, their use in instrument systems appears straightforward, since each transducer converts chemical information directly into an electrical signal. Unfortunately, few applications are found for those methods involving net current flow (e.g., amperometry) because the rate of mass transfer (and hence the current) depends on the sample flow-rate, which may vary, and on how clean the electrode surface is. This discussion will therefore be restricted to potentiometry, a zero-current technique.

The glass electrode used for measuring pH is one of the most successful examples of potentiometry in automated instruments. Modern glass electrodes are highly reliable; they give selective, sensitive, and stable response to acidity over a very wide range of pH and have been widely applied in industrial monitoring and control.

Using ion-selective electrodes in automated systems has several advantages. In general, many wide-range electrodes are available for several types of ions, and in many cases they provide the only practical method for determining ionic activities in solution [9]. They generally exhibit fast response and can be used continuously with small samples, and with many types of samples with no pretreatment (colored solutions, slurries, etc.).

The general acceptance of ion-selective electrodes in automated instruments, however, has been somewhat limited; this can be attributed to the fact that accuracy is strongly affected by chemical and environmental effects. Since these electrodes measure activity rather than concentration, factors such as ionic strength, complex formation, and pH need to be carefully controlled. In addition, few of these electrodes are perfectly selective for the ion of interest, and the presence of interfering ions must be considered before every application. The accuracy attainable may further suffer from temperature variations. For a monovalent ion, the Nernst equation shows that a change in temperature of $1°C$ causes a change in potential of 0.2 mV for a $0.1\ M$ solution of the ion of interest, and a 1 mV change for a $10^{-5}\ M$ solution of the same ion. Electrode accuracy may suffer from drift because of pressure changes, flow changes, or electrode poisoning; the relative concentration error is 3.9% per mV uncertainty in measurement for a monovalent ion. When high accuracy is required, all of the factors must be carefully controlled. A side stream and flow-through cell allowing temperature control, flow control, adjustment of pH, and reagent addition to eliminate interfering ions may be required. An example of a flow-through cell that contains pH and reference electrodes, temperature compensator, and ultrasonic cleaner is shown in Figure 24.11.

Ultrasonic electrode cleaning has contributed significantly to the use of

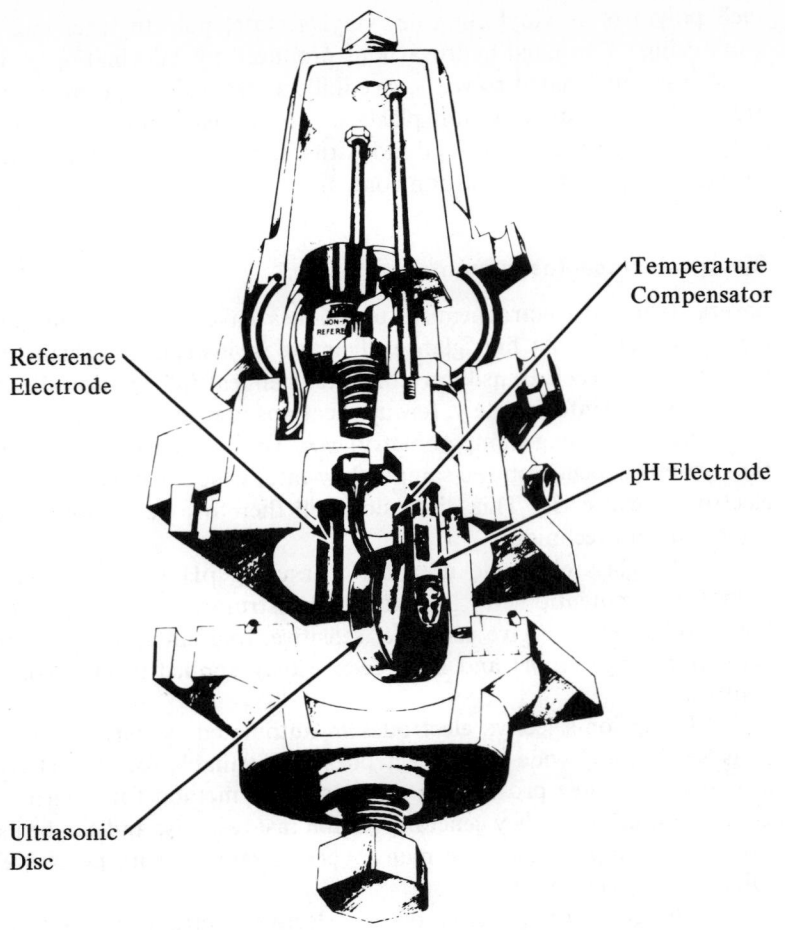

Reference
Electrode

Temperature
Compensator

pH Electrode

Ultrasonic
Disc

FIGURE 24.11. *The Foxboro Model 85A pIon Electrode Assembly. Courtesy of the Foxboro Company.*

potentiometry in automated instruments. For example, during sugar refining, the raw washed sugar liquor is treated with phosphoric acid. Subsequently, lime is added to neutralize the acid; this quickly coats the pH electrodes, increasing the response time and finally snuffing the response entirely. Ultrasonic cleaning eliminates these problems and results in a substantially improved automated instrument in terms of reduced maintenance, increased reliability, and more efficient process control.

Some important automated instruments based on ion-selective electrodes measure sodium in boiler feedwaters, fluoride in public water-supplies, and water hardness (Ca^{2+} and Mg^{2+}) in water-conditioning systems. The sulfide electrode is extensively used in the paper industry for monitoring and control of sulfidity in paper pulping liquors (for instance, the Kraft process), for waste-treatment control of excess sulfide using a process that oxidizes sulfide with air, and for monitoring the level of sulfide being discharged from the plants. Other applications include the use of the cyanide electrode for measuring free and total cyanide in metal-plating baths, the use of the silver electrode for measuring silver ion in photographic emulsions and spent fixing solutions, and many others.

In some processes, potentiometry is used for controlling ionic species for which electrodes are not available. For example, the production of chlorine and caustic soda using mercury electrolysis cells results in wastes containing toxic levels of mercury. This waste is treated by precipitating the mercury as insoluble mercurous sulfide using sodium bisulfide, and then filtering the precipitate. Both pH and S^{2-} concentration should be controlled for efficient operation. At high pH, HgS forms soluble polysulfides; at low pH, sulfide is tied up as HS^- and H_2S. The waste liquor is therefore controlled at a pH near 7.0, and sulfide is added in a controlled manner to maintain a small residual level of about 1 ppm as H_2S. In this way the very small residual concentration of mercury ion remaining in solution (governed by the common-ion effect and the solubility product of HgS) is effectively removed by means controlled by the sulfide electrode.

When the chemical composition of a stream is to be controlled using potentiometry, a significant problem is encountered because of the logarithmic relationship between the measured potential and the concentration of the species of interest. Consider a pH-control loop (a pH measurement, reagent valve, and controller); for a neutralization reaction, the gain of the pH measurement is the incremental change in pH caused by a particular quantity of added reagent. This is the slope of the titration curve; since it is inversely related to the buffer capacity of the system, it may vary over three or four orders of magnitude. It is apparent that the gain will be affected by the pH set point selected and by the type of acids or bases (that is, strong or weak) in the system. Since efficient control requires that the total gain of the loop be less than one, the extreme range of gain resulting from the potentiometric measurement must be accommodated by the other two elements in the loop. Valves are available having 50:1 rangeability which may be sequenced to achieve nearly 2500:1 rangeability, and controllers are available having complementary logarithmic control functions.

In the future, additional electrodes with improved selectivity should become available, and their use with automated instruments for process control and in biomedical applications will undoubtedly increase. The recent introduction of the microprocessor will undoubtedly have a significant impact on the sophistication of automated instruments. This device is a small, but complex, collection of integrated circuits which will perform arithmetic and logical operations according to programmed input instructions, exactly as the central processor of a full-sized computer does. When incorporated into automated instruments, microprocessors will provide versatile and economical means for performing complex timing and sequencing operations, data manipulations, and computations, thereby producing "intelligent instruments." An example of such an approach is the Princeton Applied Research Model 374 microprocessor-controlled Polarographic Analyzer.

Many other types of instruments have been utilized in addition to those described here. The reader is referred to the bibliography for references to this material.

24.5 AUTOMATION IN CLINICAL CHEMISTRY

Billions of tests are run annually in clinical chemistry laboratories; automation has therefore played a large role there. In the preceding sections, automated process-control systems were described. The first part of the present section describes the needs of the clinical chemistry laboratory as they relate to automation. The remainder will be devoted primarily to how clinical instruments are automated and which instrumental methods are most commonly used. Selected instruments will be described.

Automation Needs in Clinical Chemistry

The most significant factor that distinguishes the needs of the clinical laboratory from those of others is that the test results can directly affect the well-being and even the survival of a human being. Some of the factors influencing the design of clinical laboratory instruments are discussed below.

The Clinical Laboratory Environment. The task of the clinical chemist is to perform chemical analyses for diagnostic purposes. The concepts described in the first part of this chapter can be applied because of the common theme of automation for chemical analysis; however, the automation requirements in the clinical laboratory significantly differ from those in either process control or industrial analytical chemistry.

1. The sample is a natural biological material. It is not synthesized, and it cannot be controlled. Automation may control the testing process to some degree, but the sample itself cannot be—except perhaps for automatically rejecting a sample that is too small or has been damaged—for instance, hemolyzed (cells ruptured).

2. The most common clinical sample, blood, is probably one of the most complex substances a chemist is called upon to analyze. He or she is expected to determine the concentrations of a few specific components out of thousands present without interference from any of the other components. This selectivity requirement is usually called *specificity* by clinical chemists.

3. In interpreting the results, the clinical chemist must be aware that the components to be measured may be affected by the recent history of the patient—ingestion of food or drugs (prescribed or not), physical exertion, and the degree of physical trauma or psychological reaction to the circumstances under which the sample is obtained. This exacerbates the problem of specificity and makes the interpretation of results critically dependent on skilled judgment, which must be applied both by responsible personnel in the laboratory and by the physician requesting the analysis.

4. Partly because of the complexity of the sample and problems relating to specificity, few standards are available. An expanding number of pertinent Standard Reference Materials is becoming available from the National Bureau of Standards. Even when available, cost dictates that these be used only to calibrate other reference materials. The latter include so-called "standards" purchased from reagent suppliers and control samples that are frequently derived from a carefully stored pool of blood samples. The precision of results can be assured by good instruments,

properly selected methods, and meticulous protocol; it can be assessed by measuring replicate samples. Accuracy, however, is much more difficult to attain.

There are several strong motives for high accuracy:

1. To insure the diagnostic value of the test results
2. To monitor the progress of a patient under therapy
3. To follow the state of health of an individual, even though the tests may have been performed at different times and perhaps in different laboratories.

It is significant that, although "normal ranges" are developed statistically, these vary widely with sex, age, geographical and ethnic differences, and other factors. The situation is further complicated by the fact that the "normal range" for some components may have wide limits in the statistical population, but narrow limits in each individual biological system. Small deviations from the normal value will then indicate illness. A notable example of this is the concentration of calcium in serum, which is maintained constant to within about 1% by a healthy body, although the "normal" range for the adult population spans $\pm 13\%$.

Automation in the clinical laboratory has been spurred by the steady rise in the number of tests, an annual growth rate of about 10%. As mentioned before, about two billion tests a year are performed in clinical chemistry laboratories in the United States. This could not be physically accomplished without some automation.

A prime objective of automation is to eliminate the need for human intervention in a process. Although this may be applied literally in, for example, process control, the clinical laboratory environment described above requires more constraints. Skilled human judgment is essential for monitoring the viability of the sample and the validity and significance of the results. Therefore, automation is aimed at aiding the clinical analyst in the exercise of these skills.

Clinical Chemistry Tests. The diversity of tests that the clinical chemistry laboratory may be called upon to perform is continually expanding. Very few older tests are displaced by the newer ones developed. A reasonably sized laboratory will be prepared to perform over 60 different tests routinely, and a regional reference laboratory will offer between 200 and 300. However, many of the latter are performed infrequently and do not justify automation. Table 24.2 lists the tests that have been commonly automated.

One indication of the general level of performance achieved in clinical chemistry laboratories is the fact that control samples show a relative standard deviation of between one and three percent. Extenuating circumstances, such as a required solvent-extraction procedure, may lead to relative deviations greater than 10%. Although automation may result in improved precision, the degree attained depends on the skills and motivation of the operator and on the general quality control prevalent in the laboratory.

Automation in the Clinical Laboratory

The first automation in clinical chemistry laboratories was applied primarily to sample handling and processing in the late 1950s. This emphasis can be attributed both to the quantity of specimens and to the state of technology.

TABLE 24.2. *Blood Tests Commonly Automated*

Acid Phosphatase	Glucose
Albumin	Iodine—Protein Bound
Alcohol	Iron
Alanine Transaminase	Lactic Acid
Alkaline Phosphatase	Lactic Dehydrogenase
Aspartate Transaminase	Lithium
Bilirubin—Direct	Oxygen
Bilirubin—Total	pH
Calcium	Phosphate—Inorganic
Carbon Dioxide	Potassium
Chloride	Protein—Total
Cholesterol	Sodium
Creatine Phosphokinase	Triglycerides
Creatinine	Urea Nitrogen
Free Fatty Acids	Uric Acid

Sampling Automation. In the terminology given in the first part of the chapter, instruments that emulate manual sample handling and processing without the use of control loops are *automatic* (mechanized), but not automated. Among the automatic functions are:

1. Sample pickup (from a container such as a small cup)
2. Sample dispensing
3. Dilution
4. Deproteinization
5. Reagent addition
6. Incubation
7. Insertion of the reacted sample into the detection system

It is interesting to note that, when blood is the sample, almost all of the automatic instruments require the use of serum or plasma; none automate the separation of the serum or plasma from the whole blood.*

It is customary to refer to instruments lacking the automatic functions on the above list as *manual* instruments. If these incorporate extensive electronic data-processing, they are called *semiautomatic*.

Discrete and Continuous-Flow Sampling. In the clinical laboratory, the terms *discrete* and *continuous flow* are applied somewhat differently than in process control. In discrete sampling, each sample undergoes a reaction measured in a cuvette not shared

---

* Serum is the clear portion of blood remaining after the blood is allowed to clot and the clot containing the red cells and fibrin is separated out by centrifuging. Plasma is identical to serum except that it still contains fibrinogen, which is normally converted to the insoluble protein fibrinogen to form the clot. Plasma is obtained by adding an anticoagulating agent to prevent the clotting reaction, and then centrifuging out the red cells.

by other reactants. In continuous flow sampling, successive samples pass into the same length of tubing, reagents are added and reactions occur, and finally they flow continuously into a cuvette for detection. In order to isolate successive samples, one or more air bubbles are pumped into the flow line between samples.

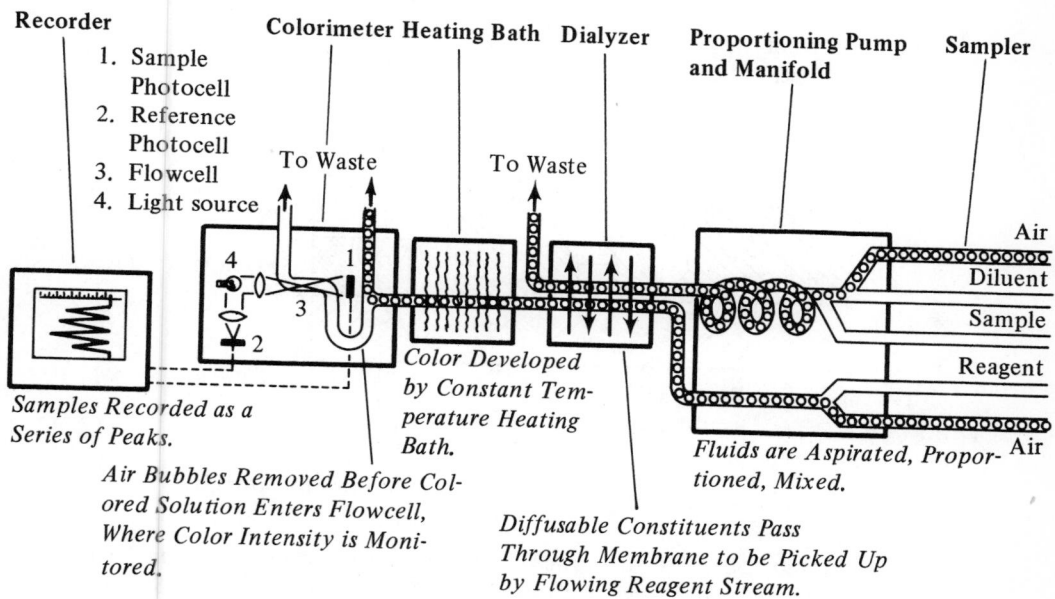

Recorder
1. Sample Photocell
2. Reference Photocell
3. Flowcell
4. Light source

Colorimeter   Heating Bath   Dialyzer   Proportioning Pump and Manifold   Sampler

To Waste

To Waste

Air
Diluent
Sample
Reagent

Air

Samples Recorded as a Series of Peaks.

Color Developed by Constant Temperature Heating Bath.

Fluids are Aspirated, Proportioned, Mixed.

Air Bubbles Removed Before Colored Solution Enters Flowcell, Where Color Intensity is Monitored.

Diffusable Constituents Pass Through Membrane to be Picked Up by Flowing Reagent Stream.

Typical Single–Channel Flow Schematic

FIGURE 24.12.   *Single-channel AutoAnalyzer®.   Courtesy of Technicon Instruments Corporation.*

Since successive samples must be kept isolated from each other in order to avoid cross-contamination, discrete sampling is the natural method for automatic clinical sample processing. Surprisingly, the first successful automation of clinical sampling was a flow-sampling system, the AutoAnalyzer®, marketed in 1957 by Technicon Instruments Corporation. A single-channel AutoAnalyzer is illustrated in Figure 24.12. A successful discrete-sampling instrument was not introduced until almost a decade later; as a result, Technicon has dominated the field of clinical chemistry automation. Only since the late 1960s have discrete sampling instruments begun to play a significant role in automated clinical chemistry.

Instrument Categories. Automatic chemical analyzers are classified by function as follows:

1. *Multi-channel.* These instruments analyze each sample for many different components—in parallel for a discrete analyzer, and sequentially for a continuous-flow analyzer.

2. *Batch.* Batch instruments analyze each sample for a single component at a time, but can be readily changed to analyze other components one at a time. These are also called *single-channel analyzers.*

3. *Parallel Fast.* Parallel-fast analyzers are a special variation of batch analyzers, based on the use of a centrifuge. They are sometimes called *centrifugal fast analyzers.* The principle is illustrated in Figure 24.13. A central, removable

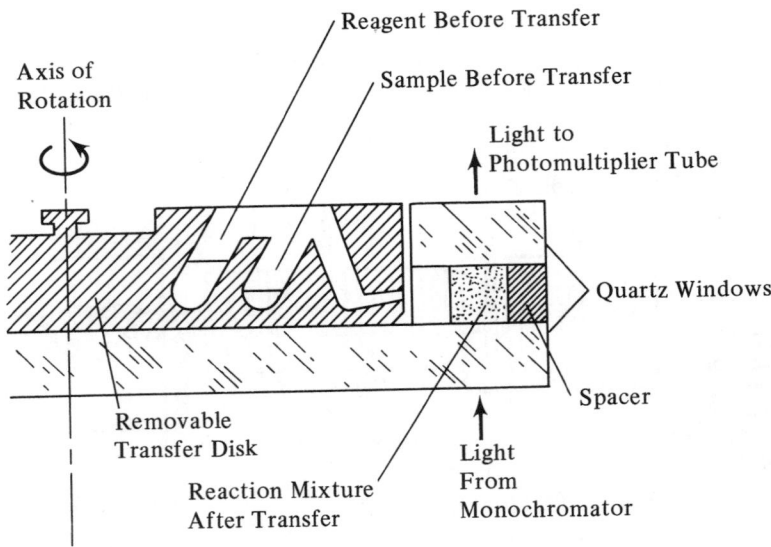

FIGURE 24.13. *Cross-section of sample disc and centrifugal-analyzer section of parallel-fast analyzer. From R. C. Coleman, W. D. Schultz, M. T. Kelly, and J. A. Dean,* Amer. Lab., *3(7), 26 (1971), by permission of International Scientific Communications, Inc.*

disc has radial slots, with two or more wells molded into each slot. An automatic pipette dispenses microsamples into the outer well and reagents into the inner wells of each slot. The disc is placed in a centrifuge rotor with the slots oriented in line with cuvettes around the outer circumference of the rotor. When the rotor spins, the reagents simultaneously wash all of the samples into the cuvettes, which rotate sequentially under a fixed photometer. The transmittance of each cell is read using an oscilloscope monitor, and the data are tabulated by a dedicated computer. The oscilloscope, like a strip-chart recorder, records the transmittance as a function of time as the different cells pass between the light source and the photomultiplier detector. Unlike a strip-chart recorder, however, the oscilloscope can expand the time scale so that transmittance changes over milliseconds or less can be seen. Hence, the transmittance is zero between cells and then increases as each cell passes through the measuring zone. The transmittance is usually read when the rotor speed is about 600 rpm. The sweep rate of the oscilloscope is keyed to the rotation rate to synchronize the readout to each cell. The system can be programmed to take readings over a period of time, say a minute, to obtain a kinetic curve for rate-limited reactions (for instance, enzyme reactions). The computer handles the data processing.

4. *Dedicated.* A dedicated instrument analyzes for only a specified component or a limited number of diagnostically related components; generally, it is not adaptable to other applications.

More examples of the above classes of analyzers will be given below.

The Impact of Modern Electronics

In the 1970s, modern electronics has led clinical automation in a completely new direction. The impact has been both on the instruments with automatic sample-handling and on the manual instruments. Some of the newer instruments are truly automated, as well as automatic. Most of the advantages of modern electronics derive from applications of microelectronic digital circuitry crammed into a remarkably small space—a boon to overcrowded laboratories.

Data Readout. Prior to this technological change, manual instruments, such as colorimeter/spectrophotometers, had meter read-outs with a linear transmittance (energy) scale and, in some cases, a nonlinear (logarithmic) absorbance scale, which in principle saved one computational step in deriving results in concentration units. The read-out of automatic instruments was generally a strip-chart recorder, which traced a series of peaks for the successive samples. In some cases, the chart had a nonlinear concentration scale, which was often shaded or otherwise marked to indicate "normal" physiological ranges. To use these features the deflection had to be calibrated with a sample of known concentration.

The most evident characteristic of modern automatic clinical instruments is the digital display of data. Most have illuminated numerical displays; an instrument that performs more than one determination simultaneously may have several. For example, a digital flame photometer commonly has two displays for the simultaneous read-out of Na and K, whereas a blood gas analyzer may have three, for pH and for the partial pressures of CO_2 and O_2.

Other types of data read-out include printer-listers, hard copy print-out with formatting, and (in some cases) data storage for later retrieval—on tape cassettes, for instance.

Data Processing. The above are superficial benefits of modern electronics. Of even greater value is the electronic processing of the raw data. A read-out directly proportional to concentration can easily be produced, although this requires a logarithmic conversion for colorimetric or spectrophotometric systems. If the instrument is calibrated with a standard of known concentration, the read-out can also be made directly in reportable units. This is a major time saver and, in addition, reduces errors in numerical manipulation and transcription.

As a further refinement, the electronics system can determine how long to wait before the readout signal is acceptably stable, and then lock the displayed result until the operator has recorded it and is ready to initiate the next reading. This type of automation is common to otherwise "manual" instruments. Other niceties are also available, such as automatic integration or averaging of the signal, automatic correction for nonlinear working curves, and automatic blank-subtraction, all of which save time and minimize the chance for human error.

One of the most valuable applications of electronic data-processing is in enzyme assays. Kinetic measurements of enzyme activity in which the rate of reaction is monitored (usually using UV measurement) are more specific than endpoint colorimetric methods, in which the development of color in a coupled reaction is measured after a fixed time. Modern systems continuously or intermittently monitor the growth in concentration of the reaction product or the decrease in concentration of one of the reactants (the substrate). From the rate of change in concentration or the average change in concentration over several fixed time-intervals, the circuitry calculates the activity in reportable units. Other ramifications of these systems will be discussed below.

Some modern clinical instruments are dedicated either to endpoint colorimetric or to kinetic determinations; others allow selection of either mode. Some program the electronic data-processing for the desired mode by means of a punched-card or other coded system that comes with the prepackaged reagents specifically made for this type of instrument. A design objective of this last type of system is to minimize the training needed by the operator.

Data Evaluation. In addition to data processing, electronic systems are being applied to evaluate the data as a further aid to the operator. For example, in an enzyme assay the system will evaluate the linearity of the reaction, which bears on the expected validity of the end result. Also, for samples of very high activity, the substrate may be prematurely exhausted. The electronics are often designed to warn of this dangerous possibility in which a low-level extraneous reaction may persist, yielding an erroneous reading of low activity for a serious case of high activity. Such samples may then yield useful answers by running a second aliquot at a much higher dilution.

In addition, the instrument may be programmed with the range of normal values so that the display will automatically *flag* abnormals. The flag may be an asterisk, or an *H* for high and an *L* for low. Before releasing the data to the requesting physician, flagged results in particular must be evaluated by the laboratory director to determine if the abnormality results from the patient, the instrument, or the reagent. This type of flagging is also helpful to the physician. Some laboratories have extended the principle of flagging by programming their own in-house computer systems to display a statistically likely diagnosis based on the out-of-normal-range data. This is an aid to the physician, who bases his diagnosis on his examination and on the patient's history, as well as on the test results.

Another type of data evaluation performed on some automatic instruments is statistical analysis of a series of data, computing such functions as standard deviation and coefficient of variation.

Instrument Monitoring. In addition to monitoring and evaluating data, circuitry may be arranged to monitor itself and other functions of the instrument. Among the variables that may be monitored are amplifier range, temperature, source operation, speed, reagent supplies, and waste level. The built-in electronics may also diagnose malperformance or dysfunction of the instrument.

A further useful feature is the automatic control and sequencing of multiple functions of the instrument by the built-in electronics, which are effectively a dedicated microcomputer. In some cases a closed loop is involved, so that certain functions are truly automated. For example, an instrument involved in enzyme determinations will monitor the temperature of the reaction cuvette and correct the assayed activity for deviations from the nominal temperature. Also, after initial calibration, an instrument may compare subsequent standards or control samples with the initial value and automatically correct for calibration drift, as well as alerting the operator to excessive drift.

Overview. The above description of automation as applied to clinical instruments leads to an interesting conclusion. Some of the current instruments that do not automate sample handling or processing, and which are referred to as manual or semiautomatic, may be more effective in saving skilled labor and time and reducing human error than some of the automatic instruments of the 1950s and 1960s.

For reference, a spectrophotometer/colorimeter with direct concentration readout costs on the order of $2000; a digital Na/K flame photometer with an automatic sample-diluter, about $4000; a flexible, computer-controlled, single-channel analyzer under $25,000; a computer-based parallel-fast analyzer, about $50,000; and a multi-channel analyzer from about $80,000 to well over $200,000.

Automatic Instrumental Methods

Because the majority of tests in the clinical chemistry laboratory are colorimetrically based, the greatest effort toward automation has been with colorimetric methods. As previously discussed, most of the automation classifies as automatic rather than automated.

A natural extension, because of similar sample-processing, is the use of a fluorimeter in place of the colorimeter. On the data-handling side, the fluorimeter usually provides a signal inherently linear with concentration, which avoids logarithmic conversion.

Enzyme Assays. More recently, the automatic colorimetric systems have been extended to provide kinetic enzyme determinations (or determinations of enzyme substrates). This required several key changes in the colorimetric systems:

1. Although sample processing is similar, temperature is a far more critical factor, since enzyme activity changes at a rate of about 7% per °C. Therefore, temperature equilibrium and constancy in the reaction cuvette are critical. Temperature control to within ± 0.1°C is commonly specified.

2. The detection system must be sensitive at 340 nm, where many enzyme

activity assays are performed. This generally requires sources, filters, gratings and detectors different from those used in colorimeters.

3. There are no recognized enzyme standards or reference materials. The accepted basis for measurement is the rate of reduction of the substrate, commonly nicotinamide adenine dinucleotide (NAD) for many reactions. The reduced form, NADH, absorbs at 340 nm, and the rate of change of this absorbance is measured in an enzyme-activity assay. The absorptivity (a in Beer's law) is known for NADH; from this and the rate of change of absorbance per unit time, the activity of the enzyme can be calculated in micromoles of substrate converted per minute. This is referred to as an *International Unit* (IU), expressing the activity as IU/liter. Therefore, an accurate, absolute absorbance scale must be established in each case in order to make a valid assay.

4. Many enzyme reactions require the measurement of high absorbance values (in the range of 1.0–1.6), in contrast to colorimetry, for which most measurements are made at absorbances no higher than 0.7. This distinction requires a more stable photometer with an increased linearity range.

5. Many reactions, particularly for samples of lower activity, cause very small changes in absorbance during a reasonable observation period. Therefore, the photometer must have high sensitivity and low noise. Some instruments have sensitivity in the range of 10^{-4} absorbance units.

Atomic Emission Spectroscopy. Another commonly automated spectroscopic method is atomic emission spectroscopy (flame photometry). Because sample processing is less elaborate—usually only a dilution—atomic emission spectroscopy was the first to be adapted to the modern methods of data read-out and processing. Instruments were available in 1964 that gave simultaneous numerical read-out of the concentrations of Na and K in directly reportable units.

Electrochemical Methods. The prime candidates for electrochemical automated methods are blood analyzers which measure pH, P_{CO_2}, and P_{O_2}. These are, by the nature of the data, "stat" instruments frequently employed in emergencies. (The term "stat" is applied to a test demanding immediate measurement and expeditious reporting of the result to the attending physician.) The pH is measured potentiometrically by means of the conventional glass electrode, P_{CO_2} is measured with a pH electrode covered with a plastic membrane that is permeable to CO_2, and P_{O_2} is measured amperometrically with a polarographic oxygen electrode (Pt wire covered with an O_2-permeable membrane). Blood gas determinations have depended heavily on the skill of the analyst, which held back the growth in demand. However, as instrumentation improved in the early part of this decade, the test volume grew accordingly. By 1974, the degree of automation of blood gas analyzers rivaled that of other automatic clinical analyzers.

Electrochemical analyzers based on the amperometric measurement of oxygen are used to measure the rate of oxidase enzyme reactions. For example, the substrate glucose is determined by measuring the rate of oxygen consumption in the presence of glucose oxidase. Results are obtained in less than a minute. Similarly, urea is determined enzymatically by measuring the rate of conductance change during urea hydrolysis in the presence of urease.

Radiochemical Methods. Radiochemical techniques are relatively new in the clinical chemistry laboratory; they are now being applied to radioimmunoassays and to determinations involving competitive protein binding, both sometimes called radio-receptor assays. Consequently, the range of automation is limited at this writing to taking radiation counts on a large number of samples—several hundred—with a sequential printout of the counts produced by each sample in a fixed length of time or of the time needed to accumulate a preset number of counts. These tests are labor intensive; new products introduced in 1975, however, are now increasing the level of automation.

Selected Automatic and Automated Clinical Chemistry Analyzers

This section will review selected examples in each of the categories of automation discussed above.

Multi-channel Analyzers. The first widely adopted multi-channel system was the SMA 12/60® (*s*equential *m*ultiple *a*nalyzer) introduced by Technicon in 1967. Built on the continuous-flow principle, it is similar in operation to the single-channel analyzer shown in Figure 24.12, but with the sample split into 12 channels. This generates 12 results sequentially on each sample at the rate of 60 samples, calibrators, and controls per hour. The 12/60 helped to establish the role of the screening battery or "profile" in diagnostic medicine.

The next generation of this product is the computer-controlled Technicon SMAC® which became available in 1974. This has 20 channels and generates results on 150 samples, calibrators, and controls per hour. The operator interacts with the system through a keyboard and an oscilloscope display. The effective rate on actual samples averages 90–100 samples per hour, after taking into account calibrators, controls, and samples that must be rerun because of out-of-range or questionable results. The rate of about 2000 diagnostically significant results per hour from the 20 channels is achieved only after following a start-up protocol taking about 90 min. Two operators are required for the care, feeding and operation of the system.

SMAC offers significant advances over its predecessors besides productivity. Less sample is consumed (about 700 μl), as well as smaller reagent volumes. The system utilizes more modern chemical methods, including kinetic assays and ion-selective electrodes for Na and K. Although the nature of continuous-flow systems precludes the selection of particular channels for a given sample, the computer system can suppress unwanted results and can automatically print out any unrequested test result that is out of the normal range.

Other multi-channel analyzers on the market are discrete sampling systems that feature test selection for each sample. The earlier generation Hycel Mark X and Mark 17 does this with a push-button panel, whereas a dedicated computer does it on the Ortho AcuChem Microanalyzer ("Basic") and the Coulter Chemistry System. All of these systems offer various combinations and degrees of the features discussed above, with 10–18 channels and nominal production rates of 40–60 samples per hour. The Hycel M, shown for the first time in 1975, displays the next step forward in flexibility and productivity because of the computer-based design.

An entirely different multi-channel analyzer, designed for a different application, is the DuPont Automatic Clinical Analyzer (ACA). This is pointed toward generating good answers whether or not the operator is highly skilled. It is well suited for automating the off-hours stat-testing in larger hospitals and for providing a wide selection of assays for smaller laboratories. Without such a system, the small laboratories would find it difficult to maintain personnel skilled in such a wide selection of assays.

The operator of the ACA loads the sample into a well in a rigid header that fits on a track. Hanging from this header is a form on which the operator may enter sample and patient ID information that is reproduced automatically with the test results. Then the operator loads a reagent pack for each test requested on that sample, placing each on the track just in front of the sample header. After separate aliquots of the sample are automatically dispensed into these packs, each enters the main body of the instrument, where the pack also serves as a purification column, as a mixing and reaction chamber, and finally as the test cuvette in the filter photometer. The operator need only prepare and dispense the serum, record ID data, and select the appropriate reagent packs. The expense of skilled labor is traded off for slow speed and the cost of reagent packs. The testing rate averages about one result every 55 sec.

Batch Analyzers. The American Monitor Programachem® 1040 does one test at a time on up to 89 samples at up to 15 results per minute. A prepunched program card automatically sets virtually all of the system variables for each method on insertion into the instrument card-reader. A second-generation instrument, the KDA, was shown in 1975. This provides an integrated system from request slip to report form, with a design heavily dependent on the dedicated minicomputer. Another feature offered is "graphics," which allows an oscilloscopic display of calibration curves, kinetic reaction-curves, quality-control points, etc.

On a much smaller scale, the Gilford 3500 is a computer-directed analyzer. For a given test, the operator must manually set the spectrophotometer wavelength and zero, as well as install the required reagents and set the required aspiration and dispensing volumes and locations. A magnetic program-card operates the system, including a dialogue on the printer, which guides the operator through the required setup and reminds him to key in the values of standards. The printed record includes all key operating data, results in reportable units, and flags where appropriate.

Parallel-Fast Analyzers. There are three commercial versions of centrifugal analyzers, which differ in such details as: (1) the number of samples accommodated on the rotor (15–30); (2) the means of setting variables for a run (manual or preprogrammed on paper tape or tape cassette); (3) the automating of such steps as the wash at the end of a run; and (4) the degree of sophistication in data generation, result listing, automatic evaluation of reaction linearity, flagging, collation of results from several runs, and so on.

In these analyzers, only one determination can be made for each sample during a given run. However, determinations are made in a matter of seconds after samples and reagents are loaded, and only microliter quantities of sample and reagents are required for each determination. Procedures can be changed simply by changing the reagents in the rotor and changing the wavelength setting.

Dedicated Analyzers. A wide choice of such systems, with varying degrees of automation, are available for clinical applications. One of the most prevalent is an atomic-emission spectrometer that generates both Na and K concentrations simultaneously on separate readouts a matter of seconds after a sample is aspirated. Automatic dilutors are commonly built in. Auto samplers and printers are generally available as optional attachments. Some of these systems are readily converted to Li assays when needed.

Beckman makes electrochemically based semiautomatic Glucose and Blood Urea Nitrogen (BUN) Analyzers. They "walk the operator" through the manually initiated steps required. The same company makes a combination Glucose/BUN Analyzer, the System I, which is more highly automated.

Another type of widely used dedicated system is the blood-gas analyzer. These are electrochemical instruments that measure pH, P_{CO_2} and P_{O_2} in whole blood, either simultaneously or sequentially. The recent, more automatic systems operate completely "hands off" after the sample is aspirated. Because the measurements are generally made under stat circumstances, these newer systems periodically recalibrate themselves while on "standby," so that a sample can be run as soon as it arrives in the laboratory.

The growing impact of ion-selective electrodes is evident in the proliferation of dedicated analyzers dependent on ISEs. For example, Technicon markets a Photovolt instrument, the Stat/Ion, which measures Na, K, Cl, and optionally CO_2; and Orion has offered an ionized-calcium analyzer and introduced a sodium/potassium analyzer, all using ion-selective electrodes.

SELECTED BIBLIOGRAPHY

Books

CLEVETT, K. J. *Handbook of Process Stream Analysis.* New York: Halsted Press, 1973. *An up-to-date handbook which describes many types of process analyzers.*

HOUSER, E. A. *Principles of Sample Handling and Sample Systems Design for Process Analysis.* Pittsburgh: Instrument Society of America, 1972. *Contains good information on the design of sample-handling systems.*

SHINSKEY, F. G. *pH and pIon Control in Process and Waste Streams.* New York: John Wiley and Sons, 1973. *Provides an excellent description of the application of potentiometry in process control.*

SHINSKEY, F. G. *Process Control Systems.* New York: McGraw-Hill, Inc., 1967. *All aspects of process control are covered.*

SMITH, D. E., and ZIMMERLI, F. H. *Electrochemical Methods of Process Analysis.* Pittsburgh: Instrument Society of America, 1972. *A good compilation of the electrochemical instrumentation available for use in industrial applications.*

Clinical Chemistry

ALPERT, N. L. *Clinical Instrument Reports.* Philadelphia: North American, 1975.

HICKS, R.; SCHENKIN, J. R.; and STEINRAUF, M. *Laboratory Instrumentation.* New York: Harper and Row, 1974.

LEE, L. W. *Elementary Principles of Laboratory Instruments*, 3rd ed. St. Louis, Mo.: C. V. Mosby, 1974.

WHITE, W. L.; ERICKSON, M. M.; and STEVENS, S. C. *Practical Automation for the Clinical Laboratory*, 2nd ed. St. Louis, Mo.: C. V. Mosby, 1972.

Articles

BOWERS, G. N., Jr. "Analytical Problems in Biomedical Research and Clinical Chemistry," in W. W. Meinke and J. K. Taylor, eds., *Analytical Chemistry: Key to Progress in National Problems*, chap. 3, National Bureau of Standards Special Publication 351. Washington, D.C.: U.S. Government Printing Office, 1972.

HOLLOWELL, C. D. and McLAUGHLIN, R. D.

"Instrumentation for Air Pollution Monitoring," *Environ. Sci. Tech.*, 7, 1011 (1973).

LIGHT, T. S. "Industrial Analysis and Control with Ion Selective Electrodes," in R. A. Durst, ed., *Ion Selective Electrodes*, chap. 10, National Bureau of Standards Special Publication 314. Washington, D.C.: U.S Government Printing Office, 1969.

Process Measurement and Control Terminology, SAMA Standard PMC20-2-1970, Scientific Apparatus Makers Association, 370 Lexington Ave., New York, New York, Pub. No. 219.

SOULE, L. M. "Basic Concepts of Industrial Process Control," *Chem. Eng.* Sept. 22, 1969.

SOULE, L. M. "Basic Control Modes," *Chem. Eng.*, Oct. 20, 1969.

REFERENCES

1. IUPAC Information Bulletin No. 26, International Union of Pure and Applied Chemistry, Oxford, England.

2. R. G. BATES, *Determination of pH: Theory and Practice*, New York: John Wiley and Sons, 1964, pp 382–83.

3. SAMA Standard PMC-20-1-1973, Scientific Apparatus Makers Association, 370 Lexington Ave., New York, N.Y.

4. F. G. SHINSKEY, *Process Control Systems*, New York: McGraw-Hill, 1967, chap. 1.

5. R. J. REYNOLDS and E. L. PIERSON, *Amer. Lab.*, 3(8), 27 (1971).

6. R. ANNINO, *J. Chromatogr. Sci.*, 8, 288 (1970).

7. R. ANNINO and L. E. BULLOCK, *Anal. Chem.*, 45, 1221 (1973).

8. R. VILLALOBOS, *Anal. Chem.*, 47(11), 983A (1975).

9. R. A. DURST, *Amer. Sci.*, 59, 353 (1971).

APPENDIX A

Units, Symbols, and Prefixes

Units in the text correspond to those in common usage. Many are gradually being replaced by the Système International (SI) or International System of Units. These recommended units, their symbols, and prefixes indicating multiples and fractions of units, are listed here.

SI Units

Quantity	Name	Symbol
Length	meter	m
Mass	kilogram	kg
Time	second	s
Electric Current	ampere	A
Thermodynamic Temperature	kelvin	K
Luminous Intensity	candela	cd
Amount of Substance	mole	mol
Plane Angle	radian	rad
Solid Angle	steradian	sr

Other Units in Use with SI

Quantity	Name	Symbol	Value in SI Unit
Time	minute	min	$1\ \text{min} = 60\ \text{s}$
	hour	h	$1\ \text{h} = 3600\ \text{s}$
	day	d	$1\ \text{d} = 86{,}400\ \text{s}$
Volume	liter	L	$1\ \text{L} = 1\ \text{dm}^3 = 10^{-3}\ \text{m}^3$

Quantity	Name	Symbol	Units	Special Multiples
Frequency	hertz	Hz	s^{-1}	——
Force	newton	N	$kg \cdot m \cdot s^{-2}$	$10^{-5} N = 1$ dyne (dyn)
Pressure [a]	pascal	Pa	$kg \cdot m^{-1} \cdot s^{-2} =$ $N \cdot m^{-2}$	10^5 Pa = 1 bar
Power, Radiant Flux	watt	W	$kg \cdot m^2 \cdot s^{-3} = J \cdot s^{-1}$	——
Electric Charge, Quantity of Electricity	coulomb	C	$A \cdot s$	——
Electric Potential, Potential Difference, Electromotive Force	volt	V	$kg \cdot m^2 \cdot s^{-3} \cdot A^{-1}$	——
Electric Resistance	ohm	Ω	$kg \cdot m^2 \cdot s^{-3} \cdot A^{-2}$	——
Electrical Capacitance	farad	F	$A^2 \cdot s^4 \cdot kg^{-1} \cdot m^{-2}$	——
Conductance	siemens	S	$kg^{-1} \cdot m^{-2} \cdot s^3 \cdot A^2 =$ Ω^{-1}	——
Energy, Work, Quantity of Heat [b]	joule	J	$kg \cdot m^2 \cdot s^{-2} = V \cdot C$	$10^{-7} J = 1$ erg
Magnetic Flux	weber	Wb	$kg \cdot m^2 \cdot s^{-2} \cdot A^{-1}$	10^{-8} Wb = 1 maxwell (Mx)
Inductance	henry	H	$kg \cdot m^2 \cdot s^{-2} \cdot A^{-2}$	——
Magnetic Flux Density	tesla	T	$kg \cdot s^{-2} \cdot A^{-1}$	10^{-4} T = 1 gauss (G)
Luminous Flux	lumen	lm	$cd \cdot sr$	——
Illumination	lux	lx	$cd \cdot sr \cdot m^{-2}$	——

a. 101,325 Pa = 1 atmosphere (atm) = 760 millimeters of mercury (mm Hg)
133.322 Pa = 1 torr = 1 millimeter of mercury (mm Hg)
b. 3.6 × 10^6 J = 1 kilowatt-hour (kWh)
1055.056 J = 1 British thermal unit (BTU)
4.184 J = 1 thermochemical calorie (cal_{th})

Prefixes Indicating Multiples and Fractions of Units

Multiple	Prefix	Symbol	Fraction	Prefix	Symbol
10^{18}	exa	E	10^{-1}	deci	d
10^{15}	peta	P	10^{-2}	centi	c
10^{12}	tera	T	10^{-3}	milli	m
10^9	giga	G	10^{-6}	micro	μ
10^6	mega	M	10^{-9}	nano	n
10^3	kilo	k	10^{-12}	pico	p
10^2	hecto	h	10^{-15}	femto	f
10	deka	da	10^{-18}	atto	a
			10^{-21}	flato	ϕ

APPENDIX B

Selected Fundamental Physical Constants

Numbers in parentheses refer to standard-deviation uncertainties in the last digit, computed on the basis of internal consistency.

Quantity	Symbol	Value	Error (ppm)	Decimal and Units SI	cgs
Velocity of Light	c	2.9979250(10)	0.33	10^8 m·s^{-1}	10^{10} cm·s^{-1}
Electron Charge	e	1.6021917(70)	4.4	10^{-19} C	10^{-20} emu
		4.803250(21)	4.4	——	10^{-10} esu
Planck's Constant	h	6.626196(50)	7.6	10^{-34} J·s	10^{-27} erg·s
	$\hbar = \dfrac{h}{2\pi}$	1.0545919(80)	7.6	10^{-34} J·s	10^{-27} erg·s
Electron Volt	eV	1.60210	——	10^{-19} J	10^{-12} erg
		3.827	——	——	10^{-20} cal
Avogadro's Number	N	6.022169(40)	6.6	10^{26} kmol^{-1}	10^{23} mol^{-1}
Atomic Mass Unit	amu	1.660531(11)	6.6	10^{-27} kg	10^{-24} g
Proton Mass	M_p	1.672614(11)	6.6	10^{-27} kg	10^{-24} g
	M_p^*	1.00727661(8)	0.08	amu	amu
Electron Mass	m_e	9.109558(54)	6.0	10^{-31} kg	10^{-28} g
	m_e^*	5.485930(34)	6.2	10^{-4} amu	10^{-4} amu
Neutron Mass	M_n	1.674920(11)	6.6	10^{-27} kg	10^{-24} kg
	M_n^*	1.00866520(10)	0.10	amu	amu
Faraday Constant	F	9.648670(54)	5.5	10^7 C·kmol^{-1}	10^3 esu·mol^{-1}
		2.892599(16)	5.5	——	10^{14} esu·mol^{-1}
Gas Constant	R	1.9872	——		cal·K^{-1}·mol^{-1}
		8.3143	——	J·K^{-1}·mol^{-1}	10^7 erg·K^{-1}·mol^{-1}
		8.2054	——		10^{-2} l·atm·K^{-1}·mol^{-1}
Rydberg Constant	R_∞	1.09737312(11)	0.10	10^7 m^{-1}	10^5 cm^{-1}
Bohr Magneton	μ_B	9.274096(65)	7.0	10^{-24} J·T^{-1}	10^{-21} erg·G^{-1}
Boltzmann Constant	k	1.380622(59)	43	10^{-23} J·K^{-1}	10^{-16} erg·K^{-1}
Stefan-Boltzmann Constant	σ	5.66961(96)	170	10^{-8} W·m^{-2}·K^{-4}	10^{-5} erg·s^{-1}·cm^{-2}·K^{-4}

Source: Adapted in part from "Reference Guide to Optical Energy Measurements," Princeton Applied Research Corp., 1974, by permission of the publisher.

APPENDIX C

Answers to Selected Problems

Chapter 2

1. $\Delta a_i / a_i = 3.89\%$ per mV uncertainty

3. (a) 0.03 M; (b) 0.05 M; (c) 0.3 M; (d) 0.006 M

4. (a) $f_{Mg^{2+}} = 0.70$, $f_{Cl^-} = 0.91$; (b) $f_{Mg^{2+}} = 0.56$, $f_{K^+} = f_{Cl^-} = 0.86$; (c) $f_{Mg^{2+}} = 0.22$, $f_{K^+} = f_{Cl^-} = 0.69$

5. (a) pH = 4.41, (b) pH = 10.70

6. +0.622 V versus SHE, +0.377 V versus SCE

7. −0.951 V

8. 160.0 g/eq

10. +7.5%

11. 3×10^{-7}, 1.2×10^{-6}, 1.6×10^{-6}, 7×10^{-5}, and 3.3×10^{-4} M; for a 10% interference level, the concentrations can be an order of magnitude higher.

12. 0.08%

13. 0.68 μgI/ml

14. $10^{\Delta E/S} = 10^{nF(E_2 - E_1)/2.303RT} = k_{ij}\left(\dfrac{a_j}{a_i}\right) + 1$

15. $k_{ij} = k_{I^-, Br^-} = 0.0015$; liquid junction potentials are constant—that is, $E_{constant}$ is constant—and $a_{Br^-}/a_{I^-} = c_{Br^-}/c_{I^-}$

16. The average of the two volumes used for ΔE (first derivative plot) or $\Delta^2 E$ (second derivative plot) is graphed on the volume axis, resulting in an estimation of 47.95 ml at the first-derivative endpoint, and 47.935 ml at the second-derivative endpoint.

17. k_{ij} for $Zn^{2+} = 50$, for $Pb^{2+} = 20$, for $Mg^{2+} = 0.01$, for $H^+ = 1000$, for $Na^+ = 0.003$, for $K^+ = 0.001$.

Chapter 3

8. (a) 3.58 (b) 8.7×10^{-6} cm²/sec

9. 3.3 mm²

10. 0.156 mM; 5.0 ppm

11. 1×10^{-6} M

12. 102 min

13. (a) $n = 2$ (b) See problem 12. Electrolyze for a known (long!) time and monitor the decrease in concentration. Using special cells that contain solution volumes as small as 1 ml or less, such experiments have been carried out in conveniently short times.

14. (a) L-shaped: $Ag \rightarrow Ag^+ + e^-$ (anode) and $Ag^+ + e^- \rightarrow Ag$ (cathode) prior to endpoint; no reactions after endpoint.
(b) V-shaped: same reactions as above prior to endpoint; $Ag + Cl^- \rightarrow AgCl + e^-$ (anode) and $2H^+ + 2e^- \rightarrow H_2$ or $2H_2O + 2e^- \rightarrow H_2 + 2OH^-$ (cathode) after endpoint.

Chapter 4

1. +1.632 V versus SHE

2. 27,900 sec

3. 0.1116%

4. 96.485 mA

5. 4.6 ppm

6. 0.0537 g Cu.   Theoretical value = 0.1742 cm³/coul

7. 3.25 μm

8. +0.202 V versus SCE

9. 7.705 mg

Chapter 5

1. 1.0×10^{-5}, 2.5×10^{-5}, 1.5×10^{-4} N

2. 890 ppm

3. (a) 25 cm⁻¹, solution resistances will vary between 73 and 86 ohm.
(b) 100,000 micromhos (midpoint equivalent to 100 ohm).

4. 110 to 1130 ohm, or 9100 to 885 μmho

5. (a) $\Lambda = 6.73$ (b) $\alpha = 0.0176$ (c) $K_a = 6.3 \times 10^{-6}$

6. 2033 ohm

7. 0.0175 N

9. $\kappa_{AgCl} = 1.81 \times 10^{-6}$ ohm⁻¹ cm⁻¹; $K_{sp,AgCl} = 1.71 \times 10^{-10}$ M^2

10. 2.4% hydrocarbon in glycol; 1.5% glycol in hydrocarbon

Chapter 7

1. 588.997 nm; 5.08960×10^{14} Hz

2. -4.9 eV, 253 nm

3. 5×10^{-10} M

4. 2.4×10^4

5. 3.7×10^{-5} M p-nitroaniline; 8.9×10^{-5} M o-nitroaniline

6. $pK_a = 6.4$

7. (a) 2.1×10^{-2} l/(g-cm) (b) 3.16×10^4 l/(mole-cm) (c) 0.03 mg X in 25.0 ml (d) 1.2 ppm X

8. 0.260% Cu

9. 0.533% Mn

10. 2×10^6

11. 122

12. (a) 1:1; (b) 2.8×10^5

13. There is probably an impurity in the "blank" which absorbs at the analytical wavelength. The impurity appears to be present at constant concentration since subtraction of the "blank" absorbance from all values results in a linear plot with zero intercept.

14. (a) 8.87 mM (b) 6.44 mM (c) 7.67

Chapter 8

1. (a) 0.7–2.5 μm; 2.5–50 μm; 50–1000 μm
(b) 14,285–4000 cm⁻¹; 4000–200 cm⁻¹; 200–10 cm⁻¹

2. (a) 14,285 cm⁻¹; (b) 0.7 μm; (c) 1.76 eV

3. (a) 1.76–0.49 eV; (b) 0.49–0.02 eV; (c) 0.02–0.001 eV

4. 2144.5 cm⁻¹; 0.265 eV; 6.11×10^3 cal/mole

5. *J. Chem. Phys.*, *47*, 4325 (1967); *49*, 2344 (1968); *Spectrochim. Acta*, *21*, 1505 (1965).

6. $A = 0.30$

7. (a) Far infrared (b) Medium infrared, Near infrared (overtone)

8. Medium and Far infrared

9. AgCl windows in a demountable cell; experiment with spacers

10. $\varepsilon = $ 40 l/(mole-cm)

11. 2740, 4110 cm⁻¹

12. 2110, 1790 cm⁻¹

13. (a) 1190, 1680, 2060 cm⁻¹; (b) About 7.5×10^5 dyne/cm, since it is midway between a single and a double carbon-carbon bond; 1460 cm⁻¹; (c) ~1650 cm⁻¹ for C=C; ~2160 cm⁻¹ for C≡C; about 1470 cm⁻¹ in benzene.

14.

$\bar{\nu}$	4880 Å	5145 Å	5682 Å	6471 Å
3374 cm⁻¹	5842	6226	7030	8278
3287 cm⁻¹	5812	6192	6987	8219
1974 cm⁻¹	5400	5727	6400	7419
729 cm⁻¹	5060	5345	5928	6791
612 cm⁻¹	5030	5312	5887	6738

15. $\rho = 0.75$ (depolarized), 0.074 (polarized), 0.016 (polarized), 0.78 (depolarized)

16. 4880 Å : 5145 Å : 5682 Å : 6471 Å = 3.09 : 2.50 : 1.68 : 1.00

Chapter 9

8. 84 ppm

9. 2.82; 1.83 μg/ml

10. (a) 30:1 (b) The cuvette and monochromators must transmit the same fraction of light at all wavelengths concerned.

11. In phosphorescence, an electron in an excited singlet state crosses over to a triplet state by intersystem crossing—a "forbidden transition" that occurs with some probability if the energy of the lowest vibrational level of the triplet state is lower than that of the excited singlet state. From here it can radiationally return to the singlet ground state. The emitted photon is phosphorescence, and it is of longer wavelength than a fluorescence wavelength produced by the same singlet state. Because the probability of triplet-singlet transitions is low, the lifetime of the triplet state is relatively long. Measurements are made at liquid nitrogen temperatures to minimize collisional deactivation during the relatively long lifetime of the triplet state.

Chapter 10

17. 1.4 ppm

18. 7.5 ppm

20. (a) 37.0 $\pm$ 1.0% Ba by weight (about 2.7% relative standard deviation). (b) Since the "pure" compound should be 32.12% Ba by weight, and the analytical result is about five standard deviations removed, it is highly unlikely that the preparation is 100% pure. Most probably, there is an excess of a barium salt in the crystalline compound.

21. (b) 25% added methanol, since this produces a 48% enhancement in the A/c ratio with only a 25% dilution factor. (c) $2.65 \times 10^{-5} M$; $1.78 \times 10^{-5} M$ (in the original aqueous solution) with 25% added methanol.

22. The enhancing effect of the potassium is due to the suppression of sodium ionization in the flame as potassium adds electrons to the flame. The result is a greater population of sodium atoms available for thermal excitation.

Chapter 11

6. Mg, Zn, Cu, Th, Zr, Mn, Ca, Si, Al (a Mg alloy)

7. 0.04 μg/ml

8. $\sigma = \pm 0.26$, r.s.d. $= \pm 5.8\%$

10. Fraction ionized at 2500 K is 1.24×10^{-9}; at 5000 K is 1.11×10^{-3}

11. 0.13% Si, 1.4% Na

Chapter 12

1. (a) $+0.86$ ppm (0.86 ppm downfield) (b) 298.4 MHz

2. A, e; B, f; C, c; D, d; E, b; F, a.

3. Acetone: singlet, 2.11 ppm. Methylethyl ketone: singlet, 2.05 ppm (area 3); quartet, 2.40 ppm (area 2); triplet, 0.99 ppm (area 3).

4. Propane: triplet, 0.99 ppm (area 6); multiplet, 1.29 ppm (area 2). 1-Nitropropane: triplet, 1.01 ppm (area 3); multiplet, 2.00 ppm (area 2); triplet, 4.31 ppm (area 2).

5. (a) 4,258 Hz/gauss (b) 100 MHz (c) 20 MHz

7. (a) 3.55 ppm (b) 3.66 ppm (c) 438 Hz

8. Hindered rotation; therefore essentially two different environments for the methyls.

11. Benzene:toluene = 2:1.

12. C_3H_7Cl = 2-chloropropane; $C_7H_{16}O_3$ = $(CH_3CH_2O)_3CH$; C_7H_7ClO = 1-chloro-4-methoxybenzene; C_9H_9ClO =

$$para\text{-isomer of } CH_3CH_2\overset{\overset{\displaystyle O}{\|}}{C}-C_6H_4-Cl$$

$C_9H_{10} = C_6H_5-CH_2CH{=}CH_2$

13. $CH_2Cl(CO)CHClCH_2COOH$

14. A = $HCFCl-CFCl_2$
B = $HCCl_2-CF_2Cl$

Chapter 13

1. 3198, 7825, and 11908 gauss for $g = 2.100$; 3377, 8262, and 12573 gauss for $g = 1.989$

2. $\Delta H = 43, 105,$ and 160 gauss for $g_1 = 1.964$, $g_2 = 1.989$; $\Delta H = 11, 27,$ and 41 gauss for $g_1 = 2.080, g_2 = 2.073$

3. 0.314, 0.767, and 1.168 cm^{-1}/molecule

T (K)	$\nu = 9.4$	23 GHz	35 GHz
4	1.26×10^{-5}	1.03×10^{-12}	5.76×10^{-19}
20	1.05×10^{-1}	4.01×10^{-3}	2.25×10^{-4}
77	5.57×10^{-1}	2.38×10^{-1}	1.13×10^{-1}
298	8.60×10^{-1}	6.90×10^{-1}	5.69×10^{-1}

5. Two equivalent Fs, 2 sets of 2 equivalent Hs: 27 lines

Two equivalent Fs, 3 sets of Hs in 2:1:1 ratio: 36 lines

Two equivalent Fs, one set of 4 equivalent Hs: 15 lines

6. 5 lines

7. Twelve lines for the Cu compound; 24 lines for the V compound.

Chapter 14

11. $d_1 = 2.51$ Å, $d_2 = 2.22$ Å, $d_3 = 2.85$ Å. $CuFeO_2$ has d values of 2.51 Å, 2.23 Å, and 2.85 Å of relative intensities 100:39:25; $NaCS_3$ had d values of 2.52 Å, 2.22 Å, and 2.84 Å with relative intensities of 100:18:15. Hence, the substance appears to be $CuFeO_2$.

12. $2\theta = 34.34°$

13. $S_1 = 68.8$ mm, $S_2 = 45.2$ mm, $S_3 = 79.6$ mm

14. $\lambda = 2.287$ Å. This corresponds to the $K\alpha$ line of chromium.

15. $\lambda = 0.248$ Å

16. $T = 0.633$

Chapter 15

1. O $2s$, 25 eV; Si $2p$, 100 eV; Si $2s$, 155 eV; C $1s$, 285 eV; Ag $3d$, 370 and 375 eV; O $1s$, 530 eV.

2. P $2p$, 135 eV; S $2p$, 165 eV; C $1s$, 285 eV; N $1s$, 400 eV; O $1s$, 530 eV; F $1s$, 690 eV

3. Binding energy for Fe $2p_{3/2}$ photoelectron = 714 eV in Fe_2O_3; 717 eV in FeF_2; 710 eV in Fe. From Table 15.1, the "nominal" $2p_{3/2}$ binding energies for Mn, Fe, and Co are 641, 710, and 779 eV, respectively.

4. See C. A. Evans, Jr., *Anal. Chem.*, *47*(9), 819A, 855A (1975).

5. (a and b) In a close-packed arrangement, one silver atom would occupy *about* 7.4×10^{-16} cm^2 of the surface area of a (flat) silicon substrate. For 0.001 monolayer, this would correspond to about 1.1×10^{10} atoms or 1.9×10^{-12} g of Ag. (c) 1.2×10^{-3} g/cm³; 520 ppm

6. (a) 1153 eV (b) 920 eV

7. C $1s$ in CH_4, CO, and CO_2; O $1s$ in CO_2, CO.

8. The peaks are probably due to aluminum $2p$ photoelectrons: the peak at lower binding energy to Al^0, that at higher energy to Al^{3+}. Aluminum metal is known to quickly form a thin protective skin of Al_2O_3. Even the short exposure to air after abrasion allowed some Al_2O_3 to form; a full week's exposure allowed a thicker skin to form, although the oxide skin must still be less than about 15 Å thick, as photoelectrons from the underlying Al^0 are still seen.

9. 83%, 68%, 30% MoO_2

Chapter 16

1. $H = 1052$ gauss, $r = 29.05$ cm

2. $H = 2975$ gauss, $r = 29.88$ cm

3. Voltage should be reduced to 1765 V to just observe $m/e = 850$ at highest magnetic field.

4. Chamber: +1765 V; exit slit: ground; repellers: 1775 V; filament: 1715 V; target: 1845 V

5. Exact mass = 220.1679; formula = $C_{11}H_{22}O_4$

6. $CO^+/C_2H_4^+$: $R = 770$; $C_{20}H_{40}^+/C_{19}H_{36}^+$: $R = 7700$

7. $C_2H_2^+$: 6.70×10^{-6} sec; $C_6H_5^+$: 1.15×10^{-5} sec; $C_6H_6^+$: 1.16×10^{-5} sec

8. 3.1×10^{-3} sec

9. 153 kHz

10. C_6H_6: 6.6%, 0.22%; $C_2H_4O_2$: 2.2%, 0.41%; $C_2H_8N_2$: 2.9%, 0.02%; C_3H_7Cl: 3.3%, 33%, 1.09%; C_4H_4S: 5.2%, 4.5%; $C_{16}H_{34}$: 17.6%, 1.5%

12. $\% \, d_3 = 90$; $\% \, d_2 = 6$; $\% \, d_1 = 4$

13. Chlorobenzene

14. *sec*-Butylamine

15. Perbromic acid (HBrO$_4$)

16. #1: 3-methyl-2-pentanone; #2: 2-methyl-3-pentanone

17. Propylphenyl ether

18. $R = \dfrac{M}{\Delta M} = \dfrac{32}{2(15.994914) - 31.972074}$

$= 1800$

19. Mother ion = CH_3O^+ ($m = 31$); daughter ion = CHO^+ ($m = 29$)

20. (A) (a) $C_2H_5O^+ \rightarrow H_3O^+ + C_2H_2$,

$m^* = 8.02$

(b) $C_2H_5O^+ \rightarrow CHO^+ + CH_4$,

$m^* = 18.69$

(B) H_3COCH_2Y, since a rearrangement is necessary to facilitate elimination of C_2H_2.

21. $m/e = 114$: molecular (parent) ion

$m/e = 99$: 114–15 (loss of CH$_3$)

$m/e = 71$: 114–43 (loss of propyl)

$m/e = 57$: $C_4H_9{}^+$ (*t*-butyl ion)

$m/e = 43$: $C_3H_7{}^+$ (*i*-propyl ion)

2,2,4-trimethylpentane spectrum is in column (a)

22. *t*-butyl amine; $C_4H_{11}N$

23. Since m/e for P is an even number, there must be 0 or an even number of nitrogens (eliminating C_4H_8NO and $C_5H_{12}N$). Among the remaining, $C_5H_{10}O$ gives the best correspondence.

24. Order of appearance = CO, N$_2$, C$_2$H$_4$; the order of increasing exact nuclidic masses.

Chapter 17

5. 2

6. CaC$_2$O$_4 \cdot$ H$_2$O $\xrightarrow{100\text{--}250°}$

$\quad$ CaC$_2$O$_4$ + H$_2$O $\quad$ (-6.2 mg)

CaC$_2$O$_4 \xrightarrow{360\text{--}500°}$

$\quad$ CaCO$_3$ + CO $\quad$ (-9.6 mg)

CaCO$_3 \xrightarrow{620\text{--}860°}$

$\quad$ CaO + CO$_2$ $\quad$ (-15.0 mg)

BaC$_2$O$_4 \cdot$ H$_2$O $\xrightarrow{100\text{--}250°}$

$\quad$ BaC$_2$O$_4$ + H$_2$O $\quad$ (-3.7 mg)

BaC$_2$O$_4 \xrightarrow{360\text{--}500°}$

$\quad$ BaCO$_3$ + CO $\quad$ (-5.7 mg)

BaCO$_3 \xrightarrow{\sim 1000°}$ BaO + CO$_2$ $\quad$ (-9.0 mg)

8. From the *Merck Index*, 1952: (1) Endotherm at $\sim 133°$C melting of urea, (2) Endo- or exotherm at $\sim 150°$C formation of biuret, (3) Endo- or exotherm at $\sim 150°$C formation of cyanuric acid, (4) Endotherm at $\sim 190°$C melting of biuret

9. Let R be the minimum rate of reaction observable via DTA or TG. Then $R = k_f[\text{Reactants}]^x - k_r[\text{Products}]^y$. Also, consider the Arrhenius equation $R = Ae^{-E_a/RT}$ which predicts a two-fold increase in rate for each 10°C rise in temperature.

(a) If product is present, $R' < R$ from the rate expression above, and temperature must be increased to get back to R.

(b) If reactant is present, the second term is zero and $R'' > R$. To decrease R'' to R, the temperature must be decreased.

(c) Since $R = k[\text{Reactants}]^x = Ae^{-E_a/RT}$ then $x \ln[\text{Reactants}] = -E_a/RT + \ln A$ A plot of $\ln[\text{Reactants}]$ versus $-1/T$ will yield x, the kinetic coefficient, which is often (but not always) the same as the stoichiometric coefficient.

13. Area = 79.8 cm^2.

14. $C_p = 151.8$ cal/°C; $R_H = 15.20$ ohms. Since heater leads and heater contribute to R_H and V_H, the V_H will be too high and the C_p will be too high.

16. $\Delta H_{ion} = +3.2$ kcal/mole

17. $K_{stab} = 4.99 \times 10^3$; $\Delta G = -5.1 \times 10^3$, $\Delta H = -10.0$ kcal; $\Delta S = -16$ cal/(mol-°C)

20. Assume $C_p = 50.0$ cal/°C (solution close to pure H$_2$O). $\Delta T_{TRISH^+} = 0.019°$C; $\Delta T_{TRIS} = 0.115°$C.

21. This appears to be a simple solid-state phase transition, and may be related to a structural change in the compound.

22. By comparing the weights obtained at 400° and 700°C, the amount of NO$_3$ lost by AgNO$_3$ is found. Therefore, the weight of Ag may be calculated. Since only Ag and CuO are present at 700°, the amount of CuO is easily found by difference. Hence, the weights of residual Ag and Cu above 950° can be calculated.

Chapter 18

1. (a) A plot of $\log(c_{t=\infty} - c_t)$ versus time is a straight line. (b) From slope, $k = 6.67 \times 10^{-5}$ sec^{-1}. From the 2nd, 4th, and 6th points, $k = 6.62$, 6.71, and 6.65×10^{-5} sec^{-1}. (c) $k_2 = 2.65 \times 10^3$ l/(mole-sec).

2. A plot of $1/c_a$ versus t is a straight line of slope k and intercept $1/c_a°$; $k = 0.196$ l/(mole-sec).

3. Azomethane $= 128$ torr; N_2 and $C_2H_6 = 72$ torr each.

4. $k = 9.29 \times 10^{-6}$ sec^{-1} at both 0.44 M and 0.167 M sucrose.

5. First order, $k = 2.60 \times 10^{-5}$ sec^{-1}; $t_{90\%} = 24.5$ hour, $t_{99\%} = 49.2$ hour.

6. Second order, 3.27×10^{-2} l/(mole-sec)

7. 7.94×10^{-6} sec^{-1}; $t_{1/2} = 24.3$ hr

8. 4.1

Chapter 19

1. 286 ppm Al

2. (a) The 5.62-MeV peak is due to the pair production interaction of the primary 6.13-MeV gamma ray with the crystal and the loss of *one* 0.511 position annihilation photon from the crystal without interaction. This is the "1st escape peak." (b) The 5.11-MeV peak is due to loss of *both* 0.511-MeV annihilation photons resulting from a pair production event in the crystal. This is the "2nd escape peak." (c) The 0.511-MeV peak is due to pair production interaction of the 6.13 MeV primary gamma ray in the *surroundings and shielding* of the detector. The 0.511-MeV position annihilation photons generated in the surrounding materials then intersect the crystal, yielding the observed 0.511-MeV peak.

3. 0.926 g Mn/g Fe

4. 0.8 ppm I$^-$

5. $N_0 = 2.60 \times 10^5$

7. Possible reactions:
   (a) $^{64}_{28}$Ni (n, γ) $^{65}_{28}$Ni

   $^{65}_{28}$Ni $\xrightarrow{2.55 \text{ hr}}$

   β^- and γ (1.48 MeV, etc.)

(b) $^{58}_{28}$Ni (n, γ) $^{59}_{28}$Ni

   $^{59}_{28}$Ni $\xrightarrow[8 \times 10^4 \text{ years}]{\text{EC}}$ $^{59}_{27}$Co

(c) $^{62}_{28}$Ni (n, γ) $^{63}_{28}$Ni

   $^{63}_{28}$Ni $\xrightarrow{92 \text{ years}}$ β^- (no γ)

(d) $^{58}_{28}$Ni (n, p) $^{58}_{27}$Co

   $^{58}_{27}$Co $\xrightarrow{71.4 \text{ days}}$ β^+ and several γs

8. 31.4% Co

9. Net Rate $= 1400 \pm 50$ counts/min

10. Ratio $A/B = 0.41 \pm 0.03$

11. 1.9×10^4 years

12. (a) 3.70×10^{10} atoms (b) 1600 years

13. (a) 1.00 microcurie (b) 2.10×10^{-6} sec^{-1} (c) 1.76×10^{10} atoms (d) 6.49×10^{-12} g

14. 725 curies

15. 1.77 disintegrations per second

16. one half-life

17. Average lifetime of an atom $= \Sigma$ (individual atomic lifetimes)/(total number of atoms) $= 1.443$ H.

Chapter 21

1. (a) $R_f = 1/(1 + k')$ (b) $k' = 2.3$ (c) Yes, $\Delta R_f = 0.03$

2. (a) k' for o-, m-, and p-nitroaniline $= 1, 2,$ and 3.5 respectively.
   (b) α for m- and p-nitroaniline $= 2.0, 3.5$

3. (a) R_f for 3'- and 2'-GMP $= 0.50$ and 0.58.
   (b) $\alpha = 1.4$

4. (a) 64,000 (b) Yes, $R = 2.7$

5. (b) Molecular weight $= 3.2 \times 10^3$ (c) about 1000

6. (a) 27.6 mg (b) 3.8 mg (c) 360 cm

7. (a) $t_r = NH(1 + k')/v$ (b) $t_r = 50$ min

8. (a) $L_2 = 26.7$, $L_1 = 26.7$ m; pressure drop $= 267$ atm (b) $t_{r_2} = t_{r_1}/0.004 = 7500$ min (c) $d_{p_2} = 8$ μm, pressure drop $= 250$ atm. Option (c) is best.

Chapter 22

3. (a) $I = 776$ (b) Only that n-butylacetate behaves in this system as if it were a hydrocarbon of 7.75 carbon-number. Structural information is better derived from the index increment ΔI ($I_{\text{polar}} - I_{\text{nonpolar}}$).

7. Toluene, 724; cyclohexane, 690.

8. (a) 1770, 2810, 3840, 4880 mm Hg (b) $j =$
0.558, 0.374, 0.280, 0.223

9. 29.6, 50.0, 64.6 ml/min

10. (a) $V_r' = 59.6$, 226.8, 606.9 ml (b) $V_n =$
16.7, 63.5, 170.0 ml (c) $V_g = 10.7$, 40.9,
109.5 ml (d) 8.7, 9.2

12. (a) 4500 (b) 6300 (c) 9800 (d) 39000
(e) 4400 (f) 0.9, 1.3, 98, and 390 m

Chapter 23

1. (a) 101 (b) 110100 (c) 110000011 (d)
10100110011100

2. (a) 13 (b) 69 (c) 170 (d) 1057

3. (a) 5 (b) 64 (c) 603 (d) 24634

4. (a) 101 (b) 101010 (c) 11000111 (d)
1000110101010

5. (a) 7 (b) 154 (c) 2566 (d) 1005

6. (a) 30 (b) 426 (c) 8863 (d) 1099039

9.

A	B	C	$X = A \cdot B + C$
0	0	0	0
0	0	1	1
0	1	0	0
0	1	1	1
1	0	0	0
1	0	1	1
1	1	0	1
1	1	1	1

10.

A	B	C	$X = A \cdot \bar{B} \cdot \bar{C}$
0	0	0	0
0	0	1	0
0	1	0	0
0	1	1	0
1	0	0	1
1	0	1	0
1	1	0	0
1	1	1	0

11. 8-bit: 20, 40, 40, 80 mV. 10-bit: 5, 10, 10,
20 mV. 12-bit: 1, 2, 2, 5 mV.

7.

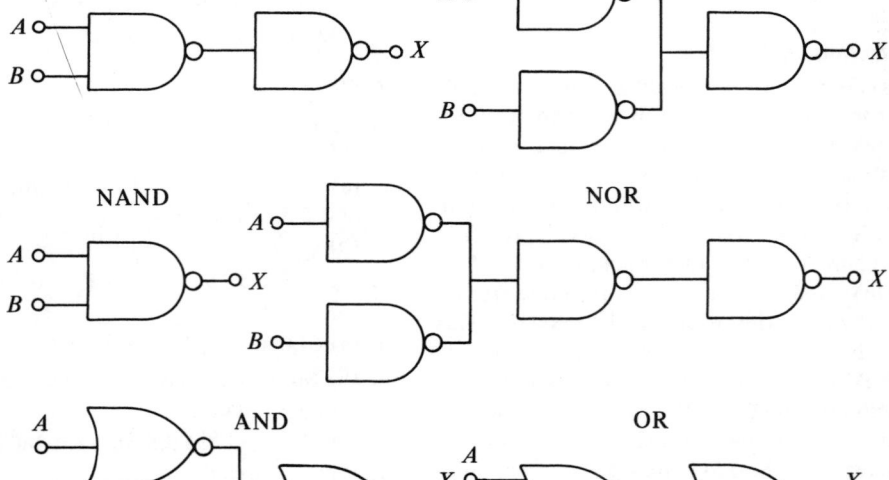

8.

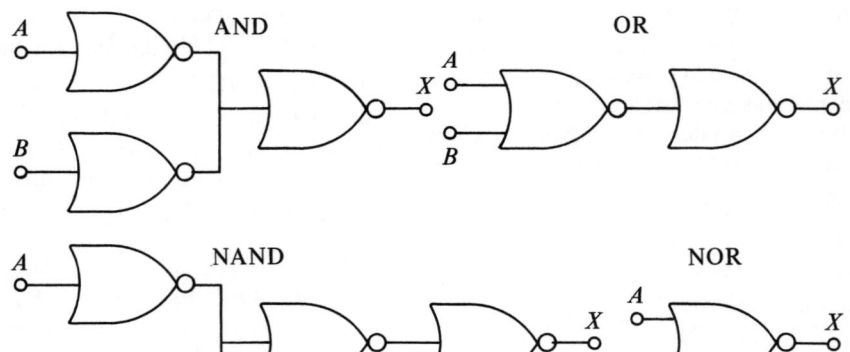

Index

Flash photolysis, 531
Flip-flop, 726
  clocked, 728
  clocked, truth table for, 729
  JK, truth table for, 731
  master-slave, 731
  reset-set, 726
  RS, truth table for, 728
Flow-proportional detectors for x-rays, 393
Fluorometric analysis, advantages and
     limitations of, 252
Fluorescence, analysis of mixtures by, 247, 249
  and structure, 243, 244
  definition of, 229
  emission, 231
  emission spectrum, 229
  excitation spectrum, 230
  in chromatography, 250
  intensity of, 233
  of inorganic compounds, 245
  of organic compounds, 243, 244
  requirements for, 243
  theory of, 230
  x-ray spectroscopy. *See* X-ray fluorescence
     spectroscopy
  x-rays, 390
Fluoride in natural water, potentiometric
     determination of, 38
Fluors, 574
Forbidden transitions, 158
Formal potential, 16
Formation constant, 615
FORTRAN, 714
Four-spin systems in NMR, 344
Fourier spectrometers, 189
Fourier spectrometry, 210
Fourier transform NMR spectroscopy, 353
Fourier transform spectra, 353
Franck-Condon principle, 158
Free energy, 488
Free induction decay, 353
Free radicals, detection of, 367
Fremy's radical, 367
Frequency factor, 528
Frequency-sweep decoupling, 347
Frontal chromatography, 623
Fructose, determination of in presence of
     glucose, 528
Full-energy peak, 574
Functional group analysis by IR, 224
Functional groups in NMR, 337

Furnace atomic absorption, direct analysis of
     solids by, 285
Furnace atomizers, 276
  detection limits for, 277

g-factor, 368
g-value, 369
  of free electron, 368
Gain, 776
Galvanic cell, 12
Gamma radiation, 565, 568
Gamma-ray spectrometry, 569
Gamma-ray spectrum, 575
  of mixtures, 576
  resolution of, 576
Gamma rays, 560
  detection of, 570
  interaction of with matter, 569
  range of in matter, 569
  shielding material for, 569
Gas analyzer, IR, 224
Gas chromatography, 625
  accuracy of, 703
  adjusted retention volume in, 679
  applications of, 703
  broadening factors in, 685
  coating of supports for, 694
  column preparation for, 694
  coulometric detector for, 107
  desired plates per meter in, 694
  detectors for, 697
  distribution coefficient in, 680
  dynamics of, 685
  effective plates in, 688
  flash-vaporization inlet for, 696
  HETP in, 633
  in automated systems, 783
  number of theoretical plates in, 686
  number of theoretical plates required for, 688
  optimizing speed of, 689
  optimum capacity factor in, 688
  optimum carrier velocity for, 686
  proposed standard stationary phases for, 693
  qualitative analysis by, 701
  quantitative analysis by, 703
  reproducibility of retention times in, 701
  required temperatures for, 689
  resolution factor in, 688
  retention vs. temperature in, 681
  retention vs. volatility in, 681

ELEMENT	SYMBOL	ATOMIC NUMBER	ATOMIC MASS
Actinium	Ac	89	(227)[a]
Aluminum	Al	13	26.98154
Americium	Am	95	(243)[a]
Antimony	Sb	51	121.75
Argon	Ar	18	39.948
Arsenic	As	33	74.9216
Astatine	At	85	(210)[a]
Barium	Ba	56	137.34
Berkelium	Bk	97	(247)[a]
Beryllium	Be	4	9.01218
Bismuth	Bi	83	208.9804
Boron	B	5	10.81
Bromine	Br	35	79.904
Cadmium	Cd	48	112.40
Calcium	Ca	20	40.08
Californium	Cf	98	(251)[a]
Carbon	C	6	12.011
Cerium	Ce	58	140.12
Cesium	Cs	55	132.9054
Chlorine	Cl	17	35.453
Chromium	Cr	24	51.996
Cobalt	Co	27	58.9332
Copper	Cu	29	63.546
Curium	Cm	96	(247)[a]
Dysprosium	Dy	66	162.50
Einsteinium	Es	99	(254)[a]
Erbium	Er	68	167.26
Europium	Eu	63	151.96
Fermium	Fm	100	(253)[a]
Fluorine	F	9	18.99840
Francium	Fr	87	(223)[a]
Gadolinium	Gd	64	157.25
Gallium	Ga	31	69.72
Germanium	Ge	32	72.59
Gold	Au	79	196.9665
Hafnium	Hf	72	178.49
Hahnium[b]	Ha	105	(260)[a]
Helium	He	2	4.00260
Holmium	Ho	67	164.9304
Hydrogen	H	1	1.0079
Indium	In	49	114.82
Iodine	I	53	126.9045
Iridium	Ir	77	192.22
Iron	Fe	26	55.847
Krypton	Kr	36	83.80
Kurchatovium[b]	Ku	104	(260)[a]
Lanthanum	La	57	138.9055
Lawrencium	Lr	103	(257)[a]
Lead	Pb	82	207.2
Lithium	Li	3	6.941
Lutetium	Lu	71	174.97
Magnesium	Mg	12	24.305

Atomic masses ($^{12}_{6}C = 12.00000$)